PETERSON'S
GRADUATE PROGRAMS
IN THE
BIOLOGICAL SCIENCES

2 0 1 2

PETERSON'S

Publishing

About Peterson's Publishing
To succeed on your lifelong educational journey, you will need accurate, dependable, and practical tools and resources. That is why Peterson's is everywhere education happens. Because whenever and however you need education content delivered, you can rely on Peterson's to provide the information, know-how, and guidance to help you reach your goals. Tools to match the right students with the right school. It's here. Personalized resources and expert guidance. It's here. Comprehensive and dependable education content—delivered whenever and however you need it. It's all here.

For more information, contact Peterson's, 2000 Lenox Drive, Lawrenceville, NJ 08648; 800-338-3282 Ext. 54229; or find us online at www.petersonspublishing.com.

© 2012 Peterson's, a Nelnet company

Previous editions © 1966, 1967, 1968, 1969, 1970, 1971, 1972, 1973, 1974, 1975, 1976, 1977, 1978, 1979, 1980, 1981, 1982, 1983, 1984, 1985, 1986, 1987, 1988, 1989, 1990, 1991, 1992, 1993, 1994, 1995, 1996, 1997, 1998, 1999, 2000, 2001, 2002, 2003, 2004, 2005, 2006, 2007, 2008, 2009, 2010, 2011

Facebook® and Facebook logos are registered trademarks of Facebook, Inc., which was not involved in the production of this book and makes no endorsement of this product.

Bernadette Webster, Director of Publishing; Jill C. Schwartz, Editor; Ken Britschge, Research Project Manager; Nicole Gallo, Amy L. Weber, Research Associates; Phyllis Johnson, Software Engineer; Ray Golaszewski, Publishing Operations Manager; Linda M. Williams, Composition Manager; Karen Mount, Fulfillment Coordinator; Danielle Vreeland, Shannon White, Client Relations Representatives

ISSN 1088-9434
ISBN-13: 978-0-7689-3282-9
ISBN-10: 0-7689-3282-3

Printed in the United States of America

10 9 8 7 6 5 4 3 2 1   14 13 12

Forty-sixth Edition

By producing this book on recycled paper (40% post consumer waste) 40 trees were saved.

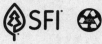

Sustainability—Its Importance to Peterson's Publishing

What does sustainability mean to Peterson's Publishing? As a leading publisher, we are aware that our business has a direct impact on vital resources—most especially the trees that are used to make our books. Peterson's Publishing is proud that its products are certified by the Sustainable Forestry Initiative (SFI) and that all of its books are printed on paper that is 40 percent post-consumer waste using vegetable-based ink.

Being a part of the Sustainable Forestry Initiative (SFI) means that all of our vendors—from paper suppliers to printers—have undergone rigorous audits to demonstrate that they are maintaining a sustainable environment.

Peterson's Publishing continuously strives to find new ways to incorporate sustainability throughout all aspects of its business.

CONTENTS

SPECIAL ADVERTISING SECTION

**Thomas Jefferson University School of
Population Health**

**University of Medicine and Dentistry of
New Jersey**

Saint Louis University

St. Mary's University

The Winston Preparatory Schools

A Note from the Peterson's Editors

The six volumes of Peterson's *Graduate and Professional Programs*, the only annually updated reference work of its kind, provide wide-ranging information on the graduate and professional programs offered by accredited colleges and universities in the United States, U.S. territories, and Canada and by those institutions outside the United States that are accredited by U.S. accrediting bodies. More than 44,000 individual academic and professional programs at more than 2,200 institutions are listed. Peterson's *Graduate and Professional Programs* have been used for more than forty years by prospective graduate and professional students, placement counselors, faculty advisers, and all others interested in postbaccalaureate education.

Graduate & Professional Programs: An Overview contains information on institutions as a whole, while the other books in the series are devoted to specific academic and professional fields:

Graduate Programs in the Humanities, Arts & Social Sciences
Graduate Programs in the Biological Sciences
Graduate Programs in the Physical Sciences, Mathematics, Agricultural Sciences, the Environment & Natural Resources
Graduate Programs in Engineering & Applied Sciences
Graduate Programs in Business, Education, Health, Information Studies, Law & Social Work

The books may be used individually or as a set. For example, if you have chosen a field of study but do not know what institution you want to attend or if you have a college or university in mind but have not chosen an academic field of study, it is best to begin with the Overview guide.

Graduate & Professional Programs: An Overview presents several directories to help you identify programs of study that might interest you; you can then research those programs further in the other books in the series by using the Directory of Graduate and Professional Programs by Field, which lists 500 fields and gives the names of those institutions that offer graduate degree programs in each.

For geographical or financial reasons, you may be interested in attending a particular institution and will want to know what it has to offer. You should turn to the Directory of Institutions and Their Offerings, which lists the degree programs available at each institution. As in the Directory of Graduate and Professional Programs by Field, the level of degrees offered is also indicated.

All books in the series include advice on graduate education, including topics such as admissions tests, financial aid, and accreditation. **The Graduate Adviser** includes two essays and information about accreditation. The first essay, "The Admissions Process," discusses general admission requirements, admission tests, factors to consider when selecting a graduate school or program, when and how to apply,

and how admission decisions are made. Special information for international students and tips for minority students are also included. The second essay, "Financial Support," is an overview of the broad range of support available at the graduate level. Fellowships, scholarships, and grants; assistantships and internships; federal and private loan programs, as well as Federal Work-Study; and the GI bill are detailed. This essay concludes with advice on applying for need-based financial aid. "Accreditation and Accrediting Agencies" gives information on accreditation and its purpose and lists institutional accrediting agencies first and then specialized accrediting agencies relevant to each volume's specific fields of study.

With information on more than 44,000 graduate programs in 500 disciplines, Peterson's *Graduate and Professional Programs* give you all the information you need about the programs that are of interest to you in three formats: **Profiles** (capsule summaries of basic information), **Displays** (information that an institution or program wants to emphasize), and **Close-Ups** (written by administrators, with more expansive information than the **Profiles**, emphasizing different aspects of the programs). By using these various formats of program information, coupled with **Appendixes** and **Indexes** covering directories and subject areas for all six books, you will find that these guides provide the most comprehensive, accurate, and up-to-date graduate study information available.

At the end of the book, you'll find a special section of ads placed by Peterson's preferred clients. Their financial support makes it possible for Peterson's Publishing to continue to provide you with the highest-quality educational exploration, test-prep, financial aid, and career-preparation resources you need to succeed on your educational journey.

Find Us on Facebook®

Join the grad school conversation on Facebook® at www.facebook.com/petersonspublishing. Peterson's expert resources are available to help you as you search for the right graduate program for you.

Peterson's publishes a full line of resources with information you need to guide you through the graduate admissions process. Peterson's publications can be found at college libraries and career centers and your local bookstore or library—or visit us on the Web at www.petersonspublishing.com. Peterson's books are now also available as eBooks.

Colleges and universities will be pleased to know that Peterson's helped you in your selection. Admissions staff members are more than happy to answer questions, address specific problems, and help in any way they can. The editors at Peterson's wish you great success in your graduate program search!

THE GRADUATE ADVISER

The Admissions Process

Generalizations about graduate admissions practices are not always helpful because each institution has its own set of guidelines and procedures. Nevertheless, some broad statements can be made about the admissions process that may help you plan your strategy.

Factors Involved in Selecting a Graduate School or Program

Selecting a graduate school and a specific program of study is a complex matter. Quality of the faculty; program and course offerings; the nature, size, and location of the institution; admission requirements; cost; and the availability of financial assistance are among the many factors that affect one's choice of institution. Other considerations are job placement and achievements of the program's graduates and the institution's resources, such as libraries, laboratories, and computer facilities. If you are to make the best possible choice, you need to learn as much as you can about the schools and programs you are considering before you apply.

The following steps may help you narrow your choices.

- Talk to alumni of the programs or institutions you are considering to get their impressions of how well they were prepared for work in their fields of study.
- Remember that graduate school requirements change, so be sure to get the most up-to-date information possible.
- Talk to department faculty members and the graduate adviser at your undergraduate institution. They often have information about programs of study at other institutions.
- Visit the Web sites of the graduate schools in which you are interested to request a graduate catalog. Contact the department chair in your chosen field of study for additional information about the department and the field.
- Visit as many campuses as possible. Call ahead for an appointment with the graduate adviser in your field of interest and be sure to check out the facilities and talk to students.

General Requirements

Graduate schools and departments have requirements that applicants for admission must meet. Typically, these requirements include undergraduate transcripts (which provide information about undergraduate grade point average and course work applied toward a major), admission test scores, and letters of recommendation. Most graduate programs also ask for an essay or personal statement that describes your personal reasons for seeking graduate study. In some fields, such as art and music, portfolios or auditions may be required in addition to other evidence of talent. Some institutions require that the applicant have an undergraduate degree in the same subject as the intended graduate major.

Most institutions evaluate each applicant on the basis of the applicant's total record, and the weight accorded any given factor varies widely from institution to institution and from program to program.

The Application Process

You should begin the application process at least one year before you expect to begin your graduate study. Find out the application deadline for each institution (many are provided in the **Profile** section of this guide). Go to the institution's Web site and find out if you can apply online. If not, request a paper application form. Fill out this form thoroughly and neatly. Assume that the school needs all the information it is requesting and that the admissions officer will be sensitive to the neatness and overall quality of what you submit. Do not supply more information than the school requires.

The institution may ask at least one question that will require a three- or four-paragraph answer. Compose your response on the assumption that the admissions officer is interested in both what you think and how you express yourself. Keep your statement brief and to the point, but, at the same time, include all pertinent information about your past experiences and your educational goals. Individual statements vary greatly in style and content, which helps admissions officers differentiate among applicants. Many graduate departments give considerable weight to the statement in making their admissions decisions, so be sure to take the time to prepare a thoughtful and concise statement.

If recommendations are a part of the admissions requirements, carefully choose the individuals you ask to write them. It is generally best to ask current or former professors to write the recommendations, provided they are able to attest to your intellectual ability and motivation for doing the work required of a graduate student. It is advisable to provide stamped, preaddressed envelopes to people being asked to submit recommendations on your behalf.

Completed applications, including references, transcripts, and admission test scores, should be received at the institution by the specified date.

Be advised that institutions do not usually make admissions decisions until all materials have been received. Enclose a self-addressed postcard with your application, requesting confirmation of receipt. Allow at least ten days for the return of the postcard before making further inquiries.

If you plan to apply for financial support, it is imperative that you file your application early.

ADMISSION TESTS

The major testing program used in graduate admissions is the Graduate Record Examinations (GRE) testing program, sponsored by the GRE Board and administered by Educational Testing Service, Princeton, New Jersey.

The Graduate Record Examinations testing program consists of a General Test and eight Subject Tests. The General Test measures critical thinking, verbal reasoning, quantitative reasoning, and analytical writing skills. It is offered as an Internet-based test (iBT) in the United States, Canada, and many other countries.

The typical computer-based General Test consists of one 30-minute verbal reasoning section, one 45-minute quantitative reasoning sections, one 45-minute issue analysis (writing) section, and one 30-minute argument analysis (writing) section. In addition, an unidentified verbal or quantitative section that doesn't count toward a score may be included and an identified research section that is not scored may also be included.

The Subject Tests measure achievement and assume undergraduate majors or extensive background in the following eight disciplines:

- Biochemistry, Cell and Molecular Biology
- Biology
- Chemistry
- Computer Science
- Literature in English
- Mathematics
- Physics
- Psychology

The Subject Tests are available three times per year as paper-based administrations around the world. Testing time is approximately 2 hours and 50 minutes. You can obtain more information about the GRE by visiting the ETS Web site at www.ets.org or consulting the *GRE Information and Registration Bulletin*. The *Bulletin* can be obtained at many undergraduate colleges. You can also download it from the ETS Web site or obtain it by contacting Graduate Record Examinations, Educational Testing Service, P.O. Box 6000, Princeton, NJ 08541-6000; phone: 609-771-7670.

If you expect to apply for admission to a program that requires any of the GRE tests, you should select a test date well in advance of the application deadline. Scores on the computer-based General Test are reported within ten to fifteen days; scores on the paper-based Subject Tests are reported within six weeks.

Another testing program, the Miller Analogies Test (MAT), is administered at more than 500 Controlled Testing Centers, licensed by Harcourt Assessment, Inc., in the United States, Canada, and other countries. The MAT computer-based test is now available. Testing time is 60 minutes. The test consists of 120 partial analogies. You can obtain the *Candidate Information Booklet,* which contains a list of test centers and instructions for taking the test, from http://www.milleranalogies.com or by calling 800-622-3231 (toll-free).

Check the specific requirements of the programs to which you are applying.

How Admission Decisions Are Made

The program you apply to is directly involved in the admissions process. Although the final decision is usually made by the graduate dean (or an associate) or the faculty admissions committee, recommendations from faculty members in your intended field are important. At some institutions, an interview is incorporated into the decision process.

A Special Note for International Students

In addition to the steps already described, there are some special considerations for international students who intend to apply for graduate study in the United States. All graduate schools require an indication of competence in English. The purpose of the Test of English as a Foreign Language (TOEFL) is to evaluate the English proficiency of people who are nonnative speakers of English and want to study at colleges and universities where English is the language of instruction. The TOEFL is administered by Educational Testing Service (ETS) under the general direction of a policy board established by the College Board and the Graduate Record Examinations Board.

The TOEFL iBT assesses the four basic language skills: listening, reading, writing, and speaking. It was administered for the first time in September 2005, and ETS continues to introduce the TOEFL iBT in selected cities. The Internet-based test is administered at secure, official test centers. The testing time is approximately 4 hours. Because the TOEFL iBT includes a speaking section, the Test of Spoken English (TSE) is no longer needed.

The TOEFL is also offered in the paper-based format in areas of the world where Internet-based testing is not available. The paper-based TOEFL consists of three sections—listening comprehension, structure and written expression, and reading comprehension. The testing time is approximately 3 hours. The Test of Written English (TWE) is also given. The TWE is a 30-minute essay that measures the examinee's ability to compose in English. Examinees receive a TWE score separate from their TOEFL score. The *Information Bulletin* contains information on local fees and registration procedures.

Additional information and registration materials are available from TOEFL Services, Educational Testing Service, P.O. Box 6151, Princeton, New Jersey 08541-6151. Phone: 609-771-7100. Web site: www.toefl.org.

International students should apply especially early because of the number of steps required to complete the admissions process. Furthermore, many United States graduate schools have a limited number of spaces for international students, and many more students apply than the schools can accommodate.

International students may find financial assistance from institutions very limited. The U.S. government requires international applicants to submit a certification of support, which is a statement attesting to the applicant's financial resources. In addition, international students *must* have health insurance coverage.

Tips for Minority Students

Indicators of a university's values in terms of diversity are found both in its recruitment programs and its resources directed to student success. Important questions: Does the institution vigorously recruit minorities for its graduate programs? Is there funding available to help with the costs associated with visiting the school? Are minorities represented in the institution's brochures or Web site or on their faculty rolls? What campus-based resources or services (including assistance in locating housing or career counseling and placement) are available? Is funding available to members of underrepresented groups?

At the program level, it is particularly important for minority students to investigate the "climate" of a program under consideration. How many minority students are enrolled and how many have graduated? What opportunities are there to work with diverse faculty and mentors whose research interests match yours? How are conflicts resolved or concerns addressed? How interested are faculty in building strong and supportive relations with students? "Climate" concerns should be addressed by posing questions to various individuals, including faculty members, current students, and alumni.

Information is also available through various organizations, such as the Hispanic Association of Colleges & Universities (HACU), and publications such as *Diverse Issues in Higher Education* and *Hispanic Outlook* magazine. There are also books devoted to this topic, such as *The Multicultural Student's Guide to Colleges* by Robert Mitchell.

Financial Support

The range of financial support at the graduate level is very broad. The following descriptions will give you a general idea of what you might expect and what will be expected of you as a financial support recipient.

Fellowships, Scholarships, and Grants

These are usually outright awards of a few hundred to many thousands of dollars with no service to the institution required in return. Fellowships and scholarships are usually awarded on the basis of merit and are highly competitive. Grants are made on the basis of financial need or special talent in a field of study. Many fellowships, scholarships, and grants not only cover tuition, fees, and supplies but also include stipends for living expenses with allowances for dependents. However, the terms of each should be examined because some do not permit recipients to supplement their income with outside work. Fellowships, scholarships, and grants may vary in the number of years for which they are awarded.

In addition to the availability of these funds at the university or program level, many excellent fellowship programs are available at the national level and may be applied for before and during enrollment in a graduate program. A listing of many of these programs can be found at the Council of Graduate Schools' Web site: http://www.cgsnet.org. There is a wealth of information in the "Programs" and "Awards" sections.

Assistantships and Internships

Many graduate students receive financial support through assistantships, particularly involving teaching or research duties. It is important to recognize that such appointments should not be viewed simply as employment relationships but rather should constitute an integral and important part of a student's graduate education. As such, the appointments should be accompanied by strong faculty mentoring and increasingly responsible apprenticeship experiences. The specific nature of these appointments in a given program should be considered in selecting that graduate program.

TEACHING ASSISTANTSHIPS

These usually provide a salary and full or partial tuition remission and may also provide health benefits. Unlike fellowships, scholarships, and grants, which require no service to the institution, teaching assistantships require recipients to provide the institution with a specific amount of undergraduate teaching, ideally related to the student's field of study. Some teaching assistants are limited to grading papers, compiling bibliographies, taking notes, or monitoring laboratories. At some graduate schools, teaching assistants must carry lighter course loads than regular full-time students.

RESEARCH ASSISTANTSHIPS

These are very similar to teaching assistantships in the manner in which financial assistance is provided. The difference is that recipients are given basic research assignments in their disciplines rather than teaching responsibilities. The work required is normally related to the student's field of study; in most instances, the assistantship supports the student's thesis or dissertation research.

ADMINISTRATIVE INTERNSHIPS

These are similar to assistantships in application of financial assistance funds, but the student is given an assignment on a part-time basis, usually as a special assistant with one of the university's administrative offices. The assignment may not necessarily be directly related to the recipient's discipline.

RESIDENCE HALL AND COUNSELING ASSISTANTSHIPS

These assistantships are frequently assigned to graduate students in psychology, counseling, and social work, but they may be offered to students in other disciplines, especially if the student has worked in this capacity during his or her undergraduate years. Duties can vary from being available in a dean's office for a specific number of hours for consultation with undergraduates to living in campus residences and being responsible for both counseling and administrative tasks or advising student activity groups. Residence hall assistantships often include a room and board allowance and, in some cases, tuition assistance and stipends. Contact the Housing and Student Life Office for more information.

Health Insurance

The availability and affordability of health insurance is an important issue and one that should be considered in an applicant's choice of institution and program. While often included with assistantships and fellowships, this is not always the case and, even if provided, the benefits may be limited. It is important to note that the U.S. government requires international students to have health insurance.

The GI Bill

This provides financial assistance for students who are veterans of the United States armed forces. If you are a veteran, contact your local Veterans Administration office to determine your eligibility and to get full details about benefits. There are a number of programs that offer educational benefits to current military enlistees. Some states have tuition assistance programs for members of the National Guard. Contact the VA office at the college for more information.

Federal Work-Study Program (FWS)

Employment is another way some students finance their graduate studies. The federally funded Federal Work-Study Program provides eligible students with employment opportunities, usually in public and private nonprofit organizations. Federal funds pay up to 75 percent of the wages, with the remainder paid by the employing agency. FWS is available to graduate students who demonstrate financial need. Not all schools have these funds, and some only award them to undergraduates. Each school sets its application deadline and work-study earnings limits. Wages vary and are related to the type of work done. You must file the Free Application for Federal Student Aid (FAFSA) to be eligible for this program.

Loans

Many graduate students borrow to finance their graduate programs when other sources of assistance (which do not have to be repaid) prove insufficient. You should always read and understand the terms of any loan program before submitting your application.

FEDERAL DIRECT LOANS

Federal Direct Stafford Loans. The Federal Direct Stafford Loan Program offers low-interest loans to students with the Department of Education acting as the lender.

There are two components of the Federal Stafford Loan program. Under the *subsidized* component of the program, the federal government pays the interest on the loan while you are enrolled in graduate school on at least a half-time basis, during the six-month grace period after you drop below half-time enrollment, as well as during any period of deferment. Under the *unsubsidized* component of the program, you pay the interest on the loan from the day proceeds are issued. Eligibility for the federal subsidy is based on demonstrated financial need as determined by the financial aid office from the information you provide on the FAFSA. A cosigner is not required, since the loan is not based on creditworthiness.

Although *unsubsidized* Federal Direct Stafford Loans may not be as desirable as *subsidized* Federal Direct Stafford Loans from the student's perspective, they are a useful source of support for those who may not qualify for the subsidized loans or who need additional financial assistance.

Graduate students may borrow up to $20,500 per year through the Direct Stafford Loan Program, up to a cumulative maximum of $138,500, including undergraduate borrowing. This may include up to $8,500 in *subsidized* Direct Stafford Loans annually, depending on eligibility, up to a cumulative maximum of $65,500, including undergraduate borrowing. The amount of the loan borrowed through the *unsubsidized* Direct Stafford Loan Program equals the total amount of the loan (as much as $20,500) minus your eligibility for a *subsidized* Direct Loan (as much as $8,500). You may borrow up to the cost of attendance at the school in which you are enrolled or will attend, minus estimated financial assistance from other federal, state, and private sources, up to a maximum of $20,500.

Direct Stafford Loans made on or after July 1, 2006, carry a fixed interest rate of 6.8% both for in-school and in-repayment borrowers.

A fee is deducted from the loan proceeds upon disbursement. Loans with a first disbursement on or after July 1, 2010, have a borrower origination fee of 1 percent. The Department of Education offers a 0.5 percent origination fee rebate incentive. Borrowers must make their first twelve payments on time in order to retain the rebate.

Under the *subsidized* Federal Direct Stafford Loan Program, repayment begins six months after your last date of enrollment on at least a half-time basis. Under the *unsubsidized* program, repayment of interest begins within thirty days from disbursement of the loan proceeds, and repayment of the principal begins six months after your last enrollment on at least a half-time basis. Some borrowers may choose to defer interest payments while they are in school. The accrued interest is added to the loan balance when the borrower begins repayment. There are several repayment options.

Federal Perkins Loans. The Federal Perkins Loan is available to students demonstrating financial need and is administered directly by the school. Not all schools have these funds, and some may award them to undergraduates only. Eligibility is determined from the information you provide on the FAFSA. The school will notify you of your eligibility.

Eligible graduate students may borrow up to $6,000 per year, up to a maximum of $40,000, including undergraduate borrowing (even if your previous Perkins Loans have been repaid). The interest rate for Federal Perkins Loans is 5 percent, and no interest accrues while you remain in school at least half-time. There are no guarantee, loan, or disbursement fees. Repayment begins nine months after your last date of enrollment on at least a half-time basis and may extend over a maximum of ten years with no prepayment penalty.

Federal Direct Graduate PLUS Loans. Effective July 1, 2006, graduate and professional students are eligible for Graduate PLUS loans. This program allows students to borrow up to the cost of attendance, less any other aid received. These loans have a fixed interest rate of 7.9 percent, and interest begins to accrue at the time of disbursement. The PLUS loans do involve a credit check; a PLUS borrower may obtain a loan with a cosigner if his or her credit is not good enough. Grad PLUS loans may be deferred while a student in school and for the six months following a drop below half-time enrollment. For more information, contact your college financial aid office.

Deferring Your Federal Loan Repayments. If you borrowed under the Federal Direct Stafford Loan Program, Federal Direct PLUS Loan Program, or the Federal Perkins Loan Program for previous undergraduate or graduate study, your payments may be deferred when you return to graduate school, depending on when you borrowed and under which program.

There are other deferment options available if you are temporarily unable to repay your loan. Information about these deferments is provided at your entrance and exit interviews. If you believe you are eligible for a deferment of your loan payments, you must contact your lender or loan servicer to request a deferment. The deferment must be filed prior to the time your payment is due, and it must be refiled when it expires if you remain eligible for deferment at that time.

SUPPLEMENTAL (PRIVATE) LOANS

Many lending institutions offer supplemental loan programs and other financing plans, such as the ones described here, to students seeking additional assistance in meeting their education expenses. Some loan programs target all types of graduate students; others are designed specifically for business, law, or medical students. In addition, you can use private loans not specifically designed for education to help finance your graduate degree.

If you are considering borrowing through a supplemental or private loan program, you should carefully consider the terms and be sure to "read the fine print." Check with the program sponsor for the most current terms that will be applicable to the amounts you intend to borrow for graduate study. Most supplemental loan programs for graduate study offer unsubsidized, credit-based loans. In general, a credit-ready borrower is one who has a satisfactory credit history or no credit history at all. A creditworthy borrower generally must pass a credit test to be eligible to borrow or act as a cosigner for the loan funds.

Many supplemental loan programs have minimum and maximum annual loan limits. Some offer amounts equal to the cost of attendance minus any other aid you will receive for graduate study. If you are planning to borrow for several years of graduate study, consider whether there is a cumulative or aggregate limit on the amount you may borrow. Often this cumulative or aggregate limit will include any amounts you borrowed and have not repaid for undergraduate or previous graduate study.

The combination of the annual interest rate, loan fees, and the repayment terms you choose will determine how much you will repay over time. Compare these features in combination before you decide which loan program to use. Some loans offer interest rates that are adjusted monthly, some quarterly, some annually. Some offer interest rates that are lower during the in-school, grace, and deferment periods and then increase when you begin repayment. Some programs include a loan "origination" fee, which is usually deducted from the principal amount you receive when the loan is disbursed and must be repaid along with the interest and other principal when you graduate, withdraw from school, or drop below half-time study. Sometimes the loan fees are reduced if you borrow with a qualified cosigner. Some programs allow you to defer interest and/or principal payments while you are enrolled in graduate school. Many programs allow you to capitalize your interest payments; the interest due on your loan is added to the outstanding balance of your loan, so you don't have to repay immediately, but this increases the amount you owe. Other programs allow you to pay the interest as you go, which reduces the amount you later have to repay. The private loan market is very competitive, and your financial aid office can help you evaluate these programs.

Applying for Need-Based Financial Aid

Schools that award federal and institutional financial assistance based on need will require you to complete the FAFSA and, in some cases, an institutional financial aid application.

If you are applying for federal student assistance, you **must** complete the FAFSA. A service of the U.S. Department of Education, the FAFSA is free to all applicants. Most applicants apply online at www.fafsa.ed.gov. Paper applications are available at the financial aid office of your local college.

After your FAFSA information has been processed, you will receive a Student Aid Report (SAR). If you provided an e-mail address on the FAFSA, this will be sent to you electronically; otherwise, it will be mailed to your home address.

Follow the instructions on the SAR if you need to correct information reported on your original application. If your situation changes after you file your FAFSA, contact your financial aid officer to discuss amending your information. You can also appeal your financial aid award if you have extenuating circumstances.

If you would like more information on federal student financial aid, visit the FAFSA Web site or download the most recent version of *Funding Education Beyond High School: The Guide to Federal Student Aid* at http://studentaid.ed.gov/students/publications/student_guide/index.html. This guide is also available in Spanish.

The U.S. Department of Education also has a toll-free number for questions concerning federal student aid programs. The number is 1-800-4-FED AID (1-800-433-3243). If you are hearing impaired, call toll-free, 1-800-730-8913.

Summary

Remember that these are generalized statements about financial assistance at the graduate level. Because each institution allots its aid differently, you should communicate directly with the school and the specific department of interest to you. It is not unusual, for example, to find that an endowment vested within a specific department supports one or more fellowships. You may fit its requirements and specifications precisely.

Accreditation and Accrediting Agencies

Colleges and universities in the United States, and their individual academic and professional programs, are accredited by nongovernmental agencies concerned with monitoring the quality of education in this country. Agencies with both regional and national jurisdictions grant accreditation to institutions as a whole, while specialized bodies acting on a nationwide basis—often national professional associations—grant accreditation to departments and programs in specific fields.

Institutional and specialized accrediting agencies share the same basic concerns: the purpose an academic unit—whether university or program—has set for itself and how well it fulfills that purpose, the adequacy of its financial and other resources, the quality of its academic offerings, and the level of services it provides. Agencies that grant institutional accreditation take a broader view, of course, and examine university-wide or college-wide services with which a specialized agency may not concern itself.

Both types of agencies follow the same general procedures when considering an application for accreditation. The academic unit prepares a self-evaluation, focusing on the concerns mentioned above and usually including an assessment of both its strengths and weaknesses; a team of representatives of the accrediting body reviews this evaluation, visits the campus, and makes its own report; and finally, the accrediting body makes a decision on the application. Often, even when accreditation is granted, the agency makes a recommendation regarding how the institution or program can improve. All institutions and programs are also reviewed every few years to determine whether they continue to meet established standards; if they do not, they may lose their accreditation.

Accrediting agencies themselves are reviewed and evaluated periodically by the U.S. Department of Education and the Council for Higher Education Accreditation (CHEA). Recognized agencies adhere to certain standards and practices, and their authority in matters of accreditation is widely accepted in the educational community.

This does not mean, however, that accreditation is a simple matter, either for schools wishing to become accredited or for students deciding where to apply. Indeed, in certain fields the very meaning and methods of accreditation are the subject of a good deal of debate. For their part, those applying to graduate school should be aware of the safeguards provided by regional accreditation, especially in terms of degree acceptance and institutional longevity. Beyond this, applicants should understand the role that specialized accreditation plays in their field, as this varies considerably from one discipline to another. In certain professional fields, it is necessary to have graduated from a program that is accredited in order to be eligible for a license to practice, and in some fields the federal government also makes this a hiring requirement. In other disciplines, however, accreditation is not as essential, and there can be excellent programs that are not accredited. In fact, some programs choose not to seek accreditation, although most do.

Institutions and programs that present themselves for accreditation are sometimes granted the status of candidate for accreditation, or what is known as "preaccreditation." This may happen, for example, when an academic unit is too new to have met all the requirements for accreditation. Such status signifies initial recognition and indicates that the school or program in question is working to fulfill all requirements; it does not, however, guarantee that accreditation will be granted.

Institutional Accrediting Agencies—Regional

MIDDLE STATES ASSOCIATION OF COLLEGES AND SCHOOLS

Accredits institutions in Delaware, District of Columbia, Maryland, New Jersey, New York, Pennsylvania, Puerto Rico, and the Virgin Islands.
Dr. Elizabeth Sibolski, President
Middle States Commission on Higher Education
3624 Market Street, Second Floor West
Philadelphia, Pennsylvania 19104
Phone: 267-284-5000
Fax: 215-662-5501
E-mail: info@msche.org
Web: www.msche.org

NEW ENGLAND ASSOCIATION OF SCHOOLS AND COLLEGES

Accredits institutions in Connecticut, Maine, Massachusetts, New Hampshire, Rhode Island, and Vermont.
Barbara E. Brittingham, Director
Commission on Institutions of Higher Education
209 Burlington Road, Suite 201
Bedford, Massachusetts 01730-1433
Phone: 781-271-0022
Fax: 781-271-0950
E-mail: kwillis@neasc.org
Web: www.neasc.org

NORTH CENTRAL ASSOCIATION OF COLLEGES AND SCHOOLS

Accredits institutions in Arizona, Arkansas, Colorado, Illinois, Indiana, Iowa, Kansas, Michigan, Minnesota, Missouri, Nebraska, New Mexico, North Dakota, Ohio, Oklahoma, South Dakota, West Virginia, Wisconsin, and Wyoming.
Dr. Sylvia Manning, President
The Higher Learning Commission
230 South LaSalle Street, Suite 7-500
Chicago, Illinois 60604-1413
Phone: 312-263-0456
Fax: 312-263-7462
E-mail: smanning@hlcommission.org
Web: www.ncahlc.org

NORTHWEST COMMISSION ON COLLEGES AND UNIVERSITIES

Accredits institutions in Alaska, Idaho, Montana, Nevada, Oregon, Utah, and Washington.
Dr. Sandra E. Elman, President
8060 165th Avenue, NE, Suite 100
Redmond, Washington 98052
Phone: 425-558-4224
Fax: 425-376-0596
E-mail: selman@nwccu.org
Web: www.nwccu.org

SOUTHERN ASSOCIATION OF COLLEGES AND SCHOOLS

Accredits institutions in Alabama, Florida, Georgia, Kentucky, Louisiana, Mississippi, North Carolina, South Carolina, Tennessee, Texas, and Virginia.
Belle S. Wheelan, President
Commission on Colleges
1866 Southern Lane
Decatur, Georgia 30033-4097
Phone: 404-679-4500
Fax: 404-679-4558
E-mail: questions@sacscoc.org
Web: www.sacscoc.org

WESTERN ASSOCIATION OF SCHOOLS AND COLLEGES

Accredits institutions in California, Guam, and Hawaii.
Ralph A. Wolff, President and Executive Director
Accrediting Commission for Senior Colleges and Universities
985 Atlantic Avenue, Suite 100
Alameda, California 94501
Phone: 510-748-9001
Fax: 510-748-9797
E-mail: www.wascsenior.org/contact
Web: www.wascweb.org/contact

Institutional Accrediting Agencies—Other

ACCREDITING COUNCIL FOR INDEPENDENT COLLEGES AND SCHOOLS
Albert C. Gray, Ph.D., Executive Director and CEO
750 First Street, NE, Suite 980
Washington, DC 20002-4241
Phone: 202-336-6780
Fax: 202-842-2593
E-mail: info@acics.org
Web: www.acics.org

DISTANCE EDUCATION AND TRAINING COUNCIL (DETC)
Accrediting Commission
Michael P. Lambert, Executive Director
1601 18th Street, NW, Suite 2
Washington, DC 20009
Phone: 202-234-5100
Fax: 202-332-1386
E-mail: Brianna@detc.org
Web: www.detc.org

Specialized Accrediting Agencies

[Only *Graduate & Professional Programs: An Overview* of *Peterson's Graduate and Professional Programs* Series includes the complete list of specialized accrediting groups recognized by the U.S. Department of Education and the Council on Higher Education Accreditation (CHEA). The list in this book is abridged.]

DIETETICS
Ulric K. Chung, Ph.D., Executive Director
American Dietetic Association
Commission on Accreditation for Dietetics Education (CADE-ADA)
120 South Riverside Plaza, Suite 2000
Chicago, Illinois 60606-6995
Phone: 800-877-1600
Fax: 312-899-4817
E-mail: cade@eatright.org
Web: www.eatright.org/cade

How to Use These Guides

As you identify the particular programs and institutions that interest you, you can use both the *Graduate & Professional Programs: An Overview* volume and the specialized volumes in the series to obtain detailed information.

- *Graduate Programs in the Physical Sciences, Mathematics, Agricultural Sciences, the Environment & Natural Resources*
- *Graduate Programs in Engineering & Applied Sciences*
- *Graduate Programs the Humanities, Arts & Social Sciences*
- *Graduate Programs in the Biological Sciences*
- *Graduate Programs in Business, Education, Health, Information Studies, Law & Social Work*

Each of the specialized volumes in the series is divided into sections that contain one or more directories devoted to programs in a particular field. If you do not find a directory devoted to your field of interest in a specific volume, consult "Directories and Subject Areas" (located at the end of each volume). After you have identified the correct volume, consult the "Directories and Subject Areas in This Book" index, which shows (as does the more general directory) what directories cover subjects not specifically named in a directory or section title.

Each of the specialized volumes in the series has a number of general directories. These directories have entries for the largest unit at an institution granting graduate degrees in that field. For example, the general Engineering and Applied Sciences directory in the *Graduate Programs in Engineering & Applied Sciences* volume consists of *Profiles* for colleges, schools, and departments of engineering and applied sciences.

General directories are followed by other directories, or sections, that give more detailed information about programs in particular areas of the general field that has been covered. The general Engineering and Applied Sciences directory, in the previous example, is followed by nineteen sections with directories in specific areas of engineering, such as Chemical Engineering, Industrial/Management Engineering, and Mechanical Engineering.

Because of the broad nature of many fields, any system of organization is bound to involve a certain amount of overlap. Environmental studies, for example, is a field whose various aspects are studied in several types of departments and schools. Readers interested in such studies will find information on relevant programs in the *Graduate Programs in the Biological Sciences* volume under Ecology and Environmental Biology; in the *Graduate Programs in the Physical Sciences, Mathematics, Agricultural Sciences, the Environment & Natural Resources* volume under Environmental Management and Policy and Natural Resources; in the *Graduate Programs in Engineering & Applied Sciences* volume under Energy Management and Policy and Environmental Engineering; and in the *Graduate Programs in Business, Education, Health, Information Studies, Law & Social Work* volume under Environmental and Occupational Health. To help you find all of the programs of interest to you, the introduction to each section within the specialized volumes includes, if applicable, a paragraph suggesting other sections and directories with information on related areas of study.

Directory of Institutions with Programs in the Biological Sciences

This directory lists institutions in alphabetical order and includes beneath each name the academic fields in which each institution offers graduate programs. The degree level in each field is also indicated, provided that the institution has supplied that information in response to Peterson's Annual Survey of Graduate and Professional Institutions. An M indicates that a master's degree program is offered; a D indicates that a doctoral degree program is offered; a P indicates that the first professional degree is offered; an O signifies that other advanced degrees (e.g., certificates or specialist degrees) are offered; and an *

(asterisk) indicates that a **Close-Up** and/or **Display** is located in this volume. See the index, "Close-Ups and Displays," for the specific page number.

Profiles of Academic and Professional Programs in the Specialized Volumes

Each section of **Profiles** has a table of contents that lists the Program Directories, **Displays**, and **Close-Ups**. Program Directories consist of the **Profiles** of programs in the relevant fields, with **Displays** following if programs have chosen to include them. **Close-Ups**, which are more individualized statements, again if programs have chosen to submit them, are also listed.

The **Profiles** found in the 500 directories in the specialized volumes provide basic data about the graduate units in capsule form for quick reference. To make these directories as useful as possible, **Profiles** are generally listed for an institution's smallest academic unit within a subject area. In other words, if an institution has a College of Liberal Arts that administers many related programs, the **Profile** for the individual program (e.g., Program in History), not the entire College, appears in the directory.

There are some programs that do not fit into any current directory and are not given individual **Profiles**. The directory structure is reviewed annually in order to keep this number to a minimum and to accommodate major trends in graduate education.

The following outline describes the **Profile** information found in the guides and explains how best to use that information. Any item that does not apply to or was not provided by a graduate unit is omitted from its listing. The format of the **Profiles** is constant, making it easy to compare one institution with another and one program with another.

Identifying Information. The institution's name, in boldface type, is followed by a complete listing of the administrative structure for that field of study. (For example, University of Akron, Buchtel College of Arts and Sciences, Department of Theoretical and Applied Mathematics, Program in Mathematics.) The last unit listed is the one to which all information in the **Profile** pertains. The institution's city, state, and zip code follow.

Offerings. Each field of study offered by the unit is listed with all postbaccalaureate degrees awarded. Degrees that are not preceded by a specific concentration are awarded in the general field listed in the unit name. Frequently, fields of study are broken down into subspecializations, and those appear following the degrees awarded; for example, "Offerings in secondary education (M.Ed.), including English education, mathematics education, science education." Students enrolled in the M.Ed. program would be able to specialize in any of the three fields mentioned.

Professional Accreditation. Some **Profiles** indicate whether a program is professionally accredited. Because it is possible for a program to receive or lose professional accreditation at any time, students entering fields in which accreditation is important to a career should verify the status of programs by contacting either the chairperson or the appropriate accrediting association.

Jointly Offered Degrees. Explanatory statements concerning programs that are offered in cooperation with other institutions are included in the list of degrees offered. This occurs most commonly on a regional basis (for example, two state universities offering a cooperative Ph.D. in special education) or where the specialized nature of the institutions encourages joint efforts (a J.D./M.B.A. offered by a law school at an institution with no formal business programs and an institution with a business school but lacking a law school). Only programs that are truly cooperative are listed; those involving only limited course work at another institution are not. Interested students should contact the heads of such units for further information.

Part-Time and Evening/Weekend Programs. When information regarding the availability of part-time or evening/weekend study appears in the **Profile**, it means that students are able to earn a degree exclusively through such study.

Postbaccalaureate Distance Learning Degrees. A post-baccalaureate distance learning degree program signifies that course requirements can be fulfilled with minimal or no on-campus study.

Faculty. Figures on the number of faculty members actively involved with graduate students through teaching or research are separated into full-and part-time as well as men and women whenever the information has been supplied.

Students. Figures for the number of students enrolled in graduate and professional programs pertain to the semester of highest enrollment from the 2010–11 academic year. These figures are broken down into full-and part-time and men and women whenever the data have been supplied. Information on the number of matriculated students enrolled in the unit who are members of a minority group or are international students appears here. The average age of the matriculated students is followed by the number of applicants, the percentage accepted, and the number enrolled for fall 2010.

Degrees Awarded. The number of degrees awarded in the calendar year is listed. Many doctoral programs offer a terminal master's degree if students leave the program after completing only part of the requirements for a doctoral degree; that is indicated here. All degrees are classified into one of four types: master's, doctoral, first professional, and other advanced degrees. A unit may award one or several degrees at a given level; however, the data are only collected by type and may therefore represent several different degree programs.

Degree Requirements. The information in this section is also broken down by type of degree, and all information for a degree level pertains to all degrees of that type unless otherwise specified. Degree requirements are collected in a simplified form to provide some very basic information on the nature of the program and on foreign language, thesis or dissertation, comprehensive exam, and registration requirements. Many units also provide a short list of additional requirements, such as fieldwork or an internship. For complete information on graduation requirements, contact the graduate school or program directly.

Entrance Requirements. Entrance requirements are broken down into the four degree levels of master's, doctoral, first professional, and other advanced degrees. Within each level, information may be provided in two basic categories: entrance exams and other requirements. The entrance exams are identified by the standard acronyms used by the testing agencies, unless they are not well known. Other entrance requirements are quite varied, but they often contain an undergraduate or graduate grade point average (GPA). Unless otherwise stated, the GPA is calculated on a 4.0 scale and is listed as a minimum required for admission. Additional exam requirements/recommendations for international students may be listed here. Application deadlines for domestic and international students, the application fee, and whether electronic applications are accepted may be listed here. Note that the deadline should be used for reference only; these dates are subject to change, and students interested in applying should always contact the graduate unit directly about application procedures and deadlines.

Expenses. The typical cost of study for the 2010–11 academic year is given in two basic categories: tuition and fees. Cost of study may be quite complex at a graduate institution. There are often sliding scales for part-time study, a different cost for first-year students, and other variables that make it impossible to completely cover the cost of study for each graduate program. To provide the most usable information, figures are given for full-time study for a full year where available and for part-time study in terms of a per-unit rate (per credit, per semester hour, etc.). Occasionally, variances may be noted in tuition and fees for reasons such as the type of program, whether courses are taken during the day or evening, whether courses are at the master's or doctoral level, or other institution-specific reasons. Expenses are usually subject to change; for exact costs at any given time, contact your chosen schools and programs directly. Keep in mind that the tuition of Canadian institutions is usually given in Canadian dollars.

Financial Support. This section contains data on the number of awards administered by the institution and given to graduate students during the 2010–11 academic year. The first figure given represents the total number of students receiving financial support enrolled in that unit. If the unit has provided information on graduate appoint-ments, these are broken down into three major categories: fellowships give money to graduate students to cover the cost of study and living expenses and are not based on a work obligation or research commitment, research assistantships provide stipends to graduate students for assistance in a formal research project with a faculty member, and teaching assistantships provide stipends to graduate students for teaching or for assisting faculty members in teaching undergraduate classes. Within each category, figures are given for the total number of awards, the average yearly amount per award, and whether full or partial tuition reimbursements are awarded. In addition to graduate appointments, the availability of several other financial aid sources is covered in this section. Tuition waivers are routinely part of a graduate appointment, but units sometimes waive part or all of a student's tuition even if a graduate appointment is not available. Federal Work-Study is made available to students who demonstrate need and meet the federal guidelines; this form of aid normally includes 10 or more hours of work per week in an office of the institution. Institutionally sponsored loans are low-interest loans available to graduate students to cover both educational and living expenses. Career-related intern-ships or fieldwork offer money to students who are participating in a formal off-campus research project or practicum. Grants, scholar-ships, traineeships, unspecified assistantships, and other awards may also be noted. The availability of financial support to part-time students is also indicated here.

Some programs list the financial aid application deadline and the forms that need to be completed for students to be eligible for financial awards. There are two forms: FAFSA, the Free Application for Federal Student Aid, which is required for federal aid, and the CSS PROFILE®.

Faculty Research. Each unit has the opportunity to list several keyword phrases describing the current research involving faculty members and graduate students. Space limitations prevent the unit from listing complete information on all research programs. The total expenditure for funded research from the previous academic year may also be included.

Unit Head and Application Contact. The head of the graduate program for each unit is listed with academic title and telephone and fax numbers and e-mail address if available. In addition to the unit head, many graduate programs list a separate contact for application and admission information, which follows the listing for the unit head. If no unit head or application contact is given, you should contact the overall institution for information on graduate admissions.

Displays and Close-Ups

The **Displays** and **Close-Ups** are supplementary insertions submitted by deans, chairs, and other administrators who wish to offer an additional, more individualized statement to readers. A number of graduate school and program administrators have attached a **Display** ad near the **Profile** listing. Here you will find information that an institution or program wants to emphasize. The **Close-Ups** are by their very nature more expansive and flexible than the **Profiles**, and the administrators who have written them may emphasize different aspects of their programs. All of the **Close-Ups** are organized in the same way (with the exception of a few that describe research and training opportunities instead of degree programs), and in each one you will find information on the same basic topics, such as programs of study, research facilities, tuition and fees, financial aid, and application procedures. If an institution or program has submitted a **Close-Up**, a boldface cross-reference appears below its **Profile**. As with the **Displays**, all of the **Close-Ups** in the guides have been submitted by choice; the absence of a **Display** or **Close-Up** does not reflect any type of editorial judgment on the part of Peterson's, and their presence in the guides should not be taken as an indication of status, quality, or approval. Statements regarding a university's objectives and accomplishments are a reflection of its own beliefs and are not the opinions of the Peterson's editors.

Appendixes

This section contains two appendixes. The first, "Institutional Changes Since the 2011 Edition," lists institutions that have closed, merged, or changed their name or status since the last edition of the guides. The second, "Abbreviations Used in the Guides," gives abbreviations of degree names, along with what those abbreviations stand for. These appendixes are identical in all six volumes of *Peterson's Graduate and Professional Programs*.

Indexes

There are three indexes presented here. The first index, "Close-Ups and Displays," gives page references for all programs that have chosen to place **Close-Ups** and **Displays** in this volume. It is arranged alphabetically by institution; within institutions, the arrangement is alphabetical by subject area. It is not an index to all programs in the book's directories of **Profiles**; readers must refer to the directories themselves for **Profile** information on programs that have not submitted the additional, more individualized statements. The second index, "Directories and Subject Areas in Other Books in This Series", gives book references for the directories in the specialized volumes and also includes cross-references for subject area names not used in the directory structure, for example, "Computing Technology (see Computer Science)." The third index, "Directories and Subject Areas in This Book," gives page references for the directories in this volume and cross-references for subject area names not used in this volume's directory structure.

Data Collection Procedures

The information published in the directories and **Profiles** of all the books is collected through Peterson's Annual Survey of Graduate and Professional Institutions. The survey is sent each spring to nearly 2,400 institutions offering postbaccalaureate degree programs, including accredited institutions in the United States, U.S. territories, and Canada and those institutions outside the United States that are accredited by U.S. accrediting bodies. Deans and other administrators complete these surveys, providing information on programs in the 500 academic and professional fields covered in the guides as well as overall institutional information. While every effort has been made to ensure the accuracy and completeness of the data, information is sometimes unavailable or changes occur after publication deadlines. All usable

information received in time for publication has been included. The omission of any particular item from a directory or **Profile** signifies either that the item is not applicable to the institution or program or that information was not available. **Profiles** of programs scheduled to begin during the 2011–12 academic year cannot, obviously, include statistics on enrollment or, in many cases, the number of faculty members. If no usable data were submitted by an institution, its name, address, and program name appear in order to indicate the availability of graduate work.

Criteria for Inclusion in This Guide

To be included in this guide, an institution must have full accreditation or be a candidate for accreditation (preaccreditation) status by an institutional or specialized accrediting body recognized by the U.S. Department of Education or the Council for Higher Education Accreditation (CHEA). Institutional accrediting bodies, which review each institution as a whole, include the six regional associations of schools and colleges (Middle States, New England, North Central, Northwest, Southern, and Western), each of which is responsible for a specified portion of the United States and its territories. Other institutional accrediting bodies are national in scope and accredit specific kinds of institutions (e.g., Bible colleges, independent colleges, and rabbinical and Talmudic schools). Program registration by the New York State Board of Regents is considered to be the equivalent of institutional accreditation, since the board requires that all programs offered by an institution meet its standards before recognition is granted. A Canadian institution must be chartered and authorized to grant degrees by the provincial government, affiliated with a chartered institution, or accredited by a recognized U.S. accrediting body. This guide also includes institutions outside the United States that are accredited by these U.S. accrediting bodies. There are recognized specialized or professional accrediting bodies in more than fifty different fields, each of which is authorized to accredit institutions or specific programs in its particular field. For specialized institutions that offer programs in one field only, we designate this to be the equivalent of institutional accreditation. A full explanation of the accrediting process and complete information on recognized institutional (regional and national) and specialized accrediting bodies can be found online at www.chea.org or at www.ed.gov/admins/finaid/accred/index.html.

DIRECTORY OF INSTITUTIONS WITH PROGRAMS IN THE BIOLOGICAL SCIENCES

ACADIA UNIVERSITY

Biological and Biomedical Sciences—General	M

ADELPHI UNIVERSITY

Biological and Biomedical Sciences—General	M*

ADLER SCHOOL OF PROFESSIONAL PSYCHOLOGY

Biopsychology	M,D,O

ALABAMA AGRICULTURAL AND MECHANICAL UNIVERSITY

Biological and Biomedical Sciences—General	M

ALABAMA STATE UNIVERSITY

Biological and Biomedical Sciences—General	M

ALBANY COLLEGE OF PHARMACY AND HEALTH SCIENCES

Cell Biology	P,M

ALBANY MEDICAL COLLEGE

Cardiovascular Sciences	M,D
Cell Biology	M,D
Immunology	M,D
Microbiology	M,D
Molecular Biology	M,D
Neuroscience	M,D
Pharmacology	M,D

ALBERT EINSTEIN COLLEGE OF MEDICINE

Anatomy	D
Biochemistry	D
Biological and Biomedical Sciences—General	D
Biophysics	D
Cell Biology	D
Developmental Biology	D
Genetics	D
Genomic Sciences	D
Immunology	D
Microbiology	D
Molecular Biology	D
Molecular Genetics	D
Molecular Pharmacology	D
Neurobiology	D
Pathology	D
Physiology	D

ALCORN STATE UNIVERSITY

Biological and Biomedical Sciences—General	M

ALLIANT INTERNATIONAL UNIVERSITY–SAN FRANCISCO

Pharmacology	M

AMERICAN UNIVERSITY

Biological and Biomedical Sciences—General	M
Biopsychology	M,D
Neuroscience	M,D
Toxicology	M,O

THE AMERICAN UNIVERSITY OF ATHENS

Biological and Biomedical Sciences—General	M

AMERICAN UNIVERSITY OF BEIRUT

Biochemistry	P,M
Biological and Biomedical Sciences—General	M
Microbiology	P,M
Neuroscience	P,M
Nutrition	M
Pharmacology	P,M
Physiology	P,M

ANDREWS UNIVERSITY

Biological and Biomedical Sciences—General	M
Nutrition	M

ANGELO STATE UNIVERSITY

Biological and Biomedical Sciences—General	M

ANTIOCH UNIVERSITY NEW ENGLAND

Conservation Biology	M

APPALACHIAN STATE UNIVERSITY

Biological and Biomedical Sciences—General	M
Cell Biology	M
Molecular Biology	M
Nutrition	M

ARGOSY UNIVERSITY, ATLANTA

Biopsychology	M,D,O

ARGOSY UNIVERSITY, CHICAGO

Neuroscience	D

ARGOSY UNIVERSITY, HAWAI'I

Pharmacology	M,O

ARGOSY UNIVERSITY, PHOENIX

Neuroscience	M,D

ARGOSY UNIVERSITY, SCHAUMBURG

Neuroscience	M,D,O

ARGOSY UNIVERSITY, TAMPA

Neuroscience	M,D

ARGOSY UNIVERSITY, TWIN CITIES

Biopsychology	M,D,O

ARIZONA STATE UNIVERSITY

Animal Behavior	M,D
Biochemistry	M,D
Biological and Biomedical Sciences—General	M,D
Cell Biology	M,D
Computational Biology	M,D
Evolutionary Biology	M,D
Microbiology	M,D
Molecular Biology	M,D
Neuroscience	M,D
Nutrition	M,D,O

ARKANSAS STATE UNIVERSITY

Biological and Biomedical Sciences—General	M,O
Molecular Biology	D,O

A.T. STILL UNIVERSITY OF HEALTH SCIENCES

Biological and Biomedical Sciences—General	P,M

AUBURN UNIVERSITY

Anatomy	M,D
Biochemistry	M,D
Biological and Biomedical Sciences—General	M,D
Botany	M,D
Cell Biology	M,D
Entomology	M,D
Microbiology	M,D
Molecular Biology	M,D
Nutrition	M,D
Pathobiology	M,D
Pharmacology	M,D
Plant Pathology	M,D
Radiation Biology	M,D
Zoology	M,D

AUSTIN PEAY STATE UNIVERSITY

Biological and Biomedical Sciences—General	M
Radiation Biology	M

BALL STATE UNIVERSITY

Biological and Biomedical Sciences—General	M,D
Physiology	M

BARRY UNIVERSITY

Anatomy	M
Biological and Biomedical Sciences—General	M

BASTYR UNIVERSITY

Nutrition	M

BAYLOR COLLEGE OF MEDICINE

Biochemistry	D
Biological and Biomedical Sciences—General	M,D
Biophysics	D
Cancer Biology/Oncology	D
Cardiovascular Sciences	D
Cell Biology	D*
Computational Biology	D*
Developmental Biology	D*
Genetics	D
Human Genetics	D*
Immunology	D
Microbiology	D
Molecular Biology	D*
Molecular Biophysics	D
Molecular Medicine	D*
Molecular Physiology	D
Neuroscience	D
Pathology	D
Pharmacology	D
Structural Biology	D
Translational Biology	D*
Virology	D

BAYLOR UNIVERSITY

Biological and Biomedical Sciences—General	M,D
Ecology	D
Environmental Biology	M,D
Nutrition	M,D

BEMIDJI STATE UNIVERSITY

Biological and Biomedical Sciences—General	M

BENEDICTINE UNIVERSITY

Nutrition	M

BLACK HILLS STATE UNIVERSITY

Genomic Sciences	M

BLOOMSBURG UNIVERSITY OF PENNSYLVANIA

Biological and Biomedical Sciences—General	M

BOISE STATE UNIVERSITY

Biological and Biomedical Sciences—General	M

BOSTON COLLEGE

Biochemistry	D
Biological and Biomedical Sciences—General	D*

BOSTON UNIVERSITY

Anatomy	M,D
Biochemistry	M,D
Biological and Biomedical Sciences—General	M,D,O
Biophysics	D
Cell Biology	M,D
Immunology	M,D
Microbiology	M,D
Molecular Biology	M,D
Molecular Medicine	D
Neuroscience	M,D
Nutrition	M
Pharmacology	M,D
Physiology	M,D

BOWLING GREEN STATE UNIVERSITY

Biological and Biomedical Sciences—General	M,D*
Nutrition	M

BRADLEY UNIVERSITY

Biological and Biomedical Sciences—General	M

BRANDEIS UNIVERSITY

Biochemistry	D
Biological and Biomedical Sciences—General	O
Biophysics	D
Cell Biology	M,D
Genetics	M,D
Microbiology	M,D
Molecular Biology	M,D
Neurobiology	M,D
Neuroscience	M,D

BRIGHAM YOUNG UNIVERSITY

Biochemistry	M,D
Biological and Biomedical Sciences—General	M,D
Developmental Biology	M,D
Microbiology	M,D
Molecular Biology	M,D
Neuroscience	M,D
Nutrition	M
Physiology	M,D

BROCK UNIVERSITY

Biological and Biomedical Sciences—General	M,D
Neuroscience	M,D

BROOKLYN COLLEGE OF THE CITY UNIVERSITY OF NEW YORK

Biological and Biomedical Sciences—General	M,D
Nutrition	M

BROWN UNIVERSITY

Biochemistry	M,D
Biological and Biomedical Sciences—General	M,D
Biopsychology	D
Cancer Biology/Oncology	M,D
Cell Biology	M,D
Developmental Biology	M,D
Ecology	D
Evolutionary Biology	D
Immunology	M,D
Microbiology	M,D
Molecular Biology	M,D
Molecular Pharmacology	M,D
Neuroscience	D
Pathobiology	M,D
Pathology	M,D
Physiology	M,D
Toxicology	M,D

BUCKNELL UNIVERSITY

Animal Behavior	M
Biological and Biomedical Sciences—General	M

BUFFALO STATE COLLEGE, STATE UNIVERSITY OF NEW YORK

Biological and Biomedical Sciences—General	M

CALIFORNIA INSTITUTE OF TECHNOLOGY

Biochemistry	M,D
Biological and Biomedical Sciences—General	D*
Biophysics	D
Cell Biology	D
Developmental Biology	D
Genetics	D
Immunology	D
Molecular Biology	D
Molecular Biophysics	M,D
Neurobiology	D
Neuroscience	M,D

CALIFORNIA POLYTECHNIC STATE UNIVERSITY, SAN LUIS OBISPO

Biochemistry	M
Biological and Biomedical Sciences—General	M

CALIFORNIA STATE POLYTECHNIC UNIVERSITY, POMONA

Biological and Biomedical Sciences—General	M

CALIFORNIA STATE UNIVERSITY, BAKERSFIELD

Biological and Biomedical Sciences—General	M

CALIFORNIA STATE UNIVERSITY, CHICO

Biological and Biomedical Sciences—General	M
Botany	M
Nutrition	M

CALIFORNIA STATE UNIVERSITY, DOMINGUEZ HILLS

Biological and Biomedical Sciences—General	M

CALIFORNIA STATE UNIVERSITY, EAST BAY

Biochemistry	M
Biological and Biomedical Sciences—General	M

CALIFORNIA STATE UNIVERSITY, FRESNO

Biological and Biomedical Sciences—General	M

CALIFORNIA STATE UNIVERSITY, FULLERTON

Biological and Biomedical Sciences—General	M

CALIFORNIA STATE UNIVERSITY, LONG BEACH

Biochemistry	M
Biological and Biomedical Sciences—General	M
Microbiology	M
Nutrition	M

CALIFORNIA STATE UNIVERSITY, LOS ANGELES

Biochemistry	M
Biological and Biomedical Sciences—General	M
Nutrition	M

CALIFORNIA STATE UNIVERSITY, NORTHRIDGE

Biochemistry	M
Biological and Biomedical Sciences—General	M

CALIFORNIA STATE UNIVERSITY, SACRAMENTO

Biological and Biomedical Sciences—General	M

CALIFORNIA STATE UNIVERSITY, SAN BERNARDINO

Biological and Biomedical Sciences—General	M

CALIFORNIA STATE UNIVERSITY, SAN MARCOS

Biological and Biomedical Sciences—General	M

CALIFORNIA STATE UNIVERSITY, STANISLAUS

Conservation Biology	M
Ecology	M

CARLETON UNIVERSITY

Biological and Biomedical Sciences—General	M,D
Neuroscience	M,D

CARNEGIE MELLON UNIVERSITY

Biochemistry	M,D
Biological and Biomedical Sciences—General	M,D
Biophysics	M,D
Biopsychology	D

(Case Western, continued)

Cell Biology	M,D
Computational Biology	M,D
Developmental Biology	M,D
Genetics	M,D
Molecular Biology	M,D
Molecular Biophysics	D
Neurobiology	M,D
Neuroscience	D
Structural Biology	D

CASE WESTERN RESERVE UNIVERSITY

Anatomy	M
Biochemistry	M,D
Biological and Biomedical Sciences—General	M,D
Biophysics	M,D
Cancer Biology/Oncology	D
Cell Biology	M,D
Genetics	D
Genomic Sciences	D
Human Genetics	D
Immunology	M,D
Microbiology	D
Molecular Biology	D
Molecular Medicine	D
Molecular Physiology	M,D
Neurobiology	D
Neuroscience	D
Nutrition	M,D*
Pathology	M,D
Pharmacology	D
Physiology	M,D*
Virology	D

THE CATHOLIC UNIVERSITY OF AMERICA

Biological and Biomedical Sciences—General	M,D
Cell Biology	M,D
Microbiology	M,D

CEDARS-SINAI MEDICAL CENTER

Biological and Biomedical Sciences—General	D
Translational Biology	D

CENTRAL CONNECTICUT STATE UNIVERSITY

Biochemistry	M,O
Biological and Biomedical Sciences—General	M,O
Molecular Biology	M

CENTRAL MICHIGAN UNIVERSITY

Biological and Biomedical Sciences—General	M
Conservation Biology	M
Neuroscience	M,D
Nutrition	M,D,O

CENTRAL WASHINGTON UNIVERSITY

Biological and Biomedical Sciences—General	M
Nutrition	M

CHAPMAN UNIVERSITY

Nutrition	M

CHATHAM UNIVERSITY

Biological and Biomedical Sciences—General	M
Environmental Biology	M

CHICAGO STATE UNIVERSITY

Biological and Biomedical Sciences—General	M

THE CITADEL, THE MILITARY COLLEGE OF SOUTH CAROLINA

Biological and Biomedical Sciences—General	M

CITY COLLEGE OF THE CITY UNIVERSITY OF NEW YORK

Biochemistry	M,D
Biological and Biomedical Sciences—General	M,D

CITY OF HOPE NATIONAL MEDICAL CENTER/BECKMAN RESEARCH INSTITUTE

Biological and Biomedical Sciences—General	D*

CLAREMONT GRADUATE UNIVERSITY

Botany	M,D
Computational Biology	M,D

CLARION UNIVERSITY OF PENNSYLVANIA

Biological and Biomedical Sciences—General	M

CLARK ATLANTA UNIVERSITY

Biological and Biomedical Sciences—General	M,D

CLARK UNIVERSITY

Biological and Biomedical Sciences—General	M,D

CLEMSON UNIVERSITY

Biochemistry	D
Biological and Biomedical Sciences—General	M,D
Biophysics	M,D
Ecology	M,D
Entomology	M,D
Evolutionary Biology	M,D
Genetics	M,D
Microbiology	M,D
Molecular Biology	D
Nutrition	M
Plant Biology	M,D

CLEVELAND STATE UNIVERSITY

Biological and Biomedical Sciences—General	M,D
Molecular Medicine	M,D

COLD SPRING HARBOR LABORATORY, WATSON SCHOOL OF BIOLOGICAL SCIENCES

Biological and Biomedical Sciences—General	D*

THE COLLEGE AT BROCKPORT, STATE UNIVERSITY OF NEW YORK

Biological and Biomedical Sciences—General	M

COLLEGE OF CHARLESTON

Marine Biology	M

*M—master's degree; P—first professional degree; D—doctorate; O—other advanced degree; *—Close-Up and / or Display*

COLLEGE OF SAINT ELIZABETH

Nutrition	M,O

COLLEGE OF STATEN ISLAND OF THE CITY UNIVERSITY OF NEW YORK

Biological and Biomedical Sciences—General	M
Neuroscience	M

THE COLLEGE OF WILLIAM AND MARY

Biological and Biomedical Sciences—General	M

COLORADO STATE UNIVERSITY

Biochemistry	M,D
Biological and Biomedical Sciences—General	M,D
Botany	M,D
Cell Biology	M,D
Conservation Biology	M,D
Ecology	M,D
Entomology	M,D
Immunology	M,D
Microbiology	M,D
Molecular Biology	M,D
Neuroscience	D
Nutrition	M,D
Pathology	M,D
Plant Pathology	M,D
Radiation Biology	M,D
Zoology	M,D

COLORADO STATE UNIVERSITY–PUEBLO

Biochemistry	M
Biological and Biomedical Sciences—General	M

COLUMBIA UNIVERSITY

Anatomy	M,D
Biochemistry	M,D
Biological and Biomedical Sciences—General	P,M,D,O
Biophysics	M,D
Biopsychology	M,D
Cell Biology	M,D
Conservation Biology	M,D,O
Developmental Biology	M,D
Ecology	M,D,O
Evolutionary Biology	M,D,O
Genetics	M,D
Microbiology	M,D
Molecular Biology	D
Neurobiology	D
Nutrition	M,D
Pathobiology	M,D
Pathology	M,D
Pharmacology	M,D
Physiology	M,D
Structural Biology	D
Toxicology	M,D

CONCORDIA UNIVERSITY (CANADA)

Biological and Biomedical Sciences—General	M,D,O
Genomic Sciences	M,D,O

CORNELL UNIVERSITY

Anatomy	M,D
Animal Behavior	D
Biochemistry	D
Biological and Biomedical Sciences—General	M,D
Biophysics	D
Biopsychology	D
Cell Biology	M,D

Computational Biology	D
Developmental Biology	M,D
Ecology	M,D
Entomology	M,D
Evolutionary Biology	D
Genetics	D
Immunology	M,D
Infectious Diseases	M,D
Microbiology	D
Molecular Biology	M,D
Molecular Medicine	M,D
Neurobiology	D
Nutrition	M,D
Pharmacology	M,D
Physiology	M,D
Plant Biology	M,D
Plant Molecular Biology	M,D
Plant Pathology	M,D
Plant Physiology	M,D
Reproductive Biology	M,D
Structural Biology	M,D
Toxicology	M,D
Zoology	M,D

CORNELL UNIVERSITY, JOAN AND SANFORD I. WEILL MEDICAL COLLEGE AND GRADUATE SCHOOL OF MEDICAL SCIENCES

Biochemistry	M,D
Biological and Biomedical Sciences—General	M,D
Biophysics	M,D
Cell Biology	M,D
Computational Biology	D
Immunology	M,D
Molecular Biology	M,D
Neuroscience	M,D
Pharmacology	M,D
Physiology	M,D
Structural Biology	M,D
Systems Biology	M,D

CREIGHTON UNIVERSITY

Anatomy	M
Biological and Biomedical Sciences—General	M,D
Immunology	M,D
Medical Microbiology	M,D
Pharmacology	M,D

DALHOUSIE UNIVERSITY

Anatomy	M,D
Biochemistry	M,D
Biological and Biomedical Sciences—General	M,D
Biophysics	M,D
Immunology	M,D
Microbiology	M,D
Neurobiology	M,D
Neuroscience	M,D
Pathology	M,D
Pharmacology	M,D
Physiology	M,D

DARTMOUTH COLLEGE

Biochemistry	D
Biological and Biomedical Sciences—General	D
Cancer Biology/Oncology	D
Cardiovascular Sciences	D
Cell Biology	D
Ecology	D
Evolutionary Biology	D
Genetics	D
Immunology	D
Microbiology	D
Molecular Biology	D
Molecular Medicine	D
Molecular Pathogenesis	D
Molecular Pharmacology	D
Neuroscience	D
Pharmacology	D

Physiology	D
Systems Biology	D
Toxicology	D

DELAWARE STATE UNIVERSITY

Biological and Biomedical Sciences—General	M
Neuroscience	M,D

DELTA STATE UNIVERSITY

Biological and Biomedical Sciences—General	M

DEPAUL UNIVERSITY

Biochemistry	M
Biological and Biomedical Sciences—General	M

DES MOINES UNIVERSITY

Anatomy	M
Biological and Biomedical Sciences—General	M

DOMINICAN UNIVERSITY OF CALIFORNIA

Biological and Biomedical Sciences—General	M

DREW UNIVERSITY

Biological and Biomedical Sciences—General	M

DREXEL UNIVERSITY

Biochemistry	M,D
Biological and Biomedical Sciences—General	M,D,O
Biopsychology	M,D
Cell Biology	M,D
Genetics	M,D
Immunology	M,D
Microbiology	M,D
Molecular Biology	M,D
Molecular Medicine	M
Neuroscience	M,D
Nutrition	M
Pathobiology	M,D
Pharmacology	M,D

DUKE UNIVERSITY

Anatomy	D
Biochemistry	D
Biological and Biomedical Sciences—General	D
Biopsychology	D
Cancer Biology/Oncology	D
Cell Biology	D,O
Developmental Biology	O
Ecology	M,D,O
Genetics	D
Immunology	D
Microbiology	D
Molecular Biology	D,O
Molecular Biophysics	O
Molecular Genetics	D
Neurobiology	D
Neuroscience	D,O
Pathology	M,D
Pharmacology	D
Structural Biology	O
Toxicology	D,O

DUQUESNE UNIVERSITY

Biochemistry	M,D
Biological and Biomedical Sciences—General	M,D
Pharmacology	M,D

D'YOUVILLE COLLEGE

Nutrition	M

EAST CAROLINA UNIVERSITY

Anatomy	D
Biochemistry	D
Biological and Biomedical Sciences—General	M,D
Biophysics	M,D
Cell Biology	D
Immunology	D
Microbiology	D
Molecular Biology	M,D
Nutrition	M
Pathology	D
Pharmacology	D
Physiology	D

EASTERN ILLINOIS UNIVERSITY

Biological and Biomedical Sciences—General	M
Nutrition	M

EASTERN KENTUCKY UNIVERSITY

Biological and Biomedical Sciences—General	M
Ecology	M
Nutrition	M

EASTERN MICHIGAN UNIVERSITY

Biological and Biomedical Sciences—General	M
Cell Biology	M
Ecology	M
Molecular Biology	M
Nutrition	M
Physiology	M

EASTERN NEW MEXICO UNIVERSITY

Biochemistry	M
Biological and Biomedical Sciences—General	M
Cell Biology	M
Ecology	M
Microbiology	M
Molecular Biology	M
Plant Biology	M
Zoology	M

EASTERN VIRGINIA MEDICAL SCHOOL

Biological and Biomedical Sciences—General	M,D
Reproductive Biology	M

EASTERN WASHINGTON UNIVERSITY

Biological and Biomedical Sciences—General	M

EAST STROUDSBURG UNIVERSITY OF PENNSYLVANIA

Biological and Biomedical Sciences—General	M

EAST TENNESSEE STATE UNIVERSITY

Anatomy	D
Biochemistry	D
Biological and Biomedical Sciences—General	M,D
Microbiology	M,D
Nutrition	M

Pharmacology	D
Physiology	D

EDINBORO UNIVERSITY OF PENNSYLVANIA

Biological and Biomedical Sciences—General	M

ELIZABETH CITY STATE UNIVERSITY

Biological and Biomedical Sciences—General	M

EMORY UNIVERSITY

Animal Behavior	D
Biochemistry	D
Biological and Biomedical Sciences—General	D
Biophysics	D
Cancer Biology/Oncology	D
Cell Biology	D
Developmental Biology	D
Ecology	D
Evolutionary Biology	D
Genetics	D
Immunology	D
Microbiology	D
Molecular Biology	D
Molecular Genetics	D
Molecular Pathogenesis	D
Neuroscience	D
Nutrition	M,D
Pharmacology	D

EMPORIA STATE UNIVERSITY

Biological and Biomedical Sciences—General	M
Botany	M
Cell Biology	M
Environmental Biology	M
Microbiology	M
Zoology	M

FAIRLEIGH DICKINSON UNIVERSITY, COLLEGE AT FLORHAM

Biological and Biomedical Sciences—General	M
Pharmacology	M,O

FAIRLEIGH DICKINSON UNIVERSITY, METROPOLITAN CAMPUS

Biological and Biomedical Sciences—General	M

FAYETTEVILLE STATE UNIVERSITY

Biological and Biomedical Sciences—General	M

FISK UNIVERSITY

Biological and Biomedical Sciences—General	M

FITCHBURG STATE UNIVERSITY

Biological and Biomedical Sciences—General	M,O

FLORIDA AGRICULTURAL AND MECHANICAL UNIVERSITY

Biological and Biomedical Sciences—General	M
Entomology	M

Pharmacology	M,D
Toxicology	M,D

FLORIDA ATLANTIC UNIVERSITY

Biological and Biomedical Sciences—General	M,D
Neuroscience	D

FLORIDA INSTITUTE OF TECHNOLOGY

Biochemistry	M,D
Biological and Biomedical Sciences—General	M,D
Cell Biology	M
Ecology	M
Marine Biology	M
Molecular Biology	M

FLORIDA INTERNATIONAL UNIVERSITY

Biological and Biomedical Sciences—General	M,D
Nutrition	M,D

FLORIDA STATE UNIVERSITY

Biochemistry	M,D
Biological and Biomedical Sciences—General	M,D
Cell Biology	M,D
Computational Biology	D
Ecology	M,D
Evolutionary Biology	M,D
Genetics	M,D
Molecular Biology	M,D
Molecular Biophysics	D
Neuroscience	M,D
Nutrition	M,D
Plant Biology	M,D
Structural Biology	M,D

FORDHAM UNIVERSITY

Biological and Biomedical Sciences—General	M,D

FORT HAYS STATE UNIVERSITY

Biological and Biomedical Sciences—General	M

FRAMINGHAM STATE UNIVERSITY

Nutrition	M

FROSTBURG STATE UNIVERSITY

Biological and Biomedical Sciences—General	M
Conservation Biology	M
Ecology	M

GENEVA COLLEGE

Cardiovascular Sciences	M

GEORGE MASON UNIVERSITY

Biochemistry	M,D
Biological and Biomedical Sciences—General	M,D,O
Computational Biology	M,D,O
Evolutionary Biology	M,D
Infectious Diseases	M,D
Microbiology	M,D
Molecular Biology	M,D
Neuroscience	M,D,O
Nutrition	M,O

GEORGETOWN UNIVERSITY

Biochemistry	M,D

Biological and Biomedical Sciences—General	M,D
Biophysics	M,D
Cell Biology	D
Immunology	M,D
Infectious Diseases	M,D
Microbiology	M,D
Molecular Biology	M,D
Neuroscience	D
Pathology	M,D
Pharmacology	M,D
Physiology	M,D
Radiation Biology	M

THE GEORGE WASHINGTON UNIVERSITY

Biochemistry	M,D
Biological and Biomedical Sciences—General	M,D
Genetics	D
Immunology	D
Infectious Diseases	M
Microbiology	M,D,O
Molecular Biology	M,D
Molecular Genetics	M,D
Molecular Medicine	D
Toxicology	M

GEORGIA CAMPUS– PHILADELPHIA COLLEGE OF OSTEOPATHIC MEDICINE

Biological and Biomedical Sciences—General	M,O

GEORGIA COLLEGE & STATE UNIVERSITY

Biological and Biomedical Sciences—General	M

GEORGIA HEALTH SCIENCES UNIVERSITY

Anatomy	M,D
Biochemistry	M,D
Biological and Biomedical Sciences—General	M,D,O
Cardiovascular Sciences	M,D
Cell Biology	M,D
Genomic Sciences	M,D
Molecular Biology	M,D
Molecular Medicine	M,D
Neuroscience	M,D
Pharmacology	M,D
Physiology	M,D

GEORGIA INSTITUTE OF TECHNOLOGY

Biochemistry	M,D
Biological and Biomedical Sciences—General	M,D
Physiology	M

GEORGIAN COURT UNIVERSITY

Biological and Biomedical Sciences—General	M,O

GEORGIA SOUTHERN UNIVERSITY

Biological and Biomedical Sciences—General	M

GEORGIA STATE UNIVERSITY

Biochemistry	M,D
Biological and Biomedical Sciences—General	M,D
Cell Biology	M,D
Environmental Biology	M,D
Microbiology	M,D

Molecular Biology	M,D
Molecular Genetics	M,D
Neurobiology	M,D
Nutrition	M
Physiology	M,D

GERSTNER SLOAN-KETTERING GRADUATE SCHOOL OF BIOMEDICAL SCIENCES

Biological and Biomedical Sciences—General	D
Cancer Biology/Oncology	D*

GOUCHER COLLEGE

Biological and Biomedical Sciences—General	O

GOVERNORS STATE UNIVERSITY

Environmental Biology	M

GRADUATE SCHOOL AND UNIVERSITY CENTER OF THE CITY UNIVERSITY OF NEW YORK

Biochemistry	D
Biological and Biomedical Sciences—General	D
Biopsychology	D
Neuroscience	D

GRAND VALLEY STATE UNIVERSITY

Biological and Biomedical Sciences—General	M
Cell Biology	M
Molecular Biology	M

HAMPTON UNIVERSITY

Biological and Biomedical Sciences—General	M
Environmental Biology	M

HARVARD UNIVERSITY

Biochemistry	D
Biological and Biomedical Sciences—General	M,D,O
Biophysics	D*
Biopsychology	D
Cell Biology	D
Evolutionary Biology	D
Genetics	D
Genomic Sciences	D
Immunology	D
Infectious Diseases	D
Microbiology	D
Molecular Biology	D
Molecular Genetics	D
Molecular Pharmacology	D
Neurobiology	D
Neuroscience	D
Nutrition	D
Pathology	D
Physiology	M,D
Structural Biology	D
Systems Biology	D

HERITAGE UNIVERSITY

Biological and Biomedical Sciences—General	M

HOFSTRA UNIVERSITY

Biological and Biomedical Sciences—General	M,O
Molecular Medicine	P,D

---

*M—master's degree; P—first professional degree; D—doctorate; O—other advanced degree; *—Close-Up and/or Display*

HOOD COLLEGE

Biological and Biomedical Sciences—General	M,O
Environmental Biology	M
Immunology	M,O
Microbiology	M,O
Molecular Biology	M,O

HOWARD UNIVERSITY

Anatomy	M,D
Biochemistry	M,D
Biological and Biomedical Sciences—General	M,D
Biophysics	D
Biopsychology	M,D
Microbiology	D
Molecular Biology	D
Nutrition	M,D
Pharmacology	M,D
Physiology	D

HUMBOLDT STATE UNIVERSITY

Biological and Biomedical Sciences—General	M

HUNTER COLLEGE OF THE CITY UNIVERSITY OF NEW YORK

Animal Behavior	M,D
Biochemistry	M,D
Biological and Biomedical Sciences—General	M,D
Biopsychology	M,D
Neuroscience	M,D
Nutrition	M

HUNTINGTON COLLEGE OF HEALTH SCIENCES

Nutrition	M

ICR GRADUATE SCHOOL

Biological and Biomedical Sciences—General	M

IDAHO STATE UNIVERSITY

Biological and Biomedical Sciences—General	M,D
Medical Microbiology	M,D
Microbiology	M,D
Nutrition	M,O
Pharmacology	M,D

ILLINOIS INSTITUTE OF TECHNOLOGY

Biochemistry	M,D
Biological and Biomedical Sciences—General	M,D
Cell Biology	M,D
Microbiology	M,D
Molecular Biology	M,D
Molecular Biophysics	M,D

ILLINOIS STATE UNIVERSITY

Animal Behavior	M,D
Bacteriology	M,D
Biochemistry	M,D
Biological and Biomedical Sciences—General	M,D
Biophysics	M,D
Botany	M,D
Cell Biology	M,D
Conservation Biology	M,D
Developmental Biology	M,D
Ecology	M,D
Entomology	M,D
Evolutionary Biology	M,D
Genetics	M,D
Immunology	M,D
Microbiology	M,D
Molecular Biology	M,D
Molecular Genetics	M,D
Neurobiology	M,D
Neuroscience	M,D
Parasitology	M,D
Physiology	M,D
Plant Biology	M,D
Plant Molecular Biology	M,D
Structural Biology	M,D
Zoology	M,D

IMMACULATA UNIVERSITY

Nutrition	M

INDIANA STATE UNIVERSITY

Biological and Biomedical Sciences—General	M,D
Ecology	M,D
Microbiology	M,D
Nutrition	M
Physiology	M,D

INDIANA UNIVERSITY BLOOMINGTON

Biochemistry	M,D
Biological and Biomedical Sciences—General	M,D
Cell Biology	M,D
Ecology	M,D
Evolutionary Biology	M,D
Genetics	M,D
Microbiology	M,D
Molecular Biology	M,D
Neuroscience	D
Nutrition	M,D
Plant Biology	M,D
Toxicology	M,D
Zoology	M,D

INDIANA UNIVERSITY OF PENNSYLVANIA

Biological and Biomedical Sciences—General	M
Nutrition	M

INDIANA UNIVERSITY–PURDUE UNIVERSITY FORT WAYNE

Biological and Biomedical Sciences—General	M

INDIANA UNIVERSITY–PURDUE UNIVERSITY INDIANAPOLIS

Anatomy	M,D
Biochemistry	M,D
Biological and Biomedical Sciences—General	M,D
Biopsychology	M,D
Cell Biology	M,D
Immunology	M,D
Microbiology	M,D
Molecular Biology	D
Molecular Genetics	M,D
Nutrition	M,D
Pathology	M,D
Pharmacology	M,D
Toxicology	M,D

INSTITUTO TECNOLOGICO DE SANTO DOMINGO

Nutrition	M,O

INTER AMERICAN UNIVERSITY OF PUERTO RICO, BAYAMÓN CAMPUS

Ecology	M

INTER AMERICAN UNIVERSITY OF PUERTO RICO, METROPOLITAN CAMPUS

Microbiology	M
Molecular Biology	M

INTER AMERICAN UNIVERSITY OF PUERTO RICO, SAN GERMÁN CAMPUS

Environmental Biology	M

IOWA STATE UNIVERSITY OF SCIENCE AND TECHNOLOGY

Biochemistry	M,D*
Biological and Biomedical Sciences—General	M,D
Biophysics	M,D*
Cell Biology	M,D
Computational Biology	M,D
Developmental Biology	M,D
Ecology	M,D
Entomology	M,D
Evolutionary Biology	M,D
Genetics	M,D
Immunology	M,D
Microbiology	M,D
Molecular Biology	M,D*
Neuroscience	M,D
Nutrition	M,D
Pathology	M,D
Plant Biology	M,D
Plant Pathology	M,D
Structural Biology	M,D
Toxicology	M,D

JACKSON STATE UNIVERSITY

Biological and Biomedical Sciences—General	M,D

JACKSONVILLE STATE UNIVERSITY

Biological and Biomedical Sciences—General	M

JAMES MADISON UNIVERSITY

Biological and Biomedical Sciences—General	M

JOHN CARROLL UNIVERSITY

Biological and Biomedical Sciences—General	M

THE JOHNS HOPKINS UNIVERSITY

Anatomy	D
Biochemistry	M,D
Biological and Biomedical Sciences—General	M,D
Biophysics	D
Cell Biology	D
Developmental Biology	D
Evolutionary Biology	D
Genetics	M,D
Human Genetics	D
Immunology	M,D
Infectious Diseases	M,D
Microbiology	M,D
Molecular Biology	M,D
Molecular Biophysics	M,D
Molecular Medicine	D
Neuroscience	D
Nutrition	M,D
Pathobiology	D
Pathology	D
Pharmacology	D
Physiology	M,D
Toxicology	M,D

KANSAS CITY UNIVERSITY OF MEDICINE AND BIOSCIENCES

Biological and Biomedical Sciences—General	M

KANSAS STATE UNIVERSITY

Biochemistry	M,D
Biological and Biomedical Sciences—General	M,D
Entomology	M,D
Genetics	M,D
Microbiology	M,D
Nutrition	M,D
Pathobiology	M,D
Physiology	D
Plant Pathology	M,D

KECK GRADUATE INSTITUTE OF APPLIED LIFE SCIENCES

Biological and Biomedical Sciences—General	M,D,O
Computational Biology	M,D,O

KENT STATE UNIVERSITY

Biochemistry	M,D
Biological and Biomedical Sciences—General	M,D
Cell Biology	M,D
Ecology	M,D
Molecular Biology	M,D
Neuroscience	M,D
Nutrition	M
Pharmacology	M,D
Physiology	M,D

LAKE ERIE COLLEGE OF OSTEOPATHIC MEDICINE

Biological and Biomedical Sciences—General	P,M,O

LAKEHEAD UNIVERSITY

Biological and Biomedical Sciences—General	M

LAMAR UNIVERSITY

Biological and Biomedical Sciences—General	M

LAURENTIAN UNIVERSITY

Biochemistry	M
Biological and Biomedical Sciences—General	M,D
Ecology	M,D

LEHIGH UNIVERSITY

Biochemistry	M,D
Biological and Biomedical Sciences—General	M,D
Molecular Biology	M,D
Neuroscience	M,D

LEHMAN COLLEGE OF THE CITY UNIVERSITY OF NEW YORK

Biological and Biomedical Sciences—General	M
Nutrition	M

LESLEY UNIVERSITY

Ecology	M,D,O

LIPSCOMB UNIVERSITY

Nutrition	M

LOGAN UNIVERSITY–COLLEGE OF CHIROPRACTIC

Nutrition	M

LOMA LINDA UNIVERSITY

Anatomy	M,D
Biochemistry	M,D
Biological and Biomedical Sciences—General	M,D
Microbiology	M,D
Nutrition	M,D
Pathology	M,D
Pharmacology	M,D
Physiology	M,D

LONG ISLAND UNIVERSITY, BROOKLYN CAMPUS

Biological and Biomedical Sciences—General	M
Pharmacology	M,D
Toxicology	M,D

LONG ISLAND UNIVERSITY, C.W. POST CAMPUS

Biological and Biomedical Sciences—General	M
Cardiovascular Sciences	M
Immunology	M
Microbiology	M
Nutrition	M,O

LOUISIANA STATE UNIVERSITY AND AGRICULTURAL AND MECHANICAL COLLEGE

Biochemistry	M,D
Biological and Biomedical Sciences—General	M,D
Biopsychology	M,D
Entomology	M,D
Plant Pathology	M,D
Toxicology	M

LOUISIANA STATE UNIVERSITY HEALTH SCIENCES CENTER

Anatomy	M,D
Biological and Biomedical Sciences—General	M,D
Cell Biology	M,D
Developmental Biology	M,D
Human Genetics	M,D
Immunology	M,D
Microbiology	M,D
Neurobiology	M,D
Neuroscience	M,D
Parasitology	M,D
Pathology	M,D
Pharmacology	M,D
Physiology	M,D

LOUISIANA STATE UNIVERSITY HEALTH SCIENCES CENTER AT SHREVEPORT

Anatomy	M,D
Biochemistry	M,D
Biological and Biomedical Sciences—General	M,D
Cell Biology	M,D
Immunology	M,D
Microbiology	M,D
Molecular Biology	M,D
Pharmacology	D
Physiology	M,D

LOUISIANA TECH UNIVERSITY

Biological and Biomedical Sciences—General	M
Nutrition	M

LOYOLA UNIVERSITY CHICAGO

Anatomy	M,D
Biochemistry	M,D
Biological and Biomedical Sciences—General	M
Cardiovascular Sciences	M,O
Cell Biology	M,D
Immunology	M,D
Infectious Diseases	M,O
Microbiology	M,D
Molecular Biology	M,D
Molecular Physiology	M,D
Neurobiology	M,D
Neuroscience	M,D
Nutrition	M,O
Pharmacology	M,D
Physiology	M,D

MARQUETTE UNIVERSITY

Biological and Biomedical Sciences—General	M,D
Cell Biology	M,D
Developmental Biology	M,D
Ecology	M,D
Genetics	M,D
Microbiology	M,D
Molecular Biology	M,D
Neuroscience	M,D
Physiology	M,D

MARSHALL UNIVERSITY

Biological and Biomedical Sciences—General	M,D
Nutrition	M

MARYWOOD UNIVERSITY

Nutrition	M,O

MASSACHUSETTS COLLEGE OF PHARMACY AND HEALTH SCIENCES

Pharmacology	M,D

MASSACHUSETTS INSTITUTE OF TECHNOLOGY

Biochemistry	D
Biological and Biomedical Sciences—General	P,M,D
Cell Biology	D
Computational Biology	D
Developmental Biology	D
Environmental Biology	M,D,O
Genetics	D
Immunology	D
Microbiology	D
Molecular Biology	D
Molecular Toxicology	D
Neurobiology	D
Neuroscience	D
Structural Biology	D
Systems Biology	D
Toxicology	M,D

MAYO GRADUATE SCHOOL

Biochemistry	D
Biological and Biomedical Sciences—General	D
Cancer Biology/Oncology	D
Cell Biology	D
Genetics	D
Immunology	D
Molecular Biology	D
Molecular Pharmacology	D
Neuroscience	D
Structural Biology	D
Virology	D

MCGILL UNIVERSITY

Anatomy	M,D
Biochemistry	M,D
Biological and Biomedical Sciences—General	M,D
Cell Biology	M,D
Entomology	M,D
Human Genetics	M,D
Immunology	M,D
Microbiology	M,D
Neuroscience	M,D
Nutrition	M,D,O
Parasitology	M,D,O
Pathology	M,D
Pharmacology	M,D
Physiology	M,D

MCMASTER UNIVERSITY

Biochemistry	M,D
Biological and Biomedical Sciences—General	M,D
Cancer Biology/Oncology	M,D
Cardiovascular Sciences	M,D
Cell Biology	M,D
Genetics	M,D
Immunology	M,D
Molecular Biology	M,D
Neuroscience	M,D
Nutrition	M,D
Pharmacology	M,D
Physiology	M,D
Virology	M,D

MCNEESE STATE UNIVERSITY

Nutrition	M

MEDICAL COLLEGE OF WISCONSIN

Biochemistry	D
Biological and Biomedical Sciences—General	M,D,O
Biophysics	D*
Microbiology	M,D
Molecular Genetics	M,D
Neuroscience	D
Pharmacology	D
Physiology	D
Toxicology	D

MEDICAL UNIVERSITY OF SOUTH CAROLINA

Biochemistry	M,D
Biological and Biomedical Sciences—General	M,D
Cancer Biology/Oncology	D
Cardiovascular Sciences	D
Cell Biology	D
Developmental Biology	D
Genetics	D
Immunology	M,D
Microbiology	M,D
Molecular Biology	M,D
Molecular Pharmacology	M,D
Neuroscience	M,D
Pathobiology	D
Pathology	M,D
Toxicology	D

MEHARRY MEDICAL COLLEGE

Biological and Biomedical Sciences—General	D
Cancer Biology/Oncology	D
Immunology	D
Microbiology	D
Neuroscience	D
Pharmacology	D

MEMORIAL UNIVERSITY OF NEWFOUNDLAND

Biochemistry	M,D
Biological and Biomedical Sciences—General	M,D,O
Biopsychology	M,D
Cancer Biology/Oncology	M,D
Cardiovascular Sciences	M,D
Human Genetics	M,D
Immunology	M,D
Marine Biology	M,D
Neuroscience	M,D

MEREDITH COLLEGE

Nutrition	M,O

MIAMI UNIVERSITY

Biochemistry	M,D
Botany	M,D
Microbiology	M,D
Plant Biology	M,D
Zoology	M,D

MICHIGAN STATE UNIVERSITY

Biochemistry	M,D
Biological and Biomedical Sciences—General	M,D
Cell Biology	M,D
Ecology	D
Entomology	M,D
Evolutionary Biology	D
Genetics	M,D
Microbiology	M,D
Molecular Biology	M,D
Molecular Genetics	M,D
Neuroscience	M,D
Nutrition	M,D
Pathobiology	M,D
Pathology	M,D
Pharmacology	M,D
Physiology	M,D
Plant Biology	M,D
Plant Pathology	M,D
Structural Biology	D
Systems Biology	D
Toxicology	M,D
Zoology	M,D

MICHIGAN TECHNOLOGICAL UNIVERSITY

Biological and Biomedical Sciences—General	M,D
Ecology	M
Plant Molecular Biology	M,D

MIDDLE TENNESSEE STATE UNIVERSITY

Biological and Biomedical Sciences—General	M
Nutrition	M

MIDWESTERN STATE UNIVERSITY

Biological and Biomedical Sciences—General	M

MIDWESTERN UNIVERSITY, DOWNERS GROVE CAMPUS

Biological and Biomedical Sciences—General	M

MIDWESTERN UNIVERSITY, GLENDALE CAMPUS

Biological and Biomedical Sciences—General	M
Cardiovascular Sciences	M

*M—master's degree; P—first professional degree; D—doctorate; O—other advanced degree; *—Close-Up and / or Display*

MILLS COLLEGE

Biological and Biomedical Sciences—General	O

MILWAUKEE SCHOOL OF ENGINEERING

Cardiovascular Sciences	M

MINNESOTA STATE UNIVERSITY MANKATO

Biological and Biomedical Sciences—General	M

MISSISSIPPI COLLEGE

Biochemistry	M
Biological and Biomedical Sciences—General	M

MISSISSIPPI STATE UNIVERSITY

Biochemistry	M,D
Biological and Biomedical Sciences—General	M,D
Entomology	M,D
Genetics	M,D
Molecular Biology	M,D
Nutrition	M,D
Plant Pathology	M,D

MISSOURI STATE UNIVERSITY

Biological and Biomedical Sciences—General	M
Cell Biology	M
Molecular Biology	M

MISSOURI UNIVERSITY OF SCIENCE AND TECHNOLOGY

Biological and Biomedical Sciences—General	M
Environmental Biology	M

MONTANA STATE UNIVERSITY

Biochemistry	M,D
Biological and Biomedical Sciences—General	M,D
Ecology	M,D
Immunology	M,D
Infectious Diseases	M,D
Microbiology	M,D
Neuroscience	M,D
Plant Pathology	M,D

MONTCLAIR STATE UNIVERSITY

Biochemistry	M,O
Biological and Biomedical Sciences—General	M,O
Ecology	M,O
Evolutionary Biology	M,O
Molecular Biology	M,O
Nutrition	M,O
Physiology	M,O

MOREHEAD STATE UNIVERSITY

Biological and Biomedical Sciences—General	M

MOREHOUSE SCHOOL OF MEDICINE

Biological and Biomedical Sciences—General	M,D*

MORGAN STATE UNIVERSITY

Biological and Biomedical Sciences—General	M,D
Environmental Biology	D

MOUNT ALLISON UNIVERSITY

Biological and Biomedical Sciences—General	M

MOUNT MARY COLLEGE

Nutrition	M

MOUNT SAINT VINCENT UNIVERSITY

Nutrition	M

MOUNT SINAI SCHOOL OF MEDICINE

Biological and Biomedical Sciences—General	M,D
Neuroscience	M,D

MURRAY STATE UNIVERSITY

Biological and Biomedical Sciences—General	M,D

NEW JERSEY INSTITUTE OF TECHNOLOGY

Biological and Biomedical Sciences—General	M,D
Computational Biology	M

NEW MEXICO INSTITUTE OF MINING AND TECHNOLOGY

Biochemistry	M,D
Biological and Biomedical Sciences—General	M

NEW MEXICO STATE UNIVERSITY

Biological and Biomedical Sciences—General	M,D
Entomology	M
Molecular Biology	M,D
Plant Pathology	M

NEW YORK CHIROPRACTIC COLLEGE

Anatomy	M
Nutrition	M

NEW YORK INSTITUTE OF TECHNOLOGY

Nutrition	M

NEW YORK MEDICAL COLLEGE

Anatomy	M,D
Biochemistry	M,D
Biological and Biomedical Sciences—General	M,D*
Cell Biology	M,D
Immunology	M,D
Microbiology	M,D
Molecular Biology	M,D
Neuroscience	M,D
Pathology	M,D
Pharmacology	M,D
Physiology	M,D

NEW YORK UNIVERSITY

Biological and Biomedical Sciences—General	M,D
Cancer Biology/Oncology	P,M,D
Cell Biology	P,M,D
Computational Biology	D
Developmental Biology	M,D
Genetics	M,D
Immunology	P,M,D
Microbiology	P,M,D
Molecular Biology	P,M,D
Molecular Genetics	M,D
Molecular Pharmacology	D
Molecular Toxicology	M,D
Neurobiology	M,D
Neuroscience	P,M,D
Nutrition	M,D
Parasitology	P,M,D
Pathobiology	P,M,D
Pharmacology	P,M,D
Physiology	P,M,D
Plant Biology	M,D
Structural Biology	P,M,D
Toxicology	M,D

NICHOLLS STATE UNIVERSITY

Environmental Biology	M
Marine Biology	M

NORTH CAROLINA AGRICULTURAL AND TECHNICAL STATE UNIVERSITY

Biological and Biomedical Sciences—General	M
Nutrition	M

NORTH CAROLINA CENTRAL UNIVERSITY

Biological and Biomedical Sciences—General	M

NORTH CAROLINA STATE UNIVERSITY

Biochemistry	D
Biological and Biomedical Sciences—General	M,D,O
Botany	M,D
Cell Biology	M,D
Entomology	M,D
Genetics	M,D
Genomic Sciences	M,D
Immunology	M,D
Infectious Diseases	M,D
Microbiology	M,D
Molecular Toxicology	M,D
Nutrition	M,D
Pathology	M,D
Pharmacology	M,D
Physiology	M,D
Plant Biology	M,D
Plant Pathology	M,D
Toxicology	M,D
Zoology	M,D

NORTH DAKOTA STATE UNIVERSITY

Biochemistry	M,D
Biological and Biomedical Sciences—General	M,D
Botany	M,D
Cell Biology	M,D
Conservation Biology	M,D
Ecology	M,D
Entomology	M,D
Genomic Sciences	M,D
Microbiology	M,D
Molecular Biology	M,D
Molecular Pathogenesis	M,D
Nutrition	M
Pathology	M,D
Plant Pathology	M,D
Zoology	M,D

NORTHEASTERN ILLINOIS UNIVERSITY

Biological and Biomedical Sciences—General	M

NORTHEASTERN UNIVERSITY

Biochemistry	M,D

NORTHERN ARIZONA UNIVERSITY

Biological and Biomedical Sciences—General	M,D
Marine Biology	M,D

NORTHERN ARIZONA UNIVERSITY

Biological and Biomedical Sciences—General	M,D

NORTHERN ILLINOIS UNIVERSITY

Biological and Biomedical Sciences—General	M,D
Nutrition	M

NORTHERN MICHIGAN UNIVERSITY

Biological and Biomedical Sciences—General	M

NORTH SHORE–LIJ GRADUATE SCHOOL OF MOLECULAR MEDICINE

Molecular Medicine	D

NORTHWESTERN UNIVERSITY

Biochemistry	D
Biological and Biomedical Sciences—General	D
Biophysics	D
Biopsychology	D
Cancer Biology/Oncology	D
Cell Biology	D
Developmental Biology	D
Evolutionary Biology	D
Genetics	D
Immunology	D
Microbiology	D
Molecular Biology	D
Neurobiology	M,D
Neuroscience	D
Pharmacology	D
Physiology	M
Reproductive Biology	D
Structural Biology	D
Toxicology	D

NORTHWEST MISSOURI STATE UNIVERSITY

Biological and Biomedical Sciences—General	M

NOTRE DAME DE NAMUR UNIVERSITY

Biological and Biomedical Sciences—General	O

NOVA SCOTIA AGRICULTURAL COLLEGE

Botany	M
Ecology	M
Environmental Biology	M
Physiology	M
Plant Pathology	M
Plant Physiology	M

NOVA SOUTHEASTERN UNIVERSITY

Biological and Biomedical Sciences—General	M,D
Marine Biology	M,D
Pharmacology	M

OAKLAND UNIVERSITY

Biological and Biomedical Sciences—General	M,D

OCCIDENTAL COLLEGE

Biological and Biomedical Sciences—General	M

OGI SCHOOL OF SCIENCE & ENGINEERING AT OREGON HEALTH & SCIENCE UNIVERSITY

Biochemistry	M,D
Molecular Biology	M,D

THE OHIO STATE UNIVERSITY

Anatomy	M,D
Biochemistry	M,D
Biological and Biomedical Sciences—General	D
Biophysics	M,D
Cell Biology	M,D
Developmental Biology	M,D
Ecology	M,D
Entomology	M,D
Evolutionary Biology	M,D
Genetics	M,D
Immunology	D
Microbiology	M,D
Molecular Biology	M,D
Molecular Genetics	M,D
Neuroscience	M,D
Nutrition	M,D
Pathobiology	M,D
Pathology	M
Pharmacology	P,M,D
Physiology	M,D
Plant Pathology	M,D
Toxicology	M,D
Virology	D

OHIO UNIVERSITY

Biochemistry	M,D
Biological and Biomedical Sciences—General	M,D
Cell Biology	M,D
Ecology	M,D
Environmental Biology	M,D
Evolutionary Biology	M,D
Microbiology	M,D
Molecular Biology	M,D
Neuroscience	M,D
Nutrition	M
Physiology	M,D
Plant Biology	M,D

OKLAHOMA STATE UNIVERSITY

Biochemistry	M,D
Botany	M,D
Entomology	M,D
Microbiology	M,D
Molecular Biology	M,D
Molecular Genetics	M,D
Nutrition	M,D
Plant Pathology	M,D
Zoology	M,D

OKLAHOMA STATE UNIVERSITY CENTER FOR HEALTH SCIENCES

Biological and Biomedical Sciences—General	M,D
Molecular Biology	M,O
Toxicology	M,O

OLD DOMINION UNIVERSITY

Biochemistry	M,D
Biological and Biomedical Sciences—General	M,D
Ecology	D

OREGON HEALTH & SCIENCE UNIVERSITY

Biochemistry	M,D
Biological and Biomedical Sciences—General	M,D,O
Biopsychology	D
Cancer Biology/Oncology	D
Cell Biology	D
Computational Biology	M,D,O
Developmental Biology	D
Genetics	D
Immunology	D
Microbiology	D
Molecular Biology	M,D
Neuroscience	D*
Nutrition	M,O
Pharmacology	D
Physiology	D

OREGON STATE UNIVERSITY

Biochemistry	M,D
Biophysics	M,D
Botany	M,D
Cell Biology	M,D
Genetics	M,D
Microbiology	M,D
Molecular Biology	M,D
Molecular Toxicology	M,D
Nutrition	M,D
Plant Pathology	M,D
Plant Physiology	M,D
Toxicology	M,D
Zoology	M,D

PALMER COLLEGE OF CHIROPRACTIC

Anatomy	M

PALO ALTO UNIVERSITY

Biopsychology	D

PENN STATE HERSHEY MEDICAL CENTER

Anatomy	M,D
Biochemistry	M,D
Biological and Biomedical Sciences—General	M,D
Cell Biology	M,D
Genetics	M,D
Immunology	M,D
Microbiology	M,D
Molecular Biology	M,D
Molecular Medicine	M,D
Molecular Toxicology	M,D
Neuroscience	M,D
Pharmacology	M,D
Physiology	M,D
Virology	M,D

PENN STATE UNIVERSITY PARK

Biochemistry	M,D
Biological and Biomedical Sciences—General	M,D
Biopsychology	D
Ecology	M,D
Entomology	M,D
Genetics	M,D
Microbiology	M,D
Molecular Biology	M,D
Nutrition	M,D
Pathobiology	D
Physiology	M,D
Plant Pathology	M,D
Plant Physiology	M,D

PHILADELPHIA COLLEGE OF OSTEOPATHIC MEDICINE

Biological and Biomedical Sciences—General	M,O

PITTSBURG STATE UNIVERSITY

Biological and Biomedical Sciences—General	M

POINT LOMA NAZARENE UNIVERSITY

Biological and Biomedical Sciences—General	M

PONCE SCHOOL OF MEDICINE

Biological and Biomedical Sciences—General	D

PONTIFICAL CATHOLIC UNIVERSITY OF PUERTO RICO

Biological and Biomedical Sciences—General	M

PORTLAND STATE UNIVERSITY

Biological and Biomedical Sciences—General	M,D

PRAIRIE VIEW A&M UNIVERSITY

Biological and Biomedical Sciences—General	M
Toxicology	M

PRINCETON UNIVERSITY

Computational Biology	D
Ecology	D
Evolutionary Biology	D
Marine Biology	D
Molecular Biology	D
Neuroscience	D

PURDUE UNIVERSITY

Anatomy	M,D
Biochemistry	M,D
Biological and Biomedical Sciences—General	M,D
Biophysics	M,D
Botany	M,D
Cell Biology	M,D
Developmental Biology	M,D
Ecology	M,D
Entomology	M,D
Evolutionary Biology	M,D
Genetics	M,D
Immunology	M,D
Microbiology	M,D
Molecular Biology	M,D
Molecular Pharmacology	M,D
Neurobiology	M,D
Nutrition	M,D
Pathobiology	M,D
Pathology	M,D
Pharmacology	M,D
Physiology	M,D
Plant Pathology	M,D
Plant Physiology	M,D
Toxicology	M,D
Virology	M,D

PURDUE UNIVERSITY CALUMET

Biological and Biomedical Sciences—General	M

QUEENS COLLEGE OF THE CITY UNIVERSITY OF NEW YORK

Biochemistry	M

Biological and Biomedical Sciences—General	M

QUEEN'S UNIVERSITY AT KINGSTON

Anatomy	M,D
Biochemistry	M,D
Biological and Biomedical Sciences—General	M,D
Cancer Biology/Oncology	M,D
Cardiovascular Sciences	M,D
Cell Biology	M,D
Immunology	M,D
Microbiology	M,D
Molecular Biology	M,D
Molecular Medicine	M,D
Neurobiology	M,D
Neuroscience	M,D
Pathology	M,D
Pharmacology	M,D
Physiology	M,D
Reproductive Biology	M,D
Toxicology	M,D

QUINNIPIAC UNIVERSITY

Biological and Biomedical Sciences—General	M
Cardiovascular Sciences	M
Cell Biology	M
Microbiology	M
Molecular Biology	M
Pathology	M

RENSSELAER POLYTECHNIC INSTITUTE

Biochemistry	M,D
Biological and Biomedical Sciences—General	M,D
Biophysics	M,D

RHODE ISLAND COLLEGE

Biological and Biomedical Sciences—General	M,O

RICE UNIVERSITY

Biochemistry	M,D
Cell Biology	M,D
Ecology	M,D
Evolutionary Biology	M,D

ROCHESTER INSTITUTE OF TECHNOLOGY

Biological and Biomedical Sciences—General	M

THE ROCKEFELLER UNIVERSITY

Biological and Biomedical Sciences—General	M,D*

ROCKY MOUNTAIN UNIVERSITY OF HEALTH PROFESSIONS

Physiology	D

ROSALIND FRANKLIN UNIVERSITY OF MEDICINE AND SCIENCE

Anatomy	M,D
Biochemistry	M,D
Biological and Biomedical Sciences—General	M,D*
Biophysics	M,D
Cell Biology	M,D
Immunology	M,D
Microbiology	M,D
Molecular Biology	M,D
Molecular Pharmacology	M,D
Neuroscience	D

*M—master's degree; P—first professional degree; D—doctorate; O—other advanced degree; *—Close-Up and/or Display*

Nutrition M
Pathology M
Physiology M,D

RUSH UNIVERSITY

Anatomy M,D
Biochemistry D
Cell Biology M,D
Immunology M,D
Microbiology M,D
Neuroscience M,D
Nutrition M
Pharmacology M,D
Physiology D
Virology M,D

RUTGERS, THE STATE UNIVERSITY OF NEW JERSEY, CAMDEN

Biological and Biomedical
  Sciences—General M

RUTGERS, THE STATE UNIVERSITY OF NEW JERSEY, NEWARK

Biochemistry M,D
Biological and Biomedical
  Sciences—General M,D
Biopsychology D
Computational Biology M
Neuroscience D

RUTGERS, THE STATE UNIVERSITY OF NEW JERSEY, NEW BRUNSWICK

Biochemistry M,D
Biological and Biomedical
  Sciences—General D
Biopsychology D
Cancer Biology/Oncology M,D
Cell Biology M,D
Computational Biology D
Developmental Biology M,D
Ecology M,D
Entomology M,D
Environmental Biology M,D
Evolutionary Biology M,D
Genetics M,D
Immunology M,D
Marine Biology M,D
Medical Microbiology M,D
Microbiology M,D
Molecular Biology M,D
Molecular Biophysics D
Molecular Genetics M,D
Molecular Pharmacology D
Molecular Physiology M,D
Neuroscience M,D
Nutrition M,D
Physiology M,D
Plant Biology M,D
Plant Molecular Biology M,D
Plant Pathology M,D
Reproductive Biology M,D
Systems Biology D
Toxicology M,D
Virology M,D

SACRED HEART UNIVERSITY

Nutrition M,D

SAGE GRADUATE SCHOOL

Nutrition M,O

ST. CLOUD STATE UNIVERSITY

Biological and Biomedical
  Sciences—General M

SAINT FRANCIS UNIVERSITY

Biological and Biomedical
  Sciences—General M

ST. FRANCIS XAVIER UNIVERSITY

Biological and Biomedical
  Sciences—General M

ST. JOHN'S UNIVERSITY (NY)

Biological and Biomedical
  Sciences—General M,D
Toxicology M

SAINT JOSEPH COLLEGE

Biochemistry M
Biological and Biomedical
  Sciences—General M
Nutrition M

SAINT JOSEPH'S UNIVERSITY

Biological and Biomedical
  Sciences—General M

SAINT LOUIS UNIVERSITY

Anatomy M,D
Biochemistry D
Biological and Biomedical
  Sciences—General M,D
Immunology D
Microbiology D
Molecular Biology D
Nutrition M
Pathology D
Pharmacology D
Physiology D

SALISBURY UNIVERSITY

Physiology M

SAM HOUSTON STATE UNIVERSITY

Biological and Biomedical
  Sciences—General M
Nutrition M

SAN DIEGO STATE UNIVERSITY

Biological and Biomedical
  Sciences—General M,D
Cell Biology M,D
Ecology M,D
Microbiology M
Molecular Biology M,D
Nutrition M
Toxicology M,D

SAN FRANCISCO STATE UNIVERSITY

Biochemistry M
Biological and Biomedical
  Sciences—General M
Cell Biology M
Conservation Biology M
Developmental Biology M
Ecology M
Marine Biology M
Microbiology M
Molecular Biology M
Physiology M

SAN JOSE STATE UNIVERSITY

Biological and Biomedical
  Sciences—General M
Ecology M
Microbiology M
Molecular Biology M
Nutrition M
Physiology M

SARAH LAWRENCE COLLEGE

Human Genetics M

SAYBROOK UNIVERSITY

Nutrition M,D,O

THE SCRIPPS RESEARCH INSTITUTE

Biological and Biomedical
  Sciences—General D

SETON HALL UNIVERSITY

Biochemistry M,D
Biological and Biomedical
  Sciences—General M,D
Microbiology M,D
Molecular Biology M,D
Neuroscience M,D

SHIPPENSBURG UNIVERSITY OF PENNSYLVANIA

Biological and Biomedical
  Sciences—General M

SIMMONS COLLEGE

Nutrition M,O

SIMON FRASER UNIVERSITY

Biochemistry M,D
Biological and Biomedical
  Sciences—General M,D
Biophysics M,D
Entomology M,D
Molecular Biology M,D
Toxicology M,D

SMITH COLLEGE

Biological and Biomedical
  Sciences—General M

SONOMA STATE UNIVERSITY

Biological and Biomedical
  Sciences—General M
Environmental Biology M

SOUTH CAROLINA STATE UNIVERSITY

Nutrition M

SOUTH DAKOTA STATE UNIVERSITY

Biological and Biomedical
  Sciences—General M,D
Microbiology M,D
Nutrition M,D

SOUTHEASTERN LOUISIANA UNIVERSITY

Biological and Biomedical
  Sciences—General M

SOUTHEAST MISSOURI STATE UNIVERSITY

Biological and Biomedical
  Sciences—General M
Nutrition M

SOUTHERN CONNECTICUT STATE UNIVERSITY

Biological and Biomedical
  Sciences—General M

SOUTHERN ILLINOIS UNIVERSITY CARBONDALE

Biochemistry M,D
Biological and Biomedical
  Sciences—General M,D
Microbiology M,D
Molecular Biology M,D
Nutrition M
Pharmacology M,D
Physiology M,D
Plant Biology M,D
Zoology M,D

SOUTHERN ILLINOIS UNIVERSITY EDWARDSVILLE

Biological and Biomedical
  Sciences—General M

SOUTHERN METHODIST UNIVERSITY

Biological and Biomedical
  Sciences—General M,D

SOUTHERN UNIVERSITY AND AGRICULTURAL AND MECHANICAL COLLEGE

Biochemistry M
Biological and Biomedical
  Sciences—General M

SOUTHWESTERN OKLAHOMA STATE UNIVERSITY

Microbiology M

STANFORD UNIVERSITY

Biochemistry D
Biological and Biomedical
  Sciences—General M,D
Biophysics D
Cancer Biology/Oncology D
Developmental Biology D
Genetics D
Immunology D
Microbiology D
Molecular Pharmacology D
Neuroscience D
Physiology D
Structural Biology D

STATE UNIVERSITY OF NEW YORK AT BINGHAMTON

Biological and Biomedical
  Sciences—General M,D
Biopsychology M,D

STATE UNIVERSITY OF NEW YORK AT FREDONIA

Biological and Biomedical
  Sciences—General M

STATE UNIVERSITY OF NEW YORK AT NEW PALTZ

Biological and Biomedical Sciences—General	M

STATE UNIVERSITY OF NEW YORK COLLEGE AT ONEONTA

Biological and Biomedical Sciences—General	M
Nutrition	M

STATE UNIVERSITY OF NEW YORK COLLEGE OF ENVIRONMENTAL SCIENCE AND FORESTRY

Biochemistry	M,D
Conservation Biology	M,D
Ecology	M,D
Entomology	M,D
Environmental Biology	M,D
Plant Pathology	M,D

STATE UNIVERSITY OF NEW YORK DOWNSTATE MEDICAL CENTER

Biological and Biomedical Sciences—General	M,D
Cell Biology	D
Molecular Biology	D
Neuroscience	D

STATE UNIVERSITY OF NEW YORK UPSTATE MEDICAL UNIVERSITY

Anatomy	M,D
Biochemistry	M,D
Biological and Biomedical Sciences—General	M,D
Cancer Biology/Oncology	
Cardiovascular Sciences	
Cell Biology	M,D
Immunology	M,D
Infectious Diseases	
Microbiology	M,D
Molecular Biology	M,D
Neuroscience	D
Pharmacology	D
Physiology	M,D

STEPHEN F. AUSTIN STATE UNIVERSITY

Biological and Biomedical Sciences—General	M

STEVENS INSTITUTE OF TECHNOLOGY

Biochemistry	M,D,O

STONY BROOK UNIVERSITY, STATE UNIVERSITY OF NEW YORK

Anatomy	D
Biochemistry	D
Biological and Biomedical Sciences—General	D
Biophysics	D
Biopsychology	D
Cell Biology	M,D
Developmental Biology	M,D
Ecology	M,D
Evolutionary Biology	M,D
Genetics	D
Immunology	M,D
Microbiology	D
Molecular Biology	M,D
Molecular Genetics	D
Molecular Physiology	D
Neuroscience	D
Pathology	M,D
Pharmacology	D

Physiology	D
Structural Biology	D

SUL ROSS STATE UNIVERSITY

Biological and Biomedical Sciences—General	M

SYRACUSE UNIVERSITY

Biochemistry	D
Biological and Biomedical Sciences—General	M,D
Biophysics	D
Nutrition	M
Structural Biology	D

TARLETON STATE UNIVERSITY

Biological and Biomedical Sciences—General	M

TEACHERS COLLEGE, COLUMBIA UNIVERSITY

Neuroscience	M
Nutrition	M,D
Physiology	M,D

TEMPLE UNIVERSITY

Anatomy	M,D
Biochemistry	M,D
Biological and Biomedical Sciences—General	M,D
Cell Biology	M,D
Genetics	M,D
Immunology	M,D
Microbiology	M,D
Molecular Biology	M,D
Neuroscience	M,D
Pathology	D
Pharmacology	D
Physiology	D

TENNESSEE STATE UNIVERSITY

Biological and Biomedical Sciences—General	M,D

TENNESSEE TECHNOLOGICAL UNIVERSITY

Biological and Biomedical Sciences—General	M,D

TEXAS A&M HEALTH SCIENCE CENTER

Biological and Biomedical Sciences—General	M,D
Cell Biology	D
Immunology	D
Microbiology	D
Molecular Biology	D
Molecular Medicine	D
Molecular Pathogenesis	D
Neuroscience	D
Systems Biology	D
Translational Biology	D
Virology	D

TEXAS A&M INTERNATIONAL UNIVERSITY

Biological and Biomedical Sciences—General	M

TEXAS A&M UNIVERSITY

Biochemistry	M,D
Biological and Biomedical Sciences—General	M,D
Biophysics	M,D
Biopsychology	D

Botany	M,D
Cell Biology	M,D
Entomology	M,D
Genetics	M,D
Microbiology	M,D
Neuroscience	M,D
Nutrition	M,D
Parasitology	M,D
Pathobiology	M,D
Pathology	M,D
Physiology	M,D
Plant Biology	M,D
Plant Pathology	M,D
Toxicology	M,D
Zoology	M,D

TEXAS A&M UNIVERSITY AT GALVESTON

Marine Biology	M,D

TEXAS A&M UNIVERSITY–COMMERCE

Biological and Biomedical Sciences—General	M

TEXAS A&M UNIVERSITY–CORPUS CHRISTI

Biological and Biomedical Sciences—General	M

TEXAS A&M UNIVERSITY–KINGSVILLE

Biological and Biomedical Sciences—General	M

TEXAS CHRISTIAN UNIVERSITY

Biochemistry	M,D
Biological and Biomedical Sciences—General	M
Neuroscience	M,D

TEXAS SOUTHERN UNIVERSITY

Biological and Biomedical Sciences—General	M
Toxicology	M,D

TEXAS STATE UNIVERSITY–SAN MARCOS

Biochemistry	M
Biological and Biomedical Sciences—General	M
Conservation Biology	M
Marine Biology	M,D
Nutrition	M

TEXAS TECH UNIVERSITY

Biological and Biomedical Sciences—General	M,D
Microbiology	M,D
Nutrition	M,D
Toxicology	M,D
Zoology	M,D

TEXAS TECH UNIVERSITY HEALTH SCIENCES CENTER

Biochemistry	M,D
Biological and Biomedical Sciences—General	M,D
Cell Biology	M,D
Medical Microbiology	M,D
Molecular Biophysics	M,D
Molecular Genetics	M,D
Molecular Pathology	M
Molecular Physiology	M,D
Neuroscience	M,D
Pharmacology	M,D

TEXAS WOMAN'S UNIVERSITY

Biological and Biomedical Sciences—General	M,D
Molecular Biology	M,D
Nutrition	M,D

THOMAS JEFFERSON UNIVERSITY

Biochemistry	D
Biological and Biomedical Sciences—General	M,D,O
Biophysics	D
Cell Biology	M,D
Developmental Biology	M,D
Genetics	D
Immunology	D
Microbiology	M,D
Molecular Biology	D
Molecular Pharmacology	D
Molecular Physiology	D
Neuroscience	D
Pharmacology	M
Structural Biology	D

TOWSON UNIVERSITY

Biological and Biomedical Sciences—General	M

TRENT UNIVERSITY

Biological and Biomedical Sciences—General	M,D

TROPICAL AGRICULTURE RESEARCH AND HIGHER EDUCATION CENTER

Conservation Biology	M,D

TRUMAN STATE UNIVERSITY

Biological and Biomedical Sciences—General	M

TUFTS UNIVERSITY

Biochemistry	D
Biological and Biomedical Sciences—General	P,M,D
Cell Biology	D
Developmental Biology	D
Genetics	D
Immunology	D
Microbiology	D
Molecular Biology	D
Molecular Physiology	D
Neuroscience	D
Nutrition	M,D
Pharmacology	D
Physiology	D

TULANE UNIVERSITY

Biochemistry	M,D
Biological and Biomedical Sciences—General	M,D
Cell Biology	M,D
Ecology	M,D
Evolutionary Biology	M,D
Human Genetics	M,D
Immunology	M,D
Infectious Diseases	M,D,O
Microbiology	M,D
Molecular Biology	M,D
Neuroscience	M,D
Nutrition	M
Parasitology	M,D,O
Pharmacology	M,D
Physiology	M,D
Structural Biology	M,D

*M—master's degree; P—first professional degree; D—doctorate; O—other advanced degree; *—Close-Up and/or Display*

TUSKEGEE UNIVERSITY

Biological and Biomedical Sciences—General	M,D
Nutrition	M

UNIFORMED SERVICES UNIVERSITY OF THE HEALTH SCIENCES

Biological and Biomedical Sciences—General	M,D
Cell Biology	D*
Immunology	D
Infectious Diseases	D*
Molecular Biology	D*
Neuroscience	D*
Zoology	M,D

UNIVERSIDAD CENTRAL DEL CARIBE

Anatomy	M,D
Biochemistry	M,D
Biological and Biomedical Sciences—General	M,D
Cell Biology	M,D
Immunology	M,D
Microbiology	M,D
Molecular Biology	M,D
Pharmacology	M,D
Physiology	M,D

UNIVERSIDAD DE CIENCIAS MEDICAS

Anatomy	P,M,O
Biological and Biomedical Sciences—General	P,M,O

UNIVERSIDAD DE IBEROAMERICA

Neuroscience	P,M,D

UNIVERSIDAD DEL TURABO

Environmental Biology	M,D

UNIVERSIDAD NACIONAL PEDRO HENRIQUEZ URENA

Ecology	M

UNIVERSITÉ DE MONCTON

Biochemistry	M
Biological and Biomedical Sciences—General	M
Nutrition	M

UNIVERSITÉ DE MONTRÉAL

Biochemistry	M,D,O
Biological and Biomedical Sciences—General	M,D
Cell Biology	M,D
Genetics	O
Immunology	M,D
Microbiology	M,D
Molecular Biology	M,D
Neuroscience	M,D
Nutrition	M,D,O
Pathology	M,D
Pharmacology	M,D
Physiology	M,D
Toxicology	O
Virology	D

UNIVERSITÉ DE SHERBROOKE

Biochemistry	M,D
Biological and Biomedical Sciences—General	M,D,O
Biophysics	M,D
Cell Biology	M,D
Immunology	M,D
Microbiology	M,D

Pharmacology	M,D
Physiology	M,D
Radiation Biology	M,D

UNIVERSITÉ DU QUÉBEC À CHICOUTIMI

Genetics	M

UNIVERSITÉ DU QUÉBEC À MONTRÉAL

Biological and Biomedical Sciences—General	M,D

UNIVERSITÉ DU QUÉBEC À TROIS-RIVIÈRES

Biophysics	M,D

UNIVERSITÉ DU QUÉBEC EN ABITIBI-TÉMISCAMINGUE

Biological and Biomedical Sciences—General	M,D

UNIVERSITÉ DU QUÉBEC, INSTITUT NATIONAL DE LA RECHERCHE SCIENTIFIQUE

Biological and Biomedical Sciences—General	M,D
Immunology	M,D
Medical Microbiology	M,D
Microbiology	M,D
Virology	M,D

UNIVERSITÉ LAVAL

Anatomy	M,D,O
Biochemistry	M,D,O
Biological and Biomedical Sciences—General	M,D,O
Cancer Biology/Oncology	O
Cardiovascular Sciences	O
Cell Biology	M,D
Immunology	M,D
Infectious Diseases	O
Microbiology	M,D
Molecular Biology	M,D
Neurobiology	M,D
Nutrition	M,D
Pathology	O
Physiology	M,D
Plant Biology	M,D

UNIVERSITY AT ALBANY, STATE UNIVERSITY OF NEW YORK

Biochemistry	M,D
Biological and Biomedical Sciences—General	M,D
Biopsychology	M,D,O
Cell Biology	M,D
Conservation Biology	M
Developmental Biology	M,D
Ecology	M,D
Evolutionary Biology	M,D
Genetics	M,D
Immunology	M,D
Molecular Biology	M,D
Molecular Pathogenesis	M,D
Neurobiology	M,D
Neuroscience	M,D
Structural Biology	M,D
Toxicology	M,D

UNIVERSITY AT BUFFALO, THE STATE UNIVERSITY OF NEW YORK

Anatomy	M,D
Biochemistry	M,D
Biological and Biomedical Sciences—General	M,D
Biophysics	M,D
Cancer Biology/Oncology	M,D

Cell Biology	D
Ecology	M,D,O
Evolutionary Biology	M,D,O
Immunology	M,D
Microbiology	M,D
Molecular Biology	D
Molecular Pharmacology	D
Neuroscience	M,D
Nutrition	M,D
Pathology	M,D
Pharmacology	M,D
Physiology	M,D
Structural Biology	M,D
Toxicology	M,D

THE UNIVERSITY OF AKRON

Biological and Biomedical Sciences—General	M,D
Nutrition	M

THE UNIVERSITY OF ALABAMA

Biological and Biomedical Sciences—General	M,D
Nutrition	M

THE UNIVERSITY OF ALABAMA AT BIRMINGHAM

Biochemistry	D
Biological and Biomedical Sciences—General	M,D*
Cell Biology	D
Genetics	D
Microbiology	D
Molecular Biology	D
Molecular Genetics	D
Molecular Physiology	D
Neurobiology	D
Nutrition	M,D
Pathology	D
Pharmacology	D
Toxicology	D

THE UNIVERSITY OF ALABAMA IN HUNTSVILLE

Biological and Biomedical Sciences—General	M

UNIVERSITY OF ALASKA ANCHORAGE

Biological and Biomedical Sciences—General	M

UNIVERSITY OF ALASKA FAIRBANKS

Biochemistry	M,D
Biological and Biomedical Sciences—General	M,D
Botany	M,D
Marine Biology	M,D
Nutrition	M,D
Zoology	M,D

UNIVERSITY OF ALBERTA

Biochemistry	M,D
Biological and Biomedical Sciences—General	P,M,D
Cancer Biology/Oncology	M,D
Cell Biology	M,D
Conservation Biology	M,D
Ecology	M,D
Environmental Biology	M,D
Evolutionary Biology	M,D
Genetics	M,D
Immunology	M,D
Medical Microbiology	M,D
Microbiology	M,D
Molecular Biology	M,D
Neuroscience	M,D
Pathology	M,D

Pharmacology	M,D
Physiology	M,D
Plant Biology	M,D

THE UNIVERSITY OF ARIZONA

Anatomy	D
Biochemistry	D
Biological and Biomedical Sciences—General	M
Cancer Biology/Oncology	D
Cell Biology	M,D
Ecology	M,D
Entomology	M,D
Evolutionary Biology	M,D
Genetics	M,D
Immunology	M,D
Microbiology	M,D
Molecular Biology	M,D
Neuroscience	D
Nutrition	M,D
Pathobiology	M,D
Pharmacology	M,D
Physiology	M,D
Plant Pathology	M,D

UNIVERSITY OF ARKANSAS

Biological and Biomedical Sciences—General	M,D
Cell Biology	M,D
Entomology	M,D
Molecular Biology	M,D
Plant Pathology	M

UNIVERSITY OF ARKANSAS AT LITTLE ROCK

Biological and Biomedical Sciences—General	M

UNIVERSITY OF ARKANSAS FOR MEDICAL SCIENCES

Anatomy	M,D
Biochemistry	M,D
Biological and Biomedical Sciences—General	M,D,O
Biophysics	M,D
Immunology	M,D
Microbiology	M,D
Molecular Biology	M,D
Neurobiology	M,D
Nutrition	M
Pathology	M
Pharmacology	M,D
Physiology	M,D
Toxicology	M,D

UNIVERSITY OF BRIDGEPORT

Nutrition	M

THE UNIVERSITY OF BRITISH COLUMBIA

Anatomy	M,D
Biochemistry	M,D
Biopsychology	M,D
Botany	M,D
Cell Biology	M,D
Genetics	M,D
Immunology	M,D
Microbiology	M,D
Molecular Biology	M,D
Neuroscience	M,D
Nutrition	M,D
Pathology	M,D
Pharmacology	M,D
Physiology	M,D
Reproductive Biology	M,D
Zoology	M,D

UNIVERSITY OF CALGARY

Biochemistry	M,D

Biological and Biomedical Sciences—General	M,D
Cancer Biology/Oncology	M,D
Cardiovascular Sciences	M,D
Immunology	M,D
Infectious Diseases	M,D
Microbiology	M,D
Molecular Biology	M,D
Neuroscience	M,D

UNIVERSITY OF CALIFORNIA, BERKELEY

Biochemistry	D
Biological and Biomedical Sciences—General	D
Biophysics	D
Cell Biology	D
Immunology	D
Infectious Diseases	M,D
Microbiology	D
Molecular Biology	D
Molecular Toxicology	D
Neuroscience	D*
Nutrition	D
Physiology	M,D
Plant Biology	D

UNIVERSITY OF CALIFORNIA, DAVIS

Animal Behavior	D
Biochemistry	M,D
Biophysics	M,D
Cell Biology	M,D
Developmental Biology	M,D
Ecology	M,D
Entomology	M,D
Evolutionary Biology	D
Genetics	M,D
Immunology	M,D
Microbiology	M,D
Molecular Biology	M,D
Neuroscience	D
Nutrition	M,D
Pathology	M,D
Pharmacology	M,D
Physiology	M,D
Plant Biology	M,D
Plant Pathology	M,D
Toxicology	M,D
Zoology	M

UNIVERSITY OF CALIFORNIA, IRVINE

Anatomy	M,D
Biochemistry	M,D
Biological and Biomedical Sciences—General	M,D
Biophysics	D
Cell Biology	M,D
Computational Biology	D
Developmental Biology	M,D
Ecology	M,D
Evolutionary Biology	M,D
Genetics	D
Microbiology	M,D
Molecular Biology	M,D
Molecular Genetics	M,D
Neurobiology	M,D
Neuroscience	D
Pathology	D
Pharmacology	M,D*
Physiology	D
Systems Biology	D
Toxicology	M,D

UNIVERSITY OF CALIFORNIA, LOS ANGELES

Anatomy	D
Biochemistry	M,D

Biological and Biomedical Sciences—General	M,D
Cell Biology	D
Developmental Biology	D
Ecology	M,D
Evolutionary Biology	M,D
Human Genetics	M,D
Immunology	M,D
Microbiology	M,D
Molecular Biology	M,D
Molecular Genetics	M,D
Molecular Toxicology	D
Neurobiology	D
Neuroscience	D
Pathology	M,D
Pharmacology	D
Physiology	M,D
Toxicology	D

UNIVERSITY OF CALIFORNIA, MERCED

Biological and Biomedical Sciences—General	M,D
Systems Biology	M,D

UNIVERSITY OF CALIFORNIA, RIVERSIDE

Biochemistry	M,D
Biological and Biomedical Sciences—General	M,D
Botany	M,D
Cell Biology	M,D
Developmental Biology	M,D
Ecology	M,D
Entomology	M,D
Evolutionary Biology	M,D
Genetics	D
Genomic Sciences	D
Microbiology	M,D
Molecular Biology	M,D
Molecular Genetics	D
Neuroscience	D
Plant Biology	M,D
Plant Pathology	M,D
Toxicology	M,D

UNIVERSITY OF CALIFORNIA, SAN DIEGO

Biochemistry	M,D
Biological and Biomedical Sciences—General	M,D
Biophysics	M,D
Cancer Biology/Oncology	D
Cardiovascular Sciences	D
Cell Biology	D
Developmental Biology	D
Ecology	D
Evolutionary Biology	D
Genetics	D
Immunology	D
Marine Biology	D
Microbiology	D
Molecular Biology	D
Molecular Pathology	D
Neurobiology	D
Neuroscience	D
Pharmacology	D
Physiology	D
Plant Biology	D
Plant Molecular Biology	D
Structural Biology	D
Systems Biology	D
Virology	D

UNIVERSITY OF CALIFORNIA, SAN FRANCISCO

Anatomy	D
Biochemistry	D

Biological and Biomedical Sciences—General	D
Biophysics	D
Cell Biology	D
Developmental Biology	D
Genetics	D
Genomic Sciences	D
Immunology	D
Microbiology	D
Molecular Biology	D
Neuroscience	D
Pathology	D
Pharmacology	D
Physiology	D

UNIVERSITY OF CALIFORNIA, SANTA BARBARA

Biochemistry	D
Biophysics	D
Cell Biology	M,D
Developmental Biology	M,D
Ecology	M,D
Evolutionary Biology	M,D
Marine Biology	M,D
Molecular Biology	M,D

UNIVERSITY OF CALIFORNIA, SANTA CRUZ

Biochemistry	M,D
Cell Biology	M,D
Developmental Biology	M,D
Ecology	M,D
Environmental Biology	M,D
Evolutionary Biology	M,D
Molecular Biology	M,D
Toxicology	M,D

UNIVERSITY OF CENTRAL ARKANSAS

Biological and Biomedical Sciences—General	M

UNIVERSITY OF CENTRAL FLORIDA

Biological and Biomedical Sciences—General	M,D,O
Conservation Biology	M,D,O

UNIVERSITY OF CENTRAL MISSOURI

Biological and Biomedical Sciences—General	M,D

UNIVERSITY OF CENTRAL OKLAHOMA

Biological and Biomedical Sciences—General	M
Nutrition	M

UNIVERSITY OF CHICAGO

Anatomy	D
Biochemistry	D
Biological and Biomedical Sciences—General	D
Biophysics	D
Cancer Biology/Oncology	D
Cell Biology	D
Developmental Biology	D
Ecology	D
Evolutionary Biology	D
Genetics	D
Genomic Sciences	D
Human Genetics	D
Immunology	D
Microbiology	D
Molecular Biology	D
Molecular Medicine	D

Molecular Pathogenesis	D
Molecular Physiology	D
Neurobiology	D
Neuroscience	D
Nutrition	D
Pathology	D
Pharmacology	D
Physiology	D
Systems Biology	D
Zoology	D

UNIVERSITY OF CINCINNATI

Biochemistry	M,D
Biological and Biomedical Sciences—General	M,D
Biophysics	D
Cancer Biology/Oncology	D
Cell Biology	D
Developmental Biology	D
Genomic Sciences	M,D
Immunology	M,D
Microbiology	M,D
Molecular Biology	M,D
Molecular Genetics	M,D
Molecular Medicine	D
Molecular Toxicology	M,D
Neuroscience	D
Nutrition	M
Pathobiology	D
Pathology	D
Pharmacology	D
Physiology	D

UNIVERSITY OF COLORADO AT COLORADO SPRINGS

Biological and Biomedical Sciences—General	M
Nutrition	M

UNIVERSITY OF COLORADO BOULDER

Animal Behavior	M,D
Biochemistry	M,D
Cell Biology	M,D
Developmental Biology	M,D
Ecology	M,D
Evolutionary Biology	M,D
Genetics	M,D
Marine Biology	M,D
Microbiology	M,D
Molecular Biology	M,D
Neurobiology	M,D
Physiology	M,D

UNIVERSITY OF COLORADO DENVER

Biochemistry	D
Biological and Biomedical Sciences—General	M,D
Cancer Biology/Oncology	D
Cell Biology	D
Computational Biology	D
Developmental Biology	D
Ecology	M
Genetics	D
Immunology	D
Microbiology	D
Molecular Biology	D
Neuroscience	D
Pharmacology	D
Physiology	D
Toxicology	D

UNIVERSITY OF CONNECTICUT

Biochemistry	M,D
Biological and Biomedical Sciences—General	D
Biophysics	M,D
Biopsychology	M,D,O

*M—master's degree; P—first professional degree; D—doctorate; O—other advanced degree; *—Close-Up and/or Display*

University of Connecticut (continued)

Botany	M,D
Cell Biology	M,D
Developmental Biology	M,D
Ecology	M,D,O
Entomology	M,D
Genetics	M,D
Genomic Sciences	M
Microbiology	M,D
Molecular Biology	M
Neurobiology	M,D*
Neuroscience	M,D,O
Nutrition	M,D
Pathobiology	M,D
Pharmacology	M,D
Physiology	M,D*
Plant Biology	M,D
Plant Molecular Biology	M,D
Structural Biology	M,D
Toxicology	M,D
Zoology	M,D

UNIVERSITY OF CONNECTICUT HEALTH CENTER

Biochemistry	D*
Biological and Biomedical Sciences—General	D*
Cell Biology	D*
Developmental Biology	D*
Genetics	D*
Immunology	D*
Molecular Biology	D*
Neuroscience	D*

UNIVERSITY OF DAYTON

Biological and Biomedical Sciences—General	M,D

UNIVERSITY OF DELAWARE

Biochemistry	M,D
Biological and Biomedical Sciences—General	M,D
Cancer Biology/Oncology	M,D
Cell Biology	M,D
Developmental Biology	M,D
Ecology	M,D
Entomology	M,D
Evolutionary Biology	M,D
Genetics	M,D
Microbiology	M,D
Molecular Biology	M,D
Neuroscience	D
Nutrition	M
Physiology	M,D

UNIVERSITY OF DENVER

Biological and Biomedical Sciences—General	M,D
Neuroscience	D

UNIVERSITY OF DETROIT MERCY

Biochemistry	M

UNIVERSITY OF FLORIDA

Biochemistry	M,D
Biological and Biomedical Sciences—General	D
Botany	M,D
Cell Biology	M,D
Ecology	M,D
Entomology	M,D
Genetics	D
Genomic Sciences	D
Immunology	D
Microbiology	M,D
Molecular Biology	M,D
Molecular Genetics	M,D
Neuroscience	M,D
Nutrition	M,D
Pathology	D

Pharmacology	M,D
Physiology	M,D
Plant Biology	M,D
Plant Molecular Biology	M,D
Plant Pathology	M,D
Toxicology	M,D,O
Zoology	M,D

UNIVERSITY OF GEORGIA

Anatomy	M
Biochemistry	M,D
Biological and Biomedical Sciences—General	D
Cell Biology	M,D
Ecology	M,D
Entomology	M,D
Genetics	M,D
Genomic Sciences	M,D
Infectious Diseases	M,D
Microbiology	M,D
Molecular Biology	M,D
Neuroscience	D
Nutrition	M,D
Pathology	M,D
Pharmacology	M,D
Physiology	M,D
Plant Biology	M,D
Plant Pathology	M,D
Toxicology	M,D

UNIVERSITY OF GUAM

Biological and Biomedical Sciences—General	M
Marine Biology	M

UNIVERSITY OF GUELPH

Anatomy	M,D
Biochemistry	M,D
Biological and Biomedical Sciences—General	M,D
Biophysics	M,D
Botany	M,D
Cardiovascular Sciences	M,D,O
Cell Biology	M,D
Ecology	M,D
Entomology	M,D
Environmental Biology	M,D
Evolutionary Biology	M,D
Immunology	M,D,O
Infectious Diseases	M,D,O
Microbiology	M,D
Molecular Biology	M,D
Molecular Genetics	M,D
Neuroscience	M,D,O
Nutrition	M,D
Pathology	M,D,O
Pharmacology	M,D
Physiology	M,D
Plant Pathology	M,D
Toxicology	M,D
Zoology	M,D

UNIVERSITY OF HARTFORD

Biological and Biomedical Sciences—General	M
Neuroscience	M

UNIVERSITY OF HAWAII AT HILO

Conservation Biology	M
Marine Biology	M

UNIVERSITY OF HAWAII AT MANOA

Biological and Biomedical Sciences—General	M,D
Botany	M,D
Conservation Biology	M,D
Developmental Biology	M,D
Ecology	M,D

Entomology	M,D
Evolutionary Biology	M,D
Genetics	M,D
Marine Biology	M,D
Medical Microbiology	M,D
Microbiology	M,D
Molecular Biology	M,D
Nutrition	M,D
Physiology	M,D
Plant Pathology	M,D
Reproductive Biology	M,D
Zoology	M,D

UNIVERSITY OF HOUSTON

Biochemistry	M,D
Biological and Biomedical Sciences—General	M,D
Nutrition	M,D
Pharmacology	P,M,D

UNIVERSITY OF HOUSTON–CLEAR LAKE

Biological and Biomedical Sciences—General	M

UNIVERSITY OF IDAHO

Biochemistry	M,D
Biological and Biomedical Sciences—General	M,D
Computational Biology	M,D
Entomology	M,D
Microbiology	M,D
Molecular Biology	M,D
Neuroscience	M,D

UNIVERSITY OF ILLINOIS AT CHICAGO

Anatomy	D
Biochemistry	D
Biological and Biomedical Sciences—General	M,D
Biophysics	M,D
Cell Biology	D
Genetics	D
Immunology	D
Microbiology	D
Molecular Biology	D
Molecular Genetics	D
Neurobiology	D
Neuroscience	D
Nutrition	M,D
Pharmacology	D
Physiology	M,D

UNIVERSITY OF ILLINOIS AT SPRINGFIELD

Biological and Biomedical Sciences—General	M

UNIVERSITY OF ILLINOIS AT URBANA–CHAMPAIGN

Biochemistry	M,D
Biological and Biomedical Sciences—General	M,D
Biophysics	M,D
Cell Biology	D
Computational Biology	M,D
Conservation Biology	M,D
Developmental Biology	D
Ecology	M,D
Entomology	M,D
Evolutionary Biology	M,D
Microbiology	M,D
Molecular Physiology	M,D
Neuroscience	D
Nutrition	M,D
Pathobiology	M,D
Physiology	M,D

Plant Biology	M,D
Zoology	M,D

UNIVERSITY OF INDIANAPOLIS

Biological and Biomedical Sciences—General	M

THE UNIVERSITY OF IOWA

Anatomy	D
Bacteriology	M,D
Biochemistry	M,D
Biological and Biomedical Sciences—General	M,D
Biophysics	M,D
Cell Biology	M,D
Computational Biology	M,D,O
Evolutionary Biology	M,D
Genetics	M,D
Immunology	M,D
Microbiology	M,D
Molecular Biology	D
Neurobiology	M,D
Neuroscience	D
Pathology	M
Pharmacology	M,D
Physiology	M,D
Radiation Biology	M,D
Toxicology	M,D
Translational Biology	M,D
Virology	M,D

THE UNIVERSITY OF KANSAS

Anatomy	M,D
Biochemistry	M,D
Biological and Biomedical Sciences—General	M,D*
Biophysics	M,D
Botany	M,D
Cell Biology	M,D
Developmental Biology	M,D
Ecology	M,D
Entomology	M,D
Evolutionary Biology	M,D
Microbiology	M,D
Molecular Biology	M,D
Neuroscience	M,D
Nutrition	M,D,O
Pathology	M,D
Pharmacology	M,D
Physiology	M,D
Toxicology	M,D

UNIVERSITY OF KENTUCKY

Anatomy	D
Biochemistry	D
Biological and Biomedical Sciences—General	M,D
Entomology	M,D
Microbiology	D
Neurobiology	D
Nutrition	M,D
Pharmacology	D
Physiology	M,D
Plant Pathology	M,D
Plant Physiology	D
Toxicology	M,D

UNIVERSITY OF LETHBRIDGE

Biochemistry	M,D
Biological and Biomedical Sciences—General	M,D
Molecular Biology	M,D
Neuroscience	M,D

UNIVERSITY OF LOUISIANA AT LAFAYETTE

Biological and Biomedical Sciences—General	M,D

Environmental Biology — M,D
Evolutionary Biology — M,D

UNIVERSITY OF LOUISIANA AT MONROE

Biological and Biomedical
  Sciences—General — M

UNIVERSITY OF LOUISVILLE

Anatomy — M,D
Biochemistry — M,D
Biological and Biomedical
  Sciences—General — M,D
Biophysics — M,D
Environmental Biology — M,D
Immunology — M,D
Microbiology — M,D
Molecular Biology — M,D
Neurobiology — M,D
Pharmacology — M,D
Physiology — M,D
Toxicology — M,D

UNIVERSITY OF MAINE

Biochemistry — M,D
Biological and Biomedical
  Sciences—General — D
Botany — M
Cell Biology — D
Ecology — M,D
Entomology — M
Genomic Sciences — D
Marine Biology — M,D
Microbiology — M,D
Molecular Biology — M,D
Neuroscience — D
Nutrition — M,D
Plant Biology — M,D
Plant Pathology — M
Toxicology — D
Zoology — M,D

THE UNIVERSITY OF MANCHESTER

Biochemistry — M,D
Biological and Biomedical
  Sciences—General — M,D
Biophysics — M,D
Cancer Biology/Oncology — M,D
Cell Biology — M,D
Developmental Biology — M,D
Ecology — M,D
Environmental Biology — M,D
Evolutionary Biology — M,D
Genetics — M,D
Immunology — M,D
Microbiology — M,D
Molecular Biology — M,D
Molecular Genetics — M,D
Neurobiology — M,D
Neuroscience — M,D
Pharmacology — M,D
Physiology — M,D
Structural Biology — M,D
Toxicology — M,D

UNIVERSITY OF MANITOBA

Anatomy — M,D
Biochemistry — M,D
Biological and Biomedical
  Sciences—General — M,D,O
Botany — M,D
Cancer Biology/Oncology — M
Ecology — M,D
Entomology — M,D
Human Genetics — M,D
Immunology — M,D
Medical Microbiology — M,D
Microbiology — M,D

Nutrition — M,D
Pathology — M
Pharmacology — M,D
Physiology — M,D
Plant Physiology — M,D
Zoology — M,D

UNIVERSITY OF MARY

Cardiovascular Sciences — M

UNIVERSITY OF MARYLAND, BALTIMORE

Biochemistry — M,D
Biological and Biomedical
  Sciences—General — M,D
Cancer Biology/Oncology — M,D
Cell Biology — M,D
Genomic Sciences — M,D
Human Genetics — M,D
Immunology — D
Microbiology — D
Molecular Biology — M,D
Molecular Medicine — M,D
Neurobiology — D
Neuroscience — D
Pathology — M
Pharmacology — M,D
Toxicology — M,D

UNIVERSITY OF MARYLAND, BALTIMORE COUNTY

Biochemistry — M,D
Biological and Biomedical
  Sciences—General — M,D
Cell Biology — D
Molecular Biology — M,D
Neuroscience — D

UNIVERSITY OF MARYLAND, COLLEGE PARK

Biochemistry — M,D
Biological and Biomedical
  Sciences—General — M,D
Biophysics — D
Cell Biology — M,D
Conservation Biology — M
Ecology — M,D
Entomology — M,D
Evolutionary Biology — M,D
Molecular Biology — D
Molecular Genetics — M,D
Neuroscience — M,D
Nutrition — M,D
Plant Biology — M,D

UNIVERSITY OF MARYLAND EASTERN SHORE

Toxicology — M,D

UNIVERSITY OF MASSACHUSETTS AMHERST

Animal Behavior — M,D
Biochemistry — M,D
Biological and Biomedical
  Sciences—General — M,D
Cell Biology — M,D
Developmental Biology — D
Ecology — M,D
Entomology — M,D
Environmental Biology — M,D
Evolutionary Biology — M,D
Genetics — M,D
Microbiology — M,D*
Molecular Biophysics — D
Neuroscience — M,D
Nutrition — M,D
Physiology — M,D
Plant Biology — M,D

Plant Molecular Biology — M,D
Plant Physiology — M,D

UNIVERSITY OF MASSACHUSETTS BOSTON

Biological and Biomedical
  Sciences—General — M
Cell Biology — D
Environmental Biology — D
Molecular Biology — D

UNIVERSITY OF MASSACHUSETTS DARTMOUTH

Biological and Biomedical
  Sciences—General — M
Marine Biology — M

UNIVERSITY OF MASSACHUSETTS LOWELL

Biochemistry — M,D
Biological and Biomedical
  Sciences—General — M,D
Nutrition — M,O
Pathology — M,O

UNIVERSITY OF MASSACHUSETTS WORCESTER

Biochemistry — M,D
Biological and Biomedical
  Sciences—General — M,D
Cancer Biology/Oncology — M,D
Cell Biology — M,D
Computational Biology — M,D
Immunology — M,D
Microbiology — M,D
Molecular Genetics — M,D
Molecular Pharmacology — M,D
Neuroscience — M,D
Virology — M,D

UNIVERSITY OF MEDICINE AND DENTISTRY OF NEW JERSEY

Biochemistry — M,D
Biological and Biomedical
  Sciences—General — M,D,O
Cancer Biology/Oncology — D,O
Cardiovascular Sciences — M,D
Cell Biology — M,D
Developmental Biology — D,O
Immunology — M,D,O
Infectious Diseases — D,O
Microbiology — M,D
Molecular Biology — M,D
Molecular Genetics — M,D
Molecular Medicine — D
Molecular Pathology — M,D,O
Molecular Pharmacology — M,D
Neuroscience — M,D
Nutrition — M,D,O
Pathology — D
Pharmacology — D
Physiology — M,D
Toxicology — M,D

UNIVERSITY OF MEMPHIS

Biological and Biomedical
  Sciences—General — M,D
Nutrition — M

UNIVERSITY OF MIAMI

Biochemistry — D
Biological and Biomedical
  Sciences—General — M,D
Biophysics — D
Cancer Biology/Oncology — D
Cell Biology — D
Developmental Biology — D

Evolutionary Biology — M,D
Genetics — M,D
Immunology — D
Marine Biology — M,D
Microbiology — D
Molecular Biology — D
Neuroscience — M,D
Pharmacology — D
Physiology — D

UNIVERSITY OF MICHIGAN

Biochemistry — D
Biological and Biomedical
  Sciences—General — M,D
Biophysics — D
Biopsychology — D
Cell Biology — M,D
Conservation Biology — M,D
Developmental Biology — M,D
Ecology — M,D
Evolutionary Biology — M,D
Human Genetics — M,D
Immunology — D
Microbiology — D
Molecular Biology — M,D
Molecular Pathology — D
Neuroscience — D
Nutrition — M,D
Pathology — D
Pharmacology — M,D
Physiology — D
Toxicology — M,D

UNIVERSITY OF MICHIGAN–FLINT

Biological and Biomedical
  Sciences—General — M

UNIVERSITY OF MINNESOTA, DULUTH

Biochemistry — M,D
Biological and Biomedical
  Sciences—General — M,D
Biophysics — M,D
Immunology — M,D
Medical Microbiology — M,D
Molecular Biology — M,D
Pharmacology — M,D
Physiology — M,D
Toxicology — M,D

UNIVERSITY OF MINNESOTA, TWIN CITIES CAMPUS

Animal Behavior — M,D
Biochemistry — D
Biological and Biomedical
  Sciences—General — M
Biophysics — M,D
Biopsychology — D
Cancer Biology/Oncology — D
Cell Biology — M,D
Conservation Biology — M,D
Developmental Biology — M,D
Ecology — M,D
Entomology — M,D
Evolutionary Biology — M,D
Genetics — M,D
Immunology — D
Infectious Diseases — M,D
Microbiology — M,D
Molecular Biology — M,D
Neurobiology — M,D
Neuroscience — M,D
Nutrition — M,D
Pharmacology — M,D
Physiology — D
Plant Biology — M,D
Plant Pathology — M,D
Structural Biology — D

*M—master's degree; P—first professional degree; D—doctorate; O—other advanced degree; *—Close-Up and / or Display*

Toxicology	M,D
Virology	D

UNIVERSITY OF MISSISSIPPI

Biological and Biomedical Sciences—General	M,D
Pharmacology	M,D

UNIVERSITY OF MISSISSIPPI MEDICAL CENTER

Anatomy	M,D
Biochemistry	M,D
Biological and Biomedical Sciences—General	M,D
Biophysics	M,D
Microbiology	M,D
Pathology	M,D
Pharmacology	M,D
Physiology	M,D
Toxicology	M,D

UNIVERSITY OF MISSOURI

Anatomy	M
Biochemistry	M,D
Biological and Biomedical Sciences—General	M,D
Cell Biology	M,D
Ecology	M,D
Entomology	M,D
Evolutionary Biology	M,D
Genetics	M,D
Immunology	M,D
Microbiology	M,D
Neurobiology	M,D
Neuroscience	M,D
Nutrition	M,D
Pathobiology	M,D
Pathology	M
Pharmacology	M,D
Physiology	M,D
Plant Biology	M,D

UNIVERSITY OF MISSOURI–KANSAS CITY

Biochemistry	D*
Biological and Biomedical Sciences—General	M,D
Biophysics	D*
Cell Biology	D*
Molecular Biology	D*

UNIVERSITY OF MISSOURI–ST. LOUIS

Biochemistry	M,D
Biological and Biomedical Sciences—General	M,D,O
Cell Biology	M,D,O
Conservation Biology	M,D,O
Ecology	M,D,O
Evolutionary Biology	M,D,O
Molecular Biology	M,D,O
Neuroscience	M,D,O

THE UNIVERSITY OF MONTANA

Animal Behavior	M,D,O
Biochemistry	M,D
Biological and Biomedical Sciences—General	M,D
Ecology	M,D
Infectious Diseases	D
Microbiology	M,D
Neuroscience	M,D
Toxicology	M,D
Zoology	M,D

UNIVERSITY OF NEBRASKA AT KEARNEY

Biological and Biomedical Sciences—General	M

UNIVERSITY OF NEBRASKA AT OMAHA

Biological and Biomedical Sciences—General	M
Biopsychology	M,D,O

UNIVERSITY OF NEBRASKA–LINCOLN

Biochemistry	M,D
Biological and Biomedical Sciences—General	M,D
Biopsychology	M,D
Entomology	M,D
Nutrition	M,D
Toxicology	M,D

UNIVERSITY OF NEBRASKA MEDICAL CENTER

Anatomy	M,D
Biochemistry	M,D
Biological and Biomedical Sciences—General	M,D
Cancer Biology/Oncology	D
Cell Biology	M,D
Genetics	M,D
Microbiology	M,D
Molecular Biology	M,D
Neuroscience	M,D
Nutrition	O
Pathology	M,D
Pharmacology	M,D
Physiology	M,D
Toxicology	M,D

UNIVERSITY OF NEVADA, LAS VEGAS

Biochemistry	M,D
Biological and Biomedical Sciences—General	M,D

UNIVERSITY OF NEVADA, RENO

Biochemistry	M,D*
Biological and Biomedical Sciences—General	M
Cell Biology	M,D
Conservation Biology	D
Ecology	D
Evolutionary Biology	D
Molecular Biology	M,D
Molecular Pharmacology	D
Nutrition	M
Physiology	D

UNIVERSITY OF NEW BRUNSWICK FREDERICTON

Biological and Biomedical Sciences—General	M,D

UNIVERSITY OF NEW BRUNSWICK SAINT JOHN

Biological and Biomedical Sciences—General	M,D

UNIVERSITY OF NEW ENGLAND

Biological and Biomedical Sciences—General	M

UNIVERSITY OF NEW HAMPSHIRE

Biochemistry	M,D
Biological and Biomedical Sciences—General	M,D
Genetics	M,D
Microbiology	M,D
Nutrition	M,D
Plant Biology	M,D
Zoology	M,D

UNIVERSITY OF NEW HAVEN

Cell Biology	M,O
Ecology	M,O
Molecular Biology	M,O
Nutrition	M

UNIVERSITY OF NEW MEXICO

Biochemistry	M,D,O
Biological and Biomedical Sciences—General	M,D,O
Biophysics	M,D
Cell Biology	M,D,O
Genetics	M,D,O
Microbiology	M,D,O
Molecular Biology	M,D,O
Neuroscience	M,D,O
Nutrition	M
Pathology	M,D,O
Physiology	M,D,O
Toxicology	M,D,O

UNIVERSITY OF NEW ORLEANS

Biological and Biomedical Sciences—General	M,D

THE UNIVERSITY OF NORTH CAROLINA AT CHAPEL HILL

Biochemistry	M,D
Biological and Biomedical Sciences—General	M,D
Biophysics	M,D
Botany	M,D
Cell Biology	M,D
Computational Biology	D
Developmental Biology	M,D
Ecology	M,D
Evolutionary Biology	M,D
Genetics	M,D
Immunology	M,D
Microbiology	M,D
Molecular Biology	M,D
Molecular Physiology	D
Neurobiology	D
Nutrition	M,D
Pathology	D
Pharmacology	D
Toxicology	M,D

THE UNIVERSITY OF NORTH CAROLINA AT CHARLOTTE

Biological and Biomedical Sciences—General	M,D

THE UNIVERSITY OF NORTH CAROLINA AT GREENSBORO

Biochemistry	M
Biological and Biomedical Sciences—General	M
Nutrition	M,D

THE UNIVERSITY OF NORTH CAROLINA WILMINGTON

Biological and Biomedical Sciences—General	M,D
Marine Biology	M,D

UNIVERSITY OF NORTH DAKOTA

Anatomy	M,D
Biochemistry	M,D
Biological and Biomedical Sciences—General	M,D
Botany	M,D
Cell Biology	M,D
Ecology	M,D
Entomology	M,D
Environmental Biology	M,D
Genetics	M,D
Immunology	M,D

UNIVERSITY OF NORTHERN COLORADO

Microbiology	M,D
Molecular Biology	M,D
Pharmacology	M,D
Physiology	M,D
Zoology	M,D

Biological and Biomedical Sciences—General	M

UNIVERSITY OF NORTHERN IOWA

Biochemistry	M
Biological and Biomedical Sciences—General	M

UNIVERSITY OF NORTH FLORIDA

Biological and Biomedical Sciences—General	M
Nutrition	M

UNIVERSITY OF NORTH TEXAS

Biochemistry	M,D
Biological and Biomedical Sciences—General	M,D
Molecular Biology	M,D

UNIVERSITY OF NORTH TEXAS HEALTH SCIENCE CENTER AT FORT WORTH

Anatomy	M,D
Biochemistry	M,D
Biological and Biomedical Sciences—General	M,D
Genetics	M,D
Immunology	M,D
Microbiology	M,D
Molecular Biology	M,D
Pharmacology	M,D
Physiology	M,D

UNIVERSITY OF NOTRE DAME

Biochemistry	M,D
Biological and Biomedical Sciences—General	M,D
Cell Biology	M,D
Ecology	M,D
Evolutionary Biology	M,D
Genetics	M,D
Molecular Biology	M,D
Parasitology	M,D
Physiology	M,D

UNIVERSITY OF OKLAHOMA

Biochemistry	M,D
Botany	M,D
Ecology	D
Evolutionary Biology	D
Microbiology	M,D
Neurobiology	M,D
Zoology	M,D

UNIVERSITY OF OKLAHOMA HEALTH SCIENCES CENTER

Biochemistry	M,D
Biological and Biomedical Sciences—General	M,D
Biopsychology	M,D
Cell Biology	M,D
Immunology	M,D
Microbiology	M,D
Molecular Biology	M,D
Neuroscience	M,D
Nutrition	M
Pathology	D
Physiology	M,D
Radiation Biology	M,D

UNIVERSITY OF OREGON

Biochemistry	M,D
Biological and Biomedical Sciences—General	M,D
Biopsychology	M,D
Ecology	M,D
Evolutionary Biology	M,D
Genetics	M,D
Marine Biology	M,D
Molecular Biology	M,D
Neuroscience	M,D
Physiology	M,D

UNIVERSITY OF OTTAWA

Biochemistry	M,D
Biological and Biomedical Sciences—General	M,D
Cell Biology	M,D
Immunology	M,D
Microbiology	M,D
Molecular Biology	M,D

UNIVERSITY OF PENNSYLVANIA

Biochemistry	D
Biological and Biomedical Sciences—General	M,D
Cancer Biology/Oncology	D
Cell Biology	D
Computational Biology	D
Developmental Biology	D
Genetics	D
Genomic Sciences	D
Immunology	D
Microbiology	D
Molecular Biology	D
Molecular Biophysics	D
Neuroscience	D
Pharmacology	D
Physiology	D
Virology	D

UNIVERSITY OF PITTSBURGH

Biological and Biomedical Sciences—General	D
Cell Biology	M,D
Computational Biology	D
Developmental Biology	M,D
Ecology	D
Evolutionary Biology	D
Human Genetics	M,D,O
Immunology	M,D
Infectious Diseases	M,D,O
Microbiology	M,D,O
Molecular Biology	D
Molecular Biophysics	D
Molecular Genetics	M,D
Molecular Pathology	M,D
Molecular Pharmacology	M,D
Molecular Physiology	M,D
Neuroscience	D
Nutrition	M
Pathology	M,D
Structural Biology	D
Systems Biology	D
Virology	M,D

UNIVERSITY OF PRINCE EDWARD ISLAND

Anatomy	M,D
Bacteriology	M,D
Biological and Biomedical Sciences—General	M
Immunology	M,D
Parasitology	M,D
Pathology	M,D
Pharmacology	M,D
Physiology	M,D
Toxicology	M,D
Virology	M,D

UNIVERSITY OF PUERTO RICO, MAYAGÜEZ CAMPUS

Biological and Biomedical Sciences—General	M

UNIVERSITY OF PUERTO RICO, MEDICAL SCIENCES CAMPUS

Anatomy	M,D
Biochemistry	M,D
Biological and Biomedical Sciences—General	M,D
Microbiology	M,D
Nutrition	M,D,O
Pharmacology	M,D
Physiology	M,D
Toxicology	M,D

UNIVERSITY OF PUERTO RICO, RÍO PIEDRAS

Biological and Biomedical Sciences—General	M,D
Cell Biology	M,D
Ecology	M,D
Evolutionary Biology	M,D
Genetics	M,D
Molecular Biology	M,D
Neuroscience	M,D
Nutrition	M

UNIVERSITY OF REGINA

Biochemistry	M,D
Biological and Biomedical Sciences—General	M,D
Biophysics	M,D
Cancer Biology/Oncology	M,D

UNIVERSITY OF RHODE ISLAND

Biochemistry	M,D
Biological and Biomedical Sciences—General	M,D
Cell Biology	M,D
Entomology	M,D
Microbiology	M,D
Molecular Biology	M,D
Molecular Genetics	M,D
Nutrition	M,D
Pharmacology	M,D
Toxicology	M,D

UNIVERSITY OF ROCHESTER

Anatomy	M,D
Biochemistry	M,D
Biological and Biomedical Sciences—General	M,D
Biophysics	M,D
Computational Biology	M,D
Genetics	M,D
Immunology	M,D
Microbiology	M,D
Neurobiology	M,D
Neuroscience	M,D
Pathology	M,D
Pharmacology	M,D
Physiology	M,D
Toxicology	M,D

UNIVERSITY OF SAN FRANCISCO

Biological and Biomedical Sciences—General	M

UNIVERSITY OF SASKATCHEWAN

Anatomy	M,D
Biochemistry	M,D
Biological and Biomedical Sciences—General	M,D
Cell Biology	M,D
Immunology	M,D

(continued column)

Microbiology	M,D
Pathology	M,D
Pharmacology	M,D
Physiology	M,D
Reproductive Biology	M,D
Toxicology	M,D,O

THE UNIVERSITY OF SCRANTON

Biochemistry	M

UNIVERSITY OF SOUTH ALABAMA

Biological and Biomedical Sciences—General	M,D
Toxicology	M

UNIVERSITY OF SOUTH CAROLINA

Biochemistry	M,D
Biological and Biomedical Sciences—General	M,D,O
Cell Biology	M,D
Developmental Biology	M,D
Ecology	M,D
Evolutionary Biology	M,D
Molecular Biology	M,D

THE UNIVERSITY OF SOUTH DAKOTA

Biological and Biomedical Sciences—General	M,D
Cardiovascular Sciences	M,D
Cell Biology	M,D
Immunology	M,D
Microbiology	M,D
Molecular Biology	M,D
Neuroscience	M,D
Pharmacology	M,D
Physiology	M,D

UNIVERSITY OF SOUTHERN CALIFORNIA

Biochemistry	M,D
Biological and Biomedical Sciences—General	M,D
Biophysics	M,D
Cell Biology	M,D
Computational Biology	D
Environmental Biology	M,D
Evolutionary Biology	D
Genetics	M,D
Immunology	M,D
Marine Biology	M,D
Microbiology	M,D
Molecular Biology	M,D
Molecular Pharmacology	M,D
Neurobiology	M,D
Neuroscience	M,D
Pathobiology	M,D*
Pathology	M,D
Physiology	M,D
Systems Biology	D
Toxicology	M,D

UNIVERSITY OF SOUTHERN MAINE

Biological and Biomedical Sciences—General	M
Immunology	M
Molecular Biology	M

UNIVERSITY OF SOUTHERN MISSISSIPPI

Biochemistry	M,D
Biological and Biomedical Sciences—General	M,D
Environmental Biology	M,D
Marine Biology	M,D

(continued column)

Microbiology	M,D
Molecular Biology	M,D
Nutrition	M,D

UNIVERSITY OF SOUTH FLORIDA

Biochemistry	M,D
Biological and Biomedical Sciences—General	M,D
Cancer Biology/Oncology	D
Cell Biology	M,D
Conservation Biology	M,D
Marine Biology	M,D
Molecular Biology	M,D
Neuroscience	D

THE UNIVERSITY OF TENNESSEE

Anatomy	M,D
Animal Behavior	M,D
Biochemistry	M,D
Biological and Biomedical Sciences—General	M,D
Ecology	M,D
Entomology	M,D
Evolutionary Biology	M,D
Genetics	M,D
Genomic Sciences	M,D
Microbiology	M,D
Nutrition	M
Physiology	M,D
Plant Pathology	M,D
Plant Physiology	M,D

THE UNIVERSITY OF TENNESSEE AT MARTIN

Nutrition	M

THE UNIVERSITY OF TENNESSEE–OAK RIDGE NATIONAL LABORATORY GRADUATE SCHOOL OF GENOME SCIENCE AND TECHNOLOGY

Biological and Biomedical Sciences—General	M,D
Genomic Sciences	M,D

THE UNIVERSITY OF TEXAS AT ARLINGTON

Biological and Biomedical Sciences—General	M,D

THE UNIVERSITY OF TEXAS AT AUSTIN

Animal Behavior	M,D
Biochemistry	M,D
Biological and Biomedical Sciences—General	M,D
Biopsychology	D
Cell Biology	D
Ecology	M,D
Evolutionary Biology	M,D
Microbiology	D
Molecular Biology	D
Neurobiology	D
Neuroscience	D
Nutrition	M,D
Plant Biology	M,D

THE UNIVERSITY OF TEXAS AT BROWNSVILLE

Biological and Biomedical Sciences—General	M

THE UNIVERSITY OF TEXAS AT DALLAS

Biological and Biomedical Sciences—General	M,D

*M—master's degree; P—first professional degree; D—doctorate; O—other advanced degree; *—Close-Up and/or Display*

Cell Biology	M,D
Molecular Biology	M,D
Neuroscience	M,D

THE UNIVERSITY OF TEXAS AT EL PASO

Biological and Biomedical Sciences—General	M,D

THE UNIVERSITY OF TEXAS AT SAN ANTONIO

Biological and Biomedical Sciences—General	M,D*
Neurobiology	M,D

THE UNIVERSITY OF TEXAS AT TYLER

Biological and Biomedical Sciences—General	M

THE UNIVERSITY OF TEXAS HEALTH SCIENCE CENTER AT HOUSTON

Biochemistry	M,D
Biological and Biomedical Sciences—General	M,D
Cancer Biology/Oncology	M,D*
Cell Biology	M,D
Developmental Biology	M,D
Genetics	M,D
Human Genetics	M,D
Immunology	M,D
Microbiology	M,D
Molecular Biology	M,D
Molecular Genetics	M,D
Molecular Pathology	M,D
Neuroscience	M,D
Virology	M,D

THE UNIVERSITY OF TEXAS HEALTH SCIENCE CENTER AT SAN ANTONIO

Biochemistry	M,D
Biological and Biomedical Sciences—General	M,D
Cell Biology	M,D
Immunology	D
Microbiology	D
Molecular Medicine	M,D
Neuroscience	D
Pharmacology	D
Physiology	M,D
Structural Biology	M,D

THE UNIVERSITY OF TEXAS MEDICAL BRANCH

Bacteriology	D
Biochemistry	D
Biological and Biomedical Sciences—General	M,D
Biophysics	D
Cell Biology	D
Computational Biology	D
Genetics	D
Immunology	M,D
Infectious Diseases	D
Microbiology	M,D
Molecular Biophysics	M,D
Neuroscience	D
Pathology	D
Pharmacology	M,D
Physiology	M,D
Structural Biology	D
Toxicology	M,D
Virology	D

THE UNIVERSITY OF TEXAS OF THE PERMIAN BASIN

Biological and Biomedical Sciences—General	M

THE UNIVERSITY OF TEXAS–PAN AMERICAN

Biological and Biomedical Sciences—General	M

THE UNIVERSITY OF TEXAS SOUTHWESTERN MEDICAL CENTER AT DALLAS

Biochemistry	D
Biological and Biomedical Sciences—General	M,D
Cancer Biology/Oncology	D
Cell Biology	D
Developmental Biology	D
Genetics	D
Immunology	D
Microbiology	D
Molecular Biophysics	D
Neuroscience	D
Nutrition	M

UNIVERSITY OF THE DISTRICT OF COLUMBIA

Cancer Biology/Oncology	M
Nutrition	M

UNIVERSITY OF THE INCARNATE WORD

Biological and Biomedical Sciences—General	M
Nutrition	M,O

UNIVERSITY OF THE PACIFIC

Biological and Biomedical Sciences—General	M

UNIVERSITY OF THE SCIENCES IN PHILADELPHIA

Biochemistry	M,D
Cell Biology	M,D
Molecular Biology	D
Pharmacology	M,D
Toxicology	M,D

THE UNIVERSITY OF TOLEDO

Biochemistry	M,D
Biological and Biomedical Sciences—General	M,D
Cancer Biology/Oncology	M,D
Cardiovascular Sciences	M,D
Cell Biology	M,D
Ecology	M,D
Genomic Sciences	M,O
Immunology	M,D
Neuroscience	M,D
Nutrition	M,O
Pathology	O
Pharmacology	M

UNIVERSITY OF TORONTO

Biochemistry	M,D
Biological and Biomedical Sciences—General	M,D
Biophysics	M,D
Cell Biology	M,D
Ecology	M,D
Evolutionary Biology	M,D
Genetics	M,D
Immunology	M,D
Nutrition	M,D
Pathobiology	M,D

UNIVERSITY OF TULSA

Biochemistry	M
Biological and Biomedical Sciences—General	M,D

UNIVERSITY OF UTAH

Anatomy	D
Biochemistry	M,D
Biological and Biomedical Sciences—General	M,D,O
Cancer Biology/Oncology	M,D
Human Genetics	M,D
Molecular Biology	D
Neurobiology	D
Neuroscience	D
Nutrition	M
Pathology	M,D
Pharmacology	D
Physiology	D
Toxicology	D

UNIVERSITY OF VERMONT

Biochemistry	M,D
Biological and Biomedical Sciences—General	M,D
Biophysics	M,D
Cell Biology	M,D
Microbiology	M,D
Molecular Biology	M,D
Molecular Genetics	M,D
Molecular Physiology	M,D
Neuroscience	D
Nutrition	M,D
Pathology	M
Pharmacology	M,D
Plant Biology	M,D

UNIVERSITY OF VICTORIA

Biochemistry	M,D
Biological and Biomedical Sciences—General	M,D
Microbiology	M,D

UNIVERSITY OF VIRGINIA

Biochemistry	D
Biological and Biomedical Sciences—General	M,D
Biophysics	M,D
Cell Biology	D
Microbiology	D
Molecular Genetics	D
Molecular Physiology	M,D
Neuroscience	D
Pathology	D
Pharmacology	D
Physiology	D

UNIVERSITY OF WASHINGTON

Animal Behavior	D
Bacteriology	D
Biochemistry	D
Biological and Biomedical Sciences—General	M,D
Biophysics	D
Cell Biology	D*
Ecology	M,D
Genetics	M,D
Genomic Sciences	D
Immunology	D
Microbiology	D
Molecular Biology	D*
Molecular Medicine	D
Neurobiology	D

Nutrition	M,D
Parasitology	D
Pathobiology	D
Pathology	D
Pharmacology	D
Physiology	D
Structural Biology	D
Toxicology	M,D

UNIVERSITY OF WATERLOO

Biochemistry	M,D
Biological and Biomedical Sciences—General	M,D

THE UNIVERSITY OF WESTERN ONTARIO

Anatomy	M,D
Biochemistry	M,D
Biophysics	M,D
Cell Biology	M,D
Immunology	M,D
Microbiology	M,D
Molecular Biology	M,D
Neuroscience	M,D
Pathology	M,D
Physiology	M,D
Plant Biology	M,D
Zoology	M,D

UNIVERSITY OF WEST FLORIDA

Biochemistry	M
Biological and Biomedical Sciences—General	M
Environmental Biology	M

UNIVERSITY OF WEST GEORGIA

Biological and Biomedical Sciences—General	M

UNIVERSITY OF WINDSOR

Biochemistry	M,D
Biological and Biomedical Sciences—General	M,D
Biopsychology	M,D

UNIVERSITY OF WISCONSIN–LA CROSSE

Biological and Biomedical Sciences—General	M
Cancer Biology/Oncology	M
Cell Biology	M
Medical Microbiology	M
Microbiology	M
Molecular Biology	M
Physiology	M

UNIVERSITY OF WISCONSIN–MADISON

Bacteriology	M
Biochemistry	M,D
Biological and Biomedical Sciences—General	M,D
Biophysics	D
Biopsychology	D
Botany	M,D
Cancer Biology/Oncology	D
Cell Biology	D
Conservation Biology	M
Ecology	M
Entomology	M,D
Environmental Biology	M,D
Genetics	M,D
Medical Microbiology	D
Microbiology	D
Molecular Biology	D
Neurobiology	D
Neuroscience	D

Nutrition — M,D
Pathology — D*
Pharmacology — D
Physiology — M,D
Plant Pathology — M,D
Toxicology — M,D
Zoology — M,D

UNIVERSITY OF WISCONSIN–MILWAUKEE
Biochemistry — M,D
Biological and Biomedical Sciences—General — M,D

UNIVERSITY OF WISCONSIN–OSHKOSH
Biological and Biomedical Sciences—General — M
Botany — M
Microbiology — M
Zoology — M

UNIVERSITY OF WISCONSIN–PARKSIDE
Molecular Biology — M

UNIVERSITY OF WISCONSIN–STEVENS POINT
Nutrition — M

UNIVERSITY OF WISCONSIN–STOUT
Nutrition — M

UNIVERSITY OF WYOMING
Botany — M,D
Cell Biology — D
Computational Biology — D
Ecology — M,D
Entomology — M,D
Genetics — D
Microbiology — D
Molecular Biology — M,D
Nutrition — M
Pathobiology — M
Physiology — M,D
Reproductive Biology — M,D
Zoology — M,D

UTAH STATE UNIVERSITY
Biochemistry — M,D
Biological and Biomedical Sciences—General — M,D
Ecology — M,D
Microbiology — M,D
Molecular Biology — M,D
Nutrition — M,D
Toxicology — M,D

VANDERBILT UNIVERSITY
Biochemistry — M,D
Biological and Biomedical Sciences—General — M,D
Biophysics — M,D
Cancer Biology/Oncology — M,D
Cell Biology — M,D
Human Genetics — D
Immunology — M,D
Microbiology — M,D
Molecular Biology — M,D
Molecular Physiology — M,D
Nutrition — M,D
Pathology — D
Pharmacology — D

VILLANOVA UNIVERSITY
Biological and Biomedical Sciences—General — M

VIRGINIA COMMONWEALTH UNIVERSITY
Anatomy — D,O
Biochemistry — M,D,O
Biological and Biomedical Sciences—General — M,D,O
Biopsychology — D
Genetics — M,D
Human Genetics — M,D,O
Immunology — M,D
Microbiology — M,D,O
Molecular Biology — M,D
Neurobiology — D
Neuroscience — M,D,O
Pathology — D
Pharmacology — M,D,O
Physiology — M,D,O
Systems Biology — D
Toxicology — M,D,O

VIRGINIA POLYTECHNIC INSTITUTE AND STATE UNIVERSITY
Biochemistry — M,D
Biological and Biomedical Sciences—General — M,D
Computational Biology — D
Entomology — M,D
Genetics — D
Microbiology — D
Molecular Biology — D
Nutrition — M,D
Plant Pathology — M,D
Plant Physiology — M,D

VIRGINIA STATE UNIVERSITY
Biological and Biomedical Sciences—General — M

WAGNER COLLEGE
Biological and Biomedical Sciences—General — M
Microbiology — M

WAKE FOREST UNIVERSITY
Anatomy — D
Biochemistry — D
Biological and Biomedical Sciences—General — M,D
Cancer Biology/Oncology — D
Genomic Sciences — D
Human Genetics — D
Immunology — D
Microbiology — D
Molecular Biology — D
Molecular Genetics — D
Molecular Medicine — M,D
Neurobiology — D
Neuroscience — D
Pathobiology — M,D
Pharmacology — D
Physiology — D

WALLA WALLA UNIVERSITY
Biological and Biomedical Sciences—General — M

WASHINGTON STATE UNIVERSITY
Biochemistry — M,D
Biological and Biomedical Sciences—General — M
Biophysics — M,D
Botany — M,D

Cell Biology — M,D
Entomology — M,D
Genetics — M,D
Microbiology — M,D
Molecular Biology — M,D
Neuroscience — M,D
Nutrition — M,D
Plant Molecular Biology — M,D
Plant Pathology — M,D
Zoology — M,D

WASHINGTON STATE UNIVERSITY TRI-CITIES
Biological and Biomedical Sciences—General — M

WASHINGTON UNIVERSITY IN ST. LOUIS
Biochemistry — D
Biological and Biomedical Sciences—General — D
Cell Biology — D
Computational Biology — D
Developmental Biology — D
Ecology — D
Environmental Biology — D
Evolutionary Biology — D
Genetics — M,D,O
Genomic Sciences — M
Immunology — D
Microbiology — D
Molecular Biology — D
Molecular Biophysics — D
Molecular Genetics — D
Molecular Pathogenesis — D
Neuroscience — D
Plant Biology — D
Translational Biology — M

WAYNE STATE UNIVERSITY
Anatomy — M,D
Biochemistry — M,D
Biological and Biomedical Sciences—General — M,D
Biopsychology — M,D
Cancer Biology/Oncology — M,D*
Genetics — M,D
Immunology — M,D
Microbiology — M,D
Molecular Biology — M,D
Neuroscience — M,D
Nutrition — M,D
Pathology — M,D
Pharmacology — P,M,D
Physiology — M,D
Toxicology — M,D

WESLEYAN UNIVERSITY
Animal Behavior — D
Biochemistry — M,D
Biological and Biomedical Sciences—General — D
Cell Biology — D
Developmental Biology — D
Ecology — D
Evolutionary Biology — D
Genetics — D
Genomic Sciences — D
Molecular Biology — D
Neurobiology — D

WEST CHESTER UNIVERSITY OF PENNSYLVANIA
Biological and Biomedical Sciences—General — M,O
Nutrition — M,O

WESTERN CAROLINA UNIVERSITY
Biological and Biomedical Sciences—General — M

WESTERN CONNECTICUT STATE UNIVERSITY
Biological and Biomedical Sciences—General — M

WESTERN ILLINOIS UNIVERSITY
Biological and Biomedical Sciences—General — M,O
Marine Biology — M,O
Zoology — M,O

WESTERN KENTUCKY UNIVERSITY
Biological and Biomedical Sciences—General — M

WESTERN MICHIGAN UNIVERSITY
Biological and Biomedical Sciences—General — M,D
Physiology — M

WESTERN UNIVERSITY OF HEALTH SCIENCES
Biological and Biomedical Sciences—General — M

WESTERN WASHINGTON UNIVERSITY
Biological and Biomedical Sciences—General — M

WEST TEXAS A&M UNIVERSITY
Biological and Biomedical Sciences—General — M

WEST VIRGINIA UNIVERSITY
Biochemistry — M,D
Biological and Biomedical Sciences—General — M,D
Cancer Biology/Oncology — M,D
Cell Biology — M,D
Developmental Biology — M,D
Entomology — M,D
Environmental Biology — M,D
Evolutionary Biology — M,D
Genetics — M,D
Genomic Sciences — M,D
Human Genetics — M,D
Immunology — M,D
Microbiology — M,D
Molecular Biology — M,D
Neurobiology — M,D
Neuroscience — D
Nutrition — M
Pharmacology — M,D
Physiology — M,D
Plant Pathology — M,D
Reproductive Biology — M,D
Teratology — M,D
Toxicology — M,D

WICHITA STATE UNIVERSITY
Biological and Biomedical Sciences—General — M

WILFRID LAURIER UNIVERSITY
Biological and Biomedical Sciences—General — M
Neuroscience — M,D

---

*M—master's degree; P—first professional degree; D—doctorate; O—other advanced degree; *—Close-Up and/or Display*

WILLIAM PATERSON UNIVERSITY OF NEW JERSEY

Biological and Biomedical Sciences—General	M

WINTHROP UNIVERSITY

Biological and Biomedical Sciences—General	M
Nutrition	M

WOODS HOLE OCEANOGRAPHIC INSTITUTION

Marine Biology	D

WORCESTER POLYTECHNIC INSTITUTE

Biochemistry	M,D
Biological and Biomedical Sciences—General	M,D

WRIGHT STATE UNIVERSITY

Anatomy	M
Biochemistry	M
Biological and Biomedical Sciences—General	M,D
Biophysics	M
Immunology	M
Microbiology	M
Molecular Biology	M
Pharmacology	M
Physiology	M
Toxicology	M

YALE UNIVERSITY

Biochemistry	D
Biological and Biomedical Sciences—General	D
Biophysics	D
Cancer Biology/Oncology	D
Cell Biology	D
Computational Biology	D
Developmental Biology	D
Ecology	D
Evolutionary Biology	D
Genetics	D
Genomic Sciences	D
Immunology	D
Infectious Diseases	D
Microbiology	D
Molecular Biology	D
Molecular Biophysics	D
Molecular Medicine	D
Molecular Pathology	D
Molecular Physiology	D
Neurobiology	D
Neuroscience	D
Pathobiology	D
Pathology	M,D
Pharmacology	D
Physiology	D
Plant Biology	D
Virology	D

YORK UNIVERSITY

Biological and Biomedical Sciences—General	M,D

YOUNGSTOWN STATE UNIVERSITY

Anatomy	M
Biochemistry	M
Biological and Biomedical Sciences—General	M
Environmental Biology	M
Microbiology	M
Molecular Biology	M
Physiology	M

ACADEMIC PROGRAMS
IN THE BIOLOGICAL SCIENCES

Section 1
Biological and Biomedical Sciences

This section contains a directory of institutions offering graduate work in biological and biomedical sciences, followed by in-depth entries submitted by institutions that chose to prepare detailed program descriptions. Additional information about programs listed in the directory but not augmented by an in-depth entry may be obtained by writing directly to the dean of a graduate school or chair of a department at the address given in the directory.

Programs in fields related to the biological and biomedical sciences may be found throughout this book. In the other guides in this series:

Graduate Programs in the Humanities, Arts & Social Sciences,

See *Psychology and Counseling* and *Sociology, Anthropology, and Archaeology*

Graduate Programs in the Physical Sciences, Mathematics, Agricultural Sciences, the Environment & Natural Resources

See *Chemistry, Marine Sciences and Oceanography,* and *Mathematical Sciences*

Graduate Programs in Engineering & Applied Sciences

See *Agricultural Engineering and Bioengineering, Biomedical Engineering and Biotechnology, Civil and Environmental Engineering, Management of Engineering and Technology,* and *Ocean Engineering*

Graduate Programs in Business, Education, Health, Information Studies, Law & Social Work

See *Allied Health, Chiropractic, Dentistry and Dental Sciences, Medicine, Nursing, Optometry and Vision Sciences, Pharmacy and Pharmaceutical Sciences, Public Health,* and *Veterinary Medicine and Sciences*

CONTENTS

Program Directory

Close-Ups and Displays

Biological and Biomedical Sciences—General

Acadia University, Faculty of Pure and Applied Science, Department of Biology, Wolfville, NS B4P 2R6, Canada. Offers M Sc. *Faculty:* 16 full-time (3 women), 24 part-time/adjunct (0 women). *Students:* 19 full-time (15 women), 10 part-time (8 women). 19 applicants, 47% accepted, 9 enrolled. In 2010, 6 master's awarded. *Degree requirements:* For master's, comprehensive exam, thesis. *Entrance requirements:* For master's, minimum B- average in last 2 years of major. Additional exam requirements/recommendations for international students: Required—TOEFL (minimum score 580 paper-based; 237 computer-based; 93 iBT), IELTS (minimum score 6.5). *Application deadline:* For fall admission, 2/1 priority date for domestic and international students. Applications are processed on a rolling basis. Application fee: $50. *Financial support:* In 2010–11, research assistantships (averaging $5,000 per year), teaching assistantships (averaging $9,000 per year) were awarded; scholarships/grants and unspecified assistantships also available. Financial award application deadline: 2/1. *Faculty research:* Respiration physiology, estuaries and fisheries, limnology, plant biology, conservation biology. *Unit head:* Dr. Soren Bondrup-Nielsen, Head, 902-585-1424, E-mail: soren.bondrup-nielsen@ acadiau.ca. *Application contact:* Lisa Taul, Administrative Secretary, 902-585-1344, Fax: 902-585-1059, E-mail: lisa.taul@acadiau.ca.

Adelphi University, College of Arts and Sciences, Department of Biology, Garden City, NY 11530-0701. Offers MS. Part-time and evening/weekend programs available. *Students:* 4 full-time (3 women), 31 part-time (18 women); includes 3 Black or African American, non-Hispanic/Latino; 1 Hispanic/Latino, 14 international. Average age 26. In 2010, 8 master's awarded. *Degree requirements:* For master's, thesis or alternative. *Entrance requirements:* For master's, 3 letters of recommendation. Additional exam requirements/recommendations for international students: Required—TOEFL (minimum score 550 paper-based; 213 computer-based; 80 iBT). *Application deadline:* For fall admission, 5/1 for international students; for spring admission, 12/1 for international students. Applications are processed on a rolling basis. Application fee: $50. Electronic applications accepted. *Financial support:* Research assistantships with full and partial tuition reimbursements, teaching assistantships, career-related internships or fieldwork, Federal Work-Study, institutionally sponsored loans, and unspecified assistantships available. Financial award application deadline: 2/15; financial award applicants required to submit FAFSA. *Faculty research:* Plant-animal interactions, physiology (plant, cornea), reproductive behavior, topics in evolution, fish biology. *Unit head:* Dr. Lawrence J. Hobbie, Director, 516-877-4198, E-mail: hobbie@adelphi.edu. *Application contact:* Christine Murphy, Director of Admissions, 516-877-3050, Fax: 516-877-3039, E-mail: graduateadmissions@ adelphi.edu.

See Close-Up on page 87.

Alabama Agricultural and Mechanical University, School of Graduate Studies, School of Arts and Sciences, Department of Biology, Huntsville, AL 35811. Offers MS. Program offered jointly with The University of Alabama in Huntsville. Part-time and evening/weekend programs available. *Degree requirements:* For master's, comprehensive exam, thesis. *Entrance requirements:* For master's, GRE General Test. Additional exam requirements/recommendations for international students: Required—TOEFL (minimum score 500 paper-based; 173 computer-based; 61 iBT). Electronic applications accepted. *Faculty research:* Radiation and chemical mutagenesis, human cytogenetics, microbial biotechnology, microbial metabolism, environmental toxicology.

Alabama State University, Department of Biological Sciences, Montgomery, AL 36101-0271. Offers MS. Part-time programs available. *Degree requirements:* For master's, one foreign language, comprehensive exam, thesis. *Entrance requirements:* For master's, GRE, GRE Subject Test, graduate writing competency test. Additional exam requirements/recommendations for international students: Required—TOEFL (minimum score 500 paper-based; 173 computer-based). *Expenses:* Tuition, state resident: part-time $312 per hour. Tuition, nonresident: part-time $624 per hour. Required fees: $213 per semester. Tuition and fees vary according to course load. *Faculty research:* Salmonella pseudomonas, cancer cells.

Albert Einstein College of Medicine, Graduate Division of Biomedical Sciences, Bronx, NY 10461. Offers PhD, MD/PhD. *Faculty:* 172 full-time, 17 part-time/adjunct. *Students:* 377 full-time; includes 13 Black or African American, non-Hispanic/Latino; 24 Asian, non-Hispanic/Latino; 8 Hispanic/Latino, 101 international. Average age 25. 213 applicants, 20% accepted. In 2010, 37 doctorates awarded. *Degree requirements:* For doctorate, thesis/dissertation. *Entrance requirements:* For doctorate, GRE General Test. Additional exam requirements/recommendations for international students: Required—TOEFL. *Application deadline:* For fall admission, 1/15 priority date for domestic students. Application fee: $0. *Financial support:* In 2010–11, 229 fellowships were awarded. *Unit head:* Dr. Victoria H. Freedman, Assistant Dean for Graduate Studies, 718-430-2345, Fax: 718-430-8655. *Application contact:* Salvatore Calabro, Assistant Director of Admissions, 718-430-2345, Fax: 718-430-8655, E-mail: phd@einstein.yu.edu.

Albert Einstein College of Medicine, Medical Scientist Training Program, Bronx, NY 10461. Offers MD/PhD.

Alcorn State University, School of Graduate Studies, School of Arts and Sciences, Department of Biology, Alcorn State, MS 39096-7500. Offers MS.

American University, College of Arts and Sciences, Department of Biology, Washington, DC 20016-8007. Offers applied science (MS); biology (MA, MS); environmental science (MS), including environmental science, marine science. Part-time programs available. *Faculty:* 9 full-time (3 women), 3 part-time/adjunct (0 women). *Students:* 8 full-time (2 women), 8 part-time (6 women); includes 3 minority (1 Black or African American, non-Hispanic/Latino; 2 Asian, non-Hispanic/Latino), 2 international. Average age 25. 40 applicants, 53% accepted, 3 enrolled. In 2010, 10 master's awarded. *Degree requirements:* For master's, comprehensive exam, thesis (for some programs). *Entrance requirements:* For master's, GRE General Test, GRE Subject Test. Additional exam requirements/recommendations for international students: Required—TOEFL. *Application deadline:* For fall admission, 2/1 for domestic students; for spring admission, 10/1 for domestic students. Application fee: $80. *Financial support:* Fellowships, research assistantships with tuition reimbursements, teaching assistantships with tuition reimbursements, career-related internships or fieldwork, Federal Work-Study, and institutionally sponsored loans available. Financial award application deadline: 2/1. *Faculty research:* Neurobiology, cave biology, population genetics, vertebrate physiology. *Unit head:* Dr. David Carlini, Chair, 202-885-2194, Fax: 202-885-2182, E-mail: carlini@american.edu. *Application contact:* Kathleen Clowery, Director, Graduate Admissions, 202-885-3621, Fax: 202-885-1505.

The American University of Athens, School of Graduate Studies, Athens, Greece. Offers biomedical sciences (MS); business (MBA); business communication (MA); computer sciences (MS); engineering and applied sciences (MS); politics and policy making (MA); systems engineering (MS); telecommunications (MS). *Entrance requirements:* For master's, resume, 2 recommendation letters. Additional exam requirements/recommendations for international students: Required—TOEFL (minimum score 550 paper-based; 213 computer-based). *Faculty research:* Nanotechnology, environmental sciences, rock mechanics, human skin studies, Monte Carlo algorithms and software.

American University of Beirut, Graduate Programs, Faculty of Arts and Sciences, Beirut, Lebanon. Offers anthropology (MA); Arabic language and literature (MA); archaeology (MA); biology (MS); chemistry (MS); computational science (MS); computer science (MS); economics (MA); education (MA); English language (MA); English literature (MA); environmental policy planning (MSES); financial economics (MAFE); geology (MS); history (MA); mathematics (MA, MS); Middle Eastern studies (MA); philosophy (MA); physics (MS); political studies (MA); psychology (MA); public administration (MA); sociology (MA); statistics (MA, MS). Part-time programs available. *Faculty:* 229 full-time (98 women), 136 part-time/adjunct (79 women). *Students:* 158 full-time (104 women), 263 part-time (171 women). Average age 25. 356

applicants, 59% accepted, 127 enrolled. In 2010, 57 master's awarded. *Degree requirements:* For master's, one foreign language, comprehensive exam, thesis (for some programs). *Entrance requirements:* For master's, GRE, letter of recommendation. Additional exam requirements/recommendations for international students: Required—TOEFL (minimum score 600 paper-based; 250 computer-based; 97 iBT), IELTS (minimum score 7). *Application deadline:* For fall admission, 4/30 for domestic and international students; for spring admission, 11/1 for domestic and international students. Application fee: $50. *Expenses:* Tuition: Full-time $12,294; part-time $683 per credit. Required fees: $499; $499 per credit. Tuition and fees vary according to course load and program. *Financial support:* In 2010–11, 33 students received support. Career-related internships or fieldwork, institutionally sponsored loans, scholarships/grants, health care benefits, and unspecified assistantships available. Financial award application deadline: 2/4; financial award applicants required to submit FAFSA. *Faculty research:* Modern and contemporary world theatre; mineralogy, petrology, and geochemistry; cell differentiation and transformation; combinatorial technologies; philosophy of action; continental philosophy; Phoenician epigraphy; nascent complex societies and urbanism; the economies of the Arab world; environmental economics; tectonophysics; host-parasite interactions; innate immunity; insect-plant interactions; history of the Ottoman archives; decentralization; transparency and corruption. Total annual research expenditures: $622,243. *Unit head:* Dr. Patrick McGreevy, Dean, 961-137-4374 Ext. 3800, Fax: 961-174-4461, E-mail: pm07@aub.edu.lb. *Application contact:* Dr. Salim Kanaan, Director, Admissions Office, 961-135-0000 Ext. 2594, Fax: 961-175-0775, E-mail: sk00@aub.edu.lb.

Andrews University, School of Graduate Studies, College of Arts and Sciences, Department of Biology, Berrien Springs, MI 49104. Offers MAT, MS. *Degree requirements:* For master's, comprehensive exam, thesis. *Entrance requirements:* For master's, GRE Subject Test. Additional exam requirements/recommendations for international students: Required—TOEFL (minimum score 550 paper-based).

Angelo State University, College of Graduate Studies, College of Sciences, Department of Biology, San Angelo, TX 76909. Offers MS. Part-time and evening/weekend programs available. *Faculty:* 8 full-time (2 women). *Students:* 10 full-time (5 women), 10 part-time (2 women). Average age 27. 10 applicants, 60% accepted, 5 enrolled. In 2010, 4 master's awarded. *Degree requirements:* For master's, comprehensive exam, thesis optional. *Entrance requirements:* For master's, GRE General Test, essay. Additional exam requirements/recommendations for international students: Required—TOEFL or IELTS. *Application deadline:* For fall admission, 7/15 priority date for domestic students, 6/10 for international students; for spring admission, 12/1 priority date for domestic students, 11/1 for international students. Applications are processed on a rolling basis. Application fee: $40 ($50 for international students). Electronic applications accepted. *Expenses:* Tuition, state resident: full-time $4560; part-time $152 per credit hour. Tuition, nonresident: full-time $13,860; part-time $462 per credit hour. Required fees: $2132. Tuition and fees vary according to course load. *Financial support:* In 2010–11, 12 students received support, including 1 research assistantship, 2 teaching assistantships (averaging $10,251 per year); career-related internships or fieldwork, Federal Work-Study, scholarships/grants, and unspecified assistantships also available. Support available to part-time students. Financial award application deadline: 3/1. *Faculty research:* Texas poppy-mallow project, Chisos hedgehog cactus, skunks, reptiles, amphibians, rodents, seed germination, mammals. *Unit head:* Dr. Kelly McCoy, Department Head, 325-942-2189 Ext. 246, Fax: 325-942-2184, E-mail: kelly.mccoy@angelo.edu. *Application contact:* Dr. Bonnie B. Amos, Graduate Advisor, 325-942-2189 Ext. 256, Fax: 325-942-2184, E-mail: bonnie.amos@ angelo.edu.

Appalachian State University, Cratis D. Williams Graduate School, Department of Biology, Boone, NC 28608. Offers cell and molecular (MS); general (MS). Part-time programs available. *Faculty:* 28 full-time (12 women), 2 part-time/adjunct (0 women). *Students:* 36 full-time (19 women), 8 part-time (3 women); includes 2 Asian, non-Hispanic/Latino; 1 Hispanic/Latino. 45 applicants, 51% accepted, 18 enrolled. In 2010, 14 master's awarded. *Degree requirements:* For master's, comprehensive exam, thesis. *Entrance requirements:* For master's, GRE General Test, 3 letters of recommendation. Additional exam requirements/recommendations for international students: Required—TOEFL (minimum score 570 paper-based; 230 computer-based; 79 iBT), IELTS (minimum score 6.5). *Application deadline:* For fall admission, 7/1 for domestic students, 2/1 for international students; for spring admission, 11/1 for domestic students, 7/1 for international students. Applications are processed on a rolling basis. Application fee: $55. Electronic applications accepted. *Expenses:* Tuition, state resident: full-time $3428; part-time $428 per unit. Tuition, nonresident: full-time $14,518; part-time $1814 per unit. Required fees: $2320; $344 per unit. Tuition and fees vary according to campus/location. *Financial support:* In 2010–11, 25 teaching assistantships (averaging $9,500 per year) were awarded; fellowships, research assistantships, career-related internships or fieldwork, Federal Work-Study, scholarships/grants, and unspecified assistantships also available. Financial award application deadline: 4/1; financial award applicants required to submit FAFSA. *Faculty research:* Aquatic and terrestrial ecology, animal and plant physiology, behavior and systematics, immunology and cell biology, molecular biology and microbiology. Total annual research expenditures: $1.3 million. *Unit head:* Dr. Steven Seagle, Chairman, 828-262-3025, E-mail: seaglesw@appstate.edu. *Application contact:* Dr. Gary Walker, Graduate Coordinator, 828-262-3025, E-mail: walkergl@ appstate.edu.

Arizona State University, College of Liberal Arts and Sciences, School of Life Sciences, Tempe, AZ 85287-4601. Offers animal behavior (PhD); applied ethics (biomedical and health ethics) (MA); biological design (PhD); biology (MS, PhD); biology (biology and society) (MS, PhD); environmental life sciences (PhD); evolutionary biology (PhD); human and social dimensions of science and technology (PhD); microbiology (PhD); molecular and cellular biology (PhD); neuroscience (PhD); philosophy (history and philosophy of science) (MA); sustainability (PhD). *Faculty:* 102 full-time (26 women), 4 part-time/adjunct (1 woman). *Students:* 188 full-time (95 women), 45 part-time (29 women); includes 31 minority (3 Black or African American, non-Hispanic/Latino; 2 American Indian or Alaska Native, non-Hispanic/Latino; 12 Asian, non-Hispanic/Latino; 12 Hispanic/Latino; 2 Two or more races, non-Hispanic/Latino), 39 international. Average age 30. 203 applicants, 41% accepted, 60 enrolled. In 2010, 17 master's, 21 doctorates awarded. Terminal master's awarded for partial completion of doctoral program. *Degree requirements:* For master's, thesis (for some programs), interactive Program of Study (iPOS) submitted before completing 50 percent of required credit hours; for doctorate, variable foreign language requirement, comprehensive exam, thesis/dissertation, interactive Program of Study (iPOS) submitted before completing 50 percent of required credit hours. *Entrance requirements:* For master's and doctorate, GRE, minimum GPA of 3.0 or equivalent in last 2 years of work leading to bachelor's degree. Additional exam requirements/recommendations for international students: Required—TOEFL (minimum score 600 paper-based; 250 computer-based; 100 iBT). *Application deadline:* For fall admission, 12/15 for domestic and international students. Application fee: $70 ($90 for international students). Electronic applications accepted. *Expenses:* Tuition, state resident: full-time $8510; part-time $608 per credit. Tuition, nonresident: full-time $16,542; part-time $919 per credit. Required fees: $339; $110 per credit. Part-time tuition and fees vary according to course load. *Financial support:* In 2010–11, 80 research assistantships with full and partial tuition reimbursements (averaging $17,888 per year), 101 teaching assistantships with full and partial tuition reimbursements (averaging $17,327 per year) were awarded; fellowships with full tuition reimbursements, career-related internships or fieldwork, Federal Work-Study, institutionally sponsored loans, scholarships/grants, and tuition waivers (full and partial) also available. Financial award application deadline: 3/1; financial award applicants required to submit FAFSA. Total annual research expenditures: $29.3 million. *Unit head:* Dr. Robert E. Page, Director, 480-965-0803, E-mail: robert.page@asu.edu. *Application contact:* Graduate Admissions, 480-965-6113.

Arizona State University, College of Technology and Innovation, Department of Applied Sciences and Mathematics, Mesa, AZ 85212. Offers applied biological sciences (MS). Part-time programs available. *Faculty:* 34 full-time (11 women). *Students:* 11 full-time (7 women), 12 part-time (7 women); includes 2 minority (1 Black or African American, non-Hispanic/Latino; 1 Hispanic/Latino), 1 international. Average age 34. 9 applicants, 100% accepted, 7 enrolled. In 2010, 6 master's awarded. *Degree requirements:* For master's, thesis, oral defense, interactive Program of Study (iPOS) submitted before completing 50 percent of required credit hours. *Entrance requirements:* For master's, GRE (minimum combined score of 1080) or MAT (minimum score of 45), minimum GPA of 3.0 or equivalent in last 2 years of work leading to bachelor's degree, 3 letters of recommendation, resume, 18 hours of biological sciences or related courses, statement of intent. Additional exam requirements/recommendations for international students: Required—TOEFL, IELTS, or Pearson Test of English. *Application deadline:* For fall admission, 3/15 for domestic and international students; for spring admission, 10/15 for domestic and international students. Applications are processed on a rolling basis. Application fee: $70 ($90 for international students). Electronic applications accepted. *Expenses:* Tuition, state resident: full-time $8510; part-time $608 per credit. Tuition, nonresident: full-time $16,542; part-time $919 per credit. Required fees: $339; $110 per credit. Part-time tuition and fees vary according to course load. *Financial support:* In 2010–11, 3 research assistantships with full and partial tuition reimbursements (averaging $8,410 per year) were awarded; fellowships with partial tuition reimbursements, teaching assistantships with full and partial tuition reimbursements, career-related internships or fieldwork, institutionally sponsored loans, scholarships/grants, traineeships, health care benefits, and tuition waivers (full and partial) also available. Support available to part-time students. Financial award application deadline: 3/1; financial award applicants required to submit FAFSA. Total annual research expenditures: $2.7 million. *Unit head:* Dr. Douglas Green, Chair, 480-727-1251, Fax: 480-727-1089, E-mail: dm.green@asu.edu. *Application contact:* Graduate Admissions, 480-965-6113.

Arizona State University, Graduate College, Program in Biological Design, Tempe, AZ 85287-5001. Offers PhD. *Faculty:* 56 full-time (16 women). *Students:* 35 full-time (10 women); includes 4 minority (2 Asian, non-Hispanic/Latino; 1 Hispanic/Latino; 1 Two or more races, non-Hispanic/Latino), 18 international. Average age 25. 56 applicants, 25% accepted, 10 enrolled. *Degree requirements:* For doctorate, comprehensive exam, thesis/dissertation, interactive Program of Study (iPOS) submitted before completing 50 percent of required credit hours. *Entrance requirements:* For doctorate, GRE, minimum GPA of 3.0 in the last 2 years of work leading to the bachelor's degree, 3 letters of recommendation, personal statement containing goals and prior/current research experience, resume. Additional exam requirements/recommendations for international students: Required—TOEFL (minimum score 550 paper-based; 213 computer-based; 80 iBT), IELTS (minimum score 6.5). *Application deadline:* For fall admission, 1/1 for domestic and international students. Application fee: $70 ($90 for international students). Electronic applications accepted. *Expenses:* Tuition, state resident: full-time $8510; part-time $608 per credit. Tuition, nonresident: full-time $16,542; part-time $919 per credit. Required fees: $339; $110 per credit. Part-time tuition and fees vary according to course load. *Financial support:* In 2010–11, 32 research assistantships with full and partial tuition reimbursements (averaging $21,283 per year) were awarded; fellowships with full and partial tuition reimbursements, teaching assistantships with full and partial tuition reimbursements, institutionally sponsored loans, scholarships/grants, and tuition waivers (full and partial) also available. Financial award application deadline: 3/1; financial award applicants required to submit FAFSA. *Unit head:* Dr. Stephen Albert Johnston, Director, 480-727-0792, E-mail: stephen.johnston@asu.edu. *Application contact:* Graduate Admissions, 480-965-6113, Fax: 480-965-5158.

Arkansas State University, Graduate School, College of Sciences and Mathematics, Department of Biological Sciences, Jonesboro, State University, AR 72467. Offers biological sciences (MA); biology (MS); biology education (MSE, SCCT). Part-time programs available. *Faculty:* 14 full-time (4 women), 1 part-time/adjunct (0 women). *Students:* 19 full-time (10 women), 21 part-time (8 women); includes 3 minority (1 American Indian or Alaska Native, non-Hispanic/Latino; 1 Native Hawaiian or other Pacific Islander, non-Hispanic/Latino; 1 Two or more races, non-Hispanic/Latino), 12 international. Average age 28. 33 applicants, 67% accepted, 14 enrolled. In 2010, 39 master's awarded. *Degree requirements:* For master's, comprehensive exam, thesis (for some programs); for SCCT, comprehensive exam. *Entrance requirements:* For master's, GRE General Test, appropriate bachelor's degree, letters of reference, interview, official transcripts, immunization records, statement of educational objectives and career goals, teaching certificate (MSE); for SCCT, GRE General Test or MAT, interview, master's degree, letters of reference, official transcript, personal statement, immunization records. Additional exam requirements/recommendations for international students: Required—TOEFL (minimum score 550 paper-based; 213 computer-based; 79 iBT), IELTS (minimum score 6), PTE: Pearson Test of English Academic (56). *Application deadline:* For fall admission, 7/1 for domestic and international students; for spring admission, 11/15 for domestic students, 11/14 for international students. Applications are processed on a rolling basis. Application fee: $30 ($40 for international students). Electronic applications accepted. *Expenses:* Tuition, state resident: full-time $3888; part-time $216 per credit hour. Tuition, nonresident: full-time $9918; part-time $551 per credit hour. International tuition: $8376 full-time. Required fees: $932; $49 per credit hour. $25 per term. One-time fee: $30. Tuition and fees vary according to course load and program. *Financial support:* In 2010–11, 21 students received support; research assistantships, career-related internships or fieldwork, scholarships/grants, and unspecified assistantships available. Financial award application deadline: 7/1; financial award applicants required to submit FAFSA. *Unit head:* Dr. Thomas Risch, Interim Chair, 870-972-3082, Fax: 870-972-2638, E-mail: trisch@astate.edu. *Application contact:* Dr. Andrew Sustich, Dean of the Graduate School, 870-972-3029, Fax: 870-972-3857, E-mail: sustich@astate.edu.

A.T. Still University of Health Sciences, Kirksville College of Osteopathic Medicine, Kirksville, MO 63501. Offers biomedical sciences (MS); osteopathic medicine (DO). *Accreditation:* AOsA. *Faculty:* 34 full-time (6 women), 17 part-time/adjunct (3 women). *Students:* 716 full-time (286 women), 9 part-time (3 women); includes 115 minority (13 Black or African American, non-Hispanic/Latino; 5 American Indian or Alaska Native, non-Hispanic/Latino; 75 Asian, non-Hispanic/Latino; 19 Hispanic/Latino; 2 Native Hawaiian or other Pacific Islander, non-Hispanic/Latino; 1 Two or more races, non-Hispanic/Latino), 11 international. Average age 26. 3,483 applicants, 11% accepted, 172 enrolled. In 2010, 165 first professional degrees, 9 master's awarded. *Degree requirements:* For master's, thesis; for DO, Level 1 and 2 COMLEX-PE and CE exams. *Entrance requirements:* For DO, MCAT, bachelor's degree with minimum undergraduate GPA of 2.5 (cumulative and science) or 90 semester hours with minimum GPA of 3.5 (cumulative and science) and minimum MCAT of 28; for master's, GRE, MCAT, or DAT, minimum undergraduate GPA of 2.5 (cumulative and science). *Application deadline:* For fall admission, 2/1 for domestic and international students. Applications are processed on a rolling basis. Application fee: $60. Electronic applications accepted. *Expenses:* Contact institution. *Financial support:* In 2010–11, 192 students received support, including 20 fellowships with full tuition reimbursements available (averaging $16,000 per year); Federal Work-Study and scholarships/grants also available. Financial award application deadline: 5/1; financial award applicants required to submit FAFSA. *Faculty research:* Osteopathic palpatory procedures, duchenne muscular dystrophy, gene array studies of pain remediation, thoracic lymphatic pump techniques, animal models of manual medicine, melanoma mestastasis. Total annual research expenditures: $362,296. *Unit head:* Dr. Jeff Suzewits, Acting Dean, 660-626-2354, Fax: 660-626-2080, E-mail: jsuzewits@atsu.edu. *Application contact:* Donna Sparks, Associate Director for Admissions, 660-626-2237, Fax: 660-626-2969, E-mail: admissions@atsu.edu.

Auburn University, College of Veterinary Medicine and Graduate School, Graduate Programs in Veterinary Medicine, Auburn University, AL 36849. Offers biomedical sciences (MS, PhD), including anatomy, physiology and pharmacology (MS), biomedical sciences (PhD), clinical sciences (MS), large animal surgery and medicine (MS), pathobiology (MS), radiology (MS), small animal surgery and medicine (MS); DVM/MS. Part-time programs available. *Faculty:* 100 full-time (40 women), 5 part-time/adjunct (1 woman). *Students:* 17 full-time (6 women), 51 part-time (35 women); includes 2 Black or African American, non-Hispanic/Latino; 1 American Indian or Alaska Native, non-Hispanic/Latino; 3 Asian, non-Hispanic/Latino; 2 Hispanic/Latino, 22 international. Average age 31. 70 applicants, 34% accepted, 10 enrolled. In 2010, 12 master's, 7 doctorates awarded. *Degree requirements:* For doctorate, thesis/dissertation. *Entrance requirements:* For master's, GRE General Test; for doctorate, GRE General Test, GRE Subject Test. *Application deadline:* For fall admission, 7/7 for domestic students; for spring admission, 11/24 for domestic students. Applications are processed on a rolling basis. Application fee: $50 ($60 for international students). Electronic applications accepted. *Expenses:* Tuition, state resident: full-time $7002. Tuition, nonresident: full-time $21,898. International tuition: $22,116 full-time. Required fees: $892. Tuition and fees vary according to course load and program. *Financial support:* Research assistantships, teaching assistantships, Federal Work-Study available. Support available to part-time students. Financial award application deadline: 3/15; financial award applicants required to submit FAFSA. *Unit head:* Dr. Timothy R. Boosinger, Dean, 334-844-4546. *Application contact:* Dr. George Flowers, Dean of the Graduate School, 334-844-2125.

Auburn University, Graduate School, College of Sciences and Mathematics, Department of Biological Sciences, Auburn University, AL 36849. Offers botany (MS, PhD); microbiology (MS, PhD); zoology (MS, PhD). *Faculty:* 33 full-time (8 women), 1 (woman) part-time/adjunct. *Students:* 42 full-time (17 women), 60 part-time (36 women); includes 4 Black or African American, non-Hispanic/Latino; 1 American Indian or Alaska Native, non-Hispanic/Latino; 3 Asian, non-Hispanic/Latino; 1 Hispanic/Latino, 21 international. Average age 28. 134 applicants, 20% accepted, 18 enrolled. In 2010, 22 master's, 11 doctorates awarded. *Entrance requirements:* For master's and doctorate, GRE General Test. Additional exam requirements/recommendations for international students: Required—TOEFL. *Application deadline:* For fall admission, 7/7 for domestic students; for spring admission, 11/24 for domestic students. Application fee: $50 ($60 for international students). Electronic applications accepted. *Expenses:* Tuition, state resident: full-time $7002. Tuition, nonresident: full-time $21,898. International tuition: $22,116 full-time. Required fees: $892. Tuition and fees vary according to course load and program. *Financial support:* Research assistantships, teaching assistantships available. Financial award applicants required to submit FAFSA. *Unit head:* Dr. James M. Barbaree, Chair, 334-844-7511, Fax: 334-844-1645. *Application contact:* Dr. George Flowers, Dean of the Graduate School, 334-844-2125.

Austin Peay State University, College of Graduate Studies, College of Science and Mathematics, Department of Biology, Clarksville, TN 37044. Offers clinical laboratory science (MS); radiologic science (MS). Part-time programs available. *Faculty:* 13 full-time (6 women). *Students:* 6 full-time (all women), 17 part-time (8 women); includes 4 minority (2 Black or African American, non-Hispanic/Latino; 2 Hispanic/Latino), 1 international. Average age 29. 15 applicants, 100% accepted, 11 enrolled. In 2010, 6 master's awarded. *Degree requirements:* For master's, comprehensive exam, thesis optional. *Entrance requirements:* For master's, GRE General Test, 3 letters of recommendation, minimum undergraduate GPA of 2.5. Additional exam requirements/recommendations for international students: Required—TOEFL (minimum score 500 paper-based; 173 computer-based). *Application deadline:* For fall admission, 7/27 priority date for domestic students; for spring admission, 12/17 priority date for domestic students. Applications are processed on a rolling basis. Application fee: $25. Electronic applications accepted. *Expenses:* Tuition, state resident: full-time $6480; part-time $324 per credit hour. Tuition, nonresident: full-time $17,960; part-time $898 per credit hour. Required fees: $1244; $61.20 per credit hour. *Financial support:* In 2010–11, research assistantships with full tuition reimbursements (averaging $5,174 per year); career-related internships or fieldwork, Federal Work-Study, institutionally sponsored loans, scholarships/grants, and unspecified assistantships also available. Support available to part-time students. Financial award application deadline: 3/1. *Faculty research:* Non-paint source pollution, amphibian biomonitoring, aquatic toxicology, biological indicators of water quality, taxonomy. *Unit head:* Dr. Don Dailey, Chair, 931-221-7781, Fax: 931-221-6323, E-mail: daileyd@apsu.edu. *Application contact:* Dr. Dixie Dennis Pinder, Dean, College of Graduate Studies, 931-221-7662, Fax: 931-221-7641, E-mail: dennisdi@apsu.edu.

Ball State University, Graduate School, College of Sciences and Humanities, Department of Biology, Muncie, IN 47306-1099. Offers biology (MA, MAE, MS); biology education (Ed D). *Faculty:* 22. *Students:* 30 full-time (17 women), 21 part-time (10 women); includes 3 minority (2 American Indian or Alaska Native, non-Hispanic/Latino; 1 Two or more races, non-Hispanic/Latino), 6 international. Average age 24. 58 applicants, 57% accepted, 29 enrolled. In 2010, 22 master's, 3 doctorates awarded. *Degree requirements:* For doctorate, thesis/dissertation. *Entrance requirements:* For master's, GRE General Test; for doctorate, GRE General Test, minimum graduate GPA of 3.2. Application fee: $50. *Expenses:* Tuition, state resident: full-time $6160; part-time $299 per credit hour. Tuition, nonresident: full-time $16,020; part-time $783 per credit hour. Required fees: $2278; $95 per credit hour. *Financial support:* In 2010–11, 3 research assistantships with full tuition reimbursements (averaging $10,967 per year), 27 teaching assistantships with full tuition reimbursements (averaging $10,780 per year) were awarded; career-related internships or fieldwork also available. Financial award application deadline: 3/1. *Faculty research:* Aquatics and fisheries, tumors, water and air pollution, developmental biology and genetics. *Unit head:* Dr. Kemuel Badger, Chairman, 765-285-8820, Fax: 765-285-8804. *Application contact:* Dr. Robert Morris, Associate Provost for Research and Dean of the Graduate School, 765-285-1300, E-mail: rmorris@bsu.edu.

Barry University, College of Health Sciences, Programs in Biology and Biomedical Sciences, Miami Shores, FL 33161-6695. Offers biology (MS); biomedical sciences (MS). Part-time and evening/weekend programs available. *Degree requirements:* For master's, comprehensive exam, thesis (for some programs). *Entrance requirements:* For master's, GRE General Test or Florida Teacher's Certification Exam (biology); GRE General Test, MCAT, or DAT (biomedical sciences). Electronic applications accepted. *Faculty research:* Genetics, immunology, anthropology.

Baylor College of Medicine, Graduate School of Biomedical Sciences, Houston, TX 77030-3498. Offers MS, PhD, MD/PhD. *Faculty:* 417 full-time (105 women). *Students:* 608 full-time (314 women); includes 25 Black or African American, non-Hispanic/Latino; 3 American Indian or Alaska Native, non-Hispanic/Latino; 63 Asian, non-Hispanic/Latino; 52 Hispanic/Latino, 221 international. Average age 28. 1,112 applicants, 20% accepted, 117 enrolled. In 2010, 11 master's, 74 doctorates awarded. Terminal master's awarded for partial completion of doctoral program. *Degree requirements:* For master's, thesis; for doctorate, thesis/dissertation, public defense. *Entrance requirements:* For doctorate, GRE General Test, GRE Subject Test (strongly recommended), minimum GPA of 3.0. Additional exam requirements/recommendations for international students: Required—TOEFL. *Application deadline:* For fall admission, 1/1 priority date for domestic students. Applications are processed on a rolling basis. Application fee: $0. Electronic applications accepted. *Expenses:* Tuition: Full-time $11,000. Required fees: $4900. *Financial support:* In 2010–11, 177 fellowships with full tuition reimbursements (averaging $26,000 per year), 431 research assistantships with full tuition reimbursements (averaging $26,000 per year) were awarded; teaching assistantships, career-related internships or fieldwork, Federal Work-Study, institutionally sponsored loans, health care benefits, and students receive a scholarship unless there are grant funds available to pay tuition also available. Financial award applicants required to submit FAFSA. *Faculty research:* Cell and molecular biology of cardiac muscle, structural biophysics, gene expression and regulation, human genomes, viruses. *Unit head:* Dr. William R. Brinkley, Dean of Graduate Sciences, 713-798-5263, Fax: 713-798-6325, E-mail: brinkley@bcm.tmc.edu. *Application contact:* Melissa Houghton, Administrator for GSBS Admissions, 713-798-4031, Fax: 713-798-6325, E-mail: melissah@bcm.edu.

Baylor University, Graduate School, College of Arts and Sciences, Department of Biology, Waco, TX 76798. Offers biology (MA, MS, PhD); environmental biology (MS); limnology (MS). Part-time programs available. *Faculty:* 13 full-time (3 women). *Students:* 34 full-time (14 women), 2 part-time (both women); includes 4 minority (2 Hispanic/Latino; 2 Two or more races, non-Hispanic/Latino), 13 international. In 2010, 6 master's, 1 doctorate awarded. *Degree requirements:* For master's, thesis (for some programs); for doctorate, thesis/dissertation. *Entrance requirements:* For master's and doctorate, GRE General Test. *Application deadline:*

Biological and Biomedical Sciences—General

Baylor University *(continued)*
For fall admission, 1/31 priority date for domestic students. Applications are processed on a rolling basis. Application fee: $25. *Financial support:* Teaching assistantships, career-related internships or fieldwork, Federal Work-Study, institutionally sponsored loans, and tuition waivers (full and partial) available. Support available to part-time students. Financial award application deadline: 2/28. *Faculty research:* Terrestrial ecology, aquatic ecology, genetics. *Unit head:* Dr. Myeongwoo Lee, Graduate Program Director, 254-710-2141, Fax: 254-710-2969, E-mail: myeongwoo_lee@baylor.edu. *Application contact:* Tamara Lehmann, Administrative Assistant, 254-710-2911, Fax: 254-710-2969, E-mail: tamara_lehmann@baylor.edu.

Baylor University, Graduate School, Institute of Biomedical Studies, Waco, TX 76798. Offers MS, PhD. *Students:* 29 full-time (17 women); includes 3 minority (1 Asian, non-Hispanic/Latino; 1 Hispanic/Latino; 1 Two or more races, non-Hispanic/Latino), 9 international. In 2010, 3 master's, 3 doctorates awarded. *Entrance requirements:* For master's and doctorate, GRE General Test. *Application deadline:* Applications are processed on a rolling basis. Application fee: $25. *Financial support:* Research assistantships, teaching assistantships available. *Unit head:* Dr. Chris Kearney, Graduate Program Director, 254-710-2131, Fax: 254-710-3878, E-mail: chris_kearney@baylor.edu. *Application contact:* Rhonda Bellert, Administrative Assistant, 254-710-2514, Fax: 254-710-3870, E-mail: rhonda_bellert@baylor.edu.

Bemidji State University, School of Graduate Studies, Bemidji, MN 56601-2699. Offers biology (MS); counseling psychology (MS); education (M Ed, MS); English (MA, MS); environmental studies (MS); mathematics (MS); mathematics (elementary and middle level education) (MS); special education (M Sp Ed, MS). Part-time programs available. Postbaccalaureate distance learning degree programs offered (no on-campus study). *Faculty:* 142 full-time (61 women), 37 part-time/adjunct (22 women). *Students:* 82 full-time (51 women), 350 part-time (210 women); includes 21 minority (6 Black or African American, non-Hispanic/Latino; 3 American Indian or Alaska Native, non-Hispanic/Latino; 6 Asian, non-Hispanic/Latino; 6 Hispanic/Latino), 8 international. Average age 35. 491 applicants, 93% accepted, 307 enrolled. In 2010, 97 master's awarded. *Degree requirements:* For master's, comprehensive exam, thesis (for some programs). *Entrance requirements:* For master's, GRE, letters of recommendation, letters of interest. Additional exam requirements/recommendations for international students: Required—TOEFL (minimum score 550 paper-based; 213 computer-based; 80 iBT). *Application deadline:* Applications are processed on a rolling basis. Application fee: $20. Electronic applications accepted. *Expenses:* Tuition, state resident: full-time $6605; part-time $330 per credit. Tuition, nonresident: full-time $6605; part-time $330 per credit. Required fees: $107.97 per credit. *Financial support:* In 2010–11, 110 students received support, including 40 research assistantships with partial tuition reimbursements available (averaging $7,196 per year), 40 teaching assistantships with partial tuition reimbursements available (averaging $7,196 per year); career-related internships or fieldwork, Federal Work-Study, scholarships/grants, health care benefits, and unspecified assistantships also available. Support available to part-time students. Financial award application deadline: 4/15; financial award applicants required to submit FAFSA. *Unit head:* Dr. Patricia Rogers, Dean, 218-755-2027, Fax: 218-755-2258, E-mail: progers@bemidjistate.edu. *Application contact:* Joan Miller, Senior Office and Administrative Specialist, 218-755-2027, Fax: 218-755-2258, E-mail: jmiller@bemidjistate.edu.

Bloomsburg University of Pennsylvania, School of Graduate Studies, College of Science and Technology, Department of Biological and Allied Health Sciences, Program in Biology, Bloomsburg, PA 17815-1301. Offers MS. *Degree requirements:* For master's, thesis or alternative. *Entrance requirements:* For master's, minimum QPA of 3.0, 2 letters of recommendation. Additional exam requirements/recommendations for international students: Required—TOEFL (minimum score 550 paper-based; 213 computer-based; 79 iBT). Electronic applications accepted.

Boise State University, Graduate College, College of Arts and Sciences, Department of Biology, Program in Biology, Boise, ID 83725-0399. Offers MA, MS. Part-time programs available. *Degree requirements:* For master's, thesis. *Entrance requirements:* For master's, GRE General Test, minimum GPA of 3.0. Electronic applications accepted.

Boston College, Graduate School of Arts and Sciences, Department of Biology, Chestnut Hill, MA 02467-3800. Offers PhD, MBA/MS. *Degree requirements:* For doctorate, thesis/dissertation. *Entrance requirements:* For doctorate, GRE General Test, GRE Subject Test. Additional exam requirements/recommendations for international students: Required—TOEFL (minimum score 600 paper-based; 250 computer-based; 100 iBT). Electronic applications accepted. *Faculty research:* DNA replication in mammalian cells, control of the cell cycle, immunology, plant genetics.

See Display below and Close-Up on page 89.

Boston University, Graduate School of Arts and Sciences, Department of Biology, Boston, MA 02215. Offers MA, PhD. *Students:* 83 full-time (47 women), 3 part-time (1 woman); includes 15 minority (3 Black or African American, non-Hispanic/Latino; 6 Asian, non-Hispanic/Latino; 3 Hispanic/Latino; 3 Two or more races, non-Hispanic/Latino), 7 international. Average age 28. 141 applicants, 27% accepted, 21 enrolled. In 2010, 206 master's, 13 doctorates awarded. Terminal master's awarded for partial completion of doctoral program. *Degree requirements:* For master's, one foreign language, thesis (for some programs); for doctorate, one foreign language, comprehensive exam, thesis/dissertation. *Entrance requirements:* For master's and doctorate, GRE General Test, GRE Subject Test, 3 letters of recommendation. Additional exam requirements/recommendations for international students: Required—TOEFL (minimum score 600 paper-based; 250 computer-based). *Application deadline:* For fall admission, 12/7 for domestic and international students. Application fee: $70. Electronic applications accepted. *Expenses:* Tuition: Full-time $39,314; part-time $1228 per credit. Required fees: $40 per semester. *Financial support:* In 2010–11, 2 fellowships with full tuition reimbursements (averaging $19,300 per year), 46 research assistantships with full tuition reimbursements (averaging $18,800 per year), 52 teaching assistantships with full tuition reimbursements (averaging $18,800 per year) were awarded; Federal Work-Study, institutionally sponsored loans, scholarships/grants, and traineeships also available. Financial award application deadline: 12/7; financial award applicants required to submit FAFSA. *Unit head:* Michael Sorenson, Chairman, 617-353-3856, Fax: 617-353-6340, E-mail: msoren@bu.edu. *Application contact:* Meredith Canode, Academic Administrator, 617-353-2432, Fax: 617-353-6340, E-mail: mcanode@bu.edu.

Boston University, School of Education, Boston, MA 02215. Offers counseling (Ed M, CAGS), including community, school, sport psychology; counseling psychology (Ed D); curriculum and teaching (Ed M, Ed D, CAGS), including early childhood (Ed D), educational media and technology (Ed D), English and language arts (Ed D), mathematics (Ed D), physical education and coaching (Ed D), science (Ed D), social studies education (Ed D), special education (Ed D); developmental studies (Ed D), including literacy and language, reading education; developmental studies in literacy and language education (Ed M, CAGS); early childhood education (Ed M, CAGS); education of the deaf (Ed M, CAGS); educational leadership and development (Ed D), including educational administration (Ed M, Ed D, CAGS), higher education administration (Ed M, Ed D, CAGS); educational media and technology (Ed M, CAGS); elementary education (Ed M); English and language arts (Ed M, CAGS); English education (MAT); health education (Ed M, CAGS); Latin and classical studies (MAT); mathematics education (Ed M, MAT, CAGS); mathematics for teaching (MMT); modern foreign language education (MAT), including French, Spanish; physical education and coaching (Ed M, CAGS); policy, planning, and administration (Ed M, CAGS), including community education leadership, educational administration (Ed M, Ed D, CAGS), higher education administration (Ed M, Ed D, CAGS); reading education (Ed M, CAGS); science education (Ed M, MAT, CAGS), including biology (MAT), chemistry (MAT), earth science (MAT), general science (MAT), physics (MAT); social studies education (Ed M, MAT, CAGS), including history (MAT), political science (MAT); special education (Ed M, Ed D, CAGS), including disability studies (Ed M), moderate disabilities (Ed M), severe disabilities (Ed M), special education administration (Ed M); teaching English as a second language (Ed M, CAGS). Part-time programs available. *Faculty:* 57

full-time, 39 part-time/adjunct. *Students:* 245 full-time (191 women), 376 part-time (274 women); includes 83 minority (14 Black or African American, non-Hispanic/Latino; 2 American Indian or Alaska Native, non-Hispanic/Latino; 28 Asian, non-Hispanic/Latino; 6 Two or more races, non-Hispanic/Latino), 79 international. Average age 30. 1,270 applicants, 66% accepted, 292 enrolled. In 2010, 273 master's, 15 doctorates, 7 other advanced degrees awarded. Terminal master's awarded for partial completion of doctoral program. *Degree requirements:* For master's, thesis (for some programs); for doctorate, comprehensive exam, thesis/dissertation; for CAGS, comprehensive exam. *Entrance requirements:* For master's and CAGS, GRE General Test or MAT; for doctorate, GRE General Test. Additional exam requirements/recommendations for international students: Required—TOEFL, IELTS. *Application deadline:* For fall admission, 1/15 priority date for domestic and international students; for spring admission, 9/15 priority date for domestic and international students. Applications are processed on a rolling basis. Application fee: $70. Electronic applications accepted. *Expenses:* Tuition: Full-time $39,314; part-time $1228 per credit. Required fees: $40 per semester. *Financial support:* In 2010–11, 276 students received support, including 31 fellowships with full tuition reimbursements available, 16 research assistantships, 26 teaching assistantships with partial tuition reimbursements available; career-related internships or fieldwork, Federal Work-Study, and scholarships/grants also available. Support available to part-time students. Financial award applicants required to submit FAFSA. *Faculty research:* Deaf studies, social emotional learning, civic engagement and education, STEM education, pre-college educational pipelines. Total annual research expenditures: $2.6 million. *Unit head:* Dr. Hardin Coleman, Dean, 617-353-3213. *Application contact:* Dana Fernandez, Director of Enrollment, 617-353-4237, Fax: 617-353-8937, E-mail: sedgrad@bu.edu.

Boston University, School of Medicine, Division of Graduate Medical Sciences, Boston, MA 02118. Offers MA, MS, PhD, MBA/MS, MD/MBA, MD/PhD, MPH/MA. Part-time programs available. *Faculty:* 1,019 full-time (460 women), 517 part-time/adjunct (212 women). *Students:* 775 full-time (432 women), 106 part-time (75 women); includes 221 minority (33 Black or African American, non-Hispanic/Latino; 2 American Indian or Alaska Native, non-Hispanic/Latino; 126 Asian, non-Hispanic/Latino; 41 Hispanic/Latino; 4 Native Hawaiian or other Pacific Islander, non-Hispanic/Latino; 15 Two or more races, non-Hispanic/Latino), 99 international. Average age 25. 2,060 applicants, 37% accepted, 373 enrolled. In 2010, 261 master's, 47 doctorates awarded. Terminal master's awarded for partial completion of doctoral program. *Degree requirements:* For master's, thesis (for some programs); for doctorate, comprehensive exam, thesis/dissertation, qualifying exam. *Entrance requirements:* For master's, GRE, MCAT; for doctorate, GRE. Additional exam requirements/recommendations for international students: Required—TOEFL; Recommended—IELTS. *Application deadline:* For fall admission, 1/31 priority date for domestic and international students; for spring admission, 10/15 priority date for domestic and international students. Applications are processed on a rolling basis. Application fee: $75. Electronic applications accepted. *Expenses:* Contact institution. *Financial support:* In 2010–11, 261 students received support, including 19 fellowships with tuition reimbursements available (averaging $30,500 per year), 157 research assistantships with full and partial tuition reimbursements available (averaging $30,500 per year), 1 teaching assistantship with tuition reimbursement available (averaging $30,500 per year); Federal Work-Study, scholarships/grants, and traineeships also available. Financial award applicants required to submit FAFSA. *Unit head:* Dr. Linda E. Hyman, Associate Provost, 617-638-5255, Fax: 617-638-5740, E-mail: askgms@bu.edu. *Application contact:* Michelle Hall, Associate Director of Admissions, 617-638-5121, Fax: 617-638-5740, E-mail: natashah@bu.edu.

Bowling Green State University, Graduate College, College of Arts and Sciences, Department of Biological Sciences, Bowling Green, OH 43403. Offers MAT, MS, PhD. Part-time programs available. *Degree requirements:* For master's, thesis or alternative; for doctorate, comprehensive exam, thesis/dissertation. *Entrance requirements:* For master's and doctorate, GRE General Test. Additional exam requirements/recommendations for international students: Required—

TOEFL. Electronic applications accepted. *Faculty research:* Aquatic ecology, endocrinology and neurophysiology, nitrogen fixation, photosynthesis.

See Display below and Close-Up on page 91.

Bradley University, Graduate School, College of Liberal Arts and Sciences, Department of Biology, Peoria, IL 61625-0002. Offers MS. Part-time programs available. *Degree requirements:* For master's, comprehensive exam, thesis. *Entrance requirements:* For master's, GRE General Test, 2 letters of recommendation. Additional exam requirements/recommendations for international students: Required—TOEFL (minimum score 550 paper-based; 213 computer-based).

Brandeis University, Graduate School of Arts and Sciences, Post-Baccalaureate Premedical Program, Waltham, MA 02454-9110. Offers Postbaccalaureate Certificate. Part-time programs available. *Students:* 2 full-time (0 women), 4 part-time (3 women); includes 1 Black or African American, non-Hispanic/Latino. 67 applicants, 34% accepted, 2 enrolled. In 2010, 5 Postbaccalaureate Certificates awarded. *Entrance requirements:* For degree, GRE or SAT, resume with paid and/or volunteer work relevant to field of medicine, letters of recommendation. Additional exam requirements/recommendations for international students: Required—TOEFL (minimum score 600 paper-based; 250 computer-based; 100 iBT); Recommended—IELTS (minimum score 7). *Application deadline:* For fall admission, 5/1 priority date for domestic students. Applications are processed on a rolling basis. Application fee: $75. Electronic applications accepted. *Financial support:* Applicants required to submit FAFSA. *Faculty research:* Health profession preparation, pre-medical, pre-veterinary, pre-dental, pre-optometry, pre-osteopathic. *Unit head:* Judith Hudson, Director of Health Professions Advising, 781-736-3470, Fax: 781-736-3469, E-mail: hudsonj@brandeis.edu. *Application contact:* David Cotter, Assistant Dean, Graduate School of Arts and Sciences, 781-736-3410, E-mail: gradschool@brandeis.edu.

Brigham Young University, Graduate Studies, College of Life Sciences, Department of Biology, Provo, UT 84602. Offers biological science education (MS); biology (MS, PhD). *Faculty:* 20 full-time (2 women). *Students:* 27 full-time (9 women), 1 part-time (0 women); includes 7 minority (1 Asian, non-Hispanic/Latino; 6 Hispanic/Latino). Average age 30. 13 applicants, 77% accepted, 8 enrolled. In 2010, 14 master's, 4 doctorates awarded. *Degree requirements:* For master's, comprehensive exam, thesis, prospectus, defense of research, defense of thesis; for doctorate, comprehensive exam, thesis/dissertation, prospectus, defense of research, defense of dissertation. *Entrance requirements:* For master's and doctorate, GRE General Test, GRE Subject Test (biology), minimum GPA of 3.0 for last 60 credit hours of course work. Additional exam requirements/recommendations for international students: Required—TOEFL (minimum score 580 paper-based; 85 iBT). *Application deadline:* For fall admission, 1/15 for domestic and international students. Application fee: $50. Electronic applications accepted. *Expenses:* Tuition: Full-time $5580; part-time $310 per credit hour. Tuition and fees vary according to program and student's religious affiliation. *Financial support:* In 2010–11, 2 students received support, including 2 fellowships with full and partial tuition reimbursements available (averaging $2,607 per year); research assistantships with full and partial tuition reimbursements available, teaching assistantships with full and partial tuition reimbursements available, career-related internships or fieldwork, institutionally sponsored loans, scholarships/grants, health care benefits, tuition waivers (full and partial), and unspecified assistantships also available. Financial award application deadline: 2/1; financial award applicants required to submit FAFSA. *Faculty research:* Systematics, bioinformatics, ecology, evolution. Total annual research expenditures: $1.4 million. *Unit head:* Dr. Keith A. Crandall, Chair, 801-422-3495, Fax: 801-422-0090, E-mail: keith_crandall@byu.edu. *Application contact:* Christina M. George, Office Manager, 801-422-7389, Fax: 801-422-0090, E-mail: biogradsec@byu.edu.

Brock University, Faculty of Graduate Studies, Faculty of Mathematics and Science, Program in Biological Sciences, St. Catharines, ON L2S 3A1, Canada. Offers M Sc, PhD. Part-time programs available. *Degree requirements:* For master's, thesis; for doctorate, thesis/dissertation.

Biological and Biomedical Sciences—General

Brock University *(continued)*
Entrance requirements: For master's, honors B Sc in biology, minimum undergraduate GPA of 3.0; for doctorate, M Sc. Additional exam requirements/recommendations for international students: Required—TOEFL (minimum score 550 paper-based; 213 computer-based; 80 iBT), IELTS (minimum score 6.5), TWE (minimum score 4). Electronic applications accepted. *Faculty research:* Viticulture, neurobiology, ecology, molecular biology, molecular genetics.

Brooklyn College of the City University of New York, Division of Graduate Studies, Department of Biology, Brooklyn, NY 11210-2889. Offers MA, PhD. *Students:* 8 full-time (5 women), 26 part-time (15 women); includes 21 minority (10 Black or African American, non-Hispanic/Latino; 7 Asian, non-Hispanic/Latino; 4 Hispanic/Latino), 6 international. Average age 28. 34 applicants, 91% accepted, 15 enrolled. In 2010, 5 master's awarded. *Degree requirements:* For master's, one foreign language, comprehensive exam, thesis. *Entrance requirements:* For master's, minimum GPA of 3.0, 2 letters of recommendation. Additional exam requirements/recommendations for international students: Required—TOEFL (minimum score 500 paper-based; 173 computer-based; 61 iBT). *Application deadline:* For fall admission, 7/31 for domestic students, 6/30 for international students; for spring admission, 12/15 for domestic students, 11/15 for international students. Applications are processed on a rolling basis. Application fee: $125. Electronic applications accepted. *Expenses:* Tuition, state resident: full-time $7360; part-time $310 per credit hour. Tuition, nonresident: full-time $13,800; part-time $575 per credit hour. Required fees: $190 per semester. *Financial support:* Federal Work-Study, institutionally sponsored loans, and scholarships/grants available. Support available to part-time students. Financial award application deadline: 5/1; financial award applicants required to submit FAFSA. *Faculty research:* Evolutionary biology, molecular biology of development, cell biology, comparative endocrinology, ecology. *Unit head:* Dr. Peter Lipke, Chairperson, 718-951-5396, E-mail: plipke@brooklyn.cuny.edu. *Application contact:* Hernan Sierra, Graduate Admissions Coordinator, 718-951-4536, Fax: 718-951-4506, E-mail: grads@brooklyn.cuny.edu.

Brooklyn College of the City University of New York, Division of Graduate Studies, School of Education, Program in Middle Childhood Education (Science), Brooklyn, NY 11210-2889. Offers biology (MA); chemistry (MA); earth science (MA); general science (MA); physics (MA). Part-time and evening/weekend programs available. *Students:* 3 full-time (1 woman), 74 part-time (46 women); includes 29 minority (12 Black or African American, non-Hispanic/Latino; 8 Asian, non-Hispanic/Latino; 9 Hispanic/Latino), 4 international. Average age 32. 29 applicants, 97% accepted, 21 enrolled. In 2010, 24 master's awarded. *Entrance requirements:* For master's, LAST, interview, previous course work in education and mathematics, resume, 2 letters of recommendation, essay. Additional exam requirements/recommendations for international students: Required—TOEFL (minimum score 500 paper-based; 173 computer-based; 61 iBT). *Application deadline:* For fall admission, 7/15 priority date for domestic students, 6/1 priority date for international students; for spring admission, 11/15 priority date for domestic students, 10/1 priority date for international students. Applications are processed on a rolling basis. Application fee: $125. Electronic applications accepted. *Expenses:* Tuition, state resident: full-time $7360; part-time $310 per credit hour. Tuition, nonresident: full-time $13,800; part-time $575 per credit hour. Required fees: $190 per semester. *Financial support:* Federal Work-Study, institutionally sponsored loans, and scholarships/grants available. Support available to part-time students. Financial award application deadline: 5/1; financial award applicants required to submit FAFSA. *Faculty research:* Geometric thinking, mastery of basic facts, problem-solving strategies, history of mathematics. *Unit head:* Dr. Jennifer Adams, Program Head, 718-951-5214, E-mail: jadams@brooklyn.cuny.edu. *Application contact:* Hernan Sierra, Graduate Admissions Coordinator, 718-951-4536, Fax: 718-951-4506, E-mail: grads@brooklyn.cuny.edu.

Brown University, Graduate School, Division of Biology and Medicine, Providence, RI 02912. Offers M Med Sc, MA, MPH, MS, Sc M, PhD, MD/PhD. Part-time programs available. Terminal master's awarded for partial completion of doctoral program. *Degree requirements:* For doctorate, thesis/dissertation. *Entrance requirements:* For master's and doctorate, GRE General Test. Additional exam requirements/recommendations for international students: Required—TOEFL. Electronic applications accepted.

Bucknell University, Graduate Studies, College of Arts and Sciences, Department of Biology, Lewisburg, PA 17837. Offers MA, MS. Part-time programs available. *Degree requirements:* For master's, thesis. *Entrance requirements:* For master's, GRE General Test, GRE Subject Test, minimum GPA of 2.8. Additional exam requirements/recommendations for international students: Required—TOEFL. *Expenses:* Tuition: Full-time $36,992; part-time $4624 per course.

Buffalo State College, State University of New York, The Graduate School, Faculty of Natural and Social Sciences, Department of Biology, Buffalo, NY 14222-1095. Offers biology (MA); secondary education (MS Ed), including biology. Evening/weekend programs available. *Degree requirements:* For master's, thesis, project. *Entrance requirements:* For master's, minimum GPA of 2.75. Additional exam requirements/recommendations for international students: Required—TOEFL (minimum score 550 paper-based; 213 computer-based).

California Institute of Technology, Division of Biology, Pasadena, CA 91125-0001. Offers biochemistry and molecular biophysics (PhD); cell biology and biophysics (PhD); developmental biology (PhD); genetics (PhD); immunology (PhD); molecular biology (PhD); neurobiology (PhD). *Faculty:* 40 full-time (9 women). *Students:* 78 full-time (41 women); includes 3 Black or African American, non-Hispanic/Latino; 5 Hispanic/Latino. 176 applicants, 18% accepted, 11 enrolled. In 2010, 18 doctorates awarded. *Degree requirements:* For doctorate, thesis/dissertation, qualifying exam. *Entrance requirements:* For doctorate, GRE General Test. Additional exam requirements/recommendations for international students: Required—TOEFL. *Application deadline:* For fall admission, 1/1 for domestic and international students. Application fee: $80. Electronic applications accepted. *Financial support:* In 2010–11, fellowships with full tuition reimbursements (averaging $23,766 per year), teaching assistantships with full tuition reimbursements (averaging $4,782 per year) were awarded; research assistantships with full tuition reimbursements, institutionally sponsored loans, scholarships/grants, and unspecified assistantships also available. Financial award application deadline: 1/1. *Faculty research:* Molecular genetics of differentiation and development, structure of biological macromolecules, molecular and integrative neurobiology. *Unit head:* Prof. Stephen L. Mayo, Chairman, 626-395-4951, Fax: 626-683-3343. *Application contact:* Elizabeth M. Ayala, Graduate Program Coordinator, 626-395-4497, Fax: 626-683-3343, E-mail: biograd@caltech.edu.

See Display below and Close-Up on page 93.

California Polytechnic State University, San Luis Obispo, College of Science and Mathematics, Department of Biological Sciences, San Luis Obispo, CA 93407. Offers MS. Part-time programs available. *Faculty:* 1 (woman) full-time, 2 part-time/adjunct (both women). *Students:* 15 full-time (9 women), 21 part-time (10 women); includes 4 minority (2 Hispanic/Latino; 2 Two or more races, non-Hispanic/Latino), 1 international. Average age 26. 34 applicants, 62% accepted, 13 enrolled. In 2010, 12 master's awarded. *Degree requirements:* For master's, comprehensive exam (for some programs), thesis (for some programs). *Entrance requirements:* For master's, GRE General Test, minimum GPA of 3.0 in last 90 quarter units. Additional exam requirements/recommendations for international students: Required—TOEFL (minimum score 550 paper-based; 213 computer-based) or IELTS (minimum score 6). *Application deadline:* For fall admission, 2/1 for domestic students, 11/30 for international students. Applications are processed on a rolling basis. Application fee: $55. Electronic applications accepted. *Expenses:* Tuition, state resident: full-time $5386; part-time $3124 per year. Tuition, nonresident: full-time $11,160; part-time $248 per unit. Required fees: $2250; $614 per term. One-time fee: $2250 full-time; $1842 part-time. *Financial support:* Research assistantships, teaching assistantships, career-related internships or fieldwork and Federal Work-Study available. Support available to part-time students. Financial award application deadline: 3/2; financial award applicants required to submit FAFSA. *Faculty research:* Ancient fossil DNA, restoration ecology microbe biodiversity indices, biological inventories. *Unit head:* Dr. Nikki Adams, Graduate Coordinator, 805-756-2943, Fax: 805-756-1419, E-mail: nadams@calpoly.edu. *Application contact:* Dr. Nikki Adams, Graduate Coordinator, 805-756-2943, Fax: 805-756-1419, E-mail: nadams@calpoly.edu.

California State Polytechnic University, Pomona, Academic Affairs, College of Science, Program in Biological Sciences, Pomona, CA 91768-2557. Offers MS. Part-time programs

California Institute of Technology (Caltech)

The mission of the California Institute of Technology is to expand human knowledge and benefit society through research integrated with education. We investigate the most challenging, fundamental problems in science and technology in a singularly collegial, interdisciplinary atmosphere, while educating outstanding students to become creative members of society.

Graduate students in the Division of Biology choose one of three options (majors): biology, biochemistry and molecular biophysics, and bioengineering.

Caltech is a vibrant intellectual community with many opportunities for self-enrichment. The flexible and lively intellectual atmosphere at Caltech nurtures a dynamic program of informal seminars, journal clubs, and joint group meetings where students and postdoctoral fellows have an opportunity to hear about recent scientific developments and to hone their public speaking skills.

Caltech faculty and alumni have received wide recognition for their achievements in science and engineering, which includes 31 Nobel Prize recipients.

Caltech occupies a beautiful campus in the center of Pasadena, a pleasant suburb of Los Angeles nestled in the foothills of the San Gabriel Mountains. The climate in Pasadena is moderate, ranging from an average temperature of 56°F in January to 75°F in July. Rainfall is infrequent and limited mostly to the winter months.

For More information contact:
Elizabeth Ayala, Biology Option Coordinator
1200 E. California Blvd. Pasadena, CA 91125
ayalae@cco.caltech.edu
http://biology.caltech.edu/graduate_program/bioinfo.html

available. *Students:* 31 full-time (16 women), 59 part-time (40 women); includes 39 minority (2 Black or African American, non-Hispanic/Latino; 1 American Indian or Alaska Native, non-Hispanic/Latino; 20 Asian, non-Hispanic/Latino; 14 Hispanic/Latino; 2 Two or more races, non-Hispanic/Latino), 11 international. Average age 27. 76 applicants, 38% accepted, 25 enrolled. In 2010, 17 master's awarded. *Degree requirements:* For master's, thesis. *Entrance requirements:* For master's, GRE General Test. *Application deadline:* For fall admission, 5/1 priority date for domestic students; for winter admission, 10/15 priority date for domestic students; for spring admission, 1/20 priority date for domestic students. Applications are processed on a rolling basis. Application fee: $55. Electronic applications accepted. *Expenses:* Tuition, state resident: full-time $5386; part-time $2850 per year. Tuition, nonresident: full-time $12,082; part-time $248 per credit. Required fees: $577; $248 per credit. $577 per year. Tuition and fees vary according to course load and program. *Financial support:* Career-related internships or fieldwork, Federal Work-Study, and institutionally sponsored loans available. Support available to part-time students. Financial award application deadline: 3/2; financial award applicants required to submit FAFSA. *Unit head:* Dr. David Moriarty, Professor, 909-869-4055, Fax: 909-869-4078, E-mail: djmoriarty@csupomona.edu. *Application contact:* Scott J. Duncan, Director, Admissions, 909-869-3258, Fax: 909-869-4529, E-mail: sjduncan@csupomona.edu.

California State University, Bakersfield, Division of Graduate Studies, School of Natural Sciences and Mathematics, Program in Biology, Bakersfield, CA 93311. Offers MS. *Entrance requirements:* For master's, GRE, minimum undergraduate GPA of 3.0 in last 90 quarter units, 3 letters of recommendation. Additional exam requirements/recommendations for international students: Required—TOEFL.

California State University, Chico, Graduate School, College of Natural Sciences, Department of Biological Sciences, Program in Biological Sciences, Chico, CA 95929-0722. Offers MS. *Students:* 16 full-time (11 women), 12 part-time (7 women); includes 1 Hispanic/Latino, 1 international. Average age 27. 31 applicants, 61% accepted, 15 enrolled. In 2010, 4 master's awarded. *Degree requirements:* For master's, thesis, oral exam. *Entrance requirements:* For master's, GRE General Test, GRE Subject Test (biology), 2 letters of recommendation. Additional exam requirements/recommendations for international students: Required—TOEFL (minimum score 550 paper-based; 213 computer-based; 80 iBT), IELTS (minimum score 6.5). *Application deadline:* For fall admission, 3/1 priority date for domestic students, 3/1 for international students; for spring admission, 9/15 priority date for domestic students, 9/15 for international students. Applications are processed on a rolling basis. Application fee: $55. Electronic applications accepted. *Financial support:* Fellowships, research assistantships, teaching assistantships, career-related internships or fieldwork available. *Unit head:* Dr. Jonathan Day, Graduate Coordinator, 530-898-6303. *Application contact:* Larry Hanne, Graduate Coordinator, 530-898-5356.

California State University, Dominguez Hills, College of Natural and Behavioral Sciences, Department of Biology, Carson, CA 90747-0001. Offers MS. Part-time and evening/weekend programs available. *Faculty:* 10 full-time (3 women), 20 part-time/adjunct (6 women). *Students:* 9 full-time (5 women), 23 part-time (13 women); includes 6 Black or African American, non-Hispanic/Latino; 7 Asian, non-Hispanic/Latino; 6 Hispanic/Latino; 2 Two or more races, non-Hispanic/Latino. Average age 30. 21 applicants, 67% accepted, 12 enrolled. In 2010, 5 master's awarded. *Degree requirements:* For master's, thesis. *Entrance requirements:* For master's, minimum GPA of 2.75. Additional exam requirements/recommendations for international students: Required—TOEFL (minimum score 550 paper-based). *Application deadline:* For fall admission, 6/1 for domestic students, 5/1 for international students; for spring admission, 12/15 for domestic students, 10/1 for international students. Application fee: $55. Electronic applications accepted. *Faculty research:* Cancer biology, infectious diseases, ecology of native plants, remediation, community ecology. *Unit head:* Dr. John Thomlinson, Chair, 310-243-3381, Fax: 310-243-2350, E-mail: jthomlinson@csudh.edu. *Application contact:* Dr. Getachew Kidane, Graduate Program Coordinator, 310-243-3564, Fax: 310-243-2350, E-mail: gkidane@csudh.edu.

California State University, East Bay, Office of Academic Programs and Graduate Studies, College of Science, Department of Biological Sciences, Hayward, CA 94542-3000. Offers biological sciences (MA, MS); marine science (MS). Part-time programs available. *Faculty:* 10 full-time (7 women). *Students:* 17 full-time (12 women), 32 part-time (23 women); includes 2 Black or African American, non-Hispanic/Latino; 10 Asian, non-Hispanic/Latino; 2 Hispanic/Latino, 7 international. Average age 31. 49 applicants, 37% accepted, 10 enrolled. In 2010, 18 master's awarded. *Degree requirements:* For master's, thesis. *Entrance requirements:* For master's, GRE General and Subject Tests, minimum GPA of 3.0 in field, 2.75 overall. Additional exam requirements/recommendations for international students: Required—TOEFL (minimum score 550 paper-based; 213 computer-based). *Application deadline:* For fall admission, 6/30 for domestic and international students. Applications are processed on a rolling basis. Application fee: $55. Electronic applications accepted. *Financial support:* Fellowships, teaching assistantships, career-related internships or fieldwork, Federal Work-Study, institutionally sponsored loans, and scholarships/grants available. Support available to part-time students. Financial award application deadline: 3/2; financial award applicants required to submit FAFSA. *Unit head:* Dr. Michael Hedrick, Chair, 510-885-3471, Fax: 510-885-4747, E-mail: michael.hedrick@csueastbay.edu. *Application contact:* Dr. Donna Wiley, Interim Associate Director, 510-885-2928, Fax: 510-885-4777, E-mail: donna.wiley@csueastbay.edu.

California State University, Fresno, Division of Graduate Studies, College of Science and Mathematics, Department of Biology, Fresno, CA 93740-8027. Offers biology (MA); biotechnology (MBT). Part-time and evening/weekend programs available. *Degree requirements:* For master's, thesis. *Entrance requirements:* For master's, GRE General Test, GRE Subject Test, minimum GPA of 2.5 in last 60 units. Additional exam requirements/recommendations for international students: Required—TOEFL. Electronic applications accepted. *Faculty research:* Genome neuroscience, ecology conflict resolution, biomechanics, cell death, vibrio cholerae.

California State University, Fullerton, Graduate Studies, College of Natural Science and Mathematics, Department of Biological Science, Fullerton, CA 92834-9480. Offers MS. Part-time programs available. *Students:* 32 full-time (17 women), 45 part-time (30 women); includes 1 Black or African American, non-Hispanic/Latino; 17 Asian, non-Hispanic/Latino; 9 Hispanic/Latino; 3 Two or more races, non-Hispanic/Latino, 11 international. Average age 29. 106 applicants, 36% accepted, 25 enrolled. In 2010, 13 master's awarded. *Degree requirements:* For master's, thesis. *Entrance requirements:* For master's, GRE General and Subject Tests, MCAT, or DAT, minimum GPA of 3.0 in biology. Application fee: $55. *Financial support:* Research assistantships, teaching assistantships, career-related internships or fieldwork, Federal Work-Study, institutionally sponsored loans, and scholarships/grants available. Support available to part-time students. Financial award application deadline: 3/1; financial award applicants required to submit FAFSA. *Faculty research:* Glycosidase release and the block to polyspermy in ascidian eggs. *Unit head:* Dr. Katherine Dickson, Chair, 657-278-3614. *Application contact:* Admissions/Applications, 657-278-2371.

California State University, Long Beach, Graduate Studies, College of Natural Sciences and Mathematics, Department of Biological Sciences, Long Beach, CA 90840. Offers biology (MS); microbiology (MS). Part-time programs available. *Faculty:* 26 full-time (10 women), 1 (woman) part-time/adjunct. *Students:* 16 full-time (9 women), 45 part-time (28 women); includes 2 Black or African American, non-Hispanic/Latino; 9 Asian, non-Hispanic/Latino; 8 Hispanic/Latino, 6 international. Average age 27. 102 applicants, 25% accepted, 12 enrolled. In 2010, 16 master's awarded. *Entrance requirements:* For master's, GRE Subject Test, minimum GPA of 3.0. *Application deadline:* For fall admission, 3/15 for domestic students. Applications are processed on a rolling basis. Application fee: $55. Electronic applications accepted. *Financial support:* Teaching assistantships, Federal Work-Study, institutionally sponsored loans, scholarships/grants, traineeships, and unspecified assistantships available. Financial award application deadline: 3/2. *Unit head:* Dr. Brian Livingston, Chair, 562-985-4807, Fax: 562-985-8878, E-mail: blivings@csulb.edu. *Application contact:* Dr. Christopher Lowe, Graduate Advisor, 562-985-4918, Fax: 562-985-8878, E-mail: clowe@csulb.edu.

California State University, Los Angeles, Graduate Studies, College of Natural and Social Sciences, Department of Biological Sciences, Los Angeles, CA 90032-8530. Offers biology (MS). Part-time and evening/weekend programs available. *Faculty:* 1 (woman) full-time, 10 part-time/adjunct (5 women). *Students:* 44 full-time (25 women), 30 part-time (21 women); includes 50 minority (2 Black or African American, non-Hispanic/Latino; 18 Asian, non-Hispanic/Latino; 29 Hispanic/Latino; 1 Two or more races, non-Hispanic/Latino), 6 international. Average age 28. 51 applicants, 100% accepted, 40 enrolled. In 2010, 24 master's awarded. *Degree requirements:* For master's, comprehensive exam or thesis. *Entrance requirements:* Additional exam requirements/recommendations for international students: Required—TOEFL (minimum score 500 paper-based; 173 computer-based). *Application deadline:* For fall admission, 5/1 for domestic and international students. Applications are processed on a rolling basis. Application fee: $55. *Financial support:* Federal Work-Study available. Support available to part-time students. Financial award application deadline: 3/1. *Faculty research:* Ecology, environmental biology, cell and molecular biology, physiology, medical microbiology. *Unit head:* Dr. Nancy McQueen, Chair, 323-343-2050, Fax: 323-343-6451, E-mail: nmcquee@exchange.calstatela.edu. *Application contact:* Dr. Alan Muchlinski, Dean of Graduate Studies, 323-343-3820, Fax: 323-343-5653, E-mail: amuchli@exchange.calstatela.edu.

California State University, Northridge, Graduate Studies, College of Science and Mathematics, Department of Biology, Northridge, CA 91330. Offers MS. *Degree requirements:* For master's, thesis, seminar. *Entrance requirements:* For master's, GRE Subject Test, GRE General Test. Additional exam requirements/recommendations for international students: Required—TOEFL. *Faculty research:* Cell adhesion, cancer research, fishery research.

California State University, Sacramento, Graduate Studies, College of Natural Sciences and Mathematics, Department of Biological Sciences, Sacramento, CA 95819. Offers biological sciences (MA, MS); immunohematology (MS); marine science (MS). Part-time programs available. *Degree requirements:* For master's, thesis, writing proficiency exam. *Entrance requirements:* For master's, bachelor's degree in biology or equivalent, minimum GPA of 3.0 in biology, minimum overall GPA of 2.75 during last 2 years of course work. Additional exam requirements/recommendations for international students: Required—TOEFL. Electronic applications accepted.

California State University, San Bernardino, Graduate Studies, College of Natural Sciences, Department of Biology, San Bernardino, CA 92407-2397. Offers MS. Part-time programs available. *Degree requirements:* For master's, thesis or alternative, advancement to candidacy. *Entrance requirements:* For master's, minimum GPA of 3.0. *Faculty research:* Ecology, molecular biology, physiology, cell biology, neurobiology.

California State University, San Marcos, College of Arts and Sciences, Program in Biological Sciences, San Marcos, CA 92096-0001. Offers MS. Part-time programs available. *Degree requirements:* For master's, thesis. *Entrance requirements:* For master's, GRE Subject Test, minimum GPA of 2.7 in mathematics and science or minimum GPA of 3.0 in the last 35 units of mathematics and science. *Faculty research:* Gene regulation of life states, carbon cycling, genetic markers of viral infection, neurobiology.

Carleton University, Faculty of Graduate Studies, Faculty of Science, Department of Biology, Ottawa, ON K1S 5B6, Canada. Offers M Sc, PhD. Programs offered jointly with University of Ottawa. *Degree requirements:* For master's, thesis, seminar; for doctorate, comprehensive exam, thesis/dissertation, seminar. *Entrance requirements:* For master's, honors degree in science; for doctorate, M Sc. Additional exam requirements/recommendations for international students: Required—TOEFL. *Faculty research:* Biochemical, structural, and genetic regulation in cells; behavioral ecology; insect taxonomy; physiology of cells.

Carnegie Mellon University, Mellon College of Science, Department of Biological Sciences, Pittsburgh, PA 15213-3891. Offers biochemistry (PhD); biophysics (PhD); cell biology (PhD); computational biology (MS, PhD); developmental biology (PhD); genetics (PhD); molecular biology (PhD); neuroscience (PhD). *Degree requirements:* For doctorate, comprehensive exam, thesis/dissertation. *Entrance requirements:* For doctorate, GRE General Test, GRE Subject Test, interview. Electronic applications accepted. *Faculty research:* Genetic structure, function, and regulation; protein structure and function; biological membranes; biological spectroscopy.

Case Western Reserve University, School of Graduate Studies, Department of Biology, Cleveland, OH 44106. Offers MS, PhD. Part-time programs available. *Faculty:* 23 full-time (9 women), 5 part-time/adjunct (2 women). *Students:* 66 full-time (31 women), 6 part-time (2 women); includes 2 Black or African American, non-Hispanic/Latino; 3 Asian, non-Hispanic/Latino; 2 Hispanic/Latino, 34 international. Average age 26. 116 applicants, 35% accepted, 17 enrolled. In 2010, 2 master's, 1 doctorate awarded. Terminal master's awarded for partial completion of doctoral program. *Degree requirements:* For master's, thesis or alternative; for doctorate, thesis/dissertation. *Entrance requirements:* For master's and doctorate, GRE General Test, GRE Subject Test. Additional exam requirements/recommendations for international students: Required—TOEFL (minimum score 550 paper-based; 213 computer-based; 79 iBT). *Application deadline:* For fall admission, 1/4 priority date for domestic students. Applications are processed on a rolling basis. Application fee: $50. Electronic applications accepted. *Financial support:* Fellowships, research assistantships, teaching assistantships, career-related internships or fieldwork, Federal Work-Study, tuition waivers, and unspecified assistantships available. Financial award application deadline: 2/15; financial award applicants required to submit FAFSA. *Faculty research:* Cellular, developmental, and molecular biology; genetics; genetic engineering; biotechnology; ecology. *Unit head:* Christopher Cullis, Chairman, 216-368-3557, Fax: 216-368-4762, E-mail: christopher.cullis@case.edu. *Application contact:* Julia Brown, Program Coordinator, 216-368-3556, Fax: 216-368-4672, E-mail: jab12@case.edu.

Case Western Reserve University, School of Medicine and School of Graduate Studies, Graduate Programs in Medicine, Biomedical Sciences Training Program, Cleveland, OH 44106. Offers PhD. *Degree requirements:* For doctorate, thesis/dissertation. *Entrance requirements:* For doctorate, GRE General Test. Additional exam requirements/recommendations for international students: Required—TOEFL. Electronic applications accepted. *Faculty research:* Biochemistry, molecular biology, immunology, genetics, neurosciences.

Case Western Reserve University, School of Medicine and School of Graduate Studies, Graduate Programs in Medicine, Department of Biochemistry, Program in RNA Biology, Cleveland, OH 44106. Offers PhD. *Degree requirements:* For doctorate, comprehensive exam, thesis/dissertation. *Entrance requirements:* For doctorate, GRE. Additional exam requirements/recommendations for international students: Required—TOEFL (minimum score 550 paper-based; 213 computer-based).

Case Western Reserve University, School of Medicine, Medical Scientist Training Program, Cleveland, OH 44106. Offers MD/PhD. Electronic applications accepted. *Faculty research:* Biomedical research.

The Catholic University of America, School of Arts and Sciences, Department of Biology, Washington, DC 20064. Offers cell and microbial biology (MS, PhD), including cell biology, microbiology; clinical laboratory science (MS, PhD); MSLS/MS. Part-time programs available. *Faculty:* 8 full-time (4 women), 2 part-time/adjunct (both women). *Students:* 10 full-time (7 women), 27 part-time (18 women); includes 2 Black or African American, non-Hispanic/Latino; 4 Asian, non-Hispanic/Latino; 3 Hispanic/Latino, 15 international. Average age 29. 39 applicants, 56% accepted, 13 enrolled. In 2010, 4 doctorates awarded. *Degree requirements:* For master's, comprehensive exam, thesis or alternative; for doctorate, comprehensive exam, thesis/dissertation. *Entrance requirements:* For master's and doctorate, GRE General Test, GRE Subject Test, statement of purpose, official copies of academic transcripts, three letters of recommendation. Additional exam requirements/recommendations for international students:

Biological and Biomedical Sciences—General

The Catholic University of America (continued)

Required—TOEFL (minimum score 580 paper-based; 237 computer-based). *Application deadline:* For fall admission, 8/1 priority date for domestic students, 7/15 for international students; for spring admission, 12/1 priority date for domestic students, 10/15 for international students. Applications are processed on a rolling basis. Application fee: $55. Electronic applications accepted. *Expenses:* Tuition: Full-time $33,580; part-time $1315 per credit hour. Required fees: $80; $40 per semester hour. One-time fee: $425. *Financial support:* Fellowships, research assistantships, teaching assistantships, Federal Work-Study, scholarships/grants, tuition waivers (full and partial), and unspecified assistantships available. Financial award application deadline: 2/1; financial award applicants required to submit FAFSA. *Faculty research:* Cell and microbiology, microbial pathogenesis, molecular biology of cell proliferation, cellular effects of electromagnetic radiation, biotechnology. Total annual research expenditures: $853,913. *Unit head:* Dr. Venigalla Rao, Chair, 202-319-5271, Fax: 202-319-5721, E-mail: rao@cua.edu. *Application contact:* Andrew Woodall, Director of Graduate Admissions, 202-319-5057, Fax: 202-319-6533, E-mail: cua-admissions@cua.edu.

Cedars-Sinai Medical Center, Graduate Program in Biomedical Sciences and Translational Medicine, Los Angeles, CA 90048. Offers PhD. *Degree requirements:* For doctorate, comprehensive exam, thesis/dissertation. *Entrance requirements:* For doctorate, GRE, 3 letters of recommendation. Additional exam requirements/recommendations for international students: Required—TOEFL (minimum score 560 paper-based; 220 computer-based; 87 iBT). *Faculty research:* Immunology and infection, neuroscience, cardiovascular science, cancer, human genetics.

Central Connecticut State University, School of Graduate Studies, School of Arts and Sciences, Department of Biology, New Britain, CT 06050-4010. Offers biological sciences (MA, MS), including anesthesia (MS), ecology and environmental sciences (MA), general biology (MA), health sciences specialization (MS), professional education program (MS); biology (Certificate). Part-time and evening/weekend programs available. *Faculty:* 13 full-time (4 women), 8 part-time/adjunct (6 women). *Students:* 121 full-time (66 women), 20 part-time (11 women); includes 28 minority (6 Black or African American, non-Hispanic/Latino; 1 American Indian or Alaska Native, non-Hispanic/Latino; 9 Asian, non-Hispanic/Latino; 9 Hispanic/Latino; 3 Two or more races, non-Hispanic/Latino). Average age 32. 41 applicants, 78% accepted, 18 enrolled. In 2010, 31 master's, 3 other advanced degrees awarded. *Degree requirements:* For master's, comprehensive exam, thesis or alternative; for Certificate, qualifying exam. *Entrance requirements:* For master's, minimum undergraduate GPA of 2.7. Additional exam requirements/recommendations for international students: Required—TOEFL. *Application deadline:* For fall admission, 7/1 for domestic students; for spring admission, 12/1 for domestic students. Applications are processed on a rolling basis. Application fee: $50. Electronic applications accepted. *Expenses:* Tuition, area resident: Full-time $5012; part-time $470 per credit. Tuition, state resident: full-time $7518; part-time $482 per credit. Tuition, nonresident: full-time $13,962; part-time $482 per credit. Required fees: $3772. One-time fee: $62 part-time. *Financial support:* In 2010–11, 10 students received support, including 7 research assistantships; career-related internships or fieldwork, Federal Work-Study, scholarships/grants, and unspecified assistantships also available. Support available to part-time students. Financial award application deadline: 2/15; financial award applicants required to submit FAFSA. *Faculty research:* Environmental science, anesthesia, health sciences, zoology, animal behavior. *Unit head:* Dr. Jeremiah Jarrett, Chair, 860-832-2645. *Application contact:* Dr. Jeremiah Jarrett, Chair, 860-832-2645.

Central Michigan University, College of Graduate Studies, College of Science and Technology, Department of Biology, Mount Pleasant, MI 48859. Offers biology (MS); conservation biology (MS). Part-time programs available. *Faculty:* 17 full-time (5 women). *Students:* 15 full-time (8 women), 44 part-time (19 women); includes 1 Black or African American, non-Hispanic/Latino; 1 American Indian or Alaska Native, non-Hispanic/Latino; 1 Hispanic/Latino, 5 international. Average age 26. *Degree requirements:* For master's, thesis or alternative. *Entrance requirements:* For master's, GRE, bachelor's degree with a major in biological science, minimum GPA of 3.0. *Application deadline:* For fall admission, 6/1 for international students; for spring admission, 10/1 for international students. Applications are processed on a rolling basis. Application fee: $35 ($45 for international students). Electronic applications accepted. *Expenses:* Tuition, state resident: full-time $8208; part-time $456 per credit hour. Tuition, nonresident: full-time $13,788; part-time $766 per credit hour. One-time fee: $25. *Financial support:* Fellowships with tuition reimbursements, research assistantships with tuition reimbursements, teaching assistantships with tuition reimbursements, career-related internships or fieldwork, Federal Work-Study, unspecified assistantships, and out-of-state merit awards, non-resident graduate awards available. *Faculty research:* Conservation biology, morphology and taxonomy of aquatic plants, molecular biology and genetics, microbials and invertebrate ecology, vertebrates. *Unit head:* Dr. Stephen Roberts, Chairperson, 989-774-3227, Fax: 989-774-3462, E-mail: rober2sp@cmich.edu. *Application contact:* Dr. Gregory Colores, Graduate Program Coordinator, 989-774-3412, Fax: 989-774-3462, E-mail: color1gm@cmich.edu.

Central Washington University, Graduate Studies and Research, College of the Sciences, Department of Biological Sciences, Ellensburg, WA 98926. Offers MS. Part-time programs available. *Degree requirements:* For master's, thesis or alternative. *Entrance requirements:* For master's, GRE General Test, minimum GPA of 3.0. Additional exam requirements/recommendations for international students: Required—TOEFL (minimum score 550 paper-based; 213 computer-based; 79 iBT).

Chatham University, Program in Biology, Pittsburgh, PA 15232-2826. Offers environmental biology-non-thesis track (MS); environmental biology-thesis track (MS); human biology-non-thesis track (MS); human biology-thesis track (MS). Part-time programs available. *Degree requirements:* For master's, thesis optional. *Entrance requirements:* For master's, 3 letters of recommendation. Additional exam requirements/recommendations for international students: Required—TOEFL (minimum score 600 paper-based; 250 computer-based; 100 iBT), IELTS (minimum score 6.5), TWE. Electronic applications accepted. *Faculty research:* Molecular evolution of iron homeostasis, characteristics of soil bacterial communities, gene flow through seed movement, role of gonadotropins in spermatogonial proliferation, phosphatid/linositol metabolism in epithelial cells.

Chicago State University, School of Graduate and Professional Studies, College of Arts and Sciences, Department of Biological Sciences, Chicago, IL 60628. Offers MS. Part-time and evening/weekend programs available. *Degree requirements:* For master's, thesis. *Entrance requirements:* For master's, minimum GPA of 2.75, 15 credit hours in biological sciences. *Faculty research:* Molecular genetics of gene complexes, mammalian immune cell function, genetics of agriculturally important microbes, environmental toxicology, neuromuscular physiology.

The Citadel, The Military College of South Carolina, Citadel Graduate College, Department of Biology, Charleston, SC 29409. Offers MA. *Accreditation:* NCATE. Part-time and evening/weekend programs available. *Faculty:* 8 full-time (4 women). *Students:* 2 full-time (1 woman), 16 part-time (9 women); includes 4 Black or African American, non-Hispanic/Latino. Average age 28. In 2010, 18 master's awarded. *Entrance requirements:* For master's, GRE (minimum score 900) or MAT (minimum score 396), minimum undergraduate GPA of 2.5. Additional exam requirements/recommendations for international students: Required—TOEFL (minimum score 550 paper-based; 213 computer-based). *Application deadline:* Applications are processed on a rolling basis. Application fee: $30. Electronic applications accepted. *Expenses:* Tuition, state resident: part-time $460 per credit hour. Tuition, nonresident: part-time $756 per credit hour. Required fees: $40 per term. *Financial support:* Health care benefits and unspecified assistantships available. Support available to part-time students. Financial award application deadline: 7/1; financial award applicants required to submit FAFSA. *Faculty research:* Genetic control of parasite-host interactions, mechanisms of development of antibiotic resistance in pseudomonas aeruginosa, interaction of visual and vocal signals in avian mate choice and competition, effects of pollutants on salt marsh animals, structure and function of mitochondrial histone H3 protein, development of cardiac conduction tissue in tadpoles with left-right axis perturbation, evolution and ecology of barnacles and marine hosts. *Unit head:* Dr. Paul Rosenblum, Department Head, 843-953-5203, Fax: 843-953-7264, E-mail: paul.rosenblum@citadel.edu. *Application contact:* Dr. Steve A. Nida, Associate Provost, The Citadel Graduate College, 843-953-5089, Fax: 843-953-7630, E-mail: cgc@citadel.edu.

City College of the City University of New York, Graduate School, College of Liberal Arts and Science, Division of Science, Department of Biology, New York, NY 10031-9198. Offers MA, PhD. PhD program offered jointly with Graduate School and University Center of the City University of New York. Part-time programs available. *Students:* 4 full-time (3 women), 19 part-time (9 women); includes 4 Black or African American, non-Hispanic/Latino; 4 Asian, non-Hispanic/Latino; 9 Hispanic/Latino, 4 international. 17 applicants, 41% accepted, 4 enrolled. In 2010, 16 master's awarded. Terminal master's awarded for partial completion of doctoral program. *Degree requirements:* For master's, thesis or alternative; for doctorate, one foreign language, thesis/dissertation, teaching experience. *Entrance requirements:* For doctorate, GRE General Test. Additional exam requirements/recommendations for international students: Required—TOEFL (minimum score 500 paper-based; 61 iBT). *Application deadline:* For fall admission, 5/1 for domestic and international students; for spring admission, 11/15 for domestic and international students. Applications are processed on a rolling basis. Application fee: $125. Electronic applications accepted. *Financial support:* Fellowships, research assistantships, teaching assistantships, career-related internships or fieldwork and scholarships/grants available. Financial award applicants required to submit FAFSA. *Faculty research:* Animal behavior, ecology, genetics, neurobiology, molecular biology. *Unit head:* Prof. Mark Pezzano, Chair, 212-650-8559, E-mail: biology@sci.ccny.cuny.edu. *Application contact:* Prof. Mark Pezzano, Chair, 212-650-8559, E-mail: biology@sci.ccny.cuny.edu.

City of Hope National Medical Center/Beckman Research Institute, Irell and Manella Graduate School of Biological Sciences, Duarte, CA 91010. Offers PhD. *Faculty:* 81 full-time (21 women). *Students:* 75 full-time (42 women); includes 1 Black or African American, non-Hispanic/Latino; 3 Asian, non-Hispanic/Latino; 3 Hispanic/Latino; 2 Native Hawaiian or other Pacific Islander, non-Hispanic/Latino; 1 Two or more races, non-Hispanic/Latino, 25 international. Average age 24. 181 applicants, 14% accepted, 15 enrolled. In 2010, 11 doctorates awarded. *Degree requirements:* For doctorate, comprehensive exam, thesis/dissertation. *Entrance requirements:* For doctorate, GRE General Test; GRE Subject Test (recommended), 2 years of course work in chemistry (general and organic); 1 year course work each in biochemistry, general biology, and general physics; 2 semesters of course work in mathematics; significant research laboratory experience. Additional exam requirements/recommendations for international students: Required—TOEFL. *Application deadline:* For fall admission, 1/1 priority date for domestic and international students. Application fee: $0. Electronic applications accepted. *Expenses:* Required fees: $150. *Financial support:* In 2010–11, 55 fellowships with full tuition reimbursements (averaging $30,000 per year) were awarded; teaching assistantships, health care benefits and tuition waivers (full) also available. Financial award application deadline: 4/15. *Faculty research:* DNA damage and repair, protein structure, cancer biology, T cells and immunology, RNA splicing and binding. Total annual research expenditures: $65 million. *Unit head:* Dr. John J. Rossi, Dean, 626-256-8775, Fax: 626-301-8105, E-mail: gradschool@coh.org. *Application contact:* Lee Ann Cornell, Graduate Education Program Director, 626-471-7396, Fax: 626-301-8105, E-mail: lcornell@coh.org.

See Display on next page and Close-Up on page 95.

Clarion University of Pennsylvania, Office of Research and Graduate Studies, College of Arts and Sciences, Department of Biology, Clarion, PA 16214. Offers MS. *Degree requirements:* For master's, thesis or alternative. *Entrance requirements:* For master's, GRE General Test, minimum QPA of 2.75. Additional exam requirements/recommendations for international students: Required—TOEFL (minimum score 600 paper-based; 250 computer-based; 100 iBT). Electronic applications accepted.

Clark Atlanta University, School of Arts and Sciences, Department of Biology, Atlanta, GA 30314. Offers MS, PhD. Part-time programs available. *Faculty:* 5 full-time (2 women). *Students:* 5 full-time (4 women), 14 part-time (10 women); includes 15 Black or African American, non-Hispanic/Latino; 2 Asian, non-Hispanic/Latino, 2 international. Average age 28. 7 applicants, 86% accepted, 2 enrolled. In 2010, 1 master's, 1 doctorate awarded. Terminal master's awarded for partial completion of doctoral program. *Degree requirements:* For master's, one foreign language, thesis; for doctorate, 2 foreign languages, thesis/dissertation. *Entrance requirements:* For master's, GRE General Test, minimum GPA of 2.5; for doctorate, GRE General Test, minimum graduate GPA of 3.0. Additional exam requirements/recommendations for international students: Required—TOEFL (minimum score 500 paper-based; 173 computer-based; 61 iBT). *Application deadline:* For fall admission, 4/1 for domestic and international students; for spring admission, 11/1 for domestic and international students. Applications are processed on a rolling basis. Application fee: $40 ($55 for international students). Electronic applications accepted. *Expenses:* Tuition: Full-time $12,942; part-time $719 per credit hour. Required fees: $710; $355 per semester. *Financial support:* In 2010–11, 6 research assistantships were awarded; career-related internships or fieldwork, Federal Work-Study, scholarships/grants, traineeships, and unspecified assistantships also available. Support available to part-time students. Financial award application deadline: 4/30; financial award applicants required to submit FAFSA. *Faculty research:* Regulation of amino-DNA, cellular regulations. *Unit head:* Dr. Marjorie Campbell, Chairperson, 404-880-6190, E-mail: mcampbell@cau.edu. *Application contact:* Michelle Clark-Davis, Graduate Program Admissions, 404-880-6605, E-mail: cauadmissions@cau.edu.

Clark University, Graduate School, Department of Biology, Worcester, MA 01610-1477. Offers MA, PhD. PhD program offered jointly with University of Massachusetts Worcester. *Faculty:* 9 full-time (4 women). *Students:* 26 full-time (8 women), 2 part-time (both women), 8 international. Average age 29. 52 applicants, 46% accepted, 16 enrolled. In 2010, 1 master's, 4 doctorates awarded. *Degree requirements:* For master's, thesis; for doctorate, thesis/dissertation. *Entrance requirements:* For master's and doctorate, GRE General Test. Additional exam requirements/recommendations for international students: Required—TOEFL. *Application deadline:* For fall admission, 2/15 priority date for domestic students. Applications are processed on a rolling basis. Application fee: $50. Electronic applications accepted. *Expenses:* Tuition: Full-time $37,000; part-time $1156 per credit hour. Required fees: $30; $1156 per credit hour. *Financial support:* In 2010–11, 3 research assistantships with full tuition reimbursements (averaging $19,825 per year), 11 teaching assistantships with full tuition reimbursements (averaging $19,825 per year) were awarded; fellowships, scholarships/grants and tuition waivers (full and partial) also available. *Faculty research:* Nitrogen assimilation in marine algae, phylogenetic relationships, fungal tree of life, ancestral plasticity, drosophi genetic analysis, cytokinesis proteins. Total annual research expenditures: $1.1 million. *Unit head:* Dr. Todd Lidvdahl, Chair, 508-793-7173. *Application contact:* Bogna Sowinska, Department Secretary, 528-793-7173, Fax: 528-793-8861, E-mail: biology@clarku.edu.

Clemson University, Graduate School, College of Agriculture, Forestry and Life Sciences, Department of Biological Sciences, Program in Biological Sciences, Clemson, SC 29634. Offers MS, PhD. *Students:* 39 full-time (26 women), 121 part-time (114 women); includes 1 Black or African American, non-Hispanic/Latino; 2 Asian, non-Hispanic/Latino, 10 international. Average age 30. 75 applicants, 44% accepted, 29 enrolled. In 2010, 6 master's, 2 doctorates awarded. *Degree requirements:* For master's, thesis optional; for doctorate, comprehensive exam, thesis/dissertation. *Entrance requirements:* For master's and doctorate, GRE General Test. Additional exam requirements/recommendations for international students: Required—TOEFL, IELTS. *Application deadline:* For fall admission, 1/15 for domestic students, 4/15 for international students. Applications are processed on a rolling basis. Application fee: $70 ($80 for international students). Electronic applications accepted. *Expenses:* Tuition, state resident: full-time $6492; part-time $400 per credit hour. Tuition, nonresident: full-time $13,634; part-time $800 per credit hour. Required fees: $262 per semester. Part-time tuition and fees vary according to course load and program. *Financial support:* In 2010–11, 38 students received support, including 9 fellowships with full and partial tuition reimbursements available (averaging

$9,389 per year), 17 research assistantships with partial tuition reimbursements available (averaging $12,632 per year), 40 teaching assistantships with partial tuition reimbursements available (averaging $10,513 per year); career-related internships or fieldwork, institutionally sponsored loans, scholarships/grants, health care benefits, and unspecified assistantships also available. Support available to part-time students. Financial award application deadline: 3/15; financial award applicants required to submit FAFSA. *Unit head:* Dr. Alfred Wheeler, Department Chair, 864-656-1415, Fax: 864-656-0435, E-mail: wheeler@clemson.edu. *Application contact:* Jay Lyn Martin, Coordinator for Graduate Program, 864-656-3587, Fax: 864-656-0435, E-mail: gradbio@clemson.edu.

Cleveland State University, College of Graduate Studies, College of Sciences and Health Professions, Department of Biological, Geological, and Environmental Sciences, Cleveland, OH 44115. Offers biology (MS); environmental science (MS); museum studies for natural historians (MS); regulatory biology (PhD); JD/MS. Part-time programs available. *Faculty:* 11 full-time (3 women), 6 part-time/adjunct (3 women). *Students:* 74 full-time (42 women), 35 part-time (19 women); includes 2 Black or African American, non-Hispanic/Latino; 2 Asian, non-Hispanic/Latino; 3 Hispanic/Latino, 41 international. Average age 30. 64 applicants, 13% accepted, 5 enrolled. In 2010, 12 master's, 2 doctorates awarded. Terminal master's awarded for partial completion of doctoral program. *Degree requirements:* For master's, comprehensive exam (for some programs), thesis (for some programs); for doctorate, comprehensive exam, thesis/dissertation. *Entrance requirements:* For master's, GRE General Test, 2 letters of recommendation; for doctorate, GRE General Test, 2 letters of recommendation; 1-2 page essay; statement of career goals and research interests. Additional exam requirements/recommendations for international students: Required—TOEFL (minimum score 525 paper-based; 197 computer-based). *Application deadline:* For fall admission, 4/1 priority date for domestic and international students; for spring admission, 12/1 priority date for domestic students. Applications are processed on a rolling basis. Application fee: $30. Electronic applications accepted. *Expenses:* Tuition, state resident: full-time $8447; part-time $469 per credit hour. Tuition, nonresident: full-time $16,020; part-time $890 per credit hour. Required fees: $50. *Financial support:* In 2010–11, 29 students received support, including research assistantships with full and partial tuition reimbursements available (averaging $16,500 per year), teaching assistantships with full and partial tuition reimbursements available (averaging $16,500 per year); institutionally sponsored loans and unspecified assistantships also available. *Faculty research:* Molecular and cell biology, immunology, urban ecology. *Unit head:* Dr. Jeffrey Dean, Chair, 216-687-2120, Fax: 216-687-6972, E-mail: j.dean@csuohio.edu. *Application contact:* Dr. Jeffrey Dean, Chair, 216-687-2120, Fax: 216-687-6972, E-mail: j.dean@csuohio.edu.

Cold Spring Harbor Laboratory, Watson School of Biological Sciences, Graduate Program, Cold Spring Harbor, NY 11724. Offers biological sciences (PhD). *Faculty:* 47 full-time (7 women). *Students:* 46 full-time (20 women); includes 6 minority (1 Black or African American, non-Hispanic/Latino; 1 Asian, non-Hispanic/Latino; 2 Hispanic/Latino; 1 Native Hawaiian or other Pacific Islander, non-Hispanic/Latino; 1 Two or more races, non-Hispanic/Latino), 25 international. Average age 23. 257 applicants. In 2010, 10 doctorates awarded. *Degree requirements:* For doctorate, comprehensive exam, thesis/dissertation, lab rotations, teaching experience, qualifying exam, postdoctoral proposals. *Entrance requirements:* Additional exam requirements/recommendations for international students: Required—TOEFL. *Application deadline:* For fall admission, 12/1 for domestic and international students. Application fee: $60. Electronic applications accepted. *Financial support:* In 2010–11, 44 students received support, including 44 fellowships with full tuition reimbursements available (averaging $30,500 per year); health care benefits and tuition waivers (full) also available. Financial award application deadline: 12/1. *Faculty research:* Genetics; neurobiology; cancer, plant, molecular, cellular, quantitative and structural biology. *Unit head:* Dr. Leemor Joshua-Tor, Dean, 516-367-6890, Fax: 516-367-6919, E-mail: gradschool@cshl.edu. *Application contact:* Dawn Pologruto, Director of Admissions, Recruitment and Student Affairs, 516-367-6911, Fax: 516-367-6919, E-mail: gradschool@cshl.edu.

See Display on next page and Close-Up on page 97.

The College at Brockport, State University of New York, School of Science and Mathematics, Department of Biology, Brockport, NY 14420-2997. Offers biological sciences (MS), including professional science masters. Part-time programs available. *Students:* 10 full-time (8 women), 3 part-time (2 women); includes 1 Black or African American, non-Hispanic/Latino. 11 applicants, 64% accepted, 7 enrolled. In 2010, 4 master's awarded. *Degree requirements:* For master's, comprehensive exam, thesis or alternative. *Entrance requirements:* For master's, GRE General or Subject Test (biology, biochemistry, cell and molecular biology), letters of recommendation, minimum GPA of 3.0, scientific writing sample, statement of objectives. Additional exam requirements/recommendations for international students: Required—TOEFL (minimum score 550 paper-based; 213 computer-based; 79 iBT). *Application deadline:* For fall admission, 7/15 priority date for domestic and international students; for spring admission, 11/15 priority date for domestic and international students. Application fee: $50. Electronic applications accepted. *Financial support:* In 2010–11, 8 teaching assistantships with full tuition reimbursements (averaging $6,000 per year) were awarded; Federal Work-Study, scholarships/grants, and unspecified assistantships also available. Support available to part-time students. Financial award application deadline: 3/15; financial award applicants required to submit FAFSA. *Faculty research:* Microbiology, molecular genetics, cellular biology developmental biology, animal physiology. *Unit head:* Dr. Stuart Tsubota, Chairperson, 585-395-2193, Fax: 585-395-2741, E-mail: stsubota@brockport.edu. *Application contact:* Dr. Adam Rich, Graduate Program Director, 585-395-5740, Fax: 585-395-2741, E-mail: arich@brockport.edu.

College of Staten Island of the City University of New York, Graduate Programs, Program in Biology, Staten Island, NY 10314-6600. Offers MS. Part-time programs available. *Faculty:* 8 full-time (4 women), 3 part-time/adjunct (1 woman). *Students:* 4 part-time (3 women); includes 1 Asian, non-Hispanic/Latino. Average age 28. 20 applicants, 15% accepted, 2 enrolled. In 2010, 3 master's awarded. *Degree requirements:* For master's, thesis. *Entrance requirements:* For master's, GRE General Test, GRE Subject Test (biology), minimum GPA of 3.0 in science and math, 2.75 overall; bachelor's degree in biology; 2 letters of recommendation (preferred). Additional exam requirements/recommendations for international students: Required—TOEFL (minimum score 550 paper-based; 213 computer-based; 79 iBT), IELTS (minimum score 6.5). *Application deadline:* For fall admission, 4/15 priority date for domestic and international students; for spring admission, 11/15 priority date for domestic and international students. Applications are processed on a rolling basis. Application fee: $125. Electronic applications accepted. *Expenses:* Tuition, state resident: full-time $7730; part-time $325 per credit. Tuition, nonresident: full-time $14,520; part-time $605 per credit. Required fees: $378. *Financial support:* Career-related internships or fieldwork, Federal Work-Study, and scholarships/grants available. Support available to part-time students. Financial award applicants required to submit FAFSA. Total annual research expenditures: $139,000. *Unit head:* Dr. Frank Burbrink, Coordinator, 718-982-3961, Fax: 718-982-3852, E-mail: biologymasters@mail.csi.cuny.edu. *Application contact:* Sasha Spence, Assistant Director of Graduate Recruitment Admissions, 718-982-2699, Fax: 718-982-2500, E-mail: sasha.spence@csi.cuny.edu.

The College of William and Mary, Faculty of Arts and Sciences, Department of Biology, Williamsburg, VA 23187-8795. Offers MS. Part-time programs available. *Students:* 21 full-time (13 women); includes 1 minority (Hispanic/Latino), 1 international. Average age 25. 47 applicants, 32% accepted, 9 enrolled. In 2010, 9 master's awarded. *Degree requirements:* For master's, comprehensive exam, thesis (for some programs). *Entrance requirements:* For master's, GRE Subject Test, GRE General Test, minimum GPA of 3.0. Additional exam requirements/recommendations for international students: Required—TOEFL. *Application deadline:* For fall admission, 2/1 priority date for domestic and international students. Application fee: $45. Electronic applications accepted. *Expenses:* Tuition, state resident: full-time $6400; part-time $345 per credit hour. Tuition, nonresident: full-time $19,720; part-time $920 per credit hour. Required fees: $4368. *Financial support:* Teaching assistantships with full tuition reimbursements, Federal Work-Study, institutionally sponsored loans, and unspecified assistantships available. Financial award application deadline: 3/1; financial award applicants required to

Biological and Biomedical Sciences—General

The College of William and Mary *(continued)*
submit FAFSA. *Faculty research:* Cellular and molecular biology, genetics, ecology, organismic biology, physiology. Total annual research expenditures: $2.4 million. *Unit head:* Dr. Lizabeth A. Allison, Chair, 757-221-2207, Fax: 757-221-6483, E-mail: laalli@wm.edu. *Application contact:* Dr. Patty Zwollo, Graduate Director, 757-221-1969, Fax: 757-221-6483, E-mail: pxzwol@wm.edu.

Colorado State University, College of Veterinary Medicine and Biomedical Sciences, Department of Biomedical Sciences, Fort Collins, CO 80523-1680. Offers MS, PhD. *Faculty:* 25 full-time (6 women), 2 part-time/adjunct (1 woman). *Students:* 72 full-time (45 women), 20 part-time (11 women); includes 10 minority (1 American Indian or Alaska Native, non-Hispanic/Latino; 1 Asian, non-Hispanic/Latino; 6 Hispanic/Latino; 1 Native Hawaiian or other Pacific Islander, non-Hispanic/Latino; 1 Two or more races, non-Hispanic/Latino), 3 international. Average age 25. 183 applicants, 50% accepted, 57 enrolled. In 2010, 58 master's, 3 doctorates awarded. Terminal master's awarded for partial completion of doctoral program. *Degree requirements:* For master's, comprehensive exam (for some programs), thesis (for some programs); for doctorate, thesis/dissertation. *Entrance requirements:* For master's, GRE General Test, GRE Subject Test, MCAT, or other standardized test or professional school entrance exam, bachelor's degree, minimum GPA of 3.0; for doctorate, GRE General Test, GRE Subject Test, bachelor's or professional degree, minimum GPA of 3.0. Additional exam requirements/recommendations for international students: Required—TOEFL (minimum score 550 paper-based; 213 computer-based; 80 iBT). *Application deadline:* For fall admission, 4/1 for domestic and international students; for winter admission, 9/1 for domestic students. Application fee: $50. Electronic applications accepted. *Expenses:* Tuition, state resident: full-time $7434; part-time $413 per credit. Tuition, nonresident: full-time $19,022; part-time $1057 per credit. Required fees: $1729; $88 per credit. *Financial support:* In 2010–11, 40 students received support, including 14 fellowships with full tuition reimbursements available (averaging $29,871 per year), 20 research assistantships with full and partial tuition reimbursements available (averaging $17,722 per year), 6 teaching assistantships with full tuition reimbursements available (averaging $8,310 per year); Federal Work-Study, scholarships/grants, traineeships, and unspecified assistantships also available. Financial award application deadline: 4/1. *Faculty research:* Developmental neurobiology, reproductive physiology, equine reproduction, molecular endocrinology, neurophysiology. Total annual research expenditures: $6.2 million. *Unit head:* Dr. Colin M. Clay, Chair, 970-491-7571, Fax: 970-491-3557, E-mail: colin.clay@colostate.edu. *Application contact:* Erin Bisenius, Graduate Education Coordinator, 970-491-6188, Fax: 970-491-7569, E-mail: erin.bisenius@colostate.edu.

Colorado State University, Graduate School, College of Natural Sciences, Department of Biology, Fort Collins, CO 80523-1878. Offers botany (MS, PhD); zoology (MS, PhD). Post-baccalaureate distance learning degree programs offered (no on-campus study). *Faculty:* 25 full-time (10 women). *Students:* 27 full-time (16 women), 22 part-time (12 women); includes 6 minority (2 Asian, non-Hispanic/Latino; 3 Hispanic/Latino; 1 Two or more races, non-Hispanic/Latino), 7 international. Average age 29. 13 applicants, 46% accepted, 5 enrolled. In 2010, 6 master's, 2 doctorates awarded. Terminal master's awarded for partial completion of doctoral program. *Degree requirements:* For master's, comprehensive exam (for some programs), thesis (for some programs); for doctorate, comprehensive exam, thesis/dissertation. *Entrance requirements:* For master's, GRE General Test, minimum GPA of 3.0; 3 letters of recommendation; for doctorate, GRE General Test, minimum GPA of 3.0; statement of purpose; 2 transcripts; 3 letters of recommendation. Additional exam requirements/recommendations for international students: Required—TOEFL (minimum score 550 paper-based; 213 computer-based; 80 iBT). *Application deadline:* For fall admission, 1/15 priority date for domestic and international students; for spring admission, 11/1 priority date for domestic and international students. Applications are processed on a rolling basis. Application fee: $50. Electronic applica-

tions accepted. *Expenses:* Tuition, state resident: full-time $7434; part-time $413 per credit. Tuition, nonresident: full-time $19,022; part-time $1057 per credit. Required fees: $1729; $88 per credit. *Financial support:* In 2010–11, 14 fellowships (averaging $31,623 per year), 36 research assistantships with full tuition reimbursements (averaging $10,921 per year), 58 teaching assistantships with full tuition reimbursements (averaging $12,196 per year) were awarded; health care benefits also available. Financial award application deadline: 1/15; financial award applicants required to submit FAFSA. *Faculty research:* Aquatic and terrestrial ecology, cell biology and genetics, plant/animal physiology, developmental biology, evolutionary biology. Total annual research expenditures: $5.9 million. *Unit head:* Dr. Daniel R. Bush, Chair, 970-491-7013, Fax: 970-491-0649, E-mail: dbush@colostate.edu. *Application contact:* Dorothy Ramirez, Graduate Coordinator, 970-491-1923, Fax: 970-491-0649, E-mail: dorothy.ramirez@colostate.edu.

Colorado State University–Pueblo, College of Science and Mathematics, Pueblo, CO 81001-4901. Offers applied natural science (MS), including biochemistry, biology, chemistry. Part-time and evening/weekend programs available. *Degree requirements:* For master's, comprehensive exam (for some programs), thesis (for some programs), internship report (if non-thesis). *Entrance requirements:* For master's, GRE General Test (minimum score 1000), 2 letters of reference, minimum GPA of 3.0. Additional exam requirements/recommendations for international students: Required—TOEFL (minimum score 500 paper-based; 173 computer-based), IELTS (minimum score 5). *Faculty research:* Fungal cell walls, molecular biology, bioactive materials synthesis, atomic force microscopy-surface chemistry, nanoscience.

Columbia University, College of Physicians and Surgeons, New York, NY 10032. Offers MD, M Phil, MA, MS, DN Sc, DPT, Ed D, PhD, Adv C, MBA/MS, MD/DDS, MD/MPH, MD/MS, MD/PhD, MPH/MS. Part-time programs available. *Entrance requirements:* For MD, MCAT; for master's and doctorate, GRE General Test. Additional exam requirements/recommendations for international students: Required—TOEFL. *Expenses:* Contact institution.

Columbia University, Graduate School of Arts and Sciences, Division of Natural Sciences, Department of Biological Sciences, New York, NY 10027. Offers M Phil, MA, PhD, MD/PhD. *Degree requirements:* For master's, teaching experience, written exam; for doctorate, thesis/dissertation. *Entrance requirements:* For master's, GRE General Test, GRE Subject Test; for doctorate, GRE General Test, GRE Subject Test (suggested). Additional exam requirements/recommendations for international students: Required—TOEFL.

See Display on next page and Close-Up on page 99.

Concordia University, School of Graduate Studies, Faculty of Arts and Science, Department of Biology, Montréal, QC H3G 1M8, Canada. Offers biology (M Sc, PhD); biotechnology and genomics (Diploma). *Degree requirements:* For master's, thesis; for doctorate, thesis/dissertation, pedagogical training. *Entrance requirements:* For master's, honors degree in biology; for doctorate, M Sc in life science. *Faculty research:* Cell biology, animal physiology, ecology, microbiology/molecular biology, plant physiology/biochemistry and biotechnology.

Cornell University, Graduate School, Graduate Fields of Comparative Biomedical Sciences, Field of Comparative Biomedical Sciences, Ithaca, NY 14853-0001. Offers cellular and molecular medicine (MS, PhD); developmental and reproductive biology (MS, PhD); infectious diseases (MS, PhD); population medicine and epidemiology (MS, PhD); structural and functional biology (MS, PhD). *Faculty:* 94 full-time (27 women). *Students:* 47 full-time (33 women); includes 2 Black or African American, non-Hispanic/Latino; 1 Asian, non-Hispanic/Latino, 23 international. Average age 30. 31 applicants, 48% accepted, 14 enrolled. In 2010, 11 doctorates awarded. *Degree requirements:* For master's, thesis; for doctorate, comprehensive exam, thesis/dissertation. *Entrance requirements:* For master's and doctorate, GRE General Test, 2 letters of recommendation. Additional exam requirements/recommendations for international students:

Watson School of Biological Sciences

Cold Spring Harbor Laboratory

The Watson School of Biological Sciences at Cold Spring Harbor Laboratory offers an innovative four-year Ph.D. program designed for exceptional students. The curriculum includes the following features:

- Approximately four years from matriculation to Ph.D. degree award
- Broad representation of the biological sciences
- A first year with course work and laboratory rotations in separate phases
- Emphasis on the principles of scientific reasoning and logic
- Continued advanced course instruction throughout graduate curriculum
- Extensive student mentoring

There is full remission of tuition fees and full stipend and research costs are provided. Summer undergraduate research program also available. Please see our websites at www.cshl.edu/gradschool and www.cshl.edu/urp.

WATSON SCHOOL OF BIOLOGICAL SCIENCES

COLD SPRING HARBOR LABORATORY

Required—TOEFL (minimum score 550 paper-based; 213 computer-based; 77 iBT). *Application deadline:* For fall admission, 12/15 for domestic students. Application fee: $70. Electronic applications accepted. *Expenses:* Tuition: Full-time $29,500. Required fees: $76. Tuition and fees vary according to degree level and program. *Financial support:* In 2010–11, 18 fellowships with full tuition reimbursements, 25 research assistantships with full tuition reimbursements were awarded; teaching assistantships with full tuition reimbursements, institutionally sponsored loans, scholarships/grants, health care benefits, tuition waivers (full and partial), and unspecified assistantships also available. Financial award applicants required to submit FAFSA. *Faculty research:* Receptors and signal transduction, viral and bacterial infectious diseases, tumor metastasis, clinical sciences/nutritional disease, developmental/neurological disorders. *Unit head:* Director of Graduate Studies, 607-253-3276, Fax: 607-253-3756. *Application contact:* Graduate Field Assistant, 607-253-3276, Fax: 607-253-3756, E-mail: graduate_edcvm@cornell.edu.

Cornell University, Joan and Sanford I. Weill Medical College and Graduate School of Medical Sciences, Weill Cornell Graduate School of Medical Sciences, New York, NY 10065. Offers MS, PhD. *Faculty:* 267 full-time (76 women). *Students:* 558 full-time (339 women); includes 16 Black or African American, non-Hispanic/Latino; 53 Asian, non-Hispanic/Latino; 26 Hispanic/Latino, 183 international. Average age 24. 682 applicants, 20% accepted, 55 enrolled. In 2010, 50 master's, 54 doctorates awarded. Terminal master's awarded for partial completion of doctoral program. *Degree requirements:* For master's, comprehensive exam; for doctorate, thesis/dissertation, final exam. *Entrance requirements:* For doctorate, GRE General Test. Additional exam requirements/recommendations for international students: Required—TOEFL. *Application deadline:* For fall admission, 12/1 for domestic students. Application fee: $60. Electronic applications accepted. *Expenses:* Contact institution. *Financial support:* In 2010–11, 48 fellowships (averaging $23,221 per year) were awarded; scholarships/grants, health care benefits, and stipends (given to all students) also available. *Unit head:* Dr. David P. Hajjar, Dean, 212-746-6900, E-mail: dphajjar@med.cornell.edu. *Application contact:* Dr. Randi Silver, Associate Dean, 212-746-6565, Fax: 212-746-8906, E-mail: gsms@med.cornell.edu.

Cornell University, Joan and Sanford I. Weill Medical College and Graduate School of Medical Sciences, Weill Cornell/Rockefeller/Sloan-Kettering Tri-Institutional MD-PhD Program, New York, NY 10065. Offers MD/PhD. Offered jointly with The Rockefeller University and Sloan-Kettering Institute. *Faculty:* 278 full-time (42 women). *Students:* 107 full-time (42 women); includes 17 Black or African American, non-Hispanic/Latino; 9 Asian, non-Hispanic/Latino; 14 Hispanic/Latino, 2 international. 477 applicants, 8% accepted, 13 enrolled. *Application deadline:* For fall admission, 10/15 for domestic and international students. Applications are processed on a rolling basis. Application fee: $0. Electronic applications accepted. *Expenses:* Contact institution. *Financial support:* In 2010–11, 107 students received support, including 107 fellowships with full tuition reimbursements available (averaging $31,600 per year); health care benefits, tuition waivers (full), and stipends, research supplements, dental insurance also available. *Faculty research:* Neuroscience, pharmacology, immunology, structural biology, genetics. *Unit head:* Dr. Olaf S. Andersen, Director, 212-746-6023, Fax: 212-746-8678, E-mail: mdphd@med.cornell.edu. *Application contact:* Ruth Gotian, Administrative Director, 212-746-6023, Fax: 212-746-8678, E-mail: mdphd@med.cornell.edu.

Creighton University, School of Medicine and Graduate School, Graduate Programs in Medicine, Department of Biomedical Sciences, Omaha, NE 68178-0001. Offers MS, PhD, MD/PhD. Terminal master's awarded for partial completion of doctoral program. *Degree requirements:* For master's, thesis; for doctorate, thesis/dissertation. *Entrance requirements:* For master's, GRE General Test (minimum 50th percentile); for doctorate, GRE General Test (minimum score: 50th percentile). Additional exam requirements/recommendations for international students: Required—TOEFL. Electronic applications accepted. *Expenses:* Tuition: Full-time $12,168; part-time $676 per credit hour. Required fees: $131 per semester. Tuition and fees vary according to program. *Faculty research:* Molecular biology and gene transfection.

Dalhousie University, Faculty of Graduate Studies and Faculty of Medicine, Graduate Programs in Medicine, Halifax, NS B3H 4R2, Canada. Offers M Sc, PhD. *Degree requirements:* For

master's, thesis; for doctorate, thesis/dissertation. *Entrance requirements:* Additional exam requirements/recommendations for international students: Required—TOEFL, IELTS, 1 of the following 5 approved tests: TOEFL, IELTS, CAEL, CANTEST, Michigan English Language Assessment Battery. Electronic applications accepted. *Expenses:* Contact institution.

Dalhousie University, Faculty of Science, Department of Biology, Halifax, NS B3H 4R2, Canada. Offers M Sc, PhD. Terminal master's awarded for partial completion of doctoral program. *Degree requirements:* For master's, thesis; for doctorate, thesis/dissertation. *Entrance requirements:* Additional exam requirements/recommendations for international students: Required—TOEFL, IELTS, CANTEST, CAEL, or Michigan English Language Assessment Battery. Electronic applications accepted. *Faculty research:* Marine biology, ecology, animal physiology, plant physiology, microbiology (cell, molecular, genetics, development).

Dartmouth College, Graduate Program in Molecular and Cellular Biology, Department of Biological Sciences, Hanover, NH 03755. Offers PhD, MD/PhD. *Entrance requirements:* For doctorate, GRE General Test, letters of recommendation. Additional exam requirements/recommendations for international students: Required—TOEFL (minimum score 450 paper-based; 90 iBT) or IELTS (minimum score 7). Electronic applications accepted.

Delaware State University, Graduate Programs, Department of Biology, Program in Biological Sciences, Dover, DE 19901-2277. Offers MS. *Entrance requirements:* For master's, GRE, prerequisite undergraduate courses. Additional exam requirements/recommendations for international students: Required—TOEFL.

Delta State University, Graduate Programs, College of Arts and Sciences, Division of Biological and Physical Sciences, Cleveland, MS 38733-0001. Offers natural sciences (MSNS). Part-time programs available. *Degree requirements:* For master's, research project or thesis. *Entrance requirements:* For master's, GRE General Test. *Expenses:* Tuition, state resident: full-time $4347; part-time $202 per credit hour. Tuition, nonresident: full-time $12,052; part-time $523 per credit hour. Required fees: $504.

DePaul University, College of Liberal Arts and Sciences, Department of Biological Sciences, Chicago, IL 60614. Offers MA, MS. *Faculty:* 10 full-time (5 women), 5 part-time/adjunct (0 women). *Students:* 14 full-time (8 women), 5 part-time (4 women); includes 4 minority (2 Black or African American, non-Hispanic/Latino; 2 Hispanic/Latino). Average age 25. 39 applicants, 21% accepted, 6 enrolled. In 2010, 4 master's awarded. *Entrance requirements:* For master's, comprehensive exam, thesis (for some programs). *Entrance requirements:* For master's, GRE, MCAT or DAT, minimum GPA of 3.0. Additional exam requirements/recommendations for international students: Required—TOEFL (minimum score 590 paper-based; 243 computer-based; 120 iBT). *Application deadline:* For fall admission, 2/15 priority date for domestic and international students. Applications are processed on a rolling basis. Application fee: $25. Electronic applications accepted. *Financial support:* In 2010–11, 10 teaching assistantships with full tuition reimbursements (averaging $9,000 per year) were awarded; Federal Work-Study, institutionally sponsored loans, scholarships/grants, and tuition waivers (partial) also available. Support available to part-time students. Financial award application deadline: 4/1. *Faculty research:* Cell motility, detoxification in plant cells, molecular biology of fungi, B-lymphocyte development, physiological ecology, traumatic brain injury, bacterial pathogenicity, cancer biology, molecular evolution, Drosophila genetics. *Unit head:* Dr. Stanley Cohn, Chair, 773-325-7595, Fax: 773-325-7596, E-mail: scohn@depaul.edu. *Application contact:* Dr. Margaret Silliker, Director of Graduate Admissions, 773-325-2194, E-mail: msillike@depaul.edu.

Des Moines University, College of Osteopathic Medicine, Program in Biomedical Sciences, Des Moines, IA 50312-4104. Offers MS. *Unit head:* Dr. Kendall Reed, Dean, 515-271-1515, Fax: 515-271-1532, E-mail: kendall.reed@dmu.edu. *Application contact:* Jamie Rehmann, Director of Admissions, 515-271-1451, Fax: 515-271-7163, E-mail: doadmit@dmu.edu.

Dominican University of California, Graduate Programs, School of Health and Natural Sciences, Program in Biology, San Rafael, CA 94901-2298. Offers MS. *Students:* 14 full-time

Biological and Biomedical Sciences—General

Dominican University of California (continued)
(6 women); includes 6 minority (2 Asian, non-Hispanic/Latino; 4 Hispanic/Latino), 1 international. Average age 26. 18 applicants, 67% accepted, 8 enrolled. In 2010, 1 master's awarded. *Entrance requirements:* For master's, GRE or MCAT, BS in biology, biological sciences or biomedical sciences; minimum GPA of 3.0 in last 60 units. Additional exam requirements/recommendations for international students: Required—TOEFL (minimum score 550 paper-based; 213 computer-based; 80 iBT), IELTS (minimum score 7). *Application deadline:* For fall admission, 3/15 priority date for domestic and international students. Applications are processed on a rolling basis. Application fee: $40. Electronic applications accepted. *Financial support:* In 2010–11, 11 students received support. Career-related internships or fieldwork, scholarships/grants, and unspecified assistantships available. Financial award application deadline: 3/2; financial award applicants required to submit FAFSA. *Unit head:* Dr. Sibdas Ghosh, Chair, Natural Science and Mathematics, 415-482-3583, Fax: 415-257-0120, E-mail: sibdas.ghosh@dominican.edu. *Application contact:* Lawrence Schwartz, Director, 415-458-3748, Fax: 415-485-3214, E-mail: larry.schwartz@dominican.edu.

Drew University, Caspersen School of Graduate Studies, Program in Education, Madison, NJ 07940-1493. Offers biology (MAT); chemistry (MAT); English (MAT); French (MAT); Italian (MAT); math (MAT); physics (MAT); social studies (MAT); Spanish (MAT); theatre arts (MAT). Part-time programs available. *Entrance requirements:* For master's, transcripts, personal statement, recommendations. Additional exam requirements/recommendations for international students: Required—TOEFL, TWE. *Expenses:* Contact institution.

Drexel University, College of Arts and Sciences, Department of Biology, Philadelphia, PA 19104-2875. Offers biological sciences (MS, PhD); human nutrition (MS). Part-time programs available. *Degree requirements:* For doctorate, thesis/dissertation. *Entrance requirements:* For master's and doctorate, GRE General Test. Additional exam requirements/recommendations for international students: Required—TOEFL. Electronic applications accepted. *Faculty research:* Genetic engineering, physiological ecology.

Drexel University, College of Medicine, Biomedical Graduate Programs, Philadelphia, PA 19129. Offers MLAS, MMS, MS, PhD, Certificate, MD/PhD. Part-time programs available. Terminal master's awarded for partial completion of doctoral program. *Degree requirements:* For master's, comprehensive exam; for doctorate, thesis/dissertation, qualifying exam. *Entrance requirements:* For master's and doctorate, GRE General Test. Additional exam requirements/recommendations for international students: Required—TOEFL. Electronic applications accepted. *Expenses:* Contact institution.

Drexel University, College of Medicine, MD/PhD Program, Philadelphia, PA 19104-2875. Offers MD/PhD. Electronic applications accepted.

Drexel University, School of Biomedical Engineering, Science and Health Systems, Program in Biomedical Science, Philadelphia, PA 19104-2875. Offers MS, PhD. *Degree requirements:* For master's, thesis (for some programs); for doctorate, thesis/dissertation. Electronic applications accepted.

Duke University, Graduate School, Department of Biology, Durham, NC 27708. Offers PhD. *Faculty:* 50 full-time. *Students:* 77 full-time (42 women); includes 6 Asian, non-Hispanic/Latino; 2 Hispanic/Latino, 24 international. 122 applicants, 11% accepted, 8 enrolled. In 2010, 10 doctorates awarded. *Degree requirements:* For doctorate, one foreign language, thesis/dissertation. *Entrance requirements:* For doctorate, GRE General Test, GRE Subject Test (recommended). Additional exam requirements/recommendations for international students: Required—TOEFL (minimum score 550 paper-based; 213 computer-based; 83 iBT), IELTS (minimum score 7). *Application deadline:* For fall admission, 12/8 priority date for domestic and international students. Application fee: $75. Electronic applications accepted. *Financial support:* Fellowships, research assistantships, teaching assistantships, Federal Work-Study available. Financial award application deadline: 12/8. *Unit head:* Sonke Johnsen, Director of Graduate Studies, 919-684-3649, Fax: 919-660-7293, E-mail: aslzoo@duke.edu. *Application contact:* Elizabeth Hutton, Director of Admissions, 919-684-3913, Fax: 919-684-2277, E-mail: grad-admissions@duke.edu.

Duquesne University, Bayer School of Natural and Environmental Sciences, Department of Biological Sciences, Pittsburgh, PA 15282-0001. Offers MS, PhD, MS/MS. Part-time programs available. *Faculty:* 14 full-time (4 women). *Students:* 33 full-time (19 women); includes 4 minority (1 Black or African American, non-Hispanic/Latino; 3 Asian, non-Hispanic/Latino), 8 international. Average age 27. 25 applicants, 32% accepted, 7 enrolled. In 2010, 2 master's, 1 doctorate awarded. Terminal master's awarded for partial completion of doctoral program. *Degree requirements:* For master's, thesis (for some programs), 32 credit hours (non-thesis); for doctorate, thesis/dissertation. *Entrance requirements:* For master's, GRE General Test; GRE Subject Test in biology, biochemistry, or cell and molecular biology (recommended), BS in biological sciences or related field, 3 letters of recommendation; for doctorate, GRE General Test; GRE Subject Test in biology, biochemistry, or cell and molecular biology (recommended), BS or MS in biological sciences or related field, 3 letters of recommendation, statement of purpose, official transcripts. Additional exam requirements/recommendations for international students: Required—TOEFL (minimum score 80 iBT). *Application deadline:* For fall admission, 2/15 for domestic and international students. Applications are processed on a rolling basis. Application fee: $0 ($40 for international students). Electronic applications accepted. *Expenses:* Contact institution. *Financial support:* In 2010–11, 31 students received support, including 1 fellowship with full tuition reimbursement available (averaging $21,650 per year), 6 research assistantships with full tuition reimbursements available (averaging $21,400 per year), 24 teaching assistantships with full tuition reimbursements available (averaging $21,400 per year); scholarships/grants, tuition waivers (partial), and unspecified assistantships also available. Financial award application deadline: 5/31. *Faculty research:* Cell and developmental biology, molecular biology and genetics, evolution, ecology, physiology and microbiology. *Unit head:* Dr. Nancy Trun, Chair, 412-396-5657, Fax: 412-396-5907, E-mail: trun@duq.edu. *Application contact:* Heather Costello, Graduate Academic Advisor, 412-396-6339, Fax: 412-396-4881, E-mail: costelloh@duq.edu.

East Carolina University, Brody School of Medicine, Graduate Programs in Medicine, Greenville, NC 27858-4353. Offers MPH, PhD. *Degree requirements:* For doctorate, comprehensive exam, thesis/dissertation. *Entrance requirements:* For doctorate, GRE General Test. Additional exam requirements/recommendations for international students: Required—TOEFL. *Expenses:* Tuition, state resident: full-time $3130; part-time $391.25 per credit hour. Tuition, nonresident: full-time $13,817; part-time $1727.13 per credit hour. Required fees: $1916; $239.50 per credit hour. Tuition and fees vary according to campus/location and program.

East Carolina University, Graduate School, Thomas Harriot College of Arts and Sciences, Department of Biology, Greenville, NC 27858-4353. Offers biology (MS); molecular biology/biotechnology (MS). Part-time programs available. *Degree requirements:* For master's, one foreign language, comprehensive exam, thesis. *Entrance requirements:* For master's, GRE General Test, GRE Subject Test. Additional exam requirements/recommendations for international students: Required—TOEFL. *Expenses:* Tuition, state resident: full-time $3130; part-time $391.25 per credit hour. Tuition, nonresident: full-time $13,817; part-time $1727.13 per credit hour. Required fees: $1916; $239.50 per credit hour. Tuition and fees vary according to campus/location and program. *Faculty research:* Biochemistry, microbiology, cell biology.

Eastern Illinois University, Graduate School, College of Sciences, Department of Biological Sciences, Charleston, IL 61920-3099. Offers MS. *Degree requirements:* For master's, exam.

Eastern Kentucky University, The Graduate School, College of Arts and Sciences, Department of Biological Sciences, Richmond, KY 40475-3102. Offers biological sciences (MS); ecology (MS). Part-time programs available. *Degree requirements:* For master's, thesis. *Entrance requirements:* For master's, GRE General Test, minimum GPA of 2.5. *Faculty research:*

Systematics, ecology, and biodiversity; animal behavior; protein structure and molecular genetics; biomonitoring and aquatic toxicology; pathogenesis of microbes and parasites.

Eastern Michigan University, Graduate School, College of Arts and Sciences, Department of Biology, Ypsilanti, MI 48197. Offers cell and molecular biology (MS); community college biology teaching (MS); ecology and organismal biology (MS); general biology (MS); water resources (MS). Part-time and evening/weekend programs available. Postbaccalaureate distance learning degree programs offered (minimal on-campus study). *Faculty:* 20 full-time (4 women). *Students:* 18 full-time (13 women), 35 part-time (19 women); includes 4 minority (2 Black or African American, non-Hispanic/Latino; 2 Two or more races, non-Hispanic/Latino), 13 international. Average age 27. 55 applicants, 47% accepted, 17 enrolled. In 2010, 10 master's awarded. *Entrance requirements:* For master's, GRE General Test, GRE Subject Test. Additional exam requirements/recommendations for international students: Required—TOEFL. *Application deadline:* Applications are processed on a rolling basis. Application fee: $35. *Financial support:* Fellowships, research assistantships with full tuition reimbursements, teaching assistantships with full tuition reimbursements, career-related internships or fieldwork, Federal Work-Study, institutionally sponsored loans, scholarships/grants, tuition waivers (partial), and unspecified assistantships available. Support available to part-time students. Financial award applicants required to submit FAFSA. *Unit head:* Dr. Marianne Laporte, Department Head, 734-487-4242, Fax: 734-487-9235, E-mail: mlaporte@emich.edu. *Application contact:* Dr. Marianne Laporte, Department Head, 734-487-4242, Fax: 734-487-9235, E-mail: mlaporte@emich.edu.

Eastern New Mexico University, Graduate School, College of Liberal Arts and Sciences, Department of Biology, Portales, NM 88130. Offers applied ecology (MS); cell, molecular biology and biotechnology (MS); education (non-thesis) (MS); microbiology (MS); plant biology (MS); zoology (MS). Part-time programs available. *Faculty:* 8 full-time (0 women). *Students:* 11 full-time (8 women), 7 part-time (4 women); includes 7 minority (5 Hispanic/Latino; 2 Two or more races, non-Hispanic/Latino), 4 international. Average age 25. 21 applicants, 14% accepted, 3 enrolled. In 2010, 4 master's awarded. *Degree requirements:* For master's, comprehensive exam, thesis optional. *Entrance requirements:* For master's, GRE, minimum GPA of 3.0, 2 letters of recommendation, statement of research interest, bachelor's degree related to field of study or proof of common knowledge. Additional exam requirements/recommendations for international students: Required—TOEFL (minimum score 550 paper-based; 213 computer-based; 79 iBT), IELTS (minimum score 6). *Application deadline:* For fall admission, 7/20 priority date for domestic students, 6/20 priority date for international students; for spring admission, 12/15 priority date for domestic students, 11/15 priority date for international students. Applications are processed on a rolling basis. Application fee: $10. Electronic applications accepted. *Expenses:* Tuition, state resident: full-time $3210; part-time $130 per credit hour. Tuition, nonresident: full-time $8652; part-time $360.50 per credit hour. Required fees: $1212; $50.50 per credit hour. Tuition and fees vary according to course load. *Financial support:* In 2010–11, 11 teaching assistantships with partial tuition reimbursements (averaging $8,500 per year) were awarded; unspecified assistantships also available. Support available to part-time students. Financial award applicants required to submit FAFSA. *Unit head:* Dr. Zach Jones, Graduate Coordinator, 575-562-2723, Fax: 575-562-2192, E-mail: zach.jones@enmu.edu. *Application contact:* Sharon Potter, Department Secretary, Biology/Physical Sciences, 575-562-2174, Fax: 575-562-2192, E-mail: sharon.potter@enmu.edu.

Eastern Virginia Medical School, Doctoral Program in Biomedical Sciences, Norfolk, VA 23501-1980. Offers PhD. Program offered jointly with Old Dominion University. *Students:* 26. 22 applicants, 27% accepted, 4 enrolled. In 2010, 6 doctorates awarded. *Degree requirements:* For doctorate, thesis/dissertation. *Entrance requirements:* For doctorate, GRE General Test. Additional exam requirements/recommendations for international students: Required—TOEFL. *Application deadline:* For fall admission, 2/1 for domestic students. Applications are processed on a rolling basis. Application fee: $60. Electronic applications accepted. *Expenses:* Contact institution. *Financial support:* Research assistantships with full tuition reimbursements available. *Faculty research:* Cancer, cardiovascular biology, diabetes, infectious disease, neuroscience, reproductive biology. Total annual research expenditures: $14 million. *Unit head:* Dr. Earl Godfrey, Director, 757-446-5609, Fax: 757-624-2255, E-mail: godfreew@evms.edu. *Application contact:* Leah Solomon, Administrative Support Coordinator, 757-446-5944, Fax: 757-446-6179, E-mail: solomolj@evms.edu.

Eastern Virginia Medical School, Master's Program in Biomedical Sciences (Medical Master's), Norfolk, VA 23501-1980. Offers MS. *Faculty:* 25. *Students:* 23 full-time (14 women); includes 6 Asian, non-Hispanic/Latino. 287 applicants, 12% accepted, 23 enrolled. In 2010, 22 master's awarded. *Entrance requirements:* For master's, MCAT. *Application deadline:* For fall admission, 4/1 for domestic students. Applications are processed on a rolling basis. Application fee: $60. Electronic applications accepted. *Expenses:* Contact institution. *Financial support:* Institutionally sponsored loans available. *Unit head:* Dr. Donald Meyer, Director, 757-446-5615, Fax: 757-446-6179, E-mail: meyerdc@evms.edu. *Application contact:* Leah Solomon, Administrative Support Coordinator, 757-446-5944, Fax: 757-446-6179, E-mail: solomolj@evms.edu.

Eastern Virginia Medical School, Master's Program in Biomedical Sciences Research, Norfolk, VA 23501-1980. Offers MS. *Faculty:* 57. *Students:* 9 full-time (7 women); includes 1 Black or African American, non-Hispanic/Latino; 2 Asian, non-Hispanic/Latino. 22 applicants, 50% accepted, 7 enrolled. In 2010, 2 master's awarded. *Degree requirements:* For master's, comprehensive exam (for some programs), thesis optional. *Entrance requirements:* For master's, GRE. Additional exam requirements/recommendations for international students: Required—TOEFL. *Application deadline:* For fall admission, 3/1 for domestic students. Applications are processed on a rolling basis. Application fee: $60. Electronic applications accepted. *Expenses:* Contact institution. *Faculty research:* Cancer, cardiovascular biology, diabetes, infectious disease, neuroscience, reproductive biology. *Unit head:* Dr. Earl Godfrey, Director, 757-446-5609, Fax: 757-624-2255, E-mail: godfreew@evms.edu. *Application contact:* Leah Solomon, Administrative Support Coordinator, 757-446-5944, Fax: 757-446-6179, E-mail: solomolj@evms.edu.

Eastern Virginia Medical School, Master's Program in Clinical Embryology and Andrology, Norfolk, VA 23501-1980. Offers MS. Postbaccalaureate distance learning degree programs offered (minimal on-campus study). *Faculty:* 12 full-time, 8 part-time/adjunct. *Students:* 66 full-time (44 women); includes 6 Black or African American, non-Hispanic/Latino; 10 Asian, non-Hispanic/Latino; 10 Hispanic/Latino. 35 applicants, 69% accepted, 23 enrolled. In 2010, 14 master's awarded. *Entrance requirements:* Additional exam requirements/recommendations for international students: Required—TOEFL (minimum score 550 paper-based; 213 computer-based; 80 iBT). *Application deadline:* For fall admission, 1/14 for domestic and international students. Applications are processed on a rolling basis. Application fee: $60. Electronic applications accepted. *Expenses:* Contact institution. *Unit head:* Dr. Jacob Mayer, Director, 757-446-5049, Fax: 757-446-5905. *Application contact:* Nancy Garcia, Administrator, 757-446-8935, Fax: 757-446-5905, E-mail: garcianw@evms.edu.

Eastern Washington University, Graduate Studies, College of Science, Health and Engineering, Department of Biology, Cheney, WA 99004-2431. Offers MS. *Degree requirements:* For master's, comprehensive exam, thesis. *Entrance requirements:* For master's, GRE General Test, minimum GPA of 3.0. *Faculty research:* Ecology of Eastern Washington Scablands, Columbia River fisheries, biotechnology applied to vaccines, role of mycorrhiza in plant nutrition, exercise and estrous cycles.

East Stroudsburg University of Pennsylvania, Graduate School, College of Arts and Sciences, Department of Biology, East Stroudsburg, PA 18301-2999. Offers M Ed, MS. Part-time and evening/weekend programs available. *Degree requirements:* For master's, comprehensive exam, thesis or alternative. *Entrance requirements:* For master's, GRE, resume, undergraduate major in life science (or equivalent), completion of organic chemistry (minimum two semesters), 3 letters of recommendation, letter of intent. Additional exam requirements/recommendations for international students: Required—TOEFL (minimum score 560 paper-based; 220 computer-based; 83 iBT) or IELTS.

East Tennessee State University, James H. Quillen College of Medicine, Biomedical Science Graduate Program, Johnson City, TN 37614. Offers anatomy (PhD); biochemistry (PhD); microbiology (PhD); pharmacology (PhD); physiology (PhD). Part-time programs available. *Faculty:* 49 full-time (12 women), 1 (woman) part-time/adjunct. *Students:* 27 full-time (14 women), 4 part-time (2 women); includes 4 minority (1 Black or African American, non-Hispanic/Latino; 1 Asian, non-Hispanic/Latino; 2 Hispanic/Latino), 5 international. Average age 32. 62 applicants, 11% accepted, 7 enrolled. In 2010, 2 doctorates awarded. Terminal master's awarded for partial completion of doctoral program. *Degree requirements:* For doctorate, thesis/dissertation, comprehensive qualifying exam. *Entrance requirements:* For doctorate, GRE General Test, GRE Subject Test. Additional exam requirements/recommendations for international students: Required—TOEFL (minimum score 550 paper-based; 213 computer-based; 79 iBT). *Application deadline:* For fall admission, 3/15 priority date for domestic students, 3/1 priority date for international students. Application fee: $25 ($35 for international students). Electronic applications accepted. *Expenses:* Contact institution. *Financial support:* In 2010–11, 7 research assistantships with full tuition reimbursements (averaging $15,000 per year) were awarded; teaching assistantships with full tuition reimbursements, career-related internships or fieldwork, institutionally sponsored loans, scholarships/grants, and unspecified assistantships also available. Financial award application deadline: 7/1; financial award applicants required to submit FAFSA. Total annual research expenditures: $2.1 million. *Unit head:* Dr. Mitchell E. Robinson, Assistant Dean/Director, 423-439-4658, E-mail: robinson@etsu.edu. *Application contact:* Edwin D. Taylor, Assistant Dean for Admissions and Records, 423-439-4753, Fax: 423-439-8206.

East Tennessee State University, School of Graduate Studies, College of Arts and Sciences, Department of Biological Sciences, Johnson City, TN 37614. Offers biology (MS); microbiology (MS); paleontology (MS). *Faculty:* 12 full-time (0 women). *Students:* 43 full-time (20 women), 9 part-time (5 women); includes 3 minority (2 Hispanic/Latino; 1 Two or more races, non-Hispanic/Latino), 17 international. Average age 26. 53 applicants, 43% accepted, 19 enrolled. In 2010, 20 master's awarded. *Degree requirements:* For master's, comprehensive exam, thesis optional. *Entrance requirements:* For master's, GRE General Test or GRE Subject Test, minimum GPA of 3.0. Additional exam requirements/recommendations for international students: Required—TOEFL (minimum score 550 paper-based; 213 computer-based; 79 iBT). *Application deadline:* For fall admission, 4/1 priority date for domestic students, 2/1 for international students; for spring admission, 9/1 for domestic students, 7/1 for international students. Application fee: $25 ($35 for international students). Electronic applications accepted. *Financial support:* In 2010–11, 1 research assistantship with full tuition reimbursement (averaging $6,000 per year), 15 teaching assistantships with full tuition reimbursements (averaging $6,000 per year) were awarded; institutionally sponsored loans, scholarships/grants, and unspecified assistantships also available. Financial award application deadline: 7/1; financial award applicants required to submit FAFSA. *Faculty research:* Vertebrate natural history, mutation rates in fruit flies, regulation of plant secondary metabolism, plant biochemistry, timekeeping in honeybees, gene expression in diapausing flies. Total annual research expenditures: $226,807. *Unit head:* Dr. Dan M. Johnson, Chair, 423-439-4329, Fax: 423-439-5958, E-mail: johnsodm@etsu.edu. *Application contact:* Admissions and Records Clerk, 423-439-4221, Fax: 423-439-5624, E-mail: gradsch@etsu.edu.

Edinboro University of Pennsylvania, College of Arts and Sciences, Department of Biology and Health Services, Edinboro, PA 16444. Offers biology (MS). Part-time and evening/weekend programs available. *Faculty:* 4 full-time (0 women). *Students:* 6 full-time (1 woman), 3 part-time (2 women); includes 1 minority (Asian, non-Hispanic/Latino). Average age 28. In 2010, 4 master's awarded. *Degree requirements:* For master's, thesis or alternative, competency exam. *Entrance requirements:* For master's, GRE or MAT, minimum QPA of 2.5. *Application deadline:* Applications are processed on a rolling basis. Application fee: $30. Electronic applications accepted. *Expenses:* Tuition, state resident: full-time $6966; part-time $387 per credit. Tuition, nonresident: full-time $11,146; part-time $619 per credit. Required fees: $2402; $96.25 per credit. *Financial support:* In 2010–11, 2 research assistantships with full and partial tuition reimbursements (averaging $4,050 per year) were awarded; Federal Work-Study, scholarships/grants, and unspecified assistantships also available. Support available to part-time students. Financial award application deadline: 2/15; financial award applicants required to submit FAFSA. *Faculty research:* Microbiology, molecular biology, zoology, botany, ecology. *Unit head:* Dr. Peter Lindeman, Program Head, 814-732-2447, E-mail: plindeman@edinboro.edu. *Application contact:* Dr. Peter Lindeman, Program Head, 814-732-2447, E-mail: plindeman@edinboro.edu.

Elizabeth City State University, School of Mathematics, Science and Technology, Program in Biology, Elizabeth City, NC 27909-7806. Offers MS. Part-time programs available. *Degree requirements:* For master's, thesis. *Entrance requirements:* For master's, GRE. Additional exam requirements/recommendations for international students: Required—TOEFL. Electronic applications accepted. *Faculty research:* Apoptosis and cancer, plant bioengineering, development of biofuels, microbial degradation, insect cell-like discovery.

Emory University, Laney Graduate School, Division of Biological and Biomedical Sciences, Atlanta, GA 30322-1100. Offers PhD. *Faculty:* 325 full-time (81 women). *Students:* 447 full-time (288 women); includes 28 Black or African American, non-Hispanic/Latino; 1 American Indian or Alaska Native, non-Hispanic/Latino; 21 Asian, non-Hispanic/Latino; 20 Hispanic/Latino, 63 international. Average age 27. 1,066 applicants, 15% accepted, 77 enrolled. In 2010, 60 doctorates awarded. *Degree requirements:* For doctorate, comprehensive exam, thesis/dissertation. *Entrance requirements:* For doctorate, GRE General Test, minimum GPA of 3.0 in science course work (recommended). Additional exam requirements/recommendations for international students: Required—TOEFL. *Application deadline:* For fall admission, 12/1 for domestic and international students. Application fee: $75. Electronic applications accepted. *Expenses:* Contact institution. *Financial support:* In 2010–11, 142 students received support, including 142 fellowships with full tuition reimbursements available (averaging $25,000 per year); institutionally sponsored loans, scholarships/grants, health care benefits, and tuition waivers (full) also available. *Faculty research:* Biochemistry, genetics and cancer; immunology and microbiology; neuroscience and pharmacology; nutrition; population biology and ecology. *Unit head:* Dr. Keith Wilkinson, Director, 404-727-2545, Fax: 404-727-3322, E-mail: genekdw@emory.edu. *Application contact:* Kathy Smith, Director of Recruitment and Admissions, 404-727-2547, Fax: 404-727-3322, E-mail: kathy.smith@emory.edu.

Emporia State University, Graduate School, College of Liberal Arts and Sciences, Department of Biological Sciences, Emporia, KS 66801-5087. Offers botany (MS); environmental biology (MS); general biology (MS); microbial and cellular biology (MS); zoology (MS). Part-time programs available. *Faculty:* 13 full-time (3 women). *Students:* 14 full-time (8 women), 19 part-time (9 women); includes 2 minority (1 Black or African American, non-Hispanic/Latino; 1 Hispanic/Latino), 6 international. 9 applicants, 100% accepted, 9 enrolled. In 2010, 4 master's awarded. *Degree requirements:* For master's, comprehensive exam or thesis. *Entrance requirements:* For master's, GRE, appropriate undergraduate degree, interview, letters of reference. Additional exam requirements/recommendations for international students: Required—TOEFL (minimum score 520 paper-based; 133 computer-based; 68 iBT). *Application deadline:* For fall admission, 8/15 priority date for domestic students. Applications are processed on a rolling basis. Application fee: $30 ($75 for international students). Electronic applications accepted. *Expenses:* Tuition, state resident: full-time $4382; part-time $183 per credit hour. Tuition, nonresident: full-time $13,572; part-time $566 per credit hour. Required fees: $1022; $62 per credit hour. Tuition and fees vary according to course level, course load and campus/location. *Financial support:* In 2010–11, 10 research assistantships with full tuition reimbursements (averaging $7,353 per year), 9 teaching assistantships with full tuition reimbursements (averaging $7,809 per year) were awarded; career-related internships or fieldwork, Federal Work-Study, institutionally sponsored loans, health care benefits, and unspecified assistantships also available. Financial award application deadline: 3/15; financial award applicants required to submit FAFSA. *Faculty research:* Fisheries, range, and wildlife management; aquatic, plant, grassland, vertebrate, and invertebrate ecology; mammalian and plant systematics, taxonomy, and evolution; immunology, virology, and molecular biology. *Unit head:* Dr. R. Brent Thomas, Chair, 620-341-5311, Fax: 620-341-5608, E-mail: rthomas2@emporia.edu. *Application contact:* Dr. Scott Crupper, Graduate Coordinator, 620-341-5621, Fax: 620-341-5607, E-mail: scrupper@emporia.edu.

Fairleigh Dickinson University, College at Florham, Maxwell Becton College of Arts and Sciences, Department of Biological and Allied Health Sciences, Program in Biology, Madison, NJ 07940-1099. Offers MS. *Students:* 3 full-time (2 women), 12 part-time (10 women). Average age 28. 9 applicants, 89% accepted, 3 enrolled. In 2010, 6 master's awarded. *Application deadline:* Applications are processed on a rolling basis. Application fee: $40. *Application contact:* Susan Brooman, University Director, Graduate Admissions, 973-443-8905, Fax: 973-443-8088, E-mail: grad@fdu.edu.

Fairleigh Dickinson University, Metropolitan Campus, University College: Arts, Sciences, and Professional Studies, School of Natural Sciences, Program in Biology, Teaneck, NJ 07666-1914. Offers MS. *Students:* 14 full-time (8 women), 10 part-time (7 women), 14 international. Average age 27. 35 applicants, 49% accepted, 5 enrolled. In 2010, 10 master's awarded. *Application deadline:* Applications are processed on a rolling basis. Application fee: $40. *Application contact:* Susan Brooman, University Director of Graduate Admissions, 201-692-2554, Fax: 201-692-2560, E-mail: globaleducation@fdu.edu.

Fayetteville State University, Graduate School, Department of Natural Sciences, Fayetteville, NC 28301-4298. Offers biology (MS). Part-time and evening/weekend programs available. *Faculty:* 9 full-time (3 women). *Students:* 5 full-time (3 women), 4 part-time (2 women); includes 4 minority (3 Black or African American, non-Hispanic/Latino; 1 Native Hawaiian or other Pacific Islander, non-Hispanic/Latino), 1 international. Average age 27. 3 applicants, 100% accepted, 3 enrolled. In 2010, 4 master's awarded. *Degree requirements:* For master's, comprehensive exam, thesis, internship. *Entrance requirements:* For master's, GRE General Test. *Application deadline:* For fall admission, 4/15 for domestic students; for spring admission, 10/15 for domestic students. Applications are processed on a rolling basis. Application fee: $35. Electronic applications accepted. *Faculty research:* Genomic science of selected plant species and pathological/industrial microorganisms, procedures to identify and eliminate defective spermatozoa in the epididymis, role of STAT3 to block gastric cancer cell proliferation and metastasis, genetic and biochemical pathways in PAO1. Total annual research expenditures: $353,280. *Unit head:* Dr. Abdelmajid Kassem, Chairperson, 910-672-1691, E-mail: mkassem@uncfsu.edu. *Application contact:* Katrina Hoffman, Graduate Admissions Officer, 910-672-1374, Fax: 910-672-1470, E-mail: khoffma1@uncfsu.edu.

Fisk University, Division of Graduate Studies, Department of Biology, Nashville, TN 37208-3051. Offers MA. Part-time programs available. *Degree requirements:* For master's, comprehensive exam, thesis. *Entrance requirements:* For master's, GRE. Electronic applications accepted. *Faculty research:* Cell biology, topographical imaging, serotonin receptors in rats, enzyme assays, developmental biology.

Fitchburg State University, Division of Graduate and Continuing Education, Programs in Biology and Teaching Biology (Secondary Level), Fitchburg, MA 01420-2697. Offers MA, MAT, Certificate. *Accreditation:* NCATE. Part-time and evening/weekend programs available. *Students:* 2 full-time (both women), 7 part-time (4 women). Average age 36. 5 applicants, 100% accepted, 3 enrolled. In 2010, 5 master's awarded. *Entrance requirements:* For master's, GRE General Test, letters of recommendation, resume. Additional exam requirements/recommendations for international students: Required—TOEFL (minimum score 550 paper-based; 213 computer-based; 79 iBT). *Application deadline:* Applications are processed on a rolling basis. Application fee: $25 ($50 for international students). *Expenses:* Tuition, area resident: Part-time $150 per credit. Tuition, state resident: part-time $150 per credit. Tuition, nonresident: part-time $150 per credit. Required fees: $127 per credit. *Financial support:* In 2010–11, research assistantships with partial tuition reimbursements (averaging $5,500 per year); Federal Work-Study, scholarships/grants, and unspecified assistantships also available. Support available to part-time students. Financial award application deadline: 3/1; financial award applicants required to submit FAFSA. *Unit head:* Dr. Christopher Cratsley, Chair, 978-665-3617, Fax: 978-665-3658, E-mail: gce@fitchburgstate.edu. *Application contact:* Director of Admissions, 978-665-3144, Fax: 978-665-4540, E-mail: admissions@fitchburgstate.edu.

Florida Agricultural and Mechanical University, Division of Graduate Studies, Research, and Continuing Education, College of Arts and Sciences, Department of Biology, Tallahassee, FL 32307-3200. Offers MS. Part-time programs available. *Degree requirements:* For master's, comprehensive exam, thesis. *Entrance requirements:* For master's, GRE General Test, minimum GPA of 3.0. Additional exam requirements/recommendations for international students: Required—TOEFL (minimum score 550 paper-based).

Florida Atlantic University, Charles E. Schmidt College of Science, Department of Biological Sciences, Boca Raton, FL 33431-0991. Offers MS, MST. Part-time programs available. *Faculty:* 26 full-time (6 women), 6 part-time/adjunct (2 women). *Students:* 93 full-time (62 women), 23 part-time (14 women); includes 19 minority (5 Black or African American, non-Hispanic/Latino; 6 Asian, non-Hispanic/Latino; 8 Hispanic/Latino), 19 international. Average age 30. 92 applicants, 36% accepted, 27 enrolled. In 2010, 18 master's awarded. *Degree requirements:* For master's, thesis (for some programs). *Entrance requirements:* For master's, GRE General Test, minimum GPA of 3.0. Additional exam requirements/recommendations for international students: Required—TOEFL. *Application deadline:* For fall admission, 3/15 for domestic and international students; for spring admission, 10/1 for domestic and international students. Application fee: $30. *Expenses:* Tuition, state resident: part-time $319.96 per credit. Tuition, nonresident: part-time $926.42 per credit. *Financial support:* Fellowships, research assistantships, teaching assistantships with tuition reimbursements, career-related internships or fieldwork and Federal Work-Study available. *Faculty research:* Ecology of the Everglades, molecular biology and biotechnology, marine biology. *Unit head:* Dr. Rodney K. Murphey, Chair, 561-297-3320, Fax: 561-297-2749. *Application contact:* Becky Dixon, Graduate Program Assistant, 561-297-3230.

Florida Atlantic University, College of Biomedical Science, Boca Raton, FL 33431-0991. Offers biomedical science (MS); integrative biology (PhD). *Faculty:* 35 full-time (14 women), 13 part-time/adjunct (2 women). *Students:* 36 full-time (25 women), 7 part-time (3 women); includes 17 minority (4 Black or African American, non-Hispanic/Latino; 3 Asian, non-Hispanic/Latino; 9 Hispanic/Latino; 1 Two or more races, non-Hispanic/Latino), 5 international. Average age 26. 61 applicants, 28% accepted, 13 enrolled. In 2010, 22 master's awarded. *Degree requirements:* For master's, thesis (for some programs). *Entrance requirements:* For master's, GRE, minimum GPA of 3.0. *Application deadline:* For fall admission, 5/1 for domestic students, 3/15 for international students; for spring admission, 10/1 for domestic and international students. Application fee: $30. *Expenses:* Tuition, state resident: part-time $319.96 per credit. Tuition, nonresident: part-time $926.42 per credit. *Financial support:* Research assistantships available. *Faculty research:* Protein engineering, biology of mind-body interaction, neuroendocrinology, gene expression, methodologies of correction of gynecomastia. *Unit head:* Dr. Michael L. Friedland, Dean, 561-297-4341. *Application contact:* Julie Sivigny, Academic Program Specialist for Graduate Studies, 561-297-2216, E-mail: jsivigny@fau.edu.

Florida Institute of Technology, Graduate Programs, College of Science, Department of Biological Sciences, Melbourne, FL 32901-6975. Offers biological sciences (PhD); biotechnology (MS); cell and molecular biology (MS); ecology and marine biology (MS), including ecology, marine biology. Part-time programs available. *Faculty:* 15 full-time (2 women), 1 part-time/adjunct (0 women). *Students:* 72 full-time (40 women), 12 part-time (7 women); includes 6 minority (1 Asian, non-Hispanic/Latino; 4 Hispanic/Latino; 1 Two or more races, non-Hispanic/Latino), 37 international. Average age 26. 227 applicants, 36% accepted, 29 enrolled. In 2010, 15 master's, 5 doctorates awarded. *Degree requirements:* For master's, thesis (for some programs), research, seminar, internship, or summer lab; for doctorate, comprehensive exam, thesis/dissertation, dissertations seminar, publications. *Entrance requirements:* For master's, GRE General Test, 3 letters of recommendation, minimum GPA of 3.0, resume, statement of objectives; for doctorate, GRE General Test, resume, 3 letters of recommendation, minimum GPA of 3.2, statement of objectives. Additional exam requirements/

Biological and Biomedical Sciences—General

Florida Institute of Technology (continued)
recommendations for international students: Required—TOEFL (minimum score 550 paper-based; 213 computer-based; 79 iBT). *Application deadline:* For fall admission, 3/1 for domestic students, 4/1 for international students; for spring admission, 9/1 for domestic and international students. Applications are processed on a rolling basis. Application fee: $50. Electronic applications accepted. *Expenses:* Tuition: Part-time $1040 per credit hour. Tuition and fees vary according to campus/location. *Financial support:* In 2010–11, 6 fellowships (averaging $20,737 per year), 15 research assistantships with full and partial tuition reimbursements (averaging $13,455 per year), 22 teaching assistantships with full and partial tuition reimbursements (averaging $13,353 per year) were awarded; career-related internships or fieldwork, institutionally sponsored loans, tuition waivers (partial), unspecified assistantships, and tuition remissions also available. Support available to part-time students. Financial award application deadline: 3/1; financial award applicants required to submit FAFSA. *Faculty research:* Initiation of protein synthesis in eukaryotic cells, fixation of radioactive carbon, changes in DNA molecule, endangered or threatened avian and mammalian species, hydroacoustics and feeding preference of the West Indian manatee. Total annual research expenditures: $1.3 million. *Unit head:* Dr. Richard B. Aronson, Department Head, 321-674-8034, Fax: 321-674-7238, E-mail: raronson@fit.edu. *Application contact:* Cheryl A. Brown, Associate Director of Graduate Admissions, 321-674-7581, Fax: 321-723-9468, E-mail: cbrown@fit.edu.

Florida International University, College of Arts and Sciences, Department of Biological Sciences, Miami, FL 33199. Offers MS, PhD. Part-time programs available. *Faculty:* 36 full-time (10 women), 16 part-time/adjunct (10 women). *Students:* 79 full-time (41 women), 13 part-time (7 women); includes 3 Black or African American, non-Hispanic/Latino; 2 Asian, non-Hispanic/Latino; 12 Hispanic/Latino, 25 international. Average age 26. 85 applicants, 33% accepted, 28 enrolled. In 2010, 7 master's, 11 doctorates awarded. *Degree requirements:* For master's, thesis; for doctorate, comprehensive exam, thesis/dissertation. *Entrance requirements:* For master's, GRE General Test, 2 letters of recommendation, minimum GPA of 3.0, faculty sponsor; for doctorate, GRE General Test, 3 letters of recommendation, faculty sponsor with dissertation advisor status, minimum GPA of 3.0. Additional exam requirements/recommendations for international students: Required—TOEFL (minimum score 550 paper-based; 80 iBT). *Application deadline:* For fall admission, 2/1 priority date for domestic and international students; for spring admission, 8/1 priority date for domestic and international students. Applications are processed on a rolling basis. Application fee: $30. Electronic applications accepted. *Financial support:* Institutionally sponsored loans and scholarships/grants available. Financial award application deadline: 3/1; financial award applicants required to submit FAFSA. *Unit head:* Dr. Laurie Richardson, Chair, 305-348-2201, Fax: 305-348-4096, E-mail: laurie.richardson@fiu.edu. *Application contact:* Nanett Rojas, Associate Director of Graduate Admissions, 305-348-7442, Fax: 305-348-7441, E-mail: gradadm@fiu.edu.

Florida State University, The Graduate School, College of Arts and Sciences, Department of Biological Science, Tallahassee, FL 32306-4295. Offers cell and molecular biology and genetics (MS, PhD); ecology and evolutionary biology (MS, PhD); neuroscience (PhD); plant biology (MS, PhD); science teaching (MST); structural biology (MS, PhD). *Faculty:* 53 full-time (16 women). *Students:* 110 full-time (51 women); includes 2 Black or African American, non-Hispanic/Latino; 2 Asian, non-Hispanic/Latino; 10 Hispanic/Latino, 13 international. 323 applicants, 12% accepted, 26 enrolled. In 2010, 5 master's, 13 doctorates awarded. Terminal master's awarded for partial completion of doctoral program. *Degree requirements:* For master's, comprehensive exam, thesis, teaching experience, seminar presentations; for doctorate, comprehensive exam, thesis/dissertation, teaching experience; seminar presentations. *Entrance requirements:* For master's, GRE General Test (minimum combined score 1100, 500 verbal, 500 quantitative), minimum upper-division GPA of 3.0; for doctorate, GRE General Test (minimum combined score 1100, Verbal 500, Quantitative 500), minimum upper-division GPA of 3.0. Additional exam requirements/recommendations for international students: Required—TOEFL (minimum score 600 paper-based; 250 computer-based; 92 iBT). *Application deadline:* For fall admission, 12/15 for domestic and international students. Application fee: $30. Electronic applications accepted. *Expenses:* Tuition, state resident: full-time $8238. *Financial support:* In 2010–11, 108 students received support, including 7 fellowships with full tuition reimbursements available (averaging $24,000 per year), 41 research assistantships with full tuition reimbursements available (averaging $21,000 per year), 56 teaching assistantships with full tuition reimbursements available (averaging $21,000 per year); traineeships also available. Financial award application deadline: 12/15; financial award applicants required to submit FAFSA. *Faculty research:* Cell and molecular biology and genetics, ecology and evolutionary biology, plant science, structural biology. *Unit head:* Dr. George W. Bates, Professor and Associate Chairman, 850-644-5749, Fax: 850-644-9829, E-mail: bates@bio.fsu.edu. *Application contact:* Judy Bowers, Coordinator, Graduate Affairs, 850-644-3023, Fax: 850-644-9829, E-mail: gradinfo@bio.fsu.edu.

Florida State University, The Graduate School, College of Arts and Sciences, Department of Mathematics, Tallahassee, FL 32306-4510. Offers applied computational mathematics (MS, PhD); biomedical mathematics (MS, PhD); financial mathematics (MS, PhD); pure mathematics (MS, PhD). Part-time programs available. *Faculty:* 46 full-time (11 women), 2 part-time/adjunct (both women). *Students:* 139 full-time (35 women), 7 part-time (0 women); includes 3 Black or African American, non-Hispanic/Latino; 3 Asian, non-Hispanic/Latino; 4 Hispanic/Latino, 92 international. Average age 26. 342 applicants, 40% accepted, 39 enrolled. In 2010, 42 master's, 8 doctorates awarded. Terminal master's awarded for partial completion of doctoral program. *Degree requirements:* For master's, comprehensive exam (for some programs), thesis optional; for doctorate, comprehensive exam (for some programs), thesis/dissertation, candidacy exam including written qualifying examinations which differ by degree concentrations. *Entrance requirements:* For master's and doctorate, GRE General Test, minimum upper-division GPA of 3.0, 4-year bachelor's degree. Additional exam requirements/recommendations for international students: Required—TOEFL (minimum score 213 computer-based; 80 iBT), IELTS (minimum score 6.5). *Application deadline:* For fall admission, 1/3 priority date for domestic students, 12/15 priority date for international students; for spring admission, 11/1 for domestic and international students. Applications are processed on a rolling basis. Application fee: $30. Electronic applications accepted. *Expenses:* Tuition, state resident: full-time $8238. *Financial support:* In 2010–11, 102 students received support, including 6 fellowships with full tuition reimbursements available (averaging $19,000 per year), 15 research assistantships with full tuition reimbursements available (averaging $20,000 per year), 75 teaching assistantships with full tuition reimbursements available (averaging $18,000 per year); career-related internships or fieldwork, institutionally sponsored loans, scholarships/grants, health care benefits, tuition waivers (full and partial), and unspecified assistantships also available. *Faculty research:* Geometric topology, algebraic geometry, fluid dynamics, financial mathematics, biomedical mathematics. *Unit head:* Dr. Philip L. Bowers, Chairperson, 850-645-3338, Fax: 850-644-4053, E-mail: bowers@math.fsu.edu. *Application contact:* Dr. Bettye Anne Case, Associate Chair for Graduate Studies, 850-644-1586, Fax: 850-644-4053, E-mail: case@math.fsu.edu.

Fordham University, Graduate School of Arts and Sciences, Department of Biological Sciences, New York, NY 10458. Offers MS, PhD. Part-time and evening/weekend programs available. *Faculty:* 18 full-time (2 women). *Students:* 38 full-time (21 women), 21 part-time (10 women); includes 2 Asian, non-Hispanic/Latino; 1 Hispanic/Latino, 17 international. Average age 27. 70 applicants, 59% accepted, 21 enrolled. In 2010, 8 master's, 5 doctorates awarded. Terminal master's awarded for partial completion of doctoral program. *Degree requirements:* For master's, one foreign language, comprehensive exam, thesis optional; for doctorate, one foreign language, comprehensive exam, thesis/dissertation. *Entrance requirements:* For master's and doctorate, GRE General Test, GRE Subject Test (recommended). Additional exam requirements/recommendations for international students: Required—TOEFL (minimum score 550 paper-based; 213 computer-based). *Application deadline:* For fall admission, 1/4 priority date for domestic students; for spring admission, 11/1 for domestic students. Application fee: $70. Electronic applications accepted. *Financial support:* In 2010–11, 28 students received support, including 3 fellowships with full and partial tuition reimbursements available (averaging $30,500 per year), 24 research assistantships with full and partial tuition reimbursements available (averaging $27,020 per year), 1 teaching assistantship with full and partial tuition reimbursement available (averaging $9,600 per year); Federal Work-Study, institutionally sponsored loans, scholarships/grants, tuition waivers (full and partial), and unspecified assistantships also available. Support available to part-time students. Financial award application deadline: 1/4; financial award applicants required to submit FAFSA. *Faculty research:* Avian ecology, behavioral ecology, and conservation biology; plant, community and ecosystem responses to invasive organisms; neurobiology and ion channel disorders; biochemical, physiological and morphological basis of pattern formation; behavioral, physiological and biochemical adaptations of mammals to extreme environments; evolutionary ecology, functional morphology and ichthyology; genotypic response to biogeographic and anthropogenic factors; community-based sustainable resource use. Total annual research expenditures: $2.7 million. *Unit head:* Dr. William Tornhill, Chair, 718-817-3642, Fax: 718-817-3645, E-mail: tornhill@fordham.edu. *Application contact:* Charlene Dundie, Director of Graduate Admissions, 718-817-4420, Fax: 718-817-3566, E-mail: dundie@fordham.edu.

Fort Hays State University, Graduate School, College of Health and Life Sciences, Department of Biological Sciences, Program in Biology, Hays, KS 67601-4099. Offers MS. Part-time programs available. *Degree requirements:* For master's, comprehensive exam, thesis optional. *Entrance requirements:* Additional exam requirements/recommendations for international students: Required—TOEFL (minimum score 550 paper-based; 213 computer-based). Electronic applications accepted.

Frostburg State University, Graduate School, College of Liberal Arts and Sciences, Department of Biology, Frostburg, MD 21532-1099. Offers applied ecology and conservation biology (MS); fisheries and wildlife management (MS). Part-time and evening/weekend programs available. *Degree requirements:* For master's, thesis. *Entrance requirements:* For master's, GRE General Test, resume. Additional exam requirements/recommendations for international students: Required—TOEFL. Electronic applications accepted. *Faculty research:* Molecular and morphological evolution, ecology and behavior of birds, conservation genetics of amphibians and fishes, biology of endangered species.

George Mason University, College of Humanities and Social Sciences, Department of Public and International Affairs, Fairfax, VA 22030. Offers association management (Certificate); biodefense (MS, PhD); emergency management and homeland security (Certificate); nonprofit management (Certificate); political science (MA, PhD); public administration (MPA); public management (Certificate). *Accreditation:* NASPAA (one or more programs are accredited). *Faculty:* 38 full-time (14 women), 31 part-time/adjunct (8 women). *Students:* 134 full-time (76 women), 319 part-time (176 women); includes 63 minority (29 Black or African American, non-Hispanic/Latino; 9 Asian, non-Hispanic/Latino; 21 Hispanic/Latino; 1 Native Hawaiian or other Pacific Islander, non-Hispanic/Latino; 3 Two or more races, non-Hispanic/Latino), 16 international. Average age 31. 574 applicants, 58% accepted, 144 enrolled. In 2010, 140 master's, 3 doctorates, 11 other advanced degrees awarded. *Entrance requirements:* For master's, GRE General Test, minimum GPA of 3.0 in last 60 hours of course work. Additional exam requirements/recommendations for international students: Required—TOEFL (minimum score 570 paper-based; 230 computer-based; 88 iBT). *Application deadline:* For fall admission, 3/1 priority date for domestic students; for spring admission, 10/15 for domestic students. Application fee: $100. Electronic applications accepted. *Expenses:* Tuition, state resident: full-time $8192; part-time $440 per credit hour. Tuition, nonresident: full-time $22,952; part-time $1055 per credit hour. Required fees: $2364; $99 per credit hour. *Financial support:* In 2010–11, 30 students received support, including 3 fellowships with full tuition reimbursements available (averaging $18,000 per year), 10 research assistantships with full and partial tuition reimbursements available (averaging $12,271 per year), 18 teaching assistantships with full and partial tuition reimbursements available (averaging $10,428 per year); career-related internships or fieldwork, Federal Work-Study, scholarships/grants, unspecified assistantships, and health care benefits (full-time research or teaching assistantship recipients) also available. Financial award application deadline: 3/1; financial award applicants required to submit FAFSA. *Faculty research:* The Rehnquist Court and economic liberties; intersection of economic development with high-tech industry, telecommunications, and entrepreneurism; political economy of development; violence, terrorism and U. S. foreign policy; international security issues. Total annual research expenditures: $696,997. *Unit head:* Dr. Priscilla Regan, Chair, 703-993-1419, Fax: 703-993-1399, E-mail: pregan@gmu.edu. *Application contact:* Peg Koback, Information Contact, 703-993-9466, E-mail: mkoback@gmu.edu.

George Mason University, College of Science, Fairfax, VA 22030. Offers advanced biomedical sciences (Certificate); bioinformatics and computational biology (MS, PhD, Certificate); biosciences (PhD); chemistry and biochemistry (MS, PhD), including chemistry (MS), chemistry and biochemistry (PhD); climate dynamics (PhD); computational and data sciences (MS, PhD, Certificate), including computational sciences (MS), computational sciences and informatics (PhD), computational techniques and applications (Certificate); environmental science and policy (MS, PhD, Certificate), including environmental management (Certificate), environmental science and policy (MS), environmental science and public policy (PhD); forensic science (MS); forensics (Certificate); geography and geoinformation science (MS, PhD, Certificate), including earth system science (MS), earth systems and geoinformation sciences (PhD), geographic and cartographic sciences (MS), geographic information sciences (Certificate), geoinformatics and geospatial intelligence (MS), geospatial intelligence (Certificate), remote sensing (Certificate); mathematical sciences (MS, PhD, Certificate), including actuarial sciences (Certificate), mathematics (MS, PhD); molecular and microbiology (MS, PhD), including biology (MS), biosciences (PhD); neuroscience (PhD); physical sciences (PhD); physics and astronomy (MS, PhD), including applied and engineering physics (MS), physics (PhD). Part-time and evening/weekend programs available. *Faculty:* 262 full-time (73 women), 62 part-time/adjunct (23 women). *Students:* 223 full-time (97 women), 716 part-time (305 women); includes 180 minority (36 Black or African American, non-Hispanic/Latino; 2 American Indian or Alaska Native, non-Hispanic/Latino; 90 Asian, non-Hispanic/Latino; 47 Hispanic/Latino; 1 Native Hawaiian or other Pacific Islander, non-Hispanic/Latino; 4 Two or more races, non-Hispanic/Latino), 144 international. Average age 33. 894 applicants, 59% accepted, 315 enrolled. In 2010, 95 master's, 32 doctorates, 27 other advanced degrees awarded. *Degree requirements:* For doctorate, comprehensive exam, thesis/dissertation. *Entrance requirements:* For master's and doctorate, GRE General Test, minimum GPA of 3.0 in last 60 hours. Additional exam requirements/recommendations for international students: Required—TOEFL (minimum score 570 paper-based; 230 computer-based; 88 iBT). *Application deadline:* For fall admission, 3/1 priority date for domestic students, 2/1 for international students; for spring admission, 11/1 priority date for domestic students. Applications are processed on a rolling basis. Application fee: $100. Electronic applications accepted. *Expenses:* Tuition, state resident: full-time $8192; part-time $440 per credit hour. Tuition, nonresident: full-time $22,952; part-time $1055 per credit hour. Required fees: $2364; $99 per credit hour. *Financial support:* In 2010–11, 233 students received support, including 26 fellowships with tuition reimbursements available (averaging $18,000 per year), 104 research assistantships with full tuition reimbursements available (averaging $15,616 per year), 107 teaching assistantships (averaging $12,215 per year); career-related internships or fieldwork, Federal Work-Study, scholarships/grants, and health care benefits (full time research or teaching assistantship recipients) also available. Support available to part-time students. Financial award application deadline: 2/1; financial award applicants required to submit FAFSA. *Faculty research:* Space sciences and astrophysics, fluid dynamics, materials modeling and simulation, bioinformatics, global changes and statistics. *Unit head:* Dr. Vikas E. Chandhoke, Director, 703-993-3622, Fax: 703-993-1993, E-mail: cosinfo@gmu.edu. *Application contact:* Dr. Tim Born, Associate Dean for Graduate Programs, 703-993-4171, Fax: 703-993-9034, E-mail: tborn@gmu.edu.

Georgetown University, Graduate School of Arts and Sciences, Department of Biology, Washington, DC 20057. Offers MS, PhD. Terminal master's awarded for partial completion of doctoral program. *Degree requirements:* For master's, comprehensive exam, thesis; for doctorate, comprehensive exam, thesis/dissertation. *Entrance requirements:* For master's and doctorate, GRE General Test, GRE Subject Test (biology). Additional exam requirements/recommendations for international students: Required—TOEFL (minimum score 550 paper-based; 213 computer-based). Electronic applications accepted. *Faculty research:* Parasitology, ecology, evaluation and behavior, neuroscience and development, cell and molecular biology, immunology.

Georgetown University, Graduate School of Arts and Sciences, Programs in Biomedical Sciences, Washington, DC 20057. Offers MS, PhD, MD/PhD, MS/PhD. *Entrance requirements:* For doctorate, GRE General Test. Additional exam requirements/recommendations for international students: Required—TOEFL.

Georgetown University, National Institutes of Health Sponsored Programs, GU-NIH Graduate Partnership Programs in Biomedical Sciences, Washington, DC 20057. Offers MS, PhD, MD/PhD, MS/PhD. *Entrance requirements:* For doctorate, GRE General Test. Additional exam requirements/recommendations for international students: Required—TOEFL.

The George Washington University, Columbian College of Arts and Sciences, Department of Anthropology, Program in Hominid Paleobiology, Washington, DC 20052. Offers MS, PhD. Part-time and evening/weekend programs available. *Students:* 9 full-time (4 women), 8 part-time (6 women); includes 1 Black or African American, non-Hispanic/Latino; 1 Hispanic/Latino, 3 international. 20 applicants, 20% accepted, 4 enrolled. In 2010, 1 doctorate awarded. Terminal master's awarded for partial completion of doctoral program. *Degree requirements:* For master's, comprehensive exam, thesis; for doctorate, thesis/dissertation, general exam. *Entrance requirements:* For master's, GRE General Test, bachelor's degree in field, minimum GPA of 3.0; for doctorate, GRE General Test, minimum GPA of 3.0. Additional exam requirements/recommendations for international students: Required—TOEFL (minimum score 550 paper-based; 213 computer-based). *Application deadline:* For fall admission, 2/1 priority date for domestic and international students; for spring admission, 10/1 priority date for domestic and international students. Applications are processed on a rolling basis. Application fee: $60. Electronic applications accepted. *Financial support:* In 2010–11, 16 students received support; fellowships with full tuition reimbursements available, teaching assistantships, tuition waivers available. Financial award application deadline: 2/1. *Unit head:* Dr. Bernard A. Wood, Director, 202-994-6077, Fax: 202-994-6097. *Application contact:* Information Contact, 202-994-6075, E-mail: anth@gwu.edu.

The George Washington University, Columbian College of Arts and Sciences, Department of Biological Sciences, Washington, DC 20052. Offers MS, PhD. Part-time and evening/weekend programs available. *Faculty:* 20 full-time (7 women). *Students:* 18 full-time (10 women), 10 part-time (8 women); includes 1 Black or African American, non-Hispanic/Latino, 12 international. Average age 30. 67 applicants, 21% accepted, 8 enrolled. In 2010, 2 master's, 5 doctorates awarded. Terminal master's awarded for partial completion of doctoral program. *Degree requirements:* For master's, comprehensive exam; for doctorate, thesis/dissertation, general exam. *Entrance requirements:* For master's and doctorate, GRE General Test, minimum GPA of 3.0. Additional exam requirements/recommendations for international students: Required—TOEFL (minimum score 550 paper-based; 213 computer-based; 80 iBT). *Application deadline:* For fall admission, 1/2 priority date for domestic and international students; for spring admission, 10/1 priority date for domestic and international students. Applications are processed on a rolling basis. Application fee: $75. Electronic applications accepted. *Financial support:* In 2010–11, 25 students received support; fellowships with full tuition reimbursements available, teaching assistantships with full tuition reimbursements available, Federal Work-Study and tuition waivers available. Financial award application deadline: 1/2. *Faculty research:* Systematics, evolution, ecology, developmental biology, cell/molecular biology. Total annual research expenditures: $900,000. *Unit head:* Dr. James M. Clark, Chair, 202-994-7144, Fax: 202-994-6100, E-mail: jclark@gwu.edu. *Application contact:* Dr. John R. Burns, Professor, 202-994-7149, Fax: 202-994-6100, E-mail: jrburns@gwu.edu.

The George Washington University, Columbian College of Arts and Sciences, Institute for Biomedical Sciences, Washington, DC 20037. Offers biochemistry and molecular genetics (PhD); microbiology and immunology (PhD); molecular medicine (PhD), including molecular and cellular oncology, neurosciences, pharmacology and physiology. Part-time and evening/weekend programs available. *Students:* 16 full-time (8 women), 32 part-time (22 women); includes 2 Black or African American, non-Hispanic/Latino; 1 American Indian or Alaska Native, non-Hispanic/Latino; 3 Asian, non-Hispanic/Latino; 1 Hispanic/Latino, 6 international. Average age 30. 203 applicants, 7% accepted, 13 enrolled. In 2010, 2 doctorates awarded. *Degree requirements:* For doctorate, thesis/dissertation. *Entrance requirements:* For doctorate, GRE General Test, minimum GPA of 3.0. Additional exam requirements/recommendations for international students: Required—TOEFL (minimum score 600 paper-based; 250 computer-based; 80 iBT). *Application deadline:* For fall admission, 12/15 priority date for domestic and international students. Applications are processed on a rolling basis. Application fee: $60. Electronic applications accepted. *Financial support:* In 2010–11, 24 students received support; fellowships with full tuition reimbursements available, Federal Work-Study, institutionally sponsored loans, and tuition waivers available. *Unit head:* Dr. Linda L. Werling, Director, 202-994-2918, Fax: 202-994-0967. *Application contact:* 202-994-2179, Fax: 202-994-0967, E-mail: gwibs@gwu.edu.

Georgia Campus–Philadelphia College of Osteopathic Medicine, Program in Biomedical Sciences, Suwanee, GA 30024. Offers MS, Certificate.

Georgia College & State University, Graduate School, College of Arts and Sciences, Department of Biology, Milledgeville, GA 31061. Offers MS. Part-time programs available. *Students:* 26 full-time (7 women), 7 part-time (4 women); includes 4 minority (1 Black or African American, non-Hispanic/Latino; 1 American Indian or Alaska Native, non-Hispanic/Latino; 1 Asian, non-Hispanic/Latino; 1 Hispanic/Latino), 8 international. Average age 26. 19 applicants, 100% accepted, 13 enrolled. In 2010, 12 master's awarded. *Degree requirements:* For master's, thesis optional. *Entrance requirements:* For master's, GRE (minimum score of 800), 30 hours undergraduate course work in biological science. Additional exam requirements/recommendations for international students: Recommended—TOEFL (minimum score 550 paper-based; 213 computer-based; 79 iBT). *Application deadline:* For fall admission, 7/1 priority date for domestic students, 4/1 for international students; for spring admission, 11/15 priority date for domestic students, 9/1 for international students. Applications are processed on a rolling basis. Application fee: $40. Electronic applications accepted. *Expenses:* Tuition, state resident: full-time $4806; part-time $267 per hour. Tuition, nonresident: full-time $17,802; part-time $989 per hour. Tuition and fees vary according to course load. *Financial support:* In 2010–11, 24 research assistantships with tuition reimbursements were awarded; career-related internships or fieldwork and unspecified assistantships also available. Support available to part-time students. Financial award application deadline: 3/1; financial award applicants required to submit FAFSA. *Faculty research:* Vertebrate collecting and monitoring, paleontologic expedition. *Unit head:* Dr. William Wall, Chair, 478-445-0818, E-mail: bill.wall@gcsu.edu. *Application contact:* Dr. Bill Wolfe, Graduate Coordinator, 478-445-3464, E-mail: bill.wolfe@gcsu.edu.

Georgia Health Sciences University, College of Graduate Studies, Augusta, GA 30912. Offers MCTS, MPH, MS, MSN, DNP, PhD, CCTS, Post-Master's Certificate. Part-time programs available. Postbaccalaureate distance learning degree programs offered (no on-campus study). *Faculty:* 225 full-time (74 women), 7 part-time/adjunct (4 women). *Students:* 471 full-time (355 women), 122 part-time (101 women); includes 60 Black or African American, non-Hispanic/Latino; 2 American Indian or Alaska Native, non-Hispanic/Latino; 33 Asian, non-Hispanic/Latino; 15 Hispanic/Latino; 12 Two or more races, non-Hispanic/Latino, 81 international. Average age 31. 451 applicants, 44% accepted, 125 enrolled. In 2010, 104 master's, 33 doctorates awarded. *Degree requirements:* For doctorate, thesis/dissertation. *Entrance requirements:* For master's and doctorate, GRE General Test. Additional exam requirements/recommendations for international students: Required—TOEFL. Application fee: $30. Electronic applications accepted. *Expenses:* Tuition, state resident: full-time $7500; part-time $313 per semester hour. Tuition, nonresident: full-time $24,772; part-time $1033 per semester hour. Required fees: $1112. *Financial support:* In 2010–11, 10 fellowships with partial tuition reimbursements (averaging $26,000 per year), 111 research assistantships with partial tuition reimburse-

ments (averaging $23,000 per year) were awarded; teaching assistantships, career-related internships or fieldwork, Federal Work-Study, institutionally sponsored loans, scholarships/grants, traineeships, and unspecified assistantships also available. Support available to part-time students. Financial award application deadline: 5/31; financial award applicants required to submit FAFSA. *Faculty research:* Cancer, cardiovascular biology, neurosciences, inflammation/infection, diabetes. Total annual research expenditures: $315,059. *Unit head:* Dr. Gretchen B. Caughman, Dean, 706-721-3278, Fax: 706-721-6829, E-mail: gcaughma@mail.mcg.edu. *Application contact:* Heather Metress, Interim Director of Admissions, 706-721-2725, Fax: 706-721-7279, E-mail: hmetress@georgiahealth.edu.

Georgia Institute of Technology, Graduate Studies and Research, College of Sciences, School of Biology, Atlanta, GA 30332-0001. Offers applied biology (MS, PhD); bioinformatics (MS, PhD); biology (MS). Part-time programs available. Terminal master's awarded for partial completion of doctoral program. *Degree requirements:* For master's, thesis; for doctorate, thesis/dissertation, qualifying exam. *Entrance requirements:* For master's, GRE General Test, minimum GPA of 2.9; for doctorate, GRE General Test, minimum GPA of 3.0. Additional exam requirements/recommendations for international students: Required—TOEFL. Electronic applications accepted. *Faculty research:* Microbiology, molecular and cell biology, ecology.

Georgian Court University, School of Arts and Sciences, Lakewood, NJ 08701-2697. Offers biology (MA); Catholic school leadership (Certificate); clinical mental health counseling (MA); holistic health studies (MA); mathematics (MA); pastoral ministry (Certificate); religious education (Certificate); school psychology (Certificate); theology (MA, Certificate). Part-time and evening/weekend programs available. *Faculty:* 19 full-time (11 women), 7 part-time/adjunct (5 women). *Students:* 61 full-time (59 women), 143 part-time (113 women); includes 20 minority (5 Black or African American, non-Hispanic/Latino; 3 Asian, non-Hispanic/Latino; 11 Hispanic/Latino; 1 Two or more races, non-Hispanic/Latino), 1 international. Average age 39. 139 applicants, 59% accepted, 50 enrolled. In 2010, 5 master's awarded. *Degree requirements:* For master's, comprehensive exam (for some programs), thesis (for some programs). *Entrance requirements:* For master's, GRE, MAT, or NTE/PRAXIS, 3 letters of recommendation. Additional exam requirements/recommendations for international students: Required—TOEFL (minimum score 550 paper-based; 213 computer-based). *Application deadline:* For fall admission, 8/1 priority date for domestic students, 4/1 for international students; for spring admission, 1/1 priority date for domestic students, 7/1 for international students. Applications are processed on a rolling basis. Application fee: $40. Electronic applications accepted. *Expenses:* Tuition: Full-time $12,510; part-time $695 per credit. Required fees: $416 per year. Tuition and fees vary according to campus/location and program. *Financial support:* Scholarships/grants, health care benefits, and unspecified assistantships available. Financial award application deadline: 4/15; financial award applicants required to submit FAFSA. *Unit head:* Dr. Linda James, Dean, 732-987-2617, Fax: 732-987-2007. *Application contact:* Patrick Givens, Assistant Director of Admissions, 732-987-2736, Fax: 732-987-2084, E-mail: graduateadmissions@georgian.edu.

Georgia Southern University, Jack N. Averitt College of Graduate Studies, Allen E. Paulson College of Science and Technology, Department of Biology, Statesboro, GA 30460. Offers MS. Part-time programs available. *Students:* 41 full-time (15 women), 6 part-time (5 women); includes 1 Black or African American, non-Hispanic/Latino; 1 American Indian or Alaska Native, non-Hispanic/Latino; 3 Asian, non-Hispanic/Latino, 3 international. Average age 25. 28 applicants, 71% accepted, 16 enrolled. In 2010, 10 master's awarded. *Degree requirements:* For master's, comprehensive exam, thesis optional, terminal exam. *Entrance requirements:* For master's, GRE General Test, GRE Subject Test, minimum GPA of 2.8, BS in biology, 2 letters of reference. Additional exam requirements/recommendations for international students: Required—TOEFL (minimum score 550 paper-based; 216 computer-based; 80 iBT). *Application deadline:* For fall admission, 3/1 priority date for domestic and international students; for spring admission, 10/1 priority date for domestic students, 10/1 for international students. Applications are processed on a rolling basis. Application fee: $50. Electronic applications accepted. *Expenses:* Tuition, state resident: full-time $6000; part-time $250 per semester hour. Tuition, nonresident: full-time $23,976; part-time $999 per semester hour. Required fees: $1644. *Financial support:* In 2010–11, 42 students received support, including research assistantships with partial tuition reimbursements available (averaging $10,000 per year), teaching assistantships with partial tuition reimbursements available (averaging $10,000 per year); career-related internships or fieldwork, Federal Work-Study, scholarships/grants, tuition waivers (partial), and unspecified assistantships also available. Support available to part-time students. Financial award application deadline: 4/15; financial award applicants required to submit FAFSA. *Faculty research:* Behavior, evolutionary and ecology, molecular biology, physiology, vector-borne diseases. Total annual research expenditures: $1.5 million. *Unit head:* Dr. Stephen Vives, Chair, 912-478-5487, Fax: 912-478-0845, E-mail: svives@georgiasouthern.edu. *Application contact:* Dr. Charles Ziglar, Coordinator for Graduate Student Recruitment, 912-478-5635, Fax: 912-478-0740, E-mail: gradadmissions@georgiasouthern.edu.

Georgia State University, College of Arts and Sciences, Department of Biology, Atlanta, GA 30302-3083. Offers applied and environmental microbiology (MS, PhD); cellular and molecular biology and physiology (MS, PhD); molecular genetics and biochemistry (MS, PhD); neurobiology and behavior (MS, PhD). Part-time programs available. Terminal master's awarded for partial completion of doctoral program. *Degree requirements:* For master's, thesis or alternative; for doctorate, thesis/dissertation, exam. *Entrance requirements:* For master's and doctorate, GRE General Test. Additional exam requirements/recommendations for international students: Required—TOEFL. Electronic applications accepted. *Faculty research:* Physiological biochemistry, gene expression, molecular virology, microbial ecology, integration in neural systems.

Georgia State University, College of Arts and Sciences, MD/PhD Program, Atlanta, GA 30302-3083. Offers MD/PhD.

Gerstner Sloan-Kettering Graduate School of Biomedical Sciences, Program in Cancer Biology, New York, NY 10021. Offers PhD. *Faculty:* 116 full-time (19 women). *Students:* 52 full-time (28 women); includes 6 minority (1 Black or African American, non-Hispanic/Latino; 4 Asian, non-Hispanic/Latino; 1 Hispanic/Latino), 4 international. *Entrance requirements:* For doctorate, GRE, transcripts, letters of recommendation. Electronic applications accepted. *Financial support:* Fellowship package including stipend ($32,637), full-tuition scholarship, first-year allowance, and comprehensive medical and dental insurance available. *Faculty research:* Biochemistry and molecular biology, biophysics/structural biology, computational biology, genetics, immunology. *Unit head:* Dr. Kenneth Marians, Dean, 212-639-5890, E-mail: kmarians@sloankettering.edu. *Application contact:* Main Office, 646-888-6639, Fax: 646-422-2351, E-mail: gradstudies@sloankettering.edu.

See Display on page 178 and Close-Up on page 225.

Goucher College, Program in Post-Baccalaureate Premedical Studies, Baltimore, MD 21204-2794. Offers Certificate. *Faculty:* 10 full-time (3 women). *Students:* 32 full-time (16 women); includes 1 Black or African American, non-Hispanic/Latino; 3 Asian, non-Hispanic/Latino; 1 Hispanic/Latino. Average age 24. In 2010, 32 Certificates awarded. *Entrance requirements:* For degree, GRE, SAT or ACT. *Application deadline:* Applications are processed on a rolling basis. Application fee: $50. *Expenses:* Contact institution. *Financial support:* In 2010–11, 5 fellowships (averaging $4,000 per year) were awarded; institutionally sponsored loans and scholarships/grants also available. Financial award application deadline: 3/1; financial award applicants required to submit FAFSA. *Unit head:* Betsy Merideth, Director, 800-414-3437, Fax: 410-337-6461, E-mail: bmerideth@goucher.edu. *Application contact:* Theresa Reifsnider, Associate Dean for Graduate and Professional Studies, 410-337-3437, Fax: 410-337-6461, E-mail: pbpm@goucher.edu.

Graduate School and University Center of the City University of New York, Graduate Studies, Program in Biology, New York, NY 10016-4039. Offers PhD. *Degree requirements:* For doctorate, thesis/dissertation, teaching experience. *Entrance requirements:* For doctorate, GRE General Test. Additional exam requirements/recommendations for international students: Required—TOEFL. Electronic applications accepted.

Biological and Biomedical Sciences—General

Grand Valley State University, College of Liberal Arts and Sciences, Biology Department, Allendale, MI 49401-9403. Offers MS. Part-time programs available. *Degree requirements:* For master's, comprehensive exam, thesis or alternative. *Entrance requirements:* For master's, GRE General Test, 3 letters of reference. Additional exam requirements/recommendations for international students: Required—TOEFL. Electronic applications accepted. *Faculty research:* Natural resources conservation biology, aquatic sciences, terrestrial ecology, behavioral biology.

Grand Valley State University, College of Liberal Arts and Sciences, Department of Biomedical Sciences, Allendale, MI 49401-9403. Offers MHS. Part-time programs available. *Degree requirements:* For master's, thesis, qualifying exam. *Entrance requirements:* For master's, GRE General Test, minimum GPA of 3.0, 3 names of references. Additional exam requirements/recommendations for international students: Required—TOEFL. Electronic applications accepted. *Faculty research:* Cell regulation, neurobiology, parasitology, virology, microbial pathogenicity.

Hampton University, Graduate College, Department of Biological Sciences, Hampton, VA 23668. Offers biology (MS); environmental science (MS); medical science (MS). Part-time and evening/weekend programs available. *Degree requirements:* For master's, thesis optional. *Entrance requirements:* For master's, GRE General Test. *Faculty research:* Marine ecology, microbial and chemical pollution, pesticide problems.

Harvard University, Extension School, Cambridge, MA 02138-3722. Offers applied sciences (CAS); biotechnology (ALM); educational technologies (ALM); educational technology (CET); English for graduate and professional studies (DGP); environmental management (ALM, CEM); information technology (ALM); journalism (ALM); liberal arts (ALM); management (ALM, CM); mathematics for teaching (ALM); museum studies (ALM); premedical studies (Diploma); publication and communication (CPC). Part-time and evening/weekend programs available. *Degree requirements:* For master's, thesis. *Entrance requirements:* For master's, 3 completed graduate courses with grade of B or higher. Additional exam requirements/recommendations for international students: Required—TOEFL (minimum score 600 paper-based; 250 computer-based), TWE (minimum score 5). *Expenses:* Contact institution.

Harvard University, Graduate School of Arts and Sciences, Department of Organismic and Evolutionary Biology, Cambridge, MA 02138. Offers biology (PhD). *Degree requirements:* For doctorate, 2 foreign languages, public presentation of thesis research, exam. *Entrance requirements:* For doctorate, GRE General Test, GRE Subject Test (recommended), 7 courses in biology, chemistry, physics, mathematics, computer science, or geology. Additional exam requirements/recommendations for international students: Required—TOEFL. *Expenses:* Tuition: Full-time $34,976. Required fees: $1166. Full-time tuition and fees vary according to program.

Harvard University, Graduate School of Arts and Sciences, Division of Medical Sciences, Boston, MA 02115. Offers biological chemistry and molecular pharmacology (PhD); cell biology (PhD); genetics (PhD); microbiology and molecular genetics (PhD); pathology (PhD), including experimental pathology. *Degree requirements:* For doctorate, thesis/dissertation. *Entrance requirements:* For doctorate, GRE General Test, GRE Subject Test. Additional exam requirements/recommendations for international students: Required—TOEFL. *Expenses:* Tuition: Full-time $34,976. Required fees: $1166. Full-time tuition and fees vary according to program.

Harvard University, Harvard Medical School and Graduate School of Arts and Sciences, Division of Health Sciences and Technology, Biomedical Enterprise Program, Cambridge, MA 02138. Offers SM. *Students:* 28 full-time (15 women); includes 1 American Indian or Alaska Native, non-Hispanic/Latino; 6 Asian, non-Hispanic/Latino; 1 Hispanic/Latino; 5 international. Average age 30. 43 applicants, 33% accepted, 13 enrolled. In 2010, 8 master's awarded. *Degree requirements:* For master's, thesis. *Entrance requirements:* For master's, GMAT or GRE, bachelor's degree in engineering or sciences, work experience in biomedical business. Additional exam requirements/recommendations for international students: Required—TOEFL. *Application deadline:* For fall admission, 12/15 for domestic and international students. Electronic applications accepted. *Expenses:* Contact institution. *Financial support:* In 2010–11, 8 students received support, including 1 fellowship (averaging $5,000 per year), 2 research assistantships with full and partial tuition reimbursements available (averaging $34,773 per year), 6 teaching assistantships with partial tuition reimbursements available (averaging $8,637 per year); institutionally sponsored loans, health care benefits, and unspecified assistantships also available. Financial award application deadline: 12/15; financial award applicants required to submit FAFSA. *Faculty research:* Entrepreneurship, technology strategy management, organizational strategies and models, epidemiology and biostatistics, biomedical research from the molecular to the whole-organism level. *Unit head:* Dr. Richard Cohen, Co-Director, 617-253-7430. *Application contact:* Traci Anderson, Academic Programs Administrator, 617-253-7470, Fax: 617-253-6692, E-mail: tanderso@mit.edu.

Harvard University, Harvard School of Public Health, PhD Program in Biological Sciences in Public Health, Boston, MA 02115. Offers PhD. *Students:* 46 full-time, 1 part-time; includes 10 minority (3 Black or African American, non-Hispanic/Latino; 5 Asian, non-Hispanic/Latino; 1 Hispanic/Latino; 1 Two or more races, non-Hispanic/Latino), 16 international. 101 applicants, 12% accepted, 9 enrolled. In 2010, 4 doctorates awarded. *Degree requirements:* For doctorate, qualifying examination, dissertation/defense. *Entrance requirements:* For doctorate, GRE General Test. Additional exam requirements/recommendations for international students: Required—TOEFL. *Application deadline:* For fall admission, 12/8 for domestic students. *Expenses:* Tuition: Full-time $34,976. Required fees: $1166. Full-time tuition and fees vary according to program. *Financial support:* Fellowships, research assistantships, teaching assistantships, institutionally sponsored loans and tuition waivers (full) available. Financial award application deadline: 1/1. *Faculty research:* Nutrition biochemistry, molecular and cellular toxicology, cardiovascular disease, cancer biology, immunology and infectious diseases, environmental health physiology. *Unit head:* Carole Knapp, Administrator, 617-432-2932. *Application contact:* Leah W. Simons, Student Contact, 617-495-1000.

Heritage University, Graduate Programs in Education, Program in Professional Studies, Toppenish, WA 98948-9599. Offers bilingual education/ESL (M Ed); biology (M Ed); English and literature (M Ed); reading/literacy (M Ed); special education (M Ed). Part-time and evening/weekend programs available. *Degree requirements:* For master's, comprehensive exam (for some programs), thesis (for some programs).

Hofstra University, College of Liberal Arts and Sciences, Department of Biology, Hempstead, NY 11549. Offers MA, MS. Part-time and evening/weekend programs available. *Faculty:* 14 full-time (7 women), 2 part-time/adjunct (1 woman). *Students:* 61 full-time (40 women), 15 part-time (11 women); includes 14 minority (5 Black or African American, non-Hispanic/Latino; 6 Asian, non-Hispanic/Latino; 3 Hispanic/Latino). Average age 25. 70 applicants, 87% accepted, 40 enrolled. In 2010, 5 master's awarded. *Degree requirements:* For master's, thesis. *Entrance requirements:* For master's, GRE, bachelor's degree in biology or equivalent; 2 letters of recommendation; essay. Additional exam requirements/recommendations for international students: Required—TOEFL (minimum score 550 paper-based; 213 computer-based; 80 iBT). *Application deadline:* Applications are processed on a rolling basis. Application fee: $70 ($75 for international students). Electronic applications accepted. *Expenses:* Tuition: Full-time $18,000; part-time $1000 per credit hour. Required fees: $970; $145 per term. Tuition and fees vary according to program. *Financial support:* In 2010–11, 19 students received support, including 8 fellowships with full and partial tuition reimbursements available (averaging $5,654 per year); research assistantships with full and partial tuition reimbursements available, Federal Work-Study, institutionally sponsored loans, scholarships/grants, and tuition waivers (full and partial) also available. Support available to part-time students. Financial award applicants required to submit FAFSA. *Faculty research:* Molecular basis of sex determination in turtles; urban ecology of invasive plant species; molecular regulation of morphological differentiation in Streptomyces; population, ecology, evolution, and behavior of mammals, reptiles, and amphibians; systematics and biology of marine polychaete worms and crustaceans. Total annual research expenditures: $180,000. *Unit head:* Dr. Maureen K. Krause, Program Director, 516-463-6178, Fax: 516-463-5112, E-mail: biomkk@hofstra.edu. *Application contact:* Carol Drummer, Dean of Graduate Admissions, 516-463-4876, Fax: 516-463-4664, E-mail: gradstudent@hofstra.edu.

Hofstra University, School of Education, Health, and Human Services, Programs in Teaching—Secondary Education, Hempstead, NY 11549. Offers business education (MS Ed); English education (MA, MS Ed); foreign language and TESOL (MS Ed); foreign language education (MA, MS Ed), including French, German, Russian, Spanish; mathematics education (MA, MS Ed); science education (MA, MS Ed), including biology, chemistry, earth science, geology, physics; secondary education (Advanced Certificate), social studies education (MA, MS Ed). Part-time and evening/weekend programs available. Postbaccalaureate distance learning degree programs offered (minimal on-campus study). *Students:* 114 full-time (74 women), 61 part-time (36 women); includes 7 Black or African American, non-Hispanic/Latino; 1 American Indian or Alaska Native, non-Hispanic/Latino; 8 Asian, non-Hispanic/Latino; 10 Hispanic/Latino; 1 Native Hawaiian or other Pacific Islander, non-Hispanic/Latino. Average age 27. 153 applicants, 90% accepted, 59 enrolled. In 2010, 102 master's, 11 other advanced degrees awarded. *Degree requirements:* For master's, one foreign language, comprehensive exam (for some programs), thesis (for some programs), exit project, electronic portfolio, student teaching, fieldwork, curriculum project; for Advanced Certificate, 3 foreign languages, comprehensive exam (for some programs), thesis project. *Entrance requirements:* For master's, 2 letters of recommendation, teacher certification (MA), essay; for Advanced Certificate, 2 letters of recommendation, essay, interview and/or portfolio. Additional exam requirements/recommendations for international students: Required—TOEFL (minimum score 550 paper-based; 213 computer-based; 80 iBT). *Application deadline:* Applications are processed on a rolling basis. Application fee: $70 ($75 for international students). Electronic applications accepted. *Expenses:* Tuition: Full-time $18,000; part-time $1000 per credit hour. Required fees: $970; $145 per term. Tuition and fees vary according to program. *Financial support:* In 2010–11, 108 students received support, including 14 fellowships with full and partial tuition reimbursements available (averaging $3,943 per year), 1 research assistantship with full and partial tuition reimbursement available (averaging $6,574 per year); career-related internships or fieldwork, Federal Work-Study, institutionally sponsored loans, scholarships/grants, tuition waivers (full and partial), unspecified assistantships, and scholarships also available. Support available to part-time students. Financial award applicants required to submit FAFSA. *Faculty research:* Appropriate content and pedagogy in secondary school disciplines, adolescent development, secondary school organization, alternative secondary school programs. *Unit head:* Dr. Esther Fusco, Chairperson, 516-463-7704, Fax: 516-463-6196, E-mail: catezf@hofstra.edu. *Application contact:* Carol Drummer, Dean of Graduate Admissions, 516-463-4876, Fax: 516-463-4664, E-mail: gradstudent@hofstra.edu.

Hood College, Graduate School, Program in Biomedical Science, Frederick, MD 21701-8575. Offers biomedical science (MS), including biotechnology/molecular biology, microbiology/immunology/virology, regulatory compliance; regulatory compliance (Certificate). Part-time and evening/weekend programs available. *Faculty:* 3 full-time (1 woman), 7 part-time/adjunct (4 women). *Students:* 9 full-time (2 women), 87 part-time (55 women); includes 16 Black or African American, non-Hispanic/Latino; 9 Asian, non-Hispanic/Latino; 3 Hispanic/Latino; 1 Two or more races, non-Hispanic/Latino, 7 international. Average age 29. 61 applicants, 64% accepted, 21 enrolled. In 2010, 9 master's, 3 other advanced degrees awarded. *Degree requirements:* For master's, comprehensive exam, thesis or alternative. *Entrance requirements:* For master's, bachelor's degree in biology; minimum GPA of 2.75; undergraduate course work in cell biology, chemistry, organic chemistry, and genetics. Additional exam requirements/recommendations for international students: Required—TOEFL (minimum score 575 paper-based; 231 computer-based; 89 iBT). *Application deadline:* For fall admission, 7/15 for domestic and international students; for spring admission, 12/15 for domestic and international students. Applications are processed on a rolling basis. Application fee: $35. Electronic applications accepted. *Expenses:* Tuition: Full-time $6480; part-time $360 per credit. Required fees: $100; $50 per term. *Financial support:* In 2010–11, 3 research assistantships with full tuition reimbursements (averaging $10,609 per year) were awarded. Financial award applicants required to submit FAFSA. *Unit head:* Dr. Oney Smith, Director, 301-696-3653, Fax: 301-696-3597, E-mail: osmith@hood.edu. *Application contact:* Dr. Allen P. Flora, Dean of Graduate School, 301-696-3811, Fax: 301-696-3597, E-mail: gofurther@hood.edu.

Howard University, Graduate School, Department of Biology, Washington, DC 20059-0002. Offers MS, PhD. Part-time programs available. *Degree requirements:* For master's, thesis, qualifying exams; for doctorate, thesis/dissertation, qualifying exams. *Entrance requirements:* For master's and doctorate, GRE General Test, minimum GPA of 3.0. Additional exam requirements/recommendations for international students: Required—TOEFL. Electronic applications accepted. *Faculty research:* Physiology, molecular biology, cell biology, microbiology, environmental biology.

Humboldt State University, Academic Programs, College of Natural Resources and Sciences, Department of Biological Sciences, Arcata, CA 95521-8299. Offers MA. *Students:* 27 full-time (13 women), 31 part-time (18 women); includes 7 minority (1 American Indian or Alaska Native, non-Hispanic/Latino; 2 Asian, non-Hispanic/Latino; 4 Hispanic/Latino), 1 international. Average age 32. 26 applicants, 77% accepted, 10 enrolled. In 2010, 9 master's awarded. *Degree requirements:* For master's, project or thesis. *Entrance requirements:* For master's, GRE General Test, appropriate bachelor's degree, minimum GPA of 2.5, 3 letters of recommendation. Additional exam requirements/recommendations for international students: Required—TOEFL (minimum score 500 paper-based; 173 computer-based). *Application deadline:* For fall admission, 2/15 for domestic and international students. Applications are processed on a rolling basis. Application fee: $55. Tuition and fees vary according to program. *Financial support:* Application deadline: 3/1. *Faculty research:* Plant ecology, DNA sequencing, invertebrates. *Unit head:* Dr. John Reiss, Chair, 707-826-3245, Fax: 707-826-3201, E-mail: jor1@humboldt.edu. *Application contact:* Dr. Michael Mesler, Coordinator, 707-826-3674, Fax: 707-826-3201, E-mail: mm1@humboldt.edu.

Hunter College of the City University of New York, Graduate School, School of Arts and Sciences, Department of Biological Sciences, New York, NY 10021-5085. Offers MA, PhD. PhD offered jointly with Graduate School and University Center of the City University of New York. Part-time programs available. *Faculty:* 12 full-time (3 women). *Students:* 8 full-time (6 women), 26 part-time (17 women); includes 4 Black or African American, non-Hispanic/Latino; 2 Asian, non-Hispanic/Latino; 8 Hispanic/Latino, 5 international. Average age 26. 41 applicants, 56% accepted, 12 enrolled. In 2010, 10 master's awarded. Terminal master's awarded for partial completion of doctoral program. *Degree requirements:* For master's, one foreign language, comprehensive exam or thesis. *Entrance requirements:* For master's, GRE, 1 year of course work in organic chemistry (including laboratory), college physics, calculus; undergraduate major in biology, botany, physiology, zoology, chemistry or physics. Additional exam requirements/recommendations for international students: Required—TOEFL. *Application deadline:* For fall admission, 4/1 for domestic students, 2/1 for international students; for spring admission, 11/1 for domestic students, 9/1 for international students. Application fee: $125. *Financial support:* Fellowships, research assistantships, teaching assistantships, scholarships/grants and tuition waivers (partial) available. Support available to part-time students. *Faculty research:* Analysis of prokaryotic and eukaryotic DNA, protein structure, mammalian DNA replication, oncogene expression, neuroscience. *Unit head:* Dr. Shirley Raps, Chairperson, 212-772-5293, E-mail: raps@genectr.hunter.cuny.edu. *Application contact:* William Zlata, Director for Graduate Admissions, 212-772-4482, Fax: 212-650-3336, E-mail: admissions@hunter.cuny.edu.

ICR Graduate School, Graduate Programs, Santee, CA 92071. Offers astro/geophysics (MS); biology (MS); geology (MS); science education (MS). Part-time programs available. *Degree requirements:* For master's, comprehensive exam (for some programs), thesis (for some programs). *Entrance requirements:* For master's, minimum undergraduate GPA of 3.0, bachelor's degree in science or science education. *Faculty research:* Age of the earth, limits of variation, catastrophe, optimum methods for teaching.

Idaho State University, Office of Graduate Studies, College of Arts and Sciences, Department of Biological Sciences, Pocatello, ID 83209-8007. Offers biology (MNS, MS, DA, PhD); clinical laboratory science (MS); microbiology (MS). Accreditation: NAACLS. Part-time programs available. *Degree requirements:* For master's, comprehensive exam, thesis; for doctorate, comprehensive exam, thesis/dissertation, 9 credits of internship (for DA). *Entrance requirements:* For master's, GRE General Test, minimum GPA of 3.0 in all upper division classes; for doctorate, GRE General Test, GRE Subject Test (biology), diagnostic exam (DA), minimum GPA of 3.0 in all upper division classes. Additional exam requirements/recommendations for international students: Required—TOEFL (minimum score 550 paper-based; 213 computer-based; 80 iBT). Electronic applications accepted. *Faculty research:* Ecology, plant and animal physiology, plant and animal developmental biology, immunology, molecular biology, bioinfomatics.

Illinois Institute of Technology, Graduate College, College of Science and Letters, Department of Biological, Chemical and Physical Sciences, Biology Division, Chicago, IL 60616. Offers biochemistry (MBS, MS); biology (PhD); biotechnology (MBS, MS); cell and molecular biology (MBS, MS); microbiology (MB, MS); molecular biochemistry and biophysics (PhD); molecular biology and biophysics (MS). Part-time and evening/weekend programs available. Post-baccalaureate distance learning degree programs offered (minimal on-campus study). *Faculty:* 13 full-time (5 women), 5 part-time/adjunct (2 women). *Students:* 121 full-time (75 women), 56 part-time (37 women); includes 16 minority (5 Black or African American, non-Hispanic/Latino; 5 Asian, non-Hispanic/Latino; 5 Hispanic/Latino; 1 Two or more races, non-Hispanic/Latino), 104 international. Average age 27. 268 applicants, 76% accepted, 62 enrolled. In 2010, 74 master's, 4 doctorates awarded. Terminal master's awarded for partial completion of doctoral program. *Degree requirements:* For master's, comprehensive exam, thesis (for some programs); for doctorate, comprehensive exam, thesis/dissertation. *Entrance requirements:* For master's, GRE General Test (minimum score 1000 Quantitative and Verbal, 2.5 Analytical Writing), minimum undergraduate GPA of 3.0; for doctorate, GRE General Test (minimum score 1200 Quantitative and Verbal, 3.0 Analytical Writing), minimum undergraduate GPA of 3.0. Additional exam requirements/recommendations for international students: Required—TOEFL (minimum score 523 paper-based; 213 computer-based; 70 iBT); Recommended—IELTS (minimum score 5.5). *Application deadline:* For fall admission, 5/1 for domestic and international students; for spring admission, 10/15 for domestic and international students. Applications are processed on a rolling basis. Application fee: $40. Electronic applications accepted. *Expenses:* Tuition: Full-time $18,576; part-time $1032 per credit hour. Required fees: $583 per semester. One-time fee: $150. Tuition and fees vary according to program and student level. *Financial support:* In 2010–11, 15 research assistantships with full and partial tuition reimbursements (averaging $6,379 per year), 14 teaching assistantships with partial tuition reimbursements (averaging $6,296 per year) were awarded; fellowships with full and partial tuition reimbursements, career-related internships or fieldwork, Federal Work-Study, institutionally sponsored loans, scholarships/grants, traineeships, health care benefits, tuition waivers (partial), and unspecified assistantships also available. Support available to part-time students. Financial award applicants required to submit FAFSA. *Faculty research:* Structure and biophysics of macromolecular systems; efficacy and mechanism of action of chemopreventive agents in experimental carcinogenesis of breast, colon, lung and prostate; study of fundamental structural biochemistry problems that have direct links to the understanding and treatment of disease; spectroscopic techniques for the study of multi-domain proteins; molecular mechanisms of cancer and cancer gene therapy. Total annual research expenditures: $2.6 million. *Unit head:* Dr. Benjamin C. Stark, Professor and Associate Chair, 312-567-3488, Fax: 312-567-3494, E-mail: starkb@iit.edu. *Application contact:* Deborah Gibson, Director, Graduate Admissions, 866-472-3448, Fax: 312-567-3138, E-mail: inquiry.grad@iit.edu.

Illinois State University, Graduate School, College of Arts and Sciences, Department of Biological Sciences, Normal, IL 61790-2200. Offers animal behavior (MS); bacteriology (MS); biochemistry (MS); biological sciences (MS); biology (PhD); biophysics (MS); biotechnology (MS); botany (MS, PhD); cell biology (MS); conservation biology (MS); developmental biology (MS); ecology (MS, PhD); entomology (MS); evolutionary biology (MS); genetics (MS, PhD); immunology (MS); microbiology (MS, PhD); molecular biology (MS); molecular genetics (MS); neurobiology (MS); neuroscience (MS); parasitology (MS); physiology (MS, PhD); plant biology (MS); plant molecular biology (MS); plant sciences (MS); structural biology (MS); zoology (MS, PhD). Part-time programs available. *Degree requirements:* For master's, thesis or alternative; for doctorate, variable foreign language requirement, thesis/dissertation, 2 terms of residency. *Entrance requirements:* For master's, GRE General Test, minimum GPA of 2.6 in last 60 hours of course work; for doctorate, GRE General Test. *Faculty research:* Redoc balance and drug development in schistosoma mansoni, control of the growth of listeria monocytogenes at low temperature, regulation of cell expansion and microtubule function by SPRI, CRUI: physiology and fitness consequences of different life history phenotypes.

Indiana State University, College of Graduate and Professional Studies, College of Arts and Sciences, Department of Biology, Terre Haute, IN 47809. Offers ecology (PhD); life sciences (MS); microbiology (PhD); physiology (PhD); science education (MS). *Degree requirements:* For master's, thesis (for some programs); for doctorate, comprehensive exam, thesis/dissertation. *Entrance requirements:* For master's and doctorate, GRE General Test. Electronic applications accepted.

Indiana University Bloomington, University Graduate School, College of Arts and Sciences, Department of Biology, Bloomington, IN 47405. Offers biology teaching (MAT); biotechnology (MA); evolution, ecology, and behavior (MA, PhD); genetics (PhD); microbiology (MA, PhD); molecular, cellular, and developmental biology (PhD); plant sciences (MA, PhD); zoology (MA, PhD). *Faculty:* 58 full-time (15 women), 21 part-time/adjunct (6 women). *Students:* 163 full-time (98 women), 7 part-time (2 women); includes 17 minority (3 Black or African American, non-Hispanic/Latino; 1 American Indian or Alaska Native, non-Hispanic/Latino; 7 Asian, non-Hispanic/Latino; 5 Hispanic/Latino; 1 Native Hawaiian or other Pacific Islander, non-Hispanic/Latino), 52 international. Average age 27. 346 applicants, 15% accepted, 24 enrolled. In 2010, 17 master's, 24 doctorates awarded. Terminal master's awarded for partial completion of doctoral program. *Degree requirements:* For master's, thesis, oral defense; for doctorate, thesis/dissertation, oral defense. *Entrance requirements:* For master's and doctorate, GRE General Test. Additional exam requirements/recommendations for international students: Required—TOEFL (minimum score 100 iBT). *Application deadline:* For fall admission, 1/5 priority date for domestic students, 12/1 priority date for international students. Application fee: $55 ($65 for international students). Electronic applications accepted. *Financial support:* In 2010–11, 170 students received support, including 64 fellowships with tuition reimbursements available (averaging $19,484 per year), 44 research assistantships with tuition reimbursements available (averaging $20,300 per year), 62 teaching assistantships with tuition reimbursements available (averaging $20,521 per year); scholarships/grants, traineeships, health care benefits, and unspecified assistantships also available. Financial award application deadline: 1/5. *Faculty research:* Evolution, ecology and behavior; microbiology; molecular biology and genetics; plant biology. *Unit head:* Dr. Roger Innes, Chair, 812-855-2219, Fax: 812-855-6082, E-mail: rinnes@indiana.edu. *Application contact:* Tracey D. Stohr, Graduate Student Recruitment Coordinator, 812-856-6303, Fax: 812-855-6082, E-mail: gradbio@indiana.edu.

Indiana University of Pennsylvania, School of Graduate Studies and Research, College of Natural Sciences and Mathematics, Department of Biology, Program in Biology, Indiana, PA 15705-1087. Offers MS. *Faculty:* 12 full-time (2 women). *Students:* 22 full-time (16 women), 3 part-time (all women), 2 international. Average age 27. 47 applicants, 32% accepted, 9 enrolled. In 2010, 11 master's awarded. *Degree requirements:* For master's, comprehensive exam, thesis optional. *Entrance requirements:* For master's, 2 letters of recommendation. Additional exam requirements/recommendations for international students: Required—TOEFL. *Application deadline:* For fall admission, 7/1 priority date for domestic students; for spring admission, 11/1 for domestic students. Applications are processed on a rolling basis. Application fee: $40. *Financial support:* In 2010–11, 7 research assistantships with full and partial tuition reimbursements (averaging $5,906 per year) were awarded; fellowships also available. Financial award application deadline: 3/15; financial award applicants required to submit FAFSA. *Unit head:* Dr. Robert Gendron, Graduate Coordinator, 724-357-2352, E-mail: robert.gendron@iup.edu. *Application contact:* Dr. Robert Hinrichsen, Graduate Coordinator, 724-357-2352, E-mail: bhinrich@iup.edu.

Indiana University–Purdue University Fort Wayne, College of Arts and Sciences, Department of Biology, Fort Wayne, IN 46805-1499. Offers MS. Part-time and evening/weekend programs available. *Faculty:* 21 full-time (4 women). *Students:* 18 full-time (7 women), 31 part-time (21 women); includes 9 minority (2 Black or African American, non-Hispanic/Latino; 1 American Indian or Alaska Native, non-Hispanic/Latino; 2 Asian, non-Hispanic/Latino; 2 Hispanic/Latino; 2 Two or more races, non-Hispanic/Latino), 4 international. Average age 26. 24 applicants, 88% accepted, 18 enrolled. In 2010, 8 master's awarded. *Degree requirements:* For master's, thesis optional. *Entrance requirements:* For master's, GRE General Test, minimum GPA of 3.0, major or minor in biology, three letters of recommendation. Additional exam requirements/recommendations for international students: Required—TOEFL (minimum score 550 paper-based; 213 computer-based; 77 iBT), TWE. *Application deadline:* For fall admission, 4/15 priority date for domestic students, 2/15 priority date for international students; for spring admission, 8/15 priority date for domestic and international students. Applications are processed on a rolling basis. Application fee: $55 ($60 for international students). Electronic applications accepted. *Expenses:* Tuition, state resident: full-time $4824; part-time $268 per credit. Tuition, nonresident: full-time $11,625; part-time $646 per credit. Required fees: $555; $30.85 per credit. Tuition and fees vary according to course load. *Financial support:* In 2010–11, 4 research assistantships with partial tuition reimbursements (averaging $12,740 per year), 15 teaching assistantships with partial tuition reimbursements (averaging $12,740 per year) were awarded; scholarships/grants and unspecified assistantships also available. Support available to part-time students. Financial award application deadline: 3/1; financial award applicants required to submit FAFSA. *Faculty research:* Copperbelly watersnakes, escape behavior challenges theory, sceloporus virgatus lizards, freshwater reptiles. Total annual research expenditures: $227,057. *Unit head:* Dr. Frank Paladino, Chair and Professor, 260-481-6305, Fax: 260-481-6087, E-mail: paladino@ipfw.edu. *Application contact:* Dr. George S. Mourad, Graduate Program Director, 260-481-5704, Fax: 260-481-6087, E-mail: mourad@ipfw.edu.

Indiana University–Purdue University Indianapolis, School of Science, Department of Biology, Indianapolis, IN 46202-2896. Offers MS, PhD. PhD offered jointly with Purdue University. Part-time and evening/weekend programs available. *Faculty:* 7 full-time (2 women). *Students:* 107 full-time (40 women), 17 part-time (10 women); includes 20 minority (1 Black or African American, non-Hispanic/Latino; 2 American Indian or Alaska Native, non-Hispanic/Latino; 8 Asian, non-Hispanic/Latino; 8 Hispanic/Latino; 1 Two or more races, non-Hispanic/Latino), 11 international. Average age 25. 203 applicants, 58% accepted, 97 enrolled. In 2010, 88 master's awarded. Terminal master's awarded for partial completion of doctoral program. *Degree requirements:* For master's, thesis (for some programs); for doctorate, thesis/dissertation. *Entrance requirements:* For master's and doctorate, GRE General Test. *Application deadline:* For fall admission, 6/1 for domestic students. Application fee: $55 ($65 for international students). *Financial support:* In 2010–11, 5 fellowships with partial tuition reimbursements (averaging $9,905 per year), 8 teaching assistantships with partial tuition reimbursements (averaging $12,773 per year) were awarded; research assistantships with partial tuition reimbursements, career-related internships or fieldwork also available. Financial award application deadline: 4/1. *Faculty research:* Cell and model membranes, cell and molecular biology, immunology, oncology, developmental biology. *Unit head:* Dr. N. Douglas Lees, Chair, 317-274-0588, Fax: 317-274-2846. *Application contact:* Dr. Sherry Queener, Director, Graduate Studies and Associate Dean, 317-274-1577, Fax: 317-278-2380.

Iowa State University of Science and Technology, College of Veterinary Medicine and Graduate College, Graduate Programs in Veterinary Medicine, Department of Biomedical Sciences, Ames, IA 50011. Offers MS, PhD. *Faculty:* 31 full-time (5 women), 4 part-time/adjunct (1 woman). *Students:* 35 full-time (7 women), 4 part-time (0 women); includes 2 Asian, non-Hispanic/Latino; 1 Hispanic/Latino, 24 international. 21 applicants, 10% accepted, 1 enrolled. *Degree requirements:* For master's, thesis or alternative; for doctorate, thesis/dissertation. *Entrance requirements:* For master's and doctorate, GRE General Test. Additional exam requirements/recommendations for international students: Required—TOEFL (minimum score 590 paper-based; 94 iBT), IELTS (minimum score 6.5). *Application deadline:* For fall admission, 3/1 priority date for domestic and international students; for spring admission, 9/1 priority date for domestic and international students. Application fee: $40 ($90 for international students). Electronic applications accepted. *Financial support:* In 2010–11, 20 research assistantships with full and partial tuition reimbursements (averaging $16,632 per year), 6 teaching assistantships with full and partial tuition reimbursements (averaging $13,303 per year) were awarded; career-related internships or fieldwork, scholarships/grants, health care benefits, and unspecified assistantships also available. *Faculty research:* Cerebella research; endocrine physiology; memory, learning and associated diseases; ion-channels and dry resistance; glia-neuron signaling; neurobiology of pain. *Unit head:* Dr. James Bloedel, Chair, 515-294-2440, Fax: 515-294-2315, E-mail: biomedsci@iastate.edu. *Application contact:* Dr. Steve Carlson, Director of Graduate Education, 515-294-2440, E-mail: biomedsci@iastate.edu.

Jackson State University, Graduate School, College of Science, Engineering and Technology, Department of Biology, Jackson, MS 39217. Offers environmental science (MS, PhD). Part-time and evening/weekend programs available. *Faculty:* 14 full-time (2 women). *Students:* 24 full-time (16 women), 26 part-time (17 women); includes 39 Black or African American, non-Hispanic/Latino, 4 international. Average age 37. In 2010, 13 master's, 7 doctorates awarded. *Degree requirements:* For master's, comprehensive exam, thesis (alternative accepted for MST); for doctorate, comprehensive exam, thesis/dissertation. *Entrance requirements:* For master's, GRE General Test; for doctorate, MAT. Additional exam requirements/recommendations for international students: Required—TOEFL (minimum score 520 paper-based; 195 computer-based; 67 iBT). *Application deadline:* For fall admission, 3/1 priority date for domestic students, 3/1 for international students; for spring admission, 10/15 for domestic students, 10/1 for international students. Applications are processed on a rolling basis. Application fee: $25. *Expenses:* Tuition, state resident: full-time $5050; part-time $281 per credit hour. Tuition, nonresident: full-time $12,380; part-time $689 per credit hour. *Financial support:* Career-related internships or fieldwork, Federal Work-Study, scholarships/grants, and unspecified assistantships available. Support available to part-time students. Financial award application deadline: 3/1; financial award applicants required to submit FAFSA. *Faculty research:* Comparative studies on the carbohydrate composition of marine macroalgae, host-parasite relationship between the spruce budworm and entomepathogen fungus. *Unit head:* Dr. Gregorio Begonia, Acting Chair, 601-979-2586, Fax: 601-979-5853, E-mail: gregorieo.begonia@jsums.edu. *Application contact:* Sharlene Wilson, Director of Graduate Admissions, 601-979-2455, Fax: 601-979-4325, E-mail: sharlene.f.wilson@jsums.edu.

Jacksonville State University, College of Graduate Studies and Continuing Education, College of Arts and Sciences, Department of Biology, Jacksonville, AL 36265-1602. Offers MS. Part-time and evening/weekend programs available. *Degree requirements:* For master's, comprehensive exam, thesis (for some programs). *Entrance requirements:* For master's, GRE General Test or MAT. Electronic applications accepted.

James Madison University, The Graduate School, College of Science and Mathematics, Department of Biology, Harrisonburg, VA 22807. Offers MS. Part-time programs available. *Faculty:* 9 full-time (3 women), 1 (woman) part-time/adjunct. *Students:* 10 full-time (7 women), 3 part-time (1 woman); includes 1 minority (Asian, non-Hispanic/Latino). Average age 27. In 2010, 5 master's awarded. *Degree requirements:* For master's, thesis (for some programs). *Entrance requirements:* For master's, GRE General Test, GRE Subject Test, 3 letters of recommendation. Additional exam requirements/recommendations for international students: Required—TOEFL. *Application deadline:* For fall admission, 2/15 for domestic students. Applications are processed on a rolling basis. Application fee: $55. Electronic applications accepted. *Financial support:* In 2010–11, 9 students received support. Federal Work-Study and 9 graduate assistantships ($7382) available. Financial award application deadline: 3/1; financial award applicants required to submit FAFSA. *Faculty research:* Evolutionary ecology, gene regulation, microbial ecology, plant development, biomechanics. *Unit head:* Dr. Judith A. Dilts, Interim Academic Unit Head, 540-568-3508, E-mail: diltsja@jmu.edu. *Application contact:* Dr. Jon Kastendiek, Interim Graduate Director, 540-568-6225.

John Carroll University, Graduate School, Department of Biology, University Heights, OH 44118-4581. Offers MA, MS. Part-time programs available. *Degree requirements:* For master's,

Biological and Biomedical Sciences—General

John Carroll University (continued)

essay or thesis, seminar. *Entrance requirements:* For master's, undergraduate major in biology, 1 semester of biochemistry, minimum 2.5 GPA. Electronic applications accepted. *Faculty research:* Algal ecology, systematics, molecular genetics, neurophysiology, behavioral ecology.

The Johns Hopkins University, National Institutes of Health Sponsored Programs, Baltimore, MD 21218-2699. Offers biology (PhD), including biochemistry, biophysics, cell biology, developmental biology, genetic biology, molecular biology; cell, molecular, and developmental biology and biophysics (PhD). *Degree requirements:* For doctorate, comprehensive exam, thesis/dissertation. *Entrance requirements:* For doctorate, GRE General Test. Additional exam requirements/recommendations for international students: Required—TOEFL (minimum score 600 paper-based; 250 computer-based), TWE. Electronic applications accepted. *Faculty research:* Protein and nucleic acid biochemistry and biophysical chemistry, molecular biology and development.

The Johns Hopkins University, School of Medicine, Graduate Programs in Medicine, Baltimore, MD 21218-2699. Offers MA, MS, PhD, MD/PhD. *Faculty:* 258 full-time (77 women), 31 part-time/adjunct (12 women). *Students:* 914 full-time (466 women); includes 211 minority (50 Black or African American, non-Hispanic/Latino; 1 American Indian or Alaska Native, non-Hispanic/Latino; 115 Asian, non-Hispanic/Latino; 33 Hispanic/Latino; 12 Two or more races, non-Hispanic/Latino), 320 international. Average age 24. 1,409 applicants, 21% accepted, 147 enrolled. In 2010, 18 master's, 90 doctorates awarded. *Degree requirements:* For doctorate, thesis/dissertation. *Entrance requirements:* Additional exam requirements/recommendations for international students: Required—TOEFL. *Application deadline:* For fall admission, 1/10 priority date for domestic and international students. Applications are processed on a rolling basis. Application fee: $85. Electronic applications accepted. *Expenses:* Contact institution. *Financial support:* In 2010–11, fellowships with full tuition reimbursements (averaging $23,000 per year); research assistantships, teaching assistantships with tuition reimbursements, career-related internships or fieldwork, Federal Work-Study, institutionally sponsored loans, and tuition waivers (full) also available. Financial award applicants required to submit FAFSA. *Unit head:* Dr. Peter Maloney, Associate Dean for Graduate Programs, 410-614-3385. *Application contact:* Dr. James Weiss, Associate Dean of Admissions, 410-955-3182.

The Johns Hopkins University, Zanvyl Krieger School of Arts and Sciences, Chemistry-Biology Interface Program, Baltimore, MD 21218-2699. Offers PhD. *Faculty:* 32 full-time (6 women). *Students:* 16 full-time (10 women); includes 5 minority (1 Black or African American, non-Hispanic/Latino; 1 American Indian or Alaska Native, non-Hispanic/Latino; 2 Asian, non-Hispanic/Latino; 1 Hispanic/Latino), 1 international. Average age 25. 77 applicants, 23% accepted, 3 enrolled. Terminal master's awarded for partial completion of doctoral program. *Degree requirements:* For doctorate, comprehensive exam, thesis/dissertation, 8 one-semester courses, literature seminar, research proposal. *Entrance requirements:* For doctorate, GRE General Test, GRE Subject Test in biochemistry, cell and molecular biology, biology or chemistry (strongly recommended), 3 letters of recommendation, interview. *Application deadline:* For fall admission, 1/15 for domestic and international students. Applications are processed on a rolling basis. Application fee: $75. Electronic applications accepted. *Financial support:* Fellowships, teaching assistantships, Federal Work-Study, scholarships/grants, health care benefits, and unspecified assistantships available. Financial award application deadline: 4/15; financial award applicants required to submit FAFSA. *Faculty research:* Enzyme mechanisms, inhibitors, and metabolic pathways; DNA replication, damaged, and repair; using small molecules to probe signal transduction, gene regulation, angiogenesis, and other biological processes; synthetic methods and medicinal chemistry; synthetic modeling of metalloenzymes. *Unit head:* Dr. Marc Greenberg, Director, 410-516-8095, Fax: 410-516-7044, E-mail: mgreenberg@jhu.edu. *Application contact:* Lauren Riker, Academic Coordinator, 410-516-7427, Fax: 410-516-8420, E-mail: lriker@jhu.edu.

The Johns Hopkins University, Zanvyl Krieger School of Arts and Sciences, Department of Biology, Baltimore, MD 21218. Offers PhD. *Faculty:* 31 full-time (11 women), 17 part-time/adjunct (5 women). *Students:* 107 full-time (59 women); includes 1 Black or African American, non-Hispanic/Latino; 16 Asian, non-Hispanic/Latino; 13 Hispanic/Latino, 16 international. Average age 25. 209 applicants, 24 enrolled. In 2010, 12 doctorates awarded. Terminal master's awarded for partial completion of doctoral program. *Degree requirements:* For doctorate, comprehensive exam, thesis/dissertation. *Entrance requirements:* For doctorate, GRE General Test. Additional exam requirements/recommendations for international students: Required—TOEFL (minimum score 600 paper-based; 250 computer-based), IELTS, TWE. *Application deadline:* For fall admission, 12/7 for domestic and international students. Application fee: $75. Electronic applications accepted. *Financial support:* In 2010–11, 95 students received support, including 4 fellowships with tuition reimbursements available (averaging $27,125 per year), 78 research assistantships with tuition reimbursements available (averaging $27,125 per year), 33 teaching assistantships with tuition reimbursements available (averaging $27,125 per year); Federal Work-Study, institutionally sponsored loans, scholarships/grants, traineeships, health care benefits, tuition waivers (full), and unspecified assistantships also available. Financial award application deadline: 4/15; financial award applicants required to submit FAFSA. *Faculty research:* Cell biology, molecular biology and development, biochemistry, developmental biology, biophysics, genetics. Total annual research expenditures: $8.3 million. *Unit head:* Dr. Beverly R. Wendland, Chair, 410-516-4693, Fax: 410-516-5213, E-mail: bwendland@jhu.edu. *Application contact:* Joan Miller, Academic Affairs Administrator, 410-516-5502, Fax: 410-516-5213, E-mail: joan@jhu.edu.

Kansas City University of Medicine and Biosciences, College of Biosciences, Kansas City, MO 64106-1453. Offers bioethics (MA); biomedical sciences (MS). Part-time programs available. *Students:* 51 full-time (29 women); includes 3 Black or African American, non-Hispanic/Latino; 4 Asian, non-Hispanic/Latino; 1 Hispanic/Latino. Average age 25. 138 applicants, 51% accepted, 51 enrolled. In 2010, 50 master's awarded. *Degree requirements:* For master's, comprehensive exam, thesis (for some programs). *Entrance requirements:* For master's, MCAT, GRE. *Application deadline:* For fall admission, 1/1 priority date for domestic students. Applications are processed on a rolling basis. Application fee: $30. *Expenses:* Tuition: Full-time $41,013. Required fees: $175. *Financial support:* Applicants required to submit FAFSA. *Unit head:* Dr. Douglas Rushing, Dean, 816-654-7252. *Application contact:* Brooke Birdsong, Associate Director of Admissions, 816-654-7160, Fax: 816-654-7161, E-mail: admissions@kcumb.edu.

Kansas State University, College of Veterinary Medicine, Department of Diagnostic Medicine/Pathobiology, Manhattan, KS 66506. Offers biomedical science (MS); diagnostic medicine/pathobiology (PhD). Terminal master's awarded for partial completion of doctoral program. *Degree requirements:* For doctorate, thesis/dissertation. *Entrance requirements:* For master's and doctorate, interviews. Additional exam requirements/recommendations for international students: Required—TOEFL (minimum score 550 paper-based; 213 computer-based). Electronic applications accepted. *Faculty research:* Infectious disease of animals, food safety and security, epidemiology and public health, toxicology, and pathology.

Kansas State University, Graduate School, College of Arts and Sciences, Division of Biology, Manhattan, KS 66506. Offers biology (MS, PhD); microbiology (PhD). Terminal master's awarded for partial completion of doctoral program. *Degree requirements:* For master's, thesis; for doctorate, thesis/dissertation. *Entrance requirements:* For master's, GRE General Test, minimum undergraduate GPA of 3.0; for doctorate, GRE General Test, minimum GPA of 3.0. Additional exam requirements/recommendations for international students: Required—TOEFL (minimum score 550 paper-based; 213 computer-based). Electronic applications accepted. *Faculty research:* Ecology, genetics, developmental biology, microbiology, cell biology.

Keck Graduate Institute of Applied Life Sciences, Bioscience Program, Claremont, CA 91711. Offers applied life science (PhD); bioscience (MBS); bioscience management (Certificate); computational systems biology (PhD). *Degree requirements:* For master's, comprehensive exam, project. *Entrance requirements:* For master's, GRE General Test or MCAT. Additional exam requirements/recommendations for international students: Required—TOEFL. Electronic

applications accepted. *Faculty research:* Computational biology, drug discovery and development, molecular and cellular biology, biomedical engineering, biomaterials and tissue engineering.

Kent State University, College of Arts and Sciences, Department of Biological Sciences, Kent, OH 44242-0001. Offers ecology (MS, PhD); physiology (MS, PhD). *Degree requirements:* For master's, thesis; for doctorate, thesis/dissertation. *Entrance requirements:* For master's, GRE General Test, minimum GPA of 3.0; for doctorate, GRE General Test, minimum GPA of 3.25. Additional exam requirements/recommendations for international students: Required—TOEFL (minimum score 600 paper-based; 257 computer-based). Electronic applications accepted. *Expenses:* Tuition, state resident: full-time $7866; part-time $437 per credit hour. Tuition, nonresident: full-time $14,022; part-time $779 per credit hour.

Kent State University, School of Biomedical Sciences, Kent, OH 44242-0001. Offers MS, PhD. Terminal master's awarded for partial completion of doctoral program. *Degree requirements:* For master's, thesis; for doctorate, thesis/dissertation. *Entrance requirements:* For master's and doctorate, GRE General Test. Electronic applications accepted. *Expenses:* Tuition, state resident: full-time $7866; part-time $437 per credit hour. Tuition, nonresident: full-time $14,022; part-time $779 per credit hour.

Lake Erie College of Osteopathic Medicine, Professional Programs, Erie, PA 16509-1025. Offers biomedical sciences (Postbaccalaureate Certificate); medical education (MS); osteopathic medicine (DO); pharmacy (Pharm D). *Accreditation:* ACPE; AOsA. *Degree requirements:* For first professional degree, comprehensive exam, National Osteopathic Medical Licensing Exam, Levels 1 and 2; for Postbaccalaureate Certificate, comprehensive exam, North American Pharmacist Licensure Examination (NAPLEX). *Entrance requirements:* For first professional degree, MCAT, minimum GPA of 3.2, letters of recommendation; for Postbaccalaureate Certificate, PCAT, letters of recommendation, minimum GPA of 3.5. Electronic applications accepted. *Faculty research:* Cardiac smooth and skeletal muscle mechanics, chemotherapeutics and vitamins, osteopathic manipulation.

Lakehead University, Graduate Studies, Faculty of Social Sciences and Humanities, Department of Biology, Thunder Bay, ON P7B 5E1, Canada. Offers M Sc. Part-time and evening/weekend programs available. *Degree requirements:* For master's, thesis, department seminary, oral examination. *Entrance requirements:* For master's, minimum B average. Additional exam requirements/recommendations for international students: Required—TOEFL. *Faculty research:* Systematics and biogeography, wildlife parasitology, plant physiology and biochemistry, plant ecology, fishery biology.

Lamar University, College of Graduate Studies, College of Arts and Sciences, Department of Biology, Beaumont, TX 77710. Offers MS. Part-time and evening/weekend programs available. *Faculty:* 9 full-time (3 women). *Students:* 9 full-time (3 women), 8 part-time (7 women); includes 1 Asian, non-Hispanic/Latino; 2 Hispanic/Latino, 2 international. Average age 30. 17 applicants, 59% accepted, 4 enrolled. In 2010, 5 master's awarded. *Degree requirements:* For master's, thesis. *Entrance requirements:* For master's, GRE General Test, minimum GPA of 2.5 in last 60 hours of undergraduate course work. Additional exam requirements/recommendations for international students: Required—TOEFL. *Application deadline:* For fall admission, 8/1 for domestic students; for spring admission, 12/1 for domestic students. Applications are processed on a rolling basis. Application fee: $25 ($50 for international students). *Expenses:* Tuition, state resident: full-time $4160; part-time $208 per credit hour. Tuition, nonresident: full-time $10,360; part-time $518 per credit hour. *Financial support:* In 2010–11, 3 teaching assistantships (averaging $6,200 per year) were awarded. Financial award application deadline: 4/1. *Faculty research:* Microbiology, limnology, vertebrate ecology, invertebrate hemoglobin, ornithology. *Unit head:* Dr. Michael E. Warren, Chair, 409-880-8262, Fax: 409-880-1827. *Application contact:* Dr. R. C. Harrel, Graduate Adviser, 409-880-8255, Fax: 409-880-1827.

Laurentian University, School of Graduate Studies and Research, Programme in Biology, Sudbury, ON P3E 2C6, Canada. Offers biology (M Sc); boreal ecology (PhD). Part-time programs available. *Degree requirements:* For master's, thesis. *Entrance requirements:* For master's, honors degree with second class or better. *Faculty research:* Recovery of acid-stressed lakes, effects of climate change, origin and maintenance of biocomplexity, radionuclide dynamics, cytogenetic studies of plants.

Lehigh University, College of Arts and Sciences, Department of Biological Sciences, Bethlehem, PA 18015. Offers biochemistry (PhD); integrative biology and neuroscience (PhD); molecular biology (MS, PhD). Part-time programs available. Postbaccalaureate distance learning degree programs offered (no on-campus study). *Faculty:* 17 full-time (7 women). *Students:* 30 full-time (14 women), 30 part-time (18 women); includes 6 minority (1 Black or African American, non-Hispanic/Latino; 1 Asian, non-Hispanic/Latino; 3 Hispanic/Latino; 1 Native Hawaiian or other Pacific Islander, non-Hispanic/Latino), 7 international. Average age 29. 79 applicants, 25% accepted, 19 enrolled. In 2010, 9 master's, 3 doctorates awarded. Terminal master's awarded for partial completion of doctoral program. *Degree requirements:* For master's, research report; for doctorate, comprehensive exam, thesis/dissertation. *Entrance requirements:* For doctorate, GRE General Test. Additional exam requirements/recommendations for international students: Required—TOEFL. *Application deadline:* For fall admission, 12/15 for domestic and international students. Applications are processed on a rolling basis. Application fee: $65. Electronic applications accepted. *Financial support:* In 2010–11, 31 students received support, including 4 fellowships with full tuition reimbursements available (averaging $24,500 per year), 6 research assistantships with full tuition reimbursements available (averaging $23,750 per year), 16 teaching assistantships with full tuition reimbursements available (averaging $23,750 per year); scholarships/grants and unspecified assistantships also available. Financial award application deadline: 12/15. *Faculty research:* Gene expression, cytoskeleton and cell structure, cell cycle and growth regulation, neuroscience, animal behavior, microbiology. Total annual research expenditures: $2.4 million. *Unit head:* Dr. Murray Itzkowitz, Chairperson, 610-758-3680, Fax: 610-758-4004, E-mail: mi00@lehigh.edu. *Application contact:* Dr. Jennifer M. Swann, Graduate Coordinator, 610-758-5484, Fax: 610-758-4004, E-mail: jms5@lehigh.edu.

Lehman College of the City University of New York, Division of Natural and Social Sciences, Department of Biological Sciences, Program in Biology, Bronx, NY 10468-1589. Offers MA.

Loma Linda University, School of Science and Technology, Department of Biological and Earth Sciences, Loma Linda, CA 92350. Offers MS, PhD. *Degree requirements:* For master's, comprehensive exam, thesis; for doctorate, comprehensive exam, thesis/dissertation. *Entrance requirements:* For master's, minimum GPA of 3.0. Additional exam requirements/recommendations for international students: Required—TOEFL (minimum score 550 paper-based; 213 computer-based).

Long Island University, Brooklyn Campus, Richard L. Conolly College of Liberal Arts and Sciences, Department of Biology, Brooklyn, NY 11201-8423. Offers MS. Part-time and evening/weekend programs available. *Degree requirements:* For master's, thesis or alternative. *Entrance requirements:* For master's, 2 letters of recommendation. Additional exam requirements/recommendations for international students: Required—TOEFL (minimum score 500 paper-based; 173 computer-based). Electronic applications accepted.

Long Island University, C.W. Post Campus, College of Liberal Arts and Sciences, Department of Biology, Brookville, NY 11548-1300. Offers biology (MS); biology education (MS); genetic counseling (MS). Part-time and evening/weekend programs available. *Degree requirements:* For master's, thesis optional. *Entrance requirements:* For master's, GRE General Test, minimum GPA of 2.75 in major. Electronic applications accepted. *Faculty research:* Immunology, molecular biology, systematics, behavioral ecology, microbiology.

Long Island University, C.W. Post Campus, School of Health Professions and Nursing, Department of Biomedical Sciences, Brookville, NY 11548-1300. Offers cardiovascular perfusion (MS); clinical laboratory management (MS); medical biology (MS), including hematology, immunology, medical biology, medical chemistry, medical microbiology. Part-time and evening/weekend programs available. Postbaccalaureate distance learning degree programs offered. *Degree requirements:* For master's, thesis. *Entrance requirements:* For master's, minimum GPA of 2.75 in major. Electronic applications accepted.

Louisiana State University and Agricultural and Mechanical College, Graduate School, College of Basic Sciences, Department of Biological Sciences, Baton Rouge, LA 70803. Offers biochemistry (MS, PhD); biological science (MS, PhD); science (MNS). Part-time programs available. *Faculty:* 61 full-time (6 women). *Students:* 133 full-time (62 women), 6 part-time (3 women); includes 1 Black or African American, non-Hispanic/Latino; 5 Asian, non-Hispanic/Latino; 3 Hispanic/Latino; 1 Two or more races, non-Hispanic/Latino, 58 international. Average age 29. 156 applicants, 16% accepted, 12 enrolled. In 2010, 6 master's, 20 doctorates awarded. Terminal master's awarded for partial completion of doctoral program. *Degree requirements:* For doctorate, thesis/dissertation. *Entrance requirements:* For master's and doctorate, GRE General Test, minimum GPA of 3.0. Additional exam requirements/recommendations for international students: Required—TOEFL (minimum score 550 paper-based; 213 computer-based; 79 iBT) or IELTS (minimum score 6.5). *Application deadline:* For fall admission, 5/15 for domestic and international students; for spring admission, 10/15 for domestic and international students. Applications are processed on a rolling basis. Application fee: $25. Electronic applications accepted. *Financial support:* In 2010–11, 138 students received support, including 15 fellowships with full and partial tuition reimbursements available (averaging $17,743 per year), 43 research assistantships with full and partial tuition reimbursements available (averaging $20,949 per year), 74 teaching assistantships with full and partial tuition reimbursements available (averaging $18,724 per year); Federal Work-Study, institutionally sponsored loans, health care benefits, and unspecified assistantships also available. Support available to part-time students. Financial award applicants required to submit FAFSA. *Faculty research:* Biochemistry and molecular biology, cell developmental and integrative biology, systematics, ecology and evolutionary biology. Total annual research expenditures: $979,438. *Unit head:* Dr. James Moroney, Chair, 225-578-1765, Fax: 225-578-2597. *Application contact:* Dr. Jacqueline Stephens, Associate Chairman, 225-578-1240, Fax: 225-578-7299, E-mail: biogradcoord@lsu.edu.

Louisiana State University Health Sciences Center, School of Graduate Studies in New Orleans, New Orleans, LA 70112-2223. Offers MPH, MS, PhD, MD/PhD. Part-time and evening/weekend programs available. Terminal master's awarded for partial completion of doctoral program. *Degree requirements:* For master's, comprehensive exam, thesis; for doctorate, comprehensive exam, thesis/dissertation. *Entrance requirements:* For master's and doctorate, GRE General Test. Additional exam requirements/recommendations for international students: Required—TOEFL.

Louisiana State University Health Sciences Center at Shreveport, Louisiana State University Health Sciences Center at Shreveport, Shreveport, LA 71130-3932. Offers MS, PhD, MD/PhD. *Accreditation:* SACS. Terminal master's awarded for partial completion of doctoral program. *Degree requirements:* For master's, thesis; for doctorate, thesis/dissertation. *Entrance requirements:* For master's and doctorate, GRE General Test. Additional exam requirements/recommendations for international students: Required—TOEFL.

Louisiana Tech University, Graduate School, College of Applied and Natural Sciences, School of Biological Sciences, Ruston, LA 71272. Offers MS. Part-time programs available. *Degree requirements:* For master's, thesis or alternative. *Entrance requirements:* For master's, GRE General Test, GRE Subject Test. *Faculty research:* Genetics, animal biology, plant biology, physiology biocontrol.

Loyola University Chicago, Graduate School, Department of Biology, Chicago, IL 60660. Offers biology (MA, MS); medical sciences (MA). *Faculty:* 23 full-time (5 women). *Students:* 80 full-time (32 women), 9 part-time (5 women); includes 23 minority (1 Black or African American, non-Hispanic/Latino; 13 Asian, non-Hispanic/Latino; 8 Hispanic/Latino; 1 Two or more races, non-Hispanic/Latino), 2 international. Average age 25. 661 applicants, 23% accepted, 65 enrolled. In 2010, 55 master's awarded. *Degree requirements:* For master's, thesis (for some programs). *Entrance requirements:* For master's, GRE General Test, 3 letters of recommendation. Additional exam requirements/recommendations for international students: Required—TOEFL. *Application deadline:* For fall admission, 6/1 for domestic and international students; for spring admission, 12/1 for domestic students. Applications are processed on a rolling basis. Application fee: $50. Electronic applications accepted. *Expenses:* Tuition: Full-time $14,940; part-time $830 per credit hour. Required fees: $87 per semester. Part-time tuition and fees vary according to course load and program. *Financial support:* In 2010–11, 7 students received support, including 7 fellowships with full tuition reimbursements available (averaging $16,000 per year); Federal Work-Study and institutionally sponsored loans also available. Financial award application deadline: 2/1; financial award applicants required to submit FAFSA. *Faculty research:* Evolution, development, aquatic biology, molecular biology and genetics, cell biology, neurobiology. Total annual research expenditures: $2.5 million. *Unit head:* Dr. Terry Grande, Graduate Program Director, 773-583-5649, Fax: 773-508-3646, E-mail: tgrande@luc.edu. *Application contact:* Dr. Terry Grande, Graduate Program Director, 773-583-5649, Fax: 773-508-3646, E-mail: tgrande@luc.edu.

Marquette University, Graduate School, College of Arts and Sciences, Department of Biology, Milwaukee, WI 53201-1881. Offers cell biology (MS, PhD); developmental biology (MS, PhD); ecology (MS, PhD); epithelial physiology (MS, PhD); genetics (MS, PhD); microbiology (MS, PhD); molecular biology (MS, PhD); muscle and exercise physiology (MS, PhD); neuroscience (PhD). *Faculty:* 25 full-time (12 women), 2 part-time/adjunct (1 woman). *Students:* 23 full-time (9 women), 12 part-time (8 women); includes 1 minority (Asian, non-Hispanic/Latino), 15 international. Average age 26. 82 applicants, 15% accepted, 5 enrolled. In 2010, 3 master's, 2 doctorates awarded. Terminal master's awarded for partial completion of doctoral program. *Degree requirements:* For master's, comprehensive exam, thesis, 1 year of teaching experience or equivalent; for doctorate, thesis/dissertation, 1 year of teaching experience or equivalent, qualifying exam. *Entrance requirements:* For master's and doctorate, GRE General Test, GRE Subject Test, official transcripts from all current and previous colleges/universities except Marquette, statement of professional goals and aspirations, three letters of recommendation. Additional exam requirements/recommendations for international students: Required—TOEFL (minimum score 530 paper-based; 78 computer-based). *Application deadline:* For fall admission, 12/15 for domestic and international students. Application fee: $50. Electronic applications accepted. *Expenses:* Tuition: Full-time $16,290; part-time $905 per credit hour. Tuition and fees vary according to program. *Financial support:* In 2010–11, 2 research assistantships, 34 teaching assistantships were awarded; fellowships, Federal Work-Study, institutionally sponsored loans, scholarships/grants, and tuition waivers (full and partial) also available. Support available to part-time students. Financial award application deadline: 2/15. *Faculty research:* Neurobiology, neuroendocrinology, epithelial physiology, neuropeptide interactions, synaptic transmission. Total annual research expenditures: $1.3 million. *Unit head:* Dr. Robert Fitts, Chair, 414-288-1748, Fax: 414-288-7357. *Application contact:* Debbie Weaver, Administrative Assistant, 414-288-7355, Fax: 414-288-7357.

Marshall University, Academic Affairs Division, College of Science, Department of Biological Science, Huntington, WV 25755. Offers MA, MS. *Faculty:* 21 full-time (4 women). *Students:* 40 full-time (17 women), 3 part-time (2 women); includes 4 Black or African American, non-Hispanic/Latino; 3 Asian, non-Hispanic/Latino, 6 international. Average age 26. In 2010, 18 master's awarded. *Degree requirements:* For master's, thesis (for some programs). *Entrance requirements:* For master's, GRE General Test, GRE Subject Test. Application fee: $40. *Financial support:* Career-related internships or fieldwork available. *Unit head:* Dr. Elmer Price, Chairperson, 304-696-3611, E-mail: pricee@marshall.edu. *Application contact:* Information Contact, 304-746-1900, Fax: 304-746-1902, E-mail: services@marshall.edu.

Marshall University, Joan C. Edwards School of Medicine and Academic Affairs Division, Program in Biomedical Sciences, Huntington, WV 25755. Offers MS, PhD. Terminal master's awarded for partial completion of doctoral program. *Degree requirements:* For master's,

comprehensive exam, thesis optional; for doctorate, thesis/dissertation, written and oral qualifying exams. *Entrance requirements:* For master's, GRE General Test or MCAT (medical science), 1 year of course work in biology, physics, chemistry, and organic chemistry and associated labs; for doctorate, GRE General Test, 1 year of course work in biology, physics, chemistry, and organic chemistry and associated labs. Additional exam requirements/recommendations for international students: Required—TOEFL (minimum score 525 paper-based; 216 computer-based). *Expenses:* Contact institution. *Faculty research:* Neurosciences, cardiopulmonary science, molecular biology, toxicology, endocrinology.

Massachusetts Institute of Technology, Harvard-MIT Division of Health Sciences and Technology, Biomedical Enterprise Program, Cambridge, MA 02139-4307. Offers SM. *Students:* 28 full-time (15 women); includes 1 American Indian or Alaska Native, non-Hispanic/Latino; 6 Asian, non-Hispanic/Latino; 1 Hispanic/Latino, 5 international. Average age 30. 43 applicants, 33% accepted, 13 enrolled. In 2010, 8 master's awarded. *Degree requirements:* For master's, thesis. *Entrance requirements:* For master's, GMAT or GRE, bachelor's degree in engineering or science, work experience in biomedical business. Additional exam requirements/recommendations for international students: Required—TOEFL. *Application deadline:* For fall admission, 12/15 for domestic and international students. Electronic applications accepted. *Expenses:* Contact institution. *Financial support:* In 2010–11, 8 students received support, including 1 fellowship (averaging $5,000 per year), 2 research assistantships with full and partial tuition reimbursements available (averaging $34,773 per year), 6 teaching assistantships with partial tuition reimbursements available (averaging $8,637 per year); institutionally sponsored loans, health care benefits, and unspecified assistantships also available. Financial award application deadline: 12/15; financial award applicants required to submit FAFSA. *Faculty research:* Entrepreneurship, technology strategy management, organizational strategies and models, epidemiology and biostatics, biomedical research from the molecular to the whole organism level. *Application contact:* Traci Anderson, Academic Programs Administrator, 617-258-7470, E-mail: tanderso@mit.edu.

Massachusetts Institute of Technology, Harvard-MIT Division of Health Sciences and Technology, Program in Medical Sciences, Cambridge, MA 02139-4307. Offers MD, MD/MS, MD/PhD. *Students:* 182 full-time (71 women); includes 4 Black or African American, non-Hispanic/Latino; 84 Asian, non-Hispanic/Latino; 5 Hispanic/Latino; 7 Two or more races, non-Hispanic/Latino, 10 international. Average age 26. 916 applicants, 5% accepted, 30 enrolled. In 2010, 28 first professional degrees awarded. *Degree requirements:* For MD, thesis/dissertation. *Entrance requirements:* MCAT. *Application deadline:* For fall admission, 10/15 for domestic students. Application fee: $85. *Expenses:* Contact institution. *Financial support:* In 2010–11, 59 students received support, including 5 fellowships with partial tuition reimbursements available (averaging $29,212 per year), 38 research assistantships with partial tuition reimbursements available (averaging $11,899 per year), 20 teaching assistantships with partial tuition reimbursements available (averaging $3,883 per year); career-related internships or fieldwork, scholarships/grants, health care benefits, and unspecified assistantships also available. Financial award application deadline: 10/15; financial award applicants required to submit FAFSA. *Unit head:* Dr. David Earl Cohen, Director, 617-726-5576. *Application contact:* Zara Smith, MD Admissions Coordinator, 617-432-7195, E-mail: zara_smith@hms.harvard.edu.

Massachusetts Institute of Technology, School of Science, Department of Biology, Cambridge, MA 02139-4307. Offers biochemistry (PhD); biological oceanography (PhD); biology (PhD); biophysical chemistry and molecular structure (PhD); cell biology (PhD); computational and systems biology (PhD); developmental biology (PhD); genetics (PhD); immunology (PhD); microbiology (PhD); molecular biology (PhD); neurobiology (PhD). *Faculty:* 56 full-time (14 women). *Students:* 251 full-time (135 women); includes 74 minority (4 Black or African American, non-Hispanic/Latino; 1 American Indian or Alaska Native, non-Hispanic/Latino; 29 Asian, non-Hispanic/Latino; 33 Hispanic/Latino; 7 Two or more races, non-Hispanic/Latino), 29 international. Average age 26. 652 applicants, 18% accepted, 58 enrolled. In 2010, 41 doctorates awarded. *Degree requirements:* For doctorate, comprehensive exam, thesis/dissertation. *Entrance requirements:* For doctorate, GRE General Test. Additional exam requirements/recommendations for international students: Required—TOEFL (minimum score 577 paper-based; 233 computer-based), IELTS (minimum score 6.5). *Application deadline:* For fall admission, 12/1 for domestic and international students. Application fee: $75. Electronic applications accepted. *Expenses:* Tuition: Full-time $38,940; part-time $605 per unit. Required fees: $272. *Financial support:* In 2010–11, 215 students received support, including 115 fellowships with tuition reimbursements available (averaging $33,090 per year), 132 research assistantships with tuition reimbursements available (averaging $31,846 per year); teaching assistantships with tuition reimbursements available, Federal Work-Study, institutionally sponsored loans, scholarships/grants, traineeships, health care benefits, and unspecified assistantships also available. *Faculty research:* DNA recombination, replication and repair; transcription and gene regulation; signal transduction; cell cycle; neuronal cell fate. Total annual research expenditures: $60.6 million. *Unit head:* Prof. Chris Kaiser, Head, 617-253-4701, E-mail: mitbio@mit.edu. *Application contact:* Biology Education Office, 617-253-3717, Fax: 617-258-9329, E-mail: gradbio@mit.edu.

Mayo Graduate School, Graduate Programs in Biomedical Sciences, Rochester, MN 55905. Offers PhD, MD/PhD. *Degree requirements:* For doctorate, oral defense of dissertation, qualifying oral and written exam. *Entrance requirements:* For doctorate, GRE, 1 year of chemistry, biology, calculus, and physics. Additional exam requirements/recommendations for international students: Required—TOEFL. Electronic applications accepted.

McGill University, Faculty of Graduate and Postdoctoral Studies, Faculty of Medicine, Department of Medicine, Montréal, QC H3A 2T5, Canada. Offers experimental medicine (M Sc, PhD), including bioethics (M Sc), experimental medicine.

McGill University, Faculty of Graduate and Postdoctoral Studies, Faculty of Science, Department of Biology, Montréal, QC H3A 2T5, Canada. Offers bioinformatics (M Sc, PhD); environment (M Sc, PhD); neo-tropical environment (M Sc, PhD).

McMaster University, Faculty of Health Sciences, Department of Biochemistry and Biomedical Sciences, Hamilton, ON L8S 4M2, Canada. Offers M Sc, PhD. Terminal master's awarded for partial completion of doctoral program. *Degree requirements:* For master's, thesis; for doctorate, comprehensive exam, thesis/dissertation. *Entrance requirements:* For master's and doctorate, minimum B+ average. Additional exam requirements/recommendations for international students: Required—TOEFL (minimum score 550 paper-based; 213 computer-based). *Faculty research:* Molecular and cell biology, biomolecular structure and function, molecular pharmacology and toxicology.

McMaster University, Faculty of Health Sciences and School of Graduate Studies, Program in Medical Sciences, Hamilton, ON L8S 4M2, Canada. Offers blood and vascular (M Sc, PhD); genetics and cancer (M Sc, PhD); immunity and infection (M Sc, PhD); metabolism and nutrition (M Sc, PhD); neurosciences and behavioral sciences (M Sc, PhD); physiology/pharmacology (M Sc, PhD); MD/PhD. *Degree requirements:* For master's, thesis; for doctorate, comprehensive exam, thesis/dissertation. *Entrance requirements:* For master's, honors B Sc, B+ average in related field; for doctorate, M Sc, minimum B+ average. Additional exam requirements/recommendations for international students: Required—TOEFL (minimum score 580 paper-based; 237 computer-based; 92 iBT).

McMaster University, School of Graduate Studies, Faculty of Science, Department of Biology, Hamilton, ON L8S 4M2, Canada. Offers M Sc, PhD. Part-time programs available. *Degree requirements:* For master's, thesis; for doctorate, comprehensive exam, thesis/dissertation. *Entrance requirements:* Additional exam requirements/recommendations for international students: Required—TOEFL (minimum score 550 paper-based; 213 computer-based).

Medical College of Wisconsin, Graduate School of Biomedical Sciences, Milwaukee, WI 53226-0509. Offers MA, MPH, MS, PhD, Graduate Certificate, MD/PhD. Part-time and evening/

Biological and Biomedical Sciences—General

Medical College of Wisconsin (continued)
weekend programs available. Postbaccalaureate distance learning degree programs offered (minimal on-campus study). *Degree requirements:* For master's, comprehensive exam (for some programs), thesis (for some programs); for doctorate, comprehensive exam, thesis/dissertation. *Entrance requirements:* For master's and doctorate, GRE General Test. Additional exam requirements/recommendations for international students: Required—TOEFL (minimum score 100 computer-based). Electronic applications accepted. *Expenses:* Tuition: Full-time $30,000; part-time $710 per credit. Required fees: $150. *Faculty research:* Clinical and translational science, genomics and proteomics, cancer.

Medical College of Wisconsin, Interdisciplinary Program in Biomedical Sciences, Milwaukee, WI 53226-0509. Offers PhD. *Expenses:* Tuition: Full-time $30,000; part-time $710 per credit. Required fees: $150.

Medical University of South Carolina, College of Graduate Studies, Charleston, SC 29425. Offers MS, PhD, DMD/PhD, MD/PhD, Pharm D/PhD. *Faculty:* 268 full-time (79 women), 20 part-time/adjunct (3 women). *Students:* 161 full-time (106 women), 41 part-time (33 women); includes 14 Black or African American, non-Hispanic/Latino; 1 American Indian or Alaska Native, non-Hispanic/Latino; 2 Asian, non-Hispanic/Latino; 6 Hispanic/Latino, 27 international. Average age 33. 272 applicants, 28% accepted, 44 enrolled. In 2010, 31 master's, 47 doctorates awarded. Terminal master's awarded for partial completion of doctoral program. *Degree requirements:* For master's, thesis; for doctorate, thesis/dissertation, oral and written exams. *Entrance requirements:* For doctorate, GRE General Test, interview. Additional exam requirements/recommendations for international students: Required—TOEFL (minimum score 600 paper-based; 250 computer-based; 100 iBT). *Application deadline:* For fall admission, 1/15 priority date for domestic and international students. Applications are processed on a rolling basis. Application fee: $85 for international students. Electronic applications accepted. *Expenses:* Contact institution. *Financial support:* In 2010–11, 114 students received support, including 114 research assistantships with partial tuition reimbursements available (averaging $23,000 per year); Federal Work-Study and scholarships/grants also available. Support available to part-time students. Financial award application deadline: 3/10; financial award applicants required to submit FAFSA. *Faculty research:* Cell signaling and cancer biology, drug discovery and toxicology, biochemistry and genetics, macromolecular structure, neurosciences, microbiology and immunology. *Unit head:* Dr. Perry V. Halushka, Dean, 843-792-3012, Fax: 843-792-6590, E-mail: halushpv@musc.edu. *Application contact:* Dr. Cynthia F. Wright, Associate Dean for Career Development and Admissions, 843-792-2564, Fax: 843-792-6590, E-mail: wrightcf@musc.edu.

Meharry Medical College, School of Graduate Studies, Program in Biomedical Sciences, Nashville, TN 37208-9989. Offers cancer biology (PhD); microbiology and immunology (PhD); neuroscience (PhD); pharmacology (PhD); MD/PhD. *Degree requirements:* For doctorate, comprehensive exam, thesis/dissertation. *Entrance requirements:* For doctorate, GRE General Test, GRE Subject Test. *Faculty research:* Molecular mechanisms of biological systems and their relationship to human diseases, regulatory biological and cellular structure and function, genetic regulation of growth and cellular metabolisms.

Memorial University of Newfoundland, Faculty of Medicine and School of Graduate Studies, Graduate Programs in Medicine, St. John's, NL A1C 5S7, Canada. Offers M Sc, PhD, Diploma, MD/PhD. Part-time programs available. *Degree requirements:* For master's, thesis; for doctorate, comprehensive exam, thesis/dissertation, oral defense of thesis. *Entrance requirements:* For master's, MD or B Sc; for doctorate, MD or M Sc; for Diploma, bachelor's degree in health-related field. Additional exam requirements/recommendations for international students: Required—TOEFL (minimum score 550 paper-based; 213 computer-based). Electronic applications accepted. *Faculty research:* Human genetics, community health, clinical epidemial, cancer, immunology, cardiovascular and immol sciences, applied health services research, neuroscience.

Memorial University of Newfoundland, School of Graduate Studies, Department of Biology, St. John's, NL A1C 5S7, Canada. Offers biology (M Sc, PhD); marine biology (M Sc, PhD). Part-time programs available. *Degree requirements:* For master's, thesis; for doctorate, comprehensive exam, thesis/dissertation, oral defense of thesis. *Entrance requirements:* For master's, honors degree (minimum 2nd class standing) in related field. Electronic applications accepted. *Faculty research:* Northern flora and fauna, especially cold ocean and boreal environments.

Michigan State University, College of Human Medicine and The Graduate School, Graduate Programs in Human Medicine, East Lansing, MI 48824. Offers biochemistry and molecular biology (MS, PhD); epidemiology (MS, PhD); microbiology (MS); microbiology and molecular genetics (PhD); pharmacology and toxicology (MS, PhD); physiology (MS, PhD); public health (MPH). *Entrance requirements:* Additional exam requirements/recommendations for international students: Required—TOEFL.

Michigan State University, College of Osteopathic Medicine and The Graduate School, Graduate Studies in Osteopathic Medicine, East Lansing, MI 48824. Offers biochemistry and molecular biology (MS, PhD); microbiology (MS); microbiology and molecular genetics (PhD); pharmacology and toxicology (MS, PhD), including integrative pharmacology (MS), pharmacology and toxicology, pharmacology and toxicology-environmental toxicology (PhD); physiology (MS, PhD).

Michigan State University, College of Veterinary Medicine and The Graduate School, Graduate Programs in Veterinary Medicine, Program in Comparative Medicine and Integrative Biology, East Lansing, MI 48824. Offers comparative medicine and integrative biology (MS, PhD); comparative medicine and integrative biology–environmental toxicology (PhD). *Entrance requirements:* Additional exam requirements/recommendations for international students: Required—TOEFL. Electronic applications accepted.

Michigan Technological University, Graduate School, College of Sciences and Arts, Department of Biological Sciences, Houghton, MI 49931. Offers MS, PhD. Part-time programs available. Terminal master's awarded for partial completion of doctoral program. *Degree requirements:* For master's, comprehensive exam (for some programs), thesis; for doctorate, comprehensive exam, thesis/dissertation. *Entrance requirements:* For master's and doctorate, GRE. Additional exam requirements/recommendations for international students: Required—TOEFL (minimum score 550 paper-based; 213 computer-based). Electronic applications accepted. *Faculty research:* Aquatic ecology, biological control, predator-prey interactions, environmental microbiology, microbial and plant biochemistry, genomics and bioinformatics.

Middle Tennessee State University, College of Graduate Studies, College of Basic and Applied Sciences, Department of Biology, Murfreesboro, TN 37132. Offers MS. Part-time and evening/weekend programs available. Postbaccalaureate distance learning degree programs offered. *Faculty:* 23 full-time (7 women). *Students:* 3 full-time (1 woman), 65 part-time (29 women); includes 2 Black or African American, non-Hispanic/Latino; 1 American Indian or Alaska Native, non-Hispanic/Latino; 3 Asian, non-Hispanic/Latino; 3 Hispanic/Latino; 2 Two or more races, non-Hispanic/Latino. Average age 30. 43 applicants, 67% accepted, 29 enrolled. In 2010, 12 master's awarded. *Degree requirements:* For master's, one foreign language, comprehensive exam, thesis. *Entrance requirements:* For master's, GRE or MAT. Additional exam requirements/recommendations for international students: Required—TOEFL (minimum score 525 paper-based; 195 computer-based; 71 iBT) or IELTS (minimum score 6). *Application deadline:* For fall admission, 6/1 for domestic and international students. Applications are processed on a rolling basis. Application fee: $25 ($30 for international students). Electronic applications accepted. *Expenses:* Tuition, state resident: full-time $4632. Tuition, nonresident: full-time $11,520. *Financial support:* In 2010–11, 30 students received support. Institutionally sponsored loans available. Support available to part-time students. Financial award application deadline: 5/1; financial award applicants required to submit FAFSA. *Unit head:* Dr. George Murphy, Chair, 615-898-2847, E-mail: gmurphy@mtsu.edu. *Application contact:* Dr. Michael Allen, Dean and Vice Provost for Research, 615-898-2840, Fax: 615-904-8020, E-mail: mallen@mtsu.edu.

Midwestern State University, Graduate Studies, College of Science and Mathematics, Program in Biology, Wichita Falls, TX 76308. Offers MS. Part-time and evening/weekend programs available. *Faculty:* 7 full-time (1 woman), 1 part-time/adjunct (0 women). *Students:* 2 full-time (1 woman), 22 part-time (14 women); includes 1 American Indian or Alaska Native, non-Hispanic/Latino; 1 Asian, non-Hispanic/Latino, 8 international. Average age 27. In 2010, 5 master's awarded. *Degree requirements:* For master's, comprehensive exam, thesis. *Entrance requirements:* For master's, GRE General Test, MAT or GMAT. Additional exam requirements/recommendations for international students: Required—TOEFL (minimum score 550 paper-based; 213 computer-based). *Application deadline:* For fall admission, 7/1 priority date for domestic students, 4/1 for international students; for spring admission, 11/1 priority date for domestic students, 8/1 for international students. Applications are processed on a rolling basis. Application fee: $35 ($50 for international students). Electronic applications accepted. *Expenses:* Tuition, state resident: full-time $1620; part-time $90 per credit hour. Tuition, nonresident: full-time $2160; part-time $120 per credit hour. International tuition: $7200 full-time. *Financial support:* In 2010–11, 11 students received support, including 3 teaching assistantships with partial tuition reimbursements available (averaging $7,500 per year); career-related internships or fieldwork, Federal Work-Study, institutionally sponsored loans, scholarships/grants, tuition waivers (partial), and unspecified assistantships also available. Support available to part-time students. Financial award application deadline: 3/1; financial award applicants required to submit FAFSA. *Faculty research:* Molecular analysis of flora and fauna, mineral toxicity in plants, embryonic patterning and cell signaling, animal physiology, mammalogy. *Unit head:* Dr. Magaly Rincon-Zachary, Graduate Coordinator, 940-397-4254, E-mail: magaly.rincon@mwsu.edu. *Application contact:* 800-842-1922, Fax: 940-397-4672, E-mail: admissions@mwsu.edu.

Midwestern University, Downers Grove Campus, College of Health Sciences, Illinois Campus, Program in Biomedical Sciences, Downers Grove, IL 60515-1235. Offers MBS. Part-time programs available. *Faculty:* 1 (woman) full-time. *Students:* 40 full-time (21 women), 18 part-time (13 women); includes 1 Black or African American, non-Hispanic/Latino; 2 Asian, non-Hispanic/Latino; 1 Hispanic/Latino, 1 international. Average age 25. 178 applicants, 63% accepted, 32 enrolled. In 2010, 13 master's awarded. *Entrance requirements:* For master's, GRE General Test, MCAT or PCAT, 2 letters of recommendation. *Application deadline:* Applications are processed on a rolling basis. Application fee: $50. *Unit head:* Dr. Michael Fay, Director, 630-515-6382. *Application contact:* Michael Laken, Director of Admissions, 630-515-6171, Fax: 630-971-6086, E-mail: admissil@midwestern.edu.

Midwestern University, Glendale Campus, College of Health Sciences, Arizona Campus, Program in Biomedical Sciences, Glendale, AZ 85308. Offers MBS. *Faculty:* 9 full-time (3 women). *Students:* 31 full-time (19 women), 2 part-time (both women); includes 4 Black or African American, non-Hispanic/Latino; 7 Asian, non-Hispanic/Latino; 2 Hispanic/Latino. Average age 25. 232 applicants, 54% accepted. In 2010, 9 master's awarded. Application fee: $50. *Expenses:* Contact institution. *Unit head:* Dr. William P. Baker, Director, 623-572-3666. *Application contact:* James Walter, Director of Admissions, 888-247-9277, Fax: 623-572-3229, E-mail: admissaz@midwestern.edu.

Midwestern University, Glendale Campus, College of Health Sciences, Arizona Campus, Program in Biomedical Sciences, Master of Arts, Glendale, AZ 85308. Offers MA. *Faculty:* 6 full-time (2 women). *Students:* 75 full-time (35 women), 1 part-time (0 women); includes 3 Black or African American, non-Hispanic/Latino; 1 American Indian or Alaska Native, non-Hispanic/Latino; 17 Asian, non-Hispanic/Latino; 4 Hispanic/Latino, 1 international. Average age 25. *Entrance requirements:* For master's, GRE General Test, MCAT, or other professional exam, bachelor's degree, minimum cumulative GPA of 2.75. *Unit head:* Leonard Bell, Program Director, 623-572-3622, Fax: 623-572-3647, E-mail: lbellx@midwestern.edu. *Application contact:* James Walter, Director of Admissions, 888-247-9277, Fax: 623-572-3229, E-mail: admissaz@midwestern.edu.

Mills College, Graduate Studies, Pre-Medical Studies Program, Oakland, CA 94613-1000. Offers Certificate. Part-time programs available. *Faculty:* 10 full-time (6 women), 10 part-time/adjunct (6 women). *Students:* 71 full-time (48 women), 2 part-time (1 woman); includes 1 American Indian or Alaska Native, non-Hispanic/Latino; 5 Asian, non-Hispanic/Latino; 2 Hispanic/Latino; 4 Two or more races, non-Hispanic/Latino. Average age 26. 157 applicants, 63% accepted, 57 enrolled. In 2010, 27 Certificates awarded. *Entrance requirements:* For degree, GRE General Test, bachelor's degree in a non-science area. Additional exam requirements/recommendations for international students: Required—TOEFL. *Application deadline:* For fall admission, 2/1 priority date for domestic students, 12/15 for international students. Applications are processed on a rolling basis. Application fee: $50. Electronic applications accepted. *Expenses:* Tuition: Full-time $28,280; part-time $7070 per course. Required fees: $1058; $1058 per year. Tuition and fees vary according to program. *Financial support:* In 2010–11, 66 students received support, including 31 fellowships (averaging $5,884 per year), 10 teaching assistantships with partial tuition reimbursements available (averaging $6,490 per year); institutionally sponsored loans and scholarships/grants also available. Support available to part-time students. Financial award application deadline: 2/1; financial award applicants required to submit FAFSA. *Faculty research:* Cell-cell and cell-extracellular matrix interactions, physiology and molecular biology of plants and photosynthetic bacteria, molecular spectroscopy, aleoceanography, antifungal compounds and their modes of action. *Unit head:* Dr. John Brabson, Head, 510-430-2203, Fax: 510-430-3314, E-mail: johnb@mills.edu. *Application contact:* Jessica King, Graduate Admission Specialist, 510-430-3305, Fax: 510-430-2159, E-mail: grad-studies@mills.edu.

Minnesota State University Mankato, College of Graduate Studies, College of Science, Engineering and Technology, Department of Biological Sciences, Mankato, MN 56001. Offers biology (MS); biology education (MS); environmental sciences (MS). Part-time programs available. *Students:* 14 full-time (9 women), 33 part-time (11 women). *Degree requirements:* For master's, one foreign language, comprehensive exam, thesis or alternative. *Entrance requirements:* For master's, minimum GPA of 3.0 during previous 2 years of course work. Additional exam requirements/recommendations for international students: Required—TOEFL. *Application deadline:* For fall admission, 7/1 priority date for domestic students; for spring admission, 11/1 for domestic students. Applications are processed on a rolling basis. Application fee: $40. Electronic applications accepted. *Financial support:* Fellowships, research assistantships with full tuition reimbursements, teaching assistantships with full tuition reimbursements, career-related internships or fieldwork, Federal Work-Study, institutionally sponsored loans, and unspecified assistantships also available. Support available to part-time students. Financial award application deadline: 3/15; financial award applicants required to submit FAFSA. *Faculty research:* Limnology, enzyme analysis, membrane engineering, converters. *Unit head:* Dr. Penny Knoblich, Graduate Coordinator, 507-389-5736. *Application contact:* 507-389-2321, E-mail: grad@mnsu.edu.

Mississippi College, Graduate School, College of Arts and Sciences, School of Science and Mathematics, Department of Biological Sciences, Clinton, MS 39058. Offers biological science (M Ed); biology (MCS); biology-biological sciences (MS); biology-medical sciences (MS). Part-time programs available. *Degree requirements:* For master's, comprehensive exam, thesis optional. *Entrance requirements:* For master's, GRE General Test, minimum GPA of 2.5. Additional exam requirements/recommendations for international students: Recommended—IELTS. Electronic applications accepted.

Mississippi State University, College of Arts and Sciences, Department of Biological Sciences, Mississippi State, MS 39762. Offers biological sciences (MS, PhD); general biology (MS); interdisciplinary sciences (MA), including biological sciences. MS (general biology), MA only offered online. Postbaccalaureate distance learning degree programs offered (minimal on-campus study). *Faculty:* 14 full-time (8 women), 1 part-time/adjunct (0 women). *Students:*

34 full-time (20 women), 135 part-time (100 women); includes 21 minority (14 Black or African American, non-Hispanic/Latino; 2 Asian, non-Hispanic/Latino; 2 Hispanic/Latino; 3 Two or more races, non-Hispanic/Latino; 12 international. Average age 33. 134 applicants, 69% accepted, 76 enrolled. In 2010, 25 master's, 3 doctorates awarded. Terminal master's awarded for partial completion of doctoral program. *Degree requirements:* For master's, one foreign language, thesis, comprehensive oral or written exam; for doctorate, one foreign language, thesis/dissertation, comprehensive oral or written exam. *Entrance requirements:* For master's, GRE General Test, minimum GPA of 2.75 on last two years of undergraduate courses; for doctorate, GRE General Test. Additional exam requirements/recommendations for international students: Required—TOEFL (minimum score 550 paper-based; 213 computer-based; 79 iBT). *Application deadline:* For fall admission, 7/1 for domestic students, 5/1 for international students; for spring admission, 11/1 for domestic students, 9/1 for international students. Applications are processed on a rolling basis. Application fee: $40. Electronic applications accepted. *Expenses:* Tuition, state resident: full-time $2731; part-time $304 per credit hour. Tuition, nonresident: full-time $6901; part-time $767 per credit hour. *Financial support:* In 2010–11, 3 research assistantships with full and partial tuition reimbursements (averaging $13,873 per year), 25 teaching assistantships with full and partial tuition reimbursements (averaging $14,491 per year) were awarded; Federal Work-Study, institutionally sponsored loans, scholarships/grants, and unspecified assistantships also available. Financial award applicants required to submit FAFSA. *Faculty research:* Botany, zoology, microbiology, ecology. Total annual research expenditures: $5 million. *Unit head:* Dr. Nancy Reichert, Professor/Head, 662-325-3483, Fax: 662-325-7939, E-mail: nreichert@biology.msstate.edu. *Application contact:* Dr. Gary Ervin, Associate Dean/Graduate Coordinator, 662-325-1203, Fax: 662-325-7939, E-mail: gervin@biology.msstate.edu.

Missouri State University, Graduate College, College of Natural and Applied Sciences, Department of Biology, Springfield, MO 65897. Offers biology (MS); natural and applied science (MNAS), including biology (MNAS, MS Ed); secondary education (MS Ed), including biology (MNAS, MS Ed). *Degree requirements:* For master's, comprehensive exam, thesis or alternative. *Entrance requirements:* For master's, GRE (MS, MNAS), 24 hours of course work in biology (MS); minimum GPA of 3.0 (MS, MNAS), 9-12 teacher certification (MS Ed). Additional exam requirements/recommendations for international students: Required—TOEFL (minimum score 550 paper-based; 213 computer-based; 79 iBT). Electronic applications accepted. *Expenses:* Tuition, state resident: full-time $3348; part-time $186 per credit hour. Tuition, nonresident: full-time $6696; part-time $372 per credit hour. Required fees: $238 per semester. Tuition and fees vary according to course level, course load and program. *Faculty research:* Hibernation physiology of bats, behavioral ecology of salamanders, mussel conservation, plant evolution and systematics, cellular/molecular mechanisms involved in migraine pathology.

Missouri University of Science and Technology, Graduate School, Department of Biological Sciences, Rolla, MO 65409. Offers applied and environmental biology (MS). *Entrance requirements:* For master's, GRE (minimum score 600 quantitative, 4 writing). Additional exam requirements/recommendations for international students: Required—TOEFL (minimum score 570 paper-based; 230 computer-based).

Montana State University, College of Graduate Studies, College of Letters and Science, Department of Cell Biology and Neuroscience, Bozeman, MT 59717. Offers biological sciences (PhD); neuroscience (MS, PhD). Part-time programs available. *Faculty:* 7 full-time (2 women), 2 part-time/adjunct (1 woman). *Students:* 4 part-time (1 woman). Average age 28. 3 applicants, 0% accepted, 0 enrolled. *Degree requirements:* For master's, comprehensive exam; for doctorate, comprehensive exam, thesis/dissertation. *Entrance requirements:* For master's and doctorate, GRE General Test. Additional exam requirements/recommendations for international students: Required—TOEFL (minimum score 550 paper-based; 213 computer-based). *Application deadline:* For fall admission, 7/15 priority date for domestic students, 5/15 priority date for international students; for spring admission, 12/1 priority date for domestic

students, 10/1 priority date for international students. Applications are processed on a rolling basis. Application fee: $30. Electronic applications accepted. *Expenses:* Tuition, state resident: full-time $5554. Tuition, nonresident: full-time $14,646. Required fees: $1233. *Financial support:* In 2010–11, 8 teaching assistantships (averaging $10,500 per year) were awarded; health care benefits and unspecified assistantships also available. Financial award application deadline: 3/1; financial award applicants required to submit FAFSA. *Faculty research:* Development of the nervous system, neuronal mechanisms of visual perception, ion channel biophysics, mechanisms of sensory coding, neuroinformatics. Total annual research expenditures: $3.4 million. *Unit head:* Dr. Thomas Hughes, Head, 406-994-5395, Fax: 406-994-7077, E-mail: thughes@montana.edu. *Application contact:* Dr. Carl A. Fox, Vice Provost for Graduate Education, 406-994-4145, Fax: 406-994-7433, E-mail: gradstudy@montana.edu.

Montclair State University, The Graduate School, College of Science and Mathematics, Department of Biology and Molecular Biology, Montclair, NJ 07043-1624. Offers biological science (Certificate); biology (MS), including biology, biology science/education, ecology and evolution, physiology; molecular biology (MS, Certificate). Part-time and evening/weekend programs available. *Faculty:* 22 full-time (9 women), 26 part-time/adjunct (13 women). *Students:* 30 full-time (20 women), 73 part-time (55 women); includes 5 Black or African American, non-Hispanic/Latino; 6 Asian, non-Hispanic/Latino; 25 Hispanic/Latino, 3 international. Average age 28. 48 applicants, 71% accepted, 24 enrolled. In 2010, 21 master's, 2 other advanced degrees awarded. *Degree requirements:* For master's, comprehensive exam, thesis or alternative. *Entrance requirements:* For master's, GRE General Test, 24 credits of course work in undergraduate biology, 2 letters of recommendation, teaching certificate (biology sciences education concentration). Additional exam requirements/recommendations for international students: Required—TOEFL (minimum iBT score of 83) or IELTS. *Application deadline:* For fall admission, 6/1 for international students; for spring admission, 10/1 for international students. Applications are processed on a rolling basis. Application fee: $60. Electronic applications accepted. *Expenses:* Tuition, state resident: part-time $501.34 per credit. Tuition, nonresident: part-time $773.88 per credit. Required fees: $71.15 per credit. *Financial support:* In 2010–11, 12 research assistantships with full tuition reimbursements (averaging $7,000 per year) were awarded; Federal Work-Study, scholarships/grants, and unspecified assistantships also available. Support available to part-time students. Financial award application deadline: 3/1; financial award applicants required to submit FAFSA. *Faculty research:* Cells, algae blooms, scallops, New Jersey bays, Barnegat Bay. Total annual research expenditures: $1.3 million. *Unit head:* Dr. Quinn Vega, Chairperson, 973-655-7178. *Application contact:* Amy Aiello, Director of Graduate Admissions and Operations, 973-655-5147, Fax: 973-655-7869, E-mail: graduate.school@montclair.edu.

Morehead State University, Graduate Programs, College of Science and Technology, Department of Biology and Chemistry, Morehead, KY 40351. Offers biology (MS); biology regional analysis (MS). Part-time programs available. *Degree requirements:* For master's, comprehensive exam, thesis optional, oral and written final exams. *Entrance requirements:* For master's, GRE General Test, minimum GPA of 3.0 in biology, 2.5 overall; undergraduate major/minor in biology, environmental science, or equivalent. Additional exam requirements/recommendations for international students: Required—TOEFL (minimum score 525 paper-based; 210 computer-based). Electronic applications accepted. *Faculty research:* Atherosclerosis, RNA evolution, cancer biology, water quality/ecology, immunoparasitology.

Morehouse School of Medicine, Graduate Programs in Biomedical Sciences, Atlanta, GA 30310-1495. Offers biomedical research (MS); biomedical sciences (PhD); biomedical technology (MS). *Faculty:* 52 full-time (17 women), 7 part-time/adjunct (2 women). *Students:* 31 full-time (19 women); includes 18 Black or African American, non-Hispanic/Latino. Average age 28. 21 applicants, 38% accepted, 6 enrolled. In 2010, 3 doctorates awarded. *Degree requirements:* For master's, thesis (for some programs); for doctorate, thesis/dissertation. *Entrance requirements:* For doctorate, GRE General Test. Additional exam requirements/recommendations for international students: Required—TOEFL (minimum score 550 paper-based; 200 computer-

Biological and Biomedical Sciences—General

Morehouse School of Medicine (continued)
based). *Application deadline:* For fall admission, 10/1 for domestic and international students; for spring admission, 2/1 for domestic and international students. Application fee: $50. Electronic applications accepted. *Expenses:* Contact institution. *Financial support:* Fellowships with full and partial tuition reimbursements, career-related internships or fieldwork, institutionally sponsored loans, scholarships/grants, traineeships, health care benefits, and tuition waivers (full) available. Financial award application deadline: 5/1; financial award applicants required to submit FAFSA. *Unit head:* Dr. Douglas Paulsen, Director, 404-752-1559. *Application contact:* Dr. Sterling Roaf, Director of Admissions, 404-752-1650, Fax: 404-752-1512, E-mail: phdadmissions@msm.edu.

See Display on previous page and Close-Up on page 101.

Morgan State University, School of Graduate Studies, School of Computer, Mathematical, and Natural Sciences, Department of Biology, Baltimore, MD 21251. Offers bioenvironmental science (PhD); biology (MS). *Degree requirements:* For master's, comprehensive exam, thesis. *Entrance requirements:* For master's, minimum GPA of 3.0.

Mount Allison University, Department of Biology, Sackville, NB E4L 1E4, Canada. Offers M Sc. *Degree requirements:* For master's, thesis. *Entrance requirements:* For master's, honors degree. *Faculty research:* Ecology, evolution, physiology, behavior, biochemistry.

Mount Sinai School of Medicine, Graduate School of Biological Sciences, New York, NY 10029-6504. Offers biomedical sciences (MS, PhD); clinical research education (MS, PhD); community medicine (MPH); genetic counseling (MS); neurosciences (PhD); MD/PhD. *Faculty:* 126 full-time (40 women). *Students:* 438 full-time (260 women); includes 29 Black or African American, non-Hispanic/Latino; 3 American Indian or Alaska Native, non-Hispanic/Latino; 86 Asian, non-Hispanic/Latino; 18 Hispanic/Latino, 99 international. 924 applicants, 29% accepted, 104 enrolled. In 2010, 58 master's, 36 doctorates awarded. Terminal master's awarded for partial completion of doctoral program. *Degree requirements:* For master's, thesis; for doctorate, comprehensive exam, thesis/dissertation. *Entrance requirements:* For master's, GRE General Test; for doctorate, GRE General Test, GRE Subject Test, 3 years of college pre-med course work. Additional exam requirements/recommendations for international students: Required—TOEFL. *Application deadline:* For fall admission, 12/15 for domestic and international students. Applications are processed on a rolling basis. Application fee: $80. Electronic applications accepted. *Expenses:* Tuition: Full-time $25,600; part-time $800 per credit hour. Required fees: $1600. Full-time tuition and fees vary according to program. *Financial support:* In 2010–11, fellowships with full tuition reimbursements (averaging $32,000 per year), research assistantships with full tuition reimbursements (averaging $32,000 per year) were awarded; Federal Work-Study, institutionally sponsored loans, scholarships/grants, health care benefits, and unspecified assistantships also available. Financial award application deadline: 4/30; financial award applicants required to submit FAFSA. *Faculty research:* Cancer, genetics and genomics, immunology, neuroscience, developmental and stem cell biology, translational research. Total annual research expenditures: $264.9 million. *Unit head:* Dr. John Morrison, Dean, 212-241-6546, Fax: 212-241-0651, E-mail: john.morrison@mssm.edu. *Application contact:* Lily Recanati, Manager, 212-241-2793, Fax: 212-241-0651, E-mail: lily.recantati@mssm.edu.

Murray State University, College of Science, Engineering and Technology, Program in Biological Sciences, Murray, KY 42071. Offers MAT, MS, PhD. PhD offered jointly with University of Louisville. Part-time programs available. *Degree requirements:* For master's, comprehensive exam, thesis optional. *Entrance requirements:* For master's, GRE General Test. Additional exam requirements/recommendations for international students: Required—TOEFL. *Faculty research:* Aquatic and terrestrial ecology, molecular systematics, micro ecology, cell biology and metabolism, palentology.

New Jersey Institute of Technology, Office of Graduate Studies, College of Science and Liberal Arts, Federated Department of Biological Sciences, Program in Biology, Newark, NJ 07102. Offers MS, PhD. Part-time and evening/weekend programs available. *Faculty:* 5 full-time (1 woman). *Students:* 12 full-time (7 women), 2 part-time (both women); includes 1 Black or African American, non-Hispanic/Latino; 2 Asian, non-Hispanic/Latino, 7 international. Average age 26. 78 applicants, 26% accepted, 4 enrolled. In 2010, 2 master's, 1 doctorate awarded. *Entrance requirements:* For master's, GRE General Test. Additional exam requirements/recommendations for international students: Required—TOEFL (minimum score 550 paper-based; 213 computer-based; 79 iBT). *Application deadline:* For fall admission, 6/5 priority date for domestic students, 4/1 for international students; for spring admission, 11/15 for domestic and international students. Applications are processed on a rolling basis. Application fee: $65. Electronic applications accepted. *Expenses:* Tuition, state resident: full-time $14,724; part-time $818 per credit. Tuition, nonresident: full-time $20,304; part-time $1128 per credit. Required fees: $2272; $209 per credit. $103 per semester. One-time fee: $312 full-time; $212 part-time. *Financial support:* Fellowships with full and partial tuition reimbursements, research assistantships with full and partial tuition reimbursements, teaching assistantships with full and partial tuition reimbursements, career-related internships or fieldwork, Federal Work-Study, institutionally sponsored loans, and unspecified assistantships available. Financial award application deadline: 3/15. *Faculty research:* Realistic building codes, optimization of training programs, effect of physical and mental fatigue of training. *Unit head:* Dr. Karen Roach, Academic Coordinator, 973-596-5612, E-mail: karen.roach@njit.edu. *Application contact:* Kathryn Kelly, Director of Admissions, 973-596-3300, Fax: 973-596-3461, E-mail: admissions@njit.edu.

New Mexico Institute of Mining and Technology, Graduate Studies, Department of Biology, Socorro, NM 87801. Offers MS. Part-time programs available. *Degree requirements:* For master's, thesis. *Entrance requirements:* For master's, GRE General Test. Additional exam requirements/recommendations for international students: Required—TOEFL (minimum score 540 paper-based; 207 computer-based). Electronic applications accepted. *Faculty research:* Molecular biology, evolution and evolutionary ecology, immunology, endocrinology.

New Mexico State University, Graduate School, College of Agricultural, Consumer and Environmental Sciences, Department of Animal and Range Sciences, Las Cruces, NM 88003-8001. Offers animal science (MS, PhD); domestic animal biology (M Ag); range science (M Ag, MS, PhD). Part-time programs available. *Faculty:* 9 full-time (2 women). *Students:* 36 full-time (23 women), 9 part-time (2 women); includes 6 minority (1 American Indian or Alaska Native, non-Hispanic/Latino; 4 Hispanic/Latino; 1 Two or more races, non-Hispanic/Latino), 7 international. Average age 27. 27 applicants, 81% accepted, 16 enrolled. In 2010, 11 master's, 2 doctorates awarded. Terminal master's awarded for partial completion of doctoral program. *Degree requirements:* For master's, thesis, seminar, experimental statistics; for doctorate, thesis/dissertation, research tool. *Entrance requirements:* For master's, minimum GPA of 3.0 in last 60 hours of undergraduate course work (MS); for doctorate, minimum graduate GPA of 3.2. Additional exam requirements/recommendations for international students: Required—TOEFL (minimum score 530 paper-based; 71 computer-based), IELTS (minimum score 6). *Application deadline:* For fall admission, 7/1 priority date for domestic students, 7/1 for international students; for spring admission, 11/1 for domestic and international students. Applications are processed on a rolling basis. Application fee: $30 ($50 for international students). Electronic applications accepted. *Expenses:* Tuition, state resident: full-time $4536; part-time $242 per credit. Tuition, nonresident: full-time $15,816; part-time $712 per credit. Required fees: $636 per term. *Financial support:* In 2010–11, 25 students received support, including 3 research assistantships (averaging $12,823 per year), 24 teaching assistantships (averaging $20,008 per year); Federal Work-Study and health care benefits also available. Support available to part-time students. Financial award application deadline: 3/1. *Faculty research:* Reproductive physiology, ruminant nutrition, nutrition toxicology, range ecology, wildland hydrology. *Unit head:* Dr. Tim Ross, Interim Head, 575-646-2514, Fax: 575-646-5441, E-mail: tross@nmsu.edu. *Application contact:* Dr. Tim Ross, Interim Head, 575-646-2514, Fax: 575-646-5441, E-mail: tross@nmsu.edu.

New Mexico State University, Graduate School, College of Arts and Sciences, Department of Biology, Las Cruces, NM 88003-8001. Offers biology (MS, PhD); biotechnology and business (MS). Part-time programs available. *Faculty:* 25 full-time (10 women). *Students:* 70 full-time (46 women), 12 part-time (8 women); includes 20 minority (3 Black or African American, non-Hispanic/Latino; 1 American Indian or Alaska Native, non-Hispanic/Latino; 16 Hispanic/Latino), 24 international. Average age 30. 71 applicants, 86% accepted, 25 enrolled. In 2010, 13 master's, 10 doctorates awarded. *Degree requirements:* For master's, thesis (for some programs), defense or oral exam; for doctorate, comprehensive exam, thesis/dissertation, qualifying exam, defense. *Entrance requirements:* Additional exam requirements/recommendations for international students: Required—TOEFL. *Application deadline:* For fall admission, 1/15 priority date for domestic students, 1/15 for international students; for spring admission, 10/4 priority date for domestic students, 10/4 for international students. Applications are processed on a rolling basis. Application fee: $30 ($50 for international students). Electronic applications accepted. *Expenses:* Tuition, state resident: full-time $4536; part-time $242 per credit. Tuition, nonresident: full-time $15,816; part-time $712 per credit. Required fees: $636 per term. *Financial support:* In 2010–11, 21 research assistantships (averaging $16,987 per year), 33 teaching assistantships (averaging $10,202 per year) were awarded; fellowships, Federal Work-Study and health care benefits also available. Support available to part-time students. Financial award application deadline: 1/15. *Faculty research:* Microbiology, cell and organismal physiology, ecology and ethology, evolution, genetics, developmental biology. *Unit head:* Dr. Michele Nishiguchi, Head, 575-646-3611, Fax: 575-646-5665, E-mail: nish@nmsu.edu. *Application contact:* Gloria Valencia, Administration Assistant, 575-646-3611, Fax: 575-646-5665, E-mail: gvalenci@nmsu.edu.

New York Medical College, Graduate School of Basic Medical Sciences, Valhalla, NY 10595-1691. Offers MS, PhD, MD/PhD. Part-time and evening/weekend programs available. *Faculty:* 91 full-time (18 women), 5 part-time/adjunct (4 women). *Students:* 170 full-time (90 women), 6 part-time (4 women); includes 92 minority (13 Black or African American, non-Hispanic/Latino; 1 American Indian or Alaska Native, non-Hispanic/Latino; 67 Asian, non-Hispanic/Latino; 11 Hispanic/Latino). Average age 26. 500 applicants, 47% accepted, 77 enrolled. In 2010, 50 master's, 8 doctorates awarded. Terminal master's awarded for partial completion of doctoral program. *Degree requirements:* For master's, thesis; for doctorate, comprehensive exam, thesis/dissertation. *Entrance requirements:* For master's and doctorate, GRE General Test. Additional exam requirements/recommendations for international students: Required—TOEFL. *Application deadline:* For fall admission, 7/1 priority date for domestic students, 5/1 priority date for international students; for spring admission, 12/1 priority date for domestic students, 10/1 priority date for international students. Applications are processed on a rolling basis. Application fee: $50 ($75 for international students). Electronic applications accepted. *Financial support:* In 2010–11, 53 research assistantships with full tuition reimbursements (averaging $24,000 per year) were awarded; Federal Work-Study, institutionally sponsored loans, scholarships/grants, tuition waivers (full), and health benefits (for PhD candidates only) also available. Financial award applicants required to submit FAFSA. *Unit head:* Dr. Francis L. Belloni, Dean, 914-594-4110, Fax: 914-594-4944, E-mail: francis_belloni@nymc.edu. *Application contact:* Valerie Romeo-Messana, Admission Coordinator, 914-594-4110, Fax: 914-594-4944, E-mail: v_romeomessana@nymc.edu.

See Display on next page and Close-Up on page 103.

New York University, Graduate School of Arts and Science, Department of Biology, New York, NY 10012-1019. Offers biology (PhD); biomedical journalism (MS); cancer and molecular biology (PhD); computational biology (PhD); computers in biological research (MS); developmental genetics (PhD); general biology (MS); immunology and microbiology (PhD); molecular genetics (PhD); neurobiology (PhD); oral biology (MS); plant biology (PhD); recombinant DNA technology (MS); MS/MBA. Part-time programs available. *Faculty:* 24 full-time (5 women). *Students:* 155 full-time (89 women), 38 part-time (24 women); includes 29 Asian, non-Hispanic/Latino; 7 Hispanic/Latino, 88 international. Average age 27. 324 applicants, 69% accepted, 63 enrolled. In 2010, 55 master's, 4 doctorates awarded. Terminal master's awarded for partial completion of doctoral program. *Degree requirements:* For master's, thesis or alternative, qualifying paper; for doctorate, comprehensive exam, thesis/dissertation. *Entrance requirements:* For master's, GRE General Test; for doctorate, GRE General Test, GRE Subject Test. Additional exam requirements/recommendations for international students: Required—TOEFL. *Application deadline:* For fall admission, 12/15 priority date for domestic students. Application fee: $90. *Financial support:* Fellowships with tuition reimbursements, research assistantships with tuition reimbursements, teaching assistantships with tuition reimbursements, career-related internships or fieldwork, Federal Work-Study, institutionally sponsored loans, scholarships/grants, health care benefits, and unspecified assistantships available. Financial award application deadline: 12/15; financial award applicants required to submit FAFSA. *Faculty research:* Genomics, molecular and cell biology, development and molecular genetics, molecular evolution of plants and animals. *Unit head:* Gloria Coruzzi, Chair, 212-998-8200, Fax: 212-995-4015, E-mail: biology@nyu.edu. *Application contact:* Justin Blau, Director of Graduate Studies, 212-998-8200, Fax: 212-995-4015, E-mail: biology@nyu.edu.

New York University, Graduate School of Arts and Science, Department of Environmental Medicine, New York, NY 10012-1019. Offers environmental health sciences (MS, PhD), including biostatistics (PhD), environmental hygiene (MS), epidemiology (PhD), ergonomics and biomechanics (PhD), exposure assessment and health effects (PhD), molecular toxicology/carcinogenesis (PhD), toxicology. Part-time programs available. *Faculty:* 26 full-time (7 women). *Students:* 53 full-time (38 women), 10 part-time (3 women); includes 3 Black or African American, non-Hispanic/Latino; 4 Asian, non-Hispanic/Latino; 5 Hispanic/Latino, 23 international. Average age 30. 60 applicants, 48% accepted, 14 enrolled. In 2010, 8 master's, 5 doctorates awarded. Terminal master's awarded for partial completion of doctoral program. *Degree requirements:* For master's, thesis or alternative; for doctorate, one foreign language, thesis/dissertation, oral and written exams. *Entrance requirements:* For master's and doctorate, GRE General Test, GRE Subject Test, minimum GPA of 3.0; bachelor's degree in biological, physical, or engineering science. Additional exam requirements/recommendations for international students: Required—TOEFL. *Application deadline:* For fall admission, 12/15 for domestic students. Application fee: $90. *Financial support:* Fellowships with tuition reimbursements, teaching assistantships with tuition reimbursements, career-related internships or fieldwork, Federal Work-Study, institutionally sponsored loans, and health care benefits available. Financial award application deadline: 12/15; financial award applicants required to submit FAFSA. *Unit head:* Dr. Max Costa, Chair, 845-731-3661, Fax: 845-351-4510, E-mail: ehs@env.med.nyu.edu. *Application contact:* Dr. Jerome J. Solomon, Director of Graduate Studies, 845-731-3661, Fax: 845-351-4510, E-mail: ehs@env.med.nyu.edu.

New York University, School of Medicine and Graduate School of Arts and Science, Medical Scientist Training Program, New York, NY 10012-1019. Offers MD/MS, MD/PhD. Students must be accepted by both the School of Medicine and the Graduate School of Arts and Science. Electronic applications accepted. *Expenses:* Contact institution. *Faculty research:* Neurosciences, cell biology and molecular genetics, structural biology, microbial pathogenesis and host defense.

North Carolina Agricultural and Technical State University, Graduate School, College of Arts and Sciences, Department of Biology, Greensboro, NC 27411. Offers biology (MS); biology education (MAT). Part-time and evening/weekend programs available. *Degree requirements:* For master's, comprehensive exam, thesis (for some programs), qualifying exam. *Entrance requirements:* For master's, GRE General Test, minimum GPA of 2.6. *Faculty research:* Physical ecology, cytochemistry, botany, parasitology, microbiology.

North Carolina Central University, Division of Academic Affairs, College of Science and Technology, Department of Biology, Durham, NC 27707-3129. Offers MS. *Degree requirements:* For master's, one foreign language, comprehensive exam, thesis. *Entrance requirements:* For master's, GRE, minimum GPA of 3.0 in major, 2.5 overall. Additional exam requirements/recommendations for international students: Required—TOEFL.

North Carolina State University, College of Veterinary Medicine, Program in Comparative Biomedical Sciences, Raleigh, NC 27695. Offers cell biology (MS, PhD); infectious disease

(MS, PhD); pathology (MS, PhD); pharmacology (MS, PhD); population medicine (MS, PhD). Part-time programs available. *Degree requirements:* For master's, thesis; for doctorate, thesis/dissertation. *Entrance requirements:* For master's and doctorate, GRE General Test. Additional exam requirements/recommendations for international students: Required—TOEFL (minimum score 550 paper-based; 213 computer-based). Electronic applications accepted. *Expenses:* Contact institution. *Faculty research:* Infectious diseases, cell biology, pharmacology and toxicology, genomics, pathology and population medicine.

North Carolina State University, Graduate School, College of Agriculture and Life Sciences, Raleigh, NC 27695. Offers M Tox, MAE, MB, MBAE, MFG, MFM, MFS, MG, MMB, MN, MP, MS, MZS, Ed D, PhD, Certificate. Part-time programs available. Electronic applications accepted.

North Dakota State University, College of Graduate and Interdisciplinary Studies, College of Science and Mathematics, Department of Biological Sciences, Fargo, ND 58108. Offers biology (MS); botany (MS, PhD); cellular and molecular biology (PhD); environmental and conservation sciences (MS, PhD); genomics (PhD); natural resources management (MS, PhD); zoology (MS, PhD). *Students:* 18 full-time (8 women), 5 part-time (3 women); includes 2 American Indian or Alaska Native, non-Hispanic/Latino, 2 international. 17 applicants, 35% accepted. In 2010, 12 master's, 9 doctorates awarded. *Degree requirements:* For master's, thesis; for doctorate, thesis/dissertation. *Entrance requirements:* For master's and doctorate, GRE General Test. Additional exam requirements/recommendations for international students: Required—TOEFL. *Application deadline:* For fall admission, 3/15 priority date for domestic students; for spring admission, 10/30 priority date for domestic students. Applications are processed on a rolling basis. Application fee: $45 ($60 for international students). Electronic applications accepted. *Financial support:* Fellowships with full tuition reimbursements, research assistantships with full tuition reimbursements, teaching assistantships with full tuition reimbursements, career-related internships or fieldwork, Federal Work-Study, institutionally sponsored loans, scholarships/grants, tuition waivers (full), and unspecified assistantships available. Support available to part-time students. Financial award application deadline: 4/15; financial award applicants required to submit FAFSA. *Faculty research:* Comparative endocrinology, physiology, behavioral ecology, plant cell biology, aquatic biology. Total annual research expenditures: $675,000. *Unit head:* Dr. Marinus L. Otte, Head, 701-231-7087, E-mail: marinus.otte@ndsu.edu. *Application contact:* Dr. Marinus L. Otte, Head, 701-231-7087, E-mail: marinus.otte@ndsu.edu.

Northeastern Illinois University, Graduate College, College of Arts and Sciences, Department of Biology, Program in Biology, Chicago, IL 60625-4699. Offers MS. Part-time and evening/weekend programs available. *Faculty:* 11 full-time (3 women), 3 part-time/adjunct (2 women). *Students:* 7 full-time (4 women), 29 part-time (16 women); includes 9 minority (7 Asian, non-Hispanic/Latino; 2 Hispanic/Latino), 4 international. Average age 30. 25 applicants, 80% accepted. In 2010, 7 master's awarded. *Degree requirements:* For master's, comprehensive exam, thesis optional. *Entrance requirements:* For master's, minimum GPA of 2.75. Additional exam requirements/recommendations for international students: Required—TOEFL (minimum score 550 paper-based; 213 computer-based; 79 iBT). *Application deadline:* For fall admission, 4/1 priority date for domestic students; for spring admission, 8/15 for domestic students. Applications are processed on a rolling basis. Application fee: $30. Electronic applications accepted. *Financial support:* In 2010–11, 18 students received support, including 10 research assistantships with full tuition reimbursements available (averaging $6,600 per year); career-related internships or fieldwork, Federal Work-Study, institutionally sponsored loans, scholarships/grants, tuition waivers (full and partial), and unspecified assistantships also available. Support available to part-time students. Financial award applicants required to submit FAFSA. *Faculty research:* Paleoecology and freshwater biology, protein biosynthesis and targeting, microbial growth and physiology, molecular biology of antibody production, reptilian neurobiology. *Unit head:* Dr. John Kasmer, Department Chair. *Application contact:* Dr. John Kasmer, Department Chair.

Northeastern University, College of Science, Department of Biology, Boston, MA 02115-5096. Offers bioinformatics (PMS); biology (MS, PhD); biotechnology (MS, PSM); marine

biology (MS). Part-time programs available. *Faculty:* 27 full-time (10 women), 5 part-time/adjunct (all women). *Students:* 112 full-time (74 women), 4 part-time (2 women). 255 applicants, 73% accepted. In 2010, 21 master's, 5 doctorates awarded. Terminal master's awarded for partial completion of doctoral program. *Degree requirements:* For master's, thesis (for some programs); for doctorate, thesis/dissertation, qualifying exam. *Entrance requirements:* For master's and doctorate, GRE General Test. Additional exam requirements/recommendations for international students: Required—TOEFL (minimum score 250 computer-based). *Application deadline:* For fall admission, 1/1 priority date for domestic and international students. Applications are processed on a rolling basis. Application fee: $50. Electronic applications accepted. *Financial support:* In 2010–11, 19 research assistantships with tuition reimbursements (averaging $18,285 per year), 41 teaching assistantships with tuition reimbursements (averaging $18,285 per year) were awarded; fellowships with tuition reimbursements, career-related internships or fieldwork, Federal Work-Study, tuition waivers (full and partial), and unspecified assistantships also available. Financial award application deadline: 3/1; financial award applicants required to submit FAFSA. *Faculty research:* Biochemistry, marine sciences, molecular biology, microbiology and immunology neurobiology, cellular and molecular biology, biochemistry, marine biochemistry and ecology, microbiology, neurobiology, biotechnology. *Unit head:* Dr. Wendy Smith, Graduate Coordinator, 617-373-2260, Fax: 617-373-3724, E-mail: gradbio@neu.edu. *Application contact:* Jo-Anne Dickinson, Admissions Assistant, 617-373-5990, Fax: 617-373-7281, E-mail: gsas@neu.edu.

Northern Arizona University, Graduate College, College of Engineering, Forestry and Natural Sciences, Department of Biological Sciences, Flagstaff, AZ 86011. Offers MS, PhD. *Faculty:* 46 full-time (15 women). *Students:* 89 full-time (56 women), 14 part-time (8 women); includes 13 minority (3 American Indian or Alaska Native, non-Hispanic/Latino; 2 Asian, non-Hispanic/Latino; 6 Hispanic/Latino; 2 Two or more races, non-Hispanic/Latino), 5 international. Average age 30. 79 applicants, 35% accepted, 22 enrolled. In 2010, 17 master's, 4 doctorates awarded. *Degree requirements:* For master's, thesis, oral exam; for doctorate, thesis/dissertation. *Entrance requirements:* For master's and doctorate, GRE General Test. Additional exam requirements/recommendations for international students: Required—TOEFL (minimum score 550 paper-based; 213 computer-based; 80 iBT), IELTS (minimum score 7). *Application deadline:* For fall admission, 2/15 priority date for domestic and international students. Application fee: $65. Electronic applications accepted. *Financial support:* In 2010–11, 17 fellowships, 20 research assistantships with partial tuition reimbursements (averaging $21,271 per year), 32 teaching assistantships with partial tuition reimbursements (averaging $13,164 per year) were awarded; Federal Work-Study, scholarships/grants, traineeships, health care benefits, tuition waivers (full and partial), and unspecified assistantships also available. Financial award applicants required to submit FAFSA. *Faculty research:* Genetic levels of trophic levels, plant hybrid zones, insect biodiversity, natural history and cognition of wild jays. Total annual research expenditures: $2.2 million. *Unit head:* Dr. Maribeth Watwood, Chair, 928-523-9322, Fax: 928-523-7500, E-mail: maribeth.watwood@nau.edu. *Application contact:* Arline Lonon, Administrative Assistant, 928-523-7164, Fax: 928-523-7500, E-mail: arline.lonon@nau.edu.

Northern Illinois University, Graduate School, College of Liberal Arts and Sciences, Department of Biological Sciences, De Kalb, IL 60115-2854. Offers MS, PhD. Part-time programs available. *Faculty:* 30 full-time (6 women), 7 part-time/adjunct (1 woman). *Students:* 48 full-time (26 women), 40 part-time (28 women); includes 7 minority (1 American Indian or Alaska Native, non-Hispanic/Latino; 2 Asian, non-Hispanic/Latino; 3 Hispanic/Latino; 1 Two or more races, non-Hispanic/Latino), 14 international. Average age 31. 101 applicants, 42% accepted, 20 enrolled. In 2010, 11 master's, 5 doctorates awarded. Terminal master's awarded for partial completion of doctoral program. *Degree requirements:* For master's, comprehensive exam, thesis optional; for doctorate, thesis/dissertation, candidacy exam, dissertation defense. *Entrance requirements:* For master's, GRE General Test, bachelor's degree in related field, minimum GPA of 2.75; for doctorate, GRE General Test, bachelor's or master's degree in related field; minimum undergraduate GPA of 2.75, graduate 3.2. Additional exam requirements/recommendations for international students: Required—TOEFL (minimum score 550 paper-based; 213 computer-based). *Application deadline:* For fall admission, 6/1 for domestic students,

Biological and Biomedical Sciences—General

Northern Illinois University (continued)
5/1 for international students; for spring admission, 11/1 for domestic students, 10/1 for international students. Applications are processed on a rolling basis. Application fee: $30. Electronic applications accepted. *Expenses:* Tuition, state resident: full-time $7200; part-time $300 per credit hour. Tuition, nonresident: full-time $14,400; part-time $600 per credit hour. Required fees: $79 per credit hour. *Financial support:* In 2010–11, 6 research assistantships with full tuition reimbursements, 38 teaching assistantships with full tuition reimbursements were awarded; fellowships with full tuition reimbursements, career-related internships or fieldwork, Federal Work-Study, scholarships/grants, tuition waivers (full), and unspecified assistantships also available. Support available to part-time students. Financial award applicants required to submit FAFSA. *Faculty research:* Plant molecular biology, neurosecretory control, ethnobotany, organellar genomes, carbon metabolism. *Unit head:* Dr. Carl VanEnde, Acting Chair, 815-753-1753, Fax: 815-753-0461, E-mail: cvonende@niu.edu. *Application contact:* Dr. Carl von Ende, Director of Graduate Studies, 815-753-7826.

Northern Michigan University, College of Graduate Studies, College of Arts and Sciences, Department of Biology, Marquette, MI 49855-5301. Offers MS. Part-time programs available. Postbaccalaureate distance learning degree programs offered (minimal on-campus study). *Degree requirements:* For master's, thesis or alternative. *Entrance requirements:* For master's, GRE, minimum GPA of 3.0. *Faculty research:* Molecular genetics of sex-linked genes, biology of protozoan parasites, wildlife ecology, organochlorines in the environment, insect development.

Northwestern University, The Graduate School, Interdepartmental Biological Sciences Program (IBiS), Evanston, IL 60208. Offers biochemistry, molecular biology, and cell biology (PhD), including biochemistry, cell and molecular biology, molecular biophysics, structural biology; biotechnology (PhD); cell and molecular biology (PhD); developmental biology and genetics (PhD); hormone action and signal transduction (PhD); neuroscience (PhD); structural biology, biochemistry, and biophysics (PhD). Program participants include the Departments of Biochemistry, Molecular Biology, and Cell Biology; Chemistry; Neurobiology and Physiology; Chemical Engineering; Civil Engineering; and Evanston Hospital. *Degree requirements:* For doctorate, thesis/dissertation, qualifying exam. *Entrance requirements:* For doctorate, GRE General Test. Additional exam requirements/recommendations for international students: Required—TOEFL (minimum score 600 paper-based). Electronic applications accepted. *Faculty research:* Developmental genetics, gene regulation, DNA-protein interactions, biological clocks, bioremediation.

Northwestern University, Northwestern University Feinberg School of Medicine, Combined MD/PhD Medical Scientist Training Program, Evanston, IL 60208. Offers MD/PhD. Application must be made to both The Graduate School and the Medical School. *Accreditation:* LCME/AMA. Electronic applications accepted. *Faculty research:* Cardiovascular epidemiology, cancer epidemiology, nutritional interventions for the prevention of cardiovascular disease and cancer, women's health, outcomes research.

Northwestern University, Northwestern University Feinberg School of Medicine and Interdepartmental Programs, Integrated Graduate Programs in the Life Sciences, Chicago, IL 60611. Offers cancer biology (PhD); cell biology (PhD); developmental biology (PhD); evolutionary biology (PhD); immunology and microbial pathogenesis (PhD); molecular biology and genetics (PhD); neurobiology (PhD); pharmacology and toxicology (PhD); structural biology and biochemistry (PhD). *Degree requirements:* For doctorate, comprehensive exam, thesis/dissertation, written and oral qualifying exams. *Entrance requirements:* For doctorate, GRE General Test. Additional exam requirements/recommendations for international students: Required—TOEFL (minimum score 600 paper-based; 250 computer-based). Electronic applications accepted.

Northwest Missouri State University, Graduate School, College of Arts and Sciences, Department of Biology, Maryville, MO 64468-6001. Offers MS. Part-time programs available. *Faculty:* 10 full-time (3 women). *Students:* 10 full-time (7 women), 9 part-time (4 women), 1 international. 9 applicants, 33% accepted, 3 enrolled. In 2010, 1 master's awarded. *Degree requirements:* For master's, comprehensive exam, thesis. *Entrance requirements:* For master's, GRE General Test, minimum GPA of 3.0 in last 60 hours or 2.75 overall, writing sample. Additional exam requirements/recommendations for international students: Required—TOEFL (minimum score 550 paper-based; 213 computer-based). *Application deadline:* For fall admission, 7/1 for domestic and international students; for spring admission, 11/15 for domestic and international students. Applications are processed on a rolling basis. Application fee: $0 ($50 for international students). *Financial support:* In 2010–11, 4 teaching assistantships with full tuition reimbursements (averaging $6,000 per year) were awarded; tutorial assistantships also available. Financial award application deadline: 4/1; financial award applicants required to submit FAFSA. *Unit head:* Dr. Gregg Dieringer, Chairperson, 660-562-1812. *Application contact:* Dr. Gregory Haddock, Dean of Graduate School, 660-562-1145, Fax: 660-562-1096, E-mail: gradsch@nwmissouri.edu.

Notre Dame de Namur University, Division of Academic Affairs, College of Arts and Sciences, Department of Natural Sciences, Belmont, CA 94002-1908. Offers premedical studies (Certificate). *Students:* 4 full-time (3 women), 13 part-time (9 women); includes 2 Black or African American, non-Hispanic/Latino; 6 Asian, non-Hispanic/Latino; 3 Hispanic/Latino. Average age 26. 28 applicants, 68% accepted, 12 enrolled.Application fee: $60. *Expenses:* Tuition: Full-time $14,220; part-time $790 per credit. Required fees: $35 per semester. Tuition and fees vary according to program. *Financial support:* Available to part-time students. Applicants required to submit FAFSA. *Unit head:* Dr. Isabelle Haithcox, Chair, 650-508-3496, E-mail: ihaithcox@ndnu.edu. *Application contact:* Candace Hallmark, Associate Director of Admissions, 650-508-3600, Fax: 650-508-3426, E-mail: grad.admit@ndnu.edu.

Nova Southeastern University, Health Professions Division, College of Allied Health and Nursing, Department of Physician Assistant Studies, Fort Lauderdale, FL 33314-7796. Offers medical science/physician assistant (MMS). Students enter program as undergraduates. *Accreditation:* ARC-PA. *Faculty:* 14 full-time (5 women). *Students:* 493 full-time (373 women), 12 part-time (10 women); includes 114 minority (8 Black or African American, non-Hispanic/Latino; 2 American Indian or Alaska Native, non-Hispanic/Latino; 40 Asian, non-Hispanic/Latino; 55 Hispanic/Latino; 9 Two or more races, non-Hispanic/Latino), 4 international. Average age 27. 710 applicants, 17% accepted, 80 enrolled. In 2010, 176 master's awarded. *Entrance requirements:* For master's, GRE, minimum GPA of 2.9. *Application deadline:* For winter admission, 12/1 for domestic students. Applications are processed on a rolling basis. Application fee: $170. Electronic applications accepted. *Expenses:* Contact institution. *Financial support:* Applicants required to submit FAFSA. *Unit head:* William H. Marquardt, Associate Dean, 954-262-1028, E-mail: marquard@nova.edu. *Application contact:* Judy Dickman, Admissions Counselor, 954-262-1109, E-mail: dickman@nova.edu.

Nova Southeastern University, Health Professions Division, College of Medical Sciences, Fort Lauderdale, FL 33314-7796. Offers biomedical sciences (MBS). *Faculty:* 32 full-time (13 women), 4 part-time/adjunct (1 woman). *Students:* 28 full-time (14 women), 1 (woman) part-time; includes 1 Black or African American, non-Hispanic/Latino; 5 Asian, non-Hispanic/Latino; 4 Hispanic/Latino; 2 Two or more races, non-Hispanic/Latino. Average age 25. 108 applicants, 23% accepted. In 2010, 11 master's awarded. *Degree requirements:* For master's, thesis. *Entrance requirements:* For master's, MCAT, DAT, minimum GPA of 2.5. *Application deadline:* For spring admission, 4/15 for domestic students. Applications are processed on a rolling basis. Application fee: $50. *Expenses:* Contact institution. *Financial support:* Applicants required to submit FAFSA. *Faculty research:* Neurophysiology, mucosal immunology, allergies involving the lungs, cardiovascular physiology parasitology. Total annual research expenditures: $125,000. *Unit head:* Dr. Harold E. Laubach, Dean, 954-262-1303, Fax: 954-262-1802, E-mail: harold@nsu.nova.edu. *Application contact:* Richard Wilson, Admissions Counselor, 954-262-1111, Fax: 954-262-1802, E-mail: rwilson@nsu.nova.edu.

Nova Southeastern University, Oceanographic Center, Fort Lauderdale, FL 33314-7796. Offers biological sciences (MS); coastal zone management (MS); marine biology (MS); marine biology and oceanography (PhD), including marine biology, oceanography; marine environmental science (MS); physical oceanography (MS). Part-time and evening/weekend programs available. *Faculty:* 15 full-time (1 woman), 5 part-time/adjunct (0 women). *Students:* 126 full-time (79 women), 109 part-time (77 women); includes 4 Black or African American, non-Hispanic/Latino; 1 American Indian or Alaska Native, non-Hispanic/Latino; 4 Asian, non-Hispanic/Latino; 21 Hispanic/Latino; 1 Two or more races, non-Hispanic/Latino, 6 international. Average age 29. 98 applicants, 82% accepted, 67 enrolled. In 2010, 40 master's, 3 doctorates awarded. *Degree requirements:* For master's, thesis; for doctorate, comprehensive exam, thesis/dissertation, departmental qualifying exam. *Entrance requirements:* For master's, GRE General Test; for doctorate, GRE General Test, master's degree. Additional exam requirements/recommendations for international students: Required—TOEFL (minimum score 550 paper-based). *Application deadline:* Applications are processed on a rolling basis. Application fee: $50. *Expenses:* Contact institution. *Financial support:* In 2010–11, 25 research assistantships (averaging $4,000 per year), 3 teaching assistantships (averaging $3,500 per year) were awarded; career-related internships or fieldwork, Federal Work-Study, scholarships/grants, tuition waivers (partial), and unspecified assistantships also available. Support available to part-time students. Financial award applicants required to submit FAFSA. *Faculty research:* Physical, geological, chemical, and biological oceanography. *Unit head:* Dr. Richard Dodge, Dean, 954-262-3600, Fax: 954-262-4020, E-mail: dodge@nsu.nova.edu. *Application contact:* Dr. Richard Spieler, Director of Academic Programs, 954-262-3600, Fax: 954-262-4020, E-mail: spieler@nova.edu.

Oakland University, Graduate Study and Lifelong Learning, College of Arts and Sciences, Department of Biological Sciences, Rochester, MI 48309-4401. Offers biological sciences (MA, MS); biomedical sciences: biological communications (PhD). *Degree requirements:* For master's, thesis. *Entrance requirements:* For master's, GRE Subject Test, GRE General Test, minimum GPA of 3.0 for unconditional admission. Additional exam requirements/recommendations for international students: Required—TOEFL (minimum score 550 paper-based; 213 computer-based). Electronic applications accepted. *Expenses:* Contact institution. *Faculty research:* Mechanism producing rhythmic beating in cilia and flagella, biochemical characterization of carbofuron hydroxylase, maize as a model system to study helitron-related transposable elements, genetic mapping of estrogen-induced endothelial growth factor on rat chromosomes.

Occidental College, Graduate Studies, Department of Biology, Los Angeles, CA 90041-3314. Offers MA. Part-time programs available. *Degree requirements:* For master's, thesis, final exam. *Entrance requirements:* For master's, GRE General Test, GRE Subject Test, minimum GPA of 3.0. Additional exam requirements/recommendations for international students: Required—TOEFL (minimum score 625 paper-based; 263 computer-based). *Expenses:* Contact institution.

The Ohio State University, College of Medicine, School of Biomedical Science, Integrated Biomedical Science Graduate Program, Columbus, OH 43210. Offers immunology (PhD); medical genetics (PhD); molecular virology (PhD); pharmacology (PhD). *Degree requirements:* For doctorate, thesis/dissertation. *Entrance requirements:* For doctorate, GRE, GRE Subject Test in biochemistry, cell and molecular biology (recommended for some). Additional exam requirements/recommendations for international students: Required—TOEFL (minimum score 600 paper-based; 250 computer-based). Electronic applications accepted. *Expenses:* Tuition, state resident: full-time $10,605. Tuition, nonresident: full-time $26,535. Tuition and fees vary according to course load and program.

Ohio University, Graduate College, College of Arts and Sciences, Department of Biological Sciences, Athens, OH 45701-2979. Offers biological sciences (MS, PhD); cell biology and physiology (MS, PhD); ecology and evolutionary biology (MS, PhD); exercise physiology and muscle biology (MS, PhD); microbiology (MS, PhD); neuroscience (MS, PhD). *Students:* 32 full-time (9 women), 5 part-time (2 women); includes 2 minority (1 Black or African American, non-Hispanic/Latino; 1 Hispanic/Latino), 9 international. 51 applicants, 37% accepted, 7 enrolled. In 2010, 2 master's, 9 doctorates awarded. Terminal master's awarded for partial completion of doctoral program. *Degree requirements:* For master's, comprehensive exam, thesis, 1 quarter of teaching experience; for doctorate, comprehensive exam, thesis/dissertation, 2 quarters of teaching experience. *Entrance requirements:* For master's, GRE General Test, names of three faculty members whose research interests most closely match the applicant's interest; for doctorate, GRE General Test, essay concerning prior training, research interest and career goals, plus names of three faculty members whose research interests most closely match the applicant's interest. Additional exam requirements/recommendations for international students: Required—TOEFL (minimum score 620 paper-based; 105 iBT) or IELTS (minimum score 7.5). *Application deadline:* For fall admission, 1/15 for domestic and international students. Application fee: $50 ($55 for international students). Electronic applications accepted. *Financial support:* In 2010–11, 1 fellowship with full tuition reimbursement (averaging $18,957 per year), 10 research assistantships with full tuition reimbursements (averaging $18,957 per year), 42 teaching assistantships with full tuition reimbursements (averaging $18,957 per year) were awarded; Federal Work-Study and institutionally sponsored loans also available. Financial award application deadline: 1/15. *Faculty research:* Ecology and evolutionary biology, exercise physiology and muscle biology, neurobiology, cell biology, physiology. Total annual research expenditures: $2.8 million. *Unit head:* Dr. Ralph DiCaprio, Chair, 740-593-2290, Fax: 740-593-0300, E-mail: dicapri@ohio.edu. *Application contact:* Dr. Patrick Hassett, Graduate Chair, 740-593-4793, Fax: 740-593-0300, E-mail: hassett@ohio.edu.

Oklahoma State University Center for Health Sciences, Program in Biomedical Sciences, Tulsa, OK 74107-1898. Offers MS, PhD, DO/PhD. *Faculty:* 25 full-time (6 women), 2 part-time/adjunct (1 woman). *Students:* 20 full-time (13 women), 10 part-time (6 women); includes 11 minority (2 Black or African American, non-Hispanic/Latino; 4 American Indian or Alaska Native, non-Hispanic/Latino; 5 Asian, non-Hispanic/Latino), 5 international. Average age 31. 36 applicants, 61% accepted, 18 enrolled. In 2010, 3 master's, 1 doctorate awarded. *Degree requirements:* For master's, thesis; for doctorate, thesis/dissertation, comprehensive, oral and written exam. *Entrance requirements:* For master's, GRE General Test, minimum GPA of 3.0; for doctorate, GRE General Test, MCAT, minimum GPA of 3.0. Additional exam requirements/recommendations for international students: Required—TOEFL (minimum score 213 computer-based). *Application deadline:* For fall admission, 2/15 for domestic students, 2/18 for international students; for winter admission, 9/15 for domestic and international students. Application fee: $40 ($75 for international students). *Financial support:* In 2010–11, 9 students received support, including 1 research assistantship with partial tuition reimbursement available (averaging $21,180 per year); scholarships/grants and tuition waivers (partial) also available. Financial award application deadline: 4/10; financial award applicants required to submit FAFSA. *Faculty research:* Neuroscience, cell biology, cell signaling, infectious disease, virology, neurotoxicology. Total annual research expenditures: $1.7 million. *Unit head:* Dr. Greg L. Sawyer, Director, 918-561-1221, Fax: 918-561-8276. *Application contact:* Patrick Anderson, Coordinator of Graduate Admissions, 800-677-1972, Fax: 918-561-8243, E-mail: patrick.anderson@okstate.edu.

Old Dominion University, College of Sciences, Master of Science in Biology Program, Norfolk, VA 23529. Offers MS. Part-time programs available. *Faculty:* 22 full-time (4 women), 23 part-time/adjunct (2 women). *Students:* 21 full-time (11 women), 20 part-time (12 women); includes 4 minority (2 Black or African American, non-Hispanic/Latino; 1 Asian, non-Hispanic/Latino; 1 Hispanic/Latino), 4 international. Average age 28. 13 applicants, 54% accepted, 3 enrolled. In 2010, 14 master's awarded. *Degree requirements:* For master's, comprehensive exam, thesis optional. *Entrance requirements:* For master's, GRE General Test, MCAT, minimum GPA of 3.0 in major, 2.7 overall. Additional exam requirements/recommendations for international students: Required—TOEFL (minimum score 550 paper-based; 213 computer-based; 79 iBT). *Application deadline:* For fall admission, 2/1 priority date for domestic and international students; for winter admission, 6/1 priority date for domestic and international students;

for spring admission, 10/1 priority date for domestic and international students. Application fee: $40. Electronic applications accepted. *Expenses:* Tuition, state resident: full-time $8592; part-time $358 per credit. Tuition, nonresident: full-time $21,672; part-time $903 per credit. Required fees: $119 per semester. One-time fee: $50. *Financial support:* In 2010–11, 2 fellowships (averaging $6,575 per year), 10 research assistantships with partial tuition reimbursements (averaging $15,000 per year), 8 teaching assistantships with partial tuition reimbursements (averaging $15,000 per year) were awarded; career-related internships or fieldwork and scholarships/grants also available. Support available to part-time students. Financial award application deadline: 2/1; financial award applicants required to submit FAFSA. *Faculty research:* Wetland ecology, systematics and ecology of vertebrates, marine biology, molecular and cellular microbiology, physiological and reproductive biology. Total annual research expenditures: $2 million. *Unit head:* Dr. Robert Ratzlaff, Graduate Program Director, 757-683-4361, Fax: 757-683-5283, E-mail: chpgpd@odu.edu. *Application contact:* Dr. Robert Ratzlaff, Graduate Program Director, 757-683-4361, Fax: 757-683-5283, E-mail: chpgpd@odu.edu.

Old Dominion University, College of Sciences, Program in Biomedical Sciences, Norfolk, VA 23529. Offers PhD. Program offered jointly with Eastern Virginia Medical School. *Faculty:* 29 full-time (8 women). *Students:* 20 full-time (10 women), 8 part-time (5 women); includes 3 minority (1 Black or African American, non-Hispanic/Latino; 2 Hispanic/Latino), 15 international. Average age 31. 14 applicants, 71% accepted, 10 enrolled. In 2010, 5 doctorates awarded. *Degree requirements:* For doctorate, comprehensive exam, thesis/dissertation. *Entrance requirements:* For doctorate, GRE General Test, minimum GPA of 3.0. Additional exam requirements/recommendations for international students: Required—TOEFL (minimum score 213 computer-based; 79 iBT). *Application deadline:* For fall admission, 2/15 priority date for domestic and international students. Application fee: $40. Electronic applications accepted. *Expenses:* Tuition, state resident: full-time $8592; part-time $358 per credit. Tuition, nonresident: full-time $21,672; part-time $903 per credit. Required fees: $119 per semester. One-time fee: $50. *Financial support:* In 2010–11, 2 fellowships with full tuition reimbursements (averaging $18,000 per year), 2 research assistantships with full tuition reimbursements (averaging $18,000 per year), 4 teaching assistantships with full tuition reimbursements (averaging $15,000 per year) were awarded; career-related internships or fieldwork, scholarships/grants, tuition waivers (partial), and unspecified assistantships also available. Support available to part-time students. Financial award application deadline: 2/15; financial award applicants required to submit FAFSA. *Faculty research:* Systems biology and biophysics, pure and applied biomedical sciences, biological chemistry, clinical chemistry, cell biology and molecular pathogenesis. Total annual research expenditures: $3.7 million. *Unit head:* Dr. Robert Ratzlaff, Graduate Program Director, 757-683-4361, Fax: 757-683-5283, E-mail: chpgpd@odu.edu. *Application contact:* Dr. Robert Ratzlaff, Graduate Program Director, 757-683-4361, Fax: 757-683-5283, E-mail: chpgpd@odu.edu.

Oregon Health & Science University, School of Medicine, Graduate Programs in Medicine, Portland, OR 97239-3098. Offers MBA, MCR, MPAS, MPH, MS, MSCNU, PhD, Certificate. Postbaccalaureate distance learning degree programs offered (minimal on-campus study). *Faculty:* 344 full-time (120 women), 205 part-time/adjunct (91 women). *Students:* 646 (342 women); includes 13 Black or African American, non-Hispanic/Latino; 8 American Indian or Alaska Native, non-Hispanic/Latino; 43 Asian, non-Hispanic/Latino; 21 Hispanic/Latino; 11 Native Hawaiian or other Pacific Islander, non-Hispanic/Latino, 88 international. Average age 33. 589 applicants, 38% accepted, 132 enrolled. In 2010, 71 master's, 36 doctorates awarded. Terminal master's awarded for partial completion of doctoral program. *Degree requirements:* For master's, thesis, capstone experience; for doctorate, comprehensive exam, thesis/dissertation, qualifying exam. *Entrance requirements:* For master's, GRE General Test (minimum scores: 500 Verbal/600 Quantitative/4.5 Analytical), MCAT or GMAT (for some programs); for doctorate, GRE General Test (minimum scores: 500 Verbal/600 Quantitative/4.5 Analytical). Additional exam requirements/recommendations for international students: Required—TOEFL. Application fee: $65. Electronic applications accepted. *Expenses:* Contact institution. *Financial support:* Fellowships, research assistantships, teaching assistantships, scholarships/grants, health care benefits, and full tuition and stipends available. *Unit head:* Dr. Allison Fryer, Associate Dean for Graduate Studies, 503-494-6222, Fax: 503-494-3400, E-mail: somgrad@ohsu.edu. *Application contact:* Lorie Gookin, Admissions Coordinator, 503-494-6222, Fax: 503-494-3400, E-mail: somgrad@ohsu.edu.

Penn State Hershey Medical Center, College of Medicine, Graduate School Programs in the Biomedical Sciences, Hershey, PA 17033. Offers MS, PhD, MD/PhD, PhD/MBA. *Students:* Average age 24.Terminal master's awarded for partial completion of doctoral program. *Degree requirements:* For master's, thesis or alternative; for doctorate, comprehensive exam, thesis/dissertation, oral exam. *Entrance requirements:* For master's, GRE; for doctorate, GRE, minimum GPA of 3.0. Additional exam requirements/recommendations for international students: Required—TOEFL (minimum score 560 paper-based; 220 computer-based). *Application deadline:* For fall admission, 1/31 priority date for domestic students, 2/1 priority date for international students. Applications are processed on a rolling basis. Application fee: $65. Electronic applications accepted. *Expenses:* Contact institution. *Financial support:* In 2010–11, 3 fellowships with full tuition reimbursements (averaging $26,500 per year), 37 research assistantships with full tuition reimbursements (averaging $22,250 per year) were awarded; career-related internships or fieldwork, scholarships/grants, health care benefits, tuition waivers (full), and unspecified assistantships also available. Financial award applicants required to submit FAFSA. *Unit head:* Dr. Michael F. Verderame, Associate Dean of Graduate Studies, 717-531-8892, Fax: 717-531-0786, E-mail: grad-hmc@psu.edu. *Application contact:* Kathleen M. Simon, Administrative Assistant, 717-531-8892, Fax: 717-531-0786, E-mail: grad-hmc@psu.edu.

Penn State University Park, Graduate School, Eberly College of Science, Department of Biology, State College, University Park, PA 16802-1503. Offers MS, PhD. *Unit head:* Dr. Douglas R. Cavener, Head, 814-865-4562, Fax: 814-865-9131, E-mail: drc9@psu.edu. *Application contact:* Kathryn McClintock, Graduate Programs Secretary, 814-863-7034, E-mail: biokat@psu.edu.

Penn State University Park, Graduate School, Intercollege Graduate Programs, Intercollege Graduate Program in Integrative Biosciences, State College, University Park, PA 16802-1503. Offers integrative biosciences (PhD), including biomolecular transport dynamics. *Unit head:* Dr. Peter J. Hudson, Director, 814-865-6057, Fax: 814-863-1357. *Application contact:* Dr. Peter J. Hudson, Director, 814-865-6057, Fax: 814-863-1357.

Philadelphia College of Osteopathic Medicine, Graduate and Professional Programs, Program in Biomedical Sciences, Philadelphia, PA 19131-1694. Offers MS, Certificate. *Degree requirements:* For master's, thesis. *Entrance requirements:* For master's, GRE, MCAT, DAT, OAT, minimum GPA of 3.0, course work in biology, chemistry, English, physics. *Faculty research:* Developmental biology, cytokines and inflammation, neurobiology of aging, pain mechanisms, cell death.

Pittsburg State University, Graduate School, College of Arts and Sciences, Department of Biology, Pittsburg, KS 66762. Offers MS. *Degree requirements:* For master's, thesis or alternative.

Point Loma Nazarene University, Program in Biology, San Diego, CA 92106-2899. Offers MA, MS. Part-time programs available. *Entrance requirements:* For master's, GRE Subject Test, BA/BS in science field, letters of recommendation, writing sample, interview, minimum GPA of 3.0.

Ponce School of Medicine, Program in Biomedical Sciences, Ponce, PR 00732-7004. Offers PhD. *Faculty:* 6 full-time (1 woman). *Students:* 33 full-time (26 women); includes 29 Hispanic/Latino. Average age 29. 9 applicants, 67% accepted, 5 enrolled. In 2010, 5 doctorates awarded. *Degree requirements:* For doctorate, one foreign language, comprehensive exam, thesis/dissertation. *Entrance requirements:* For doctorate, GRE General Test, proficiency in Spanish and English, minimum overall GPA of 3.0, 3 letters of recommendation, minimum of 35 credits in science. *Application deadline:* For fall admission, 1/15 for domestic and international students. Application fee: $100. *Expenses:* Tuition: Full-time $22,984; part-time $200 per credit. Required fees: $2729. Full-time tuition and fees vary according to course level. *Financial support:* In 2010–11, 19 students received support, including 16 fellowships with full tuition reimbursements available (averaging $145,928 per year), research assistantships with full tuition reimbursements available (averaging $47,612 per year); scholarships/grants also available. Financial award application deadline: 4/30; financial award applicants required to submit FAFSA. *Unit head:* Dr. Jose Torres, Associate Dean for Graduate Studies and Research, 787-840-2158, E-mail: jtorres@psm.edu. *Application contact:* Dr. Jose Torres, Associate Dean for Graduate Studies and Research, 787-840-2158, E-mail: jtorres@psm.edu.

Pontifical Catholic University of Puerto Rico, College of Sciences, Department of Biology, Ponce, PR 00717-0777. Offers environmental sciences (MS). *Degree requirements:* For master's, thesis. *Entrance requirements:* For master's, GRE, 2 letters of recommendation, interview, minimum GPA of 2.75.

Portland State University, Graduate Studies, College of Liberal Arts and Sciences, Department of Biology, Portland, OR 97207-0751. Offers MA, MS, PhD. *Faculty:* 21 full-time (7 women), 7 part-time/adjunct (4 women). *Students:* 65 full-time (39 women), 8 part-time (6 women); includes 1 Hispanic/Latino; 2 Two or more races, non-Hispanic/Latino, 5 international. Average age 30. 34 applicants, 71% accepted, 22 enrolled. In 2010, 11 master's awarded. *Degree requirements:* For master's, one foreign language, thesis; for doctorate, thesis/dissertation. *Entrance requirements:* For master's, GRE General Test, GRE Subject Test, minimum GPA of 3.0 in upper-division course work or 2.75 overall, 2 letters of reference; for doctorate, GRE General Test, GRE Subject Test, minimum GPA of 3.5 in science. Additional exam requirements/recommendations for international students: Required—TOEFL (minimum score 550 paper-based; 213 computer-based). *Application deadline:* For fall admission, 2/15 for domestic and international students; for winter admission, 9/1 for domestic students, 7/1 for international students; for spring admission, 11/1 for domestic and international students. Applications are processed on a rolling basis. Application fee: $50. *Expenses:* Tuition, state resident: full-time $8505; part-time $315 per credit. Tuition, nonresident: full-time $13,284; part-time $492 per credit. Required fees: $1482; $21 per credit. $99 per term. One-time fee: $120. Part-time tuition and fees vary according to course load and program. *Financial support:* In 2010–11, 3 research assistantships with full tuition reimbursements (averaging $16,699 per year) were awarded; teaching assistantships with full tuition reimbursements, Federal Work-Study, scholarships/grants, tuition waivers (partial), and unspecified assistantships also available. Support available to part-time students. Financial award application deadline: 3/1; financial award applicants required to submit FAFSA. *Faculty research:* Genetic diversity and natural population, vertebrate temperature regulation, water balance and sensory physiology, trace elements and aquatic ecology, molecular genetics. Total annual research expenditures: $2.8 million. *Unit head:* Dr. Anna Louise Reysenbach, Chair, 503-725-3864, E-mail: biochair@pdx.edu. *Application contact:* Autumn Droste, Secretary, 503-725-8757, E-mail: adroste@pdx.edu.

Prairie View A&M University, College of Arts and Sciences, Department of Biology, Prairie View, TX 77446-0519. Offers bio- environmental toxicology (MS); biology (MS). Part-time and evening/weekend programs available. *Faculty:* 5 full-time (2 women). *Students:* 6 full-time (4 women), 3 part-time (2 women); includes all Black or African American, non-Hispanic/Latino. Average age 25. 14 applicants, 86% accepted. In 2010, 1 master's awarded. *Degree requirements:* For master's, comprehensive exam, thesis optional. *Entrance requirements:* For master's, GRE General Test. Additional exam requirements/recommendations for international students: Required—TOEFL. *Application deadline:* For fall admission, 7/1 for domestic and international students; for spring admission, 11/1 for domestic and international students. Applications are processed on a rolling basis. *Expenses:* Tuition, state resident: part-time $119.06 per credit hour. Tuition, nonresident: part-time $511.23 per credit hour. *Financial support:* In 2010–11, 3 students received support, including 3 teaching assistantships (averaging $13,440 per year); Federal Work-Study and unspecified assistantships also available. Financial award application deadline: 4/1; financial award applicants required to submit FAFSA. *Faculty research:* Geonomics, hypertension, control of gene express, proteins, kigands that interact with hormone receptors, prostate cancer, renin-angiotensin yeast metabolism. *Unit head:* Dr. Harriette Howard-Lee-Block, Head, 936-261-3160, Fax: 936-261-3179, E-mail: hlblock@pvamu.edu. *Application contact:* Dr. Seab A. Smith, Associate Professor, 936-261-3169, Fax: 936-261-3179, E-mail: sasmith@pvamu.edu.

Purdue University, Graduate School, College of Science, Department of Biological Sciences, West Lafayette, IN 47907. Offers biochemistry (PhD); biophysics (PhD); cell and developmental biology (PhD); ecology, evolutionary and population biology (MS, PhD), including ecology, evolutionary biology, population biology; genetics (MS, PhD); microbiology (MS, PhD); molecular biology (PhD); neurobiology (MS, PhD); plant physiology (PhD). Terminal master's awarded for partial completion of doctoral program. *Degree requirements:* For master's, thesis (for some programs); for doctorate, thesis/dissertation, seminars, teaching experience. *Entrance requirements:* For master's and doctorate, GRE General Test. Additional exam requirements/recommendations for international students: Required—TOEFL. Electronic applications accepted.

Purdue University, Graduate School, PULSe—Purdue University Life Sciences Program, West Lafayette, IN 47907. Offers PhD. *Entrance requirements:* For doctorate, GRE. Additional exam requirements/recommendations for international students: Required—TOEFL. Electronic applications accepted.

Purdue University Calumet, Graduate Studies Office, School of Engineering, Mathematics, and Science, Department of Biological Sciences, Hammond, IN 46323-2094. Offers biology (MS); biology teaching (MS); biotechnology (MS). *Faculty:* 10 full-time (5 women). *Students:* 6 full-time (4 women), 12 part-time (6 women). 25 applicants, 60% accepted, 14 enrolled. *Entrance requirements:* For master's, GRE. Additional exam requirements/recommendations for international students: Required—TOEFL. *Application deadline:* Applications are processed on a rolling basis. Application fee: $55. Electronic applications accepted. *Expenses:* Tuition, state resident: full-time $6867. Tuition, nonresident: full-time $14,157. *Financial support:* In 2010–11, research assistantships with partial tuition reimbursements (averaging $18,000 per year), teaching assistantships with partial tuition reimbursements (averaging $15,000 per year) were awarded. Financial award application deadline: 3/1. *Faculty research:* Cell biology, molecular biology, genetics, microbiology, neurophysiology. Total annual research expenditures: $3 million. *Unit head:* Dr. Charles Tseng, Graduate Studies Advisor, Biological Sciences, 219-989-2403, E-mail: tseng@purduecal.edu. *Application contact:* Dr. Charles Tseng, Graduate Adviser, 219-989-2403, Fax: 219-989-2130, E-mail: tseng@purduecal.edu.

Queens College of the City University of New York, Division of Graduate Studies, Mathematics and Natural Sciences Division, Department of Biology, Flushing, NY 11367-1597. Offers MA. Part-time and evening/weekend programs available. *Faculty:* 18 full-time (6 women). *Students:* 3 full-time (1 woman), 29 part-time (16 women); includes 4 Black or African American, non-Hispanic/Latino; 11 Asian, non-Hispanic/Latino; 4 Hispanic/Latino, 2 international. 50 applicants, 50% accepted, 15 enrolled. In 2010, 9 master's awarded. *Degree requirements:* For master's, comprehensive exam, thesis or alternative, qualifying exam. *Entrance requirements:* For master's, minimum GPA of 3.0. Additional exam requirements/recommendations for international students: Required—TOEFL. *Application deadline:* For fall admission, 4/1 for domestic students; for spring admission, 11/1 for domestic students. Applications are processed on a rolling basis. Application fee: $125. *Financial support:* Career-related internships or fieldwork, Federal Work-Study, institutionally sponsored loans, tuition waivers (partial), and unspecified assistantships available. Support available to part-time students. Financial award application deadline: 4/1; financial award applicants required to submit FAFSA. *Faculty research:* Cell biology, evolutionary biology, environmental biology, microbiology. *Unit head:* Dr. Corrine Michels, Chairperson, 718-997-3400, E-mail: corinne_michels@qc.edu. *Application contact:* Dr. Jeanne Szalay, Graduate Adviser, 718-997-3400, E-mail: jeanne_szalay@qc.edu.

Biological and Biomedical Sciences—General

Queen's University at Kingston, School of Graduate Studies and Research, Faculty of Arts and Sciences, Department of Biology, Kingston, ON K7L 3N6, Canada. Offers M Sc, PhD. Part-time programs available. *Degree requirements:* For master's, thesis; for doctorate, comprehensive exam, thesis/dissertation. *Entrance requirements:* Additional exam requirements/ recommendations for international students: Required—TOEFL. *Faculty research:* Limnology, plant morphogenesis, nitrogen fixation, cell cycle, genetics.

Quinnipiac University, School of Health Sciences, Program in Medical Laboratory Sciences, Hamden, CT 06518-1940. Offers biomedical sciences (MHS); laboratory management (MHS); microbiology (MHS). Part-time programs available. *Faculty:* 11 full-time (5 women), 15 part-time/adjunct (7 women). *Students:* 44 full-time (21 women), 32 part-time (15 women); includes 13 minority (5 Black or African American, non-Hispanic/Latino; 6 Asian, non-Hispanic/Latino; 2 Hispanic/Latino), 25 international. 54 applicants, 70% accepted, 27 enrolled. In 2010, 17 master's awarded. *Degree requirements:* For master's, comprehensive exam, thesis optional. *Entrance requirements:* For master's, minimum GPA of 2.75; bachelor's degree in biological, medical, or health sciences. Additional exam requirements/recommendations for international students: Required—TOEFL (minimum score 575 paper-based; 233 computer-based; 90 iBT), IELTS (minimum score 6.5). *Application deadline:* For fall admission, 7/30 priority date for domestic students, 4/30 priority date for international students; for spring admission, 12/15 priority date for domestic students, 9/15 priority date for international students. Applications are processed on a rolling basis. Application fee: $45. Electronic applications accepted. *Expenses:* Tuition: Part-time $810 per credit. Required fees: $35 per credit. *Financial support:* Federal Work-Study, tuition waivers (partial), and unspecified assistantships available. Support available to part-time students. Financial award application deadline: 4/15; financial award applicants required to submit FAFSA. *Faculty research:* Microbial physiology, fermentation technology. *Unit head:* Dr. Kenneth Kaloustian, Director, 203-582-8676, Fax: 203-582-3443, E-mail: ken.kaloustian@quinnipiac.edu. *Application contact:* Kristin Parent, Assistant Director of Graduate Health Sciences Admissions, 800-462-1944, Fax: 203-582-3443, E-mail: kristin.parent@quinnipiac.edu.

Rensselaer Polytechnic Institute, Graduate School, School of Science, Program in Biology, Troy, NY 12180-3590. Offers MS, PhD. Part-time programs available. *Faculty:* 19 full-time (5 women). *Students:* 29 full-time (16 women), 1 (woman) part-time; includes 5 Asian, non-Hispanic/Latino; 1 Hispanic/Latino, 8 international. Average age 27. 94 applicants, 10% accepted, 5 enrolled. In 2010, 2 master's, 5 doctorates awarded. Terminal master's awarded for partial completion of doctoral program. *Degree requirements:* For master's, comprehensive exam, thesis optional; for doctorate, comprehensive exam, thesis/dissertation. *Entrance requirements:* Additional exam requirements/recommendations for international students: Required—TOEFL. *Application deadline:* For fall admission, 1/15 priority date for domestic students, 1/1 for international students. Applications are processed on a rolling basis. Application fee: $75. Electronic applications accepted. *Expenses:* Tuition: Full-time $39,600; part-time $1650 per credit. Required fees: $1896. *Financial support:* In 2010–11, 2 fellowships (averaging $17,500 per year), 25 research assistantships with full tuition reimbursements (averaging $17,500 per year), 30 teaching assistantships with full tuition reimbursements (averaging $17,500 per year) were awarded; career-related internships or fieldwork, institutionally sponsored loans, and tuition waivers (partial) also available. Financial award application deadline: 1/1. *Faculty research:* Bioinformatics, molecular biology/biochemistry, cell and tissue biology, environment, ecology. Total annual research expenditures: $3.2 million. *Unit head:* Dr. Susan P. Gilbert, Head, 518-276-8425, Fax: 518-276-2344, E-mail: sgilbert@rpi.edu. *Application contact:* Jody Malm, Graduate Program Coordinator, 518-276-2808, Fax: 518-276-2344, E-mail: malmj@rpi.edu.

Rhode Island College, School of Graduate Studies, Faculty of Arts and Sciences, Department of Biology, Providence, RI 02908-1991. Offers biology (MA); modern biological sciences (CGS). Part-time programs available. *Faculty:* 5 full-time (4 women). *Students:* 10 part-time (3 women); includes 2 minority (both Black or African American, non-Hispanic/Latino). Average age 31. In 2010, 2 master's awarded. *Degree requirements:* For master's, thesis. *Entrance requirements:* For master's, GRE General and Subject Tests. Additional exam requirements/recommendations for international students: Recommended—TOEFL (minimum score 550 paper-based; 213 computer-based; 79 iBT). *Application deadline:* For fall admission, 3/1 for domestic students. Applications are processed on a rolling basis. Application fee: $50. *Expenses:* Tuition, state resident: full-time $8208; part-time $342 per credit hour. Tuition, nonresident: full-time $16,080; part-time $670 per credit hour. Required fees: $554; $20 per credit. $72 per term. *Financial support:* In 2010–11, 2 teaching assistantships with full tuition reimbursements (averaging $4,550 per year) were awarded; career-related internships or fieldwork, Federal Work-Study, scholarships/grants, health care benefits, and unspecified assistantships also available. Support available to part-time students. Financial award application deadline: 5/15; financial award applicants required to submit FAFSA. *Unit head:* Dr. Eric Hall, Chair, 401-456-8010, E-mail: biology@ric.edu. *Application contact:* Graduate Studies, 401-456-8700.

Rochester Institute of Technology, Graduate Enrollment Services, College of Science, Health Sciences and Sustainability, Department of Biological Sciences, Rochester, NY 14623-5603. Offers bioinformatics (MS); environmental science (MS). Part-time programs available. *Students:* 24 full-time (8 women), 13 part-time (7 women); includes 1 Asian, non-Hispanic/Latino, 13 international. Average age 28. 89 applicants, 40% accepted, 16 enrolled. In 2010, 4 master's awarded. *Degree requirements:* For master's, thesis or alternative. *Entrance requirements:* Additional exam requirements/recommendations for international students: Required—TOEFL (minimum score 570 paper-based; 230 computer-based; 88 iBT) or IELTS (minimum score 6.5). *Application deadline:* For fall admission, 2/15 priority date for domestic and international students. Application fee: $50. *Expenses:* Tuition: Full-time $33,234; part-time $924 per credit hour. Required fees: $219. *Financial support:* In 2010–11, 24 students received support; fellowships with partial tuition reimbursements available, research assistantships with partial tuition reimbursements available, teaching assistantships with partial tuition reimbursements available, career-related internships or fieldwork, scholarships/grants, and unspecified assistantships available. Support available to part-time students. Financial award applicants required to submit FAFSA. *Faculty research:* Bioinformatic software development, bioscience, biomedical research, environmental research examining the human relationship to nature and developing solutions that prevent or reverse environmental deterioration. *Unit head:* Gary Skusse, Head, School of Biological and Medical Sciences, 585-475-6725, Fax: 585-475-2533, E-mail: biology@rit.edu. *Application contact:* Diane Ellison, Assistant Vice President, Graduate Enrollment Services, 585-475-2229, Fax: 585-475-7164, E-mail: gradinfo@rit.edu.

The Rockefeller University, Graduate Program in Biomedical Sciences, New York, NY 10021-6399. Offers MA, PhD, MD/PhD. *Faculty:* 97 full-time (21 women), 152 part-time/adjunct (39 women). *Students:* 193 full-time (90 women); includes 27 minority (8 Black or African American, non-Hispanic/Latino; 15 Asian, non-Hispanic/Latino; 4 Hispanic/Latino), 78 international. Average age 28. 732 applicants, 10% accepted, 30 enrolled. In 2010, 10 master's, 37 doctorates awarded. Terminal master's awarded for partial completion of doctoral program. *Degree requirements:* For master's, thesis; for doctorate, thesis/dissertation. *Entrance requirements:* Additional exam requirements/recommendations for international students: Required—TOEFL. *Application deadline:* For winter admission, 12/5 for domestic and international students. Application fee: $80. Electronic applications accepted. *Financial support:* In 2010–11, 193 students received support, including 193 fellowships with full tuition reimbursements available (averaging $31,600 per year); institutionally sponsored loans, scholarships/grants, traineeships, and health care benefits also available. *Unit head:* Dr. Sidney Strickland, Dean of Graduate Studies, 212-327-8086, Fax: 212-327-8505, E-mail: phd@rockefeller.edu. *Application contact:* Kristen Cullen, Graduate Admissions Administrator and Registrar, 212-327-8088, Fax: 212-327-8505, E-mail: cullenk@rockefeller.edu.

See Display on this page and Close-Up on page 105.

Rosalind Franklin University of Medicine and Science, College of Health Professions, Department of Interprofessional Healthcare Studies, Biomedical Sciences Program, North

SCIENCE FOR THE BENEFIT OF HUMANITY

The David Rockefeller Graduate Program
Ph.D. Program in the Biological Sciences

The Rockefeller University is a world-renowned center for research and graduate education in the biomedical sciences. The university's Ph.D. program, whose hallmark is learning science by doing science, offers:

- a flexible academic experience with freedom to explore different areas of science
- interdisciplinary research and collaboration
- close mentoring by faculty
- unique environment without academic departments
- modern facilities and state-of-the-art research support in its more than 70 labs.

Graduate students receive a yearly stipend, free health and dental insurance, subsidized housing on or adjacent to the university's lush 14-acre campus and an annual research allowance for travel and lab support.

Founded by John D. Rockefeller in 1901 as the nation's first institute for medical research, the university's world-class faculty, with innovative approaches to scientific discovery, have produced pioneering achievements in biology and medicine. Numerous prestigious awards have been given to Rockefeller faculty, including 24 Nobel Prizes—most recently, to the late Ralph Steinman, the 2011 recipient in Physiology and Medicine.

Chicago, IL 60064-3095. Offers MS. *Entrance requirements:* For master's, MCAT, DAT, OAT, PCAT or GRE, BS in chemistry, physics, biology. Additional exam requirements/recommendations for international students: Required—TOEFL.

Rosalind Franklin University of Medicine and Science, School of Graduate and Post-doctoral Studies—Interdisciplinary Graduate Program in Biomedical Sciences, North Chicago, IL 60064-3095. Offers MS, PhD, MD/PhD. Terminal master's awarded for partial completion of doctoral program. *Degree requirements:* For master's, comprehensive exam, thesis; for doctorate, comprehensive exam, thesis/dissertation. *Entrance requirements:* For master's and doctorate, GRE General Test. Additional exam requirements/recommendations for international students: Required—TOEFL, TWE. *Faculty research:* Extracellular matrix, nutrition and mood, neuropsychopharmacology, membrane transport, brain metabolism.

See Display below and Close-Up on page 107.

Rutgers, The State University of New Jersey, Camden, Graduate School of Arts and Sciences, Program in Biology, Camden, NJ 08102. Offers MS. Part-time and evening/weekend programs available. *Faculty:* 8 full-time (0 women), 5 part-time/adjunct (1 woman). *Students:* 12 full-time (2 women), 17 part-time (11 women); includes 1 Black or African American, non-Hispanic/Latino; 1 Asian, non-Hispanic/Latino; 1 Hispanic/Latino, 5 international. Average age 26. 43 applicants, 70% accepted, 13 enrolled. In 2010, 11 master's awarded. *Degree requirements:* For master's, comprehensive exam, thesis (for some programs), 30 credits. *Entrance requirements:* For master's, GRE General Test, GRE Subject Test (recommended), 3 letters of recommendation; statement of personal, professional and academic goals; biology or related undergraduate degree (preferred). Additional exam requirements/recommendations for international students: Required—TOEFL, IELTS. *Application deadline:* For fall admission, 3/1 priority date for domestic students, 3/1 for international students; for spring admission, 12/1 priority date for domestic students, 11/1 for international students. Applications are processed on a rolling basis. Application fee: $65. Electronic applications accepted. *Expenses:* Tuition, state resident: full-time $4963; part-time $319 per credit. Tuition, nonresident: full-time $10,493; part-time $680 per credit. *Financial support:* In 2010–11, 22 students received support, including 2 fellowships with partial tuition reimbursements available (averaging $2,600 per year), 7 teaching assistantships with full tuition reimbursements available (averaging $26,000 per year); research assistantships, Federal Work-Study, scholarships/grants, tuition waivers (partial), and unspecified assistantships also available. Financial award application deadline: 3/15; financial award applicants required to submit FAFSA. *Faculty research:* Neurobiology, biochemistry, ecology, developmental biology, biological signaling mechanisms. Total annual research expenditures: $1 million. *Unit head:* Dr. Mark Morgan, Director, 856-225-6142, Fax: 856-225-6147, E-mail: mdmorgan@camden.rutgers.edu. *Application contact:* Dr. Mark Morgan, Director, 856-225-6142, Fax: 856-225-6147, E-mail: mdmorgan@camden.rutgers.edu.

Rutgers, The State University of New Jersey, Newark, Graduate School, Program in Biology, Newark, NJ 07102. Offers MS, PhD. Part-time and evening/weekend programs available. *Faculty:* 22 full-time (5 women), 8 part-time/adjunct (1 woman). *Students:* 33 full-time (20 women), 44 part-time (28 women); includes 1 Black or African American, non-Hispanic/Latino; 30 Asian, non-Hispanic/Latino; 9 Hispanic/Latino. 116 applicants, 39% accepted, 30 enrolled. In 2010, 11 master's, 3 doctorates awarded. Terminal master's awarded for partial completion of doctoral program. *Degree requirements:* For master's, comprehensive exam, thesis optional; for doctorate, thesis/dissertation, qualifying exam. *Entrance requirements:* For master's, GRE General Test, minimum undergraduate B average; for doctorate, GRE General Test, GRE Subject Test, minimum B average. *Application deadline:* For fall admission, 2/15 priority date for domestic students; for spring admission, 12/1 for domestic students. Applications are processed on a rolling basis. Application fee: $60. Electronic applications accepted. *Expenses:* Tuition, state resident: part-time $600 per credit. Tuition, nonresident: full-time $10,694. *Financial support:* In 2010–11, 36 students received support, including 3 fellowships (averaging $18,000 per year), 2 research assistantships with full and partial tuition reimbursements available (averaging $23,112 per year), 24 teaching assistantships with full and partial

tuition reimbursements available (averaging $23,112 per year); Federal Work-Study, tuition waivers (full and partial), and unspecified assistantships also available. Support available to part-time students. Financial award application deadline: 3/1. *Faculty research:* Cell-cytoskeletal elements, development and regeneration in the nervous system, cellular trafficking, environmental stressors and their impact on development, opportunistic parasitic infections in AIDS. *Unit head:* Dr. Edward Bonder, Program Director, 973-353-1047, Fax: 973-353-5518, E-mail: ebonder@andromeda.rutgers.edu. *Application contact:* Shandell Rivera, Administrative Assistant, 973-353-1235, E-mail: sdrivera@rci.rutgers.edu.

Rutgers, The State University of New Jersey, Newark, Graduate School, Program in Computational Biology, Newark, NJ 07102. Offers MS. Program offered jointly with New Jersey Institute of Technology. *Entrance requirements:* For master's, GRE, minimum undergraduate B average. Additional exam requirements/recommendations for international students: Required—TOEFL. *Application deadline:* For fall admission, 6/1 for domestic and international students; for spring admission, 12/1 for domestic and international students. Application fee: $60. *Expenses:* Tuition, state resident: part-time $600 per credit. Tuition, nonresident: full-time $10,694. *Unit head:* Dr. Edward Bonder, Program Director, 973-353-1047, Fax: 973-353-5518, E-mail: ebonder@andromeda.rutgers.edu. *Application contact:* Dr. Edward Bonder, Program Director, 973-353-1047, Fax: 973-353-5518, E-mail: ebonder@andromeda.rutgers.edu.

Rutgers, The State University of New Jersey, New Brunswick, Graduate School-New Brunswick, BioMaPS Institute for Quantitative Biology, Piscataway, NJ 08854-8097. Offers computational biology and molecular biophysics (PhD). *Degree requirements:* For doctorate, comprehensive exam, thesis/dissertation. *Entrance requirements:* For doctorate, GRE. Additional exam requirements/recommendations for international students: Required—TOEFL. Electronic applications accepted. *Expenses:* Tuition, state resident: full-time $7200; part-time $600 per credit. Tuition, nonresident: full-time $11,124; part-time $927 per credit. *Faculty research:* Structural biology, systems biology, bioinformatics, translational medicine, genomics.

St. Cloud State University, School of Graduate Studies, College of Science and Engineering, Department of Biological Sciences, St. Cloud, MN 56301-4498. Offers MA, MS. *Degree requirements:* For master's, comprehensive exam (for some programs), thesis or alternative. *Entrance requirements:* For master's, GRE General Test, minimum GPA of 2.75. Additional exam requirements/recommendations for international students: Recommended—TOEFL (minimum score 550 paper-based; 213 computer-based), IELTS (minimum score 6.5). Electronic applications accepted.

Saint Francis University, Department of Physician Assistant Sciences, Medical Science Program, Loretto, PA 15940-0600. Offers MMS. Part-time and evening/weekend programs available. Postbaccalaureate distance learning degree programs offered (no on-campus study). *Faculty:* 1 (woman) full-time, 5 part-time/adjunct (2 women). *Students:* 99 part-time (71 women); includes 3 Black or African American, non-Hispanic/Latino; 12 Asian, non-Hispanic/Latino; 8 Hispanic/Latino. Average age 34. 73 applicants, 100% accepted, 73 enrolled. In 2010, 57 master's awarded. *Degree requirements:* For master's, thesis or alternative. *Entrance requirements:* For master's, minimum GPA of 2.5, 2 letters of reference. *Application deadline:* For fall admission, 8/1 for domestic students; for spring admission, 12/1 for domestic students. Applications are processed on a rolling basis. Application fee: $0. Electronic applications accepted. *Expenses:* Contact institution. *Financial support:* Available to part-time students. Applicants required to submit FAFSA. *Faculty research:* Health care policy, physician assistant practice roles, health promotion/disease prevention, public health epidemiology. *Unit head:* Deborah E. Budash, Director, 814-472-3919, Fax: 814-472-3137, E-mail: dbudash@francis.edu. *Application contact:* Cheryl Strittmatter, Office Assistant, 814-472-3136, Fax: 814-472-3137, E-mail: cstrittmatter@francis.edu.

St. Francis Xavier University, Graduate Studies, Department of Biology, Antigonish, NS B2G 2W5, Canada. Offers M Sc. *Degree requirements:* For master's, thesis. *Entrance requirements:* For master's, 2 letters of recommendation. Additional exam requirements/recommendations for international students: Required—TOEFL (minimum score 580 paper-based; 236 computer-

Biological and Biomedical Sciences—General

St. Francis Xavier University *(continued)*
based). *Faculty research:* Cellular, whole organism, and population levels; marine photosynthesis; biophysical mechanisms; aquatic biology.

St. John's University, St. John's College of Liberal Arts and Sciences, Department of Biological Sciences, Queens, NY 11439. Offers MS, PhD. Part-time and evening/weekend programs available. *Students:* 18 full-time (9 women), 20 part-time (9 women); includes 5 minority (2 Black or African American, non-Hispanic/Latino; 2 Asian, non-Hispanic/Latino; 1 Hispanic/Latino), 23 international. Average age 29. 54 applicants, 59% accepted, 11 enrolled. In 2010, 6 master's, 1 doctorate awarded. *Degree requirements:* For master's, comprehensive exam, thesis optional, residency; for doctorate, comprehensive exam, thesis/dissertation, residency. *Entrance requirements:* For master's, GRE General Test, GRE Subject Test, minimum GPA of 3.0, 2 letters of recommendation; for doctorate, GRE General Test, GRE Subject Test, minimum GPA of 3.0 (undergraduate), 3.5 (graduate); 2 letters of recommendation, writing sample. Additional exam requirements/recommendations for international students: Required—TOEFL (minimum score 600 paper-based; 250 computer-based; 100 iBT), IELTS (minimum score 5.5). *Application deadline:* For fall admission, 5/1 priority date for domestic and international students; for spring admission, 11/1 priority date for domestic and international students. Applications are processed on a rolling basis. Application fee: $70. Electronic applications accepted. *Expenses:* Tuition: Full-time $17,100; part-time $950 per credit. Required fees: $340; $170 per semester. Tuition and fees vary according to program. *Financial support:* Fellowships, research assistantships, scholarships/grants available. Support available to part-time students. Financial award application deadline: 3/1; financial award applicants required to submit FAFSA. *Faculty research:* Regulation of gene transcription, immunology and inflammation, cancer research, infectious diseases, molecular control of developmental processes, signal transduction. Total annual research expenditures: $200,000. *Unit head:* Dr. Ales Vancura, Chair, 718-990-6287, E-mail: vancuraa@stjohns.edu. *Application contact:* Kathleen Davis, Director of Graduate Admission, 718-990-1601, Fax: 718-990-5686, E-mail: gradhelp@stjohns.edu.

Saint Joseph College, Department of Biology, West Hartford, CT 06117-2700. Offers MS. Part-time and evening/weekend programs available. Postbaccalaureate distance learning degree programs offered (no on-campus study). *Students:* 4 full-time (3 women), 88 part-time (70 women); includes 4 Black or African American, non-Hispanic/Latino; 2 Asian, non-Hispanic/Latino. *Degree requirements:* For master's, comprehensive exam, thesis or alternative. *Entrance requirements:* For master's, 2 letters of recommendation. *Application deadline:* Applications are processed on a rolling basis. Application fee: $50. Electronic applications accepted. *Expenses:* Tuition: Full-time $11,340; part-time $630 per credit. Required fees: $540; $30 per credit. Tuition and fees vary according to course load, campus/location and program. *Financial support:* Unspecified assistantships available. Support available to part-time students. Financial award applicants required to submit FAFSA. *Application contact:* Graduate Admissions Office, 860-231-5261, E-mail: graduate@sjc.edu.

Saint Joseph's University, College of Arts and Sciences, Department of Biology, Philadelphia, PA 19131-1395. Offers MA, MS. Part-time programs available. *Faculty:* 13 full-time (5 women), 1 (woman) part-time/adjunct. *Students:* 3 full-time (2 women), 24 part-time (17 women); includes 2 Black or African American, non-Hispanic/Latino; 3 Hispanic/Latino; 1 Two or more races, non-Hispanic/Latino, 2 international. Average age 25. 32 applicants, 84% accepted, 17 enrolled. In 2010, 4 master's awarded. *Degree requirements:* For master's, comprehensive exam (for some programs), thesis (for some programs), minimum GPA of 3.0, completion of degree within 5 years. *Entrance requirements:* For master's, GRE, 2 letters of recommendation, transcript, personal statement, resume. Additional exam requirements/recommendations for international students: Required—TOEFL (minimum score 550 paper-based; 213 computer-based; 79 iBT), IELTS (minimum score 6.5). *Application deadline:* For fall admission, 7/15 priority date for domestic students, 7/15 for international students; for spring admission, 11/15 priority date for domestic students, 11/15 for international students. Applications are processed on a rolling basis. Application fee: $35. Electronic applications accepted. *Expenses:* Tuition: Part-time $729 per credit. Tuition and fees vary according to course load, degree level and program. *Financial support:* Research assistantships with tuition reimbursements, unspecified assistantships available. Financial award applicants required to submit FAFSA. *Faculty research:* Life science, undergraduate science education, confocal microscope for research and training. Total annual research expenditures: $865,347. *Unit head:* Dr. James Watrous, Director, 610-660-1829, E-mail: jwatrous@sju.edu. *Application contact:* Kate McConnell, Director, Graduate College of Arts and Sciences Admissions and Retention, 610-660-3184, Fax: 610-660-3230, E-mail: kate.mcconnell@sju.edu.

Saint Louis University, Graduate Education, College of Arts and Sciences and Graduate Education, Department of Biology, St. Louis, MO 63103-2097. Offers MS, MS-R, PhD. *Degree requirements:* For master's, comprehensive exam, thesis (for some programs); for doctorate, thesis/dissertation, preliminary exams. *Entrance requirements:* For master's, GRE General Test, letters of recommendation, resume; for doctorate, GRE General Test, letters of recommendation, resumé, statement, transcripts. Additional exam requirements/recommendations for international students: Required—TOEFL (minimum score 550 paper-based; 213 computer-based). Electronic applications accepted. *Faculty research:* Systematics, speciation, evolution, community ecology, conservation biology, molecular signaling.

Saint Louis University, Graduate Education and School of Medicine, Graduate Program in Biomedical Sciences, St. Louis, MO 63103-2097. Offers MS-R, PhD. *Degree requirements:* For doctorate, comprehensive exam, thesis/dissertation. *Entrance requirements:* For doctorate, GRE. Additional exam requirements/recommendations for international students: Required—TOEFL. Electronic applications accepted. *Faculty research:* Biochemistry and molecular biology, physiology and pharmacology, virology, pathology, immunology.

Sam Houston State University, College of Arts and Sciences, Department of Biological Sciences, Huntsville, TX 77341. Offers biology (MA, MS). Part-time programs available. *Students:* 11 full-time (5 women), 24 part-time (12 women); includes 1 Black or African American, non-Hispanic/Latino; 3 Hispanic/Latino, 2 international. Average age 26. 19 applicants, 89% accepted, 13 enrolled. In 2010, 4 master's awarded. *Degree requirements:* For master's, thesis (for some programs). *Entrance requirements:* For master's, GRE General Test. Additional exam requirements/recommendations for international students: Required—TOEFL (minimum score 550 paper-based; 213 computer-based; 79 iBT). *Application deadline:* For fall admission, 8/1 for domestic and international students; for spring admission, 12/1 for domestic and international students. Application fee: $20. *Expenses:* Tuition, state resident: full-time $1363; part-time $163 per credit hour. Tuition, nonresident: full-time $3856; part-time $473 per credit hour. *Financial support:* Research assistantships, teaching assistantships available. Financial award application deadline: 5/31; financial award applicants required to submit FAFSA. *Unit head:* Dr. Todd Primm, Chair, 936-294-1538, Fax: 936-294-3940, E-mail: tprimm@shsu.edu. *Application contact:* Dr. Anne Gaillard, Graduate Coordinator, 936-294-1549, Fax: 936-294-3940, E-mail: argaillard@shsu.edu.

San Diego State University, Graduate and Research Affairs, College of Sciences, Department of Biology, San Diego, CA 92182. Offers biology (MA, MS), including ecology (MS), molecular biology (MS), physiology (MS), systematics/evolution (MS); cell and molecular biology (PhD); ecology (MS, PhD); microbiology (MS). Terminal master's awarded for partial completion of doctoral program. *Degree requirements:* For master's, thesis; for doctorate, thesis/dissertation. *Entrance requirements:* For master's, GRE General Test, GRE Subject Test, resume or curriculum vitae, 2 letters of recommendation. Additional exam requirements/recommendations for international students: Required—TOEFL. Electronic applications accepted.

San Francisco State University, Division of Graduate Studies, College of Science and Engineering, Department of Biology, San Francisco, CA 94132-1722. Offers biomedical science (MS); cell and molecular biology (MS); conservation biology (MS); ecology and systematic biology (MS); marine biology (MS); marine science (MS); microbiology (MS); physiology and

behavioral biology (MS); science (PSM), including biotechnology, stem cell science. *Application deadline:* Applications are processed on a rolling basis. *Unit head:* Dr. Michael Goldman, Chair, 415-338-1100. *Application contact:* Dr. Robert Patterson, Graduate Coordinator, 415-338-1100, E-mail: patters@sfsu.edu.

San Jose State University, Graduate Studies and Research, College of Science, Department of Biological Sciences, San Jose, CA 95192-0001. Offers biological sciences (MA, MS); molecular biology and microbiology (MS); organismal biology, conservation and ecology (MS); physiology (MS). Part-time programs available. *Entrance requirements:* For master's, GRE. Electronic applications accepted. *Faculty research:* Systemic physiology, molecular genetics, SEM studies, toxicology, large mammal ecology.

The Scripps Research Institute, Kellogg School of Science and Technology, La Jolla, CA 92037. Offers chemical and biological sciences (PhD). *Faculty:* 163 full-time (35 women). *Students:* 222 full-time (78 women). 494 applicants, 20% accepted, 32 enrolled. *Degree requirements:* For doctorate, thesis/dissertation. *Entrance requirements:* For doctorate, GRE General Test, GRE Subject Test, 3 letters of recommendation. Additional exam requirements/recommendations for international students: Required—TOEFL. *Application deadline:* For fall admission, 12/1 for domestic and international students. Application fee: $0. Electronic applications accepted. *Expenses:* Tuition: Full-time $5000. *Financial support:* Fellowships, institutionally sponsored loans, tuition waivers (full), and annual stipends available. *Faculty research:* Molecular structure and function, plant biology, immunology, bioorganic chemistry and molecular design, synthetic organic chemistry and natural product synthesis. *Unit head:* Dr. James R. Williamson, Dean of Graduate and Postdoctoral Studies, 858-784-8469, Fax: 858-784-2802, E-mail: gradprgm@scripps.edu. *Application contact:* Marylyn Rinaldi, Administrative Director, 858-784-8469, Fax: 858-784-2802, E-mail: mrinaldi@scripps.edu.

Seton Hall University, College of Arts and Sciences, Department of Biological Sciences, South Orange, NJ 07079-2697. Offers biology (MS); biology/business administration (MS); microbiology (MS); molecular bioscience (PhD); molecular bioscience/neuroscience (PhD). Part-time and evening/weekend programs available. *Degree requirements:* For master's, thesis optional; for doctorate, comprehensive exam, thesis/dissertation. *Entrance requirements:* For master's and doctorate, GRE or MS from accredited university in the U.S. Additional exam requirements/recommendations for international students: Required—TOEFL. Electronic applications accepted. *Faculty research:* Neurobiology, genetics, immunology, molecular biology, cellular physiology, toxicology, microbiology, bioinformatics.

Shippensburg University of Pennsylvania, School of Graduate Studies, College of Arts and Sciences, Department of Biology, Shippensburg, PA 17257-2299. Offers MS. Part-time and evening/weekend programs available. *Faculty:* 11 full-time (6 women). *Students:* 14 full-time (10 women), 9 part-time (6 women); includes 3 minority (all Black or African American, non-Hispanic/Latino). Average age 29. 21 applicants, 81% accepted, 8 enrolled. In 2010, 12 master's awarded. *Degree requirements:* For master's, oral thesis defense, seminar, minimum QPA of 3.0. *Entrance requirements:* For master's, minimum GPA of 2.75; essay; 33 credits of course work in biology; minimum 4 courses/labs in chemistry including both inorganic and organic chemistry or biochemistry. Additional exam requirements/recommendations for international students: Required—TOEFL (minimum score 580 paper-based; 237 computer-based); Recommended—IELTS (minimum score 6). *Application deadline:* For fall admission, 3/1 for international students; for spring admission, 7/1 for international students. Applications are processed on a rolling basis. Application fee: $30. Electronic applications accepted. *Expenses:* Tuition, state resident: full-time $6966. Tuition, nonresident: full-time $11,146. Required fees: $1802. *Financial support:* In 2010–11, 8 research assistantships with full tuition reimbursements (averaging $5,000 per year) were awarded; career-related internships or fieldwork, scholarships/grants, unspecified assistantships, and resident hall director and student payroll positions also available. Support available to part-time students. Financial award application deadline: 3/1; financial award applicants required to submit FAFSA. *Unit head:* Dr. Theo Light, Graduate Coordinator, 717-477-1401, Fax: 717-477-4064, E-mail: tsligh@ship.edu. *Application contact:* Jeremy R. Goshorn, Associate Dean of Graduate Admissions, 717-477-1231, Fax: 717-477-4016, E-mail: jrgoshorn@ship.edu.

Simon Fraser University, Graduate Studies, Faculty of Science, Department of Biological Sciences, Burnaby, BC V5A 1S6, Canada. Offers biological sciences (M Sc, PhD); environmental toxicology (MET); pest management (MPM). *Degree requirements:* For master's, thesis; for doctorate, thesis/dissertation. *Entrance requirements:* For master's, minimum GPA of 3.0; for doctorate, minimum GPA of 3.5. Additional exam requirements/recommendations for international students: Required—TOEFL or IELTS. Electronic applications accepted. *Faculty research:* Molecular biology, marine biology, ecology, wildlife biology, endocrinology.

Smith College, Graduate and Special Programs, Department of Biological Sciences, Northampton, MA 01063. Offers MAT, MS. Part-time programs available. *Faculty:* 14 full-time (5 women), 3 part-time/adjunct (1 woman). *Students:* 1 (woman) full-time, 7 part-time (6 women); includes 1 Hispanic/Latino, 2 international. Average age 25. 8 applicants, 63% accepted, 4 enrolled. In 2010, 1 master's awarded. *Degree requirements:* For master's, one foreign language, thesis (for some programs). *Entrance requirements:* For master's, GRE General Test, GRE Subject Test. Additional exam requirements/recommendations for international students: Required—TOEFL (minimum score 590 paper-based; 243 computer-based; 97 iBT). *Application deadline:* For fall admission, 1/15 for domestic and international students; for spring admission, 12/1 for domestic students. Application fee: $60. *Expenses:* Tuition: Full-time $14,520; part-time $1210 per credit. *Financial support:* In 2010–11, 8 students received support, including 3 research assistantships with full tuition reimbursements available (averaging $11,910 per year); institutionally sponsored loans and scholarships/grants also available. Support available to part-time students. Financial award application deadline: 1/15; financial award applicants required to submit CSS PROFILE or FAFSA. *Unit head:* Stephen Tilley, Chair, 413-585-3817, E-mail: stilley@smith.edu. *Application contact:* Rob P. Dorit, Graduate Student Advisor, 413-585-3638, E-mail: rdorit@smith.edu.

Sonoma State University, School of Science and Technology, Department of Biology, Rohnert Park, CA 94928. Offers environmental biology (MA); general biology (MA). Part-time programs available. *Faculty:* 10 full-time (2 women). *Students:* 4 full-time (3 women), 16 part-time (7 women); includes 4 minority (1 American Indian or Alaska Native, non-Hispanic/Latino; 2 Hispanic/Latino; 1 Two or more races, non-Hispanic/Latino), 1 international. Average age 29. 19 applicants, 58% accepted, 9 enrolled. In 2010, 4 master's awarded. *Degree requirements:* For master's, thesis or alternative, oral exam. *Entrance requirements:* For master's, GRE General Test, GRE Subject Test, minimum GPA of 3.0. Additional exam requirements/recommendations for international students: Required—TOEFL (minimum score 500 paper-based; 173 computer-based). *Application deadline:* For fall admission, 11/30 for domestic students. Applications are processed on a rolling basis. Application fee: $55. *Financial support:* In 2010–11, 1 fellowship (averaging $2,100 per year), 15 teaching assistantships (averaging $5,343 per year) were awarded; research assistantships, career-related internships or fieldwork, Federal Work-Study, and tuition waivers (full) also available. Financial award application deadline: 3/2; financial award applicants required to submit FAFSA. *Faculty research:* Plant physiology, comparative physiology, community ecology, restoration ecology, marine ecology, conservation genetics, primate behavior, behavioral ecology, developmental biology, plant and animal systematics. Total annual research expenditures: $238,000. *Unit head:* Dr. Richard Whitkus, Chair, 707-664-2303, E-mail: james.christmann@sonoma.edu. *Application contact:* Dr. Dan Crocker, Graduate Adviser, 707-664-2995.

South Dakota State University, Graduate School, College of Agriculture and Biological Sciences, Department of Animal and Range Sciences, Brookings, SD 57007. Offers animal science (MS, PhD); biological sciences (PhD). Part-time programs available. *Degree requirements:* For master's, thesis, oral exam; for doctorate, comprehensive exam, thesis/dissertation, preliminary oral and written exams. *Entrance requirements:* Additional exam requirements/recommendations for international students: Required—TOEFL (minimum score 550 paper-based; 213 computer-based; 79 iBT). *Faculty research:* Ruminant and nonruminant nutrition, meat science, reproductive physiology, range utilization, ecology genetics, muscle biology, animal production.

South Dakota State University, Graduate School, College of Agriculture and Biological Sciences, Department of Biology and Microbiology, Brookings, SD 57007. Offers biological sciences (MS, PhD). Part-time programs available. *Degree requirements:* For master's, thesis (for some programs), oral exam; for doctorate, comprehensive exam, thesis/dissertation, oral exam. *Entrance requirements:* For master's and doctorate, GRE General Test. Additional exam requirements/recommendations for international students: Required—TOEFL (minimum score 600 paper-based; 250 computer-based; 100 iBT). *Faculty research:* Ecosystem ecology; plant, animal and microbial genomics; animal infectious disease, microbial bioproducts.

South Dakota State University, Graduate School, College of Agriculture and Biological Sciences, Department of Dairy Science, Brookings, SD 57007. Offers animal sciences (MS, PhD); biological sciences (MS, PhD). Part-time programs available. *Degree requirements:* For master's, thesis, oral exam; for doctorate, comprehensive exam, thesis/dissertation, preliminary oral and written exams. *Entrance requirements:* Additional exam requirements/recommendations for international students: Required—TOEFL (minimum score 550 paper-based; 213 computer-based). *Faculty research:* Dairy cattle nutrition, energy metabolism, food safety, dairy processing technology.

South Dakota State University, Graduate School, College of Agriculture and Biological Sciences, Department of Veterinary Science, Brookings, SD 57007. Offers biological sciences (MS, PhD). Part-time and evening/weekend programs available. *Degree requirements:* For master's, thesis (for some programs), oral exam; for doctorate, comprehensive exam, thesis/dissertation, preliminary oral and written exams. *Entrance requirements:* Additional exam requirements/recommendations for international students: Required—TOEFL (minimum score 525 paper-based; 197 computer-based; 71 iBT). *Faculty research:* Infectious disease, food animal, virology, immunology.

South Dakota State University, Graduate School, College of Engineering, Department of Agricultural and Biosystems Engineering, Brookings, SD 57007. Offers biological sciences (MS, PhD); engineering (MS). PhD offered jointly with Iowa State University of Science and Technology. Part-time programs available. *Degree requirements:* For master's, thesis (for some programs), oral exam; for doctorate, thesis/dissertation, preliminary oral and written exams. *Entrance requirements:* For master's and doctorate, engineering degree. Additional exam requirements/recommendations for international students: Required—TOEFL (minimum score 550 paper-based; 213 computer-based; 79 iBT). *Faculty research:* Water resources, food engineering, natural resources engineering, machine design, bioprocess engineering.

South Dakota State University, Graduate School, College of Pharmacy, Department of Pharmaceutical Sciences, Brookings, SD 57007. Offers biological science (MS); pharmaceutical sciences (PhD). *Degree requirements:* For master's, thesis, oral exam; for doctorate, comprehensive exam, thesis/dissertation, oral exam. *Entrance requirements:* For master's and doctorate, GRE General Test. Additional exam requirements/recommendations for international students: Required—TOEFL (minimum score 550 paper-based; 213 computer-based). *Faculty research:* Drugs of abuse, anti-cancer drugs, sustained drug delivery, drug metabolism.

Southeastern Louisiana University, College of Science and Technology, Department of Biological Sciences, Hammond, LA 70402. Offers biology (MS). Part-time programs available. *Faculty:* 8 full-time (3 women). *Students:* 14 full-time (9 women), 14 part-time (7 women); includes 1 minority (Black or African American, non-Hispanic/Latino). Average age 25. 25 applicants, 68% accepted, 8 enrolled. In 2010, 11 master's awarded. *Degree requirements:* For master's, comprehensive exam, thesis (for some programs), completion of program within six years. *Entrance requirements:* For master's, GRE General Test (minimum score 1000), minimum GPA of 3.0, 30 undergraduate hours in biology, 2 letters of reference, curriculum vitae, letter of intent. Additional exam requirements/recommendations for international students: Required—TOEFL (minimum score 500 paper-based; 173 computer-based; 61 iBT). *Application deadline:* For fall admission, 7/15 priority date for domestic students, 6/1 priority date for international students; for spring admission, 12/1 priority date for domestic students, 10/1 priority date for international students. Applications are processed on a rolling basis. Application fee: $20 ($30 for international students). Electronic applications accepted. *Expenses:* Tuition, state resident: full-time $3533. Tuition, nonresident: full-time $12,002. Required fees: $907. Tuition and fees vary according to degree level. *Financial support:* In 2010–11, 19 students received support, including 4 fellowships (averaging $10,800 per year), 5 research assistantships (averaging $12,326 per year), 10 teaching assistantships (averaging $10,100 per year); Federal Work-Study, institutionally sponsored loans, and unspecified assistantships also available. Support available to part-time students. Financial award application deadline: 5/1; financial award applicants required to submit FAFSA. *Faculty research:* Molecular and morphological evolution, environmental microbiology and microbial genetics, ecosystem diversity and wetland ecology, neurobiology, virology. Total annual research expenditures: $917,862. *Unit head:* Dr. David Sever, Department Head, 985-549-3740, Fax: 985-549-3851, E-mail: dsever@selu.edu. *Application contact:* Sandra Meyers, Graduate Admissions Analyst, 985-549-5620, Fax: 985-549-5632, E-mail: admissions@selu.edu.

Southeast Missouri State University, School of Graduate Studies, Department of Biology, Cape Girardeau, MO 63701-4799. Offers MNS. Part-time programs available. *Faculty:* 16 full-time (5 women). *Students:* 12 full-time (7 women), 15 part-time (8 women); includes 2 minority (1 Black or African American, non-Hispanic/Latino; 1 Hispanic/Latino), 3 international. Average age 25. 18 applicants, 61% accepted, 9 enrolled. In 2010, 6 master's awarded. *Degree requirements:* For master's, comprehensive exam (for some programs), thesis, scholarly paper (for some programs). *Entrance requirements:* For master's, GRE General Test, minimum undergraduate GPA of 2.75, minimum of 30 hours of undergraduate course work in science and mathematics, letter of intent declaring academic interest, 2 letters of recommendation. Additional exam requirements/recommendations for international students: Required—TOEFL (minimum score 550 paper-based; 213 computer-based; 79 iBT); Recommended—IELTS (minimum score 6). *Application deadline:* For fall admission, 8/1 for domestic students, 6/1 for international students; for spring admission, 11/21 for domestic students, 10/1 for international students. Applications are processed on a rolling basis. Application fee: $25 ($35 for international students). Electronic applications accepted. *Expenses:* Tuition, state resident: full-time $4698; part-time $261 per credit hour. Tuition, nonresident: full-time $8379; part-time $465.50 per credit hour. *Financial support:* In 2010–11, 19 students received support, including 17 teaching assistantships with full tuition reimbursements available (averaging $7,600 per year); career-related internships or fieldwork, Federal Work-Study, institutionally sponsored loans, scholarships/grants, tuition waivers (full), and unspecified assistantships also available. Financial award application deadline: 6/30; financial award applicants required to submit FAFSA. *Faculty research:* Wildlife and conservation biology; microbiology and epidemiology; ecology, animal behavior and marine biology; case-based learning; plant systematics and physiology. Total annual research expenditures: $495,425. *Unit head:* Dr. William Eddleman, Chairperson, 573-651-2171, Fax: 573-651-2382, E-mail: weddleman@semo.edu. *Application contact:* Gail Amick, Administrative Secretary, 573-651-2049, Fax: 573-651-2001, E-mail: gamick@semo.edu.

Southern Connecticut State University, School of Graduate Studies, School of Arts and Sciences, Department of Biology, New Haven, CT 06515-1355. Offers MS. Part-time and evening/weekend programs available. *Faculty:* 11 full-time (6 women). *Students:* 13 full-time (9 women), 24 part-time (16 women); includes 4 Black or African American, non-Hispanic/Latino; 3 Hispanic/Latino; 1 Two or more races, non-Hispanic/Latino. 61 applicants, 21% accepted, 9 enrolled. In 2010, 3 master's awarded. *Degree requirements:* For master's, thesis optional. *Entrance requirements:* For master's, previous course work in biology, chemistry, and mathematics; interview. *Application deadline:* Applications are processed on a rolling basis. Application fee: $50. Electronic applications accepted. *Expenses:* Tuition, state resident: full-time $5137; part-time $518 per credit. Tuition, nonresident: part-time $542 per credit. Required fees: $4008; $55 per semester. Tuition and fees vary according to program. *Financial support:* Application deadline: 4/15. *Unit head:* Dr. Dwight Smith, Chairperson, 203-392-6222, Fax: 203-392-5364, E-mail: smithd1@southernct.edu. *Application contact:* Dr. Sean Grace, Graduate Coordinator, 203-392-6216, Fax: 203-392-5364, E-mail: graces2@southernct.edu.

Southern Illinois University Carbondale, Graduate School, College of Science, Biological Sciences Program, Carbondale, IL 62901-4701. Offers MS. *Degree requirements:* For master's, thesis or alternative. *Entrance requirements:* For master's, GRE General Test, minimum GPA of 2.7. Additional exam requirements/recommendations for international students: Required—TOEFL. *Faculty research:* Molecular mechanisms of mutagenesis, reproductive endocrinology, avian energetics and nutrition, developmental plant physiology.

Southern Illinois University Carbondale, Graduate School, Graduate Program in Medicine, Carbondale, IL 62901-4701. Offers molecular, cellular and systemic physiology (MS); pharmacology (MS, PhD); physiology (MS, PhD). Terminal master's awarded for partial completion of doctoral program. *Degree requirements:* For master's, thesis; for doctorate, thesis/dissertation. *Entrance requirements:* For master's, minimum GPA of 3.0; for doctorate, minimum GPA of 3.25. Additional exam requirements/recommendations for international students: Required—TOEFL. *Faculty research:* Cardiovascular physiology, neurophysiology of hearing.

Southern Illinois University Edwardsville, Graduate School, College of Arts and Sciences, Department of Biological Sciences, Program in Biology, Edwardsville, IL 62026-0001. Offers MA, MS. Part-time programs available. *Faculty:* 26 full-time (5 women). *Students:* 18 full-time (8 women), 35 part-time (22 women); includes 4 minority (3 Black or African American, non-Hispanic/Latino; 1 Two or more races, non-Hispanic/Latino), 3 international. Average age 26. 51 applicants, 41% accepted. In 2010, 20 master's awarded. *Degree requirements:* For master's, thesis (for some programs). *Entrance requirements:* For master's, GRE. Additional exam requirements/recommendations for international students: Required—TOEFL (minimum score 550 paper-based; 213 computer-based; 79 iBT), IELTS (minimum score 6.5). *Application deadline:* For fall admission, 7/22 for domestic students, 6/1 for international students; for spring admission, 12/9 for domestic students, 10/1 for international students. Applications are processed on a rolling basis. Application fee: $30. Electronic applications accepted. *Expenses:* Tuition, state resident: full-time $6012; part-time $1503 per semester. Tuition, nonresident: full-time $15,030; part-time $3758 per semester. Required fees: $1711; $675 per semester. *Financial support:* In 2010–11, 2 research assistantships with full tuition reimbursements (averaging $8,064 per year), 33 teaching assistantships with full tuition reimbursements (averaging $8,064 per year) were awarded; fellowships with full tuition reimbursements also available. Financial award application deadline: 3/1; financial award applicants required to submit FAFSA. *Unit head:* Dr. Dave Duvernell, Director, 618-650-3468, E-mail: dduvern@siue.edu. *Application contact:* Michelle Robinson, Coordinator of Graduate Recruitment, 618-650-2811, Fax: 618-650-3523, E-mail: michero@siue.edu.

Southern Methodist University, Dedman College, Department of Biological Sciences, Dallas, TX 75275. Offers MA, MS, PhD. *Faculty:* 12 full-time (3 women), 1 (woman) part-time/adjunct. *Students:* 10 full-time (8 women), 2 part-time (both women); includes 1 Asian, non-Hispanic/Latino, 7 international. Average age 26. 23 applicants, 13% accepted. In 2010, 2 master's awarded. Terminal master's awarded for partial completion of doctoral program. *Degree requirements:* For master's, thesis (MS), oral exam; for doctorate, thesis/dissertation, qualifying exam. *Entrance requirements:* For master's, GRE General Test (minimum score 1200), minimum GPA of 3.0; for doctorate, GRE General Test (minimum score: 1200), minimum GPA of 3.0. Additional exam requirements/recommendations for international students: Required—TOEFL (minimum score 550 paper-based; 217 computer-based). *Application deadline:* For fall admission, 2/1 priority date for domestic and international students; for spring admission, 11/30 priority date for domestic and international students. Applications are processed on a rolling basis. Application fee: $60. Electronic applications accepted. *Financial support:* In 2010–11, 7 research assistantships with full tuition reimbursements (averaging $20,280 per year), 7 teaching assistantships with full tuition reimbursements (averaging $20,280 per year) were awarded; Federal Work-Study, health care benefits, and tuition waivers (partial) also available. Financial award applicants required to submit FAFSA. *Faculty research:* Free radicals and aging, protein structure, chromatin structure, signal processes, retroviral pathogenesis. Total annual research expenditures: $2 million. *Unit head:* Dr. Bill Orr, Head, 214-768-4018, Fax: 214-768-3955. *Application contact:* Dr. Pia Vogel, Graduate Advisor, 214-768-1790, Fax: 214-768-3955, E-mail: pvogel@smu.edu.

Southern University and Agricultural and Mechanical College, Graduate School, College of Sciences, Department of Biology, Baton Rouge, LA 70813. Offers MS. *Degree requirements:* For master's, comprehensive exam, thesis. *Entrance requirements:* For master's, GRE General Test. Additional exam requirements/recommendations for international students: Required—TOEFL (minimum score 525 paper-based; 193 computer-based). *Faculty research:* Toxicology, neuroendocrinology, mycotoxin, virology.

Stanford University, School of Humanities and Sciences, Department of Biological Sciences, Stanford, CA 94305-9991. Offers MS, PhD. Terminal master's awarded for partial completion of doctoral program. *Degree requirements:* For doctorate, thesis/dissertation, oral exam. *Entrance requirements:* For master's, GRE General Test; for doctorate, GRE General Test, GRE Subject Test. Additional exam requirements/recommendations for international students: Required—TOEFL. Electronic applications accepted. *Expenses:* Tuition: Full-time $38,700; part-time $860 per unit. One-time fee: $200 full-time.

Stanford University, School of Medicine, Graduate Programs in Medicine, Stanford, CA 94305-9991. Offers MS, PhD. Terminal master's awarded for partial completion of doctoral program. *Degree requirements:* For master's, thesis; for doctorate, thesis/dissertation. *Entrance requirements:* For master's, GRE General Test or MCAT. Additional exam requirements/recommendations for international students: Required—TOEFL. Electronic applications accepted. *Expenses:* Tuition: Full-time $38,700; part-time $860 per unit. One-time fee: $200 full-time.

State University of New York at Binghamton, Graduate School, School of Arts and Sciences, Department of Biological Sciences, Binghamton, NY 13902-6000. Offers MA, PhD. *Faculty:* 25 full-time (9 women), 6 part-time/adjunct (3 women). *Students:* 51 full-time (23 women), 26 part-time (13 women); includes 2 Black or African American, non-Hispanic/Latino; 7 Asian, non-Hispanic/Latino; 2 Hispanic/Latino, 19 international. Average age 27. 94 applicants, 28% accepted, 16 enrolled. In 2010, 14 master's, 2 doctorates awarded. Terminal master's awarded for partial completion of doctoral program. *Degree requirements:* For master's, thesis, oral exam, seminar presentation; for doctorate, comprehensive exam, thesis/dissertation. *Entrance requirements:* For master's and doctorate, GRE General Test, GRE Subject Test. Additional exam requirements/recommendations for international students: Required—TOEFL (minimum score 550 paper-based; 213 computer-based; 80 iBT). *Application deadline:* For fall admission, 1/15 priority date for domestic and international students; for spring admission, 10/15 priority date for domestic and international students. Applications are processed on a rolling basis. Application fee: $60. Electronic applications accepted. *Financial support:* In 2010–11, 45 students received support, including 2 fellowships with full tuition reimbursements available (averaging $17,500 per year), 6 research assistantships with full tuition reimbursements available (averaging $17,500 per year), 33 teaching assistantships with full tuition reimbursements available (averaging $17,500 per year); career-related internships or fieldwork, Federal Work-Study, institutionally sponsored loans, scholarships/grants, health care benefits, tuition waivers (full and partial), and unspecified assistantships also available. Financial award application deadline: 2/15; financial award applicants required to submit FAFSA. *Unit head:* Dr. John Titus, Chairperson, 607-777-2445, E-mail: jtitus@binghamton.edu. *Application contact:* Catherine Smith, Recruiting and Admissions Coordinator, 607-777-2151, Fax: 607-777-2501, E-mail: cmsmith@binghamton.edu.

State University of New York at Fredonia, Graduate Studies, Department of Biology, Fredonia, NY 14063-1136. Offers MS, MS Ed. Part-time and evening/weekend programs available. *Degree requirements:* For master's, thesis optional. *Expenses:* Tuition, state resident: full-time

Biological and Biomedical Sciences—General

State University of New York at Fredonia (continued)
$8370; part-time $349 per credit hour. Tuition, nonresident: full-time $13,250; part-time $552 per credit hour. Required fees: $1328; $55.15 per credit hour.

State University of New York at New Paltz, Graduate School, School of Science and Engineering, Department of Biology, New Paltz, NY 12561. Offers MA. Part-time and evening/weekend programs available. *Faculty:* 4 full-time (2 women). *Students:* 2 full-time (both women), 4 part-time (all women). Average age 29. 9 applicants, 33% accepted, 3 enrolled. In 2010, 3 master's awarded. *Degree requirements:* For master's, comprehensive exam, thesis (for some programs). *Entrance requirements:* For master's, GRE General Test, GRE Subject Test, minimum GPA of 3.0. Additional exam requirements/recommendations for international students: Required—TOEFL (minimum score 550 paper-based; 213 computer-based; 80 iBT), IELTS (minimum score 6.5). *Application deadline:* For fall admission, 5/15 for domestic and international students; for spring admission, 11/15 for domestic and international students. Application fee: $50. Electronic applications accepted. *Expenses:* Tuition, state resident: full-time $8370; part-time $349 per credit hour. Tuition, nonresident: full-time $13,780; part-time $574 per credit hour. Required fees: $1165; $33.80 per credit hour. $175 per term. Tuition and fees vary according to program. *Financial support:* In 2010–11, 3 students received support, including 3 teaching assistantships with partial tuition reimbursements available (averaging $5,000 per year); Federal Work-Study, institutionally sponsored loans, and unspecified assistantships also available. Financial award application deadline: 8/1; financial award applicants required to submit FAFSA. *Faculty research:* Neurohormonal regulation of feeding in insects. *Unit head:* Dr. Thomas Nolen, Chair, 845-257-3770, E-mail: nolent@newpaltz.edu. *Application contact:* Prof. Jeffrey Reinking, Coordinator, 845-257-3771, E-mail: reinkinj@newpaltz.edu.

State University of New York College at Oneonta, Graduate Education, Department of Biology, Oneonta, NY 13820-4015. Offers MA. Part-time and evening/weekend programs available. *Students:* 2 full-time (both women), 3 part-time (2 women). Average age 26. 5 applicants, 100% accepted, 5 enrolled. In 2010, 1 master's awarded. *Degree requirements:* For master's, comprehensive exam. *Entrance requirements:* For master's, GRE General Test, GRE Subject Test. *Application deadline:* For fall admission, 3/25 priority date for domestic students; for spring admission, 10/1 priority date for domestic students. Applications are processed on a rolling basis. Application fee: $50. *Expenses:* Tuition, state resident: full-time $8370; part-time $349 per credit hour. Tuition, nonresident: full-time $13,780; part-time $558 per credit hour. Required fees: $899; $22 per credit hour. *Unit head:* Dr. Donna Vogler, Chair, 607-436-3705, Fax: 607-436-3646, E-mail: voglerd@oneonta.edu. *Application contact:* Patrick J. Mente, Director of Graduate Studies, 607-436-2523, Fax: 607-436-3084, E-mail: gradstudies@oneonta.edu.

State University of New York Downstate Medical Center, School of Graduate Studies, Brooklyn, NY 11203-2098. Offers MS, PhD, MD/PhD. *Degree requirements:* For doctorate, thesis/dissertation. *Entrance requirements:* For doctorate, GRE. Additional exam requirements/recommendations for international students: Required—TOEFL. *Faculty research:* Cellular and molecular neurobiology, role of oncogenes in early cardiogenesis, mechanism of gene regulation, cardiovascular physiology, yeast molecular genetics.

State University of New York Upstate Medical University, College of Graduate Studies, Syracuse, NY 13210-2334. Offers MS, PhD, MD/PhD. Terminal master's awarded for partial completion of doctoral program. *Degree requirements:* For master's, thesis; for doctorate, comprehensive exam, thesis/dissertation. *Entrance requirements:* For master's, GRE General Test, interview; for doctorate, GRE General Test, telephone interview. Additional exam requirements/recommendations for international students: Required—TOEFL. Electronic applications accepted. *Faculty research:* Cancer, disorders of the nervous system, infectious diseases, diabetes/metabolic disorders/cardiovascular diseases.

Stephen F. Austin State University, Graduate School, College of Sciences and Mathematics, Department of Biology, Nacogdoches, TX 75962. Offers MS. *Degree requirements:* For master's, comprehensive exam, thesis optional. *Entrance requirements:* For master's, GRE General Test, minimum GPA of 2.8 in last 60 hours, 2.5 overall. Additional exam requirements/recommendations for international students: Required—TOEFL.

Stony Brook University, State University of New York, Stony Brook University Medical Center, School of Medicine and Graduate School, Graduate Programs in Medicine, Stony Brook, NY 11794. Offers PhD. *Students:* 77 full-time (40 women), 4 part-time (all women); includes 3 Black or African American, non-Hispanic/Latino; 10 Asian, non-Hispanic/Latino; 7 Hispanic/Latino, 20 international. 187 applicants, 24% accepted, 32 enrolled. In 2010, 16 doctorates awarded. *Degree requirements:* For doctorate, thesis/dissertation, exam. *Entrance requirements:* For doctorate, GRE General Test. Additional exam requirements/recommendations for international students: Required—TOEFL. *Application deadline:* For fall admission, 1/15 for domestic students. Application fee: $100. Electronic applications accepted. *Expenses:* Contact institution. *Financial support:* Fellowships, research assistantships, teaching assistantships, career-related internships or fieldwork and Federal Work-Study available. Financial award application deadline: 3/15. *Unit head:* Dr. Kenneth Kaushansky, Dean and Senior Vice President of Health Sciences, 631-444-2113, Fax: 631-444-6032. *Application contact:* Dr. William Jungers, Chair, 631-444-3122, Fax: 631-444-3947, E-mail: william.jungers@stonybrook.edu.

Stony Brook University, State University of New York, Stony Brook University Medical Center, School of Medicine, Medical Scientist Training Program, Stony Brook, NY 11794. Offers MD/PhD. *Application deadline:* For fall admission, 1/15 for domestic students. *Expenses:* Tuition, state resident: full-time $8370; part-time $349 per credit. Tuition, nonresident: full-time $13,780; part-time $574 per credit. Required fees: $994. *Financial support:* Tuition waivers (full) available. *Unit head:* Dr. Richard N. Fine, Dean, 631-444-2113. *Application contact:* Dr. Richard N. Fine, Dean, 631-444-2113.

Sul Ross State University, School of Arts and Sciences, Department of Biology, Alpine, TX 79832. Offers MS. Part-time programs available. *Degree requirements:* For master's, thesis optional. *Entrance requirements:* For master's, GRE General Test, minimum GPA of 2.5 in last 60 hours of undergraduate work. *Faculty research:* Plant-animal interaction, Chihuahuan desert biology, insect biological control, plant and animal systematics, wildlife biology.

Syracuse University, College of Arts and Sciences, Program in Biology, Syracuse, NY 13244. Offers MS, PhD. Part-time programs available. *Students:* 37 full-time (23 women), 4 part-time (0 women); includes 1 minority (Native Hawaiian or other Pacific Islander, non-Hispanic/Latino), 18 international. Average age 28. 90 applicants, 14% accepted, 9 enrolled. In 2010, 1 master's, 6 doctorates awarded. Terminal master's awarded for partial completion of doctoral program. *Degree requirements:* For master's, thesis; for doctorate, thesis/dissertation. *Entrance requirements:* For master's and doctorate, GRE General Test, GRE Subject Test (recommended). Additional exam requirements/recommendations for international students: Required—TOEFL (minimum score 100 iBT). *Application deadline:* For fall admission, 1/10 priority date for domestic and international students. Application fee: $75. Electronic applications accepted. *Expenses:* Tuition: Part-time $1162 per credit. *Financial support:* Fellowships with full tuition reimbursements, research assistantships with full and partial tuition reimbursements, teaching assistantships with full tuition reimbursements, tuition waivers (partial) available. Financial award application deadline: 1/10; financial award applicants required to submit FAFSA. *Faculty research:* Cell signaling, plant ecosystem ecology, aquatic ecology, genetics and molecular biology of color vision, ion transport by cell membranes. *Unit head:* Dr. Scott Pitnick, Graduate Program Director, 315-443-9145, E-mail: biology@syr.edu. *Application contact:* Evelyn Lott, Information Contact, 315-443-9154, Fax: 315-443-2012, E-mail: ealott@syr.edu.

Tarleton State University, College of Graduate Studies, College of Science and Technology, Department of Biological Sciences, Stephenville, TX 76402. Offers biology (MS). Part-time and evening/weekend programs available. *Degree requirements:* For master's, comprehensive exam, thesis (for some programs). *Entrance requirements:* For master's, GRE General Test, minimum GPA of 3.0. Additional exam requirements/recommendations for international students: Required—TOEFL (minimum score 550 paper-based; 213 computer-based; 80 iBT). Electronic applications accepted.

Temple University, College of Science and Technology, Department of Biology, Philadelphia, PA 19122-6096. Offers MS, PhD. *Faculty:* 19 full-time (5 women). *Students:* 22 full-time (16 women), 12 part-time (5 women); includes 2 Black or African American, non-Hispanic/Latino; 1 Hispanic/Latino, 15 international. 63 applicants, 25% accepted, 6 enrolled. In 2010, 5 master's, 1 doctorate awarded. Terminal master's awarded for partial completion of doctoral program. *Degree requirements:* For master's, thesis; for doctorate, thesis/dissertation. *Entrance requirements:* For master's and doctorate, GRE General Test, minimum GPA of 3.0. Additional exam requirements/recommendations for international students: Required—TOEFL (minimum score 550 paper-based; 213 computer-based; 79 iBT). *Application deadline:* For fall admission, 4/15 for domestic students, 12/15 for international students; for spring admission, 11/15 for domestic students, 8/1 for international students. Applications are processed on a rolling basis. Application fee: $50. *Financial support:* Fellowships, research assistantships, teaching assistantships, Federal Work-Study and tuition waivers (full) available. Financial award application deadline: 1/15; financial award applicants required to submit FAFSA. *Faculty research:* Membrane proteins, genetics, molecular biology, neuroscience, aquatic biology. Total annual research expenditures: $1 million. *Unit head:* Dr. Allen Nicholson, Chair, 215-204-8854, Fax: 215-204-6646, E-mail: biology@temple.edu. *Application contact:* Dr. Allen Nicholson, Chair, 215-204-8854, Fax: 215-204-6646, E-mail: biology@temple.edu.

Temple University, Health Sciences Center, School of Medicine and Graduate School, Doctor of Medicine Program, Philadelphia, PA 19122-6096. Offers MS, PhD, MD/PhD. *Faculty:* 77 full-time (13 women). *Students:* 750 full-time (353 women); includes 60 Black or African American, non-Hispanic/Latino; 15 American Indian or Alaska Native, non-Hispanic/Latino; 137 Asian, non-Hispanic/Latino; 63 Hispanic/Latino; 2 Two or more races, non-Hispanic/Latino. Terminal master's awarded for partial completion of doctoral program. *Degree requirements:* For master's, thesis; for doctorate, thesis/dissertation, research seminars. *Entrance requirements:* For master's and doctorate, GRE General Test. Additional exam requirements/recommendations for international students: Required—TOEFL. Application fee: $50. Electronic applications accepted. *Expenses:* Contact institution. *Financial support:* Fellowships, research assistantships, career-related internships or fieldwork, Federal Work-Study, institutionally sponsored loans, scholarships/grants, and tuition waivers (full and partial) available. Support available to part-time students. Financial award application deadline: 1/15; financial award applicants required to submit FAFSA. *Faculty research:* Molecular biology and biochemistry; cardiovascular, renal, and neurophysiological pharmacology; reproductive and developmental biology; immunology and microbiology; cancer research. Total annual research expenditures: $8.3 million. *Application contact:* Office of Admissions, 215-707-3656, Fax: 215-707-6932, E-mail: medadmissions@temple.edu.

Tennessee State University, The School of Graduate Studies and Research, College of Arts and Sciences, Department of Biological Sciences, Nashville, TN 37209-1561. Offers MS, PhD. *Degree requirements:* For master's, thesis optional; for doctorate, thesis/dissertation. *Entrance requirements:* For master's, GRE General Test, GRE Subject Test, minimum GPA of 2.5; for doctorate, GRE General Test, GRE Subject Test. *Faculty research:* Cellular and molecular biology and agribiology.

Tennessee Technological University, Graduate School, College of Arts and Sciences, Department of Biology, Cookeville, TN 38505. Offers fish, game, and wildlife management (MS). Part-time programs available. *Faculty:* 22 full-time (2 women). *Students:* 11 full-time (5 women), 11 part-time (6 women); includes 1 Black or African American, non-Hispanic/Latino. Average age 25. 17 applicants, 35% accepted, 4 enrolled. In 2010, 8 master's awarded. *Degree requirements:* For master's, thesis. *Entrance requirements:* For master's, GRE. Additional exam requirements/recommendations for international students: Required—TOEFL (minimum score 550 paper-based; 79 iBT), IELTS (minimum score 5.5). *Application deadline:* For fall admission, 8/1 for domestic students, 5/1 for international students; for spring admission, 12/1 for domestic students, 10/1 for international students. Application fee: $25 ($30 for international students). Electronic applications accepted. *Expenses:* Tuition, state resident: full-time $7934; part-time $388 per credit hour. Tuition, nonresident: full-time $19,758; part-time $962 per credit hour. *Financial support:* In 2010–11, 17 research assistantships (averaging $9,000 per year), 8 teaching assistantships (averaging $7,500 per year) were awarded. Financial award application deadline: 4/1. *Faculty research:* Aquatics, environmental studies. *Unit head:* Dr. Daniel Combs, Interim Chairperson, 931-372-3134, Fax: 931-372-6257, E-mail: dcombs@tntech.edu. *Application contact:* Shelia K. Kendrick, Coordinator of Graduate Admissions, 931-372-3808, Fax: 931-372-3497, E-mail: skendrick@tntech.edu.

Tennessee Technological University, Graduate School, College of Arts and Sciences, Department of Environmental Sciences, Cookeville, TN 38505. Offers biology (PhD); chemistry (PhD). *Students:* 9 full-time (4 women), 6 part-time (2 women); includes 3 Black or African American, non-Hispanic/Latino; 2 Asian, non-Hispanic/Latino; 2 Hispanic/Latino. 14 applicants, 21% accepted, 1 enrolled. In 2010, 4 doctorates awarded. *Degree requirements:* For doctorate, comprehensive exam, thesis/dissertation. *Entrance requirements:* For doctorate, GRE. Additional exam requirements/recommendations for international students: Required—TOEFL (minimum score 550 paper-based; 79 iBT), IELTS (minimum score 5.5). *Application deadline:* For fall admission, 8/1 for domestic students, 5/1 for international students; for spring admission, 12/1 for domestic students, 10/2 for international students. Application fee: $25 ($30 for international students). Electronic applications accepted. *Expenses:* Tuition, state resident: full-time $7934; part-time $388 per credit hour. Tuition, nonresident: full-time $19,758; part-time $962 per credit hour. *Financial support:* In 2010–11, 5 research assistantships (averaging $10,000 per year), 3 teaching assistantships (averaging $10,000 per year) were awarded; fellowships also available. Financial award application deadline: 4/1. *Unit head:* Dr. Dal Ensor, Director. *Application contact:* Shelia K. Kendrick, Coordinator of Graduate Admissions, 931-372-3808, Fax: 931-372-3497, E-mail: skendrick@tntech.edu.

Texas A&M Health Science Center, Baylor College of Dentistry, Graduate Division, Department of Biomedical Sciences, College Station, TX 77840. Offers MS, PhD. Part-time programs available. Terminal master's awarded for partial completion of doctoral program. *Degree requirements:* For master's, thesis; for doctorate, thesis/dissertation. *Entrance requirements:* For master's, GRE General Test; for doctorate, GRE General Test, DDS or DMD. Additional exam requirements/recommendations for international students: Required—TOEFL. *Faculty research:* Craniofacial biology, aging, neuroscience, physiology, molecular/cellular biology.

Texas A&M Health Science Center, Graduate School of Biomedical Sciences, College Station, TX 77840. Offers cell and molecular biology (PhD); microbial and molecular pathogenesis (PhD), including immunology, microbiology, molecular biology, virology; molecular and cellular medicine (PhD); neuroscience and experimental therapeutics (PhD); systems biology and translational medicine (PhD); MD/PhD. *Degree requirements:* For doctorate, thesis/dissertation. *Entrance requirements:* For doctorate, GRE General Test, minimum GPA of 3.0. Additional exam requirements/recommendations for international students: Required—TOEFL. *Faculty research:* Fetal alcohol syndrome, cardiovascular, microbial pathogenesis, cancer.

Texas A&M Health Science Center, Institute of Biosciences and Technology, Houston, TX 77030-3303. Offers medical sciences (PhD). Degree awarded by the Graduate School for Biomedical Sciences. *Degree requirements:* For doctorate, thesis/dissertation. *Entrance requirements:* For doctorate, GRE General Test. Additional exam requirements/recommendations for international students: Required—TOEFL, TWE. *Expenses:* Contact institution. *Faculty research:* Cancer biology, DNA structure, extracellular matrix biology, development, birth defects.

Texas A&M International University, Office of Graduate Studies and Research, College of Arts and Sciences, Department of Biology and Chemistry, Laredo, TX 78041-1900. Offers biology (MS). *Faculty:* 4 full-time (0 women). *Students:* 3 full-time (2 women), 20 part-time (12 women); includes 1 Asian, non-Hispanic/Latino; 20 Hispanic/Latino, 1 international. Average

age 29. 75 applicants, 84% accepted. *Application deadline:* For fall admission, 4/30 for domestic and international students; for spring admission, 11/30 for domestic students, 10/1 for international students. Application fee: $25. *Financial support:* In 2010–11, 9 students received support, including 6 research assistantships, 1 teaching assistantship. *Unit head:* Dr. Daniel Mott, Chair, 956-326-2583. *Application contact:* Suzanne Hansen-Alford, Director of Graduate Recruiting, 956-326-3023, E-mail: salford@tamiu.edu.

Texas A&M University, College of Science, Department of Biology, College Station, TX 77843. Offers biology (MS, PhD); botany (MS, PhD); microbiology (MS, PhD); molecular and cell biology (PhD); neuroscience (MS, PhD); zoology (MS, PhD). *Faculty:* 39. *Students:* 107 full-time (60 women), 4 part-time (3 women); includes 1 Black or African American, non-Hispanic/Latino; 5 Asian, non-Hispanic/Latino; 5 Hispanic/Latino, 47 international. Average age 28. In 2010, 3 master's, 6 doctorates awarded. *Degree requirements:* For master's, thesis or alternative; for doctorate, comprehensive exam, thesis/dissertation. *Entrance requirements:* For master's and doctorate, GRE General Test. Additional exam requirements/recommendations for international students: Required—TOEFL. *Application deadline:* For fall admission, 1/15 for domestic students. Applications are processed on a rolling basis. Application fee: $50 ($75 for international students). Electronic applications accepted. *Financial support:* Fellowships, research assistantships, teaching assistantships available. Financial award application deadline: 4/1; financial award applicants required to submit FAFSA. *Unit head:* Dr. Jack McMahan, Department Head, 979-845-2301, E-mail: granster@mail.bio.tamu.edu. *Application contact:* Dr. Jack McMahan, Department Head, 979-845-2301, E-mail: granster@mail.bio.tamu.edu.

Texas A&M University, College of Veterinary Medicine and Biomedical Sciences, Department of Veterinary Physiology and Pharmacology, College Station, TX 77843. Offers biomedical science (MS, PhD); toxicology (PhD). *Faculty:* 17. *Students:* 25 full-time (15 women); includes 1 Black or African American, non-Hispanic/Latino; 2 Asian, non-Hispanic/Latino; 1 Hispanic/Latino, 10 international. Average age 30. In 2010, 1 doctorate awarded. *Entrance requirements:* For master's and doctorate, GRE General Test. Additional exam requirements/recommendations for international students: Required—TOEFL. Application fee: $50 ($75 for international students). *Financial support:* Fellowships, research assistantships, teaching assistantships available. Financial award application deadline: 4/1; financial award applicants required to submit FAFSA. *Faculty research:* Gamete and embryo physiology, endocrinology, equine laminitis. *Unit head:* Glen Laine, Head, 979-845-7261, E-mail: glaine@tamu.edu. *Application contact:* Graduate Admissions, 979-845-1044, E-mail: admissions@tamu.edu.

Texas A&M University–Commerce, Graduate School, College of Arts and Sciences, Department of Biological and Earth Sciences, Commerce, TX 75429-3011. Offers M Ed, MS. *Degree requirements:* For master's, comprehensive exam, thesis (for some programs). *Entrance requirements:* For master's, GRE General Test. Electronic applications accepted. *Faculty research:* Microbiology, botany, environmental science, birds.

Texas A&M University–Corpus Christi, Graduate Studies and Research, College of Science and Technology, Program in Biology, Corpus Christi, TX 78412-5503. Offers MS.

Texas A&M University–Kingsville, College of Graduate Studies, College of Arts and Sciences, Department of Biology, Kingsville, TX 78363. Offers MS. Part-time programs available. *Degree requirements:* For master's, comprehensive exam, thesis or alternative. *Entrance requirements:* For master's, GRE General Test, minimum GPA of 3.0. Additional exam requirements/recommendations for international students: Required—TOEFL. *Faculty research:* Venom physiology, monoclonal research with venom, shore bird ecology, metabolism of foreign amino acids.

Texas Christian University, College of Science and Engineering, Department of Biology, Fort Worth, TX 76129-0002. Offers MA, MS. Part-time and evening/weekend programs available. In 2010, 5 master's awarded. *Degree requirements:* For master's, comprehensive exam, thesis (for some programs). *Entrance requirements:* For master's, GRE General Test. Additional exam requirements/recommendations for international students: Required—TOEFL. *Application deadline:* For fall admission, 1/15 priority date for domestic and international students; for spring admission, 7/15 priority date for domestic and international students. Applications are processed on a rolling basis. Application fee: $50. Electronic applications accepted. *Expenses:* Tuition: Full-time $18,720; part-time $1040 per credit hour. Tuition and fees vary according to course load and program. *Financial support:* In 2010–11, 10 students received support; teaching assistantships with full tuition reimbursements available available. Financial award application deadline: 1/15. *Unit head:* Dr. Ray Drenner, Chairperson, 817-257-7165, E-mail: r.drenner@tcu.edu. *Application contact:* Dr. Magnus Rittby, Associate Dean, College of Science and Engineering, 817-257-7729, E-mail: m.rittby@tcu.edu.

Texas Southern University, School of Science and Technology, Department of Biology, Houston, TX 77004-4584. Offers MS. Part-time and evening/weekend programs available. *Faculty:* 7 full-time (3 women). *Students:* 24 full-time (16 women), 24 part-time (20 women); includes 39 Black or African American, non-Hispanic/Latino; 5 Asian, non-Hispanic/Latino; 1 Hispanic/Latino. Average age 28. 14 applicants, 100% accepted, 11 enrolled. In 2010, 3 master's awarded. *Degree requirements:* For master's, one foreign language, comprehensive exam, thesis. *Entrance requirements:* For master's, GRE General Test, minimum GPA of 2.5. Additional exam requirements/recommendations for international students: Required—TOEFL. *Application deadline:* For fall admission, 7/1 for domestic and international students; for spring admission, 11/1 for domestic and international students. Applications are processed on a rolling basis. Application fee: $50 ($75 for international students). Electronic applications accepted. *Expenses:* Tuition, state resident: full-time $1875; part-time $100 per credit hour. Tuition, nonresident: full-time $6641; part-time $343 per credit hour. Tuition and fees vary according to course level, course load and degree level. *Financial support:* In 2010–11, 13 research assistantships (averaging $3,785 per year), 13 teaching assistantships (averaging $9,600 per year) were awarded; fellowships, career-related internships or fieldwork, scholarships/grants, and unspecified assistantships also available. Financial award application deadline: 5/1. *Faculty research:* Microbiology, cell and molecular biology, biochemistry, biochemical virology, biophysics. *Unit head:* Dr. Desiree Jackson, Acting Chair, 713-313-7778, E-mail: jackson_da@tsu.edu. *Application contact:* Helen Pittman-Cockrell, Administrative Assistant, 713-313-7005, E-mail: pittman_hj@tsu.edu.

Texas State University–San Marcos, Graduate School, College of Science, Department of Biology, Program in Biology, San Marcos, TX 78666. Offers M Ed, MA, MS. *Faculty:* 7 full-time (3 women). *Students:* 27 full-time (9 women), 17 part-time (12 women); includes 10 minority (1 Asian, non-Hispanic/Latino; 8 Hispanic/Latino; 1 Two or more races, non-Hispanic/Latino), 6 international. Average age 28. 19 applicants, 63% accepted, 10 enrolled. In 2010, 11 master's awarded. *Degree requirements:* For master's, comprehensive exam, thesis (for some programs). *Entrance requirements:* For master's, GRE General Test (minimum score 1000 preferred), minimum GPA of 3.0 in last 60 hours of undergraduate work. Additional exam requirements/recommendations for international students: Required—TOEFL (minimum score 550 paper-based; 213 computer-based; 78 iBT). *Application deadline:* For fall admission, 6/15 for domestic students, 6/1 for international students; for spring admission, 10/15 for domestic students, 10/1 for international students. Applications are processed on a rolling basis. Application fee: $40 ($90 for international students). Electronic applications accepted. *Expenses:* Tuition, state resident: full-time $6024; part-time $251 per credit hour. Tuition, nonresident: full-time $13,536; part-time $564 per credit hour. Required fees: $1776; $50 per credit hour. $306 per semester. *Financial support:* In 2010–11, 14 students received support, including 3 research assistantships (averaging $3,380 per year), 25 teaching assistantships (averaging $4,538 per year); Federal Work-Study, institutionally sponsored loans, scholarships/grants, health care benefits, and unspecified assistantships also available. Support available to part-time students. Financial award application deadline: 4/1. *Unit head:* Dr. David Lemke, Graduate Advisor, 512-245-2178, E-mail: dl10@txstate.edu. *Application contact:* Dr. J. Michael Willoughby, Dean of the Graduate School, 512-245-2581, Fax: 512-245-8365, E-mail: jw02@swt.edu.

Texas State University–San Marcos, Graduate School, Interdisciplinary Studies Program in Biology, San Marcos, TX 78666. Offers MSIS. *Degree requirements:* For master's, comprehensive exam, thesis optional. *Entrance requirements:* For master's, GRE (minimum score 1000 verbal and quantitative preferred), bachelor's degree in biology or related field, minimum GPA of 3.0 in last 60 hours of undergraduate work. Additional exam requirements/recommendations for international students: Required—TOEFL (minimum score 550 paper-based; 213 computer-based; 78 iBT). *Application deadline:* For fall admission, 6/15 priority date for domestic students, 6/1 for international students; for spring admission, 10/15 priority date for domestic students, 10/1 for international students. Applications are processed on a rolling basis. Application fee: $40 ($90 for international students). *Expenses:* Tuition, state resident: full-time $6024; part-time $251 per credit hour. Tuition, nonresident: full-time $13,536; part-time $564 per credit hour. Required fees: $1776; $50 per credit hour. $306 per semester. *Financial support:* Research assistantships, teaching assistantships, Federal Work-Study, institutionally sponsored loans, scholarships/grants, health care benefits, and unspecified assistantships available. Support available to part-time students. Financial award application deadline: 4/1; financial award applicants required to submit FAFSA. *Unit head:* Dr. David Lemker, Graduate Advisor, 512-245-2178, E-mail: dl10@txstate.edu. *Application contact:* Dr. J. Michael Willoughby, Dean of Graduate School, 512-245-2581, Fax: 512-245-8365, E-mail: gradcollege@txstate.edu.

Texas Tech University, Graduate School, College of Arts and Sciences, Department of Biological Sciences, Lubbock, TX 79409-3131. Offers biology (MS, PhD); microbiology (MS); zoology (MS, PhD). Part-time programs available. *Faculty:* 28 full-time (6 women). *Students:* 115 full-time (63 women), 12 part-time (5 women); includes 1 Asian, non-Hispanic/Latino; 6 Hispanic/Latino; 2 Two or more races, non-Hispanic/Latino, 66 international. Average age 28. 79 applicants, 32% accepted, 20 enrolled. In 2010, 14 master's, 6 doctorates awarded. *Degree requirements:* For master's, thesis or alternative; for doctorate, thesis/dissertation. *Entrance requirements:* For master's and doctorate, GRE General Test. Additional exam requirements/recommendations for international students: Required—TOEFL (minimum score 550 paper-based; 213 computer-based; 79 iBT). *Application deadline:* For fall admission, 6/1 priority date for domestic students, 1/15 priority date for international students; for spring admission, 9/1 priority date for domestic students, 6/15 priority date for international students. Applications are processed on a rolling basis. Application fee: $50 ($75 for international students). Electronic applications accepted. *Expenses:* Tuition, state resident: full-time $5496; part-time $228.99 per credit hour. Tuition, nonresident: full-time $12,936; part-time $538.99 per credit hour. Required fees: $2674; $36 per credit hour. $905 per semester. *Financial support:* In 2010–11, 123 students received support, including 14 research assistantships with partial tuition reimbursements available (averaging $6,332 per year), 49 teaching assistantships with partial tuition reimbursements available (averaging $7,121 per year). Financial award application deadline: 4/15; financial award applicants required to submit FAFSA. *Faculty research:* Biodiversity and evolution, climate change in arid ecosystems, plant biology and biotechnology, animal communication and behavior, zoonotic and emerging diseases. Total annual research expenditures: $2.3 million. *Unit head:* Dr. Llewellyn D. Densmore, Chair, 806-742-2715, Fax: 806-742-2963, E-mail: lou.densmore@ttu.edu. *Application contact:* Dr. Randall M. Jeter, Graduate Adviser, 806-742-2710 Ext. 270, Fax: 806-742-2963, E-mail: randall.jeter@ttu.edu.

Texas Tech University Health Sciences Center, Graduate School of Biomedical Sciences, Lubbock, TX 79430-0002. Offers MS, PhD, MD/PhD, MS/PhD. Terminal master's awarded for partial completion of doctoral program. *Degree requirements:* For master's, thesis; for doctorate, thesis/dissertation. *Entrance requirements:* For master's and doctorate, GRE General Test, minimum GPA of 3.0. Additional exam requirements/recommendations for international students: Required—TOEFL (minimum score 550 paper-based; 213 computer-based). Electronic applications accepted. *Faculty research:* Genetics of neurological disorders, hemodynamics to prevent DVT, toxin A synthesis, DA neurons, peroxidases.

Texas Woman's University, Graduate School, College of Arts and Sciences, Department of Biology, Denton, TX 76201. Offers biology (MS); molecular biology (PhD). Part-time programs available. *Faculty:* 13 full-time (10 women), 1 (woman) part-time/adjunct. *Students:* 26 full-time (18 women), 21 part-time (17 women); includes 3 Black or African American, non-Hispanic/Latino; 3 Asian, non-Hispanic/Latino; 4 Hispanic/Latino, 28 international. Average age 31. 37 applicants, 62% accepted, 13 enrolled. In 2010, 4 master's, 1 doctorate awarded. Terminal master's awarded for partial completion of doctoral program. *Degree requirements:* For master's, comprehensive exam, thesis (for some programs); for doctorate, comprehensive exam, thesis/dissertation, residency. *Entrance requirements:* For master's, GRE General Test (preferred minimum score 425 verbal, 425 quantitative), 3 letters of reference; letter of interest; for doctorate, GRE General Test (preferred minimum score verbal 500, quantitative 500), 3 letters of reference, letter of interest. Additional exam requirements/recommendations for international students: Required—TOEFL (minimum score 550 paper-based; 213 computer-based; 79 iBT). *Application deadline:* For fall admission, 7/1 priority date for domestic students, 3/1 for international students; for spring admission, 12/1 priority date for domestic students, 7/1 for international students. Applications are processed on a rolling basis. Application fee: $50 ($75 for international students). Electronic applications accepted. *Expenses:* Tuition, state resident: full-time $3834; part-time $213 per credit hour. Tuition, nonresident: full-time $9468; part-time $526 per credit hour. Required fees: $1247; $220 per credit hour. *Financial support:* In 2010–11, 11 students received support, including 36 research assistantships (averaging $14,418 per year); career-related internships or fieldwork, Federal Work-Study, institutionally sponsored loans, scholarships/grants, traineeships, health care benefits, and unspecified assistantships also available. Support available to part-time students. Financial award application deadline: 3/1; financial award applicants required to submit FAFSA. *Faculty research:* Computational biology, protein-protein Interactions, chromatin structure and regulation, regulation of RNA synthesis, virus-host interactions, regulation of axon growth and guidance in neurons, estrogen compounds in plants, regulation of gene expression in male reproductive tissues, female gonadal hormones in the development of anxiety and depression, electron microscopy. Total annual research expenditures: $259,701. *Unit head:* Dr. Sarah McIntire, Chair, 940-898-2351, Fax: 940-898-2382, E-mail: biology@twu.edu. *Application contact:* Dr. Samuel Wheeler, Assistant Director of Admissions, 940-898-3188, Fax: 940-898-3081, E-mail: wheelersr@twu.edu.

Thomas Jefferson University, Jefferson College of Graduate Studies, Philadelphia, PA 19107. Offers MS, PhD, Certificate, MD/PhD. Part-time and evening/weekend programs available. Postbaccalaureate distance learning degree programs offered (no on-campus study). *Faculty:* 173 full-time (45 women), 23 part-time/adjunct (8 women). *Students:* 138 full-time (77 women), 115 part-time (63 women); includes 36 minority (16 Black or African American, non-Hispanic/Latino; 19 Asian, non-Hispanic/Latino; 1 Native Hawaiian or other Pacific Islander, non-Hispanic/Latino), 38 international. Average age 29. 508 applicants, 29% accepted, 101 enrolled. In 2010, 23 master's, 20 doctorates, 6 other advanced degrees awarded. Terminal master's awarded for partial completion of doctoral program. *Degree requirements:* For master's, thesis; for doctorate, comprehensive exam, thesis/dissertation. *Entrance requirements:* For master's, GRE or MCAT; for doctorate, GRE or MCAT, minimum GPA of 3.2. Additional exam requirements/recommendations for international students: Required—TOEFL (minimum score 250 computer-based; 100 iBT). *Application deadline:* For fall admission, 1/15 priority date for domestic and international students; for winter admission, 6/1 priority date for international students; for spring admission, 9/1 priority date for international students. Applications are processed on a rolling basis. Application fee: $50. Electronic applications accepted. *Financial support:* In 2010–11, 166 students received support, including 120 fellowships with full tuition reimbursements available (averaging $54,723 per year); Federal Work-Study, institutionally sponsored loans, scholarships/grants, and traineeships also available. Support available to part-time students. Financial award application deadline: 5/1; financial award applicants required to submit FAFSA. *Unit head:* Dr. Gerald B. Grunwald, Dean, 215-503-4191, Fax: 215-503-6690, E-mail: gerald.grunwald@jefferson.edu. *Application contact:* Marc E. Stearns, Director of Admissions, 215-503-0155, Fax: 215-503-9920, E-mail: jcgs-info@jefferson.edu.

Towson University, Program in Biology, Towson, MD 21252-0001. Offers MS. Part-time and evening/weekend programs available. *Students:* 32 full-time (13 women), 26 part-time (18

Biological and Biomedical Sciences—General

Towson University (continued)
women); includes 16 minority (11 Black or African American, non-Hispanic/Latino; 4 Asian, non-Hispanic/Latino; 1 Two or more races, non-Hispanic/Latino), 5 international. Average age 27. In 2010, 28 master's awarded. *Degree requirements:* For master's, thesis optional, exam. *Entrance requirements:* For master's, GRE General Test (for thesis students), minimum GPA of 3.0, 24 credits in related course work, 3 letters of recommendation, minimum 24 units in biology, coursework in chemistry, organic chemistry, and physics. Additional exam requirements/recommendations for international students: Required—TOEFL. *Application deadline:* Applications are processed on a rolling basis. Application fee: $50. Electronic applications accepted. *Expenses:* Tuition, state resident: part-time $324 per credit. Tuition, nonresident: part-time $681 per credit. Required fees: $95 per term. *Financial support:* In 2010–11, 4 research assistantships with full tuition reimbursements (averaging $11,000 per year), 12 teaching assistantships with full tuition reimbursements (averaging $11,000 per year) were awarded; career-related internships or fieldwork, Federal Work-Study, and unspecified assistantships also available. Support available to part-time students. Financial award application deadline: 4/1; financial award applicants required to submit FAFSA. *Faculty research:* Microbiology, molecular biology, ecology, physiology, conservation biology. *Unit head:* Joel Snodgrass, Graduate Program Co-Director, 410-704-5033, Fax: 410-704-2405, E-mail: jsnodgrass@towson.edu. *Application contact:* 410-704-2501, Fax: 410-704-4675, E-mail: grads@towson.edu.

Trent University, Graduate Studies, Program in Applications of Modeling in the Natural and Social Sciences, Peterborough, ON K9J 7B8, Canada. Offers applications of modeling in the natural and social sciences (MA); biology (M Sc, PhD); chemistry (M Sc); computer studies (M Sc); geography (M Sc, PhD); physics (M Sc). Part-time programs available. *Degree requirements:* For master's, thesis. *Entrance requirements:* For master's, honours degree. *Faculty research:* Computation of heat transfer, atmospheric physics, statistical mechanics, stress and coping, evolutionary ecology.

Trent University, Graduate Studies, Program in Environmental and Life Sciences and Program in Applications of Modeling in the Natural and Social Sciences, Department of Biology, Peterborough, ON K9J 7B8, Canada. Offers M Sc, PhD. Part-time programs available. *Degree requirements:* For master's, thesis; for doctorate, thesis/dissertation. *Entrance requirements:* For master's, honours degree; for doctorate, master's degree. *Faculty research:* Aquatic and behavioral ecology, hydrology and limnology, human impact on ecosystems, behavioral ecology of birds, ecology of fish.

Truman State University, Graduate School, School of Arts and Letters, Program in Biology, Kirksville, MO 63501-4221. Offers MS. *Degree requirements:* For master's, comprehensive exam, thesis. *Entrance requirements:* For master's, GRE General Test, minimum GPA of 3.0. Additional exam requirements/recommendations for international students: Required—TOEFL (minimum score 550 paper-based; 213 computer-based). Electronic applications accepted.

Tufts University, Cummings School of Veterinary Medicine, North Grafton, MA 01536. Offers animals and public policy (MS); conservation medicine (MS); infectious diseases/digestive diseases/neuroscience/reproductive biology (PhD); veterinary medicine (DVM); DVM/MPH; DVM/MS. *Accreditation:* AVMA (one or more programs are accredited). *Faculty:* 90 full-time (39 women), 16 part-time/adjunct (7 women). *Students:* 344 full-time (291 women); includes 29 minority (3 Black or African American, non-Hispanic/Latino; 3 American Indian or Alaska Native, non-Hispanic/Latino; 10 Asian, non-Hispanic/Latino; 7 Hispanic/Latino; 1 Native Hawaiian or other Pacific Islander, non-Hispanic/Latino; 5 Two or more races, non-Hispanic/Latino), 3 international. Average age 25. 746 applicants, 35% accepted, 120 enrolled. In 2010, 74 first professional degrees, 11 master's, 1 doctorate awarded. *Degree requirements:* For master's, thesis (for some programs); for doctorate, comprehensive exam, thesis/dissertation; for DVM, thesis/dissertation optional. *Entrance requirements:* For DVM, master's, and doctorate, GRE General Test. Additional exam requirements/recommendations for international students: Required—TOEFL or IELTS. *Application deadline:* For fall admission, 11/1 for domestic and international students. Application fee: $70. Electronic applications accepted. *Expenses:* Contact institution. *Financial support:* In 2010–11, 62 students received support, including 6 research assistantships with full tuition reimbursements available (averaging $25,000 per year), 4 teaching assistantships (averaging $5,000 per year); career-related internships or fieldwork, Federal Work-Study, institutionally sponsored loans, scholarships/grants, and institutional aid awards also available. Financial award application deadline: 5/15; financial award applicants required to submit FAFSA. *Faculty research:* Oncology, veterinary ethics, international veterinary medicine, veterinary genomics, pathogenesis of Clostridium difficile. *Unit head:* Dr. Deborah T. Kochevar, Dean, 508-839-5302, Fax: 508-839-2953, E-mail: deborah.kochevar@tufts.edu. *Application contact:* Rebecca Russo, Director of Admissions, 508-839-7920, Fax: 508-887-4820, E-mail: vetadmissions@tufts.edu.

Tufts University, Graduate School of Arts and Sciences, Department of Biology, Medford, MA 02155. Offers MS, PhD. Part-time programs available. Terminal master's awarded for partial completion of doctoral program. *Degree requirements:* For master's, thesis (for some programs); for doctorate, thesis/dissertation. *Entrance requirements:* For master's and doctorate, GRE General Test. Additional exam requirements/recommendations for international students: Required—TOEFL (minimum score 550 paper-based; 213 computer-based; 80 iBT). Electronic applications accepted. *Expenses:* Tuition: Full-time $39,624; part-time $3962 per course. Required fees: $40 per year. Full-time tuition and fees vary according to degree level, program and student level. Part-time tuition and fees vary according to course load.

Tufts University, Sackler School of Graduate Biomedical Sciences, Medford, MA 02155. Offers MS, PhD, DVM/PhD, MD/PhD. *Faculty:* 173 full-time (55 women). *Students:* 194 full-time (122 women), 4 part-time (all women); includes 5 Black or African American, non-Hispanic/Latino; 19 Asian, non-Hispanic/Latino; 8 Hispanic/Latino, 33 international. Average age 29. 705 applicants, 10% accepted, 41 enrolled. In 2010, 18 master's, 38 doctorates awarded. Terminal master's awarded for partial completion of doctoral program. *Degree requirements:* For master's, thesis; for doctorate, thesis/dissertation. *Entrance requirements:* For doctorate, GRE General Test, 3 letters of reference. Additional exam requirements/recommendations for international students: Required—TOEFL. *Application deadline:* For fall admission, 12/15 priority date for domestic and international students. Applications are processed on a rolling basis. Application fee: $70. Electronic applications accepted. *Expenses:* Contact institution. *Financial support:* In 2010–11, 174 students received support, including 24 fellowships, 174 research assistantships with full tuition reimbursements available (averaging $28,500 per year); scholarships/grants and health care benefits also available. Financial award application deadline: 12/15. *Faculty research:* Cell biology, molecular biology, biochemistry, genetics, immunology. *Unit head:* Dr. Naomi Rosenberg, Dean, 617-636-6767, Fax: 617-636-0375, E-mail: naomi.rosenberg@tufts.edu. *Application contact:* Kellie Johnston, Associate Director of Admissions, 617-636-6767, Fax: 617-636-0375, E-mail: sackler-school@tufts.edu.

Tulane University, School of Medicine and School of Liberal Arts, Graduate Programs in Biomedical Sciences, New Orleans, LA 70118-5669. Offers MBS, MS, PhD, MD/MS, MD/PhD. *Degree requirements:* For doctorate, thesis/dissertation. *Entrance requirements:* For master's, GRE General Test, minimum B average in undergraduate course work; for doctorate, GRE General Test. Additional exam requirements/recommendations for international students: Required—TOEFL. *Expenses:* Contact institution.

Tuskegee University, Graduate Programs, College of Agricultural, Environmental and Natural Sciences, Department of Agricultural Sciences, Tuskegee, AL 36088. Offers agricultural and resource economics (MS); animal and poultry sciences (MS); environmental sciences (MS); integrative bio-science (PhD); plant and soil sciences (MS). *Faculty:* 26 full-time (12 women), 1 part-time/adjunct (0 women). *Students:* 77 full-time (52 women), 5 part-time (3 women); includes 54 Black or African American, non-Hispanic/Latino, 18 international. Average age 30. In 2010, 23 master's, 2 doctorates awarded. *Degree requirements:* For master's, thesis. *Entrance requirements:* For master's, GRE General Test. Additional exam requirements/recommendations for international students: Required—TOEFL (minimum score 500 paper-based; 69 computer-based). *Application deadline:* For fall admission, 7/15 for domestic students. Applications are processed on a rolling basis. Application fee: $25 ($35 for international students). *Expenses:* Tuition: Full-time $16,100; part-time $665 per credit hour. Required fees: $650. *Financial support:* In 2010–11, 5 fellowships, 4 research assistantships were awarded. Financial award application deadline: 4/15. *Unit head:* Dr. P. K. Biswas, Head, 334-727-8446. *Application contact:* Dr. Robert L. Laney, Vice President/Director of Admissions and Enrollment Management, 334-727-8580, Fax: 334-727-5750, E-mail: planey@tuskegee.edu.

Tuskegee University, Graduate Programs, College of Agricultural, Environmental and Natural Sciences, Department of Biology, Tuskegee, AL 36088. Offers MS. *Faculty:* 12 full-time (3 women). *Students:* 15 full-time (12 women), 1 (woman) part-time; includes 10 Black or African American, non-Hispanic/Latino, 3 international. Average age 27. *Degree requirements:* For master's, thesis. *Entrance requirements:* For master's, GRE General Test, GRE Subject Test. Additional exam requirements/recommendations for international students: Required—TOEFL (minimum score 500 paper-based; 69 computer-based). *Application deadline:* For fall admission, 7/15 for domestic students. Applications are processed on a rolling basis. Application fee: $25 ($35 for international students). *Expenses:* Tuition: Full-time $16,100; part-time $665 per credit hour. Required fees: $650. *Financial support:* Fellowships, teaching assistantships, Federal Work-Study and institutionally sponsored loans available. Support available to part-time students. Financial award application deadline: 4/15. *Unit head:* Dr. Roberta Troy, Head, 334-727-8829. *Application contact:* Dr. Robert L. Laney, Vice President/Director of Admissions and Enrollment Management, 334-727-8580, Fax: 334-727-5750, E-mail: planey@tuskegee.edu.

Tuskegee University, Graduate Programs, College of Agricultural, Environmental and Natural Sciences, Program in Integrative Biosciences, Tuskegee, AL 36088. Offers PhD. *Faculty:* 30. *Students:* 15 full-time (8 women); includes 12 Black or African American, non-Hispanic/Latino, 2 international. Average age 31. In 2010, 2 doctorates awarded. *Degree requirements:* For doctorate, thesis/dissertation. *Entrance requirements:* For doctorate, GRE General Test, GRE Subject Test, minimum cumulative GPA of 3.0, 3.4 in upper division courses; 3 letters of recommendation; resume or curriculum vitae. Additional exam requirements/recommendations for international students: Required—TOEFL (minimum score 500 paper-based; 69 computer-based). *Application deadline:* For fall admission, 3/30 for domestic students, 3/1 for international students. Application fee: $35. Electronic applications accepted. *Expenses:* Tuition: Full-time $16,100; part-time $665 per credit hour. Required fees: $650. *Unit head:* Dr. Deloris Alexander, Associate Director, 334-552-0690, E-mail: dalexander@tuskegee.edu. *Application contact:* Dr. Robert L. Laney, Vice President/Director of Admissions and Enrollment Management, 334-727-8580, Fax: 334-727-5750, E-mail: planey@tuskegee.edu.

Uniformed Services University of the Health Sciences, School of Medicine, Graduate Programs in the Biomedical Sciences and Public Health, Bethesda, MD 20814. Offers emerging infectious diseases (PhD); medical and clinical psychology (PhD), including clinical psychology, medical and clinical psychology (clinical/dual track), medical and clinical psychology (research track); molecular and cell biology (PhD); neuroscience (PhD); preventive medicine and biometrics (MPH, MSPH, MTMH, Dr PH, PhD), including environmental health science (PhD), medical zoology (PhD), public health (MPH, MSPH, Dr PH), tropical medicine and hygiene (MTMH). *Faculty:* 372 full-time (119 women), 4,044 part-time/adjunct (908 women). *Students:* 176 full-time (96 women); includes 6 Black or African American, non-Hispanic/Latino; 4 American Indian or Alaska Native, non-Hispanic/Latino; 14 Asian, non-Hispanic/Latino; 7 Hispanic/Latino, 11 international. Average age 28. 278 applicants, 20% accepted, 47 enrolled. In 2010, 36 master's, 17 doctorates awarded. Terminal master's awarded for partial completion of doctoral program. *Degree requirements:* For master's, comprehensive exam, thesis or alternative; for doctorate, comprehensive exam, thesis/dissertation, qualifying exam. *Entrance requirements:* For master's, GRE General Test; for doctorate, GRE General Test, minimum GPA of 3.0. Additional exam requirements/recommendations for international students: Required—TOEFL. *Application deadline:* For fall admission, 1/1 priority date for domestic and international students. Applications are processed on a rolling basis. Application fee: $0. Electronic applications accepted. *Financial support:* In 2010–11, fellowships with full tuition reimbursements (averaging $26,000 per year), research assistantships with full tuition reimbursements (averaging $26,000 per year) were awarded; career-related internships or fieldwork, scholarships/grants, health care benefits, and tuition waivers (full) also available. *Unit head:* Dr. Eleanor S. Metcalf, Associate Dean, 301-295-1104, E-mail: emetcalf@usuhs.mil. *Application contact:* Elena Marina Sherman, Graduate Program Coordinator, 301-295-3913, Fax: 301-295-6772, E-mail: elena.sherman@usuhs.mil.

Universidad Central del Caribe, School of Medicine, Program in Biomedical Sciences, Bayamón, PR 00960-6032. Offers anatomy and cell biology (MA, MS); biochemistry (MS); biomedical sciences (MA); cellular and molecular biology (PhD); microbiology and immunology (MA, MS); pharmacology (MS); physiology (MS).

Universidad de Ciencias Medicas, Graduate Programs, San Jose, Costa Rica. Offers dermatology (SP); family health (MS); health service center administration (MHA); human anatomy (MS); medical and surgery (MD); occupational medicine (MS); pharmacy (Pharm D). Part-time programs available. *Degree requirements:* For master's, thesis; for first professional degree and SP, comprehensive exam. *Entrance requirements:* For first professional degree, admissions test; for master's, MD or bachelor's degree; for SP, admissions test, MD.

Université de Moncton, Faculty of Science, Department of Biology, Moncton, NB E1A 3E9, Canada. Offers M Sc. *Degree requirements:* For master's, one foreign language, thesis. *Entrance requirements:* For master's, minimum GPA of 3.0. Electronic applications accepted. *Faculty research:* Terrestrial ecology, aquatic ecology, marine biology, aquaculture, ethology, biotechnology.

Université de Montréal, Faculty of Arts and Sciences, Department of Biological Sciences, Montréal, QC H3C 3J7, Canada. Offers M Sc, PhD. Part-time programs available. *Degree requirements:* For master's, thesis; for doctorate, thesis/dissertation, general exam. *Entrance requirements:* For doctorate, MS in biology or related field. Electronic applications accepted. *Faculty research:* Fresh water ecology, plant biotechnology, neurobiology, genetics, cell physiology.

Université de Montréal, Faculty of Medicine, Programs in Biomedical Sciences, Montréal, QC H3C 3J7, Canada. Offers M Sc, PhD. *Degree requirements:* For master's, thesis; for doctorate, thesis/dissertation, general exam. *Entrance requirements:* For master's and doctorate, proficiency in French, knowledge of English. Electronic applications accepted.

Université de Sherbrooke, Faculty of Medicine and Health Sciences, Graduate Programs in Medicine, Sherbrooke, QC J1H 5N4, Canada. Offers M Sc, PhD. Part-time programs available. Terminal master's awarded for partial completion of doctoral program. *Degree requirements:* For master's, thesis; for doctorate, thesis/dissertation. Electronic applications accepted. *Expenses:* Contact institution.

Université de Sherbrooke, Faculty of Sciences, Department of Biology, Sherbrooke, QC J1K 2R1, Canada. Offers M Sc, PhD, Diploma. *Degree requirements:* For master's, thesis; for doctorate, comprehensive exam, thesis/dissertation. *Entrance requirements:* For doctorate, master's degree. Electronic applications accepted. *Faculty research:* Microbiology, ecology, molecular biology, cell biology, biotechnology.

Université du Québec à Montréal, Graduate Programs, Program in Biology, Montréal, QC H3C 3P8, Canada. Offers M Sc, PhD. Part-time programs available. *Degree requirements:* For master's, thesis; for doctorate, thesis/dissertation. *Entrance requirements:* For master's, appropriate bachelor's degree or equivalent, proficiency in French; for doctorate, appropriate master's degree or equivalent, proficiency in French.

Université du Québec en Abitibi-Témiscamingue, Graduate Programs, Program in Environmental Sciences, Rouyn-Noranda, QC J9X 5E4, Canada. Offers biology (MS); environmental sciences (PhD); sustainable forest ecosystem management (MS).

Université du Québec, Institut National de la Recherche Scientifique, Graduate Programs, Research Center—INRS—Institut Armand-Frappier—Human Health, Québec, QC G1K 9A9, Canada. Offers applied microbiology (M Sc); biology (PhD); experimental health sciences (M Sc); virology and immunology (M Sc, PhD). Programs given in French. Part-time programs available. *Faculty:* 36. *Students:* 157 full-time (92 women), 6 part-time (4 women), 54 international. Average age 30. In 2010, 20 master's, 13 doctorates awarded. *Degree requirements:* For master's, thesis optional; for doctorate, thesis/dissertation. *Entrance requirements:* For master's and doctorate, appropriate bachelor's degree, proficiency in French. *Application deadline:* For fall admission, 3/30 for domestic and international students; for winter admission, 11/1 for domestic and international students; for spring admission, 3/1 for domestic and international students. Application fee: $30 Canadian dollars. *Financial support:* Fellowships, research assistantships, teaching assistantships available. *Faculty research:* Immunity, infection and cancer; toxicology and environmental biotechnology; molecular pharmacochemistry. *Unit head:* Charles Dozois, Director, 450-687-5010, Fax: 450-686-5501, E-mail: charles.dozois@iaf.inrs.ca. *Application contact:* Yvonne Boisvert, Registrar, 418-654-3861, Fax: 418-654-3858, E-mail: registrariat@adm.inrs.ca.

Université Laval, Faculty of Medicine, Graduate Programs in Medicine, Québec, QC G1K 7P4, Canada. Offers M Sc, PhD, Diploma. *Degree requirements:* For doctorate, comprehensive exam, thesis/dissertation. *Entrance requirements:* For doctorate, knowledge of French, comprehension of written English; for Diploma, knowledge of French. Electronic applications accepted.

Université Laval, Faculty of Sciences and Engineering, Department of Biology, Programs in Biology, Québec, QC G1K 7P4, Canada. Offers M Sc, PhD. Terminal master's awarded for partial completion of doctoral program. *Degree requirements:* For master's, thesis; for doctorate, comprehensive exam, thesis/dissertation. *Entrance requirements:* For master's and doctorate, knowledge of French and English. Electronic applications accepted.

University at Albany, State University of New York, College of Arts and Sciences, Department of Biological Sciences, Albany, NY 12222-0001. Offers biodiversity, conservation, and policy (MS); ecology, evolution, and behavior (MS, PhD); forensic molecular biology (MS); molecular, cellular, developmental, and neural biology (MS, PhD). *Degree requirements:* For master's, one foreign language; for doctorate, one foreign language, thesis/dissertation. *Entrance requirements:* For master's and doctorate, GRE General Test. Additional exam requirements/recommendations for international students: Required—TOEFL (minimum score 550 paper-based; 213 computer-based). Electronic applications accepted. *Faculty research:* Interferon, neural development, RNA self-splicing, behavioral ecology, DNA repair enzymes.

University at Albany, State University of New York, School of Public Health, Department of Biomedical Sciences, Albany, NY 12222-0001. Offers biochemistry, molecular biology, and genetics (MS, PhD); cell and molecular structure (MS, PhD); immunobiology and immunochemistry (MS, PhD); molecular pathogenesis (MS, PhD); neuroscience (MS, PhD). *Degree requirements:* For master's, thesis; for doctorate, comprehensive exam, thesis/dissertation. *Entrance requirements:* For master's and doctorate, GRE General Test, 3 letters of reference. Additional exam requirements/recommendations for international students: Required—TOEFL (minimum score 600 paper-based; 213 computer-based). Electronic applications accepted. *Faculty research:* Geno expression; RNA processing; membrane transport; immune response regulation; etiology of AIDS, Lyme disease, epilepsy.

University at Buffalo, the State University of New York, Graduate School, College of Arts and Sciences, Department of Biological Sciences, Buffalo, NY 14260. Offers MA, MS, PhD. *Faculty:* 28 full-time (7 women), 3 part-time/adjunct (1 woman). *Students:* 67 full-time (39 women), 4 part-time (1 woman); includes 2 Black or African American, non-Hispanic/Latino; 16 Asian, non-Hispanic/Latino. Average age 26. 244 applicants, 14% accepted, 27 enrolled. In 2010, 13 master's, 6 doctorates awarded. Terminal master's awarded for partial completion of doctoral program. *Degree requirements:* For master's, thesis, research rotation, seminar; for doctorate, comprehensive exam, thesis/dissertation, oral candidacy exam, research, seminar. *Entrance requirements:* For master's and doctorate, GRE General Test, 2 semesters of course work in calculus, course work in chemistry through organic chemistry, strong biology background. Additional exam requirements/recommendations for international students: Required—TOEFL (minimum score 600 paper-based; 240 computer-based; 100 iBT). *Application deadline:* For fall admission, 1/1 priority date for domestic and international students; for spring admission, 11/1 for domestic and international students. Applications are processed on a rolling basis. Application fee: $75. Electronic applications accepted. *Financial support:* In 2010–11, 51 students received support, including 15 research assistantships with full tuition reimbursements available (averaging $23,500 per year), 33 teaching assistantships with full tuition reimbursements available (averaging $22,800 per year); scholarships/grants, health care benefits, unspecified assistantships, and fellowships also available. *Faculty research:* Biochemistry, bioinformatics, biophysics, biotechnology, botany, cell biology, developmental biology, evolutionary biology, genetics, genomics, molecular biology, microbiology, neuroscience, physiology, plant physiology, plant sciences, structural biology, virology, zoology. Total annual research expenditures: $2.6 million. *Unit head:* Dr. Gerald Koudelka, Chairman, 716-645-4940, Fax: 716-645-2975, E-mail: koudelka@buffalo.edu. *Application contact:* Dr. Paul Gollnick, Director of Graduate Studies, 716-645-4972, Fax: 716-645-2975, E-mail: gollnick@buffalo.edu.

University at Buffalo, the State University of New York, Graduate School, Graduate Programs in Cancer Research and Biomedical Sciences at Roswell Park Cancer Institute, Interdisciplinary Master of Science Program in Natural and Biomedical Sciences at Roswell Park Cancer Institute, Buffalo, NY 14260. Offers biomedical sciences and cancer research (MS). Part-time programs available. *Faculty:* 8 full-time (3 women). *Students:* 62 full-time (39 women), 19 part-time (6 women); includes 5 Black or African American, non-Hispanic/Latino; 8 Asian, non-Hispanic/Latino; 4 Hispanic/Latino, 7 international. Average age 24. 100 applicants, 40% accepted, 30 enrolled. In 2010, 24 master's awarded. *Degree requirements:* For master's, thesis, defense of thesis, research project. *Entrance requirements:* For master's, GRE General Test, MCAT, DAT, PCAT. Additional exam requirements/recommendations for international students: Required—TOEFL (minimum score 600 paper-based; 250 computer-based; 100 iBT). *Application deadline:* For fall admission, 3/1 for domestic students. Applications are processed on a rolling basis. Application fee: $50. Electronic applications accepted. *Financial support:* In 2010–11, 1 fellowship with full tuition reimbursement (averaging $8,500 per year), 1 research assistantship (averaging $8,500 per year), 1 teaching assistantship with full tuition reimbursement (averaging $8,500 per year) were awarded; Federal Work-Study and institutionally sponsored loans also available. Financial award application deadline: 2/28; financial award applicants required to submit FAFSA. *Faculty research:* Biochemistry, oncology, pathology, biophysics, pharmacology, molecular biology, cellular biology, genetics, bioinformatics, immunology, therapeutic development, epidemiology. Total annual research expenditures: $1 million. *Unit head:* Dr. Adam Kisailus, Director of Graduate Studies, 716-845-2339, Fax: 716-845-8178, E-mail: adam.kisailus@roswellpark.org. *Application contact:* Craig R. Johnson, Director of Admissions, 716-845-2339, Fax: 716-845-8178, E-mail: craig.johnson@roswellpark.org.

University at Buffalo, the State University of New York, Graduate School, School of Medicine and Biomedical Sciences, Graduate Programs in Medicine and Biomedical Sciences, Buffalo, NY 14260. Offers MA, MS, PhD, MD/PhD. *Faculty:* 94 full-time (22 women), 30 part-time/adjunct (11 women). *Students:* 150 full-time (71 women), 16 part-time (10 women); includes 2 Black or African American, non-Hispanic/Latino; 8 Asian, non-Hispanic/Latino; 3 Hispanic/Latino, 60 international. Average age 25. 584 applicants, 29% accepted. In 2010, 21 master's, 27 doctorates awarded. Terminal master's awarded for partial completion of doctoral program. *Degree requirements:* For master's, comprehensive exam (for some programs), thesis (for some programs); for doctorate, comprehensive exam, thesis/dissertation. *Entrance requirements:* For master's, GRE General Test; for doctorate, GRE General Test, 3 letters of recommendation. Additional exam requirements/recommendations for international students: Required—TOEFL (minimum score 600 paper-based; 250 computer-based; 100 iBT). *Application deadline:* For fall admission, 2/1 priority date for domestic and international students. Applications are processed on a rolling basis. Application fee: $50. Electronic applications accepted. *Expenses:* Contact institution. *Financial support:* In 2010–11, 4 fellowships with full tuition reimbursements (averaging $25,000 per year), 30 research assistantships with full tuition reimbursements (averaging $21,000 per year), 31 teaching assistantships with full tuition reimbursements (averaging $2,000 per year) were awarded; career-related internships or fieldwork, Federal Work-Study, institutionally sponsored loans, scholarships/grants, traineeships, health care benefits, and unspecified assistantships also available. Financial award application deadline: 2/1; financial award applicants required to submit FAFSA. *Faculty research:* Neuroscience; molecular, cell, and structural biology; microbial pathogenesis; cardiopulmonary physiology; biochemistry, biotechnology and clinical laboratory science. Total annual research expenditures: $117.3 million. *Unit head:* Dr. Suzanne Laychock, Senior Associate Dean for Research and Graduate Studies, 716-829-3398, Fax: 716-829-2437, E-mail: laychock@acsu.buffalo.edu. *Application contact:* Amy J. Kuzdale, Staff Associate, 716-829-3399, Fax: 716-829-2437, E-mail: akuzdale@buffalo.edu.

University at Buffalo, the State University of New York, Graduate School, School of Medicine and Biomedical Sciences, Interdisciplinary Graduate Program in Biomedical Sciences, Buffalo, NY 14260. Offers PhD. *Students:* 19 full-time (8 women), 10 international. Average age 26. 303 applicants, 15% accepted, 19 enrolled. *Degree requirements:* For doctorate, comprehensive exam, thesis/dissertation. *Entrance requirements:* For doctorate, GRE General Test, 3 letters of recommendation. Additional exam requirements/recommendations for international students: Required—TOEFL (minimum score 600 paper-based; 250 computer-based; 100 iBT). *Application deadline:* For fall admission, 2/1 priority date for domestic and international students. Applications are processed on a rolling basis. Application fee: $50. Electronic applications accepted. *Financial support:* In 2010–11, 19 students received support. Federal Work-Study, scholarships/grants, traineeships, health care benefits, and unspecified assistantships available. Financial award application deadline: 2/1. *Faculty research:* Molecular, cell and structural biology; pharmacology and toxicology; neurosciences; microbiology; pathogenesis and disease. Total annual research expenditures: $117.3 million. *Unit head:* Dr. Laurie A. Read, Director, 716-829-3398, Fax: 716-829-2437, E-mail: smbs-gradprog@buffalo.edu. *Application contact:* Amy J. Kuzdale, Staff Associate, 716-829-3399, Fax: 716-829-2437, E-mail: akuzdale@buffalo.edu.

The University of Akron, Graduate School, Buchtel College of Arts and Sciences, Department of Biology, Akron, OH 44325. Offers biology (MS); integrated bioscience (PhD). Part-time programs available. *Faculty:* 21 full-time (3 women), 3 part-time/adjunct (1 woman). *Students:* 48 full-time (18 women), 5 part-time (4 women); includes 2 Black or African American, non-Hispanic/Latino; 2 Asian, non-Hispanic/Latino; 1 Hispanic/Latino, 8 international. Average age 28. 60 applicants, 43% accepted, 16 enrolled. In 2010, 6 master's awarded. *Degree requirements:* For master's, thesis optional, oral defense of thesis, oral exam, seminars; for doctorate, thesis/dissertation, oral defense of dissertation, seminars. *Entrance requirements:* For master's, GRE, baccalaureate degree in biology or the equivalent; minimum GPA of 3.0 overall and in biology; letter of interest; letter from potential biology adviser; for doctorate, GRE, minimum overall GPA of 3.0, letters of recommendation, personal statement of career goals and research interest. Additional exam requirements/recommendations for international students: Required—TOEFL (minimum score 550 paper-based; 213 computer-based; 79 iBT). *Application deadline:* Applications are processed on a rolling basis. Application fee: $30 ($40 for international students). Electronic applications accepted. *Expenses:* Tuition, state resident: full-time $6800; part-time $378 per credit hour. Tuition, nonresident: full-time $11,644; part-time $647 per credit hour. Required fees: $1265. One-time fee: $30 full-time. *Financial support:* In 2010–11, 16 teaching assistantships with full tuition reimbursements were awarded. *Faculty research:* Behavior/neuroscience, ecology-evolution, genetics, molecular biology, physiology. Total annual research expenditures: $1.1 million. *Unit head:* Dr. Monte Turner, Interim Chair, 330-972-7155, E-mail: meturner@uakron.edu. *Application contact:* Dr. Monte Turner, Interim Chair, 330-972-7155, E-mail: meturner@uakron.edu.

The University of Alabama, Graduate School, College of Arts and Sciences, Department of Biological Sciences, Tuscaloosa, AL 35487. Offers MS, PhD. *Faculty:* 36 full-time (12 women), 1 (woman) part-time/adjunct. *Students:* 74 full-time (31 women), 23 part-time (16 women); includes 16 minority (9 Black or African American, non-Hispanic/Latino; 3 Asian, non-Hispanic/Latino; 2 Hispanic/Latino; 2 Two or more races, non-Hispanic/Latino), 21 international. Average age 27. 103 applicants, 36% accepted, 31 enrolled. In 2010, 15 master's, 5 doctorates awarded. Terminal master's awarded for partial completion of doctoral program. *Degree requirements:* For master's, comprehensive exam, thesis optional; for doctorate, thesis/dissertation, preliminary written and oral exams. *Entrance requirements:* For master's and doctorate, GRE General Test, minimum GPA of 3.0. Additional exam requirements/recommendations for international students: Required—TOEFL (minimum score 550 paper-based; 79 iBT). *Application deadline:* For fall and spring admission, 12/5 priority date for domestic and international students. Applications are processed on a rolling basis. Application fee: $50 ($60 for international students). Electronic applications accepted. *Expenses:* Tuition, state resident: full-time $7900. Tuition, nonresident: full-time $20,500. *Financial support:* In 2010–11, 23 fellowships with full tuition reimbursements (averaging $15,000 per year), 21 research assistantships with full tuition reimbursements (averaging $19,000 per year), 44 teaching assistantships with full tuition reimbursements (averaging $14,454 per year) were awarded; institutionally sponsored loans, scholarships/grants, health care benefits, and unspecified assistantships also available. Financial award application deadline: 7/1; financial award applicants required to submit FAFSA. *Faculty research:* Molecular and developmental genetics, limnology, microbiology, systematics, neurobiology. Total annual research expenditures: $2.9 million. *Unit head:* Dr. Patrica A. Sobecky, Chair, 205-348-1807, Fax: 205-348-1786, E-mail: psobecky@as.ua.edu. *Application contact:* Dr. Stevan Marcus, Graduate Program Director, 205-348-8094, Fax: 205-348-1786, E-mail: smarcus@bama.ua.edu.

The University of Alabama at Birmingham, College of Arts and Sciences, Program in Biology, Birmingham, AL 35294. Offers MS, PhD. *Students:* 39 full-time (20 women), 6 part-time (4 women); includes 8 minority (3 Black or African American, non-Hispanic/Latino; 1 American Indian or Alaska Native, non-Hispanic/Latino; 3 Asian, non-Hispanic/Latino; 1 Hispanic/Latino), 7 international. Average age 30. 26 applicants, 31% accepted, 3 enrolled. In 2010, 16 master's, 3 doctorates awarded. Terminal master's awarded for partial completion of doctoral program. *Degree requirements:* For master's, thesis; for doctorate, thesis/dissertation. *Entrance requirements:* For master's and doctorate, GRE General Test, previous course work in biology, calculus, organic chemistry, and physics. Additional exam requirements/recommendations for international students: Required—TOEFL. *Application deadline:* Applications are processed on a rolling basis. Electronic applications accepted. *Expenses:* Tuition, state resident: full-time $5482. Tuition, nonresident: full-time $12,430. Tuition and fees vary according to program. *Financial support:* In 2010–11, 29 students received support, including 7 fellowships with full tuition reimbursements available (averaging $16,160 per year), 6 research assistantships with full tuition reimbursements available (averaging $16,160 per year), 16 teaching assistantships with full tuition reimbursements available (averaging $16,160 per year); career-related internships or fieldwork, Federal Work-Study, institutionally sponsored loans, scholarships/grants, traineeships, tuition waivers (full), and unspecified assistantships also available. Support available to part-time students. *Unit head:* Dr. Robert U. Fischer, Chair, 205-934-3582, Fax: 205-975-6097. *Application contact:* Juile Bryant, Director of Graduate School Operations, 205-934-8227, Fax: 205-975-6097, E-mail: sawatts@uab.edu.

See Display on next page and Close-Up on page 109.

The University of Alabama at Birmingham, Graduate Programs in Joint Health Sciences, Program in Basic Medical Sciences, Birmingham, AL 35294. Offers MSBMS. *Students:* 1 full-time (0 women). Average age 25. 1 applicant, 100% accepted, 1 enrolled. In 2010, 5 master's awarded. *Entrance requirements:* For master's, GRE. *Application deadline:* Applications are processed on a rolling basis. Electronic applications accepted. *Expenses:* Tuition,

Biological and Biomedical Sciences—General

The University of Alabama at Birmingham *(continued)*
state resident: full-time $5482. Tuition, nonresident: full-time $12,430. Tuition and fees vary according to program. *Application contact:* Julie Bryant, Director of Graduate Admissions, 205-934-8227, Fax: 205-934-8413, E-mail: jbryant@uab.edu.

The University of Alabama in Huntsville, School of Graduate Studies, College of Science, Department of Biological Sciences, Huntsville, AL 35899. Offers MS. Part-time and evening/weekend programs available. *Faculty:* 9 full-time (2 women), 2 part-time/adjunct (1 woman). *Students:* 19 full-time (8 women), 12 part-time (9 women); includes 10 minority (6 Black or African American, non-Hispanic/Latino; 4 Asian, non-Hispanic/Latino), 5 international. Average age 29. 41 applicants, 59% accepted, 17 enrolled. In 2010, 10 master's awarded. *Degree requirements:* For master's, comprehensive exam, thesis or alternative, oral and written exams. *Entrance requirements:* For master's, GRE General Test, previous course work in biochemistry and organic chemistry, minimum GPA of 3.0. Additional exam requirements/recommendations for international students: Required—TOEFL (minimum score 550 paper-based; 213 computer-based; 62 iBT). *Application deadline:* For fall admission, 7/15 for domestic students, 4/1 for international students; for spring admission, 11/30 for domestic students, 9/1 for international students. Applications are processed on a rolling basis. Application fee: $40 ($50 for international students). Electronic applications accepted. *Expenses:* Tuition, state resident: full-time $7250; part-time $407.75 per credit hour. Tuition, nonresident: full-time $17,358; part-time $970.05 per credit hour. Required fees: $246.80 per semester. Tuition and fees vary according to course load and program. *Financial support:* In 2010–11, 14 students received support, including 2 fellowships (averaging $17,250 per year), 12 teaching assistantships with full and partial tuition reimbursements available (averaging $8,392 per year); career-related internships or fieldwork, Federal Work-Study, institutionally sponsored loans, scholarships/grants, health care benefits, and unspecified assistantships also available. Support available to part-time students. Financial award application deadline: 4/1; financial award applicants required to submit FAFSA. *Faculty research:* Physiology and developmental biology, functional genomics, biotechnology, proteomics, microbiology. Total annual research expenditures: $1.3 million. *Unit head:* Dr. Debra M. Moriarity, Interim Chair, 256-824-6045, Fax: 256-824-6305, E-mail: moriard@uah.edu. *Application contact:* Kathy Biggs, Graduate Studies Admissions Manager, 256-824-6199, Fax: 256-824-6405, E-mail: deangrad@uah.edu.

University of Alaska Anchorage, College of Arts and Sciences, Department of Biological Sciences, Anchorage, AK 99508. Offers MS. Part-time programs available. *Degree requirements:* For master's, comprehensive exam, thesis. *Entrance requirements:* For master's, GRE General Test, GRE Subject Test, bachelor's degree in biology, chemistry or equivalent science. Additional exam requirements/recommendations for international students: Required—TOEFL (minimum score 550 paper-based; 213 computer-based). *Faculty research:* Taxonomy and vegetative analysis in Alaskan ecosystems, fish environment and seafood, biochemistry, arctic ecology, vertebrate ecology.

University of Alaska Fairbanks, College of Natural Sciences and Mathematics, Department of Biology and Wildlife, Fairbanks, AK 99775-6100. Offers biological sciences (MS, PhD), including biology, botany, wildlife biology (PhD); zoology; biology (MAT, MS); wildlife biology (MS). Part-time programs available. *Faculty:* 22 full-time (10 women). *Students:* 80 full-time (46 women), 42 part-time (26 women); includes 13 minority (2 American Indian or Alaska Native, non-Hispanic/Latino; 3 Asian, non-Hispanic/Latino; 2 Hispanic/Latino; 6 Two or more races, non-Hispanic/Latino), 6 international. Average age 31. 53 applicants, 30% accepted, 15 enrolled. In 2010, 11 master's, 10 doctorates awarded. *Degree requirements:* For master's, comprehensive exam, thesis, oral exam, oral defense; for doctorate, comprehensive exam, thesis/dissertation, oral exam, oral defense. *Entrance requirements:* For master's and doctorate, GRE General Test, GRE Subject Test (biology). Additional exam requirements/recommendations for international students: Required—TOEFL (minimum score 550 paper-based; 213 computer-

based; 80 iBT), TWE. *Application deadline:* For fall admission, 6/1 for domestic students, 3/1 for international students; for spring admission, 10/15 for domestic students, 9/1 for international students. Applications are processed on a rolling basis. Application fee: $60. Electronic applications accepted. *Expenses:* Tuition, state resident: full-time $5688; part-time $316 per credit. Tuition, nonresident: full-time $11,628; part-time $646 per credit. Required fees: $289 per semester. Tuition and fees vary according to course load and reciprocity agreements. *Financial support:* In 2010–11, 38 research assistantships with tuition reimbursements (averaging $11,087 per year), 20 teaching assistantships with tuition reimbursements (averaging $8,587 per year) were awarded; fellowships with tuition reimbursements, career-related internships or fieldwork, Federal Work-Study, scholarships/grants, health care benefits, and unspecified assistantships also available. Support available to part-time students. Financial award application deadline: 7/1; financial award applicants required to submit FAFSA. *Faculty research:* Plant-herbivore interactions, plant metabolic defenses, insect manufacture of glycerol, ice nucleators, structure and functions of arctic and subarctic freshwater ecosystems. *Unit head:* Christa Mulder, Department Chair, 907-474-7671, Fax: 907-474-6716, E-mail: fybio@uaf.edu. *Application contact:* Christa Mulder, Department Chair, 907-474-7671, Fax: 907-474-6716, E-mail: fybio@uaf.edu.

University of Alberta, Faculty of Graduate Studies and Research, Department of Biological Sciences, Edmonton, AB T6G 2E1, Canada. Offers environmental biology and ecology (M Sc, PhD); microbiology and biotechnology (M Sc, PhD); molecular biology and genetics (M Sc, PhD); physiology and cell biology (M Sc, PhD); plant biology (M Sc, PhD); systematics and evolution (M Sc, PhD). Terminal master's awarded for partial completion of doctoral program. *Degree requirements:* For master's, thesis; for doctorate, thesis/dissertation. *Entrance requirements:* Additional exam requirements/recommendations for international students: Required—TOEFL.

University of Alberta, Faculty of Medicine and Dentistry and Faculty of Graduate Studies and Research, Graduate Programs in Medicine, Edmonton, AB T6G 2E1, Canada. Offers MD, M Sc, PhD. Part-time programs available. Terminal master's awarded for partial completion of doctoral program. *Degree requirements:* For doctorate, thesis/dissertation. *Faculty research:* Basic, clinical, and applied biomedicine.

The University of Arizona, College of Science, Department of Molecular and Cellular Biology and Eller College of Management, Program in Applied Biosciences, Tucson, AZ 85721. Offers PSM. Part-time programs available. *Students:* 2 full-time (1 woman), 8 part-time (5 women); includes 2 Hispanic/Latino, 1 international. Average age 30. 22 applicants, 27% accepted, 4 enrolled. In 2010, 8 master's awarded. *Degree requirements:* For master's, thesis or alternative, internship, colloquium, business courses. *Entrance requirements:* For master's, 3 letters of recommendation. Additional exam requirements/recommendations for international students: Required—TOEFL (minimum score 600 paper-based; 250 computer-based; 90 iBT). *Application deadline:* For fall admission, 2/1 for domestic students, 12/1 for international students. Application fee: $75. Electronic applications accepted. *Expenses:* Tuition, state resident: full-time $7692. *Financial support:* Career-related internships or fieldwork, Federal Work-Study, scholarships/grants, health care benefits, and unspecified assistantships available. *Faculty research:* Biotechnology, bioinformatics, pharmaceuticals, agriculture, oncology. *Unit head:* Dr. Kathleen Dixon, Department Head, 520-621-7563, Fax: 520-621-3709, E-mail: dixonk@email.arizona.edu. *Application contact:* Marilyn Kramer, Graduate Coordinator, 520-621-1519, Fax: 520-621-3709, E-mail: mjkramer@u.arizona.edu.

University of Arkansas, Graduate School, J. William Fulbright College of Arts and Sciences, Department of Biological Sciences, Fayetteville, AR 72701-1201. Offers MA, MS, PhD. *Students:* 5 full-time (3 women), 40 part-time (20 women); includes 2 minority (1 Asian, non-Hispanic/Latino; 1 Hispanic/Latino), 7 international. 14 applicants, 86% accepted. In 2010, 2 master's, 9 doctorates awarded. *Degree requirements:* For doctorate, one foreign language, thesis/

dissertation. *Entrance requirements:* For master's and doctorate, GRE Subject Test. *Application deadline:* For fall admission, 4/1 for international students; for spring admission, 10/1 for international students. Applications are processed on a rolling basis. Application fee: $40 ($50 for international students). Electronic applications accepted. *Financial support:* In 2010–11, 6 fellowships with tuition reimbursements, 35 research assistantships, 6 teaching assistantships were awarded; career-related internships or fieldwork and Federal Work-Study also available. Support available to part-time students. Financial award application deadline: 4/1; financial award applicants required to submit FAFSA. *Unit head:* Dr. Fred Spiegel, Department Chairperson, 479-575-3251, Fax: 479-575-4010, E-mail: fspiegel@uark.edu. *Application contact:* Dr. David McNabb, Graduate Coordinator, 479-575-3797, Fax: 479-575-4010, E-mail: dmcnabb@uark.edu.

University of Arkansas at Little Rock, Graduate School, College of Science and Mathematics, Program in Biology, Little Rock, AR 72204-1099. Offers MS.

University of Arkansas for Medical Sciences, Graduate School, Graduate Programs in Biomedical Sciences, Little Rock, AR 72205. Offers MS, PhD, Certificate, MD/PhD. *Degree requirements:* For doctorate, thesis/dissertation. *Entrance requirements:* For master's and doctorate, GRE General Test. Additional exam requirements/recommendations for international students: Required—TOEFL. Electronic applications accepted. *Expenses:* Contact institution.

University of Calgary, Faculty of Graduate Studies, Faculty of Science, Department of Biological Sciences, Calgary, AB T2N 1N4, Canada. Offers M Sc, PhD. Part-time programs available. *Degree requirements:* For master's, thesis; for doctorate, thesis/dissertation, candidacy exam. *Entrance requirements:* Additional exam requirements/recommendations for international students: Required—TOEFL. Electronic applications accepted. *Faculty research:* Biochemistry; cellular, molecular, and microbial biology; botany; ecology; zoology.

University of Calgary, Faculty of Medicine and Faculty of Graduate Studies, Department of Medical Science, Calgary, AB T2N 1N4, Canada. Offers cancer biology (M Sc, PhD); immunology (M Sc, PhD); joint injury and arthritis research (M Sc, PhD); medical education (M Sc, PhD); medical science (M Sc, PhD); mountain medicine and high altitude physiology (M Sc). *Degree requirements:* For master's, thesis; for doctorate, thesis/dissertation, candidacy exam. *Entrance requirements:* For master's, minimum undergraduate GPA of 3.2; for doctorate, minimum graduate GPA of 3.2. Additional exam requirements/recommendations for international students: Required—TOEFL (minimum score 600 paper-based; 250 computer-based). Electronic applications accepted. *Faculty research:* Cancer biology, immunology, joint injury and arthritis, medical education, population genomics.

University of California, Berkeley, Graduate Division, College of Letters and Science, Department of Integrative Biology, Berkeley, CA 94720-1500. Offers PhD. *Degree requirements:* For doctorate, thesis/dissertation, oral qualifying exam. *Entrance requirements:* For doctorate, GRE General Test, GRE Subject Test, 3 letters of recommendation. Additional exam requirements/recommendations for international students: Required—TOEFL. *Faculty research:* Morphology, physiology, development of plants and animals, behavior, ecology.

University of California, Irvine, School of Biological Sciences, Irvine, CA 92697. Offers MS, PhD, MD/PhD. *Students:* 277 full-time (148 women), 1 (woman) part-time; includes 103 minority (3 Black or African American, non-Hispanic/Latino; 1 American Indian or Alaska Native, non-Hispanic/Latino; 54 Asian, non-Hispanic/Latino; 38 Hispanic/Latino; 7 Two or more races, non-Hispanic/Latino), 29 international. Average age 28. 749 applicants, 25% accepted, 77 enrolled. In 2010, 21 master's, 44 doctorates awarded. *Degree requirements:* For doctorate, thesis/dissertation. *Entrance requirements:* For master's and doctorate, GRE General Test, GRE Subject Test, minimum GPA of 3.0. Additional exam requirements/recommendations for international students: Required—TOEFL (minimum score 550 paper-based; 213 computer-based). *Application deadline:* For fall admission, 12/15 for domestic and international students. Applications are processed on a rolling basis. Application fee: $80 ($100 for international students). Electronic applications accepted. *Financial support:* Fellowships with full tuition reimbursements, research assistantships with full tuition reimbursements, teaching assistantships with full tuition reimbursements, career-related internships or fieldwork, institutionally sponsored loans, scholarships/grants, traineeships, health care benefits, and unspecified assistantships available. Financial award application deadline: 3/1; financial award applicants required to submit FAFSA. *Faculty research:* Molecular biology and biochemistry, developmental and cell biology, physiology and biophysics, neurosciences, ecology and evolutionary biology. *Unit head:* Prof. Albert F. Bennett, Dean, 949-824-5315, Fax: 949-824-3035, E-mail: abennett@uci.edu. *Application contact:* Prof. R. Michael Mulligan, Associate Dean, 949-824-8433, Fax: 949-824-4709, E-mail: rmmullig@uci.edu.

University of California, Los Angeles, David Geffen School of Medicine and Graduate Division, Graduate Programs in Medicine, Los Angeles, CA 90095. Offers MS, PhD, MD/PhD. *Students:* 339 full-time (164 women); includes 98 minority (5 Black or African American, non-Hispanic/Latino; 1 American Indian or Alaska Native, non-Hispanic/Latino; 58 Asian, non-Hispanic/Latino; 31 Hispanic/Latino; 1 Native Hawaiian or other Pacific Islander, non-Hispanic/Latino; 2 Two or more races, non-Hispanic/Latino), 53 international. Average age 28. 382 applicants, 19% accepted, 38 enrolled. In 2010, 22 master's, 61 doctorates awarded. Terminal master's awarded for partial completion of doctoral program. *Degree requirements:* For doctorate, thesis/dissertation, qualifying exams. *Entrance requirements:* For master's, GRE General Test. Application fee: $70 ($90 for international students). Electronic applications accepted. *Financial support:* In 2010–11, 324 fellowships, 263 research assistantships, 75 teaching assistantships were awarded; career-related internships or fieldwork, Federal Work-Study, institutionally sponsored loans, scholarships/grants, and tuition waivers (full and partial) also available. Financial award application deadline: 3/1. *Unit head:* Dr. Neil H. Parker, Senior Associate Dean for Student Affairs and Graduate Medical Education, 310-825-6774, E-mail: nhparker@mednet.ucla.edu. *Application contact:* Office of Continuing Medical Education, 310-794-2620.

University of California, Los Angeles, Graduate Division, College of Letters and Science, Department of Ecology and Evolutionary Biology, Los Angeles, CA 90095. Offers MA, PhD. *Faculty:* 25 full-time (6 women). *Students:* 65 full-time (46 women); includes 14 minority (1 Black or African American, non-Hispanic/Latino; 5 Asian, non-Hispanic/Latino; 7 Hispanic/Latino; 1 Two or more races, non-Hispanic/Latino), 8 international. Average age 29. 89 applicants, 21% accepted, 13 enrolled. In 2010, 5 master's, 13 doctorates awarded. Terminal master's awarded for partial completion of doctoral program. *Degree requirements:* For master's, comprehensive exam or thesis; for doctorate, thesis/dissertation, oral and written qualifying exams; teaching experience. *Entrance requirements:* For master's and doctorate, GRE General Test, GRE Subject Test (biology), minimum GPA of 3.0, 3 letters of recommendation. *Application deadline:* For fall admission, 12/1 for domestic and international students. Application fee: $70 ($90 for international students). Electronic applications accepted. *Financial support:* In 2010–11, 56 fellowships with full and partial tuition reimbursements, 25 research assistantships with full and partial tuition reimbursements, 43 teaching assistantships with full and partial tuition reimbursements were awarded; Federal Work-Study, institutionally sponsored loans, scholarships/grants, health care benefits, tuition waivers (full and partial), and unspecified assistantships also available. Financial award application deadline: 3/1; financial award applicants required to submit FAFSA. *Faculty research:* Molecular, cell, and developmental biology; interactive biology; organisms and populations. *Unit head:* Dr. Daniel T. Blumstein, Chair, 310-267-4746, Fax: 310-206-3987, E-mail: marmots@ucla.edu. *Application contact:* Jocelyn Yamadera, Student Affairs Officer, 310-825-1959, Fax: 310-206-5280, E-mail: jocelyny@lifesci.ucla.edu.

University of California, Merced, Division of Graduate Studies, School of Natural Sciences, Merced, CA 95343. Offers applied mathematics (MS, PhD); biological engineering and small-scale technologies (MS, PhD); environmental systems (MS, PhD); mechanical engineering and applied mechanics (MS, PhD); physics and chemistry (PhD); quantitative and systems biology (MS, PhD).

University of California, Riverside, Graduate Division, Department of Biology, Riverside, CA 92521-0102. Offers evolution, ecology and organismal biology (MS, PhD). *Faculty:* 39 full-time (9 women). *Students:* 50 full-time (24 women); includes 1 Asian, non-Hispanic/Latino; 4 Hispanic/Latino, 10 international. Average age 29. 42 applicants, 45% accepted, 6 enrolled. In 2010, 1 master's, 5 doctorates awarded. Terminal master's awarded for partial completion of doctoral program. *Degree requirements:* For master's, thesis, oral defense of thesis; for doctorate, thesis/dissertation, 3 quarters of teaching experience, qualifying exams. *Entrance requirements:* For master's and doctorate, GRE General Test, minimum GPA of 3.2. Additional exam requirements/recommendations for international students: Required—Either IELTS or TOEFL (paper-based 550, computer-based 213, iBT 80). *Application deadline:* For fall admission, 1/5 priority date for domestic students, 1/4 priority date for international students; for winter admission, 9/1 for domestic students, 7/1 for international students; for spring admission, 12/1 for domestic students, 10/1 for international students. Applications are processed on a rolling basis. Application fee: $80 ($100 for international students). Electronic applications accepted. *Financial support:* In 2010–11, fellowships with tuition reimbursements (averaging $16,000 per year), research assistantships with tuition reimbursements (averaging $18,000 per year), teaching assistantships with tuition reimbursements (averaging $16,500 per year) were awarded; career-related internships or fieldwork, Federal Work-Study, institutionally sponsored loans, and tuition waivers (full and partial) also available. Financial award application deadline: 1/5; financial award applicants required to submit FAFSA. *Faculty research:* Ecology, evolutionary biology, physiology, quantitative genetics, conservation biology. *Unit head:* Dr. Kimberly Hammond, Director, 951-827-4767, Fax: 951-827-4286, E-mail: kimberly.hammond@ucr.edu. *Application contact:* Melissa L. Gomez, Graduate Student Affairs Officer, 800-735-0717, Fax: 951-827-5913, E-mail: biograd@ucr.edu.

University of California, Riverside, Graduate Division, Program in Biomedical Sciences, Riverside, CA 92521-0102. Offers PhD, MD/PhD. *Degree requirements:* For doctorate, thesis/dissertation, qualifying exams. *Entrance requirements:* For doctorate, GRE General Test, minimum GPA of 3.2. Additional exam requirements/recommendations for international students: Required—TOEFL (minimum score 550 paper-based; 213 computer-based; 80 iBT). Electronic applications accepted. *Faculty research:* Cancer, receptor biology, developmental disorders, molecular basis of disease, neurodegeneration.

University of California, San Diego, Office of Graduate Studies, Division of Biological Sciences, La Jolla, CA 92093-0348. Offers biochemistry (PhD); biology (MS); cell and developmental biology (PhD); ecology, behavior, and evolution (PhD); genetics and molecular biology (RhD); immunology, virology, and cancer biology (PhD); molecular and cellular biology (PhD); neurobiology (PhD); plant molecular biology (PhD); plant systems biology (PhD); signal transduction (PhD). Offered in association with the Salk Institute; fall admission only. *Degree requirements:* For doctorate, thesis/dissertation, qualifying exam. *Entrance requirements:* For doctorate, GRE General Test; GRE Subject Test (recommended). Additional exam requirements/recommendations for international students: Required—TOEFL. Electronic applications accepted.

University of California, San Diego, School of Medicine and Office of Graduate Studies, Graduate Studies in Biomedical Sciences, La Jolla, CA 92093-0685. Offers molecular cell biology (PhD); pharmacology (PhD); physiology (PhD); regulatory biology (PhD). *Degree requirements:* For doctorate, thesis/dissertation, qualifying exam. *Entrance requirements:* For doctorate, GRE General Test. Additional exam requirements/recommendations for international students: Required—TOEFL. Electronic applications accepted. *Faculty research:* Molecular and cellular biology, molecular and cellular pharmacology, cell and organ physiology.

University of California, San Diego, School of Medicine, Medical Scientist Training Program, La Jolla, CA 92093. Offers MD/PhD.

University of California, San Francisco, Graduate Division, Biomedical Sciences Graduate Group, San Francisco, CA 94143. Offers anatomy (PhD); endocrinology (PhD); experimental pathology (PhD); physiology (PhD). *Degree requirements:* For doctorate, thesis/dissertation. *Entrance requirements:* For doctorate, GRE General Test.

University of Central Arkansas, Graduate School, College of Natural Sciences and Math, Department of Biological Science, Conway, AR 72035-0001. Offers MS. Part-time programs available. *Faculty:* 19 full-time (6 women). *Students:* 23 full-time (11 women), 6 part-time (3 women); includes 2 minority (1 Black or African American, non-Hispanic/Latino; 1 American Indian or Alaska Native, non-Hispanic/Latino). Average age 25. 17 applicants, 88% accepted, 11 enrolled. In 2010, 11 master's awarded. *Degree requirements:* For master's, comprehensive exam, thesis optional. *Entrance requirements:* For master's, GRE General Test, minimum GPA of 2.7. Additional exam requirements/recommendations for international students: Required—TOEFL (minimum score 550 paper-based; 213 computer-based). *Application deadline:* For fall admission, 3/1 priority date for domestic students; for spring admission, 10/1 priority date for domestic students. Applications are processed on a rolling basis. Application fee: $25 ($50 for international students). *Financial support:* In 2010–11, 4 research assistantships with partial tuition reimbursements (averaging $8,500 per year), 21 teaching assistantships with partial tuition reimbursements (averaging $8,500 per year) were awarded; unspecified assistantships also available. Financial award application deadline: 2/15; financial award applicants required to submit FAFSA. *Unit head:* Dr. Brent Hill, Chairperson, 501-450-3146, Fax: 501-450-5914, E-mail: srunge@uca.edu. *Application contact:* Susan Wood, Admissions Assistant, 501-450-3124, Fax: 501-450-5678, E-mail: swood@uca.edu.

University of Central Florida, College of Graduate Studies, Program in Biomedical Sciences, Orlando, FL 32816. Offers MS, PhD. *Faculty:* 27 full-time (7 women), 3 part-time/adjunct (1 woman). *Students:* 68 full-time (41 women), 1 part-time (0 women); includes 2 Black or African American, non-Hispanic/Latino; 1 Asian, non-Hispanic/Latino; 2 Hispanic/Latino, 32 international. Average age 29. 61 applicants, 44% accepted, 17 enrolled. In 2010, 9 doctorates awarded. *Degree requirements:* For doctorate, thesis/dissertation, qualifying exam, candidacy exam. *Entrance requirements:* For doctorate, GRE General Test, letters of recommendation. Additional exam requirements/recommendations for international students: Required—TOEFL. *Application deadline:* For fall admission, 2/1 for domestic students. Electronic applications accepted. *Expenses:* Tuition, state resident: part-time $256.56 per credit hour. Tuition, nonresident: part-time $1011.52 per credit hour. Part-time tuition and fees vary according to program. *Financial support:* In 2010–11, 61 students received support, including 12 fellowships with partial tuition reimbursements available (averaging $7,300 per year), 57 research assistantships (averaging $10,100 per year), 34 teaching assistantships with partial tuition reimbursements available (averaging $9,500 per year). *Unit head:* Dr. Pappachan Kolattukudy, Director, 407-823-5932, E-mail: pk@mail.ucf.edu. *Application contact:* Dr. Pappachan Kolattukudy, Director, 407-823-5932, E-mail: pk@mail.ucf.edu.

University of Central Florida, College of Medicine, Burnett School of Biomedical Sciences, Orlando, FL 32816. Offers biomedical sciences (MS); biotechnology (MS). *Faculty:* 27 full-time (7 women), 3 part-time/adjunct (1 woman). *Students:* 37 full-time (25 women), 7 part-time (5 women); includes 4 Asian, non-Hispanic/Latino; 4 Hispanic/Latino, 20 international. Average age 26. 105 applicants, 41% accepted, 19 enrolled. In 2010, 14 master's awarded. *Expenses:* Tuition, state resident: part-time $256.56 per credit hour. Tuition, nonresident: part-time $1011.52 per credit hour. Part-time tuition and fees vary according to program. *Financial support:* In 2010–11, 12 students received support, including 21 research assistantships (averaging $4,500 per year), 27 teaching assistantships (averaging $6,300 per year). *Unit head:* Dr. Pappachan E. Kolattukudy, Director, 407-823-1206, Fax: 407-823-0956, E-mail: pk@mail.ucf.edu. *Application contact:* Dr. Pappachan E. Kolattukudy, Director, 407-823-1206, Fax: 407-823-0956, E-mail: pk@mail.ucf.edu.

University of Central Florida, College of Sciences, Department of Biology, Orlando, FL 32816. Offers biology (MS); conservation biology (MS, PhD, Certificate). Part-time and evening/weekend programs available. *Faculty:* 22 full-time (6 women). *Students:* 47 full-time (31 women), 27 part-time (19 women); includes 1 Black or African American, non-Hispanic/Latino; 2 Asian, non-Hispanic/Latino; 3 Hispanic/Latino; 1 Native Hawaiian or other Pacific Islander,

Biological and Biomedical Sciences—General

University of Central Florida (continued)

non-Hispanic/Latino, 4 international. Average age 30. 57 applicants, 53% accepted, 15 enrolled. In 2010, 9 master's, 3 doctorates awarded. *Degree requirements:* For master's, comprehensive exam, thesis or alternative, field exam. *Entrance requirements:* For master's, GRE General Test, minimum GPA of 3.0 in last 60 hours. Additional exam requirements/recommendations for international students: Required—TOEFL. *Application deadline:* For fall admission, 3/1 priority date for domestic students; for spring admission, 10/15 for domestic students. Application fee: $30. Electronic applications accepted. *Expenses:* Tuition, state resident: part-time $256.56 per credit hour. Tuition, nonresident: part-time $1011.52 per credit hour. Part-time tuition and fees vary according to program. *Financial support:* In 2010–11, 42 students received support, including 3 fellowships with partial tuition reimbursements available (averaging $6,000 per year), 14 research assistantships with partial tuition reimbursements available (averaging $7,500 per year), 48 teaching assistantships with partial tuition reimbursements available (averaging $8,100 per year); career-related internships or fieldwork, Federal Work-Study, institutionally sponsored loans, tuition waivers (partial), and unspecified assistantships also available. Financial award application deadline: 3/1; financial award applicants required to submit FAFSA. *Unit head:* Dr. Ross Hinkle, Chair, 407-823-2976, Fax: 407-823-5769, E-mail: thinkle@mail.ucf.edu. *Application contact:* Dr. Ross Hinkle, Chair, 407-823-2976, Fax: 407-823-5769, E-mail: thinkle@mail.ucf.edu.

University of Central Missouri, The Graduate School, College of Science and Technology, Warrensburg, MO 64093. Offers applied mathematics (MS); aviation safety (MS); biology (MS); computer science (MS); environmental studies (MA); industrial management (MS); mathematics (MS); technology (MS); technology management (PhD). PhD is offered jointly with Indiana State University. Part-time programs available. Postbaccalaureate distance learning degree programs offered. *Entrance requirements:* Additional exam requirements/recommendations for international students: Required—TOEFL (minimum score 550 paper-based; 79 computer-based). Electronic applications accepted.

University of Central Oklahoma, College of Graduate Studies and Research, College of Mathematics and Science, Department of Biology, Edmond, OK 73034-5209. Offers MS. Part-time programs available. *Degree requirements:* For master's, thesis. *Entrance requirements:* For master's, GRE General Test, GRE Subject Test (biology). Additional exam requirements/recommendations for international students: Required—TOEFL (minimum score 550 paper-based; 213 computer-based). Electronic applications accepted. *Faculty research:* Environmental (*legionella*), aquatic biology (ecological), mammalogy field studies, microbiology, genetics.

University of Chicago, Division of Biological Sciences, The Interdisciplinary Scientist Training Program, Chicago, IL 60637-1513. Offers PhD. *Degree requirements:* For doctorate, thesis/dissertation, ethics class, 2 teaching assistantships. *Entrance requirements:* Additional exam requirements/recommendations for international students: Required—TOEFL (minimum score 600 paper-based; 250 computer-based; 104 iBT), IELTS (minimum score 7). Electronic applications accepted.

University of Cincinnati, Graduate School, College of Medicine, Biomedical Sciences Flex Option Program, Cincinnati, OH 45221. Offers PhD. *Degree requirements:* For doctorate, thesis/dissertation, qualifying exam. *Entrance requirements:* For doctorate, GRE, 2 letters of recommendation. Additional exam requirements/recommendations for international students: Required—TOEFL. Electronic applications accepted. *Faculty research:* Environmental health, developmental biology, cell and molecular biology, immunobiology, molecular genetics.

University of Cincinnati, Graduate School, College of Medicine, Graduate Programs in Biomedical Sciences, Cincinnati, OH 45221. Offers MS, PhD. Terminal master's awarded for partial completion of doctoral program. *Degree requirements:* For master's, thesis; for doctorate, thesis/dissertation, qualifying exam. *Entrance requirements:* For master's and doctorate, GRE General Test. Additional exam requirements/recommendations for international students: Required—TOEFL (minimum score 600 paper-based; 250 computer-based; 100 iBT). Electronic applications accepted. *Expenses:* Contact institution. *Faculty research:* Cancer, cardiovascular, metabolic disorders, neuroscience, computational medicine.

University of Cincinnati, Graduate School, College of Medicine, Physician Scientist Training Program, Cincinnati, OH 45221. Offers MD/PhD. *Entrance requirements:* Additional exam requirements/recommendations for international students: Required—TOEFL. Electronic applications accepted.

University of Cincinnati, Graduate School, McMicken College of Arts and Sciences, Department of Biological Sciences, Cincinnati, OH 45221-0006. Offers MS, PhD. Part-time programs available. Terminal master's awarded for partial completion of doctoral program. *Degree requirements:* For master's, thesis; for doctorate, comprehensive exam, thesis/dissertation. *Entrance requirements:* For master's and doctorate, GRE General Test, BS in biology, chemistry, or equivalent. Additional exam requirements/recommendations for international students: Required—TOEFL (minimum score 600 paper-based; 250 computer-based; 100 iBT). Electronic applications accepted. *Faculty research:* Physiology and development, cell and molecular, ecology and evolutionary.

University of Colorado at Colorado Springs, College of Letters, Arts and Sciences, Master of Sciences Program, Colorado Springs, CO 80933-7150. Offers applied science—bioscience (M Sc); applied science—physics (M Sc); biology (M Sc); chemistry (M Sc); health promotion (M Sc); mathematics (M Sc); physics (M Sc); sports medicine (M Sc); sports nutrition (M Sc). Part-time programs available. *Students:* 19 full-time (10 women), 11 part-time (4 women); includes 2 Asian, non-Hispanic/Latino; 3 Hispanic/Latino. Average age 34. 20 applicants, 55% accepted, 7 enrolled. In 2010, 14 master's awarded. *Degree requirements:* For master's, thesis or alternative. *Entrance requirements:* For master's, minimum GPA of 2.75. *Application deadline:* For fall admission, 6/1 priority date for domestic students; for spring admission, 12/1 for domestic students. Application fee: $60 ($75 for international students). *Expenses:* Contact institution. *Financial support:* Fellowships, research assistantships, teaching assistantships, career-related internships or fieldwork, Federal Work-Study, and scholarships/grants available. Support available to part-time students. Financial award application deadline: 3/1; financial award applicants required to submit FAFSA. *Faculty research:* Biomechanics and physiology of elite athletic training, genetic engineering in yeast and bacteria including phage display and DNA repair, immunology and cell biology, synthetic organic chemistry. *Application contact:* Michael Sanderson, Information Contact, 719-255-3417, Fax: 719-255-3037, E-mail: gradschl@uccs.edu.

University of Colorado Denver, College of Liberal Arts and Sciences, Department of Integrative Biology, Denver, CO 80217. Offers biology (MS). Part-time programs available. *Faculty:* 16 full-time (8 women). *Students:* 26 full-time (16 women), 4 part-time (3 women); includes 2 Asian, non-Hispanic/Latino; 1 Hispanic/Latino. Average age 30. 39 applicants, 69% accepted, 18 enrolled. In 2010, 15 master's awarded. *Degree requirements:* For master's, comprehensive exam, thesis or alternative, 30-32 credit hours. *Entrance requirements:* For master's, GRE General Test (minimum 50% performance in each section), BA/BS from accredited institution awarded within the last 10 years; minimum undergraduate GPA of 3.0; prerequisite courses: 1 year each of general biology and general chemistry, and 1 semester each of general genetics, general ecology, cell biology, and a structure/function course. Additional exam requirements/recommendations for international students: Required—TOEFL (minimum score 525 paper-based; 197 computer-based). *Application deadline:* For fall admission, 2/1 for domestic students, 1/15 for international students. Application fee: $50 ($75 for international students). Electronic applications accepted. *Expenses:* Tuition, state resident: full-time $7332; part-time $355 per credit hour. Tuition, nonresident: full-time $18,990; part-time $1055 per credit hour. Required fees: $998. Tuition and fees vary according to course level, course load, degree level, campus/location, program, reciprocity agreements and student level. *Financial support:* Research assistantships, teaching assistantships, Federal Work-Study, scholarships/grants, and unspecified assistantships available. Financial award application deadline: 4/1; financial award applicants required to submit FAFSA. *Faculty research:* Molecular developmental biology; quantitative ecology, biogeography, and population dynamics; environmental signaling and endocrine disruption; speciation, the evolution of reproductive isolation, and hybrid zones, evolutionary, behavioral, and conservation ecology. *Unit head:* Dr. Leo Bruederle, Chair, 303-556-3419, Fax: 303-556-4352, E-mail: leo.bruederle@ucdenver.edu. *Application contact:* Timberley Roane, Associate Professor/Associate Chair, 303-556-6592, E-mail: timberley.roane@ucdenver.edu.

University of Colorado Denver, School of Medicine, Biomedical Sciences Program, Aurora, CO 80045. Offers MS, PhD. *Students:* 10 full-time (6 women); includes 1 Asian, non-Hispanic/Latino; 1 Hispanic/Latino, 2 international. Average age 25. 117 applicants, 7% accepted, 8 enrolled. In 2010, 7 master's awarded. *Degree requirements:* For doctorate, comprehensive exam. *Entrance requirements:* For doctorate, GRE, minimum undergraduate GPA of 3.0; prerequisite coursework in organic chemistry, biology, biochemistry, physics, and calculus; letters of recommendation; interview. Additional exam requirements/recommendations for international students: Required—TOEFL (minimum score 550 paper-based; 213 computer-based). *Application deadline:* For fall admission, 1/1 for domestic students. Application fee: $65. Electronic applications accepted. *Expenses:* Contact institution. *Financial support:* Fellowships, research assistantships, teaching assistantships, health care benefits, tuition waivers (full), and stipend available. Financial award applicants required to submit FAFSA. *Unit head:* Heide Ford, Director, 303-724-3509, E-mail: heide.ford@ucdenver.edu. *Application contact:* Di Collingwood, Program Administrator, 303-724-3278, E-mail: dianna.collingwood@ucdenver.edu.

University of Connecticut, Graduate School, University of Connecticut Health Center, Field of Biomedical Science, Storrs, CT 06269. Offers PhD. *Degree requirements:* For doctorate, thesis/dissertation. *Entrance requirements:* For doctorate, GRE General Test, GRE Subject Test. Additional exam requirements/recommendations for international students: Required—TOEFL (minimum score 550 paper-based; 213 computer-based). Electronic applications accepted.

University of Connecticut Health Center, Graduate School and School of Medicine, Combined Degree Program in Biomedical Sciences, Farmington, CT 06030. Offers MD/PhD. *Faculty:* 158. *Students:* 30 full-time (12 women); includes 4 minority (1 Black or African American, non-Hispanic/Latino; 1 American Indian or Alaska Native, non-Hispanic/Latino; 2 Asian, non-Hispanic/Latino), 4 international. Average age 27. 116 applicants, 16% accepted, 4 enrolled. *Entrance requirements:* Additional exam requirements/recommendations for international students: Required—TOEFL (minimum score 600 paper-based; 250 computer-based). *Application deadline:* For fall admission, 12/15 priority date for domestic students. Applications are processed on a rolling basis. Application fee: $85. *Expenses:* Contact institution. *Financial support:* In 2010–11, 30 research assistantships with full tuition reimbursements (averaging $27,000 per year) were awarded; health care benefits and unspecified assistantships also available. *Unit head:* Dr. Barbara Kream, Director, 860-679-3849, Fax: 860-679-1258, E-mail: kream@nso1.uchc.edu. *Application contact:* Dr. Barbara Kream, Director, 860-679-3849, Fax: 860-679-1258, E-mail: kream@nso1.uchc.edu.

University of Connecticut Health Center, Graduate School, Programs in Biomedical Sciences, Farmington, CT 06030. Offers PhD, DMD/PhD, MD/PhD. *Faculty:* 158. *Students:* 152 full-time (81 women); includes 18 minority (5 Black or African American, non-Hispanic/Latino; 1 American Indian or Alaska Native, non-Hispanic/Latino; 10 Asian, non-Hispanic/Latino; 2 Hispanic/Latino), 59 international. Average age 28. 216 applicants, 22% accepted, 16 enrolled. In 2010, 27 doctorates awarded. *Degree requirements:* For doctorate, comprehensive exam, thesis/dissertation. *Entrance requirements:* For doctorate, GRE General Test. Additional exam requirements/recommendations for international students: Required—TOEFL (minimum score 600 paper-based; 250 computer-based). *Application deadline:* For fall admission, 12/15 for domestic students. Application fee: $55. Electronic applications accepted. *Financial support:* In 2010–11, 152 students received support, including 152 research assistantships with full tuition reimbursements available (averaging $27,000 per year); Federal Work-Study, traineeships, health care benefits, and unspecified assistantships also available. Total annual research expenditures: $88.2 million. *Unit head:* Dr. Barbara Kream, Associate Dean for the Graduate School, 860-679-3849, Fax: 860-679-1258, E-mail: kream@nso1.uchc.edu. *Application contact:* Tricia Avolt, Graduate Admissions Coordinator, 860-679-2175, Fax: 860-679-1899, E-mail: robertson@nso2.uchc.edu.

See Display on next page and Close-Up on page 111.

University of Connecticut Health Center, Graduate School, Programs in Biomedical Sciences—Integrated, Farmington, CT 06030. Offers PhD, DMD/PhD, MD/PhD. *Faculty:* 158. *Students:* 31 full-time (15 women); includes 3 minority (1 Black or African American, non-Hispanic/Latino; 2 Asian, non-Hispanic/Latino), 9 international. Average age 25. 216 applicants, 22% accepted, 16 enrolled. *Degree requirements:* For doctorate, comprehensive exam, thesis/dissertation. *Entrance requirements:* For doctorate, GRE General Test. Additional exam requirements/recommendations for international students: Required—TOEFL (minimum score 600 paper-based; 250 computer-based). *Application deadline:* For fall admission, 12/15 for domestic students. Application fee: $55. Electronic applications accepted. *Financial support:* In 2010–11, 31 research assistantships with full tuition reimbursements (averaging $27,000 per year) were awarded. *Unit head:* Dr. Barbara Kream, Associate Dean for the Graduate School, 860-679-3849, Fax: 860-679-1258, E-mail: kream@nso1.uchc.edu. *Application contact:* Tricia Avolt, Graduate Admissions Coordinator, 860-679-2175, Fax: 860-679-1899, E-mail: robertson@ns02.uchc.edu.

University of Dayton, Graduate School, College of Arts and Sciences, Department of Biology, Dayton, OH 45469-1300. Offers MS, PhD. *Faculty:* 20 full-time (7 women). *Students:* 20 full-time (11 women), 8 international. Average age 28. 22 applicants, 18% accepted, 4 enrolled. In 2010, 2 master's, 1 doctorate awarded. Terminal master's awarded for partial completion of doctoral program. *Degree requirements:* For master's, comprehensive exam, thesis; for doctorate, comprehensive exam, thesis/dissertation. *Entrance requirements:* For master's and doctorate, GRE General Test, minimum undergraduate GPA of 3.0. Additional exam requirements/recommendations for international students: Required—TOEFL (minimum score 550 paper-based; 213 computer-based; 80 iBT). *Application deadline:* For fall admission, 3/1 priority date for domestic and international students; for winter admission, 10/15 priority date for domestic and international students; for spring admission, 1/1 for international students. Applications are processed on a rolling basis. Application fee: $50. Electronic applications accepted. *Expenses:* Tuition: Full-time $7800; part-time $650 per credit hour. *Financial support:* In 2010–11, 3 research assistantships with full tuition reimbursements (averaging $15,036 per year), 15 teaching assistantships with full tuition reimbursements (averaging $14,601 per year) were awarded; institutionally sponsored loans, health care benefits, and unspecified assistantships also available. Financial award application deadline: 3/1; financial award applicants required to submit FAFSA. *Faculty research:* Tissue regeneration and developmental biology; cancer and stem cell biology; microbiology and immunology; molecular genetics, evolution and bioinformatics; environmental and restoration ecology. *Unit head:* Dr. Jayne B. Robinson, Chair, 937-229-2521, Fax: 937-229-2021. *Application contact:* Alexander Popovski, Associate Director of Graduate and International Admissions, 937-229-2357, Fax: 937-229-4729, E-mail: alex.popovski@notes.udayton.edu.

University of Delaware, College of Arts and Sciences, Department of Biological Sciences, Newark, DE 19716. Offers biotechnology (MS); cancer biology (MS, PhD); cell and extracellular matrix biology (MS, PhD); cell and systems physiology (MS, PhD); developmental biology (MS, PhD); ecology and evolution (MS, PhD); microbiology (MS, PhD); molecular biology and genetics (MS, PhD). Terminal master's awarded for partial completion of doctoral program. *Degree requirements:* For master's, thesis, preliminary exam; for doctorate, comprehensive exam, thesis/dissertation, preliminary exam. *Entrance requirements:* For master's and doctorate, GRE General Test. Additional exam requirements/recommendations for international students: Required—TOEFL (minimum score 600 paper-based; 250 computer-based); Recommended—TWE. Electronic applications accepted. *Faculty research:* Microorganisms, bone, cancer metastasis, developmental biology, cell biology, DNA.

University of Denver, Faculty of Natural Sciences and Mathematics, Department of Biological Sciences, Denver, CO 80208. Offers MS, PhD. Part-time programs available. *Faculty:* 19 full-time (5 women), 3 part-time/adjunct (all women). *Students:* 2 full-time (0 women), 24 part-time (20 women); includes 2 minority (1 American Indian or Alaska Native, non-Hispanic/Latino; 1 Hispanic/Latino), 3 international. Average age 27. 52 applicants, 46% accepted, 22 enrolled. In 2010, 3 master's, 1 doctorate awarded. Terminal master's awarded for partial completion of doctoral program. *Degree requirements:* For master's, comprehensive exam (for some programs), thesis; for doctorate, one foreign language, comprehensive exam (for some programs), thesis/dissertation. *Entrance requirements:* For master's, GRE General Test, BA or BS in biology or related field; for doctorate, GRE General Test, GRE Subject Test (biology). Additional exam requirements/recommendations for international students: Required—TOEFL (minimum score 570 paper-based; 88 iBT). *Application deadline:* For fall admission, 1/15 priority date for domestic students. Applications are processed on a rolling basis. Application fee: $60. Electronic applications accepted. *Expenses:* Tuition: Full-time $35,604; part-time $29,670 per year. Required fees: $687 per year. Tuition and fees vary according to program. *Financial support:* In 2010–11, 8 research assistantships with full and partial tuition reimbursements (averaging $18,300 per year), 19 teaching assistantships with full and partial tuition reimbursements (averaging $17,337 per year) were awarded; Federal Work-Study, institutionally sponsored loans, and unspecified assistantships also available. Support available to part-time students. Financial award application deadline: 3/1; financial award applicants required to submit FAFSA. *Faculty research:* Molecular biology, cell biology, neurobiology, ecology, molecular evolution. *Unit head:* Dr. Joseph Angleson, Chair, 303-871-3463, E-mail: jangleso@du.edu. *Application contact:* Randi Flageolle, Assistant to the Chair, 303-871-3457, E-mail: rflageol@du.edu.

University of Florida, College of Medicine and Graduate School, Interdisciplinary Program in Biomedical Sciences, Gainesville, FL 32611. Offers PhD, JD/MS, JD/PhD, MBA/MS, MBA/PhD, MS/M Ed. *Degree requirements:* For doctorate, thesis/dissertation. *Entrance requirements:* For doctorate, GRE General Test, minimum GPA of 3.0. Additional exam requirements/recommendations for international students: Required—TOEFL. Electronic applications accepted. *Expenses:* Contact institution.

University of Georgia, Biomedical and Health Sciences Institute, Athens, GA 30602. Offers neuroscience (PhD). *Students:* 13 full-time (9 women), 1 (woman) part-time; includes 1 Black or African American, non-Hispanic/Latino; 1 Asian, non-Hispanic/Latino; 1 Hispanic/Latino, 4 international. 23 applicants, 13% accepted, 2 enrolled. In 2010, 6 doctorates awarded. *Entrance requirements:* For doctorate, GRE, official transcripts, 3 letters of recommendation, statement of interest. Additional exam requirements/recommendations for international students: Required—TOEFL. *Expenses:* Tuition, state resident: full-time $7200; part-time $344 per credit hour. Tuition, nonresident: full-time $21,900; part-time $944 per credit hour. Tuition and fees vary according to course load and program. *Financial support:* Unspecified assistantships available. Financial award application deadline: 12/31. *Unit head:* Dr. Gaylen Edwards, Chair, 706-542-5922, Fax: 706-542-5285, E-mail: gedwards@uga.edu. *Application contact:* Philip V. Holmes, Graduate Coordinator, 706-542-5922, Fax: 706-542-5285, E-mail: pvholmes@uga.edu.

University of Guam, Office of Graduate Studies, College of Natural and Applied Sciences, Program in Biology, Mangilao, GU 96923. Offers tropical marine biology (MS). *Degree requirements:* For master's, comprehensive exam, thesis. *Entrance requirements:* For master's, GRE General Test, GRE Subject Test. Additional exam requirements/recommendations for international students: Required—TOEFL. *Faculty research:* Maintenance and ecology of coral reefs.

University of Guelph, Graduate Studies, College of Biological Science, Guelph, ON N1G 2W1, Canada. Offers M Sc, PhD. Part-time programs available. *Degree requirements:* For

master's, thesis (for some programs); for doctorate, comprehensive exam (for some programs), thesis/dissertation. *Entrance requirements:* Additional exam requirements/recommendations for international students: Required—TOEFL (minimum score 550 paper-based; 213 computer-based). Electronic applications accepted.

University of Hartford, College of Arts and Sciences, Department of Biology, West Hartford, CT 06117-1599. Offers biology (MS); neuroscience (MS). Part-time and evening/weekend programs available. *Degree requirements:* For master's, comprehensive exam, thesis optional, oral exams. *Entrance requirements:* For master's, GRE or MCAT. Additional exam requirements/recommendations for international students: Required—TOEFL (minimum score 550 paper-based; 213 computer-based). Electronic applications accepted. *Faculty research:* Neurobiology of aging, central actions of neural steroids, neuroendocrine control of reproduction, retinopathies in sharks, plasticity in the central nervous system.

University of Hawaii at Manoa, John A. Burns School of Medicine and Graduate Division, Graduate Programs in Biomedical Sciences, Honolulu, HI 96822. Offers MS, PhD. Part-time programs available. *Faculty:* 17 full-time (10 women), 1 part-time/adjunct (0 women). *Students:* 5 full-time (2 women), 6 part-time (4 women); includes 6 minority (5 Asian, non-Hispanic/Latino; 1 Two or more races, non-Hispanic/Latino), 2 international. Average age 42. 20 applicants, 55% accepted, 11 enrolled. In 2010, 1 master's, 3 doctorates awarded. Terminal master's awarded for partial completion of doctoral program. *Degree requirements:* For master's, thesis optional; for doctorate, comprehensive exam, thesis/dissertation. *Entrance requirements:* For master's and doctorate, GRE General Test. Additional exam requirements/recommendations for international students: Required—TOEFL (minimum score 500 paper-based; 173 computer-based; 61 iBT), IELTS (minimum score 5). *Application deadline:* For fall admission, 6/1 for domestic and international students. Application fee: $60. *Expenses:* Contact institution. *Financial support:* In 2010–11, 1 fellowship (averaging $18,126 per year), 1 research assistantship (averaging $23,022 per year) were awarded; career-related internships or fieldwork, Federal Work-Study, institutionally sponsored loans, and tuition waivers (full and partial) also available. Support available to part-time students. Total annual research expenditures: $989,000. *Application contact:* Rosanne Harrigan, Graduate Chairperson, 808-692-0904, Fax: 808-692-1247, E-mail: harrigan@hawaii.edu.

University of Houston, College of Natural Sciences and Mathematics, Department of Biology and Biochemistry, Houston, TX 77204. Offers biochemistry (MA, PhD); biology (MA). *Faculty:* 31 full-time (10 women), 1 (woman) part-time/adjunct. *Students:* 89 full-time (53 women), 4 part-time (1 woman); includes 3 Black or African American, non-Hispanic/Latino; 3 Asian, non-Hispanic/Latino; 2 Hispanic/Latino, 65 international. Average age 28. 144 applicants, 20% accepted, 14 enrolled. In 2010, 7 master's, 11 doctorates awarded. Terminal master's awarded for partial completion of doctoral program. *Degree requirements:* For master's, comprehensive exam (for some programs), thesis optional; for doctorate, comprehensive exam (for some programs), thesis/dissertation. *Entrance requirements:* For master's and doctorate, GRE. Additional exam requirements/recommendations for international students: Required—TOEFL (minimum score 550 paper-based; 213 computer-based; 79 iBT), IELTS (minimum score 6.5). *Application deadline:* For fall admission, 4/1 for domestic and international students; for spring admission, 10/1 for domestic and international students. Application fee: $75 for international students. Electronic applications accepted. *Expenses:* Tuition, state resident: full-time $8592; part-time $358 per credit hour. Tuition, nonresident: full-time $16,032; part-time $668 per credit hour. Required fees: $2889. Tuition and fees vary according to course load and program. *Financial support:* In 2010–11, 33 research assistantships with partial tuition reimbursements (averaging $13,776 per year), 39 teaching assistantships with partial tuition reimbursements (averaging $14,032 per year) were awarded; career-related internships or fieldwork, Federal Work-Study, institutionally sponsored loans, scholarships/grants, health care benefits, and unspecified assistantships also available. Support available to part-time students. Financial award application deadline: 2/1. *Faculty research:* Cell and molecular biology, ecology and evolution, biochemical and biophysical sciences, chemical biology. *Unit head:* Dr. Dan Wells,

Biological and Biomedical Sciences—General

University of Houston (continued)
Chairperson, 713-743-2697, Fax: 713-743-2632, E-mail: dwells@uh.edu. *Application contact:* Amanda Paul, Graduate Academic Advisor, 713-743-2633, Fax: 713-743-2636, E-mail: akpaul@central.uh.edu.

University of Houston–Clear Lake, School of Science and Computer Engineering, Program in Biological Sciences, Houston, TX 77058-1098. Offers MS. Part-time and evening/weekend programs available. *Entrance requirements:* For master's, GRE General Test. Additional exam requirements/recommendations for international students: Required—TOEFL (minimum score 550 paper-based; 213 computer-based).

University of Idaho, College of Graduate Studies, College of Science, Department of Biological Sciences, Moscow, ID 83844-2282. Offers biology (MS, PhD). *Faculty:* 13 full-time. *Students:* 24 full-time, 8 part-time. Average age 28. In 2010, 4 doctorates awarded. *Degree requirements:* For doctorate, one foreign language, thesis/dissertation. *Entrance requirements:* For master's, GRE, minimum GPA of 2.8; for doctorate, GRE, minimum undergraduate GPA of 2.8, 3.0 graduate. *Application deadline:* For fall admission, 8/1 for domestic students; for spring admission, 12/15 for domestic students. Applications are processed on a rolling basis. Application fee: $60. Electronic applications accepted. *Expenses:* Tuition, nonresident: part-time $580 per credit. Required fees: $306 per credit. *Financial support:* Research assistantships, teaching assistantships available. Financial award applicants required to submit FAFSA. *Faculty research:* Animal behavior development, germ cell development, evolutionary biology, fish reproductive biology, molecular mechanisms. *Unit head:* Joseph G. Cloud, Chair, 208-885-6280. *Application contact:* Joseph G. Cloud, Chair, 208-885-6280.

University of Illinois at Chicago, College of Medicine and Graduate College, Graduate Programs in Medicine, Chicago, IL 60607-7128. Offers MHPE, MS, PhD, MD/MS, MD/PhD. Part-time programs available. Terminal master's awarded for partial completion of doctoral program. *Degree requirements:* For master's, thesis; for doctorate, thesis/dissertation. *Entrance requirements:* For master's and doctorate, GRE General Test. *Expenses:* Contact institution.

University of Illinois at Chicago, Graduate College, College of Liberal Arts and Sciences, Department of Biological Sciences, Chicago, IL 60607-7128. Offers MS, PhD. *Degree requirements:* For master's, thesis; for doctorate, thesis/dissertation, preliminary exam. *Entrance requirements:* For master's and doctorate, GRE General Test, GRE Subject Test, previous course work in physics, calculus, and organic chemistry; minimum GPA of 2.75. Additional exam requirements/recommendations for international students: Required—TOEFL. Electronic applications accepted.

University of Illinois at Springfield, Graduate Programs, College of Liberal Arts and Sciences, Program in Biology, Springfield, IL 62703-5407. Offers MS. Part-time and evening/weekend programs available. *Degree requirements:* For master's, project or thesis. *Entrance requirements:* For master's, GRE General Test, GRE Subject Test (biology), minimum undergraduate GPA of 3.0, 3 letters of reference. Additional exam requirements/recommendations for international students: Required—TOEFL (minimum score 500 paper-based; 176 computer-based; 61 iBT). Electronic applications accepted. *Expenses:* Tuition, state resident: full-time $6774; part-time $282.25 per credit hour. Tuition, nonresident: full-time $15,078; part-time $628.25 per credit hour. Required fees: $15.25 per credit hour. $492 per term.

University of Illinois at Urbana–Champaign, Graduate College, College of Liberal Arts and Sciences, School of Chemical Sciences, Champaign, IL 61820. Offers MA, MS, PhD, MS/JD, MS/MBA. *Faculty:* 47 full-time (8 women). *Students:* 381 full-time (122 women), 8 part-time (2 women); includes 6 Black or African American, non-Hispanic/Latino; 1 American Indian or Alaska Native, non-Hispanic/Latino; 23 Asian, non-Hispanic/Latino; 13 Hispanic/Latino; 9 Two or more races, non-Hispanic/Latino, 112 international. 924 applicants, 6% accepted, 54 enrolled. In 2010, 32 master's, 60 doctorates awarded. *Entrance requirements:* For master's, minimum GPA of 3.0. *Application deadline:* Applications are processed on a rolling basis. Application fee: $75 ($90 for international students). Electronic applications accepted. *Expenses:* Contact institution. *Financial support:* In 2010–11, 137 fellowships, 216 research assistantships, 225 teaching assistantships were awarded; tuition waivers (full and partial) also available. *Unit head:* Andrew A. Gewirth, Director, 217-333-8329, Fax: 217-333-2685, E-mail: agewirth@illinois.edu. *Application contact:* Cheryl Kappes, Office Manager, 217-333-5070, Fax: 217-333-3120, E-mail: dambache@illinois.edu.

University of Illinois at Urbana–Champaign, Graduate College, College of Liberal Arts and Sciences, School of Integrative Biology, Champaign, IL 61820. Offers MS, MST, PhD. *Faculty:* 35 full-time (11 women). *Students:* 130 full-time (75 women), 20 part-time (6 women); includes 4 Black or African American, non-Hispanic/Latino; 1 American Indian or Alaska Native, non-Hispanic/Latino; 10 Asian, non-Hispanic/Latino; 2 Hispanic/Latino; 2 Two or more races, non-Hispanic/Latino, 25 international. 149 applicants, 19% accepted, 18 enrolled. In 2010, 17 master's, 14 doctorates awarded. *Application deadline:* Applications are processed on a rolling basis. Application fee: $75 ($90 for international students). Electronic applications accepted. *Financial support:* In 2010–11, 14 fellowships, 81 research assistantships, 166 teaching assistantships were awarded; tuition waivers (full and partial) also available. *Unit head:* Evan De Lucia, Director, 217-333-6177, Fax: 217-244-1224, E-mail: delucia@illinois.edu. *Application contact:* Carol Hall, Office Manager, 217-333-8208, Fax: 217-244-1224, E-mail: cahall@illinois.edu.

University of Indianapolis, Graduate Programs, College of Arts and Sciences, Department of Biology, Indianapolis, IN 46227-3697. Offers human biology (MS). Part-time and evening/weekend programs available. *Faculty:* 5 full-time (1 woman). *Students:* 11 full-time (10 women), 8 part-time (7 women); includes 2 Black or African American, non-Hispanic/Latino, 2 international. Average age 26. In 2010, 4 master's awarded. *Degree requirements:* For master's, thesis. *Entrance requirements:* For master's, GRE General Test, 3 letters of recommendation; minimum GPA of 3.0; BA/BS in anthropology, biology, human biology or closely related field, resume. Additional exam requirements/recommendations for international students: Required—TOEFL (minimum score 550 paper-based). *Application deadline:* For fall admission, 1/15 for domestic and international students. Applications are processed on a rolling basis. Application fee: $30. Tuition and fees vary according to course load, degree level and program. *Financial support:* Federal Work-Study, scholarships/grants, and tuition waivers (full and partial) available. Support available to part-time students. Financial award application deadline: 5/1; financial award applicants required to submit FAFSA. *Unit head:* Dr. L. Mark Harrison, Chairperson, 317-788-3264, E-mail: harrison@uindy.edu. *Application contact:* Dr. Stephen P. Nawrocki, Director, Graduate Program in Human Biology, 317-788-3486, Fax: 317-788-3480, E-mail: snawrocki@uindy.edu.

The University of Iowa, Graduate College, College of Liberal Arts and Sciences, Department of Biology, Iowa City, IA 52242-1324. Offers biology (MS, PhD); cell and developmental biology (MS, PhD); evolution (MS, PhD); genetics (MS, PhD); neurobiology (MS, PhD). Terminal master's awarded for partial completion of doctoral program. *Degree requirements:* For master's, thesis optional, exam; for doctorate, comprehensive exam, thesis/dissertation. *Entrance requirements:* For master's and doctorate, GRE General Test, minimum GPA of 3.0. Additional exam requirements/recommendations for international students: Required—TOEFL (minimum score 600 paper-based; 250 computer-based; 100 iBT). Electronic applications accepted. *Faculty research:* Neurobiology, evolutionary biology, genetics, cell and developmental biology.

The University of Iowa, Roy J. and Lucille A. Carver College of Medicine and Graduate College, Biosciences Program, Iowa City, IA 52242-1316. Offers anatomy and biology (PhD); biochemistry (PhD); biology (PhD); biomedical engineering (PhD); chemistry (PhD); free radical and radiation biology (PhD); genetics (PhD); human toxicology (PhD); immunology (PhD); microbiology (PhD); molecular and cellular biology (PhD); molecular physiology and biophysics (PhD); neuroscience (PhD); pharmacology (PhD); physical therapy and rehabilitation science (PhD); speech and hearing (PhD). *Faculty:* 310 full-time. *Students:* 9 full-time (5 women); includes 4 minority (1 Black or African American, non-Hispanic/Latino; 2 Asian, non-Hispanic/Latino; 1 Hispanic/Latino). 225 applicants. *Degree requirements:* For doctorate, thesis/dissertation. *Entrance requirements:* For doctorate, GRE General Test, minimum GPA of 3.0. Additional exam requirements/recommendations for international students: Required—TOEFL (minimum score 600 paper-based; 250 computer-based; 100 iBT). *Application deadline:* For fall admission, 1/15 priority date for domestic and international students. Applications are processed on a rolling basis. Application fee: $60 ($100 for international students). Electronic applications accepted. *Expenses:* Contact institution. *Financial support:* In 2010–11, 9 students received support, including 9 research assistantships with full tuition reimbursements available (averaging $25,000 per year); fellowships, teaching assistantships, health care benefits also available. *Unit head:* Dr. Andrew F. Russo, Director, 319-335-7872, Fax: 319-335-7656, E-mail: andrew-russo@uiowa.edu. *Application contact:* Jodi M. Graff, Program Associate, 319-335-8305, Fax: 319-335-7656, E-mail: biosciences-admissions@uiowa.edu.

The University of Iowa, Roy J. and Lucille A. Carver College of Medicine and Graduate College, Graduate Programs in Medicine, Iowa City, IA 52242-1316. Offers MA, MPAS, MS, DPT, PhD, JD/MHA, MBA/MHA, MD/JD, MD/PhD, MHA/MA, MHA/MS, MPH/MHA, MS/MA, MS/MS. Part-time programs available. *Faculty:* 133 full-time (30 women), 92 part-time/adjunct (42 women). *Students:* 309 full-time (176 women), 4 part-time (1 woman); includes 23 minority (4 Black or African American, non-Hispanic/Latino; 5 American Indian or Alaska Native, non-Hispanic/Latino; 9 Asian, non-Hispanic/Latino; 5 Hispanic/Latino), 30 international. 1,305 applicants, 9% accepted, 94 enrolled. In 2010, 32 master's, 27 doctorates awarded. *Degree requirements:* For doctorate, thesis/dissertation. Electronic applications accepted. *Expenses:* Contact institution. *Financial support:* In 2010–11, 160 students received support, including fellowships (averaging $25,000 per year), research assistantships (averaging $25,000 per year), teaching assistantships (averaging $25,000 per year); career-related internships or fieldwork, Federal Work-Study, institutionally sponsored loans, health care benefits, and tuition waivers (full and partial) also available. Support available to part-time students. Financial award applicants required to submit FAFSA. *Unit head:* Dr. Paul B. Rothman, Dean, 319-384-4590, Fax: 319-335-8318, E-mail: paul-rothman@uiowa.edu. *Application contact:* Dr. Paul B. Rothman, Dean, 319-384-4590, Fax: 319-335-8318, E-mail: paul-rothman@uiowa.edu.

The University of Iowa, Roy J. and Lucille A. Carver College of Medicine and Graduate College, Medical Scientist Training Program, Iowa City, IA 52242-1316. Offers MD/PhD. *Faculty:* 149 full-time (36 women), 12 part-time/adjunct (1 woman). *Students:* 67 full-time (27 women); includes 10 minority (1 American Indian or Alaska Native, non-Hispanic/Latino; 1 Asian, non-Hispanic/Latino; 7 Hispanic/Latino; 1 Native Hawaiian or other Pacific Islander, non-Hispanic/Latino). Average age 24. 151 applicants, 14% accepted, 11 enrolled. *Application deadline:* For fall admission, 12/15 priority date for domestic students. Applications are processed on a rolling basis. Application fee: $60. Electronic applications accepted. *Financial support:* In 2010–11, 33 students received support, including 7 fellowships with full tuition reimbursements available (averaging $21,180 per year), 25 research assistantships with full tuition reimbursements available (averaging $3,820 per year); scholarships/grants, traineeships, health care benefits, unspecified assistantships, and travel awards also available. *Faculty research:* Structure and function of ion channels, molecular genetics of human disease, neurobiology of pain, viral immunology and immunopathology, epidemiology of aging and cancer, human learning and memory, structural enzymology. Total annual research expenditures: $2 million. *Unit head:* Dr. Steven R. Lentz, Director, 319-356-4048, Fax: 319-335-6634, E-mail: steven-lentz@uiowa.edu. *Application contact:* Leslie Harrington, Program Associate, 319-335-8304, Fax: 319-335-6634, E-mail: mstp@uiowa.edu.

The University of Kansas, University of Kansas Medical Center, School of Medicine, Interdisciplinary Graduate Program in Biomedical Sciences (IGPBS), Kansas City, KS 66160. Offers MA, MPH, MS, PhD, MD/MPH, MD/MS, MD/PhD. *Students:* 21 full-time (13 women), 9 international. Average age 25. 222 applicants, 18% accepted, 21 enrolled.Terminal master's awarded for partial completion of doctoral program. *Degree requirements:* For master's, thesis; for doctorate, comprehensive exam, thesis/dissertation. *Entrance requirements:* For master's and doctorate, GRE. Additional exam requirements/recommendations for international students: Required—TOEFL. *Application deadline:* For fall admission, 1/15 priority date for domestic and international students. Applications are processed on a rolling basis. Application fee: $0. Electronic applications accepted. *Expenses:* Tuition, state resident: full-time $7092; part-time $295.50 per credit hour. Tuition, nonresident: full-time $16,590; part-time $691.25 per credit hour. Required fees: $858; $71.49 per credit hour. Tuition and fees vary according to course load, campus/location and program. *Financial support:* Research assistantships with full tuition reimbursements, teaching assistantships with full tuition reimbursements, scholarships/grants and unspecified assistantships available. Financial award application deadline: 2/14; financial award applicants required to submit FAFSA. *Faculty research:* Cardiovascular biology, neurosciences, signal transduction and cancer biology, molecular biology and genetics, developmental biology. *Unit head:* Dr. Michael J. Werle, Director, 913-588-7491, Fax: 913-588-2710, E-mail: mwerle@kumc.edu. *Application contact:* Miranda Olenhouse, Coordinator, 913-588-2719, Fax: 913-588-2711, E-mail: molenhouse@kumc.edu.

See Display on next page and Close-Up on page 113.

University of Kentucky, Graduate School, College of Arts and Sciences, Program in Biology, Lexington, KY 40506-0032. Offers MS, PhD. *Degree requirements:* For master's, comprehensive exam, thesis optional; for doctorate, comprehensive exam, thesis/dissertation. *Entrance requirements:* For master's, GRE General Test, minimum undergraduate GPA of 2.75; for doctorate, GRE General Test, minimum graduate GPA of 3.0. Additional exam requirements/recommendations for international students: Required—TOEFL (minimum score 550 paper-based; 213 computer-based). Electronic applications accepted. *Faculty research:* General biology, microbiology, *Drosophila* molecular genetics, molecular virology, multiple loci inheritance.

University of Kentucky, Graduate School, Graduate School Programs from the College of Medicine, Lexington, KY 40506-0032. Offers MS, PhD, MD/PhD. *Degree requirements:* For master's, comprehensive exam, thesis (for some programs); for doctorate, comprehensive exam, thesis/dissertation. *Entrance requirements:* For master's, GRE General Test, minimum undergraduate GPA of 2.75; for doctorate, GRE General Test, minimum undergraduate GPA of 3.0. Additional exam requirements/recommendations for international students: Required—TOEFL (minimum score 550 paper-based; 213 computer-based). Electronic applications accepted.

University of Lethbridge, School of Graduate Studies, Lethbridge, AB T1K 3M4, Canada. Offers accounting (MScM); addictions counseling (M Sc); agricultural biotechnology (M Sc); agricultural studies (M Sc, MA); anthropology (MA); archaeology (MA); art (MA, MFA); biochemistry (M Sc); biological sciences (M Sc); biomolecular science (PhD); biosystems and biodiversity (PhD); Canadian studies (MA); chemistry (M Sc); computer science (M Sc); computer science and geographical information science (M Sc); counseling psychology (M Ed); dramatic arts (MA); earth, space, and physical science (PhD); economics (MA); educational leadership (M Ed); English (MA); environmental science (M Sc); evolution and behavior (PhD); exercise science (M Sc); finance (MScM); French (MA); French/German (MA); French/Spanish (MA); general education (M Ed); general management (MScM); geography (M Sc, MA); German (MA); health science (M Sc); history (MA); human resource management and labour relations (MScM); individualized multidisciplinary (M Sc, MA); information systems (MScM); international management (MScM); kinesiology (M Sc, MA); management (M Sc, MA); marketing (MScM); mathematics (M Sc); music (M Mus, MA); Native American studies (MA); neuroscience (M Sc, PhD); new media (MA); nursing (M Sc); philosophy (MA); physics (M Sc); policy and strategy (MScM); political science (MA); psychology (M Sc, MA); religious studies (MA); social sciences (MA); sociology (MA); theatre and dramatic arts (MFA); theoretical and computational science (PhD); urban and regional studies (MA); women's studies (MA). Part-time and evening/weekend programs available. *Degree requirements:* For doctorate, comprehensive exam, thesis/dissertation. *Entrance requirements:* For master's, GMAT (M Sc in management), bachelor's degree in related field, minimum GPA of 3.0 during previous 20 graded semester courses, 2 years teaching or related experience (M Ed); for doctorate, master's degree, minimum graduate GPA of 3.5. Additional exam requirements/recommendations for international students: Required—TOEFL. *Faculty research:* Movement and brain plasticity, gibberellin physiology, photosynthesis, carbon cycling, molecular properties of main-group ring components.

University of Louisiana at Lafayette, College of Sciences, Department of Biology, Lafayette, LA 70504. Offers biology (MS); environmental and evolutionary biology (PhD). Terminal master's awarded for partial completion of doctoral program. *Degree requirements:* For master's, thesis; for doctorate, 2 foreign languages, comprehensive exam, thesis/dissertation. *Entrance requirements:* For master's, GRE General Test, minimum GPA of 2.75; for doctorate, GRE General Test, GRE Subject Test, minimum GPA of 3.0. Additional exam requirements/recommendations for international students: Required—TOEFL (minimum score 550 paper-based; 213 computer-based). Electronic applications accepted. *Faculty research:* Structure and ultrastructure, system biology, ecology, processes, environmental physiology.

University of Louisiana at Monroe, Graduate School, College of Arts and Sciences, Department of Biology, Monroe, LA 71209-0001. Offers MS. *Faculty:* 13 full-time (6 women). *Students:* 29 full-time (16 women), 7 part-time (4 women); includes 3 Black or African American, non-Hispanic/Latino; 2 American Indian or Alaska Native, non-Hispanic/Latino; 4 Asian, non-Hispanic/Latino, 3 international. Average age 25. In 2010, 5 master's awarded. *Entrance requirements:* For master's, GRE General Test, minimum GPA of 2.8 overall or 3.0 during last 21 hours of biology. Additional exam requirements/recommendations for international students: Required—TOEFL (minimum score 500 paper-based; 113 computer-based). *Application deadline:* For fall admission, 8/24 priority date for domestic students, 7/1 for international students; for winter admission, 12/14 priority date for domestic students; for spring admission, 1/19 for domestic students, 11/1 for international students. Applications are processed on a rolling basis. Application fee: $20 ($30 for international students). Electronic applications accepted. *Expenses:* Tuition, state resident: full-time $2991; part-time $197 per credit hour. Tuition, nonresident: full-time $2991; part-time $197 per credit hour. International tuition: $10,288 full-time. *Financial support:* In 2010–11, 3 research assistantships with full tuition reimbursements (averaging $4,000 per year), 18 teaching assistantships with full tuition reimbursements (averaging $4,000 per year) were awarded; career-related internships or fieldwork, Federal Work-Study, and unspecified assistantships also available. Financial award application deadline: 4/1; financial award applicants required to submit FAFSA. *Faculty research:* Fish systematics and zoogeography, taxonomy and distribution of Louisiana plants, aquatic biology, secondary succession, microbial ecology. *Unit head:* Dr. Sushma Krishnamurthy, Department Head, 318-342-1813, Fax: 318-342-3312, E-mail: krishnamurthy@ulm.edu. *Application contact:* Dr. Kim M. Tolson, Professor, 318-342-1805, Fax: 318-342-3312, E-mail: tolson@ulm.edu.

University of Louisville, Graduate School, College of Arts and Sciences, Department of Biology, Louisville, KY 40292-0001. Offers biology (MS); environmental biology (PhD). *Students:* 40 full-time (21 women), 9 part-time (8 women); includes 2 Black or African American, non-Hispanic/Latino; 1 Hispanic/Latino, 9 international. Average age 31. 49 applicants, 43% accepted, 13 enrolled. In 2010, 6 master's, 7 doctorates awarded. *Degree requirements:* For master's, thesis (for some programs); for doctorate, thesis/dissertation. *Entrance requirements:* For master's and doctorate, GRE General Test. *Application deadline:* Applications are processed on a rolling basis. Application fee: $50. *Expenses:* Tuition, state resident: full-time $9144; part-time $508 per credit hour. Tuition, nonresident: full-time $19,026; part-time $1057 per credit hour. Tuition and fees vary according to program and reciprocity agreements. *Unit head:* Dr. Ronald Fell, Chair, 502-852-6771, Fax: 502-852-0725, E-mail: rdfell@louisville.edu. *Application contact:* Dr. Joseph M. Steffen, Director of Graduate Studies, 502-852-6771, Fax: 502-852-0725, E-mail: joe.steffen@louisville.edu.

University of Maine, Graduate School, College of Natural Sciences, Forestry, and Agriculture, Department of Biological Sciences, Program in Biological Sciences, Orono, ME 04469. Offers PhD. *Students:* 6 full-time (3 women), 6 part-time (3 women); includes 1 minority (Asian, non-Hispanic/Latino), 1 international. Average age 31. 11 applicants, 9% accepted, 1 enrolled.

In 2010, 3 doctorates awarded. *Degree requirements:* For doctorate, thesis/dissertation. *Entrance requirements:* For doctorate, GRE General Test. Additional exam requirements/recommendations for international students: Required—TOEFL. *Application deadline:* For fall admission, 2/1 priority date for domestic students. Applications are processed on a rolling basis. Application fee: $65. Electronic applications accepted. *Expenses:* Tuition, state resident: full-time $400. Tuition, nonresident: full-time $1050. *Financial support:* Application deadline: 3/1. *Unit head:* Dr. Stellos Tavantzis, Coordinator, 207-581-2986. *Application contact:* Scott G. Delcourt, Associate Dean of the Graduate School, 207-581-3291, Fax: 207-581-3232, E-mail: graduate@maine.edu.

University of Maine, Graduate School, Program in Biomedical Sciences, Orono, ME 04469. Offers biomedical engineering (PhD); cell and molecular biology (PhD); neuroscience (PhD); toxicology (PhD). *Students:* 11 full-time (8 women), 13 part-time (6 women); includes 1 American Indian or Alaska Native, non-Hispanic/Latino, 5 international. Average age 29. 32 applicants, 19% accepted, 6 enrolled.Application fee: $60. *Expenses:* Tuition, state resident: full-time $400. Tuition, nonresident: full-time $1050. *Financial support:* In 2010–11, 8 research assistantships (averaging $25,625 per year) were awarded. *Unit head:* Dr. Carol Kim, Unit Head, 207-581-2803. *Application contact:* Dr. Carol Kim, Unit Head, 207-581-2803.

The University of Manchester, Faculty of Life Sciences, Manchester, United Kingdom. Offers adaptive organismal biology (M Phil, PhD); animal biology (M Phil, PhD); biochemistry (M Phil, PhD); bioinformatics (M Phil, PhD); biomolecular sciences (M Phil, PhD); biotechnology (M Phil, PhD); cell biology (M Phil, PhD); cell matrix research (M Phil, PhD); channels and transporters (M Phil, PhD); developmental biology (M Phil, PhD); Egyptology (M Phil, PhD); environmental biology (M Phil, PhD); evolutionary biology (M Phil, PhD); gene expression (M Phil, PhD); genetics (M Phil, PhD); history of science, technology and medicine (M Phil, PhD); immunology (M Phil, PhD); integrative neurobiology and behavior (M Phil, PhD); membrane trafficking (M Phil, PhD); microbiology (M Phil, PhD); molecular and cellular neuroscience (M Phil, PhD); molecular biology (M Phil, PhD); molecular cancer studies (M Phil, PhD); neuroscience (M Phil, PhD); ophthalmology (M Phil, PhD); optometry (M Phil, PhD); organelle function (M Phil, PhD); pharmacology (M Phil, PhD); physiology (M Phil, PhD); plant sciences (M Phil, PhD); stem cell research (M Phil, PhD); structural biology (M Phil, PhD); systems neuroscience (M Phil, PhD); toxicology (M Phil, PhD).

The University of Manchester, School of Chemical Engineering and Analytical Science, Manchester, United Kingdom. Offers biocatalysis (M Phil, PhD); chemical engineering (M Phil, PhD); chemical engineering and analytical science (M Phil, D Eng, PhD); colloids, crystals, interfaces and materials (M Phil, PhD); environment and sustainable technology (M Phil, PhD); instrumentation (M Phil, PhD); multi-scale modeling (M Phil, PhD); process integration (M Phil, PhD); systems biology (M Phil, PhD).

The University of Manchester, School of Materials, Manchester, United Kingdom. Offers advanced aerospace materials engineering (M Sc); advanced metallic systems (PhD); biomedical materials (M Phil, M Sc, PhD); ceramics and glass (M Phil, M Sc, PhD); composite materials (M Sc, PhD); corrosion and protection (M Phil, M Sc, PhD); materials (M Phil, PhD); metallic materials (M Phil, M Sc, PhD); nanostructural materials (M Phil, M Sc, PhD); paper science (M Phil, M Sc, PhD); polymer science and engineering (M Phil, M Sc, PhD); technical textiles (M Sc); textile design, fashion and management (M Phil, M Sc, PhD); textile science and technology (M Phil, M Sc, PhD); textiles (M Phil, PhD); textiles and fashion (M Ent).

The University of Manchester, School of Medicine, Manchester, United Kingdom. Offers M Phil, PhD.

University of Manitoba, Faculty of Graduate Studies, Faculty of Science, Department of Biological Sciences, Winnipeg, MB R3T 2N2, Canada. Offers botany (M Sc, PhD); ecology (M Sc, PhD); zoology (M Sc, PhD).

University of Manitoba, Faculty of Medicine and Faculty of Graduate Studies, Graduate Programs in Medicine, Winnipeg, MB R3T 2N2, Canada. Offers M Sc, MPH, PhD, G Dip, MD/PhD. *Accreditation:* LCME/AMA. Part-time programs available. *Expenses:* Contact institution.

Biological and Biomedical Sciences—General

University of Maryland, Baltimore, Graduate School, Graduate Program in Life Sciences, Baltimore, MD 21201. Offers biochemistry and molecular biology (MS, PhD), including biochemistry; epidemiology (PhD); gerontology (PhD); molecular medicine (MS, PhD), including cancer biology (PhD), cell and molecular physiology (PhD), human genetics and genomic medicine (PhD), molecular medicine (MS), molecular toxicology and pharmacology (PhD); molecular microbiology and immunology (PhD); neuroscience (PhD); physical rehabilitation science (PhD); toxicology (MS, PhD); MD/MS; MD/PhD. *Degree requirements:* For master's, comprehensive exam (for some programs), thesis (for some programs); for doctorate, comprehensive exam, thesis/dissertation. *Entrance requirements:* For master's and doctorate, GRE. Additional exam requirements/recommendations for international students: Required—TOEFL (minimum score 550 paper-based; 80 iBT); Recommended—IELTS (minimum score 7). Electronic applications accepted. Part-time tuition and fees vary according to course load, degree level and program. *Faculty research:* Cancer, reproduction, cardiovascular, immunology.

University of Maryland, Baltimore County, Graduate School, College of Arts, Humanities and Social Sciences, Department of Education, Program in Teaching, Baltimore, MD 21250. Offers early childhood education (MAT); elementary education (MAT); secondary education (MAT), including art, biology, chemistry, dance, earth/space science, English, foreign language, mathematics, music, physics, theatre; secondary science (MAT), including social studies. Part-time and evening/weekend programs available. *Faculty:* 24 full-time (18 women), 25 part-time/adjunct (19 women). *Students:* 59 full-time (46 women), 56 part-time (42 women); includes 1 Black or African American, non-Hispanic/Latino; 8 Asian, non-Hispanic/Latino; 3 Hispanic/Latino, 3 international. Average age 31. 88 applicants, 57% accepted, 39 enrolled. In 2010, 106 master's awarded. *Degree requirements:* For master's, comprehensive exam (for some programs), thesis (for some programs). *Entrance requirements:* For master's, PRAXIS I and II, minimum GPA of 3.0. Additional exam requirements/recommendations for international students: Required—TOEFL. *Application deadline:* For fall admission, 6/1 for domestic students; for spring admission, 11/1 for domestic students. Applications are processed on a rolling basis. Application fee: $50. Electronic applications accepted. *Financial support:* In 2010–11, 6 students received support, including research assistantships with full tuition reimbursements available (averaging $12,000 per year); career-related internships or fieldwork, Federal Work-Study, scholarships/grants, tuition waivers, and unspecified assistantships also available. Financial award application deadline: 3/1. *Faculty research:* STEM teacher education, culturally sensitive pedagogy, ESOL/bilingual education, early childhood education, language, literacy and culture. *Unit head:* Dr. Susan M. Blunck, Director, 410-455-2869, Fax: 410-455-3986, E-mail: blunck@umbc.edu. *Application contact:* Cheryl Johnson, 410-455-3388, E-mail: blackwel@umbc.edu.

University of Maryland, Baltimore County, Graduate School, College of Natural and Mathematical Sciences, Department of Biological Sciences, Baltimore, MD 21250. Offers applied molecular biology (MS); biological sciences (MS, PhD); molecular and cell biology (PhD); neurosciences and cognitive sciences (PhD). Part-time programs available. *Faculty:* 35 full-time (16 women). *Students:* 75 full-time (47 women), 15 part-time (8 women); includes 48 minority (10 Black or African American, non-Hispanic/Latino; 34 Asian, non-Hispanic/Latino; 4 Hispanic/Latino). Average age 26. 141 applicants, 38% accepted, 31 enrolled. In 2010, 2 master's, 10 doctorates awarded. *Entrance requirements:* For master's and doctorate, GRE General Test, minimum GPA of 3.0. Additional exam requirements/recommendations for international students: Required—TOEFL. *Application deadline:* For fall admission, 1/15 for domestic students, 12/15 for international students. Applications are processed on a rolling basis. Application fee: $50. Electronic applications accepted. *Financial support:* In 2010–11, 78 students received support, including 9 fellowships with full tuition reimbursements available (averaging $30,000 per year), 30 research assistantships with full tuition reimbursements available (averaging $22,300 per year), 39 teaching assistantships with full tuition reimbursements available (averaging $22,300 per year); career-related internships or fieldwork and tuition waivers (partial) also available. *Faculty research:* Molecular genetics, neurobiology, metabolism. *Unit head:* Dr. Lasse Lindahl, Chairman, 410-455-2261, Fax: 410-455-3875. *Application contact:* Dr. Jeff Leips, Director, 410-455-3669, Fax: 410-455-3875, E-mail: biograd@umbc.edu.

University of Maryland, College Park, Academic Affairs, College of Computer, Mathematical and Natural Sciences, Department of Biology, Program in Biology, College Park, MD 20742. Offers MS, PhD. Part-time and evening/weekend programs available. *Students:* 42 full-time (26 women), 4 part-time (3 women); includes 4 minority (3 Black or African American, non-Hispanic/Latino; 1 Asian, non-Hispanic/Latino), 14 international. In 2010, 2 master's, 3 doctorates awarded. Terminal master's awarded for partial completion of doctoral program. *Degree requirements:* For master's, comprehensive exam, thesis optional; for doctorate, thesis/dissertation, oral exam. *Entrance requirements:* For master's and doctorate, GRE General Test, GRE Subject Test, minimum GPA of 3.0, 3 letters of recommendation. Additional exam requirements/recommendations for international students: Required—TOEFL. *Application deadline:* Applications are processed on a rolling basis. Electronic applications accepted. *Expenses:* Tuition, state resident: part-time $471 per credit hour. Tuition, nonresident: part-time $1016 per credit hour. Required fees: $337 per term. *Financial support:* In 2010–11, 7 fellowships with full and partial tuition reimbursements (averaging $20,688 per year), 8 research assistantships with tuition reimbursements (averaging $19,661 per year), 12 teaching assistantships with tuition reimbursements (averaging $19,381 per year) were awarded. Financial award application deadline: 2/1; financial award applicants required to submit FAFSA. *Unit head:* Gerald Wilkinson, Chair, 301-405-6884, E-mail: wilkinso@umd.edu. *Application contact:* Gerald Wilkinson, Chair, 301-405-6884, E-mail: wilkinso@umd.edu.

University of Maryland, College Park, Academic Affairs, College of Computer, Mathematical and Natural Sciences, Program in Life Sciences, College Park, MD 20742. Offers MLS. *Students:* 2 full-time (1 woman), 96 part-time (71 women); includes 16 minority (7 Black or African American, non-Hispanic/Latino; 4 Asian, non-Hispanic/Latino; 3 Hispanic/Latino; 2 Two or more races, non-Hispanic/Latino), 2 international. 44 applicants, 95% accepted, 27 enrolled. In 2010, 36 master's awarded. *Degree requirements:* For master's, scholarly paper. *Entrance requirements:* For master's, 1 year of teaching experience, letters of recommendation. *Application deadline:* Applications are processed on a rolling basis. Application fee: $75. Electronic applications accepted. *Expenses:* Tuition, state resident: part-time $471 per credit hour. Tuition, nonresident: part-time $1016 per credit hour. Required fees: $337 per term. *Financial support:* Fellowships, research assistantships, teaching assistantships, Federal Work-Study and scholarships/grants available. Support available to part-time students. Financial award applicants required to submit FAFSA. *Faculty research:* Genetic engineering, gene therapy, ecology, biocomplexity. *Unit head:* Dr. Paul Mazzocchi, Director, 301-405-8482, E-mail: pmazzocc@deans.umd.edu. *Application contact:* Dr. Charles A. Caramello, Dean of Graduate School, 301-405-0358, Fax: 301-314-9305.

University of Massachusetts Amherst, Graduate School, College of Natural Sciences, Department of Animal Biotechnology and Biomedical Sciences, Amherst, MA 01003. Offers MS, PhD. Part-time programs available. *Faculty:* 22 full-time (9 women). *Students:* 28 full-time (17 women), 1 (woman) part-time; includes 1 minority (Hispanic/Latino), 8 international. Average age 28. 52 applicants, 21% accepted, 10 enrolled. In 2010, 3 master's, 2 doctorates awarded. Terminal master's awarded for partial completion of doctoral program. *Degree requirements:* For master's, thesis or alternative; for doctorate, comprehensive exam, thesis/dissertation. *Entrance requirements:* For master's and doctorate, GRE General Test. Additional exam requirements/recommendations for international students: Required—TOEFL (minimum score 550 paper-based; 213 computer-based; 80 iBT), IELTS (minimum score 6.5). *Application deadline:* For fall admission, 2/1 for domestic and international students; for spring admission, 10/1 for domestic and international students. Applications are processed on a rolling basis. Application fee: $50 ($65 for international students). Electronic applications accepted. *Expenses:* Tuition, state resident: full-time $2640. Required fees: $8282. One-time fee: $357 full-time. *Financial support:* In 2010–11, 1 fellowship (averaging $1,731 per year), 40 research assistantships with full tuition reimbursements (averaging $12,032 per year), 13 teaching assistantships with full tuition reimbursements (averaging $9,586 per year) were awarded; career-related internships or fieldwork, Federal Work-Study, scholarships/grants, traineeships, health care benefits, tuition waivers (full), and unspecified assistantships also available. Support available to part-time students. Financial award application deadline: 2/1; financial award applicants required to submit FAFSA. *Unit head:* Dr. Pablo E. Visconti, Graduate Program Director, 413-577-1193, Fax: 413-577-1150. *Application contact:* Jean M. Ames, Supervisor of Admissions, 413-545-0722, Fax: 413-577-0010, E-mail: gradadm@grad.umass.edu.

University of Massachusetts Boston, Office of Graduate Studies, College of Science and Mathematics, Program in Biology, Boston, MA 02125-3393. Offers MS. Part-time and evening/weekend programs available. *Degree requirements:* For master's, thesis, oral exams. *Entrance requirements:* For master's, GRE General Test, GRE Subject Test, minimum GPA of 2.75. *Faculty research:* Microbial ecology, population and conservation genetics energetics of insect locomotion, science education, evolution and ecology of marine invertebrates.

University of Massachusetts Boston, Office of Graduate Studies, College of Science and Mathematics, Program in Biotechnology and Biomedical Science, Boston, MA 02125-3393. Offers MS. Part-time and evening/weekend programs available. *Degree requirements:* For master's, comprehensive exam, thesis optional, oral exams. *Entrance requirements:* For master's, GRE General Test, GRE Subject Test, minimum GPA of 2.75, 3.0 in science and math. *Faculty research:* Evolutionary and molecular immunology, molecular genetics, tissue culture, computerized laboratory technology.

University of Massachusetts Dartmouth, Graduate School, College of Arts and Sciences, Department of Biology, North Dartmouth, MA 02747-2300. Offers biology (MS); marine biology (MS). Part-time programs available. *Faculty:* 17 full-time (7 women), 4 part-time/adjunct (1 woman). *Students:* 12 full-time (9 women), 8 part-time (4 women); includes 1 Asian, non-Hispanic/Latino; 1 Hispanic/Latino. Average age 27. 35 applicants, 29% accepted, 9 enrolled. In 2010, 6 master's awarded. *Degree requirements:* For master's, thesis. *Entrance requirements:* For master's, GRE General Test, GRE Subject Test, 3 letters of recommendation. Additional exam requirements/recommendations for international students: Required—TOEFL (minimum score 500 paper-based). *Application deadline:* For fall admission, 3/15 for domestic students, 1/15 for international students; for spring admission, 11/15 priority date for domestic students, 9/15 priority date for international students. Application fee: $40 ($60 for international students). Electronic applications accepted. *Expenses:* Tuition, state resident: full-time $2071; part-time $86 per credit. Tuition, nonresident: full-time $8099; part-time $337 per credit. Required fees: $9446; $394 per credit. One-time fee: $75. Part-time tuition and fees vary according to class time, course load, degree level and reciprocity agreements. *Financial support:* In 2010–11, 6 research assistantships with full tuition reimbursements (averaging $12,577 per year), 7 teaching assistantships with full tuition reimbursements (averaging $10,340 per year) were awarded; Federal Work-Study and unspecified assistantships also available. Support available to part-time students. Financial award application deadline: 3/1; financial award applicants required to submit FAFSA. *Faculty research:* Fish biology, antibody-mediated protection, bottlenose dolphins, adaptations in fish via genetics, evolutionary biology. Total annual research expenditures: $1.4 million. *Unit head:* Dr. Diego Bernal, Director, 508-999-8307, Fax: 508-999-8196, E-mail: dbernal@umassd.edu. *Application contact:* Elan Turcotte-Shamski, Graduate Admissions Officer, 508-999-8604, Fax: 508-999-8183, E-mail: graduate@umassd.edu.

University of Massachusetts Lowell, College of Arts and Sciences, Department of Biological Sciences, Lowell, MA 01854-2881. Offers biochemistry (PhD); biological sciences (MS); biotechnology (MS). Part-time programs available. *Degree requirements:* For master's, thesis; for doctorate, thesis/dissertation. *Entrance requirements:* For master's and doctorate, GRE General Test. Electronic applications accepted.

University of Massachusetts Worcester, Graduate School of Biomedical Sciences, Worcester, MA 01655-0115. Offers biochemistry and molecular pharmacology (PhD); bioinformatics and computational biology (PhD); cancer biology (PhD); cell biology (PhD); clinical and population health research (PhD); clinical investigation (MS); immunology and virology (PhD); interdisciplinary graduate program (PhD); molecular genetics and microbiology (PhD); neuroscience (PhD); DVM/PhD; MD/PhD. *Faculty:* 1,059 full-time (357 women), 145 part-time/adjunct (100 women). *Students:* 438 full-time (239 women), 1 (woman) part-time; includes 44 minority (9 Black or African American, non-Hispanic/Latino; 31 Asian, non-Hispanic/Latino; 4 Hispanic/Latino), 148 international. Average age 29. 687 applicants, 28% accepted, 116 enrolled. In 2010, 6 master's, 45 doctorates awarded. Terminal master's awarded for partial completion of doctoral program. *Degree requirements:* For master's, thesis; for doctorate, thesis/dissertation. *Entrance requirements:* For master's, bachelor's degree; for doctorate, GRE General Test, MS, MA, or MPH (for some programs). Additional exam requirements/recommendations for international students: Required—TOEFL (minimum score 600 paper-based; 250 computer-based). *Application deadline:* For fall admission, 12/15 for domestic and international students; for winter admission, 1/15 for domestic students; for spring admission, 5/15 for domestic students. Application fee: $35. Electronic applications accepted. *Expenses:* Contact institution. *Financial support:* In 2010–11, 439 students received support, including 439 research assistantships with full tuition reimbursements available (averaging $28,350 per year); scholarships/grants, health care benefits, tuition waivers (full), and unspecified assistantships also available. Financial award application deadline: 4/20. *Faculty research:* RNA interference, gene therapy, cell biology, bioinformatics, clinical research. Total annual research expenditures: $232 million. *Unit head:* Dr. Anthony Carruthers, Dean, 508-856-4135, E-mail: anthony.carruthers@umassmed.edu. *Application contact:* Dr. Kendall Knight, Associate Dean and Interim Director of Admissions and Recruitment, 508-856-5628, Fax: 508-856-3659, E-mail: kendall.knight@umassmed.edu.

University of Medicine and Dentistry of New Jersey, Graduate School of Biomedical Sciences, Graduate Programs in Biomedical Sciences–Newark, Newark, NJ 07107. Offers biodefense (Certificate); biomedical engineering (PhD); biomedical sciences (multidisciplinary) (PhD); cellular biology, neuroscience and physiology (PhD), including neuroscience, physiology, biophysics, cardiovascular biology, molecular pharmacology, stem cell biology; infection, immunity and inflammation (PhD), including immunology, infectious disease, microbiology, oral biology; molecular biology, genetics and cancer (PhD), including biochemistry, molecular genetics, cancer biology, radiation biology, bioinformatics; neuroscience (Certificate); pharmacological sciences (Certificate); stem cell (Certificate); DMD/PhD; MD/PhD. PhD in biomedical engineering offered jointly with New Jersey Institute of Technology. Part-time and evening/weekend programs available. *Students:* 330 full-time (199 women), 75 part-time (47 women); includes 32 Black or African American, non-Hispanic/Latino; 1 American Indian or Alaska Native, non-Hispanic/Latino; 109 Asian, non-Hispanic/Latino; 16 Hispanic/Latino, 83 international. Average age 28. 611 applicants, 52% accepted, 181 enrolled. In 2010, 24 doctorates, 2 other advanced degrees awarded. Terminal master's awarded for partial completion of doctoral program. *Degree requirements:* For doctorate, thesis/dissertation, qualifying exam. *Entrance requirements:* For doctorate, GRE General Test. Additional exam requirements/recommendations for international students: Required—TOEFL. *Application deadline:* For fall admission, 1/15 for domestic students. Applications are processed on a rolling basis. Application fee: $65. Electronic applications accepted. *Financial support:* In 2010–11, 28 fellowships (averaging $26,000 per year) were awarded; research assistantships, teaching assistantships, career-related internships or fieldwork, Federal Work-Study, institutionally sponsored loans, and tuition waivers (full and partial) also available. Financial award application deadline: 5/1. *Unit head:* Dr. Andrew Thomas, Senior Associate Dean, Graduate School of Biomedical Sciences, 973-972-4511, Fax: 973-972-7148, E-mail: thomas@umdnj.edu. *Application contact:* Dr. B. J. Wagner, 973-972-5335, Fax: 973-972-7148, E-mail: wagner@umdnj.edu.

University of Medicine and Dentistry of New Jersey, Graduate School of Biomedical Sciences, Graduate Programs in Biomedical Sciences–Piscataway, Piscataway, NJ 08854-5635. Offers biochemistry and molecular biology (MS, PhD); biomedical engineering (MS, PhD); biomedical science (MS); cellular and molecular pharmacology (MS, PhD); clinical and translational science (MS); environmental sciences/exposure assessment (PhD); molecular genetics, microbiology and immunology (MS, PhD); neuroscience (MS, PhD); physiology and integrative biology (MS, PhD); toxicology (PhD); MD/PhD. *Students:* 474 full-time (260 women),

22 part-time (7 women); includes 30 Black or African American, non-Hispanic/Latino; 89 Asian, non-Hispanic/Latino; 36 Hispanic/Latino, 158 international. Average age 28. 1,064 applicants, 18% accepted, 121 enrolled. In 2010, 32 master's, 70 doctorates awarded. Terminal master's awarded for partial completion of doctoral program. *Degree requirements:* For master's, thesis (for some programs), ethics training; for doctorate, comprehensive exam, thesis/dissertation, ethics training. *Entrance requirements:* For master's, GRE General Test, MCAT, DAT; for doctorate, GRE General Test. Additional exam requirements/recommendations for international students: Required—TOEFL. *Application deadline:* For fall admission, 1/5 for domestic students. Applications are processed on a rolling basis. Application fee: $65. Electronic applications accepted. *Financial support:* Fellowships, research assistantships, teaching assistantships, career-related internships or fieldwork, Federal Work-Study, traineeships, health care benefits, and unspecified assistantships available. *Unit head:* Dr. Terri Goss Kinzy, Senior Associate Dean, Graduate School, 732-235-5016, Fax: 732-235-4720, E-mail: gsbspisc@umdnj.edu. *Application contact:* Johanna Sierra, University Registrar, 732-235-5016, Fax: 732-235-4720.

University of Medicine and Dentistry of New Jersey, Graduate School of Biomedical Sciences, Graduate Programs in Biomedical Sciences–Stratford, Stratford, NJ 08084-5634. Offers biomedical sciences (MBS, MS); cell and molecular biology (MS, PhD); molecular pathology and immunology (MS); DO/MS; DO/PhD; MS/MPH. Part-time and evening/weekend programs available. *Students:* 79 full-time (43 women), 19 part-time (14 women); includes 21 Black or African American, non-Hispanic/Latino; 16 Asian, non-Hispanic/Latino; 7 Hispanic/Latino, 11 international. Average age 25. 128 applicants, 74% accepted, 64 enrolled. In 2010, 46 master's, 3 doctorates awarded. Terminal master's awarded for partial completion of doctoral program. *Degree requirements:* For master's, thesis (for some programs); for doctorate, thesis/dissertation, qualifying exam. *Entrance requirements:* For master's, GRE General Test, MCAT or DAT; for doctorate, GRE General Test. Additional exam requirements/recommendations for international students: Required—TOEFL. *Application deadline:* For fall admission, 2/1 for domestic and international students; for spring admission, 11/1 for domestic students. Applications are processed on a rolling basis. Application fee: $65. Electronic applications accepted. *Financial support:* Fellowships, Federal Work-Study available. Financial award application deadline: 5/1. *Unit head:* Dr. Carl E. Hock, Senior Associate Dean, Graduate School, 856-566-6282, Fax: 856-566-6232, E-mail: hock@umdnj.edu. *Application contact:* University Registrar, 973-972-5338.

University of Memphis, Graduate School, College of Arts and Sciences, Department of Biology, Memphis, TN 38152. Offers MS, PhD. *Faculty:* 23 full-time (2 women). *Students:* 49 full-time (27 women), 12 part-time (4 women); includes 8 minority (6 Black or African American, non-Hispanic/Latino; 2 Asian, non-Hispanic/Latino), 6 international. Average age 29. 23 applicants, 91% accepted, 16 enrolled. In 2010, 8 master's, 4 doctorates awarded. Terminal master's awarded for partial completion of doctoral program. *Degree requirements:* For master's, comprehensive exam, thesis (for some programs); for doctorate, one foreign language, comprehensive exam, thesis/dissertation. *Entrance requirements:* For master's, GRE General Test; for doctorate, GRE General Test, master's degree. Additional exam requirements/recommendations for international students: Required—TOEFL (minimum score 550 paper-based; 210 computer-based; 79 iBT). *Application deadline:* For fall admission, 2/1 for domestic and international students; for spring admission, 10/15 for domestic and international students. Applications are processed on a rolling basis. Application fee: $35 ($60 for international students). Electronic applications accepted. *Financial support:* In 2010–11, 16 students received support; research assistantships with full tuition reimbursements available, teaching assistantships with full tuition reimbursements available, Federal Work-Study, scholarships/grants, and unspecified assistantships available. Financial award application deadline: 2/15; financial award applicants required to submit FAFSA. *Faculty research:* Protein trafficking and signal transduction; animal behavior and communication, neurobiology, and circadian clock function; phylogenetics, evolution, and ecology; causation and prevention of cancer; reproductive biology. *Unit head:* Dr. Randall Bayer, Chairman, 901-678-2596, Fax: 901-678-4746, E-mail: rbayer@memphis.edu. *Application contact:* Dr. Melvin Beck, Professor and Graduate Studies Coordinator, 901-678-2970, Fax: 901-678-4457, E-mail: mbeck@memphis.edu.

University of Miami, Graduate School, College of Arts and Sciences, Department of Biology, Coral Gables, FL 33124. Offers biology (MS, PhD); genetics and evolution (MS, PhD). Terminal master's awarded for partial completion of doctoral program. *Degree requirements:* For master's, comprehensive exam (for some programs), thesis (for some programs); for doctorate, thesis/dissertation, oral and written qualifying exam. *Entrance requirements:* For master's, GRE General Test, 3 letters of recommendation, research papers; for doctorate, GRE General Test, 3 letters of recommendation, research papers, sponsor letter. Additional exam requirements/recommendations for international students: Required—TOEFL (minimum score 550 paper-based; 213 computer-based; 59 iBT). Electronic applications accepted. *Faculty research:* Neuroscience to ethology; plants, vertebrates and mycorrhizae; phylogenies, life histories and species interactions; molecular biology, gene expression and populations; cells, auditory neurons and vertebrate locomotion.

University of Michigan, Medical School and Rackham Graduate School, Medical Scientist Training Program, Ann Arbor, MI 48109. Offers MD/PhD. *Accreditation:* LCME/AMA. Electronic applications accepted. *Expenses:* Tuition, state resident: full-time $17,784; part-time $1116 per credit hour. Tuition, nonresident: full-time $35,944; part-time $2125 per credit hour. International tuition: $35,994 full-time. Required fees: $95 per semester. Tuition and fees vary according to course load, degree level and program.

University of Michigan, Rackham Graduate School, Program in Biomedical Sciences (PIBS), Ann Arbor, MI 48109-5619. Offers MS, PhD. *Faculty:* 464 full-time. *Students:* 100 full-time (50 women); includes 19 minority (4 Black or African American, non-Hispanic/Latino; 6 Asian, non-Hispanic/Latino; 6 Hispanic/Latino; 3 Two or more races, non-Hispanic/Latino), 14 international. Average age 24. 617 applicants, 38% accepted, 100 enrolled. *Degree requirements:* For doctorate, thesis/dissertation, oral defense of dissertation, preliminary exam. *Entrance requirements:* For doctorate, GRE General Test, 3 letters of recommendation, research experience. Additional exam requirements/recommendations for international students: Required—TOEFL (minimum score 84 iBT). *Application deadline:* For fall admission, 12/1 for domestic and international students. Application fee: $60 ($75 for international students). Electronic applications accepted. *Expenses:* Tuition, state resident: full-time $17,784; part-time $1116 per credit hour. Tuition, nonresident: full-time $35,944; part-time $2125 per credit hour. International tuition: $35,994 full-time. Required fees: $95 per semester. Tuition and fees vary according to course load, degree level and program. *Financial support:* In 2010–11, 100 students received support, including 91 fellowships with full tuition reimbursements available (averaging $26,500 per year); scholarships/grants, health care benefits, tuition waivers (full), and unspecified assistantships also available. Financial award application deadline: 12/1. *Faculty research:* Genetics, cellular and molecular biology, microbial pathogenesis, cancer biology, neuroscience. *Unit head:* Dr. Lori L. Isom, Assistant Dean/Director/Professor of Molecular and Integrative Physiology and Pharmacology, 734-615-7005, Fax: 734-647-7022, E-mail: lisom@umich.edu. *Application contact:* Michelle S. Melis, Director of Student Life, 734-615-6538, Fax: 734-647-7022, E-mail: pibs@umich.edu.

University of Michigan–Flint, College of Arts and Sciences, Program in Biology, Flint, MI 48502-1950. Offers MS. Part-time programs available. *Degree requirements:* For master's, thesis or alternative. *Entrance requirements:* For master's, GRE, minimum undergraduate GPA of 3.0 in prerequisites. Additional exam requirements/recommendations for international students: Required—TOEFL (minimum score 560 paper-based; 220 computer-based; 84 iBT), IELTS (minimum score 6.5). *Expenses:* Contact institution.

University of Minnesota, Duluth, Graduate School, Swenson College of Science and Engineering, Department of Biology, Integrated Biosciences Program, Duluth, MN 55812-2496. Offers MS, PhD. Terminal master's awarded for partial completion of doctoral program. *Degree requirements:* For master's, thesis, seminar; for doctorate, comprehensive exam,

thesis/dissertation, written and oral exam, seminar, written thesis. *Entrance requirements:* For master's, GRE, 1 year of biology, physics, and chemistry; 1 semester of calculus; for doctorate, GRE, 1 year each of chemistry, biology, physics, calculus, and advanced chemistry. Additional exam requirements/recommendations for international students: Required—TOEFL (minimum score 550 paper-based; 79 iBT). Electronic applications accepted. *Faculty research:* Ecology, organizational and population biology; cell, molecular and physiological biology.

University of Minnesota, Twin Cities Campus, Graduate School, College of Biological Sciences, Biological Science Program, Minneapolis, MN 55455-0213. Offers MBS. Part-time and evening/weekend programs available. *Entrance requirements:* For master's, 2 years of work experience. Electronic applications accepted. *Expenses:* Contact institution.

University of Minnesota, Twin Cities Campus, Graduate School, Stem Cell Biology Graduate Program, Minneapolis, MN 55455-3007. Offers MS. *Degree requirements:* For master's, thesis. *Entrance requirements:* For master's, GRE, BS, BA, or foreign equivalent in biological sciences or related field; minimum undergraduate GPA of 3.2. Additional exam requirements/recommendations for international students: Required—TOEFL (minimum scores 580 on paper-based, with a minimum score of 4 in the TWE, or 94 Internet-based, with a minimum score of 22 on each of the reading and listening, 26 on the speaking, and 26 on the writing section. *Faculty research:* Stem cell and developmental biology; embryonic stem cells; iPS cells; muscle satellite cells; hematopoietic stem cells; neuronal stem cells; cardiovascular, kidney and limb development; regenerating systems.

University of Minnesota, Twin Cities Campus, Medical School and Graduate School, Graduate Programs in Medicine, Minneapolis, MN 55455-0213. Offers MA. Part-time and evening/weekend programs available. *Expenses:* Contact institution.

University of Mississippi, Graduate School, College of Liberal Arts, Department of Biology, Oxford, University, MS 38677. Offers MS, PhD. *Students:* 32 full-time (16 women), 4 part-time (2 women); includes 5 Asian, non-Hispanic/Latino; 1 Hispanic/Latino; 1 Two or more races, non-Hispanic/Latino. In 2010, 1 master's, 2 doctorates awarded. *Degree requirements:* For master's, thesis; for doctorate, thesis/dissertation. *Entrance requirements:* For master's and doctorate, GRE General Test, GRE Subject Test, minimum GPA of 3.0. Additional exam requirements/recommendations for international students: Required—TOEFL. *Application deadline:* For fall admission, 4/1 for domestic students; for spring admission, 10/1 for domestic students. Applications are processed on a rolling basis. Application fee: $25. Electronic applications accepted. *Financial support:* Research assistantships, teaching assistantships, scholarships/grants available. Financial award application deadline: 3/1; financial award applicants required to submit FAFSA. *Faculty research:* Freshwater biology, including ecology and evolutionary biology; environmental and applied biology. *Unit head:* Dr. Paul Lago, Interim Chair, 662-915-7203, Fax: 662-915-5144, E-mail: biology@olemiss.edu. *Application contact:* Dr. Christy M. Wyandt, Associate Dean, 662-915-7474, Fax: 662-915-7577, E-mail: cwyandt@olemiss.edu.

University of Mississippi Medical Center, School of Graduate Studies in the Health Sciences, Jackson, MS 39216-4505. Offers MS, MSN, PhD, MD/PhD. Terminal master's awarded for partial completion of doctoral program. *Degree requirements:* For master's, thesis; for doctorate, thesis/dissertation, first authored publication. *Faculty research:* Immunology; protein chemistry and biosynthesis; cardiovascular, renal, and endocrine physiology; rehabilitation therapy on immune system/hypothalamic/adrenal axis interaction.

University of Missouri, Graduate School, College of Arts and Sciences, Division of Biological Sciences, Columbia, MO 65211. Offers evolutionary biology and ecology (MA, PhD); genetic, cellular and developmental biology (MA, PhD); neurobiology and behavior (MA, PhD). Terminal master's awarded for partial completion of doctoral program. *Degree requirements:* For master's, thesis; for doctorate, comprehensive exam, thesis/dissertation. *Entrance requirements:* For master's and doctorate, GRE General Test (minimum score 1200 verbal and quantitative), minimum GPA of 3.0. Additional exam requirements/recommendations for international students: Required—TOEFL (minimum score 600 paper-based; 100 iBT). Electronic applications accepted. *Faculty research:* Evolutionary biology, ecology and behavior; genetic, cellular, molecular and developmental biology; neurobiology and behavior; and plant sciences.

University of Missouri, School of Medicine and Graduate School, Graduate Programs in Medicine, Columbia, MO 65211. Offers MS, PhD. Part-time programs available. *Degree requirements:* For doctorate, thesis/dissertation. *Entrance requirements:* For master's and doctorate, GRE General Test, minimum GPA of 3.0. Additional exam requirements/recommendations for international students: Required—TOEFL. *Expenses:* Contact institution.

University of Missouri–Kansas City, School of Biological Sciences, Kansas City, MO 64110-2499. Offers biology (MA); cell biology and biophysics (PhD); cellular and molecular biology (MS); molecular biology and biochemistry (PhD). PhD (interdisciplinary) offered through the School of Graduate Studies. Part-time and evening/weekend programs available. *Faculty:* 42 full-time (11 women). *Students:* 23 full-time (14 women), 33 part-time (19 women); includes 12 minority (3 Black or African American, non-Hispanic/Latino; 6 Asian, non-Hispanic/Latino; 2 Hispanic/Latino; 1 Two or more races, non-Hispanic/Latino), 3 international. Average age 30. 56 applicants, 52% accepted, 25 enrolled. In 2010, 23 master's awarded. *Degree requirements:* For doctorate, comprehensive exam, thesis/dissertation. *Entrance requirements:* For master's, GRE, minimum GPA of 3.0; for doctorate, GRE General Test. Additional exam requirements/recommendations for international students: Required—TOEFL (minimum score 550 paper-based; 213 computer-based; 80 iBT). *Application deadline:* For fall admission, 2/15 priority date for domestic and international students. Applications are processed on a rolling basis. Application fee: $45 ($50 for international students). *Expenses:* Tuition, state resident: full-time $5522; part-time $306.80 per credit hour. Tuition, nonresident: full-time $7128; part-time $792 per credit hour. Required fees: $261.15 per term. *Financial support:* In 2010–11, 17 research assistantships with full tuition reimbursements (averaging $21,098 per year), 9 teaching assistantships with full tuition reimbursements (averaging $22,000 per year) were awarded; Federal Work-Study, institutionally sponsored loans, scholarships/grants, tuition waivers (full and partial), and unspecified assistantships also available. Support available to part-time students. Financial award application deadline: 3/1; financial award applicants required to submit FAFSA. *Faculty research:* Structural biology, molecular genetics. Total annual research expenditures: $3.5 million. *Unit head:* Dr. Lawrence A. Dreyfus, Dean, 816-235-5246, Fax: 816-235-5158, E-mail: dreyfusl@umkc.edu. *Application contact:* Laura Batenic, Information Contact, 816-235-2352, Fax: 816-235-5158, E-mail: batenicl@umkc.edu.

University of Missouri–St. Louis, College of Arts and Sciences, Department of Biology, St. Louis, MO 63121. Offers biotechnology (Certificate); cell and molecular biology (MS, PhD); ecology, evolution and systematics (MS, PhD); tropical biology and conservation (Certificate). Part-time programs available. *Faculty:* 43 full-time (13 women), 2 part-time/adjunct (1 woman). *Students:* 73 full-time (36 women), 63 part-time (36 women); includes 17 minority (6 Black or African American, non-Hispanic/Latino; 9 Asian, non-Hispanic/Latino; 2 Hispanic/Latino), 45 international. Average age 29. 193 applicants, 44% accepted, 44 enrolled. In 2010, 35 master's, 11 doctorates, 6 other advanced degrees awarded. *Degree requirements:* For master's, thesis or alternative; for doctorate, thesis/dissertation, 1 semester of teaching experience. *Entrance requirements:* For master's, 3 letters of recommendation; for doctorate, GRE General Test, 3 letters of recommendation. Additional exam requirements/recommendations for international students: Required—TOEFL. *Application deadline:* For fall admission, 12/1 priority date for domestic and international students; for spring admission, 10/15 priority date for domestic and international students. Applications are processed on a rolling basis. Application fee: $35 ($40 for international students). Electronic applications accepted. *Expenses:* Tuition, state resident: full-time $5522; part-time $306.80 per credit hour. Tuition, nonresident: full-time $14,253; part-time $792.10 per credit hour. Required fees: $658; $49 per credit hour. One-time fee: $12. Tuition and fees vary according to program. *Financial support:* In 2010–11, 30 research assistantships with full and partial tuition reimbursements (averaging $18,113 per year), 15 teaching assistantships with full and partial tuition reimbursements (averaging $17,514 per year) were awarded; fellowships with full tuition reimbursements, career-related internships or

Biological and Biomedical Sciences—General

University of Missouri–St. Louis (continued)

fieldwork and Federal Work-Study also available. Support available to part-time students. Financial award application deadline: 2/1. *Faculty research:* Molecular biology, microbial genetics, animal behavior, tropical ecology, plant systematics. *Unit head:* Dr. Peter Stevens, Director of Graduate Studies, 314-516-6200, Fax: 314-516-6233, E-mail: stevensp@umsl.edu. *Application contact:* 314-516-5458, Fax: 314-516-6996, E-mail: gradadm@umsl.edu.

The University of Montana, Graduate School, College of Arts and Sciences, Division of Biological Sciences, Missoula, MT 59812-0002. Offers biochemistry and microbiology (MS, PhD), including biochemistry (MS), integrative microbiology and biochemistry (PhD), microbial ecology, microbiology (MS); organismal biology and ecology (MS, PhD). Terminal master's awarded for partial completion of doctoral program. *Degree requirements:* For master's, thesis; for doctorate, thesis/dissertation. *Entrance requirements:* For master's and doctorate, GRE General Test. Additional exam requirements/recommendations for international students: Required—TOEFL. *Faculty research:* Biochemistry/microbiology, organismal biology, ecology.

The University of Montana, Graduate School, College of Health Professions and Biomedical Sciences, Skaggs School of Pharmacy, Department of Biomedical and Pharmaceutical Sciences, Missoula, MT 59812-0002. Offers biomedical sciences (PhD); neuroscience (MS, PhD); pharmaceutical sciences (MS); toxicology (MS, PhD). *Accreditation:* ACPE. *Degree requirements:* For master's, oral defense of thesis; for doctorate, research dissertation defense. *Entrance requirements:* For master's and doctorate, GRE General Test. Additional exam requirements/recommendations for international students: Required—TOEFL (minimum score 540 paper-based; 210 computer-based). Electronic applications accepted. *Faculty research:* Cardiovascular pharmacology, medicinal chemistry, neurosciences, environmental toxicology, pharmacogenetics, cancer.

University of Nebraska at Kearney, College of Graduate Study, College of Natural and Social Sciences, Department of Biology, Kearney, NE 68849-0001. Offers biology (MS); science education (MS Ed). Part-time and evening/weekend programs available. *Degree requirements:* For master's, thesis optional. *Entrance requirements:* For master's, GRE General Test. Additional exam requirements/recommendations for international students: Required—TOEFL (minimum score 550 paper-based; 213 computer-based). Electronic applications accepted. *Faculty research:* Pollution injury, molecular biology-viral gene expression, prairie range condition modeling, evolution of symbiotic nitrogen fixation.

University of Nebraska at Omaha, Graduate Studies, College of Arts and Sciences, Department of Biology, Omaha, NE 68182. Offers MS. Part-time programs available. *Faculty:* 18 full-time (4 women). *Students:* 11 full-time (5 women), 11 part-time (2 women); includes 1 minority (American Indian or Alaska Native, non-Hispanic/Latino), 1 international. Average age 27. 18 applicants, 28% accepted, 5 enrolled. In 2010, 7 master's awarded. *Degree requirements:* For master's, comprehensive exam (for some programs), thesis (for some programs). *Entrance requirements:* For master's, GRE General Test, minimum GPA of 3.0, 24 undergraduate biology hours, 3 letters of recommendation. Additional exam requirements/recommendations for international students: Required—TOEFL (minimum score 550 paper-based; 173 computer-based; 80 iBT). *Application deadline:* For fall admission, 3/1 priority date for domestic students; for spring admission, 10/15 priority date for domestic students. Applications are processed on a rolling basis. Application fee: $45. Electronic applications accepted. *Financial support:* In 2010–11, 18 students received support; fellowships, research assistantships with tuition reimbursements available, teaching assistantships with tuition reimbursements available, Federal Work-Study, institutionally sponsored loans, scholarships/grants, tuition waivers (partial), and unspecified assistantships available. Support available to part-time students. Financial award application deadline: 3/1; financial award applicants required to submit FAFSA. *Unit head:* Dr. William Tapprich, Chairperson, 402-554-2641. *Application contact:* Dr. La Reesa Wolfenbarger, Student Contact, 402-554-2641.

University of Nebraska–Lincoln, Graduate College, College of Agricultural Sciences and Natural Resources, Department of Veterinary and Biomedical Sciences, Lincoln, NE 68588. Offers veterinary science (MS). MS, PhD offered jointly with University of Nebraska Medical Center. Postbaccalaureate distance learning degree programs offered (minimal on-campus study). *Degree requirements:* For master's, thesis optional; for doctorate, comprehensive exam, thesis/dissertation. *Entrance requirements:* For master's, GRE General Test; for doctorate, GRE General Test, MCAT, or VCAT. Additional exam requirements/recommendations for international students: Required—TOEFL (minimum score 550 paper-based; 213 computer-based). Electronic applications accepted. *Faculty research:* Virology, immunobiology, molecular biology, mycotoxins, ocular degeneration.

University of Nebraska–Lincoln, Graduate College, College of Arts and Sciences, School of Biological Sciences, Lincoln, NE 68588. Offers MA, MS, PhD. *Degree requirements:* For master's, thesis optional; for doctorate, comprehensive exam, thesis/dissertation. *Entrance requirements:* For master's and doctorate, GRE General Test. Additional exam requirements/recommendations for international students: Required—TOEFL (minimum score 550 paper-based; 213 computer-based). Electronic applications accepted. *Faculty research:* Behavior, botany, and zoology; ecology and evolutionary biology; genetics; cellular and molecular biology; microbiology.

University of Nebraska Medical Center, Graduate Studies, Biomedical Research Training Program, Omaha, NE 68198. Offers MD/PhD. *Faculty:* 120 full-time (22 women). *Students:* 12 full-time (10 women), 1 (woman) part-time; includes 1 Hispanic/Latino. 33 applicants, 30% accepted, 10 enrolled. *Entrance requirements:* Additional exam requirements/recommendations for international students: Required—TOEFL (minimum score 600 paper-based; 250 computer-based). *Application deadline:* For fall admission, 6/1 for domestic students; for spring admission, 10/1 for domestic students. Applications are processed on a rolling basis. Application fee: $45. Electronic applications accepted. *Expenses:* Tuition, state resident: part-time $198.25 per semester hour. Required fees: $63 per semester. *Financial support:* In 2010–11, 10 research assistantships with full tuition reimbursements (averaging $21,000 per year) were awarded; career-related internships or fieldwork also available. *Faculty research:* Neuroscience, cancer, cardiovascular immunology, genetics. Total annual research expenditures: $50 million. *Unit head:* Dr. Daniel Monaghan, Program Chair, 402-559-7196, Fax: 402-559-7495, E-mail: dtmonagh@unmc.edu. *Application contact:* Jonalee Amato, Recruiting Coordinator, 402-554-3362, Fax: 402-559-3363, E-mail: brtp@unmc.edu.

University of Nebraska Medical Center, Graduate Studies, Medical Sciences Interdepartmental Area, Omaha, NE 68198. Offers MS, PhD. Part-time programs available. *Faculty:* 315. *Students:* 27 full-time (16 women), 41 part-time (28 women); includes 2 Black or African American, non-Hispanic/Latino; 1 American Indian or Alaska Native, non-Hispanic/Latino; 9 Asian, non-Hispanic/Latino; 2 Hispanic/Latino, 12 international. Average age 35. 22 applicants, 41% accepted, 9 enrolled. In 2010, 6 master's, 2 doctorates awarded. Terminal master's awarded for partial completion of doctoral program. *Degree requirements:* For master's, comprehensive exam, thesis; for doctorate, comprehensive exam, thesis/dissertation. *Entrance requirements:* For master's and doctorate, GRE General Test. Additional exam requirements/recommendations for international students: Required—TOEFL (minimum score 550 paper-based; 213 computer-based). *Application deadline:* For fall admission, 6/1 for domestic students, 4/1 for international students; for spring admission, 10/1 for domestic students, 8/1 for international students. Applications are processed on a rolling basis. Application fee: $45. *Expenses:* Tuition, state resident: part-time $198.25 per semester hour. Required fees: $63 per semester. *Financial support:* In 2010–11, 8 research assistantships with full tuition reimbursements (averaging $20,000 per year) were awarded; fellowships, teaching assistantships, institutionally sponsored loans also available. Support available to part-time students. Financial award application deadline: 3/1. *Faculty research:* Molecular genetics, oral biology, veterinary pathology, newborn medicine, immunology. *Unit head:* Dr. M. Patricia Leuschen, Graduate Committee Chair, 402-559-9291, Fax: 402-559-9333, E-mail: pleusche@unmc.edu. *Application contact:* Dan Teet, Graduate Studies Associate, 402-559-6531, Fax: 402-559-7845, E-mail: unmcgraduatestudies@unmc.edu.

University of Nevada, Las Vegas, Graduate College, College of Science, School of Life Sciences, Las Vegas, NV 89154-4004. Offers biological sciences (MS, PhD). Part-time programs available. *Faculty:* 27 full-time (5 women). *Students:* 33 full-time (18 women), 8 part-time (3 women); includes 17 minority (3 Hispanic/Latino; 1 Native Hawaiian or other Pacific Islander, non-Hispanic/Latino; 13 Two or more races, non-Hispanic/Latino), 5 international. Average age 30. 35 applicants, 37% accepted, 8 enrolled. In 2010, 4 master's, 11 doctorates awarded. *Degree requirements:* For master's, thesis, oral exam; for doctorate, one foreign language, comprehensive exam, thesis/dissertation. *Entrance requirements:* For master's and doctorate, GRE General Test. Additional exam requirements/recommendations for international students: Required—TOEFL (minimum score 550 paper-based; 213 computer-based; 80 iBT), IELTS (minimum score 7). *Application deadline:* For fall admission, 2/15 priority date for domestic and international students; for spring admission, 10/1 priority date for domestic and international students. Applications are processed on a rolling basis. Application fee: $60 ($95 for international students). Electronic applications accepted. *Expenses:* Tuition, state resident: part-time $239.50 per credit. Tuition, nonresident: part-time $503 per credit. Required fees: $108 per semester. Tuition and fees vary according to course load, program and reciprocity agreements. *Financial support:* In 2010–11, 34 students received support, including 1 fellowship with full tuition reimbursement available (averaging $20,000 per year), 10 research assistantships with full tuition reimbursements available (averaging $14,132 per year), 23 teaching assistantships with partial tuition reimbursements available (averaging $15,275 per year); institutionally sponsored loans, scholarships/grants, health care benefits, and unspecified assistantships also available. Financial award application deadline: 3/1. *Faculty research:* Environmental and medical microbiology; biodiversity, evolution, and ecological sustainability; cell and molecular biology; integrative physiology. Total annual research expenditures: $3.5 million. *Unit head:* Dr. Dennis Bazylinski, Chair, 702-895-3399, Fax: 702-895-3956, E-mail: dennis.bazylinski@unlv.edu. *Application contact:* Graduate College Admissions Evaluator, 702-895-3320, Fax: 702-895-4180, E-mail: gradcollege@unlv.edu.

University of Nevada, Reno, Graduate School, College of Science, Department of Biology, Reno, NV 89557. Offers MS. *Degree requirements:* For master's, thesis optional. *Entrance requirements:* For master's, GRE General Test, minimum GPA of 2.75. Additional exam requirements/recommendations for international students: Required—TOEFL (minimum score 500 paper-based; 173 computer-based; 61 iBT), IELTS (minimum score 6). Electronic applications accepted. *Expenses:* Tuition, state resident: full-time $2219; part-time $246 per credit. Tuition, nonresident: part-time $510 per credit. International tuition: $9009 full-time. Required fees: $59 per term. One-time fee: $101. Tuition and fees vary according to course load. *Faculty research:* Gene expression, stress protein genes, secretory proteins, conservation biology, behavioral ecology.

University of New Brunswick Fredericton, School of Graduate Studies, Faculty of Science, Department of Biology, Fredericton, NB E3B 5A3, Canada. Offers M Sc, PhD. Part-time programs available. *Faculty:* 25 full-time (6 women), 1 part-time/adjunct (0 women). *Students:* 68 full-time (35 women), 9 part-time (5 women). In 2010, 7 master's, 4 doctorates awarded. *Degree requirements:* For master's, thesis; for doctorate, thesis/dissertation. *Entrance requirements:* For master's, minimum GPA of 3.0; undergraduate degree (B Sc or equivalent preferred); for doctorate, minimum GPA of 3.0; undergraduate and/or master's degree in related discipline. Additional exam requirements/recommendations for international students: Required—TWE (minimum score 4), TOEFL (minimum score 600 paper-based; 250 computer-based) or IELTS (minimum score 7). *Application deadline:* For fall admission, 3/1 priority date for domestic students. Applications are processed on a rolling basis. Application fee: $50 Canadian dollars. Electronic applications accepted. *Expenses:* Tuition, area resident: Full-time $3708; part-time $927 per term. International tuition: $6300 full-time. Required fees: $50 per term. *Financial support:* In 2010–11, 34 fellowships (averaging $2,950 per year), 55 research assistantships with tuition reimbursements (averaging $20,170 per year), 36 teaching assistantships (averaging $3,376 per year) were awarded. *Faculty research:* Evolutionary biology, aquatic ecology, wildlife and conservation biology, marine biology, algae and plant biology. *Unit head:* Dr. Les C. Cwynar, Director of Graduate Studies, 506-452-6197, Fax: 506-453-4583, E-mail: biodogs@unb.ca. *Application contact:* Rose Comeau, Graduate Secretary, 506-452-6052, Fax: 506-453-3583, E-mail: rcomeau@unb.ca.

University of New Brunswick Saint John, Department of Biology, Saint John, NB E2L 4L5, Canada. Offers biology (M Sc, PhD). Part-time programs available. *Faculty:* 14 full-time (1 woman). *Students:* 44 full-time (26 women), 6 part-time (3 women). In 2010, 5 master's, 1 doctorate awarded. *Degree requirements:* For master's, thesis; for doctorate, comprehensive exam, thesis/dissertation. *Entrance requirements:* For master's, B Sc, minimum GPA of 3.0; for doctorate, M Sc, minimum GPA of 3.0. *Application deadline:* For fall admission, 2/15 for domestic and international students. Applications are processed on a rolling basis. Application fee: $50 Canadian dollars. *Financial support:* In 2010–11, 118 fellowships, 42 research assistantships (averaging $4,000 per year), 1 teaching assistantship (averaging $4,000 per year) were awarded; scholarships/grants and unspecified assistantships also available. *Faculty research:* Community ecology, marine biology and aquaculture, physiology, ecotoxicology, molecular/chemical ecology. *Unit head:* Dr. Kate Frego, Director of Graduate Studies, 506-648-5566, Fax: 506-648-5811, E-mail: frego@unbsj.ca. *Application contact:* Christine Robson, Secretary, 506-648-5605, Fax: 506-648-5811, E-mail: crobson@unb.ca.

University of New England, College of Arts and Sciences, Programs in Professional Science, Biddeford, ME 04005-9526. Offers applied biosciences (MS). *Expenses:* Contact institution. *Unit head:* Arthur Goldstein, Chair, Department of Marine Sciences, 207-602-2371, E-mail: agoldstein@une.edu. *Application contact:* Stacy Gato, Assistant Director of Graduate Admissions, 207-221-4225, Fax: 207-221-4898, E-mail: gradadmissions@une.edu.

University of New Hampshire, Graduate School, College of Life Sciences and Agriculture, Department of Biological Sciences, Durham, NH 03824. Offers animal science (MS); plant biology (MS, PhD); zoology (MS, PhD). Part-time programs available. *Faculty:* 31 full-time (7 women). *Students:* 30 full-time (18 women), 27 part-time (17 women); includes 1 Asian, non-Hispanic/Latino; 1 Hispanic/Latino; 2 Two or more races, non-Hispanic/Latino, 5 international. Average age 31. 51 applicants, 25% accepted, 8 enrolled. In 2010, 9 master's, 4 doctorates awarded. *Degree requirements:* For doctorate, thesis/dissertation. *Entrance requirements:* For master's and doctorate, GRE General Test. Additional exam requirements/recommendations for international students: Required—TOEFL (minimum score 550 paper-based; 215 computer-based; 80 iBT). *Application deadline:* For fall admission, 6/1 for domestic students, 4/1 for international students; for spring admission, 12/1 for domestic students. Application fee: $65. *Financial support:* In 2010–11, 40 students received support, including 2 fellowships, 8 research assistantships, 25 teaching assistantships. *Unit head:* Chris Neefus, Dean, 603-862-1990. *Application contact:* Dianne Lavalliere, Administrative Assistant, 603-862-2100, Fax: 603-862-0275, E-mail: grad.school@unh.edu.

University of New Mexico, Graduate School, College of Arts and Sciences, Department of Biology, Albuquerque, NM 87131-2039. Offers MS, PhD. *Faculty:* 73 full-time (28 women), 15 part-time/adjunct (4 women). *Students:* 87 full-time (52 women), 20 part-time (8 women); includes 2 American Indian or Alaska Native, non-Hispanic/Latino; 3 Asian, non-Hispanic/Latino; 14 Hispanic/Latino; 1 Two or more races, non-Hispanic/Latino, 8 international. Average age 32. 78 applicants, 24% accepted, 19 enrolled. In 2010, 7 master's, 9 doctorates awarded. *Degree requirements:* For master's, comprehensive exam, thesis optional; for doctorate, comprehensive exam, thesis/dissertation. *Entrance requirements:* For master's and doctorate, GRE General Test, minimum GPA of 3.2, letters of recommendation. Additional exam requirements/recommendations for international students: Required—TOEFL (minimum score 550 paper-based; 213 computer-based; 79 iBT). *Application deadline:* For fall admission, 1/2 priority date for domestic students, 1/3 priority date for international students. Application fee: $50. Electronic applications accepted. *Expenses:* Tuition, state resident: full-time $5991;

part-time $251 per credit hour. Tuition, nonresident: full-time $14,405; part-time $800.20 per credit hour. Tuition and fees vary according to course level, course load, program and reciprocity agreements. *Financial support:* In 2010–11, 94 students received support, including 5 fellowships with full tuition reimbursements available (averaging $13,267 per year), 50 research assistantships with full tuition reimbursements available (averaging $12,045 per year), 56 teaching assistantships with full tuition reimbursements available (averaging $11,214 per year); Federal Work-Study, scholarships/grants, health care benefits, and unspecified assistantships also available. Financial award application deadline: 3/1; financial award applicants required to submit FAFSA. *Faculty research:* Aquatic ecology, behavioral ecology, botany, cell biology, comparative biology, conservation biology, developmental biology, ecology, evolutionary biology, genetics, genomics, global change biology, immunology, invertebrate biology, mathematical biology, microbiology, molecular evolution, paleobiology, parasitology, physiological ecology, plant biology, systematics, vertebrate biology. Total annual research expenditures: $10.8 million. *Unit head:* Dr. Richard Cripps, Chair, 505-277-2496, Fax: 505-277-0304, E-mail: rcripps@unm.edu. *Application contact:* Cheryl Martin, Graduate Program Coordinator, 505-277-1712, Fax: 505-277-0304, E-mail: cherylm@unm.edu.

University of New Mexico, School of Medicine, Biomedical Sciences Graduate Program, Albuquerque, NM 87131-5196. Offers biochemistry and molecular biology (MS, PhD); cell biology and physiology (MS, PhD); clinical and translational science (Certificate); molecular genetics and microbiology (MS, PhD); neuroscience (MS, PhD); pathology (MS, PhD); toxicology (MS, PhD); university science teaching (Certificate). Part-time programs available. *Faculty:* 33 full-time (14 women), 3 part-time/adjunct (1 woman). *Students:* 94 full-time (57 women), 14 part-time (8 women); includes 24 minority (3 Black or African American, non-Hispanic/Latino; 1 American Indian or Alaska Native, non-Hispanic/Latino; 6 Asian, non-Hispanic/Latino; 13 Hispanic/Latino; 1 Two or more races, non-Hispanic/Latino), 20 international. Average age 30. 135 applicants, 14% accepted, 19 enrolled. In 2010, 2 master's, 19 doctorates, 3 other advanced degrees awarded. Terminal master's awarded for partial completion of doctoral program. *Degree requirements:* For master's, thesis; for doctorate, comprehensive exam, thesis/dissertation. *Entrance requirements:* For master's and doctorate, GRE General Test, minimum undergraduate GPA of 3.0. Additional exam requirements/recommendations for international students: Required—TOEFL. *Application deadline:* For fall admission, 1/1 priority date for domestic students. Applications are processed on a rolling basis. Application fee: $50. Electronic applications accepted. *Expenses:* Tuition, state resident: full-time $5991; part-time $251 per credit hour. Tuition, nonresident: full-time $14,405; part-time $800.20 per credit hour. Tuition and fees vary according to course level, course load, program and reciprocity agreements. *Financial support:* In 2010–11, 99 students received support, including 5 fellowships (averaging $75 per year), 96 research assistantships with full tuition reimbursements available (averaging $17,401 per year), 2 teaching assistantships with full tuition reimbursements available (averaging $2,415 per year); career-related internships or fieldwork, Federal Work-Study, institutionally sponsored loans, scholarships/grants, traineeships, health care benefits, and unspecified assistantships also available. Financial award application deadline: 1/1; financial award applicants required to submit FAFSA. *Faculty research:* Signal transduction, infectious disease, biology of cancer, structural biology, neuroscience. *Unit head:* Laurie G. Hudson, Director, 505-272-1887, Fax: 505-272-8738, E-mail: lhudson@salud.unm.edu. *Application contact:* Angel Cooke-Jackson, Coordinator, 505-272-1887, Fax: 505-272-8738, E-mail: acooke-jackson@salud.unm.edu.

University of New Orleans, Graduate School, College of Sciences, Department of Biological Sciences, New Orleans, LA 70148. Offers MS, PhD. *Degree requirements:* For master's, one foreign language, thesis. *Entrance requirements:* For master's, GRE General Test. Additional exam requirements/recommendations for international students: Required—TOEFL (minimum score 550 paper-based; 213 computer-based; 79 iBT). Electronic applications accepted. *Faculty research:* Biochemistry, genetics, vertebrate and invertebrate systematics and ecology, cell and mammalian physiology, morphology.

The University of North Carolina at Chapel Hill, Graduate School, College of Arts and Sciences, Department of Biology, Chapel Hill, NC 27599. Offers botany (MA, MS, PhD); cell biology, development, and physiology (MA, MS, PhD); cell motility and cytoskeleton (PhD); ecology and behavior (MA, MS, PhD); genetics and molecular biology (MA, MS, PhD); morphology, systematics, and evolution (MA, MS, PhD). Terminal master's awarded for partial completion of doctoral program. *Degree requirements:* For master's, comprehensive exam, thesis (for some programs); for doctorate, comprehensive exam, thesis/dissertation. *Entrance requirements:* For master's, GRE General Test, GRE Subject Test, 2 semesters of calculus or statistics; 2 semesters of physics, organic chemistry; 3 semesters of biology; for doctorate, GRE General Test, GRE Subject Test, 2 semesters calculus or statistics, 2 semesters physics, organic chemistry, 3 semesters of biology. Additional exam requirements/recommendations for international students: Required—TOEFL (minimum score 550 paper-based; 213 computer-based). Electronic applications accepted. *Faculty research:* Gene expression, biomechanics, yeast genetics, plant ecology, plant molecular biology.

The University of North Carolina at Chapel Hill, School of Medicine and Graduate School, Graduate Programs in Medicine, Chapel Hill, NC 27599. Offers allied health sciences (MPT, MS, Au D, DPT, PhD), including human movement science (MS, PhD), occupational science (MS, PhD), physical therapy (MPT, MS, DPT), rehabilitation counseling and psychology (MS), speech and hearing sciences (MS, Au D, PhD); biochemistry and biophysics (MS, PhD); bioinformatics and computational biology (PhD); biomedical engineering (MS, PhD); cell and developmental biology (PhD); cell and molecular physiology (PhD); genetics and molecular biology (PhD); microbiology and immunology (MS, PhD), including immunology, microbiology; neurobiology (PhD); pathology and laboratory medicine (PhD), including experimental pathology; pharmacology (PhD); MD/PhD. Postbaccalaureate distance learning degree programs offered. Terminal master's awarded for partial completion of doctoral program. *Degree requirements:* For master's, comprehensive exam; for doctorate, thesis/dissertation. Electronic applications accepted. *Expenses:* Contact institution.

The University of North Carolina at Charlotte, Graduate School, College of Arts and Sciences, Department of Biology, Charlotte, NC 28223-0001. Offers MA, MS, PhD. Part-time and evening/weekend programs available. *Faculty:* 25 full-time (9 women), 3 part-time/adjunct (1 woman). *Students:* 33 full-time (17 women), 20 part-time (13 women); includes 1 minority (Two or more races, non-Hispanic/Latino), 14 international. Average age 28. 38 applicants, 26% accepted, 9 enrolled. In 2010, 4 master's, 6 doctorates awarded. Terminal master's awarded for partial completion of doctoral program. *Degree requirements:* For master's, thesis, 30-32 semester hours with a minimum GPA of 3.0; for doctorate, thesis/dissertation. *Entrance requirements:* For master's, GRE General Test, minimum GPA of 3.0 in undergraduate major, 2.75 overall; for doctorate, GRE General Test, minimum GPA of 3.5 in biology; 3.0 in chemistry, math, and overall. Additional exam requirements/recommendations for international students: Required—TOEFL (minimum score 557 paper-based; 220 computer-based; 83 iBT). *Application deadline:* For fall admission, 7/15 for domestic students, 5/1 for international students; for spring admission, 11/15 for domestic students, 10/1 for international students. Applications are processed on a rolling basis. Application fee: $55. Electronic applications accepted. *Expenses:* Tuition, state resident: full-time $3464. Tuition, nonresident: full-time $14,297. Required fees: $2094. Tuition and fees vary according to course load. *Financial support:* In 2010–11, 48 students received support, including 4 fellowships (averaging $37,859 per year), 16 research assistantships (averaging $7,428 per year), 28 teaching assistantships (averaging $6,803 per year); career-related internships or fieldwork, institutionally sponsored loans, scholarships/grants, and administrative assistantship also available. Support available to part-time students. Financial award application deadline: 4/1; financial award applicants required to submit FAFSA. *Faculty research:* Liver blood flow in response to stress/injury, host response to bacterial and viral infection, mechanisms of cancer development and spread, stress responses in marine organisms as a measure of environmental change. Total annual research expenditures: $2.7 million. *Unit head:* Dr. Cy Knoblauch, Acting Chair, 704-687-5465, Fax: 704-687-3128, E-mail: chknobla@uncc.edu. *Application contact:* Kathy B. Giddings,

Director of Graduate Admissions, 704-687-5503, Fax: 704-687-3279, E-mail: gradadm@uncc.edu.

The University of North Carolina at Greensboro, Graduate School, College of Arts and Sciences, Department of Biology, Greensboro, NC 27412-5001. Offers MS. *Degree requirements:* For master's, thesis. *Entrance requirements:* For master's, GRE General Test, GRE Subject Test. Additional exam requirements/recommendations for international students: Required—TOEFL. Electronic applications accepted. *Faculty research:* Environmental biology, biochemistry, animal ecology, vertebrate reproduction.

The University of North Carolina Wilmington, College of Arts and Sciences, Department of Biology and Marine Biology, Wilmington, NC 28403-3297. Offers biology (MS); marine biology (MS, PhD). Part-time programs available. *Faculty:* 34 full-time (7 women). *Students:* 39 part-time (21 women); includes 1 minority (Hispanic/Latino), 1 international. Average age 28. 96 applicants, 27% accepted, 21 enrolled. In 2010, 15 master's awarded. *Degree requirements:* For master's, comprehensive exam, thesis; for doctorate, comprehensive exam, thesis/dissertation. *Entrance requirements:* For master's, GRE General Test, GRE Subject Test, minimum B average in undergraduate major; for doctorate, GRE General Test, minimum B average in undergraduate major and graduate courses. Additional exam requirements/recommendations for international students: Required—TOEFL (minimum score 550 paper-based; 217 computer-based; 79 iBT), IELTS (minimum score 6.5). *Application deadline:* For fall admission, 3/15 for domestic students. Applications are processed on a rolling basis. Application fee: $60. Electronic applications accepted. *Financial support:* In 2010–11, 24 research assistantships with full and partial tuition reimbursements (averaging $14,000 per year), 36 teaching assistantships with full and partial tuition reimbursements (averaging $14,000 per year) were awarded; career-related internships or fieldwork and Federal Work-Study also available. Support available to part-time students. Financial award application deadline: 3/15. *Faculty research:* Ecology, physiology, cell and molecular biology, systematics, biomechanics. Total annual research expenditures: $3.1 million. *Unit head:* Dr. Martin H. Posey, Chairman, 910-962-3487, E-mail: poseym@uncw.edu. *Application contact:* Dr. D. Ann Pabst, Graduate Coordinator, 910-962-7266, Fax: 910-962-4066, E-mail: pabsta@uncw.edu.

University of North Dakota, Graduate School, College of Arts and Sciences, Department of Biology, Grand Forks, ND 58202. Offers botany (MS, PhD); ecology (MS, PhD); entomology (MS, PhD); environmental biology (MS, PhD); fisheries/wildlife (MS, PhD); genetics (MS, PhD); zoology (MS, PhD). *Faculty:* 17 full-time (5 women), 6 part-time/adjunct (1 woman). *Students:* 19 full-time (6 women), 8 part-time (2 women); includes 4 minority (3 American Indian or Alaska Native, non-Hispanic/Latino; 1 Asian, non-Hispanic/Latino), 1 international. Average age 28. 21 applicants, 33% accepted, 4 enrolled. In 2010, 1 master's awarded. Terminal master's awarded for partial completion of doctoral program. *Degree requirements:* For master's, thesis, final exam; for doctorate, comprehensive exam, thesis/dissertation, final exam. *Entrance requirements:* For master's, GRE General Test, GRE Subject Test, minimum GPA of 3.0; for doctorate, GRE General Test, GRE Subject Test, minimum GPA of 3.5. Additional exam requirements/recommendations for international students: Required—TOEFL (minimum score 550 paper-based; 213 computer-based; 79 iBT), IELTS (minimum score 6.5). *Application deadline:* For fall admission, 2/15 for domestic and international students; for spring admission, 10/15 for domestic and international students. Application fee: $35. Electronic applications accepted. *Expenses:* Tuition, state resident: full-time $5857; part-time $306.74 per credit. Tuition, nonresident: full-time $15,666; part-time $729.77 per credit. Required fees: $53.42 per credit. Tuition and fees vary according to course load, program and reciprocity agreements. *Financial support:* In 2010–11, 22 students received support, including 5 research assistantships with full and partial tuition reimbursements available (averaging $11,375 per year), 17 teaching assistantships with full and partial tuition reimbursements available (averaging $10,813 per year); fellowships with full and partial tuition reimbursements available, Federal Work-Study, institutionally sponsored loans, scholarships/grants, health care benefits, tuition waivers (full and partial), and unspecified assistantships also available. Support available to part-time students. Financial award application deadline: 3/15; financial award applicants required to submit FAFSA. *Faculty research:* Population biology, wildlife ecology, RNA processing, hormonal control of behavior. Total annual research expenditures: $736,510. *Unit head:* Dr. Brett Goodwin, Graduate Director, 701-777-2621, Fax: 701-777-2623, E-mail: brett.goodwin@mail.und.edu. *Application contact:* Matthew Anderson, Admissions Specialist, 701-777-2947, Fax: 701-777-3619, E-mail: matthew.anderson@gradschool.und.edu.

University of Northern Colorado, Graduate School, College of Natural and Health Sciences, School of Biological Sciences, Program in Biological Sciences, Greeley, CO 80639. Offers MS. Part-time programs available. *Faculty:* 16 full-time (3 women). *Students:* 10 full-time (6 women), 4 part-time (1 woman); includes 1 minority (Hispanic/Latino). Average age 29. 13 applicants, 46% accepted, 4 enrolled. In 2010, 2 master's awarded. *Degree requirements:* For master's, comprehensive exam. *Entrance requirements:* For master's, GRE General Test, 3 letters of recommendation. *Application deadline:* Applications are processed on a rolling basis. Application fee: $50 ($60 for international students). Electronic applications accepted. *Expenses:* Tuition, state resident: full-time $6199; part-time $344 per credit hour. Tuition, nonresident: full-time $14,834; part-time $824 per credit hour. Required fees: $1091; $60.60 per credit hour. Tuition and fees vary according to course load, degree level and program. *Financial support:* In 2010–11, 5 research assistantships (averaging $8,507 per year), 16 teaching assistantships (averaging $11,225 per year) were awarded. Financial award application deadline: 3/1; financial award applicants required to submit FAFSA. *Unit head:* Dr. Susan Keenan, Program Coordinator, 970-351-2921, Fax: 970-951-2335. *Application contact:* Linda Sisson, Graduate Student Admission Coordinator, 970-351-1807, Fax: 970-351-2371, E-mail: linda.sisson@unco.edu.

University of Northern Iowa, Graduate College, College of Natural Sciences, Department of Biology, Cedar Falls, IA 50614. Offers biology (MA, MS); biotechnology (PSM); ecosystem management (PSM). Part-time programs available. *Students:* 21 full-time (9 women), 7 part-time (2 women); includes 2 minority (1 Hispanic/Latino; 1 Two or more races, non-Hispanic/Latino), 1 international. 39 applicants, 49% accepted, 13 enrolled. In 2010, 17 master's awarded. *Degree requirements:* For master's, comprehensive exam (for some programs), thesis or alternative. *Entrance requirements:* For master's, minimum GPA of 3.0; 3 letters of recommendation. Additional exam requirements/recommendations for international students: Required—TOEFL (minimum score 500 paper-based; 180 computer-based; 61 iBT). *Application deadline:* For fall admission, 8/1 priority date for domestic students. Applications are processed on a rolling basis. Application fee: $50 ($70 for international students). Electronic applications accepted. *Financial support:* Scholarships/grants available. Financial award application deadline: 2/1. *Unit head:* Dr. David Saunders, Head, 319-273-2456, Fax: 319-273-7125, E-mail: david.saunders@uni.edu. *Application contact:* Laurie S. Russell, Record Analyst, 319-273-2623, Fax: 319-273-2885, E-mail: laurie.russell@uni.edu.

University of North Florida, College of Arts and Sciences, Department of Biology, Jacksonville, FL 32224. Offers MA, MS. MS program has earlier application deadline of March 1. Part-time programs available. *Faculty:* 13 full-time (3 women). *Students:* 21 full-time (12 women), 12 part-time (8 women); includes 2 Black or African American, non-Hispanic/Latino; 2 Asian, non-Hispanic/Latino; 1 Hispanic/Latino. Average age 27. 27 applicants, 63% accepted, 12 enrolled. In 2010, 11 master's awarded. *Degree requirements:* For master's, thesis (for some programs). *Entrance requirements:* For master's, GRE General Test, minimum GPA of 3.0 in last 60 hours, letters of recommendation. Additional exam requirements/recommendations for international students: Required—TOEFL (minimum score 570 paper-based; 230 computer-based). *Application deadline:* For fall admission, 7/1 for domestic students, 5/1 for international students; for spring admission, 11/1 for domestic students, 10/1 for international students. Application fee: $30. Electronic applications accepted. *Expenses:* Tuition, state resident: full-time $7646; part-time $318.60 per credit hour. Tuition, nonresident: full-time $23,502; part-time $979.24 per credit hour. Required fees: $1209; $50.37 per credit hour. Tuition and fees vary according to course load and program. *Financial support:* In 2010–11, 11 students received support, including 2 research assistantships (averaging $1,626 per year), 14 teaching assistantships (averaging $5,930 per year); Federal Work-Study, scholarships/grants, and

Biological and Biomedical Sciences—General

University of North Florida (continued)

unspecified assistantships also available. Support available to part-time students. Financial award application deadline: 4/1; financial award applicants required to submit FAFSA. Total annual research expenditures: $320,082. *Unit head:* Dr. Courtney Hackney, Chair, 904-620-2830, Fax: 904-620-3885, E-mail: c.hackney@unf.edu. *Application contact:* Lillith Richardson, Assistant Director, The Graduate School, 904-620-1360, Fax: 904-620-1362, E-mail: graduateschool@unf.edu.

University of North Texas, Toulouse Graduate School, College of Arts and Sciences, Department of Biological Sciences, Program in Biology, Denton, TX 76203. Offers MA, MS, PhD. Terminal master's awarded for partial completion of doctoral program. *Degree requirements:* For master's, variable foreign language requirement, comprehensive exam, thesis (for some programs), oral defense of thesis; for doctorate, one foreign language, comprehensive exam, thesis/dissertation, oral defense of dissertation. *Entrance requirements:* For master's and doctorate, GRE General Test, letters of recommendation. *Expenses:* Tuition, state resident: full-time $4298; part-time $239 per credit hour. Tuition, nonresident: full-time $10,782; part-time $549 per credit hour. Required fees: $1292; $270 per credit hour. *Financial support:* Fellowships, research assistantships, teaching assistantships, career-related internships or fieldwork, Federal Work-Study, and institutionally sponsored loans available. Support available to part-time students. Financial award applicants required to submit FAFSA. *Faculty research:* Animal physiology, plant science, biochemistry, environmental science. *Unit head:* Professor and Chair. *Application contact:* Graduate Advisor, 940-565-2011, Fax: 940-565-3821.

University of North Texas Health Science Center at Fort Worth, Graduate School of Biomedical Sciences, Fort Worth, TX 76107-2699. Offers anatomy and cell biology (MS, PhD); biochemistry and molecular biology (MS, PhD); biomedical sciences (MS, PhD); biotechnology (MS); forensic genetics (MS); integrative physiology (MS, PhD); medical science (MS); microbiology and immunology (MS, PhD); pharmacology (MS, PhD); science education (MS); DO/MS; DO/PhD. Terminal master's awarded for partial completion of doctoral program. *Degree requirements:* For master's, thesis; for doctorate, thesis/dissertation. *Entrance requirements:* For master's and doctorate, GRE General Test. Additional exam requirements/recommendations for international students: Required—TOEFL. *Expenses:* Contact institution. *Faculty research:* Alzheimer's disease, aging, eye diseases, cancer, cardiovascular disease.

University of Notre Dame, Graduate School, College of Science, Department of Biological Sciences, Notre Dame, IN 46556. Offers aquatic ecology, evolution and environmental biology (MS, PhD); cellular and molecular biology (MS, PhD); genetics (MS, PhD); physiology (MS, PhD); vector biology and parasitology (MS, PhD). Terminal master's awarded for partial completion of doctoral program. *Degree requirements:* For master's, comprehensive exam, thesis; for doctorate, comprehensive exam, thesis/dissertation, candidacy exam. *Entrance requirements:* For master's and doctorate, GRE General Test. Additional exam requirements/recommendations for international students: Required—TOEFL (minimum score 600 paper-based; 250 computer-based; 80 iBT). Electronic applications accepted. *Faculty research:* Tropical disease, molecular genetics, neurobiology, evolutionary biology, aquatic biology.

University of Oklahoma Health Sciences Center, College of Medicine and Graduate College, Graduate Programs in Medicine, Oklahoma City, OK 73190. Offers biochemistry and molecular biology (MS, PhD), including biochemistry, molecular biology; cell biology (MS, PhD); medical sciences (MS); microbiology and immunology (MS, PhD), including immunology, microbiology; neuroscience (MS, PhD); pathology (PhD); physiology (MS, PhD); psychiatry and behavioral sciences (MS, PhD), including biological psychology; radiological sciences (MS, PhD), including medical radiation physics; MD/PhD. Part-time programs available. Terminal master's awarded for partial completion of doctoral program. *Degree requirements:* For doctorate, thesis/dissertation. *Entrance requirements:* For doctorate, GRE General Test, 3 letters of recommendation. Additional exam requirements/recommendations for international students: Required—TOEFL. *Expenses:* Contact institution. *Faculty research:* Behavior and drugs, structure and function of endothelium, genetics and behavior, gene structure and function, action of antibiotics.

University of Oregon, Graduate School, College of Arts and Sciences, Department of Biology, Eugene, OR 97403. Offers ecology and evolution (MA, MS, PhD); marine biology (MA, MS, PhD); molecular, cellular and genetic biology (PhD); neuroscience and development (PhD). Terminal master's awarded for partial completion of doctoral program. *Degree requirements:* For master's, thesis (for some programs); for doctorate, thesis/dissertation. *Entrance requirements:* For master's and doctorate, GRE General Test, minimum GPA of 3.2. Additional exam requirements/recommendations for international students: Required—TOEFL. *Faculty research:* Developmental neurobiology; evolution, population biology, and quantitative genetics; regulation of gene expression; biochemistry of marine organisms.

University of Ottawa, Faculty of Graduate and Postdoctoral Studies, Faculty of Science, Ottawa-Carleton Institute of Biology, Ottawa, ON K1N 6N5, Canada. Offers M Sc, PhD. M Sc, PhD offered jointly with Carleton University. Part-time programs available. *Degree requirements:* For master's, thesis, seminar; for doctorate, comprehensive exam, thesis/dissertation, seminar. *Entrance requirements:* For master's, honors B Sc degree or equivalent, minimum B average; for doctorate, honors B Sc with minimum B+ average or M Sc with minimum B+ average. Electronic applications accepted. *Faculty research:* Physiology/biochemistry, cellular and molecular biology, ecology, behavior and systematics.

University of Pennsylvania, Perelman School of Medicine, Biomedical Graduate Studies, Philadelphia, PA 19104. Offers MS, PhD, MD/PhD, VMD/PhD. *Faculty:* 783. *Students:* 761 full-time (392 women), 128 part-time (78 women); includes 38 Black or African American, non-Hispanic/Latino; 6 American Indian or Alaska Native, non-Hispanic/Latino; 137 Asian, non-Hispanic/Latino; 45 Hispanic/Latino, 76 international. 1,341 applicants, 25% accepted, 172 enrolled. In 2010, 52 master's, 109 doctorates awarded. Terminal master's awarded for partial completion of doctoral program. *Degree requirements:* For master's, comprehensive exam; for doctorate, thesis/dissertation. *Entrance requirements:* For master's and doctorate, GRE General Test. Additional exam requirements/recommendations for international students: Required—TOEFL. *Application deadline:* For fall admission, 12/8 priority date for domestic and international students. Applications are processed on a rolling basis. Application fee: $70. Electronic applications accepted. *Expenses:* Contact institution. *Financial support:* In 2010–11, 693 students received support; fellowships, research assistantships, scholarships/grants, traineeships, and unspecified assistantships available. Financial award application deadline: 12/8. *Unit head:* Dr. Susan R. Ross, Director, 215-898-1030. *Application contact:* Sarah Gormley, Admissions Coordinator, 215-898-1030, Fax: 215-898-2671, E-mail: gormley@mail.med.upenn.edu.

University of Pennsylvania, School of Arts and Sciences, Graduate Group in Biology, Philadelphia, PA 19104. Offers PhD. *Faculty:* 46 full-time (11 women), 7 part-time/adjunct (2 women). *Students:* 58 full-time (35 women); includes 3 Asian, non-Hispanic/Latino, 37 international. 168 applicants, 14% accepted, 7 enrolled. In 2010, 7 doctorates awarded. *Degree requirements:* For doctorate, thesis/dissertation. *Entrance requirements:* For doctorate, GRE General Test, GRE Subject Test. Additional exam requirements/recommendations for international students: Required—TOEFL. *Application deadline:* For fall admission, 12/1 priority date for domestic students. Application fee: $70. Electronic applications accepted. *Expenses:* Tuition: Full-time $25,660; part-time $4758 per course. Required fees: $2152; $270 per course. Tuition and fees vary according to course load, degree level and program. *Financial support:* Fellowships, research assistantships, teaching assistantships, institutionally sponsored loans, scholarships/grants, traineeships, health care benefits, and unspecified assistantships available. Financial award application deadline: 12/15. *Unit head:* Greg Guild, Department Chair, 215-898-3433, E-mail: gguild@sas.upenn.edu. *Application contact:* Greg Guild, Department Chair, 215-898-3433, E-mail: gguild@sas.upenn.edu.

University of Pittsburgh, School of Arts and Sciences, Department of Biological Sciences, Pittsburgh, PA 15260. Offers ecology and evolution (PhD); molecular, cellular, and developmental biology (PhD). *Faculty:* 32 full-time (8 women). *Students:* 74 full-time (40 women); includes 1 American Indian or Alaska Native, non-Hispanic/Latino; 4 Asian, non-Hispanic/Latino; 3 Hispanic/Latino, 18 international. Average age 23. 210 applicants, 14% accepted, 9 enrolled. In 2010, 6 doctorates awarded. *Degree requirements:* For doctorate, comprehensive exam, thesis/dissertation, completion of research integrity module. *Entrance requirements:* For doctorate, GRE General Test, GRE Subject Test. Additional exam requirements/recommendations for international students: Required—TOEFL (minimum score 550 paper-based; 213 computer-based; 80 iBT). *Application deadline:* For fall admission, 1/15 priority date for domestic students, 12/15 priority date for international students. Applications are processed on a rolling basis. Application fee: $0 ($50 for international students). Electronic applications accepted. *Expenses:* Tuition, state resident: full-time $17,304; part-time $701 per credit. Tuition, nonresident: full-time $29,554; part-time $1210 per credit. Required fees: $740; $214 per term. Tuition and fees vary according to program. *Financial support:* In 2010–11, 45 fellowships with full tuition reimbursements (averaging $28,382 per year), 121 research assistantships with full tuition reimbursements (averaging $25,077 per year), 38 teaching assistantships with full tuition reimbursements (averaging $24,002 per year) were awarded; Federal Work-Study, scholarships/grants, traineeships, and health care benefits also available. *Faculty research:* Molecular biology, cell biology, molecular biophysics, developmental biology, ecology and evolution. Total annual research expenditures: $9.2 million. *Unit head:* Dr. Graham F. Hatfull, Professor and Chair, 412-624-4350, Fax: 412-624-4759, E-mail: gfh@pitt.edu. *Application contact:* Cathleen M. Barr, Graduate Administrator, 412-624-4268, Fax: 412-624-4759, E-mail: cbarr@pitt.edu.

University of Pittsburgh, School of Medicine, Graduate Programs in Medicine, Interdisciplinary Biomedical Sciences Program, Pittsburgh, PA 15260. Offers PhD. *Faculty:* 301 full-time (78 women). *Students:* 28 full-time (20 women); includes 1 Asian, non-Hispanic/Latino; 1 Hispanic/Latino; 1 Two or more races, non-Hispanic/Latino, 8 international. Average age 27. 486 applicants, 14% accepted, 28 enrolled. In 2010, 43 doctorates awarded. *Degree requirements:* For doctorate, comprehensive exam, thesis/dissertation. *Entrance requirements:* For doctorate, GRE General Test, GRE Subject Test, minimum QPA of 3.0. Additional exam requirements/recommendations for international students: Required—TOEFL (minimum score 600 paper-based; 100 iBT), IELTS (minimum score 7). *Application deadline:* For fall admission, 12/15 priority date for domestic and international students. Application fee: $50. Electronic applications accepted. *Expenses:* Tuition, state resident: full-time $17,304; part-time $701 per credit. Tuition, nonresident: full-time $29,554; part-time $1210 per credit. Required fees: $740; $214 per term. Tuition and fees vary according to program. *Financial support:* In 2010–11, 28 research assistantships with full tuition reimbursements (averaging $25,500 per year) were awarded; teaching assistantships, institutionally sponsored loans, scholarships/grants, traineeships, and unspecified assistantships also available. *Faculty research:* Cell biology and molecular physiology, cellular and molecular pathology, immunology, molecular genetics and developmental biology, molecular pharmacology and molecular virology and microbiology. *Unit head:* Dr. John P. Horn, Associate Dean for Graduate Studies, 412-648-8957, Fax: 412-648-1077, E-mail: gradstudies@medschool.pitt.edu. *Application contact:* Graduate Studies Administrator, 412-648-8957, Fax: 412-648-1077, E-mail: gradstudies@medschool.pitt.edu.

University of Prince Edward Island, Faculty of Science, Charlottetown, PE C1A 4P3, Canada. Offers biology (M Sc); chemistry (M Sc). *Degree requirements:* For master's, thesis. *Entrance requirements:* Additional exam requirements/recommendations for international students: Required—TOEFL (minimum score 550 paper-based; 213 computer-based; 80 iBT), Canadian Academic English Language Assessment, Michigan English Language Assessment Battery, Canadian Test of English for Scholars and Trainees. *Faculty research:* Ecology and wildlife biology, molecular, genetics and biotechnology, organametallic, bio-organic, supramolecular and synthetic organic chemistry, neurobiology and stoke materials science.

University of Puerto Rico, Mayagüez Campus, Graduate Studies, College of Arts and Sciences, Department of Biology, Mayagüez, PR 00681-9000. Offers MS. Part-time programs available. *Students:* 83 full-time (58 women); includes 64 Hispanic/Latino, 19 international. 16 applicants, 44% accepted, 5 enrolled. In 2010, 7 master's awarded. *Degree requirements:* For master's, one foreign language, comprehensive exam, thesis. *Entrance requirements:* For master's, GRE General Test, BS in biology or its equivalent; minimum GPA of 3.0 in biology courses. Additional exam requirements/recommendations for international students: Required—TOEFL. *Application deadline:* For fall admission, 2/15 for domestic and international students; for spring admission, 9/15 for domestic and international students. Applications are processed on a rolling basis. Application fee: $25. *Expenses:* Tuition, state resident: full-time $1188. Tuition, nonresident: full-time $1188. International tuition: $6126 full-time. Tuition and fees vary according to course level and course load. *Financial support:* In 2010–11, 71 students received support, including fellowships (averaging $12,000 per year), 21 research assistantships with tuition reimbursements available (averaging $15,000 per year), 71 teaching assistantships with tuition reimbursements available (averaging $8,500 per year); Federal Work-Study and institutionally sponsored loans also available. *Faculty research:* Herpetology, entomology, microbiology, immunology, botany. Total annual research expenditures: $2.1 million. *Unit head:* Dr. Nannette Difoot, Director, 787-265-3837, Fax: 787-834-3673, E-mail: nanette.difoot@upr.edu. *Application contact:* Dr. Nannette Difoot, Director, 787-265-3837, Fax: 787-834-3673, E-mail: nanette.difoot@upr.edu.

University of Puerto Rico, Medical Sciences Campus, School of Medicine, Division of Graduate Studies, San Juan, PR 00936-5067. Offers MS, PhD. Terminal master's awarded for partial completion of doctoral program. *Degree requirements:* For master's, one foreign language, thesis; for doctorate, one foreign language, comprehensive exam, thesis/dissertation. *Entrance requirements:* For master's and doctorate, GRE General Test, GRE Subject Test, interview, 3 letters of recommendation, minimum GPA of 3.0. Electronic applications accepted. *Expenses:* Contact institution.

University of Puerto Rico, Río Piedras, College of Natural Sciences, Department of Biology, San Juan, PR 00931-3300. Offers ecology/systematics (MS, PhD); evolution/genetics (MS, PhD); molecular/cellular biology (MS, PhD); neuroscience (MS, PhD). Part-time programs available. *Degree requirements:* For master's, one foreign language, comprehensive exam, thesis; for doctorate, one foreign language, comprehensive exam, thesis/dissertation. *Entrance requirements:* For master's, GRE Subject Test, interview, minimum GPA of 3.0, letter of recommendation; for doctorate, GRE Subject Test, interview, master's degree, minimum GPA of 3.0, letter of recommendation. *Faculty research:* Environmental, poblational and systematic biology.

University of Regina, Faculty of Graduate Studies and Research, Faculty of Science, Department of Biology, Regina, SK S4S 0A2, Canada. Offers M Sc, PhD. *Faculty:* 10 full-time (1 woman). *Students:* 22 full-time (12 women), 6 part-time (4 women). 26 applicants, 54% accepted. In 2010, 8 master's, 1 doctorate awarded. *Degree requirements:* For master's, thesis; for doctorate, comprehensive exam, thesis/dissertation. *Entrance requirements:* Additional exam requirements/recommendations for international students: Required—TOEFL (minimum score 580 paper-based; 80 iBT). *Application deadline:* Applications are processed on a rolling basis. Application fee: $100. Electronic applications accepted. Tuition and fees charges are reported in Canadian dollars. *Expenses:* Tuition, area resident: Full-time $3245 Canadian dollars; part-time $180.25 Canadian dollars per credit hour. International tuition: $4745 Canadian dollars full-time. Required fees: $494 Canadian dollars; $115.25 Canadian dollars per credit hour. $115.25 Canadian dollars per semester. Tuition and fees vary according to program. *Financial support:* In 2010–11, 5 fellowships (averaging $19,200 per year), 1 research assistantship (averaging $16,500 per year), 10 teaching assistantships (averaging $6,792 per year) were awarded; scholarships/grants also available. Financial award application deadline: 6/15. *Faculty research:* Aquatic and terrestrial ecology, molecular and population genetics, developmental biology, microbiology, plant physiology and morphology. *Unit head:* Dr. Harold Weger, Head, 306-585-4479, Fax: 306-337-2410, E-mail: harold.weger@uregina.ca. *Application contact:* Dr. Harold Weger, Graduate Program Coordinator, 306-585-4479, Fax: 306-337-2410, E-mail: harold.weger@uregina.ca.

University of Rhode Island, Graduate School, College of the Environment and Life Sciences, Department of Biological Sciences, Kingston, RI 02881. Offers MS, PhD. Part-time programs available. *Faculty:* 15 full-time (8 women), 2 part-time/adjunct (0 women). *Students:* 32 full-time (21 women), 3 part-time (2 women); includes 4 minority (all Asian, non-Hispanic/Latino), 2 international. In 2010, 3 master's, 1 doctorate awarded. *Degree requirements:* For master's, comprehensive exam (for some programs), thesis optional; for doctorate, comprehensive exam, thesis/dissertation. *Entrance requirements:* For master's and doctorate, GRE, 2 letters of recommendation. Additional exam requirements/recommendations for international students: Required—TOEFL (minimum score 550 paper-based; 213 computer-based). *Application deadline:* For fall admission, 4/15 for domestic students, 1/15 for international students. Application fee: $65. Electronic applications accepted. *Expenses:* Tuition, state resident: full-time $9588; part-time $533 per credit hour. Tuition, nonresident: full-time $22,968; part-time $1276 per credit hour. Required fees: $1282; $68 per semester. Tuition and fees vary according to program. *Financial support:* In 2010–11, 1 research assistantship with partial tuition reimbursement (averaging $7,175 per year), 26 teaching assistantships with full and partial tuition reimbursements (averaging $12,054 per year) were awarded. Financial award application deadline: 1/15; financial award applicants required to submit FAFSA. *Faculty research:* Physiological constraints on predators in Antarctics, effects of CO2 absorption in salt water particularly as it impacts pteropods. *Unit head:* Dr. Marian Goldsmith, Chairperson, 401-874-2373, Fax: 401-874-2065, E-mail: mrgoldsmith@mail.uri.edu. *Application contact:* Dr. Marian Goldsmith, Chairperson, 401-874-2373, Fax: 401-874-2065, E-mail: mrgoldsmith@mail.uri.edu.

University of Rochester, School of Arts and Sciences, Department of Biology, Rochester, NY 14627. Offers MS, PhD. Terminal master's awarded for partial completion of doctoral program. *Degree requirements:* For doctorate, thesis/dissertation, qualifying exam. *Entrance requirements:* For master's and doctorate, GRE General Test, GRE Subject Test (highly recommended). Additional exam requirements/recommendations for international students: Required—TOEFL.

University of Rochester, School of Medicine and Dentistry, Graduate Programs in Medicine and Dentistry, Interdepartmental Program in Translational Biomedical Science, Rochester, NY 14627.

University of San Francisco, College of Arts and Sciences, Department of Biology, San Francisco, CA 94117-1080. Offers MS. *Faculty:* 4 full-time (all women). *Students:* 6 full-time (4 women); includes 1 Asian, non-Hispanic/Latino; 2 Two or more races, non-Hispanic/Latino. Average age 27. 34 applicants, 6% accepted, 1 enrolled. In 2010, 1 master's awarded. *Degree requirements:* For master's, thesis. *Entrance requirements:* For master's, GRE General Test, GRE Subject Test, BS in biology or the equivalent. *Application deadline:* For fall admission, 4/15 for domestic students; for spring admission, 10/15 for domestic students. Application fee: $55 ($65 for international students). *Expenses:* Tuition: Full-time $20,070; part-time $1115 per credit hour. Tuition and fees vary according to course load, degree level and program. *Financial support:* In 2010–11, 6 students received support; teaching assistantships, career-related internships or fieldwork, Federal Work-Study, institutionally sponsored loans, and tuition waivers available. Financial award application deadline: 3/2; financial award applicants required to submit FAFSA. *Unit head:* Dr. Jennifer Dever, Chair, 415-422-6755, Fax: 415-422-6363. *Application contact:* Information Contact, 415-422-5135, Fax: 415-422-2217, E-mail: asgraduate@usfca.edu.

University of Saskatchewan, College of Graduate Studies and Research, College of Arts and Sciences, Department of Biology, Saskatoon, SK S7N 5A2, Canada. Offers M Sc, PhD. *Degree requirements:* For master's, thesis (for some programs); for doctorate, comprehensive exam (for some programs), thesis/dissertation. *Entrance requirements:* Additional exam requirements/recommendations for international students: Required—TOEFL (minimum score 80 iBT); Recommended—IELTS (minimum score 6.5). Electronic applications accepted.

University of Saskatchewan, Western College of Veterinary Medicine and College of Graduate Studies and Research, Graduate Programs in Veterinary Medicine, Department of Veterinary Biomedical Sciences, Saskatoon, SK S7N 5A2, Canada. Offers veterinary anatomy (M Sc); veterinary biomedical sciences (M Vet Sc); veterinary physiological sciences (M Sc, PhD). *Faculty:* 12 full-time (4 women), 4 part-time/adjunct (0 women). *Students:* 49 full-time (24 women); includes 2 Black or African American, non-Hispanic/Latino; 47 American Indian or Alaska Native, non-Hispanic/Latino. In 2010, 8 master's, 4 doctorates awarded. *Degree requirements:* For master's, thesis; for doctorate, comprehensive exam (for some programs), thesis/dissertation. *Entrance requirements:* Additional exam requirements/recommendations for international students: Required—TOEFL (minimum score 80 iBT); Recommended—IELTS (minimum score 6.5). Electronic applications accepted. *Faculty research:* Toxicology, animal reproduction, pharmacology, chloride channels, pulmonary pathobiology. *Unit head:* Dr. Barry Blakley, Head, 306-966-7350, Fax: 306-966-7376, E-mail: barry.blakley@usask.ca. *Application contact:* Application Contact.

University of South Alabama, College of Medicine and Graduate School, Interdisciplinary Graduate Program in Basic Medical Sciences, Mobile, AL 36688-0002. Offers PhD. *Faculty:* 50 full-time (9 women), 1 part-time/adjunct (0 women). *Students:* 54 full-time (34 women), 4 part-time (3 women); includes 14 minority (5 Black or African American, non-Hispanic/Latino; 3 American Indian or Alaska Native, non-Hispanic/Latino; 3 Asian, non-Hispanic/Latino; 3 Hispanic/Latino), 11 international. 55 applicants, 20% accepted, 10 enrolled. In 2010, 6 doctorates awarded. *Degree requirements:* For doctorate, comprehensive exam. *Entrance requirements:* For doctorate, GRE, three semesters or quarters of undergraduate work in physics, general chemistry, organic chemistry, biology, English composition, and mathematics (including statistics and calculus) with minimum GPA of 3.0. Additional exam requirements/recommendations for international students: Required—TOEFL. *Application deadline:* For fall admission, 4/1 for domestic students, 3/31 for international students. Applications are processed on a rolling basis. Application fee: $35. *Expenses:* Contact institution. *Financial support:* Fellowships, research assistantships, institutionally sponsored loans available. Financial award application deadline: 4/1; financial award applicants required to submit FAFSA. *Faculty research:* Microcirculation, molecular biology, cell biology, growth control. *Unit head:* Dr. Ronald Balczon, Director of College of Medicine Graduate Studies, 251-460-6153, Fax: 251-460-6071, E-mail: rbalzon@usouthal.edu. *Application contact:* Dr. B. Keith Harrison, Dean of the Graduate School, 251-460-6310, Fax: 251-461-1513, E-mail: kharriso@usouthal.edu.

University of South Alabama, Graduate School, College of Arts and Sciences, Department of Biological Sciences, Mobile, AL 36688-0002. Offers MS. Part-time programs available. *Faculty:* 7 full-time (3 women). *Students:* 12 full-time (7 women), 5 part-time (4 women); includes 1 Black or African American, non-Hispanic/Latino; 1 Asian, non-Hispanic/Latino; 1 Hispanic/Latino, 3 international. 23 applicants, 26% accepted, 6 enrolled. In 2010, 3 master's awarded. *Degree requirements:* For master's, one foreign language, comprehensive exam, thesis optional. *Entrance requirements:* For master's, GRE Subject Test, minimum GPA of 3.0. Additional exam requirements/recommendations for international students: Required—TOEFL (minimum score 600 paper-based). *Application deadline:* For fall admission, 9/1 priority date for domestic students, 6/15 for international students; for spring admission, 11/1 for international students. Applications are processed on a rolling basis. Application fee: $35. *Expenses:* Tuition, state resident: part-time $300 per credit hour. Tuition, nonresident: part-time $600 per credit hour. Required fees: $150 per semester. *Financial support:* Fellowships, research assistantships, teaching assistantships available. Support available to part-time students. Financial award application deadline: 4/1. *Faculty research:* Aquatic and marine biology, molecular biochemistry, plant and animal taxonomy. *Unit head:* Dr. John Freeman, Chair, 251-460-6331. *Application contact:* Brian Axsmith, Graduate Coordinator, 251-460-6331.

University of South Carolina, The Graduate School, College of Arts and Sciences, Department of Biological Sciences, Columbia, SC 29208. Offers biology (MS, PhD); biology education (IMA, MAT); ecology, evolution and organismal biology (MS, PhD); molecular, cellular, and developmental biology (MS, PhD). IMA and MAT offered in cooperation with the College of Education. Terminal master's awarded for partial completion of doctoral program. *Degree requirements:* For master's, one foreign language, thesis (for some programs); for doctorate,

one foreign language, thesis/dissertation. *Entrance requirements:* For master's and doctorate, GRE General Test, minimum GPA of 3.0 in science. Electronic applications accepted. *Faculty research:* Marine ecology, population and evolutionary biology, molecular biology and genetics, development.

University of South Carolina, School of Medicine and The Graduate School, Graduate Programs in Medicine, Columbia, SC 29208. Offers biomedical science (MBS, PhD); genetic counseling (MS); nurse anesthesia (MNA); rehabilitation counseling (MRC, Certificate), including psychiatric rehabilitation (Certificate), rehabilitation counseling (MRC). Terminal master's awarded for partial completion of doctoral program. *Degree requirements:* For master's, comprehensive exam, thesis (for some programs), practicum; for doctorate, comprehensive exam, thesis/dissertation. *Entrance requirements:* For master's, doctorate, and Certificate, GRE General Test. Electronic applications accepted. *Expenses:* Contact institution. *Faculty research:* Cardiovascular diseases, oncology, neuroscience, psychiatric rehabilitation, genetics.

University of South Carolina, School of Medicine and The Graduate School, Graduate Programs in Medicine, Graduate Program in Biomedical Science, Doctoral Program in Biomedical Science, Columbia, SC 29208. Offers PhD. *Degree requirements:* For doctorate, comprehensive exam, thesis/dissertation. *Entrance requirements:* For doctorate, GRE General Test. Electronic applications accepted. *Faculty research:* Cancer, neuroscience, cardiovascular, reproductive, immunology.

University of South Carolina, School of Medicine and The Graduate School, Graduate Programs in Medicine, Graduate Program in Biomedical Science, Master's Program in Biomedical Science, Columbia, SC 29208. Offers MBS. *Degree requirements:* For master's, comprehensive exam, thesis. *Entrance requirements:* For master's, GRE General Test. Electronic applications accepted. *Faculty research:* Cardiovascular diseases, oncology, reproductive biology, neuroscience, microbiology.

The University of South Dakota, Graduate School, College of Arts and Sciences, Department of Biology, Vermillion, SD 57069-2390. Offers MA, MNS, MS, PhD. *Degree requirements:* For master's, comprehensive exam (for some programs), thesis (for some programs); for doctorate, comprehensive exam, thesis/dissertation. *Entrance requirements:* For master's, GRE Subject Test, GRE General Test, minimum GPA of 2.7; for doctorate, GRE General Test, GRE Subject Test, minimum GPA of 2.7. Additional exam requirements/recommendations for international students: Required—TOEFL (minimum score 550 paper-based; 213 computer-based; 70 iBT). Electronic applications accepted. *Faculty research:* Evolutionary and ecological informatics, neuroscience, stress physiology.

The University of South Dakota, School of Medicine and Health Sciences and Graduate School, Biomedical Sciences Graduate Program, Vermillion, SD 57069-2390. Offers cardiovascular research (MS, PhD); cellular and molecular biology (MS, PhD); molecular microbiology and immunology (MS, PhD); neuroscience (MS, PhD); physiology and pharmacology (MS, PhD). Terminal master's awarded for partial completion of doctoral program. *Degree requirements:* For master's, thesis; for doctorate, comprehensive exam, thesis/dissertation. *Entrance requirements:* For master's and doctorate, GRE General Test, minimum GPA of 3.0. Additional exam requirements/recommendations for international students: Required—TOEFL (minimum score 550 paper-based; 213 computer-based; 80 iBT), IELTS (minimum score 6). Electronic applications accepted. *Expenses:* Contact institution. *Faculty research:* Molecular biology, microbiology, neuroscience, cellular biology, physiology.

University of Southern California, Graduate School, Dana and David Dornsife College of Letters, Arts and Sciences, Department of Biological Sciences, Los Angeles, CA 90089. Offers biology (MS); computational molecular biology (MS); integrative and evolutionary biology (PhD); marine biology and biological oceanography (MS, PhD), including marine and environmental biology (MS), marine biology and biological oceanography (PhD); molecular and computational biology (PhD), including biology, computational biology and bioinformatics, molecular biology; neurobiology (PhD). *Students:* 183 full-time (93 women), 6 part-time (5 women); includes 37 minority (4 Black or African American, non-Hispanic/Latino; 19 Asian, non-Hispanic/Latino; 10 Hispanic/Latino; 4 Two or more races, non-Hispanic/Latino), 79 international. In 2010, 7 master's, 24 doctorates awarded. Terminal master's awarded for partial completion of doctoral program. *Degree requirements:* For master's, comprehensive exam (for some programs), research paper; for doctorate, thesis/dissertation, qualifying examination, dissertation defense. *Entrance requirements:* For master's, GRE, 3 letters of recommendation, personal statement, resume, minimum GPA of 3.0; for doctorate, GRE, 3 letters of recommendation, resume, minimum GPA of 3.0. Additional exam requirements/recommendations for international students: Required—TOEFL (minimum score 600 paper-based; 250 computer-based; 100 iBT). *Application deadline:* For fall admission, 12/1 priority date for domestic and international students. Application fee: $85. Electronic applications accepted. *Expenses:* Tuition: Full-time $31,240; part-time $1420 per unit. Required fees: $600. One-time fee: $35 full-time. Full-time tuition and fees vary according to degree level and program. *Financial support:* In 2010–11, 126 students received support. Scholarships/grants, traineeships, health care benefits, and tuition waivers available. *Faculty research:* Microarray data analysis, microbial ecology and genetics, integrative organismal and behavioral biology and ecology, stem cell pluipotency, cancer cell biology. *Unit head:* Dr. Douglas Capone, Chair, 213-740-2772, Fax: 213-740-8123, E-mail: capone@usc.edu. *Application contact:* Adolfo dela Rosa, Student Services Advisor, 213-821-3164, Fax: 213-740-8123, E-mail: adolfode@usc.edu.

University of Southern California, Keck School of Medicine and Graduate School, Graduate Programs in Medicine, Los Angeles, CA 90089. Offers MPAP, MPH, MS, PhD, MD/PhD. *Faculty:* 263 full-time (80 women), 16 part-time/adjunct (6 women). *Students:* 727 full-time (489 women), 3 part-time (2 women); includes 276 minority (28 Black or African American, non-Hispanic/Latino; 3 American Indian or Alaska Native, non-Hispanic/Latino; 167 Asian, non-Hispanic/Latino; 70 Hispanic/Latino; 1 Native Hawaiian or other Pacific Islander, non-Hispanic/Latino; 7 Two or more races, non-Hispanic/Latino), 225 international. Average age 27. 1,598 applicants, 26% accepted, 238 enrolled. In 2010, 153 master's, 60 doctorates awarded. *Entrance requirements:* For master's, GRE General Test, minimum GPA of 3.0; for doctorate, GRE General Test (minimum combined Verbal and Quantitative score of 1000), minimum GPA of 3.0. Additional exam requirements/recommendations for international students: Required—TOEFL (minimum score 600 paper-based; 250 computer-based; 100 iBT). Application fee: $85. Electronic applications accepted. *Expenses:* Tuition: Full-time $31,240; part-time $1420 per unit. Required fees: $600. One-time fee: $35 full-time. Full-time tuition and fees vary according to degree level and program. *Financial support:* In 2010–11, 396 students received support, including 29 fellowships with tuition reimbursements available, 243 research assistantships with tuition reimbursements available (averaging $27,060 per year), 34 teaching assistantships with tuition reimbursements available (averaging $27,060 per year); career-related internships or fieldwork, Federal Work-Study, institutionally sponsored loans, scholarships/grants, traineeships, health care benefits, and unspecified assistantships also available. Support available to part-time students. Financial award application deadline: 5/5; financial award applicants required to submit CSS PROFILE or FAFSA. *Unit head:* Dr. Debbie Johnson, Associate Dean for Graduate Affairs, 323-442-1446, Fax: 323-442-1199, E-mail: johnsond@usc.edu. *Application contact:* Marisela Zuniga, Administrative Coordinator, 323-442-1607, Fax: 323-442-1199, E-mail: mzuniga@usc.edu.

University of Southern Maine, College of Arts and Sciences, Program in Biology, Portland, ME 04104-9300. Offers MS.

University of Southern Mississippi, Graduate School, College of Science and Technology, Department of Biological Sciences, Hattiesburg, MS 39406-0001. Offers environmental biology (MS, PhD); marine biology (MS, PhD); microbiology (MS, PhD); molecular biology (MS, PhD). *Faculty:* 27 full-time (6 women). *Students:* 54 full-time (29 women), 5 part-time (4 women); includes 2 Black or African American, non-Hispanic/Latino; 4 Two or more races, non-Hispanic/Latino, 17 international. Average age 32. 54 applicants, 48% accepted, 13 enrolled. In 2010, 4

Biological and Biomedical Sciences—General

University of Southern Mississippi (continued)
master's, 4 doctorates awarded. Terminal master's awarded for partial completion of doctoral program. *Degree requirements:* For master's, comprehensive exam, thesis; for doctorate, comprehensive exam, thesis/dissertation. *Entrance requirements:* For master's, GRE General Test, minimum GPA of 3.0 on last 60 hours; for doctorate, GRE General Test, minimum GPA of 3.5. Additional exam requirements/recommendations for international students: Required—TOEFL, IELTS. *Application deadline:* For fall admission, 3/1 priority date for domestic students, 3/1 for international students; for spring admission, 1/10 priority date for domestic and international students. Applications are processed on a rolling basis. Application fee: $50. *Financial support:* In 2010–11, 25 research assistantships with full tuition reimbursements (averaging $9,700 per year), 33 teaching assistantships with full tuition reimbursements (averaging $10,600 per year) were awarded; Federal Work-Study, scholarships/grants, health care benefits, and unspecified assistantships also available. Financial award application deadline: 3/15; financial award applicants required to submit FAFSA. *Unit head:* Dr. Glenmore Shearer, Chair, 601-266-4748, Fax: 601-266-5797. *Application contact:* Dr. Jake Schaefer, Director of Graduate Studies, 601-266-4748, Fax: 601-266-5797.

University of South Florida, Graduate School, College of Arts and Sciences, Department of Biology, Tampa, FL 33620-9951. Offers cell biology and molecular biology (MS); coastal marine biology (MS); coastal marine biology and ecology (PhD); conservation biology (MS, PhD); molecular and cell biology (PhD). Part-time programs available. *Faculty:* 8 full-time (4 women). *Students:* 85 full-time (50 women), 8 part-time (all women); includes 1 Black or African American, non-Hispanic/Latino; 3 Asian, non-Hispanic/Latino; 7 Hispanic/Latino, 12 international. Average age 27. 122 applicants, 30% accepted, 34 enrolled. In 2010, 10 master's, 9 doctorates awarded. *Degree requirements:* For master's, comprehensive exam, thesis (for some programs); for doctorate, comprehensive exam, thesis/dissertation. *Entrance requirements:* For master's and doctorate, GRE General Test, minimum GPA of 3.0. Additional exam requirements/recommendations for international students: Required—TOEFL (minimum score 570 paper-based; 213 computer-based). *Application deadline:* For fall admission, 2/15 priority date for domestic students, 1/2 for international students; for spring admission, 8/1 for domestic students, 6/1 for international students. Application fee: $30. Electronic applications accepted. *Financial support:* In 2010–11, 35 research assistantships (averaging $17,940 per year), 38 teaching assistantships with tuition reimbursements (averaging $16,621 per year) were awarded; unspecified assistantships also available. Financial award application deadline: 6/30; financial award applicants required to submit FAFSA. Total annual research expenditures: $4.5 million. *Unit head:* Susan Bell, Co-Chairperson, 813-974-6210, Fax: 813-974-2876, E-mail: sbell@cas.usf.edu. *Application contact:* James Garey, Graduate Advisor, 813-974-8434, Fax: 813-974-3263, E-mail: grarey@cas.usf.edu.

University of South Florida, Graduate School, College of Medicine and Graduate School, Graduate Programs in Medical Sciences, Tampa, FL 33620-9951. Offers MS, MSMS, PhD. *Students:* 314 full-time (171 women), 90 part-time (53 women); includes 173 minority (61 Black or African American, non-Hispanic/Latino; 1 American Indian or Alaska Native, non-Hispanic/Latino; 58 Asian, non-Hispanic/Latino; 46 Hispanic/Latino; 1 Native Hawaiian or other Pacific Islander, non-Hispanic/Latino; 6 Two or more races, non-Hispanic/Latino), 17 international. Average age 29. 627 applicants, 44% accepted, 202 enrolled. In 2010, 191 master's, 17 doctorates awarded. Terminal master's awarded for partial completion of doctoral program. *Degree requirements:* For master's, comprehensive exam, thesis; for doctorate, comprehensive exam, thesis/dissertation. *Entrance requirements:* For doctorate, GRE General Test, minimum GPA of 3.0 in last 60 hours of coursework. Additional exam requirements/recommendations for international students: Required—TOEFL (minimum score 550 paper-based; 213 computer-based). *Application deadline:* For fall admission, 2/15 for domestic students, 1/2 for international students. Application fee: $30. *Expenses:* Contact institution. *Financial support:* Application deadline: 4/1. *Unit head:* Michael Barber, Program Director, 813-974-9702, Fax: 813-974-4317, E-mail: mbarber@health.usf.edu. *Application contact:* Michael Barber, Program Director, 813-974-9702, Fax: 813-974-4317, E-mail: mbarber@health.usf.edu.

The University of Tennessee, Graduate School, College of Arts and Sciences, Program in Life Sciences, Knoxville, TN 37996. Offers genome science and technology (MS, PhD); plant physiology and genetics (MS, PhD). *Degree requirements:* For doctorate, one foreign language, thesis/dissertation. *Entrance requirements:* For master's and doctorate, GRE General Test, minimum GPA of 2.7. Additional exam requirements/recommendations for international students: Required—TOEFL. Electronic applications accepted. *Expenses:* Tuition, state resident: full-time $7440; part-time $414 per credit hour. Tuition, nonresident: full-time $22,478; part-time $1250 per credit hour. Required fees: $922; $43 per credit hour. Tuition and fees vary according to program.

The University of Tennessee, Graduate School, Intercollegiate Programs, Program in Comparative and Experimental Medicine, Knoxville, TN 37996. Offers MS, PhD. *Degree requirements:* For master's, thesis; for doctorate, thesis/dissertation. *Entrance requirements:* For master's and doctorate, GRE General Test, minimum GPA of 2.7. Additional exam requirements/recommendations for international students: Required—TOEFL. Electronic applications accepted. *Expenses:* Tuition, state resident: full-time $7440; part-time $414 per credit hour. Tuition, nonresident: full-time $22,478; part-time $1250 per credit hour. Required fees: $922; $43 per credit hour. Tuition and fees vary according to program.

The University of Tennessee–Oak Ridge National Laboratory Graduate School of Genome Science and Technology, Graduate Program, Oak Ridge, TN 37830-8026. Offers life sciences (MS, PhD). *Degree requirements:* For master's, thesis; for doctorate, comprehensive exam, thesis/dissertation. *Entrance requirements:* For master's and doctorate, GRE General Test. Additional exam requirements/recommendations for international students: Required—TOEFL (minimum score 550 paper-based; 213 computer-based). Electronic applications accepted. *Faculty research:* Genetics/genomics, structural biology/proteomics, computational biology/bioinformatics, bioanalytical technologies.

The University of Texas at Arlington, Graduate School, College of Science, Department of Biology, Arlington, TX 76019. Offers biology (MS); quantitative biology (PhD). Part-time and evening/weekend programs available. *Faculty:* 24 full-time (6 women), 1 part-time/adjunct (0 women). *Students:* 66 full-time (32 women), 19 part-time (12 women); includes 17 minority (3 Black or African American, non-Hispanic/Latino; 8 Asian, non-Hispanic/Latino; 5 Hispanic/Latino; 1 Two or more races, non-Hispanic/Latino), 21 international. Average age 25. 57 applicants, 46% accepted, 21 enrolled. In 2010, 24 master's, 7 doctorates awarded. *Degree requirements:* For master's, thesis, oral defense of thesis; for doctorate, comprehensive exam, thesis/dissertation, oral defense of dissertation. *Entrance requirements:* For master's and doctorate, GRE General Test. Additional exam requirements/recommendations for international students: Required—TOEFL (minimum score 550 paper-based; 213 computer-based; 79 iBT). *Application deadline:* For fall admission, 6/15 for domestic students, 4/3 for international students; for spring admission, 10/15 for domestic students, 9/11 for international students. Applications are processed on a rolling basis. Application fee: $35 ($50 for international students). Electronic applications accepted. *Expenses:* Tuition, state resident: full-time $7500. Tuition, nonresident: full-time $13,080. International tuition: $13,250 full-time. *Financial support:* In 2010–11, 52 students received support, including 4 fellowships (averaging $1,000 per year), 4 research assistantships (averaging $15,500 per year), 26 teaching assistantships (averaging $15,500 per year); Federal Work-Study and institutionally sponsored loans also available. Financial award application deadline: 6/1; financial award applicants required to submit FAFSA. *Faculty research:* Cellular and microbiology, comparative genomics, evolution and ecology. Total annual research expenditures: $1.9 million. *Unit head:* Dr. Johnathan Campbell, Chair, 817-272-2871, Fax: 817-272-2855, E-mail: campbell@exchange.uta.edu. *Application contact:* Dr. Laura Gough, Graduate Adviser, 817-272-2871, Fax: 817-272-2855, E-mail: gough@uta.edu.

The University of Texas at Austin, Graduate School, College of Natural Sciences, School of Biological Sciences, Austin, TX 78712-1111. Offers MA, PhD. *Entrance requirements:* For master's and doctorate, GRE General Test. Electronic applications accepted.

The University of Texas at Brownsville, Graduate Studies, College of Science, Mathematics and Technology, Brownsville, TX 78520-4991. Offers biological sciences (MS, MSIS); mathematics (MS); physics (MS). Part-time and evening/weekend programs available. *Degree requirements:* For master's, comprehensive exam, thesis optional. *Entrance requirements:* For master's, GRE General Test. Additional exam requirements/recommendations for international students: Required—TOEFL. *Faculty research:* Fish, insects, barrier islands, algae, curlits.

The University of Texas at Dallas, School of Natural Sciences and Mathematics, Program in Biology, Richardson, TX 75080. Offers bioinformatics and computational biology (MS); biotechnology (MS); molecular and cell biology (MS, PhD). Part-time and evening/weekend programs available. *Faculty:* 18 full-time (3 women), 1 part-time/adjunct (0 women). *Students:* 109 full-time (61 women), 19 part-time (7 women); includes 22 minority (5 Black or African American, non-Hispanic/Latino; 14 Asian, non-Hispanic/Latino; 3 Hispanic/Latino), 82 international. Average age 26. 331 applicants, 37% accepted, 38 enrolled. In 2010, 36 master's, 5 doctorates awarded. *Degree requirements:* For master's, thesis optional; for doctorate, thesis/dissertation, publishable paper. *Entrance requirements:* For master's and doctorate, GRE (minimum combined score of 1000 on verbal and quantitative). Additional exam requirements/recommendations for international students: Required—TOEFL (minimum score 550 paper-based; 215 computer-based; 80 iBT). *Application deadline:* For fall admission, 7/15 for domestic students, 5/1 priority date for international students; for spring admission, 11/15 for domestic students, 9/1 priority date for international students. Applications are processed on a rolling basis. Application fee: $50 ($100 for international students). Electronic applications accepted. *Expenses:* Tuition, state resident: full-time $10,248; part-time $569 per credit hour. Tuition, nonresident: full-time $18,544; part-time $1030 per credit hour. Tuition and fees vary according to course load. *Financial support:* In 2010–11, 58 students received support, including 19 research assistantships with partial tuition reimbursements available (averaging $13,403 per year), 32 teaching assistantships with partial tuition reimbursements available (averaging $14,513 per year); career-related internships or fieldwork, Federal Work-Study, institutionally sponsored loans, scholarships/grants, and unspecified assistantships also available. Support available to part-time students. Financial award application deadline: 4/30; financial award applicants required to submit FAFSA. *Faculty research:* Role of mitochondria in neurodegenerative diseases, protein-DNA interactions in site-specific recombination, eukaryotic gene expression, bio-nanotechnology, sickle cell research. *Unit head:* Dr. Li Zhang, Department Head, 972-883-6032, Fax: 972-883-2502, E-mail: li.zhang@utdallas.edu. *Application contact:* Dr. Lawrence Reitzer, Graduate Advisor, 972-883-2502, Fax: 972-883-2402, E-mail: reitzer@utdallas.edu.

The University of Texas at El Paso, Graduate School, College of Science, Department of Biological Sciences, El Paso, TX 79968-0001. Offers bioinformatics (MS); biological sciences (MS, PhD). Part-time and evening/weekend programs available. *Students:* 71 (32 women); includes 4 Black or African American, non-Hispanic/Latino; 4 Asian, non-Hispanic/Latino; 31 Hispanic/Latino, 17 international. Average age 34. In 2010, 16 master's, 4 doctorates awarded. *Degree requirements:* For master's, thesis; for doctorate, thesis/dissertation. *Entrance requirements:* For master's, GRE, minimum GPA of 3.0, letters of recommendation; for doctorate, GRE, statement of purpose, letters of recommendation. Additional exam requirements/recommendations for international students: Required—TOEFL; Recommended—IELTS. *Application deadline:* For fall admission, 8/1 priority date for domestic students, 3/1 for international students; for spring admission, 11/1 priority date for domestic students, 9/1 for international students. Applications are processed on a rolling basis. Application fee: $45 ($80 for international students). Electronic applications accepted. *Financial support:* In 2010–11, research assistantships with partial tuition reimbursements (averaging $22,500 per year), teaching assistantships with partial tuition reimbursements (averaging $18,000 per year) were awarded; fellowships with partial tuition reimbursements, institutionally sponsored loans, scholarships/grants, health care benefits, tuition waivers (partial), and unspecified assistantships also available. Support available to part-time students. Financial award application deadline: 3/15; financial award applicants required to submit FAFSA. *Unit head:* Dr. Robert Kirken, Chair, 915-747-5844, Fax: 915-747-5808, E-mail: rkirken@utep.edu. *Application contact:* Dr. Patricia D. Witherspoon, Dean of Graduate School, 915-747-5491, Fax: 915-747-5788, E-mail: withersp@utep.edu.

The University of Texas at San Antonio, College of Sciences, Department of Biology, San Antonio, TX 78249-0617. Offers biology (MS, PhD); biotechnology (MS); neurobiology (PhD). Part-time programs available. *Faculty:* 36 full-time (3 women), 7 part-time/adjunct (3 women). *Students:* 143 full-time (76 women), 65 part-time (37 women); includes 73 minority (10 Black or African American, non-Hispanic/Latino; 10 Asian, non-Hispanic/Latino; 40 Hispanic/Latino; 13 Two or more races, non-Hispanic/Latino), 73 international. Average age 27. 252 applicants, 50% accepted, 69 enrolled. In 2010, 42 master's, 17 doctorates awarded. *Degree requirements:* For master's, comprehensive exam, thesis; for doctorate, comprehensive exam, thesis/dissertation. *Entrance requirements:* For master's, GRE General Test, minimum GPA of 3.0; for doctorate, GRE General Test, minimum GPA of 3.3. Additional exam requirements/recommendations for international students: Required—TOEFL (minimum score 500 paper-based; 173 computer-based; 61 iBT), IELTS (minimum score 5). *Application deadline:* For fall admission, 7/1 for domestic students, 4/1 for international students; for spring admission, 11/1 for domestic students, 9/1 for international students. Applications are processed on a rolling basis. Application fee: $45 ($80 for international students). Electronic applications accepted. *Expenses:* Tuition, state resident: full-time $4172; part-time $231.75 per credit hour. Tuition, nonresident: full-time $15,332; part-time $851.75 per credit hour. *Financial support:* In 2010–11, 66 students received support, including 25 fellowships (averaging $24,632 per year), 162 research assistantships (averaging $19,317 per year), 73 teaching assistantships (averaging $10,841 per year); career-related internships or fieldwork, scholarships/grants, and unspecified assistantships also available. Support available to part-time students. *Faculty research:* Cell and molecular biology, neurobiology, microbiology, integrative biology, environmental science. Total annual research expenditures: $1.7 million. *Unit head:* Dr. Edwin J. Barea-Rodriguez, Interim Chair, 210-458-4511, Fax: 210-458-5658, E-mail: edwin.barea@utsa.edu. *Application contact:* Veronica Ramirez, Assistant Dean of the Graduate School, 210-458-4330, Fax: 210-458-4332, E-mail: graduatestudies@utsa.edu.

See Display on next page and Close-Up on page 115.

The University of Texas at Tyler, College of Arts and Sciences, Department of Biology, Tyler, TX 75799-0001. Offers biology (MS); interdisciplinary studies (MSIS). *Degree requirements:* For master's, comprehensive exam, thesis, oral qualifying exam, thesis defense. *Entrance requirements:* For master's, GRE General Test, GRE Subject Test, bachelor's degree in biology or equivalent. Additional exam requirements/recommendations for international students: Required—TOEFL (minimum score 79 computer-based). Electronic applications accepted. *Faculty research:* Phenotypic plasticity and heritability of life history traits, invertebrate ecology and genetics, systematics and phylogenetics of reptiles, hibernation physiology in turtles, landscape ecology, host-microbe interaction, outer membrane proteins in bacteria.

The University of Texas Health Science Center at Houston, Graduate School of Biomedical Sciences, Houston, TX 77225-0036. Offers MS, PhD, MD/PhD. Terminal master's awarded for partial completion of doctoral program. *Degree requirements:* For master's, thesis; for doctorate, thesis/dissertation. *Entrance requirements:* For master's and doctorate, GRE General Test. Additional exam requirements/recommendations for international students: Required—TOEFL. Electronic applications accepted. *Faculty research:* Biomedical sciences.

The University of Texas Health Science Center at San Antonio, Graduate School of Biomedical Sciences, San Antonio, TX 78229-3900. Offers MS, MSN, PhD. *Faculty:* 203 full-time (77 women), 44 part-time/adjunct (13 women). *Students:* 368 full-time (197 women), 243 part-time (180 women); includes 27 Black or African American, non-Hispanic/Latino; 4 American Indian or Alaska Native, non-Hispanic/Latino; 41 Asian, non-Hispanic/Latino; 120 Hispanic/Latino, 144 international. Average age 33. 661 applicants, 30% accepted, 148 enrolled. In 2010, 39 master's, 39 doctorates awarded. *Degree requirements:* For master's, comprehensive exam (for some programs), thesis; for doctorate, comprehensive exam, thesis/dissertation.

Entrance requirements: For master's and doctorate, GRE General Test. Additional exam requirements/recommendations for international students: Required—TOEFL (minimum score 560 paper-based; 220 computer-based; 68 iBT). *Application deadline:* For fall admission, 1/15 priority date for domestic and international students; for spring admission, 10/1 for domestic and international students. Applications are processed on a rolling basis. Application fee: $0. Electronic applications accepted. *Expenses:* Contact institution. *Financial support:* In 2010–11, 24 fellowships (averaging $26,000 per year), 240 teaching assistantships (averaging $26,000 per year) were awarded; career-related internships or fieldwork, institutionally sponsored loans, scholarships/grants, and health care benefits also available. Financial award application deadline: 6/30; financial award applicants required to submit FAFSA. *Faculty research:* Biochemistry, cellular and structural biology, molecular medicine, microbiology and immunology, pathology, pharmacology, physiology, neuroscience, aging, cancer, genetics. Total annual research expenditures: $50.6 million. *Unit head:* Dr. David S. Weiss, Interim Dean, 210-567-3709, Fax: 210-567-3719, E-mail: weissd@uthscsa.edu. *Application contact:* Dr. Nicquet Blake, Assistant Dean for Graduate Student Recruitment, 210-567-3709, Fax: 210-567-3719, E-mail: blaken@uthscsa.edu.

The University of Texas Medical Branch, Graduate School of Biomedical Sciences, Galveston, TX 77555. Offers MA, MMS, MPH, MS, PhD, MD/PhD. Terminal master's awarded for partial completion of doctoral program. *Degree requirements:* For master's, comprehensive exam (for some programs), thesis or alternative; for doctorate, comprehensive exam, thesis/dissertation. *Entrance requirements:* For master's and doctorate, GRE General Test, 3 letters of recommendation. Additional exam requirements/recommendations for international students: Required—TOEFL (minimum score 550 paper-based; 213 computer-based; 80 iBT), IELTS (minimum score 6.5). Electronic applications accepted. *Expenses:* Contact institution.

The University of Texas of the Permian Basin, Office of Graduate Studies, College of Arts and Sciences, Department of Biology, Odessa, TX 79762-0001. Offers MS. Part-time and evening/weekend programs available. *Degree requirements:* For master's, comprehensive exam, thesis or alternative. *Entrance requirements:* For master's, GRE General Test. Additional exam requirements/recommendations for international students: Required—TOEFL (minimum score 550 paper-based; 213 computer-based).

The University of Texas–Pan American, College of Science and Engineering, Department of Biology, Edinburg, TX 78539. Offers MS. Part-time and evening/weekend programs available. *Degree requirements:* For master's, comprehensive exam. *Entrance requirements:* For master's, GRE General Test, minimum GPA of 2.75 in biology. *Faculty research:* Flora and fauna of South Padre Island, plant taxonomy of Rio Grande Valley.

The University of Texas Southwestern Medical Center at Dallas, Southwestern Graduate School of Biomedical Sciences, Division of Basic Science, Dallas, TX 75390. Offers biological chemistry (PhD); biomedical engineering (MS, PhD); cancer biology (PhD); cell regulation (PhD); genetics and development (PhD); immunology (PhD); integrative biology (PhD); molecular biophysics (PhD); molecular microbiology (PhD); neuroscience (PhD); MD/PhD. *Faculty:* 278 full-time (70 women), 10 part-time/adjunct (0 women). *Students:* 405 full-time (183 women), 22 part-time (4 women); includes 101 minority (12 Black or African American, non-Hispanic/Latino; 8 American Indian or Alaska Native, non-Hispanic/Latino; 45 Asian, non-Hispanic/Latino; 36 Hispanic/Latino), 138 international. Average age 26. 1,229 applicants, 9% accepted, 88 enrolled. In 2010, 3 master's, 50 doctorates awarded. *Degree requirements:* For doctorate, thesis/dissertation, qualifying exam. *Entrance requirements:* For doctorate, GRE General Test, research experience. Additional exam requirements/recommendations for international students: Required—TOEFL. *Application deadline:* For fall admission, 12/15 priority date for domestic and international students. Application fee: $0. Electronic applications accepted. *Financial support:* Fellowships, research assistantships, institutionally sponsored loans and traineeships available. *Unit head:* Dr. Nancy E. Street, Associate Dean, 214-648-6708, Fax: 214-648-2102, E-mail: nancy.street@utsouthwestern.edu. *Application contact:* Dr. Nancy E. Street, Associate Dean, 214-648-6708, Fax: 214-648-2102, E-mail: nancy.street@utsouthwestern.edu.

The University of Texas Southwestern Medical Center at Dallas, Southwestern Graduate School of Biomedical Sciences, Division of Clinical Science, Clinical Science Program, Dallas, TX 75390. Offers MCS, MSCS. Part-time programs available. *Students:* 1 full-time (0 women), 65 part-time (28 women); includes 24 minority (1 Black or African American, non-Hispanic/Latino; 1 American Indian or Alaska Native, non-Hispanic/Latino; 6 Hispanic/Latino; 1 Two or more races, non-Hispanic/Latino), 5 international. Average age 26. 16 applicants, 88% accepted, 14 enrolled. In 2010, 10 master's awarded. *Degree requirements:* For master's, 1 year clinical research project. *Entrance requirements:* For master's, graduate degree in biomedical science. *Application deadline:* For fall admission, 7/15 for domestic students; for spring admission, 12/15 for domestic students. Applications are processed on a rolling basis. Electronic applications accepted. *Unit head:* Dr. Milton Packer, Chair, 214-648-0491, Fax: 214-648-6417, E-mail: milton.packer@utsouthwestern.edu. *Application contact:* Dena Wheaton, Program Coordinator, 214-648-2410, Fax: 214-648-3978, E-mail: dena.wheaton@utsouthwestern.edu.

The University of Texas Southwestern Medical Center at Dallas, Southwestern Graduate School of Biomedical Sciences, Medical Scientist Training Program, Dallas, TX 75390. Offers PhD, MD/PhD. *Application deadline:* For fall admission, 11/1 for domestic students. Application fee: $0. Electronic applications accepted. *Financial support:* Application deadline: 3/1. *Unit head:* Dr. Andrew Zinn, Associate Dean, 214-648-2057, Fax: 214-648-2814, E-mail: dennis.mckearin@utsouthwestern.edu. *Application contact:* Robin Downing, Education Coordinator, 214-648-6764, Fax: 214-648-2814, E-mail: robin.downing@utsouthwestern.edu.

University of the Incarnate Word, School of Graduate Studies and Research, School of Mathematics, Science, and Engineering, Program in Biology, San Antonio, TX 78209-6397. Offers MA, MS. Part-time and evening/weekend programs available. *Faculty:* 5 full-time (3 women), 1 (woman) part-time/adjunct. *Students:* 3 full-time (2 women), 8 part-time (5 women); includes 4 Hispanic/Latino, 1 international. Average age 27. In 2010, 7 master's awarded. *Degree requirements:* For master's, comprehensive exam (for MA); thesis defense (for MS). *Entrance requirements:* For master's, GRE Subject Test (biology), minimum GPA of 3.0 in biology or GRE (minimum combined score 1,000 Verbal and Quantitative), 8 hours principles of chemistry, 6 hours organic chemistry, 12 upper-division hours in biology. Additional exam requirements/recommendations for international students: Required—TOEFL (minimum score 560 paper-based; 220 computer-based; 83 iBT). *Application deadline:* Applications are processed on a rolling basis. Application fee: $20. Electronic applications accepted. *Expenses:* Tuition: Part-time $725 per contact hour. Required fees: $890 per semester. *Financial support:* Federal Work-Study and scholarships/grants available. Financial award applicants required to submit FAFSA. *Faculty research:* Regeneration of nervous system elements, social behaviors of electric fish, gene expression in human cells, transmission of pathogenic protozoa, human DNA response to cancer fighting molecules. Total annual research expenditures: $91,351. *Unit head:* Dr. David Foglesong, 210-283-5033, Fax: 210-829-3153, E-mail: davidf@uiwtx.edu. *Application contact:* Andrea Cyterski-Acosta, Dean of Enrollment, 210-829-6005, Fax: 210-829-3921, E-mail: admis@uiwtx.edu.

University of the Pacific, College of the Pacific, Department of Biological Sciences, Stockton, CA 95211-0197. Offers MS. *Faculty:* 16 full-time (6 women), 2 part-time/adjunct (1 woman). *Students:* 1 (woman) full-time, 25 part-time (12 women); includes 2 Black or African American, non-Hispanic/Latino; 10 Asian, non-Hispanic/Latino, 1 international. Average age 24. 23 applicants, 52% accepted, 10 enrolled. In 2010, 8 master's awarded. *Degree requirements:* For master's, thesis. *Entrance requirements:* For master's, GRE General Test, GRE Subject Test. Additional exam requirements/recommendations for international students: Required—TOEFL. *Application deadline:* For fall admission, 3/1 priority date for domestic students; for spring admission, 10/1 priority date for domestic students. Applications are processed on a rolling basis. Application fee: $75. *Financial support:* In 2010–11, 22 teaching assistantships were awarded; institutionally sponsored loans also available. Support available to part-time students. Financial award application deadline: 3/1; financial award applicants required to submit FAFSA. *Unit head:* Dr. Gregg Jongeward, Chairman, 209-946-2181. *Application contact:* Information Contact, 209-946-2261.

Biological and Biomedical Sciences—General

The University of Toledo, College of Graduate Studies, College of Natural Sciences and Mathematics, Department of Biological Sciences, Toledo, OH 43606-3390. Offers cell biology (MS, PhD); ecology (MS, PhD). Part-time programs available. *Faculty:* 19. *Students:* 64 full-time (31 women), 23 part-time (5 women); includes 5 minority (2 Black or African American, non-Hispanic/Latino; 2 Asian, non-Hispanic/Latino; 1 Hispanic/Latino), 29 international. Average age 28. 110 applicants, 16% accepted, 16 enrolled. In 2010, 10 master's, 9 doctorates awarded. *Degree requirements:* For master's, thesis or alternative; for doctorate, thesis/dissertation. *Entrance requirements:* For master's and doctorate, GRE General Test, GRE Subject Test, minimum cumulative point-hour ratio of 2.7 for all previous academic work, three letters of recommendation, statement of purpose, transcripts from all prior institutions attended. Additional exam requirements/recommendations for international students: Required—TOEFL (minimum score 550 paper-based; 213 computer-based; 80 iBT), IELTS (minimum score 6.5). *Application deadline:* For fall admission, 1/15 priority date for domestic and international students. Applications are processed on a rolling basis. Application fee: $45 ($75 for international students). Electronic applications accepted. *Expenses:* Tuition, state resident: full-time $11,426; part-time $476 per credit hour. Tuition, nonresident: full-time $21,660; part-time $903 per credit hour. One-time fee: $62. *Financial support:* Fellowships, research assistantships with full tuition reimbursements, teaching assistantships with full tuition reimbursements, Federal Work-Study, scholarships/grants, tuition waivers (full), and unspecified assistantships available. Support available to part-time students. *Faculty research:* Biochemical parasitology, physiological ecology, animal physiology. *Unit head:* Dr. Doug Leaman, Chair, 419-530-1555, E-mail: douglas.leaman@utoledo.edu. *Application contact:* Graduate School Office, 419-530-4723, Fax: 419-530-4724, E-mail: grdsch@utnet.utoledo.edu.

University of Toronto, School of Graduate Studies, Life Sciences Division, Toronto, ON M5S 1A1, Canada. Offers M Sc, M Sc BMC, M Sc F, MA, MFC, MH Sc, MN, PhD, MD/PhD. Part-time programs available. *Degree requirements:* For doctorate, thesis/dissertation.

University of Tulsa, Graduate School, College of Arts and Sciences, School of Education, Program in Teaching Arts, Tulsa, OK 74104-3189. Offers art (MTA); biology (MTA); English (MTA); history (MTA); mathematics (MTA); theatre (MTA). Part-time programs available. *Students:* 2 part-time (both women); includes 1 minority (American Indian or Alaska Native, non-Hispanic/Latino). Average age 31. 1 applicant, 0% accepted, 0 enrolled. In 2010, 2 master's awarded. *Entrance requirements:* For master's, GRE General Test. Additional exam requirements/recommendations for international students: Required—TOEFL (minimum score 575 paper-based; 231 computer-based), IELTS (minimum score 6.5). *Application deadline:* Applications are processed on a rolling basis. Application fee: $40. Electronic applications accepted. *Expenses:* Tuition: Full-time $16,902; part-time $939 per credit hour. Required fees: $1020; $4 per credit hour. Tuition and fees vary according to course load. *Financial support:* In 2010–11, 2 students received support, including 2 fellowships with full and partial tuition reimbursements available (averaging $2,191 per year); research assistantships with full and partial tuition reimbursements available, teaching assistantships with full and partial tuition reimbursements available, Federal Work-Study, scholarships/grants, and tuition waivers (full and partial) also available. Support available to part-time students. Financial award application deadline: 2/1; financial award applicants required to submit FAFSA. *Unit head:* Dr. David Brown, Advisor, 918-631-2719, Fax: 918-631-2133, E-mail: david-brown@utulsa.edu. *Application contact:* Dr. David Brown, Advisor, 918-631-2719, Fax: 918-631-2133, E-mail: david-brown@utulsa.edu.

University of Tulsa, Graduate School, College of Engineering and Natural Sciences, Department of Biological Sciences, Tulsa, OK 74104-3189. Offers MS, MTA, PhD, JD/MS. Part-time programs available. *Faculty:* 14 full-time (3 women). *Students:* 15 full-time (6 women), 4 part-time (3 women); includes 2 minority (1 American Indian or Alaska Native, non-Hispanic/Latino; 1 Asian, non-Hispanic/Latino), 6 international. Average age 29. 19 applicants, 26% accepted, 2 enrolled. In 2010, 5 master's, 1 doctorate awarded. Terminal master's awarded for partial completion of doctoral program. *Degree requirements:* For master's, thesis, oral exams; for doctorate, comprehensive exam, thesis/dissertation. *Entrance requirements:* For master's and doctorate, GRE General Test. Additional exam requirements/recommendations for international students: Required—TOEFL (minimum score 550 paper-based; 213 computer-based; 80 iBT), IELTS (minimum score 6). *Application deadline:* Applications are processed on a rolling basis. Application fee: $40. Electronic applications accepted. *Expenses:* Tuition: Full-time $16,902; part-time $939 per credit hour. Required fees: $1020; $4 per credit hour. Tuition and fees vary according to course load. *Financial support:* In 2010–11, 19 students received support, including 12 fellowships with full and partial tuition reimbursements available (averaging $2,699 per year), 4 research assistantships with full and partial tuition reimbursements available (averaging $10,518 per year), 14 teaching assistantships with full and partial tuition reimbursements available (averaging $10,358 per year); career-related internships or fieldwork, Federal Work-Study, scholarships/grants, health care benefits, tuition waivers (full and partial), and unspecified assistantships also available. Support available to part-time students. Financial award application deadline: 2/1; financial award applicants required to submit FAFSA. *Faculty research:* Aerobiology, animal behavior and behavioral ecology, cell and molecular biology, ecology, developmental biology, genetics, herpetology, glycobiology, immunology, microbiology, morphology, mycology, ornithology, molecular systematic and virology. Total annual research expenditures: $3.3 million. *Unit head:* Dr. Estelle Levetin, Chairperson, 918-631-2764, Fax: 918-631-2762, E-mail: estelle-levetin@utulsa.edu. *Application contact:* Dr. Harrington Wells, Advisor, 918-631-3071, Fax: 918-631-2762, E-mail: harrington-wells@utulsa.edu.

University of Utah, Graduate School, College of Science, Department of Biology, Salt Lake City, UT 84112. Offers MS, PhD. Part-time programs available. *Faculty:* 44 full-time (9 women), 1 part-time/adjunct (0 women). *Students:* 50 full-time (20 women), 16 part-time (7 women); includes 5 minority (4 Asian, non-Hispanic/Latino; 1 Hispanic/Latino), 15 international. Average age 29. 70 applicants, 24% accepted, 8 enrolled. In 2010, 5 master's, 8 doctorates awarded. Terminal master's awarded for partial completion of doctoral program. *Degree requirements:* For master's, comprehensive exam, thesis; for doctorate, comprehensive exam, thesis/dissertation. *Entrance requirements:* For master's and doctorate, GRE General Test, minimum GPA of 3.0. Additional exam requirements/recommendations for international students: Required—TOEFL (minimum score 500 paper-based; 173 computer-based; 61 iBT). *Application deadline:* For fall admission, 1/7 for domestic and international students. Application fee: $55 ($65 for international students). *Expenses:* Tuition, area resident: Part-time $179.19 per credit hour. Tuition, state resident: full-time $4384. Tuition, nonresident: full-time $16,684; part-time $630.67 per credit hour. Required fees: $350 per semester. Tuition and fees vary according to course load, degree level and program. *Financial support:* In 2010–11, 69 students received support, including 14 fellowships with full tuition reimbursements available (averaging $25,000 per year), 25 research assistantships with full tuition reimbursements available (averaging $25,000 per year), 30 teaching assistantships with full tuition reimbursements available (averaging $16,500 per year); career-related internships or fieldwork, scholarships/grants, traineeships, and health care benefits also available. Financial award application deadline: 3/15; financial award applicants required to submit FAFSA. *Faculty research:* Ecology, evolutionary biology, cell and developmental biology, physiology and organismal biology, molecular biology, biochemistry, microbiology, plant biology, neurobiology, genetics. Total annual research expenditures: $12.8 million. *Unit head:* Dr. Neil J. Vickers, Chair, 801-585-0622, Fax: 801-585-1930, E-mail: vickers@biology.utah.edu. *Application contact:* Shannon Nielsen, Administrative Program Coordinator, 801-581-5636, Fax: 801-581-4668, E-mail: shannon.nielsen@bioscience.utah.edu.

University of Utah, School of Medicine and Graduate School, Graduate Programs in Medicine, Salt Lake City, UT 84112-1107. Offers M Phil, M Stat, MPAS, MPH, MS, MSPH, PhD, Certificate. Part-time programs available. *Degree requirements:* For doctorate, thesis/dissertation. *Entrance requirements:* For doctorate, MCAT. Electronic applications accepted. *Expenses:* Tuition, area resident: Part-time $179.19 per credit hour. Tuition, state resident: full-time $4384. Tuition, nonresident: full-time $16,684; part-time $630.67 per credit hour. Required fees: $350 per semester. Tuition and fees vary according to course load, degree level and program. *Faculty research:* Molecular biology, biochemistry, cell biology, immunology, bioengineering.

University of Vermont, College of Medicine and Graduate College, Graduate Programs in Medicine, Burlington, VT 05405. Offers biochemistry (MS, PhD); clinical and translational science (MS, PhD); microbiology and molecular genetics (MS, PhD); molecular physiology and biophysics (MS, PhD); neuroscience (PhD); pathology (MS); pharmacology (MS, PhD); MD/MS; MD/PhD. *Students:* 91 (50 women); includes 2 Asian, non-Hispanic/Latino; 6 Hispanic/Latino, 18 international. 159 applicants, 28% accepted, 21 enrolled. In 2010, 3 master's, 4 doctorates awarded. *Degree requirements:* For master's, thesis; for doctorate, thesis/dissertation. *Entrance requirements:* For master's and doctorate, GRE General Test. Additional exam requirements/recommendations for international students: Required—TOEFL (minimum score 550 paper-based; 213 computer-based; 80 iBT). *Application deadline:* For fall admission, 4/1 priority date for domestic students. Applications are processed on a rolling basis. Application fee: $40. Electronic applications accepted. *Expenses:* Tuition, state resident: part-time $537 per credit hour. Tuition, nonresident: part-time $1355 per credit hour. *Financial support:* Fellowships, research assistantships, teaching assistantships, traineeships and analytical assistantships available. Financial award application deadline: 3/1. *Unit head:* Dr. Frederick C. Morin, Dean, 802-656-2156. *Application contact:* Dr. Frederick C. Morin, Dean, 802-656-2156.

University of Vermont, Graduate College, College of Arts and Sciences, Department of Biology, Burlington, VT 05405. Offers biology (MS, PhD); biology education (MST). *Faculty:* 17. *Students:* 32 (14 women); includes 1 Black or African American, non-Hispanic/Latino; 4 Hispanic/Latino, 10 international. 36 applicants, 33% accepted, 7 enrolled. In 2010, 3 master's, 5 doctorates awarded. *Degree requirements:* For master's, thesis; for doctorate, thesis/dissertation. *Entrance requirements:* For master's and doctorate, GRE General Test. Additional exam requirements/recommendations for international students: Required—TOEFL (minimum score 550 paper-based; 213 computer-based; 80 iBT). *Application deadline:* For fall admission, 1/15 priority date for domestic students. Applications are processed on a rolling basis. Application fee: $40. Electronic applications accepted. *Expenses:* Tuition, state resident: part-time $537 per credit hour. Tuition, nonresident: part-time $1355 per credit hour. *Financial support:* Fellowships, research assistantships, teaching assistantships available. Financial award application deadline: 3/1. *Unit head:* Dr. Jim Vigoreaux, Chairperson, 802-656-2922. *Application contact:* Dr. Judith Van Houten, Coordinator, 802-656-2922.

University of Victoria, Faculty of Graduate Studies, Faculty of Science, Department of Biology, Victoria, BC V8W 2Y2, Canada. Offers M Sc, PhD. *Degree requirements:* For master's, thesis, seminar; for doctorate, thesis/dissertation, seminar, candidacy exam. *Entrance requirements:* For master's and doctorate, GRE General Test, minimum B+ average in previous 2 years of biology course work. Additional exam requirements/recommendations for international students: Required—TOEFL (minimum score 575 paper-based; 233 computer-based), IELTS (minimum score 7). Electronic applications accepted. *Faculty research:* Neurobiology of vertebrates and invertebrates, physiology, reproduction and tissue culture of forest trees, evolution and ecology, cell and molecular biology, molecular biology of environmental health.

University of Virginia, College and Graduate School of Arts and Sciences, Department of Biology, Charlottesville, VA 22903. Offers MA, MS, PhD. *Faculty:* 34 full-time (5 women), 2 part-time/adjunct (0 women). *Students:* 55 full-time (37 women); includes 1 Black or African American, non-Hispanic/Latino; 4 Asian, non-Hispanic/Latino; 2 Hispanic/Latino, 17 international. Average age 27. 93 applicants, 18% accepted, 12 enrolled. In 2010, 2 master's, 6 doctorates awarded. *Degree requirements:* For master's, thesis; for doctorate, thesis/dissertation. *Entrance requirements:* For master's and doctorate, GRE General Test, GRE Subject Test (recommended), 2 letters of recommendation. Additional exam requirements/recommendations for international students: Required—TOEFL (minimum score 600 paper-based; 250 computer-based; 90 iBT), IELTS (minimum score 7). *Application deadline:* For fall admission, 12/21 for domestic and international students. Applications are processed on a rolling basis. Application fee: $60. Electronic applications accepted. *Financial support:* Fellowships, research assistantships, teaching assistantships available. Financial award applicants required to submit FAFSA. *Faculty research:* Ecology and evolution, neurobiology and behavior, molecular genetics, cell, development. *Unit head:* Douglas Taylor, Chair, 434-982-5474, Fax: 434-982-5626, E-mail: drt3b@virginia.edu. *Application contact:* Rita Webb, Graduate Student Program Coordinator, 434-982-5474, Fax: 434-982-5626, E-mail: rea2d@virginia.edu.

University of Virginia, School of Medicine, Department of Molecular Physiology and Biological Physics, Program in Biological and Physical Sciences, Charlottesville, VA 22903. Offers MS. *Students:* 1 full-time (0 women). Average age 25. In 2010, 21 master's awarded. *Entrance requirements:* For master's, GRE General Test. Additional exam requirements/recommendations for international students: Required—TOEFL. *Application deadline:* Applications are processed on a rolling basis. Application fee: $60. Electronic applications accepted. *Financial support:* Applicants required to submit FAFSA. *Unit head:* Dr. Mark Yeager, Chair, 434-924-5108, Fax: 434-982-1616, E-mail: my3r@virginia.edu. *Application contact:* Dr. Mark Yeager, Chair, 434-924-5108, Fax: 434-982-1616, E-mail: my3r@virginia.edu.

University of Washington, Graduate School, College of Arts and Sciences, Department of Biology, Seattle, WA 98195. Offers PhD.

University of Washington, Graduate School, School of Medicine, Graduate Programs in Medicine, Seattle, WA 98195. Offers MA, MOT, MS, DPT, PhD. Part-time programs available. *Degree requirements:* For doctorate, thesis/dissertation. *Entrance requirements:* For doctorate, GRE. Electronic applications accepted. *Expenses:* Contact institution.

University of Waterloo, Graduate Studies, Faculty of Science, Department of Biology, Waterloo, ON N2L 3G1, Canada. Offers M Sc, PhD. Part-time programs available. *Degree requirements:* For master's, thesis, seminar, proposal; for doctorate, comprehensive exam, thesis/dissertation, seminar, proposal. *Entrance requirements:* For master's, honor's degree; for doctorate, master's degree. Additional exam requirements/recommendations for international students: Required—TOEFL (minimum score 580 paper-based; 237 computer-based; 90 iBT), TWE (minimum score 4). Electronic applications accepted. *Faculty research:* Biosystematics, ecology and limnology, molecular and cellular biology, biochemistry, physiology.

University of West Florida, College of Arts and Sciences: Sciences, School of Allied Health and Life Sciences, Department of Biology, Pensacola, FL 32514-5750. Offers biological chemistry (MS); biology (MS); biology education (MST); biotechnology (MS); coastal zone studies (MS); environmental biology (MS). *Faculty:* 10 full-time (2 women). *Students:* 6 full-time (4 women), 32 part-time (18 women); includes 1 Black or African American, non-Hispanic/Latino; 1 Asian, non-Hispanic/Latino; 1 Hispanic/Latino, 1 international. Average age 28. 17 applicants, 53% accepted, 7 enrolled. In 2010, 3 master's awarded. *Degree requirements:* For master's, thesis. *Entrance requirements:* For master's, GRE General Test. Additional exam requirements/recommendations for international students: Required—TOEFL (minimum score 550 paper-based; 213 computer-based). *Application deadline:* For fall admission, 6/1 for domestic students, 5/15 for international students; for spring admission, 10/1 for domestic and international students. Applications are processed on a rolling basis. Application fee: $30. *Expenses:* Tuition, state resident: full-time $4982; part-time $208 per credit hour. Tuition, nonresident: full-time $20,059; part-time $836 per credit hour. Required fees: $1365; $57 per credit hour. *Financial support:* In 2010–11, 20 fellowships with partial tuition reimbursements (averaging $523 per year), 18 research assistantships with partial tuition reimbursements (averaging $5,700 per year), 12 teaching assistantships with partial tuition reimbursements (averaging $8,042 per year) were awarded; unspecified assistantships also available. Financial award application deadline: 4/15; financial award applicants required to submit FAFSA. *Unit head:* Dr. George L. Stewart, Chairperson, 850-474-2748. *Application contact:* Terry McCray, Assistant Director of Graduate Admissions, 850-473-7718, Fax: 850-473-7714, E-mail: gradadmissions@uwf.edu.

University of West Georgia, College of Arts and Sciences, Department of Biology, Carrollton, GA 30118. Offers MS. Part-time programs available. *Faculty:* 9 full-time (2 women). *Students:* 19 full-time (9 women), 3 part-time (1 woman); includes 2 Black or African American, non-

Hispanic/Latino, 1 international. Average age 26. 17 applicants, 59% accepted, 4 enrolled. In 2010, 10 master's awarded. *Degree requirements:* For master's, comprehensive exam (for some programs), thesis (for some programs). *Entrance requirements:* For master's, GRE General Test, minimum GPA of 2.5, undergraduate degree in biology. Additional exam requirements/recommendations for international students: Required—TOEFL. *Application deadline:* For fall admission, 7/17 for domestic students; for spring admission, 11/20 for domestic students. Applications are processed on a rolling basis. Application fee: $30. Electronic applications accepted. *Expenses:* Tuition, state resident: full-time $4130; part-time $173 per semester hour. Tuition, nonresident: full-time $16,524; part-time $689 per semester hour. Required fees: $1586; $44.01 per semester hour. $397 per semester. Tuition and fees vary according to program. *Financial support:* In 2010–11, 8 teaching assistantships with full tuition reimbursements (averaging $8,000 per year) were awarded; career-related internships or fieldwork, scholarships/grants, and unspecified assistantships also available. Financial award application deadline: 7/1; financial award applicants required to submit FAFSA. *Faculty research:* Molecular systematics, animal physiology, marine ecology, plant ecology. Total annual research expenditures: $200,000. *Unit head:* Dr. Henry G. Zot, Chair, 678-839-6547, Fax: 678-839-6548, E-mail: hzot@westga.edu. *Application contact:* Dr. Charles W. Clark, Dean, 678-839-6508, E-mail: cclark@westga.edu.

University of Windsor, Faculty of Graduate Studies, Faculty of Science, Department of Biological Sciences, Windsor, ON N9B 3P4, Canada. Offers M Sc, PhD. Part-time programs available. *Degree requirements:* For master's, thesis; for doctorate, comprehensive exam, thesis/dissertation. *Entrance requirements:* For master's and doctorate, minimum B average. Additional exam requirements/recommendations for international students: Required—TOEFL (minimum score 560 paper-based; 220 computer-based). Electronic applications accepted. *Faculty research:* Great Lakes Institute: aquatic ecotoxicology, regulation and development of the olfactory system, mating system evolution, signal transduction, aquatic ecology.

University of Wisconsin–La Crosse, Office of University Graduate Studies, College of Science and Health, Department of Biology, La Crosse, WI 54601-3742. Offers aquatic sciences (MS); biology (MS); cellular and molecular biology (MS); clinical microbiology (MS); microbiology (MS); nurse anesthesia (MS); physiology (MS). Part-time programs available. *Faculty:* 31. *Students:* 23 full-time (14 women), 42 part-time (25 women); includes 4 minority (1 Asian, non-Hispanic/Latino; 3 Hispanic/Latino), 1 international. Average age 28. 100 applicants, 34% accepted, 29 enrolled. In 2010, 20 master's awarded. *Degree requirements:* For master's, comprehensive exam, thesis. *Entrance requirements:* For master's, GRE General Test, minimum GPA of 2.85. Additional exam requirements/recommendations for international students: Required—TOEFL (minimum score 550 paper-based; 213 computer-based; 79 iBT). *Application deadline:* For fall admission, 2/1 priority date for domestic and international students; for spring admission, 1/4 priority date for domestic and international students. Applications are processed on a rolling basis. Application fee: $56. Electronic applications accepted. *Expenses:* Tuition, state resident: full-time $7121; part-time $395.61 per credit. Tuition, nonresident: full-time $16,891; part-time $938.41 per credit. Part-time tuition and fees vary according to course load, program and reciprocity agreements. *Financial support:* In 2010–11, 14 research assistantships with partial tuition reimbursements (averaging $10,124 per year) were awarded; Federal Work-Study, scholarships/grants, health care benefits, and tuition waivers (partial) also available. Support available to part-time students. Financial award application deadline: 3/15; financial award applicants required to submit FAFSA. *Unit head:* Dr. Thomas Volk, Coordinator of Graduate Studies, 608-785-6972, Fax: 608-785-6959, E-mail: volk.thom@uwlax.edu. *Application contact:* Kathryn Kiefer, Director of Admissions, 608-785-8939, E-mail: admissions@uwlax.edu.

University of Wisconsin–Madison, School of Medicine and Public Health and Graduate School, Graduate Programs in Medicine, Madison, WI 53705. Offers biomolecular chemistry (MS, PhD); cancer biology (PhD); genetics and medical genetics (MS, PhD), including genetics (PhD), medical genetics (MS); medical physics (MS, PhD), including health physics (MS), medical physics; microbiology (PhD); molecular and cellular pharmacology (PhD); pathology and laboratory medicine (PhD); physiology (PhD); population health sciences (MPH, MS, PhD), including clinical research (MS, PhD), epidemiology (MS, PhD), health services research (MS, PhD), population health sciences (MPH), social and behavioral health sciences (MS, PhD); DPT/MPH; DVM/MPH; MD/MPH; MD/PhD; MPA/MPH; MS/MPH; Pharm D/MPH. Part-time programs available. Postbaccalaureate distance learning degree programs offered (minimal on-campus study). Terminal master's awarded for partial completion of doctoral program. Application fee: $45. Electronic applications accepted. *Expenses:* Contact institution. *Financial support:* Fellowships with full tuition reimbursements, research assistantships with full tuition reimbursements, teaching assistantships with full tuition reimbursements, scholarships/grants, traineeships, and tuition waivers (full) available. *Unit head:* Dr. Richard L. Moss, Senior Associate Dean for Basic Research, Biotechnology and Graduate Studies, 608-265-0523, Fax: 608-265-0522, E-mail: rlmoss@wisc.edu. *Application contact:* Information Contact, 608-262-2433, Fax: 608-262-5134, E-mail: gradadmiss@mail.bascom.wisc.edu.

University of Wisconsin–Madison, School of Medicine and Public Health, Medical Scientist Training Program, Madison, WI 53705-2221. Offers MD/PhD. *Accreditation:* LCME/AMA. *Faculty:* 380 full-time (80 women). *Students:* 76 full-time (29 women); includes 6 Black or African American, non-Hispanic/Latino; 1 American Indian or Alaska Native, non-Hispanic/Latino; 16 Asian, non-Hispanic/Latino; 1 Hispanic/Latino. 222 applicants, 13% accepted, 12 enrolled. *Application deadline:* For fall admission, 12/1 for domestic students. Applications are processed on a rolling basis. Application fee: $54. Electronic applications accepted. *Expenses:* Tuition, state resident: full-time $9887; part-time $617.96 per credit. Tuition, nonresident: full-time $24,054; part-time $1503.40 per credit. Required fees: $67.63 per credit. Tuition and fees vary according to reciprocity agreements. *Financial support:* In 2010–11, fellowships with full tuition reimbursements (averaging $24,000 per year), research assistantships with full tuition reimbursements (averaging $24,000 per year) were awarded; traineeships and health care benefits also available. *Unit head:* Dr. Deane Mosher, Director, 608-262-1576, Fax: 608-263-4969, E-mail: dfmosher@wisc.edu. *Application contact:* Paul Cook, Program Administrator, 608-262-6321, Fax: 608-262-4226, E-mail: pscook@wisc.edu.

University of Wisconsin–Milwaukee, Graduate School, College of Health Sciences, PhD Program in Health Sciences, Milwaukee, WI 53201-0413. Offers PhD. *Students:* 13 full-time (6 women), 7 part-time (4 women), 3 international. Average age 35. 11 applicants, 55% accepted. *Degree requirements:* For doctorate, comprehensive exam, thesis/dissertation. *Entrance requirements:* For doctorate, GRE. Additional exam requirements/recommendations for international students: Required—TOEFL (minimum score 600 paper-based; 250 computer-based), IELTS (minimum score 6.5). Application fee: $56 ($96 for international students). *Financial support:* In 2010–11, 4 fellowships, 5 research assistantships, 3 teaching assistantships were awarded; project assistantships also available. *Unit head:* Paula M. Rhyner, Representative, 414-229-4878, E-mail: prhyner@uwm.edu. *Application contact:* General Information Contact, 414-229-4982, Fax: 414-229-6967, E-mail: gradschool@uwm.edu.

University of Wisconsin–Milwaukee, Graduate School, College of Health Sciences, Program in Biomedical Sciences, Milwaukee, WI 53211. Offers MS. *Accreditation:* NAACLS. Part-time programs available. *Faculty:* 7 full-time (3 women). *Students:* 10 full-time (8 women), 5 part-time (all women); includes 1 Black or African American, non-Hispanic/Latino, 3 international. Average age 28. 18 applicants, 39% accepted, 3 enrolled. *Degree requirements:* For master's, thesis. *Entrance requirements:* For master's, GRE General Test. Additional exam requirements/recommendations for international students: Required—TOEFL (minimum score 550 paper-based; 79 iBT), IELTS (minimum score 6.5). *Application deadline:* For fall admission, 1/1 priority date for domestic students; for spring admission, 9/1 for domestic students. Applications are processed on a rolling basis. Application fee: $56 ($96 for international students). *Financial support:* In 2010–11, 6 teaching assistantships were awarded; fellowships, research assistantships, career-related internships or fieldwork and unspecified assistantships also available. Support available to part-time students. Financial award application deadline: 4/15. Total annual research expenditures: $222,238. *Unit head:* Janis Eells, Representative, 414-229-4505, E-mail: jeels@uwm.edu. *Application contact:* Janis Eells, Representative, 414-229-4505, E-mail: jeels@uwm.edu.

University of Wisconsin–Milwaukee, Graduate School, College of Letters and Sciences, Department of Biological Sciences, Milwaukee, WI 53201-0413. Offers MS, PhD. *Faculty:* 39 full-time (10 women). *Students:* 51 full-time (25 women), 34 part-time (23 women); includes 2 Black or African American, non-Hispanic/Latino; 2 American Indian or Alaska Native, non-Hispanic/Latino; 5 Asian, non-Hispanic/Latino; 1 Hispanic/Latino, 24 international. Average age 30. 114 applicants, 28% accepted, 11 enrolled. In 2010, 7 master's, 4 doctorates awarded. *Degree requirements:* For master's, thesis; for doctorate, thesis/dissertation, 1 foreign language or data analysis proficiency. *Entrance requirements:* For master's and doctorate, GRE General Test. Additional exam requirements/recommendations for international students: Required—TOEFL (minimum score 550 paper-based; 79 iBT), IELTS (minimum score 6.5). *Application deadline:* For fall admission, 3/1 priority date for domestic students. Applications are processed on a rolling basis. Application fee: $56 ($96 for international students). *Financial support:* In 2010–11, 3 fellowships, 9 research assistantships, 67 teaching assistantships were awarded; career-related internships or fieldwork, unspecified assistantships, and project assistantships also available. Support available to part-time students. Financial award application deadline: 4/15; financial award applicants required to submit FAFSA. Total annual research expenditures: $2.2 million. *Unit head:* Jane L. Witten, Representative, 414-229-4993, E-mail: jlw@uwm.edu. *Application contact:* General Information Contact, 414-229-4982, Fax: 414-229-6967, E-mail: gradschool@uwm.edu.

University of Wisconsin–Oshkosh, The Office of Graduate Studies, College of Letters and Science, Department of Biology and Microbiology, Oshkosh, WI 54901. Offers biology (MS), including botany, microbiology, zoology. *Degree requirements:* For master's, comprehensive exam, thesis. *Entrance requirements:* For master's, GRE General Test, minimum GPA of 3.0, BS in biology. Additional exam requirements/recommendations for international students: Required—TOEFL (minimum score 550 paper-based; 213 computer-based; 79 iBT). Electronic applications accepted.

Utah State University, School of Graduate Studies, College of Science, Department of Biology, Logan, UT 84322. Offers biology (MS, PhD); ecology (MS, PhD). Part-time programs available. *Degree requirements:* For master's, thesis; for doctorate, thesis/dissertation. *Entrance requirements:* For master's and doctorate, GRE General Test, minimum GPA of 3.0. Additional exam requirements/recommendations for international students: Required—TOEFL (minimum score 575 paper-based). *Faculty research:* Plant, insect, microbial, and animal biology.

Vanderbilt University, Graduate School, Department of Biological Sciences, Nashville, TN 37240-1001. Offers MS, PhD, MD/PhD. *Faculty:* 26 full-time (3 women), 1 (woman) part-time/adjunct. *Students:* 58 full-time (27 women); includes 11 minority (5 Black or African American, non-Hispanic/Latino; 2 Asian, non-Hispanic/Latino; 4 Hispanic/Latino). Average age 27. 118 applicants, 7% accepted, 7 enrolled. In 2010, 11 degrees awarded. Terminal master's awarded for partial completion of doctoral program. *Degree requirements:* For master's, thesis; for doctorate, thesis/dissertation, final and qualifying exams. *Entrance requirements:* For master's and doctorate, GRE General Test. Additional exam requirements/recommendations for international students: Required—TOEFL (minimum score 570 paper-based; 230 computer-based; 88 iBT). *Application deadline:* For fall admission, 1/15 for domestic and international students. Application fee: $0. Electronic applications accepted. *Financial support:* Fellowships with full and partial tuition reimbursements, research assistantships with full tuition reimbursements, teaching assistantships with full tuition reimbursements, Federal Work-Study, institutionally sponsored loans, scholarships/grants, traineeships, and health care benefits available. Financial award application deadline: 1/15; financial award applicants required to submit CSS PROFILE or FAFSA. *Faculty research:* Protein structure and function, protein transport, membrane ion channels and receptors, signal transduction, posttranscriptional control of gene expression, DNA replication and recombination, biological clocks, development, neurobiology, vector biology, insect physiology, ecology and evolution, bioinformatics. *Unit head:* Dr. Charles Singleton, Chair, 615-936-3651, E-mail: charles.k.singleton@vanderbilt.edu. *Application contact:* Dr. Katherine Friedman, Director of Graduate Studies, 615-322-5143, E-mail: katherine.friedman@vanderbilt.edu.

Vanderbilt University, School of Medicine and Graduate School, Medical Scientist Training Program, Nashville, TN 37240-1001. Offers MD/PhD. *Application deadline:* For fall admission, 11/15 for domestic and international students. Applications are processed on a rolling basis. Application fee: $50. Electronic applications accepted. *Expenses:* Contact institution. *Financial support:* Fellowships with full tuition reimbursements, traineeships, health care benefits, and tuition waivers (full) available. *Faculty research:* Cancer biology, neurosciences, microbiology, biochemistry, metabolism/diabetics. *Unit head:* Dr. Terence S. Dermody, Director, 615-343-9943. *Application contact:* Dr. Michelle Grundy, Assistant Director, 800-373-0675, E-mail: michelle.grundy@vanderbilt.edu.

Villanova University, Graduate School of Liberal Arts and Sciences, Department of Biology, Villanova, PA 19085-1699. Offers MA, MS. Part-time and evening/weekend programs available. *Faculty:* 11 full-time (2 women). *Students:* 41 full-time (23 women), 18 part-time (9 women); includes 6 minority (2 Black or African American, non-Hispanic/Latino; 1 Asian, non-Hispanic/Latino; 3 Hispanic/Latino), 5 international. Average age 27. 27 applicants, 78% accepted, 13 enrolled. In 2010, 23 master's awarded. *Degree requirements:* For master's, comprehensive exam (for some programs), thesis (for some programs). *Entrance requirements:* For master's, GRE General Test, GRE Subject Test, minimum GPA of 3.0. Additional exam requirements/recommendations for international students: Required—TOEFL. *Application deadline:* For fall admission, 2/1 priority date for domestic and international students; for spring admission, 10/15 priority date for domestic students, 11/15 priority date for international students. Applications are processed on a rolling basis. Application fee: $50. Electronic applications accepted. *Expenses:* Contact institution. *Financial support:* Research assistantships with tuition reimbursements, teaching assistantships with tuition reimbursements, Federal Work-Study, scholarships/grants, and unspecified assistantships available. Support available to part-time students. Financial award applicants required to submit FAFSA. *Unit head:* Dr. Russell Gardner, Chair, 610-519-4830. *Application contact:* Dr. Adele Lindenmeyr, Dean, Graduate School of Liberal Arts and Sciences, 610-519-7093, Fax: 610-519-7096.

Virginia Commonwealth University, Graduate School, College of Humanities and Sciences, Department of Biology, Richmond, VA 23284-9005. Offers MS. Part-time programs available. *Students:* 27 full-time (15 women), 10 part-time (5 women); includes 2 Asian, non-Hispanic/Latino, 3 international. 41 applicants, 39% accepted, 13 enrolled. In 2010, 17 master's awarded. *Degree requirements:* For master's, thesis. *Entrance requirements:* For master's, GRE General Test, BS in biology or related field. Additional exam requirements/recommendations for international students: Required—Either TOEFL (minimum score: paper-based 600, computer-based 250) or IELTS (6.5). *Application deadline:* For fall admission, 1/15 for domestic students; for spring admission, 11/15 for domestic students. Applications are processed on a rolling basis. Application fee: $50. *Expenses:* Tuition, state resident: full-time $4308; part-time $479 per credit hour. Tuition, nonresident: full-time $8942; part-time $994 per credit hour. Required fees: $2000; $85 per credit hour. Tuition and fees vary according to course level, course load, degree level, campus/location and program. *Financial support:* Fellowships, research assistantships, teaching assistantships, Federal Work-Study, institutionally sponsored loans, and tuition waivers (full and partial) available. Support available to part-time students. Financial award applicants required to submit FAFSA. *Faculty research:* Molecular and cellular biology, terrestrial and aquatic ecology, systematics, physiology and developmental biology. *Unit head:* Dr. Donald R. Young, Chair, 804-828-1562, E-mail: dyoung@vcu.edu. *Application contact:* Dr. Jennifer K. Stewart, Graduate Program Director, 804-828-1562, Fax: 804-828-0503, E-mail: jstewart@vcu.edu.

Virginia Commonwealth University, Graduate School, School of Life Sciences, Richmond, VA 23284-9005. Offers M Env Sc, MB, MS, PhD. *Students:* 61 full-time (32 women), 43 part-time (19 women); includes 15 minority (9 Black or African American, non-Hispanic/Latino;

Biological and Biomedical Sciences—General

Virginia Commonwealth University (continued)

1 American Indian or Alaska Native, non-Hispanic/Latino; 3 Asian, non-Hispanic/Latino; 1 Hispanic/Latino; 1 Two or more races, non-Hispanic/Latino), 14 international. 91 applicants, 55% accepted, 28 enrolled. In 2010, 18 master's, 3 doctorates awarded. *Entrance requirements:* For master's and doctorate, GRE. Additional exam requirements/recommendations for international students: Required—TOEFL (minimum score 600 paper-based; 250 computer-based; 100 iBT). Application fee: $50. Electronic applications accepted. *Expenses:* Tuition, state resident: full-time $4308; part-time $479 per credit hour. Tuition, nonresident: full-time $8942; part-time $994 per credit hour. Required fees: $2000; $85 per credit hour. Tuition and fees vary according to course level, course load, degree level, campus/location and program. *Financial support:* Applicants required to submit FAFSA. *Unit head:* Dr. Thomas F. Huff, Vice Provost, 804-827-5600. *Application contact:* Dr. Greg Garman, Director, Center for Environmental Studies, 804-828-1574, E-mail: ggarman@vcu.edu.

Virginia Commonwealth University, Program in Pre-Medical Basic Health Sciences, Richmond, VA 23284-9005. Offers anatomy (CBHS); biochemistry (CBHS); human genetics (CBHS); microbiology (CBHS); pharmacology (CBHS); physiology (CBHS). *Students:* 86 full-time (43 women), 2 part-time (1 woman); includes 42 minority (5 Black or African American, non-Hispanic/Latino; 29 Asian, non-Hispanic/Latino; 5 Hispanic/Latino; 3 Two or more races, non-Hispanic/Latino). 314 applicants, 64% accepted. In 2010, 70 CBHSs awarded. *Entrance requirements:* For degree, GRE, MCAT or DAT, course work in organic chemistry, minimum undergraduate GPA of 2.8. Additional exam requirements/recommendations for international students: Required—TOEFL (minimum score 600 paper-based). *Application deadline:* For fall admission, 6/1 for domestic students. Application fee: $50. Electronic applications accepted. *Expenses:* Tuition, state resident: full-time $4308; part-time $479 per credit hour. Tuition, nonresident: full-time $8942; part-time $994 per credit hour. Required fees: $2000; $85 per credit hour. Tuition and fees vary according to course level, course load, degree level, campus/location and program. *Unit head:* Dr. Louis J. De Felice, Director, 804-828-9501, E-mail: premedcert@vcu.edu. *Application contact:* Zack McDowell, Administrator, 804-828-9501, E-mail: premedcert@vcu.edu.

Virginia Polytechnic Institute and State University, Graduate School, College of Science, Department of Biological Sciences, Blacksburg, VA 24061. Offers MS, PhD. *Faculty:* 39 full-time (11 women). *Students:* 73 full-time (40 women); includes 1 Black or African American, non-Hispanic/Latino; 1 Asian, non-Hispanic/Latino; 6 Hispanic/Latino, 28 international. Average age 28. 104 applicants, 16% accepted, 12 enrolled. In 2010, 5 master's, 10 doctorates awarded. *Degree requirements:* For master's, comprehensive exam (for some programs), thesis (for some programs); for doctorate, comprehensive exam (for some programs), thesis/dissertation (for some programs). *Entrance requirements:* For master's and doctorate, GRE. Additional exam requirements/recommendations for international students: Required—TOEFL (minimum score 550 paper-based; 213 computer-based). *Application deadline:* For fall admission, 7/1 for domestic and international students; for spring admission, 12/1 for domestic and international students. Applications are processed on a rolling basis. Application fee: $65. Electronic applications accepted. *Expenses:* Tuition, state resident: full-time $9399; part-time $488 per credit hour. Tuition, nonresident: full-time $17,854; part-time $957.75 per credit hour. Required fees: $1534. Full-time tuition and fees vary according to program. *Financial support:* In 2010–11, 35 research assistantships with full tuition reimbursements (averaging $18,397 per year), 39 teaching assistantships with full tuition reimbursements (averaging $16,644 per year) were awarded; career-related internships or fieldwork, Federal Work-Study, scholarships/grants, health care benefits, and unspecified assistantships also available. Financial award application deadline: 1/15. *Faculty research:* Freshwater ecology, cell cycle regulation, behavioral ecology, motor proteins. Total annual research expenditures: $4.7 million. *Unit head:* Dr. Brenda S. Winkel, UNIT HEAD, 540-231-9514, Fax: 540-231-9307, E-mail: winkel@vt.edu. *Application contact:* Ernest Benfield, Contact, 540-231-5802, Fax: 540-231-9307, E-mail: enilsen@vt.edu.

Virginia State University, School of Graduate Studies, Research, and Outreach, School of Engineering, Science and Technology, Department of Biology, Petersburg, VA 23806-0001. Offers MS. *Degree requirements:* For master's, one foreign language, thesis. *Entrance requirements:* For master's, GRE General Test. *Expenses:* Tuition, state resident: full-time $5576; part-time $335 per credit hour. Tuition, nonresident: full-time $13,402; part-time $670 per credit hour. *Faculty research:* Schwann cell cultures, selection of apios as an alternative crop, systematic botany, flowers of three species of wild ginger.

Wagner College, Division of Graduate Studies, Department of Biological Sciences, Staten Island, NY 10301-4495. Offers advanced physician assistant studies (MS); microbiology (MS). Part-time and evening/weekend programs available. *Faculty:* 8 full-time (4 women), 13 part-time/adjunct (8 women). *Students:* 35 full-time (29 women), 3 part-time (0 women); includes 10 minority (2 Black or African American, non-Hispanic/Latino; 4 Asian, non-Hispanic/Latino; 4 Hispanic/Latino). Average age 27. 36 applicants, 97% accepted, 31 enrolled. In 2010, 25 master's awarded. *Degree requirements:* For master's, comprehensive exam or thesis. *Entrance requirements:* For master's, GRE, MCAT, minimum GPA of 2.5, proficiency in statistics, undergraduate major in science; completion of ARC-PA accredited physician assistant program with minimum GPA of 3.0 (for advanced physician assistant studies). Additional exam requirements/recommendations for international students: Required—TOEFL. *Application deadline:* For fall admission, 5/1 priority date for domestic students, 3/1 priority date for international students; for spring admission, 12/1 for domestic students, 10/1 priority date for international students. Applications are processed on a rolling basis. Application fee: $50 ($85 for international students). *Expenses:* Tuition: Full-time $15,570; part-time $865 per credit. *Financial support:* Federal Work-Study, tuition waivers, unspecified assistantships, and alumni fellowship grant available. Financial award applicants required to submit FAFSA. *Unit head:* Dr. Brian Palestis, Chair, 718-390-3197, E-mail: bpalesti@wagner.edu. *Application contact:* Patricia Clancy, Assistant Coordinator of Graduate Studies, 718-420-4464, E-mail: patricia.clancy@wagner.edu.

Wake Forest University, Graduate School of Arts and Sciences, Department of Biology, Winston-Salem, NC 27109. Offers MS, PhD. Part-time programs available. *Degree requirements:* For master's, one foreign language, thesis; for doctorate, 2 foreign languages, comprehensive exam, thesis/dissertation. *Entrance requirements:* For master's and doctorate, GRE General Test. Additional exam requirements/recommendations for international students: Required—TOEFL (minimum score 213 computer-based; 79 iBT). Electronic applications accepted. *Faculty research:* Cell biology, ecology, parasitology, immunology.

Wake Forest University, School of Medicine and Graduate School of Arts and Sciences, Graduate Programs in Medicine, Winston-Salem, NC 27109. Offers MS, PhD, MD/PhD. *Degree requirements:* For master's, thesis; for doctorate, thesis/dissertation. *Entrance requirements:* For master's and doctorate, GRE General Test. Additional exam requirements/recommendations for international students: Required—TOEFL. Electronic applications accepted. *Expenses:* Contact institution. *Faculty research:* Atherosclerosis, cardiovascular physiology, pharmacology, neuroanatomy, endocrinology.

Walla Walla University, Graduate School, Department of Biological Sciences, College Place, WA 99324-1198. Offers biology (MS). *Faculty:* 5 full-time (1 woman), 1 part-time/adjunct (0 women). *Students:* 10 full-time (5 women); includes 1 American Indian or Alaska Native, non-Hispanic/Latino; 1 Asian, non-Hispanic/Latino. Average age 24. 9 applicants, 78% accepted, 6 enrolled. In 2010, 3 master's awarded. *Degree requirements:* For master's, thesis. *Entrance requirements:* For master's, GRE General Test, GRE Subject Test, minimum GPA of 2.75. Additional exam requirements/recommendations for international students: Required—TOEFL (minimum score 550 paper-based; 213 computer-based; 79 iBT). *Application deadline:* Applications are processed on a rolling basis. Application fee: $50. Electronic applications accepted. *Financial support:* In 2010–11, 9 teaching assistantships with full tuition reimbursements (averaging $5,250 per year) were awarded; Federal Work-Study also available. Financial award application deadline: 4/1; financial award applicants required to submit FAFSA. *Faculty research:* Marine biology, plant development, neurobiology, animal physiology, behavior. *Unit head:* Dr. Robert A. Cushman, Chair, 509-527-2603, E-mail: bob.cushman@wallawalla.edu. *Application contact:* Dr. Joan Redd, Director of Graduate Program, 509-527-2482, E-mail: joan.redd@wallawalla.edu.

Washington State University, Graduate School, College of Sciences, School of Biological Sciences, Program in Biology, Pullman, WA 99164. Offers MS. *Faculty:* 33. *Students:* 2 full-time (1 woman), 1 (woman) part-time. 51 applicants, 8% accepted, 2 enrolled. *Degree requirements:* For master's, comprehensive exam (for some programs), thesis. *Entrance requirements:* For master's, GRE, three letters of recommendation, official transcripts from each university-level school attended. Additional exam requirements/recommendations for international students: Required—TOEFL, IELTS. *Application deadline:* For fall admission, 1/10 for domestic and international students; for spring admission, 7/1 for domestic and international students. Application fee: $50. *Expenses:* Tuition, state resident: full-time $8552; part-time $443 per credit. Tuition, nonresident: full-time $21,650; part-time $1083 per credit. Required fees: $846. *Financial support:* In 2010–11, 1 research assistantship with tuition reimbursement (averaging $13,917 per year), 1 teaching assistantship with tuition reimbursement (averaging $13,056 per year) were awarded. Financial award application deadline: 2/15. *Faculty research:* Inter-intra-cellular signaling in plant reproduction, biodiversity. *Unit head:* Dr. Gary Thorgaard, Director, 509-335-7438, Fax: 509-335-3184, E-mail: thorglab@wsu.edu. *Application contact:* Graduate School Admissions, 800-GRADWSU, Fax: 509-335-1949, E-mail: gradsch@wsu.edu.

Washington State University Tri-Cities, Graduate Programs, Program in Biology, Richland, WA 99354. Offers MS. *Faculty:* 17. *Students:* 1 (woman) part-time. *Degree requirements:* For master's, comprehensive exam (for some programs), thesis (for some programs), special project. *Entrance requirements:* For master's, GRE, minimum GPA of 3.0, 3 letters of recommendation. Additional exam requirements/recommendations for international students: Required—TOEFL. *Application deadline:* For fall admission, 1/10 priority date for domestic students, 1/10 for international students; for spring admission, 7/1 priority date for domestic students, 7/1 for international students. Application fee: $50. *Financial support:* Application deadline: 4/1. *Unit head:* Dr. Kate McAteer, Director, 509-372-7371, E-mail: kmcateer@tricity.wsu.edu. *Application contact:* Bonnie Bates, Academic Coordinator, 509-372-7171, Fax: 509-335-1949, E-mail: bbates@tricity.wsu.edu.

Washington University in St. Louis, Graduate School of Arts and Sciences, Division of Biology and Biomedical Sciences, St. Louis, MO 63130-4899. Offers biochemistry (PhD); chemical biology (PhD); computational biology (PhD); developmental biology (PhD); evolution, ecology and population biology (PhD), including ecology, environmental biology, evolutionary biology, genetics; immunology (PhD); molecular biophysics (PhD); molecular cell biology (PhD); molecular genetics (PhD); molecular microbiology and microbial pathogenesis (PhD); neurosciences (PhD); plant biology (PhD); MD/PhD. *Degree requirements:* For doctorate, thesis/dissertation. *Entrance requirements:* For doctorate, GRE General Test, GRE Subject Test. Electronic applications accepted.

Wayne State University, College of Liberal Arts and Sciences, Department of Biological Sciences, Detroit, MI 48202. Offers biological sciences (MA, MS, PhD); molecular biotechnology (MS). *Faculty:* 13 full-time (2 women). *Students:* 81 full-time (49 women), 9 part-time (7 women); includes 8 minority (2 Black or African American, non-Hispanic/Latino; 4 Asian, non-Hispanic/Latino; 1 Hispanic/Latino; 1 Two or more races, non-Hispanic/Latino), 54 international. Average age 28. 200 applicants, 23% accepted, 26 enrolled. In 2010, 19 master's, 2 doctorates awarded. Terminal master's awarded for partial completion of doctoral program. *Degree requirements:* For master's, thesis (for some programs); for doctorate, thesis/dissertation. *Entrance requirements:* For master's, GRE General Test, minimum GPA of 3.0; for doctorate, GRE General Test, GRE Subject Test, minimum GPA of 3.2. Additional exam requirements/recommendations for international students: Required—TOEFL; Recommended—TWE (minimum score 6). *Application deadline:* For fall admission, 7/1 for domestic students, 6/1 for international students; for winter admission, 10/1 for international students; for spring admission, 2/1 for international students. Applications are processed on a rolling basis. Application fee: $30 ($50 for international students). Electronic applications accepted. *Expenses:* Tuition, state resident: full-time $7662; part-time $478.85 per credit hour. Tuition, nonresident: full-time $16,920; part-time $1057.55 per credit hour. Required fees: $571; $35.70 per credit hour. $188.05 per semester. Tuition and fees vary according to course load and program. *Financial support:* In 2010–11, 5 fellowships with tuition reimbursements (averaging $19,224 per year), 23 research assistantships with tuition reimbursements (averaging $18,674 per year), 44 teaching assistantships with tuition reimbursements (averaging $17,824 per year) were awarded; Federal Work-Study and institutionally sponsored loans also available. *Faculty research:* Cell and developmental biology, neurobiology, molecular biology and biotechnology, evolutionary biology, ecology. *Unit head:* James D. Tucker, Chair, 313-577-2783, Fax: 313-577-6891, E-mail: ao1754@wayne.edu. *Application contact:* John Lopes, Graduate Director, 313-993-7816, Fax: 313-577-6891, E-mail: jlopes@sun.science.wayne.edu.

Wesleyan University, Graduate Programs, Department of Biology, Middletown, CT 06459. Offers animal behavior (PhD); bioformatics/genomics (PhD); cell biology (PhD); developmental biology (PhD); evolution/ecology (PhD); genetics (PhD); neurobiology (PhD); population biology (PhD). *Faculty:* 12 full-time (4 women). *Students:* 20 full-time (12 women); includes 1 Black or African American, non-Hispanic/Latino; 3 Asian, non-Hispanic/Latino. Average age 26. 24 applicants, 29% accepted, 2 enrolled. *Degree requirements:* For doctorate, variable foreign language requirement, thesis/dissertation. *Entrance requirements:* For doctorate, GRE. Additional exam requirements/recommendations for international students: Required—TOEFL. *Application deadline:* For fall admission, 1/15 for domestic and international students. Applications are processed on a rolling basis. Application fee: $0. *Expenses:* Tuition: Full-time $43,404. Required fees: $830. *Financial support:* In 2010–11, 5 research assistantships with full tuition reimbursements, 16 teaching assistantships with full tuition reimbursements were awarded; stipends also available. Financial award application deadline: 4/15; financial award applicants required to submit FAFSA. *Faculty research:* Microbial population genetics, genetic basis of evolutionary adaptation, genetic regulation of differentiation and pattern formation in *drosophila*. *Unit head:* Dr. Sonia E. Sultan, Chair/Professor, 860-685-3493, E-mail: jnaegele@wesleyan.edu. *Application contact:* Marjorie Fitzgibbons, Information Contact, 860-685-2140, E-mail: mfitzgibbons@wesleyan.edu.

West Chester University of Pennsylvania, Office of Graduate Studies, College of Arts and Sciences, Department of Biology, West Chester, PA 19383. Offers biology (MS, Teaching Certificate); biology—thesis (MS). Part-time and evening/weekend programs available. *Students:* 13 full-time (7 women), 22 part-time (10 women); includes 7 minority (2 Black or African American, non-Hispanic/Latino; 2 Asian, non-Hispanic/Latino; 3 Hispanic/Latino). Average age 28. 42 applicants, 69% accepted, 11 enrolled. In 2010, 6 master's awarded. *Degree requirements:* For master's, comprehensive exam, thesis (for some programs). *Entrance requirements:* For master's, two letters of reference. Additional exam requirements/recommendations for international students: Required—TOEFL (minimum score 550 paper-based; 213 computer-based; 80 iBT). *Application deadline:* For fall admission, 4/15 priority date for domestic students, 3/15 for international students; for spring admission, 10/15 for domestic students, 9/1 for international students. Applications are processed on a rolling basis. Application fee: $35. Electronic applications accepted. *Expenses:* Tuition, state resident: full-time $6966; part-time $387 per credit. Tuition, nonresident: full-time $11,146; part-time $619 per credit. Required fees: $1614; $133.24 per credit. Part-time tuition and fees vary according to campus/location. *Financial support:* Unspecified assistantships available. Support available to part-time students. Financial award application deadline: 2/15; financial award applicants required to submit FAFSA. *Faculty research:* Medical microbiology, molecular genetics and physiology of living systems, mammalian biomechanics, invertebrate and vertebrate animal systems, aquatic and terrestrial ecology. *Unit head:* Dr. Jack Waber, Chair, 610-436-2319, E-mail: jwaber@wcupa.edu. *Application contact:* Dr. Sharon E. Bergan, Assistant Chair and Graduate Coordinator, 610-436-2457, E-mail: sbegan@wcupa.edu.

Western Carolina University, Graduate School, College of Arts and Sciences, Department of Biology, Cullowhee, NC 28723. Offers MS. Part-time and evening/weekend programs available. *Degree requirements:* For master's, thesis. *Entrance requirements:* For master's, GRE General Test, appropriate undergraduate degree, 3 letters of recommendation. Additional exam requirements/recommendations for international students: Required—TOEFL (minimum score 550 paper-based; 270 computer-based; 79 iBT). *Faculty research:* Pathogen interactions, gene expression, plant community ecology, restoration ecology, ornithology, herpetology.

Western Connecticut State University, Division of Graduate Studies and External Programs, School of Arts and Sciences, Department of Biological and Environmental Sciences, Danbury, CT 06810-6885. Offers MA. Part-time programs available. *Students:* 1 full-time (0 women), 8 part-time (7 women); includes 1 minority (Black or African American, non-Hispanic/Latino). Average age 34. In 2010, 10 master's awarded. *Degree requirements:* For master's, comprehensive exam or thesis, completion of program in 6 years. *Entrance requirements:* For master's, minimum GPA of 2.5. Additional exam requirements/recommendations for international students: Recommended—TOEFL (minimum score 550 paper-based; 213 computer-based; 79 iBT), IELTS (minimum score 6). *Application deadline:* For fall admission, 8/5 priority date for domestic students; for spring admission, 1/5 priority date for domestic students. Applications are processed on a rolling basis. Application fee: $50. *Expenses:* Tuition, state resident: full-time $5012; part-time $417 per credit hour. Tuition, nonresident: full-time $13,962; part-time $423 per credit hour. Required fees: $3886. Full-time tuition and fees vary according to course load, degree level and program. *Financial support:* Application deadline: 5/1. *Unit head:* Dr. Richard Halliburton, Graduate Coordinator, 203-837-8233, Fax: 203-837-8525, E-mail: halliburtonr@wcsu.edu. *Application contact:* Chris Shankle, Associate Director of Graduate Studies, 203-837-9005, Fax: 203-837-8326, E-mail: shanklec@wcsu.edu.

Western Illinois University, School of Graduate Studies, College of Arts and Sciences, Department of Biological Sciences, Macomb, IL 61455-1390. Offers biological sciences (MS); environmental geographic information systems (Certificate); zoo and aquarium studies (Certificate). Part-time programs available. *Students:* 64 full-time (41 women), 31 part-time (22 women); includes 10 minority (4 Black or African American, non-Hispanic/Latino; 1 Asian, non-Hispanic/Latino; 4 Hispanic/Latino; 1 Two or more races, non-Hispanic/Latino), 7 international. Average age 26. 60 applicants, 67% accepted. In 2010, 23 master's, 15 other advanced degrees awarded. *Degree requirements:* For master's, thesis or alternative. *Entrance requirements:* Additional exam requirements/recommendations for international students: Required—TOEFL (minimum score 550 paper-based; 213 computer-based; 80 iBT); Recommended—IELTS. *Application deadline:* Applications are processed on a rolling basis. Application fee: $30. Electronic applications accepted. *Expenses:* Tuition, state resident: full-time $6370; part-time $265.40 per credit hour. Tuition, nonresident: full-time $12,740; part-time $530.80 per credit hour. Required fees: $75.67 per credit hour. *Financial support:* In 2010–11, 28 students received support, including 10 research assistantships with full tuition reimbursements available (averaging $7,280 per year), 18 teaching assistantships with full tuition reimbursements available (averaging $8,400 per year). Financial award applicants required to submit FAFSA. *Unit head:* Dr. Michael Romano, Chairperson, 309-298-1546. *Application contact:* Evelyn Hoing, Assistant Director of Graduate Studies, 309-298-1806, Fax: 309-298-2345, E-mail: grad-office@wiu.edu.

Western Kentucky University, Graduate Studies, Ogden College of Science and Engineering, Department of Biology, Bowling Green, KY 42101. Offers MS. Postbaccalaureate distance learning degree programs offered. *Degree requirements:* For master's, comprehensive exam, thesis optional, research tool. *Entrance requirements:* For master's, GRE General Test, minimum GPA of 2.75. Additional exam requirements/recommendations for international students: Required—TOEFL (minimum score 555 paper-based; 213 computer-based; 79 iBT). *Faculty research:* Phytoremediation, culturing of salt water organisms, PCR-based standards, biological monitoring (water) bioremediation, genetic diversity.

Western Michigan University, Graduate College, College of Arts and Sciences, Department of Biological Sciences, Kalamazoo, MI 49008. Offers MS, PhD. *Degree requirements:* For master's, thesis, oral exam; for doctorate, thesis/dissertation, oral exam. *Entrance requirements:* For master's and doctorate, GRE General Test.

Western University of Health Sciences, Graduate College of Biomedical Sciences, Master of Science in Biomedical Sciences Program, Pomona, CA 91766-1854. Offers MS. *Faculty:* 4 full-time (1 woman). *Students:* 4 full-time (2 women); includes 3 minority (1 Black or African American, non-Hispanic/Latino; 1 Asian, non-Hispanic/Latino; 1 Hispanic/Latino). Average age 28. 10 applicants, 0% accepted, 0 enrolled. *Degree requirements:* For master's, comprehensive exam (for some programs), thesis. *Entrance requirements:* For master's, GRE, minimum overall GPA of 3.0; letters of recommendation; personal statement; resume; BS in pharmacy, chemistry, biology or related scientific area. Additional exam requirements/recommendations for international students: Required—TOEFL. *Application deadline:* For fall admission, 5/16 for domestic students. Application fee: $50. Electronic applications accepted. *Expenses:* Tuition: Full-time $41,530. *Unit head:* Dr. Steven J. Henriksen, Founding Dean, 909-469-5299, E-mail: shenriksen@westernu.edu. *Application contact:* Information Contact, 909-469-5335, Fax: 909-469-5570, E-mail: admissions@westernu.edu.

Western University of Health Sciences, Graduate College of Biomedical Sciences, Master of Science in Medical Sciences Program, Pomona, CA 91766-1854. Offers MS. *Students:* 24 full-time (14 women); includes 12 minority (3 Black or African American, non-Hispanic/Latino; 5 Asian, non-Hispanic/Latino; 2 Hispanic/Latino; 1 Native Hawaiian or other Pacific Islander, non-Hispanic/Latino; 1 Two or more races, non-Hispanic/Latino). Average age 26. 146 applicants, 20% accepted. *Degree requirements:* For master's, comprehensive exam (for some programs). *Entrance requirements:* For master's, GRE, MCAT, OAT, or DAT, minimum overall GPA of 2.5; letters of recommendation; personal statement; resume; transcripts; bachelor's degree. Additional exam requirements/recommendations for international students: Required—TOEFL. *Application deadline:* For fall admission, 4/1 for domestic students. Application fee: $50. Electronic applications accepted. *Expenses:* Tuition: Full-time $41,530. *Unit head:* Dr. Steven J. Henriksen, Founding Dean, 909-469-5299, E-mail: shenriksen@westernu.edu. *Application contact:* Information Contact, 909-469-5335, Fax: 909-469-5570, E-mail: admissions@westernu.edu.

Western Washington University, Graduate School, College of Sciences and Technology, Department of Biology, Bellingham, WA 98225-5996. Offers MS. Part-time programs available. *Degree requirements:* For master's, thesis. *Entrance requirements:* For master's, GRE General Test, GRE Subject Test (biology), minimum GPA of 3.0 in last 60 semester hours or last 90 quarter hours. Additional exam requirements/recommendations for international students: Required—TOEFL (minimum score 567 paper-based; 227 computer-based). Electronic applications accepted. *Faculty research:* Organismal biology, ecology and evolutionary biology, marine biology, cell and molecular biology, developmental biology, larval ecology, microzoo planton, symbiosis.

West Texas A&M University, College of Agriculture, Nursing, and Natural Sciences, Department of Life, Earth, and Environmental Sciences, Program in Biology, Canyon, TX 79016-0001. Offers MS. Part-time programs available. *Degree requirements:* For master's, comprehensive exam, thesis optional. *Entrance requirements:* For master's, GRE General Test. Additional exam requirements/recommendations for international students: Required—TOEFL (minimum score 550 paper-based). Electronic applications accepted. *Faculty research:* Aeroallergen concentration, scorpions, kangaroo mice, seed anatomy with light and scanning electron microscope.

West Virginia University, Eberly College of Arts and Sciences, Department of Biology, Morgantown, WV 26506. Offers cell and molecular biology (MS, PhD); environmental and evolutionary biology (MS, PhD); forensic biology (MS, PhD); genomic biology (MS, PhD); neurobiology (MS, PhD). Terminal master's awarded for partial completion of doctoral program. *Degree requirements:* For master's, thesis, final exam; for doctorate, thesis/dissertation, preliminary and final exams. *Entrance requirements:* For master's, GRE General Test, GRE Subject Test, minimum GPA of 3.0; for doctorate, GRE General Test, minimum GPA of 3.0. Additional exam requirements/recommendations for international students: Required—TOEFL. *Faculty research:* Environmental biology, genetic engineering, developmental biology, global change, biodiversity.

West Virginia University, School of Medicine, Graduate Programs at the Health Sciences Center, Morgantown, WV 26506. Offers MS, PhD, MD/PhD. Part-time and evening/weekend programs available. Postbaccalaureate distance learning degree programs offered (minimal on-campus study). *Expenses:* Contact institution.

Wichita State University, Graduate School, Fairmount College of Liberal Arts and Sciences, Department of Biological Sciences, Wichita, KS 67260. Offers MS. Part-time programs available. *Unit head:* Dr. William J. Hendry, Chair, 316-978-3111, Fax: 316-978-3772, E-mail: william.hendry@wichita.edu. *Application contact:* Dr. Karen Brown Sullivan, Graduate Coordinator, 316-978-3111, E-mail: karen.brown@wichita.edu.

Wilfrid Laurier University, Faculty of Graduate and Postdoctoral Studies, Faculty of Science, Department of Biology, Waterloo, ON N2L 3C5, Canada. Offers integrative biology (M Sc). *Faculty:* 13 full-time (5 women), 8 part-time/adjunct (2 women). *Students:* 28 full-time (9 women), 3 international. 12 applicants, 58% accepted, 7 enrolled. In 2010, 3 master's awarded. *Degree requirements:* For master's, thesis. *Entrance requirements:* For master's, honours BA in last two years of undergraduate studies with a minimum B average. Additional exam requirements/recommendations for international students: Required—TOEFL (minimum score 89 iBT). *Application deadline:* For fall admission, 2/1 priority date for domestic and international students. Application fee: $100. Electronic applications accepted. Tuition and fees charges are reported in Canadian dollars. *Expenses:* Tuition, area resident: Full-time $15,300 Canadian dollars; part-time $1200 Canadian dollars per credit. International tuition: $21,300 Canadian dollars full-time. Required fees: $650 Canadian dollars; $100 Canadian dollars per credit. Tuition and fees vary according to course load, degree level, campus/location and program. *Financial support:* In 2010–11, 48 fellowships, 48 teaching assistantships were awarded; career-related internships or fieldwork, scholarships/grants, health care benefits, and unspecified assistantships also available. *Faculty research:* Genetic/development, anatomy/physiology, ecology/environment, evolution. *Unit head:* Dr. Frederique Guinel, Graduate Coordinator, 519-884-0710 Ext. 2230, Fax: 519-746-0677, E-mail: fguinel@wlu.ca. *Application contact:* Rosemary Springett, Graduate Admissions and Records Officer, 519-884-0710 Ext. 3078, Fax: 519-884-1020, E-mail: gradstudies@wlu.ca.

William Paterson University of New Jersey, College of Science and Health, General Biology Program, Wayne, NJ 07470-8420. Offers MS. Part-time and evening/weekend programs available. *Degree requirements:* For master's, comprehensive exam, independent study or thesis. *Entrance requirements:* For master's, GRE General Test, minimum GPA of 2.75. Electronic applications accepted.

Winthrop University, College of Arts and Sciences, Department of Biology, Rock Hill, SC 29733. Offers MS. Part-time programs available. *Degree requirements:* For master's, thesis optional. *Entrance requirements:* For master's, GRE General Test. Electronic applications accepted. *Faculty research:* Anatomy of marsupials; oxygen consumption, respiratory quotient and mechanical efficiency; bioremediation with microbial mats; floristic survey.

Worcester Polytechnic Institute, Graduate Studies, Department of Biology and Biotechnology, Worcester, MA 01609-2280. Offers biology and biotechnology (MS); biotechnology (PhD). *Faculty:* 5 full-time (3 women). *Students:* 17 full-time (13 women); includes 1 Asian, non-Hispanic/Latino, 8 international. 103 applicants, 6% accepted, 4 enrolled. In 2010, 4 master's, 1 doctorate awarded. Terminal master's awarded for partial completion of doctoral program. *Degree requirements:* For master's, thesis; for doctorate, comprehensive exam, thesis/dissertation, qualifying exam. *Entrance requirements:* For master's and doctorate, GRE General Test, 3 letters of recommendation, statement of purpose. Additional exam requirements/recommendations for international students: Required—TOEFL (minimum score 550 paper-based; 213 computer-based; 79 iBT), IELTS (minimum score 6.5). *Application deadline:* For fall admission, 1/1 priority date for domestic and international students. Application fee: $70. Electronic applications accepted. *Expenses:* Tuition: Full-time $20,862; part-time $1159 per term. One-time fee: $15. *Financial support:* Teaching assistantships, career-related internships or fieldwork, institutionally sponsored loans, scholarships/grants, and unspecified assistantships available. Financial award application deadline: 1/1; financial award applicants required to submit FAFSA. *Faculty research:* Molecular and cellular biology, developmental, neuro- and regenerative biology, behavioral and environmental biology, plant biotechnology. *Unit head:* Dr. Joseph Duffy, Head, 508-831-5538, Fax: 508-831-5936, E-mail: jduffy@wpi.edu. *Application contact:* Dr. Reeta Prusty-Rao, Graduate Coordinator, 508-831-5538, Fax: 508-831-5936, E-mail: rpr@wpi.edu.

Wright State University, School of Graduate Studies, College of Science and Mathematics, Department of Biological Sciences, Dayton, OH 45435. Offers biological sciences (MS); environmental sciences (MS). *Degree requirements:* For master's, thesis optional. *Entrance requirements:* Additional exam requirements/recommendations for international students: Required—TOEFL.

Wright State University, School of Graduate Studies, College of Science and Mathematics and School of Medicine, Program in Biomedical Sciences, Dayton, OH 45435. Offers PhD. *Degree requirements:* For doctorate, thesis/dissertation. *Entrance requirements:* For doctorate, GRE General Test. Additional exam requirements/recommendations for international students: Required—TOEFL.

Yale University, School of Medicine and Graduate School of Arts and Sciences, Combined Program in Biological and Biomedical Sciences (BBS), New Haven, CT 06520. Offers PhD, MD/PhD. *Degree requirements:* For doctorate, thesis/dissertation. *Entrance requirements:* For doctorate, GRE General Test. Additional exam requirements/recommendations for international students: Required—TOEFL. Electronic applications accepted. *Expenses:* Contact institution.

York University, Faculty of Graduate Studies, Faculty of Science and Engineering, Program in Biology, Toronto, ON M3J 1P3, Canada. Offers M Sc, PhD. Part-time and evening/weekend programs available. *Degree requirements:* For master's, thesis or alternative; for doctorate, comprehensive exam, thesis/dissertation, preliminary exam. Electronic applications accepted.

Youngstown State University, Graduate School, College of Science, Technology, Engineering and Mathematics, Department of Biological Sciences, Youngstown, OH 44555-0001. Offers environmental biology (MS); molecular biology, microbiology, and genetic (MS); physiology and anatomy (MS). Part-time programs available. *Degree requirements:* For master's, comprehensive exam, thesis, oral review. *Entrance requirements:* For master's, GRE General Test, minimum GPA of 2.7. Additional exam requirements/recommendations for international students: Required—TOEFL. *Faculty research:* Cell biology, neurophysiology, molecular biology, neurobiology, gene regulation.

ADELPHI UNIVERSITY

College of the Arts and Sciences
Program in Biology

Program of Study

Adelphi's graduate biology program prepares students for doctoral study and entrance into professional schools of medicine, dentistry, and veterinary medicine. The program also qualifies future educators for certification and expands the knowledge base of experienced teachers. Other graduates acquire the tools and skills necessary for successful careers in research, public health, and environmental law. At Adelphi, students gain a broad foundation in biology, practical experience, and the fundamental skills of scientific research. Laboratory courses emphasize contemporary scientific techniques and integrate technology into the learning experience. Faculty members work closely with students as mentors, ensuring a personal academic experience and career guidance. It is possible to fulfill degree requirements on the basis of either full- or part-time study, with completion in one to two years of full-time study.

There are two paths to the master's degree—the research thesis (33 credits) and the nonthesis option (36 credits). Requirements are subject to change. Most courses are offered in the evening for the convenience of the working student. Adelphi students have opportunities to gain professional experience through internships at many hospitals, laboratories, private medical and dental practices, and research institutions in the area.

Students seeking a graduate degree and New York State teaching certification for secondary-level teaching (grades 7 through 12) can complete required course work for a Master of Arts degree through Adelphi's graduate program in biology in conjunction with the School of Education. Students who successfully complete the program are awarded a Master of Arts from the School of Education.

Adelphi also offers a Master of Science (M.S.) degree with a concentration in biotechnology. This innovative program prepares students for careers in this rapidly expanding and dynamic discipline of biotechnology and in the related fields of pharmaceuticals, biomedical research, cancer research, and laboratory medicine. Students may pursue a research thesis track or a scholarly paper track; a limited number of teaching assistantships are available.

Research Facilities

Departmental laboratory facilities include modern equipment for the study of molecular biology, cell and tissue culture, and scanning and transmission electron microscopy. Students use these facilities for graduate research in cellular and molecular biology, immunology, genetics, evolution, and ecology.

The University's primary research holdings are at Swirbul Library and include 600,000 volumes (including bound periodicals and government publications), 806,000 items in microformats, 33,000 audiovisual items, and access to over 61,000 electronic journal titles. Online access is provided to more than 221 research databases.

Financial Aid

Adelphi University offers a wide variety of federal aid programs, state grants, scholarship and fellowship programs, on- and off-campus employment, and teaching and research assistantships.

Cost of Study

For the 2011–12 academic year, the tuition rate is $895 per credit. University fees range from $315 to $550 per semester.

Living and Housing Costs

The University assists single and married students in finding suitable accommodations whenever possible. The cost of living is dependent on location and the number of rooms rented.

Location

Located in historic Garden City, New York, 45 minutes from Manhattan and 20 minutes from Queens, Adelphi's 75-acre suburban campus is known for the beauty of its landscape and architecture. The campus is a short walk from the Long Island Rail Road and is convenient to New York's major airports and several major highways. Off-campus centers are located in Manhattan, Hauppauge, and Poughkeepsie.

The University and The College

Founded in 1896, Adelphi is a fully accredited, private university with nearly 8,000 undergraduate, graduate, and returning-adult students in the arts and sciences, business, clinical psychology, education, nursing, and social work. Students come from forty-one states and forty-eight countries. The Princeton Review named Adelphi University a Best College in the Northeastern Region, and the *Fiske Guide to Colleges* recognized Adelphi as a "Best Buy" in higher education for five years in a row. The University is one of only twenty-four private institutions in the nation to earn this recognition.

Mindful of the cultural inheritance of the past, the College of Arts and Sciences encompasses those realms of inquiry that have characterized the modern pursuit of knowledge. The faculty members of the College place a high priority on their students' intellectual development in and out of the classroom and structure programs and opportunities to foster that growth. Students analyze original research or other creative work, develop firsthand facility with creative or research methodologies, undertake collaborative work with peers and mentors, engage in serious internships, and hone communicative skills.

Applying

Applicants must hold a bachelor's degree in biology or an allied field or its equivalent and show promise of successful achievement in the field. A student must submit the completed application form, a $50 application fee, official college transcripts, and two letters of recommendation. For more information, students should contact the director of graduate studies.

Correspondence and Information

George Russell, Director
Graduate Biology Program
Science Building 103
College of Arts and Sciences
Adelphi University
Garden City, New York 11530

Phone: 516-877-4199
Fax: 516-877-4209
E-mail: russell@adelphi.edu
Web site: http://academics.adelphi.edu/artsci/bio/grad/req.php

Adelphi University

THE FACULTY AND THEIR RESEARCH

Alan Schoenfeld, Assistant Professor and Department Associate Chair; Ph.D., Yeshiva (Einstein), 1999. Cancer genetics and tumor suppressor genes, specifically, the normal cellular functions of the BRCA2 and VHL tumor suppressor genes.

George K. Russell, Professor and Director, Graduate Studies; Ph.D., Harvard, 1963. Genetics, biochemistry, and cellular physiology.

Tandra Chakraborty, Assistant Professor; Ph.D., Calcutta (India), 2000. Interplay between endocrinology and neurobiology.

Jonna Coombs, Assistant Professor; Ph.D., Penn State, 2000. Bioremediation.

Deborah F. Cooperstein, Professor; Ph.D., CUNY, 1974. Biochemistry and molecular biology; physiological and molecular aspects of nutrition; the human body.

Carol Diakow, Professor; Ph.D., NYU, 1969. Behavioral neurobiology, specifically, neurophysiological, neurochemical, neuroendocrinological, observational, anatomical, and biochemical techniques applied to the study of the neurobiological bases of behavior.

James K. Dooley, Professor; Ph.D., North Carolina, 1973. Evolution, ecology, homing behavior, and systematics of fishes; tilefish morphological and molecular systematics; fisheries/environmental science; endangered fish.

Matthias Foellmer, Assistant Professor; Ph.D., Concordia, 2004. Evolutionary ecology: significance of extreme sexual size dimorphism (SSD); mating systems; sexual cannibalism; changes in community structure in response to varying levels of human disturbances in coastal ecosystems.

Aaren Freeman, Assistant Professor, Ph.D., New Hampshire, 2007. Marine biology; evolution and ecology of marine organisms; biology of invasive species; predator-prey interactions.

Lawrence J. Hobbie, Associate Professor; Ph.D., MIT, 1989. Plant molecular genetics, specifically, the molecular mechanism of action and of transport of the plant hormone auxin and the role of auxin in plant physiology and development.

R. David Jones, Associate Professor; Ph.D., Texas, 1972. Regulatory physiology; pathophysiology.

Aram Stump, Assistant Professor; Ph.D., Notre Dame, 2005. Population variation; evolutionary processes; organismal biology using the tools of molecular genetics.

Andrea Ward, Assistant Professor; Ph.D., Massachusetts Amherst, 2005. Evoluntionary biology; functional morphology; developmental biology; evolution of the elongate body form of fishes.

Benjamin Weeks, Associate Professor; Ph.D., Connecticut, 1988. Effects of xenobiotics on the cellular mechanism of development and disease.

Adelphi's campus in historic Garden City, Long Island, New York.

A registered arboretum, Adelphi is truly a green campus.

BOSTON COLLEGE

Biology Department

Programs of Study	The Department offers a program of study leading to a Ph.D. degree in biology. Basic areas of study include biochemistry, cellular and developmental biology, genetics, cell cycle, vector biology, neurobiology, bioinformatics, and structural biology.
	The Ph.D. degree provides an in-depth training experience. Core course work is provided in cell biology, biochemistry, molecular biology, and genetics. Advanced electives are available in all areas of faculty expertise. Seminar courses provide students with ongoing training in critical thinking and oral presentation of scientific data. Research experience is provided by working in close cooperation with faculty members, postdoctoral fellows, and senior students in a collaborative, supportive environment. In cooperation with the School of Education, the Master of Science in Teaching (M.S.T.) degree in biology is also offered.
Research Facilities	The Biology Department occupies more than 30,000 square feet of research space in Higgins Hall. Faculty laboratories have state-of-the-art equipment. Shared facilities include several tissue-culture rooms; common equipment rooms; TEM, fluorescence, and confocal microscopes; X-ray diffraction and a capillary DNA sequencer; machine and electronic workshops; and state-of-the-art computers for online data analysis, production of publication-quality figures, and bioinformatic research and analysis. The university science library subscribes to more than 600 scientific journals. Access to libraries of institutions in the greater Boston area is available through consortium arrangements.
Financial Aid	Graduate assistantships (teaching and research based) are available with full tuition remission. Stipends are $28,500 per calendar year.
Cost of Study	For the 2011–12 academic year, tuition and fees for a full-time student are $1242 per credit, 100 percent of which is covered by tuition remission for students receiving financial aid.
Living and Housing Costs	The Housing Office provides an extensive list of off-campus housing options, including off-campus graduate housing. Most graduate students rent rooms or apartments near Chestnut Hill; many biology students share apartments with other students in the program. Average monthly expenses (rent, food, utilities) for the academic year (nine months) are $2105 for students.
Student Group	The enrollment at Boston College is 14,500, including 4,200 students enrolled in the various graduate schools. There are 45 graduate students in the Ph.D. program. The graduate students are geographically and ethnically diverse.
Location	Boston College is located in the Chestnut Hill section of Newton, an attractive residential area about 5 miles from the heart of Boston, with easy access to the city by public transportation. The Boston area, with its numerous educational and biomedical research institutions, offers countless outstanding seminars, lectures, colloquia, and concerts throughout the year. A wide variety of cultural and recreational opportunities can be found close to the campus.
The College	Founded in Massachusetts in 1863, Boston College currently includes the Graduate School of Arts and Sciences and graduate schools of law, social work, management, nursing, and education. Its expanding campus is graced with many attractive Gothic buildings. Boston College has a strong tradition of academic excellence and service to the community.
Applying	Preference is given to completed applications received prior to January 1. Admission is granted on the basis of academic background and demonstrated aptitude in biology and related disciplines. A year of organic chemistry, physics, and mathematics and a solid background in biology are highly recommended for admission. Scores on the Graduate Record Examinations General Test and the Subject Test in biology are required.
Correspondence and Information	Professor Charles Hoffman Director, Graduate Program Biology Department Higgins Hall Boston College Chestnut Hill, Massachusetts 02467-3961 Phone: 617-552-3540 E-mail: gradbio@bc.edu Web site: http://www.bc.edu/biology

Boston College

THE GRADUATE RESEARCH FACULTY

Anthony T. Annunziato, Professor; Ph.D., Massachusetts Amherst, 1979. Biochemistry/molecular biology; DNA replication and nucleosome assembly in mammalian cells.

David R. Burgess, Professor; Ph.D., California, Davis, 1974. Spatial and temporal regulation of cytokinesis; role of the actin- and microtubule-based cytoskeletons in early development.

Hugh P. Cam, Assistant Professor; Ph.D., Harvard 2003. Epigenetic control of higher-order genome organization and chromatin structures.

Thomas C. Chiles, Professor and Chairman of Biology; Ph.D., Florida, 1988. Cell biology, signal transduction; cell-cycle control, gene regulation in mature B lymphocytes.

Jeffrey Chuang, Assistant Professor; Ph.D., MIT, 2001. Computational approaches to comparative genomics, gene regulation, and molecular evolution.

Peter G. Clote, Professor; Ph.D., Duke, 1979. Algorithms and mathematical modeling in computational biology: genomic motif detection, protein folding on lattice models, RNA secondary structure, functional genomics via gene expression profile.

Kathleen Dunn, Associate Professor; Ph.D., North Carolina at Chapel Hill, 1982. Plant molecular biology; cloning and characterization of genes induced during alfalfa nodulation.

Marc-Jan Gubbels, Assistant Professor; Ph.D., Utrecht (Netherlands), 2000. Genetics and cell biology of the apicomplexan parasite *Toxoplasma gondii.*

Laura E. Hake, Associate Professor; Ph.D., Tufts, 1992. Molecular control of early development in *Xenopus;* protein degradation; RNA-protein interactions; translational regulation during gametogenesis.

Charles Hoffman, Professor; Ph.D., Tufts, 1986. Signal transduction and transcriptional regulation in fission yeast; analysis of PKA and MAPK signal pathways in nutrient monitoring.

Daniel Kirschner, Professor; Ph.D., Harvard, 1972. Structural biochemistry of amyloids and myelin sheath; neurodegenerative diseases; peripheral demyelinating neuropathies.

Gabor T. Marth, Assistant Professor; D.Sc., Washington (St. Louis), 1994. DNA polymorphism discovery and analysis; genomic and algorithmic approaches to population genetics; long-term human demography, haplotype structure, and medical genetics.

Michelle Meyer, Assistant Professor; Ph.D., Caltech, 2006. Bioinformatic discovery and experimental characterization of RNA-based gene regulatory mechanisms.

Junona Moroianu, Associate Professor; Ph.D., Rockefeller, 1996. Cell biology; molecular mechanisms of nucleocytoplasmic transport of cellular and viral macromolecules in mammalian cells.

Marc A. T. Muskavitch, Professor; Ph.D., Stanford, 1981. Developmental biology: intercellular signaling and cell-fate specification in *Drosophila;* host-parasite interactions in *Anopheles.*

Clare M. O'Connor, Associate Professor and Associate Chair; Ph.D., Purdue, 1977. Cellular biochemistry.

Thomas N. Seyfried, Professor; Ph.D., Illinois, 1976. Neurogenetics: use of genetics and neurochemistry in neural membrane function and developmental neurobiology.

Kenneth C. Williams, Associate Professor; Ph.D., McGill, 1993. Central nervous system macrophages; neuroAIDS; AIDS pathogenesis; monocyte/macrophage biology.

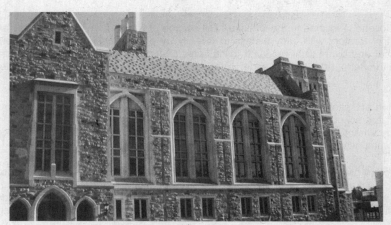

Higgins Hall, home of the Biology Department.

BOWLING GREEN STATE UNIVERSITY

Department of Biological Sciences

Programs of Study

The Department of Biological Sciences at Bowling Green State University offers graduate training for professional careers in both applied and fundamental areas of biology. Programs are available leading to the degrees of Doctor of Philosophy, Master of Science, and Master of Arts in Teaching. Major areas of specialization include ecology and conservation biology, genetics, microbiology, biochemistry and molecular biology, neuroscience and behavior, and plant science. The research interests of the individual faculty members are listed in the Faculty section of this document.

Completion of the Ph.D. program, which consists of formal and informal course work as well as dissertation research, usually takes four years after completion of the master's degree or five years after the completion of the Bachelor of Science degree. Master's programs, with both thesis and nonthesis options, take about two years to complete. The degree plan is selected by the student with the assistance of a faculty adviser and advisory committee; the program of study is flexible to allow students to pursue their individual professional goals. In addition, graduate students are expected to gain teaching experience as assistants in laboratory and lecture courses.

The Department of Biological Sciences also offers interdisciplinary research programs. Members of the Department interact with faculty members in the Departments of Chemistry, Geology, and Psychology in forming cooperative programs to meet the specialized needs and goals of graduate students.

Research Facilities

The Department of Biological Sciences is housed in the Life Sciences Building, a modern five-story, 120,000-square-foot research and teaching complex. The forty laboratories housed in the building are equipped with state-of-the-art instrumentation. Included are scanning and transmission electron microscopes, X-ray analyzers, ultracentrifuges, scanning and dual-beam spectrophotometers, PCR machines, high-performance liquid chromatography equipment, gamma and liquid scintillation counters, environmental control chambers, darkrooms, cold rooms, biochemistry and tissue-culture labs, and a biohazard work area. Other Departmental facilities include 80-acre and 100-acre forest preserves; a greenhouse complex with areas for the propagation and breeding of temperate, tropical, subtropical, and desert plants; and a herbarium containing more than 20,000 specimens. A 9,000-square-foot animal facility has thirty breeding and maintenance rooms and a P3 area.

Financial Aid

Graduate assistantship and fellowship stipends are competitive and include a waiver of tuition and out-of-state fees for a half-time appointment during the academic year. For students making good progress in their degree program, summer support with tuition is available.

Predoctoral nonservice fellowships are available to Ph.D. students, normally during the last year of study.

Renewal of assistantships and fellowships is contingent upon satisfactory completion of assignments and progress toward the degree. Research assistantships are also available through research grants to individual faculty members.

Cost of Study

For the latest information on cost of attendance, prospective students should visit the Web site at http://sfa.bgsu.edu/coa.

Living and Housing Costs

The University provides on-campus housing for a small number of graduate students at Founders Hall. However, there are numerous apartments and rooms for rent near the campus at costs comparable to those in other Midwestern cities of similar size.

Student Group

There are approximately 100 graduate students in the Department of Biological Sciences. A diverse group, they were nearly equally divided between men and women and included representatives of a dozen or more states and several countries. The majority of the Department's students receive some form of financial aid from the University.

The University enrolls 21,000 students, including more than 3,000 graduate students.

Student Outcomes

Recent Ph.D. recipients have accepted postdoctoral positions at academic institutions, including Harvard, University of California at Berkeley, University of Michigan, and Yale; or have accepted positions in government, at institutions such as the Centers for Disease Control and the Environmental Protection Agency; or have accepted positions in industry. Recent master's degree recipients have gone to graduate or medical schools, such as Ohio State, Purdue, Tufts, and University of Michigan; or have accepted positions in industry with such companies as Amgen and Wyeth Laboratories.

Location

Bowling Green is a northwestern Ohio community of approximately 29,600 residents. It is located 16 miles south of Toledo; Detroit, Cleveland, and Columbus are all within a 100-mile radius. The community offers numerous recreational and social programs that supplement the activities offered by the University.

The University

Bowling Green, a state-assisted university, was founded in 1910. The attractive campus occupies 1,250 acres and has more than 100 buildings. The atmosphere is friendly, open, and reasonably informal. Graduate faculty members in the Department of Biological Sciences and throughout the University are committed to excellence in both research and teaching.

Applying

Requirements for admission include a baccalaureate degree, normally with a major in one of the sciences; GRE scores on the verbal, quantitative, and analytical portions of the General Test; favorable grade point averages in all subjects and in the major; a short research statement including a list of up to 3 faculty members who have similar research interests; and three letters of recommendation.

Applicants can apply online at https://www.applyweb.com/apply/bgsug. Applicants should correspond directly with faculty members in their areas of interest as soon as possible. Applicants are most competitive for admission and funding if complete applications are submitted by February 1. Bowling Green State University is an Equal Opportunity/Affirmative Action employer. Women and members of minorities are encouraged to apply.

Correspondence and Information

Graduate Committee Chair
Department of Biological Sciences
Bowling Green State University
Bowling Green, Ohio 43403-0212
Fax: 419-372-2024
E-mail: kvroot@bgsu.edu
Web site: http://www.bgsu.edu/departments/biology/

Bowling Green State University

THE GRADUATE FACULTY AND THEIR RESEARCH

Gabriela Bidart-Bouzart, Assistant Professor; Ph.D., Illinois at Urbana-Champaign. Evolutionary ecology; plant-herbivore interactions; ecology of plant defenses; ecological genomics.

Juan L. Bouzat, Associate Professor; Ph.D., Illinois at Urbana-Champaign. Molecular ecology; conservation and population genetics; molecular evolution.

George S. Bullerjahn, Professor; Ph.D., Virginia. Microbial physiology; regulation of stress-induced functions in cyanobacteria.

Sheryl L. Coombs, Professor; Ph.D., Hawaii. Mechanosensory processing by auditory and lateral line systems of aquatic vertebrates; neuroethology.

Carmen F. Fioravanti, Professor; Ph.D., UCLA. Comparative biochemistry; anaerobic energetics of the parasitic helminths; mitochondrial transhydrogenase systems; electron transport mechanisms and isoprene biosynthesis.

Michael E. Geusz, Associate Professor; Ph.D., Vanderbilt. Circadian rhythms in mammalian and molluscan neurons and control of intracellular calcium.

Carol A. Heckman, Professor and Director of Electron Microscopy Center; Ph.D., Massachusetts Amherst. Cell biology; role of ruffling in growth control; image analysis; molecular biology of transforming proteins.

Robert Huber, Professor; Ph.D., Texas Tech. Neurochemistry of aggression.

Roudabeh J. Jamasbi, Professor; Ph.D., Arkansas. Biology and immunology of digestive and respiratory tract carcinomas; generation of monoclonal antibodies against carcinomas.

Ray A. Larsen, Associate Professor; Ph.D., Montana. Bacterial membrane energetics.

R. Michael McKay, Professor; Ph.D., McGill. Aquatic microbial ecology; photoplankton-trace metal interactions; inorganic carbon acquisition and assimilation; phycotoxins.

Lee A. Meserve, Distinguished Teaching Professor; Ph.D., Rutgers. Mammalian endocrinology; altered thyroid status in development and aging.

Helen Michaels, Associate Professor; Ph.D., Illinois at Urbana-Champaign. Molecular evolution; chloroplast DNA and angiosperm phylogeny; evolution and ecology of plant mating systems; ecological genetics; molecular systematics; plant ecology.

Jeffrey G. Miner, Associate Professor and Chair; Ph.D., Ohio State. Aquatic community ecology; abiotic effects on predator-prey interactions; ecology of fishes.

Paul A. Moore, Professor; Ph.D., Boston University. Marine chemical ecology; sensory ecology; physiology and behavior of marine and aquatic organisms.

Paul F. Morris, Associate Professor; Ph.D., Queen's at Kingston. Molecular plant-microbe interactions; regulation of chemoattraction in *Phytophthora* sp.

Vipaporn Phuntumart, Assistant Professor; Ph.D., Fribourg (Switzerland). Molecular biology of plant-pathogen interactions.

Scott O. Rogers, Professor; Ph.D., Washington (Seattle). Molecular biology, evolution, introns; ancient DNA, DNA preservation, biotechnology; ancient ice, plants, microbes.

Karen V. Root, Associate Professor and Graduate Coordinator; Ph.D., Florida Tech. Conservation biology and population ecology.

Karen L. Sirum, Associate Professor; Ph.D., Dartmouth. Biology education research and development; inquiry-based learning strategies.

Moira J. van Staaden, Associate Professor; Ph.D., Texas Tech. Ethology and evolution.

Daniel D. Wiegmann, Associate Professor; Ph.D., Wisconsin–Madison. Behavioral ecology; reproductive biology of fishes; animal decision making.

Ronny C. Woodruff, Distinguished Research Professor; Ph.D., Utah State. Mutagenesis and genetics of transposable DNA elements in *Drosophila;* genetics of natural populations; role of mutation in molecular evolution.

Zhaohui Xu, Assistant Professor; Ph.D., Huazhong Agricultural (China). Bacterial genetics and biotechnology; environmental microbiology.

Weidong Yang, Assistant Professor; Ph.D., Fudan (China). Single-molecule imaging and tracking; nucleocytoplasmic transport; cell cycle and nanotechnology.

Jill Zeilstra-Ryalls, Professor; Ph.D., Purdue. Gene regulation and protein structure-function relationships.

CALIFORNIA INSTITUTE OF TECHNOLOGY

Division of Biology

Program of Study	There are two principal research foci in the Division of Biology at Caltech.

The goals of research in molecular, cellular, and developmental biology and genetics are to understand the molecular mechanisms that regulate cellular proliferation, communication, and function and the mechanisms of differentiation and pattern formation that form the diverse and functionally integrated cell types in multicellular organisms. This area includes the development of the many different cell types and connections found in the nervous system.

Research in integrative neurobiology involves the analysis of the interactions of collections of neurons in behavior, both in simple insect nervous systems and in the more complex vertebrate systems. Integrative neurobiology is closely associated with computational analysis and modeling as carried out in the Computation and Neural Systems Option.

Emphasis in graduate study is on individual research under the guidance of faculty members. Normally, research is initiated during the first year of graduate study by three periods of rotation, each approximately one quarter in duration, in three different research laboratories. By the end of the first year, students will have chosen a laboratory for their thesis work. Course requirements are minimal and are limited to those that contribute to the major program of the student. Major work may be pursued in any of the seven areas: biophysics and cell biology, developmental biology, genetics, immunology, integrative neurobiology, molecular biology and biochemistry, and molecular and cellular neurobiology. Any one of these majors may be combined with biotechnology as part of a dual major. Students are admitted only for study toward the Ph.D. degree. Five to seven years are usually needed to complete the Ph.D. requirements.

Research Facilities

Caltech's Division of Biology includes the Kerckhoff, Alles, Church, Beckman, and Braun laboratories of biology; the Beckman Institute; Broad Center; and the Kerckhoff Marine Laboratory at Corona del Mar. All equipment pertinent to modern biology is available to graduate students. A complete and modern biology library is housed along with the related chemistry library in the nine-story Robert Andrews Millikan Memorial Library.

Financial Aid

Students admitted to graduate standing in biology are provided with financial support adequate to meet their normal expenses. They receive a full tuition grant and, in addition, an NIH traineeship, a fellowship, a part-time teaching assistantship, or a research assistantship. The annual stipend for 2010–11 was $29,404. There are job opportunities for spouses in the Pasadena area. Loan programs are available.

Cost of Study

Tuition costs are covered by grants, as are the fees required for participation in the health program. Funds are provided for research expenses and travel to scientific meetings.

Living and Housing Costs

A single student, or a married student whose spouse has a job, can live simply but comfortably on his or her graduate student income. University housing is available for all entering graduate students. Caltech is an informal place, and clothing costs can be kept low.

Student Group

The Division of Biology has, at any one time, approximately 90 graduate students and approximately 150 postdoctoral fellows, in addition to the 40 professors of biology. About 45 percent of the graduate students are women.

Student Outcomes

Most of the Division's graduates pursue postdoctoral research prior to joining university faculties as assistant professors. Recent examples include postdoctoral positions with the MIT Center for Genome Research and the University of California, San Francisco and a faculty position at Yonsei University in Korea.

Location

Caltech is situated in Pasadena, a city of approximately 144,000 people about 15 miles from the center of downtown Los Angeles. It is located midway between the mountains (for skiing in the winter and mountain climbing in the summer) and the sea (for swimming, surfing, and boating). Caltech offers extensive opportunities for those interested in swimming, tennis, track, and all related recreational activities. Caltech's relationship with the surrounding community is harmonious and peaceful.

The Institute

Caltech, including its Division of Biology, is an uncommon institution by virtue of its small size (about 900 undergraduate students, 1,100 graduate students, and 275 professors), its high quality, and its leadership in scientific education and research. The Division of Biology is young, having been founded in 1928, and has been able to adapt to changing circumstances in the ensuing years. Both Caltech and the Division of Biology have remarkable histories of continued important contributions in scientific research and scholarship.

Applying

To apply for admission, the applicant should write to the Dean of Graduate Studies stating an intention to apply for graduate study in biology. Application forms and related information will be mailed. There is an application fee of $80. Additional information about the research and training programs of the Division of Biology should be obtained by writing to the graduate secretary of the Division of Biology.

Applicants are normally expected to meet the following minimal requirements: mathematics through calculus and elementary differential equations; at least one year of college physics; chemistry, including organic chemistry; and elementary biology. Applications are particularly encouraged from students who have had additional course work in basic sciences and biology equivalent to the undergraduate biology option at Caltech and who have demonstrated laboratory ability and research motivation in undergraduate research projects or employment. Students may be admitted on the basis of advanced course work in psychology or other relevant subjects in lieu of some of the basic science courses normally required.

Students are usually admitted either at the beginning of the academic year in the fall or at the beginning of the summer term, July 1. Completed application materials should be received by January 1; early submission is recommended to allow ample time for a visit to the campus. Scores on the General Test of the Graduate Record Examinations should be submitted, and, if possible, the test should be taken by the November date preceding application.

Correspondence and Information

For research and training information:
Graduate Secretary
Division of Biology 156-29
California Institute of Technology
Pasadena, California 91125
Phone: 626-395-4497

For application information:
Dean of Graduate Studies 02-31
California Institute of Technology
Pasadena, California 91125

California Institute of Technology

THE FACULTY AND THEIR RESEARCH

Cellular Biology and Biophysics
Raymond J. Deshaies. Mechanisms and regulation of cell-cycle progression.
William Dunphy. Regulation of mitosis-promoting factor and the cell cycle.
Michael Elowitz. In vivo modeling: a synthetic approach to regulatory networks.
Scott E. Fraser. Developmental neurobiology; optical methods.
Alexander J. Varshavsky. Mechanics, functions, and applications of intracellular proteolysis; the ubiquitin system and the N-end rule pathway.

Molecular Biology, Biochemistry, Developmental Biology, Genetics, and Immunology
Alexei A. Aravin. Small RNAs and regulation of gene expression.
David Baltimore. Signal transduction, transcriptional regulation, and cell cycle controls.
Pamela J. Bjorkman. Crystal structures of cell-surface proteins involved in the immune response.
Marianne Bronner. Cellular and molecular studies of neural crest development.
Judith L. Campbell. Regulation of DNA replication in the yeast cell cycle: genetic and biochemical analysis.
David C. Chan. Mechanistic studies of virus entry and membrane fusion.
Eric H. Davidson. An integrated approach to the study of embryonic development in sea urchins.
Lea Goentoro. Exploring quantitative computations in cells and embryos.
Bruce Hay. Molecular genetics of cell death.
Grant Jensen. Study of structure of large protein complexes and their arrangement within living cells by cryoelectron microscopy.
Stephen L. Mayo. Protein folding and protein design.
Sarkis Mazmanian. Mechanisms of host-bacterial symbiosis during health and disease.
Elliot M. Meyerowitz. Genetics of plant development.
Dianne K. Newman. Molecular geobiology and microbial metabolism.
Ellen Rothenberg. Development of lymphocytes; changes in gene expression during T-cell maturation; lymphocyte activation pathways.
Angelike Stathopoulos. Gene regulatory network controlling gastrulation in *Drosophila;* control of gene expression; mechanisms of signal transduction.
Paul Sternberg. Molecular genetics of nematode development, behavior, and evolution; signal transduction; tumor suppressor genes.
Barbara Wold. Molecular genetic studies of the structure, function, and regulation of mammalian cell-surface receptors.

Neurobiology
Ralph Adolphs. Psychological and neurological investigations of human emotion and social cognition.
John M. Allman. Brain and behavior in primates.
Richard A. Andersen. Cortical neurophysiology, visuospatial perception, and visual-motor integration.
David J. Anderson. Genetic dissection of neural circuits controlling emotional behaviors.
Michael Dickinson. Neurobiology, aerodynamic abilities, and behavior of flies; striving to build a true robotic fly.
Mary B. Kennedy. Molecular mechanisms of central nervous system synaptic plasticity.
Christof Koch. Biophysics; computational neuroscience; computational vision.
Masakazu Konishi. Neuroethology; behavioral, neurophysiological, and neuroanatomical studies of avian auditory and vocal systems.
Gilles Laurent. Olfactory and mechanosensory processing in insects; synaptic transmission in the avian brain.
Henry A. Lester. Chemical transmission at synapses and within cells; gating of membrane channels; molecular approaches.
Paul H. Patterson. Regulation of neuronal phenotype by cytokines; interactions between the nervous and immune systems; mapping of position in the mammalian nervous system.
David A. Prober. Zebrafish as a genetic model for sleep and sleep disorders.
Erin Schuman. Mechanisms of synaptic modification; role of NO as a retrograde second messenger.
Shinsuke Shimojo. Visual psychophysics and behavioral studies of sensory-motor functions.
Athanassios Siapas. Learning and memory formation across distributed networks of neurons; multitetrode electrophysiological recordings from freely behaving rodents.
Doris Y. Tsao. Dissecting the neural machinery for face processing in the macaque monkey.
Kai Zinn. Molecular genetic studies of insect nervous system development; signal transduction in vertebrate olfaction.

CITY OF HOPE NATIONAL MEDICAL CENTER / BECKMAN RESEARCH INSTITUTE

Irell & Manella Graduate School of Biological Sciences

Programs of Study

The mission of the City of Hope Graduate School of Biological Sciences is to train students to be outstanding research scientists in chemical, molecular, and cellular biology. Graduates of this program are awarded the degree of Doctor of Philosophy in biological sciences and are equipped to address fundamental questions in the life sciences and biomedicine for careers in academia, industry, and government. The time spent in the program is devoted to full-time study and research. During the first year, the student completes the core curriculum and three laboratory rotations (ten to twelve weeks each). The core curriculum contains biochemistry, molecular biology, cell biology, and biostatistics/bioinformatics. One Advanced Topics course is taken during spring of the first year. After the first year, the student prepares and orally defends a research proposal based on an original topic not related to previous work conducted by the student, and in the second year, students prepare and defend a research proposal based on their actual thesis topic. An additional Advanced Topics course is required after the first year and students are required to take a literature-based journal club every year after the first year. Students also participate in workshops on scientific communication and on the responsible conduct of research. After successfully completing the core curriculum and research proposal, students concentrate the majority of their time on their individual dissertation laboratory research project. The written thesis/dissertation must be presented by the student for examination by 4 members of the City of Hope staff and 1 qualified member from an outside institution.

Research Facilities

City of Hope is a premier medical center, one of forty National Cancer Institute–designated Comprehensive Cancer Centers. Its Beckman Research Institute launched the biotech industry by creating the first human recombinant gene products, insulin and growth hormone, which are now used by millions of people worldwide. State-of-the-art facilities include mass spectrometry, NMR, molecular modeling, cell sorting, DNA sequencing, molecular pathology, scanning and transmission electron microscopy, confocal microscopy, and molecular imaging. The Lee Graff Medical and Scientific Library allows access to the latest biomedical information via its journal and book collection, document delivery, interlibrary loans, and searches of online databases.

Financial Aid

All students in the Graduate School receive a fellowship of $30,000 per year as well as paid health and dental insurance.

Cost of Study

There are no tuition charges. A student services fee of $50 per semester ($150 per year) is the student's only financial obligation to City of Hope.

Living and Housing Costs

The School has limited, low-cost housing available. Living in student housing provides easy access to campus resources and a connection to the vibrant campus community. Additional housing is available within the immediate area at an average cost of $700 to $1000 per month.

Student Group

The Graduate School faculty consists of 82 of City of Hope's investigators. Eighty-one graduate students are working toward the Ph.D. degree in biological sciences in 2010–11.

Student Outcomes

Graduates have gone on to work as postdoctoral fellows at California Institute of Technology; Harvard University; Scripps Research Institute; Stanford University; University of California, Los Angeles; University of California, San Diego; University of California, Irvine; University of Missouri; University of Southern California; and Washington University in St. Louis. Graduates have also found positions with Wyeth-Ayerst Research; Allergan, Inc.; and the U.S. Biodefense and its subsidiary, Stem Cell Research Institute of California, Inc.

Location

City of Hope is located 25 miles northeast of downtown Los Angeles, minutes away from Pasadena and close to beaches, mountains, and many recreational and cultural activities.

The Medical Center and The Institute

City of Hope was founded in 1913, initially as a tuberculosis sanatorium. Research programs were initiated in 1951, and, in 1983, the Beckman Research Institute of City of Hope was established with support from the Arnold and Mabel Beckman Foundation. The Institute comprises basic science research groups within the Divisions of Biology, Immunology, Molecular Medicine, and Neurosciences, among others.

Applying

The deadline for application is January 1 for classes starting in August. Applying early is advisable. Candidates must submit transcripts, three letters of recommendation, and take the Graduate Record Examination (General Test required, Subject Test recommended). For further information and an application, students should contact the School at the address listed in this description.

Correspondence and Information

City of Hope
Irell & Manuella Graduate School of Biological Sciences
1500 East Duarte Road
Duarte, California 91010
Phone: 877-715-GRAD or 626-256-4673 Ext. 63899
Fax: 626-301-8105
E-mail: gradschool@coh.org
Web site: http://www.cityofhope.org/gradschool

City of Hope National Medical Center/Beckman Research Institute

THE FACULTY AND THEIR RESEARCH

Professors

David K. Ann, Ph.D. Molecular mechanisms of maintaining genomic integrity.
Michael E. Barish, Ph.D. Imaging studies of neural progenitor and brain tumor cells.
Ravi Bhatia, M.D. Regulation of normal and malignant hematopoietic stem cell growth.
Edouard M. Cantin, Ph.D. Herpes simplex virus infections in the nervous system.
Saswati Chatterjee, Ph.D. Adeno-associated virus vector for stem-cell gene therapy.
Shiuan Chen, Ph.D. Hormones and cancer.
Yuan Chen, Ph.D., NMR spectroscopy as a tool to study biological structure.
Don J. Diamond, Ph.D. Translational research in cancer vaccines.
Richard W. Ermel, D.V.M., Ph.D. Applied animal research.
Barry Marc Forman. M.D., Ph.D. Gene regulation and drug discovery endocrinology of orphan nuclear receptors.
David Horne, Ph.D. Developing natural products as novel anticancer agents.
Richard Jove, Ph.D. Development of molecular targeted therapeutics.
Susan E. Kane, Ph.D. Drug resistance and cancer.
Theodore G. Krontiris, M.D., Ph.D. Genetic risk and disease.
Ren-Jang Lin, Ph.D. Structure and mechanisms of RNA splicing.
Chih-Pin Liu, Ph.D. Immune regulation of autoimmune disease and tumor.
Marcia M. Miller, Ph.D. Molecular immunogenetics.
Rama Natarajan, Ph.D. Diabetic vascular complications.
Susan Neuhausen, Ph.D. Genetic epidemiology of complex diseases.
Timothy R. O'Connor, Ph.D. DNA repair.
Gerd P. Pfeifer, Ph.D. Molecular mechanisms of cancer.
Arthur D. Riggs, Ph.D. Epigenetics, chromatin structure, and X chromosome inactivation.
John J. Rossi, Ph.D. The biology and applications of small RNAs.
Paul M. Salvaterra, Ph.D. Modeling Alzheimer-type neurogeneration.
Binghui Shen, Ph.D. DNA replication and repair nucleases in genome stability, cancers, and HIV life cycle.
John E. Shively, Ph.D. Structure, function, and regulation of carcinoembryonic antigen genes.
Judith Singer-Sam, Ph.D. Epigenetics and disorders of the CNS.
Steven S. Smith, Ph.D. Cancer epigenetics.
John Termini, Ph.D. Mutagenesis and carcinogenesis.
Nagarajan Vaidehi, Ph.D. Targeting G protein-coupled receptors for cancer therapy.
Jeffrey N. Weitzel, M.D. Genetic predisposition to cancer.
Jiing-Kuan Yee, Ph.D. Vectors for gene therapy.
Yun Yen, M.D., Ph.D. Novel molecular-targeted cancer therapies.
Hua Yu, Ph.D. Stat 3 and the tumor microenvironment.
John A. Zaia, M.D. Genetic and other anti-HIV therapy.

Associate and Assistant Professors

Karen S. Aboody, M.D. Neural stem cells and cancer.
Adam M. Bailis, Ph.D. Genome instability associated with aging and radiation exposure.
Wen Yong Chen, Ph.D. Epigenetics, cancer, and aging.
Warren Chow, M.D., FACP. Cell signaling and cancer.
Fong-Fong Chu, Ph.D. Role of oxidative stress in inflammatory bowel disease and cancer.
Carlotta A. Glackin, Ph.D. Understanding gene regulation from stem cells.
Wendong Huang, Ph.D. Metabolic regulation, cancer, and aging.
Janice Huss, Ph.D. Role of orphan nuclear receptors in cardiac and skeletal muscle biology.
Kazuo Ikeda, Ph.D. Synaptic transmission mechanisms.
Keiichi Itakura, Ph.D. Functions of Mrf-1 and Mrf-2.
Linda Iverson, Ph.D. Stem cells and cancer.
Jeremy Jones, Ph.D. The androgen receptor in human disease.
Markus Kalkum, Dr. rer. nat. (Ph.D.) Biodefense and emerging infectious diseases.
Mei Kong, Ph.D. Signal transduction and cancer metabolism.
Marcin Kortylewski, Ph.D. Immune cells as targets for cancer therapy.
Hsun Teresa Ku, Ph.D. Pancreatic endocrine stem cells.
Ya-Huei Kuo, Ph.D. Hematopoietic stem cell and leukemia research.
Terry D. Lee, Ph.D. Mass spectrometry of biomolecules.
Qiang Lu, Ph.D. Mechanisms that control self-renewal and differentiation of neural progenitor stem cells.
Takahiro Maeda, M.D., Ph.D. Hematological malignancies.
Edward M. Newman, Ph.D. Biochemical pharmacology of antimetabolites.
Yanhong Shi, Ph.D. Nuclear receptors in neural stem cells and adult neurogenesis.
Jeremy M. Stark, Ph.D. Pathways of chromosome break repair in mammalian cells.
Zuoming Sun, Ph.D. Signaling mechanisms that guide T cells.
Timothy W. Synold, Pharm.D. Pharmacokinetics and biomarkers of cancer.
Piroska E. Szabó, Ph.D. Mechanisms of genomic imprinting.
Toshifumi Tomoda, M.D., Ph.D. Neuronal development and degeneration.
Shizhen Emily Wang, Ph.D. Outsmarting breast cancer.
John C. Williams, Ph.D. Application of multivalency for basic science and translational medicine.
Defu Zeng, M.D. Transplantation immune tolerance.

COLD SPRING HARBOR LABORATORY

Watson School of Biological Sciences

Program of Study

The Watson School of Biological Sciences at Cold Spring Harbor Laboratory (CSHL) offers an accredited graduate training program, which leads to the Ph.D. degree, to a select group of self-motivated students of outstanding ability and intellect. The curriculum takes advantage of the unique and flexible environment of CSHL and includes the following innovative features: approximately four years from matriculation to Ph.D. degree award, broad representation of the biological sciences, a first year with course work and laboratory rotations in separate phases, emphasis on the principles of scientific reasoning and logic, continued advanced course instruction throughout the graduate curriculum, and two-tier mentoring.

The program provides an exciting and intensive educational experience. The curriculum is designed to train self-reliant students who, under their own guidance, can acquire and assimilate the knowledge that their research or career demands require. The course work is varied, involving core courses, focused topic courses, and CSHL postgraduate courses.

The current fields of research expertise of CSHL faculty members are cancer, neuroscience, quantitative biology, plant biology, and bioinformatics and genomics. The laboratories of all CSHL research faculty members are available to students in the program.

Requirements for the award of the Ph.D. degree are successful completion of all course work, laboratory rotations, teaching (at the Laboratory's Dolan DNA Learning Center), the Ph.D. qualifying exam, thesis research and postdoctoral proposals, and defense of a written thesis that describes original research. The program aims to train future leaders in the biological sciences.

Research Facilities

Cold Spring Harbor Laboratory has state-of-the-art facilities for research in cancer, neuroscience, quantitative biology, plant biology, and bioinformatics and genomics. As a National Cancer Institute–designated Cancer Center, there is an extensive set of shared resources. There are several libraries and one archive on campus. Library services, such as database searching and reference and interlibrary loan services, are available. An information technology department provides campuswide support of computing.

Financial Aid

The Watson School of Biological Sciences supports each student with an annual stipend, health benefits, affordable housing, subsidized food, and funds for tuition and research costs. To enhance their careers, students are encouraged to seek independent funding through predoctoral fellowships from federal and private sources such as the National Science Foundation.

Cost of Study

The Watson School of Biological Sciences provides full remission of all tuition fees for all accepted students. The School also supports the stipend and research costs of each student for four years.

Living and Housing Costs

The Laboratory provides affordable housing to all graduate students through a network of on-site and off-site housing. Single graduate students are offered single rooms in shared houses with house-cleaning services; married students are housed in apartments. First-year students of the Watson School are offered housing in the Townsend Knight House, a renovated house from 1810 that is located on the shore of Cold Spring Harbor opposite the Laboratory.

Student Group

The class size is approximately 10 to 15 students per year. Over the years students have come to the School from the United States, Italy, Poland, Singapore, China, England, Germany, Argentina, Mexico, Australia, Canada, India, France, and Russia. The School aims to produce graduates in the biological sciences who are likely to become ethical world leaders in science and society.

Location

The Laboratory is located on the wooded north shore of Long Island, 35 miles east of Manhattan in New York City, and offers many amenities, both cultural and recreational. Recreational activities at CSHL include a fitness room, tennis and volleyball courts, a private beach, sailboats, and many quiet back roads for running or walking. Students may also attend classical music performances and art exhibitions sponsored by the Laboratory for scientists and the neighboring community.

The Laboratory

Since its inception in 1890, CSHL has been involved in higher education and is today a world leader in biology education. The CSHL Press publishes internationally recognized books and journals. The Dolan DNA Learning Center educates students and teachers about the world of DNA. The Undergraduate Research Program, started in 1959, hosts exceptional undergraduates from around the world for a summer research experience. CSHL is also involved in education at the highest levels through a postgraduate program of twenty-five advanced courses in biology and many large and small international conferences. These meetings and courses attract 8,000 scientists annually to the Laboratory. The Laboratory has also been involved in graduate education leading to the Ph.D. degree for more than twenty-five years, particularly through shared graduate programs with Stony Brook University.

Applying

Applicants must have received a baccalaureate degree from an accredited university or college prior to matriculation. Admission is based on the perceived ability of the applicant to excel in this doctoral program, without regard to gender, race, color, ethnic origin, sexual orientation, disability, or marital status. Suitable applicants are assessed on the basis of their academic record, recommendations from their mentors, and an on-site interview. Students should ensure that the school receives all application materials (transcripts, examination scores, letters of recommendation, etc.) no later than December 1 for the following fall term. Early application is advisable. All applicants must apply online. Further information about the School and the application procedure may be requested by mail or obtained from the Web site at http://www.cshl.edu/gradschool.

Correspondence and Information

Dawn M. Pologruto
Director of Admissions and Student Affairs
Watson School of Biological Sciences
Cold Spring Harbor Laboratory
One Bungtown Road
Cold Spring Harbor, New York 11724
Phone: 516-367-6911
Fax: 516-367-6919
E-mail: gradschool@cshl.edu
Web site: http://www.cshl.edu/gradschool

Cold Spring Harbor Laboratory

THE FACULTY AND THEIR RESEARCH

Research Faculty

Dinu Florin Albeanu, Assistant Professor; Ph.D., Harvard, 2008. Neuronal circuits; sensory coding and synaptic plasticity; neuronal correlates of behavior; olfactory processing.

Gurinder Singh Atwal, Assistant Professor; Ph.D., Cornell, 2002. Population genetics; bioinformatics; cancer; stochastic processes; statistical mechanics and information theory.

Anne Churchland, Assistant Professor; Ph.D., California, San Francisco, 2003. Behavior in awake animals; neuroscience and electrophysiology.

Josh Dubnau, Assistant Professor; Ph.D., Columbia, 1995. Learning; memory; genetics; behavior.

Mikala Egeblad, Assistant Professor, Ph.D., Copenhagen, 2000. Tumor microenvironment; intravital imaging; tumor-associated myeloid cells; breast cancer.

Grigori Enikolopov, Associate Professor; Ph.D., Russian Academy of Sciences (Moscow), 1978. Signal transduction in neurons; development; gene expression; nitric oxide.

Hiro Furukawa, Assistant Professor; Ph.D., Tokyo, 2001. Structural biology; neurodegenerative diseases; intramembrane proteolysis; ion channels; membrane proteins; X-ray crystallography.

Thomas Gingeras, Professor; Ph.D., NYU, 1976. Organization and regulation of eukaryotic transcription; classification and function of non–protein coding RNAs.

Chris Hammell, Assistant Professor; Ph.D., Dartmouth, 2002. MicroRNA-mediated gene regulation of *C. elegans* developmental timing; genetics; development.

Gregory Hannon, Professor; Ph.D., Case Western Reserve, 1992. Growth control in mammalian cells.

Z. Josh Huang, Professor; Ph.D., Brandeis, 1994. Neuroscience; experience-dependent development and plasticity of the neocortex; mouse genetics.

David Jackson, Professor; Ph.D., East Anglia (England), 1991. Plant development; genetics; cell-to-cell mRNA and protein trafficking.

Leemor Joshua-Tor, Professor and Dean; Ph.D., Weizmann (Israel), 1991. Structural biology; X-ray crystallography; molecular recognition; transcription; proteases.

Adam Kepecs, Assistant Professor; Ph.D., Brandeis, 2002. Decision-making; neural circuits; behavioral electrophysiology; theoretical neuroscience; neuroeconomics.

Alexei Koulakov, Associate Professor; Ph.D., Minnesota, 1998. Theoretical neurobiology; quantitative principles of cortical design.

Adrian R. Krainer, Professor; Ph.D., Harvard, 1986. Posttranscriptional regulation of gene expression; pre-mRNA splicing mechanisms; alternative splicing; RNA-protein interactions; cell-free systems.

Alexander Krasnitz, Assistant Professor; Ph.D., Tel Aviv University, 1990. High-level analysis of microarray-derived data in cancer biology; bioinformatics.

Yuri Lazebnik, Professor; Ph.D., St. Petersburg State, 1986. Apoptosis; caspases; cancer chemotherapy; proteases.

Bo Li, Assistant Professor; Ph.D., British Columbia, 2003. Neuroscience; glutamatergic synapse; synaptic plasticity; schizophrenia; depression; rodent models of psychiatric disorders.

Zachary Lippman, Assistant Professor; Ph.D., Watson School of Biological Sciences at Cold Spring Harbor Laboratory, 2004. Plant development; genetics; flowering; inflorescence architecture; sympodial growth, phase transition, heterosis; quantitative genetics.

Robert Lucito, Assistant Professor; Ph.D., NYU, 1993. Genomic analysis of cancer.

Robert Martienssen, Professor; Ph.D., Cambridge, 1986. Plant genetics; transposons; development; gene regulation; DNA methylation.

W. Richard McCombie, Professor; Ph.D., Michigan, 1982. Genome structure; DNA sequencing; computational molecular biology; Human Genome Project.

Alea A. Mills, Associate Professor; Ph.D., California, Irvine, 1997. Functional genomics; tumorigenesis; development.

Partha P. Mitra, Professor; Ph.D., Harvard, 1993. Neuroinformatics; theoretical engineering; animal communications; neural prostheses; brain imaging; developmental linguistics.

Pavel Osten, Associate Professor; M.D., Charles University (Prague), 1991; Ph.D., SUNY Downstate Medical Center, 1995. Neurobiology of autism and schizophrenia; gene expression-based mapping of brain activity; anatomical mapping of brain connectivity; high throughput microscopy.

Darryl J. Pappin, Associate Professor; Ph.D., Leeds (United Kingdom), 1984. Proteomics; mass spectrometry; protein chemistry.

Scott Powers, Associate Professor; Ph.D., Columbia, 1983. Cancer gene discovery; cancer diagnostics and therapeutics; cancer biology.

Michael C. Schatz, Assistant Professor; Ph.D., Maryland, College Park. DNA sequence data concentrating on the alignment and assembly of short reads; bioinformatics.

Stephen Shea, Assistant Professor; Ph.D., Chicago, 2004. Olfaction; audition; communication behaviors; *in vivo* electrophysiology; individual recognition.

Raffaella Sordella, Assistant Professor; Ph.D., Turin, 1998. Molecular therapeutics; signal transduction.

David L. Spector, Professor; Ph.D., Rutgers, 1980. Cell biology; nuclear structure; microscopy; pre-mRNA splicing.

Arne Stenlund, Associate Professor; Ph.D., Uppsala (Sweden), 1984. Papillomavirus; cancer; DNA replication.

Bruce Stillman, President and CEO; Ph.D., Australian National, 1979. DNA replication; chromatin assembly; biochemistry; yeast genetics; cancer; cell cycle.

Marja Timmermans, Associate Professor; Ph.D., Rutgers, 1996. Plant development; axis specification; homeobox genes; stem cell function.

Nicholas Tonks, Professor; Ph.D., Dundee (Scotland), 1985. Posttranslational modification; phosphorylation; phosphatases; signal transduction; protein structure and function.

Lloyd Trotman, Assistant Professor; Ph.D., Zurich, 2001. Molecular mechanisms of tumor suppression; cancer modeling and treatment; molecular cancer visualization; PTEN regulation.

Glenn Turner, Assistant Professor; Ph.D., Caltech, 2000. Neural coding; learning and memory; sensory processing; *Drosophila;* electrophysiology.

Linda Van Aelst, Professor; Ph.D., Leuven (Belgium), 1991. Signal transduction; Ras and Rac proteins; tumorigenesis; metastasis.

Doreen Ware, Assistant Professor; Ph.D., Ohio State, 2000. Computational biology; comparative genomics; genome evolution; diversity; gene regulation; plant biology.

Michael Wigler, Professor; Ph.D., Columbia, 1978. Cancer; genomics; oncogenes; signal transduction; Ras; yeast genetics.

Anthony Zador, Professor; M.D./Ph.D., Yale, 1994. Computational neuroscience; synaptic plasticity; auditory processing; cortical circuitry.

Hongwu Zheng, Assistant Professor; Ph.D., Boston University, 2003. Cellular renewal and differentiation in stem cells and glioma genesis; cancer development; stem cells.

Yi Zhong, Professor; Ph.D., Iowa, 1991. Neurophysiology; *Drosophila;* learning and memory; neurofibromatosis; signal transduction.

Non-Research Faculty

Alexander A. F. Gann, Editorial Director, Cold Spring Harbor Laboratory Press; Ph.D., Edinburgh, 1989.

Terri Grodzicker, Dean, Academic Affairs; Ph.D., Columbia, 1969.

John R. Inglis, Executive Director, Cold Spring Harbor Laboratory Press; Ph.D., Edinburgh, 1976.

David A. Micklos, Executive Director, DNA Learning Center; M.A., Maryland, 1982.

David J. Stewart, Director, Meetings and Courses; Ph.D., Cambridge, 1988.

Jan A. Witkowski, Executive Director, Banbury Center; Ph.D., London, 1972.

COLUMBIA UNIVERSITY

Graduate School of Arts and Sciences
Department of Biological Sciences

Program of Study	The Department offers training leading to a Ph.D. in cellular, molecular, developmental, computational, and structural biology as well as genetics, molecular biophysics, and neurobiology. The graduate program provides each student with a solid background in contemporary biology and an in-depth knowledge of one or more of the above areas. The specific nature and scheduling of courses taken during the first two graduate years are determined by the student's consultation with the graduate student adviser, taking into account the background and specific research interests of the student. During the first year, all students take an intensive core course that provides a solid background in structural biology, cell biology, genetics, molecular biology, and bioinformatics.
	Beginning in the first year, graduate students attend advanced seminar courses, including the preresearch seminar, which is a forum for faculty-student research discussion. Important components of graduate education include the ability to analyze critically the contemporary research literature and to present such analyses effectively through oral and written presentations. Students acquire training in these skills through participation in advanced-level seminars and journal clubs, as well as through presentation and defense of original research proposals during the second year of graduate study.
	Beginning in the first year of graduate work, students also engage in research training. Students may choose laboratories in the Department of Biological Sciences on Columbia's main Morningside Heights Campus or in about twenty-five other laboratories, including many at Columbia's Health Sciences Campus. To inform incoming students of research opportunities, faculty members discuss ongoing research projects with them in the preresearch seminar held in the autumn term of the first year. All students are required to participate in ongoing research in up to three different laboratories during the first year. The choice of a dissertation sponsor is made after consultation between the student and potential faculty advisers, and intensive research begins following the spring term of the student's first year. Each student is assigned a Ph.D. Advisory Committee made up of the student's sponsor and 2 other faculty members.
Research Facilities	The Department of Biological Sciences is located in the Sherman Fairchild Center for the Life Sciences. The building provides nearly 60,000 square feet of laboratory space for the Department's laboratories, as well as extensive shared instrument facilities, including extensive sophisticated microscopy, X-ray diffraction, fluorescence-activated cell sorting (FACS), real-time PCR analysis, mass spectrometry, infrared scanning, phosphorimaging, and microinjection, as well as housing and care of research animals, including transgenic mice. In addition, several laboratories are located in the nearby new Northwest Corner interdisciplinary science building.
Financial Aid	All accepted students receive generous stipends, complete tuition exemption, and medical insurance. Special fellowships with larger stipends are also available (e.g., to members of minority groups).
Cost of Study	Tuition and fees are paid for all graduate students accepted into the Department.
Living and Housing Costs	Most students live in University-owned, subsidized apartments or dormitories within easy walking distance of the laboratories. In addition, both the Morningside and Health Sciences Campuses are easily reached by public transportation from all areas of the city.
Student Group	There are about 110 graduate students and 60 postdoctoral fellows in the Department.
Location	New York is the cultural center of the country and offers unrivaled opportunities for attending concerts, operas, plays, and sporting events, for visiting outstanding museums, and for varied, affordable dining. Many excellent beaches, ski slopes, and state and national parks are within reasonable driving distance.
The University and The Department	Columbia was established as King's College in 1754 and has grown into one of the major universities of the world. The Department is located on the beautiful main campus in Morningside Heights, which combines the advantages of an urban setting and a peaceful college-town atmosphere.
Applying	Undergraduate training in one of the natural or physical sciences is recommended, although successful students have come from computer science or engineering backgrounds, as well. It is desirable for students to have had at least one year of calculus, as well as courses in organic and physical chemistry, physics, genetics, biochemistry, and cell biology. Any deficiencies may be made up while in graduate school. The Graduate Record Examinations (GRE) is required, as is the Test of English as a Foreign Language (TOEFL) for international applicants whose native language is not English and who do not hold an undergraduate degree from a U.S. college. The GRE Subject Test in biology, biochemistry, chemistry, computer science, or physics is highly recommended. Completed applications should be returned by December 1 for admission to the fall semester. Application forms and additional information can be obtained from the Department's Web site.
	Columbia University is an Equal Opportunity/Affirmative Action institution.
Correspondence and Information	Graduate Student Adviser Department of Biological Sciences Columbia University 1212 Amsterdam Avenue, Mail Code 2402 Sherman Fairchild Center, Room 600 New York, New York 10027 Phone: 212-854-2313 Fax: 212-865-8246 E-mail: biology@columbia.edu Web site: http://www.columbia.edu/cu/biology/

Columbia University

THE FACULTY AND THEIR RESEARCH

Walter J. Bock, Professor; Ph.D., Harvard, 1959. General evolutionary theory; evolutionary and functional morphology; morphology and classification of birds; history and philosophy of evolutionary biology.

J. Chloë Bulinski, Professor; Ph.D., Wisconsin, 1980. Dynamics and functions of microtubules during myogenic differentiation and cell-cycle progression.

Harmen Bussemaker, Associate Professor; Ph.D., Utrecht (Netherlands), 1995. Data-driven modeling of transcriptional and posttranscriptional networks based on biophysical principles.

Martin Chalfie, Professor; Ph.D., Harvard, 1977; Member, National Academy of Sciences and Nobel Laureate in Chemistry 2008. Developmental genetics of identified nerve cells in *Caenorhabditis elegans;* genetic analysis of cell differentiation, mechanosensory transduction, synapse specification, and aging.

Lawrence A. Chasin, Professor; Ph.D., MIT, 1967. Pre-mRNA splicing in cultured mammalian cells.

Lars Dietrich, Assistant Professor, Ph.D., Heidelberg (Germany), 2004. Bacterial models for biological shape and pattern formation.

Julio Fernandez, Professor; Ph.D., Berkeley, 1982. Study of the cellular events that lead to the release of histamine or catecholamine-containing secretory granules from single, isolated mast cells or chromaffin cells; analysis of single-protein elasticity by atomic force microscopy (AFM).

Stuart Firestein, Professor; Ph.D., Berkeley, 1988. Cellular and molecular physiology of transduction; coding and neuronal regeneration in the vertebrate olfactory system.

Joachim Frank, Professor and Howard Hughes Medical Institute Investigator; Ph.D., Munich Technical, 1970; Member, National Academy of Sciences. Cryoelectron microscopy and three-dimensional reconstruction for the study of the mechanism of protein biosynthesis.

John F. Hunt, Associate Professor; Ph.D., Yale, 1993. Structural genomics and biophysical studies of the molecular mechanism of transmembrane transport.

Songtao Jia, Assistant Professor; Ph.D., UCLA, 2003. Epigenetic regulation of the genome.

Daniel D. Kalderon, Professor; Ph.D., London, 1984. Molecular mechanisms of cellular interactions mediated by cAMP-dependent protein kinase (PKA) in *Drosophila;* roles of PKA in hedgehog signaling and in generating anterior/posterior polarity in oocytes.

Darcy B. Kelley, Professor and Howard Hughes Medical Institute Professor; Ph.D., Rockefeller, 1975. Sexual differentiation of the nervous system; molecular analyses of androgen-regulated development in neurons and muscle; neuroethology of vocal communication; evolution of the nuclear receptor family.

James L. Manley, Professor; Ph.D., SUNY at Stony Brook, 1976. Regulation of mRNA synthesis in animal cells; biochemical and genetic analysis of mechanisms and control of mRNA transcription, splicing, and polyadenylation; developmental control of gene expression.

Elizabeth Miller, Assistant Professor; Ph.D., La Trobe (Australia), 1999. Protein folding, assembly, and the regulation of intracellular protein transport.

Dana Pe'er, Assistant Professor; Ph.D., Hebrew (Israel), 2003. Function and organization of molecular networks.

Robert E. Pollack, Professor; Ph.D., Brandeis, 1966. Critical analysis of issues involving molecular biology and religion.

Carol L. Prives, Professor; Ph.D., McGill, 1968; Member, National Academy of Sciences and National Institute of Medicine. Structure and function of the p53 tumor suppressor protein and p53 family members; studies on cell cycle and apoptosis; stress-activated signaling and control of proteolysis.

Ron Prywes, Professor; Ph.D., MIT, 1984. Normal and cancerous mechanisms of regulation of cellular proliferation and gene expression; signal transduction and activation of transcription factors; activation of transcription by the ER stress/unfolded protein response.

Ozgur Sahin, Associate Professor of Biological Sciences and Physics; Ph.D., Stanford, 2005. Mechanical investigations of biological systems for energy, environment, and biological research.

Michael P. Sheetz, Professor; Ph.D., Caltech, 1972. Motility studies of cells and microtubule motor proteins, with an emphasis on the force-dependent interactions relevant to transformed cells and neuron pathfinding, using laser tweezers.

Brent Stockwell, Associate Professor and Howard Hughes Medical Institute Investigator; Ph.D., Harvard, 1997. Diagramming disease networks with chemical and biological tools.

Liang Tong, Professor; Ph.D., Berkeley, 1989. Structural biology of proteins involved in human diseases (obesity, diabetes, cancer); structural biology of proteins involved in pre-mRNA 3'-end processing.

Alexander A. Tzagoloff, Professor of Biological Sciences; Ph.D., Columbia, 1962. Energy-coupling mechanisms; structure of membrane enzymes; biogenesis of mitochondria; genetics of mitochondria in yeast.

Jian Yang, Professor; Ph.D., Washington (Seattle), 1991. Structure and function of ion channels; molecular mechanisms of ion channel regulation and localization.

Rafael Yuste, Professor and Howard Hughes Medical Institute Investigator; M.D., Madrid, 1987; Ph.D., Rockefeller, 1992. Development and function of the cortical microcircuitry.

Additional Faculty Sponsors for Ph.D. Research

Richard Axel, Biochemistry and Molecular Biophysics/Pathology and Cell Biology; Howard Hughes Medical Institute Investigator and Nobel Laureate in Physiology or Medicine 2004; Member, National Academy of Sciences. Central and peripheral organization of the olfactory system.

Richard J. Baer, Pathology and Cell Biology. The pathogenesis of hereditary breast cancer.

Andrea Califano, Biomedical Informatics. Study of gene regulatory and signaling networks in mammalian cellular contexts using computational methods.

Virginia Cornish, Chemistry. Development of in vivo selection strategies for evolving proteins with novel catalytic properties.

Riccardo Dalla-Favera, Genetics and Development, and Microbiology and Immunology. Molecular genetics of cancer; molecular pathogenesis of lymphoma and leukemia.

Jonathan E. Dworkin, Microbiology and Immunology. Bacterial signaling and interactions with the host.

Jean Gautier, Genetics and Development/Institute for Cancer Genetics. Cell cycle and cell death during early development.

Ruben L. Gonzalez Jr., Chemistry. Single molecule biophysics.

Eric C. Greene, Biochemistry and Molecular Biophysics; Howard Hughes Medical Institute Investigator. Molecular mechanisms of DNA recombination and repair; single-molecule fluorescence microscopy and other biochemical approaches.

Lloyd Greene, Pathology and Cell Biology. Mechanisms of neuronal differentiation and degeneration and their regulation by external growth factors.

Iva Greenwald, Biochemistry and Molecular Biophysics; Howard Hughes Medical Institute Investigator; Member, National Academy of Sciences, Development and cell-cell interactions.

Wei Gu, Pathology and Cell Biology. P53 in tumor suppression and aging.

Tulle Hazelrigg, Biological Sciences. mRNA localization in *Drosophila* oocytes.

René Hen, Pharmacology. Serotonin receptors and behavior.

Wayne Hendrickson, Biochemistry and Molecular Biophysics; Howard Hughes Medical Institute Investigator; Member, National Academy of Sciences. Macromolecular structure; X-ray crystallography.

Oliver Hobert, Biochemistry and Molecular Biophysics; Howard Hughes Medical Institute Investigator. Nervous system development and function.

Thomas Jessell, Biochemistry and Molecular Biophysics; Howard Hughes Medical Institute Investigator; Member, National Academy of Sciences. Molecular mechanisms of neural differentiation.

Laura Johnston, Genetics and Development. Control of growth and cell division during development.

Eric Kandel, Physiology and Cellular Biophysics/Psychiatry/Biochemistry and Molecular Biophysics; Howard Hughes Medical Institute Investigator and Nobel Laureate in Physiology or Medicine 2000; Member, National Academy of Sciences. Cell and molecular mechanisms of associative and nonassociative learning.

Arthur Karlin, Biochemistry and Molecular Biophysics/Physiology and Cellular Biophysics/Center for Molecular Recognition; Member, National Academy of Sciences. Molecular mechanisms of receptor function.

Richard Mann, Biochemistry and Molecular Biophysics. Transcriptional control.

Ann McDermott, Chemistry/Biological Sciences/Chemical Engineering; Member, National Academy of Sciences. Solid-state NMR of enzyme active sites and model systems.

Arthur G. Palmer, Biochemistry and Molecular Biophysics. Biomolecular dynamics, structure, and function; NMR spectroscopy.

Virginia Papaioannou, Genetics and Development. Genetic control of mammalian development in the peri-implantation period.

Ramon E. Parsons, Pathology and Cell Biology. The genetics of breast cancer tumorigenesis.

Rodney Rothstein, Genetics and Development. Yeast genetics; mechanisms of genetic recombination; control of genome stability; functional genomics.

Christian Schindler, Microbiology/Medicine. JAK-STAT signaling and immune response.

Steve Siegelbaum, Pharmacology; Howard Hughes Medical Institute Investigator. Molecular studies of ion channel structure and function; synaptic transmission and plasticity in the mammalian brain.

Gary Struhl, Genetics and Development; Howard Hughes Medical Institute Investigator; Member, National Academy of Sciences. Developmental genetics in *Drosophila*.

Lorraine Symington, Microbiology. Homologous recombination in the yeast *Saccharomyces cerevisiae*.

Richard Vallee, Pathology and Cell Biology. Motor proteins in axonal transport, brain developmental disease, and synaptic function.

MOREHOUSE SCHOOL OF MEDICINE

Graduate Education in Biomedical Sciences

Program of Study

The Graduate Education in Biomedical Sciences program encompasses four degree programs. The Ph.D. in Biomedical Sciences develops independent investigators capable of assuming leadership roles in academic, corporate, and governmental biomedical research. The M.S. in Clinical Research (MSCR) develops clinical faculty members to pursue clinical research on diseases that disproportionately affect underserved populations. The M.S. in Biomedical Technology (MSBT) is a nonthesis program to enhance and document scientific background and technical expertise in the biomedical sciences in ways that improve earning power in biomedical science and technology. The M.S. in Biomedical Research (MSBR) is an interdisciplinary program that provides a foundation to prepare graduates to enter a doctoral training program (in research or the health professions) or to enter the workforce as master's-level laboratory scientists.

Students may study with graduate faculty members from basic science or clinical departments. Areas of focus within and across disciplines include HIV/AIDS and infectious disease, cancer, cardiovascular disease, cell biology, circadian biology, developmental biology, immunology, microbiology, molecular biology, neuroscience, pathology, pharmacology/toxicology, physiology, stroke, and vision research. Tracks for obtaining dual degrees, including M.D./Ph.D., M.D./MSCR, and M.D./MSBR, are available for qualified medical students. An MSCR/Ph.D. track is available for qualified Ph.D. students.

All programs begin with core course work. The core sequences for each program differ but include basic biomedical sciences, statistics, and fundamentals of basic and clinical professional science. Students select advisers, complete advanced graduate (elective) courses, and begin thesis or dissertation research in their second year. The M.S. programs generally take two years to complete. At least four years of full-time study beyond the baccalaureate degree and 3½ years in residence at Morehouse School of Medicine (MSM) are required to complete the Ph.D. program.

Research Facilities

Morehouse School of Medicine currently occupies six buildings on the main campus where most biomedical research and research-related activities take place. The Gloster Basic Medical Sciences Building and the attached Medical Education Building, with its Research Wing, provide more than 105,000 square feet of research and research support space. This includes individual, shared-use, and core facilities laboratories. The 70,000-square-foot Multi-Disciplinary Research Center currently houses the Neuroscience Institute and the Clinical Research Center. The Center for Laboratory Animal Resources, located in the Gloster building, occupies an additional 8,500 square feet, and the Medical Library comprises 10,000 square feet.

Faculty investigators currently have an average of approximately 400 square feet of individual laboratory space. In addition, many core and shared-use, state-of-the-art research technology and clinical research facilities are available to all researchers. The core support facilities and individual investigator laboratories are well equipped for biomedical research. Institutional facilities include flow cytometry/FACS, monoclonal antibody preparation, nucleic acid sequencing and DNA synthesis, Affymetrix and Agilent microarray scanners and GeneNet/GeneSpring software, SELDI and mass-spectrometry proteomics instruments, protein/peptide purification (HPLC) and two-dimensional gel electrophoresis, and imaging and image analysis facilities for brightfield, fluorescence, laser-dissection, and confocal microscopy and scanning and transmission electron microscopy. Scientific imaging and graphics preparation services are provided by Information Technology.

Additional collaborative research opportunities are available through existing links with government agencies, biotechnology companies, and other universities.

Financial Aid

The program provides stipends for all of its Ph.D. students. Stipends are a minimum of $24,000 per year. After completing the core curriculum, stipends may derive from a variety of funding sources. To continue stipend support, a student must maintain satisfactory progress in the program for which the stipend was awarded, must devote full time to study or research in the biomedical sciences, and must not engage in gainful employment outside the program. Students in all programs are eligible to apply for student loans through the financial aid office.

Cost of Study

Tuition waivers are typically provided for all full-time Ph.D. students in good academic standing who have not secured extramural grant support to cover these expenses. In addition, all fees are covered for Ph.D. students.

Tuition costs for MSBR and MSBT students are $15,860 per year, with fees ranging from approximately $4000 to $6000. The fees include a tablet/laptop computer provided to each student, health insurance, student activity, and other student support fees such as library services.

Living and Housing Costs

University housing is not currently available. Rental units are available throughout the Atlanta metropolitan area at a reasonable cost.

Student Group

Morehouse School of Medicine is a health sciences institution comprising six postbaccalaureate programs (M.D., M.P.H., MSCR, MSBT, MSBR, and Ph.D.), with a total student population approaching 300. There are currently 50 students in the Graduate Education in Biomedical Sciences program.

Location

Morehouse School of Medicine is a member of the Atlanta University Center, a consortium of five independent institutions of higher education (Clark Atlanta University, the Interdenominational Theological Center, Morehouse College, Spelman College, and Morehouse School of Medicine). Together, the center's institutions constitute the largest predominantly black private educational complex in the world. Other major educational and research institutions in Atlanta include the Centers for Disease Control and Prevention, Emory University, Georgia Institute of Technology, and Georgia State University. In addition to being a center for higher education and biotechnology in the Southeast, Atlanta offers many cultural opportunities, including the Atlanta Symphony Orchestra, the Atlanta Ballet, the Alliance Theatre, and several smaller theater companies. Other popular destinations include the Georgia Aquarium, the World of Coke (Atlanta is the international headquarters of Coca-Cola), and the Centennial Olympic Park. The High Museum of Art is an architectural masterpiece that houses an extensive collection of its own and hosts several first-rate touring collections each year. Atlanta is also known for its world-famous centers honoring Dr. Martin Luther King Jr. and former president Jimmy Carter. Sports and entertainment facilities include the Atlanta Braves' Turner Field, the Georgia Dome, broadcasting's CNN Center, the Fox Theater, the Philips Arena, and many jazz and blues clubs. It is not surprising that many of America's best-known and most respected African American businesspeople, politicians, and professionals call Atlanta home, making this city one of the premier centers of African American culture in the country.

The School

The institution was established in 1975 to address the shortage of minority physicians and related problems in medically underserved communities. Beginning as a two-year preclinical program in 1978, Morehouse School of Medicine was approved to become a four-year medical school in 1981 and granted its first M.D. degrees in 1985. The School's accreditation by the Southern Association of Colleges and Schools was expanded in 1992 to include the Ph.D. in Biomedical Sciences, and its first graduates finished in 1998. Graduates have obtained excellent positions in academic, government, and corporate biomedical research institutions. The MSCR, MSBT, and MSBR programs are more recent additions to the School's offerings.

Applying

Applications must be submitted online. Online applications, along with accompanying photos, references, and transcripts, must be received by February 1 for consideration for admission in August for Ph.D. applicants. Occasionally, student slots for the Ph.D. program become available for January entry. These slots are reserved for more advanced students, such as those with thesis-based M.S. degrees and extensive research experience. Applications for January entry must be received by October 1. Master's program applicants must complete an online application by May 1 for consideration for August admissions. MSBR, MSBT, and Ph.D. programs require applicants to have a bachelor's degree, with strong performance in science courses. GRE General Test scores are required, and scores on the Subject Test in chemistry or biology are recommended. International applicants are required to submit TOEFL scores, and third-party verification of academic records and references may be required. Application materials and information can be obtained through the Director of Admissions in the Office of Admissions and Student Affairs via phone (404-752-1650) or e-mail (gebs@msm.edu).

Correspondence and Information

Office of Graduate Education in Biomedical Sciences
Morehouse School of Medicine
720 Westview Drive
Atlanta, Georgia 30310-1495
Phone: 404-752-1580
Fax: 404-756-5220

Morehouse School of Medicine

THE FACULTY AND THEIR RESEARCH

Felix Aikhionbare, Ph.D., Nebraska. Characterizing the differences between human ovarian and colorectal cancer in normal and cancerous tissue. faikhionbare@msm.edu

Mukaila Akinbami, Ph.D., Missouri–Columbia. Cardiovascular physiology: defining the role of high blood pressure on vascular function and gene expression. makinbami@msm.edu

Leonard M. Anderson, Ph.D., Northwestern. Cardiovascular genomics; vascular smooth-muscle-cell fate determination from stem cells. landerson@msm.edu

Methode Bacanamwo, Ph.D., Illinois. Chromatin remodeling and epigenetic mechanisms in vascular gene expression. mbacanmwo@msm.edu

Mohamed A. Bayorh, Ph.D., Howard. Cardiovascular, neurochemical, and signaling pathways in actions of polyunsaturated fatty acids, vasoactive substances, and drugs of abuse. mbayorh@msm.edu

Morris Benveniste, Ph.D., Weizmann (Israel). NMDA channels in synaptic integration; scorpion toxin action on sodium channels. mbenveniste@msm.edu

Vincent C. Bond, Ph.D., Penn State. DNA virology; mammalian cell biology. vbond@msm.edu

L. DiAnne Bradford, Ph.D., Georgia Tech. Psychopharmacology; predicting clinical efficacy and safety. dbradford@msm.edu

Teh-Ching Chu, Ph.D., Louisville. Receptor pharmacology; medical acupuncture; herbal medicine. tchu@msm.edu

Margaret Colden, Ph.D., Texas Medical Branch. Cardiovascular pharmacology; membrane biophysics; cell physiology; leukocyte- and pathogen-endothelial interactions. mstanfield@msm.edu

Alec Davidson, Ph.D., Florida State. Integrative analysis of circadian systems in mammals. adavidson@msm.edu

Adam Davis, Ph.D., Clark Atlanta. Advance genomic science: expanding the racial/bio-ancestral diversity of genomic medicine datasets. adavis@msm.edu

Kamla Dutt, Ph.D., Punjab (India). Retinal cell biology; cell commitment and differentiation; tissue engineering. kdutt@msm.edu

Francis Eko, Ph.D., Vienna. Immunity and pathogenesis of *Chlamydia*, HSV-2, *Vibrio cholerae*, and related pathogens. feko@msm.edu

Martha Elks, M.D., Ph.D., North Carolina at Chapel Hill. Educational issues; teaching, and assessing professionalism; educational methodology. melks@msm.edu

Byron Ford, Ph.D., Meharry. Cellular and molecular mechanisms of atherosclerosis and stroke. bford@msm.edu

Sharon Francis-David, Ph.D., Alabama at Birmingham. Molecular physiology and vascular biology of hypertension and obesity-related vascular diseases. sfrancis-david@msm.edu

Chiaki Fukuhara, Ph.D., Sophia (Japan). Diagnostic tools for mental illnesses and sleep-wake-cycle problems. cfukuhara@msm.edu

Minerva Garcia-Barrio, Ph.D., Salamanca (Spain). Molecular biology; gene expression in vascular smooth muscle. mgarcia-barrio@msm.edu

Gary Gibbons, M.D., Harvard. Regulation of vascular remodeling. ggibbons@msm.edu

Ruben Gonzalez-Perez, Ph.D., INSA Toulouse (France). Specific signaling mechanisms involved in the leptin actions in cancer. rgonzalez@msm.edu

Sandra A. Harris-Hooker, Ph.D., Atlanta. Endothelial cells and smooth muscle in atherosclerosis; in vitro blood vessel modeling. sharris-hooker@msm.edu

Jacqueline Hibbert, Ph.D., West Indies (Jamaica). Metabolic response to disease; effects on protein and energy nutritional requirements. jhibbert@msm.edu

Ward Kirlin, Ph.D., Emory. Chemical carcinogenesis and toxicology; induction pathways in carcinogen activation and detoxification. wkirlin@msm.edu

Brenda J. Klement, Ph.D., Kansas State. Endochondral bone formation and skeletal tissue changes in microgravity. bklement@msm.edu

James Lillard Jr., Ph.D., Kentucky. Mechanisms by which chemokines enhance or suppress mucosal immunity, inflammation, and cancer cell metastasis. lillard@msm.edu

Woo-Kuen Lo, Ph.D., Wayne State. Eye ultrastructure and cell biology; intercellular junctions; cell membrane and cytoskeleton of the lens. wlo@msm.edu

Deborah A. Lyn, Ph.D., West Indies. Genetic markers and mechanisms for susceptibility to cardiovascular and infectious diseases. dlyn@msm.edu

Peter MacLeish, Ph.D., Harvard. Functional organization of the vertebrate retina; axonal regeneration; Purkinje cell viability. pmacleish@msm.edu

Julian Menter, Ph.D., George Washington. Dermatology, photobiology, and photochemistry; physical organic and physical biochemistry. jmenter@msm.edu

Shobu Namura, M.D., Ph.D., Kyoto (Japan). Cerebrovascular functions and their sequelae after stroke. snamura@msm.edu

Gale Newman, Ph.D., LSU. Pathogenesis of HIV-associated nephropathy. gnewman@msm.edu

John W. Patrickson, Ph.D., Howard. Chronobiology; neural mechanisms in the generation of circadian rhythms. jpatrickson@msm.edu

Ketema Paul, Ph.D., Georgia State. Circadian and hypothalamic coordination of sleep and wakefulness. kpaul@msm.edu

Douglas F. Paulsen, Ph.D., Wake Forest. Skeletal patterning during embryogenesis; microgravity effects on the musculoskeletal system. dpaulsen@msm.edu

Michael D. Powell, Ph.D., Texas at Dallas. Role of cellular factors in the regulation of HIV-1 reverse transcription. mpowell@msm.edu

Karen Randall, Ph.D., West Indies (Jamaica). Relationship of opioid receptors and cell signaling in the eye to identify drug targets in the design of novel drugs for the management of glaucoma. krandall@msm.edu

Veena N. Rao, Ph.D., Osmania (India). Molecular and functional dissection of ELK-1 and BRCA-1 tumor-suppressor genes in cancers. vrao@msm.edu

E. Shyam P. Reddy, Ph.D., Andhra (India). Functional role of ets, fusion onco-proteins, and tumor suppressors in cancer. ereddy@msm.edu

Gary L. Sanford, Ph.D., Brown. Lung growth, maturation, and function; vascular remodeling role of soluble lectins; cancer biology. gsanford@msm.edu

Qing Song, M.D., Peking; Ph.D., South Carolina. Molecular mechanisms of genetic susceptibility to cardiovascular disease, obesity, and diabetes. qsong@msm.edu

Rajagopala Sridaran, Ph.D., University of Health Sciences (Chicago). Reproductive endocrinology; gravity during pregnancy; GnRH in fertility; corpus luteum demise and parturition. rsridaran@msm.edu

Jonathan Stiles, Ph.D., Salford (England). Molecular and cell biology of *Trypanosoma-*, *Plasmodium-*, and *Trichomonas*-induced pathogenesis. jstiles@msm.edu

Myrtle Thierry-Palmer, Ph.D., Wisconsin–Madison. Vitamin D metabolism and function; calcium endocrine system; salt sensitivity; space biology. mtheirry-palmer@msm.edu

Kelwyn H. Thomas, Ph.D., California, San Diego. Gene regulation of cellular differentiation; germ-cell development in mouse testis. kthomas@msm.edu

Winston Thompson, Ph.D., Rutgers. Cell and reproductive biology; molecular mechanisms of ovarian follicle development and cyst formation. wthompson@msm.edu

Gianluca Tosini, Ph.D., Bristol (England). Interactions between retinal and hypothalamic circadian clocks. gtosini@msm.edu

Evan F. Williams, Ph.D., Howard. Role of nucleoside transporters in cardiovascular function; ocular purinergic systems. ewilliams@msm.edu

Lawrence E. Wineski, Ph.D., Illinois. Neural organization of craniofacial musculature; microgravity effects on the musculoskeletal system. lwineski@msm.edu

Xuebiao Yao, Ph.D., Berkeley. Mitotic chromosome segregation; establishment and maintenance of cell polarity; biophotonics. xyao@msm.edu

Xueying Zhao, M.D., Ph.D., Suzhou Medical College (China). Epoxygenase metabolites and endothelial function. xzhao@msm.edu

NEW YORK MEDICAL COLLEGE

Graduate School of Basic Medical Sciences

Programs of Study

The Graduate School of Basic Medical Sciences (GSBMS) of New York Medical College offers programs leading to the M.S. and Ph.D. degrees in biochemistry and molecular biology, cell biology, pathology, microbiology and immunology, pharmacology, and physiology plus an interdisciplinary M.S. degree in basic medical sciences. The full-time faculty of 90 basic medical scientists, with their individual and collaborative research programs, their great depth of knowledge, and their classroom experience and expertise, provide an intellectually challenging, yet supportive environment to those students with the requisite talent and motivation. These internal assets are supplemented by the College's plentiful access to other experts—in clinical research, the pharmaceutical and biotechnology industry, and public health—who can participate in the graduate school's research and educational activities.

Ph.D. degrees are awarded in six basic medical sciences. During the first year, students undertake an interdisciplinary core curriculum of courses and rotate through laboratories throughout the Graduate School. After this first year, students choose their major discipline and dissertation sponsor, complete the remaining didactic requirements in the chosen discipline, and begin intensive research training. Formal course work is usually substantially completed within two years, after which the student completes the qualifying exam, forms a dissertation advisory committee, presents a formal thesis proposal, and devotes his or her primary effort to the dissertation research project.

The M.S. degree requires completion of 30 to 32 credits, depending upon the discipline and specific track. Two M.S. degree sequences are available: (1) a research program consisting of 25 didactic (i.e., classroom-based) and up to 5 research credits and a research thesis or (2) a program consisting of 30 of 32 didactic credits and a scholarly literature review. The M.S. degree is earned full- or part-time in evening classes. The interdisciplinary M.S. program is particularly suitable for students wishing to prepare for a career in medicine, dentistry, or other health professions. An accelerated track within this program allows completion of the degree requirements within one year for highly qualified candidates.

The Department of Cell Biology offers training in cell biology and neuroscience leading to careers in academia and industry. Ongoing research includes studies of oncogene expression and cytokines; intracellular mechanisms of pulmonary arterial hypertension; modulation of neuronal and astrocytic signaling; hemorrhage and neuroprotection in the developing brain; aging and preservation of oocytes and ovarian tissue; growth control in skeletal muscle; signal transduction in a variety of tissues, including platelets, the retina, muscle cells, and the *Drosophila* nervous system; intracellular protein trafficking and degradation; cytoskeletal and receptor function; the development and regeneration of the visual system; apoptosis in glaucoma; extracellular matrices and limb development; spinal cord injury; molecular mechanisms of neuroplasticity; learning and memory; Alzheimer's disease; and modulation of seizures.

The Department of Biochemistry and Molecular Biology provides students with a solid foundation in the concepts and applications of modern biochemistry and molecular biology. Areas of research include protein structure and function, enzyme reaction mechanisms, regulation of gene expression, mechanisms of hormone action and cell signaling, enzymology, mechanisms of DNA replication and repair, cell-cycle regulation, control of cell growth, molecular biology of cancer cells and the cancer process, mechanisms of nutrition and cancer prevention, molecular neurobiology and studies of neurodegenerative disorders, and the aging process.

The Department of Pathology offers a vigorous multidisciplinary milieu for training in experimental pathology. The program's focus on the comprehensive study of pathogenic mechanisms of human disease. Areas of interest in the department include examination of the underlying mechanisms involved in biochemical toxicology, cancer cell biology, cell-cycle regulation and apoptosis, chemical carcinogenesis, hypersensitivity and chronic inflammation, molecular genetics of human hypertension, Lyme disease, tuberculosis, and tissue engineering.

In the Department of Microbiology and Immunology, the student acquires a broad acquaintance with microbiology, molecular biology, and immunology as well as depth in an elective field. Areas available for thesis research include molecular biology of tumor cells, cancer vaccines, the role of stem cells in cancer, bacterial genetics, pathogenesis of infectious disease, monoclonal antibody synthesis, immune function in AIDS, structure and function of influenza virus antigens, molecular virology, and the biochemistry and genetics of emerging bacterial pathogens.

The Department of Pharmacology emphasizes training in research methods for examining the mechanism of action of drugs at the systemic, cellular, and subcellular levels. Areas of research include investigation into the therapeutic and pathophysiologic role of bioactive lipids (eicosanoids) in cancer, ophthalmology, and cardiovascular diseases including hypertension, kidney disease, stroke, diabetes, atherosclerosis and inflammatory conditions, cytochrome P-450 function and control, patch-clamp analysis of ion transport, and the roles of vasoactive hormones and inflammatory cytokines in hypertension end-organ damage and cardiovascular function.

The Department of Physiology provides students with an understanding of the function of the body's cells and organ systems and the mechanisms for regulation of these functions. Research opportunities include cellular neurophysiology, regulation of sleep and awake states, neural and endocrine control of the heart and circulation, microcirculation, the physiology of gene expression, heart failure, cardiac metabolism, and the physiological effects of oxygen metabolites.

Research Facilities

The College has an extensive laboratory complex in the basic medical and clinical sciences. The Basic Sciences Building houses the medical sciences library, which maintains 200,000 volumes, an extensive collection of print and electronic journals, and a variety of online databases and search engines. There are also a fully accredited comparative medicine facility, a well-equipped and staffed instrumentation shop, a variety of classrooms, a bookstore, a cafeteria, and student lounges.

Financial Aid

Federal and state loan programs are available for M.S. students. Ph.D. students receive a stipend and tuition remission, medical insurance, and combinations of College fellowships and research assistantships. The Office of Financial Aid should be consulted for information on federal and state loan programs.

Cost of Study

In 2011–12, tuition is $835 per credit, or $13,360 annually, for a full-time master's student taking 8 credits per semester. The Accelerated Master's Program has an annual tuition rate of $31,680. Annual Ph.D. tuition is $20,040 before candidacy (first two years) and $4000 after candidacy. Fees range between $90 and $380 per year, depending upon options chosen. Comprehensive medical insurance is available for individual ($3708 annually), student plus spouse ($7097), or family ($10,384) coverage.

Living and Housing Costs

A limited number of rooms and apartments are available for graduate students in on-campus College housing. On-campus housing costs range from $740 to $795 per month for furnished suite-style apartments and $565 to $935 for unfurnished single-student apartments. Married housing apartment costs range from $1240 for a one-bedroom apartment, $1390 to $1445 for a two-bedroom apartment, and $1610 for a three-bedroom apartment (families with children). Private off-campus accommodations are also available. Students should contact the Director of Housing, Administration Building (phone: 914-594-4832 or e-mail: housing@nymc.edu), well in advance of arrival in order to make housing arrangements.

Student Group

The total College enrollment in fall 2101 was 1,448. There were 54 Ph.D. and 122 M.S. students in the Graduate School of Basic Medical Sciences.

Location

The College campus is located in the Westchester Medical Center campus, 5 miles from White Plains and 28 miles north of New York City.

The College

New York Medical College, one of the largest medical schools in the country, was established in 1860. Graduate education at the College began informally in 1910. Graduate degrees were offered as early as 1938, and a graduate division was established in 1963.

Applying

Applications for admission may be submitted from October 1 through July 1. For optimal review of credentials and consideration for financial aid and housing, however, applications for fall enrollment into Ph.D. programs should be received by January 15. International applicants to the master's program should complete their application no later than May 1. Specific program requirements are available on the College Web site at: http://www.nymc.edu/Academics/SchoolOfBasicMedicalSciences/Admissions/Requirements.htm. Students must apply online at the College Web site. M.S. and Ph.D. applicants must submit GRE General Test scores. Applicants for the Accelerated Master's Program must submit scores for the Medical College Admission Test (MCAT). International students are required to submit results of the TOEFL. Transcripts from all post-secondary institutions attended (undergraduate and graduate) and two letters of recommendation from teachers or scientists personally familiar with the applicant must be submitted directly by the school or recommenders separately.

Correspondence and Information

Francis L. Belloni, Ph.D., Dean
Graduate School of Basic Medical Sciences
Basic Sciences Building, Room A41
New York Medical College
Valhalla, New York 10595
E-mail: gsbms_apply@nymc.edu
Web site: http://www.nymc.edu/gsbms/

New York Medical College

THE GRADUATE FACULTY AND THEIR RESEARCH

Biochemistry and Molecular Biology. E. Y. C. Lee, Ph.D., Professor and Chairman: enzymology, structure-function relationships, and regulation of ser/thr protein phosphatases. A. J. L. Cooper, Ph.D., Professor: amino acid chemistry and biochemistry; biochemical mechanisms underlying neurological diseases. M. Y. W. Lee, Ph.D., Professor: DNA replication, polymerases, and repair; cell-cycle regulation. S. C. Olson, Ph.D., Associate Professor: signal transduction; regulation of phospholipase D pathway by protein kinase C and G proteins. J. T. Pinto, Ph.D., Professor: the effects of chemopreventive agents, dietary factors, and xenobiotic substances on oxidation/reduction capacity in human cells. E. L. Sabban, Ph.D., Professor: molecular neurobiology; molecular mechanisms of stress; cloning and regulation of gene expression for catecholamine-synthesizing enzymes and neuropeptides. Y. C. Tse-Dinh, Ph.D., Professor and Ph.D. Program Director: protein-DNA interactions; topoisomerase structure and function; gene regulation and DNA supercoiling. J. M. Wu, Ph.D., Professor and Master's Program Director: regulation of gene expression in leukemic and prostate cancer cells; cell-cycle control; chemoprevention by fenretinide and resveratrol. Z. Zhang, Ph.D., Assistant Professor: X-ray crystallography; stem cell factor; quinone reductase 2.

Cell Biology and Anatomy. J. D. Etlinger, Ph.D., Professor and Chairman: skeletal muscle growth and atrophy; intracellular proteolysis in erythroid and muscle cells; role of proteasomes and ubiquitin; spinal cord injury. P. Ballabh, M.D., Professor: germinal matrix hemorrhage, pericytes. V. A. Fried, Ph.D., Professor and Graduate Program Director: ubiquitin and cellular regulation; cytoskeletal structure and functions. F. L. Hannan, Ph.D., Assistant Professor: *Drosophila melanogaster;* neurofibromatosis; learning and memory; Res; adenylyl cyclase; expression profiles. J. Kang, M.D., Ph.D., Associate Professor: astrocyte-mediated modulation of inhibitory synaptic transmission; interplay between excitatory and inhibitory synapses; properties of gap junction, K+, and GABA-A channels. M. Kumarasiri, Ph.D., Assistant Professor: protein turnover, ubiquitin-conjugated enzymes. K. M. Lerea, Ph.D., Associate Professor and Interdisciplinary Program Director: mechanisms of signal transduction; role of protein ser/thr kinases and phosphatases in integrin functions and platelet activation. S. A. Newman, Ph.D., Professor: physical and molecular mechanisms of development and evolution; pattern formation in the vertebrate limb; collagen assembly. K. Oktay, M.D., Professor: preservation by freezing and transplantation of oocytes and ovarian tissues to protect these cells from damage due to radiation and chemotherapy. P. B. Sehgal, M.D., Ph.D., Professor: interleukin-6; p53; gene expression; signal transduction (STAT3). S. C. Sharma, Ph.D., Professor: genetic approaches to regeneration of adult CNS neurons. A. D. Springer, Ph.D., Professor: engineering models of retinal development; optic nerve regeneration. P. K. Stanton, Ph.D., Professor: neuronal plasticity; long-term depression and potentiation of synaptic strength; synaptic functional changes in epilepsy; mechanisms of ischemia-induced delayed neuronal death. L. Velíšek, M.D., Ph.D., Professor: epilepsy and epileptogenesis; epileptic syndromes of childhood; role of prenatal corticosteroids and stress in brain development and function; hypothalamic peptides and neuronal excitability. J. Velíšková, M.D., Ph.D., Associate Professor: mechanisms of estrogen effects on neuronal excitability; seizures and epilepsy; neuroprotection; and synaptic plasticity; estrogen regulation of neuropeptideY and metabotropic glutamate receptor-NR2B subunit-containing NMDA receptor interactions. R. J. Zeman, Ph.D., Associate Professor: β_2-adrenoceptors in musculoskeletal growth; mechanisms of spinal cord injury; regulation of intracellular calcium.

Pathology. J. T. Fallon, M.D., Ph.D., Professor and Chairman: cardiovascular pathology; ischemic heart disease; experimental vascular injury; immunopathology of human myocarditis and allograft rejection. A. N. Arnold, Ph.D., Assistant Professor: transplantation immunology and histocompatibility. A. Bokhari, M.B.B.S., Assistant Clinical Professor: neomatal and pediatric pathology. P. M. Chander, M.B.B.S., Professor: pathogenesis of renal and vascular damage in stroke-prone spontaneously hypertensive rats; pathogenesis of HIV-associated nephropathy. Z. Darzynkiewicz, M.D., Ph.D., Professor: development of new methods of cell analysis using flow cytometry; analysis of cell-cycle specificity of antitumor drugs. H. P. Godfrey, M.D., Ph.D., Professor and Ph.D. Program Director: mechanisms of pathogenesis in tuberculosis and Lyme disease; biomedical mechanisms of delayed hypersensitivity, chronic inflammation, and infectious disease. M. I. Iatropoulos, M.D., Research Professor: comparative mechanisms of toxicity and carcinogenesis. A. M. Jeffrey, Ph.D., Research Professor: toxicology and chronic carcinogenesis. M. Jhanwar-Uniyal, Ph.D., Research Associate Professor: signal transduction, BRCA, p53, cancer, central nervous system in obesity. A. Kumar, Ph.D., Professor: role of renin-angiotensin system in hypertension and atherosclerosis. J. M. Lombardo, M.D., Ph.D., Associate Professor: immunovirology; tuberculosis; HIV. P. A. Lucas, Ph.D., Research Associate Professor: wound healing and tissue engineering. F. H. Moy, Ph.D., Associate Professor of Clinical Pathology and Master's Program Director: biostatistics and epidemiology, methodology, and applications in environmetrics and risk assessment. F. Traganos, Ph.D., Professor: mechanisms of cell-cycle progression (checkpoints) and cell death (apoptosis) in cell cultures and clinical models. G. Wang, M.D., Clinical Assistant Professor: cytokines in Lyme carditis; antibacterial properties of treated fabrics; daptomycin-nonsusceptible enterococci. J. H. Weisburger, Ph.D., M.D. (hon.), Research Professor: mechanisms of toxicity and carcinogenicity; mechanisms and role of promoters in major human cancers; role of nutrition in human carcinogenesis; rational means of prevention of cancer, coronary heart disease, and stroke. G. M. Williams, M.D., Professor: mechanisms of carcinogenesis; metabolic and genetic effects of chemical carcinogens. R. E. Zachrau, M.D., Professor: spontaneous and induced tumor-specific, cell-mediated immunity in human breast cancer and its role in development of systemic metastasis and second primary cancers of breast and nonbreast origin. W. W. Zhang, M.D., Ph.D., Assistant Professor: molecular pathology; prostate cancer; neoplasia cancer pathogenesis; epigenetic markers for prostate cancer.

Microbiology and Immunology. I. S. Schwartz, Ph.D., Professor and Chairman: molecular pathogenesis of Lyme disease and other emerging bacterial pathogens; functional genomics. R. Banerjee, Ph.D., Assistant Professor: molecular virology and molecular oncology. D. Bessen, Ph.D., Professor: molecular pathogenesis, epidemiology, and evolutionary biology of group A *Streptococcus* (GAS); role of GAS infection in pediatric neuropsychiatric disorders. D. Bucher, Ph.D., Associate Professor: structure, function, and immunochemistry of viral antigens. F. Cabello, M.D., Professor: microbial genetics; infectious disease; recombinant DNA. R. Dattwyler, M.D., Professor. J. Geliebter, Ph.D., Professor: immunology and molecular biology of prostate cancer. C. V. Hamby, Ph.D., Associate Professor: molecular biology and immunology of human tumors. D. Mordue, Ph.D., Assistant Professor: cellular and molecular strategies used by intracellular pathogens to establish and maintain infection. M. M. Petzke, Ph.D., Assistant Professor: Lyme disease; bacterial pathogenesis; innate immunity; dendritic cells; interferons; pattern recognition receptors; functional genomics. R. K. Tiwari, Ph.D., Professor and Graduate Program Director: tumor immunology and chemoprevention; cellular immunology; immune dysregulation in disease.

Pharmacology. M. L. Schwartzman, Ph.D., Professor and Acting Chairwoman: cytochrome P-450 metabolism of arachidonic acid in inflammation and hypertension. M. A. Carroll, Ph.D., Professor: renal cytochrome P-450 metabolites of arachidonic acid. N. R. Ferreri, Ph.D., Professor: cytokine production and function in the kidney and vascular smooth muscle. M. S. Goligorsky, M.D., Ph.D., Professor: basic mechanisms of endothelial dysfunction, its prevention and reversal; translation of bench findings to clinical physiology and pharmacology. A. M. Guo, Ph.D., Assistant Professor: cytochrome P-450-derived eicosanoids (i.e., 20-HETE) in angiogenesis and cancer growth; regulation of endothelial precursor cell function. M. A. Inchiosa Jr., Ph.D., Professor: biochemical pharmacology of muscle. D. Lin, M.D., Ph.D., Research Assistant Professor: microRNA, renal K$^+$ secretion and Na$^+$ reabsorption. J. C. McGiff, M.D., Professor: neural and hormonal control of circulation and renal function. A. Nasjletti, M.D., Professor and Ph.D. Program Director: hormonal mediators of blood pressure regulation. C. A. Powers, Ph.D., Associate Professor: neuroendocrinology. J. Quilley, Ph.D., Professor: Interactions of vasoactive hormones and eicosanoids in vascular regulation in diabetes and hypertension. C. T. Stier, Ph.D., Associate Professor and M.S. Program Director: pharmacological protection against vascular damage and stroke. W. Wang, M.D., Professor: regulation of renal electrolytes transport.

Physiology. T. H. Hintze, Ph.D., Professor and Chairman: cardiovascular functions in chronically instrumented animals. Z. Bagi, M.D., Ph.D., Assistant Professor: coronary microcirculation in diabetes, obesity, and other cardiovascular diseases; flow-induced vasodilatation. F. L. Belloni, Ph.D., Professor: vascular and cardiac actions of adenosine; biomedical and research ethics. John G. Edwards, Ph.D., Associate Professor: physiological control of gene transcription; regulation of transcription factors; cardiac hypertrophy; exercise biochemistry and overload alterations of the myocardial phenotype. C. Eisenberg, Ph.D., Associate Professor: phenotypic potential of "adult" stem cells. L. Eisenberg, Ph.D., Professor: molecular mechanisms controlling the phenotypic direction of differentiating stem cells. A. Huang, M.D., Ph.D., Associate Professor of Physiology: role of estrogens in vascular function. G. Kaley, Ph.D., Professor: control of blood pressure and blood flow. A. Koller, M.D., Professor: regulation of blood flow in the microcirculation. C. S. Leonard, Ph.D., Professor: neuronal integration; synaptic and nonsynaptic neuromodulation; nitric oxide in the CNS; brain cholinergic systems; neural basis of sleep and wakefulness. N. Levine, Ph.D., Professor and Accelerated Master's Program Director: fluid and electrolyte secretion in the male reproductive system. E. J. Messina, Ph.D., Professor: microvascular control and regulation of smooth-muscle reactivity. M. Mozzor, B.A., Instructor: radiation physics. C. Ojaimi, Ph.D., Assistant Professor: gene array technology; functional genomics in vascular biology; gene expression of normal and diseased heart. S. S. Passo, Ph.D., Professor: neuroendocrine control of blood pressure. S. J. Popilskis, D.V.M., DACLAM, Assistant Professor: comparative medicine. Fabio A. Recchia, M.D., Professor and M.D./Ph.D. Program Director: control of myocardial metabolism; nitric oxide; heart failure; cardiac mechanics and efficiency; coronary circulation. W. N. Ross, Ph.D., Professor: regional properties of neurons. J. M. Stewart, M.D., Ph.D., Professor: orthostatic hypotension. D. Sun, M.D., Ph.D., Associate Professor: role of endothelial stress on coronary arteriolar function. C. I. Thompson, Ph.D., Professor and Graduate Program Director: renal hemodynamics and GFR control. M. S. Wolin, Ph.D., Professor: vascular regulation via cyclic GMP, metabolites, and oxygen tension.

THE ROCKEFELLER UNIVERSITY

Graduate Programs

Programs of Study

Graduate education leading to the Ph.D. is offered to outstanding students regarded as potential leaders in their scientific fields. The University's research covers a wide range of biomedical and related sciences, including biochemistry, structural biology, biophysics, and chemistry; molecular, cell, and developmental biology; medical sciences and human genetics; immunology and microbiology; neurosciences; and bioinformatics, biophysics, and computational neuroscience, as summarized by the faculty list in this description. Students work closely with a faculty of active scientists and are encouraged to learn through a combination of course work, tutorial guidance, and apprenticeship in research laboratories. Graduate Fellows spend the first two years engaged in a flexible combination of courses geared toward academic qualification while conducting research in laboratories pertaining to their area of scientific interest. They choose a laboratory for thesis research by the end of the first year and devote their remaining time to pursuit of significant experimental or theoretical research, culminating in a dissertation and thesis defense. Students can spend full time in research; there are no teaching or other service obligations.

The faculties of the Rockefeller University, Weill Medical College of Cornell University, the Weill Graduate School of Medical Sciences of Cornell University, and Sloan-Kettering Institute collaborate in offering a combined M.D./Ph.D. program in the biomedical sciences to about 90 students. This program, conducted on the adjacent campuses of these three institutions in New York City, normally requires six or seven years of study and leads to an M.D. degree conferred by Cornell University and a Ph.D. degree conferred by either the Rockefeller University or the Weill Graduate School of Cornell University, depending upon the organizational affiliation of the student's adviser.

Research Facilities

The University and its affiliate Howard Hughes Medical Institute maintain a full range of laboratories and services for the research activities of the professional staff and students. Facilities include clinical and animal research centers on campus, a library, computing services, a field research center in Dutchess County, the Aaron Diamond AIDS Research Center (ADARC), as well as new centers for human genetics, studies in physics and biology, biochemistry and structural biology, immunology and immune diseases, sensory neuroscience, and Alzheimer's disease research.

Financial Aid

Each student accepted into the Ph.D. program receives a stipend ($33,000 in 2011–12) that is adequate to meet all living expenses. Students also receive an annual budget of $1500 that can be used for travel, books and journals, computer purchases, and lab supplies.

Cost of Study

The University provides full remission of all tuition and fees for all accepted students.

Living and Housing Costs

On-campus housing is available for all students at subsidized rates. The stipend is designed to cover the cost of food, housing, and other basic living expenses. Students may elect to live off campus, but rents in the vicinity are very high.

Student Group

There are 198 graduate students, of whom 172 are enrolled in the Ph.D. program and 26 in the Ph.D. phase of the combined M.D./Ph.D. program. It is the policy of the Rockefeller University to support equality of educational opportunity. No individual is denied admission to the University or otherwise discriminated against with respect to any program of the University because of creed, color, national or ethnic origin, race, sex, or disability.

Student Outcomes

Graduates of the Rockefeller University have excelled in their professions. Two graduates have been awarded the Nobel Prize, and 26 graduates are members of the National Academy of Sciences. Most Ph.D. graduates move to postdoctoral positions at academic and research centers and subsequently have careers in academics, biotechnology, and the pharmaceutical industry. A few have pursued careers in medicine, law, and business. Almost all M.D./Ph.D. graduates first complete residencies in medical specialties, and most become medical scientists at major academic and research centers.

Location

The University is situated between 62nd and 68th streets in Manhattan, overlooking the East River. Despite its central metropolitan location, the 15-acre campus has a distinctive nonurban character, featuring gardens, picnic areas, fountains, and a tennis court. In addition to administrative and residential buildings, there are seven large laboratory buildings and a forty-bed hospital that serves as a clinical research center. Immediate neighbors are the New York Hospital, the Weill Medical College of Cornell University, Memorial Hospital, and the Sloan-Kettering Institute for Cancer Research. The wide range of institutions in New York City affords unlimited opportunities in research specialties, library facilities, and cultural resources.

The University

The Rockefeller University is dedicated to benefiting humankind through scientific research and its application. Founded in 1901 by John D. Rockefeller as the Rockefeller Institute for Medical Research, it rapidly became a source of major scientific innovation in treating and preventing human disease. Since 1954, the institute has extended its function by offering graduate work at the doctoral level to a select group of qualified students.

Laboratories, rather than departments, are the fundamental units of the University. The absence of departmental barriers between laboratories encourages interdisciplinary, problem-oriented approaches to research and facilitates intellectual interaction and collaboration. The collegial atmosphere fosters independence and initiative in students. In addition to the 198 doctoral students, there are 350 postdoctoral associates and fellows and a faculty of 74 full, associate, and assistant professors on campus who head laboratories.

Applying

Applications for the M.D./Ph.D. program must be completed by October 15; those for the Ph.D. program must be completed by December 5. Applicants are required to submit a personal statement describing research experience and goals as well as reasons for pursuing graduate study at the Rockefeller University. Also required are official transcripts and at least three letters of recommendation. Official GRE General Test scores are required and Subject Test scores are highly recommended for admission to the Ph.D. program. MCAT scores are required for the M.D./Ph.D. program. Further information about each program and details on application procedures may be obtained from the programs' respective Web sites. This information is also available on the University Web site, from which application forms and instructions can be downloaded.

Correspondence and Information

For the Ph.D. program:
Office of Graduate Studies
The Rockefeller University
1230 York Avenue
New York, New York 10065
Phone: 212-327-8086
E-mail: phd@rockefeller.edu
Web site: http://www.rockefeller.edu

For the M.D./Ph.D. program:
Tri-Institutional M.D./Ph.D. Program
Weill Cornell/Rockefeller/Sloan-Kettering
1300 York Avenue, Room C-103
New York, New York 10065
Phone: 212-746-6023
     888-U2-MD-PHD (toll-free)
E-mail: mdphd@mail.med.cornell.edu
Web site: http://www.med.cornell.edu/mdphd

The Rockefeller University

LABORATORY HEADS AND THEIR RESEARCH

C. David Allis, Ph.D. (Histone Modifications and Chromatin Biology). Enzymology and function of covalent histone modifications; histone code and epigenetic regulation.

Cori Bargmann, Ph.D. (Neuroscience). Genetic analysis of olfactory behavior and neural development.

Günter Blobel, M.D., Ph.D. (Cell Biology). Protein translocation across membranes; macromolecular traffic into and out of the nucleus.

Sean Brady, Ph.D. (Genetically Encoded Small Molecules). Structure and function of genetically encoded small molecules.

Jan L. Breslow, M.D. (Biochemical Genetics and Metabolism). Identifying the genes that control atherosclerosis susceptibility.

Jean-Laurent Casanova, M.D., Ph.D. (Human Genetics of Infectious Diseases). Genetics of human predisposition to pediatric infectious diseases, particularly mycobacterial diseases.

Brian T. Chait, D.Phil. (Mass Spectrometry and Gaseous Ion Chemistry). Protein mass spectrometry.

Nam-Hai Chua, Ph.D. (Plant Molecular Biology). Gene regulation and signal transduction in plants.

Joel Cohen, Ph.D., Dr.P.H. (Populations). Population dynamics; ecology; epidemiology.

Barry Coller, M.D. (Clinical Hematology). Biochemistry of platelet disorders; study of heritable coagulopathies.

Frederick P. Cross, Ph.D. (Molecular Genetics). Cell-cycle control in budding yeast.

George A. M. Cross, Ph.D. (Molecular Parasitology). Regulation of gene and surface glycoprotein expression in trypanosomes.

James E. Darnell Jr., M.D. (Molecular Cell Biology). Signal transduction and gene control in mammalian differentiation.

Robert B. Darnell, M.D., Ph.D. (Molecular Neuro-Oncology). Neuro-oncology and autoimmunity; molecular neurobiology.

Seth Darst, Ph.D. (Molecular Biophysics). Protein crystallography and electron microscopy of macromolecular assemblies.

Titia de Lange, Ph.D. (Cell Biology and Genetics). Chromosome function in vertebrates.

Mitchell J. Feigenbaum, Ph.D. (Mathematical Physics).

Vincent A. Fischetti, Ph.D. (Bacterial Pathogenesis). Pathogenesis of streptococcal diseases and mucosal vaccine development.

Jeffrey M. Friedman, M.D., Ph.D. (Molecular Genetics). Genes controlling food intake and body weight; mouse genetics.

Winrich Freiwald, Ph.D. (Neural Systems). Neural processes that form object representations, as well as those that allow attention to make those representations available for cognition.

Elaine Fuchs, Ph.D. (Mammalian Cell Biology and Development). Molecular mechanisms underlying the coordination of proliferation, transcription, and cell adhesion in tissue morphogenesis and in cancer.

Hinonori Funabiki, Ph.D. (Chromosome and Cell Biology). Mechanisms controlling accurate chromosome segregation during the cell division cycle.

David C. Gadsby, Ph.D. (Cardiac and Membrane Physiology). Mechanism and function of ion pumps and channels.

Charles D. Gilbert, M.D., Ph.D. (Neurobiology). Visual spatial integration and cortical dynamics.

Konstantin A. Goulianos, Ph.D. (Experimental High-Energy Physics).

Paul Greengard, Ph.D. (Molecular and Cellular Neuroscience). Role of phosphoproteins in signal transduction in the developing and adult nervous system.

Howard C. Hang, Ph.D. (Chemical Biology and Microbial Pathogenesis). Chemical tools for studying posttranslational modifications in living cells.

Mary E. Hatten, Ph.D. (Developmental Neurobiology). Control of CNS neuronal specification and migration during vertebrate brain development.

Nathaniel Heintz, Ph.D. (Molecular Biology). Cell-cycle regulation; molecular neurobiology; mammalian neurogenetics.

Ali Hemmati-Brivanlou, Ph.D. (Molecular Embryology). Molecular embryology of vertebrates.

David D. Ho, M.D. (Dynamics of HIV/SIV Replication). Kinetics of CD4 lymphocyte turnover; determinants of disease progression; therapy of HIV infection.

A. James Hudspeth, M.D., Ph.D. (Sensory Neuroscience). Transduction and synaptic signaling by hair cells of the inner ear.

Tarun Kapoor, Ph.D. (Chemistry and Cell Biology). Small-molecule probes of cellular processes.

Bruce W. Knight Jr. (Biophysics). Neurophysiology and applied mathematics.

M. Magda Konarska, Ph.D. (Molecular Biology and Biochemistry). Splicing of mRNA precursors and replication of hepatitis delta virus.

Mary Jeanne Kreek, M.D. (Neuroscience). Neurobiology and molecular genetics of addictive diseases; endogenous opioid system.

Daniel Kronauer, Ph.D. (Insect Social Evolution). Molecular basis of social behavior in *Cerapachys biroi*.

James G. Krueger, M.D., Ph.D. (Investigative Dermatology). Cutaneous pathobiology.

Stanislas Leibler, Ph.D. (Physics and Mathematical Biology). Analysis of biological networks.

Albert J. Libchaber, Ph.D. (Experimental Condensed-Matter Physics).

Roderick MacKinnon, M.D. (Molecular Neurobiology and Biophysics). Structure and function of ion channels and associated regulatory proteins.

Marcelo Magnasco, Ph.D. (Mathematical Physics). Stochastic processes in biology systems.

Gaby Maimon, Ph.D. (Integrative Brain Function). Neural basis of decision making in *Drosophila melanogaster*.

Luciano Marraffini, Ph.D. (Bacteriology). Mechanisms that control the traffic of DNA molecules between bacteria.

Bruce S. McEwen, Ph.D. (Neuroendocrinology). Hormonal regulation of neural plasticity.

Daniel Mucida, Ph.D. (Mucosal Immunology). Mechanisms of intestinal immunity.

Fernando Nottebohm, Ph.D. (Animal Behavior). Animal communication; mechanisms of learning, memory duration, and brain repair.

Michel C. Nussenzweig, M.D., Ph.D. (Molecular Immunology). Molecular basis of B-cell development.

Michael O'Donnell, Ph.D. (DNA Replication). Underlying principles of DNA replication in the human and *E. coli* systems.

Jürg Ott, Ph.D. (Statistical Genetics). Developing, implementing, and applying statistical methods of human genetic mapping.

F. Nina Papavasiliou, Ph.D. (Molecular Immunology). Molecular mechanisms of lymphocyte diversity.

Donald W. Pfaff, Ph.D. (Neurobiology and Behavior). Gene expression in brain; hormone action; brain control of behavior.

Jeffrey V. Ravetch, M.D., Ph.D. (Molecular Genetics and Immunology). Genetics of the humoral immune response; genetic variation in malaria parasite.

George N. Reeke Jr., Ph.D. (Biological Modeling). Theoretical models of brain functions; protein structure.

Charles Rice, Ph.D. (Virology). Molecular genetics of animal RNA viruses (alphaviruses and flaviviruses, in particular hepatitis C virus); replication and pathogenesis.

Robert G. Roeder, Ph.D. (Biochemistry and Molecular Biology). Transcriptional regulatory mechanisms in animal cells.

Michael P. Rout, Ph.D. (Structural Cell Biology). Nucleocytoplasmic transport; nuclear pore complex structure, function, and assembly.

Vanessa Ruta, Ph.D. (Neurophysiology and Behavior). Neural mechanisms and behavior modification in *Drosophila melanogaster*.

Thomas P. Sakmar, M.D. (Molecular Biology and Biochemistry). Biochemistry and molecular biology of transmembrane signal transduction and visual phototransduction.

Shai Shaham, Ph.D. (Cancer Biology). Programmed cell death in the nematode *Caenorhabditis elegans*.

Eric Siggia, Ph.D. (Theoretical Condensed-Matter Physics). Statistical physics and dynamical systems to cellular biophysics and bioinformatics.

Sanford M. Simon, Ph.D. (Cellular Biophysics). Protein biogenesis, membrane protein assembly, tumorigenesis, and drug resistance.

Agata Smogorzewska, M.D., Ph.D. (Genome Maintenance). Elucidating pathways that prevent cancer development by using Fanconi anemia as a backdrop for understanding aging and cancer.

C. Erec Stebbins, Ph.D. (Structural Microbiology). Structural studies of bacterial virulence factors and their host cell targets.

Ralph M. Steinman, M.D. (Cellular Physiology and Immunology). Antigen presenting cell function for initiating immune responses in health and disease, especially HIV-1 infection.

Hermann Steller, Ph.D. Molecular biology of apoptosis and cancer biology.

Sidney Strickland, Ph.D. (Neurobiology and Genetics). Genetics of neuronal function and dysfunction; genetics of early development.

Alexander Tarakhovsky, M.D., Ph.D. (Immunology). Mechanisms of the dynamic tuning of antigen receptor-mediated signaling in lymphocytes.

Sohail Tavazoie, M.D., Ph.D. (Systems Cancer Biology). Using a systems biological approach to identify and characterize key molecular regulators of metastasis.

Alexander Tomasz, Ph.D. (Microbiology). Mechanisms of antibiotic resistance and virulence in bacteria.

Thomas Tuschl, Ph.D. (Chemistry). Regulation of gene expression by double-stranded RNA in humans.

Leslie Vosshall, Ph.D. (Sensory Neuroscience). Molecular genetics of olfaction in *Drosophila melanogaster*.

Michael W. Young, Ph.D. (Genetics). Genes controlling behavior and development in *Drosophila;* molecular control of circadian rhythms.

ROSALIND FRANKLIN UNIVERSITY OF MEDICINE AND SCIENCE

School of Graduate and Postdoctoral Studies

Programs of Study

A student's decision as to which field of research to pursue requires careful consideration. In the School of Graduate and Postdoctoral Studies (SGPS), students explore research through hands-on laboratory experiences before selecting a mentor and research project for their doctoral degree. Students can engage in a wide array of research topics including the molecular, cellular, and structural mechanisms of diseases such as cancer, Alzheimer's, Parkinson's, cystic fibrosis, diabetes, psychiatric disorders, addiction muscular dystrophy, and many others. A more extensive list of areas of research emphasis can be found online: http://www.rosalindfranklin.edu/research. Students begin studies with the first-year core plan called the Interdisciplinary Graduate Program in Biomedical Sciences (IGPBS). This allows time for preliminary laboratory investigation while providing an education in the most current areas of the biomedical sciences before selection of a laboratory for continued research.

The Ph.D. program can lead to degrees in any of the following disciplines: biochemistry and molecular biology, cell biology and anatomy, cellular and molecular pharmacology, microbiology and immunology, physiology and biophysics, and neuroscience. The graduate school has also partnered with both Chicago Medical School and Dr. William M. Scholl College of Podiatric Medicine to create combined M.D./Ph.D. and D.P.M./Ph.D. programs in these disciplines. These programs allow individuals interested in pursuing physician/scientist careers to have a continuous balance of clinical and research training throughout all years of their education at Rosalind Franklin University of Medicine and Science (RFUMS) and then pursue research-based residency programs fostering these unique career paths.

Research Facilities

RFUMS is committed to investment in its research infrastructure to support cutting-edge biomedical research. The University's state-of-the-art facilities include fully equipped animal quarters and a spectrum of research support laboratories, such as the Midwest Proteome Center for mass spectrometry and X-ray crystallography, the Protein Structure Center for electron paramagnetic resonance (EPR), fluorescence activated cell sorting (FACS), molecular biology core facilities, confocal and electron microscopy support facilities, as well as calcium and live-cell imaging facilities.

Financial Aid

SGPS offers stipends which are awarded on a competitive basis. As of 2011–12, stipends are awarded at $26,000 annually. Additionally, full tuition waivers are provided to SGPS doctoral students. Students have access to the same health benefits as faculty members.

Cost of Study

The annual tuition for the Interdisciplinary Graduate Program in Biomedical Sciences for 2011–12 is $23,285. Tuition for SGPS doctoral programs is waived.

Living and Housing Costs

The annual cost of living in the Chicagoland area is estimated at $20,400. Moderately priced on- and off-campus housing options are available.

Student Group

The University's 2010 fall enrollment was 1,937 students in its four schools: the Chicago Medical School, School of Graduate and Postdoctoral Studies, College of Health Professions, and Dr. William M. Scholl College of Podiatric Medicine. The University's fifth school, the College of Pharmacy, will enroll its first class of 67 in the fall of 2011.

Student Outcomes

Doctoral students at RFUMS are highly competitive and are placed in excellent postdoctoral programs. The University's combined M.D./Ph.D. and D.P.M./Ph.D. graduates continue their training by placing into residency programs and postdoctoral programs. More than 16,000 degreed Rosalind Franklin University alumni are active throughout the country and internationally. To date, the School of Graduate and Postdoctoral Studies has trained 1,798 graduates.

Location

The School of Graduate and Postdoctoral Studies is part of the Rosalind Franklin University of Medicine and Science. The University is located in North Chicago, a northern suburb in Lake County, Illinois, approximately 35 miles north of downtown Chicago. Its beautiful 96.8-acre campus is home to the Basic and Health Sciences Buildings, three student residence halls, the newly constructed Interprofessional Education Center and the Rosalind Franklin University Health System.

The School

The School of Graduate and Postdoctoral Studies was established in 1968 as a further development of the Chicago Medical School, which was founded in 1912. The graduate program is directed toward the education of students who plan careers in the biomedical sciences.

Applying

Candidates for admission must have a bachelor's degree or its equivalent from a regionally accredited college or university. Applicant selection is based on, but not limited to, the following criteria: previous academic work, research experience and preparation in the proposed field of graduate study, grade point average, scores on the general Graduate Record Examination and Test of English as a Foreign Language (if applicable), and recommendations from persons involved in the student's previous educational and research experience. There is no application fee for the program.

Applications are available online at the University Web site. The priority deadline for applications and all supporting documents for the fall 2012 term is January 13, 2012. On-campus interviews are held in early March, and international interviews are held via telephone and videoconference throughout the application season. Early application is strongly encouraged. Stipends are awarded on a competitive basis, and recipients are selected by April 15. The application process may remain open after the priority deadline, but it will be closed once the class is filled.

Correspondence and Information

Office of IGPBS Admissions
Rosalind Franklin University of Medicine and Science
3333 Green Bay Road
North Chicago, Illinois 60064
Phone: 847-578-8601
    866-98-IGPBS (866-984-4727; toll-free)
E-mail: IGPBS@rosalindfranklin.edu
Web site: http://www.rosalindfranklin.edu

Rosalind Franklin University of Medicine and Science

ADMINISTRATORS OF GRADUATE PROGRAMS

School of Graduate and Postdoctoral Studies: Joseph X. DiMario, Ph.D., Dean.
Interdisciplinary Graduate Program in Biomedical Sciences: Robert Intine, Ph.D., Associate Dean for Basic Science Education Programs.

THE UNIVERSITY OF ALABAMA AT BIRMINGHAM

College of Arts and Sciences
Department of Biology

Programs of Study

The Department of Biology offers programs of study leading to the M.S. and Ph.D. degrees. Graduate students may specialize in research activities at all levels of biological organization, with emphases on ecophysiology, cellular and molecular biology, endocrinology, and ecology of aquatic organisms, plant biology, or on models related to human disease. The aim of the Department is to provide a broad background and a field of specialty that prepare the student for a professional career in research and/or teaching.

Two types of master's programs are available. A student may choose a research-based program that requires, in addition to a thesis, a minimum of 24 hours of committee-approved course work. The nonresearch plan requires a minimum of 30 hours of approved course work and a thesis incorporating a review and analysis of a topic of current or historical interest in biology. Either plan of study can be completed in approximately two years.

Course work requirements for the Ph.D. programs are individually designed to meet the needs of the student and to fulfill the aims of the Department and Graduate School. However, a dissertation embodying the results and analysis of an original experimental investigation is required.

Seminars and teaching experience are part of the training program for both the M.S. and Ph.D. degrees. To qualify for candidacy, the student in the master's program must take either a written or an oral comprehensive examination. The Ph.D. student must take both written and oral examinations. The final examination for all candidates consists of an oral defense of the research thesis.

Research Facilities

Well-equipped research laboratories for the Department are located in Campbell Hall. Facilities are available for vertebrates and invertebrates, including marine and freshwater forms, and for botanical specimens. The University operates a farm suitable for field studies. For students interested in marine biology, the University is a member of the Marine Environmental Science Program at Dauphin Island near Mobile, Alabama. The Medical Center library and the University College library have extensive holdings in biological and related sciences.

Financial Aid

Teaching assistantships, graduate assistantships, and fellowships are available. Stipends are awarded on a yearly basis; for 2010–11, they were $15,000 for the master's program and $19,000 to $21,000 for the doctoral program. Tuition and other fees are paid for all students who are awarded stipends. Health insurance is provided for qualified individuals. Fellowships can require teaching on a regular basis, and assistantships typically require teaching a maximum of 9 contact hours per week. Students not receiving stipends may teach laboratory sections on a fee-for-service basis.

Cost of Study

Graduate tuition for in-state students was $286 per credit hour in 2010–11. Out-of-state students were charged $672 per credit hour. Tuition and fees are paid for stipend recipients.

Living and Housing Costs

The cost of living in Birmingham is slightly lower than the average for major American cities. Many reasonably priced apartments are available near campus, and some University apartments are available.

Student Group

The total enrollment at the University of Alabama at Birmingham is approximately 17,000; 11,400 are undergraduates and more than 5,700 are in graduate and professional school programs. The Department of Biology averages about 50 graduate students in M.S. or Ph.D. programs.

Student Outcomes

Recent graduates have assumed professorships in departments such as biology, zoology, immunology, or marine science at various academic institutions. Some have chosen a career in the medical or dental profession. Other positions assumed recently by graduates include staff scientists at NASA, the Army Corps of Engineers, CDC, FDA, and marine research laboratories. In addition, different environmental consulting companies and biotechnology companies have employed graduates as technicians, staff scientists, or laboratory directors.

Location

The University of Alabama at Birmingham is a comprehensive urban university situated on a campus that occupies an eighty-block area in the southern section of Birmingham. Many cultural resources are available, including the Alys Robinson Stephens Performing Arts Center, museums, the Jimmy Morgan Zoo, and the Botanical Gardens. Recreational opportunities include athletic events and a variety of outdoor activities at nearby lakes and parks or along the Gulf Coast, which is 5 hours away by car. The city has a mild climate throughout the year.

The University

The University of Alabama at Birmingham has forty-six master's and thirty-three doctoral programs. Students benefit from the active research programs that attract $600 million in research funds each year, making the University one of the highest-ranked institutions in receipt of federal research support.

Applying

Application forms are available online. Other information can be obtained from the Dean of the Graduate School, the University of Alabama at Birmingham, UAB Station, Birmingham, Alabama 35294-1150. For admission in good standing, students should have a baccalaureate degree in biology or a related field, an overall B average in undergraduate courses, and a satisfactory score on the General Test of the Graduate Record Examinations or an equivalent test. It is also desirable that entering students have completed two years of chemistry (including a year of organic chemistry), a year of physics, and mathematics through calculus. A statement of career objectives, three letters of evaluation, and an official copy of transcripts should be included with the application.

Correspondence and Information

Dr. Stephen A. Watts, Program Director for Biology
Department of Biology
CH 375
The University of Alabama at Birmingham
1530 3rd Avenue South
Birmingham, Alabama 35294-1170
Phone: 205-934-2045
Fax: 205-975-6097
E-mail: sawatts@uab.edu
Web site: http://www.uab.edu/biology/

The University of Alabama at Birmingham

THE FACULTY AND THEIR RESEARCH

Charles D. Amsler, Professor; Ph.D., California, Santa Barbara. Phycology and chemical ecology.

Robert A. Angus, Professor; Ph.D., Connecticut. Aquatic ecology and toxicology.

Asim K. Bej, Professor; Ph.D., Louisville. Molecular genetics and microbial ecology.

James A. Coker, Assistant Professor; Ph.D., Penn State. Microbial biochemistry.

George F. Crozier, Adjunct Professor; Ph.D., California, San Diego. Marine vertebrate physiology.

Vithal K. Ghanta, Professor; Ph.D., Southern Illinois at Carbondale. Immunology.

David T. Jenkins, Associate Professor; Ph.D., Tennessee. *Basidiomycete* taxonomy.

Daniel D. Jones, Professor Emeritus; Ph.D., Michigan State. Plant physiology; microbial ecology.

Ken R. Marion, Professor; Ph.D., Washington (St. Louis). Vertebrate ecology.

James B. McClintock, Professor; Ph.D., South Florida. Invertebrate biology; marine chemical ecology.

Karolina M. Mukhtar, Assistant Professor; Ph.D., Max Planck Institute for Plant Breeding Research (Germany). Genetics; plant molecular biology.

Shahid M. Mukhtar, Research Assistant Professor; Ph.D., Max Planck Institute for Plant Breeding Research (Germany). Genetics; systems biology.

Timothy Nagy, Adjunct Associate Professor; Ph.D., Utah. Nutritional physiology.

Mickie L. Powell, Research Assistant Professor; Ph.D., Alabama at Birmingham. Aquatic nutritional physiology.

Robert W. Thacker, Professor; Ph.D., Michigan. Marine and freshwater ecology.

Trygve Tollefsbol, Professor; Ph.D., North Texas; D.O., North Texas Health Science at Fort Worth. Molecular biology; telomerase and DNA methylation.

R. Douglas Watson, Professor; Ph.D., Iowa. Developmental endocrinology.

Stephen A. Watts, Professor; Ph.D., South Florida. Physiology and nutrition of aquatic invertebrates; aquaculture.

Thane Wibbels, Professor; Ph.D., Texas A&M. Comparative reproductive physiology of vertebrates.

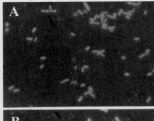

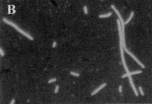

Salmonella—How expression of selected genes and their regulation enable microbes to survive in hostile environments is one area of prokaryotic research. For example, note the influence of cold temperature on morphology of *Salmonella typhimurium* LT2 grown for 78 hours at 37°C (panel A) or 10°C (panel B).

Population dynamics, reproductive ecology, and conservation of several species, including sea turtles, are studied.

Studies of marine chemical ecology are conducted in the Gulf of Mexico, the Atlantic, and, as seen here, beneath the sea ice in Antarctica.

UNIVERSITY OF CONNECTICUT HEALTH CENTER

Graduate Programs in Biomedical Sciences

Programs of Study

Work leading to the Ph.D. degree in biomedical sciences and master's degrees in dental sciences, public health, and clinical and translational research is offered through Graduate School faculty members associated with the Schools of Medicine and Dental Medicine at the University of Connecticut Health Center in Farmington. A combined-degree program with the School of Medicine offers an M.D./Ph.D. degree to qualified students interested in academic medicine and research. In addition, the Schools of Medicine and Dental Medicine, in conjunction with the Public Health Program, offer a combined program leading to the M.D./M.P.H. or D.M.D./M.P.H. The School of Dental Medicine offers a D.M.D./Ph.D. and a Combined Certificate Training Ph.D. program for students with advanced dental degrees. Ph.D. students apply to the Integrated Admissions Mode, which offers a first year of study in the basic science curriculum prior to the selection of an area of concentration in which to pursue the Ph.D. thesis work.

Research Facilities

The program offices and laboratories are part of the University of Connecticut Health Center. A wide range of general and specialized equipment and expertise in the biological, biochemical, and biophysical sciences is available. Students have access to all facilities and equipment necessary for the pursuit of their research programs. In addition, major institutional resources include central small-animal facilities and a library that contains approximately 200,000 volumes and 450 CAI programs and subscribes to more than 1,400 current periodicals.

Financial Aid

Support for doctoral students engaged in full-time degree programs at the Health Center is provided on a competitive basis. Graduate research assistantships for 2011–12 provide a stipend of $28,000 per year, which includes a waiver of tuition/University fees for the fall and spring semesters and a student health insurance plan. While financial aid is offered competitively, the Health Center makes every possible effort to address the financial needs of all doctoral students during their period of training.

Cost of Study

For 2011–12, tuition is $10,224 per year for full-time students who are Connecticut residents and $26,532 per year for full-time students who are out-of-state residents. General University fees are added to the cost of tuition for students who do not receive a tuition waiver. These costs are usually met by traineeships or research assistantships for doctoral students.

Living and Housing Costs

There is a wide range of affordable housing options in the greater Hartford area within easy commuting distance of the campus, including an extensive complex that is adjacent to the Health Center. Costs range from $600 to $900 per month for a one-bedroom unit; 2 or more students sharing an apartment usually pay less. University housing is not available at the Health Center.

Student Group

Approximately 550 students in the Schools of Medicine and Dental Medicine, 400 graduate students in the Ph.D. and master's programs, and numerous postdoctoral fellows use the facilities in Farmington.

Location

The Health Center is located in the historic town of Farmington, Connecticut. Set in the beautiful New England countryside on a hill overlooking the Farmington Valley, it is close to ski areas, hiking trails, and facilities for boating, fishing, and swimming. Connecticut's capital city of Hartford, 7 miles east of Farmington, is the center of an urban region of approximately 800,000 people. The beaches of the Long Island Sound are about 50 minutes away to the south, and the beautiful Berkshires are a short drive to the northwest. New York City and Boston can be reached within 2½ hours by car. Hartford is the home of the acclaimed Hartford Stage Company, TheatreWorks, the Hartford Symphony and Chamber orchestras, two ballet companies, an opera company, the Wadsworth Athenaeum (the oldest public art museum in the nation), the Mark Twain house, the Hartford Civic Center, and many other interesting cultural and recreational facilities. The area is also home to several branches of the University of Connecticut, Trinity College, and the University of Hartford, which includes the Hartt School of Music. Bradley International Airport (about 30 minutes from campus) serves the Hartford/Springfield area with frequent airline connections to major cities in this country and abroad. Frequent bus and rail service is also available from Hartford.

The Health Center

The 200-acre Health Center campus at Farmington houses a division of the University of Connecticut Graduate School, as well as the School of Medicine and Dental Medicine. The campus also includes the John Dempsey Hospital, associated clinics, and extensive medical research facilities, all in a centralized facility with more than 1 million square feet of floor space. The Health Center's newest research addition, the Academic Research Building, was opened in 1999. This impressive eleven-story structure provides 170,000 square feet of state-of-the-art laboratory space. The faculty at the center includes more than 260 full-time members. The institution has a strong commitment to graduate study within an environment that promotes social and intellectual interaction among the various educational programs. Graduate students are represented on various administrative committees concerned with curricular affairs, and the Graduate Student Organization (GSO) represents graduate students' needs and concerns to the faculty and administration, in addition to fostering social contact among graduate students at the Health Center.

Applying

Applications for admission should be submitted on standard forms obtained from the Graduate Admissions Office or the Web site and should be filed together with transcripts, three letters of recommendation, a personal statement, and recent results from the General Test of the Graduate Record Examinations. International students must take the Test of English as a Foreign Language (TOEFL) to satisfy Graduate School requirements. The deadline for completed applications and receipt of all supplemental materials is December 15. In accordance with the laws of the state of Connecticut and of the United States, the University of Connecticut Health Center does not discriminate against any person in its educational and employment activities on the grounds of race, color, creed, national origin, sex, age, or physical disability.

Correspondence and Information

Graduate Programs in Biomedical Sciences
Graduate Admissions Office, MC 3906
University of Connecticut Health Center
Farmington, Connecticut 06030-3906
Phone: 860-679-2175
E-mail: BiomedSciAdmissions@uchc.edu
Web site: http://grad.uchc.edu

University of Connecticut Health Center

FACULTY AND RESEARCH AREAS

The Health Center's graduate faculty of more than 150 members is drawn from both the basic and clinical departments of the Schools of Medicine and Dental Medicine.

Cell Biology. This interdisciplinary program offers the student the opportunity to bring modern molecular and physical techniques to bear on problems in cell biology. Faculty members' research spans a broad range of interests in the areas of eukaryotic cell biology and related clinical aspects. The program is particularly strong in the following areas of research: angiogenesis, cancer biology, gene expression, molecular medicine, reproductive biology, signal transduction, vascular biology, optical methods, proteomics, and computer modeling of complex biological systems. Kevin Claffey, Associate Professor of Cell Biology and Program Director; Jennifer Tirnauer, Assistant Professor of Medicine and Associate Program Director.

Genetics and Developmental Biology. This program emphasizes cellular and molecular bases of differentiation and development and includes opportunities in molecular human genetics. Research opportunities are available in the biology of human embryonic stem cells, mapping and cloning of genes responsible for human disease, RNA processing (including RNA editing, alternative splicing, antisense regulation, and RNA interference), the molecular mechanisms of aging, signal transduction pathways, microbial pathogenesis, developmental neurobiology, cell differentiation, musculoskeletal development, morphogenesis and pattern formation, reproductive biology, and endocrinology. William Mohler, Assistant Professor of Genetics and Developmental Biology and Program Director; Arthur Günzl, Professor of Genetics and Developmental Biology and Associate Program Director; Blanka Rogina, Assistant Professor of Genetics and Developmental Biology and Associate Program Director.

Immunology. The central focus of this program is to train the student to become an independent investigator and educator who will provide research and educational contributions to basic, applied, or clinical immunology through lectures, seminars, laboratory rotations, research presentations, and a concentration on laboratory research. Research in the program is focused on the cellular and molecular aspects of immune system structure and function in animal models and in humans. Areas of emphasis include molecular immunology (mechanisms of antigen presentation, major histocompatibility complex genetics and function, cytokines and cytokine receptors, and tumor antigens), cellular immunology (biochemical mechanisms and biological aspects of signal transduction of lymphocytes and granulocytes; cellular and molecular requirements for thymic T-lymphocyte development, selection, and activation; cytokines in B- and T-cell development; regulation of antitumor immunity; immunoparasitology, including parasite genetics and immune recognition of parasite antigens; and mechanisms of inflammation), organ-based immunology (immune effector mechanisms of the intestine, lymphocyte interactions in the lung, and immune regulation of the eye), immunity to infectious agents (viruses, bacteria, and parasites, including vector-borne organisms), and autoimmunity (animal models of autoimmune disease and effector mechanisms in human autoimmunity). Adam Adler, Associate Professor of Immunology and Program Director.

Molecular Biology and Biochemistry. This program uniquely bridges modern molecular biology, microbiology, biochemistry, cell biology, and structural biology. Research in this program is directed toward explaining biological phenomena at the molecular level. The program includes four major areas of concentration and research: relation of the structure of macromolecules to their function, biosynthesis of macromolecules, biochemical genetics, and assembly of macromolecules into complex cellular structures. Stephen M. King, Professor of Biochemistry and Program Director; Chris Heinen, Assistant Professor of Medicine and Associate Program Director.

Neuroscience. This interdepartmental program offers comprehensive conceptual and experimental training in molecular, systems, and behavioral neuroscience. The faculty members of the neuroscience program engage in research that involves cellular, molecular, and developmental neurobiology; neuroanatomy; neuroimaging; neurophysiology; neurochemistry; neuroendocrinology; neuropharmacology; and neuropathology. Richard Mains, Professor of Neuroscience and Program Director; Zhao-Wen Wang, Assistant Professor of Genetics and Developmental Biology and Associate Program Director.

Skeletal, Craniofacial, and Oral Biology. This program offers interdisciplinary research training in the areas of skeletal, craniofacial, and oral biology, emphasizing contemporary research technologies in cell, molecular, and developmental biology; genetics; and biochemistry. Areas of research include regulation of the formation, outgrowth, and patterning of the developing limb; control of cartilage differentiation, endochondral ossification, osteogenesis, and joint formation; molecular regulation of gene expression in bone; homeobox gene regulation of osteoblast differentiation; gene therapy of bone diseases; hormonal and cytokine regulation of bone growth, formation, and remodeling; control of craniofacial skeletogenesis and tooth development; signal transduction and intracellular signaling pathways; cellular and molecular aspects of the pathogenesis of inflammatory disease; microbiology, pathogenesis, and immunology of caries and periodontal disease; neural structure and function in the gustatory system; biomaterial development for tissue engineering; bone cell–implant interactions; differentiation of human embryonic stem cells into skeletal tissues; and analysis of oral and mucosal function and disease. Mina Mina, Professor of Orthodontics, Oral and Maxillofacial Surgery, Pediatric Dentistry, and Advanced Education and Program Director; Carol Pilbeam, Professor of Medicine and Associate Program Director.

Combined M.D./Ph.D. Program. This program is designed for students interested in careers in medical research and academic medicine. It enables students to acquire competence in both the basic science and clinical aspects of their chosen fields. The program allows a student to combine the curricula of two schools in a way that meets the specific degree requirements of each, and yet it allows the completion of both in a period less than that needed if the two curricula were taken in sequence. Entry into the program is limited to a small number of unusually well qualified students who are either currently enrolled in the medical school or who have been accepted into the first-year class. Barbara Kream, Professor of Medicine and of Genetics and Developmental Biology and Program Director.

Combined D.M.D./Ph.D. Program. This program is designed for students interested in careers in dental research and academic dental medicine. It enables students to acquire competence in both the basic science and clinical aspects of their chosen fields. The program allows a student to combine the curricula of two schools in a way that meets the specific degree requirements of each, and yet it allows the completion of both in a period less than that needed if the two curricula were taken in sequence. Entry into the program is limited to a small number of unusually well qualified students who are either currently enrolled in the dental school or who have been accepted into the first-year class. Mina Mina, Professor of Orthodontics, Oral and Maxillofacial Surgery, Pediatric Dentistry, and Advanced Education and Program Director.

Combined M.D./M.P.H. or D.M.D./M.P.H. Program. A joint-degree program leading to the Master of Public Health in addition to the Doctor of Medicine or the Doctor of Dental Medicine is sponsored by the Graduate Program in Public Health and the Schools of Medicine and Dental Medicine. The joint-degree program has been developed to prepare future physicians and dentists to deal creatively with the rapidly changing environment of medicine and health care. It is possible to complete the degree requirements for both programs during the four years of medical or dental school. David Gregorio, Professor of Community Medicine and Health Care and Program Director.

Clinical and Translational Research. The Master of Science degree program in clinical and translational research is administered in the Department of Medicine and stresses clinical research methods and research practicum in order to provide practical research training in preparation for independent research. The program is offered to individuals who have a health-related terminal degree (M.D., D.M.D., or Ph.D.) or who are involved in an M.D., D.M.D., or Ph.D. program in a health-related field and are in good standing. The master's program is based on both course work and research experience, but no research thesis is required. Students are required to sit for a final examination, which may entail the oral defense of a grant application and a manuscript. Lisa Godin (godin@nso.uchc.edu).

Dental Science. The Master of Dental Science degree program is an interdepartmental program whose primary objective is to provide instruction in dental science that will enhance the student's ability to instruct and undertake research in dental schools. This program provides an opportunity for cooperative study and research between dentistry, the basic sciences, and allied health fields. Both M.Dent.Sc. and oral biology Ph.D. students may combine their work in these programs with advanced clinical training in endodontics, orthodontics, oral pathology, pedodontics, periodontics, oral medicine, oral radiology, and oral and maxillofacial surgery. Arthur Hand, Assistant Dean for Medical and Graduate Education.

Public Health. This multidisciplinary master's program, accredited by the Council for Education in Public Health, is based in the Department of Community Medicine and Health Care. It offers a core curriculum in epidemiology, biostatistics, health administration, environmental health, the sociomedical sciences, health law, and electives in these and related areas. David Gregorio, Professor of Community Medicine and Health Care and Program Director.

THE UNIVERSITY OF KANSAS MEDICAL CENTER

Interdisciplinary Graduate Program in Biomedical Sciences

Programs of Study

Presidential and congressional commissions have identified biomedicine and biotechnology as leading growth sectors of the American and world economies. Students can pursue graduate studies on the cutting edge of biomedical research at The University of Kansas Medical Center (KUMC) and place themselves in a competitive position. Students have the opportunity to develop research skills and earn a Ph.D. degree in a broad range of biomedical research areas, including neuroscience, protein structure and function, and pharmacology and toxicology, as well as viral, microbial, molecular, cellular, developmental, reproductive, immunological, renal, and physiological biology. Research also includes many clinically related studies focusing on a wide range of human diseases. The graduate program is a partnership between KUMC (http://www.kumc.edu/igpbs) and the nearby Stowers Institute for Medical Research (http://www.stowers-institute. org), and students may conduct their research at either institution.

Graduate students pursuing a Ph.D. degree in biomedical sciences are admitted through the Interdisciplinary Graduate Program in Biomedical Sciences (IGPBS). This program is responsible for the first-year curriculum and allows each student to study in the most current areas of the biomedical sciences before selecting a laboratory in which to carry out his or her research program. Each student entering the IGPBS takes a state-of-the-art, highly integrated core curriculum. In addition to courses that provide the fundamental principles essential for understanding the biomedical sciences, students receive an introduction to practical aspects of research, including biographics, bioethics, appropriate use of animals in research, laboratory safety, and procedures for human studies research. Faculty members also present their research programs to students through a research seminar series, giving students the opportunity to evaluate each research program. Following this introduction, each student selects three laboratory rotations that are completed during the first year. Laboratory rotations expose students to potential research advisers and to the principles and procedures of cutting-edge laboratory techniques, and they allow students to decide which laboratory best fits their needs. At the beginning of the second year, each student selects a research adviser, in whose laboratory her or his doctoral research project is carried out. At this time, the student also enters one of eight graduate programs.

Research Facilities

State-of-the-art technology and equipment is available through a variety of core research facilities, including DNA microarray technology, laser capture microdissection, rodent behavioral testing facilities, bioinformatics, transgenic mouse laboratories, fluorescence-activated cell sorting, molecular neurobiology, mass spectrometry, a highly automated histological and immunohistochemistry core, FT-IR microspectroscopy, electron microscopy, confocal microscopes for live cell imaging and spectral separation, noninvasive magnetic resonance spectroscopy, functional magnetic resonance imaging, and magnetoencephalography.

Financial Aid

Teaching and research assistantships are available. Students admitted into the IGPBS are awarded $24,000 in financial support and given a tuition waiver. Student travel awards are also available as pupils progress through the program.

Cost of Study

Students accepted into the IGPBS receive a tuition waiver upon meeting enrollment requirements. Students are responsible for campus and library fees, estimated at $473 per academic year.

Living and Housing Costs

There is a multitude of options available to KUMC students near the campus. Current housing costs are between $450 and $800 per month.

Student Group

Twenty-five percent of the students enrolled in the IGPBS are from international locales. The age range of all students falls between 22 and 32 years.

Student Outcomes

Upon graduation from KUMC, students can expect to obtain a position in the biotechnology, academic, or governmental career fields.

Location

The University of Kansas Medical Center is located at 39th Avenue and Rainbow Boulevard in Kansas City, Kansas. It is on the border of Kansas and Missouri, with quick access to Westport, the Country Club Plaza, the Nelson-Atkins Museum of Art, and the Kansas City Art Institute.

The Graduate Program

The Interdisciplinary Graduate Program in Biomedical Sciences is an educational program within the School of Medicine at The University of Kansas Medical Center. It consists of eight degree-granting departments or programs. The IGPBS is made up of the Departments of Anatomy and Cell Biology; Biochemistry and Molecular Biology; Microbiology, Molecular Genetics and Immunology; Pathology and Laboratory Medicine; Molecular and Integrative Physiology; and Pharmacology, Toxicology and Therapeutics; the Neuroscience Graduate Program; and the Training Program in Environmental Toxicology.

Applying

Students who are interested in the IGPBS may apply online at http://www.kumc.edu/igpbs. Applications must be received by January 15, although applications received after that date are considered until the class is filled.

Correspondence and Information

Director
Interdisciplinary Graduate Program in Biomedical Sciences
5009 Wescoe, MS3025
The University of Kansas Medical Center
3901 Rainbow Boulevard
Kansas City, Kansas 66160-7836
Phone: 913-588-2719
        800-408-2039 (toll-free)
Fax: 913-588-2711
E-mail: igpbs@kumc.edu
Web site: http://www.kumc.edu/igpbs

The University of Kansas Medical Center

AREAS OF RESEARCH

Faculty members at KUMC have seventeen areas of research emphasis:

Cardiovascular biology
Cell and developmental biology
Imaging
Molecular and cellular biophysics
Molecular and cellular immunology
Molecular biology and genetics
Molecular pathogenesis of infectious diseases
Molecular toxicology and environmental health
Molecular virology
Muscle biology
Neurosciences
Pharmacological sciences
Proteomics
Renal biology
Reproductive biology
Signal transduction and cancer biology
Structural biology

THE UNIVERSITY OF TEXAS AT SAN ANTONIO

Department of Biology

Programs of Study

The Department of Biology currently offers the Ph.D. degree in biology, with a concentration in either neurobiology or cell and molecular biology. The Ph.D. program in neurobiology allows students to pursue research in neurobiology, neurophysiology, neuropharmacology, molecular and cellular neuroscience, neuroimaging, molecular and cellular neuroscience, and behavioral neuroscience. The Ph.D. program in cell and molecular biology allows students to pursue research in aging, bacterial pathogenesis, biochemistry, bioinformatics, bioremediation, biotechnology, cell cycle regulation, developmental biology, endocrinology, gene regulation, genetics, genomics, immunology, infectious disease, medical microbiology, physiology, reproductive biology, stem cell research, tissue engineering, tumor biology, vaccine development, virology, and other areas. Doctoral students must obtain a minimum of 90 semester hours of graduate credit beyond the bachelor's degree and must also complete three laboratory rotations. Advancement to candidacy requires doctoral students to complete not only the University and program requirements, but also to pass written and oral qualifying examinations as well as completing course requirements. Doctoral student candidates must then demonstrate their ability to conduct independent research by completing and defending an original dissertation.

The Department of Biology also offers three Master of Science degree programs in biology, biotechnology, and environmental science. The M.S. in biology program allows students to pursue research in molecular and cellular neuroscience, biochemistry, molecular cell biology, enzymology, membrane biology, molecular genetics, protein and nucleic acid structure, developmental biology, tumor biology, aging, molecular virology, medical microbiology, bioremediation, endocrinology, and parasitology. The M.S. in biotechnology program is specifically designed to enable the graduate to enter the biotechnology industry. The M.S. in environmental science program gives students the opportunity to broaden their scientific background at the graduate level into the research areas of aquatic biology and chemistry, ecology, environmental quality and remediation, and environmental management. On average, five years of full-time study are required to complete the doctoral program, while the programs leading to the M.S. degree average two years.

Research Facilities

The Department of Biology possesses state-of-the-art laboratories (both faculty research and core laboratories) for students to pursue graduate research projects. Core equipment available to the Department includes scanning and transmission electron microscopy, confocal microscopy, two-photon microscopy, fluorescence-activated cell sorting, gene chip microarray, and phosphoimagery, among many others. In addition to campuswide computing facilities, the Department has Sun Microsystems and Silicon Graphics workstations.

Financial Aid

In 2010–11, all doctoral students were supported with $21,000, which was a combination of research and teaching support. In addition to this support, all tuition and fees are paid for 21 credit hours per academic year. For qualified students, the Minority Biomedical Research Support/Research Initiative for Scientific Enhancement (MBRS/RISE) Program supports the stipend, tuition and fees, and travel to scientific meetings. Teaching and research assistantships are available to qualified M.S. students.

Cost of Study

In the 2010–11 academic year, tuition and fees for a full-time graduate degree student (9 semester hours) were approximately $3149 per semester for Texas residents and $8783 per semester for nonresidents.

Living and Housing Costs

University on-campus housing is available and includes apartment-style living at four complexes—Chisholm Hall, University Oaks, Laurel Village, and Chaparral Village. Off-campus housing is also available and includes many apartments adjacent to the University as well as a large number located within a 5-mile drive. The rate for a one-bedroom apartment is approximately $500 per month.

Student Group

In the 2010 fall semester, the University enrolled more than 30,000 students, of whom more than 3,000 were graduate students. The Department of Biology admits doctoral students in the fall semester of each academic year. Master's level students can apply for admission during the fall, spring, and summer semesters. Each year, 50–100 M.S. students are admitted each academic year. The student group is composed of both domestic and international students.

Location

San Antonio, with a population of 1.5 million, is one of the nation's major metropolitan areas. As the home of the Alamo and numerous other missions built by the Franciscans, the city is historically and culturally diverse. The Guadalupe Cultural Arts Center, McNay Art Museum, the San Antonio Museum of Art, and the Witte Museum enrich the city. The performing arts are represented by the San Antonio Symphony, the annual Tejano Music Festival and Tejano Music Awards, and performances by opera and ballet companies. Also notable are Sea World, Six Flags Fiesta Texas, Brackenridge Park, the Botanical Gardens, and the downtown Riverwalk. The San Antonio Zoo has the third-largest collection in North America. A city landmark is the Tower of the Americas, which was built for the 1968 World's Fair. San Antonio is home to the National Basketball Association's Spurs, league champions in 2000, 2003, 2005, and 2007. Numerous nearby lakes allow almost year-round outdoor activity, and the beaches of the Texas Gulf coast are within a 2-hour drive.

The University

The University was founded in 1969 and has since become a comprehensive metropolitan institution. Its research expenditures place it in the top 25 percent of public universities in Texas. The University has entered a new building and recruitment phase with a view to greatly expand the research effort in the biosciences.

Applying

To ensure full consideration, doctoral students interested in the Ph.D. program are encouraged to submit their applications for admission along with all supporting documentation by the firm February 1 deadline for acceptance the following fall semester. Information on applying may be obtained from the Office of Graduate Studies. Applications may be done on the Internet at https://apply.embark.com/grad/utsa/36. The deadlines for the M.S. domestic application are July 1 for the fall semester, November 1 for the spring semester, and May 1 for the summer semester. International M.S. applications must be submitted by April 1 for the fall semester, September 1 for the spring semester, and March 1 for the summer semester.

Correspondence and Information

For application information:
Office of Graduate Studies
The University of Texas at San Antonio
One UTSA Circle
San Antonio, Texas 78249
Phone: 210-458-4330
Web site: http://www.graduateschool.utsa.edu

For program information:
Department of Biology
The University of Texas at San Antonio
One UTSA Circle
San Antonio, Texas 78249
Phone: 210-458-4459
E-mail: Ashley.Skrobarcek@utsa.edu
Web site: http://www.bio.utsa.edu

The University of Texas at San Antonio

THE FACULTY AND THEIR RESEARCH

Deborah L. Armstrong, Professor of Neurophysiology; Ph.D., Syracuse, 1982. Hippocampal synaptic modulation.

Bernard P. Arulanandam, Associate Professor of Microbiology and Immunology; Ph.D., Medical College of Ohio, 1999. Cellular immunology; mucosal immunity.

Edwin J. Barea-Rodriguez, Associate Professor of Neurobiology; Ph.D., Southern Illinois, 1992. Neurobiology; long-term potentiation.

James Bower, Professor of Neurophysiology; Ph.D., Wisconsin–Madison, 1981. Neurocomputation; structure and function in neural circuits.

Astrid Cardona, Assistant Professor of Neuroimmunology; Ph.D., Texas Health Science Center at San Antonio, 2002. Neuroimmunology; fractalkine receptor biology.

J. Aaron Cassill, Associate Professor of Cell and Molecular Biology; Ph.D., California, San Diego, 1988. Cell and molecular biology; regulation of signal transduction cascades.

James P. Chambers, Professor of Biochemistry; Ph.D., Texas Health Science Center at San Antonio, 1975. Biochemistry.

G. Jilani Chaudry, Assistant Professor of Cell and Molecular Biology; Ph.D., Texas at Dallas, 1991. Mammalian cell intoxication by anthrax toxin.

Garry Cole, Professor of Biology; Ph.D., Waterloo, 1969. Mechanisms of fungal virulence and host immunity.

Brian E. Derrick, Professor of Neurobiology; Ph.D., Berkeley, 1993. Neurobiology; cellular/molecular mechanisms of potentiation/depression.

Jurgen E. Engelberth, Assistant Professor of Plant Biochemistry; Ph.D., Ruhr (Germany). Plant biochemistry.

Thomas Forsthuber, Professor of Immunology; Ph.D., Tübingen (Germany), 1989. Cellular immunology; T-cell immunity; autoimmune diseases.

Gary O. Gaufo, Assistant Professor of Biology; Ph.D., Berkeley, 1995. Molecular and cellular approaches to neural development.

Matthew J. Gdovin, Associate Professor of Evolutionary Biology; Ph.D., Dartmouth, 1995. Developmental aspects of the neural control of respiration.

M. Neal Guentzel, Professor of Microbiology; Ph.D., Texas at Austin, 1972. Microbiology; enteric infections; bioremediation.

Luis S. Haro, Professor of Cell and Molecular Biology; Ph.D., California, Santa Cruz, 1985. Cell and molecular biology; endocrinology; growth hormone; receptors.

Hans W. Heidner, Professor of Microbiology; Ph.D., California, Davis, 1991. Virology; genetics of alphavirus replication; virus/host cell interactions.

Brian P. Hermann, Assistant Professor of Molecular Physiology; Ph.D., Kansas Medical Center, 2005. Molecular and integrative physiology.

David B. Jaffe, Professor of Neurobiology; Ph.D., Baylor College of Medicine, 1992. Hippocampal neuron synaptic integration and plasticity.

Karl Klose, Professor of Microbiology; Ph.D., Berkeley, 1993. Bacterial pathogenesis.

Richard G. LeBaron, Professor of Cell and Molecular Biology; Ph.D., Alabama at Birmingham, 1988. Cell and molecular biology; tissue engineering; extracellular matrix biology.

Chin-Hsing Lin, Assistant Professor of Biochemistry; Ph.D., Alabama, 2005. Biochemistry; molecular genetics.

Jose Lopez-Ribot, Professor of Microbiology; M.D., Ph.D., Valencia (Spain), 1991. Study of the opportunistic pathogenic fungus *Candida albicans*.

Martha J. Lundell, Associate Professor of Molecular Genetics; Ph.D., UCLA, 1988. Specification of cell fate in the central nervous system.

Joe L. Martinez Jr., Professor of Neurobiology; Ph.D., Delaware, 1971. Neuroscience; neurobiology of learning and memory.

John McCarrey, Professor of Genetics; Ph.D., California, Davis, 1981. Cellular biology; cellular development and differentiation.

Paul Mueller, Assistant Professor of Cell and Developmental Biology; Ph.D., Caltech, 1990. Cell cycle regulation; developmental biology.

Carlos Paladini, Assistant Professor of Neuroscience; Ph.D., Rutgers, 1999. Dopamine neuron physiology and addiction.

George Perry, Dean and Professor of Biology; Ph.D., California, San Diego, 1979. Formation and physiological consequences of the cytopathology of Alzheimer's disease.

Clyde F. Phelix, Associate Professor of Anatomy and Neurobiology; Ph.D., Missouri, 1988. Anatomy; molecular neurobiology of cardiovascular disease.

Rama Ratnam, Assistant Professor of Computation and Neural Systems; Ph.D., Illinois, 1998. Sensory information processing; acoustic communication.

Robert R. Renthal, Professor of Biochemistry; Ph.D., Columbia, 1972. Membranes; protein biochemistry; sensory receptors.

Fidel Santamaria, Assistant Professor of Computation and Neural Systems; Ph.D., Caltech, 2000. Biophysical substrates of neuronal dendritic computation.

Stephen Saville, Assistant Professor of Genetics; Ph.D., Leicester, 1998. Yeast molecular genetics; mechanisms of fungal virulence and pathogenesis.

David M. Senseman, Associate Professor of Biology; Ph.D., Princeton, 1976. Neurophysiology; optical imaging; neural networks.

Janakiram Seshu, Assistant Professor of Microbiology; Ph.D., Washington State, 1996. Genetic analysis of *Borrelia burgdorferi* lp54 loci.

Valerie Sponsel, Associate Professor of Plant Physiology; Ph.D., Wales, 1972; D.Sc., Bristol (England), 1984. Regulation of plant growth and development by plant hormones.

Garry Sunter, Assistant Professor of Plant Pathology; Ph.D., Imperial College (London), 1985. DNA replication and plant-pathogen interactions.

Kelly J. Suter, Assistant Professor of Computational Biology; Ph.D., Pittsburgh, 1995. Sexual reproduction; GnRH pulse generator.

Judy Teale, Professor of Immunology; Ph.D., Virginia, 1976. Immunoparasitology; neuroimmunology; immune response to *Francisella tularensis*.

Todd Troyer, Assistant Professor of Neuroscience; Ph.D., Berkeley, 1993. Neural and behavioral dynamics.

Andrew T. C. Tsin, Professor of Biochemistry and Physiology; Ph.D., Alberta, 1979. Biochemistry and cell of the visual cycle; cell biology of the retina and the retinal pigment epithelium.

Oscar Van Auken, Professor of Plant Ecology; Ph.D., Utah, 1969. Plant ecology; species interactions; community composition and structure; rare species.

Yufeng Wang, Assistant Professor of Computational Biology; Ph.D., Iowa State, 2001. Bioinformatics.

Matthew J. Wayner, Professor of Neurobiology; Ph.D., Illinois, 1953. Hypothalamic-hippocampal interactions: learning and memory.

Tao Wei, Assistant Professor of Biotechnology; Ph.D., Uppsala (Sweden), 2000. Microbiology; instability of bacterial and yeast genomes during DNA replication and recombination.

Nicole Y. Wicha, Assistant Professor of Cognitive Science; Ph.D., California, San Diego, 2003. Cognitive neuroscience; human brain imaging and cognition.

Charles J. Wilson, Professor of Neurocomputation; Ph.D., Colorado at Boulder, 1979. Computational neuroscience; nonlinear dynamics of neurons and neuronal networks; neurocomputing; reinforcement learning.

Floyd Wormley, Assistant Professor of Microbiology/Immunology; Ph.D., LSU Health Sciences Center, 2001. Study of protective immune responses against *Cryptococcus neoformans* infections.

Section 2
Anatomy

This section contains a directory of institutions offering graduate work in anatomy. Additional information about programs listed in the directory may be obtained by writing directly to the dean of a graduate school or chair of a department at the address given in the directory.

For programs offering related work, see also in this book *Biological and Biomedical Sciences; Cell, Molecular, and Structural Biology; Genetics, Developmental Biology, and Reproductive Biology; Neuroscience and Neurobiology; Pathology and Pathobiology; Physiology;* and *Zoology.* In the other guides in this series:

Graduate Programs in the Humanities, Arts & Social Sciences
See *Sociology, Anthropology, and Archaeology*

Graduate Programs in Business, Education, Health, Information Studies, Law & Social Work
See *Allied Health, Dentistry and Dental Sciences,* and *Veterinary Medicine and Sciences*

CONTENTS

Program Directory

Anatomy

Albert Einstein College of Medicine, Graduate Division of Biomedical Sciences, Department of Anatomy and Structural Biology, Bronx, NY 10461. Offers anatomy (PhD); cell and developmental biology (PhD); MD/PhD. *Degree requirements:* For doctorate, thesis/dissertation. *Entrance requirements:* For doctorate, GRE General Test. Additional exam requirements/recommendations for international students: Required—TOEFL. Electronic applications accepted. *Faculty research:* Cell motility, cell membranes and membrane-cytoskeletal interactions as applied to processing of pancreatic hormones, mechanisms of secretion.

Auburn University, College of Veterinary Medicine and Graduate School, Graduate Programs in Veterinary Medicine, Auburn University, AL 36849. Offers biomedical sciences (MS, PhD), including anatomy, physiology and pharmacology (MS), biomedical sciences (PhD), clinical sciences (MS), large animal surgery and medicine (MS), pathobiology (MS), radiology (MS), small animal surgery and medicine (MS); DVM/MS. Part-time programs available. *Faculty:* 100 full-time (40 women), 5 part-time/adjunct (1 woman). *Students:* 17 full-time (6 women), 51 part-time (35 women); includes 2 Black or African American, non-Hispanic/Latino; 1 American Indian or Alaska Native, non-Hispanic/Latino; 3 Asian, non-Hispanic/Latino; 2 Hispanic/Latino, 22 international. Average age 31. 70 applicants, 34% accepted, 10 enrolled. In 2010, 12 master's, 7 doctorates awarded. *Degree requirements:* For doctorate, thesis/dissertation. *Entrance requirements:* For master's, GRE General Test; for doctorate, GRE General Test, GRE Subject Test. *Application deadline:* For fall admission, 7/7 for domestic students; for spring admission, 11/24 for domestic students. Applications are processed on a rolling basis. Application fee: $50 ($60 for international students). Electronic applications accepted. *Expenses:* Tuition, state resident: full-time $7002. Tuition, nonresident: full-time $21,898. International tuition: $22,116 full-time. Required fees: $892. Tuition and fees vary according to course load and program. *Financial support:* Research assistantships, teaching assistantships, Federal Work-Study available. Support available to part-time students. Financial award application deadline: 3/15; financial award applicants required to submit FAFSA. *Unit head:* Dr. Timothy R. Boosinger, Dean, 334-844-4546. *Application contact:* Dr. George Flowers, Dean of the Graduate School, 334-844-2125.

Barry University, School of Graduate Medical Sciences, Program in Anatomy, Miami Shores, FL 33161-6695. Offers MS. *Entrance requirements:* For master's, GRE.

Boston University, College of Health and Rehabilitation Sciences: Sargent College, Department of Health Sciences, Programs in Applied Anatomy and Physiology, Boston, MA 02215. Offers MS, PhD. *Faculty:* 10 full-time (9 women), 5 part-time/adjunct (2 women). *Students:* 4 full-time (2 women), 4 part-time (all women), 1 international. Average age 27. 37 applicants, 41% accepted.Terminal master's awarded for partial completion of doctoral program. *Degree requirements:* For master's, thesis or alternative; for doctorate, comprehensive exam, thesis/dissertation. *Entrance requirements:* For master's, GRE General Test, minimum GPA of 3.0; for doctorate, GRE General Test. Additional exam requirements/recommendations for international students: Required—TOEFL (minimum score 550 paper-based; 84 iBT). *Application deadline:* For fall admission, 1/15 priority date for domestic students; for spring admission, 10/1 for domestic students. Applications are processed on a rolling basis. Application fee: $70. Electronic applications accepted. *Expenses:* Tuition: Full-time $39,314; part-time $1228 per credit. Required fees: $40 per semester. *Financial support:* In 2010–11, 2 fellowships (averaging $21,000 per year), 1 research assistantship with full tuition reimbursement (averaging $18,000 per year), 3 teaching assistantships with full and partial tuition reimbursements were awarded; career-related internships or fieldwork, Federal Work-Study, institutionally sponsored loans, and scholarships/grants also available. Support available to part-time students. Financial award application deadline: 4/15; financial award applicants required to submit FAFSA. *Faculty research:* Skeletal muscle, neural systems, smooth muscle, muscular dystrophy. *Unit head:* Dr. Kathleen Morgan, Chair, 617-353-2717, E-mail: kmorgan@bu.edu. *Application contact:* Sharon Sankey, Director, Student Services, 617-353-2713, Fax: 617-353-7500, E-mail: ssankey@bu.edu.

Case Western Reserve University, School of Medicine and School of Graduate Studies, Graduate Programs in Medicine, Department of Anatomy, Cleveland, OH 44106. Offers applied anatomy (MS); biological anthropology (MS); cellular biology (MS); MD/MS. Part-time programs available. *Degree requirements:* For master's, comprehensive exam, thesis (for some programs). *Entrance requirements:* For master's, GRE General Test. Additional exam requirements/recommendations for international students: Required—TOEFL. *Faculty research:* Hypoxia, cell injury, biochemical aberration occurrences in ischemic tissue, human functional morphology, evolutionary morphology.

Columbia University, College of Physicians and Surgeons, Department of Anatomy and Cell Biology, New York, NY 10032. Offers anatomy (M Phil, MA, PhD); anatomy and cell biology (PhD); MD/PhD. Only candidates for the PhD are admitted. Terminal master's awarded for partial completion of doctoral program. *Degree requirements:* For doctorate, thesis/dissertation, oral exam. *Entrance requirements:* For master's and doctorate, GRE General Test. Additional exam requirements/recommendations for international students: Required—TOEFL. *Faculty research:* Protein sorting, membrane biophysics, muscle energetics, neuroendocrinology, developmental biology, cytoskeleton, transcription factors.

Cornell University, Graduate School, Graduate Fields of Agriculture and Life Sciences, Field of Zoology and Wildlife Conservation, Ithaca, NY 14853-0001. Offers animal cytology (MS, PhD); comparative and functional anatomy (MS, PhD); developmental biology (MS, PhD); ecology (MS, PhD); histology (MS, PhD). *Faculty:* 20 full-time (5 women). *Students:* 5 full-time (all women); includes 1 Hispanic/Latino, 1 international. Average age 31. 17 applicants, 18% accepted, 1 enrolled. *Degree requirements:* For doctorate, comprehensive exam, thesis/dissertation, 2 semesters of teaching experience. *Entrance requirements:* For doctorate, GRE General Test, GRE Subject Test (biology), 2 letters of recommendation. Additional exam requirements/recommendations for international students: Required—TOEFL (minimum score 550 paper-based; 213 computer-based; 77 iBT). *Application deadline:* For fall admission, 2/1 priority date for domestic students. Application fee: $70. Electronic applications accepted. *Expenses:* Tuition: Full-time $29,500. Required fees: $76. Tuition and fees vary according to degree level and program. *Financial support:* In 2010–11, 1 fellowship with full tuition reimbursement, 4 research assistantships with full tuition reimbursements were awarded; teaching assistantships with full tuition reimbursements, institutionally sponsored loans, scholarships/grants, health care benefits, tuition waivers (full and partial), and unspecified assistantships also available. Financial award applicants required to submit FAFSA. *Faculty research:* Organismal biology, functional morphology, biomechanics, comparative vertebrate anatomy, comparative invertebrate anatomy, paleontology. *Unit head:* Director of Graduate Studies, 607-253-3276, Fax: 607-253-3756. *Application contact:* Graduate Field Assistant, 607-253-3276, Fax: 607-253-3756, E-mail: graduate_edcvm@cornell.edu.

Creighton University, School of Medicine and Graduate School, Graduate Programs in Medicine, Program in Clinical Anatomy, Omaha, NE 68178-0001. Offers MS. *Degree requirements:* For master's, comprehensive exam, thesis or alternative. *Entrance requirements:* For master's, GRE, MCAT or DAT. Additional exam requirements/recommendations for international students: Required—TOEFL. Electronic applications accepted. *Expenses:* Tuition: Full-time $12,168; part-time $676 per credit hour. Required fees: $131 per semester. Tuition and fees vary according to program. *Faculty research:* Neural crest cell migration; ontogenetic and phylogenetic nervous system development; skeletal biology.

Dalhousie University, Faculty of Graduate Studies and Faculty of Medicine, Graduate Programs in Medicine, Department of Anatomy and Neurobiology, Halifax, NS B3H 4R2, Canada. Offers M Sc, PhD. *Degree requirements:* For master's, thesis; for doctorate, thesis/dissertation. *Entrance requirements:* For master's and doctorate, GRE (recommended), minimum A- average. Additional exam requirements/recommendations for international students: Required—TOEFL, IELTS, 1 of the following 5 approved tests: TOELF, IELTS, CANTEST, CAEL, Michigan English Language Assessment Battery. Electronic applications accepted. *Faculty research:* Neuroscience histology, cell biology, neuroendocrinology, evolutionary biology.

Des Moines University, College of Osteopathic Medicine, Program in Anatomy, Des Moines, IA 50312-4104. Offers MS. *Unit head:* Dr. Kendall Reed, Dean, 515-271-1515, Fax: 515-271-1532, E-mail: kendall.reed@dmu.edu. *Application contact:* Jamie Rehmann, Director of Admissions, 515-271-1451, Fax: 515-271-7163, E-mail: doadmit@dmu.edu.

Duke University, Graduate School, Department of Biological Anthropology and Anatomy, Durham, NC 27710. Offers cellular and molecular biology (PhD); gross anatomy and physical anthropology (PhD), including comparative morphology of human and non-human primates, primate social behavior, vertebrate paleontology; neuroanatomy (PhD). *Faculty:* 9 full-time. *Students:* 13 full-time (9 women); includes 1 Black or African American, non-Hispanic/Latino; 2 Hispanic/Latino, 1 international. 54 applicants, 9% accepted, 2 enrolled. In 2010, 2 doctorates awarded. *Degree requirements:* For doctorate, one foreign language, thesis/dissertation. *Entrance requirements:* For doctorate, GRE General Test. Additional exam requirements/recommendations for international students: Required—TOEFL (minimum score 550 paper-based; 213 computer-based; 83 iBT), IELTS (minimum score 7). *Application deadline:* For fall admission, 12/8 priority date for domestic and international students. Application fee: $75. Electronic applications accepted. *Financial support:* Fellowships, teaching assistantships, Federal Work-Study available. Financial award application deadline: 12/31. *Unit head:* Daniel Schmitt, Director of Graduate Studies, 919-684-4124, Fax: 919-684-8542, E-mail: mlsquire@duke.edu. *Application contact:* Elizabeth Hutton, Director of Admissions, 919-684-3913, Fax: 919-684-2277, E-mail: grad-admissions@duke.edu.

East Carolina University, Brody School of Medicine, Department of Anatomy and Cell Biology, Greenville, NC 27858-4353. Offers PhD. *Degree requirements:* For doctorate, comprehensive exam, thesis/dissertation. *Entrance requirements:* For doctorate, GRE General Test. Additional exam requirements/recommendations for international students: Required—TOEFL. *Expenses:* Tuition, state resident: full-time $3130; part-time $391.25 per credit hour. Tuition, nonresident: full-time $13,817; part-time $1727.13 per credit hour. Required fees: $1916; $239.50 per credit hour. Tuition and fees vary according to campus/location and program. *Faculty research:* Kinesin motors during slow matogensis, mitochondria and peroxisomes in obesity, ovarian innervation, tight junction function and regulation.

East Tennessee State University, James H. Quillen College of Medicine, Biomedical Science Graduate Program, Johnson City, TN 37614. Offers anatomy (PhD); biochemistry (PhD); microbiology (PhD); pharmacology (PhD); physiology (PhD). Part-time programs available. *Faculty:* 49 full-time (12 women), 1 (woman) part-time/adjunct. *Students:* 27 full-time (14 women), 4 part-time (2 women); includes 4 minority (1 Black or African American, non-Hispanic/Latino; 1 Asian, non-Hispanic/Latino; 2 Hispanic/Latino), 5 international. Average age 32. 62 applicants, 11% accepted, 7 enrolled. In 2010, 2 doctorates awarded. Terminal master's awarded for partial completion of doctoral program. *Degree requirements:* For doctorate, thesis/dissertation, comprehensive qualifying exam. *Entrance requirements:* For doctorate, GRE General Test, GRE Subject Test. Additional exam requirements/recommendations for international students: Required—TOEFL (minimum score 550 paper-based; 213 computer-based; 79 iBT). *Application deadline:* For fall admission, 3/15 priority date for domestic students, 3/1 priority date for international students. Application fee: $25 ($35 for international students). Electronic applications accepted. *Expenses:* Contact institution. *Financial support:* In 2010–11, 7 research assistantships with full tuition reimbursements (averaging $15,000 per year) were awarded; teaching assistantships with full tuition reimbursements, career-related internships or fieldwork, institutionally sponsored loans, scholarships/grants, and unspecified assistantships also available. Financial award application deadline: 7/1; financial award applicants required to submit FAFSA. Total annual research expenditures: $2.1 million. *Unit head:* Dr. Mitchell E. Robinson, Assistant Dean/Director, 423-439-4658, E-mail: robinson@etsu.edu. *Application contact:* Edwin D. Taylor, Assistant Dean for Admissions and Records, 423-439-4753, Fax: 423-439-8206.

Georgia Health Sciences University, College of Graduate Studies, Program in Cellular Biology and Anatomy, Augusta, GA 30912. Offers MS, PhD. *Faculty:* 16 full-time (6 women), 6 part-time/adjunct (1 woman). *Students:* 11 full-time (5 women); includes 2 Asian, non-Hispanic/Latino, 6 international. Average age 30. In 2010, 2 doctorates awarded. *Degree requirements:* For doctorate, comprehensive exam, thesis/dissertation. *Entrance requirements:* For doctorate, GRE General Test. Additional exam requirements/recommendations for international students: Required—TOEFL (minimum score 550 paper-based; 213 computer-based; 79 iBT). *Application deadline:* For fall admission, 1/15 for domestic and international students. Applications are processed on a rolling basis. Application fee: $30. *Expenses:* Tuition, state resident: full-time $7500; part-time $313 per semester hour. Tuition, nonresident: full-time $24,772; part-time $1033 per semester hour. Required fees: $1112. *Financial support:* In 2010–11, 2 students received support, including 1 fellowship with partial tuition reimbursement available (averaging $26,000 per year), 9 research assistantships with partial tuition reimbursements available (averaging $23,000 per year); teaching assistantships with partial tuition reimbursements available, Federal Work-Study, institutionally sponsored loans, and scholarships/grants also available. Support available to part-time students. Financial award application deadline: 5/31; financial award applicants required to submit FAFSA. *Faculty research:* Eye disease, developmental biology, cell injury and death, stroke and neurotoxicity, diabetic complications. Total annual research expenditures: $2.8 million. *Unit head:* Dr. Sally S. Atherton, Chair and Professor, 706-721-3731, Fax: 706-721-6120, E-mail: satherton@georgiahealth.edu. *Application contact:* Dr. Patricia L. Cameron, Acting Vice Dean, 706-721-3279, E-mail: pcameron@georgiahealth.edu.

Howard University, Graduate School, Department of Anatomy, Washington, DC 20059-0002. Offers MS, PhD. *Degree requirements:* For master's, comprehensive exam, thesis, teaching experience; for doctorate, comprehensive exam, thesis/dissertation, teaching experience. *Entrance requirements:* For master's and doctorate, GRE General Test, minimum GPA of 3.0. Additional exam requirements/recommendations for international students: Required—TOEFL (minimum score 550 paper-based; 213 computer-based). Electronic applications accepted. *Faculty research:* Neural control of function, mammalian evolution and paleontology, cellular differentiation, cellular and neuronal communication, development, cell biology, molecular biology, anatomy.

Indiana University–Purdue University Indianapolis, Indiana University School of Medicine, Department of Anatomy and Cell Biology, Indianapolis, IN 46202-2896. Offers MS, PhD, MD/PhD. *Faculty:* 14 full-time (1 woman). *Students:* 11 full-time (5 women), 1 (woman) part-time; includes 1 minority (Black or African American, non-Hispanic/Latino), 1 international. Average age 29. 17 applicants, 35% accepted, 5 enrolled. In 2010, 1 master's, 2 doctorates awarded. *Degree requirements:* For master's, thesis or alternative; for doctorate, thesis/dissertation. *Entrance requirements:* For master's and doctorate, GRE General Test. *Application deadline:* For fall admission, 1/15 priority date for domestic students. Application fee: $55 ($65 for international students). *Financial support:* In 2010–11, 1 fellowship was awarded; research assistantships, Federal Work-Study, institutionally sponsored loans, tuition waivers (partial), and stipends also available. Financial award application deadline: 2/15. *Faculty research:* Acoustic reflex control, osteoarthritis and bone disease, diabetes, kidney diseases, cellular and molecular neurobiology. *Unit head:* Dr. David B. Burr, Chairman, 317-274-7494, Fax: 317-278-2040, E-mail: dburr@indyvax.iupui.edu. *Application contact:* Dr. James Williams, Graduate Adviser, 317-274-3423, Fax: 317-278-2040, E-mail: williams@anatomy.iupui.edu.

The Johns Hopkins University, School of Medicine, Graduate Programs in Medicine, Center for Functional Anatomy and Evolution, Baltimore, MD 21218-2699. Offers PhD. *Faculty:* 5 full-time (1 woman), 2 part-time/adjunct (1 woman). *Students:* 10 full-time (7 women), 2 international. Average age 25. 26 applicants, 15% accepted, 2 enrolled. In 2010, 1 doctorate awarded. *Degree requirements:* For doctorate, comprehensive exam, thesis/dissertation, oral exams. *Entrance requirements:* For doctorate, GRE. Additional exam requirements/recommendations for international students: Required—TOEFL. *Application deadline:* For fall admission, 1/10 for domestic and international students. Application fee: $85. *Financial support:* In 2010–11, 1 fellowship with partial tuition reimbursement (averaging $30,000 per year), 8 teaching assistantships with full tuition reimbursements (averaging $26,855 per year) were awarded; career-related internships or fieldwork, institutionally sponsored loans, health care benefits, and tuition waivers (full) also available. *Faculty research:* Vertebrate evolution, functional anatomy, primate evolution, vertebrate paleobiology, vertebrate morphology. *Unit head:* Dr. Kenneth D. Rose, Director, 410-955-7172, Fax: 410-614-9030, E-mail: kdrose@jhmi.edu. *Application contact:* Catherine L. Will, Coordinator, Graduate Student Affairs, 410-614-3385, E-mail: grad_study@som.adm.jhu.edu.

Loma Linda University, School of Medicine, Department of Pathology and Human Anatomy, Loma Linda, CA 92350. Offers MS, PhD. Part-time programs available. Terminal master's awarded for partial completion of doctoral program. *Degree requirements:* For master's, thesis; for doctorate, 2 foreign languages, thesis/dissertation. *Entrance requirements:* For master's and doctorate, GRE General Test. Additional exam requirements/recommendations for international students: Required—TOEFL (minimum score 550 paper-based; 213 computer-based). *Faculty research:* Neuroendocrine system, histochemistry and image analysis, effect of age and diabetes on PNS, electron microscopy, histology.

Louisiana State University Health Sciences Center, School of Graduate Studies in New Orleans, Department of Cell Biology and Anatomy, New Orleans, LA 70112-2223. Offers cell biology and anatomy (MS, PhD), including cell biology, developmental biology, neurobiology and anatomy; MD/PhD. *Degree requirements:* For master's, comprehensive exam, thesis; for doctorate, comprehensive exam, thesis/dissertation. *Entrance requirements:* For master's and doctorate, GRE General Test, GRE Subject Test, minimum undergraduate GPA of 3.0. Additional exam requirements/recommendations for international students: Required—TOEFL. *Faculty research:* Visual system organization, neural development, plasticity of sensory systems, information processing through the nervous system, visuomotor integration.

Louisiana State University Health Sciences Center at Shreveport, Department of Cellular Biology and Anatomy, Shreveport, LA 71130-3932. Offers MS, PhD, MD/PhD. Terminal master's awarded for partial completion of doctoral program. *Degree requirements:* For master's, thesis; for doctorate, thesis/dissertation. *Entrance requirements:* For master's and doctorate, GRE General Test. Additional exam requirements/recommendations for international students: Required—TOEFL. *Faculty research:* Alcohol and immunity, neuroscience, olfactory physiology, extracellular matrix, cancer cell biology and gene therapy.

Loyola University Chicago, Graduate School, Department of Cell Biology, Neurobiology and Anatomy, Chicago, IL 60660. Offers MS, PhD. Part-time programs available. *Faculty:* 16 full-time (6 women), 9 part-time/adjunct (4 women). *Students:* 21 full-time (12 women), 2 part-time (1 woman); includes 3 minority (2 Hispanic/Latino; 1 Two or more races, non-Hispanic/Latino), 1 international. Average age 26. 25 applicants, 24% accepted, 6 enrolled. In 2010, 3 master's, 4 doctorates awarded. Terminal master's awarded for partial completion of doctoral program. *Degree requirements:* For master's, thesis; for doctorate, comprehensive exam, thesis/dissertation. *Entrance requirements:* For master's, GRE General Test, minimum GPA of 3.0; for doctorate, GRE General Test, GRE Subject Test (biology), minimum GPA of 3.0. Additional exam requirements/recommendations for international students: Required—TOEFL (minimum score 600 paper-based; 250 computer-based). *Application deadline:* For fall admission, 5/1 priority date for domestic and international students. Applications are processed on a rolling basis. Application fee: $50. Electronic applications accepted. *Expenses:* Tuition: Full-time $14,940; part-time $830 per credit hour. Required fees: $87 per semester. Part-time tuition and fees vary according to course load and program. *Financial support:* In 2010–11, 5 fellowships with full tuition reimbursements (averaging $23,000 per year), 5 research assistantships with full tuition reimbursements (averaging $23,000 per year) were awarded; Federal Work-Study and unspecified assistantships also available. Financial award application deadline: 5/1; financial award applicants required to submit FAFSA. *Faculty research:* Brain steroids, immunology, neuroregeneration, cytokines. Total annual research expenditures: $1 million. *Unit head:* Dr. Phong Le, Head, 708-216-3603, Fax: 708-216-3913, E-mail: ple@lumc.edu. *Application contact:* Ginny Hayes, Graduate Program Secretary, 708-216-3353, Fax: 708-216-3913, E-mail: vhayes@lumc.edu.

McGill University, Faculty of Graduate and Postdoctoral Studies, Faculty of Medicine, Department of Anatomy and Cell Biology, Montréal, QC H3A 2T5, Canada. Offers M Sc, PhD.

New York Chiropractic College, Program in Clinical Anatomy, Seneca Falls, NY 13148-0800. Offers MS. *Faculty:* 2 full-time (0 women). *Students:* 1 part-time (0 women). 6 applicants, 0% accepted, 0 enrolled. *Degree requirements:* For master's, thesis. *Entrance requirements:* For master's, minimum GPA of 3.0, DC, interview. *Application deadline:* Applications are processed on a rolling basis. Application fee: $0. *Expenses:* Tuition: Full-time $19,050; part-time $443 per credit hour. Required fees: $680; $340 per term. Part-time tuition and fees vary according to program. *Financial support:* In 2010–11, 1 fellowship with full tuition reimbursement (averaging $33,500 per year) was awarded. Financial award applicants required to submit FAFSA. *Faculty research:* Bone histology, biomechanics, craniofacial growth and anatomy, skeletal morphology. *Unit head:* Dr. Karen Gana, Director, 315-568-3184, E-mail: kgana@nycc.edu. *Application contact:* Dr. Karen Gana, Director, 315-568-3184, E-mail: kgana@nycc.edu.

New York Chiropractic College, Program in Human Anatomy and Physiology Instruction, Seneca Falls, NY 13148-0800. Offers MS. Postbaccalaureate distance learning degree programs offered. *Faculty:* 1 part-time/adjunct (0 women). *Students:* 30 part-time (11 women); includes 1 Hispanic/Latino, 1 international. Average age 43. *Expenses:* Tuition: Full-time $19,050; part-time $443 per credit hour. Required fees: $680; $340 per term. Part-time tuition and fees vary according to program. *Financial support:* In 2010–11, 1 student received support. Applicants required to submit FAFSA. *Unit head:* Dr. Robert A. Crocker, Director, 516-796-4800, E-mail: rcrocker@nycc.edu. *Application contact:* Michael Lynch, Director of Admissions, 315-568-3040, Fax: 315-568-3087, E-mail: mlynch@nycc.edu.

New York Medical College, Graduate School of Basic Medical Sciences, Department of Cell Biology, Valhalla, NY 10595-1691. Offers cell biology and neuroscience (MS, PhD); MD/PhD. Part-time and evening/weekend programs available. *Faculty:* 13 full-time (2 women), 2 part-time/adjunct (both women). *Students:* 6 full-time (1 woman), 3 part-time (all women); includes 1 Asian, non-Hispanic/Latino, 2 international. Average age 26. In 2010, 2 master's, 1 doctorate awarded. Terminal master's awarded for partial completion of doctoral program. *Degree requirements:* For master's, thesis; for doctorate, comprehensive exam, thesis/dissertation. *Entrance requirements:* For master's and doctorate, GRE General Test. Additional exam requirements/recommendations for international students: Required—TOEFL. *Application deadline:* For fall admission, 7/1 priority date for domestic students, 5/1 priority date for international students; for spring admission, 12/1 priority date for domestic students, 10/1 priority date for international students. Applications are processed on a rolling basis. Application fee: $50 ($75 for international students). Electronic applications accepted. *Financial support:* In 2010–11, 4 research assistantships with full tuition reimbursements (averaging $24,000 per year) were awarded; Federal Work-Study, institutionally sponsored loans, scholarships/grants, traineeships, tuition waivers (full), unspecified assistantships, and health benefits (for PhD candidates only) also available. Financial award applicants required to submit FAFSA. *Faculty research:* Mechanisms of growth control in skeletal muscle, cartilage differentiation, cytoskeletal functions, signal transduction pathways, neuronal development and plasticity. *Unit head:* Dr. Victor Fried, Director, 914-594-4036. *Application contact:* Valerie Romeo-Messana, Admission Coordinator, 914-594-4110, Fax: 914-594-4944, E-mail: v_romeomessana@nymc.edu.

The Ohio State University, College of Medicine, School of Biomedical Science, Department of Anatomy, Columbus, OH 43210. Offers MS, PhD. Terminal master's awarded for partial completion of doctoral program. *Degree requirements:* For doctorate, thesis/dissertation. *Entrance requirements:* For master's and doctorate, GRE General Test, GRE Subject Test in biology, biochemistry, chemistry, CIS, physics, or engineering. Additional exam requirements/recommendations for international students: Required—TOEFL (paper-based 600, computer-based 250) or Michigan English Language Assessment Battery (86). Electronic applications accepted. *Expenses:* Tuition, state resident: full-time $10,605. Tuition, nonresident: full-time $26,535. Tuition and fees vary according to course load and program. *Faculty research:* Cell biology, biomechanical trauma, computer-assisted instruction.

The Ohio State University, College of Veterinary Medicine, Department of Veterinary Biosciences, Columbus, OH 43210. Offers anatomy and cellular biology (MS, PhD); pathobiology (MS, PhD); pharmacology (MS, PhD); toxicology (MS, PhD); veterinary physiology (MS, PhD). *Faculty:* 45. *Students:* 4 full-time (all women), 7 part-time (5 women); includes 1 Black or African American, non-Hispanic/Latino, 3 international. Average age 30. In 2010, 2 master's, 7 doctorates awarded. *Entrance requirements:* For master's and doctorate, GRE General Test. Additional exam requirements/recommendations for international students: Required—TOEFL. *Application deadline:* Applications are processed on a rolling basis. Application fee: $40 ($50 for international students). Electronic applications accepted. *Expenses:* Tuition, state resident: full-time $10,605. Tuition, nonresident: full-time $26,535. Tuition and fees vary according to course load and program. *Faculty research:* Microvasculature, muscle biology, neonatal lung and bone development. *Unit head:* Dr. Michael J. Oglesbee, Graduate Studies Committee Chair, 614-292-5661, Fax: 614-292-6473, E-mail: oglesbee.1@osu.edu. *Application contact:* Graduate Admissions, 614-292-9444, Fax: 614-292-3895, E-mail: domestic.grad@osu.edu.

Palmer College of Chiropractic, Division of Graduate Studies, Davenport, IA 52803-5287. Offers clinical research (MS). *Faculty:* 8 full-time (3 women), 3 part-time/adjunct (2 women). *Students:* 7 full-time (2 women), 1 (woman) part-time; includes 1 Black or African American, non-Hispanic/Latino. 3 applicants, 100% accepted, 3 enrolled. In 2010, 5 master's awarded. *Degree requirements:* For master's, 2 mentored practicum projects. *Entrance requirements:* For master's, GRE General Test, minimum GPA of 2.5, bachelor's and doctoral-level health professions degrees. Additional exam requirements/recommendations for international students: Required—TOEFL. *Application deadline:* For fall admission, 8/1 for domestic and international students; for spring admission, 5/28 for domestic students. Applications are processed on a rolling basis. Application fee: $50. Electronic applications accepted. *Expenses:* Contact institution. *Financial support:* In 2010–11, 7 students received support, including 7 research assistantships with full tuition reimbursements available (averaging $30,000 per year), teaching assistantships with full and partial tuition reimbursements available (averaging $6,269 per year); tuition waivers (full) and unspecified assistantships also available. Financial award application deadline: 8/1; financial award applicants required to submit FAFSA. *Faculty research:* Chiropractic clinical research. *Unit head:* Dr. Dan Weinert, Interim Vice President for Academic Affairs, 563-884-5761, Fax: 563-884-5624, E-mail: weinert_d@palmer.edu. *Application contact:* Lori Byrd, Program Coordinator, 563-884-5198, Fax: 563-884-5227, E-mail: lori.byrd@plamer.edu.

Penn State Hershey Medical Center, College of Medicine, Graduate School Programs in the Biomedical Sciences, Program in Anatomy, Hershey, PA 17033. Offers MS, PhD. *Students:* 17 applicants, 29% accepted, 4 enrolled.Terminal master's awarded for partial completion of doctoral program. *Degree requirements:* For master's, thesis or alternative; for doctorate, comprehensive exam, thesis/dissertation. *Entrance requirements:* For master's and doctorate, GRE General Test or MCAT, minimum GPA of 3.0. Additional exam requirements/recommendations for international students: Required—TOEFL (minimum score 500 paper-based; 213 computer-based). *Application deadline:* For fall admission, 1/31 priority date for domestic students, 2/1 priority date for international students. Applications are processed on a rolling basis. Application fee: $65. Electronic applications accepted. *Financial support:* In 2010–11, research assistantships with full tuition reimbursements (averaging $22,260 per year); fellowships with full tuition reimbursements, scholarships/grants, health care benefits, and unspecified assistantships also available. Financial award applicants required to submit FAFSA. *Faculty research:* Developmental biology, stem cell, cancer-basic science and clinical application, wound healing, angiogenesis. *Unit head:* Dr. Patricia J. McLaughlin, Program Director, 717-531-6411, Fax: 717-531-5184, E-mail: grad-hmc@psu.edu. *Application contact:* Dee Clarke, Program Assistant, 717-531-8651, Fax: 717-531-8651, E-mail: grad-hmc@psu.edu.

Purdue University, School of Veterinary Medicine and Graduate School, Graduate Programs in Veterinary Medicine, Department of Basic Medical Sciences, West Lafayette, IN 47907. Offers anatomy (MS, PhD); pharmacology (MS, PhD); physiology (MS, PhD). Part-time programs available. Terminal master's awarded for partial completion of doctoral program. *Degree requirements:* For master's, thesis; for doctorate, thesis/dissertation. *Entrance requirements:* For master's and doctorate, GRE General Test. Additional exam requirements/recommendations for international students: Required—TOEFL. Electronic applications accepted. *Faculty research:* Development and regeneration, tissue injury and shock, biomedical engineering, ovarian function, bone and cartilage biology, cell and molecular biology.

Queen's University at Kingston, School of Graduate Studies and Research, Faculty of Health Sciences, Department of Anatomy and Cell Biology, Kingston, ON K7L 3N6, Canada. Offers biology of reproduction (M Sc, PhD); cancer (M Sc, PhD); cardiovascular pathophysiology (M Sc, PhD); cell and molecular biology (M Sc, PhD); drug metabolism (M Sc, PhD); endocrinology (M Sc, PhD); motor control (M Sc, PhD); neural regeneration (M Sc, PhD); neurophysiology (M Sc, PhD). Part-time programs available. *Degree requirements:* For master's, thesis; for doctorate, one foreign language, comprehensive exam, thesis/dissertation. *Entrance requirements:* Additional exam requirements/recommendations for international students: Required—TOEFL. Electronic applications accepted. *Faculty research:* Human kinetics, neuroscience, reproductive biology, cardiovascular.

Rosalind Franklin University of Medicine and Science, School of Graduate and Postdoctoral Studies—Interdisciplinary Graduate Program in Biomedical Sciences, Department of Cell Biology and Anatomy, North Chicago, IL 60064-3095. Offers MS, PhD, MD/PhD. Terminal master's awarded for partial completion of doctoral program. *Degree requirements:* For master's, comprehensive exam, thesis, qualifying exam; for doctorate, comprehensive exam, thesis/dissertation, original research project. *Entrance requirements:* For master's and doctorate, GRE General Test, minimum GPA of 3.0. Additional exam requirements/recommendations for international students: Required—TOEFL, TWE. *Faculty research:* Neuroscience, molecular biology.

Rush University, Graduate College, Division of Anatomy and Cell Biology, Chicago, IL 60612-3832. Offers MS, PhD, MD/MS, MD/PhD. Terminal master's awarded for partial completion of doctoral program. *Degree requirements:* For master's, thesis; for doctorate, comprehensive exam, thesis/dissertation, preliminary exam, dissertation proposal. *Entrance requirements:* For master's, GRE General Test, minimum GPA of 3.0, bachelor's degree in biology or chemistry (preferred), interview; for doctorate, GRE General Test, minimum GPA of 3.0, interview. Additional exam requirements/recommendations for international students: Required—TOEFL. Electronic applications accepted. *Faculty research:* Incontinence following vaginal distension, knee replacement, biomimetric materials, injured spinal motoneurons, implant fixation.

Saint Louis University, Graduate Education and School of Medicine, Graduate Program in Biomedical Sciences and Graduate Education, Center for Anatomical Science and Education, St. Louis, MO 63103-2097. Offers anatomy (MS-R, PhD). *Degree requirements:* For master's, comprehensive exam, thesis; for doctorate, comprehensive exam, thesis/dissertation, departmental qualifying exams. *Entrance requirements:* For master's, GRE General Test, letters of recommendation, resume; for doctorate, GRE General Test, letters of recommendation, resumé, goal statement, transcripts. Additional exam requirements/recommendations for international students: Required—TOEFL (minimum score 525 paper-based; 194 computer-based). *Faculty research:* Neurodegenerative diseases, cerebellar cortical circuitry, neurogenesis, evolutionary anatomy.

Anatomy

State University of New York Upstate Medical University, College of Graduate Studies, Program in Cell and Developmental Biology, Syracuse, NY 13210-2334. Offers anatomy (MS, PhD); MD/PhD. Terminal master's awarded for partial completion of doctoral program. *Degree requirements:* For master's, thesis; for doctorate, comprehensive exam, thesis/dissertation. *Entrance requirements:* For master's, GRE General Test, interview; for doctorate, GRE General Test, telephone interview. Additional exam requirements/recommendations for international students: Required—TOEFL. Electronic applications accepted. *Faculty research:* Cancer, disorders of the nervous system, infectious diseases, diabetes/metabolic disorders/cardiovascular diseases.

Stony Brook University, State University of New York, Stony Brook University Medical Center, School of Medicine and Graduate School, Graduate Programs in Medicine, Department of Anatomical Sciences, Stony Brook, NY 11794. Offers PhD. *Faculty:* 11 full-time (3 women). *Students:* 8 full-time (3 women), 1 international. Average age 30. 8 applicants, 25% accepted, 2 enrolled. *Degree requirements:* For doctorate, comprehensive exam, thesis/dissertation. *Entrance requirements:* For doctorate, GRE General Test, GRE Subject Test, BA in life sciences, minimum GPA of 3.0. Additional exam requirements/recommendations for international students: Required—TOEFL. *Application deadline:* For fall admission, 1/15 for domestic students. Application fee: $100. *Expenses:* Tuition, state resident: full-time $8370; part-time $349 per credit. Tuition, nonresident: full-time $13,780; part-time $574 per credit. Required fees: $994. *Financial support:* In 2010–11, 7 research assistantships were awarded; fellowships, teaching assistantships, Federal Work-Study also available. Financial award application deadline: 3/15. *Faculty research:* Biological membranes, biomechanics of locomotion, systematics and evolutionary history of primates. Total annual research expenditures: $895,687. *Unit head:* Dr. William Jungers, Chair, 631-444-3114, Fax: 631-444-3947, E-mail: william.jungers@stonybrook.edu. *Application contact:* Dr. Maureen Oleary, 631-444-3730, Fax: 631-444-3947, E-mail: maureen.oleary@stonybrook.edu.

Temple University, Health Sciences Center, School of Medicine and Graduate School, Doctor of Medicine Program, Department of Anatomy and Cell Biology, Philadelphia, PA 19122-6096. Offers MS, PhD. *Faculty:* 11 full-time (5 women). *Students:* 8 full-time (5 women); includes 1 Black or African American, non-Hispanic/Latino; 1 Hispanic/Latino, 3 international. 11 applicants, 45% accepted, 4 enrolled. In 2010, 3 doctorates awarded. *Degree requirements:* For doctorate, thesis/dissertation, research seminars. *Entrance requirements:* For master's and doctorate, GRE General Test, GRE Subject Test, minimum GPA of 3.0. Additional exam requirements/recommendations for international students: Required—TOEFL. *Application deadline:* For fall admission, 1/15 for domestic students, 12/15 for international students; for spring admission, 9/1 for domestic students, 8/1 for international students. Application fee: $50. Electronic applications accepted. *Financial support:* Fellowships, Federal Work-Study available. Financial award application deadline: 1/15; financial award applicants required to submit FAFSA. *Faculty research:* Neurobiology, reproductive biology, cardiovascular system, musculoskeletal biology, developmental biology. Total annual research expenditures: $632,373. *Unit head:* Dr. Steven Popoff, Chair, 215-707-3161, Fax: 215-707-2966, E-mail: spopoff@temple.edu. *Application contact:* Dr. Steven Popoff, Chair, 215-707-3161, Fax: 215-707-2966, E-mail: spopoff@temple.edu.

Universidad Central del Caribe, School of Medicine, Program in Biomedical Sciences, Bayamón, PR 00960-6032. Offers anatomy and cell biology (MA, MS); biochemistry (MS); biomedical sciences (MA); cellular and molecular biology (PhD); microbiology and immunology (MA, MS); pharmacology (MS); physiology (MS).

Universidad de Ciencias Medicas, Graduate Programs, San Jose, Costa Rica. Offers dermatology (SP); family health (MS); health service center administration (MHA); human anatomy (MS); medical and surgery (MD); occupational medicine (MS); pharmacy (Pharm D). Part-time programs available. *Degree requirements:* For master's, thesis; for first professional degree and SP, comprehensive exam. *Entrance requirements:* For first professional degree, admissions test; for master's, MD or bachelor's degree; for SP, admissions test, MD.

Université Laval, Faculty of Medicine, Department of Anatomy and Physiology, Québec, QC G1K 7P4, Canada. Offers M Sc, PhD. Terminal master's awarded for partial completion of doctoral program. *Degree requirements:* For master's, thesis (for some programs); for doctorate, comprehensive exam, thesis/dissertation. Electronic applications accepted.

Université Laval, Faculty of Medicine, Post-Professional Programs in Medical Studies, Québec, QC G1K 7P4, Canada. Offers anatomy–pathology (DESS); anesthesiology (DESS); cardiology (DESS); care of older people (Diploma); clinical research (DESS); community health (DESS); dermatology (DESS); diagnostic radiology (DESS); emergency medicine (Diploma); family medicine (DESS); general surgery (DESS); geriatrics (DESS); hematology (DESS); internal medicine (DESS); maternal and fetal medicine (Diploma); medical biochemistry (DESS); medical microbiology and infectious diseases (DESS); medical oncology (DESS); nephrology (DESS); neurology (DESS); neurosurgery (DESS); obstetrics and gynecology (DESS); ophthalmology (DESS); orthopedic surgery (DESS); oto-rhino-laryngology (DESS); palliative medicine (Diploma); pediatrics (DESS); plastic surgery (DESS); psychiatry (DESS); pulmonary medicine (DESS); radiology–oncology (DESS); thoracic surgery (DESS); urology (DESS). *Degree requirements:* For other advanced degree, comprehensive exam. *Entrance requirements:* For degree, knowledge of French. Electronic applications accepted.

University at Buffalo, the State University of New York, Graduate School, School of Medicine and Biomedical Sciences, Graduate Programs in Medicine and Biomedical Sciences, Department of Pathology and Anatomical Sciences, Buffalo, NY 14260. Offers anatomical sciences (MA, PhD); pathology (MA, PhD). *Degree requirements:* For master's, thesis; for doctorate, comprehensive exam, thesis/dissertation. *Entrance requirements:* For master's, GRE, MCAT, or DAT, 3 letters of recommendation; for doctorate, GRE, 3 letters of recommendation. Additional exam requirements/recommendations for international students: Required—TOEFL (minimum score 600 paper-based; 250 computer-based; 100 iBT). *Faculty research:* Immunopathology-immunobiology, experimental hypertension, neuromuscular disease, molecular pathology, cell motility and cytoskeleton.

The University of Arizona, College of Medicine, Department of Cell Biology and Anatomy, Tucson, AZ 85721. Offers PhD. *Faculty:* 14 full-time (3 women), 3 part-time/adjunct (1 woman). *Students:* 19 full-time (11 women), 2 part-time (1 woman); includes 8 minority (2 Black or African American, non-Hispanic/Latino; 1 Asian, non-Hispanic/Latino; 2 Hispanic/Latino; 3 Two or more races, non-Hispanic/Latino), 2 international. Average age 29. 30 applicants, 10% accepted. In 2010, 1 doctorate awarded. *Degree requirements:* For doctorate, thesis/dissertation. *Entrance requirements:* For doctorate, GRE General Test. *Application deadline:* For fall admission, 1/15 priority date for domestic students. Application fee: $45. *Expenses:* Tuition, state resident: full-time $7692. *Financial support:* In 2010–11, 11 research assistantships with partial tuition reimbursements (averaging $23,611 per year) were awarded; fellowships with full and partial tuition reimbursements, teaching assistantships, institutionally sponsored loans, scholarships/grants, traineeships, tuition waivers (full), and unspecified assistantships also available. Support available to part-time students. Financial award application deadline: 1/15. *Faculty research:* Heart development, neural development, cellular toxicology and microcirculation; membrane traffic and cytoskeleton; cell-surface receptors. Total annual research expenditures: $1.7 million. *Unit head:* Dr. Robert S. McCuskey, Head, 520-626-6084, Fax: 520-626-2097, E-mail: mccuskey@u.arizona.edu. *Application contact:* Dr. Jean M. Wilson, Chairperson, Graduate Studies Committee, 520-626-2553, Fax: 520-626-2097.

University of Arkansas for Medical Sciences, Graduate School, Graduate Programs in Biomedical Sciences, Department of Neurobiology and Developmental Sciences, Little Rock, AR 72205-7199. Offers MS, PhD, MD/PhD. *Degree requirements:* For master's, thesis; for doctorate, thesis/dissertation. *Entrance requirements:* For master's, GRE General Test; for doctorate, GRE General Test, GRE Subject Test. Additional exam requirements/recommendations for international students: Required—TOEFL. *Faculty research:* Cellular and molecular neuroscience, translation neuroscience.

The University of British Columbia, Faculty of Medicine, Department of Cellular and Physiological Sciences, Division of Anatomy and Cell Biology, Vancouver, BC V6T 1Z1, Canada. Offers M Sc, PhD. *Degree requirements:* For master's, thesis, oral defense; for doctorate, comprehensive exam, thesis/dissertation, oral defense. *Entrance requirements:* Additional exam requirements/recommendations for international students: Required—TOEFL (minimum score 550 paper-based; 213 computer-based), IELTS (minimum score 6.2). Electronic applications accepted. Tuition charges are reported in Canadian dollars. *Expenses:* Tuition, area resident: Full-time $4179 Canadian dollars. International tuition: $7344 Canadian dollars full-time. *Faculty research:* Cell and developmental biology, membrane biophysics, cellular immunology, cancer, fetal alcohol syndrome.

University of California, Irvine, School of Medicine and School of Biological Sciences, Department of Anatomy and Neurobiology, Irvine, CA 92697. Offers biological sciences (MS, PhD); MD/PhD. *Students:* 28 full-time (17 women); includes 8 minority (3 Asian, non-Hispanic/Latino; 5 Hispanic/Latino), 2 international. Average age 28. In 2010, 1 master's, 10 doctorates awarded. *Degree requirements:* For doctorate, thesis/dissertation. *Entrance requirements:* For master's and doctorate, GRE General Test, GRE Subject Test. Additional exam requirements/recommendations for international students: Required—TOEFL (minimum score 550 paper-based; 213 computer-based). *Application deadline:* For fall admission, 1/15 priority date for domestic students, 1/15 for international students. Applications are processed on a rolling basis. Application fee: $80 ($100 for international students). Electronic applications accepted. *Financial support:* Fellowships, research assistantships with full tuition reimbursements, teaching assistantships, institutionally sponsored loans, traineeships, health care benefits, and unspecified assistantships available. Financial award application deadline: 3/1; financial award applicants required to submit FAFSA. *Faculty research:* Neurotransmitter immunocytochemistry, intracellular physiology, molecular neurobiology, forebrain organization and development, structure and function of sensory and motor systems. *Unit head:* Prof. Ivan Soltesz, Professor and Chair, 949-824-3957, Fax: 949-824-9860, E-mail: isoltesz@uci.edu. *Application contact:* Debra S. Caputo, Chief Administrative Officer, 949-824-6340, Fax: 949-824-8549, E-mail: dscaputo@uci.edu.

University of California, Los Angeles, David Geffen School of Medicine and Graduate Division, Graduate Programs in Medicine, Department of Neurobiology, Los Angeles, CA 90095. Offers anatomy and cell biology (PhD). *Faculty:* 21 full-time (0 women). *Students:* 14 full-time (7 women); includes 4 minority (2 Asian, non-Hispanic/Latino; 2 Hispanic/Latino), 1 international. Average age 28. In 2010, 1 doctorate awarded. *Degree requirements:* For doctorate, thesis/dissertation, oral and written qualifying exams. *Entrance requirements:* For doctorate, GRE General Test, GRE Subject Test, bachelor's degree in physical or biological science. Application fee: $70 ($90 for international students). Electronic applications accepted. *Financial support:* In 2010–11, 15 fellowships, 10 research assistantships, 8 teaching assistantships were awarded; Federal Work-Study, institutionally sponsored loans, scholarships/grants, and tuition waivers (full and partial) also available. Financial award application deadline: 3/1. *Faculty research:* Neuroendocrinology, neurophysiology. *Unit head:* Dr. Marie-Francoise Chesselet, Chair, 310-267-1781, Fax: 310-267-1786, E-mail: mchesselet@mednet.ucla.edu. *Application contact:* UCLA Access Coordinator, 310-206-1845, Fax: 310-206-1636, E-mail: uclaaccess@mednet.ucla.edu.

University of California, San Francisco, Graduate Division, Biomedical Sciences Graduate Group, San Francisco, CA 94143. Offers anatomy (PhD); endocrinology (PhD); experimental pathology (PhD); physiology (PhD). *Degree requirements:* For doctorate, thesis/dissertation. *Entrance requirements:* For doctorate, GRE General Test.

University of Chicago, Division of Biological Sciences, Darwinian Sciences Cluster: Ecological, Integrative and Evolutionary Biology, Department of Organismal Biology and Anatomy, Chicago, IL 60637-1513. Offers functional and evolutionary biology (PhD); organismal biology and anatomy (PhD). *Degree requirements:* For doctorate, thesis/dissertation, ethics class, 2 teaching assistantships. *Entrance requirements:* For doctorate, GRE General Test. Additional exam requirements/recommendations for international students: Required—TOEFL (minimum score 600 paper-based; 250 computer-based; 104 iBT), IELTS (minimum score 7). Electronic applications accepted. *Faculty research:* Ecological physiology, evolution of fossil reptiles, vertebrate paleontology.

University of Georgia, College of Veterinary Medicine and Graduate School, Graduate Programs in Veterinary Medicine, Department of Veterinary Anatomy and Radiology, Athens, GA 30602. Offers veterinary anatomy (MS). *Faculty:* 7 full-time (3 women). *Students:* 2 full-time (1 woman). *Degree requirements:* For master's, thesis. *Entrance requirements:* For master's, GRE General Test. *Application deadline:* For fall admission, 7/1 priority date for domestic students; for spring admission, 11/15 for domestic students. Application fee: $50. Electronic applications accepted. *Expenses:* Tuition, state resident: full-time $7200; part-time $344 per credit hour. Tuition, nonresident: full-time $21,900; part-time $944 per credit hour. Tuition and fees vary according to course load and program. *Financial support:* Fellowships, research assistantships, teaching assistantships, unspecified assistantships available. *Unit head:* Dr. Steven D. Holladay, Head, 706-542-8305, E-mail: sdholl@.uga.edu. *Application contact:* Dr. Sharon Crowell-Davis, Graduate Coordinator, 706-542-8343, Fax: 706-542-0051, E-mail: scrowell@uga.edu.

University of Guelph, Ontario Veterinary College and Graduate Studies, Graduate Programs in Veterinary Sciences, Department of Biomedical Sciences, Guelph, ON N1G 2W1, Canada. Offers morphology (M Sc, DV Sc, PhD); neuroscience (M Sc, DV Sc, PhD); pharmacology (M Sc, DV Sc, PhD); physiology (M Sc, DV Sc, PhD); toxicology (M Sc, DV Sc, PhD). Part-time programs available. *Degree requirements:* For master's, thesis; for doctorate, comprehensive exam, thesis/dissertation. *Entrance requirements:* For master's, honors B Sc, minimum 75% average in last 20 courses; for doctorate, M Sc with thesis from accredited institution. Additional exam requirements/recommendations for international students: Required—TOEFL (minimum score 550 paper-based; 213 computer-based; 89 iBT). Electronic applications accepted. *Faculty research:* Cellular morphology; endocrine, vascular and reproductive physiology; clinical pharmacology; veterinary toxicology; developmental biology, neuroscience.

University of Illinois at Chicago, College of Medicine and Graduate College, Graduate Programs in Medicine, Department of Anatomy and Cell Biology, Chicago, IL 60607-7128. Offers neuroscience (PhD), including cellular and systems neuroscience and cell biology; MD/PhD. *Degree requirements:* For doctorate, preliminary oral examination, dissertation and oral defense. *Entrance requirements:* For doctorate, GRE General Test, minimum GPA of 2.75, 3 letters of recommendation, personal statement. Additional exam requirements/recommendations for international students: Required—TOEFL (minimum score 550 paper-based; 213 computer-based). Electronic applications accepted. *Faculty research:* Synapses, axonal transport, neurodegenerative diseases.

The University of Iowa, Roy J. and Lucille A. Carver College of Medicine and Graduate College, Graduate Programs in Medicine, Department of Anatomy and Cell Biology, Iowa City, IA 52242-1316. Offers PhD. *Faculty:* 22 full-time (4 women). *Students:* 14 full-time (6 women); includes 2 minority (1 American Indian or Alaska Native, non-Hispanic/Latino; 1 Asian, non-Hispanic/Latino), 1 international. Average age 28. 113 applicants, 0% accepted. In 2010, 2 doctorates awarded. *Degree requirements:* For doctorate, comprehensive exam, thesis/dissertation. *Entrance requirements:* For doctorate, GRE General Test, minimum GPA of 3.0. Additional exam requirements/recommendations for international students: Required—TOEFL (minimum score 600 paper-based; 250 computer-based; 100 iBT). *Application deadline:* For fall admission, 1/15 priority date for domestic and international students. Applications are processed on a rolling basis. Application fee: $60 ($100 for international students). Electronic applications accepted. *Financial support:* In 2010–11, 14 students received support, including 1 fellowship with full tuition reimbursement available (averaging $25,000 per year), 12 research assistantships with full tuition reimbursements available (averaging $25,000 per year), teaching assistantships with full tuition reimbursements available (averaging $25,000 per year); institutionally sponsored loans, scholarships/grants, and health care benefits also available.

Financial award application deadline: 3/1. *Faculty research:* Biology of differentiation and transformation, developmental and vascular cell biology, neurobiology. Total annual research expenditures: $3.4 million. *Unit head:* Dr. John F. Engelhardt, Professor and Head, 319-335-7744, Fax: 319-335-7770, E-mail: john-engelhardt@uiowa.edu. *Application contact:* Julie A. Stark, Program Assistant, 319-335-7744, Fax: 319-335-7770, E-mail: julie-stark@uiowa.edu.

The University of Kansas, University of Kansas Medical Center, School of Medicine, Department of Anatomy and Cell Biology, Kansas City, KS 66160. Offers MA, PhD, MD/PhD. *Faculty:* 32. *Students:* 17 full-time (12 women); includes 4 minority (1 Asian, non-Hispanic/Latino; 2 Hispanic/Latino; 1 Two or more races, non-Hispanic/Latino), 6 international. Average age 26. 2 applicants, 100% accepted, 2 enrolled. In 2010, 1 doctorate awarded. Terminal master's awarded for partial completion of doctoral program. *Degree requirements:* For doctorate, comprehensive exam, thesis/dissertation. *Entrance requirements:* For doctorate, GRE. Additional exam requirements/recommendations for international students: Required—TOEFL. *Application deadline:* For fall admission, 1/15 priority date for domestic students. Applications are processed on a rolling basis. Application fee: $0. Electronic applications accepted. *Expenses:* Tuition, state resident: full-time $7092; part-time $295.50 per credit hour. Tuition, nonresident: full-time $16,590; part-time $691.25 per credit hour. Required fees: $858; $71.49 per credit hour. Tuition and fees vary according to course load, campus/location and program. *Financial support:* Fellowships, research assistantships with full tuition reimbursements, teaching assistantships with full tuition reimbursements, institutionally sponsored loans, health care benefits, and unspecified assistantships available. Financial award application deadline: 2/14; financial award applicants required to submit FAFSA. *Faculty research:* Development of the synapse and neuromuscular junction, pain perception and diabetic neuropathies, cardiovascular and kidney development, reproductive immunology, post-fertilization signaling events. Total annual research expenditures: $9.9 million. *Unit head:* Dr. Dale R. Abrahamson, Chairman, 913-588-7000, Fax: 913-588-2710, E-mail: dabrahamson@kumc.edu. *Application contact:* Dr. Brenda Rongish, Associate Professor, 913-588-1878, Fax: 913-588-2710, E-mail: brongish@kumc.edu.

University of Kentucky, Graduate School, Graduate School Programs from the College of Medicine, Program in Anatomy and Neurobiology, Lexington, KY 40506-0032. Offers anatomy (PhD). *Degree requirements:* For doctorate, comprehensive exam, thesis/dissertation. *Entrance requirements:* For doctorate, GRE General Test, minimum undergraduate GPA of 2.75. Additional exam requirements/recommendations for international students: Required—TOEFL (minimum score 550 paper-based; 213 computer-based). Electronic applications accepted. *Faculty research:* Neuroendocrinology, developmental neurobiology, neurotrophic substances, neural plasticity and trauma, neurobiology of aging.

University of Louisville, School of Medicine, Department of Anatomical Sciences and Neurobiology, Louisville, KY 40292-0001. Offers MS, PhD, MD/PhD. *Faculty:* 20 full-time (3 women), 12 part-time/adjunct (1 woman). *Students:* 40 full-time (22 women), 3 part-time (1 woman); includes 1 Asian, non-Hispanic/Latino; 1 Hispanic/Latino; 1 Two or more races, non-Hispanic/Latino, 14 international. Average age 28. 32 applicants, 38% accepted, 12 enrolled. In 2010, 10 master's, 6 doctorates awarded. Terminal master's awarded for partial completion of doctoral program. *Degree requirements:* For master's, thesis; for doctorate, comprehensive exam, thesis/dissertation. *Entrance requirements:* For master's and doctorate, GRE General Test (minimum score of 1000 verbal and quantitative), minimum GPA of 3.0. Additional exam requirements/recommendations for international students: Required—TOEFL. *Application deadline:* For fall admission, 1/15 priority date for domestic students; for spring admission, 4/15 priority date for domestic and international students. Applications are processed on a rolling basis. Application fee: $50. Electronic applications accepted. *Expenses:* Tuition, state resident: full-time $9144; part-time $508 per credit hour. Tuition, nonresident: full-time $19,026; part-time $1057 per credit hour. Tuition and fees vary according to program and reciprocity agreements. *Financial support:* Fellowships with full tuition reimbursements, research assistantships with full tuition reimbursements, health care benefits and unspecified assistantships available. Financial award application deadline: 4/15. *Faculty research:* Human adult neural stem cells, development and plasticity of the nervous system, organization of the dorsal thalamus, electrophysiology/neuroanatomy of central neurons mediating control of reproductive and pelvic organs, normal neural mechanisms and plasticity following injury and/or chronic pain, differentiation and regeneration of motor neurons and oligodendrocytes. Total annual research expenditures: $4 million. *Unit head:* Dr. Fred J. Roisen, Chair, 502-852-5165, Fax: 502-852-6228, E-mail: fjrois01@gwise.louisville.edu. *Application contact:* Dr. Charles Hubscher, Director of Graduate Studies, 502-852-3058, Fax: 502-852-6228, E-mail: chhub01@louisville.edu.

University of Manitoba, Faculty of Medicine and Faculty of Graduate Studies, Graduate Programs in Medicine, Department of Human Anatomy and Cell Science, Winnipeg, MB R3T 2N2, Canada. Offers M Sc, PhD. *Degree requirements:* For master's, thesis; for doctorate, one foreign language, thesis/dissertation.

University of Mississippi Medical Center, School of Graduate Studies in the Health Sciences, Department of Anatomy, Jackson, MS 39216-4505. Offers MS, PhD, MD/PhD. Terminal master's awarded for partial completion of doctoral program. *Degree requirements:* For master's, thesis; for doctorate, comprehensive exam, thesis/dissertation, first authored publication. *Entrance requirements:* For master's and doctorate, GRE General Test, minimum GPA of 3.0. Additional exam requirements/recommendations for international students: Required—TOEFL. *Faculty research:* Systems neuroscience with emphasis on motor and sensory, cell biology with emphasis on cell-matrix interactions, development of cardiovascular system, biology of glial cells.

University of Missouri, School of Medicine and Graduate School, Graduate Programs in Medicine, Department of Pathology and Anatomical Sciences, Columbia, MO 65211. Offers MS.

University of Nebraska Medical Center, Graduate Studies, Department of Genetics, Cell Biology and Anatomy, Omaha, NE 68198. Offers MS, PhD. Part-time programs available. *Faculty:* 23 full-time (7 women), 1 part-time/adjunct (0 women). *Students:* 16 full-time (5 women), 5 part-time (4 women); includes 1 Asian, non-Hispanic/Latino, 2 international. Average age 25. 22 applicants, 18% accepted, 4 enrolled. In 2010, 1 master's, 5 doctorates awarded. Terminal master's awarded for partial completion of doctoral program. *Degree requirements:* For master's, comprehensive exam, thesis; for doctorate, comprehensive exam, thesis/dissertation. *Entrance requirements:* For master's and doctorate, GRE General Test. Additional exam requirements/recommendations for international students: Required—TOEFL (minimum score 550 paper-based; 213 computer-based). *Application deadline:* For fall admission, 3/1 priority date for domestic and international students; for spring admission, 10/1 for domestic students, 8/1 for international students. Applications are processed on a rolling basis. Application fee: $45. Electronic applications accepted. *Expenses:* Tuition, state resident: part-time $198.25 per semester hour. Required fees: $63 per semester. *Financial support:* In 2010–11, 3 students received support, including fellowships with full tuition reimbursements available (averaging $21,000 per year), research assistantships with full tuition reimbursements available (averaging $21,000 per year), teaching assistantships with full tuition reimbursements available (averaging $21,000 per year); institutionally sponsored loans, health care benefits, and unspecified assistantships also available. Support available to part-time students. Financial award application deadline: 3/1. *Faculty research:* Hematology, immunology, developmental biology, genetics cancer biology, neuroscience. *Unit head:* Dr. Karen Gould, Graduate Committee Chair, 402-559-2456, E-mail: kagould@unmc.edu. *Application contact:* Saralyn Fisher, Graduate Student Support, 402-559-4031, Fax: 402-559-7328, E-mail: sfisher@unmc.edu.

University of North Dakota, Graduate School and Graduate School, Graduate Programs in Medicine, Department of Anatomy and Cell Biology, Grand Forks, ND 58202. Offers MS, PhD. *Faculty:* 8 full-time (1 woman). *Students:* 8 full-time (3 women), 1 (woman) part-time, 2 international. Average age 26. 5 applicants, 20% accepted, 1 enrolled. In 2010, 1 doctorate awarded. *Degree requirements:* For master's, thesis, final exam; for doctorate, comprehensive exam, thesis/dissertation, final exam. *Entrance requirements:* For master's and doctorate, GRE General Test, minimum GPA of 3.0. Additional exam requirements/recommendations for international students: Required—TOEFL (minimum score 550 paper-based; 213 computer-based; 79 iBT), IELTS (minimum score 6.5). *Application deadline:* For fall admission, 8/1 priority date for domestic students, 5/1 priority date for international students; for spring admission, 12/1 priority date for domestic students, 9/1 priority date for international students. Applications are processed on a rolling basis. Application fee: $35. Electronic applications accepted. *Expenses:* Tuition, state resident: full-time $5857; part-time $306.74 per credit. Tuition, nonresident: full-time $15,666; part-time $729.77 per credit. Required fees: $53.42 per credit. Tuition and fees vary according to course load, program and reciprocity agreements. *Financial support:* In 2010–11, 9 students received support, including 9 research assistantships with full and partial tuition reimbursements available (averaging $14,135 per year); fellowships, teaching assistantships with full and partial tuition reimbursements available, Federal Work-Study, institutionally sponsored loans, scholarships/grants, health care benefits, tuition waivers (full and partial), and unspecified assistantships also available. Support available to part-time students. Financial award applicants required to submit FAFSA. *Faculty research:* Coronary vessel, vasculogenesis, acellular glomerular and retinal microvessel membranes, ependymal cells, cardiac muscle. Total annual research expenditures: $5,142. *Unit head:* Dr. Jane Dunlevy, Graduate Director, 701-777-2575, Fax: 701-777-3527, E-mail: jdunlevy@medicine.nodak.edu. *Application contact:* Matt Anderson, Admissions Specialist, 701-777-2947, Fax: 701-777-3619, E-mail: matthew.anderson@gradschool.und.edu.

University of North Texas Health Science Center at Fort Worth, Graduate School of Biomedical Sciences, Fort Worth, TX 76107-2699. Offers anatomy and cell biology (MS, PhD); biochemistry and molecular biology (MS, PhD); biomedical sciences (MS, PhD); biotechnology (MS); forensic genetics (MS); integrative physiology (MS, PhD); medical science (MS); microbiology and immunology (MS, PhD); pharmacology (MS, PhD); science education (MS); DO/MS; DO/PhD. Terminal master's awarded for partial completion of doctoral program. *Degree requirements:* For master's, thesis; for doctorate, thesis/dissertation. *Entrance requirements:* For master's and doctorate, GRE General Test. Additional exam requirements/recommendations for international students: Required—TOEFL. *Expenses:* Contact institution. *Faculty research:* Alzheimer's disease, aging, eye diseases, cancer, cardiovascular disease.

University of Prince Edward Island, Atlantic Veterinary College, Graduate Program in Veterinary Medicine, Charlottetown, PE C1A 4P3, Canada. Offers anatomy (M Sc, PhD); bacteriology (M Sc, PhD); clinical pharmacology (M Sc, PhD); clinical sciences (M Sc, PhD); epidemiology (M Sc, PhD), including reproduction; fish health (M Sc, PhD); food animal nutrition (M Sc, PhD); immunology (M Sc, PhD); microanatomy (M Sc, PhD); parasitology (M Sc, PhD); pathology (M Sc, PhD); pharmacology (M Sc, PhD); physiology (M Sc, PhD); toxicology (M Sc, PhD); veterinary science (M Vet Sc); virology (M Sc, PhD). Part-time programs available. *Degree requirements:* For master's, thesis; for doctorate, thesis/dissertation. *Entrance requirements:* For master's, DVM, B Sc honors degree, or equivalent; for doctorate, M Sc. Additional exam requirements/recommendations for international students: Required—TOEFL (minimum score 550 paper-based; 213 computer-based; 80 iBT). *Expenses:* Contact institution. *Faculty research:* Animal health management, infectious diseases, fin fish and shellfish health, basic biomedical sciences, ecosystem health.

University of Puerto Rico, Medical Sciences Campus, School of Medicine, Division of Graduate Studies, Department of Anatomy and Neurobiology, San Juan, PR 00936-5067. Offers anatomy (MS, PhD). *Degree requirements:* For master's, one foreign language, comprehensive exam, thesis; for doctorate, one foreign language, comprehensive exam, thesis/dissertation. *Entrance requirements:* For master's and doctorate, GRE General Test, GRE Subject Test, interview, minimum GPA of 3.0, 3 letters of recommendation. Electronic applications accepted. *Faculty research:* Neurobiology, primatology, visual system, muscle structure.

University of Rochester, School of Medicine and Dentistry, Graduate Programs in Medicine and Dentistry, Department of Neurobiology and Anatomy, Programs in Neurobiology and Anatomy, Rochester, NY 14627. Offers MS, PhD. *Degree requirements:* For doctorate, thesis/dissertation, qualifying exam. *Entrance requirements:* For master's and doctorate, GRE General Test.

University of Saskatchewan, College of Medicine, Department of Anatomy and Cell Biology, Saskatoon, SK S7N 5A2, Canada. Offers M Sc, PhD. *Degree requirements:* For master's, thesis; for doctorate, thesis/dissertation. *Entrance requirements:* Additional exam requirements/recommendations for international students: Required—TOEFL.

University of Saskatchewan, Western College of Veterinary Medicine and College of Graduate Studies and Research, Graduate Programs in Veterinary Medicine, Department of Veterinary Biomedical Sciences, Saskatoon, SK S7N 5A2, Canada. Offers veterinary anatomy (M Sc); veterinary biomedical sciences (M Vet Sc); veterinary physiological sciences (M Sc, PhD). *Faculty:* 12 full-time (4 women), 4 part-time/adjunct (0 women). *Students:* 49 full-time (24 women); includes 2 Black or African American, non-Hispanic/Latino; 47 American Indian or Alaska Native, non-Hispanic/Latino. In 2010, 8 master's, 4 doctorates awarded. *Degree requirements:* For master's, thesis; for doctorate, comprehensive exam (for some programs), thesis/dissertation. *Entrance requirements:* Additional exam requirements/recommendations for international students: Required—TOEFL (minimum score 80 iBT); Recommended—IELTS (minimum score 6.5). Electronic applications accepted. *Faculty research:* Toxicology, animal reproduction, pharmacology, chloride channels, pulmonary pathobiology. *Unit head:* Dr. Barry Blakley, Head, 306-966-7350, Fax: 306-966-7376, E-mail: barry.blakley@usask.ca. *Application contact:* Application Contact.

The University of Tennessee, Graduate School, College of Agricultural Sciences and Natural Resources, Department of Animal Science, Knoxville, TN 37996. Offers animal anatomy (PhD); breeding (MS, PhD); management (MS, PhD); nutrition (MS, PhD); physiology (MS, PhD). Part-time programs available. *Degree requirements:* For master's, thesis; for doctorate, thesis/dissertation. *Entrance requirements:* For master's and doctorate, GRE General Test, minimum GPA of 2.7. Additional exam requirements/recommendations for international students: Required—TOEFL. Electronic applications accepted. *Expenses:* Tuition, state resident: full-time $7440; part-time $414 per credit hour. Tuition, nonresident: full-time $22,478; part-time $1250 per credit hour. Required fees: $922; $43 per credit hour. Tuition and fees vary according to program.

University of Utah, School of Medicine and Graduate School, Graduate Programs in Medicine, Department of Neurobiology and Anatomy, Salt Lake City, UT 84112-1107. Offers PhD. Part-time programs available. Terminal master's awarded for partial completion of doctoral program. *Degree requirements:* For doctorate, comprehensive exam, thesis/dissertation. *Entrance requirements:* For doctorate, GRE General Test. Additional exam requirements/recommendations for international students: Required—TOEFL. *Expenses:* Tuition, area resident: Part-time $179.19 per credit hour. Tuition, state resident: full-time $4384. Tuition, nonresident: full-time $16,684; part-time $630.67 per credit hour. Required fees: $350 per semester. Tuition and fees vary according to course load, degree level and program. *Faculty research:* Neuroscience, neuroanatomy, developmental neurobiology, neurogenetics.

The University of Western Ontario, Faculty of Graduate Studies, Biosciences Division, Department of Biology, London, ON N6A 5B8, Canada. Offers M Sc, PhD. *Degree requirements:* For master's, thesis; for doctorate, comprehensive exam, thesis/dissertation. *Entrance requirements:* For master's, honors degree or equivalent in biological sciences; for doctorate, master's degree. Additional exam requirements/recommendations for international students: Required—TOEFL. *Faculty research:* Cell and molecular biology, developmental biology, neuroscience, immunobiology and cancer.

Virginia Commonwealth University, Medical College of Virginia-Professional Programs, School of Medicine, School of Medicine Graduate Programs, Department of Anatomy and Neurobiology, Program in Anatomy and Neurobiology, Richmond, VA 23284-9005. Offers PhD.

Anatomy

Virginia Commonwealth University *(continued)*
Accreditation: APTA. *Faculty:* 26 full-time (5 women). *Students:* 7 full-time (1 woman); includes 1 minority (Asian, non-Hispanic/Latino), 3 international. 27 applicants, 26% accepted, 2 enrolled. In 2010, 5 doctorates awarded. *Degree requirements:* For doctorate, thesis/dissertation. *Entrance requirements:* For doctorate, GRE, MCAT or DAT. *Application deadline:* For fall admission, 1/7 priority date for domestic students. Application fee: $50. Electronic applications accepted. *Expenses:* Tuition, state resident: full-time $4308; part-time $479 per credit hour. Tuition, nonresident: full-time $8942; part-time $994 per credit hour. Required fees: $2000; $85 per credit hour. Tuition and fees vary according to course level, course load, degree level, campus/location and program. *Unit head:* Dr. William Guido, Graduate Program Director and Recruitment Contact, 804-828-0952, E-mail: wguido@vcu.edu. *Application contact:* Dr. William Guido, Graduate Program Director and Recruitment Contact, 804-828-0952, E-mail: wguido@vcu.edu.

Virginia Commonwealth University, Program in Pre-Medical Basic Health Sciences, Richmond, VA 23284-9005. Offers anatomy (CBHS); biochemistry (CBHS); human genetics (CBHS); microbiology (CBHS); pharmacology (CBHS); physiology (CBHS). *Students:* 86 full-time (43 women), 2 part-time (1 woman); includes 42 minority (5 Black or African American, non-Hispanic/Latino; 29 Asian, non-Hispanic/Latino; 5 Hispanic/Latino; 3 Two or more races, non-Hispanic/Latino). 314 applicants, 64% accepted. In 2010, 70 CBHSs awarded. *Entrance requirements:* For degree, GRE, MCAT or DAT, course work in organic chemistry, minimum undergraduate GPA of 2.8. Additional exam requirements/recommendations for international students: Required—TOEFL (minimum score 600 paper-based). *Application deadline:* For fall admission, 6/1 for domestic students. Application fee: $50. Electronic applications accepted. *Expenses:* Tuition, state resident: full-time $4308; part-time $479 per credit hour. Tuition, nonresident: full-time $8942; part-time $994 per credit hour. Required fees: $2000; $85 per credit hour. Tuition and fees vary according to course level, course load, degree level, campus/location and program. *Unit head:* Dr. Louis J. De Felice, Director, 804-828-9501, E-mail: premedcert@vcu.edu. *Application contact:* Zack McDowell, Administrator, 804-828-9501, E-mail: premedcert@vcu.edu.

Wake Forest University, School of Medicine and Graduate School of Arts and Sciences, Graduate Programs in Medicine, Department of Neurobiology and Anatomy, Winston-Salem, NC 27109. Offers PhD, MD/PhD. *Degree requirements:* For doctorate, thesis/dissertation. *Entrance requirements:* For doctorate, GRE General Test. Additional exam requirements/ recommendations for international students: Required—TOEFL. Electronic applications accepted. *Faculty research:* Sensory neurobiology, reproductive endocrinology, regulatory processes in cell biology.

Wayne State University, School of Medicine, Department of Anatomy and Cell Biology, Detroit, MI 48202. Offers anatomy (MS, PhD); MD/PhD. *Faculty:* 4 full-time (0 women). *Students:* 15 full-time (9 women); includes 1 Asian, non-Hispanic/Latino; 1 Hispanic/Latino, 6 international. Average age 28. 11 applicants, 36% accepted, 4 enrolled. In 2010, 5 doctorates awarded. *Degree requirements:* For doctorate, thesis/dissertation. *Entrance requirements:* For master's and doctorate, GRE General Test, minimum GPA of 3.0. Additional exam requirements/ recommendations for international students: Required—TOEFL (minimum score 600 paper-based; 260 computer-based); Recommended—TWE (minimum score 6). *Application deadline:* For fall admission, 7/1 for domestic students, 6/1 for international students; for winter admission, 10/1 for international students; for spring admission, 2/1 for international students. Applications are processed on a rolling basis. Application fee: $30 ($50 for international students). Electronic applications accepted. *Expenses:* Tuition, state resident: full-time $7662; part-time $478.85 per credit hour. Tuition, nonresident: full-time $16,920; part-time $1057.55 per credit hour. Required fees: $571; $35.70 per credit hour. $188.05 per semester. Tuition and fees vary according to course load and program. *Financial support:* In 2010–11, 1 fellowship (averaging $27,638 per year), 12 research assistantships (averaging $23,914 per year) were awarded; teaching assistantships, Federal Work-Study also available. Financial award application deadline: 2/1. *Faculty research:* Inflammation and inflammatory mediators, neuronal plasticity, neural connections and glia, vision and visual neurosciences, cell signaling and receptor interactions. *Unit head:* Dr. Linda Hazlett, Chair, 313-577-1061, Fax: 313-577-3125, E-mail: aa4536@wayne.edu. *Application contact:* Dr. Roberta Pourcho, Graduate Director, 313-577-1002, Fax: 313-577-3125, E-mail: rpourcho@med.wayne.edu.

Wright State University, School of Graduate Studies, College of Science and Mathematics, Department of Neuroscience, Cell Biology, and Physiology, Dayton, OH 45435. Offers anatomy (MS); physiology and biophysics (MS). *Degree requirements:* For master's, thesis optional. *Entrance requirements:* Additional exam requirements/recommendations for international students: Required—TOEFL. *Faculty research:* Reproductive cell biology, neurobiology of pain, neurohistochemistry.

Youngstown State University, Graduate School, College of Science, Technology, Engineering and Mathematics, Department of Biological Sciences, Youngstown, OH 44555-0001. Offers environmental biology (MS); molecular biology, microbiology, and genetic (MS); physiology and anatomy (MS). Part-time programs available. *Degree requirements:* For master's, comprehensive exam, thesis, oral review. *Entrance requirements:* For master's, GRE General Test, minimum GPA of 2.7. Additional exam requirements/recommendations for international students: Required—TOEFL. *Faculty research:* Cell biology, neurophysiology, molecular biology, neurobiology, gene regulation.

Section 3
Biochemistry

This section contains a directory of institutions offering graduate work in biochemistry, followed by in-depth entries submitted by institutions that chose to prepare detailed program descriptions. Additional information about programs listed in the directory but not augmented by an in-depth entry may be obtained by writing directly to the dean of a graduate school or chair of a department at the address given in the directory.

For programs offering related work, see also in this book *Biological and Biomedical Sciences; Biophysics; Botany and Plant Biology; Cell, Molecular, and Structural Biology; Genetics, Developmental Biology, and Reproductive Biology; Microbiological Sciences; Neuroscience and Neurobiology; Nutrition; Pathology and Pathobiology; Pharmacology and Toxicology;* and *Physiology.* In the other guides in this series:

Graduate Programs in the Physical Sciences, Mathematics, Agricultural Sciences, the Environment & Natural Resources

See *Agricultural and Food Sciences, Chemistry,* and *Physics*

Graduate Programs in Engineering & Applied Sciences

See *Agricultural Engineering and Bioengineering, Biomedical Engineering and Biotechnology, Chemical Engineering,* and *Materials Sciences and Engineering*

Graduate Programs in Business, Education, Health, Information Studies, Law & Social Work

See *Allied Health, Pharmacy and Pharmaceutical Sciences,* and *Veterinary Medicine and Sciences*

CONTENTS

Biochemistry

Albert Einstein College of Medicine, Graduate Division of Biomedical Sciences, Department of Biochemistry, Bronx, NY 10461-1602. Offers PhD, MD/PhD. *Degree requirements:* For doctorate, thesis/dissertation. *Entrance requirements:* For doctorate, GRE General Test. Additional exam requirements/recommendations for international students: Required—TOEFL. *Faculty research:* Biochemical mechanisms, enzymology, protein chemistry, bio-organic chemistry, molecular genetics.

American University of Beirut, Graduate Programs, Faculty of Medicine, Beirut, Lebanon. Offers biochemistry (MS); human morphology (MS); medicine (MD); microbiology and immunology (MS); neuroscience (MS); pharmacology and therapeutics (MS); physiology (MS). Part-time programs available. *Faculty:* 222 full-time (56 women), 58 part-time/adjunct (4 women). *Students:* 346 full-time (135 women), 69 part-time (57 women). Average age 23. In 2010, 81 first professional degrees, 19 master's awarded. *Degree requirements:* For master's, one foreign language, comprehensive exam, thesis (for some programs). *Entrance requirements:* For MD, MCAT, bachelor's degree; for master's, letter of recommendation. Additional exam requirements/recommendations for international students: Required—TOEFL (minimum score 600 paper-based; 250 computer-based; 100 iBT), IELTS (minimum score 7.5). *Application deadline:* For fall admission, 4/30 for domestic and international students; for spring admission, 11/1 for domestic and international students. Application fee: $50. *Expenses:* Tuition: Full-time $12,294; part-time $683 per credit. Required fees: $499; $499 per credit. Tuition and fees vary according to course load and program. *Financial support:* In 2010–11, 4 students received support. Career-related internships or fieldwork, institutionally sponsored loans, scholarships/grants, health care benefits, and unspecified assistantships available. Financial award application deadline: 2/2. *Faculty research:* Cancer research (targeted therapy, mechanisms of leukemogenesis, tumor cell extravasation and metastasis, cancer stem cells); stem cell research (regenerative medicine, drug discovery); genetic research (neurogenetics, hereditary cardiomyopathy, hemoglobinopathies, pharmacogenomics); neuroscience research (pain, neurodegenerative disorder); metabolism (inflammation and metabolism, metabolic disorder, diabetes mellitus). Total annual research expenditures: $1.2 million. *Unit head:* Dr. Mohamed Sayegh, Dean, 961-135-0000 Ext. 4700, Fax: 961-174-4464, E-mail: msayegh@aub.edu.lb. *Application contact:* Dr. Salim Kanaan, Director, Admissions Office, 961-135-0000 Ext. 2594, Fax: 961-175-0775, E-mail: sk00@aub.edu.lb.

Arizona State University, College of Liberal Arts and Sciences, Department of Chemistry and Biochemistry, Tempe, AZ 85287-1604. Offers biochemistry (MS, PhD); chemistry (MS, PhD); nanoscience (PSM). *Faculty:* 68 full-time (16 women), 10 part-time/adjunct (6 women). *Students:* 180 full-time (59 women), 9 part-time (4 women); includes 13 minority (1 Black or African American, non-Hispanic/Latino; 10 Asian, non-Hispanic/Latino; 1 Hispanic/Latino; 1 Two or more races, non-Hispanic/Latino), 96 international. Average age 26. 505 applicants, 19% accepted, 45 enrolled. In 2010, 9 master's, 22 doctorates awarded. Terminal master's awarded for partial completion of doctoral program. *Degree requirements:* For master's, thesis, interactive Program of Study (iPOS) submitted before completing 50 percent of required credit hours; for doctorate, comprehensive exam, thesis/dissertation, interactive Program of Study (iPOS) submitted before completing 50 percent of required credit hours. *Entrance requirements:* For master's and doctorate, GRE, minimum GPA of 3.0 or equivalent in last 2 years of work leading to bachelor's degree. Additional exam requirements/recommendations for international students: Required—TOEFL, IELTS, or Pearson Test of English. *Application deadline:* For fall admission, 1/15 priority date for domestic and international students. Applications are processed on a rolling basis. Application fee: $70 ($90 for international students). Electronic applications accepted. *Expenses:* Tuition, state resident: full-time $8510; part-time $608 per credit. Tuition, nonresident: full-time $16,542; part-time $919 per credit. Required fees: $339; $110 per credit. Part-time tuition and fees vary according to course load. *Financial support:* In 2010–11, 77 research assistantships with full and partial tuition reimbursements (averaging $17,448 per year), 97 teaching assistantships with full and partial tuition reimbursements (averaging $17,637 per year) were awarded; fellowships with full tuition reimbursements, career-related internships or fieldwork, Federal Work-Study, institutionally sponsored loans, scholarships/grants, health care benefits, and tuition waivers (full and partial) also available. Financial award application deadline: 3/1. Total annual research expenditures: $18.2 million. *Unit head:* Dr. William Petuskey, Chair, 480-965-4430, Fax: 480-965-8607, E-mail: wpetuskey@asu.edu. *Application contact:* Graduate Admissions, 480-965-6113.

Auburn University, Graduate School, College of Sciences and Mathematics, Department of Chemistry and Biochemistry, Auburn University, AL 36849. Offers analytical chemistry (MS, PhD); biochemistry (MS, PhD); inorganic chemistry (MS, PhD); organic chemistry (MS, PhD); physical chemistry (MS, PhD). Part-time programs available. *Faculty:* 27 full-time (6 women). *Students:* 39 full-time (20 women), 21 part-time (8 women); includes 4 Black or African American, non-Hispanic/Latino; 1 Asian, non-Hispanic/Latino; 1 Hispanic/Latino, 41 international. Average age 28. 54 applicants, 11% accepted, 3 enrolled. In 2010, 1 master's, 13 doctorates awarded. *Degree requirements:* For master's, thesis (for some programs); for doctorate, thesis/dissertation, oral and written exams. *Entrance requirements:* For master's and doctorate, GRE General Test. *Application deadline:* For fall admission, 7/7 for domestic students; for spring admission, 11/24 for domestic students. Applications are processed on a rolling basis. Application fee: $50 ($60 for international students). Electronic applications accepted. *Expenses:* Tuition, state resident: full-time $7002. Tuition, nonresident: full-time $21,898. International tuition: $22,116 full-time. Required fees: $892. Tuition and fees vary according to course load and program. *Financial support:* Fellowships, research assistantships, teaching assistantships available. Financial award application deadline: 3/15; financial award applicants required to submit FAFSA. *Unit head:* Dr. J. V. Ortiz, Chair, 334-844-4043, Fax: 334-844-4043. *Application contact:* Dr. George Flowers, Dean of the Graduate School, 334-844-2125.

Baylor College of Medicine, Graduate School of Biomedical Sciences, Department of Biochemistry and Molecular Biology, Houston, TX 77030-3498. Offers PhD, MD/PhD. *Faculty:* 37 full-time (7 women). *Students:* 53 full-time (26 women); includes 1 Black or African American, non-Hispanic/Latino; 1 American Indian or Alaska Native, non-Hispanic/Latino; 2 Asian, non-Hispanic/Latino; 2 Hispanic/Latino, 31 international. Average age 28. 99 applicants, 15% accepted, 8 enrolled. In 2010, 6 doctorates awarded. *Degree requirements:* For doctorate, thesis/dissertation, public defense. *Entrance requirements:* For doctorate, GRE General Test, GRE Subject Test (strongly recommended), minimum GPA of 3.0. Additional exam requirements/recommendations for international students: Required—TOEFL. *Application deadline:* For fall admission, 1/1 priority date for domestic students. Application fee: $0. Electronic applications accepted. *Expenses:* Tuition: Full-time $11,000. Required fees: $4900. *Financial support:* In 2010–11, 12 fellowships with full tuition reimbursements (averaging $26,000 per year), 41 research assistantships with full tuition reimbursements (averaging $26,000 per year) were awarded; career-related internships or fieldwork, Federal Work-Study, institutionally sponsored loans, health care benefits, and students receive a scholarship unless there are grant funds available to pay tuition also available. Financial award applicants required to submit FAFSA. *Faculty research:* DNA repair, homologous recombination, gene therapy, trinucleotide repeat diseases, retinitis pigmentosa. *Unit head:* Dr. John Wilson, Director, 713-798-5760. *Application contact:* Monica Bagos, Graduate Program Administrator, 713-798-0124, Fax: 713-796-9438, E-mail: bagos@bcm.edu.

Baylor College of Medicine, Graduate School of Biomedical Sciences, Interdepartmental Program in Cell and Molecular Biology, Houston, TX 77030-3498. Offers biochemistry (PhD); cell and molecular biology (PhD); genetics (PhD); human genetics (PhD); immunology (PhD); microbiology (PhD); virology (PhD); MD/PhD. *Faculty:* 100 full-time (31 women). *Students:* 67 full-time (41 women); includes 4 Black or African American, non-Hispanic/Latino; 2 American Indian or Alaska Native, non-Hispanic/Latino; 9 Asian, non-Hispanic/Latino; 9 Hispanic/Latino, 9 international. Average age 27. 120 applicants, 27% accepted, 15 enrolled. In 2010, 7 doctorates awarded. *Degree requirements:* For doctorate, thesis/dissertation, public defense. *Entrance requirements:* For doctorate, GRE General Test, GRE Subject Test (strongly recommended), minimum GPA of 3.0. Additional exam requirements/recommendations for international students: Required—TOEFL. *Application deadline:* For fall admission, 1/1 priority date for domestic students. Applications are processed on a rolling basis. Application fee: $0. Electronic applications accepted. *Expenses:* Tuition: Full-time $11,000. Required fees: $4900. *Financial support:* In 2010–11, 67 students received support, including 24 fellowships with full tuition reimbursements available (averaging $26,000 per year), 43 research assistantships with full tuition reimbursements available (averaging $26,000 per year); teaching assistantships, Federal Work-Study, institutionally sponsored loans, health care benefits, and tuition waivers (full) also available. Financial award applicants required to submit FAFSA. *Faculty research:* Molecular and cellular biology; cancer, aging and stem cells; genomics and proteomics; microbiome, molecular microbiology; infectious disease, immunology and translational research. *Unit head:* Dr. Susan Marriott, Director, 713-798-6557. *Application contact:* Lourdes Fernandez, Graduate Program Administrator, 713-798-6557, Fax: 713-798-6325, E-mail: cmbprog@bcm.edu.

See Close-Up on page 223.

Boston College, Graduate School of Arts and Sciences, Department of Chemistry, Program in Biochemistry, Chestnut Hill, MA 02467-3800. Offers PhD. *Degree requirements:* For doctorate, 2 foreign languages, comprehensive exam, thesis/dissertation. *Entrance requirements:* For doctorate, GRE General Test, GRE Subject Test.

Boston University, Graduate School of Arts and Sciences, Molecular Biology, Cell Biology, and Biochemistry Program (MCBB), Boston, MA 02215. Offers MA, PhD. *Students:* 36 full-time (17 women), 2 part-time (both women); includes 9 minority (3 Black or African American, non-Hispanic/Latino; 3 Asian, non-Hispanic/Latino; 3 Hispanic/Latino), 6 international. Average age 28. 77 applicants, 18% accepted, 5 enrolled. In 2010, 6 master's, 20 doctorates awarded. Terminal master's awarded for partial completion of doctoral program. *Degree requirements:* For master's, one foreign language, thesis (for some programs); for doctorate, one foreign language, comprehensive exam, thesis/dissertation. *Entrance requirements:* For master's and doctorate, GRE General Test, GRE Subject Test. Additional exam requirements/recommendations for international students: Required—TOEFL (minimum score 600 paper-based; 250 computer-based). *Application deadline:* For fall admission, 12/7 for domestic and international students. Application fee: $70. Electronic applications accepted. *Expenses:* Tuition: Full-time $39,314; part-time $1228 per credit. Required fees: $40 per semester. *Financial support:* In 2010–11, 9 students received support, including 1 fellowship with full tuition reimbursement available (averaging $19,300 per year), 7 research assistantships with full tuition reimbursements available (averaging $18,800 per year), 1 teaching assistantship with full tuition reimbursement available (averaging $18,800 per year); Federal Work-Study, scholarships/grants, and traineeships also available. Financial award application deadline: 12/7; financial award applicants required to submit FAFSA. *Unit head:* Dr. Ulla Hansen, Director, 617-353-2432, Fax: 617-353-6340, E-mail: uhansen@bu.edu. *Application contact:* Meredith Canode, Academic Administrator, 617-353-2432, Fax: 617-353-6340, E-mail: mcanode@bu.edu.

Boston University, School of Medicine, Division of Graduate Medical Sciences, Department of Biochemistry, Boston, MA 02118. Offers MA, PhD, MD/PhD. Part-time programs available. *Faculty:* 41 full-time (17 women), 11 part-time/adjunct (5 women). *Students:* 31 full-time (18 women), 2 part-time (1 woman); includes 2 Asian, non-Hispanic/Latino; 1 Hispanic/Latino, 18 international. 88 applicants, 16% accepted, 7 enrolled. In 2010, 3 master's, 6 doctorates awarded. Terminal master's awarded for partial completion of doctoral program. *Degree requirements:* For master's, thesis or alternative, qualifying exam; for doctorate, thesis/dissertation, qualifying exam. *Entrance requirements:* For master's and doctorate, GRE General Test, GRE Subject Test. Additional exam requirements/recommendations for international students: Required—TOEFL. *Application deadline:* For fall admission, 1/15 priority date for domestic students; for spring admission, 10/15 priority date for domestic students. Application fee: $75. Electronic applications accepted. *Expenses:* Tuition: Full-time $39,314; part-time $1228 per credit. Required fees: $40 per semester. *Financial support:* In 2010–11, 1 fellowship (averaging $30,500 per year), 27 research assistantships (averaging $30,500 per year) were awarded; Federal Work-Study, scholarships/grants, and traineeships also available. Financial award applicants required to submit FAFSA. *Faculty research:* Extracellular matrix, gene expression, receptors, growth control. *Unit head:* Dr. David A. Harris, Chair, 617-638-5090. *Application contact:* Dr. Barbara Schreiber, Director of the Graduate Program, 617-638-5094, E-mail: schreibe@bu.edu.

Brandeis University, Graduate School of Arts and Sciences, Program in Biochemistry and Biophysics, Waltham, MA 02454. Offers PhD. Part-time programs available. *Faculty:* 9 full-time (2 women), 1 (woman) part-time/adjunct. *Students:* 37 full-time (14 women); includes 3 Asian, non-Hispanic/Latino; 2 Hispanic/Latino, 8 international. 62 applicants, 23% accepted, 7 enrolled. In 2010, 3 doctorates awarded. *Degree requirements:* For doctorate, thesis/dissertation, area exams. *Entrance requirements:* For doctorate, GRE General Test, resume, 3 letters of recommendation, statement of purpose. Additional exam requirements/recommendations for international students: Required—TOEFL (minimum score 600 paper-based; 250 computer-based; 100 iBT); Recommended—IELTS (minimum score 7). *Application deadline:* For fall admission, 1/15 priority date for domestic students. Applications are processed on a rolling basis. Application fee: $75. Electronic applications accepted. *Financial support:* In 2010–11, 16 students received support, including 9 fellowships with full tuition reimbursements available (averaging $27,500 per year), 26 research assistantships with full tuition reimbursements available (averaging $27,500 per year), teaching assistantships with partial tuition reimbursements available (averaging $3,200 per year); career-related internships or fieldwork, scholarships/grants, traineeships, health care benefits, and tuition waivers (full and partial) also available. Financial award application deadline: 4/15; financial award applicants required to submit FAFSA. *Faculty research:* Macromolecular chemistry, structure and function, biochemistry, biophysics, biological macromolecules. *Unit head:* Prof. Dorothee Kern, Director of Graduate Studies, 781-736-3100, Fax: 781-736-3107, E-mail: dkern@brandeis.edu. *Application contact:* Marcia Cabral, Department Administrator, 781-736-3100, Fax: 781-736-3107, E-mail: cabral@brandeis.edu.

Brigham Young University, Graduate Studies, College of Physical and Mathematical Sciences, Department of Chemistry and Biochemistry, Provo, UT 84602. Offers biochemistry (MS, PhD); chemistry (MS, PhD). *Faculty:* 33 full-time (2 women). *Students:* 105 full-time (44 women); includes 1 Asian, non-Hispanic/Latino; 1 Hispanic/Latino; 2 Native Hawaiian or other Pacific Islander, non-Hispanic/Latino, 44 international. Average age 28. 72 applicants, 58% accepted, 23 enrolled. In 2010, 5 master's, 11 doctorates awarded. *Degree requirements:* For master's, thesis; for doctorate, thesis/dissertation, qualifying exam. *Entrance requirements:* For master's and doctorate, GRE General Test, minimum GPA of 3.0 in last 60 hours. Additional exam requirements/recommendations for international students: Required—TOEFL (minimum score 580 paper-based; 237 computer-based; 85 iBT); Recommended—TWE. *Application deadline:* For fall admission, 2/1 priority date for domestic and international students. Applications are processed on a rolling basis. Application fee: $50. Electronic applications accepted. *Expenses:* Tuition: Full-time $5580; part-time $310 per credit hour. Tuition and fees vary according to program and student's religious affiliation. *Financial support:* In 2010–11, 105 students received support, including 10 fellowships with full tuition reimbursements available (averaging $21,250 per year), 56 research assistantships with full tuition reimbursements available (averaging $21,250 per year), 29 teaching assistantships with full tuition reimbursements available (averaging $21,250 per year); institutionally sponsored loans, scholarships/grants, health care benefits, tuition waivers (full), and unspecified assistantships also available. Financial award application deadline: 2/1. *Faculty research:* Separation science, molecular recognition, organic synthesis and biomedical application, biochemistry and molecular biology, molecular spectroscopy. Total annual research expenditures: $5.6 million. *Unit head:* Dr. Gregory F. Burton, Chair, 801-422-4917, Fax: 801-422-0153, E-mail: gburton@byu.edu.

Application contact: Dr. Matthew R. Linford, Graduate Coordinator, 801-422-1699, Fax: 801-422-0153, E-mail: mrlinford@byu.edu.

Brown University, Graduate School, Department of Chemistry, Providence, RI 02912. Offers biochemistry (PhD); chemistry (AM, Sc M, PhD). *Degree requirements:* For master's, thesis; for doctorate, one foreign language, thesis/dissertation, cumulative exam.

Brown University, Graduate School, Division of Biology and Medicine, Program in Molecular Biology, Cell Biology, and Biochemistry, Providence, RI 02912. Offers biochemistry (M Med Sc, Sc M, PhD), including biochemistry (Sc M, PhD), biology (Sc M, PhD), medical science (M Med Sc, PhD); biology (MA); cell biology (M Med Sc, Sc M, PhD), including biochemistry (Sc M, PhD), biology (Sc M, PhD), medical science (M Med Sc, PhD); developmental biology (M Med Sc, Sc M, PhD), including biochemistry (Sc M, PhD), biology (Sc M, PhD), medical science (M Med Sc, PhD); immunology (M Med Sc, Sc M, PhD), including biochemistry (Sc M, PhD), biology (Sc M, PhD), medical science (M Med Sc, PhD); molecular microbiology (M Med Sc, Sc M, PhD), including biochemistry (Sc M, PhD), biology (Sc M, PhD), medical science (M Med Sc, PhD); MD/PhD. Part-time programs available. Terminal master's awarded for partial completion of doctoral program. *Degree requirements:* For master's, thesis (for some programs); for doctorate, one foreign language, thesis/dissertation, preliminary exam. *Entrance requirements:* For master's and doctorate, GRE General Test, GRE Subject Test. Additional exam requirements/recommendations for international students: Required—TOEFL. Electronic applications accepted. *Faculty research:* Molecular genetics, gene regulation.

California Institute of Technology, Division of Biology and Division of Chemistry and Chemical Engineering, Biochemistry and Molecular Biophysics Graduate Option, Pasadena, CA 91125-0001. Offers PhD. *Degree requirements:* For doctorate, thesis/dissertation, qualifying exam. *Entrance requirements:* For doctorate, GRE General Test. Additional exam requirements/recommendations for international students: Required—TOEFL. Electronic applications accepted.

California Institute of Technology, Division of Chemistry and Chemical Engineering, Program in Biochemistry and Molecular Biophysics, Pasadena, CA 91125-0001. Offers MS, PhD. *Faculty:* 44 full-time (11 women). *Students:* 51 full-time (18 women); includes 26 minority (2 Black or African American, non-Hispanic/Latino; 15 Asian, non-Hispanic/Latino; 5 Hispanic/Latino; 1 Native Hawaiian or other Pacific Islander, non-Hispanic/Latino; 3 Two or more races, non-Hispanic/Latino). Average age 26. 115 applicants, 22% accepted, 9 enrolled. In 2010, 3 doctorates awarded. Terminal master's awarded for partial completion of doctoral program. *Degree requirements:* For master's, thesis; for doctorate, thesis/dissertation. *Entrance requirements:* For doctorate, GRE. Additional exam requirements/recommendations for international students: Required—TOEFL; Recommended—IELTS, TWE. *Application deadline:* For fall admission, 1/1 for domestic and international students. Application fee: $80. Electronic applications accepted. *Financial support:* In 2010–11, 9 students received support, including 4 fellowships with full tuition reimbursements available (averaging $23,128 per year), 5 research assistantships with full tuition reimbursements available (averaging $23,128 per year), 9 teaching assistantships with full tuition reimbursements available (averaging $4,782 per year); institutionally sponsored loans, scholarships/grants, traineeships, health care benefits, and unspecified assistantships also available. Financial award application deadline: 1/1. *Unit head:* Prof. Douglas C. Rees, Executive Officer, 626-395-8393, Fax: 626-744-9524, E-mail: dcrees@caltech.edu. *Application contact:* Alison Ross, Option Coordinator, 626-395-6446, E-mail: aross@caltech.edu.

California Polytechnic State University, San Luis Obispo, College of Science and Mathematics, Department of Chemistry and Biochemistry, San Luis Obispo, CA 93407. Offers polymers and coating science (MS). Part-time programs available. *Students:* 3 full-time (0 women), 7 part-time (3 women); includes 2 minority (1 Black or African American, non-Hispanic/Latino; 1 Asian, non-Hispanic/Latino). Average age 24. 5 applicants, 80% accepted, 1 enrolled. *Degree requirements:* For master's, comprehensive oral exam. *Entrance requirements:* For master's, minimum GPA of 2.5 in last 90 quarter units of course work. Additional exam requirements/recommendations for international students: Required—TOEFL (minimum score 550 paper-based; 213 computer-based) or IELTS (minimum score 6). *Application deadline:* For fall admission, 7/1 for domestic students, 11/30 for international students; for winter admission, 11/1 for domestic students, 6/30 for international students; for spring admission, 2/1 for domestic students. Applications are processed on a rolling basis. Application fee: $55. Electronic applications accepted. *Expenses:* Tuition, state resident: full-time $5386; part-time $3124 per year. Tuition, nonresident: full-time $11,160; part-time $248 per unit. Required fees: $2250; $614 per term. One-time fee: $2250 full-time; $1842 part-time. *Financial support:* Career-related internships or fieldwork, Federal Work-Study, and scholarships/grants available. Support available to part-time students. Financial award application deadline: 3/2; financial award applicants required to submit FAFSA. *Faculty research:* Polymer physical chemistry and analysis, polymer synthesis, coatings formulation. *Unit head:* Dr. Ray Fernando, Graduate Coordinator, 805-756-2395, Fax: 805-756-5500, E-mail: rhfernan@calpoly.edu. *Application contact:* Dr. James Maraviglia, Assistant Vice President for Admissions, Recruitment and Financial Aid, 805-756-2311, Fax: 805-756-5400, E-mail: admissions@calpoly.edu.

California State University, East Bay, Office of Academic Programs and Graduate Studies, College of Science, Department of Chemistry, Hayward, CA 94542-3000. Offers biochemistry (MS); chemistry (MS). *Faculty:* 5 full-time (3 women). *Students:* 18 full-time (10 women), 26 part-time (8 women); includes 2 Black or African American, non-Hispanic/Latino; 16 Asian, non-Hispanic/Latino; 2 Hispanic/Latino, 10 international. Average age 29. 44 applicants, 70% accepted, 18 enrolled. In 2010, 15 master's awarded. *Degree requirements:* For master's, comprehensive exam or thesis. *Entrance requirements:* For master's, minimum GPA of 2.5 in field during previous 2 years of course work. Additional exam requirements/recommendations for international students: Required—TOEFL (minimum score 550 paper-based; 213 computer-based). *Application deadline:* For fall admission, 6/30 for domestic and international students. Application fee: $55. Electronic applications accepted. *Financial support:* Fellowships, career-related internships or fieldwork, Federal Work-Study, institutionally sponsored loans, and scholarships/grants available. Support available to part-time students. Financial award application deadline: 3/2; financial award applicants required to submit FAFSA. *Unit head:* Dr. Ann McPartland, Chair, 510-885-3452, Fax: 510-885-4675, E-mail: ann.mcpartland@csueastbay.edu. *Application contact:* Dr. Donna Wiley, Interim Associate Director, 510-885-2928, Fax: 510-885-4777, E-mail: donna.wiley@csueastbay.edu.

California State University, Long Beach, Graduate Studies, College of Natural Sciences and Mathematics, Department of Chemistry and Biochemistry, Long Beach, CA 90840. Offers biochemistry (MS); chemistry (MS). Part-time programs available. *Faculty:* 14 full-time (2 women). *Students:* 17 full-time (9 women), 23 part-time (9 women); includes 1 Black or African American, non-Hispanic/Latino; 8 Asian, non-Hispanic/Latino; 4 Hispanic/Latino, 13 international. Average age 26. 74 applicants, 62% accepted, 21 enrolled. In 2010, 9 master's awarded. *Degree requirements:* For master's, thesis, departmental qualifying exam. *Application deadline:* For fall admission, 6/1 for domestic students. Applications are processed on a rolling basis. Application fee: $55. Electronic applications accepted. *Financial support:* Research assistantships, teaching assistantships, Federal Work-Study, institutionally sponsored loans, scholarships/grants, and unspecified assistantships available. Financial award application deadline: 3/2. *Faculty research:* Enzymology, organic synthesis, molecular modeling, environmental chemistry, reaction kinetics. *Unit head:* Dr. Jeffrey Cohlberg, Chair, 562-985-4944, Fax: 562-985-8557, E-mail: cohlberg@csulb.edu. *Application contact:* Dr. Lijuan Li, Graduate Advisor, 562-985-5068, Fax: 562-985-8557, E-mail: lli@csulb.edu.

California State University, Los Angeles, Graduate Studies, College of Natural and Social Sciences, Department of Chemistry and Biochemistry, Los Angeles, CA 90032-8530. Offers analytical chemistry (MS); biochemistry (MS); chemistry (MS); inorganic chemistry (MS); organic chemistry (MS); physical chemistry (MS). Part-time and evening/weekend programs available. *Faculty:* 5 part-time/adjunct (1 woman). *Students:* 19 full-time (15 women), 24 part-time (12 women); includes 21 minority (3 Black or African American, non-Hispanic/Latino; 8 Asian, non-Hispanic/Latino; 10 Hispanic/Latino), 9 international. Average age 30. 22 applicants, 100% accepted, 10 enrolled. In 2010, 7 master's awarded. *Degree requirements:* For master's, one foreign language, comprehensive exam or thesis. *Entrance requirements:* Additional exam requirements/recommendations for international students: Required—TOEFL. *Application deadline:* For fall admission, 5/1 for domestic and international students. Applications are processed on a rolling basis. Application fee: $55. *Financial support:* Federal Work-Study available. Support available to part-time students. Financial award application deadline: 3/1. *Faculty research:* Intercalation of heavy metal, carborane chemistry, conductive polymers and fabrics, titanium reagents, computer modeling and synthesis. *Unit head:* Dr. Robert L. Vellanoweth, Chair, 323-343-2300, Fax: 323-343-6490, E-mail: rvellan@calstatela.edu. *Application contact:* Dr. Allan Muchlinski, Dean of Graduate Studies, 323-343-3820 Ext. 3827, Fax: 323-343-5653, E-mail: amuchli@exchange.calstatela.edu.

California State University, Northridge, Graduate Studies, College of Science and Mathematics, Department of Chemistry and Biochemistry, Northridge, CA 91330. Offers biochemistry (MS); chemistry (MS), including chemistry, environmental chemistry. *Degree requirements:* For master's, thesis. *Entrance requirements:* For master's, GRE General Test or minimum GPA of 3.0. Additional exam requirements/recommendations for international students: Required—TOEFL. Electronic applications accepted.

Carnegie Mellon University, Mellon College of Science, Department of Biological Sciences, Pittsburgh, PA 15213-3891. Offers biochemistry (PhD); biophysics (PhD); cell biology (PhD); computational biology (MS, PhD); developmental biology (PhD); genetics (PhD); molecular biology (PhD); neuroscience (PhD). *Degree requirements:* For doctorate, comprehensive exam, thesis/dissertation. *Entrance requirements:* For doctorate, GRE General Test, GRE Subject Test, interview. Electronic applications accepted. *Faculty research:* Genetic structure, function, and regulation; protein structure and function; biological membranes; biological spectroscopy.

Case Western Reserve University, School of Medicine and School of Graduate Studies, Graduate Programs in Medicine, Department of Biochemistry, Cleveland, OH 44106. Offers biochemical research (MS); biochemistry (MS, PhD); RNA biology (PhD); MD/PhD. Part-time programs available. Terminal master's awarded for partial completion of doctoral program. *Degree requirements:* For master's, thesis (for some programs); for doctorate, thesis/dissertation. *Entrance requirements:* For master's and doctorate, GRE General Test. Additional exam requirements/recommendations for international students: Required—TOEFL. Electronic applications accepted. *Faculty research:* Regulation of metabolism, regulation of gene expression and protein synthesis, cell biology, molecular biology, structural biology.

Case Western Reserve University, School of Medicine and School of Graduate Studies, Graduate Programs in Medicine, Department of Nutrition, Cleveland, OH 44106. Offers dietetics (MS); nutrition (MS, PhD), including molecular nutrition (PhD), nutrition and biochemistry (PhD); public health nutrition (MS). Part-time programs available. Terminal master's awarded for partial completion of doctoral program. *Degree requirements:* For master's, thesis (for some programs); for doctorate, thesis/dissertation. *Entrance requirements:* For master's, GRE General Test; for doctorate, GRE General Test, GRE Subject Test. Additional exam requirements/recommendations for international students: Required—TOEFL. *Faculty research:* Fatty acid metabolism, application of gene therapy to nutritional problems, dietary intake methodology, nutrition and physical fitness, metabolism during infancy and pregnancy.

See Display on page 383 and Close-Up on page 399.

Central Connecticut State University, School of Graduate Studies, School of Arts and Sciences, Department of Chemistry and Biochemistry, New Britain, CT 06050-4010. Offers natural sciences (MS). Part-time and evening/weekend programs available. *Students:* 1 applicant, 100% accepted, 0 enrolled. In 2010, 1 other advanced degree awarded. *Degree requirements:* For Certificate, qualifying exam. *Entrance requirements:* Additional exam requirements/recommendations for international students: Required—TOEFL. *Application deadline:* For fall admission, 7/1 for domestic students; for spring admission, 12/1 for domestic students. Applications are processed on a rolling basis. Application fee: $50. Electronic applications accepted. *Expenses:* Tuition, area resident: Full-time $5012; part-time $470 per credit. Tuition, state resident: full-time $7518; part-time $482 per credit. Tuition, nonresident: full-time $13,962; part-time $482 per credit. Required fees: $3772. One-time fee: $62 part-time. *Unit head:* Dr. Thomas Burkholder, Chair, 860-832-2675. *Application contact:* Dr. Thomas Burkholder, Chair, 860-832-2675.

City College of the City University of New York, Graduate School, College of Liberal Arts and Science, Division of Science, Department of Chemistry, Program in Biochemistry, New York, NY 10031-9198. Offers MA, PhD. PhD program offered jointly with Graduate School and University Center of the City University of New York. Terminal master's awarded for partial completion of doctoral program. *Degree requirements:* For doctorate, one foreign language, thesis/dissertation. *Entrance requirements:* For doctorate, GRE. Additional exam requirements/recommendations for international students: Required—TOEFL (minimum score 550 paper-based; 79 iBT). Electronic applications accepted. *Faculty research:* Fatty acid metabolism, lectins, gene structure.

Clemson University, Graduate School, College of Agriculture, Forestry and Life Sciences, Department of Genetics and Biochemistry, Program in Biochemistry and Molecular Biology, Clemson, SC 29634. Offers PhD. *Students:* 17 full-time (11 women), 1 (woman) part-time, 9 international. Average age 29. 24 applicants, 21% accepted, 5 enrolled. In 2010, 1 doctorate awarded. *Degree requirements:* For doctorate, comprehensive exam, thesis/dissertation. *Entrance requirements:* For doctorate, GRE General Test. Additional exam requirements/recommendations for international students: Required—TOEFL. *Application deadline:* For fall admission, 1/1 for domestic students; for spring admission, 9/1 for domestic students. Applications are processed on a rolling basis. Application fee: $70 ($80 for international students). Electronic applications accepted. *Expenses:* Contact institution. *Financial support:* In 2010–11, 17 students received support, including 2 fellowships with full and partial tuition reimbursements available (averaging $9,750 per year), 9 research assistantships with partial tuition reimbursements available (averaging $16,167 per year), 12 teaching assistantships with partial tuition reimbursements available (averaging $15,875 per year); career-related internships or fieldwork, institutionally sponsored loans, scholarships/grants, health care benefits, and unspecified assistantships also available. Support available to part-time students. Financial award application deadline: 3/15; financial award applicants required to submit FAFSA. *Faculty research:* Biomembranes, protein structure, molecular biology of plants, APYA and stress response. Total annual research expenditures: $670,000. *Unit head:* Dr. Keith Murphy, Chair, 864-656-6237, Fax: 864-656-0435, E-mail: kmurph2@clemson.edu. *Application contact:* Sheryl Banks, Administrative Coordinator, 864-656-6878, E-mail: sherylb@clemson.edu.

Colorado State University, Graduate School, College of Natural Sciences, Department of Biochemistry and Molecular Biology, Fort Collins, CO 80523-1870. Offers biochemistry (MS, PhD). Postbaccalaureate distance learning degree programs offered (no on-campus study). *Faculty:* 11 full-time (5 women), 2 part-time/adjunct (0 women). *Students:* 20 full-time (9 women), 22 part-time (13 women); includes 3 minority (1 Asian, non-Hispanic/Latino; 2 Hispanic/Latino), 9 international. Average age 26. 54 applicants, 28% accepted, 12 enrolled. In 2010, 6 master's, 4 doctorates awarded. Terminal master's awarded for partial completion of doctoral program. *Degree requirements:* For master's, comprehensive exam (for some programs), thesis (for some programs); for doctorate, thesis/dissertation, comprehensive oral exam at the end of second year. *Entrance requirements:* For master's, GRE General Test, minimum GPA of 3.0; 3 letters of recommendation; resume; for doctorate, GRE General Test, minimum GPA of 3.0; one year of biology, organic chemistry, physics, calculus, and biochemistry; 3 letters of recommendation; bachelor's degree. Additional exam requirements/recommendations for international students: Required—TOEFL (minimum score 550 paper-based; 213 computer-based; 80 iBT). *Application deadline:* For fall admission, 1/7 priority date for domestic and international students; for spring admission, 9/15 priority date for domestic and international students. Applications are processed on a rolling basis. Application fee: $50. Electronic applica-

Biochemistry

Colorado State University (continued)
tions accepted. *Expenses:* Tuition, state resident: full-time $7434; part-time $413 per credit. Tuition, nonresident: full-time $19,022; part-time $1057 per credit. Required fees: $1729; $88 per credit. *Financial support:* In 2010–11, 42 students received support, including 10 fellowships (averaging $31,116 per year), 24 research assistantships with full tuition reimbursements available (averaging $19,242 per year), 9 teaching assistantships with full tuition reimbursements available (averaging $16,154 per year); health care benefits also available. Financial award application deadline: 1/15; financial award applicants required to submit FAFSA. *Faculty research:* Cellular biology, molecular gene expression, neurobiology, structural biology, yeast genetics. Total annual research expenditures: $4.3 million. *Unit head:* Dr. P. Shing Ho, Chair, 970-491-0569, Fax: 970-491-0494, E-mail: shing.ho@colostate.edu. *Application contact:* Sharon Gale, Graduate Program Assistant, 970-491-6841, Fax: 970-491-0494, E-mail: sharon.gale@colostate.edu.

Colorado State University–Pueblo, College of Science and Mathematics, Pueblo, CO 81001-4901. Offers applied natural science (MS), including biochemistry, biology, chemistry. Part-time and evening/weekend programs available. *Degree requirements:* For master's, comprehensive exam (for some programs), thesis (for some programs), internship report (if non-thesis). *Entrance requirements:* For master's, GRE General Test (minimum score 1000), 2 letters of reference, minimum GPA of 3.0. Additional exam requirements/recommendations for international students: Required—TOEFL (minimum score 500 paper-based; 173 computer-based), IELTS (minimum score 5). *Faculty research:* Fungal cell walls, molecular biology, bioactive materials synthesis, atomic force microscopy-surface chemistry, nanoscience.

Columbia University, College of Physicians and Surgeons, Department of Biochemistry and Molecular Biophysics, New York, NY 10032. Offers biochemistry and molecular biophysics (M Phil, PhD); biophysics (PhD); MD/PhD. Only candidates for the PhD are admitted. *Degree requirements:* For doctorate, one foreign language, thesis/dissertation. *Entrance requirements:* For master's and doctorate, GRE General Test. Additional exam requirements/recommendations for international students: Required—TOEFL.

Cornell University, Graduate School, Graduate Fields of Agriculture and Life Sciences, Field of Biochemistry, Molecular and Cell Biology, Ithaca, NY 14853-0001. Offers biochemistry (PhD); biophysics (PhD); cell biology (PhD); molecular and cell biology (PhD); molecular biology (PhD). *Faculty:* 59 full-time (15 women). *Students:* 90 full-time (47 women); includes 1 Black or African American, non-Hispanic/Latino; 7 Asian, non-Hispanic/Latino; 4 Hispanic/Latino, 30 international. Average age 26. 269 applicants, 9% accepted, 20 enrolled. In 2010, 12 doctorates awarded. *Degree requirements:* For doctorate, comprehensive exam, thesis/dissertation, 2 semesters of teaching experience. *Entrance requirements:* For doctorate, GRE General Test, GRE Subject Test (biology, chemistry, physics, biochemistry, cell and molecular biology), 3 letters of recommendation. Additional exam requirements/recommendations for international students: Required—TOEFL (minimum score 600 paper-based; 250 computer-based; 77 iBT). *Application deadline:* For fall admission, 1/5 for domestic students. Application fee: $70. Electronic applications accepted. *Expenses:* Tuition: Full-time $29,500. Required fees: $76. Tuition and fees vary according to degree level and program. *Financial support:* In 2010–11, 88 students received support, including 25 fellowships with full tuition reimbursements available, 48 research assistantships with full tuition reimbursements available, 15 teaching assistantships with full tuition reimbursements available; institutionally sponsored loans, scholarships/grants, health care benefits, tuition waivers (full and partial), and unspecified assistantships also available. Financial award applicants required to submit FAFSA. *Faculty research:* Biophysics, structural biology. *Unit head:* Director of Graduate Studies, 607-255-2100, Fax: 607-255-2100. *Application contact:* Graduate Field Assistant, 607-255-2100, Fax: 607-255-2100, E-mail: bmcb@cornell.edu.

Cornell University, Graduate School, Graduate Fields of Arts and Sciences, Field of Chemistry and Chemical Biology, Ithaca, NY 14853-0001. Offers analytical chemistry (PhD); bio-organic chemistry (PhD); biophysical chemistry (PhD); chemical biology (PhD); chemical physics (PhD); inorganic chemistry (PhD); materials chemistry (PhD); organic chemistry (PhD); organometallic chemistry (PhD); physical chemistry (PhD); polymer chemistry (PhD); theoretical chemistry (PhD). *Faculty:* 46 full-time (3 women). *Students:* 163 full-time (63 women); includes 10 Asian, non-Hispanic/Latino; 3 Hispanic/Latino, 49 international. Average age 24. 340 applicants, 36% accepted, 48 enrolled. In 2010, 31 doctorates awarded. *Degree requirements:* For doctorate, comprehensive exam, thesis/dissertation. *Entrance requirements:* For doctorate, GRE General Test, GRE Subject Test (chemistry), 3 letters of recommendation. Additional exam requirements/recommendations for international students: Required—TOEFL (minimum score 600 paper-based; 250 computer-based; 77 iBT). *Application deadline:* For fall admission, 1/10 for domestic students. Application fee: $80. Electronic applications accepted. *Expenses:* Tuition: Full-time $29,500. Required fees: $76. Tuition and fees vary according to degree level and program. *Financial support:* In 2010–11, 19 fellowships with full tuition reimbursements, 69 research assistantships with full tuition reimbursements, 68 teaching assistantships with full tuition reimbursements were awarded; institutionally sponsored loans, scholarships/grants, health care benefits, tuition waivers (full and partial), and unspecified assistantships also available. Financial award applicants required to submit FAFSA. *Faculty research:* Analytical, organic, inorganic, physical, materials, chemical biology. *Unit head:* Director of Graduate Studies, 607-255-4139, Fax: 607-255-4137. *Application contact:* Graduate Field Assistant, 607-255-4139, Fax: 607-255-4137, E-mail: chemgrad@cornell.edu.

Cornell University, Joan and Sanford I. Weill Medical College and Graduate School of Medical Sciences, Weill Cornell Graduate School of Medical Sciences, Biochemistry, Cell and Molecular Biology Allied Program, New York, NY 10065. Offers MS, PhD. *Faculty:* 106 full-time (30 women). *Students:* 143 full-time (91 women); includes 2 Black or African American, non-Hispanic/Latino; 8 Asian, non-Hispanic/Latino; 6 Hispanic/Latino, 73 international. Average age 22. 322 applicants, 17% accepted, 14 enrolled. In 2010, 19 doctorates awarded. Terminal master's awarded for partial completion of doctoral program. *Degree requirements:* For master's, comprehensive exam; for doctorate, thesis/dissertation, final exam. *Entrance requirements:* For doctorate, GRE General Test, background in genetics, molecular biology, chemistry, or biochemistry. Additional exam requirements/recommendations for international students: Required—TOEFL. *Application deadline:* For fall admission, 12/1 for domestic students. Application fee: $60. Electronic applications accepted. *Expenses:* Tuition: Full-time $45,545. Required fees: $2805. *Financial support:* In 2010–11, 16 fellowships (averaging $23,000 per year) were awarded; scholarships/grants, health care benefits, and stipends (given to all students) also available. *Faculty research:* Molecular structure determination, protein structure, gene structure, stem cell biology, control of gene expression, DNA replication, chromosome maintenance, RNA biosynthesis. *Unit head:* Dr. David Eliezer, Co-Director, 212-746-6557, Fax: 212-717-3047. *Application contact:* Linda Smith, Assistant Dean of Admissions, 212-746-6565, Fax: 212-746-8906, E-mail: lis2025@med.cornell.edu.

Cornell University, Joan and Sanford I. Weill Medical College and Graduate School of Medical Sciences, Weill Cornell Graduate School of Medical Sciences, Tri-Institutional Training Program in Chemical Biology, New York, NY 10065. Offers PhD. Program offered jointly with The Rockefeller University and Sloan-Kettering Institute. *Faculty:* 39 full-time (5 women). *Students:* 42 full-time (15 women); includes 20 Asian, non-Hispanic/Latino; 3 Hispanic/Latino; 1 Native Hawaiian or other Pacific Islander, non-Hispanic/Latino. Average age 23. 69 applicants, 23% accepted, 7 enrolled. In 2010, 8 doctorates awarded. *Degree requirements:* For doctorate, comprehensive exam, thesis/dissertation. *Entrance requirements:* For doctorate, GRE General Test, 3 letters of recommendation. Additional exam requirements/recommendations for international students: Required—TOEFL (minimum score 600 paper-based; 250 computer-based; 90 iBT). *Application deadline:* For winter admission, 1/1 for domestic and international students. Application fee: $80. Electronic applications accepted. *Expenses:* Tuition: Full-time $45,545. Required fees: $2805. *Financial support:* In 2010–11, 42 students received support, including 42 fellowships with full tuition reimbursements available (averaging $40,000 per year). *Faculty research:* Bio-organic chemistry, biological chemistry/biochemistry, biophysical chemistry, bioanalytical chemistry, computational chemistry and biology. *Unit head:* Kathleen E. Pickering, Executive Director, 212-746-6049, Fax: 212-746-8992, E-mail: tpcb@med.cornell.edu. *Application contact:* Margie H. Mendoza, Program Coordinator, 212-746-5267, Fax: 212-746-8992, E-mail: tpcb@med.cornell.edu.

Dalhousie University, Faculty of Medicine, Department of Biochemistry and Molecular Biology, Halifax, NS B3H 4R2, Canada. Offers M Sc, PhD. *Degree requirements:* For master's, thesis, demonstrating/teaching experience, oral defense, seminar; for doctorate, comprehensive exam, thesis/dissertation, demonstrating/teaching experience, oral defense, seminar, 2 short grant proposals in year 3. *Entrance requirements:* For master's and doctorate, GRE. Additional exam requirements/recommendations for international students: Required—TOEFL, IELTS, 1 of the following 5 approved tests: TOEFL, IELTS, CANTEST, CAEL, Michigan English Language Assessment Battery. Electronic applications accepted. *Expenses:* Contact institution. *Faculty research:* Gene expression and cell regulation; lipids, lipoproteins, and membranes; molecular evolution; proteins, molecular cell biology and molecular genetics; structure, function, and metabolism of biomolecules.

Dartmouth College, Graduate Program in Molecular and Cellular Biology, Department of Biochemistry, Hanover, NH 03755. Offers PhD, MD/PhD. *Entrance requirements:* For doctorate, GRE General Test, letters of recommendation. Additional exam requirements/recommendations for international students: Required—TOEFL (minimum score 450 paper-based; 90 iBT) or IELTS (minimum score 7). Electronic applications accepted.

DePaul University, College of Liberal Arts and Sciences, Department of Chemistry, Chicago, IL 60614. Offers biochemistry (MS); chemistry (MS); polymer chemistry and coatings technology (MS). Part-time and evening/weekend programs available. *Degree requirements:* For master's, thesis (for some programs), oral exam (for select programs). *Entrance requirements:* For master's, GRE Subject Test (chemistry), GRE General Test, BS in chemistry or equivalent. Additional exam requirements/recommendations for international students: Required—TOEFL (minimum score 590 paper-based; 243 computer-based). Electronic applications accepted. *Faculty research:* Computational chemistry, organic synthesis, inorganic synthesis, polymer synthesis, biochemistry.

Drexel University, College of Medicine, Biomedical Graduate Programs, Program in Biochemistry, Philadelphia, PA 19104-2875. Offers MS, PhD, MD/PhD. Part-time programs available. Terminal master's awarded for partial completion of doctoral program. *Degree requirements:* For master's, comprehensive exam, thesis; for doctorate, thesis/dissertation, qualifying exam. *Entrance requirements:* For master's, GRE General Test, minimum GPA of 2.75; for doctorate, GRE General Test, minimum GPA of 3.0. Additional exam requirements/recommendations for international students: Required—TOEFL. Electronic applications accepted.

Duke University, Graduate School, Department of Biochemistry, Durham, NC 27710. Offers crystallography of macromolecules (PhD); enzyme mechanisms (PhD); lipid biochemistry (PhD); membrane structure and function (PhD); molecular genetics (PhD); neurochemistry (PhD); nucleic acid structure and function (PhD); protein structure and function (PhD). *Faculty:* 28 full-time. *Students:* 75 full-time (31 women); includes 4 Black or African American, non-Hispanic/Latino; 2 Asian, non-Hispanic/Latino, 26 international. 102 applicants, 25% accepted, 15 enrolled. In 2010, 11 doctorates awarded. *Degree requirements:* For doctorate, thesis/dissertation. *Entrance requirements:* For doctorate, GRE General Test, GRE Subject Test (recommended). Additional exam requirements/recommendations for international students: Required—TOEFL (minimum score 550 paper-based; 213 computer-based; 83 iBT), IELTS (minimum score 7). *Application deadline:* For fall admission, 12/8 priority date for domestic and international students. Application fee: $75. Electronic applications accepted. *Financial support:* Fellowships, research assistantships, teaching assistantships, Federal Work-Study available. Financial award application deadline: 12/8. *Unit head:* Leonard Spicer, Director of Graduate Studies, 919-681-8770, Fax: 919-684-8885, E-mail: anorfleet@biochem.duke.edu. *Application contact:* Elizabeth Hutton, Director of Admissions, 919-684-3913, Fax: 919-684-2277, E-mail: grad-admissions@duke.edu.

Duquesne University, Bayer School of Natural and Environmental Sciences, Department of Chemistry and Biochemistry, Pittsburgh, PA 15282-0001. Offers chemistry (MS, PhD). Part-time programs available. *Faculty:* 15 full-time (4 women). *Students:* 51 full-time (22 women), 2 part-time (0 women); includes 4 minority (3 Black or African American, non-Hispanic/Latino; 1 Hispanic/Latino), 14 international. Average age 30. 53 applicants, 42% accepted, 13 enrolled. In 2010, 1 master's, 5 doctorates awarded. Terminal master's awarded for partial completion of doctoral program. *Degree requirements:* For master's, thesis (for some programs); for doctorate, thesis/dissertation. *Entrance requirements:* For master's, GRE General Test, BS in chemistry or related field, 3 letters of recommendation; for doctorate, GRE General Test, BS in chemistry or related field, statement of purpose, official transcripts, 3 letters of recommendation with recommendation forms. Additional exam requirements/recommendations for international students: Required—TOEFL (minimum score 100 iBT). *Application deadline:* For fall admission, 2/15 priority date for domestic students, 2/15 for international students; for spring admission, 10/1 priority date for domestic students, 10/1 for international students. Applications are processed on a rolling basis. Application fee: $0 ($40 for international students). Electronic applications accepted. *Expenses:* Contact institution. *Financial support:* In 2010–11, 48 students received support, including 1 fellowship with tuition reimbursement available (averaging $21,900 per year), 17 research assistantships with full tuition reimbursements available (averaging $21,400 per year), 30 teaching assistantships with full tuition reimbursements available (averaging $21,400 per year); scholarships/grants and unspecified assistantships also available. Financial award application deadline: 5/31. *Faculty research:* Computational physical chemistry, bioinorganic chemistry, analytical chemistry, biophysics, synthetic organic chemistry. *Unit head:* Dr. Ralph Wheeler, Chair, 412-396-6341, Fax: 412-396-5683, E-mail: wheeler7@duq.edu. *Application contact:* Heather Costello, Graduate Academic Advisor, 412-396-6339, Fax: 412-396-4881, E-mail: costelloh@duq.edu.

East Carolina University, Brody School of Medicine, Department of Biochemistry and Molecular Biology, Greenville, NC 27858-4353. Offers PhD. *Degree requirements:* For doctorate, comprehensive exam, thesis/dissertation. *Entrance requirements:* For doctorate, GRE General Test. Additional exam requirements/recommendations for international students: Required—TOEFL. *Expenses:* Tuition, state resident: full-time $3130; part-time $391.25 per credit hour. Tuition, nonresident: full-time $13,817; part-time $1727.13 per credit hour. Required fees: $1916; $239.50 per credit hour. Tuition and fees vary according to campus/location and program. *Faculty research:* Gene regulation, development and differentiation, contractility and motility, macromolecular interactions, cancer.

Eastern New Mexico University, Graduate School, College of Liberal Arts and Sciences, Department of Physical Sciences, Portales, NM 88130. Offers chemistry (MS), including analytical, biochemistry, inorganic, organic, physical. Part-time programs available. *Faculty:* 3 full-time (0 women). *Students:* 7 full-time (2 women), 2 part-time (1 woman), 6 international. Average age 32. 10 applicants, 40% accepted, 4 enrolled. In 2010, 3 master's awarded. *Degree requirements:* For master's, thesis optional, seminar, oral and written comprehensive exams. *Entrance requirements:* For master's, ACS placement examination, minimum GPA of 3.0; 2 letters of recommendation; personal statement of career goals; bachelor's degree with one year minimum each of general, organic, and analytical chemistry. Additional exam requirements/recommendations for international students: Required—TOEFL (minimum score 550 paper-based; 213 computer-based; 79 iBT), IELTS (minimum score 6). *Application deadline:* For fall admission, 7/20 priority date for domestic students, 6/20 priority date for international students; for spring admission, 12/15 priority date for domestic students, 11/15 priority date for international students. Applications are processed on a rolling basis. Application fee: $10. Electronic applications accepted. *Expenses:* Tuition, state resident: full-time $3210; part-time $130 per credit hour. Tuition, nonresident: full-time $8652; part-time $360.50 per credit hour. Required fees: $1212; $50.50 per credit hour. Tuition and fees vary according to course load. *Financial support:* In 2010–11, 1 research assistantship with partial tuition reimbursement (averaging $8,500 per year), 9 teaching assistantships with partial tuition reimbursements (averaging $8,500 per year) were awarded; career-related internships or fieldwork and unspecified assistantships also available. Support available to part-time students. Financial award application deadline: 3/1; financial award applicants required to submit FAFSA. *Faculty research:* Synfuel, electrochemistry, protein chemistry. *Unit head:* Dr. Juacho Yan, Graduate Coordinator, 575-562-2174, Fax: 575-562-2192, E-mail: juacho.yan@enmu.edu. *Application contact:* Sharon Potter, Department Secretary, Chemistry/Physical Sciences, 575-562-2174, Fax: 575-562-2192, E-mail: sharon.potter@enmu.edu.

East Tennessee State University, James H. Quillen College of Medicine, Biomedical Science Graduate Program, Johnson City, TN 37614. Offers anatomy (PhD); biochemistry (PhD); microbiology (PhD); pharmacology (PhD); physiology (PhD). Part-time programs available. *Faculty:* 49 full-time (12 women), 1 (woman) part-time/adjunct. *Students:* 27 full-time (14 women), 4 part-time (2 women); includes 4 minority (1 Black or African American, non-Hispanic/Latino; 1 Asian, non-Hispanic/Latino; 2 Hispanic/Latino), 5 international. Average age 32. 62 applicants, 11% accepted, 7 enrolled. In 2010, 2 doctorates awarded. Terminal master's awarded for partial completion of doctoral program. *Degree requirements:* For doctorate, thesis/dissertation, comprehensive qualifying exam. *Entrance requirements:* For doctorate, GRE General Test, GRE Subject Test. Additional exam requirements/recommendations for international students: Required—TOEFL (minimum score 550 paper-based; 213 computer-based; 79 iBT). *Application deadline:* For fall admission, 3/15 priority date for domestic students, 3/1 priority date for international students. Application fee: $25 ($35 for international students). Electronic applications accepted. *Expenses:* Contact institution. *Financial support:* In 2010–11, 7 research assistantships with full tuition reimbursements (averaging $15,000 per year) were awarded; teaching assistantships with full tuition reimbursements, career-related internships or fieldwork, institutionally sponsored loans, scholarships/grants, and unspecified assistantships also available. Financial award application deadline: 7/1; financial award applicants required to submit FAFSA. Total annual research expenditures: $2.1 million. *Unit head:* Dr. Mitchell E. Robinson, Assistant Dean/Director, 423-439-4658, E-mail: robinson@etsu.edu. *Application contact:* Edwin D. Taylor, Assistant Dean for Admissions and Records, 423-439-4753, Fax: 423-439-8206.

Emory University, Laney Graduate School, Division of Biological and Biomedical Sciences, Program in Biochemistry, Cell and Developmental Biology, Atlanta, GA 30322. Offers PhD. *Faculty:* 54 full-time (10 women). *Students:* 60 full-time (41 women); includes 3 Black or African American, non-Hispanic/Latino; 3 Asian, non-Hispanic/Latino; 1 Hispanic/Latino, 15 international. Average age 27. 214 applicants, 12% accepted, 11 enrolled. In 2010, 10 doctorates awarded. *Degree requirements:* For doctorate, comprehensive exam, thesis/dissertation. *Entrance requirements:* For doctorate, GRE General Test, minimum GPA of 3.0 in science course work (recommended). Additional exam requirements/recommendations for international students: Required—TOEFL. *Application deadline:* For fall admission, 1/3 for domestic students, 1/1 for international students. Application fee: $75. Electronic applications accepted. *Expenses:* Tuition: Full-time $33,800. Required fees: $1300. *Financial support:* In 2010–11, 19 students received support, including 19 fellowships with full tuition reimbursements available (averaging $25,000 per year); institutionally sponsored loans, scholarships/grants, health care benefits, and tuition waivers (full) also available. *Faculty research:* Signal transduction, molecular biology, enzymes and cofactors, receptor and ion channel function, membrane biology. *Unit head:* Dr. Richard Kahn, Program Director, 404-727-3561, Fax: 404-727-3746, E-mail: rkahn@emory.edu. *Application contact:* Kathy Smith, Director of Recruitment and Admissions, 404-727-2547, Fax: 404-727-3322, E-mail: kathy.smith@emory.edu.

Florida Institute of Technology, Graduate Programs, College of Science, Department of Chemistry, Melbourne, FL 32901-6975. Offers biochemistry (MS); chemistry (MS, PhD). Part-time programs available. *Faculty:* 6 full-time (0 women). *Students:* 33 full-time (13 women), 2 part-time (1 woman); includes 1 minority (Black or African American, non-Hispanic/Latino), 23 international. Average age 28. 59 applicants, 59% accepted, 14 enrolled. In 2010, 4 master's, 1 doctorate awarded. Terminal master's awarded for partial completion of doctoral program. *Degree requirements:* For master's, comprehensive exam, research proposal, thesis and oral examination in defense of the thesis, proficiency examination; for doctorate, comprehensive exam, thesis/dissertation, oral defense of dissertation, dissertation research publishable to standards, complete original research study. *Entrance requirements:* For master's, proficiency exams, minimum GPA of 3.0; for doctorate, minimum GPA of 3.3, resume, 3 letters of recommendation, statement of objectives. Additional exam requirements/recommendations for international students: Required—TOEFL (minimum score 550 paper-based; 213 computer-based; 79 iBT). *Application deadline:* For fall admission, 4/1 for international students; for spring admission, 9/30 for international students. Applications are processed on a rolling basis. Application fee: $50. Electronic applications accepted. *Expenses:* Tuition: Part-time $1040 per credit hour. Tuition and fees vary according to campus/location. *Financial support:* In 2010–11, 5 research assistantships with full and partial tuition reimbursements (averaging $13,581 per year), 15 teaching assistantships with full and partial tuition reimbursements (averaging $10,973 per year) were awarded; career-related internships or fieldwork, institutionally sponsored loans, tuition waivers (partial), unspecified assistantships, and tuition remissions also available. Support available to part-time students. Financial award application deadline: 3/1; financial award applicants required to submit FAFSA. *Faculty research:* Energy storage applications, marine and organic chemistry, stereochemistry, medicinal chemistry, environmental chemistry. Total annual research expenditures: $718,486. *Unit head:* Dr. Michael W. Babich, Department Head, 321-674-8046, Fax: 321-674-8951, E-mail: babich@fit.edu. *Application contact:* Cheryl A. Brown, Associate Director of Graduate Admissions, 321-674-7581, Fax: 321-723-9468, E-mail: cbrown@fit.edu.

Florida State University, The Graduate School, College of Arts and Sciences, Department of Chemistry and Biochemistry, Specialization in Biochemistry, Tallahassee, FL 32306-4390. Offers MS, PhD. *Faculty:* 8 full-time (3 women), 1 (woman) part-time/adjunct. *Students:* 25 full-time (11 women), 1 (woman) part-time; includes 1 Black or African American, non-Hispanic/Latino; 1 Hispanic/Latino, 14 international. Average age 25.Terminal master's awarded for partial completion of doctoral program. *Degree requirements:* For master's, comprehensive exam (for some programs), thesis (for some programs), cumulative exams; for doctorate, comprehensive exam (for some programs), thesis/dissertation, cumulative exams. *Entrance requirements:* For master's and doctorate, GRE General Test, minimum B average in undergraduate course work. Additional exam requirements/recommendations for international students: Required—TOEFL (minimum score 550 paper-based; 213 computer-based; 80 iBT). *Application deadline:* For fall admission, 12/15 priority date for domestic and international students; for spring admission, 9/15 priority date for domestic and international students. Applications are processed on a rolling basis. Application fee: $30. Electronic applications accepted. *Expenses:* Tuition, state resident: full-time $8238. *Financial support:* In 2010–11, 25 students received support, including fellowships with tuition reimbursements available (averaging $20,000 per year), research assistantships with tuition reimbursements available (averaging $20,000 per year), teaching assistantships with tuition reimbursements available (averaging $20,000 per year); traineeships also available. Financial award application deadline: 12/15; financial award applicants required to submit FAFSA. *Faculty research:* Metalloenzymes, gene regulation, DNA structure, NMR of synthetic membranes, secondary metabolites. *Unit head:* Dr. Timothy Logan, Interim Chairman, 850-644-1244, Fax: 850-644-8281, E-mail: gradinfo@chem.fsu.edu. *Application contact:* Dr. Tyler McQuade, Chair, Graduate Admissions Committee, 888-525-9281, Fax: 850-644-0465, E-mail: gradinfo@chem.fsu.edu.

Florida State University, The Graduate School, College of Arts and Sciences, Program in Molecular Biophysics, Tallahassee, FL 32306. Offers biochemistry, molecular and cell biology (PhD); computational structural biology (PhD); molecular biophysics (PhD). *Faculty:* 49 full-time (6 women). *Students:* 22 full-time (8 women); includes 5 Asian, non-Hispanic/Latino; 1 Hispanic/Latino. Average age 28. 30 applicants, 33% accepted, 7 enrolled. In 2010, 5 doctorates awarded. *Degree requirements:* For doctorate, comprehensive exam, thesis/dissertation, teaching 1 term in professor's major department. *Entrance requirements:* For doctorate, GRE General Test. Additional exam requirements/recommendations for international students: Required—TOEFL (minimum score 600 paper-based; 250 computer-based; 100 iBT). *Application deadline:* For fall admission, 2/15 for domestic students, 3/15 for international students; for spring admission, 11/2 for international students. Applications are processed on a rolling basis. Application fee: $30. Electronic applications accepted. *Expenses:* Tuition, state resident: full-time $8238. *Financial support:* In 2010–11, 21 students received support, including fellowships with partial tuition reimbursements available (averaging $21,000 per year), 18 research assistantships with partial tuition reimbursements available (averaging $21,000 per year), 4 teaching assistantships with partial tuition reimbursements available (averaging $21,000 per year); scholarships/grants, health care benefits, and unspecified assistantships also available. Financial award applicants required to submit FAFSA. *Faculty research:* Protein and nucleic acid structure and function, membrane protein structure, computational biophysics, 3-D image reconstruction. Total annual research expenditures: $1.4 million. *Unit head:* Dr. Geoffrey Strouse, Director, 850-644-0056, Fax: 850-644-7244, E-mail: strouse@chem.fsu.edu. *Application contact:* Dr. Kerry Maddox, Academic Coordinator, Graduate Programs, 850-644-1012, Fax: 850-644-7244, E-mail: bkmaddox@sb.fsu.edu.

George Mason University, College of Science, Department of Chemistry and Biochemistry, Fairfax, VA 22030. Offers chemistry (MS); chemistry and biochemistry (PhD). *Faculty:* 18 full-time (3 women), 6 part-time/adjunct (4 women). *Students:* 15 full-time (7 women), 36 part-time (15 women); includes 16 minority (1 Black or African American, non-Hispanic/Latino; 11 Asian, non-Hispanic/Latino; 4 Hispanic/Latino), 4 international. Average age 28. 49 applicants, 51% accepted, 16 enrolled. In 2010, 15 master's awarded. *Degree requirements:* For master's, thesis or alternative. *Entrance requirements:* For master's, GRE General Test, minimum GPA of 3.0 in last 60 hours of course work. Additional exam requirements/recommendations for international students: Required—TOEFL (minimum score 570 paper-based; 230 computer-based; 88 iBT). *Application deadline:* For fall admission, 5/1 for domestic students; for spring admission, 11/1 for domestic students. Application fee: $100. Electronic applications accepted. *Expenses:* Tuition, state resident: full-time $8192; part-time $440 per credit hour. Tuition, nonresident: full-time $22,952; part-time $1055 per credit hour. Required fees: $2364; $99 per credit hour. *Financial support:* In 2010–11, 13 students received support, including 2 fellowships (averaging $18,000 per year), 11 teaching assistantships (averaging $11,804 per year); career-related internships or fieldwork, Federal Work-Study, scholarships/grants, unspecified assistantships, and health care benefits (full-time research or teaching assistantship recipients) also available. Financial award application deadline: 3/1; financial award applicants required to submit FAFSA. Total annual research expenditures: $84,592. *Unit head:* Gregory Foster, Chairperson, 703-993-1070, Fax: 703-993-1055, E-mail: gfoster@gmu.edu. *Application contact:* Dr. Tim Born, Associate Dean for Graduate Programs, 703-993-4171, Fax: 703-993-9034, E-mail: tborn@gmu.edu.

Georgetown University, Graduate School of Arts and Sciences, Department of Chemistry, Washington, DC 20057. Offers analytical chemistry (PhD); biochemistry (PhD); computational chemistry (PhD); inorganic chemistry (PhD); materials chemistry (PhD); organic chemistry (PhD); physical chemistry (PhD); theoretical chemistry (PhD). Terminal master's awarded for partial completion of doctoral program. *Degree requirements:* For doctorate, comprehensive exam, thesis/dissertation. *Entrance requirements:* For doctorate, GRE General Test. Additional exam requirements/recommendations for international students: Required—TOEFL.

Georgetown University, Graduate School of Arts and Sciences, Programs in Biomedical Sciences, Department of Biochemistry and Molecular Biology, Washington, DC 20057. Offers MS, PhD. *Degree requirements:* For doctorate, comprehensive exam, thesis/dissertation. *Entrance requirements:* For doctorate, GRE General Test. Additional exam requirements/recommendations for international students: Required—TOEFL.

The George Washington University, Columbian College of Arts and Sciences, Institute for Biomedical Sciences, Program in Biochemistry and Molecular Genetics, Washington, DC 20037. Offers PhD. *Students:* 8 part-time (5 women). Average age 30. In 2010, 2 doctorates awarded. Terminal master's awarded for partial completion of doctoral program. *Degree requirements:* For doctorate, thesis/dissertation, general exam. *Entrance requirements:* For doctorate, GRE General Test, interview, minimum GPA of 3.0. Additional exam requirements/recommendations for international students: Required—TOEFL (minimum score 600 paper-based; 250 computer-based). *Application deadline:* For fall admission, 12/15 priority date for domestic and international students; for spring admission, 10/1 priority date for domestic and international students. Applications are processed on a rolling basis. Application fee: $75. Electronic applications accepted. *Financial support:* In 2010–11, 4 students received support; fellowships, Federal Work-Study, institutionally sponsored loans, and tuition waivers available. Financial award application deadline: 2/1. *Unit head:* Valerie W. Hu, Director, 202-994-8431, E-mail: valhu@gwu.edu. *Application contact:* Information Contact, 202-994-7120, Fax: 202-994-6100, E-mail: genetics@gwu.edu.

The George Washington University, School of Medicine and Health Sciences, Department of Biochemistry and Molecular Biology, Washington, DC 20037. Offers biochemistry and molecular biology (MS); biochemistry and molecular genetics (PhD); molecular biochemistry and bioinformatics (MS). *Students:* 20 full-time (9 women), 16 part-time (6 women); includes 2 Asian, non-Hispanic/Latino, 20 international. Average age 27. 57 applicants, 88% accepted, 15 enrolled. In 2010, 17 master's awarded. *Degree requirements:* For master's, comprehensive exam; for doctorate, thesis/dissertation, general exam. *Entrance requirements:* For master's, GRE General Test, interview, minimum GPA of 3.0; for doctorate, GRE General Test, minimum GPA of 3.0. Additional exam requirements/recommendations for international students: Required—TOEFL (minimum score 550 paper-based; 213 computer-based). *Application deadline:* For fall admission, 4/1 priority date for domestic and international students; for spring admission, 10/1 priority date for domestic and international students. Application fee: $60. *Financial support:* Fellowships available. Financial award application deadline: 2/1. *Unit head:* Dr. Allan L. Goldstein, Chair, 202-994-3171, E-mail: bcmalg@gwumc.edu. *Application contact:* Information Contact, 202-994-2179, Fax: 202-994-0967, E-mail: gwibs@gwu.edu.

Georgia Health Sciences University, College of Graduate Studies, Program in Biochemistry and Molecular Biology, Augusta, GA 30912. Offers MS, PhD. *Faculty:* 12 full-time (2 women). *Students:* 14 full-time (7 women), 10 international. Average age 27. In 2010, 4 doctorates awarded. *Degree requirements:* For doctorate, comprehensive exam, thesis/dissertation. *Entrance requirements:* For doctorate, GRE General Test. Additional exam requirements/recommendations for international students: Required—TOEFL (minimum score 550 paper-based; 213 computer-based; 79 iBT). *Application deadline:* For fall admission, 1/15 for domestic and international students. Application fee: $30. Electronic applications accepted. *Expenses:* Tuition, state resident: full-time $7500; part-time $313 per semester hour. Tuition, nonresident: full-time $24,772; part-time $1033 per semester hour. Required fees: $1112. *Financial support:* In 2010–11, 8 research assistantships with partial tuition reimbursements (averaging $23,000 per year) were awarded; Federal Work-Study, institutionally sponsored loans, and scholarships/grants also available. Support available to part-time students. Financial award application deadline: 5/31; financial award applicants required to submit FAFSA. *Faculty research:* Bacterial pathogenesis, eye diseases, vitamins and amino acid transporters, transcriptional control and molecular oncology, tumor biology. Total annual research expenditures: $3 million. *Unit head:* Dr. Vadivel Ganapathy, Chair/Professor, 706-721-7652, Fax: 706-721-9947, E-mail: vganapat@georgiahealth.edu. *Application contact:* Dr. Patricia L. Cameron, Acting Vice Dean, 706-721-3279, E-mail: pcameron@georgiahealth.edu.

Georgia Institute of Technology, Graduate Studies and Research, College of Sciences, School of Chemistry and Biochemistry, Atlanta, GA 30332-0001. Offers MS, MS Chem, PhD. Terminal master's awarded for partial completion of doctoral program. *Degree requirements:* For master's, thesis (for some programs); for doctorate, thesis/dissertation. *Entrance requirements:* For master's and doctorate, GRE General Test, GRE Subject Test, minimum GPA of 2.7. Additional exam requirements/recommendations for international students: Required—TOEFL. Electronic applications accepted. *Faculty research:* Inorganic, organic, physical, and analytical chemistry.

Biochemistry

Georgia State University, College of Arts and Sciences, Department of Biology, Program in Molecular Genetics and Biochemistry, Atlanta, GA 30302-3083. Offers MS, PhD. Part-time programs available. Terminal master's awarded for partial completion of doctoral program. *Degree requirements:* For master's, thesis or alternative; for doctorate, thesis/dissertation, exam. *Entrance requirements:* For master's and doctorate, GRE General Test. Additional exam requirements/recommendations for international students: Required—TOEFL. Electronic applications accepted.

Graduate School and University Center of the City University of New York, Graduate Studies, Program in Biochemistry, New York, NY 10016-4039. Offers PhD. *Degree requirements:* For doctorate, thesis/dissertation, field experience. *Entrance requirements:* For doctorate, GRE General Test. Additional exam requirements/recommendations for international students: Required—TOEFL. Electronic applications accepted.

Harvard University, Graduate School of Arts and Sciences, Department of Chemistry and Chemical Biology, Cambridge, MA 02138. Offers biochemical chemistry (PhD); inorganic chemistry (PhD); organic chemistry (PhD); physical chemistry (PhD). *Degree requirements:* For doctorate, thesis/dissertation, cumulative exams. *Entrance requirements:* For doctorate, GRE General Test, GRE Subject Test. Additional exam requirements/recommendations for international students: Required—TOEFL. *Expenses:* Tuition: Full-time $34,976. Required fees: $1166. Full-time tuition and fees vary according to program.

Harvard University, Graduate School of Arts and Sciences, Division of Medical Sciences, Boston, MA 02115. Offers biological chemistry and molecular pharmacology (PhD); cell biology (PhD); genetics (PhD); microbiology and molecular genetics (PhD); pathology (PhD), including experimental pathology. *Degree requirements:* For doctorate, thesis/dissertation. *Entrance requirements:* For doctorate, GRE General Test, GRE Subject Test. Additional exam requirements/recommendations for international students: Required—TOEFL. *Expenses:* Tuition: Full-time $34,976. Required fees: $1166. Full-time tuition and fees vary according to program.

Howard University, College of Medicine, Department of Biochemistry and Molecular Biology, Washington, DC 20059-0002. Offers biochemistry and molecular biology (PhD); biotechnology (MS); MD/PhD. Part-time programs available. *Degree requirements:* For master's, externship; for doctorate, comprehensive exam, thesis/dissertation. *Entrance requirements:* For master's and doctorate, GRE General Test, minimum GPA of 3.0. *Faculty research:* Cellular and molecular biology of olfaction, gene regulation and expression, enzymology, NMR spectroscopy of molecular structure, hormone regulation/metabolism.

Howard University, Graduate School, Department of Chemistry, Washington, DC 20059-0002. Offers analytical chemistry (MS, PhD); atmospheric (MS, PhD); biochemistry (MS, PhD); environmental (MS, PhD); inorganic chemistry (MS, PhD); organic chemistry (MS, PhD); physical chemistry (MS, PhD). Terminal master's awarded for partial completion of doctoral program. *Degree requirements:* For master's, comprehensive exam, thesis, teaching experience; for doctorate, comprehensive exam, thesis/dissertation, teaching experience. *Entrance requirements:* For master's, GRE General Test, minimum GPA of 2.7; for doctorate, GRE General Test, minimum GPA of 3.0. Additional exam requirements/recommendations for international students: Required—TOEFL. Electronic applications accepted. *Faculty research:* Synthetic organics, materials, natural products, mass spectrometry.

Hunter College of the City University of New York, Graduate School, School of Arts and Sciences, Department of Chemistry, Program in Biochemistry, New York, NY 10021-5085. Offers MA, PhD. Part-time programs available. *Faculty:* 1 (woman) full-time. *Students:* 13 part-time (7 women); includes 3 Asian, non-Hispanic/Latino; 1 Hispanic/Latino, 6 international. Average age 24. 10 applicants, 60% accepted, 2 enrolled. *Degree requirements:* For master's, comprehensive exam or thesis. *Entrance requirements:* For master's, GRE General Test, 1 year of course work in chemistry, quantitative analysis, organic chemistry, physical chemistry, biology, biochemistry lecture and laboratory. Additional exam requirements/recommendations for international students: Required—TOEFL. *Application deadline:* For fall admission, 4/1 for domestic students; for spring admission, 11/1 for domestic students. Application fee: $125. *Financial support:* Teaching assistantships, Federal Work-Study, scholarships/grants, and tuition waivers (partial) available. Support available to part-time students. *Faculty research:* Protein/nucleic acid interactions, physical properties of iron-sulfur proteins, neurotransmitter receptors and ion channels Drosophila melanogaster, requirements of DNA synthesis, oncogenes. *Unit head:* Yuiia Xu, Adviser, 212-772-4310. *Application contact:* William Zlata, Director for Graduate Admissions, 212-772-4482, Fax: 212-650-3336, E-mail: admissions@hunter.cuny.edu.

Illinois Institute of Technology, Graduate College, College of Science and Letters, Department of Biological, Chemical and Physical Sciences, Biology Division, Chicago, IL 60616. Offers biochemistry (MBS, MS); biology (PhD); biotechnology (MBS, MS); cell and molecular biology (MBS, MS); microbiology (MB, MS); molecular biochemistry and biophysics (PhD); molecular biology and biophysics (MS). Part-time and evening/weekend programs available. Postbaccalaureate distance learning degree programs offered (minimal on-campus study). *Faculty:* 13 full-time (5 women), 5 part-time/adjunct (2 women). *Students:* 121 full-time (75 women), 56 part-time (37 women); includes 16 minority (5 Black or African American, non-Hispanic/Latino; 5 Asian, non-Hispanic/Latino; 5 Hispanic/Latino; 1 Two or more races, non-Hispanic/Latino), 104 international. Average age 27. 268 applicants, 76% accepted, 62 enrolled. In 2010, 74 master's, 4 doctorates awarded. Terminal master's awarded for partial completion of doctoral program. *Degree requirements:* For master's, comprehensive exam, thesis (for some programs); for doctorate, comprehensive exam, thesis/dissertation. *Entrance requirements:* For master's, GRE General Test (minimum score 1000 Quantitative and Verbal, 2.5 Analytical Writing), minimum undergraduate GPA of 3.0; for doctorate, GRE General Test (minimum score 1200 Quantitative and Verbal, 3.0 Analytical Writing), minimum undergraduate GPA of 3.0. Additional exam requirements/recommendations for international students: Required—TOEFL (minimum score 523 paper-based; 213 computer-based; 70 iBT); Recommended—IELTS (minimum score 5.5). *Application deadline:* For fall admission, 5/1 for domestic and international students; for spring admission, 10/15 for domestic and international students. Applications are processed on a rolling basis. Application fee: $40. Electronic applications accepted. *Expenses:* Tuition: Full-time $18,576; part-time $1032 per credit hour. Required fees: $583 per semester. One-time fee: $150. Tuition and fees vary according to program and student level. *Financial support:* In 2010–11, 15 research assistantships with full and partial tuition reimbursements (averaging $6,379 per year), 14 teaching assistantships with partial tuition reimbursements (averaging $6,296 per year) were awarded; fellowships with full and partial tuition reimbursements, career-related internships or fieldwork, Federal Work-Study, institutionally sponsored loans, scholarships/grants, traineeships, health care benefits, tuition waivers (partial), and unspecified assistantships also available. Support available to part-time students. Financial award applicants required to submit FAFSA. *Faculty research:* Structure and biophysics of macromolecular systems; efficacy and mechanism of action of chemopreventive agents in experimental carcinogenesis of breast, colon, lung and prostate; study of fundamental structural biochemistry problems that have direct links to the understanding and treatment of disease; spectroscopic techniques for the study of multi-domain proteins; molecular mechanisms of cancer and cancer gene therapy. Total annual research expenditures: $2.6 million. *Unit head:* Dr. Benjamin C. Stark, Professor and Associate Chair, 312-567-3488, Fax: 312-567-3494, E-mail: starkb@iit.edu. *Application contact:* Deborah Gibson, Director, Graduate Admissions, 866-472-3448, Fax: 312-567-3138, E-mail: inquiry.grad@iit.edu.

Illinois State University, Graduate School, College of Arts and Sciences, Department of Biological Sciences, Normal, IL 61790-2200. Offers animal behavior (MS); bacteriology (MS); biochemistry (MS); biological sciences (MS); biology (PhD); biophysics (MS); biotechnology (MS); botany (MS, PhD); cell biology (MS); conservation biology (MS); developmental biology (MS); ecology (MS, PhD); entomology (MS); evolutionary biology (MS); genetics (MS, PhD); immunology (MS); microbiology (MS, PhD); molecular biology (MS); molecular genetics (MS); neurobiology (MS); neuroscience (MS); parasitology (MS); physiology (MS, PhD); plant biology (MS); plant molecular biology (MS); plant sciences (MS); structural biology (MS); zoology (MS, PhD). Part-time programs available. *Degree requirements:* For master's, thesis or alternative; for doctorate, variable foreign language requirement, thesis/dissertation, 2 terms of residency. *Entrance requirements:* For master's, GRE General Test, minimum GPA of 2.6 in last 60 hours of course work; for doctorate, GRE General Test. *Faculty research:* Redoc balance and drug development in schistosoma mansoni, control of the growth of listeria monocytogenes at low temperature, regulation of cell expansion and microtubule function by SPRI, CRUI: physiology and fitness consequences of different life history phenotypes.

Indiana University Bloomington, University Graduate School, College of Arts and Sciences, Department of Chemistry, Bloomington, IN 47405. Offers analytical chemistry (PhD); chemical biology chemistry (PhD); chemistry (MAT); inorganic chemistry (PhD); materials chemistry (PhD); organic chemistry (PhD); physical chemistry (PhD). *Faculty:* 42 full-time (4 women). *Students:* 224 full-time (77 women); includes 19 minority (7 Black or African American, non-Hispanic/Latino; 1 American Indian or Alaska Native, non-Hispanic/Latino; 8 Asian, non-Hispanic/Latino; 3 Hispanic/Latino), 68 international. Average age 27. 270 applicants, 39% accepted, 31 enrolled. In 2010, 1 master's, 20 doctorates awarded. Terminal master's awarded for partial completion of doctoral program. *Degree requirements:* For master's, thesis; for doctorate, thesis/dissertation. *Entrance requirements:* For master's and doctorate, GRE General Test, GRE Subject Test. Additional exam requirements/recommendations for international students: Required—TOEFL. *Application deadline:* For fall admission, 1/15 priority date for domestic students, 12/15 for international students. Applications are processed on a rolling basis. Application fee: $55 ($65 for international students). *Financial support:* In 2010–11, 200 students received support, including 10 fellowships with full tuition reimbursements available, 76 research assistantships with full tuition reimbursements available, 111 teaching assistantships with full tuition reimbursements available; Federal Work-Study and institutionally sponsored loans also available. *Faculty research:* Synthesis of complex natural products, organic reaction mechanisms, organic electrochemistry, transitive-metal chemistry, solid-state and surface chemistry. Total annual research expenditures: $7.7 million. *Unit head:* David Giedroc, Chairperson, 812-855-6239, E-mail: chemchair@indiana.edu. *Application contact:* Daneil Mindiola, Director of Graduate Admissions, 812-855-2069, Fax: 812-855-8385, E-mail: mindiola@indiana.edu.

Indiana University Bloomington, University Graduate School, College of Arts and Sciences, Interdisciplinary Biochemistry Graduate Program, Bloomington, IN 47405-7000. Offers PhD. *Faculty:* 52 full-time (14 women). *Students:* 56 full-time (29 women); includes 7 minority (3 Black or African American, non-Hispanic/Latino; 1 American Indian or Alaska Native, non-Hispanic/Latino; 1 Asian, non-Hispanic/Latino; 1 Hispanic/Latino; 1 Two or more races, non-Hispanic/Latino), 31 international. Average age 26. 149 applicants, 9% accepted, 2 enrolled. In 2010, 2 doctorates awarded. Terminal master's awarded for partial completion of doctoral program. *Degree requirements:* For doctorate, comprehensive exam, thesis/dissertation, Test of English Proficiency for International Associate Instructor Candidates (TEPAIC)(for international students). *Entrance requirements:* For doctorate, GRE. Additional exam requirements/recommendations for international students: Required—TOEFL (minimum score 550 paper-based; 213 computer-based; 79 iBT). *Application deadline:* For fall admission, 1/15 priority date for domestic students, 12/1 priority date for international students. Application fee: $55 ($65 for international students). Electronic applications accepted. *Financial support:* In 2010–11, 2 students received support, including 2 fellowships with full tuition reimbursements available (averaging $25,000 per year), 21 research assistantships with full tuition reimbursements available (averaging $20,500 per year), 27 teaching assistantships with full tuition reimbursements available (averaging $20,521 per year); scholarships/grants and tuition waivers (full) also available. *Faculty research:* Microbial biochemistry and virology, structural biology, chemical biology, cellular and medicinal biochemistry. *Unit head:* Dr. Carl E. Bauer, Chair, Molecular and Cellular Biochemistry Department, 812-856-0192, Fax: 812-856-5710, E-mail: bchem@indiana.edu. *Application contact:* Susanne Kindred, Administrative Assistant, 812-856-1301, Fax: 812-856-5710, E-mail: bchem@indiana.edu.

Indiana University–Purdue University Indianapolis, Indiana University School of Medicine, Department of Biochemistry and Molecular Biology, Indianapolis, IN 46202-2896. Offers PhD, MD/MS, MD/PhD. *Faculty:* 17 full-time (4 women). *Students:* 43 full-time (23 women), 13 part-time (8 women); includes 5 minority (1 Black or African American, non-Hispanic/Latino; 3 Asian, non-Hispanic/Latino; 1 Hispanic/Latino), 21 international. Average age 32. 13 applicants, 62% accepted, 8 enrolled. In 2010, 12 doctorates awarded. Terminal master's awarded for partial completion of doctoral program. *Degree requirements:* For doctorate, thesis/dissertation. *Entrance requirements:* For doctorate, GRE General Test, GRE Subject Test (recommended), previous course work in organic chemistry. *Application deadline:* For fall admission, 1/15 priority date for domestic students. Applications are processed on a rolling basis. Application fee: $55 ($65 for international students). *Financial support:* In 2010–11, 8 teaching assistantships (averaging $14,949 per year) were awarded; fellowships with tuition reimbursements, research assistantships with tuition reimbursements, Federal Work-Study, institutionally sponsored loans, scholarships/grants, and tuition waivers (partial) also available. Support available to part-time students. Financial award application deadline: 2/1. *Faculty research:* Metabolic regulation, enzymology, peptide and protein chemistry, cell biology, signal transduction. *Unit head:* Dr. Zhong-Yin Zhang, Chairman, 317-274-7151. *Application contact:* Dr. Zhong-Yin Zhang, Chairman, 317-274-7151.

Indiana University–Purdue University Indianapolis, School of Science, Department of Chemistry and Chemical Biology, Indianapolis, IN 46202-2896. Offers MS, PhD, MD/PhD. MD/PhD offered jointly with Indiana University School of Medicine and Purdue University. Part-time and evening/weekend programs available. *Faculty:* 10 full-time (2 women). *Students:* 19 full-time (7 women), 20 part-time (7 women); includes 5 minority (2 Asian, non-Hispanic/Latino; 1 Hispanic/Latino; 2 Two or more races, non-Hispanic/Latino), 8 international. Average age 31. 14 applicants, 79% accepted, 11 enrolled. In 2010, 7 master's awarded. Terminal master's awarded for partial completion of doctoral program. *Degree requirements:* For master's, thesis (for some programs); for doctorate, thesis/dissertation. *Entrance requirements:* For master's and doctorate, minimum GPA of 3.0. Additional exam requirements/recommendations for international students: Required—TOEFL. *Application deadline:* Applications are processed on a rolling basis. Application fee: $55 ($65 for international students). *Financial support:* In 2010–11, 3 fellowships with partial tuition reimbursements (averaging $13,500 per year), 13 teaching assistantships with partial tuition reimbursements (averaging $17,440 per year) were awarded; research assistantships with partial tuition reimbursements, career-related internships or fieldwork, institutionally sponsored loans, tuition waivers (partial), and cooperative positions also available. Financial award application deadline: 3/1. *Faculty research:* Analytical, biological, inorganic, organic, and physical chemistry. Total annual research expenditures: $1.6 million. *Unit head:* Jay A. Siegel, Chair, 317-274-6872. *Application contact:* Eric Long, Associate Chair, 317-274-6888, Fax: 317-274-4701, E-mail: long@chem.iupui.edu.

Iowa State University of Science and Technology, Graduate College, College of Agriculture and College of Liberal Arts and Sciences, Department of Biochemistry, Biophysics, and Molecular Biology, Ames, IA 50011. Offers biochemistry (MS, PhD); biophysics (MS, PhD); genetics (MS, PhD); molecular, cellular, and developmental biology (MS, PhD); toxicology (MS, PhD). *Faculty:* 31 full-time (7 women), 1 (woman) part-time/adjunct. *Students:* 81 full-time (33 women), 11 part-time (6 women); includes 2 Black or African American, non-Hispanic/Latino; 2 Asian, non-Hispanic/Latino, 58 international. 38 applicants, 29% accepted, 8 enrolled. In 2010, 3 master's, 9 doctorates awarded. *Degree requirements:* For master's, thesis; for doctorate, thesis/dissertation. *Entrance requirements:* For master's and doctorate, GRE General Test. Additional exam requirements/recommendations for international students: Required—TOEFL (minimum score 550 paper-based; 79 iBT), IELTS (minimum score 6.5). *Application deadline:* For fall admission, 1/15 priority date for domestic and international students; for spring admission, 10/15 for domestic and international students. Application fee: $40 ($90 for international students). Electronic applications accepted. *Financial support:* In 2010–11, 67 research assistantships with full and partial tuition reimbursements (averaging $17,228 per year) were awarded; teaching assistantships with full and partial tuition reimbursements, scholarships/grants, health care benefits, and unspecified assistantships also available. *Unit*

GRADUATE PROGRAMS IN BIOCHEMISTRY AND BIOPHYSICS

DEPARTMENT OF BIOCHEMISTRY, BIOPHYSICS, AND MOLECULAR BIOLOGY

IOWA STATE UNIVERSITY
OF SCIENCE AND TECHNOLOGY

The Department of Biochemistry, Biophysics, and Molecular Biology (BBMB) is a **research** and **teaching** organization with the overall goal of **understanding the molecular mechanisms** of living systems in terms of fundamental chemical and physical principles.

Basic research is the hallmark of the departmental mission, providing the knowledge that is essential for continued progress in the applied agricultural and biomedical sciences. Graduate students pursuing M.S. or Ph.D. degrees in our department develop into scientists capable of performing independent research, teaching, and related activities that require practical as well as theoretical applications of biochemistry, biophysics and molecular biology. Research conducted in the department covers a broad spectrum, from the isolation and characterization of biomolecules to the study of the control of processes in living organisms.

For more information contact:
BBMB Graduate Program Admissions Office
Department of Biochemistry, Biophysics & Molecular Biology
Iowa State University
1210 Molecular Biology Building
Ames, IA 50011
Phone: (515) 294-3317 or
(800) 433-3464 (toll free)
FAX: (515) 294-0453
Email: biochem0@iastate.edu

head: Dr. Guru Rao, Interim Chair, 515-294-6116, E-mail: biochem@iastate.edu. *Application contact:* Dr. Reuben Peters, Director of Graduate Education, 515-294-6116, E-mail: biochem@iastate.edu.

See Display on this page and Close-Up on page 147.

The Johns Hopkins University, Bloomberg School of Public Health, Department of Biochemistry and Molecular Biology, Baltimore, MD 21205. Offers MHS, Sc M, PhD. Part-time programs available. *Faculty:* 16 full-time (3 women), 5 part-time/adjunct (3 women). *Students:* 64 full-time (41 women), 3 part-time (1 woman); includes 1 Black or African American, non-Hispanic/Latino; 9 Asian, non-Hispanic/Latino; 3 Hispanic/Latino, 8 international. Average age 25. 108 applicants, 47% accepted, 26 enrolled. In 2010, 27 master's, 6 doctorates awarded. *Degree requirements:* For master's, thesis; for doctorate, comprehensive exam, thesis/dissertation, oral and written exams. *Entrance requirements:* For master's, MCAT or GRE, 3 letters of recommendation, curriculum vitae; for doctorate, GRE General Test, 3 letters of recommendation, curriculum vitae. Additional exam requirements/recommendations for international students: Required—TOEFL (minimum score 600 paper-based; 250 computer-based). *Application deadline:* For fall admission, 12/15 priority date for domestic students, 12/15 for international students; for spring admission, 6/1 for domestic and international students. Applications are processed on a rolling basis. Application fee: $45. Electronic applications accepted. *Financial support:* In 2010–11, 63 students received support, including 17 fellowships with tuition reimbursements available (averaging $26,800 per year), 19 research assistantships with tuition reimbursements available (averaging $26,800 per year), 7 teaching assistantships (averaging $1,000 per year); Federal Work-Study, institutionally sponsored loans, scholarships/grants, health care benefits, and stipends also available. Financial award application deadline: 3/15; financial award applicants required to submit FAFSA. *Faculty research:* DNA replication, repair, structure, carcinogenesis, protein structure, enzyme catalysts, reproductive biology. Total annual research expenditures: $6 million. *Unit head:* Dr. Pierre Coulombe, Chairman, 410-955-3671, Fax: 410-955-2926, E-mail: pcoulomb@jhsph.edu. *Application contact:* Sharon Warner, Senior Academic Program Administrator, 410-955-3672, Fax: 410-955-2926, E-mail: swarner@jhsph.edu.

The Johns Hopkins University, National Institutes of Health Sponsored Programs, Baltimore, MD 21218-2699. Offers biology (PhD), including biochemistry, biophysics, cell biology, developmental biology, genetic biology, molecular biology; cell, molecular, and developmental biology and biophysics (PhD). *Degree requirements:* For doctorate, comprehensive exam, thesis/dissertation. *Entrance requirements:* For doctorate, GRE General Test. Additional exam requirements/recommendations for international students: Required—TOEFL (minimum score 600 paper-based; 250 computer-based), TWE. Electronic applications accepted. *Faculty research:* Protein and nucleic acid biochemistry and biophysical chemistry, molecular biology and development.

The Johns Hopkins University, School of Medicine, Graduate Programs in Medicine, Department of Biological Chemistry, Baltimore, MD 21205. Offers PhD. *Faculty:* 16 full-time (5 women). *Students:* 24 full-time (11 women), 20 international. Average age 31. 66 applicants, 9% accepted, 3 enrolled. In 2010, 4 doctorates awarded. *Degree requirements:* For doctorate, thesis/dissertation. *Entrance requirements:* For doctorate, GRE General Test. Additional exam requirements/recommendations for international students: Required—TOEFL. *Application deadline:* For winter admission, 1/15 priority date for domestic and international students. Application fee: $75. Electronic applications accepted. *Financial support:* In 2010–11, 22 research assistantships (averaging $27,125 per year) were awarded; health care benefits and tuition waivers (full) also available. Financial award application deadline: 1/1. *Faculty research:* Cell adhesion, genetics, signal transduction and RNA metabolism, enzyme structure and function, gene expression. *Unit head:* Dr. Denise Montell, Co-Director, 410-614-2016, Fax: 410-614-8375, E-mail: dmontell@jhmi.edu. *Application contact:* Wendy Seno, Program Coordinator, 410-614-2976, Fax: 410-614-8375, E-mail: wendy@jnmi.edu.

The Johns Hopkins University, School of Medicine, Graduate Programs in Medicine, Program in Biochemistry, Cellular and Molecular Biology, Baltimore, MD 21205. Offers PhD. *Faculty:* 101 full-time (35 women). *Students:* 153 full-time (88 women); includes 29 minority (8 Black or African American, non-Hispanic/Latino; 1 American Indian or Alaska Native, non-Hispanic/Latino; 15 Asian, non-Hispanic/Latino; 4 Hispanic/Latino; 1 Two or more races, non-Hispanic/Latino), 54 international. Average age 25. 299 applicants, 19% accepted, 18 enrolled. In 2010, 20 doctorates awarded. *Degree requirements:* For doctorate, comprehensive exam, thesis/dissertation. *Entrance requirements:* For doctorate, GRE General Test. Additional exam requirements/recommendations for international students: Required—TOEFL. *Application deadline:* For winter admission, 1/10 for domestic and international students. Applications are processed on a rolling basis. Application fee: $80. Electronic applications accepted. *Financial support:* In 2010–11, 5 fellowships with partial tuition reimbursements (averaging $32,000 per year), 144 research assistantships with full and partial tuition reimbursements (averaging $27,125 per year) were awarded; traineeships and tuition waivers (full) also available. Financial award application deadline: 12/31. *Faculty research:* Developmental biology, genomics/proteomics, protein targeting, signal transduction, structural biology. *Unit head:* Dr. Carolyn Machamer, Director, 410-955-3466, Fax: 410-614-8842, E-mail: machamer@jhmi.edu. *Application contact:* Dr. Jeff Corden, Admissions Director, 410-955-3506, Fax: 410-614-8842, E-mail: jcorden@jhmi.edu.

Kansas State University, Graduate School, College of Arts and Sciences, Department of Biochemistry, Manhattan, KS 66506. Offers MS, PhD. Part-time programs available. *Degree requirements:* For master's, thesis; for doctorate, thesis/dissertation. *Entrance requirements:* For master's, GRE General Test, minimum GPA of 3.0 for junior and senior year; for doctorate, GRE General Test, minimum undergraduate GPA of 3.0 or an excellent postgraduate record. Additional exam requirements/recommendations for international students: Required—TOEFL (minimum score 550 paper-based; 213 computer-based). Electronic applications accepted. *Faculty research:* Protein structure/function, insect biochemistry, cellular signaling cascades, environmental biochemistry, biochemistry of vision.

Kansas State University, Graduate School, College of Arts and Sciences, Department of Chemistry, Manhattan, KS 66506. Offers analytical chemistry (MS); biological chemistry (MS); chemistry (PhD); inorganic chemistry (MS); materials chemistry (MS); organic chemistry (MS); physical chemistry (MS). Terminal master's awarded for partial completion of doctoral program. *Degree requirements:* For master's, thesis; for doctorate, thesis/dissertation. *Entrance requirements:* For master's and doctorate, GRE, minimum GPA of 3.0. Additional exam requirements/recommendations for international students: Required—TOEFL (minimum score 550 paper-based; 213 computer-based). Electronic applications accepted. *Faculty research:* Inorganic chemistry, organic and biological chemistry, analytical chemistry, physical chemistry, materials chemistry and nanotechnology.

Kent State University, College of Arts and Sciences, Department of Chemistry and Biochemistry, Kent, OH 44242-0001. Offers analytical chemistry (MS, PhD); biochemistry (MS, PhD); chemistry (MA); inorganic chemistry (MS, PhD); organic chemistry (MS, PhD); physical chemistry (MS, PhD). Terminal master's awarded for partial completion of doctoral program. *Degree requirements:* For master's, comprehensive exam, thesis; for doctorate, comprehensive exam, thesis/dissertation. *Entrance requirements:* For master's and doctorate, placement exam, GRE General Test, GRE Subject Test (recommended), minimum GPA of 2.75. Additional exam requirements/recommendations for international students: Required—TOEFL (minimum score 525 paper-based; 71 iBT). Electronic applications accepted. *Expenses:* Tuition, state resident: full-time $7866; part-time $437 per credit hour. Tuition, nonresident: full-time $14,022; part-time $779 per credit hour. *Faculty research:* Biological chemistry, materials chemistry, molecular spectroscopy.

Laurentian University, School of Graduate Studies and Research, Programme in Chemistry and Biochemistry, Sudbury, ON P3E 2C6, Canada. Offers analytical chemistry (M Sc); biochemistry (M Sc); environmental chemistry (M Sc); organic chemistry (M Sc); physical/

Biochemistry

Laurentian University (continued)
theoretical chemistry (M Sc). Part-time programs available. *Degree requirements:* For master's, thesis or alternative. *Entrance requirements:* For master's, honors degree with minimum second class. *Faculty research:* Cell cycle checkpoints, kinetic modeling, toxicology to metal stress, quantum chemistry, biogeochemistry metal speciation.

Lehigh University, College of Arts and Sciences, Department of Biological Sciences, Bethlehem, PA 18015. Offers biochemistry (PhD); integrative biology and neuroscience (PhD); molecular biology (MS, PhD). Part-time programs available. Postbaccalaureate distance learning degree programs offered (no on-campus study). *Faculty:* 17 full-time (7 women). *Students:* 30 full-time (14 women), 30 part-time (18 women); includes 6 minority (1 Black or African American, non-Hispanic/Latino; 1 Asian, non-Hispanic/Latino; 3 Hispanic/Latino; 1 Native Hawaiian or other Pacific Islander, non-Hispanic/Latino), 7 international. Average age 29. 79 applicants, 25% accepted, 19 enrolled. In 2010, 9 master's, 3 doctorates awarded. Terminal master's awarded for partial completion of doctoral program. *Degree requirements:* For master's, research report; for doctorate, comprehensive exam, thesis/dissertation. *Entrance requirements:* For doctorate, GRE General Test. Additional exam requirements/recommendations for international students: Required—TOEFL. *Application deadline:* For fall admission, 12/15 for domestic and international students. Applications are processed on a rolling basis. Application fee: $65. Electronic applications accepted. *Financial support:* In 2010–11, 31 students received support, including 4 fellowships with full tuition reimbursements available (averaging $24,500 per year), 6 research assistantships with full tuition reimbursements available (averaging $23,750 per year), 16 teaching assistantships with full tuition reimbursements available (averaging $23,750 per year); scholarships/grants and unspecified assistantships also available. Financial award application deadline: 12/15. *Faculty research:* Gene expression, cytoskeleton and cell structure, cell cycle and growth regulation, neuroscience, animal behavior, microbiology. Total annual research expenditures: $2.4 million. *Unit head:* Dr. Murray Itzkowitz, Chairperson, 610-758-3680, Fax: 610-758-4004, E-mail: mi00@lehigh.edu. *Application contact:* Dr. Jennifer M. Swann, Graduate Coordinator, 610-758-5484, Fax: 610-758-4004, E-mail: jms5@lehigh.edu.

Loma Linda University, School of Medicine, Department of Biochemistry/Microbiology, Loma Linda, CA 92350. Offers MS, PhD. Part-time programs available. *Degree requirements:* For master's, thesis or alternative; for doctorate, thesis/dissertation. *Entrance requirements:* For master's and doctorate, GRE General Test. Additional exam requirements/recommendations for international students: Required—TOEFL (minimum score 550 paper-based; 213 computer-based). *Faculty research:* Physical chemistry of macromolecules, biochemistry of endocrine system, biochemical mechanism of bone volume regulation.

Louisiana State University and Agricultural and Mechanical College, Graduate School, College of Basic Sciences, Department of Biological Sciences, Baton Rouge, LA 70803. Offers biochemistry (MS, PhD); biological science (MS, PhD); science (MNS). Part-time programs available. *Faculty:* 61 full-time (6 women). *Students:* 133 full-time (62 women), 6 part-time (3 women); includes 1 Black or African American, non-Hispanic/Latino; 5 Asian, non-Hispanic/Latino; 3 Hispanic/Latino; 1 Two or more races, non-Hispanic/Latino, 58 international. Average age 29. 156 applicants, 16% accepted, 12 enrolled. In 2010, 6 master's, 20 doctorates awarded. Terminal master's awarded for partial completion of doctoral program. *Degree requirements:* For doctorate, thesis/dissertation. *Entrance requirements:* For master's and doctorate, GRE General Test, minimum GPA of 3.0. Additional exam requirements/recommendations for international students: Required—TOEFL (minimum score 550 paper-based; 213 computer-based; 79 iBT) or IELTS (minimum score 6.5). *Application deadline:* For fall admission, 5/15 for domestic and international students; for spring admission, 10/15 for domestic and international students. Applications are processed on a rolling basis. Application fee: $25. Electronic applications accepted. *Financial support:* In 2010–11, 138 students received support, including 15 fellowships with full and partial tuition reimbursements available (averaging $17,743 per year), 43 research assistantships with full and partial tuition reimbursements available (averaging $20,949 per year), 74 teaching assistantships with full and partial tuition reimbursements available (averaging $18,724 per year); Federal Work-Study, institutionally sponsored loans, health care benefits, and unspecified assistantships also available. Support available to part-time students. Financial award applicants required to submit FAFSA. *Faculty research:* Biochemistry and molecular biology, cell developmental and integrative biology, systematics, ecology and evolutionary biology. Total annual research expenditures: $979,438. *Unit head:* Dr. James Moroney, Chair, 225-578-1765, Fax: 225-578-2597. *Application contact:* Dr. Jacqueline Stephens, Associate Chairman, 225-578-1240, Fax: 225-578-7299, E-mail: biogradcoord@lsu.edu.

Louisiana State University Health Sciences Center at Shreveport, Department of Biochemistry and Molecular Biology, Shreveport, LA 71130-3932. Offers MS, PhD, MD/PhD. *Degree requirements:* For master's, thesis; for doctorate, thesis/dissertation. *Entrance requirements:* For master's and doctorate, GRE General Test. Additional exam requirements/recommendations for international students: Required—TOEFL. *Faculty research:* Metabolite transport, regulation of translation and transcription, prokaryotic molecular genetics, cell matrix biochemistry, yeast molecular genetics, oncogenes.

Loyola University Chicago, Graduate School, Program in Molecular and Cellular Biochemistry, Chicago, IL 60660. Offers MS, PhD, MD/PhD. *Faculty:* 23 full-time (11 women). *Students:* 14 full-time (8 women); includes 1 minority (Asian, non-Hispanic/Latino), 7 international. Average age 28. 31 applicants, 13% accepted, 3 enrolled. In 2010, 1 master's, 2 doctorates awarded. *Degree requirements:* For master's, oral and written reports; for doctorate, comprehensive exam, thesis/dissertation. *Entrance requirements:* For master's and doctorate, GRE General Test. Additional exam requirements/recommendations for international students: Required—TOEFL (minimum score 600 paper-based; 250 computer-based). *Application deadline:* For fall admission, 3/30 priority date for domestic students, 3/30 for international students. Applications are processed on a rolling basis. Application fee: $50. Electronic applications accepted. *Expenses:* Tuition: Full-time $14,940; part-time $830 per credit hour. Required fees: $87 per semester. Part-time tuition and fees vary according to course load and program. *Financial support:* In 2010–11, 5 students received support, including 5 fellowships with full tuition reimbursements available, 11 research assistantships with full tuition reimbursements available; Federal Work-Study, institutionally sponsored loans, and scholarships/grants also available. Financial award application deadline: 3/30. *Faculty research:* Molecular oncology, molecular neurochemical mechanisms of brain development and alcohol addiction, biochemistry of RNA and protein synthesis and intracellular protein degradation, developmentally regulated genes, neurotransmitters and cell-cell interactions. *Unit head:* Dr. William H. Simmons, Chief, 708-216-3362, Fax: 708-216-8523, E-mail: hsimmon@lumc.edu. *Application contact:* Ashyia D. Paul, Administrative Secretary, 708-216-3360, Fax: 708-216-8523, E-mail: apaul@lumc.edu.

Massachusetts Institute of Technology, School of Science, Department of Biology, Cambridge, MA 02139-4307. Offers biochemistry (PhD); biological oceanography (PhD); biology (PhD); biophysical chemistry and molecular structure (PhD); cell biology (PhD); computational and systems biology (PhD); developmental biology (PhD); genetics (PhD); immunology (PhD); microbiology (PhD); molecular biology (PhD); neurobiology (PhD). *Faculty:* 56 full-time (14 women). *Students:* 251 full-time (135 women); includes 74 minority (4 Black or African American, non-Hispanic/Latino; 1 American Indian or Alaska Native, non-Hispanic/Latino; 29 Asian, non-Hispanic/Latino; 33 Hispanic/Latino; 7 Two or more races, non-Hispanic/Latino), 29 international. Average age 26. 652 applicants, 18% accepted, 58 enrolled. In 2010, 41 doctorates awarded. *Degree requirements:* For doctorate, comprehensive exam, thesis/dissertation. *Entrance requirements:* For doctorate, GRE General Test. Additional exam requirements/recommendations for international students: Required—TOEFL (minimum score 577 paper-based; 233 computer-based), IELTS (minimum score 6.5). *Application deadline:* For fall admission, 12/1 for domestic and international students. Application fee: $75. Electronic applications accepted. *Expenses:* Tuition: Full-time $38,940; part-time $605 per unit. Required fees: $272. *Financial support:* In 2010–11, 215 students received support, including 115 fellowships with tuition reimbursements available (averaging $33,090 per year), 132 research assistantships with tuition reimbursements available (averaging $31,846 per year); teaching assistantships with tuition reimbursements available, Federal Work-Study, institutionally sponsored loans, scholarships/grants, traineeships, health care benefits, and unspecified assistantships also available. *Faculty research:* DNA recombination, replication and repair; transcription and gene regulation; signal transduction; cell cycle; neuronal cell fate. Total annual research expenditures: $60.6 million. *Unit head:* Prof. Chris Kaiser, Head, 617-253-4701, E-mail: mitbio@mit.edu. *Application contact:* Biology Education Office, 617-253-3717, Fax: 617-258-9329, E-mail: gradbio@mit.edu.

Massachusetts Institute of Technology, School of Science, Department of Chemistry, Cambridge, MA 02139. Offers biological chemistry (PhD, Sc D); inorganic chemistry (PhD, Sc D); organic chemistry (PhD, Sc D); physical chemistry (PhD, Sc D). *Faculty:* 29 full-time (7 women). *Students:* 227 full-time (78 women); includes 44 minority (5 Black or African American, non-Hispanic/Latino; 1 American Indian or Alaska Native, non-Hispanic/Latino; 27 Asian, non-Hispanic/Latino; 9 Hispanic/Latino; 2 Two or more races, non-Hispanic/Latino), 65 international. Average age 25. 516 applicants, 25% accepted, 55 enrolled. In 2010, 34 doctorates awarded. *Degree requirements:* For doctorate, comprehensive exam, thesis/dissertation, 2 terms as a teaching assistant. *Entrance requirements:* For doctorate, GRE General Test. Additional exam requirements/recommendations for international students: Required—IELTS (minimum score 7); Recommended—TOEFL (minimum score 600 paper-based; 250 computer-based). *Application deadline:* For fall admission, 12/15 for domestic and international students. Application fee: $75. Electronic applications accepted. *Expenses:* Tuition: Full-time $38,940; part-time $605 per unit. Required fees: $272. *Financial support:* In 2010–11, 213 students received support, including 66 fellowships with tuition reimbursements available (averaging $33,072 per year), 123 research assistantships with tuition reimbursements available (averaging $29,440 per year), 38 teaching assistantships with tuition reimbursements available (averaging $31,275 per year); Federal Work-Study, institutionally sponsored loans, scholarships/grants, health care benefits, and unspecified assistantships also available. *Faculty research:* Synthetic organic and inorganic chemistry; biomolecular reactions and structure; multidimensional spectroscopy and chemical dynamics; inorganic, organometallic, and organic chemical catalysis; materials chemistry including surface science, nanoscience and polymers. Total annual research expenditures: $32.1 million. *Unit head:* Prof. Sylvia T. Ceyer, Department Head, 617-253-1803, Fax: 617-258-7500. *Application contact:* Graduate Administrator, 617-253-1845, Fax: 617-258-0241, E-mail: chemgradeducation@mit.edu.

Mayo Graduate School, Graduate Programs in Biomedical Sciences, Programs in Biochemistry, Structural Biology, Cell Biology, and Genetics, Rochester, MN 55905. Offers biochemistry and structural biology (PhD); cell biology and genetics (PhD); molecular biology (PhD). *Degree requirements:* For doctorate, oral defense of dissertation, qualifying oral and written exam. *Entrance requirements:* For doctorate, GRE, 1 year of chemistry, biology, calculus, and physics. Additional exam requirements/recommendations for international students: Required—TOEFL. Electronic applications accepted. *Faculty research:* Gene structure and function, membranes and receptors/cytoskeleton, oncogenes and growth factors, protein structure and function, steroid hormonal action.

McGill University, Faculty of Graduate and Postdoctoral Studies, Faculty of Medicine, Department of Biochemistry, Montréal, QC H3A 2T5, Canada. Offers M Sc, PhD.

McGill University, Faculty of Graduate and Postdoctoral Studies, Faculty of Science, Department of Chemistry, Montréal, QC H3A 2T5, Canada. Offers chemical biology (M Sc, PhD); chemistry (M Sc, PhD).

McMaster University, Faculty of Health Sciences, Department of Biochemistry and Biomedical Sciences, Hamilton, ON L8S 4M2, Canada. Offers M Sc, PhD. Terminal master's awarded for partial completion of doctoral program. *Degree requirements:* For master's, thesis; for doctorate, comprehensive exam, thesis/dissertation. *Entrance requirements:* For master's and doctorate, minimum B+ average. Additional exam requirements/recommendations for international students: Required—TOEFL (minimum score 550 paper-based; 213 computer-based). *Faculty research:* Molecular and cell biology, biomolecular structure and function, molecular pharmacology and toxicology.

Medical College of Wisconsin, Graduate School of Biomedical Sciences, Department of Biochemistry, Milwaukee, WI 53226-0509. Offers PhD, MD/PhD. *Degree requirements:* For doctorate, comprehensive exam, thesis/dissertation. *Entrance requirements:* For doctorate, GRE General Test, GRE Subject Test. Additional exam requirements/recommendations for international students: Required—TOEFL. *Expenses:* Tuition: Full-time $30,000; part-time $710 per credit. Required fees: $150. *Faculty research:* Enzymology, macromolecular structure and synthesis, nucleic acids, molecular and cell biology.

Medical University of South Carolina, College of Graduate Studies, Department of Biochemistry and Molecular Biology, Charleston, SC 29425. Offers MS, PhD, MD/PhD. *Faculty:* 24 full-time (9 women), 3 part-time/adjunct (1 woman). *Students:* 17 full-time (11 women), 2 part-time (0 women); includes 1 Black or African American, non-Hispanic/Latino; 2 Asian, non-Hispanic/Latino, 6 international. Average age 30. 9 applicants, 22% accepted, 2 enrolled. In 2010, 1 master's, 2 doctorates awarded. Terminal master's awarded for partial completion of doctoral program. *Degree requirements:* For master's, thesis, oral exam/thesis defense; for doctorate, thesis/dissertation, oral and written exams/dissertation defense. *Entrance requirements:* For master's, GRE General Test; for doctorate, GRE General Test, interview, minimum GPA of 3.0. Additional exam requirements/recommendations for international students: Required—TOEFL (minimum score 600 paper-based; 250 computer-based; 100 iBT). *Application deadline:* For fall admission, 1/15 priority date for domestic and international students. Applications are processed on a rolling basis. Application fee: $0 ($85 for international students). Electronic applications accepted. *Financial support:* In 2010–11, 10 research assistantships with partial tuition reimbursements (averaging $23,000 per year) were awarded; Federal Work-Study and scholarships/grants also available. Support available to part-time students. Financial award applicants required to submit FAFSA. *Faculty research:* Lipid biochemistry, DNA replication, nucleic acids, protein structure. *Unit head:* Dr. Yusuf A. Hannun, Chairman, 843-792-9318, Fax: 843-792-6590, E-mail: hannun@musc.edu. *Application contact:* Dr. Maurizio Del Poeta, Associate Professor, 843-792-8381, Fax: 843-792-6590, E-mail: delpoeta@musc.edu.

Memorial University of Newfoundland, School of Graduate Studies, Department of Biochemistry, St. John's, NL A1C 5S7, Canada. Offers biochemistry (M Sc, PhD); food science (M Sc, PhD). Part-time programs available. *Degree requirements:* For master's, thesis; for doctorate, comprehensive exam, thesis/dissertation, oral defense of thesis. *Entrance requirements:* For master's, 2nd class degree in related field; for doctorate, M Sc. Electronic applications accepted. *Faculty research:* Toxicology, cell and molecular biology, food engineering, marine biotechnology, lipid biology.

Miami University, Graduate School, College of Arts and Science, Department of Chemistry and Biochemistry, Oxford, OH 45056. Offers MS, PhD. *Students:* 68 full-time (30 women), 1 part-time (0 women); includes 4 minority (2 Black or African American, non-Hispanic/Latino; 1 Asian, non-Hispanic/Latino; 1 Hispanic/Latino), 35 international. Average age 26. In 2010, 4 master's, 7 doctorates awarded. *Entrance requirements:* For master's, minimum undergraduate GPA of 3.0 during previous 2 years or 2.75 overall; for doctorate, minimum undergraduate GPA of 2.75, 3.0 graduate. Additional exam requirements/recommendations for international students: Required—TOEFL. *Application deadline:* Applications are processed on a rolling basis. Application fee: $50. Electronic applications accepted. *Expenses:* Tuition, state resident: full-time $11,616; part-time $484 per credit hour. Tuition, nonresident: full-time $25,656; part-time $1069 per credit hour. Required fees: $528. *Financial support:* Fellowships with full tuition reimbursements, research assistantships with full tuition reimbursements, teaching assistantships with full tuition reimbursements, Federal Work-Study, institutionally sponsored loans, tuition waivers (full), and unspecified assistantships also available. Financial award application deadline: 3/1; financial award applicants required to submit FAFSA. *Unit head:* Dr. Chris

Makaroff, Chair, 513-529-1659, E-mail: makaroca@muohio.edu. *Application contact:* Dr. Michael Crowder, Professor, 513-529-7274, E-mail: crowdermw@muohio.edu.

Michigan State University, College of Human Medicine and The Graduate School, Graduate Programs in Human Medicine, East Lansing, MI 48824. Offers biochemistry and molecular biology (MS, PhD); epidemiology (MS, PhD); microbiology (MS); microbiology and molecular genetics (PhD); pharmacology and toxicology (MS, PhD); physiology (MS, PhD); public health (MPH). *Entrance requirements:* Additional exam requirements/recommendations for international students: Required—TOEFL.

Michigan State University, College of Osteopathic Medicine and The Graduate School, Graduate Studies in Osteopathic Medicine, East Lansing, MI 48824. Offers biochemistry and molecular biology (MS, PhD); microbiology (MS); microbiology and molecular genetics (PhD); pharmacology and toxicology (MS, PhD), including integrative pharmacology (MS), pharmacology and toxicology, pharmacology and toxicology-environmental toxicology (PhD); physiology (MS, PhD).

Michigan State University, The Graduate School, College of Agriculture and Natural Resources, MSU-DOE Plant Research Laboratory, East Lansing, MI 48824. Offers biochemistry and molecular biology (PhD); cellular and molecular biology (PhD); crop and soil sciences (PhD); genetics (PhD); microbiology and molecular genetics (PhD); plant biology (PhD); plant physiology (PhD). Offered jointly with the Department of Energy. *Degree requirements:* For doctorate, comprehensive exam, thesis/dissertation, laboratory rotation, defense of dissertation. *Entrance requirements:* For doctorate, GRE General Test, acceptance into one of the affiliated department programs; 3 letters of recommendation; bachelor's degree or equivalent in life sciences, chemistry, biochemistry, or biophysics; research experience. Electronic applications accepted. *Faculty research:* Role of hormones in the regulation of plant development and physiology, molecular mechanisms associated with signal recognition, development and application of genetic methods and materials, protein routing and function.

Michigan State University, The Graduate School, College of Natural Science and Graduate Programs in Human Medicine and Graduate Studies in Osteopathic Medicine, Department of Biochemistry and Molecular Biology, East Lansing, MI 48824. Offers biochemistry and molecular biology (MS, PhD); biochemistry and molecular biology/environmental toxicology (PhD). *Entrance requirements:* Additional exam requirements/recommendations for international students: Required—TOEFL. Electronic applications accepted.

Mississippi College, Graduate School, College of Arts and Sciences, School of Science and Mathematics, Department of Chemistry and Biochemistry, Clinton, MS 39058. Offers MCS, MS. Part-time programs available. *Degree requirements:* For master's, comprehensive exam, thesis (for some programs). *Entrance requirements:* For master's, GRE. Additional exam requirements/recommendations for international students: Recommended—IELTS. Electronic applications accepted.

Mississippi State University, College of Agriculture and Life Sciences, Department of Biochemistry and Molecular Biology, Mississippi State, MS 39762. Offers agriculture life sciences (MS), including biochemistry; molecular biology (PhD). *Faculty:* 6 full-time (0 women). *Students:* 23 full-time (12 women), 2 part-time (1 woman); includes 3 minority (2 Black or African American, non-Hispanic/Latino; 1 Two or more races, non-Hispanic/Latino), 11 international. Average age 27. 25 applicants, 28% accepted, 4 enrolled. In 2010, 3 master's, 4 doctorates awarded. Terminal master's awarded for partial completion of doctoral program. *Degree requirements:* For master's, thesis (for some programs), comprehensive oral or written exam; for doctorate, thesis/dissertation, comprehensive oral and written exam. *Entrance requirements:* For master's, GRE General Test, minimum GPA of 2.75; for doctorate, GRE. Additional exam requirements/recommendations for international students: Required—TOEFL (minimum score 550 paper-based; 213 computer-based; 79 iBT); Recommended—IELTS (minimum score 6.5). *Application deadline:* For fall admission, 7/1 for domestic students, 5/1 for international students; for spring admission, 11/1 for domestic students, 9/1 for international students. Applications are processed on a rolling basis. Application fee: $40. Electronic applications accepted. *Expenses:* Tuition, state resident: full-time $2731; part-time $304 per credit hour. Tuition, nonresident: full-time $6901; part-time $767 per credit hour. *Financial support:* In 2010–11, 15 research assistantships with full tuition reimbursements (averaging $13,530 per year) were awarded; Federal Work-Study, institutionally sponsored loans, and unspecified assistantships also available. Financial award application deadline: 4/1; financial award applicants required to submit FAFSA. *Faculty research:* Fish nutrition, plant and animal molecular biology, plant biochemistry, enzymology, lipid metabolism. *Unit head:* Dr. Scott T. Willard, Professor and Department Head, 662-325-2640, Fax: 662-325-8664, E-mail: swilliard@ads.msstate.edu. *Application contact:* Dr. Din-Pow Ma, Professor/Graduate Coordinator, 662-325-7739, Fax: 662-325-8664, E-mail: dm1@ra.msstate.edu.

Montana State University, College of Graduate Studies, College of Letters and Science, Department of Chemistry and Biochemistry, Bozeman, MT 59717. Offers biochemistry (MS, PhD); chemistry (MS, PhD). Part-time programs available. *Faculty:* 16 full-time (3 women), 14 part-time/adjunct (7 women). *Students:* 2 full-time (0 women), 71 part-time (25 women); includes 6 minority (1 Black or African American, non-Hispanic/Latino; 3 Asian, non-Hispanic/Latino; 2 Two or more races, non-Hispanic/Latino), 9 international. Average age 27. 42 applicants, 74% accepted, 17 enrolled. In 2010, 3 master's, 8 doctorates awarded. *Degree requirements:* For master's, comprehensive exam, thesis (for some programs); for doctorate, comprehensive exam, thesis/dissertation. *Entrance requirements:* For master's and doctorate, GRE General Test, transcripts, letter of recommendation. Additional exam requirements/recommendations for international students: Required—TOEFL (minimum score 550 paper-based; 213 computer-based), GRE Subject Test. *Application deadline:* For fall admission, 7/15 priority date for domestic students, 5/15 priority date for international students; for spring admission, 12/1 priority date for domestic students, 10/1 priority date for international students. Applications are processed on a rolling basis. Application fee: $30. Electronic applications accepted. *Expenses:* Tuition, state resident: full-time $5554. Tuition, nonresident: full-time $14,646. Required fees: $1233. *Financial support:* In 2010–11, 70 students received support, including 4 fellowships with tuition reimbursements available (averaging $22,000 per year), 31 research assistantships with tuition reimbursements available (averaging $22,000 per year), 35 teaching assistantships with tuition reimbursements available (averaging $22,000 per year); tuition waivers (full) and federal loans also available. Financial award application deadline: 3/1; financial award applicants required to submit FAFSA. *Faculty research:* Proteomics, nano-materials chemistry, computational chemistry, optical spectroscopy, photochemistry. Total annual research expenditures: $12.3 million. *Unit head:* Dr. David Singel, Interim Department Head, 406-994-3960, Fax: 406-994-5407, E-mail: rchds@montana.edu. *Application contact:* Dr. Carl A. Fox, Vice Provost for Graduate Education, 406-994-4145, Fax: 406-994-7433, E-mail: gradstudy@montana.edu.

Montclair State University, The Graduate School, College of Science and Mathematics, Department of Chemistry and Biochemistry, Montclair, NJ 07043-1624. Offers chemistry (MS, Certificate), including biochemistry (MS), chemical business (MS), chemistry (MS); pharmaceutical biochemistry (MS); MS/MBA. Part-time and evening/weekend programs available. *Faculty:* 14 full-time (2 women), 4 part-time/adjunct (3 women). *Students:* 16 full-time (9 women), 27 part-time (14 women); includes 3 Black or African American, non-Hispanic/Latino; 4 Asian, non-Hispanic/Latino; 4 Hispanic/Latino, 5 international. Average age 28. 23 applicants, 65% accepted, 12 enrolled. In 2010, 6 master's awarded. *Degree requirements:* For master's, comprehensive exam. *Entrance requirements:* For master's, GRE General Test, 24 credits of course work in undergraduate chemistry, 2 letters of recommendation. Additional exam requirements/recommendations for international students: Required—TOEFL (minimum score: 83 iBT) or IELTS. *Application deadline:* For fall admission, 6/1 for international students; for spring admission, 10/1 for international students. Applications are processed on a rolling basis. Application fee: $60. Electronic applications accepted. *Expenses:* Tuition, state resident: part-time $501.34 per credit. Tuition, nonresident: part-time $773.88 per credit. Required fees: $71.15 per credit. *Financial support:* In 2010–11, 8 research assistantships with full tuition reimbursements (averaging $7,000 per year) were awarded; Federal Work-Study, scholarships/grants, and unspecified assistantships also available. Support available to part-time students. Financial award application deadline: 3/1; financial award applicants required to submit FAFSA. *Faculty research:* Antimicrobial compounds, marine bacteria. *Unit head:* Dr. Marc Kasner, Chair, 973-655-6864. *Application contact:* Amy Aiello, Director of Graduate Admissions and Operations, 973-655-5147, E-mail: graduate.school@montclair.edu.

New Mexico Institute of Mining and Technology, Graduate Studies, Department of Chemistry, Socorro, NM 87801. Offers biochemistry (MS); chemistry (MS); environmental chemistry (PhD); explosives technology and atmospheric chemistry (PhD). Part-time programs available. *Degree requirements:* For master's, thesis; for doctorate, thesis/dissertation. *Entrance requirements:* For master's, GRE General Test; for doctorate, GRE General Test, GRE Subject Test. Additional exam requirements/recommendations for international students: Required—TOEFL (minimum score 540 paper-based; 207 computer-based). Electronic applications accepted. *Faculty research:* Organic, analytical, environmental, and explosives chemistry.

New York Medical College, Graduate School of Basic Medical Sciences, Program in Biochemistry and Molecular Biology, Valhalla, NY 10595-1691. Offers MS, PhD, MD/PhD. Part-time and evening/weekend programs available. *Faculty:* 11 full-time (5 women). *Students:* 10 full-time (9 women), 5 part-time (3 women); includes 1 American Indian or Alaska Native, non-Hispanic/Latino; 3 Asian, non-Hispanic/Latino, 2 international. Average age 27. 4 applicants, 50% accepted, 1 enrolled. In 2010, 5 master's, 2 doctorates awarded. Terminal master's awarded for partial completion of doctoral program. *Degree requirements:* For master's, thesis; for doctorate, comprehensive exam, thesis/dissertation. *Entrance requirements:* For master's and doctorate, GRE General Test. Additional exam requirements/recommendations for international students: Required—TOEFL. *Application deadline:* For fall admission, 7/1 priority date for domestic students, 5/1 priority date for international students; for spring admission, 12/1 priority date for domestic students, 10/1 priority date for international students. Applications are processed on a rolling basis. Application fee: $50 ($75 for international students). Electronic applications accepted. *Financial support:* In 2010–11, 7 research assistantships with full tuition reimbursements (averaging $24,000 per year) were awarded; Federal Work-Study, institutionally sponsored loans, scholarships/grants, traineeships, tuition waivers (full), unspecified assistantships, and health benefits (for PhD candidates only) also available. Financial award applicants required to submit FAFSA. *Faculty research:* Mechanisms of control of blood coagulation, molecular neurobiology, molecular probes for infectious disease, protein-DNA interactions, molecular biology and biochemistry of double-stranded RNA-dependent enzymes. *Unit head:* Dr. Joseph Wu, Director, 914-594-4891, Fax: 914-594-4944, E-mail: joseph_wu@nymc.edu. *Application contact:* Valerie Romeo-Messana, Admission Coordinator, 914-594-4110, Fax: 914-594-4944, E-mail: v_romeomessana@nymc.edu.

North Carolina State University, Graduate School, College of Agriculture and Life Sciences, Department of Biochemistry, Raleigh, NC 27695. Offers PhD. *Degree requirements:* For doctorate, thesis/dissertation. *Entrance requirements:* For doctorate, GRE General Test. Additional exam requirements/recommendations for international students: Required—TOEFL. Electronic applications accepted. *Faculty research:* Regulation of gene expression, structure and function of proteins and nucleic acids, molecular biology, high-field NMR, bioinorganic chemistry.

North Dakota State University, College of Graduate and Interdisciplinary Studies, College of Science and Mathematics, Department of Biochemistry and Molecular Biology, Program in Biochemistry, Fargo, ND 58108. Offers MS, PhD. Part-time programs available. *Faculty:* 5 full-time (0 women). *Students:* 15 full-time (7 women), 2 part-time (both women); includes 1 Asian, non-Hispanic/Latino, 11 international. Average age 24. 19 applicants, 32% accepted, 4 enrolled. In 2010, 1 doctorate awarded. *Degree requirements:* For master's, thesis; for doctorate, thesis/dissertation. *Entrance requirements:* Additional exam requirements/recommendations for international students: Required—TOEFL (minimum score 550 paper-based). *Application deadline:* For fall admission, 4/15 priority date for domestic students. Applications are processed on a rolling basis. Application fee: $45 ($60 for international students). *Financial support:* In 2010–11, 4 research assistantships with full tuition reimbursements (averaging $19,000 per year), 5 teaching assistantships with full tuition reimbursements (averaging $19,000 per year) were awarded; career-related internships or fieldwork, Federal Work-Study, and institutionally sponsored loans also available. Financial award application deadline: 4/15. *Unit head:* Dr. John Hershberger, Chair, 701-231-7678, Fax: 701-231-8831, E-mail: john.hershberger@ndsu.edu. *Application contact:* Dr. Seth Rasmussen, Chair, Graduate Admissions, 701-231-8747, Fax: 701-231-8831, E-mail: seth.rasmussen@ndsu.edu.

Northeastern University, College of Science, Department of Chemistry and Chemical Biology, Boston, MA 02115-5096. Offers analytical chemistry (PhD); chemistry (MS, PhD); inorganic chemistry (PhD); organic chemistry (PhD); physical chemistry (PhD). Part-time and evening/weekend programs available. *Faculty:* 24 full-time (5 women), 7 part-time/adjunct (0 women). *Students:* 98 full-time (58 women), 31 part-time (15 women). 190 applicants, 32% accepted, 34 enrolled. In 2010, 16 master's, 6 doctorates awarded. Terminal master's awarded for partial completion of doctoral program. *Degree requirements:* For master's, thesis (for some programs); for doctorate, thesis/dissertation, qualifying exam in specialty area. *Entrance requirements:* Additional exam requirements/recommendations for international students: Required—TOEFL. *Application deadline:* For fall admission, 2/1 priority date for domestic and international students. Applications are processed on a rolling basis. Application fee: $50. Electronic applications accepted. *Financial support:* In 2010–11, 41 research assistantships with tuition reimbursements (averaging $18,285 per year), 38 teaching assistantships with tuition reimbursements (averaging $18,285 per year) were awarded; fellowships with tuition reimbursements, career-related internships or fieldwork, Federal Work-Study, scholarships/grants, tuition waivers (partial), and unspecified assistantships also available. Financial award application deadline: 3/1; financial award applicants required to submit FAFSA. *Faculty research:* Bioanalysis, biorganic and medicinal chemistry, biophysical chemistry, nanomaterials, proteomics. *Unit head:* Dr. Robert Hanson, Graduate Coordinator, 617-373-3313, Fax: 617-373-8795, E-mail: chemistry-grad-info@neu.edu. *Application contact:* Jo-Anne Dickinson, Admissions Contact, 617-373-5990, Fax: 617-373-7281, E-mail: gsas@neu.edu.

Northwestern University, The Graduate School, Interdepartmental Biological Sciences Program (IBiS), Evanston, IL 60208. Offers biochemistry, molecular biology, and cell biology (PhD), including biochemistry, cell and molecular biology, molecular biophysics, structural biology; biotechnology (PhD); cell and molecular biology (PhD); developmental biology and genetics (PhD); hormone action and signal transduction (PhD); neuroscience (PhD); structural biology, biochemistry, and biophysics (PhD). Program participants include the Departments of Biochemistry, Molecular Biology, and Cell Biology; Chemistry; Neurobiology and Physiology; Chemical Engineering; Civil Engineering; and Evanston Hospital. *Degree requirements:* For doctorate, thesis/dissertation, qualifying exam. *Entrance requirements:* For doctorate, GRE General Test. Additional exam requirements/recommendations for international students: Required—TOEFL (minimum score 600 paper-based). Electronic applications accepted. *Faculty research:* Developmental genetics, gene regulation, DNA-protein interactions, biological clocks, bioremediation.

Northwestern University, Northwestern University Feinberg School of Medicine and Interdepartmental Programs, Integrated Graduate Programs in the Life Sciences, Chicago, IL 60611. Offers cancer biology (PhD); cell biology (PhD); developmental biology (PhD); evolutionary biology (PhD); immunology and microbial pathogenesis (PhD); molecular biology and genetics (PhD); neurobiology (PhD); pharmacology and toxicology (PhD); structural biology and biochemistry (PhD). *Degree requirements:* For doctorate, comprehensive exam, thesis/dissertation, written and oral qualifying exams. *Entrance requirements:* For doctorate, GRE General Test. Additional exam requirements/recommendations for international students: Required—TOEFL (minimum score 600 paper-based; 250 computer-based). Electronic applications accepted.

Biochemistry

OGI School of Science & Engineering at Oregon Health & Science University, Graduate Studies, Department of Environmental and Biomolecular Systems, Beaverton, OR 97006-8921. Offers biochemistry and molecular biology (MS, PhD); environmental health systems (MS); environmental information technology (MS, PhD); environmental science and engineering (MS, PhD). Part-time programs available. Terminal master's awarded for partial completion of doctoral program. *Degree requirements:* For master's, thesis optional; for doctorate, comprehensive exam, oral defense of dissertation. *Entrance requirements:* For master's and doctorate, GRE General Test. Additional exam requirements/recommendations for international students: Required—TOEFL. Electronic applications accepted. *Faculty research:* Air and water science, hydrogeology, estuarine and coastal modeling, environmental microbiology, contaminant transport, biochemistry, biomolecular systems.

The Ohio State University, Graduate School, College of Arts and Sciences, Division of Natural and Mathematical Sciences, Department of Biochemistry, Columbus, OH 43210. Offers MS. *Faculty:* 52. *Students:* 2 full-time. Average age 22. *Degree requirements:* For master's, comprehensive exam, thesis (for some programs). *Entrance requirements:* For master's, GRE. Additional exam requirements/recommendations for international students: Required—TOEFL (minimum score 600 paper-based; 250 computer-based). *Application deadline:* For fall admission, 8/15 priority date for domestic students, 7/1 priority date for international students; for winter admission, 12/1 priority date for domestic students, 11/1 priority date for international students; for spring admission, 3/1 priority date for domestic students, 2/1 priority date for international students. Applications are processed on a rolling basis. Application fee: $40 ($50 for international students). Electronic applications accepted. *Expenses:* Tuition, state resident: full-time $10,605. Tuition, nonresident: full-time $26,535. Tuition and fees vary according to course load and program. *Financial support:* Fellowships, research assistantships, teaching assistantships, Federal Work-Study and institutionally sponsored loans available. Support available to part-time students. *Unit head:* Mark Foster, Interim Chair, 614-292-1377, E-mail: foster.281@osu.edu. *Application contact:* Mark Foster, Interim Chair, 614-292-1377, E-mail: foster.281@osu.edu.

The Ohio State University, Graduate School, College of Arts and Sciences, Division of Natural and Mathematical Sciences, Ohio State Biochemistry Program, Columbus, OH 43210. Offers PhD. *Faculty:* 100. *Students:* 41 full-time (22 women), 48 part-time (18 women); includes 3 Black or African American, non-Hispanic/Latino; 1 Asian, non-Hispanic/Latino, 54 international. Average age 28. In 2010, 11 doctorates awarded. *Entrance requirements:* Additional exam requirements/recommendations for international students: Required—TOEFL (minimum score 620 paper-based; 250 computer-based). *Application deadline:* Applications are processed on a rolling basis. Application fee: $40 ($50 for international students). Electronic applications accepted. *Expenses:* Tuition, state resident: full-time $10,605. Tuition, nonresident: full-time $26,535. Tuition and fees vary according to course load and program. *Financial support:* Fellowships, research assistantships, teaching assistantships available. *Unit head:* Jill Rafael-Fortney, Program Director, 614-292-1463, Fax: 614-292-6511, E-mail: rafael-fortney.1@osu.edu. *Application contact:* 614-292-9444, Fax: 614-292-3895, E-mail: domestic.grad@osu.edu.

Ohio University, Graduate College, College of Arts and Sciences, Department of Chemistry and Biochemistry, Athens, OH 45701-2979. Offers MS, PhD. *Students:* 61 full-time (26 women), 3 part-time (0 women); includes 2 minority (both Two or more races, non-Hispanic/Latino), 49 international. 70 applicants, 20% accepted, 6 enrolled. In 2010, 1 master's, 12 doctorates awarded. *Degree requirements:* For master's, comprehensive exam, thesis, exam; for doctorate, comprehensive exam, thesis/dissertation, exam. *Entrance requirements:* For master's and doctorate, GRE. Additional exam requirements/recommendations for international students: Required—TOEFL (minimum score 550 paper-based; 80 iBT) or IELTS (minimum score 6.5). *Application deadline:* For fall admission, 2/1 priority date for domestic and international students. Application fee: $50 ($55 for international students). Electronic applications accepted. *Financial support:* Fellowships, research assistantships with full tuition reimbursements, teaching assistantships with full tuition reimbursements, Federal Work-Study and institutionally sponsored loans available. Financial award application deadline: 2/1. *Faculty research:* Materials, RNA, synthesis, carbohydrate, mass spectrometry. Total annual research expenditures: $3.5 million. *Unit head:* Dr. Tadeusz Malinski, Chair, 740-593-1737, Fax: 740-593-0148, E-mail: malinski@ohio.edu. *Application contact:* Dr. Stephen C. Bergmeier, Graduate Chair, 740-597-6949, Fax: 740-593-0148, E-mail: bergmeis@ohio.edu.

Oklahoma State University, College of Agricultural Science and Natural Resources, Department of Biochemistry and Molecular Biology, Stillwater, OK 74078. Offers MS, PhD. *Faculty:* 31 full-time (12 women), 2 part-time/adjunct (0 women). *Students:* 6 full-time (0 women), 26 part-time (17 women); includes 1 Black or African American, non-Hispanic/Latino; 2 American Indian or Alaska Native, non-Hispanic/Latino; 1 Hispanic/Latino, 20 international. Average age 28. 82 applicants, 18% accepted, 3 enrolled. In 2010, 5 master's, 5 doctorates awarded. *Degree requirements:* For master's, thesis, oral exam; for doctorate, comprehensive exam, thesis/dissertation. *Entrance requirements:* For master's and doctorate, GRE or GMAT. Additional exam requirements/recommendations for international students: Required—TOEFL (minimum score 550 paper-based; 79 iBT). *Application deadline:* For fall admission, 3/1 priority date for international students; for spring admission, 8/1 priority date for international students. Applications are processed on a rolling basis. Application fee: $40 ($75 for international students). Electronic applications accepted. *Expenses:* Tuition, state resident: full-time $3716; part-time $154.85 per credit hour. Tuition, nonresident: full-time $14,892; part-time $621 per credit hour. Required fees: $2044; $85.20 per credit hour. One-time fee: $50. Tuition and fees vary according to course load and campus/location. *Financial support:* In 2010–11, 30 research assistantships (averaging $19,456 per year), 2 teaching assistantships (averaging $18,699 per year) were awarded; career-related internships or fieldwork, Federal Work-Study, scholarships/grants, health care benefits, tuition waivers (partial), and unspecified assistantships also available. Support available to part-time students. Financial award application deadline: 3/1; financial award applicants required to submit FAFSA. *Unit head:* Dr. Gary Thompson, Head, 405-744-9320, Fax: 405-744-7799. *Application contact:* Dr. Gordon Emslie, Dean, 405-744-6368, Fax: 405-744-0355, E-mail: grad-i@okstate.edu.

Old Dominion University, College of Sciences, Program in Chemistry, Norfolk, VA 23529. Offers analytical chemistry (MS); biochemistry (MS); chemistry (PhD); environmental chemistry (MS); organic chemistry (MS); physical chemistry (MS). Part-time and evening/weekend programs available. *Faculty:* 14 full-time (5 women), 2 part-time/adjunct (0 women). *Students:* 36 full-time (22 women), 1 part-time (0 women); includes 3 minority (1 Black or African American, non-Hispanic/Latino; 1 Asian, non-Hispanic/Latino; 1 Hispanic/Latino), 16 international. Average age 29. 35 applicants, 60% accepted, 8 enrolled. In 2010, 6 master's, 2 doctorates awarded. *Degree requirements:* For master's, comprehensive exam, thesis. *Entrance requirements:* For master's, GRE General Test, minimum GPA of 3.0 in major, 2.5 overall; for doctorate, GRE General Test. Additional exam requirements/recommendations for international students: Required—TOEFL. *Application deadline:* For fall admission, 7/1 for domestic students, 1/15 for international students; for spring admission, 11/1 for domestic students, 8/15 for international students. Applications are processed on a rolling basis. Application fee: $30. Electronic applications accepted. *Expenses:* Tuition, state resident: full-time $8592; part-time $358 per credit. Tuition, nonresident: full-time $21,672; part-time $903 per credit. Required fees: $119 per semester. One-time fee: $50. *Financial support:* In 2010–11, 6 students received support, including fellowships (averaging $18,000 per year), research assistantships with tuition reimbursements available (averaging $21,000 per year), teaching assistantships with tuition reimbursements available (averaging $18,000 per year); career-related internships or fieldwork, scholarships/grants, and unspecified assistantships also available. Financial award application deadline: 2/15; financial award applicants required to submit FAFSA. *Faculty research:* Biogeochemistry, materials chemistry, bioanalytical chemistry, computational chemistry, organic chemistry. Total annual research expenditures: $2.6 million. *Unit head:* Dr. Craig A. Bayse, Graduate Program Director, 757-683-4097, Fax: 757-683-4628, E-mail: chemgpd@odu.edu. *Application contact:* Valerie DeCosta, Grants and Graduate Program Assistant, 757-683-6979, Fax: 757-683-4628, E-mail: chemgpd@odu.edu.

Oregon Health & Science University, School of Medicine, Graduate Programs in Medicine, Department of Environmental and Biomolecular Systems, Portland, OR 97239-3098. Offers biochemistry and molecular biology (MS, PhD); environmental science and engineering (MS, PhD). Part-time programs available. *Faculty:* 14 full-time (4 women), 1 (woman) part-time/adjunct. *Students:* 21 full-time (12 women), 25 part-time (12 women); includes 1 Black or African American, non-Hispanic/Latino; 3 American Indian or Alaska Native, non-Hispanic/Latino; 5 Asian, non-Hispanic/Latino; 3 Hispanic/Latino, 8 international. Average age 33. 45 applicants, 60% accepted, 11 enrolled. In 2010, 8 master's, 2 doctorates awarded. Terminal master's awarded for partial completion of doctoral program. *Degree requirements:* For master's, thesis (for some programs); for doctorate, comprehensive exam, thesis/dissertation. *Entrance requirements:* For master's and doctorate, GRE General Test (minimum scores: 500 Verbal/600 Quantitative/4.5 Analytical) or MCAT (for some programs). Additional exam requirements/recommendations for international students: Required—TOEFL. *Application deadline:* For fall admission, 7/15 for domestic students, 5/15 for international students; for winter admission, 10/15 for domestic students, 9/15 for international students; for spring admission, 1/15 for domestic students, 12/15 for international students. Applications are processed on a rolling basis. Application fee: $65. Electronic applications accepted. *Financial support:* Health care benefits and full tuition and stipends available. *Unit head:* Dr. Paul Tratnyek, Program Director, 503-748-1070, E-mail: info@ebs.ogi.edu. *Application contact:* Nancy Christie, Program Coordinator, 503-748-1070, E-mail: info@ebs.ogi.edu.

Oregon Health & Science University, School of Medicine, Graduate Programs in Medicine, Program in Molecular and Cellular Biosciences, Department of Biochemistry and Molecular Biology, Portland, OR 97239-3098. Offers PhD. *Faculty:* 14 full-time (4 women), 6 part-time/adjunct (3 women). *Students:* 11 full-time (6 women), 2 international. Average age 30. In 2010, 1 doctorate awarded. *Degree requirements:* For doctorate, comprehensive exam, thesis/dissertation, qualifying exam. *Entrance requirements:* For doctorate, GRE General Test (minimum scores: 500 Verbal/600 Quantitative/4.5 Analytical). Additional exam requirements/recommendations for international students: Required—TOEFL. Electronic applications accepted. *Financial support:* Health care benefits, tuition waivers (full), and full tuition and stipends available. *Faculty research:* Protein structure and function, enzymology, metabolism, membranes transport. *Unit head:* Dr. David Farrens, Program Director, 503-494-7781, E-mail: farrensd@ohsu.edu. *Application contact:* Jeni Wroblewski, Administrative Coordinator, 503-494-2541, E-mail: wroblews@ohsu.edu.

Oregon State University, Graduate School, College of Science, Department of Biochemistry and Biophysics, Corvallis, OR 97331. Offers MA, MAIS, MS, PhD. *Degree requirements:* For master's, thesis optional; for doctorate, thesis/dissertation, exams. *Entrance requirements:* For master's, GRE General Test, minimum GPA of 3.0; for doctorate, GRE Subject Test, minimum GPA of 3.0. Additional exam requirements/recommendations for international students: Required—TOEFL. *Faculty research:* DNA and deoxyribonucleotide metabolism, cell growth control, receptors and membranes, protein structure and function.

Penn State Hershey Medical Center, College of Medicine, Graduate School Programs in the Biomedical Sciences, Graduate Program in Biochemistry and Molecular Biology, Hershey, PA 17033. Offers MS, PhD, MD/PhD. *Students:* 131 applicants, 5% accepted, 3 enrolled. Terminal master's awarded for partial completion of doctoral program. *Degree requirements:* For master's, thesis or alternative; for doctorate, comprehensive exam, thesis/dissertation. *Entrance requirements:* For master's, GRE General Test; for doctorate, GRE General Test, minimum GPA of 3.0. Additional exam requirements/recommendations for international students: Required—TOEFL (minimum score 550 paper-based; 213 computer-based). *Application deadline:* For fall admission, 1/31 priority date for domestic students, 2/1 priority date for international students. Applications are processed on a rolling basis. Application fee: $65. Electronic applications accepted. *Financial support:* In 2010–11, research assistantships with full tuition reimbursements (averaging $22,260 per year); fellowships with full tuition reimbursements, scholarships/grants, health care benefits, tuition waivers, and unspecified assistantships also available. Financial award applicants required to submit FAFSA. *Faculty research:* X-ray crystallography of proteins, glycosphingolipid interactions with viruses and toxins, DNA replication and repair, tobacco and environmental carcinogenesis, gene regulation. *Unit head:* Dr. Judith S. Bond, Chair, 717-531-8585, Fax: 717-531-7072, E-mail: bchem-grad-hmc@psu.edu. *Application contact:* Ruth Dean, Administrative Assistant, 717-531-8586, Fax: 717-531-7072, E-mail: bchem-grad-hmc@psu.edu.

Penn State University Park, Graduate School, Eberly College of Science, Department of Biochemistry and Molecular Biology, Program in Biochemistry, Microbiology, and Molecular Biology, State College, University Park, PA 16802-1503. Offers MS, PhD. *Unit head:* Dr. Ronald Porter, Director of Graduate Studies, 814-863-4903, E-mail: rdp1@psu.edu. *Application contact:* Dr. Ronald Porter, Director of Graduate Studies, 814-863-4903, E-mail: rdp1@psu.edu.

Purdue University, College of Pharmacy and Pharmacal Sciences and Graduate School, Graduate Programs in Pharmacy and Pharmacal Sciences, Department of Medicinal Chemistry and Molecular Pharmacology, West Lafayette, IN 47907. Offers analytical medicinal chemistry (PhD); computational and biophysical medicinal chemistry (PhD); medicinal and bioorganic chemistry (PhD); medicinal biochemistry and molecular biology (PhD); molecular pharmacology and toxicology (PhD); natural products and pharmacognosy (PhD); nuclear pharmacy (MS); radiopharmaceutical chemistry and nuclear pharmacy (PhD); MS/PhD. Terminal master's awarded for partial completion of doctoral program. *Degree requirements:* For master's, thesis; for doctorate, thesis/dissertation. *Entrance requirements:* For master's, GRE General Test, minimum B average; BS in biology, chemistry, or pharmacy; for doctorate, GRE General Test, minimum B average; BS in biology, chemistry, or pharmacology. Additional exam requirements/recommendations for international students: Required—TOEFL. Electronic applications accepted. *Faculty research:* Drug design and development, cancer research, drug synthesis and analysis, chemical pharmacology, environmental toxicology.

Purdue University, Graduate School, College of Agriculture, Department of Biochemistry, West Lafayette, IN 47907. Offers MS, PhD. Terminal master's awarded for partial completion of doctoral program. *Degree requirements:* For master's, thesis; for doctorate, thesis/dissertation, preliminary and qualifying exams. *Entrance requirements:* For master's and doctorate, GRE General Test. Additional exam requirements/recommendations for international students: Required—TOEFL. Electronic applications accepted. *Faculty research:* Molecular biology and post-translational modifications of neuropeptides, membrane transport proteins.

Queens College of the City University of New York, Division of Graduate Studies, Mathematics and Natural Sciences Division, Department of Chemistry and Biochemistry, Flushing, NY 11367-1597. Offers biochemistry (MA); chemistry (MA). Part-time and evening/weekend programs available. *Faculty:* 14 full-time (4 women). *Students:* 2 full-time (0 women), 8 part-time (4 women); includes 1 Black or African American, non-Hispanic/Latino; 5 Asian, non-Hispanic/Latino, 2 international. 13 applicants, 38% accepted, 2 enrolled. In 2010, 6 master's awarded. *Degree requirements:* For master's, comprehensive exam. *Entrance requirements:* For master's, GRE, previous course work in calculus and physics, minimum GPA of 3.0. Additional exam requirements/recommendations for international students: Required—TOEFL. *Application deadline:* For fall admission, 4/1 for domestic students; for spring admission, 11/1 for domestic students. Applications are processed on a rolling basis. Application fee: $125. *Financial support:* Career-related internships or fieldwork, Federal Work-Study, institutionally sponsored loans, and tuition waivers (partial) available. Support available to part-time students. Financial award application deadline: 4/1; financial award applicants required to submit FAFSA. *Unit head:* Dr. William Hersh, Chairperson, 718-997-4144. *Application contact:* Graduate Adviser, 718-997-4100.

Queen's University at Kingston, School of Graduate Studies and Research, Faculty of Health Sciences, Department of Biochemistry, Kingston, ON K7L 3N6, Canada. Offers M Sc, PhD. Part-time programs available. *Degree requirements:* For master's, thesis, research proposal; for doctorate, comprehensive exam, thesis/dissertation, research proposal. *Entrance requirements:* For master's, GRE (if undergraduate degree is not from a Canadian University); for doctorate, GRE required if undergraduate degree is not from a Canadian University. Additional exam requirements/recommendations for international students: Required—TOEFL (minimum score 580 paper-based; 237 computer-based). Electronic applications accepted. *Faculty research:* Gene expression, protein structure, enzyme activity, signal transduction.

Rensselaer Polytechnic Institute, Graduate School, School of Science, Program in Biochemistry and Biophysics, Troy, NY 12180-3590. Offers MS, PhD. Part-time programs available. *Faculty:* 25 full-time (7 women). *Students:* 6 full-time (4 women), 1 international. Average age 27. 19 applicants, 21% accepted, 3 enrolled. In 2010, 1 doctorate awarded. Terminal master's awarded for partial completion of doctoral program. *Degree requirements:* For master's, thesis optional; for doctorate, comprehensive exam, thesis/dissertation. *Entrance requirements:* For doctorate, GRE General Test. Additional exam requirements/recommendations for international students: Required—TOEFL. *Application deadline:* For fall admission, 1/15 priority date for domestic students, 1/1 for international students. Applications are processed on a rolling basis. Application fee: $75. Electronic applications accepted. *Expenses:* Tuition: Full-time $39,600; part-time $1650 per credit. Required fees: $1896. *Financial support:* In 2010–11, 6 students received support, including 8 research assistantships with full tuition reimbursements available (averaging $17,500 per year), 4 teaching assistantships with full tuition reimbursements available (averaging $17,500 per year); traineeships and unspecified assistantships also available. Financial award application deadline: 1/1. *Faculty research:* Biopolymers, photosynthesis, cellular bioengineering. Total annual research expenditures: $2.5 million. *Application contact:* Jody Malm, Administrative Coordinator, 518-276-2808, Fax: 518-276-2344, E-mail: malmj@rpi.edu.

Rensselaer Polytechnic Institute, Graduate School, School of Science, Program in Chemistry, Troy, NY 12180-3590. Offers analytical chemistry (MS, PhD); biochemistry (MS, PhD); inorganic chemistry (MS, PhD); organic chemistry (MS, PhD); physical chemistry (MS, PhD); polymer chemistry (MS, PhD). Part-time and evening/weekend programs available. *Faculty:* 16 full-time (2 women). *Students:* 42 full-time (18 women), 3 part-time (1 woman); includes 1 Black or African American, non-Hispanic/Latino; 4 Asian, non-Hispanic/Latino, 16 international. Average age 24. 139 applicants, 16% accepted, 6 enrolled. In 2010, 5 master's, 8 doctorates awarded. Terminal master's awarded for partial completion of doctoral program. *Degree requirements:* For master's, thesis (for some programs); for doctorate, comprehensive exam, thesis/dissertation. *Entrance requirements:* For master's, GRE General Test, GRE Subject Test (strongly recommended); for doctorate, GRE General Test, GRE Subject Test (chemistry or biochemistry strongly recommended). Additional exam requirements/recommendations for international students: Required—TOEFL (minimum score 570 paper-based; 230 computer-based; 88 iBT). *Application deadline:* For fall admission, 2/1 priority date for domestic students; for spring admission, 11/15 for domestic students. Applications are processed on a rolling basis. Application fee: $75. Electronic applications accepted. *Expenses:* Tuition: Full-time $39,600; part-time $1650 per credit. Required fees: $1896. *Financial support:* In 2010–11, 1 fellowship with full tuition reimbursement (averaging $23,000 per year), 12 research assistantships with full tuition reimbursements (averaging $23,000 per year), 23 teaching assistantships with full tuition reimbursements (averaging $23,000 per year) were awarded; institutionally sponsored loans and tuition waivers (full and partial) also available. Financial award application deadline: 2/1. *Faculty research:* Synthetic polymer and biopolymer chemistry, physical chemistry of polymeric systems, bioanalytical chemistry, synthetic and computational drug design, protein folding and protein design. Total annual research expenditures: $1.1 million. *Unit head:* Dr. Curtis M. Breneman, Chair, 518-276-3264, Fax: 518-276-4887, E-mail: brenec@rpi.edu. *Application contact:* Sharon E. Gardner, Graduate Program Administrator, 518-276-2140, Fax: 518-276-4887, E-mail: derris@rpi.edu.

Rice University, Graduate Programs, Wiess School of Natural Sciences, Department of Biochemistry and Cell Biology, Houston, TX 77251-1892. Offers MA, PhD. Terminal master's awarded for partial completion of doctoral program. *Degree requirements:* For master's, thesis; for doctorate, thesis/dissertation. *Entrance requirements:* For master's and doctorate, GRE. Additional exam requirements/recommendations for international students: Required—TOEFL (minimum score 600 paper-based; 250 computer-based; 90 iBT). Electronic applications accepted. *Expenses:* Contact institution. *Faculty research:* Steroid metabolism, protein structure NMR, biophysics, cell growth and movement.

Rosalind Franklin University of Medicine and Science, School of Graduate and Postdoctoral Studies—Interdisciplinary Graduate Program in Biomedical Sciences, Department of Biochemistry and Molecular Biology, North Chicago, IL 60064-3095. Offers MS, PhD, MD/PhD. Terminal master's awarded for partial completion of doctoral program. *Degree requirements:* For master's, comprehensive exam, thesis; for doctorate, comprehensive exam, thesis/dissertation. *Entrance requirements:* For master's and doctorate, GRE General Test, minimum GPA of 3.0. Additional exam requirements/recommendations for international students: Required—TOEFL, TWE. Electronic applications accepted. *Faculty research:* Structure of control enzymes, extracellular matrix, glucose metabolism, gene expression, ATP synthesis.

Rush University, Graduate College, Division of Biochemistry, Chicago, IL 60612-3832. Offers PhD, MD/PhD. *Degree requirements:* For doctorate, thesis/dissertation, preliminary exam. *Entrance requirements:* For doctorate, GRE General Test. Additional exam requirements/recommendations for international students: Required—TOEFL. Electronic applications accepted. *Faculty research:* Biochemistry of extracellular matrix, connective tissue biosynthesis and degradation, molecular biology of connective tissue components, cartilage, arthritis.

Rutgers, The State University of New Jersey, Newark, Graduate School, Program in Chemistry, Newark, NJ 07102. Offers analytical chemistry (MS, PhD); biochemistry (MS, PhD); inorganic chemistry (MS, PhD); organic chemistry (MS, PhD); physical chemistry (MS, PhD). Part-time and evening/weekend programs available. *Faculty:* 13 full-time (3 women). *Students:* 29 full-time (14 women), 32 part-time (19 women); includes 2 Black or African American, non-Hispanic/Latino; 30 Asian, non-Hispanic/Latino; 3 Hispanic/Latino. 153 applicants, 45% accepted, 17 enrolled. In 2010, 4 master's, 9 doctorates awarded. Terminal master's awarded for partial completion of doctoral program. *Degree requirements:* For master's, thesis optional, cumulative exams; for doctorate, thesis/dissertation, exams, research proposal. *Entrance requirements:* For master's and doctorate, GRE General Test, minimum undergraduate B average. Additional exam requirements/recommendations for international students: Required—TOEFL. *Application deadline:* For fall admission, 7/1 priority date for domestic students; for spring admission, 12/1 for domestic students. Applications are processed on a rolling basis. Application fee: $60. Electronic applications accepted. *Expenses:* Tuition, state resident: part-time $600 per credit. Tuition, nonresident: full-time $10,694. *Financial support:* In 2010–11, 35 students received support, including 5 fellowships (averaging $18,000 per year), 6 research assistantships with full and partial tuition reimbursements available (averaging $23,112 per year), 20 teaching assistantships with full and partial tuition reimbursements available (averaging $23,112 per year); Federal Work-Study and institutionally sponsored loans also available. Financial award application deadline: 3/1. *Faculty research:* Medicinal chemistry, natural products, isotope effects, biophysics and biorganic approaches to enzyme mechanisms, organic and organometallic synthesis. *Unit head:* Prof. Frank Jordan, Chairman and Program Director, 973-353-5741, Fax: 973-353-1264, E-mail: frjordan@andromeda.rutgers.edu. *Application contact:* Jason Hand, Director of Admissions, 973-353-5205, Fax: 973-353-1440.

Rutgers, The State University of New Jersey, New Brunswick, Graduate School-New Brunswick, Department of Chemistry and Chemical Biology, Piscataway, NJ 08854-8097. Offers biological chemistry (MS, PhD); inorganic chemistry (MS, PhD); organic chemistry (MS, PhD); physical chemistry (MS, PhD). Part-time and evening/weekend programs available. Terminal master's awarded for partial completion of doctoral program. *Degree requirements:* For master's, thesis or alternative, exam; for doctorate, thesis/dissertation, 1 year residency. *Entrance requirements:* For master's and doctorate, GRE General Test, GRE Subject Test. Additional exam requirements/recommendations for international students: Required—TOEFL. Electronic applications accepted. *Expenses:* Tuition, state resident: full-time $7200; part-time $600 per credit. Tuition, nonresident: full-time $11,124; part-time $927 per credit. *Faculty research:* Biophysical organic/bioorganic, inorganic/bioinorganic, theoretical, and solid-state/surface chemistry.

Rutgers, The State University of New Jersey, New Brunswick, Graduate School-New Brunswick, Programs in the Molecular Biosciences, Program in Biochemistry, Piscataway, NJ 08854-8097. Offers PhD. Program offered jointly with University of Medicine and Dentistry of New Jersey. *Degree requirements:* For doctorate, thesis/dissertation, written qualifying exam. *Entrance requirements:* For doctorate, GRE General Test, GRE Subject Test (recommended), minimum GPA of 3.0. Additional exam requirements/recommendations for international students: Required—TOEFL. Electronic applications accepted. *Expenses:* Tuition, state resident: full-time $7200; part-time $600 per credit. Tuition, nonresident: full-time $11,124; part-time $927 per credit. *Faculty research:* DNA replication and transcription, virus gene expression, tumor biology, structural biochemistry, signal transduction and molecular targeting.

Saint Joseph College, Department of Chemistry, West Hartford, CT 06117-2700. Offers biochemistry (MS); chemistry (MS). Part-time and evening/weekend programs available. Post-baccalaureate distance learning degree programs offered. *Students:* 2 full-time (1 woman), 30 part-time (18 women); includes 3 Black or African American, non-Hispanic/Latino; 2 Asian, non-Hispanic/Latino; 2 Hispanic/Latino. *Degree requirements:* For master's, comprehensive exam, thesis optional. *Entrance requirements:* For master's, 2 letters of recommendation. *Application deadline:* Applications are processed on a rolling basis. Application fee: $50. Electronic applications accepted. *Expenses:* Tuition: Full-time $11,340; part-time $630 per credit. Required fees: $540; $30 per credit. Tuition and fees vary according to course load, campus/location and program. *Financial support:* Career-related internships or fieldwork and unspecified assistantships available. Support available to part-time students. Financial award applicants required to submit FAFSA. *Application contact:* Graduate Admissions Office, 860-231-5261, E-mail: graduate@sjc.edu.

Saint Louis University, Graduate Education and School of Medicine, Graduate Program in Biomedical Sciences and Graduate Education, Department of Biochemistry and Molecular Biology, St. Louis, MO 63103-2097. Offers PhD. *Degree requirements:* For doctorate, comprehensive exam, thesis/dissertation, departmental qualifying exams. *Entrance requirements:* For doctorate, GRE General Test, GRE Subject Test (optional), letters of recommendation, resume, interview. Additional exam requirements/recommendations for international students: Required—TOEFL (minimum score 525 paper-based; 194 computer-based). Electronic applications accepted. *Faculty research:* Transcription, chromatin modification and regulation of gene expression; structure/function of proteins and enzymes, including x-ray crystallography; inflammatory mediators in pathenogenesis of diabetes and arteriosclerosis; cellular signaling in response to growth factors, opiates and angiogenic mediators; genomics and proteomics of Cryptococcus neoformans.

San Francisco State University, Division of Graduate Studies, College of Science and Engineering, Department of Chemistry and Biochemistry, San Francisco, CA 94132-1722. Offers chemistry (MS), including biochemistry. Part-time programs available. *Application deadline:* Applications are processed on a rolling basis. Electronic applications accepted. *Unit head:* Dr. Jane DeWitt, Chair, 415-338-1288, Fax: 415-338-2384, E-mail: gradchem@sfsu.edu. *Application contact:* Dr. Bruce Manning, Graduate Coordinator, 415-338-1288, Fax: 415-338-2384, E-mail: gradchem@sfsu.edu.

Seton Hall University, College of Arts and Sciences, Department of Chemistry and Biochemistry, South Orange, NJ 07079-2697. Offers analytical chemistry (MS, PhD); biochemistry (MS, PhD); chemistry (MS); inorganic chemistry (MS, PhD); organic chemistry (MS, PhD); physical chemistry (MS, PhD). Part-time and evening/weekend programs available. Terminal master's awarded for partial completion of doctoral program. *Degree requirements:* For master's, thesis optional; for doctorate, comprehensive exam, thesis/dissertation. *Entrance requirements:* Additional exam requirements/recommendations for international students: Required—TOEFL. Electronic applications accepted. *Faculty research:* DNA metal reactions; chromatography; bioinorganic, biophysical, organometallic, polymer chemistry; heterogeneous catalyst; synthetic organic and carbohydrate chemistry.

Simon Fraser University, Graduate Studies, Faculty of Science, Department of Molecular Biology and Biochemistry, Burnaby, BC V5A 1S6, Canada. Offers M Sc, PhD. *Degree requirements:* For master's, thesis; for doctorate, thesis/dissertation. *Entrance requirements:* For master's, minimum GPA of 3.0; for doctorate, minimum GPA of 3.5. Additional exam requirements/recommendations for international students: Required—TWE or IELTS. *Faculty research:* Molecular genetics and development, biochemistry, molecular physiology, genomics, molecular phylogenetics and population genetics, bioinformation.

Southern Illinois University Carbondale, Graduate School, College of Science, Department of Chemistry and Biochemistry, Carbondale, IL 62901-4701. Offers MS, PhD. Part-time programs available. Terminal master's awarded for partial completion of doctoral program. *Degree requirements:* For master's, one foreign language, thesis; for doctorate, variable foreign language requirement, thesis/dissertation. *Entrance requirements:* For master's, minimum GPA of 2.7; for doctorate, GRE General Test, minimum GPA of 3.25. Additional exam requirements/recommendations for international students: Required—TOEFL. *Faculty research:* Materials, separations, computational chemistry, synthetics.

Southern Illinois University Carbondale, Graduate School, College of Science, Program in Molecular Biology, Microbiology, and Biochemistry, Carbondale, IL 62901-4701. Offers MS, PhD. *Degree requirements:* For master's, thesis; for doctorate, thesis/dissertation. *Entrance requirements:* For master's, GRE, minimum GPA of 2.7; for doctorate, GRE, minimum GPA of 3.25. Additional exam requirements/recommendations for international students: Required—TOEFL. *Faculty research:* Prokaryotic gene regulation and expression; eukaryotic gene regulation; microbial, phylogenetic, and metabolic diversity; immune responses to tumors, pathogens, and autoantigens; protein folding and structure.

Southern University and Agricultural and Mechanical College, Graduate School, College of Sciences, Department of Chemistry, Baton Rouge, LA 70813. Offers analytical chemistry (MS); biochemistry (MS); environmental sciences (MS); inorganic chemistry (MS); organic chemistry (MS); physical chemistry (MS). *Degree requirements:* For master's, thesis. *Entrance requirements:* For master's, GMAT or GRE General Test. Additional exam requirements/recommendations for international students: Required—TOEFL (minimum score 525 paper-based; 193 computer-based). *Faculty research:* Synthesis of macrocyclic ligands, latex accelerators, anticancer drugs, biosensors, absorption isotheums, isolation of specific enzymes from plants.

Stanford University, School of Medicine, Graduate Programs in Medicine, Department of Biochemistry, Stanford, CA 94305-9991. Offers PhD. *Degree requirements:* For doctorate, thesis/dissertation. *Entrance requirements:* For doctorate, GRE General Test, GRE Subject Test (biology or chemistry). Additional exam requirements/recommendations for international students: Required—TOEFL. Electronic applications accepted. *Expenses:* Tuition: Full-time $38,700; part-time $860 per unit. One-time fee: $200 full-time. *Faculty research:* DNA replication, recombination, and gene regulation; methods of isolating, analyzing, and altering genes and genomes; protein structure, protein folding, and protein processing; protein targeting and transport in the cell; intercellular signaling.

State University of New York College of Environmental Science and Forestry, Department of Chemistry, Syracuse, NY 13210-2779. Offers biochemistry (MPS, MS, PhD); environmental and forest chemistry (MPS, MS, PhD); organic chemistry (MPS); organic chemistry of natural products (MS, PhD); polymer chemistry (MPS, MS, PhD). *Degree requirements:* For master's, thesis; for doctorate, comprehensive exam, thesis/dissertation. *Entrance requirements:* For master's and doctorate, GRE General Test, GRE Subject Test, minimum GPA of 3.0. Additional exam requirements/recommendations for international students: Required—TOEFL (minimum

Biochemistry

State University of New York College of Environmental Science and Forestry (continued)
score 550 paper-based; 213 computer-based; 80 iBT), IELTS (minimum score 6). Electronic applications accepted. *Expenses:* Tuition, state resident: full-time $8370; part-time $349 per credit hour. Tuition, nonresident: full-time $13,780. Required fees: $30.30 per credit hour. $20 per year. *Faculty research:* Polymer chemistry, biochemistry.

State University of New York Upstate Medical University, College of Graduate Studies, Program in Biochemistry and Molecular Biology, Syracuse, NY 13210-2334. Offers biochemistry (MS); biochemistry and molecular biology (PhD); MD/PhD. Terminal master's awarded for partial completion of doctoral program. *Degree requirements:* For master's, thesis; for doctorate, comprehensive exam, thesis/dissertation. *Entrance requirements:* For master's, GRE General Test, interview; for doctorate, GRE General Test, telephone interview. Additional exam requirements/recommendations for international students: Required—TOEFL. Electronic applications accepted. *Faculty research:* Enzymology, membrane structure and functions, developmental biochemistry.

Stevens Institute of Technology, Graduate School, Charles V. Schaefer Jr. School of Engineering, Department of Chemistry, Chemical Biology and Biomedical Engineering, Hoboken, NJ 07030. Offers analytical chemistry (PhD, Certificate); bioinformatics (PhD, Certificate); biomedical chemistry (Certificate); biomedical engineering (M Eng, Certificate); chemical biology (MS, PhD, Certificate); chemical physiology (Certificate); chemistry (MS, PhD); organic chemistry (PhD); physical chemistry (PhD); polymer chemistry (PhD, Certificate). Part-time and evening/weekend programs available. Postbaccalaureate distance learning degree programs offered (no on-campus study). *Students:* 66 full-time (35 women), 25 part-time (7 women); includes 2 Black or African American, non-Hispanic/Latino; 14 Asian, non-Hispanic/Latino; 8 Hispanic/Latino, 31 international. Average age 26. 109 applicants, 68% accepted.Terminal master's awarded for partial completion of doctoral program. *Degree requirements:* For master's, thesis or alternative; for doctorate, one foreign language, thesis/dissertation; for Certificate, project or thesis. *Entrance requirements:* Additional exam requirements/recommendations for international students: Required—TOEFL. *Application deadline:* Applications are processed on a rolling basis. Application fee: $50. Electronic applications accepted. *Financial support:* Fellowships, research assistantships, teaching assistantships available. Financial award application deadline: 4/1. *Faculty research:* Biochemical reaction engineering, polymerization engineering, reactor design, biochemical process control and synthesis. *Unit head:* Philip Leopold, Director, 201-216-8957, Fax: 201-216-8196, E-mail: pleopold@stevens.edu. *Application contact:* Graduate Admissions, 800-496-4935, Fax: 201-216-8044, E-mail: gradadmissions@stevens.edu.

Stony Brook University, State University of New York, Graduate School, College of Arts and Sciences, Department of Biochemistry and Cell Biology, Molecular and Cellular Biology Program, Specialization in Biochemistry and Molecular Biology, Stony Brook, NY 11794. Offers PhD. *Degree requirements:* For doctorate, comprehensive exam, thesis/dissertation, teaching experience. *Entrance requirements:* For doctorate, GRE General Test, GRE Subject Test. Additional exam requirements/recommendations for international students: Required—TOEFL. *Application deadline:* For fall admission, 1/15 for domestic students. Application fee: $60. *Expenses:* Tuition, state resident: full-time $8370; part-time $349 per credit. Tuition, nonresident: full-time $13,780; part-time $574 per credit. Required fees: $994. *Financial support:* Fellowships, research assistantships, teaching assistantships, Federal Work-Study available. *Unit head:* Prof. Robert Haltiwanger, Chair, 631-632-8560. *Application contact:* Director, Graduate Program, 631-632-1210, E-mail: mcbprog@life.bio.sunysb.edu.

Stony Brook University, State University of New York, Graduate School, College of Arts and Sciences, Department of Biochemistry and Cell Biology, Program in Biochemistry and Structural Biology, Stony Brook, NY 11794. Offers PhD. *Students:* 28 full-time (10 women); includes 1 Black or African American, non-Hispanic/Latino; 1 Asian, non-Hispanic/Latino, 17 international. Average age 27. 92 applicants, 21% accepted, 7 enrolled. In 2010, 4 doctorates awarded. Application fee: $100. *Expenses:* Tuition, state resident: full-time $8370; part-time $349 per credit. Tuition, nonresident: full-time $13,780; part-time $574 per credit. Required fees: $994. *Financial support:* In 2010–11, 16 research assistantships, 8 teaching assistantships were awarded. *Unit head:* Prof. Robert Haltiwanger, Chair, 631-632-8560. *Application contact:* Dr. Erwin London, Director, Graduate Program, 631-632-8564, Fax: 631-632-8575, E-mail: elondon@notes.sunysb.edu.

Syracuse University, College of Arts and Sciences, Program in Structural Biology, Biochemistry and Biophysics, Syracuse, NY 13244. Offers PhD. *Students:* 6 full-time (4 women), 1 part-time (0 women); includes 1 minority (Black or African American, non-Hispanic/Latino), 4 international. Average age 30. 10 applicants, 0% accepted, 0 enrolled. In 2010, 2 doctorates awarded. *Degree requirements:* For doctorate, thesis/dissertation, exam. *Entrance requirements:* For doctorate, GRE General Test, GRE Subject Test. Additional exam requirements/recommendations for international students: Required—TOEFL (minimum score 100 iBT). *Application deadline:* For fall admission, 1/10 priority date for domestic and international students. Application fee: $75. Electronic applications accepted. *Expenses:* Tuition: Part-time $1162 per credit. *Financial support:* Fellowships with full tuition reimbursements, research assistantships with full and partial tuition reimbursements, teaching assistantships with full and partial tuition reimbursements, tuition waivers available. Financial award application deadline: 1/1; financial award applicants required to submit FAFSA. *Unit head:* Scott Pitnick, Director, 315-443-5128, Fax: 315-443-2012, E-mail: sspitnic@syr.edu. *Application contact:* Evelyn Lott, Information Contact, 315-443-9154, Fax: 315-443-2012, E-mail: ealott@syr.edu.

Temple University, Health Sciences Center, School of Medicine and Graduate School, Doctor of Medicine Program, Department of Biochemistry, Philadelphia, PA 19122-6096. Offers MS, PhD. *Faculty:* 22 full-time (6 women). *Students:* 20 full-time (8 women); includes 1 Black or African American, non-Hispanic/Latino; 2 Asian, non-Hispanic/Latino, 8 international. 21 applicants, 43% accepted, 5 enrolled. In 2010, 2 master's, 2 doctorates awarded. *Degree requirements:* For master's, thesis, research seminar; for doctorate, thesis/dissertation, research seminars. *Entrance requirements:* For master's and doctorate, GRE General Test, GRE Subject Test, minimum GPA of 3.0. Additional exam requirements/recommendations for international students: Required—TOEFL (minimum score 650 paper-based; 280 computer-based). *Application deadline:* For fall admission, 4/15 priority date for domestic students, 12/15 for international students; for spring admission, 11/15 priority date for domestic students, 8/1 for international students. Applications are processed on a rolling basis. Application fee: $50. Electronic applications accepted. *Financial support:* Fellowships, research assistantships, Federal Work-Study and institutionally sponsored loans available. Financial award application deadline: 1/15; financial award applicants required to submit FAFSA. *Faculty research:* Metabolism, enzymology, molecular biology, membranology, biophysics. *Unit head:* Dr. Donald L. Gill, Acting Chair, 215-707-3979, Fax: 215-707-7536, E-mail: dgill@temple.edu. *Application contact:* Dr. Donald L. Gill, Acting Chair, 215-707-3979, Fax: 215-707-7536, E-mail: dgill@temple.edu.

Texas A&M University, College of Agriculture and Life Sciences, Department of Biochemistry and Biophysics, College Station, TX 77843. Offers biochemistry (MS, PhD); biophysics (MS). *Faculty:* 37. *Students:* 144 full-time (55 women), 5 part-time (2 women); includes 20 minority (3 Black or African American, non-Hispanic/Latino; 1 American Indian or Alaska Native, non-Hispanic/Latino; 2 Asian, non-Hispanic/Latino; 13 Hispanic/Latino; 1 Native Hawaiian or other Pacific Islander, non-Hispanic/Latino), 55 international. Average age 27. In 2010, 5 master's, 17 doctorates awarded. *Entrance requirements:* For master's and doctorate, GRE General Test. Additional exam requirements/recommendations for international students: Required—TOEFL. *Application deadline:* For fall admission, 2/1 priority date for domestic students, 12/1 priority date for international students. Applications are processed on a rolling basis. Application fee: $50 ($75 for international students). Electronic applications accepted. *Financial support:* In 2010–11, 6 fellowships with tuition reimbursements (averaging $20,000 per year), 70 research assistantships with partial tuition reimbursements (averaging $20,000 per year) were awarded; teaching assistantships with partial tuition reimbursements, institutionally sponsored loans, scholarships/grants, traineeships, and unspecified assistantships also available. Financial award application deadline: 2/1; financial award applicants required to submit FAFSA. *Faculty research:* Enzymology, gene expression, protein structure, plant biochemistry. *Unit head:* Dr. Gregory D. Reinhart, Department Head, 979-862-2263, Fax: 979-845-9274, E-mail: gdr@tamu.edu. *Application contact:* Pat Swigert, Graduate Advisor, 979-845-1779, Fax: 979-845-9274.

Texas Christian University, College of Science and Engineering, Department of Chemistry, Fort Worth, TX 76129-0002. Offers biochemistry (MS, PhD); chemistry (MA); inorganic (MS, PhD); organic (MS, PhD); physical (MS, PhD). Part-time and evening/weekend programs available. *Faculty:* 11 full-time (2 women), 1 (woman) part-time/adjunct. *Students:* 19 full-time (9 women), 2 part-time (both women); includes 1 American Indian or Alaska Native, non-Hispanic/Latino; 3 Asian, non-Hispanic/Latino, 9 international. Average age 24. 23 applicants, 26% accepted, 5 enrolled. In 2010, 3 doctorates awarded. *Degree requirements:* For master's, thesis; for doctorate, thesis/dissertation, literature seminar, cumulative exams, research progress report, original proposal. *Entrance requirements:* For master's and doctorate, GRE General Test. Additional exam requirements/recommendations for international students: Required—TOEFL. *Application deadline:* For fall admission, 3/1 priority date for domestic and international students; for spring admission, 9/1 priority date for domestic and international students. Applications are processed on a rolling basis. Application fee: $50. Electronic applications accepted. *Expenses:* Tuition: Full-time $18,720; part-time $1040 per credit hour. Tuition and fees vary according to course load and program. *Financial support:* Fellowships, teaching assistantships, unspecified assistantships available. Financial award application deadline: 3/1. *Faculty research:* Phase transitions and transport properties of bio/macromolecular solutions, nanoscale biomaterials, electronic structure theory, synthetic methodology and total synthesis of natural products, chemistry and biology of (bio)polymers. *Unit head:* Dr. Robert Neilson, Chairperson/Professor, 817-257-7345, Fax: 817-257-5851, E-mail: r.neilson@tcu.edu. *Application contact:* Dr. Sergei V. Dzyuba, Director of Graduate Studies/Assistant Professor, 817-257-6218, Fax: 817-257-5851, E-mail: s.dzyuba@tcu.edu.

Texas State University–San Marcos, Graduate School, College of Science, Department of Chemistry and Biochemistry, Program in Biochemistry, San Marcos, TX 78666. Offers MS. *Faculty:* 5 full-time (2 women). *Students:* 20 full-time (11 women), 3 part-time (0 women); includes 9 minority (1 Black or African American, non-Hispanic/Latino; 3 Asian, non-Hispanic/Latino; 5 Hispanic/Latino). Average age 27. 19 applicants, 89% accepted, 13 enrolled. In 2010, 5 master's awarded. *Degree requirements:* For master's, thesis. *Entrance requirements:* For master's, minimum GPA of 2.75 in last 60 hours of course work. Additional exam requirements/recommendations for international students: Required—TOEFL (minimum score 550 paper-based; 213 computer-based; 78 iBT). *Application deadline:* For fall admission, 6/15 priority date for domestic students, 6/1 priority date for international students; for spring admission, 10/15 priority date for domestic students, 10/1 priority date for international students. Applications are processed on a rolling basis. Application fee: $40 ($90 for international students). Electronic applications accepted. *Expenses:* Tuition, state resident: full-time $6024; part-time $251 per credit hour. Tuition, nonresident: full-time $13,536; part-time $564 per credit hour. Required fees: $1776; $50 per credit hour. $306 per semester. *Financial support:* In 2010–11, 9 students received support, including 12 teaching assistantships (averaging $5,368 per year); research assistantships, Federal Work-Study, institutionally sponsored loans, scholarships/grants, health care benefits, and unspecified assistantships also available. Support available to part-time students. Financial award application deadline: 4/1; financial award applicants required to submit FAFSA. *Unit head:* Dr. Chad Booth, Graduate Advisor, 512-245-2156, Fax: 512-245-2374, E-mail: chadbooth@txstate.edu. *Application contact:* Dr. Chad Booth, Graduate Advisor, 512-245-2156, Fax: 512-245-2374, E-mail: chadbooth@txstate.edu.

Texas Tech University Health Sciences Center, Graduate School of Biomedical Sciences, Department of Cell Biology and Biochemistry, Program in Biochemistry and Molecular Genetics, Lubbock, TX 79430. Offers MS, PhD, MD/PhD, MS/PhD. Terminal master's awarded for partial completion of doctoral program. *Degree requirements:* For master's, comprehensive exam, thesis, preliminary, comprehensive, and final exams; for doctorate, comprehensive exam, thesis/dissertation, preliminary, comprehensive, and final exams. *Entrance requirements:* For master's and doctorate, GRE General Test, minimum GPA of 3.0. Additional exam requirements/recommendations for international students: Required—TOEFL. Electronic applications accepted. *Faculty research:* Reproductive endocrinology, immunology, developmental biochemistry, biochemistry and genetics of cancer, molecular genetics and cell cycle.

Thomas Jefferson University, Jefferson College of Graduate Studies, PhD Program in Biochemistry and Molecular Biology, Philadelphia, PA 19107. Offers PhD. *Faculty:* 48 full-time (15 women). *Students:* 15 full-time (10 women), 1 (woman) part-time; includes 1 minority (Asian, non-Hispanic/Latino), 2 international. Average age 24. 41 applicants, 20% accepted, 3 enrolled. In 2010, 3 doctorates awarded. *Degree requirements:* For doctorate, comprehensive exam, thesis/dissertation. *Entrance requirements:* For doctorate, GRE General Test or MCAT, minimum GPA of 3.2. Additional exam requirements/recommendations for international students: Required—TOEFL (minimum score 250 computer-based; 100 iBT) or IELTS. *Application deadline:* For fall admission, 1/2 priority date for domestic and international students. Applications are processed on a rolling basis. Application fee: $50. Electronic applications accepted. *Financial support:* In 2010–11, 15 students received support, including 15 fellowships with full tuition reimbursements available (averaging $54,723 per year); Federal Work-Study, institutionally sponsored loans, scholarships/grants, traineeships, and stipends also available. Financial award application deadline: 5/1; financial award applicants required to submit FAFSA. *Faculty research:* Signal transduction and molecular genetics, translational biochemistry, human mitochondrial genetics, molecular biology of protein-RNA interaction, mammalian mitochondrial biogenesis and function. Total annual research expenditures: $39.1 million. *Unit head:* Dr. Diane E. Merry, Program Director, 215-503-4907, Fax: 215-923-9162, E-mail: diane.merry@jefferson.edu. *Application contact:* Marc E. Stearns, Director of Admissions, 215-503-0155, Fax: 215-503-9920, E-mail: jcgs-info@jefferson.edu.

Tufts University, Sackler School of Graduate Biomedical Sciences, Department of Biochemistry, Medford, MA 02155. Offers PhD. *Faculty:* 28 full-time (8 women). *Students:* 16 full-time (6 women); includes 2 Asian, non-Hispanic/Latino, 5 international. Average age 29. In 2010, 5 doctorates awarded. Terminal master's awarded for partial completion of doctoral program. *Degree requirements:* For doctorate, thesis/dissertation. *Entrance requirements:* For doctorate, GRE, 3 letters of recommendation. Additional exam requirements/recommendations for international students: Required—TOEFL. *Application deadline:* For fall admission, 12/15 for domestic and international students. Applications are processed on a rolling basis. Application fee: $70. Electronic applications accepted. *Expenses:* Tuition: Full-time $39,624; part-time $3962 per course. Required fees: $40 per year. Full-time tuition and fees vary according to degree level, program and student level. Part-time tuition and fees vary according to course load. *Financial support:* In 2010–11, 16 students received support, including 16 research assistantships with full tuition reimbursements available (averaging $28,500 per year); scholarships/grants and health care benefits also available. *Faculty research:* Enzymes and mechanisms, signal transduction, NMR spectroscopy, DNA biosynthesis, membrane function. *Unit head:* Dr. Larry Feig, Program Director, 617-636-6956, Fax: 617-636-2409, E-mail: larry.feig@tufts.edu. *Application contact:* 617-636-6767, Fax: 617-636-0375, E-mail: sackler-school@tufts.edu.

Tufts University, Sackler School of Graduate Biomedical Sciences, Integrated Studies Program, Medford, MA 02155. Offers PhD. *Students:* 10 full-time (7 women); includes 1 Asian, non-Hispanic/Latino, 2 international. Average age 25. 333 applicants, 6% accepted. *Entrance requirements:* For doctorate, GRE General Test, 3 letters of reference. Additional exam requirements/recommendations for international students: Required—TOEFL. *Application deadline:* For fall admission, 12/15 for domestic and international students. Applications are processed on a rolling basis. Application fee: $70. Electronic applications accepted. *Expenses:* Tuition: Full-time $39,624; part-time $3962 per course. Required fees: $40 per year. Full-time tuition and fees vary according to degree level, program and student level. Part-time tuition and fees vary according to course load. *Financial support:* In 2010–11, 10 students received support, including 10 research assistantships with tuition reimbursements available (averaging $28,250 per year); scholarships/grants and health care benefits also available. *Unit head:* Dr. Karina Meiri, Program Director, 617-636-6707, E-mail: james.dice@tufts.edu. *Application contact:* Kellie Johnston, Associate Director of Admissions, 617-636-6767, Fax: 617-636-0375, E-mail: sackler-school@tufts.edu.

Tulane University, School of Medicine and School of Liberal Arts, Graduate Programs in Biomedical Sciences, Department of Biochemistry, New Orleans, LA 70118-5669. Offers MS, PhD, MD/PhD. MS and PhD offered through the Graduate School. *Degree requirements:* For master's, thesis; for doctorate, 2 foreign languages, thesis/dissertation. *Entrance requirements:* For master's, GRE General Test, GRE Subject Test, minimum B average in undergraduate course work; for doctorate, GRE General Test, GRE Subject Test. Additional exam requirements/recommendations for international students: Required—TOEFL. Electronic applications accepted. *Faculty research:* Nucleic acid chemistry, complex carbohydrates biochemistry.

Universidad Central del Caribe, School of Medicine, Program in Biomedical Sciences, Bayamón, PR 00960-6032. Offers anatomy and cell biology (MA, MS); biochemistry (MS); biomedical sciences (MA); cellular and molecular biology (PhD); microbiology and immunology (MA, MS); pharmacology (MS); physiology (MS).

Université de Moncton, Faculty of Science, Department of Chemistry and Biochemistry, Moncton, NB E1A 3E9, Canada. Offers biochemistry (M Sc); chemistry (M Sc). Part-time programs available. *Degree requirements:* For master's, one foreign language, thesis. *Entrance requirements:* For master's, minimum GPA of 3.0. Electronic applications accepted. *Faculty research:* Environmental contaminants, natural products synthesis, nutraceutical, organic catalysis, molecular biology of cancer.

Université de Montréal, Faculty of Medicine, Department of Biochemistry, Montréal, QC H3C 3J7, Canada. Offers biochemistry (M Sc, PhD); clinical biochemistry (DEPD). Terminal master's awarded for partial completion of doctoral program. *Degree requirements:* For master's, thesis; for doctorate, thesis/dissertation, general exam. *Entrance requirements:* For master's and doctorate, proficiency in French, knowledge of English; for DEPD, proficiency in French. Electronic applications accepted.

Université de Sherbrooke, Faculty of Medicine and Health Sciences, Graduate Programs in Medicine, Department of Biochemistry, Sherbrooke, QC J1H 5N4, Canada. Offers M Sc, PhD. Terminal master's awarded for partial completion of doctoral program. *Degree requirements:* For master's, thesis; for doctorate, thesis/dissertation. Electronic applications accepted. *Faculty research:* RNA structure-function, chromatin and gene expression, genetic diseases.

Université Laval, Faculty of Medicine, Post-Professional Programs in Medical Studies, Québec, QC G1K 7P4, Canada. Offers anatomy–pathology (DESS); anesthesiology (DESS); cardiology (DESS); care of older people (Diploma); clinical research (DESS); community health (DESS); dermatology (DESS); diagnostic radiology (DESS); emergency medicine (Diploma); family medicine (DESS); general surgery (DESS); geriatrics (DESS); hematology (DESS); internal medicine (DESS); maternal and fetal medicine (Diploma); medical biochemistry (DESS); medical microbiology and infectious diseases (DESS); medical oncology (DESS); nephrology (DESS); neurology (DESS); neurosurgery (DESS); obstetrics and gynecology (DESS); ophthalmology (DESS); orthopedic surgery (DESS); oto-rhino-laryngology (DESS); palliative medicine (Diploma); pediatrics (DESS); plastic surgery (DESS); psychiatry (DESS); pulmonary medicine (DESS); radiology–oncology (DESS); thoracic surgery (DESS); urology (DESS). *Degree requirements:* For other advanced degree, comprehensive exam. *Entrance requirements:* For degree, knowledge of French. Electronic applications accepted.

Université Laval, Faculty of Sciences and Engineering, Department of Biochemistry and Microbiology, Programs in Biochemistry, Québec, QC G1K 7P4, Canada. Offers M Sc, PhD. Terminal master's awarded for partial completion of doctoral program. *Degree requirements:* For master's, thesis; for doctorate, comprehensive exam, thesis/dissertation. *Entrance requirements:* For master's and doctorate, knowledge of French, comprehension of written English. Electronic applications accepted.

University at Albany, State University of New York, School of Public Health, Department of Biomedical Sciences, Program in Biochemistry, Molecular Biology, and Genetics, Albany, NY 12222-0001. Offers MS, PhD. *Degree requirements:* For master's, thesis; for doctorate, thesis/dissertation. *Entrance requirements:* For master's and doctorate, GRE General Test, GRE Subject Test.

University at Buffalo, the State University of New York, Graduate School, School of Medicine and Biomedical Sciences, Graduate Programs in Medicine and Biomedical Sciences, Department of Biochemistry, Buffalo, NY 14260. Offers MA, PhD. *Faculty:* 18 full-time (6 women), 1 (woman) part-time/adjunct. *Students:* 24 full-time (13 women), 5 part-time (all women); includes 1 American Indian or Alaska Native, non-Hispanic/Latino; 1 Asian, non-Hispanic/Latino, 7 international. Average age 26. 24 applicants, 50% accepted, 0 enrolled. In 2010, 2 master's, 4 doctorates awarded. Terminal master's awarded for partial completion of doctoral program. *Degree requirements:* For master's, thesis optional; for doctorate, comprehensive exam, thesis/dissertation. *Entrance requirements:* For master's, GRE General Test; for doctorate, GRE General Test, 3 letters of recommendation. Additional exam requirements/recommendations for international students: Required—TOEFL (minimum score 600 paper-based; 250 computer-based; 100 iBT). *Application deadline:* For fall admission, 2/1 priority date for domestic and international students. Applications are processed on a rolling basis. Application fee: $50. Electronic applications accepted. *Financial support:* In 2010–11, 2 fellowships with full tuition reimbursements (averaging $4,000 per year), 20 research assistantships with full tuition reimbursements (averaging $21,000 per year), 4 teaching assistantships with full tuition reimbursements (averaging $21,000 per year) were awarded; Federal Work-Study, institutionally sponsored loans, scholarships/grants, health care benefits, and unspecified assistantships also available. Financial award application deadline: 2/1; financial award applicants required to submit FAFSA. *Faculty research:* Gene expression, proteins and metalloenzymes, biochemical endocrinology. Total annual research expenditures: $3.3 million. *Unit head:* Dr. Kenneth M. Blumenthal, Chair, 716-829-2727, Fax: 716-829-2725, E-mail: kblumen@buffalo.edu. *Application contact:* Dr. Mark R. O'Brian, Director of Graduate Studies, 716-829-3200, Fax: 716-829-2725, E-mail: mrobrian@buffalo.edu.

The University of Alabama at Birmingham, Graduate Programs in Joint Health Sciences, Program in Biochemistry and Molecular Genetics, Birmingham, AL 35294. Offers PhD. *Students:* 29 full-time (9 women), 3 part-time (0 women); includes 2 minority (both Asian, non-Hispanic/Latino), 18 international. Average age 30. In 2010, 6 doctorates awarded. *Degree requirements:* For doctorate, thesis/dissertation. *Entrance requirements:* For doctorate, GRE General Test, interview. *Application deadline:* Applications are processed on a rolling basis. Electronic applications accepted. *Expenses:* Tuition, state resident: full-time $5482. Tuition, nonresident: full-time $12,430. Tuition and fees vary according to program. *Financial support:* In 2010–11, 8 fellowships were awarded. *Unit head:* Dr. Tim M. Townes, Chair, 205-934-5294, E-mail: ttownes@uab.edu. *Application contact:* Information Contact, 205-934-6034, Fax: 205-975-2547.

University of Alaska Fairbanks, College of Natural Sciences and Mathematics, Department of Chemistry and Biochemistry, Fairbanks, AK 99775-6160. Offers biochemistry and molecular biology (MS, PhD); chemistry (MA, MS); environmental chemistry (MS, PhD). Part-time programs available. *Faculty:* 9 full-time (1 woman). *Students:* 33 full-time (17 women), 4 part-time (2 women); includes 8 minority (1 Black or African American, non-Hispanic/Latino; 2 American Indian or Alaska Native, non-Hispanic/Latino; 2 Asian, non-Hispanic/Latino; 3 Two or more races, non-Hispanic/Latino), 6 international. Average age 31. 38 applicants, 34% accepted, 10 enrolled. In 2010, 3 master's, 4 doctorates awarded. *Degree requirements:* For master's, comprehensive exam, thesis or alternative; for doctorate, comprehensive exam, thesis/dissertation, oral defense. *Entrance requirements:* Additional exam requirements/recommendations for international students: Required—TOEFL (minimum score 550 paper-based; 213 computer-based). *Application deadline:* For fall admission, 6/1 for domestic students, 3/1 for international students; for spring admission, 10/15 for domestic students, 9/1 for international students. Applications are processed on a rolling basis. Application fee: $60. Electronic applications accepted. *Expenses:* Tuition, state resident: full-time $5688; part-time $316 per credit. Tuition, nonresident: full-time $11,628; part-time $646 per credit. Required fees: $289 per semester. Tuition and fees vary according to course load and reciprocity agreements. *Financial support:* In 2010–11, 15 research assistantships with tuition reimbursements (averaging $12,459 per year), 16 teaching assistantships with tuition reimbursements (averaging $14,968 per year) were awarded; fellowships with tuition reimbursements, Federal Work-Study, scholarships/grants, health care benefits, and unspecified assistantships also available. Support available to part-time students. Financial award application deadline: 7/1; financial award applicants required to submit FAFSA. *Faculty research:* Atmospheric aerosols, cold adaptation, hibernation and neuroprotection, liganogated ion channels, arctic contaminants. *Unit head:* Bill Simpson, Department Chair, 907-474-5510, Fax: 907-474-5640, E-mail: fychem@uaf.edu. *Application contact:* Bill Simpson, Department Chair, 907-474-5510, Fax: 907-474-5640, E-mail: fychem@uaf.edu.

University of Alberta, Faculty of Medicine and Dentistry and Faculty of Graduate Studies and Research, Graduate Programs in Medicine, Department of Biochemistry, Edmonton, AB T6G 2E1, Canada. Offers M Sc, PhD. Terminal master's awarded for partial completion of doctoral program. *Degree requirements:* For master's, thesis; for doctorate, thesis/dissertation. *Entrance requirements:* For master's and doctorate, minimum GPA of 3.3. Additional exam requirements/recommendations for international students: Required—TOEFL (minimum score 550 paper-based). *Faculty research:* Proteins, nucleic acids, membranes, regulation of gene expression, receptors.

The University of Arizona, College of Science, Department of Chemistry and Biochemistry, Tucson, AZ 85721. Offers biochemistry (PhD); chemistry (PhD). Part-time programs available. *Faculty:* 33 full-time (6 women), 4 part-time/adjunct (1 woman). *Students:* 201 full-time (85 women), 14 part-time (8 women); includes 25 minority (2 Black or African American, non-Hispanic/Latino; 1 American Indian or Alaska Native, non-Hispanic/Latino; 2 Asian, non-Hispanic/Latino; 9 Hispanic/Latino; 1 Native Hawaiian or other Pacific Islander, non-Hispanic/Latino; 10 Two or more races, non-Hispanic/Latino), 85 international. Average age 30. 124 applicants, 31% accepted, 34 enrolled. In 2010, 21 doctorates awarded. *Degree requirements:* For doctorate, comprehensive exam, thesis/dissertation. *Entrance requirements:* For doctorate, GRE General Test, 3 letters of recommendation, statement of purpose. Additional exam requirements/recommendations for international students: Required—TOEFL (minimum score 550 paper-based; 213 computer-based; 79 iBT). *Application deadline:* For fall admission, 2/1 for domestic students, 1/1 for international students; for spring admission, 10/15 for domestic and international students. Applications are processed on a rolling basis. Application fee: $75. Electronic applications accepted. *Expenses:* Tuition, state resident: full-time $7692. *Financial support:* In 2010–11, 66 research assistantships with full tuition reimbursements (averaging $24,083 per year), 112 teaching assistantships with full tuition reimbursements (averaging $23,402 per year) were awarded; institutionally sponsored loans, scholarships/grants, health care benefits, tuition waivers (partial), and unspecified assistantships also available. Financial award applicants required to submit FAFSA. *Faculty research:* Analytical, inorganic, organic, physical chemistry, biological chemistry. Total annual research expenditures: $11.6 million. *Unit head:* Mark A. Smith, Head, 520-621-2115, Fax: 520-621-8407, E-mail: msmith@u.arizona.edu. *Application contact:* Lori Boyd, 800-545-5814, Fax: 520-621-8407, E-mail: chemistry@arizona.edu.

University of Arkansas for Medical Sciences, Graduate School, Graduate Programs in Biomedical Sciences, Program in Biochemistry and Molecular Biology, Little Rock, AR 72205-7199. Offers MS, PhD, MD/PhD. *Degree requirements:* For master's, comprehensive exam, thesis; for doctorate, thesis/dissertation, qualifying exam. *Entrance requirements:* For master's, GRE General Test, bachelor's degree in biology, chemistry, or related field; for doctorate, GRE General Test. Additional exam requirements/recommendations for international students: Required—TOEFL. *Faculty research:* Gene regulation, growth factors, oncogenes, metabolic diseases, hormone regulation.

The University of British Columbia, Faculty of Medicine, Department of Biochemistry and Molecular Biology, Vancouver, BC V6T 1Z1, Canada. Offers M Sc, PhD. *Faculty:* 22 full-time (2 women). *Students:* 62 full-time (27 women). Average age 27. 60 applicants, 15 enrolled. In 2010, 5 master's, 6 doctorates awarded. *Degree requirements:* For master's, thesis; for doctorate, comprehensive exam, thesis/dissertation. *Entrance requirements:* For master's, first class B Sc; for doctorate, master's or first class honors bachelor's degree in biochemistry. Additional exam requirements/recommendations for international students: Required—TOEFL (minimum score 625 paper-based; 263 computer-based). *Application deadline:* For fall admission, 1/31 priority date for domestic students, 1/31 for international students; for winter admission, 5/31 priority date for domestic students, 5/31 for international students. Applications are processed on a rolling basis. Application fee: $90 ($150 for international students). Electronic applications accepted. Tuition charges are reported in Canadian dollars. *Expenses:* Tuition, area resident: Full-time $4179 Canadian dollars. International tuition: $7344 Canadian dollars full-time. *Financial support:* In 2010–11, 28 fellowships (averaging $25,074 per year), 30 research assistantships (averaging $20,600 per year), 13 teaching assistantships (averaging $2,300 per year) were awarded; institutionally sponsored loans, scholarships/grants, traineeships, tuition waivers (partial), and unspecified assistantships also available. *Faculty research:* Membrane biochemistry, protein structure/function, signal transduction, biochemistry. Total annual research expenditures: $12.6 million. *Unit head:* Dr. Roger Brownsey, Professor and Head, 604-827-4027, Fax: 604-822-5227. *Application contact:* Doris Metcalf, Graduate Secretary, 604-822-5925, Fax: 604-822-5227, E-mail: biocgrad@interchange.ubc.ca.

University of Calgary, Faculty of Medicine and Faculty of Graduate Studies, Department of Biochemistry and Molecular Biology, Calgary, AB T2N 1N4, Canada. Offers M Sc, PhD. *Degree requirements:* For master's, thesis; for doctorate, thesis/dissertation, candidacy exam. *Entrance requirements:* For master's and doctorate, GRE General Test, minimum GPA of 3.2. Additional exam requirements/recommendations for international students: Required—TOEFL. Electronic applications accepted. *Faculty research:* Molecular and developmental genetics; molecular biology of disease; genomics, proteomics and bioinformatics; ceu signaling and structure.

University of California, Berkeley, Graduate Division, Group in Comparative Biochemistry, Berkeley, CA 94720-1500. Offers PhD. *Degree requirements:* For doctorate, thesis/dissertation, qualifying exam. *Entrance requirements:* For doctorate, GRE General Test, GRE Subject Test, minimum GPA of 3.0, 3 letters of recommendation. Additional exam requirements/recommendations for international students: Required—TOEFL.

University of California, Davis, Graduate Studies, Graduate Group in Biochemistry and Molecular Biology, Davis, CA 95616. Offers MS, PhD. Terminal master's awarded for partial completion of doctoral program. *Degree requirements:* For master's, comprehensive exam (for some programs), thesis (for some programs); for doctorate, thesis/dissertation. *Entrance requirements:* For master's and doctorate, GRE General Test, GRE Subject Test. Additional exam requirements/recommendations for international students: Required—TOEFL (minimum score 550 paper-based; 213 computer-based). Electronic applications accepted. *Faculty research:* Gene expression, protein structure, molecular virology, protein synthesis, enzymology, membrane transport and structural biology.

University of California, Irvine, School of Biological Sciences, Department of Molecular Biology and Biochemistry, Irvine, CA 92697. Offers biological science (MS); biological sciences (PhD); biotechnology (MS); MD/PhD. *Students:* 61 full-time (32 women); includes 28 minority (2 Black or African American, non-Hispanic/Latino; 16 Asian, non-Hispanic/Latino; 10 Hispanic/Latino), 2 international. Average age 28. In 2010, 4 master's, 8 doctorates awarded. *Degree requirements:* For doctorate, thesis/dissertation. *Entrance requirements:* For master's, GRE, minimum GPA of 3.0; for doctorate, GRE General Test, GRE Subject Test, minimum GPA of

Biochemistry

University of California, Irvine (continued)

3.0. Additional exam requirements/recommendations for international students: Required—TOEFL (minimum score 550 paper-based; 213 computer-based). *Application deadline:* For fall admission, 12/15 priority date for domestic students, 12/15 for international students. Applications are processed on a rolling basis. Application fee: $80 ($100 for international students). Electronic applications accepted. *Financial support:* Fellowships, research assistantships with full tuition reimbursements, teaching assistantships, institutionally sponsored loans, traineeships, health care benefits, and unspecified assistantships available. Financial award application deadline: 3/1; financial award applicants required to submit FAFSA. *Faculty research:* Structure and synthesis of nucleic acids and proteins, regulation, virology, biochemical genetics, gene organization. *Unit head:* Prof. Christopher C. Hughes, Chair, 949-824-8771, Fax: 949-824-8551, E-mail: cchughes@uci.edu. *Application contact:* Judy L. Lundberg, Personnel Analyst, 949-824-4740, Fax: 949-824-8551, E-mail: jllundbe@uci.edu.

University of California, Irvine, School of Biological Sciences and School of Medicine, Graduate Program in Cellular and Molecular Biosciences, Irvine, CA 92697. Offers PhD. *Degree requirements:* For doctorate, thesis/dissertation, teaching assignment, preliminary exam. *Entrance requirements:* For doctorate, GRE General Test, minimum GPA of 3.0, research experience. Additional exam requirements/recommendations for international students: Required—TOEFL, IELTS, SPEAK test. Electronic applications accepted. *Expenses:* Contact institution. *Faculty research:* Cellular biochemistry; gene structure and expression; protein structure, function, and design; molecular genetics; pathogenesis and inherited disease.

University of California, Irvine, School of Medicine and School of Biological Sciences, Department of Biological Chemistry, Irvine, CA 92697. Offers biological sciences (MS, PhD). Students apply through the Graduate Program in Molecular Biology, Genetics, and Biochemistry. *Students:* 40 full-time (24 women); includes 11 minority (9 Asian, non-Hispanic/Latino; 2 Hispanic/Latino), 7 international. Average age 28. In 2010, 1 master's, 8 doctorates awarded. *Degree requirements:* For doctorate, thesis/dissertation. *Entrance requirements:* For master's, minimum GPA of 3.0; for doctorate, GRE General Test, GRE Subject Test, minimum GPA of 3.0. Additional exam requirements/recommendations for international students: Required—TOEFL (minimum score 550 paper-based; 213 computer-based). *Application deadline:* For fall admission, 1/15 priority date for domestic students, 1/15 for international students. Application fee: $80 ($100 for international students). Electronic applications accepted. *Financial support:* Fellowships, research assistantships with full tuition reimbursements, teaching assistantships, institutionally sponsored loans, traineeships, health care benefits, and unspecified assistantships available. Financial award application deadline: 3/1; financial award applicants required to submit FAFSA. *Faculty research:* RNA splicing, mammalian chromosomal organization, membrane-hormone interactions, regulation of protein synthesis, molecular genetics of metabolic processes. *Unit head:* Prof. Robert E. Steele, Chair, 949-824-7341, Fax: 949-824-2688, E-mail: resteele@uci.edu. *Application contact:* Aaron M. Goddman, Administrative Assistant, 949-824-6051, Fax: 949-824-2688, E-mail: amgoodma@uci.edu.

University of California, Los Angeles, David Geffen School of Medicine and Graduate Division, Graduate Programs in Medicine, Department of Biological Chemistry, Los Angeles, CA 90095. Offers MS, PhD. *Faculty:* 20 full-time (3 women). *Students:* 30 full-time (18 women); includes 1 Black or African American, non-Hispanic/Latino; 4 Asian, non-Hispanic/Latino; 1 Hispanic/Latino; 1 Native Hawaiian or other Pacific Islander, non-Hispanic/Latino, 6 international. Average age 27. 1 applicant, 0% accepted, 0 enrolled. In 2010, 3 master's, 4 doctorates awarded. *Degree requirements:* For master's, comprehensive exam or thesis; for doctorate, thesis/dissertation, oral and written qualifying exams. *Entrance requirements:* For master's and doctorate, GRE General Test. Application fee: $70 ($90 for international students). Electronic applications accepted. *Financial support:* In 2010–11, 36 fellowships, 31 research assistantships, 10 teaching assistantships were awarded; Federal Work-Study, institutionally sponsored loans, scholarships/grants, and tuition waivers (full and partial) also available. Financial award application deadline: 3/1. *Unit head:* Dr. Kelsey Catherine Martin, Head, 310-794-9502, Fax: 310-206-1929, E-mail: kcmartin@mednet.ucla.edu. *Application contact:* UCLA Access Coordinator, 310-206-1845, Fax: 310-206-1636, E-mail: uclaaccess@mednet.ucla.edu.

University of California, Los Angeles, Graduate Division, College of Letters and Science, Department of Chemistry and Biochemistry, Program in Biochemistry and Molecular Biology, Los Angeles, CA 90034. Offers MS, PhD. MS admission to program only under exceptional circumstances. *Students:* 75 full-time (31 women); includes 31 minority (1 Black or African American, non-Hispanic/Latino; 23 Asian, non-Hispanic/Latino; 7 Hispanic/Latino), 10 international. Average age 27. 109 applicants, 21% accepted, 11 enrolled. In 2010, 8 master's, 20 doctorates awarded. Terminal master's awarded for partial completion of doctoral program. *Degree requirements:* For master's, comprehensive exam or thesis; for doctorate, thesis/dissertation, oral and written exams, 1 year teaching experience. *Entrance requirements:* For master's, GRE General Test, GRE Subject Test, minimum GPA of 3.0; for doctorate, GRE General Test, GRE Subject Test, minimum undergraduate GPA of 3.0. *Application deadline:* For fall admission, 1/15 for domestic and international students. Application fee: $70 ($90 for international students). Electronic applications accepted. *Financial support:* In 2010–11, 90 fellowships with full and partial tuition reimbursements, 63 research assistantships with full and partial tuition reimbursements, 44 teaching assistantships with full and partial tuition reimbursements were awarded; Federal Work-Study, scholarships/grants, health care benefits, tuition waivers (full and partial), and unspecified assistantships also available. Financial award applicants required to submit FAFSA. *Unit head:* Dr. Albert Courey, 310-825-3958, E-mail: courey@chem.ucla.edu. *Application contact:* Departmental Office, 310-825-2645, E-mail: bmbgrad@chem.ucla.edu.

University of California, Los Angeles, Graduate Division, College of Letters and Science and David Geffen School of Medicine, UCLA ACCESS to Programs in the Molecular, Cellular and Integrative Life Sciences, Los Angeles, CA 90095. Offers biochemistry and molecular biology (PhD); biological chemistry (PhD); cellular and molecular pathology (PhD); human genetics (PhD); microbiology, immunology, and molecular genetics (PhD); molecular biology (PhD); molecular toxicology (PhD); molecular, cellular and integrative physiology (PhD); neurobiology (PhD); oral biology (PhD); physiology (PhD). ACCESS is an umbrella program for first-year coursework in 12 PhD programs. *Students:* 48 full-time (28 women), 6 international. Average age 24. 388 applicants, 27% accepted, 48 enrolled. *Degree requirements:* For doctorate, thesis/dissertation, oral and written qualifying exams. *Entrance requirements:* For doctorate, GRE General Test, minimum undergraduate GPA of 3.0. Additional exam requirements/recommendations for international students: Required—TOEFL. *Application deadline:* For fall admission, 12/15 for domestic and international students. Application fee: $70 ($90 for international students). Electronic applications accepted. *Financial support:* In 2010–11, 31 fellowships with full and partial tuition reimbursements, 13 research assistantships with full and partial tuition reimbursements, 2 teaching assistantships with full and partial tuition reimbursements were awarded; Federal Work-Study, institutionally sponsored loans, scholarships/grants, health care benefits, tuition waivers (full and partial), and unspecified assistantships also available. Financial award application deadline: 3/1; financial award applicants required to submit FAFSA. *Faculty research:* Molecular, cellular, and developmental biology; immunology; microbiology; integrative biology. *Unit head:* Jody Spillane, Project Coordinator, 310-206-1845, E-mail: jspillane@mednet.ucla.edu. *Application contact:* UCLA Access Admissions, 310-206-1845, E-mail: uclaaccess@mednet.ucla.edu.

University of California, Riverside, Graduate Division, Department of Biochemistry, Riverside, CA 92521-0102. Offers biochemistry and molecular biology (MS, PhD). Part-time programs available. Terminal master's awarded for partial completion of doctoral program. *Degree requirements:* For master's, comprehensive exams or thesis; for doctorate, comprehensive exam, thesis/dissertation, 2 quarters of teaching experience, qualifying exams. *Entrance requirements:* For master's and doctorate, GRE General Test, minimum GPA of 3.25. Additional exam requirements/recommendations for international students: Required—TOEFL (minimum score 550 paper-based; 213 computer-based; 80 iBT). Electronic applications accepted. *Faculty research:* Structural biology and molecular biophysics, signal transduction, plant biochemistry and molecular biology, gene expression and metabolic regulation, molecular toxicology and pathogenesis.

University of California, San Diego, Office of Graduate Studies, Department of Chemistry and Biochemistry, La Jolla, CA 92093. Offers chemistry (MS, PhD). *Degree requirements:* For doctorate, thesis/dissertation. *Entrance requirements:* For doctorate, GRE General Test, GRE Subject Test. Electronic applications accepted.

University of California, San Diego, Office of Graduate Studies, Division of Biological Sciences, Program in Biochemistry, La Jolla, CA 92093-0348. Offers PhD. Offered in association with the Salk Institute. *Degree requirements:* For doctorate, thesis/dissertation, qualifying exam. Electronic applications accepted.

University of California, San Francisco, Graduate Division and School of Medicine, Department of Biochemistry and Biophysics, Program in Biochemistry and Molecular Biology, San Francisco, CA 94143. Offers PhD, MD/PhD. *Degree requirements:* For doctorate, thesis/dissertation. *Entrance requirements:* For doctorate, GRE General Test, GRE Subject Test. Additional exam requirements/recommendations for international students: Required—TOEFL. *Expenses:* Contact institution. *Faculty research:* Structural biology, genetics, cell biology, cell physiology, metabolism.

University of California, San Francisco, School of Pharmacy and Graduate Division, Chemistry and Chemical Biology Graduate Program, San Francisco, CA 94143. Offers PhD. *Faculty:* 45 full-time (9 women). *Students:* 42 full-time (20 women); includes 3 Black or African American, non-Hispanic/Latino; 8 Asian, non-Hispanic/Latino; 6 Hispanic/Latino, 4 international. Average age 27. 111 applicants, 19% accepted, 9 enrolled. In 2010, 8 doctorates awarded. *Degree requirements:* For doctorate, thesis/dissertation. *Entrance requirements:* For doctorate, GRE General Test, GRE Subject Test, minimum GPA of 3.0. Additional exam requirements/recommendations for international students: Required—TOEFL (minimum score 550 paper-based; 213 computer-based; 80 iBT). *Application deadline:* For fall admission, 12/1 for domestic and international students. Applications are processed on a rolling basis. Application fee: $70 ($90 for international students). Electronic applications accepted. *Financial support:* In 2010–11, 48 students received support, including 41 fellowships with partial tuition reimbursements available (averaging $19,365 per year), 16 research assistantships with full tuition reimbursements available (averaging $27,000 per year), 2 teaching assistantships with partial tuition reimbursements available (averaging $16,000 per year); institutionally sponsored loans, scholarships/grants, traineeships, and tuition waivers (full) also available. Financial award application deadline: 5/15. *Faculty research:* Biochemistry, macromolecular structure, cellular and molecular pharmacology, physical chemistry and computational biology, synthetic chemistry. *Unit head:* Dr. Charles S. Craik, Director, 415-476-8146, E-mail: craik@cgl.ucsf.edu. *Application contact:* Christine Olson, Senior Administrative Analyst, 415-476-1914, Fax: 415-514-1546, E-mail: olson@cmp.ucsf.edu.

University of California, Santa Barbara, Graduate Division, College of Letters and Sciences, Division of Mathematics, Life, and Physical Sciences, Interdepartmental Graduate Program in Biomolecular Science and Engineering, Santa Barbara, CA 93106-2014. Offers biochemistry and molecular biology (PhD), including biochemistry and molecular biology, biophysics and bioengineering. *Faculty:* 37 full-time (4 women), 1 (woman) part-time/adjunct. *Students:* 30 full-time (13 women); includes 4 Asian, non-Hispanic/Latino. Average age 28. 59 applicants, 22% accepted, 4 enrolled. In 2010, 5 doctorates awarded. Terminal master's awarded for partial completion of doctoral program. *Degree requirements:* For doctorate, thesis/dissertation. *Entrance requirements:* For doctorate, GRE General Test. Additional exam requirements/recommendations for international students: Required—TOEFL (minimum score 630 paper-based; 109 iBT), IELTS (minimum score 7). *Application deadline:* For fall admission, 12/15 for domestic and international students. Application fee: $70 ($90 for international students). Electronic applications accepted. *Financial support:* In 2010–11, 30 students received support, including 16 fellowships with full and partial tuition reimbursements available (averaging $11,321 per year), 31 research assistantships with full and partial tuition reimbursements available (averaging $14,777 per year), 16 teaching assistantships with full and partial tuition reimbursements available (averaging $6,307 per year); Federal Work-Study, traineeships, health care benefits, tuition waivers (full and partial), and unspecified assistantships also available. Financial award application deadline: 12/15; financial award applicants required to submit FAFSA. *Faculty research:* Biochemistry and molecular biology, biophysics, biomaterials, bioengineering, systems biology. *Unit head:* Prof. Philip A. Pincus, Director/Professor, 805-893-4685, E-mail: fyl@mrl.ucsb.edu. *Application contact:* Prof. Philip A. Pincus, Director/Professor, 805-893-4685, E-mail: fyl@mrl.ucsb.edu.

University of California, Santa Cruz, Division of Graduate Studies, Division of Physical and Biological Sciences, Department of Chemistry and Biochemistry, Santa Cruz, CA 95064. Offers MS, PhD. *Students:* 87 full-time (31 women), 3 part-time (1 woman); includes 20 minority (5 Asian, non-Hispanic/Latino; 12 Hispanic/Latino; 3 Two or more races, non-Hispanic/Latino), 10 international. Average age 28. 157 applicants, 37% accepted, 23 enrolled. In 2010, 3 master's, 20 doctorates awarded. *Degree requirements:* For master's, thesis optional; for doctorate, one foreign language, thesis/dissertation, qualifying exam. *Entrance requirements:* For master's and doctorate, GRE General Test, GRE Subject Test. Additional exam requirements/recommendations for international students: Required—TOEFL (minimum score 570 paper-based; 230 computer-based; 89 iBT); Recommended—IELTS (minimum score 8). *Application deadline:* For fall admission, 12/15 for domestic and international students. Application fee: $70 ($90 for international students). Electronic applications accepted. *Financial support:* Fellowships, research assistantships, teaching assistantships, institutionally sponsored loans and tuition waivers available. Financial award applicants required to submit FAFSA. *Faculty research:* Marine chemistry; biochemistry; inorganic, organic, and physical chemistry. *Unit head:* Janet Jones, Graduate Program Coordinator, 831-459-2023, E-mail: jajones@ucsc.edu. *Application contact:* Janet Jones, Graduate Program Coordinator, 831-459-2023, E-mail: jajones@ucsc.edu.

University of Chicago, Division of Biological Sciences, Molecular Biosciences Cluster, Department of Biochemistry and Molecular Biology, Chicago, IL 60637-1513. Offers PhD, MD/PhD. *Degree requirements:* For doctorate, thesis/dissertation, ethics class, 2 teaching assistantships. *Entrance requirements:* For doctorate, GRE General Test, GRE Subject Test. Additional exam requirements/recommendations for international students: Required—TOEFL (minimum score 600 paper-based; 250 computer-based; 104 iBT), IELTS (minimum score 7). Electronic applications accepted. *Faculty research:* Molecular biology, gene expression, and DNA-protein interactions; membrane biochemistry, molecular endocrinology, and transmembrane signaling; enzyme mechanisms, physical biochemistry, and structural biology.

University of Cincinnati, Graduate School, College of Medicine, Graduate Programs in Biomedical Sciences, Department of Molecular Genetics, Biochemistry and Microbiology, Cincinnati, OH 45221. Offers MS, PhD. Terminal master's awarded for partial completion of doctoral program. *Degree requirements:* For master's, thesis or alternative; for doctorate, thesis/dissertation, qualifying exam. *Entrance requirements:* For master's and doctorate, GRE General Test. Additional exam requirements/recommendations for international students: Required—TOEFL (minimum score 600 paper-based; 250 computer-based; 100 iBT), TWE. Electronic applications accepted. *Faculty research:* Cancer biology and developmental genetics, gene regulation and chromosome structure, microbiology and pathogenic mechanisms, structural biology, membrane biochemistry and signal transduction.

University of Cincinnati, Graduate School, McMicken College of Arts and Sciences, Department of Chemistry, Cincinnati, OH 45221. Offers analytical chemistry (MS, PhD); biochemistry (MS, PhD); inorganic chemistry (MS, PhD); organic chemistry (MS, PhD); physical chemistry (MS, PhD); polymer chemistry (MS, PhD); sensors (PhD). Part-time and evening/weekend programs available. Terminal master's awarded for partial completion of doctoral program. *Degree* *requirements:* For master's, thesis optional; for doctorate, comprehensive exam, thesis/dissertation. *Entrance requirements:* For master's and doctorate, GRE General Test. Additional exam requirements/recommendations for international students: Required—TOEFL (minimum score 580 paper-based; 237 computer-based). Electronic applications accepted. *Faculty research:* Biomedical chemistry, laser chemistry, surface science, chemical sensors, synthesis.

University of Colorado Boulder, Graduate School, College of Arts and Sciences, Department of Chemistry and Biochemistry, Boulder, CO 80309. Offers biochemistry (PhD); chemistry (MS). *Faculty:* 41 full-time (7 women). *Students:* 197 full-time (82 women), 3 part-time (1 woman); includes 21 minority (3 Black or African American, non-Hispanic/Latino; 2 American Indian or Alaska Native, non-Hispanic/Latino; 8 Asian, non-Hispanic/Latino; 6 Hispanic/Latino; 2 Two or more races, non-Hispanic/Latino), 31 international. Average age 27. 639 applicants, 42 enrolled. In 2010, 9 master's, 23 doctorates awarded. *Degree requirements:* For master's, comprehensive exam or thesis; for doctorate, comprehensive exam, thesis/dissertation, cumulative exam. *Entrance requirements:* For master's, GRE General Test, GRE Subject Test, minimum undergraduate GPA of 2.75; for doctorate, GRE General Test, GRE Subject Test, minimum GPA of 3.0. *Application deadline:* For fall admission, 1/15 priority date for domestic students, 1/15 for international students. Applications are processed on a rolling basis. Application fee: $50 ($60 for international students). *Financial support:* In 2010–11, 48 fellowships with full tuition reimbursements (averaging $12,195 per year), 110 research assistantships with full tuition reimbursements (averaging $16,014 per year) were awarded; institutionally sponsored loans, traineeships, and tuition waivers (full) also available. Support available to part-time students. *Faculty research:* Analytical, atmospheric, biochemistry, biophysical, chemical physics, environmental, inorganic, organic and physical chemistry. Total annual research expenditures: $20.6 million.

University of Colorado Denver, School of Medicine, Biochemistry Program, Denver, CO 80217-3364. Offers PhD. *Students:* 29 full-time (14 women); includes 1 Asian, non-Hispanic/Latino, 5 international. Average age 30. 24 applicants, 25% accepted, 6 enrolled. In 2010, 3 doctorates awarded. *Degree requirements:* For doctorate, comprehensive exam, thesis/dissertation, 30 credit hours each of coursework and thesis research. *Entrance requirements:* For doctorate, GRE (minimum combined score of 1200 on Verbal and Quantitative portions and at least 4.0 on the Analytical Writing section), minimum of three letters of recommendation from qualified referees. Additional exam requirements/recommendations for international students: Required—TOEFL (minimum score 570 paper-based; 230 computer-based). *Application deadline:* For fall admission, 1/1 for domestic students. Applications are processed on a rolling basis. Application fee: $50. Electronic applications accepted. *Expenses:* Contact institution. *Financial support:* In 2010–11, 6 students received support; fellowships, health care benefits, tuition waivers (full), and stipend available. Financial award application deadline: 3/15; financial award applicants required to submit FAFSA. *Faculty research:* DNA damage, cancer and neurodegeneration, molecular mechanisms of pro-MRNA splicing, yeast RNA polymerases, DNA replication. Total annual research expenditures: $8.6 million. *Unit head:* Dr. Paul Megee, Associate Professor, Department of Biochemistry and Molecular Genetics, 303-724-3270, Fax: 303-724-3215, E-mail: paul.megee@ucdenver.edu. *Application contact:* Dr. Paul Megee, Associate Professor, Department of Biochemistry and Molecular Genetics, 303-724-3270, Fax: 303-724-3215, E-mail: paul.megee@ucdenver.edu.

University of Connecticut, Graduate School, College of Liberal Arts and Sciences, Department of Molecular and Cell Biology, Field of Biochemistry, Storrs, CT 06269. Offers MS, PhD. Terminal master's awarded for partial completion of doctoral program. *Degree requirements:* For master's, comprehensive exam; for doctorate, thesis/dissertation. *Entrance requirements:* For master's and doctorate, GRE General Test, GRE Subject Test. Additional exam requirements/recommendations for international students: Required—TOEFL (minimum score 550 paper-based; 213 computer-based). Electronic applications accepted.

University of Connecticut Health Center, Graduate School, Programs in Biomedical Sciences, Graduate Program in Molecular Biology and Biochemistry, Farmington, CT 06030. Offers PhD, DMD/PhD, MD/PhD. *Faculty:* 158. *Students:* 18 full-time (10 women); includes 3 minority (1 Black or African American, non-Hispanic/Latino; 2 Asian, non-Hispanic/Latino), 6 international. Average age 28. 216 applicants, 22% accepted. In 2010, 5 doctorates awarded. *Degree requirements:* For doctorate, comprehensive exam, thesis/dissertation. *Entrance requirements:* For doctorate, GRE General Test. Additional exam requirements/recommendations for international students: Required—TOEFL (minimum score 600 paper-based; 250 computer-based). *Application deadline:* For fall admission, 12/15 for domestic students. Application fee: $55. Electronic applications accepted. *Financial support:* In 2010–11, 18 research assistantships with full tuition reimbursements (averaging $27,000 per year) were awarded; health care benefits also available. *Faculty research:* Molecular biology, structural biology, protein biochemistry, microbial physiology and pathogenesis. *Unit head:* Dr. Stephen King, Director, 860-679-3347, Fax: 860-679-1239, E-mail: sking@nso2.uchc.edu. *Application contact:* Tricia Avolt, Graduate Admissions Coordinator, 860-679-2175, Fax: 860-679-1899, E-mail: robertson@nso2.uchc.edu.

See Display on page 211 and Close-Up on page 231.

University of Delaware, College of Arts and Sciences, Department of Chemistry and Biochemistry, Newark, DE 19716. Offers biochemistry (MA, MS, PhD); chemistry (MA, MS, PhD). Part-time programs available. Terminal master's awarded for partial completion of doctoral program. *Degree requirements:* For master's, one foreign language, thesis (for some programs); for doctorate, one foreign language, thesis/dissertation, cumulative exam. *Entrance requirements:* For master's and doctorate, GRE General Test. Additional exam requirements/recommendations for international students: Required—TOEFL (minimum score 600 paper-based; 260 computer-based). Electronic applications accepted. *Faculty research:* Microorganisms, bone, cancer metastosis, developmental biology, cell biology, molecular biology.

University of Detroit Mercy, College of Engineering and Science, Department of Chemistry and Biochemistry, Detroit, MI 48221. Offers chemistry (MS). Evening/weekend programs available. *Degree requirements:* For master's, thesis. *Entrance requirements:* For master's, GRE General Test, minimum GPA of 3.0. *Faculty research:* Polymer and physical chemistry, industrial aspects of chemistry.

University of Florida, College of Medicine, Department of Biochemistry and Molecular Biology, Gainesville, FL 32611. Offers biochemistry and molecular biology (MS, PhD); imaging science and technology (MS, PhD). *Degree requirements:* For doctorate, thesis/dissertation. *Entrance requirements:* For doctorate, GRE General Test, minimum GPA of 3.0. Additional exam requirements/recommendations for international students: Required—TOEFL. Electronic applications accepted. *Expenses:* Tuition, state resident: full-time $10,916. Tuition, nonresident: full-time $28,309. *Faculty research:* Gene expression, metabolic regulation, structural biology, enzyme mechanism, membrane transporters.

University of Florida, College of Medicine and Graduate School, Interdisciplinary Program in Biomedical Sciences, Concentration in Biochemistry and Molecular Biology, Gainesville, FL 32611. Offers PhD. *Degree requirements:* For doctorate, thesis/dissertation. *Entrance requirements:* For doctorate, GRE General Test, minimum GPA of 3.0. Additional exam requirements/recommendations for international students: Required—TOEFL. Electronic applications accepted. *Expenses:* Tuition, state resident: full-time $10,916. Tuition, nonresident: full-time $28,309. *Faculty research:* Gene expression, metabolic regulation, structural biology, enzyme mechanism, membrane transporters.

University of Georgia, College of Arts and Sciences, Department of Biochemistry and Molecular Biology, Athens, GA 30602. Offers MS, PhD. *Faculty:* 36 full-time (4 women). *Students:* 68 full-time (25 women), 2 part-time (1 woman); includes 6 Black or African American, non-Hispanic/Latino; 1 Asian, non-Hispanic/Latino; 1 Hispanic/Latino; 1 Two or more races, non-Hispanic/Latino, 23 international. 105 applicants, 20% accepted, 14 enrolled. In 2010, 4 master's, 10 doctorates awarded. *Degree requirements:* For master's, one foreign language, thesis; for doctorate, one foreign language, thesis/dissertation. *Entrance requirements:* For master's and doctorate, GRE General Test. Additional exam requirements/recommendations for international students: Required—TOEFL. *Application deadline:* For fall admission, 1/1 priority date for domestic and international students. Application fee: $50. Electronic applications accepted. *Expenses:* Tuition, state resident: full-time $7200; part-time $344 per credit hour. Tuition, nonresident: full-time $21,900; part-time $944 per credit hour. Tuition and fees vary according to course load and program. *Financial support:* Fellowships, research assistantships, teaching assistantships, scholarships/grants and unspecified assistantships available. Financial award application deadline: 1/1. *Unit head:* Dr. Stephen L. Hajduk, Head, 706-542-1676, Fax: 706-542-0182, E-mail: shajduk@bmb.uga.edu. *Application contact:* Dr. Lance Wells, Graduate Coordinator, 706-583-7806, Fax: 706-542-1738, E-mail: lwells@ccr.uga.edu.

University of Guelph, Graduate Studies, College of Biological Science, Department of Molecular and Cellular Biology, Guelph, ON N1G 2W1, Canada. Offers biochemistry (M Sc, PhD); biophysics (M Sc, PhD); botany (M Sc, PhD); microbiology (M Sc, PhD); molecular biology and genetics (M Sc, PhD). *Degree requirements:* For master's, thesis, research proposal; for doctorate, comprehensive exam, thesis/dissertation, research proposal. *Entrance requirements:* For master's, minimum B-average during previous 2 years of coursework; for doctorate, minimum A-average. Additional exam requirements/recommendations for international students: Required—TOEFL (minimum score 550 paper-based; 213 computer-based), IELTS (minimum score 6.5). Electronic applications accepted. *Faculty research:* Physiology, structure, genetics, and ecology of microbes; virology and microbial technology.

University of Guelph, Graduate Studies, College of Physical and Engineering Science, Guelph-Waterloo Centre for Graduate Work in Chemistry and Biochemistry, Guelph, ON N1G 2W1, Canada. Offers M Sc, PhD. M Sc, PhD offered jointly with University of Waterloo. Part-time programs available. *Degree requirements:* For master's, thesis; for doctorate, thesis/dissertation. *Faculty research:* Inorganic, analytical, biological, physical/theoretical, polymer, and organic chemistry.

University of Houston, College of Natural Sciences and Mathematics, Department of Biology and Biochemistry, Houston, TX 77204. Offers biochemistry (MA, PhD); biology (MA). *Faculty:* 31 full-time (10 women), 1 (woman) part-time/adjunct. *Students:* 89 full-time (53 women), 4 part-time (1 woman); includes 3 Black or African American, non-Hispanic/Latino; 3 Asian, non-Hispanic/Latino; 2 Hispanic/Latino, 65 international. Average age 28. 144 applicants, 20% accepted, 14 enrolled. In 2010, 7 master's, 11 doctorates awarded. Terminal master's awarded for partial completion of doctoral program. *Degree requirements:* For master's, comprehensive exam (for some programs), thesis optional; for doctorate, comprehensive exam (for some programs), thesis/dissertation. *Entrance requirements:* For master's and doctorate, GRE. Additional exam requirements/recommendations for international students: Required—TOEFL (minimum score 550 paper-based; 213 computer-based; 79 iBT), IELTS (minimum score 6.5). *Application deadline:* For fall admission, 4/1 for domestic and international students; for spring admission, 10/1 for domestic and international students. Application fee: $75 for international students. Electronic applications accepted. *Expenses:* Tuition, state resident: full-time $8592; part-time $358 per credit hour. Tuition, nonresident: full-time $16,032; part-time $668 per credit hour. Required fees: $2889. Tuition and fees vary according to course load and program. *Financial support:* In 2010–11, 33 research assistantships with partial tuition reimbursements (averaging $13,776 per year), 39 teaching assistantships with partial tuition reimbursements (averaging $14,032 per year) were awarded; career-related internships or fieldwork, Federal Work-Study, institutionally sponsored loans, scholarships/grants, health care benefits, and unspecified assistantships also available. Support available to part-time students. Financial award application deadline: 2/1. *Faculty research:* Cell and molecular biology, ecology and evolution, biochemical and biophysical sciences, chemical biology. *Unit head:* Dr. Dan Wells, Chairperson, 713-743-2697, Fax: 713-743-2632, E-mail: dwells@uh.edu. *Application contact:* Amanda Paul, Graduate Academic Advisor, 713-743-2633, Fax: 713-743-2636, E-mail: akpaul@central.uh.edu.

University of Idaho, College of Graduate Studies, College of Agricultural and Life Sciences, Department of Microbiology, Molecular Biology and Biochemistry, Moscow, ID 83844-2282. Offers MS, PhD. *Faculty:* 16 full-time. *Students:* 13 full-time, 6 part-time. Average age 30. In 2010, 4 master's, 3 doctorates awarded. *Degree requirements:* For master's, thesis; for doctorate, one foreign language, thesis/dissertation. *Entrance requirements:* For master's, minimum GPA of 2.8; for doctorate, minimum undergraduate GPA of 2.8, 3.0 graduate. *Application deadline:* For fall admission, 8/1 for domestic students; for spring admission, 12/15 for domestic students. Applications are processed on a rolling basis. Application fee: $60. Electronic applications accepted. *Expenses:* Tuition, nonresident: part-time $580 per credit. Required fees: $306 per credit. *Financial support:* Research assistantships, teaching assistantships available. Financial award applicants required to submit FAFSA. *Unit head:* Bruce L. Miller, Interim Chair, 208-885-7247, Fax: 208-885-6518, E-mail: mmbb@uidaho.edu. *Application contact:* Bruce L. Miller, Interim Chair, 208-885-7247, Fax: 208-885-6518, E-mail: mmbb@uidaho.edu.

University of Illinois at Chicago, College of Medicine and Graduate College, Graduate Programs in Medicine, Department of Biochemistry and Molecular Genetics, Chicago, IL 60607-7128. Offers PhD, MD/PhD. Terminal master's awarded for partial completion of doctoral program. *Degree requirements:* For doctorate, thesis/dissertation. *Entrance requirements:* For doctorate, GRE General Test. Additional exam requirements/recommendations for international students: Required—TOEFL. Electronic applications accepted. *Faculty research:* Nature of cellular components, control of metabolic processes, regulation of gene expression.

University of Illinois at Urbana–Champaign, Graduate College, College of Liberal Arts and Sciences, School of Chemical Sciences, Champaign, IL 61820. Offers MA, MS, PhD, MS/JD, MS/MBA. *Faculty:* 47 full-time (8 women). *Students:* 381 full-time (122 women), 8 part-time (2 women); includes 6 Black or African American, non-Hispanic/Latino; 1 American Indian or Alaska Native, non-Hispanic/Latino; 23 Asian, non-Hispanic/Latino; 13 Hispanic/Latino; 9 Two or more races, non-Hispanic/Latino, 112 international. 924 applicants, 6% accepted, 54 enrolled. In 2010, 32 master's, 60 doctorates awarded. *Entrance requirements:* For master's, minimum GPA of 3.0. *Application deadline:* Applications are processed on a rolling basis. Application fee: $75 ($90 for international students). Electronic applications accepted. *Expenses:* Contact institution. *Financial support:* In 2010–11, 137 fellowships, 216 research assistantships, 225 teaching assistantships were awarded; tuition waivers (full and partial) also available. *Unit head:* Andrew A. Gewirth, Director, 217-333-8329, Fax: 217-333-2685, E-mail: agewirth@illinois.edu. *Application contact:* Cheryl Kappes, Office Manager, 217-333-5070, Fax: 217-333-3120, E-mail: dambache@illinois.edu.

University of Illinois at Urbana–Champaign, Graduate College, College of Liberal Arts and Sciences, School of Molecular and Cellular Biology, Department of Biochemistry, Champaign, IL 61820. Offers MS, PhD. *Faculty:* 10 full-time (1 woman). *Students:* 66 full-time (32 women); includes 10 Asian, non-Hispanic/Latino; 4 Hispanic/Latino; 2 Two or more races, non-Hispanic/Latino, 27 international. In 2010, 2 master's, 19 doctorates awarded. *Entrance requirements:* For master's, GRE General Test, minimum GPA of 3.0; for doctorate, GRE General Test, minimum GPA of 3.0. Additional exam requirements/recommendations for international students: Required—TOEFL (minimum score 590 paper-based; 243 computer-based; 96 iBT). *Application deadline:* Applications are processed on a rolling basis. Application fee: $75 ($90 for international students). Electronic applications accepted. *Financial support:* In 2010–11, 14 fellowships, 46 research assistantships, 27 teaching assistantships were awarded; tuition waivers (full and partial) also available. *Unit head:* Colin A. Wraight, Head, 217-333-3945, Fax: 217-333-8920, E-mail: cwraight@illinois.edu. *Application contact:* Jeff M. Goldberg, Coordinator for Student Academic Affairs, 217-244-3149, Fax: 217-244-5858, E-mail: jmgoldbe@illinois.edu.

The University of Iowa, Roy J. and Lucille A. Carver College of Medicine and Graduate College, Graduate Programs in Medicine, Department of Biochemistry, Iowa City, IA 52242-1316. Offers MS, PhD, MD/PhD. *Faculty:* 21 full-time (7 women), 6 part-time/adjunct (2 women). *Students:* 19 full-time (5 women), 10 international. Average age 27. 97 applicants,

Biochemistry

The University of Iowa (continued)

9% accepted, 9 enrolled. In 2010, 3 doctorates awarded. Terminal master's awarded for partial completion of doctoral program. *Degree requirements:* For master's, thesis; for doctorate, comprehensive exam, thesis/dissertation, research project, one semester of teaching. *Entrance requirements:* For master's and doctorate, GRE General Test. Additional exam requirements/recommendations for international students: Required—TOEFL (minimum score 600 paper-based; 250 computer-based; 100 iBT). *Application deadline:* For winter admission, 11/15 priority date for domestic students, 12/15 priority date for international students. Applications are processed on a rolling basis. Application fee: $30 ($67 for international students). Electronic applications accepted. *Financial support:* In 2010–11, research assistantships with full tuition reimbursements (averaging $25,500 per year); institutionally sponsored loans, scholarships/grants, traineeships, tuition waivers, and unspecified assistantships also available. *Faculty research:* Regulation of gene expression, protein structure, membrane structure/function, DNA structure and replication. Total annual research expenditures: $6.7 million. *Unit head:* Dr. Charles M. Brenner, Head, 319-335-7934, Fax: 319-335-9570, E-mail: charles-brenner@uiowa.edu. *Application contact:* Admissions Committee, 319-335-7932, Fax: 319-335-9570, E-mail: biochem@uiowa.edu.

The University of Kansas, Graduate Studies, College of Liberal Arts and Sciences, Department of Molecular Biosciences, Lawrence, KS 66044. Offers biochemistry and biophysics (MA, PhD); microbiology (MA, PhD); molecular, cellular, and developmental biology (MA, PhD). *Faculty:* 34. *Students:* 65 full-time (31 women), 1 part-time (0 women); includes 7 minority (2 Asian, non-Hispanic/Latino; 4 Hispanic/Latino; 1 Two or more races, non-Hispanic/Latino), 24 international. Average age 27. 34 applicants, 47% accepted, 10 enrolled. In 2010, 1 master's, 5 doctorates awarded. Terminal master's awarded for partial completion of doctoral program. *Degree requirements:* For master's, comprehensive exam, thesis; for doctorate, comprehensive exam, thesis/dissertation. *Entrance requirements:* For master's and doctorate, GRE General Test. Additional exam requirements/recommendations for international students: Required—TOEFL (minimum score 24 iBT), OR IELTS Speaking: 8. *Application deadline:* For fall admission, 12/15 for domestic and international students. Application fee: $55 ($65 for international students). Electronic applications accepted. *Expenses:* Tuition, state resident: full-time $7092; part-time $295.50 per credit hour. Tuition, nonresident: full-time $16,590; part-time $691.25 per credit hour. Required fees: $858; $71.49 per credit hour. Tuition and fees vary according to course load, campus/location and program. *Financial support:* Fellowships with tuition reimbursements, research assistantships with tuition reimbursements, teaching assistantships with tuition reimbursements, health care benefits and unspecified assistantships available. Financial award application deadline: 3/1. *Faculty research:* Structure and function of proteins, genetics of organism development, molecular genetics, neurophysiology, molecular virology and pathogenics, developmental biology, cell biology. *Unit head:* Dr. Mark Richter, Chair, 785-864-3334, Fax: 785-864-5294, E-mail: richter@ku.edu. *Application contact:* John P. Connolly, Graduate Program Assistant, 785-864-4311, Fax: 785-864-5294, E-mail: jconnolly@ku.edu.

The University of Kansas, University of Kansas Medical Center, School of Medicine, Department of Biochemistry and Molecular Biology, Kansas City, KS 66160. Offers MS, PhD, MD/PhD. *Faculty:* 18. *Students:* 6 full-time (0 women), 4 international. Average age 29. Terminal master's awarded for partial completion of doctoral program. *Degree requirements:* For master's, thesis, oral defense of thesis; for doctorate, thesis/dissertation, comprehensive oral and written exam. *Entrance requirements:* Additional exam requirements/recommendations for international students: Required—TOEFL. Application fee: $0. Electronic applications accepted. *Expenses:* Tuition, state resident: full-time $7092; part-time $295.50 per credit hour. Tuition, nonresident: full-time $16,590; part-time $691.25 per credit hour. Required fees: $858; $71.49 per credit hour. Tuition and fees vary according to course load, campus/location and program. *Financial support:* In 2010–11, 5 teaching assistantships with full and partial tuition reimbursements were awarded; fellowships, research assistantships with partial tuition reimbursements, traineeships, health care benefits, and unspecified assistantships also available. Financial award application deadline: 2/14; financial award applicants required to submit FAFSA. *Faculty research:* Determination of portion structure, underlying bases for interaction of proteins with their target, mapping allosteric circuiting within proteins, mechanism of action of transcription factors, renal signal transduction. Total annual research expenditures: $3.4 million. *Unit head:* Dr. Gerald M. Carlson, Chairman, 913-588-6574, Fax: 913-588-7007, E-mail: gcarlson@kumc.edu. *Application contact:* Dr. Liskin Swint-Kruse, Associate Professor, 913-588-0399, Fax: 913-588-9896, E-mail: lswint-kruse@kumc.edu.

University of Kentucky, Graduate School, Graduate School Programs from the College of Medicine, Program in Molecular and Cellular Biochemistry, Lexington, KY 40506-0032. Offers biochemistry (PhD); MD/PhD. *Degree requirements:* For doctorate, comprehensive exam, thesis/dissertation. *Entrance requirements:* For doctorate, GRE General Test, minimum undergraduate GPA of 2.75. Additional exam requirements/recommendations for international students: Required—TOEFL (minimum score 550 paper-based; 213 computer-based). Electronic applications accepted.

University of Lethbridge, School of Graduate Studies, Lethbridge, AB T1K 3M4, Canada. Offers accounting (MScM); addictions counseling (M Sc); agricultural biotechnology (M Sc); agricultural studies (M Sc, MA); anthropology (MA); archaeology (MA); art (MA, MFA); biochemistry (M Sc); biological sciences (M Sc); biomolecular science (PhD); biosystems and biodiversity (PhD); Canadian studies (MA); chemistry (M Sc); computer science (M Sc); computer science and geographical information science (M Sc); counseling psychology (M Ed); dramatic arts (MA); earth, space, and physical science (PhD); economics (MA); educational leadership (M Ed); English (MA); environmental science (M Sc); evolution and behavior (PhD); exercise science (M Sc); finance (MScM); French (MA); French/German (MA); French/Spanish (MA); general education (M Ed); general management (MScM); geography (M Sc, MA); German (MA); health science (M Sc); history (MA); human resource management and labour relations (MScM); individualized multidisciplinary (M Sc, MA); information systems (MScM); international management (MScM); kinesiology (M Sc, MA); management (M Sc, MA); marketing (MScM); mathematics (M Sc); music (M Mus, MA); Native American studies (MA); neuroscience (M Sc, PhD); new media (MA); nursing (M Sc); philosophy (MA); physics (M Sc); policy and strategy (MScM); political science (MA); psychology (M Sc, MA); religious studies (MA); social sciences (MA); sociology (MA); theatre and dramatic arts (MFA); theoretical and computational science (PhD); urban and regional studies (MA); women's studies (MA). Part-time and evening/weekend programs available. *Degree requirements:* For doctorate, comprehensive exam, thesis/dissertation. *Entrance requirements:* For master's, GMAT (M Sc in management), bachelor's degree in related field, minimum GPA of 3.0 during previous 20 graded semester courses, 2 years teaching or related experience (M Ed); for doctorate, master's degree, minimum graduate GPA of 3.5. Additional exam requirements/recommendations for international students: Required—TOEFL. *Faculty research:* Movement and brain plasticity, gibberellin physiology, photosynthesis, carbon cycling, molecular properties of main-group ring components.

University of Louisville, Graduate School, College of Arts and Sciences, Department of Chemistry, Louisville, KY 40292-0001. Offers analytical chemistry (MS, PhD); biochemistry (MS, PhD); chemical physics (PhD); inorganic chemistry (MS, PhD); organic chemistry (MS, PhD); physical chemistry (MS, PhD). *Faculty:* 21 full-time (4 women). *Students:* 55 full-time (24 women), 4 part-time (0 women); includes 1 Black or African American, non-Hispanic/Latino; 1 Asian, non-Hispanic/Latino, 42 international. Average age 29. 79 applicants, 27% accepted, 7 enrolled. In 2010, 7 master's, 5 doctorates awarded. Terminal master's awarded for partial completion of doctoral program. *Degree requirements:* For master's, variable foreign language requirement, comprehensive exam, thesis optional; for doctorate, variable foreign language requirement, comprehensive exam, thesis/dissertation. *Entrance requirements:* For master's and doctorate, BA or BS coursework. Additional exam requirements/recommendations for international students: Required—TOEFL. *Application deadline:* For fall admission, 3/15 for domestic and international students; for winter admission, 9/15 for domestic and international students. Applications are processed on a rolling basis. Application fee: $50. Electronic applications accepted. *Expenses:* Tuition, state resident: full-time $9144; part-time $508 per credit hour. Tuition, nonresident: full-time $19,026; part-time $1057 per credit hour. Tuition and fees vary according to program and reciprocity agreements. *Financial support:* In 2010–11, 33 teaching assistantships with full tuition reimbursements (averaging $22,000 per year) were awarded; fellowships with full tuition reimbursements, research assistantships with full tuition reimbursements, career-related internships or fieldwork, scholarships/grants, traineeships, health care benefits, and unspecified assistantships also available. Support available to part-time students. Financial award application deadline: 3/15. *Faculty research:* Computational chemistry, biophysics nuclear magnetic resonance, synthetic organic chemistry, synthetic inorganic chemistry, chemistry, medicinal chemistry, protein chemistry, enzymology, nanochemistry, electrochemistry, analytical chemistry, synthetic biology, bioinformatics. Total annual research expenditures: $2.5 million. *Unit head:* Dr. Richard J. Wittebort, Professor/Chair, 502-852-6613. *Application contact:* Sherry Nalley, Administrator, 502-852-6798.

University of Louisville, School of Medicine, Department of Biochemistry and Molecular Biology, Louisville, KY 40292-0001. Offers MS, PhD, MD/PhD. *Faculty:* 33 full-time (7 women), 2 part-time/adjunct (1 woman). *Students:* 39 full-time (19 women), 2 part-time (both women); includes 1 Black or African American, non-Hispanic/Latino; 2 Asian, non-Hispanic/Latino; 1 Hispanic/Latino, 10 international. Average age 29. 37 applicants, 41% accepted, 11 enrolled. In 2010, 3 master's, 7 doctorates awarded. Terminal master's awarded for partial completion of doctoral program. *Degree requirements:* For master's, thesis; for doctorate, comprehensive exam, thesis/dissertation, one first author publication. *Entrance requirements:* For master's and doctorate, GRE General Test (minimum score of 1000 verbal and quantitative), minimum GPA of 3.0. Additional exam requirements/recommendations for international students: Required—TOEFL. *Application deadline:* For fall admission, 4/15 for domestic and international students. Applications are processed on a rolling basis. Application fee: $50. Electronic applications accepted. *Expenses:* Tuition, state resident: full-time $9144; part-time $508 per credit hour. Tuition, nonresident: full-time $19,026; part-time $1057 per credit hour. Tuition and fees vary according to program and reciprocity agreements. *Financial support:* In 2010–11, 12 fellowships with full tuition reimbursements (averaging $22,000 per year), 23 research assistantships with full tuition reimbursements (averaging $22,000 per year) were awarded; teaching assistantships with tuition reimbursements, scholarships/grants, traineeships, tuition waivers (full and partial), and unspecified assistantships also available. Financial award application deadline: 4/15. *Faculty research:* Genetic regulatory mechanisms, microRNAs, vesicular trafficking in cancer metastasis and angiogenesis, ribosome biogenesis and disease, regulation of foreign compound metabolism/lipid and steroid metabolism. *Unit head:* Dr. Ronald G. Gregg, Chair, 502-852-5217, Fax: 502-852-6222, E-mail: rggreg02@gwise.louisville.edu. *Application contact:* Dr. William L. Dean, Information Contact, 502-852-5227, Fax: 502-852-6222, E-mail: wldean01@gwise.louisville.edu.

University of Maine, Graduate School, College of Natural Sciences, Forestry, and Agriculture, Department of Biochemistry, Molecular Biology, and Microbiology, Orono, ME 04469. Offers biochemistry (MPS, MS); biochemistry and molecular biology (PhD); microbiology (MPS, MS, PhD). *Faculty:* 9 full-time (5 women), 3 part-time/adjunct (2 women). *Students:* 19 full-time (12 women), 21 part-time (15 women); includes 5 minority (1 American Indian or Alaska Native, non-Hispanic/Latino; 2 Asian, non-Hispanic/Latino; 1 Hispanic/Latino; 1 Two or more races, non-Hispanic/Latino), 6 international. Average age 30. 39 applicants, 26% accepted, 9 enrolled. In 2010, 6 master's, 3 doctorates awarded. *Degree requirements:* For doctorate, thesis/dissertation. *Entrance requirements:* For master's and doctorate, GRE General Test. Additional exam requirements/recommendations for international students: Required—TOEFL. *Application deadline:* For fall admission, 2/1 priority date for domestic students. Applications are processed on a rolling basis. Application fee: $65. Electronic applications accepted. *Expenses:* Tuition, state resident: full-time $400. Tuition, nonresident: full-time $1050. *Financial support:* In 2010–11, 5 research assistantships with tuition reimbursements (averaging $20,893 per year), 12 teaching assistantships with tuition reimbursements (averaging $19,296 per year) were awarded; tuition waivers (full and partial) also available. Financial award application deadline: 3/1. *Unit head:* Dr. Robert Gundersen, Chair, 207-581-2802, Fax: 207-581-2801. *Application contact:* Scott G. Delcourt, Associate Dean of the Graduate School, 207-581-3291, Fax: 207-581-3232, E-mail: graduate@maine.edu.

The University of Manchester, Faculty of Life Sciences, Manchester, United Kingdom. Offers adaptive organismal biology (M Phil, PhD); animal biology (M Phil, PhD); biochemistry (M Phil, PhD); bioinformatics (M Phil, PhD); biomolecular sciences (M Phil, PhD); biotechnology (M Phil, PhD); cell biology (M Phil, PhD); cell matrix research (M Phil, PhD); channels and transporters (M Phil, PhD); developmental biology (M Phil, PhD); Egyptology (M Phil, PhD); environmental biology (M Phil, PhD); evolutionary biology (M Phil, PhD); gene expression (M Phil, PhD); genetics (M Phil, PhD); history of science, technology and medicine (M Phil, PhD); immunology (M Phil, PhD); integrative neurobiology and behavior (M Phil, PhD); membrane trafficking (M Phil, PhD); microbiology (M Phil, PhD); molecular and cellular neuroscience (M Phil, PhD); molecular biology (M Phil, PhD); molecular cancer studies (M Phil, PhD); neuroscience (M Phil, PhD); ophthalmology (M Phil, PhD); optometry (M Phil, PhD); organelle function (M Phil, PhD); pharmacology (M Phil, PhD); physiology (M Phil, PhD); plant sciences (M Phil, PhD); stem cell research (M Phil, PhD); structural biology (M Phil, PhD); systems neuroscience (M Phil, PhD); toxicology (M Phil, PhD).

The University of Manchester, School of Chemistry, Manchester, United Kingdom. Offers biological chemistry (PhD); chemistry (M Ent, M Phil, M Sc, D Ent, PhD); inorganic chemistry (PhD); materials chemistry (PhD); nanoscience (PhD); nuclear fission (PhD); organic chemistry (PhD); physical chemistry (PhD); theoretical chemistry (PhD).

University of Manitoba, Faculty of Medicine and Faculty of Graduate Studies, Graduate Programs in Medicine, Department of Biochemistry and Medical Genetics, Winnipeg, MB R3T 2N2, Canada. Offers M Sc, PhD. Terminal master's awarded for partial completion of doctoral program. *Degree requirements:* For master's, thesis; for doctorate, thesis/dissertation. *Faculty research:* Cancer, gene expression, membrane lipids, metabolic control, genetic diseases.

University of Maryland, Baltimore, Graduate School, Graduate Program in Life Sciences, Program in Biochemistry and Molecular Biology, Baltimore, MD 21201. Offers biochemistry (MS, PhD); MD/PhD. *Entrance requirements:* For doctorate, GRE General Test. Additional exam requirements/recommendations for international students: Required—TOEFL (minimum score 550 paper-based; 80 iBT); Recommended—IELTS (minimum score 7). Electronic applications accepted. Part-time tuition and fees vary according to course load, degree level and program. *Faculty research:* Membrane transport, hormonal regulation, protein structure, molecular virology.

University of Maryland, Baltimore County, Graduate School, College of Natural and Mathematical Sciences, Department of Chemistry and Biochemistry, Program in Biochemistry, Baltimore, MD 21201. Offers MS, PhD. *Faculty:* 60 full-time (7 women). *Students:* 35 full-time (21 women); includes 5 Black or African American, non-Hispanic/Latino; 1 American Indian or Alaska Native, non-Hispanic/Latino; 4 Asian, non-Hispanic/Latino; 4 Hispanic/Latino, 3 international. Average age 25. 70 applicants, 16% accepted, 9 enrolled. In 2010, 90 doctorates awarded. Terminal master's awarded for partial completion of doctoral program. *Degree requirements:* For master's, comprehensive exam (for some programs), thesis (for some programs); for doctorate, comprehensive exam, thesis/dissertation. *Entrance requirements:* For master's and doctorate, GRE General Test, minimum GPA of 3.0. Additional exam requirements/recommendations for international students: Required—TOEFL (minimum score 550 paper-based; 213 computer-based). *Application deadline:* For fall admission, 1/31 priority date for domestic and international students. Applications are processed on a rolling basis. Application fee: $50. Electronic applications accepted. *Financial support:* In 2010–11, 9 fellowships with full tuition reimbursements (averaging $26,000 per year), 26 research assistantships with full tuition reimbursements (averaging $26,000 per year) were awarded; health care benefits and tuition waivers (full) also available. *Faculty research:* Protein structure, metabolism, molecular biology, physical biochemistry, enzymology. *Unit head:* Dr. Michael F. Summers, Professor, 410-455-2880, Fax: 410-455-1174, E-mail: summers@hhmi.umbc.edu. *Application* *contact:* Foyeke A. Daramola, Coordinator, 410-706-8417, Fax: 410-706-8297, E-mail: fdaramola@som.umaryland.edu.

University of Maryland, College Park, Academic Affairs, College of Computer, Mathematical and Natural Sciences, Department of Chemistry and Biochemistry, Biochemistry Program, College Park, MD 20742. Offers MS, PhD. Part-time and evening/weekend programs available. *Students:* 48 full-time (25 women); includes 3 Black or African American, non-Hispanic/Latino; 4 Asian, non-Hispanic/Latino; 1 Hispanic/Latino, 18 international. 97 applicants, 20% accepted, 8 enrolled. In 2010, 1 master's, 5 doctorates awarded. Terminal master's awarded for partial completion of doctoral program. *Degree requirements:* For master's, thesis or alternative; for doctorate, thesis/dissertation, 2 seminar presentations, oral exam. *Entrance requirements:* For master's and doctorate, GRE General Test, GRE Subject Test (recommended), minimum GPA of 3.0, 3 letters of recommendation. Additional exam requirements/recommendations for international students: Required—TOEFL. *Application deadline:* For fall admission, 2/1 for domestic and international students. Applications are processed on a rolling basis. Application fee: $75. Electronic applications accepted. *Expenses:* Tuition, state resident: part-time $471 per credit hour. Tuition, nonresident: part-time $1016 per credit hour. Required fees: $337 per term. *Financial support:* In 2010–11, 16 research assistantships (averaging $19,022 per year), 30 teaching assistantships with tuition reimbursements (averaging $19,239 per year) were awarded; Federal Work-Study also available. Support available to part-time students. Financial award applicants required to submit FAFSA. *Faculty research:* Analytical biochemistry, immunochemistry, drug metabolism, biosynthesis of proteins, mass spectrometry. *Unit head:* Dr. Michael Doyle, Chairperson, 301-405-1795, Fax: 301-314-2779, E-mail: mdoyle3@umd.edu. *Application contact:* Dean of Graduate School, 301-405-0358, Fax: 301-314-9305.

University of Massachusetts Amherst, Graduate School, College of Natural Sciences, Department of Biochemistry and Molecular Biology, Amherst, MA 01003. Offers biochemistry (MS). Part-time programs available. *Faculty:* 17 full-time (7 women). *Students:* 2 full-time (0 women). Average age 23. 2 applicants, 50% accepted, 1 enrolled. In 2010, 1 master's awarded. Terminal master's awarded for partial completion of doctoral program. *Degree requirements:* For master's, thesis or alternative. *Entrance requirements:* Additional exam requirements/recommendations for international students: Required—TOEFL (minimum score 550 paper-based; 213 computer-based; 80 iBT), IELTS (minimum score 6.5). *Application deadline:* For fall admission, 2/1 for domestic and international students. Applications are processed on a rolling basis. Application fee: $50 ($65 for international students). Electronic applications accepted. *Expenses:* Tuition, state resident: full-time $2640. Required fees: $8282. One-time fee: $357 full-time. *Financial support:* In 2010–11, 1 fellowship (averaging $2,000 per year), 28 research assistantships with full tuition reimbursements (averaging $11,519 per year), 6 teaching assistantships with full tuition reimbursements (averaging $13,946 per year) were awarded; career-related internships or fieldwork, Federal Work-Study, scholarships/grants, traineeships, health care benefits, tuition waivers (full), and unspecified assistantships also available. Support available to part-time students. Financial award application deadline: 2/1; financial award applicants required to submit FAFSA. *Unit head:* Dr. Lila M. Gierasch, Graduate Program Director, 413-545-0353, Fax: 413-545-3291. *Application contact:* Jean M. Ames, Supervisor of Admissions, 413-545-0722, Fax: 413-577-0010, E-mail: gradadm@grad.umass.edu.

University of Massachusetts Amherst, Graduate School, Interdisciplinary Programs, Program in Molecular and Cellular Biology, Amherst, MA 01003. Offers biological chemistry and molecular biophysics (PhD); biomedicine (PhD); cellular and developmental biology (PhD). Part-time programs available. *Students:* 76 full-time (42 women), 3 part-time (2 women); includes 13 minority (3 Black or African American, non-Hispanic/Latino; 4 Asian, non-Hispanic/Latino; 5 Hispanic/Latino; 1 Two or more races, non-Hispanic/Latino), 23 international. Average age 27. 179 applicants, 25% accepted, 22 enrolled. In 2010, 8 doctorates awarded. Terminal master's awarded for partial completion of doctoral program. *Degree requirements:* For doctorate, comprehensive exam, thesis/dissertation. *Entrance requirements:* For doctorate, GRE General Test. Additional exam requirements/recommendations for international students: Required—TOEFL (minimum score 550 paper-based; 213 computer-based; 80 iBT), IELTS (minimum score 6.5). *Application deadline:* For fall admission, 12/1 for domestic and international students. Applications are processed on a rolling basis. Application fee: $50 ($65 for international students). Electronic applications accepted. *Expenses:* Tuition, state resident: full-time $2640. Required fees: $8282. One-time fee: $357 full-time. *Financial support:* In 2010–11, 11 research assistantships with full tuition reimbursements (averaging $2,590 per year), 3 teaching assistantships with full tuition reimbursements (averaging $3,303 per year) were awarded; fellowships, career-related internships or fieldwork, Federal Work-Study, scholarships/grants, traineeships, health care benefits, tuition waivers (full), and unspecified assistantships also available. Support available to part-time students. Financial award application deadline: 12/1; financial award applicants required to submit FAFSA. *Unit head:* Dr. Barbara Osborne, Graduate Program Director, 413-545-3246, Fax: 413-545-1812. *Application contact:* Jean M. Ames, Supervisor of Admissions, 413-545-0722, Fax: 413-577-0010, E-mail: gradadm@grad.umass.edu.

University of Massachusetts Amherst, Graduate School, Interdisciplinary Programs, Program in Plant Biology, Amherst, MA 01003. Offers biochemistry and metabolism (MS, PhD); cell biology and physiology (MS, PhD); environmental, ecological and integrative (PhD); environmental, ecological and integrative biology (MS); genetics and evolution (MS, PhD). *Students:* 18 full-time (8 women); includes 1 minority (Asian, non-Hispanic/Latino), 7 international. Average age 29. 27 applicants, 41% accepted, 6 enrolled. In 2010, 3 doctorates awarded. *Degree requirements:* For master's, thesis; for doctorate, 2 foreign languages, comprehensive exam, thesis/dissertation. *Entrance requirements:* For master's and doctorate, GRE General Test. Additional exam requirements/recommendations for international students: Required—TOEFL (minimum score 550 paper-based; 213 computer-based; 80 iBT), IELTS (minimum score 6.5). *Application deadline:* For fall admission, 12/15 for domestic and international students; for spring admission, 10/1 for domestic and international students. Applications are processed on a rolling basis. Application fee: $50 ($65 for international students). Electronic applications accepted. *Expenses:* Tuition, state resident: full-time $2640. Required fees: $8282. One-time fee: $357 full-time. *Financial support:* In 2010–11, 12 research assistantships with full tuition reimbursements (averaging $11,651 per year) were awarded; fellowships, teaching assistantships, career-related internships or fieldwork, Federal Work-Study, scholarships/grants, traineeships, health care benefits, tuition waivers (full), and unspecified assistantships also available. Support available to part-time students. Financial award application deadline: 12/15; financial award applicants required to submit FAFSA. *Unit head:* Dr. Elsbeth L. Walker, Graduate Program Director, 413-577-3217, Fax: 413-545-3243. *Application contact:* Jean M. Ames, Supervisor of Admissions, 413-545—0722, Fax: 413-577-0010, E-mail: gradadm@grad.umass.edu.

University of Massachusetts Lowell, College of Arts and Sciences, Department of Biological Sciences, Lowell, MA 01854-2881. Offers biochemistry (PhD); biological sciences (MS); biotechnology (MS). Part-time programs available. *Degree requirements:* For master's, thesis; for doctorate, thesis/dissertation. *Entrance requirements:* For master's and doctorate, GRE General Test. Electronic applications accepted.

University of Massachusetts Lowell, College of Arts and Sciences, Department of Chemistry, Lowell, MA 01854-2881. Offers analytical chemistry (PhD); biochemistry (PhD); chemistry (MS, PhD); environmental studies (PhD); green chemistry (PhD); inorganic chemistry (PhD); organic chemistry (PhD); polymer science (MS). Terminal master's awarded for partial completion of doctoral program. *Degree requirements:* For master's, thesis; for doctorate, 2 foreign languages, thesis/dissertation. *Entrance requirements:* For master's and doctorate, GRE General Test. Electronic applications accepted.

University of Massachusetts Worcester, Graduate School of Biomedical Sciences, Worcester, MA 01655-0115. Offers biochemistry and molecular pharmacology (PhD); bioinformatics and computational biology (PhD); cancer biology (PhD); cell biology (PhD); clinical and population health research (PhD); clinical investigation (MS); immunology and virology (PhD); interdisciplinary

graduate program (PhD); molecular genetics and microbiology (PhD); neuroscience (PhD); DVM/PhD; MD/PhD. *Faculty:* 1,059 full-time (357 women), 145 part-time/adjunct (100 women). *Students:* 438 full-time (239 women), 1 (woman) part-time; includes 44 minority (9 Black or African American, non-Hispanic/Latino; 31 Asian, non-Hispanic/Latino; 4 Hispanic/Latino), 148 international. Average age 29. 687 applicants, 28% accepted, 116 enrolled. In 2010, 6 master's, 45 doctorates awarded. Terminal master's awarded for partial completion of doctoral program. *Degree requirements:* For master's, thesis; for doctorate, thesis/dissertation. *Entrance requirements:* For master's, bachelor's degree; for doctorate, GRE General Test, MS, MA, or MPH (for some programs). Additional exam requirements/recommendations for international students: Required—TOEFL (minimum score 600 paper-based; 250 computer-based). *Application deadline:* For fall admission, 12/15 for domestic and international students; for winter admission, 1/15 for domestic students; for spring admission, 5/15 for domestic students. Application fee: $35. Electronic applications accepted. *Expenses:* Contact institution. *Financial support:* In 2010–11, 439 students received support, including 439 research assistantships with full tuition reimbursements available (averaging $28,350 per year); scholarships/grants, health care benefits, tuition waivers (full), and unspecified assistantships also available. Financial award application deadline: 4/20. *Faculty research:* RNA interference, gene therapy, cell biology, bioinformatics, clinical research. Total annual research expenditures: $232 million. *Unit head:* Dr. Anthony Carruthers, Dean, 508-856-4135, E-mail: anthony.carruthers@umassmed.edu. *Application contact:* Dr. Kendall Knight, Associate Dean and Interim Director of Admissions and Recruitment, 508-856-5628, Fax: 508-856-3659, E-mail: kendall.knight@umassmed.edu.

University of Medicine and Dentistry of New Jersey, Graduate School of Biomedical Sciences, Graduate Programs in Biomedical Sciences–Newark, Department of Biochemistry and Molecular Biology, Newark, NJ 07107. Offers MS, PhD. *Degree requirements:* For master's, thesis; for doctorate, thesis/dissertation, qualifying exam. *Entrance requirements:* For master's and doctorate, GRE General Test. Additional exam requirements/recommendations for international students: Required—TOEFL. Electronic applications accepted.

University of Medicine and Dentistry of New Jersey, Graduate School of Biomedical Sciences, Graduate Programs in Biomedical Sciences–Piscataway, Program in Biochemistry and Molecular Biology, Piscataway, NJ 08854-5635. Offers MS, PhD, MD/PhD. PhD, MS offered jointly with Rutgers, The State University of New Jersey, New Brunswick. Terminal master's awarded for partial completion of doctoral program. *Degree requirements:* For master's, thesis, qualifying exam; for doctorate, thesis/dissertation, qualifying exam. *Entrance requirements:* For master's and doctorate, GRE General Test. Additional exam requirements/recommendations for international students: Required—TOEFL. Electronic applications accepted. *Faculty research:* Signal transduction, regulation of RNA, polymerase II transcribed genes, developmental gene expression.

University of Miami, Graduate School, Miller School of Medicine, Graduate Programs in Medicine, Department of Biochemistry and Molecular Biology, Coral Gables, FL 33124. Offers PhD, MD/PhD. *Degree requirements:* For doctorate, comprehensive exam, thesis/dissertation, proposition exams. *Faculty research:* Macromolecule metabolism, molecular genetics, protein folding and 3-D structure, regulation of gene expression and enzyme function, signal transduction and developmental biology.

University of Michigan, Rackham Graduate School, Chemical Biology Program, Ann Arbor, MI 48109. Offers PhD. *Degree requirements:* For doctorate, thesis/dissertation. *Entrance requirements:* Additional exam requirements/recommendations for international students: Required—TOEFL (minimum score 600 paper-based; 250 computer-based; 102 iBT). Electronic applications accepted. *Expenses:* Tuition, state resident: full-time $17,784; part-time $1116 per credit hour. Tuition, nonresident: full-time $35,944; part-time $2125 per credit hour. International tuition: $35,994 full-time. Required fees: $95 per semester. Tuition and fees vary according to course load, degree level and program. *Faculty research:* Chemical genetics, structural enzymology, signal transduction, biological catalysis, biomolecular structure, function and recognition.

University of Michigan, Rackham Graduate School, College of Literature, Science, and the Arts, Department of Chemistry, Ann Arbor, MI 48109-1055. Offers analytical chemistry (PhD); chemical biology (PhD); inorganic chemistry (PhD); material chemistry (PhD); organic chemistry (PhD); physical chemistry (PhD). *Faculty:* 39 full-time (8 women). *Students:* 201 full-time (106 women); includes 19 minority (1 Black or African American, non-Hispanic/Latino; 12 Asian, non-Hispanic/Latino; 4 Hispanic/Latino; 2 Two or more races, non-Hispanic/Latino), 60 international. Average age 26. 565 applicants, 38% accepted, 39 enrolled. In 2010, 58 doctorates awarded. *Degree requirements:* For doctorate, thesis/dissertation, oral defense of dissertation, organic cumulative proficiency exams. *Entrance requirements:* For doctorate, GRE General Test, GRE Subject Test (recommended), 3 letters of recommendation. Additional exam requirements/recommendations for international students: Required—TOEFL (minimum score 560 paper-based; 220 computer-based; 84 iBT). *Application deadline:* For fall admission, 1/15 for domestic students, 12/15 for international students. Applications are processed on a rolling basis. Application fee: $0 ($75 for international students). Electronic applications accepted. *Expenses:* Tuition, state resident: full-time $17,784; part-time $1116 per credit hour. Tuition, nonresident: full-time $35,944; part-time $2125 per credit hour. International tuition: $35,994 full-time. Required fees: $95 per semester. Tuition and fees vary according to course load, degree level and program. *Financial support:* In 2010–11, 201 students received support, including 23 fellowships with full tuition reimbursements available (averaging $25,905 per year), 54 research assistantships with full tuition reimbursements available (averaging $25,905 per year), 118 teaching assistantships with full tuition reimbursements available (averaging $25,905 per year); career-related internships or fieldwork, scholarships/grants, traineeships, health care benefits, and unspecified assistantships also available. *Faculty research:* Biological catalysis, protein engineering, chemical sensors, de novo metalloprotein design, supra-molecular architecture. *Unit head:* Dr. Carol A. Fierke, Chair, 734-763-9681, Fax: 734-647-4847. *Application contact:* Margarita Bekiares, Graduate Program Coordinator, 734-764-7278, Fax: 734-647-4865, E-mail: chemadmissions@umich.edu.

University of Michigan, Rackham Graduate School, Program in Biomedical Sciences (PIBS), Department of Biological Chemistry, Ann Arbor, MI 48109. Offers PhD. *Faculty:* 46 full-time (10 women), 1 part-time/adjunct (0 women). *Students:* 37 full-time (20 women); includes 9 minority (4 Black or African American, non-Hispanic/Latino; 1 Asian, non-Hispanic/Latino; 2 Hispanic/Latino; 2 Two or more races, non-Hispanic/Latino), 5 international. Average age 27. 45 applicants, 71% accepted, 11 enrolled. In 2010, 7 doctorates awarded. *Degree requirements:* For doctorate, comprehensive exam, thesis/dissertation. *Entrance requirements:* For doctorate, GRE General Test, bachelor's degree. Additional exam requirements/recommendations for international students: Required—TOEFL (minimum score 84 iBT). *Application deadline:* For fall admission, 12/1 for domestic and international students. Application fee: $65 ($75 for international students). Electronic applications accepted. *Expenses:* Contact institution. *Financial support:* In 2010–11, 1 student received support, including 1 fellowship with full tuition reimbursement available (averaging $27,000 per year), 32 research assistantships with full tuition reimbursements available (averaging $26,500 per year), 4 teaching assistantships with partial tuition reimbursements available; traineeships, health care benefits, and unspecified assistantships also available. *Faculty research:* Regulation of gene expression, structural enzymology, protein processing and folding, biochemical signaling. Total annual research expenditures: $9.2 million. *Unit head:* Craig A. Reynolds, Administrative Director, 734-763-1085, Fax: 734-763-4581, E-mail: creyno@umich.edu. *Application contact:* Beth Goodwin, Graduate Program Manager, 734-764-8594, Fax: 734-763-4581, E-mail: egoodwin@umich.edu.

University of Minnesota, Duluth, Graduate School, Swenson College of Science and Engineering, Department of Chemistry and Biochemistry, Duluth, MN 55812-2496. Offers MS. Part-time programs available. *Degree requirements:* For master's, thesis. *Entrance requirements:* For master's, bachelor's degree in chemistry, minimum GPA of 3.0. Additional exam requirements/recommendations for international students: Required—TOEFL (minimum score

Biochemistry

University of Minnesota, Duluth (continued)

550 paper-based; 213 computer-based; 79 iBT), IELTS (minimum score 6.5). *Faculty research:* Physical, inorganic, organic, and analytical chemistry; biochemistry and molecular biology.

University of Minnesota, Duluth, Medical School, Department of Biochemistry, Molecular Biology and Biophysics, Duluth, MN 55812-2496. Offers biochemistry, molecular biology and biophysics (MS); biology and biophysics (PhD); social, administrative, and clinical pharmacy (MS, PhD); toxicology (MS, PhD). *Faculty:* 10 full-time (3 women). *Students:* 16 full-time (5 women); includes 3 Asian, non-Hispanic/Latino. Average age 29. 7 applicants, 29% accepted, 2 enrolled. In 2010, 1 master's, 1 doctorate awarded. Terminal master's awarded for partial completion of doctoral program. *Degree requirements:* For master's, comprehensive exam, thesis; for doctorate, comprehensive exam, thesis/dissertation. *Entrance requirements:* For master's and doctorate, GRE General Test. Additional exam requirements/recommendations for international students: Required—TOEFL. *Application deadline:* For winter admission, 1/3 for domestic students, 1/2 for international students; for spring admission, 3/15 priority date for domestic and international students. Application fee: $75 ($95 for international students). Electronic applications accepted. *Financial support:* In 2010–11, 8 students received support, including research assistantships with full tuition reimbursements available (averaging $27,300 per year), teaching assistantships with full tuition reimbursements available (averaging $27,300 per year); career-related internships or fieldwork, scholarships/grants, health care benefits, and unspecified assistantships also available. Financial award application deadline: 9/1. *Faculty research:* Intestinal cancer biology; hepatotoxins and mitochondriopathies; toxicology; cell cycle regulation in stem cells; neurobiology of brain development, trace metal function and blood-brain barrier; hibernation biology. Total annual research expenditures: $1.5 million. *Unit head:* Dr. Lester R. Drewes, Professor/Head, 218-726-7925, Fax: 218-726-8014, E-mail: ldrewes@d.umn.edu. *Application contact:* Cheryl Beeman, Executive Office and Administrative Assistant, 218-726-6354, Fax: 218-726-8014, E-mail: ahcd@d.umn.edu.

University of Minnesota, Twin Cities Campus, Graduate School, College of Biological Sciences, Biochemistry, Molecular Biology and Biophysics Graduate Program, Minneapolis, MN 55455-0213. Offers PhD. *Degree requirements:* For doctorate, thesis/dissertation. *Entrance requirements:* For doctorate, GRE, 3 letters of recommendation, more than 1 semester of laboratory experience. Additional exam requirements/recommendations for international students: Required—TOEFL (minimum score 625 paper-based; 263 computer-based; 108 iBT with writing subsection 25 and reading subsection 25) or IELTS (minimum score 7). Electronic applications accepted. *Faculty research:* Microbial biochemistry, biotechnology, molecular biology, regulatory biochemistry, structural biology and biophysics, physical biochemistry, enzymology, physiological chemistry.

University of Mississippi Medical Center, School of Graduate Studies in the Health Sciences, Department of Biochemistry, Jackson, MS 39216-4505. Offers MS, PhD, MD/PhD. Terminal master's awarded for partial completion of doctoral program. *Degree requirements:* For master's, thesis; for doctorate, thesis/dissertation, first authored publication. *Entrance requirements:* For doctorate, GRE General Test, minimum GPA of 3.0. Additional exam requirements/recommendations for international students: Required—TOEFL. *Faculty research:* Structural biology, regulation of gene expression, enzymology of redox reactions, mechanism of anti cancer drugs, function of nuclear substructure.

University of Missouri, Graduate School, College of Agriculture, Food and Natural Resources, Department of Biochemistry, Columbia, MO 65211. Offers MS, PhD. *Faculty:* 40 full-time (20 women), 3 part-time/adjunct (1 woman). *Students:* 42 full-time (15 women), 2 part-time (0 women); includes 4 minority (2 Asian, non-Hispanic/Latino; 1 Hispanic/Latino; 1 Two or more races, non-Hispanic/Latino), 16 international. Average age 25. 26 applicants, 42% accepted, 11 enrolled. In 2010, 2 master's, 2 doctorates awarded. Terminal master's awarded for partial completion of doctoral program. *Degree requirements:* For master's, thesis; for doctorate, comprehensive exam, thesis/dissertation. *Entrance requirements:* For master's and doctorate, minimum GPA of 3.0; undergraduate research. Additional exam requirements/recommendations for international students: Required—TOEFL (minimum score 620 paper-based; 95 iBT). *Application deadline:* For fall admission, 1/15 priority date for domestic students, 1/15 for international students. Application fee: $45 ($60 for international students). Electronic applications accepted. *Financial support:* Fellowships with tuition reimbursements, research assistantships with tuition reimbursements, teaching assistantships with tuition reimbursements, institutionally sponsored loans, scholarships/grants, health care benefits, and unspecified assistantships available. Support available to part-time students. *Faculty research:* Gene expression; molecular medicine; plant sciences; receptors and signaling; macromolecular synthesis, assembly and localization; structural and chemical biology; proteomics, genomics and combinatorial chemistry; enzymology, nutrition and metabolism. *Unit head:* Dr. Gerald Hazelbauer, Department Chair, 573-882-4845, E-mail: hazelbauerg@missouri.edu. *Application contact:* Ryan Duncan, Executive Staff Assistant, 573-882-4845, E-mail: duncancd@missouri.edu.

University of Missouri–Kansas City, School of Biological Sciences, Program in Molecular Biology and Biochemistry, Kansas City, MO 64110-2499. Offers PhD. Offered through the School of Graduate Studies. *Faculty:* 42 full-time (11 women). *Students:* 9 full-time (4 women), 6 part-time (4 women); includes 6 minority (4 Asian, non-Hispanic/Latino; 1 Hispanic/Latino; 1 Two or more races, non-Hispanic/Latino), 3 international. Average age 25. 34 applicants, 32% accepted, 10 enrolled. *Degree requirements:* For doctorate, comprehensive exam, thesis/dissertation. *Entrance requirements:* For doctorate, GRE General Test, bachelor's degree in chemistry, biology, or a related discipline; minimum GPA of 3.0. Additional exam requirements/recommendations for international students: Required—TOEFL (minimum score 550 paper-based; 213 computer-based; 80 iBT). *Application deadline:* For fall admission, 2/15 priority date for domestic and international students. Application fee: $45 ($50 for international students). *Expenses:* Tuition, state resident: full-time $5522; part-time $306.80 per credit hour. Tuition, nonresident: full-time $7128; part-time $792 per credit hour. Required fees: $261.15 per term. *Financial support:* Research assistantships with full tuition reimbursements, teaching assistantships with full and partial tuition reimbursements, scholarships/grants, tuition waivers (full and partial), and unspecified assistantships available. Financial award application deadline: 3/1; financial award applicants required to submit FAFSA. *Unit head:* Dr. Henry Miziorko, Head, 816-235-2235, E-mail: miziorkoh@umkc.edu. *Application contact:* Laura Batenic, Information Contact, 816-235-2352, Fax: 816-235-5158, E-mail: batenicl@umkc.edu.

See Display on page 214 and Close-Up on page 237.

University of Missouri–St. Louis, College of Arts and Sciences, Department of Chemistry and Biochemistry, St. Louis, MO 63121. Offers chemistry (MS, PhD), including biochemistry, inorganic chemistry, organic chemistry, physical chemistry. Part-time and evening/weekend programs available. *Faculty:* 19 full-time (3 women), 7 part-time/adjunct (1 woman). *Students:* 24 full-time (11 women), 37 part-time (13 women); includes 1 Black or African American, non-Hispanic/Latino; 2 Asian, non-Hispanic/Latino; 1 Hispanic/Latino, 24 international. Average age 30. 75 applicants, 29% accepted, 7 enrolled. In 2010, 13 master's, 7 doctorates awarded. Terminal master's awarded for partial completion of doctoral program. *Degree requirements:* For master's, thesis optional; for doctorate, thesis/dissertation. *Entrance requirements:* For master's, 2 letters of recommendation; for doctorate, GRE General Test, 3 letters of recommendation. Additional exam requirements/recommendations for international students: Required—TOEFL (minimum score 550 paper-based; 213 computer-based). *Application deadline:* For fall admission, 7/1 priority date for domestic and international students; for spring admission, 12/1 priority date for domestic and international students. Applications are processed on a rolling basis. Application fee: $35 ($40 for international students). Electronic applications accepted. *Expenses:* Tuition, state resident: full-time $5522; part-time $306.80 per credit hour. Tuition, nonresident: full-time $14,253; part-time $792.10 per credit hour. Required fees: $658; $49 per credit hour. One-time fee: $12. Tuition and fees vary according to program. *Financial support:* In 2010–11, 18 research assistantships with full and partial tuition reimbursements (averaging $13,104 per year), 18 teaching assistantships with full and partial tuition reimbursements (averaging $13,270 per year) were awarded; fellowships with full and partial tuition reimbursements also available. *Faculty research:* Metallaborane chemistry, serum transferrin chemistry, natural products chemistry, organic synthesis. *Unit head:* Dr. Cynthia Dupureur, Director of Graduate Studies, 314-516-5311, Fax: 314-516-5342, E-mail: gradchem@umsl.edu. *Application contact:* Graduate Admissions, 314-516-5458, Fax: 314-516-6996, E-mail: gradadm@umsl.edu.

The University of Montana, Graduate School, College of Arts and Sciences, Division of Biological Sciences, Program in Biochemistry and Microbiology, Missoula, MT 59812-0002. Offers biochemistry (MS); integrative microbiology and biochemistry (PhD); microbial ecology (MS, PhD); microbiology (MS). Terminal master's awarded for partial completion of doctoral program. *Degree requirements:* For master's, thesis; for doctorate, variable foreign language requirement, thesis/dissertation. *Entrance requirements:* For master's and doctorate, GRE General Test. *Faculty research:* Ribosome structure, medical microbiology/pathogenesis, microbial ecology/environmental microbiology.

University of Nebraska–Lincoln, Graduate College, College of Agricultural Sciences and Natural Resources and College of Arts and Sciences, Department of Biochemistry, Lincoln, NE 68588. Offers MS, PhD. Terminal master's awarded for partial completion of doctoral program. *Degree requirements:* For master's, thesis optional; for doctorate, comprehensive exam, thesis/dissertation. *Entrance requirements:* For master's and doctorate, GRE General Test, GRE Subject Test. Additional exam requirements/recommendations for international students: Required—TOEFL (minimum score 550 paper-based; 213 computer-based). Electronic applications accepted. *Faculty research:* Molecular genetics, enzymology, photosynthesis, molecular virology, structural biology.

University of Nebraska–Lincoln, Graduate College, College of Arts and Sciences, Department of Chemistry, Lincoln, NE 68588. Offers analytical chemistry (PhD); biochemistry (PhD); chemistry (MS); inorganic chemistry (PhD); materials chemistry (PhD); organic chemistry (PhD); physical chemistry (PhD). *Degree requirements:* For master's, one foreign language, thesis optional, departmental qualifying exam; for doctorate, one foreign language, comprehensive exam, thesis/dissertation, departmental qualifying exams. *Entrance requirements:* For master's and doctorate, GRE. Additional exam requirements/recommendations for international students: Required—TOEFL (minimum score 550 paper-based; 213 computer-based). Electronic applications accepted. *Faculty research:* Bioorganic and bioinorganic chemistry, biophysical and bioanalytical chemistry, structure-function of DNA and proteins, organometallics, mass spectrometry.

University of Nebraska Medical Center, Graduate Studies, Department of Biochemistry and Molecular Biology, Omaha, NE 68198. Offers MS, PhD. *Faculty:* 17 full-time (2 women), 28 part-time/adjunct (5 women). *Students:* 28 full-time (13 women), 9 part-time (7 women); includes 1 Asian, non-Hispanic/Latino; 1 Hispanic/Latino, 19 international. Average age 27. 30 applicants, 37% accepted, 11 enrolled. In 2010, 1 master's, 5 doctorates awarded. Terminal master's awarded for partial completion of doctoral program. *Degree requirements:* For master's, comprehensive exam, thesis; for doctorate, comprehensive exam, thesis/dissertation. *Entrance requirements:* For master's and doctorate, GRE General Test. Additional exam requirements/recommendations for international students: Required—TOEFL (minimum score 550 paper-based; 213 computer-based). *Application deadline:* For fall admission, 6/1 for domestic students, 4/1 for international students; for spring admission, 10/1 for domestic students, 8/1 for international students. Application fee: $45. Electronic applications accepted. *Expenses:* Tuition, state resident: part-time $198.25 per semester hour. Required fees: $63 per semester. *Financial support:* In 2010–11, 10 students received support, including fellowships with full tuition reimbursements available (averaging $21,000 per year), research assistantships with full tuition reimbursements available (averaging $21,000 per year); institutionally sponsored loans also available. Support available to part-time students. Financial award application deadline: 2/15. *Faculty research:* Recombinant DNA, cancer biology, diabetes and drug metabolism, biochemical endocrinology. Total annual research expenditures: $2.5 million. *Unit head:* Dr. Surinder K. Batra, Chairman, Graduate Committee, 402-559-5455, Fax: 402-559-6650, E-mail: biochem@unmc.edu. *Application contact:* Jennifer Pace, Office Associate, 402-559-4417.

University of Nevada, Las Vegas, Graduate College, College of Science, Department of Chemistry, Las Vegas, NV 89154-4003. Offers biochemistry (MS); chemistry (MS, PhD); radiochemistry (PhD). Part-time programs available. *Faculty:* 18 full-time (3 women), 1 part-time/adjunct (0 women). *Students:* 41 full-time (21 women), 8 part-time (3 women); includes 21 minority (2 Black or African American, non-Hispanic/Latino; 2 Asian, non-Hispanic/Latino; 2 Hispanic/Latino; 1 Native Hawaiian or other Pacific Islander, non-Hispanic/Latino; 14 Two or more races, non-Hispanic/Latino), 13 international. Average age 30. 39 applicants, 49% accepted, 9 enrolled. In 2010, 3 master's, 4 doctorates awarded. *Degree requirements:* For master's, thesis. *Entrance requirements:* For master's and doctorate, GRE General Test. Additional exam requirements/recommendations for international students: Required—TOEFL (minimum score 550 paper-based; 213 computer-based; 80 iBT), IELTS (minimum score 7). *Application deadline:* For fall admission, 2/1 priority date for domestic and international students; for spring admission, 10/1 priority date for domestic and international students. Applications are processed on a rolling basis. Application fee: $60 ($95 for international students). Electronic applications accepted. *Expenses:* Tuition, state resident: part-time $239.50 per credit. Tuition, nonresident: part-time $503 per credit. Required fees: $108 per semester. Tuition and fees vary according to course load, program and reciprocity agreements. *Financial support:* In 2010–11, 23 students received support, including 7 research assistantships with partial tuition reimbursements available (averaging $17,957 per year), 16 teaching assistantships with partial tuition reimbursements available (averaging $11,250 per year); institutionally sponsored loans, scholarships/grants, health care benefits, and unspecified assistantships also available. Financial award application deadline: 3/1. *Faculty research:* Material science, biochemistry, chemical education, physical chemistry and theoretical computation, analytical and organic chemistry. Total annual research expenditures: $1.8 million. *Unit head:* Dr. Dennis Lindle, Chair/Professor, 702-895-4426, Fax: 702-895-4072, E-mail: lindle@unlv.nevada.edu. *Application contact:* Graduate Coordinator, 702-895-3320, Fax: 702-895-4180, E-mail: gradcollege@unlv.edu.

University of Nevada, Reno, Graduate School, College of Agriculture, Biotechnology and Natural Resources, Program in Biochemistry, Reno, NV 89557. Offers MS, PhD. Terminal master's awarded for partial completion of doctoral program. *Degree requirements:* For master's, thesis; for doctorate, thesis/dissertation. *Entrance requirements:* For master's, GRE General Test, minimum GPA of 2.75; for doctorate, GRE General Test, minimum GPA of 3.0. Additional exam requirements/recommendations for international students: Required—TOEFL (minimum score 500 paper-based; 173 computer-based; 61 iBT), IELTS (minimum score 6). Electronic applications accepted. *Expenses:* Tuition, state resident: full-time $2219; part-time $246 per credit. Tuition, nonresident: part-time $510 per credit. International tuition: $9009 full-time. Required fees: $59 per term. One-time fee: $101. Tuition and fees vary according to course load. *Faculty research:* Cancer research, insect biochemistry, plant biochemistry, enzymology.

See Display on next page and Close-Up on page 149.

University of New Hampshire, Graduate School, College of Life Sciences and Agriculture, Department of Molecular, Cellular and Biomedical Sciences, Program in Biochemistry, Durham, NH 03824. Offers MS, PhD. Part-time programs available. *Faculty:* 12 full-time. *Students:* 12 full-time (2 women), 7 part-time (3 women); includes 2 Asian, non-Hispanic/Latino; 2 Hispanic/Latino, 7 international. Average age 29. 46 applicants, 24% accepted, 3 enrolled. In 2010, 2 master's awarded. Terminal master's awarded for partial completion of doctoral program. *Degree requirements:* For master's, thesis; for doctorate, one foreign language, thesis/dissertation. *Entrance requirements:* For master's and doctorate, GRE General Test. Additional exam requirements/recommendations for international students: Required—TOEFL (minimum score 550 paper-based; 213 computer-based; 80 iBT). *Application deadline:* For fall admission, 6/1 priority date for domestic students, 4/1 for international students; for spring admission, 12/1 for domestic students. Applications are processed on a rolling basis. Application fee: $65.

Electronic applications accepted. *Financial support:* In 2010–11, 15 students received support, including 5 research assistantships, 10 teaching assistantships; fellowships, career-related internships or fieldwork, Federal Work-Study, scholarships/grants, and tuition waivers (full and partial) also available. Support available to part-time students. Financial award application deadline: 2/15. *Faculty research:* Developmental biochemistry, biochemistry of natural products, physical biochemistry, biochemical genetics, structure and metabolism of macromolecules. *Unit head:* Rick Cote, Chairperson, 603-862-2470. *Application contact:* Flora Joyal, Administrative Assistant, 603-862-2103, E-mail: biochemistry.dept@unh.edu.

University of New Mexico, School of Medicine, Biomedical Sciences Graduate Program, Albuquerque, NM 87131-5196. Offers biochemistry and molecular biology (MS, PhD); cell biology and physiology (MS, PhD); clinical and translational science (Certificate); molecular genetics and microbiology (MS, PhD); neuroscience (MS, PhD); pathology (MS, PhD); toxicology (MS, PhD); university science teaching (Certificate). Part-time programs available. *Faculty:* 33 full-time (14 women), 3 part-time/adjunct (1 woman). *Students:* 94 full-time (57 women), 14 part-time (8 women); includes 24 minority (3 Black or African American, non-Hispanic/Latino; 1 American Indian or Alaska Native, non-Hispanic/Latino; 6 Asian, non-Hispanic/Latino; 13 Hispanic/Latino; 1 Two or more races, non-Hispanic/Latino), 20 international. Average age 30. 135 applicants, 14% accepted, 19 enrolled. In 2010, 2 master's, 19 doctorates, 3 other advanced degrees awarded. Terminal master's awarded for partial completion of doctoral program. *Degree requirements:* For master's, thesis; for doctorate, comprehensive exam, thesis/dissertation. *Entrance requirements:* For master's and doctorate, GRE General Test, minimum undergraduate GPA of 3.0. Additional exam requirements/recommendations for international students: Required—TOEFL. *Application deadline:* For fall admission, 1/1 priority date for domestic students. Applications are processed on a rolling basis. Application fee: $50. Electronic applications accepted. *Expenses:* Tuition, state resident: full-time $5991; part-time $251 per credit hour. Tuition, nonresident: full-time $14,405; part-time $800.20 per credit hour. Tuition and fees vary according to course level, course load, program and reciprocity agreements. *Financial support:* In 2010–11, 99 students received support, including 5 fellowships (averaging $75 per year), 96 research assistantships with full tuition reimbursements available (averaging $17,401 per year), 2 teaching assistantships with full tuition reimbursements available (averaging $2,415 per year); career-related internships or fieldwork, Federal Work-Study, institutionally sponsored loans, scholarships/grants, traineeships, health care benefits, and unspecified assistantships also available. Financial award application deadline: 1/1; financial award applicants required to submit FAFSA. *Faculty research:* Signal transduction, infectious disease, biology of cancer, structural biology, neuroscience. *Unit head:* Laurie G. Hudson, Director, 505-272-1887, Fax: 505-272-8738, E-mail: lhudson@salud.unm.edu. *Application contact:* Angel Cooke-Jackson, Coordinator, 505-272-1887, Fax: 505-272-8738, E-mail: acooke-jackson@salud.unm.edu.

The University of North Carolina at Chapel Hill, School of Medicine and Graduate School, Graduate Programs in Medicine, Department of Biochemistry and Biophysics, Chapel Hill, NC 27599. Offers MS, PhD. Terminal master's awarded for partial completion of doctoral program. *Degree requirements:* For master's, comprehensive exam, thesis; for doctorate, comprehensive exam, thesis/dissertation. *Entrance requirements:* For master's and doctorate, GRE General Test, GRE Subject Test (recommended), minimum GPA of 3.0. Additional exam requirements/recommendations for international students: Required—TOEFL. Electronic applications accepted.

The University of North Carolina at Greensboro, Graduate School, College of Arts and Sciences, Department of Chemistry and Biochemistry, Greensboro, NC 27412-5001. Offers biochemistry (MS); chemistry (MS). *Degree requirements:* For master's, one foreign language, thesis. *Entrance requirements:* For master's, GRE General Test. Additional exam requirements/recommendations for international students: Required—TOEFL. Electronic applications accepted. *Faculty research:* Synthesis of novel cyclopentadienes, molybdenum hydroxylase-cata ladder polymers, vinyl silicones.

University of North Dakota, Graduate School and Graduate School, Graduate Programs in Medicine, Department of Biochemistry and Molecular Biology, Grand Forks, ND 58202. Offers MS, PhD. *Faculty:* 8 full-time (4 women). *Students:* 16 full-time (8 women), 4 part-time (3 women); includes 1 minority (Black or African American, non-Hispanic/Latino), 7 international. Average age 26. 19 applicants, 26% accepted, 5 enrolled. In 2010, 2 master's, 3 doctorates awarded. *Degree requirements:* For master's, thesis, final exam; for doctorate, comprehensive exam, thesis/dissertation, final exam. *Entrance requirements:* For master's and doctorate, GRE General Test, minimum GPA of 3.0. Additional exam requirements/recommendations for international students: Required—TOEFL (minimum score 550 paper-based; 213 computer-based; 79 iBT), IELTS (minimum score 6.5). *Application deadline:* For fall admission, 2/15 priority date for domestic and international students. Application fee: $35. Electronic applications accepted. *Expenses:* Tuition, state resident: full-time $5857; part-time $306.74 per credit. Tuition, nonresident: full-time $15,666; part-time $729.77 per credit. Required fees: $53.42 per credit. Tuition and fees vary according to course load, program and reciprocity agreements. *Financial support:* In 2010–11, 17 students received support, including 12 research assistantships with full and partial tuition reimbursements available (averaging $13,997 per year), 5 teaching assistantships with full and partial tuition reimbursements available (averaging $13,997 per year); fellowships with full and partial tuition reimbursements available, Federal Work-Study, institutionally sponsored loans, scholarships/grants, health care benefits, tuition waivers (full and partial), and unspecified assistantships also available. Support available to part-time students. Financial award application deadline: 3/15; financial award applicants required to submit FAFSA. *Faculty research:* Glucose-6-phosphatase, guanine nucleotides, carbohydrate and lipid metabolism, cytoskeletal proteins, chromatin structure. Total annual research expenditures: $741,346. *Unit head:* Dr. Min Wu, Graduate Director, 701-777-4875, Fax: 701-777-3527, E-mail: minwu@medicine.nodak.edu. *Application contact:* Matt Anderson, Admissions Specialist, 701-777-2947, Fax: 701-777-3619, E-mail: matthew.anderson@gradschool.und.edu.

University of Northern Iowa, Graduate College, College of Natural Sciences, Department of Chemistry, Cedar Falls, IA 50614. Offers applied chemistry and biochemistry (PSM); chemistry (MA, MS). Part-time programs available. *Students:* 4 full-time (1 woman), 3 part-time (all women), 2 international. 14 applicants, 21% accepted, 3 enrolled. In 2010, 3 master's awarded. *Degree requirements:* For master's, comprehensive exam (for some programs), thesis (for some programs). *Entrance requirements:* For master's, minimum GPA of 3.0, 3 letters of recommendation. Additional exam requirements/recommendations for international students: Required—TOEFL (minimum score 500 paper-based; 180 computer-based; 61 iBT). *Application deadline:* For fall admission, 8/1 priority date for domestic students. Applications are processed on a rolling basis. Application fee: $50 ($70 for international students). Electronic applications accepted. *Financial support:* Career-related internships or fieldwork, Federal Work-Study, scholarships/grants, and tuition waivers (full and partial) available. Support available to part-time students. Financial award application deadline: 2/1. *Unit head:* Dr. William S. Harwood, Head, 319-273-2437, Fax: 319-273-7127, E-mail: bill.harwood@uni.edu. *Application contact:* Laurie S. Russell, Record Analyst, 319-273-2623, Fax: 319-273-2885, E-mail: laurie.russell@uni.edu.

University of North Texas, Toulouse Graduate School, College of Arts and Sciences, Department of Biological Sciences, Program in Biochemistry, Denton, TX 76203. Offers MS, PhD. Terminal master's awarded for partial completion of doctoral program. *Degree requirements:* For master's, comprehensive exam, thesis (for some programs), oral defense of thesis; for doctorate, one foreign language, comprehensive exam, thesis/dissertation, oral defense of dissertation. *Entrance requirements:* For master's, GRE General Test, placement exams in 3 areas, letters of recommendation; for doctorate, GRE General Test, placement exams in 4 areas. Additional exam requirements/recommendations for international students: Recommended—TOEFL (minimum score 550 paper-based; 213 computer-based; 79 iBT). *Application deadline:* For fall admission, 7/15 for domestic students; for spring admission, 11/15 for domestic students. *Expenses:* Tuition, state resident: full-time $4298; part-time $239 per credit hour. Tuition, nonresident: full-time $10,782; part-time $549 per credit hour. Required fees: $1292; $270 per credit hour. *Financial support:* Career-related internships or fieldwork, Federal Work-Study, institutionally sponsored loans, scholarships/grants, health care benefits, and unspecified assistantships available. Support available to part-time students. Financial award application deadline: 4/1; financial award applicants required to submit FAFSA. *Faculty research:* Microbial and plant metabolism, regulation of prokaryotic and eukaryotic gene expression, protein

Graduate Program in Biochemistry (BCH)

The University of Nevada, Reno ranks among the top 100 Public Research Schools in the U.S. according to a recent survey by U.S. News and World Report. Biochemistry graduate students have opportunities to conduct research either in the College of Agriculture, Biotechnology and Natural Resources (CABNR) or the School of Medicine (SOM) with access to state-of-the-art federally funded research centers in genomics, proteomics, bioinformatics, flow cytometry and *in vivo* imaging. Graduate student have a broad range of research areas from which to choose spanning human biomedicine and disease, insect biochemistry and signaling, and plant and microbial genomics and biotechnology.

The University is situated within an unusually attractive natural setting on the eastern slopes of the majestic Sierra Nevada mountain range. Reno-Sparks benefits from a comfortable climate marked by generally cool and dry weather with more than 300 sunny days per year. The area is a haven for those who love the four seasons, an active live style, and it offers many diverse recreational activities including Lake Tahoe and many world-class ski resorts.

Interdisciplinary Graduate Programs in Molecular Biosciences (MB)

All first year Ph.D. candidates are provided research stipends and have the opportunity to conduct research rotations within interdisciplinary graduate programs in the molecular biosciences with more than 65 active research faculty.

Contact: John C. Cushman, Ph.D.
Professor, Graduate Program Director
Department of Biochemistry & Molecular Biology
Reno, NV 89557
Email: jcushman@unr.edu
BCH: http://www.cabnr.unr.edu/bmb/default.aspx
MB: http://www.unr.edu/mb/index.html

University of Nevada, Reno

Biochemistry

University of North Texas (continued)
interaction. *Application contact:* Dr. Dan Kunz, Graduate Advisor, 940-565-2011, Fax: 940-565-3821, E-mail: kunz@unt.edu.

University of North Texas Health Science Center at Fort Worth, Graduate School of Biomedical Sciences, Fort Worth, TX 76107-2699. Offers anatomy and cell biology (MS, PhD); biochemistry and molecular biology (MS, PhD); biomedical sciences (MS, PhD); biotechnology (MS); forensic genetics (MS); integrative physiology (MS, PhD); medical science (MS); microbiology and immunology (MS, PhD); pharmacology (MS, PhD); science education (MS); DO/MS; DO/PhD. Terminal master's awarded for partial completion of doctoral program. *Degree requirements:* For master's, thesis; for doctorate, thesis/dissertation. *Entrance requirements:* For master's and doctorate, GRE General Test. Additional exam requirements/recommendations for international students: Required—TOEFL. *Expenses:* Contact institution. *Faculty research:* Alzheimer's disease, aging, eye diseases, cancer, cardiovascular disease.

University of Notre Dame, Graduate School, College of Science, Department of Chemistry and Biochemistry, Notre Dame, IN 46556. Offers biochemistry (MS, PhD); inorganic chemistry (MS, PhD); organic chemistry (MS, PhD); physical chemistry (MS, PhD). Terminal master's awarded for partial completion of doctoral program. *Degree requirements:* For master's, comprehensive exam, thesis; for doctorate, thesis/dissertation, qualifying exam. *Entrance requirements:* For master's and doctorate, GRE General Test, GRE Subject Test (strongly recommended). Additional exam requirements/recommendations for international students: Required—TOEFL (minimum score 600 paper-based; 250 computer-based; 80 iBT). Electronic applications accepted. *Faculty research:* Reaction design and mechanistic studies; reactive intermediates; synthesis, structure and reactivity of organometallic cluster complexes and biologically active natural products; bioorganic chemistry; enzymology.

University of Oklahoma, College of Arts and Sciences, Department of Chemistry and Biochemistry, Norman, OK 73019. Offers chemistry and biochemistry (MS, PhD), including bioinformatics, cellular and behavioral neurobiology (PhD), chemistry. Part-time programs available. *Faculty:* 27 full-time (6 women). *Students:* 72 full-time (27 women), 26 part-time (11 women); includes 12 minority (6 Black or African American, non-Hispanic/Latino; 1 American Indian or Alaska Native, non-Hispanic/Latino; 2 Asian, non-Hispanic/Latino; 1 Hispanic/Latino; 2 Two or more races, non-Hispanic/Latino), 50 international. Average age 28. 31 applicants, 61% accepted, 16 enrolled. In 2010, 17 master's, 17 doctorates awarded. Terminal master's awarded for partial completion of doctoral program. *Degree requirements:* For master's, thesis optional; for doctorate, thesis/dissertation. *Entrance requirements:* For master's, GRE, BS in chemistry; for doctorate, GRE. Additional exam requirements/recommendations for international students: Required—TOEFL (minimum score 550 paper-based; 213 computer-based; 79 iBT). *Application deadline:* For fall admission, 4/1 priority date for domestic students, 4/1 for international students; for spring admission, 9/1 priority date for domestic students, 9/1 for international students. Applications are processed on a rolling basis. Application fee: $40 ($90 for international students). Electronic applications accepted. *Expenses:* Tuition, state resident: full-time $3893; part-time $162.20 per credit hour. Tuition, nonresident: full-time $14,167; part-time $590.30 per credit hour. Required fees: $2523; $94.60 per credit hour. Tuition and fees vary according to course load and degree level. *Financial support:* In 2010–11, 1 fellowship with full tuition reimbursement (averaging $5,000 per year), 24 research assistantships with partial tuition reimbursements (averaging $14,788 per year), 62 teaching assistantships with partial tuition reimbursements (averaging $16,444 per year) were awarded; scholarships/grants and unspecified assistantships also available. Financial award application deadline: 4/1; financial award applicants required to submit FAFSA. *Faculty research:* Structural biology, synthesis and catalysis, biomaterials, membrane biochemistry, genomics. Total annual research expenditures: $6.8 million. *Unit head:* Dr. George Richter-Addo, Chair, 405-325-4811, Fax: 405-325-6111, E-mail: grichteraddo@ou.edu. *Application contact:* Angela Link-Perez, Graduate Program Assistant, 405-325-4811 Ext. 62946, Fax: 405-325-6111, E-mail: alperez@ou.edu.

University of Oklahoma Health Sciences Center, College of Medicine and Graduate College, Graduate Programs in Medicine, Department of Biochemistry and Molecular Biology, Oklahoma City, OK 73190. Offers biochemistry (MS, PhD); molecular biology (MS, PhD). Part-time programs available. Terminal master's awarded for partial completion of doctoral program. *Degree requirements:* For master's, thesis; for doctorate, thesis/dissertation. *Entrance requirements:* For master's, GRE General Test, 2 letters of recommendation; for doctorate, GRE General Test, 3 letters of recommendation. Additional exam requirements/recommendations for international students: Required—TOEFL. *Faculty research:* Gene expression, regulation of transcription, enzyme evolution, melanogenesis, signal transduction.

University of Oregon, Graduate School, College of Arts and Sciences, Department of Chemistry, Eugene, OR 97403. Offers biochemistry (MA, MS, PhD); chemistry (MA, MS, PhD). Terminal master's awarded for partial completion of doctoral program. *Degree requirements:* For doctorate, thesis/dissertation. *Entrance requirements:* For master's and doctorate, GRE General Test, minimum GPA of 3.0. Additional exam requirements/recommendations for international students: Required—TOEFL. *Faculty research:* Organic chemistry, organometallic chemistry, inorganic chemistry, physical chemistry, materials science, biochemistry, chemical physics, molecular or cell biology.

University of Ottawa, Faculty of Graduate and Postdoctoral Studies, Faculty of Medicine, Department of Biochemistry, Microbiology and Immunology, Ottawa, ON K1N 6N5, Canada. Offers biochemistry (M Sc, PhD); microbiology and immunology (M Sc, PhD). *Degree requirements:* For master's, thesis; for doctorate, comprehensive exam, thesis/dissertation, seminar. *Entrance requirements:* For master's, honors degree or equivalent, minimum B average; for doctorate, master's degree, minimum B+ average. Electronic applications accepted. *Faculty research:* General biochemistry, molecular biology, microbiology, host biology, nutrition and metabolism.

University of Pennsylvania, Perelman School of Medicine, Biomedical Graduate Studies, Graduate Group in Biochemistry and Molecular Biophysics, Philadelphia, PA 19104. Offers PhD, MD/PhD, VMD/PhD. *Faculty:* 77. *Students:* 73 full-time (28 women); includes 4 Black or African American, non-Hispanic/Latino; 8 Asian, non-Hispanic/Latino; 8 Hispanic/Latino, 9 international. 145 applicants, 25% accepted, 10 enrolled. In 2010, 11 doctorates awarded. *Degree requirements:* For doctorate, thesis/dissertation. *Entrance requirements:* For doctorate, GRE General Test. Additional exam requirements/recommendations for international students: Required—TOEFL. *Application deadline:* For fall admission, 12/8 priority date for domestic and international students. Applications are processed on a rolling basis. Application fee: $70. Electronic applications accepted. *Expenses:* Tuition: Full-time $25,660; part-time $4758 per course. Required fees: $2152; $270 per course. Tuition and fees vary according to course load, degree level and program. *Financial support:* In 2010–11, 73 students received support; fellowships, research assistantships, scholarships/grants, traineeships, and unspecified assistantships available. *Faculty research:* Biochemistry of cell differentiation, tissue culture, intermediary metabolism, structure of proteins and nucleic acids, biochemical genetics. *Unit head:* Dr. Kathryn Ferguson, Chairperson, 215-573-7288. *Application contact:* Ruth Keris, Administrator, 215-898-4639, Fax: 215-573-2085, E-mail: keris@mail.med.upenn.edu.

University of Puerto Rico, Medical Sciences Campus, School of Medicine, Division of Graduate Studies, Department of Biochemistry, San Juan, PR 00936-5067. Offers MS, PhD. *Degree requirements:* For master's, thesis; for doctorate, comprehensive exam, thesis/dissertation. *Entrance requirements:* For master's and doctorate, GRE General Test, GRE Subject Test, interview, minimum GPA of 3.0. Electronic applications accepted. *Faculty research:* Genetics, cell and molecular biology, cancer biology, protein structure/function, glycosilation of proteins.

University of Regina, Faculty of Graduate Studies and Research, Faculty of Science, Department of Chemistry and Biochemistry, Regina, SK S4S 0A2, Canada. Offers analytical/environmental chemistry (M Sc, PhD); biophysics of biological interfaces (M Sc, PhD); enzymology/chemical biology (M Sc, PhD); inorganic/organometallic chemistry (M Sc, PhD); signal transduction and mechanisms of cancer cell regulation (M Sc, PhD); supramolecular organic photochemistry and photophysics (M Sc, PhD); synthetic organic chemistry (M Sc, PhD); theoretical/computational chemistry (M Sc, PhD). *Faculty:* 10 full-time (2 women). *Students:* 19 full-time (9 women), 2 part-time (1 woman). 20 applicants, 40% accepted. In 2010, 2 master's, 1 doctorate awarded. *Degree requirements:* For master's, thesis; for doctorate, thesis/dissertation. *Entrance requirements:* Additional exam requirements/recommendations for international students: Required—TOEFL (minimum score 580 paper-based; 80 iBT). *Application deadline:* Applications are processed on a rolling basis. Application fee: $100. Electronic applications accepted. Tuition and fees charges are reported in Canadian dollars. *Expenses:* Tuition, area resident: Full-time $3245 Canadian dollars; part-time $180.25 Canadian dollars per credit hour. International tuition: $4745 Canadian dollars full-time. Required fees: $494 Canadian dollars; $115.25 Canadian dollars per credit hour. $115.25 Canadian dollars per semester. Tuition and fees vary according to program. *Financial support:* In 2010–11, 3 fellowships (averaging $20,000 per year), 2 research assistantships (averaging $17,250 per year), 8 teaching assistantships (averaging $6,965 per year) were awarded; scholarships/grants also available. Financial award application deadline: 6/15. *Faculty research:* Asymmetric synthesis and methodology, theoretical and computational chemistry, biophysical biochemistry, analytical and environmental chemistry, chemical biology. *Unit head:* Dr. Lynn Mihichuk, Head, 306-585-4793, Fax: 306-337-2409, E-mail: lynn.mihichuk@uregina.ca. *Application contact:* Dr. Tanya Dahms, Graduate Program Coordinator, 306-585-4246, Fax: 306-337-2409, E-mail: tanya.dahms@uregina.ca.

University of Rhode Island, Graduate School, College of the Environment and Life Sciences, Department of Cell and Molecular Biology, Kingston, RI 02881. Offers biochemistry (MS, PhD); clinical laboratory sciences (MS), including biotechnology, clinical laboratory science, cytopathology; microbiology (MS, PhD); molecular genetics (MS, PhD). Part-time programs available. *Faculty:* 13 full-time (5 women), 2 part-time/adjunct (1 woman). *Students:* 32 full-time (15 women), 37 part-time (23 women); includes 10 minority (5 Black or African American, non-Hispanic/Latino; 2 Asian, non-Hispanic/Latino; 3 Hispanic/Latino), 4 international. In 2010, 29 master's, 3 doctorates awarded. *Degree requirements:* For master's, comprehensive exam (for some programs); for doctorate, comprehensive exam. *Entrance requirements:* For master's and doctorate, GRE, 2 letters of recommendation. Additional exam requirements/recommendations for international students: Required—TOEFL (minimum score 550 paper-based; 213 computer-based). *Application deadline:* For fall admission, 7/15 for domestic students, 2/1 for international students; for spring admission, 11/15 for domestic students, 7/15 for international students. Application fee: $65. Electronic applications accepted. *Expenses:* Tuition, state resident: full-time $9588; part-time $533 per credit hour. Tuition, nonresident: full-time $22,968; part-time $1276 per credit hour. Required fees: $1282; $68 per semester. Tuition and fees vary according to program. *Financial support:* In 2010–11, 3 research assistantships with full and partial tuition reimbursements (averaging $11,653 per year), 12 teaching assistantships with full and partial tuition reimbursements (averaging $12,379 per year) were awarded. Financial award application deadline: 7/15; financial award applicants required to submit FAFSA. *Faculty research:* Genomics and Sequencing Center: an interdisciplinary genomics research and undergraduate and graduate student training program which provides researchers access to cutting-edge technologies in the field of genomics. Total annual research expenditures: $3.5 million. *Unit head:* Dr. Jay Sperry, Chairperson, 401-874-2201, Fax: 401-874-2202, E-mail: jsperry@mail.uri.edu. *Application contact:* Dr. Jay Sperry, Chairperson, 401-874-2201, Fax: 401-874-2202, E-mail: jsperry@mail.uri.edu.

University of Rochester, School of Medicine and Dentistry, Graduate Programs in Medicine and Dentistry, Department of Biochemistry and Biophysics, Programs in Biochemistry, Rochester, NY 14627. Offers MS, PhD. Terminal master's awarded for partial completion of doctoral program. *Degree requirements:* For doctorate, thesis/dissertation, qualifying exam. *Entrance requirements:* For master's and doctorate, GRE General Test.

University of Saskatchewan, College of Medicine, Department of Biochemistry, Saskatoon, SK S7N 5A2, Canada. Offers M Sc, PhD. *Degree requirements:* For master's, thesis; for doctorate, thesis/dissertation. *Entrance requirements:* Additional exam requirements/recommendations for international students: Required—TOEFL.

The University of Scranton, College of Graduate and Continuing Education, Department of Chemistry, Program in Biochemistry, Scranton, PA 18510. Offers MA, MS. Part-time and evening/weekend programs available. *Faculty:* 10 full-time (3 women), 1 part-time/adjunct (0 women). *Students:* 25 full-time (8 women), 5 part-time (1 woman); includes 2 Asian, non-Hispanic/Latino; 1 Hispanic/Latino, 8 international. Average age 24. 59 applicants, 69% accepted. In 2010, 13 master's awarded. *Degree requirements:* For master's, comprehensive exam (for some programs), thesis (for some programs), capstone experience. *Entrance requirements:* For master's, minimum GPA of 2.75. Additional exam requirements/recommendations for international students: Required—TOEFL (minimum score 500 paper-based; 173 computer-based), IELTS (minimum score 5.5). *Application deadline:* Applications are processed on a rolling basis. Application fee: $0. *Financial support:* Fellowships, teaching assistantships with full and partial tuition reimbursements, career-related internships or fieldwork, Federal Work-Study, and unspecified assistantships available. Support available to part-time students. Financial award application deadline: 3/1. *Unit head:* Dr. Christopher A. Baumann, Director, 570-941-6389, Fax: 570-941-7510, E-mail: cab@scranton.edu. *Application contact:* Dr. Christopher A. Baumann, Director, 570-941-6389, Fax: 570-941-7510, E-mail: cab@scranton.edu.

University of South Carolina, The Graduate School, College of Arts and Sciences, Department of Chemistry and Biochemistry, Columbia, SC 29208. Offers IMA, MAT, MS, PhD. IMA and MAT offered in cooperation with the College of Education. Part-time programs available. Terminal master's awarded for partial completion of doctoral program. *Degree requirements:* For master's, comprehensive exam, thesis; for doctorate, comprehensive exam, thesis/dissertation. *Entrance requirements:* For master's and doctorate, GRE General Test. Additional exam requirements/recommendations for international students: Required—TOEFL. Electronic applications accepted. *Faculty research:* Spectroscopy, crystallography, organic and organometallic synthesis, analytical chemistry, materials.

University of Southern California, Keck School of Medicine and Graduate School, Graduate Programs in Medicine, Department of Biochemistry and Molecular Biology, Los Angeles, CA 90089. Offers MS, PhD. *Faculty:* 24 full-time (6 women). *Students:* 28 full-time (15 women); includes 7 minority (1 Black or African American, non-Hispanic/Latino; 5 Asian, non-Hispanic/Latino; 1 Hispanic/Latino), 19 international. Average age 24. 29 applicants, 93% accepted, 13 enrolled. In 2010, 7 master's, 18 doctorates awarded. Terminal master's awarded for partial completion of doctoral program. *Degree requirements:* For master's, thesis; for doctorate, comprehensive exam, thesis/dissertation. *Entrance requirements:* For master's and doctorate, GRE General Test, minimum GPA of 3.0. Additional exam requirements/recommendations for international students: Required—TOEFL (minimum score 600 paper-based; 250 computer-based; 100 iBT). *Application deadline:* For fall admission, 4/15 priority date for domestic and international students. Applications are processed on a rolling basis. Application fee: $85 for international students. Electronic applications accepted. *Expenses:* Tuition: Full-time $31,240; part-time $1420 per unit. Required fees: $600. One-time fee: $35 full-time. Full-time tuition and fees vary according to degree level and program. *Financial support:* In 2010–11, 5 students received support, including 1 fellowship with tuition reimbursement available (averaging $27,600 per year), 12 research assistantships with tuition reimbursements available (averaging $27,600 per year), 3 teaching assistantships with tuition reimbursements available (averaging $27,600 per year); Federal Work-Study, institutionally sponsored loans, scholarships/grants, health care benefits, and unspecified assistantships also available. Financial award application deadline: 5/5. *Faculty research:* Molecular genetics, gene expression, membrane biochemistry, metabolic regulation, cancer biology. *Unit head:* Dr. Michael R. Stallcup, Chair, 323-442-1145, Fax: 323-442-1224, E-mail: stallcup@usc.edu. *Application contact:* Anne L. Rice, Student Services Coordinator, 323-442-1145, Fax: 323-442-1224, E-mail: annvazqu@usc.edu.

University of Southern Mississippi, Graduate School, College of Science and Technology, Department of Chemistry and Biochemistry, Hattiesburg, MS 39406-0001. Offers analytical chemistry (MS, PhD); biochemistry (MS, PhD); inorganic chemistry (MS, PhD); organic chemistry (MS, PhD); physical chemistry (MS, PhD). *Faculty:* 16 full-time (4 women). *Students:* 23 full-time (11 women), 1 part-time (0 women); includes 1 Black or African American, non-Hispanic/Latino, 11 international. Average age 29. 35 applicants, 20% accepted, 5 enrolled. In 2010, 3 master's, 8 doctorates awarded. *Degree requirements:* For master's, comprehensive exam, thesis; for doctorate, comprehensive exam, thesis/dissertation. *Entrance requirements:* For master's, GRE General Test, minimum GPA of 2.75 in last 60 hours; for doctorate, GRE General Test, minimum GPA of 3.5. Additional exam requirements/recommendations for international students: Required—TOEFL, IELTS. *Application deadline:* For fall admission, 3/1 priority date for domestic students, 3/1 for international students. Applications are processed on a rolling basis. Application fee: $50. *Financial support:* In 2010–11, 3 research assistantships with full tuition reimbursements (averaging $17,000 per year), 19 teaching assistantships with full tuition reimbursements (averaging $20,700 per year) were awarded; fellowships, Federal Work-Study, institutionally sponsored loans, scholarships/grants, health care benefits, and unspecified assistantships also available. Support available to part-time students. Financial award application deadline: 3/15; financial award applicants required to submit FAFSA. *Faculty research:* Plant biochemistry, photo chemistry, polymer chemistry, x-ray analysis, enzyme chemistry. *Unit head:* Dr. Sabine Heinhorst, Chair, 601-266-4701, Fax: 601-266-6075. *Application contact:* Dr. Sabine Heinhorst, Graduate Coordinator, 601-266-4702, Fax: 601-266-6075.

University of South Florida, Graduate School, College of Arts and Sciences, Department of Chemistry, Tampa, FL 33620-9951. Offers analytical chemistry (MS, PhD); biochemistry (MS, PhD); computational chemistry (MS, PhD); environmental chemistry (MS, PhD); inorganic chemistry (MS, PhD); organic chemistry (MS); physical chemistry (MS, PhD); polymer chemistry (PhD). Part-time programs available. *Faculty:* 15 full-time (1 woman). *Students:* 120 full-time (42 women), 9 part-time (2 women); includes 7 Black or African American, non-Hispanic/Latino; 8 Asian, non-Hispanic/Latino; 8 Hispanic/Latino, 62 international. Average age 29. 1,118 applicants, 4% accepted, 20 enrolled. In 2010, 4 master's, 14 doctorates awarded. Terminal master's awarded for partial completion of doctoral program. *Degree requirements:* For master's, comprehensive exam, thesis (for some programs); for doctorate, 2 foreign languages, comprehensive exam, thesis/dissertation. *Entrance requirements:* For master's, GRE General Test or GMAT, minimum GPA of 3.0. Additional exam requirements/recommendations for international students: Required—TOEFL (minimum score 550 paper-based; 213 computer-based). *Application deadline:* For fall admission, 2/15 priority date for domestic students, 1/2 priority date for international students; for spring admission, 10/1 priority date for domestic students, 6/1 priority date for international students. Applications are processed on a rolling basis. Application fee: $30. Electronic applications accepted. *Financial support:* In 2010–11, 39 research assistantships (averaging $14,359 per year), 99 teaching assistantships with tuition reimbursements (averaging $15,094 per year) were awarded; unspecified assistantships also available. Financial award application deadline: 6/30. *Faculty research:* Synthesis, bio-organic chemistry, bioinorganic chemistry, environmental chemistry, NMR. Total annual research expenditures: $3.9 million. *Unit head:* Dr. Randy Larsen, Chairperson, 813-974-4129, Fax: 813-974-3203, E-mail: rlarsen@cas.usf.edu. *Application contact:* Patricia Muisener, Director, 813-974-1730, Fax: 813-974-3203, E-mail: muisener@cas.usf.edu.

The University of Tennessee, Graduate School, College of Arts and Sciences, Department of Biochemistry, Cellular and Molecular Biology, Knoxville, TN 37996. Offers MS, PhD. Terminal master's awarded for partial completion of doctoral program. *Degree requirements:* For master's, thesis; for doctorate, thesis/dissertation. *Entrance requirements:* For master's and doctorate, GRE General Test, minimum GPA of 2.7. Additional exam requirements/recommendations for international students: Required—TOEFL. Electronic applications accepted. *Expenses:* Tuition, state resident: full-time $7440; part-time $414 per credit hour. Tuition, nonresident: full-time $22,478; part-time $1250 per credit hour. Required fees: $922; $43 per credit hour. Tuition and fees vary according to program.

The University of Texas at Austin, Graduate School, College of Natural Sciences, Department of Chemistry and Biochemistry, Program in Biochemistry, Austin, TX 78712-1111. Offers MA, PhD. *Entrance requirements:* For master's and doctorate, GRE General Test.

The University of Texas Health Science Center at Houston, Graduate School of Biomedical Sciences, Program in Biochemistry and Molecular Biology, Houston, TX 77225-0036. Offers MS, PhD, MD/PhD. Terminal master's awarded for partial completion of doctoral program. *Degree requirements:* For master's, thesis; for doctorate, thesis/dissertation. *Entrance requirements:* For master's and doctorate, GRE General Test. Additional exam requirements/recommendations for international students: Required—TOEFL. Electronic applications accepted. *Faculty research:* Biochemistry, membrane biology, macromolecular structure, structural biophysics, molecular models of human disease, molecular biology of the cell.

The University of Texas Health Science Center at San Antonio, Graduate School of Biomedical Sciences, Department of Biochemistry, San Antonio, TX 78229. Offers MS, PhD. *Faculty:* 23 full-time (5 women), 2 part-time/adjunct (1 woman). *Students:* 24 full-time (9 women); includes 5 Asian, non-Hispanic/Latino, 18 international. Average age 24. In 2010, 1 master's, 2 doctorates awarded. *Degree requirements:* For master's, thesis; for doctorate, comprehensive exam, thesis/dissertation. *Entrance requirements:* For master's and doctorate, GRE General Test. Additional exam requirements/recommendations for international students: Required—TOEFL (minimum score 560 paper-based; 220 computer-based; 68 iBT). *Application deadline:* For fall admission, 1/15 priority date for domestic and international students. Applications are processed on a rolling basis. Application fee: $0. Electronic applications accepted. *Expenses:* Tuition, state resident: full-time $3072; part-time $128 per credit hour. Tuition, nonresident: full-time $11,928; part-time $497 per credit hour. Required fees: $1078; $1078 per year. One-time fee: $60. *Financial support:* In 2010–11, 7 fellowships (averaging $26,000 per year), 17 teaching assistantships (averaging $26,000 per year) were awarded; scholarships/grants and health care benefits also available. Financial award application deadline: 6/30; financial award applicants required to submit FAFSA. *Faculty research:* Protein structure and function, lipid biochemistry, metabolic regulation, immunology, membrane assembly. Total annual research expenditures: $9.4 million. *Unit head:* Dr. Bruce J. Nicholson, Professor and Chair, 210-567-3770, Fax: 210-567-6595, E-mail: nicholsonb@uthscsa.edu. *Application contact:* Dr. Neal C. Robinson, Chairman, Committee on Graduate Studies, 210-567-3754, E-mail: robinson@uthscsa.edu.

The University of Texas Medical Branch, Graduate School of Biomedical Sciences, Program in Biochemistry and Molecular Biology, Galveston, TX 77555. Offers biochemistry (PhD); bioinformatics (PhD); biophysics (PhD); cell biology (PhD); computational biology (PhD); structural biology (PhD). *Degree requirements:* For doctorate, thesis/dissertation. *Entrance requirements:* Additional exam requirements/recommendations for international students: Required—TOEFL (minimum score 550 paper-based; 213 computer-based). Electronic applications accepted.

The University of Texas Southwestern Medical Center at Dallas, Southwestern Graduate School of Biomedical Sciences, Division of Basic Science, Program in Biological Chemistry, Dallas, TX 75390. Offers PhD. *Faculty:* 44 full-time (9 women), 1 part-time/adjunct (0 women). *Students:* 40 full-time (15 women), 4 part-time (0 women); includes 10 minority (1 American Indian or Alaska Native, non-Hispanic/Latino; 6 Asian, non-Hispanic/Latino; 3 Hispanic/Latino), 12 international. Average age 26. In 2010, 9 doctorates awarded. *Degree requirements:* For doctorate, thesis/dissertation, qualifying exam. *Entrance requirements:* For doctorate, GRE General Test, minimum GPA of 3.0. Additional exam requirements/recommendations for international students: Required—TOEFL. *Application deadline:* For fall admission, 12/15 priority date for domestic students. Application fee: $0. Electronic applications accepted. *Financial support:* Fellowships, research assistantships, institutionally sponsored loans available. *Faculty research:* Regulation of gene expression, protein trafficking, molecular neurobiology, protein structure and function, metabolic regulation. *Unit head:* Adam de Pencier. *Application contact:* Dr. Nancy E. Street, Associate Dean, 214-648-6708, Fax: 214-648-2102, E-mail: nancy.street@utsouthwestern.edu.

University of the Sciences in Philadelphia, College of Graduate Studies, Program in Chemistry, Biochemistry and Pharmacognosy, Philadelphia, PA 19104-4495. Offers biochemistry (MS, PhD); chemistry (MS, PhD); pharmacognosy (MS, PhD). Part-time programs available. *Degree requirements:* For master's, thesis, qualifying exams; for doctorate, comprehensive exam, thesis/dissertation, qualifying exams. *Entrance requirements:* For master's and doctorate, GRE General Test, GRE Subject Test. Additional exam requirements/recommendations for international students: Required—TOEFL, TWE. *Expenses:* Contact institution. *Faculty research:* Organic and medicinal synthesis, mass spectroscopy use in protein analysis, study of analogues of taxol, cholesteryl esters.

The University of Toledo, College of Graduate Studies, College of Natural Sciences and Mathematics, Department of Chemistry, Toledo, OH 43606-3390. Offers analytical chemistry (MS, PhD); biological chemistry (MS, PhD); inorganic chemistry (MS, PhD); organic chemistry (MS, PhD); physical chemistry (MS, PhD). Part-time programs available. *Faculty:* 24. *Students:* 63 full-time (22 women), 4 part-time (2 women); includes 2 minority (1 Asian, non-Hispanic/Latino; 1 Hispanic/Latino), 45 international. Average age 27. 111 applicants, 17% accepted, 16 enrolled. In 2010, 4 master's, 6 doctorates awarded. *Degree requirements:* For master's, thesis; for doctorate, thesis/dissertation. *Entrance requirements:* For master's and doctorate, GRE General Test, GRE Subject Test, minimum cumulative point-hour ratio of 2.7 for all previous academic work, three letters of recommendation, statement of purpose, transcripts from all prior institutions attended. Additional exam requirements/recommendations for international students: Required—TOEFL (minimum score 550 paper-based; 213 computer-based; 80 iBT), IELTS (minimum score 6.5). *Application deadline:* For fall admission, 1/15 priority date for domestic and international students. Applications are processed on a rolling basis. Application fee: $45 ($75 for international students). Electronic applications accepted. *Expenses:* Tuition, state resident: full-time $11,426; part-time $476 per credit hour. Tuition, nonresident: full-time $21,660; part-time $903 per credit hour. One-time fee: $62. *Financial support:* Fellowships with tuition reimbursements, research assistantships with full tuition reimbursements, teaching assistantships with full tuition reimbursements, Federal Work-Study, institutionally sponsored loans, scholarships/grants, tuition waivers (full), and unspecified assistantships available. Support available to part-time students. *Faculty research:* Enzymology, materials chemistry, crystallography, theoretical chemistry. *Unit head:* Dr. Alan Pinkerton, Chair, 419-530-7902, Fax: 419-530-4033, E-mail: alan.pinkerton@utoledo.edu. *Application contact:* Graduate School Office, 419-530-4723, Fax: 419-530-4724, E-mail: grdsch@utnet.utoledo.edu.

The University of Toledo, College of Graduate Studies, College of Pharmacy, Program in Medicinal and Biological Chemistry, Toledo, OH 43606-3390. Offers MS, PhD. Terminal master's awarded for partial completion of doctoral program. *Degree requirements:* For master's, thesis; for doctorate, thesis/dissertation. *Entrance requirements:* For master's and doctorate, GRE General Test. Additional exam requirements/recommendations for international students: Required—TOEFL (minimum score 550 paper-based; 213 computer-based; 80 iBT). Electronic applications accepted. *Expenses:* Tuition, state resident: full-time $11,426; part-time $476 per credit hour. Tuition, nonresident: full-time $21,660; part-time $903 per credit hour. One-time fee: $62. *Faculty research:* Neuroscience, molecular modeling, immunotoxicology, organic synthesis, peptide biochemistry.

University of Toronto, School of Graduate Studies, Life Sciences Division, Department of Biochemistry, Toronto, ON M5S 1A1, Canada. Offers M Sc, PhD. *Degree requirements:* For master's, thesis, oral examination of thesis; for doctorate, thesis/dissertation, oral defense of thesis. *Entrance requirements:* For master's, GRE General Test and GRE Subject Test in biochemistry/molecular biology (international applicants only), B Sc in biochemistry or molecular biology, minimum B+ average, letters of reference. Additional exam requirements/recommendations for international students: Required—TOEFL (minimum score 580 paper-based; 237 computer-based), TWE (minimum score 5).

University of Tulsa, Graduate School, College of Engineering and Natural Sciences, Department of Chemistry and Biochemistry, Program in Biochemistry, Tulsa, OK 74104-3189. Offers MS. Part-time programs available. *Faculty:* 2 full-time (0 women). *Students:* 7 full-time (5 women); includes 2 minority (both American Indian or Alaska Native, non-Hispanic/Latino), 4 international. Average age 26. 4 applicants, 100% accepted, 3 enrolled. In 2010, 1 master's awarded. *Degree requirements:* For master's, thesis (for some programs). *Entrance requirements:* For master's, GRE General Test. Additional exam requirements/recommendations for international students: Required—TOEFL (minimum score 550 paper-based; 213 computer-based; 80 iBT), IELTS (minimum score 6). *Application deadline:* Applications are processed on a rolling basis. Application fee: $40. Electronic applications accepted. *Expenses:* Tuition: Full-time $16,902; part-time $939 per credit hour. Required fees: $1020; $4 per credit hour. Tuition and fees vary according to course load. *Financial support:* In 2010–11, 3 students received support, including 1 research assistantship (averaging $12,000 per year), 2 teaching assistantships (averaging $11,942 per year); career-related internships or fieldwork, Federal Work-Study, scholarships/grants, health care benefits, and unspecified assistantships also available. Support available to part-time students. Financial award application deadline: 2/1; financial award applicants required to submit FAFSA. *Unit head:* Dr. Dale C. Teeters, Chairperson and Advisor, 918-631-2515, Fax: 918-631-3404, E-mail: dale-teeters@utulsa.edu. *Application contact:* Dr. Robert Sheaff, Advisor, 918-631-2319, Fax: 918-631-3404, E-mail: robert-sheaff@utulsa.edu.

University of Utah, Graduate School and Graduate Programs in Medicine, Program in Biological Chemistry, Salt Lake City, UT 84112-1107. Offers PhD. *Faculty:* 48 full-time (9 women). *Students:* 13 full-time (4 women), 6 international. Average age 24. 210 applicants, 13% accepted, 13 enrolled. *Degree requirements:* For doctorate, thesis/dissertation. *Entrance requirements:* For doctorate, GRE General Test. Additional exam requirements/recommendations for international students: Required—TOEFL (minimum score 500 paper-based; 173 computer-based; 60 iBT). *Application deadline:* For fall admission, 12/15 for domestic and international students. Application fee: $0. *Expenses:* Tuition, area resident: Part-time $179.19 per credit hour. Tuition, state resident: full-time $4384. Tuition, nonresident: full-time $16,684; part-time $630.67 per credit hour. Required fees: $350 per semester. Tuition and fees vary according to course load, degree level and program. *Financial support:* In 2010–11, 12 research assistantships with full tuition reimbursements (averaging $25,000 per year) were awarded; health care benefits also available. *Faculty research:* Protein structure, nucleic acid, enzymes, proteolysis, HIV. *Unit head:* Dr. Dennis Winge, Director, 801-581-5207, Fax: 801-585-2465. *Application contact:* Barb Saffel, Administrative Program Coordinator, 801-581-5207, E-mail: bsaffel@genetics.utah.edu.

University of Utah, School of Medicine and Graduate School, Graduate Programs in Medicine, Department of Biochemistry, Salt Lake City, UT 84112-1107. Offers MS, PhD. Terminal master's awarded for partial completion of doctoral program. *Degree requirements:* For master's, thesis; for doctorate, thesis/dissertation. *Entrance requirements:* For doctorate, GRE Subject Test, minimum GPA of 3.0. Additional exam requirements/recommendations for international students: Required—TOEFL. Electronic applications accepted. *Expenses:* Tuition, area resident: Part-time $179.19 per credit hour. Tuition, state resident: full-time $4384. Tuition, nonresident: full-time $16,684; part-time $630.67 per credit hour. Required fees: $350 per semester. Tuition and fees vary according to course load, degree level and program. *Faculty research:* Protein structure and function, nucleic acid structure and function, nucleic acid enzymology, RNA modification, protein turnover.

University of Vermont, College of Medicine and Graduate College, Graduate Programs in Medicine, Department of Biochemistry, Burlington, VT 05405. Offers MS, PhD, MD/MS, MD/PhD. *Students:* 15 (8 women), 4 international. 38 applicants, 16% accepted, 1 enrolled. In 2010, 1 master's awarded. *Degree requirements:* For master's, thesis; for doctorate, thesis/dissertation. *Entrance requirements:* For master's and doctorate, GRE General Test. Additional exam requirements/recommendations for international students: Required—TOEFL (minimum score

Biochemistry

University of Vermont (continued)
550 paper-based; 213 computer-based; 80 iBT). *Application deadline:* For fall admission, 3/1 priority date for domestic students, 3/1 for international students. Applications are processed on a rolling basis. Application fee: $40. Electronic applications accepted. *Expenses:* Tuition, state resident: part-time $537 per credit hour. Tuition, nonresident: part-time $1355 per credit hour. *Financial support:* Fellowships, research assistantships, teaching assistantships, analytical assistantships available. Financial award application deadline: 3/1. *Faculty research:* Endocrinology, protein chemistry, cell-surface signaling. *Unit head:* Dr. Paula Tracy, Interim Chairperson, 802-656-2220. *Application contact:* Dr. Christopher Francklyn, Coordinator, 802-656-2220.

University of Victoria, Faculty of Graduate Studies, Faculty of Science, Department of Biochemistry and Microbiology, Victoria, BC V8W 2Y2, Canada. Offers biochemistry (M Sc, PhD); microbiology (M Sc, PhD). *Degree requirements:* For master's, thesis, seminar; for doctorate, thesis/dissertation, seminar, candidacy exam. *Entrance requirements:* For master's, GRE General Test, minimum B+ average; for doctorate, GRE General Test, minimum B+ average, M Sc. Additional exam requirements/recommendations for international students: Required—TOEFL (minimum score 600 paper-based; 250 computer-based). Electronic applications accepted. *Faculty research:* Molecular pathogenesis, prokaryotic, eukaryotic, macromolecular interactions, microbial surfaces, virology, molecular genetics.

University of Virginia, School of Medicine, Department of Biochemistry and Molecular Genetics, Charlottesville, VA 22903. Offers biochemistry (PhD); MD/PhD. *Faculty:* 26 full-time (5 women), 1 (woman) part-time/adjunct. *Students:* 36 full-time (15 women); includes 1 Black or African American, non-Hispanic/Latino, 11 international. Average age 27. In 2010, 7 doctorates awarded. *Degree requirements:* For doctorate, thesis/dissertation, written research proposal and defense. *Entrance requirements:* For doctorate, GRE General Test, 3 letters of recommendation. Additional exam requirements/recommendations for international students: Recommended—TOEFL (minimum score 630 paper-based; 250 computer-based; 90 iBT). Application fee: $60. Electronic applications accepted. *Financial support:* Fellowships, health care benefits and tuition waivers (full) available. Financial award applicants required to submit FAFSA. *Unit head:* Joyce L. Hamlin, Chair, 434-924-1940, Fax: 434-924-5069. *Application contact:* Associate Dean for Graduate Programs and Research.

University of Washington, Graduate School, School of Medicine, Graduate Programs in Medicine, Department of Biochemistry, Seattle, WA 98195. Offers PhD. *Degree requirements:* For doctorate, thesis/dissertation. *Entrance requirements:* For doctorate, GRE General Test, GRE Subject Test (biology, chemistry, biochemistry, or cell and molecular biology), minimum GPA of 3.0. Additional exam requirements/recommendations for international students: Required—TOEFL. Electronic applications accepted. *Faculty research:* Blood coagulation, structure and function of enzymes, fertilization events, interaction of plants with bacteria, protein structure.

University of Waterloo, Graduate Studies, Faculty of Science, Guelph-Waterloo Centre for Graduate Work in Chemistry and Biochemistry, Waterloo, ON N2L 3G1, Canada. Offers M Sc, PhD. M Sc, PhD offered jointly with University of Guelph. Part-time programs available. *Degree requirements:* For master's and doctorate, project or thesis. *Entrance requirements:* For master's, GRE, honors degree, minimum B average; for doctorate, GRE, master's degree, minimum B average. Additional exam requirements/recommendations for international students: Required—TOEFL, TWE. Electronic applications accepted. *Faculty research:* Polymer, physical, inorganic, organic, and theoretical chemistry.

The University of Western Ontario, Faculty of Graduate Studies, Biosciences Division, Department of Biochemistry, London, ON N6A 5B8, Canada. Offers M Sc, PhD. *Degree requirements:* For master's, thesis; for doctorate, thesis/dissertation. *Entrance requirements:* For master's, minimum B+ average in last 2 years of undergraduate study; for doctorate, M Sc or an external scholarship winner.

University of West Florida, College of Arts and Sciences: Sciences, School of Allied Health and Life Sciences, Department of Biology, Pensacola, FL 32514-5750. Offers biological chemistry (MS); biology (MS); biology education (MST); biotechnology (MS); coastal zone studies (MS); environmental biology (MS). *Faculty:* 10 full-time (2 women). *Students:* 6 full-time (4 women), 32 part-time (18 women); includes 1 Black or African American, non-Hispanic/Latino; 1 Asian, non-Hispanic/Latino; 1 Hispanic/Latino, 1 international. Average age 28. 17 applicants, 53% accepted, 7 enrolled. In 2010, 3 master's awarded. *Degree requirements:* For master's, thesis. *Entrance requirements:* For master's, GRE General Test. Additional exam requirements/recommendations for international students: Required—TOEFL (minimum score 550 paper-based; 213 computer-based). *Application deadline:* For fall admission, 6/1 for domestic students, 5/15 for international students; for spring admission, 10/1 for domestic and international students. Applications are processed on a rolling basis. Application fee: $30. *Expenses:* Tuition, state resident: full-time $4982; part-time $208 per credit hour. Tuition, nonresident: full-time $20,059; part-time $836 per credit hour. Required fees: $1365; $57 per credit hour. *Financial support:* In 2010–11, 20 fellowships with partial tuition reimbursements (averaging $523 per year), 18 research assistantships with partial tuition reimbursements (averaging $5,700 per year), 12 teaching assistantships with partial tuition reimbursements (averaging $8,042 per year) were awarded; unspecified assistantships also available. Financial award application deadline: 4/15; financial award applicants required to submit FAFSA. *Unit head:* Dr. George L. Stewart, Chairperson, 850-474-2748. *Application contact:* Terry McCray, Assistant Director of Graduate Admissions, 850-473-7718, Fax: 850-473-7714, E-mail: gradadmissions@uwf.edu.

University of Windsor, Faculty of Graduate Studies, Faculty of Science, Department of Chemistry and Biochemistry, Windsor, ON N9B 3P4, Canada. Offers M Sc, PhD. Part-time programs available. *Degree requirements:* For master's, thesis; for doctorate, comprehensive exam, thesis/dissertation. *Entrance requirements:* For master's and doctorate, minimum B average. Additional exam requirements/recommendations for international students: Required—TOEFL (minimum score 560 paper-based; 220 computer-based), GRE. Electronic applications accepted. *Faculty research:* Molecular biology/recombinant DNA techniques (PCR, cloning mutagenesis), No/02 detectors, western immunoblotting and detection, CD/NMR protein/peptide structure determination, confocal/electron microscopes.

University of Wisconsin–Madison, Graduate School, College of Agricultural and Life Sciences, Department of Biochemistry, Madison, WI 53706. Offers PhD. *Faculty:* 49 full-time (11 women). *Students:* 104 full-time (51 women), 17 international. 306 applicants, 9% accepted, 28 enrolled. In 2010, 6 doctorates awarded. Terminal master's awarded for partial completion of doctoral program. *Degree requirements:* For doctorate, thesis/dissertation. *Entrance requirements:* For doctorate, GRE General Test, GRE Subject Test (recommended). Additional exam requirements/recommendations for international students: Required—TOEFL. *Application deadline:* For fall admission, 12/15 priority date for domestic and international students. Applications are processed on a rolling basis. Application fee: $56. Electronic applications accepted. *Expenses:* Tuition, state resident: full-time $9887; part-time $617.96 per credit. Tuition, nonresident: full-time $24,054; part-time $1503.40 per credit. Required fees: $67.63 per credit. Tuition and fees vary according to reciprocity agreements. *Financial support:* In 2010–11, fellowships with full tuition reimbursements (averaging $24,000 per year), research assistantships with full tuition reimbursements (averaging $24,000 per year) were awarded; traineeships, health care benefits, and tuition waivers (full) also available. Financial award application deadline: 12/15. *Faculty research:* Molecular structure of vitamins and hormones, enzymology, NMR spectroscopy, protein structure, molecular genetics. Total annual research expenditures: $18 million. *Unit head:* Dr. Elizabeth A. Craig, Chair, 608-262-3040, Fax: 608-262-3453, E-mail: chair@biochem.wisc.edu. *Application contact:* Brad A. Clark, Graduate Program Coordinator, 608-265-2281, Fax: 608-262-3453, E-mail: bradclark@wisc.edu.

University of Wisconsin–Madison, School of Medicine and Public Health and Graduate School, Graduate Programs in Medicine, Department of Biomolecular Chemistry, Madison, WI 53706-1380. Offers MS, PhD. *Faculty:* 13 full-time (3 women). *Students:* 36 full-time (16 women), 5 international. Average age 25. 280 applicants, 16% accepted, 22 enrolled. In 2010, 10 doctorates awarded. Terminal master's awarded for partial completion of doctoral program. *Degree requirements:* For master's, thesis; for doctorate, thesis/dissertation. *Entrance requirements:* For doctorate, GRE. *Application deadline:* For fall admission, 12/1 priority date for domestic students. Application fee: $56. Electronic applications accepted. *Expenses:* Tuition, state resident: full-time $9887; part-time $617.96 per credit. Tuition, nonresident: full-time $24,054; part-time $1503.40 per credit. Required fees: $67.63 per credit. Tuition and fees vary according to reciprocity agreements. *Financial support:* In 2010–11, fellowships with full tuition reimbursements (averaging $20,000 per year), research assistantships with full tuition reimbursements (averaging $24,000 per year), teaching assistantships with full tuition reimbursements (averaging $27,640 per year) were awarded; traineeships, health care benefits, and tuition waivers (full) also available. *Faculty research:* Membrane biochemistry, protein folding and translocation, gene expression, signal transduction, cell growth and differentiation. Total annual research expenditures: $3.4 million. *Unit head:* Dr. Robert H. Fillingame, Chair, 608-262-1347, Fax: 608-262-5253, E-mail: rhfillin@wisc.edu. *Application contact:* Elyse Meuer, Student Services Coordinator, 608-262-1347, Fax: 608-262-5253, E-mail: eemeuer@wisc.edu.

University of Wisconsin–Milwaukee, Graduate School, College of Letters and Sciences, Department of Chemistry, Milwaukee, WI 53201-0413. Offers biogeochemistry (PhD); chemistry (MS, PhD). *Faculty:* 22 full-time (4 women). *Students:* 58 full-time (20 women), 16 part-time (10 women); includes 3 Black or African American, non-Hispanic/Latino; 3 Asian, non-Hispanic/Latino, 27 international. Average age 30. 52 applicants, 33% accepted, 5 enrolled. In 2010, 5 master's, 10 doctorates awarded. *Degree requirements:* For master's, thesis or alternative; for doctorate, thesis/dissertation. *Entrance requirements:* For doctorate, GRE General Test. Additional exam requirements/recommendations for international students: Required—TOEFL (minimum score 600 paper-based; 79 iBT), IELTS (minimum score 6.5). *Application deadline:* For fall admission, 1/1 priority date for domestic students; for spring admission, 9/1 for domestic students. Applications are processed on a rolling basis. Application fee: $56 ($96 for international students). *Financial support:* In 2010–11, 3 fellowships, 30 research assistantships, 46 teaching assistantships were awarded; career-related internships or fieldwork, unspecified assistantships, and project assistantships also available. Support available to part-time students. Financial award application deadline: 4/15; financial award applicants required to submit FAFSA. *Faculty research:* Analytical chemistry, biochemistry, inorganic chemistry, organic chemistry, physical chemistry. Total annual research expenditures: $3 million. *Unit head:* Peter Geissinger, Representative, 414-229-5230, Fax: 414-229-5530, E-mail: geissing@uwm.edu. *Application contact:* General Information Contact, 414-229-4982, Fax: 414-229-6967, E-mail: gradschool@uwm.edu.

Utah State University, School of Graduate Studies, College of Science, Department of Chemistry and Biochemistry, Logan, UT 84322. Offers biochemistry (MS, PhD); chemistry (MS, PhD). Part-time programs available. Terminal master's awarded for partial completion of doctoral program. *Degree requirements:* For master's, thesis, oral and written exams; for doctorate, thesis/dissertation, oral and written exams. *Entrance requirements:* For master's and doctorate, GRE General Test, minimum GPA of 3.0. Additional exam requirements/recommendations for international students: Required—TOEFL. *Faculty research:* Analytical, inorganic, organic, and physical chemistry; iron in asbestos chemistry and carcinogenicity; dicopper complexes; photothermal spectrometry; metal molecule clusters.

Vanderbilt University, Graduate School and School of Medicine, Department of Biochemistry, Nashville, TN 37240-1001. Offers MS, PhD, MD/PhD. *Faculty:* 22 full-time (2 women). *Students:* 38 full-time (21 women), 1 part-time (0 women); includes 3 minority (1 Black or African American, non-Hispanic/Latino; 1 Asian, non-Hispanic/Latino; 1 Hispanic/Latino). Average age 27. In 2010, 2 master's, 7 doctorates awarded. Terminal master's awarded for partial completion of doctoral program. *Degree requirements:* For master's, thesis; for doctorate, thesis/dissertation, preliminary, qualifying, and final exams. *Entrance requirements:* For master's, GRE General Test; for doctorate, GRE General Test, GRE Subject Test (recommended). Additional exam requirements/recommendations for international students: Required—TOEFL (minimum score 570 paper-based; 230 computer-based; 88 iBT). *Application deadline:* For fall admission, 1/15 for domestic and international students. Application fee: $0. Electronic applications accepted. *Financial support:* Fellowships with full tuition reimbursements, research assistantships with full tuition reimbursements, Federal Work-Study, institutionally sponsored loans, scholarships/grants, traineeships, and tuition waivers (partial) available. Financial award application deadline: 1/15; financial award applicants required to submit CSS PROFILE or FAFSA. *Faculty research:* Protein chemistry, carcinogenesis, metabolism, toxicology, receptors and signaling, DNA recognition and transcription. *Unit head:* Dr. Peter F. Guengerich, Interim Chair, 615-322-2261, E-mail: f.guengerich@vanderbilt.edu. *Application contact:* Dr. Marlene Jayne, Administrator, 615-322-3318, E-mail: marlene.jayne@vanderbilt.edu.

Vanderbilt University, School of Medicine, Program in Chemical and Physical Biology, Nashville, TN 37240-1001. Offers PhD. *Degree requirements:* For doctorate, comprehensive exam, thesis/dissertation, dissertation defense. *Entrance requirements:* For doctorate, GRE, 3 letters of recommendation, official transcripts. Additional exam requirements/recommendations for international students: Required—TOEFL. *Application deadline:* For fall admission, 1/15 priority date for domestic students, 1/15 for international students. Applications are processed on a rolling basis. Application fee: $0. Electronic applications accepted. *Financial support:* Fellowships with full tuition reimbursements, traineeships, health care benefits, and tuition waivers (full) available. *Faculty research:* Mathematical modeling, enzyme kinetics, structural biology, genomics, proteomics and mass spectrometry. *Unit head:* Dave Piston, Chair, 615-322-7030, Fax: 615-343-0490, E-mail: dave.piston@vanderbilt.edu. *Application contact:* Lindsay Meyers, Education Manager, 615-322-3770, E-mail: lindsay.meyers@vanderbilt.edu.

Virginia Commonwealth University, Medical College of Virginia-Professional Programs, School of Medicine, School of Medicine Graduate Programs, Department of Biochemistry, Richmond, VA 23284-9005. Offers biochemistry (MS, PhD); molecular biology (MS, PhD); MD/PhD. *Faculty:* 28 full-time (3 women). *Students:* 42 full-time (21 women), 5 part-time (3 women); includes 13 minority (4 Black or African American, non-Hispanic/Latino; 7 Asian, non-Hispanic/Latino; 1 Hispanic/Latino; 1 Two or more races, non-Hispanic/Latino), 8 international. 34 applicants, 41% accepted, 7 enrolled. In 2010, 11 master's, 7 doctorates awarded. *Degree requirements:* For master's, thesis; for doctorate, thesis/dissertation, comprehensive oral and written exams. *Entrance requirements:* For master's and doctorate, GRE, MCAT or DAT. *Application deadline:* For fall admission, 2/15 priority date for domestic students. Application fee: $50. Electronic applications accepted. *Expenses:* Tuition, state resident: full-time $4308; part-time $479 per credit hour. Tuition, nonresident: full-time $8942; part-time $994 per credit hour. Required fees: $2000; $85 per credit hour. Tuition and fees vary according to course level, course load, degree level, campus/location and program. *Financial support:* Fellowships, research assistantships available. *Faculty research:* Molecular biology, peptide/protein chemistry, neurochemistry, enzyme mechanisms, macromolecular structure determination. Total annual research expenditures: $3.5 million. *Unit head:* Dr. Sarah Spiegel, Chair, 804-828-6971, Fax: 804-828-1473, E-mail: sspiegel@vcu.edu. *Application contact:* Dr. Tomasz Kordula, Graduate Program Director, 804-828-0771, Fax: 804-828-1473, E-mail: tkordula@vcu.edu.

Virginia Commonwealth University, Program in Pre-Medical Basic Health Sciences, Richmond, VA 23284-9005. Offers anatomy (CBHS); biochemistry (CBHS); human genetics (CBHS); microbiology (CBHS); pharmacology (CBHS); physiology (CBHS). *Students:* 86 full-time (43 women), 2 part-time (1 woman); includes 42 minority (5 Black or African American, non-Hispanic/Latino; 29 Asian, non-Hispanic/Latino; 5 Hispanic/Latino; 3 Two or more races, non-Hispanic/Latino). 314 applicants, 64% accepted. In 2010, 70 CBHSs awarded. *Entrance requirements:* For degree, GRE, MCAT or DAT, course work in organic chemistry, minimum undergraduate GPA of 2.8. Additional exam requirements/recommendations for international students: Required—TOEFL (minimum score 600 paper-based). *Application deadline:* For fall admission, 6/1 for domestic students. Application fee: $50. Electronic applications accepted. *Expenses:* Tuition, state resident: full-time $4308; part-time $479 per credit hour. Tuition, nonresident: full-time $8942; part-time $994 per credit hour. Required fees: $2000; $85 per credit hour. Tuition and fees vary according to course level, course load, degree level, campus/location and program. *Unit head:* Dr. Louis J. De Felice, Director, 804-828-9501, E-mail: premedcert@vcu.edu. *Application contact:* Zack McDowell, Administrator, 804-828-9501, E-mail: premedcert@vcu.edu.

Virginia Polytechnic Institute and State University, Graduate School, College of Agriculture and Life Sciences, Department of Biochemistry, Blacksburg, VA 24061. Offers MSLFS, PhD. *Faculty:* 14 full-time (3 women). *Students:* 25 full-time (12 women), 1 part-time (0 women); includes 1 Black or African American, non-Hispanic/Latino; 1 Asian, non-Hispanic/Latino; 3 Hispanic/Latino, 10 international. Average age 27. 51 applicants, 10% accepted, 5 enrolled. In 2010, 3 master's, 6 doctorates awarded. *Degree requirements:* For master's, comprehensive exam (for some programs), thesis (for some programs); for doctorate, comprehensive exam (for some programs), thesis/dissertation (for some programs). *Entrance requirements:* For master's and doctorate, GRE. Additional exam requirements/recommendations for international students: Required—TOEFL (minimum score 550 paper-based; 213 computer-based). *Application deadline:* For fall admission, 7/1 for domestic and international students; for spring admission, 12/1 for domestic and international students. Applications are processed on a rolling basis. Application fee: $65. Electronic applications accepted. *Expenses:* Contact institution. *Financial support:* In 2010–11, 4 research assistantships with full tuition reimbursements (averaging $20,741 per year), 13 teaching assistantships with full tuition reimbursements (averaging $18,237 per year) were awarded; career-related internships or fieldwork, Federal Work-Study, scholarships/grants, health care benefits, and unspecified assistantships also available. Financial award application deadline: 1/15. *Faculty research:* Molecular biology, molecular entomology, enzymology, signal transduction, protein structure-function. Total annual research expenditures: $4.3 million. *Unit head:* Dr. Peter J. Kennelly, UNIT HEAD, 540-231-6315, Fax: 540-231-6315, E-mail: dgerrard@vt.edu. *Application contact:* Tim Larson, Contact, 540-231-7060, Fax: 540-231-6315, E-mail: tilarson@vt.edu.

Wake Forest University, School of Medicine and Graduate School of Arts and Sciences, Graduate Programs in Medicine, Department of Biochemistry, Winston-Salem, NC 27109. Offers PhD, MD/PhD. *Degree requirements:* For doctorate, thesis/dissertation. *Entrance requirements:* For doctorate, GRE General Test. Additional exam requirements/recommendations for international students: Required—TOEFL. Electronic applications accepted. *Faculty research:* Biomembranes, cancer, biophysics.

Washington State University, Graduate School, College of Sciences, School of Molecular Biosciences, Program of Biochemistry and Biophysics, Pullman, WA 99164. Offers MS, PhD. *Faculty:* 23 full-time (5 women), 21 part-time/adjunct (4 women). *Students:* 26 full-time (9 women), 1 (woman) part-time; includes 1 Hispanic/Latino, 12 international. Average age 27. 231 applicants, 18% accepted, 13 enrolled. In 2010, 1 master's, 2 doctorates awarded. Terminal master's awarded for partial completion of doctoral program. *Degree requirements:* For master's, thesis or alternative, oral exam; for doctorate, comprehensive exam, thesis/dissertation, oral exam, written exam. *Entrance requirements:* For master's and doctorate, GRE General Test, minimum GPA of 3.0. Additional exam requirements/recommendations for international students: Required—TOEFL (minimum score 550 paper-based; 213 computer-based). *Application deadline:* For fall admission, 12/15 for domestic and international students. Application fee: $50. Electronic applications accepted. *Expenses:* Tuition, state resident: full-time $8552; part-time $443 per credit. Tuition, nonresident: full-time $21,650; part-time $1083 per credit. Required fees: $846. *Financial support:* In 2010–11, 5 fellowships with full tuition reimbursements (averaging $18,384 per year), 11 research assistantships with full tuition reimbursements (averaging $18,384 per year), 10 teaching assistantships with full tuition reimbursements (averaging $18,384 per year) were awarded; career-related internships or fieldwork, Federal Work-Study, institutionally sponsored loans, traineeships, and health care benefits also available. Financial award application deadline: 4/1; financial award applicants required to submit FAFSA. *Faculty research:* Gene regulation, signal transduction, protein export, reproductive biology, DNA repair. Total annual research expenditures: $5.8 million. *Unit head:* Dr. John H. Nilson, Director, 509-335-8724, Fax: 509-335-9688, E-mail: jhn@wsu.edu. *Application contact:* Kelly G. McGovern, 509-335-6424, E-mail: mcgnerk@wsu.edu.

Washington University in St. Louis, Graduate School of Arts and Sciences, Division of Biology and Biomedical Sciences, Program in Biochemistry, St. Louis, MO 63130-4899. Offers PhD. *Degree requirements:* For doctorate, thesis/dissertation. *Entrance requirements:* For doctorate, GRE General Test, GRE Subject Test. Electronic applications accepted.

Washington University in St. Louis, Graduate School of Arts and Sciences, Division of Biology and Biomedical Sciences, Program in Chemical Biology, St. Louis, MO 63130-4899. Offers PhD. *Degree requirements:* For doctorate, thesis/dissertation. *Entrance requirements:* For doctorate, GRE General Test, GRE Subject Test. Electronic applications accepted.

Wayne State University, School of Medicine, Department of Biochemistry and Molecular Biology, Detroit, MI 48202. Offers MS, PhD. *Faculty:* 3 full-time (1 woman). *Students:* 30 full-time (17 women), 2 part-time (0 women); includes 1 Black or African American, non-Hispanic/Latino; 2 Asian, non-Hispanic/Latino, 16 international. Average age 26. 52 applicants, 35% accepted, 14 enrolled. In 2010, 6 doctorates awarded. Terminal master's awarded for partial completion of doctoral program. *Degree requirements:* For master's, thesis; for doctorate, one foreign language, thesis/dissertation. *Entrance requirements:* For master's and doctorate, GRE General Test, GRE Subject Test. Additional exam requirements/recommendations for international students: Required—TOEFL (minimum score 550 paper-based; 213 computer-based); Recommended—TWE (minimum score 6). *Application deadline:* For fall admission, 6/1 for international students; for winter admission, 10/1 for international students; for spring admission, 2/1 for international students. Applications are processed on a rolling basis. Application fee: $30 ($50 for international students). Electronic applications accepted. *Expenses:* Tuition, state resident: full-time $7662; part-time $478.85 per credit hour. Tuition, nonresident: full-time $16,920; part-time $1057.55 per credit hour. Required fees: $571; $35.70 per credit hour. $188.05 per semester. Tuition and fees vary according to course load and program. *Financial support:* In 2010–11, 18 research assistantships (averaging $21,580 per year) were awarded; fellowships, teaching assistantships also available. *Faculty research:* Protein structure, molecular biology, molecular genetics, enzymology, x-ray crystallography. *Unit head:* Dr. Barry P. Rosen, Chair, 313-577-1512, Fax: 313-577-2765, E-mail: aa1133@wayne.edu. *Application contact:* Marilyn Doscher, Graduate Director, 313-577-1295, E-mail: mdoscher@med.wayne.edu.

Wesleyan University, Graduate Programs, Department of Chemistry, Middletown, CT 06459. Offers biochemistry (MA, PhD); chemical physics (MA, PhD); inorganic chemistry (MA, PhD); organic chemistry (MA, PhD); physical chemistry (MA, PhD); theoretical chemistry (MA, PhD). *Faculty:* 12 full-time (2 women). *Students:* 29 full-time (9 women); includes 3 Black or African American, non-Hispanic/Latino; 7 Asian, non-Hispanic/Latino; 2 Hispanic/Latino. Average age 26. 48 applicants, 23% accepted, 5 enrolled. In 2010, 6 master's, 6 doctorates awarded. Terminal master's awarded for partial completion of doctoral program. *Degree requirements:* For master's, thesis, proposal; for doctorate, thesis/dissertation, proposal. *Entrance requirements:* For doctorate, GRE General Test, 3 recommendations. Additional exam requirements/recommendations for international students: Required—TOEFL. *Application deadline:* Applications are processed on a rolling basis. Application fee: $0. Electronic applications accepted. *Expenses:* Tuition: Full-time $43,404. Required fees: $830. *Financial support:* In 2010–11, 9 research assistantships with full tuition reimbursements, 18 teaching assistantships with full tuition reimbursements were awarded; institutionally sponsored loans also available. Financial award application deadline: 4/15; financial award applicants required to submit FAFSA. *Unit head:* Dr. Joseph Knee, Chair, 860-685-2210. *Application contact:* Cait Zinser, Information Contact, 860-685-2573, Fax: 860-685-2211, E-mail: czinser@wesleyan.edu.

Wesleyan University, Graduate Programs, Department of Molecular Biology and Biochemistry, Middletown, CT 06459. Offers biochemistry (PhD); molecular biology (PhD). *Faculty:* 8 full-time (3 women). *Students:* 19 full-time (13 women); includes 9 Asian, non-Hispanic/Latino; 1 Hispanic/Latino. Average age 28. 37 applicants, 22% accepted, 3 enrolled. In 2010, 3 doctorates awarded. *Degree requirements:* For doctorate, comprehensive exam, thesis/dissertation. *Entrance requirements:* For doctorate, GRE General Test, GRE Subject Test. Additional exam requirements/recommendations for international students: Required—TOEFL. *Application deadline:* For fall admission, 2/15 for domestic and international students. Applications are processed on a rolling basis. Application fee: $0. Electronic applications accepted. *Expenses:* Tuition: Full-time $43,404. Required fees: $830. *Financial support:* In 2010–11, 13 research assistantships with full tuition reimbursements, 9 teaching assistantships with full tuition reimbursements were awarded; institutionally sponsored loans also available. Financial award application deadline: 4/15; financial award applicants required to submit FAFSA. *Faculty research:* Genome organization, regulation of gene expression, molecular biology of development, physical biochemistry. *Unit head:* Dr. Michael McAlear, Chair, 860-685-2443, E-mail: mmcalear@wesleyan.edu. *Application contact:* Information Contact, 860-685-2640, E-mail: mbbgrad@wesleyan.edu.

West Virginia University, School of Medicine, Graduate Programs at the Health Sciences Center, Interdisciplinary Graduate Programs in Biomedical Sciences, Program in Biochemistry and Molecular Biology, Morgantown, WV 26506. Offers MS, PhD, MD/PhD. *Degree requirements:* For doctorate, comprehensive exam, thesis/dissertation. *Entrance requirements:* For doctorate, GRE General Test, minimum GPA of 3.0. Additional exam requirements/recommendations for international students: Required—TOEFL. Electronic applications accepted. *Faculty research:* Regulation of gene expression, cell survival mechanisms, signal transduction, regulation of metabolism, sensory neuroscience.

Worcester Polytechnic Institute, Graduate Studies, Department of Chemistry and Biochemistry, Worcester, MA 01609-2280. Offers biochemistry (MS, PhD); chemistry (MS, PhD). Evening/weekend programs available. *Faculty:* 6 full-time (0 women). *Students:* 15 full-time (8 women); includes 1 Native Hawaiian or other Pacific Islander, non-Hispanic/Latino, 7 international. 80 applicants, 6% accepted, 4 enrolled. In 2010, 1 master's, 2 doctorates awarded. *Degree requirements:* For master's, thesis; for doctorate, comprehensive exam, thesis/dissertation. *Entrance requirements:* For master's, GRE General Test, 3 letters of recommendation; for doctorate, GRE General Test, 3 letters of recommendation, statement of purpose. Additional exam requirements/recommendations for international students: Required—TOEFL (minimum score 550 paper-based; 213 computer-based; 79 iBT), IELTS (minimum score 6.5). *Application deadline:* For fall admission, 1/1 priority date for domestic and international students; for spring admission, 10/1 priority date for domestic and international students. Applications are processed on a rolling basis. Application fee: $70. Electronic applications accepted. *Expenses:* Tuition: Full-time $20,862; part-time $1159 per term. One-time fee: $15. *Financial support:* Career-related internships or fieldwork, institutionally sponsored loans, scholarships/grants, and unspecified assistantships available. Financial award application deadline: 1/1; financial award applicants required to submit FAFSA. *Faculty research:* Catalysis experimental and computational protein biophysics, biological metals, synthetic methods, surface chemistry, computational chemistry. *Unit head:* Dr. Kristin K. Wobbe, Interim Head, 508-831-5371, Fax: 508-831-5933, E-mail: kwobbe@wpi.edu. *Application contact:* Dr. James Dittami, Graduate Coordinator, 508-831-5371, Fax: 508-831-5933, E-mail: jdittami@wpi.edu.

Wright State University, School of Graduate Studies, College of Science and Mathematics, Department of Biochemistry and Molecular Biology, Dayton, OH 45435. Offers MS. *Degree requirements:* For master's, thesis. *Entrance requirements:* Additional exam requirements/recommendations for international students: Required—TOEFL. *Faculty research:* Regulation of gene expression, macromolecular structural function, NMR imaging, visual biochemistry.

Yale University, Graduate School of Arts and Sciences, Department of Geology and Geophysics, New Haven, CT 06520. Offers biogeochemistry (PhD); climate dynamics (PhD); geochemistry (PhD); geophysics (PhD); meteorology (PhD); oceanography (PhD); paleontology (PhD); paleooceanography (PhD); petrology (PhD); tectonics (PhD). *Degree requirements:* For doctorate, thesis/dissertation. *Entrance requirements:* For doctorate, GRE General Test. Additional exam requirements/recommendations for international students: Required—TOEFL.

Yale University, Graduate School of Arts and Sciences, Department of Molecular Biophysics and Biochemistry, New Haven, CT 06520. Offers PhD. *Degree requirements:* For doctorate, thesis/dissertation. *Entrance requirements:* For doctorate, GRE General Test, GRE Subject Test.

Yale University, Graduate School of Arts and Sciences, Department of Molecular, Cellular, and Developmental Biology, Program in Biochemistry, Molecular Biology and Chemical Biology, New Haven, CT 06520. Offers PhD. *Degree requirements:* For doctorate, thesis/dissertation. *Entrance requirements:* For doctorate, GRE General Test, GRE Subject Test.

Yale University, School of Medicine and Graduate School of Arts and Sciences, Combined Program in Biological and Biomedical Sciences (BBS), Molecular Biophysics and Biochemistry Track, New Haven, CT 06520. Offers PhD, MD/PhD. *Degree requirements:* For doctorate, thesis/dissertation. *Entrance requirements:* For doctorate, GRE General Test. Additional exam requirements/recommendations for international students: Required—TOEFL. Electronic applications accepted.

Youngstown State University, Graduate School, College of Science, Technology, Engineering and Mathematics, Department of Chemistry, Youngstown, OH 44555-0001. Offers analytical chemistry (MS); biochemistry (MS); chemistry education (MS); inorganic chemistry (MS); organic chemistry (MS); physical chemistry (MS). Part-time programs available. *Degree requirements:* For master's, thesis. *Entrance requirements:* For master's, bachelor's degree in chemistry, minimum GPA of 2.7. Additional exam requirements/recommendations for international students: Required—TOEFL. *Faculty research:* Analysis of antioxidants, chromatography, defects and disorder in crystalline oxides, hydrogen bonding, novel organic and organometallic materials.

IOWA STATE UNIVERSITY
OF SCIENCE AND TECHNOLOGY
Department of Biochemistry, Biophysics, and Molecular Biology

Programs of Study

The Department of Biochemistry, Biophysics, and Molecular Biology (BBMB) offers programs leading to M.S. and Ph.D. degrees with majors in the fields of biochemistry; bioinformatics and computational biology; biophysics; genetics; immunobiology; molecular, cellular, and developmental biology; plant physiology; and toxicology. Students enter a rotation program that lasts through the end of the first semester. By the second semester, students have identified their area of research and begun work on their research project with their chosen mentor. A minimum of 30 credits is required for the M.S. degree. For the Ph.D. degree, a minimum of three years of full-time study, at least half of which must be spent in residence, is required. Preliminary examinations in the field of specialization are required for admission to candidacy for the Ph.D. degree. The final examination for M.S. and Ph.D. candidates is an oral defense of the thesis. At some time during graduate work, each student is expected to serve as a teaching assistant. More information about individual faculty members' research activities is available on request or from the Departmental Web site (http://www.bbmb.iastate.edu).

Research Facilities

The Department is housed in the Molecular Biology Building, a unique structure that integrates 204,000 square feet of research laboratories and classrooms with artwork inspired by genetic engineering and crafted by award-winning national artists. The modular design of the laboratories allows scientists to quickly reconfigure their space as research needs change. State-of-the-art instrumentation facilities for protein chemistry, nucleic acids, flow cytometry, antibody and hybridoma production, and macromolecular structure determination (X ray and NMR) support life sciences research on campus and throughout the state. The W. M. Keck Metabolomics Research Facility is the most recent addition. Supporting instrument services, a fabrication shop, and chemical stores are conveniently located in a nearby building. Molecular Biology Building classrooms are fitted with the latest instructional technology equipment. Students are linked to the University's high-speed computing network through approximately thirty workstations strategically placed throughout the building. For students and faculty members who prefer it, wireless networking is available in all classrooms and other public areas.

Financial Aid

Financial aid is available to graduate students in the form of research assistantships, teaching assistantships, and fellowships. Most Ph.D. students are supported by research assistantships that currently provide $22,500 per year along with a 100 percent tuition credit. Students are eligible for additional fellowships on a competitive basis.

Cost of Study

In 2011–12, tuition for graduate students is $3738 per semester for fall and spring. Ph.D. students on assistantships receive a 100 percent tuition credit; M.S. students on assistantships receive up to a 50 percent tuition credit. Computer fees ($46 per semester), health center fees ($106 per semester), and activities and service fees ($317.80 per semester) are paid by the student. Health insurance for graduate students on assistantships is paid by the Graduate College.

Living and Housing Costs

University student apartments are available at rates of $505 for single occupancy to $612 per month for two-person occupancy. Rooms on the top two floors in an upperclass dorm are reserved for graduate students if there is a demand; rent is $5942 annually for a single suite. Please refer to the Department of Residence Web site for more information. Private, off-campus rooms and apartments are available in the vicinity of the campus.

Student Group

The current enrollment of the University is around 27,000 students, including about 4,700 graduate students. More than 3,000 of the graduate students come from all areas of the United States; the remainder are international students representing nearly 100 countries. There are approximately 90 graduate students enrolled in the Department; most are preparing for research careers in industry or academia.

Student Outcomes

Ph.D. graduates typically pursue careers in research as directors of academic, industry, or government laboratories. Ph.D. graduates normally go on to postdoctoral research appointments prior to seeking assistant professor/laboratory director positions. Other career courses include college/university teaching or research-related administration. M.S. graduates normally go on to Ph.D. programs or research associate positions in industry or academic laboratories.

Location

Ames is a city of about 50,000 residents, including the student body of Iowa State University. The city is located in a rural area 30 miles north of Des Moines, the capital of Iowa. An active cultural life is provided in Ames by local musical and theatrical groups and by the many internationally acclaimed artists who perform on campus. Athletic events at the University provide a year-round focus of interest. The University has a scenic golf course adjacent to the campus and offers facilities for numerous indoor and outdoor sports. The climate is typical of the Midwest: warm to hot in the summer, generally quite cold in the winter, and mild in spring and fall.

The University

Iowa State University of Science and Technology was founded in 1858 as Iowa State College, one of the first land-grant institutions in the nation. Besides the Graduate College, the University has seven undergraduate colleges—Agriculture, Business, Design, Engineering, Human Sciences, Liberal Arts and Sciences, and Veterinary Medicine. The scenic campus is a point of pride for students and faculty members and offers a fitting environment for the varied activities of those who work and study at the University.

Applying

Applicants must be graduates of an accredited institution and must normally rank in the upper half of his or her class. GRE General Test scores are required; the Subject Test in biochemistry, cell and molecular biology; chemistry; biology; or physics is recommended. Undergraduate preparation should include emphasis in chemistry, physics, mathematics, and biology. Visits to the Department are encouraged. Preapplications are required and can be requested by sending e-mail to biochem@iastate.edu.

Correspondence and Information

Department of Biochemistry, Biophysics, and Molecular Biology
1210 Molecular Biology Building
Iowa State University of Science and Technology
Ames, Iowa 50011
Phone: 515-294-3317
      800-433-3464 (toll-free from within the United States)
Fax: 515-294-0453
E-mail: biochem@iastate.edu
Web site: http://www.bbmb.iastate.edu/

Iowa State University of Science and Technology

THE FACULTY AND THEIR RESEARCH

Senior Staff of the Department

Gaya Amarasinghe, Associate Professor; Ph.D., Maryland, Baltimore County, 2001. Biophysical and biochemical studies of protein-RNA interactions.

Linda Ambrosio, Associate Professor; Ph.D., Princeton, 1985. Mechanisms of signal transduction; molecular and genetic characterization of *D-raf;* pattern formation and cellular differentiation in development.

Amy H. Andreotti, Professor of Biochemistry; Ph.D., Princeton, 1994. Nuclear magnetic resonance; macromolecular structure and recognition.

Donald C. Beitz, Distinguished Professor of Biochemistry and Animal Science; Ph.D., Michigan State, 1967. Lipid metabolism; cholesterol homeostasis in animals and humans; nutritional and genetic control of animal-derived food quality; etiology and prevention of fatty liver disease.

Thomas Bobik, Professor of Biochemistry; Ph.D., Illinois at Urbana-Champaign, 1990. Conversion of inactive cobalamins to coenzyme B12.

Alan DiSpirito, Professor; Ph.D., Ohio State, 1983. Bioenergetics of chemoautotrophic and methanotrophic bacteria.

Jack Girton, University Professor; Ph.D., Alberta, 1979. Chromatin structure and function; regulation of cell determination.

Mark S. Hargrove, Professor of Biochemistry and Biophysics; Ph.D., Rice, 1995. Heme protein structure and function; regulation of cell determination.

Richard B. Honzatko, Professor of Biochemistry and Biophysics; Ph.D., Harvard, 1982. X-ray crystallography of proteins; enzyme structure-function.

Ted W. Huiatt, Associate Professor of Biochemistry and Animal Science; Ph.D., Iowa State, 1979. Growth and determination of striated muscle during embryonic development.

Robert L. Jernigan, Professor of Biochemistry and Director, Laurence H. Baker Center for Bioinformatics and Biological Statistics; Ph.D., Stanford, 1968. Bioinformatics; genomics; computational biology; interfaces between structure, function, and sequence; motions of proteins and large assemblages; protein and drug design.

Jorgen Johansen, Professor; Ph.D., Copenhagen, 1984. Regulation of nuclear organization and function.

Kristen M. Johansen, Professor; Ph.D., Yale, 1989. Regulation of nuclear organization and function.

Gustavo MacIntosh, Assistant Professor; Ph.D., Buenos Aires, 1997. Gene expression and metabolic changes during plant defense responses to pests; functional genomics of plant nucleases.

Alan M. Myers, Professor of Biochemistry; Ph.D., Duke, 1983. Molecular mechanisms of starch assembly and disassembly.

Scott Nelson, Assistant Professor of Biochemistry; Ph.D., Iowa State, 2002. Molecular mechanisms of DNA replication and repair.

Basil J. Nikolau, Francis M. Craig Professor of Biochemistry; Director, Center for Metabolic Biology; Director, W. M. Keck Metabolomics Research Laboratory; and Deputy Director, Center for Biorenewable Chemicals; Ph.D., Massey (New Zealand), 1981. Biochemistry and functional genomics of plant metabolism.

Marit Nilsen-Hamilton, Professor of Biochemistry; Ph.D., Cornell, 1973. Nucleic acid, aptamer-based analytical technology; Growth factor function.

Reuben J. Peters, Professor; Ph.D., California, San Francisco, 1998. Enzymatic/metabolic engineering of terpenoid biosynthesis.

Guru Rao, Professor/Chair of Biochemistry; Ph.D., Mysore (India), 1980. Structure-function relationships of plant proteins; protein-protein interactions in plant signal transduction; protein engineering.

Richard M. Robson, Professor of Biochemistry, Molecular Biology, and Animal Science; Ph.D., Iowa State, 1969. Structure and function of muscle contractile and cytosketal proteins.

John F. Robyt, Professor of Biochemistry; Ph.D., Iowa State, 1962. Carbohydrate chemistry and enzymology.

Yeon-Kyun Shin, Professor of Biophysics; Ph.D., Cornell, 1990. SNARE complex assembly and mechanisms of membrane fusion; EPR methods.

Michael Shogren-Knaak, Associate Professor of Biochemistry; Ph.D., Stanford, 1994. Role and establishment of histone modifications; chromatin structure.

Robert Thornburg, Professor of Biochemistry; Ph.D., South Carolina, 1981. Eukaryotic gene regulations and expression; plant response to insect attack.

Olga Zabotina, Assistant Professor; Ph.D., Russian Academy of Sciences, 1987. Plant cell wall structure; polysaccharide biosynthesis, modification, and degredation; bioactive carbohydrates.

Affiliates and Collaborators Primarily Associated with This Department

Kanwarpal Dhugga, Collaborator Associate Professor; Ph.D., Research Fellow, DuPont Agricultural Biotechnology, Pioneer Hi-Bred International, Johnsont, Iowa. Plant cell-wall biochemistry.

Martha G. James, Adjunct Associate Professor of Biochemistry; Ph.D., Iowa State, 1989. Plant starch metabolism; functional interactions and genetic engineering.

Andrzej Kloczkowski, Collaborator Professor; Ph.D., Polish Academy of Sciences, 1980. Computational molecular biology; structural bioinformatics; prediction of protein structure, function, and dynamics; biomolecular simulations.

Terry Meyer, Collaborator, Senior Research Manager and Deputy for the AgBiotech Program Management Office, Pioneer Hi-Bred International, Johnston, Iowa.

Louisa B. Tabatabai, USDA-ARS Collaborator, Professor of Biochemistry, and Research Chemist, National Animal Disease Center; Ph.D., Iowa State, 1976. Protein chemistry and proteomics; vaccines and diagnostics for animal diseases.

Faculty with Joint ISU Appointments

Michael Cho, Associate Professor and Lloyd Chair in Biomedical Sciences, College of Veterinary Medicine, ISU; Ph.D., Utah. Development of vaccines against infectious diseases.

W. Allen Miller, Professor of Plant Pathology and Microbiology; Ph.D., Wisconsin–Madison, 1984. RNA virus replication and gene expression; translation mechanisms; barley yellow dwarf virus genomics.

Edward Yu, Associate Professor of Physics and Astronomy; Ph.D., Michigan, 1997. Structural and mechanistic aspects of membrane transport; X-ray crystallography of membrane proteins; biophysics.

The skylit atrium of the Molecular Biology Building provides natural light for its forty-eight research laboratories and eight instrumentation centers.

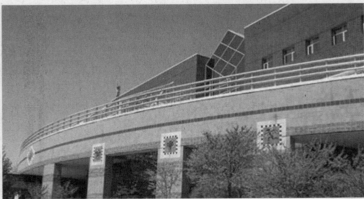

The 204,000-square-foot Molecular Biology Building is home to the Department of Biochemistry, Biophysics, and Molecular Biology.

UNIVERSITY OF NEVADA, RENO

Department of Biochemistry and Molecular Biology
Graduate Programs in Biochemistry

Programs of Study

The Department of Biochemistry and Molecular Biology at the University of Nevada, Reno (UNR), offers a challenging and broad-based graduate program of research and course studies leading to the M.S. or Ph.D. in biochemistry. The aim of the graduate program is to train scientists for critical analysis and solution of biochemical problems at the molecular level. The diverse research areas represented by the faculty have the common theme of understanding the structures and roles of macromolecules in complex biological systems. Students benefit from exposure to faculty members appointed in both the College of Agriculture, Biotechnology and Natural Resources (CABNR) and the School of Medicine. They have an opportunity for multidisciplinary interactions with graduate students and faculty members in related departments, including the Departments of Physiology and Anatomy, Microbiology and Immunology, Pharmacology and Cell Biology, Chemistry, Biology, and Animal Biotechnology. The academic environment is lively and highly interactive, as represented by a diverse, interdisciplinary seminar program sponsored in conjunction with other related departments. The program of study includes lecture courses, laboratory rotations, journal club presentations and discussion groups, a qualifying written and oral examination, dissertation research, and one or more semesters of teaching experience. First-year students take a core curriculum and gain research experience by rotating through student-selected research laboratories. Laboratory rotations facilitate the choice of a dissertation adviser. Doctoral and master's research projects are selected by the student in consultation with a major dissertation adviser and an advisory committee. The requirements for the Ph.D. can generally be completed in four or five years. The program, which is designed to prepare students for careers in research and/or teaching, emphasizes a cooperative, personal working environment between students and members of the faculty.

Faculty interests cover a wide range of disciplines in the biomedical sciences and life sciences. Research interests include metagenomics analysis of extreme microbial ecosystems; environmental and biotic stress functional genomics, rubber, and vitamin biosynthesis, and biofuel feedstock production in plants and algae; functional genomics of insect peptide and lipid hormones and pheromones, and lipid metabolism; insect chromatin structure and remodeling; muscle protein enzymology, structure, and signaling; muscle contraction and excitation-contraction coupling; cell motility; insulin signaling pathways and glucose transport; receptor structure and transmembrane signal transduction mechanisms; membrane-cytoskeletal interactions; oxygen toxicity; mammalian lipid metabolism in cancer; receptor-mediated endocytosis; and computational methods in database mining and macromolecular structure. Each faculty member directs an active research program and is dedicated to training postdoctoral associates and doctoral- and master's-level graduate students as well as undergraduate students. Faculty members are funded by the National Institutes of Health, National Science Foundation, Department of Energy, Department of Transportation, United States Department of Agriculture, and other extramural sources of about $4 million per year.

Research Facilities

Research in UNR's Department of Biochemistry and Molecular Biology is supported by state-of-the-art approaches to genomics, proteomics, gene transfer, recombinant techniques, bioinformatics, computational biology, electrophysiology, spectroscopy, single-molecule biophysics, protein analytical biochemistry, and mass spectrometry, among others. Facilities and technical staff members are available for analysis of samples by electron, confocal, two-photon confocal, single-molecule, and atomic force microscopy; flow cytometry; mass spectrometry; high-throughput DNA sequence and mRNA, and protein expression analysis. In addition, research centers for genomics, monoclonal antibody production, construction of viral vectors, calcium imaging, proteomics analysis, bioinformatics and molecular modeling including more than 1 TB of RAM for computational use through the University Research Grid. Transgenic mouse generation and housing are also available.

A new Knowledge Center that integrates a modern library with extensive digital retrieval of information serves as the primary center for information resources and services in support of teaching and research. The Savitt Medical Library is located in close proximity to the Biochemistry Department. The libraries' Web-based information delivery system provides access to the libraries' physical collections (more than 1 million books, 5,000 print journals, 12,000 videos and DVDs, and 3.3 million microforms); course reserves, most of which are available online; full-text articles from a growing number of electronic journals and magazines (currently around 15,000); approximately 13,000 electronic books; more than 200 general and specialized databases; and high-quality Internet resources selected and organized for the UNR community.

Financial Aid

Graduate fellowships, assistantships, and research awards are available to students admitted to the Graduate School on a competitive basis. Both fellowships and assistantships carry a stipend and a tuition waiver. Assistantship stipends currently start at $22,000 and vary upward depending upon year of study. Information is available from the Graduate School (http://www.unr.edu/grad/) or the Department of Biochemistry and Molecular Biology (http://www.ag.unr.edu/biochemistry/).

Cost of Study

Nevada residents pay registration fees only. The registration fee is $246 per credit. Nonresidents pay tuition in addition to registration fees. In 2011–12, part-time tuition (1–6 credits) is $263 per credit and full-time tuition (7 credits or more) is $6645 per semester. Students awarded research fellowships or teaching assistantships are entitled to a partial fee waiver of nonresident tuition rates and pay only $63 per credit. Residents of neighboring Arizona and California counties are eligible for reduced "Good Neighbor" nonresident tuition fees of $482 per credit. Additional fees and student insurance costs also apply.

Living and Housing Costs

A room in the residence halls ranges from $4750 to $6610 per academic year, depending on location. Meal plans range from $3539 to $4768. A listing of off-campus housing—including rooms, apartments, and houses—is also available.

Student Group

There are approximately 30 students enrolled in the graduate biochemistry programs.

Student Outcomes

Ph.D. graduates from the Department of Biochemistry and Molecular Biology now hold professional positions in universities, industry, and government, including federal science administration. These include faculty members at leading universities and medical schools and research scientists at pharmaceutical companies. Many other former students hold positions in biotechnology start-up companies.

Location

The University of Nevada, Reno, is a center of innovation and energy for the thriving Reno-Sparks metropolitan area. Its 290-acre campus of rolling hills features a blend of ivy-covered buildings, sweeping lawns, and functional, progressive architecture. Reno-Sparks is in an unusually attractive natural setting. It is bounded on the west by the majestic Sierra Nevada range and on the east by a rolling basin and range province. Reno-Sparks benefits from a comfortable climate marked by generally cool and dry weather with more than 300 sunny days per year. The area is a haven for those who love the four seasons and outdoor activities. Recreational activities are easy to find. Students are within less than an hour's driving distance of the many world-class ski resorts of Lake Tahoe and the historic Western realm of Virginia City.

The University

The University of Nevada, Reno, is a constitutionally established land-grant university founded in 1874. The University served the state of Nevada as its only state-supported institution of higher education for almost seventy-five years. In that historical role, it has emerged as a doctoral-granting university that focuses its resources on doing a select number of things well. A diverse student body strengthens the academic atmosphere for the cultural and intellectual development of the student. By fostering creative and scholarly activity, the University encourages and supports faculty research and the application of that research to state and national problems. UNR is growing rapidly and currently enrolls more than 17,000 students, including 3,300 enrolled in graduate programs. The University houses a School of Medicine with a class of 65 medical students. The Northwest Commission on Colleges and Universities (NWCCU) accredits the University.

Applying

There is a $90 nonrefundable graduate program application fee. All GPA and test score information must be included on the application. Interested students should submit two copies of their official undergraduate and graduate school transcripts directly from the institutions previously attended to the University of Nevada, Reno. Applicants who are applying for a graduate assistantship must send three letters of recommendation and a statement of purpose directly to the program director.

Correspondence and Information

Dr. John C. Cushman
Graduate Program Director
Department of Biochemistry and Molecular Biology
University of Nevada, Reno
1664 North Virginia Street, MS 330
Reno, Nevada 89557-0330
Phone: 775-784-1918
Fax: 775-784-1419
E-mail: jcushman@unr.edu
Web site: http://www.ag.unr.edu/biochemistry/

University of Nevada, Reno

THE FACULTY AND THEIR RESEARCH

Josh E. Baker, Assistant Professor; Ph.D., Minnesota, Twin Cities, 1999. Use of optical traps, fluorescence microscopy, and single-molecule imaging techniques to study the molecular basis for cell motility.

Gary Blomquist, Professor and Department Chair; Ph.D., Montana State, 1973. Biosynthesis and molecular biology of pheromone production; insect hydrocarbons and lipid metabolism.

Grant R. Cramer, Professor; Ph.D., California, Davis, 1985. Systems biology of grapes; abiotic stress effects on vines and berries; influence of water deficit on wine flavors.

Christine Cremo, Professor; Ph.D., Oregon State, 1983. Structure, function, and regulation of motor proteins in smooth muscle.

John C. Cushman, Professor; Ph.D., Rutgers, 1987. Molecular and evolutionary genetics of Crassulacean acid metabolism; functional genomics of environmental stress tolerance in plants; biofuel production from algal and plant feedstocks.

Hanna Damke, Research Assistant Professor; Ph.D., Marburg (Germany), 1992. Role of the signaling GTPase dynamin in coordinating endocytosis with other cellular functions to maintain homeostasis.

Patricia Ellison, Research Assistant Professor; Ph.D., Sheffield, 1981. Regulation of smooth muscle myosins by phosphorylation and dephosphorylation; interaction between myosin and actin, myosin light chain kinase, and phosphatase.

Kevin Facemyer, Research Assistant Professor; Ph.D., Washington State, 1996. Computational analysis of motor proteins; development of novel computational methods of detecting and quantifying interfacial binding energy.

Joseph J. Grzymski, Assistant Research Professor, Desert Research Institute; Ph.D., Rutgers, 2002. Computational and synthetic biology; genome and protein adaptations to the environment; protein cost minimization.

Jeffrey Harper, Professor; Ph.D., Washington (St. Louis), 1985. Calcium signaling in plants; engineering plants to better tolerate abiotic and biotic stress; plant mineral nutrition.

Susan W. Liebman, Research Professor; Ph.D., Rochester, 1974. Using yeast genetics and molecular biology to study protein misfolding diseases.

Cynthia Corley Mastick, Associate Professor; Ph.D., Carnegie Mellon, 1990. Cellular mechanisms of insulin actions on maturity-onset or type 2 diabetes; molecular mechanisms of signal transduction and signaling specificity; cellular basis of insulin action and peripheral insulin resistance; regulation of glucose and lipid uptake/metabolism; cell biology of adipocytes and muscle.

Grant Mastick, Assistant Professor; Ph.D., Carnegie Mellon, 1992. Molecular signals that guide neuronal connections in the embryonic brain; developmental neurobiology.

Kunio Misono, Professor; Ph.D., Vanderbilt, 1978. Structure of cell membrane receptors and signal transduction mechanisms.

Alison Murray, Associate Research Professor, Desert Research Institute; Ph.D., California, Santa Barbara, 1998. Metagenomics of aquatic and symbiotic microbial communities in Antarctic and deep sea environments; environmental adaptation, biogeochemical cycling, and metabolic plasticity.

Chi-Yun Pai, Assistant Professor, Department of Biological Sciences; Ph.D., National Yang-Ming University (Taiwan), 1996. Transcriptional regulation of gene expression; chromatin and nucleolar structural organization in Drosophila melanogaster.

Ronald S. Pardini, Professor and Interim Dean of the College of Agriculture, Biotechnology, and Natural Resources; and Director, Nevada Agriculture Experiment Station; Ph.D., Illinois, 1965. Nutritional intervention with omega-3 fatty acids in the treatment of cancer; understanding mechanisms of omega-3 fatty acid–induced growth inhibition and enhanced response to cancer therapy.

David Quilici, Manager, Nevada Proteomics Center; Ph.D., Nevada, Reno, 1997. Identifying unknown compounds; quantifying known compounds; elucidating structure and chemical properties of molecules.

Kathleen M. Schegg, Research Biochemist, Nevada Proteomics Center; Ph.D., Nevada, Reno, 1980. Proteomics; 2-D gel separation of proteins; amino acid analysis; protein sequencing; peptide synthesis.

Karen A. Schlauch, Associate Professor; Ph.D., New Mexico State, 1998. Bioinformatic analysis of gene interactions and biological expression data using novel clustering algorithms and graph-theoretic approaches, mathematical models.

David A. Schooley, Professor; Ph.D., Stanford, 1968. Structural, biosynthetic, and metabolic studies on physiologically active materials, chiefly, insect juvenile hormones and peptide hormones; mechanism of signal transduction of peptide hormones.

David Shintani, Associate Professor; Ph.D., Michigan State, 1996. Plant biochemistry and genome research; metabolic and developmental regulation of plant isoprenoid metabolism; vitamin and cofactor biosynthesis in plants.

Claus Tittiger, Associate Professor; Ph.D., Queen's at Kingston, 1994. Insect molecular biology and genomics; isoprenoid metabolism and pheromone biosynthesis; cytochromes P450; hydrocarbon and lipid metabolism.

Maria L. Valencik, Assistant Professor; Ph.D., UCLA, 1991. Cardiovascular research; integrins and natriuretic peptides in cardiac myocytes.

William H. Welch, Professor (Emeritus); Ph.D., Kansas, 1968. Molecular modeling of enzymes and ion channels; enzymology; ryanodine receptor function; immunology of pathogen capsules.

Section 4
Biophysics

This section contains a directory of institutions offering graduate work in biophysics, followed by in-depth entries submitted by institutions that chose to prepare detailed program descriptions. Additional information about programs listed in the directory but not augmented by an in-depth entry may be obtained by writing directly to the dean of a graduate school or chair of a department at the address given in the directory.

For programs offering related work, see also in this book *Biochemistry; Biological and Biomedical Sciences; Cell, Molecular, and Structural Biology; Neuroscience and Neurobiology;* and *Physiology.* In the other guides in this series:

Graduate Programs in the Physical Sciences, Mathematics, Agricultural Sciences, the Environment & Natural Resources
See *Chemistry* and *Physics*

Graduate Programs in Engineering & Applied Sciences
See *Agricultural Engineering and Bioengineering* and *Biomedical Engineering and Biotechnology*

Graduate Programs in Business, Education, Health, Information Studies, Law & Social Work
See *Allied Health, Optometry and Vision Sciences,* and *Public Health*

CONTENTS

Biophysics

Albert Einstein College of Medicine, Graduate Division of Biomedical Sciences, Department of Physiology and Biophysics, Bronx, NY 10461. Offers PhD, MD/PhD. *Degree requirements:* For doctorate, thesis/dissertation. *Entrance requirements:* For doctorate, GRE General Test. Additional exam requirements/recommendations for international students: Required—TOEFL. *Faculty research:* Biophysical and biochemical basis of body function at the subcellular, cellular, organ, and whole-body level.

Baylor College of Medicine, Graduate School of Biomedical Sciences, Department of Molecular Physiology and Biophysics, Houston, TX 77030-3498. Offers PhD, MD/PhD. *Faculty:* 34 full-time (10 women). *Students:* 20 full-time (10 women); includes 1 Black or African American, non-Hispanic/Latino; 1 Asian, non-Hispanic/Latino; 1 Hispanic/Latino, 8 international. Average age 27. 22 applicants, 32% accepted, 5 enrolled. In 2010, 3 doctorates awarded. *Degree requirements:* For doctorate, thesis/dissertation, public defense. *Entrance requirements:* For doctorate, GRE General Test, GRE Subject Test (strongly recommended), minimum GPA of 3.0. Additional exam requirements/recommendations for international students: Required—TOEFL. *Application deadline:* For fall admission, 1/1 priority date for domestic students. Electronic applications accepted. *Expenses:* Tuition: Full-time $11,000. Required fees: $4900. *Financial support:* In 2010–11, 8 fellowships with full tuition reimbursements (averaging $26,000 per year), 12 research assistantships with full tuition reimbursements (averaging $26,000 per year) were awarded; career-related internships or fieldwork, Federal Work-Study, institutionally sponsored loans, health care benefits, and students receive a scholarship unless there are grant funds available to pay tuition also available. Financial award applicants required to submit FAFSA. *Faculty research:* Biophysics, cardiovascular biology, imaging, muscle physiology, ion channels. *Unit head:* Dr. Robia Pautler, Director, 713-798-5630, Fax: 713-798-3475. *Application contact:* Cherrie McGlory, Graduate Program Administrator, 713-798-5109, Fax: 713-798-3475, E-mail: molphysgrad@bcm.edu.

Boston University, Graduate School of Arts and Sciences, Program in Cellular Biophysics, Boston, MA 02215. Offers PhD. *Students:* 2 full-time (0 women), 1 international. Average age 28. 4 applicants, 0% accepted. In 2010, 4 doctorates awarded. *Degree requirements:* For doctorate, one foreign language, comprehensive exam, thesis/dissertation. *Entrance requirements:* For doctorate, GRE General Test, GRE Subject Test, 3 letters of recommendation. Additional exam requirements/recommendations for international students: Required—TOEFL (minimum score 550 paper-based; 213 computer-based; 84 iBT). *Application deadline:* For fall admission, 7/1 for domestic and international students; for spring admission, 10/15 for domestic and international students. Application fee: $70. Electronic applications accepted. *Expenses:* Tuition: Full-time $39,314; part-time $1228 per credit. Required fees: $40 per semester. *Financial support:* Career-related internships or fieldwork available. Support available to part-time students. Financial award application deadline: 1/15; financial award applicants required to submit FAFSA. *Unit head:* Dr. M. Carter Cornwall, Director, 617-638-4256, Fax: 617-638-4273, E-mail: cornwall@bu.edu. *Application contact:* Rebekah Alexander, Assistant Director of Admissions and Financial Aid, 617-353-2696, Fax: 617-358-5492, E-mail: grs@bu.edu.

Brandeis University, Graduate School of Arts and Sciences, Program in Biochemistry and Biophysics, Waltham, MA 02454. Offers PhD. Part-time programs available. *Faculty:* 9 full-time (2 women), 1 (woman) part-time/adjunct. *Students:* 37 full-time (14 women); includes 3 Asian, non-Hispanic/Latino; 2 Hispanic/Latino, 8 international. 62 applicants, 23% accepted, 7 enrolled. In 2010, 3 doctorates awarded. *Degree requirements:* For doctorate, thesis/dissertation, area exams. *Entrance requirements:* For doctorate, GRE General Test, resume, 3 letters of recommendation, statement of purpose. Additional exam requirements/recommendations for international students: Required—TOEFL (minimum score 600 paper-based; 250 computer-based; 100 iBT); Recommended—IELTS (minimum score 7). *Application deadline:* For fall admission, 1/15 priority date for domestic students. Applications are processed on a rolling basis. Application fee: $75. Electronic applications accepted. *Financial support:* In 2010–11, 16 students received support, including 9 fellowships with full tuition reimbursements available (averaging $27,500 per year), 26 research assistantships with full tuition reimbursements available (averaging $27,500 per year), teaching assistantships with partial tuition reimbursements available (averaging $3,200 per year); career-related internships or fieldwork, scholarships/grants, traineeships, health care benefits, and tuition waivers (full and partial) also available. Financial award application deadline: 4/15; financial award applicants required to submit FAFSA. *Faculty research:* Macromolecular chemistry, structure and function, biochemistry, biophysics, biological macromolecules. *Unit head:* Prof. Dorothee Kern, Director of Graduate Studies, 781-736-3100, Fax: 781-736-3107, E-mail: dkern@brandeis.edu. *Application contact:* Marcia Cabral, Department Administrator, 781-736-3100, Fax: 781-736-3107, E-mail: cabral@brandeis.edu.

California Institute of Technology, Division of Biology, Program in Cell Biology and Biophysics, Pasadena, CA 91125-0001. Offers PhD. *Degree requirements:* For doctorate, thesis/dissertation, qualifying exam. *Entrance requirements:* For doctorate, GRE General Test.

Carnegie Mellon University, Mellon College of Science, Department of Biological Sciences, Pittsburgh, PA 15213-3891. Offers biochemistry (PhD); biophysics (PhD); cell biology (PhD); computational biology (MS, PhD); developmental biology (PhD); genetics (PhD); molecular biology (PhD); neuroscience (PhD). *Degree requirements:* For doctorate, comprehensive exam, thesis/dissertation. *Entrance requirements:* For doctorate, GRE General Test, GRE Subject Test, interview. Electronic applications accepted. *Faculty research:* Genetic structure, function, and regulation; protein structure and function; biological membranes; biological spectroscopy.

Carnegie Mellon University, Mellon College of Science, Department of Chemistry, Pittsburgh, PA 15213-3891. Offers biotechnology and management (MS); chemistry (PhD), including bioinorganic, bioorganic, organic and materials, biophysics and spectroscopy, computational and theoretical, polymer; colloids, polymers and surfaces (MS). Part-time programs available. Terminal master's awarded for partial completion of doctoral program. *Degree requirements:* For doctorate, thesis/dissertation, departmental qualifying and oral exams, teaching experience. *Entrance requirements:* For master's, GRE General Test; for doctorate, GRE General Test, GRE Subject Test. Additional exam requirements/recommendations for international students: Required—TOEFL. Electronic applications accepted. *Faculty research:* Physical and theoretical chemistry, chemical synthesis, biophysical/bioinorganic chemistry.

Case Western Reserve University, School of Medicine and School of Graduate Studies, Graduate Programs in Medicine, Department of Physiology and Biophysics, Cleveland, OH 44106. Offers cell and molecular physiology (MS); cell physiology (PhD); molecular/cellular biophysics (PhD); physiology and biophysics (PhD); systems physiology (PhD); MD/PhD. Terminal master's awarded for partial completion of doctoral program. *Degree requirements:* For master's, thesis; for doctorate, thesis/dissertation. *Entrance requirements:* For master's, GRE General Test, minimum GPA of 3.28; for doctorate, GRE General Test, minimum GPA of 3.6. Additional exam requirements/recommendations for international students: Required—TOEFL. Electronic applications accepted. *Faculty research:* Cardiovascular physiology, calcium metabolism, epithelial cell biology.

See Display on pae 443 and Close-Up on page 453.

Clemson University, Graduate School, College of Engineering and Science, Department of Physics and Astronomy, Clemson, SC 29634. Offers physics (MS, PhD), including astronomy and astrophysics, atmospheric physics, biophysics. Part-time programs available. *Faculty:* 25 full-time (4 women), 2 part-time/adjunct (0 women). *Students:* 63 full-time (19 women); includes 3 Black or African American, non-Hispanic/Latino, 26 international. Average age 27. 66 applicants, 92% accepted, 21 enrolled. In 2010, 2 master's, 6 doctorates awarded. Terminal master's awarded for partial completion of doctoral program. *Degree requirements:* For master's, thesis or alternative; for doctorate, thesis/dissertation. *Entrance requirements:* For master's and doctorate, GRE General Test. Additional exam requirements/recommendations for international students: Required—TOEFL. *Application deadline:* For fall admission, 1/15 priority date for domestic students; for spring admission, 9/15 priority date for domestic students. Applications are processed on a rolling basis. Application fee: $70 ($80 for international students). Electronic applications accepted. *Expenses:* Tuition, state resident: full-time $6492; part-time $400 per credit hour. Tuition, nonresident: full-time $13,634; part-time $800 per credit hour. Required fees: $262 per semester. Part-time tuition and fees vary according to course load and program. *Financial support:* In 2010–11, 58 students received support, including 1 fellowship with full and partial tuition reimbursement available (averaging $16,000 per year), 26 research assistantships with partial tuition reimbursements available (averaging $13,559 per year), 43 teaching assistantships with partial tuition reimbursements available (averaging $14,097 per year); career-related internships or fieldwork, institutionally sponsored loans, scholarships/grants, health care benefits, and unspecified assistantships also available. Support available to part-time students. Financial award application deadline: 6/1; financial award applicants required to submit FAFSA. *Faculty research:* Radiation physics, solid-state physics, nuclear physics, radar and lidar studies of atmosphere. Total annual research expenditures: $2.4 million. *Unit head:* Dr. Peter Barnes, Chair, 864-656-3419, Fax: 864-656-0805, E-mail: peterb@clemson.edu. *Application contact:* Dr. Murray Daw, Graduate Coordinator, 864-656-6702, Fax: 864-656-0805, E-mail: physgradinfo-l@clemson.edu.

Columbia University, College of Physicians and Surgeons, Department of Biochemistry and Molecular Biophysics, New York, NY 10032. Offers biochemistry and molecular biophysics (M Phil, PhD); biophysics (PhD); MD/PhD. Only candidates for the PhD are admitted. *Degree requirements:* For doctorate, one foreign language, thesis/dissertation. *Entrance requirements:* For master's and doctorate, GRE General Test. Additional exam requirements/recommendations for international students: Required—TOEFL.

Columbia University, College of Physicians and Surgeons, Department of Physiology and Cellular Biophysics, New York, NY 10032. Offers M Phil, MA, PhD, MD/PhD. Only candidates for the PhD are admitted. Terminal master's awarded for partial completion of doctoral program. *Degree requirements:* For doctorate, thesis/dissertation. *Entrance requirements:* For master's and doctorate, GRE General Test. Additional exam requirements/recommendations for international students: Required—TOEFL. *Faculty research:* Membrane physiology, cellular biology, cardiovascular physiology, neurophysiology.

Columbia University, College of Physicians and Surgeons, Integrated Program in Cellular, Molecular, Structural and Genetic Studies, New York, NY 10032. Offers PhD. Terminal master's awarded for partial completion of doctoral program. *Degree requirements:* For doctorate, thesis/dissertation. *Entrance requirements:* For doctorate, GRE General Test, GRE Subject Test. Additional exam requirements/recommendations for international students: Required—TOEFL. *Expenses:* Contact institution. *Faculty research:* Transcription, macromolecular sorting, gene expression during development, cellular interaction.

Cornell University, Graduate School, Graduate Fields of Agriculture and Life Sciences, Field of Biochemistry, Molecular and Cell Biology, Ithaca, NY 14853-0001. Offers biochemistry (PhD); biophysics (PhD); cell biology (PhD); molecular and cell biology (PhD); molecular biology (PhD). *Faculty:* 59 full-time (15 women). *Students:* 90 full-time (47 women); includes 1 Black or African American, non-Hispanic/Latino; 7 Asian, non-Hispanic/Latino; 4 Hispanic/Latino, 30 international. Average age 26. 269 applicants, 9% accepted, 20 enrolled. In 2010, 12 doctorates awarded. *Degree requirements:* For doctorate, comprehensive exam, thesis/dissertation, 2 semesters of teaching experience. *Entrance requirements:* For doctorate, GRE General Test, GRE Subject Test (biology, chemistry, physics, biochemistry, cell and molecular biology), 3 letters of recommendation. Additional exam requirements/recommendations for international students: Required—TOEFL (minimum score 600 paper-based; 250 computer-based; 77 iBT). *Application deadline:* For fall admission, 1/5 for domestic students. Application fee: $70. Electronic applications accepted. *Expenses:* Tuition: Full-time $29,500. Required fees: $76. Tuition and fees vary according to degree level and program. *Financial support:* In 2010–11, 88 students received support, including 25 fellowships with full tuition reimbursements available, 48 research assistantships with full tuition reimbursements available, 15 teaching assistantships with full tuition reimbursements available; institutionally sponsored loans, scholarships/grants, health care benefits, tuition waivers (full and partial), and unspecified assistantships also available. Financial award applicants required to submit FAFSA. *Faculty research:* Biophysics, structural biology. *Unit head:* Director of Graduate Studies, 607-255-2100, Fax: 607-255-2100. *Application contact:* Graduate Field Assistant, 607-255-2100, Fax: 607-255-2100, E-mail: bmcb@cornell.edu.

Cornell University, Graduate School, Graduate Fields of Agriculture and Life Sciences, Graduate Field of Biophysics, Ithaca, NY 14853-0001. Offers PhD. *Faculty:* 28 full-time (4 women). *Students:* 21 full-time (7 women); includes 2 Asian, non-Hispanic/Latino, 9 international. Average age 26. 17 applicants, 35% accepted, 5 enrolled. In 2010, 4 doctorates awarded. *Degree requirements:* For doctorate, comprehensive exam, thesis/dissertation. *Entrance requirements:* For doctorate, GRE General Test, GRE Subject Test (physics or chemistry preferred), 3 letters of recommendation. Additional exam requirements/recommendations for international students: Required—TOEFL (minimum score 550 paper-based; 213 computer-based; 77 iBT). *Application deadline:* For fall admission, 1/15 for domestic students. Application fee: $70. Electronic applications accepted. *Expenses:* Tuition: Full-time $29,500. Required fees: $76. Tuition and fees vary according to degree level and program. *Financial support:* In 2010–11, 10 fellowships with full tuition reimbursements, 10 research assistantships with full tuition reimbursements were awarded; teaching assistantships with full tuition reimbursements, institutionally sponsored loans, scholarships/grants, health care benefits, tuition waivers (full and partial), and unspecified assistantships also available. Financial award applicants required to submit FAFSA. *Faculty research:* Protein structure and function, biomolecular and cellular function, membrane biophysics, signal transduction, computational biology. *Unit head:* Director of Graduate Studies, 607-255-2100, E-mail: biophysics@cornell.edu. *Application contact:* Graduate Field Assistant, 610-255-2100, E-mail: biophysics@cornell.edu.

Cornell University, Joan and Sanford I. Weill Medical College and Graduate School of Medical Sciences, Weill Cornell Graduate School of Medical Sciences, Physiology, Biophysics and Systems Biology Program, New York, NY 10065. Offers MS, PhD. *Faculty:* 35 full-time (9 women). *Students:* 51 full-time (20 women); includes 2 Black or African American, non-Hispanic/Latino; 5 Asian, non-Hispanic/Latino; 1 Hispanic/Latino, 24 international. Average age 23. 44 applicants, 59% accepted, 13 enrolled. In 2010, 5 doctorates awarded. Terminal master's awarded for partial completion of doctoral program. *Degree requirements:* For master's, comprehensive exam; for doctorate, thesis/dissertation, final exam. *Entrance requirements:* For doctorate, GRE General Test, introductory courses in biology, inorganic and organic chemistry, physics, and mathematics. Additional exam requirements/recommendations for international students: Required—TOEFL. *Application deadline:* For fall admission, 12/1 for domestic students. Application fee: $60. *Expenses:* Tuition: Full-time $45,545. Required fees: $2805. *Financial support:* In 2010–11, 4 fellowships (averaging $24,735 per year) were awarded; scholarships/grants, health care benefits, and stipends (given to all students) also available. *Faculty research:* Receptor-mediated regulation of cell function, molecular properties of channels or receptors, bioinformatics, mathematical modeling. *Unit head:* Dr. Emre Aksay, Co-Director, 212-746-6207, E-mail: ema2004@med.cornell.edu. *Application contact:* Audrey Rivera, Program Coordinator, 212-746-6361, E-mail: ajr2004@med.cornell.edu.

Dalhousie University, Faculty of Medicine, Department of Physiology and Biophysics, Halifax, NS B3H 1X5, Canada. Offers M Sc, PhD, M Sc/PhD. *Degree requirements:* For master's, thesis; for doctorate, thesis/dissertation. *Entrance requirements:* For master's and doctorate, GRE Subject Test (for international students). Additional exam requirements/recommendations for international students: Required—TOEFL, IELTS, 1 of the following 5 approved tests: TOEFL, IELTS, CANTEST, CAEL, Michigan English Language Assessment Battery. Electronic applications accepted. *Faculty research:* Computer modeling, reproductive and endocrine physiology, cardiovascular physiology, neurophysiology, membrane biophysics.

East Carolina University, Graduate School, Thomas Harriot College of Arts and Sciences, Department of Physics, Greenville, NC 27858-4353. Offers applied and biomedical physics (MS); medical physics (MS); physics (PhD). Part-time programs available. *Degree requirements:* For master's, one foreign language, comprehensive exam. *Entrance requirements:* For master's, GRE General Test. Additional exam requirements/recommendations for international students: Required—TOEFL. *Expenses:* Tuition, state resident: full-time $3130; part-time $391.25 per credit hour. Tuition, nonresident: full-time $13,817; part-time $1727.13 per credit hour. Required fees: $1916; $239.50 per credit hour. Tuition and fees vary according to campus/location and program.

Emory University, Laney Graduate School, Department of Physics, Atlanta, GA 30322-1100. Offers biophysics (PhD); condensed matter physics (PhD); non-linear physics (PhD); radiological physics (PhD); soft condensed matter physics (PhD); solid-state physics (PhD); statistical physics (PhD); MS/PhD. *Degree requirements:* For doctorate, thesis/dissertation, qualifier proposal (PhD). *Entrance requirements:* For doctorate, GRE General Test, minimum GPA of 3.0. Additional exam requirements/recommendations for international students: Required— TOEFL (minimum score 600 paper-based). Electronic applications accepted. *Expenses:* Tuition: Full-time $33,800. Required fees: $1300. *Faculty research:* Experimental studies of the structure and function of metalloproteins, soft condensed matter, granular materials, biophotonics and fluorescence correlation spectroscopy, single molecule studies of DNA-protein systems.

Georgetown University, Graduate School of Arts and Sciences, Programs in Biomedical Sciences, Department of Physiology and Biophysics, Washington, DC 20057. Offers MS, PhD, MD/PhD. *Degree requirements:* For doctorate, thesis/dissertation. *Entrance requirements:* For master's, GRE General Test, MCAT; for doctorate, GRE General Test. Additional exam requirements/recommendations for international students: Required—TOEFL.

Harvard University, Graduate School of Arts and Sciences, Committee on Biophysics, Cambridge, MA 02138. Offers PhD. *Degree requirements:* For doctorate, thesis/dissertation, exam, qualifying paper. *Entrance requirements:* For doctorate, GRE General Test, GRE Subject Test (recommended). Additional exam requirements/recommendations for international students: Required—TOEFL. *Expenses:* Tuition: Full-time $34,976. Required fees: $1166. Full-time tuition and fees vary according to program. *Faculty research:* Structural molecular biology, cell and membrane biophysics, molecular genetics, physical biochemistry, mathematical biophysics.

See Display on this page and Close-Up on page 161.

Howard University, Graduate School, Department of Physiology and Biophysics, Washington, DC 20059-0002. Offers biophysics (PhD); physiology (PhD). *Degree requirements:* For doctorate, comprehensive exam, thesis/dissertation. *Entrance requirements:* For doctorate, GRE General Test, minimum B average in field. *Faculty research:* Cardiovascular physiology, pulmonary physiology, renal physiology, neurophysiology, endocrinology.

Illinois State University, Graduate School, College of Arts and Sciences, Department of Biological Sciences, Normal, IL 61790-2200. Offers animal behavior (MS); bacteriology (MS); biochemistry (MS); biological sciences (MS); biology (PhD); biophysics (MS); biotechnology (MS); botany (MS, PhD); cell biology (MS); conservation biology (MS); developmental biology (MS); ecology (MS, PhD); entomology (MS); evolutionary biology (MS); genetics (MS, PhD); immunology (MS); microbiology (MS, PhD); molecular biology (MS); molecular genetics (MS); neurobiology (MS); neuroscience (MS); parasitology (MS); physiology (MS, PhD); plant biology (MS); plant molecular biology (MS); plant sciences (MS); structural biology (MS); zoology (MS, PhD). Part-time programs available. *Degree requirements:* For master's, thesis or alternative; for doctorate, variable foreign language requirement, thesis/dissertation, 2 terms of residency. *Entrance requirements:* For master's, GRE General Test, minimum GPA of 2.6 in last 60 hours of course work; for doctorate, GRE General Test. *Faculty research:* Redoc balance and drug development in schistosoma mansoni, control of the growth of listeria monocytogenes at low temperature, regulation of cell expansion and microtubule function by SPRI, CRUI: physiology and fitness consequences of different life history phenotypes.

Iowa State University of Science and Technology, Graduate College, College of Agriculture and College of Liberal Arts and Sciences, Department of Biochemistry, Biophysics, and Molecular Biology, Ames, IA 50011. Offers biochemistry (MS, PhD); biophysics (MS, PhD); genetics (MS, PhD); molecular, cellular, and developmental biology (MS, PhD); toxicology (MS, PhD). *Faculty:* 31 full-time (7 women), 1 (woman) part-time/adjunct. *Students:* 81 full-time (33 women), 11 part-time (6 women); includes 2 Black or African American, non-Hispanic/ Latino; 2 Asian, non-Hispanic/Latino, 58 international. 38 applicants, 29% accepted, 8 enrolled. In 2010, 3 master's, 9 doctorates awarded. *Degree requirements:* For master's, thesis; for doctorate, thesis/dissertation. *Entrance requirements:* For master's and doctorate, GRE General Test. Additional exam requirements/recommendations for international students: Required— TOEFL (minimum score 550 paper-based; 79 iBT), IELTS (minimum score 6.5). *Application deadline:* For fall admission, 1/15 priority date for domestic and international students; for spring admission, 10/15 for domestic and international students. Application fee: $40 ($90 for international students). Electronic applications accepted. *Financial support:* In 2010–11, 67 research assistantships with full and partial tuition reimbursements (averaging $17,228 per year) were awarded; teaching assistantships with full and partial tuition reimbursements, scholarships/grants, health care benefits, and unspecified assistantships also available. *Unit head:* Dr. Guru Rao, Interim Chair, 515-294-6116, E-mail: biochem@iastate.edu. *Application contact:* Dr. Reuben Peters, Director of Graduate Education, 515-294-6116, E-mail: biochem@iastate.edu.

See Display on page 129 and Close-Up on page 147.

The Johns Hopkins University, National Institutes of Health Sponsored Programs, Baltimore, MD 21218-2699. Offers biology (PhD), including biochemistry, biophysics, cell biology, developmental biology, genetic biology, molecular biology; cell, molecular, and developmental biology and biophysics (PhD). *Degree requirements:* For doctorate, comprehensive exam, thesis/dissertation. *Entrance requirements:* For doctorate, GRE General Test. Additional exam requirements/recommendations for international students: Required—TOEFL (minimum score 600 paper-based; 250 computer-based), TWE. Electronic applications accepted. *Faculty research:* Protein and nucleic acid biochemistry and biophysical chemistry, molecular biology and development.

The Johns Hopkins University, Zanvyl Krieger School of Arts and Sciences, Program in Molecular Biophysics, Baltimore, MD 21218-2699. Offers PhD. *Faculty:* 9 full-time (3 women). *Students:* 43 full-time (16 women); includes 6 minority (4 Asian, non-Hispanic/Latino; 2 Hispanic/ Latino), 11 international. Average age 26. 73 applicants, 15% accepted, 11 enrolled. In 2010, 7 doctorates awarded. *Degree requirements:* For doctorate, comprehensive exam, thesis/ dissertation. *Entrance requirements:* For doctorate, GRE General Test. Additional exam requirements/recommendations for international students: Required—TOEFL (minimum score 600 paper-based; 250 computer-based), IELTS; Recommended—TWE. *Application deadline:* For fall admission, 1/2 priority date for domestic and international students. Applications are processed on a rolling basis. Application fee: $75. Electronic applications accepted. *Financial support:* In 2010–11, 2 students received support, including fellowships with full tuition reimbursements available (averaging $27,532 per year), research assistantships with full tuition reimbursements available (averaging $27,532 per year); teaching assistantships, institutionally sponsored loans, scholarships/grants, traineeships, health care benefits, tuition waivers (full), and unspecified assistantships also available. Financial award application deadline: 4/15; financial award applicants required to submit FAFSA. *Faculty research:* Protein folding and dynamics, membranes and membrane proteins, structural biology and prediction, RNA biophysics, enzymes and metabolic pathways, single molecule studies, DNA-protein interactions. Total annual research expenditures: $3.7 million. *Unit head:* Dr. Juliette Lecomte, Director, 410-516-5197,

Harvard University
Graduate Program in Biophysics

Initiated in 1959, the Committee on Higher Degrees in Biophysics at Harvard University has a long history of important research achievements.

Designed to nurture independent, creative scientists, the program is for students with sound preliminary training in a physical or quantitative science; such as chemistry, physics, mathematics, or computer science. The primary objective of the program is to educate and train individuals with this background to apply the concepts and methods of the physical sciences to the solution of biological problems.

Structural Biology
- X-ray crystallography
- NMR
- Electron microscopy
- Computational chemistry

Imaging
- Medical Imaging
  fMRI
  Magnetoencephalography
- Cellular Imaging
  Confocal microscopy
  Multiphoton microscopy
  Advance sub-Rayleigh approaches
- Molecular imaging
  Single molecule methods

Computational Biology
- Bioinformatics
- Genomics
- Proteomics

Computational Modeling
- Molecules
- Networks

Neurobiology
- Molecular
- Cellular
- Systems

Biophysics Program
HMS Campus, 240 Longwood Ave, Boston, MA 02115
Phone: 617-495-3360 Fax: 617-432-4360
http://www.fas.harvard.edu/~biophys/

Application Information:
http://www.gsas.harvard.edu/

Biophysics

The Johns Hopkins University (continued)
Fax: 410-516-4118, E-mail: juliette@jhu.edu. *Application contact:* Ranice Crosby, Coordinator, Graduate Admissions, 410-516-5197, Fax: 410-516-4118, E-mail: crosbyr@jhu.edu.

Medical College of Wisconsin, Graduate School of Biomedical Sciences, Department of Biophysics, Milwaukee, WI 53226-0509. Offers PhD, MD/PhD. *Degree requirements:* For doctorate, comprehensive exam, thesis/dissertation. *Entrance requirements:* For doctorate, GRE. Additional exam requirements/recommendations for international students: Required—TOEFL. Electronic applications accepted. *Expenses:* Tuition: Full-time $30,000; part-time $710 per credit. Required fees: $150.

Medical College of Wisconsin, Graduate School of Biomedical Sciences, Program in Biophysics, Milwaukee, WI 53226-0509. Offers PhD, MD/PhD. Part-time programs available. *Degree requirements:* For doctorate, thesis/dissertation, oral exam. *Entrance requirements:* For doctorate, GRE General Test. Additional exam requirements/recommendations for international students: Required—TOEFL. Electronic applications accepted. *Expenses:* Tuition: Full-time $30,000; part-time $710 per credit. Required fees: $150. *Faculty research:* X-ray crystallography, electron spin resonance and membrane structure, protein and membrane dynamics, magnetic resonance imaging, free radical biology.

See Display below and Close-Up on page 163.

Northwestern University, The Graduate School, Interdepartmental Biological Sciences Program (IBiS), Evanston, IL 60208. Offers biochemistry, molecular biology, and cell biology (PhD), including biochemistry, cell and molecular biology, molecular biophysics, structural biology; biotechnology (PhD); cell and molecular biology (PhD); developmental biology and genetics (PhD); hormone action and signal transduction (PhD); neuroscience (PhD); structural biology, biochemistry, and biophysics (PhD). Program participants include the Departments of Biochemistry, Molecular Biology, and Cell Biology; Chemistry; Neurobiology and Physiology; Chemical Engineering; Civil Engineering; and Evanston Hospital. *Degree requirements:* For doctorate, thesis/dissertation, qualifying exam. *Entrance requirements:* For doctorate, GRE General Test. Additional exam requirements/recommendations for international students: Required—TOEFL (minimum score 600 paper-based). Electronic applications accepted. *Faculty research:* Developmental genetics, gene regulation, DNA-protein interactions, biological clocks, bioremediation.

The Ohio State University, Graduate School, College of Arts and Sciences, Division of Natural and Mathematical Sciences, Program in Biophysics, Columbus, OH 43210. Offers MS, PhD. *Faculty:* 57. *Students:* 24 full-time (10 women), 25 part-time (9 women), 26 international. Average age 28. In 2010, 4 master's, 5 doctorates awarded. *Degree requirements:* For master's, thesis optional; for doctorate, thesis/dissertation. *Entrance requirements:* For master's and doctorate, GRE General Test. Additional exam requirements/recommendations for international students: Required—TOEFL (minimum score 600 paper-based; 250 computer-based). *Application deadline:* For fall admission, 8/15 priority date for domestic students, 7/1 priority date for international students; for winter admission, 12/1 priority date for domestic students, 11/1 priority date for international students; for spring admission, 3/1 priority date for domestic students, 2/1 priority date for international students. Applications are processed on a rolling basis. Application fee: $40 ($50 for international students). Electronic applications accepted. *Expenses:* Tuition, state resident: full-time $10,605. Tuition, nonresident: full-time $26,535. Tuition and fees vary according to course load and program. *Financial support:* Fellowships, research assistantships, teaching assistantships, Federal Work-Study and institutionally sponsored loans available. Support available to part-time students. *Unit head:* Richard Swenson, Chair, 614-292-9428, E-mail: swenson.1@osu.edu. *Application contact:* 614-292-9444, Fax: 614-292-3895, E-mail: domestic.grad@osu.edu.

Oregon State University, Graduate School, College of Science, Department of Biochemistry and Biophysics, Corvallis, OR 97331. Offers MA, MAIS, MS, PhD. *Degree requirements:* For master's, thesis optional; for doctorate, thesis/dissertation, exams. *Entrance requirements:* For master's, GRE General Test, minimum GPA of 3.0; for doctorate, GRE Subject Test, minimum GPA of 3.0. Additional exam requirements/recommendations for international students:

Required—TOEFL. *Faculty research:* DNA and deoxyribonucleotide metabolism, cell growth control, receptors and membranes, protein structure and function.

Purdue University, Graduate School, College of Science, Department of Biological Sciences, West Lafayette, IN 47907. Offers biochemistry (PhD); biophysics (PhD); cell and developmental biology (PhD); ecology, evolutionary and population biology (MS, PhD), including ecology, evolutionary biology, population biology; genetics (MS, PhD); microbiology (MS, PhD); molecular biology (PhD); neurobiology (MS, PhD); plant physiology (PhD). Terminal master's awarded for partial completion of doctoral program. *Degree requirements:* For master's, thesis (for some programs); for doctorate, thesis/dissertation, seminars, teaching experience. *Entrance requirements:* For master's and doctorate, GRE General Test. Additional exam requirements/recommendations for international students: Required—TOEFL. Electronic applications accepted.

Rensselaer Polytechnic Institute, Graduate School, School of Science, Program in Biochemistry and Biophysics, Troy, NY 12180-3590. Offers MS, PhD. Part-time programs available. *Faculty:* 25 full-time (7 women). *Students:* 6 full-time (4 women), 1 international. Average age 27. 19 applicants, 21% accepted, 3 enrolled. In 2010, 1 doctorate awarded. Terminal master's awarded for partial completion of doctoral program. *Degree requirements:* For master's, thesis optional; for doctorate, comprehensive exam, thesis/dissertation. *Entrance requirements:* For doctorate, GRE General Test. Additional exam requirements/recommendations for international students: Required—TOEFL. *Application deadline:* For fall admission, 1/15 priority date for domestic students, 1/1 for international students. Applications are processed on a rolling basis. Application fee: $75. Electronic applications accepted. *Expenses:* Tuition: Full-time $39,600; part-time $1650 per credit. Required fees: $1896. *Financial support:* In 2010–11, 6 students received support, including 8 research assistantships with full tuition reimbursements available (averaging $17,500 per year), 4 teaching assistantships with full tuition reimbursements available (averaging $17,500 per year); traineeships and unspecified assistantships also available. Financial award application deadline: 1/1. *Faculty research:* Biopolymers, photosynthesis, cellular bioengineering. Total annual research expenditures: $2.5 million. *Application contact:* Jody Malm, Administrative Coordinator, 518-276-2808, Fax: 518-276-2344, E-mail: malmj@rpi.edu.

Rosalind Franklin University of Medicine and Science, School of Graduate and Postdoctoral Studies—Interdisciplinary Graduate Program in Biomedical Sciences, Department of Physiology and Biophysics, North Chicago, IL 60064-3095. Offers MS, PhD, MD/PhD. Terminal master's awarded for partial completion of doctoral program. *Degree requirements:* For master's, comprehensive exam, thesis; for doctorate, comprehensive exam, thesis/dissertation. *Entrance requirements:* For master's and doctorate, GRE General Test. Additional exam requirements/recommendations for international students: Required—TOEFL, TWE. *Faculty research:* Membrane transport, mechanisms of cellular regulation, brain metabolism, peptide metabolism.

Simon Fraser University, Graduate Studies, Faculty of Science, Department of Physics, Burnaby, BC V5A 1S6, Canada. Offers biophysics (M Sc, PhD); chemical physics (M Sc, PhD); physics (M Sc, PhD). *Degree requirements:* For master's, thesis; for doctorate, thesis/dissertation. *Entrance requirements:* For master's, minimum GPA of 3.0; for doctorate, minimum GPA of 3.5. Additional exam requirements/recommendations for international students: Required—TOEFL or IELTS. *Faculty research:* Solid-state physics, magnetism, energy research, superconductivity, nuclear physics.

Stanford University, School of Humanities and Sciences, Program in Biophysics, Stanford, CA 94305-9991. Offers PhD. *Degree requirements:* For doctorate, thesis/dissertation, oral exam. *Entrance requirements:* For doctorate, GRE General Test, GRE Subject Test. Additional exam requirements/recommendations for international students: Required—TOEFL. Electronic applications accepted. *Expenses:* Tuition: Full-time $38,700; part-time $860 per unit. One-time fee: $200 full-time.

Stony Brook University, State University of New York, Stony Brook University Medical Center, School of Medicine and Graduate School, Graduate Programs in Medicine, Department of Physiology and Biophysics, Stony Brook, NY 11794. Offers PhD. *Faculty:* 16 full-time (5 women). *Students:* 11 full-time (6 women); includes 1 Black or African American, non-Hispanic/

Latino, 4 international. Average age 29. 46 applicants, 33% accepted. In 2010, 2 doctorates awarded. *Degree requirements:* For doctorate, comprehensive exam, thesis/dissertation. *Entrance requirements:* For doctorate, GRE General Test, GRE Subject Test, BS in related field, minimum GPA of 3.0. Additional exam requirements/recommendations for international students: Required—TOEFL. *Application deadline:* For fall admission, 1/15 for domestic students. Application fee: $100. *Expenses:* Tuition, state resident: full-time $8370; part-time $349 per credit. Tuition, nonresident: full-time $13,780; part-time $574 per credit. Required fees: $994. *Financial support:* In 2010–11, 10 research assistantships, 1 teaching assistantship were awarded; fellowships, Federal Work-Study also available. Financial award application deadline: 3/15. *Faculty research:* Cellular electrophysiology, membrane permeation and transport, metabolic endocrinology. Total annual research expenditures: $5.1 million. *Unit head:* Dr. Peter Brink, Chair, 631-444-2299, Fax: 631-444-3432, E-mail: peter.brink@stonybrook.edu. *Application contact:* Dr. Raafat El-Maghrabi, Graduate Program Director, 631-444-3049, Fax: 631-444-3432, E-mail: raafat.el-maghrabi@stonybrook.edu.

Syracuse University, College of Arts and Sciences, Program in Structural Biology, Biochemistry and Biophysics, Syracuse, NY 13244. Offers PhD. *Students:* 6 full-time (4 women), 1 part-time (0 women); includes 1 minority (Black or African American, non-Hispanic/Latino), 4 international. Average age 30. 10 applicants, 0% accepted, 0 enrolled. In 2010, 2 doctorates awarded. *Degree requirements:* For doctorate, thesis/dissertation, exam. *Entrance requirements:* For doctorate, GRE General Test, GRE Subject Test. Additional exam requirements/recommendations for international students: Required—TOEFL (minimum score 100 iBT). *Application deadline:* For fall admission, 1/10 priority date for domestic and international students. Application fee: $75. Electronic applications accepted. *Expenses:* Tuition: Part-time $1162 per credit. *Financial support:* Fellowships with full tuition reimbursements, research assistantships with full and partial tuition reimbursements, teaching assistantships with full and partial tuition reimbursements, tuition waivers available. Financial award application deadline: 1/1; financial award applicants required to submit FAFSA. *Unit head:* Scott Pitnick, Director, 315-443-5128, Fax: 315-443-2012, E-mail: sspitnic@syr.edu. *Application contact:* Evelyn Lott, Information Contact, 315-443-9154, Fax: 315-443-2012, E-mail: ealott@syr.edu.

Texas A&M University, College of Agriculture and Life Sciences, Department of Biochemistry and Biophysics, College Station, TX 77843. Offers biochemistry (MS, PhD); biophysics (MS). *Faculty:* 37. *Students:* 144 full-time (55 women), 5 part-time (2 women); includes 20 minority (3 Black or African American, non-Hispanic/Latino; 1 American Indian or Alaska Native, non-Hispanic/Latino; 2 Asian, non-Hispanic/Latino; 13 Hispanic/Latino; 1 Native Hawaiian or other Pacific Islander, non-Hispanic/Latino), 55 international. Average age 27. In 2010, 5 master's, 17 doctorates awarded. *Entrance requirements:* For master's and doctorate, GRE General Test. Additional exam requirements/recommendations for international students: Required—TOEFL. *Application deadline:* For fall admission, 2/1 priority date for domestic students, 12/1 priority date for international students. Applications are processed on a rolling basis. Application fee: $50 ($75 for international students). Electronic applications accepted. *Financial support:* In 2010–11, 6 fellowships with tuition reimbursements (averaging $20,000 per year), 70 research assistantships with partial tuition reimbursements (averaging $20,000 per year) were awarded; teaching assistantships with partial tuition reimbursements, institutionally sponsored loans, scholarships/grants, traineeships, and unspecified assistantships also available. Financial award application deadline: 2/1; financial award applicants required to submit FAFSA. *Faculty research:* Enzymology, gene expression, protein structure, plant biochemistry. *Unit head:* Dr. Gregory D. Reinhart, Department Head, 979-862-2263, Fax: 979-845-9274, E-mail: gdr@tamu.edu. *Application contact:* Pat Swigert, Graduate Advisor, 979-845-1779, Fax: 979-845-9274.

Thomas Jefferson University, Jefferson College of Graduate Studies, Program in Molecular Physiology and Biophysics, Philadelphia, PA 19107. Offers PhD. *Faculty:* 13 full-time (5 women). *Students:* 2 full-time (1 woman). 4 applicants, 0% accepted. *Degree requirements:* For doctorate, comprehensive exam, thesis/dissertation. *Entrance requirements:* For doctorate, GRE General Test, minimum GPA of 3.2. Additional exam requirements/recommendations for international students: Required—TOEFL (minimum score 250 computer-based; 100 iBT). *Application deadline:* For fall admission, 1/15 priority date for domestic and international students. Applications are processed on a rolling basis. Application fee: $50. Electronic applications accepted. *Financial support:* In 2010–11, 2 students received support, including 2 fellowships with full tuition reimbursements available (averaging $52,883 per year); Federal Work-Study, institutionally sponsored loans, scholarships/grants, traineeships, and stipends also available. Support available to part-time students. Financial award application deadline: 5/1; financial award applicants required to submit FAFSA. *Faculty research:* Cardiovascular physiology, smooth muscle physiology, pathophysiology of myocardial ischemia, endothelial cell physiology, molecular biology of ion channel physiology. Total annual research expenditures: $3.2 million. *Unit head:* Dr. Thomas M. Butler, Program Director, 215-503-6583, E-mail: thomas.butler@jefferson.edu. *Application contact:* Marc E. Stearns, Director of Admissions, 215-503-0155, Fax: 215-503-9920, E-mail: jcgs-info@jefferson.edu.

Université de Sherbrooke, Faculty of Medicine and Health Sciences, Graduate Programs in Medicine, Department of Physiology and Biophysics, Sherbrooke, QC J1H 5N4, Canada. Offers M Sc, PhD. Terminal master's awarded for partial completion of doctoral program. *Degree requirements:* For master's, thesis; for doctorate, thesis/dissertation. Electronic applications accepted. *Faculty research:* Ion channels, neurological basis of pain, insulin resistance, obesity.

Université du Québec à Trois-Rivières, Graduate Programs, Program in Biophysics and Cellular Biology, Trois-Rivières, QC G9A 5H7, Canada. Offers M Sc, PhD. Part-time programs available. *Degree requirements:* For master's, thesis; for doctorate, thesis/dissertation. *Entrance requirements:* For master's, appropriate bachelor's degree, proficiency in French; for doctorate, appropriate master's degree, proficiency in French.

University at Buffalo, the State University of New York, Graduate School, Graduate Programs in Cancer Research and Biomedical Sciences at Roswell Park Cancer Institute, Department of Molecular and Cellular Biophysics and Biochemistry at Roswell Park Cancer Institute, Buffalo, NY 14260. Offers PhD. *Faculty:* 25 full-time (3 women). *Students:* 17 full-time (10 women), 1 part-time (0 women); includes 2 Black or African American, non-Hispanic/Latino; 1 Asian, non-Hispanic/Latino, 8 international. Average age 25. 20 applicants, 40% accepted, 4 enrolled. In 2010, 3 doctorates awarded. *Degree requirements:* For doctorate, comprehensive exam, thesis/dissertation. *Entrance requirements:* For doctorate, GRE General Test. Additional exam requirements/recommendations for international students: Required—TOEFL (minimum score 600 paper-based; 250 computer-based; 100 iBT). *Application deadline:* For fall admission, 2/1 priority date for domestic students. Applications are processed on a rolling basis. Application fee: $50. Electronic applications accepted. *Financial support:* In 2010–11, 4 fellowships with full tuition reimbursements (averaging $24,000 per year), 21 research assistantships with full tuition reimbursements (averaging $24,000 per year) were awarded; Federal Work-Study, institutionally sponsored loans, and health care benefits also available. Financial award application deadline: 2/1; financial award applicants required to submit FAFSA. *Faculty research:* MRI research, structural and function of biomolecules, photodynamic therapy, DNA damage and repair, heat-shock proteins and vaccine research. Total annual research expenditures: $5.5 million. *Unit head:* Dr. Eugene Kandel, Director of Graduate Studies, 716-845-3530, E-mail: eugene.kandel@roswellpark.org. *Application contact:* Craig R. Johnson, Director of Admissions, 716-845-2339, Fax: 716-845-8178, E-mail: craig.johnson@roswellpark.org.

University at Buffalo, the State University of New York, Graduate School, School of Medicine and Biomedical Sciences, Graduate Programs in Medicine and Biomedical Sciences, Department of Physiology and Biophysics, Buffalo, NY 14260. Offers biophysics (MS, PhD); physiology (MA, PhD). Terminal master's awarded for partial completion of doctoral program. *Degree requirements:* For master's, thesis, oral exam, project; for doctorate, thesis/dissertation, oral and written qualifying exam or 2 research proposals. *Entrance requirements:*

For master's and doctorate, GRE General Test. Additional exam requirements/recommendations for international students: Required—TOEFL (minimum score 600 paper-based; 250 computer-based; 100 iBT). Electronic applications accepted. *Faculty research:* Neurosciences, ion channels, cardiac physiology, renal/epithelial transport, cardiopulmonary exercise.

University of Arkansas for Medical Sciences, Graduate School, Graduate Programs in Biomedical Sciences, Department of Physiology and Biophysics, Little Rock, AR 72205-7199. Offers MS, PhD, MD/PhD. *Degree requirements:* For master's, thesis; for doctorate, thesis/dissertation. *Entrance requirements:* For master's and doctorate, GRE General Test. Additional exam requirements/recommendations for international students: Required—TOEFL. *Faculty research:* Gene transcription, protein targeting, membrane biology, cell-cell communication.

University of California, Berkeley, Graduate Division, College of Letters and Science, Group in Biophysics, Berkeley, CA 94720-1500. Offers PhD. *Degree requirements:* For doctorate, thesis/dissertation, qualifying exam. *Entrance requirements:* For doctorate, GRE General Test, minimum GPA of 3.0, 3 letters of recommendation.

University of California, Davis, Graduate Studies, Graduate Group in Biophysics, Davis, CA 95616. Offers MS, PhD. *Degree requirements:* For doctorate, thesis/dissertation. *Entrance requirements:* For master's and doctorate, GRE General Test, GRE Subject Test. Additional exam requirements/recommendations for international students: Required—TOEFL (minimum score 550 paper-based; 213 computer-based). Electronic applications accepted. *Faculty research:* Molecular structure, protein structure/function relationships, spectroscopy.

University of California, Irvine, School of Medicine and School of Biological Sciences, Department of Physiology and Biophysics, Irvine, CA 92697. Offers biological sciences (PhD); MD/PhD. Students apply through the Graduate Program in Molecular Biology, Genetics, and Biochemistry. *Students:* 11 full-time (6 women); includes 5 minority (4 Asian, non-Hispanic/Latino; 1 Hispanic/Latino). Average age 28. In 2010, 1 doctorate awarded. *Degree requirements:* For doctorate, thesis/dissertation. *Entrance requirements:* For doctorate, GRE General Test, GRE Subject Test, minimum GPA of 3.0. Additional exam requirements/recommendations for international students: Required—TOEFL (minimum score 550 paper-based; 213 computer-based). *Application deadline:* For fall admission, 1/15 priority date for domestic students, 1/15 for international students. Application fee: $80 ($100 for international students). Electronic applications accepted. *Financial support:* Fellowships, research assistantships with full tuition reimbursements, teaching assistantships, institutionally sponsored loans, traineeships, health care benefits, and unspecified assistantships available. Financial award application deadline: 3/1; financial award applicants required to submit FAFSA. *Faculty research:* Membrane physiology, exercise physiology, regulation of hormone biosynthesis and action, endocrinology, ion channels and signal transduction. *Unit head:* Prof. Michael Cahalan, Chairman, 949-824-7776, Fax: 949-824-3143, E-mail: mcahalan@uci.edu. *Application contact:* Vicki C. Ledray, Chief Administrative Officer, 949-824-5865, Fax: 949-824-0019, E-mail: ledray@uci.edu.

University of California, San Diego, Office of Graduate Studies, Department of Physics, La Jolla, CA 92093. Offers biophysics (MS, PhD); physics (MS, PhD); physics/materials physics (MS). *Degree requirements:* For doctorate, thesis/dissertation. *Entrance requirements:* For master's and doctorate, GRE General Test, GRE Subject Test. Additional exam requirements/recommendations for international students: Required—TOEFL. Electronic applications accepted.

University of California, San Francisco, School of Pharmacy and School of Medicine, Graduate Group in Biophysics, San Francisco, CA 94143. Offers PhD. *Faculty:* 44 full-time (11 women). *Students:* 46 full-time (15 women); includes 7 Asian, non-Hispanic/Latino; 4 Hispanic/Latino, 5 international. Average age 25. 140 applicants, 20% accepted, 8 enrolled. In 2010, 6 doctorates awarded. *Degree requirements:* For doctorate, thesis/dissertation. *Entrance requirements:* For doctorate, GRE General Test; GRE Subject Test (recommended). Additional exam requirements/recommendations for international students: Required—TOEFL. *Application deadline:* For fall admission, 12/1 for domestic students. Application fee: $70 ($90 for international students). Electronic applications accepted. *Financial support:* In 2010–11, fellowships with full tuition reimbursements (averaging $29,500 per year), research assistantships with full tuition reimbursements (averaging $29,500 per year) were awarded; traineeships, health care benefits, tuition waivers (full), unspecified assistantships, and stipends also available. *Faculty research:* Structural and computational biology; proteomic, genomic, and cell biology; chemistry; systems biology. *Unit head:* Dr. Matthew Jacobson, Program Director, 415-514-9881, E-mail: matt.jacobson@ucsf.edu. *Application contact:* Rebecca Brown, Program Administrator, 415-514-0249, Fax: 415-514-0502, E-mail: rbrown@cgl.ucsf.edu.

University of California, Santa Barbara, Graduate Division, College of Letters and Sciences, Division of Mathematics, Life, and Physical Sciences, Interdepartmental Graduate Program in Biomolecular Science and Engineering, Santa Barbara, CA 93106-2014. Offers biochemistry and molecular biology (PhD), including biochemistry and molecular biology, biophysics and bioengineering. *Faculty:* 37 full-time (4 women), 1 (woman) part-time/adjunct. *Students:* 30 full-time (13 women); includes 4 Asian, non-Hispanic/Latino. Average age 28. 59 applicants, 22% accepted, 4 enrolled. In 2010, 5 doctorates awarded. Terminal master's awarded for partial completion of doctoral program. *Degree requirements:* For doctorate, thesis/dissertation. *Entrance requirements:* For doctorate, GRE General Test. Additional exam requirements/recommendations for international students: Required—TOEFL (minimum score 630 paper-based; 109 iBT), IELTS (minimum score 7). *Application deadline:* For fall admission, 12/15 for domestic and international students. Application fee: $70 ($90 for international students). Electronic applications accepted. *Financial support:* In 2010–11, 30 students received support, including 16 fellowships with full and partial tuition reimbursements available (averaging $11,321 per year), 31 research assistantships with full and partial tuition reimbursements available (averaging $14,777 per year), 16 teaching assistantships with full and partial tuition reimbursements available (averaging $6,307 per year); Federal Work-Study, traineeships, health care benefits, tuition waivers (full and partial), and unspecified assistantships also available. Financial award application deadline: 12/15; financial award applicants required to submit FAFSA. *Faculty research:* Biochemistry and molecular biology, biophysics, biomaterials, bioengineering, systems biology. *Unit head:* Prof. Philip A. Pincus, Director/Professor, 805-893-4685, E-mail: fyl@mrl.ucsb.edu. *Application contact:* Prof. Philip A. Pincus, Director/Professor, 805-893-4685, E-mail: fyl@mrl.ucsb.edu.

University of Chicago, Division of the Physical Sciences, Graduate Program in Biophysical Science, Chicago, IL 60637-1513. Offers PhD. *Degree requirements:* For doctorate, comprehensive exam, thesis/dissertation, ethics class, 2 teaching assistantships. *Entrance requirements:* Additional exam requirements/recommendations for international students: Required—IELTS (minimum score 7); Recommended—TOEFL (minimum score 600 paper-based; 250 computer-based; 104 iBT). Electronic applications accepted.

University of Cincinnati, Graduate School, College of Medicine, Graduate Programs in Biomedical Sciences, Department of Pharmacology and Cell Biophysics, Cincinnati, OH 45221. Offers cell biophysics (PhD); pharmacology (PhD). *Degree requirements:* For doctorate, thesis/dissertation, qualifying exam. *Entrance requirements:* For doctorate, GRE General Test. Additional exam requirements/recommendations for international students: Required—TOEFL. Electronic applications accepted. *Faculty research:* Lipoprotein research, enzyme regulation, electrophysiology, gene actuation.

University of Connecticut, Graduate School, College of Liberal Arts and Sciences, Department of Molecular and Cell Biology, Field of Biophysics and Structural Biology, Storrs, CT 06269. Offers MS, PhD. Terminal master's awarded for partial completion of doctoral program. *Degree requirements:* For master's, comprehensive exam; for doctorate, thesis/dissertation. *Entrance requirements:* For master's and doctorate, GRE General Test, GRE Subject Test. Additional exam requirements/recommendations for international students: Required—TOEFL (minimum score 550 paper-based; 213 computer-based). Electronic applications accepted.

University of Guelph, Graduate Studies, Biophysics Interdepartmental Group, Guelph, ON N1G 2W1, Canada. Offers M Sc, PhD. *Degree requirements:* For master's, thesis; for doctorate,

Biophysics

University of Guelph (continued)
comprehensive exam, thesis/dissertation. *Entrance requirements:* For master's, minimum B average during previous 2 years of course work; for doctorate, minimum B+ average. Additional exam requirements/recommendations for international students: Required—TOEFL (minimum score 550 paper-based; 213 computer-based). Electronic applications accepted. *Faculty research:* Molecular, cellular, structural, and computational biophysics.

University of Guelph, Graduate Studies, College of Biological Science, Department of Molecular and Cellular Biology, Guelph, ON N1G 2W1, Canada. Offers biochemistry (M Sc, PhD); biophysics (M Sc, PhD); botany (M Sc, PhD); microbiology (M Sc, PhD); molecular biology and genetics (M Sc, PhD). *Degree requirements:* For master's, thesis, research proposal; for doctorate, comprehensive exam, thesis/dissertation, research proposal. *Entrance requirements:* For master's, minimum B-average during previous 2 years of coursework; for doctorate, minimum A-average. Additional exam requirements/recommendations for international students: Required—TOEFL (minimum score 550 paper-based; 213 computer-based), IELTS (minimum score 6.5). Electronic applications accepted. *Faculty research:* Physiology, structure, genetics, and ecology of microbes; virology and microbial technology.

University of Illinois at Chicago, College of Medicine and Graduate College, Graduate Programs in Medicine, Department of Physiology and Biophysics, Chicago, IL 60607-7128. Offers MS, PhD. Terminal master's awarded for partial completion of doctoral program. *Degree requirements:* For master's, thesis; for doctorate, thesis/dissertation. *Entrance requirements:* For master's and doctorate, GRE General Test. Additional exam requirements/recommendations for international students: Required—TOEFL. Electronic applications accepted. *Faculty research:* Neuroscience, endocrinology and reproduction, cell physiology, exercise physiology, NMR.

University of Illinois at Urbana–Champaign, Graduate College, College of Liberal Arts and Sciences, School of Molecular and Cellular Biology, Center for Biophysics and Computational Biology, Champaign, IL 61820. Offers MS, PhD. *Students:* 67 full-time (12 women), 1 (woman) part-time; includes 9 minority (6 Asian, non-Hispanic/Latino; 2 Hispanic/Latino; 1 Two or more races, non-Hispanic/Latino), 42 international. 74 applicants, 14% accepted, 10 enrolled. In 2010, 12 doctorates awarded. *Entrance requirements:* For doctorate, GRE, minimum GPA of 3.0. Additional exam requirements/recommendations for international students: Required—TOEFL. *Application deadline:* Applications are processed on a rolling basis. Application fee: $75 ($90 for international students). Electronic applications accepted. *Financial support:* In 2010–11, 12 fellowships, 59 research assistantships, 22 teaching assistantships were awarded; tuition waivers (full and partial) also available. *Unit head:* Martin Gruebele, Director, 217-333-1624, Fax: 217-244-3186, E-mail: mgruebel@illinois.edu. *Application contact:* Cynthia Dodds, Office Administrator, 217-333-1630, Fax: 217-244-6615, E-mail: dodds@illinois.edu.

The University of Iowa, Roy J. and Lucille A. Carver College of Medicine and Graduate College, Graduate Programs in Medicine, Department of Molecular Physiology and Biophysics, Iowa City, IA 52242-1316. Offers MS, PhD. *Faculty:* 17 full-time (3 women), 16 part-time/adjunct (2 women). *Students:* 20 full-time (6 women); includes 3 Asian, non-Hispanic/Latino, 3 international. Average age 25. 8 applicants, 100% accepted, 8 enrolled. In 2010, 1 master's, 8 doctorates awarded. Terminal master's awarded for partial completion of doctoral program. *Degree requirements:* For master's, comprehensive exam; for doctorate, comprehensive exam, thesis/dissertation, teaching experience. *Entrance requirements:* For master's, GRE; for doctorate, GRE General Test, minimum GPA of 3.0. Additional exam requirements/recommendations for international students: Required—TOEFL. *Application deadline:* For fall admission, 4/1 for domestic students, 3/1 for international students; for spring admission, 10/1 for domestic students, 9/1 for international students. Applications are processed on a rolling basis. Application fee: $60 ($80 for international students). Electronic applications accepted. *Financial support:* In 2010–11, 4 fellowships with full tuition reimbursements (averaging $24,250 per year), 13 research assistantships with full tuition reimbursements (averaging $24,250 per year) were awarded; traineeships also available. Financial award application deadline: 4/1. *Faculty research:* Cellular and molecular endocrinology, membrane structure and function, cardiac cell electrophysiology, regulation of gene expression, neurophysiology. *Unit head:* Dr. Kevin P. Campbell, Head, 319-335-7800, Fax: 319-335-7330, E-mail: kevin-campbell@uiowa.edu. *Application contact:* Dr. Michael Anderson, Director of Graduate Studies, 319-335-7839, Fax: 319-335-7330, E-mail: michael-g-anderson@uiowa.edu.

The University of Kansas, Graduate Studies, College of Liberal Arts and Sciences, Department of Molecular Biosciences, Lawrence, KS 66044. Offers biochemistry and biophysics (MA, PhD); microbiology (MA, PhD); molecular, cellular, and developmental biology (MA, PhD). *Faculty:* 34. *Students:* 65 full-time (31 women), 1 part-time (0 women); includes 7 minority (2 Asian, non-Hispanic/Latino; 4 Hispanic/Latino; 1 Two or more races, non-Hispanic/Latino), 24 international. Average age 27. 34 applicants, 47% accepted, 10 enrolled. In 2010, 1 master's, 5 doctorates awarded. Terminal master's awarded for partial completion of doctoral program. *Degree requirements:* For master's, comprehensive exam, thesis; for doctorate, comprehensive exam, thesis/dissertation. *Entrance requirements:* For master's and doctorate, GRE General Test. Additional exam requirements/recommendations for international students: Required—TOEFL (minimum score 24 iBT), OR IELTS Speaking: 8. *Application deadline:* For fall admission, 12/15 for domestic and international students. Application fee: $55 ($65 for international students). Electronic applications accepted. *Expenses:* Tuition, state resident: full-time $7092; part-time $295.50 per credit hour. Tuition, nonresident: full-time $16,590; part-time $691.25 per credit hour. Required fees: $858; $71.49 per credit hour. Tuition and fees vary according to course load, campus/location and program. *Financial support:* Fellowships with tuition reimbursements, research assistantships with tuition reimbursements, teaching assistantships with tuition reimbursements, health care benefits and unspecified assistantships available. Financial award application deadline: 3/1. *Faculty research:* Structure and function of proteins, genetics of organism development, molecular genetics, neurophysiology, molecular virology and pathogenics, developmental biology, cell biology. *Unit head:* Dr. Mark Richter, Chair, 785-864-3334, Fax: 785-864-5294, E-mail: richter@ku.edu. *Application contact:* John P. Connolly, Graduate Program Assistant, 785-864-4311, Fax: 785-864-5294, E-mail: jconnolly@ku.edu.

University of Louisville, School of Medicine, Department of Physiology and Biophysics, Louisville, KY 40292-0001. Offers MS, PhD, MD/PhD. *Faculty:* 23 full-time (0 women). *Students:* 31 full-time (17 women), 6 part-time (1 woman); includes 6 Black or African American, non-Hispanic/Latino; 4 Asian, non-Hispanic/Latino; 1 Hispanic/Latino; 1 Two or more races, non-Hispanic/Latino, 6 international. Average age 27. 36 applicants, 58% accepted, 18 enrolled. In 2010, 13 master's, 8 doctorates awarded. Terminal master's awarded for partial completion of doctoral program. *Degree requirements:* For master's, thesis; for doctorate, comprehensive exam, thesis/dissertation. *Entrance requirements:* For master's and doctorate, GRE General Test (minimum score of 1000 verbal and quantitative), minimum GPA of 3.0. Additional exam requirements/recommendations for international students: Required—TOEFL. *Application deadline:* For fall admission, 1/15 priority date for domestic students. Applications are processed on a rolling basis. Application fee: $50. Electronic applications accepted. *Expenses:* Tuition, state resident: full-time $9144; part-time $508 per credit hour. Tuition, nonresident: full-time $19,026; part-time $1057 per credit hour. Tuition and fees vary according to program and reciprocity agreements. *Financial support:* Fellowships with full tuition reimbursements, research assistantships with full tuition reimbursements available. Financial award application deadline: 4/15. *Faculty research:* Control of microvascular function during normal and disease states; mechanisms of cellular adhesive interactions on endothelial cells lining blood vessels; changes in blood rheological properties and mechanisms associated with increased blood fibrinogen content; role of nutrition in microvascular control mechanisms; mechanism of cardiovascular-renal remodeling in hypertension, diabetes, and heart failure. *Unit head:* Dr. Irving G. Joshua, Chair, 502-852-5371, Fax: 502-852-6239, E-mail: igjosh01@gwise.louisville.edu. *Application contact:* Dr. William Wead, Director of Admissions, 502-852-7571, Fax: 502-852-6849, E-mail: wbwead01@gwise.louisville.edu.

The University of Manchester, School of Physics and Astronomy, Manchester, United Kingdom. Offers astronomy and astrophysics (M Sc, PhD); biological physics (M Sc, PhD); condensed matter physics (M Sc, PhD); nonlinear and liquid crystals physics (M Sc, PhD); nuclear physics (M Sc, PhD); particle physics (M Sc, PhD); photon physics (M Sc, PhD); physics (M Sc, PhD); theoretical physics (M Sc, PhD).

University of Maryland, College Park, Academic Affairs, College of Computer, Mathematical and Natural Sciences, Institute for Physical Science and Technology, Program in Biophysics, College Park, MD 20742. Offers PhD. *Students:* 8 full-time (3 women), 1 (woman) part-time, 7 international. 18 applicants, 56% accepted, 2 enrolled. *Application deadline:* For fall admission, 1/15 for domestic and international students. Application fee: $75. *Expenses:* Tuition, state resident: part-time $471 per credit hour. Tuition, nonresident: part-time $1016 per credit hour. Required fees: $337 per term. *Financial support:* In 2010–11, 3 research assistantships (averaging $19,094 per year), 6 teaching assistantships (averaging $17,532 per year) were awarded; Federal Work-Study and scholarships/grants also available. Support available to part-time students. Financial award applicants required to submit FAFSA. *Unit head:* Dr. Devarajan Thirumalai, Director, 301-405-4803. *Application contact:* Dr. Charles A. Caramello, Dean of the Graduate School, 301-405-0376.

University of Miami, Graduate School, Miller School of Medicine, Graduate Programs in Medicine, Department of Physiology and Biophysics, Coral Gables, FL 33124. Offers PhD, MD/PhD. *Degree requirements:* For doctorate, thesis/dissertation, qualifying exam. *Entrance requirements:* For doctorate, GRE General Test, minimum GPA of 3.0 in sciences. Additional exam requirements/recommendations for international students: Required—TOEFL. *Faculty research:* Cell and membrane physiology, cell-to-cell communication, molecular neurobiology, neuroimmunology, neural development.

University of Michigan, Rackham Graduate School, College of Literature, Science, and the Arts, Department of Biophysics, Ann Arbor, MI 48109. Offers PhD. *Faculty:* 43 full-time (7 women). *Students:* 34 full-time (11 women); includes 2 Black or African American, non-Hispanic/Latino; 4 Asian, non-Hispanic/Latino; 2 Hispanic/Latino, 9 international. Average age 22. 41 applicants, 20% accepted, 4 enrolled. In 2010, 2 doctorates awarded. *Degree requirements:* For doctorate, thesis/dissertation, oral defense of dissertation, preliminary exam. *Entrance requirements:* For doctorate, GRE General Test, GRE Subject Test. Additional exam requirements/recommendations for international students: Required—TOEFL. *Application deadline:* For fall admission, 1/11 for domestic students, 1/10 for international students. Application fee: $65 ($75 for international students). Electronic applications accepted. *Expenses:* Tuition, state resident: full-time $17,784; part-time $1116 per credit hour. Tuition, nonresident: full-time $35,944; part-time $2125 per credit hour. International tuition: $35,994 full-time. Required fees: $95 per semester. Tuition and fees vary according to course load, degree level and program. *Financial support:* In 2010–11, 14 fellowships with full tuition reimbursements (averaging $26,000 per year), 6 research assistantships with full tuition reimbursements (averaging $26,000 per year), teaching assistantships with full tuition reimbursements (averaging $26,000 per year) were awarded; scholarships/grants, traineeships, health care benefits, and unspecified assistantships also available. Financial award application deadline: 3/15. *Faculty research:* Structural biology, computational biophysics, physical chemistry, cellular biophysics. *Unit head:* Dr. Jens-Christian Meiners, Program Director, 734-764-1146, E-mail: meiners@umich.edu. *Application contact:* Sara Grosky, Student Services Administrator, 734-763-6722, E-mail: saramin@umich.edu.

University of Minnesota, Duluth, Medical School, Department of Biochemistry, Molecular Biology and Biophysics, Duluth, MN 55812-2496. Offers biochemistry, molecular biology and biophysics (MS); biology and biophysics (PhD); social, administrative, and clinical pharmacy (MS, PhD); toxicology (MS, PhD). *Faculty:* 10 full-time (3 women). *Students:* 16 full-time (5 women); includes 3 Asian, non-Hispanic/Latino. Average age 29. 7 applicants, 29% accepted, 2 enrolled. In 2010, 1 master's, 1 doctorate awarded. Terminal master's awarded for partial completion of doctoral program. *Degree requirements:* For master's, comprehensive exam, thesis; for doctorate, comprehensive exam, thesis/dissertation. *Entrance requirements:* For master's and doctorate, GRE General Test. Additional exam requirements/recommendations for international students: Required—TOEFL. *Application deadline:* For winter admission, 1/3 for domestic students, 1/2 for international students; for spring admission, 3/15 priority date for domestic and international students. Application fee: $75 ($95 for international students). Electronic applications accepted. *Financial support:* In 2010–11, 8 students received support, including research assistantships with full tuition reimbursements available (averaging $27,300 per year), teaching assistantships with full tuition reimbursements available (averaging $27,300 per year); career-related internships or fieldwork, scholarships/grants, health care benefits, and unspecified assistantships also available. Financial award application deadline: 9/1. *Faculty research:* Intestinal cancer biology; hepatotoxins and mitochondriopathies; toxicology; cell cycle regulation in stem cells; neurobiology of brain development, trace metal function and blood-brain barrier; hibernation biology. Total annual research expenditures: $1.5 million. *Unit head:* Dr. Lester R. Drewes, Professor/Head, 218-726-7925, Fax: 218-726-8014, E-mail: ldrewes@d.umn.edu. *Application contact:* Cheryl Beeman, Executive Office and Administrative Assistant, 218-726-6354, Fax: 218-726-8014, E-mail: ahcd@d.umn.edu.

University of Minnesota, Twin Cities Campus, Graduate School, College of Biological Sciences, Biochemistry, Molecular Biology and Biophysics Graduate Program, Minneapolis, MN 55455-0213. Offers PhD. *Degree requirements:* For doctorate, thesis/dissertation. *Entrance requirements:* For doctorate, GRE, 3 letters of recommendation, more than 1 semester of laboratory experience. Additional exam requirements/recommendations for international students: Required—TOEFL (minimum score 625 paper-based; 263 computer-based; 108 iBT with writing subsection 25 and reading subsection 25) or IELTS (minimum score 7). Electronic applications accepted. *Faculty research:* Microbial biochemistry, biotechnology, molecular biology, regulatory biochemistry, structural biology and biophysics, physical biochemistry, enzymology, physiological chemistry.

University of Minnesota, Twin Cities Campus, Graduate School, Program in Biophysical Sciences and Medical Physics, Minneapolis, MN 55455-0213. Offers MS, PhD. Part-time programs available. *Degree requirements:* For master's, thesis optional, research paper, oral exam; for doctorate, thesis/dissertation, oral/written preliminary exam, oral final exam. *Faculty research:* Theoretical biophysics, radiological physics, cellular and molecular biophysics.

University of Mississippi Medical Center, School of Graduate Studies in the Health Sciences, Department of Physiology and Biophysics, Jackson, MS 39216-4505. Offers MS, PhD, MD/PhD. *Degree requirements:* For master's, thesis; for doctorate, thesis/dissertation, first authored publication. *Entrance requirements:* For master's and doctorate, GRE General Test, minimum GPA of 3.0. *Faculty research:* Cardiovascular, renal, endocrine, and cellular neurophysiology; molecular physiology.

University of Missouri–Kansas City, School of Biological Sciences, Program in Cell Biology and Biophysics, Kansas City, MO 64110-2499. Offers PhD. Offered through the School of Graduate Studies. *Faculty:* 42 full-time (11 women). *Students:* 14 full-time (10 women), 27 part-time (15 women); includes 6 minority (3 Black or African American, non-Hispanic/Latino; 2 Asian, non-Hispanic/Latino; 1 Hispanic/Latino). Average age 32. 56 applicants, 52% accepted, 25 enrolled. *Degree requirements:* For doctorate, comprehensive exam, thesis/dissertation. *Entrance requirements:* For doctorate, GRE General Test, bachelor's degree in chemistry, biology or related field; minimum GPA of 3.0. Additional exam requirements/recommendations for international students: Required—TOEFL (minimum score 550 paper-based; 213 computer-based; 80 iBT). *Application deadline:* For fall admission, 2/15 priority date for domestic and international students. Applications are processed on a rolling basis. Application fee: $45 ($50 for international students). Electronic applications accepted. *Expenses:* Tuition, state resident: full-time $5522; part-time $306.80 per credit hour. Tuition, nonresident: full-time $7128; part-time $792 per credit hour. Required fees: $261.15 per term. *Financial support:* Fellowships with full tuition reimbursements, research assistantships with full tuition reimbursements, teaching assistantships with full and partial tuition reimbursements, scholarships/grants, tuition waivers (full and partial), and unspecified assistantships available. Financial award application deadline: 3/1; financial award applicants required to submit FAFSA. *Unit head:* Dr. Theodore White,

Head, 816-235-2538, E-mail: sbsgradrecruit@umkc.edu. *Application contact:* Laura Batenic, Information Contact, 816-235-2352, Fax: 816-235-5158, E-mail: batenicl@umkc.edu.

See Display on page 195 and Close-Up on page 235.

University of New Mexico, Graduate School, College of Arts and Sciences, Department of Physics and Astronomy, Albuquerque, NM 87131-2039. Offers biomedical physics (MS, PhD); physics (MS, PhD). Part-time programs available. *Faculty:* 48 full-time (5 women), 9 part-time/adjunct (1 woman). *Students:* 78 full-time (16 women), 9 part-time (2 women); includes 2 Black or African American, non-Hispanic/Latino; 1 American Indian or Alaska Native, non-Hispanic/Latino; 4 Asian, non-Hispanic/Latino; 4 Hispanic/Latino; 1 Native Hawaiian or other Pacific Islander, non-Hispanic/Latino, 25 international. Average age 29. 97 applicants, 24% accepted, 19 enrolled. In 2010, 6 master's, 2 doctorates awarded. Terminal master's awarded for partial completion of doctoral program. *Degree requirements:* For master's, comprehensive exam (for some programs), thesis optional, preliminary exams (for non-thesis option); for doctorate, comprehensive exam, thesis/dissertation. *Entrance requirements:* For master's, GRE; for doctorate, GRE General Test; GRE Subject Test (physics). Additional exam requirements/recommendations for international students: Required—TOEFL (minimum score 550 paper-based; 213 computer-based; 80 iBT), IELTS (minimum score 7). *Application deadline:* For fall admission, 1/15 for domestic students, 1/15 priority date for international students; for spring admission, 8/1 for domestic students, 8/1 priority date for international students. Application fee: $50. Electronic applications accepted. *Expenses:* Tuition, state resident: full-time $5991; part-time $251 per credit hour. Tuition, nonresident: full-time $14,405; part-time $800.20 per credit hour. Tuition and fees vary according to course level, course load, program and reciprocity agreements. *Financial support:* In 2010–11, 82 students received support, including 3 fellowships with full tuition reimbursements available (averaging $8,333 per year), 64 research assistantships with full tuition reimbursements available (averaging $16,189 per year), 41 teaching assistantships with full tuition reimbursements available (averaging $7,637 per year); career-related internships or fieldwork, scholarships/grants, traineeships, health care benefits, and unspecified assistantships also available. Support available to part-time students. Financial award application deadline: 2/1; financial award applicants required to submit FAFSA. *Faculty research:* Astronomy and astrophysics, biological physics, condensed-matter physics, nonlinear science and complexity, optics and photonics, quantum information, subatomic physics. Total annual research expenditures: $6 million. *Unit head:* Dr. Bernd Bassalleck, Chair, 505-277-1517, Fax: 505-277-1520, E-mail: bossek@unm.edu. *Application contact:* Alisa Gibson, Program Advisement Coordinator, 505-277-1514, Fax: 505-277-1520, E-mail: agibson@unm.edu.

The University of North Carolina at Chapel Hill, School of Medicine and Graduate School, Graduate Programs in Medicine, Department of Biochemistry and Biophysics, Chapel Hill, NC 27599. Offers MS, PhD. Terminal master's awarded for partial completion of doctoral program. *Degree requirements:* For master's, comprehensive exam, thesis; for doctorate, comprehensive exam, thesis/dissertation. *Entrance requirements:* For master's and doctorate, GRE General Test, GRE Subject Test (recommended), minimum GPA of 3.0. Additional exam requirements/recommendations for international students: Required—TOEFL. Electronic applications accepted.

University of Regina, Faculty of Graduate Studies and Research, Faculty of Science, Department of Chemistry and Biochemistry, Regina, SK S4S 0A2, Canada. Offers analytical/environmental chemistry (M Sc, PhD); biophysics of biological interfaces (M Sc, PhD); enzymology/chemical biology (M Sc, PhD); inorganic/organometallic chemistry (M Sc, PhD); signal transduction and mechanisms of cancer cell regulation (M Sc, PhD); supramolecular organic photochemistry and photophysics (M Sc, PhD); synthetic organic chemistry (M Sc, PhD); theoretical/computational chemistry (M Sc, PhD). *Faculty:* 10 full-time (2 women). *Students:* 19 full-time (9 women), 2 part-time (1 woman). 20 applicants, 40% accepted. In 2010, 2 master's, 1 doctorate awarded. *Degree requirements:* For master's, thesis; for doctorate, thesis/dissertation. *Entrance requirements:* Additional exam requirements/recommendations for international students: Required—TOEFL (minimum score 580 paper-based; 80 iBT). *Application deadline:* Applications are processed on a rolling basis. Application fee: $100. Electronic applications accepted. Tuition and fees charges are reported in Canadian dollars. *Expenses:* Tuition, area resident: Full-time $3245 Canadian dollars; part-time $180.25 Canadian dollars per credit hour. International tuition: $4745 Canadian dollars full-time. Required fees: $494 Canadian dollars; $115.25 Canadian dollars per credit hour. $115.25 Canadian dollars per semester. Tuition and fees vary according to program. *Financial support:* In 2010–11, 3 fellowships (averaging $20,000 per year), 2 research assistantships (averaging $17,250 per year), 8 teaching assistantships (averaging $6,965 per year) were awarded; scholarships/grants also available. Financial award application deadline: 6/15. *Faculty research:* Asymmetric synthesis and methodology, theoretical and computational chemistry, biophysical biochemistry, analytical and environmental chemistry, chemical biology. *Unit head:* Dr. Lynn Mihichuk, Head, 306-585-4793, Fax: 306-337-2409, E-mail: lynn.mihichuk@uregina.ca. *Application contact:* Dr. Tanya Dahms, Graduate Program Coordinator, 306-585-4246, Fax: 306-337-2409, E-mail: tanya.dahms@uregina.ca.

University of Rochester, School of Medicine and Dentistry, Graduate Programs in Medicine and Dentistry, Department of Biochemistry and Biophysics, Programs in Biophysics, Rochester, NY 14627. Offers MS, PhD. Terminal master's awarded for partial completion of doctoral program. *Degree requirements:* For doctorate, thesis/dissertation, qualifying exam. *Entrance requirements:* For master's and doctorate, GRE General Test.

University of Southern California, Keck School of Medicine and Graduate School, Graduate Programs in Medicine, Department of Physiology and Biophysics, Los Angeles, CA 90089. Offers MS, PhD, MD/PhD. *Faculty:* 16 full-time (5 women). *Students:* 7 full-time (3 women); includes 1 Asian, non-Hispanic/Latino, 5 international. Average age 28. 12 applicants, 17% accepted, 1 enrolled.Terminal master's awarded for partial completion of doctoral program. *Degree requirements:* For master's, thesis optional; for doctorate, comprehensive exam, thesis/dissertation. *Entrance requirements:* For master's and doctorate, GRE General Test, minimum GPA of 3.0. Additional exam requirements/recommendations for international students: Required—TOEFL (minimum score 600 paper-based; 250 computer-based; 100 iBT). *Application deadline:* For fall admission, 2/1 priority date for domestic and international students. Application fee: $85. Electronic applications accepted. *Expenses:* Tuition: Full-time $31,240; part-time $1420 per unit. Required fees: $600. One-time fee: $35 full-time. Full-time tuition and fees vary according to degree level and program. *Financial support:* In 2010–11, 1 student received support, including 5 research assistantships with full tuition reimbursements available; Federal Work-Study, institutionally sponsored loans, scholarships/grants, traineeships, health care benefits, and unspecified assistantships also available. Financial award application deadline: 5/5. *Faculty research:* Endocrinology and metabolism, neurophysiology, mathematical modeling, cell transport, autoimmunity and cancer immunotherapy. Total annual research expenditures: $2.1 million. *Unit head:* Dr. Richard N. Bergman, Chair, 323-442-1920, Fax: 323-442-1918, E-mail: rbergman@usc.edu. *Application contact:* Elena Camarena, Graduate Coordinator, 323-442-1039, Fax: 323-442-2283, E-mail: physiol@hsc.usc.edu.

The University of Texas Medical Branch, Graduate School of Biomedical Sciences, Program in Biochemistry and Molecular Biology, Galveston, TX 77555. Offers biochemistry (PhD); bioinformatics (PhD); biophysics (PhD); cell biology (PhD); computational biology (PhD); structural biology (PhD). *Degree requirements:* For doctorate, thesis/dissertation. *Entrance requirements:* Additional exam requirements/recommendations for international students: Required—TOEFL (minimum score 550 paper-based; 213 computer-based). Electronic applications accepted.

University of Toronto, School of Graduate Studies, Life Sciences Division, Department of Medical Biophysics, Toronto, ON M5S 1A1, Canada. Offers M Sc, PhD. *Degree requirements:* For master's, thesis; for doctorate, thesis/dissertation. *Entrance requirements:* For master's, resume, 2 letters of reference; for doctorate, resumé, 2 letters of reference. Additional exam requirements/recommendations for international students: Required—TOEFL (minimum score 620 paper-based; 260 computer-based), TWE (minimum score 5), GRE General Test, GRE Subject Test.

University of Vermont, College of Medicine and Graduate College, Graduate Programs in Medicine, Department of Molecular Physiology and Biophysics, Burlington, VT 05405. Offers MS, PhD, MD/MS, MD/PhD. *Students:* 4 (2 women), 1 international. 8 applicants, 38% accepted, 2 enrolled. *Degree requirements:* For master's, thesis; for doctorate, thesis/dissertation. *Entrance requirements:* For master's and doctorate, GRE General Test. Additional exam requirements/recommendations for international students: Required—TOEFL (minimum score 550 paper-based; 213 computer-based; 80 iBT). *Application deadline:* For fall admission, 4/1 priority date for domestic students, 4/1 for international students. Applications are processed on a rolling basis. Application fee: $40. Electronic applications accepted. *Expenses:* Tuition, state resident: part-time $537 per credit hour. Tuition, nonresident: part-time $1355 per credit hour. *Financial support:* Fellowships, research assistantships, teaching assistantships available. Financial award application deadline: 3/1. *Unit head:* Dr. D. Warshaw, Chairperson, 802-656-2540. *Application contact:* Dr. Terese Ruiz, Coordinator, 802-656-2540.

University of Virginia, School of Medicine, Department of Molecular Physiology and Biological Physics, Charlottesville, VA 22903. Offers biological and physical sciences (MS); physiology (PhD); MD/PhD. *Faculty:* 30 full-time (5 women), 1 part-time/adjunct (0 women). *Students:* 14 full-time (6 women), 1 part-time (0 women); includes 2 Black or African American, non-Hispanic/Latino. Average age 29. In 2010, 21 master's, 1 doctorate awarded. *Entrance requirements:* For doctorate, GRE General Test, GRE Subject Test. Additional exam requirements/recommendations for international students: Required—TOEFL. *Application deadline:* For fall admission, 2/15 for domestic and international students. Applications are processed on a rolling basis. Application fee: $60. Electronic applications accepted. *Financial support:* Fellowships, research assistantships, teaching assistantships available. Financial award applicants required to submit FAFSA. *Unit head:* Dr. Mark Yeager, Chair, 434-924-5108, Fax: 434-982-1616, E-mail: my3r@virginia.edu. *Application contact:* Dr. Mark Yeager, Chair, 434-924-5108, Fax: 434-982-1616, E-mail: my3r@virginia.edu.

University of Virginia, School of Medicine, Interdisciplinary Program in Biophysics, Charlottesville, VA 22908. Offers PhD. *Students:* 16 full-time (4 women); includes 2 Asian, non-Hispanic/Latino, 10 international. Average age 28. In 2010, 5 doctorates awarded. *Degree requirements:* For doctorate, thesis/dissertation, research proposal, oral defense. *Entrance requirements:* For doctorate, GRE General Test, GRE Subject Test (recommended), 2 or more letters of recommendation. Additional exam requirements/recommendations for international students: Required—TOEFL. *Application deadline:* For fall admission, 4/15 for domestic and international students. Applications are processed on a rolling basis. Application fee: $60. Electronic applications accepted. *Financial support:* Fellowships with full tuition reimbursements, research assistantships with full tuition reimbursements, teaching assistantships with full tuition reimbursements, tuition waivers (full) available. Financial award application deadline: 1/15; financial award applicants required to submit FAFSA. *Faculty research:* Structural biology and structural genomics, structural biology of membrane proteins and membrane biophysics, spectroscopy and thermodynamics of macromolecular interactions, high resolution imaging and cell biophysics. *Unit head:* Robert K. Nakamoto, Director, 434-982-6390. *Application contact:* Pam Mullinex, Graduate Program Administrator, 434-243-7248, Fax: 434-982-1616, E-mail: prm8b@virginia.edu.

University of Washington, Graduate School, School of Medicine, Graduate Programs in Medicine, Department of Physiology and Biophysics, Seattle, WA 98195. Offers PhD. *Degree requirements:* For doctorate, thesis/dissertation. *Entrance requirements:* For doctorate, GRE General Test. Additional exam requirements/recommendations for international students: Required—TOEFL (minimum score 580 paper-based; 237 computer-based; 70 iBT). *Faculty research:* Membrane and cell biophysics, neuroendocrinology, cardiovascular and respiratory physiology, systems neurophysiology and behavior, molecular physiology.

The University of Western Ontario, Faculty of Graduate Studies, Biosciences Division, Department of Medical Biophysics, London, ON N6A 5B8, Canada. Offers M Sc, PhD. *Degree requirements:* For master's, thesis; for doctorate, thesis/dissertation. *Entrance requirements:* Additional exam requirements/recommendations for international students: Required—TOEFL. *Faculty research:* Haemodynamics and cardiovascular biomechanics, microcirculation, orthopedic biomechanics, radiobiology, medical imaging.

University of Wisconsin–Madison, Graduate School, Program in Biophysics, Madison, WI 53706-1380. Offers PhD. *Degree requirements:* For doctorate, comprehensive exam, thesis/dissertation. *Entrance requirements:* For doctorate, GRE General Test, minimum GPA of 3.0. Additional exam requirements/recommendations for international students: Required—TOEFL (minimum score 600 paper-based). Electronic applications accepted. *Expenses:* Tuition, state resident: full-time $9887; part-time $617.96 per credit. Tuition, nonresident: full-time $24,054; part-time $1503.40 per credit. Required fees: $67.63 per credit. Tuition and fees vary according to reciprocity agreements. *Faculty research:* NMR spectroscopy, high-speed automated DNA sequencing, x-ray crystallography, neuronal signaling and exocytosis, protein structure.

Vanderbilt University, Graduate School and School of Medicine, Department of Molecular Physiology and Biophysics, Nashville, TN 37240-1001. Offers MS, PhD, MD/PhD. *Faculty:* 38 full-time (11 women). *Students:* 33 full-time (25 women), 9 part-time (3 women); includes 2 Black or African American, non-Hispanic/Latino; 1 American Indian or Alaska Native, non-Hispanic/Latino; 3 Hispanic/Latino; 2 Two or more races, non-Hispanic/Latino. Average age 28. In 2010, 8 doctorates awarded. *Degree requirements:* For doctorate, comprehensive exam, thesis/dissertation, preliminary, qualifying, and final exams. *Entrance requirements:* For doctorate, GRE General Test, GRE Subject Test (recommended). Additional exam requirements/recommendations for international students: Required—TOEFL (minimum score 570 paper-based; 230 computer-based; 88 iBT). *Application deadline:* For fall admission, 1/15 for domestic and international students. Application fee: $0. Electronic applications accepted. *Financial support:* Fellowships with full tuition reimbursements, research assistantships with full tuition reimbursements, Federal Work-Study, institutionally sponsored loans, scholarships/grants, traineeships, health care benefits, and tuition waivers (partial) available. Financial award application deadline: 1/15; financial award applicants required to submit CSS PROFILE or FAFSA. *Faculty research:* Biophysics, cell signaling and gene regulation, human genetics, diabetes and obesity, neuroscience. *Unit head:* Roger Cone, Chair, 615-322-7000, Fax: 615-343-0490. *Application contact:* Michelle Grundy, Assistant Director, 800-373-0675, E-mail: michelle.grundy@vanderbilt.edu.

Vanderbilt University, School of Medicine, Program in Chemical and Physical Biology, Nashville, TN 37240-1001. Offers PhD. *Degree requirements:* For doctorate, comprehensive exam, thesis/dissertation, dissertation defense. *Entrance requirements:* For doctorate, GRE, 3 letters of recommendation, official transcripts. Additional exam requirements/recommendations for international students: Required—TOEFL. *Application deadline:* For fall admission, 1/15 priority date for domestic students, 1/15 for international students. Applications are processed on a rolling basis. Application fee: $0. Electronic applications accepted. *Financial support:* Fellowships with full tuition reimbursements, traineeships, health care benefits, and tuition waivers (full) available. *Faculty research:* Mathematical modeling, enzyme kinetics, structural biology, genomics, proteomics and mass spectrometry. *Unit head:* Dave Piston, Chair, 615-322-7030, Fax: 615-343-0490, E-mail: dave.piston@vanderbilt.edu. *Application contact:* Lindsay Meyers, Education Manager, 615-322-3770, E-mail: lindsay.meyers@vanderbilt.edu.

Washington State University, Graduate School, College of Sciences, School of Molecular Biosciences, Program of Biochemistry and Biophysics, Pullman, WA 99164. Offers MS, PhD. *Faculty:* 23 full-time (5 women), 21 part-time/adjunct (4 women). *Students:* 26 full-time (9 women), 1 (woman) part-time; includes 1 Hispanic/Latino, 12 international. Average age 27. 231 applicants, 18% accepted, 13 enrolled. In 2010, 1 master's, 2 doctorates awarded. Terminal master's awarded for partial completion of doctoral program. *Degree requirements:* For master's, thesis or alternative, oral exam; for doctorate, comprehensive exam, thesis/dissertation, oral exam, written exam. *Entrance requirements:* For master's and doctorate, GRE General Test, minimum GPA of 3.0. Additional exam requirements/recommendations for international students: Required—TOEFL (minimum score 550 paper-based; 213 computer-

Biophysics

Washington State University (continued)

based). *Application deadline:* For fall admission, 12/15 for domestic and international students. Application fee: $50. Electronic applications accepted. *Expenses:* Tuition, state resident: full-time $8552; part-time $443 per credit. Tuition, nonresident: full-time $21,650; part-time $1083 per credit. Required fees: $846. *Financial support:* In 2010–11, 5 fellowships with full tuition reimbursements (averaging $18,384 per year), 11 research assistantships with full tuition reimbursements (averaging $18,384 per year), 10 teaching assistantships with full tuition reimbursements (averaging $18,384 per year) were awarded; career-related internships or fieldwork, Federal Work-Study, institutionally sponsored loans, traineeships, and health care benefits also available. Financial award application deadline: 4/1; financial award applicants required to submit FAFSA. *Faculty research:* Gene regulation, signal transduction, protein export, reproductive biology, DNA repair. Total annual research expenditures: $5.8 million. *Unit head:* Dr. John H. Nilson, Director, 509-335-8724, Fax: 509-335-9688, E-mail: jhn@wsu.edu. *Application contact:* Kelly G. McGovern, 509-335-6424, E-mail: mcgnerk@wsu.edu.

Wright State University, School of Graduate Studies, College of Science and Mathematics, Department of Neuroscience, Cell Biology, and Physiology, Dayton, OH 45435. Offers anatomy (MS); physiology and biophysics (MS). *Degree requirements:* For master's, thesis optional. *Entrance requirements:* Additional exam requirements/recommendations for international students: Required—TOEFL. *Faculty research:* Reproductive cell biology, neurobiology of pain, neurohistochemistry.

Yale University, Graduate School of Arts and Sciences, Department of Molecular Biophysics and Biochemistry, New Haven, CT 06520. Offers PhD. *Degree requirements:* For doctorate, thesis/dissertation. *Entrance requirements:* For doctorate, GRE General Test, GRE Subject Test.

Molecular Biophysics

Baylor College of Medicine, Graduate School of Biomedical Sciences, Program in Structural and Computational Biology and Molecular Biophysics, Houston, TX 77030-3498. Offers PhD, MD/PhD. MD/PhD offered jointly with Rice University and University of Houston. *Faculty:* 83 full-time (10 women). *Students:* 36 full-time (10 women); includes 2 Asian, non-Hispanic/Latino; 1 Hispanic/Latino, 17 international. Average age 28. 78 applicants, 12% accepted, 5 enrolled. In 2010, 6 doctorates awarded. *Degree requirements:* For doctorate, thesis/dissertation, public defense. *Entrance requirements:* For doctorate, GRE General Test, GRE Subject Test (strongly recommended), minimum GPA of 3.0. Additional exam requirements/recommendations for international students: Required—TOEFL. *Application deadline:* For fall admission, 1/1 for domestic students. Application fee: $0. Electronic applications accepted. *Expenses:* Tuition: Full-time $11,000. Required fees: $4900. *Financial support:* In 2010–11, 36 students received support, including 14 fellowships with full tuition reimbursements available (averaging $26,000 per year), 22 research assistantships with full tuition reimbursements available (averaging $26,000 per year); career-related internships or fieldwork, Federal Work-Study, institutionally sponsored loans, health care benefits, and students receive a scholarship unless there are grant funds available to pay tuition also available. Financial award applicants required to submit FAFSA. *Faculty research:* Computational biology, structural biology, biophysics. *Unit head:* Dr. Wah Chiu, Director, 713-798-6985. *Application contact:* Lourdes Fernandez, Graduate Program Administrator, 713-798-6557, Fax: 713-798-6325, E-mail: lourdesf@bcm.edu.

See Close-Up on page 251.

California Institute of Technology, Division of Biology and Division of Chemistry and Chemical Engineering, Biochemistry and Molecular Biophysics Graduate Option, Pasadena, CA 91125-0001. Offers PhD. *Degree requirements:* For doctorate, thesis/dissertation, qualifying exam. *Entrance requirements:* For doctorate, GRE General Test. Additional exam requirements/recommendations for international students: Required—TOEFL. Electronic applications accepted.

California Institute of Technology, Division of Chemistry and Chemical Engineering, Program in Biochemistry and Molecular Biophysics, Pasadena, CA 91125-0001. Offers MS, PhD. *Faculty:* 14 full-time (11 women). *Students:* 51 full-time (18 women); includes 26 minority (2 Black or African American, non-Hispanic/Latino; 15 Asian, non-Hispanic/Latino; 5 Hispanic/Latino; 1 Native Hawaiian or other Pacific Islander, non-Hispanic/Latino; 3 Two or more races, non-Hispanic/Latino). Average age 26. 115 applicants, 22% accepted, 9 enrolled. In 2010, 3 doctorates awarded. Terminal master's awarded for partial completion of doctoral program. *Degree requirements:* For master's, thesis; for doctorate, thesis/dissertation. *Entrance requirements:* For doctorate, GRE. Additional exam requirements/recommendations for international students: Required—TOEFL; Recommended—IELTS, TWE. *Application deadline:* For fall admission, 1/1 for domestic and international students. Application fee: $80. Electronic applications accepted. *Financial support:* In 2010–11, 9 students received support, including 4 fellowships with full tuition reimbursements available (averaging $23,128 per year), 5 research assistantships with full tuition reimbursements available (averaging $23,128 per year), 9 teaching assistantships with full tuition reimbursements available (averaging $4,782 per year); institutionally sponsored loans, scholarships/grants, traineeships, health care benefits, and unspecified assistantships also available. Financial award application deadline: 1/1. *Unit head:* Prof. Douglas C. Rees, Executive Officer, 626-395-8393, Fax: 626-744-9524, E-mail: dcrees@caltech.edu. *Application contact:* Alison Ross, Option Coordinator, 626-395-6446, E-mail: aross@caltech.edu.

Carnegie Mellon University, Mellon College of Science, Joint Pitt + CMU Molecular Biophysics and Structural Biology Graduate Program, Pittsburgh, PA 15213-3891. Offers PhD. Program offered jointly with University of Pittsburgh. *Degree requirements:* For doctorate, comprehensive exam, thesis/dissertation. *Entrance requirements:* For doctorate, GRE General Test. Additional exam requirements/recommendations for international students: Required—TOEFL (minimum score 600 paper-based; 250 computer-based; 100 iBT), IELTS (minimum score 7). Electronic applications accepted. *Faculty research:* Structural biology, protein dynamics and folding, computational biophysics, molecular informatics, membrane biophysics and ion channels, NMR, x-ray crystallography cryaelectron microscopy.

Duke University, Graduate School, Program in Structural Biology and Biophysics, Durham, NC 27710. Offers Certificate. Students must be enrolled in a participating Ph D program (biochemistry, cell biology, chemistry, molecular genetics, neurobiology, pharmacology). *Faculty:* 25 full-time. *Students:* 5 full-time (2 women), 2 international. 31 applicants, 29% accepted, 4 enrolled. *Entrance requirements:* For degree, GRE General Test. Additional exam requirements/recommendations for international students: Required—TOEFL (minimum score 550 paper-based; 213 computer-based; 83 iBT), IELTS (minimum score 7). *Application deadline:* For fall admission, 12/8 priority date for domestic and international students. Application fee: $75. *Financial support:* Application deadline: 12/8. *Unit head:* David Richardson, Director of Graduate Studies, 919-684-6559, Fax: 919-684-8346, E-mail: cmbtgp@biochem.duke.edu. *Application contact:* Elizabeth Hutton, Director of Admissions, 919-684-3913, Fax: 919-684-2277, E-mail: grad-admissions@duke.edu.

Florida State University, The Graduate School, College of Arts and Sciences, Program in Molecular Biophysics, Tallahassee, FL 32306. Offers biochemistry, molecular and cell biology (PhD); computational structural biology (PhD); molecular biophysics (PhD). *Faculty:* 49 full-time (6 women). *Students:* 22 full-time (8 women); includes 5 Asian, non-Hispanic/Latino; 1 Hispanic/Latino. Average age 28. 30 applicants, 33% accepted, 7 enrolled. In 2010, 5 doctorates awarded. *Degree requirements:* For doctorate, comprehensive exam, thesis/dissertation, teaching 1 term in professor's major department. *Entrance requirements:* For doctorate, GRE General Test. Additional exam requirements/recommendations for international students: Required—TOEFL (minimum score 600 paper-based; 250 computer-based; 100 iBT). *Application deadline:* For fall admission, 2/15 for domestic students, 3/15 for international students; for spring admission, 11/2 for international students. Applications are processed on a rolling basis. Application fee: $30. Electronic applications accepted. *Expenses:* Tuition, state resident: full-time $8238. *Financial support:* In 2010–11, 21 students received support, including fellowships with partial tuition reimbursements available (averaging $21,000 per year), 18 research assistantships with partial tuition reimbursements available (averaging $21,000 per year), 4 teaching assistantships with partial tuition reimbursements available (averaging $21,000 per year); scholarships/grants, health care benefits, and unspecified assistantships also available. Financial award applicants required to submit FAFSA. *Faculty research:* Protein and nucleic acid structure and function, membrane protein structure, computational biophysics, 3-D image reconstruction. Total annual research expenditures: $1.4 million. *Unit head:* Dr. Geoffrey Strouse, Director, 850-644-0056, Fax: 850-644-7244, E-mail: strouse@chem.fsu.edu. *Application contact:* Dr. Kerry Maddox, Academic Coordinator, Graduate Programs, 850-644-1012, Fax: 850-644-7244, E-mail: bkmaddox@sb.fsu.edu.

Illinois Institute of Technology, Graduate College, College of Science and Letters, Department of Biological, Chemical and Physical Sciences, Biology Division, Chicago, IL 60616. Offers biochemistry (MBS, MS); biology (PhD); biotechnology (MBS, MS); cell and molecular biology (MBS, MS); microbiology (MB, MS); molecular biochemistry and biophysics (PhD); molecular biology and biophysics (MS). Part-time and evening/weekend programs available. Postbaccalaureate distance learning degree programs offered (minimal on-campus study). *Faculty:* 13 full-time (5 women), 5 part-time/adjunct (2 women). *Students:* 121 full-time (75 women), 56 part-time (37 women); includes 16 minority (5 Black or African American, non-Hispanic/Latino; 5 Asian, non-Hispanic/Latino; 5 Hispanic/Latino; 1 Two or more races, non-Hispanic/Latino), 104 international. Average age 27. 268 applicants, 76% accepted, 62 enrolled. In 2010, 74 master's, 4 doctorates awarded. Terminal master's awarded for partial completion of doctoral program. *Degree requirements:* For master's, comprehensive exam, thesis (for some programs); for doctorate, comprehensive exam, thesis/dissertation. *Entrance requirements:* For master's, GRE General Test (minimum score 1000 Quantitative and Verbal, 2.5 Analytical Writing), minimum undergraduate GPA of 3.0; for doctorate, GRE General Test (minimum score 1200 Quantitative and Verbal, 3.0 Analytical Writing), minimum undergraduate GPA of 3.0. Additional exam requirements/recommendations for international students: Required—TOEFL (minimum score 523 paper-based; 213 computer-based; 70 iBT); Recommended—IELTS (minimum score 5.5). *Application deadline:* For fall admission, 5/1 for domestic and international students; for spring admission, 10/15 for domestic and international students. Applications are processed on a rolling basis. Application fee: $40. Electronic applications accepted. *Expenses:* Tuition: Full-time $18,576; part-time $1032 per credit hour. Required fees: $583 per semester. One-time fee: $150. Tuition and fees vary according to program and student level. *Financial support:* In 2010–11, 15 research assistantships with full and partial tuition reimbursements (averaging $6,379 per year), 14 teaching assistantships with partial tuition reimbursements (averaging $6,296 per year) were awarded; fellowships with full and partial tuition reimbursements, career-related internships or fieldwork, Federal Work-Study, institutionally sponsored loans, scholarships/grants, traineeships, health care benefits, tuition waivers (partial), and unspecified assistantships also available. Support available to part-time students. Financial award applicants required to submit FAFSA. *Faculty research:* Structure and biophysics of macromolecular systems; efficacy and mechanism of action of chemopreventive agents in experimental carcinogenesis of breast, colon, lung and prostate; study of fundamental structural biochemistry problems that have direct links to the understanding and treatment of disease; spectroscopic techniques for the study of multi-domain proteins; molecular mechanisms of cancer and cancer gene therapy. Total annual research expenditures: $2.6 million. *Unit head:* Dr. Benjamin C. Stark, Professor and Associate Chair, 312-567-3488, Fax: 312-567-3494, E-mail: starkb@iit.edu. *Application contact:* Deborah Gibson, Director, Graduate Admissions, 866-472-3448, Fax: 312-567-3138, E-mail: inquiry.grad@iit.edu.

The Johns Hopkins University, School of Medicine, Graduate Programs in Medicine, Program in Molecular Biophysics, Baltimore, MD 21218-2699. Offers MS, PhD. Program held jointly with Zanvyl Krieger School of Arts and Sciences and G. W. C. Whiting School of Engineering. *Faculty:* 48 full-time (10 women). *Students:* 42 full-time (13 women); includes 8 Asian, non-Hispanic/Latino; 4 Hispanic/Latino. Average age 25. 87 applicants, 21% accepted, 9 enrolled. In 2010, 3 master's, 14 doctorates awarded. *Degree requirements:* For doctorate, comprehensive exam, thesis/dissertation, oral exam, thesis defense. *Entrance requirements:* For doctorate, GRE. Additional exam requirements/recommendations for international students: Required—TOEFL (minimum score 600 paper-based; 250 computer-based), IELTS; Recommended—TWE. *Application deadline:* For fall admission, 1/5 for domestic students. Applications are processed on a rolling basis. Application fee: $75. Electronic applications accepted. *Financial support:* In 2010–11, 21 fellowships with full tuition reimbursements (averaging $28,083 per year), 21 research assistantships (averaging $28,083 per year) were awarded; scholarships/grants, traineeships, health care benefits, and tuition waivers (full) also available. *Faculty research:* Protein folding and dynamics; membranes and membrane proteins; structural biology; RNA biophysics; enzymes and metabolic pathways; computation, theory and prediction; DNA protein interactions; single molecule studies; protein design and evolution. *Unit head:* Dr. Juliette Lecomte, Professor and Director, 410-516-7109, Fax: 410-516-4118, E-mail: lecomte_jtj@jhu.edu. *Application contact:* Ranice H. Crosby, Administrative Coordinator, 410-516-5197, Fax: 410-516-5199, E-mail: crosbyr@jhu.edu.

Rutgers, The State University of New Jersey, New Brunswick, Graduate School-New Brunswick, BioMaPS Institute for Quantitative Biology, Piscataway, NJ 08854-8097. Offers computational biology and molecular biophysics (PhD). *Degree requirements:* For doctorate, comprehensive exam, thesis/dissertation. *Entrance requirements:* For doctorate, GRE. Additional exam requirements/recommendations for international students: Required—TOEFL. Electronic applications accepted. *Expenses:* Tuition, state resident: full-time $7200; part-time $600 per credit. Tuition, nonresident: full-time $11,124; part-time $927 per credit. *Faculty research:* Structural biology, systems biology, bioinformatics, translational medicine, genomics.

Texas Tech University Health Sciences Center, Graduate School of Biomedical Sciences, Department of Cell Physiology and Molecular Biophysics, Lubbock, TX 79430. Offers MS, PhD, MD/PhD. Terminal master's awarded for partial completion of doctoral program. *Degree requirements:* For master's, thesis; for doctorate, thesis/dissertation. *Entrance requirements:* For master's and doctorate, GRE General Test, minimum GPA of 3.4. Additional exam requirements/recommendations for international students: Required—TOEFL. Electronic applications accepted. *Faculty research:* Cardiovascular physiology, neurophysiology, renal physiology, respiratory physiology.

University of Massachusetts Amherst, Graduate School, Interdisciplinary Programs, Program in Molecular and Cellular Biology, Amherst, MA 01003. Offers biological chemistry and molecular biophysics (PhD); biomedicine (PhD); cellular and developmental biology (PhD). Part-time programs available. *Students:* 76 full-time (42 women), 3 part-time (2 women); includes 13 minority (3 Black or African American, non-Hispanic/Latino; 4 Asian, non-Hispanic/Latino; 5 Hispanic/Latino; 1 Two or more races, non-Hispanic/Latino), 23 international. Average age 27. 179 applicants, 25% accepted, 22 enrolled. In 2010, 8 doctorates awarded. Terminal master's awarded for partial completion of doctoral program. *Degree requirements:* For doctorate, comprehensive exam, thesis/dissertation. *Entrance requirements:* For doctorate, GRE General Test. Additional exam requirements/recommendations for international students: Required—TOEFL (minimum score 550 paper-based; 213 computer-based; 80 iBT), IELTS (minimum score 6.5). *Application deadline:* For fall admission, 12/1 for domestic and international students. Applications are processed on a rolling basis. Application fee: $50 ($65 for international students). Electronic applications accepted. *Expenses:* Tuition, state resident: full-time $2640. Required fees: $8282. One-time fee: $357 full-time. *Financial support:* In 2010–11, 11 research assistantships with full tuition reimbursements (averaging $2,590 per year), 3 teaching assistantships with full tuition reimbursements (averaging $3,303 per year) were awarded; fellowships, career-related internships or fieldwork, Federal Work-Study, scholarships/grants, traineeships, health care benefits, tuition waivers (full), and unspecified assistantships also available. Support available to part-time students. Financial award application deadline: 12/1; financial award applicants required to submit FAFSA. *Unit head:* Dr. Barbara Osborne, Graduate Program Director, 413-545-3246, Fax: 413-545-1812. *Application contact:* Jean M. Ames, Supervisor of Admissions, 413-545-0722, Fax: 413-577-0010, E-mail: gradadm@grad.umass.edu.

University of Pennsylvania, Perelman School of Medicine, Biomedical Graduate Studies, Graduate Group in Biochemistry and Molecular Biophysics, Philadelphia, PA 19104. Offers PhD, MD/PhD, VMD/PhD. *Faculty:* 77. *Students:* 73 full-time (28 women); includes 4 Black or African American, non-Hispanic/Latino; 8 Asian, non-Hispanic/Latino; 8 Hispanic/Latino, 9 international. 145 applicants, 25% accepted, 10 enrolled. In 2010, 11 doctorates awarded. *Degree requirements:* For doctorate, thesis/dissertation. *Entrance requirements:* For doctorate, GRE General Test. Additional exam requirements/recommendations for international students: Required—TOEFL. *Application deadline:* For fall admission, 12/8 priority date for domestic and international students. Applications are processed on a rolling basis. Application fee: $70. Electronic applications accepted. *Expenses:* Tuition: Full-time $25,660; part-time $4758 per course. Required fees: $2152; $270 per course. Tuition and fees vary according to course load, degree level and program. *Financial support:* In 2010–11, 73 students received support; fellowships, research assistantships, scholarships/grants, traineeships, and unspecified assistantships available. *Faculty research:* Biochemistry of cell differentiation, tissue culture, intermediary metabolism, structure of proteins and nucleic acids, biochemical genetics. *Unit head:* Dr. Kathryn Ferguson, Chairperson, 215-573-7288. *Application contact:* Ruth Keris, Administrator, 215-898-4639, Fax: 215-573-2085, E-mail: keris@mail.med.upenn.edu.

University of Pittsburgh, School of Medicine and School of Arts and Sciences, Joint Pitt + CMU Molecular Biophysics and Structural Biology Graduate Program, Pittsburgh, PA 15260. Offers PhD. *Faculty:* 52 full-time (15 women). *Students:* 20 full-time (5 women); includes 1 Asian, non-Hispanic/Latino; 1 Hispanic/Latino; 1 Native Hawaiian or other Pacific Islander, non-Hispanic/Latino, 5 international. Average age 26. 70 applicants, 13% accepted, 4 enrolled. In 2010, 2 doctorates awarded. *Degree requirements:* For doctorate, comprehensive exam, thesis/dissertation. *Entrance requirements:* For doctorate, GRE General Test. Additional exam requirements/recommendations for international students: Required—TOEFL (minimum score 600 paper-based; 250 computer-based; 100 iBT), IELTS (minimum score 7). *Application deadline:* For fall admission, 12/15 priority date for domestic and international students. Application fee: $0. Electronic applications accepted. *Expenses:* Tuition, state resident: full-time $17,304; part-time $701 per credit. Tuition, nonresident: full-time $29,554; part-time $1210 per credit. Required fees: $740; $214 per term. Tuition and fees vary according to program. *Financial support:* In 2010–11, 3 fellowships with full tuition reimbursements (averaging $27,326 per year), 13 research assistantships with full tuition reimbursements (averaging $24,650 per year) were awarded; institutionally sponsored loans, scholarships/grants, traineeships, and unspecified assistantships also available. *Faculty research:* Structural biology, protein dynamics and folding, computational biophysics, molecular informatics, membrane biophysics and ion channels, x-ray crystallography cryaelectron microscopy. *Unit head:* Dr. Angela M. Gronenborn, Director, 412-648-8957, Fax: 412-648-1077, E-mail: mbsbinfo@medschool.pitt.edu. *Application contact:* Jennifer L. Walker, Program Coordinator, 412-648-8957, Fax: 412-648-1077, E-mail: mbsbinfo@medschool.pitt.edu.

The University of Texas Medical Branch, Graduate School of Biomedical Sciences, Program in Cellular Physiology and Molecular Biophysics, Galveston, TX 77555. Offers MS, PhD. *Degree requirements:* For master's, thesis or alternative; for doctorate, thesis/dissertation. *Entrance requirements:* For master's and doctorate, GRE General Test. Additional exam requirements/recommendations for international students: Required—TOEFL (minimum score 550 paper-based; 213 computer-based). Electronic applications accepted.

The University of Texas Southwestern Medical Center at Dallas, Southwestern Graduate School of Biomedical Sciences, Division of Basic Science, Program in Molecular Biophysics, Dallas, TX 75390. Offers PhD. *Faculty:* 34 full-time (6 women). *Students:* 40 full-time (15 women), 1 (woman) part-time; includes 7 minority (1 Black or African American, non-Hispanic/Latino; 3 Asian, non-Hispanic/Latino; 3 Hispanic/Latino), 19 international. Average age 26. In 2010, 3 doctorates awarded. *Degree requirements:* For doctorate, thesis/dissertation, qualifying exam. *Entrance requirements:* For doctorate, GRE General Test, minimum GPA of 3.0. Additional exam requirements/recommendations for international students: Required—TOEFL. *Application deadline:* For fall admission, 12/15 priority date for domestic students. Applications are processed on a rolling basis. Application fee: $0. Electronic applications accepted. *Financial support:* Fellowships, research assistantships, institutionally sponsored loans and traineeships available. *Faculty research:* Optical spectroscopy, x-ray crystallography, protein chemistry, ion channels, contractile and cytoskeletal proteins. *Unit head:* Dr. Kevin Gardner, Chair, 214-645-6365, Fax: 214-645-6353, E-mail: kevin.gardner@utsouthwestern.edu. *Application contact:* Dr. Nancy E. Street, Associate Dean, 214-648-6708, Fax: 214-648-2102, E-mail: nancy.street@utsouthwestern.edu.

Washington University in St. Louis, Graduate School of Arts and Sciences, Division of Biology and Biomedical Sciences, Program in Molecular Biophysics, St. Louis, MO 63130-4899. Offers PhD. *Degree requirements:* For doctorate, thesis/dissertation. *Entrance requirements:* For doctorate, GRE General Test, GRE Subject Test. Electronic applications accepted.

Yale University, School of Medicine and Graduate School of Arts and Sciences, Combined Program in Biological and Biomedical Sciences (BBS), Molecular Biophysics and Biochemistry Track, New Haven, CT 06520. Offers PhD, MD/PhD. *Degree requirements:* For doctorate, thesis/dissertation. *Entrance requirements:* For doctorate, GRE General Test. Additional exam requirements/recommendations for international students: Required—TOEFL. Electronic applications accepted.

Radiation Biology

Auburn University, College of Veterinary Medicine and Graduate School, Graduate Programs in Veterinary Medicine, Auburn University, AL 36849. Offers biomedical sciences (MS, PhD), including anatomy, physiology and pharmacology (MS), biomedical sciences (PhD), clinical sciences (MS), large animal surgery and medicine (MS), pathobiology (MS), radiology (MS), small animal surgery and medicine (MS); DVM/MS. Part-time programs available. *Faculty:* 100 full-time (40 women), 5 part-time/adjunct (1 woman). *Students:* 17 full-time (6 women), 51 part-time (35 women); includes 2 Black or African American, non-Hispanic/Latino; 1 American Indian or Alaska Native, non-Hispanic/Latino; 3 Asian, non-Hispanic/Latino; 2 Hispanic/Latino, 22 international. Average age 31. 70 applicants, 34% accepted, 10 enrolled. In 2010, 12 master's, 7 doctorates awarded. *Degree requirements:* For doctorate, thesis/dissertation. *Entrance requirements:* For master's, GRE General Test; for doctorate, GRE General Test, GRE Subject Test. *Application deadline:* For fall admission, 7/7 for domestic students; for spring admission, 11/24 for domestic students. Applications are processed on a rolling basis. Application fee: $50 ($60 for international students). Electronic applications accepted. *Expenses:* Tuition, state resident: full-time $7002. Tuition, nonresident: full-time $21,898. International tuition: $22,116 full-time. Required fees: $892. Tuition and fees vary according to course load and program. *Financial support:* Research assistantships, teaching assistantships, Federal Work-Study available. Support available to part-time students. Financial award application deadline: 3/15; financial award applicants required to submit FAFSA. *Unit head:* Dr. Timothy R. Boosinger, Dean, 334-844-4546. *Application contact:* Dr. George Flowers, Dean of the Graduate School, 334-844-2125.

Austin Peay State University, College of Graduate Studies, College of Science and Mathematics, Department of Biology, Clarksville, TN 37044. Offers clinical laboratory science (MS); radiologic science (MS). Part-time programs available. *Faculty:* 13 full-time (6 women). *Students:* 6 full-time (all women), 17 part-time (8 women); includes 4 minority (2 Black or African American, non-Hispanic/Latino; 2 Hispanic/Latino), 1 international. Average age 29. 15 applicants, 100% accepted, 11 enrolled. In 2010, 6 master's awarded. *Degree requirements:* For master's, comprehensive exam, thesis optional. *Entrance requirements:* For master's, GRE General Test, 3 letters of recommendation, minimum undergraduate GPA of 2.5. Additional exam requirements/recommendations for international students: Required—TOEFL (minimum score 500 paper-based; 173 computer-based). *Application deadline:* For fall admission, 7/27 priority date for domestic students; for spring admission, 12/17 priority date for domestic students. Applications are processed on a rolling basis. Application fee: $25. Electronic applications accepted. *Expenses:* Tuition, state resident: full-time $6480; part-time $324 per credit hour. Tuition, nonresident: full-time $17,960; part-time $898 per credit hour. Required fees: $1244; $61.20 per credit hour. *Financial support:* In 2010–11, research assistantships with full tuition reimbursements (averaging $5,174 per year); career-related internships or fieldwork, Federal Work-Study, institutionally sponsored loans, scholarships/grants, and unspecified assistantships also available. Support available to part-time students. Financial award application deadline: 3/1. *Faculty research:* Non-paint source pollution, amphibian biomonitoring, aquatic toxicology, biological indicators of water quality, taxonomy. *Unit head:* Dr. Don Dailey, Chair, 931-221-7781, Fax: 931-221-6323, E-mail: daileyd@apsu.edu. *Application contact:* Dr. Dixie Dennis Pinder, Dean, College of Graduate Studies, 931-221-7662, Fax: 931-221-7641, E-mail: dennisdi@apsu.edu.

Colorado State University, College of Veterinary Medicine and Biomedical Sciences, Department of Environmental and Radiological Health Sciences, Fort Collins, CO 80523-1681. Offers environmental health (MS, PhD); radiological health sciences (MS, PhD). Part-time programs available. *Faculty:* 23 full-time (8 women), 3 part-time/adjunct (0 women). *Students:* 87 full-time (49 women), 31 part-time (19 women); includes 1 Black or African American, non-Hispanic/Latino; 1 American Indian or Alaska Native, non-Hispanic/Latino; 3 Asian, non-Hispanic/Latino; 4 Hispanic/Latino; 2 Two or more races, non-Hispanic/Latino, 8 international. Average age 28. 83 applicants, 73% accepted, 48 enrolled. In 2010, 25 master's, 2 doctorates awarded. Terminal master's awarded for partial completion of doctoral program. *Degree requirements:* For master's, comprehensive exam (for some programs), thesis (for some programs), publishable paper; for doctorate, comprehensive exam, thesis/dissertation, publishable paper. *Entrance requirements:* For master's, GRE General Test, 1 year of course work in biology lab and chemistry lab, 1 semester of course work in organic chemistry, course work in calculus, resume, letters of recommendation; for doctorate, GRE General Test, 1 year of course work in biology lab and chemistry lab, 1 semester of course work in organic chemistry, course work in calculus, resume, letters of recommendation, evidence of research capability. Additional exam requirements/recommendations for international students: Required—TOEFL (minimum score 550 paper-based; 213 computer-based). *Application deadline:* For fall admission, 6/1 for domestic students, 6/1 priority date for international students; for spring admission, 11/1 for domestic and international students. Applications are processed on a rolling basis. Application fee: $50. Electronic applications accepted. *Expenses:* Tuition, state resident: full-time $7434; part-time $413 per credit. Tuition, nonresident: full-time $19,022; part-time $1057 per credit. Required fees: $1729; $88 per credit. *Financial support:* In 2010–11, 22 students received support, including 7 fellowships with full and partial tuition reimbursements available (averaging $30,357 per year), 11 research assistantships with full and partial tuition reimbursements available (averaging $21,422 per year), 4 teaching assistantships with full and partial tuition reimbursements available (averaging $12,032 per year); career-related internships or fieldwork, Federal Work-Study, institutionally sponsored loans, traineeships, and unspecified assistantships also available. Support available to part-time students. Financial award application deadline: 2/1; financial award applicants required to submit FAFSA. *Faculty research:* Epidemiology, toxicology, industrial hygiene, occupational health, radiation therapy. Total annual research expenditures: $8.4 million. *Unit head:* Dr. Jac A. Nickoloff, Head, 970-491-6674, Fax: 970-491-0623, E-mail: j.nickoloff@colostate.edu. *Application contact:* Jeanne A. Brockway, Graduate Program Coordinator, 970-491-5003, Fax: 970-491-0623, E-mail: jeanne.brockway@colostate.edu.

Georgetown University, Graduate School of Arts and Sciences, Programs in Biomedical Sciences, Department of Health Physics, Washington, DC 20057. Offers health physics (MS); radiobiology (MS). *Degree requirements:* For master's, thesis. *Entrance requirements:* Additional exam requirements/recommendations for international students: Required—TOEFL.

Université de Sherbrooke, Faculty of Medicine and Health Sciences, Graduate Programs in Medicine, Program in Radiobiology, Sherbrooke, QC J1H 5N4, Canada. Offers M Sc, PhD. Terminal master's awarded for partial completion of doctoral program. *Degree requirements:* For master's, thesis; for doctorate, thesis/dissertation. Electronic applications accepted. *Faculty research:* DNA repair, physiochemical actions of radiation, radiopharmacy, phototherapy, imaging.

The University of Iowa, Roy J. and Lucille A. Carver College of Medicine and Graduate College, Graduate Programs in Medicine, Program in Free Radical and Radiation Biology, Iowa City, IA 52242-1316. Offers MS, PhD. Part-time programs available. *Faculty:* 5 full-time (1 woman). *Students:* 17 full-time (4 women). Average age 26. 6 applicants, 67% accepted, 4 enrolled. In 2010, 1 doctorate awarded. *Degree requirements:* For doctorate, thesis/dissertation. *Entrance requirements:* For master's and doctorate, GRE. Additional exam requirements/recommendations for international students: Required—TOEFL. *Application deadline:* For fall admission, 5/31 priority date for domestic and international students; for spring admission, 10/31 for domestic and international students. Applications are processed on a rolling basis. Application fee: $60 ($85 for international students). *Financial support:* In 2010–11, fellowships with partial tuition reimbursements (averaging $25,000 per year), research assistantships with

Radiation Biology

The University of Iowa (continued)

tuition reimbursements (averaging $25,000 per year) were awarded; traineeships, health care benefits, tuition waivers (partial), and unspecified assistantships also available. *Faculty research:* Radiation injury and cellular repair, cell proliferation kinetics, free radical biology, tumor control, PET imaging, EPR. Total annual research expenditures: $1 million. *Unit head:* Dr. Douglas R. Spitz, Head, 319-335-8019, Fax: 319-335-8039. *Application contact:* Jennifer K. DeWitte, Grant/Program Administrator, 319-335-8164, Fax: 319-335-8039, E-mail: jennifer-dewitte@uiowa.edu.

University of Oklahoma Health Sciences Center, College of Medicine and Graduate College, Graduate Programs in Medicine, Department of Radiological Sciences, Oklahoma City, OK 73190. Offers medical radiation physics (MS, PhD), including diagnostic radiology, nuclear medicine, radiation therapy, ultrasound. Part-time programs available. Terminal master's awarded for partial completion of doctoral program. *Degree requirements:* For master's, thesis; for doctorate, thesis/dissertation. *Entrance requirements:* For master's, GRE General Test; for doctorate, GRE General Test, 3 letters of recommendation. Additional exam requirements/recommendations for international students: Required—TOEFL. *Faculty research:* Monte Carlo applications in radiation therapy, observer-performed studies in diagnostic radiology, error analysis in gated cardiac nuclear medicine studies, nuclear medicine absorbed fraction determinations.

HARVARD UNIVERSITY

Biophysics Program

Program of Study

The Committee on Higher Degrees in Biophysics offers a program of study leading to the Ph.D. degree. The committee comprises senior representatives of the Departments of Chemistry and Chemical Biology, Physics, and Molecular and Cellular Biology; the School of Engineering and Applied Physics; and the Division of Medical Sciences. Students receive sufficient training in physics, biology, and chemistry to enable them to apply the concepts and methods of the physical sciences to the solution of biological problems.

An initial goal of the Biophysics Program is to provide an introduction through courses and seminars to several of the diverse areas of biophysics, such as structural molecular biology, cell and membrane biophysics, neurobiology, molecular genetics, physical biochemistry, and theoretical biophysics. The program is flexible, and special effort has been devoted to minimizing course work and other formal requirements. Students engage in several research rotations during their first two years. The qualifying examination is taken at the end of the second year to determine admission to candidacy. Students undertake dissertation research as early as possible in the field and subject of their choice. Opportunities for dissertation research are available in a number of special fields. The Ph.D. requires not less than three years devoted to advanced studies, including dissertation research and the dissertation. The Committee on Higher Degrees in Biophysics anticipates that it takes an average of five years, with the maximum being six years, to complete this program.

Research Facilities

Many more of the University's modern research facilities are available to the biophysics student because of the interdepartmental nature of the program. Research programs may be pursued in the Departments of Chemistry and Chemical Biology, Molecular and Cellular Biology, Applied Physics, and Engineering Sciences in Cambridge as well as in the Departments of Biological Chemistry and Molecular Pharmacology, Genetics, Microbiology and Molecular Genetics, Neurobiology, Virology, and Cell Biology in the Harvard Medical School Division of Medical Sciences. Research may also be pursued in the Harvard School of Public Health, the Dana Farber Cancer Institute, Children's Hospital, Massachusetts General Hospital, Beth Israel Hospital, and more than ten other Harvard-affiliated institutions located throughout the cities.

Financial Aid

In 2011–12, all graduate students receive a stipend ($31,512 for twelve months) and full tuition and health fees ($39,324). A semester of teaching is required in the second year. Students are strongly encouraged to apply for fellowships from such sources as the National Science Foundation, the NDSEG, the Hertz Foundation, and the Ford Foundation. Full-time Ph.D. candidates in good academic standing are guaranteed full financial support through their sixth year of study or throughout their academic program if less than six years.

Cost of Study

Tuition and health fees for the 2011–12 academic year are $39,324. After two years in residence, students are eligible for a reduced rate (currently $12,460).

Living and Housing Costs

Accommodations in graduate residence halls are available at rents ranging from $5674 to $8910 per academic year. In addition, there are approximately 1,500 apartments available for graduate students in Harvard-owned buildings. Applications may be obtained from the Harvard University Housing Office, which also maintains a list of available private rooms, houses, and apartments in the vicinity.

Student Group

On average, the program enrolls 50 students annually. Currently, 20 women and 8 international students are enrolled in the program. Biophysics students intermingle in both their research and their social life with graduate students from the many other departments where research in the biophysical sciences is carried out.

Location

The Biophysics Program maintains a dual-campus orientation in the neighboring cities of Cambridge and Boston. Their proximity provides for a wide range of academic, cultural, extracurricular, and recreational opportunities, and the large numbers of theaters, museums, libraries, and universities contribute to enrich the scientific and cultural life of students. Because New England is compact in area, it is easy to reach countryside, mountains, and seacoast for winter and summer sports or just for a change of scenery.

The University

Established in 1636 in the Massachusetts Bay Colony, Harvard has grown to become a complex of many facilities whose educational vitality, social commitment, and level of cultural achievement contribute to make the University a leader in the academic world. Comprising more than 15,000 students and 3,000 faculty members, Harvard appeals to self-directed, resourceful students of diverse beliefs and backgrounds.

Applying

Students must apply by December 1, 2011, to be considered for admission in September 2012. Scores on the General Test of the Graduate Record Examinations are required except in rare circumstances. GRE Subject Tests are recommended. Due to the early application deadline, applicants should plan to take the GRE test no later than October to ensure that original scores are received by December 1. Information about Graduate School fellowships and scholarships, admission procedures, and graduate study at Harvard may be obtained by writing to the Admissions Office.

Correspondence and Information

For information on the program:
Harvard Biophysics Program
Building C2, Room 122
Harvard Medical School Campus
240 Longwood Avenue
Boston, Massachusetts 02115
E-mail: biophys@fas.harvard.edu
Web site: http://fas.harvard.edu/~biophys

For application forms for admission and financial aid:
Admissions Office
Graduate School of Arts and Sciences
Holyoke Center
Harvard University
1350 Massachusetts Avenue
Cambridge, Massachusetts 02138
E-mail: admiss@fas.harvard.edu
Web site: http://www.gsas.harvard.edu

Harvard University

THE FACULTY AND THEIR RESEARCH

The following faculty members accept students for degree work in biophysics. Thesis research with other faculty members is possible by arrangement.

John Assad, Ph.D., Professor of Neurobiology. Mechanisms of visual processing in the visual cortex of awake behaving monkeys.

Frederick M. Ausubel, Ph.D., Professor of Genetics. Molecular biology of microbial pathogenesis in plants and animals.

Howard Berg, Ph.D., Herchel Smith Professor of Physics and Professor of Molecular and Cellular Biology. Motile behavior of bacteria.

Stephen C. Blacklow, M.D., Ph.D., Professor of Pathology. Molecular basis for specificity in protein folding and protein-protein interactions.

Martha L. Bulyk, Ph.D., Associate Professor of Medicine and Health Sciences and Technology and of Pathology. Computational methods; genomic and proteomic technologies in the study of DNA-protein interactions.

Lewis Cantley, Ph.D., Professor of Cell Biology and Systems Biology. Structural basis for specificity in eukaryotic signal transduction pathways.

James J. Chou, Ph.D., Associate Professor of Biological Chemistry and Molecular Pharmacology. NMR spectroscopy on membrane-associated proteins and peptides.

George McDonald Church, Ph.D., Professor of Genetics. Human and microbial functional genomics; genotyping; gene expression regulatory network models.

David E. Clapham, M.D., Ph.D., Professor of Pediatrics and of Neurobiology. Intracellular signal transduction.

Jon Clardy, Ph.D., Professor of Biological Chemistry and Molecular Pharmacology. Chemical ecology; biosynthesis; structure-based design.

Adam E. Cohen, Ph.D., Assistant Professor of Chemistry and Chemical Biology and of Physics. Analysis of structure and function of nicotinic acetylcholine receptors.

Jonathan B. Cohen, Ph.D., Professor of Neurobiology. Structure and function of ligand-gated ion channels.

David P. Corey, Ph.D., Professor of Neurobiology. Ion channels in neural cell membranes.

Vladimir Denic, Ph.D., Assistant Professor of Molecular and Cellular Biology. Structural diversification of very long-chain fatty acids.

Michael M. Desai, Ph.D., Assistant Professor of Organismic and Evolutionary Biology and of Physics. Theoretical and experimental approaches to study genetic variation within populations.

Jacques Dumais, Ph.D., Associate Professor of Organismic and Evolutionary Biology. Mechanics and morphogenesis of plant development.

Michael J. Eck, M.D., Ph.D., Professor of Biological Chemistry and Molecular Pharmacology. Structural studies of proteins involved in signal transduction pathways.

Conor L. Evans, Ph.D., Assistant Professor of Dermatology. Development and application of optical detection, treatment, and monitoring approaches targeting major human diseases.

Florian Engert, Ph.D., Associate Professor of Molecular and Cellular Biology. Synaptic plasticity and neuronal networks.

Rachelle Gaudet, Ph.D., Associate Professor of Molecular and Cellular Biology. Structural studies of the stereochemistry of signaling and transport through biological membranes.

David E. Golan, M.D., Ph.D., Professor of Biological Chemistry and Molecular Pharmacology and of Medicine. Membrane dynamics; membrane structure; cellular adhesion.

Stephen C. Harrison, Ph.D., Professor of Biological Chemistry and Molecular Pharmacology. Structure of viruses and viral membranes; protein-DNA interactions; structural aspects of signal transduction and membrane traffic; X-ray diffraction.

James M. Hogle, Ph.D., Professor of Biological Chemistry and Molecular Pharmacology. Structure and function of viruses and virus-related proteins; X-ray crystallography.

Sun Hur, Ph.D., Assistant Professor of Biological Chemistry and Molecular Pharmacology. Principles of self versus nonself RNA discrimination by the immune system.

Donald E. Ingber, M.D., Ph.D., Professor of Bioengineering and Judah Folkman Professor of Vascular Biology. Research in integrin signaling, cytoskeleton, and control of angiogenesis.

Tomas Kirchhausen, Ph.D., Professor of Cell Biology. Molecular mechanisms of membrane traffic; X-ray crystallography; chemical genetics.

Andrew J. M. Kiruluta, Ph.D., Associate Professor of Radiology. Novel theory and experiments in NMR spectroscopy.

Roy Kishony, Ph.D., Associate Professor of Systems Biology. System-level genetic networks.

Nancy Kleckner, Ph.D., Herchel Smith Professor of Molecular Biology. Chromosome metabolism in bacteria and yeast.

Roberto G. Kolter, Ph.D., Professor of Microbiology and Molecular Genetics. DNA protection from oxidative damage; cell-cell communication in biofilms; microbial evolution.

Gabriel Kreiman, Ph.D., Assistant Professor of Neurology. Transcriptional regulatory circuits and neuronal circuits in visual recognition.

Galit Lahav, Ph.D., Assistant Professor of Systems Biology. Dynamics of network motifs in single living human cells.

Andres Leschziner, Ph.D., Assistant Professor of Molecular and Cellular Biology. Structural biology of ATP-dependent chromatin remodeling.

Erel Levine, Ph.D., Assistant Professor of Physics. Communication in and between cells and organisms.

David R. Liu, Ph.D., Professor of Chemistry and Chemical Biology. Organic chemistry and chemical biology.

Jun S. Liu, Ph.D., Professor of Statistics. Stochastic processes, probability theory, and statistical inference.

Joseph J. Loparo, Ph.D., Assistant Professor of Biological Chemistry and Molecular Pharmacology. Developing novel single-molecule methods to study multiprotein complexes.

Markus Meister, Ph.D., Jeff C. Tarr Professor of Molecular and Cellular Biology. Function of neuronal circuits.

Keith W. Miller, Ph.D., Mallinckrodt Professor of Pharmacology, Department of Anesthesia. Molecular mechanisms of regulatory conformation changes and drug action on membrane receptors and channels, using rapid kinetics, time-resolved photolabeling, and spectroscopy (EPR, fluorescence, NMR); characterization of lipid-protein interactions in membrane proteins.

Timothy Mitchison, Ph.D., Hasib Sabbagh Professor of Systems Biology. Cytoskeleton dynamics; mechanism of mitosis and cell locomotion; small-molecule inhibitors.

Venkatesh N. Murthy, Ph.D., Morris Khan Associate Professor of Molecular and Cellular Biology. Mechanisms of synaptic transmission and plasticity.

Daniel J. Needleman, Ph.D., Assistant Professor of Applied Physics. Physics of macromolecular assemblies and subcellular organization.

Bence P. Olveczky, Ph.D., Assistant Professor of Organismic and Evolutionary Biology. Neurobiology of vocal learning.

Erin K. O'Shea, Ph.D., Professor of Molecular and Cellular Biology and of Chemistry and Chemical Biology. Quantitative analysis of regulatory networks.

David Pellman, M.D., Professor of Cell Biology. The mechanics and regulation of mitosis.

Mara Prentiss, Ph.D., Professor of Physics. Exploitation of optical manipulation to measure adhesion properties, including virus cell binding.

Tom A. Rapoport, Ph.D., Professor of Cell Biology. Mechanism of how proteins are transported across the endoplasmic reticulum membrane.

Samara L. Reck-Peterson, Ph.D., Assistant Professor of Cell Biology. Single molecule studies of cellular motors.

Gary Ruvkun, Ph.D., Professor of Genetics. Genetic control of developmental timing, neurogenesis, and neural function.

Bernardo L. Sabatini, Ph.D., Associate Professor of Neurobiology. Regulation of synaptic transmission and dendritic function in the mammalian brain.

Aravinthan D. T. Samuel, Ph.D., Associate Professor of Physics. Topics in biophysics, neurobiology, and animal behavior.

Stuart L. Schreiber, Ph.D., Morris Loeb Professor of Chemistry and Chemical Biology. Forward and reverse chemical genetics: using small molecules to explore biology.

Brian Seed, Ph.D., Professor of Genetics. Genetic analysis of signal transduction in the immune system.

Eugene Shakhnovich, Ph.D., Professor of Chemistry and Chemical Biology. Theory and experiments in protein folding and design; theory of molecular evolution; rational drug design and physical chemistry of protein-ligand interactions; theory of complex systems.

William Shih, Ph.D., Assistant Professor of Biological Chemistry and Molecular Pharmacology. Biomolecular nanotechnology.

Steven E. Shoelson, M.D., Ph.D., Professor of Medicine. Structural and cellular study of insulin signal transduction, insulin, resistance, diabetes, and obesity.

Pamela Silver, Ph.D., Professor of Systems Biology. Nucleocytoplasmic transport; RNA-protein interactions; protein methylation; cell-based small-molecule screens.

Timothy A. Springer, Ph.D., Latham Family Professor of Pathology. Molecular biology of immune cell interactions.

Shamil R. Sunyaev, Ph.D., Assistant Professor of Medicine. Population genetic variation and genomic divergence, with a focus on protein coding regions.

Jack W. Szostak, Ph.D., Professor of Genetics. Directed evolution; information content and molecular function; self-replicating systems.

Gregory L. Verdine, Ph.D., Erving Professor of Chemistry. Protein–nucleic acid interactions; transcriptional regulation; X-ray crystallography.

Gerhard Wagner, Ph.D., Elkan Blout Professor of Biological Chemistry and Molecular Pharmacology. Protein and nucleic acid structure, interaction, and mobility; NMR spectroscopy.

John R. Wakeley, Ph.D., Professor of Organismic and Evolutionary Biology. Theoretical population genetics.

Thomas Walz, Ph.D., Professor of Cell Biology. High-resolution electron microscopy.

George M. Whitesides, Ph.D., Mallinckrodt Professor of Chemistry. Molecular pharmacology; biosurface chemistry; virology.

Xiaoliang Sunney Xie, Ph.D., Mallinckrodt Professor of Chemistry and Chemical Biology. Single-molecule spectroscopy and dynamics; molecular interaction and chemical dynamics in biological systems.

Gary Yellen, Ph.D., Professor of Neurobiology. Molecular physiology of ion channels: functional motions, drug interactions, and electrophysiological mechanisms.

Xaiowei Zhuang, Ph.D., Professor of Chemistry and Chemical Biology and of Physics. Single-molecule biophysics.

MEDICAL COLLEGE OF WISCONSIN

Graduate School of Biomedical Sciences
Biophysics Graduate Program

Programs of Study	The Biophysics Graduate Program has two tracks, each leading to the Ph.D. degree: Molecular Biophysics and Magnetic Resonance Biophysics. The Molecular Biophysics track encompasses the investigation, detection, and use of free radicals and paramagnetic metal ions in biological systems. Free radicals are involved in many disease processes and yet are also an integral part of cellular communication. Free radicals can also be used to label proteins and to map out protein structure, providing information on protein dynamics and conformational changes that cannot be obtained from crystal structure data. In addition, free-radical labels can be used to probe the dynamics of biological membranes. Paramagnetic metal ions are central to most biological processes and electron transfer systems. A major technique used in the above studies is electron paramagnetic resonance (EPR), and the Department of Biophysics houses one of the few National Centers for EPR-related research. Students with a more physical background may specialize in EPR instrumentation.
	In the Magnetic Resonance Biophysics track, particular emphasis is placed on magnetic resonance imaging (MRI) and magnetic resonance spectroscopy (MRS). Functional magnetic resonance imaging (fMRI) of the human brain is an active research area (neuroscience, contrast mechanisms, technical development). Other opportunities exist in both tracks, as is evident from the research interests of the faculty.
	All students are expected to be comfortable with mathematical approaches to biological problems. Molecular biophysics students must demonstrate general proficiency at an undergraduate level in chemistry, biology, and mathematics prior to advancement to candidacy. Magnetic resonance biophysics students must demonstrate proficiency in neuroscience, physics, and mathematics prior to advancement to candidacy. The biophysics program offers a number of core courses as well as courses in each of the two tracks. All graduate students in biophysics are required to take the biophysics seminar and a journal club. Additional courses may be taken from the basic science and clinical departments throughout the Medical College and also from Marquette University and the University of Wisconsin–Milwaukee. Every effort is made to tailor the formal course work to the particular needs of the student.
Research Facilities	The program is composed of faculty members actively involved in research in clinical and basic science departments. This diversity provides excellent research opportunities in a large number of areas. Most faculty members have external research support to provide the most up-to-date equipment and facilities. Students also have access to the National Biomedical EPR Center, the Allen-Bradley Animal Laboratory, the Animal Resource Center, the Todd Wehr Library, the research laboratories at the Clement J. Zablocki VA Medical Center, and the Magnetic Resonance Imaging Center. A 3-Tesla human MRI scanner and a 9.4-Tesla animal MRI scanner are available for research involving human subjects and animal models.
Financial Aid	Every full-time Ph.D. candidate in good academic standing is guaranteed a full scholarship, including tuition and stipend, throughout the academic program. Candidates are only accepted when financial support is available. This support may come from any of several sources, such as the department or program, the graduate school, or an extramural funding agency. Most students are classified as fellows, trainees, or research assistants and spend no time during their academic programs working as teaching assistants.
Cost of Study	All full-time degree candidates in good standing receive a full scholarship, as explained in the Financial Aid section, for at least five years.
Living and Housing Costs	Living accommodations, for both single and married students, are available nearby and in the regional Milwaukee area.
Student Group	The total enrollment in the Graduate School of the Medical College is about 620. Approximately 800 medical students are enrolled in the College. The Biophysics Graduate Program has 30 students.
Location	The Medical College is located on the suburban grounds of the Milwaukee Regional Medical Center. The center houses hospitals, other medical institutions, and several small companies devoted to the development of new medical devices. Milwaukee offers numerous cultural events in music, art, and theater. The city is rich in old-world tradition and has a diverse ethnic heritage leading to an abundant variety of fine restaurants in the area. Milwaukee County has an excellent park system, with more than 125 parks scattered throughout the city and metropolitan area, and an extensive bicycle trail system. The city is bordered on the east by Lake Michigan and lies within commuting distance of 200 inland lakes, which provide recreation throughout the year.
The Medical College	Medical College of Wisconsin was originally chartered as the Marquette University School of Medicine in 1913 and became a freestanding, private corporation in 1967. The Medical College moved into its quarters on the grounds of the Milwaukee Regional Medical Center in 1978; the College now neighbors the majority of its clinical teaching facilities. The major teaching hospitals of the Medical College—Froedtert Memorial Lutheran Hospital, Veterans Administration Medical Center, Children's Hospital of Wisconsin, and the Milwaukee County Mental Health Complex—constitute the core of the Medical Center of southeastern Wisconsin. The faculty members of the clinical and basic science departments frequently interact and have numerous collaborative research investigations.
Applying	Prospective students can apply online or download the application form by visiting the Web site at http://www.mcw.edu/gradschool. Students with an undergraduate major in mathematics, science, or engineering are invited to apply. Applications are also invited from students interested in a biophysical approach to neuroscience. Students interested in the molecular biophysics track should apply to the Interdisciplinary Program in Biomedical Sciences. Students interested in the MRI track should apply directly to the Department of Biophysics.
Correspondence and Information	Biophysics Graduate Program Medical College of Wisconsin 8701 Watertown Plank Road P.O. Box 26509 Milwaukee, Wisconsin 53226-0509 Phone: 414-955-4000 Fax: 414-955-6512 E-mail: gradschool@mcw.edu Web site: http://www.biophysics.mcw.edu

Medical College of Wisconsin

THE FACULTY AND THEIR RESEARCH

Molecular Biophysics

William E. Antholine, Associate Professor, Department of Biophysics; Ph.D., Iowa State, 1971. Uptake studies of metal antitumor agents; development of radiosensitizing agents.

Brian Bennett, Associate Professor, Department of Biophysics; Ph.D., Sussex (England), 1994. Transition metal–containing enzymes and electron-transfer proteins: the roles of transition icon catalytic and redox-active centers in life-threatening conditions.

Jimmy B. Feix, Professor, Department of Biophysics; Ph.D., Kentucky, 1981. Electron spin resonance studies of model and biological membranes; membrane interactions of photosensitizing dyes; effects of oxidative stress; preparation and use of liposomes.

Neil Hogg, Professor, Department of Biophysics; Ph.D., Essex (England), 1993. Biological chemistry of nitric oxide and its oxidation products in pathophysiology.

James S. Hyde, Professor, Department of Biophysics; Ph.D., MIT, 1959. Spin label probes of rotational, lateral, and transverse diffusion of synthetic and biological membranes; magnetic resonance imaging; functional neuroimaging.

Balaraman Kalyanaraman, Professor and Chairman, Department of Biophysics; Ph.D., Alabama, 1978. Free-radical metabolites in the biological system; detection of free radicals by EPR spin-trapping, fluorescence, optical stopped-flow, and HPLC techniques.

Candice S. Klug, Associate Professor, Department of Biophysics; Ph.D., Medical College of Wisconsin, 1999. Protein structure and functional dynamics studies using site-directed spin labeling electron paramagnetic resonance spectroscopy.

Witold K. Subczynski, Associate Professor, Department of Biophysics; Ph.D., Moscow, 1976. Spin label studies on membrane dynamics and organization (raft-domain formation), spin label oximetry and NO-metry.

Jeannette Vásquez Vivar, Associate Professor, Department of Biophysics; Ph.D., São Paulo, 1992. Mechanisms regulating superoxide and nitric oxide formation from nitric oxide synthase; tetrahydrobiopterin metabolism; applications of electron paramagnetic resonance spin trapping methodology.

MRI/MRS

Jeffrey R. Binder, Professor, Department of Neurology; M.D., Nebraska, 1986. Functional magnetic resonance imaging; human brain auditory and language systems; fMRI in epilepsy patients.

Edgar A. DeYoe III, Professor, Department of Radiology; Ph.D., Rochester, 1983. Functional magnetic resonance imaging mapping of the human visual cortex.

Andrew S. Greene, Professor, Department of Physiology; Ph.D., Johns Hopkins, 1985. Mathematical modeling and simulation of complex biological systems.

Anthony D. Hudetz, Professor, Department of Anesthesiology; Ph.D., Semmelweis (Hungary), 1985. Cerebral microcirculation control.

James S. Hyde, Professor, Department of Biophysics; Ph.D., MIT, 1959. Spin label probes of rotational, lateral, and transverse diffusion of synthetic and biological membranes; magnetic resonance imaging; functional neuroimaging.

Andrzej Jesmanowicz, Associate Professor, Department of Biophysics; Ph.D., Copernicus (Poland), 1975. MRI physics and image processing.

Shi-Jiang Li, Professor, Department of Biophysics; Ph.D., Ohio, 1985. Magnetic resonance imaging and magnetic resonance spectroscopy studies of tumor hypoxia and oxygenation.

Kathleen M. Schmainda, Associate Professor, Department of Radiology; Ph.D., Harvard–MIT Division of Health Sciences and Technology, 1993. Quantification of biologically relevant parameters with exogenous, contrast-enhanced MRI; development of MRI methods to diagnose disease, with a focus on diabetes and cancer.

Section 5
Botany and Plant Biology

This section contains a directory of institutions offering graduate work in botany and plant biology. Additional information about programs listed in the directory may be obtained by writing directly to the dean of a graduate school or chair of a department at the address given in the directory.

For programs offering related work, see also in this book *Biochemistry; Biological and Biomedical Sciences; Cell, Molecular, and Structural Biology; Ecology, Environmental Biology, and Evolutionary Biology; Entomology; Genetics, Developmental Biology, and Reproductive Biology;* and *Microbiological Sciences.* In the other guides in this series:

Graduate Programs in the Humanities, Arts & Social Sciences
See *Architecture (Landscape Architecture)* and *Economics (Agricultural Economics and Agribusiness)*

Graduate Programs in the Physical Sciences, Mathematics, Agricultural Sciences, the Environment & Natural Resources
See *Agricultural and Food Sciences*

Graduate Programs in Engineering & Applied Sciences
See *Agricultural Engineering* and *Bioengineering*

CONTENTS

Program Directories

Botany

Auburn University, Graduate School, College of Sciences and Mathematics, Department of Biological Sciences, Auburn University, AL 36849. Offers botany (MS, PhD); microbiology (MS, PhD); zoology (MS, PhD). *Faculty:* 33 full-time (8 women), 1 (woman) part-time/adjunct. *Students:* 42 full-time (17 women), 60 part-time (36 women); includes 4 Black or African American, non-Hispanic/Latino; 1 American Indian or Alaska Native, non-Hispanic/Latino; 3 Asian, non-Hispanic/Latino; 1 Hispanic/Latino, 21 international. Average age 28. 134 applicants, 20% accepted, 18 enrolled. In 2010, 22 master's, 11 doctorates awarded. *Entrance requirements:* For master's and doctorate, GRE General Test. Additional exam requirements/recommendations for international students: Required—TOEFL. *Application deadline:* For fall admission, 7/7 for domestic students; for spring admission, 11/24 for domestic students. Application fee: $50 ($60 for international students). Electronic applications accepted. *Expenses:* Tuition, state resident: full-time $7002. Tuition, nonresident: full-time $21,898. International tuition: $22,116 full-time. Required fees: $892. Tuition and fees vary according to course load and program. *Financial support:* Research assistantships, teaching assistantships available. Financial award applicants required to submit FAFSA. *Unit head:* Dr. James M. Barbaree, Chair, 334-844-7511, Fax: 334-844-1645. *Application contact:* Dr. George Flowers, Dean of the Graduate School, 334-844-2125.

California State University, Chico, Graduate School, College of Natural Sciences, Department of Biological Sciences, Program in Botany, Chico, CA 95929-0722. Offers MS. *Students:* 1 (woman) full-time, 1 (woman) part-time. Average age 32. *Degree requirements:* For master's, thesis, seminar presentation. *Entrance requirements:* For master's, GRE General Test, GRE Subject Test (biology), 2 letters of recommendation. Additional exam requirements/recommendations for international students: Required—TOEFL (minimum score 550 paper-based; 213 computer-based; 80 iBT), IELTS (minimum score 6.5). *Application deadline:* For fall admission, 3/1 priority date for domestic students, 3/1 for international students; for spring admission, 9/15 priority date for domestic students, 9/15 for international students. Applications are processed on a rolling basis. Application fee: $55. Electronic applications accepted. *Financial support:* Fellowships, career-related internships or fieldwork available. *Unit head:* Dr. Jonathan Day, Graduate Coordinator, 530-898-6303. *Application contact:* Larry Hanne, Graduate Coordinator, 530-898-5356.

Claremont Graduate University, Graduate Programs, Program in Botany, Claremont, CA 91711-6160. Offers MS, PhD. Part-time programs available. *Faculty:* 5 full-time (3 women). *Students:* 12 full-time (9 women), 1 (woman) part-time; includes 1 Asian, non-Hispanic/Latino; 1 Hispanic/Latino, 4 international. Average age 30. In 2010, 1 master's, 2 doctorates awarded. Terminal master's awarded for partial completion of doctoral program. *Entrance requirements:* For master's and doctorate, GRE General Test. Additional exam requirements/recommendations for international students: Required—TOEFL (minimum score 550 paper-based; 213 computer-based; 80 iBT). *Application deadline:* For fall admission, 2/1 priority date for domestic students. Applications are processed on a rolling basis. Application fee: $60. Electronic applications accepted. *Expenses:* Tuition: Full-time $35,748; part-time $1554 per unit. Required fees: $215 per semester. *Financial support:* Fellowships, research assistantships, Federal Work-Study, institutionally sponsored loans, scholarships/grants, and tuition waivers (full) available. Support available to part-time students. Financial award application deadline: 2/15; financial award applicants required to submit FAFSA. *Unit head:* Lucinda McDade, Director of Research/Chair, 909-625-8767 Ext. 234, Fax: 909-626-3489, E-mail: lucinda.mcdade@cgu.edu. *Application contact:* Linda Worlow, Program Coordinator, 909-625-8767 Ext. 241, Fax: 909-626-3489, E-mail: botany@cgu.edu.

Colorado State University, Graduate School, College of Natural Sciences, Department of Biology, Fort Collins, CO 80523-1878. Offers botany (MS, PhD); zoology (MS, PhD). Post-baccalaureate distance learning degree programs offered (no on-campus study). *Faculty:* 25 full-time (10 women). *Students:* 27 full-time (16 women), 22 part-time (12 women); includes 6 minority (2 Asian, non-Hispanic/Latino; 3 Hispanic/Latino; 1 Two or more races, non-Hispanic/Latino), 7 international. Average age 29. 13 applicants, 46% accepted, 5 enrolled. In 2010, 6 master's, 2 doctorates awarded. Terminal master's awarded for partial completion of doctoral program. *Degree requirements:* For master's, comprehensive exam (for some programs), thesis (for some programs); for doctorate, comprehensive exam, thesis/dissertation. *Entrance requirements:* For master's, GRE General Test, minimum GPA of 3.0; 3 letters of recommendation; for doctorate, GRE General Test, minimum GPA of 3.0; statement of purpose; 2 transcripts; 3 letters of recommendation. Additional exam requirements/recommendations for international students: Required—TOEFL (minimum score 550 paper-based; 213 computer-based; 80 iBT). *Application deadline:* For fall admission, 1/15 priority date for domestic and international students; for spring admission, 11/1 priority date for domestic and international students. Applications are processed on a rolling basis. Application fee: $50. Electronic applications accepted. *Expenses:* Tuition, state resident: full-time $7434; part-time $413 per credit. Tuition, nonresident: full-time $19,022; part-time $1057 per credit. Required fees: $1729; $88 per credit. *Financial support:* In 2010–11, 14 fellowships (averaging $31,623 per year), 36 research assistantships with full tuition reimbursements (averaging $10,921 per year), 58 teaching assistantships with full tuition reimbursements (averaging $12,196 per year) were awarded; health care benefits also available. Financial award application deadline: 1/15; financial award applicants required to submit FAFSA. *Faculty research:* Aquatic and terrestrial ecology, cell biology and genetics, plant/animal physiology, developmental biology, evolutionary biology. Total annual research expenditures: $5.9 million. *Unit head:* Dr. Daniel R. Bush, Chair, 970-491-7013, Fax: 970-491-0649, E-mail: dbush@colostate.edu. *Application contact:* Dorothy Ramirez, Graduate Coordinator, 970-491-1923, Fax: 970-491-0649, E-mail: dorothy.ramirez@colostate.edu.

Emporia State University, Graduate School, College of Liberal Arts and Sciences, Department of Biological Sciences, Emporia, KS 66801-5087. Offers botany (MS); environmental biology (MS); general biology (MS); microbial and cellular biology (MS); zoology (MS). Part-time programs available. *Faculty:* 13 full-time (3 women). *Students:* 14 full-time (8 women), 19 part-time (9 women); includes 2 minority (1 Black or African American, non-Hispanic/Latino; 1 Hispanic/Latino), 6 international. 9 applicants, 100% accepted, 9 enrolled. In 2010, 4 master's awarded. *Degree requirements:* For master's, comprehensive exam or thesis. *Entrance requirements:* For master's, GRE, appropriate undergraduate degree, interview, letters of reference. Additional exam requirements/recommendations for international students: Required—TOEFL (minimum score 520 paper-based; 133 computer-based; 68 iBT). *Application deadline:* For fall admission, 8/15 priority date for domestic students. Applications are processed on a rolling basis. Application fee: $30 ($75 for international students). Electronic applications accepted. *Expenses:* Tuition, state resident: full-time $4382; part-time $183 per credit hour. Tuition, nonresident: full-time $13,572; part-time $566 per credit hour. Required fees: $1022; $62 per credit hour. Tuition and fees vary according to course level, course load and campus/location. *Financial support:* In 2010–11, 10 research assistantships with full tuition reimbursements (averaging $7,353 per year), 9 teaching assistantships with full tuition reimbursements (averaging $7,809 per year) were awarded; career-related internships or fieldwork, Federal Work-Study, institutionally sponsored loans, health care benefits, and unspecified assistantships also available. Financial award application deadline: 3/15; financial award applicants required to submit FAFSA. *Faculty research:* Fisheries, range, and wildlife management; aquatic, plant, grassland, vertebrate, and invertebrate ecology; mammalian and plant systematics, taxonomy, and evolution; immunology, virology, and molecular biology. *Unit head:* Dr. R. Brent Thomas, Chair, 620-341-5311, Fax: 620-341-5608, E-mail: rthomas2@emporia.edu. *Application contact:* Dr. Scott Crupper, Graduate Coordinator, 620-341-5621, Fax: 620-341-5607, E-mail: scrupper@emporia.edu.

Illinois State University, Graduate School, College of Arts and Sciences, Department of Biological Sciences, Normal, IL 61790-2200. Offers animal behavior (MS); bacteriology (MS); biochemistry (MS); biological sciences (MS); biology (PhD); biophysics (MS); biotechnology (MS); botany (MS, PhD); cell biology (MS); conservation biology (MS); developmental biology (MS); ecology (MS, PhD); entomology (MS); evolutionary biology (MS); genetics (MS, PhD); immunology (MS); microbiology (MS, PhD); molecular biology (MS); molecular genetics (MS); neurobiology (MS); neuroscience (MS); parasitology (MS); physiology (MS, PhD); plant biology (MS); plant molecular biology (MS); plant sciences (MS); structural biology (MS); zoology (MS, PhD). Part-time programs available. *Degree requirements:* For master's, thesis or alternative; for doctorate, variable foreign language requirement, thesis/dissertation, 2 terms of residency. *Entrance requirements:* For master's, GRE General Test, minimum GPA of 2.6 in last 60 hours of course work; for doctorate, GRE General Test. *Faculty research:* Redoc balance and drug development in schistosoma mansoni, control of the growth of listeria monocytogenes at low temperature, regulation of cell expansion and microtubule function by SPRI, CRUI: physiology and fitness consequences of different life history phenotypes.

Miami University, Graduate School, College of Arts and Science, Department of Botany, Oxford, OH 45056. Offers MA, MAT, MS, PhD. *Students:* 48 full-time (28 women), 131 part-time (96 women); includes 6 minority (2 Black or African American, non-Hispanic/Latino; 2 Asian, non-Hispanic/Latino; 2 Two or more races, non-Hispanic/Latino), 15 international. Average age 35. In 2010, 17 master's, 4 doctorates awarded. *Entrance requirements:* For master's, GRE General Test, GRE Subject Test (recommended), minimum undergraduate GPA of 3.0 during previous 2 years or 2.75 overall; for doctorate, GRE General Test, GRE Subject Test (recommended), minimum undergraduate GPA of 2.75, 3.0 graduate. Additional exam requirements/recommendations for international students: Required—TOEFL (minimum score 550 paper-based). *Application deadline:* Applications are processed on a rolling basis. Application fee: $50. Electronic applications accepted. *Expenses:* Tuition, state resident: full-time $11,616; part-time $484 per credit hour. Tuition, nonresident: full-time $25,656; part-time $1069 per credit hour. Required fees: $528. *Financial support:* Research assistantships, teaching assistantships with full tuition reimbursements, Federal Work-Study, institutionally sponsored loans, health care benefits, and unspecified assistantships available. Financial award application deadline: 3/1; financial award applicants required to submit FAFSA. *Faculty research:* Evolution of plants, fungi and algae; bioinformatics; molecular biology of plants and cyanobacteria; food web dynamics; plant science education. *Unit head:* Dr. John Kiss, Chair, 513-529-4200, E-mail: kissjz@muohio.edu. *Application contact:* Dr. Richard C. Moore, Graduate Coordinator, 513-529-4278, E-mail: moorerc@muohio.edu.

North Carolina State University, Graduate School, College of Agriculture and Life Sciences, Department of Plant Biology, Raleigh, NC 27695. Offers MS, PhD. Part-time programs available. Terminal master's awarded for partial completion of doctoral program. *Degree requirements:* For master's, thesis (for some programs); for doctorate, thesis/dissertation. *Entrance requirements:* For master's and doctorate, GRE. Additional exam requirements/recommendations for international students: Required—TOEFL. Electronic applications accepted. *Faculty research:* Plant molecular and cell biology, aquatic ecology, community ecology, restoration, systematics plant pathogen and environmental interactions.

North Dakota State University, College of Graduate and Interdisciplinary Studies, College of Science and Mathematics, Department of Biological Sciences, Fargo, ND 58108. Offers biology (MS); botany (MS, PhD); cellular and molecular biology (PhD); environmental and conservation sciences (MS, PhD); genomics (PhD); natural resources management (MS, PhD); zoology (MS, PhD). *Students:* 18 full-time (8 women), 5 part-time (3 women); includes 2 American Indian or Alaska Native, non-Hispanic/Latino, 2 international. 17 applicants, 35% accepted. In 2010, 12 master's, 9 doctorates awarded. *Degree requirements:* For master's, thesis; for doctorate, thesis/dissertation. *Entrance requirements:* For master's and doctorate, GRE General Test. Additional exam requirements/recommendations for international students: Required—TOEFL. *Application deadline:* For fall admission, 3/15 priority date for domestic students; for spring admission, 10/30 priority date for domestic students. Applications are processed on a rolling basis. Application fee: $45 ($60 for international students). Electronic applications accepted. *Financial support:* Fellowships with full tuition reimbursements, research assistantships with full tuition reimbursements, teaching assistantships with full tuition reimbursements, career-related internships or fieldwork, Federal Work-Study, institutionally sponsored loans, scholarships/grants, tuition waivers (full), and unspecified assistantships available. Support available to part-time students. Financial award application deadline: 4/15; financial award applicants required to submit FAFSA. *Faculty research:* Comparative endocrinology, physiology, behavioral ecology, plant cell biology, aquatic biology. Total annual research expenditures: $675,000. *Unit head:* Dr. Marinus L. Otte, Head, 701-231-7087, E-mail: marinus.otte@ndsu.edu. *Application contact:* Dr. Marinus L. Otte, Head, 701-231-7087, E-mail: marinus.otte@ndsu.edu.

Nova Scotia Agricultural College, Research and Graduate Studies, Truro, NS B2N 5E3, Canada. Offers agriculture (M Sc), including air quality, animal behavior, animal molecular genetics, animal nutrition, animal technology, aquaculture, botany, crop management, crop physiology, ecology, environmental microbiology, food science, horticulture, nutrient management, pest management, physiology, plant biotechnology, plant pathology, soil chemistry, soil fertility, waste management and composting, water quality. Program offered jointly with Dalhousie University. Part-time programs available. *Degree requirements:* For master's, thesis, ATC Exam Teaching Assistantship. *Entrance requirements:* For master's, honors B Sc, minimum GPA of 3.0. Additional exam requirements/recommendations for international students: Required—TOEFL (minimum score 580 paper-based; 237 computer-based; 92 iBT), IELTS, Michigan English Language Assessment Battery, CanTEST, CAEL. *Faculty research:* Bio-product development, organic agriculture, nutrient management, air and water quality, agricultural biotechnology.

Oklahoma State University, College of Arts and Sciences, Department of Botany, Stillwater, OK 74078. Offers botany (MS); environmental science (MS, PhD); plant science (PhD). *Faculty:* 13 full-time (4 women), 1 (woman) part-time/adjunct. *Students:* 12 part-time (5 women); includes 1 American Indian or Alaska Native, non-Hispanic/Latino; 1 Hispanic/Latino, 2 international. Average age 29. 5 applicants, 80% accepted, 3 enrolled. In 2010, 3 master's awarded. *Degree requirements:* For master's, thesis; for doctorate, comprehensive exam, thesis/dissertation. *Entrance requirements:* For master's and doctorate, GRE or GMAT. Additional exam requirements/recommendations for international students: Required—TOEFL (minimum score 550 paper-based; 79 iBT). *Application deadline:* For fall admission, 3/1 priority date for international students; for spring admission, 8/1 priority date for international students. Applications are processed on a rolling basis. Application fee: $40 ($75 for international students). Electronic applications accepted. *Expenses:* Tuition, state resident: full-time $3716; part-time $154.85 per credit hour. Tuition, nonresident: full-time $14,892; part-time $621 per credit hour. Required fees: $2044; $85.20 per credit hour. One-time fee: $50. Tuition and fees vary according to course load and campus/location. *Financial support:* In 2010–11, 4 research assistantships (averaging $16,635 per year), 12 teaching assistantships (averaging $14,896 per year) were awarded; career-related internships or fieldwork, Federal Work-Study, scholarships/grants, health care benefits, tuition waivers (partial), and unspecified assistantships also available. Support available to part-time students. Financial award application deadline: 3/1; financial award applicants required to submit FAFSA. *Faculty research:* Ethnobotany, developmental genetics of Arabidopsis, biological roles of Plasmodesmata, community ecology and biodiversity, nutrient cycling in grassland ecosystems. *Unit head:* Dr. Linda Watson, Head, 405-744-5559, Fax: 405-744-7074. *Application contact:* Dr. Gordon Emslie, Dean, 405-744-6368, Fax: 405-744-0355, E-mail: grad-i@okstate.edu.

Oregon State University, Graduate School, College of Science, Department of Botany and Plant Pathology, Corvallis, OR 97331. Offers ecology (MA, MAIS, MS, PhD); genetics (MA, MAIS, MS, PhD); molecular and cellular biology (MA, MAIS, MS, PhD); mycology (MA, MAIS, MS, PhD); plant pathology (MA, MAIS, MS, PhD); plant physiology (MA, MAIS, MS, PhD); structural botany (MA, MAIS, MS, PhD); systematics (MA, MAIS, MS, PhD). Part-time programs available. *Degree requirements:* For master's, variable foreign language requirement, thesis optional; for doctorate, thesis/dissertation. *Entrance requirements:* For master's and doctorate, GRE General Test, minimum GPA of 3.0 in last 90 hours. Additional exam requirements/recommendations for international students: Required—TOEFL. *Faculty research:* Plant ecology, plant molecular biology, systematic botany, epidemiology, host-pathogen interaction.

Purdue University, Graduate School, College of Agriculture, Department of Botany and Plant Pathology, West Lafayette, IN 47907. Offers MS, PhD. Part-time programs available. Terminal master's awarded for partial completion of doctoral program. *Degree requirements:* For master's, thesis; for doctorate, thesis/dissertation. *Entrance requirements:* For master's and doctorate, GRE. Additional exam requirements/recommendations for international students: Required—TOEFL. Electronic applications accepted. *Faculty research:* Biotechnology, plant growth, weed control, crop improvement, plant physiology.

Texas A&M University, College of Science, Department of Biology, College Station, TX 77843. Offers biology (MS, PhD); botany (MS, PhD); microbiology (MS, PhD); molecular and cell biology (PhD); neuroscience (MS, PhD); zoology (MS, PhD). *Faculty:* 39. *Students:* 107 full-time (60 women), 4 part-time (3 women); includes 1 Black or African American, non-Hispanic/Latino; 5 Asian, non-Hispanic/Latino; 5 Hispanic/Latino, 47 international. Average age 28. In 2010, 3 master's, 6 doctorates awarded. *Degree requirements:* For master's, thesis or alternative; for doctorate, comprehensive exam, thesis/dissertation. *Entrance requirements:* For master's and doctorate, GRE General Test. Additional exam requirements/recommendations for international students: Required—TOEFL. *Application deadline:* For fall admission, 1/15 for domestic students. Applications are processed on a rolling basis. Application fee: $50 ($75 for international students). Electronic applications accepted. *Financial support:* Fellowships, research assistantships, teaching assistantships available. Financial award application deadline: 4/1; financial award applicants required to submit FAFSA. *Unit head:* Dr. Jack McMahan, Department Head, 979-845-2301, E-mail: granster@mail.bio.tamu.edu. *Application contact:* Dr. Jack McMahan, Department Head, 979-845-2301, E-mail: granster@mail.bio.tamu.edu.

University of Alaska Fairbanks, College of Natural Sciences and Mathematics, Department of Biology and Wildlife, Fairbanks, AK 99775-6100. Offers biological sciences (MS, PhD), including biology, botany, wildlife biology (PhD), zoology; biology (MAT, MS); wildlife biology (MS). Part-time programs available. *Faculty:* 22 full-time (10 women). *Students:* 80 full-time (46 women), 42 part-time (26 women); includes 13 minority (2 American Indian or Alaska Native, non-Hispanic/Latino; 3 Asian, non-Hispanic/Latino; 2 Hispanic/Latino; 6 Two or more races, non-Hispanic/Latino), 6 international. Average age 31. 53 applicants, 30% accepted, 15 enrolled. In 2010, 11 master's, 10 doctorates awarded. *Degree requirements:* For master's, comprehensive exam, thesis, oral exam, oral defense; for doctorate, comprehensive exam, thesis/dissertation, oral exam, oral defense. *Entrance requirements:* For master's and doctorate, GRE General Test, GRE Subject Test (biology). Additional exam requirements/recommendations for international students: Required—TOEFL (minimum score 550 paper-based; 213 computer-based; 80 iBT), TWE. *Application deadline:* For fall admission, 6/1 for domestic students, 3/1 for international students; for spring admission, 10/15 for domestic students, 9/1 for international students. Applications are processed on a rolling basis. Application fee: $60. Electronic applications accepted. *Expenses:* Tuition, state resident: full-time $5688; part-time $316 per credit. Tuition, nonresident: full-time $11,628; part-time $646 per credit. Required fees: $289 per semester. Tuition and fees vary according to course load and reciprocity agreements. *Financial support:* In 2010–11, 38 research assistantships with tuition reimbursements (averaging $11,087 per year), 20 teaching assistantships with tuition reimbursements (averaging $8,587 per year) were awarded; fellowships with tuition reimbursements, career-related internships or fieldwork, Federal Work-Study, scholarships/grants, health care benefits, and unspecified assistantships also available. Support available to part-time students. Financial award application deadline: 7/1; financial award applicants required to submit FAFSA. *Faculty research:* Plant-herbivore interactions, plant metabolic defenses, insect manufacture of glycerol, ice nucleators, structure and functions of arctic and subarctic freshwater ecosystems. *Unit head:* Christa Mulder, Department Chair, 907-474-7671, Fax: 907-474-6716, E-mail: fybio@uaf.edu. *Application contact:* Christa Mulder, Department Chair, 907-474-7671, Fax: 907-474-6716, E-mail: fybio@uaf.edu.

The University of British Columbia, Faculty of Science, Department of Botany, Vancouver, BC V6T 1Z1, Canada. Offers M Sc, PhD. *Faculty:* 34 full-time (9 women), 10 part-time/adjunct (3 women). *Students:* 75 full-time (41 women). 38 applicants, 47% accepted, 15 enrolled. In 2010, 5 master's, 6 doctorates awarded. *Degree requirements:* For master's, thesis; for doctorate, comprehensive exam, thesis/dissertation. *Entrance requirements:* Additional exam requirements/recommendations for international students: Required—TOEFL. *Application deadline:* For fall admission, 3/31 for domestic and international students; for winter admission, 9/30 for domestic and international students. Applications are processed on a rolling basis. Application fee: $90 Canadian dollars ($150 Canadian dollars for international students). Electronic applications accepted. Tuition charges are reported in Canadian dollars. *Expenses:* Tuition, area resident: Full-time $4179 Canadian dollars. International tuition: $7344 Canadian dollars full-time. *Financial support:* In 2010–11, 75 students received support, including 25 fellowships (averaging $17,000 per year), 72 research assistantships (averaging $12,000 per year), 48 teaching assistantships (averaging $11,120 per year); institutionally sponsored loans, scholarships/grants, and tuition waivers also available. *Faculty research:* Plant ecology, evolution and systematics, cell and developmental biology, plant physiology/biochemistry, genetics. Total annual research expenditures: $5.7 million Canadian dollars. *Unit head:* Dr. Fred Sack, Head, 604-822-2133, Fax: 604-822-6089, E-mail: botagrad@interchange.ubc.ca. *Application contact:* Dr. Reinhard Jetter, Chairman, Graduate Admissions, 604-822-2133, Fax: 604-822-6089, E-mail: botagrad@interchange.ubc.ca.

University of California, Riverside, Graduate Division, Department of Botany and Plant Sciences, Riverside, CA 92521-0102. Offers plant biology (MS, PhD), including plant genetics (PhD). Part-time programs available. Terminal master's awarded for partial completion of doctoral program. *Degree requirements:* For master's, comprehensive exams or thesis; for doctorate, thesis/dissertation, qualifying exams. *Entrance requirements:* For master's and doctorate, GRE General Test, minimum GPA of 3.2. Additional exam requirements/recommendations for international students: Required—TOEFL (minimum score 550 paper-based; 213 computer-based; 80 iBT). Electronic applications accepted. *Faculty research:* Agricultural plant biology; biochemistry and physiology; cellular, molecular and developmental biology; ecology, evolution, systematics and ethnobotany; genetics, genomics and bioinformatics.

University of Connecticut, Graduate School, College of Liberal Arts and Sciences, Department of Ecology and Evolutionary Biology, Storrs, CT 06269. Offers botany (MS, PhD); ecology (MS, PhD); entomology (MS, PhD); zoology (MS, PhD). Terminal master's awarded for partial completion of doctoral program. *Degree requirements:* For master's, comprehensive exam; for doctorate, thesis/dissertation. *Entrance requirements:* For master's and doctorate, GRE General Test, GRE Subject Test. Additional exam requirements/recommendations for international students: Required—TOEFL (minimum score 550 paper-based; 213 computer-based). Electronic applications accepted.

University of Florida, Graduate School, College of Liberal Arts and Sciences and College of Agricultural and Life Sciences, Department of Botany, Gainesville, FL 32611. Offers M Ag, MS, MST, PhD. Part-time programs available. *Entrance requirements:* Additional exam requirements/recommendations for international students: Required—TOEFL, IELTS. *Application deadline:* Applications are processed on a rolling basis. Electronic applications accepted. *Expenses:* Tuition, state resident: full-time $10,916. Tuition, nonresident: full-time $28,309. *Financial support:* Federal Work-Study and institutionally sponsored loans available. Support available to part-time students. *Unit head:* Dr. Alice Harmon, Chair, 352-273-0127, E-mail: harmon@ufl.edu. *Application contact:* Dr. Rebecca T. Kimball, Graduate Coordinator, 352-846-3737, E-mail: rkimball@ufl.edu.

University of Florida, Graduate School, College of Liberal Arts and Sciences, Department of Zoology, Gainesville, FL 32611. Offers botany (MS, MST); zoology (MS, MST, PhD). *Faculty:* 37 full-time (9 women), 1 part-time/adjunct (0 women). *Students:* 79 full-time (40 women), 5 part-time (2 women); includes 2 Asian, non-Hispanic/Latino; 8 Hispanic/Latino, 20 international. Average age 29. 102 applicants, 29% accepted, 22 enrolled. In 2010, 8 master's, 11 doctorates awarded. *Degree requirements:* For master's, comprehensive exam (for some programs), thesis; for doctorate, comprehensive exam, thesis/dissertation, teaching experience. *Entrance requirements:* For master's and doctorate, GRE General Test (minimum score of 1000), minimum GPA of 3.0. Additional exam requirements/recommendations for international students: Required—TOEFL (minimum score 550 paper-based; 213 computer-based; 80 iBT), IELTS (minimum score 6). *Application deadline:* For fall admission, 12/1 for domestic and international students. Applications are processed on a rolling basis. Application fee: $30. Electronic applications accepted. *Expenses:* Tuition, state resident: full-time $10,916. Tuition, nonresident: full-time $28,309. *Financial support:* In 2010–11, 95 students received support, including 39 fellowships, 14 research assistantships (averaging $23,199 per year), 42 teaching assistantships (averaging $22,469 per year); unspecified assistantships also available. Financial award application deadline: 12/15; financial award applicants required to submit FAFSA. *Faculty research:* Ecology, evolution, genetics, molecular and cellular biology, physiology. Total annual research expenditures: $4.8 million. *Unit head:* Dr. Alice Harmon, Chair, 352-273-0127, E-mail: harmon@ufl.edu. *Application contact:* Dr. Rebecca T. Kimball, Graduate Coordinator, 352-846-3737, Fax: 352-392-3704, E-mail: rkimball@ufl.edu.

University of Guelph, Graduate Studies, College of Biological Science, Department of Integrative Biology, Botany and Zoology, Guelph, ON N1G 2W1, Canada. Offers botany (M Sc, PhD); zoology (M Sc, PhD). Part-time programs available. *Degree requirements:* For master's, thesis, research proposal; for doctorate, thesis/dissertation, research proposal, qualifying exam. *Entrance requirements:* For master's, minimum B average during previous 2 years of course work. Additional exam requirements/recommendations for international students: Required—TOEFL (minimum score 550 paper-based; 213 computer-based), IELTS (minimum score 6.5). Electronic applications accepted. *Faculty research:* Aquatic science, environmental physiology, parasitology, wildlife biology, management.

University of Guelph, Graduate Studies, College of Biological Science, Department of Molecular and Cellular Biology, Guelph, ON N1G 2W1, Canada. Offers biochemistry (M Sc, PhD); biophysics (M Sc, PhD); botany (M Sc, PhD); microbiology (M Sc, PhD); molecular biology and genetics (M Sc, PhD). *Degree requirements:* For master's, thesis, research proposal; for doctorate, comprehensive exam, thesis/dissertation, research proposal. *Entrance requirements:* For master's, minimum B-average during previous 2 years of coursework; for doctorate, minimum A-average. Additional exam requirements/recommendations for international students: Required—TOEFL (minimum score 550 paper-based; 213 computer-based), IELTS (minimum score 6.5). Electronic applications accepted. *Faculty research:* Physiology, structure, genetics, and ecology of microbes; virology and microbial technology.

University of Hawaii at Manoa, Graduate Division, College of Natural Sciences, Department of Botany, Honolulu, HI 96822. Offers MS, PhD. Part-time programs available. *Faculty:* 23 full-time (8 women), 6 part-time/adjunct (0 women). *Students:* 47 full-time (26 women), 10 part-time (4 women); includes 18 minority (1 American Indian or Alaska Native, non-Hispanic/Latino; 4 Asian, non-Hispanic/Latino; 2 Hispanic/Latino; 6 Native Hawaiian or other Pacific Islander, non-Hispanic/Latino; 5 Two or more races, non-Hispanic/Latino), 11 international. Average age 33. 40 applicants, 18% accepted, 5 enrolled. In 2010, 10 master's, 4 doctorates awarded. Terminal master's awarded for partial completion of doctoral program. *Degree requirements:* For master's, one foreign language, thesis optional, presentation; for doctorate, one foreign language, comprehensive exam, thesis/dissertation, presentation. *Entrance requirements:* For master's and doctorate, GRE General Test, GRE Subject Test (biology). Additional exam requirements/recommendations for international students: Required—TOEFL (minimum score 540 paper-based; 207 computer-based; 76 iBT), IELTS (minimum score 5). *Application deadline:* For fall admission, 2/1 for domestic students, 1/15 for international students. Application fee: $60. *Financial support:* In 2010–11, 2 students received support, including 15 fellowships (averaging $1,563 per year), 18 research assistantships (averaging $20,869 per year), 14 teaching assistantships (averaging $16,409 per year); tuition waivers (full and partial) also available. *Faculty research:* Plant ecology, evolution, systematics, conservation biology, ethnobotany. Total annual research expenditures: $14.3 million. *Application contact:* Tom Ranker, Graduate Field Chair, 808-956-3930, Fax: 808-956-3923, E-mail: ranker@hawaii.edu.

The University of Kansas, Graduate Studies, College of Liberal Arts and Sciences, Department of Ecology and Evolutionary Biology, Lawrence, KS 66045. Offers botany (MA, PhD); ecology and evolutionary biology (MA, PhD); entomology (MA, PhD). *Faculty:* 13 full-time (6 women), 29 part-time/adjunct (7 women). *Students:* 62 full-time (30 women); includes 1 minority (Hispanic/Latino), 16 international. Average age 29. 52 applicants, 42% accepted, 14 enrolled. In 2010, 9 master's, 8 doctorates awarded. Terminal master's awarded for partial completion of doctoral program. *Degree requirements:* For master's, comprehensive exam, thesis (for some programs), 30-36 credits, thesis presentation; for doctorate, comprehensive exam, thesis/dissertation, residency, responsible scholarship and research skills, final exam, dissertation defense. *Entrance requirements:* For master's, GRE General Test, bachelor's degree with minimum undergraduate GPA of 3.0; for doctorate, GRE General Test, bachelor's degree; minimum undergraduate/graduate GPA of 3.0. Additional exam requirements/recommendations for international students: Required—TOEFL, IELTS, Score requirements in EEB are the same as those set by Graduate Studies. *Application deadline:* For fall admission, 12/15 for domestic and international students; for spring admission, 9/15 for domestic and international students. Application fee: $55 ($65 for international students). Electronic applications accepted. *Expenses:* Tuition, state resident: full-time $7092; part-time $295.50 per credit hour. Tuition, nonresident: full-time $16,590; part-time $691.25 per credit hour. Required fees: $858; $71.49 per credit hour. Tuition and fees vary according to course load, campus/location and program. *Financial support:* Fellowships with tuition reimbursements, research assistantships with full and partial tuition reimbursements, teaching assistantships with full and partial tuition reimbursements, scholarships/grants, traineeships, health care benefits, and unspecified assistantships available. Financial award application deadline: 12/15. *Faculty research:* Biodiversity and macroevolution, ecology and global change, evolutionary mechanisms. *Unit head:* Dr. Christopher H. Haufler, Chair, 785-864-3255, Fax: 785-864-5860, E-mail: vulgare@ku.edu. *Application contact:* Jaime Rochelle Keeler, Graduate Coordinator, 785-864-2362, Fax: 785-864-5860, E-mail: jrkeeler@ku.edu.

University of Maine, Graduate School, College of Natural Sciences, Forestry, and Agriculture, Department of Biological Sciences, Program in Botany and Plant Pathology, Orono, ME 04469. Offers MS. Part-time programs available. *Students:* 1 (woman) full-time, 1 (woman) part-time, 1 international. Average age 26. 6 applicants, 0% accepted, 0 enrolled. In 2010, 1 master's awarded. *Degree requirements:* For master's, thesis. *Entrance requirements:* For master's, GRE General Test. Additional exam requirements/recommendations for international students: Required—TOEFL. *Application deadline:* For fall admission, 2/1 priority date for domestic students. Applications are processed on a rolling basis. Application fee: $65. Electronic applications accepted. *Expenses:* Tuition, state resident: full-time $400. Tuition, nonresident: full-time $1050. *Financial support:* Career-related internships or fieldwork, Federal Work-Study, institutionally sponsored loans, and tuition waivers (full) available. Financial award application deadline: 3/1. *Faculty research:* Molecular biology of viral and fungal pathogens, marine ecology, paleoecology and acid systematics and evolution. *Unit head:* Dr. Stellos Tavantiz, Coordinator, 207-581-2986. *Application contact:* Scott G. Delcourt, Associate Dean of the Graduate School, 207-581-3291, Fax: 207-581-3232, E-mail: graduate@maine.edu.

University of Manitoba, Faculty of Graduate Studies, Faculty of Science, Department of Biological Sciences, Winnipeg, MB R3T 2N2, Canada. Offers botany (M Sc, PhD); ecology (M Sc, PhD); zoology (M Sc, PhD).

The University of North Carolina at Chapel Hill, Graduate School, College of Arts and Sciences, Department of Biology, Chapel Hill, NC 27599. Offers botany (MA, MS, PhD); cell biology, development, and physiology (MA, MS, PhD); cell motility and cytoskeleton (PhD); ecology and behavior (MA, MS, PhD); genetics and molecular biology (MA, MS, PhD);

Botany

The University of North Carolina at Chapel Hill (continued)
morphology, systematics, and evolution (MA, MS, PhD). Terminal master's awarded for partial completion of doctoral program. *Degree requirements:* For master's, comprehensive exam, thesis (for some programs); for doctorate, comprehensive exam, thesis/dissertation. *Entrance requirements:* For master's, GRE General Test, GRE Subject Test, 2 semesters of calculus or statistics; 2 semesters of physics, organic chemistry; 3 semesters of biology; for doctorate, GRE General Test, GRE Subject Test, 2 semesters calculus or statistics, 2 semesters physics, organic chemistry, 3 semesters of biology. Additional exam requirements/recommendations for international students: Required—TOEFL (minimum score 550 paper-based; 213 computer-based). Electronic applications accepted. *Faculty research:* Gene expression, biomechanics, yeast genetics, plant ecology, plant molecular biology.

University of North Dakota, Graduate School, College of Arts and Sciences, Department of Biology, Grand Forks, ND 58202. Offers botany (MS, PhD); ecology (MS, PhD); entomology (MS, PhD); environmental biology (MS, PhD); fisheries/wildlife (MS, PhD); genetics (MS, PhD); zoology (MS, PhD). *Faculty:* 17 full-time (5 women), 6 part-time/adjunct (1 woman). *Students:* 19 full-time (6 women), 8 part-time (2 women); includes 4 minority (3 American Indian or Alaska Native, non-Hispanic/Latino; 1 Asian, non-Hispanic/Latino), 1 international. Average age 28. 21 applicants, 33% accepted, 4 enrolled. In 2010, 1 master's awarded. Terminal master's awarded for partial completion of doctoral program. *Degree requirements:* For master's, thesis, final exam; for doctorate, comprehensive exam, thesis/dissertation, final exam. *Entrance requirements:* For master's, GRE General Test, GRE Subject Test, minimum GPA of 3.0; for doctorate, GRE General Test, GRE Subject Test, minimum GPA of 3.5. Additional exam requirements/recommendations for international students: Required—TOEFL (minimum score 550 paper-based; 213 computer-based; 79 iBT), IELTS (minimum score 6.5). *Application deadline:* For fall admission, 2/15 for domestic and international students; for spring admission, 10/15 for domestic and international students. Application fee: $35. Electronic applications accepted. *Expenses:* Tuition, state resident: full-time $5857; part-time $306.74 per credit. Tuition, nonresident: full-time $15,666; part-time $729.77 per credit. Required fees: $53.42 per credit. Tuition and fees vary according to course load, program and reciprocity agreements. *Financial support:* In 2010–11, 22 students received support, including 5 research assistantships with full and partial tuition reimbursements available (averaging $11,375 per year), 17 teaching assistantships with full and partial tuition reimbursements available (averaging $10,813 per year); fellowships with full and partial tuition reimbursements available, Federal Work-Study, institutionally sponsored loans, scholarships/grants, health care benefits, tuition waivers (full and partial), and unspecified assistantships also available. Support available to part-time students. Financial award application deadline: 3/15; financial award applicants required to submit FAFSA. *Faculty research:* Population biology, wildlife ecology, RNA processing, hormonal control of behavior. Total annual research expenditures: $736,510. *Unit head:* Dr. Brett Goodwin, Graduate Director, 701-777-2621, Fax: 701-777-2623, E-mail: brett.goodwin@mail.und.edu. *Application contact:* Matthew Anderson, Admissions Specialist, 701-777-2947, Fax: 701-777-3619, E-mail: matthew.anderson@gradschool.und.edu.

University of Oklahoma, College of Arts and Sciences, Department of Botany and Microbiology, Program in Botany, Norman, OK 73019. Offers MS, PhD. *Students:* 13 full-time (5 women), 2 part-time (both women); includes 2 minority (1 Asian, non-Hispanic/Latino; 1 Hispanic/Latino), 10 international. Average age 28. 11 applicants, 73% accepted, 7 enrolled. In 2010, 2 master's, 2 doctorates awarded. Terminal master's awarded for partial completion of doctoral program. *Degree requirements:* For master's, thesis, oral exam; for doctorate, one foreign language, thesis/dissertation, general exam. *Entrance requirements:* Additional exam requirements/recommendations for international students: Required—TOEFL (minimum score 550 paper-based; 213 computer-based; 79 iBT). *Application deadline:* For fall admission, 4/1 for domestic and international students; for spring admission, 12/1 for domestic students, 9/1 for international students. Applications are processed on a rolling basis. Application fee: $40 ($90 for international students). Electronic applications accepted. *Expenses:* Tuition, state resident: full-time $3893; part-time $162.20 per credit hour. Tuition, nonresident: full-time $14,167; part-time $590.30 per credit hour. Required fees: $2523; $94.60 per credit hour. Tuition and fees vary according to course load and degree level. *Financial support:* Federal Work-Study, institutionally sponsored loans, scholarships/grants, health care benefits, and unspecified assistantships available. Support available to part-time students. Financial award applicants required to submit FAFSA. *Faculty research:* Global change biology, plant molecular biology, systematics and evolution of plant species, plant reproductive biology, science education. *Unit head:* Dr. Gordon Uno, Chair, 405-325-4321, Fax: 405-325-7619, E-mail: guno@ou.edu. *Application contact:* Adell Hopper, Staff Assistant, 405-325-4322, Fax: 405-325-7619, E-mail: ahopper@ou.edu.

University of Wisconsin–Madison, Graduate School, College of Letters and Science, Department of Botany, Madison, WI 53706-1380. Offers MS, PhD. Part-time programs available. Terminal master's awarded for partial completion of doctoral program. *Degree requirements:* For master's, thesis; for doctorate, one foreign language, thesis/dissertation. *Entrance requirements:* For master's and doctorate, GRE General Test. Electronic applications accepted. *Expenses:* Tuition, state resident: full-time $9887; part-time $617.96 per credit. Tuition, nonresident: full-time $24,054; part-time $1503.40 per credit. Required fees: $67.63 per credit. Tuition and fees vary according to reciprocity agreements. *Faculty research:* Taxonomy and systematics; ecology; structural botany; physiological, cellular, and molecular biology.

University of Wisconsin–Oshkosh, The Office of Graduate Studies, College of Letters and Science, Department of Biology and Microbiology, Oshkosh, WI 54901. Offers biology (MS), including botany, microbiology, zoology. *Degree requirements:* For master's, comprehensive exam, thesis. *Entrance requirements:* For master's, GRE General Test, minimum GPA of 3.0, BS in biology. Additional exam requirements/recommendations for international students: Required—TOEFL (minimum score 550 paper-based; 213 computer-based; 79 iBT). Electronic applications accepted.

University of Wyoming, College of Arts and Sciences, Department of Botany, Laramie, WY 82070. Offers botany (MS, PhD); botany/water resources (MS). Part-time programs available. Terminal master's awarded for partial completion of doctoral program. *Degree requirements:* For master's, thesis; for doctorate, thesis/dissertation. *Entrance requirements:* For master's and doctorate, GRE General Test, minimum GPA of 3.0. Additional exam requirements/recommendations for international students: Required—TOEFL. Electronic applications accepted. *Faculty research:* Ecology, systematics, physiology, mycology, genetics.

Washington State University, Graduate School, College of Sciences, School of Biological Sciences, Department of Botany, Pullman, WA 99164. Offers MS, PhD. *Faculty:* 33. *Students:* 22 full-time (11 women). Average age 30. 27 applicants, 26% accepted, 7 enrolled. In 2010, 1 master's, 6 doctorates awarded. *Degree requirements:* For master's, comprehensive exam (for some programs), thesis (for some programs), oral exam; for doctorate, comprehensive exam, thesis/dissertation, oral exam. *Entrance requirements:* For master's and doctorate, GRE General Test, GRE Subject Test (recommended), three letters of recommendation, official transcripts from each university-level school attended, minimum GPA of 3.0. Additional exam requirements/recommendations for international students: Required—TOEFL, IELTS. *Application deadline:* For fall admission, 1/10 priority date for domestic students, 1/15 for international students; for spring admission, 9/15 for domestic students, 7/1 for international students. Applications are processed on a rolling basis. Application fee: $50. *Expenses:* Tuition, state resident: full-time $8552; part-time $443 per credit. Tuition, nonresident: full-time $21,650; part-time $1083 per credit. Required fees: $846. *Financial support:* In 2010–11, 3 fellowships (averaging $4,000 per year), 4 research assistantships with full and partial tuition reimbursements (averaging $13,917 per year), 21 teaching assistantships with full and partial tuition reimbursements (averaging $13,056 per year) were awarded; career-related internships or fieldwork, Federal Work-Study, institutionally sponsored loans, health care benefits, and tuition waivers (partial) also available. Financial award application deadline: 2/15; financial award applicants required to submit FAFSA. *Unit head:* Dr. Gary Thorgaard, Director, 509-335-3553, Fax: 509-335-3184, E-mail: sbs@wsu.edu. *Application contact:* Graduate School Admissions, 800-GRADWSU, Fax: 509-335-1949, E-mail: gradsch@wsu.edu.

Plant Biology

Clemson University, Graduate School, College of Agriculture, Forestry and Life Sciences, Department of Forestry and Natural Resources, Program in Plant and Environmental Sciences, Clemson, SC 29634. Offers MS, PhD. *Students:* 34 full-time (10 women), 10 part-time (2 women); includes 1 Hispanic/Latino, 14 international. Average age 31. 32 applicants, 53% accepted, 12 enrolled. In 2010, 7 master's awarded. *Degree requirements:* For master's, thesis; for doctorate, thesis/dissertation. *Entrance requirements:* For master's, GRE General Test, bachelor's degree in biological science or chemistry; for doctorate, GRE General Test. Additional exam requirements/recommendations for international students: Required—TOEFL, IELTS. *Application deadline:* Applications are processed on a rolling basis. Application fee: $70 ($80 for international students). Electronic applications accepted. *Expenses:* Contact institution. *Financial support:* In 2010–11, 31 students received support, including 4 fellowships with full and partial tuition reimbursements available (averaging $6,635 per year), 26 research assistantships with partial tuition reimbursements available (averaging $16,445 per year), 8 teaching assistantships with partial tuition reimbursements available (averaging $11,000 per year); career-related internships or fieldwork, institutionally sponsored loans, scholarships/grants, health care benefits, and unspecified assistantships also available. Support available to part-time students. Financial award application deadline: 3/15; financial award applicants required to submit FAFSA. *Faculty research:* Systematics, aquatic botany, plant ecology, plant-fungus interactions, plant developmental genetics. *Unit head:* Dr. Patricia A. Zungoli, Chair, 864-656-3137, Fax: 864-656-5065, E-mail: pzngl@clemson.edu. *Application contact:* Dr. Halina Knap, Coordinator, 864-656-3102, Fax: 864-656-5065, E-mail: hskrpsk@clemson.edu.

Cornell University, Graduate School, Graduate Fields of Agriculture and Life Sciences, Field of Plant Biology, Ithaca, NY 14853-0001. Offers cytology (MS, PhD); paleobotany (MS, PhD); plant cell biology (MS, PhD); plant ecology (MS, PhD); plant molecular biology (MS, PhD); plant morphology, anatomy and biomechanics (MS, PhD); plant physiology (MS, PhD); systematic botany (MS, PhD). *Faculty:* 48 full-time (13 women). *Students:* 33 full-time (18 women); includes 2 Black or African American, non-Hispanic/Latino; 1 Hispanic/Latino, 10 international. Average age 26. 48 applicants, 33% accepted, 7 enrolled. In 2010, 8 doctorates awarded. *Degree requirements:* For doctorate, comprehensive exam, thesis/dissertation. *Entrance requirements:* For doctorate, GRE General Test, GRE Subject Test in biology (recommended), 3 letters of recommendation. Additional exam requirements/recommendations for international students: Required—TOEFL (minimum score 610 paper-based; 253 computer-based; 77 iBT). *Application deadline:* For fall admission, 1/15 priority date for domestic students. Application fee: $70. Electronic applications accepted. *Expenses:* Tuition: Full-time $29,500. Required fees: $76. Tuition and fees vary according to degree level and program. *Financial support:* In 2010–11, 7 fellowships with full tuition reimbursements, 13 research assistantships with full tuition reimbursements, 13 teaching assistantships with full tuition reimbursements were awarded; institutionally sponsored loans, scholarships/grants, health care benefits, tuition waivers (full and partial), and unspecified assistantships also available. Financial award applicants required to submit FAFSA. *Faculty research:* Plant cell biology/cytology; plant molecular biology; plant morphology/anatomy/biomechanics; plant physiology, systematic botany, paleobotany; plant ecology, ethnobotany, plant biochemistry, photosynthesis. *Unit head:* Director of Graduate Studies, 607-255-2131. *Application contact:* Graduate Field Assistant, 607-255-2131, E-mail: plbio@cornell.edu.

Eastern New Mexico University, Graduate School, College of Liberal Arts and Sciences, Department of Biology, Portales, NM 88130. Offers applied ecology (MS); cell, molecular biology and biotechnology (MS); education (non-thesis) (MS); microbiology (MS); plant biology (MS); zoology (MS). Part-time programs available. *Faculty:* 8 full-time (0 women). *Students:* 11 full-time (8 women), 7 part-time (4 women); includes 7 minority (5 Hispanic/Latino; 2 Two or more races, non-Hispanic/Latino), 4 international. Average age 25. 21 applicants, 14% accepted, 3 enrolled. In 2010, 4 master's awarded. *Degree requirements:* For master's, comprehensive exam, thesis optional. *Entrance requirements:* For master's, GRE, minimum GPA of 3.0, 2 letters of recommendation, statement of research interest, bachelor's degree related to field of study or proof of common knowledge. Additional exam requirements/recommendations for international students: Required—TOEFL (minimum score 550 paper-based; 213 computer-based; 79 iBT), IELTS (minimum score 6). *Application deadline:* For fall admission, 7/20 priority date for domestic students, 6/20 priority date for international students; for spring admission, 12/15 priority date for domestic students, 11/15 priority date for international students. Applications are processed on a rolling basis. Application fee: $10. Electronic applications accepted. *Expenses:* Tuition, state resident: full-time $3210; part-time $130 per credit hour. Tuition, nonresident: full-time $8652; part-time $360.50 per credit hour. Required fees: $1212; $50.50 per credit hour. Tuition and fees vary according to course load. *Financial support:* In 2010–11, 11 teaching assistantships with partial tuition reimbursements (averaging $8,500 per year) were awarded; unspecified assistantships also available. Support available to part-time students. Financial award applicants required to submit FAFSA. *Unit head:* Dr. Zach Jones, Graduate Coordinator, 575-562-2723, Fax: 575-562-2192, E-mail: zach.jones@enmu.edu. *Application contact:* Sharon Potter, Department Secretary, Biology/Physical Sciences, 575-562-2174, Fax: 575-562-2192, E-mail: sharon.potter@enmu.edu.

Florida State University, The Graduate School, College of Arts and Sciences, Department of Biological Science, Specialization in Plant Biology, Tallahassee, FL 32306-4295. Offers MS, PhD. *Faculty:* 10 full-time (5 women). *Students:* 20 full-time (11 women); includes 1 Asian, non-Hispanic/Latino; 2 Hispanic/Latino, 2 international. In 2010, 1 master's awarded. Terminal master's awarded for partial completion of doctoral program. *Degree requirements:* For master's, comprehensive exam, thesis, teaching experience, seminar presentation; for doctorate, comprehensive exam, thesis/dissertation, teaching experience, seminar presentation. *Entrance requirements:* For master's and doctorate, GRE General Test (minimum combined score 1100; 500 verbal, 500 quantitative), minimum upper-division GPA of 3.0. Additional exam requirements/recommendations for international students: Required—TOEFL (minimum score 600 paper-based; 250 computer-based; 92 iBT). *Application deadline:* For fall admission, 12/15 for domestic and international students. Application fee: $30. Electronic applications accepted. *Expenses:* Tuition, state resident: full-time $8238. *Financial support:* In 2010–11, 19 students received support, including 4 research assistantships with full tuition reimbursements available (averaging $21,000 per year), 15 teaching assistantships with full tuition reimbursements available (averaging $21,000 per year). Financial award application deadline: 12/15; financial award applicants required to submit FAFSA. *Faculty research:* Plant cell and molecular biology; plant population ecology and evolution; meiosis in higher plants; 7pPlant systematics, evolution, ecology, and biogeography; plant-environment interaction; community ecology; plant-insect interactions; rhizobial/plant symbiotic interactions; cell fate specification and reprogramming in plants; evolutionary and developmental biology; plant-environment interaction. *Unit head:* Professor and Associate Chairman for Graduate Studies. *Application contact:* Judy Bowers, Coordinator, Graduate Affairs, 850-644-3023, Fax: 850-644-9829, E-mail: gradinfo@bio.fsu.edu.

Illinois State University, Graduate School, College of Arts and Sciences, Department of Biological Sciences, Normal, IL 61790-2200. Offers animal behavior (MS); bacteriology (MS); biochemistry (MS); biological sciences (MS); biology (PhD); biophysics (MS); biotechnology (MS); botany (MS, PhD); cell biology (MS); conservation biology (MS); developmental biology (MS); ecology (MS, PhD); entomology (MS); evolutionary biology (MS); genetics (MS, PhD); immunology (MS); microbiology (MS, PhD); molecular biology (MS); molecular genetics (MS); neurobiology (MS); neuroscience (MS); parasitology (MS); physiology (MS, PhD); plant biology (MS); plant molecular biology (MS); plant sciences (MS); structural biology (MS); zoology (MS, PhD). Part-time programs available. *Degree requirements:* For master's, thesis or alternative; for doctorate, variable foreign language requirement, thesis/dissertation, 2 terms of residency. *Entrance requirements:* For master's, GRE General Test, minimum GPA of 2.6 in last 60 hours of course work; for doctorate, GRE General Test. *Faculty research:* Redoc balance and drug development in schistosoma mansoni, control of the growth of listeria monocytogenes at low temperature, regulation of cell expansion and microtubule function by SPRI, CRUI: physiology and fitness consequences of different life history phenotypes.

Indiana University Bloomington, University Graduate School, College of Arts and Sciences, Department of Biology, Bloomington, IN 47405. Offers biology teaching (MAT); biotechnology (MA); evolution, ecology, and behavior (MA, PhD); genetics (PhD); microbiology (MA, PhD); molecular, cellular, and developmental biology (PhD); plant sciences (MA, PhD); zoology (MA, PhD). *Faculty:* 58 full-time (15 women), 21 part-time/adjunct (6 women). *Students:* 163 full-time (98 women), 7 part-time (2 women); includes 17 minority (3 Black or African American, non-Hispanic/Latino; 1 American Indian or Alaska Native, non-Hispanic/Latino; 7 Asian, non-Hispanic/Latino; 5 Hispanic/Latino; 1 Native Hawaiian or other Pacific Islander, non-Hispanic/Latino), 52 international. Average age 27. 346 applicants, 15% accepted, 24 enrolled. In 2010, 17 master's, 24 doctorates awarded. Terminal master's awarded for partial completion of doctoral program. *Degree requirements:* For master's, thesis, oral defense; for doctorate, thesis/dissertation, oral defense. *Entrance requirements:* For master's and doctorate, GRE General Test. Additional exam requirements/recommendations for international students: Required—TOEFL (minimum score 100 iBT). *Application deadline:* For fall admission, 1/5 priority date for domestic students, 12/1 priority date for international students. Application fee: $55 ($65 for international students). Electronic applications accepted. *Financial support:* In 2010–11, 170 students received support, including 64 fellowships with tuition reimbursements available (averaging $19,484 per year), 44 research assistantships with tuition reimbursements available (averaging $20,300 per year), 62 teaching assistantships with tuition reimbursements available (averaging $20,521 per year); scholarships/grants, traineeships, health care benefits, and unspecified assistantships also available. Financial award application deadline: 1/5. *Faculty research:* Evolution, ecology and behavior; microbiology; molecular biology and genetics; plant biology. *Unit head:* Dr. Roger Innes, Chair, 812-855-2219, Fax: 812-855-6082, E-mail: rinnes@indiana.edu. *Application contact:* Tracey D. Stohr, Graduate Student Recruitment Coordinator, 812-856-6303, Fax: 812-855-6082, E-mail: gradbio@indiana.edu.

Iowa State University of Science and Technology, Graduate College, Interdisciplinary Programs, Program in Plant Biology, Ames, IA 50011. Offers MS, PhD. *Students:* 19 full-time (7 women), 3 part-time (1 woman); includes 1 Black or African American, non-Hispanic/Latino; 1 Asian, non-Hispanic/Latino, 14 international. In 2010, 2 master's, 5 doctorates awarded. *Degree requirements:* For master's, thesis; for doctorate, thesis/dissertation. *Entrance requirements:* For master's and doctorate, GRE General Test. Additional exam requirements/recommendations for international students: Required—TOEFL (minimum score 550 paper-based; 79 iBT), IELTS (minimum score 6.5). *Application deadline:* For fall admission, 1/15 priority date for domestic students, 1/16 priority date for international students. Applications are processed on a rolling basis. Application fee: $40 ($90 for international students). Electronic applications accepted. *Financial support:* In 2010–11, 19 research assistantships with full and partial tuition reimbursements (averaging $19,808 per year), 1 teaching assistantship with full and partial tuition reimbursement (averaging $10,050 per year) were awarded; scholarships/grants, health care benefits, and unspecified assistantships also available. *Unit head:* Dr. Steven Whitman, Supervisory Committee Chair, 515-294-9052, E-mail: ippm@iastate.edu. *Application contact:* Information Contact, 515-294-5836, Fax: 515-294-2592, E-mail: grad_admissions@iastate.edu.

Miami University, Graduate School, College of Arts and Science, Department of Botany, Oxford, OH 45056. Offers MA, MAT, MS, PhD. *Students:* 48 full-time (28 women), 131 part-time (96 women); includes 6 minority (2 Black or African American, non-Hispanic/Latino; 2 Asian, non-Hispanic/Latino; 2 Two or more races, non-Hispanic/Latino), 15 international. Average age 35. In 2010, 17 master's, 4 doctorates awarded. *Entrance requirements:* For master's, GRE General Test, GRE Subject Test (recommended), minimum undergraduate GPA of 3.0 during previous 2 years or 2.75 overall; for doctorate, GRE General Test, GRE Subject Test (recommended), minimum undergraduate GPA of 2.75, 3.0 graduate. Additional exam requirements/recommendations for international students: Required—TOEFL (minimum score 550 paper-based). *Application deadline:* Applications are processed on a rolling basis. Application fee: $50. Electronic applications accepted. *Expenses:* Tuition, state resident: full-time $11,616; part-time $484 per credit hour. Tuition, nonresident: full-time $25,656; part-time $1069 per credit hour. Required fees: $528. *Financial support:* Research assistantships, teaching assistantships with full tuition reimbursements, Federal Work-Study, institutionally sponsored loans, health care benefits, and unspecified assistantships available. Financial award application deadline: 3/1; financial award applicants required to submit FAFSA. *Faculty research:* Evolution of plants, fungi and algae; bioinformatics; molecular biology of plants and cyanobacteria; food web dynamics; plant science education. *Unit head:* Dr. John Kiss, Chair, 513-529-4200, E-mail: kissjz@muohio.edu. *Application contact:* Dr. Richard C. Moore, Graduate Coordinator, 513-529-4278, E-mail: moorerc@muohio.edu.

Michigan State University, The Graduate School, College of Agriculture and Natural Resources, MSU-DOE Plant Research Laboratory, East Lansing, MI 48824. Offers biochemistry and molecular biology (PhD); cellular and molecular biology (PhD); crop and soil sciences (PhD); genetics (PhD); microbiology and molecular genetics (PhD); plant biology (PhD); plant physiology (PhD). Offered jointly with the Department of Energy. *Degree requirements:* For doctorate, comprehensive exam, thesis/dissertation, laboratory rotation, defense of dissertation. *Entrance requirements:* For doctorate, GRE General Test, acceptance into one of the affiliated department programs; 3 letters of recommendation; bachelor's degree or equivalent in life sciences, chemistry, biochemistry, or biophysics; research experience. Electronic applications accepted. *Faculty research:* Role of hormones in the regulation of plant development and physiology, molecular mechanisms associated with signal recognition, development and application of genetic methods and materials, protein routing and function.

Michigan State University, The Graduate School, College of Natural Science and College of Agriculture and Natural Resources, Department of Plant Biology, East Lansing, MI 48824. Offers plant biology (MS, PhD); plant breeding, genetics and biotechnology—plant biology (MS, PhD). *Entrance requirements:* Additional exam requirements/recommendations for international students: Required—TOEFL. Electronic applications accepted. *Faculty research:* Physiological, molecular, and biochemical mechanisms; systematics; inheritance; ecology and geohistory.

New York University, Graduate School of Arts and Science, Department of Biology, New York, NY 10012-1019. Offers biology (PhD); biomedical journalism (MS); cancer and molecular biology (PhD); computational biology (PhD); computers in biological research (MS); developmental genetics (PhD); general biology (MS); immunology and microbiology (PhD); molecular genetics (PhD); neurobiology (PhD); oral biology (MS); plant biology (PhD); recombinant DNA technology (MS); MS/MBA. Part-time programs available. *Faculty:* 24 full-time (5 women). *Students:* 155 full-time (89 women), 38 part-time (24 women); includes 29 Asian, non-Hispanic/Latino; 7 Hispanic/Latino, 88 international. Average age 27. 324 applicants, 69% accepted, 63 enrolled. In 2010, 55 master's, 4 doctorates awarded. Terminal master's awarded for partial completion of doctoral program. *Degree requirements:* For master's, thesis or alternative, qualifying paper; for doctorate, comprehensive exam, thesis/dissertation. *Entrance requirements:* For master's, GRE General Test; for doctorate, GRE General Test, GRE Subject Test. Additional exam requirements/recommendations for international students: Required—TOEFL. *Application deadline:* For fall admission, 12/15 priority date for domestic students. Application fee: $90. *Financial support:* Fellowships with tuition reimbursements, research assistantships with tuition reimbursements, teaching assistantships with tuition reimbursements, career-related internships or fieldwork, Federal Work-Study, institutionally sponsored loans, scholarships/grants, health care benefits, and unspecified assistantships available. Financial award application deadline: 12/15; financial award applicants required to submit FAFSA. *Faculty research:* Genomics, molecular and cell biology, development and molecular genetics, molecular evolution of plants and animals. *Unit head:* Gloria Coruzzi, Chair, 212-998-8200, Fax: 212-995-4015, E-mail: biology@nyu.edu. *Application contact:* Justin Blau, Director of Graduate Studies, 212-998-8200, Fax: 212-995-4015, E-mail: biology@nyu.edu.

North Carolina State University, Graduate School, College of Agriculture and Life Sciences, Department of Plant Biology, Raleigh, NC 27695. Offers MS, PhD. Part-time programs available. Terminal master's awarded for partial completion of doctoral program. *Degree requirements:* For master's, thesis (for some programs); for doctorate, thesis/dissertation. *Entrance requirements:* For master's and doctorate, GRE. Additional exam requirements/recommendations for international students: Required—TOEFL. Electronic applications accepted. *Faculty research:* Plant molecular and cell biology, aquatic ecology, community ecology, restoration, systematics, plant pathogen and environmental interactions.

Ohio University, Graduate College, College of Arts and Sciences, Department of Environmental and Plant Biology, Athens, OH 45701-2979. Offers MS, PhD. Part-time programs available. *Students:* 19 full-time (5 women), 1 part-time (0 women); includes 2 minority (1 Black or African American, non-Hispanic/Latino; 1 Two or more races, non-Hispanic/Latino), 2 international. Average age 25. 17 applicants, 47% accepted, 7 enrolled. In 2010, 2 master's, 2 doctorates awarded. *Degree requirements:* For master's, thesis, 2 quarters of teaching experience; for doctorate, comprehensive exam, thesis/dissertation, 2 quarters of teaching experience. *Entrance requirements:* For master's, GRE General Test, minimum GPA of 3.0; for doctorate, GRE General Test, minimum GPA of 3.2. Additional exam requirements/recommendations for international students: Required—TOEFL (minimum score 620 paper-based; 260 computer-based; 105 iBT) or IELTS (minimum score 7.5). *Application deadline:* For fall admission, 1/15 priority date for domestic and international students. Applications are processed on a rolling basis. Application fee: $50 ($55 for international students). Electronic applications accepted. *Financial support:* Fellowships with full tuition reimbursements, research assistantships with full tuition reimbursements, teaching assistantships with full tuition reimbursements, Federal Work-Study, institutionally sponsored loans, and scholarships/grants available. Financial award application deadline: 1/15. *Faculty research:* Eastern deciduous forest ecology, evolutionary developmental plant biology, phylogenetic systematics, plant cell wall biotechnology. Total annual research expenditures: $859,166. *Unit head:* Dr. Brian C. McCarthy, Chair, 740-593-1615, Fax: 740-593-1130, E-mail: mccarthy@ohio.edu. *Application contact:* Dr. Allan Showalter, Graduate Chair, 740-593-1135, Fax: 740-593-1130, E-mail: showalte@ohio.edu.

Rutgers, The State University of New Jersey, New Brunswick, Graduate School-New Brunswick, Program in Plant Biology, Piscataway, NJ 08854-8097. Offers horticulture and plant technology (MS, PhD); molecular and cellular biology (MS, PhD); organismal and population biology (MS, PhD); plant pathology (MS, PhD). Part-time programs available. Terminal master's awarded for partial completion of doctoral program. *Degree requirements:* For master's, comprehensive exam, thesis or alternative; for doctorate, comprehensive exam, thesis/dissertation. *Entrance requirements:* For master's and doctorate, GRE General Test, GRE Subject Test (recommended). Additional exam requirements/recommendations for international students: Required—TOEFL (minimum score 600 paper-based; 250 computer-based). Electronic applications accepted. *Expenses:* Tuition, state resident: full-time $7200; part-time $600 per credit. Tuition, nonresident: full-time $11,124; part-time $927 per credit. *Faculty research:* Molecular biology and biochemistry of plants, plant development and genomics, plant protection, plant improvement, plant management of horticultural and field crops.

Southern Illinois University Carbondale, Graduate School, College of Science, Department of Plant Biology, Carbondale, IL 62901-4701. Offers MS, PhD. *Degree requirements:* For master's, thesis; for doctorate, one foreign language, thesis/dissertation. *Entrance requirements:* For master's, GRE General Test, minimum GPA of 2.7; for doctorate, GRE General Test, minimum GPA of 3.25. Additional exam requirements/recommendations for international students: Required—TOEFL. *Faculty research:* Algal toxins, ethnobotany, community and wetland ecology, morphogenesis, systematics and evolution.

Texas A&M University, College of Agriculture and Life Sciences, Department of Soil and Crop Sciences, College Station, TX 77843. Offers agronomy (M Agr, MS, PhD); food science and technology (MS, PhD); genetics (PhD); molecular and environmental plant sciences (MS, PhD); plant breeding (MS, PhD); soil science (MS, PhD). *Faculty:* 36. *Students:* 94 full-time (35 women), 30 part-time (7 women); includes 14 minority (3 Black or African American, non-Hispanic/Latino; 1 American Indian or Alaska Native, non-Hispanic/Latino; 3 Asian, non-Hispanic/Latino; 7 Hispanic/Latino), 36 international. Average age 26. In 2010, 11 master's, 3 doctorates awarded. *Degree requirements:* For master's, thesis; for doctorate, thesis/dissertation. *Entrance requirements:* For master's and doctorate, GRE General Test. Additional exam requirements/recommendations for international students: Required—TOEFL. *Application deadline:* For fall admission, 3/1 priority date for domestic students; for spring admission, 8/1 for domestic students. Applications are processed on a rolling basis. Application fee: $50 ($75 for international students). *Financial support:* In 2010–11, fellowships (averaging $16,000 per year), research assistantships with partial tuition reimbursements (averaging $15,000 per year) were awarded; career-related internships or fieldwork, Federal Work-Study, and institutionally sponsored loans also available. *Faculty research:* Soil and crop management, turfgrass science, weed science, cereal chemistry, food protein chemistry. *Unit head:* Dr. David D. Baltensperger, Department Head, 979-845-3001, E-mail: dbaltensperger@ag.tamu.edu. *Application contact:* Dr. David D. Baltensperger, Department Head, 979-845-3001, E-mail: dbaltensperger@ag.tamu.edu.

Université Laval, Faculty of Agricultural and Food Sciences, Program in Plant Biology, Québec, QC G1K 7P4, Canada. Offers M Sc, PhD. Terminal master's awarded for partial completion of doctoral program. *Degree requirements:* For master's, thesis (for some programs); for doctorate, comprehensive exam, thesis/dissertation. *Entrance requirements:* For master's and doctorate, knowledge of French and English. Electronic applications accepted.

University of Alberta, Faculty of Graduate Studies and Research, Department of Biological Sciences, Edmonton, AB T6G 2E1, Canada. Offers environmental biology and ecology (M Sc, PhD); microbiology and biotechnology (M Sc, PhD); molecular biology and genetics (M Sc, PhD); physiology and cell biology (M Sc, PhD); plant biology (M Sc, PhD); systematics and evolution (M Sc, PhD). Terminal master's awarded for partial completion of doctoral program. *Degree requirements:* For master's, thesis; for doctorate, thesis/dissertation. *Entrance requirements:* Additional exam requirements/recommendations for international students: Required—TOEFL.

University of California, Berkeley, Graduate Division, College of Natural Resources, Department of Plant and Microbial Biology, Berkeley, CA 94720-1500. Offers plant biology (PhD). *Degree requirements:* For doctorate, thesis/dissertation, qualifying exam, seminar

Plant Biology

University of California, Berkeley (continued)
presentation. *Entrance requirements:* For doctorate, GRE General Test, minimum GPA of 3.0, 3 letters of recommendation. *Faculty research:* Development, molecular biology, genetics, microbial biology, mycology.

University of California, Davis, Graduate Studies, Graduate Group in Plant Biology, Davis, CA 95616. Offers MS, PhD. *Degree requirements:* For master's, comprehensive exam (for some programs), thesis (for some programs); for doctorate, thesis/dissertation. *Entrance requirements:* For master's, GRE General Test, GRE Subject Test (biology), minimum GPA of 3.0; for doctorate, GRE General Test, GRE Subject Test (biology). Additional exam requirements/recommendations for international students: Required—TOEFL (minimum score 550 paper-based; 213 computer-based). Electronic applications accepted. *Faculty research:* Cell and molecular biology, ecology, systematics and evolution, integrative plant and crop physiology, plant development and structure.

University of California, Riverside, Graduate Division, Department of Botany and Plant Sciences, Riverside, CA 92521-0102. Offers plant biology (MS, PhD), including plant genetics (PhD). Part-time programs available. Terminal master's awarded for partial completion of doctoral program. *Degree requirements:* For master's, comprehensive exams or thesis; for doctorate, thesis/dissertation, qualifying exams. *Entrance requirements:* For master's and doctorate, GRE General Test, minimum GPA of 3.2. Additional exam requirements/recommendations for international students: Required—TOEFL (minimum score 550 paper-based; 213 computer-based; 80 iBT). Electronic applications accepted. *Faculty research:* Agricultural plant biology; biochemistry and physiology; cellular, molecular and developmental biology; ecology, evolution, systematics and ethnobotany; genetics, genomics and bioinformatics.

University of California, San Diego, Office of Graduate Studies, Division of Biological Sciences, Program in Plant Systems Biology, La Jolla, CA 92093. Offers PhD.

University of Connecticut, Graduate School, College of Liberal Arts and Sciences, Department of Molecular and Cell Biology, Field of Plant Cell and Molecular Biology, Storrs, CT 06269. Offers MS, PhD. *Degree requirements:* For doctorate, thesis/dissertation. *Entrance requirements:* For master's and doctorate, GRE General Test, GRE Subject Test. Additional exam requirements/recommendations for international students: Required—TOEFL.

University of Florida, Graduate School, College of Agricultural and Life Sciences and College of Liberal Arts and Sciences, Program in Plant Molecular and Cellular Biology, Gainesville, FL 32611. Offers MS, PhD. *Students:* 23 full-time (9 women), 1 (woman) part-time; includes 2 Asian, non-Hispanic/Latino, 13 international. Average age 27. 44 applicants, 16% accepted, 7 enrolled. In 2010, 1 master's, 7 doctorates awarded. *Degree requirements:* For master's, thesis; for doctorate, comprehensive exam, thesis/dissertation, first author peer-reviewed publication. *Entrance requirements:* For master's and doctorate, GRE General Test (minimum combined score 1100 verbal and quantitative), minimum GPA of 3.0. Additional exam requirements/recommendations for international students: Required—TOEFL (minimum score 550 paper-based; 213 computer-based; 80 iBT), IELTS (minimum score 6). *Application deadline:* For fall admission, 1/1 priority date for domestic students, 1/1 for international students; for spring admission, 8/1 for domestic and international students. Applications are processed on a rolling basis. Application fee: $30. Electronic applications accepted. *Expenses:* Tuition, state resident: full-time $10,916. Tuition, nonresident: full-time $28,309. *Financial support:* In 2010–11, 29 students received support, including 7 fellowships, 22 research assistantships (averaging $22,751 per year); unspecified assistantships also available. Financial award applicants required to submit FAFSA. *Faculty research:* The understanding of molecular and cellular mechanisms that mediate plant development, adaptation, and evolution including bioinformatics, genomics, proteomics, genetics, biochemistry, breeding, physiology and molecular and cellular biology. *Unit head:* Dr. Gary F. Peter, Director, 352-846-0896, E-mail: gfpeter@ufl.edu. *Application contact:* Dr. A. Mark Settles, Graduate Coordinator, 352-392-7571, E-mail: settles@ufl.edu.

University of Georgia, College of Arts and Sciences, Department of Plant Biology, Athens, GA 30602. Offers MS, PhD. *Faculty:* 22 full-time (9 women). *Students:* 35 full-time (16 women), 2 part-time (1 woman); includes 2 Hispanic/Latino, 12 international. 34 applicants, 35% accepted, 6 enrolled. In 2010, 7 doctorates awarded. *Degree requirements:* For master's, thesis; for doctorate, one foreign language, thesis/dissertation. *Entrance requirements:* For master's and doctorate, GRE General Test. *Application deadline:* For fall admission, 1/1 priority date for domestic students. Application fee: $50. Electronic applications accepted. *Expenses:* Tuition, state resident: full-time $7200; part-time $344 per credit hour. Tuition, nonresident: full-time $21,900; part-time $944 per credit hour. Tuition and fees vary according to course load and program. *Financial support:* Fellowships, research assistantships, teaching assistantships, unspecified assistantships available. *Unit head:* Dr. Michelle Momany, Head, 706-542-1811, Fax: 706-542-1805, E-mail: depthead@plantbio.uga.edu. *Application contact:* Dr. Lisa Donovan, Graduate Coordinator, 706-542-2969, Fax: 706-542-1805, E-mail: donovan@plantbio.uga.edu.

University of Illinois at Urbana–Champaign, Graduate College, College of Liberal Arts and Sciences, School of Integrative Biology, Department of Plant Biology, Champaign, IL 61820. Offers MS, PhD. *Faculty:* 15 full-time (3 women). *Students:* 37 full-time (22 women), 3 part-time (1 woman); includes 1 Black or African American, non-Hispanic/Latino; 1 American Indian or Alaska Native, non-Hispanic/Latino; 2 Asian, non-Hispanic/Latino, 4 international. 37 applicants, 8% accepted, 3 enrolled. In 2010, 2 master's, 1 doctorate awarded. *Entrance requirements:* For master's, GRE General Test, minimum GPA of 3.0; for doctorate, GRE, minimum GPA of 3.0. Additional exam requirements/recommendations for international students: Required—TOEFL (minimum score 600 paper-based; 250 computer-based; 102 iBT). *Application deadline:* Applications are processed on a rolling basis. Application fee: $75 ($90 for international students). Electronic applications accepted. *Financial support:* In 2010–11, 3 fellowships, 24 research assistantships, 22 teaching assistantships were awarded; tuition waivers (full and partial) also available. *Unit head:* Feng Sheng Hu, Head, 217-244-2982, Fax: 217-244-7246, E-mail: fhu@illinois.edu. *Application contact:* Lisa Boise, Office Administrator, 217-333-3261, Fax: 217-244-7246, E-mail: boise@illinois.edu.

University of Illinois at Urbana–Champaign, Graduate College, College of Liberal Arts and Sciences, School of Integrative Biology, Program in Physiological and Molecular Plant Biology, Champaign, IL 61820. Offers PhD. *Students:* 7 full-time (3 women), 5 international. 1 applicant, 0% accepted, 0 enrolled. In 2010, 3 doctorates awarded. *Entrance requirements:* For doctorate, GRE, minimum GPA of 3.0. Additional exam requirements/recommendations for international students: Required—TOEFL (minimum score 570 paper-based; 230 computer-based; 89 iBT). *Application deadline:* Applications are processed on a rolling basis. Application fee: $75 ($90 for international students). Electronic applications accepted. *Financial support:* In 2010–11, 1 fellowship, 4 research assistantships, 4 teaching assistantships were awarded; tuition waivers (full and partial) also available. *Unit head:* Stephen Moose, Director, 217-244-6308, Fax: 217-244-1224, E-mail: smoose@illinois.edu. *Application contact:* Carol Hall, Office Manager, 217-333-8208, Fax: 217-244-1224, E-mail: cahall@illinois.edu.

University of Maine, Graduate School, College of Natural Sciences, Forestry, and Agriculture, Department of Biological Sciences, Program in Plant Science, Orono, ME 04469. Offers PhD. Part-time programs available. *Students:* 1 full-time (0 women), 1 (woman) part-time, 1 international. Average age 28. 5 applicants, 20% accepted, 1 enrolled. In 2010, 1 degree awarded. *Degree requirements:* For doctorate, thesis/dissertation. *Entrance requirements:* For doctorate, GRE General Test. Additional exam requirements/recommendations for international students: Required—TOEFL. *Application deadline:* For fall admission, 2/1 priority date for domestic students. Applications are processed on a rolling basis. Application fee: $65. Electronic applications accepted. *Expenses:* Tuition, state resident: full-time $400. Tuition, nonresident: full-time $1050. *Financial support:* Career-related internships or fieldwork, Federal Work-Study, institutionally sponsored loans, and tuition waivers (full) available. Financial award application deadline: 3/1. *Unit head:* Dr. Stellos Tavantiz, Coordinator, 207-581-2986. *Application contact:* Scott G. Delcourt, Associate Dean of the Graduate School, 207-581-3291, Fax: 207-581-3232, E-mail: graduate@maine.edu.

University of Maine, Graduate School, College of Natural Sciences, Forestry, and Agriculture, Department of Plant, Soil, and Environmental Sciences, Orono, ME 04469. Offers biological sciences (PhD); ecology and environmental sciences (MS, PhD); forest resources (PhD); horticulture (MS); plant science (PhD); plant, soil, and environmental sciences (MS); resource utilization (MS). *Faculty:* 9 full-time (3 women), 7 part-time/adjunct (3 women). *Students:* 6 full-time (2 women), 2 part-time (1 woman), 2 international. Average age 31. 9 applicants, 22% accepted, 0 enrolled. In 2010, 2 master's awarded. *Entrance requirements:* For master's and doctorate, GRE General Test. Additional exam requirements/recommendations for international students: Required—TOEFL. *Application deadline:* Applications are processed on a rolling basis. Application fee: $65. Electronic applications accepted. *Expenses:* Tuition, state resident: full-time $400. Tuition, nonresident: full-time $1050. *Financial support:* In 2010–11, 16 research assistantships with tuition reimbursements (averaging $16,260 per year), 3 teaching assistantships with tuition reimbursements (averaging $12,790 per year) were awarded; scholarships/grants, tuition waivers (full and partial), and unspecified assistantships also available. *Unit head:* Dr. Gregory Porter, Chair, 207-581-2943, Fax: 207-581-3207. *Application contact:* Scott G. Delcourt, Associate Dean of the Graduate School, 207-581-3291, Fax: 207-581-3232, E-mail: graduate@maine.edu.

University of Maryland, College Park, Academic Affairs, College of Computer, Mathematical and Natural Sciences, Department of Cell Biology and Molecular Genetics, College Park, MD 20742. Offers cell biology and molecular genetics (MS, PhD); molecular and cellular biology (PhD); plant biology (MS, PhD). Part-time and evening/weekend programs available. *Faculty:* 78 full-time (30 women), 3 part-time/adjunct (all women). *Students:* 96 full-time (57 women), 5 part-time (4 women); includes 16 minority (4 Black or African American, non-Hispanic/Latino; 7 Asian, non-Hispanic/Latino; 5 Hispanic/Latino), 42 international. In 2010, 3 master's, 7 doctorates awarded. Terminal master's awarded for partial completion of doctoral program. *Degree requirements:* For master's, thesis; for doctorate, thesis/dissertation. *Entrance requirements:* For master's, GRE General Test, minimum GPA of 3.0, 3 letters of recommendation; for doctorate, GRE General Test. Additional exam requirements/recommendations for international students: Required—TOEFL. *Application deadline:* Applications are processed on a rolling basis. Application fee: $75. Electronic applications accepted. *Expenses:* Tuition, state resident: part-time $471 per credit hour. Tuition, nonresident: part-time $1016 per credit hour. Required fees: $337 per term. *Financial support:* In 2010–11, 7 fellowships with full and partial tuition reimbursements (averaging $24,904 per year), 30 research assistantships (averaging $19,503 per year), 46 teaching assistantships (averaging $19,224 per year) were awarded; Federal Work-Study and scholarships/grants also available. Support available to part-time students. Financial award applicants required to submit FAFSA. *Faculty research:* Cytoskeletal activity, membrane biology, cell division, genetics and genomics, virology. Total annual research expenditures: $7.2 million. *Unit head:* Dr. Norma Andrews, Chair, 301-405-8414, E-mail: andrewsn@umd.edu. *Application contact:* Dr. Charles A. Caramello, Dean of Graduate School, 301-405-0358, Fax: 301-314-9305.

University of Massachusetts Amherst, Graduate School, Interdisciplinary Programs, Program in Plant Biology, Amherst, MA 01003. Offers biochemistry and metabolism (MS, PhD); cell biology and physiology (MS, PhD); environmental, ecological and integrative (PhD); environmental, ecological and integrative biology (MS); genetics and evolution (MS, PhD). *Students:* 18 full-time (8 women); includes 1 minority (Asian, non-Hispanic/Latino), 7 international. Average age 29. 27 applicants, 41% accepted, 6 enrolled. In 2010, 3 doctorates awarded. *Degree requirements:* For master's, thesis; for doctorate, 2 foreign languages, comprehensive exam, thesis/dissertation. *Entrance requirements:* For master's and doctorate, GRE General Test. Additional exam requirements/recommendations for international students: Required—TOEFL (minimum score 550 paper-based; 213 computer-based; 80 iBT), IELTS (minimum score 6.5). *Application deadline:* For fall admission, 12/15 for domestic and international students; for spring admission, 10/1 for domestic and international students. Applications are processed on a rolling basis. Application fee: $50 ($65 for international students). Electronic applications accepted. *Expenses:* Tuition, state resident: full-time $2640. Required fees: $8282. One-time fee: $357 full-time. *Financial support:* In 2010–11, 12 research assistantships with full tuition reimbursements (averaging $11,651 per year) were awarded; fellowships, teaching assistantships, career-related internships or fieldwork, Federal Work-Study, scholarships/grants, traineeships, health care benefits, tuition waivers (full), and unspecified assistantships also available. Support available to part-time students. Financial award application deadline: 12/15; financial award applicants required to submit FAFSA. *Unit head:* Dr. Elsbeth L. Walker, Graduate Program Director, 413-577-3217, Fax: 413-545-3243. *Application contact:* Jean M. Ames, Supervisor of Admissions, 413-545—0722, Fax: 413-577-0010, E-mail: gradadm@grad.umass.edu.

University of Minnesota, Twin Cities Campus, Graduate School, College of Biological Sciences, Program in Plant Biological Sciences, Minneapolis, MN 55455-0213. Offers MS, PhD. Part-time programs available. Terminal master's awarded for partial completion of doctoral program. *Degree requirements:* For master's, thesis or alternative; for doctorate, thesis/dissertation, written and oral preliminary exams. *Entrance requirements:* For master's and doctorate, GRE General Test. Additional exam requirements/recommendations for international students: Required—TOEFL. Electronic applications accepted. *Faculty research:* Cell and molecular biology; plant physiology; plant structure, diversity, and development; ecology, systematics, evolution and genomics.

University of Missouri, Graduate School, College of Agriculture, Food and Natural Resources, Division of Plant Sciences, Program in Plant Biology and Genetics, Columbia, MO 65211. Offers MS, PhD. Terminal master's awarded for partial completion of doctoral program. *Degree requirements:* For master's, thesis; for doctorate, thesis/dissertation. *Entrance requirements:* For master's and doctorate, GRE General Test, minimum GPA of 3.0. *Application deadline:* For fall admission, 3/1 priority date for domestic students. Applications are processed on a rolling basis. Application fee: $45 ($60 for international students). *Financial support:* Research assistantships, teaching assistantships, institutionally sponsored loans available. *Unit head:* Dr. Jeanne Mihail, Director of Graduate Studies, 573-882-0574, E-mail: mihailj@missouri.edu. *Application contact:* Dr. Jeanne Mihail, Director of Graduate Studies, 573-882-0574, E-mail: mihailj@missouri.edu.

University of New Hampshire, Graduate School, College of Life Sciences and Agriculture, Department of Biological Sciences, Program in Plant Biology, Durham, NH 03824. Offers MS, PhD. Part-time programs available. *Faculty:* 22 full-time. *Students:* 9 full-time (6 women), 10 part-time (6 women); includes 1 Asian, non-Hispanic/Latino; 2 Two or more races, non-Hispanic/Latino, 3 international. Average age 33. 14 applicants, 21% accepted, 2 enrolled. In 2010, 2 master's awarded. Terminal master's awarded for partial completion of doctoral program. *Degree requirements:* For master's, thesis; for doctorate, thesis/dissertation. *Entrance requirements:* For master's and doctorate, GRE General Test, GRE Subject Test. Additional exam requirements/recommendations for international students: Required—TOEFL (minimum score 550 paper-based; 213 computer-based; 80 iBT). *Application deadline:* For fall admission, 6/1 priority date for domestic students, 4/1 for international students; for spring admission, 12/1 for domestic students. Applications are processed on a rolling basis. Application fee: $65. Electronic applications accepted. *Financial support:* In 2010–11, 15 students received support, including 1 fellowship, 3 research assistantships, 9 teaching assistantships; career-related internships or fieldwork, Federal Work-Study, scholarships/grants, and tuition waivers (full and partial) also available. Support available to part-time students. Financial award application deadline: 2/15. *Unit head:* Christopher Neefus, Chairperson, 603-862-3205. *Application contact:* Diane Lavalliere, Administrative Assistant, 603-862-4095, E-mail: diane.lavallier@unh.edu.

The University of Texas at Austin, Graduate School, College of Natural Sciences, School of Biological Sciences, Program in Plant Biology, Austin, TX 78712-1111. Offers MA, PhD. *Entrance requirements:* For master's and doctorate, GRE General Test, minimum GPA of 3.0.

Additional exam requirements/recommendations for international students: Required—TOEFL. Electronic applications accepted. *Faculty research:* Systematics, plant molecular biology, psychology, ecology, evolution.

University of Vermont, Graduate College, College of Agriculture and Life Sciences, Department of Plant Biology, Plant Biology Program, Burlington, VT 05405. Offers MS, PhD. *Faculty:* 11 full-time (4 women). *Students:* 12 (6 women), 1 international. 39 applicants, 21% accepted, 0 enrolled. In 2010, 3 master's awarded. *Degree requirements:* For master's, comprehensive exam, thesis; for doctorate, comprehensive exam, thesis/dissertation. *Entrance requirements:* For master's and doctorate, GRE General Test. Additional exam requirements/recommendations for international students: Required—TOEFL (minimum score 550 paper-based; 213 computer-based; 80 iBT). *Application deadline:* For fall admission, 1/1 priority date for domestic and international students. Applications are processed on a rolling basis. Application fee: $40. Electronic applications accepted. *Expenses:* Tuition, state resident: part-time $537 per credit hour. Tuition, nonresident: part-time $1355 per credit hour. *Financial support:* In 2010–11, research assistantships with full tuition reimbursements (averaging $21,800 per year), teaching assistantships with full tuition reimbursements (averaging $21,800 per year) were awarded; fellowships, health care benefits, tuition waivers (full and partial), and stipends also available. Financial award application deadline: 1/1. *Faculty research:* Systematics, biochemistry, ecology and evolution, physiology, development and molecular genetics. Total annual research expenditures: $739,761. *Unit head:* Dr. Thomas Vogelmann, Chairperson, 802-656-2930, Fax: 802-656-0440. *Application contact:* Dr. C. Paris, Coordinator, 802-656-2930, Fax: 802-656-0440.

The University of Western Ontario, Faculty of Graduate Studies, Biosciences Division, Department of Plant Sciences, London, ON N6A 5B8, Canada. Offers plant and environmental sciences (M Sc); plant sciences (M Sc, PhD); plant sciences and environmental sciences (PhD); plant sciences and molecular biology (M Sc, PhD). *Degree requirements:* For master's, thesis; for doctorate, thesis/dissertation. *Entrance requirements:* For doctorate, M Sc or equivalent. Additional exam requirements/recommendations for international students: Required—TOEFL. *Faculty research:* Ecology systematics, plant biochemistry and physiology, yeast genetics, molecular biology.

Washington University in St. Louis, Graduate School of Arts and Sciences, Division of Biology and Biomedical Sciences, Program in Plant Biology, St. Louis, MO 63130-4899. Offers PhD. *Degree requirements:* For doctorate, thesis/dissertation. *Entrance requirements:* For doctorate, GRE General Test, GRE Subject Test. Electronic applications accepted.

Yale University, Graduate School of Arts and Sciences, Department of Molecular, Cellular, and Developmental Biology, Program in Plant Sciences, New Haven, CT 06520. Offers PhD. *Degree requirements:* For doctorate, thesis/dissertation. *Entrance requirements:* For doctorate, GRE General Test, GRE Subject Test.

Plant Molecular Biology

Cornell University, Graduate School, Graduate Fields of Agriculture and Life Sciences, Field of Plant Biology, Ithaca, NY 14853-0001. Offers cytology (MS, PhD); paleobotany (MS, PhD); plant cell biology (MS, PhD); plant ecology (MS, PhD); plant molecular biology (MS, PhD); plant morphology, anatomy and biomechanics (MS, PhD); plant physiology (MS, PhD); systematic botany (MS, PhD). *Faculty:* 48 full-time (13 women). *Students:* 33 full-time (18 women); includes 2 Black or African American, non-Hispanic/Latino; 1 Hispanic/Latino, 10 international. Average age 26. 48 applicants, 33% accepted, 7 enrolled. In 2010, 8 doctorates awarded. *Degree requirements:* For doctorate, comprehensive exam, thesis/dissertation. *Entrance requirements:* For doctorate, GRE General Test, GRE Subject Test in biology (recommended), 3 letters of recommendation. Additional exam requirements/recommendations for international students: Required—TOEFL (minimum score 610 paper-based; 253 computer-based; 77 iBT). *Application deadline:* For fall admission, 1/15 priority date for domestic students. Application fee: $70. Electronic applications accepted. *Expenses:* Tuition: Full-time $29,500. Required fees: $76. Tuition and fees vary according to degree level and program. *Financial support:* In 2010–11, 7 fellowships with full tuition reimbursements, 13 research assistantships with full tuition reimbursements, 13 teaching assistantships with full tuition reimbursements were awarded; institutionally sponsored loans, scholarships/grants, health care benefits, tuition waivers (full and partial), and unspecified assistantships also available. Financial award applicants required to submit FAFSA. *Faculty research:* Plant cell biology/cytology; plant molecular biology; plant morphology/anatomy/biomechanics; plant physiology, systematic botany, paleobotany; plant ecology, ethnobotany, plant biochemistry, photosynthesis. *Unit head:* Director of Graduate Studies, 607-255-2131. *Application contact:* Graduate Field Assistant, 607-255-2131, E-mail: plbio@cornell.edu.

Illinois State University, Graduate School, College of Arts and Sciences, Department of Biological Sciences, Normal, IL 61790-2200. Offers animal behavior (MS); bacteriology (MS); biochemistry (MS); biological sciences (MS); biology (PhD); biophysics (MS); biotechnology (MS); botany (MS, PhD); cell biology (MS); conservation biology (MS); developmental biology (MS); ecology (MS, PhD); entomology (MS); evolutionary biology (MS); genetics (MS, PhD); immunology (MS); microbiology (MS, PhD); molecular biology (MS); molecular genetics (MS); neurobiology (MS); neuroscience (MS); parasitology (MS); physiology (MS, PhD); plant biology (MS); plant molecular biology (MS); plant sciences (MS); structural biology (MS); zoology (MS, PhD). Part-time programs available. *Degree requirements:* For master's, thesis or alternative; for doctorate, variable foreign language requirement, thesis/dissertation, 2 terms of residency. *Entrance requirements:* For master's, GRE General Test, minimum GPA of 2.6 in last 60 hours of course work; for doctorate, GRE General Test. *Faculty research:* Redoc balance and drug development in schistosoma mansoni, control of the growth of listeria monocytogenes at low temperature, regulation of cell expansion and microtubule function by SPRI, CRUI: physiology and fitness consequences of different life history phenotypes.

Michigan Technological University, Graduate School, School of Forest Resources and Environmental Science, Program in Forest Molecular Genetics and Biotechnology, Houghton, MI 49931. Offers MS, PhD. Part-time programs available. Terminal master's awarded for partial completion of doctoral program. *Degree requirements:* For master's, thesis (for some programs); for doctorate, comprehensive exam, thesis/dissertation. *Entrance requirements:* For master's, GRE. Additional exam requirements/recommendations for international students: Required—TOEFL (minimum score 550 paper-based; 213 computer-based). Electronic applications accepted.

Rutgers, The State University of New Jersey, New Brunswick, Graduate School-New Brunswick, Program in Plant Biology, Piscataway, NJ 08854-8097. Offers horticulture and plant technology (MS, PhD); molecular and cellular biology (MS, PhD); organismal and population biology (MS, PhD); plant pathology (MS, PhD). Part-time programs available. Terminal master's awarded for partial completion of doctoral program. *Degree requirements:* For master's, comprehensive exam, thesis or alternative; for doctorate, comprehensive exam, thesis/dissertation. *Entrance requirements:* For master's and doctorate, GRE General Test, GRE Subject Test (recommended). Additional exam requirements/recommendations for international students: Required—TOEFL (minimum score 600 paper-based; 250 computer-based). Electronic applications accepted. *Expenses:* Tuition, state resident: full-time $7200; part-time $600 per credit. Tuition, nonresident: full-time $11,124; part-time $927 per credit. *Faculty research:* Molecular biology and biochemistry of plants, plant development and genomics, plant protection, plant improvement, plant management of horticultural and field crops.

University of California, San Diego, Office of Graduate Studies, Division of Biological Sciences, Program in Plant Molecular Biology, La Jolla, CA 92093. Offers PhD. Offered in association with the Salk Institute. *Degree requirements:* For doctorate, thesis/dissertation, qualifying exam. Electronic applications accepted.

University of Connecticut, Graduate School, College of Liberal Arts and Sciences, Department of Molecular and Cell Biology, Field of Plant Cell and Molecular Biology, Storrs, CT 06269. Offers MS, PhD. *Degree requirements:* For doctorate, thesis/dissertation. *Entrance requirements:* For master's and doctorate, GRE General Test, GRE Subject Test. Additional exam requirements/recommendations for international students: Required—TOEFL.

University of Florida, Graduate School, College of Agricultural and Life Sciences and College of Liberal Arts and Sciences, Program in Plant Molecular and Cellular Biology, Gainesville, FL 32611. Offers MS, PhD. *Students:* 23 full-time (9 women), 1 (woman) part-time; includes 2 Asian, non-Hispanic/Latino, 13 international. Average age 27. 44 applicants, 16% accepted, 7 enrolled. In 2010, 1 master's, 7 doctorates awarded. *Degree requirements:* For master's, thesis; for doctorate, comprehensive exam, thesis/dissertation, first author peer-reviewed publication. *Entrance requirements:* For master's and doctorate, GRE General Test (minimum combined score 1100 verbal and quantitative), minimum GPA of 3.0. Additional exam requirements/recommendations for international students: Required—TOEFL (minimum score 550 paper-based; 213 computer-based; 80 iBT), IELTS (minimum score 6). *Application deadline:* For fall admission, 1/1 priority date for domestic students, 1/1 for international students; for spring admission, 8/1 for domestic and international students. Applications are processed on a rolling basis. Application fee: $30. Electronic applications accepted. *Expenses:* Tuition, state resident: full-time $10,916. Tuition, nonresident: full-time $28,309. *Financial support:* In 2010–11, 29 students received support, including 7 fellowships, 22 research assistantships (averaging $22,751 per year); unspecified assistantships also available. Financial award applicants required to submit FAFSA. *Faculty research:* The understanding of molecular and cellular mechanisms that mediate plant development, adaptation, and evolution including bioinformatics, genomics, proteomics, genetics, biochemistry, breeding, physiology and molecular and cellular biology. *Unit head:* Dr. Gary F. Peter, Director, 352-846-0896, E-mail: gfpeter@ufl.edu. *Application contact:* Dr. A. Mark Settles, Graduate Coordinator, 352-392-7571, E-mail: settles@ufl.edu.

University of Massachusetts Amherst, Graduate School, Interdisciplinary Programs, Program in Plant Biology, Amherst, MA 01003. Offers biochemistry and metabolism (MS, PhD); cell biology and physiology (MS, PhD); environmental, ecological and integrative (PhD); environmental, ecological and integrative biology (MS); genetics and evolution (MS, PhD). *Students:* 18 full-time (8 women); includes 1 minority (Asian, non-Hispanic/Latino), 7 international. Average age 29. 27 applicants, 41% accepted, 6 enrolled. In 2010, 3 doctorates awarded. *Degree requirements:* For master's, thesis; for doctorate, 2 foreign languages, comprehensive exam, thesis/dissertation. *Entrance requirements:* For master's and doctorate, GRE General Test. Additional exam requirements/recommendations for international students: Required—TOEFL (minimum score 550 paper-based; 213 computer-based; 80 iBT), IELTS (minimum score 6.5). *Application deadline:* For fall admission, 12/15 for domestic and international students; for spring admission, 10/1 for domestic and international students. Applications are processed on a rolling basis. Application fee: $50 ($65 for international students). Electronic applications accepted. *Expenses:* Tuition, state resident: full-time $2640. Required fees: $8282. One-time fee: $357 full-time. *Financial support:* In 2010–11, 12 research assistantships with full tuition reimbursements (averaging $11,651 per year) were awarded; fellowships, teaching assistantships, career-related internships or fieldwork, Federal Work-Study, scholarships/grants, traineeships, health care benefits, tuition waivers (full), and unspecified assistantships also available. Support available to part-time students. Financial award application deadline: 12/15; financial award applicants required to submit FAFSA. *Unit head:* Dr. Elsbeth L. Walker, Graduate Program Director, 413-577-3217, Fax: 413-545-3243. *Application contact:* Jean M. Ames, Supervisor of Admissions, 413-545—0722, Fax: 413-577-0010, E-mail: gradadm@grad.umass.edu.

Washington State University, Graduate School, College of Agricultural, Human, and Natural Resource Sciences, Program in Molecular Plant Sciences, Pullman, WA 99164. Offers MS, PhD. *Faculty:* 28. *Students:* 48 full-time (20 women), 1 part-time (0 women); includes 2 minority (1 Asian, non-Hispanic/Latino; 1 Native Hawaiian or other Pacific Islander, non-Hispanic/Latino), 21 international. Average age 27. 80 applicants, 16% accepted, 11 enrolled. In 2010, 2 master's, 5 doctorates awarded. Terminal master's awarded for partial completion of doctoral program. *Degree requirements:* For master's, comprehensive exam (for some programs), thesis (for some programs), oral exam, written exam; for doctorate, comprehensive exam, thesis/dissertation, oral exam, written exam. *Entrance requirements:* For master's and doctorate, GRE General Test. Additional exam requirements/recommendations for international students: Required—TOEFL, IELTS. *Application deadline:* For fall admission, 1/1 priority date for domestic students, 1/1 for international students. Applications are processed on a rolling basis. Application fee: $50. *Expenses:* Tuition, state resident: full-time $8552; part-time $443 per credit. Tuition, nonresident: full-time $21,650; part-time $1083 per credit. Required fees: $846. *Financial support:* In 2010–11, 40 research assistantships with full and partial tuition reimbursements (averaging $18,204 per year), 5 teaching assistantships with full and partial tuition reimbursements (averaging $18,204 per year) were awarded; career-related internships or fieldwork, Federal Work-Study, institutionally sponsored loans, and tuition waivers (partial) also available. Financial award application deadline: 4/1; financial award applicants required to submit FAFSA. *Faculty research:* Cell response to environmental signals, transport of amino acids, regulation of synthesis of defense proteins. *Unit head:* Dr. Michael Neff, Chair, 509-335-7705, Fax: 509-335-1949, E-mail: mmneff@wsu.edu. *Application contact:* Graduate School Admissions, 800-GRADWSU, Fax: 509-335-1949, E-mail: gradsch@wsu.edu.

Plant Pathology

Auburn University, Graduate School, College of Agriculture, Department of Entomology and Plant Pathology, Auburn University, AL 36849. Offers entomology (M Ag, MS, PhD); plant pathology (M Ag, MS, PhD). Part-time programs available. *Faculty:* 17 full-time (6 women). *Students:* 24 full-time (10 women), 11 part-time (4 women); includes 1 Black or African American, non-Hispanic/Latino; 2 Asian, non-Hispanic/Latino, 17 international. Average age 30. 21 applicants, 57% accepted, 7 enrolled. In 2010, 3 master's, 2 doctorates awarded. *Degree requirements:* For master's, thesis (for some programs); for doctorate, one foreign language, thesis/dissertation. *Entrance requirements:* For master's, GRE General Test; for doctorate, GRE General Test, GRE Subject Test, master's degree with thesis. *Application deadline:* For fall admission, 7/7 for domestic students; for spring admission, 11/24 for domestic students. Applications are processed on a rolling basis. Application fee: $50 ($60 for international students). Electronic applications accepted. *Expenses:* Tuition, state resident: full-time $7002. Tuition, nonresident: full-time $21,898. International tuition: $22,116 full-time. Required fees: $892. Tuition and fees vary according to course load and program. *Financial support:* Research assistantships, teaching assistantships, Federal Work-Study available. Support available to part-time students. Financial award application deadline: 3/15; financial award applicants required to submit FAFSA. *Faculty research:* Pest management, biological control, systematics, medical entomology. *Unit head:* Dr. Arthur Appel, Chair, 334-844-5006. *Application contact:* Dr. George Flowers, Dean of the Graduate School, 334-844-2125.

Colorado State University, Graduate School, College of Agricultural Sciences, Department of Bioagricultural Sciences and Pest Management, Fort Collins, CO 80523-1177. Offers entomology (MS, PhD); plant pathology and weed science (MS, PhD). Part-time programs available. *Faculty:* 19 full-time (4 women). *Students:* 20 full-time (9 women), 21 part-time (10 women); includes 4 minority (2 American Indian or Alaska Native, non-Hispanic/Latino; 1 Hispanic/Latino; 1 Two or more races, non-Hispanic/Latino), 4 international. Average age 32. 15 applicants, 73% accepted, 9 enrolled. In 2010, 5 master's, 1 doctorate awarded. *Degree requirements:* For master's, comprehensive exam, thesis; for doctorate, comprehensive exam, thesis/dissertation. *Entrance requirements:* For master's, GRE General Test, minimum GPA of 3.0, letters of recommendation; for doctorate, GRE General Test, minimum GPA of 3.0, letters of recommendation, essay. Additional exam requirements/recommendations for international students: Required—TOEFL (minimum score 550 paper-based; 213 computer-based; 80 iBT). *Application deadline:* For fall admission, 1/15 priority date for domestic students, 1/1 priority date for international students; for spring admission, 9/1 priority date for domestic and international students. Applications are processed on a rolling basis. Application fee: $50. Electronic applications accepted. *Expenses:* Tuition, state resident: full-time $7434; part-time $413 per credit. Tuition, nonresident: full-time $19,022; part-time $1057 per credit. Required fees: $1729; $88 per credit. *Financial support:* In 2010–11, 8 fellowships with partial tuition reimbursements (averaging $32,474 per year), 27 research assistantships with full tuition reimbursements (averaging $15,270 per year), 12 teaching assistantships with full tuition reimbursements (averaging $9,900 per year) were awarded; unspecified assistantships and fellowships also available. Financial award application deadline: 1/15; financial award applicants required to submit FAFSA. *Faculty research:* Entomology specialization, plant pathology specialization, weed science specialization, ecology and biodiversity, integrated pest management. Total annual research expenditures: $2.7 million. *Unit head:* Dr. Thomas O. Holtzer, Head, 970-491-5261, Fax: 970-491-3862, E-mail: tholtzer@lamar.colostate.edu. *Application contact:* Janet Dill, Education Coordinator, 970-491-0402, Fax: 970-491-3862, E-mail: janet.dill@colostate.edu.

Cornell University, Graduate School, Graduate Fields of Agriculture and Life Sciences, Field of Plant Pathology and Plant-Microbe Biology, Ithaca, NY 14853-0001. Offers ecological and environmental plant pathology (MPS, MS, PhD); epidemiological plant pathology (MPS, MS, PhD); molecular plant pathology (MPS, MS, PhD); mycology (MPS, MS, PhD); plant disease epidemiology (MPS, MS, PhD); plant pathology (MPS, MS, PhD). *Faculty:* 43 full-time (13 women). *Students:* 29 full-time (17 women); includes 2 Hispanic/Latino, 8 international. Average age 29. 44 applicants, 18% accepted, 6 enrolled. In 2010, 2 master's, 4 doctorates awarded. *Degree requirements:* For master's, thesis (MS), project paper (MPS); for doctorate, comprehensive exam, thesis/dissertation. *Entrance requirements:* For master's and doctorate, GRE General Test, GRE Subject Test (biology recommended), 3 letters of recommendation. Additional exam requirements/recommendations for international students: Required—TOEFL (minimum score 550 paper-based; 213 computer-based; 77 iBT). *Application deadline:* For fall admission, 1/15 priority date for domestic students. Applications are processed on a rolling basis. Application fee: $70. Electronic applications accepted. *Expenses:* Tuition: Full-time $29,500. Required fees: $76. Tuition and fees vary according to degree level and program. *Financial support:* In 2010–11, 5 fellowships with full tuition reimbursements, 20 research assistantships with full tuition reimbursements, 4 teaching assistantships with full tuition reimbursements were awarded; institutionally sponsored loans, scholarships/grants, health care benefits, tuition waivers (full and partial), and unspecified assistantships also available. Financial award applicants required to submit FAFSA. *Faculty research:* Plant pathology; mycology; molecular plant pathology; plant disease epidemiology, ecological and environmental plant pathology; plant disease epidemiology and simulation modeling. *Unit head:* Director of Graduate Studies, 607-255-3259, Fax: 607-255-4471. *Application contact:* Graduate Field Assistant, 607-255-3259, Fax: 607-255-4471, E-mail: plpathology@cornell.edu.

Iowa State University of Science and Technology, Graduate College, College of Agriculture, Department of Plant Pathology, Ames, IA 50011. Offers MS, PhD. *Faculty:* 18 full-time (4 women). *Students:* 31 full-time (15 women), 5 part-time (2 women); includes 1 Black or African American, non-Hispanic/Latino; 2 Asian, non-Hispanic/Latino; 1 Hispanic/Latino, 13 international. 25 applicants, 20% accepted, 4 enrolled. In 2010, 2 master's, 2 doctorates awarded. *Degree requirements:* For master's, thesis or alternative; for doctorate, thesis/dissertation. *Entrance requirements:* For master's and doctorate, GRE General Test, resume. Additional exam requirements/recommendations for international students: Required—TOEFL (minimum score 550 paper-based; 79 iBT), IELTS (minimum score 6.5). *Application deadline:* For fall admission, 3/15 priority date for domestic and international students; for spring admission, 9/1 for domestic and international students. Applications are processed on a rolling basis. Application fee: $40 ($90 for international students). Electronic applications accepted. *Financial support:* In 2010–11, 34 research assistantships with full and partial tuition reimbursements (averaging $18,405 per year), 2 teaching assistantships with full and partial tuition reimbursements (averaging $10,000 per year) were awarded; fellowships, scholarships/grants, health care benefits, and unspecified assistantships also available. *Unit head:* Dr. Thomas Baum, Chair, 515-294-1741, Fax: 515-294-9420, E-mail: plantpath@iastate.edu. *Application contact:* Information Contact, 515-294-5836, Fax: 515-294-2592, E-mail: grad_admissions@iastate.edu.

Kansas State University, Graduate School, College of Agriculture, Department of Plant Pathology, Manhattan, KS 66506. Offers genetics (MS, PhD); plant pathology (MS, PhD). Terminal master's awarded for partial completion of doctoral program. *Degree requirements:* For master's, thesis, oral exam; for doctorate, thesis/dissertation, preliminary exams. *Entrance requirements:* For master's and doctorate, minimum undergraduate GPA of 3.0. Additional exam requirements/recommendations for international students: Required—TOEFL (minimum score 550 paper-based; 213 computer-based). Electronic applications accepted. *Faculty research:* Applied microbiology, microbial genetics, microbial ecology/epidemiology, integrated pest management, plant genetics/genomics/molecular biology.

Louisiana State University and Agricultural and Mechanical College, Graduate School, College of Agriculture, Department of Plant Pathology and Crop Physiology, Baton Rouge, LA 70803. Offers plant health (MS, PhD). *Faculty:* 19 full-time (1 woman). *Students:* 25 full-time (7 women), 2 part-time (0 women); includes 2 Hispanic/Latino, 16 international. Average age 31. 18 applicants, 39% accepted, 6 enrolled. In 2010, 5 master's, 2 doctorates awarded. Terminal master's awarded for partial completion of doctoral program. *Degree requirements:* For master's, thesis; for doctorate, thesis/dissertation. *Entrance requirements:* For master's and doctorate, GRE General Test, minimum GPA of 3.0. Additional exam requirements/recommendations for international students: Required—TOEFL (minimum score 550 paper-based; 213 computer-based; 79 iBT) or IELTS (minimum score 6.5). *Application deadline:* For fall admission, 1/25 priority date for domestic students, 5/15 for international students; for spring admission, 10/15 for international students. Applications are processed on a rolling basis. Application fee: $50 ($70 for international students). Electronic applications accepted. *Financial support:* In 2010–11, 27 students received support, including 24 research assistantships with partial tuition reimbursements available (averaging $17,787 per year); fellowships, teaching assistantships with partial tuition reimbursements available, career-related internships or fieldwork, Federal Work-Study, health care benefits, and tuition waivers (full) also available. Support available to part-time students. Financial award applicants required to submit FAFSA. *Faculty research:* Plant health and protection, weed biology and management, crop physiology and biotechnology. Total annual research expenditures: $80,397. *Unit head:* Dr. Lawrence Datnoff, Head, 225-765-2876, Fax: 225-578-1415, E-mail: ldatno1@lsu.edu. *Application contact:* Dr. Raymond Schneider, Graduate Adviser, 225-578-4880, Fax: 225-578-1415, E-mail: rschneider@agcenter.lsu.edu.

Michigan State University, The Graduate School, College of Agriculture and Natural Resources and College of Natural Science, Department of Plant Pathology, East Lansing, MI 48824. Offers MS, PhD. *Entrance requirements:* Additional exam requirements/recommendations for international students: Required—TOEFL.

Mississippi State University, College of Agriculture and Life Sciences, Department of Entomology and Plant Pathology, Mississippi State, MS 39762. Offers agricultural life sciences (MS), including entomology and plant pathology (MS, PhD); life sciences (PhD), including entomology and plant pathology (MS, PhD). *Faculty:* 20 full-time (1 woman). *Students:* 19 full-time (4 women), 10 part-time (5 women); includes 2 minority (1 Black or African American, non-Hispanic/Latino; 1 Hispanic/Latino), 2 international. Average age 32. 17 applicants, 47% accepted, 7 enrolled. In 2010, 2 master's, 4 doctorates awarded. *Degree requirements:* For master's, thesis; for doctorate, thesis/dissertation. *Entrance requirements:* For master's, GRE General Test, minimum GPA of 2.75; for doctorate, GRE General Test. Additional exam requirements/recommendations for international students: Required—TOEFL (minimum score 475 paper-based; 153 computer-based; 53 iBT); Recommended—IELTS (minimum score 4.5). *Application deadline:* For fall admission, 7/1 for domestic students, 5/1 for international students; for spring admission, 11/1 for domestic students, 9/1 for international students. Applications are processed on a rolling basis. Application fee: $40. Electronic applications accepted. *Expenses:* Tuition, state resident: full-time $2731; part-time $304 per credit hour. Tuition, nonresident: full-time $6901; part-time $767 per credit hour. *Financial support:* In 2010–11, 20 research assistantships (averaging $16,783 per year) were awarded; Federal Work-Study, institutionally sponsored loans, and unspecified assistantships also available. Financial award application deadline: 4/1; financial award applicants required to submit FAFSA. *Unit head:* Dr. Scott T. Willard, Professor and Department Head, 662-325-2640, Fax: 662-325-8837, E-mail: swillard@bch.msstate.edu. *Application contact:* Dr. Michael Caprio, Professor and Graduate Coordinator, 662-325-2085, Fax: 662-325-8837, E-mail: mcaprio@entomology.msstate.edu.

Montana State University, College of Graduate Studies, College of Agriculture, Department of Plant Sciences and Plant Pathology, Bozeman, MT 59717. Offers plant pathology (MS); plant sciences (MS, PhD), including plant genetics (PhD), plant pathology (PhD). Part-time programs available. *Faculty:* 24 full-time (5 women), 2 part-time/adjunct (0 women). *Students:* 3 full-time (1 woman), 14 part-time (6 women); includes 2 minority (1 Asian, non-Hispanic/Latino; 1 Two or more races, non-Hispanic/Latino), 5 international. Average age 29. 17 applicants, 41% accepted, 6 enrolled. In 2010, 5 master's awarded. *Degree requirements:* For master's, comprehensive exam; for doctorate, comprehensive exam, thesis/dissertation. *Entrance requirements:* For master's, GRE General Test, minimum GPA of 3.0; for doctorate, GRE General Test. Additional exam requirements/recommendations for international students: Required—TOEFL (minimum score 550 paper-based; 213 computer-based). *Application deadline:* For fall admission, 7/15 priority date for domestic students, 5/15 priority date for international students; for spring admission, 12/1 priority date for domestic students, 10/1 priority date for international students. Applications are processed on a rolling basis. Application fee: $30. Electronic applications accepted. *Expenses:* Tuition, state resident: full-time $5554. Tuition, nonresident: full-time $14,646. Required fees: $1233. *Financial support:* In 2010–11, 9 students received support, including 4 research assistantships with tuition reimbursements available (averaging $32,665 per year), 5 teaching assistantships with tuition reimbursements available (averaging $16,271 per year); health care benefits and unspecified assistantships also available. Financial award application deadline: 3/1; financial award applicants required to submit FAFSA. *Faculty research:* Plant genetics, plant metabolism, plant microbe interactions, plant pathology, entomology research. Total annual research expenditures: $3.2 million. *Unit head:* Dr. John Sherwood, Head, 406-994-5153, Fax: 406-994-7600, E-mail: sherwood@montana.edu. *Application contact:* Dr. Carl A. Fox, Vice Provost for Graduate Education, 406-994-4145, Fax: 406-994-7433, E-mail: gradstudy@montana.edu.

New Mexico State University, Graduate School, College of Agricultural, Consumer and Environmental Sciences, Department of Entomology, Plant Pathology and Weed Science, Las Cruces, NM 88003-8001. Offers agricultural biology (MS). Part-time programs available. *Faculty:* 7 full-time (2 women). *Students:* 11 full-time (5 women), 4 part-time (2 women); includes 5 minority (4 Hispanic/Latino; 1 Two or more races, non-Hispanic/Latino), 2 international. Average age 27. 14 applicants, 79% accepted, 9 enrolled. In 2010, 5 master's awarded. *Degree requirements:* For master's, comprehensive exam, thesis. *Entrance requirements:* For master's, GRE General Test. *Application deadline:* For fall admission, 7/1 priority date for domestic students; for spring admission, 11/1 priority date for domestic students. Applications are processed on a rolling basis. Application fee: $30 ($50 for international students). Electronic applications accepted. *Expenses:* Tuition, state resident: full-time $4536; part-time $242 per credit. Tuition, nonresident: full-time $15,816; part-time $712 per credit. Required fees: $636 per term. *Financial support:* In 2010–11, 8 students received support, including 6 research assistantships with full tuition reimbursements available (averaging $20,550 per year), 2 teaching assistantships with partial tuition reimbursements available (averaging $14,225 per year); career-related internships or fieldwork and health care benefits also available. Financial award application deadline: 3/1. *Faculty research:* Integrated pest management, pesticide application and safety, livestock ectoparasite research, biotechnology, nematology. *Unit head:* Dr. Jill Schroeder, Interim Head, 575-646-3225, Fax: 575-646-8087, E-mail: jischroe@nmsu.edu. *Application contact:* Cindy Bullard, Intermediate Administrative Assistant, 575-646-1145, Fax: 575-646-8087, E-mail: cbullard@nmsu.edu.

North Carolina State University, Graduate School, College of Agriculture and Life Sciences, Department of Plant Pathology, Raleigh, NC 27695. Offers MS, PhD. Terminal master's awarded for partial completion of doctoral program. *Degree requirements:* For master's, thesis (for some programs); for doctorate, thesis/dissertation. *Entrance requirements:* For master's and doctorate, GRE. Additional exam requirements/recommendations for international students: Required—TOEFL. Electronic applications accepted. *Faculty research:* Microbe-plant interactions, biology of plant pathogens, pathogen evaluation, host-plant resistance, genomics.

North Dakota State University, College of Graduate and Interdisciplinary Studies, College of Agriculture, Food Systems, and Natural Resources, Department of Plant Pathology, Fargo, ND 58108. Offers MS, PhD. Part-time programs available. *Faculty:* 14 full-time (1 woman), 4 part-time/adjunct (0 women). *Students:* 19 full-time (7 women), 8 part-time (4 women); includes 1 Black or African American, non-Hispanic/Latino; 10 Asian, non-Hispanic/Latino; 4 Hispanic/Latino. Average age 23. 4 applicants, 50% accepted, 2 enrolled. In 2010, 1 master's, 1 doctorate awarded. *Degree requirements:* For master's, thesis; for doctorate, thesis/dissertation. *Entrance requirements:* Additional exam requirements/recommendations for international students: Required—TOEFL (minimum score 550 paper-based; 213 computer-based; 79 iBT). *Application deadline:* Applications are processed on a rolling basis. Application fee: $45 ($60 for international students). Electronic applications accepted. *Financial support:* In 2010–11, 19 research assistantships with full tuition reimbursements were awarded; Federal Work-Study and institutionally sponsored loans also available. Financial award application deadline: 4/15. *Faculty research:* Electron microscopy, disease physiology, molecular biology, genetic resistance, tissue culture. *Unit head:* Dr. Jack Rasmussen, Chair, 701-231-8362, Fax: 701-231-7851, E-mail: jack.rasmussen@ndsu.edu. *Application contact:* Dr. Jack Rasmussen, Chair, 701-231-8362, Fax: 701-231-7851, E-mail: jack.rasmussen@ndsu.edu.

Nova Scotia Agricultural College, Research and Graduate Studies, Truro, NS B2N 5E3, Canada. Offers agriculture (M Sc), including air quality, animal behavior, animal molecular genetics, animal nutrition, animal technology, aquaculture, botany, crop management, crop physiology, ecology, environmental microbiology, food science, horticulture, nutrient management, pest management, physiology, plant biotechnology, plant pathology, soil chemistry, soil fertility, waste management and composting, water quality. Program offered jointly with Dalhousie University. Part-time programs available. *Degree requirements:* For master's, thesis, ATC Exam Teaching Assistantship. *Entrance requirements:* For master's, honors B Sc, minimum GPA of 3.0. Additional exam requirements/recommendations for international students: Required—TOEFL (minimum score 580 paper-based; 237 computer-based; 92 iBT), IELTS, Michigan English Language Assessment Battery, CanTEST, CAEL. *Faculty research:* Bio-product development, organic agriculture, nutrient management, air and water quality, agricultural biotechnology.

The Ohio State University, Graduate School, College of Food, Agricultural, and Environmental Sciences, Department of Plant Pathology, Columbus, OH 43210. Offers MS, PhD. *Faculty:* 26. *Students:* 23 full-time (13 women), 9 part-time (5 women); includes 1 Hispanic/Latino, 18 international. Average age 27. In 2010, 11 master's awarded. *Degree requirements:* For master's, thesis optional; for doctorate, thesis/dissertation. *Entrance requirements:* For master's and doctorate, GRE General Test. Additional exam requirements/recommendations for international students: Required—TOEFL (minimum score 550 paper-based; 213 computer-based), IELTS (minimum score 7), or Michigan English Language Assessment Battery (minimum score 88). *Application deadline:* For fall admission, 8/15 priority date for domestic students, 7/1 priority date for international students; for winter admission, 12/1 priority date for domestic students, 11/1 priority date for international students; for spring admission, 3/1 priority date for domestic students, 2/1 priority date for international students. Applications are processed on a rolling basis. Application fee: $40 ($50 for international students). Electronic applications accepted. *Expenses:* Tuition, state resident: full-time $10,605. Tuition, nonresident: full-time $26,535. Tuition and fees vary according to course load and program. *Financial support:* Fellowships, research assistantships, teaching assistantships, Federal Work-Study and institutionally sponsored loans available. Support available to part-time students. *Unit head:* Laurence Madden, Chair, 330-263-3839, E-mail: madden.1@osu.edu. *Application contact:* Graduate Admissions, 614-292-9444, Fax: 614-292-3895, E-mail: domestic.grad@osu.edu.

Oklahoma State University, College of Agricultural Science and Natural Resources, Department of Entomology and Plant Pathology, Stillwater, OK 74078. Offers entomology (PhD); entomology and plant pathology (MS); plant pathology (PhD). *Faculty:* 33 full-time (12 women). *Students:* 5 full-time (2 women), 30 part-time (16 women); includes 1 American Indian or Alaska Native, non-Hispanic/Latino; 1 Asian, non-Hispanic/Latino, 14 international. Average age 29. 17 applicants, 29% accepted, 5 enrolled. In 2010, 10 master's, 3 doctorates awarded. *Degree requirements:* For master's, thesis or alternative; for doctorate, comprehensive exam, thesis/dissertation. *Entrance requirements:* For master's and doctorate, GRE or GMAT. Additional exam requirements/recommendations for international students: Required—TOEFL (minimum score 550 paper-based; 79 iBT). *Application deadline:* For fall admission, 3/1 priority date for international students; for spring admission, 8/1 priority date for international students. Applications are processed on a rolling basis. Application fee: $40 ($75 for international students). Electronic applications accepted. *Expenses:* Tuition, state resident: full-time $3716; part-time $154.85 per credit hour. Tuition, nonresident: full-time $14,892; part-time $621 per credit hour. Required fees: $2044; $85.20 per credit hour. One-time fee: $50. Tuition and fees vary according to course load and campus/location. *Financial support:* In 2010–11, 29 research assistantships (averaging $17,167 per year), 2 teaching assistantships (averaging $16,584 per year) were awarded; career-related internships or fieldwork, Federal Work-Study, scholarships/grants, health care benefits, tuition waivers (partial), and unspecified assistantships also available. Support available to part-time students. Financial award application deadline: 3/1; financial award applicants required to submit FAFSA. *Unit head:* Dr. Phil Mulder, Head, 405-744-5527, Fax: 405-744-6039. *Application contact:* Dr. Brad Kard, Graduate Coordinator, 405-744-2142, Fax: 405-744-6039, E-mail: brad.kard@okstate.edu.

Oregon State University, Graduate School, College of Science, Department of Botany and Plant Pathology, Corvallis, OR 97331. Offers ecology (MA, MAIS, MS, PhD); genetics (MA, MAIS, MS, PhD); molecular and cellular biology (MA, MAIS, MS, PhD); mycology (MA, MAIS, MS, PhD); plant pathology (MA, MAIS, MS, PhD); plant physiology (MA, MAIS, MS, PhD); structural botany (MA, MAIS, MS, PhD); systematics (MA, MAIS, MS, PhD). Part-time programs available. *Degree requirements:* For master's, variable foreign language requirement, thesis optional; for doctorate, thesis/dissertation. *Entrance requirements:* For master's and doctorate, GRE General Test, minimum GPA of 3.0 in last 90 hours. Additional exam requirements/recommendations for international students: Required—TOEFL. *Faculty research:* Plant ecology, plant molecular biology, systematic botany, epidemiology, host-pathogen interaction.

Penn State University Park, Graduate School, College of Agricultural Sciences, Department of Plant Pathology, State College, University Park, PA 16802-1503. Offers MS, PhD.

Purdue University, Graduate School, College of Agriculture, Department of Botany and Plant Pathology, West Lafayette, IN 47907. Offers MS, PhD. Part-time programs available. Terminal master's awarded for partial completion of doctoral program. *Degree requirements:* For master's, thesis; for doctorate, thesis/dissertation. *Entrance requirements:* For master's and doctorate, GRE. Additional exam requirements/recommendations for international students: Required—TOEFL. Electronic applications accepted. *Faculty research:* Biotechnology, plant growth, weed control, crop improvement, plant physiology.

Rutgers, The State University of New Jersey, New Brunswick, Graduate School-New Brunswick, Program in Plant Biology, Piscataway, NJ 08854-8097. Offers horticulture and plant technology (MS, PhD); molecular and cellular biology (MS, PhD); organismal and population biology (MS, PhD); plant pathology (MS, PhD). Part-time programs available. Terminal master's awarded for partial completion of doctoral program. *Degree requirements:* For master's, comprehensive exam, thesis or alternative; for doctorate, comprehensive exam, thesis/dissertation. *Entrance requirements:* For master's and doctorate, GRE General Test, GRE Subject Test (recommended). Additional exam requirements/recommendations for international students: Required—TOEFL (minimum score 600 paper-based; 250 computer-based). Electronic applications accepted. *Expenses:* Tuition, state resident: full-time $7200; part-time $600 per credit. Tuition, nonresident: full-time $11,124; part-time $927 per credit. *Faculty research:* Molecular biology and biochemistry of plants, plant development and genomics, plant protection, plant improvement, plant management of horticultural and field crops.

State University of New York College of Environmental Science and Forestry, Department of Environmental and Forest Biology, Syracuse, NY 13210-2779. Offers applied ecology (MPS); chemical ecology (MPS, MS, PhD); conservation biology (MPS, MS, PhD); ecology (MPS, MS, PhD); entomology (MPS, MS, PhD); environmental interpretation (MPS, MS, PhD); environmental physiology (MPS, MS, PhD); fish and wildlife biology and management (MPS, MS, PhD); forest pathology and mycology (MPS, MS, PhD); plant biotechnology (MPS); plant science and biotechnology (MPS, MS, PhD). *Degree requirements:* For master's, thesis (for some programs); for doctorate, comprehensive exam, thesis/dissertation. *Entrance requirements:* For master's and doctorate, GRE General Test, GRE Subject Test, minimum GPA of 3.0. Additional exam requirements/recommendations for international students: Required—TOEFL (minimum score 550 paper-based; 213 computer-based; 80 iBT), IELTS (minimum score 6). *Expenses:* Tuition, state resident: full-time $8370; part-time $349 per credit hour. Tuition,

nonresident: full-time $13,780. Required fees: $30.30 per credit hour. $20 per year. *Faculty research:* Ecology, fish and wildlife biology and management, plant science, entomology.

Texas A&M University, College of Agriculture and Life Sciences, Department of Plant Pathology and Microbiology, College Station, TX 77843. Offers M Agr, MS, PhD. Part-time programs available. Postbaccalaureate distance learning degree programs offered. *Faculty:* 16. *Students:* 32 full-time (17 women), 3 part-time (2 women); includes 8 minority (1 Black or African American, non-Hispanic/Latino; 7 Hispanic/Latino), 16 international. Average age 31. In 2010, 3 master's awarded. *Degree requirements:* For master's, comprehensive exam (for some programs), thesis; for doctorate, comprehensive exam, thesis/dissertation. *Entrance requirements:* For master's and doctorate, GRE General Test, letters of recommendation, BS/BA in biological sciences. *Application deadline:* Applications are processed on a rolling basis. Application fee: $50 ($75 for international students). *Financial support:* In 2010–11, research assistantships with partial tuition reimbursements (averaging $16,800 per year), teaching assistantships with partial tuition reimbursements (averaging $16,800 per year) were awarded; fellowships, career-related internships or fieldwork, Federal Work-Study, institutionally sponsored loans, and unspecified assistantships also available. Support available to part-time students. Financial award application deadline: 4/1; financial award applicants required to submit FAFSA. *Faculty research:* Plant disease control, population biology of plant pathogens, disease epidemiology, molecular genetics of host/parasite interactions. *Unit head:* Leland S. Pierson, Professor and Head, 979-845-8288, Fax: 979-845-6483, E-mail: lspierson@tamu.edu. *Application contact:* Leland S. Pierson, Professor and Head, 979-845-8288, Fax: 979-845-6483, E-mail: lspierson@tamu.edu.

The University of Arizona, College of Agriculture and Life Sciences, Department of Plant Sciences, Program in Plant Pathology, Tucson, AZ 85721. Offers MS, PhD. Part-time programs available. *Students:* 12 full-time (8 women); includes 1 Asian, non-Hispanic/Latino, 7 international. Average age 31. 6 applicants. In 2010, 1 master's, 4 doctorates awarded. *Degree requirements:* For master's, thesis optional; for doctorate, thesis/dissertation. *Entrance requirements:* For master's, GRE (recommended), minimum GPA of 3.0, academic resume, 3 letters of recommendation; for doctorate, GRE (recommended), minimum GPA of 3.0, academic resume, statement of purpose, 3 letters of recommendation. Additional exam requirements/recommendations for international students: Required—TOEFL. *Application deadline:* For fall admission, 12/1 for domestic and international students; for spring admission, 6/1 for domestic and international students. Applications are processed on a rolling basis. Application fee: $75. *Expenses:* Tuition, state resident: full-time $7692. *Financial support:* Fellowships, research assistantships, teaching assistantships, Federal Work-Study and institutionally sponsored loans available. *Faculty research:* Fungal molecular biology, ecology of soil-borne plant pathogens, plant virology, plant bacteriology, plant/pathogen interactions. *Unit head:* Dr. Leland S. Pierson, Chair, 520-621-1828, E-mail: lsp@u.arizona.edu. *Application contact:* Dr. Rachel W. Pfister, Graduate Coordinator/Advisor, 520-621-8423, Fax: 520-621-7186, E-mail: pfister@ag.arizona.edu.

University of Arkansas, Graduate School, Dale Bumpers College of Agricultural, Food and Life Sciences, Department of Plant Pathology, Fayetteville, AR 72701-1201. Offers MS. *Students:* 2 full-time (both women), 9 part-time (6 women), 3 international. 6 applicants, 33% accepted. In 2010, 6 master's awarded. *Degree requirements:* For master's, thesis. *Application deadline:* For fall admission, 4/1 for international students; for spring admission, 10/1 for international students. Applications are processed on a rolling basis. Application fee: $40 ($50 for international students). Electronic applications accepted. *Financial support:* In 2010–11, 8 research assistantships were awarded; fellowships, teaching assistantships, career-related internships or fieldwork and Federal Work-Study also available. Support available to part-time students. Financial award application deadline: 4/1; financial award applicants required to submit FAFSA. *Unit head:* Dr. A. Rick Bennett, Department Head, 479-575-2445, E-mail: rbennett@uark.edu. *Application contact:* Dr. Ioannis Tzanetakis, Graduate Coordinator, 479-575-3180, E-mail: itzaneta@uark.edu.

University of California, Davis, Graduate Studies, Program in Plant Pathology, Davis, CA 95616. Offers MS, PhD. Terminal master's awarded for partial completion of doctoral program. *Degree requirements:* For master's, comprehensive exam (for some programs), thesis (for some programs); for doctorate, thesis/dissertation. *Entrance requirements:* For master's and doctorate, GRE General Test. Additional exam requirements/recommendations for international students: Required—TOEFL (minimum score 550 paper-based; 213 computer-based). Electronic applications accepted. *Faculty research:* Soil microbiology; diagnosis etiology and control of plant diseases; genomics and molecular biology of plant microbe interactions; biotechnology, ecology of plant pathogens and epidemiology of diseases in agricultural and native ecosystems.

University of California, Riverside, Graduate Division, Department of Plant Pathology, Riverside, CA 92521-0102. Offers MS, PhD. Terminal master's awarded for partial completion of doctoral program. *Degree requirements:* For master's, comprehensive exams or thesis; for doctorate, thesis/dissertation, qualifying exams. *Entrance requirements:* For master's and doctorate, GRE General Test (minimum score 1100), minimum GPA of 3.2. Additional exam requirements/recommendations for international students: Required—TOEFL (minimum score 550 paper-based; 213 computer-based; 80 iBT). Electronic applications accepted. *Faculty research:* Host-pathogen interactions, biological control and integrated approaches to disease management, fungicide behavior, molecular genetics.

University of Florida, Graduate School, College of Agricultural and Life Sciences, Department of Plant Pathology, Gainesville, FL 32611. Offers MS, PhD. Part-time programs available. *Faculty:* 13 full-time (3 women). *Students:* 30 full-time (15 women), 6 part-time (2 women); includes 1 Asian, non-Hispanic/Latino; 2 Hispanic/Latino, 21 international. Average age 31. 31 applicants, 19% accepted, 6 enrolled. In 2010, 3 master's, 4 doctorates awarded. Terminal master's awarded for partial completion of doctoral program. *Degree requirements:* For master's, comprehensive exam (for some programs), thesis optional; for doctorate, comprehensive exam, thesis/dissertation. *Entrance requirements:* For master's and doctorate, GRE General Test, minimum GPA of 3.0. Additional exam requirements/recommendations for international students: Required—TOEFL (minimum score 550 paper-based; 213 computer-based; 80 iBT), IELTS (minimum score 6). *Application deadline:* For fall admission, 2/1 priority date for domestic students, 2/1 for international students; for winter admission, 2/1 for domestic and international students; for spring admission, 10/1 for domestic students, 9/1 for international students. Applications are processed on a rolling basis. Application fee: $30. Electronic applications accepted. *Expenses:* Tuition, state resident: full-time $10,916. Tuition, nonresident: full-time $28,309. *Financial support:* In 2010–11, 29 students received support, including 3 fellowships, 26 research assistantships (averaging $18,073 per year); career-related internships or fieldwork also available. Financial award application deadline: 2/1; financial award applicants required to submit FAFSA. *Faculty research:* Epidemiology, molecular biology of host-parasite interactions, bacteriology, virology, post-harvest diseases. Total annual research expenditures: $4.3 million. *Unit head:* Dr. Eric Triplett, Chair, 352-392-5430, E-mail: ewt@ufl.edu. *Application contact:* Dr. Robert J. McGovern, Graduate Coordinator, 352-392-3631 Ext. 213, Fax: 352-392-6532, E-mail: rjmcgov@ufl.edu.

University of Georgia, College of Agricultural and Environmental Sciences, Department of Plant Pathology, Athens, GA 30602. Offers MS, PhD. *Faculty:* 19 full-time (4 women), 3 part-time/adjunct (1 woman). *Students:* 34 full-time (17 women), 3 part-time (all women); includes 1 Black or African American, non-Hispanic/Latino, 16 international. 31 applicants, 42% accepted, 9 enrolled. In 2010, 9 master's, 2 doctorates awarded. *Degree requirements:* For master's, thesis (MS); for doctorate, one foreign language, thesis/dissertation. *Entrance requirements:* For master's and doctorate, GRE General Test. *Application deadline:* For fall admission, 7/1 priority date for domestic students; for spring admission, 11/15 for domestic students. Application fee: $50. Electronic applications accepted. *Expenses:* Tuition, state resident: full-time $7200; part-time $344 per credit hour. Tuition, nonresident: full-time $21,900; part-time $944 per credit hour. Tuition and fees vary according to course load and program.

Plant Pathology

University of Georgia *(continued)*
Financial support: Fellowships, research assistantships, teaching assistantships, unspecified assistantships available. *Unit head:* Dr. John L. Sherwood, Head, 706-542-1246, E-mail: sherwood@uga.edu. *Application contact:* Dr. Harald Scherm, Graduate Coordinator, 706-542-1258, Fax: 706-542-1262, E-mail: scherm@uga.edu.

University of Guelph, Graduate Studies, Ontario Agricultural College, Department of Environmental Biology, Guelph, ON N1G 2W1, Canada. Offers entomology (M Sc, PhD); environmental microbiology and biotechnology (M Sc, PhD); environmental toxicology (M Sc, PhD); plant and forest systems (M Sc, PhD); plant pathology (M Sc, PhD). Part-time programs available. *Degree requirements:* For master's, thesis; for doctorate, comprehensive exam, thesis/dissertation. *Entrance requirements:* For master's, minimum 75% average during previous 2 years of course work; for doctorate, minimum 75% average. Additional exam requirements/recommendations for international students: Required—TOEFL or IELTS. Electronic applications accepted. *Faculty research:* Entomology, environmental microbiology and biotechnology, environmental toxicology, forest ecology, plant pathology.

University of Hawaii at Manoa, Graduate Division, College of Tropical Agriculture and Human Resources, Department of Plant and Environmental Protection Sciences, Program in Tropical Plant Pathology, Honolulu, HI 96822. Offers MS, PhD. Part-time programs available. *Faculty:* 34 full-time (6 women), 10 part-time/adjunct (5 women). *Students:* 10 full-time (4 women), 3 part-time (1 woman); includes 2 Asian, non-Hispanic/Latino, 10 international. Average age 34. 13 applicants, 85% accepted, 4 enrolled. In 2010, 2 master's awarded. *Degree requirements:* For master's, thesis optional; for doctorate, comprehensive exam, thesis/dissertation. *Entrance requirements:* For master's and doctorate, GRE General Test. Additional exam requirements/recommendations for international students: Required—TOEFL (minimum score 540 paper-based; 207 computer-based; 76 iBT), IELTS (minimum score 5). *Application deadline:* For fall admission, 3/1 for domestic and international students; for spring admission, 9/1 for domestic and international students. Application fee: $60. *Financial support:* In 2010–11, 2 fellowships (averaging $2,237 per year), 8 research assistantships (averaging $17,609 per year) were awarded. Total annual research expenditures: $1.8 million. *Application contact:* Dr. Brent Sipes, Graduate Chairperson, 808-956-7076, Fax: 808-956-2832, E-mail: sipes@hawaii.edu.

University of Kentucky, Graduate School, College of Agriculture, Program in Plant Pathology, Lexington, KY 40506-0032. Offers MS, PhD. *Degree requirements:* For master's, comprehensive exam, thesis; for doctorate, comprehensive exam, thesis/dissertation. *Entrance requirements:* For master's, GRE General Test, minimum undergraduate GPA of 2.75; for doctorate, GRE General Test, minimum graduate GPA of 3.0. Additional exam requirements/recommendations for international students: Required—TOEFL (minimum score 550 paper-based; 213 computer-based). Electronic applications accepted. *Faculty research:* Molecular biology of viruses and fungi, biochemistry and physiology of disease resistance, plant transformation, disease ecology, forest pathology.

University of Maine, Graduate School, College of Natural Sciences, Forestry, and Agriculture, Department of Biological Sciences, Program in Botany and Plant Pathology, Orono, ME 04469. Offers MS. Part-time programs available. *Students:* 1 (woman) full-time, 1 (woman) part-time, 1 international. Average age 26. 6 applicants, 0% accepted, 0 enrolled. In 2010, 1 master's awarded. *Degree requirements:* For master's, thesis. *Entrance requirements:* For master's, GRE General Test. Additional exam requirements/recommendations for international students: Required—TOEFL. *Application deadline:* For fall admission, 2/1 priority date for domestic students. Applications are processed on a rolling basis. Application fee: $65. Electronic applications accepted. *Expenses:* Tuition, state resident: full-time $400. Tuition, nonresident: full-time $1050. *Financial support:* Career-related internships or fieldwork, Federal Work-Study, institutionally sponsored loans, and tuition waivers (full) available. Financial award application deadline: 3/1. *Faculty research:* Molecular biology of viral and fungal pathogens, marine ecology, paleoecology and acid systematics and evolution. *Unit head:* Dr. Stellos Tavantiz, Coordinator, 207-581-2986. *Application contact:* Scott G. Delcourt, Associate Dean of the Graduate School, 207-581-3291, Fax: 207-581-3232, E-mail: graduate@maine.edu.

University of Minnesota, Twin Cities Campus, Graduate School, College of Food, Agricultural and Natural Resource Sciences, Department of Plant Pathology, Saint Paul, MN 55108. Offers MS, PhD. Part-time programs available. *Faculty:* 26 full-time (7 women). *Students:* 19 full-time (6 women); includes 1 minority (Asian, non-Hispanic/Latino), 7 international. Average age 30. 18 applicants, 33% accepted, 4 enrolled. In 2010, 1 master's, 5 doctorates awarded. Terminal master's awarded for partial completion of doctoral program. *Degree requirements:* For master's, comprehensive exam, thesis; for doctorate, comprehensive exam, thesis/dissertation. *Entrance requirements:* For master's and doctorate, GRE General Test. Additional exam requirements/recommendations for international students: Required—TOEFL (minimum score 550 paper-based; 213 computer-based; 79 iBT). *Application deadline:* For fall admission, 1/10 priority date for domestic and international students; for spring admission, 5/1 priority date for domestic students, 5/10 priority date for international students. Applications are processed on a rolling basis. Application fee: $75 ($95 for international students). Electronic applications accepted. *Financial support:* In 2010–11, 3 students received support, including fellowships with full tuition reimbursements available (averaging $23,500 per year), research assistantships with full and partial tuition reimbursements available (averaging $18,000 per year), teaching assistantships with full and partial tuition reimbursements available (averaging $18,000 per year); scholarships/grants, health care benefits, and unspecified assistantships also available. Support available to part-time students. Financial award application deadline: 1/10. *Faculty research:* Plant disease management, disease resistance, product deterioration, international agriculture, molecular biology. Total annual research expenditures: $4.9 million. *Unit head:* Dr. Robert Blanchette, Director of Graduate Studies, 612-625-4735, Fax: 612-625-0202, E-mail: robertb@umn.edu. *Application contact:* Anne Lageson, Program Coordinator, 612-625-8200, Fax: 612-625-9728, E-mail: anna@umn.edu.

The University of Tennessee, Graduate School, College of Agricultural Sciences and Natural Resources, Department of Entomology and Plant Pathology, Knoxville, TN 37996. Offers entomology (MS, PhD); integrated pest management and bioactive natural products (PhD); plant pathology (MS, PhD). Part-time programs available. *Degree requirements:* For master's, thesis, seminar. *Entrance requirements:* For master's, GRE General Test, minimum GPA of 2.7, 3 reference letters, letter of intent; for doctorate, GRE General Test, minimum GPA of 2.7, 3 reference letters, letter of intent, proposed dissertation research. Additional exam requirements/recommendations for international students: Required—TOEFL. Electronic applications accepted. *Expenses:* Tuition, state resident: full-time $7440; part-time $414 per credit hour. Tuition, nonresident: full-time $22,478; part-time $1250 per credit hour. Required fees: $922; $43 per credit hour. Tuition and fees vary according to program.

University of Wisconsin–Madison, Graduate School, College of Agricultural and Life Sciences, Department of Plant Pathology, Madison, WI 53706-1380. Offers MS, PhD. Part-time programs available. Terminal master's awarded for partial completion of doctoral program. *Degree requirements:* For master's, thesis; for doctorate, thesis/dissertation. *Entrance requirements:* For master's and doctorate, GRE. Additional exam requirements/recommendations for international students: Required—TOEFL. Electronic applications accepted. *Expenses:* Tuition, state resident: full-time $9887; part-time $617.96 per credit. Tuition, nonresident: full-time $24,054; part-time $1503.40 per credit. Required fees: $67.63 per credit. Tuition and fees vary according to reciprocity agreements. *Faculty research:* Plant disease, plant health, plant-microbe interactions, plant disease management, biological control.

Virginia Polytechnic Institute and State University, Graduate School, College of Agriculture and Life Sciences, Department of Plant Pathology, Physiology and Weed Science, Blacksburg, VA 24061. Offers MS, PhD. *Faculty:* 15 full-time (5 women), 1 (woman) part-time/adjunct. *Students:* 33 full-time (15 women); includes 2 Asian, non-Hispanic/Latino, 12 international. Average age 28. 21 applicants, 48% accepted, 9 enrolled. In 2010, 3 master's, 3 doctorates awarded. *Degree requirements:* For master's, comprehensive exam (for some programs), thesis (for some programs); for doctorate, comprehensive exam (for some programs), thesis/dissertation (for some programs). *Entrance requirements:* For master's and doctorate, GRE. Additional exam requirements/recommendations for international students: Required—TOEFL (minimum score 550 paper-based; 213 computer-based). *Application deadline:* For fall admission, 7/1 for domestic and international students; for spring admission, 12/1 for domestic students, 12/15 for international students. Applications are processed on a rolling basis. Application fee: $65. Electronic applications accepted. *Expenses:* Tuition, state resident: full-time $9399; part-time $488 per credit hour. Tuition, nonresident: full-time $17,854; part-time $957.75 per credit hour. Required fees: $1534. Full-time tuition and fees vary according to program. *Financial support:* In 2010–11, 15 research assistantships with full tuition reimbursements (averaging $21,551 per year) were awarded; career-related internships or fieldwork, Federal Work-Study, scholarships/grants, health care benefits, and unspecified assistantships also available. Financial award application deadline: 1/15. *Faculty research:* Biotechnology, Dutch elm disease, weed control, plant pathogenic microorganisms, agronomic crop resistance to fungal and viral pathogens. Total annual research expenditures: $2.2 million. *Unit head:* Dr. Elizabeth A. Grabau, UNIT HEAD, 540-231-6361, Fax: 540-231-7477, E-mail: egrabau@vt.edu. *Application contact:* Anton Baudoin, Contact, 540-231-5757, Fax: 540-231-7477, E-mail: abaudoin@vt.edu.

Washington State University, Graduate School, College of Agricultural, Human, and Natural Resource Sciences, Department of Plant Pathology, Pullman, WA 99164. Offers MS, PhD. *Faculty:* 11. *Students:* 42 full-time (23 women), 2 part-time (0 women); includes 6 minority (5 Asian, non-Hispanic/Latino; 1 Hispanic/Latino), 25 international. Average age 31. 78 applicants, 18% accepted, 14 enrolled. In 2010, 4 doctorates awarded. Terminal master's awarded for partial completion of doctoral program. *Degree requirements:* For master's, comprehensive exam (for some programs), thesis (for some programs), oral exam; for doctorate, comprehensive exam, thesis/dissertation, oral exam. *Entrance requirements:* For master's and doctorate, GRE, statement of purpose. Additional exam requirements/recommendations for international students: Required—TOEFL (minimum score 550 paper-based; 213 computer-based), IELTS. *Application deadline:* For fall admission, 1/10 priority date for domestic students, 1/10 for international students; for spring admission, 7/1 for domestic and international students. Applications are processed on a rolling basis. Application fee: $50. Electronic applications accepted. *Expenses:* Tuition, state resident: full-time $8552; part-time $443 per credit. Tuition, nonresident: full-time $21,650; part-time $1083 per credit. Required fees: $846. *Financial support:* In 2010–11, 25 students received support, including 16 research assistantships with full and partial tuition reimbursements available (averaging $18,204 per year), 1 teaching assistantship with full and partial tuition reimbursement available (averaging $18,204 per year); career-related internships or fieldwork, Federal Work-Study, institutionally sponsored loans, scholarships/grants, and teaching associateships also available. Financial award application deadline: 4/1; financial award applicants required to submit FAFSA. *Faculty research:* Biology of fungi, bacteria, and viruses; diseases of plants; genetics of fungi, bacteria, and viruses. Total annual research expenditures: $4.6 million. *Unit head:* Dr. Hanu R. Pappu, Chair, 509-335-9541, Fax: 509-335-9581, E-mail: hrp@wsu.edu. *Application contact:* Graduate School Admissions, 800-GRADWSU, Fax: 509-335-1949, E-mail: gradsch@wsu.edu.

West Virginia University, Davis College of Agriculture, Forestry and Consumer Sciences, Division of Plant and Soil Sciences, Morgantown, WV 26506. Offers agricultural sciences (PhD), including animal and food sciences, plant and soil sciences; agronomy (MS); entomology (MS); environmental microbiology (MS); horticulture (MS); plant pathology (MS). *Degree requirements:* For master's, thesis. *Entrance requirements:* For master's, GRE, minimum GPA of 2.5. Additional exam requirements/recommendations for international students: Required—TOEFL. *Faculty research:* Water quality, reclamation of disturbed land, crop production, pest control, environmental protection.

Plant Physiology

Cornell University, Graduate School, Graduate Fields of Agriculture and Life Sciences, Field of Plant Biology, Ithaca, NY 14853-0001. Offers cytology (MS, PhD); paleobotany (MS, PhD); plant cell biology (MS, PhD); plant ecology (MS, PhD); plant molecular biology (MS, PhD); plant morphology, anatomy and biomechanics (MS, PhD); plant physiology (MS, PhD); systematic botany (MS, PhD). *Faculty:* 48 full-time (13 women). *Students:* 33 full-time (18 women); includes 2 Black or African American, non-Hispanic/Latino; 1 Hispanic/Latino, 10 international. Average age 26. 48 applicants, 33% accepted, 7 enrolled. In 2010, 8 doctorates awarded. *Degree requirements:* For doctorate, comprehensive exam, thesis/dissertation. *Entrance requirements:* For doctorate, GRE General Test, GRE Subject Test in biology (recommended), 3 letters of recommendation. Additional exam requirements/recommendations for international students: Required—TOEFL (minimum score 610 paper-based; 253 computer-based; 77 iBT). *Application deadline:* For fall admission, 1/15 priority date for domestic students. Application fee: $70. Electronic applications accepted. *Expenses:* Tuition: Full-time $29,500. Required fees: $76. Tuition and fees vary according to degree level and program. *Financial support:* In 2010–11, 7 fellowships with full tuition reimbursements, 13 research assistantships with full tuition reimbursements, 13 teaching assistantships with full tuition reimbursements were awarded; institutionally sponsored loans, scholarships/grants, health care benefits, tuition waivers (full and partial), and unspecified assistantships also available. Financial award applicants required to submit FAFSA. *Faculty research:* Plant cell biology/cytology; plant molecular biology; plant morphology/anatomy/biomechanics; plant physiology, systematic botany, paleobotany; plant ecology, ethnobotany, plant biochemistry, photosynthesis. *Unit head:* Director of Graduate Studies, 607-255-2131. *Application contact:* Graduate Field Assistant, 607-255-2131, E-mail: plbio@cornell.edu.

Nova Scotia Agricultural College, Research and Graduate Studies, Truro, NS B2N 5E3, Canada. Offers agriculture (M Sc), including air quality, animal behavior, animal molecular genetics, animal nutrition, animal technology, aquaculture, botany, crop management, crop physiology, ecology, environmental microbiology, food science, horticulture, nutrient management, pest management, physiology, plant biotechnology, plant pathology, soil chemistry, soil fertility, waste management and composting, water quality. Program offered jointly with Dalhousie University. Part-time programs available. *Degree requirements:* For master's, thesis, ATC Exam Teaching Assistantship. *Entrance requirements:* For master's, honors B Sc, minimum GPA of 3.0. Additional exam requirements/recommendations for international students: Required—TOEFL (minimum score 580 paper-based; 237 computer-based; 92 iBT), IELTS, Michigan English Language Assessment Battery, CanTEST, CAEL. *Faculty research:* Bio-product development, organic agriculture, nutrient management, air and water quality, agricultural biotechnology.

Oregon State University, Graduate School, College of Science, Department of Botany and Plant Pathology, Corvallis, OR 97331. Offers ecology (MA, MAIS, MS, PhD); genetics (MA, MAIS, MS, PhD); molecular and cellular biology (MA, MAIS, MS, PhD); mycology (MA, MAIS, MS, PhD); plant pathology (MA, MAIS, MS, PhD); plant physiology (MA, MAIS, MS, PhD); structural botany (MA, MAIS, MS, PhD); systematics (MA, MAIS, MS, PhD). Part-time programs available. *Degree requirements:* For master's, variable foreign language requirement, thesis optional; for doctorate, thesis/dissertation. *Entrance requirements:* For master's and doctorate, GRE General Test, minimum GPA of 3.0 in last 90 hours. Additional exam requirements/recommendations for international students: Required—TOEFL. *Faculty research:* Plant ecology, plant molecular biology, systematic botany, epidemiology, host-pathogen interaction.

Oregon State University, Graduate School, Program in Plant Physiology, Corvallis, OR 97331. Offers MS, PhD. *Degree requirements:* For master's, thesis; for doctorate, thesis/dissertation. *Entrance requirements:* For master's, BS in related area; for doctorate, BS or MS in related area, minimum GPA of 3.0 in last 90 hours of course work. Additional exam requirements/recommendations for international students: Required—TOEFL. *Faculty research:* Nitrogen metabolism, physiological ecology, phloem transport, mineral nutrition, plant hormones.

Penn State University Park, Graduate School, Intercollege Graduate Programs, Intercollege Graduate Program in Plant Physiology, State College, University Park, PA 16802-1503. Offers MS, PhD. *Unit head:* Dr. Teh-hui Kao, Head, 814-823-1042, Fax: 814-863-9416, E-mail: txk3@psu.edu. *Application contact:* Dr. Teh-hui Kao, Head, 814-823-1042, Fax: 814-863-9416, E-mail: txk3@psu.edu.

Purdue University, Graduate School, College of Science, Department of Biological Sciences, West Lafayette, IN 47907. Offers biochemistry (PhD); biophysics (PhD); cell and developmental biology (PhD); ecology, evolutionary and population biology (MS, PhD), including ecology, evolutionary biology, population biology; genetics (MS, PhD); microbiology (MS, PhD); molecular biology (PhD); neurobiology (MS, PhD); plant physiology (PhD). Terminal master's awarded for partial completion of doctoral program. *Degree requirements:* For master's, thesis (for some programs); for doctorate, thesis/dissertation, seminars, teaching experience. *Entrance requirements:* For master's and doctorate, GRE General Test. Additional exam requirements/recommendations for international students: Required—TOEFL. Electronic applications accepted.

University of Kentucky, Graduate School, College of Agriculture, Program in Plant Physiology, Lexington, KY 40506-0032. Offers PhD. *Degree requirements:* For doctorate, comprehensive exam, thesis/dissertation. *Entrance requirements:* For doctorate, GRE General Test, minimum graduate GPA of 3.0, undergraduate 2.75. Additional exam requirements/recommendations for international students: Required—TOEFL (minimum score 550 paper-based; 213 computer-based). Electronic applications accepted. *Faculty research:* Biochemistry and biophysics of photosynthesis, biochemical and molecular basis for resistance of plants to pathogens, plant gene expression, physiological aspects of crop production.

University of Manitoba, Faculty of Graduate Studies, Faculty of Agricultural and Food Sciences, Department of Plant Science, Winnipeg, MB R3T 2N2, Canada. Offers agronomy and plant protection (M Sc, PhD); horticulture (M Sc, PhD); plant breeding and genetics (M Sc, PhD); plant physiology-biochemistry (M Sc, PhD). *Degree requirements:* For master's, thesis; for doctorate, one foreign language, thesis/dissertation.

University of Massachusetts Amherst, Graduate School, Interdisciplinary Programs, Program in Plant Biology, Amherst, MA 01003. Offers biochemistry and metabolism (MS, PhD); cell biology and physiology (MS, PhD); environmental, ecological and integrative (PhD); environmental, ecological and integrative biology (MS); genetics and evolution (MS, PhD). *Students:* 18 full-time (8 women); includes 1 minority (Asian, non-Hispanic/Latino), 7 international. Average age 29. 27 applicants, 41% accepted, 6 enrolled. In 2010, 3 doctorates awarded. *Degree requirements:* For master's, thesis; for doctorate, 2 foreign languages, comprehensive exam, thesis/dissertation. *Entrance requirements:* For master's and doctorate, GRE General Test. Additional exam requirements/recommendations for international students: Required—TOEFL (minimum score 550 paper-based; 213 computer-based; 80 iBT), IELTS (minimum score 6.5). *Application deadline:* For fall admission, 12/15 for domestic and international students; for spring admission, 10/1 for domestic and international students. Applications are processed on a rolling basis. Application fee: $50 ($65 for international students). Electronic applications accepted. *Expenses:* Tuition, state resident: full-time $2640. Required fees: $8282. One-time fee: $357 full-time. *Financial support:* In 2010–11, 12 research assistantships with full tuition reimbursements (averaging $11,651 per year) were awarded; fellowships, teaching assistantships, career-related internships or fieldwork, Federal Work-Study, scholarships/grants, traineeships, health care benefits, tuition waivers (full), and unspecified assistantships also available. Support available to part-time students. Financial award application deadline: 12/15; financial award applicants required to submit FAFSA. *Unit head:* Dr. Elsbeth L. Walker, Graduate Program Director, 413-577-3217, Fax: 413-545-3243. *Application contact:* Jean M. Ames, Supervisor of Admissions, 413-545—0722, Fax: 413-577-0010, E-mail: gradadm@grad.umass.edu.

The University of Tennessee, Graduate School, College of Arts and Sciences, Program in Life Sciences, Knoxville, TN 37996. Offers genome science and technology (MS, PhD); plant physiology and genetics (MS, PhD). *Degree requirements:* For doctorate, one foreign language, thesis/dissertation. *Entrance requirements:* For master's and doctorate, GRE General Test, minimum GPA of 2.7. Additional exam requirements/recommendations for international students: Required—TOEFL. Electronic applications accepted. *Expenses:* Tuition, state resident: full-time $7440; part-time $414 per credit hour. Tuition, nonresident: full-time $22,478; part-time $922 per credit hour. Required fees: $922; $43 per credit hour. Tuition and fees vary according to program.

Virginia Polytechnic Institute and State University, Graduate School, College of Agriculture and Life Sciences, Department of Plant Pathology, Physiology and Weed Science, Blacksburg, VA 24061. Offers MS, PhD. *Faculty:* 15 full-time (5 women), 1 (woman) part-time/adjunct. *Students:* 33 full-time (15 women); includes 2 Asian, non-Hispanic/Latino, 12 international. Average age 28. 21 applicants, 48% accepted, 9 enrolled. In 2010, 3 master's, 3 doctorates awarded. *Degree requirements:* For master's, comprehensive exam (for some programs), thesis (for some programs); for doctorate, comprehensive exam (for some programs), thesis/dissertation (for some programs). *Entrance requirements:* For master's and doctorate, GRE. Additional exam requirements/recommendations for international students: Required—TOEFL (minimum score 550 paper-based; 213 computer-based). *Application deadline:* For fall admission, 7/1 for domestic and international students; for spring admission, 12/1 for domestic students, 12/15 for international students. Applications are processed on a rolling basis. Application fee: $65. Electronic applications accepted. *Expenses:* Tuition, state resident: full-time $9399; part-time $488 per credit hour. Tuition, nonresident: full-time $17,854; part-time $957.75 per credit hour. Required fees: $1534. Full-time tuition and fees vary according to program. *Financial support:* In 2010–11, 15 research assistantships with full tuition reimbursements (averaging $21,551 per year) were awarded; career-related internships or fieldwork, Federal Work-Study, scholarships/grants, health care benefits, and unspecified assistantships also available. Financial award application deadline: 1/15. *Faculty research:* Biotechnology, Dutch elm disease, weed control, plant pathogenic microorganisms, agronomic crop resistance to fungal and viral pathogens. Total annual research expenditures: $2.2 million. *Unit head:* Dr. Elizabeth A. Grabau, Unit Head, 540-231-6361, Fax: 540-231-7477, E-mail: egrabau@vt.edu. *Application contact:* Anton Baudoin, Contact, 540-231-5757, Fax: 540-231-7477, E-mail: abaudoin@vt.edu.

Section 6
Cell, Molecular, and Structural Biology

This section contains a directory of institutions offering graduate work in cell, molecular, and structural biology, followed by in-depth entries submitted by institutions that chose to prepare detailed program descriptions. Additional information about programs listed in the directory but not augmented by an in-depth entry may be obtained by writing directly to the dean of a graduate school or chair of a department at the address given in the directory.

For programs offering related work, see also in this book *Anatomy; Biochemistry; Biological and Biomedical Sciences; Biophysics; Botany and Plant Biology; Genetics, Developmental Biology, and Reproductive Biology; Microbiological Sciences; Pathology and Pathobiology; Pharmacology and Toxicology;* and *Physiology.* In the other guides in this series:

Graduate Programs in the Physical Sciences, Mathematics, Agricultural Sciences, the Environment & Natural Resources
See *Chemistry*

Graduate Programs in Engineering & Applied Sciences
See *Agricultural Engineering and Bioengineering* and *Biomedical Engineering and Biotechnology*

Graduate Programs in Business, Education, Health, Information Studies, Law & Social Work
See *Pharmacy and Pharmaceutical Sciences* and *Veterinary Medicine and Sciences*

CONTENTS

Program Directories

Cancer Biology/Oncology

Baylor College of Medicine, Graduate School of Biomedical Sciences, Program in Translational Biology and Molecular Medicine, Houston, TX 77030-3498. Offers PhD. *Faculty:* 173 full-time (54 women). *Students:* 58 full-time (28 women); includes 6 Black or African American, non-Hispanic/Latino; 6 Hispanic/Latino, 16 international. Average age 27. 88 applicants, 32% accepted, 13 enrolled. In 2010, 1 doctorate awarded. *Degree requirements:* For doctorate, thesis/dissertation, public defense. *Entrance requirements:* For doctorate, GRE, minimum GPA of 3.0. Additional exam requirements/recommendations for international students: Required—TOEFL. *Application deadline:* For fall admission, 1/1 for domestic students. Application fee: $0. Electronic applications accepted. *Expenses:* Tuition: Full-time $11,000. Required fees: $4900. *Financial support:* In 2010–11, 58 students received support, including 24 fellowships with full tuition reimbursements available (averaging $26,000 per year), 34 research assistantships with full tuition reimbursements available (averaging $26,000 per year); career-related internships or fieldwork, Federal Work-Study, health care benefits, and students receive a scholarship unless there are grant funds available to pay tuition also available. Financial award applicants required to submit FAFSA. *Faculty research:* Molecular medicine, translational biology, human disease biology and therapy. *Unit head:* Dr. Mary Estes, Director, 713-798-3585, Fax: 713-798-3586, E-mail: tbmm@bcm.edu. *Application contact:* Wanda Waguespack, Graduate Program Administrator, 713-798-1077, Fax: 713-798-3586, E-mail: wandaw@bcm.edu.

See Close-Up on page 253.

Brown University, Graduate School, Division of Biology and Medicine, Program in Pathology and Laboratory Medicine, Providence, RI 02912. Offers biology (PhD); cancer biology (PhD); immunology and infection (PhD); medical science (PhD); pathobiology (Sc M); toxicology and environmental pathology (PhD). Terminal master's awarded for partial completion of doctoral program. *Degree requirements:* For doctorate, thesis/dissertation, preliminary exam. *Entrance requirements:* For master's and doctorate, GRE General Test, GRE Subject Test. Additional exam requirements/recommendations for international students: Required—TOEFL. Electronic applications accepted. *Faculty research:* Environmental pathology, carcinogenesis, immunopathology, signal transduction, innate immunity.

Case Western Reserve University, School of Medicine and School of Graduate Studies, Graduate Programs in Medicine, Programs in Molecular and Cellular Basis of Disease/ Pathology, Cancer Biology Training Program, Cleveland, OH 44106. Offers PhD, MD/PhD. *Degree requirements:* For doctorate, comprehensive exam, thesis/dissertation. *Entrance requirements:* For doctorate, GRE. Additional exam requirements/recommendations for international students: Required—TOEFL (minimum score 550 paper-based; 213 computer-based).

Dartmouth College, Program in Experimental and Molecular Medicine, Cancer Biology and Molecular Therapeutics Track, Hanover, NH 03755. Offers PhD.

Duke University, Graduate School, University Program in Molecular Cancer Biology, Durham, NC 27710. Offers PhD. *Faculty:* 50 full-time. *Students:* 44 full-time (24 women); includes 3 Asian, non-Hispanic/Latino; 1 Hispanic/Latino, 16 international. 71 applicants, 14% accepted, 5 enrolled. In 2010, 11 doctorates awarded. *Degree requirements:* For doctorate, thesis/ dissertation. *Entrance requirements:* For doctorate, GRE General Test, GRE Subject Test in biology or biochemistry, cell and molecular biology (recommended). Additional exam requirements/recommendations for international students: Required—TOEFL (minimum score 550 paper-based; 213 computer-based; 83 iBT), IELTS (minimum score 7). *Application deadline:* For fall admission, 12/8 priority date for domestic and international students. Application fee: $75. Electronic applications accepted. *Financial support:* Fellowships, research assistantships available. Financial award application deadline: 12/31. *Unit head:* Ann Marie Pendergast, Director of Graduate Studies, 919-613-8600, Fax: 919-681-7767, E-mail: baize@duke.edu.

Application contact: Elizabeth Hutton, Director of Admissions, 919-684-3913, Fax: 919-684-2277, E-mail: grad-admissions@duke.edu.

Emory University, Laney Graduate School, Division of Biological and Biomedical Sciences, Program in Cancer Biology, Atlanta, GA 30322. Offers PhD. *Faculty:* 26 full-time (4 women). *Entrance requirements:* For doctorate, GRE General Test, minimum GPA of 3.0 in science course work (recommended). Additional exam requirements/recommendations for international students: Required—TOEFL. *Application deadline:* For fall admission, 12/1 for domestic and international students. Application fee: $75. Electronic applications accepted. *Expenses:* Contact institution. *Financial support:* Fellowships with tuition reimbursements, institutionally sponsored loans, scholarships/grants, health care benefits, and tuition waivers available. *Faculty research:* Basic and translational cancer research, molecular and cellular biology, genetics and epigenetics, signal transduction, genetic engineering and nanotechnologies. *Unit head:* Dr. Erwin Van Meir, Program Director, 404-778-5563, Fax: 404-778-5550, E-mail: evanmei@emory.edu. *Application contact:* Kathy Smith, Director of Recruitment and Admissions, 404-727-2547, Fax: 404-727-3322, E-mail: kathy.smith@emory.edu.

Gerstner Sloan-Kettering Graduate School of Biomedical Sciences, Program in Cancer Biology, New York, NY 10021. Offers PhD. *Faculty:* 116 full-time (19 women). *Students:* 52 full-time (28 women); includes 6 Black or African American, non-Hispanic/Latino; 4 Asian, non-Hispanic/Latino; 1 Hispanic/Latino, 4 international. *Entrance requirements:* For doctorate, GRE, transcripts, letters of recommendation. Electronic applications accepted. *Financial support:* Fellowship package including stipend ($32,637), full-tuition scholarship, first-year allowance, and comprehensive medical and dental insurance available. *Faculty research:* Biochemistry and molecular biology, biophysics/structural biology, computational biology, genetics, immunology. *Unit head:* Dr. Kenneth Marians, Dean, 212-639-5890, E-mail: kmarians@sloankettering.edu. *Application contact:* Main Office, 646-888-6639, Fax: 646-422-2351, E-mail: gradstudies@sloankettering.edu.

See Display below and Close-Up on page 225.

Mayo Graduate School, Graduate Programs in Biomedical Sciences, Program in Tumor Biology, Rochester, MN 55905. Offers PhD. *Degree requirements:* For doctorate, oral defense of dissertation, qualifying oral and written exam. *Entrance requirements:* For doctorate, GRE, 1 year of chemistry, biology, calculus, and physics. Additional exam requirements/ recommendations for international students: Required—TOEFL. Electronic applications accepted.

McMaster University, Faculty of Health Sciences and School of Graduate Studies, Program in Medical Sciences, Genetics and Cancer Area, Hamilton, ON L8S 4M2, Canada. Offers M Sc, PhD, MD/PhD. *Degree requirements:* For master's, thesis; for doctorate, comprehensive exam, thesis/dissertation. *Entrance requirements:* For master's, honors B Sc, B+ average in related field; for doctorate, M Sc, minimum B+ average, students with proven research experience and an A average may be admitted with a B Sc degree. Additional exam requirements/recommendations for international students: Required—TOEFL (minimum score 580 paper-based; 237 computer-based; 92 iBT).

Medical University of South Carolina, College of Graduate Studies, Program in Molecular and Cellular Biology and Pathobiology, Charleston, SC 29425. Offers cancer biology (PhD); cardiovascular biology (PhD); cardiovascular imaging (PhD); cell regulation (PhD); craniofacial biology (PhD); genetics and development (PhD); marine biomedicine (PhD); DMD/PhD; MD/PhD. *Faculty:* 137 full-time (33 women). *Students:* 27 full-time (20 women); includes 3 Black or African American, non-Hispanic/Latino; 1 Hispanic/Latino, 6 international. Average age 30. In 2010, 16 doctorates awarded. *Degree requirements:* For doctorate, thesis/dissertation, oral and written exams. *Entrance requirements:* For doctorate, GRE General Test, interview, minimum GPA of 3.0. Additional exam requirements/recommendations for international students: Required—TOEFL (minimum score 600 paper-based; 250 computer-based; 100 iBT). *Application*

deadline: For fall admission, 1/15 priority date for domestic and international students. Applications are processed on a rolling basis. Application fee: $0 ($85 for international students). Electronic applications accepted. *Financial support:* In 2010–11, 39 research assistantships with partial tuition reimbursements (averaging $23,000 per year) were awarded; Federal Work-Study and scholarships/grants also available. Support available to part-time students. Financial award application deadline: 3/10; financial award applicants required to submit FAFSA. *Unit head:* Dr. Donald R. Menick, Director, 843-876-5045, Fax: 843-792-6590, E-mail: menickd@musc.edu. *Application contact:* Dr. Cynthia F. Wright, Associate Dean for Admissions and Career Development, 843-792-2564, Fax: 843-792-6590, E-mail: wrightcf@musc.edu.

Meharry Medical College, School of Graduate Studies, Program in Biomedical Sciences, Cancer Biology Emphasis, Nashville, TN 37208-9989. Offers PhD, MD/PhD. *Degree requirements:* For doctorate, comprehensive exam, thesis/dissertation. *Entrance requirements:* For doctorate, GRE. *Faculty research:* Regulation of metabolism, enzymology, signal transduction, physical biochemistry.

Memorial University of Newfoundland, Faculty of Medicine and School of Graduate Studies, Graduate Programs in Medicine, Division of Biomedical Sciences, St. John's, NL A1C 5S7, Canada. Offers cancer (M Sc, PhD); cardiovascular (M Sc, PhD); immunology (M Sc, PhD); neuroscience (M Sc, PhD). Part-time programs available. *Degree requirements:* For master's, thesis; for doctorate, comprehensive exam, thesis/dissertation, oral defense of thesis. *Entrance requirements:* For master's, MD or B Sc; for doctorate, MD or M Sc. Additional exam requirements/recommendations for international students: Required—TOEFL. *Faculty research:* Neuroscience, immunology, cardiovascular, and cancer.

New York University, Graduate School of Arts and Science, Department of Biology, New York, NY 10012-1019. Offers biology (PhD); biomedical journalism (MS); cancer and molecular biology (PhD); computational biology (PhD); computers in biological research (MS); developmental genetics (PhD); general biology (MS); immunology and microbiology (PhD); molecular genetics (PhD); neurobiology (PhD); oral biology (MS); plant biology (PhD); recombinant DNA technology (MS); MS/MBA. Part-time programs available. *Faculty:* 24 full-time (5 women). *Students:* 155 full-time (89 women), 38 part-time (24 women); includes 29 Asian, non-Hispanic/Latino; 7 Hispanic/Latino, 88 international. Average age 27. 324 applicants, 69% accepted, 63 enrolled. In 2010, 55 master's, 4 doctorates awarded. Terminal master's awarded for partial completion of doctoral program. *Degree requirements:* For master's, thesis or alternative, qualifying paper; for doctorate, comprehensive exam, thesis/dissertation. *Entrance requirements:* For master's, GRE General Test; for doctorate, GRE General Test, GRE Subject Test. Additional exam requirements/recommendations for international students: Required—TOEFL. *Application deadline:* For fall admission, 12/15 priority date for domestic students. Application fee: $90. *Financial support:* Fellowships with tuition reimbursements, research assistantships with tuition reimbursements, teaching assistantships with tuition reimbursements, career-related internships or fieldwork, Federal Work-Study, institutionally sponsored loans, scholarships/grants, health care benefits, and unspecified assistantships available. Financial award application deadline: 12/15; financial award applicants required to submit FAFSA. *Faculty research:* Genomics, molecular and cell biology, development and molecular genetics, molecular evolution of plants and animals. *Unit head:* Gloria Coruzzi, Chair, 212-998-8200, Fax: 212-995-4015, E-mail: biology@nyu.edu. *Application contact:* Justin Blau, Director of Graduate Studies, 212-998-8200, Fax: 212-995-4015, E-mail: biology@nyu.edu.

New York University, School of Medicine, New York, NY 10012-1019. Offers biomedical sciences (PhD), including biomedical imaging, cellular and molecular biology, computational biology, developmental genetics, medical and molecular parasitology, microbiology, molecular oncobiology and immunology, neuroscience and physiology, pathobiology, pharmacology, structural biology; clinical investigation (MS); medicine (MD); MD/MA; MD/MPA; MD/MS; MD/PhD. *Accreditation:* LCME/AMA (one or more programs are accredited). *Degree requirements:* For master's, comprehensive exam, thesis; for doctorate, comprehensive exam, thesis/dissertation. *Entrance requirements:* MCAT. Additional exam requirements/recommendations for international students: Required—TOEFL. *Expenses:* Contact institution. *Faculty research:* AIDS, cancer, neuroscience, molecular biology, neuroscience, cell biology and molecular genetics, structural biology, microbial pathogenesis and host defense, pharmacology, molecular oncology and immunology.

New York University, School of Medicine and Graduate School of Arts and Science, Sackler Institute of Graduate Biomedical Sciences, Programs in Molecular Oncology and Immunology, New York, NY 10012-1019. Offers immunology (PhD); molecular oncology (PhD); MD/PhD. *Degree requirements:* For doctorate, one foreign language, thesis/dissertation, qualifying exam. *Entrance requirements:* For doctorate, GRE General Test, GRE Subject Test. Additional exam requirements/recommendations for international students: Required—TOEFL. Electronic applications accepted. *Faculty research:* Stem cells, immunology, genome instability, DNA damage checkpoints.

Northwestern University, Northwestern University Feinberg School of Medicine and Interdepartmental Programs, Integrated Graduate Programs in the Life Sciences, Chicago, IL 60611. Offers cancer biology (PhD); cell biology (PhD); developmental biology (PhD); evolutionary biology (PhD); immunology and microbial pathogenesis (PhD); molecular biology and genetics (PhD); neurobiology (PhD); pharmacology and toxicology (PhD); structural biology and biochemistry (PhD). *Degree requirements:* For doctorate, comprehensive exam, thesis/dissertation, written and oral qualifying exams. *Entrance requirements:* For doctorate, GRE General Test. Additional exam requirements/recommendations for international students: Required—TOEFL (minimum score 600 paper-based; 250 computer-based). Electronic applications accepted.

Oregon Health & Science University, School of Medicine, Graduate Programs in Medicine, Cancer Biology Program, Portland, OR 97239-3098. Offers PhD. *Faculty:* 21. *Students:* 8 full-time (4 women); includes 1 Black or African American, non-Hispanic/Latino, 2 international. Average age 29. *Degree requirements:* For doctorate, comprehensive exam, thesis/dissertation. *Entrance requirements:* For doctorate, GRE. Additional exam requirements/recommendations for international students: Required—TOEFL. Electronic applications accepted. *Financial support:* Health care benefits and full tuition and stipends available. *Unit head:* Dr. Matthew Thayer, Program Leader, 503-494-2447, E-mail: thayerm@ohsu.edu. *Application contact:* Jeni Wroblewski, Program Coordinator, 503-494-2541, Fax: 503-494-8393, E-mail: wroblews@ohsu.edu.

Queen's University at Kingston, School of Graduate Studies and Research, Faculty of Health Sciences, Department of Anatomy and Cell Biology, Kingston, ON K7L 3N6, Canada. Offers biology of reproduction (M Sc, PhD); cancer (M Sc, PhD); cardiovascular pathophysiology (M Sc, PhD); cell and molecular biology (M Sc, PhD); drug metabolism (M Sc, PhD); endocrinology (M Sc, PhD); motor control (M Sc, PhD); neural regeneration (M Sc, PhD); neurophysiology (M Sc, PhD). Part-time programs available. *Degree requirements:* For master's, thesis; for doctorate, one foreign language, comprehensive exam, thesis/dissertation. *Entrance requirements:* Additional exam requirements/recommendations for international students: Required—TOEFL. Electronic applications accepted. *Faculty research:* Human kinetics, neuroscience, reproductive biology, cardiovascular.

Rutgers, The State University of New Jersey, New Brunswick, Graduate School-New Brunswick, Program in Endocrinology and Animal Biosciences, Piscataway, NJ 08854-8097. Offers MS, PhD. Terminal master's awarded for partial completion of doctoral program. *Degree requirements:* For master's, thesis; for doctorate, comprehensive exam, thesis/dissertation. *Entrance requirements:* For master's and doctorate, GRE General Test. Additional exam requirements/recommendations for international students: Required—TOEFL. Electronic applications accepted. *Expenses:* Tuition, state resident: full-time $7200; part-time $600 per credit. Tuition, nonresident: full-time $11,124; part-time $927 per credit. *Faculty research:* Comparative and behavioral endocrinology, epigenetic regulation of the endocrine system, exercise physiology

and immunology, fetal and neonatal developmental programming, mammary gland biology and breast cancer, neuroendocrinology and alcohol studies, reproductive and developmental toxicology.

Stanford University, School of Medicine, Graduate Programs in Medicine, Program in Cancer Biology, Stanford, CA 94305-9991. Offers PhD. *Degree requirements:* For doctorate, thesis/dissertation, qualifying examination. *Entrance requirements:* For doctorate, GRE General Test, GRE Subject Test. Additional exam requirements/recommendations for international students: Required—TOEFL. Electronic applications accepted. *Expenses:* Tuition: Full-time $38,700; part-time $860 per unit. One-time fee: $200 full-time.

State University of New York Upstate Medical University, College of Graduate Studies, Major Research Areas of the College of Graduate Studies, Syracuse, NY 13210-2334.

Université Laval, Faculty of Medicine, Post-Professional Programs in Medical Studies, Québec, QC G1K 7P4, Canada. Offers anatomy–pathology (DESS); anesthesiology (DESS); cardiology (DESS); care of older people (Diploma); clinical research (DESS); community health (DESS); dermatology (DESS); diagnostic radiology (DESS); emergency medicine (Diploma); family medicine (DESS); general surgery (DESS); geriatrics (DESS); hematology (DESS); internal medicine (DESS); maternal and fetal medicine (Diploma); medical biochemistry (DESS); medical microbiology and infectious diseases (DESS); medical oncology (DESS); nephrology (DESS); neurology (DESS); neurosurgery (DESS); obstetrics and gynecology (DESS); ophthalmology (DESS); orthopedic surgery (DESS); oto-rhino-laryngology (DESS); palliative medicine (Diploma); pediatrics (DESS); plastic surgery (DESS); psychiatry (DESS); pulmonary medicine (DESS); radiology–oncology (DESS); thoracic surgery (DESS); urology (DESS). *Degree requirements:* For other advanced degree, comprehensive exam. *Entrance requirements:* For degree, knowledge of French. Electronic applications accepted.

University at Buffalo, the State University of New York, Graduate School, Graduate Programs in Cancer Research and Biomedical Sciences at Roswell Park Cancer Institute, Department of Molecular Pharmacology and Cancer Therapeutics at Roswell Park Cancer Institute, Buffalo, NY 14260. Offers molecular pharmacology and cancer therapeutics (PhD). *Faculty:* 21 full-time (5 women). *Students:* 24 full-time (16 women), 1 part-time (0 women); includes 1 Black or African American, non-Hispanic/Latino; 1 Asian, non-Hispanic/Latino; 2 Hispanic/Latino, 13 international. Average age 26. 30 applicants, 33% accepted, 5 enrolled. In 2010, 3 doctorates awarded. *Degree requirements:* For doctorate, comprehensive exam, thesis/dissertation. *Entrance requirements:* For doctorate, GRE. Additional exam requirements/recommendations for international students: Required—TOEFL (minimum score 600 paper-based; 250 computer-based; 100 iBT), IELTS (minimum score 7), TWE (minimum score 4). *Application deadline:* For fall admission, 2/1 priority date for domestic and international students. Applications are processed on a rolling basis. Application fee: $50. Electronic applications accepted. *Financial support:* In 2010–11, 25 students received support, including 25 research assistantships with full tuition reimbursements available (averaging $24,000 per year); Federal Work-Study and health care benefits also available. Financial award application deadline: 2/1. *Faculty research:* Cell cycle regulation, apoptosis, signal transduction, k+s signaling pathway, drug development. Total annual research expenditures: $6.5 million. *Unit head:* Dr. David Goodrich, Chair, 716-845-8225, Fax: 716-845-3879, E-mail: david.goodrich@roswellpark.org. *Application contact:* Dr. Moray Campbell, Director of Graduate Studies, 716-845-8225, Fax: 716-845-8857, E-mail: theresa.skurzewski@roswellpark.org.

University at Buffalo, the State University of New York, Graduate School, Graduate Programs in Cancer Research and Biomedical Sciences at Roswell Park Cancer Institute, Interdisciplinary Master of Science Program in Natural and Biomedical Sciences at Roswell Park Cancer Institute, Buffalo, NY 14260. Offers biomedical sciences and cancer research (MS). Part-time programs available. *Faculty:* 8 full-time (3 women). *Students:* 62 full-time (39 women), 19 part-time (6 women); includes 5 Black or African American, non-Hispanic/Latino; 8 Asian, non-Hispanic/Latino; 4 Hispanic/Latino, 7 international. Average age 24. 100 applicants, 40% accepted, 30 enrolled. In 2010, 24 master's awarded. *Degree requirements:* For master's, thesis, defense of thesis, research project. *Entrance requirements:* For master's, GRE General Test, MCAT, DAT, PCAT. Additional exam requirements/recommendations for international students: Required—TOEFL (minimum score 600 paper-based; 250 computer-based; 100 iBT). *Application deadline:* For fall admission, 3/1 for domestic students. Applications are processed on a rolling basis. Application fee: $50. Electronic applications accepted. *Financial support:* In 2010–11, 1 fellowship with full tuition reimbursement (averaging $8,500 per year), 1 research assistantship (averaging $8,500 per year), 1 teaching assistantship with full tuition reimbursement (averaging $8,500 per year) were awarded; Federal Work-Study and institutionally sponsored loans also available. Financial award application deadline: 2/28; financial award applicants required to submit FAFSA. *Faculty research:* Biochemistry, oncology, pathology, biophysics, pharmacology, molecular biology, cellular biology, genetics, bioinformatics, immunology, therapeutic development, epidemiology. Total annual research expenditures: $1 million. *Unit head:* Dr. Adam Kisailus, Director of Graduate Studies, 716-845-2339, Fax: 716-845-8178, E-mail: adam.kisailus@roswellpark.org. *Application contact:* Craig R. Johnson, Director of Admissions, 716-845-2339, Fax: 716-845-8178, E-mail: craig.johnson@roswellpark.org.

University of Alberta, Faculty of Medicine and Dentistry and Faculty of Graduate Studies and Research, Graduate Programs in Medicine, Department of Oncology, Edmonton, AB T6G 2E1, Canada. Offers M Sc, PhD. Terminal master's awarded for partial completion of doctoral program. *Degree requirements:* For master's, thesis; for doctorate, thesis/dissertation. *Entrance requirements:* For master's and doctorate, minimum GPA of 7.0 on a 9.0 scale, B SC. Additional exam requirements/recommendations for international students: Required—TOEFL (minimum score 600 paper-based). Electronic applications accepted. *Faculty research:* Experimental oncology, radiation oncology, medical physics, medical oncology.

The University of Arizona, Graduate Interdisciplinary Programs, Graduate Interdisciplinary Program in Cancer Biology, Tucson, AZ 85721. Offers PhD. *Students:* 16 full-time (12 women), 1 part-time (0 women); includes 1 Black or African American, non-Hispanic/Latino; 3 Hispanic/Latino; 2 Two or more races, non-Hispanic/Latino, 2 international. Average age 32. 49 applicants, 6% accepted, 3 enrolled. In 2010, 6 doctorates awarded. *Degree requirements:* For doctorate, comprehensive exam, thesis/dissertation. *Entrance requirements:* For doctorate, GRE General Test, 3 letters of recommendation. Additional exam requirements/recommendations for international students: Required—TOEFL (minimum score 550 paper-based; 213 computer-based; 79 iBT). *Application deadline:* For fall admission, 12/1 for domestic and international students. Applications are processed on a rolling basis. Application fee: $65. Electronic applications accepted. *Expenses:* Tuition, state resident: full-time $7692. *Financial support:* Institutionally sponsored loans, scholarships/grants, traineeships, health care benefits, tuition waivers (full), and unspecified assistantships available. *Faculty research:* Differential gene expression, DNA-protein cross linking, cell growth regulation steroid, receptor proteins. *Unit head:* Dr. G. Tim Bowden, Chairman, 520-626-7479, E-mail: bowden@azcc.arizona.edu. *Application contact:* Anne Cione, Senior Program Coordinator, 520-626-7479, Fax: 520-626-4979, E-mail: acione@azcc.arizona.edu.

University of Calgary, Faculty of Medicine and Faculty of Graduate Studies, Department of Medical Science, Calgary, AB T2N 1N4, Canada. Offers cancer biology (M Sc, PhD); immunology (M Sc, PhD); joint injury and arthritis research (M Sc, PhD); medical education (M Sc, PhD); medical science (M Sc, PhD); mountain medicine and high altitude physiology (M Sc). *Degree requirements:* For master's, thesis; for doctorate, thesis/dissertation, candidacy exam. *Entrance requirements:* For master's, minimum undergraduate GPA of 3.2; for doctorate, minimum graduate GPA of 3.2. Additional exam requirements/recommendations for international students: Required—TOEFL (minimum score 600 paper-based; 250 computer-based). Electronic applications accepted. *Faculty research:* Cancer biology, immunology, joint injury and arthritis, medical education, population genomics.

Cancer Biology/Oncology

University of California, San Diego, Office of Graduate Studies, Division of Biological Sciences, Program in Immunology, Virology, and Cancer Biology, La Jolla, CA 92093. Offers PhD. Offered in association with the Salk Institute. *Degree requirements:* For doctorate, thesis/dissertation, qualifying exam. Electronic applications accepted.

University of California, San Diego, School of Medicine and Office of Graduate Studies, Molecular Pathology Program, La Jolla, CA 92093. Offers bioinformatics (PhD); cancer biology/oncology (PhD); cardiovascular sciences and disease (PhD); microbiology (PhD); molecular pathology (PhD); neurological disease (PhD); stem cell and developmental biology (PhD); structural biology/drug design (PhD). *Entrance requirements:* For doctorate, GRE General Test, GRE Subject Test. Additional exam requirements/recommendations for international students: Required—TOEFL. Electronic applications accepted.

University of Chicago, Division of Biological Sciences, Biomedical Sciences Cluster: Cancer Biology, Immunology, Molecular Metabolism and Nutrition, Pathology, and Microbiology, Committee on Cancer Biology, Chicago, IL 60637-1513. Offers PhD. *Degree requirements:* For doctorate, thesis/dissertation, ethics class, 2 teaching assistantships. *Entrance requirements:* For doctorate, GRE General Test. Additional exam requirements/recommendations for international students: Required—TOEFL (minimum score 600 paper-based; 250 computer-based; 104 iBT), IELTS (minimum score 7). Electronic applications accepted. *Faculty research:* Cancer genetics, apoptosis, signal transduction, tumor biology, cell cycle regulation.

University of Cincinnati, Graduate School, College of Medicine, Graduate Programs in Biomedical Sciences, Graduate Program in Cell and Cancer Biology, Cincinnati, OH 45221. Offers PhD. *Degree requirements:* For doctorate, thesis/dissertation, qualifying exam. *Entrance requirements:* For doctorate, GRE General Test. Additional exam requirements/recommendations for international students: Required—TOEFL. Electronic applications accepted. *Faculty research:* Cancer biology; cell and molecular biology, breast cancer, pancreatic cancer, drug discovery.

University of Colorado Denver, School of Medicine, Program in Cancer Biology, Denver, CO 80217-3364. Offers PhD. *Students:* 16 full-time (12 women); includes 1 Hispanic/Latino, 1 international. Average age 25. 32 applicants, 9% accepted, 2 enrolled. In 2010, 2 doctorates awarded. *Degree requirements:* For doctorate, comprehensive exam, thesis/dissertation, 3 laboratory rotations. *Entrance requirements:* For doctorate, GRE General Test, interview, minimum undergraduate GPA of 3.0. Additional exam requirements/recommendations for international students: Required—TOEFL (minimum score 550 paper-based; 213 computer-based). *Application deadline:* For fall admission, 1/1 for domestic students. Application fee: $50 ($75 for international students). Electronic applications accepted. *Expenses:* Contact institution. *Financial support:* In 2010–11, 2 students received support; fellowships with full tuition reimbursements available, health care benefits, tuition waivers (full), and stipend available. Financial award application deadline: 3/15; financial award applicants required to submit FAFSA. *Faculty research:* Signal transduction by tyrosine kinases, estrogen and progesterone receptors in breast cancer, mechanism of mitochondrial DNA replication in the mammalian cell. Total annual research expenditures: $9 million. *Unit head:* Dr. Mary Reyland, Director, 303-724-4572, E-mail: mary.reyland@ucdenver.edu. *Application contact:* Jamie Kean, Program Administrator, 303-724-3905, E-mail: cancer.biology@ucdenver.edu.

University of Delaware, College of Arts and Sciences, Department of Biological Sciences, Newark, DE 19716. Offers biotechnology (MS); cancer biology (MS, PhD); cell and extracellular matrix biology (MS, PhD); cell and systems physiology (MS, PhD); developmental biology (MS, PhD); ecology and evolution (MS, PhD); microbiology (MS, PhD); molecular biology and genetics (MS, PhD). Terminal master's awarded for partial completion of doctoral program. *Degree requirements:* For master's, thesis, preliminary exam; for doctorate, comprehensive exam, thesis/dissertation, preliminary exam. *Entrance requirements:* For master's and doctorate, GRE General Test. Additional exam requirements/recommendations for international students: Required—TOEFL (minimum score 600 paper-based; 250 computer-based); Recommended—TWE. Electronic applications accepted. *Faculty research:* Microorganisms, bone, cancer metastasis, developmental biology, cell biology, DNA.

The University of Manchester, Faculty of Life Sciences, Manchester, United Kingdom. Offers adaptive organismal biology (M Phil, PhD); animal biology (M Phil, PhD); biochemistry (M Phil, PhD); bioinformatics (M Phil, PhD); biomolecular sciences (M Phil, PhD); biotechnology (M Phil, PhD); cell biology (M Phil, PhD); cell matrix research (M Phil, PhD); channels and transporters (M Phil, PhD); developmental biology (M Phil, PhD); Egyptology (M Phil, PhD); environmental biology (M Phil, PhD); evolutionary biology (M Phil, PhD); gene expression (M Phil, PhD); genetics (M Phil, PhD); history of science, technology and medicine (M Phil, PhD); immunology (M Phil, PhD); integrative neurobiology and behavior (M Phil, PhD); membrane trafficking (M Phil, PhD); microbiology (M Phil, PhD); molecular and cellular neuroscience (M Phil, PhD); molecular biology (M Phil, PhD); molecular cancer studies (M Phil, PhD); neuroscience (M Phil, PhD); ophthalmology (M Phil, PhD); optometry (M Phil, PhD); organelle function (M Phil, PhD); pharmacology (M Phil, PhD); physiology (M Phil, PhD); plant sciences (M Phil, PhD); stem cell research (M Phil, PhD); structural biology (M Phil, PhD); systems neuroscience (M Phil, PhD); toxicology (M Phil, PhD).

The University of Manchester, School of Dentistry, Manchester, United Kingdom. Offers basic dental sciences (cancer studies) (M Phil, PhD); basic dental sciences (molecular genetics) (M Phil, PhD); basic dental sciences (stem cell biology) (M Phil, PhD); biomaterials sciences and dental technology (M Phil, PhD); dental public health/community dentistry (M Phil, PhD); dental science (clinical) (PhD); endodontology (M Phil, PhD); fixed and removable prosthodontics (M Phil, PhD); operative dentistry (M Phil, PhD); oral and maxillofacial surgery (M Phil, PhD); oral radiology (M Phil, PhD); orthodontics (M Phil, PhD); restorative dentistry (M Phil, PhD).

University of Manitoba, Faculty of Graduate Studies, Faculty of Nursing, Winnipeg, MB R3T 2N2, Canada. Offers cancer nursing (MN); nursing (MN). *Degree requirements:* For master's, thesis.

University of Maryland, Baltimore, Graduate School, Graduate Program in Life Sciences, Program in Molecular Medicine, Baltimore, MD 21201. Offers cancer biology (PhD); cell and molecular physiology (PhD); human genetics and genomic medicine (PhD); molecular medicine (MS); molecular toxicology and pharmacology (PhD); MD/PhD. *Entrance requirements:* Additional exam requirements/recommendations for international students: Required—TOEFL (minimum score 600 paper-based; 100 iBT); Recommended—IELTS (minimum score 7). Electronic applications accepted. Part-time tuition and fees vary according to course load, degree level and program.

University of Massachusetts Worcester, Graduate School of Biomedical Sciences, Worcester, MA 01655-0115. Offers biochemistry and molecular pharmacology (PhD); bioinformatics and computational biology (PhD); cancer biology (PhD); cell biology (PhD); clinical and population health research (PhD); clinical investigation (MS); immunology and virology (PhD); interdisciplinary graduate program (PhD); molecular genetics and microbiology (PhD); neuroscience (PhD); DVM/PhD; MD/PhD. *Faculty:* 1,059 full-time (357 women), 145 part-time/adjunct (100 women). *Students:* 438 full-time (239 women), 1 (woman) part-time; includes 44 minority (9 Black or African American, non-Hispanic/Latino; 31 Asian, non-Hispanic/Latino; 4 Hispanic/Latino), 148 international. Average age 29. 687 applicants, 28% accepted, 116 enrolled. In 2010, 6 master's, 45 doctorates awarded. Terminal master's awarded for partial completion of doctoral program. *Degree requirements:* For master's, thesis; for doctorate, thesis/dissertation. *Entrance requirements:* For master's, bachelor's degree; for doctorate, GRE General Test, MS, MA, or MPH (for some programs). Additional exam requirements/recommendations for international students: Required—TOEFL (minimum score 600 paper-based; 250 computer-based). *Application deadline:* For fall admission, 12/15 for domestic and international students; for winter admission, 1/15 for domestic students; for spring admission, 5/15 for domestic students. Application fee: $35. Electronic applications accepted. *Expenses:* Contact institution. *Financial support:* In 2010–11, 439 students received support, including 439 research assistantships with full tuition reimbursements available (averaging $28,350 per year); scholarships/grants,

health care benefits, tuition waivers (full), and unspecified assistantships also available. Financial award application deadline: 4/20. *Faculty research:* RNA interference, gene therapy, cell biology, bioinformatics, clinical research. Total annual research expenditures: $232 million. *Unit head:* Dr. Anthony Carruthers, Dean, 508-856-4135, E-mail: anthony.carruthers@umassmed.edu. *Application contact:* Dr. Kendall Knight, Associate Dean and Interim Director of Admissions and Recruitment, 508-856-5628, Fax: 508-856-3659, E-mail: kendall.knight@umassmed.edu.

University of Medicine and Dentistry of New Jersey, Graduate School of Biomedical Sciences, Graduate Programs in Biomedical Sciences–Newark, Newark, NJ 07107. Offers biodefense (Certificate); biomedical engineering (PhD); biomedical sciences (multidisciplinary) (PhD); cellular biology, neuroscience and physiology (PhD), including neuroscience, physiology, biophysics, cardiovascular biology, molecular pharmacology, stem cell biology; infection, immunity and inflammation (PhD), including immunology, infectious disease, microbiology, oral biology; molecular biology, genetics and cancer (PhD), including biochemistry, molecular genetics, cancer biology, radiation biology, bioinformatics; neuroscience (Certificate); pharmacological sciences (Certificate); stem cell (Certificate); DMD/PhD; MD/PhD. PhD in biomedical engineering offered jointly with New Jersey Institute of Technology. Part-time and evening/weekend programs available. *Students:* 330 full-time (199 women), 75 part-time (47 women); includes 32 Black or African American, non-Hispanic/Latino; 1 American Indian or Alaska Native, non-Hispanic/Latino; 109 Asian, non-Hispanic/Latino; 16 Hispanic/Latino, 83 international. Average age 28. 611 applicants, 52% accepted, 181 enrolled. In 2010, 24 doctorates, 2 other advanced degrees awarded. Terminal master's awarded for partial completion of doctoral program. *Degree requirements:* For doctorate, thesis/dissertation, qualifying exam. *Entrance requirements:* For doctorate, GRE General Test. Additional exam requirements/recommendations for international students: Required—TOEFL. *Application deadline:* For fall admission, 1/15 for domestic students. Applications are processed on a rolling basis. Application fee: $65. Electronic applications accepted. *Financial support:* In 2010–11, 28 fellowships (averaging $26,000 per year) were awarded; research assistantships, teaching assistantships, career-related internships or fieldwork, Federal Work-Study, institutionally sponsored loans, and tuition waivers (full and partial) also available. Financial award application deadline: 5/1. *Unit head:* Dr. Andrew Thomas, Senior Associate Dean, Graduate School of Biomedical Sciences, 973-972-4511, Fax: 973-972-7148, E-mail: thomas@umdnj.edu. *Application contact:* Dr. B. J. Wagner, 973-972-5335, Fax: 973-972-7148, E-mail: wagner@umdnj.edu.

University of Miami, Graduate School, Miller School of Medicine, Program in Cancer Biology, Coral Gables, FL 33124. Offers PhD, MD/PhD.

University of Minnesota, Twin Cities Campus, Graduate School, PhD Program in Microbiology, Immunology and Cancer Biology, Minneapolis, MN 55455-0213. Offers PhD. *Degree requirements:* For doctorate, thesis/dissertation. *Entrance requirements:* For doctorate, GRE General Test. Additional exam requirements/recommendations for international students: Required—TOEFL (minimum score 600 paper-based; 250 computer-based). Electronic applications accepted. *Faculty research:* Virology, microbiology, cancer biology, immunology.

University of Nebraska Medical Center, Graduate Studies, Program in Cancer Research, Omaha, NE 68198. Offers PhD. *Faculty:* 33 full-time (8 women). *Students:* 33 full-time (14 women), 15 part-time (12 women); includes 2 Hispanic/Latino, 19 international. Average age 28. 48 applicants, 4% accepted, 2 enrolled. In 2010, 2 doctorates awarded. Terminal master's awarded for partial completion of doctoral program. *Degree requirements:* For doctorate, comprehensive exam, thesis/dissertation. *Entrance requirements:* For doctorate, GRE, 3 letters of reference; course work in chemistry, biology, physics and mathematics. Additional exam requirements/recommendations for international students: Required—TOEFL (minimum score 550 paper-based; 213 computer-based). *Application deadline:* For fall admission, 6/1 for domestic students, 5/1 for international students; for spring admission, 10/1 for domestic students, 8/1 for international students. Applications are processed on a rolling basis. Application fee: $45. Electronic applications accepted. *Expenses:* Tuition, state resident: part-time $198.25 per semester hour. Required fees: $63 per semester. *Financial support:* In 2010–11, 7 fellowships with tuition reimbursements (averaging $21,000 per year), 13 research assistantships with tuition reimbursements (averaging $21,000 per year) were awarded; health care benefits also available. *Faculty research:* DNA repair, tumor immunology, signal transduction, structural biology, gene expression. Total annual research expenditures: $18.1 million. *Unit head:* Dr. Joyce Solheim, Graduate Committee Chair, 402-559-4539, Fax: 402-559-8270, E-mail: jsolheim@unmc.edu.

University of Pennsylvania, Perelman School of Medicine, Biomedical Graduate Studies, Graduate Group in Cell and Molecular Biology, Philadelphia, PA 19104. Offers cancer biology (PhD); cell biology and physiology (PhD); developmental stem cell regenerative biology (PhD); gene therapy and vaccines (PhD); genetics and gene regulation (PhD); microbiology, virology, and parasitology (PhD); MD/PhD; VMD/PhD. *Faculty:* 299. *Students:* 315 full-time (166 women); includes 13 Black or African American, non-Hispanic/Latino; 1 American Indian or Alaska Native, non-Hispanic/Latino; 44 Asian, non-Hispanic/Latino; 18 Hispanic/Latino, 37 international. 579 applicants, 21% accepted, 49 enrolled. In 2010, 53 doctorates awarded. *Degree requirements:* For doctorate, thesis/dissertation. *Entrance requirements:* For doctorate, GRE General Test. Additional exam requirements/recommendations for international students: Required—TOEFL. *Application deadline:* For fall admission, 12/8 priority date for domestic and international students. Applications are processed on a rolling basis. Application fee: $70. Electronic applications accepted. *Expenses:* Tuition: Full-time $25,660; part-time $4758 per course. Required fees: $2152; $270 per course. Tuition and fees vary according to course load, degree level and program. *Financial support:* In 2010–11, 315 students received support; fellowships, research assistantships, scholarships/grants, traineeships, and unspecified assistantships available. Financial award application deadline: 12/8. *Unit head:* Dr. Daniel Kessler, Graduate Group Chair, 215-898-2180, E-mail: raperj@mail.med.upenn.edu. *Application contact:* Meagan Schofer, Coordinator, 215-898-9536, Fax: 215-573-2104, E-mail: camb@mailmed.upenn.edu.

University of Regina, Faculty of Graduate Studies and Research, Faculty of Science, Department of Chemistry and Biochemistry, Regina, SK S4S 0A2, Canada. Offers analytical/environmental chemistry (M Sc, PhD); biophysics of biological interfaces (M Sc, PhD); enzymology/chemical biology (M Sc, PhD); inorganic/organometallic chemistry (M Sc, PhD); signal transduction and mechanisms of cancer cell regulation (M Sc, PhD); supramolecular organic photochemistry and photophysics (M Sc, PhD); synthetic organic chemistry (M Sc, PhD); theoretical/computational chemistry (M Sc, PhD). *Faculty:* 10 full-time (2 women). *Students:* 19 full-time (9 women), 2 part-time (1 woman). 20 applicants, 40% accepted. In 2010, 2 master's, 1 doctorate awarded. *Degree requirements:* For master's, thesis; for doctorate, thesis/dissertation. *Entrance requirements:* Additional exam requirements/recommendations for international students: Required—TOEFL (minimum score 580 paper-based; 80 iBT). *Application deadline:* Applications are processed on a rolling basis. Application fee: $100. Electronic applications accepted. Tuition and fees charges are reported in Canadian dollars. *Expenses:* Tuition, area resident: Full-time $3245 Canadian dollars; part-time $180.25 Canadian dollars per credit hour. International tuition: $4745 Canadian dollars full-time. Required fees: $494 Canadian dollars; $115.25 Canadian dollars per credit hour. $115.25 Canadian dollars per semester. Tuition and fees vary according to program. *Financial support:* In 2010–11, 3 fellowships (averaging $20,000 per year), 2 research assistantships (averaging $17,250 per year), 8 teaching assistantships (averaging $6,965 per year) were awarded; scholarships/grants also available. Financial award application deadline: 6/15. *Faculty research:* Asymmetric synthesis and methodology, theoretical and computational chemistry, biophysical biochemistry, analytical and environmental chemistry, chemical biology. *Unit head:* Dr. Lynn Mihichuk, Head, 306-585-4793, Fax: 306-337-2409, E-mail: lynn.mihichuk@uregina.ca. *Application contact:* Dr. Tanya Dahms, Graduate Program Coordinator, 306-585-4246, Fax: 306-337-2409, E-mail: tanya.dahms@uregina.ca.

University of South Florida, Graduate School, College of Arts and Sciences, Program in Cancer Biology, Tampa, FL 33620-9951. Offers PhD. *Students:* 34 full-time (22 women), 1 (woman) part-time; includes 2 Hispanic/Latino, 8 international. Average age 29. 9 applicants, 100% accepted, 9 enrolled. *Entrance requirements:* For doctorate, GRE General Test. Additional exam requirements/recommendations for international students: Required—TOEFL (minimum score 550 paper-based; 213 computer-based). *Application deadline:* For fall admission, 2/1 for domestic students, 1/1 for international students. Application fee: $30. *Financial support:* Career-related internships or fieldwork, health care benefits, and unspecified assistantships available. Financial award application deadline: 4/1. *Faculty research:* Immunology, cancer control, signal transduction, drug discovery, genomics. *Unit head:* Kenneth Wright, Director, 813-745-6876, Fax: 813-745-7264, E-mail: ken.wright@moffitt.org. *Application contact:* Kenneth Wright, Director, 813-745-6876, Fax: 813-745-7264, E-mail: ken.wright@moffitt.org.

The University of Texas Health Science Center at Houston, Graduate School of Biomedical Sciences, Program in Cancer Biology, Houston, TX 77225-0036. Offers MS, PhD, MD/PhD. Terminal master's awarded for partial completion of doctoral program. *Degree requirements:* For master's, thesis; for doctorate, thesis/dissertation. *Entrance requirements:* For master's and doctorate, GRE General Test. Additional exam requirements/recommendations for international students: Required—TOEFL. Electronic applications accepted. *Faculty research:* Cancer metastasis, signal transduction, therapeutic resistance, cell cycle deregulation, cancer markers and target.

See Display below and Close-Up on page 239.

The University of Texas Health Science Center at Houston, Graduate School of Biomedical Sciences, Program in Molecular Carcinogenesis, Houston, TX 77225-0036. Offers MS, PhD, MD/PhD. Terminal master's awarded for partial completion of doctoral program. *Degree requirements:* For master's, thesis; for doctorate, thesis/dissertation. *Entrance requirements:* For master's and doctorate, GRE General Test. Additional exam requirements/recommendations for international students: Required—TOEFL. Electronic applications accepted. *Faculty research:* Carcinogenesis, mutagenesis, epigenetics, mouse models, cancer prevention.

The University of Texas Southwestern Medical Center at Dallas, Southwestern Graduate School of Biomedical Sciences, Division of Basic Science, Program in Cancer Biology, Dallas, TX 75390. Offers PhD. *Faculty:* 85 full-time (16 women), 2 part-time/adjunct (0 women). *Students:* 51 full-time (28 women); includes 17 minority (1 Black or African American, non-Hispanic/Latino; 9 Asian, non-Hispanic/Latino; 7 Hispanic/Latino), 11 international. Average age 26. In 2010, 7 doctorates awarded. *Degree requirements:* For doctorate, thesis/dissertation, qualifying examination. *Unit head:* Jerry Shay, Chair, 214-648-3282, E-mail: jerry.shay@utsouthwestern.edu. *Application contact:* Jerry Shay, Chair, 214-648-3282, E-mail: jerry.shay@utsouthwestern.edu.

University of the District of Columbia, College of Arts and Sciences, Department of Biological and Environmental Sciences, Program in Cancer Biology, Prevention and Control, Washington, DC 20008-1175. Offers MS. Program offered in partnership with Lombardi Comprehensive Cancer Center at Georgetown University. *Expenses:* Tuition, state resident: full-time $7580; part-time $421 per credit. Tuition, nonresident: full-time $14,580; part-time $810 per credit. Required fees: $620; $30 per credit. One-time fee: $100 part-time.

The University of Toledo, College of Graduate Studies, College of Medicine and Life Sciences, Department of Biochemistry and Cancer Biology, Toledo, OH 43606-3390. Offers MSBS, PhD. *Students:* 21 full-time (14 women), 7 part-time (3 women); includes 1 Hispanic/Latino, 22 international. 12 applicants, 83% accepted, 6 enrolled. In 2010, 1 master's, 1 doctorate awarded. Application fee: $45. *Expenses:* Tuition, state resident: full-time $11,426; part-time $476 per credit hour. Tuition, nonresident: full-time $21,660; part-time $903 per credit hour. One-time fee: $62. *Financial support:* In 2010–11, 2 research assistantships with full tuition reimbursements (averaging $20,772 per year) were awarded; fellowships with tuition reimbursements, Federal Work-Study, scholarships/grants, tuition waivers (full), and unspecified assistantships also available. *Unit head:* Dr. James Trempe, Track Director, 419-383-4103, E-mail: james.trempe@utoledo.edu.

University of Utah, School of Medicine and Graduate School, Graduate Programs in Medicine, Department of Oncological Sciences, Salt Lake City, UT 84112-1107. Offers M Phil, MS, PhD. Terminal master's awarded for partial completion of doctoral program. *Degree requirements:* For master's, thesis (for some programs); for doctorate, thesis/dissertation. *Entrance requirements:* For master's and doctorate, GRE General Test, GRE Subject Test, minimum GPA of 3.0. Additional exam requirements/recommendations for international students: Required—TOEFL. *Expenses:* Tuition, area resident: Part-time $179.19 per credit hour. Tuition, state resident: full-time $4384. Tuition, nonresident: full-time $16,684; part-time $630.67 per credit hour. Required fees: $350 per semester. Tuition and fees vary according to course load, degree level and program. *Faculty research:* Molecular basis of cell growth and differences, regulation of gene expression, biochemical mechanics of DNA replication, molecular biology and biochemistry of signal transduction, somatic cell genetics.

University of Wisconsin–La Crosse, Office of University Graduate Studies, College of Science and Health, Department of Health Professions, Program in Medical Dosimetry, La Crosse, WI 54601-3742. Offers MS. Postbaccalaureate distance learning degree programs offered (no on-campus study). *Students:* 12 full-time (7 women); includes 3 minority (2 Black or African American, non-Hispanic/Latino; 1 Asian, non-Hispanic/Latino). Average age 32. 25 applicants, 60% accepted, 12 enrolled. *Entrance requirements:* For master's, Amercian Registry of Radiologic Technologists test, Medical Dosimetrist Certification Board Exam. Additional exam requirements/recommendations for international students: Required—TOEFL (minimum score 600 paper-based; 250 computer-based; 100 iBT). *Application deadline:* For fall admission, 12/1 priority date for domestic students, 11/1 priority date for international students. Application fee: $56. Electronic applications accepted. *Expenses:* Contact institution. *Financial support:* Federal Work-Study and scholarships/grants available. Support available to part-time students. Financial award applicants required to submit FAFSA. *Unit head:* Nishele Lenards, Program Director, 608-785-8470, E-mail: lenards.nish@uwlax.edu. *Application contact:* Kathryn Kiefer, Director of Admissions, 608-785-8939, E-mail: admissions@uwlax.edu.

University of Wisconsin–Madison, School of Medicine and Public Health and Graduate School, Graduate Programs in Medicine, Program in Cancer Biology, Madison, WI 53706. Offers PhD. *Faculty:* 43 full-time (14 women). *Students:* 32 full-time (15 women), 10 international. 246 applicants, 6% accepted, 5 enrolled. In 2010, 12 doctorates awarded. *Degree requirements:* For doctorate, comprehensive exam, thesis/dissertation. *Entrance requirements:* For doctorate, GRE General Test. Additional exam requirements/recommendations for international students: Required—TOEFL (minimum score 580 paper-based; 237 computer-based; 92 iBT). *Application deadline:* For fall admission, 12/1 priority date for domestic and international students. Applications are processed on a rolling basis. Application fee: $56. Electronic applications accepted. *Expenses:* Tuition, state resident: full-time $9887; part-time $617.96 per credit. Tuition, nonresident: full-time $24,054; part-time $1503.40 per credit. Required fees: $67.63 per credit. Tuition and fees vary according to reciprocity agreements. *Financial support:* In 2010–11, 28 students received support, including 4 fellowships with full tuition reimbursements available (averaging $24,000 per year), 24 research assistantships with full tuition reimbursements available (averaging $24,000 per year); traineeships, health care benefits, and unspecified assistantships also available. Financial award application deadline: 12/1. *Faculty research:* Cancer genetics, tumor virology, chemical carcinogenesis, signal transduction, cell cycle. Total annual research expenditures: $18 million. *Unit head:* Dr. James Shull, Director, 608-262-2177, Fax: 608-262-2824, E-mail: shull@oncology.wisc.edu. *Application contact:* Bette Sheehan, Administrative Program Manager, 608-262-8651, Fax: 608-262-2824, E-mail: bsheehan@oncology.wisc.edu.

Vanderbilt University, Graduate School, Department of Cancer Biology, Nashville, TN 37240-1001. Offers MS, PhD, MD/PhD. *Faculty:* 13 full-time (8 women). *Students:* 49 full-time (34 women); includes 15 minority (6 Black or African American, non-Hispanic/Latino; 6 Asian, non-Hispanic/Latino; 2 Hispanic/Latino; 1 Two or more races, non-Hispanic/Latino). Average age 28. In 2010, 14 degrees awarded. *Degree requirements:* For doctorate, thesis/dissertation, final and qualifying exams. *Entrance requirements:* For master's and doctorate, GRE General

Cancer Biology/Oncology

Vanderbilt University (continued)

Test. Additional exam requirements/recommendations for international students: Required—TOEFL (minimum score 570 paper-based; 230 computer-based; 88 iBT). *Application deadline:* For fall admission, 1/15 for domestic and international students. Application fee: $0. Electronic applications accepted. *Financial support:* Fellowships with full and partial tuition reimbursements, research assistantships with full and partial tuition reimbursements, Federal Work-Study, institutionally sponsored loans, scholarships/grants, traineeships, and health care benefits available. Financial award application deadline: 1/15; financial award applicants required to submit CSS PROFILE or FAFSA. *Faculty research:* Microenvironmental influences on cellular phenotype, in particular as it relates to host/tumor interactions, tumor-stroma interactions, angiogenesis, growth factor and cytokine signaling, oncogenes, tumor suppressors, matrix and matrix degradation, cell adhesion, metastasis. *Unit head:* Dr. Lynn M. Matrisian, Chair, 615-322-0375, Fax: 615-936-2911, E-mail: lynn.matrisian@vanderbilt.edu. *Application contact:* Jin Chen, Director of Graduate Studies, 615-322-0375, Fax: 615-936-2911, E-mail: jin.chen@vanderbilt.edu.

Wake Forest University, School of Medicine and Graduate School of Arts and Sciences, Graduate Programs in Medicine, Department of Cancer Biology, Winston-Salem, NC 27109. Offers PhD, MD/PhD. *Degree requirements:* For doctorate, thesis/dissertation. *Entrance requirements:* For doctorate, GRE General Test. Additional exam requirements/recommendations for international students: Required—TOEFL. Electronic applications accepted. *Faculty research:* Cancer research, mechanisms of carcinogenesis, signal transduction and regulation of cell growth.

Wayne State University, School of Medicine, Cancer Biology Graduate Program, Detroit, MI 48202. Offers MS, PhD. *Students:* 26 full-time (18 women); includes 3 Black or African American, non-Hispanic/Latino; 1 American Indian or Alaska Native, non-Hispanic/Latino, 4 international. Average age 27. 66 applicants, 11% accepted, 6 enrolled. In 2010, 1 master's awarded. *Degree requirements:* For doctorate, thesis/dissertation. *Entrance requirements:* For doctorate, GRE General Test. Additional exam requirements/recommendations for international students: Required—TOEFL (minimum score 550 paper-based; 213 computer-based); Recommended—TWE (minimum score 6). *Application deadline:* For fall admission, 3/1 for international students. Applications are processed on a rolling basis. Application fee: $50. Electronic applications accepted. *Expenses:* Tuition, state resident: full-time $7662; part-time $478.85 per credit hour. Tuition, nonresident: full-time $16,920; part-time $1057.55 per credit hour. Required fees: $571; $35.70 per credit hour. $188.05 per semester. Tuition and fees vary according to course load and program. *Financial support:* In 2010–11, 7 fellowships (averaging $22,249 per year), 18 research assistantships (averaging $21,172 per year) were awarded; 4 external fellowships (averaging over $20,000 per year), 5 training grant appointments also available. *Faculty research:* Molecular oncology and carcinogenesis, cellular interactions and signaling, proteases in neoplasia, therapeutics and prevention, translational research. *Unit head:* Dr. Robert Pauley, Director, 313-577-1065, Fax: 313-577-4112, E-mail: 1a4407@wayne.edu. *Application contact:* Dr. Kenneth C. Palmer, Assistant Dean, 313-577-1455, E-mail: kpalmer@med.wayne.edu.

See Close-Up on page 243.

Wayne State University, School of Medicine, Graduate Programs in Medicine, Department of Radiation Oncology, Detroit, MI 48202. Offers medical physics (PhD); radiological physics (MS). Part-time and evening/weekend programs available. *Faculty:* 4 full-time (0 women). *Students:* 4 full-time (1 woman), 2 part-time (0 women); includes 1 minority (Asian, non-Hispanic/Latino), 1 international. Average age 33. 24 applicants, 29% accepted, 2 enrolled. In 2010, 1 doctorate awarded. Terminal master's awarded for partial completion of doctoral program. *Degree requirements:* For master's, thesis, essay, exit exam; for doctorate, thesis/dissertation, qualifying exam. *Entrance requirements:* For master's, GRE General Test, BS in physics or related area; for doctorate, GRE General Test, GRE Subject Test, BS in physics or related area. Additional exam requirements/recommendations for international students: Required—TOEFL (minimum score 550 paper-based; 213 computer-based); Recommended—TWE (minimum score 6). *Application deadline:* For fall admission, 1/15 for domestic students, 6/1 for international students; for winter admission, 10/1 for international students; for spring admission, 2/1 for international students. Applications are processed on a rolling basis. Application fee: $30 ($50 for international students). Electronic applications accepted. *Expenses:* Tuition, state resident: full-time $7662; part-time $478.85 per credit hour. Tuition, nonresident: full-time $16,920; part-time $1057.55 per credit hour. Required fees: $571; $35.70 per credit hour. $188.05 per semester. Tuition and fees vary according to course load and program. *Financial support:* In 2010–11, 1 research assistantship (averaging $20,787 per year) was awarded; fellowships, teaching assistantships, career-related internships or fieldwork also available. Support available to part-time students. Financial award application deadline: 1/15. *Unit head:* Maria Vlachaki, Chair, 313-966-2774, Fax: 313-745-2314, E-mail: 661250@wayne.edu. *Application contact:* Michael Joiner, Professor, 313-745-2489, E-mail: joinerm@kci.wayne.edu.

West Virginia University, Davis College of Agriculture, Forestry and Consumer Sciences, Interdisciplinary Program in Genetics and Developmental Biology, Morgantown, WV 26506. Offers animal breeding (MS, PhD); biochemical and molecular genetics (MS, PhD); cytogenetics (MS, PhD); descriptive embryology (MS, PhD); developmental genetics (MS); experimental morphogenesis/teratology (MS); human genetics (MS, PhD); immunogenetics (MS, PhD); life cycles of animals and plants (MS, PhD); molecular aspects of development (MS, PhD); mutagenesis (MS, PhD); oncology (MS, PhD); plant genetics (MS, PhD); population and quantitative genetics (MS, PhD); regeneration (MS, PhD); teratology (PhD); toxicology (MS, PhD). *Degree requirements:* For master's, thesis; for doctorate, comprehensive exam, thesis/dissertation. *Entrance requirements:* For master's, GRE or MCAT, minimum GPA of 2.75. Additional exam requirements/recommendations for international students: Required—TOEFL.

West Virginia University, School of Medicine, Graduate Programs at the Health Sciences Center, Interdisciplinary Graduate Programs in Biomedical Sciences, Program in Cancer Cell Biology, Morgantown, WV 26506. Offers PhD, MD/PhD. *Degree requirements:* For doctorate, comprehensive exam, thesis/dissertation. *Entrance requirements:* For doctorate, GRE General Test, minimum GPA of 3.0. Additional exam requirements/recommendations for international students: Required—TOEFL. Electronic applications accepted. *Faculty research:* Cellular signaling, tumor microenvironment, cancer therapeutics.

Yale University, School of Medicine and Graduate School of Arts and Sciences, Combined Program in Biological and Biomedical Sciences (BBS), Pharmacological Sciences and Molecular Medicine Track, New Haven, CT 06520. Offers PhD, MD/PhD. *Degree requirements:* For doctorate, thesis/dissertation. *Entrance requirements:* For doctorate, GRE General Test. Additional exam requirements/recommendations for international students: Required—TOEFL. Electronic applications accepted.

Cell Biology

Albany College of Pharmacy and Health Sciences, Program in Pharmacy, Albany, NY 12208. Offers biotechnology (MS); cytotechnology (MS); health outcomes research (MS); pharmaceutical sciences (MS); pharmacy (Pharm D); pharmacy administration (MS). *Accreditation:* ACPE. *Faculty:* 59 full-time (25 women), 9 part-time/adjunct (3 women). *Students:* 467 full-time (251 women), 2 part-time (both women); includes 19 Black or African American, non-Hispanic/Latino; 60 Asian, non-Hispanic/Latino; 3 Hispanic/Latino; 6 Two or more races, non-Hispanic/Latino, 52 international. Average age 26. 1,648 applicants, 8% accepted, 76 enrolled. In 2010, 216 first professional degrees awarded. *Degree requirements:* For master's, thesis (for some programs); for Pharm D, comprehensive exam (for some programs), practice experience. *Entrance requirements:* For Pharm D, PCAT, minimum GPA of 3.0; for master's, GRE, minimum GPA of 3.0. Additional exam requirements/recommendations for international students: Required—TOEFL (minimum score 600 paper-based; 250 computer-based; 100 iBT). *Application deadline:* For fall admission, 3/1 for domestic and international students. Applications are processed on a rolling basis. Application fee: $75. Electronic applications accepted. *Expenses:* Tuition: Full-time $28,830; part-time $815 per credit hour. Required fees: $670. *Financial support:* Federal Work-Study and scholarships/grants available. Support available to part-time students. Financial award application deadline: 3/1; financial award applicants required to submit FAFSA. *Faculty research:* Therapeutic use of drugs, pharmacokinetics, drug delivery and design. *Unit head:* Dr. Mehdi Boroujerdi, Provost, 518-694-7212, Fax: 518-694-7063. *Application contact:* Donna Myers, Pharmacy and Graduate Admissions Counselor, 518-694-7149, Fax: 518-694-7063.

Albany Medical College, Center for Cell Biology and Cancer Research, Albany, NY 12208-3479. Offers MS, PhD. Part-time programs available. *Faculty:* 14 full-time (4 women). *Students:* 22 full-time (19 women); includes 7 minority (1 Black or African American, non-Hispanic/Latino; 5 Asian, non-Hispanic/Latino; 1 Hispanic/Latino). Average age 26. 25 applicants, 44% accepted, 9 enrolled. In 2010, 1 master's, 5 doctorates awarded. Terminal master's awarded for partial completion of doctoral program. *Degree requirements:* For master's, thesis; for doctorate, comprehensive exam, thesis/dissertation. *Entrance requirements:* For master's and doctorate, GRE General Test, all transcripts, letters of recommendation. Additional exam requirements/recommendations for international students: Required—TOEFL. *Application deadline:* For fall admission, 3/15 priority date for domestic and international students. Applications are processed on a rolling basis. *Financial support:* In 2010–11, 10 research assistantships (averaging $24,000 per year) were awarded; Federal Work-Study, scholarships/grants, and tuition waivers (full) also available. Financial award applicants required to submit FAFSA. *Faculty research:* Cancer cell biology, tissue remodeling, signal transduction, gene regulation, cell adhesion, angiogenesis. *Unit head:* Dr. C. Michael DiPersio, Graduate Director, 518-262-5916, Fax: 518-262-5669, E-mail: dipersm@mail.amc.edu. *Application contact:* Dr. C. Michael DiPersio, Graduate Director, 518-262-5916, Fax: 518-262-5669, E-mail: dipersm@mail.amc.edu.

Albert Einstein College of Medicine, Graduate Division of Biomedical Sciences, Department of Anatomy and Structural Biology, Bronx, NY 10461. Offers anatomy (PhD); cell and developmental biology (PhD); MD/PhD. *Degree requirements:* For doctorate, thesis/dissertation. *Entrance requirements:* For doctorate, GRE General Test. Additional exam requirements/recommendations for international students: Required—TOEFL. Electronic applications accepted. *Faculty research:* Cell motility, cell membranes and membrane-cytoskeletal interactions as applied to processing of pancreatic hormones, mechanisms of secretion.

Albert Einstein College of Medicine, Graduate Division of Biomedical Sciences, Division of Biological Sciences, Department of Cell Biology, Bronx, NY 10461. Offers PhD, MD/PhD. *Degree requirements:* For doctorate, thesis/dissertation. *Entrance requirements:* For doctorate, GRE General Test. Additional exam requirements/recommendations for international students: Required—TOEFL. *Faculty research:* Molecular and genetic basis of gene expression in animal cells; expression of differentiated traits of albumin, hemoglobin, myosin, and immunoglobin.

Appalachian State University, Cratis D. Williams Graduate School, Department of Biology, Boone, NC 28608. Offers cell and molecular (MS); general (MS). Part-time programs available. *Faculty:* 28 full-time (12 women), 2 part-time/adjunct (0 women). *Students:* 36 full-time (19 women), 8 part-time (3 women); includes 2 Asian, non-Hispanic/Latino; 1 Hispanic/Latino. 45 applicants, 51% accepted, 18 enrolled. In 2010, 14 master's awarded. *Degree requirements:* For master's, comprehensive exam, thesis. *Entrance requirements:* For master's, GRE General Test, 3 letters of recommendation. Additional exam requirements/recommendations for international students: Required—TOEFL (minimum score 570 paper-based; 230 computer-based; 79 iBT), IELTS (minimum score 6.5). *Application deadline:* For fall admission, 7/1 for domestic students, 2/1 for international students; for spring admission, 11/1 for domestic students, 7/1 for international students. Applications are processed on a rolling basis. Application fee: $55. Electronic applications accepted. *Expenses:* Tuition, state resident: full-time $3428; part-time $428 per unit. Tuition, nonresident: full-time $14,518; part-time $1814 per unit. Required fees: $2320; $344 per unit. Tuition and fees vary according to campus/location. *Financial support:* In 2010–11, 25 teaching assistantships (averaging $9,500 per year) were awarded; fellowships, research assistantships, career-related internships or fieldwork, Federal Work-Study, scholarships/grants, and unspecified assistantships also available. Financial award application deadline: 4/1; financial award applicants required to submit FAFSA. *Faculty research:* Aquatic and terrestrial ecology, animal and plant physiology, behavior and systematics, immunology and cell biology, molecular biology and microbiology. Total annual research expenditures: $1.3 million. *Unit head:* Dr. Steven Seagle, Chairman, 828-262-3025, E-mail: seaglesw@appstate.edu. *Application contact:* Dr. Gary Walker, Graduate Coordinator, 828-262-3025, E-mail: walkergl@appstate.edu.

Arizona State University, College of Liberal Arts and Sciences, School of Life Sciences, Tempe, AZ 85287-4601. Offers animal behavior (PhD); applied ethics (biomedical and health ethics) (MA); biological design (PhD); biology (MS, PhD); biology (biology and society) (MS, PhD); environmental life sciences (PhD); evolutionary biology (PhD); human and social dimensions of science and technology (PhD); microbiology (PhD); molecular and cellular biology (PhD); neuroscience (PhD); philosophy (history and philosophy of science) (MA); sustainability (PhD). *Faculty:* 102 full-time (26 women), 4 part-time/adjunct (1 woman). *Students:* 188 full-time (95 women), 45 part-time (29 women); includes 31 minority (3 Black or African American, non-Hispanic/Latino; 2 American Indian or Alaska Native, non-Hispanic/Latino; 12 Asian, non-Hispanic/Latino; 12 Hispanic/Latino; 2 Two or more races, non-Hispanic/Latino), 39 international. Average age 30. 203 applicants, 41% accepted, 60 enrolled. In 2010, 17 master's, 21 doctorates awarded. Terminal master's awarded for partial completion of doctoral program. *Degree requirements:* For master's, thesis (for some programs), interactive Program of Study (iPOS) submitted before completing 50 percent of required credit hours; for doctorate, variable foreign language requirement, comprehensive exam, thesis/dissertation, interactive Program of Study (iPOS) submitted before completing 50 percent of required credit hours. *Entrance requirements:* For master's and doctorate, GRE, minimum GPA of 3.0 or equivalent in last 2 years of work leading to bachelor's degree. Additional exam requirements/recommendations for international students: Required—TOEFL (minimum score 600 paper-based; 250 computer-based; 100 iBT). *Application deadline:* For fall admission, 12/15 for domestic and international students. Application fee: $70 ($90 for international students). Electronic applications accepted. *Expenses:* Tuition, state resident: full-time $8510; part-time $608 per credit. Tuition, nonresident: full-time $16,542; part-time $919 per credit. Required fees: $339; $110 per credit. Part-time tuition and fees vary according to course load. *Financial support:* In 2010–11, 80 research assistantships with full and partial tuition reimbursements (averaging $17,888 per year), 101 teaching assistantships with full and partial tuition reimbursements (averaging $17,327 per year) were awarded; fellowships with full tuition reimbursements, career-related internships or fieldwork, Federal Work-Study, institutionally sponsored loans, scholarships/grants, and tuition waivers (full and partial) also available. Financial award application deadline: 3/1; financial award applicants required to submit FAFSA. Total annual research expenditures: $29.3 million. *Unit head:* Dr. Robert E. Page, Director, 480-965-0803, E-mail: robert.page@asu.edu. *Application contact:* Graduate Admissions, 480-965-6113.

Auburn University, Graduate School, Interdepartmental Programs, Auburn University, AL 36849. Offers cell and molecular biology (PhD); integrated textile and apparel sciences (PhD); sociology and rural sociology (MA, MS), including rural sociology (MS), sociology. Part-time programs available. *Students:* 25 full-time (12 women), 19 part-time (13 women); includes 1 Black or African American, non-Hispanic/Latino; 1 American Indian or Alaska Native, non-Hispanic/Latino; 2 Asian, non-Hispanic/Latino, 26 international. Average age 28. 88 applicants, 35% accepted, 12 enrolled. In 2010, 4 master's, 3 doctorates awarded. *Entrance requirements:* For master's, GRE General Test. *Application deadline:* For fall admission, 7/7 for domestic students; for spring admission, 11/24 for domestic students. Applications are processed on a rolling basis. Application fee: $50 ($60 for international students). Electronic applications accepted. *Expenses:* Tuition, state resident: full-time $7002. Tuition, nonresident: full-time $21,898. International tuition: $22,116 full-time. Required fees: $892. Tuition and fees vary according to course load and program. *Financial support:* Fellowships, research assistantships, teaching assistantships, Federal Work-Study available. Support available to part-time students. Financial award application deadline: 3/15; financial award applicants required to submit FAFSA. *Unit head:* Interim Dean of the Graduate School. *Application contact:* Dr. George Flowers, Dean of the Graduate School, 334-844-2125.

Baylor College of Medicine, Graduate School of Biomedical Sciences, Department of Molecular and Cellular Biology, Houston, TX 77030-3498. Offers PhD, MD/PhD. *Faculty:* 75 full-time (21 women). *Students:* 63 full-time (36 women); includes 1 Black or African American, non-Hispanic/Latino; 6 Asian, non-Hispanic/Latino; 6 Hispanic/Latino, 19 international. Average age 27. 127 applicants, 17% accepted, 8 enrolled. In 2010, 12 doctorates awarded. *Degree requirements:* For doctorate, thesis/dissertation, public defense, qualifying exam. *Entrance requirements:* For doctorate, GRE General Test, GRE Subject Test (strongly recommended), minimum GPA of 3.0. Additional exam requirements/recommendations for international students: Required—TOEFL. *Application deadline:* For fall admission, 1/1 priority date for domestic students. Application fee: $0. Electronic applications accepted. *Expenses:* Tuition: Full-time $11,000. Required fees: $4900. *Financial support:* In 2010–11, 14 fellowships with full tuition reimbursements (averaging $26,000 per year), 49 research assistantships with full tuition reimbursements (averaging $26,000 per year) were awarded; career-related internships or fieldwork, Federal Work-Study, institutionally sponsored loans, health care benefits, and tuition waivers (full) also available. Financial award applicants required to submit FAFSA. *Faculty research:* Hormone action, development, cancer, gene therapy, neurobiology. *Unit head:* Dr. JoAnne Richards, Director, 713-798-4598. *Application contact:* Caroline Kosnik, Graduate Program Administrator, 713-798-4598, Fax: 713-790-0545, E-mail: ckosnik@bcm.edu.

Baylor College of Medicine, Graduate School of Biomedical Sciences, Interdepartmental Program in Cell and Molecular Biology, Houston, TX 77030-3498. Offers biochemistry (PhD); cell and molecular biology (PhD); genetics (PhD); human genetics (PhD); immunology (PhD); microbiology (PhD); virology (PhD); MD/PhD. *Faculty:* 100 full-time (31 women). *Students:* 67 full-time (41 women); includes 4 Black or African American, non-Hispanic/Latino; 2 American Indian or Alaska Native, non-Hispanic/Latino; 9 Asian, non-Hispanic/Latino; 9 Hispanic/Latino, 9 international. Average age 27. 120 applicants, 27% accepted, 15 enrolled. In 2010, 7 doctorates awarded. *Degree requirements:* For doctorate, thesis/dissertation, public defense. *Entrance requirements:* For doctorate, GRE General Test, GRE Subject Test (strongly recommended), minimum GPA of 3.0. Additional exam requirements/recommendations for international students: Required—TOEFL. *Application deadline:* For fall admission, 1/1 priority date for domestic students. Applications are processed on a rolling basis. Application fee: $0. Electronic applications accepted. *Expenses:* Tuition: Full-time $11,000. Required fees: $4900. *Financial support:* In 2010–11, 67 students received support, including 24 fellowships with full tuition reimbursements available (averaging $26,000 per year), 43 research assistantships with full tuition reimbursements available (averaging $26,000 per year); teaching assistantships, Federal Work-Study, institutionally sponsored loans, health care benefits, and tuition waivers (full) also available. Financial award applicants required to submit FAFSA. *Faculty research:* Molecular and cellular biology; cancer, aging and stem cells; genomics and proteomics; microbiome, molecular microbiology; infectious disease, immunology and translational research. *Unit head:* Dr. Susan Marriott, Director, 713-798-6557. *Application contact:* Lourdes Fernandez, Graduate Program Administrator, 713-798-6557, Fax: 713-798-6325, E-mail: cmbprog@bcm.edu.

See Close-Up on page 223.

Baylor College of Medicine, Graduate School of Biomedical Sciences, Program in Developmental Biology, Houston, TX 77030-3498. Offers PhD, MD/PhD. *Faculty:* 63 full-time (19 women). *Students:* 55 full-time (26 women); includes 5 Asian, non-Hispanic/Latino; 3 Hispanic/Latino, 35 international. Average age 28. 73 applicants, 18% accepted, 10 enrolled. In 2010, 5 doctorates awarded. *Degree requirements:* For doctorate, thesis/dissertation, public defense. *Entrance requirements:* For doctorate, GRE General Test, GRE Subject Test (strongly recommended), minimum GPA of 3.0. Additional exam requirements/recommendations for international students: Required—TOEFL. *Application deadline:* For fall admission, 1/1 priority date for domestic students. Application fee: $0. Electronic applications accepted. *Expenses:* Tuition: Full-time $11,000. Required fees: $4900. *Financial support:* In 2010–11, 55 students received support, including 15 fellowships with full tuition reimbursements available (averaging $26,000 per year), 40 research assistantships with full tuition reimbursements available (averaging $26,000 per year); career-related internships or fieldwork, Federal Work-Study, institutionally sponsored loans, health care benefits, tuition waivers (full), and stipends also available. *Faculty research:* Stem cells, cancer, neurobiology, organogenesis, genetics of model organisms. *Unit head:* Dr. Hugo Bellen, Director, 713-798-6410. *Application contact:* Catherine Tasnier, Graduate Program Administrator, 713-798-6410, Fax: 713-798-5386, E-mail: cat@bcm.edu.

See Display on page 282 and Close-Up on page 307.

Baylor College of Medicine, Program in Cell and Molecular Biology of Aging, Houston, TX 77030-3498. Offers PhD, MD/PhD. *Expenses:* Tuition: Full-time $11,000. Required fees: $4900. *Application contact:* Dr. Lloyd H. Michael, Senior Associate Dean of the Medical School, 713-798-4842, Fax: 713-798-5563, E-mail: lmichael@bcm.edu.

Boston University, Graduate School of Arts and Sciences, Molecular Biology, Cell Biology, and Biochemistry Program (MCBB), Boston, MA 02215. Offers MA, PhD. *Students:* 36 full-time (17 women), 2 part-time (both women); includes 9 minority (3 Black or African American, non-Hispanic/Latino; 3 Asian, non-Hispanic/Latino; 3 Hispanic/Latino), 6 international. Average age 28. 77 applicants, 18% accepted, 5 enrolled. In 2010, 6 master's, 20 doctorates awarded. Terminal master's awarded for partial completion of doctoral program. *Degree requirements:* For master's, one foreign language, thesis (for some programs); for doctorate, one foreign language, comprehensive exam, thesis/dissertation. *Entrance requirements:* For master's and doctorate, GRE General Test, GRE Subject Test. Additional exam requirements/recommendations for international students: Required—TOEFL (minimum score 600 paper-based; 250 computer-based). *Application deadline:* For fall admission, 12/7 for domestic and international students. Application fee: $70. Electronic applications accepted. *Expenses:* Tuition: Full-time $39,314; part-time $1228 per credit. Required fees: $40 per semester. *Financial support:* In 2010–11, 9 students received support, including 1 fellowship with full tuition reimbursement available (averaging $19,300 per year), 7 research assistantships with full tuition reimbursements available (averaging $18,800 per year), 1 teaching assistantship with full tuition reimbursement available (averaging $18,800 per year); Federal Work-Study, scholarships/grants, and traineeships also available. Financial award application deadline: 12/7; financial award applicants required to submit FAFSA. *Unit head:* Dr. Ulla Hansen, Director, 617-353-2432, Fax: 617-353-6340, E-mail: uhansen@bu.edu. *Application contact:* Meredith Canode, Academic Administrator, 617-353-2432, Fax: 617-353-6340, E-mail: mcanode@bu.edu.

Boston University, School of Medicine, Division of Graduate Medical Sciences, Department of Biochemistry, Boston, MA 02118. Offers MA, PhD, MD/PhD. Part-time programs available. *Faculty:* 41 full-time (17 women), 11 part-time/adjunct (5 women). *Students:* 31 full-time (18 women), 2 part-time (1 woman); includes 2 Asian, non-Hispanic/Latino; 1 Hispanic/Latino, 18 international. 88 applicants, 16% accepted, 7 enrolled. In 2010, 3 master's, 6 doctorates awarded. Terminal master's awarded for partial completion of doctoral program. *Degree requirements:* For master's, thesis or alternative, qualifying exam; for doctorate, thesis/dissertation, qualifying exam. *Entrance requirements:* For master's and doctorate, GRE General Test, GRE Subject Test. Additional exam requirements/recommendations for international students: Required—TOEFL. *Application deadline:* For fall admission, 1/15 priority date for domestic students; for spring admission, 10/15 priority date for domestic students. Application fee: $75. Electronic applications accepted. *Expenses:* Tuition: Full-time $39,314; part-time $1228 per credit. Required fees: $40 per semester. *Financial support:* In 2010–11, 1 fellowship (averaging $30,500 per year), 27 research assistantships (averaging $30,500 per year) were awarded; Federal Work-Study, scholarships/grants, and traineeships also available. Financial award applicants required to submit FAFSA. *Faculty research:* Extracellular matrix, gene expression, receptors, growth control. *Unit head:* Dr. David A. Harris, Chair, 617-638-5090. *Application contact:* Dr. Barbara Schreiber, Director of the Graduate Program, 617-638-5094, E-mail: schreibe@bu.edu.

Boston University, School of Medicine, Division of Graduate Medical Sciences, Program in Cell and Molecular Biology, Boston, MA 02118. Offers PhD, MD/PhD. *Faculty:* 10 full-time (5 women). *Students:* 35 full-time (18 women); includes 1 Asian, non-Hispanic/Latino; 1 Two or more races, non-Hispanic/Latino, 11 international. 102 applicants, 14% accepted, 4 enrolled. In 2010, 9 doctorates awarded. *Degree requirements:* For doctorate, thesis/dissertation. *Entrance requirements:* For doctorate, GRE General Test, GRE Subject Test. Additional exam requirements/recommendations for international students: Required—TOEFL. *Application deadline:* For fall admission, 1/15 priority date for domestic students; for spring admission, 10/15 priority date for domestic students. Application fee: $75. Electronic applications accepted. *Expenses:* Tuition: Full-time $39,314; part-time $1228 per credit. Required fees: $40 per semester. *Financial support:* In 2010–11, 3 fellowships (averaging $30,500 per year), 29 research assistantships (averaging $30,500 per year) were awarded; Federal Work-Study, scholarships/grants, and traineeships also available. Financial award applicants required to submit FAFSA. *Unit head:* Dr. Vickery Trinkaus Randall, Director, 617-638-6099, Fax: 617-638-5337, E-mail: vickery@bu.edu. *Application contact:* Dr. Vickery Trinkaus-Randall, Program Director, 617-638-6099, Fax: 617-638-5337, E-mail: vickery@bu.edu.

Brandeis University, Graduate School of Arts and Sciences, Program in Molecular and Cell Biology, Waltham, MA 02454-9110. Offers genetics (PhD); microbiology (PhD); molecular and cell biology (MS, PhD); molecular biology (PhD); neurobiology (PhD). *Faculty:* 30 full-time (13 women), 1 (woman) part-time/adjunct. *Students:* 55 full-time (31 women); includes 1 Black or African American, non-Hispanic/Latino; 1 American Indian or Alaska Native, non-Hispanic/Latino; 1 Asian, non-Hispanic/Latino; 2 Hispanic/Latino, 12 international. 138 applicants, 32% accepted, 17 enrolled. In 2010, 3 master's, 3 doctorates awarded. Terminal master's awarded for partial completion of doctoral program. *Degree requirements:* For master's, thesis optional, research project; for doctorate, comprehensive exam, thesis/dissertation, teaching assistant experience. *Entrance requirements:* For master's and doctorate, GRE General Test, official transcript(s), resume, 3 letters of recommendation, statement of purpose. Additional exam requirements/recommendations for international students: Required—TOEFL (minimum score 600 paper-based; 250 computer-based; 100 iBT); Recommended—IELTS (minimum score 7). *Application deadline:* For fall admission, 1/15 priority date for domestic students. Applications are processed on a rolling basis. Application fee: $75. Electronic applications accepted. *Financial support:* In 2010–11, 41 students received support, including 13 fellowships with full tuition reimbursements available (averaging $27,500 per year), 27 research assistantships with full tuition reimbursements available (averaging $27,500 per year), 1 teaching assistantship with partial tuition reimbursement available (averaging $3,200 per year); scholarships/grants, traineeships, health care benefits, and tuition waivers (full and partial) also available. Financial award application deadline: 4/15; financial award applicants required to submit FAFSA. *Faculty research:* Molecular biology, cell biology, biology, structural biology, immunology, developmental biology, neurobiology, DNA, RNA. *Unit head:* Dr. Piali Sengupta, Chair, 781-736-2686, Fax: 781-736-3107, E-mail: piali@brandeis.edu. *Application contact:* Marcia Cabral, Department Administrator, 781-736-3100, Fax: 781-736-3107, E-mail: cabral@brandeis.edu.

Brown University, Graduate School, Division of Biology and Medicine, Program in Molecular Biology, Cell Biology, and Biochemistry, Providence, RI 02912. Offers biochemistry (M Med Sc, Sc M, PhD), including biochemistry (Sc M, PhD), biology (Sc M, PhD), medical science (M Med Sc, PhD); biology (MA); cell biology (M Med Sc, Sc M, PhD), including biochemistry (Sc M, PhD), biology (Sc M, PhD), medical science (M Med Sc, PhD); developmental biology (M Med Sc, Sc M, PhD), including biochemistry (Sc M, PhD), biology (Sc M, PhD), medical science (M Med Sc, PhD); immunology (M Med Sc, Sc M, PhD), including biochemistry (Sc M, PhD), biology (Sc M, PhD), medical science (M Med Sc, PhD); molecular microbiology (M Med Sc, Sc M, PhD), including biochemistry (Sc M, PhD), biology (Sc M, PhD), medical science (M Med Sc, PhD); MD/PhD. Part-time programs available. Terminal master's awarded for partial completion of doctoral program. *Degree requirements:* For master's, thesis (for some programs); for doctorate, one foreign language, thesis/dissertation, preliminary exam. *Entrance requirements:* For master's and doctorate, GRE General Test, GRE Subject Test. Additional exam requirements/recommendations for international students: Required—TOEFL. Electronic applications accepted. *Faculty research:* Molecular genetics, gene regulation.

California Institute of Technology, Division of Biology, Program in Cell Biology and Biophysics, Pasadena, CA 91125-0001. Offers PhD. *Degree requirements:* For doctorate, thesis/dissertation, qualifying exam. *Entrance requirements:* For doctorate, GRE General Test.

Carnegie Mellon University, Mellon College of Science, Department of Biological Sciences, Pittsburgh, PA 15213-3891. Offers biochemistry (PhD); biophysics (PhD); cell biology (PhD); computational biology (MS, PhD); developmental biology (PhD); genetics (PhD); molecular biology (PhD); neuroscience (PhD). *Degree requirements:* For doctorate, comprehensive exam, thesis/dissertation. *Entrance requirements:* For doctorate, GRE General Test, GRE Subject Test, interview. Electronic applications accepted. *Faculty research:* Genetic structure, function, and regulation; protein structure and function; biological membranes; biological spectroscopy.

Case Western Reserve University, School of Medicine and School of Graduate Studies, Graduate Programs in Medicine, Department of Anatomy, Cleveland, OH 44106. Offers applied anatomy (MS); biological anthropology (MS); cellular biology (MS); MD/MS. Part-time programs available. *Degree requirements:* For master's, comprehensive exam, thesis (for some programs). *Entrance requirements:* For master's, GRE General Test. Additional exam requirements/recommendations for international students: Required—TOEFL. *Faculty research:* Hypoxia, cell injury, biochemical aberration occurrences in ischemic tissue, human functional morphology, evolutionary morphology.

Case Western Reserve University, School of Medicine and School of Graduate Studies, Graduate Programs in Medicine, Department of Molecular Biology and Microbiology, Cleveland, OH 44106-4960. Offers cellular biology (PhD); microbiology (PhD); molecular biology (PhD); molecular virology (PhD); MD/PhD. Students are admitted to an integrated Biomedical Sciences Training Program involving 11 basic science programs at Case Western Reserve University. *Degree requirements:* For doctorate, thesis/dissertation. *Entrance requirements:* For doctorate, GRE General Test, GRE Subject Test. Additional exam requirements/recommendations for international students: Required—TOEFL. Electronic applications accepted.

Cell Biology

Case Western Reserve University *(continued)*
Faculty research: Gene expression in eukaryotic and prokaryotic systems; microbial physiology; intracellular transport and signaling; mechanisms of oncogenesis; molecular mechanisms of RNA processing, editing, and catalysis.

Case Western Reserve University, School of Medicine and School of Graduate Studies, Graduate Programs in Medicine, Program in Cell Biology, Cleveland, OH 44106. Offers PhD. *Degree requirements:* For doctorate, thesis/dissertation. *Entrance requirements:* For doctorate, GRE General Test, GRE Subject Test, previous course work in biochemistry. Additional exam requirements/recommendations for international students: Required—TOEFL. Electronic applications accepted. *Faculty research:* Macromolecular transport, membrane traffic, signal transduction, nuclear organization, lipid metabolism.

Case Western Reserve University, School of Medicine and School of Graduate Studies, Graduate Programs in Medicine, Programs in Molecular and Cellular Basis of Disease/Pathology, Cleveland, OH 44106. Offers cancer biology (PhD); cell biology (MS, PhD); immunology (MS, PhD); pathology (MS, PhD); MD/PhD. Terminal master's awarded for partial completion of doctoral program. *Degree requirements:* For master's, thesis; for doctorate, thesis/dissertation. *Entrance requirements:* For master's and doctorate, GRE General Test, GRE Subject Test. Additional exam requirements/recommendations for international students: Required—TOEFL (minimum score 550 paper-based; 213 computer-based). Electronic applications accepted. *Faculty research:* Neurobiology, molecular biology, cancer biology, biomaterials, biocompatibility.

The Catholic University of America, School of Arts and Sciences, Department of Biology, Washington, DC 20064. Offers cell and microbial biology (MS, PhD), including cell biology, microbiology; clinical laboratory science (MS, PhD); MSLS/MS. Part-time programs available. *Faculty:* 8 full-time (4 women), 2 part-time/adjunct (both women). *Students:* 10 full-time (7 women), 27 part-time (18 women); includes 2 Black or African American, non-Hispanic/Latino; 4 Asian, non-Hispanic/Latino; 3 Hispanic/Latino, 15 international. Average age 29. 39 applicants, 56% accepted, 13 enrolled. In 2010, 4 doctorates awarded. *Degree requirements:* For master's, comprehensive exam, thesis or alternative; for doctorate, comprehensive exam, thesis/dissertation. *Entrance requirements:* For master's and doctorate, GRE General Test, GRE Subject Test, statement of purpose, official copies of academic transcripts, three letters of recommendation. Additional exam requirements/recommendations for international students: Required—TOEFL (minimum score 580 paper-based; 237 computer-based). *Application deadline:* For fall admission, 8/1 priority date for domestic students, 7/15 for international students; for spring admission, 12/1 priority date for domestic students, 10/15 for international students. Applications are processed on a rolling basis. Application fee: $55. Electronic applications accepted. *Expenses:* Tuition: Full-time $33,580; part-time $1315 per credit hour. Required fees: $80; $40 per semester hour. One-time fee: $425. *Financial support:* Fellowships, research assistantships, teaching assistantships, Federal Work-Study, scholarships/grants, tuition waivers (full and partial), and unspecified assistantships available. Financial award application deadline: 2/1; financial award applicants required to submit FAFSA. *Faculty research:* Cell and microbiology, microbial pathogenesis, molecular biology of cell proliferation, cellular effects of electromagnetic radiation, biotechnology. Total annual research expenditures: $853,913. *Unit head:* Dr. Venigalla Rao, Chair, 202-319-5271, Fax: 202-319-5721, E-mail: rao@cua.edu. *Application contact:* Andrew Woodall, Director of Graduate Admissions, 202-319-5057, Fax: 202-319-6533, E-mail: cua-admissions@cua.edu.

Colorado State University, Graduate School, Program in Cell and Molecular Biology, Fort Collins, CO 80523-1618. Offers MS, PhD. *Students:* 25 full-time (16 women), 31 part-time (14 women); includes 12 minority (1 Black or African American, non-Hispanic/Latino; 1 American Indian or Alaska Native, non-Hispanic/Latino; 3 Asian, non-Hispanic/Latino; 6 Hispanic/Latino; 1 Two or more races, non-Hispanic/Latino), 11 international. Average age 30. 57 applicants, 19% accepted, 9 enrolled. In 2010, 2 master's, 7 doctorates awarded. *Degree requirements:* For master's, comprehensive exam, thesis; for doctorate, comprehensive exam, thesis/dissertation. *Entrance requirements:* For master's and doctorate, GRE General Test, GRE Subject Test in biology (strongly recommended), minimum GPA of 3.0; BA/BS in biology, biochemistry, physics; calculus sequence, letters of recommendation. Additional exam requirements/recommendations for international students: Required—TOEFL (minimum score 625 paper-based; 263 computer-based; 107 iBT). *Application deadline:* For fall admission, 1/1 priority date for domestic and international students. Application fee: $50. Electronic applications accepted. *Expenses:* Tuition, state resident: full-time $7434; part-time $413 per credit. Tuition, nonresident: full-time $19,022; part-time $1057 per credit. Required fees: $1729; $88 per credit. *Financial support:* In 2010–11, 5 students received support, including 2 research assistantships with full tuition reimbursements available (averaging $12,152 per year), 3 teaching assistantships with full tuition reimbursements available (averaging $16,962 per year); fellowships with partial tuition reimbursements available, traineeships and unspecified assistantships also available. Financial award application deadline: 1/1; financial award applicants required to submit FAFSA. *Faculty research:* Regulation of gene expression, cancer biology, plant molecular genetics, reproductive physiology, infectious diseases. Total annual research expenditures: $2,353. *Unit head:* Dr. Paul J. Laybourn, Director, 970-491-5100, Fax: 970-491-0623, E-mail: paul.laybourn@colostate.edu. *Application contact:* Lori Williams, Administrative Assistant, 970-491-0241, Fax: 970-491-0623, E-mail: cmb@colostate.edu.

Columbia University, College of Physicians and Surgeons, Department of Anatomy and Cell Biology, New York, NY 10032. Offers anatomy (M Phil, MA, PhD); anatomy and cell biology (PhD); MD/PhD. Only candidates for the PhD are admitted. Terminal master's awarded for partial completion of doctoral program. *Degree requirements:* For doctorate, thesis/dissertation, oral exam. *Entrance requirements:* For master's and doctorate, GRE General Test. Additional exam requirements/recommendations for international students: Required—TOEFL. *Faculty research:* Protein sorting, membrane biophysics, muscle energetics, neuroendocrinology, developmental biology, cytoskeleton, transcription factors.

Columbia University, College of Physicians and Surgeons, Integrated Program in Cellular, Molecular, Structural and Genetic Studies, New York, NY 10032. Offers PhD. Terminal master's awarded for partial completion of doctoral program. *Degree requirements:* For doctorate, thesis/dissertation. *Entrance requirements:* For doctorate, GRE General Test, GRE Subject Test. Additional exam requirements/recommendations for international students: Required—TOEFL. *Expenses:* Contact institution. *Faculty research:* Transcription, macromolecular sorting, gene expression during development, cellular interaction.

Cornell University, Graduate School, Graduate Fields of Agriculture and Life Sciences, Field of Biochemistry, Molecular and Cell Biology, Ithaca, NY 14853-0001. Offers biochemistry (PhD); biophysics (PhD); cell biology (PhD); molecular and cell biology (PhD); molecular biology (PhD). *Faculty:* 59 full-time (15 women). *Students:* 90 full-time (47 women); includes 1 Black or African American, non-Hispanic/Latino; 7 Asian, non-Hispanic/Latino; 4 Hispanic/Latino, 30 international. Average age 26. 269 applicants, 9% accepted, 20 enrolled. In 2010, 12 doctorates awarded. *Degree requirements:* For doctorate, comprehensive exam, thesis/dissertation, 2 semesters of teaching experience. *Entrance requirements:* For doctorate, GRE General Test, GRE Subject Test (biology, chemistry, physics, biochemistry, cell and molecular biology), 3 letters of recommendation. Additional exam requirements/recommendations for international students: Required—TOEFL (minimum score 600 paper-based; 250 computer-based; 77 iBT). *Application deadline:* For fall admission, 1/5 for domestic students. Application fee: $70. Electronic applications accepted. *Expenses:* Tuition: Full-time $29,500. Required fees: $76. Tuition and fees vary according to degree level and program. *Financial support:* In 2010–11, 88 students received support, including 25 fellowships with full tuition reimbursements available, 48 research assistantships with full tuition reimbursements available, 15 teaching assistantships with full tuition reimbursements available; institutionally sponsored loans, scholarships/grants, health care benefits, tuition waivers (full and partial), and unspecified assistantships also available. Financial award applicants required to submit FAFSA. *Faculty research:* Biophysics, structural biology. *Unit head:* Director of Graduate Studies, 607-255-

2100, Fax: 607-255-2100. *Application contact:* Graduate Field Assistant, 607-255-2100, Fax: 607-255-2100, E-mail: bmcb@cornell.edu.

Cornell University, Graduate School, Graduate Fields of Agriculture and Life Sciences, Field of Computational Biology, Ithaca, NY 14853-0001. Offers computational behavioral biology (PhD); computational biology (PhD); computational cell biology (PhD); computational ecology (PhD); computational macromolecular biology (PhD); computational organismal biology (PhD). *Faculty:* 32 full-time (5 women). *Students:* 21 full-time (6 women); includes 4 Asian, non-Hispanic/Latino, 9 international. Average age 25. 128 applicants, 7% accepted, 9 enrolled. In 2010, 3 doctorates awarded. *Degree requirements:* For doctorate, comprehensive exam, thesis/dissertation, 2 semesters of teaching experience. *Entrance requirements:* For doctorate, GRE General Test, GRE Subject Test (biology), 2 letters of recommendation. Additional exam requirements/recommendations for international students: Required—TOEFL (minimum score 550 paper-based; 213 computer-based; 77 iBT). *Application deadline:* For fall admission, 2/1 priority date for domestic students. Application fee: $70. Electronic applications accepted. *Expenses:* Tuition: Full-time $29,500. Required fees: $76. Tuition and fees vary according to degree level and program. *Financial support:* In 2010–11, 15 fellowships with full tuition reimbursements, 4 research assistantships with full tuition reimbursements, 2 teaching assistantships with full tuition reimbursements were awarded; institutionally sponsored loans, scholarships/grants, health care benefits, tuition waivers (full and partial), and unspecified assistantships also available. Financial award applicants required to submit FAFSA. *Faculty research:* Computational behavioral biology, computational biology, computational cell biology, computational ecology, computational genetics, computational macromolecular biology, computational organismal biology. *Unit head:* Dr. Andrew Clark, Director of Graduate Studies, 607-255-5488, E-mail: ac347@cornell.edu. *Application contact:* Graduate School Application Requests, 607-255-5816, E-mail: gradadmissions@cornell.edu.

Cornell University, Graduate School, Graduate Fields of Agriculture and Life Sciences, Field of Zoology and Wildlife Conservation, Ithaca, NY 14853-0001. Offers animal cytology (MS, PhD); comparative and functional anatomy (MS, PhD); developmental biology (MS, PhD); ecology (MS, PhD); histology (MS, PhD). *Faculty:* 20 full-time (5 women). *Students:* 5 full-time (all women); includes 1 Hispanic/Latino, 1 international. Average age 31. 17 applicants, 18% accepted, 1 enrolled. *Degree requirements:* For doctorate, comprehensive exam, thesis/dissertation, 2 semesters of teaching experience. *Entrance requirements:* For doctorate, GRE General Test, GRE Subject Test (biology), 2 letters of recommendation. Additional exam requirements/recommendations for international students: Required—TOEFL (minimum score 550 paper-based; 213 computer-based; 77 iBT). *Application deadline:* For fall admission, 2/1 priority date for domestic students. Application fee: $70. Electronic applications accepted. *Expenses:* Tuition: Full-time $29,500. Required fees: $76. Tuition and fees vary according to degree level and program. *Financial support:* In 2010–11, 1 fellowship with full tuition reimbursement, 4 research assistantships with full tuition reimbursements were awarded; teaching assistantships with full tuition reimbursements, institutionally sponsored loans, scholarships/grants, health care benefits, tuition waivers (full and partial), and unspecified assistantships also available. Financial award applicants required to submit FAFSA. *Faculty research:* Organismal biology, functional morphology, biomechanics, comparative vertebrate anatomy, comparative invertebrate anatomy, paleontology. *Unit head:* Director of Graduate Studies, 607-253-3276, Fax: 607-253-3756. *Application contact:* Graduate Field Assistant, 607-253-3276, Fax: 607-253-3756, E-mail: graduate_edcvm@cornell.edu.

Cornell University, Joan and Sanford I. Weill Medical College and Graduate School of Medical Sciences, Weill Cornell Graduate School of Medical Sciences, Biochemistry, Cell and Molecular Biology Allied Program, New York, NY 10065. Offers MS, PhD. *Faculty:* 106 full-time (30 women). *Students:* 143 full-time (91 women); includes 2 Black or African American, non-Hispanic/Latino; 8 Asian, non-Hispanic/Latino; 6 Hispanic/Latino, 73 international. Average age 22. 322 applicants, 17% accepted, 14 enrolled. In 2010, 19 doctorates awarded. Terminal master's awarded for partial completion of doctoral program. *Degree requirements:* For master's, comprehensive exam; for doctorate, thesis/dissertation, final exam. *Entrance requirements:* For doctorate, GRE General Test, background in genetics, molecular biology, chemistry, or biochemistry. Additional exam requirements/recommendations for international students: Required—TOEFL. *Application deadline:* For fall admission, 12/1 for domestic students. Application fee: $60. Electronic applications accepted. *Expenses:* Tuition: Full-time $45,545. Required fees: $2805. *Financial support:* In 2010–11, 16 fellowships (averaging $23,000 per year) were awarded; scholarships/grants, health care benefits, and stipends (given to all students) also available. *Faculty research:* Molecular structure determination, protein structure, gene structure, stem cell biology, control of gene expression, DNA replication, chromosome maintenance, RNA biosynthesis. *Unit head:* Dr. David Eliezer, Co-Director, 212-746-6557, Fax: 212-717-3047. *Application contact:* Linda Smith, Assistant Dean of Admissions, 212-746-6565, Fax: 212-746-8906, E-mail: lis2025@med.cornell.edu.

Dartmouth College, Graduate Program in Molecular and Cellular Biology, Hanover, NH 03755. Offers PhD, MD/PhD. *Entrance requirements:* For doctorate, GRE General Test, letters of recommendation. Additional exam requirements/recommendations for international students: Required—TOEFL (minimum score 450 paper-based; 90 iBT) or IELTS (minimum score 7). Electronic applications accepted.

Drexel University, College of Medicine, Biomedical Graduate Programs, Interdisciplinary Program in Molecular and Cell Biology and Genetics, Philadelphia, PA 19104-2875. Offers MS, PhD, MD/PhD. Terminal master's awarded for partial completion of doctoral program. *Degree requirements:* For master's, comprehensive exam, thesis; for doctorate, thesis/dissertation, qualifying exam. *Entrance requirements:* For master's, GRE General Test, minimum GPA of 2.75; for doctorate, GRE General Test, minimum GPA of 3.0. Additional exam requirements/recommendations for international students: Required—TOEFL. Electronic applications accepted. *Faculty research:* Molecular anatomy, biochemistry, medical biotechnology, molecular pathology, microbiology and immunology.

Duke University, Graduate School, Department of Biological Anthropology and Anatomy, Durham, NC 27710. Offers cellular and molecular biology (PhD); gross anatomy and physical anthropology (PhD), including comparative morphology of human and non-human primates, primate social behavior, vertebrate paleontology; neuroanatomy (PhD). *Faculty:* 9 full-time. *Students:* 13 full-time (9 women); includes 1 Black or African American, non-Hispanic/Latino; 2 Hispanic/Latino, 1 international. 54 applicants, 9% accepted, 2 enrolled. In 2010, 2 doctorates awarded. *Degree requirements:* For doctorate, one foreign language, thesis/dissertation. *Entrance requirements:* For doctorate, GRE General Test. Additional exam requirements/recommendations for international students: Required—TOEFL (minimum score 550 paper-based; 213 computer-based; 83 iBT), IELTS (minimum score 7). *Application deadline:* For fall admission, 12/8 priority date for domestic and international students. Application fee: $75. Electronic applications accepted. *Financial support:* Fellowships, teaching assistantships, Federal Work-Study available. Financial award application deadline: 12/31. *Unit head:* Daniel Schmitt, Director of Graduate Studies, 919-684-4124, Fax: 919-684-8542, E-mail: mlsquire@duke.edu. *Application contact:* Elizabeth Hutton, Director of Admissions, 919-684-3913, Fax: 919-684-2277, E-mail: grad-admissions@duke.edu.

Duke University, Graduate School, Department of Cell Biology, Durham, NC 27710. Offers PhD. *Faculty:* 21 full-time. *Students:* 37 full-time (24 women); includes 1 Black or African American, non-Hispanic/Latino; 3 Asian, non-Hispanic/Latino; 1 Hispanic/Latino, 7 international. In 2010, 8 doctorates awarded. *Degree requirements:* For doctorate, thesis/dissertation. *Entrance requirements:* For doctorate, GRE General Test, GRE Subject Test in biology, chemistry, cell and molecular biology (recommended). Additional exam requirements/recommendations for international students: Required—TOEFL or IELTS. Application fee: $75. *Financial support:* Fellowships, research assistantships, teaching assistantships, Federal Work-Study available. Financial award application deadline: 12/8. *Unit head:* Chris Nicchitta, Director of Graduate Studies, 919-684-8085, Fax: 919-684-8592, E-mail: teresa.jenkins@duke.edu. *Application* *contact:* Elizabeth Hutton, Director of Admissions, 919-684-3913, Fax: 919-684-2277, E-mail: grad-admissions@duke.edu.

Duke University, Graduate School, Program in Cellular and Molecular Biology, Durham, NC 27710. Offers Certificate. Students must be enrolled in a participating Ph D program (biology, cell biology, immunology, molecular genetics, neurobiology, pathology, pharmacology). *Faculty:* 144 full-time. *Students:* 22 full-time (10 women); includes 2 Hispanic/Latino, 6 international. 198 applicants, 24% accepted, 19 enrolled. *Entrance requirements:* Additional exam requirements/recommendations for international students: Required—TOEFL (minimum score 550 paper-based; 213 computer-based; 83 iBT), IELTS (minimum score 7). *Application deadline:* For fall admission, 12/8 priority date for domestic and international students. Application fee: $75. Electronic applications accepted. *Financial support:* Fellowships available. Financial award application deadline: 12/8. *Unit head:* Dr. Margarethe Kuehn, Director of Graduate Studies, 919-684-6559, Fax: 919-684-8346, E-mail: carol.richardson@duke.edu. *Application contact:* Elizabeth Hutton, Director of Admissions, 919-684-3913, Fax: 919-684-3913, E-mail: grad-admissions@duke.edu.

East Carolina University, Brody School of Medicine, Department of Anatomy and Cell Biology, Greenville, NC 27858-4353. Offers PhD. *Degree requirements:* For doctorate, comprehensive exam, thesis/dissertation. *Entrance requirements:* For doctorate, GRE General Test. Additional exam requirements/recommendations for international students: Required—TOEFL. *Expenses:* Tuition, state resident: full-time $3130; part-time $391.25 per credit hour. Tuition, nonresident: full-time $13,817; part-time $1727.13 per credit hour. Required fees: $1916; $239.50 per credit hour. Tuition and fees vary according to campus/location and program. *Faculty research:* Kinesin motors during slow matogensis, mitochondria and peroxisomes in obesity, ovarian innervation, tight junction function and regulation.

Eastern Michigan University, Graduate School, College of Arts and Sciences, Department of Biology, Ypsilanti, MI 48197. Offers cell and molecular biology (MS); community college biology teaching (MS); ecology and organismal biology (MS); general biology (MS); water resources (MS). Part-time and evening/weekend programs available. Postbaccalaureate distance learning degree programs offered (minimal on-campus study). *Faculty:* 20 full-time (4 women). *Students:* 18 full-time (13 women), 35 part-time (19 women); includes 4 minority (2 Black or African American, non-Hispanic/Latino; 2 Two or more races, non-Hispanic/Latino), 13 international. Average age 27. 55 applicants, 47% accepted, 17 enrolled. In 2010, 10 master's awarded. *Entrance requirements:* For master's, GRE General Test, GRE Subject Test. Additional exam requirements/recommendations for international students: Required—TOEFL. *Application deadline:* Applications are processed on a rolling basis. Application fee: $35. *Financial support:* Fellowships, research assistantships with full tuition reimbursements, teaching assistantships with full tuition reimbursements, career-related internships or fieldwork, Federal Work-Study, institutionally sponsored loans, scholarships/grants, tuition waivers (partial), and unspecified assistantships available. Support available to part-time students. Financial award applicants required to submit FAFSA. *Unit head:* Dr. Marianne Laporte, Department Head, 734-487-4242, Fax: 734-487-9235, E-mail: mlaporte@emich.edu. *Application contact:* Dr. Marianne Laporte, Department Head, 734-487-4242, Fax: 734-487-9235, E-mail: mlaporte@emich.edu.

Eastern New Mexico University, Graduate School, College of Liberal Arts and Sciences, Department of Biology, Portales, NM 88130. Offers applied ecology (MS); cell, molecular biology and biotechnology (MS); education (non-thesis) (MS); microbiology (MS); plant biology (MS); zoology (MS). Part-time programs available. *Faculty:* 8 full-time (0 women). *Students:* 11 full-time (8 women), 7 part-time (4 women); includes 7 minority (5 Hispanic/Latino; 2 Two or more races, non-Hispanic/Latino), 4 international. Average age 25. 21 applicants, 14% accepted, 3 enrolled. In 2010, 4 master's awarded. *Degree requirements:* For master's, comprehensive exam, thesis optional. *Entrance requirements:* For master's, GRE, minimum GPA of 3.0, 2 letters of recommendation, statement of research interest, bachelor's degree related to field of study or proof of common knowledge. Additional exam requirements/recommendations for international students: Required—TOEFL (minimum score 550 paper-based; 213 computer-based; 79 iBT), IELTS (minimum score 6). *Application deadline:* For fall admission, 7/20 priority date for domestic students, 6/20 priority date for international students; for spring admission, 12/15 priority date for domestic students, 11/15 priority date for international students. Applications are processed on a rolling basis. Application fee: $10. Electronic applications accepted. *Expenses:* Tuition, state resident: full-time $3210; part-time $130 per credit hour. Tuition, nonresident: full-time $8652; part-time $360.50 per credit hour. Required fees: $1212; $50.50 per credit hour. Tuition and fees vary according to course load. *Financial support:* In 2010–11, 11 teaching assistantships with partial tuition reimbursements (averaging $8,500 per year) were awarded; unspecified assistantships also available. Support available to part-time students. Financial award applicants required to submit FAFSA. *Unit head:* Dr. Zach Jones, Graduate Coordinator, 575-562-2723, Fax: 575-562-2192, E-mail: zach.jones@enmu.edu. *Application contact:* Sharon Potter, Department Secretary, Biology/Physical Sciences, 575-562-2174, Fax: 575-562-2192, E-mail: sharon.potter@enmu.edu.

Emory University, Laney Graduate School, Division of Biological and Biomedical Sciences, Program in Biochemistry, Cell and Developmental Biology, Atlanta, GA 30322. Offers PhD. *Faculty:* 54 full-time (10 women). *Students:* 60 full-time (41 women); includes 3 Black or African American, non-Hispanic/Latino; 3 Asian, non-Hispanic/Latino; 1 Hispanic/Latino, 15 international. Average age 27. 214 applicants, 12% accepted, 11 enrolled. In 2010, 10 doctorates awarded. *Degree requirements:* For doctorate, comprehensive exam, thesis/dissertation. *Entrance requirements:* For doctorate, GRE General Test, minimum GPA of 3.0 in science course work (recommended). Additional exam requirements/recommendations for international students: Required—TOEFL. *Application deadline:* For fall admission, 1/3 for domestic students, 1/1 for international students. Application fee: $75. Electronic applications accepted. *Expenses:* Tuition: Full-time $33,800. Required fees: $1300. *Financial support:* In 2010–11, 19 students received support, including 19 fellowships with full tuition reimbursements available (averaging $25,000 per year); institutionally sponsored loans, scholarships/grants, health care benefits, and tuition waivers (full) also available. *Faculty research:* Signal transduction, molecular biology, enzymes and cofactors, receptor and ion channel function, membrane biology. *Unit head:* Dr. Richard Kahn, Program Director, 404-727-3561, Fax: 404-727-3746, E-mail: rkahn@emory.edu. *Application contact:* Kathy Smith, Director of Recruitment and Admissions, 404-727-2547, Fax: 404-727-3322, E-mail: kathy.smith@emory.edu.

Emporia State University, Graduate School, College of Liberal Arts and Sciences, Department of Biological Sciences, Emporia, KS 66801-5087. Offers botany (MS); environmental biology (MS); general biology (MS); microbial and cellular biology (MS); zoology (MS). Part-time programs available. *Faculty:* 13 full-time (3 women). *Students:* 14 full-time (8 women), 19 part-time (9 women); includes 2 minority (1 Black or African American, non-Hispanic/Latino; 1 Hispanic/Latino), 6 international. 9 applicants, 100% accepted, 9 enrolled. In 2010, 4 master's awarded. *Degree requirements:* For master's, comprehensive exam or thesis. *Entrance requirements:* For master's, GRE, appropriate undergraduate degree, interview, letters of reference. Additional exam requirements/recommendations for international students: Required—TOEFL (minimum score 520 paper-based; 133 computer-based; 68 iBT). *Application deadline:* For fall admission, 8/15 priority date for domestic students. Applications are processed on a rolling basis. Application fee: $30 ($75 for international students). Electronic applications accepted. *Expenses:* Tuition, state resident: full-time $4382; part-time $183 per credit hour. Tuition, nonresident: full-time $13,572; part-time $566 per credit hour. Required fees: $1022; $62 per credit hour. Tuition and fees vary according to course level, course load and campus/location. *Financial support:* In 2010–11, 10 research assistantships with full tuition reimbursements (averaging $7,353 per year), 9 teaching assistantships with full tuition reimbursements (averaging $7,809 per year) were awarded; career-related internships or fieldwork, Federal Work-Study, institutionally sponsored loans, health care benefits, and unspecified assistantships also available. Financial award application deadline: 3/15; financial award applicants required to submit FAFSA. *Faculty research:* Fisheries, range, and wildlife management; aquatic, plant, grassland, vertebrate, and invertebrate ecology; mammalian and plant systematics, taxonomy, and evolution; immunology, virology, and molecular biology. *Unit head:* Dr. R. Brent Thomas, Chair, 620-341-5311, Fax: 620-341-5608, E-mail: rthomas2@emporia.edu. *Application contact:* Dr. Scott Crupper, Graduate Coordinator, 620-341-5621, Fax: 620-341-5607, E-mail: scrupper@emporia.edu.

Florida Institute of Technology, Graduate Programs, College of Science, Department of Biological Sciences, Program in Cell and Molecular Biology, Melbourne, FL 32901-6975. Offers MS. Part-time programs available. *Faculty:* 15 full-time (2 women), 1 part-time/adjunct (0 women). *Students:* 5 full-time (2 women), 1 (woman) part-time; includes 2 Hispanic/Latino. Average age 28. 43 applicants, 7% accepted, 1 enrolled. In 2010, 2 degrees awarded. *Degree requirements:* For master's, research, seminar, internship, or summer lab. *Entrance requirements:* For master's, GRE General Test, 3 letters of recommendation, minimum GPA of 3.0, resume, statement of objectives. Additional exam requirements/recommendations for international students: Required—TOEFL (minimum score 550 paper-based; 213 computer-based; 79 iBT). *Application deadline:* Applications are processed on a rolling basis. Application fee: $50. Electronic applications accepted. *Expenses:* Tuition: Part-time $1040 per credit hour. Tuition and fees vary according to campus/location. *Financial support:* In 2010–11, 6 fellowships with full and partial tuition reimbursements (averaging $20,737 per year), 15 research assistantships with full and partial tuition reimbursements (averaging $13,455 per year), 22 teaching assistantships with full and partial tuition reimbursements (averaging $13,353 per year) were awarded; career-related internships or fieldwork, institutionally sponsored loans, tuition waivers (partial), unspecified assistantships, and tuition remissions also available. Support available to part-time students. Financial award application deadline: 3/1; financial award applicants required to submit FAFSA. *Faculty research:* Changes in DNA molecule and differential expression of genetic information during aging. Total annual research expenditures: $1.3 million. *Unit head:* Dr. Richard B. Aronson, Department Head, 321-674-8034, Fax: 321-674-7238, E-mail: raronson@fit.edu. *Application contact:* Cheryl A. Brown, Associate Director of Graduate Admission, 321-674-7581, Fax: 321-723-9468, E-mail: cbrown@fit.edu.

Florida State University, The Graduate School, College of Arts and Sciences, Department of Biological Science, Specialization in Cell and Molecular Biology and Genetics, Tallahassee, FL 32306-4295. Offers MS, PhD. *Faculty:* 27 full-time (7 women). *Students:* 46 full-time (21 women); includes 2 Black or African American, non-Hispanic/Latino; 6 Hispanic/Latino, 10 international. 162 applicants, 10% accepted, 8 enrolled. In 2010, 3 master's, 3 doctorates awarded. Terminal master's awarded for partial completion of doctoral program. *Degree requirements:* For master's, comprehensive exam, thesis, teaching experience, seminar presentation; for doctorate, comprehensive exam, thesis/dissertation, teaching experience; seminar presentation. *Entrance requirements:* For master's, GRE General Test (minimum combined score 1100, 500 verbal, 500 quantitative), minimum upper-division GPA of 3.0; for doctorate, GRE General Test (minimum combined score 1100, Verbal 500, Quantitative 500), minimum upper-division GPA of 3.0. Additional exam requirements/recommendations for international students: Required—TOEFL (minimum score 600 paper-based; 250 computer-based; 92 iBT). *Application deadline:* For fall admission, 12/15 for domestic and international students. Application fee: $30. Electronic applications accepted. *Expenses:* Tuition, state resident: full-time $8238. *Financial support:* In 2010–11, 14 research assistantships with full tuition reimbursements (averaging $21,000 per year), 30 teaching assistantships with full tuition reimbursements (averaging $21,000 per year) were awarded; unspecified assistantships also available. Financial award application deadline: 12/15; financial award applicants required to submit FAFSA. *Faculty research:* Molecular biology; genetics and genomics; developmental biology and gene expression; cell structure, function, and motility; cellular and organismal physiology; biophysical and structural biology. *Application contact:* Judy Bowers, Coordinator, Graduate Affairs, 850-644-3023, Fax: 850-644-9829, E-mail: gradinfo@bio.fsu.edu.

Georgetown University, Graduate School of Arts and Sciences, Programs in Biomedical Sciences, Department of Cell Biology, Washington, DC 20057. Offers PhD, MD/PhD. *Degree requirements:* For doctorate, comprehensive exam, thesis/dissertation. *Entrance requirements:* For doctorate, GRE General Test. Additional exam requirements/recommendations for international students: Required—TOEFL.

Georgia Health Sciences University, College of Graduate Studies, Program in Cellular Biology and Anatomy, Augusta, GA 30912. Offers MS, PhD. *Faculty:* 16 full-time (6 women), 6 part-time/adjunct (1 woman). *Students:* 11 full-time (5 women); includes 2 Asian, non-Hispanic/Latino, 6 international. Average age 30. In 2010, 2 doctorates awarded. *Degree requirements:* For doctorate, comprehensive exam, thesis/dissertation. *Entrance requirements:* For doctorate, GRE General Test. Additional exam requirements/recommendations for international students: Required—TOEFL (minimum score 550 paper-based; 213 computer-based; 79 iBT). *Application deadline:* For fall admission, 1/15 for domestic and international students. Applications are processed on a rolling basis. Application fee: $30. *Expenses:* Tuition, state resident: full-time $7500; part-time $313 per semester hour. Tuition, nonresident: full-time $24,772; part-time $1033 per semester hour. Required fees: $1112. *Financial support:* In 2010–11, 2 students received support, including 1 fellowship with partial tuition reimbursement available (averaging $26,000 per year), 9 research assistantships with partial tuition reimbursements available (averaging $23,000 per year); teaching assistantships with partial tuition reimbursements available, Federal Work-Study, institutionally sponsored loans, and scholarships/grants also available. Support available to part-time students. Financial award application deadline: 5/31; financial award applicants required to submit FAFSA. *Faculty research:* Eye disease, developmental biology, cell injury and death, stroke and neurotoxicity, diabetic complications. Total annual research expenditures: $2.8 million. *Unit head:* Dr. Sally S. Atherton, Chair and Professor, 706-721-3731, Fax: 706-721-6120, E-mail: satherton@georgiahealth.edu. *Application contact:* Dr. Patricia L. Cameron, Acting Vice Dean, 706-721-3279, E-mail: pcameron@georgiahealth.edu.

Georgia State University, College of Arts and Sciences, Department of Biology, Program in Cellular and Molecular Biology and Physiology, Atlanta, GA 30302-3083. Offers MS, PhD. Part-time programs available. Terminal master's awarded for partial completion of doctoral program. *Degree requirements:* For master's, thesis or alternative; for doctorate, thesis/dissertation, exam. *Entrance requirements:* For master's and doctorate, GRE General Test. Additional exam requirements/recommendations for international students: Required—TOEFL.

Grand Valley State University, College of Liberal Arts and Sciences, Program in Cell and Molecular Biology, Allendale, MI 49401-9403. Offers MS. *Entrance requirements:* For master's, minimum GPA of 3.0. *Faculty research:* Plant cell biology, plant development, cell/signal integration.

Harvard University, Graduate School of Arts and Sciences, Department of Molecular and Cellular Biology, Cambridge, MA 02138. Offers PhD. *Degree requirements:* For doctorate, thesis/dissertation, oral exam. *Entrance requirements:* For doctorate, GRE General Test, GRE Subject Test (recommended). Additional exam requirements/recommendations for international students: Required—TOEFL. *Expenses:* Tuition: Full-time $34,976. Required fees: $1166. Full-time tuition and fees vary according to program.

Harvard University, Graduate School of Arts and Sciences, Division of Medical Sciences, Boston, MA 02115. Offers biological chemistry and molecular pharmacology (PhD); cell biology (PhD); genetics (PhD); microbiology and molecular genetics (PhD); pathology (PhD), including experimental pathology. *Degree requirements:* For doctorate, thesis/dissertation. *Entrance requirements:* For doctorate, GRE General Test, GRE Subject Test. Additional exam requirements/recommendations for international students: Required—TOEFL. *Expenses:* Tuition: Full-time $34,976. Required fees: $1166. Full-time tuition and fees vary according to program.

Illinois Institute of Technology, Graduate College, College of Science and Letters, Department of Biological, Chemical and Physical Sciences, Biology Division, Chicago, IL 60616. Offers biochemistry (MBS, MS); biology (PhD); biotechnology (MBS, MS); cell and molecular biology (MBS, MS); microbiology (MB, MS); molecular biochemistry and biophysics (PhD); molecular biology and biophysics (MS). Part-time and evening/weekend programs available. Postbaccalaureate distance learning degree programs offered (minimal on-campus study). *Faculty:*

Cell Biology

Illinois Institute of Technology (continued)
13 full-time (5 women), 5 part-time/adjunct (2 women). *Students:* 121 full-time (75 women), 56 part-time (37 women); includes 16 minority (5 Black or African American, non-Hispanic/Latino; 5 Asian, non-Hispanic/Latino; 5 Hispanic/Latino; 1 Two or more races, non-Hispanic/Latino), 104 international. Average age 27. 268 applicants, 76% accepted, 62 enrolled. In 2010, 74 master's, 4 doctorates awarded. Terminal master's awarded for partial completion of doctoral program. *Degree requirements:* For master's, comprehensive exam, thesis (for some programs); for doctorate, comprehensive exam, thesis/dissertation. *Entrance requirements:* For master's, GRE General Test (minimum score 1000 Quantitative and Verbal, 2.5 Analytical Writing), minimum undergraduate GPA of 3.0; for doctorate, GRE General Test (minimum score 1200 Quantitative and Verbal, 3.0 Analytical Writing), minimum undergraduate GPA of 3.0. Additional exam requirements/recommendations for international students: Required—TOEFL (minimum score 523 paper-based; 213 computer-based; 70 iBT); Recommended—IELTS (minimum score 5.5). *Application deadline:* For fall admission, 5/1 for domestic and international students; for spring admission, 10/15 for domestic and international students. Applications are processed on a rolling basis. Application fee: $40. Electronic applications accepted. *Expenses:* Tuition: Full-time $18,576; part-time $1032 per credit hour. Required fees: $583 per semester. One-time fee: $150. Tuition and fees vary according to program and student level. *Financial support:* In 2010–11, 15 research assistantships with full and partial tuition reimbursements (averaging $6,379 per year), 14 teaching assistantships with partial tuition reimbursements (averaging $6,296 per year) were awarded; fellowships with full and partial tuition reimbursements, career-related internships or fieldwork, Federal Work-Study, institutionally sponsored loans, scholarships/grants, traineeships, health care benefits, tuition waivers (partial), and unspecified assistantships also available. Support available to part-time students. Financial award applicants required to submit FAFSA. *Faculty research:* Structure and biophysics of macromolecular systems; efficacy and mechanism of action of chemopreventive agents in experimental carcinogenesis of breast, colon, lung and prostate; study of fundamental structural biochemistry problems that have direct links to the understanding and treatment of disease; spectroscopic techniques for the study of multi-domain proteins; molecular mechanisms of cancer and cancer gene therapy. Total annual research expenditures: $2.6 million. *Unit head:* Dr. Benjamin C. Stark, Professor and Associate Chair, 312-567-3488, Fax: 312-567-3494, E-mail: starkb@iit.edu. *Application contact:* Deborah Gibson, Director, Graduate Admissions, 866-472-3448, Fax: 312-567-3138, E-mail: inquiry.grad@iit.edu.

Illinois State University, Graduate School, College of Arts and Sciences, Department of Biological Sciences, Normal, IL 61790-2200. Offers animal behavior (MS); bacteriology (MS); biochemistry (MS); biological sciences (MS); biology (PhD); biophysics (MS); biotechnology (MS); botany (MS, PhD); cell biology (MS); conservation biology (MS); developmental biology (MS); ecology (MS, PhD); entomology (MS); evolutionary biology (MS); genetics (MS, PhD); immunology (MS); microbiology (MS, PhD); molecular biology (MS); molecular genetics (MS); neurobiology (MS); neuroscience (MS); parasitology (MS); physiology (MS, PhD); plant biology (MS); plant molecular biology (MS); plant sciences (MS); structural biology (MS); zoology (MS, PhD). Part-time programs available. *Degree requirements:* For master's, thesis or alternative; for doctorate, variable foreign language requirement, thesis/dissertation, 2 terms of residency. *Entrance requirements:* For master's, GRE General Test, minimum GPA of 2.6 in last 60 hours of course work; for doctorate, GRE General Test. *Faculty research:* Redoc balance and drug development in schistosoma mansoni, control of the growth of listeria monocytogenes at low temperature, regulation of cell expansion and microtubule function by SPRI, CRUI: physiology and fitness consequences of different life history phenotypes.

Indiana University Bloomington, University Graduate School, College of Arts and Sciences, Department of Biology, Bloomington, IN 47405. Offers biology teaching (MAT); biotechnology (MA); evolution, ecology, and behavior (MA, PhD); genetics (PhD); microbiology (MA, PhD); molecular, cellular, and developmental biology (PhD); plant sciences (MA, PhD); zoology (MA, PhD). *Faculty:* 58 full-time (15 women), 21 part-time/adjunct (6 women). *Students:* 163 full-time (98 women), 7 part-time (2 women); includes 17 minority (3 Black or African American, non-Hispanic/Latino; 1 American Indian or Alaska Native, non-Hispanic/Latino; 7 Asian, non-Hispanic/Latino; 5 Hispanic/Latino; 1 Native Hawaiian or other Pacific Islander, non-Hispanic/Latino), 52 international. Average age 27. 346 applicants, 15% accepted, 24 enrolled. In 2010, 17 master's, 24 doctorates awarded. Terminal master's awarded for partial completion of doctoral program. *Degree requirements:* For master's, thesis, oral defense; for doctorate, thesis/dissertation, oral defense. *Entrance requirements:* For master's and doctorate, GRE General Test. Additional exam requirements/recommendations for international students: Required—TOEFL (minimum score 100 iBT). *Application deadline:* For fall admission, 1/5 priority date for domestic students, 12/1 priority date for international students. Application fee: $55 ($65 for international students). Electronic applications accepted. *Financial support:* In 2010–11, 170 students received support, including 64 fellowships with tuition reimbursements available (averaging $19,484 per year), 44 research assistantships with tuition reimbursements available (averaging $20,300 per year), 62 teaching assistantships with tuition reimbursements available (averaging $20,521 per year); scholarships/grants, traineeships, health care benefits, and unspecified assistantships also available. Financial award application deadline: 1/5. *Faculty research:* Evolution, ecology and behavior; microbiology; molecular biology and genetics; plant biology. *Unit head:* Dr. Roger Innes, Chair, 812-855-2219, Fax: 812-855-6082, E-mail: rinnes@indiana.edu. *Application contact:* Tracey D. Stohr, Graduate Student Recruitment Coordinator, 812-856-6303, Fax: 812-855-6082, E-mail: gradbio@indiana.edu.

Indiana University–Purdue University Indianapolis, Indiana University School of Medicine, Department of Anatomy and Cell Biology, Indianapolis, IN 46202-2896. Offers MS, PhD, MD/PhD. *Faculty:* 14 full-time (1 woman). *Students:* 11 full-time (5 women), 1 (woman) part-time; includes 1 minority (Black or African American, non-Hispanic/Latino), 1 international. Average age 29. 17 applicants, 35% accepted, 5 enrolled. In 2010, 1 master's, 2 doctorates awarded. *Degree requirements:* For master's, thesis or alternative; for doctorate, thesis/dissertation. *Entrance requirements:* For master's and doctorate, GRE General Test. *Application deadline:* For fall admission, 1/15 priority date for domestic students. Application fee: $55 ($65 for international students). *Financial support:* In 2010–11, 1 fellowship was awarded; research assistantships, Federal Work-Study, institutionally sponsored loans, tuition waivers (partial), and stipends also available. Financial award application deadline: 2/15. *Faculty research:* Acoustic reflex control, osteoarthritis and bone disease, diabetes, kidney diseases, cellular and molecular neurobiology. *Unit head:* Dr. David B. Burr, Chairman, 317-274-7494, Fax: 317-278-2040, E-mail: dburr@indyvax.iupui.edu. *Application contact:* Dr. James Williams, Graduate Adviser, 317-274-3423, Fax: 317-278-2040, E-mail: williams@anatomy.iupui.edu.

Iowa State University of Science and Technology, Graduate College, College of Agriculture and College of Liberal Arts and Sciences, Department of Biochemistry, Biophysics, and Molecular Biology, Ames, IA 50011. Offers biochemistry (MS, PhD); biophysics (MS, PhD); genetics (MS, PhD); molecular, cellular, and developmental biology (MS, PhD); toxicology (MS, PhD). *Faculty:* 31 full-time (7 women), 1 (woman) part-time/adjunct. *Students:* 81 full-time (33 women), 11 part-time (6 women); includes 2 Black or African American, non-Hispanic/Latino; 2 Asian, non-Hispanic/Latino, 58 international. 38 applicants, 29% accepted, 8 enrolled. In 2010, 3 master's, 9 doctorates awarded. *Degree requirements:* For master's, thesis; for doctorate, thesis/dissertation. *Entrance requirements:* For master's and doctorate, GRE General Test. Additional exam requirements/recommendations for international students: Required—TOEFL (minimum score 550 paper-based; 79 iBT), IELTS (minimum score 6.5). *Application deadline:* For fall admission, 1/15 priority date for domestic and international students; for spring admission, 10/15 for domestic and international students. Application fee: $40 ($90 for international students). Electronic applications accepted. *Financial support:* In 2010–11, 67 research assistantships with full and partial tuition reimbursements (averaging $17,228 per year) were awarded; teaching assistantships with full and partial tuition reimbursements, scholarships/grants, health care benefits, and unspecified assistantships also available. *Unit head:* Dr. Guru Rao, Interim Chair, 515-294-6116, E-mail: biochem@iastate.edu. *Application contact:* Dr. Reuben Peters, Director of Graduate Education, 515-294-6116, E-mail: biochem@iastate.edu.

See Close-Up on page 147.

Iowa State University of Science and Technology, Graduate College, College of Liberal Arts and Sciences and College of Agriculture, Department of Genetics, Developmental and Cell Biology, Ames, IA 50011. Offers MS, PhD. *Faculty:* 43 full-time (8 women), 4 part-time/adjunct (2 women). *Students:* 52 full-time (25 women), 5 part-time (2 women); includes 1 Black or African American, non-Hispanic/Latino, 42 international. 1 applicant, 100% accepted, 1 enrolled. *Degree requirements:* For master's, thesis; for doctorate, thesis/dissertation. *Entrance requirements:* Additional exam requirements/recommendations for international students: Required—TOEFL (minimum score 570 paper-based), IELTS (minimum score 6.5). Application fee: $40 ($90 for international students). *Financial support:* In 2010–11, 42 research assistantships with full and partial tuition reimbursements (averaging $18,008 per year), 9 teaching assistantships with full and partial tuition reimbursements (averaging $9,115 per year) were awarded; fellowships with full tuition reimbursements, scholarships/grants, health care benefits, and unspecified assistantships also available. Financial award application deadline: 2/1. *Faculty research:* Animal behavior, animal models of gene therapy, cell biology, comparative physiology, developmental biology. *Unit head:* Dr. Martin Spalding, Chair, 515-294-1749. *Application contact:* Information Contact, 515-294-5836, Fax: 515-294-2592, E-mail: grad_admissions@iastate.edu.

Iowa State University of Science and Technology, Graduate College, Interdisciplinary Programs, Program in Molecular, Cellular, and Developmental Biology, Ames, IA 50011. Offers MS, PhD. *Students:* 31 full-time (17 women), 4 part-time (2 women), 23 international. In 2010, 2 master's, 3 doctorates awarded. *Degree requirements:* For master's, thesis or alternative; for doctorate, thesis/dissertation. *Entrance requirements:* For master's and doctorate, GRE General Test. Additional exam requirements/recommendations for international students: Required—TOEFL (minimum score 580 paper-based; 85 iBT), IELTS (minimum score 7). *Application deadline:* For fall admission, 1/15 priority date for domestic and international students. Application fee: $40 ($90 for international students). Electronic applications accepted. *Financial support:* In 2010–11, 30 research assistantships with full and partial tuition reimbursements (averaging $20,962 per year), 1 teaching assistantship with full and partial tuition reimbursement (averaging $11,366 per year) were awarded; scholarships/grants, health care benefits, and unspecified assistantships also available. *Unit head:* Dr. Jeff Beetham, Supervisory Committee Chair, 515-294-7252, E-mail: idgp@iastate.edu. *Application contact:* Katie Blair, Information Contact, 515-294-7252, Fax: 515-924-6790, E-mail: idgp@iastate.edu.

The Johns Hopkins University, National Institutes of Health Sponsored Programs, Baltimore, MD 21218-2699. Offers biology (PhD), including biochemistry, biophysics, cell biology, developmental biology, genetic biology, molecular biology; cell, molecular, and developmental biology and biophysics (PhD). *Degree requirements:* For doctorate, comprehensive exam, thesis/dissertation. *Entrance requirements:* For doctorate, GRE General Test. Additional exam requirements/recommendations for international students: Required—TOEFL (minimum score 600 paper-based; 250 computer-based), TWE. Electronic applications accepted. *Faculty research:* Protein and nucleic acid biochemistry and biophysical chemistry, molecular biology and development.

The Johns Hopkins University, School of Medicine, Graduate Programs in Medicine, Graduate Program in Cellular and Molecular Medicine, Baltimore, MD 21218-2699. Offers PhD. *Faculty:* 125 full-time (29 women). *Students:* 130 full-time (80 women); includes 43 minority (12 Black or African American, non-Hispanic/Latino; 22 Asian, non-Hispanic/Latino; 7 Hispanic/Latino; 2 Two or more races, non-Hispanic/Latino), 30 international. Average age 24. 243 applicants, 16% accepted, 21 enrolled. In 2010, 13 doctorates awarded. *Degree requirements:* For doctorate, comprehensive exam, thesis/dissertation, oral exam. *Entrance requirements:* For doctorate, GRE. Additional exam requirements/recommendations for international students: Required—TOEFL. *Application deadline:* For winter admission, 1/1 for domestic students. Application fee: $85. Electronic applications accepted. *Financial support:* In 2010–11, 17 fellowships with tuition reimbursements (averaging $27,125 per year) were awarded; scholarships/grants, health care benefits, and tuition waivers (full) also available. *Faculty research:* Cellular and molecular basis of disease. Total annual research expenditures: $100 million. *Unit head:* Dr. Rajini Rao, Director, 410-955-4732, Fax: 410-614-7294, E-mail: rrao@jhmi.edu. *Application contact:* Leslie Lichter-Mason, Admissions Administrator, 410-614-0391, Fax: 410-614-7294, E-mail: llichte2@jhmi.edu.

The Johns Hopkins University, School of Medicine, Graduate Programs in Medicine, Program in Biochemistry, Cellular and Molecular Biology, Baltimore, MD 21205. Offers PhD. *Faculty:* 101 full-time (35 women). *Students:* 153 full-time (88 women); includes 29 minority (8 Black or African American, non-Hispanic/Latino; 1 American Indian or Alaska Native, non-Hispanic/Latino; 15 Asian, non-Hispanic/Latino; 4 Hispanic/Latino; 1 Two or more races, non-Hispanic/Latino), 54 international. Average age 25. 299 applicants, 19% accepted, 18 enrolled. In 2010, 20 doctorates awarded. *Degree requirements:* For doctorate, comprehensive exam, thesis/dissertation. *Entrance requirements:* For doctorate, GRE General Test. Additional exam requirements/recommendations for international students: Required—TOEFL. *Application deadline:* For winter admission, 1/10 for domestic and international students. Applications are processed on a rolling basis. Application fee: $80. Electronic applications accepted. *Financial support:* In 2010–11, 5 fellowships with partial tuition reimbursements (averaging $32,000 per year), 144 research assistantships with full and partial tuition reimbursements (averaging $27,125 per year) were awarded; traineeships and tuition waivers (full) also available. Financial award application deadline: 12/31. *Faculty research:* Developmental biology, genomics/proteomics, protein targeting, signal transduction, structural biology. *Unit head:* Dr. Carolyn Machamer, Director, 410-955-3466, Fax: 410-614-8842, E-mail: machamer@jhmi.edu. *Application contact:* Dr. Jeff Corden, Admissions Director, 410-955-3506, Fax: 410-614-8842, E-mail: jcorden@jhmi.edu.

Kent State University, School of Biomedical Sciences, Program in Cellular and Molecular Biology, Kent, OH 44242-0001. Offers MS, PhD. Offered in cooperation with Northeastern Ohio Universities College of Medicine. Terminal master's awarded for partial completion of doctoral program. *Degree requirements:* For master's, thesis; for doctorate, thesis/dissertation. *Entrance requirements:* For master's, GRE General Test, letter of recommendation, minimum GPA of 3.0; for doctorate, GRE General Test, letter of recommendation, minimum GPA of 3.0, MS. Additional exam requirements/recommendations for international students: Required—TOEFL. Electronic applications accepted. *Expenses:* Tuition, state resident: full-time $7866; part-time $437 per credit hour. Tuition, nonresident: full-time $14,022; part-time $779 per credit hour. *Faculty research:* Molecular genetics, molecular endocrinology, virology and tumor biology, P450 enzymology and catalysis, membrane structure and function.

Louisiana State University Health Sciences Center, School of Graduate Studies in New Orleans, Department of Cell Biology and Anatomy, New Orleans, LA 70112-2223. Offers cell biology and anatomy (MS, PhD), including cell biology, developmental biology, neurobiology and anatomy; MD/PhD. *Degree requirements:* For master's, comprehensive exam, thesis; for doctorate, comprehensive exam, thesis/dissertation. *Entrance requirements:* For master's and doctorate, GRE General Test, GRE Subject Test, minimum undergraduate GPA of 3.0. Additional exam requirements/recommendations for international students: Required—TOEFL. *Faculty research:* Visual system organization, neural development, plasticity of sensory systems, information processing through the nervous system, visuomotor integration.

Louisiana State University Health Sciences Center at Shreveport, Department of Cellular Biology and Anatomy, Shreveport, LA 71130-3932. Offers MS, PhD, MD/PhD. Terminal master's awarded for partial completion of doctoral program. *Degree requirements:* For master's, thesis; for doctorate, thesis/dissertation. *Entrance requirements:* For master's and doctorate, GRE General Test. Additional exam requirements/recommendations for international students: Required—TOEFL. *Faculty research:* Alcohol and immunity, neuroscience, olfactory physiology, extracellular matrix, cancer cell biology and gene therapy.

Loyola University Chicago, Graduate School, Department of Cell Biology, Neurobiology and Anatomy, Chicago, IL 60660. Offers MS, PhD. Part-time programs available. *Faculty:* 16 full-time (6 women), 9 part-time/adjunct (4 women). *Students:* 21 full-time (12 women), 2 part-time (1 woman); includes 3 minority (2 Hispanic/Latino; 1 Two or more races, non-Hispanic/

Latino), 1 international. Average age 26. 25 applicants, 24% accepted, 6 enrolled. In 2010, 3 master's, 4 doctorates awarded. Terminal master's awarded for partial completion of doctoral program. *Degree requirements:* For master's, thesis; for doctorate, comprehensive exam, thesis/dissertation. *Entrance requirements:* For master's, GRE General Test, minimum GPA of 3.0; for doctorate, GRE General Test, GRE Subject Test (biology), minimum GPA of 3.0. Additional exam requirements/recommendations for international students: Required—TOEFL (minimum score 600 paper-based; 250 computer-based). *Application deadline:* For fall admission, 5/1 priority date for domestic and international students. Applications are processed on a rolling basis. Application fee: $50. Electronic applications accepted. *Expenses:* Tuition: Full-time $14,940; part-time $830 per credit hour. Required fees: $87 per semester. Part-time tuition and fees vary according to course load and program. *Financial support:* In 2010–11, 5 fellowships with full tuition reimbursements (averaging $23,000 per year), 5 research assistantships with full tuition reimbursements (averaging $23,000 per year) were awarded; Federal Work-Study and unspecified assistantships also available. Financial award application deadline: 5/1; financial award applicants required to submit FAFSA. *Faculty research:* Brain steroids, immunology, neuroregeneration, cytokines. Total annual research expenditures: $1 million. *Unit head:* Dr. Phong Le, Head, 708-216-3603, Fax: 708-216-3913, E-mail: ple@lumc.edu. *Application contact:* Ginny Hayes, Graduate Program Secretary, 708-216-3353, Fax: 708-216-3913, E-mail: vhayes@lumc.edu.

Marquette University, Graduate School, College of Arts and Sciences, Department of Biology, Milwaukee, WI 53201-1881. Offers cell biology (MS, PhD); developmental biology (MS, PhD); ecology (MS, PhD); epithelial physiology (MS, PhD); genetics (MS, PhD); microbiology (MS, PhD); molecular biology (MS, PhD); muscle and exercise physiology (MS, PhD); neuroscience (PhD). *Faculty:* 25 full-time (12 women), 2 part-time/adjunct (1 woman). *Students:* 23 full-time (9 women), 12 part-time (8 women); includes 1 minority (Asian, non-Hispanic/Latino), 15 international. Average age 26. 82 applicants, 15% accepted, 5 enrolled. In 2010, 3 master's, 2 doctorates awarded. Terminal master's awarded for partial completion of doctoral program. *Degree requirements:* For master's, comprehensive exam, thesis, 1 year of teaching experience or equivalent; for doctorate, thesis/dissertation, 1 year of teaching experience or equivalent, qualifying exam. *Entrance requirements:* For master's and doctorate, GRE General Test, GRE Subject Test, official transcripts from all current and previous colleges/universities except Marquette, statement of professional goals and aspirations, three letters of recommendation. Additional exam requirements/recommendations for international students: Required—TOEFL (minimum score 530 paper-based; 78 computer-based). *Application deadline:* For fall admission, 12/15 for domestic and international students. Application fee: $50. Electronic applications accepted. *Expenses:* Tuition: Full-time $16,290; part-time $905 per credit hour. Tuition and fees vary according to program. *Financial support:* In 2010–11, 2 research assistantships, 34 teaching assistantships were awarded; fellowships, Federal Work-Study, institutionally sponsored loans, scholarships/grants, and tuition waivers (full and partial) also available. Support available to part-time students. Financial award application deadline: 2/15. *Faculty research:* Neurobiology, neuroendocrinology, epithelial physiology, neuropeptide interactions, synaptic transmission. Total annual research expenditures: $1.3 million. *Unit head:* Dr. Robert Fitts, Chair, 414-288-1748, Fax: 414-288-7357. *Application contact:* Debbie Weaver, Administrative Assistant, 414-288-7355, Fax: 414-288-7357.

Massachusetts Institute of Technology, School of Science, Department of Biology, Cambridge, MA 02139-4307. Offers biochemistry (PhD); biological oceanography (PhD); biology (PhD); biophysical chemistry and molecular structure (PhD); cell biology (PhD); computational and systems biology (PhD); developmental biology (PhD); genetics (PhD); immunology (PhD); microbiology (PhD); molecular biology (PhD); neurobiology (PhD). *Faculty:* 56 full-time (14 women). *Students:* 251 full-time (135 women); includes 74 minority (4 Black or African American, non-Hispanic/Latino; 1 American Indian or Alaska Native, non-Hispanic/Latino; 29 Asian, non-Hispanic/Latino; 33 Hispanic/Latino; 7 Two or more races, non-Hispanic/Latino), 29 international. Average age 26. 652 applicants, 18% accepted, 58 enrolled. In 2010, 41 doctorates awarded. *Degree requirements:* For doctorate, comprehensive exam, thesis/dissertation. *Entrance requirements:* For doctorate, GRE General Test. Additional exam requirements/recommendations for international students: Required—TOEFL (minimum score 577 paper-based; 233 computer-based), IELTS (minimum score 6.5). *Application deadline:* For fall admission, 12/1 for domestic and international students. Application fee: $75. Electronic applications accepted. *Expenses:* Tuition: Full-time $38,940; part-time $605 per unit. Required fees: $272. *Financial support:* In 2010–11, 215 students received support, including 115 fellowships with tuition reimbursements available (averaging $33,090 per year), 132 research assistantships with tuition reimbursements available (averaging $31,846 per year); teaching assistantships with tuition reimbursements available, Federal Work-Study, institutionally sponsored loans, scholarships/grants, traineeships, health care benefits, and unspecified assistantships also available. *Faculty research:* DNA recombination, replication and repair; transcription and gene regulation; signal transduction; cell cycle; neuronal cell fate. Total annual research expenditures: $60.6 million. *Unit head:* Prof. Chris Kaiser, Head, 617-253-4701, E-mail: mitbio@mit.edu. *Application contact:* Biology Education Office, 617-253-3717, Fax: 617-258-9329, E-mail: gradbio@mit.edu.

Mayo Graduate School, Graduate Programs in Biomedical Sciences, Programs in Biochemistry, Structural Biology, Cell Biology, and Genetics, Rochester, MN 55905. Offers biochemistry and structural biology (PhD); cell biology and genetics (PhD); molecular biology (PhD). *Degree requirements:* For doctorate, oral defense of dissertation, qualifying oral and written exam. *Entrance requirements:* For doctorate, GRE, 1 year of chemistry, biology, calculus, and physics. Additional exam requirements/recommendations for international students: Required—TOEFL. Electronic applications accepted. *Faculty research:* Gene structure and function, membranes and receptors/cytoskeleton, oncogenes and growth factors, protein structure and function, steroid hormonal action.

McGill University, Faculty of Graduate and Postdoctoral Studies, Faculty of Medicine, Department of Anatomy and Cell Biology, Montréal, QC H3A 2T5, Canada. Offers M Sc, PhD.

McMaster University, Faculty of Health Sciences and School of Graduate Studies, Program in Medical Sciences, Metabolism and Nutrition Area, Hamilton, ON L8S 4M2, Canada. Offers M Sc, PhD, MD/PhD. *Degree requirements:* For master's, thesis; for doctorate, comprehensive exam, thesis/dissertation. *Entrance requirements:* For master's, honors B Sc, B+ average in related field; for doctorate, M Sc, minimum B+ average, students with proven research experience and an A average may be admitted with a B Sc degree. Additional exam requirements/recommendations for international students: Required—TOEFL (minimum score 580 paper-based; 237 computer-based; 92 iBT).

Medical University of South Carolina, College of Graduate Studies, Program in Molecular and Cellular Biology and Pathobiology, Charleston, SC 29425. Offers cancer biology (PhD); cardiovascular biology (PhD); cardiovascular imaging (PhD); cell regulation (PhD); craniofacial biology (PhD); genetics and development (PhD); marine biomedicine (PhD); DMD/PhD; MD/PhD. *Faculty:* 137 full-time (33 women). *Students:* 27 full-time (20 women); includes 3 Black or African American, non-Hispanic/Latino; 1 Hispanic/Latino, 6 international. Average age 30. In 2010, 16 doctorates awarded. *Degree requirements:* For doctorate, thesis/dissertation, oral and written exams. *Entrance requirements:* For doctorate, GRE General Test, interview, minimum GPA of 3.0. Additional exam requirements/recommendations for international students: Required—TOEFL (minimum score 600 paper-based; 250 computer-based; 100 iBT). *Application deadline:* For fall admission, 1/15 priority date for domestic and international students. Applications are processed on a rolling basis. Application fee: $0 ($85 for international students). Electronic applications accepted. *Financial support:* In 2010–11, 39 research assistantships with partial tuition reimbursements (averaging $23,000 per year) were awarded; Federal Work-Study and scholarships/grants also available. Support available to part-time students. Financial award application deadline: 3/10; financial award applicants required to submit FAFSA. *Unit head:* Dr. Donald R. Menick, Director, 843-876-5045, Fax: 843-792-6590, E-mail: menickd@musc.edu. *Application contact:* Dr. Cynthia F. Wright, Associate Dean for Admissions and Career Development, 843-792-2564, Fax: 843-792-6590, E-mail: wrightcf@musc.edu.

Michigan State University, The Graduate School, College of Agriculture and Natural Resources, MSU-DOE Plant Research Laboratory, East Lansing, MI 48824. Offers biochemistry and molecular biology (PhD); cellular and molecular biology (PhD); crop and soil sciences (PhD); genetics (PhD); microbiology and molecular genetics (PhD); plant biology (PhD); plant physiology (PhD). Offered jointly with the Department of Energy. *Degree requirements:* For doctorate, comprehensive exam, thesis/dissertation, laboratory rotation, defense of dissertation. *Entrance requirements:* For doctorate, GRE General Test, acceptance into one of the affiliated department programs; 3 letters of recommendation; bachelor's degree or equivalent in life sciences, chemistry, biochemistry, or biophysics; research experience. Electronic applications accepted. *Faculty research:* Role of hormones in the regulation of plant development and physiology, molecular mechanisms associated with signal recognition, development and application of genetic methods and materials, protein routing and function.

Michigan State University, The Graduate School, College of Natural Science, Program in Cell and Molecular Biology, East Lansing, MI 48824. Offers cell and molecular biology (MS, PhD); cell and molecular biology/environmental toxicology (PhD). *Entrance requirements:* Additional exam requirements/recommendations for international students: Required—TOEFL. Electronic applications accepted.

Missouri State University, Graduate College, College of Health and Human Services, Department of Biomedical Sciences, Program in Cell and Molecular Biology, Springfield, MO 65897. Offers MS. Part-time programs available. *Degree requirements:* For master's, thesis or alternative, oral and written exams. *Entrance requirements:* For master's, GRE General Test, 2 semesters of course work in organic chemistry and physics, 1 semester of course work in calculus, minimum GPA of 3.0 in last 60 hours of course work. Additional exam requirements/recommendations for international students: Required—TOEFL (minimum score 550 paper-based; 213 computer-based; 79 iBT). Electronic applications accepted. *Expenses:* Tuition, state resident: full-time $3348; part-time $186 per credit hour. Tuition, nonresident: full-time $6696; part-time $372 per credit hour. Required fees: $238 per semester. Tuition and fees vary according to course level, course load and program. *Faculty research:* Extracellular matrix membrane protein, P2 nucleotide receptors, double stranded RNA viruses.

New York Medical College, Graduate School of Basic Medical Sciences, Department of Cell Biology, Valhalla, NY 10595-1691. Offers cell biology and neuroscience (MS, PhD); MD/PhD. Part-time and evening/weekend programs available. *Faculty:* 13 full-time (2 women), 2 part-time/adjunct (both women). *Students:* 6 full-time (1 woman), 3 part-time (all women); includes 1 Asian, non-Hispanic/Latino, 2 international. Average age 26. In 2010, 2 master's, 1 doctorate awarded. Terminal master's awarded for partial completion of doctoral program. *Degree requirements:* For master's, thesis; for doctorate, comprehensive exam, thesis/dissertation. *Entrance requirements:* For master's and doctorate, GRE General Test. Additional exam requirements/recommendations for international students: Required—TOEFL. *Application deadline:* For fall admission, 7/1 priority date for domestic students, 5/1 priority date for international students; for spring admission, 12/1 priority date for domestic students, 10/1 priority date for international students. Applications are processed on a rolling basis. Application fee: $50 ($75 for international students). Electronic applications accepted. *Financial support:* In 2010–11, 4 research assistantships with full tuition reimbursements (averaging $24,000 per year) were awarded; Federal Work-Study, institutionally sponsored loans, scholarships/grants, traineeships, tuition waivers (full), unspecified assistantships, and health benefits (for PhD candidates only) also available. Financial award applicants required to submit FAFSA. *Faculty research:* Mechanisms of growth control in skeletal muscle, cartilage differentiation, cytoskeletal functions, signal transduction pathways, neuronal development and plasticity. *Unit head:* Dr. Victor Fried, Director, 914-594-4036. *Application contact:* Valerie Romeo-Messana, Admission Coordinator, 914-594-4110, Fax: 914-594-4944, E-mail: v_romeomessana@nymc.edu.

New York University, School of Medicine, New York, NY 10012-1019. Offers biomedical sciences (PhD), including biomedical imaging, cellular and molecular biology, computational biology, developmental genetics, medical and molecular parasitology, microbiology, molecular oncobiology and immunology, neuroscience and physiology, pathobiology, pharmacology, structural biology; clinical investigation (MS); medicine (MD); MD/MA; MD/MPA; MD/MS; MD/PhD. *Accreditation:* LCME/AMA (one or more programs are accredited). *Degree requirements:* For master's, comprehensive exam, thesis; for doctorate, comprehensive exam, thesis/dissertation. *Entrance requirements:* MCAT. Additional exam requirements/recommendations for international students: Required—TOEFL. *Expenses:* Contact institution. *Faculty research:* AIDS, cancer, neuroscience, molecular biology, neuroscience, cell biology and molecular genetics, structural biology, microbial pathogenesis and host defense, pharmacology, molecular oncology and immunology.

New York University, School of Medicine and Graduate School of Arts and Science, Sackler Institute of Graduate Biomedical Sciences, Program in Cellular and Molecular Biology, New York, NY 10012-1019. Offers PhD, MD/PhD. *Degree requirements:* For doctorate, comprehensive exam, thesis/dissertation, qualifying exams. *Entrance requirements:* For doctorate, GRE General Test. Additional exam requirements/recommendations for international students: Required—TOEFL. *Faculty research:* Membrane and organelle structure and biogenesis, intracellular transport and processing of proteins, cellular recognition and cell adhesion, oncogene structure and function, action of growth factors.

North Carolina State University, College of Veterinary Medicine, Program in Comparative Biomedical Sciences, Raleigh, NC 27695. Offers cell biology (MS, PhD); infectious disease (MS, PhD); pathology (MS, PhD); pharmacology (MS, PhD); population medicine (MS, PhD). Part-time programs available. *Degree requirements:* For master's, thesis; for doctorate, thesis/dissertation. *Entrance requirements:* For master's and doctorate, GRE General Test. Additional exam requirements/recommendations for international students: Required—TOEFL (minimum score 550 paper-based; 213 computer-based). Electronic applications accepted. *Expenses:* Contact institution. *Faculty research:* Infectious diseases, cell biology, pharmacology and toxicology, genomics, pathology and population medicine.

North Dakota State University, College of Graduate and Interdisciplinary Studies, College of Science and Mathematics, Department of Biological Sciences, Fargo, ND 58108. Offers biology (MS); botany (MS, PhD); cellular and molecular biology (PhD); environmental and conservation sciences (MS, PhD); genomics (PhD); natural resources management (MS, PhD); zoology (MS, PhD). *Students:* 18 full-time (8 women), 5 part-time (3 women); includes 2 American Indian or Alaska Native, non-Hispanic/Latino, 2 international. 17 applicants, 35% accepted. In 2010, 12 master's, 9 doctorates awarded. *Degree requirements:* For master's, thesis; for doctorate, thesis/dissertation. *Entrance requirements:* For master's and doctorate, GRE General Test. Additional exam requirements/recommendations for international students: Required—TOEFL. *Application deadline:* For fall admission, 3/15 priority date for domestic students; for spring admission, 10/30 priority date for domestic students. Applications are processed on a rolling basis. Application fee: $45 ($60 for international students). Electronic applications accepted. *Financial support:* Fellowships with full tuition reimbursements, research assistantships with full tuition reimbursements, teaching assistantships with full tuition reimbursements, career-related internships or fieldwork, Federal Work-Study, institutionally sponsored loans, scholarships/grants, tuition waivers (full), and unspecified assistantships available. Support available to part-time students. Financial award application deadline: 4/15; financial award applicants required to submit FAFSA. *Faculty research:* Comparative endocrinology, physiology, behavioral ecology, plant cell biology, aquatic biology. Total annual research expenditures: $675,000. *Unit head:* Dr. Marinus L. Otte, Head, 701-231-7087, E-mail: marinus.otte@ndsu.edu. *Application contact:* Dr. Marinus L. Otte, Head, 701-231-7087, E-mail: marinus.otte@ndsu.edu.

North Dakota State University, College of Graduate and Interdisciplinary Studies, Interdisciplinary Program in Cellular and Molecular Biology, Fargo, ND 58108. Offers PhD. PhD offered in cooperation with 11 departments in the university. *Students:* 11 full-time (8 women), 1 part-time (0 women), 7 international. 24 applicants, 21% accepted, 5 enrolled. *Degree requirements:* For doctorate, thesis/dissertation. *Entrance requirements:* For doctorate, GRE. Additional exam

Cell Biology

North Dakota State University (continued)
requirements/recommendations for international students: Required—TOEFL (minimum score 525 paper-based; 197 computer-based; 71 iBT). *Application deadline:* Applications are processed on a rolling basis. Application fee: $45 ($60 for international students). Electronic applications accepted. *Financial support:* Fellowships with full tuition reimbursements, research assistantships with full tuition reimbursements, teaching assistantships with full tuition reimbursements, unspecified assistantships available. Financial award application deadline: 3/15. *Faculty research:* Plant and animal cell biology, gene regulation, molecular genetics, plant and animal virology. *Unit head:* Dr. Mark Sheridan, Director, 701-231-7087, E-mail: ndsu.cmb@ndsu.edu. *Application contact:* Dr. Mark Sheridan, Director, 701-231-7087, E-mail: ndsu.cmb@ndsu.edu.

Northwestern University, The Graduate School, Interdepartmental Biological Sciences Program (IBiS), Evanston, IL 60208. Offers biochemistry, molecular biology, and cell biology (PhD), including biochemistry, cell and molecular biology, molecular biophysics, structural biology; biotechnology (PhD); cell and molecular biology (PhD); developmental biology and genetics (PhD); hormone action and signal transduction (PhD); neuroscience (PhD); structural biology, biochemistry, and biophysics (PhD). Program participants include the Departments of Biochemistry, Molecular Biology, and Cell Biology; Chemistry; Neurobiology and Physiology; Chemical Engineering; Civil Engineering; and Evanston Hospital. *Degree requirements:* For doctorate, thesis/dissertation, qualifying exam. *Entrance requirements:* For doctorate, GRE General Test. Additional exam requirements/recommendations for international students: Required—TOEFL (minimum score 600 paper-based). Electronic applications accepted. *Faculty research:* Developmental genetics, gene regulation, DNA-protein interactions, biological clocks, bioremediation.

Northwestern University, Northwestern University Feinberg School of Medicine and Interdepartmental Programs, Integrated Graduate Programs in the Life Sciences, Chicago, IL 60611. Offers cancer biology (PhD); cell biology (PhD); developmental biology (PhD); evolutionary biology (PhD); immunology and microbial pathogenesis (PhD); molecular biology and genetics (PhD); neurobiology (PhD); pharmacology and toxicology (PhD); structural biology and biochemistry (PhD). *Degree requirements:* For doctorate, comprehensive exam, thesis/dissertation, written and oral qualifying exams. *Entrance requirements:* For doctorate, GRE General Test. Additional exam requirements/recommendations for international students: Required—TOEFL (minimum score 600 paper-based; 250 computer-based). Electronic applications accepted.

The Ohio State University, College of Veterinary Medicine, Department of Veterinary Biosciences, Columbus, OH 43210. Offers anatomy and cellular biology (MS, PhD); pathobiology (MS, PhD); pharmacology (MS, PhD); toxicology (MS, PhD); veterinary physiology (MS, PhD). *Faculty:* 45. *Students:* 4 full-time (all women), 7 part-time (5 women); includes 1 Black or African American, non-Hispanic/Latino, 3 international. Average age 30. In 2010, 2 master's, 7 doctorates awarded. *Entrance requirements:* For master's and doctorate, GRE General Test. Additional exam requirements/recommendations for international students: Required—TOEFL. *Application deadline:* Applications are processed on a rolling basis. Application fee: $40 ($50 for international students). Electronic applications accepted. *Expenses:* Tuition, state resident: full-time $10,605. Tuition, nonresident: full-time $26,535. Tuition and fees vary according to course load and program. *Faculty research:* Microvasculature, muscle biology, neonatal lung and bone development. *Unit head:* Dr. Michael J. Oglesbee, Graduate Studies Committee Chair, 614-292-5661, Fax: 614-292-6473, E-mail: oglesbee.1@osu.edu. *Application contact:* Graduate Admissions, 614-292-9444, Fax: 614-292-3895, E-mail: domestic.grad@osu.edu.

The Ohio State University, Graduate School, College of Arts and Sciences, Division of Natural and Mathematical Sciences, Department of Molecular Genetics, Columbus, OH 43210. Offers cell and developmental biology (MS, PhD); genetics (MS, PhD); molecular biology (MS, PhD). *Faculty:* 26. *Students:* 7 full-time (3 women), 25 part-time (14 women), 16 international. Average age 27. In 2010, 1 master's, 1 doctorate awarded. *Degree requirements:* For master's, thesis; for doctorate, thesis/dissertation. *Entrance requirements:* For master's and doctorate, GRE General Test, GRE Subject Test in biology or biochemistry (recommended). Additional exam requirements/recommendations for international students: Required—TOEFL (minimum score 600 paper-based; 250 computer-based). *Application deadline:* For fall admission, 8/15 priority date for domestic students, 7/1 priority date for international students; for winter admission, 12/1 priority date for domestic students, 11/1 priority date for international students; for spring admission, 3/1 priority date for domestic students, 2/1 priority date for international students. Applications are processed on a rolling basis. Application fee: $40 ($50 for international students). Electronic applications accepted. *Expenses:* Tuition, state resident: full-time $10,605. Tuition, nonresident: full-time $26,535. Tuition and fees vary according to course load and program. *Financial support:* Fellowships, research assistantships, teaching assistantships, Federal Work-Study and institutionally sponsored loans available. Support available to part-time students. *Unit head:* Dr. Anna Hopper, Chair, 614-688-3306, Fax: 614-247-2594, E-mail: hopper.64@osu.edu. *Application contact:* 614-292-9444, Fax: 614-292-3895, E-mail: domestic.grad@osu.edu.

The Ohio State University, Graduate School, College of Arts and Sciences, Division of Natural and Mathematical Sciences, Program in Molecular, Cellular and Developmental Biology, Columbus, OH 43210. Offers MS, PhD. *Students:* 70 full-time (40 women), 64 part-time (35 women); includes 8 Asian, non-Hispanic/Latino; 7 Hispanic/Latino, 75 international. Average age 28. In 2010, 4 master's, 17 doctorates awarded. *Degree requirements:* For master's, thesis; for doctorate, thesis/dissertation. *Entrance requirements:* For master's and doctorate, GRE General Test, GRE Subject Test (biology or biochemistry, cell and molecular biology). Additional exam requirements/recommendations for international students: Required—TOEFL (minimum score 573 paper-based; 230 computer-based). *Application deadline:* For fall admission, 8/15 priority date for domestic students, 7/1 priority date for international students; for winter admission, 12/1 priority date for domestic students, 11/1 priority date for international students; for spring admission, 3/1 priority date for domestic students, 2/1 priority date for international students. Applications are processed on a rolling basis. Application fee: $40 ($50 for international students). Electronic applications accepted. *Expenses:* Tuition, state resident: full-time $10,605. Tuition, nonresident: full-time $26,535. Tuition and fees vary according to course load and program. *Unit head:* David M. Bisaro, Director, 614-292-3281, Fax: 614-292-4466, E-mail: bisaro.1@osu.edu. *Application contact:* Graduate Admissions, 614-292-9444, Fax: 614-292-3895, E-mail: domestic.grad@osu.edu.

Ohio University, Graduate College, College of Arts and Sciences, Department of Biological Sciences, Athens, OH 45701-2979. Offers biological sciences (MS, PhD); cell biology and physiology (MS, PhD); ecology and evolutionary biology (MS, PhD); exercise physiology and muscle biology (MS, PhD); microbiology (MS, PhD); neuroscience (MS, PhD). *Students:* 32 full-time (9 women), 5 part-time (2 women); includes 2 minority (1 Black or African American, non-Hispanic/Latino; 1 Hispanic/Latino), 9 international. 51 applicants, 37% accepted, 7 enrolled. In 2010, 2 master's, 9 doctorates awarded. Terminal master's awarded for partial completion of doctoral program. *Degree requirements:* For master's, comprehensive exam, thesis, 1 quarter of teaching experience; for doctorate, comprehensive exam, thesis/dissertation, 2 quarters of teaching experience. *Entrance requirements:* For master's, GRE General Test, names of three faculty members whose research interests most closely match the applicant's interest; for doctorate, GRE General Test, essay concerning prior training, research interest and career goals, plus names of three faculty members whose research interests most closely match the applicant's interest. Additional exam requirements/recommendations for international students: Required—TOEFL (minimum score 620 paper-based; 105 iBT) or IELTS (minimum score 7.5). *Application deadline:* For fall admission, 1/15 for domestic and international students. Application fee: $50 ($55 for international students). Electronic applications accepted. *Financial support:* In 2010–11, 1 fellowship with full tuition reimbursement (averaging $18,957 per year), 10 research assistantships with full tuition reimbursements (averaging $18,957 per year), 42 teaching assistantships with full tuition reimbursements (averaging $18,957 per year) were awarded; Federal Work-Study and institutionally sponsored loans also available. Financial award application deadline: 1/15. *Faculty research:* Ecology and evolutionary biology, exercise physiology and muscle biology, neurobiology, cell biology, physiology. Total annual research expenditures: $2.8 million. *Unit head:* Dr. Ralph DiCaprio, Chair, 740-593-2290, Fax: 740-593-0300, E-mail: dicapri@ohio.edu. *Application contact:* Dr. Patrick Hassett, Graduate Chair, 740-593-4793, Fax: 740-593-0300, E-mail: hassett@ohio.edu.

Ohio University, Graduate College, College of Arts and Sciences, Interdisciplinary Graduate Program in Molecular and Cellular Biology, Athens, OH 45701-2979. Offers MS, PhD. *Students:* 27 full-time (17 women), 3 part-time (1 woman); includes 1 minority (Hispanic/Latino), 24 international. Average age 28. 34 applicants, 18% accepted, 1 enrolled. In 2010, 4 doctorates awarded. *Degree requirements:* For master's, comprehensive exam, thesis, research proposal, teaching experience; for doctorate, comprehensive exam, thesis/dissertation, research proposal, teaching experience. *Entrance requirements:* For master's and doctorate, GRE General Test. Additional exam requirements/recommendations for international students: Required—TOEFL (minimum score 620 paper-based; 260 computer-based; 105 iBT); Recommended—TWE. *Application deadline:* For fall admission, 12/30 priority date for domestic students, 12/30 for international students. Application fee: $50 ($55 for international students). Electronic applications accepted. *Financial support:* In 2010–11, 25 students received support, including research assistantships with full tuition reimbursements available (averaging $19,500 per year), teaching assistantships with full tuition reimbursements available (averaging $19,500 per year); Federal Work-Study, institutionally sponsored loans, traineeships, and unspecified assistantships also available. Financial award application deadline: 12/30. *Faculty research:* Animal biotechnology, plant molecular biology RNA, immunology, cellular genetics, biochemistry of signal transduction, cancer research, membrane transport, bioinformatics, bioengineering, chemical biology and drug discovery, diabetes, microbiology, neuroscience. Total annual research expenditures: $4.4 million. *Unit head:* Dr. Robert A. Colvin, Chair, 740-593-0198, Fax: 740-593-1569, E-mail: colvin@ohio.edu. *Application contact:* Dr. Xiaozhuo Chen, Graduate Chair, 740-593-9699, Fax: 740-593-1569, E-mail: chenx@ohio.edu.

Oregon Health & Science University, School of Medicine, Graduate Programs in Medicine, Program in Molecular and Cellular Biosciences, Department of Cell and Developmental Biology, Portland, OR 97239-3098. Offers PhD. *Faculty:* 30 full-time (8 women). *Students:* 29 full-time (18 women); includes 1 Asian, non-Hispanic/Latino; 1 Native Hawaiian or other Pacific Islander, non-Hispanic/Latino, 9 international. Average age 28. In 2010, 5 doctorates awarded. *Degree requirements:* For doctorate, comprehensive exam, thesis/dissertation. *Entrance requirements:* For doctorate, GRE General Test, GRE Subject Test, MCAT. Additional exam requirements/recommendations for international students: Required—TOEFL. *Financial support:* Health care benefits, tuition waivers (full), and full tuition and stipends available. *Faculty research:* Developmental mechanisms, molecular biology of cancer, molecular neurobiology, intracellular signaling, growth factors and development. *Unit head:* Dr. Richard Maurer, Interim Chair/Program Director, 503-494-7811, E-mail: maurerr@ohsu.edu. *Application contact:* Elaine Offield, Program Coordinator, 503-494-5824, E-mail: offielde@ohsu.edu.

Oregon State University, Graduate School, Program in Molecular and Cellular Biology, Corvallis, OR 97331. Offers MS, PhD. *Degree requirements:* For doctorate, thesis/dissertation, oral and written qualifying exams. *Entrance requirements:* For doctorate, minimum GPA of 3.0 in last 90 hours. Additional exam requirements/recommendations for international students: Required—TOEFL.

Penn State Hershey Medical Center, College of Medicine, Graduate School Programs in the Biomedical Sciences, Interdepartmental Graduate Program in Cell and Molecular Biology, Hershey, PA 17033. Offers MS, PhD, MD/PhD. *Students:* 37 applicants, 38% accepted, 4 enrolled. In 2010, 4 doctorates awarded. Terminal master's awarded for partial completion of doctoral program. *Degree requirements:* For master's, thesis or alternative; for doctorate, comprehensive exam, thesis/dissertation, oral exam. *Entrance requirements:* For master's, GRE General Test or MCAT; for doctorate, GRE General Test or MCAT, minimum GPA of 3.0. Additional exam requirements/recommendations for international students: Required—TOEFL (minimum score 500 paper-based; 213 computer-based). *Application deadline:* For fall admission, 1/31 priority date for domestic students, 2/1 priority date for international students. Applications are processed on a rolling basis. Application fee: $65. Electronic applications accepted. *Financial support:* In 2010–11, research assistantships with full tuition reimbursements (averaging $22,260 per year); fellowships with full tuition reimbursements, career-related internships or fieldwork, scholarships/grants, health care benefits, and unspecified assistantships also available. Financial award applicants required to submit FAFSA. *Faculty research:* Membrane structure, function and modulators; cell division, differentiation and gene expression; metastasis; intracellular events in the immune system. *Unit head:* Dr. Henry Donahue, Program Director, 717-531-1045, Fax: 717-531-4139, E-mail: cmb-grad-hmc@psu.edu. *Application contact:* Lori Coover, Program Assistant, 717-531-1045, Fax: 717-531-0786, E-mail: cmb-grad-hmc@psu.edu.

Purdue University, Graduate School, College of Science, Department of Biological Sciences, West Lafayette, IN 47907. Offers biochemistry (PhD); biophysics (PhD); cell and developmental biology (PhD); ecology, evolutionary and population biology (MS, PhD), including ecology, evolutionary biology, population biology; genetics (MS, PhD); microbiology (MS, PhD); molecular biology (PhD); neurobiology (MS, PhD); plant physiology (PhD). Terminal master's awarded for partial completion of doctoral program. *Degree requirements:* For master's, thesis (for some programs); for doctorate, thesis/dissertation, seminars, teaching experience. *Entrance requirements:* For master's and doctorate, GRE General Test. Additional exam requirements/recommendations for international students: Required—TOEFL. Electronic applications accepted.

Queen's University at Kingston, School of Graduate Studies and Research, Faculty of Health Sciences, Department of Anatomy and Cell Biology, Kingston, ON K7L 3N6, Canada. Offers biology of reproduction (M Sc, PhD); cancer (M Sc, PhD); cardiovascular pathophysiology (M Sc, PhD); cell and molecular biology (M Sc, PhD); drug metabolism (M Sc, PhD); endocrinology (M Sc, PhD); motor control (M Sc, PhD); neural regeneration (M Sc, PhD); neurophysiology (M Sc, PhD). Part-time programs available. *Degree requirements:* For master's, thesis; for doctorate, one foreign language, comprehensive exam, thesis/dissertation. *Entrance requirements:* Additional exam requirements/recommendations for international students: Required—TOEFL. Electronic applications accepted. *Faculty research:* Human kinetics, neuroscience, reproductive biology, cardiovascular.

Quinnipiac University, School of Health Sciences, Program in Molecular and Cell Biology, Hamden, CT 06518-1940. Offers MS. Part-time programs available. *Faculty:* 10 full-time (4 women), 12 part-time/adjunct (5 women). *Students:* 16 full-time (11 women), 21 part-time (15 women); includes 8 minority (3 Black or African American, non-Hispanic/Latino; 4 Asian, non-Hispanic/Latino; 1 Hispanic/Latino), 4 international. Average age 26. 37 applicants, 89% accepted, 19 enrolled. In 2010, 8 master's awarded. *Degree requirements:* For master's, thesis optional. *Entrance requirements:* For master's, bachelor's degree in biological, medical, or health sciences; minimum GPA of 2.75. Additional exam requirements/recommendations for international students: Required—TOEFL (minimum score 575 paper-based; 233 computer-based; 90 iBT), IELTS (minimum score 6.5). *Application deadline:* For fall admission, 7/30 priority date for domestic students, 4/30 priority date for international students; for spring admission, 12/15 priority date for domestic students, 9/15 priority date for international students. Applications are processed on a rolling basis. Application fee: $45. Electronic applications accepted. *Expenses:* Tuition: Part-time $810 per credit. Required fees: $35 per credit. *Financial support:* Federal Work-Study, tuition waivers, and unspecified assistantships available. Support available to part-time students. Financial award application deadline: 4/15; financial award applicants required to submit FAFSA. *Unit head:* Dr. Gene Wong, Director, 203-582-8467, E-mail: gene.wong@quinnipiac.edu. *Application contact:* Kristin Parent, Assistant Director of Graduate Health Sciences Admissions, 800-462-1944, Fax: 203-582-3443, E-mail: kristin.parent@quinnipiac.edu.

Rice University, Graduate Programs, Wiess School of Natural Sciences, Department of Biochemistry and Cell Biology, Houston, TX 77251-1892. Offers MA, PhD. Terminal master's awarded for partial completion of doctoral program. *Degree requirements:* For master's, thesis; for doctorate, thesis/dissertation. *Entrance requirements:* For master's and doctorate, GRE. Additional exam requirements/recommendations for international students: Required—TOEFL (minimum score 600 paper-based; 250 computer-based; 90 iBT). Electronic applications accepted. *Expenses:* Contact institution. *Faculty research:* Steroid metabolism, protein structure NMR, biophysics, cell growth and movement.

Rosalind Franklin University of Medicine and Science, School of Graduate and Postdoctoral Studies—Interdisciplinary Graduate Program in Biomedical Sciences, Department of Cell Biology and Anatomy, North Chicago, IL 60064-3095. Offers MS, PhD, MD/PhD. Terminal master's awarded for partial completion of doctoral program. *Degree requirements:* For master's, comprehensive exam, thesis, qualifying exam; for doctorate, comprehensive exam, thesis/dissertation, original research project. *Entrance requirements:* For master's and doctorate, GRE General Test, minimum GPA of 3.0. Additional exam requirements/recommendations for international students: Required—TOEFL, TWE. *Faculty research:* Neuroscience, molecular biology.

Rush University, Graduate College, Division of Anatomy and Cell Biology, Chicago, IL 60612-3832. Offers MS, PhD, MD/MS, MD/PhD. Terminal master's awarded for partial completion of doctoral program. *Degree requirements:* For master's, thesis; for doctorate, comprehensive exam, thesis/dissertation, preliminary exam, dissertation proposal. *Entrance requirements:* For master's, GRE General Test, minimum GPA of 3.0, bachelor's degree in biology or chemistry (preferred), interview; for doctorate, GRE General Test, minimum GPA of 3.0, interview. Additional exam requirements/recommendations for international students: Required—TOEFL. Electronic applications accepted. *Faculty research:* Incontinence following vaginal distension, knee replacement, biomimetric materials, injured spinal motoneurons, implant fixation.

Rutgers, The State University of New Jersey, New Brunswick, Graduate School-New Brunswick, Programs in the Molecular Biosciences, Program in Cell and Developmental Biology, Piscataway, NJ 08854-8097. Offers MS, PhD. MS, PhD offered jointly with University of Medicine and Dentistry of New Jersey. Part-time programs available. Terminal master's awarded for partial completion of doctoral program. *Degree requirements:* For master's, thesis; for doctorate, thesis/dissertation, written qualifying exam. *Entrance requirements:* For master's, GRE General Test; for doctorate, GRE General Test, GRE Subject Test (recommended), minimum GPA of 3.0. Additional exam requirements/recommendations for international students: Required—TOEFL. Electronic applications accepted. *Expenses:* Tuition, state resident: full-time $7200; part-time $600 per credit. Tuition, nonresident: full-time $11,124; part-time $927 per credit. *Faculty research:* Signal transduction and regulation of gene expression, developmental biology, cellular biology, developmental genetics, neurobiology.

San Diego State University, Graduate and Research Affairs, College of Sciences, Department of Biology, San Diego, CA 92182. Offers biology (MA, MS), including ecology (MS), molecular biology (MS), physiology (MS), systematics/evolution (MS); cell and molecular biology (PhD); ecology (MS, PhD); microbiology (MS). Terminal master's awarded for partial completion of doctoral program. *Degree requirements:* For master's, thesis; for doctorate, thesis/dissertation. *Entrance requirements:* For master's, GRE General Test, GRE Subject Test, resume or curriculum vitae, 2 letters of recommendation. Additional exam requirements/recommendations for international students: Required—TOEFL. Electronic applications accepted.

San Diego State University, Graduate and Research Affairs, College of Sciences, Molecular Biology Institute, Program in Cell and Molecular Biology, San Diego, CA 92182. Offers PhD. Program offered jointly with University of California, San Diego. *Degree requirements:* For doctorate, thesis/dissertation, oral comprehensive qualifying exam. *Entrance requirements:* For doctorate, GRE General Test, GRE Subject Test, resumé or curriculum vitae, 3 letters of recommendation. Electronic applications accepted. *Faculty research:* Structure/dynamics of protein kinesis, chromatin structure and DNA methylation membrane biochemistry, secretory protein targeting, molecular biology of cardiac myocytes.

San Francisco State University, Division of Graduate Studies, College of Science and Engineering, Department of Biology, Program in Cell and Molecular Biology, San Francisco, CA 94132-1722. Offers MS. *Application deadline:* Applications are processed on a rolling basis. *Unit head:* Dr. Diana Chu, Program Coordinator, 415-405-3487, E-mail: chud@sfsu.edu. *Application contact:* Dr. Robert Patterson, Graduate Coordinator, 415-338-1100, E-mail: patters@sfsu.edu.

State University of New York Downstate Medical Center, School of Graduate Studies, Program in Molecular and Cellular Biology, Brooklyn, NY 11203-2098. Offers PhD, MD/PhD. Affiliation with a particular PhD degree-granting program is deferred to the second year. *Degree requirements:* For doctorate, comprehensive exam, thesis/dissertation. *Entrance requirements:* For doctorate, GRE General Test. *Faculty research:* Mechanism of gene regulation, molecular virology.

State University of New York Upstate Medical University, College of Graduate Studies, Program in Cell and Developmental Biology, Syracuse, NY 13210-2334. Offers anatomy (MS, PhD); MD/PhD. Terminal master's awarded for partial completion of doctoral program. *Degree requirements:* For master's, thesis; for doctorate, comprehensive exam, thesis/dissertation. *Entrance requirements:* For master's, GRE General Test, interview; for doctorate, GRE General Test, telephone interview. Additional exam requirements/recommendations for international students: Required—TOEFL. Electronic applications accepted. *Faculty research:* Cancer, disorders of the nervous system, infectious diseases, diabetes/metabolic disorders/cardiovascular diseases.

Stony Brook University, State University of New York, Graduate School, College of Arts and Sciences, Department of Biochemistry and Cell Biology, Molecular and Cellular Biology Program, Stony Brook, NY 11794. Offers biochemistry and molecular biology (PhD); biological sciences (MA); cellular and developmental biology (PhD); immunology and pathology (PhD); molecular and cellular biology (PhD). *Faculty:* 22 full-time (7 women). *Students:* 106 full-time (65 women); includes 2 Black or African American, non-Hispanic/Latino; 9 Asian, non-Hispanic/Latino; 1 Hispanic/Latino, 58 international. Average age 30. 320 applicants, 16% accepted, 26 enrolled. In 2010, 5 master's, 16 doctorates awarded. *Degree requirements:* For doctorate, comprehensive exam, thesis/dissertation, teaching experience. *Entrance requirements:* For doctorate, GRE General Test, GRE Subject Test. Additional exam requirements/recommendations for international students: Required—TOEFL. *Application deadline:* For fall admission, 1/15 for domestic students. Application fee: $100. *Expenses:* Tuition, state resident: full-time $8370; part-time $349 per credit. Tuition, nonresident: full-time $13,780; part-time $574 per credit. Required fees: $994. *Financial support:* In 2010–11, 42 research assistantships, 19 teaching assistantships were awarded; fellowships, Federal Work-Study also available. *Unit head:* Prof. Robert Haltiwanger, Chair, 631-632-8560. *Application contact:* Prof. Robert Haltiwanger, Chair, 631-632-8560.

Temple University, Health Sciences Center, School of Medicine and Graduate School, Doctor of Medicine Program, Department of Anatomy and Cell Biology, Philadelphia, PA 19122-6096. Offers MS, PhD. *Faculty:* 11 full-time (5 women). *Students:* 8 full-time (5 women); includes 1 Black or African American, non-Hispanic/Latino; 1 Hispanic/Latino, 3 international. 11 applicants, 45% accepted, 4 enrolled. In 2010, 3 doctorates awarded. *Degree requirements:* For doctorate, thesis/dissertation, research seminars. *Entrance requirements:* For master's and doctorate, GRE General Test, GRE Subject Test, minimum GPA of 3.0. Additional exam requirements/recommendations for international students: Required—TOEFL. *Application deadline:* For fall admission, 1/15 for domestic students, 12/15 for international students; for spring admission, 9/1 for domestic students, 8/1 for international students. Application fee: $50. Electronic applications accepted. *Financial support:* Fellowships, Federal Work-Study available. Financial award application deadline: 1/15; financial award applicants required to submit FAFSA. *Faculty research:* Neurobiology, reproductive biology, cardiovascular system, musculoskeletal biology, developmental biology. Total annual research expenditures: $632,373. *Unit head:* Dr. Steven

Popoff, Chair, 215-707-3161, Fax: 215-707-2966, E-mail: spopoff@temple.edu. *Application contact:* Dr. Steven Popoff, Chair, 215-707-3161, Fax: 215-707-2966, E-mail: spopoff@temple.edu.

Texas A&M Health Science Center, Graduate School of Biomedical Sciences, Department of Molecular and Cellular Medicine, College Station, TX 77840. Offers PhD. *Degree requirements:* For doctorate, thesis/dissertation. *Entrance requirements:* For doctorate, GRE General Test. *Faculty research:* Immunology, cell and membrane biology, protein biochemistry, molecular genetics, parasitology, vertebrate embryogenesis and microbiology.

Texas A&M Health Science Center, Graduate School of Biomedical Sciences, Program in Cell and Molecular Biology, College Station, TX 77840. Offers PhD.

Texas A&M University, College of Science, Department of Biology, College Station, TX 77843. Offers biology (MS, PhD); botany (MS, PhD); microbiology (MS, PhD); molecular and cell biology (PhD); neuroscience (MS, PhD); zoology (MS, PhD). *Faculty:* 39. *Students:* 107 full-time (60 women), 4 part-time (3 women); includes 1 Black or African American, non-Hispanic/Latino; 5 Asian, non-Hispanic/Latino; 5 Hispanic/Latino, 47 international. Average age 28. In 2010, 3 master's, 6 doctorates awarded. *Degree requirements:* For master's, thesis or alternative; for doctorate, comprehensive exam, thesis/dissertation. *Entrance requirements:* For master's and doctorate, GRE General Test. Additional exam requirements/recommendations for international students: Required—TOEFL. *Application deadline:* For fall admission, 1/15 for domestic students. Applications are processed on a rolling basis. Application fee: $50 ($75 for international students). Electronic applications accepted. *Financial support:* Fellowships, research assistantships, teaching assistantships available. Financial award application deadline: 4/1; financial award applicants required to submit FAFSA. *Unit head:* Dr. Jack McMahan, Department Head, 979-845-2301, E-mail: granster@mail.bio.tamu.edu. *Application contact:* Dr. Jack McMahan, Department Head, 979-845-2301, E-mail: granster@mail.bio.tamu.edu.

Texas Tech University Health Sciences Center, Graduate School of Biomedical Sciences, Department of Cell Biology and Biochemistry, Program in Cell and Molecular Biology, Lubbock, TX 79430. Offers MS, PhD, MD/PhD, MS/PhD. Terminal master's awarded for partial completion of doctoral program. *Degree requirements:* For master's, comprehensive exam, thesis; for doctorate, comprehensive exam, thesis/dissertation. *Entrance requirements:* For master's and doctorate, GRE General Test, minimum GPA of 3.0. Additional exam requirements/recommendations for international students: Required—TOEFL. *Faculty research:* Biochemical endocrinology, neurobiology, molecular biology, reproductive biology, biology of developing systems.

Thomas Jefferson University, Jefferson College of Graduate Studies, MS Program in Cell and Developmental Biology, Philadelphia, PA 19107. Offers MS. Part-time and evening/weekend programs available. *Faculty:* 19 full-time (6 women). *Students:* 9 part-time (8 women); includes 2 minority (1 Black or African American, non-Hispanic/Latino; 1 Asian, non-Hispanic/Latino), 1 international. 14 applicants, 50% accepted, 7 enrolled. In 2010, 3 master's awarded. *Degree requirements:* For master's, thesis, clerkship. *Entrance requirements:* For master's, GRE General Test or MCAT, minimum GPA of 3.0. Additional exam requirements/recommendations for international students: Required—TOEFL (minimum score 250 computer-based; 100 iBT) or IELTS. *Application deadline:* For fall admission, 8/1 priority date for domestic students, 3/1 priority date for international students; for winter admission, 12/1 priority date for domestic students, 6/1 priority date for international students; for spring admission, 4/1 priority date for domestic students. Applications are processed on a rolling basis. Application fee: $50. Electronic applications accepted. *Financial support:* In 2010–11, 4 students received support. Federal Work-Study and institutionally sponsored loans available. Support available to part-time students. Financial award application deadline: 5/1; financial award applicants required to submit FAFSA. *Unit head:* Dr. Gerald B. Grunwald, Dean and Program Director, 215-503-4191, Fax: 215-503-6690, E-mail: gerald.grunwald@jefferson.edu. *Application contact:* Eleanor M. Gorman, Assistant Coordinator, Graduate Center Programs, 215-503-5799, Fax: 215-503-3433, E-mail: eleanor.gorman@jefferson.edu.

Thomas Jefferson University, Jefferson College of Graduate Studies, PhD Program in Cell and Developmental Biology, Philadelphia, PA 19107. Offers PhD. *Faculty:* 57 full-time (13 women). *Students:* 24 full-time (11 women); includes 1 minority (Black or African American, non-Hispanic/Latino), 4 international. 27 applicants, 41% accepted, 6 enrolled. In 2010, 6 doctorates awarded. *Degree requirements:* For doctorate, comprehensive exam, thesis/dissertation. *Entrance requirements:* For doctorate, GRE General Test, minimum GPA of 3.2. Additional exam requirements/recommendations for international students: Required—TOEFL (minimum score 250 computer-based; 100 iBT). *Application deadline:* For fall admission, 1/5 priority date for domestic and international students. Applications are processed on a rolling basis. Application fee: $50. Electronic applications accepted. *Financial support:* In 2010–11, 24 students received support, including 24 fellowships with full tuition reimbursements available (averaging $54,723 per year); Federal Work-Study, institutionally sponsored loans, scholarships/grants, traineeships, and stipends also available. Support available to part-time students. Financial award application deadline: 5/1; financial award applicants required to submit FAFSA. Total annual research expenditures: $35.5 million. *Unit head:* Dr. Theodore F. Taraschi, Program Director, 215-503-5020, Fax: 215-503-0206, E-mail: theodore.taraschi@jefferson.edu. *Application contact:* Marc E. Stearns, Director of Admissions, 215-503-0155, Fax: 215-503-9920, E-mail: jcgs-info@jefferson.edu.

Tufts University, Sackler School of Graduate Biomedical Sciences, Integrated Studies Program, Medford, MA 02155. Offers PhD. *Students:* 10 full-time (7 women); includes 1 Asian, non-Hispanic/Latino, 2 international. Average age 25. 333 applicants, 6% accepted. *Entrance requirements:* For doctorate, GRE General Test, 3 letters of reference. Additional exam requirements/recommendations for international students: Required—TOEFL. *Application deadline:* For fall admission, 12/15 for domestic and international students. Applications are processed on a rolling basis. Application fee: $70. Electronic applications accepted. *Expenses:* Tuition: Full-time $39,624; part-time $3962 per course. Required fees: $40 per year. Full-time tuition and fees vary according to degree level, program and student level. Part-time tuition and fees vary according to course load. *Financial support:* In 2010–11, 10 students received support, including 10 research assistantships with tuition reimbursements available (averaging $28,250 per year); scholarships/grants and health care benefits also available. *Unit head:* Dr. Karina Meiri, Program Director, 617-636-6707, E-mail: james.dice@tufts.edu. *Application contact:* Kellie Johnston, Associate Director of Admissions, 617-636-6767, Fax: 617-636-0375, E-mail: sackler-school@tufts.edu.

Tufts University, Sackler School of Graduate Biomedical Sciences, Program in Cell, Molecular and Developmental Biology, Medford, MA 02155. Offers PhD. *Faculty:* 35 full-time (11 women). *Students:* 25 full-time (13 women); includes 2 Asian, non-Hispanic/Latino, 2 international. Average age 29. In 2010, 8 doctorates awarded. Terminal master's awarded for partial completion of doctoral program. *Degree requirements:* For doctorate, thesis/dissertation. *Entrance requirements:* For doctorate, GRE General Test, 3 letters of reference. Additional exam requirements/recommendations for international students: Required—TOEFL. *Application deadline:* For fall admission, 12/15 for domestic and international students. Applications are processed on a rolling basis. Application fee: $70. Electronic applications accepted. *Expenses:* Tuition: Full-time $39,624; part-time $3962 per course. Required fees: $40 per year. Full-time tuition and fees vary according to degree level, program and student level. Part-time tuition and fees vary according to course load. *Financial support:* In 2010–11, 25 students received support, including 25 research assistantships with full tuition reimbursements available (averaging $28,500 per year); fellowships, scholarships/grants, health care benefits, and tuition waivers (full) also available. *Faculty research:* Reproduction and hormone action, control of gene expression, cell-matrix and cell-cell interactions, growth control and tumorigenesis, cytoskeleton and contractile proteins. *Unit head:* Dr. John Castellot, Program Director, 617-636-0303, Fax: 617-636-0375, E-mail: john.castellot@tufts.edu. *Application contact:* Kellie Johnston, Associate Director of Admissions, 617-636-6767, Fax: 617-636-0375, E-mail: sackler-school@tufts.edu.

Cell Biology

Tulane University, School of Medicine and School of Liberal Arts, Graduate Programs in Biomedical Sciences, Department of Structural and Cellular Biology, New Orleans, LA 70118-5669. Offers MS, PhD, MD/PhD. MS and PhD offered through the Graduate School. *Degree requirements:* For master's, one foreign language, thesis; for doctorate, 2 foreign languages, thesis/dissertation. *Entrance requirements:* For master's, GRE General Test, minimum B average in undergraduate course work; for doctorate, GRE General Test. Additional exam requirements/recommendations for international students: Required—TOEFL. Electronic applications accepted. *Faculty research:* Reproductive endocrinology, visual neuroscience, neural response to altered hormones.

Tulane University, School of Medicine and School of Liberal Arts, Graduate Programs in Biomedical Sciences, Interdisciplinary Graduate Program in Molecular and Cellular Biology, New Orleans, LA 70118-5669. Offers PhD, MD/PhD. PhD offered through the Graduate School. *Degree requirements:* For doctorate, thesis/dissertation. *Entrance requirements:* For doctorate, GRE General Test, GRE Subject Test. Additional exam requirements/recommendations for international students: Required—TOEFL. Electronic applications accepted. *Faculty research:* Developmental biology, neuroscience, virology.

Tulane University, School of Science and Engineering, Department of Cell and Molecular Biology, New Orleans, LA 70118-5669. Offers MS, PhD. Terminal master's awarded for partial completion of doctoral program. *Degree requirements:* For doctorate, thesis/dissertation. *Entrance requirements:* For master's, GRE General Test, minimum B average in undergraduate course work; for doctorate, GRE General Test. Additional exam requirements/recommendations for international students: Required—TOEFL. Electronic applications accepted.

Uniformed Services University of the Health Sciences, School of Medicine, Graduate Programs in the Biomedical Sciences and Public Health, Graduate Program in Molecular and Cell Biology, Bethesda, MD 20814-4799. Offers PhD. *Faculty:* 43 full-time (11 women), 3 part-time/adjunct (0 women). *Students:* 22 full-time (11 women); includes 5 Asian, non-Hispanic/Latino; 5 Hispanic/Latino, 6 international. Average age 26. 30 applicants, 43% accepted, 8 enrolled. In 2010, 2 doctorates awarded. *Degree requirements:* For doctorate, comprehensive exam, thesis/dissertation, qualifying exam. *Entrance requirements:* For doctorate, GRE General Test, minimum GPA of 3.0. Additional exam requirements/recommendations for international students: Required—TOEFL. *Application deadline:* For fall admission, 1/1 priority date for domestic and international students. Applications are processed on a rolling basis. Application fee: $0. Electronic applications accepted. *Financial support:* In 2010–11, fellowships with full tuition reimbursements (averaging $27,000 per year); scholarships/grants, health care benefits, and tuition waivers (full) also available. *Faculty research:* Immunology, biochemistry, cancer biology, stem cell biology. *Unit head:* Dr. Mary Lou Cutler, Graduate Program Director, 301-295-3453, Fax: 301-295-1996. *Application contact:* Tina Finley, Graduate Program Coordinator, 301-295-3642, Fax: 301-295-1996, E-mail: nfinley@usuhs.mil.

See Display on page 208 and Close-Up on page 227.

Universidad Central del Caribe, School of Medicine, Program in Biomedical Sciences, Bayamón, PR 00960-6032. Offers anatomy and cell biology (MA, MS); biochemistry (MS); biomedical sciences (MA); cellular and molecular biology (PhD); microbiology and immunology (MA, MS); pharmacology (MS); physiology (MS).

Université de Montréal, Faculty of Medicine, Department of Pathology and Cellular Biology, Montréal, QC H3C 3J7, Canada. Offers M Sc, PhD. Terminal master's awarded for partial completion of doctoral program. *Degree requirements:* For master's, thesis; for doctorate, thesis/dissertation, general exam. *Entrance requirements:* For master's and doctorate, proficiency in French, knowledge of English. Electronic applications accepted. *Faculty research:* Immunopathology, cardiovascular pathology, oncogenetics, cellular neurocytology, muscular dystrophy.

Université de Sherbrooke, Faculty of Medicine and Health Sciences, Graduate Programs in Medicine, Department of Anatomy and Cell Biology, Sherbrooke, QC J1H 5N4, Canada. Offers cell biology (M Sc, PhD). Terminal master's awarded for partial completion of doctoral program. *Degree requirements:* For master's, thesis; for doctorate, thesis/dissertation. Electronic applications accepted. *Faculty research:* Biology of the gut epithelium, signal transduction, gene expression and differentiation, intestinal inflammation, vascular and skeletal muscle cell biology.

Université Laval, Faculty of Medicine, Graduate Programs in Medicine, Programs in Cellular and Molecular Biology, Québec, QC G1K 7P4, Canada. Offers M Sc, PhD. Terminal master's awarded for partial completion of doctoral program. *Degree requirements:* For master's, thesis; for doctorate, comprehensive exam, thesis/dissertation. *Entrance requirements:* For master's and doctorate, knowledge of French, comprehension of written English. Electronic applications accepted. *Faculty research:* Oral bacterial metabolism, sugar transport.

University at Albany, State University of New York, College of Arts and Sciences, Department of Biological Sciences, Specialization in Molecular, Cellular, Developmental, and Neural Biology, Albany, NY 12222-0001. Offers MS, PhD. *Degree requirements:* For master's, one foreign language; for doctorate, one foreign language, thesis/dissertation. *Entrance requirements:* For master's and doctorate, GRE General Test.

University at Albany, State University of New York, School of Public Health, Department of Biomedical Sciences, Program in Cell and Molecular Structure, Albany, NY 12222-0001. Offers MS, PhD. *Degree requirements:* For master's, thesis; for doctorate, thesis/dissertation. *Entrance requirements:* For master's and doctorate, GRE General Test, GRE Subject Test.

University at Buffalo, the State University of New York, Graduate School, Graduate Programs in Cancer Research and Biomedical Sciences at Roswell Park Cancer Institute, Department of Cellular and Molecular Biology at Roswell Park Cancer Institute, Buffalo, NY 14260. Offers cellular molecular biology/genetics (PhD). *Faculty:* 26 full-time (6 women). *Students:* 22 full-time (12 women); includes 4 minority (1 Black or African American, non-Hispanic/Latino; 1 Asian, non-Hispanic/Latino; 2 Native Hawaiian or other Pacific Islander, non-Hispanic/Latino), 2 international. Average age 25. 45 applicants, 13% accepted, 4 enrolled. In 2010, 1 doctorate awarded. *Degree requirements:* For doctorate, thesis/dissertation, exam, project. *Entrance requirements:* For doctorate, GRE General Test, minimum B average in undergraduate coursework. Additional exam requirements/recommendations for international students: Required—TOEFL, TOEFL (minimum score 600 paper-based; 250 computer-based; 100 iBT) or IELTS. *Application deadline:* For winter admission, 12/30 priority date for domestic and international students. Applications are processed on a rolling basis. Application fee: $55. Electronic applications accepted. *Financial support:* In 2010–11, 22 students received support, including 4 fellowships with full tuition reimbursements available (averaging $24,000 per year), 17 research assistantships with full tuition reimbursements available (averaging $24,000 per year); health care benefits also available. Financial award application deadline: 2/1; financial award applicants required to submit FAFSA. *Faculty research:* Cancer genetics, chromatin structure and replication, regulation of transcription, human gene mapping, genetic and structural approaches to regulation of gene expression. Total annual research expenditures: $5.5 million. *Unit head:* Dr. Dominic James Smiraglia, Director of Graduate Studies, 716-845-1347, Fax: 716-845-1698, E-mail: dominic.smiraglia@roswellpark.org. *Application contact:* Craig R. Johnson, Director of Admissions, 716-845-3063, Fax: 716-845-8178, E-mail: craig.johnson@roswellpark.org.

The University of Alabama at Birmingham, Graduate Programs in Joint Health Sciences, Program in Cell Biology, Birmingham, AL 35294. Offers PhD. *Students:* 41 full-time (20 women), 3 part-time (0 women); includes 6 minority (3 Black or African American, non-Hispanic/Latino; 1 American Indian or Alaska Native, non-Hispanic/Latino; 1 Asian, non-Hispanic/Latino; 1 Hispanic/Latino), 19 international. Average age 29. In 2010, 16 doctorates awarded. *Degree requirements:* For doctorate, variable foreign language requirement, thesis/dissertation, qualifying exam. *Entrance requirements:* For doctorate, GRE General Test, interview. *Application deadline:* Applications are processed on a rolling basis. Electronic applications accepted. *Expenses:* Tuition, state resident: full-time $5482. Tuition, nonresident: full-time $12,430. Tuition and fees vary according to program. *Financial support:* In 2010–11, 4 fellowships were awarded. *Unit head:* Dr. Etty Benveniste, Chair, 205-934-7667, Fax: 205-975-6748. *Application contact:* Information Contact, 205-975-7145, Fax: 205-975-6748.

The University of Alabama at Birmingham, Graduate Programs in Joint Health Sciences, Program in Cellular and Molecular Physiology, Birmingham, AL 35294. Offers PhD. *Students:* 15 full-time (3 women), 1 part-time (0 women); includes 2 minority (1 Black or African American, non-Hispanic/Latino; 1 Hispanic/Latino), 3 international. Average age 28. In 2010, 8 doctorates awarded. Application fee: $35 ($60 for international students). *Expenses:* Tuition, state resident: full-time $5482. Tuition, nonresident: full-time $12,430. Tuition and fees vary according to program. *Unit head:* Dr. Ray L. Watts, Vice President/Dean, School of Medicine, 205-934-1111, Fax: 205-943-0333. *Application contact:* Julie Bryant, Director of Graduate Admissions, 205-934-8227, Fax: 205-934-8413, E-mail: jbryant@uab.edu.

University of Alberta, Faculty of Graduate Studies and Research, Department of Biological Sciences, Edmonton, AB T6G 2E1, Canada. Offers environmental biology and ecology (M Sc, PhD); microbiology and biotechnology (M Sc, PhD); molecular biology and genetics (M Sc, PhD); physiology and cell biology (M Sc, PhD); plant biology (M Sc, PhD); systematics and evolution (M Sc, PhD). Terminal master's awarded for partial completion of doctoral program. *Degree requirements:* For master's, thesis; for doctorate, thesis/dissertation. *Entrance requirements:* Additional exam requirements/recommendations for international students: Required—TOEFL.

University of Alberta, Faculty of Medicine and Dentistry and Faculty of Graduate Studies and Research, Graduate Programs in Medicine, Department of Cell Biology, Edmonton, AB T6G 2E1, Canada. Offers cell and molecular biology (M Sc, PhD). Terminal master's awarded for partial completion of doctoral program. *Degree requirements:* For master's, thesis; for doctorate, thesis/dissertation. *Entrance requirements:* For master's and doctorate, 3 letters of reference, curriculum vitae. Additional exam requirements/recommendations for international students: Required—TOEFL (minimum score 600 paper-based; 250 computer-based). *Faculty research:* Protein targeting, membrane trafficking, signal transduction, cell growth and division, cell-cell interaction and development.

The University of Arizona, College of Medicine, Department of Cell Biology and Anatomy, Tucson, AZ 85721. Offers PhD. *Faculty:* 14 full-time (3 women), 3 part-time/adjunct (1 woman). *Students:* 19 full-time (11 women), 2 part-time (1 woman); includes 8 minority (2 Black or African American, non-Hispanic/Latino; 1 Asian, non-Hispanic/Latino; 2 Hispanic/Latino; 3 Two or more races, non-Hispanic/Latino), 2 international. Average age 29. 30 applicants, 10% accepted. In 2010, 1 doctorate awarded. *Degree requirements:* For doctorate, thesis/dissertation. *Entrance requirements:* For doctorate, GRE General Test. *Application deadline:* For fall admission, 1/15 priority date for domestic students. Application fee: $45. *Expenses:* Tuition, state resident: full-time $7692. *Financial support:* In 2010–11, 11 research assistantships with partial tuition reimbursements (averaging $23,611 per year) were awarded; fellowships with full and partial tuition reimbursements, teaching assistantships, institutionally sponsored loans, scholarships/grants, traineeships, tuition waivers (full), and unspecified assistantships also available. Support available to part-time students. Financial award application deadline: 1/15. *Faculty research:* Heart development, neural development, cellular toxicology and microcirculation; membrane traffic and cytoskeleton; cell-surface receptors. Total annual research expenditures: $1.7 million. *Unit head:* Dr. Robert S. McCuskey, Head, 520-626-6084, Fax: 520-626-2097, E-mail: mccuskey@u.arizona.edu. *Application contact:* Dr. Jean M. Wilson, Chairperson, Graduate Studies Committee, 520-626-2553, Fax: 520-626-2097.

The University of Arizona, College of Science, Department of Molecular and Cellular Biology, Tucson, AZ 85721. Offers applied biosciences (PSM); molecular and cellular biology (MS, PhD). Evening/weekend programs available. *Faculty:* 12 full-time (4 women), 2 part-time/adjunct (1 woman). *Students:* 23 full-time (10 women), 3 part-time (1 woman); includes 2 Hispanic/Latino; 5 Two or more races, non-Hispanic/Latino, 4 international. Average age 31. 160 applicants, 11% accepted, 9 enrolled. In 2010, 10 master's, 10 doctorates awarded. Terminal master's awarded for partial completion of doctoral program. *Degree requirements:* For master's, thesis; for doctorate, thesis/dissertation. *Entrance requirements:* For master's, 3 letters of recommendation; for doctorate, 3 letters of recommendation, statement of purpose. Additional exam requirements/recommendations for international students: Required—TOEFL (minimum score 600 paper-based; 250 computer-based; 90 iBT), IELTS (minimum score 7). *Application deadline:* For fall admission, 1/1 for domestic and international students. Applications are processed on a rolling basis. Application fee: $75. Electronic applications accepted. *Expenses:* Tuition, state resident: full-time $7692. *Financial support:* In 2010–11, 14 research assistantships with full tuition reimbursements (averaging $23,390 per year), 8 teaching assistantships with full tuition reimbursements (averaging $22,929 per year) were awarded; career-related internships or fieldwork, scholarships/grants, health care benefits, and unspecified assistantships also available. *Faculty research:* Plant molecular biology, cellular and molecular aspects of development, genetics of bacteria and lower eukaryotes. Total annual research expenditures: $7 million. *Unit head:* Kathleen Dixon, Department Head, 520-621-7563, Fax: 520-621-3709, E-mail: dixonk@email.arizona.edu. *Application contact:* Kathleen Dixon, Department Head, 520-621-7563, Fax: 520-621-3709, E-mail: dixonk@email.arizona.edu.

University of Arkansas, Graduate School, Interdisciplinary Program in Cell and Molecular Biology, Fayetteville, AR 72701-1201. Offers MS, PhD. *Students:* 16 full-time (8 women), 42 part-time (26 women); includes 3 minority (all Asian, non-Hispanic/Latino), 41 international. 28 applicants, 21% accepted. In 2010, 1 master's, 6 doctorates awarded. *Degree requirements:* For doctorate, thesis/dissertation. *Application deadline:* For fall admission, 4/1 for international students; for spring admission, 10/1 for international students. Applications are processed on a rolling basis. Application fee: $40 ($50 for international students). Electronic applications accepted. *Financial support:* In 2010–11, 4 fellowships with tuition reimbursements, 33 research assistantships, 10 teaching assistantships were awarded. Financial award application deadline: 4/1; financial award applicants required to submit FAFSA. *Unit head:* Dr. Douglas Rhoads, Head, 479-575-7396, Fax: 479-575-5908, E-mail: drhoads@uark.edu. *Application contact:* Graduate Admissions, 479-575-6246, Fax: 479-575-5908, E-mail: gradinfo@uark.edu.

The University of British Columbia, Faculty of Medicine, Department of Cellular and Physiological Sciences, Division of Anatomy and Cell Biology, Vancouver, BC V6T 1Z1, Canada. Offers M Sc, PhD. *Degree requirements:* For master's, thesis, oral defense; for doctorate, comprehensive exam, thesis/dissertation, oral defense. *Entrance requirements:* Additional exam requirements/recommendations for international students: Required—TOEFL (minimum score 550 paper-based; 213 computer-based), IELTS (minimum score 6.2). Electronic applications accepted. Tuition charges are reported in Canadian dollars. *Expenses:* Tuition, area resident: Full-time $4179 Canadian dollars. International tuition: $7344 Canadian dollars full-time. *Faculty research:* Cell and developmental biology, membrane biophysics, cellular immunology, cancer, fetal alcohol syndrome.

University of California, Berkeley, Graduate Division, College of Letters and Science, Department of Molecular and Cell Biology, Berkeley, CA 94720-1500. Offers PhD. *Degree requirements:* For doctorate, comprehensive exam, thesis/dissertation, qualifying exam, 2 semesters of teaching, 3 seminars. *Entrance requirements:* For doctorate, GRE General Test, GRE Subject Test (recommended), minimum GPA of 3.0. Additional exam requirements/recommendations for international students: Required—TOEFL (minimum score 570 paper-based; 230 computer-based; 68 iBT), IELTS (minimum score 7). Electronic applications accepted. *Faculty research:* Biochemistry and molecular biology, cell and developmental biology, genetics, immunology, neurobiology, genomics.

University of California, Davis, Graduate Studies, Graduate Group in Cell and Developmental Biology, Davis, CA 95616. Offers MS, PhD. *Degree requirements:* For master's, comprehensive exam (for some programs), thesis (for some programs); for doctorate, thesis/dissertation. *Entrance requirements:* For doctorate, GRE General Test, GRE Subject Test. Additional exam requirements/recommendations for international students: Required—TOEFL (minimum score 550 paper-based; 213 computer-based). Electronic applications accepted. *Faculty research:* Molecular basis of cell function and development.

University of California, Irvine, School of Biological Sciences, Department of Developmental and Cell Biology, Irvine, CA 92697. Offers biological sciences (MS, PhD). Students apply through the Graduate Program in Molecular Biology, Genetics, and Biochemistry. *Students:* 40 full-time (20 women); includes 21 minority (1 Black or African American, non-Hispanic/Latino; 1 American Indian or Alaska Native, non-Hispanic/Latino; 11 Asian, non-Hispanic/Latino; 8 Hispanic/Latino), 3 international. Average age 28. 1 applicant, 100% accepted, 1 enrolled. In 2010, 3 master's, 14 doctorates awarded. *Degree requirements:* For doctorate, thesis/dissertation. *Entrance requirements:* For master's and doctorate, GRE General Test, GRE Subject Test, minimum GPA of 3.0. Additional exam requirements/recommendations for international students: Required—TOEFL (minimum score 550 paper-based; 213 computer-based). *Application deadline:* For fall admission, 12/15 priority date for domestic and international students. Application fee: $80 ($100 for international students). Electronic applications accepted. *Financial support:* Fellowships, research assistantships with full tuition reimbursements, teaching assistantships, institutionally sponsored loans, traineeships, health care benefits, and unspecified assistantships available. Financial award application deadline: 3/1; financial award applicants required to submit FAFSA. *Faculty research:* Genetics and development, oncogene signaling pathways, gene regulation, tissue regeneration and molecular genetics. *Unit head:* Prof. Ken W. Cho, Chair, 949-824-7950, Fax: 949-824-4709, E-mail: kwcho@uci.edu. *Application contact:* Renee Marie Frigo, Program Manager, 949-824-8145, Fax: 949-824-1965, E-mail: rfrigo@uci.edu.

University of California, Irvine, School of Biological Sciences and School of Medicine, Graduate Program in Cellular and Molecular Biosciences, Irvine, CA 92697. Offers PhD. *Degree requirements:* For doctorate, thesis/dissertation, teaching assignment, preliminary exam. *Entrance requirements:* For doctorate, GRE General Test, minimum GPA of 3.0, research experience. Additional exam requirements/recommendations for international students: Required—TOEFL, IELTS, SPEAK test. Electronic applications accepted. *Expenses:* Contact institution. *Faculty research:* Cellular biochemistry; gene structure and expression; protein structure, function, and design; molecular genetics; pathogenesis and inherited disease.

University of California, Los Angeles, David Geffen School of Medicine and Graduate Division, Graduate Programs in Medicine, Department of Neurobiology, Los Angeles, CA 90095. Offers anatomy and cell biology (PhD). *Faculty:* 21 full-time (0 women). *Students:* 14 full-time (7 women); includes 4 minority (2 Asian, non-Hispanic/Latino; 2 Hispanic/Latino), 1 international. Average age 28. In 2010, 1 doctorate awarded. *Degree requirements:* For doctorate, thesis/dissertation, oral and written qualifying exams. *Entrance requirements:* For doctorate, GRE General Test, GRE Subject Test, bachelor's degree in physical or biological science. Application fee: $70 ($90 for international students). Electronic applications accepted. *Financial support:* In 2010–11, 15 fellowships, 10 research assistantships, 8 teaching assistantships were awarded; Federal Work-Study, institutionally sponsored loans, scholarships/grants, and tuition waivers (full and partial) also available. Financial award application deadline: 3/1. *Faculty research:* Neuroendocrinology, neurophysiology. *Unit head:* Dr. Marie-Francoise Chesselet, Chair, 310-267-1781, Fax: 310-267-1786, E-mail: mchesselet@mednet.ucla.edu. *Application contact:* UCLA Access Coordinator, 310-206-1845, Fax: 310-206-1636, E-mail: uclaaccess@mednet.ucla.edu.

University of California, Los Angeles, Graduate Division, College of Letters and Science, Department of Molecular, Cell and Developmental Biology, Los Angeles, CA 90095. Offers PhD. *Faculty:* 6 full-time (1 woman). *Students:* 34 full-time (20 women); includes 12 minority (3 Black or African American, non-Hispanic/Latino; 6 Asian, non-Hispanic/Latino; 3 Hispanic/Latino), 6 international. Average age 27. 3 applicants, 67% accepted, 2 enrolled. In 2010, 4 doctorates awarded. *Degree requirements:* For doctorate, thesis/dissertation, qualifying exams. *Entrance requirements:* For doctorate, GRE General Test, GRE Subject Test. Additional exam requirements/recommendations for international students: Required—TOEFL. Application fee: $70 ($90 for international students). Electronic applications accepted. *Financial support:* In 2010–11, 26 fellowships, 26 research assistantships, 14 teaching assistantships were awarded; scholarships/grants, traineeships, and unspecified assistantships also available. Financial award application deadline: 3/1. *Unit head:* Dr. Utpal Banerjee, Chair, 310-206-5439, Fax: 310-206-3987, E-mail: banerjee@mbi.ucla.edu. *Application contact:* UCLA Access Coordinator, 310-206-1845, Fax: 310-206-1636, E-mail: uclaaccess@mednet.ucla.edu.

University of California, Los Angeles, Graduate Division, College of Letters and Science and David Geffen School of Medicine, UCLA ACCESS to Programs in the Molecular, Cellular and Integrative Life Sciences, Los Angeles, CA 90095. Offers biochemistry and molecular biology (PhD); biological chemistry (PhD); cellular and molecular pathology (PhD); human genetics (PhD); microbiology, immunology, and molecular genetics (PhD); molecular biology (PhD); molecular toxicology (PhD); molecular, cellular and integrative physiology (PhD); neurobiology (PhD); oral biology (PhD); physiology (PhD). ACCESS is an umbrella program for first-year coursework in 12 PhD programs. *Students:* 48 full-time (28 women), 6 international. Average age 24. 388 applicants, 27% accepted, 48 enrolled. *Degree requirements:* For doctorate, thesis/dissertation, oral and written qualifying exams. *Entrance requirements:* For doctorate, GRE General Test, minimum undergraduate GPA of 3.0. Additional exam requirements/recommendations for international students: Required—TOEFL. *Application deadline:* For fall admission, 12/15 for domestic and international students. Application fee: $70 ($90 for international students). Electronic applications accepted. *Financial support:* In 2010–11, 31 fellowships with full and partial tuition reimbursements, 13 research assistantships with full and partial tuition reimbursements, 2 teaching assistantships with full and partial tuition reimbursements were awarded; Federal Work-Study, institutionally sponsored loans, scholarships/grants, health care benefits, tuition waivers (full and partial), and unspecified assistantships also available. Financial award application deadline: 3/1; financial award applicants required to submit FAFSA. *Faculty research:* Molecular, cellular, and developmental biology; immunology; microbiology; integrative biology. *Unit head:* Jody Spillane, Project Coordinator, 310-206-1845, E-mail: jspillane@mednet.ucla.edu. *Application contact:* UCLA Access Admissions, 310-206-1845, E-mail: uclaaccess@mednet.ucla.edu.

University of California, Riverside, Graduate Division, Program in Cell, Molecular, and Developmental Biology, Riverside, CA 92521-0102. Offers MS, PhD. Terminal master's awarded for partial completion of doctoral program. *Degree requirements:* For master's, thesis, oral defense of thesis; for doctorate, thesis/dissertation, oral defense of thesis, qualifying exams, 2 quarters of teaching experience. *Entrance requirements:* For master's and doctorate, GRE General Test, minimum GPA of 3.2. Additional exam requirements/recommendations for international students: Required—TOEFL (minimum score 550 paper-based; 213 computer-based; 80 iBT). Electronic applications accepted.

University of California, San Diego, Office of Graduate Studies, Division of Biological Sciences, Program in Cell and Developmental Biology, La Jolla, CA 92093-0348. Offers PhD. Offered in association with the Salk Institute. *Degree requirements:* For doctorate, thesis/dissertation, qualifying exam. Electronic applications accepted.

University of California, San Diego, Office of Graduate Studies, Division of Biological Sciences, Program in Molecular and Cellular Biology, La Jolla, CA 92093. Offers PhD. Offered in association with the Salk Institute. *Degree requirements:* For doctorate, thesis/dissertation, qualifying exam. Electronic applications accepted.

University of California, San Diego, School of Medicine and Office of Graduate Studies, Graduate Studies in Biomedical Sciences, Program in Molecular Cell Biology, La Jolla, CA 92093. Offers PhD. *Degree requirements:* For doctorate, thesis/dissertation, qualifying exam. *Entrance requirements:* For doctorate, GRE General Test. Additional exam requirements/recommendations for international students: Required—TOEFL. Electronic applications accepted. *Faculty research:* Molecular and cellular pharmacology, cell and organ physiology.

University of California, San Diego, School of Medicine and Office of Graduate Studies, Graduate Studies in Biomedical Sciences, Regulatory Biology Program, La Jolla, CA 92093. Offers PhD. *Degree requirements:* For doctorate, thesis/dissertation, 2 qualifying exams. *Entrance requirements:* For doctorate, GRE General Test, GRE Subject Test. Additional exam requirements/recommendations for international students: Required—TOEFL. Electronic applications accepted. *Faculty research:* Eukaryotic regulatory and molecular biology, molecular and cellular pharmacology, cell and organ physiology.

University of California, San Francisco, Graduate Division and School of Medicine, Department of Biochemistry and Biophysics, Program in Cell Biology, San Francisco, CA 94143. Offers PhD, MD/PhD. *Degree requirements:* For doctorate, thesis/dissertation. *Entrance requirements:* For doctorate, GRE General Test, GRE Subject Test. Additional exam requirements/recommendations for international students: Required—TOEFL. *Expenses:* Contact institution.

University of California, Santa Barbara, Graduate Division, College of Letters and Sciences, Division of Mathematics, Life, and Physical Sciences, Department of Molecular, Cellular, and Developmental Biology, Santa Barbara, CA 93106-9625. Offers MA, PhD, MA/PhD. *Faculty:* 21 full-time (3 women), 7 part-time/adjunct (2 women). *Students:* 57 full-time (35 women); includes 1 Black or African American, non-Hispanic/Latino; 6 Asian, non-Hispanic/Latino; 3 Hispanic/Latino. Average age 28. 64 applicants, 41% accepted, 14 enrolled. In 2010, 8 master's, 7 doctorates awarded. *Degree requirements:* For master's, comprehensive exam (for some programs), thesis (for some programs); for doctorate, comprehensive exam, thesis/dissertation. *Entrance requirements:* For master's, GRE General Test, GRE Subject Test, 3 letters of recommendation, resume/curriculum vitae; for doctorate, GRE General Test, GRE Subject Test, 3 letters of recommendation, statement of purpose, personal achievements/contributions statement, resume/curriculum vitae, transcripts for post-secondary institutions attended. Additional exam requirements/recommendations for international students: Required—TOEFL (minimum score 610 paper-based; 102 iBT), IELTS (minimum score 7). *Application deadline:* For fall admission, 12/15 for domestic and international students. Application fee: $70 ($90 for international students). Electronic applications accepted. *Financial support:* In 2010–11, 55 students received support, including 13 fellowships with full and partial tuition reimbursements available (averaging $6,150 per year), 37 research assistantships with full and partial tuition reimbursements available (averaging $14,365 per year), 44 teaching assistantships with partial tuition reimbursements available (averaging $10,340 per year); career-related internships or fieldwork, Federal Work-Study, institutionally sponsored loans, scholarships/grants, traineeships, health care benefits, and unspecified assistantships also available. Financial award application deadline: 12/15; financial award applicants required to submit FAFSA. *Faculty research:* Microbiology, neurobiology (including stem cell research), developmental, virology, cell biology. *Unit head:* Dr. Dennis O. Clegg, Chair, 805-893-8490, Fax: 805-893-4724, E-mail: clegg@lifesci.ucsb.edu. *Application contact:* Nicole McCoy, Graduate Program Advisor, 805-893-8499, Fax: 805-893-4724, E-mail: nicole.mccoy@lifesci.ucsb.edu.

University of California, Santa Cruz, Division of Graduate Studies, Division of Physical and Biological Sciences, Program in Molecular, Cellular, and Developmental Biology, Santa Cruz, CA 95064. Offers MA, PhD. *Students:* 51 full-time (24 women); includes 9 minority (1 Black or African American, non-Hispanic/Latino; 4 Asian, non-Hispanic/Latino; 2 Hispanic/Latino; 1 Native Hawaiian or other Pacific Islander, non-Hispanic/Latino; 1 Two or more races, non-Hispanic/Latino), 4 international. Average age 28. 137 applicants, 21% accepted, 15 enrolled. In 2010, 5 doctorates awarded. Terminal master's awarded for partial completion of doctoral program. *Degree requirements:* For master's, thesis; for doctorate, thesis/dissertation, qualifying exam. *Entrance requirements:* For master's and doctorate, GRE General Test, 3 letters of recommendation, interview. Additional exam requirements/recommendations for international students: Required—TOEFL (minimum score 550 paper-based; 220 computer-based; 83 iBT); Recommended—IELTS (minimum score 8). *Application deadline:* For fall admission, 12/3 for domestic and international students. Application fee: $70 ($90 for international students). Electronic applications accepted. *Financial support:* Fellowships, research assistantships, teaching assistantships, institutionally sponsored loans and tuition waivers available. Financial award applicants required to submit FAFSA. *Faculty research:* RNA biology, chromatin and chromosome biology, neurobiology, stem cell biology and differentiation, cell structure and function. *Unit head:* Teel Lopez, Graduate Program Coordinator, 831-459-2385, E-mail: tablack@ucsc.edu. *Application contact:* Teel Lopez, Graduate Program Coordinator, 831-459-2385, E-mail: tablack@ucsc.edu.

University of Chicago, Division of Biological Sciences, Molecular Biosciences Cluster, Graduate Program in Cell and Molecular Biology, Chicago, IL 60637-1513. Offers PhD. *Degree requirements:* For doctorate, thesis/dissertation, ethics class, 2 teaching assistantships. *Entrance requirements:* For doctorate, GRE General Test. Additional exam requirements/recommendations for international students: Required—TOEFL (minimum score 600 paper-based; 250 computer-based; 104 iBT), IELTS (minimum score 7). Electronic applications accepted. *Faculty research:* Gene expression, chromosome structure, animal viruses, plant molecular genetics.

University of Cincinnati, Graduate School, College of Medicine, Graduate Programs in Biomedical Sciences, Graduate Program in Cell and Cancer Biology, Cincinnati, OH 45221. Offers PhD. *Degree requirements:* For doctorate, thesis/dissertation, qualifying exam. *Entrance requirements:* For doctorate, GRE General Test. Additional exam requirements/recommendations for international students: Required—TOEFL. Electronic applications accepted. *Faculty research:* Cancer biology, cell and molecular biology, breast cancer, pancreatic cancer, drug discovery.

University of Colorado Boulder, Graduate School, College of Arts and Sciences, Department of Molecular, Cellular, and Developmental Biology, Boulder, CO 80309. Offers cellular structure and function (MA, PhD); developmental biology (MA, PhD); molecular biology (MA, PhD). *Faculty:* 27 full-time (7 women). *Students:* 72 full-time (37 women), 1 part-time (0 women); includes 5 minority (1 American Indian or Alaska Native, non-Hispanic/Latino; 1 Asian, non-Hispanic/Latino; 3 Hispanic/Latino), 15 international. Average age 28. 257 applicants, 9 enrolled. In 2010, 4 master's, 9 doctorates awarded. Terminal master's awarded for partial completion of doctoral program. *Degree requirements:* For master's, comprehensive exam, thesis or alternative; for doctorate, comprehensive exam, thesis/dissertation. *Entrance requirements:* For master's, GRE General Test, GRE Subject Test, minimum undergraduate GPA of 3.0; for doctorate, GRE General Test, GRE Subject Test. *Application deadline:* For fall admission, 1/1 for domestic students, 12/1 for international students. Application fee: $50 ($60 for international students). *Financial support:* In 2010–11, 40 fellowships (averaging $11,628 per year), 53 research assistantships (averaging $14,700 per year) were awarded; tuition waivers (full) also available. Financial award application deadline: 2/1. *Faculty research:* Molecular biology of RNA and DNA, molecular genetics, cell motility and cytoskeleton, cell membranes, developmental genetics, human genetics. Total annual research expenditures: $16.4 million.

University of Colorado Denver, School of Medicine, Program in Cell Biology, Stem Cells, and Developmental Biology, Denver, CO 80217-3364. Offers PhD. *Students:* 26 full-time (16 women); includes 1 Asian, non-Hispanic/Latino; 1 Hispanic/Latino, 6 international. Average age 27. 39 applicants, 5% accepted, 2 enrolled. In 2010, 1 doctorate awarded. *Degree requirements:* For doctorate, comprehensive exam, thesis/dissertation, at least 30 credit hours of coursework and 30 credit hours of thesis research; laboratory rotations. *Entrance requirements:* For doctorate, GRE, minimum GPA of 3.0; 3 letters of reference; prerequisite coursework in organic chemistry, biology, biochemistry, physics and calculus; research experience (highly recommended). Additional exam requirements/recommendations for international students: Required—TOEFL (minimum score 550 paper-based; 213 computer-based). *Application deadline:* For fall admission, 1/1 for domestic students. Application fee: $65. Electronic applications accepted. *Expenses:* Contact institution. *Financial support:* Fellowships, research assistantships, teaching assistantships, health care benefits, tuition waivers (full), and stipend available. Financial award application deadline: 3/15; financial award applicants required to submit FAFSA. *Faculty research:* Development and repair of the vertebrate nervous system; molecular, genetic and developmental mechanisms involved in the patterning of the

Cell Biology

University of Colorado Denver *(continued)*
early spinal cord (neural plate) during vertebrate embryogenesis; structural analysis of protein glycosylation using NMR and mass spectrometry; small RNAs and post-transcriptional gene regulation during nematode gametogenesis and early development; diabetes-mediated changes in cardiovascular gene expression and functional exercise capacity. Total annual research expenditures: $5.7 million. *Unit head:* Dr. Wendy Macklin, Department Chair, 303-724-3426, E-mail: wendy.macklin@ucdenver.edu. *Application contact:* Jennifer Thurston, Program Manager, 303-724-5902, Fax: 303-724-3420, E-mail: jennifer.thurston@ucdenver.edu.

University of Connecticut, Graduate School, College of Liberal Arts and Sciences, Department of Molecular and Cell Biology, Field of Cell and Developmental Biology, Storrs, CT 06269. Offers MS, PhD. *Degree requirements:* For doctorate, thesis/dissertation. *Entrance requirements:* For master's and doctorate, GRE General Test, GRE Subject Test. Additional exam requirements/recommendations for international students: Required—TOEFL (minimum score 550 paper-based; 213 computer-based). Electronic applications accepted.

University of Connecticut Health Center, Graduate School, Graduate Program in Cell Analysis and Modeling, Farmington, CT 06030. Offers PhD. *Students:* 1 (woman) full-time, 1 international. Average age 28. 216 applicants, 22% accepted. *Degree requirements:* For doctorate, comprehensive exam, thesis/dissertation. *Entrance requirements:* For doctorate, GRE General Test. Additional exam requirements/recommendations for international students: Required—TOEFL (minimum score 600 paper-based; 250 computer-based). *Application deadline:* For fall admission, 12/15 for domestic students. Electronic applications accepted. *Financial support:* In 2010–11, 1 student received support, including 1 research assistantship with full tuition reimbursement available (averaging $27,000 per year). *Unit head:* Dr. Charles Wolgemuth, Program Director, 860-679-1452, E-mail: cwolgemuth@uchc.edu. *Application contact:* Tricia Avolt, Graduate Admissions Coordinator, 860-679-2175, Fax: 860-679-1899, E-mail: robertson@nso2.uchc.edu.

See Display below and Close-Up on page 233.

University of Connecticut Health Center, Graduate School, Programs in Biomedical Sciences, Graduate Program in Cell Biology, Farmington, CT 06030. Offers PhD, DMD/PhD, MD/PhD. *Faculty:* 158. *Students:* 25 full-time (14 women); includes 2 minority (1 American Indian or Alaska Native, non-Hispanic/Latino; 1 Asian, non-Hispanic/Latino), 11 international. Average age 27. 216 applicants, 22% accepted. In 2010, 6 doctorates awarded. *Degree requirements:* For doctorate, comprehensive exam, thesis/dissertation. *Entrance requirements:* For doctorate, GRE General Test. Additional exam requirements/recommendations for international students: Required—TOEFL (minimum score 600 paper-based; 250 computer-based). *Application deadline:* For fall admission, 12/15 for domestic students. Application fee: $55. Electronic applications accepted. *Financial support:* In 2010–11, 24 research assistantships with full tuition reimbursements (averaging $27,000 per year) were awarded; health care benefits also available. *Faculty research:* Vascular biology, computational biology, cytoskeleton and molecular motors, reproductive biology, signal transduction. *Unit head:* Dr. Kevin Claffey, Director, 860-679-8713, Fax: 860-679-1201, E-mail: claffey@nso2.uchc.edu. *Application contact:* Tricia Avolt, Graduate Admissions Coordinator, 860-679-2175, Fax: 860-679-1899, E-mail: robertson@nso2.uchc.edu.

See Display below and Close-Up on page 229.

University of Delaware, College of Arts and Sciences, Department of Biological Sciences, Newark, DE 19716. Offers biotechnology (MS); cancer biology (MS, PhD); cell and extracellular matrix biology (MS, PhD); cell and systems physiology (MS, PhD); developmental biology (MS, PhD); ecology and evolution (MS, PhD); microbiology (MS, PhD); molecular biology and genetics (MS, PhD). Terminal master's awarded for partial completion of doctoral program. *Degree requirements:* For master's, thesis, preliminary exam; for doctorate, comprehensive exam, thesis/dissertation, preliminary exam. *Entrance requirements:* For master's

and doctorate, GRE General Test. Additional exam requirements/recommendations for international students: Required—TOEFL (minimum score 600 paper-based; 250 computer-based); Recommended—TWE. Electronic applications accepted. *Faculty research:* Microorganisms, bone, cancer metastasis, developmental biology, cell biology, DNA.

University of Florida, College of Medicine and Graduate School, Interdisciplinary Program in Biomedical Sciences, Concentration in Molecular Cell Biology, Gainesville, FL 32611. Offers PhD. *Degree requirements:* For doctorate, thesis/dissertation. *Entrance requirements:* For doctorate, GRE General Test, minimum GPA of 3.0. Additional exam requirements/recommendations for international students: Required—TOEFL. Electronic applications accepted. *Expenses:* Tuition, state resident: full-time $10,916. Tuition, nonresident: full-time $28,309.

University of Florida, Graduate School, College of Agricultural and Life Sciences, Department of Microbiology and Cell Science, Gainesville, FL 32611. Offers biochemistry and molecular biology (MS, PhD); microbiology and cell science (MS, PhD). *Faculty:* 22 full-time (7 women), 1 part-time/adjunct (0 women). *Students:* 45 full-time (21 women), 1 part-time (0 women); includes 2 Black or African American, non-Hispanic/Latino; 6 Asian, non-Hispanic/Latino; 4 Hispanic/Latino, 13 international. Average age 26. 67 applicants, 27% accepted, 10 enrolled. In 2010, 2 master's, 6 doctorates awarded. *Degree requirements:* For master's, comprehensive exam, thesis (for some programs); for doctorate, comprehensive exam, thesis/dissertation. *Entrance requirements:* For master's and doctorate, GRE General Test (minimum score 1000), minimum GPA of 3.0. Additional exam requirements/recommendations for international students: Required—TOEFL (minimum score 550 paper-based; 213 computer-based; 80 iBT), IELTS (minimum score 6). *Application deadline:* For fall admission, 6/1 priority date for domestic students. Applications are processed on a rolling basis. Application fee: $30. Electronic applications accepted. *Expenses:* Tuition, state resident: full-time $10,916. Tuition, nonresident: full-time $28,309. *Financial support:* In 2010–11, 49 students received support, including 13 fellowships, 27 research assistantships (averaging $22,767 per year), 9 teaching assistantships (averaging $23,678 per year). Financial award applicants required to submit FAFSA. *Faculty research:* Biomass conversion, membrane and cell wall chemistry, plant biochemistry and genetics. *Unit head:* Dr. Eric Triplett, Chair, 352-392-1906, Fax: 352-392-5922, E-mail: ewt@ufl.edu. *Application contact:* Dr. Tony Romeo, Graduate Coordinator, 352-392-2400, Fax: 352-392-5922, E-mail: tromeo@ufl.edu.

University of Florida, Interdisciplinary Concentration in Animal Molecular and Cellular Biology, Gainesville, FL 32611. Offers MS, PhD. Program offered jointly with College of Agricultural and Life Sciences, College of Liberal Arts and Sciences, College of Medicine, and College of Veterinary Medicine. *Students:* 2 full-time (both women), both international. Average age 27. 5 applicants, 80% accepted, 2 enrolled. *Entrance requirements:* For master's and doctorate, GRE General Test (minimum score 1000), minimum GPA of 3.0. Additional exam requirements/recommendations for international students: Required—TOEFL (minimum score 550 paper-based; 213 computer-based; 80 iBT), IELTS (minimum score 6). Application fee: $30. Electronic applications accepted. *Expenses:* Tuition, state resident: full-time $10,916. Tuition, nonresident: full-time $28,309. *Financial support:* In 2010–11, 2 students received support, including 1 fellowship, 1 research assistantship (averaging $25,749 per year). Financial award applicants required to submit FAFSA. *Unit head:* Dr. Geoffrey E. Dahl, Chair, Animal Sciences, 352-392-1981 Ext. 221, Fax: 352-392-5595, E-mail: gdahl@ufl.edu. *Application contact:* Dr. Joel H. Brendemuhl, Assistant Chair, 352-392-8073, Fax: 352-392-5595, E-mail: brendj@ufl.edu.

University of Georgia, College of Arts and Sciences, Department of Cellular Biology, Athens, GA 30602. Offers MS, PhD. *Faculty:* 16 full-time (5 women), 2 part-time/adjunct (1 woman). *Students:* 41 full-time (19 women); includes 5 Black or African American, non-Hispanic/Latino; 1 Hispanic/Latino, 19 international. 58 applicants, 28% accepted, 10 enrolled. In 2010, 1 master's, 3 doctorates awarded. *Degree requirements:* For master's, thesis; for doctorate, one foreign language, thesis/dissertation. *Entrance requirements:* For master's and doctorate, GRE General Test. *Application deadline:* For fall admission, 7/1 priority date for domestic students; for spring admission, 11/15 for domestic students. Application fee: $50. Electronic applications accepted. *Expenses:* Tuition, state resident: full-time $7200; part-time $344 per credit hour. Tuition, nonresident: full-time $21,900; part-time $944 per credit hour. Tuition and fees vary according to course load and program. *Financial support:* Fellowships, research assistantships, teaching assistantships, unspecified assistantships available. *Unit head:* Dr. Kojo Mensa-Wilmot, Head, 706-542-3383, E-mail: head@cb.uga.edu. *Application contact:* Dr. Marcus Fechheimer, Graduate Coordinator, 706-542-3338, Fax: 706-542-4271, E-mail: fechheim@cb.uga.edu.

University of Guelph, Graduate Studies, College of Biological Science, Department of Molecular and Cellular Biology, Guelph, ON N1G 2W1, Canada. Offers biochemistry (M Sc, PhD); biophysics (M Sc, PhD); botany (M Sc, PhD); microbiology (M Sc, PhD); molecular biology and genetics (M Sc, PhD). *Degree requirements:* For master's, thesis, research proposal; for doctorate, comprehensive exam, thesis/dissertation, research proposal. *Entrance requirements:* For master's, minimum B-average during previous 2 years of coursework; for doctorate, minimum A-average. Additional exam requirements/recommendations for international students: Required—TOEFL (minimum score 550 paper-based; 213 computer-based), IELTS (minimum score 6.5). Electronic applications accepted. *Faculty research:* Physiology, structure, genetics, and ecology of microbes; virology and microbial technology.

University of Illinois at Chicago, College of Medicine and Graduate College, Graduate Programs in Medicine, Department of Anatomy and Cell Biology, Chicago, IL 60607-7128. Offers neuroscience (PhD), including cellular and systems neuroscience and cell biology; MD/PhD. *Degree requirements:* For doctorate, preliminary oral examination, dissertation and oral defense. *Entrance requirements:* For doctorate, GRE General Test, minimum GPA of 2.75, 3 letters of recommendation, personal statement. Additional exam requirements/recommendations for international students: Required—TOEFL (minimum score 550 paper-based; 213 computer-based). Electronic applications accepted. *Faculty research:* Synapses, axonal transport, neurodegenerative diseases.

University of Illinois at Urbana–Champaign, Graduate College, College of Liberal Arts and Sciences, School of Molecular and Cellular Biology, Department of Cell and Developmental Biology, Champaign, IL 61820. Offers PhD. *Faculty:* 13 full-time (4 women), 1 (woman) part-time/adjunct. *Students:* 47 full-time (20 women); includes 4 Asian, non-Hispanic/Latino; 1 Hispanic/Latino, 25 international. In 2010, 9 doctorates awarded. *Entrance requirements:* For doctorate, GRE, minimum GPA of 3.0. Additional exam requirements/recommendations for international students: Required—TOEFL (minimum score 590 paper-based; 243 computer-based). *Application deadline:* Applications are processed on a rolling basis. Application fee: $75 ($90 for international students). Electronic applications accepted. *Financial support:* In 2010–11, 7 fellowships, 41 research assistantships, 20 teaching assistantships were awarded; tuition waivers (full and partial) also available. *Unit head:* Andrew Belmont, Head, 217-244-2311, Fax: 217-244-1648, E-mail: asbel@illinois.edu. *Application contact:* Delynn Carter, Assistant to the Head, 217-244-8116, Fax: 217-244-1648, E-mail: dmcarter@illinois.edu.

The University of Iowa, Graduate College, College of Liberal Arts and Sciences, Department of Biology, Iowa City, IA 52242-1324. Offers biology (MS, PhD); cell and developmental biology (MS, PhD); evolution (MS, PhD); genetics (MS, PhD); neurobiology (MS, PhD). Terminal master's awarded for partial completion of doctoral program. *Degree requirements:* For master's, thesis optional, exam; for doctorate, comprehensive exam, thesis/dissertation. *Entrance requirements:* For master's and doctorate, GRE General Test, minimum GPA of 3.0. Additional exam requirements/recommendations for international students: Required—TOEFL (minimum score 600 paper-based; 250 computer-based; 100 iBT). Electronic applications accepted. *Faculty research:* Neurobiology, evolutionary biology, genetics, cell and developmental biology.

The University of Iowa, Graduate College, Program in Molecular and Cellular Biology, Iowa City, IA 52242-1316. Offers PhD, MD/PhD. *Degree requirements:* For doctorate, comprehensive exam, thesis/dissertation. *Entrance requirements:* For doctorate, GRE General Test, minimum GPA of 3.0. Additional exam requirements/recommendations for international students: Required—TOEFL (minimum score 600 paper-based; 250 computer-based; 100 iBT). Electronic applications accepted. *Faculty research:* Regulation of gene expression, inherited human genetic diseases, signal transduction mechanisms, structural biology and function.

The University of Iowa, Roy J. and Lucille A. Carver College of Medicine and Graduate College, Graduate Programs in Medicine, Department of Anatomy and Cell Biology, Iowa City, IA 52242-1316. Offers PhD. *Faculty:* 22 full-time (4 women). *Students:* 14 full-time (6 women); includes 2 minority (1 American Indian or Alaska Native, non-Hispanic/Latino; 1 Asian, non-Hispanic/Latino), 1 international. Average age 28. 113 applicants, 0% accepted. In 2010, 2 doctorates awarded. *Degree requirements:* For doctorate, comprehensive exam, thesis/dissertation. *Entrance requirements:* For doctorate, GRE General Test, minimum GPA of 3.0. Additional exam requirements/recommendations for international students: Required—TOEFL (minimum score 600 paper-based; 250 computer-based; 100 iBT). *Application deadline:* For fall admission, 1/15 priority date for domestic and international students. Applications are processed on a rolling basis. Application fee: $60 ($100 for international students). Electronic applications accepted. *Financial support:* In 2010–11, 14 students received support, including 1 fellowship with full tuition reimbursement available (averaging $25,000 per year), 12 research assistantships with full tuition reimbursements available (averaging $25,000 per year), teaching assistantships with full tuition reimbursements available (averaging $25,000 per year); institutionally sponsored loans, scholarships/grants, and health care benefits also available. Financial award application deadline: 3/1. *Faculty research:* Biology of differentiation and transformation, developmental and vascular cell biology, neurobiology. Total annual research expenditures: $3.4 million. *Unit head:* Dr. John F. Engelhardt, Professor and Head, 319-335-7744, Fax: 319-335-7770, E-mail: john-engelhardt@uiowa.edu. *Application contact:* Julie A. Stark, Program Assistant, 319-335-7744, Fax: 319-335-7770, E-mail: julie-stark@uiowa.edu.

The University of Kansas, Graduate Studies, College of Liberal Arts and Sciences, Department of Molecular Biosciences, Lawrence, KS 66044. Offers biochemistry and biophysics (MA, PhD); microbiology (MA, PhD); molecular, cellular, and developmental biology (MA, PhD). *Faculty:* 34. *Students:* 65 full-time (31 women), 1 part-time (0 women); includes 7 minority (2 Asian, non-Hispanic/Latino; 4 Hispanic/Latino; 1 Two or more races, non-Hispanic/Latino), 24 international. Average age 27. 34 applicants, 47% accepted, 10 enrolled. In 2010, 1 master's, 5 doctorates awarded. Terminal master's awarded for partial completion of doctoral program. *Degree requirements:* For master's, comprehensive exam, thesis; for doctorate, comprehensive exam, thesis/dissertation. *Entrance requirements:* For master's and doctorate, GRE General Test. Additional exam requirements/recommendations for international students: Required—TOEFL (minimum score 24 iBT), OR IELTS Speaking: 8. *Application deadline:* For fall admission, 12/15 for domestic and international students. Application fee: $55 ($65 for international students). Electronic applications accepted. *Expenses:* Tuition, state resident: full-time $7092; part-time $295.50 per credit hour. Tuition, nonresident: full-time $16,590; part-time $691.25 per credit hour. Required fees: $858; $71.49 per credit hour. Tuition and fees vary according to course load, campus/location and program. *Financial support:* Fellowships with tuition reimbursements, research assistantships with tuition reimbursements, teaching assistantships with tuition reimbursements, health care benefits and unspecified assistantships available. Financial award application deadline: 3/1. *Faculty research:* Structure and function of proteins, genetics of organism development, molecular genetics, neurophysiology, molecular virology and pathogenics, developmental biology, cell biology. *Unit head:* Dr. Mark Richter, Chair, 785-864-3334, Fax: 785-864-5294, E-mail: richter@ku.edu. *Application contact:* John P. Connolly, Graduate Program Assistant, 785-864-4311, Fax: 785-864-5294, E-mail: jconnolly@ku.edu.

The University of Kansas, University of Kansas Medical Center, School of Medicine, Department of Anatomy and Cell Biology, Kansas City, KS 66160. Offers MA, PhD, MD/PhD. *Faculty:* 32. *Students:* 17 full-time (12 women); includes 4 minority (1 Asian, non-Hispanic/Latino; 2 Hispanic/Latino; 1 Two or more races, non-Hispanic/Latino), 6 international. Average age 26. 2 applicants, 100% accepted, 2 enrolled. In 2010, 1 doctorate awarded. Terminal master's awarded for partial completion of doctoral program. *Degree requirements:* For doctorate, comprehensive exam, thesis/dissertation. *Entrance requirements:* For doctorate, GRE. Additional exam requirements/recommendations for international students: Required—TOEFL. *Application deadline:* For fall admission, 1/15 priority date for domestic students. Applications are processed on a rolling basis. Application fee: $0. Electronic applications accepted. *Expenses:* Tuition, state resident: full-time $7092; part-time $295.50 per credit hour. Tuition, nonresident: full-time $16,590; part-time $691.25 per credit hour. Required fees: $858; $71.49 per credit hour. Tuition and fees vary according to course load, campus/location and program. *Financial support:* Fellowships, research assistantships with full tuition reimbursements, teaching assistantships with full tuition reimbursements, institutionally sponsored loans, health care benefits, and unspecified assistantships available. Financial award application deadline: 2/14; financial award applicants required to submit FAFSA. *Faculty research:* Development of the synapse and neuromuscular junction, pain perception and diabetic neuropathies, cardiovascular and kidney development, reproductive immunology, post-fertilization signaling events. Total annual research expenditures: $9.9 million. *Unit head:* Dr. Dale R. Abrahamson, Chairman, 913-588-7000, Fax: 913-588-2710, E-mail: dabrahamson@kumc.edu. *Application contact:* Dr. Brenda Rongish, Associate Professor, 913-588-1878, Fax: 913-588-2710, E-mail: brongish@kumc.edu.

University of Maine, Graduate School, Program in Biomedical Sciences, Orono, ME 04469. Offers biomedical engineering (PhD); cell and molecular biology (PhD); neuroscience (PhD); toxicology (PhD). *Students:* 11 full-time (8 women), 13 part-time (6 women); includes 1 American Indian or Alaska Native, non-Hispanic/Latino, 5 international. Average age 29. 32 applicants, 19% accepted, 6 enrolled.Application fee: $60. *Expenses:* Tuition, state resident: full-time $400. Tuition, nonresident: full-time $1050. *Financial support:* In 2010–11, 8 research assistantships (averaging $25,625 per year) were awarded. *Unit head:* Dr. Carol Kim, Unit Head, 207-581-2803. *Application contact:* Dr. Carol Kim, Unit Head, 207-581-2803.

The University of Manchester, Faculty of Life Sciences, Manchester, United Kingdom. Offers adaptive organismal biology (M Phil, PhD); animal biology (M Phil, PhD); biochemistry (M Phil, PhD); bioinformatics (M Phil, PhD); biomolecular sciences (M Phil, PhD); biotechnology (M Phil, PhD); cell biology (M Phil, PhD); cell matrix research (M Phil, PhD); channels and transporters (M Phil, PhD); developmental biology (M Phil, PhD); Egyptology (M Phil, PhD); environmental biology (M Phil, PhD); evolutionary biology (M Phil, PhD); gene expression (M Phil, PhD); genetics (M Phil, PhD); history of science, technology and medicine (M Phil, PhD); immunology (M Phil, PhD); integrative neurobiology and behavior (M Phil, PhD); membrane trafficking (M Phil, PhD); microbiology (M Phil, PhD); molecular and cellular neuroscience (M Phil, PhD); molecular biology (M Phil, PhD); molecular cancer studies (M Phil, PhD); neuroscience (M Phil, PhD); ophthalmology (M Phil, PhD); optometry (M Phil, PhD); organelle function (M Phil, PhD); pharmacology (M Phil, PhD); physiology (M Phil, PhD); plant sciences (M Phil, PhD); stem cell research (M Phil, PhD); structural biology (M Phil, PhD); systems neuroscience (M Phil, PhD); toxicology (M Phil, PhD).

University of Maryland, Baltimore, Graduate School, Graduate Program in Life Sciences, Program in Molecular Medicine, Baltimore, MD 21201. Offers cancer biology (PhD); cell and molecular physiology (PhD); human genetics and genomic medicine (PhD); molecular medicine (MS); molecular toxicology and pharmacology (PhD); MD/PhD. *Entrance requirements:* Additional exam requirements/recommendations for international students: Required—TOEFL (minimum score 600 paper-based; 100 iBT); Recommended—IELTS (minimum score 7). Electronic applications accepted. Part-time tuition and fees vary according to course load, degree level and program.

University of Maryland, Baltimore County, Graduate School, College of Natural and Mathematical Sciences, Department of Biological Sciences, Program in Molecular and Cell Biology, Baltimore, MD 21250. Offers PhD. *Faculty:* 24 full-time (10 women), 1 part-time/adjunct (0 women). *Students:* 18 full-time (12 women); includes 2 Black or African American, non-Hispanic/Latino; 7 Asian, non-Hispanic/Latino. Average age 27. 36 applicants, 28% accepted, 5 enrolled. In 2010, 1 doctorate awarded. *Degree requirements:* For doctorate, thesis/dissertation. *Entrance requirements:* For doctorate, GRE General Test, GRE Subject Test, minimum GPA of 3.0. Additional exam requirements/recommendations for international students: Required—TOEFL. *Application deadline:* For fall admission, 1/15 for domestic students, 12/15 for international students. Applications are processed on a rolling basis. Application fee: $50. Electronic applications accepted. *Financial support:* In 2010–11, fellowships with full tuition reimbursements (averaging $23,000 per year), research assistantships with full tuition reimbursements (averaging $22,300 per year), teaching assistantships with full tuition reimbursements (averaging $22,300 per year) were awarded. *Unit head:* Dr. Jeff Leips, Director, 410-455-3669, Fax: 410-455-3875, E-mail: biograd@umbc.edu. *Application contact:* Dr. Phyllis Robinson, Director, 410-455-3669, Fax: 410-455-3875, E-mail: biograd@umbc.edu.

University of Maryland, College Park, Academic Affairs, College of Computer, Mathematical and Natural Sciences, Department of Cell Biology and Molecular Genetics, Program in Cell Biology and Molecular Genetics, College Park, MD 20742. Offers MS, PhD. *Faculty:* 78 full-time (30 women), 3 part-time/adjunct (all women). *Students:* 58 full-time (31 women), 2 part-time (1 woman); includes 3 Black or African American, non-Hispanic/Latino; 4 Asian, non-Hispanic/Latino; 3 Hispanic/Latino, 19 international. 226 applicants, 13% accepted, 15 enrolled. In 2010, 3 master's, 6 doctorates awarded. *Degree requirements:* For master's, thesis; for doctorate, thesis/dissertation, exams. *Entrance requirements:* For master's and doctorate, GRE General Test, 3 letters of recommendation, minimum GPA of 3.0. Additional exam requirements/recommendations for international students: Required—TOEFL. *Application deadline:* For fall admission, 1/6 for domestic and international students. Application fee: $75. *Expenses:* Tuition, state resident: part-time $471 per credit hour. Tuition, nonresident: part-time $1016 per credit hour. Required fees: $337 per term. *Financial support:* In 2010–11, 7 fellowships with full and partial tuition reimbursements (averaging $24,904 per year), 16 research assistantships (averaging $19,428 per year), 30 teaching assistantships (averaging $19,352 per year) were awarded. Financial award applicants required to submit FAFSA. *Faculty research:* Cytoskeletal activity, membrane biology, cell division, genetics and genomics, virology. *Unit head:* Norma Andrews, Chair, 301-405-1605, Fax: 301-314-9489, E-mail: andrewsn@umd.edu. *Application contact:* Dean of Graduate School, 301-405-0358, Fax: 301-314-9305.

University of Maryland, College Park, Academic Affairs, College of Computer, Mathematical and Natural Sciences, Department of Cell Biology and Molecular Genetics, Program in Molecular and Cellular Biology, College Park, MD 20742. Offers PhD. Part-time and evening/weekend programs available. *Students:* 38 full-time (26 women), 3 part-time (all women); includes 1 Black or African American, non-Hispanic/Latino; 3 Asian, non-Hispanic/Latino; 2 Hispanic/Latino, 23 international. 97 applicants, 15% accepted, 6 enrolled. In 2010, 1 doctorate awarded. *Degree requirements:* For doctorate, thesis/dissertation, exam, public service. *Entrance requirements:* For doctorate, GRE General Test, 3 letters of reference. Additional exam requirements/recommendations for international students: Required—TOEFL. *Application deadline:* For fall admission, 1/6 for domestic and international students. Applications are processed on a rolling basis. Application fee: $75. Electronic applications accepted. *Expenses:* Tuition, state resident: part-time $471 per credit hour. Tuition, nonresident: part-time $1016 per credit hour. Required fees: $337 per term. *Financial support:* In 2010–11, 14 research assistantships (averaging $19,589 per year), 16 teaching assistantships (averaging $18,983 per year) were awarded. Financial award applicants required to submit FAFSA. *Faculty research:* Monoclonal antibody production, oligonucleotide synthesis, macronolular processing, signal transduction, developmental biology. *Unit head:* Norma Andrews, 301-405-1605, E-mail: andrewsn@umd.edu. *Application contact:* Dean of Graduate School, 301-405-0358, Fax: 301-314-9305.

University of Massachusetts Amherst, Graduate School, Interdisciplinary Programs, Program in Molecular and Cellular Biology, Amherst, MA 01003. Offers biological chemistry and molecular biophysics (PhD); biomedicine (PhD); cellular and developmental biology (PhD). Part-time programs available. *Students:* 76 full-time (42 women), 3 part-time (2 women); includes 13 minority (3 Black or African American, non-Hispanic/Latino; 4 Asian, non-Hispanic/Latino; 5

Cell Biology

University of Massachusetts Amherst (continued)

Hispanic/Latino; 1 Two or more races, non-Hispanic/Latino), 23 international. Average age 27. 179 applicants, 25% accepted, 22 enrolled. In 2010, 8 doctorates awarded. Terminal master's awarded for partial completion of doctoral program. *Degree requirements:* For doctorate, comprehensive exam, thesis/dissertation. *Entrance requirements:* For doctorate, GRE General Test. Additional exam requirements/recommendations for international students: Required—TOEFL (minimum score 550 paper-based; 213 computer-based; 80 iBT), IELTS (minimum score 6.5). *Application deadline:* For fall admission, 12/1 for domestic and international students. Applications are processed on a rolling basis. Application fee: $50 ($65 for international students). Electronic applications accepted. *Expenses:* Tuition, state resident: full-time $2640. Required fees: $8282. One-time fee: $357 full-time. *Financial support:* In 2010–11, 11 research assistantships with full tuition reimbursements (averaging $2,590 per year), 3 teaching assistantships with full tuition reimbursements (averaging $3,303 per year) were awarded; fellowships, career-related internships or fieldwork, Federal Work-Study, scholarships/grants, traineeships, health care benefits, tuition waivers (full), and unspecified assistantships also available. Support available to part-time students. Financial award application deadline: 12/1; financial award applicants required to submit FAFSA. *Unit head:* Dr. Barbara Osborne, Graduate Program Director, 413-545-3246, Fax: 413-545-1812. *Application contact:* Jean M. Ames, Supervisor of Admissions, 413-545-0722, Fax: 413-577-0010, E-mail: gradadm@grad.umass.edu.

University of Massachusetts Amherst, Graduate School, Interdisciplinary Programs, Program in Plant Biology, Amherst, MA 01003. Offers biochemistry and metabolism (MS, PhD); cell biology and physiology (MS, PhD); environmental, ecological and integrative (PhD); environmental, ecological and integrative biology (MS); genetics and evolution (MS, PhD). *Students:* 18 full-time (8 women); includes 1 minority (Asian, non-Hispanic/Latino), 7 international. Average age 29. 27 applicants, 41% accepted, 6 enrolled. In 2010, 3 doctorates awarded. *Degree requirements:* For master's, thesis; for doctorate, 2 foreign languages, comprehensive exam, thesis/dissertation. *Entrance requirements:* For master's and doctorate, GRE General Test. Additional exam requirements/recommendations for international students: Required—TOEFL (minimum score 550 paper-based; 213 computer-based; 80 iBT), IELTS (minimum score 6.5). *Application deadline:* For fall admission, 12/15 for domestic and international students; for spring admission, 10/1 for domestic and international students. Applications are processed on a rolling basis. Application fee: $50 ($65 for international students). Electronic applications accepted. *Expenses:* Tuition, state resident: full-time $2640. Required fees: $8282. One-time fee: $357 full-time. *Financial support:* In 2010–11, 12 research assistantships with full tuition reimbursements (averaging $11,651 per year) were awarded; fellowships, teaching assistantships, career-related internships or fieldwork, Federal Work-Study, scholarships/grants, traineeships, health care benefits, tuition waivers (full), and unspecified assistantships also available. Support available to part-time students. Financial award application deadline: 12/15; financial award applicants required to submit FAFSA. *Unit head:* Dr. Elsbeth L. Walker, Graduate Program Director, 413-577-3217, Fax: 413-545-3243. *Application contact:* Jean M. Ames, Supervisor of Admissions, 413-545—0722, Fax: 413-577-0010, E-mail: gradadm@grad.umass.edu.

University of Massachusetts Boston, Office of Graduate Studies, College of Science and Mathematics, Track in Molecular, Cellular and Organismal Biology, Boston, MA 02125-3393. Offers PhD.

University of Massachusetts Worcester, Graduate School of Biomedical Sciences, Worcester, MA 01655-0115. Offers biochemistry and molecular pharmacology (PhD); bioinformatics and computational biology (PhD); cancer biology (PhD); cell biology (PhD); clinical and population health research (PhD); clinical investigation (MS); immunology and virology (PhD); interdisciplinary graduate program (PhD); molecular genetics and microbiology (PhD); neuroscience (PhD); DVM/PhD; MD/PhD. *Faculty:* 1,059 full-time (357 women), 145 part-time/adjunct (100 women). *Students:* 438 full-time (239 women), 1 (woman) part-time; includes 44 minority (9 Black or African American, non-Hispanic/Latino; 31 Asian, non-Hispanic/Latino; 4 Hispanic/Latino), 148 international. Average age 29. 687 applicants, 28% accepted, 116 enrolled. In 2010, 6 master's, 45 doctorates awarded. Terminal master's awarded for partial completion of doctoral program. *Degree requirements:* For master's, thesis; for doctorate, thesis/dissertation. *Entrance requirements:* For master's, bachelor's degree; for doctorate, GRE General Test, MS, MA, or MPH (for some programs). Additional exam requirements/recommendations for international students: Required—TOEFL (minimum score 600 paper-based; 250 computer-based). *Application deadline:* For fall admission, 12/15 for domestic and international students; for winter admission, 1/15 for domestic students; for spring admission, 5/15 for domestic students. Application fee: $35. Electronic applications accepted. *Expenses:* Contact institution. *Financial support:* In 2010–11, 439 students received support, including 439 research assistantships with full tuition reimbursements available (averaging $28,350 per year); scholarships/grants, health care benefits, tuition waivers (full), and unspecified assistantships also available. Financial award application deadline: 4/20. *Faculty research:* RNA interference, gene therapy, cell biology, bioinformatics, clinical research. Total annual research expenditures: $232 million. *Unit head:* Dr. Anthony Carruthers, Dean, 508-856-4135, E-mail: anthony.carruthers@umassmed.edu. *Application contact:* Dr. Kendall Knight, Associate Dean and Interim Director of Admissions and Recruitment, 508-856-5628, Fax: 508-856-3659, E-mail: kendall.knight@umassmed.edu.

University of Medicine and Dentistry of New Jersey, Graduate School of Biomedical Sciences, Graduate Programs in Biomedical Sciences–Newark, Department of Cell Biology and Molecular Medicine, Newark, NJ 07107. Offers PhD. *Degree requirements:* For doctorate, thesis/dissertation, qualifying exam. *Entrance requirements:* For doctorate, GRE General Test. Additional exam requirements/recommendations for international students: Required—TOEFL. Electronic applications accepted.

University of Medicine and Dentistry of New Jersey, Graduate School of Biomedical Sciences, Graduate Programs in Biomedical Sciences–Stratford, Program in Cell and Molecular Biology, Stratford, NJ 08084-5634. Offers MS, PhD, DO/PhD. *Degree requirements:* For master's, thesis; for doctorate, thesis/dissertation, qualifying exam. *Entrance requirements:* For master's and doctorate, GRE General Test. Additional exam requirements/recommendations for international students: Required—TOEFL. Electronic applications accepted.

University of Miami, Graduate School, Miller School of Medicine, Graduate Programs in Medicine, Department of Cell Biology and Anatomy, Coral Gables, FL 33124. Offers molecular cell and developmental biology (PhD); MD/PhD. *Degree requirements:* For doctorate, thesis/dissertation. *Entrance requirements:* For doctorate, GRE General Test, GRE Subject Test. Additional exam requirements/recommendations for international students: Required—TOEFL. Electronic applications accepted.

University of Michigan, Rackham Graduate School, College of Literature, Science, and the Arts, Department of Molecular, Cellular, and Developmental Biology, Ann Arbor, MI 48109. Offers MS, PhD. Part-time programs available. *Faculty:* 33 full-time (8 women). *Students:* 69 full-time (35 women), 7 part-time (5 women); includes 4 minority (3 Asian, non-Hispanic/Latino; 1 Hispanic/Latino), 35 international. Average age 27. 122 applicants, 16% accepted, 6 enrolled. In 2010, 5 master's, 7 doctorates awarded. Terminal master's awarded for partial completion of doctoral program. *Degree requirements:* For master's, 24 credits with at least 16 in molecular, cellular, and developmental biology and 4 in a cognate field; for doctorate, thesis/dissertation, preliminary exam, oral defense. *Entrance requirements:* For master's and doctorate, GRE General Test. Additional exam requirements/recommendations for international students: Required—TOEFL (minimum score 560 paper-based; 220 computer-based; 83 iBT). *Application deadline:* For fall admission, 1/5 for domestic and international students; for winter admission, 11/1 for domestic and international students. Applications are processed on a rolling basis. Application fee: $65 ($75 for international students). Electronic applications accepted. *Expenses:* Tuition, state resident: full-time $17,784; part-time $1116 per credit hour. Tuition, nonresident: full-time $35,944; part-time $2125 per credit hour. International tuition: $35,994 full-time. Required fees: $95 per semester. Tuition and fees vary according to course load, degree level and program. *Financial support:* In 2010–11, 61 students received support, including 13 fellowships with full tuition reimbursements available (averaging $26,500 per year), 28 research assistantships with full tuition reimbursements available (averaging $26,500 per year), 21 teaching assistantships with full tuition reimbursements available (averaging $26,500 per year); health care benefits also available. *Faculty research:* Cell biology, microbiology, neurobiology and physiology, developmental biology and plant molecular biology. *Unit head:* Patrick J. Flannery, Administrative Manager, 734-936-2997, Fax: 734-615-6337, E-mail: pjflan@umich.edu. *Application contact:* Mary Carr, Graduate Coordinator, 734-615-1635, Fax: 734-764-0884, E-mail: carrmm@umich.edu.

University of Michigan, Rackham Graduate School, Program in Biomedical Sciences (PIBS), Department of Cell and Developmental Biology, Ann Arbor, MI 48109. Offers PhD. *Faculty:* 29 full-time (10 women). *Students:* 17 full-time (10 women); includes 1 Asian, non-Hispanic/Latino, 9 international. Average age 30. 28 applicants, 25% accepted, 4 enrolled. In 2010, 6 doctorates awarded. *Degree requirements:* For doctorate, thesis/dissertation, oral defense of dissertation, preliminary exam. *Entrance requirements:* For doctorate, GRE General Test, 3 letters of recommendation, research experience. Additional exam requirements/recommendations for international students: Required—TOEFL (minimum score 84 iBT). *Application deadline:* For fall admission, 12/1 for domestic and international students. Application fee: $60 ($75 for international students). Electronic applications accepted. *Expenses:* Tuition, state resident: full-time $17,784; part-time $1116 per credit hour. Tuition, nonresident: full-time $35,944; part-time $2125 per credit hour. International tuition: $35,994 full-time. Required fees: $95 per semester. Tuition and fees vary according to course load, degree level and program. *Financial support:* In 2010–11, 21 students received support, including 21 fellowships (averaging $26,500 per year); scholarships/grants, health care benefits, tuition waivers (full), and unspecified assistantships also available. Financial award application deadline: 12/1. *Faculty research:* Small stress proteins, cellular stress response, muscle, male reproductive, toxicology, cell cytoskeleton. Total annual research expenditures: $3.8 million. *Unit head:* Dr. James Douglas Engel, Chair, 734-615-7509, Fax: 734-763-1166, E-mail: engel@umich.edu. *Application contact:* Michelle S. Melis, Director of Student Life, 734-615-6538, Fax: 734-647-7022, E-mail: msmtegan@umich.edu.

University of Michigan, Rackham Graduate School, Program in Biomedical Sciences (PIBS), Interdisciplinary Program in Cellular and Molecular Biology, Ann Arbor, MI 48109. Offers PhD. *Faculty:* 153 part-time/adjunct (43 women). *Students:* 74 full-time (37 women); includes 19 minority (1 Black or African American, non-Hispanic/Latino; 1 American Indian or Alaska Native, non-Hispanic/Latino; 9 Asian, non-Hispanic/Latino; 8 Hispanic/Latino). Average age 26. In 2010, 9 doctorates awarded. *Degree requirements:* For doctorate, comprehensive exam, thesis/dissertation, oral defense of dissertation, preliminary exam. *Entrance requirements:* For doctorate, GRE General Test, GRE Subject Test. *Expenses:* Tuition, state resident: full-time $17,784; part-time $1116 per credit hour. Tuition, nonresident: full-time $35,944; part-time $2125 per credit hour. International tuition: $35,994 full-time. Required fees: $95 per semester. Tuition and fees vary according to course load, degree level and program. *Financial support:* In 2010–11, 74 students received support, including 21 fellowships with tuition reimbursements available (averaging $26,500 per year), 53 research assistantships with tuition reimbursements available (averaging $26,500 per year); teaching assistantships, scholarships/grants also available. *Faculty research:* Genetics, genomics, gene regulation, models of disease, microbes. Total annual research expenditures: $20 million. *Unit head:* Dr. Jessica Schwartz, Director, 734-764-5428, Fax: 734-647-6232, E-mail: jeschwar@umich.edu. *Application contact:* Catherine A. Mitchell, Student Services Associate I, 734-764-5428, Fax: 734-647-6232, E-mail: cmbgrad@umich.edu.

University of Minnesota, Twin Cities Campus, Graduate School, Program in Molecular, Cellular, Developmental Biology and Genetics, Minneapolis, MN 55455-0213. Offers genetic counseling (MS); molecular, cellular, developmental biology and genetics (PhD). Terminal master's awarded for partial completion of doctoral program. *Degree requirements:* For master's, thesis optional; for doctorate, thesis/dissertation. *Entrance requirements:* For master's and doctorate, GRE General Test. Additional exam requirements/recommendations for international students: Required—TOEFL (minimum score 625 paper-based; 263 computer-based; 80 iBT). Electronic applications accepted. *Faculty research:* Membrane receptors and membrane transport, cell interactions, cytoskeleton and cell mobility, regulation of gene expression, plant cell and molecular biology.

University of Minnesota, Twin Cities Campus, Graduate School, Stem Cell Biology Graduate Program, Minneapolis, MN 55455-3007. Offers MS. *Degree requirements:* For master's, thesis. *Entrance requirements:* For master's, GRE, BS, BA, or foreign equivalent in biological sciences or related field; minimum undergraduate GPA of 3.2. Additional exam requirements/recommendations for international students: Required—TOEFL (minimum scores 580 on paper-based, with a minimum score of 4 in the TWE, or 94 Internet-based, with a minimum score of 22 on each of the reading and listening, 26 on the speaking, and 26 on the writing section. *Faculty research:* Stem cell and developmental biology; embryonic stem cells; iPS cells; muscle satellite cells; hematopoietic stem cells; neuronal stem cells; cardiovascular, kidney and limb development; regenerating systems.

University of Missouri, Graduate School, College of Arts and Sciences, Division of Biological Sciences, Program in Genetic, Cellular and Developmental Biology, Columbia, MO 65211. Offers MA, PhD.

University of Missouri–Kansas City, School of Biological Sciences, Program in Cell Biology and Biophysics, Kansas City, MO 64110-2499. Offers PhD. Offered through the School of Graduate Studies. *Faculty:* 42 full-time (11 women). *Students:* 14 full-time (10 women), 27 part-time (15 women); includes 6 minority (3 Black or African American, non-Hispanic/Latino; 2 Asian, non-Hispanic/Latino; 1 Hispanic/Latino). Average age 32. 56 applicants, 52% accepted, 25 enrolled. *Degree requirements:* For doctorate, comprehensive exam, thesis/dissertation. *Entrance requirements:* For doctorate, GRE General Test, bachelor's degree in chemistry, biology or related field; minimum GPA of 3.0. Additional exam requirements/recommendations for international students: Required—TOEFL (minimum score 550 paper-based; 213 computer-based; 80 iBT). *Application deadline:* For fall admission, 2/15 priority date for domestic and international students. Applications are processed on a rolling basis. Application fee: $45 ($50 for international students). Electronic applications accepted. *Expenses:* Tuition, state resident: full-time $5522; part-time $306.80 per credit hour. Tuition, nonresident: full-time $7128; part-time $792 per credit hour. Required fees: $261.15 per term. *Financial support:* Fellowships with full tuition reimbursements, research assistantships with full tuition reimbursements, teaching assistantships with full and partial tuition reimbursements, scholarships/grants, tuition waivers (full and partial), and unspecified assistantships available. Financial award application deadline: 3/1; financial award applicants required to submit FAFSA. *Unit head:* Dr. Theodore White, Head, 816-235-2538, E-mail: sbsgradrecruit@umkc.edu. *Application contact:* Laura Batenic, Information Contact, 816-235-2352, Fax: 816-235-5158, E-mail: batenicl@umkc.edu.

See Display on next page and Close-Up on page 235.

University of Missouri–St. Louis, College of Arts and Sciences, Department of Biology, St. Louis, MO 63121. Offers biotechnology (Certificate); cell and molecular biology (MS, PhD); ecology, evolution and systematics (MS, PhD); tropical biology and conservation (Certificate). Part-time programs available. *Faculty:* 43 full-time (13 women), 2 part-time/adjunct (1 woman). *Students:* 73 full-time (36 women), 63 part-time (36 women); includes 17 minority (6 Black or African American, non-Hispanic/Latino; 9 Asian, non-Hispanic/Latino; 2 Hispanic/Latino), 45 international. Average age 29. 193 applicants, 44% accepted, 44 enrolled. In 2010, 35 master's, 11 doctorates, 6 other advanced degrees awarded. *Degree requirements:* For master's, thesis or alternative; for doctorate, thesis/dissertation, 1 semester of teaching experience. *Entrance requirements:* For master's, 3 letters of recommendation; for doctorate, GRE General Test, 3 letters of recommendation. Additional exam requirements/recommendations for international students: Required—TOEFL. *Application deadline:* For fall admission, 12/1 priority date for domestic and international students; for spring admission, 10/15 priority date for domestic and

Cell Biology

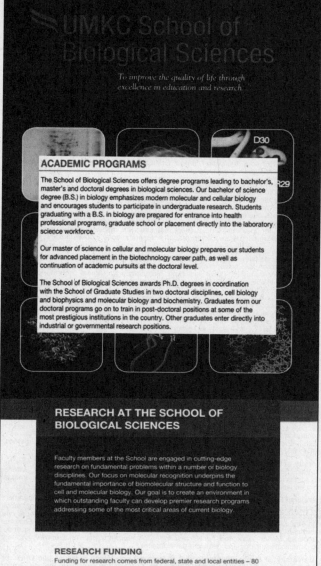
international students. Applications are processed on a rolling basis. Application fee: $35 ($40 for international students). Electronic applications accepted. *Expenses:* Tuition, state resident: full-time $5522; part-time $306.80 per credit hour. Tuition, nonresident: full-time $14,253; part-time $792.10 per credit hour. Required fees: $658; $49 per credit hour. One-time fee: $12. Tuition and fees vary according to program. *Financial support:* In 2010–11, 30 research assistantships with full and partial tuition reimbursements (averaging $18,113 per year), 15 teaching assistantships with full and partial tuition reimbursements (averaging $17,514 per year) were awarded; fellowships with full tuition reimbursements, career-related internships or fieldwork and Federal Work-Study also available. Support available to part-time students. Financial award application deadline: 2/1. *Faculty research:* Molecular biology, microbial genetics, animal behavior, tropical ecology, plant systematics. *Unit head:* Dr. Peter Stevens, Director of Graduate Studies, 314-516-6200, Fax: 314-516-6233, E-mail: stevensp@umsl.edu. *Application contact:* 314-516-5458, Fax: 314-516-6996, E-mail: gradadm@umsl.edu.

University of Nebraska Medical Center, Graduate Studies, Department of Genetics, Cell Biology and Anatomy, Omaha, NE 68198. Offers MS, PhD. Part-time programs available. *Faculty:* 23 full-time (7 women), 1 part-time/adjunct (0 women). *Students:* 16 full-time (5 women), 5 part-time (4 women); includes 1 Asian, non-Hispanic/Latino, 2 international. Average age 25. 22 applicants, 18% accepted, 4 enrolled. In 2010, 1 master's, 5 doctorates awarded. Terminal master's awarded for partial completion of doctoral program. *Degree requirements:* For master's, comprehensive exam, thesis; for doctorate, comprehensive exam, thesis/dissertation. *Entrance requirements:* For master's and doctorate, GRE General Test. Additional exam requirements/recommendations for international students: Required—TOEFL (minimum score 550 paper-based; 213 computer-based). *Application deadline:* For fall admission, 3/1 priority date for domestic and international students; for spring admission, 10/1 for domestic students, 8/1 for international students. Applications are processed on a rolling basis. Application fee: $45. Electronic applications accepted. *Expenses:* Tuition, state resident: part-time $198.25 per semester hour. Required fees: $63 per semester. *Financial support:* In 2010–11, 3 students received support, including fellowships with full tuition reimbursements available (averaging $21,000 per year), research assistantships with full tuition reimbursements available (averaging $21,000 per year), teaching assistantships with full tuition reimbursements available (averaging $21,000 per year); institutionally sponsored loans, health care benefits, and unspecified assistantships also available. Support available to part-time students. Financial award application deadline: 3/1. *Faculty research:* Hematology, immunology, developmental biology, genetics cancer biology, neuroscience. *Unit head:* Dr. Karen Gould, Graduate Committee Chair, 402-559-2456, E-mail: kagould@unmc.edu. *Application contact:* Saralyn Fisher, Graduate Student Support, 402-559-4031, Fax: 402-559-7328, E-mail: sfisher@unmc.edu.

University of Nevada, Reno, Graduate School, Interdisciplinary Program in Cell and Molecular Biology, Reno, NV 89557. Offers MS, PhD. Terminal master's awarded for partial completion of doctoral program. *Degree requirements:* For master's, thesis; for doctorate, thesis/dissertation. *Entrance requirements:* For master's, GRE Subject Test (recommended), minimum GPA of 2.75; for doctorate, GRE Subject Test (recommended), minimum GPA of 3.0. Additional exam requirements/recommendations for international students: Required—TOEFL (minimum score 500 paper-based; 173 computer-based; 61 iBT), IELTS (minimum score 6). Electronic applications accepted. *Expenses:* Tuition, state resident: full-time $2219; part-time $246 per credit. Tuition, nonresident: part-time $510 per credit. International tuition: $9009 full-time. Required fees: $59 per term. One-time fee: $101. Tuition and fees vary according to course load. *Faculty research:* Cellular biology, biophysics, cancer, microbiology, insect biochemistry.

University of New Haven, Graduate School, College of Arts and Sciences, Program in Cellular and Molecular Biology, West Haven, CT 06516-1916. Offers cellular and molecular biology (MS). *Faculty:* 6 full-time (3 women), 8 part-time/adjunct (2 women). *Students:* 34 full-time (25 women), 20 part-time (13 women); includes 1 Black or African American, non-Hispanic/Latino; 1 Asian, non-Hispanic/Latino; 1 Hispanic/Latino, 28 international. Average age 28. 91 applicants, 99% accepted, 27 enrolled. In 2010, 15 master's awarded. *Degree requirements:* For master's, thesis optional. *Entrance requirements:* Additional exam requirements/recommendations for international students: Required—TOEFL (minimum score 520 paper-based; 190 computer-based; 70 iBT), IELTS (minimum score 5.5). *Application deadline:* For fall admission, 5/31 for international students; for winter admission, 10/15 for international students; for spring admission, 1/15 for international students. Applications are processed on a rolling basis. Application fee: $50. Electronic applications accepted. *Financial support:* Career-related internships or fieldwork and Federal Work-Study available. Financial award application deadline: 5/1; financial award applicants required to submit FAFSA. *Unit head:* Dr. Eva Sapi, Coordinator, 203-479-4552. *Application contact:* Eloise Gormley, Director of Graduate Admissions, 203-932-7449, Fax: 203-932-7137, E-mail: gradinfo@newhaven.edu.

University of New Mexico, School of Medicine, Biomedical Sciences Graduate Program, Albuquerque, NM 87131-5196. Offers biochemistry and molecular biology (MS, PhD); cell biology and physiology (MS, PhD); clinical and translational science (Certificate); molecular genetics and microbiology (MS, PhD); neuroscience (MS, PhD); pathology (MS, PhD); toxicology (MS, PhD); university science teaching (Certificate). Part-time programs available. *Faculty:* 33 full-time (14 women), 3 part-time/adjunct (1 woman). *Students:* 94 full-time (57 women), 14 part-time (8 women); includes 24 minority (3 Black or African American, non-Hispanic/Latino; 1 American Indian or Alaska Native, non-Hispanic/Latino; 6 Asian, non-Hispanic/Latino; 13 Hispanic/Latino; 1 Two or more races, non-Hispanic/Latino), 20 international. Average age 30. 135 applicants, 14% accepted, 19 enrolled. In 2010, 2 master's, 19 doctorates, 3 other advanced degrees awarded. Terminal master's awarded for partial completion of doctoral program. *Degree requirements:* For master's, thesis; for doctorate, comprehensive exam, thesis/dissertation. *Entrance requirements:* For master's and doctorate, GRE General Test, minimum undergraduate GPA of 3.0. Additional exam requirements/recommendations for international students: Required—TOEFL. *Application deadline:* For fall admission, 1/1 priority date for domestic students. Applications are processed on a rolling basis. Application fee: $50. Electronic applications accepted. *Expenses:* Tuition, state resident: full-time $5991; part-time $251 per credit hour. Tuition, nonresident: full-time $14,405; part-time $800.20 per credit hour. Tuition and fees vary according to course level, course load, program and reciprocity agreements. *Financial support:* In 2010–11, 99 students received support, including 5 fellowships (averaging $75 per year), 96 research assistantships with full tuition reimbursements available (averaging $17,401 per year), 2 teaching assistantships with full tuition reimbursements available (averaging $2,415 per year); career-related internships or fieldwork, Federal Work-Study, institutionally sponsored loans, scholarships/grants, traineeships, health care benefits, and unspecified assistantships also available. Financial award application deadline: 1/1; financial award applicants required to submit FAFSA. *Faculty research:* Signal transduction, infectious disease, biology of cancer, structural biology, neuroscience. *Unit head:* Laurie G. Hudson, Director, 505-272-1887, Fax: 505-272-8738, E-mail: lhudson@salud.unm.edu. *Application contact:* Angel Cooke-Jackson, Coordinator, 505-272-1887, Fax: 505-272-8738, E-mail: acooke-jackson@salud.unm.edu.

The University of North Carolina at Chapel Hill, Graduate School, College of Arts and Sciences, Department of Biology, Chapel Hill, NC 27599. Offers botany (MA, MS, PhD); cell biology, development, and physiology (MA, MS, PhD); cell motility and cytoskeleton (PhD); ecology and behavior (MA, MS, PhD); genetics and molecular biology (MA, MS, PhD); morphology, systematics, and evolution (MA, MS, PhD). Terminal master's awarded for partial completion of doctoral program. *Degree requirements:* For master's, comprehensive exam, thesis (for some programs); for doctorate, comprehensive exam, thesis/dissertation. *Entrance requirements:* For master's, GRE General Test, GRE Subject Test, 2 semesters of calculus or statistics; 2 semesters of physics, organic chemistry; 3 semesters of biology; for doctorate, GRE General Test, GRE Subject Test, 2 semesters calculus or statistics, 2 semesters physics, organic chemistry, 3 semesters of biology. Additional exam requirements/recommendations for international students: Required—TOEFL (minimum score 550 paper-based; 213 computer-based). Electronic applications accepted. *Faculty research:* Gene expression, biomechanics, yeast genetics, plant ecology, plant molecular biology.

Cell Biology

The University of North Carolina at Chapel Hill, School of Medicine and Graduate School, Graduate Programs in Medicine, Department of Cell and Developmental Biology, Chapel Hill, NC 27599. Offers PhD. *Faculty:* 16 full-time (2 women). *Students:* 35 full-time (19 women); includes 2 Black or African American, non-Hispanic/Latino; 3 Asian, non-Hispanic/Latino, 7 international. Average age 24. 23 applicants, 9% accepted, 2 enrolled. In 2010, 5 doctorates awarded. *Degree requirements:* For doctorate, comprehensive exam, thesis/dissertation. *Entrance requirements:* For doctorate, GRE General Test, GRE Subject Test. *Application deadline:* For fall admission, 1/1 priority date for domestic and international students. Applications are processed on a rolling basis. Application fee: $73. Electronic applications accepted. *Financial support:* In 2010–11, 6 fellowships with tuition reimbursements (averaging $21,180 per year), 29 research assistantships with full tuition reimbursements (averaging $27,000 per year) were awarded; teaching assistantships with full tuition reimbursements, tuition waivers (full) and unspecified assistantships also available. Financial award application deadline: 2/1; financial award applicants required to submit FAFSA. *Faculty research:* Cell adhesion, motility and cytoskeleton; molecular analysis of signal transduction; development biology and toxicology; reproductive biology; cell and molecular imaging. Total annual research expenditures: $8 million. *Unit head:* Dr. Vytas A. Bankaitis, Chair, 919-966-3026, Fax: 919-966-1856, E-mail: vytas@med.unc.edu. *Application contact:* Dr. Douglas Cyr, Director of Graduate Studies, 919-843-4805, E-mail: dmcyr@med.unc.edu.

University of North Dakota, Graduate School and Graduate School, Graduate Programs in Medicine, Department of Anatomy and Cell Biology, Grand Forks, ND 58202. Offers MS, PhD. *Faculty:* 8 full-time (1 woman). *Students:* 8 full-time (3 women), 1 (woman) part-time, 2 international. Average age 26. 5 applicants, 20% accepted, 1 enrolled. In 2010, 1 doctorate awarded. *Degree requirements:* For master's, thesis, final exam; for doctorate, comprehensive exam, thesis/dissertation, final exam. *Entrance requirements:* For master's and doctorate, GRE General Test, minimum GPA of 3.0. Additional exam requirements/recommendations for international students: Required—TOEFL (minimum score 550 paper-based; 213 computer-based; 79 iBT), IELTS (minimum score 6.5). *Application deadline:* For fall admission, 8/1 priority date for domestic students, 5/1 priority date for international students; for spring admission, 12/1 priority date for domestic students, 9/1 priority date for international students. Applications are processed on a rolling basis. Application fee: $35. Electronic applications accepted. *Expenses:* Tuition: state resident: full-time $5857; part-time $306.74 per credit. Tuition, nonresident: full-time $15,666; part-time $729.77 per credit. Required fees: $53.42 per credit. Tuition and fees vary according to course load, program and reciprocity agreements. *Financial support:* In 2010–11, 9 students received support, including 9 research assistantships with full and partial tuition reimbursements available (averaging $14,135 per year); fellowships, teaching assistantships with full and partial tuition reimbursements available, Federal Work-Study, institutionally sponsored loans, scholarships/grants, health care benefits, tuition waivers (full and partial), and unspecified assistantships also available. Support available to part-time students. Financial award applicants required to submit FAFSA. *Faculty research:* Coronary vessel, vasculogenesis, acellular glomerular and retinal microvessel membranes, ependymal cells, cardiac muscle. Total annual research expenditures: $5,142. *Unit head:* Dr. Jane Dunlevy, Graduate Director, 701-777-2575, Fax: 701-777-3527, E-mail: jdunlevy@medicine.nodak.edu. *Application contact:* Matt Anderson, Admissions Specialist, 701-777-2947, Fax: 701-777-3619, E-mail: matthew.anderson@gradschool.und.edu.

University of Notre Dame, Graduate School, College of Science, Department of Biological Sciences, Notre Dame, IN 46556. Offers aquatic ecology, evolution and environmental biology (MS, PhD); cellular and molecular biology (MS, PhD); genetics (MS, PhD); physiology (MS, PhD); vector biology and parasitology (MS, PhD). Terminal master's awarded for partial completion of doctoral program. *Degree requirements:* For master's, comprehensive exam, thesis; for doctorate, comprehensive exam, thesis/dissertation, candidacy exam. *Entrance requirements:* For master's and doctorate, GRE General Test. Additional exam requirements/recommendations for international students: Required—TOEFL (minimum score 600 paper-based; 250 computer-based; 80 iBT). Electronic applications accepted. *Faculty research:* Tropical disease, molecular genetics, neurobiology, evolutionary biology, aquatic biology.

University of Oklahoma Health Sciences Center, College of Medicine and Graduate College, Graduate Programs in Medicine, Department of Cell Biology, Oklahoma City, OK 73190. Offers MS, PhD. *Degree requirements:* For master's, thesis; for doctorate, thesis/dissertation. *Entrance requirements:* For doctorate, GRE General Test, GRE Subject Test, 3 letters of recommendation. Additional exam requirements/recommendations for international students: Required—TOEFL. *Faculty research:* Neurobiology, reproductive, neuronal plasticity, extracellular matrix, neuroendocrinology.

University of Ottawa, Faculty of Graduate and Postdoctoral Studies, Faculty of Medicine, Department of Cellular and Molecular Medicine, Ottawa, ON K1H 8M5, Canada. Offers M Sc, PhD. *Degree requirements:* For master's, thesis, seminar; for doctorate, comprehensive exam, thesis/dissertation, seminar. *Entrance requirements:* For master's, honors degree or equivalent, minimum B average; for doctorate, master's degree, minimum B+ average. Electronic applications accepted. *Faculty research:* Physiology, pharmacology, growth and development.

University of Pennsylvania, Perelman School of Medicine, Biomedical Graduate Studies, Graduate Group in Cell and Molecular Biology, Philadelphia, PA 19104. Offers cancer biology (PhD); cell biology and physiology (PhD); developmental stem cell regenerative biology (PhD); gene therapy and vaccines (PhD); genetics and gene regulation (PhD); microbiology, virology, and parasitology (PhD); MD/PhD; VMD/PhD. *Faculty:* 299. *Students:* 315 full-time (166 women); includes 13 Black or African American, non-Hispanic/Latino; 1 American Indian or Alaska Native, non-Hispanic/Latino; 44 Asian, non-Hispanic/Latino; 18 Hispanic/Latino, 37 international. 579 applicants, 21% accepted, 49 enrolled. In 2010, 53 doctorates awarded. *Degree requirements:* For doctorate, thesis/dissertation. *Entrance requirements:* For doctorate, GRE General Test. Additional exam requirements/recommendations for international students: Required—TOEFL. *Application deadline:* For fall admission, 12/8 priority date for domestic and international students. Applications are processed on a rolling basis. Application fee: $70. Electronic applications accepted. *Expenses:* Tuition: Full-time $25,660; part-time $4758 per course. Required fees: $2152; $270 per course. Tuition and fees vary according to course load, degree level and program. *Financial support:* In 2010–11, 315 students received support; fellowships, research assistantships, scholarships/grants, traineeships, and unspecified assistantships available. Financial award application deadline: 12/8. *Unit head:* Dr. Daniel Kessler, Graduate Group Chair, 215-898-2180, E-mail: raperj@mail.med.upenn.edu. *Application contact:* Meagan Schofer, Coordinator, 215-898-9536, Fax: 215-573-2104, E-mail: camb@mailmed.upenn.edu.

University of Pittsburgh, School of Arts and Sciences, Department of Biological Sciences, Program in Molecular, Cellular, and Developmental Biology, Pittsburgh, PA 15260. Offers PhD. *Faculty:* 25 full-time (6 women). *Students:* 56 full-time (35 women); includes 3 Asian, non-Hispanic/Latino, 17 international. Average age 23. 181 applicants, 11% accepted, 7 enrolled. In 2010, 6 doctorates awarded. *Degree requirements:* For doctorate, comprehensive exam, thesis/dissertation, completion of research integrity module. *Entrance requirements:* For doctorate, GRE General Test, GRE Subject Test. Additional exam requirements/recommendations for international students: Required—TOEFL (minimum score 550 paper-based; 213 computer-based; 80 iBT). *Application deadline:* For fall admission, 1/15 priority date for domestic students, 12/15 priority date for international students. Applications are processed on a rolling basis. Application fee: $0 ($50 for international students). Electronic applications accepted. *Expenses:* Tuition, state resident: full-time $17,304; part-time $701 per credit. Tuition, nonresident: full-time $29,554; part-time $1210 per credit. Required fees: $740; $214 per term. Tuition and fees vary according to program. *Financial support:* In 2010–11, 25 fellowships with full tuition reimbursements (averaging $28,382 per year), 116 research assistantships with full tuition reimbursements (averaging $25,058 per year), 22 teaching assistantships with full tuition reimbursements (averaging $23,907 per year) were awarded; Federal Work-Study, scholarships/grants, traineeships, health care benefits, and tuition waivers (full) also available. *Unit head:* Dr. Gerard L. Campbell, Associate Professor, 412-624-6812, Fax: 412-

624-4759, E-mail: camp@pitt.edu. *Application contact:* Cathleen M. Barr, Graduate Administrator, 412-624-4268, Fax: 412-624-4759, E-mail: cbarr@pitt.edu.

University of Pittsburgh, School of Medicine, Graduate Programs in Medicine, Program in Cell Biology and Molecular Physiology, Pittsburgh, PA 15260. Offers MS, PhD. *Faculty:* 43 full-time (12 women). *Students:* 11 full-time (6 women); includes 1 Asian, non-Hispanic/Latino, 5 international. Average age 27. 486 applicants, 14% accepted. In 2010, 4 doctorates awarded. *Degree requirements:* For doctorate, comprehensive exam, thesis/dissertation. *Entrance requirements:* For doctorate, GRE General Test, GRE Subject Test, minimum QPA of 3.0. Additional exam requirements/recommendations for international students: Required—TOEFL (minimum score 600 paper-based; 100 iBT), IELTS (minimum score 7). *Application deadline:* For fall admission, 12/15 priority date for domestic and international students. Application fee: $50. Electronic applications accepted. *Expenses:* Tuition, state resident: full-time $17,304; part-time $701 per credit. Tuition, nonresident: full-time $29,554; part-time $1210 per credit. Required fees: $740; $214 per term. Tuition and fees vary according to program. *Financial support:* In 2010–11, 4 research assistantships with full tuition reimbursements (averaging $25,500 per year), 7 teaching assistantships with full tuition reimbursements (averaging $25,500 per year) were awarded; institutionally sponsored loans, scholarships/grants, traineeships, health care benefits, and unspecified assistantships also available. *Faculty research:* Genetic disorders of ion channels, regulation of gene expression/development, membrane traffic of proteins and lipids, reproductive biology, signal transduction in diabetes and metabolism. *Unit head:* Dr. William H. Walker, Graduate Program Director, 412-641-7672, Fax: 412-641-7676, E-mail: walkerw@pitt.edu. *Application contact:* Graduate Studies Administrator, 412-648-8957, Fax: 412-648-1077, E-mail: gradstudies@medschool.pitt.edu.

University of Puerto Rico, Río Piedras, College of Natural Sciences, Department of Biology, San Juan, PR 00931-3300. Offers ecology/systematics (MS, PhD); evolution/genetics (MS, PhD); molecular/cellular biology (MS, PhD); neuroscience (MS, PhD). Part-time programs available. *Degree requirements:* For master's, one foreign language, comprehensive exam, thesis; for doctorate, one foreign language, comprehensive exam, thesis/dissertation. *Entrance requirements:* For master's, GRE Subject Test, interview, minimum GPA of 3.0, letter of recommendation; for doctorate, GRE Subject Test, interview, master's degree, minimum GPA of 3.0, letter of recommendation. *Faculty research:* Environmental, poblational and systematic biology.

University of Rhode Island, Graduate School, College of the Environment and Life Sciences, Department of Cell and Molecular Biology, Kingston, RI 02881. Offers biochemistry (MS, PhD); clinical laboratory sciences (MS), including biotechnology, clinical laboratory science, cytopathology; microbiology (MS, PhD); molecular genetics (MS, PhD). Part-time programs available. *Faculty:* 13 full-time (5 women), 2 part-time/adjunct (1 woman). *Students:* 32 full-time (15 women), 37 part-time (23 women); includes 10 minority (5 Black or African American, non-Hispanic/Latino; 2 Asian, non-Hispanic/Latino; 3 Hispanic/Latino), 4 international. In 2010, 29 master's, 3 doctorates awarded. *Degree requirements:* For master's, comprehensive exam (for some programs); for doctorate, comprehensive exam. *Entrance requirements:* For master's and doctorate, GRE, 2 letters of recommendation. Additional exam requirements/recommendations for international students: Required—TOEFL (minimum score 550 paper-based; 213 computer-based). *Application deadline:* For fall admission, 7/15 for domestic students, 2/1 for international students; for spring admission, 11/15 for domestic students, 7/15 for international students. Application fee: $65. Electronic applications accepted. *Expenses:* Tuition, state resident: full-time $9588; part-time $533 per credit hour. Tuition, nonresident: full-time $22,968; part-time $1276 per credit hour. Required fees: $1282; $68 per semester. Tuition and fees vary according to program. *Financial support:* In 2010–11, 3 research assistantships with full and partial tuition reimbursements (averaging $11,653 per year), 12 teaching assistantships with full and partial tuition reimbursements (averaging $12,379 per year) were awarded. Financial award application deadline: 7/15; financial award applicants required to submit FAFSA. *Faculty research:* Genomics and Sequencing Center: an interdisciplinary genomics research and undergraduate and graduate student training program which provides researchers access to cutting-edge technologies in the field of genomics. Total annual research expenditures: $3.5 million. *Unit head:* Dr. Jay Sperry, Chairperson, 401-874-2201, Fax: 401-874-2202, E-mail: jsperry@mail.uri.edu. *Application contact:* Dr. Jay Sperry, Chairperson, 401-874-2201, Fax: 401-874-2202, E-mail: jsperry@mail.uri.edu.

University of Saskatchewan, College of Medicine, Department of Anatomy and Cell Biology, Saskatoon, SK S7N 5A2, Canada. Offers M Sc, PhD. *Degree requirements:* For master's, thesis; for doctorate, thesis/dissertation. *Entrance requirements:* Additional exam requirements/recommendations for international students: Required—TOEFL.

University of South Carolina, The Graduate School, College of Arts and Sciences, Department of Biological Sciences, Graduate Training Program in Molecular, Cellular, and Developmental Biology, Columbia, SC 29208. Offers MS, PhD. *Degree requirements:* For master's, one foreign language, thesis; for doctorate, one foreign language, thesis/dissertation. *Entrance requirements:* For master's and doctorate, GRE General Test, minimum GPA of 3.0 in science. Electronic applications accepted. *Faculty research:* Marine ecology, population and evolutionary biology, molecular biology and genetics, development.

The University of South Dakota, School of Medicine and Health Sciences and Graduate School, Biomedical Sciences Graduate Program, Cellular and Molecular Biology Group, Vermillion, SD 57069-2390. Offers MS, PhD. Terminal master's awarded for partial completion of doctoral program. *Degree requirements:* For master's, thesis; for doctorate, comprehensive exam, thesis/dissertation. *Entrance requirements:* For master's and doctorate, GRE General Test, GRE Subject Test, minimum GPA of 3.0. Additional exam requirements/recommendations for international students: Required—TOEFL (minimum score 550 paper-based; 213 computer-based; 80 iBT), IELTS (minimum score 6). Electronic applications accepted. *Expenses:* Contact institution. *Faculty research:* Molecular aspects of protein and DNA, neurochemistry and energy transduction, gene regulation, cellular development.

University of Southern California, Keck School of Medicine and Graduate School, Graduate Programs in Medicine, Department of Cell and Neurobiology, Los Angeles, CA 90089. Offers MS, PhD. *Faculty:* 29 full-time (11 women), 3 part-time/adjunct (1 woman). *Students:* 3 full-time (2 women); includes 1 Asian, non-Hispanic/Latino. Average age 24. 3 applicants, 0% accepted, 0 enrolled. Terminal master's awarded for partial completion of doctoral program. *Degree requirements:* For master's, thesis or alternative; for doctorate, thesis/dissertation. *Entrance requirements:* For master's, GRE General Test, minimum GPA of 3.0; for doctorate, GRE General Test. *Application deadline:* For fall admission, 3/1 priority date for domestic and international students. Application fee: $85. Electronic applications accepted. *Expenses:* Tuition: Full-time $31,240; part-time $1420 per unit. Required fees: $600. One-time fee: $35 full-time. Full-time tuition and fees vary according to degree level and program. *Financial support:* In 2010–11, 1 student received support, including 1 fellowship (averaging $27,060 per year), 4 research assistantships (averaging $27,060 per year); teaching assistantships, Federal Work-Study and institutionally sponsored loans also available. Support available to part-time students. *Faculty research:* Neurobiology and development, gene therapy in vision, lachrymal glands, neuroendocrinology, signal transduction mechanisms. *Unit head:* Dr. Mikel Henry Snow, Vice-Chair, 323-442-1881, Fax: 323-442-3466. *Application contact:* Darlene Marie Campbell, Project Specialist, 323-442-2843, Fax: 323-442-0466, E-mail: dmc@usc.edu.

University of South Florida, Graduate School, College of Arts and Sciences, Department of Biology, Tampa, FL 33620-9951. Offers cell biology and molecular biology (MS); coastal marine biology (MS); coastal marine biology and ecology (PhD); conservation biology (MS, PhD); molecular and cell biology (PhD). Part-time programs available. *Faculty:* 8 full-time (4 women). *Students:* 85 full-time (50 women), 8 part-time (all women); includes 1 Black or African American, non-Hispanic/Latino; 3 Asian, non-Hispanic/Latino; 7 Hispanic/Latino, 12 international. Average age 27. 122 applicants, 30% accepted, 34 enrolled. In 2010, 10 master's, 9 doctorates awarded. *Degree requirements:* For master's, comprehensive exam, thesis (for some programs); for doctorate, comprehensive exam, thesis/dissertation. *Entrance requirements:*

For master's and doctorate, GRE General Test, minimum GPA of 3.0. Additional exam requirements/recommendations for international students: Required—TOEFL (minimum score 570 paper-based; 213 computer-based). *Application deadline:* For fall admission, 2/15 priority date for domestic students, 1/2 for international students; for spring admission, 8/1 for domestic students, 6/1 for international students. Application fee: $30. Electronic applications accepted. *Financial support:* In 2010–11, 35 research assistantships (averaging $17,940 per year), 38 teaching assistantships with tuition reimbursements (averaging $16,621 per year) were awarded; unspecified assistantships also available. Financial award application deadline: 6/30; financial award applicants required to submit FAFSA. Total annual research expenditures: $4.5 million. *Unit head:* Susan Bell, Co-Chairperson, 813-974-6210, Fax: 813-974-2876, E-mail: sbell@cas.usf.edu. *Application contact:* James Garey, Graduate Advisor, 813-974-8434, Fax: 813-974-3263, E-mail: grarey@cas.usf.edu.

The University of Texas at Austin, Graduate School, Institute for Cellular and Molecular Biology, Austin, TX 78712-1111. Offers PhD.

The University of Texas at Dallas, School of Natural Sciences and Mathematics, Program in Biology, Richardson, TX 75080. Offers bioinformatics and computational biology (MS); biotechnology (MS); molecular and cell biology (MS, PhD). Part-time and evening/weekend programs available. *Faculty:* 18 full-time (3 women), 1 part-time/adjunct (0 women). *Students:* 109 full-time (61 women), 19 part-time (7 women); includes 22 minority (5 Black or African American, non-Hispanic/Latino; 14 Asian, non-Hispanic/Latino; 3 Hispanic/Latino), 82 international. Average age 26. 331 applicants, 37% accepted, 38 enrolled. In 2010, 36 master's, 5 doctorates awarded. *Degree requirements:* For master's, thesis optional; for doctorate, thesis/dissertation, publishable paper. *Entrance requirements:* For master's and doctorate, GRE (minimum combined score of 1000 on verbal and quantitative). Additional exam requirements/recommendations for international students: Required—TOEFL (minimum score 550 paper-based; 215 computer-based; 80 iBT). *Application deadline:* For fall admission, 7/15 for domestic students, 5/1 priority date for international students; for spring admission, 11/15 for domestic students, 9/1 priority date for international students. Applications are processed on a rolling basis. Application fee: $50 ($100 for international students). Electronic applications accepted. *Expenses:* Tuition, state resident: full-time $10,248; part-time $569 per credit hour. Tuition, nonresident: full-time $18,544; part-time $1030 per credit hour. Tuition and fees vary according to course load. *Financial support:* In 2010–11, 58 students received support, including 19 research assistantships with partial tuition reimbursements available (averaging $13,403 per year), 32 teaching assistantships with partial tuition reimbursements available (averaging $14,513 per year); career-related internships or fieldwork, Federal Work-Study, institutionally sponsored loans, scholarships/grants, and unspecified assistantships also available. Support available to part-time students. Financial award application deadline: 4/30; financial award applicants required to submit FAFSA. *Faculty research:* Role of mitochondria in neurodegenerative diseases, protein-DNA interactions in site-specific recombination, eukaryotic gene expression, bio-nanotechnology, sickle cell research. *Unit head:* Dr. Li Zhang, Department Head, 972-883-6032, Fax: 972-883-2502, E-mail: li.zhang@utdallas.edu. *Application contact:* Dr. Lawrence Reitzer, Graduate Advisor, 972-883-2502, Fax: 972-883-2402, E-mail: reitzer@utdallas.edu.

The University of Texas Health Science Center at Houston, Graduate School of Biomedical Sciences, Program in Cell and Regulatory Biology, Houston, TX 77225-0036. Offers MS, PhD, MD/PhD. Terminal master's awarded for partial completion of doctoral program. *Degree requirements:* For master's, thesis; for doctorate, thesis/dissertation. *Entrance requirements:* For master's and doctorate, GRE General Test. Additional exam requirements/recommendations for international students: Required—TOEFL. Electronic applications accepted. *Faculty research:* Pharmacology, cell biology, physiology, signal transduction, systems biology.

The University of Texas Health Science Center at San Antonio, Graduate School of Biomedical Sciences, Department of Cellular and Structural Biology, San Antonio, TX 78229-3900. Offers MS, PhD. *Faculty:* 55 full-time (20 women). *Students:* 67 full-time (49 women); includes 2 Black or African American, non-Hispanic/Latino; 7 Asian, non-Hispanic/Latino; 9 Hispanic/Latino, 20 international. Average age 27. In 2010, 2 master's, 3 doctorates awarded. *Degree requirements:* For master's, thesis; for doctorate, comprehensive exam, thesis/dissertation. *Entrance requirements:* For doctorate, GRE General Test, previous course work in biology, chemistry, physics, and calculus. Additional exam requirements/recommendations for international students: Required—TOEFL (minimum score 550 paper-based; 213 computer-based; 68 iBT). *Application deadline:* For fall admission, 3/1 priority date for domestic and international students. Applications are processed on a rolling basis. Application fee: $0. Electronic applications accepted. *Expenses:* Tuition, state resident: full-time $3072; part-time $128 per credit hour. Tuition, nonresident: full-time $11,928; part-time $497 per credit hour. Required fees: $1078; $1078 per year. One-time fee: $60. *Financial support:* In 2010–11, 55 students received support, including 14 fellowships with partial tuition reimbursements available (averaging $26,000 per year), 41 teaching assistantships (averaging $26,000 per year). Financial award application deadline: 6/30; financial award applicants required to submit FAFSA. *Faculty research:* Human/molecular genetics, endocrinology and neurobiology, cell biology, stem cell biology, cancer biology, biology of aging. Total annual research expenditures: $11.5 million. *Unit head:* Christi A. Walter, Professor and Chair, 210-567-3800, Fax: 210-567-0073, E-mail: walter@uthscsa.edu. *Application contact:* Susan Naylor, Chair, Committee on Graduate Studies, 210-567-3842, Fax: 210-567-3803, E-mail: naylor@uthscsa.edu.

The University of Texas Medical Branch, Graduate School of Biomedical Sciences, Program in Biochemistry and Molecular Biology, Galveston, TX 77555. Offers biochemistry (PhD); bioinformatics (PhD); biophysics (PhD); cell biology (PhD); computational biology (PhD); structural biology (PhD). *Degree requirements:* For doctorate, thesis/dissertation. *Entrance requirements:* Additional exam requirements/recommendations for international students: Required—TOEFL (minimum score 550 paper-based; 213 computer-based). Electronic applications accepted.

The University of Texas Southwestern Medical Center at Dallas, Southwestern Graduate School of Biomedical Sciences, Division of Basic Science, Program in Cell Regulation, Dallas, TX 75390. Offers PhD. *Degree requirements:* For doctorate, thesis/dissertation, qualifying exam. *Entrance requirements:* For doctorate, GRE General Test, minimum GPA of 3.0. Additional exam requirements/recommendations for international students: Required—TOEFL. *Application deadline:* For fall admission, 12/15 priority date for domestic students. Applications are processed on a rolling basis. Application fee: $0. Electronic applications accepted. *Financial support:* Fellowships, research assistantships, institutionally sponsored loans and traineeships available. *Faculty research:* Molecular and cellular approaches to regulatory biology, receptor-effector coupling, membrane structure, function, and assembly. *Unit head:* Dr. Paul Sternweis, Chair, 214-645-6149, Fax: 214-645-6131, E-mail: paul.sternweis@utsouthwestern.edu. *Application contact:* Dr. Paul Sternweis, Chair, 214-645-6149, Fax: 214-645-6131, E-mail: paul.sternweis@utsouthwestern.edu.

University of the Sciences in Philadelphia, College of Graduate Studies, Misher College of Arts and Sciences, Program in Cell and Molecular Biology, Philadelphia, PA 19104-4495. Offers PhD.

University of the Sciences in Philadelphia, College of Graduate Studies, Program in Cell Biology and Biotechnology, Philadelphia, PA 19104-4495. Offers cell and molecular biology (PhD); cell biology (MS). Part-time and evening/weekend programs available. *Degree requirements:* For master's, thesis (for some programs). *Entrance requirements:* For master's, GRE General Test. Additional exam requirements/recommendations for international students: Required—TOEFL, TWE. *Expenses:* Contact institution. *Faculty research:* Invertebrate cell adhesion, plant-microbe interactions, natural product mechanisms, cell signal transduction, gene regulation and organization.

The University of Toledo, College of Graduate Studies, College of Natural Sciences and Mathematics, Department of Biological Sciences, Toledo, OH 43606-3390. Offers cell biology (MS, PhD); ecology (MS, PhD). Part-time programs available. *Faculty:* 19. *Students:* 64 full-time (31 women), 23 part-time (5 women); includes 5 minority (2 Black or African American, non-Hispanic/Latino; 2 Asian, non-Hispanic/Latino; 1 Hispanic/Latino), 29 international. Average age 28. 110 applicants, 16% accepted, 16 enrolled. In 2010, 10 master's, 9 doctorates awarded. *Degree requirements:* For master's, thesis or alternative; for doctorate, thesis/dissertation. *Entrance requirements:* For master's and doctorate, GRE General Test, GRE Subject Test, minimum cumulative point-hour ratio of 2.7 for all previous academic work, three letters of recommendation, statement of purpose, transcripts from all prior institutions attended. Additional exam requirements/recommendations for international students: Required—TOEFL (minimum score 550 paper-based; 213 computer-based; 80 iBT), IELTS (minimum score 6.5). *Application deadline:* For fall admission, 1/15 priority date for domestic and international students. Applications are processed on a rolling basis. Application fee: $45 ($75 for international students). Electronic applications accepted. *Expenses:* Tuition, state resident: full-time $11,426; part-time $476 per credit hour. Tuition, nonresident: full-time $21,660; part-time $903 per credit hour. One-time fee: $62. *Financial support:* Fellowships, research assistantships with full tuition reimbursements, teaching assistantships with full tuition reimbursements, Federal Work-Study, scholarships/grants, tuition waivers (full), and unspecified assistantships available. Support available to part-time students. *Faculty research:* Biochemical parasitology, physiological ecology, animal physiology. *Unit head:* Dr. Doug Leaman, Chair, 419-530-1555, E-mail: douglas.leaman@utoledo.edu. *Application contact:* Graduate School Office, 419-530-4723, Fax: 419-530-4724, E-mail: grdsch@utnet.utoledo.edu.

University of Toronto, School of Graduate Studies, Life Sciences Division, Department of Cell and Systems Biology, Toronto, ON M5S 1A1, Canada. Offers M Sc, PhD. *Degree requirements:* For master's, thesis, thesis defense; for doctorate, thesis/dissertation, thesis defense, oral thesis examination. *Entrance requirements:* For master's, minimum B+ average in final year, B overall, 3 letters of reference. Additional exam requirements/recommendations for international students: Required—TOEFL (minimum score 580 paper-based; 237 computer-based), TWE (minimum score 5).

University of Vermont, Graduate College, Cell and Molecular Biology Program, Burlington, VT 05405. Offers MS, PhD. *Students:* 39; includes 3 Asian, non-Hispanic/Latino; 6 Hispanic/Latino, 7 international. 63 applicants, 29% accepted, 7 enrolled. In 2010, 1 master's, 8 doctorates awarded. *Degree requirements:* For master's, thesis; for doctorate, thesis/dissertation. *Entrance requirements:* For master's and doctorate, GRE General Test. Additional exam requirements/recommendations for international students: Required—TOEFL (minimum score 550 paper-based; 213 computer-based; 80 iBT). *Application deadline:* For fall admission, 1/15 priority date for domestic students. Applications are processed on a rolling basis. Application fee: $40. Electronic applications accepted. *Expenses:* Tuition, state resident: part-time $537 per credit hour. Tuition, nonresident: part-time $1355 per credit hour. *Financial support:* Fellowships, research assistantships, teaching assistantships, career-related internships or fieldwork available. Financial award application deadline: 3/1. *Unit head:* Dr. Karen Lounsbury, Coordinator, 802-656-9673. *Application contact:* Dr. Karen Lounsbury, Coordinator, 802-656-9673.

University of Virginia, School of Medicine, Department of Cell Biology, Charlottesville, VA 22903. Offers PhD, MD/PhD. *Faculty:* 23 full-time (8 women), 3 part-time/adjunct (1 woman). *Students:* 30 full-time (19 women); includes 2 Black or African American, non-Hispanic/Latino; 2 Asian, non-Hispanic/Latino; 1 Hispanic/Latino, 9 international. Average age 28. In 2010, 1 doctorate awarded. *Degree requirements:* For doctorate, one foreign language, thesis/dissertation. *Entrance requirements:* For doctorate, GRE General Test, GRE Subject Test (recommended), 2 letters of recommendation. Additional exam requirements/recommendations for international students: Required—TOEFL. *Application deadline:* For fall admission, 4/15 for domestic and international students. Applications are processed on a rolling basis. Application fee: $60. Electronic applications accepted. *Financial support:* Application deadline: 1/15. *Unit head:* Dr. Barry M. Gumbiner, Chairman, 434-924-2731, Fax: 434-982-3912. *Application contact:* Dr. Barry M. Gumbiner, Chairman, 434-924-2731, Fax: 434-982-3912.

University of Washington, Graduate School, School of Medicine, Graduate Programs in Medicine, Program in Molecular and Cellular Biology, Seattle, WA 98195. Offers PhD. Offered jointly with Fred Hutchinson Cancer Research Center. *Degree requirements:* For doctorate, thesis/dissertation. *Entrance requirements:* For doctorate, GRE General Test, GRE Subject Test. Additional exam requirements/recommendations for international students: Required—TOEFL. Electronic applications accepted.

See Display on next page and Close-Up on page 241.

The University of Western Ontario, Faculty of Graduate Studies, Biosciences Division, Department of Biology, London, ON N6A 5B8, Canada. Offers M Sc, PhD. *Degree requirements:* For master's, thesis; for doctorate, comprehensive exam, thesis/dissertation. *Entrance requirements:* For master's, honors degree or equivalent in biological sciences; for doctorate, master's degree. Additional exam requirements/recommendations for international students: Required—TOEFL. *Faculty research:* Cell and molecular biology, developmental biology, neuroscience, immunobiology and cancer.

University of Wisconsin–La Crosse, Office of University Graduate Studies, College of Science and Health, Department of Biology, La Crosse, WI 54601-3742. Offers aquatic sciences (MS); biology (MS); cellular and molecular biology (MS); clinical microbiology (MS); microbiology (MS); nurse anesthesia (MS); physiology (MS). Part-time programs available. *Faculty:* 31. *Students:* 23 full-time (14 women), 42 part-time (25 women); includes 4 minority (1 Asian, non-Hispanic/Latino; 3 Hispanic/Latino), 1 international. Average age 28. 100 applicants, 34% accepted, 29 enrolled. In 2010, 20 master's awarded. *Degree requirements:* For master's, comprehensive exam, thesis. *Entrance requirements:* For master's, GRE General Test, minimum GPA of 2.85. Additional exam requirements/recommendations for international students: Required—TOEFL (minimum score 550 paper-based; 213 computer-based; 79 iBT). *Application deadline:* For fall admission, 2/1 priority date for domestic and international students; for spring admission, 1/4 priority date for domestic and international students. Applications are processed on a rolling basis. Application fee: $56. Electronic applications accepted. *Expenses:* Tuition, state resident: full-time $7121; part-time $395.61 per credit. Tuition, nonresident: full-time $16,891; part-time $938.41 per credit. Part-time tuition and fees vary according to course load, program and reciprocity agreements. *Financial support:* In 2010–11, 14 research assistantships with partial tuition reimbursements (averaging $10,124 per year) were awarded; Federal Work-Study, scholarships/grants, health care benefits, and tuition waivers (partial) also available. Support available to part-time students. Financial award application deadline: 3/15; financial award applicants required to submit FAFSA. *Unit head:* Dr. Thomas Volk, Coordinator of Graduate Studies, 608-785-6972, Fax: 608-785-6959, E-mail: volk.thom@uwlax.edu. *Application contact:* Kathryn Kiefer, Director of Admissions, 608-785-8939, E-mail: admissions@uwlax.edu.

University of Wisconsin–Madison, Graduate School, Program in Cellular and Molecular Biology, Madison, WI 53706-1596. Offers PhD. *Degree requirements:* For doctorate, comprehensive exam, thesis/dissertation. *Entrance requirements:* For doctorate, GRE General Test, GRE Subject Test (recommended), minimum GPA of 3.0, lab experience. Additional exam requirements/recommendations for international students: Required—TOEFL (minimum score 580 paper-based; 237 computer-based; 92 iBT). Electronic applications accepted. *Expenses:* Tuition, state resident: full-time $9887; part-time $617.96 per credit. Tuition, nonresident: full-time $24,054; part-time $1503.40 per credit. Required fees: $67.63 per credit. Tuition and fees vary according to reciprocity agreements. *Faculty research:* Virology, cancer biology, transcriptional mechanisms, plant biology, immunology.

University of Wyoming, Graduate Program in Molecular and Cellular Life Sciences, Laramie, WY 82070. Offers PhD. *Degree requirements:* For doctorate, thesis/dissertation, four eight-week laboratory rotations, comprehensive basic practical exam, two-part qualifying exam, seminars, symposium.

Cell Biology

W

UNIVERSITY *of* WASHINGTON

www.mcb-seattle.org

Molecular & Cellular Biology

A PhD Program in Seattle Washington

MCB is an interdisciplinary research program fostering an innovative and flexible graduate program with a broad range of research in all areas of biomedical science.

Partners:
FRED HUTCHINSON CANCER RESEARCH CENTER
SEATTLE BIOMEDICAL RESEARCH CENTER
INSTITUTE FOR SYSTEMS BIOLOGY
UNIVERSITY OF WASHINGTON

Vanderbilt University, Graduate School and School of Medicine, Department of Cell and Developmental Biology, Nashville, TN 37240-1001. Offers MS, PhD, MD/PhD. *Faculty:* 20 full-time (9 women). *Students:* 87 full-time (45 women); includes 11 minority (3 Black or African American, non-Hispanic/Latino; 5 Asian, non-Hispanic/Latino; 3 Two or more races, non-Hispanic/Latino). Average age 27. In 2010, 3 master's, 20 doctorates awarded. Terminal master's awarded for partial completion of doctoral program. *Degree requirements:* For master's, thesis or alternative; for doctorate, thesis/dissertation, preliminary, qualifying, and final exams. *Entrance requirements:* For master's, GRE General Test; for doctorate, GRE General Test, GRE Subject Test (recommended). Additional exam requirements/recommendations for international students: Required—TOEFL (minimum score 570 paper-based; 230 computer-based; 88 iBT). *Application deadline:* For fall admission, 1/15 for domestic and international students. Application fee: $0. Electronic applications accepted. *Financial support:* Fellowships with full and partial tuition reimbursements, research assistantships with full and partial tuition reimbursements, career-related internships or fieldwork, Federal Work-Study, institutionally sponsored loans, scholarships/grants, traineeships, health care benefits, and tuition waivers (partial) available. Financial award application deadline: 1/15; financial award applicants required to submit CSS PROFILE or FAFSA. *Faculty research:* Cancer biology, cell cycle regulation, cell signaling, cytoskeletal biology, developmental biology, neurobiology, proteomics, stem cell biology, structural biology, reproductive biology, trafficking and transport, medical education and gross anatomy. *Unit head:* Dr. Susan R. Wente, Chair, 615-936-3455, Fax: 615-343-4539, E-mail: susan.wente@vanderbilt.edu. *Application contact:* Dr. Kathy Gould, Director of Graduate Studies, 615-322-2134, Fax: 615-343-4539, E-mail: kathy.gould@vanderbilt.edu.

Washington State University, Graduate School, College of Sciences, School of Molecular Biosciences, Program in Genetics and Cell Biology, Pullman, WA 99164. Offers MS, PhD. *Faculty:* 23 full-time (5 women), 21 part-time/adjunct (4 women). *Students:* 23 full-time (15 women), 1 (woman) part-time; includes 1 American Indian or Alaska Native, non-Hispanic/Latino; 1 Asian, non-Hispanic/Latino, 7 international. Average age 26. 231 applicants, 18% accepted, 13 enrolled. In 2010, 3 master's, 4 doctorates awarded. Terminal master's awarded for partial completion of doctoral program. *Degree requirements:* For master's, thesis or alternative, oral exam; for doctorate, comprehensive exam, thesis/dissertation, oral exam. *Entrance requirements:* For master's and doctorate, GRE General Test, minimum GPA of 3.0. Additional exam requirements/recommendations for international students: Required—TOEFL (minimum score 550 paper-based; 213 computer-based). *Application deadline:* For fall admission, 12/15 for domestic and international students. Application fee: $50. Electronic applications accepted. *Expenses:* Tuition, state resident: full-time $8552; part-time $443 per credit. Tuition, nonresident: full-time $21,650; part-time $1083 per credit. Required fees: $846. *Financial support:* In 2010–11, 1 fellowship with full tuition reimbursement (averaging $18,852 per year), 16 research assistantships with full tuition reimbursements (averaging $18,852 per year), 6 teaching assistantships with full tuition reimbursements (averaging $18,852 per year) were awarded; Federal Work-Study, institutionally sponsored loans, health care benefits, and unspecified assistantships also available. Financial award application deadline: 4/1; financial award applicants required to submit FAFSA. *Faculty research:* Plant molecular biology, growth factors, cancer induction and DNA repair, gene regulation and genetic engineering. Total annual research expenditures: $5.8 million. *Unit head:* Dr. John H. Nilson, Director, 509-335-8724, Fax: 509-335-9688, E-mail: jhn@wsu.edu. *Application contact:* Kelly G. McGovern, Academic Coordinator, 509-335-4566, Fax: 509-335-1907, E-mail: smbgrad@wsu.edu.

Washington University in St. Louis, Graduate School of Arts and Sciences, Division of Biology and Biomedical Sciences, Program in Molecular Cell Biology, St. Louis, MO 63130-4899. Offers PhD. *Degree requirements:* For doctorate, thesis/dissertation. *Entrance requirements:* For doctorate, GRE General Test, GRE Subject Test. Electronic applications accepted.

Wesleyan University, Graduate Programs, Department of Biology, Middletown, CT 06459. Offers animal behavior (PhD); bioformatics/genomics (PhD); cell biology (PhD); developmental biology (PhD); evolution/ecology (PhD); genetics (PhD); neurobiology (PhD); population biology (PhD). *Faculty:* 12 full-time (4 women). *Students:* 20 full-time (12 women); includes 1 Black or African American, non-Hispanic/Latino; 3 Asian, non-Hispanic/Latino. Average age 26. 24 applicants, 29% accepted, 2 enrolled. *Degree requirements:* For doctorate, variable foreign language requirement, thesis/dissertation. *Entrance requirements:* For doctorate, GRE. Additional exam requirements/recommendations for international students: Required—TOEFL. *Application deadline:* For fall admission, 1/15 for domestic and international students. Applications are processed on a rolling basis. Application fee: $0. *Expenses:* Tuition: Full-time $43,404. Required fees: $830. *Financial support:* In 2010–11, 5 research assistantships with full tuition reimbursements, 16 teaching assistantships with full tuition reimbursements were awarded; stipends also available. Financial award application deadline: 4/15; financial award applicants required to submit FAFSA. *Faculty research:* Microbial population genetics, genetic basis of evolutionary adaptation, genetic regulation of differentiation and pattern formation in *drosophila*. *Unit head:* Dr. Sonia E. Sultan, Chair/Professor, 860-685-3493, E-mail: jnaegele@wesleyan.edu. *Application contact:* Marjorie Fitzgibbons, Information Contact, 860-685-2140, E-mail: mfitzgibbons@wesleyan.edu.

West Virginia University, Eberly College of Arts and Sciences, Department of Biology, Morgantown, WV 26506. Offers cell and molecular biology (MS, PhD); environmental and evolutionary biology (MS, PhD); forensic biology (MS, PhD); genomic biology (MS, PhD); neurobiology (MS, PhD). Terminal master's awarded for partial completion of doctoral program. *Degree requirements:* For master's, thesis, final exam; for doctorate, thesis/dissertation, preliminary and final exams. *Entrance requirements:* For master's, GRE General Test, GRE Subject Test, minimum GPA of 3.0; for doctorate, GRE General Test, minimum GPA of 3.0. Additional exam requirements/recommendations for international students: Required—TOEFL. *Faculty research:* Environmental biology, genetic engineering, developmental biology, global change, biodiversity.

Yale University, Graduate School of Arts and Sciences, Department of Cell Biology, New Haven, CT 06520. Offers PhD. *Degree requirements:* For doctorate, thesis/dissertation. *Entrance requirements:* For doctorate, GRE General Test. *Expenses:* Contact institution.

Yale University, Graduate School of Arts and Sciences, Department of Molecular, Cellular, and Developmental Biology, Program in Cellular and Developmental Biology, New Haven, CT 06520. Offers PhD. *Degree requirements:* For doctorate, thesis/dissertation. *Entrance requirements:* For doctorate, GRE General Test, GRE Subject Test.

Yale University, School of Medicine and Graduate School of Arts and Sciences, Combined Program in Biological and Biomedical Sciences (BBS), Molecular Cell Biology, Genetics, and Development Track, New Haven, CT 06520. Offers PhD, MD/PhD. *Entrance requirements:* Additional exam requirements/recommendations for international students: Required—TOEFL.

Molecular Biology

Albany Medical College, Center for Cell Biology and Cancer Research, Albany, NY 12208-3479. Offers MS, PhD. Part-time programs available. *Faculty:* 14 full-time (4 women). *Students:* 22 full-time (19 women); includes 7 minority (1 Black or African American, non-Hispanic/Latino; 5 Asian, non-Hispanic/Latino; 1 Hispanic/Latino). Average age 26. 25 applicants, 44% accepted, 9 enrolled. In 2010, 1 master's, 5 doctorates awarded. Terminal master's awarded for partial completion of doctoral program. *Degree requirements:* For master's, thesis; for doctorate, comprehensive exam, thesis/dissertation. *Entrance requirements:* For master's and doctorate, GRE General Test, all transcripts, letters of recommendation. Additional exam requirements/recommendations for international students: Required—TOEFL. *Application deadline:* For fall admission, 3/15 priority date for domestic and international students. Applications are processed on a rolling basis. *Financial support:* In 2010–11, 10 research assistantships (averaging $24,000 per year) were awarded; Federal Work-Study, scholarships/grants, and tuition waivers (full) also available. Financial award applicants required to submit FAFSA. *Faculty research:* Cancer cell biology, tissue remodeling, signal transduction, gene regulation, cell adhesion, angiogenesis. *Unit head:* Dr. C. Michael DiPersio, Graduate Director, 518-262-5916, Fax: 518-262-5669, E-mail: dipersm@mail.amc.edu. *Application contact:* Dr. C. Michael DiPersio, Graduate Director, 518-262-5916, Fax: 518-262-5669, E-mail: dipersm@mail.amc.edu.

Albert Einstein College of Medicine, Graduate Division of Biomedical Sciences, Division of Biological Sciences, Department of Developmental and Molecular Biology, Bronx, NY 10461. Offers PhD, MD/PhD. *Degree requirements:* For doctorate, thesis/dissertation. *Entrance requirements:* For doctorate, GRE General Test. Additional exam requirements/recommendations for international students: Required—TOEFL. *Faculty research:* DNA, RNA, and protein synthesis in prokaryotes and eukaryotes; chemical and enzymatic alteration of RNA; glycoproteins.

Appalachian State University, Cratis D. Williams Graduate School, Department of Biology, Boone, NC 28608. Offers cell and molecular (MS); general (MS). Part-time programs available. *Faculty:* 28 full-time (12 women), 2 part-time/adjunct (0 women). *Students:* 36 full-time (19 women), 8 part-time (3 women); includes 2 Asian, non-Hispanic/Latino; 1 Hispanic/Latino. 45 applicants, 51% accepted, 18 enrolled. In 2010, 14 master's awarded. *Degree requirements:* For master's, comprehensive exam, thesis. *Entrance requirements:* For master's, GRE General Test, 3 letters of recommendation. Additional exam requirements/recommendations for international students: Required—TOEFL (minimum score 570 paper-based; 230 computer-based; 79 iBT), IELTS (minimum score 6.5). *Application deadline:* For fall admission, 7/1 for domestic students, 2/1 for international students; for spring admission, 11/1 for domestic students, 7/1 for international students. Applications are processed on a rolling basis. Application fee: $55. Electronic applications accepted. *Expenses:* Tuition, state resident: full-time $3428; part-time $428 per unit. Tuition, nonresident: full-time $14,518; part-time $1814 per unit. Required fees: $2320; $344 per unit. Tuition and fees vary according to campus/location. *Financial support:* In 2010–11, 25 teaching assistantships (averaging $9,500 per year) were awarded; fellowships, research assistantships, career-related internships or fieldwork, Federal Work-Study, scholarships/grants, and unspecified assistantships also available. Financial award application deadline: 4/1; financial award applicants required to submit FAFSA. *Faculty research:* Aquatic and terrestrial ecology, animal and plant physiology, behavior and systematics, immunology and cell biology, molecular biology and microbiology. Total annual research expenditures: $1.3 million. *Unit head:* Dr. Steven Seagle, Chairman, 828-262-3025, E-mail: seaglesw@appstate.edu. *Application contact:* Dr. Gary Walker, Graduate Coordinator, 828-262-3025, E-mail: walkergl@appstate.edu.

Arizona State University, College of Liberal Arts and Sciences, School of Life Sciences, Tempe, AZ 85287-4601. Offers animal behavior (PhD); applied ethics (biomedical and health ethics) (MA); biological design (PhD); biology (MS, PhD); biology (biology and society) (MS, PhD); environmental life sciences (PhD); evolutionary biology (PhD); human and social dimensions of science and technology (PhD); microbiology (PhD); molecular and cellular biology (PhD); neuroscience (PhD); philosophy (history and philosophy of science) (MA); sustainability (PhD). *Faculty:* 102 full-time (26 women), 4 part-time/adjunct (1 woman). *Students:* 188 full-time (95 women), 45 part-time (29 women); includes 31 minority (3 Black or African American, non-Hispanic/Latino; 2 American Indian or Alaska Native, non-Hispanic/Latino; 12 Asian, non-Hispanic/Latino; 12 Hispanic/Latino; 2 Two or more races, non-Hispanic/Latino), 39 international. Average age 30. 203 applicants, 41% accepted, 60 enrolled. In 2010, 17 master's, 21 doctorates awarded. Terminal master's awarded for partial completion of doctoral program. *Degree requirements:* For master's, thesis (for some programs), interactive Program of Study (iPOS) submitted before completing 50 percent of required credit hours; for doctorate, variable foreign language requirement, comprehensive exam, thesis/dissertation, interactive Program of Study (iPOS) submitted before completing 50 percent of required credit hours. *Entrance requirements:* For master's and doctorate, GRE, minimum GPA of 3.0 or equivalent in last 2 years of work leading to bachelor's degree. Additional exam requirements/recommendations for international students: Required—TOEFL (minimum score 600 paper-based; 250 computer-based; 100 iBT). *Application deadline:* For fall admission, 12/15 for domestic and international students. Application fee: $70 ($90 for international students). Electronic applications accepted. *Expenses:* Tuition, state resident: full-time $8510; part-time $608 per credit. Tuition, nonresident: full-time $16,542; part-time $919 per credit. Required fees: $339; $110 per credit. Part-time tuition and fees vary according to course load. *Financial support:* In 2010–11, 80 research assistantships with full and partial tuition reimbursements (averaging $17,888 per year), 101 teaching assistantships with full and partial tuition reimbursements (averaging $17,327 per year) were awarded; fellowships with full tuition reimbursements, career-related internships or fieldwork, Federal Work-Study, institutionally sponsored loans, scholarships/grants, and tuition waivers (full and partial) also available. Financial award application deadline: 3/1; financial award applicants required to submit FAFSA. Total annual research expenditures: $29.3 million. *Unit head:* Dr. Robert E. Page, Director, 480-965-0803, E-mail: robert.page@asu.edu. *Application contact:* Graduate Admissions, 480-965-6113.

Arkansas State University, Graduate School, College of Sciences and Mathematics, Program in Molecular Biosciences, Jonesboro, State University, AR 72467. Offers biotechnology (Certificate); molecular biosciences (PhD). Part-time programs available. *Faculty:* 2 full-time (1 woman), 3 part-time/adjunct (1 woman). *Students:* 18 full-time (5 women), 1 (woman) part-time; includes 3 minority (1 American Indian or Alaska Native, non-Hispanic/Latino; 1 Asian, non-Hispanic/Latino; 1 Two or more races, non-Hispanic/Latino), 11 international. Average age 29. 4 applicants, 50% accepted, 2 enrolled. *Degree requirements:* For doctorate, comprehensive exam, thesis/dissertation. *Entrance requirements:* For doctorate, GRE, appropriate bachelor's or master's degree, interview, letters of reference, official transcripts, personal statement, immunization records. Additional exam requirements/recommendations for international students: Required—TOEFL (minimum score 550 paper-based; 213 computer-based; 79 iBT), IELTS (minimum score 6), PTE: Pearson Test of English Academic (56). *Application deadline:* For fall admission, 2/15 for domestic and international students; for spring admission, 11/15 for domestic students, 11/14 for international students. Applications are processed on a rolling basis. Application fee: $50. Electronic applications accepted. *Expenses:* Tuition, state resident: full-time $3888; part-time $216 per credit hour. Tuition, nonresident: full-time $9918; part-time $551 per credit hour. International tuition: $8376 full-time. Required fees: $932; $49 per credit hour. $25 per term. One-time fee: $30. Tuition and fees vary according to course load and program. *Financial support:* In 2010–11, 14 students received support; fellowships, research assistantships, teaching assistantships, career-related internships or fieldwork, scholarships/grants, and unspecified assistantships available. Financial award application deadline: 7/1; financial award applicants required to submit FAFSA. *Unit head:* Dr. Roger Buchanan, Director, 870-972-2007, Fax: 870-972-2008, E-mail: rbuck@astate.edu. *Application contact:* Dr. Andrew Sustich, Dean of the Graduate School, 870-972-3029, Fax: 870-972-3857, E-mail: sustich@astate.edu.

Auburn University, Graduate School, Interdepartmental Programs, Auburn University, AL 36849. Offers cell and molecular biology (PhD); integrated textile and apparel sciences (PhD); sociology and rural sociology (MA, MS), including rural sociology (MS), sociology. Part-time programs available. *Students:* 25 full-time (12 women), 19 part-time (13 women); includes 1 Black or African American, non-Hispanic/Latino; 1 American Indian or Alaska Native, non-Hispanic/Latino; 2 Asian, non-Hispanic/Latino, 26 international. Average age 28. 88 applicants, 35% accepted, 12 enrolled. In 2010, 4 master's, 3 doctorates awarded. *Entrance requirements:* For master's, GRE General Test. *Application deadline:* For fall admission, 7/7 for domestic students; for spring admission, 11/24 for domestic students. Applications are processed on a rolling basis. Application fee: $50 ($60 for international students). Electronic applications accepted. *Expenses:* Tuition, state resident: full-time $7002. Tuition, nonresident: full-time $21,898. International tuition: $22,116 full-time. Required fees: $892. Tuition and fees vary according to course load and program. *Financial support:* Fellowships, research assistantships, teaching assistantships, Federal Work-Study available. Support available to part-time students. Financial award application deadline: 3/15; financial award applicants required to submit FAFSA. *Unit head:* Interim Dean of the Graduate School. *Application contact:* Dr. George Flowers, Dean of the Graduate School, 334-844-2125.

Baylor College of Medicine, Graduate School of Biomedical Sciences, Department of Biochemistry and Molecular Biology, Houston, TX 77030-3498. Offers PhD, MD/PhD. *Faculty:* 37 full-time (7 women). *Students:* 53 full-time (26 women); includes 1 Black or African American, non-Hispanic/Latino; 1 American Indian or Alaska Native, non-Hispanic/Latino; 2 Asian, non-Hispanic/Latino; 2 Hispanic/Latino, 31 international. Average age 28. 99 applicants, 15% accepted, 8 enrolled. In 2010, 6 doctorates awarded. *Degree requirements:* For doctorate, thesis/dissertation, public defense. *Entrance requirements:* For doctorate, GRE General Test, GRE Subject Test (strongly recommended), minimum GPA of 3.0. Additional exam requirements/recommendations for international students: Required—TOEFL. *Application deadline:* For fall admission, 1/1 priority date for domestic students. Application fee: $0. Electronic applications accepted. *Expenses:* Tuition: Full-time $11,000. Required fees: $4900. *Financial support:* In 2010–11, 12 fellowships with full tuition reimbursements (averaging $26,000 per year), 41 research assistantships with full tuition reimbursements (averaging $26,000 per year) were awarded; career-related internships or fieldwork, Federal Work-Study, institutionally sponsored loans, health care benefits, and students receive a scholarship unless there are grant funds available to pay tuition also available. Financial award applicants required to submit FAFSA. *Faculty research:* DNA repair, homologous recombination, gene therapy, trinucleotide repeat diseases, retinitis pigmentosa. *Unit head:* Dr. John Wilson, Director, 713-798-5760. *Application contact:* Monica Bagos, Graduate Program Administrator, 713-798-0124, Fax: 713-796-9438, E-mail: bagos@bcm.edu.

Baylor College of Medicine, Graduate School of Biomedical Sciences, Department of Molecular and Cellular Biology, Houston, TX 77030-3498. Offers PhD, MD/PhD. *Faculty:* 75 full-time (21 women). *Students:* 63 full-time (36 women); includes 1 Black or African American, non-Hispanic/Latino; 6 Asian, non-Hispanic/Latino; 6 Hispanic/Latino, 19 international. Average age 27. 127 applicants, 17% accepted, 8 enrolled. In 2010, 12 doctorates awarded. *Degree requirements:* For doctorate, thesis/dissertation, public defense, qualifying exam. *Entrance requirements:* For doctorate, GRE General Test, GRE Subject Test (strongly recommended), minimum GPA of 3.0. Additional exam requirements/recommendations for international students: Required—TOEFL. *Application deadline:* For fall admission, 1/1 priority date for domestic students. Application fee: $0. Electronic applications accepted. *Expenses:* Tuition: Full-time $11,000. Required fees: $4900. *Financial support:* In 2010–11, 14 fellowships with full tuition reimbursements (averaging $26,000 per year), 49 research assistantships with full tuition reimbursements (averaging $26,000 per year) were awarded; career-related internships or fieldwork, Federal Work-Study, institutionally sponsored loans, health care benefits, and tuition waivers (full) also available. Financial award applicants required to submit FAFSA. *Faculty research:* Hormone action, development, cancer, gene therapy, neurobiology. *Unit head:* Dr. JoAnne Richards, Director, 713-798-4598. *Application contact:* Caroline Kosnik, Graduate Program Administrator, 713-798-4598, Fax: 713-790-0545, E-mail: ckosnik@bcm.edu.

Baylor College of Medicine, Graduate School of Biomedical Sciences, Interdepartmental Program in Cell and Molecular Biology, Houston, TX 77030-3498. Offers biochemistry (PhD); cell and molecular biology (PhD); genetics (PhD); human genetics (PhD); immunology (PhD); microbiology (PhD); virology (PhD); MD/PhD. *Faculty:* 100 full-time (31 women). *Students:* 67 full-time (41 women); includes 4 Black or African American, non-Hispanic/Latino; 2 American Indian or Alaska Native, non-Hispanic/Latino; 9 Asian, non-Hispanic/Latino; 9 Hispanic/Latino, 9 international. Average age 27. 120 applicants, 27% accepted, 15 enrolled. In 2010, 7 doctorates awarded. *Degree requirements:* For doctorate, thesis/dissertation, public defense. *Entrance requirements:* For doctorate, GRE General Test, GRE Subject Test (strongly recommended), minimum GPA of 3.0. Additional exam requirements/recommendations for international students: Required—TOEFL. *Application deadline:* For fall admission, 1/1 priority date for domestic students. Applications are processed on a rolling basis. Application fee: $0. Electronic applications accepted. *Expenses:* Tuition: Full-time $11,000. Required fees: $4900. *Financial support:* In 2010–11, 67 students received support, including 24 fellowships with full tuition reimbursements available (averaging $26,000 per year), 43 research assistantships with full tuition reimbursements available (averaging $26,000 per year); teaching assistantships, Federal Work-Study, institutionally sponsored loans, health care benefits, and tuition waivers (full) also available. Financial award applicants required to submit FAFSA. *Faculty research:* Molecular and cellular biology; cancer, aging and stem cells; genomics and proteomics; microbiome, molecular microbiology; infectious disease, immunology and translational research. *Unit head:* Dr. Susan Marriott, Director, 713-798-6557. *Application contact:* Lourdes Fernandez, Graduate Program Administrator, 713-798-6557, Fax: 713-798-6325, E-mail: cmbprog@bcm.edu.

See Close-Up on page 223.

Baylor College of Medicine, Graduate School of Biomedical Sciences, Program in Developmental Biology, Houston, TX 77030-3498. Offers PhD, MD/PhD. *Faculty:* 63 full-time (19 women). *Students:* 55 full-time (26 women); includes 5 Asian, non-Hispanic/Latino; 3 Hispanic/Latino, 35 international. Average age 28. 73 applicants, 18% accepted, 10 enrolled. In 2010, 5 doctorates awarded. *Degree requirements:* For doctorate, thesis/dissertation, public defense. *Entrance requirements:* For doctorate, GRE General Test, GRE Subject Test (strongly recommended), minimum GPA of 3.0. Additional exam requirements/recommendations for international students: Required—TOEFL. *Application deadline:* For fall admission, 1/1 priority date for domestic students. Application fee: $0. Electronic applications accepted. *Expenses:* Tuition: Full-time $11,000. Required fees: $4900. *Financial support:* In 2010–11, 55 students received support, including 15 fellowships with full tuition reimbursements available (averaging $26,000 per year), 40 research assistantships with full tuition reimbursements available (averaging $26,000 per year); career-related internships or fieldwork, Federal Work-Study, institutionally sponsored loans, health care benefits, tuition waivers (full), and stipends also available. *Faculty research:* Stem cells, cancer, neurobiology, organogenesis, genetics of model organisms. *Unit head:* Dr. Hugo Bellen, Director, 713-798-6410. *Application contact:* Catherine Tasnier, Graduate Program Administrator, 713-798-6410, Fax: 713-798-5386, E-mail: cat@bcm.edu.

See Display on page 282 and Close-Up on page 307.

Boston University, Graduate School of Arts and Sciences, Molecular Biology, Cell Biology, and Biochemistry Program (MCBB), Boston, MA 02215. Offers MA, PhD. *Students:* 36 full-time (17 women), 2 part-time (both women); includes 9 minority (3 Black or African American, non-Hispanic/Latino; 3 Asian, non-Hispanic/Latino; 3 Hispanic/Latino), 6 international. Average age 28. 77 applicants, 18% accepted, 5 enrolled. In 2010, 6 master's, 20 doctorates awarded. Terminal master's awarded for partial completion of doctoral program. *Degree requirements:* For master's, one foreign language, thesis (for some programs); for doctorate, one foreign language, comprehensive exam, thesis/dissertation. *Entrance requirements:* For master's and

Molecular Biology

Boston University (continued)
doctorate, GRE General Test, GRE Subject Test. Additional exam requirements/recommendations for international students: Required—TOEFL (minimum score 600 paper-based; 250 computer-based). *Application deadline:* For fall admission, 12/7 for domestic and international students. Application fee: $70. Electronic applications accepted. *Expenses:* Tuition: Full-time $39,314; part-time $1228 per credit. Required fees: $40 per semester. *Financial support:* In 2010–11, 9 students received support, including 1 fellowship with full tuition reimbursement available (averaging $19,300 per year), 7 research assistantships with full tuition reimbursements available (averaging $18,800 per year), 1 teaching assistantship with full tuition reimbursement available (averaging $18,800 per year); Federal Work-Study, scholarships/grants, and traineeships also available. Financial award application deadline: 12/7; financial award applicants required to submit FAFSA. *Unit head:* Dr. Ulla Hansen, Director, 617-353-2432, Fax: 617-353-6340, E-mail: uhansen@bu.edu. *Application contact:* Meredith Canode, Academic Administrator, 617-353-2432, Fax: 617-353-6340, E-mail: mcanode@bu.edu.

Boston University, School of Medicine, Division of Graduate Medical Sciences, Department of Biochemistry, Boston, MA 02118. Offers MA, PhD, MD/PhD. Part-time programs available. *Faculty:* 41 full-time (17 women), 11 part-time/adjunct (5 women). *Students:* 31 full-time (18 women), 2 part-time (1 woman); includes 2 Asian, non-Hispanic/Latino; 1 Hispanic/Latino, 18 international. 88 applicants, 16% accepted, 7 enrolled. In 2010, 3 master's, 6 doctorates awarded. Terminal master's awarded for partial completion of doctoral program. *Degree requirements:* For master's, thesis or alternative, qualifying exam; for doctorate, thesis/dissertation, qualifying exam. *Entrance requirements:* For master's and doctorate, GRE General Test, GRE Subject Test. Additional exam requirements/recommendations for international students: Required—TOEFL. *Application deadline:* For fall admission, 1/15 priority date for domestic students; for spring admission, 10/15 priority date for domestic students. Application fee: $75. Electronic applications accepted. *Expenses:* Tuition: Full-time $39,314; part-time $1228 per credit. Required fees: $40 per semester. *Financial support:* In 2010–11, 1 fellowship (averaging $30,500 per year), 27 research assistantships (averaging $30,500 per year) were awarded; Federal Work-Study, scholarships/grants, and traineeships also available. Financial award applicants required to submit FAFSA. *Faculty research:* Extracellular matrix, gene expression, receptors, growth control. *Unit head:* Dr. David A. Harris, Chair, 617-638-5090. *Application contact:* Dr. Barbara Schreiber, Director of the Graduate Program, 617-638-5094, E-mail: schreibe@bu.edu.

Boston University, School of Medicine, Division of Graduate Medical Sciences, Program in Cell and Molecular Biology, Boston, MA 02118. Offers PhD, MD/PhD. *Faculty:* 10 full-time (5 women). *Students:* 35 full-time (18 women); includes 1 Asian, non-Hispanic/Latino; 1 Two or more races, non-Hispanic/Latino, 11 international. 102 applicants, 14% accepted, 4 enrolled. In 2010, 9 doctorates awarded. *Degree requirements:* For doctorate, thesis/dissertation. *Entrance requirements:* For doctorate, GRE General Test, GRE Subject Test. Additional exam requirements/recommendations for international students: Required—TOEFL. *Application deadline:* For fall admission, 1/15 priority date for domestic students; for spring admission, 10/15 priority date for domestic students. Application fee: $75. Electronic applications accepted. *Expenses:* Tuition: Full-time $39,314; part-time $1228 per credit. Required fees: $40 per semester. *Financial support:* In 2010–11, 3 fellowships (averaging $30,500 per year), 29 research assistantships (averaging $30,500 per year) were awarded; Federal Work-Study, scholarships/grants, and traineeships also available. Financial award applicants required to submit FAFSA. *Unit head:* Dr. Vickery Trinkaus Randall, Director, 617-638-6099, Fax: 617-638-5337, E-mail: vickery@bu.edu. *Application contact:* Dr. Vickery Trinkaus-Randall, Program Director, 617-638-6099, Fax: 617-638-5337, E-mail: vickery@bu.edu.

Brandeis University, Graduate School of Arts and Sciences, Program in Molecular and Cell Biology, Waltham, MA 02454-9110. Offers genetics (PhD); microbiology (PhD); molecular and cell biology (MS, PhD); molecular biology (PhD); neurobiology (PhD). *Faculty:* 30 full-time (13 women), 1 (woman) part-time/adjunct. *Students:* 55 full-time (31 women); includes 1 Black or African American, non-Hispanic/Latino; 1 American Indian or Alaska Native, non-Hispanic/Latino; 1 Asian, non-Hispanic/Latino; 2 Hispanic/Latino, 12 international. 138 applicants, 32% accepted, 17 enrolled. In 2010, 3 master's, 3 doctorates awarded. Terminal master's awarded for partial completion of doctoral program. *Degree requirements:* For master's, thesis optional, research project; for doctorate, comprehensive exam, thesis/dissertation, teaching assistant experience. *Entrance requirements:* For master's and doctorate, GRE General Test, official transcript(s), resume, 3 letters of recommendation, statement of purpose. Additional exam requirements/recommendations for international students: Required—TOEFL (minimum score 600 paper-based; 250 computer-based; 100 iBT); Recommended—IELTS (minimum score 7). *Application deadline:* For fall admission, 1/15 priority date for domestic students. Applications are processed on a rolling basis. Application fee: $75. Electronic applications accepted. *Financial support:* In 2010–11, 41 students received support, including 13 fellowships with full tuition reimbursements available (averaging $27,500 per year), 27 research assistantships with full tuition reimbursements available (averaging $27,500 per year), 1 teaching assistantship with partial tuition reimbursement available (averaging $3,200 per year); scholarships/grants, traineeships, health care benefits, and tuition waivers (full and partial) also available. Financial award application deadline: 4/15; financial award applicants required to submit FAFSA. *Faculty research:* Molecular biology, cell biology, biology, structural biology, immunology, developmental biology, neurobiology, DNA, RNA. *Unit head:* Dr. Piali Sengupta, Chair, 781-736-2686, Fax: 781-736-3107, E-mail: piali@brandeis.edu. *Application contact:* Marcia Cabral, Department Administrator, 781-736-3100, Fax: 781-736-3107, E-mail: cabral@brandeis.edu.

Brigham Young University, Graduate Studies, College of Life Sciences, Department of Microbiology and Molecular Biology, Provo, UT 84602-1001. Offers microbiology (MS, PhD); molecular biology (MS, PhD). *Faculty:* 17 full-time (3 women), 2 part-time/adjunct (1 woman). *Students:* 21 full-time (9 women); includes 3 Asian, non-Hispanic/Latino; 3 Hispanic/Latino, 1 international. Average age 28. 17 applicants, 47% accepted, 7 enrolled. In 2010, 3 master's, 1 doctorate awarded. Terminal master's awarded for partial completion of doctoral program. *Degree requirements:* For master's, comprehensive exam, thesis; for doctorate, comprehensive exam, thesis/dissertation. *Entrance requirements:* For master's, GRE General Test, minimum GPA of 3.0 during previous 2 years; for doctorate, GRE General Test, minimum GPA of 3.0. Additional exam requirements/recommendations for international students: Required—TOEFL (minimum score 580 paper-based; 85 iBT), IELTS (minimum score 7). *Application deadline:* For fall admission, 12/15 priority date for domestic and international students. Application fee: $50. Electronic applications accepted. *Expenses:* Tuition: Full-time $5580; part-time $310 per credit hour. Tuition and fees vary according to program and student's religious affiliation. *Financial support:* In 2010–11, 17 students received support, including 8 research assistantships with full and partial tuition reimbursements available (averaging $18,000 per year), 7 teaching assistantships with full and partial tuition reimbursements available (averaging $18,000 per year); institutionally sponsored loans, scholarships/grants, health care benefits, and unspecified assistantships also available. Financial award application deadline: 2/1. *Faculty research:* Immunobiology, molecular genetics, molecular virology, cancer biology, pathogenic and environmental microbiology. Total annual research expenditures: $414,278. *Unit head:* Dr. Brent L. Nielsen, Chair, 801-422-1102, Fax: 801-422-0519, E-mail: brent_nielsen@byu.edu. *Application contact:* Dr. Richard A. Robison, Graduate Coordinator, 801-422-2416, Fax: 801-422-0519, E-mail: richard_robison@byu.edu.

Brown University, Graduate School, Division of Biology and Medicine, Program in Molecular Biology, Cell Biology, and Biochemistry, Providence, RI 02912. Offers biochemistry (M Med Sc, Sc M, PhD), including biochemistry (Sc M, PhD), biology (Sc M, PhD), medical science (M Med Sc, PhD); biology (MA); cell biology (M Med Sc, Sc M, PhD), including biochemistry (Sc M, PhD), biology (Sc M, PhD), medical science (M Med Sc, PhD); developmental biology (M Med Sc, Sc M, PhD), including biochemistry (Sc M, PhD), biology (Sc M, PhD), medical science (M Med Sc, PhD); immunology (M Med Sc, Sc M, PhD), including biochemistry (Sc M, PhD), biology (Sc M, PhD), medical science (M Med Sc, PhD); molecular microbiology (M Med Sc, Sc M, PhD), including biochemistry (Sc M, PhD), biology (Sc M, PhD), medical science (M Med Sc, PhD); MD/PhD. Part-time programs available. Terminal master's awarded for partial completion of doctoral program. *Degree requirements:* For master's, thesis (for some programs); for doctorate, one foreign language, thesis/dissertation, preliminary exam. *Entrance requirements:* For master's and doctorate, GRE General Test, GRE Subject Test. Additional exam requirements/recommendations for international students: Required—TOEFL. Electronic applications accepted. *Faculty research:* Molecular genetics, gene regulation.

California Institute of Technology, Division of Biology, Program in Molecular Biology, Pasadena, CA 91125-0001. Offers PhD. *Degree requirements:* For doctorate, thesis/dissertation, qualifying exam. *Entrance requirements:* For doctorate, GRE General Test.

Carnegie Mellon University, Mellon College of Science, Department of Biological Sciences, Pittsburgh, PA 15213-3891. Offers biochemistry (PhD); biophysics (PhD); cell biology (PhD); computational biology (MS, PhD); developmental biology (PhD); genetics (PhD); molecular biology (PhD); neuroscience (PhD). *Degree requirements:* For doctorate, comprehensive exam, thesis/dissertation. *Entrance requirements:* For doctorate, GRE General Test, GRE Subject Test, interview. Electronic applications accepted. *Faculty research:* Genetic structure, function, and regulation; protein structure and function; biological membranes; biological spectroscopy.

Case Western Reserve University, School of Medicine and School of Graduate Studies, Graduate Programs in Medicine, Department of Molecular Biology and Microbiology, Cleveland, OH 44106-4960. Offers cellular biology (PhD); microbiology (PhD); molecular biology (PhD); molecular virology (PhD); MD/PhD. Students are admitted to an integrated Biomedical Sciences Training Program involving 11 basic science programs at Case Western Reserve University. *Degree requirements:* For doctorate, thesis/dissertation. *Entrance requirements:* For doctorate, GRE General Test, GRE Subject Test. Additional exam requirements/recommendations for international students: Required—TOEFL. Electronic applications accepted. *Faculty research:* Gene expression in eukaryotic and prokaryotic systems; microbial physiology; intracellular transport and signaling; mechanisms of oncogenesis; molecular mechanisms of RNA processing, editing, and catalysis.

Central Connecticut State University, School of Graduate Studies, School of Technology, Department of Biomolecular Sciences, New Britain, CT 06050-4010. Offers MS. Part-time and evening/weekend programs available. *Faculty:* 8 full-time (3 women), 6 part-time/adjunct (5 women). *Students:* 17 full-time (9 women), 18 part-time (12 women); includes 12 minority (1 Black or African American, non-Hispanic/Latino; 8 Asian, non-Hispanic/Latino; 3 Hispanic/Latino), 1 international. Average age 27. 18 applicants, 89% accepted, 15 enrolled. In 2010, 9 master's awarded. *Degree requirements:* For master's, comprehensive exam, thesis or alternative. *Entrance requirements:* For master's, minimum undergraduate GPA of 2.7. Additional exam requirements/recommendations for international students: Required—TOEFL. *Application deadline:* For fall admission, 7/1 for domestic students; for spring admission, 12/1 for domestic students. Applications are processed on a rolling basis. Application fee: $50. Electronic applications accepted. *Expenses:* Tuition, area resident: Full-time $5012; part-time $470 per credit. Tuition, state resident: full-time $7518; part-time $482 per credit. Tuition, nonresident: full-time $13,962; part-time $482 per credit. Required fees: $3772. One-time fee: $62 part-time. *Financial support:* In 2010–11, 4 students received support, including 3 research assistantships; career-related internships or fieldwork, Federal Work-Study, scholarships/grants, and unspecified assistantships also available. Support available to part-time students. Financial award application deadline: 2/15; financial award applicants required to submit FAFSA. *Unit head:* Dr. James Mulrooney, Chair, 860-832-3560. *Application contact:* Dr. James Mulrooney, Chair, 860-832-3560.

Clemson University, Graduate School, College of Agriculture, Forestry and Life Sciences, Department of Genetics and Biochemistry, Program in Biochemistry and Molecular Biology, Clemson, SC 29634. Offers PhD. *Students:* 17 full-time (11 women), 1 (woman) part-time, 9 international. Average age 29. 24 applicants, 21% accepted, 5 enrolled. In 2010, 1 doctorate awarded. *Degree requirements:* For doctorate, comprehensive exam, thesis/dissertation. *Entrance requirements:* For doctorate, GRE General Test. Additional exam requirements/recommendations for international students: Required—TOEFL. *Application deadline:* For fall admission, 1/1 for domestic students; for spring admission, 9/1 for domestic students. Applications are processed on a rolling basis. Application fee: $70 ($80 for international students). Electronic applications accepted. *Expenses:* Contact institution. *Financial support:* In 2010–11, 17 students received support, including 2 fellowships with full and partial tuition reimbursements available (averaging $9,750 per year), 9 research assistantships with partial tuition reimbursements available (averaging $16,167 per year), 12 teaching assistantships with partial tuition reimbursements available (averaging $15,875 per year); career-related internships or fieldwork, institutionally sponsored loans, scholarships/grants, health care benefits, and unspecified assistantships also available. Support available to part-time students. Financial award application deadline: 3/15; financial award applicants required to submit FAFSA. *Faculty research:* Biomembranes, protein structure, molecular biology of plants, APYA and stress response. Total annual research expenditures: $670,000. *Unit head:* Dr. Keith Murphy, Chair, 864-656-6237, Fax: 864-656-0435, E-mail: kmurph2@clemson.edu. *Application contact:* Sheryl Banks, Administrative Coordinator, 864-656-6878, E-mail: sherylb@clemson.edu.

Colorado State University, Graduate School, Program in Cell and Molecular Biology, Fort Collins, CO 80523-1618. Offers MS, PhD. *Students:* 25 full-time (16 women), 31 part-time (14 women); includes 12 minority (1 Black or African American, non-Hispanic/Latino; 1 American Indian or Alaska Native, non-Hispanic/Latino; 3 Asian, non-Hispanic/Latino; 6 Hispanic/Latino; 1 Two or more races, non-Hispanic/Latino), 11 international. Average age 30. 57 applicants, 19% accepted, 9 enrolled. In 2010, 2 master's, 7 doctorates awarded. *Degree requirements:* For master's, comprehensive exam, thesis; for doctorate, comprehensive exam, thesis/dissertation. *Entrance requirements:* For master's and doctorate, GRE General Test, GRE Subject Test in biology (strongly recommended), minimum GPA of 3.0; BA/BS in biology, biochemistry, physics; calculus sequence, letters of recommendation. Additional exam requirements/recommendations for international students: Required—TOEFL (minimum score 625 paper-based; 263 computer-based; 107 iBT). *Application deadline:* For fall admission, 1/1 priority date for domestic and international students. Application fee: $50. Electronic applications accepted. *Expenses:* Tuition, state resident: full-time $7434; part-time $413 per credit. Tuition, nonresident: full-time $19,022; part-time $1057 per credit. Required fees: $1729; $88 per credit. *Financial support:* In 2010–11, 5 students received support, including 2 research assistantships with full tuition reimbursements available (averaging $12,152 per year), 3 teaching assistantships with full tuition reimbursements available (averaging $16,962 per year); fellowships with partial tuition reimbursements available, traineeships and unspecified assistantships also available. Financial award application deadline: 1/1; financial award applicants required to submit FAFSA. *Faculty research:* Regulation of gene expression, cancer biology, plant molecular genetics, reproductive physiology, infectious diseases. Total annual research expenditures: $2,353. *Unit head:* Dr. Paul J. Laybourn, Director, 970-491-5100, Fax: 970-491-0623, E-mail: paul.laybourn@colostate.edu. *Application contact:* Lori Williams, Administrative Assistant, 970-491-0241, Fax: 970-491-0623, E-mail: cmb@colostate.edu.

Columbia University, College of Physicians and Surgeons, Integrated Program in Cellular, Molecular, Structural and Genetic Studies, New York, NY 10032. Offers PhD. Terminal master's awarded for partial completion of doctoral program. *Degree requirements:* For doctorate, thesis/dissertation. *Entrance requirements:* For doctorate, GRE General Test, GRE Subject Test. Additional exam requirements/recommendations for international students: Required—TOEFL. *Expenses:* Contact institution. *Faculty research:* Transcription, macromolecular sorting, gene expression during development, cellular interaction.

Cornell University, Graduate School, Graduate Fields of Agriculture and Life Sciences, Field of Biochemistry, Molecular and Cell Biology, Ithaca, NY 14853-0001. Offers biochemistry (PhD); biophysics (PhD); cell biology (PhD); molecular and cell biology (PhD); molecular biology (PhD). *Faculty:* 59 full-time (15 women). *Students:* 90 full-time (47 women); includes 1

Black or African American, non-Hispanic/Latino; 7 Asian, non-Hispanic/Latino; 4 Hispanic/Latino, 30 international. Average age 26. 269 applicants, 9% accepted, 20 enrolled. In 2010, 12 doctorates awarded. *Degree requirements:* For doctorate, comprehensive exam, thesis/dissertation, 2 semesters of teaching experience. *Entrance requirements:* For doctorate, GRE General Test, GRE Subject Test (biology, chemistry, physics, biochemistry, cell and molecular biology), 3 letters of recommendation. Additional exam requirements/recommendations for international students: Required—TOEFL (minimum score 600 paper-based; 250 computer-based; 77 iBT). *Application deadline:* For fall admission, 1/5 for domestic students. Application fee: $70. Electronic applications accepted. *Expenses:* Tuition: Full-time $29,500. Required fees: $76. Tuition and fees vary according to degree level and program. *Financial support:* In 2010–11, 88 students received support, including 25 fellowships with full tuition reimbursements available, 48 research assistantships with full tuition reimbursements available, 15 teaching assistantships with full tuition reimbursements available; institutionally sponsored loans, scholarships/grants, health care benefits, tuition waivers (full and partial), and unspecified assistantships also available. Financial award applicants required to submit FAFSA. *Faculty research:* Biophysics, structural biology. *Unit head:* Director of Graduate Studies, 607-255-2100, Fax: 607-255-2100. *Application contact:* Graduate Field Assistant, 607-255-2100, Fax: 607-255-2100, E-mail: bmcb@cornell.edu.

Cornell University, Joan and Sanford I. Weill Medical College and Graduate School of Medical Sciences, Weill Cornell Graduate School of Medical Sciences, Biochemistry, Cell and Molecular Biology Allied Program, New York, NY 10065. Offers MS, PhD. *Faculty:* 106 full-time (30 women). *Students:* 143 full-time (91 women); includes 2 Black or African American, non-Hispanic/Latino; 8 Asian, non-Hispanic/Latino; 6 Hispanic/Latino, 73 international. Average age 22. 322 applicants, 17% accepted, 14 enrolled. In 2010, 19 doctorates awarded. Terminal master's awarded for partial completion of doctoral program. *Degree requirements:* For master's, comprehensive exam; for doctorate, thesis/dissertation, final exam. *Entrance requirements:* For doctorate, GRE General Test, background in genetics, molecular biology, chemistry, or biochemistry. Additional exam requirements/recommendations for international students: Required—TOEFL. *Application deadline:* For fall admission, 12/1 for domestic students. Application fee: $60. Electronic applications accepted. *Expenses:* Tuition: Full-time $45,545. Required fees: $2805. *Financial support:* In 2010–11, 16 fellowships (averaging $23,000 per year) were awarded; scholarships/grants, health care benefits, and stipends (given to all students) also available. *Faculty research:* Molecular structure determination, protein structure, gene structure, stem cell biology, control of gene expression, DNA replication, chromosome maintenance, RNA biosynthesis. *Unit head:* Dr. David Eliezer, Co-Director, 212-746-6557, Fax: 212-717-3047. *Application contact:* Linda Smith, Assistant Dean of Admissions, 212-746-6565, Fax: 212-746-8906, E-mail: lis2025@med.cornell.edu.

Dartmouth College, Graduate Program in Molecular and Cellular Biology, Hanover, NH 03755. Offers PhD, MD/PhD. *Entrance requirements:* For doctorate, GRE General Test, letters of recommendation. Additional exam requirements/recommendations for international students: Required—TOEFL (minimum score 450 paper-based; 90 iBT) or IELTS (minimum score 7). Electronic applications accepted.

Drexel University, College of Medicine, Biomedical Graduate Programs, Interdisciplinary Program in Molecular and Cell Biology and Genetics, Philadelphia, PA 19104-2875. Offers MS, PhD, MD/PhD. Terminal master's awarded for partial completion of doctoral program. *Degree requirements:* For master's, comprehensive exam, thesis; for doctorate, thesis/dissertation, qualifying exam. *Entrance requirements:* For master's, GRE General Test, minimum GPA of 2.75; for doctorate, GRE General Test, minimum GPA of 3.0. Additional exam requirements/recommendations for international students: Required—TOEFL. Electronic applications accepted. *Faculty research:* Molecular anatomy, biochemistry, medical biotechnology, molecular pathology, microbiology and immunology.

Duke University, Graduate School, Department of Biological Anthropology and Anatomy, Durham, NC 27710. Offers cellular and molecular biology (PhD); gross anatomy and physical anthropology (PhD), including comparative morphology of human and non-human primates, primate social behavior, vertebrate paleontology; neuroanatomy (PhD). *Faculty:* 9 full-time. *Students:* 13 full-time (9 women); includes 1 Black or African American, non-Hispanic/Latino; 2 Hispanic/Latino, 1 international. 54 applicants, 9% accepted, 2 enrolled. In 2010, 2 doctorates awarded. *Degree requirements:* For doctorate, one foreign language, thesis/dissertation. *Entrance requirements:* For doctorate, GRE General Test. Additional exam requirements/recommendations for international students: Required—TOEFL (minimum score 550 paper-based; 213 computer-based; 83 iBT), IELTS (minimum score 7). *Application deadline:* For fall admission, 12/8 priority date for domestic and international students. Application fee: $75. Electronic applications accepted. *Financial support:* Fellowships, teaching assistantships, Federal Work-Study available. Financial award application deadline: 12/31. *Unit head:* Daniel Schmitt, Director of Graduate Studies, 919-684-4124, Fax: 919-684-8542, E-mail: mlsquire@duke.edu. *Application contact:* Elizabeth Hutton, Director of Admissions, 919-684-3913, Fax: 919-684-2277, E-mail: grad-admissions@duke.edu.

Duke University, Graduate School, Program in Cellular and Molecular Biology, Durham, NC 27710. Offers Certificate. Students must be enrolled in a participating Ph D program (biology, cell biology, immunology, molecular genetics, neurobiology, pathology, pharmacology). *Faculty:* 144 full-time. *Students:* 22 full-time (10 women); includes 2 Hispanic/Latino, 6 international. 198 applicants, 24% accepted, 19 enrolled. *Entrance requirements:* Additional exam requirements/recommendations for international students: Required—TOEFL (minimum score 550 paper-based; 213 computer-based; 83 iBT), IELTS (minimum score 7). *Application deadline:* For fall admission, 12/8 priority date for domestic and international students. Application fee: $75. Electronic applications accepted. *Financial support:* Fellowships available. Financial award application deadline: 12/8. *Unit head:* Dr. Margarethe Kuehn, Director of Graduate Studies, 919-684-6559, Fax: 919-684-8346, E-mail: carol.richardson@duke.edu. *Application contact:* Elizabeth Hutton, Director of Admissions, 919-684-3913, Fax: 919-684-3913, E-mail: grad-admissions@duke.edu.

East Carolina University, Brody School of Medicine, Department of Biochemistry and Molecular Biology, Greenville, NC 27858-4353. Offers PhD. *Degree requirements:* For doctorate, comprehensive exam, thesis/dissertation. *Entrance requirements:* For doctorate, GRE General Test. Additional exam requirements/recommendations for international students: Required—TOEFL. *Expenses:* Tuition, state resident: full-time $3130; part-time $391.25 per credit hour. Tuition, nonresident: full-time $13,817; part-time $1727.13 per credit hour. Required fees: $1916; $239.50 per credit hour. Tuition and fees vary according to campus/location and program. *Faculty research:* Gene regulation, development and differentiation, contractility and motility, macromolecular interactions, cancer.

East Carolina University, Graduate School, Thomas Harriot College of Arts and Sciences, Department of Biology, Greenville, NC 27858-4353. Offers biology (MS); molecular biology/biotechnology (MS). Part-time programs available. *Degree requirements:* For master's, one foreign language, comprehensive exam, thesis. *Entrance requirements:* For master's, GRE General Test, GRE Subject Test. Additional exam requirements/recommendations for international students: Required—TOEFL. *Expenses:* Tuition, state resident: full-time $3130; part-time $391.25 per credit hour. Tuition, nonresident: full-time $13,817; part-time $1727.13 per credit hour. Required fees: $1916; $239.50 per credit hour. Tuition and fees vary according to campus/location and program. *Faculty research:* Biochemistry, microbiology, cell biology.

Eastern Michigan University, Graduate School, College of Arts and Sciences, Department of Biology, Ypsilanti, MI 48197. Offers cell and molecular biology (MS); community college biology teaching (MS); ecology and organismal biology (MS); general biology (MS); water resources (MS). Part-time and evening/weekend programs available. Postbaccalaureate distance learning degree programs offered (minimal on-campus study). *Faculty:* 20 full-time (4 women). *Students:* 18 full-time (13 women), 35 part-time (19 women); includes 4 minority (2 Black or African American, non-Hispanic/Latino; 2 Two or more races, non-Hispanic/Latino), 13 international. Average age 27. 55 applicants, 47% accepted, 17 enrolled. In 2010, 10 master's awarded. *Entrance requirements:* For master's, GRE General Test, GRE Subject Test. Additional exam requirements/recommendations for international students: Required—TOEFL. *Application deadline:* Applications are processed on a rolling basis. Application fee: $35. *Financial support:* Fellowships, research assistantships with full tuition reimbursements, teaching assistantships with full tuition reimbursements, career-related internships or fieldwork, Federal Work-Study, institutionally sponsored loans, scholarships/grants, tuition waivers (partial), and unspecified assistantships available. Support available to part-time students. Financial award applicants required to submit FAFSA. *Unit head:* Dr. Marianne Laporte, Department Head, 734-487-4242, Fax: 734-487-9235, E-mail: mlaporte@emich.edu. *Application contact:* Dr. Marianne Laporte, Department Head, 734-487-4242, Fax: 734-487-9235, E-mail: mlaporte@emich.edu.

Eastern New Mexico University, Graduate School, College of Liberal Arts and Sciences, Department of Biology, Portales, NM 88130. Offers applied ecology (MS); cell, molecular biology and biotechnology (MS); education (non-thesis) (MS); microbiology (MS); plant biology (MS); zoology (MS). Part-time programs available. *Faculty:* 8 full-time (0 women). *Students:* 11 full-time (8 women), 7 part-time (4 women); includes 7 minority (5 Hispanic/Latino; 2 Two or more races, non-Hispanic/Latino), 4 international. Average age 25. 21 applicants, 14% accepted, 3 enrolled. In 2010, 4 master's awarded. *Degree requirements:* For master's, comprehensive exam, thesis optional. *Entrance requirements:* For master's, GRE, minimum GPA of 3.0, 2 letters of recommendation, statement of research interest, bachelor's degree related to field of study or proof of common knowledge. Additional exam requirements/recommendations for international students: Required—TOEFL (minimum score 550 paper-based; 213 computer-based; 79 iBT), IELTS (minimum score 6). *Application deadline:* For fall admission, 7/20 priority date for domestic students, 6/20 priority date for international students; for spring admission, 12/15 priority date for domestic students, 11/15 priority date for international students. Applications are processed on a rolling basis. Application fee: $10. Electronic applications accepted. *Expenses:* Tuition, state resident: full-time $3210; part-time $130 per credit hour. Tuition, nonresident: full-time $8652; part-time $360.50 per credit hour. Required fees: $1212; $50.50 per credit hour. Tuition and fees vary according to course load. *Financial support:* In 2010–11, 11 teaching assistantships with partial tuition reimbursements (averaging $8,500 per year) were awarded; unspecified assistantships also available. Support available to part-time students. Financial award applicants required to submit FAFSA. *Unit head:* Dr. Zach Jones, Graduate Coordinator, 575-562-2723, Fax: 575-562-2192, E-mail: zach.jones@enmu.edu. *Application contact:* Sharon Potter, Department Secretary, Biology/Physical Sciences, 575-562-2174, Fax: 575-562-2192, E-mail: sharon.potter@enmu.edu.

Emory University, Laney Graduate School, Division of Biological and Biomedical Sciences, Program in Genetics and Molecular Biology, Atlanta, GA 30322-1100. Offers PhD. *Faculty:* 47 full-time (8 women). *Students:* 56 full-time (35 women); includes 5 Black or African American, non-Hispanic/Latino; 1 Hispanic/Latino, 13 international. Average age 27. 144 applicants, 11% accepted, 10 enrolled. In 2010, 10 doctorates awarded. *Degree requirements:* For doctorate, comprehensive exam, thesis/dissertation. *Entrance requirements:* For doctorate, GRE General Test, minimum GPA of 3.0 in science course work (recommended). Additional exam requirements/recommendations for international students: Required—TOEFL. *Application deadline:* For fall admission, 12/1 for domestic and international students. Application fee: $75. Electronic applications accepted. *Expenses:* Tuition: Full-time $33,800. Required fees: $1300. *Financial support:* In 2010–11, 16 students received support, including 16 fellowships with full tuition reimbursements available (averaging $25,000 per year); institutionally sponsored loans, scholarships/grants, health care benefits, and tuition waivers (full) also available. *Faculty research:* Gene regulation, genetic combination, developmental regulation. *Unit head:* Dr. Andreas Fritz, Director, 404-727-9012, Fax: 404-727-2880, E-mail: afritz@biology.emory.edu. *Application contact:* Kathy Smith, Director of Recruitment and Admissions, 404-727-2547, Fax: 404-727-3322, E-mail: kathy.smith@emory.edu.

Florida Institute of Technology, Graduate Programs, College of Science, Department of Biological Sciences, Program in Cell and Molecular Biology, Melbourne, FL 32901-6975. Offers MS. Part-time programs available. *Faculty:* 15 full-time (2 women), 1 part-time/adjunct (0 women). *Students:* 5 full-time (2 women), 1 (woman) part-time; includes 2 Hispanic/Latino. Average age 28. 43 applicants, 7% accepted, 1 enrolled. In 2010, 2 degrees awarded. *Degree requirements:* For master's, research, seminar, internship, or summer lab. *Entrance requirements:* For master's, GRE General Test, 3 letters of recommendation, minimum GPA of 3.0, resume, statement of objectives. Additional exam requirements/recommendations for international students: Required—TOEFL (minimum score 550 paper-based; 213 computer-based; 79 iBT). *Application deadline:* Applications are processed on a rolling basis. Application fee: $50. Electronic applications accepted. *Expenses:* Tuition: Part-time $1040 per credit hour. Tuition and fees vary according to campus/location. *Financial support:* In 2010–11, 6 fellowships with full and partial tuition reimbursements (averaging $20,737 per year), 15 research assistantships with full and partial tuition reimbursements (averaging $13,455 per year), 22 teaching assistantships with full and partial tuition reimbursements (averaging $13,353 per year) were awarded; career-related internships or fieldwork, institutionally sponsored loans, tuition waivers (partial), unspecified assistantships, and tuition remissions also available. Support available to part-time students. Financial award application deadline: 3/1; financial award applicants required to submit FAFSA. *Faculty research:* Changes in DNA molecule and differential expression of genetic information during aging. Total annual research expenditures: $1.3 million. *Unit head:* Dr. Richard B. Aronson, Department Head, 321-674-8034, Fax: 321-674-7238, E-mail: raronson@fit.edu. *Application contact:* Cheryl A. Brown, Associate Director of Graduate Admission, 321-674-7581, Fax: 321-723-9468, E-mail: cbrown@fit.edu.

Florida State University, The Graduate School, College of Arts and Sciences, Department of Biological Science, Specialization in Cell and Molecular Biology and Genetics, Tallahassee, FL 32306-4295. Offers MS, PhD. *Faculty:* 27 full-time (7 women). *Students:* 46 full-time (21 women); includes 2 Black or African American, non-Hispanic/Latino; 6 Hispanic/Latino, 10 international. 162 applicants, 10% accepted, 8 enrolled. In 2010, 3 master's, 3 doctorates awarded. Terminal master's awarded for partial completion of doctoral program. *Degree requirements:* For master's, comprehensive exam, thesis, teaching experience, seminar presentation; for doctorate, comprehensive exam, thesis/dissertation, teaching experience; seminar presentation. *Entrance requirements:* For master's, GRE General Test (minimum combined score 1100, 500 verbal, 500 quantitative), minimum upper-division GPA of 3.0; for doctorate, GRE General Test (minimum combined score 1100, Verbal 500, Quantitative 500), minimum upper-division GPA of 3.0. Additional exam requirements/recommendations for international students: Required—TOEFL (minimum score 600 paper-based; 250 computer-based; 92 iBT). *Application deadline:* For fall admission, 12/15 for domestic and international students. Application fee: $30. Electronic applications accepted. *Expenses:* Tuition, state resident: full-time $8238. *Financial support:* In 2010–11, 14 research assistantships with full tuition reimbursements (averaging $21,000 per year), 30 teaching assistantships with full tuition reimbursements (averaging $21,000 per year) were awarded; unspecified assistantships also available. Financial award application deadline: 12/15; financial award applicants required to submit FAFSA. *Faculty research:* Molecular biology; genetics and genomics; developmental biology and gene expression; cell structure, function, and motility; cellular and organismal physiology; biophysical and structural biology. *Application contact:* Judy Bowers, Coordinator, Graduate Affairs, 850-644-3023, Fax: 850-644-9829, E-mail: gradinfo@bio.fsu.edu.

Florida State University, The Graduate School, College of Arts and Sciences, Program in Molecular Biophysics, Tallahassee, FL 32306. Offers biochemistry, molecular and cell biology (PhD); computational structural biology (PhD); molecular biophysics (PhD). *Faculty:* 49 full-time (6 women). *Students:* 22 full-time (8 women); includes 5 Asian, non-Hispanic/Latino; 1 Hispanic/Latino. Average age 28. 30 applicants, 33% accepted, 7 enrolled. In 2010, 5 doctorates awarded. *Degree requirements:* For doctorate, comprehensive exam, thesis/dissertation, teaching 1 term in professor's major department. *Entrance requirements:* For doctorate, GRE General Test. Additional exam requirements/recommendations for international students: Required—TOEFL (minimum score 600 paper-based; 250 computer-based; 100 iBT). *Application deadline:* For fall admission, 2/15 for domestic students, 3/15 for international students; for spring admission, 11/2 for international students. Applications are processed on a rolling basis.

Molecular Biology

Florida State University (continued)

Application fee: $30. Electronic applications accepted. *Expenses:* Tuition, state resident: full-time $8238. *Financial support:* In 2010–11, 21 students received support, including fellowships with partial tuition reimbursements available (averaging $21,000 per year), 18 research assistantships with partial tuition reimbursements available (averaging $21,000 per year), 4 teaching assistantships with partial tuition reimbursements available (averaging $21,000 per year); scholarships/grants, health care benefits, and unspecified assistantships also available. Financial award applicants required to submit FAFSA. *Faculty research:* Protein and nucleic acid structure and function, membrane protein structure, computational biophysics, 3-D image reconstruction. Total annual research expenditures: $1.4 million. *Unit head:* Dr. Geoffrey Strouse, Director, 850-644-0056, Fax: 850-644-7244, E-mail: strouse@chem.fsu.edu. *Application contact:* Dr. Kerry Maddox, Academic Coordinator, Graduate Programs, 850-644-1012, Fax: 850-644-7244, E-mail: bkmaddox@sb.fsu.edu.

George Mason University, College of Science, Department of Molecular and Microbiology, Fairfax, VA 22030. Offers biology (MS), including bioinformatics and computational biology, general biology, microbiology and infectious disease, molecular biology, systematics and evolutionary biology; biosciences (PhD). *Faculty:* 10 full-time (5 women). *Students:* 12 full-time (6 women), 63 part-time (36 women); includes 2 Black or African American, non-Hispanic/Latino; 1 American Indian or Alaska Native, non-Hispanic/Latino; 8 Asian, non-Hispanic/Latino; 1 Hispanic/Latino, 16 international. Average age 31. 98 applicants, 37% accepted, 19 enrolled. In 2010, 7 master's, 7 doctorates awarded. *Entrance requirements:* Additional exam requirements/recommendations for international students: Required—TOEFL (minimum score 570 paper-based; 230 computer-based; 88 iBT). Application fee: $100. *Expenses:* Tuition, state resident: full-time $8192; part-time $440 per credit hour. Tuition, nonresident: full-time $22,952; part-time $1055 per credit hour. Required fees: $2364; $99 per credit hour. *Financial support:* In 2010–11, 32 students received support, including 3 fellowships (averaging $18,000 per year), 6 research assistantships (averaging $14,073 per year), 23 teaching assistantships (averaging $12,194 per year); career-related internships or fieldwork, Federal Work-Study, scholarships/grants, unspecified assistantships, and health care benefits (full-time research or teaching assistantship recipients) also available. Financial award applicants required to submit FAFSA. Total annual research expenditures: $457,760. *Unit head:* Dr. James Willett, Director, 703-993-8311, Fax: 703-993-8976, E-mail: jwillett@gmu.edu. *Application contact:* Daniel Cox, Associate Dean for Graduate Programs, 703-993-4971, Fax: 703-993-4325, E-mail: dcox5@gmu.edu.

Georgetown University, Graduate School of Arts and Sciences, Programs in Biomedical Sciences, Department of Biochemistry and Molecular Biology, Washington, DC 20057. Offers MS, PhD. *Degree requirements:* For doctorate, comprehensive exam, thesis/dissertation. *Entrance requirements:* For doctorate, GRE General Test. Additional exam requirements/recommendations for international students: Required—TOEFL.

The George Washington University, School of Medicine and Health Sciences, Department of Biochemistry and Molecular Biology, Washington, DC 20037. Offers biochemistry and molecular biology (MS); biochemistry and molecular genetics (PhD); molecular biochemistry and bioinformatics (MS). *Students:* 20 full-time (9 women), 16 part-time (6 women); includes 2 Asian, non-Hispanic/Latino, 20 international. Average age 27. 57 applicants, 88% accepted, 15 enrolled. In 2010, 17 master's awarded. *Degree requirements:* For master's, comprehensive exam; for doctorate, thesis/dissertation, general exam. *Entrance requirements:* For master's, GRE General Test, interview, minimum GPA of 3.0; for doctorate, GRE General Test, minimum GPA of 3.0. Additional exam requirements/recommendations for international students: Required—TOEFL (minimum score 550 paper-based; 213 computer-based). *Application deadline:* For fall admission, 4/1 priority date for domestic and international students; for spring admission, 10/1 priority date for domestic and international students. Application fee: $60. *Financial support:* Fellowships available. Financial award application deadline: 2/1. *Unit head:* Dr. Allan L. Goldstein, Chair, 202-994-3171, E-mail: bcmalg@gwumc.edu. *Application contact:* Information Contact, 202-994-2179, Fax: 202-994-0967, E-mail: gwibs@gwu.edu.

Georgia Health Sciences University, College of Graduate Studies, Program in Biochemistry and Molecular Biology, Augusta, GA 30912. Offers MS, PhD. *Faculty:* 12 full-time (2 women). *Students:* 14 full-time (7 women), 10 international. Average age 27. In 2010, 4 doctorates awarded. *Degree requirements:* For doctorate, comprehensive exam, thesis/dissertation. *Entrance requirements:* For doctorate, GRE General Test. Additional exam requirements/recommendations for international students: Required—TOEFL (minimum score 550 paper-based; 213 computer-based; 79 iBT). *Application deadline:* For fall admission, 1/15 for domestic and international students. Application fee: $30. Electronic applications accepted. *Expenses:* Tuition, state resident: full-time $7500; part-time $313 per semester hour. Tuition, nonresident: full-time $24,772; part-time $1033 per semester hour. Required fees: $1112. *Financial support:* In 2010–11, 8 research assistantships with partial tuition reimbursements (averaging $23,000 per year) were awarded; Federal Work-Study, institutionally sponsored loans, and scholarships/grants also available. Support available to part-time students. Financial award application deadline: 5/31; financial award applicants required to submit FAFSA. *Faculty research:* Bacterial pathogenesis, eye diseases, vitamins and amino acid transporters, transcriptional control and molecular oncology, tumor biology. Total annual research expenditures: $3 million. *Unit head:* Dr. Vadivel Ganapathy, Chair/Professor, 706-721-7652, Fax: 706-721-9947, E-mail: vganapat@georgiahealth.edu. *Application contact:* Dr. Patricia L. Cameron, Acting Vice Dean, 706-721-3279, E-mail: pcameron@georgiahealth.edu.

Georgia State University, College of Arts and Sciences, Department of Biology, Program in Cellular and Molecular Biology and Physiology, Atlanta, GA 30302-3083. Offers MS, PhD. Part-time programs available. Terminal master's awarded for partial completion of doctoral program. *Degree requirements:* For master's, thesis or alternative; for doctorate, thesis/dissertation, exam. *Entrance requirements:* For master's and doctorate, GRE General Test. Additional exam requirements/recommendations for international students: Required—TOEFL.

Grand Valley State University, College of Liberal Arts and Sciences, Program in Cell and Molecular Biology, Allendale, MI 49401-9403. Offers MS. *Entrance requirements:* For master's, minimum GPA of 3.0. *Faculty research:* Plant cell biology, plant development, cell/signal integration.

Harvard University, Graduate School of Arts and Sciences, Department of Molecular and Cellular Biology, Cambridge, MA 02138. Offers PhD. *Degree requirements:* For doctorate, thesis/dissertation, oral exam. *Entrance requirements:* For doctorate, GRE General Test, GRE Subject Test (recommended). Additional exam requirements/recommendations for international students: Required—TOEFL. *Expenses:* Tuition: Full-time $34,976. Required fees: $1166. Full-time tuition and fees vary according to program.

Harvard University, Graduate School of Arts and Sciences, Program in Chemical Biology, Cambridge, MA 02138. Offers PhD. *Expenses:* Tuition: Full-time $34,976. Required fees: $1166. Full-time tuition and fees vary according to program.

Hood College, Graduate School, Program in Biomedical Science, Frederick, MD 21701-8575. Offers biomedical science (MS), including biotechnology/molecular biology, microbiology/immunology/virology, regulatory compliance; regulatory compliance (Certificate). Part-time and evening/weekend programs available. *Faculty:* 3 full-time (1 woman), 7 part-time/adjunct (4 women). *Students:* 9 full-time (2 women), 87 part-time (55 women); includes 16 Black or African American, non-Hispanic/Latino; 9 Asian, non-Hispanic/Latino; 3 Hispanic/Latino; 1 Two or more races, non-Hispanic/Latino, 7 international. Average age 29. 61 applicants, 64% accepted, 21 enrolled. In 2010, 9 master's, 3 other advanced degrees awarded. *Degree requirements:* For master's, comprehensive exam, thesis or alternative. *Entrance requirements:* For master's, bachelor's degree in biology; minimum GPA of 2.75; undergraduate course work in cell biology, chemistry, organic chemistry, and genetics. Additional exam requirements/recommendations for international students: Required—TOEFL (minimum score 575 paper-based; 231 computer-based; 89 iBT). *Application deadline:* For fall admission, 7/15 for domestic and international students; for spring admission, 12/15 for domestic and international students. Applications are processed on a rolling basis. Application fee: $35. Electronic applications accepted. *Expenses:* Tuition: Full-time $6480; part-time $360 per credit. Required fees: $100; $50 per term. *Financial support:* In 2010–11, 3 research assistantships with full tuition reimbursements (averaging $10,609 per year) were awarded. Financial award applicants required to submit FAFSA. *Unit head:* Dr. Oney Smith, Director, 301-696-3653, Fax: 301-696-3597, E-mail: osmith@hood.edu. *Application contact:* Dr. Allen P. Flora, Dean of Graduate School, 301-696-3811, Fax: 301-696-3597, E-mail: gofurther@hood.edu.

Howard University, College of Medicine, Department of Biochemistry and Molecular Biology, Washington, DC 20059-0002. Offers biochemistry and molecular biology (PhD); biotechnology (MS); MD/PhD. Part-time programs available. *Degree requirements:* For master's, externship; for doctorate, comprehensive exam, thesis/dissertation. *Entrance requirements:* For master's and doctorate, GRE General Test, minimum GPA of 3.0. *Faculty research:* Cellular and molecular biology of olfaction, gene regulation and expression, enzymology, NMR spectroscopy of molecular structure, hormone regulation/metabolism.

Illinois Institute of Technology, Graduate College, College of Science and Letters, Department of Biological, Chemical and Physical Sciences, Biology Division, Chicago, IL 60616. Offers biochemistry (MBS, MS); biology (PhD); biotechnology (MBS, MS); cell and molecular biology (MBS, MS); microbiology (MB, MS); molecular biochemistry and biophysics (PhD); molecular biology and biophysics (MS). Part-time and evening/weekend programs available. Post-baccalaureate distance learning degree programs offered (minimal on-campus study). *Faculty:* 13 full-time (5 women), 5 part-time/adjunct (2 women). *Students:* 121 full-time (75 women), 56 part-time (37 women); includes 16 minority (5 Black or African American, non-Hispanic/Latino; 5 Asian, non-Hispanic/Latino; 5 Hispanic/Latino; 1 Two or more races, non-Hispanic/Latino), 104 international. Average age 27. 268 applicants, 76% accepted, 62 enrolled. In 2010, 74 master's, 4 doctorates awarded. Terminal master's awarded for partial completion of doctoral program. *Degree requirements:* For master's, comprehensive exam, thesis (for some programs); for doctorate, comprehensive exam, thesis/dissertation. *Entrance requirements:* For master's, GRE General Test (minimum score 1000 Quantitative and Verbal, 2.5 Analytical Writing), minimum undergraduate GPA of 3.0; for doctorate, GRE General Test (minimum score 1200 Quantitative and Verbal, 3.0 Analytical Writing), minimum undergraduate GPA of 3.0. Additional exam requirements/recommendations for international students: Required—TOEFL (minimum score 523 paper-based; 213 computer-based; 70 iBT); Recommended—IELTS (minimum score 5.5). *Application deadline:* For fall admission, 5/1 for domestic and international students; for spring admission, 10/15 for domestic and international students. Applications are processed on a rolling basis. Application fee: $40. Electronic applications accepted. *Expenses:* Tuition: Full-time $18,576; part-time $1032 per credit hour. Required fees: $583 per semester. One-time fee: $150. Tuition and fees vary according to program and student level. *Financial support:* In 2010–11, 15 research assistantships with full and partial tuition reimbursements (averaging $6,379 per year), 14 teaching assistantships with partial tuition reimbursements (averaging $6,296 per year) were awarded; fellowships with full and partial tuition reimbursements, career-related internships or fieldwork, Federal Work-Study, institutionally sponsored loans, scholarships/grants, traineeships, health care benefits, tuition waivers (partial), and unspecified assistantships also available. Support available to part-time students. Financial award applicants required to submit FAFSA. *Faculty research:* Structure and biophysics of macromolecular systems; efficacy and mechanism of action of chemopreventive agents in experimental carcinogenesis of breast, colon, lung and prostate; study of fundamental structural biochemistry problems that have direct links to the understanding and treatment of disease; spectroscopic techniques for the study of multi-domain proteins; molecular mechanisms of cancer and cancer gene therapy. Total annual research expenditures: $2.6 million. *Unit head:* Dr. Benjamin C. Stark, Professor and Associate Chair, 312-567-3488, Fax: 312-567-3494, E-mail: starkb@iit.edu. *Application contact:* Deborah Gibson, Director, Graduate Admissions, 866-472-3448, Fax: 312-567-3138, E-mail: inquiry.grad@iit.edu.

Illinois State University, Graduate School, College of Arts and Sciences, Department of Biological Sciences, Normal, IL 61790-2200. Offers animal behavior (MS); bacteriology (MS); biochemistry (MS); biological sciences (MS); biology (PhD); biophysics (MS); biotechnology (MS); botany (MS, PhD); cell biology (MS); conservation biology (MS); developmental biology (MS); ecology (MS, PhD); entomology (MS); evolutionary biology (MS); genetics (MS, PhD); immunology (MS); microbiology (MS, PhD); molecular biology (MS); molecular genetics (MS); neurobiology (MS); neuroscience (MS); parasitology (MS); physiology (MS, PhD); plant biology (MS); plant molecular biology (MS); plant sciences (MS); structural biology (MS); zoology (MS, PhD). Part-time programs available. *Degree requirements:* For master's, thesis or alternative; for doctorate, variable foreign language requirement, thesis/dissertation, 2 terms of residency. *Entrance requirements:* For master's, GRE General Test, minimum GPA of 2.6 in last 60 hours of course work; for doctorate, GRE General Test. *Faculty research:* Redoc balance and drug development in schistosoma mansoni, control of the growth of listeria monocytogenes at low temperature, regulation of cell expansion and microtubule function by SPRI, CRUI: physiology and fitness consequences of different life history phenotypes.

Indiana University Bloomington, University Graduate School, College of Arts and Sciences, Department of Biology, Bloomington, IN 47405. Offers biology teaching (MAT); biotechnology (MA); evolution, ecology, and behavior (MA, PhD); genetics (PhD); microbiology (MA, PhD); molecular, cellular, and developmental biology (PhD); plant sciences (MA, PhD); zoology (MA, PhD). *Faculty:* 58 full-time (15 women), 21 part-time/adjunct (6 women). *Students:* 163 full-time (98 women), 7 part-time (2 women); includes 17 minority (3 Black or African American, non-Hispanic/Latino; 1 American Indian or Alaska Native, non-Hispanic/Latino; 7 Asian, non-Hispanic/Latino; 5 Hispanic/Latino; 1 Native Hawaiian or other Pacific Islander, non-Hispanic/Latino), 52 international. Average age 27. 346 applicants, 15% accepted, 24 enrolled. In 2010, 17 master's, 24 doctorates awarded. Terminal master's awarded for partial completion of doctoral program. *Degree requirements:* For master's, thesis, oral defense; for doctorate, thesis/dissertation, oral defense. *Entrance requirements:* For master's and doctorate, GRE General Test. Additional exam requirements/recommendations for international students: Required—TOEFL (minimum score 100 iBT). *Application deadline:* For fall admission, 1/5 priority date for domestic students, 12/1 priority date for international students. Application fee: $55 ($65 for international students). Electronic applications accepted. *Financial support:* In 2010–11, 170 students received support, including 64 fellowships with tuition reimbursements available (averaging $19,484 per year), 44 research assistantships with tuition reimbursements available (averaging $20,300 per year), 62 teaching assistantships with tuition reimbursements available (averaging $20,521 per year); scholarships/grants, traineeships, health care benefits, and unspecified assistantships also available. Financial award application deadline: 1/5. *Faculty research:* Evolution, ecology and behavior; microbiology; molecular biology and genetics; plant biology. *Unit head:* Dr. Roger Innes, Chair, 812-855-2219, Fax: 812-855-6082, E-mail: rinnes@indiana.edu. *Application contact:* Tracey D. Stohr, Graduate Student Recruitment Coordinator, 812-856-6303, Fax: 812-855-6082, E-mail: gradbio@indiana.edu.

Indiana University–Purdue University Indianapolis, Indiana University School of Medicine, Department of Biochemistry and Molecular Biology, Indianapolis, IN 46202-2896. Offers PhD, MD/MS, MD/PhD. *Faculty:* 17 full-time (4 women). *Students:* 43 full-time (23 women), 13 part-time (8 women); includes 5 minority (1 Black or African American, non-Hispanic/Latino; 3 Asian, non-Hispanic/Latino; 1 Hispanic/Latino), 21 international. Average age 32. 13 applicants, 62% accepted, 8 enrolled. In 2010, 12 doctorates awarded. Terminal master's awarded for partial completion of doctoral program. *Degree requirements:* For doctorate, thesis/dissertation. *Entrance requirements:* For doctorate, GRE General Test, GRE Subject Test (recommended), previous course work in organic chemistry. *Application deadline:* For fall admission, 1/15 priority date for domestic students. Applications are processed on a rolling basis. Application fee: $55 ($65 for international students). *Financial support:* In 2010–11, 8 teaching assistantships (averaging $14,949 per year) were awarded; fellowships with tuition reimbursements, research assistantships with tuition reimbursements, Federal Work-Study, institutionally sponsored loans, scholarships/grants, and tuition waivers (partial) also available. Support available to part-time students. Financial award application deadline: 2/1. *Faculty research:* Metabolic regulation, enzymology, peptide and protein chemistry, cell biology, signal transduction. *Unit head:* Dr. Zhong-Yin Zhang, Chairman, 317-274-7151. *Application contact:* Dr. Zhong-Yin Zhang, Chairman, 317-274-7151.

Inter American University of Puerto Rico, Metropolitan Campus, Graduate Programs, Program in Medical Technology, San Juan, PR 00919-1293. Offers administration of clinical laboratories (MS); molecular microbiology (MS). *Accreditation:* NAACLS. Part-time programs available. *Degree requirements:* For master's, comprehensive exam. *Entrance requirements:* For master's, BS in medical technology, minimum GPA of 2.5. Electronic applications accepted.

Iowa State University of Science and Technology, Graduate College, College of Agriculture and College of Liberal Arts and Sciences, Department of Biochemistry, Biophysics, and Molecular Biology, Ames, IA 50011. Offers biochemistry (MS, PhD); biophysics (MS, PhD); genetics (MS, PhD); molecular, cellular, and developmental biology (MS, PhD); toxicology (MS, PhD). *Faculty:* 31 full-time (7 women), 1 (woman) part-time/adjunct. *Students:* 81 full-time (33 women), 11 part-time (6 women); includes 2 Black or African American, non-Hispanic/Latino; 2 Asian, non-Hispanic/Latino, 58 international. 38 applicants, 29% accepted, 8 enrolled. In 2010, 3 master's, 9 doctorates awarded. *Degree requirements:* For master's, thesis; for doctorate, thesis/dissertation. *Entrance requirements:* For master's and doctorate, GRE General Test. Additional exam requirements/recommendations for international students: Required—TOEFL (minimum score 550 paper-based; 79 iBT), IELTS (minimum score 6.5). *Application deadline:* For fall admission, 1/15 priority date for domestic and international students; for spring admission, 10/15 for domestic and international students. Application fee: $40 ($90 for international students). Electronic applications accepted. *Financial support:* In 2010–11, 67 research assistantships with full and partial tuition reimbursements (averaging $17,228 per year) were awarded; teaching assistantships with full and partial tuition reimbursements, scholarships/grants, health care benefits, and unspecified assistantships also available. *Unit head:* Dr. Guru Rao, Interim Chair, 515-294-6116, E-mail: biochem@iastate.edu. *Application contact:* Dr. Reuben Peters, Director of Graduate Education, 515-294-6116, E-mail: biochem@iastate.edu.

See Display on page 129 and Close-Up on page 147.

Iowa State University of Science and Technology, Graduate College, Interdisciplinary Programs, Bioinformatics and Computational Biology Program, Ames, IA 50011. Offers MS, PhD. *Students:* 54 full-time (22 women), 34 international. In 2010, 1 master's, 5 doctorates awarded. *Degree requirements:* For doctorate, thesis/dissertation. *Entrance requirements:* For master's and doctorate, GRE General Test. Additional exam requirements/recommendations for international students: Recommended—IELTS. *Application deadline:* For fall admission, 1/15 priority date for domestic students, 1/15 for international students; for spring admission, 10/15 for domestic and international students. Application fee: $40 ($90 for international students). Electronic applications accepted. *Financial support:* In 2010–11, 47 research assistantships with full and partial tuition reimbursements (averaging $22,000 per year), 3 teaching assistantships (averaging $20,000 per year) were awarded; fellowships with full tuition reimbursements, scholarships/grants, traineeships, health care benefits, and unspecified assistantships also available. *Faculty research:* Functional and structural genomics, genome evolution, macromolecular structure and function, mathematical biology and biological statistics, metabolic and developmental networks. *Unit head:* Dr. Julie Dickerson, Chair, Supervising Committee, 515-294-5122, Fax: 515-294-6790, E-mail: bcb@iastate.edu. *Application contact:* Dr. Julie Dickerson, Chair, Supervising Committee, 515-294-5122, Fax: 515-294-6790, E-mail: bcb@iastate.edu.

Iowa State University of Science and Technology, Graduate College, Interdisciplinary Programs, Program in Molecular, Cellular, and Developmental Biology, Ames, IA 50011. Offers MS, PhD. *Students:* 31 full-time (17 women), 4 part-time (2 women), 23 international. In 2010, 2 master's, 3 doctorates awarded. *Degree requirements:* For master's, thesis or alternative; for doctorate, thesis/dissertation. *Entrance requirements:* For master's and doctorate, GRE General Test. Additional exam requirements/recommendations for international students: Required—TOEFL (minimum score 580 paper-based; 85 iBT), IELTS (minimum score 7). *Application deadline:* For fall admission, 1/15 priority date for domestic and international students. Application fee: $40 ($90 for international students). Electronic applications accepted. *Financial support:* In 2010–11, 30 research assistantships with full and partial tuition reimbursements (averaging $20,962 per year), 1 teaching assistantship with full and partial tuition reimbursement (averaging $11,366 per year) were awarded; scholarships/grants, health care benefits, and unspecified assistantships also available. *Unit head:* Dr. Jeff Beetham, Supervisory Committee Chair, 515-294-7252, E-mail: idgp@iastate.edu. *Application contact:* Katie Blair, Information Contact, 515-294-7252, Fax: 515-924-6790, E-mail: idgp@iastate.edu.

The Johns Hopkins University, Bloomberg School of Public Health, Department of Biochemistry and Molecular Biology, Baltimore, MD 21205. Offers MHS, Sc M, PhD. Part-time programs available. *Faculty:* 16 full-time (3 women), 5 part-time/adjunct (3 women). *Students:* 64 full-time (41 women), 3 part-time (1 woman); includes 1 Black or African American, non-Hispanic/Latino; 9 Asian, non-Hispanic/Latino; 3 Hispanic/Latino, 8 international. Average age 25. 108 applicants, 47% accepted, 26 enrolled. In 2010, 27 master's, 6 doctorates awarded. *Degree requirements:* For master's, thesis; for doctorate, comprehensive exam, thesis/dissertation, oral and written exams. *Entrance requirements:* For master's, MCAT or GRE, 3 letters of recommendation, curriculum vitae; for doctorate, GRE General Test, 3 letters of recommendation, curriculum vitae. Additional exam requirements/recommendations for international students: Required—TOEFL (minimum score 600 paper-based; 250 computer-based). *Application deadline:* For fall admission, 12/15 priority date for domestic students, 12/15 for international students; for spring admission, 6/1 for domestic and international students. Applications are processed on a rolling basis. Application fee: $45. Electronic applications accepted. *Financial support:* In 2010–11, 63 students received support, including 17 fellowships with tuition reimbursements available (averaging $26,800 per year), 19 research assistantships with tuition reimbursements available (averaging $26,800 per year), 7 teaching assistantships (averaging $1,000 per year); Federal Work-Study, institutionally sponsored loans, scholarships/grants, health care benefits, and stipends also available. Financial award application deadline: 3/15; financial award applicants required to submit FAFSA. *Faculty research:* DNA replication, repair, structure, carcinogenesis, protein structure, enzyme catalysts, reproductive biology. Total annual research expenditures: $6 million. *Unit head:* Dr. Pierre Coulombe, Chairman, 410-955-3671, Fax: 410-955-2926, E-mail: pcoulomb@jhsph.edu. *Application contact:* Sharon Warner, Senior Academic Program Administrator, 410-955-3672, Fax: 410-955-2926, E-mail: swarner@jhsph.edu.

The Johns Hopkins University, National Institutes of Health Sponsored Programs, Baltimore, MD 21218-2699. Offers biology (PhD), including biochemistry, biophysics, cell biology, developmental biology, genetic biology, molecular biology; cell, molecular, and developmental biology and biophysics (PhD). *Degree requirements:* For doctorate, comprehensive exam, thesis/dissertation. *Entrance requirements:* For doctorate, GRE General Test. Additional exam requirements/recommendations for international students: Required—TOEFL (minimum score 600 paper-based; 250 computer-based), TWE. Electronic applications accepted. *Faculty research:* Protein and nucleic acid biochemistry and biophysical chemistry, molecular biology and development.

The Johns Hopkins University, School of Medicine, Graduate Programs in Medicine, Department of Pharmacology and Molecular Sciences, Baltimore, MD 21205. Offers PhD. *Faculty:* 42 full-time (8 women). *Students:* 60 full-time (28 women); includes 15 minority (5 Black or African American, non-Hispanic/Latino; 9 Asian, non-Hispanic/Latino; 1 Hispanic/Latino), 16 international. 180 applicants, 10% accepted, 9 enrolled. In 2010, 10 doctorates awarded. *Degree requirements:* For doctorate, comprehensive exam, thesis/dissertation, departmental seminar. *Entrance requirements:* For doctorate, GRE General Test. Additional exam requirements/recommendations for international students: Required—TOEFL. *Application deadline:* For fall admission, 1/10 for domestic and international students. Application fee: $85. Electronic applications accepted. *Unit head:* Dr. Philip A. Cole, Chairman, 410-614-0540, Fax:

410-614-7717, E-mail: pcole@jhmi.edu. *Application contact:* Dr. James T. Stivers, Director of Admissions, 410-955-7117, Fax: 410-955-3023, E-mail: jstivers@jhmi.edu.

The Johns Hopkins University, School of Medicine, Graduate Programs in Medicine, Predoctoral Training Program in Human Genetics, Baltimore, MD 21218-2699. Offers PhD, MD/PhD. *Faculty:* 59 full-time (14 women). *Students:* 77 full-time (55 women); includes 8 Black or African American, non-Hispanic/Latino; 11 Asian, non-Hispanic/Latino; 5 Hispanic/Latino, 15 international. Average age 24. 172 applicants, 11% accepted, 10 enrolled. In 2010, 9 doctorates awarded. Terminal master's awarded for partial completion of doctoral program. *Degree requirements:* For doctorate, comprehensive exam, thesis/dissertation. *Entrance requirements:* For doctorate, GRE General Test, GRE Subject Test. *Application deadline:* For fall admission, 12/31 priority date for domestic and international students. Application fee: $85. Electronic applications accepted. *Financial support:* In 2010–11, 1 fellowship with full tuition reimbursement (averaging $26,855 per year) was awarded; teaching assistantships with full tuition reimbursements, health care benefits also available. *Faculty research:* Human, mammalian, and molecular genetics, bioinformatics, genomics. *Unit head:* Dr. David Valle, Director, 410-955-4260, Fax: 410-955-7397, E-mail: muscelli@jhmi.edu. *Application contact:* Sandy Muscelli, Program Administrator, 410-955-4260, Fax: 410-955-7397, E-mail: muscelli@jhmi.edu.

The Johns Hopkins University, School of Medicine, Graduate Programs in Medicine, Program in Biochemistry, Cellular and Molecular Biology, Baltimore, MD 21205. Offers PhD. *Faculty:* 101 full-time (35 women). *Students:* 153 full-time (88 women); includes 29 minority (8 Black or African American, non-Hispanic/Latino; 1 American Indian or Alaska Native, non-Hispanic/Latino; 15 Asian, non-Hispanic/Latino; 4 Hispanic/Latino; 1 Two or more races, non-Hispanic/Latino), 54 international. Average age 25. 299 applicants, 19% accepted, 18 enrolled. In 2010, 20 doctorates awarded. *Degree requirements:* For doctorate, comprehensive exam, thesis/dissertation. *Entrance requirements:* For doctorate, GRE General Test. Additional exam requirements/recommendations for international students: Required—TOEFL. *Application deadline:* For winter admission, 1/10 for domestic and international students. Applications are processed on a rolling basis. Application fee: $80. Electronic applications accepted. *Financial support:* In 2010–11, 5 fellowships with partial tuition reimbursements (averaging $32,000 per year), 144 research assistantships with full and partial tuition reimbursements (averaging $27,125 per year) were awarded; traineeships and tuition waivers (full) also available. Financial award application deadline: 12/31. *Faculty research:* Developmental biology, genomics/proteomics, protein targeting, signal transduction, structural biology. *Unit head:* Dr. Carolyn Machamer, Director, 410-955-3466, Fax: 410-614-8842, E-mail: machamer@jhmi.edu. *Application contact:* Dr. Jeff Corden, Admissions Director, 410-955-3506, Fax: 410-614-8842, E-mail: jcorden@jhmi.edu.

Kent State University, School of Biomedical Sciences, Program in Cellular and Molecular Biology, Kent, OH 44242-0001. Offers MS, PhD. Offered in cooperation with Northeastern Ohio Universities College of Medicine. Terminal master's awarded for partial completion of doctoral program. *Degree requirements:* For master's, thesis; for doctorate, thesis/dissertation. *Entrance requirements:* For master's, GRE General Test, letter of recommendation, minimum GPA of 3.0; for doctorate, GRE General Test, letter of recommendation, minimum GPA of 3.0, MS. Additional exam requirements/recommendations for international students: Required—TOEFL. Electronic applications accepted. *Expenses:* Tuition, state resident: full-time $7866; part-time $437 per credit hour. Tuition, nonresident: full-time $14,022; part-time $779 per credit hour. *Faculty research:* Molecular genetics, molecular endocrinology, virology and tumor biology, P450 enzymology and catalysis, membrane structure and function.

Lehigh University, College of Arts and Sciences, Department of Biological Sciences, Bethlehem, PA 18015. Offers biochemistry (PhD); integrative biology and neuroscience (PhD); molecular biology (MS, PhD). Part-time programs available. Postbaccalaureate distance learning degree programs offered (no on-campus study). *Faculty:* 17 full-time (7 women). *Students:* 30 full-time (14 women), 30 part-time (18 women); includes 6 minority (1 Black or African American, non-Hispanic/Latino; 1 Asian, non-Hispanic/Latino; 3 Hispanic/Latino; 1 Native Hawaiian or other Pacific Islander, non-Hispanic/Latino), 7 international. Average age 29. 79 applicants, 25% accepted, 19 enrolled. In 2010, 9 master's, 3 doctorates awarded. Terminal master's awarded for partial completion of doctoral program. *Degree requirements:* For master's, research report; for doctorate, comprehensive exam, thesis/dissertation. *Entrance requirements:* For doctorate, GRE General Test. Additional exam requirements/recommendations for international students: Required—TOEFL. *Application deadline:* For fall admission, 12/15 for domestic and international students. Applications are processed on a rolling basis. Application fee: $65. Electronic applications accepted. *Financial support:* In 2010–11, 31 students received support, including 4 fellowships with full tuition reimbursements available (averaging $24,500 per year), 6 research assistantships with full tuition reimbursements available (averaging $23,750 per year), 16 teaching assistantships with full tuition reimbursements available (averaging $23,750 per year); scholarships/grants and unspecified assistantships also available. Financial award application deadline: 12/15. *Faculty research:* Gene expression, cytoskeleton and cell structure, cell cycle and growth regulation, neuroscience, animal behavior, microbiology. Total annual research expenditures: $2.4 million. *Unit head:* Dr. Murray Itzkowitz, Chairperson, 610-758-3680, Fax: 610-758-4004, E-mail: mi00@lehigh.edu. *Application contact:* Dr. Jennifer M. Swann, Graduate Coordinator, 610-758-5484, Fax: 610-758-4004, E-mail: jms5@lehigh.edu.

Louisiana State University Health Sciences Center at Shreveport, Department of Biochemistry and Molecular Biology, Shreveport, LA 71130-3932. Offers MS, PhD, MD/PhD. *Degree requirements:* For master's, thesis; for doctorate, thesis/dissertation. *Entrance requirements:* For master's and doctorate, GRE General Test. Additional exam requirements/recommendations for international students: Required—TOEFL. *Faculty research:* Metabolite transport, regulation of translation and transcription, prokaryotic molecular genetics, cell matrix biochemistry, yeast molecular genetics, oncogenes.

Loyola University Chicago, Graduate School, Program in Molecular Biology, Maywood, IL 60153. Offers MS, PhD, MD/PhD. *Faculty:* 28 full-time (5 women). *Students:* 18 full-time (13 women); includes 3 minority (1 American Indian or Alaska Native, non-Hispanic/Latino; 1 Asian, non-Hispanic/Latino; 1 Two or more races, non-Hispanic/Latino), 8 international. Average age 27. 40 applicants, 15% accepted, 4 enrolled. In 2010, 3 doctorates awarded. Terminal master's awarded for partial completion of doctoral program. *Degree requirements:* For master's, comprehensive exam (for some programs), thesis; for doctorate, comprehensive exam, thesis/dissertation, 48 credit hours. *Entrance requirements:* For master's, GRE General Test, statement of purpose, transcripts, 3 letters of recommendation; for doctorate, GRE General Test, 3 letters of recommendation. Additional exam requirements/recommendations for international students: Required—TOEFL (minimum score 600 paper-based; 250 computer-based). *Application deadline:* For fall admission, 3/1 for domestic and international students. Applications are processed on a rolling basis. Application fee: $40. Electronic applications accepted. *Expenses:* Tuition: Full-time $14,940; part-time $830 per credit hour. Required fees: $87 per semester. Part-time tuition and fees vary according to course load and program. *Financial support:* In 2010–11, 7 students received support, including fellowships (averaging $23,000 per year); research assistantships, Federal Work-Study, institutionally sponsored loans, scholarships/grants, and health care benefits also available. Financial award application deadline: 2/15; financial award applicants required to submit FAFSA. *Faculty research:* Cell cycle regulation, molecular immunology, molecular genetics, molecular oncology, molecular virology. Total annual research expenditures: $3,500. *Unit head:* Dr. Manuel O. Diaz, Director, 708-327-3172, Fax: 708-216-6505, E-mail: mdiaz@luc.edu. *Application contact:* Dr. Mitchell Denning, Graduate Program Director, 708-327-3358, E-mail: mdennin@lumc.edu.

Marquette University, Graduate School, College of Arts and Sciences, Department of Biology, Milwaukee, WI 53201-1881. Offers cell biology (MS, PhD); developmental biology (MS, PhD); ecology (MS, PhD); epithelial physiology (MS, PhD); genetics (MS, PhD); microbiology (MS, PhD); molecular biology (MS, PhD); muscle and exercise physiology (MS, PhD); neuroscience (PhD). *Faculty:* 25 full-time (12 women), 2 part-time/adjunct (1 woman). *Students:* 23 full-time (9 women), 12 part-time (8 women); includes 1 minority (Asian, non-Hispanic/Latino), 15

Molecular Biology

Marquette University (continued)

international. Average age 26. 82 applicants, 15% accepted, 5 enrolled. In 2010, 3 master's, 2 doctorates awarded. Terminal master's awarded for partial completion of doctoral program. *Degree requirements:* For master's, comprehensive exam, thesis, 1 year of teaching experience or equivalent; for doctorate, thesis/dissertation, 1 year of teaching experience or equivalent, qualifying exam. *Entrance requirements:* For master's and doctorate, GRE General Test, GRE Subject Test, official transcripts from all current and previous colleges/universities except Marquette, statement of professional goals and aspirations, three letters of recommendation. Additional exam requirements/recommendations for international students: Required—TOEFL (minimum score 530 paper-based; 78 computer-based). *Application deadline:* For fall admission, 12/15 for domestic and international students. Application fee: $50. Electronic applications accepted. *Expenses:* Tuition: Full-time $16,290; part-time $905 per credit hour. Tuition and fees vary according to program. *Financial support:* In 2010–11, 2 research assistantships, 34 teaching assistantships were awarded; fellowships, Federal Work-Study, institutionally sponsored loans, scholarships/grants, and tuition waivers (full and partial) also available. Support available to part-time students. Financial award application deadline: 2/15. *Faculty research:* Neurobiology, neuroendocrinology, epithelial physiology, neuropeptide interactions, synaptic transmission. Total annual research expenditures: $1.3 million. *Unit head:* Dr. Robert Fitts, Chair, 414-288-1748, Fax: 414-288-7357. *Application contact:* Debbie Weaver, Administrative Assistant, 414-288-7355, Fax: 414-288-7357.

Massachusetts Institute of Technology, School of Science, Department of Biology, Cambridge, MA 02139-4307. Offers biochemistry (PhD); biological oceanography (PhD); biology (PhD); biophysical chemistry and molecular structure (PhD); cell biology (PhD); computational and systems biology (PhD); developmental biology (PhD); genetics (PhD); immunology (PhD); microbiology (PhD); molecular biology (PhD); neurobiology (PhD). *Faculty:* 56 full-time (14 women). *Students:* 251 full-time (135 women); includes 74 minority (4 Black or African American, non-Hispanic/Latino; 1 American Indian or Alaska Native, non-Hispanic/Latino; 29 Asian, non-Hispanic/Latino; 33 Hispanic/Latino; 7 Two or more races, non-Hispanic/Latino), 29 international. Average age 26. 652 applicants, 18% accepted, 58 enrolled. In 2010, 41 doctorates awarded. *Degree requirements:* For doctorate, comprehensive exam, thesis/dissertation. *Entrance requirements:* For doctorate, GRE General Test. Additional exam requirements/recommendations for international students: Required—TOEFL (minimum score 577 paper-based; 233 computer-based), IELTS (minimum score 6.5). *Application deadline:* For fall admission, 12/1 for domestic and international students. Application fee: $75. Electronic applications accepted. *Expenses:* Tuition: Full-time $38,940; part-time $605 per unit. Required fees: $272. *Financial support:* In 2010–11, 215 students received support, including 115 fellowships with tuition reimbursements available (averaging $33,090 per year), 132 research assistantships with tuition reimbursements available (averaging $31,846 per year); teaching assistantships with tuition reimbursements available, Federal Work-Study, institutionally sponsored loans, scholarships/grants, traineeships, health care benefits, and unspecified assistantships also available. *Faculty research:* DNA recombination, replication and repair; transcription and gene regulation; signal transduction; cell cycle; neuronal cell fate. Total annual research expenditures: $60.6 million. *Unit head:* Prof. Chris Kaiser, Head, 617-253-4701, E-mail: mitbio@mit.edu. *Application contact:* Biology Education Office, 617-253-3717, Fax: 617-258-9329, E-mail: gradbio@mit.edu.

Mayo Graduate School, Graduate Programs in Biomedical Sciences, Programs in Biochemistry, Structural Biology, Cell Biology, and Genetics, Rochester, MN 55905. Offers biochemistry and structural biology (PhD); cell biology and genetics (PhD); molecular biology (PhD). *Degree requirements:* For doctorate, oral defense of dissertation, qualifying oral and written exam. *Entrance requirements:* For doctorate, GRE, 1 year of chemistry, biology, calculus, and physics. Additional exam requirements/recommendations for international students: Required—TOEFL. Electronic applications accepted. *Faculty research:* Gene structure and function, membranes and receptors/cytoskeleton, oncogenes and growth factors, protein structure and function, steroid hormonal action.

McMaster University, Faculty of Health Sciences and School of Graduate Studies, Program in Medical Sciences, Hamilton, ON L8S 4M2, Canada. Offers blood and vascular (M Sc, PhD); genetics and cancer (M Sc, PhD); immunity and infection (M Sc, PhD); metabolism and nutrition (M Sc, PhD); neurosciences and behavioral sciences (M Sc, PhD); physiology/pharmacology (M Sc, PhD); MD/PhD. *Degree requirements:* For master's, thesis; for doctorate, comprehensive exam, thesis/dissertation. *Entrance requirements:* For master's, honors B Sc, B+ average in related field; for doctorate, M Sc, minimum B+ average. Additional exam requirements/recommendations for international students: Required—TOEFL (minimum score 580 paper-based; 237 computer-based; 92 iBT).

Medical University of South Carolina, College of Graduate Studies, Department of Biochemistry and Molecular Biology, Charleston, SC 29425. Offers MS, PhD, MD/PhD. *Faculty:* 24 full-time (9 women), 3 part-time/adjunct (1 woman). *Students:* 17 full-time (11 women), 2 part-time (0 women); includes 1 Black or African American, non-Hispanic/Latino; 2 Asian, non-Hispanic/Latino, 6 international. Average age 30. 9 applicants, 22% accepted, 2 enrolled. In 2010, 1 master's, 2 doctorates awarded. Terminal master's awarded for partial completion of doctoral program. *Degree requirements:* For master's, thesis, oral exam/thesis defense; for doctorate, thesis/dissertation, oral and written exams/dissertation defense. *Entrance requirements:* For master's, GRE General Test; for doctorate, GRE General Test, interview, minimum GPA of 3.0. Additional exam requirements/recommendations for international students: Required—TOEFL (minimum score 600 paper-based; 250 computer-based; 100 iBT). *Application deadline:* For fall admission, 1/15 priority date for domestic and international students. Applications are processed on a rolling basis. Application fee: $0 ($85 for international students). Electronic applications accepted. *Financial support:* In 2010–11, 10 research assistantships with partial tuition reimbursements (averaging $23,000 per year) were awarded; Federal Work-Study and scholarships/grants also available. Support available to part-time students. Financial award applicants required to submit FAFSA. *Faculty research:* Lipid biochemistry, DNA replication, nucleic acids, protein structure. *Unit head:* Dr. Yusuf A. Hannun, Chairman, 843-792-9318, Fax: 843-792-6590, E-mail: hannun@musc.edu. *Application contact:* Dr. Maurizio Del Poeta, Associate Professor, 843-792-8381, Fax: 843-792-6590, E-mail: delpoeta@musc.edu.

Medical University of South Carolina, College of Graduate Studies, Program in Molecular and Cellular Biology and Pathobiology, Charleston, SC 29425. Offers cancer biology (PhD); cardiovascular biology (PhD); cardiovascular imaging (PhD); cell regulation (PhD); craniofacial biology (PhD); genetics and development (PhD); marine biomedicine (PhD); DMD/PhD; MD/PhD. *Faculty:* 137 full-time (33 women). *Students:* 27 full-time (20 women); includes 3 Black or African American, non-Hispanic/Latino; 1 Hispanic/Latino, 6 international. Average age 30. In 2010, 16 doctorates awarded. *Degree requirements:* For doctorate, thesis/dissertation, oral and written exams. *Entrance requirements:* For doctorate, GRE General Test, interview, minimum GPA of 3.0. Additional exam requirements/recommendations for international students: Required—TOEFL (minimum score 600 paper-based; 250 computer-based; 100 iBT). *Application deadline:* For fall admission, 1/15 priority date for domestic and international students. Applications are processed on a rolling basis. Application fee: $0 ($85 for international students). Electronic applications accepted. *Financial support:* In 2010–11, 39 research assistantships with partial tuition reimbursements (averaging $23,000 per year) were awarded; Federal Work-Study and scholarships/grants also available. Support available to part-time students. Financial award application deadline: 3/10; financial award applicants required to submit FAFSA. *Unit head:* Dr. Donald R. Menick, Director, 843-876-5045, Fax: 843-792-6590, E-mail: menickd@musc.edu. *Application contact:* Dr. Cynthia F. Wright, Associate Dean for Admissions and Career Development, 843-792-2564, Fax: 843-792-6590, E-mail: wrightcf@musc.edu.

Michigan State University, The Graduate School, College of Agriculture and Natural Resources, MSU-DOE Plant Research Laboratory, East Lansing, MI 48824. Offers biochemistry and molecular biology (PhD); cellular and molecular biology (PhD); crop and soil sciences (PhD); genetics (PhD); microbiology and molecular genetics (PhD); plant biology (PhD); plant physiology (PhD). Offered jointly with the Department of Energy. *Degree requirements:* For doctorate, comprehensive exam, thesis/dissertation, laboratory rotation, defense of dissertation. *Entrance requirements:* For doctorate, GRE General Test, acceptance into one of the affiliated department programs; 3 letters of recommendation; bachelor's degree or equivalent in life sciences, chemistry, biochemistry, or biophysics; research experience. Electronic applications accepted. *Faculty research:* Role of hormones in the regulation of plant development and physiology, molecular mechanisms associated with signal recognition, development and application of genetic methods and materials, protein routing and function.

Michigan State University, The Graduate School, College of Natural Science and Graduate Programs in Human Medicine and Graduate Studies in Osteopathic Medicine, Department of Biochemistry and Molecular Biology, East Lansing, MI 48824. Offers biochemistry and molecular biology (MS, PhD); biochemistry and molecular biology/environmental toxicology (PhD). *Entrance requirements:* Additional exam requirements/recommendations for international students: Required—TOEFL. Electronic applications accepted.

Michigan State University, The Graduate School, College of Natural Science, Program in Cell and Molecular Biology, East Lansing, MI 48824. Offers cell and molecular biology (MS, PhD); cell and molecular biology/environmental toxicology (PhD). *Entrance requirements:* Additional exam requirements/recommendations for international students: Required—TOEFL. Electronic applications accepted.

Mississippi State University, College of Agriculture and Life Sciences, Department of Biochemistry and Molecular Biology, Mississippi State, MS 39762. Offers agriculture life sciences (MS), including biochemistry; molecular biology (PhD). *Faculty:* 6 full-time (0 women). *Students:* 23 full-time (12 women), 2 part-time (1 woman); includes 3 minority (2 Black or African American, non-Hispanic/Latino; 1 Two or more races, non-Hispanic/Latino), 11 international. Average age 27. 25 applicants, 28% accepted, 4 enrolled. In 2010, 3 master's, 4 doctorates awarded. Terminal master's awarded for partial completion of doctoral program. *Degree requirements:* For master's, thesis (for some programs), comprehensive oral or written exam; for doctorate, thesis/dissertation, comprehensive oral and written exam. *Entrance requirements:* For master's, GRE General Test, minimum GPA of 2.75; for doctorate, GRE. Additional exam requirements/recommendations for international students: Required—TOEFL (minimum score 550 paper-based; 213 computer-based; 79 iBT); Recommended—IELTS (minimum score 6.5). *Application deadline:* For fall admission, 7/1 for domestic students, 5/1 for international students; for spring admission, 11/1 for domestic students, 9/1 for international students. Applications are processed on a rolling basis. Application fee: $40. Electronic applications accepted. *Expenses:* Tuition, state resident: full-time $2731; part-time $304 per credit hour. Tuition, nonresident: full-time $6901; part-time $767 per credit hour. *Financial support:* In 2010–11, 15 research assistantships with full tuition reimbursements (averaging $13,530 per year) were awarded; Federal Work-Study, institutionally sponsored loans, and unspecified assistantships also available. Financial award application deadline: 4/1; financial award applicants required to submit FAFSA. *Faculty research:* Fish nutrition, plant and animal molecular biology, plant biochemistry, enzymology, lipid metabolism. *Unit head:* Dr. Scott T. Willard, Professor and Department Head, 662-325-2640, Fax: 662-325-8664, E-mail: swilliard@ads.msstate.edu. *Application contact:* Dr. Din-Pow Ma, Professor/Graduate Coordinator, 662-325-7739, Fax: 662-325-8664, E-mail: dm1@ra.msstate.edu.

Missouri State University, Graduate College, College of Health and Human Services, Department of Biomedical Sciences, Program in Cell and Molecular Biology, Springfield, MO 65897. Offers MS. Part-time programs available. *Degree requirements:* For master's, thesis or alternative, oral and written exams. *Entrance requirements:* For master's, GRE General Test, 2 semesters of course work in organic chemistry and physics, 1 semester of course work in calculus, minimum GPA of 3.0 in last 60 hours of course work. Additional exam requirements/recommendations for international students: Required—TOEFL (minimum score 550 paper-based; 213 computer-based; 79 iBT). Electronic applications accepted. *Expenses:* Tuition, state resident: full-time $3348; part-time $186 per credit hour. Tuition, nonresident: full-time $6696; part-time $372 per credit hour. Required fees: $238 per semester. Tuition and fees vary according to course level, course load and program. *Faculty research:* Extracellular matrix membrane protein, P2 nucleotide receptors, double stranded RNA viruses.

Montclair State University, The Graduate School, College of Science and Mathematics, Department of Biology and Molecular Biology, Montclair, NJ 07043-1624. Offers biological science (Certificate); biology (MS), including biology, biology science/education, ecology and evolution, physiology; molecular biology (MS, Certificate). Part-time and evening/weekend programs available. *Faculty:* 22 full-time (9 women), 26 part-time/adjunct (13 women). *Students:* 30 full-time (20 women), 73 part-time (55 women); includes 5 Black or African American, non-Hispanic/Latino; 6 Asian, non-Hispanic/Latino; 25 Hispanic/Latino, 3 international. Average age 28. 48 applicants, 71% accepted, 24 enrolled. In 2010, 21 master's, 2 other advanced degrees awarded. *Degree requirements:* For master's, comprehensive exam, thesis or alternative. *Entrance requirements:* For master's, GRE General Test, 24 credits of course work in undergraduate biology, 2 letters of recommendation, teaching certificate (biology sciences education concentration). Additional exam requirements/recommendations for international students: Required—TOEFL (minimum iBT score of 83) or IELTS. *Application deadline:* For fall admission, 6/1 for international students; for spring admission, 10/1 for international students. Applications are processed on a rolling basis. Application fee: $60. Electronic applications accepted. *Expenses:* Tuition, state resident: part-time $501.34 per credit. Tuition, nonresident: part-time $773.88 per credit. Required fees: $71.15 per credit. *Financial support:* In 2010–11, 12 research assistantships with full tuition reimbursements (averaging $7,000 per year) were awarded; Federal Work-Study, scholarships/grants, and unspecified assistantships also available. Support available to part-time students. Financial award application deadline: 3/1; financial award applicants required to submit FAFSA. *Faculty research:* Cells, algae blooms, scallops, New Jersey bays, Barnegat Bay. Total annual research expenditures: $1.3 million. *Unit head:* Dr. Quinn Vega, Chairperson, 973-655-7178. *Application contact:* Amy Aiello, Director of Graduate Admissions and Operations, 973-655-5147, Fax: 973-655-7869, E-mail: graduate.school@montclair.edu.

New Mexico State University, Graduate School, Program in Molecular Biology, Las Cruces, NM 88003-8001. Offers MS, PhD. *Students:* 20 full-time (8 women), 6 part-time (3 women); includes 7 minority (1 Black or African American, non-Hispanic/Latino; 1 American Indian or Alaska Native, non-Hispanic/Latino; 5 Hispanic/Latino), 12 international. Average age 31. 13 applicants, 100% accepted, 8 enrolled. In 2010, 1 master's, 6 doctorates awarded. *Degree requirements:* For master's, thesis, oral seminars; for doctorate, comprehensive exam, thesis/dissertation, oral seminars. *Entrance requirements:* For master's and doctorate, GRE General Test, minimum GPA of 3.3. Additional exam requirements/recommendations for international students: Required—TOEFL. *Application deadline:* For fall admission, 12/15 for domestic and international students; for spring admission, 1/15 for domestic and international students. Applications are processed on a rolling basis. Application fee: $30 ($50 for international students). Electronic applications accepted. *Expenses:* Tuition, state resident: full-time $4536; part-time $242 per credit. Tuition, nonresident: full-time $15,816; part-time $712 per credit. Required fees: $636 per term. *Financial support:* In 2010–11, 10 research assistantships (averaging $16,865 per year), 8 teaching assistantships (averaging $10,222 per year) were awarded; fellowships, career-related internships or fieldwork, health care benefits, and unspecified assistantships also available. Financial award application deadline: 3/1. *Faculty research:* Emerging pathogens, plant-molecular biology and virology, molecular symbiotic interactions, cell and organismal biology, applied and environmental microbiology. *Unit head:* Dr. Rebecca Creamer, Director, 575-646-3068, Fax: 575-646-8087, E-mail: creamer@nmsu.edu. *Application contact:* Nancy McDow, Program Secretary, 575-646-3437, Fax: 575-646-5170, E-mail: nancyt@nmsu.edu.

New York Medical College, Graduate School of Basic Medical Sciences, Program in Biochemistry and Molecular Biology, Valhalla, NY 10595-1691. Offers MS, PhD, MD/PhD. Part-time and evening/weekend programs available. *Faculty:* 11 full-time (5 women). *Students:*

10 full-time (9 women), 5 part-time (3 women); includes 1 American Indian or Alaska Native, non-Hispanic/Latino; 3 Asian, non-Hispanic/Latino, 2 international. Average age 27. 4 applicants, 50% accepted, 1 enrolled. In 2010, 5 master's, 2 doctorates awarded. Terminal master's awarded for partial completion of doctoral program. *Degree requirements:* For master's, thesis; for doctorate, comprehensive exam, thesis/dissertation. *Entrance requirements:* For master's and doctorate, GRE General Test. Additional exam requirements/recommendations for international students: Required—TOEFL. *Application deadline:* For fall admission, 7/1 priority date for domestic students, 5/1 priority date for international students; for spring admission, 12/1 priority date for domestic students, 10/1 priority date for international students. Applications are processed on a rolling basis. Application fee: $50 ($75 for international students). Electronic applications accepted. *Financial support:* In 2010–11, 7 research assistantships with full tuition reimbursements (averaging $24,000 per year) were awarded; Federal Work-Study, institutionally sponsored loans, scholarships/grants, traineeships, tuition waivers (full), unspecified assistantships, and health benefits (for PhD candidates only) also available. Financial award applicants required to submit FAFSA. *Faculty research:* Mechanisms of control of blood coagulation, molecular neurobiology, molecular probes for infectious disease, protein-DNA interactions, molecular biology and biochemistry of double-stranded RNA-dependent enzymes. *Unit head:* Dr. Joseph Wu, Director, 914-594-4891, Fax: 914-594-4944, E-mail: joseph_wu@nymc.edu. *Application contact:* Valerie Romeo-Messana, Admission Coordinator, 914-594-4110, Fax: 914-594-4944, E-mail: v_romeomessana@nymc.edu.

New York University, Graduate School of Arts and Science, Department of Biology, New York, NY 10012-1019. Offers biology (PhD); biomedical journalism (MS); cancer and molecular biology (PhD); computational biology (PhD); computers in biological research (MS); developmental genetics (PhD); general biology (MS); immunology and microbiology (PhD); molecular genetics (PhD); neurobiology (PhD); oral biology (MS); plant biology (PhD); recombinant DNA technology (MS); MS/MBA. Part-time programs available. *Faculty:* 24 full-time (5 women). *Students:* 155 full-time (89 women), 38 part-time (24 women); includes 29 Asian, non-Hispanic/Latino; 7 Hispanic/Latino, 88 international. Average age 27. 324 applicants, 69% accepted, 63 enrolled. In 2010, 55 master's, 4 doctorates awarded. Terminal master's awarded for partial completion of doctoral program. *Degree requirements:* For master's, thesis or alternative, qualifying paper; for doctorate, comprehensive exam, thesis/dissertation. *Entrance requirements:* For master's, GRE General Test; for doctorate, GRE General Test, GRE Subject Test. Additional exam requirements/recommendations for international students: Required—TOEFL. *Application deadline:* For fall admission, 12/15 priority date for domestic students. Application fee: $90. *Financial support:* Fellowships with tuition reimbursements, research assistantships with tuition reimbursements, teaching assistantships with tuition reimbursements, career-related internships or fieldwork, Federal Work-Study, institutionally sponsored loans, scholarships/grants, health care benefits, and unspecified assistantships available. Financial award application deadline: 12/15; financial award applicants required to submit FAFSA. *Faculty research:* Genomics, molecular and cell biology, development and molecular genetics, molecular evolution of plants and animals. *Unit head:* Gloria Coruzzi, Chair, 212-998-8200, Fax: 212-995-4015, E-mail: biology@nyu.edu. *Application contact:* Justin Blau, Director of Graduate Studies, 212-998-8200, Fax: 212-995-4015, E-mail: biology@nyu.edu.

New York University, School of Medicine, New York, NY 10012-1019. Offers biomedical sciences (PhD), including biomedical imaging, cellular and molecular biology, computational biology, developmental genetics, medical and molecular parasitology, microbiology, molecular oncobiology and immunology, neuroscience and physiology, pathobiology, pharmacology, structural biology; clinical investigation (MS); medicine (MD); MD/MA; MD/MPA; MD/MS; MD/PhD. *Accreditation:* LCME/AMA (one or more programs are accredited). *Degree requirements:* For master's, comprehensive exam, thesis; for doctorate, comprehensive exam, thesis/dissertation. *Entrance requirements:* MCAT. Additional exam requirements/recommendations for international students: Required—TOEFL. *Expenses:* Contact institution. *Faculty research:* AIDS, cancer, neuroscience, molecular biology, neuroscience, cell biology and molecular genetics, structural biology, microbial pathogenesis and host defense, pharmacology, molecular oncology and immunology.

New York University, School of Medicine and Graduate School of Arts and Science, Sackler Institute of Graduate Biomedical Sciences, Program in Cellular and Molecular Biology, New York, NY 10012-1019. Offers PhD, MD/PhD. *Degree requirements:* For doctorate, comprehensive exam, thesis/dissertation, qualifying exams. *Entrance requirements:* For doctorate, GRE General Test. Additional exam requirements/recommendations for international students: Required—TOEFL. *Faculty research:* Membrane and organelle structure and biogenesis, intracellular transport and processing of proteins, cellular recognition and cell adhesion, oncogene structure and function, action of growth factors.

North Dakota State University, College of Graduate and Interdisciplinary Studies, College of Science and Mathematics, Department of Biological Sciences, Fargo, ND 58108. Offers biology (MS); botany (MS, PhD); cellular and molecular biology (PhD); environmental and conservation sciences (MS, PhD); genomics (PhD); natural resources management (MS, PhD); zoology (MS, PhD). *Students:* 18 full-time (8 women), 5 part-time (3 women); includes 2 American Indian or Alaska Native, non-Hispanic/Latino, 2 international. 17 applicants, 35% accepted. In 2010, 12 master's, 9 doctorates awarded. *Degree requirements:* For master's, thesis; for doctorate, thesis/dissertation. *Entrance requirements:* For master's and doctorate, GRE General Test. Additional exam requirements/recommendations for international students: Required—TOEFL. *Application deadline:* For fall admission, 3/15 priority date for domestic students; for spring admission, 10/30 priority date for domestic students. Applications are processed on a rolling basis. Application fee: $45 ($60 for international students). Electronic applications accepted. *Financial support:* Fellowships with full tuition reimbursements, research assistantships with full tuition reimbursements, teaching assistantships with full tuition reimbursements, career-related internships or fieldwork, Federal Work-Study, institutionally sponsored loans, scholarships/grants, tuition waivers (full), and unspecified assistantships available. Support available to part-time students. Financial award application deadline: 4/15; financial award applicants required to submit FAFSA. *Faculty research:* Comparative endocrinology, physiology, behavioral ecology, plant cell biology, aquatic biology. Total annual research expenditures: $675,000. *Unit head:* Dr. Marinus L. Otte, Head, 701-231-7087, E-mail: marinus.otte@ndsu.edu. *Application contact:* Dr. Marinus L. Otte, Head, 701-231-7087, E-mail: marinus.otte@ndsu.edu.

North Dakota State University, College of Graduate and Interdisciplinary Studies, Interdisciplinary Program in Cellular and Molecular Biology, Fargo, ND 58108. Offers PhD. PhD offered in cooperation with 11 departments in the university. *Students:* 11 full-time (8 women), 1 part-time (0 women), 7 international. 24 applicants, 21% accepted, 5 enrolled. *Degree requirements:* For doctorate, thesis/dissertation. *Entrance requirements:* For doctorate, GRE. Additional exam requirements/recommendations for international students: Required—TOEFL (minimum score 525 paper-based; 197 computer-based; 71 iBT). *Application deadline:* Applications are processed on a rolling basis. Application fee: $45 ($60 for international students). Electronic applications accepted. *Financial support:* Fellowships with full tuition reimbursements, research assistantships with full tuition reimbursements, teaching assistantships with full tuition reimbursements, unspecified assistantships available. Financial award application deadline: 3/15. *Faculty research:* Plant and animal cell biology, gene regulation, molecular genetics, plant and animal virology. *Unit head:* Dr. Mark Sheridan, Director, 701-231-7087, E-mail: ndsu.cmb@ndsu.edu. *Application contact:* Dr. Mark Sheridan, Director, 701-231-7087, E-mail: ndsu.cmb@ndsu.edu.

Northwestern University, The Graduate School, Interdepartmental Biological Sciences Program (IBiS), Evanston, IL 60208. Offers biochemistry, molecular biology, and cell biology (PhD), including biochemistry, cell and molecular biology, molecular biophysics, structural biology; biotechnology (PhD); cell and molecular biology (PhD); developmental biology and genetics (PhD); hormone action and signal transduction (PhD); neuroscience (PhD); structural biology, biochemistry, and biophysics (PhD). Program participants include the Departments of Biochemistry, Molecular Biology, and Cell Biology; Chemistry; Neurobiology and Physiology; Chemical Engineering; Civil Engineering; and Evanston Hospital. *Degree requirements:* For

doctorate, thesis/dissertation, qualifying exam. *Entrance requirements:* For doctorate, GRE General Test. Additional exam requirements/recommendations for international students: Required—TOEFL (minimum score 600 paper-based). Electronic applications accepted. *Faculty research:* Developmental genetics, gene regulation, DNA-protein interactions, biological clocks, bioremediation.

Northwestern University, Northwestern University Feinberg School of Medicine and Interdepartmental Programs, Integrated Graduate Programs in the Life Sciences, Chicago, IL 60611. Offers cancer biology (PhD); cell biology (PhD); developmental biology (PhD); evolutionary biology (PhD); immunology and microbial pathogenesis (PhD); molecular biology and genetics (PhD); neurobiology (PhD); pharmacology and toxicology (PhD); structural biology and biochemistry (PhD). *Degree requirements:* For doctorate, comprehensive exam, thesis/dissertation, written and oral qualifying exams. *Entrance requirements:* For doctorate, GRE General Test. Additional exam requirements/recommendations for international students: Required—TOEFL (minimum score 600 paper-based; 250 computer-based). Electronic applications accepted.

OGI School of Science & Engineering at Oregon Health & Science University, Graduate Studies, Department of Environmental and Biomolecular Systems, Beaverton, OR 97006-8921. Offers biochemistry and molecular biology (MS, PhD); environmental health systems (MS); environmental information technology (MS, PhD); environmental science and engineering (MS, PhD). Part-time programs available. Terminal master's awarded for partial completion of doctoral program. *Degree requirements:* For master's, thesis optional; for doctorate, comprehensive exam, oral defense of dissertation. *Entrance requirements:* For master's and doctorate, GRE General Test. Additional exam requirements/recommendations for international students: Required—TOEFL. Electronic applications accepted. *Faculty research:* Air and water science, hydrogeology, estuarine and coastal modeling, environmental microbiology, contaminant transport, biochemistry, biomolecular systems.

The Ohio State University, Graduate School, College of Arts and Sciences, Division of Natural and Mathematical Sciences, Department of Molecular Genetics, Columbus, OH 43210. Offers cell and developmental biology (MS, PhD); genetics (MS, PhD); molecular biology (MS, PhD). *Faculty:* 26. *Students:* 7 full-time (3 women), 25 part-time (14 women), 16 international. Average age 27. In 2010, 1 master's, 1 doctorate awarded. *Degree requirements:* For master's, thesis; for doctorate, thesis/dissertation. *Entrance requirements:* For master's and doctorate, GRE General Test, GRE Subject Test in biology or biochemistry (recommended). Additional exam requirements/recommendations for international students: Required—TOEFL (minimum score 600 paper-based; 250 computer-based). *Application deadline:* For fall admission, 8/15 priority date for domestic students, 7/1 priority date for international students; for winter admission, 12/1 priority date for domestic students, 11/1 priority date for international students; for spring admission, 3/1 priority date for domestic students, 2/1 priority date for international students. Applications are processed on a rolling basis. Application fee: $40 ($50 for international students). Electronic applications accepted. *Expenses:* Tuition, state resident: full-time $10,605. Tuition, nonresident: full-time $26,535. Tuition and fees vary according to course load and program. *Financial support:* Fellowships, research assistantships, teaching assistantships, Federal Work-Study and institutionally sponsored loans available. Support available to part-time students. *Unit head:* Dr. Anna Hopper, Chair, 614-688-3306, Fax: 614-247-2594, E-mail: hopper.64@osu.edu. *Application contact:* 614-292-9444, Fax: 614-292-3895, E-mail: domestic.grad@osu.edu.

The Ohio State University, Graduate School, College of Arts and Sciences, Division of Natural and Mathematical Sciences, Program in Molecular, Cellular and Developmental Biology, Columbus, OH 43210. Offers MS, PhD. *Students:* 70 full-time (40 women), 64 part-time (35 women); includes 8 Asian, non-Hispanic/Latino; 7 Hispanic/Latino, 75 international. Average age 28. In 2010, 4 master's, 17 doctorates awarded. *Degree requirements:* For master's, thesis; for doctorate, thesis/dissertation. *Entrance requirements:* For master's and doctorate, GRE General Test, GRE Subject Test (biology or biochemistry, cell and molecular biology). Additional exam requirements/recommendations for international students: Required—TOEFL (minimum score 573 paper-based; 230 computer-based). *Application deadline:* For fall admission, 8/15 priority date for domestic students, 7/1 priority date for international students; for winter admission, 12/1 priority date for domestic students, 11/1 priority date for international students; for spring admission, 3/1 priority date for domestic students, 2/1 priority date for international students. Applications are processed on a rolling basis. Application fee: $40 ($50 for international students). Electronic applications accepted. *Expenses:* Tuition, state resident: full-time $10,605. Tuition, nonresident: full-time $26,535. Tuition and fees vary according to course load and program. *Unit head:* David M. Bisaro, Director, 614-292-3281, Fax: 614-292-4466, E-mail: bisaro.1@osu.edu. *Application contact:* Graduate Admissions, 614-292-9444, Fax: 614-292-3895, E-mail: domestic.grad@osu.edu.

Ohio University, Graduate College, College of Arts and Sciences, Interdisciplinary Graduate Program in Molecular and Cellular Biology, Athens, OH 45701-2979. Offers MS, PhD. *Students:* 27 full-time (17 women), 3 part-time (1 woman); includes 1 minority (Hispanic/Latino), 24 international. Average age 28. 34 applicants, 18% accepted, 1 enrolled. In 2010, 4 doctorates awarded. *Degree requirements:* For master's, comprehensive exam, thesis, research proposal, teaching experience; for doctorate, comprehensive exam, thesis/dissertation, research proposal, teaching experience. *Entrance requirements:* For master's and doctorate, GRE General Test. Additional exam requirements/recommendations for international students: Required—TOEFL (minimum score 620 paper-based; 260 computer-based; 105 iBT); Recommended—TWE. *Application deadline:* For fall admission, 12/30 priority date for domestic students, 12/30 for international students. Application fee: $50 ($55 for international students). Electronic applications accepted. *Financial support:* In 2010–11, 25 students received support, including research assistantships with full tuition reimbursements available (averaging $19,500 per year), teaching assistantships with full tuition reimbursements available (averaging $19,500 per year); Federal Work-Study, institutionally sponsored loans, traineeships, and unspecified assistantships also available. Financial award application deadline: 12/30. *Faculty research:* Animal biotechnology, plant molecular biology RNA, immunology, cellular genetics, biochemistry of signal transduction, cancer research, membrane transport, bioinformatics, bioengineering, chemical biology and drug discovery, diabetes, microbiology, neuroscience. Total annual research expenditures: $4.4 million. *Unit head:* Dr. Robert A. Colvin, Chair, 740-593-0198, Fax: 740-593-1569, E-mail: colvin@ohio.edu. *Application contact:* Dr. Xiaozhuo Chen, Graduate Chair, 740-593-9699, Fax: 740-593-1569, E-mail: chenx@ohio.edu.

Oklahoma State University, College of Agricultural Science and Natural Resources, Department of Biochemistry and Molecular Biology, Stillwater, OK 74078. Offers MS, PhD. *Faculty:* 31 full-time (12 women), 2 part-time/adjunct (0 women). *Students:* 6 full-time (0 women), 26 part-time (17 women); includes 1 Black or African American, non-Hispanic/Latino; 2 American Indian or Alaska Native, non-Hispanic/Latino; 1 Hispanic/Latino, 20 international. Average age 28. 82 applicants, 18% accepted, 3 enrolled. In 2010, 5 master's, 5 doctorates awarded. *Degree requirements:* For master's, thesis, oral exam; for doctorate, comprehensive exam, thesis/dissertation. *Entrance requirements:* For master's and doctorate, GRE or GMAT. Additional exam requirements/recommendations for international students: Required—TOEFL (minimum score 550 paper-based; 79 iBT). *Application deadline:* For fall admission, 3/1 priority date for international students; for spring admission, 8/1 priority date for international students. Applications are processed on a rolling basis. Application fee: $40 ($75 for international students). Electronic applications accepted. *Expenses:* Tuition, state resident: full-time $3716; part-time $154.85 per credit hour. Tuition, nonresident: full-time $14,892; part-time $621 per credit hour. Required fees: $2044; $85.20 per credit hour. One-time fee: $50. Tuition and fees vary according to course load and campus/location. *Financial support:* In 2010–11, 30 research assistantships (averaging $19,456 per year), 2 teaching assistantships (averaging $18,699 per year) were awarded; career-related internships or fieldwork, Federal Work-Study, scholarships/grants, health care benefits, tuition waivers (partial), and unspecified assistantships also available. Support available to part-time students. Financial award application deadline: 3/1; financial award applicants required to submit FAFSA. *Unit head:* Dr. Gary

Molecular Biology

Oklahoma State University (continued)

Thompson, Head, 405-744-9320, Fax: 405-744-7799. *Application contact:* Dr. Gordon Emslie, Dean, 405-744-6368, Fax: 405-744-0355, E-mail: grad-i@okstate.edu.

Oklahoma State University Center for Health Sciences, Graduate Program in Forensic Sciences, Tulsa, OK 74107-1898. Offers forensic DNA/molecular biology (MS); forensic examination of questioned documents (Certificate); forensic pathology (MS); forensic psychology (MS); forensic toxicology (MS). Part-time and evening/weekend programs available. Post-baccalaureate distance learning degree programs offered (no on-campus study). *Faculty:* 2 full-time (0 women), 14 part-time/adjunct (5 women). *Students:* 7 full-time (6 women), 21 part-time (12 women); includes 5 minority (2 Black or African American, non-Hispanic/Latino; 2 Asian, non-Hispanic/Latino; 1 Hispanic/Latino). Average age 34. 21 applicants, 57% accepted, 7 enrolled. In 2010, 6 master's awarded. *Degree requirements:* For master's, comprehensive exam (for some programs), thesis (for some programs). *Entrance requirements:* For master's, MAT (MFSA) or GRE General Test, professional experience (MFSA). Additional exam requirements/recommendations for international students: Required—TOEFL (minimum score 600 paper-based; 250 computer-based), TWE (minimum score 5). *Application deadline:* For fall admission, 3/1 for domestic and international students; for spring admission, 10/1 for domestic and international students. Application fee: $40 ($75 for international students). *Financial support:* In 2010–11, 10 students received support, including 10 research assistantships (averaging $29,000 per year); career-related internships or fieldwork, Federal Work-Study, and tuition waivers (partial) also available. Support available to part-time students. Financial award application deadline: 4/1; financial award applicants required to submit FAFSA. *Faculty research:* DNA typing, DNA polymorphism, identification through DNA, disease transmission, forensic dentistry, neurotoxicity of HIV, forensic toxicology method development, toxin detection and characterization. Total annual research expenditures: $58,000. *Unit head:* Dr. Robert T. Allen, Director, 918-561-1108, Fax: 918-561-8414. *Application contact:* Cathy Newsome, Coordinator, 918-561-1108, Fax: 918-561-8414, E-mail: cathy.newsome@okstate.edu.

Oregon Health & Science University, School of Medicine, Graduate Programs in Medicine, Department of Environmental and Biomolecular Systems, Portland, OR 97239-3098. Offers biochemistry and molecular biology (MS, PhD); environmental science and engineering (MS, PhD). Part-time programs available. *Faculty:* 14 full-time (4 women), 1 (woman) part-time/adjunct. *Students:* 21 full-time (12 women), 25 part-time (12 women); includes 1 Black or African American, non-Hispanic/Latino; 3 American Indian or Alaska Native, non-Hispanic/Latino; 5 Asian, non-Hispanic/Latino; 3 Hispanic/Latino, 8 international. Average age 33. 45 applicants, 60% accepted, 11 enrolled. In 2010, 8 master's, 2 doctorates awarded. Terminal master's awarded for partial completion of doctoral program. *Degree requirements:* For master's, thesis (for some programs); for doctorate, comprehensive exam, thesis/dissertation. *Entrance requirements:* For master's and doctorate, GRE General Test (minimum scores: 500 Verbal/600 Quantitative/4.5 Analytical) or MCAT (for some programs). Additional exam requirements/recommendations for international students: Required—TOEFL. *Application deadline:* For fall admission, 7/15 for domestic students, 5/15 for international students; for winter admission, 10/15 for domestic students, 9/15 for international students; for spring admission, 1/15 for domestic students, 12/15 for international students. Applications are processed on a rolling basis. Application fee: $65. Electronic applications accepted. *Financial support:* Health care benefits and full tuition and stipends available. *Unit head:* Dr. Paul Tratnyek, Program Director, 503-748-1070, E-mail: info@ebs.ogi.edu. *Application contact:* Nancy Christie, Program Coordinator, 503-748-1070, E-mail: info@ebs.ogi.edu.

Oregon Health & Science University, School of Medicine, Graduate Programs in Medicine, Program in Molecular and Cellular Biosciences, Department of Biochemistry and Molecular Biology, Portland, OR 97239-3098. Offers PhD. *Faculty:* 14 full-time (4 women), 6 part-time/adjunct (3 women). *Students:* 11 full-time (6 women), 2 international. Average age 30. In 2010, 1 doctorate awarded. *Degree requirements:* For doctorate, comprehensive exam, thesis/dissertation, qualifying exam. *Entrance requirements:* For doctorate, GRE General Test (minimum scores: 500 Verbal/600 Quantitative/4.5 Analytical). Additional exam requirements/recommendations for international students: Required—TOEFL. Electronic applications accepted. *Financial support:* Health care benefits, tuition waivers (full), and full tuition and stipends available. *Faculty research:* Protein structure and function, enzymology, metabolism, membranes transport. *Unit head:* Dr. David Farrens, Program Director, 503-494-7781, E-mail: farrensd@ohsu.edu. *Application contact:* Jeni Wroblewski, Administrative Coordinator, 503-494-2541, E-mail: wroblews@ohsu.edu.

Oregon State University, Graduate School, Program in Molecular and Cellular Biology, Corvallis, OR 97331. Offers MS, PhD. *Degree requirements:* For doctorate, thesis/dissertation, oral and written qualifying exams. *Entrance requirements:* For doctorate, minimum GPA of 3.0 in last 90 hours. Additional exam requirements/recommendations for international students: Required—TOEFL.

Penn State Hershey Medical Center, College of Medicine, Graduate School Programs in the Biomedical Sciences, Graduate Program in Biochemistry and Molecular Biology, Hershey, PA 17033. Offers MS, PhD, MD/PhD. *Students:* 131 applicants, 5% accepted, 3 enrolled. Terminal master's awarded for partial completion of doctoral program. *Degree requirements:* For master's, thesis or alternative; for doctorate, comprehensive exam, thesis/dissertation. *Entrance requirements:* For master's, GRE General Test; for doctorate, GRE General Test, minimum GPA of 3.0. Additional exam requirements/recommendations for international students: Required—TOEFL (minimum score 550 paper-based; 213 computer-based). *Application deadline:* For fall admission, 1/31 priority date for domestic students, 2/1 priority date for international students. Applications are processed on a rolling basis. Application fee: $65. Electronic applications accepted. *Financial support:* In 2010–11, research assistantships with full tuition reimbursements (averaging $22,260 per year); fellowships with full tuition reimbursements, scholarships/grants, health care benefits, tuition waivers, and unspecified assistantships also available. Financial award applicants required to submit FAFSA. *Faculty research:* X-ray crystallography of proteins, glycosphingolipid interactions with viruses and toxins, DNA replication and repair, tobacco and environmental carcinogenesis, gene regulation. *Unit head:* Dr. Judith S. Bond, Chair, 717-531-8585, Fax: 717-531-7072, E-mail: bchem-grad-hmc@psu.edu. *Application contact:* Ruth Dean, Administrative Assistant, 717-531-8586, Fax: 717-531-7072, E-mail: bchem-grad-hmc@psu.edu.

Penn State Hershey Medical Center, College of Medicine, Graduate School Programs in the Biomedical Sciences, Graduate Program in Microbiology and Immunology, Hershey, PA 17033. Offers genetics (PhD); immunology (MS, PhD); microbiology (MS); microbiology/virology (PhD); molecular biology (PhD); MD/PhD. *Students:* 12 applicants, 75% accepted, 3 enrolled. In 2010, 1 doctorate awarded. Terminal master's awarded for partial completion of doctoral program. *Degree requirements:* For master's, thesis or alternative; for doctorate, comprehensive exam, thesis/dissertation, oral exam. *Entrance requirements:* For doctorate, GRE General Test, minimum GPA of 3.0. Additional exam requirements/recommendations for international students: Required—TOEFL. *Application deadline:* For fall admission, 1/31 priority date for domestic students, 2/1 priority date for international students. Applications are processed on a rolling basis. Application fee: $45. Electronic applications accepted. *Financial support:* In 2010–11, research assistantships with full tuition reimbursements (averaging $22,260 per year); fellowships with full tuition reimbursements, scholarships/grants, health care benefits, and unspecified assistantships also available. Financial award applicants required to submit FAFSA. *Faculty research:* Virus replication and assembly, oncogenesis, interactions of viruses with host cells and animal model systems. *Unit head:* Dr. Richard J. Courtney, Chair, 717-531-7659, Fax: 717-531-6522, E-mail: micro-grad-hmc@psu.edu. *Application contact:* Billie Burns, Secretary, 717-531-7659, Fax: 717-531-6522, E-mail: micro-grad-hmc@psu.edu.

Penn State Hershey Medical Center, College of Medicine, Graduate School Programs in the Biomedical Sciences, Interdepartmental Graduate Program in Cell and Molecular Biology, Hershey, PA 17033. Offers MS, PhD, MD/PhD. *Students:* 37 applicants, 38% accepted, 4 enrolled. In 2010, 4 doctorates awarded. Terminal master's awarded for partial completion of doctoral program. *Degree requirements:* For master's, thesis or alternative; for doctorate, comprehensive exam, thesis/dissertation, oral exam. *Entrance requirements:* For master's, GRE General Test or MCAT; for doctorate, GRE General Test or MCAT, minimum GPA of 3.0. Additional exam requirements/recommendations for international students: Required—TOEFL (minimum score 500 paper-based; 213 computer-based). *Application deadline:* For fall admission, 1/31 priority date for domestic students, 2/1 priority date for international students. Applications are processed on a rolling basis. Application fee: $65. Electronic applications accepted. *Financial support:* In 2010–11, research assistantships with full tuition reimbursements (averaging $22,260 per year); fellowships with full tuition reimbursements, career-related internships or fieldwork, scholarships/grants, health care benefits, and unspecified assistantships also available. Financial award applicants required to submit FAFSA. *Faculty research:* Membrane structure, function and modulators; cell division, differentiation and gene expression; metastasis; intra-cellular events in the immune system. *Unit head:* Dr. Henry Donahue, Program Director, 717-531-1045, Fax: 717-531-4139, E-mail: cmb-grad-hmc@psu.edu. *Application contact:* Lori Coover, Program Assistant, 717-531-1045, Fax: 717-531-0786, E-mail: cmb-grad-hmc@psu.edu.

Penn State University Park, Graduate School, Eberly College of Science, Department of Biochemistry and Molecular Biology, Program in Biochemistry, Microbiology, and Molecular Biology, State College, University Park, PA 16802-1503. Offers MS, PhD. *Unit head:* Dr. Ronald Porter, Director of Graduate Studies, 814-863-4903, E-mail: rdp1@psu.edu. *Application contact:* Dr. Ronald Porter, Director of Graduate Studies, 814-863-4903, E-mail: rdp1@psu.edu.

Princeton University, Graduate School, Department of Molecular Biology, Princeton, NJ 08544-1019. Offers PhD. *Degree requirements:* For doctorate, thesis/dissertation. *Entrance requirements:* For doctorate, GRE General Test. Additional exam requirements/recommendations for international students: Required—TOEFL (minimum score 600 paper-based; 250 computer-based). Electronic applications accepted. *Faculty research:* Genetics, virology, biochemistry.

Purdue University, College of Pharmacy and Pharmacal Sciences and Graduate School, Graduate Programs in Pharmacy and Pharmacal Sciences, Department of Medicinal Chemistry and Molecular Pharmacology, West Lafayette, IN 47907. Offers analytical medicinal chemistry (PhD); computational and biophysical medicinal chemistry (PhD); medicinal and bioorganic chemistry (PhD); medicinal biochemistry and molecular biology (PhD); molecular pharmacology and toxicology (PhD); natural products and pharmacognosy (PhD); nuclear pharmacy (MS); radiopharmaceutical chemistry and nuclear pharmacy (PhD); MS/PhD. Terminal master's awarded for partial completion of doctoral program. *Degree requirements:* For master's, thesis; for doctorate, thesis/dissertation. *Entrance requirements:* For master's, GRE General Test, minimum B average; BS in biology, chemistry, or pharmacy; for doctorate, GRE General Test, minimum B average; BS in biology, chemistry, or pharmacology. Additional exam requirements/recommendations for international students: Required—TOEFL. Electronic applications accepted. *Faculty research:* Drug design and development, cancer research, drug synthesis and analysis, chemical pharmacology, environmental toxicology.

Purdue University, Graduate School, College of Science, Department of Biological Sciences, West Lafayette, IN 47907. Offers biochemistry (PhD); biophysics (PhD); cell and developmental biology (PhD); ecology, evolutionary and population biology (MS, PhD), including ecology, evolutionary biology, population biology; genetics (MS, PhD); microbiology (MS, PhD); molecular biology (PhD); neurobiology (MS, PhD); plant physiology (PhD). Terminal master's awarded for partial completion of doctoral program. *Degree requirements:* For master's, thesis (for some programs); for doctorate, thesis/dissertation, seminars, teaching experience. *Entrance requirements:* For master's and doctorate, GRE General Test. Additional exam requirements/recommendations for international students: Required—TOEFL. Electronic applications accepted.

Queen's University at Kingston, School of Graduate Studies and Research, Faculty of Health Sciences, Department of Anatomy and Cell Biology, Kingston, ON K7L 3N6, Canada. Offers biology of reproduction (M Sc, PhD); cancer (M Sc, PhD); cardiovascular pathophysiology (M Sc, PhD); cell and molecular biology (M Sc, PhD); drug metabolism (M Sc, PhD); endocrinology (M Sc, PhD); motor control (M Sc, PhD); neural regeneration (M Sc, PhD); neurophysiology (M Sc, PhD). Part-time programs available. *Degree requirements:* For master's, thesis; for doctorate, one foreign language, comprehensive exam, thesis/dissertation. *Entrance requirements:* Additional exam requirements/recommendations for international students: Required—TOEFL. Electronic applications accepted. *Faculty research:* Human kinetics, neuroscience, reproductive biology, cardiovascular.

Quinnipiac University, School of Health Sciences, Program in Molecular and Cell Biology, Hamden, CT 06518-1940. Offers MS. Part-time programs available. *Faculty:* 10 full-time (4 women), 12 part-time/adjunct (5 women). *Students:* 16 full-time (11 women), 21 part-time (15 women); includes 8 minority (3 Black or African American, non-Hispanic/Latino; 4 Asian, non-Hispanic/Latino; 1 Hispanic/Latino), 4 international. Average age 26. 37 applicants, 89% accepted, 19 enrolled. In 2010, 8 master's awarded. *Degree requirements:* For master's, thesis optional. *Entrance requirements:* For master's, bachelor's degree in biological, medical, or health sciences; minimum GPA of 2.75. Additional exam requirements/recommendations for international students: Required—TOEFL (minimum score 575 paper-based; 233 computer-based; 90 iBT), IELTS (minimum score 6.5). *Application deadline:* For fall admission, 7/30 priority date for domestic students, 4/30 priority date for international students; for spring admission, 12/15 priority date for domestic students, 9/15 priority date for international students. Applications are processed on a rolling basis. Application fee: $45. Electronic applications accepted. *Expenses:* Tuition: Part-time $810 per credit. Required fees: $35 per credit. *Financial support:* Federal Work-Study, tuition waivers, and unspecified assistantships available. Support available to part-time students. Financial award application deadline: 4/15; financial award applicants required to submit FAFSA. *Unit head:* Dr. Gene Wong, Director, 203-582-8467, E-mail: gene.wong@quinnipiac.edu. *Application contact:* Kristin Parent, Assistant Director of Graduate Health Sciences Admissions, 800-462-1944, Fax: 203-582-3443, E-mail: kristin.parent@quinnipiac.edu.

Rosalind Franklin University of Medicine and Science, School of Graduate and Post-doctoral Studies—Interdisciplinary Graduate Program in Biomedical Sciences, Department of Biochemistry and Molecular Biology, North Chicago, IL 60064-3095. Offers MS, PhD, MD/PhD. Terminal master's awarded for partial completion of doctoral program. *Degree requirements:* For master's, comprehensive exam, thesis; for doctorate, comprehensive exam, thesis/dissertation. *Entrance requirements:* For master's and doctorate, GRE General Test, minimum GPA of 3.0. Additional exam requirements/recommendations for international students: Required—TOEFL, TWE. Electronic applications accepted. *Faculty research:* Structure of control enzymes, extracellular matrix, glucose metabolism, gene expression, ATP synthesis.

Rutgers, The State University of New Jersey, New Brunswick, Graduate School-New Brunswick, Programs in the Molecular Biosciences, Piscataway, NJ 08854-8097. Offers biochemistry (PhD); cell and developmental biology (MS, PhD); microbiology and molecular genetics (MS, PhD), including applied microbiology, clinical microbiology (MS), clinical mircobiology (PhD), computational molecular biology (PhD), immunology, microbial biochemistry, molecular genetics, virology. MS, PhD offered jointly with University of Medicine and Dentistry of New Jersey. *Expenses:* Tuition, state resident: full-time $7200; part-time $600 per credit. Tuition, nonresident: full-time $11,124; part-time $927 per credit.

Saint Louis University, Graduate Education and School of Medicine, Graduate Program in Biomedical Sciences and Graduate Education, Department of Biochemistry and Molecular Biology, St. Louis, MO 63103-2097. Offers PhD. *Degree requirements:* For doctorate, comprehensive exam, thesis/dissertation, departmental qualifying exams. *Entrance requirements:* For doctorate, GRE General Test, GRE Subject Test (optional), letters of recommendation, resume, interview. Additional exam requirements/recommendations for international students: Required—TOEFL (minimum score 525 paper-based; 194 computer-based). Electronic applications accepted. *Faculty research:* Transcription, chromatin modification and regulation of gene expression; structure/function of proteins and enzymes, including x-ray crystallography; inflammatory mediators in pathenogenesis of diabetes and arteriosclerosis; cellular signaling in response to growth factors, opiates and angiogenic mediators; genomics and proteomics of Cryptococcus neoformans.

San Diego State University, Graduate and Research Affairs, College of Sciences, Department of Biology, San Diego, CA 92182. Offers biology (MA, MS), including ecology (MS), molecular biology (MS), physiology (MS), systematics/evolution (MS); cell and molecular biology (PhD); ecology (MS, PhD); microbiology (MS). Terminal master's awarded for partial completion of doctoral program. *Degree requirements:* For master's, thesis; for doctorate, thesis/dissertation. *Entrance requirements:* For master's, GRE General Test, GRE Subject Test, resume or curriculum vitae, 2 letters of recommendation. Additional exam requirements/recommendations for international students: Required—TOEFL. Electronic applications accepted.

San Diego State University, Graduate and Research Affairs, College of Sciences, Molecular Biology Institute, Program in Cell and Molecular Biology, San Diego, CA 92182. Offers PhD. Program offered jointly with University of California, San Diego. *Degree requirements:* For doctorate, thesis/dissertation, oral comprehensive qualifying exam. *Entrance requirements:* For doctorate, GRE General Test, GRE Subject Test, resumé or curriculum vitae, 3 letters of recommendation. Electronic applications accepted. *Faculty research:* Structure/dynamics of protein kinesis, chromatin structure and DNA methylation membrane biochemistry, secretory protein targeting, molecular biology of cardiac myocytes.

San Francisco State University, Division of Graduate Studies, College of Science and Engineering, Department of Biology, Program in Cell and Molecular Biology, San Francisco, CA 94132-1722. Offers MS. *Application deadline:* Applications are processed on a rolling basis. *Unit head:* Dr. Diana Chu, Program Coordinator, 415-405-3487, E-mail: chud@sfsu.edu. *Application contact:* Dr. Robert Patterson, Graduate Coordinator, 415-338-1100, E-mail: patters@sfsu.edu.

San Jose State University, Graduate Studies and Research, College of Science, Department of Biological Sciences, San Jose, CA 95192-0001. Offers biological sciences (MA, MS); molecular biology and microbiology (MS); organismal biology, conservation and ecology (MS); physiology (MS). Part-time programs available. *Entrance requirements:* For master's, GRE. Electronic applications accepted. *Faculty research:* Systemic physiology, molecular genetics, SEM studies, toxicology, large mammal ecology.

Seton Hall University, College of Arts and Sciences, Department of Biological Sciences, South Orange, NJ 07079-2697. Offers biology (MS); biology/business administration (MS); microbiology (MS); molecular bioscience (PhD); molecular bioscience/neuroscience (PhD). Part-time and evening/weekend programs available. *Degree requirements:* For master's, thesis optional; for doctorate, comprehensive exam, thesis/dissertation. *Entrance requirements:* For master's and doctorate, GRE or MS from accredited university in the U.S. Additional exam requirements/recommendations for international students: Required—TOEFL. Electronic applications accepted. *Faculty research:* Neurobiology, genetics, immunology, molecular biology, cellular physiology, toxicology, microbiology, bioinformatics.

Simon Fraser University, Graduate Studies, Faculty of Science, Department of Molecular Biology and Biochemistry, Burnaby, BC V5A 1S6, Canada. Offers M Sc, PhD. *Degree requirements:* For master's, thesis; for doctorate, thesis/dissertation. *Entrance requirements:* For master's, minimum GPA of 3.0; for doctorate, minimum GPA of 3.5. Additional exam requirements/recommendations for international students: Required—TWE or IELTS. *Faculty research:* Molecular genetics and development, biochemistry, molecular physiology, genomics, molecular phylogenetics and population genetics, bioinformation.

Southern Illinois University Carbondale, Graduate School, College of Science, Program in Molecular Biology, Microbiology, and Biochemistry, Carbondale, IL 62901-4701. Offers MS, PhD. *Degree requirements:* For master's, thesis; for doctorate, thesis/dissertation. *Entrance requirements:* For master's, GRE, minimum GPA of 2.7; for doctorate, GRE, minimum GPA of 3.25. Additional exam requirements/recommendations for international students: Required—TOEFL. *Faculty research:* Prokaryotic gene regulation and expression; eukaryotic gene regulation; microbial, phylogenetic, and metabolic diversity; immune responses to tumors, pathogens, and autoantigens; protein folding and structure.

State University of New York Downstate Medical Center, School of Graduate Studies, Program in Molecular and Cellular Biology, Brooklyn, NY 11203-2098. Offers PhD, MD/PhD. Affiliation with a particular PhD degree-granting program is deferred to the second year. *Degree requirements:* For doctorate, comprehensive exam, thesis/dissertation. *Entrance requirements:* For doctorate, GRE General Test. *Faculty research:* Mechanism of gene regulation, molecular virology.

State University of New York Upstate Medical University, College of Graduate Studies, Program in Biochemistry and Molecular Biology, Syracuse, NY 13210-2334. Offers biochemistry (MS); biochemistry and molecular biology (PhD); MD/PhD. Terminal master's awarded for partial completion of doctoral program. *Degree requirements:* For master's, thesis; for doctorate, comprehensive exam, thesis/dissertation. *Entrance requirements:* For master's, GRE General Test, interview; for doctorate, GRE General Test, telephone interview. Additional exam requirements/recommendations for international students: Required—TOEFL. Electronic applications accepted. *Faculty research:* Enzymology, membrane structure and functions, developmental biochemistry.

Stony Brook University, State University of New York, Graduate School, College of Arts and Sciences, Department of Biochemistry and Cell Biology, Molecular and Cellular Biology Program, Stony Brook, NY 11794. Offers biochemistry and molecular biology (PhD); biological sciences (MA); cellular and developmental biology (PhD); immunology and pathology (PhD); molecular and cellular biology (PhD). *Faculty:* 22 full-time (7 women). *Students:* 106 full-time (65 women); includes 2 Black or African American, non-Hispanic/Latino; 9 Asian, non-Hispanic/Latino; 1 Hispanic/Latino, 58 international. Average age 30. 320 applicants, 16% accepted, 26 enrolled. In 2010, 5 master's, 16 doctorates awarded. *Degree requirements:* For doctorate, comprehensive exam, thesis/dissertation, teaching experience. *Entrance requirements:* For doctorate, GRE General Test, GRE Subject Test. Additional exam requirements/recommendations for international students: Required—TOEFL. *Application deadline:* For fall admission, 1/15 for domestic students. Application fee: $100. *Expenses:* Tuition, state resident: full-time $8370; part-time $349 per credit. Tuition, nonresident: full-time $13,780; part-time $574 per credit. Required fees: $994. *Financial support:* In 2010–11, 42 research assistantships, 19 teaching assistantships were awarded; fellowships, Federal Work-Study also available. *Unit head:* Prof. Robert Haltiwanger, Chair, 631-632-8560. *Application contact:* Prof. Robert Haltiwanger, Chair, 631-632-8560.

Temple University, Health Sciences Center, School of Medicine and Graduate School, Doctor of Medicine Program, Program in Molecular Biology and Genetics, Philadelphia, PA 19122-6096. Offers MS, PhD, MD/PhD. *Students:* 22 full-time (13 women); includes 1 Black or African American, non-Hispanic/Latino; 1 Asian, non-Hispanic/Latino, 11 international. 35 applicants, 26% accepted, 4 enrolled. In 2010, 1 master's, 2 doctorates awarded. *Degree requirements:* For doctorate, thesis/dissertation, presentation research/literature seminars distinct from area of concentration. *Entrance requirements:* For doctorate, GRE General Test, GRE Subject Test, minimum GPA of 3.0. Additional exam requirements/recommendations for international students: Required—TOEFL (minimum score 620 paper-based; 260 computer-based). *Application deadline:* For fall admission, 1/15 for domestic students, 12/15 for international students. Application fee: $50. Electronic applications accepted. *Financial support:* Fellowships, research assistantships, Federal Work-Study, institutionally sponsored loans, and tuition waivers (full) available. Financial award application deadline: 1/15; financial award applicants required to submit FAFSA. *Faculty research:* Molecular genetics of normal and malignant cell growth, regulation of gene expression, DNA repair systems and carcinogenesis, hormone-receptor interactions and signal transduction systems, structural biology. *Unit head:* Dr. Scott Shore, Chair, 215-707-3359, Fax: 215-707-2805, E-mail: sks@temple.edu. *Application contact:* Dr. Scott Shore, Chair, 215-707-3359, Fax: 215-707-2805, E-mail: sks@temple.edu.

Texas A&M Health Science Center, Graduate School of Biomedical Sciences, Department of Microbial and Molecular Pathogenesis, College Station, TX 77840. Offers immunology (PhD); microbiology (PhD); molecular biology (PhD); virology (PhD). *Degree requirements:* For doctorate, thesis/dissertation. *Entrance requirements:* For doctorate, GRE General Test, minimum GPA of 3.0. *Faculty research:* Molecular pathogenesis, microbial therapeutics.

Texas A&M Health Science Center, Graduate School of Biomedical Sciences, Program in Cell and Molecular Biology, College Station, TX 77840. Offers PhD.

Texas Woman's University, Graduate School, College of Arts and Sciences, Department of Biology, Denton, TX 76201. Offers biology (MS); molecular biology (PhD). Part-time programs available. *Faculty:* 13 full-time (10 women), 1 (woman) part-time/adjunct. *Students:* 26 full-time (18 women), 21 part-time (17 women); includes 3 Black or African American, non-Hispanic/Latino; 3 Asian, non-Hispanic/Latino; 4 Hispanic/Latino, 28 international. Average age 31. 37 applicants, 62% accepted, 13 enrolled. In 2010, 4 master's, 1 doctorate awarded. Terminal master's awarded for partial completion of doctoral program. *Degree requirements:* For master's, comprehensive exam, thesis (for some programs); for doctorate, comprehensive exam, thesis/dissertation, residency. *Entrance requirements:* For master's, GRE General Test (preferred minimum score 425 verbal, 425 quantitative), 3 letters of reference; letter of interest; for doctorate, GRE General Test (preferred minimum score verbal 500, quantitative 500), 3 letters of reference, letter of interest. Additional exam requirements/recommendations for international students: Required—TOEFL (minimum score 550 paper-based; 213 computer-based; 79 iBT). *Application deadline:* For fall admission, 7/1 priority date for domestic students, 3/1 for international students; for spring admission, 12/1 priority date for domestic students, 7/1 for international students. Applications are processed on a rolling basis. Application fee: $50 ($75 for international students). Electronic applications accepted. *Expenses:* Tuition, state resident: full-time $3834; part-time $213 per credit hour. Tuition, nonresident: full-time $9468; part-time $526 per credit hour. Required fees: $1247; $220 per credit hour. *Financial support:* In 2010–11, 11 students received support, including 36 research assistantships (averaging $14,418 per year); career-related internships or fieldwork, Federal Work-Study, institutionally sponsored loans, scholarships/grants, traineeships, health care benefits, and unspecified assistantships also available. Support available to part-time students. Financial award application deadline: 3/1; financial award applicants required to submit FAFSA. *Faculty research:* Computational biology, protein-protein Interactions, chromatin structure and regulation, regulation of RNA synthesis, virus-host interactions, regulation of axon growth and guidance in neurons, estrogen compounds in plants, regulation of gene expression in male reproductive tissues, female gonadal hormones in the development of anxiety and depression, electron microscopy. Total annual research expenditures: $259,701. *Unit head:* Dr. Sarah McIntire, Chair, 940-898-2351, Fax: 940-898-2382, E-mail: biology@twu.edu. *Application contact:* Dr. Samuel Wheeler, Assistant Director of Admissions, 940-898-3188, Fax: 940-898-3081, E-mail: wheelersr@twu.edu.

Thomas Jefferson University, Jefferson College of Graduate Studies, PhD Program in Biochemistry and Molecular Biology, Philadelphia, PA 19107. Offers PhD. *Faculty:* 48 full-time (15 women). *Students:* 15 full-time (10 women), 1 (woman) part-time; includes 1 minority (Asian, non-Hispanic/Latino), 2 international. Average age 24. 41 applicants, 20% accepted, 3 enrolled. In 2010, 3 doctorates awarded. *Degree requirements:* For doctorate, comprehensive exam, thesis/dissertation. *Entrance requirements:* For doctorate, GRE General Test or MCAT, minimum GPA of 3.2. Additional exam requirements/recommendations for international students: Required—TOEFL (minimum score 250 computer-based; 100 iBT) or IELTS. *Application deadline:* For fall admission, 1/2 priority date for domestic and international students. Applications are processed on a rolling basis. Application fee: $50. Electronic applications accepted. *Financial support:* In 2010–11, 15 students received support, including 15 fellowships with full tuition reimbursements available (averaging $54,723 per year); Federal Work-Study, institutionally sponsored loans, scholarships/grants, traineeships, and stipends also available. Financial award application deadline: 5/1; financial award applicants required to submit FAFSA. *Faculty research:* Signal transduction and molecular genetics, translational biochemistry, human mitochondrial genetics, molecular biology of protein-RNA interaction, mammalian mitochondrial biogenesis and function. Total annual research expenditures: $39.1 million. *Unit head:* Dr. Diane E. Merry, Program Director, 215-503-4907, Fax: 215-923-9162, E-mail: diane.merry@jefferson.edu. *Application contact:* Marc E. Stearns, Director of Admissions, 215-503-0155, Fax: 215-503-9920, E-mail: jcgs-info@jefferson.edu.

Tufts University, Sackler School of Graduate Biomedical Sciences, Department of Molecular Biology and Microbiology, Medford, MA 02155. Offers molecular microbiology (PhD), including microbiology, molecular biology, molecular microbiology. *Faculty:* 18 full-time (7 women). *Students:* 29 full-time (21 women); includes 2 Black or African American, non-Hispanic/Latino; 4 Asian, non-Hispanic/Latino; 2 Hispanic/Latino, 1 international. Average age 27. 80 applicants, 18% accepted, 5 enrolled. In 2010, 4 doctorates awarded. Terminal master's awarded for partial completion of doctoral program. *Degree requirements:* For doctorate, comprehensive exam, thesis/dissertation. *Entrance requirements:* For doctorate, GRE General Test, 3 letters of reference. Additional exam requirements/recommendations for international students: Required—TOEFL. *Application deadline:* For fall admission, 12/15 priority date for domestic and international students. Applications are processed on a rolling basis. Application fee: $70. Electronic applications accepted. *Expenses:* Tuition: Full-time $39,624; part-time $3962 per course. Required fees: $40 per year. Full-time tuition and fees vary according to degree level, program and student level. Part-time tuition and fees vary according to course load. *Financial support:* In 2010–11, 29 students received support, including 29 research assistantships with full tuition reimbursements available (averaging $28,500 per year); scholarships/grants, health care benefits, and tuition waivers (full) also available. Financial award application deadline: 12/15. *Faculty research:* Fundamental problems of molecular biology of prokaryotes, eukaryotes and their viruses. *Unit head:* Dr. Michael Malamy, Director, 617-636-6750, Fax: 617-636-0337, E-mail: michael.malamy@tufts.edu. *Application contact:* Kellie Johnston, Associate Director of Admissions, 617-636-6767, Fax: 617-633-0375, E-mail: sackler-school@tufts.edu.

Tufts University, Sackler School of Graduate Biomedical Sciences, Program in Cell, Molecular and Developmental Biology, Medford, MA 02155. Offers PhD. *Faculty:* 35 full-time (11 women). *Students:* 25 full-time (13 women); includes 2 Asian, non-Hispanic/Latino, 2 international. Average age 29. In 2010, 8 doctorates awarded. Terminal master's awarded for partial completion of doctoral program. *Degree requirements:* For doctorate, thesis/dissertation. *Entrance requirements:* For doctorate, GRE General Test, 3 letters of reference. Additional exam requirements/recommendations for international students: Required—TOEFL. *Application deadline:* For fall admission, 12/15 for domestic and international students. Applications are processed on a rolling basis. Application fee: $70. Electronic applications accepted. *Expenses:* Tuition: Full-time $39,624; part-time $3962 per course. Required fees: $40 per year. Full-time tuition and fees vary according to degree level, program and student level. Part-time tuition and fees vary according to course load. *Financial support:* In 2010–11, 25 students received support, including 25 research assistantships with full tuition reimbursements available (averaging $28,500 per year); fellowships, scholarships/grants, health care benefits, and tuition waivers (full) also available. *Faculty research:* Reproduction and hormone action, control of gene expression, cell-matrix and cell-cell interactions, growth control and tumorigenesis, cytoskeleton and contractile proteins. *Unit head:* Dr. John Castellot, Program Director, 617-636-0303, Fax: 617-636-0375, E-mail: john.castellot@tufts.edu. *Application contact:* Kellie Johnston, Associate Director of Admissions, 617-636-6767, Fax: 617-636-0375, E-mail: sackler-school@tufts.edu.

Tulane University, School of Medicine and School of Liberal Arts, Graduate Programs in Biomedical Sciences, Interdisciplinary Graduate Program in Molecular and Cellular Biology, New Orleans, LA 70118-5669. Offers PhD, MD/PhD. PhD offered through the Graduate School. *Degree requirements:* For doctorate, thesis/dissertation. *Entrance requirements:* For

Molecular Biology

Tulane University (continued)

doctorate, GRE General Test, GRE Subject Test. Additional exam requirements/recommendations for international students: Required—TOEFL. Electronic applications accepted. *Faculty research:* Developmental biology, neuroscience, virology.

Tulane University, School of Science and Engineering, Department of Cell and Molecular Biology, New Orleans, LA 70118-5669. Offers MS, PhD. Terminal master's awarded for partial completion of doctoral program. *Degree requirements:* For doctorate, thesis/dissertation. *Entrance requirements:* For master's, GRE General Test, minimum B average in undergraduate course work; for doctorate, GRE General Test. Additional exam requirements/recommendations for international students: Required—TOEFL. Electronic applications accepted.

Uniformed Services University of the Health Sciences, School of Medicine, Graduate Programs in the Biomedical Sciences and Public Health, Graduate Program in Molecular and Cell Biology, Bethesda, MD 20814-4799. *Faculty:* 43 full-time (11 women), 3 part-time/adjunct (0 women). *Students:* 22 full-time (11 women); includes 5 Asian, non-Hispanic/Latino; 5 Hispanic/Latino, 6 international. Average age 26. 30 applicants, 43% accepted, 8 enrolled. In 2010, 2 doctorates awarded. *Degree requirements:* For doctorate, comprehensive exam, thesis/dissertation, qualifying exam. *Entrance requirements:* For doctorate, GRE General Test, minimum GPA of 3.0. Additional exam requirements/recommendations for international students: Required—TOEFL. *Application deadline:* For fall admission, 1/1 priority date for domestic and international students. Applications are processed on a rolling basis. Application fee: $0. Electronic applications accepted. *Financial support:* In 2010–11, fellowships with full tuition reimbursements (averaging $27,000 per year); scholarships/grants, health care benefits, and tuition waivers (full) also available. *Faculty research:* Immunology, biochemistry, cancer biology, stem cell biology. *Unit head:* Dr. Mary Lou Cutler, Graduate Program Director, 301-295-3453, Fax: 301-295-1996. *Application contact:* Tina Finley, Graduate Program Coordinator, 301-295-3642, Fax: 301-295-1996, E-mail: nfinley@usuhs.mil.

See Display below and Close-Up on page 227.

Universidad Central del Caribe, School of Medicine, Program in Biomedical Sciences, Bayamón, PR 00960-6032. Offers anatomy and cell biology (MA, MS); biochemistry (MS); biomedical sciences (MA); cellular and molecular biology (PhD); microbiology and immunology (MA, MS); pharmacology (MS); physiology (MS).

Université de Montréal, Faculty of Medicine, Program in Molecular Biology, Montréal, QC H3C 3J7, Canada. Offers M Sc, PhD. Terminal master's awarded for partial completion of doctoral program. *Degree requirements:* For master's, thesis; for doctorate, thesis/dissertation, general exam. *Entrance requirements:* For master's and doctorate, proficiency in French, knowledge of English. Electronic applications accepted. *Faculty research:* Protein interactions, intracellular signaling, development and differentiation, hematopoiesis, stem cells.

Université Laval, Faculty of Medicine, Graduate Programs in Medicine, Programs in Cellular and Molecular Biology, Québec, QC G1K 7P4, Canada. Offers M Sc, PhD. Terminal master's awarded for partial completion of doctoral program. *Degree requirements:* For master's, thesis; for doctorate, comprehensive exam, thesis/dissertation. *Entrance requirements:* For master's and doctorate, knowledge of French, comprehension of written English. Electronic applications accepted. *Faculty research:* Oral bacterial metabolism, sugar transport.

University at Albany, State University of New York, College of Arts and Sciences, Department of Biological Sciences, Specialization in Molecular, Cellular, Developmental, and Neural Biology, Albany, NY 12222-0001. Offers MS, PhD. *Degree requirements:* For master's, one foreign language; for doctorate, one foreign language, thesis/dissertation. *Entrance requirements:* For master's and doctorate, GRE General Test.

University at Albany, State University of New York, School of Public Health, Department of Biomedical Sciences, Program in Biochemistry, Molecular Biology, and Genetics, Albany, NY

12222-0001. Offers MS, PhD. *Degree requirements:* For master's, thesis; for doctorate, thesis/dissertation. *Entrance requirements:* For master's and doctorate, GRE General Test, GRE Subject Test.

University at Buffalo, the State University of New York, Graduate School, Graduate Programs in Cancer Research and Biomedical Sciences at Roswell Park Cancer Institute, Department of Cellular and Molecular Biology at Roswell Park Cancer Institute, Buffalo, NY 14260. Offers cellular molecular biology/genetics (PhD). *Faculty:* 26 full-time (6 women). *Students:* 22 full-time (12 women); includes 4 minority (1 Black or African American, non-Hispanic/Latino; 1 Asian, non-Hispanic/Latino; 2 Native Hawaiian or other Pacific Islander, non-Hispanic/Latino), 2 international. Average age 25. 45 applicants, 13% accepted, 4 enrolled. In 2010, 1 doctorate awarded. *Degree requirements:* For doctorate, thesis/dissertation, exam, project. *Entrance requirements:* For doctorate, GRE General Test, minimum B average in undergraduate coursework. Additional exam requirements/recommendations for international students: Required—TOEFL, TOEFL (minimum score 600 paper-based; 250 computer-based; 100 iBT) or IELTS. *Application deadline:* For winter admission, 12/30 priority date for domestic and international students. Applications are processed on a rolling basis. Application fee: $55. Electronic applications accepted. *Financial support:* In 2010–11, 22 students received support, including 4 fellowships with full tuition reimbursements available (averaging $24,000 per year), 17 research assistantships with full tuition reimbursements available (averaging $24,000 per year); health care benefits also available. Financial award application deadline: 2/1; financial award applicants required to submit FAFSA. *Faculty research:* Cancer genetics, chromatin structure and replication, regulation of transcription, human gene mapping, genetic and structural approaches to regulation of gene expression. Total annual research expenditures: $5.5 million. *Unit head:* Dr. Dominic James Smiraglia, Director of Graduate Studies, 716-845-1347, Fax: 716-845-1698, E-mail: dominic.smiraglia@roswellpark.org. *Application contact:* Craig R. Johnson, Director of Admissions, 716-845-3063, Fax: 716-845-8178, E-mail: craig.johnson@roswellpark.org.

The University of Alabama at Birmingham, Graduate Programs in Joint Health Sciences, Program in Cellular and Molecular Physiology, Birmingham, AL 35294. Offers PhD. *Students:* 15 full-time (3 women), 1 part-time (0 women); includes 2 minority (1 Black or African American, non-Hispanic/Latino; 1 Hispanic/Latino), 3 international. Average age 28. In 2010, 8 doctorates awarded. Application fee: $35 ($60 for international students). *Expenses:* Tuition, state resident: full-time $5482. Tuition, nonresident: full-time $12,430. Tuition and fees vary according to program. *Unit head:* Dr. Ray L. Watts, Vice President/Dean, School of Medicine, 205-934-1111, Fax: 205-943-0333. *Application contact:* Julie Bryant, Director of Graduate Admissions, 205-934-8227, Fax: 205-934-8413, E-mail: jbryant@uab.edu.

University of Alberta, Faculty of Graduate Studies and Research, Department of Biological Sciences, Edmonton, AB T6G 2E1, Canada. Offers environmental biology and ecology (M Sc, PhD); microbiology and biotechnology (M Sc, PhD); molecular biology and genetics (M Sc, PhD); physiology and cell biology (M Sc, PhD); plant biology (M Sc, PhD); systematics and evolution (M Sc, PhD). Terminal master's awarded for partial completion of doctoral program. *Degree requirements:* For master's, thesis; for doctorate, thesis/dissertation. *Entrance requirements:* Additional exam requirements/recommendations for international students: Required—TOEFL.

University of Alberta, Faculty of Medicine and Dentistry and Faculty of Graduate Studies and Research, Graduate Programs in Medicine, Department of Cell Biology, Edmonton, AB T6G 2E1, Canada. Offers cell and molecular biology (M Sc, PhD). Terminal master's awarded for partial completion of doctoral program. *Degree requirements:* For master's, thesis; for doctorate, thesis/dissertation. *Entrance requirements:* For master's and doctorate, 3 letters of reference, curriculum vitae. Additional exam requirements/recommendations for international students: Required—TOEFL (minimum score 600 paper-based; 250 computer-based). *Faculty research:* Protein targeting, membrane trafficking, signal transduction, cell growth and division, cell-cell interaction and development.

The University of Arizona, College of Science, Department of Molecular and Cellular Biology, Tucson, AZ 85721. Offers applied biosciences (PSM); molecular and cellular biology (MS, PhD). Evening/weekend programs available. *Faculty:* 12 full-time (4 women), 2 part-time/adjunct (1 woman). *Students:* 23 full-time (10 women), 3 part-time (1 woman); includes 2 Hispanic/Latino; 5 Two or more races, non-Hispanic/Latino, 4 international. Average age 31. 160 applicants, 11% accepted, 9 enrolled. In 2010, 10 master's, 10 doctorates awarded. Terminal master's awarded for partial completion of doctoral program. *Degree requirements:* For master's, thesis; for doctorate, thesis/dissertation. *Entrance requirements:* For master's, 3 letters of recommendation; for doctorate, 3 letters of recommendation, statement of purpose. Additional exam requirements/recommendations for international students: Required—TOEFL (minimum score 600 paper-based; 250 computer-based; 90 iBT), IELTS (minimum score 7). *Application deadline:* For fall admission, 1/1 for domestic and international students. Applications are processed on a rolling basis. Application fee: $75. Electronic applications accepted. *Expenses:* Tuition, state resident: full-time $7692. *Financial support:* In 2010–11, 14 research assistantships with full tuition reimbursements (averaging $23,390 per year), 8 teaching assistantships with full tuition reimbursements (averaging $22,929 per year) were awarded; career-related internships or fieldwork, scholarships/grants, health care benefits, and unspecified assistantships also available. *Faculty research:* Plant molecular biology, cellular and molecular aspects of development, genetics of bacteria and lower eukaryotes. Total annual research expenditures: $7 million. *Unit head:* Kathleen Dixon, Department Head, 520-621-7563, Fax: 520-621-3709, E-mail: dixonk@email.arizona.edu. *Application contact:* Kathleen Dixon, Department Head, 520-621-7563, Fax: 520-621-3709, E-mail: dixonk@email.arizona.edu.

University of Arkansas, Graduate School, Interdisciplinary Program in Cell and Molecular Biology, Fayetteville, AR 72701-1201. Offers MS, PhD. *Students:* 16 full-time (8 women), 42 part-time (26 women); includes 3 minority (all Asian, non-Hispanic/Latino), 41 international. 28 applicants, 21% accepted. In 2010, 1 master's, 6 doctorates awarded. *Degree requirements:* For doctorate, thesis/dissertation. *Application deadline:* For fall admission, 4/1 for international students; for spring admission, 10/1 for international students. Applications are processed on a rolling basis. Application fee: $40 ($50 for international students). Electronic applications accepted. *Financial support:* In 2010–11, 4 fellowships with tuition reimbursements, 33 research assistantships, 10 teaching assistantships were awarded. Financial award application deadline: 4/1; financial award applicants required to submit FAFSA. *Unit head:* Dr. Douglas Rhoads, Head, 479-575-7396, Fax: 479-575-5908, E-mail: drhoads@uark.edu. *Application contact:* Graduate Admissions, 479-575-6246, Fax: 479-575-5908, E-mail: gradinfo@uark.edu.

University of Arkansas for Medical Sciences, Graduate School, Graduate Programs in Biomedical Sciences, Program in Biochemistry and Molecular Biology, Little Rock, AR 72205-7199. Offers MS, PhD, MD/PhD. *Degree requirements:* For master's, comprehensive exam, thesis; for doctorate, thesis/dissertation, qualifying exam. *Entrance requirements:* For master's, GRE General Test, bachelor's degree in biology, chemistry, or related field; for doctorate, GRE General Test. Additional exam requirements/recommendations for international students: Required—TOEFL. *Faculty research:* Gene regulation, growth factors, oncogenes, metabolic diseases, hormone regulation.

The University of British Columbia, Faculty of Medicine, Department of Biochemistry and Molecular Biology, Vancouver, BC V6T 1Z1, Canada. Offers M Sc, PhD. *Faculty:* 22 full-time (2 women). *Students:* 62 full-time (27 women). Average age 27. 60 applicants, 15 enrolled. In 2010, 5 master's, 6 doctorates awarded. *Degree requirements:* For master's, thesis; for doctorate, comprehensive exam, thesis/dissertation. *Entrance requirements:* For master's, first class B Sc; for doctorate, master's or first class honors bachelor's degree in biochemistry. Additional exam requirements/recommendations for international students: Required—TOEFL (minimum score 625 paper-based; 263 computer-based). *Application deadline:* For fall admission, 1/31 priority date for domestic students, 1/31 for international students; for winter admission, 5/31 priority date for domestic students, 5/31 for international students. Applications are processed on a rolling basis. Application fee: $90 ($150 for international students). Electronic applications accepted. Tuition charges are reported in Canadian dollars. *Expenses:* Tuition, area resident: Full-time $4179 Canadian dollars. International tuition: $7344 Canadian dollars full-time. *Financial support:* In 2010–11, 28 fellowships (averaging $25,074 per year), 30 research assistantships (averaging $20,600 per year), 13 teaching assistantships (averaging $2,300 per year) were awarded; institutionally sponsored loans, scholarships/grants, traineeships, tuition waivers (partial), and unspecified assistantships also available. *Faculty research:* Membrane biochemistry, protein structure/function, signal transduction, biochemistry. Total annual research expenditures: $12.6 million. *Unit head:* Dr. Roger Brownsey, Professor and Head, 604-827-4027, Fax: 604-822-5227. *Application contact:* Doris Metcalf, Graduate Secretary, 604-822-5925, Fax: 604-822-5227, E-mail: biocgrad@interchange.ubc.ca.

University of Calgary, Faculty of Medicine and Faculty of Graduate Studies, Department of Biochemistry and Molecular Biology, Calgary, AB T2N 1N4, Canada. Offers M Sc, PhD. *Degree requirements:* For master's, thesis; for doctorate, thesis/dissertation, candidacy exam. *Entrance requirements:* For master's and doctorate, GRE General Test, minimum GPA of 3.2. Additional exam requirements/recommendations for international students: Required—TOEFL. Electronic applications accepted. *Faculty research:* Molecular and developmental genetics; molecular biology of disease; genomics, proteomics and bioinformatics; ceu signaling and structure.

University of California, Berkeley, Graduate Division, College of Letters and Science, Department of Molecular and Cell Biology, Berkeley, CA 94720-1500. Offers PhD. *Degree requirements:* For doctorate, comprehensive exam, thesis/dissertation, qualifying exam, 2 semesters of teaching, 3 seminars. *Entrance requirements:* For doctorate, GRE General Test, GRE Subject Test (recommended), minimum GPA of 3.0. Additional exam requirements/recommendations for international students: Required—TOEFL (minimum score 570 paper-based; 230 computer-based; 68 iBT), IELTS (minimum score 7). Electronic applications accepted. *Faculty research:* Biochemistry and molecular biology, cell and developmental biology, genetics, immunology, neurobiology, genomics.

University of California, Davis, Graduate Studies, Graduate Group in Biochemistry and Molecular Biology, Davis, CA 95616. Offers MS, PhD. Terminal master's awarded for partial completion of doctoral program. *Degree requirements:* For master's, comprehensive exam (for some programs), thesis (for some programs); for doctorate, thesis/dissertation. *Entrance requirements:* For master's and doctorate, GRE General Test, GRE Subject Test. Additional exam requirements/recommendations for international students: Required—TOEFL (minimum score 550 paper-based; 213 computer-based). Electronic applications accepted. *Faculty research:* Gene expression, protein structure, molecular virology, protein synthesis, enzymology, membrane transport and structural biology.

University of California, Irvine, School of Biological Sciences, Department of Molecular Biology and Biochemistry, Irvine, CA 92697. Offers biological science (MS); biological sciences (PhD); biotechnology (MS); MD/PhD. *Students:* 61 full-time (32 women); includes 28 minority (2 Black or African American, non-Hispanic/Latino; 16 Asian, non-Hispanic/Latino; 10 Hispanic/Latino), 2 international. Average age 28. In 2010, 4 master's, 8 doctorates awarded. *Degree requirements:* For doctorate, thesis/dissertation. *Entrance requirements:* For master's, GRE, minimum GPA of 3.0; for doctorate, GRE General Test, GRE Subject Test, minimum GPA of 3.0. Additional exam requirements/recommendations for international students: Required—TOEFL (minimum score 550 paper-based; 213 computer-based). *Application deadline:* For fall admission, 12/15 priority date for domestic students, 12/15 for international students. Applications are processed on a rolling basis. Application fee: $80 ($100 for international students). Electronic applications accepted. *Financial support:* Fellowships, research assistantships with full tuition reimbursements, teaching assistantships, institutionally sponsored loans, traineeships, health care benefits, and unspecified assistantships available. Financial award application deadline: 3/1; financial award applicants required to submit FAFSA. *Faculty research:* Structure and synthesis of nucleic acids and proteins, regulation, virology, biochemical genetics, gene organization. *Unit head:* Prof. Christopher C. Hughes, Chair, 949-824-8771, Fax: 949-824-8551, E-mail: cchughes@uci.edu. *Application contact:* Judy L. Lundberg, Personnel Analyst, 949-824-4740, Fax: 949-824-8551, E-mail: jllundbe@uci.edu.

University of California, Irvine, School of Biological Sciences and School of Medicine, Graduate Program in Cellular and Molecular Biosciences, Irvine, CA 92697. Offers PhD. *Degree requirements:* For doctorate, thesis/dissertation, teaching assignment, preliminary exam. *Entrance requirements:* For doctorate, GRE General Test, minimum GPA of 3.0, research experience. Additional exam requirements/recommendations for international students: Required—TOEFL, IELTS, SPEAK test. Electronic applications accepted. *Expenses:* Contact institution. *Faculty research:* Cellular biochemistry; gene structure and expression; protein structure, function, and design; molecular genetics; pathogenesis and inherited disease.

University of California, Los Angeles, Graduate Division, College of Letters and Science, Department of Chemistry and Biochemistry, Program in Biochemistry and Molecular Biology, Los Angeles, CA 90034. Offers MS, PhD. MS admission to program only under exceptional circumstances. *Students:* 75 full-time (31 women); includes 31 minority (1 Black or African American, non-Hispanic/Latino; 23 Asian, non-Hispanic/Latino; 7 Hispanic/Latino), 10 international. Average age 27. 109 applicants, 21% accepted, 11 enrolled. In 2010, 8 master's, 20 doctorates awarded. Terminal master's awarded for partial completion of doctoral program. *Degree requirements:* For master's, comprehensive exam or thesis; for doctorate, thesis/dissertation, oral and written exams, 1 year teaching experience. *Entrance requirements:* For master's, GRE General Test, GRE Subject Test, minimum GPA of 3.0; for doctorate, GRE General Test, GRE Subject Test, minimum undergraduate GPA of 3.0. *Application deadline:* For fall admission, 1/15 for domestic and international students. Application fee: $70 ($90 for international students). Electronic applications accepted. *Financial support:* In 2010–11, 90 fellowships with full and partial tuition reimbursements, 63 research assistantships with full and partial tuition reimbursements, 44 teaching assistantships with full and partial tuition reimbursements were awarded; Federal Work-Study, scholarships/grants, health care benefits, tuition waivers (full and partial), and unspecified assistantships also available. Financial award applicants required to submit FAFSA. *Unit head:* Dr. Albert Courey, 310-825-3958, E-mail: courey@chem.ucla.edu. *Application contact:* Departmental Office, 310-825-2645, E-mail: bmbgrad@chem.ucla.edu.

University of California, Los Angeles, Graduate Division, College of Letters and Science, Department of Molecular, Cell and Developmental Biology, Los Angeles, CA 90095. Offers PhD. *Faculty:* 6 full-time (1 woman). *Students:* 34 full-time (20 women); includes 12 minority (3 Black or African American, non-Hispanic/Latino; 6 Asian, non-Hispanic/Latino; 3 Hispanic/Latino), 6 international. Average age 27. 3 applicants, 67% accepted, 2 enrolled. In 2010, 4 doctorates awarded. *Degree requirements:* For doctorate, thesis/dissertation, qualifying exams. *Entrance requirements:* For doctorate, GRE General Test, GRE Subject Test. Additional exam requirements/recommendations for international students: Required—TOEFL. Application fee: $70 ($90 for international students). Electronic applications accepted. *Financial support:* In 2010–11, 26 fellowships, 26 research assistantships, 14 teaching assistantships were awarded; scholarships/grants, traineeships, and unspecified assistantships also available. Financial award application deadline: 3/1. *Unit head:* Dr. Utpal Banerjee, Chair, 310-206-5439, Fax: 310-206-3987, E-mail: banerjee@mbi.ucla.edu. *Application contact:* UCLA Access Coordinator, 310-206-1845, Fax: 310-206-1636, E-mail: uclaaccess@mednet.ucla.edu.

University of California, Los Angeles, Graduate Division, College of Letters and Science, Program in Molecular Biology, Los Angeles, CA 90095. Offers PhD, MD/PhD. *Students:* 77 full-time (35 women); includes 27 minority (2 Black or African American, non-Hispanic/Latino; 1 American Indian or Alaska Native, non-Hispanic/Latino; 19 Asian, non-Hispanic/Latino; 5 Hispanic/Latino), 9 international. Average age 27. 9 applicants, 33% accepted, 3 enrolled. In 2010, 10 doctorates awarded. *Degree requirements:* For doctorate, thesis/dissertation, oral and written qualifying exams, teaching experience. *Entrance requirements:* For doctorate, GRE General Test, GRE Subject Test (biochemistry, chemistry, biology, or physics). *Application deadline:* For fall admission, 1/10 for domestic and international students. Application fee: $70 ($90 for international students). Electronic applications accepted. *Financial support:* In 2010–11, 72 fellowships with full and partial tuition reimbursements, 56 research assistantships with full and partial tuition reimbursements, 30 teaching assistantships with full and partial tuition reimbursements were awarded; Federal Work-Study, institutionally sponsored loans, scholarships/grants, health care benefits, tuition waivers (full and partial), and unspecified assistantships also available. Financial award application deadline: 3/1; financial award applicants required to submit FAFSA. *Unit head:* Dr. James Tidball, Director, 310-206-3395, E-mail: jtidball@physci.ucla.edu. *Application contact:* Department Office, 800-206-3395, E-mail: mbigrad@mednet.ucla.edu.

University of California, Los Angeles, Graduate Division, College of Letters and Science, Program in Molecular, Cellular and Integrative Physiology, Los Angeles, CA 90095. Offers PhD. *Students:* 39 full-time (22 women); includes 8 minority (1 Black or African American, non-Hispanic/Latino; 5 Asian, non-Hispanic/Latino; 2 Hispanic/Latino), 13 international. Average age 28. 17 applicants, 53% accepted, 9 enrolled. In 2010, 5 doctorates awarded. *Degree requirements:* For doctorate, thesis/dissertation, oral and written exams, student teaching. *Entrance requirements:* For doctorate, GRE General Test, GRE Subject Test (biology or applicant's undergraduate major), minimum GPA of 3.0, bachelor's degree in biological or physical sciences. Application fee: $70 ($90 for international students). Electronic applications accepted. *Financial support:* In 2010–11, 32 fellowships with full and partial tuition reimbursements, 30 research assistantships with full and partial tuition reimbursements, 8 teaching assistantships with full and partial tuition reimbursements were awarded; Federal Work-Study, institutionally sponsored loans, scholarships/grants, health care benefits, tuition waivers (full and partial), and unspecified assistantships also available. Financial award applicants required to submit FAFSA. *Unit head:* Dr. James Tidball, Chair, 310-825-3891, E-mail: jtidball@physci.ucla.edu. *Application contact:* Department Office, 310-825-3891, E-mail: mcarr@physci.ucla.edu.

University of California, Los Angeles, Graduate Division, College of Letters and Science and David Geffen School of Medicine, UCLA ACCESS to Programs in the Molecular, Cellular and Integrative Life Sciences, Los Angeles, CA 90095. Offers biochemistry and molecular biology (PhD); biological chemistry (PhD); cellular and molecular pathology (PhD); human genetics (PhD); microbiology, immunology, and molecular genetics (PhD); molecular biology (PhD); molecular toxicology (PhD); molecular, cellular and integrative physiology (PhD); neurobiology (PhD); oral biology (PhD); physiology (PhD). ACCESS is an umbrella program for first-year coursework in 12 PhD programs. *Students:* 48 full-time (28 women), 6 international. Average age 24. 388 applicants, 27% accepted, 48 enrolled. *Degree requirements:* For doctorate, thesis/dissertation, oral and written qualifying exams. *Entrance requirements:* For doctorate, GRE General Test, minimum undergraduate GPA of 3.0. Additional exam requirements/recommendations for international students: Required—TOEFL. *Application deadline:* For fall admission, 12/15 for domestic and international students. Application fee: $70 ($90 for international students). Electronic applications accepted. *Financial support:* In 2010–11, 31 fellowships with full and partial tuition reimbursements, 13 research assistantships with full and partial tuition reimbursements, 2 teaching assistantships with full and partial tuition reimbursements were awarded; Federal Work-Study, institutionally sponsored loans, scholarships/grants, health care benefits, tuition waivers (full and partial), and unspecified assistantships also available. Financial award application deadline: 3/1; financial award applicants required to submit FAFSA. *Faculty research:* Molecular, cellular, and developmental biology; immunology; microbiology; integrative biology. *Unit head:* Jody Spillane, Project Coordinator, 310-206-1845, E-mail: jspillane@mednet.ucla.edu. *Application contact:* UCLA Access Admissions, 310-206-1845, E-mail: uclaaccess@mednet.ucla.edu.

University of California, Riverside, Graduate Division, Program in Cell, Molecular, and Developmental Biology, Riverside, CA 92521-0102. Offers MS, PhD. Terminal master's awarded for partial completion of doctoral program. *Degree requirements:* For master's, thesis, oral defense of thesis; for doctorate, thesis/dissertation, oral defense of thesis, qualifying exams, 2

Molecular Biology

University of California, Riverside (continued)
quarters of teaching experience. *Entrance requirements:* For master's and doctorate, GRE General Test, minimum GPA of 3.2. Additional exam requirements/recommendations for international students: Required—TOEFL (minimum score 550 paper-based; 213 computer-based; 80 iBT). Electronic applications accepted.

University of California, San Diego, Office of Graduate Studies, Division of Biological Sciences, Program in Genetics and Molecular Biology, La Jolla, CA 92093-0348. Offers PhD. Offered in association with the Salk Institute. *Degree requirements:* For doctorate, thesis/dissertation, qualifying exam. Electronic applications accepted.

University of California, San Diego, Office of Graduate Studies, Division of Biological Sciences, Program in Molecular and Cellular Biology, La Jolla, CA 92093. Offers PhD. Offered in association with the Salk Institute. *Degree requirements:* For doctorate, thesis/dissertation, qualifying exam. Electronic applications accepted.

University of California, San Diego, School of Medicine and Office of Graduate Studies, Graduate Studies in Biomedical Sciences, Program in Molecular Cell Biology, La Jolla, CA 92093. Offers PhD. *Degree requirements:* For doctorate, thesis/dissertation, qualifying exam. *Entrance requirements:* For doctorate, GRE General Test. Additional exam requirements/recommendations for international students: Required—TOEFL. Electronic applications accepted. *Faculty research:* Molecular and cellular pharmacology, cell and organ physiology.

University of California, San Diego, School of Medicine and Office of Graduate Studies, Graduate Studies in Biomedical Sciences, Regulatory Biology Program, La Jolla, CA 92093. Offers PhD. *Degree requirements:* For doctorate, thesis/dissertation, 2 qualifying exams. *Entrance requirements:* For doctorate, GRE General Test, GRE Subject Test. Additional exam requirements/recommendations for international students: Required—TOEFL. Electronic applications accepted. *Faculty research:* Eukaryotic regulatory and molecular biology, molecular and cellular pharmacology, cell and organ physiology.

University of California, San Francisco, Graduate Division and School of Medicine, Department of Biochemistry and Biophysics, Program in Biochemistry and Molecular Biology, San Francisco, CA 94143. Offers PhD, MD/PhD. *Degree requirements:* For doctorate, thesis/dissertation. *Entrance requirements:* For doctorate, GRE General Test, GRE Subject Test. Additional exam requirements/recommendations for international students: Required—TOEFL. *Expenses:* Contact institution. *Faculty research:* Structural biology, genetics, cell biology, cell physiology, metabolism.

University of California, Santa Barbara, Graduate Division, College of Letters and Sciences, Division of Mathematics, Life, and Physical Sciences, Department of Molecular, Cellular, and Developmental Biology, Santa Barbara, CA 93106-9625. Offers MA, PhD, MA/PhD. *Faculty:* 21 full-time (3 women), 7 part-time/adjunct (2 women). *Students:* 57 full-time (35 women); includes 1 Black or African American, non-Hispanic/Latino; 6 Asian, non-Hispanic/Latino; 3 Hispanic/Latino. Average age 28. 64 applicants, 41% accepted, 14 enrolled. In 2010, 8 master's, 7 doctorates awarded. *Degree requirements:* For master's, comprehensive exam (for some programs), thesis (for some programs); for doctorate, comprehensive exam, thesis/dissertation. *Entrance requirements:* For master's, GRE General Test, GRE Subject Test, 3 letters of recommendation, resume/curriculum vitae; for doctorate, GRE General Test, GRE Subject Test, 3 letters of recommendation, statement of purpose, personal achievements/contributions statement, resume/curriculum vitae, transcripts for post-secondary institutions attended. Additional exam requirements/recommendations for international students: Required—TOEFL (minimum score 610 paper-based; 102 iBT), IELTS (minimum score 7). *Application deadline:* For fall admission, 12/15 for domestic and international students. Application fee: $70 ($90 for international students). Electronic applications accepted. *Financial support:* In 2010–11, 55 students received support, including 13 fellowships with full and partial tuition reimbursements available (averaging $6,150 per year), 37 research assistantships with full and partial tuition reimbursements available (averaging $14,365 per year), 44 teaching assistantships with partial tuition reimbursements available (averaging $10,340 per year); career-related internships or fieldwork, Federal Work-Study, institutionally sponsored loans, scholarships/grants, traineeships, health care benefits, and unspecified assistantships also available. Financial award application deadline: 12/15; financial award applicants required to submit FAFSA. *Faculty research:* Microbiology, neurobiology (including stem cell research), developmental, virology, cell biology. *Unit head:* Dr. Dennis O. Clegg, Chair, 805-893-8490, Fax: 805-893-4724, E-mail: clegg@lifesci.ucsb.edu. *Application contact:* Nicole McCoy, Graduate Program Advisor, 805-893-8499, Fax: 805-893-4724, E-mail: nicole.mccoy@lifesci.ucsb.edu.

University of California, Santa Barbara, Graduate Division, College of Letters and Sciences, Division of Mathematics, Life, and Physical Sciences, Interdepartmental Graduate Program in Biomolecular Science and Engineering, Santa Barbara, CA 93106-2014. Offers biochemistry and molecular biology (PhD), including biochemistry and molecular biology, biophysics and bioengineering. *Faculty:* 37 full-time (4 women), 1 (woman) part-time/adjunct. *Students:* 30 full-time (13 women); includes 4 Asian, non-Hispanic/Latino. Average age 28. 59 applicants, 22% accepted, 4 enrolled. In 2010, 5 doctorates awarded. Terminal master's awarded for partial completion of doctoral program. *Degree requirements:* For doctorate, thesis/dissertation. *Entrance requirements:* For doctorate, GRE General Test. Additional exam requirements/recommendations for international students: Required—TOEFL (minimum score 630 paper-based; 109 iBT), IELTS (minimum score 7). *Application deadline:* For fall admission, 12/15 for domestic and international students. Application fee: $70 ($90 for international students). Electronic applications accepted. *Financial support:* In 2010–11, 30 students received support, including 16 fellowships with full and partial tuition reimbursements available (averaging $11,321 per year), 31 research assistantships with full and partial tuition reimbursements available (averaging $14,777 per year), 16 teaching assistantships with full and partial tuition reimbursements available (averaging $6,307 per year); Federal Work-Study, traineeships, health care benefits, tuition waivers (full and partial), and unspecified assistantships also available. Financial award application deadline: 12/15; financial award applicants required to submit FAFSA. *Faculty research:* Biochemistry and molecular biology, biophysics, biomaterials, bioengineering, systems biology. *Unit head:* Prof. Philip A. Pincus, Director/Professor, 805-893-4685, E-mail: fyl@mrl.ucsb.edu. *Application contact:* Prof. Philip A. Pincus, Director/Professor, 805-893-4685, E-mail: fyl@mrl.ucsb.edu.

University of California, Santa Cruz, Division of Graduate Studies, Division of Physical and Biological Sciences, Program in Molecular, Cellular, and Developmental Biology, Santa Cruz, CA 95064. Offers MA, PhD. *Students:* 51 full-time (24 women); includes 9 minority (1 Black or African American, non-Hispanic/Latino; 4 Asian, non-Hispanic/Latino; 2 Hispanic/Latino; 1 Native Hawaiian or other Pacific Islander, non-Hispanic/Latino; 1 Two or more races, non-Hispanic/Latino), 4 international. Average age 28. 137 applicants, 21% accepted, 15 enrolled. In 2010, 5 doctorates awarded. Terminal master's awarded for partial completion of doctoral program. *Degree requirements:* For master's, thesis; for doctorate, thesis/dissertation, qualifying exam. *Entrance requirements:* For master's and doctorate, GRE General Test, 3 letters of recommendation, interview. Additional exam requirements/recommendations for international students: Required—TOEFL (minimum score 550 paper-based; 220 computer-based; 83 iBT); Recommended—IELTS (minimum score 8). *Application deadline:* For fall admission, 12/3 for domestic and international students. Application fee: $70 ($90 for international students). Electronic applications accepted. *Financial support:* Fellowships, research assistantships, teaching assistantships, institutionally sponsored loans and tuition waivers available. Financial award applicants required to submit FAFSA. *Faculty research:* RNA biology, chromatin and chromosome biology, neurobiology, stem cell biology and differentiation, cell structure and function. *Unit head:* Teel Lopez, Graduate Program Coordinator, 831-459-2385, E-mail: tablack@ucsc.edu. *Application contact:* Teel Lopez, Graduate Program Coordinator, 831-459-2385, E-mail: tablack@ucsc.edu.

University of Chicago, Division of Biological Sciences, Molecular Biosciences Cluster, Department of Biochemistry and Molecular Biology, Chicago, IL 60637-1513. Offers PhD, MD/PhD. *Degree requirements:* For doctorate, thesis/dissertation, ethics class, 2 teaching assistantships. *Entrance requirements:* For doctorate, GRE General Test, GRE Subject Test. Additional exam requirements/recommendations for international students: Required—TOEFL (minimum score 600 paper-based; 250 computer-based; 104 iBT), IELTS (minimum score 7). Electronic applications accepted. *Faculty research:* Molecular biology, gene expression, and DNA-protein interactions; membrane biochemistry, molecular endocrinology, and transmembrane signaling; enzyme mechanisms, physical biochemistry, and structural biology.

University of Chicago, Division of Biological Sciences, Molecular Biosciences Cluster, Graduate Program in Cell and Molecular Biology, Chicago, IL 60637-1513. Offers PhD. *Degree requirements:* For doctorate, thesis/dissertation, ethics class, 2 teaching assistantships. *Entrance requirements:* For doctorate, GRE General Test. Additional exam requirements/recommendations for international students: Required—TOEFL (minimum score 600 paper-based; 250 computer-based; 104 iBT), IELTS (minimum score 7). Electronic applications accepted. *Faculty research:* Gene expression, chromosome structure, animal viruses, plant molecular genetics.

University of Cincinnati, Graduate School, College of Medicine, Graduate Programs in Biomedical Sciences, Department of Environmental Health, Programs in Environmental Genetics and Molecular Toxicology, Cincinnati, OH 45221. Offers MS, PhD. *Degree requirements:* For doctorate, thesis/dissertation. *Entrance requirements:* For master's, GRE, minimum GPA of 3.0, 3 letters of recommendation. Additional exam requirements/recommendations for international students: Required—TOEFL (minimum score 520 paper-based; 190 computer-based).

University of Cincinnati, Graduate School, College of Medicine, Graduate Programs in Biomedical Sciences, Department of Molecular Genetics, Biochemistry and Microbiology, Cincinnati, OH 45221. Offers MS, PhD. Terminal master's awarded for partial completion of doctoral program. *Degree requirements:* For master's, thesis or alternative; for doctorate, thesis/dissertation, qualifying exam. *Entrance requirements:* For master's and doctorate, GRE General Test. Additional exam requirements/recommendations for international students: Required—TOEFL (minimum score 600 paper-based; 250 computer-based; 100 iBT), TWE. Electronic applications accepted. *Faculty research:* Cancer biology and developmental genetics, gene regulation and chromosome structure, microbiology and pathogenic mechanisms, structural biology, membrane biochemistry and signal transduction.

University of Cincinnati, Graduate School, College of Medicine, Graduate Programs in Biomedical Sciences, Department of Pediatrics, Program in Molecular and Developmental Biology, Cincinnati, OH 45221. Offers PhD. *Degree requirements:* For doctorate, thesis/dissertation, qualifying exam. *Entrance requirements:* For doctorate, GRE General Test, minimum GPA of 3.2. Additional exam requirements/recommendations for international students: Required—TOEFL (minimum score 520 paper-based; 190 computer-based). Electronic applications accepted. *Faculty research:* Cancer biology, cardiovascular biology, developmental biology, human genetics, gene therapy, genomics and bioinformatics, immunobiology, molecular medicine, neuroscience, pulmonary biology, reproductive biology, stem cell biology.

University of Colorado Boulder, Graduate School, College of Arts and Sciences, Department of Molecular, Cellular, and Developmental Biology, Boulder, CO 80309. Offers cellular structure and function (MA, PhD); developmental biology (MA, PhD); molecular biology (MA, PhD). *Faculty:* 27 full-time (7 women). *Students:* 72 full-time (37 women), 1 part-time (0 women); includes 5 minority (1 American Indian or Alaska Native, non-Hispanic/Latino; 1 Asian, non-Hispanic/Latino; 3 Hispanic/Latino), 15 international. Average age 28. 257 applicants, 9 enrolled. In 2010, 4 master's, 9 doctorates awarded. Terminal master's awarded for partial completion of doctoral program. *Degree requirements:* For master's, comprehensive exam, thesis or alternative; for doctorate, comprehensive exam, thesis/dissertation. *Entrance requirements:* For master's, GRE General Test, GRE Subject Test, minimum undergraduate GPA of 3.0; for doctorate, GRE General Test, GRE Subject Test. *Application deadline:* For fall admission, 1/1 for domestic students, 12/1 for international students. Application fee: $50 ($60 for international students). *Financial support:* In 2010–11, 40 fellowships (averaging $11,628 per year), 53 research assistantships (averaging $14,700 per year) were awarded; tuition waivers (full) also available. Financial award application deadline: 2/1. *Faculty research:* Molecular biology of RNA and DNA, molecular genetics, cell motility and cytoskeleton, cell membranes, developmental genetics, human genetics. Total annual research expenditures: $16.4 million.

University of Colorado Denver, School of Medicine, Program in Molecular Biology, Denver, CO 80217-3364. Offers biomolecular structure (PhD); molecular biology (PhD). *Students:* 40 full-time (24 women); includes 2 Asian, non-Hispanic/Latino; 2 Hispanic/Latino, 3 international. Average age 28. 5 applicants, 80% accepted, 4 enrolled. In 2010, 3 doctorates awarded. *Degree requirements:* For doctorate, comprehensive exam, thesis/dissertation. *Entrance requirements:* For doctorate, GRE, organic chemistry (2 semesters, including 1 semester of laboratory), biology, general physics, college-level mathematics through calculus. Additional exam requirements/recommendations for international students: Required—TOEFL (minimum score 550 paper-based; 213 computer-based). *Application deadline:* For fall admission, 1/1 for domestic students. Application fee: $50 ($75 for international students). Electronic applications accepted. *Expenses:* Contact institution. *Financial support:* Fellowships, research assistantships, teaching assistantships, health care benefits, tuition waivers (full), and stipend available. Financial award application deadline: 3/15; financial award applicants required to submit FAFSA. *Faculty research:* Gene transcription, RNA processing, chromosome dynamics, DNA damage and repair, chromatin assembly. *Unit head:* Dr. James DeGregori, Director, 303-724-3245, E-mail: james.degregori@uchsc.edu. *Application contact:* Jean Sibley, Administrator, 303-724-3245, Fax: 303-724-3247, E-mail: jean.sibley@uchsc.edu.

University of Colorado Denver, School of Medicine, Program in Pharmacology, Denver, CO 80217-3364. Offers bioinformatics (PhD); biomolecular structure (PhD); pharmacology (PhD). *Students:* 25 full-time (13 women); includes 1 Black or African American, non-Hispanic/Latino; 2 Asian, non-Hispanic/Latino; 1 Hispanic/Latino. Average age 28. 31 applicants, 16% accepted, 5 enrolled. In 2010, 3 doctorates awarded. *Degree requirements:* For doctorate, comprehensive exam, thesis/dissertation, major seminar, 3 research rotations, 30 hours each of course work and thesis. *Entrance requirements:* For doctorate, GRE General Test. Additional exam requirements/recommendations for international students: Required—TOEFL (minimum score 550 paper-based; 213 computer-based; 80 iBT). *Application deadline:* For fall admission, 1/1 priority date for domestic students. Application fee: $50 ($75 for international students). Electronic applications accepted. *Expenses:* Contact institution. *Financial support:* Fellowships, research assistantships, teaching assistantships, health care benefits, tuition waivers (full), and stipend available. Financial award application deadline: 3/15; financial award applicants required to submit FAFSA. *Faculty research:* Cancer biology, drugs of abuse, neuroscience, signal transduction, structural biology. Total annual research expenditures: $16.7 million. *Unit head:* Dr. Andrew Thorburn, Interim Chair, 303-724-3290, Fax: 303-724-3663, E-mail: andrew.thorburn@ucdenver.edu. *Application contact:* Graduate Training Coordinator, 303-724-3565, E-mail: grad.pharm@ucdenver.edu.

University of Connecticut, Graduate School, College of Liberal Arts and Sciences, Department of Molecular and Cell Biology, Field of Microbial Systems Analysis, Storrs, CT 06269. Offers MS, PSM. *Degree requirements:* For master's, comprehensive exam. *Entrance requirements:* For master's, GRE General Test, GRE Subject Test. Additional exam requirements/recommendations for international students: Required—TOEFL (minimum score 550 paper-based; 213 computer-based). Electronic applications accepted.

University of Connecticut Health Center, Graduate School, Programs in Biomedical Sciences, Graduate Program in Molecular Biology and Biochemistry, Farmington, CT 06030. Offers PhD, DMD/PhD, MD/PhD. *Faculty:* 158. *Students:* 18 full-time (10 women); includes 3 minority (1 Black or African American, non-Hispanic/Latino; 2 Asian, non-Hispanic/Latino), 6 international. Average age 28. 216 applicants, 22% accepted. In 2010, 5 doctorates awarded.

Degree requirements: For doctorate, comprehensive exam, thesis/dissertation. *Entrance requirements:* For doctorate, GRE General Test. Additional exam requirements/recommendations for international students: Required—TOEFL (minimum score 600 paper-based; 250 computer-based). *Application deadline:* For fall admission, 12/15 for domestic students. Application fee: $55. Electronic applications accepted. *Financial support:* In 2010–11, 18 research assistantships with full tuition reimbursements (averaging $27,000 per year) were awarded; health care benefits also available. *Faculty research:* Molecular biology, structural biology, protein biochemistry, microbial physiology and pathogenesis. *Unit head:* Dr. Stephen King, Director, 860-679-3347, Fax: 860-679-1239, E-mail: sking@nso2.uchc.edu. *Application contact:* Tricia Avolt, Graduate Admissions Coordinator, 860-679-2175, Fax: 860-679-1899, E-mail: robertson@nso2.uchc.edu.

See Display below and Close-Up on page 231.

University of Delaware, College of Arts and Sciences, Department of Biological Sciences, Newark, DE 19716. Offers biotechnology (MS); cancer biology (MS, PhD); cell and extracellular matrix biology (MS, PhD); cell and systems physiology (MS, PhD); developmental biology (MS, PhD); ecology and evolution (MS, PhD); microbiology (MS, PhD); molecular biology and genetics (MS, PhD). Terminal master's awarded for partial completion of doctoral program. *Degree requirements:* For master's, thesis, preliminary exam; for doctorate, comprehensive exam, thesis/dissertation, preliminary exam. *Entrance requirements:* For master's and doctorate, GRE General Test. Additional exam requirements/recommendations for international students: Required—TOEFL (minimum score 600 paper-based; 250 computer-based); Recommended—TWE. Electronic applications accepted. *Faculty research:* Microorganisms, bone, cancer metastasis, developmental biology, cell biology, DNA.

University of Florida, College of Medicine, Department of Biochemistry and Molecular Biology, Gainesville, FL 32611. Offers biochemistry and molecular biology (MS, PhD); imaging science and technology (MS, PhD). *Degree requirements:* For doctorate, thesis/dissertation. *Entrance requirements:* For doctorate, GRE General Test, minimum GPA of 3.0. Additional exam requirements/recommendations for international students: Required—TOEFL. Electronic applications accepted. *Expenses:* Tuition, state resident: full-time $10,916. Tuition, nonresident: full-time $28,309. *Faculty research:* Gene expression, metabolic regulation, structural biology, enzyme mechanism, membrane transporters.

University of Florida, College of Medicine and Graduate School, Interdisciplinary Program in Biomedical Sciences, Concentration in Biochemistry and Molecular Biology, Gainesville, FL 32611. Offers PhD. *Degree requirements:* For doctorate, thesis/dissertation. *Entrance requirements:* For doctorate, GRE General Test, minimum GPA of 3.0. Additional exam requirements/recommendations for international students: Required—TOEFL. Electronic applications accepted. *Expenses:* Tuition, state resident: full-time $10,916. Tuition, nonresident: full-time $28,309. *Faculty research:* Gene expression, metabolic regulation, structural biology, enzyme mechanism, membrane transporters.

University of Florida, Interdisciplinary Concentration in Animal Molecular and Cellular Biology, Gainesville, FL 32611. Offers MS, PhD. Program offered jointly with College of Agricultural and Life Sciences, College of Liberal Arts and Sciences, College of Medicine, and College of Veterinary Medicine. *Students:* 2 full-time (both women), both international. Average age 27. 5 applicants, 80% accepted, 2 enrolled. *Entrance requirements:* For master's and doctorate, GRE General Test (minimum score 1000), minimum GPA of 3.0. Additional exam requirements/recommendations for international students: Required—TOEFL (minimum score 550 paper-based; 213 computer-based; 80 iBT), IELTS (minimum score 6). Application fee: $30. Electronic applications accepted. *Expenses:* Tuition, state resident: full-time $10,916. Tuition, nonresident: full-time $28,309. *Financial support:* In 2010–11, 2 students received support, including 1 fellowship, 1 research assistantship (averaging $25,749 per year). Financial award applicants required to submit FAFSA. *Unit head:* Dr. Geoffrey E. Dahl, Chair, Animal Sciences, 352-

392-1981 Ext. 221, Fax: 352-392-5595, E-mail: gdahl@ufl.edu. *Application contact:* Dr. Joel H. Brendemuhl, Assistant Chair, 352-392-8073, Fax: 352-392-5595, E-mail: brendj@ufl.edu.

University of Georgia, College of Arts and Sciences, Department of Biochemistry and Molecular Biology, Athens, GA 30602. Offers MS, PhD. *Faculty:* 36 full-time (4 women). *Students:* 68 full-time (25 women), 2 part-time (1 woman); includes 6 Black or African American, non-Hispanic/Latino; 1 Asian, non-Hispanic/Latino; 1 Hispanic/Latino; 1 Two or more races, non-Hispanic/Latino, 23 international. 105 applicants, 20% accepted, 14 enrolled. In 2010, 4 master's, 10 doctorates awarded. *Degree requirements:* For master's, one foreign language, thesis; for doctorate, one foreign language, thesis/dissertation. *Entrance requirements:* For master's and doctorate, GRE General Test. Additional exam requirements/recommendations for international students: Required—TOEFL. *Application deadline:* For fall admission, 1/1 priority date for domestic and international students. Application fee: $50. Electronic applications accepted. *Expenses:* Tuition, state resident: full-time $7200; part-time $344 per credit hour. Tuition, nonresident: full-time $21,900; part-time $944 per credit hour. Tuition and fees vary according to course load and program. *Financial support:* Fellowships, research assistantships, teaching assistantships, scholarships/grants and unspecified assistantships available. Financial award application deadline: 1/1. *Unit head:* Dr. Stephen L. Hajduk, Head, 706-542-1676, Fax: 706-542-0182, E-mail: shajduk@bmb.uga.edu. *Application contact:* Dr. Lance Wells, Graduate Coordinator, 706-583-7806, Fax: 706-542-1738, E-mail: lwells@ccr.uga.edu.

University of Guelph, Graduate Studies, College of Biological Science, Department of Molecular and Cellular Biology, Guelph, ON N1G 2W1, Canada. Offers biochemistry (M Sc, PhD); biophysics (M Sc, PhD); botany (M Sc, PhD); microbiology (M Sc, PhD); molecular biology and genetics (M Sc, PhD). *Degree requirements:* For master's, thesis, research proposal; for doctorate, comprehensive exam, thesis/dissertation, research proposal. *Entrance requirements:* For master's, minimum B-average during previous 2 years of coursework; for doctorate, minimum A-average. Additional exam requirements/recommendations for international students: Required—TOEFL (minimum score 600 paper-based; 213 computer-based), IELTS (minimum score 6.5). Electronic applications accepted. *Faculty research:* Physiology, structure, genetics, and ecology of microbes; virology and microbial technology.

University of Hawaii at Manoa, Graduate Division, College of Tropical Agriculture and Human Resources, Department of Molecular Biosciences and Bioengineering, Honolulu, HI 96822. Offers bioengineering (MS); molecular bioscience and bioengineering (MS); molecular biosciences and bioengineering (PhD). Part-time programs available. *Faculty:* 71 full-time (18 women), 10 part-time/adjunct (4 women). *Students:* 81 full-time (34 women), 9 part-time (6 women); includes 32 minority (1 Black or African American, non-Hispanic/Latino; 1 American Indian or Alaska Native, non-Hispanic/Latino; 20 Asian, non-Hispanic/Latino; 1 Hispanic/Latino; 5 Native Hawaiian or other Pacific Islander, non-Hispanic/Latino; 4 Two or more races, non-Hispanic/Latino), 36 international. Average age 31. 52 applicants, 77% accepted, 31 enrolled. In 2010, 14 master's, 5 doctorates awarded. *Degree requirements:* For master's, thesis optional; for doctorate, comprehensive exam, thesis/dissertation. *Entrance requirements:* For master's and doctorate, GRE General Test. Additional exam requirements/recommendations for international students: Required—TOEFL (minimum score 550 paper-based; 213 computer-based; 79 iBT), IELTS (minimum score 5). *Application deadline:* For fall admission, 5/30 for domestic students, 4/30 for international students; for spring admission, 10/30 for domestic students, 9/30 for international students. Application fee: $60. *Financial support:* In 2010–11, 11 fellowships (averaging $1,927 per year), 52 research assistantships (averaging $18,421 per year), 11 teaching assistantships (averaging $15,788 per year) were awarded; Federal Work-Study, institutionally sponsored loans, and tuition waivers (full) also available. *Faculty research:* Mechanization, agricultural systems, waste management, water management, cell culture. Total annual research expenditures: $1.4 million. *Application contact:* Dulal Borthakur, Graduate Chair, 808-956-6660, Fax: 808-956-3542, E-mail: dulal@hawaii.edu.

University of Hawaii at Manoa, John A. Burns School of Medicine, Department of Cell and Molecular Biology, Honolulu, HI 96813. Offers MS, PhD. Part-time programs available. *Faculty:*

Molecular Biology

University of Hawaii at Manoa *(continued)*
55 full-time (16 women), 5 part-time/adjunct (1 woman). *Students:* 38 full-time (20 women), 2 part-time (1 woman); includes 16 minority (8 Asian, non-Hispanic/Latino; 2 Hispanic/Latino; 1 Native Hawaiian or other Pacific Islander, non-Hispanic/Latino; 5 Two or more races, non-Hispanic/Latino), 4 international. Average age 31. 63 applicants, 35% accepted, 12 enrolled. In 2010, 5 doctorates awarded. Terminal master's awarded for partial completion of doctoral program. *Degree requirements:* For master's, thesis optional; for doctorate, comprehensive exam, thesis/dissertation. *Entrance requirements:* For master's and doctorate, GRE General Test, minimum GPA of 3.0. Additional exam requirements/recommendations for international students: Required—TOEFL (minimum score 500 paper-based; 173 computer-based; 61 iBT), IELTS (minimum score 5). *Application deadline:* For fall admission, 1/15 for domestic and international students. Applications are processed on a rolling basis. Application fee: $60. *Financial support:* In 2010–11, 19 fellowships (averaging $824 per year), 36 research assistantships (averaging $20,351 per year), 1 teaching assistantship (averaging $16,824 per year) were awarded; Federal Work-Study and institutionally sponsored loans also available. Financial award application deadline: 2/1. Total annual research expenditures: $2.7 million. *Application contact:* Marla Berry, Graduate Co-Chair, 808-692-1506, Fax: 808-692-1968, E-mail: mberry@hawaii.edu.

University of Idaho, College of Graduate Studies, College of Agricultural and Life Sciences, Department of Microbiology, Molecular Biology and Biochemistry, Moscow, ID 83844-2282. Offers MS, PhD. *Faculty:* 16 full-time. *Students:* 13 full-time, 6 part-time. Average age 30. In 2010, 4 master's, 3 doctorates awarded. *Degree requirements:* For master's, thesis; for doctorate, one foreign language, thesis/dissertation. *Entrance requirements:* For master's, minimum GPA of 2.8; for doctorate, minimum undergraduate GPA of 2.8, 3.0 graduate. *Application deadline:* For fall admission, 8/1 for domestic students; for spring admission, 12/15 for domestic students. Applications are processed on a rolling basis. Application fee: $60. Electronic applications accepted. *Expenses:* Tuition, nonresident: part-time $580 per credit. Required fees: $306 per credit. *Financial support:* Research assistantships, teaching assistantships available. Financial award applicants required to submit FAFSA. *Unit head:* Bruce L. Miller, Interim Chair, 208-885-7247, Fax: 208-885-6518, E-mail: mmbb@uidaho.edu. *Application contact:* Bruce L. Miller, Interim Chair, 208-885-7247, Fax: 208-885-6518, E-mail: mmbb@uidaho.edu.

University of Illinois at Chicago, College of Medicine and Graduate College, Graduate Programs in Medicine, Department of Biochemistry and Molecular Genetics, Chicago, IL 60607-7128. Offers PhD, MD/PhD. Terminal master's awarded for partial completion of doctoral program. *Degree requirements:* For doctorate, thesis/dissertation. *Entrance requirements:* For doctorate, GRE General Test. Additional exam requirements/recommendations for international students: Required—TOEFL. Electronic applications accepted. *Faculty research:* Nature of cellular components, control of metabolic processes, regulation of gene expression.

The University of Iowa, Graduate College, Program in Molecular and Cellular Biology, Iowa City, IA 52242-1316. Offers PhD, MD/PhD. *Degree requirements:* For doctorate, comprehensive exam, thesis/dissertation. *Entrance requirements:* For doctorate, GRE General Test, minimum GPA of 3.0. Additional exam requirements/recommendations for international students: Required—TOEFL (minimum score 600 paper-based; 250 computer-based; 100 iBT). Electronic applications accepted. *Faculty research:* Regulation of gene expression, inherited human genetic diseases, signal transduction mechanisms, structural biology and function.

The University of Kansas, Graduate Studies, College of Liberal Arts and Sciences, Department of Molecular Biosciences, Lawrence, KS 66044. Offers biochemistry and biophysics (MA, PhD); microbiology (MA, PhD); molecular, cellular, and developmental biology (MA, PhD). *Faculty:* 34. *Students:* 65 full-time (31 women), 1 part-time (0 women); includes 7 minority (2 Asian, non-Hispanic/Latino; 4 Hispanic/Latino; 1 Two or more races, non-Hispanic/Latino), 24 international. Average age 27. 34 applicants, 47% accepted, 10 enrolled. In 2010, 1 master's, 5 doctorates awarded. Terminal master's awarded for partial completion of doctoral program. *Degree requirements:* For master's, comprehensive exam, thesis; for doctorate, comprehensive exam, thesis/dissertation. *Entrance requirements:* For master's and doctorate, GRE General Test. Additional exam requirements/recommendations for international students: Required—TOEFL (minimum score 24 iBT), OR IELTS Speaking: 8. *Application deadline:* For fall admission, 12/15 for domestic and international students. Application fee: $55 ($65 for international students). Electronic applications accepted. *Expenses:* Tuition, state resident: full-time $7092; part-time $295.50 per credit hour. Tuition, nonresident: full-time $16,590; part-time $691.25 per credit hour. Required fees: $858; $71.49 per credit hour. Tuition and fees vary according to course load, campus/location and program. *Financial support:* Fellowships with tuition reimbursements, research assistantships with tuition reimbursements, teaching assistantships with tuition reimbursements, health care benefits and unspecified assistantships available. Financial award application deadline: 3/1. *Faculty research:* Structure and function of proteins, genetics of organism development, molecular genetics, neurophysiology, molecular virology and pathogenics, developmental biology, cell biology. *Unit head:* Dr. Mark Richter, Chair, 785-864-3334, Fax: 785-864-5294, E-mail: richter@ku.edu. *Application contact:* John P. Connolly, Graduate Program Assistant, 785-864-4311, Fax: 785-864-5294, E-mail: jconnolly@ku.edu.

The University of Kansas, University of Kansas Medical Center, School of Medicine, Department of Biochemistry and Molecular Biology, Kansas City, KS 66160. Offers MS, PhD, MD/PhD. *Faculty:* 18. *Students:* 6 full-time (0 women), 4 international. Average age 29. Terminal master's awarded for partial completion of doctoral program. *Degree requirements:* For master's, thesis, oral defense of thesis; for doctorate, thesis/dissertation, comprehensive oral and written exam. *Entrance requirements:* Additional exam requirements/recommendations for international students: Required—TOEFL. Application fee: $0. Electronic applications accepted. *Expenses:* Tuition, state resident: full-time $7092; part-time $295.50 per credit hour. Tuition, nonresident: full-time $16,590; part-time $691.25 per credit hour. Required fees: $858; $71.49 per credit hour. Tuition and fees vary according to course load, campus/location and program. *Financial support:* In 2010–11, 5 teaching assistantships with full and partial tuition reimbursements were awarded; fellowships, research assistantships with partial tuition reimbursements, traineeships, health care benefits, and unspecified assistantships also available. Financial award application deadline: 2/14; financial award applicants required to submit FAFSA. *Faculty research:* Determination of portion structure, underlying bases for interaction of proteins with their target, mapping allosteric circuiting within proteins, mechanism of action of transcription factors, renal signal transduction. Total annual research expenditures: $3.4 million. *Unit head:* Dr. Gerald M. Carlson, Chairman, 913-588-6574, Fax: 913-588-7007, E-mail: gcarlson@kumc.edu. *Application contact:* Dr. Liskin Swint-Kruse, Associate Professor, 913-588-0399, Fax: 913-588-9896, E-mail: lswint-kruse@kumc.edu.

University of Lethbridge, School of Graduate Studies, Lethbridge, AB T1K 3M4, Canada. Offers accounting (MScM); addictions counseling (M Sc); agricultural biotechnology (M Sc); agricultural studies (M Sc, MA); anthropology (MA); archaeology (MA); art (MA, MFA); biochemistry (M Sc); biological sciences (M Sc); biomolecular science (PhD); biosystems and biodiversity (PhD); Canadian studies (MA); chemistry (M Sc); computer science (M Sc); computer science and geographical information science (M Sc); counseling psychology (M Ed); dramatic arts (MA); earth, space, and physical science (PhD); economics (MA); educational leadership (M Ed); English (MA); environmental science (M Sc); evolution and behavior (PhD); exercise science (M Sc); finance (MScM); French (MA); French/German (MA); French/Spanish (MA); general education (M Ed); general management (MScM); geography (M Sc, MA); German (MA); health science (M Sc); history (MA); human resource management and labour relations (MScM); individualized multidisciplinary (M Sc, MA); information systems (MScM); international management (MScM); kinesiology (M Sc, MA); management (M Sc, MA); marketing (MScM); mathematics (M Sc); music (M Mus, MA); Native American studies (MA); neuroscience (M Sc, PhD); new media (MA); nursing (M Sc); philosophy (MA); physics (M Sc); policy and strategy (MScM); political science (MA); psychology (M Sc, MA); religious studies (MA); social sciences (MA); sociology (MA); theatre and dramatic arts (MFA); theoretical and

computational science (PhD); urban and regional studies (MA); women's studies (MA). Part-time and evening/weekend programs available. *Degree requirements:* For doctorate, comprehensive exam, thesis/dissertation. *Entrance requirements:* For master's, GMAT (M Sc in management), bachelor's degree in related field, minimum GPA of 3.0 during previous 20 graded semester courses, 2 years teaching or related experience (M Ed); for doctorate, master's degree, minimum graduate GPA of 3.5. Additional exam requirements/recommendations for international students: Required—TOEFL. *Faculty research:* Movement and brain plasticity, gibberellin physiology, photosynthesis, carbon cycling, molecular properties of main-group ring components.

University of Louisville, School of Medicine, Department of Biochemistry and Molecular Biology, Louisville, KY 40292-0001. Offers MS, PhD, MD/PhD. *Faculty:* 33 full-time (7 women), 2 part-time/adjunct (1 woman). *Students:* 39 full-time (19 women), 2 part-time (both women); includes 1 Black or African American, non-Hispanic/Latino; 2 Asian, non-Hispanic/Latino; 1 Hispanic/Latino, 10 international. Average age 29. 37 applicants, 41% accepted, 11 enrolled. In 2010, 3 master's, 7 doctorates awarded. Terminal master's awarded for partial completion of doctoral program. *Degree requirements:* For master's, thesis; for doctorate, comprehensive exam, thesis/dissertation, one first author publication. *Entrance requirements:* For master's and doctorate, GRE General Test (minimum score of 1000 verbal and quantitative), minimum GPA of 3.0. Additional exam requirements/recommendations for international students: Required—TOEFL. *Application deadline:* For fall admission, 4/15 for domestic and international students. Applications are processed on a rolling basis. Application fee: $50. Electronic applications accepted. *Expenses:* Tuition, state resident: full-time $9144; part-time $508 per credit hour. Tuition, nonresident: full-time $19,026; part-time $1057 per credit hour. Tuition and fees vary according to program and reciprocity agreements. *Financial support:* In 2010–11, 12 fellowships with full tuition reimbursements (averaging $22,000 per year), 23 research assistantships with full tuition reimbursements (averaging $22,000 per year) were awarded; teaching assistantships with tuition reimbursements, scholarships/grants, traineeships, tuition waivers (full and partial), and unspecified assistantships also available. Financial award application deadline: 4/15. *Faculty research:* Genetic regulatory mechanisms, microRNAs, vesicular trafficking in cancer metastasis and angiogenesis, ribosome biogenesis and disease, regulation of foreign compound metabolism/lipid and steroid metabolism. *Unit head:* Dr. Ronald G. Gregg, Chair, 502-852-5217, Fax: 502-852-6222, E-mail: rggreg02@gwise.louisville.edu. *Application contact:* Dr. William L. Dean, Information Contact, 502-852-5227, Fax: 502-852-6222, E-mail: wldean01@gwise.louisville.edu.

University of Maine, Graduate School, College of Natural Sciences, Forestry, and Agriculture, Department of Biochemistry, Molecular Biology, and Microbiology, Orono, ME 04469. Offers biochemistry (MPS, MS); biochemistry and molecular biology (PhD); microbiology (MPS, MS, PhD). *Faculty:* 9 full-time (5 women), 3 part-time/adjunct (2 women). *Students:* 19 full-time (12 women), 21 part-time (15 women); includes 5 minority (1 American Indian or Alaska Native, non-Hispanic/Latino; 2 Asian, non-Hispanic/Latino; 1 Hispanic/Latino; 1 Two or more races, non-Hispanic/Latino), 6 international. Average age 30. 39 applicants, 26% accepted, 9 enrolled. In 2010, 6 master's, 3 doctorates awarded. *Degree requirements:* For doctorate, thesis/dissertation. *Entrance requirements:* For master's and doctorate, GRE General Test. Additional exam requirements/recommendations for international students: Required—TOEFL. *Application deadline:* For fall admission, 2/1 priority date for domestic students. Applications are processed on a rolling basis. Application fee: $65. Electronic applications accepted. *Expenses:* Tuition, state resident: full-time $400. Tuition, nonresident: full-time $1050. *Financial support:* In 2010–11, 5 research assistantships with tuition reimbursements (averaging $20,893 per year), 12 teaching assistantships with tuition reimbursements (averaging $19,296 per year) were awarded; tuition waivers (full and partial) also available. Financial award application deadline: 3/1. *Unit head:* Dr. Robert Gundersen, Chair, 207-581-2802, Fax: 207-581-2801. *Application contact:* Scott G. Delcourt, Associate Dean of the Graduate School, 207-581-3291, Fax: 207-581-3232, E-mail: graduate@maine.edu.

University of Maine, Graduate School, Program in Biomedical Sciences, Orono, ME 04469. Offers biomedical engineering (PhD); cell and molecular biology (PhD); neuroscience (PhD); toxicology (PhD). *Students:* 11 full-time (8 women), 13 part-time (6 women); includes 1 American Indian or Alaska Native, non-Hispanic/Latino, 5 international. Average age 29. 32 applicants, 19% accepted, 6 enrolled. Application fee: $60. *Expenses:* Tuition, state resident: full-time $400. Tuition, nonresident: full-time $1050. *Financial support:* In 2010–11, 8 research assistantships (averaging $25,625 per year) were awarded. *Unit head:* Dr. Carol Kim, Unit Head, 207-581-2803. *Application contact:* Dr. Carol Kim, Unit Head, 207-581-2803.

The University of Manchester, Faculty of Life Sciences, Manchester, United Kingdom. Offers adaptive organismal biology (M Phil, PhD); animal biology (M Phil, PhD); biochemistry (M Phil, PhD); bioinformatics (M Phil, PhD); biomolecular sciences (M Phil, PhD); biotechnology (M Phil, PhD); cell biology (M Phil, PhD); cell matrix research (M Phil, PhD); channels and transporters (M Phil, PhD); developmental biology (M Phil, PhD); Egyptology (M Phil, PhD); environmental biology (M Phil, PhD); evolutionary biology (M Phil, PhD); gene expression (M Phil, PhD); genetics (M Phil, PhD); history of science, technology and medicine (M Phil, PhD); immunology (M Phil, PhD); integrative neurobiology and behavior (M Phil, PhD); membrane trafficking (M Phil, PhD); microbiology (M Phil, PhD); molecular and cellular neuroscience (M Phil, PhD); molecular biology (M Phil, PhD); molecular cancer studies (M Phil, PhD); neuroscience (M Phil, PhD); ophthalmology (M Phil, PhD); optometry (M Phil, PhD); organelle function (M Phil, PhD); pharmacology (M Phil, PhD); physiology (M Phil, PhD); plant sciences (M Phil, PhD); stem cell research (M Phil, PhD); structural biology (M Phil, PhD); systems neuroscience (M Phil, PhD); toxicology (M Phil, PhD).

The University of Manchester, School of Dentistry, Manchester, United Kingdom. Offers basic dental sciences (cancer studies) (M Phil, PhD); basic dental sciences (molecular genetics) (M Phil, PhD); basic dental sciences (stem cell biology) (M Phil, PhD); biomaterials sciences and dental technology (M Phil, PhD); dental public health/community dentistry (M Phil, PhD); dental science (clinical) (PhD); endodontology (M Phil, PhD); fixed and removable prosthodontics (M Phil, PhD); operative dentistry (M Phil, PhD); oral and maxillofacial surgery (M Phil, PhD); oral radiology (M Phil, PhD); orthodontics (M Phil, PhD); restorative dentistry (M Phil, PhD).

University of Maryland, Baltimore, Graduate School, Graduate Program in Life Sciences, Program in Biochemistry and Molecular Biology, Baltimore, MD 21201. Offers biochemistry (MS, PhD); MD/PhD. *Entrance requirements:* For doctorate, GRE General Test. Additional exam requirements/recommendations for international students: Required—TOEFL (minimum score 550 paper-based; 80 iBT); Recommended—IELTS (minimum score 7). Electronic applications accepted. Part-time tuition and fees vary according to course load, degree level and program. *Faculty research:* Membrane transport, hormonal regulation, protein structure, molecular virology.

University of Maryland, Baltimore, Graduate School, Graduate Program in Life Sciences, Program in Molecular Medicine, Baltimore, MD 21201. Offers cancer biology (PhD); cell and molecular physiology (PhD); human genetics and genomic medicine (PhD); molecular medicine (MS); molecular toxicology and pharmacology (PhD); MD/PhD. *Entrance requirements:* Additional exam requirements/recommendations for international students: Required—TOEFL (minimum score 600 paper-based; 100 iBT); Recommended—IELTS (minimum score 7). Electronic applications accepted. Part-time tuition and fees vary according to course load, degree level and program.

University of Maryland, Baltimore County, Graduate School, College of Natural and Mathematical Sciences, Department of Biological Sciences, Program in Applied Molecular Biology, Baltimore, MD 21250. Offers MS. *Faculty:* 25 full-time (10 women). *Students:* 7 full-time (5 women), 2 part-time (both women); includes 5 Asian, non-Hispanic/Latino; 1 Hispanic/Latino. Average age 24. 30 applicants, 47% accepted, 9 enrolled. In 2010, 8 master's awarded. *Entrance requirements:* For master's, GRE General Test, GRE Subject Test (recommended), minimum GPA of 3.0. Additional exam requirements/recommendations for international students: Required—TOEFL. *Application deadline:* For fall admission, 4/1 priority date for domestic and international students. Applications are processed on a rolling basis. Application fee: $50. Electronic applications accepted. *Financial support:* In 2010–11, 4 students received support, including 4 teaching assistantships with full and partial tuition reimbursements available (averaging $12,000 per year); tuition waivers (partial) also available. *Faculty research:* Structure-function of RNA, genetics and molecular biology, biological chemistry. *Unit head:* Dr. Richard E. Wolf, Director, Graduate Program, 410-455-3669, Fax: 410-455-3875, E-mail: biograd@umbc.edu. *Application contact:* Dr. Richard E. Wolf, Director, Graduate Program, 410-455-3669, Fax: 410-455-3875, E-mail: biograd@umbc.edu.

University of Maryland, Baltimore County, Graduate School, College of Natural and Mathematical Sciences, Department of Biological Sciences, Program in Molecular and Cell Biology, Baltimore, MD 21250. Offers PhD. *Faculty:* 24 full-time (10 women), 1 part-time/adjunct (0 women). *Students:* 18 full-time (12 women); includes 2 Black or African American, non-Hispanic/Latino; 7 Asian, non-Hispanic/Latino. Average age 27. 36 applicants, 28% accepted, 5 enrolled. In 2010, 1 doctorate awarded. *Degree requirements:* For doctorate, thesis/dissertation. *Entrance requirements:* For doctorate, GRE General Test, GRE Subject Test, minimum GPA of 3.0. Additional exam requirements/recommendations for international students: Required—TOEFL. *Application deadline:* For fall admission, 1/15 for domestic students, 12/15 for international students. Applications are processed on a rolling basis. Application fee: $50. Electronic applications accepted. *Financial support:* In 2010–11, fellowships with full tuition reimbursements (averaging $23,000 per year), research assistantships with full tuition reimbursements (averaging $22,300 per year), teaching assistantships with full tuition reimbursements (averaging $22,300 per year) were awarded. *Unit head:* Dr. Jeff Leips, Director, 410-455-3669, Fax: 410-455-3875, E-mail: biograd@umbc.edu. *Application contact:* Dr. Phyllis Robinson, Director, 410-455-3669, Fax: 410-455-3875, E-mail: biograd@umbc.edu.

University of Maryland, College Park, Academic Affairs, College of Computer, Mathematical and Natural Sciences, Department of Cell Biology and Molecular Genetics, Program in Molecular and Cellular Biology, College Park, MD 20742. Offers PhD. Part-time and evening/weekend programs available. *Students:* 38 full-time (26 women), 3 part-time (all women); includes 1 Black or African American, non-Hispanic/Latino; 3 Asian, non-Hispanic/Latino; 2 Hispanic/Latino, 23 international. 97 applicants, 15% accepted, 6 enrolled. In 2010, 1 doctorate awarded. *Degree requirements:* For doctorate, thesis/dissertation, exam, public service. *Entrance requirements:* For doctorate, GRE General Test, 3 letters of reference. Additional exam requirements/recommendations for international students: Required—TOEFL. *Application deadline:* For fall admission, 1/6 for domestic and international students. Applications are processed on a rolling basis. Application fee: $75. Electronic applications accepted. *Expenses:* Tuition, state resident: part-time $471 per credit hour. Tuition, nonresident: part-time $1016 per credit hour. Required fees: $337 per term. *Financial support:* In 2010–11, 14 research assistantships (averaging $19,589 per year), 16 teaching assistantships (averaging $18,983 per year) were awarded. Financial award applicants required to submit FAFSA. *Faculty research:* Monoclonal antibody production, oligonucleotide synthesis, macromolecular processing, signal transduction, developmental biology. *Unit head:* Norma Andrews, 301-405-1605, E-mail: andrewsn@umd.edu. *Application contact:* Dean of Graduate School, 301-405-0358, Fax: 301-314-9305.

University of Massachusetts Boston, Office of Graduate Studies, College of Science and Mathematics, Track in Molecular, Cellular and Organismal Biology, Boston, MA 02125-3393. Offers PhD.

University of Medicine and Dentistry of New Jersey, Graduate School of Biomedical Sciences, Graduate Programs in Biomedical Sciences–Newark, Department of Biochemistry and Molecular Biology, Newark, NJ 07107. Offers MS, PhD. *Degree requirements:* For master's, thesis; for doctorate, thesis/dissertation, qualifying exam. *Entrance requirements:* For master's and doctorate, GRE General Test. Additional exam requirements/recommendations for international students: Required—TOEFL. Electronic applications accepted.

University of Medicine and Dentistry of New Jersey, Graduate School of Biomedical Sciences, Graduate Programs in Biomedical Sciences–Piscataway, Program in Biochemistry and Molecular Biology, Piscataway, NJ 08854-5635. Offers MS, PhD, MD/PhD. PhD, MS offered jointly with Rutgers, The State University of New Jersey, New Brunswick. Terminal master's awarded for partial completion of doctoral program. *Degree requirements:* For master's, thesis, qualifying exam; for doctorate, thesis/dissertation, qualifying exam. *Entrance requirements:* For master's and doctorate, GRE General Test. Additional exam requirements/recommendations for international students: Required—TOEFL. Electronic applications accepted. *Faculty research:* Signal transduction, regulation of RNA, polymerase II transcribed genes, developmental gene expression.

University of Medicine and Dentistry of New Jersey, Graduate School of Biomedical Sciences, Graduate Programs in Biomedical Sciences–Stratford, Program in Cell and Molecular Biology, Stratford, NJ 08084-5634. Offers MS, PhD, DO/PhD. *Degree requirements:* For master's, thesis; for doctorate, thesis/dissertation, qualifying exam. *Entrance requirements:* For master's and doctorate, GRE General Test. Additional exam requirements/recommendations for international students: Required—TOEFL. Electronic applications accepted.

University of Medicine and Dentistry of New Jersey, Graduate School of Biomedical Sciences, Programs in the Molecular Biosciences, Piscataway, NJ 08854-5696. Offers PhD. Program offered jointly with Rutgers, The State University of New Jersey, New Brunswick. *Entrance requirements:* Additional exam requirements/recommendations for international students: Required—TOEFL. Electronic applications accepted.

University of Miami, Graduate School, Miller School of Medicine, Graduate Programs in Medicine, Department of Biochemistry and Molecular Biology, Coral Gables, FL 33124. Offers PhD, MD/PhD. *Degree requirements:* For doctorate, comprehensive exam, thesis/dissertation, proposition exams. *Faculty research:* Macromolecule metabolism, molecular genetics, protein folding and 3-D structure, regulation of gene expression and enzyme function, signal transduction and developmental biology.

University of Miami, Graduate School, Miller School of Medicine, Graduate Programs in Medicine, Department of Cell Biology and Anatomy, Coral Gables, FL 33124. Offers molecular cell and developmental biology (PhD); MD/PhD. *Degree requirements:* For doctorate, thesis/dissertation. *Entrance requirements:* For doctorate, GRE General Test, GRE Subject Test. Additional exam requirements/recommendations for international students: Required—TOEFL. Electronic applications accepted.

University of Michigan, Rackham Graduate School, College of Literature, Science, and the Arts, Department of Molecular, Cellular, and Developmental Biology, Ann Arbor, MI 48109. Offers MS, PhD. Part-time programs available. *Faculty:* 33 full-time (8 women). *Students:* 69 full-time (35 women), 7 part-time (5 women); includes 4 minority (3 Asian, non-Hispanic/Latino; 1 Hispanic/Latino), 35 international. Average age 27. 122 applicants, 16% accepted, 6 enrolled. In 2010, 5 master's, 7 doctorates awarded. Terminal master's awarded for partial completion of doctoral program. *Degree requirements:* For master's, 24 credits with at least 16 in molecular, cellular, and developmental biology and 4 in a cognate field; for doctorate, thesis/dissertation, preliminary exam, oral defense. *Entrance requirements:* For master's and doctorate, GRE General Test. Additional exam requirements/recommendations for international students: Required—TOEFL (minimum score 560 paper-based; 220 computer-based; 83 iBT). *Application deadline:* For fall admission, 1/5 for domestic and international students; for winter admission, 11/1 for domestic and international students. Applications are processed on a rolling basis. Application fee: $65 ($75 for international students). Electronic applications accepted. *Expenses:* Tuition, state resident: full-time $17,784; part-time $1116 per credit hour. Tuition, nonresident: full-time $35,944; part-time $2125 per credit hour. International tuition: $35,994 full-time. Required fees: $95 per semester. Tuition and fees vary according to course load, degree level and program. *Financial support:* In 2010–11, 61 students received support, including 13 fellowships with full tuition reimbursements available (averaging $26,500 per year), 28 research assistantships with full tuition reimbursements available (averaging $26,500 per year), 21 teaching assistantships with full tuition reimbursements available (averaging $26,500 per year); health care benefits also available. *Faculty research:* Cell biology, microbiology, neurobiology and physiology, developmental biology and plant molecular biology. *Unit head:* Patrick J. Flannery, Administrative Manager, 734-936-2997, Fax: 734-615-6337, E-mail: pjflan@umich.edu. *Application contact:* Mary Carr, Graduate Coordinator, 734-615-1635, Fax: 734-764-0884, E-mail: carrmm@umich.edu.

University of Michigan, Rackham Graduate School, Program in Biomedical Sciences (PIBS), Interdisciplinary Program in Cellular and Molecular Biology, Ann Arbor, MI 48109. Offers PhD. *Faculty:* 153 part-time/adjunct (43 women). *Students:* 74 full-time (37 women); includes 19 minority (1 Black or African American, non-Hispanic/Latino; 1 American Indian or Alaska Native, non-Hispanic/Latino; 9 Asian, non-Hispanic/Latino; 8 Hispanic/Latino). Average age 26. In 2010, 9 doctorates awarded. *Degree requirements:* For doctorate, comprehensive exam, thesis/dissertation, oral defense of dissertation, preliminary exam. *Entrance requirements:* For doctorate, GRE General Test, GRE Subject Test. *Expenses:* Tuition, state resident: full-time $17,784; part-time $1116 per credit hour. Tuition, nonresident: full-time $35,944; part-time $2125 per credit hour. International tuition: $35,994 full-time. Required fees: $95 per semester. Tuition and fees vary according to course load, degree level and program. *Financial support:* In 2010–11, 74 students received support, including 21 fellowships with tuition reimbursements available (averaging $26,500 per year), 53 research assistantships with tuition reimbursements available (averaging $26,500 per year); teaching assistantships, scholarships/grants also available. *Faculty research:* Genetics, genomics, gene regulation, models of disease, microbes. Total annual research expenditures: $20 million. *Unit head:* Dr. Jessica Schwartz, Director, 734-764-5428, Fax: 734-647-6232, E-mail: jeschwar@umich.edu. *Application contact:* Catherine A. Mitchell, Student Services Associate I, 734-764-5428, Fax: 734-647-6232, E-mail: cmbgrad@umich.edu.

University of Minnesota, Duluth, Medical School, Department of Biochemistry, Molecular Biology and Biophysics, Duluth, MN 55812-2496. Offers biochemistry, molecular biology and biophysics (MS); biology and biophysics (PhD); social, administrative, and clinical pharmacy (MS, PhD); toxicology (MS, PhD). *Faculty:* 10 full-time (3 women). *Students:* 16 full-time (5 women); includes 3 Asian, non-Hispanic/Latino. Average age 29. 7 applicants, 29% accepted, 2 enrolled. In 2010, 1 master's, 1 doctorate awarded. Terminal master's awarded for partial completion of doctoral program. *Degree requirements:* For master's, comprehensive exam, thesis; for doctorate, comprehensive exam, thesis/dissertation. *Entrance requirements:* For master's and doctorate, GRE General Test. Additional exam requirements/recommendations for international students: Required—TOEFL. *Application deadline:* For winter admission, 1/3 for domestic students, 1/2 for international students; for spring admission, 3/15 priority date for domestic and international students. Application fee: $75 ($95 for international students). Electronic applications accepted. *Financial support:* In 2010–11, 8 students received support, including research assistantships with full tuition reimbursements available (averaging $27,300 per year), teaching assistantships with full tuition reimbursements available (averaging $27,300 per year); career-related internships or fieldwork, scholarships/grants, health care benefits, and unspecified assistantships also available. Financial award application deadline: 9/1. *Faculty research:* Intestinal cancer biology; hepatotoxins and mitochondriopathies; toxicology; cell cycle regulation in stem cells; neurobiology of brain development, trace metal function and blood-brain barrier; hibernation biology. Total annual research expenditures: $1.5 million. *Unit head:* Dr. Lester R. Drewes, Professor/Head, 218-726-7925, Fax: 218-726-8014, E-mail: ldrewes@d.umn.edu. *Application contact:* Cheryl Beeman, Executive Office and Administrative Assistant, 218-726-6354, Fax: 218-726-8014, E-mail: ahcd@d.umn.edu.

University of Minnesota, Twin Cities Campus, Graduate School, College of Biological Sciences, Biochemistry, Molecular Biology and Biophysics Graduate Program, Minneapolis, MN 55455-0213. Offers PhD. *Degree requirements:* For doctorate, thesis/dissertation. *Entrance requirements:* For doctorate, GRE, 3 letters of recommendation, more than 1 semester of laboratory experience. Additional exam requirements/recommendations for international students: Required—TOEFL (minimum score 625 paper-based; 263 computer-based; 108 iBT with writing subsection 25 and reading subsection 25) or IELTS (minimum score 7). Electronic applications accepted. *Faculty research:* Microbial biochemistry, biotechnology, molecular biology, regulatory biochemistry, structural biology and biophysics, physical biochemistry, enzymology, physiological chemistry.

University of Minnesota, Twin Cities Campus, Graduate School, Program in Molecular, Cellular, Developmental Biology and Genetics, Minneapolis, MN 55455-0213. Offers genetic counseling (MS); molecular, cellular, developmental biology and genetics (PhD). Terminal master's awarded for partial completion of doctoral program. *Degree requirements:* For master's, thesis optional; for doctorate, thesis/dissertation. *Entrance requirements:* For master's and doctorate, GRE General Test. Additional exam requirements/recommendations for international students: Required—TOEFL (minimum score 625 paper-based; 263 computer-based; 80 iBT). Electronic applications accepted. *Faculty research:* Membrane receptors and membrane transport, cell interactions, cytoskeleton and cell mobility, regulation of gene expression, plant cell and molecular biology.

University of Missouri–Kansas City, School of Biological Sciences, Program in Molecular Biology and Biochemistry, Kansas City, MO 64110-2499. Offers PhD. Offered through the School of Graduate Studies. *Faculty:* 42 full-time (11 women). *Students:* 9 full-time (4 women), 6 part-time (4 women); includes 6 minority (4 Asian, non-Hispanic/Latino; 1 Hispanic/Latino; 1 Two or more races, non-Hispanic/Latino), 3 international. Average age 25. 34 applicants, 32% accepted, 10 enrolled. *Degree requirements:* For doctorate, comprehensive exam, thesis/dissertation. *Entrance requirements:* For doctorate, GRE General Test, bachelor's degree in chemistry, biology, or a related discipline; minimum GPA of 3.0. Additional exam requirements/recommendations for international students: Required—TOEFL (minimum score 550 paper-based; 213 computer-based; 80 iBT). *Application deadline:* For fall admission, 2/15 priority date for domestic and international students. Application fee: $45 ($50 for international students). *Expenses:* Tuition, state resident: full-time $5522; part-time $306.80 per credit hour. Tuition, nonresident: full-time $7128; part-time $792 per credit hour. Required fees: $261.15 per term. *Financial support:* Research assistantships with full tuition reimbursements, teaching assistantships with full and partial tuition reimbursements, scholarships/grants, tuition waivers (full and partial), and unspecified assistantships available. Financial award application deadline: 3/1; financial award applicants required to submit FAFSA. *Unit head:* Dr. Henry Miziorko, Head, 816-235-2235, E-mail: miziorkoh@umkc.edu. *Application contact:* Laura Batenic, Information Contact, 816-235-2352, Fax: 816-235-5158, E-mail: batenicl@umkc.edu.

See Display on next page and Close-Up on page 237.

University of Missouri–St. Louis, College of Arts and Sciences, Department of Biology, St. Louis, MO 63121. Offers biotechnology (Certificate); cell and molecular biology (MS, PhD); ecology, evolution and systematics (MS, PhD); tropical biology and conservation (Certificate). Part-time programs available. *Faculty:* 43 full-time (13 women), 2 part-time/adjunct (1 woman). *Students:* 73 full-time (36 women), 63 part-time (36 women); includes 17 minority (6 Black or African American, non-Hispanic/Latino; 9 Asian, non-Hispanic/Latino; 2 Hispanic/Latino), 45 international. Average age 29. 193 applicants, 44% accepted, 44 enrolled. In 2010, 35 master's, 11 doctorates, 6 other advanced degrees awarded. *Degree requirements:* For master's, thesis or alternative; for doctorate, thesis/dissertation, 1 semester of teaching experience. *Entrance requirements:* For master's, 3 letters of recommendation; for doctorate, GRE General Test, 3 letters of recommendation. Additional exam requirements/recommendations for international students: Required—TOEFL. *Application deadline:* For fall admission, 12/1 priority date for domestic and international students; for spring admission, 10/15 priority date for domestic and international students. Applications are processed on a rolling basis. Application fee: $35 ($40 for international students). Electronic applications accepted. *Expenses:* Tuition, state resident: full-time $5522; part-time $306.80 per credit hour. Tuition, nonresident: full-time $14,253; part-time $792.10 per credit hour. Required fees: $658; $49 per credit hour. One-time fee: $12. Tuition and fees vary according to program. *Financial support:* In 2010–11, 30 research

Molecular Biology

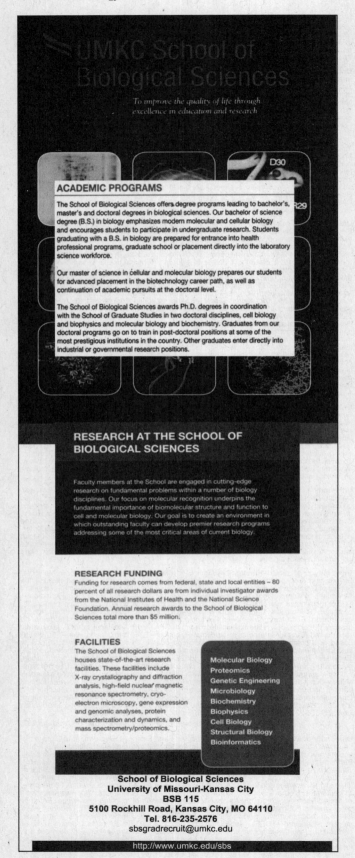

assistantships with full and partial tuition reimbursements (averaging $18,113 per year), 15 teaching assistantships with full and partial tuition reimbursements (averaging $17,514 per year) were awarded; fellowships with full tuition reimbursements, career-related internships or fieldwork and Federal Work-Study also available. Support available to part-time students. Financial award application deadline: 2/1. *Faculty research:* Molecular biology, microbial genetics, animal behavior, tropical ecology, plant systematics. *Unit head:* Dr. Peter Stevens, Director of Graduate Studies, 314-516-6200, Fax: 314-516-6233, E-mail: stevensp@umsl.edu. *Application contact:* 314-516-5458, Fax: 314-516-6996, E-mail: gradadm@umsl.edu.

University of Nebraska Medical Center, Graduate Studies, Department of Biochemistry and Molecular Biology, Omaha, NE 68198. Offers MS, PhD. *Faculty:* 17 full-time (2 women), 28 part-time/adjunct (5 women). *Students:* 28 full-time (13 women), 9 part-time (7 women); includes 1 Asian, non-Hispanic/Latino; 1 Hispanic/Latino, 19 international. Average age 27. 30 applicants, 37% accepted, 11 enrolled. In 2010, 1 master's, 5 doctorates awarded. Terminal master's awarded for partial completion of doctoral program. *Degree requirements:* For master's, comprehensive exam, thesis; for doctorate, comprehensive exam, thesis/dissertation. *Entrance requirements:* For master's and doctorate, GRE General Test. Additional exam requirements/ recommendations for international students: Required—TOEFL (minimum score 550 paper-based; 213 computer-based). *Application deadline:* For fall admission, 6/1 for domestic students, 4/1 for international students; for spring admission, 10/1 for domestic students, 8/1 for international students. Application fee: $45. Electronic applications accepted. *Expenses:* Tuition, state resident: part-time $198.25 per semester hour. Required fees: $63 per semester. *Financial support:* In 2010–11, 10 students received support, including fellowships with full tuition reimbursements available (averaging $21,000 per year), research assistantships with full tuition reimbursements available (averaging $21,000 per year); institutionally sponsored loans also available. Support available to part-time students. Financial award application deadline: 2/15. *Faculty research:* Recombinant DNA, cancer biology, diabetes and drug metabolism, biochemical endocrinology. Total annual research expenditures: $2.5 million. *Unit head:* Dr. Surinder K. Batra, Chairman, Graduate Committee, 402-559-5455, Fax: 402-559-6650, E-mail: biochem@unmc.edu. *Application contact:* Jennifer Pace, Office Associate, 402-559-4417.

University of Nevada, Reno, Graduate School, Interdisciplinary Program in Cell and Molecular Biology, Reno, NV 89557. Offers MS, PhD. Terminal master's awarded for partial completion of doctoral program. *Degree requirements:* For master's, thesis; for doctorate, thesis/dissertation. *Entrance requirements:* For master's, GRE Subject Test (recommended), minimum GPA of 2.75; for doctorate, GRE Subject Test (recommended), minimum GPA of 3.0. Additional exam requirements/recommendations for international students: Required—TOEFL (minimum score 500 paper-based; 173 computer-based; 61 iBT), IELTS (minimum score 6). Electronic applications accepted. *Expenses:* Tuition, state resident: full-time $2219; part-time $246 per credit. Tuition, nonresident: part-time $510 per credit. International tuition: $9009 full-time. Required fees: $59 per term. One-time fee: $101. Tuition and fees vary according to course load. *Faculty research:* Cellular biology, biophysics, cancer, microbiology, insect biochemistry.

University of New Haven, Graduate School, College of Arts and Sciences, Program in Cellular and Molecular Biology, West Haven, CT 06516-1916. Offers cellular and molecular biology (MS). *Faculty:* 6 full-time (3 women), 8 part-time/adjunct (2 women). *Students:* 34 full-time (25 women), 20 part-time (13 women); includes 1 Black or African American, non-Hispanic/Latino; 1 Asian, non-Hispanic/Latino; 1 Hispanic/Latino, 28 international. Average age 28. 91 applicants, 99% accepted, 27 enrolled. In 2010, 15 master's awarded. *Degree requirements:* For master's, thesis optional. *Entrance requirements:* Additional exam requirements/recommendations for international students: Required—TOEFL (minimum score 520 paper-based; 190 computer-based; 70 iBT), IELTS (minimum score 5.5). *Application deadline:* For fall admission, 5/31 for international students; for winter admission, 10/15 for international students; for spring admission, 1/15 for international students. Applications are processed on a rolling basis. Application fee: $50. Electronic applications accepted. *Financial support:* Career-related internships or fieldwork and Federal Work-Study available. Financial award application deadline: 5/1; financial award applicants required to submit FAFSA. *Unit head:* Dr. Eva Sapi, Coordinator, 203-479-4552. *Application contact:* Eloise Gormley, Director of Graduate Admissions, 203-932-7449, Fax: 203-932-7137, E-mail: gradinfo@newhaven.edu.

University of New Mexico, School of Medicine, Biomedical Sciences Graduate Program, Albuquerque, NM 87131-5196. Offers biochemistry and molecular biology (MS, PhD); cell biology and physiology (MS, PhD); clinical and translational science (Certificate); molecular genetics and microbiology (MS, PhD); neuroscience (MS, PhD); pathology (MS, PhD); toxicology (MS, PhD); university science teaching (Certificate). Part-time programs available. *Faculty:* 33 full-time (14 women), 3 part-time/adjunct (1 woman). *Students:* 94 full-time (57 women), 14 part-time (8 women); includes 24 minority (3 Black or African American, non-Hispanic/Latino; 1 American Indian or Alaska Native, non-Hispanic/Latino; 6 Asian, non-Hispanic/Latino; 13 Hispanic/Latino; 1 Two or more races, non-Hispanic/Latino), 20 international. Average age 30. 135 applicants, 14% accepted, 19 enrolled. In 2010, 2 master's, 19 doctorates, 3 other advanced degrees awarded. Terminal master's awarded for partial completion of doctoral program. *Degree requirements:* For master's, thesis; for doctorate, comprehensive exam, thesis/dissertation. *Entrance requirements:* For master's and doctorate, GRE General Test, minimum undergraduate GPA of 3.0. Additional exam requirements/recommendations for international students: Required—TOEFL. *Application deadline:* For fall admission, 1/1 priority date for domestic students. Applications are processed on a rolling basis. Application fee: $50. Electronic applications accepted. *Expenses:* Tuition, state resident: full-time $5991; part-time $251 per credit hour. Tuition, nonresident: full-time $14,405; part-time $800.20 per credit hour. Tuition and fees vary according to course level, course load, program and reciprocity agreements. *Financial support:* In 2010–11, 99 students received support, including 5 fellowships (averaging $75 per year), 96 research assistantships with full tuition reimbursements available (averaging $17,401 per year), 2 teaching assistantships with full tuition reimbursements available (averaging $2,415 per year); career-related internships or fieldwork, Federal Work-Study, institutionally sponsored loans, scholarships/grants, traineeships, health care benefits, and unspecified assistantships also available. Financial award application deadline: 1/1; financial award applicants required to submit FAFSA. *Faculty research:* Signal transduction, infectious disease, biology of cancer, structural biology, neuroscience. *Unit head:* Laurie G. Hudson, Director, 505-272-1887, Fax: 505-272-8738, E-mail: lhudson@salud.unm.edu. *Application contact:* Angel Cooke-Jackson, Coordinator, 505-272-1887, Fax: 505-272-8738, E-mail: acooke-jackson@salud.unm.edu.

The University of North Carolina at Chapel Hill, Graduate School, College of Arts and Sciences, Department of Biology, Chapel Hill, NC 27599. Offers botany (MA, MS, PhD); cell biology, development, and physiology (MA, MS, PhD); cell motility and cytoskeleton (PhD); ecology and behavior (MA, MS, PhD); genetics and molecular biology (MA, MS, PhD); morphology, systematics, and evolution (MA, MS, PhD). Terminal master's awarded for partial completion of doctoral program. *Degree requirements:* For master's, comprehensive exam, thesis (for some programs); for doctorate, comprehensive exam, thesis/dissertation. *Entrance requirements:* For master's, GRE General Test, GRE Subject Test, 2 semesters of calculus or statistics; 2 semesters of physics, organic chemistry; 3 semesters of biology; for doctorate, GRE General Test, GRE Subject Test, 2 semesters calculus or statistics, 2 semesters physics, organic chemistry, 3 semesters of biology. Additional exam requirements/recommendations for international students: Required—TOEFL (minimum score 550 paper-based; 213 computer-based). Electronic applications accepted. *Faculty research:* Gene expression, biomechanics, yeast genetics, plant ecology, plant molecular biology.

The University of North Carolina at Chapel Hill, School of Medicine and Graduate School, Graduate Programs in Medicine, Curriculum in Genetics and Molecular Biology, Chapel Hill, NC 27599. Offers MS, PhD. *Faculty:* 82 full-time (26 women). *Students:* 78 full-time (45 women); includes 5 Black or African American, non-Hispanic/Latino; 2 Asian, non-Hispanic/Latino; 7 Hispanic/Latino, 4 international. Average age 26. In 2010, 19 doctorates awarded. *Degree requirements:* For doctorate, comprehensive exam, thesis/dissertation. *Entrance requirements:* For doctorate, GRE, minimum GPA of 3.0. Additional exam requirements/

recommendations for international students: Required—TOEFL. *Application deadline:* For fall admission, 1/1 priority date for domestic and international students. Applications are processed on a rolling basis. Application fee: $77. Electronic applications accepted. *Financial support:* In 2010–11, 8 fellowships with full tuition reimbursements (averaging $26,000 per year), 72 research assistantships with full tuition reimbursements (averaging $26,000 per year), 6 teaching assistantships with full tuition reimbursements (averaging $26,000 per year) were awarded; traineeships and tuition waivers (full) also available. *Faculty research:* Telomere replication and germline immortality, experimental evolution in microorganisms, genetic vulnerabilities in tumor genomes, genetics of cell cycle control during Drosophila development, mammalian genetics. *Unit head:* Dr. Robert J. Duronio, Director, 919-962-7749, E-mail: duronio@med.unc.edu. *Application contact:* Sausyty A. Hermreck, Graduate Student Coordinator, 919-966-2681, Fax: 919-966-0401, E-mail: sausytyh@med.unc.edu.

University of North Dakota, Graduate School and Graduate School, Graduate Programs in Medicine, Department of Biochemistry and Molecular Biology, Grand Forks, ND 58202. Offers MS, PhD. *Faculty:* 8 full-time (4 women). *Students:* 16 full-time (8 women), 4 part-time (3 women); includes 1 minority (Black or African American, non-Hispanic/Latino), 7 international. Average age 26. 19 applicants, 26% accepted, 5 enrolled. In 2010, 2 master's, 3 doctorates awarded. *Degree requirements:* For master's, thesis, final exam; for doctorate, comprehensive exam, thesis/dissertation, final exam. *Entrance requirements:* For master's and doctorate, GRE General Test, minimum GPA of 3.0. Additional exam requirements/recommendations for international students: Required—TOEFL (minimum score 550 paper-based; 213 computer-based; 79 iBT), IELTS (minimum score 6.5). *Application deadline:* For fall admission, 2/15 priority date for domestic and international students. Application fee: $35. Electronic applications accepted. *Expenses:* Tuition, state resident: full-time $5857; part-time $306.74 per credit. Tuition, nonresident: full-time $15,666; part-time $729.77 per credit. Required fees: $53.42 per credit. Tuition and fees vary according to course load, program and reciprocity agreements. *Financial support:* In 2010–11, 17 students received support, including 12 research assistantships with full and partial tuition reimbursements available (averaging $13,997 per year), 5 teaching assistantships with full and partial tuition reimbursements available (averaging $13,997 per year); fellowships with full and partial tuition reimbursements available, Federal Work-Study, institutionally sponsored loans, scholarships/grants, health care benefits, tuition waivers (full and partial), and unspecified assistantships also available. Support available to part-time students. Financial award application deadline: 3/15; financial award applicants required to submit FAFSA. *Faculty research:* Glucose-6-phosphatase, guanine nucleotides, carbohydrate and lipid metabolism, cytoskeletal proteins, chromatin structure. Total annual research expenditures: $741,346. *Unit head:* Dr. Min Wu, Graduate Director, 701-777-4875, Fax: 701-777-3527, E-mail: minwu@medicine.nodak.edu. *Application contact:* Matt Anderson, Admissions Specialist, 701-777-2947, Fax: 701-777-3619, E-mail: matthew.anderson@gradschool.und.edu.

University of North Texas, Toulouse Graduate School, College of Arts and Sciences, Department of Biological Sciences, Program in Molecular Biology, Denton, TX 76203. Offers MA, MS, PhD. *Degree requirements:* For master's, variable foreign language requirement, comprehensive exam, thesis (for some programs), oral defense of thesis; for doctorate, one foreign language, comprehensive exam, thesis/dissertation, oral defense of dissertation. *Entrance requirements:* For master's and doctorate, GRE General Test, letters of recommendation. Additional exam requirements/recommendations for international students: Recommended—TOEFL (minimum score 550 paper-based; 213 computer-based). *Application deadline:* Applications are processed on a rolling basis. *Expenses:* Tuition, state resident: full-time $4298; part-time $239 per credit hour. Tuition, nonresident: full-time $10,782; part-time $549 per credit hour. Required fees: $1292; $270 per credit hour. *Financial support:* Applicants required to submit FAFSA. *Faculty research:* Pyrimidine metabolism, enzymology mammalian/plant gene structure, organization and expression. *Application contact:* Graduate Advisor, 940-565-2011, Fax: 940-565-3821.

University of North Texas Health Science Center at Fort Worth, Graduate School of Biomedical Sciences, Fort Worth, TX 76107-2699. Offers anatomy and cell biology (MS, PhD); biochemistry and molecular biology (MS, PhD); biomedical sciences (MS, PhD); biotechnology (MS); forensic genetics (MS); integrative physiology (MS, PhD); medical science (MS); microbiology and immunology (MS, PhD); pharmacology (MS, PhD); science education (MS); DO/MS; DO/PhD. Terminal master's awarded for partial completion of doctoral program. *Degree requirements:* For master's, thesis; for doctorate, thesis/dissertation. *Entrance requirements:* For master's and doctorate, GRE General Test. Additional exam requirements/recommendations for international students: Required—TOEFL. *Expenses:* Contact institution. *Faculty research:* Alzheimer's disease, aging, eye diseases, cancer, cardiovascular disease.

University of Notre Dame, Graduate School, College of Science, Department of Biological Sciences, Notre Dame, IN 46556. Offers aquatic ecology, evolution and environmental biology (MS, PhD); cellular and molecular biology (MS, PhD); genetics (MS, PhD); physiology (MS, PhD); vector biology and parasitology (MS, PhD). Terminal master's awarded for partial completion of doctoral program. *Degree requirements:* For master's, comprehensive exam, thesis; for doctorate, comprehensive exam, thesis/dissertation, candidacy exam. *Entrance requirements:* For master's and doctorate, GRE General Test. Additional exam requirements/recommendations for international students: Required—TOEFL (minimum score 600 paper-based; 250 computer-based; 80 iBT). Electronic applications accepted. *Faculty research:* Tropical disease, molecular genetics, neurobiology, evolutionary biology, aquatic biology.

University of Oklahoma Health Sciences Center, College of Medicine and Graduate College, Graduate Programs in Medicine, Department of Biochemistry and Molecular Biology, Oklahoma City, OK 73190. Offers biochemistry (MS, PhD); molecular biology (MS, PhD). Part-time programs available. Terminal master's awarded for partial completion of doctoral program. *Degree requirements:* For master's, thesis; for doctorate, thesis/dissertation. *Entrance requirements:* For master's, GRE General Test, 2 letters of recommendation; for doctorate, GRE General Test, 3 letters of recommendation. Additional exam requirements/recommendations for international students: Required—TOEFL. *Faculty research:* Gene expression, regulation of transcription, enzyme evolution, melanogenesis, signal transduction.

University of Oregon, Graduate School, College of Arts and Sciences, Department of Biology, Eugene, OR 97403. Offers ecology and evolution (MA, MS, PhD); marine biology (MA, MS, PhD); molecular, cellular and genetic biology (PhD); neuroscience and development (PhD). Terminal master's awarded for partial completion of doctoral program. *Degree requirements:* For master's, thesis (for some programs); for doctorate, thesis/dissertation. *Entrance requirements:* For master's and doctorate, GRE General Test, minimum GPA of 3.2. Additional exam requirements/recommendations for international students: Required—TOEFL. *Faculty research:* Developmental neurobiology; evolution, population biology, and quantitative genetics; regulation of gene expression; biochemistry of marine organisms.

University of Ottawa, Faculty of Graduate and Postdoctoral Studies, Faculty of Medicine, Department of Cellular and Molecular Medicine, Ottawa, ON K1H 8M5, Canada. Offers M Sc, PhD. *Degree requirements:* For master's, thesis, seminar; for doctorate, comprehensive exam, thesis/dissertation, seminar. *Entrance requirements:* For master's, honors degree or equivalent, minimum B average; for doctorate, master's degree, minimum B+ average. Electronic applications accepted. *Faculty research:* Physiology, pharmacology, growth and development.

University of Pennsylvania, Perelman School of Medicine, Biomedical Graduate Studies, Graduate Group in Cell and Molecular Biology, Philadelphia, PA 19104. Offers cancer biology (PhD); cell biology and physiology (PhD); developmental stem cell regenerative biology (PhD); gene therapy and vaccines (PhD); genetics and gene regulation (PhD); microbiology, virology, and parasitology (PhD); MD/PhD; VMD/PhD. *Faculty:* 299. *Students:* 315 full-time (166 women); includes 13 Black or African American, non-Hispanic/Latino; 1 American Indian or Alaska Native, non-Hispanic/Latino; 44 Asian, non-Hispanic/Latino; 18 Hispanic/Latino, 37 international. 579 applicants, 21% accepted, 49 enrolled. In 2010, 53 doctorates awarded. *Degree requirements:* For doctorate, thesis/dissertation. *Entrance requirements:* For doctorate, GRE

General Test. Additional exam requirements/recommendations for international students: Required—TOEFL. *Application deadline:* For fall admission, 12/8 priority date for domestic and international students. Applications are processed on a rolling basis. Application fee: $70. Electronic applications accepted. *Expenses:* Tuition: Full-time $25,660; part-time $4758 per course. Required fees: $2152; $270 per course. Tuition and fees vary according to course load, degree level and program. *Financial support:* In 2010–11, 315 students received support; fellowships, research assistantships, scholarships/grants, traineeships, and unspecified assistantships available. Financial award application deadline: 12/8. *Unit head:* Dr. Daniel Kessler, Graduate Group Chair, 215-898-2180, E-mail: raperj@mail.med.upenn.edu. *Application contact:* Meagan Schofer, Coordinator, 215-898-9536, Fax: 215-573-2104, E-mail: camb@mailmed.upenn.edu.

University of Pittsburgh, School of Arts and Sciences, Department of Biological Sciences, Program in Molecular, Cellular, and Developmental Biology, Pittsburgh, PA 15260. Offers PhD. *Faculty:* 25 full-time (6 women). *Students:* 56 full-time (35 women); includes 3 Asian, non-Hispanic/Latino, 17 international. Average age 23. 181 applicants, 11% accepted, 7 enrolled. In 2010, 6 doctorates awarded. *Degree requirements:* For doctorate, comprehensive exam, thesis/dissertation, completion of research integrity module. *Entrance requirements:* For doctorate, GRE General Test, GRE Subject Test. Additional exam requirements/recommendations for international students: Required—TOEFL (minimum score 550 paper-based; 213 computer-based; 80 iBT). *Application deadline:* For fall admission, 1/15 priority date for domestic students, 12/15 priority date for international students. Applications are processed on a rolling basis. Application fee: $0 ($50 for international students). Electronic applications accepted. *Expenses:* Tuition, state resident: full-time $17,304; part-time $701 per credit. Tuition, nonresident: full-time $29,554; part-time $1210 per credit. Required fees: $740; $214 per term. Tuition and fees vary according to program. *Financial support:* In 2010–11, 25 fellowships with full tuition reimbursements (averaging $28,382 per year), 116 research assistantships with full tuition reimbursements (averaging $25,058 per year), 22 teaching assistantships with full tuition reimbursements (averaging $23,907 per year) were awarded; Federal Work-Study, scholarships/grants, traineeships, health care benefits, and tuition waivers (full) also available. *Unit head:* Dr. Gerard L. Campbell, Associate Professor, 412-624-6812, Fax: 412-624-4759, E-mail: camp@pitt.edu. *Application contact:* Cathleen M. Barr, Graduate Administrator, 412-624-4268, Fax: 412-624-4759, E-mail: cbarr@pitt.edu.

University of Pittsburgh, School of Medicine and School of Arts and Sciences, Program in Integrative Molecular Biology, Pittsburgh, PA 15260. Offers PhD. *Faculty:* 29 full-time (10 women). *Students:* 19 full-time (12 women); includes 1 Asian, non-Hispanic/Latino, 10 international. Average age 25. 43 applicants, 16% accepted, 4 enrolled. In 2010, 3 doctorates awarded. *Degree requirements:* For doctorate, comprehensive exam, thesis/dissertation. *Entrance requirements:* For doctorate, GRE, minimum GPA of 3.7, 3 letters of reference. Additional exam requirements/recommendations for international students: Required—TOEFL (minimum score 650 paper-based; 280 computer-based; 114 iBT), IELTS (minimum score 7.5). *Application deadline:* For fall admission, 1/7 for domestic and international students. Application fee: $0. Electronic applications accepted. *Expenses:* Tuition, state resident: full-time $17,304; part-time $701 per credit. Tuition, nonresident: full-time $29,554; part-time $1210 per credit. Required fees: $740; $214 per term. Tuition and fees vary according to program. *Financial support:* In 2010–11, 5 fellowships with full tuition reimbursements (averaging $27,326 per year), 12 research assistantships with full tuition reimbursements (averaging $24,650 per year) were awarded; institutionally sponsored loans, scholarships/grants, traineeships, and unspecified assistantships also available. *Faculty research:* Cellular, molecular, developmental biology; genomics; proteomics and gene function. *Unit head:* Dr. Alan Wells, Program Director, 412-648-8975, Fax: 412-648-1077, E-mail: pimbinfo@medschool.pitt.edu. *Application contact:* Jennifer L. Walker, Program Coordinator, 412-648-8957, Fax: 412-648-1077, E-mail: pimbinfo@medschool.pitt.edu.

University of Puerto Rico, Río Piedras, College of Natural Sciences, Department of Biology, San Juan, PR 00931-3300. Offers ecology/systematics (MS, PhD); evolution/genetics (MS, PhD); molecular/cellular biology (MS, PhD); neuroscience (MS, PhD). Part-time programs available. *Degree requirements:* For master's, one foreign language, comprehensive exam, thesis; for doctorate, one foreign language, comprehensive exam, thesis/dissertation. *Entrance requirements:* For master's, GRE Subject Test, interview, minimum GPA of 3.0, letter of recommendation; for doctorate, GRE Subject Test, interview, master's degree, minimum GPA of 3.0, letter of recommendation. *Faculty research:* Environmental, poblational and systematic biology.

University of Rhode Island, Graduate School, College of the Environment and Life Sciences, Department of Cell and Molecular Biology, Kingston, RI 02881. Offers biochemistry (MS, PhD); clinical laboratory sciences (MS), including biotechnology, clinical laboratory science, cytopathology; microbiology (MS, PhD); molecular genetics (MS, PhD). Part-time programs available. *Faculty:* 13 full-time (5 women), 2 part-time/adjunct (1 woman). *Students:* 32 full-time (15 women), 37 part-time (23 women); includes 10 minority (5 Black or African American, non-Hispanic/Latino; 2 Asian, non-Hispanic/Latino; 3 Hispanic/Latino), 4 international. In 2010, 29 master's, 3 doctorates awarded. *Degree requirements:* For master's, comprehensive exam (for some programs); for doctorate, comprehensive exam. *Entrance requirements:* For master's and doctorate, GRE, 2 letters of recommendation. Additional exam requirements/recommendations for international students: Required—TOEFL (minimum score 550 paper-based; 213 computer-based). *Application deadline:* For fall admission, 7/15 for domestic students, 2/1 for international students; for spring admission, 11/15 for domestic students, 7/15 for international students. Application fee: $65. Electronic applications accepted. *Expenses:* Tuition, state resident: full-time $9588; part-time $533 per credit hour. Tuition, nonresident: full-time $22,968; part-time $1276 per credit hour. Required fees: $1282; $68 per semester. Tuition and fees vary according to program. *Financial support:* In 2010–11, 3 research assistantships with full and partial tuition reimbursements (averaging $11,653 per year), 12 teaching assistantships with full and partial tuition reimbursements (averaging $12,379 per year) were awarded. Financial award application deadline: 7/15; financial award applicants required to submit FAFSA. *Faculty research:* Genomics and Sequencing Center: an interdisciplinary genomics research and undergraduate and graduate student training program which provides researchers access to cutting-edge technologies in the field of genomics. Total annual research expenditures: $3.5 million. *Unit head:* Dr. Jay Sperry, Chairperson, 401-874-2201, Fax: 401-874-2202, E-mail: jsperry@mail.uri.edu. *Application contact:* Dr. Jay Sperry, Chairperson, 401-874-2201, Fax: 401-874-2202, E-mail: jsperry@mail.uri.edu.

University of South Carolina, The Graduate School, College of Arts and Sciences, Department of Biological Sciences, Graduate Training Program in Molecular, Cellular, and Developmental Biology, Columbia, SC 29208. Offers MS, PhD. *Degree requirements:* For master's, one foreign language, thesis; for doctorate, one foreign language, thesis/dissertation. *Entrance requirements:* For master's and doctorate, GRE General Test, minimum GPA of 3.0 in science. Electronic applications accepted. *Faculty research:* Marine ecology, population and evolutionary biology, molecular biology and genetics, development.

The University of South Dakota, School of Medicine and Health Sciences and Graduate School, Biomedical Sciences Graduate Program, Cellular and Molecular Biology Group, Vermillion, SD 57069-2390. Offers MS, PhD. Terminal master's awarded for partial completion of doctoral program. *Degree requirements:* For master's, thesis; for doctorate, comprehensive exam, thesis/dissertation. *Entrance requirements:* For master's and doctorate, GRE General Test, GRE Subject Test, minimum GPA of 3.0. Additional exam requirements/recommendations for international students: Required—TOEFL (minimum score 550 paper-based; 213 computer-based; 80 iBT), IELTS (minimum score 6). Electronic applications accepted. *Expenses:* Contact institution. *Faculty research:* Molecular aspects of protein and DNA, neurochemistry and energy transduction, gene regulation, cellular development.

University of Southern California, Graduate School, Dana and David Dornsife College of Letters, Arts and Sciences, Department of Biological Sciences, Program in Molecular and

Molecular Biology

University of Southern California (continued)
Computational Biology, Los Angeles, CA 90089. Offers computational biology and bioinformatics (PhD); molecular biology (PhD). *Faculty:* 40 full-time (7 women). *Students:* 100 full-time (48 women), 3 part-time (2 women); includes 19 minority (3 Black or African American, non-Hispanic/Latino; 10 Asian, non-Hispanic/Latino; 4 Hispanic/Latino; 2 Two or more races, non-Hispanic/Latino), 58 international. 178 applicants, 25% accepted, 24 enrolled. In 2010, 15 doctorates awarded. *Median time to degree:* Of those who began their doctoral program in fall 2002, 100% received their degree in 8 years or less. *Degree requirements:* For doctorate, comprehensive exam, thesis/dissertation, qualifying examination, dissertation defense. *Entrance requirements:* For doctorate, GRE, 3 letters of recommendation, personal statement, resume, minimum GPA of 3.0. Additional exam requirements/recommendations for international students: Required—TOEFL (minimum score 600 paper-based; 250 computer-based; 100 iBT). *Application deadline:* For fall admission, 12/1 priority date for domestic students, 11/1 priority date for international students. Application fee: $85. Electronic applications accepted. *Expenses:* Tuition: Full-time $31,240; part-time $1420 per unit. Required fees: $600. One-time fee: $35 full-time. Full-time tuition and fees vary according to degree level and program. *Financial support:* In 2010–11, 100 students received support, including 31 fellowships with full tuition reimbursements available (averaging $29,000 per year), 48 research assistantships with full tuition reimbursements available (averaging $28,000 per year), 21 teaching assistantships with full tuition reimbursements available (averaging $28,000 per year); career-related internships or fieldwork, scholarships/grants, traineeships, health care benefits, and unspecified assistantships also available. Financial award application deadline: 12/1. *Faculty research:* Biochemistry and molecular biology; genomics; computational biology and bioinformatics; cell and developmental biology, and genetics; DNA replication and repair, and cancer biology. *Unit head:* Dr. Myron Goodman, Professor of Biological Sciences and Chemistry/Director of the MCB Research Section, 213-740-5190, E-mail: mgoodman@usc.edu. *Application contact:* Catherine Atienza, Student Services Advisor I, 213-740-5188, E-mail: catherine.atienza@usc.edu.

University of Southern California, Keck School of Medicine and Graduate School, Graduate Programs in Medicine, Department of Biochemistry and Molecular Biology, Los Angeles, CA 90089. Offers MS, PhD. *Faculty:* 24 full-time (6 women). *Students:* 28 full-time (15 women); includes 7 minority (1 Black or African American, non-Hispanic/Latino; 5 Asian, non-Hispanic/Latino; 1 Hispanic/Latino), 19 international. Average age 24. 29 applicants, 93% accepted, 13 enrolled. In 2010, 7 master's, 18 doctorates awarded. Terminal master's awarded for partial completion of doctoral program. *Degree requirements:* For master's, thesis; for doctorate, comprehensive exam, thesis/dissertation. *Entrance requirements:* For master's and doctorate, GRE General Test, minimum GPA of 3.0. Additional exam requirements/recommendations for international students: Required—TOEFL (minimum score 600 paper-based; 250 computer-based; 100 iBT). *Application deadline:* For fall admission, 4/15 priority date for domestic and international students. Applications are processed on a rolling basis. Application fee: $85 for international students. Electronic applications accepted. *Expenses:* Tuition: Full-time $31,240; part-time $1420 per unit. Required fees: $600. One-time fee: $35 full-time. Full-time tuition and fees vary according to degree level and program. *Financial support:* In 2010–11, 5 students received support, including 1 fellowship with tuition reimbursement available (averaging $27,600 per year), 12 research assistantships with tuition reimbursements available (averaging $27,600 per year), 3 teaching assistantships with tuition reimbursements available (averaging $27,600 per year); Federal Work-Study, institutionally sponsored loans, scholarships/grants, health care benefits, and unspecified assistantships also available. Financial award application deadline: 5/5. *Faculty research:* Molecular genetics, gene expression, membrane biochemistry, metabolic regulation, cancer biology. *Unit head:* Dr. Michael R. Stallcup, Chair, 323-442-1145, Fax: 323-442-1224, E-mail: stallcup@usc.edu. *Application contact:* Anne L. Rice, Student Services Coordinator, 323-442-1145, Fax: 323-442-1224, E-mail: annvazqu@usc.edu.

University of Southern California, Keck School of Medicine and Graduate School, Graduate Programs in Medicine, Department of Preventive Medicine, Division of Biostatistics, Los Angeles, CA 90089. Offers applied biostatistics/epidemiology (MS); biostatistics (MS, PhD); epidemiology (PhD); genetic epidemiology and statistical genetics (PhD); molecular epidemiology (MS, PhD). *Faculty:* 71 full-time (30 women). *Students:* 103 full-time (63 women); includes 21 Asian, non-Hispanic/Latino; 4 Hispanic/Latino, 55 international. Average age 29. 79 applicants, 52% accepted, 18 enrolled. In 2010, 6 master's, 4 doctorates awarded. Terminal master's awarded for partial completion of doctoral program. *Degree requirements:* For master's, thesis; for doctorate, thesis/dissertation. *Entrance requirements:* For master's and doctorate, GRE General Test, GRE Subject Test, minimum GPA of 3.0. Additional exam requirements/recommendations for international students: Required—TOEFL (minimum score 600 paper-based; 250 computer-based; 100 iBT). *Application deadline:* For fall admission, 12/1 priority date for domestic students, 12/1 for international students. Application fee: $85. Electronic applications accepted. *Expenses:* Tuition: Full-time $31,240; part-time $1420 per unit. Required fees: $600. One-time fee: $35 full-time. Full-time tuition and fees vary according to degree level and program. *Financial support:* In 2010–11, 3 fellowships with full tuition reimbursements (averaging $27,600 per year), 50 research assistantships with full tuition reimbursements (averaging $27,600 per year), 24 teaching assistantships with full and partial tuition reimbursements (averaging $15,525 per year) were awarded; career-related internships or fieldwork, Federal Work-Study, institutionally sponsored loans, scholarships/grants, health care benefits, and unspecified assistantships also available. Financial award application deadline: 5/3. *Faculty research:* Clinical trials in ophthalmology and cancer research, methods of analysis for epidemiological studies, genetic epidemiology. Total annual research expenditures: $1.3 million. *Unit head:* Dr. Stanley P. Azen, Co-Director, 323-442-1810, Fax: 323-442-2993, E-mail: mtrujill@usc.edu. *Application contact:* Mary L. Trujillo, Student Adviser, 323-442-1810, Fax: 323-442-2993, E-mail: mtrujill@usc.edu.

University of Southern California, Keck School of Medicine and Graduate School, Program in Genetic, Molecular and Cellular Biology, Los Angeles, CA 90089. Offers PhD. *Faculty:* 234 full-time (64 women). *Students:* 132 full-time (75 women); includes 4 Black or African American, non-Hispanic/Latino; 19 Asian, non-Hispanic/Latino; 4 Hispanic/Latino, 78 international. Average age 29. 350 applicants, 27% accepted, 43 enrolled. In 2010, 16 doctorates awarded. *Degree requirements:* For doctorate, comprehensive exam, thesis/dissertation. *Entrance requirements:* For doctorate, GRE, minimum GPA of 3.0. Additional exam requirements/recommendations for international students: Required—TOEFL (minimum score 600 paper-based; 250 computer-based; 100 iBT). *Application deadline:* For fall admission, 12/1 priority date for domestic and international students. Application fee: $85. Electronic applications accepted. *Expenses:* Tuition: Full-time $31,240; part-time $1420 per unit. Required fees: $600. One-time fee: $35 full-time. Full-time tuition and fees vary according to degree level and program. *Financial support:* In 2010–11, 122 students received support, including 8 fellowships (averaging $27,600 per year), 122 research assistantships with full tuition reimbursements available (averaging $27,600 per year), 2 teaching assistantships with full tuition reimbursements available (averaging $27,600 per year); institutionally sponsored loans, scholarships/grants, traineeships, health care benefits, and unspecified assistantships also available. Financial award application deadline: 5/5; financial award applicants required to submit FAFSA. *Unit head:* Dr. Henry Sucov, Director, 323-442-1475, Fax: 323-442-1199, E-mail: sucov@usc.edu. *Application contact:* Dawn Burke, Student Program Coordinator, 323-442-1475, Fax: 323-442-1199, E-mail: pibbs@usc.edu.

University of Southern Maine, School of Applied Science, Engineering, and Technology, Program in Applied Medical Sciences, Portland, ME 04104-9300. Offers MS. Part-time programs available. *Degree requirements:* For master's, thesis. *Entrance requirements:* For master's, GRE General Test, minimum GPA of 3.0. Additional exam requirements/recommendations for international students: Required—TOEFL. Electronic applications accepted. *Faculty research:* Flow cytometry, cancer, epidemiology, monoclonal antibodies, DNA diagnostics.

University of Southern Mississippi, Graduate School, College of Science and Technology, Department of Biological Sciences, Hattiesburg, MS 39406-0001. Offers environmental biology (MS, PhD); marine biology (MS, PhD); microbiology (MS, PhD); molecular biology (MS, PhD).

Faculty: 27 full-time (6 women). *Students:* 54 full-time (29 women), 5 part-time (4 women); includes 2 Black or African American, non-Hispanic/Latino; 4 Two or more races, non-Hispanic/Latino, 17 international. Average age 32. 54 applicants, 48% accepted, 13 enrolled. In 2010, 4 master's, 4 doctorates awarded. Terminal master's awarded for partial completion of doctoral program. *Degree requirements:* For master's, comprehensive exam, thesis; for doctorate, comprehensive exam, thesis/dissertation. *Entrance requirements:* For master's, GRE General Test, minimum GPA of 3.0 on last 60 hours; for doctorate, GRE General Test, minimum GPA of 3.5. Additional exam requirements/recommendations for international students: Required—TOEFL, IELTS. *Application deadline:* For fall admission, 3/1 priority date for domestic students, 3/1 for international students; for spring admission, 1/10 priority date for domestic and international students. Applications are processed on a rolling basis. Application fee: $50. *Financial support:* In 2010–11, 25 research assistantships with full tuition reimbursements (averaging $9,700 per year), 33 teaching assistantships with full tuition reimbursements (averaging $10,600 per year) were awarded; Federal Work-Study, scholarships/grants, health care benefits, and unspecified assistantships also available. Financial award application deadline: 3/15; financial award applicants required to submit FAFSA. *Unit head:* Dr. Glenmore Shearer, Chair, 601-266-4748, Fax: 601-266-5797. *Application contact:* Dr. Jake Schaefer, Director of Graduate Studies, 601-266-4748, Fax: 601-266-5797.

University of South Florida, Graduate School, College of Arts and Sciences, Department of Biology, Tampa, FL 33620-9951. Offers cell biology and molecular biology (MS); coastal marine biology (MS); coastal marine biology and ecology (PhD); conservation biology (MS, PhD); molecular and cell biology (PhD). Part-time programs available. *Faculty:* 8 full-time (4 women). *Students:* 85 full-time (50 women), 8 part-time (all women); includes 1 Black or African American, non-Hispanic/Latino; 3 Asian, non-Hispanic/Latino; 7 Hispanic/Latino, 12 international. Average age 27. 122 applicants, 30% accepted, 34 enrolled. In 2010, 10 master's, 9 doctorates awarded. *Degree requirements:* For master's, comprehensive exam, thesis (for some programs); for doctorate, comprehensive exam, thesis/dissertation. *Entrance requirements:* For master's and doctorate, GRE General Test, minimum GPA of 3.0. Additional exam requirements/recommendations for international students: Required—TOEFL (minimum score 570 paper-based; 213 computer-based). *Application deadline:* For fall admission, 2/15 priority date for domestic students, 1/2 for international students; for spring admission, 8/1 for domestic students, 6/1 for international students. Application fee: $30. Electronic applications accepted. *Financial support:* In 2010–11, 35 research assistantships (averaging $17,940 per year), 38 teaching assistantships with tuition reimbursements (averaging $16,621 per year) were awarded; unspecified assistantships also available. Financial award application deadline: 6/30; financial award applicants required to submit FAFSA. Total annual research expenditures: $4.5 million. *Unit head:* Susan Bell, Co-Chairperson, 813-974-6210, Fax: 813-974-2876, E-mail: sbell@cas.usf.edu. *Application contact:* James Garey, Graduate Advisor, 813-974-8434, Fax: 813-974-3263, E-mail: grarey@cas.usf.edu.

The University of Texas at Austin, Graduate School, Institute for Cellular and Molecular Biology, Austin, TX 78712-1111. Offers PhD.

The University of Texas at Dallas, School of Natural Sciences and Mathematics, Program in Biology, Richardson, TX 75080. Offers bioinformatics and computational biology (MS); biotechnology (MS); molecular and cell biology (MS, PhD). Part-time and evening/weekend programs available. *Faculty:* 18 full-time (3 women), 1 part-time/adjunct (0 women). *Students:* 109 full-time (61 women), 19 part-time (7 women); includes 22 minority (5 Black or African American, non-Hispanic/Latino; 14 Asian, non-Hispanic/Latino; 3 Hispanic/Latino), 82 international. Average age 26. 331 applicants, 37% accepted, 38 enrolled. In 2010, 36 master's, 5 doctorates awarded. *Degree requirements:* For master's, thesis optional; for doctorate, thesis/dissertation, publishable paper. *Entrance requirements:* For master's and doctorate, GRE (minimum combined score of 1000 on verbal and quantitative). Additional exam requirements/recommendations for international students: Required—TOEFL (minimum score 550 paper-based; 215 computer-based; 80 iBT). *Application deadline:* For fall admission, 7/15 for domestic students, 5/1 priority date for international students; for spring admission, 11/15 for domestic students, 9/1 priority date for international students. Applications are processed on a rolling basis. Application fee: $50 ($100 for international students). Electronic applications accepted. *Expenses:* Tuition, state resident: full-time $10,248; part-time $569 per credit hour. Tuition, nonresident: full-time $18,544; part-time $1030 per credit hour. Tuition and fees vary according to course load. *Financial support:* In 2010–11, 58 students received support, including 19 research assistantships with partial tuition reimbursements available (averaging $13,403 per year), 32 teaching assistantships with partial tuition reimbursements available (averaging $14,513 per year); career-related internships or fieldwork, Federal Work-Study, institutionally sponsored loans, scholarships/grants, and unspecified assistantships also available. Support available to part-time students. Financial award application deadline: 4/30; financial award applicants required to submit FAFSA. *Faculty research:* Role of mitochondria in neurodegenerative diseases, protein-DNA interactions in site-specific recombination, eukaryotic gene expression, bio-nanotechnology, sickle cell research. *Unit head:* Dr. Li Zhang, Department Head, 972-883-6032, Fax: 972-883-2502, E-mail: li.zhang@utdallas.edu. *Application contact:* Dr. Lawrence Reitzer, Graduate Advisor, 972-883-2502, Fax: 972-883-2402, E-mail: reitzer@utdallas.edu.

The University of Texas Health Science Center at Houston, Graduate School of Biomedical Sciences, Program in Biochemistry and Molecular Biology, Houston, TX 77225-0036. Offers MS, PhD, MD/PhD. Terminal master's awarded for partial completion of doctoral program. *Degree requirements:* For master's, thesis; for doctorate, thesis/dissertation. *Entrance requirements:* For master's and doctorate, GRE General Test. Additional exam requirements/recommendations for international students: Required—TOEFL. Electronic applications accepted. *Faculty research:* Biochemistry, membrane biology, macromolecular structure, structural biophysics, molecular models of human disease, molecular biology of the cell.

The University of Texas Health Science Center at Houston, Graduate School of Biomedical Sciences, Program in Cell and Regulatory Biology, Houston, TX 77225-0036. Offers MS, PhD, MD/PhD. Terminal master's awarded for partial completion of doctoral program. *Degree requirements:* For master's, thesis; for doctorate, thesis/dissertation. *Entrance requirements:* For master's and doctorate, GRE General Test. Additional exam requirements/recommendations for international students: Required—TOEFL. Electronic applications accepted. *Faculty research:* Pharmacology, cell biology, physiology, signal transduction, systems biology.

University of the Sciences in Philadelphia, College of Graduate Studies, Misher College of Arts and Sciences, Program in Cell and Molecular Biology, Philadelphia, PA 19104-4495. Offers PhD.

University of Utah, School of Medicine, Program in Molecular Biology, Salt Lake City, UT 84132. Offers PhD. *Degree requirements:* For doctorate, thesis/dissertation, preliminary exams. *Entrance requirements:* For doctorate, GRE General Test, minimum GPA of 3.0. Additional exam requirements/recommendations for international students: Required—TOEFL (minimum score 500 paper-based; 173 computer-based; 60 iBT). Electronic applications accepted. *Expenses:* Tuition, area resident: Part-time $179.19 per credit hour. Tuition, state resident: full-time $4384. Tuition, nonresident: full-time $16,684; part-time $630.67 per credit hour. Required fees: $350 per semester. Tuition and fees vary according to course load, degree level and program. *Faculty research:* Biochemistry; cellular, viral, and molecular biology; human genetics; pathology; procaryotic development.

University of Vermont, Graduate College, Cell and Molecular Biology Program, Burlington, VT 05405. Offers MS, PhD. *Students:* 39; includes 3 Asian, non-Hispanic/Latino; 6 Hispanic/Latino, 7 international. 63 applicants, 29% accepted, 7 enrolled. In 2010, 1 master's, 8 doctorates awarded. *Degree requirements:* For master's, thesis; for doctorate, thesis/dissertation. *Entrance requirements:* For master's and doctorate, GRE General Test. Additional exam requirements/recommendations for international students: Required—TOEFL (minimum score 550 paper-based; 213 computer-based; 80 iBT). *Application deadline:* For fall admission, 1/15 priority date for domestic students. Applications are processed on a rolling basis. Application fee: $40. Electronic applications accepted. *Expenses:* Tuition, state resident: part-time $537 per credit hour. Tuition, nonresident: part-time $1355 per credit hour. *Financial support:* Fellowships, research assistantships, teaching assistantships, career-related internships or fieldwork available. Financial award application deadline: 3/1. *Unit head:* Dr. Karen Lounsbury, Coordinator, 802-656-9673. *Application contact:* Dr. Karen Lounsbury, Coordinator, 802-656-9673.

University of Washington, Graduate School, School of Medicine, Graduate Programs in Medicine, Program in Molecular and Cellular Biology, Seattle, WA 98195. Offers PhD. Offered jointly with Fred Hutchinson Cancer Research Center. *Degree requirements:* For doctorate, thesis/dissertation. *Entrance requirements:* For doctorate, GRE General Test, GRE Subject Test. Additional exam requirements/recommendations for international students: Required—TOEFL. Electronic applications accepted.

See Display on page 198 and Close-Up on page 241.

The University of Western Ontario, Faculty of Graduate Studies, Biosciences Division, Department of Plant Sciences, London, ON N6A 5B8, Canada. Offers plant and environmental sciences (M Sc); plant sciences (M Sc, PhD); plant sciences and environmental sciences (PhD); plant sciences and molecular biology (M Sc, PhD). *Degree requirements:* For master's, thesis; for doctorate, thesis/dissertation. *Entrance requirements:* For doctorate, M Sc or equivalent. Additional exam requirements/recommendations for international students: Required—TOEFL. *Faculty research:* Ecology systematics, plant biochemistry and physiology, yeast genetics, molecular biology.

University of Wisconsin–La Crosse, Office of University Graduate Studies, College of Science and Health, Department of Biology, La Crosse, WI 54601-3742. Offers aquatic sciences (MS); biology (MS); cellular and molecular biology (MS); clinical microbiology (MS); microbiology (MS); nurse anesthesia (MS); physiology (MS). Part-time programs available. *Faculty:* 31. *Students:* 23 full-time (14 women), 42 part-time (25 women); includes 4 minority (1 Asian, non-Hispanic/Latino; 3 Hispanic/Latino), 1 international. Average age 28. 100 applicants, 34% accepted, 29 enrolled. In 2010, 20 master's awarded. *Degree requirements:* For master's, comprehensive exam, thesis. *Entrance requirements:* For master's, GRE General Test, minimum GPA of 2.85. Additional exam requirements/recommendations for international students: Required—TOEFL (minimum score 550 paper-based; 213 computer-based; 79 iBT). *Application deadline:* For fall admission, 2/1 priority date for domestic and international students; for spring admission, 1/4 priority date for domestic and international students. Applications are processed on a rolling basis. Application fee: $56. Electronic applications accepted. *Expenses:* Tuition, state resident: full-time $7121; part-time $395.61 per credit. Tuition, nonresident: full-time $16,891; part-time $938.41 per credit. Part-time tuition and fees vary according to course load, program and reciprocity agreements. *Financial support:* In 2010–11, 14 research assistantships with partial tuition reimbursements (averaging $10,124 per year) were awarded; Federal Work-Study, scholarships/grants, health care benefits, and tuition waivers (partial) also available. Support available to part-time students. Financial award application deadline: 3/15; financial award applicants required to submit FAFSA. *Unit head:* Dr. Thomas Volk, Coordinator of Graduate Studies, 608-785-6972, Fax: 608-785-6959, E-mail: volk.thom@uwlax.edu. *Application contact:* Kathryn Kiefer, Director of Admissions, 608-785-8939, E-mail: admissions@uwlax.edu.

University of Wisconsin–Madison, Graduate School, Program in Cellular and Molecular Biology, Madison, WI 53706-1596. Offers PhD. *Degree requirements:* For doctorate, comprehensive exam, thesis/dissertation. *Entrance requirements:* For doctorate, GRE General Test, GRE Subject Test (recommended), minimum GPA of 3.0, lab experience. Additional exam requirements/recommendations for international students: Required—TOEFL (minimum score 580 paper-based; 237 computer-based; 92 iBT). Electronic applications accepted. *Expenses:* Tuition, state resident: full-time $9887; part-time $617.96 per credit. Tuition, nonresident: full-time $24,054; part-time $1503.40 per credit. Required fees: $67.63 per credit. Tuition and fees vary according to reciprocity agreements. *Faculty research:* Virology, cancer biology, transcriptional mechanisms, plant biology, immunology.

University of Wisconsin–Parkside, College of Arts and Sciences, Program in Applied Molecular Biology, Kenosha, WI 53141-2000. Offers MAMB. Part-time programs available. *Faculty:* 9 full-time (3 women). *Students:* 10 full-time (5 women), 4 part-time (1 woman); includes 2 Asian, non-Hispanic/Latino, 2 international. Average age 25. 22 applicants, 64% accepted, 8 enrolled. In 2010, 3 master's awarded. *Degree requirements:* For master's, thesis, oral exam. *Entrance requirements:* For master's, GRE General Test, minimum GPA of 3.0; course work in biology, chemistry, math, physics. Additional exam requirements/recommendations for international students: Required—TOEFL (minimum score 550 paper-based; 213 computer-based). *Application deadline:* For fall admission, 7/1 priority date for domestic students. Applications are processed on a rolling basis. Application fee: $65 ($110 for international students). Electronic applications accepted. *Financial support:* Career-related internships or fieldwork and Federal Work-Study available. Financial award application deadline: 7/1. *Faculty research:* Gene cloning, genome structure, cell cycle effects on gene expression, molecular biology of plant hormones, laboratory toxin production and resistance, RNA stability, pathogencity. Total annual research expenditures: $200,000. *Unit head:* Dr. Daphne Pham, Chair of Molecular Biology Programs, 262-595-2172, Fax: 262-595-2056, E-mail: daphne.pham@uwp.edu. *Application contact:* Dr. Daphne Pham, Chair of Molecular Biology Programs, 262-595-2172, Fax: 262-595-2056, E-mail: daphne.pham@uwp.edu.

University of Wyoming, College of Agriculture and Natural Resources, Department of Molecular Biology, Laramie, WY 82070. Offers MA, MS, PhD. Terminal master's awarded for partial completion of doctoral program. *Degree requirements:* For master's, comprehensive exam (for some programs), thesis; for doctorate, comprehensive exam, thesis/dissertation. *Entrance requirements:* For master's and doctorate, GRE General Test, GRE Subject Test (recommended), minimum GPA of 3.0. Additional exam requirements/recommendations for international students: Required—TOEFL. Electronic applications accepted. *Faculty research:* Protein structure/function, developmental regulation, yeast genetics, bacterial pathogenesis.

University of Wyoming, Graduate Program in Molecular and Cellular Life Sciences, Laramie, WY 82070. Offers PhD. *Degree requirements:* For doctorate, thesis/dissertation, four eight-week laboratory rotations, comprehensive basic practical exam, two-part qualifying exam, seminars, symposium.

Utah State University, School of Graduate Studies, College of Agriculture, Department of Nutrition and Food Sciences, Logan, UT 84322. Offers dietetic administration (MDA); food microbiology and safety (MFMS); nutrition and food sciences (MS, PhD); nutrition science (MS, PhD), including molecular biology. Postbaccalaureate distance learning degree programs offered. *Degree requirements:* For master's, thesis; for doctorate, comprehensive exam, thesis/dissertation, teaching experience. *Entrance requirements:* For master's, GRE General Test, minimum GPA of 3.0, course work in chemistry, biochemistry, physics, math, bacteriology, physiology; for doctorate, GRE General Test, minimum GPA of 3.2, course work in chemistry, MS or manuscript in referred journal. Additional exam requirements/recommendations for international students: Required—TOEFL (minimum score 550 paper-based). Electronic applications accepted. *Faculty research:* Mineral balance, meat microbiology and nitrate interactions, milk ultrafiltration, lactic culture, milk coagulation.

Vanderbilt University, Graduate School and School of Medicine, Department of Molecular Physiology and Biophysics, Nashville, TN 37240-1001. Offers MS, PhD, MD/PhD. *Faculty:* 38 full-time (11 women). *Students:* 33 full-time (25 women), 9 part-time (3 women); includes 2 Black or African American, non-Hispanic/Latino; 1 American Indian or Alaska Native, non-Hispanic/Latino; 3 Hispanic/Latino; 2 Two or more races, non-Hispanic/Latino. Average age 28. In 2010, 8 doctorates awarded. *Degree requirements:* For doctorate, comprehensive exam, thesis/dissertation, preliminary, qualifying, and final exams. *Entrance requirements:* For doctorate, GRE General Test, GRE Subject Test (recommended). Additional exam requirements/recommendations for international students: Required—TOEFL (minimum score 570 paper-based; 230 computer-based; 88 iBT). *Application deadline:* For fall admission, 1/15 for domestic

and international students. Application fee: $0. Electronic applications accepted. *Financial support:* Fellowships with full tuition reimbursements, research assistantships with full tuition reimbursements, Federal Work-Study, institutionally sponsored loans, scholarships/grants, traineeships, health care benefits, and tuition waivers (partial) available. Financial award application deadline: 1/15; financial award applicants required to submit CSS PROFILE or FAFSA. *Faculty research:* Biophysics, cell signaling and gene regulation, human genetics, diabetes and obesity, neuroscience. *Unit head:* Roger Cone, Chair, 615-322-7000, Fax: 615-343-0490. *Application contact:* Michelle Grundy, Assistant Director, 800-373-0675, E-mail: michelle.grundy@vanderbilt.edu.

Virginia Commonwealth University, Medical College of Virginia-Professional Programs, School of Medicine, School of Medicine Graduate Programs, Department of Biochemistry, Richmond, VA 23284-9005. Offers biochemistry (MS, PhD); molecular biology (MS, PhD); MD/PhD. *Faculty:* 28 full-time (3 women). *Students:* 42 full-time (21 women), 5 part-time (3 women); includes 13 minority (4 Black or African American, non-Hispanic/Latino; 7 Asian, non-Hispanic/Latino; 1 Hispanic/Latino; 1 Two or more races, non-Hispanic/Latino), 8 international. 34 applicants, 41% accepted, 7 enrolled. In 2010, 11 master's, 7 doctorates awarded. *Degree requirements:* For master's, thesis; for doctorate, thesis/dissertation, comprehensive oral and written exams. *Entrance requirements:* For master's and doctorate, GRE, MCAT or DAT. *Application deadline:* For fall admission, 2/15 priority date for domestic students. Application fee: $50. Electronic applications accepted. *Expenses:* Tuition, state resident: full-time $4308; part-time $479 per credit hour. Tuition, nonresident: full-time $8942; part-time $994 per credit hour. Required fees: $2000; $85 per credit hour. Tuition and fees vary according to course level, course load, degree level, campus/location and program. *Financial support:* Fellowships, research assistantships available. *Faculty research:* Molecular biology, peptide/protein chemistry, neurochemistry, enzyme mechanisms, macromolecular structure determination. Total annual research expenditures: $3.5 million. *Unit head:* Dr. Sarah Spiegel, Chair, 804-828-6971, Fax: 804-828-1473, E-mail: sspiegel@vcu.edu. *Application contact:* Dr. Tomasz Kordula, Graduate Program Director, 804-828-0771, Fax: 804-828-1473, E-mail: tkordula@vcu.edu.

Virginia Commonwealth University, Medical College of Virginia-Professional Programs, School of Medicine, School of Medicine Graduate Programs, Department of Human and Molecular Genetics, Richmond, VA 23284-9005. Offers genetic counseling (MS); human genetics (PhD); molecular biology and genetics (MS, PhD); MD/PhD. *Faculty:* 25 full-time (14 women). *Students:* 37 full-time (21 women), 1 (woman) part-time; includes 5 minority (1 Black or African American, non-Hispanic/Latino; 4 Asian, non-Hispanic/Latino), 14 international. 51 applicants, 33% accepted, 10 enrolled. In 2010, 3 master's, 5 doctorates awarded. *Degree requirements:* For master's, thesis; for doctorate, thesis/dissertation, comprehensive oral and written exams. *Entrance requirements:* For master's, GRE; for doctorate, GRE General Test. Additional exam requirements/recommendations for international students: Required—TOEFL (minimum score 600 paper-based; 250 computer-based; 100 iBT). *Application deadline:* For fall admission, 12/15 priority date for domestic students. Application fee: $50. Electronic applications accepted. *Expenses:* Tuition, state resident: full-time $4308; part-time $479 per credit hour. Tuition, nonresident: full-time $8942; part-time $994 per credit hour. Required fees: $2000; $85 per credit hour. Tuition and fees vary according to course level, course load, degree level, campus/location and program. *Financial support:* Fellowships available. *Faculty research:* Genetic epidemiology, biochemical genetics, quantitative genetics, human cytogenetics, molecular genetics. *Unit head:* Dr. Paul B. Fisher, Chair, 804-628-3506, Fax: 804-827-1124, E-mail: pbfisher@vcu.edu. *Application contact:* Dr. Linda A. Corey, Graduate Program Director, 804-628-4514, E-mail: corey@vcu.edu.

Virginia Polytechnic Institute and State University, Graduate School, Intercollege, Program in Molecular Plant Sciences, Blacksburg, VA 24061. Offers PhD. *Students:* 62 full-time (32 women), 399 part-time (161 women); includes 33 Black or African American, non-Hispanic/Latino; 1 American Indian or Alaska Native, non-Hispanic/Latino; 32 Asian, non-Hispanic/Latino; 16 Hispanic/Latino, 49 international. Average age 33. 501 applicants, 88% accepted, 289 enrolled. *Degree requirements:* For doctorate, comprehensive exam (for some programs), thesis/dissertation (for some programs). *Entrance requirements:* For doctorate, GRE. Additional exam requirements/recommendations for international students: Required—TOEFL (minimum score 550 paper-based; 213 computer-based). *Application deadline:* For fall admission, 7/1 for domestic and international students; for spring admission, 12/1 for domestic and international students. Application fee: $65. *Expenses:* Tuition, state resident: full-time $9399; part-time $488 per credit hour. Tuition, nonresident: full-time $17,854; part-time $957.75 per credit hour. Required fees: $1534. Full-time tuition and fees vary according to program. *Financial support:* Career-related internships or fieldwork, Federal Work-Study, scholarships/grants, health care benefits, and unspecified assistantships available. Financial award application deadline: 1/15. *Unit head:* By Program. *Application contact:* By Program.

Wake Forest University, School of Medicine and Graduate School of Arts and Sciences, Graduate Programs in Medicine, Molecular Genetics and Genomics Program, Winston-Salem, NC 27109. Offers PhD, MD/PhD. *Degree requirements:* For doctorate, thesis/dissertation. *Entrance requirements:* For doctorate, GRE General Test. Additional exam requirements/recommendations for international students: Required—TOEFL. Electronic applications accepted. *Faculty research:* Control of gene expression, molecular pathogenesis, protein biosynthesis, cell development, clinical cytogenetics.

Washington State University, Graduate School, College of Sciences, School of Molecular Biosciences, Pullman, WA 99164. Offers MS, PhD. *Faculty:* 30. *Students:* 24 full-time (14 women); includes 1 American Indian or Alaska Native, non-Hispanic/Latino; 1 Asian, non-Hispanic/Latino; 1 Hispanic/Latino, 3 international. 194 applicants, 15% accepted, 16 enrolled. In 2010, 8 master's, 10 doctorates awarded. *Entrance requirements:* For master's and doctorate, GRE, personal statement describing qualifications, goals, and objectives in pursuing graduate research in molecular biosciences; official transcripts from all colleges attended; three letters of recommendation. Additional exam requirements/recommendations for international students: Required—TOEFL, IELTS. *Application deadline:* For fall admission, 12/15 for domestic students. Application fee: $50. *Expenses:* Tuition, state resident: full-time $8552; part-time $443 per credit. Tuition, nonresident: full-time $21,650; part-time $1083 per credit. Required fees: $846. *Financial support:* In 2010–11, research assistantships (averaging $13,917 per year), teaching assistantships (averaging $13,056 per year) were awarded. Financial award application deadline: 2/15; financial award applicants required to submit FAFSA. Total annual research expenditures: $8 million. *Unit head:* Dr. John H. Nilson, Director, 509-335-8724, Fax: 509-335-9688, E-mail: jhn@wsu.edu. *Application contact:* Graduate School Admissions, 800-GRADWSU, Fax: 509-335-1949, E-mail: gradsch@wsu.edu.

Washington University in St. Louis, Graduate School of Arts and Sciences, Division of Biology and Biomedical Sciences, Program in Molecular Cell Biology, St. Louis, MO 63130-4899. Offers PhD. *Degree requirements:* For doctorate, thesis/dissertation. *Entrance requirements:* For doctorate, GRE General Test, GRE Subject Test. Electronic applications accepted.

Wayne State University, Graduate School, Program in Molecular Biology and Genetics, Detroit, MI 48202. Offers MS, PhD. *Faculty:* 2 full-time (0 women). *Students:* 23 full-time (10 women); includes 2 Asian, non-Hispanic/Latino, 6 international. Average age 27. 29 applicants, 52% accepted, 6 enrolled. In 2010, 1 master's, 3 doctorates awarded. Terminal master's awarded for partial completion of doctoral program. *Degree requirements:* For master's, thesis; for doctorate, thesis/dissertation. *Entrance requirements:* For master's and doctorate, GRE General Test, references. Additional exam requirements/recommendations for international students: Required—TOEFL (minimum score 550 paper-based; 213 computer-based); Recommended—TWE (minimum score 6). *Application deadline:* For fall admission, 6/1 for international students; for winter admission, 10/1 for international students; for spring admission, 2/1 for international students. Applications are processed on a rolling basis. Application fee: $30 ($50 for international students). Electronic applications accepted. *Expenses:*

Molecular Biology

Wayne State University (continued)

Tuition, state resident: full-time $7662; part-time $478.85 per credit hour. Tuition, nonresident: full-time $16,920; part-time $1057.55 per credit hour. Required fees: $571; $35.70 per credit hour. $188.05 per semester. Tuition and fees vary according to course load and program. *Financial support:* In 2010–11, 4 fellowships (averaging $16,133 per year), 18 research assistantships (averaging $22,252 per year) were awarded; teaching assistantships. *Faculty research:* Human gene mapping, genome organization and sequencing, gene regulation, molecular evolution. *Unit head:* Dr. David Womble, Director, 313-577-2374, Fax: 313-577-5218, E-mail: aa3330@wayne.edu. *Application contact:* Alexander Gow, Associate Professor, 313-577-9401, E-mail: agow@genetics.wayne.edu.

Wayne State University, School of Medicine, Department of Biochemistry and Molecular Biology, Detroit, MI 48202. Offers MS, PhD. *Faculty:* 3 full-time (1 woman). *Students:* 30 full-time (17 women), 2 part-time (0 women); includes 1 Black or African American, non-Hispanic/Latino; 2 Asian, non-Hispanic/Latino, 16 international. Average age 26. 52 applicants, 35% accepted, 14 enrolled. In 2010, 6 doctorates awarded. Terminal master's awarded for partial completion of doctoral program. *Degree requirements:* For master's, thesis; for doctorate, one foreign language, thesis/dissertation. *Entrance requirements:* For master's and doctorate, GRE General Test, GRE Subject Test. Additional exam requirements/recommendations for international students: Required—TOEFL (minimum score 550 paper-based; 213 computer-based); Recommended—TWE (minimum score 6). *Application deadline:* For fall admission, 6/1 for international students; for winter admission, 10/1 for international students; for spring admission, 2/1 for international students. Applications are processed on a rolling basis. Application fee: $30 ($50 for international students). Electronic applications accepted. *Expenses:* Tuition, state resident: full-time $7662; part-time $478.85 per credit hour. Tuition, nonresident: full-time $16,920; part-time $1057.55 per credit hour. Required fees: $571; $35.70 per credit hour. $188.05 per semester. Tuition and fees vary according to course load and program. *Financial support:* In 2010–11, 18 research assistantships (averaging $21,580 per year) were awarded; fellowships, teaching assistantships also available. *Faculty research:* Protein structure, molecular biology, molecular genetics, enzymology, x-ray crystallography. *Unit head:* Dr. Barry P. Rosen, Chair, 313-577-1512, Fax: 313-577-2765, E-mail: aa1133@wayne.edu. *Application contact:* Marilyn Doscher, Graduate Director, 313-577-1295, E-mail: mdoscher@med.wayne.edu.

Wesleyan University, Graduate Programs, Department of Molecular Biology and Biochemistry, Middletown, CT 06459. Offers biochemistry (PhD); molecular biology (PhD). *Faculty:* 8 full-time (3 women). *Students:* 19 full-time (13 women); includes 9 Asian, non-Hispanic/Latino; 1 Hispanic/Latino. Average age 28. 37 applicants, 22% accepted, 3 enrolled. In 2010, 3 doctorates awarded. *Degree requirements:* For doctorate, comprehensive exam, thesis/dissertation. *Entrance requirements:* For doctorate, GRE General Test, GRE Subject Test. Additional exam requirements/recommendations for international students: Required—TOEFL. *Application deadline:* For fall admission, 2/15 for domestic and international students. Applications are processed on a rolling basis. Application fee: $0. Electronic applications accepted. *Expenses:* Tuition: Full-time $43,404. Required fees: $830. *Financial support:* In 2010–11, 13 research assistantships with full tuition reimbursements, 9 teaching assistantships with full tuition reimbursements were awarded; institutionally sponsored loans also available. Financial award application deadline: 4/15; financial award applicants required to submit FAFSA. *Faculty research:* Genome organization, regulation of gene expression, molecular biology of development, physical biochemistry. *Unit head:* Dr. Michael McAlear, Chair, 860-685-2443, E-mail: mmcalear@wesleyan.edu. *Application contact:* Information Contact, 860-685-2640, E-mail: mbbgrad@wesleyan.edu.

West Virginia University, Eberly College of Arts and Sciences, Department of Biology, Morgantown, WV 26506. Offers cell and molecular biology (MS, PhD); environmental and evolutionary biology (MS, PhD); forensic biology (MS, PhD); genomic biology (MS, PhD); neurobiology (MS, PhD). Terminal master's awarded for partial completion of doctoral program. *Degree requirements:* For master's, thesis, final exam; for doctorate, thesis/dissertation, preliminary and final exams. *Entrance requirements:* For master's, GRE General Test, GRE Subject Test, minimum GPA of 3.0; for doctorate, GRE General Test, minimum GPA of 3.0. Additional exam requirements/recommendations for international students: Required—TOEFL. *Faculty research:* Environmental biology, genetic engineering, developmental biology, global change, biodiversity.

West Virginia University, School of Medicine, Graduate Programs at the Health Sciences Center, Interdisciplinary Graduate Programs in Biomedical Sciences, Program in Biochemistry and Molecular Biology, Morgantown, WV 26506. Offers MS, PhD, MD/PhD. *Degree requirements:* For doctorate, comprehensive exam, thesis/dissertation. *Entrance requirements:* For doctorate, GRE General Test, minimum GPA of 3.0. Additional exam requirements/recommendations for international students: Required—TOEFL. Electronic applications accepted. *Faculty research:* Regulation of gene expression, cell survival mechanisms, signal transduction, regulation of metabolism, sensory neuroscience.

Wright State University, School of Graduate Studies, College of Science and Mathematics, Department of Biochemistry and Molecular Biology, Dayton, OH 45435. Offers MS. *Degree requirements:* For master's, thesis. *Entrance requirements:* Additional exam requirements/recommendations for international students: Required—TOEFL. *Faculty research:* Regulation of gene expression, macromolecular structural function, NMR imaging, visual biochemistry.

Yale University, Graduate School of Arts and Sciences, Department of Molecular, Cellular, and Developmental Biology, Program in Biochemistry, Molecular Biology and Chemical Biology, New Haven, CT 06520. Offers PhD. *Degree requirements:* For doctorate, thesis/dissertation. *Entrance requirements:* For doctorate, GRE General Test, GRE Subject Test.

Yale University, School of Medicine and Graduate School of Arts and Sciences, Combined Program in Biological and Biomedical Sciences (BBS), Molecular Cell Biology, Genetics, and Development Track, New Haven, CT 06520. Offers PhD, MD/PhD. *Entrance requirements:* Additional exam requirements/recommendations for international students: Required—TOEFL.

Youngstown State University, Graduate School, College of Science, Technology, Engineering and Mathematics, Department of Biological Sciences, Youngstown, OH 44555-0001. Offers environmental biology (MS); molecular biology, microbiology, and genetic (MS); physiology and anatomy (MS). Part-time programs available. *Degree requirements:* For master's, comprehensive exam, thesis, oral review. *Entrance requirements:* For master's, GRE General Test, minimum GPA of 2.7. Additional exam requirements/recommendations for international students: Required—TOEFL. *Faculty research:* Cell biology, neurophysiology, molecular biology, neurobiology, gene regulation.

Molecular Medicine

Baylor College of Medicine, Graduate School of Biomedical Sciences, Program in Translational Biology and Molecular Medicine, Houston, TX 77030-3498. Offers PhD. *Faculty:* 173 full-time (54 women). *Students:* 58 full-time (28 women); includes 6 Black or African American, non-Hispanic/Latino; 6 Hispanic/Latino, 16 international. Average age 27. 88 applicants, 32% accepted, 13 enrolled. In 2010, 1 doctorate awarded. *Degree requirements:* For doctorate, thesis/dissertation, public defense. *Entrance requirements:* For doctorate, GRE, minimum GPA of 3.0. Additional exam requirements/recommendations for international students: Required—TOEFL. *Application deadline:* For fall admission, 1/1 for domestic students. Application fee: $0. Electronic applications accepted. *Expenses:* Tuition: Full-time $11,000. Required fees: $4900. *Financial support:* In 2010–11, 58 students received support, including 24 fellowships with full tuition reimbursements available (averaging $26,000 per year), 34 research assistantships with full tuition reimbursements available (averaging $26,000 per year); career-related internships or fieldwork, Federal Work-Study, health care benefits, and students receive a scholarship unless there are grant funds available to pay tuition also available. Financial award applicants required to submit FAFSA. *Faculty research:* Molecular medicine, translational biology, human disease biology and therapy. *Unit head:* Dr. Mary Estes, Director, 713-798-3585, Fax: 713-798-3586, E-mail: tbmm@bcm.edu. *Application contact:* Wanda Waguespack, Graduate Program Administrator, 713-798-1077, Fax: 713-798-3586, E-mail: wandaw@bcm.edu.

See Close-Up on page 253.

Boston University, School of Medicine, Division of Graduate Medical Sciences, Program in Molecular Medicine, Boston, MA 02215. Offers PhD, MD/PhD. *Faculty:* 76 full-time (25 women), 1 (woman) part-time/adjunct. *Students:* 38 full-time (25 women), 1 part-time; includes 2 Black or African American, non-Hispanic/Latino; 2 Asian, non-Hispanic/Latino; 1 Hispanic/Latino, 6 international. 56 applicants, 9% accepted, 4 enrolled. In 2010, 7 doctorates awarded. *Degree requirements:* For doctorate, thesis/dissertation, qualifying exam. *Entrance requirements:* For doctorate, GRE. Additional exam requirements/recommendations for international students: Required—TOEFL. *Application deadline:* For fall admission, 1/15 priority date for domestic students; for spring admission, 10/15 priority date for domestic students. Application fee: $75. Electronic applications accepted. *Expenses:* Tuition: Full-time $39,314; part-time $1228 per credit. Required fees: $40 per semester. *Financial support:* In 2010–11, 7 fellowships with full tuition reimbursements (averaging $30,500 per year), 26 research assistantships with full and partial tuition reimbursements (averaging $30,500 per year) were awarded; Federal Work-Study, scholarships/grants, and traineeships also available. Financial award applicants required to submit FAFSA. *Unit head:* Dr. Herbert Cohen, Director, 617-638-7322, E-mail: gpmm@med-med1.bu.edu. *Application contact:* Mary-Kathleen Delooge, Administrative Coordinator, 617-414-1519, E-mail: mkdeloge@bu.edu.

Case Western Reserve University, School of Graduate Studies, Cleveland Clinic Lerner Research Institute–Molecular Medicine PhD Program, Cleveland, OH 44106. Offers PhD. *Faculty:* 137 full-time (41 women). *Students:* 16 full-time (7 women), 17 part-time (11 women); includes 6 Black or African American, non-Hispanic/Latino; 4 Asian, non-Hispanic/Latino; 1 Hispanic/Latino, 7 international. Average age 26. 79 applicants, 22% accepted, 7 enrolled. In 2010, 1 doctorate awarded. *Degree requirements:* For doctorate, comprehensive exam, thesis/dissertation, seminar. *Entrance requirements:* For doctorate, MCAT, 3 letters of reference, prior research experience, interview. Additional exam requirements/recommendations for international students: Required—TOEFL (minimum score 550 paper-based; 213 computer-based; 79 iBT). *Application deadline:* For fall admission, 11/1 priority date for domestic students, 11/1 for international students. Application fee: $50. Electronic applications accepted. *Financial support:* Fellowships with full tuition reimbursements, health care benefits and stipends available. *Faculty research:* Cancer, cardiovascular disease, neuroscience, molecular biology, genetics. *Unit head:* Dr. Martha Cathcart, Program Director, 216-444-5222, E-mail: molmedphd@ccf.org. *Application contact:* John Pounardjian, Recruiting and Development Coordinator, 216-445-9417, E-mail: molmedphd@ccf.org.

Case Western Reserve University, School of Medicine and School of Graduate Studies, Graduate Programs in Medicine, Department of Molecular Medicine at the Lerner Research Institute, Cleveland, OH 44106. Offers PhD. *Degree requirements:* For doctorate, comprehensive exam, thesis/dissertation. *Entrance requirements:* For doctorate, GRE. Additional exam requirements/recommendations for international students: Required—TOEFL. Electronic applications accepted.

Cleveland State University, College of Graduate Studies, College of Sciences and Health Professions, Department of Chemistry, Cleveland, OH 44115. Offers analytical chemistry (MS); clinical chemistry (MS); clinical/bioanalytical chemistry (PhD), including cellular and molecular medicine, clinical chemistry, clinical/bioanalytical chemistry; environmental chemistry (MS); inorganic chemistry (MS); pharmaceutical/organic chemistry (MS); physical chemistry (MS). Part-time and evening/weekend programs available. *Faculty:* 13 full-time (0 women), 1 (woman) part-time/adjunct. *Students:* 58 full-time (29 women), 42 part-time (17 women); includes 4 Black or African American, non-Hispanic/Latino; 3 Asian, non-Hispanic/Latino; 1 Hispanic/Latino, 70 international. Average age 28. 76 applicants, 74% accepted, 16 enrolled. In 2010, 4 master's, 15 doctorates awarded. *Degree requirements:* For master's, thesis optional; for doctorate, comprehensive exam, thesis/dissertation. *Entrance requirements:* For master's and doctorate, GRE General Test. Additional exam requirements/recommendations for international students: Required—TOEFL (minimum score 525 paper-based; 197 computer-based; 65 iBT). *Application deadline:* For fall admission, 1/15 priority date for domestic and international students. Applications are processed on a rolling basis. Application fee: $30. Electronic applications accepted. *Expenses:* Tuition, state resident: full-time $8447; part-time $469 per credit hour. Tuition, nonresident: full-time $16,020; part-time $890 per credit hour. Required fees: $50. *Financial support:* In 2010–11, 44 students received support, including 5 fellowships with full tuition reimbursements available (averaging $30,000 per year), 13 research assistantships with full tuition reimbursements available (averaging $20,000 per year), 24 teaching assistantships with full tuition reimbursements available (averaging $18,500 per year); scholarships/grants and unspecified assistantships also available. Financial award application deadline: 1/15. *Faculty research:* Bioanalytical techniques and molecular diagnostics, glycoproteomics and antithrombotic agents, drug discovery and innovation, analytical pharmacology, inflammatory disease research. Total annual research expenditures: $3 million. *Unit head:* Dr. David J. Anderson, Interim Chair, 216-687-2467, Fax: 216-687-9298, E-mail: d.anderson@csuohio.edu. *Application contact:* Richelle P. Emery, Administrative Coordinator, 216-687-2457, Fax: 216-687-9298, E-mail: r.emery@csuohio.edu.

Cornell University, Graduate School, Graduate Fields of Comparative Biomedical Sciences, Field of Comparative Biomedical Sciences, Ithaca, NY 14853-0001. Offers cellular and molecular medicine (MS, PhD); developmental and reproductive biology (MS, PhD); infectious diseases (MS, PhD); population medicine and epidemiology (MS, PhD); structural and functional biology (MS, PhD). *Faculty:* 94 full-time (27 women). *Students:* 47 full-time (33 women); includes 2 Black or African American, non-Hispanic/Latino; 1 Asian, non-Hispanic/Latino, 23 international. Average age 30. 31 applicants, 48% accepted, 14 enrolled. In 2010, 11 doctorates awarded. *Degree requirements:* For master's, thesis; for doctorate, comprehensive exam, thesis/dissertation. *Entrance requirements:* For master's and doctorate, GRE General Test, 2 letters of recommendation. Additional exam requirements/recommendations for international students: Required—TOEFL (minimum score 550 paper-based; 213 computer-based; 77 iBT). *Application deadline:* For fall admission, 12/15 for domestic students. Application fee: $70. Electronic applications accepted. *Expenses:* Tuition: Full-time $29,500. Required fees: $76. Tuition and fees vary according to degree level and program. *Financial support:* In 2010–11, 18 fellowships with full tuition reimbursements, 25 research assistantships with full tuition reimbursements were awarded; teaching assistantships with full tuition reimbursements, institutionally sponsored loans, scholarships/grants, health care benefits, tuition waivers (full and partial), and unspecified assistantships also available. Financial award applicants required to submit FAFSA. *Faculty research:* Receptors and signal transduction, viral and bacterial infectious diseases, tumor metastasis, clinical sciences/nutritional disease, developmental/neurological disorders. *Unit head:* Director of Graduate Studies, 607-253-3276, Fax: 607-253-3756. *Application contact:* Graduate Field Assistant, 607-253-3276, Fax: 607-253-3756, E-mail: graduate_edcvm@cornell.edu.

Dartmouth College, Arts and Sciences Graduate Programs, Program in Experimental and Molecular Medicine, Hanover, NH 03755. Offers biomedical physiology (PhD); cancer biology and molecular therapeutics (PhD); cardiovascular diseases (PhD); molecular pharmacology, toxicology and experimental therapeutics (PhD); neuroscience (PhD); MD/PhD. *Degree requirements:* For doctorate, comprehensive exam, thesis/dissertation. *Entrance requirements:* For doctorate, GRE, 3 letters of recommendation, interview, minimum GPA of 3.0. Additional exam requirements/recommendations for international students: Required—TOEFL (minimum score 620 paper-based; 260 computer-based; 105 iBT). Electronic applications accepted.

Dartmouth College, Program in Experimental and Molecular Medicine, Hanover, NH 03755. Offers biomedical physiology (PhD); cancer biology and molecular therapeutics (PhD); cardiovascular diseases (PhD); molecular pharmacology, toxicology and experimental therapeutics (PhD); neuroscience (PhD); MD/PhD. *Degree requirements:* For doctorate, comprehensive exam, thesis/dissertation. *Entrance requirements:* For doctorate, GRE General Test, 3 letters of recommendation. Additional exam requirements/recommendations for international students: Required—TOEFL (minimum score 620 paper-based; 260 computer-based; 105 iBT). Electronic applications accepted.

Drexel University, College of Medicine, Biomedical Graduate Programs, Molecular Medicine Program, Philadelphia, PA 19129. Offers MS.

The George Washington University, Columbian College of Arts and Sciences, Institute for Biomedical Sciences, Program in Molecular Medicine, Washington, DC 20037. Offers molecular and cellular oncology (PhD); neurosciences (PhD); pharmacology and physiology (PhD). *Students:* 12 full-time (6 women), 21 part-time (13 women); includes 1 Black or African American, non-Hispanic/Latino; 2 Asian, non-Hispanic/Latino, 5 international. Average age 31. In 2010, 7 doctorates awarded. *Degree requirements:* For doctorate, comprehensive exam, thesis/dissertation, general exams. *Entrance requirements:* For doctorate, GRE General Test, interview, minimum GPA of 3.0. Additional exam requirements/recommendations for international students: Required—TOEFL (minimum score 600 paper-based; 250 computer-based). *Application deadline:* For fall admission, 12/15 priority date for domestic and international students. Applications are processed on a rolling basis. Application fee: $75. Electronic applications accepted. *Financial support:* In 2010–11, 10 students received support; fellowships with tuition reimbursements available, Federal Work-Study, institutionally sponsored loans, and tuition waivers available. Financial award application deadline: 2/1. *Unit head:* Dr. Norman Lee, Director, 202-994-2114, E-mail: beb@gwu.edu. *Application contact:* 202-994-2179, Fax: 202-994-0967, E-mail: gwibs@gwu.edu.

Georgia Health Sciences University, College of Graduate Studies, Program in Molecular Medicine, Augusta, GA 30912. Offers MS, PhD. *Faculty:* 38 full-time (7 women), 1 part-time/adjunct (0 women). *Students:* 17 full-time (10 women), 1 part-time (0 women); includes 2 Black or African American, non-Hispanic/Latino; 1 Asian, non-Hispanic/Latino, 10 international. Average age 29. In 2010, 3 doctorates awarded. *Degree requirements:* For doctorate, comprehensive exam, thesis/dissertation. *Entrance requirements:* For doctorate, GRE General Test. Additional exam requirements/recommendations for international students: Required—TOEFL (minimum score 550 paper-based; 213 computer-based; 79 iBT). *Application deadline:* For fall admission, 1/15 for domestic and international students. Application fee: $30. Electronic applications accepted. *Expenses:* Tuition, state resident: full-time $7500; part-time $313 per semester hour. Tuition, nonresident: full-time $24,772; part-time $1033 per semester hour. Required fees: $1112. *Financial support:* In 2010–11, 4 students received support, including fellowships with partial tuition reimbursements available (averaging $26,000 per year), 17 research assistantships with partial tuition reimbursements available (averaging $23,000 per year); teaching assistantships, Federal Work-Study, institutionally sponsored loans, and scholarships/grants also available. Support available to part-time students. Financial award application deadline: 5/31; financial award applicants required to submit FAFSA. *Faculty research:* Developmental neurobiology, cancer, regenerative medicine, molecular chaperones, molecular immunology. Total annual research expenditures: $10.4 million. *Unit head:* Dr. Lin Mei, Director of Institute of Molecular Medicine and Genetics, 706-721-8775, Fax: 706-721-8685, E-mail: lmie@georgiahealth.edu. *Application contact:* Dr. Patricia L. Cameron, Associate Dean, 706-721-3279, E-mail: pcameron@georgiahealth.edu.

Hofstra University, School of Medicine, Hempstead, NY 11549. Offers medicine (MD); molecular basis of medicine (PhD); MD/PhD. *Accreditation:* LCME/AMA. *Entrance requirements:* Additional exam requirements/recommendations for international students: Required—TOEFL (minimum score 600 paper-based; 250 computer-based; 100 iBT). *Application deadline:* For fall admission, 12/1 priority date for domestic students. Application fee: $100. *Expenses:* Contact institution. *Financial support:* Fellowships with full and partial tuition reimbursements, research assistantships with full and partial tuition reimbursements, Federal Work-Study, institutionally sponsored loans, scholarships/grants, and tuition waivers (full and partial) available. Support available to part-time students. Financial award applicants required to submit FAFSA. *Faculty research:* Pathogenesis of sepsis, autoimmune disease, schizophrenia and movement disorder, pathogenesis and treatment of chronic leukemia, population health: healthcare quality and effectiveness. *Unit head:* Dr. Lawrence Smith, Dean, 516-463-7577, Fax: 516-463-5631, E-mail: medlgs@hofstra.edu. *Application contact:* Carol Drummer, Dean of Graduate Admissions, 516-463-4876, Fax: 516-463-4664, E-mail: gradstudent@hofstra.edu.

The Johns Hopkins University, School of Medicine, Graduate Programs in Medicine, Graduate Program in Cellular and Molecular Medicine, Baltimore, MD 21218-2699. Offers PhD. *Faculty:* 125 full-time (29 women). *Students:* 130 full-time (80 women); includes 43 minority (12 Black or African American, non-Hispanic/Latino; 22 Asian, non-Hispanic/Latino; 7 Hispanic/Latino; 2 Two or more races, non-Hispanic/Latino), 30 international. Average age 24. 243 applicants, 16% accepted, 21 enrolled. In 2010, 13 doctorates awarded. *Degree requirements:* For doctorate, comprehensive exam, thesis/dissertation, oral exam. *Entrance requirements:* For doctorate, GRE. Additional exam requirements/recommendations for international students: Required—TOEFL. *Application deadline:* For winter admission, 1/1 for domestic students. Application fee: $85. Electronic applications accepted. *Financial support:* In 2010–11, 17 fellowships with tuition reimbursements (averaging $27,125 per year) were awarded; scholarships/grants, health care benefits, and tuition waivers (full) also available. *Faculty research:* Cellular and molecular basis of disease. Total annual research expenditures: $100 million. *Unit head:* Dr. Rajini Rao, Director, 410-955-4732, Fax: 410-614-7294, E-mail: rrao@jhmi.edu. *Application contact:* Leslie Lichter-Mason, Admissions Administrator, 410-614-0391, Fax: 410-614-7294, E-mail: llichte2@jhmi.edu.

North Shore–LIJ Graduate School of Molecular Medicine, Graduate Program, Manhasset, NY 11030. Offers PhD. *Faculty:* 38 full-time (14 women). *Students:* 12 full-time (4 women), 11 international. Average age 30. 8 applicants, 25% accepted, 2 enrolled. In 2010, 1 doctorate awarded. *Degree requirements:* For doctorate, comprehensive exam, thesis/dissertation. *Entrance requirements:* For doctorate, MD or equivalent. *Application deadline:* Applications are processed on a rolling basis. Application fee: $25. *Financial support:* In 2010–11, 12 students received support, including 12 fellowships with full tuition reimbursements available (averaging $55,000 per year); health care benefits and tuition waivers (full) also available. *Faculty research:* Cardiopulmonary disease, cancer, inflammation, genetics of complex disorders, cytokine biology. Total annual research expenditures: $64 million. *Unit head:* Dr. Bettie M. Steinberg, Dean, 516-562-1159, Fax: 516-562-1022, E-mail: bsteinbe@lij.edu. *Application contact:* Emilia C. Hristis, Education Coordinator, 516-562-3405, Fax: 516-562-1022, E-mail: ehristis@nshs.edu.

Penn State Hershey Medical Center, College of Medicine, Graduate School Programs in the Biomedical Sciences, The Huck Institutes of the Life Sciences, Intercollege Graduate Program in Molecular Medicine, Hershey, PA 17033. Offers MS, PhD, MD/PhD. *Students:* 57 applicants, 5% accepted, 3 enrolled. In 2010, 9 master's awarded. Terminal master's awarded for partial completion of doctoral program. *Degree requirements:* For master's, thesis or alternative; for doctorate, comprehensive exam, thesis/dissertation. *Application deadline:* For fall admission, 1/31 for domestic students, 2/1 priority date for international students. Applications are processed on a rolling basis. Application fee: $65. Electronic applications accepted. *Financial support:* In 2010–11, research assistantships with full tuition reimbursements (averaging $22,260 per year); fellowships with full tuition reimbursements, career-related internships or fieldwork, scholarships/grants, health care benefits, and unspecified assistantships also available. *Faculty research:* Transitional research, diabetes and retinal vessels, stem cell differentiation/osteogenesis, cancer, malaria. *Unit head:* Dr. Charles Lang, Head, 717-531-8982, E-mail: grad-hmc@psu.edu. *Application contact:* Kathy Shuey, Administrative Assistant, 717-531-8982, Fax: 717-531-0786, E-mail: grad-hmc@psu.edu.

Queen's University at Kingston, School of Graduate Studies and Research, Faculty of Health Sciences, Department of Pathology and Molecular Medicine, Kingston, ON K7L 3N6, Canada. Offers M Sc, PhD. Part-time programs available. *Degree requirements:* For master's, thesis; for doctorate, comprehensive exam, thesis/dissertation. *Entrance requirements:* Additional exam requirements/recommendations for international students: Required—TOEFL. *Faculty research:* Immunopathology, cancer biology, immunology and metastases, cell differentiation, blood coagulation.

Texas A&M Health Science Center, Graduate School of Biomedical Sciences, Department of Molecular and Cellular Medicine, College Station, TX 77840. Offers PhD. *Degree requirements:* For doctorate, thesis/dissertation. *Entrance requirements:* For doctorate, GRE General Test. *Faculty research:* Immunology, cell and membrane biology, protein biochemistry, molecular genetics, parasitology, vertebrate embryogenesis and microbiology.

University of Chicago, Division of Biological Sciences, Biomedical Sciences Cluster: Cancer Biology, Immunology, Molecular Metabolism and Nutrition, Pathology, and Microbiology, Department of Pathology, Chicago, IL 60637-1513. Offers molecular pathogenesis and molecular medicine (PhD). *Degree requirements:* For doctorate, thesis/dissertation, ethics class, 2 teaching assistantships. *Entrance requirements:* For doctorate, GRE General Test. Additional exam requirements/recommendations for international students: Required—IELTS (minimum score 7); Recommended—TOEFL (minimum score 600 paper-based; 250 computer-based; 104 iBT). Electronic applications accepted. *Faculty research:* Vascular biology, apolipoproteins, cardiovascular disease, immunopathology.

University of Cincinnati, Graduate School, College of Medicine, Graduate Programs in Biomedical Sciences, Program in Pathobiology and Molecular Medicine, Cincinnati, OH 45221. Offers pathology (PhD), including anatomic pathology, laboratory medicine, pathobiology and molecular medicine. *Degree requirements:* For doctorate, thesis/dissertation, qualifying exam. *Entrance requirements:* For doctorate, GRE General Test. Additional exam requirements/recommendations for international students: Required—TOEFL (minimum score 620 paper-based; 260 computer-based). Electronic applications accepted. *Faculty research:* Cardiovascular and lipid disorders, digestive and kidney disease, endocrine and metabolic disorders, hematologic and oncogenic, immunology and infectious disease.

University of Maryland, Baltimore, Graduate School, Graduate Program in Life Sciences, Program in Molecular Medicine, Baltimore, MD 21201. Offers cancer biology (PhD); cell and molecular physiology (PhD); human genetics and genomic medicine (PhD); molecular medicine (MS); molecular toxicology and pharmacology (PhD); MD/PhD. *Entrance requirements:* Additional exam requirements/recommendations for international students: Required—TOEFL (minimum score 600 paper-based; 100 iBT); Recommended—IELTS (minimum score 7). Electronic applications accepted. Part-time tuition and fees vary according to course load, degree level and program.

University of Medicine and Dentistry of New Jersey, Graduate School of Biomedical Sciences, Graduate Programs in Biomedical Sciences–Newark, Department of Cell Biology and Molecular Medicine, Newark, NJ 07107. Offers PhD. *Degree requirements:* For doctorate, thesis/dissertation, qualifying exam. *Entrance requirements:* For doctorate, GRE General Test. Additional exam requirements/recommendations for international students: Required—TOEFL. Electronic applications accepted.

The University of Texas Health Science Center at San Antonio, Graduate School of Biomedical Sciences, Program in Molecular Medicine, San Antonio, TX 78245-3207. Offers MS, PhD. *Faculty:* 11 full-time (5 women). *Students:* 34 full-time (13 women); includes 1 Asian, non-Hispanic/Latino; 1 Hispanic/Latino, 24 international. Average age 24. 50 applicants, 18% accepted, 4 enrolled. In 2010, 1 master's, 7 doctorates awarded. Terminal master's awarded for partial completion of doctoral program. *Degree requirements:* For master's, comprehensive exam, thesis, written and oral qualifying exam; for doctorate, comprehensive exam, thesis/dissertation, written and oral qualifying exam. *Entrance requirements:* For master's and doctorate, GRE General Test. Additional exam requirements/recommendations for international students: Required—TOEFL (minimum score 560 paper-based; 220 computer-based; 68 iBT). *Application deadline:* For fall admission, 2/1 priority date for domestic and international students; for spring admission, 10/1 for domestic and international students. Applications are processed on a rolling basis. Application fee: $0. Electronic applications accepted. *Expenses:* Tuition, state resident: full-time $3072; part-time $128 per credit hour. Tuition, nonresident: full-time $11,928; part-time $497 per credit hour. Required fees: $1078; $1078 per year. One-time fee: $60. *Financial support:* In 2010–11, 2 fellowships with full and partial tuition reimbursements (averaging $30,000 per year), 32 teaching assistantships (averaging $26,000 per year) were awarded; career-related internships or fieldwork, health care benefits, and unspecified assistantships also available. Financial award application deadline: 6/30; financial award applicants required to submit FAFSA. *Faculty research:* DNA repair, tumor suppressor genes, vision in drosophila, gene expression (nervous system), cell-type specific gene regulation and development. Total annual research expenditures: $3.6 million. *Unit head:* Dr. Zelton Dave Sharp, Chair, 210-567-7200, Fax: 210-567-7277, E-mail: sharp@uthscsa.edu. *Application contact:* Dr. Barbara A. Christy, Chair, Committee on Graduate Studies, 210-567-7227, Fax: 210-567-7277, E-mail: christy@uthscsa.edu.

University of Washington, Graduate School, School of Public Health, Department of Global Health, Graduate Program in Pathobiology, Seattle, WA 98195. Offers PhD. *Students:* 34 full-time (27 women), 1 part-time (0 women); includes 2 Black or African American, non-Hispanic/Latino; 3 Asian, non-Hispanic/Latino; 2 Hispanic/Latino, 6 international. Average age 29. 59 applicants, 24% accepted, 6 enrolled. In 2010, 3 doctorates awarded. *Degree requirements:* For doctorate, comprehensive exam, thesis/dissertation, published paper from thesis work. *Entrance requirements:* For doctorate, GRE General Test, minimum GPA of 3.0. *Application deadline:* For fall admission, 12/1 for domestic students, 11/1 for international students. Application fee: $75. Electronic applications accepted. *Financial support:* In 2010–11, 32 students received support, including 2 fellowships with full tuition reimbursements available (averaging $27,348 per year), 30 research assistantships with full tuition reimbursements available (averaging $27,348 per year); career-related internships or fieldwork, institutionally sponsored loans, scholarships/grants, traineeships, and unspecified assistantships also available. *Faculty research:* Malaria, immunological response to mycobacteria infections, HIV-cell interaction and the development of an anti-HIV vaccine, regulation of intercellular communication via gap junctions, genetic and nutritional regulation of proteins involved in lipid transport. *Unit head:* Dr. King Holmes, Chair, 206-744-3620, Fax: 206-744-3694. *Application contact:* Rachel Reichert, Program Manager, 206-543-4338, Fax: 206-543-3873, E-mail: pabio@u.washington.edu.

Molecular Medicine

Wake Forest University, School of Medicine and Graduate School of Arts and Sciences, Graduate Programs in Medicine, Molecular Genetics and Genomics Program, Winston-Salem, NC 27109. Offers PhD, MD/PhD. *Degree requirements:* For doctorate, thesis/dissertation. *Entrance requirements:* For doctorate, GRE General Test. Additional exam requirements/ recommendations for international students: Required—TOEFL. Electronic applications accepted. *Faculty research:* Control of gene expression, molecular pathogenesis, protein biosynthesis, cell development, clinical cytogenetics.

Wake Forest University, School of Medicine and Graduate School of Arts and Sciences, Graduate Programs in Medicine, Program in Molecular Medicine, Winston-Salem, NC 27109. Offers MS, PhD, MD/PhD. *Degree requirements:* For master's, thesis; for doctorate, thesis/ dissertation. *Entrance requirements:* For master's and doctorate, GRE General Test. Additional exam requirements/recommendations for international students: Required—TOEFL. Electronic applications accepted. *Faculty research:* Human biology and disease, scientific basis of medicine, cellular and molecular mechanisms of health and disease.

Yale University, School of Medicine and Graduate School of Arts and Sciences, Combined Program in Biological and Biomedical Sciences (BBS), Pharmacological Sciences and Molecular Medicine Track, New Haven, CT 06520. Offers PhD, MD/PhD. *Degree requirements:* For doctorate, thesis/dissertation. *Entrance requirements:* For doctorate, GRE General Test. Additional exam requirements/recommendations for international students: Required—TOEFL. Electronic applications accepted.

Structural Biology

Baylor College of Medicine, Graduate School of Biomedical Sciences, Program in Structural and Computational Biology and Molecular Biophysics, Houston, TX 77030-3498. Offers PhD, MD/PhD. MD/PhD offered jointly with Rice University and University of Houston. *Faculty:* 83 full-time (10 women). *Students:* 36 full-time (10 women); includes 2 Asian, non-Hispanic/ Latino; 1 Hispanic/Latino, 17 international. Average age 28. 78 applicants, 12% accepted, 5 enrolled. In 2010, 6 doctorates awarded. *Degree requirements:* For doctorate, thesis/ dissertation, public defense. *Entrance requirements:* For doctorate, GRE General Test, GRE Subject Test (strongly recommended), minimum GPA of 3.0. Additional exam requirements/ recommendations for international students: Required—TOEFL. *Application deadline:* For fall admission, 1/1 for domestic students. Application fee: $0. Electronic applications accepted. *Expenses:* Tuition: Full-time $11,000. Required fees: $4900. *Financial support:* In 2010–11, 36 students received support, including 14 fellowships with full tuition reimbursements available (averaging $26,000 per year), 22 research assistantships with full tuition reimbursements available (averaging $26,000 per year); career-related internships or fieldwork, Federal Work-Study, institutionally sponsored loans, health care benefits, and students receive a scholarship unless there are grant funds available to pay tuition also available. Financial award applicants required to submit FAFSA. *Faculty research:* Computational biology, structural biology, biophysics. *Unit head:* Dr. Wah Chiu, Director, 713-798-6985. *Application contact:* Lourdes Fernandez, Graduate Program Administrator, 713-798-6557, Fax: 713-798-6325, E-mail: lourdesf@bcm.edu.

See Close-Up on page 251.

Carnegie Mellon University, Mellon College of Science, Joint Pitt + CMU Molecular Biophysics and Structural Biology Graduate Program, Pittsburgh, PA 15213-3891. Offers PhD. Program offered jointly with University of Pittsburgh. *Degree requirements:* For doctorate, comprehensive exam, thesis/dissertation. *Entrance requirements:* For doctorate, GRE General Test. Additional exam requirements/recommendations for international students: Required—TOEFL (minimum score 600 paper-based; 250 computer-based; 100 iBT), IELTS (minimum score 7). Electronic applications accepted. *Faculty research:* Structural biology, protein dynamics and folding, computational biophysics, molecular informatics, membrane biophysics and ion channels, NMR, x-ray crystallography cryaelectron microscopy.

Columbia University, College of Physicians and Surgeons, Integrated Program in Cellular, Molecular, Structural and Genetic Studies, New York, NY 10032. Offers PhD. Terminal master's awarded for partial completion of doctoral program. *Degree requirements:* For doctorate, thesis/dissertation. *Entrance requirements:* For doctorate, GRE General Test, GRE Subject Test. Additional exam requirements/recommendations for international students: Required—TOEFL. *Expenses:* Contact institution. *Faculty research:* Transcription, macromolecular sorting, gene expression during development, cellular interaction.

Cornell University, Graduate School, Graduate Fields of Comparative Biomedical Sciences, Field of Comparative Biomedical Sciences, Ithaca, NY 14853-0001. Offers cellular and molecular medicine (MS, PhD); developmental and reproductive biology (MS, PhD); infectious diseases (MS, PhD); population medicine and epidemiology (MS, PhD); structural and functional biology (MS, PhD). *Faculty:* 94 full-time (27 women). *Students:* 47 full-time (33 women); includes 2 Black or African American, non-Hispanic/Latino; 1 Asian, non-Hispanic/Latino, 23 international. Average age 30. 31 applicants, 48% accepted, 14 enrolled. In 2010, 11 doctorates awarded. *Degree requirements:* For master's, thesis; for doctorate, comprehensive exam, thesis/ dissertation. *Entrance requirements:* For master's and doctorate, GRE General Test, 2 letters of recommendation. Additional exam requirements/recommendations for international students: Required—TOEFL (minimum score 550 paper-based; 213 computer-based; 77 iBT). *Application deadline:* For fall admission, 12/15 for domestic students. Application fee: $70. Electronic applications accepted. *Expenses:* Tuition: Full-time $29,500. Required fees: $76. Tuition and fees vary according to degree level and program. *Financial support:* In 2010–11, 18 fellowships with full tuition reimbursements, 25 research assistantships with full tuition reimbursements were awarded; teaching assistantships with full tuition reimbursements, institutionally sponsored loans, scholarships/grants, health care benefits, tuition waivers (full and partial), and unspecified assistantships also available. Financial award applicants required to submit FAFSA. *Faculty research:* Receptors and signal transduction, viral and bacterial infectious diseases, tumor metastasis, clinical sciences/nutritional disease, developmental/neurological disorders. *Unit head:* Director of Graduate Studies, 607-253-3276, Fax: 607-253-3756. *Application contact:* Graduate Field Assistant, 607-253-3276, Fax: 607-253-3756, E-mail: graduate_edcvm@cornell.edu.

Cornell University, Joan and Sanford I. Weill Medical College and Graduate School of Medical Sciences, Weill Cornell Graduate School of Medical Sciences, Biochemistry, Cell and Molecular Biology Allied Program, New York, NY 10065. Offers MS, PhD. *Faculty:* 106 full-time (30 women). *Students:* 143 full-time (91 women); includes 2 Black or African American, non-Hispanic/Latino; 8 Asian, non-Hispanic/Latino; 6 Hispanic/Latino, 73 international. Average age 22. 322 applicants, 17% accepted, 14 enrolled. In 2010, 19 doctorates awarded. Terminal master's awarded for partial completion of doctoral program. *Degree requirements:* For master's, comprehensive exam; for doctorate, thesis/dissertation, final exam. *Entrance requirements:* For doctorate, GRE General Test, background in genetics, molecular biology, chemistry, or biochemistry. Additional exam requirements/recommendations for international students: Required—TOEFL. *Application deadline:* For fall admission, 12/1 for domestic students. Application fee: $60. Electronic applications accepted. *Expenses:* Tuition: Full-time $45,545. Required fees: $2805. *Financial support:* In 2010–11, 16 fellowships (averaging $23,000 per year) were awarded; scholarships/grants, health care benefits, and stipends (given to all students) also available. *Faculty research:* Molecular structure determination, protein structure, gene structure, stem cell biology, control of gene expression, DNA replication, chromosome maintenance, RNA biosynthesis. *Unit head:* Dr. David Eliezer, Co-Director, 212-746-6557, Fax: 212-717-3047. *Application contact:* Linda Smith, Assistant Dean of Admissions, 212-746-6565, Fax: 212-746-8906, E-mail: lis2025@med.cornell.edu.

Duke University, Graduate School, Program in Structural Biology and Biophysics, Durham, NC 27710. Offers Certificate. Students must be enrolled in a participating Ph D program (biochemistry, cell biology, chemistry, molecular genetics, neurobiology, pharmacology). *Faculty:* 25 full-time. *Students:* 5 full-time (2 women), 2 international. 31 applicants, 29% accepted, 4 enrolled. *Entrance requirements:* For degree, GRE General Test. Additional exam requirements/ recommendations for international students: Required—TOEFL (minimum score 550 paper-based; 213 computer-based; 83 iBT), IELTS (minimum score 7). *Application deadline:* For fall admission, 12/8 priority date for domestic and international students. Application fee: $75. *Financial support:* Application deadline: 12/8. *Unit head:* David Richardson, Director of Graduate Studies, 919-684-6559, Fax: 919-684-8346, E-mail: cmbtgp@biochem.duke.edu. *Application contact:* Elizabeth Hutton, Director of Admissions, 919-684-3913, Fax: 919-684-2277, E-mail: grad-admissions@duke.edu.

Florida State University, The Graduate School, College of Arts and Sciences, Department of Biological Science, Specialization in Structural Biology, Tallahassee, FL 32306-4295. Offers MS, PhD. *Faculty:* 14 full-time (4 women). *Students:* 21 full-time (9 women); includes 2 Black or African American, non-Hispanic/Latino; 2 Hispanic/Latino, 4 international. In 2010, 1 master's, 1 doctorate awarded. Terminal master's awarded for partial completion of doctoral program. *Degree requirements:* For master's, comprehensive exam, thesis, teaching experience, seminar presentation; for doctorate, comprehensive exam, thesis/dissertation, teaching experience, seminar presentation. *Entrance requirements:* For master's and doctorate, GRE General Test (minimum combined score 1100; 500 verbal, 500 quantitative), minimum upper-division GPA of 3.0. Additional exam requirements/recommendations for international students: Required—TOEFL (minimum score 600 paper-based; 250 computer-based; 92 iBT). *Application deadline:* For fall admission, 12/15 for domestic and international students. Application fee: $30. Electronic applications accepted. *Expenses:* Tuition, state resident: full-time $8238. *Financial support:* In 2010–11, 21 students received support, including 1 fellowship with full tuition reimbursement available (averaging $24,000 per year), 10 research assistantships with full tuition reimbursements available (averaging $21,000 per year), 10 teaching assistantships with full tuition reimbursements available (averaging $21,000 per year). Financial award application deadline: 12/15; financial award applicants required to submit FAFSA. *Faculty research:* Molecular genetics, signal transduction and regulation of gene expression, cell and molecular biology of the cytoskeleton, olfactory signal transduction, ion channel structure-function, neuromodulation, 3-D electron microscopy and x-ray crystallography of protein complexes involved in mRNA and sulfur metabolism, olfaction, synaptic physiology and plasticity, ion channel modulation, biomechanics of cardiac and skeletal muscle, magnetic resonance of proteins. *Unit head:* Professor and Associate Chairman for Graduate Studies. *Application contact:* Judy Bowers, Coordinator, Graduate Affairs, 850-644-3023, Fax: 850-644-9829, E-mail: gradinfo@bio.fsu.edu.

Florida State University, The Graduate School, College of Arts and Sciences, Program in Molecular Biophysics, Tallahassee, FL 32306. Offers biochemistry, molecular and cell biology (PhD); computational structural biology (PhD); molecular biophysics (PhD). *Faculty:* 49 full-time (6 women). *Students:* 22 full-time (8 women); includes 5 Asian, non-Hispanic/Latino; 1 Hispanic/ Latino. Average age 28. 30 applicants, 33% accepted, 7 enrolled. In 2010, 5 doctorates awarded. *Degree requirements:* For doctorate, comprehensive exam, thesis/dissertation, teaching 1 term in professor's major department. *Entrance requirements:* For doctorate, GRE General Test. Additional exam requirements/recommendations for international students: Required—TOEFL (minimum score 600 paper-based; 250 computer-based; 100 iBT). *Application deadline:* For fall admission, 2/15 for domestic students, 3/15 for international students; for spring admission, 11/2 for international students. Applications are processed on a rolling basis. Application fee: $30. Electronic applications accepted. *Expenses:* Tuition, state resident: full-time $8238. *Financial support:* In 2010–11, 21 students received support, including fellowships with partial tuition reimbursements available (averaging $21,000 per year), 18 research assistantships with partial tuition reimbursements available (averaging $21,000 per year), 4 teaching assistantships with partial tuition reimbursements available (averaging $21,000 per year); scholarships/grants, health care benefits, and unspecified assistantships also available. Financial award applicants required to submit FAFSA. *Faculty research:* Protein and nucleic acid structure and function, membrane protein structure, computational biophysics, 3-D image reconstruction. Total annual research expenditures: $1.4 million. *Unit head:* Dr. Geoffrey Strouse, Director, 850-644-0056, Fax: 850-644-7244, E-mail: strouse@chem.fsu.edu. *Application contact:* Dr. Kerry Maddox, Academic Coordinator, Graduate Programs, 850-644-1012, Fax: 850-644-7244, E-mail: bkmaddox@sb.fsu.edu.

Harvard University, Graduate School of Arts and Sciences, Department of Systems Biology, Cambridge, MA 02138. Offers PhD. *Degree requirements:* For doctorate, thesis/dissertation, lab rotation, qualifying examination. *Entrance requirements:* For doctorate, GRE. Additional exam requirements/recommendations for international students: Required—TOEFL. Electronic applications accepted. *Expenses:* Tuition: Full-time $34,976. Required fees: $1166. Full-time tuition and fees vary according to program.

Illinois State University, Graduate School, College of Arts and Sciences, Department of Biological Sciences, Normal, IL 61790-2200. Offers animal behavior (MS); bacteriology (MS); biochemistry (MS); biological sciences (MS); biology (PhD); biophysics (MS); biotechnology (MS); botany (MS, PhD); cell biology (MS); conservation biology (MS); developmental biology (MS); ecology (MS, PhD); entomology (MS); evolutionary biology (MS); genetics (MS, PhD); immunology (MS); microbiology (MS, PhD); molecular biology (MS); molecular genetics (MS); neurobiology (MS); neuroscience (MS); parasitology (MS); physiology (MS, PhD); plant biology (MS); plant molecular biology (MS); plant sciences (MS); structural biology (MS); zoology (MS, PhD). Part-time programs available. *Degree requirements:* For master's, thesis or alternative; for doctorate, variable foreign language requirement, thesis/dissertation, 2 terms of residency. *Entrance requirements:* For master's, GRE General Test, minimum GPA of 2.6 in last 60 hours of course work; for doctorate, GRE General Test. *Faculty research:* Redoc balance and drug development in schistosoma mansoni, control of the growth of listeria monocytogenes at low temperature, regulation of cell expansion and microtubule function by SPRI, CRUI: physiology and fitness consequences of different life history phenotypes.

Iowa State University of Science and Technology, Graduate College, Interdisciplinary Programs, Bioinformatics and Computational Biology Program, Ames, IA 50011. Offers MS, PhD. *Students:* 54 full-time (22 women), 34 international. In 2010, 1 master's, 5 doctorates awarded. *Degree requirements:* For doctorate, thesis/dissertation. *Entrance requirements:* For master's and doctorate, GRE General Test. Additional exam requirements/recommendations for international students: Recommended—IELTS. *Application deadline:* For fall admission, 1/15 priority date for domestic students, 1/15 for international students; for spring admission, 10/15 for domestic and international students. Application fee: $40 ($90 for international students). Electronic applications accepted. *Financial support:* In 2010–11, 47 research assistantships with full and partial tuition reimbursements (averaging $22,000 per year), 3 teaching assistantships (averaging $20,000 per year) were awarded; fellowships with full tuition reimbursements, scholarships/grants, traineeships, health care benefits, and unspecified assistantships also available. *Faculty research:* Functional and structural genomics, genome evolution, macromolecular structure and function, mathematical biology and biological statistics, metabolic and developmental networks. *Unit head:* Dr. Julie Dickerson, Chair, Supervising Committee, 515-294-5122, Fax: 515-294-6790, E-mail: bcb@iastate.edu. *Application contact:* Dr. Julie Dickerson, Chair, Supervising Committee, 515-294-5122, Fax: 515-294-6790, E-mail: bcb@iastate.edu.

Massachusetts Institute of Technology, School of Science, Department of Biology, Cambridge, MA 02139-4307. Offers biochemistry (PhD); biological oceanography (PhD); biology (PhD); biophysical chemistry and molecular structure (PhD); cell biology (PhD); computational and systems biology (PhD); developmental biology (PhD); genetics (PhD); immunology (PhD); microbiology (PhD); molecular biology (PhD); neurobiology (PhD). *Faculty:* 56 full-time (14 women). *Students:* 251 full-time (135 women); includes 74 minority (4 Black or African American, non-Hispanic/Latino; 1 American Indian or Alaska Native, non-Hispanic/Latino; 29 Asian, non-Hispanic/Latino; 33 Hispanic/Latino; 7 Two or more races, non-Hispanic/Latino), 29 international. Average age 26. 652 applicants, 18% accepted, 58 enrolled. In 2010, 41 doctorates awarded. *Degree requirements:* For doctorate, comprehensive exam, thesis/dissertation. *Entrance requirements:* For doctorate, GRE General Test. Additional exam requirements/recommendations for international students: Required—TOEFL (minimum score 577 paper-based; 233 computer-based), IELTS (minimum score 6.5). *Application deadline:* For fall admission, 12/1 for domestic and international students. Application fee: $75. Electronic applications accepted. *Expenses:* Tuition: Full-time $38,940; part-time $605 per unit. Required fees: $272. *Financial support:* In 2010–11, 215 students received support, including 115 fellowships with tuition reimbursements available (averaging $33,090 per year), 132 research assistantships with tuition reimbursements available (averaging $31,846 per year); teaching assistantships with tuition reimbursements available, Federal Work-Study, institutionally sponsored loans, scholarships/grants, traineeships, health care benefits, and unspecified assistantships also available. *Faculty research:* DNA recombination, replication and repair; transcription and gene regulation; signal transduction; cell cycle; neuronal cell fate. Total annual research expenditures: $60.6 million. *Unit head:* Prof. Chris Kaiser, Head, 617-253-4701, E-mail: mitbio@mit.edu. *Application contact:* Biology Education Office, 617-253-3717, Fax: 617-258-9329, E-mail: gradbio@mit.edu.

Mayo Graduate School, Graduate Programs in Biomedical Sciences, Programs in Biochemistry, Structural Biology, Cell Biology, and Genetics, Rochester, MN 55905. Offers biochemistry and structural biology (PhD); cell biology and genetics (PhD); molecular biology (PhD). *Degree requirements:* For doctorate, oral defense of dissertation, qualifying oral and written exam. *Entrance requirements:* For doctorate, GRE, 1 year of chemistry, biology, calculus, and physics. Additional exam requirements/recommendations for international students: Required—TOEFL. Electronic applications accepted. *Faculty research:* Gene structure and function, membranes and receptors/cytoskeleton, oncogenes and growth factors, protein structure and function, steroid hormonal action.

Michigan State University, The Graduate School, College of Natural Science, Quantitative Biology Program, East Lansing, MI 48824. Offers PhD.

New York University, School of Medicine, New York, NY 10012-1019. Offers biomedical sciences (PhD), including biomedical imaging, cellular and molecular biology, computational biology, developmental genetics, medical and molecular parasitology, microbiology, molecular oncobiology and immunology, neuroscience and physiology, pathobiology, pharmacology, structural biology; clinical investigation (MS); medicine (MD); MD/MA; MD/MPA; MD/MS; MD/PhD. *Accreditation:* LCME/AMA (one or more programs are accredited). *Degree requirements:* For master's, comprehensive exam, thesis; for doctorate, comprehensive exam, thesis/dissertation. *Entrance requirements:* MCAT. Additional exam requirements/recommendations for international students: Required—TOEFL. *Expenses:* Contact institution. *Faculty research:* AIDS, cancer, neuroscience, molecular biology, neuroscience, cell biology and molecular genetics, structural biology, microbial pathogenesis and host defense, pharmacology, molecular oncology and immunology.

New York University, School of Medicine and Graduate School of Arts and Science, Sackler Institute of Graduate Biomedical Sciences, Program in Structural Biology, New York, NY 10012-1019. Offers PhD. *Degree requirements:* For doctorate, thesis/dissertation, qualifying examination. *Entrance requirements:* For doctorate, GRE General Test, GRE Subject Test in biology or chemistry (recommended). Additional exam requirements/recommendations for international students: Required—TOEFL.

Northwestern University, The Graduate School, Interdepartmental Biological Sciences Program (IBiS), Evanston, IL 60208. Offers biochemistry, molecular biology, and cell biology (PhD), including biochemistry, cell and molecular biology, molecular biophysics, structural biology; biotechnology (PhD); cell and molecular biology (PhD); developmental biology and genetics (PhD); hormone action and signal transduction (PhD); neuroscience (PhD); structural biology, biochemistry, and biophysics (PhD). Program participants include the Departments of Biochemistry, Molecular Biology, and Cell Biology; Chemistry; Neurobiology and Physiology; Chemical Engineering; Civil Engineering; and Evanston Hospital. *Degree requirements:* For doctorate, thesis/dissertation, qualifying exam. *Entrance requirements:* For doctorate, GRE General Test. Additional exam requirements/recommendations for international students: Required—TOEFL (minimum score 600 paper-based). Electronic applications accepted. *Faculty research:* Developmental genetics, gene regulation, DNA-protein interactions, biological clocks, bioremediation.

Northwestern University, Northwestern University Feinberg School of Medicine and Interdepartmental Programs, Integrated Graduate Programs in the Life Sciences, Chicago, IL 60611. Offers cancer biology (PhD); cell biology (PhD); developmental biology (PhD); evolutionary biology (PhD); immunology and microbial pathogenesis (PhD); molecular biology and genetics (PhD); neurobiology (PhD); pharmacology and toxicology (PhD); structural biology and biochemistry (PhD). *Degree requirements:* For doctorate, comprehensive exam, thesis/dissertation, written and oral qualifying exams. *Entrance requirements:* For doctorate, GRE General Test. Additional exam requirements/recommendations for international students: Required—TOEFL (minimum score 600 paper-based; 250 computer-based). Electronic applications accepted.

Stanford University, School of Medicine, Graduate Programs in Medicine, Department of Structural Biology, Stanford, CA 94305-9991. Offers PhD. *Degree requirements:* For doctorate, thesis/dissertation. *Entrance requirements:* For doctorate, GRE General Test, GRE Subject Test. Additional exam requirements/recommendations for international students: Required—TOEFL. Electronic applications accepted. *Expenses:* Tuition: Full-time $38,700; part-time $860 per unit. One-time fee: $200 full-time.

Stony Brook University, State University of New York, Graduate School, College of Arts and Sciences, Department of Biochemistry and Cell Biology, Program in Biochemistry and Structural Biology, Stony Brook, NY 11794. Offers PhD. *Students:* 28 full-time (10 women); includes 1 Black or African American, non-Hispanic/Latino; 1 Asian, non-Hispanic/Latino, 17 international. Average age 27. 92 applicants, 21% accepted, 7 enrolled. In 2010, 4 doctorates awarded. Application fee: $100. *Expenses:* Tuition, state resident: full-time $8370; part-time $349 per credit. Tuition, nonresident: full-time $13,780; part-time $574 per credit. Required fees: $994. *Financial support:* In 2010–11, 16 research assistantships, 8 teaching assistantships were awarded. *Unit head:* Prof. Robert Haltiwanger, Chair, 631-632-8560. *Application contact:* Dr. Erwin London, Director, Graduate Program, 631-632-8564, Fax: 631-632-8575, E-mail: elondon@notes.sunysb.edu.

Syracuse University, College of Arts and Sciences, Program in Structural Biology, Biochemistry and Biophysics, Syracuse, NY 13244. Offers PhD. *Students:* 6 full-time (4 women), 1 part-time (0 women); includes 1 minority (Black or African American, non-Hispanic/Latino), 4 international. Average age 30. 10 applicants, 0% accepted, 0 enrolled. In 2010, 2 doctorates awarded. *Degree requirements:* For doctorate, thesis/dissertation, exam. *Entrance requirements:* For doctorate, GRE General Test, GRE Subject Test. Additional exam requirements/recommendations for international students: Required—TOEFL (minimum score 100 iBT). *Application deadline:* For fall admission, 1/10 priority date for domestic and international students. Application fee: $75. Electronic applications accepted. *Expenses:* Tuition: Part-time $1162 per credit. *Financial support:* Fellowships with full tuition reimbursements, research assistantships with full and partial tuition reimbursements, teaching assistantships with full and partial tuition reimbursements, tuition waivers available. Financial award application deadline: 1/1; financial award applicants required to submit FAFSA. *Unit head:* Scott Pitnick, Director, 315-443-5128, Fax: 315-443-2012, E-mail: sspitnic@syr.edu. *Application contact:* Evelyn Lott, Information Contact, 315-443-9154, Fax: 315-443-2012, E-mail: ealott@syr.edu.

Thomas Jefferson University, Jefferson College of Graduate Studies, Graduate Program in Molecular Pharmacology and Structural Biology, Philadelphia, PA 19107. Offers PhD. *Faculty:* 37 full-time (7 women). *Students:* 15 full-time (6 women); includes 4 minority (all Asian, non-Hispanic/Latino), 3 international. 20 applicants, 35% accepted, 3 enrolled. In 2010, 4 doctorates awarded. *Degree requirements:* For doctorate, comprehensive exam, thesis/dissertation. *Entrance requirements:* For doctorate, GRE General Test, minimum GPA of 3.2. Additional exam requirements/recommendations for international students: Required—TOEFL (minimum score 250 computer-based; 100 iBT) or IELTS. *Application deadline:* For fall admission, 1/2 priority date for domestic and international students. Applications are processed on a rolling basis. Application fee: $50. Electronic applications accepted. *Financial support:* In 2010–11, 15 students received support, including 15 fellowships with full tuition reimbursements available (averaging $54,723 per year); Federal Work-Study, institutionally sponsored loans, scholarships/grants, traineeships, and stipends also available. Support available to part-time students. Financial award application deadline: 5/1; financial award applicants required to submit FAFSA. *Faculty research:* Biochemistry and cell, molecular and structural biology of cell-surface and intracellular receptors, molecular modeling, signal transduction. Total annual research expenditures: $36.7 million. *Unit head:* Dr. Philip Wedegaertner, Program Director, 215-503-3137, Fax: 215-923-2117, E-mail: philip.wedegaertner@mail.tju.edu. *Application contact:* Marc E. Stearns, Director of Admissions, 215-503-0155, Fax: 215-503-9920, E-mail: jcgs-info@jefferson.edu.

Tulane University, School of Medicine and School of Liberal Arts, Graduate Programs in Biomedical Sciences, Department of Structural and Cellular Biology, New Orleans, LA 70118-5669. Offers MS, PhD, MD/PhD. MS and PhD offered through the Graduate School. *Degree requirements:* For master's, one foreign language, thesis; for doctorate, 2 foreign languages, thesis/dissertation. *Entrance requirements:* For master's, GRE General Test, minimum B average in undergraduate course work; for doctorate, GRE General Test. Additional exam requirements/recommendations for international students: Required—TOEFL. Electronic applications accepted. *Faculty research:* Reproductive endocrinology, visual neuroscience, neural response to altered hormones.

University at Albany, State University of New York, School of Public Health, Department of Biomedical Sciences, Program in Cell and Molecular Structure, Albany, NY 12222-0001. Offers MS, PhD. *Degree requirements:* For master's, thesis; for doctorate, thesis/dissertation. *Entrance requirements:* For master's and doctorate, GRE General Test, GRE Subject Test.

University at Buffalo, the State University of New York, Graduate School, School of Medicine and Biomedical Sciences, Graduate Programs in Medicine and Biomedical Sciences, Department of Structural Biology, Buffalo, NY 14260. Offers MS, PhD. *Faculty:* 6 part-time/adjunct (1 woman). *Students:* 7 full-time (0 women), 1 (woman) part-time; includes 1 Hispanic/Latino. Average age 27. 4 applicants, 75% accepted. In 2010, 2 doctorates awarded. *Degree requirements:* For master's, comprehensive exam, thesis; for doctorate, comprehensive exam, thesis/dissertation. *Entrance requirements:* For master's, BS or BA in science, engineering, or math; for doctorate, GRE General Test, BS or BA in science, engineering, or math. Additional exam requirements/recommendations for international students: Required—TOEFL (minimum score 600 paper-based; 250 computer-based; 100 iBT). *Application deadline:* For fall admission, 2/1 priority date for domestic and international students. Applications are processed on a rolling basis. Application fee: $50. Electronic applications accepted. *Financial support:* Federal Work-Study, scholarships/grants, traineeships, and unspecified assistantships available. Financial award application deadline: 2/1; financial award applicants required to submit FAFSA. *Faculty research:* Biomacromolecular structure and function at the level of three-dimensional atomic architecture. Total annual research expenditures: $3.5 million. *Unit head:* Dr. Robert H. Blessing, Interim Department Chair and Professor, 716-898-8613, Fax: 716-898-8660, E-mail: blessing@hwi.buffalo.edu. *Application contact:* Dr. Robert H. Blessing, Director of Graduate Studies, 716-898-8613, Fax: 716-898-8660, E-mail: blessing@hwi.buffalo.edu.

University of California, San Diego, School of Medicine and Office of Graduate Studies, Molecular Pathology Program, La Jolla, CA 92093. Offers bioinformatics (PhD); cancer biology/oncology (PhD); cardiovascular sciences and disease (PhD); microbiology (PhD); molecular pathology (PhD); neurological disease (PhD); stem cell and developmental biology (PhD); structural biology/drug design (PhD). *Entrance requirements:* For doctorate, GRE General Test, GRE Subject Test. Additional exam requirements/recommendations for international students: Required—TOEFL. Electronic applications accepted.

University of Connecticut, Graduate School, College of Liberal Arts and Sciences, Department of Molecular and Cell Biology, Field of Biophysics and Structural Biology, Storrs, CT 06269. Offers MS, PhD. Terminal master's awarded for partial completion of doctoral program. *Degree requirements:* For master's, comprehensive exam; for doctorate, thesis/dissertation. *Entrance requirements:* For master's and doctorate, GRE General Test, GRE Subject Test. Additional exam requirements/recommendations for international students: Required—TOEFL (minimum score 550 paper-based; 213 computer-based). Electronic applications accepted.

The University of Manchester, Faculty of Life Sciences, Manchester, United Kingdom. Offers adaptive organismal biology (M Phil, PhD); animal biology (M Phil, PhD); biochemistry (M Phil, PhD); bioinformatics (M Phil, PhD); biomolecular sciences (M Phil, PhD); biotechnology (M Phil, PhD); cell biology (M Phil, PhD); cell matrix research (M Phil, PhD); channels and transporters (M Phil, PhD); developmental biology (M Phil, PhD); Egyptology (M Phil, PhD); environmental biology (M Phil, PhD); evolutionary biology (M Phil, PhD); gene expression (M Phil, PhD); genetics (M Phil, PhD); history of science, technology and medicine (M Phil, PhD); immunology (M Phil, PhD); integrative neurobiology and behavior (M Phil, PhD); membrane trafficking (M Phil, PhD); microbiology (M Phil, PhD); molecular and cellular neuroscience (M Phil, PhD); molecular biology (M Phil, PhD); molecular cancer studies (M Phil, PhD); neuroscience (M Phil, PhD); ophthalmology (M Phil, PhD); optometry (M Phil, PhD); organelle function (M Phil, PhD); pharmacology (M Phil, PhD); physiology (M Phil, PhD); plant sciences (M Phil, PhD); stem cell research (M Phil, PhD); structural biology (M Phil, PhD); systems neuroscience (M Phil, PhD); toxicology (M Phil, PhD).

University of Minnesota, Twin Cities Campus, Graduate School, College of Biological Sciences, Biochemistry, Molecular Biology and Biophysics Graduate Program, Minneapolis, MN 55455-0213. Offers PhD. *Degree requirements:* For doctorate, thesis/dissertation. *Entrance requirements:* For doctorate, GRE, 3 letters of recommendation, more than 1 semester of laboratory experience. Additional exam requirements/recommendations for international students: Required—TOEFL (minimum score 625 paper-based; 263 computer-based; 108 iBT with writing subsection 25 and reading subsection 25) or IELTS (minimum score 7). Electronic applications accepted. *Faculty research:* Microbial biochemistry, biotechnology, molecular biology, regulatory biochemistry, structural biology and biophysics, physical biochemistry, enzymology, physiological chemistry.

University of Pittsburgh, School of Medicine and School of Arts and Sciences, Joint Pitt + CMU Molecular Biophysics and Structural Biology Graduate Program, Pittsburgh, PA 15260. Offers PhD. *Faculty:* 52 full-time (15 women). *Students:* 20 full-time (5 women); includes 1

Structural Biology

University of Pittsburgh (continued)

Asian, non-Hispanic/Latino; 1 Hispanic/Latino; 1 Native Hawaiian or other Pacific Islander, non-Hispanic/Latino, 5 international. Average age 26. 70 applicants, 13% accepted, 4 enrolled. In 2010, 2 doctorates awarded. *Degree requirements:* For doctorate, comprehensive exam, thesis/dissertation. *Entrance requirements:* For doctorate, GRE General Test. Additional exam requirements/recommendations for international students: Required—TOEFL (minimum score 600 paper-based; 250 computer-based; 100 iBT), IELTS (minimum score 7). *Application deadline:* For fall admission, 12/15 priority date for domestic and international students. Application fee: $0. Electronic applications accepted. *Expenses:* Tuition, state resident: full-time $17,304; part-time $701 per credit. Tuition, nonresident: full-time $29,554; part-time $1210 per credit. Required fees: $740; $214 per term. Tuition and fees vary according to program. *Financial support:* In 2010–11, 3 fellowships with full tuition reimbursements (averaging $27,326 per year), 13 research assistantships with full tuition reimbursements (averaging $24,650 per year) were awarded; institutionally sponsored loans, scholarships/grants, traineeships, and unspecified assistantships also available. *Faculty research:* Structural biology, protein dynamics and folding, computational biophysics, molecular informatics, membrane biophysics and ion channels, x-ray crystallography cryaelectron microscopy. *Unit head:* Dr. Angela M. Gronenborn, Director, 412-648-8957, Fax: 412-648-1077, E-mail: mbsbinfo@medschool.pitt.edu. *Application contact:* Jennifer L. Walker, Program Coordinator, 412-648-8957, Fax: 412-648-1077, E-mail: mbsbinfo@medschool.pitt.edu.

The University of Texas Health Science Center at San Antonio, Graduate School of Biomedical Sciences, Department of Cellular and Structural Biology, San Antonio, TX 78229-3900. Offers MS, PhD. *Faculty:* 55 full-time (20 women). *Students:* 67 full-time (49 women); includes 2 Black or African American, non-Hispanic/Latino; 7 Asian, non-Hispanic/Latino; 9 Hispanic/Latino, 20 international. Average age 27. In 2010, 2 master's, 3 doctorates awarded. *Degree requirements:* For master's, thesis; for doctorate, comprehensive exam, thesis/dissertation. *Entrance requirements:* For doctorate, GRE General Test, previous course work in biology, chemistry, physics, and calculus. Additional exam requirements/recommendations for international students: Required—TOEFL (minimum score 550 paper-based; 213 computer-based; 68 iBT). *Application deadline:* For fall admission, 3/1 priority date for domestic and international students. Applications are processed on a rolling basis. Application fee: $0. Electronic applications accepted. *Expenses:* Tuition, state resident: full-time $3072; part-time $128 per credit hour. Tuition, nonresident: full-time $11,928; part-time $497 per credit hour. Required fees: $1078; $1078 per year. One-time fee: $60. *Financial support:* In 2010–11, 55 students received support, including 14 fellowships with partial tuition reimbursements available (averaging $26,000 per year), 41 teaching assistantships (averaging $26,000 per year). Financial award application deadline: 6/30; financial award applicants required to submit FAFSA. *Faculty research:* Human/molecular genetics, endocrinology and neurobiology, cell biology, stem cell biology, cancer biology, biology of aging. Total annual research expenditures: $11.5 million. *Unit head:* Christi A. Walter, Professor and Chair, 210-567-3800, Fax: 210-567-0073, E-mail: walter@uthscsa.edu. *Application contact:* Susan Naylor, Chair, Committee on Graduate Studies, 210-567-3842, Fax: 210-567-3803, E-mail: naylor@uthscsa.edu.

The University of Texas Medical Branch, Graduate School of Biomedical Sciences, Program in Biochemistry and Molecular Biology, Galveston, TX 77555. Offers biochemistry (PhD); bioinformatics (PhD); biophysics (PhD); cell biology (PhD); computational biology (PhD); structural biology (PhD). *Degree requirements:* For doctorate, thesis/dissertation. *Entrance requirements:* Additional exam requirements/recommendations for international students: Required—TOEFL (minimum score 550 paper-based; 213 computer-based). Electronic applications accepted.

University of Washington, Graduate School, School of Medicine, Graduate Programs in Medicine, Department of Biological Structure, Seattle, WA 98195. Offers PhD. *Degree requirements:* For doctorate, thesis/dissertation. *Faculty research:* Cellular and developmental biology, experimental immunology and hematology, molecular structure and molecular biology, neurobiology, x-rays.

Baylor College of Medicine

BAYLOR COLLEGE OF MEDICINE

Interdepartmental Program in Cell and Molecular Biology

Program of Study

In 1988, a group of faculty members at Baylor College of Medicine set out to design the ideal biomedical graduate program from a student's perspective. This effort has produced a multidisciplinary environment that provides the brightest and most ambitious students with the skills needed to navigate overlapping scientific disciplines. More than 100 participating faculty members from eleven different departments provide students in the Interdepartmental Program in Cell and Molecular Biology (CMB) with a diverse set of choices for thesis research, leading to the Ph.D. degree. The range of research interests includes molecular mechanisms of inherited diseases, cancer and cell-cycle regulation, biology of aging, human gene therapy, signal transduction and membrane biology, large-scale genome sequencing and bioinformatics, functional genomics, structural and computational biology, gene expression and regulation, developmental biology, molecular virology, and immunology.

A wide range of courses are available during the first year. Core courses (taught by the Graduate School) and specialty courses (offered by individual departments) allow students to acquire depth and breadth in a number of different areas. These courses are combined with advanced courses that allow intensive investigation into topics of particular interest to each student. Course selection is flexible, with multiple choices for each requirement. Course requirements can be easily fulfilled by the end of the first year. This means that, during the second year, no required courses stand in the way of conducting research.

An additional unique feature of the CMB program is the first-year Director's Course. In this small seminar course, consisting of 10 to 15 students and taught by 4 faculty members (one for each term), students develop both practical and intellectual skills as they learn to critically evaluate the primary scientific literature, design and interpret experiments, and give lucid presentations. The intimate format also enables students to get to know the CMB Co-Directors at the beginning of their graduate career, and encourages close working relationships with fellow first-year CMB classmates. The program is supported by a competitive training grant from the National Institute of General Medical Sciences (GM 008231), which is in its eighteenth consecutive year.

Research Facilities

The participating faculty members in the program occupy extensive research space with state-of-the-art equipment and core facilities. In addition to a large number of common laboratory instruments such as ultracentrifuges, scintillation counters, spectrophotometers, and cell-culture facilities, the faculty members are also in charge of sophisticated equipment for transmission and scanning electron microscopy, protein sequencing, mass spectrometry, microarray construction and data analysis, peptide and nucleic acid synthesis, genome sequencing and analysis, knockout and transgenic mouse facilities, flow cytometry, and X-ray diffraction. There are also extensive computing and imaging facilities.

Financial Aid

All students in the CMB program receive competitive stipends of $29,000 per year. This stipend is provided during each year of study, and there are no linked teaching requirements. In addition, full health insurance and tuition are completely covered. Top-performing students each receive a $500 Claude W. Smith Fellowship Award. Although the stipend is always guaranteed, students are also encouraged to apply for outside funding. The Dean recognizes every student who receives outside funding with an additional $3000-per-year supplement to the $29,000 yearly stipend.

Cost of Study

Tuition is supported by Baylor College of Medicine and the training grant. Students pay a one-time matriculation fee of $25, a one-time graduation fee of $190, and an annual Education Resource Center fee of $150 for the first year and $20 for each subsequent year.

Living and Housing Costs

Most students and faculty members live within a few miles of the Medical Center. Housing is not provided for graduate students because a variety of affordable outstanding housing options are readily available. Some CMB students pool their resources to rent a nearby private house, while others choose to rent their own one-bedroom apartments. Numerous apartment complexes are located very close to the Texas Medical Center. Because the cost of living in Houston is well below that of every major city in the U.S., graduate students can afford to enjoy the many recreational and cultural opportunities available in Houston and even buy their own condo or town house.

Student Group

Unlike other interdisciplinary programs, the CMB program accepts only 10 to 15 carefully selected students each year. This means that training, particularly during the first year, involves one-on-one interactions with some of the best scientists in the world in an intimate environment that teaches students how to think like a scientist. Starting in the second year, CMB students present their research once a year in a formal seminar setting. This seminar course, which is attended by CMB students at all stages of training, helps students develop intellectual vigor as well as learn how to present research in a lucid way. CMB students leave Baylor with seminar skills that rival those of any Ph.D. student in the country.

Student Outcomes

Following graduation from this program, students have pursued postdoctoral training in excellent laboratories and high-quality institutions throughout the U.S. and abroad.

Location

Houston is a dynamic city that is both affordable and fun for graduate student life. Symphony concerts, opera, ballet, live theater, year-round major-league sports, and great restaurants are all a part of living in Houston, the fourth-largest city in the United States. From fall through spring, the average temperature ranges between 50°F and 75°F, with the temperatures rarely dropping below freezing, and it does not snow. Average highs during the summer are in the 90s, although it cools down into the 70s each evening, and air conditioning is present in virtually all homes, the Medical Center, indoor sporting events, etc.

The College

Baylor College of Medicine was established as an independent, private university committed to excellence in the training and education of scholars and physicians. The major area of growth for the College continues to be research. The College is located in the Texas Medical Center, which comprises more than 675 acres and includes forty-two independent institutions. The University of Texas Health Science Center, the School of Public Health, and the M. D. Anderson Cancer Center are also on campus. The Texas Medical Center is one of the most actively growing science centers in the country. The influx of new colleagues and the opportunities created by an atmosphere of expansion provide a stimulating academic environment. More information on Baylor College of Medicine can be found on the College's Web site at http://www.bcm.edu/.

Applying

Applicants are required to have a bachelor's degree or the equivalent in a relevant area of science. Most students who join the CMB program have an undergraduate degree in some aspect of the biological sciences or in chemistry, although students with degrees in other areas, such as engineering, have also joined the program. Applications are due on January 1 and should be accompanied by three letters of recommendation from people who are familiar with the applicant's scholastic qualifications and/or research abilities, as well as a personal statement that describes research experience and career goals. Official GRE scores (not more than three years old) and transcripts from all colleges and universities attended must also be provided. Applications can be made online through the Graduate School Web site at http://www.bcm.edu/gradschool/ or the CMB Web site at http://www.bcm.edu/cmb/. There is no fee for online applications. Applicants are invited to visit Baylor to meet with the participating faculty members and students, in order to have a firsthand look at the research and educational opportunities available to students in the CMB program. Expenses for travel and accommodations during the visit are provided by Baylor College of Medicine. Questions regarding the application process can be directed through e-mail to cmbprog@bcm.edu.

Correspondence and Information

Interdepartmental Program in Cell and Molecular Biology
Graduate School of Biomedical Sciences
Baylor College of Medicine
One Baylor Plaza, MS: BCM215
Houston, Texas 77030

Phone: 713-798-6557
E-mail: cmbprog@bcm.edu
Web site: http://www.bcm.edu/cmb/

Baylor College of Medicine

THE FACULTY AND THEIR RESEARCH

Department of Biochemistry and Molecular Biology
Wah Chiu, Ph.D. Structural and computational biology of macromolecular machines and cells.
Ido Golding, Ph.D. Decision-making in living cells: Lessons from simple systems.
Adam Kuspa, Ph.D. Molecular genetics of development in *Dictyostelium*.
Jianpeng Ma, Ph.D. Computational molecular biophysics; structural biology.
B. V. Venkataram Prasad, Ph.D. Structural biology of viruses and viral proteins.
Jun Qin, Ph.D. Network analysis proteomics.
Florante A. Quiocho, Ph.D. Protein structure, molecular recognition, and function; structural biophysics and biology: X-ray crystallography of proteins.
Shelley Sazer, Ph.D. Eukaryotic cell-cycle control; spindle assembly checkpoint; Ran GTPase; nuclear division.
Anna Sokac, Ph.D. Shaping cells, shaping embryos: Coordinated actin and membrane dynamics in flies and frogs.
Zhou Songyang, Ph.D. Molecular mechanisms of signal transduction.
Francis T. F. Tsai, D.Phil. Structural and functional studies of protein complexes and macromolecular assemblies.
Salih Wakil, Ph.D. Mechanism and regulation of fatty acid metabolism.
Theodore G. Wensel, Ph.D. G-protein signaling in neurons.
Thomas Westbrook, Ph.D. RNAi-based strategies to cancer gene discovery; REST tumor suppressor pathway.
John H. Wilson, Ph.D. Instability of trinucleotide repeats; knock-in mouse models for retinitis pigmentosa; gene therapy of dominant rhodopsin mutations.
Zheng Zhou, Ph.D. Molecular genetic studies of clearance of apoptotic cells in *C. elegans*.

Department of Medicine
Lawrence Chan, D.Sc. Molecular biology, genetics, and gene therapy of atherosclerosis; lipid disorders and diabetes mellitus.
N. Tony Eissa, M.D. Innate immunity and inflammation.
Henry Pownall, Ph.D. Identification of the molecular basis of disorders associated with atherosclerosis, obesity, alcoholic hepatitis, and hypertriglyceridemia; dietary studies in human subjects and in animal models; cell culture and gene regulation.
Matthew H. Wilson, M.D., Ph.D. Transposons and kidney gene therapy.
Li-Yuan Yu-Lee, Ph.D. Signaling pathways in immune and inflammatory responses and cancer.

Department of Molecular and Cellular Biology
William (B. R.) Brinkley, Ph.D. Factors in the nucleus and mitotic apparatus affecting genomic instability in cancer.
Keith Syson Chan, Ph.D., Department of Urology. Bladder cancer stem cells in invasion and metastasis.
Eric Chang, Ph.D. Growth and signaling regulation by Ras G-proteins.
Orla Conneely, Ph.D. Developmental control mechanisms.
Francesco J. DeMayo, Ph.D. Molecular and developmental biology of the lung and uterus.
Xin-Hua Feng, Ph.D. Protein modifications and cell signaling in cell fate determination, development, and cancer.
Loning Fu, Ph.D. Role of the circadian clock in cancer development and therapy.
Suzanne A.W. Fuqua, Ph.D., Department of Medicine. The role of estrogen receptors and estrogen-regulated proteins in breast tumor progression.
Milan A. Jamrich, Ph.D. Role of homeobox and forkhead genes in vertebrate eye development.
Weei-Chin Lin, M.D., Ph.D., Department of Medicine. Cell-cycle regulators and novel cancer therapeutic targets.
David D. Moore, Ph.D. Nuclear hormone receptors regulate metabolism and cancer.
Hoang Nguyen, Ph.D. Skin epithelial stem cell fate maintenance and lineage determination.
Bert W. O'Malley, M.D. Steroid receptors and coactivators regulate gene expression in normal and disease states.
Paul Overbeek, Ph.D. Cell fate determination.
Fred A. Pereira, Ph.D. Signaling pathways in auditory development, aging, and cancer.
JoAnne S. Richards, Ph.D. Hormonal control of ovarian gene expression.
Jeffrey M. Rosen, Ph.D. Mammary gland development and breast cancer.
David R. Rowley, Ph.D. The tumor microenvironment in cancer progression.
Ming-Jer Tsai, Ph.D. Transcription factors in development and diseases.
Li Xin, Ph.D. Prostate stem cells and cells of origin for prostate cancer.
Thomas P. Zwaka, M.D., Ph.D. The nature of embryonic stem cell pluripotency.

Department of Molecular and Human Genetics
David B. Bates, Ph.D. Chromosome dynamics, molecular mechanisms of DNA replication, and cell cycle control in *E. coli*.
Arthur L. Beaudet, M.D. Role of genomic imprinting and epigenetics in disease, including Prader-Willi and Angelman syndromes and autism; hepatocyte gene therapy.
Richard A. Gibbs, Ph.D. Genomics; genome sequencing; molecular basis of human genetic diseases.
Xiangwei He, Ph.D. Chromosome segregation: Interaction between spindle and kinetochores.
Christophe Herman, Ph.D. Regulation of cellular processes and quality control by an ATP dependent membrane protease.
Grzegorz Ira, Ph.D. DNA recombination is ubiquitous and essential for DNA-based life.
Monica Justice, Ph.D. Genetic analysis of mouse development and disease.
Brendan Lee, M.D., Ph.D. Genetic pathways that specify development and homeostasis: Translational studies of skeletal development and urea cycle disorders, and therapy for metabolic diseases.
Olivier Lichtarge, M.D., Ph.D. Computational and systems biology; rational protein engineering; inhibition of protein interactions and drug design.
James R. Lupski, M.D., Ph.D. Molecular genetics of Charcot-Marie-Tooth disease and related inherited neuropathies; molecular mechanisms for human DNA rearrangements; genomic disorders, copy number variation (CNV), and disease.
David L. Nelson, Ph.D. Human genetic disorders; fragile X syndrome; unstable DNA and neurodegeneration.

Susan Rosenberg, Ph.D. Genome instability in evolution; cancer and antibiotic resistance.
Kenneth Scott, Ph.D. Cancer gene discovery; pathways governing tumor metastasis; animal models for cancer.
Gad Shaulsky, Ph.D. Allorecognition, evolution of sociality, and functional genomics in *Dictyostelium*.
Jue D. Wang, Ph.D. Elongation of DNA replication and implications for genomic stability.
Meng Wang, Ph.D. Systemic studies of endocrine and metabolic signaling in promoting healthy aging.
Hui Zheng, Ph.D. Molecular genetics of Alzheimer's disease and age-related disorders.

Department of Molecular Physiology and Biophysics
Mary Dickinson, Ph.D. Imaging the role of fluid mechanics in early cardiovascular development.
Steen E. Pedersen, Ph.D. Ion channel function and structure.
Xander H. T. Wehrens, M.D., Ph.D. Regulation of cardiac ion channels in normal and diseased hearts.
Pumin Zhang, Ph.D. Cell-cycle regulation in development and disease.

Department of Molecular Virology and Microbiology
Janet S. Butel, Ph.D. Polyomaviruses and pathogenesis of infection and disease.
Lawrence A. Donehower, Ph.D. Tumor suppressors and mouse cancer and aging models.
Mary K. Estes, Ph.D. Molecular mechanisms regulating virus–intestinal cell interactions and pathogenesis.
Ronald Javier, Ph.D. Adenoviruses and viral oncology.
Jason T. Kimata, Ph.D. Retroviral replication and pathogenesis.
Richard E. Lloyd, Ph.D. Translation regulation in cancer, apoptosis, and viral infection.
Anthony W. Maresso, Ph.D. Pathogenesis of bacterial infections.
Susan J. Marriott, Ph.D. Cellular transformation mediated by human retroviruses.
Joseph F. Petrosino, Ph.D., Functional genomics of biodefense and emerging infectious disease pathogens.
Robert F. (Frank) Ramig, Ph.D. Genetics, replication, and pathogenesis of *Reoviridae*.
Betty L. Slagle, Ph.D. Hepatitis B virus pathogenesis.
Lynn Zechiedrich, Ph.D. Protein-DNA interactions, genomic instability, and antibiotic resistance.

Department of Neurology
Jeffrey L. Noebels, M.D., Ph.D. Gene control of neuronal excitability.

Department of Neuroscience
Andrew K. Groves, Ph.D. Development and regeneration of the inner ear.
Kimberley R. Tolias, Ph.D. Molecular signaling pathways in structural development and plasticity of dendrites and synapses.

Department of Pathology and Immunology
Thomas A. Cooper, M.D. Alternative splicing regulation in development and disease.
Shuhua Han, M.D. B-cell activation and differentiation; inflammation; autoimmunity.
H. Daniel Lacorazza, Ph.D. Genetic control of hematopoiesis and developmental immunology.
Dario Marchetti, Ph.D. Invasive, angiogenic, and metastatic mechanisms of brain cancers; brain invasion/metastasis in breast, melanoma, and medulloblastoma; the biology of circulating tumor cells.
Graeme Mardon, Ph.D. Molecular mechanisms controlling retinal development.
Richard N. Sifers, Ph.D. Glycobiology; posttranslational disease modifiers; conformational disease.
David M. Spencer, Ph.D. Prostate cancer progression and immunotherapy; gene therapy.
Tse-Hua Tan, Ph.D. Signal transduction by MAP kinases and phosphatases in cancer and immunity.
Nikolai A. Timchenko, Ph.D. Role of C/EBP proteins and RNA binding proteins in liver biology.
James Versalovic, M.D., Ph.D. The human microbiome; beneficial microbes and host interactions; probiotics, innate immunity, and intestinal inflammation.
Jin Wang, Ph.D. Molecular regulation of immune responses by apoptosis and autophagy.
Laising Yen, Ph.D. RNA-based molecular switches and biosensors; cancer biomarker discovery.
Biao Zheng, M.D., Ph.D. Somatic genetics and development of immune responses; immunosenescence; autoimmunity.

Department of Pediatrics
Alison Bertuch, M.D., Ph.D. Telomere structure, maintenance and function, and DNA double-strand break repair.
Margaret A. Goodell, Ph.D. Hematopoietic stem cells: basic biology and gene therapy.
Kendal Hirschi, Ph.D. Plant biology related to human nutrition and environmental issues.
Sharon E. Plon, M.D., Ph.D. Genetic susceptibility to cancer; molecular mechanisms that control genomic stability.
Yong Xu, M.D., Ph.D. Understanding CNS control of body weight, glucose balance and cardiovascular functions.
Jason T. Yustein, M.D., Ph.D. Insights into molecular pathogenesis of pediatric sarcomas.
Huda Y. Zoghbi, M.D. Molecular pathogenesis of neurodegenerative and neurodevelopmental disorders.

Department of Pharmacology
Pui-Kwong Chan, Ph.D. Antitumor agents and mechanism
Timothy G. Palzkill, Ph.D. Protein structure-function; protein-protein interactions.

Interinstitutional Faculty
Michael J. Galko, Ph.D. U.T. M.D. Anderson Cancer Center. Molecular genetics of tissue repair responses in *Drosophila*.
Stephen Wong, Ph.D., The Methodist Hospital. Computational biology; high throughput cell imaging and medical imaging.

GERSTNER SLOAN-KETTERING
GRADUATE SCHOOL OF BIOMEDICAL SCIENCES
Ph.D. in Cancer Biology Program

Program of Study

The mission of the Gerstner Sloan-Kettering Graduate School is to advance the frontiers of knowledge by providing an interactive, innovative, and collegial environment that educates and trains students to make new discoveries in the biological sciences. The recent explosion in new knowledge about the biological functions of disease, including cancer, is rooted in fundamental laboratory discoveries. Research in genetics, cell biology, immunology, and other disciplines contributes to the understanding of the pathogenesis of disease.

The curriculum places special emphasis on the development of a self-reliant research approach, critical analysis, and the integration of basic science knowledge with human disease physiology. During the first year, students complete a thirty-two-week core course (sixteen weeks per semester) that introduces recent findings in relevant topics through didactic lecture and discussion; three laboratory rotations, with each one culminating in a written summary and oral presentation of their findings; four visits with clinicians in the clinic; course work in logic and critical analysis and responsible conduct of research; and two semesters of the President's Research Seminar Series Journal Club, which introduces students to the published works of world-renowned speakers. Following the end of the spring semester, students are expected to choose a research mentor.

During the second year, students begin their full-time dissertation research and present a written and oral thesis proposal. They are also expected to take part in the Current Topics Journal Club as well as the Graduate Student Seminar, in which students present their own research. At the beginning of the third year, students can select a clinical mentor who serves as a conduit for hospital-based academic activities.

Research Facilities

The library subscribes to a full range of databases that encompass key science, medical, and health-care information. Students have access to more than 1,100 journal titles, with over 80 percent of these titles accessible and available electronically. The library's Web site provides access to an extensive collection of resources, including an online catalog, databases, electronic books, and electronic journals.

Sloan-Kettering Institute's thirty-nine cutting-edge research core facilities serve both basic and clinical research needs, offering state-of-the-art instruments and technical staff support to students as they train and conduct research. These facilities include the High-Throughput Screening Facility, which screens potential anticancer compounds against targets; the Genomics Core Laboratory, which extracts and analyzes microarrays; the Stem Cell Research Facility, which characterizes and distributes human embryonic stem cells; the Gene Transfer and Somatic Cell Engineering Facility, which develops, validates, and implements procedures critical to gene transfer–related clinical research; the Antitumor Assessment Facility, which provides advisory services related to the evaluation of agents with potential antitumor activity; and the Pathology Core Facility, which performs research involving human tissue.

Financial Aid

All students receive a fellowship package that includes an annual stipend ($33,127 for 2011–12); a first-year allowance to be used for books, journals, and other school expenses; a scholarship that covers tuition and fees; comprehensive medical and dental insurance; a laptop computer; relocation costs of up to $500; and membership in the New York Academy of Sciences. Students may also apply for independent funding from agencies such as the National Institutes of Health and the National Science Foundation. Recipients of one of these fellowships receive an additional award of $5000 from the school; this is in addition to any supplement necessary to bring the stipend to the common level. Travel awards are given to students who present a poster or a short talk at a scientific meeting.

Cost of Study

As highlighted in the Financial Aid section, all tuition expenses are covered by a full fellowship, which is awarded to all students who matriculate in the school. Students are also provided with health insurance at no cost to them.

Living and Housing Costs

Affordable housing in proximity to the research buildings is provided to all students by Memorial Sloan-Kettering. There is a wide range of costs, which vary depending on the size of the housing unit.

Student Group

The graduate students enrolled at Gerstner Sloan-Kettering are drawn from a pool of applicants who comprise a variety of backgrounds and nationalities. Applicants are expected to hold an undergraduate degree from an accredited institution and must have completed sufficient course work in biology, chemistry, genetics, molecular biology, etc.

Student Outcomes

Graduates of the program are expected to enter into careers as researchers, scientists, and educators in excellent laboratories, hospitals, medical schools, and research institutions throughout the country and around the world.

Location

The campus is located on Manhattan's Upper East Side, home to some of New York City's best shopping and dining. Several world-famous museums are within walking distance, and Central Park is a few blocks away. New York also offers theater, live music, outdoor recreation, and cultural attractions such as the Metropolitan Museum of Art, all accessible by public transportation.

The Graduate School

The Gerstner Sloan-Kettering Graduate School of Biomedical Sciences offers the next generation of basic scientists an intensive Ph.D. program to study the biological sciences through the lens of cancer—while giving students the tools they need to put them in the vanguard of research that can be applied in any area of human disease. The faculty members of the School have the exceptional ability to present novel perspectives on the molecular pathophysiology of disease to gifted young men and women eager to be part of shaping the future of research and treatment.

Applying

Prospective students must complete and submit the online application form and submit the following: official transcripts from all colleges previously attended; three letters of recommendation from advisers and/or research mentors; and official GRE scores. An in-person interview is requested from those applicants being seriously considered for admission, but the requirement may be waived if geographical constraints are overwhelming and may be substituted with video interviews. The deadline to apply is December 10, and interviews take place the following January.

Correspondence and Information

Gerstner Sloan-Kettering Graduate School of Biomedical Sciences
1275 York Avenue, Box 441
New York, New York 10065
Phone: 646-888-6639
Fax: 646-422-2351
E-mail: gradstudies@sloankettering.edu
Web site: http://www.sloankettering.edu

Gerstner Sloan-Kettering Graduate School of Biomedical Sciences

THE FACULTY AND THEIR RESEARCH

C. David Allis, Molecular Biology. The histone code and its impact on gene regulation and chromosome dynamics.
James P. Allison, Immunology. Regulation of T-cell responses and new approaches to cancer and immunotherapy.
Grégoire Altan-Bonnet, Computational Biology. Robustness and adaptability in T-cell ligand discrimination.
Kathryn V. Anderson, Developmental Biology. Genetic pathways that direct embryonic patterning and morphogenesis in the mouse embryo.
Zhirong Bao, Developmental Biology. How the genome dictates development, with *C. elegans* as model.
Boris C. Bastian, Human Oncology and Pathogenesis. Genetic and biologic characterization of cutaneous neoplasia.
Mary K. Baylies, Developmental Biology. Mechanisms underlying the specification and morphogenesis of organ systems.
Robert Benezra, Cancer Biology and Genetics. Molecular mechanisms of tumor growth and progression, using mouse Id1 and Id3 knockout models and analysis of the mitotic checkpoint.
Peter Besmer, Developmental Biology. Normal and oncogenic receptor tyrosine kinase signaling in vitro and in vivo in mice.
Ronald G. Blasberg, Molecular Pharmacology and Chemistry. Development of noninvasive imaging paradigms in living organisms, using radionuclide and optical reporter systems.
Jacqueline Bromberg, Medicine. Aberrantly activated Stat3 and the mechanisms of Stat3-mediated transformation.
Luca Cartegni, Molecular Pharmacology and Chemistry. Role of alternative splicing and other post-transcriptional events in the development and/or maintenance of cancer and their therapeutic modulation.
Raju S. K. Chaganti, Cell Biology. Genomic instability in cancer cells and its implications for clinical behavior of tumors and normal cellular developmental pathways.
Timothy A. Chan, Human Oncology and Pathogenesis. Identification and characterization of tumor suppressors in human cancers.
Jayanta Chaudhuri, Immunology. Mechanistic elucidation of immunoglobulin gene diversification.
Emily Cheng, Human Oncology and Pathogenesis. Molecular mechanisms of cell death.
Nai-Kong V. Cheung, Pediatrics. Development of curative therapies for the treatment of metastatic childhood solid tumors, with special emphasis on antibody-based strategies.
Gabriela Chiosis, Molecular Pharmacology and Chemistry. Pharmacological modulation of molecular chaperones in transformed biological systems.
Samuel J. Danishefsky, Molecular Pharmacology and Chemistry. Synthesis of antitumor natural products and of fully synthetic carbohydrate-based vaccines.
Bo Dupont, Immunology. Receptor-ligand interactions regulating NK cell activation/inhibition; signal transduction pathways in NK cells; NK cells in tumor immunosurveillance and hematopoietic stem cell transplantation.
James Fagin, Human Oncology and Pathogenesis. Oncogenic kinases in pathogenesis and therapeutic targeting of thyroid cancer.
Yuman Fong, Surgery. Oncolytic viral therapies in the treatment of malignancy.
Zvi Fuks, Molecular Pharmacology and Chemistry. Mechanisms of radiation-induced damage and the clinical basis of radiation resistance.
Hironori Funabiki, Cell Biology. Spatial and temporal control of mitosis and chromosome-mediated signaling.
Filippo Giancotti, Cell Biology. Molecular mechanisms underlying tumor initiation and progression to metastasis.
Michael Glickman, Immunology. Molecular mechanisms underlying the pathogenesis of *Mycobacterium tuberculosis* and mechanisms of nonhomologous end-joining in mycobacteria.
Jonathan Goldberg, Structural Biology. Structural and biochemical characterization of intracellular vesicle transport.
Mary Goll, Developmental Biology. Epigenetic regulation of transcription using zebrafish as a model.
Jan Grimm, Molecular Pharmacology and Chemistry. Developing novel imaging approaches for improved detection and monitoring of disease.
Anna-Katerina Hadjantonakis, Developmental Biology. Using mouse genetics and high-resolution imaging of living samples to study developmental pathways that direct and orchestrate establishment of the mammalian body plan.
Alan Hall, Cell Biology. Rho and Ras GTPases in cell migration, morphogenesis, polarity and cell cycle.
Ulrich G. Hammerling, Immunology. Mechanisms underlying immunodeficiency caused by vitamin A deprivation.
Cole Haynes, Cell Biology. Molecular mechanisms that protect mitochondrial function, molecular chaperones, and proteases.
Eric C. Holland, Cancer Biology and Genetics. Molecular mechanisms underlying pathogenesis of CNS tumors and modeling of these cancers in mice.
Alan N. Houghton, Immunology. Immune response to cancer; immune recognition of self and mutated molecules; development of new immunotherapies.
Hedvig Hricak, Radiology. Methodologies of molecular imaging of prostate and gynecologic tumors.
James Hsieh, Human Oncology and Pathogenesis. Cancer cell proliferation and death, cancer drug development, and kidney cancer.
Danwei Huangfu, Developmental Biology. Developing therapies for diabetes using stem cell and regenerative biology.
Jerard Hurwitz, Molecular Biology. Mechanisms of eukaryotic DNA replication and the isolation and characterization of proteins involved.
Morgan Huse, Immunology. Study of intracellular signaling dynamics in lymphocytes.
Prasad V. Jallepalli, Molecular Biology. Mechanisms of high-fidelity chromosome segregation in human cells.
Maria Jasin, Developmental Biology. Double-strand break repair and genomic integrity in mammalian cells and the relationship to tumor suppression.
Xuejun Jiang, Cell Biology. Programmed cell death, molecular mechanisms, and its roles in tumorigenesis.
Johanna Joyce, Cancer Biology and Genetics. Understanding how a tumor cell co-opts its environment to promote its growth and progression.
Alexandra L. Joyner, Developmental Biology. Genetic and cellular regulation of neural development and adult stem cell biology.
Julia A. Kaltschmidt, Developmental Biology. Understanding the mechanisms of synaptic specificity underlying neuronal circuit formation.
Scott N. Keeney, Molecular Biology. Molecular mechanisms of the initiation of meiotic recombination.
Thomas J. Kelly, Molecular Biology. Regulatory mechanisms that control DNA replication during the cell cycle of eukaryotic cells.
Robert J. Klein, Cancer Biology and Genetics. Identification of genes responsible for inherited predisposition to cancer.
Andrew Koff, Molecular Biology. Role of cell-cycle inhibitors in differentiation and how their loss affects tumorigenesis.
Richard N. Kolesnick, Molecular Pharmacology and Chemistry. Role of ceramide signaling in radiation-induced vascular dysfunction and tumor regression.
Jason A. Koutcher, Medicine. Application of magnetic resonance spectroscopy and imaging to enhance therapeutic gain of different antineoplastic modalities.
Elizabeth H. Lacy, Developmental Biology. Mechanisms of gastrulation and organogenesis during mouse development.
Marc Ladanyi, Human Oncology and Pathogenesis. Genetics and molecular pathogenesis of sarcomas and thoracic malignancies.
Eric Lai, Developmental Biology. Control of developmental patterning by notch signaling and microRNAs.
Steven M. Larson, Molecular Pharmacology and Chemistry. Molecular imaging in animals and humans, using high-resolution diagnostic instruments such as PET and single-photon emission tomography.
Christina Leslie, Computational Biology. Machine learning algorithms for computational and systems biology.
Ross L. Levine, Human Oncology and Pathogenesis. Investigation of genetic basis of hematopoietic malignancies.
Jason S. Lewis, Molecular Pharmacology and Chemistry. Development of radiopharmaceuticals for the imaging and therapy of cancer.
Ming Li, Immunology. Mechanisms of T-cell homeostasis, tolerance, and immunity and their relevance to autoimmune diseases and cancer.
Yueming Li, Molecular Pharmacology and Chemistry. Function and regulation of transmembrane proteases; development of novel protease-based cancer therapies.
Christopher D. Lima, Structural Biology. Structural biology of posttranslational protein modification; RNA processing and decay.
Jidong Liu, Cell Biology. Molecular mechanism of RNA interference, function, and regulation of mammalian cytoplasmic processing bodies.
Philip O. Livingston, Medicine. Tumor vaccinology; approaches to augmenting antibody and T-cell responses to defined cancer antigens.
Stephen B. Long, Structural Biology. Structural biology of ion channels and enzymatic membrane proteins.
Minkui Luo, Molecular Pharmacology and Chemistry. Developing chemical tools to elucidate protein posttranslational modification and designing inhibitors for cancer therapies.
Kenneth J. Marians, Molecular Biology. Mechanisms of replication restart and chromosome segregation.
Joan Massagué, Cancer Biology and Genetics. Control of cell growth and phenotype; delineating mechanisms of relevance to tumor progression, metastasis, and response to therapy.
Christine Mayr, Cancer Biology and Genetics. Role of the 3' UTR for gene regulation.
Ingo K. Mellinghoff, Human Oncology and Pathogenesis. Molecular determinants in drug response and growth factor signaling.
Malcolm A. S. Moore, Cell Biology. Biology of hematopoietic stem cells in normal and malignant lymphohematopoiesis.
Philipp Niethammer, Cell Biology. Regulation of wound detection in tissues.
Dimitar B. Nikolov, Structural Biology. Structural, biophysical, and biochemical characterization of molecular mechanisms of cell-cell interactions and signal transduction in the nervous system.
Stephen D. Nimer, Molecular Pharmacology and Chemistry. Defining molecular and biological abnormalities and underlying transcriptional regulation mechanisms involved in development and growth of hematologic cancers.
Kenneth Offit, Medicine. Population genetics of cancer-susceptibility: genomic approaches to characterization of novel cancer-risk alleles.
Richard J. O'Reilly, Immunology. Genetic disparities and cellular interactions between donor and host that affect allogeneic hematopoietic cell transplantation.
Michael Overholtzer, Cell Biology. Mechanisms of tumor initiation/progression; cell adhesion; cell death.
Eric G. Pamer, Immunology. T-cell and innate inflammatory responses to bacterial and fungal infections.
Christopher Park, Human Oncology and Pathogenesis. Normal and malignant stem cells in the hematopoietic system.
Gavril W. Pasternak, Molecular Pharmacology and Chemistry. Molecular mechanisms of opioid receptor actions, analgesics, and G-protein–coupled receptors.
Dinshaw Patel, Structural Biology. Structural biology of macromolecular recognition, regulation, and catalysis.
Nikola P. Pavletich, Structural Biology. Structural biology of oncogenes and tumor suppressors.
Alexandros Pertsinidis, Structural Biology. Structural biology of the principles of gene regulation and synaptic physiology, using sophisticated optical techniques.
John H. J. Petrini, Molecular Biology. Repair of chromosomal breaks and activation of DNA damage-induced cell-cycle checkpoints.
Simon N. Powell, Molecular Biology, Radiation Oncology. DNA replication and recombination; chromosome dynamics; human genetics.
Mark S. Ptashne, Molecular Biology. Mechanisms of gene regulation as studied in yeast.
Dirk Remus, Molecular Biology. Molecular mechanism of the initiation of DNA replication in eukaryotes.
Marilyn Resh, Cell Biology. Regulation of protein function by fatty acylation; mechanism of retroviral particle assembly; mechanisms of normal and malignant glial cell growth.
Neal Rosen, Molecular Pharmacology and Chemistry. Understanding biochemical mechanisms underlying phenotypes and the development of new therapeutic strategies.
Alexander Y. Rudensky, Immunology. Immunological tolerance; T cell differentiation and function.
Michael Sadelain, Immunology. Mechanisms governing transgene expression, stem cell engineering, and genetic strategies to enhance immunity against cancer.
Chris Sander, Computational Biology. Computational and systems biology of molecules, pathways, and processes.
Charles L. Sawyers, Human Oncology and Pathogenesis. Molecular basis of prostate cancer progression.
David A. Scheinberg, Molecular Pharmacology and Chemistry. Discovery and development of novel, specific immunotherapeutic agents, vaccines, and targeted nanodevices for cancer therapy.
Gary K. Schwartz, Medicine. Identification of cell-cycle inhibitors that promote chemotherapy-induced apoptosis and their use in cancer therapy.
Songhai Shi, Developmental Biology. Molecular and cellular mechanisms underlying mammalian neuronal development and circuit formation.
Stewart Shuman, Molecular Biology. Mechanisms and structures of mRNA cap-forming enzymes and means by which capping is coupled to transcription.
Samuel Singer, Surgery. Development of a novel clinically relevant biochemical and molecular system of prognostic determinants for soft-tissue sarcoma.
David Solit, Human Oncology and Pathogenesis. Human oncology and pathogenesis; genomics; oncogenes and tumor suppressors; cancer therapeutics; clinical trials.
David R. Spriggs, Medicine. Molecular mechanisms of drug resistance in ovarian cancer.
Lorenz P. Studer, Developmental Biology. Stem cells as a tool to understand normal and pathological development in CNS and to develop cell-based strategies for neural repair.
Joseph Sun, Immunology. Natural killer cell development and responses against infection.
Viviane Tabar, Neurosurgery. In vivo applications of neural derivatives of pluripotent stem cells (iPS, ES); cancer stem cells in human brain tumors.
Derek S. Tan, Molecular Pharmacology and Chemistry. Diversity-oriented synthesis and rational design for cancer chemical biology and drug discovery.
Paul J. Tempst, Molecular Biology. Development of proteomic technologies and approaches for studying eukaryotic transcriptional machineries and for cancer biomarker discovery.
Craig B. Thompson, Cancer Biology and Genetics. Regulation of cancer cell metabolism; immune cell activation and transformation; delineation of the roles of autophagy and apoptosis in health and disease.
Meng-Fu Bryan Tsou, Cell Biology. Cell cycle control of centrosome duplication and degeneration.
Marcel van den Brink, Immunology. Immunology of bone marrow transplantation.
Andrea Ventura, Cancer Biology and Genetics. Biological functions of cancer-relevant microRNAs.
Harel Weinstein, Computational Biology. Structural, dynamic, and integrative determinants of molecular and cellular mechanisms underlying physiological function and pharmacological activity.
Hans-Guido Wendel, Cancer Biology and Genetics. Modeling genetics of tumor initiation, progression, and treatment response in vivo.
Iestyn Whitehouse, Molecular Biology. Chromatin structure and the function of ATP-dependent chromatin remodeling enzymes.
Joao Xavier, Computational Biology. Computational models and quantitative experiments of biofilm and cancer growth.
James W. Young, Medicine. Innate and adaptive immunity against tumors and viruses stimulated by human dendritic cells.
Jennifer A. Zallen, Developmental Biology. Generation of tissue structure through the collective action of cell populations.
Xiaolan Zhao, Molecular Biology. Chromosome structure and protein modification in the maintenance of genomic integrity.

UNIFORMED SERVICES UNIVERSITY OF THE HEALTH SCIENCES

F. Edward Hébert School of Medicine
Graduate Program in Molecular and Cell Biology

Program of Study

The program of study is designed for full-time students who wish to obtain a Ph.D. degree in the area of molecular and cell biology. This interdepartmental graduate program, which includes faculty members from both basic and clinical departments, offers research expertise in a wide range of areas, including bacteriology, immunology, genetics, biochemistry, regulation of gene expression, and cancer biology. The program includes core courses in molecular and cell biology that provide necessary knowledge for modern biomedical research, as well as advanced electives in areas of faculty expertise. The first-year curriculum includes courses in biochemistry, cell biology, experimental methodology, genetics, and immunology. During the first summer, students participate in laboratory rotations in two laboratories of their choice, leading to the choice of a mentor for their doctoral research. The second-year curriculum offers advanced elective courses in a variety of disciplines, including biochemistry, cell biology, immunology, molecular endocrinology, and virology, and marks the transition from classwork to original laboratory research. Throughout their graduate experience, students participate in journal clubs designed to foster interaction across disciplines and to develop the critical skills needed for data presentation and analysis. A year-round seminar series brings renowned scientists to the Uniformed Services University of the Health Sciences (USUHS) to share their results and to meet with students and faculty members. Students may also take advantage of seminars hosted by other programs and departments as well as those presented at the National Institutes of Health. Completion of the research project and preparation and successful defense of a written dissertation leads to the degree of Doctor of Philosophy.

Research Facilities

The University possesses outstanding facilities for research in molecular and cell biology. Well-equipped laboratories and extramurally funded faculty members provide an outstanding environment in which to pursue state-of-the-art research. Shared equipment in a modern biomedical instrumentation core facility includes oligonucleotide and peptide synthesizers and sequencers; a variety of imaging equipment, including laser confocal and electron microscopes; fluorescent-activated cell sorters; and an ACAS workstation. A recently added proteomics facility contains both MADLI-TOF and ESI tandem mass spectrometers. All offices, laboratories, and the Learning Resource Center are equipped with high-speed Internet connectivity and have access to an extensive online journal collection.

Financial Aid

Stipends are available for civilian applicants. Awards of stipends are competitive and may be renewed. For the 2011–12 academic year, stipends for entering students begin at $27,000. Outstanding students may be nominated for the Dean's Special Fellowship, which supports a stipend of $32,000.

Cost of Study

Graduate students are not required to pay tuition. Civilian graduate students do not incur any obligation to the United States government for service after completion of their graduate training programs. Active-duty military personnel incur an obligation for additional military service by Department of Defense regulations that govern sponsored graduate education. Students are required to maintain health insurance.

Living and Housing Costs

The University does not have housing for graduate students. However, there is an abundant supply of rental housing in the area. Living costs in the greater Washington, D.C., area are comparable to those of other East Coast metropolitan areas.

Student Group

The first graduate students in the interdisciplinary Graduate Program in Molecular and Cell Biology at USUHS were admitted in 1995. Over the last decade, the Graduate Program in Molecular and Cell Biology has grown significantly; 23 students are currently enrolled. Twenty-five Ph.D. degrees in molecular and cell biology have been awarded over the past nine years.

Location

Metropolitan Washington has a population of about 2.7 million residents in the District of Columbia and the surrounding areas of Maryland and Virginia. The region is a center of education and research and is home to five major universities, four medical schools, the National Library of Medicine and the National Institutes of Health (next to the USUHS campus), Walter Reed Army Medical Center, the Armed Forces Institute of Pathology, the Library of Congress, the Smithsonian Institution, the National Bureau of Standards, and many other private and government research centers. Many cultural advantages of the area include the theater, a major symphony orchestra, major-league sports, and world-famous museums. The Metro subway system has a station near campus and provides a convenient connection from the University to the museums and cultural attractions of downtown Washington. For outdoor activities, the Blue Ridge Mountains, the Chesapeake Bay, and the Atlantic coast beaches are all within a few hours' drive.

The University

USUHS is located just outside Washington, D.C., in Bethesda, Maryland. The campus is situated on an attractive, wooded site at the National Naval Medical Center and is close to several major federal health research facilities. Through various affiliation agreements, these institutes provide additional resources to enhance the educational experience of graduate students at USUHS.

Applying

Both civilians and military personnel are eligible to apply for graduate study at USUHS. Before matriculation, each applicant must complete a baccalaureate degree that includes college-level courses in biology, inorganic chemistry, mathematics, organic chemistry, and physics. Advanced courses in biology, chemistry, or related fields, such as biochemistry, cell biology, genetics, immunology, microbiology, molecular biology, and physical chemistry, are desirable but not essential. Each applicant must submit a USUHS graduate training application form, complete academic transcripts of postsecondary education, GRE scores (in addition to the aptitude sections, one advanced examination is recommended), three letters of recommendation from individuals familiar with the academic achievements or research experience of the applicant, and a personal statement expressing the applicant's career objectives. Active-duty military personnel must obtain the approval and sponsorship of their parent military department in addition to acceptance from USUHS. USUHS subscribes fully to the policy of equal educational opportunity and selects students on a competitive basis without regard to race, sex, creed, or national origin. Application forms may be obtained from the Web site at http://www.usuhs.mil/mcb/gradapp.html#applynow. Completed applications must be received before January 1 for matriculation in August.

Correspondence and Information

Associate Dean for Graduate Education
Uniformed Services University of the Health Sciences
4301 Jones Bridge Road
Bethesda, Maryland 20814
Phone: 301-295-3913
     800-772-1747 (toll-free)
Web site: http://www.usuhs.mil/graded/

For an application and information about the molecular and cell biology program:

Dr. Mary Lou Cutler, Director
Graduate Program in Molecular and Cell Biology
Uniformed Services University of the Health Sciences
4301 Jones Bridge Road
Bethesda, Maryland 20814

Phone: 301-295-3642
Fax: 301-295-1996
E-mail: nfinley@usuhs.mil
Web site: http://www.usuhs.mil/mcb/

Uniformed Services University of the Health Sciences

THE FACULTY AND THEIR RESEARCH

Regina C. Armstrong, Professor; Ph.D., North Carolina at Chapel Hill, 1987. Cellular and molecular mechanisms of neural stem/progenitor cell development and regeneration in demyelinating diseases and brain injury models.
Roopa Biswas, Adjunct Assistant Professor, PhD. Ohio State, 1997. Mechanisms of regulation of inflammation; http://www.usuhs.mil/gsn/abdellah/faculty.html.
Jorge Blanco, Adjunct Assistant Professor; Ph.D., Buenos Aires, 1991. Molecular mechanisms of pathogenesis of respiratory viruses. *J. Infect. Dis.* 185(12):1780–5, 2002.
Christopher C. Broder, Professor and Director; Ph.D., Florida, 1989. Virus-host cell interactions; vaccines and therapeutics; HIV, Hendra and Nipah viruses, Australian bat lyssavirus.
Teodor Brumeanu, Professor; M.D., Carol Davila (Romania), 1978. Medicine.
Rolf Bünger, Professor; M.D./Ph.D., Munich, 1979. Cellular, molecular, and metabolic mechanisms of heart and brain circulation and resuscitation at various levels of organization: intact animal/isolated perfused organs/subcellular compartments of cytosol and mitochondria. *NMR Biomed.,* doi: 10.1002/nbm.1717; *Exp. Biol. Med. 234(12):1395–416, 2009; in Recent Research Developments in Physiology, Vol. 4, ed. S. G. Pandalai, 2006;Exerc. Sport Sci. Rev.* 32(4):174–9, 2004.
Rachel Cox, Assistant Professor, Ph.D., North Carolina at Chapel Hill, 1998. Mitochondrial dynamics and inheritance during development. *Disease Models & Mechanisms* 2(9/10):490–9, 2009.
Mary Lou Cutler, Professor and Director; Ph.D., Hahnemann, 1980. Role of molecules that suppress transformation by the Ras oncogene; Ras signal transduction and human carcinogenesis. *Eur. J. Cell Biol.* 87:721–34, 2008; *J. Cell. Physiol.* 214:38–46, 2007; *BMC Cell Biol.* 7:34, 2006; *Exp. Cell Res.* 306:168–79, 2005.
Clifton Dalgard, Assistant Professor; Ph.D., Uniformed Services University of the Health Sciences, 2005. Molecular mechanisms of damage-associated inflammation.
Michael Daly, Professor; Ph.D., London, 1988. Pathology.
Thomas N. Darling, Professor; M.D./Ph.D., Duke, 1990. *Ann. Intern. Med.* 154(12):806–13, 2011; *Nat. Commun.* doi: 10.1038/ncomms1236, 2011.
Stephen Davies, Assistant Professor; Ph.D., Cornell. Microbiology.
Regina Day, Associate Professor; Ph.D., Tufts, 1995. Angiotensin-II-induced apoptosis requires regulation of nucleolin and Bcl-xLTag subscript by SHP-2 in primary lung endothelial cells*J. Cell Sci.* 123(10):1634–43, 2010.
Saibal Dey, Associate Professor; Ph.D., Wayne State (Michigan), 1995. Allosteric modulation of the human multidrug transporter P-glycoprotein (MDR1 or ABCB1), which confers multidrug resistance in cancer cells and alters bioavailability of many anticancer and antimicrobial agents. *J. Biol. Chem.* 281(16):10699–777, 2006; *Biochemistry* 45:2739–51, 2006; *J. Biol. Chem.* 278(20):18132–9, 2003.
Yang Du, Assistant Professor; Ph.D., Texas Tech, 2000. Leukemia development mechanisms.
Teresa M. Dunn, Professor; Ph.D., Brandeis, 1984. Sphingolipid synthesis and function. *J. Biol. Chem.* 277:11481–8, 2002 and 277:10194–200, 2002; *Mol. Cell Biol.* 21:109–25, 2001; *Methods Enzymol.* 312:317–30, 2000.
Gabriela S. Dveksler, Professor; Ph.D., Uniformed Services University of the Health Sciences, 1991. *J. Biol. Chem.* 286(9):7577–86, 2011; *Biol. Reprod.* 83(1):27–35, 2010.
Ying-Hong Feng, Associate Professor; Ph.D., Oxford, 1993. Pharmacology.
Zygmund Galdzicki, Assistant Professor, Ph.D., Wroclaw (Poland), 1982. Molecular and electrophysiological approach to understanding mental retardation in trisomy 21/Down syndrome
Chou Zen Giam, Professor; Ph.D., Connecticut Health Center, 1983. Human T-lymphotropic virus type I, Kaposi's sarcoma herpes virus, and hepatitis C virus; cellular senescence, cell-cycle controls, I-kappa B kinases, cell transformation, viral oncogenesis, HTLV-1 pathogenesis, and transcriptional regulation. *PLoS Pathog.* 7(4):e1002025, 2011; *J. Virol.* 85(6):3001–9, 2011; *J. Virol.* 82(17):8442–55, 2008; *EMBO J.* 25:1741–52, 2006.
David A. Grahame, Professor; Ph.D., Ohio State, 1984. Metalloenzyme structure and function in Archaea. *J. Biol. Chem.* 285(20):15450–63, 2010; *Biochemistry* 47:5544–55, 2008; *Arch. Microbiol.* 184:32–40, 2005; *J. Am. Chem. Soc.* 126:88–95, 2004; *J. Biol. Chem.* 278:6101–10, 2003.
Philip M. Grimley, Professor; M.D., Albany Medical College, 1961. Population studies relevant to the pathogenesis and molecular biology of ovarian and mammary epithelial cancers.
Jeffrey M. Harmon, Professor and Chair of Pharmacology; Ph.D., Rochester, 1976. Mechanism(s) by which steroid hormones regulate gene expression and the role of steroid hormones in the development and treatment of malignant tumors. *Cancer Res.* 60:2056–62, 2000.
David Horowitz, Associate Professor; Ph.D., Harvard, 1986. Biochemistry of pre-mRNA splicing.
Ann E. Jerse, Associate Professor; Ph.D., Maryland, Baltimore, 1991. Estradiol-treated female mice as surrogate hosts for *Neisseria gonorrhoeae* genital-tract infections. *Front. Microbio.* 2:107, 2011, doi: 10.3389/fmicb.2011.00107.
Sharon L. Juliano, Professor; Ph.D., Pennsylvania, 1982. Mechanisms of development and plasticity in the cerebral cortex, with particular emphasis on the migration of neurons into the cortical plate; factors maintaining the function and morphology of radial glia and Cajal-Retzius cells.
Johnan Kaleeba, Assistant Professor, Ph.D. Mechanisms of infection and disease pathogenesis of oncogenic viruses (EBV and HHV-8); epidemiology and genetic markers of virus-induced cancer in high-risk populations; influences of parasitic inflammation on viral oncogenesis. *PLoS Pathog.* 6(1):e1000742, 2010; *Science* 311(5769):1921–24, 2006.
Radha K. Maheshwari, Professor; Ph.D., Kanpur (India), 1974. Alphaviruses as biothreat agents: Novel approaches for studying the pathogenesis for the development of diagnostic biomarkers, antivirals, and vaccines.
Joseph Mattapallil, Assistant Professor; Ph.D., California Davis, 1997. Molecular and cellular mechanisms of HIV and EBV pathogenesis using nonhuman primate models. *AIDS Res. Hum. Retroviruses* 27(7):763–75, 2011; *Mucosal Immunol.* 2(5):439–49, 2009; *J. Immunol.* 182(3):1439–48, 2009; *J. Virol.* 82(22):11467–71, 2008; *Nature* 434(7037):1093–7, 2005.
Anthony T. Maurelli, Professor; Ph.D., Alabama at Birmingham, 1983. Molecular genetics of bacterial pathogens; molecular biology and pathogenesis of the intracellular pathogens *Shigella* and *Chlamydia*. *BMC Genom.* 11:272, 2010; *Proc. Natl. Acad. Sci. U.S.A.* 106:292–7, 2009.
Ernest Maynard, Assistant Professor; Ph.D., Texas A&M, 2001. Zinc binding to the HCCH motif of HIV-1 virion infectivity factor induces a conformational change that mediates protein-protein interactions. *Proc. Natl. Acad. Sci. U.S.A.* 103:18475–80, 2006.
Joseph T. McCabe, Professor and Vice Chair; Ph.D., CUNY Graduate Center, 1983. Diazoxide, as a postconditioning and delayed preconditioner trigger, increases HSP25 and HSP70 in the central nervous system following combined cerebral stroke and hemorrhagic shock. *J. Neurotrauma* 24(3):532–46. 2007.
D. Scott Merrell, Associate Professor; Ph.D., Tufts, 2001. *H. pylori,* gene regulation and gastric cancer; http://www.usuhs.mil/mic/Merrell/index.html. *Infect. Immun.* 78(7):3073–82, 2010.
Eleanor S. Metcalf, Associate Dean; Ph.D., Pennsylvania, 1976. *J. Immun.,* in press; *Infect. Immun.* 72(5):2843–9, 2004.
Alexandra C. Miller, Assistant Professor; Ph.D., SUNY, 1986. Radiation and heavy metal exposure induced late effects: mechanisms and prevention. A review of depleted uranium biological effects: In vitro and in vivo studies. *Rev. Environ. Health* 22(1):75–94, 2007.
Edward Mitre, Assistant Professor; M.D., Johns Hopkins, 1995. Immune modulation by parasitic helminthes; www.usuhs.mil/mic/mitre.html.
Paul Mongan, Associate Professor and Chair; M.D., Uniformed Services University of the Health Sciences, 1987. Anesthesiology.
Aryan Namboodiri, Assistant Professor; Ph.D., Indian Institute of Science, 1977. Anatomy, physiology, and genetics.
Alison D. O'Brien, Professor and Chair; Ph.D., Ohio State, 1976. The role of *E. coli* shiga toxins in the pathogenesis of hemorrhagic colitis and the hemolytic uremic syndrome; analysis of the mode of action of the Rho-modifying cytotoxic necrotizing factor and its role in the pathogenesis of *E. coli*–mediated urinary-tract infections; identification of spore-surface antigens of *Bacillus anthracis* as potential vaccine candidates. *Infect. Immun.* 79(8):3012–9, 2011.
Galina Petukhova, Assistant Professor, Ph.D., Shemyakin & Ovchinnikov Institute of Bioorganic Chemistry, Moscow, 1994. Molecular mechanisms of genetic recombination in mammals. *Nature* 472:375–78, 2011.
Harvey Pollard, Professor and Chair; Ph.D., 1969, M.D., 1973, Chicago. Molecular biology of secretory processes. *Proc. Natl. Acad. Sci. U.S.A.* 98:4575–80, 2001.
Gerald Quinnan, Professor; M.D., Saint Louis, 1973. Understanding the significance of mutations in the envelope gene of HIV in determining the resistance of virus to neutralization; induction of neutralizing antibody responses using novel HIV-1 envelope glycoproteins and methods of administration with the goal of inducing protection against infection; attempting to understand the factors that limit B cell responses to neutralization epitopes on HIV envelope glycoproteins.
Brian C. Schaefer, Associate Professor; Ph.D., Harvard, 1995. Biology of lymphocyte activation, particularly the antigen regulated NF-kappa B pathway; role of inflammation in traumatic brain injury; imaging, biochemical, and cellular approaches to elucidate signal transduction mechanisms. *J. Immunol.* 185:4520–4, 2010; *J. Immunol.* 181(9):6244–54, 2008; *Mol. Biol. Cell* 17:2166–76, 2006.
Michael J. Schell, Assistant Professor; Ph.D., Johns Hopkins, 1996.
Michael Shamblott, Assistant Professor; Ph.D., Johns Hopkins, 2001. Human stem cells and regenerative medicine; development of new tools for bioinformatic research. *Proc. Natl. Acad. Sci. U.S.A.* 98:113–8, 2001.
Ishaiahu Shechter, Professor and Chair; Ph.D., UCLA, 1969. Regulation of cholesterogenesis both in hepatic and nonhepatic cells/tissues; cholesterol homeostasis. *J. Lipid Res.* 37:1406–21, 1996.
Frank Shewmaker, Assistant Professor, Ph.D., Tulane.
Vijay K. Singh, Assistant Professor, Ph.D. Preclinical development of a bridging therapy for radiation casualties. *Exp. Hematol.* 38(1):61–70, 2010.
Clifford M. Snapper, Professor; M.D., Albany Medical College, 1981. In vivo regulation of protein- and polysaccharide-specific humoral immunity to extracellular bacteria and conjugate vaccines. *J. Immunol.* 183(3):1551–59, 2009.
Andrew Snow, Assistant Professor; Ph.D., Stanford, 2005. Control of human lymphocyte homeostasis via antigen receptor signaling and apoptosis. *J. Clin. Investig.* 119(10): 2976–89, 2009.
Shiv Srivastava, Professor and Co-Director, Center for Prostate Disease Research, Department of Surgery; Ph.D., Indian Institute of Technology (New Delhi), 1980. Molecular genetics of human cancer; prostate cancer. *Clin. Chem.* 51:102–12, 2005; *Oncogene* 23:605–11, 2004; *Cancer Res.* 63:4299–304, 2003.
Tharun Sundaresan, Assistant Professor; Ph.D., Centre for Cellular and Molecular Biology (India), 1995. Mechanism of eukaryotic mRNA decay, with particular focus on the role of Lsm1p-7p-Pat1p complex.
Viqar Syed, Assistant Professor, Ph.D., Karolinska Institute, Stockholm.
Aviva Symes, Associate Professor; Ph.D., University College (London), 1990. The role of the TGF-beta superfamily of cytokines in the central nervous system after injury. *J. Mol. Neurosci.* 41:383–96, 2010.
Charles S. Via, Professor; M.D., Virginia, 1973.
Shuishu Wang, Assistant Professor, Ph.D., Purdue, 1999. Structural and functional studies of potential drug target proteins from *Mycobacterium tuberculosis* by x-ray crystallography and biochemical techniques.
Robert W. Williams, Associate Professor; Ph.D., Washington State, 1980. Inelastic neutron scattering, Raman, vibrational analysis with anharmonic corrections, and scaled quantum mechanical force field for polycrystalline L-alanine. *Chem. Phys.* 343(1):1–18, 2008.
T. John Wu, Associate Professor; Ph.D., Texas A&M, 1991. Molecular and cellular neuroendocrinology of reproduction and stress. *Reproduction* 139(2):319–30, 2010; *Endocrinology* 150(4):1817–25, 2009; *Endocrinology* 146:280–6, 2005.
Xin Xiang, Associate Professor; Ph.D., University of Medicine and Dentistry of New Jersey, 1991. The p25 subunit of the dynactin complex is required for dynein–early endosome interaction. *J. Cell Biol.* 193(7):1245–55, 2011.

UNIVERSITY OF CONNECTICUT HEALTH CENTER

Graduate Program in Cell Biology

Program of Study

The program offers training leading to a Ph.D. in biomedical sciences and includes faculty members from the Department of Cell Biology as well as eight other Health Center departments. Faculty members' research spans a broad range of interests in the areas of eukaryotic cell biology and related clinical aspects. The program is particularly strong in the following areas of research: angiogenesis, cancer biology, gene expression, molecular medicine, reproductive biology, signal transduction, vascular biology, optical methods, proteomics, and computer modeling of complex biological systems. The curriculum for the first year is tailored to the individual student and can include core courses in the basic biomedical sciences that have been specially formulated to acquaint the student with the principles and practice of modern biomedical research as well as more specialized, analytical courses. In consultation with their advisory committee, students work out a supplementary program of advanced courses, laboratory experiences, and independent study designed to prepare them for general examinations near the end of their second year. Thesis research begins in the second or third year, and research and thesis writing normally occupy the third and fourth years.

Research Facilities

The program is situated in the modern Health Center in Farmington. This complex provides excellent physical facilities for research in both basic and clinical sciences, a computer center, and the Lyman Maynard Stowe Library. The program provides research facilities and guidance for graduate and postdoctoral work in cell biology—particularly membrane and surface function, membrane protein synthesis and turnover, cytoskeleton structure and function, stimulus-response coupling, gene expression and regulation, vascular biology, fertilization, bone biology, molecular medicine, early development, signal transduction, angiogenesis, computer modeling, and tumor biology. Facilities for training in cell culture, electron microscopy, electrophysiology, fluorescence spectroscopy, molecular biology, molecular modeling, fluorescence imaging, and intravital microscopy are available.

Financial Aid

Support for doctoral students engaged in full-time degree programs at the Health Center is provided on a competitive basis. Graduate research assistantships for 2011–12 provide a stipend of $28,000 per year, which includes a waiver of tuition/University fees for the fall and spring semesters and a student health insurance plan. While financial aid is offered competitively, the Health Center makes every possible effort to address the financial needs of all students during their period of training.

Cost of Study

For 2011–12, tuition is $10,224 per year for full-time students who are Connecticut residents and $26,532 per year for full-time students who are out-of-state residents. General University fees are added to the cost of tuition for students who do not receive a tuition waiver. These costs are usually met by traineeships or research assistantships for doctoral students.

Living and Housing Costs

There is a wide range of affordable housing options in the greater Hartford area within easy commuting distance of the campus, including an extensive complex that is adjacent to the Health Center. Costs range from $600 to $900 per month for a one-bedroom unit; 2 or more students sharing an apartment usually pay less. University housing is not available at the Health Center.

Student Group

Currently, 20 students are pursuing doctoral studies in the program. The total number of Ph.D. students at the Health Center is approximately 150, while the medical and dental schools combined currently enroll 130 students per class.

Location

The Health Center is located in the historic town of Farmington, Connecticut. Set in the beautiful New England countryside on a hill overlooking the Farmington Valley, it is close to ski areas, hiking trails, and facilities for boating, fishing, and swimming. Connecticut's capital city of Hartford, 7 miles east of Farmington, is the center of an urban region of approximately 800,000 people. The beaches of the Long Island Sound are about 50 minutes away to the south, and the beautiful Berkshires are a short drive to the northwest. New York City and Boston can be reached within 2½ hours by car. Hartford is the home of the acclaimed Hartford Stage Company, TheatreWorks, the Hartford Symphony and Chamber orchestras, two ballet companies, an opera company, the Wadsworth Atheneum (the oldest public art museum in the nation), the Mark Twain house, the Hartford Civic Center, and many other interesting cultural and recreational facilities. The area is also home to several branches of the University of Connecticut, Trinity College, and the University of Hartford, which includes the Hartt School of Music. Bradley International Airport (about 30 minutes from campus) serves the Hartford/Springfield area with frequent airline connections to major cities in this country and abroad. Frequent bus and rail service is also available from Hartford.

The Health Center

The 200-acre Health Center campus at Farmington houses a division of the University of Connecticut Graduate School, as well as the School of Medicine and Dental Medicine. The campus also includes the John Dempsey Hospital, associated clinics, and extensive medical research facilities, all in a centralized facility with more than 1 million square feet of floor space. The Health Center's newest research addition, the Academic Research Building, was opened in 1999. This impressive eleven-story structure provides 170,000 square feet of state-of-the-art laboratory space. The faculty at the center includes more than 260 full-time members. The institution has a strong commitment to graduate study within an environment that promotes social and intellectual interaction among the various educational programs. Graduate students are represented on various administrative committees concerned with curricular affairs, and the Graduate Student Organization (GSO) represents graduate students' needs and concerns to the faculty and administration, in addition to fostering social contact among graduate students in the Health Center.

Applying

Applications for admission should be submitted on standard forms obtained from the Graduate Admissions Office at the UConn Health Center or on the Web site. The application should be filed together with transcripts, three letters of recommendation, a personal statement, and recent results from the General Test of the Graduate Record Examinations. International students must take the Test of English as a Foreign Language (TOEFL) to satisfy Graduate School requirements. The deadline for completed applications and receipt of all supplemental materials is December 15. In accordance with the laws of the state of Connecticut and of the United States, the University of Connecticut Health Center does not discriminate against any person in its educational and employment activities on the grounds of race, color, creed, national origin, sex, age, or physical disability.

Correspondence and Information

Dr. Kevin Claffey
Director, Cell Biology Graduate Program
MC 3501
University of Connecticut Health Center
Farmington, Connecticut 06030-3501
Phone: 860-679-8713
E-mail: claffey@nso2.uchc.edu
Web site: http://grad.uchc.edu

University of Connecticut Health Center

THE FACULTY AND THEIR RESEARCH

Andrew Arnold, Professor and Director, Center for Molecular Medicine; M.D., Harvard, 1978. Structure and function of the cyclin D1 oncogene and cell-cycle regulator; molecular genetics and biology of endocrine tumors; inherited endocrine neoplastic diseases.

Rashmi Bansal, Associate Professor of Neuroscience; Ph.D., Central Drug Research Institute, 1976. Developmental, cellular, and molecular biology of oligodendrocytes (OLs), the cells that synthesize myelin membrane in the central nervous system.

Gordon G. Carmichael, Professor of Microbiology; Ph.D., Harvard, 1975. Regulation of gene expression in eukaryotes.

Joan M. Caron, Assistant Professor of Cell Biology; Ph.D., Connecticut, 1982. Biochemistry and cell biology of microtubules; palmitoylation of tubulin and cell function; functional role of palmitoylation of signaling proteins.

Kevin P. Claffey, Associate Professor of Cell Biology and Center for Vascular Biology; Ph.D., Boston University, 1989. Angiogenesis in human cancer progression and metastasis; vascular endothelial growth factor (VEGF) expression; hypoxia-mediated gene regulation.

Robert B. Clark, Associate Professor of Medicine, Division of Rheumatic Diseases; M.D., Stanford, 1975. Basic T-lymphocyte biology, especially as it relates to autoimmune diseases, such as multiple sclerosis and rheumatoid arthritis; molecular biology and structure of the T-cell antigen receptor; T-cell function; T-cell activation.

Ann Cowan, Assistant Professor of Biochemistry and Deputy Director of the Center for Biomedical Imaging Technology; Ph.D., Colorado, 1984. Mammalian sperm development.

Anne Delany, Assistant Professor of Medicine; Ph.D., Dartmouth, 1991. Function and regulation of the noncollagen matrix protein osteonectin/SPARC in bone; regulation of osteoblast gene expression by microRNAs; exploring how the extracellular matrix regulates gene expression in bone-metastatic prostate carcinoma.

Kimberly Dodge-Kafka, Assistant Professor of Cell Biology, Center for Cardiology and Cardiovascular Research; Ph.D., Texas–Houston Health Science Center, 1999. Molecular mechanism of signaling pathways in the heart.

David I. Dorsky, Assistant Professor of Medicine; M.D./Ph.D., Harvard, 1982. The structure and function of herpesvirus DNA polymerases and their roles in viral DNA replication.

Paul Epstein, Associate Professor of Cell Biology; Ph.D., Yeshiva (Einstein), 1975. Signal transduction in relation to leukemia and breast cancer; purification and cloning of cyclic nucleotide phosphodiesterases.

Alan Fein, Professor of Cell Biology; Ph.D., Johns Hopkins, 1973. Molecular basis of visual excitation and adaptation; signal transduction and calcium homeostasis in platelets.

Guo-Hua Fong, Associate Professor of Cell Biology and Center for Vascular Biology; Ph.D., Illinois, 1988. Cardiovascular biology.

Brenton R. Graveley, Assistant Professor, Department of Genetics and Developmental Biology; Ph.D., Vermont, 1996. Regulation of alternative splicing in the mammalian nervous system and mechanisms of alternative splicing.

David Han, Associate Professor of Cell Biology and Center for Vascular Biology; Ph.D., George Washington, 1994. Proteomic analysis of complex protein mixtures.

Arthur R. Hand, Professor of Craniofacial Sciences and Cell Biology; D.D.S., UCLA, 1968. Study of protein and gene expression in rodent salivary glands during normal growth and development and in various experimental conditions employing morphological, immunological, and biochemical methodology.

Marc Hansen, Professor of Medicine; Ph.D., Cincinnati, 1986. Analysis of genes involved in the development of the bone tumor osteosarcoma.

Greg Huber, Assistant Professor of Cell Biology; Ph.D., Boston University. Problems in biological physics, with an emphasis on the interplay of statistical mechanics, biomechanics, and fluid dynamics.

Marja Hurley, Professor of Medicine; M.D., Connecticut Health Center, 1972. Molecular mechanisms by which members of the fibroblast growth factor (FGFs) and fibroblast growth factor receptor (FGFR) families (produced by osteoblasts, osteoclasts, and stromal cells) regulate bone development, remodeling, and disorders of bone: Fgf2 knockout and Fgf2 transgenic mice are utilized in loss and gain of function experiments to elucidate the role of FGF-2 in disorders of bone, including osteoporosis.

Laurinda A. Jaffe, Professor of Cell Biology; Ph.D., UCLA, 1977. Physiology of fertilization, in particular the mechanisms by which membrane potential regulates sperm-egg fusion; transduction mechanisms coupling sperm-egg interaction to egg exocytosis; opening of ion channels in the egg membrane.

Ingela Jansson, Assistant Professor of Cell Biology; Ph.D., Stockholm. DNA-binding proteins in metallothionine induction and cytochrome P450–cytochrome b5 interactions.

Stephen M. King, Associate Professor of Biochemistry; Ph.D., London, 1982. Cell biology; biochemistry and function of molecular motors; dynein structure and function.

Dennis E. Koppel, Professor of Biochemistry; Ph.D., Columbia, 1973. Application of biophysical techniques to membrane dynamics; mechanisms by which specialized cell-surface domains are produced and maintained.

Eric S. Levine, Associate Professor of Neuroscience; Ph.D., Princeton. Synaptic physiology and plasticity; roles of nerve growth factors and endogenous cannabinoids in hippocampus and cortex.

Bruce Liang, Professor of Cardiopulmonary Medicine; M.D., Harvard, 1982. Signal transduction; cardiac and vascular cell biology; receptors; G proteins; transgenic mice.

Leslie M. Loew, Professor of Cell Biology and Director, Center for Cell Analysis and Modeling; Ph.D., Cornell, 1974. Spectroscopic methods for measuring spatial and temporal variations in membrane potential; electric field effects on cell membranes; membrane pores induced by toxins and antibiotics.

Nilanjana Maulik, Associate Professor of Surgery; Ph.D., Calcutta, 1990. Molecular and cellular signaling during myocardial ischemia and reperfusion.

Lisa Mehlman, Assistant Professor of Cell Biology; Ph.D., Kent State, 1996. Cell signaling events that regulate oocyte maturation and fertilization; maintenance of oocyte meiotic arrest by G-protein receptors; hormonal regulation of oocyte maturation.

Ion I. Moraru, Associate Professor of Cell Biology; M.D., Ph.D., Carol Davila (Romania). Understanding signal transduction mechanisms, in particular related to calcium and phosphoinositides.

Flavia O'Rourke, Assistant Professor of Cell Biology; Ph.D., Connecticut, 1976. Signal transduction in human platelets, with specific interest in the inositol phosphate signaling pathway and its regulation.

Joel Pachter, Professor of Cell Biology; Ph.D., NYU, 1983. Elucidating the mechanisms by which leukocytes and pathogens invade the central nervous system.

Achilles Pappano, Professor of Cell Biology; Ph.D., Pennsylvania. Cardiac membrane receptors and regulation of ion channels.

John J. Peluso, Professor of Cell Biology and Obstetrics and Gynecology; Ph.D., West Virginia, 1974. Cell and molecular mechanisms involving the regulating ovarian cell mitosis and apoptosis; cell-cell interaction as a regulator of ovarian cell function; identification and characterization of a putative membrane receptor for progesterone.

Carol C. Pilbeam, Associate Professor of Medicine; M.D./Ph.D., Yale, 1982. Regulation and function of prostaglandins in bone; transcriptional regulation of cyclooxygenase-2; role of cytokines and estrogen in bone physiology and osteoporosis.

Vladimir Rodionov, Assistant Professor of Cell Biology; Ph.D., Moscow, 1980. Dynamics of cytoskeleton; self-organization of microtubule arrays; regulation of the activity of microtubule motors.

Daniel Rosenberg, Professor of Medicine; Ph.D., Michigan. Molecular genetics of colorectal cancer; signaling pathways in the development of tumors; toxicogenomics.

John B. Schenkman, Professor of Pharmacology; Ph.D., SUNY Upstate Medical Center, 1964. The cytochrome P450 monooxygenase system; homeostatic control of the hepatic microsomal enzymes.

Linda H. Shapiro, Associate Professor of Cell Biology and Center for Vascular Biology; Ph.D., Michigan, 1984. Regulation and function of CD 13/aminopeptidase N in angiogenic vasculature and early myeloid cells; control of tumor and myocardial angiogenesis by peptidases; inflammatory regulation of angiogenesis.

Mark R. Terasaki, Assistant Professor of Cell Biology; Ph.D., Berkeley, 1983. Structure and function of the endoplasmic reticulum; confocal microscopy.

Jennifer Tirnauer, Assistant Professor of Medicine, Center for Molecular Medicine; M.D., Maryland, 1989. Role of the microtubule cytoskeleton in cancer biology; molecular mechanisms of microtubule regulation.

James Watras, Associate Professor of Medicine; Ph.D., Washington State, 1979. The mechanisms by which the sarcoplasmic reticulum regulates intracellular calcium concentration in vascular smooth muscle.

Bruce A. White, Professor of Cell Biology; Ph.D., Berkeley, 1980. Regulation of prolactin gene expression by Ca and calmodulin in rat pituitary tumor cells; examination of nuclear DNA-binding proteins, nuclear calmodulin-binding proteins, and nuclear Ca-calmodulin-dependent protein kinase activity.

Charles Wolgemuth, Assistant Professor of Cell Biology; Ph.D., Arizona. Using physics to understand biological systems; morphology; propulsion; growth and fluid dynamics.

Catherine H.-y. Wu, Associate Professor of Medicine; Ph.D., CUNY, Brooklyn, 1976. Mechanisms of procollagen propeptide feedback inhibition of collagen synthesis; pretranslational control.

George Y. Wu, Professor of Medicine; M.D./Ph.D., Yeshiva (Einstein), 1976. Receptor-mediated endocytosis of glycoproteins; drug delivery by endocytic targeting; targeted gene delivery and expression.

Lixia Yue, Assistant Professor of Cell Biology and Center for Cardiovascular Research; Ph.D., McGill, 1999. TRP channels and Ca^{2+} signaling mechanisms in cardiac remodeling.

UNIVERSITY OF CONNECTICUT HEALTH CENTER

Graduate Program in Molecular Biology and Biochemistry

Program of Study	The Graduate Program in Molecular Biology and Biochemistry uniquely bridges modern molecular biology, microbiology, biochemistry, cell biology, and structural biology, leading to a Ph.D. in the biomedical sciences. The goals of the graduate program are to provide rigorous research training in an environment dedicated to advancing excellence in teaching and research. Whether graduates enter academic research, the biotechnology industry, liberal arts college teaching, patent law, or other disciplines, they bring to that career a solid base of knowledge, an ability to learn independently and think independently, and an enduring desire to use their full range of professional skills and experience in creative ways. Graduates are expected to have demonstrated a high degree of competence in research, as judged by publications in first-rank journals, and to have developed essential skills in identifying important research problems, planning research projects and scientific writing. In addition, students are expected to have incorporated ethical principles of scientific conduct into their professional attitudes and activities and to be sensitive to such issues throughout their careers. The success of this training approach is indicated by the high percentage of students who have developed successful independent careers in biomedical research. The current program offers an unparalleled opportunity to study a wide variety of biological problems at the biochemical, molecular, cellular, and structural levels. The interests of the faculty are summarized below.
Research Facilities	In addition to the general facilities of the Health Center (see page describing programs in the Biological and Biomedical Sciences), the program offers complete physical research facilities. There is research equipment, as well as expertise, for all areas of genetic, biochemical, molecular, cellular, and biophysical investigation. The department houses the UConn Health Center NMR Structural Biology Facility (http://structbio.uchc.edu), which includes a 400-MHz NMR spectrometer and cryoprobe-equipped 500- and 600-MHz NMR spectrometers, as well as a circular dichroism spectropolarimeter, isothermal titration calorimeter, and multi-angle laser light scattering facilities. An 800-MHz NMR spectrometer and X-ray crystallography facilities are planned. The department also houses the UConn Health Center Structural Biology Computational Facility, which includes a bank of Mac and Linux desktop computers connected to ultrafast servers with the latest structural biology software. Facilities are also available for electron and confocal laser scanning microscopy, low-light-level imaging microscopy (in the state-of-the-art Center for Cell Analysis and Modeling), protein purification and sequencing, cell culture, monoclonal antibody production, DNA oligonucleotide and peptide synthesis and sequencing, and gene silencing using RNAI.
Financial Aid	Support for doctoral students engaged in full-time degree programs at the Health Center is provided on a competitive basis. Graduate research assistantships for 2011–12 provide a stipend of $28,000 per year, which includes a waiver of tuition/University fees for the fall and spring semesters and a student health insurance plan. While financial aid is offered competitively, the Health Center makes every possible effort to address the financial needs of all students during their period of training.
Cost of Study	For 2011–12, tuition is $10,224 per year for full-time students who are Connecticut residents and $26,532 per year for full-time out-of-state residents. General University fees are added to the cost of tuition for students who do not receive a tuition waiver. These costs are usually met by traineeships or research assistantships for doctoral students.
Living and Housing Costs	There is a wide range of affordable housing options in the greater Hartford area within easy commuting distance of the campus, including an extensive complex that is adjacent to the Health Center. Costs range from $600 to $900 per month for a one-bedroom unit; 2 or more students sharing an apartment usually pay less. University housing is not available at the Health Center.
Student Group	There are approximately 20 graduate students in the molecular biology and biochemistry program. There are approximately 150 graduate students in Ph.D. programs on the Health Center campus, and the total enrollment is about 1,000.
Location	The Health Center is located in the historic town of Farmington, Connecticut. Set in the beautiful New England countryside on a hill overlooking the Farmington Valley, it is close to ski areas, hiking trails, and facilities for boating, fishing, and swimming. Connecticut's capital city of Hartford, 7 miles east of Farmington, is the center of an urban region of approximately 800,000 people. The beaches of the Long Island Sound are about 50 minutes away to the south, and the beautiful Berkshires are a short drive to the northwest. New York City and Boston can be reached within 2½ hours by car. Hartford is the home of the acclaimed Hartford Stage Company, TheatreWorks, the Hartford Symphony and Chamber orchestras, two ballet companies, an opera company, the Wadsworth Athenaeum (the oldest public art museum in the nation), the Mark Twain house, the Hartford Civic Center, and many other interesting cultural and recreational facilities. The area is also home to several branches of the University of Connecticut, Trinity College, and the University of Hartford, which includes the Hartt School of Music. Bradley International Airport (about 30 minutes from campus) serves the Hartford/Springfield area with frequent airline connections to major cities in this country and abroad. Frequent bus and rail service is also available from Hartford.
The Health Center	The 200-acre Health Center campus at Farmington houses a division of the University of Connecticut Graduate School, as well as the School of Medicine and Dental Medicine. The campus also includes the John Dempsey Hospital, associated clinics, and extensive medical research facilities, all in a centralized facility with more than 1 million square feet of floor space. The Health Center's newest research addition, the Academic Research Building, was opened in 1999. This impressive eleven-story structure provides 170,000 square feet of state-of-the-art laboratory space. The faculty at the center includes more than 260 full-time members. The institution has a strong commitment to graduate study within an environment that promotes social and intellectual interaction among the various educational programs. Graduate students are represented on various administrative committees concerned with curricular affairs, and the Graduate Student Organization (GSO) represents graduate students' needs and concerns to the faculty and administration, in addition to fostering social contact among graduate students in the Health Center.
Applying	Applications should be submitted on standard forms obtained from the Graduate Admissions Office at the UConn Health Center or the Web site. The application should be filed together with transcripts, three letters of recommendation, a personal statement, and recent results from the General Test of the Graduate Record Examinations. International students must take the Test of English as a Foreign Language (TOEFL) to satisfy Graduate School requirements. The deadline for completed applications and receipt of all supplemental materials is December 15. In accordance with the laws of the state of Connecticut and of the United States, the University of Connecticut Health Center does not discriminate against any person in its educational and employment activities on the grounds of race, color, creed, national origin, sex, age, or physical disability.
Correspondence and Information	Dr. Stephen King Program Director for Molecular Biology and Biochemistry University of Connecticut Health Center Farmington, Connecticut 06030-3305 Phone: 860-679-3347 Fax: 860-679-1862 E-mail: sking@nso2.uchc.edu Web site: http://grad.uchc.edu

University of Connecticut Health Center

THE FACULTY AND THEIR RESEARCH

Gordon G. Carmichael, Professor; Ph.D., Harvard. Regulation of viral gene expression and function.

John H. Carson, Professor; Ph.D., MIT. RNA transport in cells of the nervous system.

Ann Cowan, Associate Professor; Ph.D., Colorado at Boulder. Plasma membrane proteins in sperm.

Asis Das, Professor; Ph.D., Calcutta. Gene control in bacterial adaptive response.

Kimberly Dodge-Kafka, Assistant Professor of Cell Biology/Center for Cardiology and Cardiovascular Research; Ph.D., Texas Health Science Center at Houston, 1999. Molecular mechanism of signaling pathways in the heart.

Betty Eipper, Professor; Ph.D., Harvard. Biosynthesis and secretion of peptides by neurons and endocrine cells.

Shlomo Eisenberg, Professor; Ph.D., McGill. Biochemistry of DNA replication in yeast.

Richard Everson, Deputy Director for Cancer Prevention and Control, Neag Comprehensive Cancer Center; M.D., Rochester; M.P.H., North Carolina at Chapel Hill. Conducting large-scale cancer genomic clinical research and population studies by developing a statewide biorepository of tumor tissue with analysis by high-throughput arrays and next-generation sequencing.

Michael Gryk, Assistant Professor; Ph.D., Stanford. Three-dimensional structure and function of proteins involved in DNA repair.

Arthur Günzl, Associate Professor; Ph.D., Tübingen (Germany). Transcription and antigenic variation in the mammalian parasite *Trypanosoma brucei.*

Bing Hao, Assistant Professor of Molecular, Microbial, and Structural Biology; Ph.D., Ohio State. Understanding how the cell cycle is regulated by ubiquitin-mediated proteolysis using X-ray crystallography as a primary tool.

Christopher Heinen, Assistant Professor of Medicine; Ph.D., Cincinnati. Biochemical and cellular defects of the DNA mismatch repair pathway during tumorigenesis.

Jeffrey Hoch, Associate Professor; Ph.D., Harvard. Biophysical chemistry of proteins.

Stephen M. King, Associate Professor; Ph.D., University College, London. Structure and function of microtubule-based molecular motor proteins.

Lawrence A. Klobutcher, Professor and Associate Dean of the Graduate School; Ph.D., Yale. DNA rearrangement, programmed translational frameshifting, and phagocytosis in ciliated protozoa.

Dennis E. Koppel, Professor; Ph.D., Columbia. Biophysical studies of membrane dynamics.

Dmitry Korzhnev, Assistant Professor, Molecular, Microbial, and Structural Biology; Ph.D., Moscow Institute of Physics and Technology. Liquid-state nuclear magnetic resonance (NMR) studies of structure and dynamics of proteins and their assemblies; multiprotein complexes involved in DNA replication and repair; protein folding.

Mark Maciejewski, Assistant Professor; Ph.D., Ohio State. Enzymes of DNA replication, repair, and recombination.

Mary Jane Osborn, Professor, Department of Microbiology; Ph.D., Washington (Seattle). Biogenesis of the outer membrane of *Salmonella.*

Juris Ozols, Professor; Ph.D., Washington (Seattle). Isolation and structure of membranous proteins.

Lawrence I. Rothfield, Professor; Ph.D., NYU. Membrane biology and biochemistry; bacterial cell division.

Peter Setlow, Professor; Ph.D., Brandeis. Biochemistry of bacterial spore germination.

Aziz Taghbalout, Assistant Professor of Molecular, Microbial, and Structural Biology; Ph.D., Hassan II University (Morocco). Understanding the molecular organization of the RNA degradosome, a multiprotein complex that plays essential role in the normal RNA degradation and processing in *Escherichia coli.*

Jennifer Tirnauer, Assistant Professor of Medicine, Center for Molecular Medicine; M.D., Maryland, Baltimore. Role of the microtubule cytoskeleton in cancer biology; molecular mechanisms of microtubule regulation.

Sandra K. Weller, Professor and Department Head; Ph.D., Wisconsin. Mechanisms of DNA replication and DNA encapsidation in herpes simplex virus; virus-host interactions.

UNIVERSITY OF CONNECTICUT HEALTH CENTER
Program in Cell Analysis and Modeling

Program of Study

The University of Connecticut Health Center's (UCHC) quantitative cell biology research has expanded into the area in cell analysis and modeling. Faculty members associated with this area explore complex biological systems using computational cell biology, optical imaging, and other quantitative approaches to analyze processes in living cells. The program in cell analysis and modeling is designed to train students from diverse disciplinary backgrounds in the cutting-edge research techniques that comprise the interdisciplinary research of modern cell biology. Students are provided with rigorous cross-training in areas of mathematical, physical, and computational sciences as well as biology. Students in the program take courses, attend seminars, and work on interdisciplinary research projects to broaden and strengthen their abilities to conduct quantitative cell biology research.

The cell analysis and modeling (CAM) area of concentration is based at the Richard D. Berlin Center for Cell Analysis and Modeling (CCAM) at UCHC. Established in 1994, CCAM has emerged as a center that promotes the application of physics, chemistry, and computation to cell biology. The environment of CCAM is designed to promote interdisciplinary interactions and its cadre of physical scientists are supported and valued in a way that is unique for a medical school.

The CAM program is particularly strong in the following areas of research: cellular modeling (analysis and simulation, data integration, modeling movies boundaries, modularity and multistate complexes, molecular flux in crowded spaces, stochastic modeling and discrete particles); biophysics (biological signaling platforms, in vivo nanofabrication); optical imaging (fluorescent correlation spectroscopy, optical probe development, second harmonic generation, single-molecule imaging); cell biology (cellular tissues and development, cytoskeletal dynamics, RNA trafficking, signal transduction, molecular medicine).

Research Facilities

The program is situated in the modern Health Center in Farmington. This complex provides excellent physical facilities for research in both basic and clinical sciences, a computer center, and the Lyman Maynard Stowe Library. The program provides research facilities and guidance for graduate and postdoctoral work in cell biology—particularly membrane and surface function, membrane protein synthesis and turnover, cytoskeleton structure and function, stimulus-response coupling, gene expression and regulation, vascular biology, fertilization, bone biology, molecular medicine, early development, signal transduction, angiogenesis, computer modeling, and tumor biology. Facilities for training in cell culture, electron microscopy, electrophysiology, fluorescence spectroscopy, molecular biology, molecular modeling, fluorescence imaging, and intravital microscopy are available.

Financial Aid

Support for doctoral students engaged in full-time degree programs at the Health Center is provided on a competitive basis. Graduate research assistantships for 2011–12 provide a stipend of $28,000 per year, which includes a waiver of tuition/University fees for the fall and spring semesters and a student health insurance plan. While financial aid is offered competitively, the Health Center makes every possible effort to address the financial needs of all students during their period of training.

Cost of Study

For 2011–12, tuition is $10,224 per year for full-time students who are Connecticut residents and $26,532 per year for full-time students who are out-of-state residents. General University fees are added to the cost of tuition for students who do not receive a tuition waiver. These costs are usually met by traineeships or research assistantships for doctoral students.

Living and Housing Costs

There is a wide range of affordable housing options in the greater Hartford area within easy commuting distance of the campus, including an extensive complex that is adjacent to the Health Center. Costs range from $600 to $900 per month for a one-bedroom unit; 2 or more students sharing an apartment usually pay less. University housing is not available at the Health Center.

Student Group

The total number of Ph.D. students at the Health Center is approximately 150, while the medical and dental schools combined currently enroll 130 students per class.

Location

The Health Center is located in the historic town of Farmington, Connecticut. Set in the beautiful New England countryside on a hill overlooking the Farmington Valley, it is close to ski areas, hiking trails, and facilities for boating, fishing, and swimming. Connecticut's capital city of Hartford, 7 miles east of Farmington, is the center of an urban region of approximately 800,000 people. The beaches of the Long Island Sound are about 50 minutes away to the south, and the beautiful Berkshires are a short drive to the northwest. New York City and Boston can be reached within 2½ hours by car. Hartford is the home of the acclaimed Hartford Stage Company, TheatreWorks, the Hartford Symphony and Chamber orchestras, two ballet companies, an opera company, the Wadsworth Athenaeum (the oldest public art museum in the nation), the Mark Twain house, the Hartford Civic Center, and many other interesting cultural and recreational facilities. The area is also home to several branches of the University of Connecticut, Trinity College, and the University of Hartford, which includes the Hartt School of Music. Bradley International Airport (about 30 minutes from campus) serves the Hartford/Springfield area with frequent airline connections to major cities in this country and abroad. Frequent bus and rail service is also available from Hartford.

The Health Center

The 200-acre Health Center campus at Farmington houses a division of the University of Connecticut Graduate School, as well as the School of Medicine and Dental Medicine. The campus also includes the John Dempsey Hospital, associated clinics, and extensive medical research facilities, all in a centralized facility with more than 1 million square feet of floor space. The Health Center's newest research addition, the Academic Research Building, was opened in 1999. This impressive eleven-story structure provides 170,000 square feet of state-of-the-art laboratory space. The faculty at the center includes more than 260 full-time members. The institution has a strong commitment to graduate study within an environment that promotes social and intellectual interaction among the various educational programs. Graduate students are represented on various administrative committees concerned with curricular affairs, and the Graduate Student Organization (GSO) represents graduate students' needs and concerns to the faculty and administration, in addition to fostering social contact among graduate students in the Health Center.

Applying

Applications for admission should be submitted on standard forms obtained from the Graduate Admissions Office at the UConn Health Center or on the Web site. The application should be filed together with transcripts, three letters of recommendation, a personal statement, and recent results from the General Test of the Graduate Record Examinations. International students must take the Test of English as a Foreign Language (TOEFL) to satisfy Graduate School requirements. The deadline for completed applications and receipt of all supplemental materials is December 15. In accordance with the laws of the state of Connecticut and of the United States, the University of Connecticut Health Center does not discriminate against any person in its educational and employment activities on the grounds of race, color, creed, national origin, sex, age, or physical disability.

Correspondence and Information

Dr. Charles Wolgemuth, Program Director
Cell Analysis and Modeling
University of Connecticut Health Center Graduate School
263 Farmington Avenue, MC 6406
Farmington, Connecticut 06030-6406
Phone: 860-679-1452
E-mail: cwolgemuth@uchc.edu
Web site: http://grad.uchc.edu
　　　　　http://www.ccam.uchc.edu

University of Connecticut Health Center

THE FACULTY AND THEIR RESEARCH

Michael Blinov, Assistant Professor of Genetics and Developmental Biology; Ph.D., Weizmann Institute (Israel). Computational biology: modeling of signal transcription systems and protein-DNA interactions; bioinformatics: data mining and visualization; developing software tools and mathematical methods for rule-based modeling of signal transduction systems.

John H. Carson, Professor of Molecular, Microbial and Structural Biology; Ph.D., MIT. RNA transport in cells of the nervous system.

Ann E. Cowan, Associate Professor of Molecular, Microbial, and Structural Biology; Deputy Director, Center for Biomedical Imaging Technology; Ph.D., Colorado, 1984. Research encompassing several areas of mammalian sperm development.

Greg Huber, Assistant Professor of Cell Biology; Ph.D., Boston University. Problems in biological physics, with an emphasis on the interplay of statistical mechanics, biomechanics, and fluid dynamics.

Leslie M. Loew, Professor of Cell Biology and of Computer Science and Engineering; Ph.D., Cornell, 1974. Morphological determinants of cell physiology; image-based computational models of cellular biology; spatial variations of cell membrane electrophysiology; new optical methods for probing living cells.

Bruce J. Mayer, Associate Professor of Genetics and Developmental Biology; Ph.D., Rockefeller. Mechanisms of signal transduction.

William A. Mohler, Ph.D., Stanford. Assistant Professor of Genetics and Developmental Biology. Developmental cell fusion; *C. elegans* genetics; multidimensional imaging of developmental and cell biological processes.

Ion I. Moraru, Associate Professor of Cell Biology; M.D., Ph.D., Carol Davila (Romania). Understanding signal transduction mechanisms, in particular those related to calcium and phosphoinositides.

Vladimir Rodionov, Assistant Professor of Cell Biology; Ph.D., Moscow, 1980. Molecular mechanisms of intracellular transport; organization of microtubule cytoskeleton.

Charles Wolgemuth, Associate Professor of Cell Biology; Ph.D., Arizona. Physical underpinnings of biological processes; how forces are produced inside cells to handle processes such as creating and maintaining cell shape and driving cell motility and cell growth; wound healing, cancer metastatsis, and pathogen-host interactions in Lyme disease.

Ji Yu, Assistant Professor of Genetics and Developmental Biology; Ph.D., Texas at Austin. Optical imaging technology; regulation mechanisms in dendritic RNA translation; cytoskeletal dynamics.

UNIVERSITY OF MISSOURI–KANSAS CITY

School of Biological Sciences
Program in Cell Biology and Biophysics

Program of Study	The graduate program in cell biology and biophysics at the University of Missouri–Kansas City (UMKC) leads to the Ph.D. degree. The program functions within the interdisciplinary Ph.D. framework of the University and is associated with the M.S. program in cell and molecular biology. The graduate program is designed to prepare students for research-oriented careers in academia, government, or the private sector. An original independent research project under the supervision of a faculty adviser is the core of these programs.
	Programs of study provide a background of course work tailored to the interests of each student. Opportunity for research experience begins immediately as a component of the first-year curriculum, with each student being assigned short research projects. By the end of the first academic year, the student is also expected to have acquired a general understanding of the basis of molecular and cellular biology. At that time, the student selects a faculty research adviser and makes further course selections. To qualify for doctoral degree candidacy, students take a written comprehensive examination and prepare and defend an original research proposal. The culmination of the graduate degree programs is the preparation and oral defense of a research dissertation, typically five years after entry into the program.
	The areas of research interest of participating faculty members are included in the Faculty and Their Research section. Extensive possibilities for collaboration exist with the School's program in molecular biology and biochemistry and with regional research associates. Opportunities for postdoctoral research are abundant.
Research Facilities	Research facilities for cell, molecular and structural biology, and biochemistry are primarily located in the Biological Sciences and Chemistry buildings. Modern research is conducted in laboratories assigned to individual faculty members and in specialized central facilities. Sophisticated instrumentation in these facilities includes automated DNA and protein synthesizers and sequencers, mass spectrometers, macromolecular X-ray, low-intensity electron microscope and 600-MHz NMR imaging facilities, molecular graphics equipment, and Fourier-transform infrared and EPR spectrometers. Raman and UV-resonance Raman spectrometers, differential scanning and titration microcalorimeters, analytical ultracentrifuge, HPLCs, amino acid and carbohydrate analyzers, low-intensity fluorescence imaging and confocal microscopes, and a large assortment of scanning spectrophotometers, ELISA readers, gel scanners, centrifuges, and related instrumentation associated with modern biochemical research are available. Students also enjoy the use of Linda Hall Library, one of the country's premier private science libraries; central animal facilities; and a fully integrated computer network with on-site and off-site access to national and international databases and the Internet.
Financial Aid	All fully admitted U.S. citizen and resident doctoral students receive financial support as teaching or research assistants. Support is provided for up to five years for students who are progressing satisfactorily. For the 2011–12 year, stipends are $23,000. Other forms of financial aid may be available through the Student Financial Aid Office. The metropolitan area offers many career and educational opportunities for spouses and other family members.
Cost of Study	In 2011–12, in-state tuition is about $6700 per year, while out-of-state fees are approximately $16,000 per year. Full-time doctoral students, as a general rule, receive basic tuition support.
Living and Housing Costs	A wide variety of off-campus housing is available in every price range. The overall cost of living in Kansas City is low compared with metropolitan areas in other parts of the country.
Student Group	The cell biology and biophysics graduate program has a very active graduate student organization. UMKC has approximately 10,000 students, of whom about half are graduate and professional students. The School of Biological Sciences currently has about 80 graduate students and 15 postdoctoral fellows as well as more than 200 undergraduate majors. Eight to 12 new doctoral students are admitted each year.
Student Outcomes	The majority of doctoral graduates transfer to nationally known research institutions, typically as postdoctoral associates, or undertake advanced professional training. A short transitional postdoctoral research period within the School is not uncommon.
Location	Kansas City, "The Heart of America," is the center of a metropolitan area with a population of more than 1 million. The University is adjacent to the elegant Country Club Plaza, the city's entertainment and shopping center. Major-league sports, historical and art museums, and many musical, theatrical, and cultural events as well as an extensive parks system provide entertainment throughout the year. A relaxed, Midwestern lifestyle is also an advantage of the setting, which, with its many fountains, boulevards, unusually clean air, and more days of sunshine than in most large U.S. cities, provides an enjoyable quality of life.
The University and The School	UMKC is part of the four-campus University of Missouri System, and it is the only comprehensive research university in western Missouri. It has a strong life science mission. The School of Biological Sciences was established in 1985 to develop strong research and graduate programs in the modern life sciences. The School has been cited by the Board of Curators of the University of Missouri System as an area of eminence for its programs in molecular biology and biochemistry and in cell biology and biophysics. Program improvement funds have facilitated the hiring of many research-oriented faculty members and the creation of excellent research facilities. An innovative interdisciplinary doctoral program has also been initiated, creating a stimulating environment that offers outstanding research opportunities to graduate students.
Applying	The deadline for applications from U.S. applicants is July 1, but applications received before March 1 have priority for financial support. The deadline for international applications is February 15. A bachelor's degree in biology, chemistry, physics, or a related discipline with a minimum 3.0 grade point average is required for full admission. The General Test of the Graduate Record Examinations is also required. The TOEFL is required for international applicants whose native language is not English.
Correspondence and Information	Graduate Adviser School of Biological Sciences University of Missouri–Kansas City Kansas City, Missouri 64110-2499 Phone: 816-235-2352 Fax: 816-235-5158 E-mail: sbs-grad@umkc.edu Web site: http://sbs.umkc.edu/graduate/

University of Missouri–Kansas City

THE FACULTY AND THEIR RESEARCH

Professors
Lawrence A. Dreyfus, Ph.D., Kansas. Molecular biology; bacterial toxin structure-function.
Henry M. Miziorko, Ph.D., Pennsylvania. Study of enzyme catalysis and regulation using chemical, biophysical, and molecular biology approaches; lipid biosynthesis; enzymes in inherited disease.
Anthony J. Persechini, Ph.D., Carnegie Mellon. Calcium-calmodulin signaling pathways; intracellular interactions.
G. Sullivan Read, Ph.D., Penn State. RNA turnover control; gene regulation; herpes virus.
Ann Smith, Ph.D., London. Receptor-mediated endocytosis; protein-receptor interactions; intercellular heme transport.
Theodore White, Ph.D., Michigan. Virulence and drug resistance in medically important fungi.

Associate Professors
Karen J. Bame, Ph.D., UCLA. Metabolism of heparan sulfate proteoglycans.
Leonard L. Dobens Jr., Ph.D., Dartmouth. Pattern formation; cell-cell signaling.
Brian Geisbrecht, Ph.D., Johns Hopkins. Structure and function studies of bacterial virulence factors; X-ray crystallography.
Edward P. Gogol, Ph.D., Yale. Structure of macromolecular assemblies; cryoelectron microscopy.
Saul M. Honigberg, Ph.D., Yale. Signal transduction; cell-cycle control and cell differentiation.
Chi-ming Huang, Ph.D., UCLA. Evolution neurobiology of the cerebellum.
John H. Laity, Ph.D., Cornell. Molecular recognition; NMR spectroscopy; protein biophysical chemistry.
Thomas M. Menees, Ph.D., Yale. Replication of retroviral elements and transposons; yeast molecular genetics.
Michael O'Connor, Ph.D., Ireland. Structure and function of the bacterial ribosome, ribosomal subunits, and the translational reading frame.
Lynda S. Plamann, Ph.D., Iowa. Cell-cell communication during fruiting body formation and sporulation in the soil bacterium *Myxococcus xanthus*.
Michael D. Plamann, Ph.D., Iowa. Microtubule-associated motors; organelle movement; growth polarity; cytoskeleton.
Jeffrey L. Price, Ph.D., Johns Hopkins. *Drosophila* genes involved in chronobiology and circadian rhythms.
Garth Resch, Ph.D., Missouri–Columbia. Neurophysiology and behavior patterns of alcoholism.
Jakob H. Waterborg, Ph.D., Nijmegen (Netherlands). Plant histones; chromatin conformation and gene expression.
Gerald J. Wyckoff, Ph.D., Chicago. Bioinformatics and study of molecular evolution through large-scale comparative genomics in sexual selection.
Marilyn D. Yoder, Ph.D., California, Riverside. X-ray crystallography; protein structure.
Xiao-Qiang Yu, Ph.D., Kansas State. Insect molecular biology and biochemistry of immune responses, pattern recognition proteins, and protein-protein–protein-ligand interactions.

Assistant Professors
Samuel Bouyain, D.Phil., Oxford. Structure and function of the protein tyrosine phosphatase family of cell surface receptors; X-ray crystallography.
Julia Chekanova, Ph.D. Moscow State. Relationships between mRNA quality control, processing, and export in *Saccharomyces cerevisiae*.
Erika Geisbrecht, Ph.D., Johns Hopkins. Myoblast fusion in *Drosophila* embryogenesis.
Alexander Idnurm, Ph.D., Melbourne. Molecular pathogenesis of fungal parasites.
Xiaolan Yao, Ph.D., Iowa State. Structure and dynamic bases of protein function; NMR spectroscopy.

Regional Associates
Mark Fisher, Ph.D., Illinois. Chaperonin-assisted protein folding and oligomer assembly.

UNIVERSITY OF MISSOURI–KANSAS CITY

School of Biological Sciences
Program in Molecular Biology and Biochemistry

Programs of Study

The graduate program in molecular biology and biochemistry at the University of Missouri–Kansas City (UMKC) leads to the Ph.D. degree. The program functions within the interdisciplinary Ph.D. framework of the University and is associated with the M.S. program in cell and molecular biology. The graduate program is designed to prepare students for research-oriented careers in academia, government, or the private sector. An original independent research project under the supervision of a faculty adviser is the core of these programs.

Programs of study provide a background of course work tailored to the interests of each student. Opportunity for research experience begins immediately as a component of the first-year curriculum, with each student being assigned short research projects. By the end of the first academic year, the student is also expected to have acquired a general understanding of the basis of molecular and cellular biology. At that time, the student selects a faculty research adviser and makes further course selections. To qualify for doctoral degree candidacy, students take a written comprehensive examination and prepare and defend an original research proposal. The culmination of the graduate degree programs is the preparation and oral defense of a research dissertation, typically five years after entry into the program.

The areas of research interest of participating faculty members are included in the Faculty and Their Research section. Extensive possibilities for collaboration exist with the School's program in cell biology and biophysics and with regional research associates. Opportunities for postdoctoral research are abundant.

Research Facilities

Research facilities for cell, molecular, and structural biology and biochemistry are located primarily in the Biological Sciences and Chemistry buildings. Modern research is done in laboratories assigned to individual faculty members or in specialized central facilities. Sophisticated instrumentation in these facilities includes automated DNA and protein synthesizers and sequencers, mass spectrometers, macromolecular X-ray, low-intensity electron microscope and 600-MHz NMR imaging facilities, molecular graphics equipment, and Fourier-transform infrared and EPR spectrometers. Raman and UV-resonance Raman spectrometers, differential scanning and titration microcalorimeters, analytical ultracentrifuge, HPLCs, amino-acid and carbohydrate analyzers, low-intensity fluorescence imaging and confocal microscopes, and a large assortment of scanning spectrophotometers, ELISA readers, gel scanners, centrifuges, and related instrumentation associated with modern biochemical research are also available. Students enjoy the use of Linda Hall Library, one of the country's premier private science libraries; central animal facilities; and a fully integrated computer network with on-site and off-site access to national and international databases and the Internet.

Financial Aid

All fully admitted U.S. citizen and resident doctoral students receive financial support as teaching or research assistants. Support is provided up to five years for students who are progressing satisfactorily. For the 2011–12 year, stipends are $23,000. Other forms of financial aid may be available through the Student Financial Aid Office. The metropolitan area offers many career and educational opportunities for spouses and other family members.

Cost of Study

In 2011–12, in-state tuition is about $6700 per year, while out-of-state fees are approximately $16,000 per year. Full-time doctoral students, as a general rule, receive basic tuition support.

Living and Housing Costs

A wide variety of off-campus housing is available in every price range. The overall cost of living in Kansas City is low compared with metropolitan areas in other parts of the country.

Student Group

The molecular biology and biochemistry graduate program has a very active graduate student organization. UMKC has approximately 10,000 students, of whom about half are graduate and professional students. The School of Biological Sciences currently has about 80 graduate students and 15 postdoctoral fellows as well as more than 200 undergraduate majors. Eight to 12 new doctoral students are admitted each year.

Student Outcomes

The majority of doctoral graduates transfer to nationally known research institutions, typically as postdoctoral associates, or undertake advanced professional training. A short transitional postdoctoral research period within the School is not uncommon.

Location

Kansas City, "The Heart of America," is the center of a metropolitan area with a population of more than 1 million. The University is adjacent to the elegant Country Club Plaza, the city's entertainment and shopping center. Major-league sports, historical and art museums, and many musical, theatrical, and cultural events as well as an extensive parks system provide entertainment throughout the year. A relaxed, Midwestern lifestyle is also an advantage of the setting, which, with its many fountains, boulevards, unusually clean air, and more days of sunshine than in most large U.S. cities, provides an enjoyable quality of life.

The University and The School

UMKC is part of the four-campus University of Missouri System, and it is the only comprehensive research university in western Missouri. It has a strong life science mission. The School of Biological Sciences was established in 1985 to develop strong research and graduate programs in the modern life sciences. The School has been cited by the Board of Curators of the University of Missouri System as an area of eminence for its programs in molecular biology and biochemistry and in cell biology and biophysics. Program improvement funds have facilitated the hiring of many research-oriented faculty members and the creation of excellent research facilities. An innovative interdisciplinary doctoral program has also been initiated, creating a stimulating environment that offers outstanding research opportunities to graduate students.

Applying

The deadline for applications from U.S. applicants is July 1, but applications received before March 1 have priority for financial support. The deadline for international applications is February 15. A bachelor's degree in biology, chemistry, physics, or a related discipline with a minimum 3.0 grade point average is required for full admission. The General Test of the Graduate Record Examinations is also required. The TOEFL is required for international applicants whose native language is not English.

Correspondence and Information

Graduate Adviser
School of Biological Sciences
University of Missouri–Kansas City
Kansas City, Missouri 64110-2499

Phone: 816-235-2352
Fax: 816-235-5158
E-mail: sbs-grad@umkc.edu
Web site: http://sbs.umkc.edu/graduate/

University of Missouri–Kansas City

THE FACULTY AND THEIR RESEARCH

Professors

Lawrence A. Dreyfus, Ph.D., Kansas. Molecular biology; bacterial toxin structure-function.

Henry M. Miziorko, Ph.D., Pennsylvania. Study of enzyme catalysis and regulation using chemical, biophysical, and molecular biology approaches; lipid biosynthesis; enzymes in inherited disease.

Anthony J. Persechini, Ph.D., Carnegie Mellon. Calcium-calmodulin signaling pathways; intracellular interactions.

G. Sullivan Read, Ph.D., Penn State. RNA turnover control; gene regulation; herpes virus.

Ann Smith, Ph.D., London. Receptor-mediated endocytosis; protein-receptor interactions; intercellular heme transport.

Theodore White, Ph.D., Michigan. Virulence and drug resistance in medically important fungi.

Associate Professors

Karen J. Bame, Ph.D., UCLA. Metabolism of heparan sulfate proteoglycans.

Leonard L. Dobens Jr., Ph.D., Dartmouth. Pattern formation; cell-cell signaling.

Brian Geisbrecht, Ph.D., Johns Hopkins. Structure and function studies of bacterial virulence factors; X-ray crystallography.

Edward P. Gogol, Ph.D., Yale. Structure of macromolecular assemblies; cryoelectron microscopy.

Saul M. Honigberg, Ph.D., Yale. Signal transduction; cell-cycle control and cell differentiation.

Chi-ming Huang, Ph.D., UCLA. Evolution neurobiology of the cerebellum.

John H. Laity, Ph.D., Cornell. Molecular recognition; NMR spectroscopy; protein biophysical chemistry.

Thomas M. Menees, Ph.D., Yale. Replication of retroviral elements and transposons; yeast molecular genetics.

Michael O'Connor, Ph.D., Ireland. Structure and function of the bacterial ribosome, ribosomal subunits, and the translational reading frame.

Lynda S. Plamann, Ph.D., Iowa. Cell-cell communication during fruiting body formation and sporulation in the soil bacterium *Myxococcus xanthus*.

Michael D. Plamann, Ph.D., Iowa. Microtubule-associated motors; organelle movement; growth polarity; cytoskeleton.

Jeffrey L. Price, Ph.D., Johns Hopkins. *Drosophila* genes involved in chronobiology and circadian rhythms.

Garth Resch, Ph.D., Missouri–Columbia. Neurophysiology and behavior patterns of alcoholism.

Jakob H. Waterborg, Ph.D., Nijmegen (Netherlands). Plant histones; chromatin conformation and gene expression.

Gerald J. Wyckoff, Ph.D., Chicago. Bioinformatics and study of molecular evolution through large-scale comparative genomics in sexual selection.

Marilyn D. Yoder, Ph.D., California, Riverside. X-ray crystallography; protein structure.

Xiao-Qiang Yu, Ph.D., Kansas State. Insect molecular biology and biochemistry of immune responses, pattern recognition proteins, and protein-protein–protein-ligand interactions.

Assistant Professors

Samuel Bouyain, D.Phil., Oxford. Structure and function of the protein tyrosine phosphatase family of cell surface receptors; X-ray crystallography.

Julia Chekanova, Ph.D. Moscow State. Relationships between mRNA quality control, processing, and export in *Saccharomyces cerevisiae*.

Erika Geisbrecht, Ph.D., Johns Hopkins. Myoblast fusion in *Drosophila* embryogenesis.

Alexander Idnurm, Ph.D., Melbourne. Molecular pathogenesis of fungal parasites.

Xiaolan Yao, Ph.D., Iowa State. Structure and dynamic bases of protein function; NMR spectroscopy.

Regional Associates

Gerald M. Carlson, Ph.D., Iowa State. Biophysical, biochemical, and chemical approaches in the study of macromolecular assemblies.

THE UNIVERSITY OF TEXAS HEALTH SCIENCE CENTER AT HOUSTON/ MD ANDERSON CANCER CENTER

Graduate School of Biomedical Sciences
Cancer Biology Program

Program of Study	The Cancer Biology Program (CBP) offers a graduate program of study and research leading to the Ph.D. degree from the Graduate School of Biomedical Sciences. The CBP provides training on all aspects of cancer biology, including tumor/host interactions, metastasis and invasion, tumor cell biology and biochemistry, tumor heterogeneity, cell surfaces, cancer genetics, retroviruses, cancer stem cells, and development. The CBP encompasses multidisciplinary interests of a diverse group of faculty whose research focuses on cancer-oriented problems.
	The mission of CBP is to provide a unique multidisciplinary training environment for highly qualified students to prepare them for independent careers in both basic and translational cancer research, education, and biotechnology. An important aspect of the program is its interactions and collaborations among faculty members and students from different disciplines and different institutions. Such collaborations are keys to research excellence. The total number of Ph.D. degrees awarded by the CBP for 2007–08, 2008–09, and 2009–10 academic years was 7, 11, and 11 respectively, with an average time-to-degree of 5.3, 5.2, and 5.8 years respectively. The CBP was ranked in the top tier (between 2 to 9) in the "Cell and Developmental Biology" category by the National Research Council in 2010, alongside Harvard, Stanford, and Johns Hopkins—only behind MIT.
Research Facilities	The Cancer Biology Program is dedicated to the highest level of education and research. Its faculty, classrooms, and laboratories are drawn from two major institutions: The University of Texas Health Science Center at Houston and The University of Texas MD Anderson Cancer Center, including its Science Park Division, with additional faculty and resources drawn from the Texas A&M University Health Science Center's Institute of Biosciences and Technology in Houston—together, a unique interdisciplinary and inter-institutional collaboration.
	Located in the renowned Texas Medical Center, the largest comprehensive medical center in the world, the laboratories are modern and well equipped, with state-of-the-art instrumentation. In addition, there are many core facilities or central support facilities available to all members of the research community. The Houston Academy of Medicine/Texas Medical Center Library serves the entire medical center. Other specialized libraries exist, including University of Texas MD Anderson Cancer Center Research Medical Library, University of Texas School of Dentistry at Houston Library, and others.
Financial Aid	Graduate Research Assistantships, Fellowships, and Training grants: All entering Ph.D. students receive a stipend of $26,000 per annum plus tuition and health insurance.
	Scholarships: A wide variety of scholarships, from $500–$5000, are available to GSBS students on the basis of academic and research excellence, in addition to the standard graduate research stipend.
	Travel: Each year, GSBS awards travel funds in excess of $30,000 to nearly 100 students to enable them to attend scientific meetings at which they present their research.
	Loans: Short-term and long-term loans are available through the UT- Houston Student Financial Aid.
Cost of Study	Research assistantships are provided to virtually all Ph.D. students. Students entering with funding from GSBS are offered assistantships for the first two years of study. These awards require no service other than degree-related academic activities. They include a stipend of $26,000 per annum (in 2010–11), payment of the student's tuition and required fees (valued at over $3000 for a full-time student who registered for the 12-month academic year in 2010–11), and multiple health insurance plans from which to choose.
Living and Housing Costs	Houston has the most affordable housing of the ten largest U.S. metropolitan areas and the second lowest cost of living among major American cities. Safe, attractive, and affordable housing is available in the TMC area, and many GSBS students choose to live in the UT-H Student Apartments. The stipend provided by GSBS is sufficient to meet the costs associated with obtaining a graduate education in Houston.
Student Group	The Cancer Biology Program is the largest program among the 14 Ph.D. programs of GSBS in terms of student size. Approximately one third of the student body of GSBS is from Texas, one third is from the rest of the United States, and the final third are international students. In the 2009–10 academic year, there were 37 men and 59 women in the Cancer Biology Program. There are no part-time Ph.D. students. The ratio of students enrolled to core faculty members for the 2007–08, 2008–09, and 2009–10 academic years was 1.0, 1.3 and 1.5 respectively. All doctoral students receive an identical stipend, tuition, and medical benefits.
Student Outcomes	Most graduates of the Cancer Biology Program are employed in discipline-related fields, including academic and industry.
Location	The campus of the GSBS is the Texas Medical Center (TMC), among the world's largest, most modern, and best equipped facilities for training in the basic biomedical sciences as well as translational and clinical research. The TMC occupies 675 acres on an attractive site, 2 miles southwest of downtown Houston, and it includes more than twenty academic institutions plus hospitals and patient-care facilities.
The University	The University of Texas Graduate School of Biomedical Sciences at Houston is fully accredited by the Southern Association of Colleges and Schools through both its parent institutions: The University of Texas Health Science Center at Houston and The University of Texas MD Anderson Cancer Center.
	In 1962, there was a movement, led by then MD Anderson Hospital President, R. Lee Clark, M.D., to establish The University of Texas Graduate School of Biomedical Sciences in Houston. The University of Texas Graduate School of Biomedical Sciences at Houston was established in1963 and activated by the Board of Regents of the University of Texas in the same year. The Cancer Biology Program was established in 1984.
	The mission of The University of Texas Graduate School of Biomedical Sciences at Houston is to train and educate research scientists and scientist-educators, to generate new knowledge in the biomedical sciences, and to increase public understanding of science. Given the unique environment of the Texas Medical Center, the philosophy of the Cancer Biology Program is to supplement traditional graduate school training with both depth and breadth of knowledge in cancer biology.
Applying	GSBS Admissions Office handles admissions of all of the graduate students irrespective of their choices of program affiliation. Therefore, students interested in CBP should apply to GSBS directly but not to the CBP. All application materials are collected via GSBS' new online application system. No paper application materials are accepted. To see all application requirements and instructions, visit http://www.uthouston.edu/gsbs/future-students/admissions/requirements/.
	Prospective students who seek more information about the Graduate School and/or the application process should visit the University of Texas Graduate School of Biomedical Sciences Web site at http://www.uthouston.edu/gsbs/.
Correspondence and Information	Cancer Biology Program The University of Texas Graduate School of Biomedical Sciences at Houston/ The University of Texas MD Anderson Cancer Center Houston, Texas 77030 Phone: 713-792-8969 E-mail: xllin@mdanderson.org Web site: http://www.mdanderson.org/departments/canbioprogram

The University of Texas Health Science Center at Houston / MD Anderson Cancer Center

THE FACULTY AND THEIR RESEARCH

Hesham Amin, M.D., Professor. Research interests: Signal transduction; apoptosis, cell cycle, cytokines molecular targets.

Michael Andreeff, M.D., Ph.D., Professor. Research interests: Apoptosis; drug resistance; cell cycle; gene therapy.

Menashe Bar-Eli, Ph.D., Professor. Research interests: Melanoma; tumor metastasis; gene expression; tumor suppressor genes.

Robert C. Bast Jr., M.D., Professor. Research interests: Biomarkers (antigens and autoantibodies) for early detection of ovarian cancer; kinase regulation of paclitaxel sensitivity; imprinted tumor suppressor genes (ARHI/DIRAS, PEG3, SNRPN, NDN); autophagy; tumor dormancy.

Oliver Bögler, Ph.D., Professor. Research interests: Molecular and cellular biology of gliomas; signal transduction; phosphoproteomics; mass spectrometry; receptor tyrosine kinase regulation; nuclear signaling by receptor Tyrosine Kinases; glial transformation; novel platinum chemotherapeutics.

Douglas Boyd, Ph.D., Professor. Research interests: Transcription; tumor cell invasion; metastases.

Joya Chandra, Ph.D., Associate Professor. Research interests: Oxidative stress-dependent signaling; induction of oxidative stress by biologically targeted agents; apoptosis induction as a consequence of proteasome inhibition; biology of pediatric; adult leukemias..

Junjie Chen, Ph.D., Professor. Research interests: Biochemical and molecular aspects of breast/ovarian cancers; the roles of tumor suppressor genes in DNA damage-signaling pathways; mitotic regulation and potential link between dynamic regulation of chromatin structures and tumorigenesis.

Paul Chiao, Ph.D., Professor. Research interests: Signal transduction; regulation of NF-B family of transcription factors; pancreatic cancers.

François X. Claret, Ph.D., Associate Professor. Research interests: Signal transduction; cell cycle control; oncogenes.

Jiale Dai, Ph.D. Research interests: Tumor suppressor genes, oncogenes; signal transduction.

Lee Ellis, M.D., Professor. Research interests: Angiogenesis; colon cancer.

Zhen Fan, M.D., Professor. Research interests: Breast cancer therapeutics; breast cancer development signaling and resistance to molecular-targeted therapies.

Bingliang Fang, M.D., Ph.D., Professor. Research interests: Tumor specific transgene expression; apoptotic genes; cancer gene therapy.

Isaiah Fidler, D.V.M./Ph.D., Professor. Research interests: Cancer metastasis, angiogenesis, immunotherapy.

Elsa Flores, Ph.D., Associate Professor. Research interests: Tumor suppressor genes; DNA damage; apoptosis; gene expression; transcriptional regulation; mouse genetics.

Gary Gallick, Ph.D., Professor. Research interests: Tyrosine kinases; malignant transformation.

Jeffrey Gershenwald, M.D., Professor. Research interests: Melanoma; metastasis; gene expression and gene expression profiling; gene regulation; lymphatic metastases; lymphangiogenesis.

Candelaria Gomez-Manzano, Ph.D., Assistant Professor. Research interests: Cancer stem cells; brain tumors; tie2-multicompartmental role; tumor microenvironment; mechanisms of tumor resistance.

Elizabeth Grimm, Ph.D., Professor. Research interests: Interleukins; cytotoxic lymphocytes; macrophages; kinases.

Walter Hittelman, Ph.D., Professor. Research interests: Genomic instability; cell cycle; chemoprevention.

Peng Huang, M.D., Ph.D., Professor. Research interests: Mechanisms of cancer therapeutics; anticancer agents; cancer cell energy metabolism; role of mitochondria in ROS generation and drug-induced apoptosis; free radical/redox regulation and signaling; role of p53 in DNA.

Suyun Huang, M.D., Ph.D., Associate Professor. Research interests: Molecular mechanisms of tumor metastasis; angiogenesis; transcriptional factors; molecular diagnosis and therapy.

Dennis P.M. Hughes, M.D., Ph.D., Associate Professor. Research interests: Cell signaling; small molecule inhibitors; ERBB family members (EGFR, Her-2, Her-4, etc.); nuclear trafficking of receptors; osteosarcoma; Ewing sarcoma; clinical monitoring.

Mien-Chie Hung, Ph.D., Professor. Research interests: Oncogenes; cell cycle; signal transduction; gene expression.

Jean Pierre Issa, M.D., Professor. Affiliation: MD Anderson Cancer Center, Leukemia Department. Research interests: DNA methylation; aging and cancer; epigenetic silencing.

Randy Johnson, Ph.D., Professor, Department of Biochemistry and Molecular Biology. Research interests: Modeling human disease and development in the mouse.

Khandan Keyomarsi, Ph.D., Professor. Research interests: Breast cancer; cell cycle control; drug-targeting.

Eugenie Kleinerman, M.D., Professor. Research interests: Fas/FasL, angiogenesis, vasculogenesis, biologic response modifiers; liposome drug delivery.

Mikhail G. Kolonin, Ph.D., Assistant Professor. Research interests: Mesenchymal stem cells; mechanisms of adult stem cell; mobilization/migration/engraftment; role of mesenchymal stem cells in cancer vasculogenesis.

Ja Seok Koo, Ph.D., Associate Professor. Research interests: Mucous and squamous differentiation of bronchial epithelium Retinoids; CREB, Mucin, Inflammation, cytokine; airway secretions; lung cancer.

Razelle Kurzrock, M.D., Professor. Research interests: Cytokine deregulation; chromosomal translocation.

Ju-Seog Lee, Ph.D., Assistant Professor. Research interests: Systems biology; gene expression profile; cancer genomics; microarray; proteomics; integromics.

Min Gyu Lee, Ph.D., Assistant Professor. Research interests: Histone modifications; histone-modifying enzymes; gene regulation.

Mong-Hong Lee, Ph.D., Professor. Research interests: Cell cycle regulation; gene knock-out; gene expression.

Dina Chelouche Lev, M.D., Associate Professor. Research interests: Soft tissue sarcoma; chemoresistance; angiogensis; lymphangiogenesis, metastasis, preclinical therapeutic models; tumor microenvironment; gene therapy.

Hui-Kuan Lin, Ph.D., Associate Professor. Research interests: Tumor suppressor gene/oncogene in cancer development; protein phosphorylation.

Shiaw-Yih Lin, Ph.D., Associate Professor. Research interests: Cellular immortalization; genomic instability; metastasis.

Xin Lin, Ph.D., Professor. Research interests: Signal transduction; activation of NF-B family of transcription factors; protein phosphorylation; lymphocyte activation; development and differentiation; cell proliferation and tumorigenesis.

Mingyao Liu, Ph.D., Professor. Research interests: G-protein coupled receptors; G-proteins; molecular basis of signal transduction; mechanism of human stem cell differentiation.

Craig D. Logsdon, Ph.D., Professor. Research interests: Pancreatic disease; biomarker discovery; cancer cell biology; molecular biology, gene therapy, inflammation.

Xiongbin Lu, Ph.D., Assistant Professor. Research interests: DNA damage signaling pathways; MicroRNA biogenesis; p53 tumor suppressor; protein phosphatases and deubiquitinases.

Zhimin Lu, M.D., Ph.D., Associate Professor. Research interests: Signal transduction; oncogenesis; tumor cell migration; Invasion and metastasis; cancer metabolism.

Li Ma, Ph.D., Assistant Professor. Research interests: MicroRNA-mediated regulation of metastasis; epithelial-mesenchymal transition (EMT); stem cells molecularly targeted therapeutics.

Sendurai A. Mani, Ph.D., Assistant Professor. Research interests: Metastasis; EMT; normal/cancer stem cells.

Joseph McCarty, Ph.D., Assistant Professor. Research interests: Cerebrovascular disease; angiogenesis; cell adhesion and signaling; blood-brain barrier; brain cancer and metastasis.

David McConkey, Ph.D., Professor. Research interests: Apoptosis; tumor metastasis.

Kapil Mehta, Ph.D., Professor. Research interests: Mechanisms of retinoid action and drug resistance.

Funda Meric-Bernstam, M.D., Professor. Research interests: Breast cancer; cancer biology; molecular oncology; gene expression; translational regulation; signal transduction; molecular therapeutics.

Gordon Mills, M.D., Ph.D., Professor. Research interests: Ovarian cancer; signal transduction; human cancer genetics.

Jeff Myers, M.D./Ph.D., Professor. Research interests: Orthotopic models of oral cancer; anoikis; tumor progression.

Honami Naora, Ph.D., Associate Professor. Research interests: Cell differentiation; embryonic patterning; tumor histogenesis and tumor behavior; cancers of female reproductive organs.

Nora Navone, M.D./Ph.D., Associate Professor. Research interests: Prostate cancer; p53; TGF-beta; tumor progression.

Jae-Il Park, Ph.D., Assistant Professor. Research interests: Telomerase dynamics; telomerase regulation; cells of origin in cancer; stem cells, Wnt pathway in cancer and stem cell regulation.

Raphael Pollock, M.D., Ph.D., Professor. Research interests: Oncogenes and tumor suppressor genes in soft tissue sarcoma.

Dos Sarbassov, Ph.D., Assistant Professor. Research interests: Cell signaling; cell growth regulation, proliferation, survival, and migration; rapamycin and the mTOR (mammalian Target Of Rapamycin) pathway; kinases and phosphatases; anti-cancer drug development.

Anil K. Sood, M.D., Professor. Research interests: Vascular development in cancer; receptor tyrosine kinase regulation, invasion, metastasis.

Shao-Cong Sun, Ph.D., Professor. Research interests: NF-B signaling, protein ubiquitination, autoimmunity, inflammation and cancer

Elizabeth Travis, Ph.D., Professor. Research interests: Molecular genetics, radiosensitivity.

Kenneth Tsai, M.D., Ph.D., Assistant Professor. Research interests: Skin cancer; targeted and personalized therapy for cancer; cancer immunology.

Jessica Tyler, Ph.D., Professor. Research interests: Epigenetics; cancer; aging; DNA repair; chromati; transcription.

T. Naoto Ueno, M.D., Ph.D., FACP, Professor. Research interests: Gene therapy; cell cycle; apoptosis; breast cancer; ovarian cancer; kidney cancer.

Zhengxin Wang, Ph.D., Associate Professor. Research interests: Mechanisms of action of androgen receptor in the regulation of prostate-specific gene expression with an emphasis on how de-regulation leads to prostate cancer.

Kwong-Kwok Wong, Ph.D., Professor. Research interests: Molecular pathogenesis of ovarian cancers; next generation sequencing; cancer cell signaling pathways.

Xiangwei Wu, Ph.D., Associate Professor. Research interests: Mechanisms of p53 and death receptor-mediated apoptosis and applications in chemoprevention and cancer therapy.

Keping Xie, M.D., Ph.D., Professor. Research interests: Cancer metastasis; angiogenesis; gene regulation; molecular diagnosis and therapy.

Xiaochun Xu, M.D., Ph.D., Associate Professor. Research Interests: Retinoids and their nuclear receptors in cell differentiation; carcinogenesis, and chemoprevention; nonsteroidal anti-inflammatory drugs (NSAIDs) in carcinogenesis and chemoprevention; biomarkers for carcinogenesis and tumor promotion.

Dihua Yu, M.D./Ph.D., Professor. Research interests: cancer metastasis; drug resistance; oncogenes; suppressor genes.

Wei Zhang, Ph.D., Professor. Research interests: Cell cycle; cell death; signal transduction; radiotherapy.

Patrick Zweidler-McKay, M.D., Ph.D., Associate Professor. Research interests: Leukemias; neuroblastoma molecular therapeutics; Xenograft models.

UNIVERSITY OF WASHINGTON / FRED HUTCHINSON CANCER RESEARCH CENTER
Molecular and Cellular Biology Program

Program of Study

The University of Washington and the Fred Hutchinson Cancer Research Center offer a program of graduate studies in molecular and cellular biology leading to the Ph.D. degree. More than 200 faculty members participate in the program and are located on the University of Washington campus in the Departments of Biochemistry, Bioengineering, Biological Structure, Biology, Genome Sciences, Immunology, Microbiology, Pathobiology, Pathology, Pharmacology, and Physiology and Biophysics, as well as on the Day campus at the Hutchinson Center, primarily in the Division of Basic Sciences and the Division of Human Biology. Recently, the Institute for Systems Biology (ISB), a nonprofit research institute headed by Dr. Leroy Hood, and the Seattle Biomedical Research Institute (SBRI), an infectious disease research center led by Dr. Ken Stuart, have joined the Molecular and Cellular Biology (MCB) program.

The goals of the program are to give the student a sound background in molecular and cellular biology and to provide access to the research expertise of all faculty members and laboratories working in this area. These goals are accomplished through the basic elements of the program, which include three quarters of core conjoint courses, a two-quarter literature review course, one quarter of grant writing, three or more quarter-long lab rotations, advanced elective courses in molecular and cellular biology, and a series of informal workshops and seminars on topics in diverse areas of molecular biology and cellular biology. Emphasis is placed on critical evaluation of the literature, exposure to current research methods, and creative thinking through independent research. Students are expected to begin active research in their first year through their lab rotations and to choose a permanent thesis adviser at the end of their first year.

Research Facilities

The program uses the research facilities of the individual departments, Hutchinson Center, ISB, and SBRI. The School of Medicine is housed in the Health Sciences Center and the South Lake Union research hub (SLU). The University Hospital and the College of Arts and Sciences are located in adjoining or nearby buildings. The Hutchinson Center's Day campus and SLU are a 15-minute shuttle ride from the University. The laboratories of participating faculty members are well equipped with the latest in research equipment and are funded by external support. The ISB and the SBRI are located within easy commuting distance. Some of the other facilities available are two Howard Hughes Medical Institute research units, the Markey Molecular Medicine Center, animal quarters, shared major instrument facilities, oligonucleotide and peptide synthesis facilities, a marine biology station at Friday Harbor in the San Juan Islands, and an extensive Health Sciences Library.

Financial Aid

The program offers a salary of approximately $27,348 for twelve months. Students with satisfactory academic progress can anticipate funding that includes tuition and health insurance for the duration of their studies.

Cost of Study

Tuition, salary, and medical, dental, and vision benefits are funded for the duration of the program for students in good standing.

Living and Housing Costs

The University has a wide variety of housing available for single and married students as well as families. Students should call the University Housing Office at 206-543-4059 for further information. Private accommodations may be found within easy walking or bicycling distance.

Student Group

At the University of Washington, approximately 2,500 full-time faculty members serve a student population of 35,000 that is drawn from all over the United States and many other countries.

More than 20 new students are admitted to the program each year. There are approximately 500 graduate students in the biological sciences at the University of Washington.

Student Outcomes

The Molecular and Cellular Biology Program received degree-granting status in 1994. The majority of students, upon earning Ph.D. degrees, secure postdoctoral research positions.

Location

All around Seattle, there is an abundance of opportunity for outdoor recreation. Unsurpassed sailing, hiking, mountain climbing, skiing, and camping are all a short distance away. Because of the saltwater expanse of the Puget Sound and the mountains both to the east and to the west, Seattle enjoys a moderate climate, with precipitation averaging 32 inches per year, mostly during the winter and early spring. The city's downtown area offers many cultural and educational advantages, including theater, museums, symphony, films, and opera, while the waterfront is home to a large marketplace, galleries, and fresh seafood restaurants. The University itself sponsors many public lectures, concerts, exhibits, film festivals, and theatrical performances.

The University

The University of Washington is located in a residential section of Seattle near the downtown area. It is bordered by two lakes and is one of the largest and most scenic institutions of higher education in the country. The University is a research-intensive institution, regularly ranking first overall among public universities in externally funded research programs. It is recognized for graduate instruction of high quality, offering more than ninety graduate and professional programs that enroll more than 7,300 graduate students on campus. The Hutchinson Center's research laboratories are located near Lake Union just north of downtown Seattle. It is the largest independent cancer research center in the country.

Applying

Applicants must have completed a baccalaureate or advanced degree by the time of matriculation; degrees emphasizing biology, physical or natural sciences, and mathematics are preferred. It is advisable to take the GRE (the General Test) no later than October so that scores can be recorded before the deadline (code for MCB is 0206, code for UW is 4854, on the GRE registration form). New students enter the graduate program in the autumn quarter. The deadline for completion of applications is currently December 1 of the academic year preceding entrance. Students must apply via the online application available at the MCB Program Web site (http://depts.washington.edu/mcb/applicantsinfo.php).

Correspondence and Information

Graduate Program Specialist
Molecular and Cellular Biology Program, Box 357275
University of Washington
Seattle, Washington 98195-7275
Phone: 206-685-3155
Fax: 206-685-8174
E-mail: mcb@u.washington.edu
Web site: http://www.mcb-seattle.edu

University of Washington/Fred Hutchinson Cancer Research Center

THE FACULTY AND THEIR RESEARCH

UNIVERSITY OF WASHINGTON

Cancer Biology
Charles Asbury, Richard Gardner, Philip Greenberg, Brian Iritani, Lawrence Loeb, Nancy Maizels, Raymond Monnat, Junko Oshima, Stephen Plymate, Bradley Preston, Peter Rabinovitch, Timothy Rose, Judit Villen, Edith Wang, Alejandro Wolf-Yadlin, Linda Wordeman.

Cell Signaling and Cell/Environment Interactions
John Aitchison, Charles Asbury, Sandra Bajjalieh, Nitin Baliga, Joseph Beavo, Celeste Berg, Karol Bomsztyk, Karin Bornfeldt, Mark Bothwell, Susan Brockerhoff, Peter Byers, Steven Carlson, John Clark, Trisha Davis, Jeremy Duffield, Andrew Farr, Elaine Faustman, Stanley Froehner, Clement Furlong, Richard Gardner, Michael Gelb, Cecilia Giachelli, Sharona Gordon, E. Peter Greenberg, Ted Gross, Chris Hague, Bertil Hille, Takato Imaizumi, Matthew Kaeberlein, David Kimelman, Michael Laflamme, John Leigh, Weiqing Li, Jaisri Lingappa, Qinghang Liu, Stanley McKnight, Alexey Merz, Dana Miller, Samuel Miller, Neil Nathanson, Jennifer Nemhauser, Leo Pallanck, William Parks, Marilyn Parsons, Stephen Plymate, Christine Queitsch, Peter Rabinovitch, Hannele Ruohola-Baker, Ram Samudrala, Andrew Scharenberg, Lynn Schnapp, Debra Schwinn, John Scott, Daniel Storm, Rong Tian, Keiko Torii, Judit Villen, Edith Wang, Norman Wolf, Alejandro Wolf-Yadlin, Zhengui Xia, Wenqing Xu, Zipora Yablonka-Reuveni, William Zagotta, Ning Zheng.

Developmental Biology, Stem Cells, and Aging
Chris Amemiya, Celeste Berg, C. Tony Blau, Mark Bothwell, Steven Carlson, Jeffrey Chamberlain, Michael Cunningham, Ajay Dhaka, Christine Disteche, Cecilia Giachelli, Robert Hevner, Merrill Hille, Michael Horwitz, David Kimelman, Michael Laflamme, Weiqing Li, Alexey Merz, Raymond Monnat, William Moody, Randall Moon, Charles Murry, Jennifer Nemhauser, David Parichy, Jay Parrish, David Raible, Thomas Reh, Hannele Ruohola-Baker, Billie Swalla, Keiko Torii, Barbara Wakimoto, Robert Waterston, Norman Wolf, Zhengui Xia, Zipora Yablonka-Reuveni.

Gene Expression, Cell Cycle, and Chromosome Biology
John Aitchison, Charles Asbury, Karol Bomsztyk, Bonita Brewer, Daniel Campbell, RoseAnn Cattolico, Christine Disteche, Maitreya Dunham, Stanley Fields, Richard Gardner, Takato Imaizumi, Weiqing Li, Raymond Monnat, David Morris, Peter Myler, Jennifer Nemhauser, Shao-En Ong, Peter Rabinovitch, Debra Schwinn, Keiko Torii, Gabriele Varani, Judit Villen, Edith Wang, Robert Waterston, Alan Weiner, Amy Weinmann, Norman Wolf, Linda Wordeman, Zipora Yablonka-Reuveni.

Genetics, Genomics, and Evolution
Chris Amemiya, Nitin Baliga, Celeste Berg, Elhanan Borenstein, Bonita Brewer, Peter Byers, Jeffrey Chamberlain, Michael Cunningham, Trisha Davis, Christine Disteche, Aimee Dudley, Maitreya Dunham, Stanley Fields, Richard Gardner, Marshall Horwitz, Matthew Kaeberlein, Mary-Claire King, Charles Laird, John Leigh, Weiqing Li, Mary Lidstrom, Dana Miller, Samuel Miller, Raymond Monnat, Shao-En Ong, Junko Oshima, Leo Pallanck, David Parichy, Jay Parrish, Bradley Preston, Christine Queitsch, David Raible, Lalita Ramakrishnan, Hannele Ruohola-Baker, Ram Samudrala, Debra Schwinn, Jay Shendure, David Sherman, Ilya Shmulevich, Kenneth Stuart, Billie Swalla, Bruce Tempel, Rong Tian, Keiko Torii, Jeffrey Vieira, Judit Villen, Barbara Wakimoto, Robert Waterston, Alan Weiner,, Norman Wolf, Zipora Yablonka-Reuveni.

Microbiology, Infection, and Immunity
Alan Aderem, Elhanan Borenstein, Daniel Campbell, Lee Ann Campbell, James Champoux, Edward Clark, Brad Cookson, Nicholas Crispe, Richard Darveau, Sharon Doty, Jeremy Duffield, Ferric Fang, Pamela Fink, Clement Furlong, Michael Gale, Michael Gelb, E. Peter Greenberg, Philip Greenberg, Christoph Grundner, Jessica Hamerman, Caroline Harwood, Jay Heinecke, Helen Horton, Brian Iritani, Michael Katze, Michael Lagunoff, Mary Lidstrom, Jaisri Lingappa, Nancy Maizels, Samuel Miller, Steven Moseley, Joseph Mougous, James Mullins, William Parks, Matthew Parsek, Marilyn Parsons, Lakshmi Rajgopal, Lalita Ramakrishnan, David Rawlings, Marilyn Roberts, Timothy Rose, Ram Samudrala, Jay Shendure, David Sherman, Pradeep Singh, Jason Smith, Joseph Smith, Kelly Smith, Donald Sodora, Leonidas Stamatatos, Daniel Stetson, Kenneth Stuart, Kenneth Urdahl, Wesley Van Voorhis, Amy Weinmann, Tuofu Zhu, Steven Ziegler.

Molecular Structure and Computational Biology
John Aitchison, Charles Asbury, David Baker, Elhanan Borenstein, Roger Bumgarner, James Champoux, John Clark, Clement Furlong, Michael Gelb, Jay Heinecke, Bertil Hille, Wim Hol, Rachel Klevit, Michael MacCoss, Samuel Miller, Raymond Monnat, Peter Myler, Shao-En Ong, Ram Samudrala, Ilya Shmulevich, Leonidas Stamatatos, Gabriele Varani, Liguo Wang, Wenqing Xu, Ning Zheng.

Neuroscience
Sandra Bajjalieh, Andres Barria, Joseph Beavo, Olivia Bermingham-McDonogh, Eliot Brenowitz, Susan Brockerhoff, Steven Carlson, William Catterall, Jeffrey Chamberlain, Charles Chavkin, Horacio de la Iglesia, Ajay Dhaka, Clement Furlong, Sharona Gordon, James Hurley, Matthew Kaeberlein, Stanley McKnight, William Moody, David Morris, Neil Nathanson, John Neumaier, Leo Pallanck, Richard Palmiter, Jay Parrish, Paul Phillips, Nicholas Poolos, David Raible, Thomas Reh, Fred Rieke, Hannele Ruohola-Baker, Debra Schwinn, Robert Steiner, Nephi Stella, Daniel Storm, Bruce Tempel, Rachel Wong, Zhengui Xia, William Zagotta.

FRED HUTCHINSON CANCER RESEARCH CENTER

Cancer Biology
Antonio Bedalov, Laura Beretta, Jason Bielas, William Carter, Bruce Clurman, Steven Collins, Robert Eisenman, Matthew Fero, Denise Galloway, William Grady, David Hockenbery, Christopher Kemp, Paul Lampe, A. Dusty Miller, Peter Nelson, James Olson, Amanda Paulovich, Peggy Porter, James Roberts, Nina Salama, Akiko Shimamura, Julian Simon, Toshiyasu Taniguchi, Stephen Tapscott, Muneesh Tewari, Valeri Vasioukhin, Edus Warren, Cassian Yee.

Cell Signaling and Cell/Environment Interactions
Linda Breeden, William Carter, Steven Collins, Jonathan Cooper, Robert Eisenman, Daniel Gottschling, David Hockenbery, Paul Lampe, Susan Parkhurst, James Priess, Mark Roth, Wenying Shou, Valeri Vasioukhin.

Developmental Biology, Stem Cells, and Aging
Jonathan Cooper, Robert Eisenman, Cecilia Moens, Patrick Paddison, Susan Parkhurst, James Priess.

Gene Expression, Cell Cycle, and Chromosome Biology
Antonio Bedalov, Sue Biggins, Robert Bradley, Linda Breeden, Robert Eisenman, Matthew Fero, Adam Geballe, Daniel Gottschling, William Grady, Mark Groudine, Steven Hahn, Steven Henikoff, Amanda Paulovich, James Roberts, Mark Roth, Gerald Smith, Stephen Tapscott, Toshio Tsukiyama.

Genetics, Genomics, and Evolution
Antonio Bedalov, Jesse Bloom, Robert Bradley, Michael Emerman, Adam Geballe, Daniel Gottschling, Steven Hahn, Steven Henikoff, Harmit Malik, J. Lee Nelson, Peter Nelson, Amanda Paulovich, Katie Peichel, Wenying Shou, Muneesh Tewari.

Microbiology, Infection, and Immunity
Laura Beretta, Jesse Bloom, William Carter, Lawrence Corey, Michael Emerman, David Fredricks, Denise Galloway, Adam Geballe, Keith Jerome, Hans-Peter Kiem, Julie McElrath, Dusty Miller, Julie Overbaugh, Nina Salama, Roland Strong, Edus Warren.

Molecular Structure and Computational Biology
Jesse Bloom, Robert Bradley, Steven Hahn, Barry Stoddard, Roland Strong.

Neuroscience
Jihong Bai, Linda Buck, Cecilia Moens, James Olson.

WAYNE STATE UNIVERSITY

WAYNE STATE UNIVERSITY

School of Medicine
Graduate Program in Cancer Biology

Program of Study

This nationally recognized Ph.D. in Cancer Biology–granting program was established in 1989. The program's multidisciplinary and interdisciplinary faculty is mostly in the School of Medicine and the Barbara Ann Karmanos Cancer Institute (BAKCI). The program's faculty members are from basic and clinical science departments, their research is well supported with national competitive funding, and they are experienced in graduate student/Ph.D. candidate education and research training. The scope of the faculty's cutting-edge cancer biology research is broad, encompassing basic and translational cancer biology research in areas including drug discovery and development, proteases and metastasis, molecular oncology and human genetics, breast cancer, chemical carcinogenesis and toxicology, and prevention. Their research is on specific topics, such as mechanisms of cell proliferation control, apoptosis, DNA repair, cell-cell interactions, invasion, and metastasis.

Cancer biology is a new multi- and interdisciplinary field that requires education and research training in many disciplines, including cellular biology, molecular biology, pharmacology, and oncology. Students' first year is devoted primarily to courses, research explorations, and seminars, and by the end, the student chooses a graduate adviser who guides the initial research. During the second year, each student completes most of the course requirements, progresses to dissertation research, and fulfills the dissertation prospectus requirement. Subsequent years as a predoctoral candidate are devoted primarily to dissertation research. Additional details are available at the program's Web site. The average time to degree is less than five years.

Research Facilities

The cancer biology faculty has more than 100,000 square feet of modern laboratory space. Besides typical laboratory instruments, there are many specialized core facilities (e.g., molecular biology and genetics, biostatistics, flow cytometry/cell sorting, and confocal imaging) equipment (e.g., DNA and protein synthesis and sequencing, X-ray crystallography, and spectroscopy), science libraries, and computer facilities.

Financial Aid

Support is awarded on a competitive basis to first-year graduate students, who receive full financial support until completion provided the program's standards of progress are met. A significant addition to the stipend is available to U.S. citizens and permanent residents who can qualify for support from training grants and individual fellowships. Support includes full tuition (see Cost of Study section), insurances (medical, dental, and vision) and annual stipend of more than $20,389, for an approximate total value of at least $37,000 for Michigan residents and $47,500 for nonresidents. Applicants who are U.S. citizens or permanent residents are encouraged to also apply for an Undergraduate Summer Cancer Biology Research Fellowship.

Cost of Study

Supported students have their tuition and fees covered (approximately $11,300 and $23,500 per year for Michigan and nonresident students, respectively).

Living and Housing Costs

WSU has a variety of furnished and unfurnished graduate student apartments. The metropolitan area has high-quality housing within a modest price range. The University Housing Office assists students in locating housing. Living costs, food, and recreation are modest. There are abundant employment opportunities for spouses.

Student Group

The program annually has over 25 enrolled students and Ph.D. candidates. Current students are from several states (Michigan, Minnesota, Mississippi, New York, Washington D.C., Wisconsin, Utah) and other countries (Canada, India, Thailand). They are a significant component of the School of Medicine's approximately 180 Ph.D. students.

Student Outcomes

The vast majority of the program's over 60 Ph.D. in Cancer Biology alumni progressed to postdoctoral training in excellent laboratories at prestigious institutions such as Duke, Harvard, Johns Hopkins, Yale, University of Michigan, National Institutes of Health, and Scripps Research Institute. Many graduates have progressed to faculty appointments (e.g., Grand Valley State, Loma Linda, Michigan State, Northwestern, and Wake Forest Universities) or to investigator positions at research institutes (e.g., Scripps Research Institute) or pharmaceutical enterprises (e.g., Millennium Pharmaceuticals).

Location

WSU is in the University Cultural Center with the Institute of Arts, Orchestra Hall, Public Library, theaters, schools of art and music, and the African-American Museum. Nearby are major sports (baseball, hockey, football) facilities. The riverfront, lakes, and parks are in driving distance.

The University

WSU is a major public urban research university with nine major schools and colleges. BAKCI is a National Cancer Institute–designated Comprehensive Cancer Center, a nationally recognized institution of basic, translational, and clinical cancer research excellence.

Applying

Applications are encouraged from U.S. citizens or permanent residents, particularly diverse individuals, as well as international students. A copy of official transcripts from all previously attended institutions must include one that reports at least a bachelor's degree from an accredited school or evidence that the degree requirements will be completed before matriculation. The cumulative degree posted grade point average should be at least 3.0 (on a 4.0 scale). Transcripts must report one full year each of general/inorganic chemistry, organic chemistry, and biology; one full year of calculus and of physics are recommended but not required. The GRE General Test is required, and a score report is mandatory. International applicants must provide a copy of the TOEFL or an equivalent exam score report. Three letters of evaluation are required; they may be mailed directly or submitted via the online application mechanism. A brief (one-page) Statement of Purpose is required (a description of the applicant's background, goals, and objectives). A brief description of research experiences should be detailed in a one-page addendum. Complete applications should be submitted well in advance of March 1.

Correspondence and Information

Dr. Robert J. Pauley, Director
Graduate Program in Cancer Biology
School of Medicine
Wayne State University
550 East Canfield Avenue, Room 329
Detroit, Michigan 48202
Phone: 313-577-1065
E-mail: rpauley@med.wayne.edu
        ad3340@wayne.edu (to send applications)
Web site: http://www.med.wayne.edu/cancer/

Wayne State University

THE FACULTY AND THEIR RESEARCH

Ayad M. Al-Katib, Professor of Medicine; M.D., Mosul Medical College (Iraq), 1974. Biology and experimental therapeutics of human lymphoid tumors.

Julie L. Boerner, Assistant Professor of Pharmacology, Karmanos Cancer Institute; Ph.D., Mayo, 2000. Ligand-independent EGFR signaling.

George S. Brush, Associate Professor of Pathology, Karmanos Cancer Institute; Ph.D., Johns Hopkins, 1991. DNA damage and DNA replication checkpoints.

Angelika M. Burger, Professor of Pharmacology, Karmanos Cancer Institute; Ph.D., Johannes Gutenberg (Germany), 1992; Ph.D., Bradford (UK), 2005. Molecular targets and cancer therapeutics.

Ben D.-M. Chen, Professor of Medicine; Ph.D., Vanderbilt, 1977. Regulation of macrophage production and differentiation by hematopoietic growth factor; growth-factor receptor; signal transduction.

Michael L. Cher, Professor of Urology and Pathology, Karmanos Cancer Institute; M.D., Washington (St. Louis), 1986. Biology of prostate cancer bone metastasis.

Sreenivasa R. Chinni, Assistant Professor, Departments of Urology and Pathology and Karmanos Cancer Institute; Ph.D., Louisville, 1997. Chemokine signaling; prostate cancer bone metastasis.

Q. Ping Dou, Professor of Pathology; Ph.D., Rutgers, 1988. Chemoprevention and molecular targeting.

James F. Eliason, Associate Professor of Medicine and Oncology; Ph.D., Chicago, 1978. Mechanisms of drug resistance and prediction of patient response to therapy.

Stephen P. Ethier, Professor of Pathology; Associate Center Director, Basic Research; and Deputy Director, Karmanos Cancer Institute; Ph.D., Tennessee–Oak Ridge, 1982. Breast cancer genetics, cell biology, and cell signaling.

David R. Evans, Professor of Biochemistry; Ph.D., Wayne State, 1968. Structure and control mechanisms of enzymes that regulate mammalian pyrimidine biosynthesis.

Joseph A. Fontana, Professor of Medicine; Ph.D., Johns Hopkins, 1969; M.D., Pennsylvania, 1975. Retinoids and their signaling pathways.

Rafael Fridman, Professor of Pathology; Ph.D., Jerusalem, 1986. Role of tumor proteases in tumor cell invasion.

Craig N. Giroux, Associate Professor of Institute of Environmental Health; Ph.D., MIT, 1979. Molecular biology of germ line differentiation; genome stability; developmental genetics; mechanisms of mutation and tumor prevention.

David H. Gorski, Associate Professor of Surgery, Karmanos Cancer Institute; M.D., Michigan, 1988; Ph.D., Case Western Reserve, 1994. Breast cancer and regulation of tumor angiogenesis.

Miriam L. Greenberg, Professor of Biological Sciences; Ph.D., Yeshiva (Einstein), 1980. Regulation of membrane biogenesis; genetic control of phospholipid biosynthesis; inositol phosphate metabolism in yeast.

Ahmad R. Heydari, Associate Professor of Nutrition and Food Science; Ph.D., Illinois State, 1990. Nutrient-gene interactions in aging and neoplasia; nutrients and DNA damage and repair.

Kenneth V. Honn, Professor of Radiation Oncology and Pathology; Ph.D., Wayne State, 1977. Cancer biology: role of kinases, eicosanoids, and integrin receptors in tumor invasion/metastasis.

Michael C. Joiner, Professor of Radiation Oncology; Ph.D., London, 1980. Mechanisms underlying variation in response to ionizing radiation.

David H. Kessel, Professor of Pharmacology and of Medicine; Ph.D., Michigan, 1959. Photosensitization of neoplastic cells; photobiology; mechanisms of drug resistance.

Hyeong-Reh C. Kim, Professor of Pathology; Ph.D., Northwestern, 1989. Growth factor signaling and regulation of apoptosis.

Thomas A. Kocarek, Associate Professor, Institute of Chemical Toxicology; Ph.D., Ohio State, 1988. Regulation of cytochrome P-450 gene expression

Adhip N. Majumdar, Professor of Internal Medicine; Ph.D., London, 1968. Aging and carcinogenesis of the gastrointestinal tract, in particular, the role of EGF-receptor family in regulating growth and transformation.

Larry H. Matherly, Professor of Pharmacology and Associate Member, Karmanos Cancer Institute; Ph.D., Penn State, 1981. Cancer chemotherapy: mechanisms of action of antitumor agents; mechanisms of drug resistance.

Raymond R. Mattingly, Associate Professor of Pharmacology; Ph.D., Virginia, 1993. Signal transduction through Ras and heterotrimeric GTP-binding proteins.

Fred R. Miller, Professor, Karmanos Cancer Institute; Ph.D., Wisconsin–Madison, 1976. Progression of preneoplastic breast disease; stromal-epithelial interactions; mechanisms of metastasis.

Ramzi Mohammad, Professor of Hematology and Oncology; Ph.D., Utah State, 1987. Developmental therapeutic program.

Raymond F. Novak, Professor of Pharmacology and Director, Institute of Environmental Health Sciences; Ph.D., Case Western Reserve, 1973. Role of intracellular and extracellular matrix signaling in gene expression; cell function and tumorigenesis; microarray analysis and global gene expression profiling.

Robert J. Pauley, Professor; Ph.D., Marquette, 1975. Molecular oncology: Mtv (mammary tumor virus) and oncogenes; human breast neoplasia.

Izabela Podgorski, Assistant Professor, Department of Pharmacology and Karmanos Cancer Institute; Ph.D., Oakland, 2001. Obesity; inflammation; prostate cancer.

Venuprasad K. Poojary, Assistant Professor, Karmanos Cancer Institute and Department of Immunology and Microbiology; Ph.D., National Center for Cell Science (India), 2002. Cell signaling in the immune system; regulation of inflammation; anti-tumor immune response.

Avraham Raz, Professor of Radiation Oncology and Pathology and Director, Cancer Metastasis Program, Karmanos Cancer Institute; Ph.D., Weizmann (Israel), 1978. Tumor metastasis: role of adhesion molecule in tumor spread

John J. Reiners Jr., Professor of Pharmacology and Associate Professor, Environmental Health Science; Ph.D., Purdue, 1977. Mechanisms of chemical-induced carcinogenesis, signal transduction, and immunomodulation.

James H. Rigby, Professor of Chemistry; Ph.D., Wisconsin–Madison, 1977. Total synthesis and structure-activity studies on tumor-promoting diterpenes and alkaloids; total synthesis of antitumor natural products.

Arun K. Rishi, Associate Professor of Internal Medicine; Ph.D., London, 1987. Retinoid-dependent and -independent cell-cycle and apoptosis regulatory pathways.

Louis J. Romano, Professor of Chemistry; Ph.D., Rutgers, 1976. Chemical carcinogenesis; mutagenesis; replication of damaged DNA.

Melissa Runge-Morris, Associate Professor, Institute of Chemical Toxicology; M.D., Michigan, 1979. Molecular regulation of the sulfotransferase multigene family.

Fazlul H. Sarkar, Professor of Pathology; Ph.D., Banaras Hindu (India), 1978. Molecular biology of human adenocarcinoma; gene expression and regulation, activation and inactivation, and mutation; tumor angiogenesis; invasion and metastasis.

Ann G. Schwartz, Professor, Internal Medicine and Cancer Institute, and Associate Center Director, Population Sciences, Karmanos Cancer Institute; Ph.D., Michigan, 1986. Genetic epidemiology of lung cancer.

Malathy Shekhar, Associate Professor of Pathology; Ph.D., Indian Institute of Science, 1985. Breast cancer.

Shijie Sheng, Associate Professor of Pathology; Ph.D., Florida, 1993. Tumor invasion and metastasis/proteolysis.

Anthony Shields, Professor of Internal Medicine; M.D., Harvard, 1979; Ph.D., MIT, 1979. Positron emission tomography.

Debra F. Skafar, Associate Professor of Physiology; Ph.D., Vanderbilt, 1983. Estrogen receptor signaling mechanisms.

Bonnie F. Sloane, Professor and Chair of Pharmacology; Ph.D., Rutgers, 1976. Cancer biology: role of cysteine proteinases and their inhibitors in malignant progression.

Michael A. Tainsky, Professor of Pathology and Member, Karmanos Cancer Institute; Ph.D., Cornell, 1977. Molecular oncology and genetics.

Jeffrey W. Taub, M.D., Associate Professor of Pediatrics; M.D., Western Ontario, 1987. Molecular epidemiology and pharmacology of childhood leukemia.

Wei-Zen Wei, Professor of Immunology, Karmanos Cancer Institute; Ph.D., Brown, 1978. Host immunity in mammary tumorigenesis; modulation of mammary-tumor progression.

Gen Sheng Wu, Assistant Professor of Cancer Biology and Immunology; Ph.D., Chinese Academy of Medical Sciences (Beijing), 1992. Tumor suppressor genes and chemosensitivity.

Guojun Wu, Assistant Professor of Pathology, Karmanos Cancer Institute; Ph.D., Fudan (China), 1998. Oncogene, tumor suppressor gene, and breast cancer metastasis.

Hai-Young Wu, Associate Professor of Pharmacology; Ph.D., CUNY Graduate Center, 1985. DNA topology; DNA conformation; gene expression regulation.

Youming Xie, Assistant Professor of Pathology, Karmanos Cancer Institute; Ph.D., Texas, 1996. The ubiquitin-proteasome system.

Fayth Yoshimura, Associate Professor of Immunology and Microbiology; Ph.D., Yale, 1972. Pathogenesis of oncogenic murine retroviruses.

Section 7
Computational, Systems, and Translational Biology

This section contains a directory of institutions offering graduate work in computational, systems, and translational biology, followed by in-depth entries submitted by an institution that chose to prepare detailed program descriptions. Additional information about programs listed in the directory but not augmented by an in-depth entry may be obtained by writing directly to the dean of a graduate school or chair of a department at the address given in the directory.

CONTENTS

Program Directories

Close-Ups and Display

Computational Biology

Arizona State University, College of Liberal Arts and Sciences, Department of Mathematics and Statistics, Tempe, AZ 85287-1804. Offers applied mathematics (PhD); computational biosciences (PhD); mathematics (MA, MNS, PhD); mathematics education (PhD); statistics (PhD). Part-time programs available. *Faculty:* 94 full-time (32 women), 4 part-time/adjunct (1 woman). *Students:* 72 full-time (21 women), 23 part-time (10 women); includes 9 minority (2 Black or African American, non-Hispanic/Latino; 3 Asian, non-Hispanic/Latino; 4 Hispanic/Latino), 24 international. Average age 30. 168 applicants, 48% accepted, 26 enrolled. In 2010, 17 master's, 19 doctorates awarded. Terminal master's awarded for partial completion of doctoral program. *Median time to degree:* Of those who began their doctoral program in fall 2002, 69% received their degree in 8 years or less. *Degree requirements:* For master's, thesis or alternative, interactive Program of Study (iPOS) submitted before completing 50 percent of required credit hours; for doctorate, comprehensive exam, thesis/dissertation, interactive Program of Study (iPOS) submitted before completing 50 percent of required credit hours. *Entrance requirements:* For master's and doctorate, GRE General Test, minimum GPA of 3.0 or equivalent in last 2 years of work leading to bachelor's degree. Additional exam requirements/recommendations for international students: Required—TOEFL, IELTS, or Pearson Test of English. *Application deadline:* For fall admission, 1/1 for domestic and international students. Applications are processed on a rolling basis. Application fee: $70 ($90 for international students). Electronic applications accepted. *Expenses:* Contact institution. *Financial support:* In 2010–11, 12 research assistantships with full and partial tuition reimbursements (averaging $18,559 per year), 55 teaching assistantships with full and partial tuition reimbursements (averaging $17,743 per year) were awarded; fellowships with full tuition reimbursements, career-related internships or fieldwork, Federal Work-Study, institutionally sponsored loans, scholarships/grants, and tuition waivers (partial) also available. Financial award application deadline: 3/1; financial award applicants required to submit FAFSA. Total annual research expenditures: $4.5 million. *Unit head:* Dr. Wayne Raskind, Director, 480-965-3951, E-mail: raskind@asu.edu. *Application contact:* Graduate Admissions, 480-965-6113.

Baylor College of Medicine, Graduate School of Biomedical Sciences, Program in Structural and Computational Biology and Molecular Biophysics, Houston, TX 77030-3498. Offers PhD, MD/PhD. MD/PhD offered jointly with Rice University and University of Houston. *Faculty:* 83 full-time (10 women). *Students:* 36 full-time (10 women); includes 2 Asian, non-Hispanic/Latino; 1 Hispanic/Latino, 17 international. Average age 28. 78 applicants, 12% accepted, 5 enrolled. In 2010, 6 doctorates awarded. *Degree requirements:* For doctorate, thesis/dissertation, public defense. *Entrance requirements:* For doctorate, GRE General Test, GRE Subject Test (strongly recommended), minimum GPA of 3.0. Additional exam requirements/recommendations for international students: Required—TOEFL. *Application deadline:* For fall admission, 1/1 for domestic students. Application fee: $0. Electronic applications accepted. *Expenses:* Tuition: Full-time $11,000. Required fees: $4900. *Financial support:* In 2010–11, 36 students received support, including 14 fellowships with full tuition reimbursements available (averaging $26,000 per year), 22 research assistantships with full tuition reimbursements available (averaging $26,000 per year); career-related internships or fieldwork, Federal Work-Study, institutionally sponsored loans, health care benefits, and students receive a scholarship unless there are grant funds available to pay tuition also available. Financial award applicants required to submit FAFSA. *Faculty research:* Computational biology, structural biology, biophysics. *Unit head:* Dr. Wah Chiu, Director, 713-798-6985. *Application contact:* Lourdes Fernandez, Graduate Program Administrator, 713-798-6557, Fax: 713-798-6325, E-mail: lourdesf@bcm.edu.

See Close-Up on page 251.

Carnegie Mellon University, Joint CMU-Pitt PhD Program in Computational Biology, Pittsburgh, PA 15213-3891. Offers PhD.

Carnegie Mellon University, Mellon College of Science, Department of Biological Sciences, Program in Computational Biology, Pittsburgh, PA 15213-3891. Offers MS. *Entrance requirements:* For master's, GRE General Test, GRE Subject Test, interview.

Claremont Graduate University, Graduate Programs, School of Mathematical Sciences, Claremont, CA 91711-6160. Offers computational and systems biology (PhD); computational mathematics and numerical analysis (MA, MS); computational science (PhD); engineering and industrial applied mathematics (PhD); mathematics (PhD); operations research and statistics (MA, MS); physical applied mathematics (MA, MS); pure mathematics (MA, MS); scientific computing (MA, MS); systems and control theory (MA, MS). Part-time programs available. *Faculty:* 6 full-time (0 women). *Students:* 50 full-time (15 women), 11 part-time (1 woman); includes 2 Black or African American, non-Hispanic/Latino; 9 Asian, non-Hispanic/Latino; 7 Hispanic/Latino; 3 Two or more races, non-Hispanic/Latino, 13 international. Average age 36. In 2010, 17 master's, 11 doctorates awarded. Terminal master's awarded for partial completion of doctoral program. *Entrance requirements:* For master's and doctorate, GRE General Test. Additional exam requirements/recommendations for international students: Required—TOEFL (minimum score 550 paper-based; 213 computer-based; 80 iBT). *Application deadline:* For fall admission, 2/1 priority date for domestic students. Applications are processed on a rolling basis. Application fee: $60. Electronic applications accepted. *Expenses:* Tuition: Full-time $35,748; part-time $1554 per unit. Required fees: $215 per semester. *Financial support:* Fellowships, research assistantships, Federal Work-Study, institutionally sponsored loans, scholarships/grants, and tuition waivers (full and partial) available. Support available to part-time students. Financial award application deadline: 2/15; financial award applicants required to submit FAFSA. *Unit head:* John Angus, Dean, 909-621-8080, Fax: 909-607-8261, E-mail: john.angus@cgu.edu. *Application contact:* Susan Townzen, Program Coordinator, 909-621-8080, Fax: 909-607-8261, E-mail: susan.n.townzen@cgu.edu.

Cornell University, Graduate School, Graduate Fields of Agriculture and Life Sciences, Field of Computational Biology, Ithaca, NY 14853-0001. Offers computational behavioral biology (PhD); computational biology (PhD); computational cell biology (PhD); computational ecology (PhD); computational macromolecular biology (PhD); computational organismal biology (PhD). *Faculty:* 32 full-time (5 women). *Students:* 21 full-time (6 women); includes 4 Asian, non-Hispanic/Latino, 9 international. Average age 25. 128 applicants, 7% accepted, 9 enrolled. In 2010, 3 doctorates awarded. *Degree requirements:* For doctorate, comprehensive exam, thesis/dissertation, 2 semesters of teaching experience. *Entrance requirements:* For doctorate, GRE General Test, GRE Subject Test (biology), 2 letters of recommendation. Additional exam requirements/recommendations for international students: Required—TOEFL (minimum score 550 paper-based; 213 computer-based; 77 iBT). *Application deadline:* For fall admission, 2/1 priority date for domestic students. Application fee: $70. Electronic applications accepted. *Expenses:* Tuition: Full-time $29,500. Required fees: $76. Tuition and fees vary according to degree level and program. *Financial support:* In 2010–11, 15 fellowships with full tuition reimbursements, 4 research assistantships with full tuition reimbursements, 2 teaching assistantships with full tuition reimbursements were awarded; institutionally sponsored loans, scholarships/grants, health care benefits, tuition waivers (full and partial), and unspecified assistantships also available. Financial award applicants required to submit FAFSA. *Faculty research:* Computational behavioral biology, computational biology, computational cell biology, computational ecology, computational genetics, computational macromolecular biology, computational organismal biology. *Unit head:* Dr. Andrew Clark, Director of Graduate Studies, 607-255-5488, E-mail: ac347@cornell.edu. *Application contact:* Graduate School Application Requests, 607-255-5816, E-mail: gradadmissions@cornell.edu.

Cornell University, Joan and Sanford I. Weill Medical College and Graduate School of Medical Sciences, Weill Cornell Graduate School of Medical Sciences, Tri-Institutional Training Program in Computational Biology and Medicine, New York, NY 10065. Offers PhD. *Faculty:* 44 full-time (6 women). *Students:* 34 full-time (11 women); includes 3 Black or African American, non-Hispanic/Latino; 10 Asian, non-Hispanic/Latino; 1 Hispanic/Latino. Average age 23. 129 applicants, 13% accepted, 7 enrolled. In 2010, 6 doctorates awarded. Terminal master's awarded for partial completion of doctoral program. *Degree requirements:* For doctorate, comprehensive exam, thesis/dissertation. *Entrance requirements:* For doctorate, GRE. Additional exam requirements/recommendations for international students: Required—TOEFL. *Application deadline:* For winter admission, 1/1 for domestic and international students. Application fee: $70. Electronic applications accepted. *Expenses:* Tuition: Full-time $45,545. Required fees: $2805. *Financial support:* In 2010–11, 34 students received support, including 34 fellowships with full tuition reimbursements available (averaging $37,000 per year), 1 teaching assistantship with full tuition reimbursement available (averaging $18,500 per year). *Faculty research:* Biophysics/structural biology, genomics/bioinformatics, modeling/systems biology, neuroscience, cancer biology. *Unit head:* Kathleen E. Pickering, Executive Director, 212-746-6049, Fax: 212-746-8992, E-mail: cbm@triiprograms.org. *Application contact:* Margie H. Mendoza, Program Administrator, 212-746-5267, Fax: 212-746-8992, E-mail: cbm@triiprograms.org.

Florida State University, The Graduate School, College of Arts and Sciences, Program in Molecular Biophysics, Tallahassee, FL 32306. Offers biochemistry, molecular and cell biology (PhD); computational structural biology (PhD); molecular biophysics (PhD). *Faculty:* 49 full-time (6 women). *Students:* 22 full-time (8 women); includes 5 Asian, non-Hispanic/Latino; 1 Hispanic/Latino. Average age 28. 30 applicants, 33% accepted, 7 enrolled. In 2010, 5 doctorates awarded. *Degree requirements:* For doctorate, comprehensive exam, thesis/dissertation, teaching 1 term in professor's major department. *Entrance requirements:* For doctorate, GRE General Test. Additional exam requirements/recommendations for international students: Required—TOEFL (minimum score 600 paper-based; 250 computer-based; 100 iBT). *Application deadline:* For fall admission, 2/15 for domestic students, 3/15 for international students; for spring admission, 11/2 for international students. Applications are processed on a rolling basis. Application fee: $30. Electronic applications accepted. *Expenses:* Tuition, state resident: full-time $8238. *Financial support:* In 2010–11, 21 students received support, including fellowships with partial tuition reimbursements available (averaging $21,000 per year), 18 research assistantships with partial tuition reimbursements available (averaging $21,000 per year), 4 teaching assistantships with partial tuition reimbursements available (averaging $21,000 per year); scholarships/grants, health care benefits, and unspecified assistantships also available. Financial award applicants required to submit FAFSA. *Faculty research:* Protein and nucleic acid structure and function, membrane protein structure, computational biophysics, 3-D image reconstruction. Total annual research expenditures: $1.4 million. *Unit head:* Dr. Geoffrey Strouse, Director, 850-644-0056, Fax: 850-644-7244, E-mail: strouse@chem.fsu.edu. *Application contact:* Dr. Kerry Maddox, Academic Coordinator, Graduate Programs, 850-644-1012, Fax: 850-644-7244, E-mail: bkmaddox@sb.fsu.edu.

George Mason University, College of Science, Department of Bioinformatics and Computational Biology, Fairfax, VA 22030. Offers MS, PhD, Certificate. *Faculty:* 7 full-time (0 women), 2 part-time/adjunct (0 women). *Students:* 22 full-time (10 women), 38 part-time (18 women); includes 1 Black or African American, non-Hispanic/Latino; 12 Asian, non-Hispanic/Latino, 28 international. Average age 33. 92 applicants, 46% accepted, 11 enrolled. In 2010, 14 master's, 4 doctorates awarded. *Entrance requirements:* For master's, GRE General Test, resume, three letters of recommendation. Additional exam requirements/recommendations for international students: Required—TOEFL (minimum score 570 paper-based; 230 computer-based; 88 iBT). Application fee: $100. *Expenses:* Tuition, state resident: full-time $8192; part-time $440 per credit hour. Tuition, nonresident: full-time $22,952; part-time $1055 per credit hour. Required fees: $2364; $99 per credit hour. *Financial support:* In 2010–11, 15 students received support, including 3 fellowships (averaging $18,000 per year), 10 research assistantships (averaging $11,824 per year), 2 teaching assistantships (averaging $12,105 per year); career-related internships or fieldwork, Federal Work-Study, scholarships/grants, unspecified assistantships, and health care benefits (full-time research or teaching assistantship recipients) also available. Financial award applicants required to submit FAFSA. Total annual research expenditures: $824,761. *Unit head:* Dr. Saleer Jofri, Head, 703-993-8420. *Application contact:* Dr. Tim Born, Associate Dean for Graduate Programs, 703-993-4171, Fax: 703-993-9034, E-mail: tborn@gmu.edu.

George Mason University, College of Science, Department of Molecular and Microbiology, Fairfax, VA 22030. Offers biology (MS), including bioinformatics and computational biology, general biology, microbiology and infectious disease, molecular biology, systematics and evolutionary biology; biosciences (PhD). *Faculty:* 10 full-time (5 women). *Students:* 12 full-time (6 women), 63 part-time (36 women); includes 2 Black or African American, non-Hispanic/Latino; 1 American Indian or Alaska Native, non-Hispanic/Latino; 8 Asian, non-Hispanic/Latino; 1 Hispanic/Latino, 16 international. Average age 31. 98 applicants, 37% accepted, 19 enrolled. In 2010, 7 master's, 7 doctorates awarded. *Entrance requirements:* Additional exam requirements/recommendations for international students: Required—TOEFL (minimum score 570 paper-based; 230 computer-based; 88 iBT). Application fee: $100. *Expenses:* Tuition, state resident: full-time $8192; part-time $440 per credit hour. Tuition, nonresident: full-time $22,952; part-time $1055 per credit hour. Required fees: $2364; $99 per credit hour. *Financial support:* In 2010–11, 32 students received support, including 3 fellowships (averaging $18,000 per year), 6 research assistantships (averaging $14,073 per year), 23 teaching assistantships (averaging $12,194 per year); career-related internships or fieldwork, Federal Work-Study, scholarships/grants, unspecified assistantships, and health care benefits (full-time research or teaching assistantship recipients) also available. Financial award applicants required to submit FAFSA. Total annual research expenditures: $457,760. *Unit head:* Dr. James Willett, Director, 703-993-8311, Fax: 703-993-8976, E-mail: jwillett@gmu.edu. *Application contact:* Daniel Cox, Associate Dean for Graduate Programs, 703-993-4971, Fax: 703-993-4325, E-mail: dcox5@gmu.edu.

Iowa State University of Science and Technology, Graduate College, Interdisciplinary Programs, Bioinformatics and Computational Biology Program, Ames, IA 50011. Offers MS, PhD. *Students:* 54 full-time (22 women), 34 international. In 2010, 1 master's, 5 doctorates awarded. *Degree requirements:* For doctorate, thesis/dissertation. *Entrance requirements:* For master's and doctorate, GRE General Test. Additional exam requirements/recommendations for international students: Recommended—IELTS. *Application deadline:* For fall admission, 1/15 priority date for domestic students, 1/15 for international students; for spring admission, 10/15 for domestic and international students. Application fee: $40 ($90 for international students). Electronic applications accepted. *Financial support:* In 2010–11, 47 research assistantships with full and partial tuition reimbursements (averaging $22,000 per year), 3 teaching assistantships (averaging $20,000 per year) were awarded; fellowships with full tuition reimbursements, scholarships/grants, traineeships, health care benefits, and unspecified assistantships also available. *Faculty research:* Functional and structural genomics, genome evolution, macromolecular structure and function, mathematical biology and biological statistics, metabolic and developmental networks. *Unit head:* Dr. Julie Dickerson, Chair, Supervising Committee, 515-294-5122, Fax: 515-294-6790, E-mail: bcb@iastate.edu. *Application contact:* Dr. Julie Dickerson, Chair, Supervising Committee, 515-294-5122, Fax: 515-294-6790, E-mail: bcb@iastate.edu.

Keck Graduate Institute of Applied Life Sciences, Bioscience Program, Claremont, CA 91711. Offers applied life science (PhD); bioscience (MBS); bioscience management (Certificate); computational systems biology (PhD). *Degree requirements:* For master's, comprehensive exam, project. *Entrance requirements:* For master's, GRE General Test or MCAT. Additional exam requirements/recommendations for international students: Required—TOEFL. Electronic applications accepted. *Faculty research:* Computational biology, drug discovery and development, molecular and cellular biology, biomedical engineering, biomaterials and tissue engineering.

Massachusetts Institute of Technology, School of Engineering and School of Science, Program in Computational and Systems Biology, Cambridge, MA 02139-4307. Offers PhD. *Faculty:* 100 full-time (19 women). *Students:* 36 full-time (15 women); includes 8 minority (1 Black or African American, non-Hispanic/Latino; 6 Asian, non-Hispanic/Latino; 1 Hispanic/

Latino), 17 international. Average age 26. 130 applicants, 9% accepted, 6 enrolled. In 2010, 3 doctorates awarded. *Degree requirements:* For doctorate, comprehensive exam, thesis/dissertation. *Entrance requirements:* For doctorate, GRE General Test. Additional exam requirements/recommendations for international students: Required—IELTS (minimum score 6). *Application deadline:* For fall admission, 12/15 for domestic and international students. Application fee: $75. Electronic applications accepted. *Expenses:* Tuition: Full-time $38,940; part-time $605 per unit. Required fees: $272. *Financial support:* In 2010–11, 36 students received support, including 16 fellowships (averaging $35,926 per year), 20 research assistantships (averaging $30,848 per year); teaching assistantships, Federal Work-Study, institutionally sponsored loans, scholarships/grants, health care benefits, and unspecified assistantships also available. *Faculty research:* Computational biology and bioinformatics, biological design and synthetic biology, gene and protein networks, systems biology of cancer, nanobiology and microsystems. *Unit head:* Prof. Douglas A. Lauffenberger, Director, 617-252-1629, E-mail: csbi@mit.edu. *Application contact:* Academic Office, 617-324-0055, Fax: 617-253-8699, E-mail: csbphd@mit.edu.

Massachusetts Institute of Technology, School of Science, Department of Biology, Cambridge, MA 02139-4307. Offers biochemistry (PhD); biological oceanography (PhD); biology (PhD); biophysical chemistry and molecular structure (PhD); cell biology (PhD); computational and systems biology (PhD); developmental biology (PhD); genetics (PhD); immunology (PhD); microbiology (PhD); molecular biology (PhD); neurobiology (PhD). *Faculty:* 56 full-time (14 women). *Students:* 251 full-time (135 women); includes 74 minority (4 Black or African American, non-Hispanic/Latino; 1 American Indian or Alaska Native, non-Hispanic/Latino; 29 Asian, non-Hispanic/Latino; 33 Hispanic/Latino; 7 Two or more races, non-Hispanic/Latino), 29 international. Average age 26. 652 applicants, 18% accepted, 58 enrolled. In 2010, 41 doctorates awarded. *Degree requirements:* For doctorate, comprehensive exam, thesis/dissertation. *Entrance requirements:* For doctorate, GRE General Test. Additional exam requirements/recommendations for international students: Required—TOEFL (minimum score 577 paper-based; 233 computer-based), IELTS (minimum score 6.5). *Application deadline:* For fall admission, 12/1 for domestic and international students. Application fee: $75. Electronic applications accepted. *Expenses:* Tuition: Full-time $38,940; part-time $605 per unit. Required fees: $272. *Financial support:* In 2010–11, 215 students received support, including 115 fellowships with tuition reimbursements available (averaging $33,090 per year), 132 research assistantships with tuition reimbursements available (averaging $31,846 per year); teaching assistantships with tuition reimbursements available, Federal Work-Study, institutionally sponsored loans, scholarships/grants, traineeships, health care benefits, and unspecified assistantships also available. *Faculty research:* DNA recombination, replication and repair; transcription and gene regulation; signal transduction; cell cycle; neuronal cell fate. Total annual research expenditures: $60.6 million. *Unit head:* Prof. Chris Kaiser, Head, 617-253-4701, E-mail: mitbio@mit.edu. *Application contact:* Biology Education Office, 617-253-3717, Fax: 617-258-9329, E-mail: gradbio@mit.edu.

New Jersey Institute of Technology, Office of Graduate Studies, College of Science and Liberal Arts, Department of Mathematical Science, Program in Computational Biology, Newark, NJ 07102. Offers MS. Part-time and evening/weekend programs available. *Students:* 1 full-time; includes Asian, non-Hispanic/Latino. Average age 24. 5 applicants, 40% accepted, 0 enrolled. *Entrance requirements:* For master's, GRE General Test. Additional exam requirements/recommendations for international students: Required—TOEFL (minimum score 550 paper-based; 213 computer-based; 79 iBT). *Application deadline:* For fall admission, 6/5 priority date for domestic students; for spring admission, 10/15 for domestic students. Applications are processed on a rolling basis. Application fee: $65. Electronic applications accepted. *Expenses:* Tuition, state resident: full-time $14,724; part-time $818 per credit. Tuition, nonresident: full-time $20,304; part-time $1128 per credit. Required fees: $2272; $209 per credit. $103 per semester. One-time fee: $312 full-time; $212 part-time. *Financial support:* Fellowships with full and partial tuition reimbursements, research assistantships with full and partial tuition reimbursements, teaching assistantships with full and partial tuition reimbursements, career-related internships or fieldwork, Federal Work-Study, institutionally sponsored loans, and unspecified assistantships available. Financial award application deadline: 3/15. *Faculty research:* Technological, computational, and mathematical aspects of biology and bioengineering. *Unit head:* Dr. Daljit S. Ahluwalia, Chair, 973-596-8465, E-mail: daljit.ahluwalia@njit.edu. *Application contact:* Kathryn Kelly, Director of Admissions, 973-596-3300, Fax: 973-596-3461, E-mail: admissions@njit.edu.

New York University, Graduate School of Arts and Science, Department of Biology, Program in Computational Biology, New York, NY 10012-1019. Offers PhD. *Students:* 19 full-time (5 women), 5 part-time (all women); includes 2 Asian, non-Hispanic/Latino, 8 international. Average age 31. 75 applicants, 11% accepted, 4 enrolled. In 2010, 1 doctorate awarded. *Entrance requirements:* For doctorate, GRE. Additional exam requirements/recommendations for international students: Required—TOEFL. Application fee: $90. *Financial support:* Fellowships, research assistantships, teaching assistantships, Federal Work-Study, institutionally sponsored loans, scholarships/grants, health care benefits, and unspecified assistantships available. *Unit head:* Mike Shelley, Director, 212-998-4856, Fax: 212-995-4121, E-mail: fas.computational.biology@nyu.edu. *Application contact:* Susan Mrsic, Program Administrator, 212-998-4856, Fax: 212-995-4121, E-mail: fas.computational.biology@nyu.edu.

New York University, School of Medicine and Graduate School of Arts and Science, Sackler Institute of Graduate Biomedical Sciences, New York, NY 10012-1019. Offers cellular and molecular biology (PhD); computational biology (PhD); developmental genetics (PhD); medical and molecular parasitology (PhD); microbiology (PhD); molecular oncology and immunology (PhD), including immunology, molecular oncology; neuroscience and physiology (PhD); pathobiology (PhD); pharmacology (PhD), including molecular pharmacology; structural biology (PhD); MD/PhD. *Degree requirements:* For doctorate, comprehensive exam, thesis/dissertation, qualifying exam. *Entrance requirements:* For doctorate, GRE General Test. Additional exam requirements/recommendations for international students: Required—TOEFL. Electronic applications accepted. *Expenses:* Contact institution.

Oregon Health & Science University, School of Medicine, Graduate Programs in Medicine, Department of Medical Informatics and Clinical Epidemiology, Portland, OR 97239-3098. Offers clinical informatics (MS, PhD, Certificate); computational biology (MS, PhD); health information management (Certificate). Part-time programs available. Postbaccalaureate distance learning degree programs offered (minimal on-campus study). *Faculty:* 26. *Students:* 111 (34 women); includes 3 Black or African American, non-Hispanic/Latino; 1 American Indian or Alaska Native, non-Hispanic/Latino; 8 Asian, non-Hispanic/Latino; 4 Hispanic/Latino; 4 Native Hawaiian or other Pacific Islander, non-Hispanic/Latino, 12 international. Average age 42. 46 applicants, 70% accepted, 28 enrolled. In 2010, 11 master's, 1 doctorate awarded. Terminal master's awarded for partial completion of doctoral program. *Degree requirements:* For master's, thesis; for doctorate, comprehensive exam, thesis/dissertation. *Entrance requirements:* For master's and doctorate, GRE General Test, coursework in computer programming, human anatomy and physiology. Additional exam requirements/recommendations for international students: Required—TOEFL. *Application deadline:* For fall admission, 12/1 for domestic students; for winter admission, 11/1 for domestic students; for spring admission, 2/1 for domestic students. Applications are processed on a rolling basis. Application fee: $65. Electronic applications accepted. *Expenses:* Contact institution. *Financial support:* Fellowships with full tuition reimbursements, research assistantships, Federal Work-Study, institutionally sponsored loans, scholarships/grants, and full tuition and stipends available. Financial award application deadline: 3/1; financial award applicants required to submit FAFSA. *Faculty research:* Information retrieval, telemedicine, consumer health informatics, information needs assessment, healthcare quality. *Unit head:* Andrea Ilg, 503-494-2547, E-mail: informat@ohsu.edu. *Application contact:* Diane Doctor, 503-494-2547, E-mail: informat@ohsu.edu.

Princeton University, Graduate School, Department of Molecular Biology, Princeton, NJ 08544-1019. Offers PhD. *Degree requirements:* For doctorate, thesis/dissertation. *Entrance requirements:* For doctorate, GRE General Test. Additional exam requirements/recommendations for international students: Required—TOEFL (minimum score 600 paper-based; 250 computer-based). Electronic applications accepted. *Faculty research:* Genetics, virology, biochemistry.

Rutgers, The State University of New Jersey, Newark, Graduate School, Program in Computational Biology, Newark, NJ 07102. Offers MS. Program offered jointly with New Jersey Institute of Technology. *Entrance requirements:* For master's, GRE, minimum undergraduate B average. Additional exam requirements/recommendations for international students: Required—TOEFL. *Application deadline:* For fall admission, 6/1 for domestic and international students; for spring admission, 12/1 for domestic and international students. Application fee: $60. *Expenses:* Tuition, state resident: part-time $600 per credit. Tuition, nonresident: full-time $10,694. *Unit head:* Dr. Edward Bonder, Program Director, 973-353-1047, Fax: 973-353-5518, E-mail: ebonder@andromeda.rutgers.edu. *Application contact:* Dr. Edward Bonder, Program Director, 973-353-1047, Fax: 973-353-5518, E-mail: ebonder@andromeda.rutgers.edu.

Rutgers, The State University of New Jersey, New Brunswick, Graduate School-New Brunswick, BioMaPS Institute for Quantitative Biology, Piscataway, NJ 08854-8097. Offers computational biology and molecular biophysics (PhD). *Degree requirements:* For doctorate, comprehensive exam, thesis/dissertation. *Entrance requirements:* For doctorate, GRE. Additional exam requirements/recommendations for international students: Required—TOEFL. Electronic applications accepted. *Expenses:* Tuition, state resident: full-time $7200; part-time $600 per credit. Tuition, nonresident: full-time $11,124; part-time $927 per credit. *Faculty research:* Structural biology, systems biology, bioinformatics, translational medicine, genomics.

University of California, Irvine, School of Biological Sciences, Program in Mathematical, Computational and Systems Biology, Irvine, CA 92697. Offers PhD. *Students:* 13 full-time (3 women); includes 5 minority (4 Asian, non-Hispanic/Latino; 1 Hispanic/Latino), 4 international. Average age 28. 64 applicants, 31% accepted, 11 enrolled.Application fee: $80 ($100 for international students). *Unit head:* Prof. Frederic Yui-Ming Wan, Director, 949-824-5529, Fax: 949-824-7993, E-mail: fwan@math.uci.edu. *Application contact:* Prof. Frederic Yui-Ming Wan, Director, 949-824-5529, Fax: 949-824-7993, E-mail: fwan@math.uci.edu.

University of Colorado Denver, School of Medicine, Program in Computational Bioscience, Aurora, CO 80045-0511. Offers PhD. Part-time programs available. *Students:* 9 full-time (1 woman), 3 part-time (1 woman); includes 2 Black or African American, non-Hispanic/Latino; 1 Hispanic/Latino, 1 international. Average age 33. 12 applicants, 33% accepted, 4 enrolled. In 2010, 1 doctorate awarded. *Degree requirements:* For doctorate, comprehensive exam, thesis/dissertation, minimum of 30 semester credit hours each of course work (including academic credits transferred from other programs) and doctoral dissertation research. *Entrance requirements:* For doctorate, GRE, demonstrated adequate computational and biological backgrounds. Additional exam requirements/recommendations for international students: Required—TOEFL. *Application deadline:* For fall admission, 1/1 for domestic students. Application fee: $65. Electronic applications accepted. *Expenses:* Contact institution. *Financial support:* Fellowships, research assistantships, teaching assistantships, scholarships/grants, health care benefits, tuition waivers (full), unspecified assistantships, and stipend available. Financial award application deadline: 4/1; financial award applicants required to submit FAFSA. *Faculty research:* Physical simulations of biological macromolecules and their dynamics, gene expression array analysis and interpretation of expression data, natural language processing in the biomedical literature, metabolic and signaling pathway analysis, evolutionary reconstruction and disease gene finding. *Unit head:* Dr. Larry Hunter, Director, 303-724-3574, E-mail: larry.hunter@ucdenver.edu. *Application contact:* Liz Pruett, Student Coordinator, 303-724-3399, E-mail: liz.pruett@ucdenver.edu.

University of Idaho, College of Graduate Studies, Program in Bioinformatics and Computational Biology, Moscow, ID 83844-2282. Offers MS, PhD. *Faculty:* 13 full-time. *Students:* 12 full-time, 1 part-time. Average age 28. In 2010, 4 doctorates awarded. *Entrance requirements:* For master's, GRE, minimum GPA of 2.8. *Application deadline:* For fall admission, 8/1 for domestic students; for spring admission, 12/15 for domestic students. Applications are processed on a rolling basis. Application fee: $60. Electronic applications accepted. *Expenses:* Tuition, nonresident: part-time $580 per credit. Required fees: $306 per credit. *Financial support:* Applicants required to submit FAFSA. *Unit head:* Dr. Paul Joyce, Director, 208-885-6010, E-mail: bcb@uidaho.edu. *Application contact:* Dr. Paul Joyce, Director, 208-885-6010, E-mail: bcb@uidaho.edu.

University of Illinois at Urbana–Champaign, Graduate College, College of Liberal Arts and Sciences, School of Molecular and Cellular Biology, Center for Biophysics and Computational Biology, Champaign, IL 61820. Offers MS, PhD. *Students:* 67 full-time (12 women), 1 (woman) part-time; includes 9 minority (6 Asian, non-Hispanic/Latino; 2 Hispanic/Latino; 1 Two or more races, non-Hispanic/Latino), 42 international. 74 applicants, 14% accepted, 10 enrolled. In 2010, 12 doctorates awarded. *Entrance requirements:* For doctorate, GRE, minimum GPA of 3.0. Additional exam requirements/recommendations for international students: Required—TOEFL. *Application deadline:* Applications are processed on a rolling basis. Application fee: $75 ($90 for international students). Electronic applications accepted. *Financial support:* In 2010–11, 12 fellowships, 59 research assistantships, 22 teaching assistantships were awarded; tuition waivers (full and partial) also available. *Unit head:* Martin Gruebele, Director, 217-333-1624, Fax: 217-244-3186, E-mail: mgruebel@illinois.edu. *Application contact:* Cynthia Dodds, Office Administrator, 217-333-1630, Fax: 217-244-6615, E-mail: dodds@illinois.edu.

The University of Iowa, Graduate College, Program in Informatics, Iowa City, IA 52242-1316. Offers bioinformatics and computational biology (Certificate); health informatics (MS, PhD, Certificate); information science (MS, PhD, Certificate). *Degree requirements:* For master's, thesis optional; for doctorate, comprehensive exam, thesis/dissertation. *Entrance requirements:* For master's and doctorate, GRE General Test, minimum GPA of 3.0. Additional exam requirements/recommendations for international students: Required—TOEFL (minimum score 550 paper-based; 213 computer-based; 81 iBT). Electronic applications accepted.

University of Massachusetts Worcester, Graduate School of Biomedical Sciences, Worcester, MA 01655-0115. Offers biochemistry and molecular pharmacology (PhD); bioinformatics and computational biology (PhD); cancer biology (PhD); cell biology (PhD); clinical and population health research (PhD); clinical investigation (MS); immunology and virology (PhD); interdisciplinary graduate program (PhD); molecular genetics and microbiology (PhD); neuroscience (PhD); DVM/PhD; MD/PhD. *Faculty:* 1,059 full-time (357 women), 145 part-time/adjunct (100 women). *Students:* 438 full-time (239 women), 1 (woman) part-time; includes 44 minority (9 Black or African American, non-Hispanic/Latino; 31 Asian, non-Hispanic/Latino; 4 Hispanic/Latino), 148 international. Average age 29. 687 applicants, 28% accepted, 116 enrolled. In 2010, 6 master's, 45 doctorates awarded. Terminal master's awarded for partial completion of doctoral program. *Degree requirements:* For master's, thesis; for doctorate, thesis/dissertation. *Entrance requirements:* For master's, bachelor's degree; for doctorate, GRE General Test, MS, MA, or MPH (for some programs). Additional exam requirements/recommendations for international students: Required—TOEFL (minimum score 600 paper-based; 250 computer-based). *Application deadline:* For fall admission, 12/15 for domestic and international students; for winter admission, 1/15 for domestic students; for spring admission, 5/15 for domestic students. Application fee: $35. Electronic applications accepted. *Expenses:* Contact institution. *Financial support:* In 2010–11, 439 students received support, including 439 research assistantships with full tuition reimbursements available (averaging $28,350 per year); scholarships/grants, health care benefits, tuition waivers (full), and unspecified assistantships also available. Financial award application deadline: 4/20. *Faculty research:* RNA interference, gene therapy, cell biology, bioinformatics, clinical research. Total annual research expenditures: $232 million. *Unit head:* Dr. Anthony Carruthers, Dean, 508-856-4135, E-mail: anthony.carruthers@umassmed.edu. *Application contact:* Dr. Kendall Knight, Associate Dean and Interim Director of Admissions and Recruitment, 508-856-5628, Fax: 508-856-3659, E-mail: kendall.knight@umassmed.edu.

Computational Biology

The University of North Carolina at Chapel Hill, School of Medicine and Graduate School, Graduate Programs in Medicine, Curriculum in Bioinformatics and Computational Biology, Chapel Hill, NC 27599. Offers PhD. *Faculty:* 40 full-time (6 women). *Students:* 11 full-time (6 women); includes 1 Black or African American, non-Hispanic/Latino; 1 Asian, non-Hispanic/Latino, 3 international. Average age 27. In 2010, 1 doctorate awarded. *Degree requirements:* For doctorate, comprehensive exam, thesis/dissertation. *Entrance requirements:* For doctorate, GRE, minimum GPA of 3.0. Additional exam requirements/recommendations for international students: Required—TOEFL. *Application deadline:* For fall admission, 1/1 for domestic and international students. Applications are processed on a rolling basis. Application fee: $77. Electronic applications accepted. *Financial support:* In 2010–11, 2 fellowships with full tuition reimbursements (averaging $26,000 per year), 9 research assistantships with full tuition reimbursements (averaging $26,000 per year) were awarded; tuition waivers (full) also available. *Faculty research:* Protein folding, design and evolution and molecular biophysics of disease; mathematical modeling of signaling pathways and regulatory networks; bioinformatics, medical informatics, user interface design; statistical genetics and genetic epidemiology datamining, classification and clustering analysis of gene-expression data. *Unit head:* Dr. Tim C. Elston, Director, 919-843-7670, E-mail: telston@med.unc.edu. *Application contact:* Sausyty A. Hermreck, Graduate Student Coordinator, 919-966-2681, Fax: 919-966-0401, E-mail: sausytyh@med.unc.edu.

University of Pennsylvania, Perelman School of Medicine, Biomedical Graduate Studies, Graduate Group in Genomics and Computational Biology, Philadelphia, PA 19104. Offers PhD, MD/PhD, VMD/PhD. *Faculty:* 59. *Students:* 33 full-time (9 women); includes 2 Black or African American, non-Hispanic/Latino; 9 Asian, non-Hispanic/Latino; 2 Hispanic/Latino, 6 international. 77 applicants, 22% accepted, 4 enrolled. In 2010, 6 doctorates awarded. *Degree requirements:* For doctorate, thesis/dissertation optional. *Entrance requirements:* For doctorate, GRE. Additional exam requirements/recommendations for international students: Required—TOEFL. *Application deadline:* For fall admission, 12/8 priority date for domestic and international students. Applications are processed on a rolling basis. Application fee: $70. Electronic applications accepted. *Expenses:* Tuition: Full-time $25,660; part-time $4758 per course. Required fees: $2152; $270 per course. Tuition and fees vary according to course load, degree level and program. *Financial support:* In 2010–11, 33 students received support; fellowships, research assistantships, scholarships/grants, traineeships, and unspecified assistantships available. *Unit head:* Dr. Maja Bucan, Chairperson, 215-898-0020. *Application contact:* Hannah Chervitz, Graduate Coordinator, 215-746-2807, E-mail: gcbcoord@pcbi.upenn.edu.

University of Pittsburgh, Joint CMU-Pitt PhD Program in Computational and Systems Biology, Pittsburgh, PA 15260. Offers PhD. *Faculty:* 78 full-time (17 women). *Students:* 46 full-time (9 women); includes 22 Asian, non-Hispanic/Latino; 2 Hispanic/Latino; 1 Native Hawaiian or other Pacific Islander, non-Hispanic/Latino, 18 international. Average age 25. 133 applicants, 16% accepted, 7 enrolled. *Degree requirements:* For doctorate, comprehensive exam, thesis/dissertation, ethics training service as course assistant, seminar. *Entrance requirements:* For doctorate, GRE Subject Test (recommended), GRE General Test, 3 letters of recommendation, resume. Additional exam requirements/recommendations for international students: Required—TOEFL (minimum score 600 paper-based; 250 computer-based; 100 iBT). *Application deadline:* For fall admission, 1/15 priority date for domestic and international students. Application fee: $50. Electronic applications accepted. *Expenses:* Tuition, state resident: full-time $17,304; part-time $701 per credit. Tuition, nonresident: full-time $29,554; part-time $1210 per credit. Required fees: $740; $214 per term. Tuition and fees vary according to program. *Financial support:* In 2010–11, 46 students received support, including 10 fellowships with full tuition reimbursements available, 36 research assistantships with full tuition reimbursements available (averaging $25,500 per year). *Faculty research:* Computational structural biology, computational genomics, cell and systems modeling, bioimage informatics, computational neurobiology. *Unit head:* Dr. Takis Benos, Director, 412-648-3315, Fax: 412-648-3163, E-mail: benos@pitt.edu. *Application contact:* Kelly Gentille, Assistant Programs Coordinator, 412-648-8107, Fax: 412-648-3163, E-mail: kmg120@pitt.edu.

University of Rochester, School of Medicine and Dentistry, Graduate Programs in Medicine and Dentistry, Department of Biostatistics and Computational Biology, Program in Medical Statistics, Rochester, NY 14627. Offers medical statistics (MS).

University of Rochester, School of Medicine and Dentistry, Graduate Programs in Medicine and Dentistry, Department of Biostatistics and Computational Biology, Programs in Statistics, Rochester, NY 14627. Offers MA, PhD.

University of Southern California, Graduate School, Dana and David Dornsife College of Letters, Arts and Sciences, Department of Biological Sciences, Program in Molecular and Computational Biology, Los Angeles, CA 90089. Offers computational biology and bioinformatics (PhD); molecular biology (PhD). *Faculty:* 40 full-time (7 women). *Students:* 100 full-time (48 women), 3 part-time (2 women); includes 19 minority (3 Black or African American, non-Hispanic/Latino; 10 Asian, non-Hispanic/Latino; 4 Hispanic/Latino; 2 Two or more races, non-Hispanic/Latino), 58 international. 178 applicants, 25% accepted, 24 enrolled. In 2010, 15 doctorates awarded. *Median time to degree:* Of those who began their doctoral program in fall 2002, 100% received their degree in 8 years or less. *Degree requirements:* For doctorate, comprehensive exam, thesis/dissertation, qualifying examination, dissertation defense. *Entrance requirements:* For doctorate, GRE, 3 letters of recommendation, personal statement, resume, minimum GPA of 3.0. Additional exam requirements/recommendations for international students: Required—TOEFL (minimum score 600 paper-based; 250 computer-based; 100 iBT). *Application deadline:* For fall admission, 12/1 priority date for domestic students, 11/1 priority date for international students. Application fee: $85. Electronic applications accepted. *Expenses:* Tuition: Full-time $31,240; part-time $1420 per unit. Required fees: $600. One-time fee: $35 full-time. Full-time tuition and fees vary according to degree level and program. *Financial support:* In 2010–11, 100 students received support, including 31 fellowships with full tuition reimbursements available (averaging $29,000 per year), 48 research assistantships with full tuition reimbursements available (averaging $28,000 per year), 21 teaching assistantships with full tuition reimbursements available (averaging $28,000 per year); career-related internships or fieldwork, scholarships/grants, traineeships, health care benefits, and unspecified assistantships also available. Financial award application deadline: 12/1. *Faculty research:* Biochemistry and molecular biology; genomics; computational biology and bioinformatics; cell and developmental biology, and genetics; DNA replication and repair, and cancer biology. *Unit head:* Dr. Myron Goodman, Professor of Biological Sciences and Chemistry/Director of the MCB Research Section, 213-740-5190, E-mail: mgoodman@usc.edu. *Application contact:* Catherine Atienza, Student Services Advisor I, 213-740-5188, E-mail: catherine.atienza@usc.edu.

The University of Texas Medical Branch, Graduate School of Biomedical Sciences, Program in Biochemistry and Molecular Biology, Galveston, TX 77555. Offers biochemistry (PhD); bioinformatics (PhD); biophysics (PhD); cell biology (PhD); computational biology (PhD); structural biology (PhD). *Degree requirements:* For doctorate, thesis/dissertation. *Entrance requirements:* Additional exam requirements/recommendations for international students: Required—TOEFL (minimum score 550 paper-based; 213 computer-based). Electronic applications accepted.

University of Wyoming, Graduate Program in Molecular and Cellular Life Sciences, Laramie, WY 82070. Offers PhD. *Degree requirements:* For doctorate, thesis/dissertation, four eight-week laboratory rotations, comprehensive basic practical exam, two-part qualifying exam, seminars, symposium.

Virginia Polytechnic Institute and State University, Graduate School, Intercollege, Program in Genetics, Bioinformatics and Computational Biology, Blacksburg, VA 24061. Offers PhD. *Students:* 42 full-time (18 women), 5 part-time (1 woman); includes 5 Black or African American, non-Hispanic/Latino; 2 Asian, non-Hispanic/Latino; 1 Hispanic/Latino, 27 international. Average age 30. 50 applicants, 22% accepted, 7 enrolled. In 2010, 4 doctorates awarded. *Degree requirements:* For doctorate, comprehensive exam (for some programs), thesis/dissertation (for some programs). *Entrance requirements:* For doctorate, GRE. Additional exam requirements/recommendations for international students: Required—TOEFL (minimum score 550 paper-based; 213 computer-based). *Application deadline:* For fall admission, 7/1 for domestic and international students; for spring admission, 12/1 for international students. Applications are processed on a rolling basis. Application fee: $65. Electronic applications accepted. *Expenses:* Tuition, state resident: full-time $9399; part-time $488 per credit hour. Tuition, nonresident: full-time $17,854; part-time $957.75 per credit hour. Required fees: $1534. Full-time tuition and fees vary according to program. *Financial support:* Career-related internships or fieldwork, Federal Work-Study, scholarships/grants, health care benefits, and unspecified assistantships available. Financial award application deadline: 1/15. *Unit head:* Dr. David R. Bevan, UNIT HEAD, 540-231-5040, Fax: 540-231-3010, E-mail: drbevan@vt.edu. *Application contact:* Dennie Munson, Contact, 540-231-1928, Fax: 540-231-3010, E-mail: dennie@vt.edu.

Washington University in St. Louis, Graduate School of Arts and Sciences, Division of Biology and Biomedical Sciences, Program in Computational Biology, St. Louis, MO 63130-4899. Offers PhD. *Degree requirements:* For doctorate, thesis/dissertation. Electronic applications accepted.

Yale University, School of Medicine and Graduate School of Arts and Sciences, Combined Program in Biological and Biomedical Sciences (BBS), Computational Biology and Bioinformatics Track, New Haven, CT 06520. Offers PhD, MD/PhD. *Entrance requirements:* Additional exam requirements/recommendations for international students: Required—TOEFL.

Systems Biology

Cornell University, Joan and Sanford I. Weill Medical College and Graduate School of Medical Sciences, Weill Cornell Graduate School of Medical Sciences, Physiology, Biophysics and Systems Biology Program, New York, NY 10065. Offers MS, PhD. *Faculty:* 35 full-time (9 women). *Students:* 51 full-time (20 women); includes 2 Black or African American, non-Hispanic/Latino; 5 Asian, non-Hispanic/Latino; 1 Hispanic/Latino, 24 international. Average age 23. 44 applicants, 59% accepted, 13 enrolled. In 2010, 5 doctorates awarded. Terminal master's awarded for partial completion of doctoral program. *Degree requirements:* For master's, comprehensive exam; for doctorate, thesis/dissertation, final exam. *Entrance requirements:* For doctorate, GRE General Test, introductory courses in biology, inorganic and organic chemistry, physics, and mathematics. Additional exam requirements/recommendations for international students: Required—TOEFL. *Application deadline:* For fall admission, 12/1 for domestic students. Application fee: $60. *Expenses:* Tuition: Full-time $45,545. Required fees: $2805. *Financial support:* In 2010–11, 4 fellowships (averaging $24,735 per year) were awarded; scholarships/grants, health care benefits, and stipends (given to all students) also available. *Faculty research:* Receptor-mediated regulation of cell function, molecular properties of channels or receptors, bioinformatics, mathematical modeling. *Unit head:* Dr. Emre Aksay, Co-Director, 212-746-6207, E-mail: ema2004@med.cornell.edu. *Application contact:* Audrey Rivera, Program Coordinator, 212-746-6361, E-mail: ajr2004@med.cornell.edu.

Dartmouth College, Program in Experimental and Molecular Medicine, Biomedical Physiology Track, Hanover, NH 03755. Offers PhD.

Harvard University, Graduate School of Arts and Sciences, Department of Systems Biology, Cambridge, MA 02138. Offers PhD. *Degree requirements:* For doctorate, thesis/dissertation, lab rotation, qualifying examination. *Entrance requirements:* For doctorate, GRE. Additional exam requirements/recommendations for international students: Required—TOEFL. Electronic applications accepted. *Expenses:* Tuition: Full-time $34,976. Required fees: $1166. Full-time tuition and fees vary according to program.

Massachusetts Institute of Technology, School of Engineering and School of Science, Program in Computational and Systems Biology, Cambridge, MA 02139-4307. Offers PhD. *Faculty:* 100 full-time (19 women). *Students:* 36 full-time (15 women); includes 8 minority (1 Black or African American, non-Hispanic/Latino; 6 Asian, non-Hispanic/Latino; 1 Hispanic/Latino), 17 international. Average age 26. 130 applicants, 9% accepted, 6 enrolled. In 2010, 3 doctorates awarded. *Degree requirements:* For doctorate, comprehensive exam, thesis/dissertation. *Entrance requirements:* For doctorate, GRE General Test. Additional exam requirements/recommendations for international students: Required—IELTS (minimum score 6). *Application deadline:* For fall admission, 12/15 for domestic and international students. Application fee: $75. Electronic applications accepted. *Expenses:* Tuition: Full-time $38,940; part-time $605 per unit. Required fees: $272. *Financial support:* In 2010–11, 36 students received support, including 16 fellowships (averaging $35,926 per year), 20 research assistantships (averaging $30,848 per year); teaching assistantships, Federal Work-Study, institutionally sponsored loans, scholarships/grants, health care benefits, and unspecified assistantships also available. *Faculty research:* Computational biology and bioinformatics, biological design and synthetic biology, gene and protein networks, systems biology of cancer, nanobiology and microsystems. *Unit head:* Prof. Douglas A. Lauffenberger, Director, 617-252-1629, E-mail: csbi@mit.edu. *Application contact:* Academic Office, 617-324-0055, Fax: 617-253-8699, E-mail: csbphd@mit.edu.

Michigan State University, The Graduate School, College of Natural Science, Quantitative Biology Program, East Lansing, MI 48824. Offers PhD.

Rutgers, The State University of New Jersey, New Brunswick, Graduate School-New Brunswick, BioMaPS Institute for Quantitative Biology, Piscataway, NJ 08854-8097. Offers computational biology and molecular biophysics (PhD). *Degree requirements:* For doctorate, comprehensive exam, thesis/dissertation. *Entrance requirements:* For doctorate, GRE. Additional exam requirements/recommendations for international students: Required—TOEFL. Electronic applications accepted. *Expenses:* Tuition, state resident: full-time $7200; part-time $600 per credit. Tuition, nonresident: full-time $11,124; part-time $927 per credit. *Faculty research:* Structural biology, systems biology, bioinformatics, translational medicine, genomics.

Texas A&M Health Science Center, Graduate School of Biomedical Sciences, Department of Systems Biology and Translational Medicine, College Station, TX 77840. Offers PhD. *Degree requirements:* For doctorate, thesis/dissertation. *Entrance requirements:* For doctorate, GRE General Test. *Faculty research:* Cardiovascular physiology, vascular cell and molecular biology.

University of California, Irvine, School of Biological Sciences, Program in Mathematical, Computational and Systems Biology, Irvine, CA 92697. Offers PhD. *Students:* 13 full-time (3 women); includes 5 minority (4 Asian, non-Hispanic/Latino; 1 Hispanic/Latino), 4 international. Average age 28. 64 applicants, 31% accepted, 11 enrolled.Application fee: $80 ($100 for international students). *Unit head:* Prof. Frederic Yui-Ming Wan, Director, 949-824-5529, Fax: 949-824-7993, E-mail: fwan@math.uci.edu. *Application contact:* Prof. Frederic Yui-Ming Wan, Director, 949-824-5529, Fax: 949-824-7993, E-mail: fwan@math.uci.edu.

University of California, Merced, Division of Graduate Studies, School of Natural Sciences, Merced, CA 95343. Offers applied mathematics (MS, PhD); biological engineering and small-scale technologies (MS, PhD); environmental systems (MS, PhD); mechanical engineering and applied mechanics (MS, PhD); physics and chemistry (PhD); quantitative and systems biology (MS, PhD).

University of California, San Diego, Office of Graduate Studies, Division of Biological Sciences, Program in Plant Systems Biology, La Jolla, CA 92093. Offers PhD.

University of Chicago, Division of Biological Sciences, Molecular Biosciences Cluster, Committee on Genetics, Genomics and Systems Biology, Chicago, IL 60637-1513. Offers PhD. *Degree requirements:* For doctorate, thesis/dissertation, ethics class, 2 teaching assistantships. *Entrance requirements:* For doctorate, GRE General Test, minimum GPA of 3.0. Additional exam requirements/recommendations for international students: Required—TOEFL (minimum score 600 paper-based; 250 computer-based; 104 iBT), IELTS (minimum score 7). Electronic applications accepted. *Faculty research:* Molecular genetics, developmental genetics, population genetics, human genetics.

University of Pittsburgh, Joint CMU-Pitt PhD Program in Computational and Systems Biology, Pittsburgh, PA 15260. Offers PhD. *Faculty:* 78 full-time (17 women). *Students:* 46 full-time (9 women); includes 22 Asian, non-Hispanic/Latino; 2 Hispanic/Latino; 1 Native Hawaiian or other Pacific Islander, non-Hispanic/Latino, 18 international. Average age 25. 133 applicants, 16% accepted, 7 enrolled. *Degree requirements:* For doctorate, comprehensive exam, thesis/dissertation, ethics training service as course assistant, seminar. *Entrance requirements:* For doctorate, GRE Subject Test (recommended), GRE General Test, 3 letters of recommendation, resume. Additional exam requirements/recommendations for international students: Required—TOEFL (minimum score 600 paper-based; 250 computer-based; 100 iBT). *Application deadline:* For fall admission, 1/15 priority date for domestic and international students. Application fee: $50. Electronic applications accepted. *Expenses:* Tuition, state resident: full-time $17,304; part-time $701 per credit. Tuition, nonresident: full-time $29,554; part-time $1210 per credit. Required fees: $740; $214 per term. Tuition and fees vary according to program. *Financial support:* In 2010–11, 46 students received support, including 10 fellowships with full tuition reimbursements available, 36 research assistantships with full tuition reimbursements available (averaging $25,500 per year). *Faculty research:* Computational structural biology, computational genomics, cell and systems modeling, bioimage informatics, computational neurobiology. *Unit head:* Dr. Takis Benos, Director, 412-648-3315, Fax: 412-648-3163, E-mail: benos@pitt.edu. *Application contact:* Kelly Gentille, Assistant Programs Coordinator, 412-648-8107, Fax: 412-648-3163, E-mail: kmg120@pitt.edu.

University of Southern California, Keck School of Medicine and Graduate School, Program in Systems Biology and Disease, Los Angeles, CA 90089. Offers PhD. *Faculty:* 234 full-time (64 women). *Students:* 27 full-time (14 women); includes 1 Black or African American, non-Hispanic/Latino; 4 Asian, non-Hispanic/Latino; 4 Hispanic/Latino, 6 international. Average age 30. 5 applicants, 60% accepted, 1 enrolled. In 2010, 8 doctorates awarded. *Degree requirements:* For doctorate, comprehensive exam, thesis/dissertation. *Entrance requirements:* For doctorate, GRE, minimum GPA of 3.0. Additional exam requirements/recommendations for international students: Required—TOEFL (minimum score 600 paper-based; 250 computer-based; 100 iBT). *Application deadline:* For fall admission, 12/1 priority date for domestic and international students. Application fee: $85. Electronic applications accepted. *Expenses:* Tuition: Full-time $31,240; part-time $1420 per unit. Tuition and fees vary according to degree level and program. *Financial support:* In 2010–11, 27 students received support, including 3 fellowships (averaging $27,600 per year), 23 research assistantships with full tuition reimbursements available (averaging $27,600 per year), 1 teaching assistantship with full tuition reimbursement available (averaging $27,600 per year); institutionally sponsored loans, scholarships/grants, traineeships, health care benefits, and unspecified assistantships also available. Financial award application deadline: 5/5; financial award applicants required to submit FAFSA. *Unit head:* Dr. Alicia McDonough, Director, 323-442-1475, Fax: 323-442-1199, E-mail: mcdonoug@usc.edu. *Application contact:* Dawn Burke, Student Program Coordinator, 323-442-1475, Fax: 323-442-1199, E-mail: pibbs@usc.edu.

University of Toronto, School of Graduate Studies, Life Sciences Division, Department of Cell and Systems Biology, Toronto, ON M5S 1A1, Canada. Offers M Sc, PhD. *Degree requirements:* For master's, thesis, thesis defense; for doctorate, thesis/dissertation, thesis defense, oral thesis examination. *Entrance requirements:* For master's, minimum B+ average in final year, B overall, 3 letters of reference. Additional exam requirements/recommendations for international students: Required—TOEFL (minimum score 580 paper-based; 237 computer-based), TWE (minimum score 5).

Virginia Commonwealth University, Graduate School, School of Life Sciences, Doctoral Program in Integrative Life Sciences, Richmond, VA 23284-9005. Offers PhD. *Students:* 32 full-time (18 women), 6 part-time (3 women); includes 3 minority (2 Black or African American, non-Hispanic/Latino; 1 American Indian or Alaska Native, non-Hispanic/Latino), 11 international. 35 applicants, 26% accepted, 6 enrolled. In 2010, 3 doctorates awarded. *Entrance requirements:* For doctorate, GRE, minimum GPA of 3.0 in last 60 credits of undergraduate work or in graduate degree, 3 letters of recommendation. Additional exam requirements/recommendations for international students: Required—TOEFL (minimum score 600 paper-based; 250 computer-based; 100 iBT). *Application deadline:* For fall admission, 2/1 for domestic students. Application fee: $50. Electronic applications accepted. *Expenses:* Tuition, state resident: full-time $4308; part-time $479 per credit hour. Tuition, nonresident: full-time $8942; part-time $994 per credit hour. Required fees: $2000; $85 per credit hour. Tuition and fees vary according to course level, course load, degree level, campus/location and program. *Financial support:* Applicants required to submit FAFSA. *Unit head:* Dr. Robert M. Tombes, Director, 804-827-0141, E-mail: rtombes@vcu.edu. *Application contact:* Dr. Robert M. Tombes, Director, 804-827-0141, E-mail: rtombes@vcu.edu.

Translational Biology

Baylor College of Medicine, Graduate School of Biomedical Sciences, Program in Translational Biology and Molecular Medicine, Houston, TX 77030-3498. Offers PhD. *Faculty:* 173 full-time (54 women). *Students:* 58 full-time (28 women); includes 6 Black or African American, non-Hispanic/Latino; 6 Hispanic/Latino, 16 international. Average age 27. 88 applicants, 32% accepted, 13 enrolled. In 2010, 1 doctorate awarded. *Degree requirements:* For doctorate, thesis/dissertation, public defense. *Entrance requirements:* For doctorate, GRE, minimum GPA of 3.0. Additional exam requirements/recommendations for international students: Required—TOEFL. *Application deadline:* For fall admission, 1/1 for domestic students. Application fee: $0. Electronic applications accepted. *Expenses:* Tuition: Full-time $11,000. Required fees: $4900. *Financial support:* In 2010–11, 58 students received support, including 24 fellowships with full tuition reimbursements available (averaging $26,000 per year), 34 research assistantships with full tuition reimbursements available (averaging $26,000 per year); career-related internships or fieldwork, Federal Work-Study, health care benefits, and students receive a scholarship unless there are grant funds available to pay tuition also available. Financial award applicants required to submit FAFSA. *Faculty research:* Molecular medicine, translational biology, human disease biology and therapy. *Unit head:* Dr. Mary Estes, Director, 713-798-3585, Fax: 713-798-3586, E-mail: tbmm@bcm.edu. *Application contact:* Wanda Waguespack, Graduate Program Administrator, 713-798-1077, Fax: 713-798-3586, E-mail: wandaw@bcm.edu.

See Display on this page and Close-Up on page 253.

Cedars-Sinai Medical Center, Graduate Program in Biomedical Sciences and Translational Medicine, Los Angeles, CA 90048. Offers PhD. *Degree requirements:* For doctorate, comprehensive exam, thesis/dissertation. *Entrance requirements:* For doctorate, GRE, 3 letters of recommendation. Additional exam requirements/recommendations for international students: Required—TOEFL (minimum score 560 paper-based; 220 computer-based; 87 iBT). *Faculty research:* Immunology and infection, neuroscience, cardiovascular science, cancer, human genetics.

Texas A&M Health Science Center, Graduate School of Biomedical Sciences, Department of Systems Biology and Translational Medicine, College Station, TX 77840. Offers PhD. *Degree requirements:* For doctorate, thesis/dissertation. *Entrance requirements:* For doctorate, GRE General Test. *Faculty research:* Cardiovascular physiology, vascular cell and molecular biology.

The University of Iowa, Graduate College, Program in Translational Biomedicine, Iowa City, IA 52242-1316. Offers MS, PhD. Terminal master's awarded for partial completion of doctoral program. *Degree requirements:* For master's, comprehensive exam; for doctorate, comprehensive exam, thesis/dissertation. *Entrance requirements:* For master's and doctorate, minimum GPA of 3.0. Additional exam requirements/recommendations for international students: Required—TOEFL (minimum score 550 paper-based; 213 computer-based; 81 iBT). Electronic applications accepted.

Washington University in St. Louis, School of Medicine, Program in Clinical Investigation, St. Louis, MO 63130-4899. Offers clinical investigation (MS), including genetics/genomics, translational medicine. Part-time programs available. *Faculty:* 54 full-time (14 women), 5 part-time/adjunct (3 women). *Students:* 13 full-time (8 women), 23 part-time (10 women); includes 13 minority (1 Black or African American, non-Hispanic/Latino; 9 Asian, non-Hispanic/Latino; 2 Hispanic/Latino; 1 Two or more races, non-Hispanic/Latino). Average age 32. In 2010, 13 master's awarded. *Entrance requirements:* For master's, doctoral level degree or in process of obtaining doctoral level degree. Additional exam requirements/recommendations for international students: Required—TOEFL. *Application deadline:* For fall admission, 3/1 for domestic students. Application fee: $0. Electronic applications accepted. *Faculty research:* Neurology, otolaryngology, pediatrics, obstetrics/gynecology, occupational therapy, physical therapy. *Unit head:* Dr. David Warren, Associate Professor of Medicine, 314-454-8225, Fax: 314-454-5392, E-mail: dwarren@dom.wustl.edu. *Application contact:* Sarah E. Zalud-Cerrato, Curriculum Coordinator, 314-362-0916, Fax: 314-454-8279, E-mail: szalud@dom.wustl.edu.

BAYLOR COLLEGE OF MEDICINE

Structural and Computational Biology and Molecular Biophysics

Program of Study

The Structural and Computational Biology and Molecular Biophysics (SCBMB) program is an interdisciplinary and interdepartmental program that offers a Ph.D. in structural and computational biology and molecular biophysics. This program is designed to train students by employing a strong research emphasis in these areas while also providing a solid background in biochemistry and cellular and molecular biology.

Faculty research activities cover development of state-of-the-art structural and computational techniques, protein design and engineering, biophysical chemistry of macromolecules, DNA structure and topology, membrane biophysics, and genome informatics. Over 70 faculty members in this program, from different departments at Baylor College of Medicine (BCM), Rice University, the University of Houston (UH), the University of Texas–Houston Health Science Center (UT–HSC), the University of Texas–M. D. Anderson Cancer Center (MDACC), and the University of Texas Medical Branch in Galveston (UTMB) are involved in teaching and supervising students' research.

The program seeks applicants with undergraduate degrees in physical, chemical, mathematical, computational, and engineering sciences as well as students with traditional backgrounds in biochemistry and molecular biology. The first-year curriculum is tailored to each student's background; undergraduate courses in science, mathematics, and engineering are available at Rice University and the University of Houston. Courses not available at Baylor can be taken free of charge at the other institutions. Students participate in three to five laboratory rotations to experience different research areas. Seminars of student research and distinguished scientists enhance the educational experience.

Research Facilities

Through participating faculty members, students have access to a number of research centers, each uniquely equipped and staffed. These include the W. M. Keck Center for Computational and Structural Biology, Howard Hughes Medical Institute, Human Genome Sequencing Center, National Center for Macromolecular Imaging, Institute for Molecular Design, Center for Research on Parallel Computation, Bioinformatics Research Laboratory, Human Neuroimaging Laboratory, Center for Protein Folding Machinery, and the Gulf Coast Consortia. These facilities offer students access to state-of-the-art hardware and software for X-ray and electron crystallography, magnetic resonance spectroscopy, genomics, proteomics, computational biophysics, and MRI and advanced optical imaging techniques.

Financial Aid

All students enrolled in the program receive an annual stipend for $29,000 and paid individual health insurance. Separate offices assist students with additional needs.

Cost of Study

Full-tuition scholarships are supported by Baylor College of Medicine. Students pay a one-time matriculation fee of $25, a graduation fee of $190 (due in the fourth year), and an Educational Resource Center fee of $150 for the first year and $20 for each following year. International students pay additional yearly visa fees: $75 for an F-1 and $100 for a J-1.

Living and Housing Costs

There are numerous apartment complexes located very close to the Texas Medical Center. Students frequently bike or walk to the campus from these apartments. The cost of living in Houston is less than in most major U.S. cities. The cost for food and recreation is modest, and there are many opportunities for employment of spouses in the Texas Medical Center.

Student Group

The SCBMB program currently has 40 graduate students and enrolls 6 to 8 students per year. Approximately 550 students are enrolled in the graduate school. Students interact with predoctoral and postdoctoral fellows and with staff members in a variety of research centers. These centers sponsor annual symposia, workshops, seminars, and informal discussion groups.

Location

Houston is a dynamic city, with a population of approximately 5 million people. With its large seaport and modern airport, it is a center of international travel. Mexico City is 90 minutes away by air, and the Gulf of Mexico is only an hour's ride by car. The climate offers very pleasant cool and dry weather from fall through spring. The temperature during winter rarely drops below freezing, and it does not normally snow. Although summer temperatures are in the 90s with moderately high humidity, comfort is ensured by air-conditioning in all homes and workplaces. Symphony, opera, ballet, live theater, year-round major-league sports, and a large number of diverse ethnic groups and restaurants help to make Houston an entertaining and exciting city in which to live and work.

The College

Baylor College of Medicine was established as an independent, private university committed to excellence in the training and education of scholars and physicians. The College is located in the Texas Medical Center, which is composed of more than 1,000 acres and includes forty-nine independent institutions. The University of Texas Health Science Center, the School of Public Health, and the M. D. Anderson Cancer Center are also on the campus, together with numerous hospitals and research institutes. The Texas Medical Center is one of the most actively growing science centers in the country. The influx of new colleagues and the opportunities created by an atmosphere of expansion provide a stimulating academic environment. More information on Baylor College of Medicine can be found on the College's Web site at http://www.bcm.edu.

Applying

Applicants must be in excellent academic standing and have a bachelor's degree, with extensive course work in biology, chemistry, physics, and mathematics. GRE scores less than three years old at the time of application must be provided. Applications should be accompanied by transcripts from all colleges and universities attended, plus three letters of recommendation and a statement of research interest and career goals.

Applications, catalogs, and instructions can be obtained via the Internet through the graduate school's Web site at http://www.bcm.edu/gradschool/ or the SCBMB Web site. There is no application fee for electronic submission. The application deadline is January 1 for fall admission. Successful candidates are invited for either a phone interview or a visit BCM to meet with the participating faculty members and students in order to have a firsthand look at the SCBMB program. Expenses for travel and accommodations during the visit are provided by Baylor College of Medicine. Questions regarding the application process can be directed to the admissions e-mail address at gradappboss@bcm.edu.

Correspondence and Information

Dr. Wah Chiu, Director
Graduate Program in Structural and Computational Biology and Molecular Biophysics
Graduate School of Biomedical Sciences, Room N204S
Baylor College of Medicine
One Baylor Plaza, MS: BCM 215
Houston, Texas 77030
Phone: 713-798-5197
Fax: 713-798-6325
E-mail: scb@bcm.edu
Web site: http://www.bcm.edu/scbmb

Baylor College of Medicine

THE FACULTY AND THEIR RESEARCH

Genevera Allen, Ph.D.; Neurology at BCM. Statistical modeling of dependences in high-dimensional biological data.

Patrick Barth, Ph.D.; Pharmacology and Biochemistry and Molecular Biology at BCM. Signaling mechanisms across biological membranes by computational modeling, design, and experimental biophysics.

Hugo Bellen, Ph.D.; Molecular and Human Genetics at BCM. Genetic and molecular analysis of neurotransmitter release and nervous system development in *Drosophila*.

John Belmont, M.D., Ph.D.; Molecular and Human Genetics at BCM. Structural congenital heart defects including abnormalities in laterality and hypoplastic left heart syndrome; functional studies of Zic3; genetics of human immune responses; medical population genetics.

Elmer V. Bernstam, M.D., Ph.D.; Internal Medicine at UT–HSC. Biomedical informatics.

Penelope Bonnen, Ph.D., Molecular and Human Genetics at BCM. Genomics and population genetics; genetics of infectious disease; genetics of metabolic disease.

Aladin M. Boriek, Ph.D.; Medicine and Molecular Physiology and Biophysics at BCM. Respiratory muscle mechanics; computational models of tissue mechanics; mechanical role of structural proteins in skeletal and smooth muscles; mechanical signal transduction in skeletal and smooth muscles.

James M. Briggs, Ph.D.; Biology and Biochemistry at UH. Computer-aided drug design; molecular modeling; computational biophysics.

William R. Brinkley, Ph.D.; Molecular and Cellular Biology at BCM. Structure and assembly of the mitotic apparatus; molecular mechanisms for aneuploidy and genomic instability in tumor cells.

William E. Brownell, Ph.D.; Otorhinolaryngology and Communicative Sciences at BCM. Cochlear biophysics and the mechanism of outer hair cell electromotility.

Rui Chen, Ph.D.; Molecular and Human Genetics at BCM. Functioning genomics of visual system development and diseases; high-throughput technology; bioinformatics.

Wah Chiu, Ph.D.; Biochemistry and Molecular Biology at BCM. Structural and computational biology of biological machines.

John W. Clark Jr., Ph.D.; Electrical and Computer Engineering at Rice. Cell modeling; engineering in critical care medicine.

Cecilia Clementi, Ph.D.; Chemistry at Rice. Theory of protein folding; protein modeling and simulations; folding/function relationship.

John A. Dani, Ph.D.; Neuroscience at BCM. In vivo, cellular, and molecular studies of synaptic communication and of circuits underlying reward and behavior.

Anne H. Delcour, Ph.D.; Biology and Biochemistry at UH. Molecular mechanisms of bacterial ion channels.

Mary E. Dickinson, Ph.D.; Molecular Physiology and Molecular Biophysics at BCM. In vivo optical microscopy; analysis of vascular networks; role of mechanical forces in vertebrate development.

Henry F. Epstein, M.D.; Neuroscience and Cell Biology at UTMB. Structural biology of myosin filaments, molecular chaperones, and protein kinase complexes.

Mary K. Estes, Ph.D.; Molecular Virology and Microbiology at BCM. Molecular biology and structure of virus assembly.

Mauro Ferrari, Ph.D.; Biomedical Engineering at UT–HSC. Nanotechnology in Biomedical Applications.

George E. Fox, Ph.D.; Biology and Biochemistry at UH. RNA structure, function, and evolution; bioinformatics.

Fabrizio Gabbiani, Ph.D.; Neuroscience at BCM. Biophysics of information processing in the nervous system.

Xiaolian Gao, Ph.D.; Biology and Biochemistry at UH. Biophysical and bioorganic chemistry of nucleic acids; NMR of nucleic acids, proteins, antitumor antibiotics, and their complexes; development of biochips for genetic screening.

Richard A. Gibbs, Ph.D.; Molecular and Human Genetics at BCM. Human Genome Project; molecular basis of human genetic diseases; molecular evolution.

Hiram F. Gilbert, Ph.D.; Biochemistry and Molecular Biology at BCM. Protein folding and catalysis of disulfide formation during protein secretion in yeast.

Ido Golding, Ph.D. Biochemistry and Molecular Biology at BCM. Spatiotemporal dynamics in living cells.

David Gorenstein, Ph.D.; Biochemistry and Molecular Biology at UT–HSC. Proteomics and nanomedicine for both diagnostics and therapeutics in cancer and infectious diseases.

Dan Graur, Ph.D.; Biology and Biochemistry at UH. Theoretical, statistical, and analytical topics within the area of molecular evolution.

Rudy Guerra, Ph.D.; Statistics at Rice. Meta-analysis for genetic linkage studies; case-control studies using haplotype blocks; identification of multiple genetic markers influencing a single trait.

Susan L. Hamilton, Ph.D.; Molecular Physiology and Biophysics at BCM. Calcium release channel structure and function.

Frank Horrigan, Ph.D.; Molecular Physiology and Biophysics at BCM. Molecular and biophysical mechanisms of ion channel gating. Allosteric regulation of BK potassium channel function.

S. Lennart Johnsson, Ph.D.; Computer Science at UH. Computational science.

Lydia E. Kavraki, Ph.D.; Computer Science and Bioengineering at Rice. Computation of shape and motion in biology; computer-assisted drug design.

Ching-Hwa Kiang, Ph.D.; Physics and Astronomy at Rice. Single-molecule force spectroscopy of biomolecules.

Choel Kim, Ph.D.; Pharmacology and Biochemistry and Molecular Biology at BCM Signal transduction; protein-protein recognition; assembly of higher order signal transduction complexes; localized cyclic nucleotide signaling.

Marek Kimmel, Ph.D.; Statistics at Rice. Informatics and statistical modeling of genome dynamics.

Ching C. Lau, M.D., Ph.D.; Pediatrics and Cancer Genomics Program at BCM. Genomics and proteomics of cancer, bioinformatics, and development of targeted therapy.

Suzanne M. Leal, Ph.D.; Molecular and Human Genetics at BCM. Statistical genetics and genetic epidemiology.

Wei Li, Ph.D.; Molecular and Cellular Biology at BCM. A genomic view of epigenetic and transcriptional regulation.

Han Liang, Ph.D.; Bioinformatics and Computational Biology at UT–MDACC. Next-generation sequencing; microRNA regulation; regulatory network; evolutionary genomics.

Olivier Lichtarge, M.D., Ph.D.; Molecular and Human Genetics at BCM. Annotation and designed perturbation of protein function and pathways.

Jun Liu, Ph.D.; Pathology and Laboratory Medicine at UT–HSC. Three-dimensional structure/function of macromolecular assemblies; intact bacteria and enveloped viruses; AIDS virus; viral entry and antibody neutralization.

Steven Ludtke, Ph.D.; Biochemistry and Molecular Biology at BCM. Cryoelectron microscopy and single particle reconstruction.

Jianpeng Ma, Ph.D.; Biochemistry and Molecular Biology at BCM. Computational molecular biophysics and structural biology.

Whee Ky "Wei Ji" Ma, Ph.D.; Neuroscience at BCM. Theoretical and behavioral studies of perceptual computation.

Michael A. Mancini, Ph.D.; Molecular and Cellular Biology at BCM. Transcription analyses at the single-cell level.

Aleksandar Milosavljevic, Ph.D.; Molecular and Human Genetics at BCM. Bioinformatics and comparative genomics.

Joel D. Morrisett, Ph.D.; Medicine and Biochemistry and Molecular Biology at BCM. Imaging, genomics, and proteomics of human atherosclerosis.

Luay Nakhleh, Ph.D.; Computer Science at Rice. Computational biology and bioinformatics.

Timothy G. Palzkill, Ph.D.; Molecular Virology and Microbiology at BCM. Molecular basis of antibiotic resistance; functional genomics of bacterial pathogens.

Steen E. Pedersen, Ph.D.; Molecular Physiology and Biophysics at BCM. Allosteric mechanisms of ion channel function.

Pawel A. Penczek, Ph.D.; Biochemistry and Molecular Biology at UT–HSC. Structural determination of proteins and molecular assemblies.

B. Montgomery Pettitt, Ph.D.; Chemistry at UH. Theoretical and computational biology and biochemistry.

Paul J. Pfaffinger, Ph.D.; Neuroscience at BCM. Molecular biology and biophysics of potassium ion channels.

Henry J. Pownall, Ph.D.; Medicine at BCM. Structures of native and model plasma lipoproteins.

B. V. Venkataram Prasad, Ph.D.; Biochemistry and Molecular Biology at BCM. Structural biology of replication mechanisms in pathogens such as rotavirus, norovirus, and influenza virus.

Jun Qin, Ph.D.; Biochemistry and Molecular Biology at BCM. Network analysis proteomics: the human DNA damage-signaling network.

Florante A. Quiocho, Ph.D.; Biochemistry and Molecular Biology at BCM. Protein atomic structure; molecular recognition and function.

Robert Raphael, Ph.D.; Bioengineering at Rice. Cell membrane mechanics; thermodynamics and biophysics.

Peter Saggau, Ph.D.; Neuroscience at BCM. Mechanisms and modulation of synaptic transmission; single neuron computation; advanced optical imaging techniques in neuroscience.

Michael F. Schmid, Ph.D.; Biochemistry and Molecular Biology at BCM. Image processing and electron crystallography of macromolecular machines.

Gad Shaulsky, Ph.D.; Molecular and Human Genetics at BCM. Allorecognition; evolution of sociality; functional genomics in *Dictyostelium*.

Chad Shaw, Ph.D.; Molecular and Human Genetics at BCM. Devising new statistical methods for genome scale data using a systems biology approach.

Richard N. Sifers, Ph.D.; Pathology and Molecular and Cellular Biology at BCM. Glycobiology; regulation of endoplasmic reticulum degradation; conformational disease; alpha1-antitrypsin deficiency.

Stelios Manolis Smirnakis, Ph.D.; Neurology and Neuroscience at BCM. In vivo functional magnetic resonance imaging, electrophysiology, and two-photon techniques in the study of cortical network function in health and disease.

Jack W. Smith, M.D., Ph.D.; Health Informatics at UT–HSC. Decision support systems and intelligent tutoring.

Yongcheng Song, Ph.D.; Pharmacology at BCM. Rational design and development of small molecule inhibitors of novel, biologically important enzymes.

John L. Spudich, Ph.D.; Center for Membrane Biology at UT–MS. Photosensory receptors and signal transduction/microbial rhodopsins.

David States, M.D., Ph.D; School of Health Information Sciences at UT–HSC. Multidisciplinary computational applications for biomedicine.

Andreas Tolias, Ph.D. Neuroscience at BCM. Electrophysiological, computational, and functional imaging approaches to processing of visual information in the cerebral cortex of alert-behaving primates.

Francis T. F. Tsai, D.Phil.; Biochemistry and Molecular Biology at BCM. Structure and function of macromolecular complexes and supramolecular assemblies.

Salih J. Wakil, Ph.D.; Biochemistry and Molecular Biology at BCM. Structure, function, and regulation of the multifunctional enzymes, acetyl-CoA carboxylase, and fatty acid synthase.

Ted Wensel, Ph.D.; Biochemistry and Ophthalmology at BCM. Structure and dynamics of signal transducing membranes.

Richard Willson, Ph.D.; Chemical Engineering and Biochemical and Biophysical Sciences at UH. Biology and biochemistry.

John H. Wilson, Ph.D.; Biochemistry and Molecular Biology at BCM. Instability of trinucleotide repeats in human disease; gene therapy for diseases of the eye.

Steve Wong, Ph.D.; Chief Research Informatics Officer at The Methodist Hospital. Computational biology; high throughput cell imaging and medical imaging.

Samuel M. Wu, Ph.D.; Ophthalmology at BCM. Retinal neurophysiology.

E. Lynn Zechiedrich, Ph.D.; Molecular Virology and Microbiology at BCM. DNA topoisomererases and antimicrobial resistance.

BAYLOR COLLEGE OF MEDICINE

Translational Biology and Molecular Medicine Graduate Program

Program of Study	The interdepartmental Translational Biology and Molecular Medicine (TBMM) graduate program is a new complimentary approach to train individuals in translational biology and to promote collaborations between more than 150 clinical and basic science faculty members. The Ph.D. program aims to develop a new workforce with firsthand experience in translational research and leadership training to serve as a catalyst to move discoveries effectively between bench and bedside. One of the unique aspects of the program is that students have 2 mentors, 1 basic scientist and 1 clinical scientist. The courses have been created to teach molecular mechanisms and clinical aspects of human health problems in an integrated fashion. During their second year, students participate in clinical rotations, which provide them with direct knowledge of human health issues. Journal clubs emphasize in-depth discussions of disease mechanisms. In addition, the program provides training in ethics, the approval process for human health research, grant writing, statistics, and high-throughput technologies.
	The Translational Biology and Molecular Medicine graduate program emphasizes research in human health problems and diseases and is closely aligned with centers and other areas of translational research strength at Baylor College of Medicine. The first-year courses are designed to provide the background. In the second year, the clinical rotations and electives are specifically targeted to health and diseases, including cancer, digestive system disorders, diseases of cardiac muscle, diseases of skeletal muscle, endocrine diseases and diabetes, genetic disorders, hemodynamic disorders, thrombosis and shock, infectious diseases, inflammation and immune disorders, neurological disorders, psychiatric disorders, renal system disorders, reproductive disorders, respiratory system disorders, and vascular system diseases. Students participate in at least three laboratory rotations and select their mentor pairs and thesis project by the end of their first year. The program is supported in part by the Howard Hughes Medical Research Institute Med into Grad Initiative.
Research Facilities	Baylor College of Medicine is one of several biomedical institutions within the Texas Medical Center. The participating faculty members in the program utilize state-of-the-art research facilities housed in one of the seventy nationally recognized research centers. More than 1 million square feet of space is devoted to the research and teaching activities of the 1,700 full-time faculty members, who conduct more than $400 million worth of sponsored research annually.
Financial Aid	All students in the TBMM program receive competitive stipends of $29,000 per year. This stipend is provided to students for each year of study, without any teaching assistantship requirements. In addition, full health insurance and tuition are completely covered. Although the stipend is always guaranteed, applying for outside funding is encouraged. Students who receive outside funding are recognized with a Dean's award, which is an additional $3000-per-year supplement to the $29,000 yearly stipend.
Cost of Study	Tuition is supported by the College. Students pay a one-time matriculation fee of $25, a one-time graduation fee of $190 during the fourth year, and an annual student fee of $150 for the first year and $20 for subsequent years. Students on temporary visas also pay an annual international services fee of $75 for an F-1 visa or $100 for a J-1 visa.
Living and Housing Costs	Most students live within a few miles of the Medical Center. Housing is not provided for graduate students because a variety of affordable excellent housing options are readily available. Some students choose to rent a private house nearby, while others choose to rent or buy a one-bedroom apartment or condo of their own. Numerous apartment complexes are located very close to the Medical Center. Houston's cost of living is well below that of every major city in the U.S., so graduate students can afford to enjoy the many recreational and cultural opportunities available.
Student Group	The TBMM program accepts 10 to 12 carefully selected students per year. The smaller class size allows for a more personalized one-on-one approach to learning and training in an environment with some of the best scientists in the country. Several specialized courses in the area of translational biology are part of the curriculum.
Student Outcomes	Graduates typically go on to postdoctoral research appointments, followed by careers in academics, medicine, and industry. Other options include careers in science education and government.
Location	Houston is a young and dynamic city that is both fun and affordable for graduate student life. Extensive and affordable cultural and recreational facilities and opportunities are available, including symphony concerts, operas, ballets, live theaters, museums, professional year-round sports, and numerous restaurants, which are all part of living in Houston, the fourth-largest city in the United States. From fall through spring, temperatures average between 50°F and 75°F, with temperatures rarely dropping below freezing, and it does not snow. Average highs during the summer are in the 90s, although it cools down in the evenings, and air conditioning is present in virtually all homes, the Medical Center, indoor sporting venues, etc.
The College	Baylor College of Medicine was established as an independent, private university committed to excellence in the training and education of scholars and physicians. The College is located in the heart of the Texas Medical Center, one of the largest medical centers in the world. The Medical Center, adjacent to residential areas, covers more than 675 acres and includes forty-two independent institutions. The Graduate School is committed to excellence in graduate training. There is a high degree of interdisciplinary cooperation not only among the faculty members in basic science areas but also with clinical investigators in the College and associated institutions in the Texas Medical Center. Ongoing research programs carried out by productive and widely recognized investigators in both the basic sciences and the clinical faculty, coupled with the favorable faculty-student ratio, permit students to be directly involved in and contribute to significant research projects.
Applying	Applicants must hold a bachelor's degree or the equivalent in a relevant area of science. Most of the students who join the program have a variety of undergraduate degrees in any area of the biological sciences, as well as in chemistry, engineering, and physics. Applications are due by January 1 each year and should be accompanied by three letters of recommendation from people who are familiar with the applicant's scholastic qualifications and/or research abilities, as well as a personal statement that describes research experience and career goals. Official GRE scores (not more than three years old) and transcripts from all colleges and universities attended must also be provided. Applications can be made online through the Graduate School Web site at http://www.bcm.edu/gradschool or the TBMM Web site at http://www.bcm.edu/tbmm/. There is no fee for online applications. Top applicants are invited to visit Baylor to meet with the participating faculty members and students, in order to have a firsthand look at the research and educational opportunities available to students in the TBMM program. Expenses for travel and accommodations during the visit are provided by Baylor College of Medicine. Applications from members of underrepresented populations, including women, are encouraged. Questions regarding the application process can be directed through e-mail to tbmm@bcm.edu.
Correspondence and Information	Translational Biology and Molecular Medicine Graduate Program Baylor College of Medicine One Baylor Plaza Mail Stop: BCM215 Houston, Texas 77030 Phone: 713-798-1077 Fax: 713-798-6325 E-mail: tbmm@bcm.edu Web site: http://www.bcm.edu/tbmm/

Baylor College of Medicine

THE FACULTY AND THEIR RESEARCH

Department of Biochemistry and Molecular Biology
Francis T. F. Tsai, D.Phil. Structural biochemistry of protein quality control systems.
John H. Wilson, Ph.D. Neurological diseases: genomic instability and gene therapy.

Department of Medicine
Roberto C. Arduino, M.D. HIV treatment strategies and new antiretroviral drugs.
Robert Atmar, M.D. Respiratory and enteric viruses, therapeutics and vaccines.
Mandeep Bajaj, M.D. Obesity and insulin resistance.
Ashok Balasubramanyam, M.D. Diabetes; molecular pathology; mouse models; human metabolic studies.
Christie Ballantyne, M.D. Inflammation; vascular disease; genetics; biomarkers; obesity.
Biykem Bozkurt, M.D., Ph.D. Predictors of outcome and remodeling in heart failure.
Malcolm K. Brenner, M.B., Ch.B., Ph.D. Cell and gene therapy of cancer.
Lawrence C. B. Chan, M.B., D.Sc. Diabetes: molecular cell biology, physiology and therapy.
David B. Corry, M.D. Asthma; cytokine receptors; T cells; microRNAs; proteases.
Farhad R. Danesh, M.D. RhoA and stem cell regulation in kidney diseases.
Jing-Fei Dong, M.D., Ph.D. Platelets and adhesion ligands in hemostasis and thrombosis.
Gianpietro Dotti, M.D. Immunotherapy and T-cell therapy of human malignancies.
Tony N. Eissa, M.D. Airway inflammation; innate immunity; lung diseases; autophagy; nitric oxide.
Mark L. Entman, M.D. Molecular mechanisms of cardiac injury and repair.
Suzanne A. Fuqua, Ph.D. Estrogen receptors; microarray profiling; metastasis; hormone resistance.
David Y. Graham, M.D. *Helicobacter pylori;* virulence; treatment; epidemiology; vaccines; resistance.
Teresa Hayes, M.D., Ph.D. Cancer prevention; cancer clinical research.
Helen E. Heslop, M.D., M.B., Ch.B. Adoptive immunotherapy; lymphoproliferative disorders.
Susan G. Hilsenbeck, Ph.D. Design/statistical analysis of translational/clinical experiments.
Farrah Kheradmand, M.D. Lung inflammation; asthma; COPD; infection; autoimmunity.
Weei-Chin Lin, M.D., Ph.D. Cell cycle regulators; novel cancer therapeutic targets.
Martha P. Mims, M.D., Ph.D. Genetic markers of prostate cancer risk in African Americans.
William E. Mitch, M.D. Control of protein metabolism in catabolic conditions.
C. Kent Osborne, M.D. Molecular mechanisms of treatment resistance in breast cancer.
Mothaffar F. Rimawi, M.D. Targeted therapy and biomarkers in breast cancer.
Rolando E. Rumbaut, M.D., Ph.D. Microvascular dysfunction in inflammation.
Susan L. Samson, M.D., Ph.D. The role of Wnt signaling in diabetes, both through its effects on beta cell function and maintenance in the face of insulin resistance.
Rachel Schiff, Ph.D. Breast cancer endocrine; targeted therapies.
David Sheikh-Hamad, M.D. Stanniocalcin; inflammation; SMADs; cardiac failure; osmoregulation; dysnatremias.
George E. Taffet, M.D. Aging and cardiovascular function; arterial rigidity; mouse models.
David J. Tweardy, M.D. STAT 3 function, activation, and specific inhibitors; hemorrhagic shock; cancer.
Vinod K. Vijayan, M.D. Serine/threonine phosphatases in platelet and endothelial cell activation.
Matthew H. Wilson, M.D., Ph.D. Transposons and gene therapy for renal diseases.
Li-Yuan Yu-Lee, Ph.D. Immune-inflammatory responses; mitotic regulators; cancer.

Department of Molecular and Cellular Biology
Karl-Dimiter Bissig, M.D., Ph.D. Cell therapy for liver disease utilizing novel stem cell or cellular engineering technologies.
Francisco J. DeMayo, Ph.D. Molecular regulation of cellular differentiation and physiology.
Yi Li, Ph.D. Breast cancer; stem cells; Wnt; differentiation.
Daniel Medina, M.D. Mammary premalignant progression; mechanisms of cancer chemoprevention.
Hoang Nguyen, Ph.D. Skin stem cell maintenance, differentiation, and tumorigenesis.
Bert W. O'Malley, M.D. Steroid hormone action; gene regulation; transcription factors.
Frederick A. Pereira, Ph.D. Signaling pathways in auditory development, aging, and cancer.
Jeffrey M. Rosen, Ph.D. Mammary gland development; stem cells and breast cancer.
David R. Rowley, Ph.D. Tumor microenvironment regulation of cancer progression.
Carolyn L. Smith, Ph.D. Estrogen receptor molecular pharmacology; breast/bladder cancer.
Nancy L. Weigel, Ph.D. Nuclear receptors and coactivators in prostate cancer.
Li Xin, Ph.D. Prostate stem cells, development and carcinogenesis.

Department of Molecular and Human Genetics
Carlos A. Bacino, M.D. Clinical studies in patients with imprinting disorders (Angelman syndrome), skeletal dysplasias, and genomic disorders.
Arthur L. Beaudet, M.D. Epigenetics; autism; clinical array CGH; hepatocyte gene therapy.
John W. Belmont, M.D., Ph.D. Cardiovascular malformations; infectious disease; complex traits.
William J. Craigen, M.D., Ph.D. Energy metabolism; mitochondrial function; transgenic models.
Richard A. Gibbs, Ph.D. Genomic sequencing; haplotype maps; rare genetic variation.
Brett H. Graham, M.D., Ph.D. Models of mitochondrial disease in fly/mouse.
Monica J. Justice, Ph.D. Mouse molecular genetics; blood diseases; leukemia.
Brendan Lee, M.D., Ph.D. Gene therapy; skeletal dysplasias; biochemical genetics.
James R. Lupski, M.D., Ph.D. Genomic disorders; gene dosage and recombination.
Aleksandar Milosavljevic, Ph.D. Bioinformatics and comparative genomics.
Philip Ng, Ph.D. Gene therapy for genetic diseases.
Donald W. Parsons, M.D., Ph.D. Genomic analysis of pediatric cancers for identification of biologically and clinically relevant molecular targets.
Richard E. Paylor, Ph.D. Behavioral analysis of mutant mouse models of human disease.
Antony Rodriguez, Ph.D. Role of microRNAs in pathophysiology of cardiac disease in mice.
Susan M. Rosenberg, Ph.D. Genomic instability in evolution, cancer, and antibiotic resistance.
Pawel Stankiewicz, M.D., Ph.D. Better understanding the molecular mechanisms and phenotypic effects of genomic rearrangements.
Lee-Jun C. Wong, Ph.D. Genetics and pathogenic mechanism of mitochondrial disorders.
Hui Zheng, Ph.D. Genetic studies of Alzheimer's disease using mouse models.
Huda Y. Zoghbi, M.D. Neurodegenerative disease; ataxia; Rett syndrome; autism; mouse models.

Department of Molecular Physiology and Biophysics
Christine Beeton, Ph.D. Ion channels in chronic inflammatory diseases.
Mary Dickinson, Ph.D. Hemodynamic forces in vascular development and remodeling.
Susan L. Hamilton, Ph.D. Mechanisms of malignant hyperthermia and central core diseases.
Robia Pautler, Ph.D. MRI; Nanotechnology; technology development; Alzheimer's disease.
Xander Wehrens, M.D., Ph.D. Molecular mechanisms of cardiac arrhythmias and heart failure.
Pumin Zhang, Ph.D. Cell-cycle regulation; myogenesis; lens development; rhabdomyosarcoma.

Department of Molecular Virology and Microbiology
Janet S. Butel, Ph.D. SV40 pathogenesis of infection and cancer; hamster model.
Margaret E. Conner, Ph.D. Mucosal immunity; rotavirus pathogenesis; intestinal intussusception.
Lawrence A. Donehower, Ph.D. The p53 tumor suppressor gene in cancer and aging.
Hana M. El Sahli, M.D. Clinical development of vaccines for use against human diseases.
Mary K. Estes, Ph.D. GI virus-host interactions: pathogenesis, immunity, and vaccines.
Wendy A. Keitel, M.D. Immunization; vaccine evaluation; infection and immunity.
Jason T. Kimata, Ph.D. HIV replication and pathogenesis; HIV model development.
Joseph Petrosino, Ph.D. Human microbiome and infectious disease systems biology.
Andrew P. Rice, Ph.D. Viral gene expression and pathogenesis.
Lynn Zechiedrich, Ph.D. DNA structure-function; gene therapy vectors; fluoroquinolone and multidrug resistance.

Department of Neurology
Rachelle Doody, M.D., Ph.D. Progression and treatment of Alzheimer's disease and mild cognitive impairment.
Thomas A. Kent, M.D. Translational stroke models; cerebrovascular regulation; oxygen radicals.
Jeffrey L. Noebels, M.D., Ph.D. Epilepsy; ion channel genes; mutant gene expression.

Department of Neuroscience
Mauro Costa-Mattioli, Ph.D. Molecular and cellular mechanisms underlying memory formation and its disorders.
John A. Dani, Ph.D. Addiction; learning and memory; degenerative dysfunction.
Mariella De Biasi, Ph.D. Molecular basis of nicotine addiction; mouse models; ubiquitin-like proteins; receptor trafficking.
Benjamin Deneen, Ph.D. Glial cell development and the generation of gliomas.
Joanna L. Jankowsky, Ph.D. Pathogenesis and treatment of Alzheimer's disease.

Department of Neurosurgery
Robert G. Grossman, M.D. Clinical trials of immunotherapy for the treatment of malignant brain tumors.
Claudia S. Robertson, M.D. Cerebral vascular flow; brain injury; imaging; biomarkers.
H. David Shine, Ph.D. Gene therapy and nervous system repair.

Department of Obstetrics and Gynecology
Kjersti M. Aagaard-Tillery, M.D., Ph.D. The in-utero environment and epigenetics in fetal programming and development.
Matthew L. Anderson, M.D., Ph.D. Noncoding RNAs in reproductive tract cancers; novel miRNA-based therapeutics.
Creighton L. Edwards, M.D. Clinical trials; drug discovery; genetics of cancer and immunotherapy.
William E. Gibbons, M.D. Folliculogenesis; endometrial function; ART outcomes; fertility preservation.
Shannon M. Hawkins, M.D., Ph.D. The role of microRNAs and genomic variants in endometriosis.
Ignatia B. Van den Veyver, M.D. Genetic and epigenetic developmental disorders; prenatal genetic diagnosis.

Department of Ophthalmology
Patricia Chevez-Barrios, M.D. Retinoblastoma biology, predictive factors, and targeted therapies.
Stephen C. Pflugfelder, M.D. Pathogenesis of dessication-induced autoimmunity on the ocular surface.

Department of Orthopedic Surgery
Michael H. Heggeness, M.D., Ph.D. Pathophysiology of the spine during degenerative disease states.

Department of Otolaryngology
William E. Brownell, Ph.D. Electromechanics of hearing: membrane-based motor mechanisms.

Department of Pathology and Immunology
Thomas A. Cooper, M.D. Myotonic dystrophy pathogenesis; pre-mRNA alternative splicing.
Milton Finegold, M.D. Molecular genetics of liver cancer.
Michael M. Ittman, M.D., Ph.D. Molecular genetics of prostate cancer.
H. Daniel Lacorazza, Ph.D. Transcriptional control of hematopoiesis and development of immunity.
Dario Marchetti, Ph.D. Mechanisms and molecular determinants of brain metastasis.
Martin M. Matzuk, M.D., Ph.D. Ovarian and testicular function; dysfunction in mammals.
Richard N. Sifers, Ph.D. Glycoprotein quality control as disease modifier.
David M. Spencer, Ph.D. Immunogenetic therapy; DCs; prostate cancer; signaling; apoptosis.
James Versalovic, M.D., Ph.D. Probiotics; intestinal inflammation; human microbiome and metagenomics.
Jin Wang, Ph.D. Molecular regulation of immune responses by apoptosis and autophagy.
Rongfu Wang, Ph.D. Cancer immunology; inflammation; immune regulation.
Laising Yen, Ph.D. Investigating mutational events in cancer RNA and secreted proteins.

Department of Pediatrics
Nabil M. Ahmed, M.D., M.P.H. Immunotherapy for brain tumors.
Anne Anderson, M.D. Signaling mechanisms in epilepsy; potassium channels; transcription.
Susan M. Blaney, M.D. Novel therapies for pediatric cancer.
Catherine Bollard, M.B., Ch.B., M.D. Developing immunotherapies for viral and malignant diseases.
Malcolm K. Brenner, M.B., Ch.B., Ph.D. Cell and gene therapy of cancer.
Douglas Burrin, Ph.D. Translational research in pediatric nutrition and gastroenterology.
Murali M. Chintagumpala, M.D. Clinical research in brain tumors, retinoblastoma, and Wilms' tumor.
Alan R. Davis, Ph.D. Bone stem cell recruitment, function, and differentiation; tissue engineering.
Elizabeth A. Davis, Ph.D. Tissue engineering of endochondral bone.
George D. Ferry, M.D. Inflammatory bowel disease.
Aaron E. Foster, Ph.D. Identification and immunotherapeutic targeting of cancer stem cells.
M. Waleed Gaber, Ph.D. Animal imaging of microvascular changes caused by tumors and radiotherapy.
Daniel G. Glaze, M.D. Neurophysiology of Rett syndrome.
Margaret A. Goodell, Ph.D. Regulation of hematopoietic stem cells.
Stephen M. G. Gottschalk, M.D. Immunotherapy for malignancies and viral-associated diseases.
Xinfu Guan, Ph.D. Neuropeptide receptor-mediated cell function and signaling network.
Terzah M. Horton, M.D., Ph.D. Treatment therapies for childhood leukemias and lymphomas.
Richard L. Hurwitz, M.D. Gene therapy; retinoblastoma; retinal degeneration.
Jeffrey J. Kim, M.D. Molecular mechanisms of sudden death and arrhythmias in heart failure and primary arrhythmia syndromes.
Mark W. Kline, M.D. International pediatric HIV/AIDS care and treatment.
Ann M. Leen, Ph.D. T-cell immunotherapy for viruses and cancer.
Bhagavatula Moorthy, Ph.D. Cytochrome P450 regulation; hyperoxia; lung injury; carcinogenesis.
Jeffrey N. Neul, M.D., Ph.D. Models of neurodevelopmental diseases; Rett syndrome.
Debananda Pati, Ph.D. Molecular basis of aneuploidy and apoptosis; mammary carcinogenesis; pediatric tumors; immunotherapy.
Mary E. Paul, M.D. Pediatric and adolescent HIV/AIDS and clinical trials.
David G. Poplack, M.D. Childhood leukemia; cancer survivorship; clinical pharmacology of anticancer agents in children.
Cliona M. Rooney, Ph.D. T cell therapy for virus infections and cancer; tumor immune evasion strategies.
Jason M. Shohet, M.D., Ph.D. Apoptosis pathways and oncogenes in pediatric cancers.
Yuxiang Sun, M.D., Ph.D. Nutritional regulation; glucose - and energy-homeostasis; pathophysiology of obesity, diabetes, and aging.
John W. Swann, Ph.D. Molecular mechanisms of early-onset epilepsy.
Sundararajah Thevananther, Ph.D. Molecular mechanisms of liver regeneration.
Qiang Tong, Ph.D. Molecular mechanisms of metabolic regulation and aging.
Lisa L. Wang, M.D. Molecular basis of osteosarcoma, RECQL4.
Yong Xu, M.D., Ph.D. CNS control of body weight, glucose, and blood pressure.
Jianhua Yang, Ph.D. Molecular targets in cancer.
Jason T. Yustein, M.D., Ph.D. Investigations into the molecular pathogenesis of pediatric sarcomas.

Department of Pharmacology
Timothy G. Palzkill, Ph.D. Role of beta-lactamase mutations in antibiotic resistance.

Department of Psychiatry and Behavioral Sciences
Thomas R. Kosten, M.D. Neurobiology of mental health and addictions.

Department of Radiology
Juliet A. Wendt, M.D. Multimodality molecular imaging.

Department of Surgery
David H. Berger, M.D. Impact of obesity and diabetes on survival in colorectal cancer; epithelial motility; colon cancer.
Changyi (Johnny) Chen, M.D., Ph.D. Vascular tissue engineering; HIV; endothelial dysfunction.
Xin-Hua Feng, Ph.D. Cell signaling; protein modifications; cancer.
John A. Goss, M.D. Genomics or hepatocellular carcinoma.
Mimi Leong, M.D. Role of immune system in abnormal or impaired wound healing.
Peter H. Lin, M.D. Endovascular treatment outcome; vascular disease progression.
Vijay Nambi, M.D. Vascular disease; atherosclerosis; atherosclerosis imaging; preventive cardiology.
Qizhi (Cathy) Yao, M.D., Ph.D. Vaccines for HIV, cardiovascular disease, and cancers.

Department of Urology
Keith S. Chan, Ph.D. Role of cancer stem cells in tumor progression.
Dolores J. Lamb, Ph.D. Male infertility; genitourinary defects; prostate cancer; receptors.
Seth P. Lerner, M.D. Bladder cancer; estrogen receptor–targeted therapy.
Kevin M. Slawin, M.D. Urologic oncology; benign and malignant diseases of the prostate.

Section 8
Ecology, Environmental Biology, and Evolutionary Biology

This section contains a directory of institutions offering graduate work in ecology, environmental biology, and evolutionary biology. Additional information about programs listed in the directory may be obtained by writing directly to the dean of a graduate school or chair of a department at the address given in the directory.

For programs offering related work, see also in this book *Biological and Biomedical Sciences; Botany and Plant Biology; Entomology; Genetics, Developmental Biology, and Reproductive Biology; Microbiological Sciences; Pharmacology and Toxicology;* and *Zoology.* In the other guides in this series:

Graduate Programs in the Humanities, Arts & Social Sciences
See *Sociology, Anthropology, and Archaeology*

Graduate Programs in the Physical Sciences, Mathematics, Agricultural Sciences, the Environment & Natural Resources

See *Agricultural and Food Sciences, Geosciences, Marine Sciences and Oceanography,* and *Mathematical Sciences*

Graduate Programs in Engineering & Applied Sciences

See *Civil and Environmental Engineering, Management of Engineering and Technology,* and *Ocean Engineering*

Graduate Programs in Business, Education, Health, Information Studies, Law & Social Work

See *Public Health*

CONTENTS

Program Directories

Conservation Biology

Antioch University New England, Graduate School, Department of Environmental Studies, Program in Conservation Biology, Keene, NH 03431-3552. Offers MS. *Degree requirements:* For master's, thesis or project. *Entrance requirements:* For master's, resume, 3 letters of recommendation.

California State University, Stanislaus, College of Natural Sciences, Program in Ecology and Sustainability (MS), Turlock, CA 95382. Offers ecological conservation (MS); ecological economics (MS). Part-time programs available. *Faculty:* 9 full-time (3 women), 1 (woman) part-time/adjunct. *Students:* 7 full-time (1 woman), 8 part-time (6 women); includes 6 minority (1 Black or African American, non-Hispanic/Latino; 4 Hispanic/Latino; 1 Two or more races, non-Hispanic/Latino). Average age 33. 10 applicants, 70% accepted, 4 enrolled. *Degree requirements:* For master's, thesis. *Entrance requirements:* For master's, GRE, minimum GPA of 3.0, 3 letters of recommendation, personal statement. Additional exam requirements/recommendations for international students: Required—TOEFL (minimum score 550 paper-based; 213 computer-based). *Application deadline:* For fall admission, 5/1 for domestic students; for spring admission, 1/7 for domestic students. Application fee: $55. Electronic applications accepted. Tuition and fees vary according to program. *Financial support:* In 2010–11, 4 teaching assistantships (averaging $4,500 per year) were awarded. Financial award application deadline: 3/1; financial award applicants required to submit FAFSA. *Unit head:* Dr. Matthew Cover, Program Director, 209-667-3153, E-mail: mcover@biology.csustan.edu. *Application contact:* Graduate School, 209-667-3129, Fax: 209-664-7025, E-mail: graduate_school@csustan.edu.

Central Michigan University, College of Graduate Studies, College of Science and Technology, Department of Biology, Mount Pleasant, MI 48859. Offers biology (MS); conservation biology (MS). Part-time programs available. *Faculty:* 17 full-time (5 women). *Students:* 15 full-time (8 women), 44 part-time (19 women); includes 1 Black or African American, non-Hispanic/Latino; 1 American Indian or Alaska Native, non-Hispanic/Latino; 1 Hispanic/Latino, 5 international. Average age 26. *Degree requirements:* For master's, thesis or alternative. *Entrance requirements:* For master's, GRE, bachelor's degree with a major in biological science, minimum GPA of 3.0. *Application deadline:* For fall admission, 6/1 for international students; for spring admission, 10/1 for international students. Applications are processed on a rolling basis. Application fee: $35 ($45 for international students). Electronic applications accepted. *Expenses:* Tuition, state resident: full-time $8208; part-time $456 per credit hour. Tuition, nonresident: full-time $13,788; part-time $766 per credit hour. One-time fee: $25. *Financial support:* Fellowships with tuition reimbursements, research assistantships with tuition reimbursements, teaching assistantships with tuition reimbursements, career-related internships or fieldwork, Federal Work-Study, unspecified assistantships, and out-of-state merit awards, non-resident graduate awards available. *Faculty research:* Conservation biology, morphology and taxonomy of aquatic plants, molecular biology and genetics, microbials and invertebrate ecology, vertebrates. *Unit head:* Dr. Stephen Roberts, Chairperson, 989-774-3227, Fax: 989-774-3462, E-mail: rober2sp@cmich.edu. *Application contact:* Dr. Gregory Colores, Graduate Program Coordinator, 989-774-3412, Fax: 989-774-3462, E-mail: color1gm@cmich.edu.

Colorado State University, Graduate School, Warner College of Natural Resources, Department of Fishery and Wildlife Biology, Fort Collins, CO 80523-1474. Offers fish, wildlife and conservation biology (MFWCB); fishery and wildlife biology (MFWB, MS, PhD). *Faculty:* 15 full-time (4 women). *Students:* 13 full-time (3 women), 15 part-time (5 women); includes 1 minority (Hispanic/Latino). Average age 31. 7 applicants, 86% accepted, 6 enrolled. In 2010, 4 master's, 1 doctorate awarded. Terminal master's awarded for partial completion of doctoral program. *Degree requirements:* For master's, comprehensive exam, thesis (for some programs); for doctorate, comprehensive exam, thesis/dissertation. *Entrance requirements:* For master's, GRE General Test (combined minimum score of 1200 on the Verbal and Quantitative sections), minimum GPA of 3.0, BA or BS in related field, letters of recommendation, personal narrative, resume, transcripts; for doctorate, GRE General Test (minimum score 1000 verbal and quantitative), minimum GPA of 3.0, MS in related field. Additional exam requirements/recommendations for international students: Required—TOEFL (minimum score 550 paper-based; 213 computer-based; 80 iBT). *Application deadline:* For fall admission, 2/15 priority date for domestic and international students. Applications are processed on a rolling basis. Application fee: $50. Electronic applications accepted. *Expenses:* Tuition, state resident: full-time $7434; part-time $413 per credit. Tuition, nonresident: full-time $19,022; part-time $1057 per credit. Required fees: $1729; $88 per credit. *Financial support:* In 2010–11, 4 fellowships with full and partial tuition reimbursements (averaging $37,058 per year), 17 research assistantships with full and partial tuition reimbursements (averaging $12,477 per year), 11 teaching assistantships with full and partial tuition reimbursements (averaging $7,568 per year) were awarded; tuition waivers (full and partial) and unspecified assistantships also available. Financial award application deadline: 2/15; financial award applicants required to submit FAFSA. *Faculty research:* Conservation biology, aquatic ecology, animal behavior, population modeling, habitat evaluation and management. Total annual research expenditures: $3.6 million. *Unit head:* Dr. Kenneth R. Wilson, Head, 970-491-7755, Fax: 970-491-5091, E-mail: kenneth.wilson@colostate.edu. *Application contact:* Joyce Pratt, Graduate Contact, 970-491-5020, Fax: 970-491-5091, E-mail: joyce.pratt@colostate.edu.

Columbia University, Graduate School of Arts and Sciences, Division of Natural Sciences, Department of Ecology, Evolution and Environmental Biology, New York, NY 10027. Offers conservation biology (MA, Certificate); ecology and evolutionary biology (PhD); environmental policy (Certificate); evolutionary primatology (PhD). *Degree requirements:* For doctorate, one foreign language, thesis/dissertation, teaching experience. *Entrance requirements:* For doctorate, GRE General Test, previous course work in biology. Additional exam requirements/recommendations for international students: Required—TOEFL. Electronic applications accepted. *Faculty research:* Tropical ecology, ethnobotany, global change, systematics.

Columbia University, Graduate School of Arts and Sciences, Program in Conservation Biology, New York, NY 10027. Offers MA. *Degree requirements:* For master's, thesis.

Frostburg State University, Graduate School, College of Liberal Arts and Sciences, Department of Biology, Program in Applied Ecology and Conservation Biology, Frostburg, MD 21532-1099. Offers MS. *Degree requirements:* For master's, thesis. *Entrance requirements:* For master's, GRE General Test, resume. Additional exam requirements/recommendations for international students: Required—TOEFL. Electronic applications accepted. *Faculty research:* Forest ecology, microbiology of man-made wetlands, invertebrate zoology and entomology, wildlife and carnivore ecology, aquatic pollution ecology.

Illinois State University, Graduate School, College of Arts and Sciences, Department of Biological Sciences, Normal, IL 61790-2200. Offers animal behavior (MS); bacteriology (MS); biochemistry (MS); biological sciences (MS); biology (PhD); biophysics (MS); biotechnology (MS); botany (MS, PhD); cell biology (MS); conservation biology (MS); developmental biology (MS); ecology (MS, PhD); entomology (MS); evolutionary biology (MS); genetics (MS, PhD); immunology (MS); microbiology (MS, PhD); molecular biology (MS); molecular genetics (MS); neurobiology (MS); neuroscience (MS); parasitology (MS); physiology (MS, PhD); plant biology (MS); plant molecular biology (MS); plant sciences (MS); structural biology (MS); zoology (MS, PhD). Part-time programs available. *Degree requirements:* For master's, thesis or alternative; for doctorate, variable foreign language requirement, thesis/dissertation, 2 terms of residency. *Entrance requirements:* For master's, GRE General Test, minimum GPA of 2.6 in last 60 hours of course work; for doctorate, GRE General Test. *Faculty research:* Redoc balance and drug development in schistosoma mansoni, control of the growth of listeria monocytogenes at low temperature, regulation of cell expansion and microtubule function by SPRI, CRUI: physiology and fitness consequences of different life history phenotypes.

North Dakota State University, College of Graduate and Interdisciplinary Studies, College of Agriculture, Food Systems, and Natural Resources, Department of Entomology, Fargo, ND 58108. Offers entomology (MS, PhD); environment and conservation science (MS, PhD); natural resource management (MS, PhD). Part-time programs available. *Faculty:* 7 full-time (3 women), 8 part-time/adjunct (0 women). *Students:* 6 full-time (3 women), 5 part-time (2 women), 3 international. Average age 34. 2 applicants, 50% accepted, 0 enrolled. In 2010, 1 master's; 1 doctorate awarded. *Degree requirements:* For master's, thesis; for doctorate, comprehensive exam, thesis/dissertation. *Entrance requirements:* For master's and doctorate, minimum GPA of 3.0. Additional exam requirements/recommendations for international students: Required—TOEFL (minimum score 550 paper-based; 213 computer-based; 79 iBT). *Application deadline:* Applications are processed on a rolling basis. Application fee: $45 ($60 for international students). Electronic applications accepted. *Financial support:* In 2010–11, 11 research assistantships with full tuition reimbursements (averaging $13,800 per year) were awarded; Federal Work-Study, institutionally sponsored loans, and unspecified assistantships also available. Financial award application deadline: 4/15. *Faculty research:* Insect systematics, conservation biology, integrated pest management, insect behavior, insect biology. *Unit head:* Dr. David A. Rider, Chair, 701-231-7908, Fax: 701-231-8557, E-mail: david.rider@ndsu.edu. *Application contact:* Dr. David A. Rider, Chair, 701-231-7908, Fax: 701-231-8557, E-mail: david.rider@ndsu.edu.

North Dakota State University, College of Graduate and Interdisciplinary Studies, College of Science and Mathematics, Department of Biological Sciences, Fargo, ND 58108. Offers biology (MS); botany (MS, PhD); cellular and molecular biology (PhD); environmental and conservation sciences (MS, PhD); genomics (PhD); natural resources management (MS, PhD); zoology (MS, PhD). *Students:* 18 full-time (8 women), 5 part-time (3 women); includes 2 American Indian or Alaska Native, non-Hispanic/Latino, 2 international. 17 applicants, 35% accepted. In 2010, 12 master's, 9 doctorates awarded. *Degree requirements:* For master's, thesis; for doctorate, thesis/dissertation. *Entrance requirements:* For master's and doctorate, GRE General Test. Additional exam requirements/recommendations for international students: Required—TOEFL. *Application deadline:* For fall admission, 3/15 priority date for domestic students; for spring admission, 10/30 priority date for domestic students. Applications are processed on a rolling basis. Application fee: $45 ($60 for international students). Electronic applications accepted. *Financial support:* Fellowships with full tuition reimbursements, research assistantships with full tuition reimbursements, teaching assistantships with full tuition reimbursements, career-related internships or fieldwork, Federal Work-Study, institutionally sponsored loans, scholarships/grants, tuition waivers (full), and unspecified assistantships available. Support available to part-time students. Financial award application deadline: 4/15; financial award applicants required to submit FAFSA. *Faculty research:* Comparative endocrinology, physiology, behavioral ecology, plant cell biology, aquatic biology. Total annual research expenditures: $675,000. *Unit head:* Dr. Marinus L. Otte, Head, 701-231-7087, E-mail: marinus.otte@ndsu.edu. *Application contact:* Dr. Marinus L. Otte, Head, 701-231-7087, E-mail: marinus.otte@ndsu.edu.

San Francisco State University, Division of Graduate Studies, College of Science and Engineering, Department of Biology, Program in Conservation Biology, San Francisco, CA 94132-1722. Offers MS. *Application deadline:* Applications are processed on a rolling basis. *Unit head:* Dr. Robert Patterson, Program Coordinator, 415-338-1100, E-mail: patters@sfsu.edu. *Application contact:* Dr. Robert Patterson, Program Coordinator, 415-338-1100, E-mail: patters@sfsu.edu.

State University of New York College of Environmental Science and Forestry, Department of Environmental and Forest Biology, Syracuse, NY 13210-2779. Offers applied ecology (MPS); chemical ecology (MPS, MS, PhD); conservation biology (MPS, MS, PhD); ecology (MPS, MS, PhD); entomology (MPS, MS, PhD); environmental interpretation (MPS, MS, PhD); environmental physiology (MPS, MS, PhD); fish and wildlife biology and management (MPS, MS, PhD); forest pathology and mycology (MPS, MS, PhD); plant biotechnology (MPS); plant science and biotechnology (MPS, MS, PhD). *Degree requirements:* For master's, thesis (for some programs); for doctorate, comprehensive exam, thesis/dissertation. *Entrance requirements:* For master's and doctorate, GRE General Test, GRE Subject Test, minimum GPA of 3.0. Additional exam requirements/recommendations for international students: Required—TOEFL (minimum score 550 paper-based; 213 computer-based; 80 iBT), IELTS (minimum score 6). *Expenses:* Tuition, state resident: full-time $8370; part-time $349 per credit hour. Tuition, nonresident: full-time $13,780. Required fees: $30.30 per credit hour. $20 per year. *Faculty research:* Ecology, fish and wildlife biology and management, plant science, entomology.

Texas State University–San Marcos, Graduate School, College of Science, Department of Biology, Program in Population and Conservation Biology, San Marcos, TX 78666. Offers MS. *Faculty:* 4 full-time (1 woman). *Students:* 14 full-time (8 women), 7 part-time (5 women); includes 5 minority (3 Asian, non-Hispanic/Latino; 2 Hispanic/Latino). Average age 28. 4 applicants, 100% accepted, 4 enrolled. In 2010, 5 master's awarded. *Degree requirements:* For master's, thesis. *Entrance requirements:* For master's, GRE (preferred minimum combined score of 1000 Verbal and Quantitative), bachelor's degree in biology or related discipline, minimum GPA of 3.0 in last 60 hours of undergraduate course work. Additional exam requirements/recommendations for international students: Required—TOEFL (minimum score 550 paper-based; 213 computer-based; 78 iBT). *Application deadline:* For fall admission, 6/15 for domestic students, 6/1 for international students; for spring admission, 10/15 for domestic students, 10/1 for international students. Applications are processed on a rolling basis. Application fee: $40 ($90 for international students). Electronic applications accepted. *Expenses:* Tuition, state resident: full-time $6024; part-time $251 per credit hour. Tuition, nonresident: full-time $13,536; part-time $564 per credit hour. Required fees: $1776; $50 per credit hour. $306 per semester. *Financial support:* In 2010–11, 10 students received support, including 18 teaching assistantships (averaging $4,862 per year); research assistantships, Federal Work-Study, institutionally sponsored loans, scholarships/grants, health care benefits, and unspecified assistantships also available. Support available to part-time students. Financial award application deadline: 4/1; financial award applicants required to submit FAFSA. *Unit head:* Dr. Chris Nice, Graduate Advisor, 512-245-2321, E-mail: ccnice@txstate.edu. *Application contact:* Dr. J. Michael Willoughby, Dean of the Graduate School, 512-245-2581, Fax: 512-245-8365, E-mail: jw02@swt.edu.

Tropical Agriculture Research and Higher Education Center, Graduate School, Turrialba, Costa Rica. Offers agribusiness management (MS); agroforestry systems (PhD); development practices (MS); ecological agriculture (MS); environmental socioeconomics (MS); forestry in tropical and subtropical zones (PhD); integrated watershed management (MS); international sustainable tourism (MS); management and conservation of tropical rainforests and biodiversity (MS); tropical agriculture (PhD); tropical agroforestry (MS). *Entrance requirements:* For master's, GRE, 2 years of related professional experience, letters of recommendation; for doctorate, GRE, 4 letters of recommendation, letter of support from employing organization, master's degree in agronomy, biological sciences, forestry, natural resources or related field. Additional exam requirements/recommendations for international students: Required—TOEFL (minimum score 550 paper-based; 213 computer-based). Electronic applications accepted. *Faculty research:* Biodiversity in fragmented landscapes, ecosystem management, integrated pest management, environmental livestock production, biotechnology carbon balances in diverse land uses.

University at Albany, State University of New York, College of Arts and Sciences, Department of Biological Sciences, Program in Biodiversity, Conservation, and Policy, Albany, NY 12222-0001. Offers MS. *Degree requirements:* For master's, one foreign language. *Entrance requirements:* For master's, GRE General Test. *Faculty research:* Aquatic ecology, plant community ecology, biodiversity and public policy, restoration ecology, coastal and estuarine science.

University of Alberta, Faculty of Graduate Studies and Research, Department of Renewable Resources, Edmonton, AB T6G 2E1, Canada. Offers agroforestry (M Ag, M Sc, MF);

conservation biology (M Sc, PhD); forest biology and management (M Sc, PhD); land reclamation and remediation (M Sc, PhD); protected areas and wildlands management (M Sc, PhD); soil science (M Ag, M Sc, PhD); water and land resources (M Ag, M Sc, PhD); wildlife ecology and management (M Sc, PhD); MBA/M Ag; MBA/MF. Part-time programs available. *Degree requirements:* For master's, thesis (for some programs); for doctorate, comprehensive exam, thesis/dissertation. *Entrance requirements:* For master's, minimum 2 years of relevant professional experiences, minimum GPA of 3.0; for doctorate, minimum GPA of 3.0. Additional exam requirements/recommendations for international students: Required—TOEFL (minimum score 550 paper-based; 213 computer-based). Electronic applications accepted. *Faculty research:* Natural and managed landscapes.

University of Central Florida, College of Sciences, Department of Biology, Orlando, FL 32816. Offers biology (MS); conservation biology (MS, PhD, Certificate). Part-time and evening/weekend programs available. *Faculty:* 22 full-time (6 women). *Students:* 47 full-time (31 women), 27 part-time (19 women); includes 1 Black or African American, non-Hispanic/Latino; 2 Asian, non-Hispanic/Latino; 3 Hispanic/Latino; 1 Native Hawaiian or other Pacific Islander, non-Hispanic/Latino, 4 international. Average age 30. 57 applicants, 53% accepted, 15 enrolled. In 2010, 9 master's, 3 doctorates awarded. *Degree requirements:* For master's, comprehensive exam, thesis or alternative, field exam. *Entrance requirements:* For master's, GRE General Test, minimum GPA of 3.0 in last 60 hours. Additional exam requirements/recommendations for international students: Required—TOEFL. *Application deadline:* For fall admission, 3/1 priority date for domestic students; for spring admission, 10/15 for domestic students. Application fee: $30. Electronic applications accepted. *Expenses:* Tuition, state resident: part-time $256.56 per credit hour. Tuition, nonresident: part-time $1011.52 per credit hour. Part-time tuition and fees vary according to program. *Financial support:* In 2010–11, 42 students received support, including 3 fellowships with partial tuition reimbursements available (averaging $6,000 per year), 14 research assistantships with partial tuition reimbursements available (averaging $7,500 per year), 48 teaching assistantships with partial tuition reimbursements available (averaging $8,100 per year); career-related internships or fieldwork, Federal Work-Study, institutionally sponsored loans, tuition waivers (partial), and unspecified assistantships also available. Financial award application deadline: 3/1; financial award applicants required to submit FAFSA. *Unit head:* Dr. Ross Hinkle, Chair, 407-823-2976, Fax: 407-823-5769, E-mail: thinkle@mail.ucf.edu. *Application contact:* Dr. Ross Hinkle, Chair, 407-823-2976, Fax: 407-823-5769, E-mail: thinkle@mail.ucf.edu.

University of Hawaii at Hilo, Program in Tropical Conservation Biology and Environmental Science, Hilo, HI 96720-4091. Offers MS.

University of Hawaii at Manoa, Graduate Division, Interdisciplinary Specialization in Ecology, Evolution and Conservation Biology, Honolulu, HI 96822. Offers MS, PhD. *Faculty:* 6 part-time/adjunct (1 woman). *Degree requirements:* For doctorate, thesis/dissertation. *Application deadline:* For fall admission, 2/1 for domestic students; for spring admission, 10/15 for domestic students. Application fee: $50. *Financial support:* Fellowships, research assistantships, teaching assistantships, career-related internships or fieldwork and tuition waivers (full) available. *Faculty research:* Agronomy and soil science, zoology, entomology, genetics and molecular biology, botanical sciences. *Unit head:* Robert H. Cowie, Chair, 808-956-4909, Fax: 808-956-2647, E-mail: cowie@hawaii.edu. *Application contact:* Robert H. Cowie, Chair, 808-956-4909, Fax: 808-956-2647, E-mail: cowie@hawaii.edu.

University of Illinois at Urbana–Champaign, Graduate College, College of Liberal Arts and Sciences, School of Integrative Biology, Program in Ecology, Evolution and Conservation Biology, Champaign, IL 61820. Offers MS, PhD. *Students:* 25 full-time (14 women), 10 part-time (8 women); includes 1 Black or African American, non-Hispanic/Latino; 2 Asian, non-Hispanic/Latino; 1 Hispanic/Latino, 2 international. 40 applicants, 23% accepted, 6 enrolled. In 2010, 1 master's, 4 doctorates awarded. *Entrance requirements:* For master's and doctorate, GRE. Additional exam requirements/recommendations for international students: Required—TOEFL (minimum score 613 paper-based; 257 computer-based; 103 iBT). *Application deadline:* Applications are processed on a rolling basis. Application fee: $75 ($90 for international students). Electronic applications accepted. *Financial support:* In 2010–11, 8 fellowships, 16 research assistantships, 15 teaching assistantships were awarded; tuition waivers (full and partial) also available. *Unit head:* Carla E. Caceres, Director, 217-244-2139, Fax: 217-244-1224, E-mail: cecacere@illinois.edu. *Application contact:* Carol Hall, Secretary, 217-333-8208, Fax: 217-244-1224, E-mail: cahall@illinois.edu.

University of Maryland, College Park, Academic Affairs, College of Computer, Mathematical and Natural Sciences, Department of Biology, Program in Sustainable Development and Conservation Biology, College Park, MD 20742. Offers MS. Part-time and evening/weekend programs available. *Students:* 20 full-time (11 women), 3 part-time (2 women); includes 1 Hispanic/Latino, 5 international. 105 applicants, 22% accepted, 13 enrolled. In 2010, 14 master's awarded. *Degree requirements:* For master's, internship, scholarly paper. *Entrance requirements:* For master's, GRE General Test, minimum GPA of 3.0, 3 letters of recommendation. *Application deadline:* For fall admission, 1/15 priority date for domestic students, 2/1 for international students. Applications are processed on a rolling basis. Application fee: $75. Electronic applications accepted. *Expenses:* Tuition, state resident: part-time $471 per credit hour. Tuition, nonresident: part-time $1016 per credit hour. Required fees: $337 per term. *Financial support:* In 2010–11, 14 teaching assistantships (averaging $18,659 per year) were awarded. Financial award application deadline: 2/1; financial award applicants required to submit FAFSA. *Faculty research:* Biodiversity, global change, conservation. *Unit head:* Dr. David W. Inouye, Director, 301-405-9358, Fax: 301-314-9358, E-mail: inouye@umd.edu. *Application contact:* Dean of Graduate School, 301-405-0358, Fax: 301-314-9305.

University of Michigan, School of Natural Resources and Environment, Program in Natural Resources and Environment, Ann Arbor, MI 48109. Offers aquatic sciences: research and management (MS); behavior, education and communication (MS); conservation biology (MS); conservation ecology (MS); environmental informatics (MS); environmental justice (MS); environmental policy and planning (MS); natural resources and environment (PhD); sustainable systems (MS); terrestrial ecosystems (MS); MS/AM; MS/JD; MS/MBA. *Faculty:* 42 full-time, 23 part-time/adjunct. *Students:* 450 full-time (254 women); includes 7 Black or African American, non-Hispanic/Latino; 2 American Indian or Alaska Native, non-Hispanic/Latino; 35 Asian, non-Hispanic/Latino; 13 Hispanic/Latino; 6 Two or more races, non-Hispanic/Latino, 50 international. Average age 27. 692 applicants. In 2010, 133 master's, 11 doctorates awarded. Terminal master's awarded for partial completion of doctoral program. *Degree requirements:* For master's, practicum or group project; for doctorate, comprehensive exam, thesis/dissertation, oral defense of dissertation, preliminary exam. *Entrance requirements:* For master's, GRE General Test; for doctorate, GRE General Test, master's degree. Additional exam requirements/recommendations for international students: Required—TOEFL (minimum score 560 paper-based; 220 computer-based; 84 iBT). *Application deadline:* For fall admission, 1/5 priority date for domestic and international students. Applications are processed on a rolling basis. Application fee: $65 ($75 for international students). Electronic applications accepted. *Expenses:* Tuition, state resident: full-time $17,784; part-time $1116 per credit hour. Tuition, nonresident: full-time $35,944; part-time $2125 per credit hour. International tuition: $35,994 full-time. Required fees: $95 per semester. Tuition and fees vary according to course load, degree level and program. *Financial support:* Fellowships with tuition reimbursements, research assistantships with tuition reimbursements, teaching assistantships with tuition reimbursements, career-related internships or fieldwork, Federal Work-Study, institutionally sponsored loans, scholarships/grants, health care benefits, and unspecified assistantships available. Support available to part-time students. Financial award application deadline: 1/5; financial award applicants required to submit FAFSA. *Faculty research:* Stream ecology, plant-insect interactions, fish biology, resource control and reproductive success, remote sensing, conservation ecology. *Application*

contact: Graduate Admissions Team, 734-764-6453, Fax: 734-936-2195, E-mail: snre.admissions@umich.edu.

University of Minnesota, Twin Cities Campus, Graduate School, College of Food, Agricultural and Natural Resource Sciences, Program in Conservation Biology, Minneapolis, MN 55455-0213. Offers MS, PhD. Part-time programs available. *Faculty:* 111 full-time (30 women). *Students:* 51 full-time (27 women), 2 part-time (0 women); includes 4 minority (1 Hispanic/Latino; 3 Two or more races, non-Hispanic/Latino), 6 international. Average age 28. 91 applicants, 15% accepted, 13 enrolled. In 2010, 5 master's, 6 doctorates awarded. Terminal master's awarded for partial completion of doctoral program. *Degree requirements:* For master's, comprehensive exam, thesis; for doctorate, comprehensive exam, thesis/dissertation. *Entrance requirements:* For master's and doctorate, GRE, advanced ecology course. Additional exam requirements/recommendations for international students: Required—TOEFL (minimum score 550 paper-based; 213 computer-based; 79 iBT). *Application deadline:* For fall admission, 12/15 priority date for domestic and international students; for spring admission, 10/15 for domestic and international students. Applications are processed on a rolling basis. Application fee: $75 ($95 for international students). Electronic applications accepted. *Financial support:* In 2010–11, fellowships with full tuition reimbursements (averaging $23,500 per year), research assistantships with full and partial tuition reimbursements (averaging $18,000 per year), teaching assistantships with full and partial tuition reimbursements (averaging $18,000 per year) were awarded; scholarships/grants, health care benefits, and unspecified assistantships also available. *Faculty research:* Wildlife conservation, fisheries and aquatic biology, invasive species, human dimensions, GIS, restoration ecology. *Unit head:* Dr. Karen Oberhauser, Co-Director of Graduate Studies, 612-642-8706, E-mail: oberh001@umn.edu. *Application contact:* Anup Joshi, Program Coordinator, 612-524-7751, E-mail: consbio@umn.edu.

University of Missouri–St. Louis, College of Arts and Sciences, Department of Biology, St. Louis, MO 63121. Offers biotechnology (Certificate); cell and molecular biology (MS, PhD); ecology, evolution and systematics (MS, PhD); tropical biology and conservation (Certificate). Part-time programs available. *Faculty:* 43 full-time (13 women), 2 part-time/adjunct (1 woman). *Students:* 73 full-time (36 women), 63 part-time (36 women); includes 17 minority (6 Black or African American, non-Hispanic/Latino; 9 Asian, non-Hispanic/Latino; 2 Hispanic/Latino), 45 international. Average age 29. 193 applicants, 44% accepted, 44 enrolled. In 2010, 35 master's, 11 doctorates, 6 other advanced degrees awarded. *Degree requirements:* For master's, thesis or alternative; for doctorate, thesis/dissertation, 1 semester of teaching experience. *Entrance requirements:* For master's, 3 letters of recommendation; for doctorate, GRE General Test, 3 letters of recommendation. Additional exam requirements/recommendations for international students: Required—TOEFL. *Application deadline:* For fall admission, 12/1 priority date for domestic and international students; for spring admission, 10/15 priority date for domestic and international students. Applications are processed on a rolling basis. Application fee: $35 ($40 for international students). Electronic applications accepted. *Expenses:* Tuition, state resident: full-time $5522; part-time $306.80 per credit hour. Tuition, nonresident: full-time $14,253; part-time $792.10 per credit hour. Required fees: $658; $49 per credit hour. One-time fee: $12. Tuition and fees vary according to program. *Financial support:* In 2010–11, 30 research assistantships with full and partial tuition reimbursements (averaging $18,113 per year), 15 teaching assistantships with full and partial tuition reimbursements (averaging $17,514 per year) were awarded; fellowships with full tuition reimbursements, career-related internships or fieldwork and Federal Work-Study also available. Support available to part-time students. Financial award application deadline: 2/1. *Faculty research:* Molecular biology, microbial genetics, animal behavior, tropical ecology, plant systematics. *Unit head:* Dr. Peter Stevens, Director of Graduate Studies, 314-516-6200, Fax: 314-516-6233, E-mail: stevensp@umsl.edu. *Application contact:* 314-516-5458, Fax: 314-516-6996, E-mail: gradadm@umsl.edu.

University of Nevada, Reno, Graduate School, Interdisciplinary Program in Ecology, Evolution, and Conservation Biology, Reno, NV 89557. Offers PhD. Offered through the College of Arts and Science, the M. C. Fleischmann College of Agriculture, and the Desert Research Institute. *Degree requirements:* For doctorate, thesis/dissertation. *Entrance requirements:* For doctorate, GRE General Test, GRE Subject Test, minimum GPA of 3.0. Additional exam requirements/recommendations for international students: Required—TOEFL (minimum score 500 paper-based; 173 computer-based; 61 iBT), IELTS (minimum score 6). Electronic applications accepted. *Expenses:* Tuition, state resident: full-time $2219; part-time $246 per credit. Tuition, nonresident: part-time $510 per credit. International tuition: $9009 full-time. Required fees: $59 per term. One-time fee: $101. Tuition and fees vary according to course load. *Faculty research:* Population biology, behavioral ecology, plant response to climate change, conservation of endangered species, restoration of natural ecosystems.

University of South Florida, Graduate School, College of Arts and Sciences, Department of Biology, Tampa, FL 33620-9951. Offers cell biology and molecular biology (MS); coastal marine biology (MS); coastal marine biology and ecology (PhD); conservation biology (MS, PhD); molecular and cell biology (PhD). Part-time programs available. *Faculty:* 8 full-time (4 women). *Students:* 85 full-time (50 women), 8 part-time (all women); includes 1 Black or African American, non-Hispanic/Latino; 3 Asian, non-Hispanic/Latino; 7 Hispanic/Latino, 12 international. Average age 27. 122 applicants, 30% accepted, 34 enrolled. In 2010, 10 master's, 9 doctorates awarded. *Degree requirements:* For master's, comprehensive exam, thesis (for some programs); for doctorate, comprehensive exam, thesis/dissertation. *Entrance requirements:* For master's and doctorate, GRE General Test, minimum GPA of 3.0. Additional exam requirements/recommendations for international students: Required—TOEFL (minimum score 570 paper-based; 213 computer-based). *Application deadline:* For fall admission, 2/15 priority date for domestic students, 1/2 for international students; for spring admission, 8/1 for domestic students, 6/1 for international students. Application fee: $30. Electronic applications accepted. *Financial support:* In 2010–11, 35 research assistantships (averaging $17,940 per year), 38 teaching assistantships with tuition reimbursements (averaging $16,621 per year) were awarded; unspecified assistantships also available. Financial award application deadline: 6/30; financial award applicants required to submit FAFSA. Total annual research expenditures: $4.5 million. *Unit head:* Susan Bell, Co-Chairperson, 813-974-6210, Fax: 813-974-2876, E-mail: sbell@cas.usf.edu. *Application contact:* James Garey, Graduate Advisor, 813-974-8434, Fax: 813-974-3263, E-mail: grarey@cas.usf.edu.

University of Wisconsin–Madison, Graduate School, Gaylord Nelson Institute for Environmental Studies, Conservation Biology and Sustainable Development Program, Madison, WI 53706-1380. Offers MS. Part-time programs available. *Faculty:* 3 full-time (1 woman), 15 part-time/adjunct (4 women). *Students:* 26 (22 women); includes 1 Asian, non-Hispanic/Latino. Average age 27. 54 applicants, 35% accepted, 11 enrolled. In 2010, 7 master's awarded. *Degree requirements:* For master's, thesis or alternative, exit seminar. *Entrance requirements:* For master's, GRE General Test. Additional exam requirements/recommendations for international students: Required—TOEFL (minimum score 550 paper-based; 213 computer-based; 80 iBT). *Application deadline:* For fall admission, 1/15 for domestic and international students; for spring admission, 10/15 for domestic and international students. Application fee: $56. Electronic applications accepted. *Expenses:* Tuition, state resident: full-time $9887; part-time $617.96 per credit. Tuition, nonresident: full-time $24,054; part-time $1503.40 per credit. Required fees: $67.63 per credit. Tuition and fees vary according to reciprocity agreements. *Financial support:* In 2010–11, 19 students received support, including 3 fellowships with full tuition reimbursements available (averaging $18,756 per year), 3 research assistantships with full tuition reimbursements available (averaging $14,960 per year), 7 teaching assistantships with full tuition reimbursements available (averaging $9,392 per year); career-related internships or fieldwork, Federal Work-Study, scholarships/grants, health care benefits, unspecified assistantships, and project assistantships also available. Financial award application deadline: 1/2. *Faculty research:* Ornithology, forestry, sociology, rural sociology, plant ecology, biodiversity, sustainability, sustainable development. *Unit head:* Janet M. Silbernagel, Chair, 608-890-2600, Fax: 608-262-2273, E-mail: jmsilber@wisc.edu. *Application contact:* Jim Miller, Student Services Coordinator, 608-263-4373, Fax: 608-262-2273, E-mail: jemiller@wisc.edu.

Ecology

Baylor University, Graduate School, College of Arts and Sciences, The Institute of Ecological, Earth and Environmental Sciences, Waco, TX 76798. Offers PhD. *Students:* 7 full-time (3 women); includes 1 minority (Two or more races, non-Hispanic/Latino), 5 international. In 2010, 1 doctorate awarded. *Unit head:* Dr. Joseph D. White, Director, 254-710-2911, E-mail: joseph_d_white@baylor.edu. *Application contact:* Suzanne Keener, Administrative Assistant, 254-710-3588, Fax: 254-710-3870.

Brown University, Graduate School, Division of Biology and Medicine, Program in Ecology and Evolutionary Biology, Providence, RI 02912. Offers PhD. *Degree requirements:* For doctorate, thesis/dissertation, preliminary exam. *Entrance requirements:* For doctorate, GRE General Test, GRE Subject Test. Additional exam requirements/recommendations for international students: Required—TOEFL. Electronic applications accepted. *Faculty research:* Marine ecology, behavioral ecology, population genetics, evolutionary morphology, plant ecology.

California State University, Stanislaus, College of Natural Sciences, Program in Ecology and Sustainability (MS), Turlock, CA 95382. Offers ecological conservation (MS); ecological economics (MS). Part-time programs available. *Faculty:* 9 full-time (3 women), 1 (woman) part-time/adjunct. *Students:* 7 full-time (1 woman), 8 part-time (6 women); includes 6 minority (1 Black or African American, non-Hispanic/Latino; 4 Hispanic/Latino; 1 Two or more races, non-Hispanic/Latino). Average age 33. 10 applicants, 70% accepted, 4 enrolled. *Degree requirements:* For master's, thesis. *Entrance requirements:* For master's, GRE, minimum GPA of 3.0, 3 letters of recommendation, personal statement. Additional exam requirements/recommendations for international students: Required—TOEFL (minimum score 550 paper-based; 213 computer-based). *Application deadline:* For fall admission, 5/1 for domestic students; for spring admission, 1/7 for domestic students. Application fee: $55. Electronic applications accepted. Tuition and fees vary according to program. *Financial support:* In 2010–11, 4 teaching assistantships (averaging $4,500 per year) were awarded. Financial award application deadline: 3/1; financial award applicants required to submit FAFSA. *Unit head:* Dr. Matthew Cover, Program Director, 209-667-3153, E-mail: mcover@biology.csustan.edu. *Application contact:* Graduate School, 209-667-3129, Fax: 209-664-7025, E-mail: graduate_school@csustan.edu.

Clemson University, Graduate School, College of Agriculture, Forestry and Life Sciences, Department of Biological Sciences, Program in Biological Sciences, Clemson, SC 29634. Offers MS, PhD. *Students:* 39 full-time (26 women), 121 part-time (114 women); includes 1 Black or African American, non-Hispanic/Latino; 2 Asian, non-Hispanic/Latino, 10 international. Average age 30. 75 applicants, 44% accepted, 29 enrolled. In 2010, 6 master's, 2 doctorates awarded. *Degree requirements:* For master's, thesis optional; for doctorate, comprehensive exam, thesis/dissertation. *Entrance requirements:* For master's and doctorate, GRE General Test. Additional exam requirements/recommendations for international students: Required—TOEFL, IELTS. *Application deadline:* For fall admission, 1/15 for domestic students, 4/15 for international students. Applications are processed on a rolling basis. Application fee: $70 ($80 for international students). Electronic applications accepted. *Expenses:* Tuition, state resident: full-time $6492; part-time $400 per credit hour. Tuition, nonresident: full-time $13,634; part-time $800 per credit hour. Required fees: $262 per semester. Part-time tuition and fees vary according to course load and program. *Financial support:* In 2010–11, 38 students received support, including 9 fellowships with full and partial tuition reimbursements available (averaging $9,389 per year), 17 research assistantships with partial tuition reimbursements available (averaging $12,632 per year), 40 teaching assistantships with partial tuition reimbursements available (averaging $10,513 per year); career-related internships or fieldwork, institutionally sponsored loans, scholarships/grants, health care benefits, and unspecified assistantships also available. Support available to part-time students. Financial award application deadline: 3/15; financial award applicants required to submit FAFSA. *Unit head:* Dr. Alfred Wheeler, Department Chair, 864-656-1415, Fax: 864-656-0435, E-mail: wheeler@clemson.edu. *Application contact:* Jay Lyn Martin, Coordinator for Graduate Program, 864-656-3587, Fax: 864-656-0435, E-mail: gradbio@clemson.edu.

Colorado State University, Graduate School, Graduate Degree Program in Ecology, Fort Collins, CO 80523-1401. Offers MS, PhD. Part-time programs available. *Students:* 55 full-time (24 women), 73 part-time (41 women); includes 12 minority (1 Black or African American, non-Hispanic/Latino; 1 American Indian or Alaska Native, non-Hispanic/Latino; 4 Asian, non-Hispanic/Latino; 4 Hispanic/Latino; 2 Two or more races, non-Hispanic/Latino), 9 international. Average age 32. 115 applicants, 23% accepted, 25 enrolled. In 2010, 9 master's, 7 doctorates awarded. Terminal master's awarded for partial completion of doctoral program. *Degree requirements:* For master's, comprehensive exam, thesis; for doctorate, comprehensive exam, thesis/dissertation. *Entrance requirements:* For master's, GRE General Test, minimum GPA of 3.0, BA/BS in agriculture, anthropology, biology, biochemistry, math or physical sciences (preferred), letters of recommendation; for doctorate, GRE General Test, minimum GPA of 3.0, BA/BS in agriculture, anthropology, biology, biochemistry, math or physical sciences (preferred), letters of recommendation, personal statement. Additional exam requirements/recommendations for international students: Required—TOEFL (minimum score 550 paper-based; 213 computer-based; 80 iBT). *Application deadline:* For fall admission, 1/1 priority date for domestic and international students. Application fee: $50. Electronic applications accepted. *Expenses:* Tuition, state resident: full-time $7434; part-time $413 per credit. Tuition, nonresident: full-time $19,022; part-time $1057 per credit. Required fees: $1729; $88 per credit. *Financial support:* Fellowships, research assistantships, teaching assistantships with full tuition reimbursements available. Financial award application deadline: 1/1; financial award applicants required to submit FAFSA. *Faculty research:* Plant and animal ecology at organismal, population, community, and ecosystem levels. *Unit head:* Dr. N. Leroy Poff, Interim Director, 970-491-2079, Fax: 970-491-2796, E-mail: poff@lamar.colostate.edu. *Application contact:* Jeri Morgan, Program Assistant, 970-491-4373, Fax: 970-491-2796, E-mail: ecology@colostate.edu.

Columbia University, Graduate School of Arts and Sciences, Division of Natural Sciences, Department of Ecology, Evolution and Environmental Biology, New York, NY 10027. Offers conservation biology (MA, Certificate); ecology and evolutionary biology (PhD); environmental policy (Certificate); evolutionary primatology (PhD). *Degree requirements:* For doctorate, one foreign language, thesis/dissertation, teaching experience. *Entrance requirements:* For doctorate, GRE General Test, previous course work in biology. Additional exam requirements/recommendations for international students: Required—TOEFL. Electronic applications accepted. *Faculty research:* Tropical ecology, ethnobotany, global change, systematics.

Cornell University, Graduate School, Graduate Fields of Agriculture and Life Sciences, Field of Computational Biology, Ithaca, NY 14853-0001. Offers computational behavioral biology (PhD); computational biology (PhD); computational cell biology (PhD); computational ecology (PhD); computational macromolecular biology (PhD); computational organismal biology (PhD). *Faculty:* 32 full-time (5 women). *Students:* 21 full-time (6 women); includes 4 Asian, non-Hispanic/Latino, 9 international. Average age 25. 128 applicants, 7% accepted, 9 enrolled. In 2010, 3 doctorates awarded. *Degree requirements:* For doctorate, comprehensive exam, thesis/dissertation, 2 semesters of teaching experience. *Entrance requirements:* For doctorate, GRE General Test, GRE Subject Test (biology), 2 letters of recommendation. Additional exam requirements/recommendations for international students: Required—TOEFL (minimum score 550 paper-based; 213 computer-based; 77 iBT). *Application deadline:* For fall admission, 2/1 priority date for domestic students. Application fee: $70. Electronic applications accepted. *Expenses:* Tuition: Full-time $29,500. Required fees: $76. Tuition and fees vary according to degree level and program. *Financial support:* In 2010–11, 15 fellowships with full tuition reimbursements, 4 research assistantships with full tuition reimbursements, 2 teaching assistantships with full tuition reimbursements were awarded; institutionally sponsored loans, scholarships/grants, health care benefits, tuition waivers (full and partial), and unspecified assistantships also available. Financial award applicants required to submit FAFSA. *Faculty research:* Computational behavioral biology, computational biology, computational cell biology, computational ecology, computational genetics, computational macromolecular biology, computational organismal biology. *Unit head:* Dr. Andrew Clark, Director of Graduate Studies, 607-255-5488, E-mail: ac347@cornell.edu. *Application contact:* Graduate School Application Requests, 607-255-5816, E-mail: gradadmissions@cornell.edu.

Cornell University, Graduate School, Graduate Fields of Agriculture and Life Sciences, Field of Ecology and Evolutionary Biology, Ithaca, NY 14853-0001. Offers ecology (PhD), including animal ecology, applied ecology, biogeochemistry, community and ecosystem ecology, limnology, oceanography, physiological ecology, plant ecology, population ecology, theoretical ecology, vertebrate zoology; evolutionary biology (PhD), including ecological genetics, paleobiology, population biology, systematics. *Faculty:* 48 full-time (13 women). *Students:* 51 full-time (37 women); includes 1 Asian, non-Hispanic/Latino; 3 Hispanic/Latino, 8 international. Average age 27. 108 applicants, 12% accepted, 10 enrolled. In 2010, 16 doctorates awarded. *Degree requirements:* For doctorate, comprehensive exam, thesis/dissertation, 2 semesters of teaching experience. *Entrance requirements:* For doctorate, GRE General Test, GRE Subject Test (biology), 2 letters of recommendation. Additional exam requirements/recommendations for international students: Required—TOEFL (minimum score 550 paper-based; 213 computer-based; 77 iBT). *Application deadline:* For fall admission, 12/15 for domestic students. Application fee: $70. Electronic applications accepted. *Expenses:* Tuition: Full-time $29,500. Required fees: $76. Tuition and fees vary according to degree level and program. *Financial support:* In 2010–11, 23 fellowships with full tuition reimbursements, 5 research assistantships with full tuition reimbursements, 21 teaching assistantships with full tuition reimbursements were awarded; institutionally sponsored loans, scholarships/grants, health care benefits, tuition waivers (full and partial), and unspecified assistantships also available. Financial award applicants required to submit FAFSA. *Faculty research:* Population and organismal biology, population and evolutionary genetics, systematics and macroevolution, biochemistry, conservation biology. *Unit head:* Director of Graduate Studies, 607-254-4230. *Application contact:* Graduate Field Assistant, 607-254-4230, E-mail: eeb_grad_req@cornell.edu.

Cornell University, Graduate School, Graduate Fields of Agriculture and Life Sciences, Field of Zoology and Wildlife Conservation, Ithaca, NY 14853-0001. Offers animal cytology (MS, PhD); comparative and functional anatomy (MS, PhD); developmental biology (MS, PhD); ecology (MS, PhD); histology (MS, PhD). *Faculty:* 20 full-time (5 women). *Students:* 5 full-time (all women); includes 1 Hispanic/Latino, 1 international. Average age 31. 17 applicants, 18% accepted, 1 enrolled. *Degree requirements:* For doctorate, comprehensive exam, thesis/dissertation, 2 semesters of teaching experience. *Entrance requirements:* For doctorate, GRE General Test, GRE Subject Test (biology), 2 letters of recommendation. Additional exam requirements/recommendations for international students: Required—TOEFL (minimum score 550 paper-based; 213 computer-based; 77 iBT). *Application deadline:* For fall admission, 2/1 priority date for domestic students. Application fee: $70. Electronic applications accepted. *Expenses:* Tuition: Full-time $29,500. Required fees: $76. Tuition and fees vary according to degree level and program. *Financial support:* In 2010–11, 1 fellowship with full tuition reimbursement, 4 research assistantships with full tuition reimbursements were awarded; teaching assistantships with full tuition reimbursements, institutionally sponsored loans, scholarships/grants, health care benefits, tuition waivers (full and partial), and unspecified assistantships also available. Financial award applicants required to submit FAFSA. *Faculty research:* Organismal biology, functional morphology, biomechanics, comparative vertebrate anatomy, comparative invertebrate anatomy, paleontology. *Unit head:* Director of Graduate Studies, 607-253-3276, Fax: 607-253-3756. *Application contact:* Graduate Field Assistant, 607-253-3276, Fax: 607-253-3756, E-mail: graduate_edcvm@cornell.edu.

Dartmouth College, Arts and Sciences Graduate Programs, Program in Ecology and Evolutionary Biology, Hanover, NH 03755. Offers PhD. *Entrance requirements:* For doctorate, GRE General Test, GRE Subject Test in biology (highly recommended). Additional exam requirements/recommendations for international students: Required—TOEFL.

Duke University, Graduate School, Department of Ecology, Durham, NC 27708-0342. Offers PhD, Certificate. *Faculty:* 31 full-time. *Students:* 28 full-time (16 women); includes 1 Black or African American, non-Hispanic/Latino; 2 Asian, non-Hispanic/Latino; 2 Hispanic/Latino, 2 international. 61 applicants, 11% accepted, 4 enrolled. In 2010, 6 doctorates awarded. *Degree requirements:* For doctorate, thesis/dissertation. *Entrance requirements:* For doctorate, GRE General Test. Additional exam requirements/recommendations for international students: Required—TOEFL (minimum score 550 paper-based; 213 computer-based; 83 iBT), IELTS (minimum score 7). *Application deadline:* For fall admission, 12/8 priority date for domestic and international students. Application fee: $75. Electronic applications accepted. *Financial support:* Fellowships, research assistantships, teaching assistantships available. Financial award application deadline: 12/8. *Unit head:* Dan Richter, Director of Graduate Studies, 919-613-8002, Fax: 919-613-8061, E-mail: meg.stephens@duke.edu. *Application contact:* Elizabeth Hutton, Director, Graduate Admissions, 919-684-3913, Fax: 919-684-2277, E-mail: grad-admissions@duke.edu.

Duke University, Graduate School, Department of Environment, Durham, NC 27708. Offers natural resource economics/policy (PhD); natural resource science/ecology (PhD); natural resource systems science (PhD); JD/AM. Part-time programs available. *Faculty:* 28 full-time. *Students:* 59 full-time (33 women); includes 2 Black or African American, non-Hispanic/Latino; 1 Asian, non-Hispanic/Latino, 17 international. 84 applicants, 13% accepted, 6 enrolled. In 2010, 14 doctorates awarded. *Degree requirements:* For doctorate, variable foreign language requirement, thesis/dissertation. *Entrance requirements:* For doctorate, GRE General Test. Additional exam requirements/recommendations for international students: Required—TOEFL (minimum score 550 paper-based; 213 computer-based; 83 iBT), IELTS (minimum score 7). *Application deadline:* For fall admission, 12/8 priority date for domestic and international students. Application fee: $75. Electronic applications accepted. *Financial support:* Fellowships, research assistantships, teaching assistantships, Federal Work-Study available. Financial award application deadline: 12/8. *Unit head:* Gaby Katul, Director of Graduate Studies, 919-613-8002, Fax: 919-613-8061, E-mail: meg.stephens@duke.edu. *Application contact:* Elizabeth Hutton, Director, Graduate Admissions, 919-684-3913, Fax: 919-684-2277, E-mail: grad-admissions@duke.edu.

Duke University, Nicholas School of the Environment, Durham, NC 27708-0328. Offers coastal environmental management (MEM); DEL-environmental leadership (MEM); energy and environment (MEM); environmental economics and policy (MEM); environmental health and security (MEM); forest resource management (MF); global environmental change (MEM); resource ecology (MEM); water and air resources (MEM); JD/AM; JD/MEM; JD/MF; MAT/MEM; MBA/MEM; MBA/MF; MEM/MPP; MF/MPP. *Accreditation:* SAF (one or more programs are accredited). Part-time programs available. *Degree requirements:* For master's, thesis. *Entrance requirements:* For master's, GRE General Test, previous course work in biology or ecology, calculus, statistics, and microeconomics; computer familiarity with word processing and data analysis. Additional exam requirements/recommendations for international students: Required—TOEFL (minimum score 550 paper-based; 213 computer-based). Electronic applications accepted. *Expenses:* Contact institution. *Faculty research:* Ecosystem management, conservation ecology, earth systems, risk assessment.

Eastern Kentucky University, The Graduate School, College of Arts and Sciences, Department of Biological Sciences, Richmond, KY 40475-3102. Offers biological sciences (MS); ecology (MS). Part-time programs available. *Degree requirements:* For master's, thesis. *Entrance requirements:* For master's, GRE General Test, minimum GPA of 2.5. *Faculty research:* Systematics, ecology, and biodiversity; animal behavior; protein structure and molecular genetics; biomonitoring and aquatic toxicology; pathogenesis of microbes and parasites.

Eastern Michigan University, Graduate School, College of Arts and Sciences, Department of Biology, Ypsilanti, MI 48197. Offers cell and molecular biology (MS); community college biology teaching (MS); ecology and organismal biology (MS); general biology (MS); water resources (MS). Part-time and evening/weekend programs available. Postbaccalaureate distance learning degree programs offered (minimal on-campus study). *Faculty:* 20 full-time (4 women). *Students:* 18 full-time (13 women), 35 part-time (19 women); includes 4 minority (2 Black or African American, non-Hispanic/Latino; 2 Two or more races, non-Hispanic/Latino), 13 international. Average age 27. 55 applicants, 47% accepted, 17 enrolled. In 2010, 10 master's awarded. *Entrance requirements:* For master's, GRE General Test, GRE Subject Test. Additional exam requirements/recommendations for international students: Required—TOEFL. *Application deadline:* Applications are processed on a rolling basis. Application fee: $35. *Financial support:* Fellowships, research assistantships with full tuition reimbursements, teaching assistantships with full tuition reimbursements, career-related internships or fieldwork, Federal Work-Study, institutionally sponsored loans, scholarships/grants, tuition waivers (partial), and unspecified assistantships available. Support available to part-time students. Financial award applicants required to submit FAFSA. *Unit head:* Dr. Marianne Laporte, Department Head, 734-487-4242, Fax: 734-487-9235, E-mail: mlaporte@emich.edu. *Application contact:* Dr. Marianne Laporte, Department Head, 734-487-4242, Fax: 734-487-9235, E-mail: mlaporte@emich.edu.

Eastern New Mexico University, Graduate School, College of Liberal Arts and Sciences, Department of Biology, Portales, NM 88130. Offers applied ecology (MS); cell, molecular biology and biotechnology (MS); education (non-thesis) (MS); microbiology (MS); plant biology (MS); zoology (MS). Part-time programs available. *Faculty:* 8 full-time (0 women). *Students:* 11 full-time (8 women), 7 part-time (4 women); includes 7 minority (5 Hispanic/Latino; 2 Two or more races, non-Hispanic/Latino), 4 international. Average age 25. 21 applicants, 14% accepted, 3 enrolled. In 2010, 4 master's awarded. *Degree requirements:* For master's, comprehensive exam, thesis optional. *Entrance requirements:* For master's, GRE, minimum GPA of 3.0, 2 letters of recommendation, statement of research interest, bachelor's degree related to field of study or proof of common knowledge. Additional exam requirements/recommendations for international students: Required—TOEFL (minimum score 550 paper-based; 213 computer-based; 79 iBT), IELTS (minimum score 6). *Application deadline:* For fall admission, 7/20 priority date for domestic students, 6/20 priority date for international students; for spring admission, 12/15 priority date for domestic students, 11/15 priority date for international students. Applications are processed on a rolling basis. Application fee: $10. Electronic applications accepted. *Expenses:* Tuition, state resident: full-time $3210; part-time $130 per credit hour. Tuition, nonresident: full-time $8652; part-time $360.50 per credit hour. Required fees: $1212; $50.50 per credit hour. Tuition and fees vary according to course load. *Financial support:* In 2010–11, 11 teaching assistantships with partial tuition reimbursements (averaging $8,500 per year) were awarded; unspecified assistantships also available. Support available to part-time students. Financial award applicants required to submit FAFSA. *Unit head:* Dr. Zach Jones, Graduate Coordinator, 575-562-2723, Fax: 575-562-2192, E-mail: zach.jones@enmu.edu. *Application contact:* Sharon Potter, Department Secretary, Biology/Physical Sciences, 575-562-2174, Fax: 575-562-2192, E-mail: sharon.potter@enmu.edu.

Emory University, Laney Graduate School, Division of Biological and Biomedical Sciences, Program in Population Biology, Ecology and Evolution, Atlanta, GA 30322-1100. Offers PhD. *Faculty:* 35 full-time (6 women). *Students:* 29 full-time (20 women); includes 1 Asian, non-Hispanic/Latino; 4 Hispanic/Latino, 6 international. Average age 27. 40 applicants, 38% accepted, 5 enrolled. In 2010, 4 doctorates awarded. *Degree requirements:* For doctorate, comprehensive exam, thesis/dissertation. *Entrance requirements:* For doctorate, GRE General Test, minimum GPA of 3.0 in science course work (recommended). Additional exam requirements/recommendations for international students: Required—TOEFL. *Application deadline:* For fall admission, 12/1 for domestic and international students. Application fee: $75. Electronic applications accepted. *Expenses:* Tuition: Full-time $33,800. Required fees: $1300. *Financial support:* In 2010–11, 12 students received support, including 12 fellowships with full tuition reimbursements available (averaging $25,000 per year); institutionally sponsored loans, scholarships/grants, health care benefits, and tuition waivers (full) also available. *Faculty research:* Evolution of microbes, infectious disease, the immune system, genetic disease in humans, evolution of behavior. *Unit head:* Dr. Michael Zwick, Director, 404-727-9924, Fax: 404-727-3949, E-mail: mzwick@emory.edu. *Application contact:* Kathy Smith, Director of Recruitment and Admissions, 404-727-2547, Fax: 404-727-3322, E-mail: kathy.smith@emory.edu.

Florida Institute of Technology, Graduate Programs, College of Science, Department of Biological Sciences, Programs in Ecology and Marine Biology, Melbourne, FL 32901-6975. Offers ecology (MS); marine biology (MS). Part-time programs available. *Faculty:* 15 full-time (2 women), 1 part-time/adjunct (0 women). *Students:* 24 full-time (17 women), 3 part-time (all women); includes 1 American Indian or Alaska Native, non-Hispanic/Latino; 1 Asian, non-Hispanic/Latino; 2 Hispanic/Latino, 1 international. Average age 25. 52 applicants, 23% accepted, 11 enrolled. In 2010, 4 master's awarded. *Degree requirements:* For master's, thesis, research, seminar, internship or summer lab. *Entrance requirements:* For master's, GRE General Test, minimum GPA of 3.0, 3 letters of recommendation, statement of objectives. Additional exam requirements/recommendations for international students: Required—TOEFL (minimum score 550 paper-based; 213 computer-based; 79 iBT). *Application deadline:* For fall admission, 3/15 for domestic students; for spring admission, 10/1 for domestic students. Applications are processed on a rolling basis. Application fee: $50. Electronic applications accepted. *Expenses:* Tuition: Part-time $1040 per credit hour. Tuition and fees vary according to campus/location. *Financial support:* In 2010–11, 6 fellowships (averaging $20,737 per year), 15 research assistantships with full and partial tuition reimbursements (averaging $13,455 per year), 22 teaching assistantships with full and partial tuition reimbursements (averaging $13,353 per year) were awarded; career-related internships or fieldwork, institutionally sponsored loans, tuition waivers (partial), unspecified assistantships, and tuition remissions also available. Support available to part-time students. Financial award application deadline: 3/1; financial award applicants required to submit FAFSA. *Faculty research:* Endangered or threatened avian and mammalian species, hydroacoustics and feeding preference of the West Indian manatee, habitat preference of the Florida scrub jay. Total annual research expenditures: $1.3 million. *Unit head:* Dr. Richard B. Aronson, Department Head, 321-674-8034, Fax: 321-674-7238, E-mail: raronson@fit.edu. *Application contact:* Cheryl A. Brown, Associate Director of Graduate Admission, 321-674-7581, Fax: 321-723-9468, E-mail: cbrown@fit.edu.

Florida State University, The Graduate School, College of Arts and Sciences, Department of Biological Science, Specialization in Ecology and Evolutionary Biology, Tallahassee, FL 32306-4295. Offers MS, PhD. *Faculty:* 26 full-time (9 women). *Students:* 61 full-time (30 women); includes 2 Asian, non-Hispanic/Latino; 4 Hispanic/Latino, 4 international. 133 applicants, 13% accepted, 14 enrolled. In 2010, 3 master's, 6 doctorates awarded. Terminal master's awarded for partial completion of doctoral program. *Degree requirements:* For master's, comprehensive exam, thesis, teaching experience, seminar presentation; for doctorate, comprehensive exam, thesis/dissertation, teaching experience; seminar presentation. *Entrance requirements:* For master's, GRE General Test (minimum combined score 1100, 500 verbal, 500 quantitative), minimum upper-division GPA of 3.0; for doctorate, GRE General Test (minimum combined score 1100, Verbal 500, Quantitative 500), minimum upper-division GPA of 3.0. Additional exam requirements/recommendations for international students: Required—TOEFL (minimum score 600 paper-based; 250 computer-based; 92 iBT). *Application deadline:* For fall admission, 12/15 for domestic and international students. Application fee: $30. Electronic applications accepted. *Expenses:* Tuition, state resident: full-time $8238. *Financial support:* In 2010–11, 55 students received support, including 3 fellowships with full tuition reimbursements available (averaging $24,000 per year), 21 research assistantships with full tuition reimbursements available (averaging $21,000 per year), 31 teaching assistantships with full tuition reimbursements available (averaging $21,000 per year). Financial award application deadline: 12/15; financial award applicants required to submit FAFSA. *Faculty research:* Ecology and conservation biology; evolution; marine biology; phylogeny and systematics; theoretical, computational and mathematical biology. *Application contact:* Judy Bowers, Coordinator, Graduate Affairs, 850-644-3023, Fax: 850-644-9829, E-mail: gradinfo@bio.fsu.edu.

Frostburg State University, Graduate School, College of Liberal Arts and Sciences, Department of Biology, Program in Applied Ecology and Conservation Biology, Frostburg, MD 21532-1099. Offers MS. *Degree requirements:* For master's, thesis. *Entrance requirements:* For master's, GRE General Test, resume. Additional exam requirements/recommendations for international students: Required—TOEFL. Electronic applications accepted. *Faculty research:* Forest ecology, microbiology of man-made wetlands, invertebrate zoology and entomology, wildlife and carnivore ecology, aquatic pollution ecology.

Illinois State University, Graduate School, College of Arts and Sciences, Department of Biological Sciences, Normal, IL 61790-2200. Offers animal behavior (MS); bacteriology (MS); biochemistry (MS); biological sciences (MS); biology (PhD); biophysics (MS); biotechnology (MS); botany (MS, PhD); cell biology (MS); conservation biology (MS); developmental biology (MS); ecology (MS, PhD); entomology (MS); evolutionary biology (MS); genetics (MS, PhD); immunology (MS); microbiology (MS, PhD); molecular biology (MS); molecular genetics (MS); neurobiology (MS); neuroscience (MS); parasitology (MS); physiology (MS, PhD); plant biology (MS); plant molecular biology (MS); plant sciences (MS); structural biology (MS); zoology (MS, PhD). Part-time programs available. *Degree requirements:* For master's, thesis or alternative; for doctorate, variable foreign language requirement, thesis/dissertation, 2 terms of residency. *Entrance requirements:* For master's, GRE General Test, minimum GPA of 2.6 in last 60 hours of course work; for doctorate, GRE General Test. *Faculty research:* Redoc balance and drug development in schistosoma mansoni, control of the growth of listeria monocytogenes at low temperature, regulation of cell expansion and microtubule function by SPRI, CRUI: physiology and fitness consequences of different life history phenotypes.

Indiana State University, College of Graduate and Professional Studies, College of Arts and Sciences, Department of Biology, Terre Haute, IN 47809. Offers ecology (PhD); life sciences (MS); microbiology (PhD); physiology (PhD); science education (MS). *Degree requirements:* For master's, thesis (for some programs); for doctorate, comprehensive exam, thesis/dissertation. *Entrance requirements:* For master's and doctorate, GRE General Test. Electronic applications accepted.

Indiana University Bloomington, School of Public and Environmental Affairs, Environmental Science Programs, Bloomington, IN 47405-7000. Offers applied ecology (MSES); energy (MSES); environmental chemistry, toxicology, and risk assessment (MSES); environmental science (PhD); specialized environmental science (MSES); water resources (MSES); JD/MSES; MSES/MS. Part-time programs available. *Faculty:* 17 full-time, 8 part-time/adjunct. *Students:* 87 full-time (49 women), 2 part-time (1 woman); includes 1 Black or African American, non-Hispanic/Latino; 1 American Indian or Alaska Native, non-Hispanic/Latino; 10 Asian, non-Hispanic/Latino; 3 Hispanic/Latino, 11 international. Average age 26. 79 applicants, 29 enrolled. In 2010, 53 master's, 10 doctorates awarded. Terminal master's awarded for partial completion of doctoral program. *Degree requirements:* For master's, thesis optional; for doctorate, comprehensive exam, thesis/dissertation. *Entrance requirements:* For master's, GRE General Test or GMAT, official transcripts, 3 letters of recommendation, resume, personal statement, departmental questions; for doctorate, GRE General Test or LSAT, official transcripts, 3 letters of recommendation, resume or curriculum vitae, statement of purpose. Additional exam requirements/recommendations for international students: Required—TOEFL (minimum score 600 paper-based; 96 iBT); Recommended—IELTS (minimum score 7). *Application deadline:* For fall admission, 5/1 for domestic students, 12/1 for international students; for spring admission, 11/1 for domestic and international students. Applications are processed on a rolling basis. Application fee: $55 ($65 for international students). Electronic applications accepted. *Financial support:* Fellowships with partial tuition reimbursements, research assistantships with partial tuition reimbursements, teaching assistantships with partial tuition reimbursements, career-related internships or fieldwork, Federal Work-Study, scholarships/grants, health care benefits, and unspecified assistantships available. Financial award application deadline: 2/1; financial award applicants required to submit FAFSA. *Faculty research:* Applied ecology, bio-geo chemistry, toxicology, wetlands ecology, environmental microbiology, forest ecology, environmental chemistry. *Unit head:* Jennifer J. Forney, Director, Graduate Student Services, 812-855-9485, Fax: 812-856-3665, E-mail: speampo@indiana.edu. *Application contact:* Audrey Whittaker, Admissions Assistant, 812-855-2840, Fax: 812-856-3665, E-mail: speaapps@indiana.edu.

Indiana University Bloomington, University Graduate School, College of Arts and Sciences, Department of Biology, Bloomington, IN 47405. Offers biology teaching (MAT); biotechnology (MA); evolution, ecology, and behavior (MA, PhD); genetics (PhD); microbiology (MA, PhD); molecular, cellular, and developmental biology (PhD); plant sciences (MA, PhD); zoology (MA, PhD). *Faculty:* 58 full-time (15 women), 21 part-time/adjunct (6 women). *Students:* 163 full-time (98 women), 7 part-time (2 women); includes 17 minority (3 Black or African American, non-Hispanic/Latino; 1 American Indian or Alaska Native, non-Hispanic/Latino; 7 Asian, non-Hispanic/Latino; 5 Hispanic/Latino; 1 Native Hawaiian or other Pacific Islander, non-Hispanic/Latino), 52 international. Average age 27. 346 applicants, 15% accepted, 24 enrolled. In 2010, 17 master's, 24 doctorates awarded. Terminal master's awarded for partial completion of doctoral program. *Degree requirements:* For master's, thesis, oral defense; for doctorate, thesis/dissertation, oral defense. *Entrance requirements:* For master's and doctorate, GRE General Test. Additional exam requirements/recommendations for international students: Required—TOEFL (minimum score 100 iBT). *Application deadline:* For fall admission, 1/5 priority date for domestic students, 12/1 priority date for international students. Application fee: $55 ($65 for international students). Electronic applications accepted. *Financial support:* In 2010–11, 170 students received support, including 64 fellowships with tuition reimbursements available (averaging $19,484 per year), 44 research assistantships with tuition reimbursements available (averaging $20,300 per year), 62 teaching assistantships with tuition reimbursements available (averaging $20,521 per year); scholarships/grants, traineeships, health care benefits, and unspecified assistantships also available. Financial award application deadline: 1/5. *Faculty research:* Evolution, ecology and behavior; microbiology; molecular biology and genetics; plant biology. *Unit head:* Dr. Roger Innes, Chair, 812-855-2219, Fax: 812-855-6082, E-mail: rinnes@indiana.edu. *Application contact:* Tracey D. Stohr, Graduate Student Recruitment Coordinator, 812-856-6303, Fax: 812-855-6082, E-mail: gradbio@indiana.edu.

Inter American University of Puerto Rico, Bayamón Campus, Graduate School, Bayamón, PR 00957. Offers biology (MS), including environmental sciences and ecology, molecular biotechnology; electronic commerce (MBA); human resources (MBA). Part-time and evening/weekend programs available. *Faculty:* 4 full-time (1 woman), 5 part-time/adjunct (4 women). *Students:* 115 part-time (84 women); includes 49 Hispanic/Latino. Average age 31. *Degree requirements:* For master's, comprehensive exam, research project. *Entrance requirements:* For master's, EXADEP, GRE General Test, letters of recommendation. *Application deadline:* For fall admission, 7/1 for domestic students, 5/1 priority date for international students; for winter admission, 11/15 priority date for domestic and international students; for spring admission, 2/15 priority date for domestic and international students. Application fee: $31. *Expenses:* Tuition: Full-time $4424; part-time $202 per credit. Required fees: $180 per trimester. *Unit head:* Prof. Juan F. Martinez, Chancellor, 787-279-1200 Ext. 2295, Fax: 787-279-2205, E-mail: jmartinez@bc.inter.edu. *Application contact:* Carlos Alicea, Director of Admission, 787-279-1200 Ext. 2017, Fax: 787-279-2205, E-mail: calicea@bc.inter.edu.

Iowa State University of Science and Technology, Graduate College, College of Liberal Arts and Sciences, Department of Ecology, Evolution, and Organismal Biology, Ames, IA 50011. Offers MS, PhD. *Faculty:* 31 full-time (9 women), 6 part-time/adjunct (4 women). *Students:* 49 full-time (23 women), 9 part-time (3 women); includes 1 American Indian or Alaska Native, non-Hispanic/Latino; 1 Asian, non-Hispanic/Latino; 1 Hispanic/Latino, 14 international. 8 applicants, 100% accepted, 5 enrolled. *Degree requirements:* For master's, thesis or alternative; for doctorate, thesis/dissertation. *Entrance requirements:* For master's and doctorate, GRE General Test. Additional exam requirements/recommendations for international students: Required—TOEFL. Application fee: $40 ($90 for international students). Electronic applications accepted. *Financial support:* In 2010–11, 28 research assistantships with partial tuition reimbursements (averaging $17,245 per year), 18 teaching assistantships with partial tuition reimbursements (averaging $14,619 per year) were awarded; fellowships, scholarships/grants, health care benefits, and unspecified assistantships also available. *Faculty*

Ecology

Iowa State University of Science and Technology (continued)

research: Aquatic and wetland ecology, cytology, ecology, physiology and molecular biology, systematics and evolution. *Unit head:* Dr. Jonathan Wendel, Chair, 515-294-7172. *Application contact:* Information Contact, 515-294-5836, Fax: 515-294-2592, E-mail: grad_admissions@iastate.edu.

Iowa State University of Science and Technology, Graduate College, Interdisciplinary Programs, Program in Ecology and Evolutionary Biology, Ames, IA 50011. Offers MS, PhD. *Students:* 55 full-time (25 women), 7 part-time (2 women); includes 1 American Indian or Alaska Native, non-Hispanic/Latino; 1 Asian, non-Hispanic/Latino; 1 Hispanic/Latino, 11 international. In 2010, 4 master's, 5 doctorates awarded. *Degree requirements:* For master's, thesis or alternative; for doctorate, thesis/dissertation. *Entrance requirements:* For master's and doctorate, GRE General Test, application to cooperating department. Additional exam requirements/recommendations for international students: Required—TOEFL (minimum score 550 paper-based; 79 iBT), IELTS (minimum score 6.5). *Application deadline:* For fall admission, 1/1 priority date for domestic and international students; for spring admission, 5/1 priority date for domestic and international students. Application fee: $40 ($90 for international students). Electronic applications accepted. *Financial support:* In 2010–11, 32 research assistantships with full and partial tuition reimbursements (averaging $17,573 per year), 17 teaching assistantships with full and partial tuition reimbursements (averaging $12,241 per year) were awarded; scholarships/grants, health care benefits, and unspecified assistantships also available. *Faculty research:* Landscape ecology, aquatic and method ecology, physiological ecology, population genetics and evolution, systematics. *Unit head:* Dr. Kirk Moloney, Supervisory Committee Chair, 515-294-6518, E-mail: eeboffice@iastate.edu. *Application contact:* Charles Sauer, Information Contact, 515-294-6518, E-mail: eeboffice@iastate.edu.

Kent State University, College of Arts and Sciences, Department of Biological Sciences, Program in Ecology, Kent, OH 44242-0001. Offers MS, PhD. *Degree requirements:* For master's, thesis; for doctorate, thesis/dissertation. *Entrance requirements:* For master's, GRE General Test, minimum GPA of 3.0; for doctorate, GRE General Test, minimum GPA of 3.25. Additional exam requirements/recommendations for international students: Required—TOEFL (minimum score 600 paper-based; 287 computer-based). Electronic applications accepted. *Expenses:* Tuition, state resident: full-time $7866; part-time $437 per credit hour. Tuition, nonresident: full-time $14,022; part-time $779 per credit hour.

Laurentian University, School of Graduate Studies and Research, Programme in Biology, Sudbury, ON P3E 2C6, Canada. Offers biology (M Sc); boreal ecology (PhD). Part-time programs available. *Degree requirements:* For master's, thesis. *Entrance requirements:* For master's, honors degree with second class or better. *Faculty research:* Recovery of acid-stressed lakes, effects of climate change, origin and maintenance of biocomplexity, radionuclide dynamics, cytogenetic studies of plants.

Lesley University, Graduate School of Arts and Social Sciences, Cambridge, MA 02138-2790. Offers clinical mental health counseling (MA), including expressive therapies counseling, holistic counseling, school and community counseling; counseling psychology (MA, CAGS), including professional counseling (MA), school counseling (MA); creative arts in learning (CAGS); creative writing (MFA); ecological teaching and learning (MS); environmental education (MS); expressive therapies (MA, PhD, CAGS), including art (MA), dance (MA), expressive therapies, music (MA); independent studies (CAGS); independent study (MA); intercultural relations (MA, CAGS); interdisciplinary studies (MA), including individualized studies, integrative holistic health, women's studies; urban environmental leadership (MA); visual arts (MFA). Part-time and evening/weekend programs available. Postbaccalaureate distance learning degree programs offered (minimal on-campus study). *Degree requirements:* For master's, internship, practicum, thesis (expressive therapies); for doctorate, thesis/dissertation, arts apprenticeship, field placement; for CAGS, thesis, internship (counseling psychology, expressive therapies). *Entrance requirements:* For master's, MAT (counseling psychology), interview, writing samples, art portfolio; for doctorate, GRE or MAT; for CAGS, interview, master's degree. Additional exam requirements/recommendations for international students: Required—TOEFL (minimum score 550 paper-based; 213 computer-based; 80 iBT). Electronic applications accepted. *Faculty research:* Psychotherapy and culture; psychotherapy and psychological trauma; women's issues in art, teaching and psychotherapy; community based art, psycho-spiritual inquiry.

Marquette University, Graduate School, College of Arts and Sciences, Department of Biology, Milwaukee, WI 53201-1881. Offers cell biology (MS, PhD); developmental biology (MS, PhD); ecology (MS, PhD); epithelial physiology (MS, PhD); genetics (MS, PhD); microbiology (MS, PhD); molecular biology (MS, PhD); muscle and exercise physiology (MS, PhD); neuroscience (PhD). *Faculty:* 25 full-time (12 women), 2 part-time/adjunct (1 woman). *Students:* 23 full-time (9 women), 12 part-time (8 women); includes 1 minority (Asian, non-Hispanic/Latino), 15 international. Average age 26. 82 applicants, 15% accepted, 5 enrolled. In 2010, 3 master's, 2 doctorates awarded. Terminal master's awarded for partial completion of doctoral program. *Degree requirements:* For master's, comprehensive exam, thesis, 1 year of teaching experience or equivalent; for doctorate, thesis/dissertation, 1 year of teaching experience or equivalent, qualifying exam. *Entrance requirements:* For master's and doctorate, GRE General Test, GRE Subject Test, official transcripts from all current and previous colleges/universities except Marquette, statement of professional goals and aspirations, three letters of recommendation. Additional exam requirements/recommendations for international students: Required—TOEFL (minimum score 530 paper-based; 78 computer-based). *Application deadline:* For fall admission, 12/15 for domestic and international students. Application fee: $50. Electronic applications accepted. *Expenses:* Tuition: Full-time $16,290; part-time $905 per credit hour. Tuition and fees vary according to program. *Financial support:* In 2010–11, 2 research assistantships, 34 teaching assistantships were awarded; fellowships, Federal Work-Study, institutionally sponsored loans, scholarships/grants, and tuition waivers (full and partial) also available. Support available to part-time students. Financial award application deadline: 2/15. *Faculty research:* Neurobiology, neuroendocrinology, epithelial physiology, neuropeptide interactions, synaptic transmission. Total annual research expenditures: $1.3 million. *Unit head:* Dr. Robert Fitts, Chair, 414-288-1748, Fax: 414-288-7357. *Application contact:* Debbie Weaver, Administrative Assistant, 414-288-7355, Fax: 414-288-7357.

Michigan State University, The Graduate School, College of Natural Science, Interdepartmental Program in Ecology, Evolutionary Biology and Behavior, East Lansing, MI 48824. Offers PhD. *Entrance requirements:* Additional exam requirements/recommendations for international students: Required—TOEFL. Electronic applications accepted.

Michigan Technological University, Graduate School, School of Forest Resources and Environmental Science, Program in Applied Ecology, Houghton, MI 49931. Offers MS. Part-time programs available. *Degree requirements:* For master's, thesis (for some programs). *Entrance requirements:* For master's, GRE. Additional exam requirements/recommendations for international students: Required—TOEFL (minimum score 550 paper-based; 213 computer-based). Electronic applications accepted.

Montana State University, College of Graduate Studies, College of Letters and Science, Department of Ecology, Bozeman, MT 59717. Offers ecological and environmental statistics (MS); ecology and environmental sciences (PhD); fish and wildlife biology (PhD); fish and wildlife management (MS). Part-time programs available. *Faculty:* 12 full-time (2 women), 2 part-time/adjunct (0 women). *Students:* 3 full-time (2 women), 46 part-time (16 women). Average age 31. 11 applicants, 27% accepted, 3 enrolled. In 2010, 3 master's, 1 doctorate awarded. *Degree requirements:* For master's, comprehensive exam, thesis (for some programs); for doctorate, comprehensive exam, thesis/dissertation. *Entrance requirements:* For master's and doctorate, GRE, minimum GPA of 3.0, letters of recommendation, essay. Additional exam requirements/recommendations for international students: Required—TOEFL (minimum score 550 paper-based; 213 computer-based). *Application deadline:* For fall admission, 7/15 priority date for domestic students, 5/15 priority date for international students; for spring admission, 12/1 priority date for domestic students, 10/1 priority date for international students. Applications are processed on a rolling basis. Application fee: $30. Electronic applications accepted. *Expenses:* Tuition, state resident: full-time $5554. Tuition, nonresident: full-time $14,646. Required fees: $1233. *Financial support:* In 2010–11, 46 students received support, including 1 fellowship with full and partial tuition reimbursement available (averaging $19,200 per year), 32 research assistantships with full and partial tuition reimbursements available (averaging $18,000 per year), 16 teaching assistantships with full tuition reimbursements available (averaging $10,862 per year); career-related internships or fieldwork, institutionally sponsored loans, scholarships/grants, traineeships, health care benefits, tuition waivers (partial), and unspecified assistantships also available. Support available to part-time students. Financial award application deadline: 3/1; financial award applicants required to submit FAFSA. *Faculty research:* Community ecology, population ecology, land-use effects, management and conservation, environmental modeling. Total annual research expenditures: $2.6 million. *Unit head:* Dr. David Roberts, Head, 406-994-4548, Fax: 406-994-3190, E-mail: droberts@montana.edu. *Application contact:* Dr. Carl A. Fox, Vice Provost for Graduate Education, 406-994-4145, Fax: 406-994-7433, E-mail: gradstudy@montana.edu.

Montclair State University, The Graduate School, College of Science and Mathematics, Department of Biology and Molecular Biology, Montclair, NJ 07043-1624. Offers biological science (Certificate); biology (MS), including biology, biology science/education, ecology and evolution, physiology; molecular biology (MS, Certificate). Part-time and evening/weekend programs available. *Faculty:* 22 full-time (9 women), 26 part-time/adjunct (13 women). *Students:* 30 full-time (20 women), 73 part-time (55 women); includes 5 Black or African American, non-Hispanic/Latino; 6 Asian, non-Hispanic/Latino; 25 Hispanic/Latino, 3 international. Average age 28. 48 applicants, 71% accepted, 24 enrolled. In 2010, 21 master's, 2 other advanced degrees awarded. *Degree requirements:* For master's, comprehensive exam, thesis or alternative. *Entrance requirements:* For master's, GRE General Test, 24 credits of course work in undergraduate biology, 2 letters of recommendation, teaching certificate (biology sciences education concentration). Additional exam requirements/recommendations for international students: Required—TOEFL (minimum iBT score of 83) or IELTS. *Application deadline:* For fall admission, 6/1 for international students; for spring admission, 10/1 for international students. Applications are processed on a rolling basis. Application fee: $60. Electronic applications accepted. *Expenses:* Tuition, state resident: part-time $501.34 per credit. Tuition, nonresident: part-time $773.88 per credit. Required fees: $71.15 per credit. *Financial support:* In 2010–11, 12 research assistantships with full tuition reimbursements (averaging $7,000 per year) were awarded; Federal Work-Study, scholarships/grants, and unspecified assistantships also available. Support available to part-time students. Financial award application deadline: 3/1; financial award applicants required to submit FAFSA. *Faculty research:* Cells, algae blooms, scallops, New Jersey bays, Barnegat Bay. Total annual research expenditures: $1.3 million. *Unit head:* Dr. Quinn Vega, Chairperson, 973-655-7178. *Application contact:* Amy Aiello, Director of Graduate Admissions and Operations, 973-655-5147, Fax: 973-655-7869, E-mail: graduate.school@montclair.edu.

North Dakota State University, College of Graduate and Interdisciplinary Studies, Interdisciplinary Program in Environmental and Conservation Sciences, Fargo, ND 58108. Offers MS, PhD. *Faculty:* 59. *Students:* 27 full-time (12 women), 9 part-time (3 women), 18 international. 12 applicants, 92% accepted, 9 enrolled. In 2010, 3 master's awarded. *Degree requirements:* For master's, comprehensive exam, thesis. *Entrance requirements:* Additional exam requirements/recommendations for international students: Required—TOEFL (minimum score 550 paper-based; 213 computer-based; 79 iBT). *Application deadline:* For fall admission, 5/1 for international students; for spring admission, 8/1 for international students. Application fee: $35. *Unit head:* Dr. Craig Stockwell, Director, 701-231-8449, Fax: 701-231-7149, E-mail: craig.stockwell@ndsu.edu. *Application contact:* Madonna Fitzgerald, Administrative Assistant, 701-231-6456, E-mail: madonna.fitzgerald@ndsu.edu.

Nova Scotia Agricultural College, Research and Graduate Studies, Truro, NS B2N 5E3, Canada. Offers agriculture (M Sc), including air quality, animal behavior, animal molecular genetics, animal nutrition, animal technology, aquaculture, botany, crop management, crop physiology, ecology, environmental microbiology, food science, horticulture, nutrient management, pest management, physiology, plant biotechnology, plant pathology, soil chemistry, soil fertility, waste management and composting, water quality. Program offered jointly with Dalhousie University. Part-time programs available. *Degree requirements:* For master's, thesis, ATC Exam Teaching Assistantship. *Entrance requirements:* For master's, honors B Sc, minimum GPA of 3.0. Additional exam requirements/recommendations for international students: Required—TOEFL (minimum score 580 paper-based; 237 computer-based; 92 iBT), IELTS, Michigan English Language Assessment Battery, CanTEST, CAEL. *Faculty research:* Bio-product development, organic agriculture, nutrient management, air and water quality, agricultural biotechnology.

The Ohio State University, Graduate School, College of Arts and Sciences, Division of Natural and Mathematical Sciences, Department of Evolution, Ecology, and Organismal Biology, Columbus, OH 43210. Offers MS, PhD. *Faculty:* 43. *Students:* 21 full-time (11 women), 40 part-time (21 women); includes 2 Black or African American, non-Hispanic/Latino, 9 international. Average age 29. In 2010, 9 master's, 4 doctorates awarded. *Degree requirements:* For master's, thesis optional; for doctorate, thesis/dissertation. *Entrance requirements:* For master's and doctorate, GRE General Test. Additional exam requirements/recommendations for international students: Required—TOEFL (minimum score 600 paper-based; 250 computer-based). *Application deadline:* For fall admission, 8/15 priority date for domestic students, 7/1 priority date for international students; for winter admission, 12/1 priority date for domestic students, 11/1 priority date for international students; for spring admission, 3/1 priority date for domestic students, 2/1 priority date for international students. Applications are processed on a rolling basis. Application fee: $40 ($50 for international students). Electronic applications accepted. *Expenses:* Tuition, state resident: full-time $10,605. Tuition, nonresident: full-time $26,535. Tuition and fees vary according to course load and program. *Financial support:* Fellowships, research assistantships, teaching assistantships, Federal Work-Study and institutionally sponsored loans available. Support available to part-time students. *Unit head:* Peter S. Curtis, Chair, 614-292-8280, Fax: 614-292-2030, E-mail: curtis.7@osu.edu. *Application contact:* 614-292-9444, Fax: 614-292-3895, E-mail: domestic.grad@osu.edu.

Ohio University, Graduate College, College of Arts and Sciences, Department of Biological Sciences, Athens, OH 45701-2979. Offers biological sciences (MS, PhD); cell biology and physiology (MS, PhD); ecology and evolutionary biology (MS, PhD); exercise physiology and muscle biology (MS, PhD); microbiology (MS, PhD); neuroscience (MS, PhD). *Students:* 32 full-time (9 women), 5 part-time (2 women); includes 2 minority (1 Black or African American, non-Hispanic/Latino; 1 Hispanic/Latino), 9 international. 51 applicants, 37% accepted, 7 enrolled. In 2010, 2 master's, 9 doctorates awarded. Terminal master's awarded for partial completion of doctoral program. *Degree requirements:* For master's, comprehensive exam, thesis, 1 quarter of teaching experience; for doctorate, comprehensive exam, thesis/dissertation, 2 quarters of teaching experience. *Entrance requirements:* For master's, GRE General Test, names of three faculty members whose research interests most closely match the applicant's interest; for doctorate, GRE General Test, essay concerning prior training, research interest and career goals, plus names of three faculty members whose research interests most closely match the applicant's interest. Additional exam requirements/recommendations for international students: Required—TOEFL (minimum score 620 paper-based; 105 iBT) or IELTS (minimum score 7.5). *Application deadline:* For fall admission, 1/15 for domestic and international students. Application fee: $50 ($55 for international students). Electronic applications accepted. *Financial support:* In 2010–11, 1 fellowship with full tuition reimbursement (averaging $18,957 per year), 10 research assistantships with full tuition reimbursements (averaging $18,957 per year), 42 teaching assistantships with full tuition reimbursements (averaging $18,957 per year) were awarded; Federal Work-Study and institutionally sponsored loans also available. Financial award application deadline: 1/15. *Faculty research:* Ecology and evolutionary biology, exercise physiology and muscle biology, neurobiology, cell biology, physiology. Total annual research expenditures: $2.8 million. *Unit head:* Dr. Ralph DiCaprio, Chair, 740-593-2290, Fax: 740-593-

0300, E-mail: dicaprir@ohio.edu. *Application contact:* Dr. Patrick Hassett, Graduate Chair, 740-593-4793, Fax: 740-593-0300, E-mail: hassett@ohio.edu.

Old Dominion University, College of Sciences, Program in Ecological Sciences, Norfolk, VA 23529. Offers PhD. *Faculty:* 13 full-time (3 women), 41 part-time/adjunct (7 women). *Students:* 10 full-time (5 women), 9 part-time (4 women), 3 international. Average age 31. 12 applicants, 25% accepted, 2 enrolled. In 2010, 4 doctorates awarded. *Degree requirements:* For doctorate, one foreign language, comprehensive exam, thesis/dissertation. *Entrance requirements:* For doctorate, GRE General Test, 3 letters of recommendation. Additional exam requirements/recommendations for international students: Required—TOEFL (minimum score 550 paper-based; 213 computer-based; 79 iBT). *Application deadline:* For fall admission, 2/1 priority date for domestic and international students. Applications are processed on a rolling basis. Application fee: $40. Electronic applications accepted. *Expenses:* Tuition, state resident: full-time $8592; part-time $358 per credit. Tuition, nonresident: full-time $21,672; part-time $903 per credit. Required fees: $119 per semester. One-time fee: $50. *Financial support:* In 2010–11, 3 fellowships with full tuition reimbursements (averaging $17,000 per year), 4 research assistantships with full tuition reimbursements (averaging $15,750 per year), 9 teaching assistantships with full tuition reimbursements (averaging $15,000 per year) were awarded; scholarships/grants also available. Financial award application deadline: 2/15; financial award applicants required to submit FAFSA. *Faculty research:* Marine ecology, physiological ecology, systematics and speciation, ecological and evolutionary processes, molecular genetics. Total annual research expenditures: $2 million. *Unit head:* Dr. Ian Bartol, Graduate Program Director, 757-683-4737, Fax: 757-683-5283, E-mail: ecolgpd@odu.edu. *Application contact:* Dr. Ian Bartol, Graduate Program Director, 757-683-4737, Fax: 757-683-5283, E-mail: ecolgpd@odu.edu.

Penn State University Park, Graduate School, Intercollege Graduate Programs, Intercollege Graduate Program in Ecology, State College, University Park, PA 16802-1503. Offers MS, PhD. *Unit head:* Dr. David Eissenstat, Chair, 814-863-3371, Fax: 814-865-9451. *Application contact:* Dr. David Eissenstat, Chair, 814-863-3371, Fax: 814-865-9451.

Princeton University, Graduate School, Department of Ecology and Evolutionary Biology, Princeton, NJ 08544-1019. Offers PhD. *Degree requirements:* For doctorate, thesis/dissertation. *Entrance requirements:* For doctorate, GRE General Test, GRE Subject Test. Additional exam requirements/recommendations for international students: Required—TOEFL (minimum score 600 paper-based; 250 computer-based). Electronic applications accepted.

Purdue University, Graduate School, College of Science, Department of Biological Sciences, West Lafayette, IN 47907. Offers biochemistry (PhD); biophysics (PhD); cell and developmental biology (PhD); ecology, evolutionary and population biology (MS, PhD), including ecology, evolutionary biology, population biology; genetics (MS, PhD); microbiology (MS, PhD); molecular biology (PhD); neurobiology (MS, PhD); plant physiology (PhD). Terminal master's awarded for partial completion of doctoral program. *Degree requirements:* For master's, thesis (for some programs); for doctorate, thesis/dissertation, seminars, teaching experience. *Entrance requirements:* For master's and doctorate, GRE General Test. Additional exam requirements/recommendations for international students: Required—TOEFL. Electronic applications accepted.

Rice University, Graduate Programs, Wiess School of Natural Sciences, Department of Ecology and Evolutionary Biology, Houston, TX 77251-1892. Offers MA, MS, PhD. Terminal master's awarded for partial completion of doctoral program. *Degree requirements:* For master's, comprehensive exam (for some programs), thesis (for some programs); for doctorate, comprehensive exam, thesis/dissertation. *Entrance requirements:* For master's and doctorate, GRE General Test, GRE Subject Test. Additional exam requirements/recommendations for international students: Required—TOEFL (minimum score 600 paper-based; 250 computer-based; 90 iBT). Electronic applications accepted. *Faculty research:* Trace gas emissions, wetlands, biology, community ecology of forests and grasslands, conservation biology specialization.

Rutgers, The State University of New Jersey, New Brunswick, Graduate School-New Brunswick, Program in Ecology and Evolution, Piscataway, NJ 08854-8097. Offers MS, PhD. Part-time programs available. Terminal master's awarded for partial completion of doctoral program. *Degree requirements:* For master's, comprehensive exam; for doctorate, comprehensive exam, thesis/dissertation. *Entrance requirements:* For master's and doctorate, GRE General Test, minimum GPA of 3.0. Additional exam requirements/recommendations for international students: Required—TOEFL (minimum score 550 paper-based; 213 computer-based). Electronic applications accepted. *Expenses:* Tuition, state resident: full-time $7200; part-time $600 per credit. Tuition, nonresident: full-time $11,124; part-time $927 per credit. *Faculty research:* Population and community ecology, population genetics, evolutionary biology, conservation biology, ecosystem ecology.

San Diego State University, Graduate and Research Affairs, College of Sciences, Department of Biology, Program in Ecology, San Diego, CA 92182. Offers MS, PhD. PhD offered jointly with University of California, Davis. *Degree requirements:* For master's, thesis; for doctorate, thesis/dissertation. *Entrance requirements:* For master's, GRE General Test, resumé or curriculum vitae, 2 letters of recommendation; for doctorate, GRE General Test, GRE Subject Test, resume or curriculum vitae, 3 letters of recommendation. Electronic applications accepted. *Faculty research:* Conservation and restoration ecology, coastal and marine ecology, global change and ecosystem ecology.

San Francisco State University, Division of Graduate Studies, College of Science and Engineering, Department of Biology, Program in Ecology and Systematic Biology, San Francisco, CA 94132-1722. Offers MS. *Application deadline:* Applications are processed on a rolling basis. *Unit head:* Dr. Robert Patterson, Program Coordinator, 415-338-1237, E-mail: patters@sfsu.edu. *Application contact:* Dr. Robert Patterson, Graduate Coordinator, 415-338-1100, E-mail: patters@sfsu.edu.

San Jose State University, Graduate Studies and Research, College of Science, Department of Biological Sciences, San Jose, CA 95192-0001. Offers biological sciences (MA, MS); molecular biology and microbiology (MS); organismal biology, conservation and ecology (MS); physiology (MS). Part-time programs available. *Entrance requirements:* For master's, GRE. Electronic applications accepted. *Faculty research:* Systemic physiology, molecular genetics, SEM studies, toxicology, large mammal ecology.

State University of New York College of Environmental Science and Forestry, Department of Environmental and Forest Biology, Syracuse, NY 13210-2779. Offers applied ecology (MPS); chemical ecology (MPS, MS, PhD); conservation biology (MPS, MS, PhD); ecology (MPS, MS, PhD); entomology (MPS, MS, PhD); environmental interpretation (MPS, MS, PhD); environmental physiology (MPS, MS, PhD); fish and wildlife biology and management (MPS, MS, PhD); forest pathology and mycology (MPS, MS, PhD); plant biotechnology (MPS); plant science and biotechnology (MPS, MS, PhD). *Degree requirements:* For master's, thesis (for some programs); for doctorate, comprehensive exam, thesis/dissertation. *Entrance requirements:* For master's and doctorate, GRE General Test, GRE Subject Test, minimum GPA of 3.0. Additional exam requirements/recommendations for international students: Required—TOEFL (minimum score 550 paper-based; 213 computer-based; 80 iBT), IELTS (minimum score 6). *Expenses:* Tuition, state resident: full-time $8370; part-time $349 per credit hour. Tuition, nonresident: full-time $13,780. Required fees: $30.30 per credit hour. $20 per year. *Faculty research:* Ecology, fish and wildlife biology and management, plant science, entomology.

State University of New York College of Environmental Science and Forestry, Department of Forest and Natural Resources Management, Syracuse, NY 13210-2779. Offers ecology and ecosystems (MPS, MS, PhD); economics, governance and human dimensions (MPS, MS, PhD); environmental and natural resource policy (PhD); forest resources management (MF); monitoring, analysis and modeling (MPS, MS, PhD); natural resources management (MPS, MS, PhD). *Accreditation:* SAF. *Degree requirements:* For master's, thesis (for some programs); for doctorate, comprehensive exam, thesis/dissertation. *Entrance requirements:* For master's and doctorate, GRE General Test, minimum GPA of 3.0. Additional exam requirements/recommendations for international students: Required—TOEFL (minimum score 550 paper-based; 213 computer-based; 80 iBT), IELTS (minimum score 6). *Expenses:* Tuition, state resident: full-time $8370; part-time $349 per credit hour. Tuition, nonresident: full-time $13,780. Required fees: $30.30 per credit hour. $20 per year. *Faculty research:* Silviculture recreation management, tree improvement, operations management, economics.

Stony Brook University, State University of New York, Graduate School, College of Arts and Sciences, Department of Ecology and Evolution, Stony Brook, NY 11794. Offers applied ecology (MA); ecology and evolution (PhD). *Faculty:* 17 full-time (5 women). *Students:* 46 full-time (23 women); includes 3 Asian, non-Hispanic/Latino; 4 Hispanic/Latino, 6 international. Average age 28. 90 applicants, 38% accepted, 10 enrolled. In 2010, 6 doctorates awarded. *Degree requirements:* For doctorate, one foreign language, comprehensive exam, thesis/dissertation, teaching experience. *Entrance requirements:* For doctorate, GRE General Test, GRE Subject Test. Additional exam requirements/recommendations for international students: Required—TOEFL. *Application deadline:* For fall admission, 1/15 for domestic students. Application fee: $100. *Expenses:* Tuition, state resident: full-time $8370; part-time $349 per credit. Tuition, nonresident: full-time $13,780; part-time $574 per credit. Required fees: $994. *Financial support:* In 2010–11, 9 research assistantships, 29 teaching assistantships were awarded; fellowships, Federal Work-Study also available. *Faculty research:* Theoretical and experimental population genetics, numerical taxonomy, biostatistics, population and community ecology, plant ecology. Total annual research expenditures: $1.4 million. *Unit head:* Dr. Jessica Gurevitch, Chair, 631-632-8600. *Application contact:* Dr. Dan Dykhuizen, Director, 631-246-8604, E-mail: dandyk@life.bio.sunysb.edu.

Tulane University, School of Science and Engineering, Department of Ecology and Evolutionary Biology, New Orleans, LA 70118-5669. Offers MS, PhD. Terminal master's awarded for partial completion of doctoral program. *Degree requirements:* For master's, thesis or alternative; for doctorate, thesis/dissertation. *Entrance requirements:* For master's, GRE General Test, minimum B average in undergraduate course work; for doctorate, GRE General Test. Additional exam requirements/recommendations for international students: Required—TOEFL. Electronic applications accepted. *Faculty research:* Ichthyology, plant systematics, crustacean endocrinology, ecotoxicology, ornithology.

Universidad Nacional Pedro Henriquez Urena, Graduate School, Santo Domingo, Dominican Republic. Offers agricultural diversity (MS), including horticultural/fruit production, tropical animal production; conservation of monuments and cultural assets (M Arch); ecology and environment (MS); environmental engineering (MEE); international relations (MA); natural resource management (MS); political science (MA); project optimization (MPM); project feasibility (MPM); project management (MPM); sanitation engineering (ME); science for teachers (MS); tropical Caribbean architecture (M Arch).

University at Albany, State University of New York, College of Arts and Sciences, Department of Biological Sciences, Specialization in Ecology, Evolution, and Behavior, Albany, NY 12222-0001. Offers MS, PhD. *Degree requirements:* For master's, one foreign language; for doctorate, one foreign language, thesis/dissertation. *Entrance requirements:* For master's and doctorate, GRE General Test.

University at Buffalo, the State University of New York, Graduate School, College of Arts and Sciences, Program in Evolution, Ecology and Behavior, Buffalo, NY 14260. Offers MS, PhD, Certificate. *Faculty:* 13 full-time (3 women). *Students:* 14 full-time (8 women); includes 1 Black or African American, non-Hispanic/Latino, 1 international. Average age 25. 23 applicants, 35% accepted, 3 enrolled. In 2010, 3 master's, 1 doctorate awarded. Terminal master's awarded for partial completion of doctoral program. *Degree requirements:* For master's, project; for doctorate, comprehensive exam, thesis/dissertation. *Entrance requirements:* For master's, GRE, minimum undergraduate GPA of 3.0; for doctorate, GRE, minimum GPA of 3.0. Additional exam requirements/recommendations for international students: Required—TOEFL (minimum score 79 iBT). *Application deadline:* For fall admission, 1/15 priority date for domestic and international students. Applications are processed on a rolling basis. Application fee: $75. Electronic applications accepted. *Financial support:* In 2010–11, 2 fellowships with full tuition reimbursements (averaging $6,000 per year), 4 research assistantships with full tuition reimbursements (averaging $20,000 per year), 3 teaching assistantships with full tuition reimbursements (averaging $17,000 per year) were awarded; Federal Work-Study, scholarships/grants, health care benefits, and unspecified assistantships also available. Financial award application deadline: 1/15; financial award applicants required to submit FAFSA. *Faculty research:* Coral reef ecology, evolution and ecology of aquatic invertebrates, animal communication, paleobiology, primate behavior. *Unit head:* Dr. Howard Lasker, Program Director, 716-645-4870, Fax: 716-645-3999, E-mail: ub-evb@buffalo.edu. *Application contact:* Marty Roth, Secretary, 716-645-3489, Fax: 716-345-3999, E-mail: mlroth@buffalo.edu.

University of Alberta, Faculty of Graduate Studies and Research, Department of Biological Sciences, Edmonton, AB T6G 2E1, Canada. Offers environmental biology and ecology (M Sc, PhD); microbiology and biotechnology (M Sc, PhD); molecular biology and genetics (M Sc, PhD); physiology and cell biology (M Sc, PhD); plant biology (M Sc, PhD); systematics and evolution (M Sc, PhD). Terminal master's awarded for partial completion of doctoral program. *Degree requirements:* For master's, thesis; for doctorate, thesis/dissertation. *Entrance requirements:* Additional exam requirements/recommendations for international students: Required—TOEFL.

The University of Arizona, College of Science, Department of Ecology and Evolutionary Biology, Tucson, AZ 85721. Offers MS, PhD. *Faculty:* 19 full-time (5 women), 2 part-time/adjunct (0 women). *Students:* 30 full-time (10 women), 19 part-time (10 women); includes 1 American Indian or Alaska Native, non-Hispanic/Latino; 1 Hispanic/Latino; 2 Two or more races, non-Hispanic/Latino, 11 international. Average age 29. 87 applicants, 15% accepted, 9 enrolled. In 2010, 3 master's, 5 doctorates awarded. Terminal master's awarded for partial completion of doctoral program. *Degree requirements:* For master's, thesis optional; for doctorate, one foreign language, comprehensive exam, thesis/dissertation. *Entrance requirements:* For master's, GRE General Test, GRE Subject Test, statement of purpose, curriculum vitae, 3 letters of recommendation; for doctorate, GRE General Test, GRE Subject Test, curriculum vitae, 3 letters of recommendation. Additional exam requirements/recommendations for international students: Required—TOEFL (minimum score 550 paper-based; 213 computer-based; 79 iBT). *Application deadline:* For fall admission, 12/1 for domestic students, 12/8 for international students. Application fee: $75. *Expenses:* Tuition, state resident: full-time $7692. *Financial support:* In 2010–11, 8 research assistantships with full tuition reimbursements (averaging $21,303 per year), 38 teaching assistantships with full tuition reimbursements (averaging $21,555 per year) were awarded; career-related internships or fieldwork, scholarships/grants, health care benefits, and unspecified assistantships also available. *Faculty research:* Biological diversity, evolutionary history, evolutionary mechanisms, community structure. Total annual research expenditures: $4.5 million. *Unit head:* Dr. Richard E. Michod, Head, 520-621-7509, Fax: 520-621-9190, E-mail: michod@email.arizona.edu. *Application contact:* Carol Burleson, Administrative Associate, 520-621-1165, Fax: 520-621-9190, E-mail: burleson@email.arizona.edu.

University of California, Davis, Graduate Studies, Graduate Group in Ecology, Davis, CA 95616. Offers MS, PhD. PhD offered jointly with San Diego State University. *Degree requirements:* For master's, comprehensive exam (for some programs), thesis (for some programs); for doctorate, thesis/dissertation. *Entrance requirements:* For master's and doctorate, GRE General Test. Additional exam requirements/recommendations for international students: Required—TOEFL (minimum score 550 paper-based; 213 computer-based). Electronic applications accepted. *Faculty research:* Agricultural conservation, physiological restoration, environmental policy, ecotoxicology.

University of California, Irvine, School of Biological Sciences, Department of Ecology and Evolutionary Biology, Irvine, CA 92697. Offers biological sciences (MS, PhD). *Students:* 45 full-time (30 women); includes 6 minority (2 Asian, non-Hispanic/Latino; 4 Hispanic/Latino), 7

Ecology

University of California, Irvine (continued)
international. Average age 28. 69 applicants, 23% accepted, 6 enrolled. In 2010, 9 doctorates awarded. *Degree requirements:* For master's, thesis; for doctorate, thesis/dissertation. *Entrance requirements:* For master's and doctorate, GRE General Test, GRE Subject Test, minimum GPA of 3.0. Additional exam requirements/recommendations for international students: Required—TOEFL (minimum score 550 paper-based; 213 computer-based). *Application deadline:* For fall admission, 1/15 priority date for domestic students, 1/15 for international students. Applications are processed on a rolling basis. Application fee: $80 ($100 for international students). Electronic applications accepted. *Financial support:* Fellowships, research assistantships with full tuition reimbursements, teaching assistantships, career-related internships or fieldwork, institutionally sponsored loans, traineeships, health care benefits, and unspecified assistantships available. Financial award application deadline: 3/1; financial award applicants required to submit FAFSA. *Faculty research:* Ecological energetics, quantitative genetics, life history evolution, plant-herbivore and plant-pollinator interactions, molecular evolution. *Unit head:* Prof. Brandon Gaut, Chair, 949-824-2564, Fax: 949-824-2181, E-mail: bgaut@uci.edu. *Application contact:* Pam McDonald, Student Affairs Officer, 949-824-4743, Fax: 949-824-2181, E-mail: pmcdonal@uci.edu.

University of California, Los Angeles, Graduate Division, College of Letters and Science, Department of Ecology and Evolutionary Biology, Los Angeles, CA 90095. Offers MA, PhD. *Faculty:* 25 full-time (6 women). *Students:* 65 full-time (46 women); includes 14 minority (1 Black or African American, non-Hispanic/Latino; 5 Asian, non-Hispanic/Latino; 7 Hispanic/Latino; 1 Two or more races, non-Hispanic/Latino), 8 international. Average age 29. 89 applicants, 21% accepted, 13 enrolled. In 2010, 5 master's, 13 doctorates awarded. Terminal master's awarded for partial completion of doctoral program. *Degree requirements:* For master's, comprehensive exam or thesis; for doctorate, thesis/dissertation, oral and written qualifying exams; teaching experience. *Entrance requirements:* For master's and doctorate, GRE General Test, GRE Subject Test (biology), minimum GPA of 3.0, 3 letters of recommendation. *Application deadline:* For fall admission, 12/1 for domestic and international students. Application fee: $70 ($90 for international students). Electronic applications accepted. *Financial support:* In 2010–11, 56 fellowships with full and partial tuition reimbursements, 25 research assistantships with full and partial tuition reimbursements, 43 teaching assistantships with full and partial tuition reimbursements were awarded; Federal Work-Study, institutionally sponsored loans, scholarships/grants, health care benefits, tuition waivers (full and partial), and unspecified assistantships also available. Financial award application deadline: 3/1; financial award applicants required to submit FAFSA. *Faculty research:* Molecular, cell, and developmental biology; interactive biology; organisms and populations. *Unit head:* Dr. Daniel T. Blumstein, Chair, 310-267-4746, Fax: 310-206-3987, E-mail: marmots@ucla.edu. *Application contact:* Jocelyn Yamadera, Student Affairs Officer, 310-825-1959, Fax: 310-206-5280, E-mail: jocelyny@lifesci.ucla.edu.

University of California, Riverside, Graduate Division, Department of Entomology, Riverside, CA 92521-0102. Offers entomology (MS, PhD); evolution and ecology (PhD). Part-time programs available. *Faculty:* 27 full-time (4 women). *Students:* 39 full-time (20 women); includes 1 Black or African American, non-Hispanic/Latino; 3 Asian, non-Hispanic/Latino; 2 Hispanic/Latino, 8 international. Average age 29. 27 applicants, 44% accepted, 11 enrolled. In 2010, 5 master's, 7 doctorates awarded. Terminal master's awarded for partial completion of doctoral program. *Degree requirements:* For master's, thesis; for doctorate, thesis/dissertation, qualifying exams. *Entrance requirements:* For master's and doctorate, GRE General Test, minimum GPA of 3.2. Additional exam requirements/recommendations for international students: Required—Either IELTS or TOEFL (paper-based 550, computer-based 213, iBT 80). *Application deadline:* For fall admission, 5/1 for domestic students, 2/1 for international students; for winter admission, 9/1 for domestic students, 7/1 for international students; for spring admission, 12/1 for domestic students, 10/1 for international students. Applications are processed on a rolling basis. Application fee: $80 ($100 for international students). Electronic applications accepted. *Financial support:* In 2010–11, fellowships with tuition reimbursements (averaging $15,000 per year), research assistantships with tuition reimbursements (averaging $18,000 per year), teaching assistantships with tuition reimbursements (averaging $16,640 per year) were awarded; career-related internships or fieldwork, Federal Work-Study, institutionally sponsored loans, and tuition waivers (full and partial) also available. Financial award application deadline: 1/5; financial award applicants required to submit FAFSA. *Faculty research:* Agricultural, urban, medical, and veterinary entomology; biological control; chemical ecology; insect pathogens; novel toxicants. *Unit head:* Dr. Richard Redak, Chair, 951-827-7250, Fax: 951-827-3086, E-mail: richard.redak@ucr.edu. *Application contact:* Melissa L. Gomez, Graduate Student Affairs Officer, 800-735-0717, Fax: 951-827-5913, E-mail: insects@ucr.edu.

University of California, San Diego, Office of Graduate Studies, Division of Biological Sciences, Program in Ecology, Behavior, and Evolution, La Jolla, CA 92093. Offers PhD. *Degree requirements:* For doctorate, thesis/dissertation, qualifying exam. Electronic applications accepted.

University of California, Santa Barbara, Graduate Division, College of Letters and Sciences, Division of Mathematics, Life, and Physical Sciences, Department of Ecology, Evolution, and Marine Biology, Santa Barbara, CA 93106-9620. Offers computational science and engineering (MA); computational sciences and engineering (PhD); ecology, evolution, and marine biology (MA, PhD); MA/PhD. *Faculty:* 27 full-time (7 women). *Students:* 59 full-time (38 women); includes 2 Black or African American, non-Hispanic/Latino; 5 Asian, non-Hispanic/Latino; 2 Hispanic/Latino. Average age 29. 119 applicants, 11% accepted, 8 enrolled. In 2010, 5 master's, 3 doctorates awarded. *Degree requirements:* For master's, comprehensive exam (for some programs), thesis (for some programs); for doctorate, comprehensive exam, thesis/dissertation. *Entrance requirements:* For master's and doctorate, GRE General Test. Additional exam requirements/recommendations for international students: Required—TOEFL (minimum score 550 paper-based; 80 iBT), IELTS. *Application deadline:* For fall admission, 12/15 for domestic and international students. Application fee: $70 ($90 for international students). Electronic applications accepted. *Financial support:* In 2010–11, 54 students received support, including 35 fellowships with full and partial tuition reimbursements available (averaging $10,812 per year), 21 research assistantships with full and partial tuition reimbursements available (averaging $8,441 per year), 43 teaching assistantships with partial tuition reimbursements available (averaging $9,346 per year); Federal Work-Study, scholarships/grants, traineeships, health care benefits, and tuition waivers (full and partial) also available. Financial award application deadline: 12/15; financial award applicants required to submit FAFSA. *Faculty research:* Community ecology, evolution, marine biology, population genetics, stream ecology. *Unit head:* Dr. Cheryl Briggs, Chair, 805-893-2415, Fax: 805-893-5885. *Application contact:* Melanie Fujii, Staff Graduate Advisor, 805-893-2979, Fax: 805-893-5885, E-mail: eemb-info@lifesci.ucsb.edu.

University of California, Santa Cruz, Division of Graduate Studies, Division of Physical and Biological Sciences, Department of Ecology and Evolutionary Biology, Santa Cruz, CA 95064. Offers MA, PhD. *Students:* 61 full-time (44 women), 1 part-time (0 women); includes 12 minority (2 Black or African American, non-Hispanic/Latino; 1 American Indian or Alaska Native, non-Hispanic/Latino; 1 Asian, non-Hispanic/Latino; 5 Hispanic/Latino; 1 Native Hawaiian or other Pacific Islander, non-Hispanic/Latino; 2 Two or more races, non-Hispanic/Latino), 2 international. Average age 29. 159 applicants, 12% accepted, 15 enrolled. In 2010, 3 master's, 11 doctorates awarded. *Degree requirements:* For master's, thesis; for doctorate, comprehensive exam, thesis/dissertation. *Entrance requirements:* For master's and doctorate, GRE General Test, GRE Subject Test, 3 letters of recommendation. Additional exam requirements/recommendations for international students: Required—TOEFL (minimum score 550 paper-based; 220 computer-based; 83 iBT); Recommended—IELTS (minimum score 8). *Application deadline:* For fall admission, 12/15 for domestic and international students. Application fee: $70 ($90 for international students). Electronic applications accepted. *Financial support:* Fellowships, research assistantships, teaching assistantships, institutionally sponsored loans and tuition waivers available. Financial award applicants required to submit FAFSA. *Faculty research:* Population and community ecology, evolutionary biology, physiology and behavior (marine and terrestrial), systematics and biodiversity. *Unit head:* Debbie Inferrera, Graduate Program Coordinator, 831-459-2193, E-mail: deborain@ucsc.edu. *Application contact:* Debbie Inferrera, Graduate Program Coordinator, 831-459-2193, E-mail: deborain@ucsc.edu.

University of Chicago, Division of Biological Sciences, Darwinian Sciences Cluster: Ecological, Integrative and Evolutionary Biology, Department of Ecology and Evolution, Chicago, IL 60637-1513. Offers PhD. *Degree requirements:* For doctorate, thesis/dissertation, ethics class, 2 teaching assistantships. *Entrance requirements:* For doctorate, GRE General Test. Additional exam requirements/recommendations for international students: Required—TOEFL (minimum score 600 paper-based; 250 computer-based; 104 iBT), IELTS (minimum score 7). Electronic applications accepted. *Faculty research:* Population genetics, molecular evolution, behavior.

University of Colorado Boulder, Graduate School, College of Arts and Sciences, Department of Ecology and Evolutionary Biology, Boulder, CO 80309. Offers animal behavior (MA); biology (MA, PhD); environmental biology (MA, PhD); evolutionary biology (MA, PhD); neurobiology (MA); population biology (MA); population genetics (PhD). *Faculty:* 32 full-time (10 women). *Students:* 71 full-time (36 women), 17 part-time (11 women); includes 10 minority (1 American Indian or Alaska Native, non-Hispanic/Latino; 2 Asian, non-Hispanic/Latino; 7 Hispanic/Latino), 4 international. Average age 30. 176 applicants, 20 enrolled. In 2010, 11 master's, 8 doctorates awarded. Terminal master's awarded for partial completion of doctoral program. *Degree requirements:* For master's, comprehensive exam, thesis or alternative; for doctorate, comprehensive exam, thesis/dissertation. *Entrance requirements:* For master's, GRE General Test, GRE Subject Test, minimum undergraduate GPA of 3.0; for doctorate, GRE General Test, GRE Subject Test. *Application deadline:* For fall admission, 12/30 priority date for domestic students, 12/1 for international students. Application fee: $50 ($60 for international students). *Financial support:* In 2010–11, 25 fellowships (averaging $17,876 per year), 27 research assistantships (averaging $15,070 per year) were awarded; Federal Work-Study, institutionally sponsored loans, and tuition waivers (full) also available. *Faculty research:* Behavior, ecology, genetics, morphology, endocrinology, physiology, systematics. Total annual research expenditures: $3.5 million.

University of Colorado Denver, College of Liberal Arts and Sciences, Department of Geography and Environmental Sciences, Denver, CO 80217. Offers environmental sciences (MS), including air quality, ecosystems, environmental health, environmental science education, environmental sciences, geo-spatial analysis, hazardous waste, water quality. Part-time and evening/weekend programs available. *Students:* 48 full-time (28 women), 4 part-time (3 women); includes 2 Black or African American, non-Hispanic/Latino; 2 Asian, non-Hispanic/Latino; 3 Hispanic/Latino, 8 international. Average age 29. 44 applicants, 52% accepted, 14 enrolled. In 2010, 17 master's awarded. *Degree requirements:* For master's, thesis or alternative. *Entrance requirements:* For master's, GRE General Test, BA in one of the natural/physical sciences or engineering (or equivalent background); prerequisite coursework in calculus and physics (one semester each), general chemistry with lab and general biology with lab (two semesters each). Additional exam requirements/recommendations for international students: Required—TOEFL (minimum score 525 paper-based; 197 computer-based). *Application deadline:* For fall admission, 4/1 for domestic students; for spring admission, 10/1 for domestic students. Application fee: $50 ($75 for international students). Electronic applications accepted. *Expenses:* Tuition, state resident: full-time $7332; part-time $355 per credit hour. Tuition, nonresident: full-time $18,990; part-time $1055 per credit hour. Required fees: $998. Tuition and fees vary according to course level, course load, degree level, campus/location, program, reciprocity agreements and student level. *Financial support:* Research assistantships, teaching assistantships, Federal Work-Study available. Financial award application deadline: 4/1; financial award applicants required to submit FAFSA. *Faculty research:* Air quality, environmental health, ecosystems, hazardous waste, water quality, geo-spatial analysis and environmental science education. *Unit head:* Dr. John Wyckoff, Director, 303-556-2590, Fax: 303-556-6197, E-mail: john.wyckoff@cudenver.edu. *Application contact:* Dr. John Wyckoff, Director, 303-556-2590, Fax: 303-556-6197, E-mail: john.wyckoff@cudenver.edu.

University of Connecticut, Graduate School, College of Liberal Arts and Sciences, Department of Ecology and Evolutionary Biology, Storrs, CT 06269. Offers botany (MS, PhD); ecology (MS, PhD); entomology (MS, PhD); zoology (MS, PhD). Terminal master's awarded for partial completion of doctoral program. *Degree requirements:* For master's, comprehensive exam; for doctorate, thesis/dissertation. *Entrance requirements:* For master's and doctorate, GRE General Test, GRE Subject Test. Additional exam requirements/recommendations for international students: Required—TOEFL (minimum score 550 paper-based; 213 computer-based). Electronic applications accepted.

University of Connecticut, Graduate School, College of Liberal Arts and Sciences, Department of Psychology, Storrs, CT 06269. Offers behavioral neuroscience (PhD); biopsychology (PhD); clinical psychology (MA, PhD); cognition and instruction (PhD); developmental psychology (MA, PhD); ecological psychology (PhD); experimental psychology (PhD); general psychology (MA, PhD); health psychology (Graduate Certificate); industrial/organizational psychology (PhD); language and cognition (PhD); neuroscience (PhD); occupational health psychology (Graduate Certificate); social psychology (MA, PhD). *Accreditation:* APA. Terminal master's awarded for partial completion of doctoral program. *Degree requirements:* For master's, comprehensive exam; for doctorate, thesis/dissertation. *Entrance requirements:* For master's and doctorate, GRE General Test, GRE Subject Test. Additional exam requirements/recommendations for international students: Required—TOEFL (minimum score 550 paper-based; 213 computer-based). Electronic applications accepted.

University of Delaware, College of Agriculture and Natural Resources, Department of Entomology and Wildlife Ecology, Newark, DE 19716. Offers entomology and applied ecology (MS, PhD), including avian ecology, evolution and taxonomy, insect biological control, insect ecology and behavior (MS), insect genetics, pest management, plant-insect interactions, wildlife ecology and management. Part-time programs available. *Degree requirements:* For master's, comprehensive exam, thesis, oral exam, seminar; for doctorate, comprehensive exam, thesis/dissertation, qualifying exam, seminar. *Entrance requirements:* For master's, GRE General Test, minimum GPA of 3.0 in field, 2.8 overall; for doctorate, GRE General Test, GRE Subject Test (biology), minimum GPA of 3.0 in field, 2.8 overall. Additional exam requirements/recommendations for international students: Required—TOEFL. Electronic applications accepted. *Faculty research:* Ecology and evolution of plant-insect interactions, ecology of wildlife conservation management, habitat restoration, biological control, applied ecosystem management.

University of Delaware, College of Arts and Sciences, Department of Biological Sciences, Newark, DE 19716. Offers biotechnology (MS); cancer biology (MS, PhD); cell and extracellular matrix biology (MS, PhD); cell and systems physiology (MS, PhD); developmental biology (MS, PhD); ecology and evolution (MS, PhD); microbiology (MS, PhD); molecular biology and genetics (MS, PhD). Terminal master's awarded for partial completion of doctoral program. *Degree requirements:* For master's, thesis, preliminary exam; for doctorate, comprehensive exam, thesis/dissertation, preliminary exam. *Entrance requirements:* For master's and doctorate, GRE General Test. Additional exam requirements/recommendations for international students: Required—TOEFL (minimum score 600 paper-based; 250 computer-based); Recommended—TWE. Electronic applications accepted. *Faculty research:* Microorganisms, bone, cancer metastasis, developmental biology, cell biology, DNA.

University of Florida, Graduate School, College of Agricultural and Life Sciences, Department of Wildlife Ecology and Conservation, Gainesville, FL 32611. Offers MS, PhD. *Faculty:* 16 full-time (4 women), 1 part-time/adjunct (0 women). *Students:* 36 full-time (19 women), 9 part-time (4 women); includes 1 Black or African American, non-Hispanic/Latino; 1 Asian, non-Hispanic/Latino; 3 Hispanic/Latino, 11 international. Average age 31. 50 applicants, 8% accepted, 4 enrolled. In 2010, 11 master's, 7 doctorates awarded. *Degree requirements:* For master's, comprehensive exam, thesis optional; for doctorate, comprehensive exam, thesis/dissertation. *Entrance requirements:* For master's and doctorate, GRE General Test, minimum GPA of 3.3. Additional exam requirements/recommendations for international students:

Required—TOEFL (minimum score 550 paper-based; 213 computer-based; 80 iBT), IELTS (minimum score 6). *Application deadline:* For fall admission, 6/1 priority date for domestic students; for spring admission, 12/1 for domestic students. Applications are processed on a rolling basis. Application fee: $30. Electronic applications accepted. *Expenses:* Tuition, state resident: full-time $10,916. Tuition, nonresident: full-time $28,309. *Financial support:* In 2010–11, 33 students received support, including 8 fellowships, 16 research assistantships (averaging $21,203 per year), 9 teaching assistantships (averaging $21,685 per year); institutionally sponsored loans also available. Financial award applicants required to submit FAFSA. *Faculty research:* Wildlife biology and management, tropical ecology and conservation, conservation biology, landscape ecology and restoration, conservation education. *Unit head:* Dr. John P. Hayes, Department Chair, 352-846-0552, E-mail: hayesj@ufl.edu. *Application contact:* Dr. Wiley Kitchens, Graduate Coordinator, 352-846-0536, Fax: 352-846-0841, E-mail: wiley01@ufl.edu.

University of Florida, Graduate School, School of Natural Resources and Environment, Gainesville, FL 32611. Offers interdisciplinary ecology (MS, PhD). *Students:* 101 full-time (55 women), 29 part-time (15 women); includes 2 Black or African American, non-Hispanic/Latino; 1 American Indian or Alaska Native, non-Hispanic/Latino; 4 Asian, non-Hispanic/Latino; 7 Hispanic/Latino, 38 international. 65 applicants, 34% accepted, 18 enrolled. In 2010, 12 master's, 11 doctorates awarded. *Degree requirements:* For master's, comprehensive exam, thesis; for doctorate, comprehensive exam, thesis/dissertation. *Entrance requirements:* For master's and doctorate, GRE General Test, minimum GPA of 3.0. Additional exam requirements/recommendations for international students: Required—TOEFL (minimum score 550 paper-based; 213 computer-based; 80 iBT), IELTS (minimum score 6). *Application deadline:* For fall admission, 2/1 priority date for domestic students, 2/1 for international students. Applications are processed on a rolling basis. Application fee: $30. Electronic applications accepted. *Expenses:* Tuition, state resident: full-time $10,916. Tuition, nonresident: full-time $28,309. *Financial support:* In 2010–11, 96 students received support, including 27 fellowships, 50 research assistantships (averaging $12,679 per year), 19 teaching assistantships (averaging $17,101 per year). Financial award applicants required to submit FAFSA. *Faculty research:* Natural sciences, social sciences, sustainability studies, research design and methods. *Unit head:* Dr. Stephen R. Humphrey, Director and Graduate Coordinator, 352-392-9230, Fax: 352-392-9748, E-mail: humphrey@ufl.edu. *Application contact:* Dr. Stephen R. Humphrey, Director and Graduate Coordinator, 352-392-9230, Fax: 352-392-9748, E-mail: humphrey@ufl.edu.

University of Georgia, School of Ecology, Athens, GA 30602. Offers conservation ecology and sustainable development (MS); ecology (MS, PhD). *Faculty:* 19 full-time (5 women), 4 part-time/adjunct (1 woman). *Students:* 62 full-time (35 women), 19 part-time (10 women); includes 1 Black or African American, non-Hispanic/Latino; 4 Hispanic/Latino; 1 Two or more races, non-Hispanic/Latino, 3 international. 93 applicants, 24% accepted, 14 enrolled. In 2010, 4 master's, 9 doctorates awarded. *Degree requirements:* For master's, thesis; for doctorate, one foreign language, thesis/dissertation. *Entrance requirements:* For master's and doctorate, GRE General Test. *Application deadline:* For fall admission, 7/1 priority date for domestic students; for spring admission, 11/15 for domestic students. Application fee: $50. Electronic applications accepted. *Expenses:* Tuition, state resident: full-time $7200; part-time $344 per credit hour. Tuition, nonresident: full-time $21,900; part-time $944 per credit hour. Tuition and fees vary according to course load and program. *Financial support:* Fellowships, research assistantships, teaching assistantships, unspecified assistantships available. *Unit head:* Dr. John L. Gittleman, Dean, 706-542-2968, Fax: 706-542-4819, E-mail: ecohead@uga.edu. *Application contact:* Dr. James Byers, Graduate Coordinator, 706-338-0012, Fax: 706-542-4819, E-mail: jebyers@uga.edu.

University of Guelph, Graduate Studies, College of Biological Science, Department of Integrative Biology, Botany and Zoology, Guelph, ON N1G 2W1, Canada. Offers botany (M Sc, PhD); zoology (M Sc, PhD). Part-time programs available. *Degree requirements:* For master's, thesis, research proposal; for doctorate, thesis/dissertation, research proposal, qualifying exam. *Entrance requirements:* For master's, minimum B average during previous 2 years of course work. Additional exam requirements/recommendations for international students: Required—TOEFL (minimum score 550 paper-based; 213 computer-based), IELTS (minimum score 6.5). Electronic applications accepted. *Faculty research:* Aquatic science, environmental physiology, parasitology, wildlife biology, management.

University of Hawaii at Manoa, Graduate Division, Interdisciplinary Specialization in Ecology, Evolution and Conservation Biology, Honolulu, HI 96822. Offers MS, PhD. *Faculty:* 6 part-time/adjunct (1 woman). *Degree requirements:* For doctorate, thesis/dissertation. *Application deadline:* For fall admission, 2/1 for domestic students; for spring admission, 10/15 for domestic students. Application fee: $50. *Financial support:* Fellowships, research assistantships, teaching assistantships, career-related internships or fieldwork and tuition waivers (full) available. *Faculty research:* Agronomy and soil science, zoology, entomology, genetics and molecular biology, botanical sciences. *Unit head:* Robert H. Cowie, Chair, 808-956-4909, Fax: 808-956-2647, E-mail: cowie@hawaii.edu. *Application contact:* Robert H. Cowie, Chair, 808-956-4909, Fax: 808-956-2647, E-mail: cowie@hawaii.edu.

University of Illinois at Urbana–Champaign, Graduate College, College of Liberal Arts and Sciences, School of Integrative Biology, Department of Animal Biology, Champaign, IL 61820. Offers animal biology (ecology, ethology and evolution) (MS, PhD). *Faculty:* 9 full-time (5 women). *Students:* 14 full-time (10 women), 3 part-time (1 woman); includes 1 minority (Two or more races, non-Hispanic/Latino), 3 international. 11 applicants, 27% accepted, 1 enrolled. *Entrance requirements:* For master's and doctorate, GRE. Additional exam requirements/recommendations for international students: Required—TOEFL (minimum score 570 paper-based; 230 computer-based; 88 iBT). *Application deadline:* Applications are processed on a rolling basis. Application fee: $75 ($90 for international students). Electronic applications accepted. *Financial support:* In 2010–11, 2 fellowships, 8 research assistantships, 13 teaching assistantships were awarded; tuition waivers (full and partial) also available. *Unit head:* Ken Paige, Head, 217-244-6606, Fax: 217-244-4565, E-mail: k-paige@illinois.edu. *Application contact:* Lisa Smith, Office Administrator, 217-333-7802, Fax: 217-244-4565, E-mail: ljsmith1@illinois.edu.

University of Illinois at Urbana–Champaign, Graduate College, College of Liberal Arts and Sciences, School of Integrative Biology, Program in Ecology, Evolution and Conservation Biology, Champaign, IL 61820. Offers MS, PhD. *Students:* 25 full-time (14 women), 10 part-time (8 women); includes 1 Black or African American, non-Hispanic/Latino; 2 Asian, non-Hispanic/Latino; 1 Hispanic/Latino, 2 international. 40 applicants, 23% accepted, 6 enrolled. In 2010, 1 master's, 4 doctorates awarded. *Entrance requirements:* For master's and doctorate, GRE. Additional exam requirements/recommendations for international students: Required—TOEFL (minimum score 613 paper-based; 257 computer-based; 103 iBT). *Application deadline:* Applications are processed on a rolling basis. Application fee: $75 ($90 for international students). Electronic applications accepted. *Financial support:* In 2010–11, 8 fellowships, 16 research assistantships, 15 teaching assistantships were awarded; tuition waivers (full and partial) also available. *Unit head:* Carla E. Caceres, Director, 217-244-2139, Fax: 217-244-1224, E-mail: cecacere@illinois.edu. *Application contact:* Carol Hall, Secretary, 217-333-8208, Fax: 217-244-1224, E-mail: cahall@illinois.edu.

The University of Kansas, Graduate Studies, College of Liberal Arts and Sciences, Department of Ecology and Evolutionary Biology, Lawrence, KS 66045. Offers botany (MA, PhD); ecology and evolutionary biology (MA, PhD); entomology (MA, PhD). *Faculty:* 13 full-time (6 women), 29 part-time/adjunct (7 women). *Students:* 62 full-time (30 women); includes 1 minority (Hispanic/Latino), 16 international. Average age 29. 52 applicants, 42% accepted, 14 enrolled. In 2010, 9 master's, 8 doctorates awarded. Terminal master's awarded for partial completion of doctoral program. *Degree requirements:* For master's, comprehensive exam, thesis (for some programs), 30-36 credits, thesis presentation; for doctorate, comprehensive exam, thesis/dissertation, residency, responsible scholarship and research skills, final exam, dissertation defense. *Entrance requirements:* For master's, GRE General Test, bachelor's degree with minimum undergraduate GPA of 3.0; for doctorate, GRE General Test, bachelor's degree; minimum undergraduate/graduate GPA of 3.0. Additional exam requirements/recommendations for international students: Required—TOEFL, IELTS, Score requirements in EEB are the same as those set by Graduate Studies. *Application deadline:* For fall admission, 12/15 for domestic and international students; for spring admission, 9/15 for domestic and international students. Application fee: $55 ($65 for international students). Electronic applications accepted. *Expenses:* Tuition, state resident: full-time $7092; part-time $295.50 per credit hour. Tuition, nonresident: full-time $16,590; part-time $691.25 per credit hour. Required fees: $858; $71.49 per credit hour. Tuition and fees vary according to course load, campus/location and program. *Financial support:* Fellowships with tuition reimbursements, research assistantships with full and partial tuition reimbursements, teaching assistantships with full and partial tuition reimbursements, scholarships/grants, traineeships, health care benefits, and unspecified assistantships available. Financial award application deadline: 12/15. *Faculty research:* Biodiversity and macroevolution, ecology and global change, evolutionary mechanisms. *Unit head:* Dr. Christopher H. Haufler, Chair, 785-864-3255, Fax: 785-864-5860, E-mail: vulgare@ku.edu. *Application contact:* Jaime Rochelle Keeler, Graduate Coordinator, 785-864-2362, Fax: 785-864-5860, E-mail: jrkeeler@ku.edu.

University of Maine, Graduate School, College of Natural Sciences, Forestry, and Agriculture, Department of Biological Sciences, Program in Ecology and Environmental Science, Orono, ME 04469. Offers water resources (PhD). Part-time programs available. *Students:* 41 full-time (30 women), 11 part-time (6 women), 1 international. Average age 31. 84 applicants, 20% accepted, 15 enrolled. In 2010, 11 master's, 4 doctorates awarded. *Degree requirements:* For doctorate, thesis/dissertation. *Entrance requirements:* For master's and doctorate, GRE General Test. Additional exam requirements/recommendations for international students: Required—TOEFL. *Application deadline:* For fall admission, 2/1 priority date for domestic students. Applications are processed on a rolling basis. Application fee: $65. Electronic applications accepted. *Expenses:* Tuition, state resident: full-time $400. Tuition, nonresident: full-time $1050. *Financial support:* Career-related internships or fieldwork, Federal Work-Study, institutionally sponsored loans, and tuition waivers (full) available. Financial award application deadline: 3/1. *Unit head:* Dr. Chris Cronan, Coordinator, 207-581-3235. *Application contact:* Scott G. Delcourt, Associate Dean of the Graduate School, 207-581-3291, Fax: 207-581-3232, E-mail: graduate@maine.edu.

University of Maine, Graduate School, College of Natural Sciences, Forestry, and Agriculture, Department of Plant, Soil, and Environmental Sciences, Orono, ME 04469. Offers biological sciences (PhD); ecology and environmental sciences (MS, PhD); forest resources (PhD); horticulture (MS); plant science (PhD); plant, soil, and environmental sciences (MS); resource utilization (MS). *Faculty:* 9 full-time (3 women), 7 part-time/adjunct (3 women). *Students:* 6 full-time (2 women), 2 part-time (1 woman), 2 international. Average age 31. 9 applicants, 22% accepted, 0 enrolled. In 2010, 2 master's awarded. *Entrance requirements:* For master's and doctorate, GRE General Test. Additional exam requirements/recommendations for international students: Required—TOEFL. *Application deadline:* Applications are processed on a rolling basis. Application fee: $65. Electronic applications accepted. *Expenses:* Tuition, state resident: full-time $400. Tuition, nonresident: full-time $1050. *Financial support:* In 2010–11, 16 research assistantships with tuition reimbursements (averaging $16,260 per year), 3 teaching assistantships with tuition reimbursements (averaging $12,790 per year) were awarded; scholarships/grants, tuition waivers (full and partial), and unspecified assistantships also available. *Unit head:* Dr. Gregory Porter, Chair, 207-581-2943, Fax: 207-581-3207. *Application contact:* Scott G. Delcourt, Associate Dean of the Graduate School, 207-581-3291, Fax: 207-581-3232, E-mail: graduate@maine.edu.

The University of Manchester, Faculty of Life Sciences, Manchester, United Kingdom. Offers adaptive organismal biology (M Phil, PhD); animal biology (M Phil, PhD); biochemistry (M Phil, PhD); bioinformatics (M Phil, PhD); biomolecular sciences (M Phil, PhD); biotechnology (M Phil, PhD); cell biology (M Phil, PhD); cell matrix research (M Phil, PhD); channels and transporters (M Phil, PhD); developmental biology (M Phil, PhD); Egyptology (M Phil, PhD); environmental biology (M Phil, PhD); evolutionary biology (M Phil, PhD); gene expression (M Phil, PhD); genetics (M Phil, PhD); history of science, technology and medicine (M Phil, PhD); immunology (M Phil, PhD); integrative neurobiology and behavior (M Phil, PhD); membrane trafficking (M Phil, PhD); microbiology (M Phil, PhD); molecular and cellular neuroscience (M Phil, PhD); molecular biology (M Phil, PhD); molecular cancer studies (M Phil, PhD); neuroscience (M Phil, PhD); ophthalmology (M Phil, PhD); optometry (M Phil, PhD); organelle function (M Phil, PhD); pharmacology (M Phil, PhD); physiology (M Phil, PhD); plant sciences (M Phil, PhD); stem cell research (M Phil, PhD); structural biology (M Phil, PhD); systems neuroscience (M Phil, PhD); toxicology (M Phil, PhD).

University of Manitoba, Faculty of Graduate Studies, Faculty of Science, Department of Biological Sciences, Winnipeg, MB R3T 2N2, Canada. Offers botany (M Sc, PhD); ecology (M Sc, PhD); zoology (M Sc, PhD).

University of Maryland, College Park, Academic Affairs, College of Computer, Mathematical and Natural Sciences, Department of Biology, Behavior, Ecology, Evolution, and Systematics Program, College Park, MD 20742. Offers MS, PhD. *Students:* 24 full-time (15 women), 2 part-time (0 women); includes 3 minority (2 Asian, non-Hispanic/Latino; 1 Two or more races, non-Hispanic/Latino), 2 international. In 2010, 1 master's, 8 doctorates awarded. *Degree requirements:* For master's, thesis, oral defense, seminar; for doctorate, thesis/dissertation, exam, 4 seminars. *Entrance requirements:* For master's and doctorate, GRE General Test, GRE Subject Test (biology), 3 letters of recommendation. Additional exam requirements/recommendations for international students: Required—TOEFL. *Application deadline:* Applications are processed on a rolling basis. Application fee: $75. Electronic applications accepted. *Expenses:* Tuition, state resident: part-time $471 per credit hour. Tuition, nonresident: part-time $1016 per credit hour. Required fees: $337 per term. *Financial support:* In 2010–11, 4 fellowships with full and partial tuition reimbursements (averaging $20,932 per year), 3 research assistantships (averaging $19,727 per year), 12 teaching assistantships (averaging $19,483 per year) were awarded; Federal Work-Study and scholarships/grants also available. Support available to part-time students. Financial award applicants required to submit FAFSA. *Faculty research:* Animal behavior, biostatistics, ecology, evolution, neurothology. *Unit head:* Dr. Michele Dudash, Director, 301-405-1642, Fax: 301-314-9358, E-mail: mdudash@umd.edu. *Application contact:* Dr. Michele Dudash, Director, 301-405-1642, Fax: 301-314-9358, E-mail: mdudash@umd.edu.

University of Massachusetts Amherst, Graduate School, Interdisciplinary Programs, Program in Organismic and Evolutionary Biology, Amherst, MA 01003. Offers animal behavior (PhD); ecology (PhD); evolutionary biology (PhD); organismal biology (PhD); organismic and evolutionary biology (MS). Part-time programs available. *Students:* 30 full-time (16 women), 3 part-time (all women); includes 4 minority (3 Hispanic/Latino; 1 Native Hawaiian or other Pacific Islander, non-Hispanic/Latino), 6 international. Average age 29. 51 applicants, 33% accepted, 6 enrolled. In 2010, 2 master's, 5 doctorates awarded. Terminal master's awarded for partial completion of doctoral program. *Degree requirements:* For master's, thesis or alternative; for doctorate, comprehensive exam, thesis/dissertation. *Entrance requirements:* For master's and doctorate, GRE General Test, 3 letters of recommendation. Additional exam requirements/recommendations for international students: Required—TOEFL (minimum score 550 paper-based; 213 computer-based; 80 iBT), IELTS (minimum score 6.5). *Application deadline:* For fall admission, 12/1 for domestic and international students. Applications are processed on a rolling basis. Application fee: $50 ($65 for international students). Electronic applications accepted. *Expenses:* Tuition, state resident: full-time $2640. Required fees: $8282. One-time fee: $357 full-time. *Financial support:* In 2010–11, 4 fellowships (averaging $2,657 per year), 2 teaching assistantships with full tuition reimbursements (averaging $7,607 per year) were awarded; research assistantships, career-related internships or fieldwork, Federal Work-Study, scholarships/grants, traineeships, health care benefits, tuition waivers (full), and unspecified assistantships also available. Support available to part-time students. Financial award application deadline: 12/1; financial award applicants required to submit FAFSA. *Unit*

Ecology

University of Massachusetts Amherst (continued)

head: Dr. Elizabeth M. Jakob, Graduate Program Director, 413-545-0928, Fax: 413-545-3243. *Application contact:* Jean M. Ames, Supervisor of Admissions, 413-545-0722, Fax: 413-577-0010, E-mail: gradadm@grad.umass.edu.

University of Michigan, Rackham Graduate School, College of Literature, Science, and the Arts, Department of Ecology and Evolutionary Biology, Ann Arbor, MI 48109. Offers ecology and evolutionary biology (MS, PhD); ecology and evolutionary biology-Frontiers (MS). Part-time programs available. Terminal master's awarded for partial completion of doctoral program. *Degree requirements:* For master's, thesis (for some programs), two seminars; for doctorate, comprehensive exam, thesis/dissertation, 2 semesters of teaching. *Entrance requirements:* For master's and doctorate, GRE. Additional exam requirements/recommendations for international students: Required—TOEFL (minimum score 560 paper-based; 220 computer-based; 84 iBT). Electronic applications accepted. *Expenses:* Tuition, state resident: full-time $17,784; part-time $1116 per credit hour. Tuition, nonresident: full-time $35,944; part-time $2125 per credit hour. International tuition: $35,994 full-time. Required fees: $95 per semester. Tuition and fees vary according to course load, degree level and program. *Faculty research:* Community ecology, molecular evolution, theoretical ecology, systematics, evolutionary genetics.

University of Michigan, School of Natural Resources and Environment, Program in Natural Resources and Environment, Ann Arbor, MI 48109. Offers aquatic sciences: research and management (MS); behavior, education and communication (MS); conservation biology (MS); conservation ecology (MS); environmental informatics (MS); environmental justice (MS); environmental policy and planning (MS); natural resources and environment (PhD); sustainable systems (MS); terrestrial ecosystems (MS); MS/AM; MS/JD; MS/MBA. *Faculty:* 42 full-time, 23 part-time/adjunct. *Students:* 450 full-time (254 women); includes 7 Black or African American, non-Hispanic/Latino; 2 American Indian or Alaska Native, non-Hispanic/Latino; 35 Asian, non-Hispanic/Latino; 13 Hispanic/Latino; 6 Two or more races, non-Hispanic/Latino, 50 international. Average age 27. 692 applicants. In 2010, 133 master's, 11 doctorates awarded. Terminal master's awarded for partial completion of doctoral program. *Degree requirements:* For master's, practicum or group project; for doctorate, comprehensive exam, thesis/dissertation, oral defense of dissertation, preliminary exam. *Entrance requirements:* For master's, GRE General Test; for doctorate, GRE General Test, master's degree. Additional exam requirements/recommendations for international students: Required—TOEFL (minimum score 560 paper-based; 220 computer-based; 84 iBT). *Application deadline:* For fall admission, 1/5 priority date for domestic and international students. Applications are processed on a rolling basis. Application fee: $65 ($75 for international students). Electronic applications accepted. *Expenses:* Tuition, state resident: full-time $17,784; part-time $1116 per credit hour. Tuition, nonresident: full-time $35,944; part-time $2125 per credit hour. International tuition: $35,994 full-time. Required fees: $95 per semester. Tuition and fees vary according to course load, degree level and program. *Financial support:* Fellowships with tuition reimbursements, research assistantships with tuition reimbursements, teaching assistantships with tuition reimbursements, career-related internships or fieldwork, Federal Work-Study, institutionally sponsored loans, scholarships/grants, health care benefits, and unspecified assistantships available. Support available to part-time students. Financial award application deadline: 1/5; financial award applicants required to submit FAFSA. *Faculty research:* Stream ecology, plant-insect interactions, fish biology, resource control and reproductive success, remote sensing, conservation ecology. *Application contact:* Graduate Admissions Team, 734-764-6453, Fax: 734-936-2195, E-mail: snre.admissions@umich.edu.

University of Minnesota, Twin Cities Campus, Graduate School, College of Biological Sciences, Department of Ecology, Evolution, and Behavior, St. Paul, MN 55418. Offers MS, PhD. Terminal master's awarded for partial completion of doctoral program. *Degree requirements:* For master's, comprehensive exam, thesis or projects; for doctorate, comprehensive exam, thesis/dissertation. *Entrance requirements:* For master's and doctorate, GRE General Test, minimum GPA of 3.0. Additional exam requirements/recommendations for international students: Required—TOEFL (minimum score 550 paper-based; 79 iBT), Michigan English Language Assessment Battery. Electronic applications accepted. *Faculty research:* Behavioral ecology, community ecology, community genetics, ecosystem and global change, evolution and systematics.

University of Missouri, Graduate School, College of Arts and Sciences, Division of Biological Sciences, Program in Evolutionary Biology and Ecology, Columbia, MO 65211. Offers MA, PhD.

University of Missouri–St. Louis, College of Arts and Sciences, Department of Biology, St. Louis, MO 63121. Offers biotechnology (Certificate); cell and molecular biology (MS, PhD); ecology, evolution and systematics (MS, PhD); tropical biology and conservation (Certificate). Part-time programs available. *Faculty:* 43 full-time (13 women), 2 part-time/adjunct (1 woman). *Students:* 73 full-time (36 women), 63 part-time (36 women); includes 17 minority (6 Black or African American, non-Hispanic/Latino; 9 Asian, non-Hispanic/Latino; 2 Hispanic/Latino), 45 international. Average age 29. 193 applicants, 44% accepted, 44 enrolled. In 2010, 35 master's, 11 doctorates, 6 other advanced degrees awarded. *Degree requirements:* For master's, thesis or alternative; for doctorate, thesis/dissertation, 1 semester of teaching experience. *Entrance requirements:* For master's, 3 letters of recommendation; for doctorate, GRE General Test, 3 letters of recommendation. Additional exam requirements/recommendations for international students: Required—TOEFL. *Application deadline:* For fall admission, 12/1 priority date for domestic and international students; for spring admission, 10/15 priority date for domestic and international students. Applications are processed on a rolling basis. Application fee: $35 ($40 for international students). Electronic applications accepted. *Expenses:* Tuition, state resident: full-time $5522; part-time $306.80 per credit hour. Tuition, nonresident: full-time $14,253; part-time $792.10 per credit hour. Required fees: $658; $49 per credit hour. One-time fee: $12. Tuition and fees vary according to program. *Financial support:* In 2010–11, 30 research assistantships with full and partial tuition reimbursements (averaging $18,113 per year), 15 teaching assistantships with full and partial tuition reimbursements (averaging $17,514 per year) were awarded; fellowships with full tuition reimbursements, career-related internships or fieldwork and Federal Work-Study also available. Support available to part-time students. Financial award application deadline: 2/1. *Faculty research:* Molecular biology, microbial genetics, animal behavior, tropical ecology, plant systematics. *Unit head:* Dr. Peter Stevens, Director of Graduate Studies, 314-516-6200, Fax: 314-516-6233, E-mail: stevensp@umsl.edu. *Application contact:* 314-516-5458, Fax: 314-516-6996, E-mail: gradadm@umsl.edu.

The University of Montana, Graduate School, College of Arts and Sciences, Division of Biological Sciences, Program in Ecology of Infectious Disease, Missoula, MT 59812-0002. Offers PhD.

The University of Montana, Graduate School, College of Arts and Sciences, Division of Biological Sciences, Program in Organismal Biology and Ecology, Missoula, MT 59812-0002. Offers MS, PhD. Terminal master's awarded for partial completion of doctoral program. *Degree requirements:* For master's, one foreign language, thesis; for doctorate, 2 foreign languages, thesis/dissertation. *Entrance requirements:* For master's and doctorate, GRE General Test. *Faculty research:* Conservation biology, ecology and behavior, evolutionary genetics, avian biology.

University of Nevada, Reno, Graduate School, Interdisciplinary Program in Ecology, Evolution, and Conservation Biology, Reno, NV 89557. Offers PhD. Offered through the College of Arts and Science, the M. C. Fleischmann College of Agriculture, and the Desert Research Institute. *Degree requirements:* For doctorate, thesis/dissertation. *Entrance requirements:* For doctorate, GRE General Test, GRE Subject Test, minimum GPA of 3.0. Additional exam requirements/recommendations for international students: Required—TOEFL (minimum score 500 paper-based; 173 computer-based; 61 iBT), IELTS (minimum score 6). Electronic applications accepted. *Expenses:* Tuition, state resident: full-time $2219; part-time $246 per credit. Tuition, nonresident: part-time $510 per credit. International tuition: $9009 full-time. Required fees: $59 per term. One-time fee: $101. Tuition and fees vary according to course load. *Faculty research:* Population biology, behavioral ecology, plant response to climate change, conservation of endangered species, restoration of natural ecosystems.

University of New Haven, Graduate School, College of Arts and Sciences, Program in Environmental Sciences, West Haven, CT 06516-1916. Offers environmental ecology (Certificate); environmental geoscience (MS); environmental health and management (MS); environmental science (MS); geographical information systems (Certificate). Part-time and evening/weekend programs available. *Students:* 13 full-time (5 women), 24 part-time (10 women); includes 2 Black or African American, non-Hispanic/Latino; 1 American Indian or Alaska Native, non-Hispanic/Latino; 1 Asian, non-Hispanic/Latino; 1 Hispanic/Latino, 4 international. Average age 27. 29 applicants, 100% accepted, 14 enrolled. In 2010, 13 master's, 1 other advanced degree awarded. *Degree requirements:* For master's, thesis or alternative. *Application deadline:* For fall admission, 5/31 for international students; for winter admission, 10/15 for international students; for spring admission, 1/15 for international students. Applications are processed on a rolling basis. Application fee: $50. Electronic applications accepted. *Financial support:* Research assistantships with partial tuition reimbursements, teaching assistantships with partial tuition reimbursements, career-related internships or fieldwork, Federal Work-Study, scholarships/grants, tuition waivers, and unspecified assistantships available. Support available to part-time students. Financial award applicants required to submit FAFSA. *Faculty research:* Mapping and assessing geological and living resources in Long Island Sound, geology, San Salvador Island, Bahamas. *Unit head:* Dr. Roman Zajac, Coordinator, 203-932-7108. *Application contact:* Eloise Gormley, Director of Graduate Admissions, 203-932-7449, Fax: 203-932-7137, E-mail: gradinfo@newhaven.edu.

The University of North Carolina at Chapel Hill, Graduate School, College of Arts and Sciences, Curriculum in Ecology, Chapel Hill, NC 27599. Offers MA, MS, PhD. *Degree requirements:* For master's, comprehensive exam, thesis (for some programs), oral defense of thesis; for doctorate, comprehensive exam, thesis/dissertation, oral exams, oral defense of dissertation. *Entrance requirements:* For master's and doctorate, GRE General Test. Additional exam requirements/recommendations for international students: Required—TOEFL (minimum score 550 paper-based; 213 computer-based). Electronic applications accepted. *Faculty research:* Community and population ecology and ecosystems, human ecology, landscape ecology, conservation ecology, marine ecology.

The University of North Carolina at Chapel Hill, Graduate School, College of Arts and Sciences, Department of Biology, Chapel Hill, NC 27599. Offers botany (MA, MS, PhD); cell biology, development, and physiology (MA, MS, PhD); cell motility and cytoskeleton (PhD); ecology and behavior (MA, MS, PhD); genetics and molecular biology (MA, MS, PhD); morphology, systematics, and evolution (MA, MS, PhD). Terminal master's awarded for partial completion of doctoral program. *Degree requirements:* For master's, comprehensive exam, thesis (for some programs); for doctorate, comprehensive exam, thesis/dissertation. *Entrance requirements:* For master's, GRE General Test, GRE Subject Test, 2 semesters of calculus or statistics; 2 semesters of physics, organic chemistry; 3 semesters of biology; for doctorate, GRE General Test, GRE Subject Test, 2 semesters calculus or statistics, 2 semesters physics, organic chemistry, 3 semesters of biology. Additional exam requirements/recommendations for international students: Required—TOEFL (minimum score 550 paper-based; 213 computer-based). Electronic applications accepted. *Faculty research:* Gene expression, biomechanics, yeast genetics, plant ecology, plant molecular biology.

University of North Dakota, Graduate School, College of Arts and Sciences, Department of Biology, Grand Forks, ND 58202. Offers botany (MS, PhD); ecology (MS, PhD); entomology (MS, PhD); environmental biology (MS, PhD); fisheries/wildlife (MS, PhD); genetics (MS, PhD); zoology (MS, PhD). *Faculty:* 17 full-time (5 women), 6 part-time/adjunct (1 woman). *Students:* 19 full-time (6 women), 8 part-time (2 women); includes 4 minority (3 American Indian or Alaska Native, non-Hispanic/Latino; 1 Asian, non-Hispanic/Latino), 1 international. Average age 28. 21 applicants, 33% accepted, 4 enrolled. In 2010, 1 master's awarded. Terminal master's awarded for partial completion of doctoral program. *Degree requirements:* For master's, thesis, final exam; for doctorate, comprehensive exam, thesis/dissertation, final exam. *Entrance requirements:* For master's, GRE General Test, GRE Subject Test, minimum GPA of 3.0; for doctorate, GRE General Test, GRE Subject Test, minimum GPA of 3.5. Additional exam requirements/recommendations for international students: Required—TOEFL (minimum score 550 paper-based; 213 computer-based; 79 iBT), IELTS (minimum score 6.5). *Application deadline:* For fall admission, 2/15 for domestic and international students; for spring admission, 10/15 for domestic and international students. Application fee: $35. Electronic applications accepted. *Expenses:* Tuition, state resident: full-time $5857; part-time $306.74 per credit. Tuition, nonresident: full-time $15,666; part-time $729.77 per credit. Required fees: $53.42 per credit. Tuition and fees vary according to course load, program and reciprocity agreements. *Financial support:* In 2010–11, 22 students received support, including 5 research assistantships with full and partial tuition reimbursements available (averaging $11,375 per year), 17 teaching assistantships with full and partial tuition reimbursements available (averaging $10,813 per year); fellowships with full and partial tuition reimbursements available, Federal Work-Study, institutionally sponsored loans, scholarships/grants, health care benefits, tuition waivers (full and partial), and unspecified assistantships also available. Support available to part-time students. Financial award application deadline: 3/15; financial award applicants required to submit FAFSA. *Faculty research:* Population biology, wildlife ecology, RNA processing, hormonal control of behavior. Total annual research expenditures: $736,510. *Unit head:* Dr. Brett Goodwin, Graduate Director, 701-777-2621, Fax: 701-777-2623, E-mail: brett.goodwin@mail.und.edu. *Application contact:* Matthew Anderson, Admissions Specialist, 701-777-2947, Fax: 701-777-3619, E-mail: matthew.anderson@gradschool.und.edu.

University of Notre Dame, Graduate School, College of Science, Department of Biological Sciences, Notre Dame, IN 46556. Offers aquatic ecology, evolution and environmental biology (MS, PhD); cellular and molecular biology (MS, PhD); genetics (MS, PhD); physiology (MS, PhD); vector biology and parasitology (MS, PhD). Terminal master's awarded for partial completion of doctoral program. *Degree requirements:* For master's, comprehensive exam, thesis; for doctorate, comprehensive exam, thesis/dissertation, candidacy exam. *Entrance requirements:* For master's and doctorate, GRE General Test. Additional exam requirements/recommendations for international students: Required—TOEFL (minimum score 600 paper-based; 250 computer-based; 80 iBT). Electronic applications accepted. *Faculty research:* Tropical disease, molecular genetics, neurobiology, evolutionary biology, aquatic biology.

University of Oklahoma, College of Arts and Sciences, Department of Botany and Microbiology, Program in Ecology and Evolutionary Biology, Norman, OK 73019. Offers PhD. *Students:* 3 full-time (1 woman), 2 part-time (0 women), 4 international. Average age 30. 3 applicants, 33% accepted, 0 enrolled. *Entrance requirements:* Additional exam requirements/recommendations for international students: Required—TOEFL (minimum score 550 paper-based; 213 computer-based; 79 iBT). *Application deadline:* For fall admission, 4/1 for domestic and international students; for spring admission, 11/1 for domestic students, 9/1 for international students. Applications are processed on a rolling basis. Application fee: $40 ($90 for international students). Electronic applications accepted. *Expenses:* Tuition, state resident: full-time $3893; part-time $162.20 per credit hour. Tuition, nonresident: full-time $14,167; part-time $590.30 per credit hour. Required fees: $2523; $94.60 per credit hour. Tuition and fees vary according to course load and degree level. *Financial support:* Career-related internships or fieldwork, scholarships/grants, traineeships, health care benefits, tuition waivers (partial), and unspecified assistantships available. *Faculty research:* Ecology of climate change, microbial ecology, evolution of behavior, community ecology. *Unit head:* Dr. Gordon Uno, Chair, 405-325-4321, Fax: 405-325-7619, E-mail: guno@ou.edu. *Application contact:* Adell Hopper, Staff Assistant, 405-325-4322, Fax: 405-325-7619, E-mail: ahopper@ou.edu.

University of Oklahoma, College of Arts and Sciences, Department of Zoology, Program in Ecology and Evolutionary Biology, Norman, OK 73019. Offers PhD. *Students:* 14 full-time (5 women), 4 part-time (2 women), 5 international. Average age 28. 9 applicants, 67% accepted,

5 enrolled. In 2010, 2 doctorates awarded. *Entrance requirements:* Additional exam requirements/recommendations for international students: Required—TOEFL (minimum score 550 paper-based; 213 computer-based; 79 iBT). *Application deadline:* For fall admission, 12/15 for domestic students, 4/1 for international students; for spring admission, 10/1 for domestic students, 9/1 for international students. Applications are processed on a rolling basis. Application fee: $40 ($90 for international students). Electronic applications accepted. *Expenses:* Tuition, state resident: full-time $3893; part-time $162.20 per credit hour. Tuition, nonresident: full-time $14,167; part-time $590.30 per credit hour. Required fees: $2523; $94.60 per credit hour. Tuition and fees vary according to course load and degree level. *Financial support:* Career-related internships or fieldwork, institutionally sponsored loans, scholarships/grants, traineeships, health care benefits, tuition waivers (partial), and unspecified assistantships available. *Faculty research:* Ecology of climate change, microbial ecology, evolution of behavior, community ecology. *Unit head:* Bill Mathhews, Chair, 405-325-4712, Fax: 405-325-6202, E-mail: wmatthews@ou.edu. *Application contact:* Bill Mathhews, Chair, 405-325-4712, Fax: 405-325-6202, E-mail: wmatthews@ou.edu.

University of Oregon, Graduate School, College of Arts and Sciences, Department of Biology, Eugene, OR 97403. Offers ecology and evolution (MA, MS, PhD); marine biology (MA, MS, PhD); molecular, cellular and genetic biology (PhD); neuroscience and development (PhD). Terminal master's awarded for partial completion of doctoral program. *Degree requirements:* For master's, thesis (for some programs); for doctorate, thesis/dissertation. *Entrance requirements:* For master's and doctorate, GRE General Test, minimum GPA of 3.2. Additional exam requirements/recommendations for international students: Required—TOEFL. *Faculty research:* Developmental neurobiology; evolution, population biology, and quantitative genetics; regulation of gene expression; biochemistry of marine organisms.

University of Pittsburgh, School of Arts and Sciences, Department of Biological Sciences, Program in Ecology and Evolution, Pittsburgh, PA 15260. Offers PhD. *Faculty:* 7 full-time (2 women). *Students:* 18 full-time (5 women); includes 12 Black or African American, non-Hispanic/Latino; 1 American Indian or Alaska Native, non-Hispanic/Latino; 1 Asian, non-Hispanic/Latino; 2 Hispanic/Latino, 1 international. Average age 23. 29 applicants, 31% accepted, 2 enrolled. *Degree requirements:* For doctorate, comprehensive exam, thesis/dissertation, completion of research integrity module. *Entrance requirements:* For doctorate, GRE General Test, GRE Subject Test. Additional exam requirements/recommendations for international students: Required—TOEFL (minimum score 550 paper-based; 213 computer-based; 80 iBT). *Application deadline:* For fall admission, 1/15 priority date for domestic students, 12/15 priority date for international students. Applications are processed on a rolling basis. Application fee: $0 ($50 for international students). Electronic applications accepted. *Expenses:* Tuition, state resident: full-time $17,304; part-time $701 per credit. Tuition, nonresident: full-time $29,554; part-time $1210 per credit. Required fees: $740; $214 per term. Tuition and fees vary according to program. *Financial support:* In 2010–11, 20 fellowships with full tuition reimbursements (averaging $28,382 per year), 5 research assistantships with full tuition reimbursements (averaging $25,500 per year), 17 teaching assistantships with full tuition reimbursements (averaging $24,125 per year) were awarded; Federal Work-Study, scholarships/grants, traineeships, health care benefits, and tuition waivers (full) also available. *Unit head:* Dr. Gerard L. Campbell, Associate Professor, 412-624-6812, Fax: 412-624-4759, E-mail: camp@pitt.edu. *Application contact:* Cathleen M. Barr, Graduate Administrator, 412-624-4268, Fax: 412-624-4759, E-mail: cbarr@pitt.edu.

University of Puerto Rico, Río Piedras, College of Natural Sciences, Department of Biology, San Juan, PR 00931-3300. Offers ecology/systematics (MS, PhD); evolution/genetics (MS, PhD); molecular/cellular biology (MS, PhD); neuroscience (MS, PhD). Part-time programs available. *Degree requirements:* For master's, one foreign language, comprehensive exam, thesis; for doctorate, one foreign language, comprehensive exam, thesis/dissertation. *Entrance requirements:* For master's, GRE Subject Test, interview, minimum GPA of 3.0, letter of recommendation; for doctorate, GRE Subject Test, interview, master's degree, minimum GPA of 3.0, letter of recommendation. *Faculty research:* Environmental, poblational and systematic biology.

University of South Carolina, The Graduate School, College of Arts and Sciences, Department of Biological Sciences, Graduate Training Program in Ecology, Evolution, and Organismal Biology, Columbia, SC 29208. Offers MS, PhD. *Degree requirements:* For master's, one foreign language, comprehensive exam, thesis; for doctorate, one foreign language, comprehensive exam, thesis/dissertation. *Entrance requirements:* For master's and doctorate, GRE General Test, minimum GPA of 3.0 in science. Additional exam requirements/recommendations for international students: Required—TOEFL (minimum score 570 paper-based; 230 computer-based). Electronic applications accepted.

The University of Tennessee, Graduate School, College of Arts and Sciences, Department of Ecology and Evolutionary Biology, Knoxville, TN 37996. Offers behavior (MS, PhD); ecology (MS, PhD); evolutionary biology (MS, PhD). Part-time programs available. *Degree requirements:* For master's, thesis; for doctorate, thesis/dissertation. *Entrance requirements:* For master's and doctorate, GRE General Test, minimum GPA of 2.7. Additional exam requirements/recommendations for international students: Required—TOEFL. Electronic applications accepted. *Expenses:* Tuition, state resident: full-time $7440; part-time $414 per credit hour. Tuition, nonresident: full-time $22,478; part-time $1250 per credit hour. Required fees: $922; $43 per credit hour. Tuition and fees vary according to program.

The University of Tennessee, Graduate School, College of Arts and Sciences, Department of Mathematics, Knoxville, TN 37996. Offers applied mathematics (MS); mathematical ecology (PhD); mathematics (M Math, MS, PhD). Part-time programs available. *Degree requirements:* For master's, thesis or alternative; for doctorate, one foreign language, thesis/dissertation. *Entrance requirements:* For master's and doctorate, minimum GPA of 2.7. Additional exam requirements/recommendations for international students: Required—TOEFL. Electronic applications accepted. *Expenses:* Tuition, state resident: full-time $7440; part-time $414 per credit hour. Tuition, nonresident: full-time $22,478; part-time $1250 per credit hour. Required fees: $922; $43 per credit hour. Tuition and fees vary according to program.

The University of Texas at Austin, Graduate School, College of Natural Sciences, School of Biological Sciences, Program in Ecology, Evolution and Behavior, Austin, TX 78712-1111. Offers MA, PhD. *Entrance requirements:* For doctorate, GRE General Test. Additional exam requirements/recommendations for international students: Required—TOEFL. Electronic applications accepted.

The University of Toledo, College of Graduate Studies, College of Natural Sciences and Mathematics, Department of Biological Sciences, Toledo, OH 43606-3390. Offers cell biology (MS, PhD); ecology (MS, PhD). Part-time programs available. *Faculty:* 19. *Students:* 64 full-time (31 women), 23 part-time (5 women); includes 5 minority (2 Black or African American, non-Hispanic/Latino; 2 Asian, non-Hispanic/Latino; 1 Hispanic/Latino), 29 international. Average age 28. 110 applicants, 16% accepted, 16 enrolled. In 2010, 10 master's, 9 doctorates awarded. *Degree requirements:* For master's, thesis or alternative; for doctorate, thesis/dissertation. *Entrance requirements:* For master's and doctorate, GRE General Test, GRE Subject Test, minimum cumulative point-hour ratio of 2.7 for all previous academic work, three letters of recommendation, statement of purpose, transcripts from all prior institutions attended. Additional exam requirements/recommendations for international students: Required—TOEFL (minimum score 550 paper-based; 213 computer-based; 80 iBT), IELTS (minimum score 6.5). *Application deadline:* For fall admission, 1/15 priority date for domestic and international students. Applications are processed on a rolling basis. Application fee: $45 ($75 for international students). Electronic applications accepted. *Expenses:* Tuition, state resident: full-time $11,426; part-time $476 per credit hour. Tuition, nonresident: full-time $21,660; part-time $903 per credit hour. One-time fee: $62. *Financial support:* Fellowships, research assistantships with full tuition reimbursements, teaching assistantships with full tuition reimbursements, Federal Work-Study, scholarships/grants, tuition waivers (full), and unspecified assistantships available. Support available to part-time students. *Faculty research:* Biochemical parasitology, physiological ecology, animal physiology. *Unit head:* Dr. Doug Leaman, Chair, 419-530-1555, E-mail: douglas.leaman@utoledo.edu. *Application contact:* Graduate School Office, 419-530-4723, Fax: 419-530-4724, E-mail: grdsch@utnet.utoledo.edu.

The University of Toledo, College of Graduate Studies, College of Natural Sciences and Mathematics, Department of Environmental Sciences, Toledo, OH 43606-3390. Offers geology (MS), including earth surface processes, general geology. Part-time programs available. *Faculty:* 30. *Students:* 9 full-time (5 women), 1 (woman) part-time; includes 1 minority (Black or African American, non-Hispanic/Latino), 1 international. Average age 30. 9 applicants, 56% accepted, 5 enrolled. In 2010, 2 master's awarded. *Degree requirements:* For master's, thesis. *Entrance requirements:* For master's, GRE General Test, minimum cumulative point-hour ratio of 2.7 for all previous academic work, three letters of recommendation, statement of purpose, transcripts from all prior institutions attended. Additional exam requirements/recommendations for international students: Required—TOEFL (minimum score 550 paper-based; 213 computer-based; 80 iBT), IELTS (minimum score 6.5). *Application deadline:* For fall admission, 1/15 priority date for domestic and international students. Applications are processed on a rolling basis. Application fee: $45 ($75 for international students). Electronic applications accepted. *Expenses:* Tuition, state resident: full-time $11,426; part-time $476 per credit hour. Tuition, nonresident: full-time $21,660; part-time $903 per credit hour. One-time fee: $62. *Financial support:* Research assistantships with tuition reimbursements, teaching assistantships with tuition reimbursements, Federal Work-Study, institutionally sponsored loans, scholarships/grants, tuition waivers (full), and unspecified assistantships available. Support available to part-time students. *Faculty research:* Environmental geochemistry, geophysics, petrology and mineralogy, paleontology, geohydrology. *Unit head:* Dr. Timothy G. Fisher, Chair, 419-530-2883, E-mail: timothy.fisher@utoledo.edu. *Application contact:* Graduate School Office, 419-530-4723, Fax: 419-530-4724, E-mail: grdsch@utnet.utoledo.edu.

University of Toronto, School of Graduate Studies, Life Sciences Division, Department of Ecology and Evolutionary Biology, Toronto, ON M5S 1A1, Canada. Offers M Sc, PhD. *Degree requirements:* For master's, thesis, thesis defense; for doctorate, thesis/dissertation, thesis defense. *Entrance requirements:* For master's, minimum B average in last 2 years; knowledge of physics, chemistry, and biology.

University of Washington, Graduate School, College of Forest Resources, Seattle, WA 98195. Offers bioresource science and engineering (MS, PhD); environmental horticulture (MEH); environmental horticulture and urban forestry (MS, PhD); forest ecology (MS, PhD); forest management (MFR); forest soils (MS, PhD); forest systems and bioenergy (MS, PhD); restoration ecology (MS, PhD); social sciences (MS, PhD); sustainable resource management (MS, PhD); wildlife science (MS, PhD); MFR/MAIS; MPA/MS. *Accreditation:* SAF. *Degree requirements:* For master's, thesis (for some programs); for doctorate, comprehensive exam (for some programs), thesis/dissertation. *Entrance requirements:* For master's and doctorate, GRE, minimum GPA of 3.0. Additional exam requirements/recommendations for international students: Required—TOEFL. Electronic applications accepted. *Faculty research:* Ecosystem analysis, silviculture and forest protection, paper science and engineering, environmental horticulture and urban forestry, natural resource policy and economics.

University of Wisconsin–Madison, Graduate School, College of Agricultural and Life Sciences, Agroecology Program, Madison, WI 53706-1380. Offers MS. *Degree requirements:* For master's, thesis (for some programs). *Entrance requirements:* For master's, GRE. Additional exam requirements/recommendations for international students: Required—TOEFL (minimum score 580 paper-based; 237 computer-based; 92 iBT), IELTS (minimum score 7). Electronic applications accepted. *Expenses:* Tuition, state resident: full-time $9887; part-time $617.96 per credit. Tuition, nonresident: full-time $24,054; part-time $1503.40 per credit. Required fees: $67.63 per credit. Tuition and fees vary according to reciprocity agreements. *Faculty research:* Multifunctional landscape, socio-ecological systems, participatory solutions to environmental problems.

University of Wyoming, Program in Ecology, Laramie, WY 82070. Offers MS, PhD. *Entrance requirements:* For master's and doctorate, GRE.

Utah State University, School of Graduate Studies, College of Natural Resources, Department of Aquatic, Watershed, and Earth Resources, Logan, UT 84322. Offers ecology (MS, PhD); fisheries biology (MS, PhD); watershed science (MS, PhD). *Degree requirements:* For master's, thesis (for some programs); for doctorate, thesis/dissertation. *Entrance requirements:* For master's and doctorate, GRE General Test, minimum GPA of 3.2. Additional exam requirements/recommendations for international students: Required—TOEFL. Electronic applications accepted. *Faculty research:* Behavior, population ecology, habitat, conservation biology, restoration, aquatic ecology, fisheries management, fluvial geomorphology, remote sensing, conservation biology.

Utah State University, School of Graduate Studies, College of Natural Resources, Department of Environment and Society, Logan, UT 84322. Offers bioregional planning (MS); geography (MA, MS); human dimensions of ecosystem science and management (MS, PhD); recreation resource management (MS, PhD). *Degree requirements:* For master's, comprehensive exam, thesis (for some programs). *Entrance requirements:* For master's and doctorate, GRE General Test, minimum GPA of 3.0. Additional exam requirements/recommendations for international students: Required—TOEFL. Electronic applications accepted. *Faculty research:* Geographic information systems/geographic and environmental education, bioregional planning, natural resource and environmental policy, outdoor recreation and tourism, natural resource and environmental management.

Utah State University, School of Graduate Studies, College of Natural Resources, Department of Wildland Resources, Logan, UT 84322. Offers ecology (MS, PhD); forestry (MS, PhD); range science (MS, PhD); wildlife biology (MS, PhD). Part-time programs available. *Degree requirements:* For master's, thesis; for doctorate, comprehensive exam, thesis/dissertation. *Entrance requirements:* For master's and doctorate, GRE General Test, minimum GPA of 3.0. Additional exam requirements/recommendations for international students: Required—TOEFL. *Faculty research:* Range plant ecophysiology, plant community ecology, ruminant nutrition, population ecology.

Utah State University, School of Graduate Studies, College of Science, Department of Biology, Logan, UT 84322. Offers biology (MS, PhD); ecology (MS, PhD). Part-time programs available. *Degree requirements:* For master's, thesis; for doctorate, thesis/dissertation. *Entrance requirements:* For master's and doctorate, GRE General Test, minimum GPA of 3.0. Additional exam requirements/recommendations for international students: Required—TOEFL (minimum score 575 paper-based). *Faculty research:* Plant, insect, microbial, and animal biology.

Washington University in St. Louis, Graduate School of Arts and Sciences, Division of Biology and Biomedical Sciences, Program in Evolution, Ecology and Population Biology, St. Louis, MO 63130-4899. Offers ecology (PhD); environmental biology (PhD); evolutionary biology (PhD); genetics (PhD). *Degree requirements:* For doctorate, thesis/dissertation. *Entrance requirements:* For doctorate, GRE General Test, GRE Subject Test. Electronic applications accepted.

Wesleyan University, Graduate Programs, Department of Biology, Middletown, CT 06459. Offers animal behavior (PhD); bioformatics/genomics (PhD); cell biology (PhD); developmental biology (PhD); evolution/ecology (PhD); genetics (PhD); neurobiology (PhD); population biology (PhD). *Faculty:* 12 full-time (4 women). *Students:* 20 full-time (12 women); includes 1 Black or African American, non-Hispanic/Latino; 3 Asian, non-Hispanic/Latino. Average age 26. 24 applicants, 29% accepted, 2 enrolled. *Degree requirements:* For doctorate, variable foreign language requirement, thesis/dissertation. *Entrance requirements:* For doctorate, GRE. Additional exam requirements/recommendations for international students: Required—TOEFL. *Application deadline:* For fall admission, 1/15 for domestic and international students. Applications are processed on a rolling basis. Application fee: $0. *Expenses:* Tuition: Full-time $43,404. Required

Wesleyan University (continued)
fees: $830. *Financial support:* In 2010–11, 5 research assistantships with full tuition reimbursements, 16 teaching assistantships with full tuition reimbursements were awarded; stipends also available. Financial award application deadline: 4/15; financial award applicants required to submit FAFSA. *Faculty research:* Microbial population genetics, genetic basis of evolutionary adaptation, genetic regulation of differentiation and pattern formation in *drosophila*. *Unit head:* Dr. Sonia E. Sultan, Chair/Professor, 860-685-3493, E-mail: jnaegele@wesleyan.edu. *Application contact:* Marjorie Fitzgibbons, Information Contact, 860-685-2140, E-mail: mfitzgibbons@wesleyan.edu.

Yale University, Graduate School of Arts and Sciences, Department of Ecology and Evolutionary Biology, New Haven, CT 06520. Offers PhD. *Entrance requirements:* For doctorate, GRE General Test, GRE Subject Test (biology).

Environmental Biology

Baylor University, Graduate School, College of Arts and Sciences, Department of Biology, Waco, TX 76798. Offers biology (MA, MS, PhD); environmental biology (MS); limnology (MS). Part-time programs available. *Faculty:* 13 full-time (3 women). *Students:* 34 full-time (14 women), 2 part-time (both women); includes 4 minority (2 Hispanic/Latino; 2 Two or more races, non-Hispanic/Latino), 13 international. In 2010, 6 master's, 1 doctorate awarded. *Degree requirements:* For master's, thesis (for some programs); for doctorate, thesis/dissertation. *Entrance requirements:* For master's and doctorate, GRE General Test. *Application deadline:* For fall admission, 1/31 priority date for domestic students. Applications are processed on a rolling basis. Application fee: $25. *Financial support:* Teaching assistantships, career-related internships or fieldwork, Federal Work-Study, institutionally sponsored loans, and tuition waivers (full and partial) available. Support available to part-time students. Financial award application deadline: 2/28. *Faculty research:* Terrestrial ecology, aquatic ecology, genetics. *Unit head:* Dr. Myeongwoo Lee, Graduate Program Director, 254-710-2141, Fax: 254-710-2969, E-mail: myeongwoo_lee@baylor.edu. *Application contact:* Tamara Lehmann, Administrative Assistant, 254-710-2911, Fax: 254-710-2969, E-mail: tamara_lehmann@baylor.edu.

Chatham University, Program in Biology, Pittsburgh, PA 15232-2826. Offers environmental biology-non-thesis track (MS); environmental biology-thesis track (MS); human biology-non-thesis track (MS); human biology-thesis track (MS). Part-time programs available. *Degree requirements:* For master's, thesis optional. *Entrance requirements:* For master's, 3 letters of recommendation. Additional exam requirements/recommendations for international students: Required—TOEFL (minimum score 600 paper-based; 250 computer-based; 100 iBT), IELTS (minimum score 6.5), TWE. Electronic applications accepted. *Faculty research:* Molecular evolution of iron homeostasis, characteristics of soil bacterial communities, gene flow through seed movement, role of gonadotropins in spermatogonial proliferation, phosphatid/linositol metabolism in epithelial cells.

Emporia State University, Graduate School, College of Liberal Arts and Sciences, Department of Biological Sciences, Emporia, KS 66801-5087. Offers botany (MS); environmental biology (MS); general biology (MS); microbial and cellular biology (MS); zoology (MS). Part-time programs available. *Faculty:* 13 full-time (3 women). *Students:* 14 full-time (8 women), 19 part-time (9 women); includes 2 minority (1 Black or African American, non-Hispanic/Latino; 1 Hispanic/Latino), 6 international. 9 applicants, 100% accepted, 9 enrolled. In 2010, 4 master's awarded. *Degree requirements:* For master's, comprehensive exam or thesis. *Entrance requirements:* For master's, GRE, appropriate undergraduate degree, interview, letters of reference. Additional exam requirements/recommendations for international students: Required—TOEFL (minimum score 520 paper-based; 133 computer-based; 68 iBT). *Application deadline:* For fall admission, 8/15 priority date for domestic students. Applications are processed on a rolling basis. Application fee: $30 ($75 for international students). Electronic applications accepted. *Expenses:* Tuition, state resident: full-time $4382; part-time $183 per credit hour. Tuition, nonresident: full-time $13,572; part-time $566 per credit hour. Required fees: $1022; $62 per credit hour. Tuition and fees vary according to course level, course load and campus/location. *Financial support:* In 2010–11, 10 research assistantships with full tuition reimbursements (averaging $7,353 per year), 9 teaching assistantships with full tuition reimbursements (averaging $7,809 per year) were awarded; career-related internships or fieldwork, Federal Work-Study, institutionally sponsored loans, health care benefits, and unspecified assistantships also available. Financial award application deadline: 3/15; financial award applicants required to submit FAFSA. *Faculty research:* Fisheries, range, and wildlife management; aquatic, plant, grassland, vertebrate, and invertebrate ecology; mammalian and plant systematics, taxonomy, and evolution; immunology, virology, and molecular biology. *Unit head:* Dr. R. Brent Thomas, Chair, 620-341-5311, Fax: 620-341-5608, E-mail: rthomas2@emporia.edu. *Application contact:* Dr. Scott Crupper, Graduate Coordinator, 620-341-5621, Fax: 620-341-5607, E-mail: scrupper@emporia.edu.

Georgia State University, College of Arts and Sciences, Department of Biology, Program in Applied and Environmental Microbiology, Atlanta, GA 30302-3083. Offers MS, PhD. Part-time programs available. Terminal master's awarded for partial completion of doctoral program. *Degree requirements:* For master's, thesis or alternative; for doctorate, thesis/dissertation, exam. *Entrance requirements:* For master's and doctorate, GRE General Test. Additional exam requirements/recommendations for international students: Required—TOEFL. Electronic applications accepted.

Governors State University, College of Arts and Sciences, Program in Environmental Biology, University Park, IL 60466-0975. Offers MS. Part-time and evening/weekend programs available. *Degree requirements:* For master's, thesis or alternative. *Expenses:* Tuition, state resident: full-time $5400; part-time $225 per credit hour. Tuition, nonresident: full-time $16,200; part-time $675 per credit hour. Required fees: $1358; $46 per credit hour. $126 per term. Tuition and fees vary according to degree level and program. *Faculty research:* Animal physiology, cell biology, animal behavior, plant physiology, plant populations.

Hampton University, Graduate College, Department of Biological Sciences, Hampton, VA 23668. Offers biology (MS); environmental science (MS); medical science (MS). Part-time and evening/weekend programs available. *Degree requirements:* For master's, thesis optional. *Entrance requirements:* For master's, GRE General Test. *Faculty research:* Marine ecology, microbial and chemical pollution, pesticide problems.

Hood College, Graduate School, Program in Environmental Biology, Frederick, MD 21701-8575. Offers MS. Part-time and evening/weekend programs available. *Faculty:* 3 full-time (1 woman), 3 part-time/adjunct (1 woman). *Students:* 3 full-time (2 women), 63 part-time (47 women); includes 2 Black or African American, non-Hispanic/Latino; 1 Asian, non-Hispanic/Latino; 2 Hispanic/Latino; 2 Two or more races, non-Hispanic/Latino. Average age 32. 23 applicants, 91% accepted, 18 enrolled. In 2010, 11 master's awarded. *Degree requirements:* For master's, thesis or alternative. *Entrance requirements:* For master's, minimum GPA of 2.75, 1 year of undergraduate biology and chemistry, 1 semester of mathematics. Additional exam requirements/recommendations for international students: Required—TOEFL (minimum score 575 paper-based; 231 computer-based; 89 iBT). *Application deadline:* For fall admission, 7/15 for domestic and international students; for spring admission, 12/15 for domestic and international students. Applications are processed on a rolling basis. Application fee: $35. Electronic applications accepted. *Expenses:* Tuition: Full-time $6480; part-time $360 per credit. Required fees: $100; $50 per term. *Financial support:* Applicants required to submit FAFSA. *Unit head:* Dr. April Boulton, Director, 301-696-3649, Fax: 301-694-3597, E-mail: dferrier@hood.edu. *Application contact:* Dr. Allen P. Flora, Dean of Graduate School, 301-696-3811, Fax: 301-696-3597, E-mail: gofurther@hood.edu.

Inter American University of Puerto Rico, San Germán Campus, Graduate Studies Center, Program in Environmental Sciences, San Germán, PR 00683-5008. Offers environmental biology (MS); environmental chemistry (MS); water analysis (MS). Part-time and evening/weekend programs available. *Degree requirements:* For master's, comprehensive exam, thesis. *Entrance requirements:* For master's, GRE General Test or EXADEP, minimum GPA of 3.0. *Expenses:* Tuition: Part-time $202 per credit. Required fees: $258 per semester. *Faculty research:* Environmental biology, environmental chemistry, water resources and unit operations.

Massachusetts Institute of Technology, School of Engineering, Department of Civil and Environmental Engineering, Cambridge, MA 02139. Offers biological oceanography (PhD, Sc D); chemical oceanography (PhD, Sc D); civil and environmental engineering (M Eng, SM, PhD, Sc D); civil and environmental systems (PhD, Sc D); civil engineering (PhD, Sc D, CE); coastal engineering (PhD, Sc D); construction engineering and management (PhD, Sc D); environmental biology (PhD, Sc D); environmental chemistry (PhD, Sc D); environmental engineering (PhD, Sc D); environmental fluid mechanics (PhD, Sc D); geotechnical and geoenvironmental engineering (PhD, Sc D); hydrology (PhD, Sc D); information technology (PhD, Sc D); oceanographic engineering (PhD, Sc D); structures and materials (PhD, Sc D); transportation (PhD, Sc D); SM/MBA. *Faculty:* 36 full-time (6 women). *Students:* 181 full-time (56 women); includes 27 minority (3 Black or African American, non-Hispanic/Latino; 10 Asian, non-Hispanic/Latino; 10 Hispanic/Latino; 4 Two or more races, non-Hispanic/Latino), 93 international. Average age 26. 525 applicants, 29% accepted, 74 enrolled. In 2010, 85 master's, 18 doctorates, 2 other advanced degrees awarded. *Degree requirements:* For master's and CE, thesis; for doctorate, comprehensive exam, thesis/dissertation. *Entrance requirements:* For master's and doctorate, GRE General Test. Additional exam requirements/recommendations for international students: Required—TOEFL (minimum score 577 paper-based; 233 computer-based; 90 iBT), IELTS (minimum score 7). *Application deadline:* For fall admission, 1/2 for domestic and international students. Application fee: $75. Electronic applications accepted. *Expenses:* Tuition: Full-time $38,940; part-time $605 per unit. Required fees: $272. *Financial support:* In 2010–11, 146 students received support, including 50 fellowships with tuition reimbursements available (averaging $21,808 per year), 90 research assistantships with tuition reimbursements available (averaging $28,452 per year), 20 teaching assistantships with tuition reimbursements available (averaging $27,842 per year); career-related internships or fieldwork, Federal Work-Study, institutionally sponsored loans, scholarships/grants, health care benefits, and unspecified assistantships also available. *Faculty research:* Environmental chemistry, environmental microbiology, environmental fluid mechanics and coastal engineering, geotechnical engineering and geomechanics, hydrology and hydroclimatology, mechanics of materials and structures, operations research/supply chain, transportation. Total annual research expenditures: $19.5 million. *Unit head:* Prof. Andrew Whittle, Department Head, 617-253-7101. *Application contact:* Patricia Glidden, Graduate Admissions Coordinator, 617-253-7119, Fax: 617-258-6775, E-mail: cee-admissions@mit.edu.

Missouri University of Science and Technology, Graduate School, Department of Biological Sciences, Rolla, MO 65409. Offers applied and environmental biology (MS). *Entrance requirements:* For master's, GRE (minimum score 600 quantitative, 4 writing). Additional exam requirements/recommendations for international students: Required—TOEFL (minimum score 570 paper-based; 230 computer-based).

Morgan State University, School of Graduate Studies, School of Computer, Mathematical, and Natural Sciences, Department of Biology, Program in Bioenvironmental Science, Baltimore, MD 21251. Offers PhD. *Degree requirements:* For doctorate, comprehensive exam, thesis/dissertation, oral defense of dissertation. *Entrance requirements:* For doctorate, GRE General Test, GRE Subject Test (biology, chemistry, or related science), bachelor's or master's degree in biology, chemistry, physics or related field; minimum GPA of 3.0. Additional exam requirements/recommendations for international students: Required—TOEFL (minimum score 550 paper-based; 213 computer-based).

Nicholls State University, Graduate Studies, College of Arts and Sciences, Department of Biological Sciences, Thibodaux, LA 70310. Offers marine and environmental biology (MS). Part-time programs available. *Degree requirements:* For master's, comprehensive exam, thesis. *Entrance requirements:* For master's, GRE. Additional exam requirements/recommendations for international students: Required—TOEFL (minimum score 600 paper-based). *Faculty research:* Bioremediation, ecology, public health, biotechnology, physiology.

Nova Scotia Agricultural College, Research and Graduate Studies, Truro, NS B2N 5E3, Canada. Offers agriculture (M Sc), including air quality, animal behavior, animal molecular genetics, animal nutrition, animal technology, aquaculture, botany, crop management, crop physiology, ecology, environmental microbiology, food science, horticulture, nutrient management, pest management, physiology, plant biotechnology, plant pathology, soil chemistry, soil fertility, waste management and composting, water quality. Program offered jointly with Dalhousie University. Part-time programs available. *Degree requirements:* For master's, thesis, ATC Exam Teaching Assistantship. *Entrance requirements:* For master's, honors B Sc, minimum GPA of 3.0. Additional exam requirements/recommendations for international students: Required—TOEFL (minimum score 580 paper-based; 237 computer-based; 92 iBT), IELTS, Michigan English Language Assessment Battery, CanTEST, CAEL. *Faculty research:* Bio-product development, organic agriculture, nutrient management, air and water quality, agricultural biotechnology.

Ohio University, Graduate College, College of Arts and Sciences, Department of Environmental and Plant Biology, Athens, OH 45701-2979. Offers MS, PhD. Part-time programs available. *Students:* 19 full-time (5 women), 1 part-time (0 women); includes 2 minority (1 Black or African American, non-Hispanic/Latino; 1 Two or more races, non-Hispanic/Latino), 2 international. Average age 25. 17 applicants, 47% accepted, 7 enrolled. In 2010, 2 master's, 2 doctorates awarded. *Degree requirements:* For master's, thesis, 2 quarters of teaching experience; for doctorate, comprehensive exam, thesis/dissertation, 2 quarters of teaching experience. *Entrance requirements:* For master's, GRE General Test, minimum GPA of 3.0; for doctorate, GRE General Test, minimum GPA of 3.2. Additional exam requirements/recommendations for international students: Required—TOEFL (minimum score 620 paper-based; 260 computer-based; 105 iBT) or IELTS (minimum score 7.5). *Application deadline:* For fall admission, 1/15 priority date for domestic and international students. Applications are processed on a rolling basis. Application fee: $50 ($55 for international students). Electronic applications accepted. *Financial support:* Fellowships with full tuition reimbursements, research assistantships with full tuition reimbursements, teaching assistantships with full tuition reimbursements, Federal Work-Study, institutionally sponsored loans, and scholarships/grants available. Financial award application deadline: 1/15. *Faculty research:* Eastern deciduous forest ecology, evolutionary developmental plant biology, phylogenetic systematics, plant cell wall biotechnology. Total annual research expenditures: $859,166. *Unit head:* Dr. Brian C. McCarthy, Chair,

740-593-1615, Fax: 740-593-1130, E-mail: mccarthy@ohio.edu. *Application contact:* Dr. Allan Showalter, Graduate Chair, 740-593-1135, Fax: 740-593-1130, E-mail: showalte@ohio.edu.

Rutgers, The State University of New Jersey, New Brunswick, Graduate School-New Brunswick, Department of Environmental Sciences, Piscataway, NJ 08854-8097. Offers air pollution and resources (MS, PhD); aquatic biology (MS, PhD); aquatic chemistry (MS, PhD); atmospheric science (MS, PhD); chemistry and physics of aerosol and hydrosol systems (MS, PhD); environmental chemistry (MS, PhD); environmental microbiology (MS, PhD); environmental toxicology (PhD); exposure assessment (PhD); fate and effects of pollutants (MS, PhD); pollution prevention and control (MS, PhD); water and wastewater treatment (MS, PhD); water resources (MS, PhD). Terminal master's awarded for partial completion of doctoral program. *Degree requirements:* For master's, comprehensive exam, thesis or alternative, oral final exam; for doctorate, comprehensive exam, thesis/dissertation, thesis defense, qualifying exam. *Entrance requirements:* For master's and doctorate, GRE General Test. Additional exam requirements/recommendations for international students: Required—TOEFL. Electronic applications accepted. *Expenses:* Tuition, state resident: full-time $7200; part-time $600 per credit. Tuition, nonresident: full-time $11,124; part-time $927 per credit. *Faculty research:* Biological waste treatment; contaminant fate and transport; air, soil and water quality.

Sonoma State University, School of Science and Technology, Department of Biology, Rohnert Park, CA 94928. Offers environmental biology (MA); general biology (MA). Part-time programs available. *Faculty:* 10 full-time (2 women). *Students:* 4 full-time (3 women), 16 part-time (7 women); includes 4 minority (1 American Indian or Alaska Native, non-Hispanic/Latino; 2 Hispanic/Latino; 1 Two or more races, non-Hispanic/Latino), 1 international. Average age 29. 19 applicants, 58% accepted, 9 enrolled. In 2010, 4 master's awarded. *Degree requirements:* For master's, thesis or alternative, oral exam. *Entrance requirements:* For master's, GRE General Test, GRE Subject Test, minimum GPA of 3.0. Additional exam requirements/recommendations for international students: Required—TOEFL (minimum score 500 paper-based; 173 computer-based). *Application deadline:* For fall admission, 11/30 for domestic students. Applications are processed on a rolling basis. Application fee: $55. *Financial support:* In 2010–11, 1 fellowship (averaging $2,100 per year), 15 teaching assistantships (averaging $5,343 per year) were awarded; research assistantships, career-related internships or fieldwork, Federal Work-Study, and tuition waivers (full) also available. Financial award application deadline: 3/2; financial award applicants required to submit FAFSA. *Faculty research:* Plant physiology, comparative physiology, community ecology, restoration ecology, marine ecology, conservation genetics, primate behavior, behavioral ecology, developmental biology, plant and animal systematics. Total annual research expenditures: $238,000. *Unit head:* Dr. Richard Whitkus, Chair, 707-664-2303, E-mail: james.christmann@sonoma.edu. *Application contact:* Dr. Dan Crocker, Graduate Adviser, 707-664-2995.

State University of New York College of Environmental Science and Forestry, Department of Environmental and Forest Biology, Syracuse, NY 13210-2779. Offers applied ecology (MPS); chemical ecology (MPS, MS, PhD); conservation biology (MPS, MS, PhD); ecology (MPS, MS, PhD); entomology (MPS, MS, PhD); environmental interpretation (MPS, MS, PhD); environmental physiology (MPS, MS, PhD); fish and wildlife biology and management (MPS, MS, PhD); forest pathology and mycology (MPS, MS, PhD); plant biotechnology (MPS); plant science and biotechnology (MPS, MS, PhD). *Degree requirements:* For master's, thesis (for some programs); for doctorate, comprehensive exam, thesis/dissertation. *Entrance requirements:* For master's and doctorate, GRE General Test, GRE Subject Test, minimum GPA of 3.0. Additional exam requirements/recommendations for international students: Required—TOEFL (minimum score 550 paper-based; 213 computer-based; 80 iBT), IELTS (minimum score 6). *Expenses:* Tuition, state resident: full-time $8370; part-time $349 per credit hour. Tuition, nonresident: full-time $13,780. Required fees: $30.30 per credit hour. $20 per year. *Faculty research:* Ecology, fish and wildlife biology and management, plant science, entomology.

Universidad del Turabo, Graduate Programs, Programs in Science and Technology, Gurabo, PR 00778-3030. Offers environmental analysis (MSE), including environmental chemistry; environmental management (MSE), including pollution management; environmental science (D Sc), including environmental biology. *Entrance requirements:* For master's, GRE, EXADEP, interview.

University of Alberta, Faculty of Graduate Studies and Research, Department of Biological Sciences, Edmonton, AB T6G 2E1, Canada. Offers environmental biology and ecology (M Sc, PhD); microbiology and biotechnology (M Sc, PhD); molecular biology and genetics (M Sc, PhD); physiology and cell biology (M Sc, PhD); plant biology (M Sc, PhD); systematics and evolution (M Sc, PhD). Terminal master's awarded for partial completion of doctoral program. *Degree requirements:* For master's, thesis; for doctorate, thesis/dissertation. *Entrance requirements:* Additional exam requirements/recommendations for international students: Required—TOEFL.

University of California, Santa Cruz, Division of Graduate Studies, Division of Physical and Biological Sciences, Environmental Toxicology Department, Santa Cruz, CA 95064. Offers MS, PhD. *Students:* 18 full-time (9 women); includes 8 minority (2 Black or African American, non-Hispanic/Latino; 2 Asian, non-Hispanic/Latino; 4 Hispanic/Latino), 1 international. Average age 27. 45 applicants, 18% accepted, 7 enrolled. In 2010, 3 doctorates awarded. Terminal master's awarded for partial completion of doctoral program. *Degree requirements:* For master's, comprehensive exam, thesis; for doctorate, thesis/dissertation, qualifying exams. *Entrance requirements:* For master's and doctorate, GRE. Additional exam requirements/recommendations for international students: Required—TOEFL (minimum score 550 paper-based; 220 computer-based; 83 iBT); Recommended—IELTS (minimum score 8). *Application deadline:* For fall admission, 12/3 for domestic and international students. Application fee: $70 ($90 for international students). Electronic applications accepted. *Financial support:* Fellowships, research assistantships, teaching assistantships, institutionally sponsored loans and tuition waivers available. Financial award applicants required to submit FAFSA. *Faculty research:* Molecular mechanisms of reactive DNA methylation toxicity, anthropogenic perturbations of biogeochemical cycles, anaerobic microbiology and biotransformation of pollutants and toxic metals, organismal responses and therapeutic treatment of toxins, microbiology, molecular genetics, genomics. *Unit head:* Claudia McClure, Graduate Program Coordinator, 831-459-4719, E-mail: clmcclur@ucsc.edu. *Application contact:* Claudia McClure, Graduate Program Coordinator, 831-459-4719, E-mail: clmcclur@ucsc.edu.

University of Guelph, Graduate Studies, Ontario Agricultural College, Department of Environmental Biology, Guelph, ON N1G 2W1, Canada. Offers entomology (M Sc, PhD); environmental microbiology and biotechnology (M Sc, PhD); environmental toxicology (M Sc, PhD); plant and forest systems (M Sc, PhD); plant pathology (M Sc, PhD). Part-time programs available. *Degree requirements:* For master's, thesis; for doctorate, comprehensive exam, thesis/dissertation. *Entrance requirements:* For master's, minimum 75% average during previous 2 years of course work; for doctorate, minimum 75% average. Additional exam requirements/recommendations for international students: Required—TOEFL or IELTS. Electronic applications accepted. *Faculty research:* Entomology, environmental microbiology and biotechnology, environmental toxicology, forest ecology, plant pathology.

University of Louisiana at Lafayette, College of Sciences, Department of Biology, Lafayette, LA 70504. Offers biology (MS); environmental and evolutionary biology (PhD). Terminal master's awarded for partial completion of doctoral program. *Degree requirements:* For master's, thesis; for doctorate, 2 foreign languages, comprehensive exam, thesis/dissertation. *Entrance requirements:* For master's, GRE General Test, minimum GPA of 2.75; for doctorate, GRE General Test, GRE Subject Test, minimum GPA of 3.0. Additional exam requirements/recommendations for international students: Required—TOEFL (minimum score 550 paper-based; 213 computer-based). Electronic applications accepted. *Faculty research:* Structure and ultrastructure, system biology, ecology, processes, environmental physiology.

University of Louisville, Graduate School, College of Arts and Sciences, Department of Biology, Louisville, KY 40292-0001. Offers biology (MS); environmental biology (PhD). *Students:*

40 full-time (21 women), 9 part-time (8 women); includes 2 Black or African American, non-Hispanic/Latino; 1 Hispanic/Latino, 9 international. Average age 31. 49 applicants, 43% accepted, 13 enrolled. In 2010, 6 master's, 7 doctorates awarded. *Degree requirements:* For master's, thesis (for some programs); for doctorate, thesis/dissertation. *Entrance requirements:* For master's and doctorate, GRE General Test. *Application deadline:* Applications are processed on a rolling basis. Application fee: $50. *Expenses:* Tuition, state resident: full-time $9144; part-time $508 per credit hour. Tuition, nonresident: full-time $19,026; part-time $1057 per credit hour. Tuition and fees vary according to program and reciprocity agreements. *Unit head:* Dr. Ronald Fell, Chair, 502-852-6771, Fax: 502-852-0725, E-mail: rdfell@louisville.edu. *Application contact:* Dr. Joseph M. Steffen, Director of Graduate Studies, 502-852-6771, Fax: 502-852-0725, E-mail: joe.steffen@louisville.edu.

The University of Manchester, Faculty of Life Sciences, Manchester, United Kingdom. Offers adaptive organismal biology (M Phil, PhD); animal biology (M Phil, PhD); biochemistry (M Phil, PhD); bioinformatics (M Phil, PhD); biomolecular sciences (M Phil, PhD); biotechnology (M Phil, PhD); cell biology (M Phil, PhD); cell matrix research (M Phil, PhD); channels and transporters (M Phil, PhD); developmental biology (M Phil, PhD); Egyptology (M Phil, PhD); environmental biology (M Phil, PhD); evolutionary biology (M Phil, PhD); gene expression (M Phil, PhD); genetics (M Phil, PhD); history of science, technology and medicine (M Phil, PhD); immunology (M Phil, PhD); integrative neurobiology and behavior (M Phil, PhD); membrane trafficking (M Phil, PhD); microbiology (M Phil, PhD); molecular and cellular neuroscience (M Phil, PhD); molecular biology (M Phil, PhD); molecular cancer studies (M Phil, PhD); neuroscience (M Phil, PhD); ophthalmology (M Phil, PhD); optometry (M Phil, PhD); organelle function (M Phil, PhD); pharmacology (M Phil, PhD); physiology (M Phil, PhD); plant sciences (M Phil, PhD); stem cell research (M Phil, PhD); structural biology (M Phil, PhD); systems neuroscience (M Phil, PhD); toxicology (M Phil, PhD).

University of Massachusetts Amherst, Graduate School, College of Natural Sciences, Department of Environmental Conservation, Program in Wildlife and Fisheries Conservation, Amherst, MA 01003. Offers MS, PhD. Part-time programs available. *Students:* 32 full-time (17 women), 32 part-time (11 women); includes 1 Black or African American, non-Hispanic/Latino; 1 American Indian or Alaska Native, non-Hispanic/Latino, 10 international. Average age 32. 43 applicants, 26% accepted, 9 enrolled. In 2010, 8 master's, 3 doctorates awarded. Terminal master's awarded for partial completion of doctoral program. *Degree requirements:* For master's, thesis optional; for doctorate, comprehensive exam, thesis/dissertation. *Entrance requirements:* For master's and doctorate, GRE General Test. Additional exam requirements/recommendations for international students: Required—TOEFL (minimum score 550 paper-based; 213 computer-based; 80 iBT), IELTS (minimum score 6.5). *Application deadline:* For fall admission, 2/1 for domestic and international students; for spring admission, 10/1 for domestic and international students. Applications are processed on a rolling basis. Application fee: $50 ($65 for international students). Electronic applications accepted. *Expenses:* Tuition, state resident: full-time $2640. Required fees: $8282. One-time fee: $357 full-time. *Financial support:* Fellowships, research assistantships, teaching assistantships, career-related internships or fieldwork, Federal Work-Study, scholarships/grants, traineeships, health care benefits, tuition waivers (full), and unspecified assistantships available. Support available to part-time students. Financial award application deadline: 2/1. *Unit head:* Dr. Kevin McGarigal, Graduate Program Director, 413-545-2666, Fax: 413-545-4358. *Application contact:* Jean M. Ames, Supervisor of Admissions, 413-545-0722, Fax: 413-577-0010, E-mail: gradadm@grad.umass.edu.

University of Massachusetts Boston, Office of Graduate Studies, College of Science and Mathematics, Department of Environmental, Earth and Ocean Sciences, Program in Environmental Biology, Boston, MA 02125-3393. Offers PhD. Part-time and evening/weekend programs available. *Degree requirements:* For doctorate, comprehensive exam, thesis/dissertation, oral exams. *Entrance requirements:* For doctorate, GRE General Test, minimum GPA of 2.75. *Faculty research:* Polychoets biology, predator and prey relationships, population and evolutionary biology, neurobiology, biodiversity.

University of North Dakota, Graduate School, College of Arts and Sciences, Department of Biology, Grand Forks, ND 58202. Offers botany (MS, PhD); ecology (MS, PhD); entomology (MS, PhD); environmental biology (MS, PhD); fisheries/wildlife (MS, PhD); genetics (MS, PhD); zoology (MS, PhD). *Faculty:* 17 full-time (5 women), 6 part-time/adjunct (1 woman). *Students:* 19 full-time (6 women), 8 part-time (2 women); includes 4 minority (3 American Indian or Alaska Native, non-Hispanic/Latino; 1 Asian, non-Hispanic/Latino), 1 international. Average age 28. 21 applicants, 33% accepted, 4 enrolled. In 2010, 1 master's awarded. Terminal master's awarded for partial completion of doctoral program. *Degree requirements:* For master's, thesis, final exam; for doctorate, comprehensive exam, thesis/dissertation, final exam. *Entrance requirements:* For master's, GRE General Test, GRE Subject Test, minimum GPA of 3.0; for doctorate, GRE General Test, GRE Subject Test, minimum GPA of 3.5. Additional exam requirements/recommendations for international students: Required—TOEFL (minimum score 550 paper-based; 213 computer-based; 79 iBT), IELTS (minimum score 6.5). *Application deadline:* For fall admission, 2/15 for domestic and international students; for spring admission, 10/15 for domestic and international students. Application fee: $35. Electronic applications accepted. *Expenses:* Tuition, state resident: full-time $5857; part-time $306.74 per credit. Tuition, nonresident: full-time $15,666; part-time $729.77 per credit. Required fees: $53.42 per credit. Tuition and fees vary according to course load, program and reciprocity agreements. *Financial support:* In 2010–11, 22 students received support, including 5 research assistantships with full and partial tuition reimbursements available (averaging $11,375 per year), 17 teaching assistantships with full and partial tuition reimbursements available (averaging $10,813 per year), fellowships with full and partial tuition reimbursements available, Federal Work-Study, institutionally sponsored loans, scholarships/grants, health care benefits, tuition waivers (full and partial), and unspecified assistantships also available. Support available to part-time students. Financial award application deadline: 3/15; financial award applicants required to submit FAFSA. *Faculty research:* Population biology, wildlife ecology, RNA processing, hormonal control of behavior. Total annual research expenditures: $736,510. *Unit head:* Dr. Brett Goodwin, Graduate Director, 701-777-2621, Fax: 701-777-2623, E-mail: brett.goodwin@mail.und.edu. *Application contact:* Matthew Anderson, Admissions Specialist, 701-777-2947, Fax: 701-777-3619, E-mail: matthew.anderson@gradschool.und.edu.

University of Southern California, Graduate School, Dana and David Dornsife College of Letters, Arts and Sciences, Department of Biological Sciences, Program in Marine Biology and Biological Oceanography, Los Angeles, CA 90089. Offers marine and environmental biology (MS); marine biology and biological oceanography (PhD). *Faculty:* 21 full-time (6 women), 11 part-time/adjunct (4 women). *Students:* 10 full-time (7 women); includes 6 minority (1 Black or African American, non-Hispanic/Latino; 3 Asian, non-Hispanic/Latino; 1 Hispanic/Latino; 1 Two or more races, non-Hispanic/Latino), 1 international. 35 applicants, 37% accepted, 10 enrolled. In 2010, 1 master's awarded. Terminal master's awarded for partial completion of doctoral program. *Degree requirements:* For master's, research paper; for doctorate, comprehensive exam, thesis/dissertation, qualifying examination, dissertation defense. *Entrance requirements:* For master's and doctorate, GRE, 3 letters of recommendation, personal statement, resume, minimum GPA of 3.0. Additional exam requirements/recommendations for international students: Required—TOEFL (minimum score 600 paper-based; 250 computer-based; 100 iBT). *Application deadline:* For fall admission, 12/1 priority date for domestic and international students. Application fee: $85. Electronic applications accepted. *Expenses:* Tuition: Full-time $31,240; part-time $1420 per unit. Required fees: $600. One-time fee: $35 full-time. Full-time tuition and fees vary according to degree level and program. *Financial support:* In 2010–11, 49 students received support, including 15 fellowships with full tuition reimbursements available (averaging $28,500 per year), 14 research assistantships with full tuition reimbursements available (averaging $26,700 per year), 13 teaching assistantships with full tuition reimbursements available (averaging $26,700 per year); scholarships/grants, traineeships, health care benefits, and tuition waivers also available. *Faculty research:* Microbial ecology, biogeochemistry, and geobiology; biodiversity and molecular ecology; integrative organismal biology; conservation biology; marine genomics. *Unit head:* Dr. David A. Caron, Professor of Biological Sciences/

Environmental Biology

University of Southern California (continued)
Director, 213-740-0203, E-mail: dcaron@usc.edu. *Application contact:* Adolfo dela Rosa, Student Services Advisor I, 213-821-3164, Fax: 213-740-1380, E-mail: adolfode@usc.edu.

University of Southern Mississippi, Graduate School, College of Science and Technology, Department of Biological Sciences, Hattiesburg, MS 39406-0001. Offers environmental biology (MS, PhD); marine biology (MS, PhD); microbiology (MS, PhD); molecular biology (MS, PhD). *Faculty:* 27 full-time (6 women). *Students:* 54 full-time (29 women), 5 part-time (4 women); includes 2 Black or African American, non-Hispanic/Latino; 4 Two or more races, non-Hispanic/Latino, 17 international. Average age 32. 54 applicants, 48% accepted, 13 enrolled. In 2010, 4 master's, 4 doctorates awarded. Terminal master's awarded for partial completion of doctoral program. *Degree requirements:* For master's, comprehensive exam, thesis; for doctorate, comprehensive exam, thesis/dissertation. *Entrance requirements:* For master's, GRE General Test, minimum GPA of 3.0 on last 60 hours; for doctorate, GRE General Test, minimum GPA of 3.5. Additional exam requirements/recommendations for international students: Required—TOEFL, IELTS. *Application deadline:* For fall admission, 3/1 priority date for domestic students, 3/1 for international students; for spring admission, 1/10 priority date for domestic and international students. Applications are processed on a rolling basis. Application fee: $50. *Financial support:* In 2010–11, 25 research assistantships with full tuition reimbursements (averaging $9,700 per year), 33 teaching assistantships with full tuition reimbursements (averaging $10,600 per year) were awarded; Federal Work-Study, scholarships/grants, health care benefits, and unspecified assistantships also available. Financial award application deadline: 3/15; financial award applicants required to submit FAFSA. *Unit head:* Dr. Glenmore Shearer, Chair, 601-266-4748, Fax: 601-266-5797. *Application contact:* Dr. Jake Schaefer, Director of Graduate Studies, 601-266-4748, Fax: 601-266-5797.

University of West Florida, College of Arts and Sciences: Sciences, School of Allied Health and Life Sciences, Department of Biology, Pensacola, FL 32514-5750. Offers biological chemistry (MS); biology (MS); biology education (MST); biotechnology (MS); coastal zone studies (MS); environmental biology (MS). *Faculty:* 10 full-time (2 women). *Students:* 6 full-time (4 women), 32 part-time (18 women); includes 1 Black or African American, non-Hispanic/Latino; 1 Asian, non-Hispanic/Latino; 1 Hispanic/Latino, 1 international. Average age 28. 17 applicants, 53% accepted, 7 enrolled. In 2010, 3 master's awarded. *Degree requirements:* For master's, thesis. *Entrance requirements:* For master's, GRE General Test. Additional exam requirements/recommendations for international students: Required—TOEFL (minimum score 550 paper-based; 213 computer-based). *Application deadline:* For fall admission, 6/1 for domestic students, 5/15 for international students; for spring admission, 10/1 for domestic and international students. Applications are processed on a rolling basis. Application fee: $30. *Expenses:* Tuition, state resident: full-time $4982; part-time $208 per credit hour. Tuition, nonresident: full-time $20,059; part-time $836 per credit hour. Required fees: $1365; $57 per credit hour. *Financial support:* In 2010–11, 20 fellowships with partial tuition reimbursements (averaging $523 per year), 18 research assistantships with partial tuition reimbursements (averaging $5,700 per year), 12 teaching assistantships with partial tuition reimbursements (averaging $8,042 per year) were awarded; unspecified assistantships also available. Financial award application deadline: 4/15; financial award applicants required to submit FAFSA. *Unit head:* Dr. George L. Stewart, Chairperson, 850-474-2748. *Application contact:* Terry McCray, Assistant Director of Graduate Admissions, 850-473-7718, Fax: 850-473-7714, E-mail: gradadmissions@uwf.edu.

University of Wisconsin–Madison, School of Medicine and Public Health, Molecular and Environmental Toxicology Center, Madison, WI 53706. Offers MS, PhD. *Faculty:* 77 full-time (25 women), 1 part-time/adjunct (0 women). *Students:* 34 full-time (20 women); includes 1 American Indian or Alaska Native, non-Hispanic/Latino; 1 Asian, non-Hispanic/Latino; 3 Hispanic/Latino; 2 Native Hawaiian or other Pacific Islander, non-Hispanic/Latino, 8 international. Average age 28. 51 applicants, 31% accepted, 5 enrolled. In 2010, 1 master's, 10 doctorates awarded. Terminal master's awarded for partial completion of doctoral program. *Degree requirements:* For master's, thesis; for doctorate, thesis/dissertation. *Entrance requirements:* For master's and doctorate, bachelor's degree in science-related field. Additional exam requirements/recommendations for international students: Required—TOEFL. *Application deadline:* For fall admission, 12/15 priority date for domestic and international students. Application fee: $56. Electronic applications accepted. *Expenses:* Tuition, state resident: full-time $9887; part-time $617.96 per credit. Tuition, nonresident: full-time $24,054; part-time $1503.40 per credit. Required fees: $67.63 per credit. Tuition and fees vary according to reciprocity agreements. *Financial support:* In 2010–11, 5 research assistantships with tuition reimbursements (averaging $23,500 per year) were awarded; fellowships with tuition reimbursements, traineeships, health care benefits, and unspecified assistantships also available. *Faculty research:* Toxicology cancer, genetics, cell cycle, xenobotic metabolism. *Unit head:* Dr. Christopher Bradfield, Director, 608-262-2024, E-mail: bradfield@oncology.wisc.edu. *Application contact:* Eileen M. Stevens, Program Administrator, 608-263-4580, Fax: 608-262-5245, E-mail: emstevens@wisc.edu.

Washington University in St. Louis, Graduate School of Arts and Sciences, Division of Biology and Biomedical Sciences, Program in Evolution, Ecology and Population Biology, St. Louis, MO 63130-4899. Offers ecology (PhD); environmental biology (PhD); evolutionary biology (PhD); genetics (PhD). *Degree requirements:* For doctorate, thesis/dissertation. *Entrance requirements:* For doctorate, GRE General Test, GRE Subject Test. Electronic applications accepted.

West Virginia University, Davis College of Agriculture, Forestry and Consumer Sciences, Division of Plant and Soil Sciences, Morgantown, WV 26506. Offers agricultural sciences (PhD), including animal and food sciences, plant and soil sciences; agronomy (MS); entomology (MS); environmental microbiology (MS); horticulture (MS); plant pathology (MS). *Degree requirements:* For master's, thesis. *Entrance requirements:* For master's, GRE, minimum GPA of 2.5. Additional exam requirements/recommendations for international students: Required—TOEFL. *Faculty research:* Water quality, reclamation of disturbed land, crop production, pest control, environmental protection.

West Virginia University, Eberly College of Arts and Sciences, Department of Biology, Morgantown, WV 26506. Offers cell and molecular biology (MS, PhD); environmental and evolutionary biology (MS, PhD); forensic biology (MS, PhD); genomic biology (MS, PhD); neurobiology (MS, PhD). Terminal master's awarded for partial completion of doctoral program. *Degree requirements:* For master's, thesis, final exam; for doctorate, thesis/dissertation, preliminary and final exams. *Entrance requirements:* For master's, GRE General Test, GRE Subject Test, minimum GPA of 3.0; for doctorate, GRE General Test, minimum GPA of 3.0. Additional exam requirements/recommendations for international students: Required—TOEFL. *Faculty research:* Environmental biology, genetic engineering, developmental biology, global change, biodiversity.

Youngstown State University, Graduate School, College of Science, Technology, Engineering and Mathematics, Department of Biological Sciences, Youngstown, OH 44555-0001. Offers environmental biology (MS); molecular biology, microbiology, and genetic (MS); physiology and anatomy (MS). Part-time programs available. *Degree requirements:* For master's, comprehensive exam, thesis, oral review. *Entrance requirements:* For master's, GRE General Test, minimum GPA of 2.7. Additional exam requirements/recommendations for international students: Required—TOEFL. *Faculty research:* Cell biology, neurophysiology, molecular biology, neurobiology, gene regulation.

Evolutionary Biology

Arizona State University, College of Liberal Arts and Sciences, School of Life Sciences, Tempe, AZ 85287-4601. Offers animal behavior (PhD); applied ethics (biomedical and health ethics) (MA); biological design (PhD); biology (MS, PhD); biology (biology and society) (MS, PhD); environmental life sciences (PhD); evolutionary biology (PhD); human and social dimensions of science and technology (PhD); microbiology (PhD); molecular and cellular biology (PhD); neuroscience (PhD); philosophy (history and philosophy of science) (MA); sustainability (PhD). *Faculty:* 102 full-time (26 women), 4 part-time/adjunct (1 woman). *Students:* 188 full-time (95 women), 45 part-time (29 women); includes 31 minority (3 Black or African American, non-Hispanic/Latino; 2 American Indian or Alaska Native, non-Hispanic/Latino; 12 Asian, non-Hispanic/Latino; 12 Hispanic/Latino; 2 Two or more races, non-Hispanic/Latino, 39 international. Average age 30. 203 applicants, 41% accepted, 60 enrolled. In 2010, 17 master's, 21 doctorates awarded. Terminal master's awarded for partial completion of doctoral program. *Degree requirements:* For master's, thesis (for some programs), interactive Program of Study (iPOS) submitted before completing 50 percent of required credit hours; for doctorate, variable foreign language requirement, comprehensive exam, thesis/dissertation, interactive Program of Study (iPOS) submitted before completing 50 percent of required credit hours. *Entrance requirements:* For master's and doctorate, GRE, minimum GPA of 3.0 or equivalent in last 2 years of work leading to bachelor's degree. Additional exam requirements/recommendations for international students: Required—TOEFL (minimum score 600 paper-based; 250 computer-based; 100 iBT). *Application deadline:* For fall admission, 12/15 for domestic and international students. Application fee: $70 ($90 for international students). Electronic applications accepted. *Expenses:* Tuition, state resident: full-time $8510; part-time $608 per credit. Tuition, nonresident: full-time $16,542; part-time $919 per credit. Required fees: $339; $110 per credit. Part-time tuition and fees vary according to course load. *Financial support:* In 2010–11, 80 research assistantships with full and partial tuition reimbursements (averaging $17,888 per year), 101 teaching assistantships with full and partial tuition reimbursements (averaging $17,327 per year) were awarded; fellowships with full tuition reimbursements, career-related internships or fieldwork, Federal Work-Study, institutionally sponsored loans, scholarships/grants, and tuition waivers (full and partial) also available. Financial award application deadline: 3/1; financial award applicants required to submit FAFSA. Total annual research expenditures: $29.3 million. *Unit head:* Dr. Robert E. Page, Director, 480-965-0803, E-mail: robert.page@asu.edu. *Application contact:* Graduate Admissions, 480-965-6113.

Brown University, Graduate School, Division of Biology and Medicine, Program in Ecology and Evolutionary Biology, Providence, RI 02912. Offers PhD. *Degree requirements:* For doctorate, thesis/dissertation, preliminary exam. *Entrance requirements:* For doctorate, GRE General Test, GRE Subject Test. Additional exam requirements/recommendations for international students: Required—TOEFL. Electronic applications accepted. *Faculty research:* Marine ecology, behavioral ecology, population genetics, evolutionary morphology, plant ecology.

Clemson University, Graduate School, College of Agriculture, Forestry and Life Sciences, Department of Biological Sciences, Program in Biological Sciences, Clemson, SC 29634. Offers MS, PhD. *Students:* 39 full-time (26 women), 121 part-time (114 women); includes 1 Black or African American, non-Hispanic/Latino; 2 Asian, non-Hispanic/Latino, 10 international. Average age 30. 75 applicants, 44% accepted, 29 enrolled. In 2010, 6 master's, 2 doctorates awarded. *Degree requirements:* For master's, thesis optional; for doctorate, comprehensive exam, thesis/dissertation. *Entrance requirements:* For master's and doctorate, GRE General Test. Additional exam requirements/recommendations for international students: Required— TOEFL, IELTS. *Application deadline:* For fall admission, 1/15 for domestic students, 4/15 for international students. Applications are processed on a rolling basis. Application fee: $70 ($80 for international students). Electronic applications accepted. *Expenses:* Tuition, state resident: full-time $6492; part-time $400 per credit hour. Tuition, nonresident: full-time $13,634; part-time $800 per credit hour. Required fees: $262 per semester. Part-time tuition and fees vary according to course load and program. *Financial support:* In 2010–11, 38 students received support, including 9 fellowships with full and partial tuition reimbursements available (averaging $9,389 per year), 17 research assistantships with partial tuition reimbursements available (averaging $12,632 per year), 40 teaching assistantships with partial tuition reimbursements available (averaging $10,513 per year); career-related internships or fieldwork, institutionally sponsored loans, scholarships/grants, health care benefits, and unspecified assistantships also available. Support available to part-time students. Financial award application deadline: 3/15; financial award applicants required to submit FAFSA. *Unit head:* Dr. Alfred Wheeler, Department Chair, 864-656-1415, Fax: 864-656-0435, E-mail: wheeler@clemson.edu. *Application contact:* Jay Lyn Martin, Coordinator for Graduate Program, 864-656-3587, Fax: 864-656-0435, E-mail: gradbio@clemson.edu.

Columbia University, Graduate School of Arts and Sciences, Division of Natural Sciences, Department of Ecology, Evolution and Environmental Biology, New York, NY 10027. Offers conservation biology (MA, Certificate); ecology and evolutionary biology (PhD); environmental policy (Certificate); evolutionary primatology (PhD). *Degree requirements:* For doctorate, one foreign language, thesis/dissertation, teaching experience. *Entrance requirements:* For doctorate, GRE General Test, previous course work in biology. Additional exam requirements/recommendations for international students: Required—TOEFL. Electronic applications accepted. *Faculty research:* Tropical ecology, ethnobotany, global change, systematics.

Cornell University, Graduate School, Graduate Fields of Agriculture and Life Sciences, Field of Ecology and Evolutionary Biology, Ithaca, NY 14853-0001. Offers ecology (PhD), including animal ecology, applied ecology, biogeochemistry, community and ecosystem ecology, limnology, oceanography, physiological ecology, plant ecology, population ecology, theoretical ecology, vertebrate zoology; evolutionary biology (PhD), including ecological genetics, paleobiology, population biology, systematics. *Faculty:* 48 full-time (13 women). *Students:* 51 full-time (37 women); includes 1 Asian, non-Hispanic/Latino; 3 Hispanic/Latino, 8 international. Average age 27. 108 applicants, 12% accepted, 10 enrolled. In 2010, 16 doctorates awarded. *Degree requirements:* For doctorate, comprehensive exam, thesis/dissertation, 2 semesters of teaching experience. *Entrance requirements:* For doctorate, GRE General Test, GRE Subject Test (biology), 2 letters of recommendation. Additional exam requirements/recommendations for international students: Required—TOEFL (minimum score 550 paper-based; 213 computer-based; 77 iBT). *Application deadline:* For fall admission, 12/15 for domestic students. Application fee: $70. Electronic applications accepted. *Expenses:* Tuition: Full-time $29,500. Required fees: $76. Tuition and fees vary according to degree level and program. *Financial support:* In 2010–11, 23 fellowships with full tuition reimbursements, 5 research assistantships with full tuition reimbursements, 21 teaching assistantships with full tuition reimbursements were awarded; institutionally sponsored loans, scholarships/grants, health care benefits, tuition waivers (full and partial), and unspecified assistantships also available. Financial award applicants required to submit FAFSA. *Faculty research:* Population and organismal biology, population and evolutionary genetics, systematics and macroevolution, biochemistry, conservation biology. *Unit head:* Director of Graduate Studies, 607-254-4230. *Application contact:* Graduate Field Assistant, 607-254-4230, E-mail: eeb_grad_req@cornell.edu.

Dartmouth College, Arts and Sciences Graduate Programs, Program in Ecology and Evolutionary Biology, Hanover, NH 03755. Offers PhD. *Entrance requirements:* For doctorate, GRE General Test, GRE Subject Test in biology (highly recommended). Additional exam requirements/recommendations for international students: Required—TOEFL.

Emory University, Laney Graduate School, Division of Biological and Biomedical Sciences, Program in Population Biology, Ecology and Evolution, Atlanta, GA 30322-1100. Offers PhD. *Faculty:* 35 full-time (6 women). *Students:* 29 full-time (20 women); includes 1 Asian, non-Hispanic/Latino; 4 Hispanic/Latino, 6 international. Average age 27. 40 applicants, 38% accepted, 5 enrolled. In 2010, 4 doctorates awarded. *Degree requirements:* For doctorate, comprehensive exam, thesis/dissertation. *Entrance requirements:* For doctorate, GRE General Test, minimum GPA of 3.0 in science course work (recommended). Additional exam requirements/recommendations for international students: Required—TOEFL. *Application deadline:* For fall admission, 12/1 for domestic and international students. Application fee: $75. Electronic applications accepted. *Expenses:* Tuition: Full-time $33,800. Required fees: $1300. *Financial support:* In 2010–11, 12 students received support, including 12 fellowships with full tuition reimbursements available (averaging $25,000 per year); institutionally sponsored loans, scholarships/grants, health care benefits, and tuition waivers (full) also available. *Faculty research:* Evolution of microbes, infectious disease, the immune system, genetic disease in humans, evolution of behavior. *Unit head:* Dr. Michael Zwick, Director, 404-727-9924, Fax: 404-727-3949, E-mail: mzwick@emory.edu. *Application contact:* Kathy Smith, Director of Recruitment and Admissions, 404-727-2547, Fax: 404-727-3322, E-mail: kathy.smith@emory.edu.

Florida State University, The Graduate School, College of Arts and Sciences, Department of Biological Science, Specialization in Ecology and Evolutionary Biology, Tallahassee, FL 32306-4295. Offers MS, PhD. *Faculty:* 26 full-time (9 women). *Students:* 61 full-time (30 women); includes 2 Asian, non-Hispanic/Latino; 4 Hispanic/Latino, 4 international. 133 applicants, 13% accepted, 14 enrolled. In 2010, 3 master's, 6 doctorates awarded. Terminal master's awarded for partial completion of doctoral program. *Degree requirements:* For master's, comprehensive exam, thesis, teaching experience, seminar presentation; for doctorate, comprehensive exam, thesis/dissertation, teaching experience; seminar presentation. *Entrance requirements:* For master's, GRE General Test (minimum combined score 1100, 500 verbal, 500 quantitative), minimum upper-division GPA of 3.0; for doctorate, GRE General Test (minimum combined score 1100, Verbal 500, Quantitative 500), minimum upper-division GPA of 3.0. Additional exam requirements/recommendations for international students: Required—TOEFL (minimum score 600 paper-based; 250 computer-based; 92 iBT). *Application deadline:* For fall admission, 12/15 for domestic and international students. Application fee: $30. Electronic applications accepted. *Expenses:* Tuition, state resident: full-time $8238. *Financial support:* In 2010–11, 55 students received support, including 3 fellowships with full tuition reimbursements available (averaging $24,000 per year), 21 research assistantships with full tuition reimbursements available (averaging $21,000 per year), 31 teaching assistantships with full tuition reimbursements available (averaging $21,000 per year). Financial award application deadline: 12/15; financial award applicants required to submit FAFSA. *Faculty research:* Ecology and conservation biology; evolution; marine biology; phylogeny and systematics; theoretical, computational and mathematical biology. *Application contact:* Judy Bowers, Coordinator, Graduate Affairs, 850-644-3023, Fax: 850-644-9829, E-mail: gradinfo@bio.fsu.edu.

George Mason University, College of Science, Department of Molecular and Microbiology, Fairfax, VA 22030. Offers biology (MS), including bioinformatics and computational biology, general biology, microbiology and infectious disease, molecular biology, systematics and evolutionary biology; biosciences (PhD). *Faculty:* 10 full-time (5 women). *Students:* 12 full-time (6 women), 63 part-time (36 women); includes 2 Black or African American, non-Hispanic/Latino; 1 American Indian or Alaska Native, non-Hispanic/Latino; 8 Asian, non-Hispanic/Latino; 1 Hispanic/Latino, 16 international. Average age 31. 98 applicants, 37% accepted, 19 enrolled. In 2010, 7 master's, 7 doctorates awarded. *Entrance requirements:* Additional exam requirements/recommendations for international students: Required—TOEFL (minimum score 570 paper-based; 230 computer-based; 88 iBT). Application fee: $100. *Expenses:* Tuition, state resident: full-time $8192; part-time $440 per credit hour. Tuition, nonresident: full-time $22,952; part-time $1055 per credit hour. Required fees: $2364; $99 per credit hour. *Financial support:* In 2010–11, 32 students received support, including 3 fellowships (averaging $18,000 per year), 6 research assistantships (averaging $14,073 per year), 23 teaching assistantships (averaging $12,194 per year); career-related internships or fieldwork, Federal Work-Study, scholarships/grants, unspecified assistantships, and health care benefits (full-time research or teaching assistantship recipients) also available. Financial award applicants required to submit FAFSA. Total annual research expenditures: $457,760. *Unit head:* Dr. James Willett, Director, 703-993-8311, Fax: 703-993-8976, E-mail: jwillett@gmu.edu. *Application contact:* Daniel Cox, Associate Dean for Graduate Programs, 703-993-4971, Fax: 703-993-4325, E-mail: dcox5@gmu.edu.

Harvard University, Graduate School of Arts and Sciences, Department of Organismic and Evolutionary Biology, Cambridge, MA 02138. Offers biology (PhD). *Degree requirements:* For doctorate, 2 foreign languages, public presentation of thesis research, exam. *Entrance requirements:* For doctorate, GRE General Test, GRE Subject Test (recommended), 7 courses in biology, chemistry, physics, mathematics, computer science, or geology. Additional exam requirements/recommendations for international students: Required—TOEFL. *Expenses:* Tuition: Full-time $34,976. Required fees: $1166. Full-time tuition and fees vary according to program.

Illinois State University, Graduate School, College of Arts and Sciences, Department of Biological Sciences, Normal, IL 61790-2200. Offers animal behavior (MS); bacteriology (MS); biochemistry (MS); biological sciences (MS); biology (PhD); biophysics (MS); biotechnology (MS); botany (MS, PhD); cell biology (MS); conservation biology (MS); developmental biology (MS); ecology (MS, PhD); entomology (MS); evolutionary biology (MS); genetics (MS, PhD); immunology (MS); microbiology (MS, PhD); molecular biology (MS); molecular genetics (MS); neurobiology (MS); neuroscience (MS); parasitology (MS); physiology (MS, PhD); plant biology (MS); plant molecular biology (MS); plant sciences (MS); structural biology (MS); zoology (MS, PhD). Part-time programs available. *Degree requirements:* For master's, thesis or alternative; for doctorate, variable foreign language requirement, thesis/dissertation, 2 terms of residency. *Entrance requirements:* For master's, GRE General Test, minimum GPA of 2.6 in last 60 hours of course work; for doctorate, GRE General Test. *Faculty research:* Redoc balance and drug development in schistosoma mansoni, control of the growth of listeria monocytogenes at low temperature, regulation of cell expansion and microtubule function by SPRI, CRUI: physiology and fitness consequences of different life history phenotypes.

Indiana University Bloomington, University Graduate School, College of Arts and Sciences, Department of Biology, Bloomington, IN 47405. Offers biology teaching (MAT); biotechnology (MA); evolution, ecology, and behavior (MA, PhD); genetics (PhD); microbiology (MA, PhD); molecular, cellular, and developmental biology (PhD); plant sciences (MA, PhD); zoology (MA, PhD). *Faculty:* 58 full-time (15 women), 21 part-time/adjunct (6 women). *Students:* 163 full-time (98 women), 7 part-time (2 women); includes 17 minority (3 Black or African American, non-Hispanic/Latino; 1 American Indian or Alaska Native, non-Hispanic/Latino; 7 Asian, non-Hispanic/Latino; 5 Hispanic/Latino; 1 Native Hawaiian or other Pacific Islander, non-Hispanic/Latino), 52 international. Average age 27. 346 applicants, 15% accepted, 24 enrolled. In 2010, 17 master's, 24 doctorates awarded. Terminal master's awarded for partial completion of doctoral program. *Degree requirements:* For master's, thesis, oral defense; for doctorate, thesis/dissertation, oral defense. *Entrance requirements:* For master's and doctorate, GRE General Test. Additional exam requirements/recommendations for international students: Required—TOEFL (minimum score 100 iBT). *Application deadline:* For fall admission, 1/5 priority date for domestic students, 12/1 priority date for international students. Application fee: $55 ($65 for international students). Electronic applications accepted. *Financial support:* In 2010–11, 170 students received support, including 64 fellowships with tuition reimbursements available (averaging $19,484 per year), 44 research assistantships with tuition reimbursements available (averaging $20,300 per year), 62 teaching assistantships with tuition reimbursements available (averaging $20,521 per year); scholarships/grants, traineeships, health care benefits, and unspecified assistantships also available. Financial award application deadline: 1/5. *Faculty research:* Evolution, ecology and behavior; microbiology; molecular biology and genetics; plant biology. *Unit head:* Dr. Roger Innes, Chair, 812-855-2219, Fax: 812-855-6082, E-mail: rinnes@indiana.edu. *Application contact:* Tracey D. Stohr, Graduate Student Recruitment Coordinator, 812-856-6303, Fax: 812-855-6082, E-mail: gradbio@indiana.edu.

Iowa State University of Science and Technology, Graduate College, College of Liberal Arts and Sciences, Department of Ecology, Evolution, and Organismal Biology, Ames, IA 50011. Offers MS, PhD. *Faculty:* 31 full-time (9 women), 6 part-time/adjunct (4 women). *Students:* 49 full-time (23 women), 9 part-time (3 women); includes 1 American Indian or Alaska Native, non-Hispanic/Latino; 1 Asian, non-Hispanic/Latino; 1 Hispanic/Latino, 14 international. 8 applicants, 100% accepted, 5 enrolled. *Degree requirements:* For master's, thesis or alternative; for doctorate, thesis/dissertation. *Entrance requirements:* For master's and doctorate, GRE General Test. Additional exam requirements/recommendations for international students: Required—TOEFL. Application fee: $40 ($90 for international students). Electronic applications accepted. *Financial support:* In 2010–11, 28 research assistantships with partial tuition reimbursements (averaging $17,245 per year), 18 teaching assistantships with partial tuition reimbursements (averaging $14,619 per year) were awarded; fellowships, scholarships/grants, health care benefits, and unspecified assistantships also available. *Faculty research:* Aquatic and wetland ecology, cytology, ecology, physiology and molecular biology, systematics and evolution. *Unit head:* Dr. Jonathan Wendel, Chair, 515-294-7172. *Application contact:* Information Contact, 515-294-5836, Fax: 515-294-2592, E-mail: grad_admissions@iastate.edu.

Iowa State University of Science and Technology, Graduate College, Interdisciplinary Programs, Program in Ecology and Evolutionary Biology, Ames, IA 50011. Offers MS, PhD. *Students:* 55 full-time (25 women), 7 part-time (2 women); includes 1 American Indian or Alaska Native, non-Hispanic/Latino; 1 Asian, non-Hispanic/Latino; 1 Hispanic/Latino, 11 international. In 2010, 4 master's, 5 doctorates awarded. *Degree requirements:* For master's, thesis or alternative; for doctorate, thesis/dissertation. *Entrance requirements:* For master's and doctorate, GRE General Test, application to cooperating department. Additional exam requirements/recommendations for international students: Required—TOEFL (minimum score 550 paper-based; 79 iBT), IELTS (minimum score 6.5). *Application deadline:* For fall admission, 1/1 priority date for domestic and international students; for spring admission, 5/1 priority date for domestic and international students. Application fee: $40 ($90 for international students). Electronic applications accepted. *Financial support:* In 2010–11, 32 research assistantships with full and partial tuition reimbursements (averaging $17,573 per year), 17 teaching assistantships with full and partial tuition reimbursements (averaging $12,241 per year) were awarded; scholarships/grants, health care benefits, and unspecified assistantships also available. *Faculty research:* Landscape ecology, aquatic and method ecology, physiological ecology, population genetics and evolution, systematics. *Unit head:* Dr. Kirk Moloney, Supervisory Committee Chair, 515-294-6518, E-mail: eeboffice@iastate.edu. *Application contact:* Charles Sauer, Information Contact, 515-294-6518, E-mail: eeboffice@iastate.edu.

The Johns Hopkins University, School of Medicine, Graduate Programs in Medicine, Center for Functional Anatomy and Evolution, Baltimore, MD 21218-2699. Offers PhD. *Faculty:* 5 full-time (1 woman), 2 part-time/adjunct (1 woman). *Students:* 10 full-time (7 women), 2 international. Average age 25. 26 applicants, 15% accepted, 2 enrolled. In 2010, 1 doctorate awarded. *Degree requirements:* For doctorate, comprehensive exam, thesis/dissertation, oral exams. *Entrance requirements:* For doctorate, GRE. Additional exam requirements/recommendations for international students: Required—TOEFL. *Application deadline:* For fall admission, 1/10 for domestic and international students. Application fee: $85. *Financial support:* In 2010–11, 1 fellowship with partial tuition reimbursement (averaging $30,000 per year), 8 teaching assistantships with full tuition reimbursements (averaging $26,855 per year) were awarded; career-related internships or fieldwork, institutionally sponsored loans, health care benefits, and tuition waivers (full) also available. *Faculty research:* Vertebrate evolution, functional anatomy, primate evolution, vertebrate paleobiology, vertebrate morphology. *Unit head:* Dr. Kenneth D. Rose, Director, 410-955-7172, Fax: 410-614-9030, E-mail: kdrose@jhmi.edu. *Application contact:* Catherine L. Will, Coordinator, Graduate Student Affairs, 410-614-3385, E-mail: grad_study@som.adm.jhu.edu.

Michigan State University, The Graduate School, College of Natural Science, Interdepartmental Program in Ecology, Evolutionary Biology and Behavior, East Lansing, MI 48824. Offers PhD. *Entrance requirements:* Additional exam requirements/recommendations for international students: Required—TOEFL. Electronic applications accepted.

Montclair State University, The Graduate School, College of Science and Mathematics, Department of Biology and Molecular Biology, Montclair, NJ 07043-1624. Offers biological science (Certificate); biology (MS), including biology, biology science/education, ecology and evolution, physiology; molecular biology (MS, Certificate). Part-time and evening/weekend programs available. *Faculty:* 22 full-time (9 women), 26 part-time/adjunct (13 women). *Students:* 30 full-time (20 women), 73 part-time (55 women); includes 5 Black or African American, non-Hispanic/Latino; 6 Asian, non-Hispanic/Latino; 25 Hispanic/Latino, 3 international. Average age 28. 48 applicants, 71% accepted, 24 enrolled. In 2010, 21 master's, 2 other advanced degrees awarded. *Degree requirements:* For master's, comprehensive exam, thesis or alternative. *Entrance requirements:* For master's, GRE General Test, 24 credits of course work in undergraduate biology, 2 letters of recommendation, teaching certificate (biology sciences education concentration). Additional exam requirements/recommendations for international students: Required—TOEFL (minimum iBT score of 83) or IELTS. *Application deadline:* For fall admission, 6/1 for international students; for spring admission, 10/1 for international students. Applications are processed on a rolling basis. Application fee: $60. Electronic applications accepted. *Expenses:* Tuition, state resident: part-time $501.34 per credit. Tuition, nonresident: part-time $773.88 per credit. Required fees: $71.15 per credit. *Financial support:* In 2010–11, 12 research assistantships with full tuition reimbursements (averaging $7,000 per year) were awarded; Federal Work-Study, scholarships/grants, and unspecified assistantships also available. Support available to part-time students. Financial award application deadline: 3/1; financial award applicants required to submit FAFSA. *Faculty research:* Cells, algae blooms, scallops, New Jersey bays, Barnegat Bay. Total annual research expenditures: $1.3 million. *Unit head:* Dr. Quinn Vega, Chairperson, 973-655-7178. *Application contact:* Amy Aiello, Director of Graduate Admissions and Operations, 973-655-5147, Fax: 973-655-7869, E-mail: graduate.school@montclair.edu.

Northwestern University, Northwestern University Feinberg School of Medicine and Interdepartmental Programs, Integrated Graduate Programs in the Life Sciences, Chicago, IL 60611. Offers cancer biology (PhD); cell biology (PhD); developmental biology (PhD); evolutionary biology (PhD); immunology and microbial pathogenesis (PhD); molecular biology and genetics (PhD); neurobiology (PhD); pharmacology and toxicology (PhD); structural biology and biochemistry (PhD). *Degree requirements:* For doctorate, comprehensive exam, thesis/dissertation, written and oral qualifying exams. *Entrance requirements:* For doctorate, GRE General Test. Additional exam requirements/recommendations for international students: Required—TOEFL (minimum score 600 paper-based; 250 computer-based). Electronic applications accepted.

The Ohio State University, Graduate School, College of Arts and Sciences, Division of Natural and Mathematical Sciences, Department of Evolution, Ecology, and Organismal Biology, Columbus, OH 43210. Offers MS, PhD. *Faculty:* 43. *Students:* 21 full-time (11 women), 40 part-time (21 women); includes 2 Black or African American, non-Hispanic/Latino, 9 international. Average age 29. In 2010, 9 master's, 4 doctorates awarded. *Degree requirements:* For master's, thesis optional; for doctorate, thesis/dissertation. *Entrance requirements:* For master's and doctorate, GRE General Test. Additional exam requirements/recommendations for international students: Required—TOEFL (minimum score 600 paper-based; 250 computer-based). *Application deadline:* For fall admission, 8/15 priority date for domestic students, 7/1

Evolutionary Biology

The Ohio State University (continued)
priority date for international students; for winter admission, 12/1 priority date for domestic students, 11/1 priority date for international students; for spring admission, 3/1 priority date for domestic students, 2/1 priority date for international students. Applications are processed on a rolling basis. Application fee: $40 ($50 for international students). Electronic applications accepted. *Expenses:* Tuition, state resident: full-time $10,605. Tuition, nonresident: full-time $26,535. Tuition and fees vary according to course load and program. *Financial support:* Fellowships, research assistantships, teaching assistantships, Federal Work-Study and institutionally sponsored loans available. Support available to part-time students. *Unit head:* Peter S. Curtis, Chair, 614-292-8280, Fax: 614-292-2030, E-mail: curtis.7@osu.edu. *Application contact:* 614-292-9444, Fax: 614-292-3895, E-mail: domestic.grad@osu.edu.

Ohio University, Graduate College, College of Arts and Sciences, Department of Biological Sciences, Athens, OH 45701-2979. Offers biological sciences (MS, PhD); cell biology and physiology (MS, PhD); ecology and evolutionary biology (MS, PhD); exercise physiology and muscle biology (MS, PhD); microbiology (MS, PhD); neuroscience (MS, PhD). *Students:* 32 full-time (9 women), 5 part-time (2 women); includes 2 minority (1 Black or African American, non-Hispanic/Latino; 1 Hispanic/Latino), 9 international. 51 applicants, 37% accepted, 7 enrolled. In 2010, 2 master's, 9 doctorates awarded. Terminal master's awarded for partial completion of doctoral program. *Degree requirements:* For master's, comprehensive exam, thesis, 1 quarter of teaching experience; for doctorate, comprehensive exam, thesis/dissertation, 2 quarters of teaching experience. *Entrance requirements:* For master's, GRE General Test, names of three faculty members whose research interests most closely match the applicant's interest; for doctorate, GRE General Test, essay concerning prior training, research interest and career goals, plus names of three faculty members whose research interests most closely match the applicant's interest. Additional exam requirements/recommendations for international students: Required—TOEFL (minimum score 620 paper-based; 105 iBT) or IELTS (minimum score 7.5). *Application deadline:* For fall admission, 1/15 for domestic and international students. Application fee: $50 ($55 for international students). Electronic applications accepted. *Financial support:* In 2010–11, 1 fellowship with full tuition reimbursement (averaging $18,957 per year), 10 research assistantships with full tuition reimbursements (averaging $18,957 per year), 42 teaching assistantships with full tuition reimbursements (averaging $18,957 per year) were awarded; Federal Work-Study and institutionally sponsored loans also available. Financial award application deadline: 1/15. *Faculty research:* Ecology and evolutionary biology, exercise physiology and muscle biology, neurobiology, cell biology, physiology. Total annual research expenditures: $2.8 million. *Unit head:* Dr. Ralph DiCaprio, Chair, 740-593-2290, Fax: 740-593-0300, E-mail: dicaprir@ohio.edu. *Application contact:* Dr. Patrick Hassett, Graduate Chair, 740-593-4793, Fax: 740-593-0300, E-mail: hassett@ohio.edu.

Princeton University, Graduate School, Department of Ecology and Evolutionary Biology, Princeton, NJ 08544-1019. Offers PhD. *Degree requirements:* For doctorate, thesis/dissertation. *Entrance requirements:* For doctorate, GRE General Test, GRE Subject Test. Additional exam requirements/recommendations for international students: Required—TOEFL (minimum score 600 paper-based; 250 computer-based). Electronic applications accepted.

Purdue University, Graduate School, College of Science, Department of Biological Sciences, West Lafayette, IN 47907. Offers biochemistry (PhD); biophysics (PhD); cell and developmental biology (PhD); ecology, evolutionary and population biology (MS, PhD), including ecology, evolutionary biology, population biology; genetics (MS, PhD); microbiology (MS, PhD); molecular biology (PhD); neurobiology (MS, PhD); plant physiology (PhD). Terminal master's awarded for partial completion of doctoral program. *Degree requirements:* For master's, thesis (for some programs); for doctorate, thesis/dissertation, seminars, teaching experience. *Entrance requirements:* For master's and doctorate, GRE General Test. Additional exam requirements/recommendations for international students: Required—TOEFL. Electronic applications accepted.

Rice University, Graduate Programs, Wiess School of Natural Sciences, Department of Ecology and Evolutionary Biology, Houston, TX 77251-1892. Offers MA, MS, PhD. Terminal master's awarded for partial completion of doctoral program. *Degree requirements:* For master's, comprehensive exam (for some programs), thesis (for some programs); for doctorate, comprehensive exam, thesis/dissertation. *Entrance requirements:* For master's and doctorate, GRE General Test, GRE Subject Test. Additional exam requirements/recommendations for international students: Required—TOEFL (minimum score 600 paper-based; 250 computer-based; 90 iBT). Electronic applications accepted. *Faculty research:* Trace gas emissions, wetlands, biology, community ecology of forests and grasslands, conservation biology specialization.

Rutgers, The State University of New Jersey, New Brunswick, Graduate School-New Brunswick, Program in Ecology and Evolution, Piscataway, NJ 08854-8097. Offers MS, PhD. Part-time programs available. Terminal master's awarded for partial completion of doctoral program. *Degree requirements:* For master's, comprehensive exam; for doctorate, comprehensive exam, thesis/dissertation. *Entrance requirements:* For master's and doctorate, GRE General Test, minimum GPA of 3.0. Additional exam requirements/recommendations for international students: Required—TOEFL (minimum score 550 paper-based; 213 computer-based). Electronic applications accepted. *Expenses:* Tuition, state resident: full-time $7200; part-time $600 per credit. Tuition, nonresident: full-time $11,124; part-time $927 per credit. *Faculty research:* Population and community ecology, population genetics, evolutionary biology, conservation biology, ecosystem ecology.

Rutgers, The State University of New Jersey, New Brunswick, Graduate School-New Brunswick, Program in Plant Biology, Piscataway, NJ 08854-8097. Offers horticulture and plant technology (MS, PhD); molecular and cellular biology (MS, PhD); organismal and population biology (MS, PhD); plant pathology (MS, PhD). Part-time programs available. Terminal master's awarded for partial completion of doctoral program. *Degree requirements:* For master's, comprehensive exam, thesis or alternative; for doctorate, comprehensive exam, thesis/dissertation. *Entrance requirements:* For master's and doctorate, GRE General Test, GRE Subject Test (recommended). Additional exam requirements/recommendations for international students: Required—TOEFL (minimum score 600 paper-based; 250 computer-based). Electronic applications accepted. *Expenses:* Tuition, state resident: full-time $7200; part-time $600 per credit. Tuition, nonresident: full-time $11,124; part-time $927 per credit. *Faculty research:* Molecular biology and biochemistry of plants, plant development and genomics, plant protection, plant improvement, plant management of horticultural and field crops.

Stony Brook University, State University of New York, Graduate School, College of Arts and Sciences, Department of Ecology and Evolution, Stony Brook, NY 11794. Offers applied ecology (MA); ecology and evolution (PhD). *Faculty:* 17 full-time (5 women). *Students:* 46 full-time (23 women); includes 3 Asian, non-Hispanic/Latino; 4 Hispanic/Latino, 6 international. Average age 28. 90 applicants, 38% accepted, 10 enrolled. In 2010, 6 doctorates awarded. *Degree requirements:* For doctorate, one foreign language, comprehensive exam, thesis/dissertation, teaching experience. *Entrance requirements:* For doctorate, GRE General Test, GRE Subject Test. Additional exam requirements/recommendations for international students: Required—TOEFL. *Application deadline:* For fall admission, 1/15 for domestic students. Application fee: $100. *Expenses:* Tuition, state resident: full-time $8370; part-time $349 per credit. Tuition, nonresident: full-time $13,780; part-time $574 per credit. Required fees: $994. *Financial support:* In 2010–11, 9 research assistantships, 29 teaching assistantships were awarded; fellowships, Federal Work-Study also available. *Faculty research:* Theoretical and experimental population genetics, numerical taxonomy, biostatistics, population and community ecology, plant ecology. Total annual research expenditures: $1.4 million. *Unit head:* Dr. Jessica Gurevitch, Chair, 631-632-8600. *Application contact:* Dr. Dan Dykhuizen, Director, 631-246-8604, E-mail: dandyk@life.bio.sunysb.edu.

Tulane University, School of Science and Engineering, Department of Ecology and Evolutionary Biology, New Orleans, LA 70118-5669. Offers MS, PhD. Terminal master's awarded for partial completion of doctoral program. *Degree requirements:* For master's, thesis or alternative; for

doctorate, thesis/dissertation. *Entrance requirements:* For master's, GRE General Test, minimum B average in undergraduate course work; for doctorate, GRE General Test. Additional exam requirements/recommendations for international students: Required—TOEFL. Electronic applications accepted. *Faculty research:* Ichthyology, plant systematics, crustacean endocrinology, ecotoxicology, ornithology.

University at Albany, State University of New York, College of Arts and Sciences, Department of Biological Sciences, Specialization in Ecology, Evolution, and Behavior, Albany, NY 12222-0001. Offers MS, PhD. *Degree requirements:* For master's, one foreign language; for doctorate, one foreign language, thesis/dissertation. *Entrance requirements:* For master's and doctorate, GRE General Test.

University at Buffalo, the State University of New York, Graduate School, College of Arts and Sciences, Program in Evolution, Ecology and Behavior, Buffalo, NY 14260. Offers MS, PhD, Certificate. *Faculty:* 13 full-time (3 women). *Students:* 14 full-time (8 women); includes 1 Black or African American, non-Hispanic/Latino, 1 international. Average age 25. 23 applicants, 35% accepted, 3 enrolled. In 2010, 3 master's, 1 doctorate awarded. Terminal master's awarded for partial completion of doctoral program. *Degree requirements:* For master's, project; for doctorate, comprehensive exam, thesis/dissertation. *Entrance requirements:* For master's, GRE, minimum undergraduate GPA of 3.0; for doctorate, GRE, minimum GPA of 3.0. Additional exam requirements/recommendations for international students: Required—TOEFL (minimum score 79 iBT). *Application deadline:* For fall admission, 1/15 priority date for domestic and international students. Applications are processed on a rolling basis. Application fee: $75. Electronic applications accepted. *Financial support:* In 2010–11, 2 fellowships with full tuition reimbursements (averaging $6,000 per year), 4 research assistantships with full tuition reimbursements (averaging $20,000 per year), 3 teaching assistantships with full tuition reimbursements (averaging $17,000 per year) were awarded; Federal Work-Study, scholarships/grants, health care benefits, and unspecified assistantships also available. Financial award application deadline: 1/15; financial award applicants required to submit FAFSA. *Faculty research:* Coral reef ecology, evolution and ecology of aquatic invertebrates, animal communication, paleobiology, primate behavior. *Unit head:* Dr. Howard Lasker, Program Director, 716-645-4870, Fax: 716-645-3999, E-mail: ub-evb@buffalo.edu. *Application contact:* Marty Roth, Secretary, 716-645-3489, Fax: 716-345-3999, E-mail: mlroth@buffalo.edu.

University of Alberta, Faculty of Graduate Studies and Research, Department of Biological Sciences, Edmonton, AB T6G 2E1, Canada. Offers environmental biology and ecology (M Sc, PhD); microbiology and biotechnology (M Sc, PhD); molecular biology and genetics (M Sc, PhD); physiology and cell biology (M Sc, PhD); plant biology (M Sc, PhD); systematics and evolution (M Sc, PhD). Terminal master's awarded for partial completion of doctoral program. *Degree requirements:* For master's, thesis; for doctorate, thesis/dissertation. *Entrance requirements:* Additional exam requirements/recommendations for international students: Required—TOEFL.

The University of Arizona, College of Science, Department of Ecology and Evolutionary Biology, Tucson, AZ 85721. Offers MS, PhD. *Faculty:* 19 full-time (5 women), 2 part-time/adjunct (0 women). *Students:* 30 full-time (10 women), 19 part-time (10 women); includes 1 American Indian or Alaska Native, non-Hispanic/Latino; 1 Hispanic/Latino; 2 Two or more races, non-Hispanic/Latino, 11 international. Average age 29. 87 applicants, 15% accepted, 9 enrolled. In 2010, 3 master's, 5 doctorates awarded. Terminal master's awarded for partial completion of doctoral program. *Degree requirements:* For master's, thesis optional; for doctorate, one foreign language, comprehensive exam, thesis/dissertation. *Entrance requirements:* For master's, GRE General Test, GRE Subject Test, statement of purpose, curriculum vitae, 3 letters of recommendation; for doctorate, GRE General Test, GRE Subject Test, curriculum vitae, 3 letters of recommendation. Additional exam requirements/recommendations for international students: Required—TOEFL (minimum score 550 paper-based; 213 computer-based; 79 iBT). *Application deadline:* For fall admission, 12/1 for domestic students, 12/8 for international students. Application fee: $75. *Expenses:* Tuition, state resident: full-time $7692. *Financial support:* In 2010–11, 8 research assistantships with full tuition reimbursements (averaging $21,303 per year), 38 teaching assistantships with full tuition reimbursements (averaging $21,555 per year) were awarded; career-related internships or fieldwork, scholarships/grants, health care benefits, and unspecified assistantships also available. *Faculty research:* Biological diversity, evolutionary history, evolutionary mechanisms, community structure. Total annual research expenditures: $4.5 million. *Unit head:* Dr. Richard E. Michod, Head, 520-621-7509, Fax: 520-621-9190, E-mail: michod@email.arizona.edu. *Application contact:* Carol Burleson, Administrative Associate, 520-621-1165, Fax: 520-621-9190, E-mail: burleson@email.arizona.edu.

University of California, Davis, Graduate Studies, Graduate Group in Population Biology, Davis, CA 95616. Offers PhD. *Degree requirements:* For doctorate, thesis/dissertation. *Entrance requirements:* For doctorate, GRE General Test, GRE Subject Test. Additional exam requirements/recommendations for international students: Required—TOEFL (minimum score 550 paper-based; 213 computer-based). Electronic applications accepted. *Faculty research:* Population ecology, population genetics, systematics, evolution, community ecology.

University of California, Irvine, School of Biological Sciences, Department of Ecology and Evolutionary Biology, Irvine, CA 92697. Offers biological sciences (MS, PhD). *Students:* 45 full-time (30 women); includes 6 minority (2 Asian, non-Hispanic/Latino; 4 Hispanic/Latino), 7 international. Average age 28. 69 applicants, 23% accepted, 6 enrolled. In 2010, 9 doctorates awarded. *Degree requirements:* For master's, thesis; for doctorate, thesis/dissertation. *Entrance requirements:* For master's and doctorate, GRE General Test, GRE Subject Test, minimum GPA of 3.0. Additional exam requirements/recommendations for international students: Required—TOEFL (minimum score 550 paper-based; 213 computer-based). *Application deadline:* For fall admission, 1/15 priority date for domestic students, 1/15 for international students. Applications are processed on a rolling basis. Application fee: $80 ($100 for international students). Electronic applications accepted. *Financial support:* Fellowships, research assistantships with full tuition reimbursements, teaching assistantships, career-related internships or fieldwork, institutionally sponsored loans, traineeships, health care benefits, and unspecified assistantships available. Financial award application deadline: 3/1; financial award applicants required to submit FAFSA. *Faculty research:* Ecological energetics, quantitative genetics, life history evolution, plant-herbivore and plant-pollinator interactions, molecular evolution. *Unit head:* Prof. Brandon Gaut, Chair, 949-824-2564, Fax: 949-824-2181, E-mail: bgaut@uci.edu. *Application contact:* Pam McDonald, Student Affairs Officer, 949-824-4743, Fax: 949-824-2181, E-mail: pmcdonal@uci.edu.

University of California, Los Angeles, Graduate Division, College of Letters and Science, Department of Ecology and Evolutionary Biology, Los Angeles, CA 90095. Offers MA, PhD. *Faculty:* 25 full-time (6 women). *Students:* 65 full-time (46 women); includes 14 minority (1 Black or African American, non-Hispanic/Latino; 5 Asian, non-Hispanic/Latino; 7 Hispanic/Latino; 1 Two or more races, non-Hispanic/Latino), 8 international. Average age 29. 89 applicants, 21% accepted, 13 enrolled. In 2010, 5 master's, 13 doctorates awarded. Terminal master's awarded for partial completion of doctoral program. *Degree requirements:* For master's, comprehensive exam or thesis; for doctorate, thesis/dissertation, oral and written qualifying exams; teaching experience. *Entrance requirements:* For master's and doctorate, GRE General Test, GRE Subject Test (biology), minimum GPA of 3.0, 3 letters of recommendation. *Application deadline:* For fall admission, 12/1 for domestic and international students. Application fee: $70 ($90 for international students). Electronic applications accepted. *Financial support:* In 2010–11, 56 fellowships with full and partial tuition reimbursements, 25 research assistantships with full and partial tuition reimbursements, 43 teaching assistantships with full and partial tuition reimbursements were awarded; Federal Work-Study, institutionally sponsored loans, scholarships/grants, health care benefits, tuition waivers (full and partial), and unspecified assistantships also available. Financial award application deadline: 3/1; financial award applicants required to submit FAFSA. *Faculty research:* Molecular, cell, and developmental biology; interactive biology; organisms and populations. *Unit head:* Dr. Daniel T. Blumstein, Chair, 310-267-4746, Fax:

310-206-3987, E-mail: marmots@ucla.edu. *Application contact:* Jocelyn Yamadera, Student Affairs Officer, 310-825-1959, Fax: 310-206-5280, E-mail: jocelyny@lifesci.ucla.edu.

University of California, Riverside, Graduate Division, Department of Biology, Riverside, CA 92521-0102. Offers evolution, ecology and organismal biology (MS, PhD). *Faculty:* 39 full-time (9 women). *Students:* 50 full-time (24 women); includes 1 Asian, non-Hispanic/Latino; 4 Hispanic/Latino, 10 international. Average age 29. 42 applicants, 45% accepted, 6 enrolled. In 2010, 1 master's, 5 doctorates awarded. Terminal master's awarded for partial completion of doctoral program. *Degree requirements:* For master's, thesis, oral defense of thesis; for doctorate, thesis/dissertation, 3 quarters of teaching experience, qualifying exams. *Entrance requirements:* For master's and doctorate, GRE General Test, minimum GPA of 3.2. Additional exam requirements/recommendations for international students: Required—Either IELTS or TOEFL (paper-based 550, computer-based 213, iBT 80). *Application deadline:* For fall admission, 1/5 priority date for domestic students, 1/4 priority date for international students; for winter admission, 9/1 for domestic students, 7/1 for international students; for spring admission, 12/1 for domestic students, 10/1 for international students. Applications are processed on a rolling basis. Application fee: $80 ($100 for international students). Electronic applications accepted. *Financial support:* In 2010–11, fellowships with tuition reimbursements (averaging $16,000 per year), research assistantships with tuition reimbursements (averaging $18,000 per year), teaching assistantships with tuition reimbursements (averaging $16,500 per year) were awarded; career-related internships or fieldwork, Federal Work-Study, institutionally sponsored loans, and tuition waivers (full and partial) also available. Financial award application deadline: 1/5; financial award applicants required to submit FAFSA. *Faculty research:* Ecology, evolutionary biology, physiology, quantitative genetics, conservation biology. *Unit head:* Dr. Kimberly Hammond, Director, 951-827-4767, Fax: 951-827-4286, E-mail: kimberly.hammond@ucr.edu. *Application contact:* Melissa L. Gomez, Graduate Student Affairs Officer, 800-735-0717, Fax: 951-827-5913, E-mail: biograd@ucr.edu.

University of California, Riverside, Graduate Division, Department of Entomology, Riverside, CA 92521-0102. Offers entomology (MS, PhD); evolution and ecology (PhD). Part-time programs available. *Faculty:* 27 full-time (4 women). *Students:* 39 full-time (20 women); includes 1 Black or African American, non-Hispanic/Latino; 3 Asian, non-Hispanic/Latino; 2 Hispanic/Latino, 8 international. Average age 29. 27 applicants, 44% accepted, 11 enrolled. In 2010, 5 master's, 7 doctorates awarded. Terminal master's awarded for partial completion of doctoral program. *Degree requirements:* For master's, thesis; for doctorate, thesis/dissertation, qualifying exams. *Entrance requirements:* For master's and doctorate, GRE General Test, minimum GPA of 3.2. Additional exam requirements/recommendations for international students: Required—Either IELTS or TOEFL (paper-based 550, computer-based 213, iBT 80). *Application deadline:* For fall admission, 5/1 for domestic students, 2/1 for international students; for winter admission, 9/1 for domestic students, 7/1 for international students; for spring admission, 12/1 for domestic students, 10/1 for international students. Applications are processed on a rolling basis. Application fee: $80 ($100 for international students). Electronic applications accepted. *Financial support:* In 2010–11, fellowships with tuition reimbursements (averaging $15,000 per year), research assistantships with tuition reimbursements (averaging $18,000 per year), teaching assistantships with tuition reimbursements (averaging $16,640 per year) were awarded; career-related internships or fieldwork, Federal Work-Study, institutionally sponsored loans, and tuition waivers (full and partial) also available. Financial award application deadline: 1/5; financial award applicants required to submit FAFSA. *Faculty research:* Agricultural, urban, medical, and veterinary entomology; biological control; chemical ecology; insect pathogens; novel toxicants. *Unit head:* Dr. Richard Redak, Chair, 951-827-7250, Fax: 951-827-3086, E-mail: richard.redak@ucr.edu. *Application contact:* Melissa L. Gomez, Graduate Student Affairs Officer, 800-735-0717, Fax: 951-827-5913, E-mail: insects@ucr.edu.

University of California, San Diego, Office of Graduate Studies, Division of Biological Sciences, Program in Ecology, Behavior, and Evolution, La Jolla, CA 92093. Offers PhD. *Degree requirements:* For doctorate, thesis/dissertation, qualifying exam. Electronic applications accepted.

University of California, Santa Barbara, Graduate Division, College of Letters and Sciences, Division of Mathematics, Life, and Physical Sciences, Department of Ecology, Evolution, and Marine Biology, Santa Barbara, CA 93106-9620. Offers computational science and engineering (MA); computational sciences and engineering (PhD); ecology, evolution, and marine biology (MA, PhD); MA/PhD. *Faculty:* 27 full-time (7 women). *Students:* 59 full-time (38 women); includes 2 Black or African American, non-Hispanic/Latino; 5 Asian, non-Hispanic/Latino; 2 Hispanic/Latino. Average age 29. 119 applicants, 11% accepted, 8 enrolled. In 2010, 5 master's, 3 doctorates awarded. *Degree requirements:* For master's, comprehensive exam (for some programs), thesis (for some programs); for doctorate, comprehensive exam, thesis/dissertation. *Entrance requirements:* For master's and doctorate, GRE General Test. Additional exam requirements/recommendations for international students: Required—TOEFL (minimum score 550 paper-based; 80 iBT), IELTS. *Application deadline:* For fall admission, 12/15 for domestic and international students. Application fee: $70 ($90 for international students). Electronic applications accepted. *Financial support:* In 2010–11, 54 students received support, including 35 fellowships with full and partial tuition reimbursements available (averaging $10,812 per year), 21 research assistantships with full and partial tuition reimbursements available (averaging $8,441 per year), 43 teaching assistantships with partial tuition reimbursements available (averaging $9,346 per year); Federal Work-Study, scholarships/grants, traineeships, health care benefits, and tuition waivers (full and partial) also available. Financial award application deadline: 12/15; financial award applicants required to submit FAFSA. *Faculty research:* Community ecology, evolution, marine biology, population genetics, stream ecology. *Unit head:* Dr. Cheryl Briggs, Chair, 805-893-2415, Fax: 805-893-5885. *Application contact:* Melanie Fujii, Staff Graduate Advisor, 805-893-2979, Fax: 805-893-5885, E-mail: eemb-info@lifesci.ucsb.edu.

University of California, Santa Cruz, Division of Graduate Studies, Division of Physical and Biological Sciences, Department of Ecology and Evolutionary Biology, Santa Cruz, CA 95064. Offers MA, PhD. *Students:* 61 full-time (44 women), 1 part-time (0 women); includes 12 minority (2 Black or African American, non-Hispanic/Latino; 1 American Indian or Alaska Native, non-Hispanic/Latino; 1 Asian, non-Hispanic/Latino; 5 Hispanic/Latino; 1 Native Hawaiian or other Pacific Islander, non-Hispanic/Latino; 2 Two or more races, non-Hispanic/Latino), 2 international. Average age 29. 159 applicants, 12% accepted, 15 enrolled. In 2010, 3 master's, 11 doctorates awarded. *Degree requirements:* For master's, thesis; for doctorate, comprehensive exam, thesis/dissertation. *Entrance requirements:* For master's and doctorate, GRE General Test, GRE Subject Test, 3 letters of recommendation. Additional exam requirements/recommendations for international students: Required—TOEFL (minimum score 550 paper-based; 220 computer-based; 83 iBT); Recommended—IELTS (minimum score 8). *Application deadline:* For fall admission, 12/15 for domestic and international students. Application fee: $70 ($90 for international students). Electronic applications accepted. *Financial support:* Fellowships, research assistantships, teaching assistantships, institutionally sponsored loans and tuition waivers available. Financial award applicants required to submit FAFSA. *Faculty research:* Population and community ecology, evolutionary biology, physiology and behavior (marine and terrestrial), systematics and biodiversity. *Unit head:* Debbie Inferrera, Graduate Program Coordinator, 831-459-2193, E-mail: deborain@ucsc.edu. *Application contact:* Debbie Inferrera, Graduate Program Coordinator, 831-459-2193, E-mail: deborain@ucsc.edu.

University of Chicago, Division of Biological Sciences, Darwinian Sciences Cluster: Ecological, Integrative and Evolutionary Biology, Committee on Evolutionary Biology, Chicago, IL 60637-1513. Offers functional and evolutionary biology (PhD). Terminal master's awarded for partial completion of doctoral program. *Degree requirements:* For doctorate, thesis/dissertation, ethics class, 2 teaching assistantships. *Entrance requirements:* For doctorate, GRE General Test. Additional exam requirements/recommendations for international students: Required—TOEFL (minimum score 600 paper-based; 250 computer-based; 104 iBT), IELTS (minimum score 7). Electronic applications accepted. *Faculty research:* Systematics and evolutionary theory, genetics, functional morphology and physiology, behavior, ecology and biogeography.

University of Colorado Boulder, Graduate School, College of Arts and Sciences, Department of Ecology and Evolutionary Biology, Boulder, CO 80309. Offers animal behavior (MA); biology (MA, PhD); environmental biology (MA, PhD); evolutionary biology (MA, PhD); neurobiology (MA); population biology (MA); population genetics (PhD). *Faculty:* 32 full-time (10 women). *Students:* 71 full-time (36 women), 17 part-time (11 women); includes 10 minority (1 American Indian or Alaska Native, non-Hispanic/Latino; 2 Asian, non-Hispanic/Latino; 7 Hispanic/Latino), 4 international. Average age 30. 176 applicants, 20 enrolled. In 2010, 11 master's, 8 doctorates awarded. Terminal master's awarded for partial completion of doctoral program. *Degree requirements:* For master's, comprehensive exam, thesis or alternative; for doctorate, comprehensive exam, thesis/dissertation. *Entrance requirements:* For master's, GRE General Test, GRE Subject Test, minimum undergraduate GPA of 3.0; for doctorate, GRE General Test, GRE Subject Test. *Application deadline:* For fall admission, 12/30 priority date for domestic students, 12/1 for international students. Application fee: $50 ($60 for international students). *Financial support:* In 2010–11, 25 fellowships (averaging $17,876 per year), 27 research assistantships (averaging $15,070 per year) were awarded; Federal Work-Study, institutionally sponsored loans, and tuition waivers (full) also available. *Faculty research:* Behavior, ecology, genetics, morphology, endocrinology, physiology, systematics. Total annual research expenditures: $3.5 million.

University of Delaware, College of Arts and Sciences, Department of Biological Sciences, Newark, DE 19716. Offers biotechnology (MS); cancer biology (MS, PhD); cell and extracellular matrix biology (MS, PhD); cell and systems physiology (MS, PhD); developmental biology (MS, PhD); ecology and evolution (MS, PhD); microbiology (MS, PhD); molecular biology and genetics (MS, PhD). Terminal master's awarded for partial completion of doctoral program. *Degree requirements:* For master's, thesis, preliminary exam; for doctorate, comprehensive exam, thesis/dissertation, preliminary exam. *Entrance requirements:* For master's and doctorate, GRE General Test. Additional exam requirements/recommendations for international students: Required—TOEFL (minimum score 600 paper-based; 250 computer-based); Recommended—TWE. Electronic applications accepted. *Faculty research:* Microorganisms, bone, cancer metastasis, developmental biology, cell biology, DNA.

University of Guelph, Graduate Studies, College of Biological Science, Department of Integrative Biology, Botany and Zoology, Guelph, ON N1G 2W1, Canada. Offers botany (M Sc, PhD); zoology (M Sc, PhD). Part-time programs available. *Degree requirements:* For master's, thesis, research proposal; for doctorate, thesis/dissertation, research proposal, qualifying exam. *Entrance requirements:* For master's, minimum B average during previous 2 years of course work. Additional exam requirements/recommendations for international students: Required—TOEFL (minimum score 550 paper-based; 213 computer-based), IELTS (minimum score 6.5). Electronic applications accepted. *Faculty research:* Aquatic science, environmental physiology, parasitology, wildlife biology, management.

University of Hawaii at Manoa, Graduate Division, Interdisciplinary Specialization in Ecology, Evolution and Conservation Biology, Honolulu, HI 96822. Offers MS, PhD. *Faculty:* 6 part-time/adjunct (1 woman). *Degree requirements:* For doctorate, thesis/dissertation. *Application deadline:* For fall admission, 2/1 for domestic students; for spring admission, 10/15 for domestic students. Application fee: $50. *Financial support:* Fellowships, research assistantships, teaching assistantships, career-related internships or fieldwork and tuition waivers (full) available. *Faculty research:* Agronomy and soil science, zoology, entomology, genetics and molecular biology, botanical sciences. *Unit head:* Robert H. Cowie, Chair, 808-956-4909, Fax: 808-956-2647, E-mail: cowie@hawaii.edu. *Application contact:* Robert H. Cowie, Chair, 808-956-4909, Fax: 808-956-2647, E-mail: cowie@hawaii.edu.

University of Illinois at Urbana–Champaign, Graduate College, College of Liberal Arts and Sciences, School of Integrative Biology, Department of Animal Biology, Champaign, IL 61820. Offers animal biology (ecology, ethology and evolution) (MS, PhD). *Faculty:* 9 full-time (5 women). *Students:* 14 full-time (10 women), 3 part-time (1 woman); includes 1 minority (Two or more races, non-Hispanic/Latino), 3 international. 11 applicants, 27% accepted, 1 enrolled. *Entrance requirements:* For master's and doctorate, GRE. Additional exam requirements/recommendations for international students: Required—TOEFL (minimum score 570 paper-based; 230 computer-based; 88 iBT). *Application deadline:* Applications are processed on a rolling basis. Application fee: $75 ($90 for international students). Electronic applications accepted. *Financial support:* In 2010–11, 2 fellowships, 8 research assistantships, 13 teaching assistantships were awarded; tuition waivers (full and partial) also available. *Unit head:* Ken Paige, Head, 217-244-6606, Fax: 217-244-4565, E-mail: k-paige@illinois.edu. *Application contact:* Lisa Smith, Office Administrator, 217-333-7802, Fax: 217-244-4565, E-mail: ljsmith1@illinois.edu.

University of Illinois at Urbana–Champaign, Graduate College, College of Liberal Arts and Sciences, School of Integrative Biology, Program in Ecology, Evolution and Conservation Biology, Champaign, IL 61820. Offers MS, PhD. *Students:* 25 full-time (14 women), 10 part-time (8 women); includes 1 Black or African American, non-Hispanic/Latino; 2 Asian, non-Hispanic/Latino; 1 Hispanic/Latino, 2 international. 40 applicants, 23% accepted, 6 enrolled. In 2010, 1 master's, 4 doctorates awarded. *Entrance requirements:* For master's and doctorate, GRE. Additional exam requirements/recommendations for international students: Required—TOEFL (minimum score 613 paper-based; 257 computer-based; 103 iBT). *Application deadline:* Applications are processed on a rolling basis. Application fee: $75 ($90 for international students). Electronic applications accepted. *Financial support:* In 2010–11, 8 fellowships, 16 research assistantships, 15 teaching assistantships were awarded; tuition waivers (full and partial) also available. *Unit head:* Carla E. Caceres, Director, 217-244-2139, Fax: 217-244-1224, E-mail: cecacere@illinois.edu. *Application contact:* Carol Hall, Secretary, 217-333-8208, Fax: 217-244-1224, E-mail: cahall@illinois.edu.

The University of Iowa, Graduate College, College of Liberal Arts and Sciences, Department of Biology, Iowa City, IA 52242-1324. Offers biology (MS, PhD); cell and developmental biology (MS, PhD); evolution (MS, PhD); genetics (MS, PhD); neurobiology (MS, PhD). Terminal master's awarded for partial completion of doctoral program. *Degree requirements:* For master's, thesis optional, exam; for doctorate, comprehensive exam, thesis/dissertation. *Entrance requirements:* For master's and doctorate, GRE General Test, minimum GPA of 3.0. Additional exam requirements/recommendations for international students: Required—TOEFL (minimum score 600 paper-based; 250 computer-based; 100 iBT). Electronic applications accepted. *Faculty research:* Neurobiology, evolutionary biology, genetics, cell and developmental biology.

The University of Kansas, Graduate Studies, College of Liberal Arts and Sciences, Department of Ecology and Evolutionary Biology, Lawrence, KS 66045. Offers botany (MA, PhD); ecology and evolutionary biology (MA, PhD); entomology (MA, PhD). *Faculty:* 13 full-time (6 women), 29 part-time/adjunct (7 women). *Students:* 62 full-time (30 women); includes 1 minority (Hispanic/Latino), 16 international. Average age 29. 52 applicants, 42% accepted, 14 enrolled. In 2010, 9 master's, 8 doctorates awarded. Terminal master's awarded for partial completion of doctoral program. *Degree requirements:* For master's, comprehensive exam, thesis (for some programs), 30-36 credits, thesis presentation; for doctorate, comprehensive exam, thesis/dissertation, residency, responsible scholarship and research skills, final exam, dissertation defense. *Entrance requirements:* For master's, GRE General Test, bachelor's degree with minimum undergraduate GPA of 3.0; for doctorate, GRE General Test, bachelor's degree; minimum undergraduate/graduate GPA of 3.0. Additional exam requirements/recommendations for international students: Required—TOEFL, IELTS, Score requirements in EEB are the same as those set by Graduate Studies. *Application deadline:* For fall admission, 12/15 for domestic and international students; for spring admission, 9/15 for domestic and international students. Application fee: $55 ($65 for international students). Electronic applications accepted. *Expenses:* Tuition, state resident: full-time $7092; part-time $295.50 per credit hour. Tuition, nonresident: full-time $16,590; part-time $691.25 per credit hour. Required fees: $858; $71.49 per credit hour. Tuition and fees vary according to course load, campus/location and program. *Financial support:* Fellowships with tuition reimbursements, research assistantships with full and partial tuition reimbursements, teaching assistantships with full and partial tuition reimbursements, scholarships/

Evolutionary Biology

The University of Kansas (continued)

grants, traineeships, health care benefits, and unspecified assistantships available. Financial award application deadline: 12/15. *Faculty research:* Biodiversity and macroevolution, ecology and global change, evolutionary mechanisms. *Unit head:* Dr. Christopher H. Haufler, Chair, 785-864-3255, Fax: 785-864-5860, E-mail: vulgare@ku.edu. *Application contact:* Jaime Rochelle Keeler, Graduate Coordinator, 785-864-2362, Fax: 785-864-5860, E-mail: jrkeeler@ku.edu.

University of Louisiana at Lafayette, College of Sciences, Department of Biology, Lafayette, LA 70504. Offers biology (MS); environmental and evolutionary biology (PhD). Terminal master's awarded for partial completion of doctoral program. *Degree requirements:* For master's, thesis; for doctorate, 2 foreign languages, comprehensive exam, thesis/dissertation. *Entrance requirements:* For master's, GRE General Test, minimum GPA of 2.75; for doctorate, GRE General Test, GRE Subject Test, minimum GPA of 3.0. Additional exam requirements/recommendations for international students: Required—TOEFL (minimum score 550 paper-based; 213 computer-based). Electronic applications accepted. *Faculty research:* Structure and ultrastructure, system biology, ecology, processes, environmental physiology.

The University of Manchester, Faculty of Life Sciences, Manchester, United Kingdom. Offers adaptive organismal biology (M Phil, PhD); animal biology (M Phil, PhD); biochemistry (M Phil, PhD); bioinformatics (M Phil, PhD); biomolecular sciences (M Phil, PhD); biotechnology (M Phil, PhD); cell biology (M Phil, PhD); cell matrix research (M Phil, PhD); channels and transporters (M Phil, PhD); developmental biology (M Phil, PhD); Egyptology (M Phil, PhD); environmental biology (M Phil, PhD); evolutionary biology (M Phil, PhD); gene expression (M Phil, PhD); genetics (M Phil, PhD); history of science, technology and medicine (M Phil, PhD); immunology (M Phil, PhD); integrative neurobiology and behavior (M Phil, PhD); membrane trafficking (M Phil, PhD); microbiology (M Phil, PhD); molecular and cellular neuroscience (M Phil, PhD); molecular biology (M Phil, PhD); molecular cancer studies (M Phil, PhD); neuroscience (M Phil, PhD); ophthalmology (M Phil, PhD); optometry (M Phil, PhD); organelle function (M Phil, PhD); pharmacology (M Phil, PhD); physiology (M Phil, PhD); plant sciences (M Phil, PhD); stem cell research (M Phil, PhD); structural biology (M Phil, PhD); systems neuroscience (M Phil, PhD); toxicology (M Phil, PhD).

University of Maryland, College Park, Academic Affairs, College of Computer, Mathematical and Natural Sciences, Department of Biology, Behavior, Ecology, Evolution, and Systematics Program, College Park, MD 20742. Offers MS, PhD. *Students:* 24 full-time (15 women), 2 part-time (0 women); includes 3 minority (2 Asian, non-Hispanic/Latino; 1 Two or more races, non-Hispanic/Latino), 2 international. In 2010, 1 master's, 8 doctorates awarded. *Degree requirements:* For master's, thesis, oral defense, seminar; for doctorate, thesis/dissertation, exam, 4 seminars. *Entrance requirements:* For master's and doctorate, GRE General Test, GRE Subject Test (biology), 3 letters of recommendation. Additional exam requirements/recommendations for international students: Required—TOEFL. *Application deadline:* Applications are processed on a rolling basis. Application fee: $75. Electronic applications accepted. *Expenses:* Tuition, state resident: part-time $471 per credit hour. Tuition, nonresident: part-time $1016 per credit hour. Required fees: $337 per term. *Financial support:* In 2010–11, 4 fellowships with full and partial tuition reimbursements (averaging $20,932 per year), 3 research assistantships (averaging $19,727 per year), 12 teaching assistantships (averaging $19,483 per year) were awarded; Federal Work-Study and scholarships/grants also available. Support available to part-time students. Financial award applicants required to submit FAFSA. *Faculty research:* Animal behavior, biostatistics, ecology, evolution, neurothology. *Unit head:* Dr. Michele Dudash, Director, 301-405-1642, Fax: 301-314-9358, E-mail: mdudash@umd.edu. *Application contact:* Dr. Michele Dudash, Director, 301-405-1642, Fax: 301-314-9358, E-mail: mdudash@umd.edu.

University of Massachusetts Amherst, Graduate School, Interdisciplinary Programs, Program in Organismic and Evolutionary Biology, Amherst, MA 01003. Offers animal behavior (PhD); ecology (PhD); evolutionary biology (PhD); organismal biology (PhD); organismic and evolutionary biology (MS). Part-time programs available. *Students:* 30 full-time (16 women), 3 part-time (all women); includes 4 minority (3 Hispanic/Latino; 1 Native Hawaiian or other Pacific Islander, non-Hispanic/Latino), 6 international. Average age 29. 51 applicants, 33% accepted, 6 enrolled. In 2010, 2 master's, 5 doctorates awarded. Terminal master's awarded for partial completion of doctoral program. *Degree requirements:* For master's, thesis or alternative; for doctorate, comprehensive exam, thesis/dissertation. *Entrance requirements:* For master's and doctorate, GRE General Test, 3 letters of recommendation. Additional exam requirements/recommendations for international students: Required—TOEFL (minimum score 550 paper-based; 213 computer-based; 80 iBT), IELTS (minimum score 6.5). *Application deadline:* For fall admission, 12/1 for domestic and international students. Applications are processed on a rolling basis. Application fee: $50 ($65 for international students). Electronic applications accepted. *Expenses:* Tuition, state resident: full-time $2640. Required fees: $8282. One-time fee: $357 full-time. *Financial support:* In 2010–11, 4 fellowships (averaging $2,657 per year), 2 teaching assistantships with full tuition reimbursements (averaging $7,607 per year) were awarded; research assistantships, career-related internships or fieldwork, Federal Work-Study, scholarships/grants, traineeships, health care benefits, tuition waivers (full), and unspecified assistantships also available. Support available to part-time students. Financial award application deadline: 12/1; financial award applicants required to submit FAFSA. *Unit head:* Dr. Elizabeth M. Jakob, Graduate Program Director, 413-545-0928, Fax: 413-545-3243. *Application contact:* Jean M. Ames, Supervisor of Admissions, 413-545-0722, Fax: 413-577-0010, E-mail: gradadm@grad.umass.edu.

University of Massachusetts Amherst, Graduate School, Interdisciplinary Programs, Program in Plant Biology, Amherst, MA 01003. Offers biochemistry and metabolism (MS, PhD); cell biology and physiology (MS, PhD); environmental, ecological and integrative (PhD); environmental, ecological and integrative biology (MS); genetics and evolution (MS, PhD). *Students:* 18 full-time (8 women); includes 1 minority (Asian, non-Hispanic/Latino), 7 international. Average age 29. 27 applicants, 41% accepted, 6 enrolled. In 2010, 3 doctorates awarded. *Degree requirements:* For master's, thesis; for doctorate, 2 foreign languages, comprehensive exam, thesis/dissertation. *Entrance requirements:* For master's and doctorate, GRE General Test. Additional exam requirements/recommendations for international students: Required—TOEFL (minimum score 550 paper-based; 213 computer-based; 80 iBT), IELTS (minimum score 6.5). *Application deadline:* For fall admission, 12/15 for domestic and international students; for spring admission, 10/1 for domestic and international students. Applications are processed on a rolling basis. Application fee: $50 ($65 for international students). Electronic applications accepted. *Expenses:* Tuition, state resident: full-time $2640. Required fees: $8282. One-time fee: $357 full-time. *Financial support:* In 2010–11, 12 research assistantships with full tuition reimbursements (averaging $11,651 per year) were awarded; fellowships, teaching assistantships, career-related internships or fieldwork, Federal Work-Study, scholarships/grants, traineeships, health care benefits, tuition waivers (full), and unspecified assistantships also available. Support available to part-time students. Financial award application deadline: 12/15; financial award applicants required to submit FAFSA. *Unit head:* Dr. Elsbeth L. Walker, Graduate Program Director, 413-577-3217, Fax: 413-545-3243. *Application contact:* Jean M. Ames, Supervisor of Admissions, 413-545—0722, Fax: 413-577-0010, E-mail: gradadm@grad.umass.edu.

University of Miami, Graduate School, College of Arts and Sciences, Department of Biology, Coral Gables, FL 33124. Offers biology (MS, PhD); genetics and evolution (MS, PhD). Terminal master's awarded for partial completion of doctoral program. *Degree requirements:* For master's, comprehensive exam (for some programs), thesis (for some programs); for doctorate, thesis/dissertation, oral and written qualifying exam. *Entrance requirements:* For master's, GRE General Test, 3 letters of recommendation, research papers; for doctorate, GRE General Test, 3 letters of recommendation, research papers, sponsor letter. Additional exam requirements/recommendations for international students: Required—TOEFL (minimum score 550 paper-based; 213 computer-based; 59 iBT). Electronic applications accepted. *Faculty research:* Neuroscience to ethology; plants, vertebrates and mycorrhizae; phylogenies, life histories and species interactions; molecular biology, gene expression and populations; cells, auditory neurons and vertebrate locomotion.

University of Michigan, Rackham Graduate School, College of Literature, Science, and the Arts, Department of Ecology and Evolutionary Biology, Ann Arbor, MI 48109. Offers ecology and evolutionary biology (MS, PhD); ecology and evolutionary biology-Frontiers (MS). Part-time programs available. Terminal master's awarded for partial completion of doctoral program. *Degree requirements:* For master's, thesis (for some programs), two seminars; for doctorate, comprehensive exam, thesis/dissertation, 2 semesters of teaching. *Entrance requirements:* For master's and doctorate, GRE. Additional exam requirements/recommendations for international students: Required—TOEFL (minimum score 560 paper-based; 220 computer-based; 84 iBT). Electronic applications accepted. *Expenses:* Tuition, state resident: full-time $17,784; part-time $1116 per credit hour. Tuition, nonresident: full-time $35,944; part-time $2125 per credit hour. International tuition: $35,994 full-time. Required fees: $95 per semester. Tuition and fees vary according to course load, degree level and program. *Faculty research:* Community ecology, molecular evolution, theoretical ecology, systematics, evolutionary genetics.

University of Minnesota, Twin Cities Campus, Graduate School, College of Biological Sciences, Department of Ecology, Evolution, and Behavior, St. Paul, MN 55418. Offers MS, PhD. Terminal master's awarded for partial completion of doctoral program. *Degree requirements:* For master's, comprehensive exam, thesis or projects; for doctorate, comprehensive exam, thesis/dissertation. *Entrance requirements:* For master's and doctorate, GRE General Test, minimum GPA of 3.0. Additional exam requirements/recommendations for international students: Required—TOEFL (minimum score 550 paper-based; 79 iBT), Michigan English Language Assessment Battery. Electronic applications accepted. *Faculty research:* Behavioral ecology, community ecology, community genetics, ecosystem and global change, evolution and systematics.

University of Missouri, Graduate School, College of Arts and Sciences, Division of Biological Sciences, Program in Evolutionary Biology and Ecology, Columbia, MO 65211. Offers MA, PhD.

University of Missouri–St. Louis, College of Arts and Sciences, Department of Biology, St. Louis, MO 63121. Offers biotechnology (Certificate); cell and molecular biology (MS, PhD); ecology, evolution and systematics (MS, PhD); tropical biology and conservation (Certificate). Part-time programs available. *Faculty:* 43 full-time (13 women), 2 part-time/adjunct (1 woman). *Students:* 73 full-time (36 women), 63 part-time (36 women); includes 17 minority (6 Black or African American, non-Hispanic/Latino; 9 Asian, non-Hispanic/Latino; 2 Hispanic/Latino), 45 international. Average age 29. 193 applicants, 44% accepted, 44 enrolled. In 2010, 35 master's, 11 doctorates, 6 other advanced degrees awarded. *Degree requirements:* For master's, thesis or alternative; for doctorate, thesis/dissertation, 1 semester of teaching experience. *Entrance requirements:* For master's, 3 letters of recommendation; for doctorate, GRE General Test, 3 letters of recommendation. Additional exam requirements/recommendations for international students: Required—TOEFL. *Application deadline:* For fall admission, 12/1 priority date for domestic and international students; for spring admission, 10/15 priority date for domestic and international students. Applications are processed on a rolling basis. Application fee: $35 ($40 for international students). Electronic applications accepted. *Expenses:* Tuition, state resident: full-time $5522; part-time $306.80 per credit hour. Tuition, nonresident: full-time $14,253; part-time $792.10 per credit hour. Required fees: $658; $49 per credit hour. One-time fee: $12. Tuition and fees vary according to program. *Financial support:* In 2010–11, 30 research assistantships with full and partial tuition reimbursements (averaging $18,113 per year), 15 teaching assistantships with full and partial tuition reimbursements (averaging $17,514 per year) were awarded; fellowships with full tuition reimbursements, career-related internships or fieldwork and Federal Work-Study also available. Support available to part-time students. Financial award application deadline: 2/1. *Faculty research:* Molecular biology, microbial genetics, animal behavior, tropical ecology, plant systematics. *Unit head:* Dr. Peter Stevens, Director of Graduate Studies, 314-516-6200, Fax: 314-516-6233, E-mail: stevensp@umsl.edu. *Application contact:* 314-516-5458, Fax: 314-516-6996, E-mail: gradadm@umsl.edu.

University of Nevada, Reno, Graduate School, Interdisciplinary Program in Ecology, Evolution, and Conservation Biology, Reno, NV 89557. Offers PhD. Offered through the College of Arts and Science, the M. C. Fleischmann College of Agriculture, and the Desert Research Institute. *Degree requirements:* For doctorate, thesis/dissertation. *Entrance requirements:* For doctorate, GRE General Test, GRE Subject Test, minimum GPA of 3.0. Additional exam requirements/recommendations for international students: Required—TOEFL (minimum score 500 paper-based; 173 computer-based; 61 iBT), IELTS (minimum score 6). Electronic applications accepted. *Expenses:* Tuition, state resident: full-time $2219; part-time $246 per credit. Tuition, nonresident: part-time $510 per credit. International tuition: $9009 full-time. Required fees: $59 per term. One-time fee: $101. Tuition and fees vary according to course load. *Faculty research:* Population biology, behavioral ecology, plant response to climate change, conservation of endangered species, restoration of natural ecosystems.

The University of North Carolina at Chapel Hill, Graduate School, College of Arts and Sciences, Department of Biology, Chapel Hill, NC 27599. Offers botany (MA, MS, PhD); cell biology, development, and physiology (MA, MS, PhD); cell motility and cytoskeleton (PhD); ecology and behavior (MA, MS, PhD); genetics and molecular biology (MA, MS, PhD); morphology, systematics, and evolution (MA, MS, PhD). Terminal master's awarded for partial completion of doctoral program. *Degree requirements:* For master's, comprehensive exam, thesis (for some programs); for doctorate, comprehensive exam, thesis/dissertation. *Entrance requirements:* For master's, GRE General Test, GRE Subject Test, 2 semesters of calculus or statistics; 2 semesters of physics, organic chemistry; 3 semesters of biology; for doctorate, GRE General Test, GRE Subject Test, 2 semesters calculus or statistics, 2 semesters physics, organic chemistry, 3 semesters of biology. Additional exam requirements/recommendations for international students: Required—TOEFL (minimum score 550 paper-based; 213 computer-based). Electronic applications accepted. *Faculty research:* Gene expression, biomechanics, yeast genetics, plant ecology, plant molecular biology.

University of Notre Dame, Graduate School, College of Science, Department of Biological Sciences, Notre Dame, IN 46556. Offers aquatic ecology, evolution and environmental biology (MS, PhD); cellular and molecular biology (MS, PhD); genetics (MS, PhD); physiology (MS, PhD); vector biology and parasitology (MS, PhD). Terminal master's awarded for partial completion of doctoral program. *Degree requirements:* For master's, comprehensive exam, thesis; for doctorate, comprehensive exam, thesis/dissertation, candidacy exam. *Entrance requirements:* For master's and doctorate, GRE General Test. Additional exam requirements/recommendations for international students: Required—TOEFL (minimum score 600 paper-based; 250 computer-based; 80 iBT). Electronic applications accepted. *Faculty research:* Tropical disease, molecular genetics, neurobiology, evolutionary biology, aquatic biology.

University of Oklahoma, College of Arts and Sciences, Department of Botany and Microbiology, Program in Ecology and Evolutionary Biology, Norman, OK 73019. Offers PhD. *Students:* 3 full-time (1 woman), 2 part-time (0 women), 4 international. Average age 30. 3 applicants, 33% accepted, 0 enrolled. *Entrance requirements:* Additional exam requirements/recommendations for international students: Required—TOEFL (minimum score 550 paper-based; 213 computer-based; 79 iBT). *Application deadline:* For fall admission, 4/1 for domestic and international students; for spring admission, 11/1 for domestic students, 9/1 for international students. Applications are processed on a rolling basis. Application fee: $40 ($90 for international students). Electronic applications accepted. *Expenses:* Tuition, state resident: full-time $3893; part-time $162.20 per credit hour. Tuition, nonresident: full-time $14,167; part-time $590.30 per credit hour. Required fees: $2523; $94.60 per credit hour. Tuition and fees vary according to course load and degree level. *Financial support:* Career-related internships or fieldwork, scholarships/grants, traineeships, health care benefits, tuition waivers (partial), and unspecified assistantships available. *Faculty research:* Ecology of climate change, microbial ecology, evolution of behavior, community ecology. *Unit head:* Dr. Gordon Uno,

Chair, 405-325-4321, Fax: 405-325-7619, E-mail: guno@ou.edu. *Application contact:* Adell Hopper, Staff Assistant, 405-325-4322, Fax: 405-325-7619, E-mail: ahopper@ou.edu.

University of Oklahoma, College of Arts and Sciences, Department of Zoology, Program in Ecology and Evolutionary Biology, Norman, OK 73019. Offers PhD. *Students:* 14 full-time (5 women), 4 part-time (2 women), 5 international. Average age 28. 9 applicants, 67% accepted, 5 enrolled. In 2010, 2 doctorates awarded. *Entrance requirements:* Additional exam requirements/recommendations for international students: Required—TOEFL (minimum score 550 paper-based; 213 computer-based; 79 iBT). *Application deadline:* For fall admission, 12/15 for domestic students, 4/1 for international students; for spring admission, 10/1 for domestic students, 9/1 for international students. Applications are processed on a rolling basis. Application fee: $40 ($90 for international students). Electronic applications accepted. *Expenses:* Tuition, state resident: full-time $3893; part-time $162.20 per credit hour. Tuition, nonresident: full-time $14,167; part-time $590.30 per credit hour. Required fees: $2523; $94.60 per credit hour. Tuition and fees vary according to course load and degree level. *Financial support:* Career-related internships or fieldwork, institutionally sponsored loans, scholarships/grants, traineeships, health care benefits, tuition waivers (partial), and unspecified assistantships available. *Faculty research:* Ecology of climate change, microbial ecology, evolution of behavior, community ecology. *Unit head:* Bill Mathhews, Chair, 405-325-4712, Fax: 405-325-6202, E-mail: wmatthews@ou.edu. *Application contact:* Bill Mathhews, Chair, 405-325-4712, Fax: 405-325-6202, E-mail: wmatthews@ou.edu.

University of Oregon, Graduate School, College of Arts and Sciences, Department of Biology, Eugene, OR 97403. Offers ecology and evolution (MA, MS, PhD); marine biology (MA, MS, PhD); molecular, cellular and genetic biology (PhD); neuroscience and development (PhD). Terminal master's awarded for partial completion of doctoral program. *Degree requirements:* For master's, thesis (for some programs); for doctorate, thesis/dissertation. *Entrance requirements:* For master's and doctorate, GRE General Test, minimum GPA of 3.2. Additional exam requirements/recommendations for international students: Required—TOEFL. *Faculty research:* Developmental neurobiology; evolution, population biology, and quantitative genetics; regulation of gene expression; biochemistry of marine organisms.

University of Pittsburgh, School of Arts and Sciences, Department of Biological Sciences, Program in Ecology and Evolution, Pittsburgh, PA 15260. Offers PhD. *Faculty:* 7 full-time (2 women). *Students:* 18 full-time (5 women); includes 12 Black or African American, non-Hispanic/Latino; 1 American Indian or Alaska Native, non-Hispanic/Latino; 1 Asian, non-Hispanic/Latino; 2 Hispanic/Latino, 1 international. Average age 23. 29 applicants, 31% accepted, 2 enrolled. *Degree requirements:* For doctorate, comprehensive exam, thesis/dissertation, completion of research integrity module. *Entrance requirements:* For doctorate, GRE General Test, GRE Subject Test. Additional exam requirements/recommendations for international students: Required—TOEFL (minimum score 550 paper-based; 213 computer-based; 80 iBT). *Application deadline:* For fall admission, 1/15 priority date for domestic students, 12/15 priority date for international students. Applications are processed on a rolling basis. Application fee: $0 ($50 for international students). Electronic applications accepted. *Expenses:* Tuition, state resident: full-time $17,304; part-time $701 per credit. Tuition, nonresident: full-time $29,554; part-time $1210 per credit. Required fees: $740; $214 per term. Tuition and fees vary according to program. *Financial support:* In 2010–11, 20 fellowships with full tuition reimbursements (averaging $28,382 per year), 5 research assistantships with full tuition reimbursements (averaging $25,500 per year), 17 teaching assistantships with full tuition reimbursements (averaging $24,125 per year) were awarded; Federal Work-Study, scholarships/grants, traineeships, health care benefits, and tuition waivers (full) also available. *Unit head:* Dr. Gerard L. Campbell, Associate Professor, 412-624-6812, Fax: 412-624-4759, E-mail: camp@pitt.edu. *Application contact:* Cathleen M. Barr, Graduate Administrator, 412-624-4268, Fax: 412-624-4759, E-mail: cbarr@pitt.edu.

University of Puerto Rico, Río Piedras, College of Natural Sciences, Department of Biology, San Juan, PR 00931-3300. Offers ecology/systematics (MS, PhD); evolution/genetics (MS, PhD); molecular/cellular biology (MS, PhD); neuroscience (MS, PhD). Part-time programs available. *Degree requirements:* For master's, one foreign language, comprehensive exam, thesis; for doctorate, one foreign language, comprehensive exam, thesis/dissertation. *Entrance requirements:* For master's, GRE Subject Test, interview, minimum GPA of 3.0, letter of recommendation; for doctorate, GRE Subject Test, interview, master's degree, minimum GPA of 3.0, letter of recommendation. *Faculty research:* Environmental, poblational and systematic biology.

University of South Carolina, The Graduate School, College of Arts and Sciences, Department of Biological Sciences, Graduate Training Program in Ecology, Evolution, and Organismal Biology, Columbia, SC 29208. Offers MS, PhD. *Degree requirements:* For master's, one foreign language, comprehensive exam, thesis; for doctorate, one foreign language, comprehensive exam, thesis/dissertation. *Entrance requirements:* For master's and doctorate, GRE General Test, minimum GPA of 3.0 in science. Additional exam requirements/recommendations for international students: Required—TOEFL (minimum score 570 paper-based; 230 computer-based). Electronic applications accepted.

University of Southern California, Graduate School, Dana and David Dornsife College of Letters, Arts and Sciences, Department of Biological Sciences, Program in Integrative and Evolutionary Biology, Los Angeles, CA 90089. Offers PhD. M.S. in Biology is a terminal degree only. *Faculty:* 24 full-time (5 women), 3 part-time/adjunct (0 women). *Students:* 20 full-time (8 women); includes 3 minority (2 Asian, non-Hispanic/Latino; 1 Hispanic/Latino), 7 international. 24 applicants, 21% accepted, 3 enrolled.Terminal master's awarded for partial completion of doctoral program. *Degree requirements:* For doctorate, comprehensive exam, thesis/dissertation, qualifying examination, dissertation defense. *Entrance requirements:* For doctorate, GRE, 3 letters of recommendation, personal statement, resume, minimum GPA of 3.0. Additional exam requirements/recommendations for international students: Required—TOEFL (minimum score 600 paper-based; 250 computer-based; 100 iBT). *Application deadline:* For fall admission, 12/1 priority date for domestic and international students. Application fee: $85. Electronic applications accepted. *Expenses:* Tuition: Full-time $31,240; part-time $1420 per unit. Required fees: $600. One-time fee: $35 full-time. Full-time tuition and fees vary according to degree level and program. *Financial support:* In 2010–11, 17 students received support, including 6 fellowships with full tuition reimbursements available (averaging $26,700 per year), 2 research assistantships with full tuition reimbursements available (averaging $26,700 per year), 9 teaching assistantships with full tuition reimbursements available (averaging $26,700 per year); scholarships/grants, traineeships, health care benefits, tuition waivers, and unspecified assistantships also available. *Faculty research:* Organisms and their interaction with the environment, evolution and life history, integration of the control and dynamics of physiological processes, biomechanics and rehabilitation engineering, primate behavior and ecology. *Unit head:* Dr. Jill L. McNitt-Gray, Professor of Kinesiology, Biological Sciences, and Biomedical Engineering/Director, 213-740-7902, E-mail: mcnitt@usc.edu. *Application contact:* Adolfo dela Rosa, Student Services Advisor I, 213-821-3164, Fax: 213-740-1380, E-mail: adolfode@usc.edu.

The University of Tennessee, Graduate School, College of Arts and Sciences, Department of Ecology and Evolutionary Biology, Knoxville, TN 37996. Offers behavior (MS, PhD); ecology (MS, PhD); evolutionary biology (MS, PhD). Part-time programs available. *Degree requirements:* For master's, thesis; for doctorate, thesis/dissertation. *Entrance requirements:* For master's and doctorate, GRE General Test, minimum GPA of 2.7. Additional exam requirements/recommendations for international students: Required—TOEFL. Electronic applications accepted. *Expenses:* Tuition, state resident: full-time $7440; part-time $414 per credit hour. Tuition, nonresident: full-time $22,478; part-time $1250 per credit hour. Required fees: $922; $43 per credit hour. Tuition and fees vary according to program.

The University of Texas at Austin, Graduate School, College of Natural Sciences, School of Biological Sciences, Program in Ecology, Evolution and Behavior, Austin, TX 78712-1111. Offers MA, PhD. *Entrance requirements:* For doctorate, GRE General Test. Additional exam requirements/recommendations for international students: Required—TOEFL. Electronic applications accepted.

University of Toronto, School of Graduate Studies, Life Sciences Division, Department of Ecology and Evolutionary Biology, Toronto, ON M5S 1A1, Canada. Offers M Sc, PhD. *Degree requirements:* For master's, thesis, thesis defense; for doctorate, thesis/dissertation, thesis defense. *Entrance requirements:* For master's, minimum B average in last 2 years; knowledge of physics, chemistry, and biology.

Washington University in St. Louis, Graduate School of Arts and Sciences, Division of Biology and Biomedical Sciences, Program in Evolution, Ecology and Population Biology, St. Louis, MO 63130-4899. Offers ecology (PhD); environmental biology (PhD); evolutionary biology (PhD); genetics (PhD). *Degree requirements:* For doctorate, thesis/dissertation. *Entrance requirements:* For doctorate, GRE General Test, GRE Subject Test. Electronic applications accepted.

Wesleyan University, Graduate Programs, Department of Biology, Middletown, CT 06459. Offers animal behavior (PhD); bioformatics/genomics (PhD); cell biology (PhD); developmental biology (PhD); evolution/ecology (PhD); genetics (PhD); neurobiology (PhD); population biology (PhD). *Faculty:* 12 full-time (4 women). *Students:* 20 full-time (12 women); includes 1 Black or African American, non-Hispanic/Latino; 3 Asian, non-Hispanic/Latino. Average age 26. 24 applicants, 29% accepted, 2 enrolled. *Degree requirements:* For doctorate, variable foreign language requirement, thesis/dissertation. *Entrance requirements:* For doctorate, GRE. Additional exam requirements/recommendations for international students: Required—TOEFL. *Application deadline:* For fall admission, 1/15 for domestic and international students. Applications are processed on a rolling basis. Application fee: $0. *Expenses:* Tuition: Full-time $43,404. Required fees: $830. *Financial support:* In 2010–11, 5 research assistantships with full tuition reimbursements, 16 teaching assistantships with full tuition reimbursements were awarded; stipends also available. Financial award application deadline: 4/15; financial award applicants required to submit FAFSA. *Faculty research:* Microbial population genetics, genetic basis of evolutionary adaptation, genetic regulation of differentiation and pattern formation in *drosophila*. *Unit head:* Dr. Sonia E. Sultan, Chair/Professor, 860-685-3493, E-mail: jnaegele@wesleyan.edu. *Application contact:* Marjorie Fitzgibbons, Information Contact, 860-685-2140, E-mail: mfitzgibbons@wesleyan.edu.

West Virginia University, Eberly College of Arts and Sciences, Department of Biology, Morgantown, WV 26506. Offers cell and molecular biology (MS, PhD); environmental and evolutionary biology (MS, PhD); forensic biology (MS, PhD); genomic biology (MS, PhD); neurobiology (MS, PhD). Terminal master's awarded for partial completion of doctoral program. *Degree requirements:* For master's, thesis, final exam; for doctorate, thesis/dissertation, preliminary and final exams. *Entrance requirements:* For master's, GRE General Test, GRE Subject Test, minimum GPA of 3.0; for doctorate, GRE General Test, minimum GPA of 3.0. Additional exam requirements/recommendations for international students: Required—TOEFL. *Faculty research:* Environmental biology, genetic engineering, developmental biology, global change, biodiversity.

Yale University, Graduate School of Arts and Sciences, Department of Ecology and Evolutionary Biology, New Haven, CT 06520. Offers PhD. *Entrance requirements:* For doctorate, GRE General Test, GRE Subject Test (biology).

Section 9
Entomology

This section contains a directory of institutions offering graduate work in entomology. Additional information about programs listed in the directory may be obtained by writing directly to the dean of a graduate school or chair of a department at the address given in the directory.

For programs offering related work, see also in this book *Biochemistry; Biological and Biomedical Sciences; Botany and Plant Biology; Ecology, Environmental Biology, and Evolutionary Biology; Genetics, Developmental Biology, and Reproductive Biology; Microbiological Sciences; Physiology;* and *Zoology.* In the other guides in this series:

Graduate Programs in the Humanities, Arts & Social Sciences
See *Economics (Agricultural Economics and Agribusiness)*

Graduate Programs in the Physical Sciences, Mathematics, Agricultural Sciences, the Environment & Natural Resources
See *Agricultural and Food Sciences* and *Environmental Sciences and Management*

Graduate Programs in Engineering & Applied Sciences
See *Agricultural Engineering* and *Bioengineering*

CONTENTS

Program Directory

Entomology

Auburn University, Graduate School, College of Agriculture, Department of Entomology and Plant Pathology, Auburn University, AL 36849. Offers entomology (M Ag, MS, PhD); plant pathology (M Ag, MS, PhD). Part-time programs available. *Faculty:* 17 full-time (6 women). *Students:* 24 full-time (10 women), 11 part-time (4 women); includes 1 Black or African American, non-Hispanic/Latino; 2 Asian, non-Hispanic/Latino, 17 international. Average age 30. 21 applicants, 57% accepted, 7 enrolled. In 2010, 3 master's, 2 doctorates awarded. *Degree requirements:* For master's, thesis (for some programs); for doctorate, one foreign language, thesis/dissertation. *Entrance requirements:* For master's, GRE General Test; for doctorate, GRE General Test, GRE Subject Test, master's degree with thesis. *Application deadline:* For fall admission, 7/7 for domestic students; for spring admission, 11/24 for domestic students. Applications are processed on a rolling basis. Application fee: $50 ($60 for international students). Electronic applications accepted. *Expenses:* Tuition, state resident: full-time $7002. Tuition, nonresident: full-time $21,898. International tuition: $22,116 full-time. Required fees: $892. Tuition and fees vary according to course load and program. *Financial support:* Research assistantships, teaching assistantships, Federal Work-Study available. Support available to part-time students. Financial award application deadline: 3/15; financial award applicants required to submit FAFSA. *Faculty research:* Pest management, biological control, systematics, medical entomology. *Unit head:* Dr. Arthur Appel, Chair, 334-844-5006. *Application contact:* Dr. George Flowers, Dean of the Graduate School, 334-844-2125.

Clemson University, Graduate School, College of Agriculture, Forestry and Life Sciences, Department of Forestry and Natural Resources, Program in Entomology, Clemson, SC 29634. Offers MS, PhD. Part-time programs available. *Students:* 19 full-time (11 women); includes 1 Black or African American, non-Hispanic/Latino; 1 Asian, non-Hispanic/Latino, 4 international. Average age 28. 20 applicants, 85% accepted, 10 enrolled. In 2010, 2 master's awarded. *Degree requirements:* For master's, thesis, peer-reviewed manuscript submission; conference presentation; for doctorate, thesis/dissertation, peer-reviewed manuscript submission; conference presentation; one semester of teaching. *Entrance requirements:* For master's, GRE General Test, bachelor's degree in biological science or chemistry (recommended); for doctorate, GRE General Test, master's degree in science and/or independent research experience (recommended). Additional exam requirements/recommendations for international students: Required—TOEFL. *Application deadline:* Applications are processed on a rolling basis. Application fee: $70 ($80 for international students). Electronic applications accepted. *Expenses:* Contact institution. *Financial support:* In 2010–11, 18 students received support, including 5 fellowships with full and partial tuition reimbursements available (averaging $8,840 per year), 16 research assistantships with partial tuition reimbursements available (averaging $15,400 per year), 4 teaching assistantships with partial tuition reimbursements available (averaging $9,370 per year); career-related internships or fieldwork, institutionally sponsored loans, scholarships/grants, health care benefits, and unspecified assistantships also available. Support available to part-time students. Financial award application deadline: 3/1. *Faculty research:* Biodiversity, urban entomology, applied ecology, agricultural entomology. *Unit head:* Dr. Patricia A. Zungoli, Chair, 864-656-3137, Fax: 864-656-5065, E-mail: pzngl@clemson.edu. *Application contact:* Dr. Matthew Turnbull, Coordinator, 864-656-5038, Fax: 864-656-5065, E-mail: turnbul@clemson.edu.

Colorado State University, Graduate School, College of Agricultural Sciences, Department of Bioagricultural Sciences and Pest Management, Fort Collins, CO 80523-1177. Offers entomology (MS, PhD); plant pathology and weed science (MS, PhD). Part-time programs available. *Faculty:* 19 full-time (4 women). *Students:* 20 full-time (9 women), 21 part-time (10 women); includes 4 minority (2 American Indian or Alaska Native, non-Hispanic/Latino; 1 Hispanic/Latino; 1 Two or more races, non-Hispanic/Latino), 4 international. Average age 32. 15 applicants, 73% accepted, 9 enrolled. In 2010, 5 master's, 1 doctorate awarded. *Degree requirements:* For master's, comprehensive exam, thesis; for doctorate, comprehensive exam, thesis/dissertation. *Entrance requirements:* For master's, GRE General Test, minimum GPA of 3.0, letters of recommendation; for doctorate, GRE General Test, minimum GPA of 3.0, letters of recommendation, essay. Additional exam requirements/recommendations for international students: Required—TOEFL (minimum score 550 paper-based; 213 computer-based; 80 iBT). *Application deadline:* For fall admission, 1/15 priority date for domestic students, 1/1 priority date for international students; for spring admission, 9/1 priority date for domestic and international students. Applications are processed on a rolling basis. Application fee: $50. Electronic applications accepted. *Expenses:* Tuition, state resident: full-time $7434; part-time $413 per credit. Tuition, nonresident: full-time $19,022; part-time $1057 per credit. Required fees: $1729; $88 per credit. *Financial support:* In 2010–11, 8 fellowships with partial tuition reimbursements (averaging $32,474 per year), 27 research assistantships with full tuition reimbursements (averaging $15,270 per year), 12 teaching assistantships with full tuition reimbursements (averaging $9,900 per year) were awarded; unspecified assistantships and fellowships also available. Financial award application deadline: 1/15; financial award applicants required to submit FAFSA. *Faculty research:* Entomology specialization, plant pathology specialization, weed science specialization, ecology and biodiversity, integrated pest management. Total annual research expenditures: $2.7 million. *Unit head:* Dr. Thomas O. Holtzer, Head, 970-491-5261, Fax: 970-491-3862, E-mail: tholtzer@lamar.colostate.edu. *Application contact:* Janet Dill, Education Coordinator, 970-491-0402, Fax: 970-491-3862, E-mail: janet.dill@colostate.edu.

Cornell University, Graduate School, Graduate Fields of Agriculture and Life Sciences, Field of Entomology, Ithaca, NY 14853-0001. Offers acarology (MS, PhD); apiculture (MS, PhD); applied entomology (MS, PhD); aquatic entomology (MS, PhD); biological control (MS, PhD); insect behavior (MS, PhD); insect biochemistry (MS, PhD); insect ecology (MS, PhD); insect genetics (MS, PhD); insect morphology (MS, PhD); insect pathology (MS, PhD); insect physiology (MS, PhD); insect systematics (MS, PhD); insect toxicology and insecticide chemistry (MS, PhD); integrated pest management (MS, PhD); medical and veterinary entomology (MS, PhD). *Faculty:* 39 full-time (6 women). *Students:* 32 full-time (17 women); includes 2 Asian, non-Hispanic/Latino; 1 Hispanic/Latino, 11 international. Average age 28. 31 applicants, 16% accepted, 5 enrolled. In 2010, 5 doctorates awarded. *Degree requirements:* For master's, thesis; for doctorate, comprehensive exam, thesis/dissertation. *Entrance requirements:* For master's and doctorate, GRE General Test, GRE Subject Test (biology), 3 letters of recommendation. Additional exam requirements/recommendations for international students: Required—TOEFL (minimum score 550 paper-based; 213 computer-based; 77 iBT). *Application deadline:* For fall admission, 12/1 for domestic students. Application fee: $70. Electronic applications accepted. *Expenses:* Tuition: Full-time $29,500. Required fees: $76. Tuition and fees vary according to degree level and program. *Financial support:* In 2010–11, 7 fellowships with full tuition reimbursements, 14 research assistantships with full tuition reimbursements, 10 teaching assistantships with full tuition reimbursements were awarded; institutionally sponsored loans, scholarships/grants, health care benefits, tuition waivers (full and partial), and unspecified assistantships also available. Financial award applicants required to submit FAFSA. *Faculty research:* Systematics and biodiversity, integrated pest management, pathology and biological control, toxicology and physiology, ecology and behavior. *Unit head:* Director of Graduate Studies, 607-255-6198, Fax: 607-255-0939. *Application contact:* Graduate Field Assistant, 607-255-6198, Fax: 607-255-0939, E-mail: fieldofent2@cornell.edu.

Florida Agricultural and Mechanical University, Division of Graduate Studies, Research, and Continuing Education, College of Engineering Science, Technology, and Agriculture, Division of Agricultural Sciences, Tallahassee, FL 32307-3200. Offers agribusiness (MS); animal science (MS); engineering technology (MS); entomology (MS); food science (MS); international programs (MS); plant science (MS). *Degree requirements:* For master's, thesis. *Entrance requirements:* For master's, GRE General Test, minimum GPA of 3.0. Additional exam requirements/recommendations for international students: Required—TOEFL (minimum score 500 paper-based).

Illinois State University, Graduate School, College of Arts and Sciences, Department of Biological Sciences, Normal, IL 61790-2200. Offers animal behavior (MS); bacteriology (MS); biochemistry (MS); biological sciences (MS); biology (PhD); biophysics (MS); biotechnology (MS); botany (MS, PhD); cell biology (MS); conservation biology (MS); developmental biology (MS); ecology (MS, PhD); entomology (MS); evolutionary biology (MS); genetics (MS, PhD); immunology (MS); microbiology (MS, PhD); molecular biology (MS); molecular genetics (MS); neurobiology (MS); neuroscience (MS); parasitology (MS); physiology (MS, PhD); plant biology (MS); plant molecular biology (MS); plant sciences (MS); structural biology (MS); zoology (MS, PhD). Part-time programs available. *Degree requirements:* For master's, thesis or alternative; for doctorate, variable foreign language requirement, thesis/dissertation, 2 terms of residency. *Entrance requirements:* For master's, GRE General Test, minimum GPA of 2.6 in last 60 hours of course work; for doctorate, GRE General Test. *Faculty research:* Redoc balance and drug development in schistosoma mansoni, control of the growth of listeria monocytogenes at low temperature, regulation of cell expansion and microtubule function by SPRI, CRUI: physiology and fitness consequences of different life history phenotypes.

Iowa State University of Science and Technology, Graduate College, College of Agriculture, Department of Entomology, Ames, IA 50011. Offers MS, PhD. *Faculty:* 15 full-time (5 women), 2 part-time/adjunct (1 woman). *Students:* 25 full-time (10 women), 6 part-time (3 women); includes 1 Black or African American, non-Hispanic/Latino, 4 international. 9 applicants, 33% accepted, 1 enrolled. In 2010, 7 master's, 2 doctorates awarded. *Degree requirements:* For master's, thesis; for doctorate, thesis/dissertation. *Entrance requirements:* For master's and doctorate, GRE General Test, GRE Subject Test (biology). Additional exam requirements/recommendations for international students: Required—TOEFL (minimum score 550 paper-based; 79 iBT), IELTS (minimum score 6.5). *Application deadline:* Applications are processed on a rolling basis. Application fee: $40 ($90 for international students). Electronic applications accepted. *Financial support:* In 2010–11, 27 research assistantships with full and partial tuition reimbursements (averaging $17,913 per year) were awarded; fellowships, teaching assistantships with full and partial tuition reimbursements, scholarships/grants, health care benefits, and unspecified assistantships also available. *Unit head:* Dr. Leslie Lewis, Chair, 515-294-7400, Fax: 515-294-2125, E-mail: entomology@iastate.edu. *Application contact:* Dr. Joel Coats, Director of Graduate Education, 515-294-7400, E-mail: entomology@iastate.edu.

Kansas State University, Graduate School, College of Agriculture, Department of Entomology, Manhattan, KS 66506. Offers MS, PhD. *Degree requirements:* For master's, thesis, oral exam; for doctorate, thesis/dissertation, written and oral exams. Electronic applications accepted. *Faculty research:* Molecular genetics, biologically-based pest management, host plant resistance, ecological genomics, stored product entomology.

Louisiana State University and Agricultural and Mechanical College, Graduate School, College of Agriculture, Department of Entomology, Baton Rouge, LA 70803. Offers MS, PhD. *Faculty:* 20 full-time (4 women). *Students:* 24 full-time (5 women), 6 part-time (1 woman); includes 1 American Indian or Alaska Native, non-Hispanic/Latino; 1 Hispanic/Latino, 9 international. Average age 31. 12 applicants, 42% accepted, 2 enrolled. In 2010, 3 master's, 1 doctorate awarded. *Degree requirements:* For master's, thesis; for doctorate, thesis/dissertation. *Entrance requirements:* For master's and doctorate, GRE General Test, minimum GPA of 3.0. Additional exam requirements/recommendations for international students: Required—TOEFL (minimum score 550 paper-based; 213 computer-based; 79 iBT) or IELTS (minimum score 6.5). *Application deadline:* For fall admission, 1/25 priority date for domestic students, 5/15 for international students; for spring admission, 10/15 for international students. Applications are processed on a rolling basis. Application fee: $50 ($70 for international students). Electronic applications accepted. *Financial support:* In 2010–11, 26 students received support, including 22 research assistantships with partial tuition reimbursements available (averaging $18,041 per year); fellowships, teaching assistantships with partial tuition reimbursements available, Federal Work-Study, institutionally sponsored loans, scholarships/grants, health care benefits, and unspecified assistantships also available. Support available to part-time students. Financial award applicants required to submit FAFSA. *Faculty research:* Conservation biology, insect systematics, insect ecology, urban entomology, agricultural pest management, insect genomics. Total annual research expenditures: $10,414. *Unit head:* Dr. Timothy Schowalter, Head, 225-578-1628, Fax: 225-578-2257, E-mail: tschowalter@agcenter.lsu.edu. *Application contact:* Paula Beecher, Recruiting Coordinator, 225-578-2468, E-mail: pbeeche@lsu.edu.

McGill University, Faculty of Graduate and Postdoctoral Studies, Faculty of Agricultural and Environmental Sciences, Department of Natural Resource Sciences, Montréal, QC H3A 2T5, Canada. Offers entomology (M Sc, PhD); environmental assessment (M Sc); forest science (M Sc, PhD); microbiology (M Sc, PhD); micrometeorology (M Sc, PhD); neotropical environment (M Sc, PhD); soil science (M Sc, PhD); wildlife biology (M Sc, PhD).

Michigan State University, The Graduate School, College of Agriculture and Natural Resources and College of Natural Science, Department of Entomology, East Lansing, MI 48824. Offers entomology (MS, PhD); integrated pest management (MS). *Entrance requirements:* Additional exam requirements/recommendations for international students: Required—TOEFL (minimum score 550 paper-based; 213 computer-based), Michigan State University ELT (minimum score 85), Michigan English Language Assessment Battery (minimum score 83). Electronic applications accepted.

Mississippi State University, College of Agriculture and Life Sciences, Department of Entomology and Plant Pathology, Mississippi State, MS 39762. Offers agricultural life sciences (MS), including entomology and plant pathology (MS, PhD); life sciences (PhD), including entomology and plant pathology (MS, PhD). *Faculty:* 20 full-time (1 woman). *Students:* 19 full-time (4 women), 10 part-time (5 women); includes 2 minority (1 Black or African American, non-Hispanic/Latino; 1 Hispanic/Latino), 2 international. Average age 32. 17 applicants, 47% accepted, 7 enrolled. In 2010, 2 master's, 4 doctorates awarded. *Degree requirements:* For master's, thesis; for doctorate, thesis/dissertation. *Entrance requirements:* For master's, GRE General Test, minimum GPA of 2.75; for doctorate, GRE General Test. Additional exam requirements/recommendations for international students: Required—TOEFL (minimum score 475 paper-based; 153 computer-based; 53 iBT); Recommended—IELTS (minimum score 4.5). *Application deadline:* For fall admission, 7/1 for domestic students, 5/1 for international students; for spring admission, 11/1 for domestic students, 9/1 for international students. Applications are processed on a rolling basis. Application fee: $40. Electronic applications accepted. *Expenses:* Tuition, state resident: full-time $2731; part-time $304 per credit hour. Tuition, nonresident: full-time $6901; part-time $767 per credit hour. *Financial support:* In 2010–11, 20 research assistantships (averaging $16,783 per year) were awarded; Federal Work-Study, institutionally sponsored loans, and unspecified assistantships also available. Financial award application deadline: 4/1; financial award applicants required to submit FAFSA. *Unit head:* Dr. Scott T. Willard, Professor and Department Head, 662-325-2640, Fax: 662-325-8837, E-mail: swillard@bch.msstate.edu. *Application contact:* Dr. Michael Caprio, Professor and Graduate Coordinator, 662-325-2085, Fax: 662-325-8837, E-mail: mcaprio@entomology.msstate.edu.

New Mexico State University, Graduate School, College of Agricultural, Consumer and Environmental Sciences, Department of Entomology, Plant Pathology and Weed Science, Las Cruces, NM 88003-8001. Offers agricultural biology (MS). Part-time programs available. *Faculty:* 7 full-time (2 women). *Students:* 11 full-time (5 women), 4 part-time (2 women); includes 5 minority (4 Hispanic/Latino; 1 Two or more races, non-Hispanic/Latino), 2 international. Average age 27. 14 applicants, 79% accepted, 9 enrolled. In 2010, 5 master's awarded. *Degree requirements:* For master's, comprehensive exam, thesis. *Entrance requirements:* For master's, GRE General Test. *Application deadline:* For fall admission, 7/1 priority date for domestic students; for spring admission, 11/1 priority date for domestic students. Applications are processed on a rolling basis. Application fee: $30 ($50 for international students). Electronic applications accepted. *Expenses:* Tuition, state resident: full-time $4536; part-time $242 per credit. Tuition, nonresident: full-time $15,816; part-time $712 per credit. Required fees: $636 per term. *Financial support:* In 2010–11, 8 students received support, including 6 research assistantships with full tuition reimbursements available (averaging $20,550 per year), 2 teaching assistantships with partial tuition reimbursements available (averaging $14,225 per year); career-related internships or fieldwork and health care benefits also available. Financial award application deadline: 3/1. *Faculty research:* Integrated pest management, pesticide application and safety, livestock ectoparasite research, biotechnology, nematology. *Unit head:* Dr. Jill Schroeder, Interim Head, 575-646-3225, Fax: 575-646-8087, E-mail: jischroe@nmsu.edu. *Application contact:* Cindy Bullard, Intermediate Administrative Assistant, 575-646-1145, Fax: 575-646-8087, E-mail: cbullard@nmsu.edu.

North Carolina State University, Graduate School, College of Agriculture and Life Sciences, Department of Entomology, Raleigh, NC 27695. Offers MS, PhD. Terminal master's awarded for partial completion of doctoral program. *Degree requirements:* For master's, thesis (for some programs); for doctorate, thesis/dissertation. *Entrance requirements:* For master's and doctorate, GRE General Test. Electronic applications accepted. *Faculty research:* Physiology, biocontrol, ecology, forest entomology, apiculture.

North Dakota State University, College of Graduate and Interdisciplinary Studies, College of Agriculture, Food Systems, and Natural Resources, Department of Entomology, Fargo, ND 58108. Offers entomology (MS, PhD); environment and conservation science (MS, PhD); natural resource management (MS, PhD). Part-time programs available. *Faculty:* 7 full-time (3 women), 8 part-time/adjunct (0 women). *Students:* 6 full-time (3 women), 5 part-time (2 women), 3 international. Average age 34. 2 applicants, 50% accepted, 0 enrolled. In 2010, 1 master's, 1 doctorate awarded. *Degree requirements:* For master's, thesis; for doctorate, comprehensive exam, thesis/dissertation. *Entrance requirements:* For master's and doctorate, minimum GPA of 3.0. Additional exam requirements/recommendations for international students: Required—TOEFL (minimum score 550 paper-based; 213 computer-based; 79 iBT). *Application deadline:* Applications are processed on a rolling basis. Application fee: $45 ($60 for international students). Electronic applications accepted. *Financial support:* In 2010–11, 11 research assistantships with full tuition reimbursements (averaging $13,800 per year) were awarded; Federal Work-Study, institutionally sponsored loans, and unspecified assistantships also available. Financial award application deadline: 4/15. *Faculty research:* Insect systematics, conservation biology, integrated pest management, insect behavior, insect biology. *Unit head:* Dr. David A. Rider, Chair, 701-231-7908, Fax: 701-231-8557, E-mail: david.rider@ndsu.edu. *Application contact:* Dr. David A. Rider, Chair, 701-231-7908, Fax: 701-231-8557, E-mail: david.rider@ndsu.edu.

The Ohio State University, Graduate School, College of Food, Agricultural, and Environmental Sciences, Department of Entomology, Columbus, OH 43210. Offers MS, PhD. *Faculty:* 33. *Students:* 20 full-time (11 women), 8 part-time (4 women), 13 international. Average age 27. In 2010, 2 master's, 2 doctorates awarded. *Degree requirements:* For master's, variable foreign language requirement, thesis optional; for doctorate, variable foreign language requirement, thesis/dissertation. *Entrance requirements:* For master's and doctorate, GRE General Test. Additional exam requirements/recommendations for international students: Required—TOEFL (minimum score 600 paper-based; 250 computer-based). *Application deadline:* For fall admission, 8/15 priority date for domestic students, 7/1 priority date for international students; for winter admission, 12/1 priority date for domestic students, 11/1 priority date for international students; for spring admission, 3/1 priority date for domestic students, 2/1 priority date for international students. Applications are processed on a rolling basis. Application fee: $40 ($50 for international students). Electronic applications accepted. *Expenses:* Tuition, state resident: full-time $10,605. Tuition, nonresident: full-time $26,535. Tuition and fees vary according to course load and program. *Financial support:* Fellowships, research assistantships, teaching assistantships, Federal Work-Study and institutionally sponsored loans available. Support available to part-time students. *Faculty research:* Acarology, insect systematics, soil ecology, integrated pest management, chemical ecology. *Unit head:* Susan Fisher, Chair, 614-292-1617, Fax: 614-292-2180, E-mail: fisher.14@osu.edu. *Application contact:* 614-292-9444, Fax: 614-292-3895, E-mail: domestic.grad@osu.edu.

Oklahoma State University, College of Agricultural Science and Natural Resources, Department of Entomology and Plant Pathology, Stillwater, OK 74078. Offers entomology (PhD); entomology and plant pathology (MS); plant pathology (PhD). *Faculty:* 33 full-time (12 women). *Students:* 5 full-time (2 women), 30 part-time (16 women); includes 1 American Indian or Alaska Native, non-Hispanic/Latino; 1 Asian, non-Hispanic/Latino, 14 international. Average age 29. 17 applicants, 29% accepted, 5 enrolled. In 2010, 10 master's, 3 doctorates awarded. *Degree requirements:* For master's, thesis or alternative; for doctorate, comprehensive exam, thesis/dissertation. *Entrance requirements:* For master's and doctorate, GRE or GMAT. Additional exam requirements/recommendations for international students: Required—TOEFL (minimum score 550 paper-based; 79 iBT). *Application deadline:* For fall admission, 3/1 priority date for international students; for spring admission, 8/1 priority date for international students. Applications are processed on a rolling basis. Application fee: $40 ($75 for international students). Electronic applications accepted. *Expenses:* Tuition, state resident: full-time $3716; part-time $154.85 per credit hour. Tuition, nonresident: full-time $14,892; part-time $621 per credit hour. Required fees: $2044; $85.20 per credit hour. One-time fee: $50. Tuition and fees vary according to course load and campus/location. *Financial support:* In 2010–11, 29 research assistantships (averaging $17,167 per year), 2 teaching assistantships (averaging $16,584 per year) were awarded; career-related internships or fieldwork, Federal Work-Study, scholarships/grants, health care benefits, tuition waivers (partial), and unspecified assistantships also available. Support available to part-time students. Financial award application deadline: 3/1; financial award applicants required to submit FAFSA. *Unit head:* Dr. Phil Mulder, Head, 405-744-5527, Fax: 405-744-6039. *Application contact:* Dr. Brad Kard, Graduate Coordinator, 405-744-2142, Fax: 405-744-6039, E-mail: brad.kard@okstate.edu.

Penn State University Park, Graduate School, College of Agricultural Sciences, Department of Entomology, State College, University Park, PA 16802-1503. Offers MS, PhD.

Purdue University, Graduate School, College of Agriculture, Department of Entomology, West Lafayette, IN 47907. Offers MS, PhD. Part-time programs available. *Degree requirements:* For master's, thesis (for some programs), seminar; for doctorate, thesis/dissertation, seminar. *Entrance requirements:* For master's and doctorate, GRE. Additional exam requirements/recommendations for international students: Required—TOEFL. Electronic applications accepted. *Faculty research:* Insect biochemistry, nematology, aquatic diptera, behavioral ecology, insect physiology.

Rutgers, The State University of New Jersey, New Brunswick, Graduate School-New Brunswick, Program in Entomology, Piscataway, NJ 08854-8097. Offers MS, PhD. *Degree requirements:* For master's, thesis or alternative; for doctorate, thesis/dissertation. *Entrance requirements:* For master's and doctorate, GRE General Test, GRE Subject Test (recommended). Additional exam requirements/recommendations for international students: Required—TOEFL. Electronic applications accepted. *Expenses:* Tuition, state resident: full-time $7200; part-time $600 per credit. Tuition, nonresident: full-time $11,124; part-time $927 per credit. *Faculty research:* Insect toxicology, biolorial control, pathology, IPM and ecology, insect systematics.

Simon Fraser University, Graduate Studies, Faculty of Science, Department of Biological Sciences, Burnaby, BC V5A 1S6, Canada. Offers biological sciences (M Sc, PhD); environmental toxicology (MET); pest management (MPM). *Degree requirements:* For master's, thesis; for doctorate, thesis/dissertation. *Entrance requirements:* For master's, minimum GPA of 3.0; for doctorate, minimum GPA of 3.5. Additional exam requirements/recommendations for international students: Required—TOEFL or IELTS. Electronic applications accepted. *Faculty research:* Molecular biology, marine biology, ecology, wildlife biology, endocrinology.

State University of New York College of Environmental Science and Forestry, Department of Environmental and Forest Biology, Syracuse, NY 13210-2779. Offers applied ecology (MPS); chemical ecology (MPS, MS, PhD); conservation biology (MPS, MS, PhD); ecology (MPS, MS, PhD); entomology (MPS, MS, PhD); environmental interpretation (MPS, MS, PhD); environmental physiology (MPS, MS, PhD); fish and wildlife biology and management (MPS,

MS, PhD); forest pathology and mycology (MPS, MS, PhD); plant biotechnology (MPS); plant science and biotechnology (MPS, MS, PhD). *Degree requirements:* For master's, thesis (for some programs); for doctorate, comprehensive exam, thesis/dissertation. *Entrance requirements:* For master's and doctorate, GRE General Test, GRE Subject Test, minimum GPA of 3.0. Additional exam requirements/recommendations for international students: Required—TOEFL (minimum score 550 paper-based; 213 computer-based; 80 iBT), IELTS (minimum score 6). *Expenses:* Tuition, state resident: full-time $8370; part-time $349 per credit hour. Tuition, nonresident: full-time $13,780. Required fees: $30.30 per credit hour. $20 per year. *Faculty research:* Ecology, fish and wildlife biology and management, plant science, entomology.

Texas A&M University, College of Agriculture and Life Sciences, Department of Entomology, College Station, TX 77843. Offers M Agr, MS, PhD. *Faculty:* 21. *Students:* 49 full-time (25 women), 7 part-time (2 women); includes 8 minority (1 Black or African American, non-Hispanic/Latino; 7 Hispanic/Latino), 14 international. Average age 34. In 2010, 7 master's, 5 doctorates awarded. *Degree requirements:* For master's, comprehensive exam, thesis (for some programs); for doctorate, comprehensive exam, thesis/dissertation. *Entrance requirements:* For master's and doctorate, GRE General Test. Additional exam requirements/recommendations for international students: Required—TOEFL. *Application deadline:* For fall admission, 2/1 priority date for domestic students; for spring admission, 10/1 for domestic students. Applications are processed on a rolling basis. Application fee: $50 ($75 for international students). Electronic applications accepted. *Financial support:* In 2010–11, research assistantships with partial tuition reimbursements (averaging $16,500 per year), teaching assistantships with partial tuition reimbursements (averaging $16,500 per year) were awarded; fellowships, Federal Work-Study also available. Financial award application deadline: 3/1; financial award applicants required to submit FAFSA. *Faculty research:* Biology, biological control, integrated pest management, systematics, host plant resistance. *Unit head:* David Ragsdale, Head, 979-845-2510, Fax: 979-845-6305, E-mail: dragsdale@tamu.edu. *Application contact:* David Ragsdale, Head, 979-845-2510, Fax: 979-845-6305, E-mail: dragsdale@tamu.edu.

The University of Arizona, Graduate Interdisciplinary Programs, Graduate Interdisciplinary Program in Entomology and Insect Science, Tucson, AZ 85721. Offers MS, PhD. Part-time programs available. *Faculty:* 9. *Students:* 19 full-time (8 women), 2 part-time (1 woman); includes 1 Black or African American, non-Hispanic/Latino; 2 Asian, non-Hispanic/Latino; 2 Hispanic/Latino; 2 Two or more races, non-Hispanic/Latino, 8 international. Average age 28. 21 applicants, 10% accepted, 1 enrolled. In 2010, 3 master's, 2 doctorates awarded. *Degree requirements:* For master's, thesis; for doctorate, comprehensive exam, thesis/dissertation. *Entrance requirements:* For master's, GRE General Test, GRE Subject Test, minimum GPA of 3.0, 3 letters of recommendation; for doctorate, GRE General Test, GRE Subject Test, minimum GPA of 3.0, 3 letters of recommendation, statement of purpose. Additional exam requirements/recommendations for international students: Required—TOEFL (minimum score 550 paper-based; 213 computer-based). *Application deadline:* For fall admission, 1/1 for domestic students, 12/1 for international students. Applications are processed on a rolling basis. Application fee: $75. *Expenses:* Tuition, state resident: full-time $7692. *Financial support:* In 2010–11, 1 student received support, including 5 research assistantships with full and partial tuition reimbursements available (averaging $17,954 per year); fellowships, teaching assistantships, Federal Work-Study, institutionally sponsored loans, scholarships/grants, health care benefits, tuition waivers (full and partial), and unspecified assistantships also available. Financial award application deadline: 3/1. *Faculty research:* Toxicology and physiology, plant/insect relations, vector biology, insect pest management, chemical ecology. Total annual research expenditures: $2.4 million. *Unit head:* Dr. Bruce E. Tabashnik, Professor and Head, 520-621-1141, Fax: 520-621-1150, E-mail: brucet@ag.arizona.edu. *Application contact:* Patricia L. Baldewiez, Graduate Coordinator, 520-621-1151, Fax: 520-621-1150, E-mail: pbaldewi@ag.arizona.edu.

University of Arkansas, Graduate School, Dale Bumpers College of Agricultural, Food and Life Sciences, Department of Entomology, Fayetteville, AR 72701-1201. Offers MS, PhD. *Faculty:* 14 full-time (0 women). *Students:* 4 full-time (1 woman), 13 part-time (6 women); includes 2 minority (both Asian, non-Hispanic/Latino), 1 international. 5 applicants, 80% accepted. In 2010, 1 master's, 2 doctorates awarded. *Degree requirements:* For master's, thesis; for doctorate, one foreign language, thesis/dissertation. *Entrance requirements:* For master's, GRE, minimum GPA of 3.0; for doctorate, GRE, minimum GPA of 3.25. *Application deadline:* For fall admission, 4/1 for international students; for spring admission, 10/1 for international students. Applications are processed on a rolling basis. Application fee: $40 ($50 for international students). Electronic applications accepted. *Financial support:* In 2010–11, 4 fellowships with tuition reimbursements, 17 research assistantships were awarded; teaching assistantships, career-related internships or fieldwork and Federal Work-Study also available. Support available to part-time students. Financial award application deadline: 4/1; financial award applicants required to submit FAFSA. *Faculty research:* Integrated pest management, insect virology, insect taxonomy. *Unit head:* Dr. Robert Wiedenmann, Chair, 479-575-6628, E-mail: rwieden@uark.edu. *Application contact:* Janet Funk, Administrative Assistant I, 479-575-6628, E-mail: jfunk@uark.edu.

University of California, Davis, Graduate Studies, Graduate Group in Integrated Pest Management, Davis, CA 95616. Offers MS. *Degree requirements:* For master's, comprehensive exam (for some programs), thesis (for some programs). *Entrance requirements:* For master's, GRE General Test, GRE Subject Test (biology), minimum GPA of 3.0. Additional exam requirements/recommendations for international students: Required—TOEFL (minimum score 550 paper-based; 213 computer-based). Electronic applications accepted.

University of California, Davis, Graduate Studies, Program in Entomology, Davis, CA 95616. Offers MS, PhD. Terminal master's awarded for partial completion of doctoral program. *Degree requirements:* For master's, comprehensive exam (for some programs), thesis (for some programs); for doctorate, thesis/dissertation. *Entrance requirements:* For master's and doctorate, GRE General Test, GRE Subject Test (biology). Additional exam requirements/recommendations for international students: Required—TOEFL (minimum score 550 paper-based; 213 computer-based). Electronic applications accepted. *Faculty research:* Bee biology, biological control, systematics, medical/veterinary entomology, pest management.

University of California, Riverside, Graduate Division, Department of Entomology, Riverside, CA 92521-0102. Offers entomology (MS, PhD); evolution and ecology (PhD). Part-time programs available. *Faculty:* 27 full-time (4 women). *Students:* 39 full-time (20 women); includes 1 Black or African American, non-Hispanic/Latino; 3 Asian, non-Hispanic/Latino; 2 Hispanic/Latino, 8 international. Average age 29. 27 applicants, 44% accepted, 11 enrolled. In 2010, 5 master's, 7 doctorates awarded. Terminal master's awarded for partial completion of doctoral program. *Degree requirements:* For master's, thesis; for doctorate, thesis/dissertation, qualifying exams. *Entrance requirements:* For master's and doctorate, GRE General Test, minimum GPA of 3.2. Additional exam requirements/recommendations for international students: Required—Either IELTS or TOEFL (paper-based 550, computer-based 213, iBT 80). *Application deadline:* For fall admission, 5/1 for domestic students, 2/1 for international students; for winter admission, 9/1 for domestic students, 7/1 for international students; for spring admission, 12/1 for domestic students, 10/1 for international students. Applications are processed on a rolling basis. Application fee: $80 ($100 for international students). Electronic applications accepted. *Financial support:* In 2010–11, fellowships with tuition reimbursements (averaging $15,000 per year), research assistantships with tuition reimbursements (averaging $18,000 per year), teaching assistantships with tuition reimbursements (averaging $16,640 per year) were awarded; career-related internships or fieldwork, Federal Work-Study, institutionally sponsored loans, and tuition waivers (full and partial) also available. Financial award application deadline: 1/5; financial award applicants required to submit FAFSA. *Faculty research:* Agricultural, urban, medical, and veterinary entomology; biological control; chemical ecology; insect pathogens; novel toxicants. *Unit head:* Dr. Richard Redak, Chair, 951-827-7250, Fax: 951-827-3086, E-mail: richard.redak@ucr.edu. *Application contact:* Melissa L. Gomez, Graduate Student Affairs Officer, 800-735-0717, Fax: 951-827-5913, E-mail: insects@ucr.edu.

University of Connecticut, Graduate School, College of Liberal Arts and Sciences, Department of Ecology and Evolutionary Biology, Storrs, CT 06269. Offers botany (MS, PhD); ecology

Entomology

University of Connecticut (continued)
(MS, PhD); entomology (MS, PhD); zoology (MS, PhD). Terminal master's awarded for partial completion of doctoral program. *Degree requirements:* For master's, comprehensive exam; for doctorate, thesis/dissertation. *Entrance requirements:* For master's and doctorate, GRE General Test, GRE Subject Test. Additional exam requirements/recommendations for international students: Required—TOEFL (minimum score 550 paper-based; 213 computer-based). Electronic applications accepted.

University of Delaware, College of Agriculture and Natural Resources, Department of Entomology and Wildlife Ecology, Newark, DE 19716. Offers entomology and applied ecology (MS, PhD), including avian ecology, evolution and taxonomy, insect biological control, insect ecology and behavior (MS), insect genetics, pest management, plant-insect interactions, wildlife ecology and management. Part-time programs available. *Degree requirements:* For master's, comprehensive exam, thesis, oral exam, seminar; for doctorate, comprehensive exam, thesis/dissertation, qualifying exam, seminar. *Entrance requirements:* For master's, GRE General Test, minimum GPA of 3.0 in field, 2.8 overall; for doctorate, GRE General Test, GRE Subject Test (biology), minimum GPA of 3.0 in field, 2.8 overall. Additional exam requirements/recommendations for international students: Required—TOEFL. Electronic applications accepted. *Faculty research:* Ecology and evolution of plant-insect interactions, ecology of wildlife conservation management, habitat restoration, biological control, applied ecosystem management.

University of Florida, Graduate School, College of Agricultural and Life Sciences, Department of Entomology and Nematology, Gainesville, FL 32611. Offers MS, PhD. Cooperative Ph D program available with Florida A&M University. Part-time and evening/weekend programs available. *Faculty:* 30 full-time (8 women). *Students:* 71 full-time (32 women), 31 part-time (21 women); includes 3 Black or African American, non-Hispanic/Latino; 3 Asian, non-Hispanic/Latino; 4 Hispanic/Latino, 29 international. Average age 31. 52 applicants, 54% accepted, 20 enrolled. In 2010, 16 master's, 19 doctorates awarded. *Degree requirements:* For master's, comprehensive exam (for some programs), thesis (for some programs); for doctorate, comprehensive exam, thesis/dissertation. *Entrance requirements:* For master's and doctorate, GRE General Test, GRE Subject Test (biology), minimum GPA of 3.0. Additional exam requirements/recommendations for international students: Required—TOEFL (minimum score 550 paper-based; 213 computer-based; 80 iBT), IELTS (minimum score 6). *Application deadline:* For fall admission, 7/15 priority date for domestic students; for spring admission, 11/15 for domestic students. Applications are processed on a rolling basis. Application fee: $30. Electronic applications accepted. *Expenses:* Tuition, state resident: full-time $10,916. Tuition, nonresident: full-time $28,309. *Financial support:* In 2010–11, 62 students received support, including 5 fellowships, 56 research assistantships (averaging $16,962 per year), 1 teaching assistantship (averaging $16,800 per year); career-related internships or fieldwork also available. Financial award applicants required to submit FAFSA. *Faculty research:* Biological control, pest management, genetics, ecology, physiology, toxicology, systematics and taxonomy, medical and veterinary entomology, urban entomology, nematology. Total annual research expenditures: $5 million. *Unit head:* Dr. John L. Capinera, Department Chair, 352-273-3905, Fax: 352-392-0190, E-mail: capinera@ufl.edu. *Application contact:* Dr. Heather J. McAuslane, Graduate Coordinator, 352-273-3923, Fax: 352-392-0190, E-mail: hjmca@ufl.edu.

University of Georgia, College of Agricultural and Environmental Sciences, Department of Entomology, Athens, GA 30602. Offers entomology (MS, PhD); plant protection and pest management (MPPPM). *Faculty:* 26 full-time (3 women). *Students:* 33 full-time (15 women), 6 part-time (2 women); includes 1 Black or African American, non-Hispanic/Latino; 1 Hispanic/Latino; 1 Two or more races, non-Hispanic/Latino, 14 international. 27 applicants, 52% accepted, 13 enrolled. In 2010, 5 master's, 6 doctorates awarded. *Degree requirements:* For master's, thesis (MS); for doctorate, one foreign language, thesis/dissertation. *Entrance requirements:* For master's and doctorate, GRE General Test. *Application deadline:* For fall admission, 7/1 priority date for domestic students; for spring admission, 11/15 for domestic students. Application fee: $50. Electronic applications accepted. *Expenses:* Tuition, state resident: full-time $7200; part-time $344 per credit hour. Tuition, nonresident: full-time $21,900; part-time $944 per credit hour. Tuition and fees vary according to course load and program. *Financial support:* Unspecified assistantships available. *Faculty research:* Apiculture, acarology, aquatic and soil biology, ecology, systematics. *Unit head:* Dr. Raymond Noblet, Head, 706-542-2816, Fax: 706-542-2279, E-mail: rnoblet@bugs.ent.uga.edu. *Application contact:* Dr. Mark Brown, Graduate Coordinator, 706-542-2317, E-mail: mbrown@uga.edu.

University of Guelph, Graduate Studies, Ontario Agricultural College, Department of Environmental Biology, Guelph, ON N1G 2W1, Canada. Offers entomology (M Sc, PhD); environmental microbiology and biotechnology (M Sc, PhD); environmental toxicology (M Sc, PhD); plant and forest systems (M Sc, PhD); plant pathology (M Sc, PhD). Part-time programs available. *Degree requirements:* For master's, thesis; for doctorate, comprehensive exam, thesis/dissertation. *Entrance requirements:* For master's, minimum 75% average during previous 2 years of course work; for doctorate, minimum 75% average. Additional exam requirements/recommendations for international students: Required—TOEFL or IELTS. Electronic applications accepted. *Faculty research:* Entomology, environmental microbiology and biotechnology, environmental toxicology, forest ecology, plant pathology.

University of Hawaii at Manoa, Graduate Division, College of Tropical Agriculture and Human Resources, Department of Plant and Environmental Protection Sciences, Program in Entomology, Honolulu, HI 96822. Offers MS, PhD. Part-time programs available. *Faculty:* 14 full-time (3 women), 2 part-time/adjunct (1 woman). *Students:* 16 full-time (9 women), 2 part-time (0 women); includes 4 minority (1 Asian, non-Hispanic/Latino; 3 Two or more races, non-Hispanic/Latino), 6 international. Average age 32. 15 applicants, 47% accepted, 5 enrolled. *Degree requirements:* For master's, thesis optional; for doctorate, comprehensive exam, thesis/dissertation. *Entrance requirements:* For master's and doctorate, GRE General Test, GRE Subject Test (biology). Additional exam requirements/recommendations for international students: Required—TOEFL (minimum score 500 paper-based; 173 computer-based; 61 iBT), IELTS (minimum score 5). *Application deadline:* For fall admission, 3/1 for domestic and international students; for spring admission, 10/1 for domestic and international students. Application fee: $50. *Financial support:* In 2010–11, 5 fellowships (averaging $1,148 per year), 16 research assistantships (averaging $19,580 per year) were awarded; tuition waivers (full) also available. *Faculty research:* Integrated pest management, biological control, urban entomology, medical/forensic entomology resistance. Total annual research expenditures: $200,000. *Application contact:* Mark Wright, Graduate Chair, 808-956-6747, Fax: 808-956-2458, E-mail: markwrig@hawaii.edu.

University of Idaho, College of Graduate Studies, College of Agricultural and Life Sciences, Department of Plant, Soil, and Entomological Sciences, Program in Entomology, Moscow, ID 83844-2282. Offers MS, PhD. *Students:* 11 full-time, 1 part-time. Average age 29. *Degree requirements:* For master's, thesis (for some programs); for doctorate, one foreign language, thesis/dissertation. *Entrance requirements:* For master's and doctorate, GRE General Test, minimum GPA of 3.0. *Application deadline:* For fall admission, 8/1 for domestic students; for spring admission, 12/15 for domestic students. Applications are processed on a rolling basis. Application fee: $60. Electronic applications accepted. *Expenses:* Tuition, nonresident: part-time $580 per credit. Required fees: $306 per credit. *Financial support:* Applicants required to submit FAFSA. *Faculty research:* Biological control of insect pests/weeds, aquatic entomology-resource management, hop pest management, mosquito reproductive physiology, landscape ecology for sustainability and biological conservation. *Unit head:* Dr. James B. Johnson, Department Head, 208-885-6274, E-mail: nthompson@uidaho.edu. *Application contact:* Dr. James B. Johnson, Department Head, 208-885-6274, E-mail: nthompson@uidaho.edu.

University of Illinois at Urbana–Champaign, Graduate College, College of Liberal Arts and Sciences, School of Integrative Biology, Department of Entomology, Champaign, IL 61820. Offers MS, PhD. *Faculty:* 11 full-time (3 women). *Students:* 30 full-time (18 women), 3 part-time (1 woman); includes 1 Black or African American, non-Hispanic/Latino; 2 Asian, non-Hispanic/Latino; 1 Hispanic/Latino, 10 international. 23 applicants, 22% accepted, 5 enrolled. In 2010, 4 master's, 5 doctorates awarded. Terminal master's awarded for partial completion of doctoral program. *Entrance requirements:* For master's and doctorate, GRE General Test, GRE Subject Test, minimum GPA of 3.0. Additional exam requirements/recommendations for international students: Required—TOEFL (minimum score 550 paper-based). *Application deadline:* Applications are processed on a rolling basis. Application fee: $75 ($90 for international students). Electronic applications accepted. *Financial support:* In 2010–11, 1 fellowship, 27 research assistantships, 17 teaching assistantships were awarded; tuition waivers (full and partial) also available. *Unit head:* Dr. May R. Berenbaum, Head, 217-333-7784, Fax: 217-244-3499, E-mail: maybe@illinois.edu. *Application contact:* Audra Weinstein, Office Administrator, 217-244-2888, Fax: 217-244-3499, E-mail: audra@illinois.edu.

The University of Kansas, Graduate Studies, College of Liberal Arts and Sciences, Department of Ecology and Evolutionary Biology, Lawrence, KS 66045. Offers botany (MA, PhD); ecology and evolutionary biology (MA, PhD); entomology (MA, PhD). *Faculty:* 13 full-time (6 women), 29 part-time/adjunct (7 women). *Students:* 62 full-time (30 women); includes 1 minority (Hispanic/Latino), 16 international. Average age 29. 52 applicants, 42% accepted, 14 enrolled. In 2010, 9 master's, 8 doctorates awarded. Terminal master's awarded for partial completion of doctoral program. *Degree requirements:* For master's, comprehensive exam, thesis (for some programs), 30-36 credits, thesis presentation; for doctorate, comprehensive exam, thesis/dissertation, residency, responsible scholarship and research skills, final exam, dissertation defense. *Entrance requirements:* For master's, GRE General Test, bachelor's degree with minimum undergraduate GPA of 3.0; for doctorate, GRE General Test, bachelor's degree; minimum undergraduate/graduate GPA of 3.0. Additional exam requirements/recommendations for international students: Required—TOEFL, IELTS, Score requirements in EEB are the same as those set by Graduate Studies. *Application deadline:* For fall admission, 12/15 for domestic and international students; for spring admission, 9/15 for domestic and international students. Application fee: $55 ($65 for international students). Electronic applications accepted. *Expenses:* Tuition, state resident: full-time $7092; part-time $295.50 per credit hour. Tuition, nonresident: full-time $16,590; part-time $691.25 per credit hour. Required fees: $858; $71.49 per credit hour. Tuition and fees vary according to course load, campus/location and program. *Financial support:* Fellowships with tuition reimbursements, research assistantships with full and partial tuition reimbursements, teaching assistantships with full and partial tuition reimbursements, scholarships/grants, traineeships, health care benefits, and unspecified assistantships available. Financial award application deadline: 12/15. *Faculty research:* Biodiversity and macroevolution, ecology and global change, evolutionary mechanisms. *Unit head:* Dr. Christopher H. Haufler, Chair, 785-864-3255, Fax: 785-864-5860, E-mail: vulgare@ku.edu. *Application contact:* Jaime Rochelle Keeler, Graduate Coordinator, 785-864-2362, Fax: 785-864-5860, E-mail: jrkeeler@ku.edu.

University of Kentucky, Graduate School, College of Agriculture, Program in Entomology, Lexington, KY 40506-0032. Offers MS, PhD. *Degree requirements:* For master's, comprehensive exam, thesis optional; for doctorate, comprehensive exam, thesis/dissertation. *Entrance requirements:* For master's, GRE General Test, minimum undergraduate GPA of 2.75; for doctorate, GRE General Test, minimum graduate GPA of 3.0. Additional exam requirements/recommendations for international students: Required—TOEFL (minimum score 550 paper-based; 213 computer-based). Electronic applications accepted. *Faculty research:* Applied entomology, behavior, insect biology and ecology, biological control, insect physiology and molecular biology.

University of Maine, Graduate School, College of Natural Sciences, Forestry, and Agriculture, Department of Biological Sciences, Program in Entomology, Orono, ME 04469. Offers MS. Part-time programs available. *Students:* 1 (woman) full-time, all international. Average age 22. 2 applicants, 50% accepted, 1 enrolled. *Entrance requirements:* For master's, GRE General Test. Additional exam requirements/recommendations for international students: Required—TOEFL. *Application deadline:* For fall admission, 2/1 priority date for domestic students. Applications are processed on a rolling basis. Application fee: $65. Electronic applications accepted. *Expenses:* Tuition, state resident: full-time $400. Tuition, nonresident: full-time $1050. *Financial support:* Career-related internships or fieldwork, Federal Work-Study, institutionally sponsored loans, and tuition waivers (full) available. Financial award application deadline: 3/1. *Unit head:* Dr. Stellos Tavantiz, Coordinator, 207-581-2986. *Application contact:* Scott G. Delcourt, Associate Dean of the Graduate School, 207-581-3291, Fax: 207-581-3232, E-mail: graduate@maine.edu.

University of Manitoba, Faculty of Graduate Studies, Faculty of Agricultural and Food Sciences, Department of Entomology, Winnipeg, MB R3T 2N2, Canada. Offers M Sc, PhD. *Degree requirements:* For master's, thesis; for doctorate, one foreign language, thesis/dissertation.

University of Maryland, College Park, Academic Affairs, College of Computer, Mathematical and Natural Sciences, Department of Entomology, College Park, MD 20742. Offers MS, PhD. Part-time and evening/weekend programs available. *Faculty:* 38 full-time (18 women), 2 part-time/adjunct (both women). *Students:* 13 full-time (3 women), 2 part-time (both women); includes 4 minority (1 Black or African American, non-Hispanic/Latino; 1 Asian, non-Hispanic/Latino; 1 Hispanic/Latino; 1 Two or more races, non-Hispanic/Latino), 4 international. 26 applicants, 19% accepted, 3 enrolled. In 2010, 1 master's, 4 doctorates awarded. Terminal master's awarded for partial completion of doctoral program. *Degree requirements:* For master's, thesis; for doctorate, thesis/dissertation, oral qualifying exam. *Entrance requirements:* For master's and doctorate, GRE General Test, minimum GPA of 3.0, 3 letters of recommendation. *Application deadline:* For fall admission, 1/1 for domestic and international students. Applications are processed on a rolling basis. Application fee: $75. Electronic applications accepted. *Expenses:* Tuition, state resident: part-time $471 per credit hour. Tuition, nonresident: part-time $1016 per credit hour. Required fees: $337 per term. *Financial support:* In 2010–11, 1 fellowship with full tuition reimbursement (averaging $15,000 per year), 14 teaching assistantships (averaging $19,222 per year) were awarded; career-related internships or fieldwork and Federal Work-Study also available. Support available to part-time students. Financial award applicants required to submit FAFSA. *Faculty research:* Pest management, biosystematics, physiology and morphology, toxicology. Total annual research expenditures: $1.5 million. *Unit head:* Dr. Charles Mitter, Chair, 301-405-3912, Fax: 301-314-9290, E-mail: cmitter@umd.edu. *Application contact:* Dr. Charles A. Caramello, Dean of Graduate School, 301-405-0358, Fax: 301-314-9305.

University of Massachusetts Amherst, Graduate School, College of Natural Sciences, Department of Plant, Soil and Insect Sciences, Program in Entomology, Amherst, MA 01003. Offers MS, PhD. Part-time programs available. *Faculty:* 9 full-time (2 women). *Students:* 5 full-time (3 women), 2 part-time (1 woman), 2 international. Average age 27. 15 applicants, 53% accepted, 3 enrolled. In 2010, 1 master's, 1 doctorate awarded. Terminal master's awarded for partial completion of doctoral program. *Degree requirements:* For master's, thesis or alternative; for doctorate, comprehensive exam, thesis/dissertation. *Entrance requirements:* For master's and doctorate, GRE General Test. Additional exam requirements/recommendations for international students: Required—TOEFL (minimum score 550 paper-based; 213 computer-based; 80 iBT), IELTS (minimum score 6.5). *Application deadline:* For fall admission, 1/2 for domestic and international students; for spring admission, 10/1 for domestic and international students. Applications are processed on a rolling basis. Application fee: $50 ($65 for international students). Electronic applications accepted. *Expenses:* Tuition, state resident: full-time $2640. Required fees: $8282. One-time fee: $357 full-time. *Financial support:* Fellowships, research assistantships, teaching assistantships, career-related internships or fieldwork, Federal Work-Study, scholarships/grants, traineeships, health care benefits, tuition waivers (full), and unspecified assistantships available. Support available to part-time students. Financial award application deadline: 1/2; financial award applicants required to submit FAFSA. *Unit head:* Dr. Benjamin Normark, Graduate Program Director, 413-545-1059, Fax: 413-545-2115. *Application contact:* Jean M. Ames, Supervisor of Admissions, 413-545-0722, Fax: 413-577-0010, E-mail: gradadm@grad.umass.edu.

University of Minnesota, Twin Cities Campus, Graduate School, College of Food, Agricultural and Natural Resource Sciences, Entomology Graduate Program, Saint Paul, MN 55108. Offers MS, PhD. Part-time programs available. *Faculty:* 27 full-time (8 women). *Students:* 27 full-time (15 women); includes 6 minority (2 Asian, non-Hispanic/Latino; 3 Hispanic/Latino; 1 Two or more races, non-Hispanic/Latino), 3 international. Average age 30. 25 applicants, 64% accepted, 14 enrolled. In 2010, 1 master's, 1 doctorate awarded. *Degree requirements:* For master's, comprehensive exam, thesis; for doctorate, comprehensive exam, thesis/dissertation. *Entrance requirements:* For master's, GRE, minimum undergraduate GPA of 3.0; for doctorate, GRE, minimum undergraduate GPA of 3.0, graduate 3.5. Additional exam requirements/recommendations for international students: Required—TOEFL (minimum score 550 paper-based; 213 computer-based; 79 iBT). *Application deadline:* For fall admission, 12/15 priority date for domestic and international students; for spring admission, 10/15 priority date for domestic students, 12/15 priority date for international students. Applications are processed on a rolling basis. Application fee: $75 ($95 for international students). Electronic applications accepted. *Financial support:* In 2010–11, fellowships with full tuition reimbursements (averaging $23,500 per year), research assistantships with full tuition reimbursements (averaging $18,000 per year), teaching assistantships with full tuition reimbursements (averaging $18,000 per year) were awarded; scholarships/grants, health care benefits, and unspecified assistantships also available. *Faculty research:* Behavior, ecology, molecular genetics, physiology, systematics and taxonomy. Total annual research expenditures: $2.2 million. *Unit head:* Dr. George Heimpel, Director of Graduate Studies, 612-624-3480, Fax: 612-625-5299, E-mail: heimp001@umn.edu. *Application contact:* Felicia Christy Horan, Program Coordinator, 612-624-3278, Fax: 612-625-5299, E-mail: christy@umn.edu.

University of Missouri, Graduate School, College of Agriculture, Food and Natural Resources, Division of Plant Sciences, Program in Entomology, Columbia, MO 65211. Offers MS, PhD. *Degree requirements:* For doctorate, thesis/dissertation. *Application deadline:* Applications are processed on a rolling basis. *Financial support:* Research assistantships, teaching assistantships, institutionally sponsored loans available. *Application contact:* Dr. Jeanne Mihail, Director of Graduate Studies, 573-882-0574, E-mail: mihailj@missouri.edu.

University of Nebraska–Lincoln, Graduate College, College of Agricultural Sciences and Natural Resources, Department of Entomology, Lincoln, NE 68588. Offers MS, PhD. Post-baccalaureate distance learning degree programs offered (no on-campus study). *Degree requirements:* For master's, thesis optional; for doctorate, comprehensive exam, thesis/dissertation. *Entrance requirements:* For master's and doctorate, GRE General Test. Additional exam requirements/recommendations for international students: Required—TOEFL (minimum score 550 paper-based; 213 computer-based). Electronic applications accepted. *Faculty research:* Ecology and behavior, insect-plant interactions, integrated pest management, genetics, urban entomology.

University of North Dakota, Graduate School, College of Arts and Sciences, Department of Biology, Grand Forks, ND 58202. Offers botany (MS, PhD); ecology (MS, PhD); entomology (MS, PhD); environmental biology (MS, PhD); fisheries/wildlife (MS, PhD); genetics (MS, PhD); zoology (MS, PhD). *Faculty:* 17 full-time (5 women), 6 part-time/adjunct (1 woman). *Students:* 19 full-time (6 women), 8 part-time (2 women); includes 4 minority (3 American Indian or Alaska Native, non-Hispanic/Latino; 1 Asian, non-Hispanic/Latino), 1 international. Average age 28. 21 applicants, 33% accepted, 4 enrolled. In 2010, 1 master's awarded. Terminal master's awarded for partial completion of doctoral program. *Degree requirements:* For master's, thesis, final exam; for doctorate, comprehensive exam, thesis/dissertation, final exam. *Entrance requirements:* For master's, GRE General Test, GRE Subject Test, minimum GPA of 3.0; for doctorate, GRE General Test, GRE Subject Test, minimum GPA of 3.5. Additional exam requirements/recommendations for international students: Required—TOEFL (minimum score 550 paper-based; 213 computer-based; 79 iBT), IELTS (minimum score 6.5). *Application deadline:* For fall admission, 2/15 for domestic and international students; for spring admission, 10/15 for domestic and international students. Application fee: $35. Electronic applications accepted. *Expenses:* Tuition, state resident: full-time $5857; part-time $306.74 per credit. Tuition, nonresident: full-time $15,666; part-time $729.77 per credit. Required fees: $53.42 per credit. Tuition and fees vary according to course load, program and reciprocity agreements. *Financial support:* In 2010–11, 22 students received support, including 5 research assistantships with full and partial tuition reimbursements available (averaging $11,375 per year), 17 teaching assistantships with full and partial tuition reimbursements available (averaging $10,813 per year); fellowships with full and partial tuition reimbursements available, Federal Work-Study, institutionally sponsored loans, scholarships/grants, health care benefits, tuition waivers (full and partial), and unspecified assistantships also available. Support available to part-time students. Financial award application deadline: 3/15; financial award applicants required to submit FAFSA. *Faculty research:* Population biology, wildlife ecology, RNA processing, hormonal control of behavior. Total annual research expenditures: $736,510. *Unit head:* Dr. Brett Goodwin, Graduate Director, 701-777-2621, Fax: 701-777-2623, E-mail: brett.goodwin@mail.und.edu. *Application contact:* Matthew Anderson, Admissions Specialist, 701-777-2947, Fax: 701-777-3619, E-mail: matthew.anderson@gradschool.und.edu.

University of Rhode Island, Graduate School, College of the Environment and Life Sciences, Department of Plant Sciences, Kingston, RI 02881. Offers entomology (MS, PhD); plant sciences (MS, PhD). Part-time programs available. *Faculty:* 9 full-time (2 women), 1 part-time/adjunct (0 women). *Degree requirements:* For master's, comprehensive exam (for some programs), thesis optional; for doctorate, comprehensive exam, thesis/dissertation. *Entrance requirements:* For master's and doctorate, GRE, 2 letters of recommendation. Additional exam requirements/recommendations for international students: Required—TOEFL (minimum score 550 paper-based; 213 computer-based). *Application deadline:* For fall admission, 7/15 for domestic students, 2/1 for international students; for spring admission, 11/15 for domestic students, 7/15 for international students. Application fee: $65. Electronic applications accepted. *Expenses:* Tuition, state resident: full-time $9588; part-time $533 per credit hour. Tuition, nonresident: full-time $22,968; part-time $1276 per credit hour. Required fees: $1282; $68 per semester. Tuition and fees vary according to program. *Financial support:* In 2010–11, 3 research assistantships with full and partial tuition reimbursements (averaging $10,612 per year), 1 teaching assistantship with full and partial tuition reimbursement (averaging $6,974 per year) were awarded. Financial award application deadline: 7/15; financial award applicants required to submit FAFSA. *Faculty research:* Plant development and management; pest management; tick biology, ecology, and control; identification and replacement of invasive ornamentals. Total annual research expenditures: $1.3 million. *Unit head:* Dr. Brian K. Maynard, Interim Chair, 401-874-2928, Fax: 401-874-2494, E-mail: bmaynard@uri.edu. *Application contact:*

Dr. Thomas Mather, Director of Graduate Studies, 401-874-5616, Fax: 401-874-2494, E-mail: tmather@uri.edu.

The University of Tennessee, Graduate School, College of Agricultural Sciences and Natural Resources, Department of Entomology and Plant Pathology, Knoxville, TN 37996. Offers entomology (MS, PhD); integrated pest management and bioactive natural products (PhD); plant pathology (MS, PhD). Part-time programs available. *Degree requirements:* For master's, thesis, seminar. *Entrance requirements:* For master's, GRE General Test, minimum GPA of 2.7, 3 reference letters, letter of intent; for doctorate, GRE General Test, minimum GPA of 2.7, 3 reference letters, letter of intent, proposed dissertation research. Additional exam requirements/recommendations for international students: Required—TOEFL. Electronic applications accepted. *Expenses:* Tuition, state resident: full-time $7440; part-time $414 per credit hour. Tuition, nonresident: full-time $22,478; part-time $1250 per credit hour. Required fees: $922; $43 per credit hour. Tuition and fees vary according to program.

University of Wisconsin–Madison, Graduate School, College of Agricultural and Life Sciences, Department of Entomology, Madison, WI 53706-1380. Offers MS, PhD. *Degree requirements:* For master's, thesis; for doctorate, thesis/dissertation. *Entrance requirements:* For master's and doctorate, GRE General Test, minimum GPA of 3.0. Additional exam requirements/recommendations for international students: Required—TOEFL (minimum score 237 computer-based). Electronic applications accepted. *Expenses:* Tuition, state resident: full-time $9887; part-time $617.96 per credit. Tuition, nonresident: full-time $24,054; part-time $1503.40 per credit. Required fees: $67.63 per credit. Tuition and fees vary according to reciprocity agreements. *Faculty research:* Ecology, biocontrol, molecular.

University of Wyoming, College of Agriculture and Natural Resources, Department of Renewable Resources, Program in Entomology, Laramie, WY 82070. Offers MS, PhD. *Degree requirements:* For master's, thesis; for doctorate, thesis/dissertation. *Entrance requirements:* For master's and doctorate, GRE General Test, minimum GPA of 3.0. Additional exam requirements/recommendations for international students: Required—TOEFL. Electronic applications accepted. *Faculty research:* Insect pest management, taxonomy, biocontrol of weeds, forest insects, insects affecting humans and animals.

Virginia Polytechnic Institute and State University, Graduate School, College of Agriculture and Life Sciences, Department of Entomology, Blacksburg, VA 24061. Offers MSLFS, PhD. *Faculty:* 12 full-time (2 women). *Students:* 35 full-time (20 women), 3 part-time (1 woman); includes 3 Black or African American, non-Hispanic/Latino; 1 Asian, non-Hispanic/Latino; 3 Hispanic/Latino, 8 international. Average age 30. 8 applicants, 75% accepted, 3 enrolled. In 2010, 4 master's, 5 doctorates awarded. *Degree requirements:* For master's, comprehensive exam (for some programs), thesis (for some programs); for doctorate, comprehensive exam (for some programs), thesis/dissertation (for some programs). *Entrance requirements:* For master's and doctorate, GRE. Additional exam requirements/recommendations for international students: Required—TOEFL (minimum score 550 paper-based; 213 computer-based). *Application deadline:* For fall admission, 7/1 for domestic and international students; for spring admission, 12/1 for domestic and international students. Applications are processed on a rolling basis. Application fee: $65. Electronic applications accepted. *Expenses:* Tuition, state resident: full-time $9399; part-time $488 per credit hour. Tuition, nonresident: full-time $17,854; part-time $957.75 per credit hour. Required fees: $1534. Full-time tuition and fees vary according to program. *Financial support:* In 2010–11, 16 research assistantships with full tuition reimbursements (averaging $17,187 per year), 9 teaching assistantships with full tuition reimbursements (averaging $14,742 per year) were awarded; career-related internships or fieldwork, Federal Work-Study, scholarships/grants, health care benefits, and unspecified assistantships also available. Financial award application deadline: 1/15. *Faculty research:* Physiology, ecology, biocontrol, genetics, taxonomy. Total annual research expenditures: $3.3 million. *Unit head:* Dr. Loke T. Kok, UNIT HEAD, 540-231-6341, Fax: 540-231-9131, E-mail: ltkok@vt.edu. *Application contact:* J. Reese, Contact, 540-231-5707, Fax: 540-231-9131, E-mail: rvoshell@vt.edu.

Washington State University, Graduate School, College of Agricultural, Human, and Natural Resource Sciences, Department of Entomology, Pullman, WA 99164. Offers MS, PhD. Part-time programs available. *Faculty:* 25. *Students:* 27 full-time (13 women), 2 part-time (1 woman), 5 international. Average age 28. 24 applicants, 46% accepted, 11 enrolled. In 2010, 5 master's, 2 doctorates awarded. Terminal master's awarded for partial completion of doctoral program. *Degree requirements:* For master's, comprehensive exam (for some programs), thesis (for some programs), oral exam; for doctorate, comprehensive exam, thesis/dissertation, oral exam, written exam. *Entrance requirements:* For master's, GRE General Test, GRE Subject Test in advanced biology (recommended), minimum GPA of 3.0, 3 letters of recommendation; for doctorate, GRE General Test, minimum GPA of 3.0, 3 letters of recommendation. Additional exam requirements/recommendations for international students: Required—TOEFL (minimum score 550 paper-based; 213 computer-based), IELTS. *Application deadline:* For fall admission, 1/10 priority date for domestic and international students; for spring admission, 7/1 priority date for domestic and international students. Applications are processed on a rolling basis. Application fee: $50. Electronic applications accepted. *Expenses:* Tuition, state resident: full-time $8552; part-time $443 per credit. Tuition, nonresident: full-time $21,650; part-time $1083 per credit. Required fees: $846. *Financial support:* In 2010–11, fellowships (averaging $5,306 per year), research assistantships with full and partial tuition reimbursements (averaging $18,204 per year), teaching assistantships with full and partial tuition reimbursements (averaging $18,204 per year) were awarded; career-related internships or fieldwork, Federal Work-Study, institutionally sponsored loans, tuition waivers (partial), unspecified assistantships, and teaching associateships also available. Financial award application deadline: 2/5; financial award applicants required to submit FAFSA. *Faculty research:* Apiculture, biological control of arthropods, integrated pest management, ecology, physiology and systematics of insects. Total annual research expenditures: $4.3 million. *Unit head:* Dr. W. Steve Sheppard, Chair, 509-335-5180, Fax: 509-335-1009, E-mail: shepp@wsu.edu. *Application contact:* Graduate School Admissions, 800-GRADWSU, Fax: 509-335-1949, E-mail: gradsch@wsu.edu.

West Virginia University, Davis College of Agriculture, Forestry and Consumer Sciences, Division of Plant and Soil Sciences, Morgantown, WV 26506. Offers agricultural sciences (PhD), including animal and food sciences, plant and soil sciences; agronomy (MS); entomology (MS); environmental microbiology (MS); horticulture (MS); plant pathology (MS). *Degree requirements:* For master's, thesis. *Entrance requirements:* For master's, GRE, minimum GPA of 2.5. Additional exam requirements/recommendations for international students: Required—TOEFL. *Faculty research:* Water quality, reclamation of disturbed land, crop production, pest control, environmental protection.

Section 10
Genetics, Developmental Biology, and Reproductive Biology

This section contains a directory of institutions offering graduate work in genetics, developmental biology, and reproductive biology, followed by in-depth entries submitted by institutions that chose to prepare detailed program descriptions. Additional information about programs listed in the directory but not augmented by an in-depth entry may be obtained by writing directly to the dean of a graduate school or chair of a department at the address given in the directory.

For programs offering related work, see also all other sections of this book. In the other guides in this series:

Graduate Programs in the Physical Sciences, Mathematics, Agricultural Sciences, the Environment & Natural Resources
See *Agricultural and Food Sciences, Chemistry,* and *Environmental Sciences and Management*

Graduate Programs in Engineering & Applied Sciences
See *Agricultural Engineering and Bioengineering* and *Biomedical Engineering and Biotechnology*

Graduate Programs in Business, Education, Health, Information Studies, Law & Social Work
See *Veterinary Medicine and Sciences*

CONTENTS

Close-Ups and Displays

Developmental Biology

Albert Einstein College of Medicine, Graduate Division of Biomedical Sciences, Department of Anatomy and Structural Biology, Bronx, NY 10461. Offers anatomy (PhD); cell and developmental biology (PhD); MD/PhD. *Degree requirements:* For doctorate, thesis/dissertation. *Entrance requirements:* For doctorate, GRE General Test. Additional exam requirements/recommendations for international students: Required—TOEFL. Electronic applications accepted. *Faculty research:* Cell motility, cell membranes and membrane-cytoskeletal interactions as applied to processing of pancreatic hormones, mechanisms of secretion.

Albert Einstein College of Medicine, Graduate Division of Biomedical Sciences, Division of Biological Sciences, Department of Developmental and Molecular Biology, Bronx, NY 10461. Offers PhD, MD/PhD. *Degree requirements:* For doctorate, thesis/dissertation. *Entrance requirements:* For doctorate, GRE General Test. Additional exam requirements/recommendations for international students: Required—TOEFL. *Faculty research:* DNA, RNA, and protein synthesis in prokaryotes and eukaryotes; chemical and enzymatic alteration of RNA; glycoproteins.

Baylor College of Medicine, Graduate School of Biomedical Sciences, Program in Developmental Biology, Houston, TX 77030-3498. Offers PhD, MD/PhD. *Faculty:* 63 full-time (19 women). *Students:* 55 full-time (26 women); includes 5 Asian, non-Hispanic/Latino; 3 Hispanic/Latino, 35 international. Average age 28. 73 applicants, 18% accepted, 10 enrolled. In 2010, 5 doctorates awarded. *Degree requirements:* For doctorate, thesis/dissertation, public defense. *Entrance requirements:* For doctorate, GRE General Test, GRE Subject Test (strongly recommended), minimum GPA of 3.0. Additional exam requirements/recommendations for international students: Required—TOEFL. *Application deadline:* For fall admission, 1/1 priority date for domestic students. Application fee: $0. Electronic applications accepted. *Expenses:* Tuition: Full-time $11,000. Required fees: $4900. *Financial support:* In 2010–11, 55 students received support, including 15 fellowships with full tuition reimbursements available (averaging $26,000 per year), 40 research assistantships with full tuition reimbursements available (averaging $26,000 per year); career-related internships or fieldwork, Federal Work-Study, institutionally sponsored loans, health care benefits, tuition waivers (full), and stipends also available. *Faculty research:* Stem cells, cancer, neurobiology, organogenesis, genetics of model organisms. *Unit head:* Dr. Hugo Bellen, Director, 713-798-6410. *Application contact:* Catherine Tasnier, Graduate Program Administrator, 713-798-6410, Fax: 713-798-5386, E-mail: cat@bcm.edu.

See Display on this page and Close-Up on page 307.

Brigham Young University, Graduate Studies, College of Life Sciences, Department of Physiology and Developmental Biology, Provo, UT 84602. Offers neuroscience (MS, PhD); physiology and developmental biology (MS, PhD). Part-time programs available. *Faculty:* 19 full-time (0 women). *Students:* 25 full-time (11 women); includes 6 minority (1 American Indian or Alaska Native, non-Hispanic/Latino; 3 Asian, non-Hispanic/Latino; 2 Hispanic/Latino). Average age 29. 17 applicants, 47% accepted, 7 enrolled. In 2010, 5 master's, 2 doctorates awarded. Terminal master's awarded for partial completion of doctoral program. *Degree requirements:* For master's, thesis; for doctorate, thesis/dissertation. *Entrance requirements:* For master's, GRE General Test, minimum GPA of 3.0 during previous 2 years; for doctorate, GRE General Test, minimum GPA of 3.0 overall. Additional exam requirements/recommendations for international students: Required—TOEFL. *Application deadline:* For fall admission, 2/1 priority date for domestic and international students; for winter admission, 9/10 priority date for domestic and international students. Application fee: $50. Electronic applications accepted. *Expenses:* Tuition: Full-time $5580; part-time $310 per credit hour. Tuition and fees vary according to program and student's religious affiliation. *Financial support:* In 2010–11, 25 students received support, including 1 fellowship with partial tuition reimbursement available (averaging $7,100 per year), 12 research assistantships with full tuition reimbursements available (averaging $15,500 per year), 13 teaching assistantships with partial tuition reimbursements available (averaging $14,900 per year); career-related internships or fieldwork, institutionally sponsored loans, scholarships/grants, tuition waivers (full and partial), unspecified assistantships, and tuition awards also available. Financial award application deadline: 2/1. *Faculty research:* Sex differentiation of the brain, exercise physiology, developmental biology, membrane biophysics, neuroscience. Total annual research expenditures: $827,031. *Unit head:* Dr. William W. Winder, Chair, 801-422-3093, Fax: 801-422-0700, E-mail: william_winder@byu.edu. *Application contact:* Dr. Dixon J. Woodbury, Graduate Coordinator, 801-422-7562, Fax: 801-422-0700, E-mail: dixon_woodbury@byu.edu.

Brown University, Graduate School, Division of Biology and Medicine, Program in Molecular Biology, Cell Biology, and Biochemistry, Providence, RI 02912. Offers biochemistry (M Med Sc, Sc M, PhD), including biochemistry (Sc M, PhD), biology (Sc M, PhD), medical science (M Med Sc, PhD); biology (MA); cell biology (M Med Sc, Sc M, PhD), including biochemistry (Sc M, PhD), biology (Sc M, PhD), medical science (M Med Sc, PhD); developmental biology (M Med Sc, Sc M, PhD), including biochemistry (Sc M, PhD), biology (Sc M, PhD), medical science (M Med Sc, PhD); immunology (M Med Sc, Sc M, PhD), including biochemistry (Sc M, PhD), biology (Sc M, PhD), medical science (M Med Sc, PhD); molecular microbiology (M Med Sc, Sc M, PhD), including biochemistry (Sc M, PhD), biology (Sc M, PhD), medical science (M Med Sc, PhD); MD/PhD. Part-time programs available. Terminal master's awarded for partial completion of doctoral program. *Degree requirements:* For master's, thesis (for some programs); for doctorate, one foreign language, thesis/dissertation, preliminary exam. *Entrance requirements:* For master's and doctorate, GRE General Test, GRE Subject Test. Additional exam requirements/recommendations for international students: Required—TOEFL. Electronic applications accepted. *Faculty research:* Molecular genetics, gene regulation.

California Institute of Technology, Division of Biology, Program in Developmental Biology, Pasadena, CA 91125-0001. Offers PhD. *Degree requirements:* For doctorate, thesis/dissertation, qualifying exam. *Entrance requirements:* For doctorate, GRE General Test.

Carnegie Mellon University, Mellon College of Science, Department of Biological Sciences, Pittsburgh, PA 15213-3891. Offers biochemistry (PhD); biophysics (PhD); cell biology (PhD); computational biology (MS, PhD); developmental biology (PhD); genetics (PhD); molecular biology (PhD); neuroscience (PhD). *Degree requirements:* For doctorate, comprehensive exam, thesis/dissertation. *Entrance requirements:* For doctorate, GRE General Test, GRE Subject Test, interview. Electronic applications accepted. *Faculty research:* Genetic structure, function, and regulation; protein structure and function; biological membranes; biological spectroscopy.

Columbia University, College of Physicians and Surgeons, Department of Genetics and Development, New York, NY 10032. Offers genetics (M Phil, MA, PhD); MD/PhD. Only candidates for the PhD are admitted. Terminal master's awarded for partial completion of doctoral program. *Degree requirements:* For doctorate, thesis/dissertation. *Entrance requirements:* For master's and doctorate, GRE General Test. Additional exam requirements/recommendations for international students: Required—TOEFL. *Faculty research:* Mammalian cell differentiation and meiosis, developmental genetics, yeast and human genetics, chromosome structure, molecular and cellular biology.

Cornell University, Graduate School, Graduate Fields of Agriculture and Life Sciences, Field of Genetics and Development, Ithaca, NY 14853-0001. Offers developmental biology (PhD); genetics (PhD). *Faculty:* 54 full-time (12 women). *Students:* 58 full-time (36 women); includes 1 Black or African American, non-Hispanic/Latino; 2 Asian, non-Hispanic/Latino; 2 Hispanic/Latino, 24 international. Average age 25. 90 applicants, 12% accepted, 11 enrolled. In 2010, 10 doctorates awarded. *Degree requirements:* For doctorate, comprehensive exam, thesis/dissertation, 2 semesters of teaching experience. *Entrance requirements:* For doctorate, GRE General Test, GRE Subject Test in biology or biochemistry (recommended), 2 letters of recommendation. Additional exam requirements/recommendations for international students: Required—TOEFL (minimum score 550 paper-based; 213 computer-based; 77 iBT). *Application*

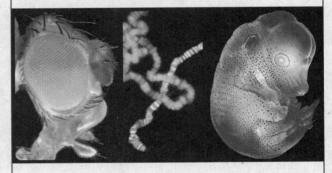

deadline: For fall admission, 1/5 for domestic students. Application fee: $70. Electronic applications accepted. *Expenses:* Tuition: Full-time $29,500. Required fees: $76. Tuition and fees vary according to degree level and program. *Financial support:* In 2010–11, 16 fellowships with full tuition reimbursements, 28 research assistantships with full tuition reimbursements, 13 teaching assistantships with full tuition reimbursements were awarded; institutionally sponsored loans, scholarships/grants, health care benefits, tuition waivers (full and partial), and unspecified assistantships also available. Financial award applicants required to submit FAFSA. *Faculty research:* Molecular and general genetics, developmental biology and developmental genetics, evolution and population genetics, plant genetics, microbial genetics. *Unit head:* Director of Graduate Studies, 607-254-2100. *Application contact:* Graduate Field Assistant, 607-254-2100, E-mail: gendev@cornell.edu.

Cornell University, Graduate School, Graduate Fields of Agriculture and Life Sciences, Field of Zoology and Wildlife Conservation, Ithaca, NY 14853-0001. Offers animal cytology (MS, PhD); comparative and functional anatomy (MS, PhD); developmental biology (MS, PhD); ecology (MS, PhD); histology (MS, PhD). *Faculty:* 20 full-time (5 women). *Students:* 5 full-time (all women); includes 1 Hispanic/Latino, 1 international. Average age 31. 17 applicants, 18% accepted, 1 enrolled. *Degree requirements:* For doctorate, comprehensive exam, thesis/dissertation, 2 semesters of teaching experience. *Entrance requirements:* For doctorate, GRE General Test, GRE Subject Test (biology), 2 letters of recommendation. Additional exam requirements/recommendations for international students: Required—TOEFL (minimum score 550 paper-based; 213 computer-based; 77 iBT). *Application deadline:* For fall admission, 2/1 priority date for domestic students. Application fee: $70. Electronic applications accepted. *Expenses:* Tuition: Full-time $29,500. Required fees: $76. Tuition and fees vary according to degree level and program. *Financial support:* In 2010–11, 1 fellowship with full tuition reimbursement, 4 research assistantships with full tuition reimbursements were awarded; teaching assistantships with full tuition reimbursements, institutionally sponsored loans, scholarships/grants, health care benefits, tuition waivers (full and partial), and unspecified assistantships also available. Financial award applicants required to submit FAFSA. *Faculty research:* Organismal biology, functional morphology, biomechanics, comparative vertebrate anatomy, comparative invertebrate anatomy, paleontology. *Unit head:* Director of Graduate Studies, 607-253-3276, Fax: 607-253-3756. *Application contact:* Graduate Field Assistant, 607-253-3276, Fax: 607-253-3756, E-mail: graduate_edcvm@cornell.edu.

Cornell University, Graduate School, Graduate Fields of Comparative Biomedical Sciences, Field of Comparative Biomedical Sciences, Ithaca, NY 14853-0001. Offers cellular and molecular medicine (MS, PhD); developmental and reproductive biology (MS, PhD); infectious diseases (MS, PhD); population medicine and epidemiology (MS, PhD); structural and functional biology (MS, PhD). *Faculty:* 94 full-time (27 women). *Students:* 47 full-time (33 women); includes 2 Black or African American, non-Hispanic/Latino; 1 Asian, non-Hispanic/Latino, 23 international. Average age 30. 31 applicants, 48% accepted, 14 enrolled. In 2010, 11 doctorates awarded. *Degree requirements:* For master's, thesis; for doctorate, comprehensive exam, thesis/dissertation. *Entrance requirements:* For master's and doctorate, GRE General Test, 2 letters of recommendation. Additional exam requirements/recommendations for international students: Required—TOEFL (minimum score 550 paper-based; 213 computer-based; 77 iBT). *Application deadline:* For fall admission, 12/15 for domestic students. Application fee: $70. Electronic applications accepted. *Expenses:* Tuition: Full-time $29,500. Required fees: $76. Tuition and fees vary according to degree level and program. *Financial support:* In 2010–11, 18 fellowships with full tuition reimbursements, 25 research assistantships with full tuition reimbursements were awarded; teaching assistantships with full tuition reimbursements, institutionally sponsored loans, scholarships/grants, health care benefits, tuition waivers (full and partial), and unspecified assistantships also available. Financial award applicants required to submit FAFSA. *Faculty research:* Receptors and signal transduction, viral and bacterial infectious diseases, tumor metastasis, clinical sciences/nutritional disease, developmental/neurological disorders. *Unit head:* Director of Graduate Studies, 607-253-3276, Fax: 607-253-3756. *Application contact:* Graduate Field Assistant, 607-253-3276, Fax: 607-253-3756, E-mail: graduate_edcvm@cornell.edu.

Duke University, Graduate School, Program in Developmental Biology, Durham, NC 27710. Offers Certificate. *Faculty:* 45 full-time. *Students:* 12 full-time (7 women); includes 1 Black or African American, non-Hispanic/Latino; 1 Asian, non-Hispanic/Latino; 1 Hispanic/Latino, 2 international. 69 applicants, 32% accepted, 7 enrolled. *Entrance requirements:* For degree, GRE General Test. Additional exam requirements/recommendations for international students: Required—TOEFL (minimum score 550 paper-based; 213 computer-based; 83 iBT), IELTS (minimum score 7). *Application deadline:* For fall admission, 12/8 priority date for domestic and international students. Application fee: $75. *Financial support:* Application deadline: 12/8. *Unit head:* John Klingensmith, Head, 919-684-6629, Fax: 919-684-8346, E-mail: andrea.lanahan@duke.edu. *Application contact:* Elizabeth Hutton, Director of Admissions, 919-684-3913, Fax: 919-684-2277, E-mail: grad-admissions@duke.edu.

Emory University, Laney Graduate School, Division of Biological and Biomedical Sciences, Program in Biochemistry, Cell and Developmental Biology, Atlanta, GA 30322. Offers PhD. *Faculty:* 54 full-time (10 women). *Students:* 60 full-time (41 women); includes 3 Black or African American, non-Hispanic/Latino; 3 Asian, non-Hispanic/Latino; 1 Hispanic/Latino, 15 international. Average age 27. 214 applicants, 12% accepted, 11 enrolled. In 2010, 10 doctorates awarded. *Degree requirements:* For doctorate, comprehensive exam, thesis/dissertation. *Entrance requirements:* For doctorate, GRE General Test, minimum GPA of 3.0 in science course work (recommended). Additional exam requirements/recommendations for international students: Required—TOEFL. *Application deadline:* For fall admission, 1/3 for domestic students, 1/1 for international students. Application fee: $75. Electronic applications accepted. *Expenses:* Tuition: Full-time $33,800. Required fees: $1300. *Financial support:* In 2010–11, 19 students received support, including 19 fellowships with full tuition reimbursements available (averaging $25,000 per year); institutionally sponsored loans, scholarships/grants, health care benefits, and tuition waivers (full) also available. *Faculty research:* Signal transduction, molecular biology, enzymes and cofactors, receptor and ion channel function, membrane biology. *Unit head:* Dr. Richard Kahn, Program Director, 404-727-3561, Fax: 404-727-3746, E-mail: rkahn@emory.edu. *Application contact:* Kathy Smith, Director of Recruitment and Admissions, 404-727-2547, Fax: 404-727-3322, E-mail: kathy.smith@emory.edu.

Illinois State University, Graduate School, College of Arts and Sciences, Department of Biological Sciences, Normal, IL 61790-2200. Offers animal behavior (MS); bacteriology (MS); biochemistry (MS); biological sciences (MS); biology (PhD); biophysics (MS); biotechnology (MS); botany (MS, PhD); cell biology (MS); conservation biology (MS); developmental biology (MS); ecology (MS, PhD); entomology (MS); evolutionary biology (MS); genetics (MS, PhD); immunology (MS); microbiology (MS, PhD); molecular biology (MS); molecular genetics (MS); neurobiology (MS); neuroscience (MS); parasitology (MS); physiology (MS, PhD); plant biology (MS); plant molecular biology (MS); plant sciences (MS); structural biology (MS); zoology (MS, PhD). Part-time programs available. *Degree requirements:* For master's, thesis or alternative; for doctorate, variable foreign language requirement, thesis/dissertation, 2 terms of residency. *Entrance requirements:* For master's, GRE General Test, minimum GPA of 2.6 in last 60 hours of course work; for doctorate, GRE General Test. *Faculty research:* Redoc balance and drug development in schistosoma mansoni, control of the growth of listeria monocytogenes at low temperature, regulation of cell expansion and microtubule function by SPRI, CRUI: physiology and fitness consequences of different life history phenotypes.

Iowa State University of Science and Technology, Graduate College, College of Liberal Arts and Sciences and College of Agriculture, Department of Genetics, Developmental and Cell Biology, Ames, IA 50011. Offers MS, PhD. *Faculty:* 43 full-time (8 women), 4 part-time/adjunct (2 women). *Students:* 52 full-time (25 women), 5 part-time (2 women); includes 1 Black or African American, non-Hispanic/Latino, 42 international. 1 applicant, 100% accepted, 1 enrolled. *Degree requirements:* For master's, thesis; for doctorate, thesis/dissertation. *Entrance requirements:* Additional exam requirements/recommendations for international students: Required—TOEFL (minimum score 570 paper-based), IELTS (minimum score 6.5). Application

fee: $40 ($90 for international students). *Financial support:* In 2010–11, 42 research assistantships with full and partial tuition reimbursements (averaging $18,008 per year), 9 teaching assistantships with full and partial tuition reimbursements (averaging $9,115 per year) were awarded; fellowships with full tuition reimbursements, scholarships/grants, health care benefits, and unspecified assistantships also available. Financial award application deadline: 2/1. *Faculty research:* Animal behavior, animal models of gene therapy, cell biology, comparative physiology, developmental biology. *Unit head:* Dr. Martin Spalding, Chair, 515-294-1749. *Application contact:* Information Contact, 515-294-5836, Fax: 515-294-2592, E-mail: grad_admissions@iastate.edu.

Iowa State University of Science and Technology, Graduate College, Interdisciplinary Programs, Program in Molecular, Cellular, and Developmental Biology, Ames, IA 50011. Offers MS, PhD. *Students:* 31 full-time (17 women), 4 part-time (2 women), 23 international. In 2010, 2 master's, 3 doctorates awarded. *Degree requirements:* For master's, thesis or alternative; for doctorate, thesis/dissertation. *Entrance requirements:* For master's and doctorate, GRE General Test. Additional exam requirements/recommendations for international students: Required—TOEFL (minimum score 580 paper-based; 85 iBT), IELTS (minimum score 7). *Application deadline:* For fall admission, 1/15 priority date for domestic and international students. Application fee: $40 ($90 for international students). Electronic applications accepted. *Financial support:* In 2010–11, 30 research assistantships with full and partial tuition reimbursements (averaging $20,962 per year), 1 teaching assistantship with full and partial tuition reimbursement (averaging $11,366 per year) were awarded; scholarships/grants, health care benefits, and unspecified assistantships also available. *Unit head:* Dr. Jeff Beetham, Supervisory Committee Chair, 515-294-7252, E-mail: idgp@iastate.edu. *Application contact:* Katie Blair, Information Contact, 515-294-7252, Fax: 515-924-6790, E-mail: idgp@iastate.edu.

The Johns Hopkins University, National Institutes of Health Sponsored Programs, Baltimore, MD 21218-2699. Offers biology (PhD), including biochemistry, biophysics, cell biology, developmental biology, genetic biology, molecular biology; cell, molecular, and developmental biology and biophysics (PhD). *Degree requirements:* For doctorate, comprehensive exam, thesis/dissertation. *Entrance requirements:* For doctorate, GRE General Test. Additional exam requirements/recommendations for international students: Required—TOEFL (minimum score 600 paper-based; 250 computer-based), TWE. Electronic applications accepted. *Faculty research:* Protein and nucleic acid biochemistry and biophysical chemistry, molecular biology and development.

Louisiana State University Health Sciences Center, School of Graduate Studies in New Orleans, Department of Cell Biology and Anatomy, New Orleans, LA 70112-2223. Offers cell biology and anatomy (MS, PhD), including cell biology, developmental biology, neurobiology and anatomy; MD/PhD. *Degree requirements:* For master's, comprehensive exam, thesis; for doctorate, comprehensive exam, thesis/dissertation. *Entrance requirements:* For master's and doctorate, GRE General Test, GRE Subject Test, minimum undergraduate GPA of 3.0. Additional exam requirements/recommendations for international students: Required—TOEFL. *Faculty research:* Visual system organization, neural development, plasticity of sensory systems, information processing through the nervous system, visuomotor integration.

Marquette University, Graduate School, College of Arts and Sciences, Department of Biology, Milwaukee, WI 53201-1881. Offers cell biology (MS, PhD); developmental biology (MS, PhD); ecology (MS, PhD); epithelial physiology (MS, PhD); genetics (MS, PhD); microbiology (MS, PhD); molecular biology (MS, PhD); muscle and exercise physiology (MS, PhD); neuroscience (PhD). *Faculty:* 25 full-time (12 women), 2 part-time/adjunct (1 woman). *Students:* 23 full-time (9 women), 12 part-time (8 women); includes 1 minority (Asian, non-Hispanic/Latino), 15 international. Average age 26. 82 applicants, 15% accepted, 5 enrolled. In 2010, 3 master's, 2 doctorates awarded. Terminal master's awarded for partial completion of doctoral program. *Degree requirements:* For master's, comprehensive exam, thesis, 1 year of teaching experience or equivalent; for doctorate, thesis/dissertation, 1 year of teaching experience or equivalent, qualifying exam. *Entrance requirements:* For master's and doctorate, GRE General Test, GRE Subject Test, official transcripts from all current and previous colleges/universities except Marquette, statement of professional goals and aspirations, three letters of recommendation. Additional exam requirements/recommendations for international students: Required—TOEFL (minimum score 530 paper-based; 78 computer-based). *Application deadline:* For fall admission, 12/15 for domestic and international students. Application fee: $50. Electronic applications accepted. *Expenses:* Tuition: Full-time $16,290; part-time $905 per credit hour. Tuition and fees vary according to program. *Financial support:* In 2010–11, 2 research assistantships, 34 teaching assistantships were awarded; fellowships, Federal Work-Study, institutionally sponsored loans, scholarships/grants, and tuition waivers (full and partial) also available. Support available to part-time students. Financial award application deadline: 2/15. *Faculty research:* Neurobiology, neuroendocrinology, epithelial physiology, neuropeptide interactions, synaptic transmission. Total annual research expenditures: $1.3 million. *Unit head:* Dr. Robert Fitts, Chair, 414-288-1748, Fax: 414-288-7357. *Application contact:* Debbie Weaver, Administrative Assistant, 414-288-7355, Fax: 414-288-7357.

Massachusetts Institute of Technology, School of Science, Department of Biology, Cambridge, MA 02139-4307. Offers biochemistry (PhD); biological oceanography (PhD); biology (PhD); biophysical chemistry and molecular structure (PhD); cell biology (PhD); computational and systems biology (PhD); developmental biology (PhD); genetics (PhD); immunology (PhD); microbiology (PhD); molecular biology (PhD); neurobiology (PhD). *Faculty:* 56 full-time (14 women). *Students:* 251 full-time (135 women); includes 74 minority (4 Black or African American, non-Hispanic/Latino; 1 American Indian or Alaska Native, non-Hispanic/Latino; 29 Asian, non-Hispanic/Latino; 33 Hispanic/Latino; 7 Two or more races, non-Hispanic/Latino), 29 international. Average age 26. 652 applicants, 18% accepted, 58 enrolled. In 2010, 41 doctorates awarded. *Degree requirements:* For doctorate, comprehensive exam, thesis/dissertation. *Entrance requirements:* For doctorate, GRE General Test. Additional exam requirements/recommendations for international students: Required—TOEFL (minimum score 577 paper-based; 233 computer-based), IELTS (minimum score 6.5). *Application deadline:* For fall admission, 12/1 for domestic and international students. Application fee: $75. Electronic applications accepted. *Expenses:* Tuition: Full-time $38,940; part-time $605 per unit. Required fees: $272. *Financial support:* In 2010–11, 215 students received support, including 115 fellowships with tuition reimbursements available (averaging $33,090 per year), 132 research assistantships with tuition reimbursements available (averaging $31,846 per year); teaching assistantships with tuition reimbursements available, Federal Work-Study, institutionally sponsored loans, scholarships/grants, traineeships, health care benefits, and unspecified assistantships also available. *Faculty research:* DNA recombination, replication and repair; transcription and gene regulation; signal transduction; cell cycle; neuronal cell fate. Total annual research expenditures: $60.6 million. *Unit head:* Prof. Chris Kaiser, Head, 617-253-4701, E-mail: mitbio@mit.edu. *Application contact:* Biology Education Office, 617-253-3717, Fax: 617-258-9329, E-mail: gradbio@mit.edu.

Medical University of South Carolina, College of Graduate Studies, Program in Molecular and Cellular Biology and Pathobiology, Charleston, SC 29425. Offers cancer biology (PhD); cardiovascular biology (PhD); cardiovascular imaging (PhD); cell regulation (PhD); craniofacial biology (PhD); genetics and development (PhD); marine biomedicine (PhD); DMD/PhD; MD/PhD. *Faculty:* 137 full-time (33 women). *Students:* 27 full-time (20 women); includes 3 Black or African American, non-Hispanic/Latino; 1 Hispanic/Latino, 6 international. Average age 30. In 2010, 16 doctorates awarded. *Degree requirements:* For doctorate, thesis/dissertation, oral and written exams. *Entrance requirements:* For doctorate, GRE General Test, interview, minimum GPA of 3.0. Additional exam requirements/recommendations for international students: Required—TOEFL (minimum score 600 paper-based; 250 computer-based; 100 iBT). *Application deadline:* For fall admission, 1/15 priority date for domestic and international students. Applications are processed on a rolling basis. Application fee: $0 ($85 for international students). Electronic applications accepted. *Financial support:* In 2010–11, 39 research assistantships with partial tuition reimbursements (averaging $23,000 per year) were awarded; Federal Work-Study and scholarships/grants also available. Support available to part-time students. Financial award application deadline: 3/10; financial award applicants required to submit

Developmental Biology

Medical University of South Carolina (continued)

FAFSA. *Unit head:* Dr. Donald R. Menick, Director, 843-876-5045, Fax: 843-792-6590, E-mail: menickd@musc.edu. *Application contact:* Dr. Cynthia F. Wright, Associate Dean for Admissions and Career Development, 843-792-2564, Fax: 843-792-6590, E-mail: wrightcf@musc.edu.

New York University, Graduate School of Arts and Science, Department of Biology, New York, NY 10012-1019. Offers biology (PhD); biomedical journalism (MS); cancer and molecular biology (PhD); computational biology (PhD); computers in biological research (MS); developmental genetics (PhD); general biology (MS); immunology and microbiology (PhD); molecular genetics (PhD); neurobiology (PhD); oral biology (MS); plant biology (PhD); recombinant DNA technology (MS); MS/MBA. Part-time programs available. *Faculty:* 24 full-time (5 women). *Students:* 155 full-time (89 women), 38 part-time (24 women); includes 29 Asian, non-Hispanic/Latino; 7 Hispanic/Latino, 88 international. Average age 27. 324 applicants, 69% accepted, 63 enrolled. In 2010, 55 master's, 4 doctorates awarded. Terminal master's awarded for partial completion of doctoral program. *Degree requirements:* For master's, thesis or alternative, qualifying paper; for doctorate, comprehensive exam, thesis/dissertation. *Entrance requirements:* For master's, GRE General Test; for doctorate, GRE General Test, GRE Subject Test. Additional exam requirements/recommendations for international students: Required—TOEFL. *Application deadline:* For fall admission, 12/15 priority date for domestic students. Application fee: $90. *Financial support:* Fellowships with tuition reimbursements, research assistantships with tuition reimbursements, teaching assistantships with tuition reimbursements, career-related internships or fieldwork, Federal Work-Study, institutionally sponsored loans, scholarships/grants, health care benefits, and unspecified assistantships available. Financial award application deadline: 12/15; financial award applicants required to submit FAFSA. *Faculty research:* Genomics, molecular and cell biology, development and molecular genetics, molecular evolution of plants and animals. *Unit head:* Gloria Coruzzi, Chair, 212-998-8200, Fax: 212-995-4015, E-mail: biology@nyu.edu. *Application contact:* Justin Blau, Director of Graduate Studies, 212-998-8200, Fax: 212-995-4015, E-mail: biology@nyu.edu.

New York University, School of Medicine and Graduate School of Arts and Science, Sackler Institute of Graduate Biomedical Sciences, New York, NY 10012-1019. Offers cellular and molecular biology (PhD); computational biology (PhD); developmental genetics (PhD); medical and molecular parasitology (PhD); microbiology (PhD); molecular oncology and immunology (PhD), including immunology, molecular oncology; neuroscience and physiology (PhD); pathobiology (PhD); pharmacology (PhD), including molecular pharmacology; structural biology (PhD); MD/PhD. *Degree requirements:* For doctorate, comprehensive exam, thesis/dissertation, qualifying exam. *Entrance requirements:* For doctorate, GRE General Test. Additional exam requirements/recommendations for international students: Required—TOEFL. Electronic applications accepted. *Expenses:* Contact institution.

Northwestern University, The Graduate School, Interdepartmental Biological Sciences Program (IBiS), Evanston, IL 60208. Offers biochemistry, molecular biology, and cell biology (PhD), including biochemistry, cell and molecular biology, molecular biophysics, structural biology; biotechnology (PhD); cell and molecular biology (PhD); developmental biology and genetics (PhD); hormone action and signal transduction (PhD); neuroscience (PhD); structural biology, biochemistry, and biophysics (PhD). Program participants include the Departments of Biochemistry, Molecular Biology, and Cell Biology; Chemistry; Neurobiology and Physiology; Chemical Engineering; Civil Engineering; and Evanston Hospital. *Degree requirements:* For doctorate, thesis/dissertation, qualifying exam. *Entrance requirements:* For doctorate, GRE General Test. Additional exam requirements/recommendations for international students: Required—TOEFL (minimum score 600 paper-based). Electronic applications accepted. *Faculty research:* Developmental genetics, gene regulation, DNA-protein interactions, biological clocks, bioremediation.

Northwestern University, Northwestern University Feinberg School of Medicine and Interdepartmental Programs, Integrated Graduate Programs in the Life Sciences, Chicago, IL 60611. Offers cancer biology (PhD); cell biology (PhD); developmental biology (PhD); evolutionary biology (PhD); immunology and microbial pathogenesis (PhD); molecular biology and genetics (PhD); neurobiology (PhD); pharmacology and toxicology (PhD); structural biology and biochemistry (PhD). *Degree requirements:* For doctorate, comprehensive exam, thesis/dissertation, written and oral qualifying exams. *Entrance requirements:* For doctorate, GRE General Test. Additional exam requirements/recommendations for international students: Required—TOEFL (minimum score 600 paper-based; 250 computer-based). Electronic applications accepted.

The Ohio State University, Graduate School, College of Arts and Sciences, Division of Natural and Mathematical Sciences, Department of Molecular Genetics, Columbus, OH 43210. Offers cell and developmental biology (MS, PhD); genetics (MS, PhD); molecular biology (MS, PhD). *Faculty:* 26. *Students:* 7 full-time (3 women), 25 part-time (14 women), 16 international. Average age 27. In 2010, 1 master's, 1 doctorate awarded. *Degree requirements:* For master's, thesis; for doctorate, thesis/dissertation. *Entrance requirements:* For master's and doctorate, GRE General Test, GRE Subject Test in biology or biochemistry (recommended). Additional exam requirements/recommendations for international students: Required—TOEFL (minimum score 600 paper-based; 250 computer-based). *Application deadline:* For fall admission, 8/15 priority date for domestic students, 7/1 priority date for international students; for winter admission, 12/1 priority date for domestic students, 11/1 priority date for international students; for spring admission, 3/1 priority date for domestic students, 2/1 priority date for international students. Applications are processed on a rolling basis. Application fee: $40 ($50 for international students). Electronic applications accepted. *Expenses:* Tuition, state resident: full-time $10,605. Tuition, nonresident: full-time $26,535. Tuition and fees vary according to course load and program. *Financial support:* Fellowships, research assistantships, teaching assistantships, Federal Work-Study and institutionally sponsored loans available. Support available to part-time students. *Unit head:* Dr. Anna Hopper, Chair, 614-688-3306, Fax: 614-247-2594, E-mail: hopper.64@osu.edu. *Application contact:* 614-292-9444, Fax: 614-292-3895, E-mail: domestic.grad@osu.edu.

The Ohio State University, Graduate School, College of Arts and Sciences, Division of Natural and Mathematical Sciences, Program in Molecular, Cellular and Developmental Biology, Columbus, OH 43210. Offers MS, PhD. *Students:* 70 full-time (40 women), 64 part-time (35 women); includes 8 Asian, non-Hispanic/Latino; 7 Hispanic/Latino, 75 international. Average age 28. In 2010, 4 master's, 17 doctorates awarded. *Degree requirements:* For master's, thesis; for doctorate, thesis/dissertation. *Entrance requirements:* For master's and doctorate, GRE General Test, GRE Subject Test (biology or biochemistry, cell and molecular biology). Additional exam requirements/recommendations for international students: Required—TOEFL (minimum score 573 paper-based; 230 computer-based). *Application deadline:* For fall admission, 8/15 priority date for domestic students, 7/1 priority date for international students; for winter admission, 12/1 priority date for domestic students, 11/1 priority date for international students; for spring admission, 3/1 priority date for domestic students, 2/1 priority date for international students. Applications are processed on a rolling basis. Application fee: $40 ($50 for international students). Electronic applications accepted. *Expenses:* Tuition, state resident: full-time $10,605. Tuition, nonresident: full-time $26,535. Tuition and fees vary according to course load and program. *Unit head:* David M. Bisaro, Director, 614-292-3281, Fax: 614-292-4466, E-mail: bisaro.1@osu.edu. *Application contact:* Graduate Admissions, 614-292-9444, Fax: 614-292-3895, E-mail: domestic.grad@osu.edu.

Oregon Health & Science University, School of Medicine, Graduate Programs in Medicine, Program in Molecular and Cellular Biosciences, Department of Cell and Developmental Biology, Portland, OR 97239-3098. Offers PhD. *Faculty:* 30 full-time (8 women). *Students:* 29 full-time (18 women); includes 1 Asian, non-Hispanic/Latino; 1 Native Hawaiian or other Pacific Islander, non-Hispanic/Latino, 9 international. Average age 28. In 2010, 5 doctorates awarded. *Degree requirements:* For doctorate, comprehensive exam, thesis/dissertation. *Entrance requirements:* For doctorate, GRE General Test, GRE Subject Test, MCAT. Additional exam requirements/recommendations for international students: Required—TOEFL. *Financial support:* Health care benefits, tuition waivers (full), and full tuition and stipends available. *Faculty research:* Developmental mechanisms, molecular biology of cancer, molecular neurobiology, intracellular signaling, growth factors and development. *Unit head:* Dr. Richard Maurer, Interim Chair/Program Director, 503-494-7811, E-mail: maurerr@ohsu.edu. *Application contact:* Elaine Offield, Program Coordinator, 503-494-5824, E-mail: offielde@ohsu.edu.

Purdue University, Graduate School, College of Science, Department of Biological Sciences, West Lafayette, IN 47907. Offers biochemistry (PhD); biophysics (PhD); cell and developmental biology (PhD); ecology, evolutionary and population biology (MS, PhD), including ecology, evolutionary biology, population biology; genetics (MS, PhD); microbiology (MS, PhD); molecular biology (PhD); neurobiology (MS, PhD); plant physiology (PhD). Terminal master's awarded for partial completion of doctoral program. *Degree requirements:* For master's, thesis (for some programs); for doctorate, thesis/dissertation, seminars, teaching experience. *Entrance requirements:* For master's and doctorate, GRE General Test. Additional exam requirements/recommendations for international students: Required—TOEFL. Electronic applications accepted.

Rutgers, The State University of New Jersey, New Brunswick, Graduate School-New Brunswick, Programs in the Molecular Biosciences, Program in Cell and Developmental Biology, Piscataway, NJ 08854-8097. Offers MS, PhD. MS, PhD offered jointly with University of Medicine and Dentistry of New Jersey. Part-time programs available. Terminal master's awarded for partial completion of doctoral program. *Degree requirements:* For master's, thesis; for doctorate, thesis/dissertation, written qualifying exam. *Entrance requirements:* For master's, GRE General Test; for doctorate, GRE General Test, GRE Subject Test (recommended), minimum GPA of 3.0. Additional exam requirements/recommendations for international students: Required—TOEFL. Electronic applications accepted. *Expenses:* Tuition, state resident: full-time $7200; part-time $600 per credit. Tuition, nonresident: full-time $11,124; part-time $927 per credit. *Faculty research:* Signal transduction and regulation of gene expression, developmental biology, cellular biology, developmental genetics, neurobiology.

San Francisco State University, Division of Graduate Studies, College of Science and Engineering, Department of Biology, Professional Science Master's Program, San Francisco, CA 94132-1722. Offers biotechnology (PSM); stem cell science (PSM). *Unit head:* Dr. Lily Chen, Director, 415-338-6763, E-mail: lilychen@sfsu.edu. *Application contact:* Dr. Linda H. Chen, Program Coordinator, 415-338-1696, E-mail: psm@sfsu.edu.

Stanford University, School of Medicine, Graduate Programs in Medicine, Department of Developmental Biology, Stanford, CA 94305-9991. Offers PhD. *Degree requirements:* For doctorate, thesis/dissertation, qualifying examination. *Entrance requirements:* For doctorate, GRE General Test, GRE Subject Test. Additional exam requirements/recommendations for international students: Required—TOEFL. Electronic applications accepted. *Expenses:* Tuition: Full-time $38,700; part-time $860 per unit. One-time fee: $200 full-time. *Faculty research:* Mammalian embryology, developmental genetics with particular emphasis on microbial systems, *Dictyostelium*, *Drosophila*, the nematode, and the mouse.

Stony Brook University, State University of New York, Graduate School, College of Arts and Sciences, Department of Biochemistry and Cell Biology, Stony Brook, NY 11794. Offers biochemistry and structural biology (PhD); molecular and cellular biology (MA, PhD), including biochemistry and molecular biology (PhD), biological sciences (MA), cellular and developmental biology (PhD), immunology and pathology (PhD), molecular and cellular biology (PhD). *Faculty:* 22 full-time (7 women). *Students:* 134 full-time (75 women); includes 3 Black or African American, non-Hispanic/Latino; 10 Asian, non-Hispanic/Latino; 2 Hispanic/Latino, 75 international. Average age 28. 412 applicants, 17% accepted, 37 enrolled. In 2010, 6 master's, 19 doctorates awarded. *Degree requirements:* For doctorate, comprehensive exam, thesis/dissertation, teaching experience. *Entrance requirements:* For doctorate, GRE General Test, GRE Subject Test. Additional exam requirements/recommendations for international students: Required—TOEFL. *Application deadline:* For fall admission, 1/15 for domestic students. Application fee: $100. *Expenses:* Tuition, state resident: full-time $8370; part-time $349 per credit. Tuition, nonresident: full-time $13,780; part-time $574 per credit. Required fees: $994. *Financial support:* In 2010–11, 58 research assistantships, 27 teaching assistantships were awarded; fellowships, Federal Work-Study also available. *Faculty research:* Genome organization and replication, cell surface dynamics, enzyme structure and mechanism, developmental and regulatory biology. Total annual research expenditures: $10.2 million. *Unit head:* Prof. Robert Haltiwanger, Chair, 631-632-8560, E-mail: rhaltiwanger@ms.cc.sunysb.edu. *Application contact:* Director, Graduate Program, 631-632-8533, Fax: 631-632-9730, E-mail: mcbprog@life.bio.sunysb.edu.

Stony Brook University, State University of New York, Graduate School, College of Arts and Sciences, Department of Biochemistry and Cell Biology, Molecular and Cellular Biology Program, Specialization in Cellular and Developmental Biology, Stony Brook, NY 11794. Offers PhD. *Degree requirements:* For doctorate, one foreign language, comprehensive exam, thesis/dissertation, teaching experience. *Entrance requirements:* For doctorate, GRE General Test, GRE Subject Test. Additional exam requirements/recommendations for international students: Required—TOEFL. *Application deadline:* For fall admission, 1/15 for domestic students. Application fee: $100. *Expenses:* Tuition, state resident: full-time $8370; part-time $349 per credit. Tuition, nonresident: full-time $13,780; part-time $574 per credit. Required fees: $994. *Financial support:* Fellowships, research assistantships, teaching assistantships available. *Unit head:* Director, Graduate Program, 631-632-8533, Fax: 631-632-9730, E-mail: mcbprog@life.bio.sunysb.edu. *Application contact:* Director, Graduate Program, 631-632-8533, Fax: 631-632-9730, E-mail: mcbprog@life.bio.sunysb.edu.

Thomas Jefferson University, Jefferson College of Graduate Studies, MS Program in Cell and Developmental Biology, Philadelphia, PA 19107. Offers MS. Part-time and evening/weekend programs available. *Faculty:* 19 full-time (6 women). *Students:* 9 part-time (8 women); includes 2 minority (1 Black or African American, non-Hispanic/Latino; 1 Asian, non-Hispanic/Latino), 1 international. 14 applicants, 50% accepted, 7 enrolled. In 2010, 3 master's awarded. *Degree requirements:* For master's, thesis, clerkship. *Entrance requirements:* For master's, GRE General Test or MCAT, minimum GPA of 3.0. Additional exam requirements/recommendations for international students: Required—TOEFL (minimum score 250 computer-based; 100 iBT) or IELTS. *Application deadline:* For fall admission, 8/1 priority date for domestic students, 3/1 priority date for international students; for winter admission, 12/1 priority date for domestic students, 6/1 priority date for international students; for spring admission, 4/1 priority date for domestic students. Applications are processed on a rolling basis. Application fee: $50. Electronic applications accepted. *Financial support:* In 2010–11, 4 students received support. Federal Work-Study and institutionally sponsored loans available. Support available to part-time students. Financial award application deadline: 5/1; financial award applicants required to submit FAFSA. *Unit head:* Dr. Gerald B. Grunwald, Dean and Program Director, 215-503-4191, Fax: 215-503-6690, E-mail: gerald.grunwald@jefferson.edu. *Application contact:* Eleanor M. Gorman, Assistant Coordinator, Graduate Center Programs, 215-503-5799, Fax: 215-503-3433, E-mail: eleanor.gorman@jefferson.edu.

Thomas Jefferson University, Jefferson College of Graduate Studies, PhD Program in Cell and Developmental Biology, Philadelphia, PA 19107. Offers PhD. *Faculty:* 57 full-time (13 women). *Students:* 24 full-time (11 women); includes 1 minority (Black or African American, non-Hispanic/Latino), 4 international. 27 applicants, 41% accepted, 6 enrolled. In 2010, 6 doctorates awarded. *Degree requirements:* For doctorate, comprehensive exam, thesis/dissertation. *Entrance requirements:* For doctorate, GRE General Test, minimum GPA of 3.2. Additional exam requirements/recommendations for international students: Required—TOEFL (minimum score 250 computer-based; 100 iBT). *Application deadline:* For fall admission, 1/5 priority date for domestic and international students. Applications are processed on a rolling basis. Application fee: $50. Electronic applications accepted. *Financial support:* In 2010–11, 24 students received support, including 24 fellowships with full tuition reimbursements available (averaging $54,723 per year); Federal Work-Study, institutionally sponsored loans, scholarships/grants, traineeships, and stipends also available. Support available to part-time students. Financial award application deadline: 5/1; financial award applicants required to submit FAFSA.

Total annual research expenditures: $35.5 million. *Unit head:* Dr. Theodore F. Taraschi, Program Director, 215-503-5020, Fax: 215-503-0206, E-mail: theodore.taraschi@jefferson.edu. *Application contact:* Marc E. Stearns, Director of Admissions, 215-503-0155, Fax: 215-503-9920, E-mail: jcgs-info@jefferson.edu.

Tufts University, Sackler School of Graduate Biomedical Sciences, Program in Cell, Molecular and Developmental Biology, Medford, MA 02155. Offers PhD. *Faculty:* 35 full-time (11 women). *Students:* 25 full-time (13 women); includes 2 Asian, non-Hispanic/Latino, 2 international. Average age 29. In 2010, 8 doctorates awarded. Terminal master's awarded for partial completion of doctoral program. *Degree requirements:* For doctorate, thesis/dissertation. *Entrance requirements:* For doctorate, GRE General Test, 3 letters of reference. Additional exam requirements/recommendations for international students: Required—TOEFL. *Application deadline:* For fall admission, 12/15 for domestic and international students. Applications are processed on a rolling basis. Application fee: $70. Electronic applications accepted. *Expenses:* Tuition: Full-time $39,624; part-time $3962 per course. Required fees: $40 per year. Full-time tuition and fees vary according to degree level, program and student level. Part-time tuition and fees vary according to course load. *Financial support:* In 2010–11, 25 students received support, including 25 research assistantships with full tuition reimbursements available (averaging $28,500 per year); fellowships, scholarships/grants, health care benefits, and tuition waivers (full) also available. *Faculty research:* Reproduction and hormone action, control of gene expression, cell-matrix and cell-cell interactions, growth control and tumorigenesis, cytoskeleton and contractile proteins. *Unit head:* Dr. John Castellot, Program Director, 617-636-0303, Fax: 617-636-0375, E-mail: john.castellot@tufts.edu. *Application contact:* Kellie Johnston, Associate Director of Admissions, 617-636-6767, Fax: 617-636-0375, E-mail: sackler-school@tufts.edu.

University at Albany, State University of New York, College of Arts and Sciences, Department of Biological Sciences, Specialization in Molecular, Cellular, Developmental, and Neural Biology, Albany, NY 12222-0001. Offers MS, PhD. *Degree requirements:* For master's, one foreign language; for doctorate, one foreign language, thesis/dissertation. *Entrance requirements:* For master's and doctorate, GRE General Test.

University of California, Davis, Graduate Studies, Graduate Group in Cell and Developmental Biology, Davis, CA 95616. Offers MS, PhD. *Degree requirements:* For master's, comprehensive exam (for some programs), thesis (for some programs); for doctorate, thesis/dissertation. *Entrance requirements:* For doctorate, GRE General Test, GRE Subject Test. Additional exam requirements/recommendations for international students: Required—TOEFL (minimum score 550 paper-based; 213 computer-based). Electronic applications accepted. *Faculty research:* Molecular basis of cell function and development.

University of California, Irvine, School of Biological Sciences, Department of Developmental and Cell Biology, Irvine, CA 92697. Offers biological sciences (MS, PhD). Students apply through the Graduate Program in Molecular Biology, Genetics, and Biochemistry. *Students:* 40 full-time (20 women); includes 21 minority (1 Black or African American, non-Hispanic/Latino; 1 American Indian or Alaska Native, non-Hispanic/Latino; 11 Asian, non-Hispanic/Latino; 8 Hispanic/Latino), 3 international. Average age 28. 1 applicant, 100% accepted, 1 enrolled. In 2010, 3 master's, 14 doctorates awarded. *Degree requirements:* For doctorate, thesis/dissertation. *Entrance requirements:* For master's and doctorate, GRE General Test, GRE Subject Test, minimum GPA of 3.0. Additional exam requirements/recommendations for international students: Required—TOEFL (minimum score 550 paper-based; 213 computer-based). *Application deadline:* For fall admission, 12/15 priority date for domestic and international students. Application fee: $80 ($100 for international students). Electronic applications accepted. *Financial support:* Fellowships, research assistantships with full tuition reimbursements, teaching assistantships, institutionally sponsored loans, traineeships, health care benefits, and unspecified assistantships available. Financial award application deadline: 3/1; financial award applicants required to submit FAFSA. *Faculty research:* Genetics and development, oncogene signaling pathways, gene regulation, tissue regeneration and molecular genetics. *Unit head:* Prof. Ken W. Cho, Chair, 949-824-7950, Fax: 949-824-4709, E-mail: kwcho@uci.edu. *Application contact:* Renee Marie Frigo, Program Manager, 949-824-8145, Fax: 949-824-1965, E-mail: rfrigo@uci.edu.

University of California, Los Angeles, Graduate Division, College of Letters and Science, Department of Molecular, Cell and Developmental Biology, Los Angeles, CA 90095. Offers PhD. *Faculty:* 6 full-time (1 woman). *Students:* 34 full-time (20 women); includes 12 minority (3 Black or African American, non-Hispanic/Latino; 6 Asian, non-Hispanic/Latino; 3 Hispanic/Latino), 6 international. Average age 27. 3 applicants, 67% accepted, 2 enrolled. In 2010, 4 doctorates awarded. *Degree requirements:* For doctorate, thesis/dissertation, qualifying exams. *Entrance requirements:* For doctorate, GRE General Test, GRE Subject Test. Additional exam requirements/recommendations for international students: Required—TOEFL. Application fee: $70 ($90 for international students). Electronic applications accepted. *Financial support:* In 2010–11, 26 fellowships, 26 research assistantships, 14 teaching assistantships were awarded; scholarships/grants, traineeships, and unspecified assistantships also available. Financial award application deadline: 3/1. *Unit head:* Dr. Utpal Banerjee, Chair, 310-206-5439, Fax: 310-206-3987, E-mail: banerjee@mbi.ucla.edu. *Application contact:* UCLA Access Coordinator, 310-206-1845, Fax: 310-206-1636, E-mail: uclaaccess@mednet.ucla.edu.

University of California, Riverside, Graduate Division, Program in Cell, Molecular, and Developmental Biology, Riverside, CA 92521-0102. Offers MS, PhD. Terminal master's awarded for partial completion of doctoral program. *Degree requirements:* For master's, thesis, oral defense of thesis; for doctorate, thesis/dissertation, oral defense of thesis, qualifying exams, 2 quarters of teaching experience. *Entrance requirements:* For master's and doctorate, GRE General Test, minimum GPA of 3.2. Additional exam requirements/recommendations for international students: Required—TOEFL (minimum score 550 paper-based; 213 computer-based; 80 iBT). Electronic applications accepted.

University of California, San Diego, Office of Graduate Studies, Division of Biological Sciences, Program in Cell and Developmental Biology, La Jolla, CA 92093-0348. Offers PhD. Offered in association with the Salk Institute. *Degree requirements:* For doctorate, thesis/dissertation, qualifying exam. Electronic applications accepted.

University of California, San Diego, School of Medicine and Office of Graduate Studies, Molecular Pathology Program, La Jolla, CA 92093. Offers bioinformatics (PhD); cancer biology/oncology (PhD); cardiovascular sciences and disease (PhD); microbiology (PhD); molecular pathology (PhD); neurological disease (PhD); stem cell and developmental biology (PhD); structural biology/drug design (PhD). *Entrance requirements:* For doctorate, GRE General Test, GRE Subject Test. Additional exam requirements/recommendations for international students: Required—TOEFL. Electronic applications accepted.

University of California, San Francisco, Graduate Division and School of Medicine, Department of Biochemistry and Biophysics, San Francisco, CA 94143. Offers biochemistry and molecular biology (PhD); cell biology (PhD); developmental biology (PhD); genetics (PhD); MD/PhD. *Degree requirements:* For doctorate, thesis/dissertation. *Entrance requirements:* For doctorate, GRE General Test, GRE Subject Test. Additional exam requirements/recommendations for international students: Required—TOEFL. *Expenses:* Contact institution.

University of California, Santa Barbara, Graduate Division, College of Letters and Sciences, Division of Mathematics, Life, and Physical Sciences, Department of Molecular, Cellular, and Developmental Biology, Santa Barbara, CA 93106-9625. Offers MA, PhD, MA/PhD. *Faculty:* 21 full-time (3 women), 7 part-time/adjunct (2 women). *Students:* 57 full-time (35 women); includes 1 Black or African American, non-Hispanic/Latino; 6 Asian, non-Hispanic/Latino; 3 Hispanic/Latino. Average age 28. 64 applicants, 41% accepted, 14 enrolled. In 2010, 8 master's, 7 doctorates awarded. *Degree requirements:* For master's, comprehensive exam (for some programs), thesis (for some programs); for doctorate, comprehensive exam, thesis/dissertation. *Entrance requirements:* For master's, GRE General Test, GRE Subject Test, 3 letters of recommendation, resume/curriculum vitae; for doctorate, GRE General Test, GRE Subject Test, 3 letters of recommendation, statement of purpose, personal achievements/contributions statement, resume/curriculum vitae, transcripts for post-secondary institutions attended. Additional exam requirements/recommendations for international students: Required—TOEFL (minimum score 610 paper-based; 102 iBT), IELTS (minimum score 7). *Application deadline:* For fall admission, 12/15 for domestic and international students. Application fee: $70 ($90 for international students). Electronic applications accepted. *Financial support:* In 2010–11, 55 students received support, including 13 fellowships with full and partial tuition reimbursements available (averaging $6,150 per year), 37 research assistantships with full and partial tuition reimbursements available (averaging $14,365 per year), 44 teaching assistantships with partial tuition reimbursements available (averaging $10,340 per year); career-related internships or fieldwork, Federal Work-Study, institutionally sponsored loans, scholarships/grants, traineeships, health care benefits, and unspecified assistantships also available. Financial award application deadline: 12/15; financial award applicants required to submit FAFSA. *Faculty research:* Microbiology, neurobiology (including stem cell research), developmental, virology, cell biology. *Unit head:* Dr. Dennis O. Clegg, Chair, 805-893-8490, Fax: 805-893-4724, E-mail: clegg@lifesci.ucsb.edu. *Application contact:* Nicole McCoy, Graduate Program Advisor, 805-893-8499, Fax: 805-893-4724, E-mail: nicole.mccoy@lifesci.ucsb.edu.

University of California, Santa Cruz, Division of Graduate Studies, Division of Physical and Biological Sciences, Program in Molecular, Cellular, and Developmental Biology, Santa Cruz, CA 95064. Offers MA, PhD. *Students:* 51 full-time (24 women); includes 9 minority (1 Black or African American, non-Hispanic/Latino; 4 Asian, non-Hispanic/Latino; 2 Hispanic/Latino; 1 Native Hawaiian or other Pacific Islander, non-Hispanic/Latino; 1 Two or more races, non-Hispanic/Latino), 4 international. Average age 28. 137 applicants, 21% accepted, 15 enrolled. In 2010, 5 doctorates awarded. Terminal master's awarded for partial completion of doctoral program. *Degree requirements:* For master's, thesis; for doctorate, thesis/dissertation, qualifying exam. *Entrance requirements:* For master's and doctorate, GRE General Test, 3 letters of recommendation, interview. Additional exam requirements/recommendations for international students: Required—TOEFL (minimum score 550 paper-based; 220 computer-based; 83 iBT); Recommended—IELTS (minimum score 8). *Application deadline:* For fall admission, 12/3 for domestic and international students. Application fee: $70 ($90 for international students). Electronic applications accepted. *Financial support:* Fellowships, research assistantships, teaching assistantships, institutionally sponsored loans and tuition waivers available. Financial award applicants required to submit FAFSA. *Faculty research:* RNA biology, chromatin and chromosome biology, neurobiology, stem cell biology and differentiation, cell structure and function. *Unit head:* Teel Lopez, Graduate Program Coordinator, 831-459-2385, E-mail: tablack@ucsc.edu. *Application contact:* Teel Lopez, Graduate Program Coordinator, 831-459-2385, E-mail: tablack@ucsc.edu.

University of Chicago, Division of Biological Sciences, Molecular Biosciences Cluster, Committee on Developmental Biology, Chicago, IL 60637-1513. Offers cellular differentiation (PhD); developmental endocrinology (PhD); developmental genetics (PhD); developmental neurobiology (PhD); gene expression (PhD). *Degree requirements:* For doctorate, thesis/dissertation, ethics class, 2 teaching assistantships. *Entrance requirements:* For doctorate, GRE General Test. Additional exam requirements/recommendations for international students: Required—TOEFL (minimum score 600 paper-based; 250 computer-based; 104 iBT), IELTS (minimum score 7). Electronic applications accepted. *Faculty research:* Epidermal differentiation, neural lineages, pattern formation.

University of Cincinnati, Graduate School, College of Medicine, Graduate Programs in Biomedical Sciences, Department of Pediatrics, Program in Molecular and Developmental Biology, Cincinnati, OH 45221. Offers PhD. *Degree requirements:* For doctorate, thesis/dissertation, qualifying exam. *Entrance requirements:* For doctorate, GRE General Test, minimum GPA of 3.2. Additional exam requirements/recommendations for international students: Required—TOEFL (minimum score 520 paper-based; 190 computer-based). Electronic applications accepted. *Faculty research:* Cancer biology, cardiovascular biology, developmental biology, human genetics, gene therapy, genomics and bioinformatics, immunobiology, molecular medicine, neuroscience, pulmonary biology, reproductive biology, stem cell biology.

University of Colorado Boulder, Graduate School, College of Arts and Sciences, Department of Molecular, Cellular, and Developmental Biology, Boulder, CO 80309. Offers cellular structure and function (MA, PhD); developmental biology (MA, PhD); molecular biology (MA, PhD). *Faculty:* 27 full-time (7 women). *Students:* 72 full-time (37 women), 1 part-time (0 women); includes 5 minority (1 American Indian or Alaska Native, non-Hispanic/Latino; 1 Asian, non-Hispanic/Latino; 3 Hispanic/Latino), 15 international. Average age 28. 257 applicants, 9 enrolled. In 2010, 4 master's, 9 doctorates awarded. Terminal master's awarded for partial completion of doctoral program. *Degree requirements:* For master's, comprehensive exam, thesis or alternative; for doctorate, comprehensive exam, thesis/dissertation. *Entrance requirements:* For master's, GRE General Test, GRE Subject Test, minimum undergraduate GPA of 3.0; for doctorate, GRE General Test, GRE Subject Test. *Application deadline:* For fall admission, 1/1 for domestic students, 12/1 for international students. Application fee: $50 ($60 for international students). *Financial support:* In 2010–11, 40 fellowships (averaging $11,628 per year), 53 research assistantships (averaging $14,700 per year) were awarded; tuition waivers (full) also available. Financial award application deadline: 2/1. *Faculty research:* Molecular biology of RNA and DNA, molecular genetics, cell motility and cytoskeleton, cell membranes, developmental genetics, human genetics. Total annual research expenditures: $16.4 million.

University of Colorado Denver, School of Medicine, Program in Cell Biology, Stem Cells, and Developmental Biology, Denver, CO 80217-3364. Offers PhD. *Students:* 26 full-time (16 women); includes 1 Asian, non-Hispanic/Latino; 1 Hispanic/Latino, 6 international. Average age 27. 39 applicants, 5% accepted, 2 enrolled. In 2010, 1 doctorate awarded. *Degree requirements:* For doctorate, comprehensive exam, thesis/dissertation, at least 30 credit hours of coursework and 30 credit hours of thesis research; laboratory rotations. *Entrance requirements:* For doctorate, GRE, minimum GPA of 3.0; 3 letters of reference; prerequisite coursework in organic chemistry, biology, biochemistry, physics and calculus; research experience (highly recommended). Additional exam requirements/recommendations for international students: Required—TOEFL (minimum score 550 paper-based; 213 computer-based). *Application deadline:* For fall admission, 1/1 for domestic students. Application fee: $65. Electronic applications accepted. *Expenses:* Contact institution. *Financial support:* Fellowships, research assistantships, teaching assistantships, health care benefits, tuition waivers (full), and stipend available. Financial award application deadline: 3/15; financial award applicants required to submit FAFSA. *Faculty research:* Development and repair of the vertebrate nervous system; molecular, genetic and developmental mechanisms involved in the patterning of the early spinal cord (neural plate) during vertebrate embryogenesis; structural analysis of protein glycosylation using NMR and mass spectrometry; small RNAs and post-transcriptional gene regulation during nematode gametogenesis and early development; diabetes-mediated changes in cardiovascular gene expression and functional exercise capacity. Total annual research expenditures: $5.7 million. *Unit head:* Dr. Wendy Macklin, Department Chair, 303-724-3426, E-mail: wendy.macklin@ucdenver.edu. *Application contact:* Jennifer Thurston, Program Manager, 303-724-5902, Fax: 303-724-3420, E-mail: jennifer.thurston@ucdenver.edu.

University of Connecticut, Graduate School, College of Liberal Arts and Sciences, Department of Molecular and Cell Biology, Storrs, CT 06269. Offers applied genomics (MS, PSM); biochemistry (MS, PhD); biophysics and structural biology (MS, PhD); cell and developmental biology (MS, PhD); genetics, genomics, and bioinformatics (MS, PhD); microbial systems analysis (MS, PSM); microbiology (MS, PhD); plant cell and molecular biology (MS, PhD). Terminal master's awarded for partial completion of doctoral program. *Degree requirements:* For master's, comprehensive exam; for doctorate, thesis/dissertation. *Entrance requirements:* For master's and doctorate, GRE General Test, GRE Subject Test. Additional exam requirements/recommendations for international students: Required—TOEFL (minimum score 550 paper-based; 213 computer-based). Electronic applications accepted.

Developmental Biology

University of Connecticut Health Center, Graduate School, Programs in Biomedical Sciences, Program in Genetics and Developmental Biology, Farmington, CT 06030. Offers PhD, DMD/PhD, MD/PhD. *Faculty:* 158. *Students:* 21 full-time (10 women); includes 1 minority (Asian, non-Hispanic/Latino), 7 international. Average age 29. 216 applicants, 22% accepted. In 2010, 4 doctorates awarded. *Degree requirements:* For doctorate, comprehensive exam, thesis/dissertation. *Entrance requirements:* For doctorate, GRE General Test, GRE Subject Test. Additional exam requirements/recommendations for international students: Required—TOEFL (minimum score 600 paper-based; 250 computer-based). *Application deadline:* For fall admission, 12/15 for domestic students. Application fee: $55. Electronic applications accepted. *Financial support:* In 2010–11, 21 research assistantships with full tuition reimbursements (averaging $27,000 per year) were awarded; health care benefits also available. *Faculty research:* Developmental biology, genomic imprinting, RNA biology, RNA alternative splicing, human embryonic stem cells. *Unit head:* Dr. William Mohler, Director, 860-679-7947, E-mail: wmohler@neuron.uchc.edu. *Application contact:* Tricia Avolt, Graduate Admissions Coordinator, 860-679-2175, Fax: 860-679-1899, E-mail: robertson@nso2.uchc.edu.

See Display on page 293 and Close-Up on page 309.

University of Delaware, College of Arts and Sciences, Department of Biological Sciences, Newark, DE 19716. Offers biotechnology (MS); cancer biology (MS, PhD); cell and extracellular matrix biology (MS, PhD); cell and systems physiology (MS, PhD); developmental biology (MS, PhD); ecology and evolution (MS, PhD); microbiology (MS, PhD); molecular biology and genetics (MS, PhD). Terminal master's awarded for partial completion of doctoral program. *Degree requirements:* For master's, thesis, preliminary exam; for doctorate, comprehensive exam, thesis/dissertation, preliminary exam. *Entrance requirements:* For master's and doctorate, GRE General Test. Additional exam requirements/recommendations for international students: Required—TOEFL (minimum score 600 paper-based; 250 computer-based); Recommended—TWE. Electronic applications accepted. *Faculty research:* Microorganisms, bone, cancer metastasis, developmental biology, cell biology, DNA.

University of Hawaii at Manoa, John A. Burns School of Medicine, Program in Developmental and Reproductive Biology, Honolulu, HI 96813. Offers MS, PhD. Part-time programs available. *Faculty:* 24 full-time (7 women). *Students:* 12 full-time (7 women), 8 part-time (3 women); includes 12 minority (8 Asian, non-Hispanic/Latino; 3 Native Hawaiian or other Pacific Islander, non-Hispanic/Latino; 1 Two or more races, non-Hispanic/Latino), 3 international. Average age 29. 22 applicants, 68% accepted, 11 enrolled. In 2010, 1 master's, 1 doctorate awarded. *Degree requirements:* For doctorate, thesis/dissertation. *Entrance requirements:* For doctorate, GRE General Test, GRE Subject Test. Additional exam requirements/recommendations for international students: Recommended—TOEFL (minimum score 560 paper-based; 83 computer-based), IELTS (minimum score 5). *Application deadline:* For fall admission, 3/1 for domestic and international students. Application fee: $50. *Financial support:* In 2010–11, 2 fellowships (averaging $4,577 per year), 10 research assistantships (averaging $16,328 per year) were awarded; teaching assistantships. *Faculty research:* Biology of gametes and fertilization, reproductive endocrinology. Total annual research expenditures: $5.4 million. *Application contact:* Steve Ward, Graduate Chair, 808-956-1412, Fax: 808-956-9722, E-mail: wward@hawaii.edu.

University of Illinois at Urbana–Champaign, Graduate College, College of Liberal Arts and Sciences, School of Molecular and Cellular Biology, Department of Cell and Developmental Biology, Champaign, IL 61820. Offers PhD. *Faculty:* 13 full-time (4 women), 1 (woman) part-time/adjunct. *Students:* 47 full-time (20 women); includes 4 Asian, non-Hispanic/Latino; 1 Hispanic/Latino, 25 international. In 2010, 9 doctorates awarded. *Entrance requirements:* For doctorate, GRE, minimum GPA of 3.0. Additional exam requirements/recommendations for international students: Required—TOEFL (minimum score 590 paper-based; 243 computer-based). *Application deadline:* Applications are processed on a rolling basis. Application fee: $75 ($90 for international students). Electronic applications accepted. *Financial support:* In 2010–11, 7 fellowships, 41 research assistantships, 20 teaching assistantships were awarded; tuition waivers (full and partial) also available. *Unit head:* Andrew Belmont, Head, 217-244-2311, Fax: 217-244-1648, E-mail: asbel@illinois.edu. *Application contact:* Delynn Carter, Assistant to the Head, 217-244-8116, Fax: 217-244-1648, E-mail: dmcarter@illinois.edu.

The University of Kansas, Graduate Studies, College of Liberal Arts and Sciences, Department of Molecular Biosciences, Lawrence, KS 66044. Offers biochemistry and biophysics (MA, PhD); microbiology (MA, PhD); molecular, cellular, and developmental biology (MA, PhD). *Faculty:* 34. *Students:* 65 full-time (31 women), 1 part-time (0 women); includes 7 minority (2 Asian, non-Hispanic/Latino; 4 Hispanic/Latino; 1 Two or more races, non-Hispanic/Latino), 24 international. Average age 27. 34 applicants, 47% accepted, 10 enrolled. In 2010, 1 master's, 5 doctorates awarded. Terminal master's awarded for partial completion of doctoral program. *Degree requirements:* For master's, comprehensive exam, thesis; for doctorate, comprehensive exam, thesis/dissertation. *Entrance requirements:* For master's and doctorate, GRE General Test. Additional exam requirements/recommendations for international students: Required—TOEFL (minimum score 24 iBT), OR IELTS Speaking: 8. *Application deadline:* For fall admission, 12/15 for domestic and international students. Application fee: $55 ($65 for international students). Electronic applications accepted. *Expenses:* Tuition, state resident: full-time $7092; part-time $295.50 per credit hour. Tuition, nonresident: full-time $16,590; part-time $691.25 per credit hour. Required fees: $858; $71.49 per credit hour. Tuition and fees vary according to course load, campus/location and program. *Financial support:* Fellowships with tuition reimbursements, research assistantships with tuition reimbursements, teaching assistantships with tuition reimbursements, health care benefits and unspecified assistantships available. Financial award application deadline: 3/1. *Faculty research:* Structure and function of proteins, genetics of organism development, molecular genetics, neurophysiology, molecular virology and pathogenics, developmental biology, cell biology. *Unit head:* Dr. Mark Richter, Chair, 785-864-3334, Fax: 785-864-5294, E-mail: richter@ku.edu. *Application contact:* John P. Connolly, Graduate Program Assistant, 785-864-4311, Fax: 785-864-5294, E-mail: jconnolly@ku.edu.

The University of Manchester, Faculty of Life Sciences, Manchester, United Kingdom. Offers adaptive organismal biology (M Phil, PhD); animal biology (M Phil, PhD); biochemistry (M Phil, PhD); bioinformatics (M Phil, PhD); biomolecular sciences (M Phil, PhD); biotechnology (M Phil, PhD); cell biology (M Phil, PhD); cell matrix research (M Phil, PhD); channels and transporters (M Phil, PhD); developmental biology (M Phil, PhD); Egyptology (M Phil, PhD); environmental biology (M Phil, PhD); evolutionary biology (M Phil, PhD); gene expression (M Phil, PhD); genetics (M Phil, PhD); history of science, technology and medicine (M Phil, PhD); immunology (M Phil, PhD); integrative neurobiology and behavior (M Phil, PhD); membrane trafficking (M Phil, PhD); microbiology (M Phil, PhD); molecular and cellular neuroscience (M Phil, PhD); molecular biology (M Phil, PhD); molecular cancer studies (M Phil, PhD); neuroscience (M Phil, PhD); ophthalmology (M Phil, PhD); optometry (M Phil, PhD); organelle function (M Phil, PhD); pharmacology (M Phil, PhD); physiology (M Phil, PhD); plant sciences (M Phil, PhD); stem cell research (M Phil, PhD); structural biology (M Phil, PhD); systems neuroscience (M Phil, PhD); toxicology (M Phil, PhD).

The University of Manchester, School of Dentistry, Manchester, United Kingdom. Offers basic dental sciences (cancer studies) (M Phil, PhD); basic dental sciences (molecular genetics) (M Phil, PhD); basic dental sciences (stem cell biology) (M Phil, PhD); biomaterials sciences and dental technology (M Phil, PhD); dental public health/community dentistry (M Phil, PhD); dental science (clinical) (PhD); endodontology (M Phil, PhD); fixed and removable prosthodontics (M Phil, PhD); operative dentistry (M Phil, PhD); oral and maxillofacial surgery (M Phil, PhD); oral radiology (M Phil, PhD); orthodontics (M Phil, PhD); restorative dentistry (M Phil, PhD).

University of Massachusetts Amherst, Graduate School, Interdisciplinary Programs, Program in Molecular and Cellular Biology, Amherst, MA 01003. Offers biological chemistry and molecular biophysics (PhD); biomedicine (PhD); cellular and developmental biology (PhD). Part-time programs available. *Students:* 76 full-time (42 women), 3 part-time (2 women); includes 13 minority (3 Black or African American, non-Hispanic/Latino; 4 Asian, non-Hispanic/Latino; 5 Hispanic/Latino; 1 Two or more races, non-Hispanic/Latino), 23 international. Average age 27. 179 applicants, 25% accepted, 22 enrolled. In 2010, 8 doctorates awarded. Terminal master's awarded for partial completion of doctoral program. *Degree requirements:* For doctorate, comprehensive exam, thesis/dissertation. *Entrance requirements:* For doctorate, GRE General Test. Additional exam requirements/recommendations for international students: Required—TOEFL (minimum score 550 paper-based; 213 computer-based; 80 iBT), IELTS (minimum score 6.5). *Application deadline:* For fall admission, 12/1 for domestic and international students. Applications are processed on a rolling basis. Application fee: $50 ($65 for international students). Electronic applications accepted. *Expenses:* Tuition, state resident: full-time $2640. Required fees: $8282. One-time fee: $357 full-time. *Financial support:* In 2010–11, 11 research assistantships with full tuition reimbursements (averaging $2,590 per year), 3 teaching assistantships with full tuition reimbursements (averaging $3,303 per year) were awarded; fellowships, career-related internships or fieldwork, Federal Work-Study, scholarships/grants, traineeships, health care benefits, tuition waivers (full), and unspecified assistantships also available. Support available to part-time students. Financial award application deadline: 12/1; financial award applicants required to submit FAFSA. *Unit head:* Dr. Barbara Osborne, Graduate Program Director, 413-545-3246, Fax: 413-545-1812. *Application contact:* Jean M. Ames, Supervisor of Admissions, 413-545-0722, Fax: 413-577-0010, E-mail: gradadm@grad.umass.edu.

University of Medicine and Dentistry of New Jersey, Graduate School of Biomedical Sciences, Graduate Programs in Biomedical Sciences–Newark, Newark, NJ 07107. Offers biodefense (Certificate); biomedical engineering (PhD); biomedical sciences (multidisciplinary) (PhD); cellular biology, neuroscience and physiology (PhD), including neuroscience, physiology, biophysics, cardiovascular biology, molecular pharmacology, stem cell biology; infection, immunity and inflammation (PhD), including immunology, infectious disease, microbiology, oral biology; molecular biology, genetics and cancer (PhD), including biochemistry, molecular genetics, cancer biology, radiation biology, bioinformatics; neuroscience (Certificate); pharmacological sciences (Certificate); stem cell (Certificate); DMD/PhD; MD/PhD. PhD in biomedical engineering offered jointly with New Jersey Institute of Technology. Part-time and evening/weekend programs available. *Students:* 330 full-time (199 women), 75 part-time (47 women); includes 32 Black or African American, non-Hispanic/Latino; 1 American Indian or Alaska Native, non-Hispanic/Latino; 109 Asian, non-Hispanic/Latino; 16 Hispanic/Latino, 83 international. Average age 28. 611 applicants, 52% accepted, 181 enrolled. In 2010, 24 doctorates, 2 other advanced degrees awarded. Terminal master's awarded for partial completion of doctoral program. *Degree requirements:* For doctorate, thesis/dissertation, qualifying exam. *Entrance requirements:* For doctorate, GRE General Test. Additional exam requirements/recommendations for international students: Required—TOEFL. *Application deadline:* For fall admission, 1/15 for domestic students. Applications are processed on a rolling basis. Application fee: $65. Electronic applications accepted. *Financial support:* In 2010–11, 28 fellowships (averaging $26,000 per year) were awarded; research assistantships, teaching assistantships, career-related internships or fieldwork, Federal Work-Study, institutionally sponsored loans, and tuition waivers (full and partial) also available. Financial award application deadline: 5/1. *Unit head:* Dr. Andrew Thomas, Senior Associate Dean, Graduate School of Biomedical Sciences, 973-972-4511, Fax: 973-972-7148, E-mail: thomas@umdnj.edu. *Application contact:* Dr. B. J. Wagner, 973-972-5335, Fax: 973-972-7148, E-mail: wagner@umdnj.edu.

University of Miami, Graduate School, Miller School of Medicine, Graduate Programs in Medicine, Department of Cell Biology and Anatomy, Coral Gables, FL 33124. Offers molecular cell and developmental biology (PhD); MD/PhD. *Degree requirements:* For doctorate, thesis/dissertation. *Entrance requirements:* For doctorate, GRE General Test, GRE Subject Test. Additional exam requirements/recommendations for international students: Required—TOEFL. Electronic applications accepted.

University of Michigan, Rackham Graduate School, College of Literature, Science, and the Arts, Department of Molecular, Cellular, and Developmental Biology, Ann Arbor, MI 48109. Offers MS, PhD. Part-time programs available. *Faculty:* 33 full-time (8 women). *Students:* 69 full-time (35 women), 7 part-time (5 women); includes 4 minority (3 Asian, non-Hispanic/Latino; 1 Hispanic/Latino), 35 international. Average age 27. 122 applicants, 16% accepted, 6 enrolled. In 2010, 5 master's, 7 doctorates awarded. Terminal master's awarded for partial completion of doctoral program. *Degree requirements:* For master's, 24 credits with at least 16 in molecular, cellular, and developmental biology and 4 in a cognate field; for doctorate, thesis/dissertation, preliminary exam, oral defense. *Entrance requirements:* For master's and doctorate, GRE General Test. Additional exam requirements/recommendations for international students: Required—TOEFL (minimum score 560 paper-based; 220 computer-based; 83 iBT). *Application deadline:* For fall admission, 1/5 for domestic and international students; for winter admission, 11/1 for domestic and international students. Applications are processed on a rolling basis. Application fee: $65 ($75 for international students). Electronic applications accepted. *Expenses:* Tuition, state resident: full-time $17,784; part-time $1116 per credit hour. Tuition, nonresident: full-time $35,944; part-time $2125 per credit hour. International tuition: $35,994 full-time. Required fees: $95 per semester. Tuition and fees vary according to course load, degree level and program. *Financial support:* In 2010–11, 61 students received support, including 13 fellowships with full tuition reimbursements available (averaging $26,500 per year), 28 research assistantships with full tuition reimbursements available (averaging $26,500 per year), 21 teaching assistantships with full tuition reimbursements available (averaging $26,500 per year); health care benefits also available. *Faculty research:* Cell biology, microbiology, neurobiology and physiology, developmental biology and plant molecular biology. *Unit head:* Patrick J. Flannery, Administrative Manager, 734-936-2997, Fax: 734-615-6337, E-mail: pjflan@umich.edu. *Application contact:* Mary Carr, Graduate Coordinator, 734-615-1635, Fax: 734-764-0884, E-mail: carrmm@umich.edu.

University of Michigan, Rackham Graduate School, Program in Biomedical Sciences (PIBS), Department of Cell and Developmental Biology, Ann Arbor, MI 48109. Offers PhD. *Faculty:* 29 full-time (10 women). *Students:* 17 full-time (10 women); includes 1 Asian, non-Hispanic/Latino, 9 international. Average age 30. 28 applicants, 25% accepted, 4 enrolled. In 2010, 6 doctorates awarded. *Degree requirements:* For doctorate, thesis/dissertation, oral defense of dissertation, preliminary exam. *Entrance requirements:* For doctorate, GRE General Test, 3 letters of recommendation, research experience. Additional exam requirements/recommendations for international students: Required—TOEFL (minimum score 84 iBT). *Application deadline:* For fall admission, 12/1 for domestic and international students. Application fee: $60 ($75 for international students). Electronic applications accepted. *Expenses:* Tuition, state resident: full-time $17,784; part-time $1116 per credit hour. Tuition, nonresident: full-time $35,944; part-time $2125 per credit hour. International tuition: $35,994 full-time. Required fees: $95 per semester. Tuition and fees vary according to course load, degree level and program. *Financial support:* In 2010–11, 21 students received support, including 21 fellowships (averaging $26,500 per year); scholarships/grants, health care benefits, tuition waivers (full), and unspecified assistantships also available. Financial award application deadline: 12/1. *Faculty research:* Small stress proteins, cellular stress response, muscle, male reproductive, toxicology, cell cytoskeleton. Total annual research expenditures: $3.8 million. *Unit head:* Dr. James Douglas Engel, Chair, 734-615-7509, Fax: 734-763-1166, E-mail: engel@umich.edu. *Application contact:* Michelle S. Melis, Director of Student Life, 734-615-6538, Fax: 734-647-7022, E-mail: msmtegan@umich.edu.

University of Minnesota, Twin Cities Campus, Graduate School, Program in Molecular, Cellular, Developmental Biology and Genetics, Minneapolis, MN 55455-0213. Offers genetic counseling (MS); molecular, cellular, developmental biology and genetics (PhD). Terminal master's awarded for partial completion of doctoral program. *Degree requirements:* For master's, thesis optional; for doctorate, thesis/dissertation. *Entrance requirements:* For master's and doctorate, GRE General Test. Additional exam requirements/recommendations for international students: Required—TOEFL (minimum score 625 paper-based; 263 computer-based; 80 iBT). Electronic applications accepted. *Faculty research:* Membrane receptors and membrane transport, cell interactions, cytoskeleton and cell mobility, regulation of gene expression, plant cell and molecular biology.

University of Minnesota, Twin Cities Campus, Graduate School, Stem Cell Biology Graduate Program, Minneapolis, MN 55455-3007. Offers MS. *Degree requirements:* For master's, thesis.

Entrance requirements: For master's, GRE, BS, BA, or foreign equivalent in biological sciences or related field; minimum undergraduate GPA of 3.2. Additional exam requirements/recommendations for international students: Required—TOEFL (minimum scores 580 on paper-based, with a minimum score of 4 in the TWE, or 94 Internet-based, with a minimum score of 22 on each of the reading and listening, 26 on the speaking, and 26 on the writing section. *Faculty research:* Stem cell and developmental biology; embryonic stem cells; iPS cells; muscle satellite cells; hematopoietic stem cells; neuronal stem cells; cardiovascular, kidney and limb development; regenerating systems.

The University of North Carolina at Chapel Hill, Graduate School, College of Arts and Sciences, Department of Biology, Chapel Hill, NC 27599. Offers botany (MA, MS, PhD); cell biology, development, and physiology (MA, MS, PhD); cell motility and cytoskeleton (PhD); ecology and behavior (MA, MS, PhD); genetics and molecular biology (MA, MS, PhD); morphology, systematics, and evolution (MA, MS, PhD). Terminal master's awarded for partial completion of doctoral program. *Degree requirements:* For master's, comprehensive exam, thesis (for some programs); for doctorate, comprehensive exam, thesis/dissertation. *Entrance requirements:* For master's, GRE General Test, GRE Subject Test, 2 semesters of calculus or statistics; 2 semesters of physics, organic chemistry; 3 semesters of biology; for doctorate, GRE General Test, GRE Subject Test, 2 semesters calculus or statistics, 2 semesters physics, organic chemistry, 3 semesters of biology. Additional exam requirements/recommendations for international students: Required—TOEFL (minimum score 550 paper-based; 213 computer-based). Electronic applications accepted. *Faculty research:* Gene expression, biomechanics, yeast genetics, plant ecology, plant molecular biology.

The University of North Carolina at Chapel Hill, School of Medicine and Graduate School, Graduate Programs in Medicine, Department of Cell and Developmental Biology, Chapel Hill, NC 27599. Offers PhD. *Faculty:* 16 full-time (2 women). *Students:* 35 full-time (19 women); includes 2 Black or African American, non-Hispanic/Latino; 3 Asian, non-Hispanic/Latino, 7 international. Average age 24. 23 applicants, 9% accepted, 2 enrolled. In 2010, 5 doctorates awarded. *Degree requirements:* For doctorate, comprehensive exam, thesis/dissertation. *Entrance requirements:* For doctorate, GRE General Test, GRE Subject Test. *Application deadline:* For fall admission, 1/1 priority date for domestic and international students. Applications are processed on a rolling basis. Application fee: $73. Electronic applications accepted. *Financial support:* In 2010–11, 6 fellowships with tuition reimbursements (averaging $21,180 per year), 29 research assistantships with full tuition reimbursements (averaging $27,000 per year) were awarded; teaching assistantships with full tuition reimbursements, tuition waivers (full) and unspecified assistantships also available. Financial award application deadline: 2/1; financial award applicants required to submit FAFSA. *Faculty research:* Cell adhesion, motility and cytoskeleton; molecular analysis of signal transduction; development biology and toxicology; reproductive biology; cell and molecular imaging. Total annual research expenditures: $8 million. *Unit head:* Dr. Vytas A. Bankaitis, Chair, 919-966-3026, Fax: 919-966-1856, E-mail: vytas@med.unc.edu. *Application contact:* Dr. Douglas Cyr, Director of Graduate Studies, 919-843-4805, E-mail: dmcyr@med.unc.edu.

University of Pennsylvania, Perelman School of Medicine, Biomedical Graduate Studies, Graduate Group in Cell and Molecular Biology, Philadelphia, PA 19104. Offers cancer biology (PhD); cell biology and physiology (PhD); developmental stem cell regenerative biology (PhD); gene therapy and vaccines (PhD); genetics and gene regulation (PhD); microbiology, virology, and parasitology (PhD); MD/PhD; VMD/PhD. *Faculty:* 299. *Students:* 315 full-time (166 women); includes 13 Black or African American, non-Hispanic/Latino; 1 American Indian or Alaska Native, non-Hispanic/Latino; 44 Asian, non-Hispanic/Latino; 18 Hispanic/Latino, 37 international. 579 applicants, 21% accepted, 49 enrolled. In 2010, 53 doctorates awarded. *Degree requirements:* For doctorate, thesis/dissertation. *Entrance requirements:* For doctorate, GRE General Test. Additional exam requirements/recommendations for international students: Required—TOEFL. *Application deadline:* For fall admission, 12/8 priority date for domestic and international students. Applications are processed on a rolling basis. Application fee: $70. Electronic applications accepted. *Expenses:* Tuition: Full-time $25,660; part-time $4758 per course. Required fees: $2152; $270 per course. Tuition and fees vary according to course load, degree level and program. *Financial support:* In 2010–11, 315 students received support; fellowships, research assistantships, scholarships/grants, traineeships, and unspecified assistantships available. Financial award application deadline: 12/8. *Unit head:* Dr. Daniel Kessler, Graduate Group Chair, 215-898-2180, E-mail: raperj@mail.med.upenn.edu. *Application contact:* Meagan Schofer, Coordinator, 215-898-9536, Fax: 215-573-2104, E-mail: camb@mailmed.upenn.edu.

University of Pittsburgh, School of Arts and Sciences, Department of Biological Sciences, Program in Molecular, Cellular, and Developmental Biology, Pittsburgh, PA 15260. Offers PhD. *Faculty:* 25 full-time (6 women). *Students:* 56 full-time (35 women); includes 3 Asian, non-Hispanic/Latino, 17 international. Average age 23. 181 applicants, 11% accepted, 7 enrolled. In 2010, 6 doctorates awarded. *Degree requirements:* For doctorate, comprehensive exam, thesis/dissertation, completion of research integrity module. *Entrance requirements:* For doctorate, GRE General Test, GRE Subject Test. Additional exam requirements/recommendations for international students: Required—TOEFL (minimum score 550 paper-based; 213 computer-based; 80 iBT). *Application deadline:* For fall admission, 1/15 priority date for domestic students, 12/15 priority date for international students. Applications are processed on a rolling basis. Application fee: $0 ($50 for international students). Electronic applications accepted. *Expenses:* Tuition, state resident: full-time $17,304; part-time $701 per credit. Tuition, nonresident: full-time $29,554; part-time $1210 per credit. Required fees: $740; $214 per term. Tuition and fees vary according to program. *Financial support:* In 2010–11, 25 fellowships with full tuition reimbursements (averaging $28,382 per year), 116 research assistantships with full tuition reimbursements (averaging $25,058 per year), 22 teaching assistantships with full tuition reimbursements (averaging $23,907 per year) were awarded; Federal Work-Study, scholarships/grants, traineeships, health care benefits, and tuition waivers (full) also available. *Unit head:* Dr. Gerard L. Campbell, Associate Professor, 412-624-6812, Fax: 412-624-4759, E-mail: camp@pitt.edu. *Application contact:* Cathleen M. Barr, Graduate Administrator, 412-624-4268, Fax: 412-624-4759, E-mail: cbarr@pitt.edu.

University of Pittsburgh, School of Medicine, Graduate Programs in Medicine, Molecular Genetics and Developmental Biology Program, Pittsburgh, PA 15260. Offers MS, PhD. *Faculty:* 35 full-time (10 women). *Students:* 14 full-time (8 women); includes 2 Asian, non-Hispanic/Latino, 4 international. Average age 27. 486 applicants, 14% accepted. In 2010, 6 doctorates awarded. *Degree requirements:* For doctorate, comprehensive exam, thesis/dissertation. *Entrance requirements:* For doctorate, GRE General Test, GRE Subject Test, minimum QPA of 3.0. Additional exam requirements/recommendations for international students: Required—TOEFL (minimum score 600 paper-based; 100 iBT), IELTS (minimum score 7). *Application deadline:* For fall admission, 12/15 priority date for domestic and international students. Application fee: $50. Electronic applications accepted. *Expenses:* Tuition, state resident: full-time $17,304; part-time $701 per credit. Tuition, nonresident: full-time $29,554; part-time $1210 per credit. Required fees: $740; $214 per term. Tuition and fees vary according to program. *Financial support:* In 2010–11, 14 research assistantships with full tuition reimbursements (averaging $25,500 per year) were awarded; institutionally sponsored loans, scholarships/grants, traineeships, health care benefits, and unspecified assistantships also available. *Faculty research:* Developmental and stem cell biology, DNA replication and repair, gene regulation and signal transduction, oncogenes and tumor suppressor genes, protein structure and molecular dynamics. *Unit head:* Dr. Neil A. Hukriede, Graduate Program Director, 412-648-9918, Fax: 412-624-1401, E-mail: hukriede@pitt.edu. *Application contact:* Graduate Studies Administrator, 412-648-8957, Fax: 412-648-1077, E-mail: gradstudies@medschool.pitt.edu.

University of South Carolina, The Graduate School, College of Arts and Sciences, Department of Biological Sciences, Graduate Training Program in Molecular, Cellular, and Developmental Biology, Columbia, SC 29208. Offers MS, PhD. *Degree requirements:* For master's, one foreign language, thesis; for doctorate, one foreign language, thesis/dissertation. *Entrance requirements:* For master's and doctorate, GRE General Test, minimum GPA of 3.0 in science. Electronic applications accepted. *Faculty research:* Marine ecology, population and evolutionary biology, molecular biology and genetics, development.

The University of Texas Health Science Center at Houston, Graduate School of Biomedical Sciences, Program in Genes and Development, Houston, TX 77030. Offers MS, PhD, MD/PhD. Terminal master's awarded for partial completion of doctoral program. *Degree requirements:* For master's, thesis; for doctorate, thesis/dissertation. *Entrance requirements:* For master's and doctorate, GRE General Test. Additional exam requirements/recommendations for international students: Required—TOEFL. Electronic applications accepted. *Faculty research:* Developmental biology, genetics, cell biology, structural biology, cancer.

The University of Texas Southwestern Medical Center at Dallas, Southwestern Graduate School of Biomedical Sciences, Division of Basic Science, Program in Genetics and Development, Dallas, TX 75390. Offers PhD. *Faculty:* 85 full-time (16 women), 2 part-time/adjunct (0 women). *Students:* 59 full-time (22 women), 1 part-time (0 women); includes 13 minority (1 American Indian or Alaska Native, non-Hispanic/Latino; 8 Asian, non-Hispanic/Latino; 4 Hispanic/Latino), 24 international. Average age 26. In 2010, 12 doctorates awarded. *Degree requirements:* For doctorate, thesis/dissertation, qualifying exam. *Entrance requirements:* For doctorate, GRE General Test, minimum GPA of 3.0. Additional exam requirements/recommendations for international students: Required—TOEFL. *Application deadline:* For fall admission, 12/15 priority date for domestic students. Application fee: $0. Electronic applications accepted. *Financial support:* Fellowships, research assistantships, institutionally sponsored loans available. *Faculty research:* Human molecular genetics, chromosome structure, gene regulation, molecular biology, gene expression. *Unit head:* Dr. Nancy E. Street, Associate Dean, 214-648-6708, Fax: 214-648-2102, E-mail: nancy.street@utsouthwestern.edu. *Application contact:* Dr. Nancy E. Street, Associate Dean, 214-648-6708, Fax: 214-648-2102, E-mail: nancy.street@utsouthwestern.edu.

Washington University in St. Louis, Graduate School of Arts and Sciences, Division of Biology and Biomedical Sciences, Program in Developmental Biology, St. Louis, MO 63130-4899. Offers PhD. *Degree requirements:* For doctorate, thesis/dissertation. *Entrance requirements:* For doctorate, GRE General Test, GRE Subject Test. Electronic applications accepted.

Wesleyan University, Graduate Programs, Department of Biology, Middletown, CT 06459. Offers animal behavior (PhD); bioformatics/genomics (PhD); cell biology (PhD); developmental biology (PhD); evolution/ecology (PhD); genetics (PhD); neurobiology (PhD); population biology (PhD). *Faculty:* 12 full-time (4 women). *Students:* 20 full-time (12 women); includes 1 Black or African American, non-Hispanic/Latino; 3 Asian, non-Hispanic/Latino. Average age 26. 24 applicants, 29% accepted, 2 enrolled. *Degree requirements:* For doctorate, variable foreign language requirement, thesis/dissertation. *Entrance requirements:* For doctorate, GRE. Additional exam requirements/recommendations for international students: Required—TOEFL. *Application deadline:* For fall admission, 1/15 for domestic and international students. Applications are processed on a rolling basis. Application fee: $0. *Expenses:* Tuition: Full-time $43,404. Required fees: $830. *Financial support:* In 2010–11, 5 research assistantships with full tuition reimbursements, 16 teaching assistantships with full tuition reimbursements were awarded; stipends also available. Financial award application deadline: 4/15; financial award applicants required to submit FAFSA. *Faculty research:* Microbial population genetics, genetic basis of evolutionary adaptation, genetic regulation of differentiation and pattern formation in *drosophila*. *Unit head:* Dr. Sonia E. Sultan, Chair/Professor, 860-685-3493, E-mail: jnaegele@wesleyan.edu. *Application contact:* Marjorie Fitzgibbons, Information Contact, 860-685-2140, E-mail: mfitzgibbons@wesleyan.edu.

West Virginia University, Davis College of Agriculture, Forestry and Consumer Sciences, Interdisciplinary Program in Genetics and Developmental Biology, Morgantown, WV 26506. Offers animal breeding (MS, PhD); biochemical and molecular genetics (MS, PhD); cytogenetics (MS, PhD); descriptive embryology (MS, PhD); developmental genetics (MS); experimental morphogenesis/teratology (MS); human genetics (MS, PhD); immunogenetics (MS, PhD); life cycles of animals and plants (MS, PhD); molecular aspects of development (MS, PhD); mutagenesis (MS, PhD); oncology (MS, PhD); plant genetics (MS, PhD); population and quantitative genetics (MS, PhD); regeneration (MS, PhD); teratology (PhD); toxicology (MS, PhD). *Degree requirements:* For master's, thesis; for doctorate, comprehensive exam, thesis/dissertation. *Entrance requirements:* For master's, GRE or MCAT, minimum GPA of 2.75. Additional exam requirements/recommendations for international students: Required—TOEFL.

Yale University, Graduate School of Arts and Sciences, Department of Molecular, Cellular, and Developmental Biology, New Haven, CT 06520. Offers biochemistry, molecular biology and chemical biology (PhD); cellular and developmental biology (PhD); genetics (PhD); neurobiology (PhD); plant sciences (PhD). *Degree requirements:* For doctorate, thesis/dissertation. *Entrance requirements:* For doctorate, GRE General Test, GRE Subject Test.

Genetics

Albert Einstein College of Medicine, Graduate Division of Biomedical Sciences, Division of Biological Sciences, Department of Genetics, Bronx, NY 10461. Offers computational genetics (PhD); molecular genetics (PhD); translational genetics (PhD); MD/PhD. *Degree requirements:* For doctorate, thesis/dissertation. *Entrance requirements:* For doctorate, GRE General Test. Additional exam requirements/recommendations for international students: Required—TOEFL. *Faculty research:* Neurologic genetics in *Drosophila*, biochemical genetics of yeast, developmental genetics in the mouse.

Baylor College of Medicine, Graduate School of Biomedical Sciences, Department of Molecular and Human Genetics, Houston, TX 77030-3498. Offers PhD, MD/PhD. *Faculty:* 67 full-time (14 women). *Students:* 77 full-time (45 women); includes 2 Black or African American, non-Hispanic/Latino; 2 Asian, non-Hispanic/Latino; 3 Hispanic/Latino, 36 international. Average age 26. 130 applicants, 20% accepted, 16 enrolled. In 2010, 15 doctorates awarded. *Degree requirements:* For doctorate, thesis/dissertation, public defense. *Entrance requirements:* For doctorate, GRE General Test, GRE Subject Test (strongly recommended), minimum GPA of 3.0. Additional exam requirements/recommendations for international students: Required—TOEFL. *Application deadline:* For fall admission, 1/1 priority date for domestic students. Application fee: $0. Electronic applications accepted. *Expenses:* Tuition: Full-time $11,000. Required fees: $4900. *Financial support:* In 2010–11, 18 fellowships with full tuition reimbursements (averaging $26,000 per year), 59 research assistantships with full tuition reimburse-

Genetics

Baylor College of Medicine (continued)

ments (averaging $26,009 per year) were awarded; career-related internships or fieldwork, Federal Work-Study, institutionally sponsored loans, health care benefits, and students receive a scholarship unless there are grant funds available to pay tuition also available. Financial award applicants required to submit FAFSA. *Faculty research:* Human genetics, genome biology, epigenetics, gene therapy, model organisms. *Unit head:* Dr. Gad Shaulsky, Director, 713-798-5056. *Application contact:* Judi Coleman, Graduate Program Administrator, 713-798-5056, Fax: 713-798-8597, E-mail: genetics-gradprm@bcm.edu.

See Close-Up on page 305.

Baylor College of Medicine, Graduate School of Biomedical Sciences, Interdepartmental Program in Cell and Molecular Biology, Houston, TX 77030-3498. Offers biochemistry (PhD); cell and molecular biology (PhD); genetics (PhD); human genetics (PhD); immunology (PhD); microbiology (PhD); virology (PhD); MD/PhD. *Faculty:* 100 full-time (31 women). *Students:* 67 full-time (41 women); includes 4 Black or African American, non-Hispanic/Latino; 2 American Indian or Alaska Native, non-Hispanic/Latino; 9 Asian, non-Hispanic/Latino; 9 Hispanic/Latino, 9 international. Average age 27. 120 applicants, 27% accepted, 15 enrolled. In 2010, 7 doctorates awarded. *Degree requirements:* For doctorate, thesis/dissertation, public defense. *Entrance requirements:* For doctorate, GRE General Test, GRE Subject Test (strongly recommended), minimum GPA of 3.0. Additional exam requirements/recommendations for international students: Required—TOEFL. *Application deadline:* For fall admission, 1/1 priority date for domestic students. Applications are processed on a rolling basis. Application fee: $0. Electronic applications accepted. *Expenses:* Tuition: Full-time $11,000. Required fees: $4900. *Financial support:* In 2010–11, 67 students received support, including 24 fellowships with full tuition reimbursements available (averaging $26,000 per year), 43 research assistantships with full tuition reimbursements available (averaging $26,000 per year); teaching assistantships, Federal Work-Study, institutionally sponsored loans, health care benefits, and tuition waivers (full) also available. Financial award applicants required to submit FAFSA. *Faculty research:* Molecular and cellular biology; cancer, aging and stem cells; genomics and proteomics; microbiome, molecular microbiology; infectious disease, immunology and translational research. *Unit head:* Dr. Susan Marriott, Director, 713-798-6557. *Application contact:* Lourdes Fernandez, Graduate Program Administrator, 713-798-6557, Fax: 713-798-6325, E-mail: cmbprog@bcm.edu.

See Close-Up on page 223.

Baylor College of Medicine, Graduate School of Biomedical Sciences, Program in Developmental Biology, Houston, TX 77030-3498. Offers PhD, MD/PhD. *Faculty:* 63 full-time (19 women). *Students:* 55 full-time (26 women); includes 5 Asian, non-Hispanic/Latino; 3 Hispanic/Latino, 35 international. Average age 28. 73 applicants, 18% accepted, 10 enrolled. In 2010, 5 doctorates awarded. *Degree requirements:* For doctorate, thesis/dissertation, public defense. *Entrance requirements:* For doctorate, GRE General Test, GRE Subject Test (strongly recommended), minimum GPA of 3.0. Additional exam requirements/recommendations for international students: Required—TOEFL. *Application deadline:* For fall admission, 1/1 priority date for domestic students. Application fee: $0. Electronic applications accepted. *Expenses:* Tuition: Full-time $11,000. Required fees: $4900. *Financial support:* In 2010–11, 55 students received support, including 15 fellowships with full tuition reimbursements available (averaging $26,000 per year), 40 research assistantships with full tuition reimbursements available (averaging $26,000 per year); career-related internships or fieldwork, Federal Work-Study, institutionally sponsored loans, health care benefits, tuition waivers (full), and stipends also available. *Faculty research:* Stem cells, cancer, neurobiology, organogenesis, genetics of model organisms. *Unit head:* Dr. Hugo Bellen, Director, 713-798-6410. *Application contact:* Catherine Tasnier, Graduate Program Administrator, 713-798-6410, Fax: 713-798-5386, E-mail: cat@bcm.edu.

See Display on page 282 and Close-Up on page 307.

Baylor College of Medicine, Graduate School of Biomedical Sciences, Program in Translational Biology and Molecular Medicine, Houston, TX 77030-3498. Offers PhD. *Faculty:* 173 full-time (54 women). *Students:* 58 full-time (28 women); includes 6 Black or African American, non-Hispanic/Latino; 6 Hispanic/Latino, 16 international. Average age 27. 88 applicants, 32% accepted, 13 enrolled. In 2010, 1 doctorate awarded. *Degree requirements:* For doctorate, thesis/dissertation, public defense. *Entrance requirements:* For doctorate, GRE, minimum GPA of 3.0. Additional exam requirements/recommendations for international students: Required—TOEFL. *Application deadline:* For fall admission, 1/1 for domestic students. Application fee: $0. Electronic applications accepted. *Expenses:* Tuition: Full-time $11,000. Required fees: $4900. *Financial support:* In 2010–11, 58 students received support, including 24 fellowships with full tuition reimbursements available (averaging $26,000 per year), 34 research assistantships with full tuition reimbursements available (averaging $26,000 per year); career-related internships or fieldwork, Federal Work-Study, health care benefits, and students receive a scholarship unless there are grant funds available to pay tuition also available. Financial award applicants required to submit FAFSA. *Faculty research:* Molecular medicine, translational biology, human disease biology and therapy. *Unit head:* Dr. Mary Estes, Director, 713-798-3585, Fax: 713-798-3586, E-mail: tbmm@bcm.edu. *Application contact:* Wanda Waguespack, Graduate Program Administrator, 713-798-1077, Fax: 713-798-3586, E-mail: wandaw@bcm.edu.

See Display on page 250 and Close-Up on page 253.

Brandeis University, Graduate School of Arts and Sciences, Program in Molecular and Cell Biology, Waltham, MA 02454-9110. Offers genetics (PhD); microbiology (PhD); molecular and cell biology (MS, PhD); molecular biology (PhD); neurobiology (PhD). *Faculty:* 30 full-time (13 women), 1 (woman) part-time/adjunct. *Students:* 55 full-time (31 women); includes 1 Black or African American, non-Hispanic/Latino; 1 American Indian or Alaska Native, non-Hispanic/Latino; 1 Asian, non-Hispanic/Latino; 2 Hispanic/Latino, 12 international. 138 applicants, 32% accepted, 17 enrolled. In 2010, 3 master's, 3 doctorates awarded. Terminal master's awarded for partial completion of doctoral program. *Degree requirements:* For master's, thesis optional, research project; for doctorate, comprehensive exam, thesis/dissertation, teaching assistant experience. *Entrance requirements:* For master's and doctorate, GRE General Test, official transcript(s), resume, 3 letters of recommendation, statement of purpose. Additional exam requirements/recommendations for international students: Required—TOEFL (minimum score 600 paper-based; 250 computer-based; 100 iBT); Recommended—IELTS (minimum score 7). *Application deadline:* For fall admission, 1/15 priority date for domestic students. Applications are processed on a rolling basis. Application fee: $75. Electronic applications accepted. *Financial support:* In 2010–11, 41 students received support, including 13 fellowships with full tuition reimbursements available (averaging $27,500 per year), 27 research assistantships with full tuition reimbursements available (averaging $27,500 per year), 1 teaching assistantship with partial tuition reimbursement available (averaging $3,200 per year); scholarships/grants, traineeships, health care benefits, and tuition waivers (full and partial) also available. Financial award application deadline: 4/15; financial award applicants required to submit FAFSA. *Faculty research:* Molecular biology, cell biology, biology, structural biology, immunology, developmental biology, neurobiology, DNA, RNA. *Unit head:* Dr. Piali Sengupta, Chair, 781-736-2686, Fax: 781-736-3107, E-mail: piali@brandeis.edu. *Application contact:* Marcia Cabral, Department Administrator, 781-736-3100, Fax: 781-736-3107, E-mail: cabral@brandeis.edu.

California Institute of Technology, Division of Biology, Program in Genetics, Pasadena, CA 91125-0001. Offers PhD. *Degree requirements:* For doctorate, thesis/dissertation, qualifying exam. *Entrance requirements:* For doctorate, GRE General Test.

Carnegie Mellon University, Mellon College of Science, Department of Biological Sciences, Pittsburgh, PA 15213-3891. Offers biochemistry (PhD); biophysics (PhD); cell biology (PhD); computational biology (MS, PhD); developmental biology (PhD); genetics (PhD); molecular biology (PhD); neuroscience (PhD). *Degree requirements:* For doctorate, comprehensive exam, thesis/dissertation. *Entrance requirements:* For doctorate, GRE General Test, GRE Subject Test, interview. Electronic applications accepted. *Faculty research:* Genetic structure, function, and regulation; protein structure and function; biological membranes; biological spectroscopy.

Case Western Reserve University, School of Medicine and School of Graduate Studies, Graduate Programs in Medicine, Department of Genetics, Program in Human, Molecular, and Developmental Genetics and Genomics, Cleveland, OH 44106. Offers PhD, MD/PhD. *Degree requirements:* For doctorate, comprehensive exam, thesis/dissertation. *Entrance requirements:* For doctorate, GRE General Test, GRE Subject Test. Additional exam requirements/recommendations for international students: Required—TOEFL. *Faculty research:* Regulation of gene expression, molecular control of development, genomics.

Clemson University, Graduate School, College of Agriculture, Forestry and Life Sciences, Department of Genetics and Biochemistry, Program in Genetics, Clemson, SC 29634. Offers PhD. *Students:* 19 full-time (12 women), 1 (woman) part-time, 5 international. Average age 30. 22 applicants, 18% accepted, 3 enrolled. In 2010, 5 doctorates awarded. *Degree requirements:* For doctorate, thesis/dissertation. *Entrance requirements:* For doctorate, GRE General Test, minimum GPA of 3.2. Additional exam requirements/recommendations for international students: Required—TOEFL, IELTS. *Application deadline:* For fall admission, 1/1 for domestic students; for spring admission, 9/1 for domestic students. Applications are processed on a rolling basis. Application fee: $70 ($80 for international students). Electronic applications accepted. *Expenses:* Contact institution. *Financial support:* In 2010–11, 19 students received support, including 5 fellowships with full and partial tuition reimbursements available (averaging $11,900 per year), 14 research assistantships with partial tuition reimbursements available (averaging $13,865 per year), 14 teaching assistantships with partial tuition reimbursements available (averaging $11,855 per year). Financial award application deadline: 3/15; financial award applicants required to submit FAFSA. *Faculty research:* Animal, plant, microbial, molecular, and biometrical genetics. *Unit head:* Dr. Keith Murphy, Chair, 864-656-6237, E-mail: kmurph2@clemson.edu. *Application contact:* Sheryl Banks, Administrative Coordinator, 866-656-6878, E-mail: sherylb@clemson.edu.

Clemson University, Graduate School, College of Health, Education, and Human Development, School of Nursing, Clemson, SC 29634. Offers healthcare genetics (PhD); nursing (MS). *Accreditation:* AACN. Part-time programs available. Postbaccalaureate distance learning degree programs offered. *Faculty:* 15 full-time (14 women). *Students:* 42 full-time (all women), 48 part-time (40 women); includes 8 Black or African American, non-Hispanic/Latino; 2 Hispanic/Latino, 3 international. Average age 35. 90 applicants, 72% accepted, 54 enrolled. In 2010, 30 master's awarded. *Degree requirements:* For master's, thesis or alternative; for doctorate, comprehensive exam, thesis/dissertation. *Entrance requirements:* For master's, GRE General Test, RN license; for doctorate, GRE General Test. Additional exam requirements/recommendations for international students: Required—TOEFL. *Application deadline:* For fall admission, 4/1 for domestic students; for spring admission, 10/1 for domestic students. Applications are processed on a rolling basis. Application fee: $70 ($80 for international students). Electronic applications accepted. *Expenses:* Contact institution. *Financial support:* In 2010–11, 26 students received support, including 2 research assistantships with partial tuition reimbursements available (averaging $5,600 per year), 22 teaching assistantships with partial tuition reimbursements available (averaging $5,922 per year); fellowships with full and partial tuition reimbursements available, career-related internships or fieldwork, institutionally sponsored loans, scholarships/grants, health care benefits, and unspecified assistantships also available. Support available to part-time students. Financial award applicants required to submit FAFSA. *Faculty research:* Risk behaviors and chronic risk-taking in early adolescents, stress in older caregivers, home care of elderly, cancer awareness, pain. Total annual research expenditures: $174,787. *Unit head:* Dr. Rosanne Pruitt, Director, 864-656-7622, Fax: 864-656-5488, E-mail: prosan@clemson.edu. *Application contact:* Dr. Margaret Ann Wetsel, Graduate Studies Coordinator, 864-656-5527, Fax: 864-656-5488, E-mail: mwetsel@clemson.edu.

Columbia University, College of Physicians and Surgeons, Department of Genetics and Development, New York, NY 10032. Offers genetics (M Phil, MA, PhD); MD/PhD. Only candidates for the PhD are admitted. Terminal master's awarded for partial completion of doctoral program. *Degree requirements:* For doctorate, thesis/dissertation. *Entrance requirements:* For master's and doctorate, GRE General Test. Additional exam requirements/recommendations for international students: Required—TOEFL. *Faculty research:* Mammalian cell differentiation and meiosis, developmental genetics, yeast and human genetics, chromosome structure, molecular and cellular biology.

Columbia University, College of Physicians and Surgeons, Integrated Program in Cellular, Molecular, Structural and Genetic Studies, New York, NY 10032. Offers PhD. Terminal master's awarded for partial completion of doctoral program. *Degree requirements:* For doctorate, thesis/dissertation. *Entrance requirements:* For doctorate, GRE General Test, GRE Subject Test. Additional exam requirements/recommendations for international students: Required—TOEFL. *Expenses:* Contact institution. *Faculty research:* Transcription, macromolecular sorting, gene expression during development, cellular interaction.

Cornell University, Graduate School, Graduate Fields of Agriculture and Life Sciences, Field of Genetics and Development, Ithaca, NY 14853-0001. Offers developmental biology (PhD); genetics (PhD). *Faculty:* 54 full-time (12 women). *Students:* 58 full-time (36 women); includes 1 Black or African American, non-Hispanic/Latino; 2 Asian, non-Hispanic/Latino; 2 Hispanic/Latino, 24 international. Average age 25. 90 applicants, 12% accepted, 11 enrolled. In 2010, 10 doctorates awarded. *Degree requirements:* For doctorate, comprehensive exam, thesis/dissertation, 2 semesters of teaching experience. *Entrance requirements:* For doctorate, GRE General Test, GRE Subject Test in biology or biochemistry (recommended), 2 letters of recommendation. Additional exam requirements/recommendations for international students: Required—TOEFL (minimum score 550 paper-based; 213 computer-based; 77 iBT). *Application deadline:* For fall admission, 1/5 for domestic students. Application fee: $70. Electronic applications accepted. *Expenses:* Tuition: Full-time $29,500. Required fees: $76. Tuition and fees vary according to degree level and program. *Financial support:* In 2010–11, 16 fellowships with full tuition reimbursements, 28 research assistantships with full tuition reimbursements, 13 teaching assistantships with full tuition reimbursements were awarded; institutionally sponsored loans, scholarships/grants, health care benefits, tuition waivers (full and partial), and unspecified assistantships also available. Financial award applicants required to submit FAFSA. *Faculty research:* Molecular and general genetics, developmental biology and developmental genetics, evolution and population genetics, plant genetics, microbial genetics. *Unit head:* Director of Graduate Studies, 607-254-2100. *Application contact:* Graduate Field Assistant, 607-254-2100, E-mail: gendev@cornell.edu.

Dartmouth College, Graduate Program in Molecular and Cellular Biology, Department of Genetics, Hanover, NH 03755. Offers PhD, MD/PhD. *Entrance requirements:* For doctorate, GRE General Test, letters of recommendation. Additional exam requirements/recommendations for international students: Required—TOEFL (minimum score 450 paper-based; 90 iBT) or IELTS (minimum score 7). Electronic applications accepted.

Drexel University, College of Medicine, Biomedical Graduate Programs, Interdisciplinary Program in Molecular and Cell Biology and Genetics, Philadelphia, PA 19104-2875. Offers MS, PhD, MD/PhD. Terminal master's awarded for partial completion of doctoral program. *Degree requirements:* For master's, comprehensive exam, thesis; for doctorate, thesis/dissertation, qualifying exam. *Entrance requirements:* For master's, GRE General Test, minimum GPA of 2.75; for doctorate, GRE General Test, minimum GPA of 3.0. Additional exam requirements/recommendations for international students: Required—TOEFL. Electronic applications accepted. *Faculty research:* Molecular anatomy, biochemistry, medical biotechnology, molecular pathology, microbiology and immunology.

Duke University, Graduate School, Department of Biochemistry, Durham, NC 27710. Offers crystallography of macromolecules (PhD); enzyme mechanisms (PhD); lipid biochemistry

(PhD); membrane structure and function (PhD); molecular genetics (PhD); neurochemistry (PhD); nucleic acid structure and function (PhD); protein structure and function (PhD). *Faculty:* 28 full-time. *Students:* 75 full-time (31 women); includes 4 Black or African American, non-Hispanic/Latino; 2 Asian, non-Hispanic/Latino, 26 international. 102 applicants, 25% accepted, 15 enrolled. In 2010, 11 doctorates awarded. *Degree requirements:* For doctorate, thesis/dissertation. *Entrance requirements:* For doctorate, GRE General Test, GRE Subject Test (recommended). Additional exam requirements/recommendations for international students: Required—TOEFL (minimum score 550 paper-based; 213 computer-based; 83 iBT), IELTS (minimum score 7). *Application deadline:* For fall admission, 12/8 priority date for domestic and international students. Application fee: $75. Electronic applications accepted. *Financial support:* Fellowships, research assistantships, teaching assistantships, Federal Work-Study available. Financial award application deadline: 12/8. *Unit head:* Leonard Spicer, Director of Graduate Studies, 919-681-8770, Fax: 919-684-8885, E-mail: anorfleet@biochem.duke.edu. *Application contact:* Elizabeth Hutton, Director of Admissions, 919-684-3913, Fax: 919-684-2277, E-mail: grad-admissions@duke.edu.

Duke University, Graduate School, Program in Genetics and Genomics, Durham, NC 27710. Offers PhD. *Faculty:* 115 full-time. *Students:* 85 full-time (57 women); includes 5 Black or African American, non-Hispanic/Latino; 5 Asian, non-Hispanic/Latino; 1 Hispanic/Latino, 13 international. 97 applicants, 25% accepted, 5 enrolled. In 2010, 11 doctorates awarded. *Degree requirements:* For doctorate, variable foreign language requirement, thesis/dissertation. *Entrance requirements:* For doctorate, GRE General Test. Additional exam requirements/recommendations for international students: Required—TOEFL (minimum score 550 paper-based; 213 computer-based; 83 iBT), IELTS (minimum score 7). *Application deadline:* For fall admission, 12/8 priority date for domestic and international students. Application fee: $75. *Financial support:* Fellowships available. Financial award application deadline: 12/8. *Unit head:* Dr. Michael Hauser, Director of Graduate Studies, 919-684-6629, Fax: 919-684-8346, E-mail: genetics@biochem.duke.edu. *Application contact:* Elizabeth Hutton, Director of Admissions, 919-684-3913, Fax: 919-684-2277, E-mail: grad-admissions@duke.edu.

Emory University, Laney Graduate School, Division of Biological and Biomedical Sciences, Program in Genetics and Molecular Biology, Atlanta, GA 30322-1100. Offers PhD. *Faculty:* 47 full-time (8 women). *Students:* 56 full-time (35 women); includes 5 Black or African American, non-Hispanic/Latino; 1 Hispanic/Latino, 13 international. Average age 27. 144 applicants, 11% accepted, 10 enrolled. In 2010, 10 doctorates awarded. *Degree requirements:* For doctorate, comprehensive exam, thesis/dissertation. *Entrance requirements:* For doctorate, GRE General Test, minimum GPA of 3.0 in science course work (recommended). Additional exam requirements/recommendations for international students: Required—TOEFL. *Application deadline:* For fall admission, 12/1 for domestic and international students. Application fee: $75. Electronic applications accepted. *Expenses:* Tuition: Full-time $33,800. Required fees: $1300. *Financial support:* In 2010–11, 16 students received support, including 16 fellowships with full tuition reimbursements available (averaging $25,000 per year); institutionally sponsored loans, scholarships/grants, health care benefits, and tuition waivers (full) also available. *Faculty research:* Gene regulation, genetic combination, developmental regulation. *Unit head:* Dr. Andreas Fritz, Director, 404-727-9012, Fax: 404-727-2880, E-mail: afritz@biology.emory.edu. *Application contact:* Kathy Smith, Director of Recruitment and Admissions, 404-727-2547, Fax: 404-727-3322, E-mail: kathy.smith@emory.edu.

Florida State University, The Graduate School, College of Arts and Sciences, Department of Biological Science, Specialization in Cell and Molecular Biology and Genetics, Tallahassee, FL 32306-4295. Offers MS, PhD. *Faculty:* 27 full-time (7 women). *Students:* 46 full-time (21 women); includes 2 Black or African American, non-Hispanic/Latino; 6 Hispanic/Latino, 10 international. 162 applicants, 10% accepted, 8 enrolled. In 2010, 3 master's, 3 doctorates awarded. Terminal master's awarded for partial completion of doctoral program. *Degree requirements:* For master's, comprehensive exam, thesis, teaching experience, seminar presentation; for doctorate, comprehensive exam, thesis/dissertation, teaching experience; seminar presentation. *Entrance requirements:* For master's, GRE General Test (minimum combined score 1100, 500 verbal, 500 quantitative), minimum upper-division GPA of 3.0; for doctorate, GRE General Test (minimum combined score 1100, Verbal 500, Quantitative 500), minimum upper-division GPA of 3.0. Additional exam requirements/recommendations for international students: Required—TOEFL (minimum score 600 paper-based; 250 computer-based; 92 iBT). *Application deadline:* For fall admission, 12/15 for domestic and international students. Application fee: $30. Electronic applications accepted. *Expenses:* Tuition, state resident: full-time $8238. *Financial support:* In 2010–11, 14 research assistantships with full tuition reimbursements (averaging $21,000 per year), 30 teaching assistantships with full tuition reimbursements (averaging $21,000 per year) were awarded; unspecified assistantships also available. Financial award application deadline: 12/15; financial award applicants required to submit FAFSA. *Faculty research:* Molecular biology; genetics and genomics; developmental biology and gene expression; cell structure, function, and motility; cellular and organismal physiology; biophysical and structural biology. *Application contact:* Judy Bowers, Coordinator, Graduate Affairs, 850-644-3023, Fax: 850-644-9829, E-mail: gradinfo@bio.fsu.edu.

The George Washington University, Columbian College of Arts and Sciences, Institute for Biomedical Sciences, Program in Biochemistry and Molecular Genetics, Washington, DC 20037. Offers PhD. *Students:* 8 part-time (5 women). Average age 30. In 2010, 2 doctorates awarded. Terminal master's awarded for partial completion of doctoral program. *Degree requirements:* For doctorate, thesis/dissertation, general exam. *Entrance requirements:* For doctorate, GRE General Test, interview, minimum GPA of 3.0. Additional exam requirements/recommendations for international students: Required—TOEFL (minimum score 600 paper-based; 250 computer-based). *Application deadline:* For fall admission, 12/15 priority date for domestic and international students; for spring admission, 10/1 priority date for domestic and international students. Applications are processed on a rolling basis. Application fee: $75. Electronic applications accepted. *Financial support:* In 2010–11, 4 students received support; fellowships, Federal Work-Study, institutionally sponsored loans, and tuition waivers available. Financial award application deadline: 2/1. *Unit head:* Valerie W. Hu, Director, 202-994-8431, E-mail: valhu@gwu.edu. *Application contact:* Information Contact, 202-994-7120, Fax: 202-994-6100, E-mail: genetics@gwu.edu.

Harvard University, Graduate School of Arts and Sciences, Division of Medical Sciences, Boston, MA 02115. Offers biological chemistry and molecular pharmacology (PhD); cell biology (PhD); genetics (PhD); microbiology and molecular genetics (PhD); pathology (PhD), including experimental pathology. *Degree requirements:* For doctorate, thesis/dissertation. *Entrance requirements:* For doctorate, GRE General Test, GRE Subject Test. Additional exam requirements/recommendations for international students: Required—TOEFL. *Expenses:* Tuition: Full-time $34,976. Required fees: $1166. Full-time tuition and fees vary according to program.

Harvard University, Harvard School of Public Health, Department of Genetics and Complex Diseases, Boston, MA 02115-6096. Offers PhD. *Faculty:* 9 full-time (3 women). *Degree requirements:* For doctorate, thesis/dissertation, qualifying exam. *Entrance requirements:* For doctorate, GRE. Additional exam requirements/recommendations for international students: Required—TOEFL (minimum score 600 paper-based; 240 computer-based; 100 iBT); Recommended—IELTS (minimum score 7). *Application deadline:* For fall admission, 12/8 for domestic and international students. Application fee: $115. Electronic applications accepted. *Expenses:* Tuition: Full-time $34,976. Required fees: $1166. Full-time tuition and fees vary according to program. *Financial support:* Fellowships, research assistantships, Federal Work-Study, scholarships/grants, traineeships, tuition waivers (partial), and unspecified assistantships available. Financial award application deadline: 2/8; financial award applicants required to submit FAFSA. *Faculty research:* Toxicology, radiation biology. *Unit head:* Dr. Gokhan Hotamisligil, Chair, 617-432-0054, Fax: 617-432-5236, E-mail: ghotamis@hsph.harvard.edu. *Application contact:* Vincent W. James, Director of Admissions, 617-432-1031, Fax: 617-432-7080, E-mail: admissions@hsph.harvard.edu.

Illinois State University, Graduate School, College of Arts and Sciences, Department of Biological Sciences, Normal, IL 61790-2200. Offers animal behavior (MS); bacteriology (MS); biochemistry (MS); biological sciences (MS); biology (PhD); biophysics (MS); biotechnology (MS); botany (MS, PhD); cell biology (MS); conservation biology (MS); developmental biology (MS); ecology (MS, PhD); entomology (MS); evolutionary biology (MS); genetics (MS, PhD); immunology (MS); microbiology (MS, PhD); molecular biology (MS); molecular genetics (MS); neurobiology (MS); neuroscience (MS); parasitology (MS); physiology (MS, PhD); plant biology (MS); plant molecular biology (MS); plant sciences (MS); structural biology (MS); zoology (MS, PhD). Part-time programs available. *Degree requirements:* For master's, thesis or alternative; for doctorate, variable foreign language requirement, thesis/dissertation, 2 terms of residency. *Entrance requirements:* For master's, GRE General Test, minimum GPA of 2.6 in last 60 hours of course work; for doctorate, GRE General Test. *Faculty research:* Redoc balance and drug development in schistosoma mansoni, control of the growth of listeria monocytogenes at low temperature, regulation of cell expansion and microtubule function by SPRI, CRUI: physiology and fitness consequences of different life history phenotypes.

Indiana University Bloomington, University Graduate School, College of Arts and Sciences, Department of Biology, Bloomington, IN 47405. Offers biology teaching (MAT); biotechnology (MA); evolution, ecology, and behavior (MA, PhD); genetics (PhD); microbiology (MA, PhD); molecular, cellular, and developmental biology (PhD); plant sciences (MA, PhD); zoology (MA, PhD). *Faculty:* 58 full-time (15 women), 21 part-time/adjunct (6 women). *Students:* 163 full-time (98 women), 7 part-time (2 women); includes 17 minority (3 Black or African American, non-Hispanic/Latino; 1 American Indian or Alaska Native, non-Hispanic/Latino; 7 Asian, non-Hispanic/Latino; 5 Hispanic/Latino; 1 Native Hawaiian or other Pacific Islander, non-Hispanic/Latino), 52 international. Average age 27. 346 applicants, 15% accepted, 24 enrolled. In 2010, 17 master's, 24 doctorates awarded. Terminal master's awarded for partial completion of doctoral program. *Degree requirements:* For master's, thesis, oral defense; for doctorate, thesis/dissertation, oral defense. *Entrance requirements:* For master's and doctorate, GRE General Test. Additional exam requirements/recommendations for international students: Required—TOEFL (minimum score 100 iBT). *Application deadline:* For fall admission, 1/5 priority date for domestic students, 12/1 priority date for international students. Application fee: $55 ($65 for international students). Electronic applications accepted. *Financial support:* In 2010–11, 170 students received support, including 64 fellowships with tuition reimbursements available (averaging $19,484 per year), 44 research assistantships with tuition reimbursements available (averaging $20,300 per year), 62 teaching assistantships with tuition reimbursements available (averaging $20,521 per year); scholarships/grants, traineeships, health care benefits, and unspecified assistantships also available. Financial award application deadline: 1/5. *Faculty research:* Evolution, ecology and behavior; microbiology; molecular biology and genetics; plant biology. *Unit head:* Dr. Roger Innes, Chair, 812-855-2219, Fax: 812-855-6082, E-mail: rinnes@indiana.edu. *Application contact:* Tracey D. Stohr, Graduate Student Recruitment Coordinator, 812-856-6303, Fax: 812-855-6082, E-mail: gradbio@indiana.edu.

Iowa State University of Science and Technology, Graduate College, College of Liberal Arts and Sciences and College of Agriculture, Department of Genetics, Developmental and Cell Biology, Ames, IA 50011. Offers MS, PhD. *Faculty:* 43 full-time (8 women), 4 part-time/adjunct (2 women). *Students:* 52 full-time (25 women), 5 part-time (2 women); includes 1 Black or African American, non-Hispanic/Latino, 42 international. 1 applicant, 100% accepted, 1 enrolled. *Degree requirements:* For master's, thesis; for doctorate, thesis/dissertation. *Entrance requirements:* Additional exam requirements/recommendations for international students: Required—TOEFL (minimum score 570 paper-based), IELTS (minimum score 6.5). Application fee: $40 ($90 for international students). *Financial support:* In 2010–11, 42 research assistantships with full and partial tuition reimbursements (averaging $18,008 per year), 9 teaching assistantships with full and partial tuition reimbursements (averaging $9,115 per year) were awarded; fellowships with full tuition reimbursements, scholarships/grants, health care benefits, and unspecified assistantships also available. Financial award application deadline: 2/1. *Faculty research:* Animal behavior, animal models of gene therapy, cell biology, comparative physiology, developmental biology. *Unit head:* Dr. Martin Spalding, Chair, 515-294-1749. *Application contact:* Information Contact, 515-294-5836, Fax: 515-294-2592, E-mail: grad_admissions@iastate.edu.

Iowa State University of Science and Technology, Graduate College, Interdisciplinary Programs, Bioinformatics and Computational Biology Program, Ames, IA 50011. Offers MS, PhD. *Students:* 54 full-time (22 women), 34 international. In 2010, 1 master's, 5 doctorates awarded. *Degree requirements:* For doctorate, thesis/dissertation. *Entrance requirements:* For master's and doctorate, GRE General Test. Additional exam requirements/recommendations for international students: Recommended—IELTS. *Application deadline:* For fall admission, 1/15 priority date for domestic students, 1/15 for international students; for spring admission, 10/15 for domestic and international students. Application fee: $40 ($90 for international students). Electronic applications accepted. *Financial support:* In 2010–11, 47 research assistantships with full and partial tuition reimbursements (averaging $22,000 per year), 3 teaching assistantships (averaging $20,000 per year) were awarded; fellowships with full tuition reimbursements, scholarships/grants, traineeships, health care benefits, and unspecified assistantships also available. *Faculty research:* Functional and structural genomics, genome evolution, macromolecular structure and function, mathematical biology and biological statistics, metabolic and developmental networks. *Unit head:* Dr. Julie Dickerson, Chair, Supervising Committee, 515-294-5122, Fax: 515-294-6790, E-mail: bcb@iastate.edu. *Application contact:* Dr. Julie Dickerson, Chair, Supervising Committee, 515-294-5122, Fax: 515-294-6790, E-mail: bcb@iastate.edu.

Iowa State University of Science and Technology, Graduate College, Interdisciplinary Programs, Program in Genetics, Ames, IA 50011. Offers MS, PhD. *Students:* 89 full-time (49 women), 13 part-time (11 women); includes 4 Black or African American, non-Hispanic/Latino; 1 American Indian or Alaska Native, non-Hispanic/Latino; 3 Hispanic/Latino, 58 international. In 2010, 4 master's, 16 doctorates awarded. Terminal master's awarded for partial completion of doctoral program. *Degree requirements:* For master's, thesis; for doctorate, thesis/dissertation. *Entrance requirements:* For master's and doctorate, GRE General Test. Additional exam requirements/recommendations for international students: Required—TOEFL (minimum score 550 paper-based; 79 iBT), IELTS (minimum score 6.5). *Application deadline:* For fall admission, 2/1 priority date for domestic and international students; for spring admission, 9/1 priority date for domestic and international students. Applications are processed on a rolling basis. Application fee: $40 ($90 for international students). *Financial support:* In 2010–11, 78 research assistantships with full and partial tuition reimbursements (averaging $18,612 per year), 11 teaching assistantships with full and partial tuition reimbursements (averaging $11,494 per year) were awarded; fellowships, scholarships/grants, health care benefits, and unspecified assistantships also available. *Unit head:* Dr. Phil Becraft, Supervisory Committee Chair, 515-294-7697, Fax: 515-294-6669, E-mail: genetics@iastate.edu. *Application contact:* Linda Wild, Program Coordinator, 800-499-1972, Fax: 515-294-6669, E-mail: genetics@iastate.edu.

The Johns Hopkins University, Bloomberg School of Public Health, Department of Epidemiology, Baltimore, MD 21205. Offers cancer epidemiology (MHS, Sc M, PhD, Sc D); cardiovascular disease epidemiology (MHS, Sc M, PhD, Sc D); clinical epidemiology (MHS, Sc M, PhD, Sc D); clinical trials (PhD, Sc D); epidemiology (Dr PH); epidemiology (general) (MHS, Sc M, PhD, Sc D); epidemiology of aging (MHS, Sc M, PhD, Sc D); human genetics/genetic epidemiology (MHS, Sc M, PhD, Sc D); infectious disease epidemiology (MHS, Sc M, PhD, Sc D); occupational/environmental epidemiology (MHS, Sc M, PhD, Sc D). Part-time programs available. *Faculty:* 80 full-time (44 women), 82 part-time/adjunct (36 women). *Students:* 143 full-time (108 women), 24 part-time (17 women); includes 43 minority (14 Black or African American, non-Hispanic/Latino; 1 American Indian or Alaska Native, non-Hispanic/Latino; 19 Asian, non-Hispanic/Latino; 3 Hispanic/Latino; 6 Two or more races, non-Hispanic/Latino), 36 international. Average age 30. 263 applicants, 41% accepted, 52 enrolled. In 2010, 30 master's, 33 doctorates awarded. *Degree requirements:* For master's, comprehensive exam, thesis, 1 year full-time residency; for doctorate, comprehensive exam, thesis/dissertation, 2 years full-time residency, oral and written exams, student teaching. *Entrance requirements:* For master's, GRE General Test or MCAT, 3 letters of recommendation, curriculum vitae; for doctorate, GRE General Test, minimum 1 year of work experience, 3 letters of recommendation, curriculum vitae, academic records from all schools. Additional exam requirements/recommendations for international students: Required—TOEFL (minimum score 600 paper-based; 250 computer-

Genetics

The Johns Hopkins University (continued)

based; 100 iBT); Recommended—IELTS (minimum score 7.5), TWE. *Application deadline:* For fall admission, 12/1 priority date for domestic students. Applications are processed on a rolling basis. Application fee: $45. Electronic applications accepted. *Financial support:* In 2010–11, 2 fellowships (averaging $28,859 per year) were awarded; Federal Work-Study, institutionally sponsored loans, scholarships/grants, traineeships, tuition waivers (partial), and stipends also available. Support available to part-time students. Financial award application deadline: 3/15; financial award applicants required to submit FAFSA. *Faculty research:* Cancer and congenital malformations, nutritional epidemiology, AIDS, tuberculosis, cardiovascular disease, risk assessment. Total annual research expenditures: $70.1 million. *Unit head:* Dr. David D. Celentano, Chair, 410-955-3286, Fax: 410-955-0863, E-mail: dcelenta@jhsph.edu. *Application contact:* Frances S. Burman, Academic Program Manager, 410-955-3926, Fax: 410-955-0863, E-mail: fburman@jhsph.edu.

The Johns Hopkins University, National Institutes of Health Sponsored Programs, Baltimore, MD 21218-2699. Offers biology (PhD), including biochemistry, biophysics, cell biology, developmental biology, genetic biology, molecular biology; cell, molecular, and developmental biology and biophysics (PhD). *Degree requirements:* For doctorate, comprehensive exam, thesis/dissertation. *Entrance requirements:* For doctorate, GRE General Test. Additional exam requirements/recommendations for international students: Required—TOEFL (minimum score 600 paper-based; 250 computer-based), TWE. Electronic applications accepted. *Faculty research:* Protein and nucleic acid biochemistry and biophysical chemistry, molecular biology and development.

Kansas State University, Graduate School, College of Agriculture, Department of Plant Pathology, Manhattan, KS 66506. Offers genetics (MS, PhD); plant pathology (MS, PhD). Terminal master's awarded for partial completion of doctoral program. *Degree requirements:* For master's, thesis, oral exam; for doctorate, thesis/dissertation, preliminary exams. *Entrance requirements:* For master's and doctorate, minimum undergraduate GPA of 3.0. Additional exam requirements/recommendations for international students: Required—TOEFL (minimum score 550 paper-based; 213 computer-based). Electronic applications accepted. *Faculty research:* Applied microbiology, microbial genetics, microbial ecology/epidemiology, integrated pest management, plant genetics/genomics/molecular biology.

Marquette University, Graduate School, College of Arts and Sciences, Department of Biology, Milwaukee, WI 53201-1881. Offers cell biology (MS, PhD); developmental biology (MS, PhD); ecology (MS, PhD); epithelial physiology (MS, PhD); genetics (MS, PhD); microbiology (MS, PhD); molecular biology (MS, PhD); muscle and exercise physiology (MS, PhD); neuroscience (PhD). *Faculty:* 25 full-time (12 women), 2 part-time/adjunct (1 woman). *Students:* 23 full-time (9 women), 12 part-time (8 women); includes 1 minority (Asian, non-Hispanic/Latino), 15 international. Average age 26. 82 applicants, 15% accepted, 5 enrolled. In 2010, 3 master's, 2 doctorates awarded. Terminal master's awarded for partial completion of doctoral program. *Degree requirements:* For master's, comprehensive exam, thesis, 1 year of teaching experience or equivalent; for doctorate, thesis/dissertation, 1 year of teaching experience or equivalent, qualifying exam. *Entrance requirements:* For master's and doctorate, GRE General Test, GRE Subject Test, official transcripts from all current and previous colleges/universities except Marquette, statement of professional goals and aspirations, three letters of recommendation. Additional exam requirements/recommendations for international students: Required—TOEFL (minimum score 530 paper-based; 78 computer-based). *Application deadline:* For fall admission, 12/15 for domestic and international students. Application fee: $50. Electronic applications accepted. *Expenses:* Tuition: Full-time $16,290; part-time $905 per credit hour. Tuition and fees vary according to program. *Financial support:* In 2010–11, 2 research assistantships, 34 teaching assistantships were awarded; fellowships, Federal Work-Study, institutionally sponsored loans, scholarships/grants, and tuition waivers (full and partial) also available. Support available to part-time students. Financial award application deadline: 2/15. *Faculty research:* Neurobiology, neuroendocrinology, epithelial physiology, neuropeptide interactions, synaptic transmission. Total annual research expenditures: $1.3 million. *Unit head:* Dr. Robert Fitts, Chair, 414-288-1748, Fax: 414-288-7357. *Application contact:* Debbie Weaver, Administrative Assistant, 414-288-7355, Fax: 414-288-7357.

Massachusetts Institute of Technology, School of Science, Department of Biology, Cambridge, MA 02139-4307. Offers biochemistry (PhD); biological oceanography (PhD); biology (PhD); biophysical chemistry and molecular structure (PhD); cell biology (PhD); computational and systems biology (PhD); developmental biology (PhD); genetics (PhD); immunology (PhD); microbiology (PhD); molecular biology (PhD); neurobiology (PhD). *Faculty:* 56 full-time (14 women). *Students:* 251 full-time (135 women); includes 74 minority (4 Black or African American, non-Hispanic/Latino; 1 American Indian or Alaska Native, non-Hispanic/Latino; 29 Asian, non-Hispanic/Latino; 33 Hispanic/Latino; 7 Two or more races, non-Hispanic/Latino), 29 international. Average age 26. 652 applicants, 18% accepted, 58 enrolled. In 2010, 41 doctorates awarded. *Degree requirements:* For doctorate, comprehensive exam, thesis/dissertation. *Entrance requirements:* For doctorate, GRE General Test. Additional exam requirements/recommendations for international students: Required—TOEFL (minimum score 577 paper-based; 233 computer-based), IELTS (minimum score 6.5). *Application deadline:* For fall admission, 12/1 for domestic and international students. Application fee: $75. Electronic applications accepted. *Expenses:* Tuition: Full-time $38,940; part-time $605 per unit. Required fees: $272. *Financial support:* In 2010–11, 215 students received support, including 115 fellowships with tuition reimbursements available (averaging $33,090 per year), 132 research assistantships with tuition reimbursements available (averaging $31,846 per year); teaching assistantships with tuition reimbursements available, Federal Work-Study, institutionally sponsored loans, scholarships/grants, health care benefits, and unspecified assistantships also available. *Faculty research:* DNA recombination, replication and repair; transcription and gene regulation; signal transduction; cell cycle; neuronal cell fate. Total annual research expenditures: $60.6 million. *Unit head:* Prof. Chris Kaiser, Head, 617-253-4701, E-mail: mitbio@mit.edu. *Application contact:* Biology Education Office, 617-253-3717, Fax: 617-258-9329, E-mail: gradbio@mit.edu.

Mayo Graduate School, Graduate Programs in Biomedical Sciences, Program in Virology and Gene Therapy, Rochester, MN 55905. Offers PhD.

Mayo Graduate School, Graduate Programs in Biomedical Sciences, Programs in Biochemistry, Structural Biology, Cell Biology, and Genetics, Rochester, MN 55905. Offers biochemistry and structural biology (PhD); cell biology and genetics (PhD); molecular biology (PhD). *Degree requirements:* For doctorate, oral defense of dissertation, qualifying oral and written exam. *Entrance requirements:* For doctorate, GRE, 1 year of chemistry, biology, calculus, and physics. Additional exam requirements/recommendations for international students: Required—TOEFL. Electronic applications accepted. *Faculty research:* Gene structure and function, membranes and receptors/cytoskeleton, oncogenes and growth factors, protein structure and function, steroid hormonal action.

McMaster University, Faculty of Health Sciences and School of Graduate Studies, Program in Medical Sciences, Genetics and Cancer Area, Hamilton, ON L8S 4M2, Canada. Offers M Sc, PhD, MD/PhD. *Degree requirements:* For master's, thesis; for doctorate, comprehensive exam, thesis/dissertation. *Entrance requirements:* For master's, honors B Sc, B+ average in related field; for doctorate, M Sc, minimum B+ average, students with proven research experience and an A average may be admitted with a B Sc degree. Additional exam requirements/recommendations for international students: Required—TOEFL (minimum score 580 paper-based; 237 computer-based; 92 iBT).

Medical University of South Carolina, College of Graduate Studies, Program in Molecular and Cellular Biology and Pathobiology, Charleston, SC 29425. Offers cancer biology (PhD); cardiovascular biology (PhD); cardiovascular imaging (PhD); cell regulation (PhD); craniofacial biology (PhD); genetics and development (PhD); marine biomedicine (PhD); DMD/PhD; MD/PhD. *Faculty:* 137 full-time (33 women). *Students:* 27 full-time (20 women); includes 3 Black or African American, non-Hispanic/Latino; 1 Hispanic/Latino, 6 international. Average age 30. In 2010, 16 doctorates awarded. *Degree requirements:* For doctorate, thesis/dissertation, oral and written exams. *Entrance requirements:* For doctorate, GRE General Test, interview, minimum GPA of 3.0. Additional exam requirements/recommendations for international students: Required—TOEFL (minimum score 600 paper-based; 250 computer-based; 100 iBT). *Application deadline:* For fall admission, 1/15 priority date for domestic and international students. Applications are processed on a rolling basis. Application fee: $0 ($85 for international students). Electronic applications accepted. *Financial support:* In 2010–11, 39 research assistantships with partial tuition reimbursements (averaging $23,000 per year) were awarded; Federal Work-Study and scholarships/grants also available. Support available to part-time students. Financial award application deadline: 3/10; financial award applicants required to submit FAFSA. *Unit head:* Dr. Donald R. Menick, Director, 843-876-5045, Fax: 843-792-6590, E-mail: menickd@musc.edu. *Application contact:* Dr. Cynthia F. Wright, Associate Dean for Admissions and Career Development, 843-792-2564, Fax: 843-792-6590, E-mail: wrightcf@musc.edu.

Michigan State University, College of Veterinary Medicine and The Graduate School, Graduate Programs in Veterinary Medicine and College of Natural Science and Graduate Programs in Human Medicine, Department of Microbiology and Molecular Genetics, East Lansing, MI 48824. Offers industrial microbiology (MS, PhD); microbiology (MS, PhD); microbiology and molecular genetics (MS, PhD); microbiology–environmental toxicology (PhD). *Entrance requirements:* For master's, GRE General Test. Additional exam requirements/recommendations for international students: Required—TOEFL (minimum score 550 paper-based; 213 computer-based), Michigan State University ELT (minimum score 85), Michigan English Language Assessment Battery (minimum score 83). Electronic applications accepted.

Michigan State University, The Graduate School, College of Agriculture and Natural Resources, MSU-DOE Plant Research Laboratory, East Lansing, MI 48824. Offers biochemistry and molecular biology (PhD); cellular and molecular biology (PhD); crop and soil sciences (PhD); genetics (PhD); microbiology and molecular genetics (PhD); plant biology (PhD); plant physiology (PhD). Offered jointly with the Department of Energy. *Degree requirements:* For doctorate, comprehensive exam, thesis/dissertation, laboratory rotation, defense of dissertation. *Entrance requirements:* For doctorate, GRE General Test, acceptance into one of the affiliated department programs; 3 letters of recommendation; bachelor's degree or equivalent in life sciences, chemistry, biochemistry, or biophysics; research experience. Electronic applications accepted. *Faculty research:* Role of hormones in the regulation of plant development and physiology, molecular mechanisms associated with signal recognition, development and application of genetic methods and materials, protein routing and function.

Michigan State University, The Graduate School, College of Natural Science, Program in Genetics, East Lansing, MI 48824. Offers genetics (MS, PhD); genetics–environmental toxicology (PhD). *Entrance requirements:* Additional exam requirements/recommendations for international students: Required—TOEFL. Electronic applications accepted.

Mississippi State University, College of Agriculture and Life Sciences, Department of Animal Dairy Sciences, Mississippi State, MS 39762. Offers agricultural life sciences (MS), including animal physiology (MS, PhD), genetics (MS, PhD); agricultural science (PhD), including animal dairy sciences, animal nutrition (MS, PhD); agriculture (MS), including animal dairy science, animal nutrition (MS, PhD); life sciences (PhD), including animal physiology (MS, PhD), genetics (MS, PhD). *Faculty:* 12 full-time (5 women). *Students:* 24 full-time (12 women), 11 part-time (6 women); includes 4 minority (2 Black or African American, non-Hispanic/Latino; 2 Hispanic/Latino), 6 international. Average age 29. 22 applicants, 55% accepted, 7 enrolled. In 2010, 6 master's, 1 doctorate awarded. *Degree requirements:* For master's, thesis, comprehensive oral or written exam; for doctorate, thesis/dissertation, comprehensive oral or written exam. *Entrance requirements:* For master's, GRE General Test, minimum GPA of 3.0; for doctorate, GRE General Test. Additional exam requirements/recommendations for international students: Required—TOEFL (minimum score 575 paper-based). *Application deadline:* For fall admission, 7/1 for domestic students, 5/1 for international students; for spring admission, 11/1 for domestic students, 9/1 for international students. Applications are processed on a rolling basis. Application fee: $40. Electronic applications accepted. *Expenses:* Tuition, state resident: full-time $2731; part-time $304 per credit hour. Tuition, nonresident: full-time $6901; part-time $767 per credit hour. *Financial support:* In 2010–11, 16 research assistantships (averaging $12,464 per year), 2 teaching assistantships (averaging $10,324 per year) were awarded; Federal Work-Study, institutionally sponsored loans, and unspecified assistantships also available. Financial award application deadline: 4/1; financial award applicants required to submit FAFSA. *Faculty research:* Ecology and population dynamics, physiology, biochemistry and behavior, systematics. *Unit head:* Dr. Terry Kiser, Professor and Department Head, 662-325-2802, Fax: 662-325-8873, E-mail: tkiser@ads.msstate.edu. *Application contact:* Dr. Peter Ryan, Graduate Coordinator, 662-325-2802, Fax: 662-325-8873, E-mail: ryan@cvm.msstate.edu.

New York University, Graduate School of Arts and Science, Department of Biology, New York, NY 10012-1019. Offers biology (PhD); biomedical journalism (MS); cancer and molecular biology (PhD); computational biology (PhD); computers in biological research (MS); developmental genetics (PhD); general biology (MS); immunology and microbiology (PhD); molecular genetics (PhD); neurobiology (PhD); oral biology (MS); plant biology (PhD); recombinant DNA technology (MS); MS/MBA. Part-time programs available. *Faculty:* 24 full-time (5 women). *Students:* 155 full-time (89 women), 38 part-time (24 women); includes 29 Asian, non-Hispanic/Latino; 7 Hispanic/Latino, 88 international. Average age 27. 324 applicants, 69% accepted, 63 enrolled. In 2010, 55 master's, 4 doctorates awarded. Terminal master's awarded for partial completion of doctoral program. *Degree requirements:* For master's, thesis or alternative, qualifying paper; for doctorate, comprehensive exam, thesis/dissertation. *Entrance requirements:* For master's, GRE General Test; for doctorate, GRE General Test, GRE Subject Test. Additional exam requirements/recommendations for international students: Required—TOEFL. *Application deadline:* For fall admission, 12/15 priority date for domestic students. Application fee: $90. *Financial support:* Fellowships with tuition reimbursements, research assistantships with tuition reimbursements, teaching assistantships with tuition reimbursements, career-related internships or fieldwork, Federal Work-Study, institutionally sponsored loans, scholarships/grants, health care benefits, and unspecified assistantships available. Financial award application deadline: 12/15; financial award applicants required to submit FAFSA. *Faculty research:* Genomics, molecular and cell biology, development and molecular genetics, molecular evolution of plants and animals. *Unit head:* Gloria Coruzzi, Chair, 212-998-8200, Fax: 212-995-4015, E-mail: biology@nyu.edu. *Application contact:* Justin Blau, Director of Graduate Studies, 212-998-8200, Fax: 212-995-4015, E-mail: biology@nyu.edu.

North Carolina State University, Graduate School, College of Agriculture and Life Sciences, Department of Genetics, Raleigh, NC 27695. Offers MG, MS, PhD. Terminal master's awarded for partial completion of doctoral program. *Degree requirements:* For master's, thesis (for some programs); for doctorate, thesis/dissertation. *Entrance requirements:* For master's and doctorate, GRE General Test, minimum GPA of 3.0. Electronic applications accepted. *Faculty research:* Population and quantitative genetics, plant molecular genetics, developmental genetics.

Northwestern University, The Graduate School, Interdepartmental Biological Sciences Program (IBiS), Evanston, IL 60208. Offers biochemistry, molecular biology, and cell biology (PhD), including biochemistry, cell and molecular biology, molecular biophysics, structural biology; biotechnology (PhD); cell and molecular biology (PhD); developmental biology and genetics (PhD); hormone action and signal transduction (PhD); neuroscience (PhD); structural biology, biochemistry, and biophysics (PhD). Program participants include the Departments of Biochemistry, Molecular Biology, and Cell Biology; Chemistry; Neurobiology and Physiology; Chemical Engineering; Civil Engineering; and Evanston Hospital. *Degree requirements:* For doctorate, thesis/dissertation, qualifying exam. *Entrance requirements:* For doctorate, GRE General Test. Additional exam requirements/recommendations for international students: Required—TOEFL (minimum score 600 paper-based). Electronic applications accepted. *Faculty research:* Developmental genetics, gene regulation, DNA-protein interactions, biological clocks, bioremediation.

Northwestern University, Northwestern University Feinberg School of Medicine and Interdepartmental Programs, Integrated Graduate Programs in the Life Sciences, Chicago, IL 60611. Offers cancer biology (PhD); cell biology (PhD); developmental biology (PhD); evolutionary biology (PhD); immunology and microbial pathogenesis (PhD); molecular biology and genetics (PhD); neurobiology (PhD); pharmacology and toxicology (PhD); structural biology and biochemistry (PhD). *Degree requirements:* For doctorate, comprehensive exam, thesis/dissertation, written and oral qualifying exams. *Entrance requirements:* For doctorate, GRE General Test. Additional exam requirements/recommendations for international students: Required—TOEFL (minimum score 600 paper-based; 250 computer-based). Electronic applications accepted.

The Ohio State University, College of Medicine, School of Biomedical Science, Integrated Biomedical Science Graduate Program, Columbus, OH 43210. Offers immunology (PhD); medical genetics (PhD); molecular virology (PhD); pharmacology (PhD). *Degree requirements:* For doctorate, thesis/dissertation. *Entrance requirements:* For doctorate, GRE, GRE Subject Test in biochemistry, cell and molecular biology (recommended for some). Additional exam requirements/recommendations for international students: Required—TOEFL (minimum score 600 paper-based; 250 computer-based). Electronic applications accepted. *Expenses:* Tuition, state resident: full-time $10,605. Tuition, nonresident: full-time $26,535. Tuition and fees vary according to course load and program.

The Ohio State University, Graduate School, College of Arts and Sciences, Division of Natural and Mathematical Sciences, Department of Molecular Genetics, Columbus, OH 43210. Offers cell and developmental biology (MS, PhD); genetics (MS, PhD); molecular biology (MS, PhD). *Faculty:* 26. *Students:* 7 full-time (3 women), 25 part-time (14 women), 16 international. Average age 27. In 2010, 1 master's, 1 doctorate awarded. *Degree requirements:* For master's, thesis; for doctorate, thesis/dissertation. *Entrance requirements:* For master's and doctorate, GRE General Test, GRE Subject Test in biology or biochemistry (recommended). Additional exam requirements/recommendations for international students: Required—TOEFL (minimum score 600 paper-based; 250 computer-based). *Application deadline:* For fall admission, 8/15 priority date for domestic students, 7/1 priority date for international students; for winter admission, 12/1 priority date for domestic students, 11/1 priority date for international students; for spring admission, 3/1 priority date for domestic students, 2/1 priority date for international students. Applications are processed on a rolling basis. Application fee: $40 ($50 for international students). Electronic applications accepted. *Expenses:* Tuition, state resident: full-time $10,605. Tuition, nonresident: full-time $26,535. Tuition and fees vary according to course load and program. *Financial support:* Fellowships, research assistantships, teaching assistantships, Federal Work-Study and institutionally sponsored loans available. Support available to part-time students. *Unit head:* Dr. Anna Hopper, Chair, 614-688-3306, Fax: 614-247-2594, E-mail: hopper.64@osu.edu. *Application contact:* 614-292-9444, Fax: 614-292-3895, E-mail: domestic.grad@osu.edu.

Oregon Health & Science University, School of Medicine, Graduate Programs in Medicine, Program in Molecular and Cellular Biosciences, Department of Molecular and Medical Genetics, Portland, OR 97239-3098. Offers PhD. *Faculty:* 11 full-time (7 women), 3 part-time/adjunct (2 women). *Students:* 10 full-time (5 women), 2 international. Average age 30. In 2010, 6 doctorates awarded. Terminal master's awarded for partial completion of doctoral program. *Degree requirements:* For doctorate, comprehensive exam, thesis/dissertation. *Entrance requirements:* For doctorate, GRE General Test (minimum scores: 500 Verbal/600 Quantitative/4.5 Analytical) or MCAT (for some programs). Additional exam requirements/recommendations for international students: Required—TOEFL. Electronic applications accepted. *Financial support:* Health care benefits and full tuition and stipends available. *Faculty research:* Molecular studies of metabolic diseases, gene therapy, control of mycogenesis, regulation of gene expression, DNA replication and repair. *Unit head:* Dr. Susan Olson, Program Director, 503-494-7703, E-mail: olsonsu@oshsu.edu. *Application contact:* Anne Huntzicker, Program Coordinator, 503-494-1771, E-mail: utter@ohsu.edu.

Oregon State University, Graduate School, College of Agricultural Sciences, Program in Genetics, Corvallis, OR 97331. Offers MA, MAIS, MS, PhD. Part-time programs available. Terminal master's awarded for partial completion of doctoral program. *Degree requirements:* For master's, variable foreign language requirement, thesis or alternative; for doctorate, thesis/dissertation. *Entrance requirements:* For master's and doctorate, GRE General Test, minimum GPA of 3.0 in last 90 hours. Additional exam requirements/recommendations for international students: Required—TOEFL. *Faculty research:* Molecular genetics, cytogenetics, population and quantitative genetics, microbial genetics, plant genetics.

Penn State Hershey Medical Center, College of Medicine, Graduate School Programs in the Biomedical Sciences, Graduate Program in Microbiology and Immunology, Hershey, PA 17033. Offers genetics (PhD); immunology (MS, PhD); microbiology (MS); microbiology/virology (PhD); molecular biology (PhD); MD/PhD. *Students:* 12 applicants, 75% accepted, 3 enrolled. In 2010, 1 doctorate awarded. Terminal master's awarded for partial completion of doctoral program. *Degree requirements:* For master's, thesis or alternative; for doctorate, comprehensive exam, thesis/dissertation, oral exam. *Entrance requirements:* For doctorate, GRE General Test, minimum GPA of 3.0. Additional exam requirements/recommendations for international students: Required—TOEFL. *Application deadline:* For fall admission, 1/31 priority date for domestic students, 2/1 priority date for international students. Applications are processed on a rolling basis. Application fee: $45. Electronic applications accepted. *Financial support:* In 2010–11, research assistantships with full tuition reimbursements (averaging $22,260 per year); fellowships with full tuition reimbursements, scholarships/grants, health care benefits, and unspecified assistantships also available. Financial award applicants required to submit FAFSA. *Faculty research:* Virus replication and assembly, oncogenesis, interactions of viruses with host cells and animal model systems. *Unit head:* Dr. Richard J. Courtney, Chair, 717-531-7659, Fax: 717-531-6522, E-mail: micro-grad-hmc@psu.edu. *Application contact:* Billie Burns, Secretary, 717-531-7659, Fax: 717-531-6522, E-mail: micro-grad-hmc@psu.edu.

Penn State Hershey Medical Center, College of Medicine, Graduate School Programs in the Biomedical Sciences, The Huck Institutes of the Life Sciences, Intercollege Graduate Program in Genetics, Hershey, PA 17033. Offers MS, PhD, MD/PhD. *Students:* 173 applicants, 4% accepted, 2 enrolled. In 2010, 4 doctorates awarded. Terminal master's awarded for partial completion of doctoral program. *Degree requirements:* For master's, thesis or alternative; for doctorate, comprehensive exam, thesis/dissertation, oral exam. *Entrance requirements:* For master's, GRE General Test; for doctorate, GRE General Test, minimum GPA of 3.0. Additional exam requirements/recommendations for international students: Required—TOEFL (minimum score 500 paper-based; 213 computer-based). *Application deadline:* For fall admission, 1/31 priority date for domestic students, 2/1 priority date for international students. Applications are processed on a rolling basis. Application fee: $65. Electronic applications accepted. *Financial support:* In 2010–11, research assistantships with full tuition reimbursements (averaging $22,260 per year); fellowships with full tuition reimbursements, scholarships/grants, health care benefits, and unspecified assistantships also available. Financial award applicants required to submit FAFSA. *Faculty research:* Genome structure/stability, gene expression, cellular sorting of macromolecules, signal transduction, stem cell differentiation. *Unit head:* Dr. Ralph Keil, Co-Director, 717-531-8982, E-mail: grad-hmc@psu.edu. *Application contact:* Kathy Shuey, Administrative Assistant, 717-531-8982, Fax: 717-531-0786, E-mail: grad-hmc@psu.edu.

Penn State University Park, Graduate School, Intercollege Graduate Programs, Intercollege Graduate Program in Genetics, State College, University Park, PA 16802-1503. Offers MS, PhD. *Unit head:* Dr. Richard Ordway, Chair, 814-863-5693, Fax: 814-865-9131, E-mail: rordway@psu.edu. *Application contact:* Cynthia E. Nicosia, Director, Graduate Enrollment Services, 814-865-1795, Fax: 814-865-4627, E-mail: cey1@psu.edu.

Purdue University, Graduate School, College of Science, Department of Biological Sciences, West Lafayette, IN 47907. Offers biochemistry (PhD); biophysics (PhD); cell and developmental biology (PhD); ecology, evolutionary and population biology (MS, PhD), including ecology, evolutionary biology, population biology; genetics (MS, PhD); microbiology (MS, PhD); molecular

biology (PhD); neurobiology (MS, PhD); plant physiology (PhD). Terminal master's awarded for partial completion of doctoral program. *Degree requirements:* For master's, thesis (for some programs); for doctorate, thesis/dissertation, seminars, teaching experience. *Entrance requirements:* For master's and doctorate, GRE General Test. Additional exam requirements/recommendations for international students: Required—TOEFL. Electronic applications accepted.

Rutgers, The State University of New Jersey, New Brunswick, Graduate School-New Brunswick, Programs in the Molecular Biosciences, Program in Microbiology and Molecular Genetics, Piscataway, NJ 08854-8097. Offers applied microbiology (MS, PhD); clinical microbiology (MS, PhD); computational molecular biology (PhD); immunology (MS, PhD); microbial biochemistry (MS, PhD); molecular genetics (MS, PhD); virology (MS, PhD). MS, PhD offered jointly with University of Medicine and Dentistry of New Jersey. Part-time programs available. Terminal master's awarded for partial completion of doctoral program. *Degree requirements:* For master's, comprehensive exam, thesis or alternative; for doctorate, comprehensive exam, thesis/dissertation, written qualifying exam. *Entrance requirements:* For master's, GRE General Test, minimum GPA of 3.0; for doctorate, GRE General Test, GRE Subject Test (recommended), minimum GPA of 3.0. Additional exam requirements/recommendations for international students: Required—TOEFL. Electronic applications accepted. *Expenses:* Tuition, state resident: full-time $7200; part-time $600 per credit. Tuition, nonresident: full-time $11,124; part-time $927 per credit. *Faculty research:* Molecular genetics and microbial physiology; virology and pathogenic microbiology; applied, environmental and industrial microbiology; computers in molecular biology.

Stanford University, School of Medicine, Graduate Programs in Medicine, Department of Genetics, Stanford, CA 94305-9991. Offers PhD. *Degree requirements:* For doctorate, thesis/dissertation, qualifying examination. *Entrance requirements:* For doctorate, GRE General Test, GRE Subject Test. Additional exam requirements/recommendations for international students: Required—TOEFL. Electronic applications accepted. *Expenses:* Tuition: Full-time $38,700; part-time $860 per unit. One-time fee: $200 full-time. *Faculty research:* Molecular biology of DNA replication in human cells, analysis of existing and search for new DNA polymorphisms in humans, molecular genetics of prokaryotic and eukaryotic genetic elements, proteins in DNA replication.

Stony Brook University, State University of New York, Graduate School, College of Arts and Sciences, Graduate Program in Genetics, Stony Brook, NY 11794. Offers PhD. *Faculty:* 20 full-time (4 women). *Students:* 47 full-time (24 women); includes 2 Black or African American, non-Hispanic/Latino; 1 Asian, non-Hispanic/Latino; 6 Hispanic/Latino, 12 international. Average age 27. 127 applicants, 13% accepted, 12 enrolled. In 2010, 11 doctorates awarded. *Degree requirements:* For doctorate, comprehensive exam, thesis/dissertation, teaching experience. *Entrance requirements:* For doctorate, GRE General Test, GRE Subject Test. Additional exam requirements/recommendations for international students: Required—TOEFL. *Application deadline:* For fall admission, 1/15 for domestic students. Application fee: $100. *Expenses:* Tuition, state resident: full-time $8370; part-time $349 per credit. Tuition, nonresident: full-time $13,780; part-time $574 per credit. Required fees: $994. *Financial support:* In 2010–11, 17 research assistantships, 12 teaching assistantships were awarded; fellowships, Federal Work-Study also available. *Faculty research:* Gene structure, gene regulation. *Application contact:* Dr. Kent Marks, Assistant Dean, Admissions and Records, 631-632-4723, Fax: 631-632-7243, E-mail: kmarks@notes.cc.sunysb.edu.

Temple University, Health Sciences Center, School of Medicine and Graduate School, Doctor of Medicine Program, Program in Molecular Biology and Genetics, Philadelphia, PA 19122-6096. Offers MS, PhD, MD/PhD. *Students:* 22 full-time (13 women); includes 1 Black or African American, non-Hispanic/Latino; 1 Asian, non-Hispanic/Latino, 11 international. 35 applicants, 26% accepted, 4 enrolled. In 2010, 1 master's, 2 doctorates awarded. *Degree requirements:* For doctorate, thesis/dissertation, presentation research/literature seminars distinct from area of concentration. *Entrance requirements:* For doctorate, GRE General Test, GRE Subject Test, minimum GPA of 3.0. Additional exam requirements/recommendations for international students: Required—TOEFL (minimum score 620 paper-based; 260 computer-based). *Application deadline:* For fall admission, 1/15 for domestic students, 12/15 for international students. Application fee: $50. Electronic applications accepted. *Financial support:* Fellowships, research assistantships, Federal Work-Study, institutionally sponsored loans, and tuition waivers (full) available. Financial award application deadline: 1/15; financial award applicants required to submit FAFSA. *Faculty research:* Molecular genetics of normal and malignant cell growth, regulation of gene expression, DNA repair systems and carcinogenesis, hormone-receptor interactions and signal transduction systems, structural biology. *Unit head:* Dr. Scott Shore, Chair, 215-707-3359, Fax: 215-707-2805, E-mail: sks@temple.edu. *Application contact:* Dr. Scott Shore, Chair, 215-707-3359, Fax: 215-707-2805, E-mail: sks@temple.edu.

Texas A&M University, College of Veterinary Medicine and Biomedical Sciences, Department of Veterinary Pathobiology, College Station, TX 77843. Offers genetics (MS, PhD); veterinary microbiology (MS, PhD); veterinary parasitology (MS, PhD); veterinary pathology (MS, PhD). Part-time programs available. Postbaccalaureate distance learning degree programs offered. *Faculty:* 26. *Students:* 25 full-time (17 women), 18 part-time (14 women); includes 1 Black or African American, non-Hispanic/Latino; 3 Asian, non-Hispanic/Latino; 2 Hispanic/Latino, 10 international. Average age 33. In 2010, 1 master's, 5 doctorates awarded. Terminal master's awarded for partial completion of doctoral program. *Degree requirements:* For master's, thesis, seminars; for doctorate, thesis/dissertation, seminars. *Entrance requirements:* For master's and doctorate, GRE General Test, minimum GPA of 3.0 in last 60 hours. Additional exam requirements/recommendations for international students: Required—TOEFL. *Application deadline:* For fall admission, 3/1 priority date for domestic students; for spring admission, 8/1 priority date for domestic students. Applications are processed on a rolling basis. Application fee: $50 ($75 for international students). Electronic applications accepted. *Financial support:* In 2010–11, fellowships with partial tuition reimbursements (averaging $16,000 per year), research assistantships with partial tuition reimbursements (averaging $15,400 per year), teaching assistantships with partial tuition reimbursements (averaging $16,000 per year) were awarded; Federal Work-Study, institutionally sponsored loans, scholarships/grants, traineeships, health care benefits, and unspecified assistantships also available. Support available to part-time students. Financial award applicants required to submit FAFSA. *Faculty research:* Infectious and noninfectious diseases of animals and birds, animal genetics, molecular biology, immunology, virology. *Unit head:* Dr. Linda Logan, Head, 979-862-6559, Fax: 979-845-9231, E-mail: llogan@cvm.tamu.edu. *Application contact:* Dr. Patricia Holman, Graduate Advisor, 979-845-4202, Fax: 979-862-1147, E-mail: pholman@cvm.tamu.edu.

Thomas Jefferson University, Jefferson College of Graduate Studies, Graduate Program in Genetics, Philadelphia, PA 19107. Offers PhD. *Faculty:* 37 full-time (11 women), 2 part-time/adjunct (both women). *Students:* 24 full-time (14 women); includes 3 minority (all Black or African American, non-Hispanic/Latino), 5 international. 22 applicants, 23% accepted, 3 enrolled. In 2010, 3 doctorates awarded. *Degree requirements:* For doctorate, comprehensive exam, thesis/dissertation. *Entrance requirements:* For doctorate, GRE General Test, minimum GPA of 3.2. Additional exam requirements/recommendations for international students: Required—TOEFL (minimum score 250 computer-based; 100 iBT) or IELTS. *Application deadline:* For fall admission, 1/5 priority date for domestic and international students. Applications are processed on a rolling basis. Application fee: $50. Electronic applications accepted. *Financial support:* In 2010–11, 24 students received support, including 24 fellowships with full tuition reimbursements available (averaging $54,723 per year); Federal Work-Study, institutionally sponsored loans, scholarships/grants, traineeships, and stipends also available. Support available to part-time students. Financial award application deadline: 5/1; financial award applicants required to submit FAFSA. *Faculty research:* Functional genomics, cancer susceptibility, cell cycle, regulation oncogenes and tumor suppressor genes, genetics of neoplastic disease. Total annual research expenditures: $37.9 million. *Unit head:* Dr. Linda D. Siracusa, Program Director, 215-503-4536, E-mail: linda.siracusa@jefferson.edu. *Application contact:* Marc E. Stearns, Director of Admissions, 215-503-0155, Fax: 215-503-9920, E-mail: jcgs-info@jefferson.edu.

Genetics

Tufts University, Sackler School of Graduate Biomedical Sciences, Graduate Program in Genetics, Medford, MA 02155. Offers PhD. *Faculty:* 47 full-time (17 women). *Students:* 29 full-time (20 women); includes 1 Black or African American, non-Hispanic/Latino; 3 Asian, non-Hispanic/Latino; 1 Hispanic/Latino, 6 international. Average age 28. 77 applicants, 10% accepted, 3 enrolled. In 2010, 3 doctorates awarded. Terminal master's awarded for partial completion of doctoral program. *Degree requirements:* For doctorate, thesis/dissertation, qualifying exam. *Entrance requirements:* For doctorate, GRE General Test, 3 letters of reference. Additional exam requirements/recommendations for international students: Required—TOEFL. *Application deadline:* For fall admission, 12/15 for domestic and international students. Applications are processed on a rolling basis. Application fee: $70. Electronic applications accepted. *Expenses:* Tuition: Full-time $39,624; part-time $3962 per course. Required fees: $40 per year. Full-time tuition and fees vary according to degree level, program and student level. Part-time tuition and fees vary according to course load. *Financial support:* In 2010–11, 29 students received support, including 29 research assistantships with full tuition reimbursements available (averaging $28,250 per year); scholarships/grants and health care benefits also available. *Faculty research:* Cancer, human and developmental genetics. *Unit head:* Dr. Erik Selsing, Program Director, 617-636-0467, E-mail: erik.selsing@tufts.edu. *Application contact:* Kellie Johnston, Associate Director of Admissions, 617-636-6767, Fax: 617-636-0375.

Université de Montréal, Faculty of Medicine, Program in Medical Genetics, Montréal, QC H3C 3J7, Canada. Offers DESS.

Université du Québec à Chicoutimi, Graduate Programs, Program in Experimental Medicine, Chicoutimi, QC G7H 2B1, Canada. Offers genetics (M Sc). *Degree requirements:* For master's, thesis. *Entrance requirements:* For master's, appropriate bachelor's degree, proficiency in French.

University at Albany, State University of New York, School of Public Health, Department of Biomedical Sciences, Program in Biochemistry, Molecular Biology, and Genetics, Albany, NY 12222-0001. Offers MS, PhD. *Degree requirements:* For master's, thesis; for doctorate, thesis/dissertation. *Entrance requirements:* For master's and doctorate, GRE General Test, GRE Subject Test.

The University of Alabama at Birmingham, Graduate Programs in Joint Health Sciences, Program in Genetics, Birmingham, AL 35294. Offers PhD. *Students:* 20 full-time (10 women), 1 (woman) part-time, 8 international. Average age 27. In 2010, 3 doctorates awarded. *Degree requirements:* For doctorate, thesis/dissertation. *Entrance requirements:* For doctorate, GRE, interview. *Application deadline:* Applications are processed on a rolling basis. Application fee: $35 ($60 for international students). Electronic applications accepted. *Expenses:* Tuition, state resident: full-time $5482. Tuition, nonresident: full-time $12,430. Tuition and fees vary according to program. *Financial support:* In 2010–11, 2 fellowships were awarded. *Faculty research:* Clinical cytogenetics, cancer cytogenetics, prenatal diagnosis. *Unit head:* Dr. Bruce R. Korf, Chair, 205-934-9411. *Application contact:* Julie Bryant, Director of Graduate Admissions, 205-934-8227, Fax: 205-934-8413, E-mail: jbryant@uab.edu.

University of Alberta, Faculty of Graduate Studies and Research, Department of Biological Sciences, Edmonton, AB T6G 2E1, Canada. Offers environmental biology and ecology (M Sc, PhD); microbiology and biotechnology (M Sc, PhD); molecular biology and genetics (M Sc, PhD); physiology and cell biology (M Sc, PhD); plant biology (M Sc, PhD); systematics and evolution (M Sc, PhD). Terminal master's awarded for partial completion of doctoral program. *Degree requirements:* For master's, thesis; for doctorate, thesis/dissertation. *Entrance requirements:* Additional exam requirements/recommendations for international students: Required—TOEFL.

University of Alberta, Faculty of Medicine and Dentistry and Faculty of Graduate Studies and Research, Graduate Programs in Medicine, Department of Medical Genetics, Edmonton, AB T6G 2E1, Canada. Offers M Sc, PhD. *Degree requirements:* For master's, comprehensive exam, thesis; for doctorate, comprehensive exam, thesis/dissertation. *Entrance requirements:* For master's and doctorate, minimum GPA of 3.2. *Faculty research:* Clinical and molecular cytogenetics, ocular genetics, Prader-Willi syndrome, genomic instability, developmental genetics.

The University of Arizona, Graduate Interdisciplinary Programs, Graduate Interdisciplinary Program in Genetics, Tucson, AZ 85719. Offers MS, PhD. *Students:* 15 full-time (8 women); includes 2 Two or more races, non-Hispanic/Latino, 2 international. Average age 29. 15 applicants, 13% accepted, 1 enrolled. In 2010, 1 doctorate awarded. Terminal master's awarded for partial completion of doctoral program. *Degree requirements:* For master's, thesis; for doctorate, one foreign language, comprehensive exam, thesis/dissertation. *Entrance requirements:* For master's, GRE General Test, 3 letters of recommendation; for doctorate, GRE General Test, statement of purpose, 3 letters of recommendation. Additional exam requirements/recommendations for international students: Required—TOEFL (minimum score 550 paper-based; 213 computer-based; 79 iBT). *Application deadline:* For fall admission, 6/1 for domestic students, 12/1 for international students. Applications are processed on a rolling basis. Application fee: $65. Electronic applications accepted. *Expenses:* Tuition, state resident: full-time $7692. *Financial support:* Career-related internships or fieldwork, scholarships/grants, health care benefits, and unspecified assistantships available. *Faculty research:* Cancer research; DNA repair; plant and animal cytogenetics; molecular, population, and ecological genetics. *Unit head:* Dr. Murray Brilliant, Chairman, 520-626-3305, Fax: 520-626-5097, E-mail: mhb@peds.arizona.edu. *Application contact:* Lori Taylor, Program Coordinator, 520-626-9821, Fax: 520-626-5097, E-mail: lltaylor@arizona.edu.

The University of British Columbia, Faculty of Medicine, Department of Medical Genetics, Medical Genetics Graduate Program, Vancouver, BC V6T 1Z1, Canada. Offers M Sc, PhD. *Students:* 62 full-time (43 women), 1 part-time (0 women). In 2010, 9 master's, 9 doctorates awarded. *Degree requirements:* For master's, thesis, 18 credits of coursework; for doctorate, comprehensive exam, thesis/dissertation, 18 credits of coursework. *Application deadline:* For fall admission, 3/1 for domestic students, 2/1 for international students; for winter admission, 7/1 for domestic students, 6/1 for international students. Electronic applications accepted. Tuition charges are reported in Canadian dollars. *Expenses:* Tuition, area resident: Full-time $4179 Canadian dollars. International tuition: $7344 Canadian dollars full-time. *Unit head:* Dr. Carolyn Brown, Head, Department of Medical Genetics, 604-822-5312. *Application contact:* Cheryl Bishop, Graduate Program Assistant, 604-822-5312, Fax: 604-822-5348, E-mail: medgen@interchange.ubc.ca.

The University of British Columbia, Genetics Graduate Program, Vancouver, BC V6T 1Z1, Canada. Offers M Sc, PhD. *Degree requirements:* For master's, comprehensive exam, thesis, thesis defense; for doctorate, comprehensive exam, thesis/dissertation, qualifying exam, oral and written comprehensive exams. *Entrance requirements:* Additional exam requirements/recommendations for international students: Required—TOEFL (minimum score 600 paper-based; 250 computer-based; 100 iBT). Tuition charges are reported in Canadian dollars. *Expenses:* Tuition, area resident: Full-time $4179 Canadian dollars. International tuition: $7344 Canadian dollars full-time. *Faculty research:* Prokaryote and eukaryote genetics.

University of California, Davis, Graduate Studies, Graduate Group in Genetics, Davis, CA 95616. Offers MS, PhD. Terminal master's awarded for partial completion of doctoral program. *Degree requirements:* For master's, comprehensive exam (for some programs), thesis (for some programs); for doctorate, thesis/dissertation. *Entrance requirements:* For master's and doctorate, GRE General Test, GRE Subject Test. Additional exam requirements/recommendations for international students: Required—TOEFL (minimum score 550 paper-based; 213 computer-based). Electronic applications accepted. *Faculty research:* Molecular, quantitative, and developmental genetics; cytogenetics; plant breeding.

University of California, Irvine, School of Biological Sciences and School of Medicine, Graduate Program in Cellular and Molecular Biosciences, Irvine, CA 92697. Offers PhD. *Degree requirements:* For doctorate, thesis/dissertation, teaching assignment, preliminary exam. *Entrance requirements:* For doctorate, GRE General Test, minimum GPA of 3.0, research experience. Additional exam requirements/recommendations for international students: Required—TOEFL, IELTS, SPEAK test. Electronic applications accepted. *Expenses:* Contact institution. *Faculty research:* Cellular biochemistry; gene structure and expression; protein structure, function, and design; molecular genetics; pathogenesis and inherited disease.

University of California, Riverside, Graduate Division, Graduate Program in Genetics, Genomics, and Bioinformatics, Riverside, CA 92521-0102. Offers genomics and bioinformatics (PhD); molecular genetics (PhD); population and evolutionary genetics (PhD). *Degree requirements:* For doctorate, thesis/dissertation, qualifying exams, teaching experience. *Entrance requirements:* For doctorate, GRE General Test, minimum GPA of 3.2. Additional exam requirements/recommendations for international students: Required—TOEFL (minimum score 550 paper-based; 213 computer-based; 80 iBT). Electronic applications accepted. *Faculty research:* Molecular Genetics, Evolution and Population Genetics, Genomics and Bioinformatics.

University of California, San Diego, Office of Graduate Studies, Division of Biological Sciences, Program in Genetics and Molecular Biology, La Jolla, CA 92093-0348. Offers PhD. Offered in association with the Salk Institute. *Degree requirements:* For doctorate, thesis/dissertation, qualifying exam. Electronic applications accepted.

University of California, San Francisco, Graduate Division and School of Medicine, Department of Biochemistry and Biophysics, Program in Genetics, San Francisco, CA 94143. Offers PhD, MD/PhD. *Degree requirements:* For doctorate, thesis/dissertation. *Entrance requirements:* For doctorate, GRE General Test, GRE Subject Test. Additional exam requirements/recommendations for international students: Required—TOEFL. *Expenses:* Contact institution. *Faculty research:* Gene expression; chromosome structure and mechanics; medical, somatic cell, and radiation genetics.

University of Chicago, Division of Biological Sciences, Molecular Biosciences Cluster, Committee on Genetics, Genomics and Systems Biology, Chicago, IL 60637-1513. Offers PhD. *Degree requirements:* For doctorate, thesis/dissertation, ethics class, 2 teaching assistantships. *Entrance requirements:* For doctorate, GRE General Test, minimum GPA of 3.0. Additional exam requirements/recommendations for international students: Required—TOEFL (minimum score 600 paper-based; 250 computer-based; 104 iBT), IELTS (minimum score 7). Electronic applications accepted. *Faculty research:* Molecular genetics, developmental genetics, population genetics, human genetics.

University of Colorado Boulder, Graduate School, College of Arts and Sciences, Department of Ecology and Evolutionary Biology, Boulder, CO 80309. Offers animal behavior (MA); biology (MA, PhD); environmental biology (MA, PhD); evolutionary biology (MA, PhD); neurobiology (MA); population biology (MA); population genetics (PhD). *Faculty:* 32 full-time (10 women). *Students:* 71 full-time (36 women), 17 part-time (11 women); includes 10 minority (1 American Indian or Alaska Native, non-Hispanic/Latino; 2 Asian, non-Hispanic/Latino; 7 Hispanic/Latino), 4 international. Average age 30. 176 applicants, 20 enrolled. In 2010, 11 master's, 8 doctorates awarded. Terminal master's awarded for partial completion of doctoral program. *Degree requirements:* For master's, comprehensive exam, thesis or alternative; for doctorate, comprehensive exam, thesis/dissertation. *Entrance requirements:* For master's, GRE General Test, GRE Subject Test, minimum undergraduate GPA of 3.0; for doctorate, GRE General Test, GRE Subject Test. *Application deadline:* For fall admission, 12/30 priority date for domestic students, 12/1 for international students. Application fee: $50 ($60 for international students). *Financial support:* In 2010–11, 25 fellowships (averaging $17,876 per year), 27 research assistantships (averaging $15,070 per year) were awarded; Federal Work-Study, institutionally sponsored loans, and tuition waivers (full) also available. *Faculty research:* Behavior, ecology, genetics, morphology, endocrinology, physiology, systematics. Total annual research expenditures: $3.5 million.

University of Colorado Denver, School of Medicine, Program in Medical Genetics and Genetic Counseling, Denver, CO 80217-3364. Offers human medical genetics (PhD). *Students:* 9 full-time (3 women); includes 1 American Indian or Alaska Native, non-Hispanic/Latino. Average age 30. 19 applicants, 11% accepted, 2 enrolled. In 2010, 1 doctorate awarded. *Degree requirements:* For doctorate, comprehensive exam, thesis/dissertation, at least 30 semester hours in course work (rotations and research courses taken prior to the completion of the comprehensive examination) and 30 semester hours of thesis/didactic credits prior to defending. *Entrance requirements:* For doctorate, GRE General Test (minimum combined score of 1205), minimum GPA of 3.0, 4 letters of recommendation; prerequisite courses in biology, chemistry (general and organic), physics, genetics, calculus, and statistics (recommended). Additional exam requirements/recommendations for international students: Required—TOEFL (minimum score 570 paper-based; 230 computer-based; 80 iBT). *Application deadline:* For fall admission, 1/1 for domestic students. Application fee: $50. Electronic applications accepted. *Expenses:* Contact institution. *Financial support:* Fellowships, research assistantships, teaching assistantships, Federal Work-Study available. Financial award application deadline: 3/15; financial award applicants required to submit FAFSA. *Faculty research:* Mapping, discovery, and function of disease genes affecting skin and craniofacial development and autoimmunity; genetics of colon cancer; clinical proteomics; biochemical markers of disease, including cancer; modeling human genetic diseases with patient-derived induced pluripotent stem cells; cell cycle control of DNA replication and mutagenesis in yeast and human cancer cells; mechanisms of cancer chemoprevention. *Unit head:* Dr. Richard A. Spritz, Director, 303-724-3107, E-mail: richard.spritz@ucdenver.edu. *Application contact:* M. J. Stewart, Administrator, 303-724-3102, Fax: 303-724-3100, E-mail: mj.stewart@ucdenver.edu.

University of Connecticut, Graduate School, College of Liberal Arts and Sciences, Department of Molecular and Cell Biology, Field of Genetics, Genomics, and Bioinformatics, Storrs, CT 06269. Offers MS, PhD. Terminal master's awarded for partial completion of doctoral program. *Degree requirements:* For master's, comprehensive exam; for doctorate, thesis/dissertation. *Entrance requirements:* For master's and doctorate, GRE General Test, GRE Subject Test. Additional exam requirements/recommendations for international students: Required—TOEFL (minimum score 550 paper-based; 213 computer-based). Electronic applications accepted.

University of Connecticut Health Center, Graduate School, Programs in Biomedical Sciences, Graduate Program in Molecular Biology and Biochemistry, Farmington, CT 06030. Offers PhD, DMD/PhD, MD/PhD. *Faculty:* 158. *Students:* 18 full-time (10 women); includes 3 minority (1 Black or African American, non-Hispanic/Latino; 2 Asian, non-Hispanic/Latino), 6 international. Average age 28. 216 applicants, 22% accepted. In 2010, 5 doctorates awarded. *Degree requirements:* For doctorate, comprehensive exam, thesis/dissertation. *Entrance requirements:* For doctorate, GRE General Test. Additional exam requirements/recommendations for international students: Required—TOEFL (minimum score 600 paper-based; 250 computer-based). *Application deadline:* For fall admission, 12/15 for domestic students. Application fee: $55. Electronic applications accepted. *Financial support:* In 2010–11, 18 research assistantships with full tuition reimbursements (averaging $27,000 per year) were awarded; health care benefits also available. *Faculty research:* Molecular biology, structural biology, protein biochemistry, microbial physiology and pathogenesis. *Unit head:* Dr. Stephen King, Director, 860-679-3347, Fax: 860-679-1239, E-mail: sking@nso2.uchc.edu. *Application contact:* Tricia Avolt, Graduate Admissions Coordinator, 860-679-2175, Fax: 860-679-1899, E-mail: robertson@nso2.uchc.edu.

See Display on next page and Close-Up on page 231.

University of Connecticut Health Center, Graduate School, Programs in Biomedical Sciences, Program in Genetics and Developmental Biology, Farmington, CT 06030. Offers PhD, DMD/PhD, MD/PhD. *Faculty:* 158. *Students:* 21 full-time (10 women); includes 1 minority (Asian, non-Hispanic/Latino), 7 international. Average age 29. 216 applicants, 22% accepted. In 2010, 4 doctorates awarded. *Degree requirements:* For doctorate, comprehensive exam, thesis/dissertation. *Entrance requirements:* For doctorate, GRE General Test, GRE Subject Test. Additional exam requirements/recommendations for international students: Required—TOEFL (minimum score 600 paper-based; 250 computer-based). *Application deadline:* For fall admission, 12/15 for domestic students. Application fee: $55. Electronic applications accepted. *Financial support:* In 2010–11, 21 research assistantships with full tuition reimbursements (averaging $27,000 per year) were awarded; health care benefits also available. *Faculty research:* Developmental biology, genomic imprinting, RNA biology, RNA alternative splicing, human embryonic stem cells. *Unit head:* Dr. William Mohler, Director, 860-679-7947, E-mail: wmohler@neuron.uchc.edu. *Application contact:* Tricia Avolt, Graduate Admissions Coordinator, 860-679-2175, Fax: 860-679-1899, E-mail: robertson@nso2.uchc.edu.

See Display below and Close-Up on page 309.

University of Delaware, College of Arts and Sciences, Department of Biological Sciences, Newark, DE 19716. Offers biotechnology (MS); cancer biology (MS, PhD); cell and extracellular matrix biology (MS, PhD); cell and systems physiology (MS, PhD); developmental biology (MS, PhD); ecology and evolution (MS, PhD); microbiology (MS, PhD); molecular biology and genetics (MS, PhD). Terminal master's awarded for partial completion of doctoral program. *Degree requirements:* For master's, thesis, preliminary exam; for doctorate, comprehensive exam, thesis/dissertation, preliminary exam. *Entrance requirements:* For master's and doctorate, GRE General Test. Additional exam requirements/recommendations for international students: Required—TOEFL (minimum score 600 paper-based; 250 computer-based); Recommended—TWE. Electronic applications accepted. *Faculty research:* Microorganisms, bone, cancer metastasis, developmental biology, cell biology, DNA.

University of Florida, College of Medicine and Graduate School, Interdisciplinary Program in Biomedical Sciences, Concentration in Genetics, Gainesville, FL 32611. Offers PhD. *Degree requirements:* For doctorate, thesis/dissertation. *Entrance requirements:* For doctorate, GRE General Test, minimum GPA of 3.0. Additional exam requirements/recommendations for international students: Required—TOEFL. Electronic applications accepted. *Expenses:* Tuition, state resident: full-time $10,916. Tuition, nonresident: full-time $28,309.

University of Georgia, College of Agricultural and Environmental Sciences, Institute of Plant Breeding, Genetics and Genomics, Athens, GA 30602. Offers MS, PhD. *Students:* 22 full-time (7 women), 5 part-time (1 woman), 12 international. 17 applicants, 24% accepted, 3 enrolled. In 2010, 3 master's awarded. *Expenses:* Tuition, state resident: full-time $7200; part-time $344 per credit hour. Tuition, nonresident: full-time $21,900; part-time $944 per credit hour. Tuition and fees vary according to course load and program. *Financial support:* Tuition waivers and unspecified assistantships available. *Unit head:* Dr. E. Charles Brummer, Director, 706-542-8847, Fax: 706-583-8120, E-mail: pbgg@uga.edu. *Application contact:* Dr. Dayton Wilde, Graduate Coordinator, 706-542-5607, E-mail: pbgg@uga.edu.

University of Georgia, College of Arts and Sciences, Department of Genetics, Athens, GA 30602. Offers MS, PhD. *Faculty:* 17 full-time (5 women). *Students:* 54 full-time (42 women); includes 1 Black or African American, non-Hispanic/Latino; 2 Hispanic/Latino, 9 international. 70 applicants, 30% accepted, 13 enrolled. In 2010, 1 master's, 3 doctorates awarded. Terminal master's awarded for partial completion of doctoral program. *Degree requirements:* For master's, thesis; for doctorate, comprehensive exam, thesis/dissertation. *Entrance requirements:* For master's and doctorate, GRE General Test. Additional exam requirements/recommendations for international students: Required—TOEFL. *Application deadline:* For fall admission, 1/1 priority date for domestic and international students; for spring admission, 11/15 for domestic students. Application fee: $50. Electronic applications accepted. *Expenses:* Tuition, state resident: full-time $7200; part-time $344 per credit hour. Tuition, nonresident: full-time $21,900; part-time $944 per credit hour. Tuition and fees vary according to course load and program. *Financial support:* In 2010–11, fellowships with full tuition reimbursements (averaging $19,000 per year), research assistantships with full tuition reimbursements (averaging $19,000 per year), teaching assistantships with full tuition reimbursements (averaging $19,000 per year) were awarded; scholarships/grants and unspecified assistantships also available. *Unit head:* Dr. Jeffrey L. Bennetzen, Head, 706-542-3698, E-mail: maize@uga.edu. *Application contact:*

Dr. R. Kelly Dawe, Director of Graduate Studies, 706-542-0288, Fax: 706-542-3910, E-mail: gencoord@uga.edu.

University of Hawaii at Manoa, John A. Burns School of Medicine, Department of Cell and Molecular Biology, Honolulu, HI 96813. Offers MS, PhD. Part-time programs available. *Faculty:* 55 full-time (16 women), 5 part-time/adjunct (1 woman). *Students:* 38 full-time (20 women), 2 part-time (1 woman); includes 16 minority (8 Asian, non-Hispanic/Latino; 2 Hispanic/Latino; 1 Native Hawaiian or other Pacific Islander, non-Hispanic/Latino; 5 Two or more races, non-Hispanic/Latino), 4 international. Average age 31. 63 applicants, 35% accepted, 12 enrolled. In 2010, 5 doctorates awarded. Terminal master's awarded for partial completion of doctoral program. *Degree requirements:* For master's, thesis optional; for doctorate, comprehensive exam, thesis/dissertation. *Entrance requirements:* For master's and doctorate, GRE General Test, minimum GPA of 3.0. Additional exam requirements for international students: Required—TOEFL (minimum score 500 paper-based; 173 computer-based; 61 iBT), IELTS (minimum score 5). *Application deadline:* For fall admission, 1/15 for domestic and international students. Applications are processed on a rolling basis. Application fee: $60. *Financial support:* In 2010–11, 19 fellowships (averaging $824 per year), 36 research assistantships (averaging $20,351 per year), 1 teaching assistantship (averaging $16,824 per year) were awarded; Federal Work-Study and institutionally sponsored loans also available. Financial award application deadline: 2/1. Total annual research expenditures: $2.7 million. *Application contact:* Marla Berry, Graduate Co-Chair, 808-692-1506, Fax: 808-692-1968, E-mail: mberry@hawaii.edu.

University of Illinois at Chicago, College of Medicine and Graduate College, Graduate Programs in Medicine, Department of Biochemistry and Molecular Genetics, Chicago, IL 60607-7128. Offers PhD, MD/PhD. Terminal master's awarded for partial completion of doctoral program. *Degree requirements:* For doctorate, thesis/dissertation. *Entrance requirements:* For doctorate, GRE General Test. Additional exam requirements/recommendations for international students: Required—TOEFL. Electronic applications accepted. *Faculty research:* Nature of cellular components, control of metabolic processes, regulation of gene expression.

The University of Iowa, Graduate College, College of Liberal Arts and Sciences, Department of Biology, Iowa City, IA 52242-1324. Offers biology (MS, PhD); cell and developmental biology (MS, PhD); evolution (MS, PhD); genetics (MS, PhD); neurobiology (MS, PhD). Terminal master's awarded for partial completion of doctoral program. *Degree requirements:* For master's, thesis optional; exam; for doctorate, comprehensive exam, thesis/dissertation. *Entrance requirements:* For master's and doctorate, GRE General Test, minimum GPA of 3.0. Additional exam requirements/recommendations for international students: Required—TOEFL (minimum score 600 paper-based; 250 computer-based; 100 iBT). Electronic applications accepted. *Faculty research:* Neurobiology, evolutionary biology, genetics, cell and developmental biology.

The University of Iowa, Graduate College, Program in Genetics, Iowa City, IA 52242-1316. Offers PhD, MD/PhD. *Degree requirements:* For doctorate, comprehensive exam, thesis/dissertation. *Entrance requirements:* For doctorate, GRE General Test, minimum GPA of 3.0. Additional exam requirements/recommendations for international students: Required—TOEFL (minimum score 600 paper-based; 250 computer-based; 100 iBT). Electronic applications accepted. *Expenses:* Contact institution. *Faculty research:* Developmental genetics, eukaryotic gene expression, human genetics, molecular and biochemical genetics, evolutionary genetics.

The University of Iowa, Roy J. and Lucille A. Carver College of Medicine and Graduate College, Graduate Programs in Medicine, Department of Microbiology, Iowa City, IA 52242-1316. Offers general microbiology and microbial physiology (MS, PhD); immunology (MS, PhD); microbial genetics (MS, PhD); pathogenic bacteriology (MS, PhD); virology (MS, PhD). *Faculty:* 23 full-time (4 women), 11 part-time/adjunct (5 women). *Students:* 35 full-time (20 women); includes 2 American Indian or Alaska Native, non-Hispanic/Latino; 1 Hispanic/Latino, 5 international. Average age 25. 71 applicants, 20% accepted, 8 enrolled. In 2010, 1 master's, 5 doctorates awarded. *Degree requirements:* For master's, thesis; for doctorate, comprehensive

Genetics

The University of Iowa (continued)

exam, thesis/dissertation. *Entrance requirements:* For master's and doctorate, GRE General Test. Additional exam requirements/recommendations for international students: Required—TOEFL (minimum score 600 paper-based; 250 computer-based). *Application deadline:* For fall admission, 2/1 for domestic and international students. Application fee: $60 ($85 for international students). Electronic applications accepted. *Financial support:* In 2010–11, 4 fellowships with full tuition reimbursements (averaging $25,000 per year), 31 research assistantships with full tuition reimbursements (averaging $25,000 per year) were awarded; institutionally sponsored loans, scholarships/grants, traineeships, and health care benefits also available. *Faculty research:* Gene regulation, processing and transport of HIV, retroviral pathogenesis, biodegradation, biofilm. Total annual research expenditures: $12.6 million. *Unit head:* Dr. Michael A. Apicella, Head, 319-335-7810, E-mail: grad-micro-info@uiowa.edu. *Application contact:* Dr. Michael A. Apicella, Head, 319-335-7810, E-mail: grad-micro-info@uiowa.edu.

The University of Manchester, Faculty of Life Sciences, Manchester, United Kingdom. Offers adaptive organismal biology (M Phil, PhD); animal biology (M Phil, PhD); biochemistry (M Phil, PhD); bioinformatics (M Phil, PhD); biomolecular sciences (M Phil, PhD); biotechnology (M Phil, PhD); cell biology (M Phil, PhD); cell matrix research (M Phil, PhD); channels and transporters (M Phil, PhD); developmental biology (M Phil, PhD); Egyptology (M Phil, PhD); environmental biology (M Phil, PhD); evolutionary biology (M Phil, PhD); gene expression (M Phil, PhD); genetics (M Phil, PhD); history of science, technology and medicine (M Phil, PhD); immunology (M Phil, PhD); integrative neurobiology and behavior (M Phil, PhD); membrane trafficking (M Phil, PhD); microbiology (M Phil, PhD); molecular and cellular neuroscience (M Phil, PhD); molecular biology (M Phil, PhD); molecular cancer studies (M Phil, PhD); neuroscience (M Phil, PhD); ophthalmology (M Phil, PhD); optometry (M Phil, PhD); organelle function (M Phil, PhD); pharmacology (M Phil, PhD); physiology (M Phil, PhD); plant sciences (M Phil, PhD); stem cell research (M Phil, PhD); structural biology (M Phil, PhD); systems neuroscience (M Phil, PhD); toxicology (M Phil, PhD).

University of Massachusetts Amherst, Graduate School, Interdisciplinary Programs, Program in Plant Biology, Amherst, MA 01003. Offers biochemistry and metabolism (MS, PhD); cell biology and physiology (MS, PhD); environmental, ecological and integrative (PhD); environmental, ecological and integrative biology (MS); genetics and evolution (MS, PhD). *Students:* 18 full-time (8 women); includes 1 minority (Asian, non-Hispanic/Latino), 7 international. Average age 29. 27 applicants, 41% accepted, 6 enrolled. In 2010, 3 doctorates awarded. *Degree requirements:* For master's, thesis; for doctorate, 2 foreign languages, comprehensive exam, thesis/dissertation. *Entrance requirements:* For master's and doctorate, GRE General Test. Additional exam requirements/recommendations for international students: Required—TOEFL (minimum score 550 paper-based; 213 computer-based; 80 iBT), IELTS (minimum score 6.5). *Application deadline:* For fall admission, 12/15 for domestic and international students; for spring admission, 10/1 for domestic and international students. Applications are processed on a rolling basis. Application fee: $50 ($65 for international students). Electronic applications accepted. *Expenses:* Tuition, state resident: full-time $2640. Required fees: $8282. One-time fee: $357 full-time. *Financial support:* In 2010–11, 12 research assistantships with full tuition reimbursements (averaging $11,651 per year) were awarded; fellowships, teaching assistantships, career-related internships or fieldwork, Federal Work-Study, scholarships/grants, traineeships, health care benefits, tuition waivers (full), and unspecified assistantships also available. Support available to part-time students. Financial award application deadline: 12/15; financial award applicants required to submit FAFSA. *Unit head:* Dr. Elsbeth L. Walker, Graduate Program Director, 413-577-3217, Fax: 413-545-3243. *Application contact:* Jean M. Ames, Supervisor of Admissions, 413-545—0722, Fax: 413-577-0010, E-mail: gradadm@grad.umass.edu.

University of Miami, Graduate School, College of Arts and Sciences, Department of Biology, Coral Gables, FL 33124. Offers biology (MS, PhD); genetics and evolution (MS, PhD). Terminal master's awarded for partial completion of doctoral program. *Degree requirements:* For master's, comprehensive exam (for some programs), thesis (for some programs); for doctorate, thesis/dissertation, oral and written qualifying exam. *Entrance requirements:* For master's, GRE General Test, 3 letters of recommendation, research papers; for doctorate, GRE General Test, 3 letters of recommendation, research papers, sponsor letter. Additional exam requirements/recommendations for international students: Required—TOEFL (minimum score 550 paper-based; 213 computer-based; 59 iBT). Electronic applications accepted. *Faculty research:* Neuroscience to ethology; plants, vertebrates and mycorrhizae; phylogenies, life histories and species interactions; molecular biology, gene expression and populations; cells, auditory neurons and vertebrate locomotion.

University of Minnesota, Twin Cities Campus, Graduate School, Program in Molecular, Cellular, Developmental Biology and Genetics, Minneapolis, MN 55455-0213. Offers genetic counseling (MS); molecular, cellular, developmental biology and genetics (PhD). Terminal master's awarded for partial completion of doctoral program. *Degree requirements:* For master's, thesis optional; for doctorate, thesis/dissertation. *Entrance requirements:* For master's and doctorate, GRE General Test. Additional exam requirements/recommendations for international students: Required—TOEFL (minimum score 625 paper-based; 263 computer-based; 80 iBT). Electronic applications accepted. *Faculty research:* Membrane receptors and membrane transport, cell interactions, cytoskeleton and cell mobility, regulation of gene expression, plant cell and molecular biology.

University of Missouri, Graduate School, College of Arts and Sciences, Division of Biological Sciences, Program in Genetic, Cellular and Developmental Biology, Columbia, MO 65211. Offers MA, PhD.

University of Missouri, Graduate School, Genetics Area Program, Columbia, MO 65211. Offers PhD. *Degree requirements:* For doctorate, comprehensive exam, thesis/dissertation. *Entrance requirements:* For doctorate, GRE General Test, minimum GPA of 3.0. Additional exam requirements/recommendations for international students: Required—TOEFL (minimum score 580 paper-based; 237 computer-based; 92 iBT).

University of Nebraska Medical Center, Graduate Studies, Department of Genetics, Cell Biology and Anatomy, Omaha, NE 68198. Offers MS, PhD. Part-time programs available. *Faculty:* 23 full-time (7 women), 1 part-time/adjunct (0 women). *Students:* 16 full-time (5 women), 5 part-time (4 women); includes 1 Asian, non-Hispanic/Latino, 2 international. Average age 25. 22 applicants, 18% accepted, 4 enrolled. In 2010, 1 master's, 5 doctorates awarded. Terminal master's awarded for partial completion of doctoral program. *Degree requirements:* For master's, comprehensive exam, thesis; for doctorate, comprehensive exam, thesis/dissertation. *Entrance requirements:* For master's and doctorate, GRE General Test. Additional exam requirements/recommendations for international students: Required—TOEFL (minimum score 550 paper-based; 213 computer-based). *Application deadline:* For fall admission, 3/1 priority date for domestic and international students; for spring admission, 10/1 for domestic students, 8/1 for international students. Applications are processed on a rolling basis. Application fee: $45. Electronic applications accepted. *Expenses:* Tuition, state resident: part-time $198.25 per semester hour. Required fees: $63 per semester. *Financial support:* In 2010–11, 3 students received support, including fellowships with full tuition reimbursements available (averaging $21,000 per year), research assistantships with full tuition reimbursements available (averaging $21,000 per year), teaching assistantships with full tuition reimbursements available (averaging $21,000 per year); institutionally sponsored loans, health care benefits, and unspecified assistantships also available. Support available to part-time students. Financial award application deadline: 3/1. *Faculty research:* Hematology, immunology, developmental biology, genetics cancer biology, neuroscience. *Unit head:* Dr. Karen Gould, Graduate Committee Chair, 402-559-2456, E-mail: kagould@unmc.edu. *Application contact:* Saralyn Fisher, Graduate Student Support, 402-559-4031, Fax: 402-559-7328, E-mail: sfisher@unmc.edu.

University of New Hampshire, Graduate School, College of Life Sciences and Agriculture, Department of Molecular, Cellular and Biomedical Sciences, Program in Genetics, Durham, NH 03824. Offers MS, PhD. Part-time programs available. *Faculty:* 12 full-time. *Students:* 10 full-time (8 women), 6 part-time (3 women), 6 international. Average age 33. 21 applicants, 19% accepted, 1 enrolled. In 2010, 3 master's awarded. *Degree requirements:* For master's, thesis; for doctorate, thesis/dissertation. *Entrance requirements:* For master's and doctorate, GRE General Test, GRE Subject Test. Additional exam requirements/recommendations for international students: Required—TOEFL (minimum score 550 paper-based; 213 computer-based; 80 iBT). *Application deadline:* For fall admission, 6/1 priority date for domestic students; 4/1 for international students; for spring admission, 12/1 for domestic students. Applications are processed on a rolling basis. Application fee: $65. Electronic applications accepted. *Financial support:* In 2010–11, 12 students received support, including 6 research assistantships, 6 teaching assistantships; fellowships, career-related internships or fieldwork, Federal Work-Study, and scholarships/grants also available. Support available to part-time students. Financial award application deadline: 2/15. *Unit head:* Dr. Rick Cote, Chair, 603-862-3217. *Application contact:* Flora Joyal, Administrative Assistant, 603-862-2250, E-mail: genetics.dept@unh.edu.

University of New Mexico, School of Medicine, Biomedical Sciences Graduate Program, Albuquerque, NM 87131-5196. Offers biochemistry and molecular biology (MS, PhD); cell biology and physiology (MS, PhD); clinical and translational science (Certificate); molecular genetics and microbiology (MS, PhD); neuroscience (MS, PhD); pathology (MS, PhD); toxicology (MS, PhD); university science teaching (Certificate). Part-time programs available. *Faculty:* 33 full-time (14 women), 3 part-time/adjunct (1 woman). *Students:* 94 full-time (57 women), 14 part-time (8 women); includes 24 minority (3 Black or African American, non-Hispanic/Latino; 1 American Indian or Alaska Native, non-Hispanic/Latino; 6 Asian, non-Hispanic/Latino; 13 Hispanic/Latino; 1 Two or more races, non-Hispanic/Latino), 20 international. Average age 30. 135 applicants, 14% accepted, 19 enrolled. In 2010, 2 master's, 19 doctorates, 3 other advanced degrees awarded. Terminal master's awarded for partial completion of doctoral program. *Degree requirements:* For master's, thesis; for doctorate, comprehensive exam, thesis/dissertation. *Entrance requirements:* For master's and doctorate, GRE General Test, minimum undergraduate GPA of 3.0. Additional exam requirements/recommendations for international students: Required—TOEFL. *Application deadline:* For fall admission, 1/1 priority date for domestic students. Applications are processed on a rolling basis. Application fee: $50. Electronic applications accepted. *Expenses:* Tuition, state resident: full-time $5991; part-time $251 per credit hour. Tuition, nonresident: full-time $14,405; part-time $800.20 per credit hour. Tuition and fees vary according to course level, course load, program and reciprocity agreements. *Financial support:* In 2010–11, 99 students received support, including 5 fellowships (averaging $75 per year), 96 research assistantships with full tuition reimbursements available (averaging $17,401 per year), 2 teaching assistantships with full tuition reimbursements available (averaging $2,415 per year); career-related internships or fieldwork, Federal Work-Study, institutionally sponsored loans, scholarships/grants, traineeships, health care benefits, and unspecified assistantships also available. Financial award application deadline: 1/1; financial award applicants required to submit FAFSA. *Faculty research:* Signal transduction, infectious disease, biology of cancer, structural biology, neuroscience. *Unit head:* Laurie G. Hudson, Director, 505-272-1887, Fax: 505-272-8738, E-mail: lhudson@salud.unm.edu. *Application contact:* Angel Cooke-Jackson, Coordinator, 505-272-1887, Fax: 505-272-8738, E-mail: acooke-jackson@salud.unm.edu.

The University of North Carolina at Chapel Hill, Graduate School, College of Arts and Sciences, Department of Biology, Chapel Hill, NC 27599. Offers botany (MA, MS, PhD); cell biology, development, and physiology (MA, MS, PhD); cell motility and cytoskeleton (PhD); ecology and behavior (MA, MS, PhD); genetics and molecular biology (MA, MS, PhD); morphology, systematics, and evolution (MA, MS, PhD). Terminal master's awarded for partial completion of doctoral program. *Degree requirements:* For master's, comprehensive exam, thesis (for some programs); for doctorate, comprehensive exam, thesis/dissertation. *Entrance requirements:* For master's, GRE General Test, GRE Subject Test, 2 semesters of calculus or statistics; 2 semesters of physics, organic chemistry; 3 semesters of biology; for doctorate, GRE General Test, GRE Subject Test, 2 semesters calculus or statistics, 2 semesters physics, organic chemistry, 3 semesters of biology. Additional exam requirements/recommendations for international students: Required—TOEFL (minimum score 550 paper-based; 213 computer-based). Electronic applications accepted. *Faculty research:* Gene expression, biomechanics, yeast genetics, plant ecology, plant molecular biology.

The University of North Carolina at Chapel Hill, School of Medicine and Graduate School, Graduate Programs in Medicine, Curriculum in Genetics and Molecular Biology, Chapel Hill, NC 27599. Offers MS, PhD. *Faculty:* 82 full-time (26 women). *Students:* 78 full-time (45 women); includes 5 Black or African American, non-Hispanic/Latino; 2 Asian, non-Hispanic/Latino; 7 Hispanic/Latino, 4 international. Average age 26. In 2010, 19 doctorates awarded. *Degree requirements:* For doctorate, comprehensive exam, thesis/dissertation. *Entrance requirements:* For doctorate, GRE, minimum GPA of 3.0. Additional exam requirements/recommendations for international students: Required—TOEFL. *Application deadline:* For fall admission, 1/1 priority date for domestic and international students. Applications are processed on a rolling basis. Application fee: $77. Electronic applications accepted. *Financial support:* In 2010–11, 8 fellowships with full tuition reimbursements (averaging $26,000 per year), 72 research assistantships with full tuition reimbursements (averaging $26,000 per year), 6 teaching assistantships with full tuition reimbursements (averaging $26,000 per year) were awarded; traineeships and tuition waivers (full) also available. *Faculty research:* Telomere replication and germline immortality, experimental evolution in microorganisms, genetic vulnerabilities in tumor genomes, genetics of cell cycle control during Drosophila development, mammalian genetics. *Unit head:* Dr. Robert J. Duronio, Director, 919-962-7749, E-mail: duronio@med.unc.edu. *Application contact:* Sausyty A. Hermreck, Graduate Student Coordinator, 919-966-2681, Fax: 919-966-0401, E-mail: sausytyh@med.unc.edu.

University of North Dakota, Graduate School, College of Arts and Sciences, Department of Biology, Grand Forks, ND 58202. Offers botany (MS, PhD); ecology (MS, PhD); entomology (MS, PhD); environmental biology (MS, PhD); fisheries/wildlife (MS, PhD); genetics (MS, PhD); zoology (MS, PhD). *Faculty:* 17 full-time (5 women), 6 part-time/adjunct (1 woman). *Students:* 19 full-time (6 women), 8 part-time (2 women); includes 4 minority (3 American Indian or Alaska Native, non-Hispanic/Latino; 1 Asian, non-Hispanic/Latino), 1 international. Average age 28. 21 applicants, 33% accepted, 4 enrolled. In 2010, 1 master's awarded. Terminal master's awarded for partial completion of doctoral program. *Degree requirements:* For master's, thesis, final exam; for doctorate, comprehensive exam, thesis/dissertation, final exam. *Entrance requirements:* For master's, GRE General Test, GRE Subject Test, minimum GPA of 3.0; for doctorate, GRE General Test, GRE Subject Test, minimum GPA of 3.5. Additional exam requirements/recommendations for international students: Required—TOEFL (minimum score 550 paper-based; 213 computer-based; 79 iBT), IELTS (minimum score 6.5). *Application deadline:* For fall admission, 2/15 for domestic and international students; for spring admission, 10/15 for domestic and international students. Application fee: $35. Electronic applications accepted. *Expenses:* Tuition, state resident: full-time $5857; part-time $306.74 per credit. Tuition, nonresident: full-time $15,666; part-time $729.77 per credit. Required fees: $53.42 per credit. Tuition and fees vary according to course load, program and reciprocity agreements. *Financial support:* In 2010–11, 22 students received support, including 5 research assistantships with full and partial tuition reimbursements available (averaging $11,375 per year), 17 teaching assistantships with full and partial tuition reimbursements available (averaging $10,813 per year); fellowships with full and partial tuition reimbursements available, Federal Work-Study, institutionally sponsored loans, scholarships/grants, health care benefits, tuition waivers (full and partial), and unspecified assistantships also available. Support available to part-time students. Financial award application deadline: 3/15; financial award applicants required to submit FAFSA. *Faculty research:* Population biology, wildlife ecology, RNA processing, hormonal control of behavior. Total annual research expenditures: $736,510. *Unit head:* Dr. Brett Goodwin, Graduate Director, 701-777-2621, Fax: 701-777-2623, E-mail: brett.goodwin@mail.und.edu. *Application contact:* Matthew Anderson, Admissions Specialist, 701-777-2947, Fax: 701-777-3619, E-mail: matthew.anderson@gradschool.und.edu.

University of North Texas Health Science Center at Fort Worth, Graduate School of Biomedical Sciences, Fort Worth, TX 76107-2699. Offers anatomy and cell biology (MS, PhD); biochemistry and molecular biology (MS, PhD); biomedical sciences (MS, PhD); biotechnology (MS); forensic genetics (MS); integrative physiology (MS, PhD); medical science (MS); microbiology and immunology (MS, PhD); pharmacology (MS, PhD); science education (MS); DO/MS; DO/PhD. Terminal master's awarded for partial completion of doctoral program. *Degree requirements:* For master's, thesis; for doctorate, thesis/dissertation. *Entrance requirements:* For master's and doctorate, GRE General Test. Additional exam requirements/recommendations for international students: Required—TOEFL. *Expenses:* Contact institution. *Faculty research:* Alzheimer's disease, aging, eye diseases, cancer, cardiovascular disease.

University of Notre Dame, Graduate School, College of Science, Department of Biological Sciences, Notre Dame, IN 46556. Offers aquatic ecology, evolution and environmental biology (MS, PhD); cellular and molecular biology (MS, PhD); genetics (MS, PhD); physiology (MS, PhD); vector biology and parasitology (MS, PhD). Terminal master's awarded for partial completion of doctoral program. *Degree requirements:* For master's, comprehensive exam, thesis; for doctorate, comprehensive exam, thesis/dissertation, candidacy exam. *Entrance requirements:* For master's and doctorate, GRE General Test. Additional exam requirements/recommendations for international students: Required—TOEFL (minimum score 600 paper-based; 250 computer-based; 80 iBT). Electronic applications accepted. *Faculty research:* Tropical disease, molecular genetics, neurobiology, evolutionary biology, aquatic biology.

University of Oregon, Graduate School, College of Arts and Sciences, Department of Biology, Eugene, OR 97403. Offers ecology and evolution (MA, MS, PhD); marine biology (MA, MS, PhD); molecular, cellular and genetic biology (PhD); neuroscience and development (PhD). Terminal master's awarded for partial completion of doctoral program. *Degree requirements:* For master's, thesis (for some programs); for doctorate, thesis/dissertation. *Entrance requirements:* For master's and doctorate, GRE General Test, minimum GPA of 3.2. Additional exam requirements/recommendations for international students: Required—TOEFL. *Faculty research:* Developmental neurobiology; evolution, population biology, and quantitative genetics; regulation of gene expression; biochemistry of marine organisms.

University of Pennsylvania, Perelman School of Medicine, Biomedical Graduate Studies, Graduate Group in Cell and Molecular Biology, Philadelphia, PA 19104. Offers cancer biology (PhD); cell biology and physiology (PhD); developmental stem cell regenerative biology (PhD); gene therapy and vaccines (PhD); genetics and gene regulation (PhD); microbiology, virology, and parasitology (PhD); MD/PhD; VMD/PhD. *Faculty:* 299. *Students:* 315 full-time (166 women); includes 13 Black or African American, non-Hispanic/Latino; 1 American Indian or Alaska Native, non-Hispanic/Latino; 44 Asian, non-Hispanic/Latino; 18 Hispanic/Latino, 37 international. 579 applicants, 21% accepted, 49 enrolled. In 2010, 53 doctorates awarded. *Degree requirements:* For doctorate, thesis/dissertation. *Entrance requirements:* For doctorate, GRE General Test. Additional exam requirements/recommendations for international students: Required—TOEFL. *Application deadline:* For fall admission, 12/8 priority date for domestic and international students. Applications are processed on a rolling basis. Application fee: $70. Electronic applications accepted. *Expenses:* Tuition: Full-time $25,660; part-time $4758 per course. Required fees: $2152; $270 per course. Tuition and fees vary according to course load, degree level and program. *Financial support:* In 2010–11, 315 students received support; fellowships, research assistantships, scholarships/grants, traineeships, and unspecified assistantships available. Financial award application deadline: 12/8. *Unit head:* Dr. Daniel Kessler, Graduate Group Chair, 215-898-2180, E-mail: raperj@mail.med.upenn.edu. *Application contact:* Meagan Schofer, Coordinator, 215-898-9536, Fax: 215-573-2104, E-mail: camb@mailmed.upenn.edu.

University of Puerto Rico, Río Piedras, College of Natural Sciences, Department of Biology, San Juan, PR 00931-3300. Offers ecology/systematics (MS, PhD); evolution/genetics (MS, PhD); molecular/cellular biology (MS, PhD); neuroscience (MS, PhD). Part-time programs available. *Degree requirements:* For master's, one foreign language, comprehensive exam, thesis; for doctorate, one foreign language, comprehensive exam, thesis/dissertation. *Entrance requirements:* For master's, GRE Subject Test, interview, minimum GPA of 3.0, letter of recommendation; for doctorate, GRE Subject Test, interview, master's degree, minimum GPA of 3.0, letter of recommendation. *Faculty research:* Environmental, poblational and systematic biology.

University of Rochester, School of Medicine and Dentistry, Graduate Programs in Medicine and Dentistry, Department of Biomedical Genetics, Rochester, NY 14627. Offers MS, PhD. *Degree requirements:* For doctorate, thesis/dissertation, qualifying exam. *Entrance requirements:* For doctorate, GRE General Test.

University of Southern California, Keck School of Medicine and Graduate School, Graduate Programs in Medicine, Department of Preventive Medicine, Division of Biostatistics, Los Angeles, CA 90089. Offers applied biostatistics/epidemiology (MS); biostatistics (MS, PhD); epidemiology (PhD); genetic epidemiology and statistical genetics (PhD); molecular epidemiology (MS, PhD). *Faculty:* 71 full-time (30 women). *Students:* 103 full-time (63 women); includes 21 Asian, non-Hispanic/Latino; 4 Hispanic/Latino, 55 international. Average age 29. 79 applicants, 52% accepted, 18 enrolled. In 2010, 6 master's, 4 doctorates awarded. Terminal master's awarded for partial completion of doctoral program. *Degree requirements:* For master's, thesis; for doctorate, thesis/dissertation. *Entrance requirements:* For master's and doctorate, GRE General Test, GRE Subject Test, minimum GPA of 3.0. Additional exam requirements/recommendations for international students: Required—TOEFL (minimum score 600 paper-based; 250 computer-based; 100 iBT). *Application deadline:* For fall admission, 12/1 priority date for domestic students, 12/1 for international students. Application fee: $85. Electronic applications accepted. *Expenses:* Tuition: Full-time $31,240; part-time $1420 per unit. Required fees: $600. One-time fee: $35 full-time. Full-time tuition and fees vary according to degree level and program. *Financial support:* In 2010–11, 3 fellowships with full tuition reimbursements (averaging $27,600 per year), 50 research assistantships with full tuition reimbursements (averaging $27,600 per year), 24 teaching assistantships with full and partial tuition reimbursements (averaging $15,525 per year) were awarded; career-related internships or fieldwork, Federal Work-Study, institutionally sponsored loans, scholarships/grants, health care benefits, and unspecified assistantships also available. Financial award application deadline: 5/3. *Faculty research:* Clinical trials in ophthalmology and cancer research, methods of analysis for epidemiological studies, genetic epidemiology. Total annual research expenditures: $1.3 million. *Unit head:* Dr. Stanley P. Azen, Co-Director, 323-442-1810, Fax: 323-442-2993, E-mail: mtrujill@usc.edu. *Application contact:* Mary L. Trujillo, Student Adviser, 323-442-1810, Fax: 323-442-2993, E-mail: mtrujill@usc.edu.

University of Southern California, Keck School of Medicine and Graduate School, Program in Genetic, Molecular and Cellular Biology, Los Angeles, CA 90089. Offers PhD. *Faculty:* 234 full-time (64 women). *Students:* 132 full-time (75 women); includes 4 Black or African American, non-Hispanic/Latino; 19 Asian, non-Hispanic/Latino; 4 Hispanic/Latino, 78 international. Average age 29. 350 applicants, 27% accepted, 43 enrolled. In 2010, 16 doctorates awarded. *Degree requirements:* For doctorate, comprehensive exam, thesis/dissertation. *Entrance requirements:* For doctorate, GRE, minimum GPA of 3.0. Additional exam requirements/recommendations for international students: Required—TOEFL (minimum score 600 paper-based; 250 computer-based; 100 iBT). *Application deadline:* For fall admission, 12/1 priority date for domestic and international students. Application fee: $85. Electronic applications accepted. *Expenses:* Tuition: Full-time $31,240; part-time $1420 per unit. Required fees: $600. One-time fee: $35 full-time. Full-time tuition and fees vary according to degree level and program. *Financial support:* In 2010–11, 122 students received support, including 8 fellowships (averaging $27,600 per year), 122 research assistantships with full tuition reimbursements available (averaging $27,600 per year), 2 teaching assistantships with full tuition reimbursements available (averaging $27,600 per year); institutionally sponsored loans, scholarships/grants, traineeships, health care benefits, and unspecified assistantships also available. Financial award application deadline: 5/5; financial award applicants required to submit FAFSA. *Unit head:* Dr. Henry Sucov, Director, 323-442-

1475, Fax: 323-442-1199, E-mail: sucov@usc.edu. *Application contact:* Dawn Burke, Student Program Coordinator, 323-442-1475, Fax: 323-442-1199, E-mail: pibbs@usc.edu.

The University of Tennessee, Graduate School, College of Arts and Sciences, Program in Life Sciences, Knoxville, TN 37996. Offers genome science and technology (MS, PhD); plant physiology and genetics (MS, PhD). *Degree requirements:* For doctorate, one foreign language, thesis/dissertation. *Entrance requirements:* For master's and doctorate, GRE General Test, minimum GPA of 2.7. Additional exam requirements/recommendations for international students: Required—TOEFL. Electronic applications accepted. *Expenses:* Tuition: state resident: full-time $7440; part-time $414 per credit hour. Tuition, nonresident: full-time $22,478; part-time $1250 per credit hour. Required fees: $922; $43 per credit hour. Tuition and fees vary according to program.

The University of Texas Health Science Center at Houston, Graduate School of Biomedical Sciences, Program in Genes and Development, Houston, TX 77030. Offers MS, PhD, MD/PhD. Terminal master's awarded for partial completion of doctoral program. *Degree requirements:* For master's, thesis; for doctorate, thesis/dissertation. *Entrance requirements:* For master's and doctorate, GRE General Test. Additional exam requirements/recommendations for international students: Required—TOEFL. Electronic applications accepted. *Faculty research:* Developmental biology, genetics, cell biology, structural biology, cancer.

The University of Texas Medical Branch, Graduate School of Biomedical Sciences, Program in Biochemistry and Molecular Biology, Galveston, TX 77555. Offers biochemistry (PhD); bioinformatics (PhD); biophysics (PhD); cell biology (PhD); computational biology (PhD); structural biology (PhD). *Degree requirements:* For doctorate, thesis/dissertation. *Entrance requirements:* Additional exam requirements/recommendations for international students: Required—TOEFL (minimum score 550 paper-based; 213 computer-based). Electronic applications accepted.

The University of Texas Southwestern Medical Center at Dallas, Southwestern Graduate School of Biomedical Sciences, Division of Basic Science, Program in Genetics and Development, Dallas, TX 75390. Offers PhD. *Faculty:* 85 full-time (16 women), 2 part-time/adjunct (0 women). *Students:* 59 full-time (22 women), 1 part-time (0 women); includes 13 minority (1 American Indian or Alaska Native, non-Hispanic/Latino; 8 Asian, non-Hispanic/Latino; 4 Hispanic/Latino), 24 international. Average age 26. In 2010, 12 doctorates awarded. *Degree requirements:* For doctorate, thesis/dissertation, qualifying exam. *Entrance requirements:* For doctorate, GRE General Test, minimum GPA of 3.0. Additional exam requirements/recommendations for international students: Required—TOEFL. *Application deadline:* For fall admission, 12/15 priority date for domestic students. Application fee: $0. Electronic applications accepted. *Financial support:* Fellowships, research assistantships, institutionally sponsored loans available. *Faculty research:* Human molecular genetics, chromosome structure, gene regulation, molecular biology, gene expression. *Unit head:* Dr. Nancy E. Street, Associate Dean, 214-648-6708, Fax: 214-648-2102, E-mail: nancy.street@utsouthwestern.edu. *Application contact:* Dr. Nancy E. Street, Associate Dean, 214-648-6708, Fax: 214-648-2102, E-mail: nancy.street@utsouthwestern.edu.

University of Toronto, School of Graduate Studies, Life Sciences Division, Department of Molecular and Medical Genetics, Toronto, ON M5S 1A1, Canada. Offers genetic counseling (M Sc); molecular and medical genetics (M Sc, PhD). *Degree requirements:* For master's, thesis; for doctorate, thesis/dissertation. *Entrance requirements:* For master's, B Sc or equivalent; for doctorate, M Sc or equivalent, minimum B+ average. Additional exam requirements/recommendations for international students: Required—TOEFL, IELTS (minimum score: 7), Michigan English Language Assessment Battery (minimum score: 85) or COPE (minimum score: 4). *Faculty research:* Structural biology, developmental genetics, molecular medicine, genetic counseling.

University of Washington, Graduate School, School of Public Health, Department of Epidemiology, Institute for Public Health Genetics, Seattle, WA 98195. Offers genetic epidemiology (MS); public health genetics (MPH, PhD). Part-time programs available. *Students:* 25 full-time (22 women), 6 part-time (3 women); includes 5 Asian, non-Hispanic/Latino; 2 Hispanic/Latino. Average age 31. 54 applicants, 39% accepted, 9 enrolled. In 2010, 9 master's, 1 doctorate awarded. Terminal master's awarded for partial completion of doctoral program. *Degree requirements:* For master's, thesis, practicum (MPH); for doctorate, comprehensive exam, thesis/dissertation. *Entrance requirements:* For master's, GRE General Test, experience in health sciences (preferred), minimum GPA of 3.0; for doctorate, GRE General Test, experience in health sciences (preferred), master's degree (preferred), minimum GPA of 3.0. Additional exam requirements/recommendations for international students: Required—TOEFL (minimum score 580 paper-based; 237 computer-based; 92 iBT). *Application deadline:* For fall admission, 12/15 for domestic and international students. Application fee: $75. Electronic applications accepted. *Financial support:* In 2010–11, 5 students received support, including 4 research assistantships with full tuition reimbursements available (averaging $13,725 per year), 1 teaching assistantship with full tuition reimbursement available (averaging $13,725 per year). Financial award application deadline: 1/15; financial award applicants required to submit FAFSA. *Faculty research:* Genetic epidemiology; ethical, legal, social issues of genetics; ecogenetics; health policy. *Unit head:* Dr. Melissa A. Austin, Director, 206-616-9286. *Application contact:* Barb Snyder, Student Services Advisor, 206-616-9286, Fax: 206-685-9651, E-mail: phgen@u.washington.edu.

University of Wisconsin–Madison, Graduate School, College of Agricultural and Life Sciences and Graduate Programs in Medicine, Department of Genetics, Program in Genetics, Madison, WI 53706-1380. Offers PhD. *Degree requirements:* For doctorate, thesis/dissertation. *Expenses:* Tuition, state resident: full-time $9887; part-time $617.96 per credit. Tuition, nonresident: full-time $24,054; part-time $1503.40 per credit. Required fees: $67.63 per credit. Tuition and fees vary according to reciprocity agreements.

University of Wisconsin–Madison, School of Medicine and Public Health and Graduate School, Graduate Programs in Medicine, Madison, WI 53705. Offers biomolecular chemistry (MS, PhD); cancer biology (PhD); genetics and medical genetics (MS, PhD), including genetics (PhD), medical genetics (MS); medical physics (MS, PhD), including health physics (MS), medical physics; microbiology (PhD); molecular and cellular pharmacology (PhD); pathology and laboratory medicine (PhD); physiology (PhD); population health sciences (MPH, MS, PhD), including clinical research (MS, PhD), epidemiology (MS, PhD), health services research (MS, PhD), population health sciences (MPH), social and behavioral health sciences (MS, PhD); DPT/MPH; DVM/MPH; MD/MPH; MD/PhD; MPA/MPH; MS/MPH; Pharm D/MPH. Part-time programs available. Postbaccalaureate distance learning degree programs offered (minimal on-campus study). Terminal master's awarded for partial completion of doctoral program. Application fee: $45. Electronic applications accepted. *Expenses:* Contact institution. *Financial support:* Fellowships with full tuition reimbursements, research assistantships with full tuition reimbursements, teaching assistantships with full tuition reimbursements, scholarships/grants, traineeships, and tuition waivers (full) available. *Unit head:* Dr. Richard L. Moss, Senior Associate Dean for Basic Research, Biotechnology and Graduate Studies, 608-265-0523, Fax: 608-265-0522, E-mail: rlmoss@wisc.edu. *Application contact:* Information Contact, 608-262-2433, Fax: 608-262-5134, E-mail: gradadmiss@mail.bascom.wisc.edu.

University of Wyoming, Graduate Program in Molecular and Cellular Life Sciences, Laramie, WY 82070. Offers PhD. *Degree requirements:* For doctorate, thesis/dissertation, four eight-week laboratory rotations, comprehensive basic practical exam, two-part qualifying exam, seminars, symposium.

Virginia Commonwealth University, Medical College of Virginia-Professional Programs, School of Medicine, School of Medicine Graduate Programs, Department of Human and Molecular Genetics, Richmond, VA 23284-9005. Offers genetic counseling (MS); human genetics (PhD); molecular biology and genetics (MS, PhD); MD/PhD. *Faculty:* 25 full-time (14 women). *Students:* 37 full-time (21 women), 1 (woman) part-time; includes 5 minority (1 Black or African

Genetics

Virginia Commonwealth University *(continued)*
American, non-Hispanic/Latino; 4 Asian, non-Hispanic/Latino, 14 international. 51 applicants, 33% accepted, 10 enrolled. In 2010, 3 master's, 5 doctorates awarded. *Degree requirements:* For master's, thesis; for doctorate, thesis/dissertation, comprehensive oral and written exams. *Entrance requirements:* For master's, GRE; for doctorate, GRE General Test. Additional exam requirements/recommendations for international students: Required—TOEFL (minimum score 600 paper-based; 250 computer-based; 100 iBT). *Application deadline:* For fall admission, 12/15 priority date for domestic students. Application fee: $50. Electronic applications accepted. *Expenses:* Tuition, state resident: full-time $4308; part-time $479 per credit hour. Tuition, nonresident: full-time $8942; part-time $994 per credit hour. Required fees: $2000; $85 per credit hour. Tuition and fees vary according to course level, course load, degree level, campus/location and program. *Financial support:* Fellowships available. *Faculty research:* Genetic epidemiology, biochemical genetics, quantitative genetics, human cytogenetics, molecular genetics. *Unit head:* Dr. Paul B. Fisher, Chair, 804-628-3506, Fax: 804-827-1124, E-mail: pbfisher@vcu.edu. *Application contact:* Dr. Linda A. Corey, Graduate Program Director, 804-628-4514, E-mail: corey@vcu.edu.

Virginia Polytechnic Institute and State University, Graduate School, Intercollege, Program in Genetics, Bioinformatics and Computational Biology, Blacksburg, VA 24061. Offers PhD. *Students:* 42 full-time (18 women), 5 part-time (1 woman); includes 5 Black or African American, non-Hispanic/Latino; 2 Asian, non-Hispanic/Latino; 1 Hispanic/Latino, 27 international. Average age 30. 50 applicants, 22% accepted, 7 enrolled. In 2010, 4 doctorates awarded. *Degree requirements:* For doctorate, comprehensive exam (for some programs), thesis/dissertation (for some programs). *Entrance requirements:* For doctorate, GRE. Additional exam requirements/recommendations for international students: Required—TOEFL (minimum score 550 paper-based; 213 computer-based). *Application deadline:* For fall admission, 7/1 for domestic and international students; for spring admission, 12/1 for international students. Applications are processed on a rolling basis. Application fee: $65. Electronic applications accepted. *Expenses:* Tuition, state resident: full-time $9399; part-time $488 per credit hour. Tuition, nonresident: full-time $17,854; part-time $957.75 per credit hour. Required fees: $1534. Full-time tuition and fees vary according to program. *Financial support:* Career-related internships or fieldwork, Federal Work-Study, scholarships/grants, health care benefits, and unspecified assistantships available. Financial award application deadline: 1/15. *Unit head:* Dr. David R. Bevan, UNIT HEAD, 540-231-5040, Fax: 540-231-3010, E-mail: drbevan@vt.edu. *Application contact:* Dennie Munson, Contact, 540-231-1928, Fax: 540-231-3010, E-mail: dennie@vt.edu.

Washington State University, Graduate School, College of Sciences, School of Molecular Biosciences, Program in Genetics and Cell Biology, Pullman, WA 99164. Offers MS, PhD. *Faculty:* 23 full-time (5 women), 21 part-time/adjunct (4 women). *Students:* 23 full-time (15 women), 1 (woman) part-time; includes 1 American Indian or Alaska Native, non-Hispanic/Latino; 1 Asian, non-Hispanic/Latino, 7 international. Average age 26. 231 applicants, 18% accepted, 13 enrolled. In 2010, 3 master's, 4 doctorates awarded. Terminal master's awarded for partial completion of doctoral program. *Degree requirements:* For master's, thesis or alternative, oral exam; for doctorate, comprehensive exam, thesis/dissertation, oral exam. *Entrance requirements:* For master's and doctorate, GRE General Test, minimum GPA of 3.0. Additional exam requirements/recommendations for international students: Required—TOEFL (minimum score 550 paper-based; 213 computer-based). *Application deadline:* For fall admission, 12/15 for domestic and international students. Application fee: $50. Electronic applications accepted. *Expenses:* Tuition, state resident: full-time $8552; part-time $443 per credit. Tuition, nonresident: full-time $21,650; part-time $1083 per credit. Required fees: $846. *Financial support:* In 2010–11, 1 fellowship with full tuition reimbursement (averaging $18,852 per year), 16 research assistantships with full tuition reimbursements (averaging $18,852 per year), 6 teaching assistantships with full tuition reimbursements (averaging $18,852 per year) were awarded; Federal Work-Study, institutionally sponsored loans, health care benefits, and unspecified assistantships also available. Financial award application deadline: 4/1; financial award applicants required to submit FAFSA. *Faculty research:* Plant molecular biology, growth factors, cancer induction and DNA repair, gene regulation and genetic engineering. Total annual research expenditures: $5.8 million. *Unit head:* Dr. John H. Nilson, Director, 509-335-8724, Fax: 509-335-9688, E-mail: jhn@wsu.edu. *Application contact:* Kelly G. McGovern, Academic Coordinator, 509-335-4566, Fax: 509-335-1907, E-mail: smbgrad@wsu.edu.

Washington University in St. Louis, Graduate School of Arts and Sciences, Division of Biology and Biomedical Sciences, Program in Evolution, Ecology and Population Biology, St. Louis, MO 63130-4899. Offers ecology (PhD); environmental biology (PhD); evolutionary biology (PhD); genetics (PhD). *Degree requirements:* For doctorate, thesis/dissertation. *Entrance requirements:* For doctorate, GRE General Test, GRE Subject Test. Electronic applications accepted.

Washington University in St. Louis, School of Medicine, Program in Clinical Investigation, St. Louis, MO 63130-4899. Offers clinical investigation (MS), including genetics/genomics, translational medicine. Part-time programs available. *Faculty:* 54 full-time (14 women), 5 part-time/adjunct (3 women). *Students:* 13 full-time (8 women), 23 part-time (10 women); includes 13 minority (1 Black or African American, non-Hispanic/Latino; 9 Asian, non-Hispanic/Latino; 2 Hispanic/Latino; 1 Two or more races, non-Hispanic/Latino). Average age 32. In 2010, 13 master's awarded. *Entrance requirements:* For master's, doctoral level degree or in process of obtaining doctoral level degree. Additional exam requirements/recommendations for international students: Required—TOEFL. *Application deadline:* For fall admission, 3/1 for domestic students. Application fee: $0. Electronic applications accepted. *Faculty research:* Neurology, otolaryngology, pediatrics, obstetrics/gynecology, occupational therapy, physical therapy. *Unit head:* Dr. David Warren, Associate Professor of Medicine, 314-454-8225, Fax: 314-454-5392, E-mail: dwarren@dom.wustl.edu. *Application contact:* Sarah E. Zalud-Cerrato, Curriculum Coordinator, 314-362-0916, Fax: 314-454-8279, E-mail: szalud@dom.wustl.edu.

Washington University in St. Louis, School of Medicine, Program in Genetic Epidemiology, St. Louis, MO 63130-4899. Offers computational (MS); genetic epidemiology (Certificate).

Part-time programs available. *Faculty:* 15 full-time (4 women), 9 part-time/adjunct (6 women). *Students:* 9 full-time (5 women), 3 part-time (all women); includes 1 Black or African American, non-Hispanic/Latino; 5 Asian, non-Hispanic/Latino; 2 Hispanic/Latino. Average age 30. 16 applicants, 75% accepted, 9 enrolled. In 2010, 8 master's awarded. *Degree requirements:* For master's, thesis, research paper. *Entrance requirements:* For master's, proficiency in computer programming, statistics and biology/genetics. Additional exam requirements/recommendations for international students: Required—TOEFL (minimum score 600 paper-based; 250 computer-based; 100 iBT). *Application deadline:* Applications are processed on a rolling basis. Application fee: $50. *Expenses:* Contact institution. *Financial support:* In 2010–11, 2 research assistantships (averaging $16,000 per year) were awarded; Federal Work-Study, scholarships/grants, health care benefits, tuition waivers (partial), and unspecified assistantships also available. Financial award applicants required to submit FAFSA. *Faculty research:* Biostatistics, clinical trials, cardiovascular diseases, genetics, genetic epidemiology. *Unit head:* Dr. Dabeeru C. Rao, Professor/Director of Biostatistics, 314-362-3608, Fax: 314-362-2693, E-mail: rao@wubios.wustl.edu. *Application contact:* June C. Mueller, Program Manager, 314-362-1052, Fax: 314-362-2693, E-mail: june@wubios.wustl.edu.

Wayne State University, Graduate School, Program in Molecular Biology and Genetics, Detroit, MI 48202. Offers MS, PhD. *Faculty:* 2 full-time (0 women). *Students:* 23 full-time (10 women); includes 2 Asian, non-Hispanic/Latino, 6 international. Average age 27. 29 applicants, 52% accepted, 6 enrolled. In 2010, 1 master's, 3 doctorates awarded. Terminal master's awarded for partial completion of doctoral program. *Degree requirements:* For master's, thesis; for doctorate, thesis/dissertation. *Entrance requirements:* For master's and doctorate, GRE General Test, references. Additional exam requirements/recommendations for international students: Required—TOEFL (minimum score 550 paper-based; 213 computer-based); Recommended—TWE (minimum score 6). *Application deadline:* For fall admission, 6/1 for international students; for winter admission, 10/1 for international students; for spring admission, 2/1 for international students. Applications are processed on a rolling basis. Application fee: $30 ($50 for international students). Electronic applications accepted. *Expenses:* Tuition, state resident: full-time $7662; part-time $478.85 per credit hour. Tuition, nonresident: full-time $16,920; part-time $1057.55 per credit hour. Required fees: $571; $35.70 per credit hour. $188.05 per semester. Tuition and fees vary according to course load and program. *Financial support:* In 2010–11, 4 fellowships (averaging $16,133 per year), 18 research assistantships (averaging $22,252 per year) were awarded; teaching assistantships. *Faculty research:* Human gene mapping, genome organization and sequencing, gene regulation, molecular evolution. *Unit head:* Dr. David Womble, Director, 313-577-2374, Fax: 313-577-5218, E-mail: aa3330@wayne.edu. *Application contact:* Alexander Gow, Associate Professor, 313-577-9401, E-mail: agow@genetics.wayne.edu.

Wesleyan University, Graduate Programs, Department of Biology, Middletown, CT 06459. Offers animal behavior (PhD); bioformatics/genomics (PhD); cell biology (PhD); developmental biology (PhD); evolution/ecology (PhD); genetics (PhD); neurobiology (PhD); population biology (PhD). *Faculty:* 12 full-time (4 women). *Students:* 20 full-time (12 women); includes 1 Black or African American, non-Hispanic/Latino; 3 Asian, non-Hispanic/Latino. Average age 26. 24 applicants, 29% accepted, 2 enrolled. *Degree requirements:* For doctorate, variable foreign language requirement, thesis/dissertation. *Entrance requirements:* For doctorate, GRE. Additional exam requirements/recommendations for international students: Required—TOEFL. *Application deadline:* For fall admission, 1/15 for domestic and international students. Applications are processed on a rolling basis. Application fee: $0. *Expenses:* Tuition: Full-time $43,404. Required fees: $830. *Financial support:* In 2010–11, 5 research assistantships with full tuition reimbursements, 16 teaching assistantships with full tuition reimbursements were awarded; stipends also available. Financial award application deadline: 4/15; financial award applicants required to submit FAFSA. *Faculty research:* Microbial population genetics, genetic basis of evolutionary adaptation, genetic regulation of differentiation and pattern formation in *drosophila*. *Unit head:* Dr. Sonia E. Sultan, Chair/Professor, 860-685-3493, E-mail: jnaegele@wesleyan.edu. *Application contact:* Marjorie Fitzgibbons, Information Contact, 860-685-2140, E-mail: mfitzgibbons@wesleyan.edu.

West Virginia University, Davis College of Agriculture, Forestry and Consumer Sciences, Interdisciplinary Program in Genetics and Developmental Biology, Morgantown, WV 26506. Offers animal breeding (MS, PhD); biochemical and molecular genetics (MS, PhD); cytogenetics (MS, PhD); descriptive embryology (MS, PhD); developmental genetics (MS); experimental morphogenesis/teratology (MS); human genetics (MS, PhD); immunogenetics (MS, PhD); life cycles of animals and plants (MS, PhD); molecular aspects of development (MS, PhD); mutagenesis (MS, PhD); oncology (MS, PhD); plant genetics (MS, PhD); population and quantitative genetics (MS, PhD); regeneration (MS, PhD); teratology (PhD); toxicology (MS, PhD). *Degree requirements:* For master's, thesis; for doctorate, comprehensive exam, thesis/dissertation. *Entrance requirements:* For master's, GRE or MCAT, minimum GPA of 2.75. Additional exam requirements/recommendations for international students: Required—TOEFL.

Yale University, Graduate School of Arts and Sciences, Department of Genetics, New Haven, CT 06520. Offers PhD, MD/PhD. *Degree requirements:* For doctorate, thesis/dissertation. *Entrance requirements:* For doctorate, GRE General Test, GRE Subject Test.

Yale University, Graduate School of Arts and Sciences, Department of Molecular, Cellular, and Developmental Biology, Program in Genetics, New Haven, CT 06520. Offers PhD. *Degree requirements:* For doctorate, thesis/dissertation. *Entrance requirements:* For doctorate, GRE General Test, GRE Subject Test.

Yale University, School of Medicine and Graduate School of Arts and Sciences, Combined Program in Biological and Biomedical Sciences (BBS), Molecular Cell Biology, Genetics, and Development Track, New Haven, CT 06520. Offers PhD, MD/PhD. *Entrance requirements:* Additional exam requirements/recommendations for international students: Required—TOEFL.

Genomic Sciences

Albert Einstein College of Medicine, Graduate Division of Biomedical Sciences, Division of Biological Sciences, Department of Genetics, Bronx, NY 10461. Offers computational genetics (PhD); molecular genetics (PhD); translational genetics (PhD); MD/PhD. *Degree requirements:* For doctorate, thesis/dissertation. *Entrance requirements:* For doctorate, GRE General Test. Additional exam requirements/recommendations for international students: Required—TOEFL. *Faculty research:* Neurologic genetics in Drosophila, biochemical genetics of yeast, developmental genetics in the mouse.

Black Hills State University, Graduate Studies, Program in Integrative Genomics, Spearfish, SD 57799. Offers MS. *Entrance requirements:* Additional exam requirements/recommendations for international students: Required—TOEFL (minimum score 500 paper-based; 171 computer-based; 60 iBT).

Case Western Reserve University, School of Medicine and School of Graduate Studies, Graduate Programs in Medicine, Department of Genetics, Program in Human, Molecular, and Developmental Genetics and Genomics, Cleveland, OH 44106. Offers PhD, MD/PhD. *Degree requirements:* For doctorate, comprehensive exam, thesis/dissertation. *Entrance requirements:* For doctorate, GRE General Test, GRE Subject Test. Additional exam requirements/

recommendations for international students: Required—TOEFL. *Faculty research:* Regulation of gene expression, molecular control of development, genomics.

Concordia University, School of Graduate Studies, Faculty of Arts and Science, Department of Biology, Montréal, QC H3G 1M8, Canada. Offers biology (M Sc, PhD); biotechnology and genomics (Diploma). *Degree requirements:* For master's, thesis; for doctorate, thesis/dissertation, pedagogical training. *Entrance requirements:* For master's, honors degree in biology; for doctorate, M Sc in life science. *Faculty research:* Cell biology, animal physiology, ecology, microbiology/molecular biology, plant physiology/biochemistry and biotechnology.

Georgia Health Sciences University, College of Graduate Studies, Program in Genomic Medicine, Augusta, GA 30912. Offers MS, PhD. *Faculty:* 5 full-time (1 woman). *Students:* 2 full-time (1 woman), 1 (woman) part-time; includes 1 Black or African American, non-Hispanic/Latino; 1 Asian, non-Hispanic/Latino. Average age 29. *Degree requirements:* For doctorate, comprehensive exam, thesis/dissertation. *Entrance requirements:* For doctorate, GRE General Test. Additional exam requirements/recommendations for international students: Required—TOEFL (minimum score 550 paper-based; 213 computer-based; 79 iBT). *Application deadline:* For fall admission, 1/15 for domestic and international students. Application fee: $30. Electronic applications accepted. *Expenses:* Tuition, state resident: full-time $7500; part-time $313 per semester hour. Tuition, nonresident: full-time $24,772; part-time $1033 per semester hour. Required fees: $1112. *Financial support:* In 2010–11, 2 research assistantships with partial tuition reimbursements (averaging $23,000 per year) were awarded; Federal Work-Study, institutionally sponsored loans, and scholarships/grants also available. Support available to part-time students. Financial award application deadline: 5/31; financial award applicants required to submit FAFSA. *Faculty research:* Genetic and genomic basis of diseases (diabetes, cancer, autoimmunity), development of diagnostic markers, bioinformatics, computational biology. Total annual research expenditures: $7.3 million. *Unit head:* Dr. Jin-Xiong She, Professor, Chair and Eminent Scholar, 706-721-3540, E-mail: jshe@georgiahealth.edu. *Application contact:* Dr. Patricia L. Cameron, Associate Dean, 706-721-3279, Fax: 706-721-6829, E-mail: pcameron@georgiahealth.edu.

Harvard University, Graduate School of Arts and Sciences, Department of Systems Biology, Cambridge, MA 02138. Offers PhD. *Degree requirements:* For doctorate, thesis/dissertation, lab rotation, qualifying examination. *Entrance requirements:* For doctorate, GRE. Additional exam requirements/recommendations for international students: Required—TOEFL. Electronic applications accepted. *Expenses:* Tuition: Full-time $34,976. Required fees: $1166. Full-time tuition and fees vary according to program.

North Carolina State University, Graduate School, College of Agriculture and Life Sciences, Graduate Program in Genomic Sciences, Raleigh, NC 27695. Offers MS, PhD.

North Carolina State University, Graduate School, College of Agriculture and Life Sciences, Program in Functional Genomics, Raleigh, NC 27695. Offers MFG, MS, PhD. *Degree requirements:* For master's, thesis (for some programs); for doctorate, thesis/dissertation. *Entrance requirements:* For master's and doctorate, GRE, minimum B average. Additional exam requirements/recommendations for international students: Required—TOEFL. Electronic applications accepted. *Faculty research:* Genome structure, genome expression, molecular evolution, nucleic acid structure/function, proteomics.

North Dakota State University, College of Graduate and Interdisciplinary Studies, College of Science and Mathematics, Department of Biological Sciences, Fargo, ND 58108. Offers biology (MS); botany (MS, PhD); cellular and molecular biology (PhD); environmental and conservation sciences (MS, PhD); genomics (PhD); natural resources management (MS, PhD); zoology (MS, PhD). *Students:* 18 full-time (8 women), 5 part-time (3 women); includes 2 American Indian or Alaska Native, non-Hispanic/Latino, 2 international. 17 applicants, 35% accepted. In 2010, 12 master's, 9 doctorates awarded. *Degree requirements:* For master's, thesis; for doctorate, thesis/dissertation. *Entrance requirements:* For master's and doctorate, GRE General Test. Additional exam requirements/recommendations for international students: Required—TOEFL. *Application deadline:* For fall admission, 3/15 priority date for domestic students; for spring admission, 10/30 priority date for domestic students. Applications are processed on a rolling basis. Application fee: $45 ($60 for international students). Electronic applications accepted. *Financial support:* Fellowships with full tuition reimbursements, research assistantships with full tuition reimbursements, teaching assistantships with full tuition reimbursements, career-related internships or fieldwork, Federal Work-Study, institutionally sponsored loans, scholarships/grants, tuition waivers (full), and unspecified assistantships available. Support available to part-time students. Financial award application deadline: 4/15; financial award applicants required to submit FAFSA. *Faculty research:* Comparative endocrinology, physiology, behavioral ecology, plant cell biology, aquatic biology. Total annual research expenditures: $675,000. *Unit head:* Dr. Marinus L. Otte, Head, 701-231-7087, E-mail: marinus.otte@ndsu.edu. *Application contact:* Dr. Marinus L. Otte, Head, 701-231-7087, E-mail: marinus.otte@ndsu.edu.

North Dakota State University, College of Graduate and Interdisciplinary Studies, Interdisciplinary Program in Genomics and Bioinformatics, Fargo, ND 58108. Offers MS, PhD. Part-time programs available. *Faculty:* 21 full-time (3 women). *Students:* 5 full-time (3 women), 7 part-time (3 women), 10 international. 8 applicants, 38% accepted, 2 enrolled. In 2010, 1 doctorate awarded. *Degree requirements:* For master's, thesis; for doctorate, comprehensive exam, thesis/dissertation. *Entrance requirements:* For master's and doctorate, minimum GPA of 3.0. Additional exam requirements/recommendations for international students: Required—TOEFL (minimum score 525 paper-based; 197 computer-based; 71 iBT). *Application deadline:* For fall admission, 5/1 for international students; for spring admission, 8/1 for international students. Applications are processed on a rolling basis. Application fee: $45 ($60 for international students). Electronic applications accepted. *Financial support:* In 2010–11, 12 research assistantships with full tuition reimbursements (averaging $15,000 per year) were awarded; unspecified assistantships also available. *Faculty research:* Genome evolution, genome mapping, genome expression, bioinformatics, data mining. Total annual research expenditures: $300,000. *Unit head:* Dr. Phillip E. McClean, Director, 701-231-8443, Fax: 701-231-8474. *Application contact:* Dr. Phillip E. McClean, Director, 701-231-8443, Fax: 701-231-8474.

University of California, Riverside, Graduate Division, Graduate Program in Genetics, Genomics, and Bioinformatics, Riverside, CA 92521-0102. Offers genomics and bioinformatics (PhD); molecular genetics (PhD); population and evolutionary genetics (PhD). *Degree requirements:* For doctorate, thesis/dissertation, qualifying exams, teaching experience. *Entrance requirements:* For doctorate, GRE General Test, minimum GPA of 3.2. Additional exam requirements/recommendations for international students: Required—TOEFL (minimum score 550 paper-based; 213 computer-based; 80 iBT). Electronic applications accepted. *Faculty research:* Molecular Genetics, Evolution and Population Genetics, Genomics and Bioinformatics.

University of California, San Francisco, School of Pharmacy and Graduate Division, Pharmaceutical Sciences and Pharmacogenomics Graduate Group, San Francisco, CA 94158-0775. Offers PhD. *Faculty:* 52 full-time (14 women). *Students:* 48 full-time (24 women); includes 15 Asian, non-Hispanic/Latino; 1 Hispanic/Latino. Average age 24. 92 applicants, 15% accepted, 8 enrolled. In 2010, 7 doctorates awarded. *Degree requirements:* For doctorate, comprehensive exam, thesis/dissertation. *Entrance requirements:* For doctorate, GRE General Test, minimum GPA of 3.0. Additional exam requirements/recommendations for international students: Required—TOEFL. *Application deadline:* For fall admission, 12/1 for domestic and international students. Application fee: $70 ($90 for international students). Electronic applications accepted. *Financial support:* In 2010–11, 6 fellowships with full tuition reimbursements (averaging $28,000 per year), 34 research assistantships with full tuition reimbursements (averaging $28,000 per year), 8 teaching assistantships with full tuition reimbursements (averaging $28,000 per year) were awarded; career-related internships or fieldwork, institutionally sponsored loans, scholarships/grants, traineeships, tuition waivers (full), and unspecified assistantships also available. Financial award application deadline: 4/6. *Faculty research:* Drug development, drug delivery, molecular pharmacology. *Unit head:* Deanna L. Kroetz, Program Director, 415-476-1153, Fax: 415-476-6022, E-mail: deanna.kroetz@ucsf.edu. *Application contact:* Debbie Acoba-Idlebi, Program Coordinator, 415-476-1947, Fax: 415-476-6022, E-mail: debbie.acoba@ucsf.edu.

University of Chicago, Division of Biological Sciences, Molecular Biosciences Cluster, Committee on Genetics, Genomics and Systems Biology, Chicago, IL 60637-1513. Offers PhD. *Degree requirements:* For doctorate, thesis/dissertation, ethics class, 2 teaching assistantships. *Entrance requirements:* For doctorate, GRE General Test, minimum GPA of 3.0. Additional exam requirements/recommendations for international students: Required—TOEFL (minimum score 600 paper-based; 250 computer-based; 104 iBT), IELTS (minimum score 7). Electronic applications accepted. *Faculty research:* Molecular genetics, developmental genetics, population genetics, human genetics.

University of Cincinnati, Graduate School, College of Medicine, Graduate Programs in Biomedical Sciences, Department of Environmental Health, Programs in Environmental Genetics and Molecular Toxicology, Cincinnati, OH 45221. Offers MS, PhD. *Degree requirements:* For doctorate, thesis/dissertation. *Entrance requirements:* For master's, GRE, minimum GPA of 3.0, 3 letters of recommendation. Additional exam requirements/recommendations for international students: Required—TOEFL (minimum score 520 paper-based; 190 computer-based).

University of Connecticut, Graduate School, College of Liberal Arts and Sciences, Department of Molecular and Cell Biology, Field of Applied Genomics, Storrs, CT 06269. Offers MS, PSM. *Degree requirements:* For master's, comprehensive exam. *Entrance requirements:* For master's, GRE General Test, GRE Subject Test. Additional exam requirements/recommendations for international students: Required—TOEFL (minimum score 550 paper-based; 213 computer-based). Electronic applications accepted.

University of Florida, College of Medicine, Department of Physiology and Functional Genomics, Gainesville, FL 32611. Offers PhD. *Degree requirements:* For doctorate, thesis/dissertation. *Entrance requirements:* For doctorate, GRE General Test, minimum GPA of 3.0. Additional exam requirements/recommendations for international students: Required—TOEFL. Electronic applications accepted. *Expenses:* Tuition, state resident: full-time $10,916. Tuition, nonresident: full-time $28,309. *Faculty research:* Cell and general endocrinology, neuroendocrinology, neurophysiology, respiration, membrane transport and ion channels.

University of Georgia, College of Agricultural and Environmental Sciences, Institute of Plant Breeding, Genetics and Genomics, Athens, GA 30602. Offers MS, PhD. *Students:* 22 full-time (7 women), 5 part-time (1 woman), 12 international. 17 applicants, 24% accepted, 3 enrolled. In 2010, 3 master's awarded. *Expenses:* Tuition, state resident: full-time $7200; part-time $344 per credit hour. Tuition, nonresident: full-time $21,900; part-time $944 per credit hour. Tuition and fees vary according to course load and program. *Financial support:* Tuition waivers and unspecified assistantships available. *Unit head:* Dr. E. Charles Brummer, Director, 706-542-8847, Fax: 706-583-8120, E-mail: pbgg@uga.edu. *Application contact:* Dr. Dayton Wilde, Graduate Coordinator, 706-542-5607, E-mail: pbgg@uga.edu.

University of Maine, Graduate School, Interdisciplinary Doctoral Program, Orono, ME 04469. Offers communication (PhD); functional genomics (PhD); mass communication (PhD); ocean engineering (PhD). Part-time and evening/weekend programs available. *Students:* 22 full-time (13 women), 25 part-time (14 women); includes 2 minority (1 Black or African American, non-Hispanic/Latino; 1 Asian, non-Hispanic/Latino), 4 international. Average age 37. 17 applicants, 41% accepted, 7 enrolled. In 2010, 10 doctorates awarded. *Degree requirements:* For doctorate, comprehensive exam, thesis/dissertation. *Entrance requirements:* For doctorate, GRE General Test. Additional exam requirements/recommendations for international students: Required—TOEFL. *Application deadline:* For fall admission, 4/1 for domestic students; for spring admission, 11/1 for domestic students. Applications are processed on a rolling basis. Application fee: $65. Electronic applications accepted. *Expenses:* Tuition, state resident: full-time $400. Tuition, nonresident: full-time $1050. *Unit head:* Scott G. Delcourt, Associate Dean of the Graduate School, 207-581-3291, Fax: 207-581-3232, E-mail: graduate@maine.edu. *Application contact:* Scott G. Delcourt, Associate Dean of the Graduate School, 207-581-3291, Fax: 207-581-3232, E-mail: graduate@maine.edu.

University of Maryland, Baltimore, School of Medicine, Department of Epidemiology and Preventive Medicine, Baltimore, MD 21201. Offers biostatistics (MS); clinical research (MS); epidemiology and preventative medicine (PhD); epidemiology and preventive medicine (MPH, MS); gerontology (PhD); human genetics and genomic (PhD); human genetics and genomic medicine (MS); molecular epidemiology (MS, PhD); toxicology (MS, PhD); JD/MS; MD/PhD; MS/PhD. *Accreditation:* CEPH. Part-time programs available. *Students:* 84 full-time (57 women), 64 part-time (46 women); includes 17 Black or African American, non-Hispanic/Latino; 23 Asian, non-Hispanic/Latino; 4 Hispanic/Latino, 18 international. Average age 32. In 2010, 21 master's, 10 doctorates awarded. *Entrance requirements:* For master's and doctorate, GRE General Test. Additional exam requirements/recommendations for international students: Required—TOEFL (minimum score 550 paper-based; 213 computer-based; 80 iBT); Recommended—IELTS. *Application deadline:* For fall admission, 1/15 for domestic and international students. Electronic applications accepted. *Expenses:* Contact institution. *Financial support:* In 2010–11, research assistantships with partial tuition reimbursements (averaging $25,000 per year); fellowships, Federal Work-Study, scholarships/grants, and unspecified assistantships also available. Financial award application deadline: 3/1; financial award applicants required to submit FAFSA. *Unit head:* Dr. Patricia Langenberg, Program Director, 410-706-3251, Fax: 410-706-8013. *Application contact:* Danielle Fitzpatrick, Program Coordinator, 410-706-8492, Fax: 410-706-4225, E-mail: dfitzpatrick@epi.umaryland.edu.

University of Pennsylvania, Perelman School of Medicine, Biomedical Graduate Studies, Graduate Group in Genomics and Computational Biology, Philadelphia, PA 19104. Offers PhD, MD/PhD, VMD/PhD. *Faculty:* 59. *Students:* 33 full-time (9 women); includes 2 Black or African American, non-Hispanic/Latino; 9 Asian, non-Hispanic/Latino; 2 Hispanic/Latino, 6 international. 77 applicants, 22% accepted, 4 enrolled. In 2010, 6 doctorates awarded. *Degree requirements:* For doctorate, thesis/dissertation optional. *Entrance requirements:* For doctorate, GRE. Additional exam requirements/recommendations for international students: Required—TOEFL. *Application deadline:* For fall admission, 12/8 priority date for domestic and international students. Applications are processed on a rolling basis. Application fee: $70. Electronic applications accepted. *Expenses:* Tuition: Full-time $25,660; part-time $4758 per course. Required fees: $2152; $270 per course. Tuition and fees vary according to course load, degree level and program. *Financial support:* In 2010–11, 33 students received support; fellowships, research assistantships, scholarships/grants, traineeships, and unspecified assistantships available. *Unit head:* Dr. Maja Bucan, Chairperson, 215-898-0020. *Application contact:* Hannah Chervitz, Graduate Coordinator, 215-746-2807, E-mail: gcbcoord@pcbi.upenn.edu.

The University of Tennessee, Graduate School, College of Arts and Sciences, Program in Life Sciences, Knoxville, TN 37996. Offers genome science and technology (MS, PhD); plant physiology and genetics (MS, PhD). *Degree requirements:* For doctorate, one foreign language, thesis/dissertation. *Entrance requirements:* For master's and doctorate, GRE General Test, minimum GPA of 2.7. Additional exam requirements/recommendations for international students: Required—TOEFL. Electronic applications accepted. *Expenses:* Tuition, state resident: full-time $7440; part-time $414 per credit hour. Tuition, nonresident: full-time $22,478; part-time $1250 per credit hour. Required fees: $922; $43 per credit hour. Tuition and fees vary according to program.

The University of Tennessee–Oak Ridge National Laboratory Graduate School of Genome Science and Technology, Graduate Program, Oak Ridge, TN 37830-8026. Offers life sciences (MS, PhD). *Degree requirements:* For master's, thesis; for doctorate, comprehensive exam, thesis/dissertation. *Entrance requirements:* For master's and doctorate, GRE General Test. Additional exam requirements/recommendations for international students: Required—TOEFL (minimum score 550 paper-based; 213 computer-based). Electronic applications accepted. *Faculty research:* Genetics/genomics, structural biology/proteomics, computational biology/bioinformatics, bioanalytical technologies.

The University of Toledo, College of Graduate Studies, College of Medicine and Life Sciences, Interdepartmental Programs, Toledo, OH 43606-3390. Offers bioinformatics/proteomics/genomics (MSBS, Certificate); human donation sciences (MSBS). *Expenses:* Tuition, state resident: full-time $11,426; part-time $476 per credit hour. Tuition, nonresident: full-time $21,660; part-time $903 per credit hour. One-time fee: $62.

University of Washington, Graduate School, School of Medicine, Graduate Programs in Medicine, Department of Genome Sciences, Seattle, WA 98195. Offers PhD. *Degree requirements:* For doctorate, thesis/dissertation, general exam. *Entrance requirements:* For doctorate, GRE General Test, minimum GPA of 3.0. Additional exam requirements/recommendations for international students: Required—TOEFL. Electronic applications accepted. *Faculty research:* Model organism genetics, human and medical genetics, genomics and proteomics, computational biology.

Genomic Sciences

Wake Forest University, School of Medicine and Graduate School of Arts and Sciences, Graduate Programs in Medicine, Molecular Genetics and Genomics Program, Winston-Salem, NC 27109. Offers PhD, MD/PhD. *Degree requirements:* For doctorate, thesis/dissertation. *Entrance requirements:* For doctorate, GRE General Test. Additional exam requirements/recommendations for international students: Required—TOEFL. Electronic applications accepted. *Faculty research:* Control of gene expression, molecular pathogenesis, protein biosynthesis, cell development, clinical cytogenetics.

Washington University in St. Louis, School of Medicine, Program in Clinical Investigation, St. Louis, MO 63130-4899. Offers clinical investigation (MS), including genetics/genomics, translational medicine. Part-time programs available. *Faculty:* 54 full-time (14 women), 5 part-time/adjunct (3 women). *Students:* 13 full-time (8 women), 23 part-time (10 women); includes 13 minority (1 Black or African American, non-Hispanic/Latino; 9 Asian, non-Hispanic/Latino; 2 Hispanic/Latino; 1 Two or more races, non-Hispanic/Latino). Average age 32. In 2010, 13 master's awarded. *Entrance requirements:* For master's, doctoral level degree or in process of obtaining doctoral level degree. Additional exam requirements/recommendations for international students: Required—TOEFL. *Application deadline:* For fall admission, 3/1 for domestic students. Application fee: $0. Electronic applications accepted. *Faculty research:* Neurology, otolaryngology, pediatrics, obstetrics/gynecology, occupational therapy, physical therapy. *Unit head:* Dr. David Warren, Associate Professor of Medicine, 314-454-8225, Fax: 314-454-5392, E-mail: dwarren@dom.wustl.edu. *Application contact:* Sarah E. Zalud-Cerrato, Curriculum Coordinator, 314-362-0916, Fax: 314-454-8279, E-mail: szalud@dom.wustl.edu.

Wesleyan University, Graduate Programs, Department of Biology, Middletown, CT 06459. Offers animal behavior (PhD); bioformatics/genomics (PhD); cell biology (PhD); developmental biology (PhD); evolution/ecology (PhD); genetics (PhD); neurobiology (PhD); population biology (PhD). *Faculty:* 12 full-time (4 women). *Students:* 20 full-time (12 women); includes 1 Black or African American, non-Hispanic/Latino; 3 Asian, non-Hispanic/Latino. Average age 26. 24 applicants, 29% accepted, 2 enrolled. *Degree requirements:* For doctorate, variable foreign language requirement, thesis/dissertation. *Entrance requirements:* For doctorate, GRE. Additional exam requirements/recommendations for international students: Required—TOEFL. *Application deadline:* For fall admission, 1/15 for domestic and international students. Applications are processed on a rolling basis. Application fee: $0. *Expenses:* Tuition: Full-time $43,404. Required fees: $830. *Financial support:* In 2010–11, 5 research assistantships with full tuition reimbursements, 16 teaching assistantships with full tuition reimbursements were awarded; stipends also available. Financial award application deadline: 4/15; financial award applicants required to submit FAFSA. *Faculty research:* Microbial population genetics, genetic basis of evolutionary adaptation, genetic regulation of differentiation and pattern formation in *drosophila*. *Unit head:* Dr. Sonia E. Sultan, Chair/Professor, 860-685-3493, E-mail: jnaegele@wesleyan.edu. *Application contact:* Marjorie Fitzgibbons, Information Contact, 860-685-2140, E-mail: mfitzgibbons@wesleyan.edu.

West Virginia University, Eberly College of Arts and Sciences, Department of Biology, Morgantown, WV 26506. Offers cell and molecular biology (MS, PhD); environmental and evolutionary biology (MS, PhD); forensic biology (MS, PhD); genomic biology (MS, PhD); neurobiology (MS, PhD). Terminal master's awarded for partial completion of doctoral program. *Degree requirements:* For master's, thesis, final exam; for doctorate, thesis/dissertation, preliminary and final exams. *Entrance requirements:* For master's, GRE General Test, GRE Subject Test, minimum GPA of 3.0; for doctorate, GRE General Test, minimum GPA of 3.0. Additional exam requirements/recommendations for international students: Required—TOEFL. *Faculty research:* Environmental biology, genetic engineering, developmental biology, global change, biodiversity.

Yale University, School of Medicine and Graduate School of Arts and Sciences, Combined Program in Biological and Biomedical Sciences (BBS), Computational Biology and Bioinformatics Track, New Haven, CT 06520. Offers PhD, MD/PhD. *Entrance requirements:* Additional exam requirements/recommendations for international students: Required—TOEFL.

Human Genetics

Baylor College of Medicine, Graduate School of Biomedical Sciences, Department of Molecular and Human Genetics, Houston, TX 77030-3498. Offers PhD, MD/PhD. *Faculty:* 67 full-time (14 women). *Students:* 77 full-time (45 women); includes 2 Black or African American, non-Hispanic/Latino; 2 Asian, non-Hispanic/Latino; 3 Hispanic/Latino, 36 international. Average age 26. 130 applicants, 20% accepted, 16 enrolled. In 2010, 15 doctorates awarded. *Degree requirements:* For doctorate, thesis/dissertation, public defense. *Entrance requirements:* For doctorate, GRE General Test, GRE Subject Test (strongly recommended), minimum GPA of 3.0. Additional exam requirements/recommendations for international students: Required—TOEFL. *Application deadline:* For fall admission, 1/1 priority date for domestic students. Application fee: $0. Electronic applications accepted. *Expenses:* Tuition: Full-time $11,000. Required fees: $4900. *Financial support:* In 2010–11, 18 fellowships with full tuition reimbursements (averaging $26,000 per year), 59 research assistantships with full tuition reimbursements (averaging $26,009 per year) were awarded; career-related internships or fieldwork, Federal Work-Study, institutionally sponsored loans, health care benefits, and students receive a scholarship unless there are grant funds available to pay tuition also available. Financial award applicants required to submit FAFSA. *Faculty research:* Human genetics, genome biology, epigenetics, gene therapy, model organisms. *Unit head:* Dr. Gad Shaulsky, Director, 713-798-5056. *Application contact:* Judi Coleman, Graduate Program Administrator, 713-798-5056, Fax: 713-798-8597, E-mail: genetics-gradprm@bcm.edu.

See Close-Up on page 305.

Baylor College of Medicine, Graduate School of Biomedical Sciences, Interdepartmental Program in Cell and Molecular Biology, Houston, TX 77030-3498. Offers biochemistry (PhD); cell and molecular biology (PhD); genetics (PhD); human genetics (PhD); immunology (PhD); microbiology (PhD); virology (PhD); MD/PhD. *Faculty:* 100 full-time (31 women). *Students:* 67 full-time (41 women); includes 4 Black or African American, non-Hispanic/Latino; 2 American Indian or Alaska Native, non-Hispanic/Latino; 9 Asian, non-Hispanic/Latino; 9 Hispanic/Latino, 9 international. Average age 27. 120 applicants, 27% accepted, 15 enrolled. In 2010, 7 doctorates awarded. *Degree requirements:* For doctorate, thesis/dissertation, public defense. *Entrance requirements:* For doctorate, GRE General Test, GRE Subject Test (strongly recommended), minimum GPA of 3.0. Additional exam requirements/recommendations for international students: Required—TOEFL. *Application deadline:* For fall admission, 1/1 priority date for domestic students. Applications are processed on a rolling basis. Application fee: $0. Electronic applications accepted. *Expenses:* Tuition: Full-time $11,000. Required fees: $4900. *Financial support:* In 2010–11, 67 students received support, including 24 fellowships with full tuition reimbursements available (averaging $26,000 per year), 43 research assistantships with full tuition reimbursements available (averaging $26,000 per year); teaching assistantships, Federal Work-Study, institutionally sponsored loans, health care benefits, and tuition waivers (full) also available. Financial award applicants required to submit FAFSA. *Faculty research:* Molecular and cellular biology; cancer, aging and stem cells; genomics and proteomics; microbiome, molecular microbiology; infectious disease, immunology and translational research. *Unit head:* Dr. Susan Marriott, Director, 713-798-6557. *Application contact:* Lourdes Fernandez, Graduate Program Administrator, 713-798-6557, Fax: 713-798-6325, E-mail: cmbprog@bcm.edu.

See Close-Up on page 223.

Case Western Reserve University, School of Medicine and School of Graduate Studies, Graduate Programs in Medicine, Department of Genetics, Program in Human, Molecular, and Developmental Genetics and Genomics, Cleveland, OH 44106. Offers PhD, MD/PhD. *Degree requirements:* For doctorate, comprehensive exam, thesis/dissertation. *Entrance requirements:* For doctorate, GRE General Test, GRE Subject Test. Additional exam requirements/recommendations for international students: Required—TOEFL. *Faculty research:* Regulation of gene expression, molecular control of development, genomics.

The Johns Hopkins University, School of Medicine, Graduate Programs in Medicine, Predoctoral Training Program in Human Genetics, Baltimore, MD 21218-2699. Offers PhD, MD/PhD. *Faculty:* 59 full-time (14 women). *Students:* 77 full-time (55 women); includes 8 Black or African American, non-Hispanic/Latino; 11 Asian, non-Hispanic/Latino; 5 Hispanic/Latino, 15 international. Average age 24. 172 applicants, 11% accepted, 10 enrolled. In 2010, 9 doctorates awarded. Terminal master's awarded for partial completion of doctoral program. *Degree requirements:* For doctorate, comprehensive exam, thesis/dissertation. *Entrance requirements:* For doctorate, GRE General Test, GRE Subject Test. *Application deadline:* For fall admission, 12/31 priority date for domestic and international students. Application fee: $85. Electronic applications accepted. *Financial support:* In 2010–11, 1 fellowship with full tuition reimbursement (averaging $26,855 per year) was awarded; teaching assistantships with full tuition reimbursements, health care benefits also available. *Faculty research:* Human, mammalian, and molecular genetics, bioinformatics, genomics. *Unit head:* Dr. David Valle, Director, 410-955-4260, Fax: 410-955-7397, E-mail: muscelli@jhmi.edu. *Application contact:* Sandy Muscelli, Program Administrator, 410-955-4260, Fax: 410-955-7397, E-mail: muscelli@jhmi.edu.

Louisiana State University Health Sciences Center, School of Graduate Studies in New Orleans, Department of Human Genetics, New Orleans, LA 70112-2223. Offers MS, PhD, MD/PhD. Part-time programs available. Terminal master's awarded for partial completion of doctoral program. *Degree requirements:* For master's, comprehensive exam, thesis; for doctorate, comprehensive exam, thesis/dissertation. *Entrance requirements:* For master's and doctorate, GRE General Test. Additional exam requirements/recommendations for international students: Required—TOEFL. *Faculty research:* Genetic epidemiology, segregation and linkage analysis, gene mapping.

McGill University, Faculty of Graduate and Postdoctoral Studies, Faculty of Medicine, Department of Human Genetics, Montréal, QC H3A 2T5, Canada. Offers genetic counseling (M Sc); human genetics (M Sc, PhD).

Memorial University of Newfoundland, Faculty of Medicine and School of Graduate Studies, Graduate Programs in Medicine, Division of Human Genetics, St. John's, NL A1C 5S7, Canada. Offers M Sc, PhD, MD/PhD. Part-time programs available. *Degree requirements:* For master's, thesis; for doctorate, comprehensive exam, thesis/dissertation, oral defense of thesis. *Entrance requirements:* For master's, MD or B Sc; for doctorate, MD or M Sc. Additional exam requirements/recommendations for international students: Required—TOEFL. *Faculty research:* Cancer genetics, gene mapping, medical genetics, birth defects, population genetics.

Sarah Lawrence College, Graduate Studies, Joan H. Marks Graduate Program in Human Genetics, Bronxville, NY 10708-5999. Offers MS. Part-time programs available. *Degree requirements:* For master's, thesis, fieldwork. *Entrance requirements:* For master's, previous course work in biology, chemistry, developmental biology, genetics, probability and statistics. *Expenses:* Contact institution.

Tulane University, School of Medicine and School of Liberal Arts, Graduate Programs in Biomedical Sciences, Program in Human Genetics, New Orleans, LA 70118-5669. Offers MBS, PhD, MD/PhD. MS and PhD offered through the Graduate School. *Degree requirements:* For master's, thesis; for doctorate, thesis/dissertation. *Entrance requirements:* For master's, GRE, MCAT; for doctorate, GRE General Test. Additional exam requirements/recommendations for international students: Required—TOEFL. Electronic applications accepted. *Faculty research:* Inborn errors of metabolism, DNA methylation, gene therapy.

University of California, Los Angeles, David Geffen School of Medicine and Graduate Division, Graduate Programs in Medicine, Department of Human Genetics, Los Angeles, CA 90095. Offers MS, PhD. *Faculty:* 14 full-time (6 women). *Students:* 18 full-time (13 women); includes 4 minority (2 Asian, non-Hispanic/Latino; 2 Hispanic/Latino), 6 international. Average age 29. 13 applicants, 0% accepted, 0 enrolled. In 2010, 5 doctorates awarded. *Entrance requirements:* For master's and doctorate, GRE General Test. Application fee: $70 ($90 for international students). Electronic applications accepted. *Financial support:* In 2010–11, 19 fellowships, 19 research assistantships, 6 teaching assistantships were awarded. *Unit head:* Dr. Kenneth L. Lange, Chair, 310-206-8076, Fax: 310-825-8685, E-mail: klange@ucla.edu. *Application contact:* Departmental Information Contact for Admission, 310-206-0920, Fax: 310-794-5446, E-mail: humgen@mednet.ucla.edu.

University of California, Los Angeles, Graduate Division, College of Letters and Science and David Geffen School of Medicine, UCLA ACCESS to Programs in the Molecular, Cellular and Integrative Life Sciences, Los Angeles, CA 90095. Offers biochemistry and molecular biology (PhD); biological chemistry (PhD); cellular and molecular pathology (PhD); human genetics (PhD); microbiology, immunology, and molecular genetics (PhD); molecular biology (PhD); molecular toxicology (PhD); molecular, cellular and integrative physiology (PhD); neurobiology (PhD); oral biology (PhD); physiology (PhD). ACCESS is an umbrella program for first-year coursework in 12 PhD programs. *Students:* 48 full-time (28 women), 6 international. Average age 24. 388 applicants, 27% accepted, 48 enrolled. *Degree requirements:* For doctorate, thesis/dissertation, oral and written qualifying exams. *Entrance requirements:* For doctorate, GRE General Test, minimum undergraduate GPA of 3.0. Additional exam requirements/recommendations for international students: Required—TOEFL. *Application deadline:* For fall admission, 12/15 for domestic and international students. Application fee: $70 ($90 for international students). Electronic applications accepted. *Financial support:* In 2010–11, 31 fellowships with full and partial tuition reimbursements, 13 research assistantships with full and partial tuition reimbursements, 2 teaching assistantships with full and partial tuition reimbursements were awarded; Federal Work-Study, institutionally sponsored loans, scholarships/grants, health care benefits, tuition waivers (full and partial), and unspecified assistantships also available. Financial award application deadline: 3/1; financial award applicants required to submit FAFSA. *Faculty research:* Molecular, cellular, and developmental biology; immunology; microbiology; integrative biology. *Unit head:* Jody Spillane, Project Coordinator, 310-206-1845, E-mail: jspillane@mednet.ucla.edu. *Application contact:* UCLA Access Admissions, 310-206-1845, E-mail: uclaaccess@mednet.ucla.edu.

University of Chicago, Division of Biological Sciences, Department of Human Genetics, Chicago, IL 60637-1513. Offers PhD. *Degree requirements:* For doctorate, thesis/dissertation, ethics class, 2 teaching assistantships. *Entrance requirements:* For doctorate, GRE General Test. Additional exam requirements/recommendations for international students: Required—

TOEFL (minimum score 600 paper-based; 250 computer-based; 104 iBT), IELTS (minimum score 7). Electronic applications accepted.

University of Chicago, Division of Biological Sciences, Molecular Biosciences Cluster, Chicago, IL 60637-1513. Offers biochemistry and molecular biology (PhD); cell and molecular biology (PhD); developmental biology (PhD), including cellular differentiation, developmental endocrinology, developmental genetics, developmental neurobiology, gene expression; genetics, genomics and systems biology (PhD); human genetics (PhD); MD/PhD. *Degree requirements:* For doctorate, thesis/dissertation, ethics class, 2 teaching assistantships. *Entrance requirements:* For doctorate, GRE General Test. Additional exam requirements/recommendations for international students: Required—TOEFL (minimum score 600 paper-based; 250 computer-based; 104 iBT), IELTS (minimum score 7). Electronic applications accepted.

University of Manitoba, Faculty of Medicine and Faculty of Graduate Studies, Graduate Programs in Medicine, Department of Biochemistry and Medical Genetics, Winnipeg, MB R3T 2N2, Canada. Offers M Sc, PhD. Terminal master's awarded for partial completion of doctoral program. *Degree requirements:* For master's, thesis; for doctorate, thesis/dissertation. *Faculty research:* Cancer, gene expression, membrane lipids, metabolic control, genetic diseases.

University of Maryland, Baltimore, School of Medicine, Department of Epidemiology and Preventive Medicine, Baltimore, MD 21201. Offers biostatistics (MS); clinical research (MS); epidemiology and preventative medicine (PhD); epidemiology and preventive medicine (MPH, MS); gerontology (PhD); human genetics and genomic (PhD); human genetics and genomic medicine (MS); molecular epidemiology (MS, PhD); toxicology (MS, PhD); JD/MS; MD/PhD; MS/PhD. *Accreditation:* CEPH. Part-time programs available. *Students:* 84 full-time (57 women), 64 part-time (46 women); includes 17 Black or African American, non-Hispanic/Latino; 23 Asian, non-Hispanic/Latino; 4 Hispanic/Latino, 18 international. Average age 32. In 2010, 21 master's, 10 doctorates awarded. *Entrance requirements:* For master's and doctorate, GRE General Test. Additional exam requirements/recommendations for international students: Required—TOEFL (minimum score 550 paper-based; 213 computer-based; 80 iBT); Recommended—IELTS. *Application deadline:* For fall admission, 1/15 for domestic and international students. Electronic applications accepted. *Expenses:* Contact institution. *Financial support:* In 2010–11, research assistantships with partial tuition reimbursements (averaging $25,000 per year); fellowships, Federal Work-Study, scholarships/grants, and unspecified assistantships also available. Financial award application deadline: 3/1; financial award applicants required to submit FAFSA. *Unit head:* Dr. Patricia Langenberg, Program Director, 410-706-3251, Fax: 410-706-8013. *Application contact:* Danielle Fitzpatrick, Program Coordinator, 410-706-8492, Fax: 410-706-4225, E-mail: dfitzpatrick@epi.umaryland.edu.

University of Michigan, Rackham Graduate School, Program in Biomedical Sciences (PIBS), Department of Human Genetics, Ann Arbor, MI 48109. Offers genetic counseling (MS); human genetics (MS, PhD). *Faculty:* 33 full-time (14 women). *Students:* 38 full-time (29 women); includes 8 minority (1 Black or African American, non-Hispanic/Latino; 5 Asian, non-Hispanic/Latino; 1 Hispanic/Latino; 1 Two or more races, non-Hispanic/Latino). Average age 28. 187 applicants, 16 enrolled. In 2010, 8 master's, 3 doctorates awarded. Terminal master's awarded for partial completion of doctoral program. *Degree requirements:* For master's, research project; for doctorate, thesis/dissertation, oral preliminary exam, oral defense of dissertation. *Entrance requirements:* For master's, GRE General Test, 3 letters of recommendation, advocacy experience; for doctorate, GRE General Test, 3 letters of recommendation. Additional exam requirements/recommendations for international students: Required—TOEFL (minimum score 84 iBT). *Application deadline:* For fall admission, 12/1 for domestic students, 12/1 priority date for international students. Application fee: $65 ($75 for international students). Electronic applications accepted. *Expenses:* Tuition, state resident: full-time $17,784; part-time $1116 per credit hour. Tuition, nonresident: full-time $35,944; part-time $2125 per credit hour. International tuition: $35,994 full-time. Required fees: $95 per semester. Tuition and fees vary according to course load, degree level and program. *Financial support:* In 2010–11, 32 students received support, including 24 fellowships with full tuition reimbursements available (averaging $26,500 per year), 3 teaching assistantships with full tuition reimbursements available (averaging $17,270 per year); scholarships/grants, traineeships, health care benefits, and unspecified assistantships also available. Financial award application deadline: 12/1; financial award applicants required to submit FAFSA. *Faculty research:* Molecular, developmental, statistical, and population genetics. Total annual research expenditures: $8.4 million. *Unit head:* Dr. Sally A. Camper, Chair, 734-763-0682, Fax: 734-763-3784, E-mail: scamper@umich.edu. *Application contact:* Michelle S. Melis, Director of Student Life, 734-615-6538, Fax: 734-647-7022, E-mail: msmtegan@umich.edu.

University of Pittsburgh, Graduate School of Public Health, Department of Human Genetics, Pittsburgh, PA 15260. Offers genetic counseling (MS); human genetics (MS, PhD); public health genetics (MPH, Certificate). *Faculty:* 9 full-time (5 women), 5 part-time/adjunct (2 women). *Students:* 40 full-time (31 women), 27 part-time (23 women); includes 5 Asian, non-Hispanic/Latino; 1 Hispanic/Latino, 22 international. Average age 28. 111 applicants, 53% accepted, 21 enrolled. In 2010, 14 master's, 7 doctorates awarded. Terminal master's awarded for partial completion of doctoral program. *Degree requirements:* For master's, thesis (for some programs); for doctorate, thesis/dissertation. *Entrance requirements:* For master's, GRE General Test, previous course work in biochemistry, calculus, and genetics; for doctorate, GRE General Test. Additional exam requirements/recommendations for international students: Required—TOEFL (minimum score 550 paper-based; 213 computer-based; 80 iBT). *Application deadline:* For fall admission, 4/1 for international students; for winter admission, 9/1 for international students; for spring admission, 2/1 for international students. Applications are processed on a rolling basis. Application fee: $115. Electronic applications accepted. *Expenses:* Tuition, state resident: full-time $17,304; part-time $701 per credit. Tuition, nonresident: full-time $29,554; part-time $1210 per credit. Required fees: $740; $214 per term. Tuition and fees vary according to program. *Financial support:* In 2010–11, 20 students received support, including 20 research assistantships with full tuition reimbursements available (averaging $21,834 per year). *Faculty research:* Genetic mechanisms related to the transition from normal to disease states, how genes and the environment interact to affect the distribution of health and disease in human populations. Total annual research expenditures: $5.8 million. *Unit head:* Dr. Mohammad Kamboh, Chairman, 412-624-3066, Fax: 412-624-3020, E-mail: kamboh@pitt.edu. *Application contact:* Jeanette Norbut, Administrative Secretary, 412-624-3018, Fax: 412-624-3020, E-mail: jeanette.norbut@hgen.pitt.edu.

The University of Texas Health Science Center at Houston, Graduate School of Biomedical Sciences, Program in Human and Molecular Genetics, Houston, TX 77225-0036. Offers MS, PhD, MD/PhD. Terminal master's awarded for partial completion of doctoral program. *Degree requirements:* For master's, thesis; for doctorate, thesis/dissertation. *Entrance requirements:* For master's and doctorate, GRE General Test. Additional exam requirements/recommendations for international students: Required—TOEFL. Electronic applications accepted. *Faculty research:* Computational genomics, cancer genetics, complex disease genetics, medical genetics.

University of Utah, School of Medicine and Graduate School, Graduate Programs in Medicine, Department of Human Genetics, Salt Lake City, UT 84112-1107. Offers MS, PhD. Terminal master's awarded for partial completion of doctoral program. *Degree requirements:* For master's, comprehensive exam, thesis optional; for doctorate, comprehensive exam, thesis/dissertation. Electronic applications accepted. *Expenses:* Tuition, area resident: Part-time $179.19 per credit hour. Tuition, state resident: full-time $4384. Tuition, nonresident: full-time $16,684; part-time $630.67 per credit hour. Required fees: $350 per semester. Tuition and fees vary according to course load, degree level and program. *Faculty research:* RNA metabolism, drosophilia genetics, mouse genetics, protein synthesis.

Vanderbilt University, Graduate School, Program in Human Genetics, Nashville, TN 37240-1001. Offers PhD, MD/PhD. *Students:* 23 full-time (12 women); includes 2 Black or African American, non-Hispanic/Latino; 1 Two or more races, non-Hispanic/Latino. Average age 28. In 2010, 3 doctorates awarded. *Degree requirements:* For doctorate, comprehensive exam, thesis/dissertation. *Entrance requirements:* For doctorate, GRE General Test. Additional exam requirements/recommendations for international students: Required—TOEFL (minimum score 570 paper-based; 230 computer-based; 88 iBT). *Application deadline:* For fall admission, 1/15 for domestic and international students. Application fee: $0. Electronic applications accepted. *Financial support:* Fellowships with full and partial tuition reimbursements, research assistantships with full and partial tuition reimbursements, Federal Work-Study, institutionally sponsored loans, traineeships, and health care benefits available. Financial award application deadline: 1/15; financial award applicants required to submit CSS PROFILE or FAFSA. *Faculty research:* Disease gene discovery, computational genomics, translational genetics. *Unit head:* Dr. Jonathan L. Haines, Director, The Center for Human Genetics Research, 615-343-5851, Fax: 615-343-8619, E-mail: jonathan.haines@vanderbilt.edu. *Application contact:* Scott M. Williams, Director of Graduate Studies, 615-343-5851, Fax: 615-343-8619, E-mail: scott.m.williams@vanderbilt.edu.

Virginia Commonwealth University, Medical College of Virginia-Professional Programs, School of Medicine, School of Medicine Graduate Programs, Department of Human and Molecular Genetics, Richmond, VA 23284-9005. Offers genetic counseling (MS); human genetics (PhD); molecular biology and genetics (MS, PhD); MD/PhD. *Faculty:* 25 full-time (14 women). *Students:* 37 full-time (21 women), 1 (woman) part-time; includes 5 minority (1 Black or African American, non-Hispanic/Latino; 4 Asian, non-Hispanic/Latino), 14 international. 51 applicants, 33% accepted, 10 enrolled. In 2010, 3 master's, 5 doctorates awarded. *Degree requirements:* For master's, thesis; for doctorate, thesis/dissertation, comprehensive oral and written exams. *Entrance requirements:* For master's, GRE; for doctorate, GRE General Test. Additional exam requirements/recommendations for international students: Required—TOEFL (minimum score 600 paper-based; 250 computer-based; 100 iBT). *Application deadline:* For fall admission, 12/15 priority date for domestic students. Application fee: $50. Electronic applications accepted. *Expenses:* Tuition, state resident: full-time $4308; part-time $479 per credit hour. Tuition, nonresident: full-time $8942; part-time $994 per credit hour. Required fees: $2000; $85 per credit hour. Tuition and fees vary according to course level, course load, degree level, campus/location and program. *Financial support:* Fellowships available. *Faculty research:* Genetic epidemiology, biochemical genetics, quantitative genetics, human cytogenetics, molecular genetics. *Unit head:* Dr. Paul B. Fisher, Chair, 804-628-3506, Fax: 804-827-1124, E-mail: pbfisher@vcu.edu. *Application contact:* Dr. Linda A. Corey, Graduate Program Director, 804-628-4514, E-mail: corey@vcu.edu.

Virginia Commonwealth University, Program in Pre-Medical Basic Health Sciences, Richmond, VA 23284-9005. Offers anatomy (CBHS); biochemistry (CBHS); human genetics (CBHS); microbiology (CBHS); pharmacology (CBHS); physiology (CBHS). *Students:* 86 full-time (43 women), 2 part-time (1 woman); includes 42 minority (5 Black or African American, non-Hispanic/Latino; 29 Asian, non-Hispanic/Latino; 5 Hispanic/Latino; 3 Two or more races, non-Hispanic/Latino). 314 applicants, 64% accepted. In 2010, 70 CBHSs awarded. *Entrance requirements:* For degree, GRE, MCAT or DAT, course work in organic chemistry, minimum undergraduate GPA of 2.8. Additional exam requirements/recommendations for international students: Required—TOEFL (minimum score 600 paper-based). *Application deadline:* For fall admission, 6/1 for domestic students. Application fee: $50. Electronic applications accepted. *Expenses:* Tuition, state resident: full-time $4308; part-time $479 per credit hour. Tuition, nonresident: full-time $8942; part-time $994 per credit hour. Required fees: $2000; $85 per credit hour. Tuition and fees vary according to course level, course load, degree level, campus/location and program. *Unit head:* Dr. Louis J. De Felice, Director, 804-828-9501, E-mail: premedcert@vcu.edu. *Application contact:* Zack McDowell, Administrator, 804-828-9501, E-mail: premedcert@vcu.edu.

Wake Forest University, School of Medicine and Graduate School of Arts and Sciences, Graduate Programs in Medicine, Molecular Genetics and Genomics Program, Winston-Salem, NC 27109. Offers PhD, MD/PhD. *Degree requirements:* For doctorate, thesis/dissertation. *Entrance requirements:* For doctorate, GRE General Test. Additional exam requirements/recommendations for international students: Required—TOEFL. Electronic applications accepted. *Faculty research:* Control of gene expression, molecular pathogenesis, protein biosynthesis, cell development, clinical cytogenetics.

West Virginia University, Davis College of Agriculture, Forestry and Consumer Sciences, Interdisciplinary Program in Genetics and Developmental Biology, Morgantown, WV 26506. Offers animal breeding (MS, PhD); biochemical and molecular genetics (MS, PhD); cytogenetics (MS, PhD); descriptive embryology (MS, PhD); developmental genetics (MS); experimental morphogenesis/teratology (MS); human genetics (MS, PhD); immunogenetics (MS, PhD); life cycles of animals and plants (MS, PhD); molecular aspects of development (MS, PhD); mutagenesis (MS, PhD); oncology (MS, PhD); plant genetics (MS, PhD); population and quantitative genetics (MS, PhD); regeneration (MS, PhD); teratology (PhD); toxicology (MS, PhD). *Degree requirements:* For master's, thesis; for doctorate, comprehensive exam, thesis/dissertation. *Entrance requirements:* For master's, GRE or MCAT, minimum GPA of 2.75. Additional exam requirements/recommendations for international students: Required—TOEFL.

Molecular Genetics

Albert Einstein College of Medicine, Graduate Division of Biomedical Sciences, Division of Biological Sciences, Department of Genetics, Bronx, NY 10461. Offers computational genetics (PhD); molecular genetics (PhD); translational genetics (PhD); MD/PhD. *Degree requirements:* For doctorate, thesis/dissertation. *Entrance requirements:* For doctorate, GRE General Test. Additional exam requirements/recommendations for international students: Required—TOEFL. *Faculty research:* Neurologic genetics in *Drosophila*, biochemical genetics of yeast, developmental genetics in the mouse.

Duke University, Graduate School, Department of Molecular Genetics and Microbiology, Durham, NC 27710. Offers PhD. *Faculty:* 25 full-time. *Students:* 41 full-time (23 women); includes 2 Black or African American, non-Hispanic/Latino; 1 American Indian or Alaska Native, non-Hispanic/Latino; 2 Asian, non-Hispanic/Latino, 11 international. 73 applicants, 29% accepted, 15 enrolled. In 2010, 11 doctorates awarded. *Degree requirements:* For doctorate, thesis/dissertation. *Entrance requirements:* For doctorate, GRE General Test, GRE Subject Test in biology, chemistry, or biochemistry, cell and molecular biology (recommended). Additional exam requirements/recommendations for international students: Required—TOEFL (minimum score 550 paper-based; 213 computer-based; 83 iBT), IELTS (minimum score 7). *Application deadline:* For fall admission, 12/8 priority date for domestic and international students. Application fee: $75. Electronic applications accepted. *Financial support:* Fellow-

Molecular Genetics

Duke University (continued)

ships with full tuition reimbursements, research assistantships with full tuition reimbursements, Federal Work-Study available. Financial award application deadline: 12/31. *Unit head:* Dr. Raphael Valdivia, Director of Graduate Studies, 919-684-6629, Fax: 919-684-8346, E-mail: andrea.lanahan@duke.edu. *Application contact:* Elizabeth Hutton, Director of Admissions, 919-684-3913, Fax: 919-684-2277, E-mail: grad-admissions@duke.edu.

Emory University, Laney Graduate School, Division of Biological and Biomedical Sciences, Program in Microbiology and Molecular Genetics, Atlanta, GA 30322-1100. Offers PhD. *Faculty:* 36 full-time (7 women). *Students:* 44 full-time (31 women); includes 3 Black or African American, non-Hispanic/Latino; 2 Hispanic/Latino, 5 international. Average age 27. 104 applicants, 19% accepted, 7 enrolled. In 2010, 7 doctorates awarded. *Degree requirements:* For doctorate, comprehensive exam, thesis/dissertation. *Entrance requirements:* For doctorate, GRE General Test, minimum GPA of 3.0 in science course work (recommended). Additional exam requirements/recommendations for international students: Required—TOEFL. *Application deadline:* For fall admission, 12/1 for domestic and international students. Application fee: $75. Electronic applications accepted. *Expenses:* Tuition: Full-time $33,800. Required fees: $1300. *Financial support:* In 2010–11, 12 students received support, including 12 fellowships with full tuition reimbursements available (averaging $25,000 per year); institutionally sponsored loans, scholarships/grants, health care benefits, and tuition waivers (full) also available. *Faculty research:* Bacterial genetics and physiology, microbial development, molecular biology of viruses and bacterial pathogens, DNA recombination. *Unit head:* Dr. Phil Rather, Program Director, 404-728-5079, Fax: 404-728-7780, E-mail: prather@emory.edu. *Application contact:* Kathy Smith, Director of Recruitment and Admissions, 404-727-2547, Fax: 404-727-3322, E-mail: kathy.smith@emory.edu.

The George Washington University, Columbian College of Arts and Sciences, Institute for Biomedical Sciences, Program in Biochemistry and Molecular Genetics, Washington, DC 20037. Offers PhD. *Students:* 8 part-time (5 women). Average age 30. In 2010, 2 doctorates awarded. Terminal master's awarded for partial completion of doctoral program. *Degree requirements:* For doctorate, thesis/dissertation, general exam. *Entrance requirements:* For doctorate, GRE General Test, interview, minimum GPA of 3.0. Additional exam requirements/recommendations for international students: Required—TOEFL (minimum score 600 paper-based; 250 computer-based). *Application deadline:* For fall admission, 12/15 priority date for domestic and international students; for spring admission, 10/1 priority date for domestic and international students. Applications are processed on a rolling basis. Application fee: $75. Electronic applications accepted. *Financial support:* In 2010–11, 4 students received support; fellowships, Federal Work-Study, institutionally sponsored loans, and tuition waivers available. Financial award application deadline: 2/1. *Unit head:* Valerie W. Hu, Director, 202-994-8431, E-mail: valhu@gwu.edu. *Application contact:* Information Contact, 202-994-7120, Fax: 202-994-6100, E-mail: genetics@gwu.edu.

The George Washington University, School of Medicine and Health Sciences, Department of Biochemistry and Molecular Biology, Washington, DC 20037. Offers biochemistry and molecular biology (MS); biochemistry and molecular genetics (PhD); molecular biochemistry and bioinformatics (MS). *Students:* 20 full-time (9 women), 16 part-time (6 women); includes 2 Asian, non-Hispanic/Latino, 20 international. Average age 27. 57 applicants, 88% accepted, 15 enrolled. In 2010, 17 master's awarded. *Degree requirements:* For master's, comprehensive exam; for doctorate, thesis/dissertation, general exam. *Entrance requirements:* For master's, GRE General Test, interview, minimum GPA of 3.0; for doctorate, GRE General Test, minimum GPA of 3.0. Additional exam requirements/recommendations for international students: Required—TOEFL (minimum score 550 paper-based; 213 computer-based). *Application deadline:* For fall admission, 4/1 priority date for domestic and international students; for spring admission, 10/1 priority date for domestic and international students. Application fee: $60. *Financial support:* Fellowships available. Financial award application deadline: 2/1. *Unit head:* Dr. Allan L. Goldstein, Chair, 202-994-3171, E-mail: bcmalg@gwumc.edu. *Application contact:* Information Contact, 202-994-2179, Fax: 202-994-0967, E-mail: gwibs@gwu.edu.

Georgia State University, College of Arts and Sciences, Department of Biology, Program in Molecular Genetics and Biochemistry, Atlanta, GA 30302-3083. Offers MS, PhD. Part-time programs available. Terminal master's awarded for partial completion of doctoral program. *Degree requirements:* For master's, thesis or alternative; for doctorate, thesis/dissertation, exam. *Entrance requirements:* For master's and doctorate, GRE General Test. Additional exam requirements/recommendations for international students: Required—TOEFL. Electronic applications accepted.

Harvard University, Graduate School of Arts and Sciences, Division of Medical Sciences, Boston, MA 02115. Offers biological chemistry and molecular pharmacology (PhD); cell biology (PhD); genetics (PhD); microbiology and molecular genetics (PhD); pathology (PhD), including experimental pathology. *Degree requirements:* For doctorate, thesis/dissertation. *Entrance requirements:* For doctorate, GRE General Test, GRE Subject Test. Additional exam requirements/recommendations for international students: Required—TOEFL. *Expenses:* Tuition: Full-time $34,976. Required fees: $1166. Full-time tuition and fees vary according to program.

Illinois State University, Graduate School, College of Arts and Sciences, Department of Biological Sciences, Normal, IL 61790-2200. Offers animal behavior (MS); bacteriology (MS); biochemistry (MS); biological sciences (MS); biology (PhD); biophysics (MS); biotechnology (MS); botany (MS, PhD); cell biology (MS); conservation biology (MS); developmental biology (MS); ecology (MS, PhD); entomology (MS); evolutionary biology (MS); genetics (MS, PhD); immunology (MS); microbiology (MS, PhD); molecular biology (MS); molecular genetics (MS); neurobiology (MS); neuroscience (MS); parasitology (MS); physiology (MS, PhD); plant biology (MS); plant molecular biology (MS); plant sciences (MS); structural biology (MS); zoology (MS, PhD). Part-time programs available. *Degree requirements:* For master's, thesis or alternative; for doctorate, variable foreign language requirement, thesis/dissertation, 2 terms of residency. *Entrance requirements:* For master's, GRE General Test, minimum GPA of 2.6 in last 60 hours of course work; for doctorate, GRE General Test. *Faculty research:* Redoc balance and drug development in schistosoma mansoni, control of the growth of listeria monocytogenes at low temperature, regulation of cell expansion and microtubule function by SPRI, CRUI: physiology and fitness consequences of different life history phenotypes.

Indiana University–Purdue University Indianapolis, Indiana University School of Medicine, Department of Medical and Molecular Genetics, Indianapolis, IN 46202-2896. Offers genetic counseling (MS); medical and molecular genetics (MS, PhD); MD/MS; MD/PhD. Part-time programs available. *Faculty:* 8 full-time (2 women). *Students:* 34 full-time (23 women), 2 part-time (both women); includes 3 minority (1 Black or African American, non-Hispanic/Latino; 1 Asian, non-Hispanic/Latino; 1 Hispanic/Latino), 7 international. Average age 26. 125 applicants, 26% accepted, 18 enrolled. In 2010, 8 master's, 2 doctorates awarded. Terminal master's awarded for partial completion of doctoral program. *Degree requirements:* For master's, thesis optional; for doctorate, thesis/dissertation, research ethics. *Entrance requirements:* For master's and doctorate, GRE General Test, minimum GPA of 3.2. *Application deadline:* For fall admission, 1/15 priority date for domestic students. Application fee: $55 ($65 for international students). *Financial support:* In 2010–11, 11 students received support, including 2 fellowships with tuition reimbursements available (averaging $12,750 per year), 2 teaching assistantships (averaging $22,000 per year); research assistantships with tuition reimbursements available, Federal Work-Study and institutionally sponsored loans also available. Support available to part-time students. Financial award application deadline: 1/15. *Faculty research:* Twins, human gene mapping, chromosomes and malignancy, clinical genetics. Total annual research expenditures: $2.1 million. *Unit head:* Dr. Joe Christian, Chairman, 317-274-2241. *Application contact:* Kathleen Wilhelm, Admissions Secretary, 317-274-2241, Fax: 317-274-2387, E-mail: medgen@iupui.edu.

Medical College of Wisconsin, Graduate School of Biomedical Sciences, Department of Microbiology and Molecular Genetics, Milwaukee, WI 53226-0509. Offers MS, PhD, MD/PhD. *Degree requirements:* For doctorate, comprehensive exam, thesis/dissertation. *Entrance requirements:* For doctorate, GRE General Test. Additional exam requirements/recommendations for international students: Required—TOEFL. *Expenses:* Tuition: Full-time $30,000; part-time $710 per credit. Required fees: $150. *Faculty research:* Virology, immunology, bacterial toxins, regulation of gene expression.

Michigan State University, College of Human Medicine and The Graduate School, Graduate Programs in Human Medicine, East Lansing, MI 48824. Offers biochemistry and molecular biology (MS, PhD); epidemiology (MS, PhD); microbiology (MS); microbiology and molecular genetics (PhD); pharmacology and toxicology (MS, PhD); physiology (MS, PhD); public health (MPH). *Entrance requirements:* Additional exam requirements/recommendations for international students: Required—TOEFL.

Michigan State University, College of Osteopathic Medicine and The Graduate School, Graduate Studies in Osteopathic Medicine, East Lansing, MI 48824. Offers biochemistry and molecular biology (MS, PhD); microbiology (MS); microbiology and molecular genetics (PhD); pharmacology and toxicology (MS, PhD), including integrative pharmacology (MS), pharmacology and toxicology, pharmacology and toxicology-environmental toxicology (PhD); physiology (MS, PhD).

New York University, Graduate School of Arts and Science, Department of Biology, New York, NY 10012-1019. Offers biology (PhD); biomedical journalism (MS); cancer and molecular biology (PhD); computational biology (PhD); computers in biological research (MS); developmental genetics (PhD); general biology (MS); immunology and microbiology (PhD); molecular genetics (PhD); neurobiology (PhD); oral biology (MS); plant biology (PhD); recombinant DNA technology (MS); MS/MBA. Part-time programs available. *Faculty:* 24 full-time (5 women). *Students:* 155 full-time (89 women), 38 part-time (24 women); includes 29 Asian, non-Hispanic/Latino; 7 Hispanic/Latino, 88 international. Average age 27. 324 applicants, 69% accepted, 63 enrolled. In 2010, 55 master's, 4 doctorates awarded. Terminal master's awarded for partial completion of doctoral program. *Degree requirements:* For master's, thesis or alternative, qualifying paper; for doctorate, comprehensive exam, thesis/dissertation. *Entrance requirements:* For master's, GRE General Test; for doctorate, GRE General Test, GRE Subject Test. Additional exam requirements/recommendations for international students: Required—TOEFL. *Application deadline:* For fall admission, 12/15 priority date for domestic students. Application fee: $90. *Financial support:* Fellowships with tuition reimbursements, research assistantships with tuition reimbursements, teaching assistantships with tuition reimbursements, career-related internships or fieldwork, Federal Work-Study, institutionally sponsored loans, scholarships/grants, health care benefits, and unspecified assistantships available. Financial award application deadline: 12/15; financial award applicants required to submit FAFSA. *Faculty research:* Genomics, molecular and cell biology, development and molecular genetics, molecular evolution of plants and animals. *Unit head:* Gloria Coruzzi, Chair, 212-998-8200, Fax: 212-995-4015, E-mail: biology@nyu.edu. *Application contact:* Justin Blau, Director of Graduate Studies, 212-998-8200, Fax: 212-995-4015, E-mail: biology@nyu.edu.

The Ohio State University, Graduate School, College of Arts and Sciences, Division of Natural and Mathematical Sciences, Department of Molecular Genetics, Columbus, OH 43210. Offers cell and developmental biology (MS, PhD); genetics (MS, PhD); molecular biology (MS, PhD). *Faculty:* 26. *Students:* 7 full-time (3 women), 25 part-time (14 women), 16 international. Average age 27. In 2010, 1 master's, 1 doctorate awarded. *Degree requirements:* For master's, thesis; for doctorate, thesis/dissertation. *Entrance requirements:* For master's and doctorate, GRE General Test, GRE Subject Test in biology or biochemistry (recommended). Additional exam requirements/recommendations for international students: Required—TOEFL (minimum score 600 paper-based; 250 computer-based). *Application deadline:* For fall admission, 8/15 priority date for domestic students, 7/1 priority date for international students; for winter admission, 12/1 priority date for domestic students, 11/1 priority date for international students; for spring admission, 3/1 priority date for domestic students, 2/1 priority date for international students. Applications are processed on a rolling basis. Application fee: $40 ($50 for international students). Electronic applications accepted. *Expenses:* Tuition, state resident: full-time $10,605. Tuition, nonresident: full-time $26,535. Tuition and fees vary according to course load and program. *Financial support:* Fellowships, research assistantships, teaching assistantships, Federal Work-Study and institutionally sponsored loans available. Support available to part-time students. *Unit head:* Dr. Anna Hopper, Chair, 614-688-3306, Fax: 614-247-2594, E-mail: hopper.64@osu.edu. *Application contact:* 614-292-9444, Fax: 614-292-3895, E-mail: domestic.grad@osu.edu.

Oklahoma State University, College of Arts and Sciences, Department of Microbiology and Molecular Genetics, Stillwater, OK 74078. Offers MS, PhD. *Faculty:* 22 full-time (4 women). *Students:* 7 full-time (4 women), 20 part-time (10 women); includes 1 American Indian or Alaska Native, non-Hispanic/Latino; 1 Asian, non-Hispanic/Latino, 14 international. Average age 28. 81 applicants, 9% accepted, 3 enrolled. In 2010, 1 master's, 2 doctorates awarded. *Degree requirements:* For master's, thesis; for doctorate, comprehensive exam, thesis/dissertation. *Entrance requirements:* For master's, GRE General Test; for doctorate, GRE General Test. Additional exam requirements/recommendations for international students: Required—TOEFL (minimum score 550 paper-based; 79 iBT). *Application deadline:* For fall admission, 3/1 priority date for international students; for spring admission, 8/1 priority date for international students. Applications are processed on a rolling basis. Application fee: $40 ($75 for international students). Electronic applications accepted. *Expenses:* Tuition, state resident: full-time $3716; part-time $154.85 per credit hour. Tuition, nonresident: full-time $14,892; part-time $621 per credit hour. Required fees: $2044; $85.20 per credit hour. One-time fee: $50. Tuition and fees vary according to course load and campus/location. *Financial support:* In 2010–11, 16 research assistantships (averaging $17,685 per year), 11 teaching assistantships (averaging $17,044 per year) were awarded; career-related internships or fieldwork, Federal Work-Study, scholarships/grants, health care benefits, tuition waivers (partial), and unspecified assistantships also available. Support available to part-time students. Financial award application deadline: 3/1; financial award applicants required to submit FAFSA. *Faculty research:* Bioinformatics, genomics-genetics, virology, environmental microbiology, development-molecular mechanisms. *Unit head:* Dr. Bill Picking, Head, 405-744-7180, Fax: 405-744-6790. *Application contact:* Dr. Gordon Emslie, Dean, 405-744-6368, Fax: 405-744-0355, E-mail: grad-i@okstate.edu.

Rutgers, The State University of New Jersey, New Brunswick, Graduate School-New Brunswick, Programs in the Molecular Biosciences, Program in Microbiology and Molecular Genetics, Piscataway, NJ 08854-8097. Offers applied microbiology (MS, PhD); clinical microbiology (MS, PhD); computational molecular biology (PhD); immunology (MS, PhD); microbial biochemistry (MS, PhD); molecular genetics (MS, PhD); virology (MS, PhD). MS, PhD offered jointly with University of Medicine and Dentistry of New Jersey. Part-time programs available. Terminal master's awarded for partial completion of doctoral program. *Degree requirements:* For master's, comprehensive exam, thesis or alternative; for doctorate, comprehensive exam, thesis/dissertation, written qualifying exam. *Entrance requirements:* For master's, GRE General Test, minimum GPA of 3.0; for doctorate, GRE General Test, GRE Subject Test (recommended), minimum GPA of 3.0. Additional exam requirements/recommendations for international students: Required—TOEFL. Electronic applications accepted. *Expenses:* Tuition, state resident: full-time $7200; part-time $600 per credit. Tuition, nonresident: full-time $11,124; part-time $927 per credit. *Faculty research:* Molecular genetics and microbial physiology; virology and pathogenic microbiology; applied, environmental and industrial microbiology; computers in molecular biology.

Stony Brook University, State University of New York, Stony Brook University Medical Center, School of Medicine and Graduate School, Graduate Programs in Medicine, Department of Molecular Genetics and Microbiology, Stony Brook, NY 11794. Offers molecular microbiology (PhD). *Faculty:* 18 full-time (6 women). *Students:* 26 full-time (16 women); includes 2 Asian, non-Hispanic/Latino; 1 Hispanic/Latino, 9 international. Average age 27. 85 applicants, 20% accepted, 5 enrolled. In 2010, 9 doctorates awarded. *Degree requirements:* For doctorate, comprehensive exam, thesis/dissertation. *Entrance requirements:* For doctorate, GRE General Test, GRE Subject Test. Additional exam requirements/recommendations for international students: Required—TOEFL. *Application deadline:* For fall admission, 1/15 for domestic students. Application fee: $100. *Expenses:* Tuition, state resident: full-time $8370; part-time $349 per credit. Tuition, nonresident: full-time $13,780; part-time $574 per credit. Required fees: $994. *Financial support:* In 2010–11, 19 research assistantships were awarded; fellowships, teaching assistantships, Federal Work-Study also available. Financial award application deadline: 3/15. *Faculty research:* Adenovirus molecular genetics, molecular biology of tumors, virus SV40, mechanism of tumor infection by SAV virus. Total annual research expenditures: $9.8 million. *Unit head:* Dr. Jorge Benach, Interim Chair, 631-632-8800, Fax: 631-632-9797. *Application contact:* Dr. Janet Hearing, Director, 631-632-8778, Fax: 631-632-9797, E-mail: jhearing@ms.cc.sunysb.edu.

Texas Tech University Health Sciences Center, Graduate School of Biomedical Sciences, Department of Cell Biology and Biochemistry, Program in Biochemistry and Molecular Genetics, Lubbock, TX 79430. Offers MS, PhD, MD/PhD, MS/PhD. Terminal master's awarded for partial completion of doctoral program. *Degree requirements:* For master's, comprehensive exam, thesis, preliminary, comprehensive, and final exams; for doctorate, comprehensive exam, thesis/dissertation, preliminary, comprehensive, and final exams. *Entrance requirements:* For master's and doctorate, GRE General Test, minimum GPA of 3.0. Additional exam requirements/recommendations for international students: Required—TOEFL. Electronic applications accepted. *Faculty research:* Reproductive endocrinology, immunology, developmental biochemistry, biochemistry and genetics of cancer, molecular genetics and cell cycle.

The University of Alabama at Birmingham, Graduate Programs in Joint Health Sciences, Program in Biochemistry and Molecular Genetics, Birmingham, AL 35294. Offers PhD. *Students:* 29 full-time (9 women), 3 part-time (0 women); includes 2 minority (both Asian, non-Hispanic/Latino), 18 international. Average age 30. In 2010, 6 doctorates awarded. *Degree requirements:* For doctorate, thesis/dissertation. *Entrance requirements:* For doctorate, GRE General Test, interview. *Application deadline:* Applications are processed on a rolling basis. Electronic applications accepted. *Expenses:* Tuition, state resident: full-time $5482. Tuition, nonresident: full-time $12,430. Tuition and fees vary according to program. *Financial support:* In 2010–11, 8 fellowships were awarded. *Unit head:* Dr. Tim M. Townes, Chair, 205-934-5294, E-mail: ttownes@uab.edu. *Application contact:* Information Contact, 205-934-6034, Fax: 205-975-2547.

University of California, Irvine, School of Medicine and School of Biological Sciences, Department of Microbiology and Molecular Genetics, Irvine, CA 92697. Offers biological sciences (MS, PhD); MD/PhD. Students apply through the Graduate Program in Molecular Biology, Genetics, and Biochemistry. *Students:* 31 full-time (18 women); includes 16 minority (1 Black or African American, non-Hispanic/Latino; 9 Asian, non-Hispanic/Latino; 6 Hispanic/Latino). Average age 28. In 2010, 1 master's, 10 doctorates awarded. *Degree requirements:* For doctorate, thesis/dissertation. *Entrance requirements:* For doctorate, GRE General Test, GRE Subject Test, minimum GPA of 3.0. Additional exam requirements/recommendations for international students: Required—TOEFL (minimum score 550 paper-based; 213 computer-based). *Application deadline:* For fall admission, 12/15 priority date for domestic students, 12/15 for international students. Application fee: $80 ($100 for international students). Electronic applications accepted. *Financial support:* Fellowships, research assistantships with full tuition reimbursements, teaching assistantships, institutionally sponsored loans, traineeships, health care benefits, and unspecified assistantships available. Financial award applicants required to submit FAFSA. *Faculty research:* Molecular biology and genetics of viruses, bacteria, and yeast; immune response; molecular biology of cultured animal cells; genetic basis of cancer; genetics and physiology of infectious agents. *Unit head:* Rozanne M. Sandri-Goldin, Chair, 949-824-7570, Fax: 949-824-8598, E-mail: rmsandri@uci.edu. *Application contact:* Renee Marie Frigo, Program Manager, 949-824-8145, Fax: 949-824-1965, E-mail: rfrigo@uci.edu.

University of California, Los Angeles, David Geffen School of Medicine and Graduate Division, Graduate Programs in Medicine, Department of Microbiology, Immunology and Molecular Genetics, Los Angeles, CA 90095. Offers MS, PhD. *Faculty:* 31 full-time (6 women). *Students:* 51 full-time (19 women); includes 19 minority (1 Black or African American, non-Hispanic/Latino; 9 Asian, non-Hispanic/Latino; 9 Hispanic/Latino), 6 international. Average age 28. 5 applicants, 100% accepted, 4 enrolled. In 2010, 4 master's, 14 doctorates awarded. *Degree requirements:* For doctorate, thesis/dissertation, oral and written qualifying exams. *Entrance requirements:* For doctorate, GRE General Test, GRE Subject Test. Additional exam requirements/recommendations for international students: Required—TOEFL. Application fee: $70 ($90 for international students). Electronic applications accepted. *Financial support:* In 2010–11, 50 fellowships, 47 research assistantships, 20 teaching assistantships were awarded; Federal Work-Study, institutionally sponsored loans, and tuition waivers (full and partial) also available. Financial award application deadline: 3/1. *Unit head:* Dr. Jeff F. Miller, Chair, 310-206-7926, Fax: 310-267-2774, E-mail: jfmiller@ucla.edu. *Application contact:* Bridget Wolfgang, Graduate Student Affairs, 310-825-8482, Fax: 310-206-5231, E-mail: bridgetw@microbio.ucla.edu.

University of California, Riverside, Graduate Division, Graduate Program in Genetics, Genomics, and Bioinformatics, Riverside, CA 92521-0102. Offers genomics and bioinformatics (PhD); molecular genetics (PhD); population and evolutionary genetics (PhD). *Degree requirements:* For doctorate, thesis/dissertation, qualifying exams, teaching experience. *Entrance requirements:* For doctorate, GRE General Test, minimum GPA of 3.2. Additional exam requirements/recommendations for international students: Required—TOEFL (minimum score 550 paper-based; 213 computer-based; 80 iBT). Electronic applications accepted. *Faculty research:* Molecular Genetics, Evolution and Population Genetics, Genomics and Bioinformatics.

University of Cincinnati, Graduate School, College of Medicine, Graduate Programs in Biomedical Sciences, Department of Molecular Genetics, Biochemistry and Microbiology, Cincinnati, OH 45221. Offers MS, PhD. Terminal master's awarded for partial completion of doctoral program. *Degree requirements:* For master's, thesis or alternative; for doctorate, thesis/dissertation, qualifying exam. *Entrance requirements:* For master's and doctorate, GRE General Test. Additional exam requirements/recommendations for international students: Required—TOEFL (minimum score 600 paper-based; 250 computer-based; 100 iBT), TWE. Electronic applications accepted. *Faculty research:* Cancer biology and developmental genetics, gene regulation and chromosome structure, microbiology and pathogenic mechanisms, structural biology, membrane biochemistry and signal transduction.

University of Florida, College of Medicine, Department of Molecular Genetics and Microbiology, Gainesville, FL 32611. Offers MS, PhD. Terminal master's awarded for partial completion of doctoral program. *Degree requirements:* For master's, thesis; for doctorate, thesis/dissertation. *Entrance requirements:* For master's and doctorate, GRE General Test, minimum GPA of 3.0. Additional exam requirements/recommendations for international students: Required—TOEFL. Electronic applications accepted. *Expenses:* Tuition, state resident: full-time $10,916. Tuition, nonresident: full-time $28,309.

University of Guelph, Graduate Studies, College of Biological Science, Department of Molecular and Cellular Biology, Guelph, ON N1G 2W1, Canada. Offers biochemistry (M Sc, PhD); biophysics (M Sc, PhD); botany (M Sc, PhD); microbiology (M Sc, PhD); molecular biology and genetics (M Sc, PhD). *Degree requirements:* For master's, thesis, research proposal; for doctorate, comprehensive exam, thesis/dissertation, research proposal. *Entrance requirements:* For master's, minimum B-average during previous 2 years of coursework; for doctorate, minimum A-average. Additional exam requirements/recommendations for international students: Required—TOEFL (minimum score 550 paper-based; 213 computer-based), IELTS (minimum score 6.5). Electronic applications accepted. *Faculty research:* Physiology, structure, genetics, and ecology of microbes; virology and microbial technology.

University of Illinois at Chicago, College of Medicine and Graduate College, Graduate Programs in Medicine, Department of Biochemistry and Molecular Genetics, Chicago, IL 60607-7128. Offers PhD, MD/PhD. Terminal master's awarded for partial completion of doctoral program. *Degree requirements:* For doctorate, thesis/dissertation. *Entrance requirements:* For doctorate, GRE General Test. Additional exam requirements/recommendations for international students: Required—TOEFL. Electronic applications accepted. *Faculty research:* Nature of cellular components, control of metabolic processes, regulation of gene expression.

The University of Manchester, Faculty of Life Sciences, Manchester, United Kingdom. Offers adaptive organismal biology (M Phil, PhD); animal biology (M Phil, PhD); biochemistry (M Phil, PhD); bioinformatics (M Phil, PhD); biomolecular sciences (M Phil, PhD); biotechnology (M Phil, PhD); cell biology (M Phil, PhD); cell matrix research (M Phil, PhD); channels and transporters (M Phil, PhD); developmental biology (M Phil, PhD); Egyptology (M Phil, PhD); environmental biology (M Phil, PhD); evolutionary biology (M Phil, PhD); gene expression (M Phil, PhD); genetics (M Phil, PhD); history of science, technology and medicine (M Phil, PhD); immunology (M Phil, PhD); integrative neurobiology and behavior (M Phil, PhD); membrane trafficking (M Phil, PhD); microbiology (M Phil, PhD); molecular and cellular neuroscience (M Phil, PhD); molecular biology (M Phil, PhD); molecular cancer studies (M Phil, PhD); neuroscience (M Phil, PhD); ophthalmology (M Phil, PhD); optometry (M Phil, PhD); organelle function (M Phil, PhD); pharmacology (M Phil, PhD); physiology (M Phil, PhD); plant sciences (M Phil, PhD); stem cell research (M Phil, PhD); structural biology (M Phil, PhD); systems neuroscience (M Phil, PhD); toxicology (M Phil, PhD).

University of Maryland, College Park, Academic Affairs, College of Computer, Mathematical and Natural Sciences, Department of Cell Biology and Molecular Genetics, Program in Cell Biology and Molecular Genetics, College Park, MD 20742. Offers MS, PhD. *Faculty:* 78 full-time (30 women), 3 part-time/adjunct (all women). *Students:* 58 full-time (31 women), 2 part-time (1 woman); includes 3 Black or African American, non-Hispanic/Latino; 4 Asian, non-Hispanic/Latino; 3 Hispanic/Latino, 19 international. 226 applicants, 13% accepted, 15 enrolled. In 2010, 3 master's, 6 doctorates awarded. *Degree requirements:* For master's, thesis; for doctorate, thesis/dissertation, exams. *Entrance requirements:* For master's and doctorate, GRE General Test, 3 letters of recommendation, minimum GPA of 3.0. Additional exam requirements/recommendations for international students: Required—TOEFL. *Application deadline:* For fall admission, 1/6 for domestic and international students. Application fee: $75. *Expenses:* Tuition, state resident: part-time $471 per credit hour. Tuition, nonresident: part-time $1016 per credit hour. Required fees: $337 per term. *Financial support:* In 2010–11, 7 fellowships with full and partial tuition reimbursements (averaging $24,904 per year), 16 research assistantships (averaging $19,428 per year), 30 teaching assistantships (averaging $19,352 per year) were awarded. Financial award applicants required to submit FAFSA. *Faculty research:* Cytoskeletal activity, membrane biology, cell division, genetics and genomics, virology. *Unit head:* Norma Andrews, Chair, 301-405-1605, Fax: 301-314-9489, E-mail: andrewsn@umd.edu. *Application contact:* Dean of Graduate School, 301-405-0358, Fax: 301-314-9305.

University of Massachusetts Worcester, Graduate School of Biomedical Sciences, Worcester, MA 01655-0115. Offers biochemistry and molecular pharmacology (PhD); bioinformatics and computational biology (PhD); cancer biology (PhD); cell biology (PhD); clinical and population health research (PhD); clinical investigation (MS); immunology and virology (PhD); interdisciplinary graduate program (PhD); molecular genetics and microbiology (PhD); neuroscience (PhD); DVM/PhD; MD/PhD. *Faculty:* 1,059 full-time (357 women), 145 part-time/adjunct (100 women). *Students:* 438 full-time (239 women), 1 (woman) part-time; includes 44 minority (9 Black or African American, non-Hispanic/Latino; 31 Asian, non-Hispanic/Latino; 4 Hispanic/Latino), 148 international. Average age 29. 687 applicants, 28% accepted, 116 enrolled. In 2010, 6 master's, 45 doctorates awarded. Terminal master's awarded for partial completion of doctoral program. *Degree requirements:* For master's, thesis; for doctorate, thesis/dissertation. *Entrance requirements:* For master's, bachelor's degree; for doctorate, GRE General Test, MS, MA, or MPH (for some programs). Additional exam requirements/recommendations for international students: Required—TOEFL (minimum score 600 paper-based; 250 computer-based). *Application deadline:* For fall admission, 12/15 for domestic and international students; for winter admission, 1/15 for domestic students; for spring admission, 5/15 for domestic students. Application fee: $35. Electronic applications accepted. *Expenses:* Contact institution. *Financial support:* In 2010–11, 439 students received support, including 439 research assistantships with full tuition reimbursements available (averaging $28,350 per year); scholarships/grants, health care benefits, tuition waivers (full), and unspecified assistantships also available. Financial award application deadline: 4/20. *Faculty research:* RNA interference, gene therapy, cell biology, bioinformatics, clinical research. Total annual research expenditures: $232 million. *Unit head:* Dr. Anthony Carruthers, Dean, 508-856-4135, E-mail: anthony.carruthers@umassmed.edu. *Application contact:* Dr. Kendall Knight, Associate Dean and Interim Director of Admissions and Recruitment, 508-856-5628, Fax: 508-856-3659, E-mail: kendall.knight@umassmed.edu.

University of Medicine and Dentistry of New Jersey, Graduate School of Biomedical Sciences, Graduate Programs in Biomedical Sciences–Newark, Department of Microbiology and Molecular Genetics, Newark, NJ 07107. Offers PhD. *Degree requirements:* For doctorate, thesis/dissertation, qualifying exam. *Entrance requirements:* For doctorate, GRE General Test. Additional exam requirements/recommendations for international students: Required—TOEFL. Electronic applications accepted. *Faculty research:* Molecular genetics of yeast, mutagenesis and carcinogenesis of DNA, bacterial protein synthesis, mammalian cell genetics, adenovirus gene expression.

University of Medicine and Dentistry of New Jersey, Graduate School of Biomedical Sciences, Graduate Programs in Biomedical Sciences–Piscataway, Program in Molecular Genetics, Microbiology and Immunology, Piscataway, NJ 08854-5635. Offers MS, PhD, MD/PhD. Terminal master's awarded for partial completion of doctoral program. *Degree requirements:* For master's, thesis, qualifying exam; for doctorate, thesis/dissertation, qualifying exam. *Entrance requirements:* For master's and doctorate, GRE General Test. Additional exam requirements/recommendations for international students: Required—TOEFL. *Application deadline:* For fall admission, 1/5 for domestic students. Applications are processed on a rolling basis. Application fee: $40. Electronic applications accepted. *Financial support:* Fellowships, research assistantships, teaching assistantships available. Financial award application deadline: 5/1. *Faculty research:* Interferon, receptors, retrovirus evolution, Arbo virus/host cell interactions. *Unit head:* Dr. Michael J. Leibowitz, Director, 732-235-4795, Fax: 732-235-5223, E-mail: leibowit@umdnj.edu. *Application contact:* Johanna Sierra, University Registrar, 732-235-5016, Fax: 732-235-4720.

University of Pittsburgh, School of Medicine, Graduate Programs in Medicine, Molecular Genetics and Developmental Biology Program, Pittsburgh, PA 15260. Offers MS, PhD. *Faculty:* 35 full-time (10 women). *Students:* 14 full-time (8 women); includes 2 Asian, non-Hispanic/Latino, 4 international. Average age 27. 486 applicants, 14% accepted. In 2010, 6 doctorates awarded. *Degree requirements:* For doctorate, comprehensive exam, thesis/dissertation. *Entrance requirements:* For doctorate, GRE General Test, GRE Subject Test, minimum QPA of 3.0. Additional exam requirements/recommendations for international students: Required—TOEFL (minimum score 600 paper-based; 100 iBT), IELTS (minimum score 7). *Application deadline:* For fall admission, 12/15 priority date for domestic and international students. Application fee: $50. Electronic applications accepted. *Expenses:* Tuition, state resident: full-time $17,304; part-time $701 per credit. Tuition, nonresident: full-time $29,554; part-time $1210 per credit. Required fees: $740; $214 per term. Tuition and fees vary according to program. *Financial support:* In 2010–11, 14 research assistantships with full tuition reimbursements (averaging $25,500 per year) were awarded; institutionally sponsored loans, scholarships/grants, traineeships, health care benefits, and unspecified assistantships also available. *Faculty research:* Developmental and stem cell biology, DNA replication and repair, gene regulation and signal transduction, oncogenes and tumor suppressor genes, protein structure and molecular dynamics. *Unit head:* Dr. Neil A. Hukriede, Graduate Program Director, 412-648-9918, Fax: 412-624-1401, E-mail: hukriede@pitt.edu. *Application contact:* Graduate Studies Administrator, 412-648-8957, Fax: 412-648-1077, E-mail: gradstudies@medschool.pitt.edu.

Molecular Genetics

University of Rhode Island, Graduate School, College of the Environment and Life Sciences, Department of Cell and Molecular Biology, Kingston, RI 02881. Offers biochemistry (MS, PhD); clinical laboratory sciences (MS), including biotechnology, clinical laboratory science, cytopathology; microbiology (MS, PhD); molecular genetics (MS, PhD). Part-time programs available. *Faculty:* 13 full-time (5 women), 2 part-time/adjunct (1 woman). *Students:* 32 full-time (15 women), 37 part-time (23 women); includes 10 minority (5 Black or African American, non-Hispanic/Latino; 2 Asian, non-Hispanic/Latino; 3 Hispanic/Latino), 4 international. In 2010, 29 master's, 3 doctorates awarded. *Degree requirements:* For master's, comprehensive exam (for some programs); for doctorate, comprehensive exam. *Entrance requirements:* For master's and doctorate, GRE, 2 letters of recommendation. Additional exam requirements/recommendations for international students: Required—TOEFL (minimum score 550 paper-based; 213 computer-based). *Application deadline:* For fall admission, 7/15 for domestic students, 2/1 for international students; for spring admission, 11/15 for domestic students, 7/15 for international students. Application fee: $65. Electronic applications accepted. *Expenses:* Tuition, state resident: full-time $9588; part-time $533 per credit hour. Tuition, nonresident: full-time $22,968; part-time $1276 per credit hour. Required fees: $1282; $68 per semester. Tuition and fees vary according to program. *Financial support:* In 2010–11, 3 research assistantships with full and partial tuition reimbursements (averaging $11,653 per year), 12 teaching assistantships with full and partial tuition reimbursements (averaging $12,379 per year) were awarded. Financial award application deadline: 7/15; financial award applicants required to submit FAFSA. *Faculty research:* Genomics and Sequencing Center: an interdisciplinary genomics research and undergraduate and graduate student training program which provides researchers access to cutting-edge technologies in the field of genomics. Total annual research expenditures: $3.5 million. *Unit head:* Dr. Jay Sperry, Chairperson, 401-874-2201, Fax: 401-874-2202, E-mail: jsperry@mail.uri.edu. *Application contact:* Dr. Jay Sperry, Chairperson, 401-874-2201, Fax: 401-874-2202, E-mail: jsperry@mail.uri.edu.

The University of Texas Health Science Center at Houston, Graduate School of Biomedical Sciences, Program in Human and Molecular Genetics, Houston, TX 77225-0036. Offers MS, PhD, MD/PhD. Terminal master's awarded for partial completion of doctoral program. *Degree requirements:* For master's, thesis; for doctorate, thesis/dissertation. *Entrance requirements:* For master's and doctorate, GRE General Test. Additional exam requirements/recommendations for international students: Required—TOEFL. Electronic applications accepted. *Faculty research:* Computational genomics, cancer genetics, complex disease genetics, medical genetics.

The University of Texas Health Science Center at Houston, Graduate School of Biomedical Sciences, Program in Microbiology and Molecular Genetics, Houston, TX 77225-0036. Offers MS, PhD, MD/PhD. Terminal master's awarded for partial completion of doctoral program. *Degree requirements:* For master's, thesis; for doctorate, thesis/dissertation. *Entrance requirements:* For master's and doctorate, GRE General Test. Additional exam requirements/recommendations for international students: Required—TOEFL. Electronic applications accepted. *Faculty research:* Disease causation, environmental signaling, gene regulation, cell growth and division, cell structure and architecture.

University of Vermont, College of Medicine and Graduate College, Graduate Programs in Medicine, Department of Microbiology and Molecular Genetics, Burlington, VT 05405. Offers MS, PhD, MD/MS, MD/PhD. *Faculty:* 18 full-time (5 women). *Students:* 26 (15 women); includes 1 Hispanic/Latino, 10 international. 47 applicants, 30% accepted, 5 enrolled. In 2010, 2 doctorates awarded. *Degree requirements:* For master's, thesis; for doctorate, thesis/

dissertation. *Entrance requirements:* For master's and doctorate, GRE General Test. Additional exam requirements/recommendations for international students: Required—TOEFL (minimum score 550 paper-based; 213 computer-based; 80 iBT). *Application deadline:* For fall admission, 1/16 priority date for domestic students, 1/16 for international students. Applications are processed on a rolling basis. Application fee: $40. Electronic applications accepted. *Expenses:* Tuition, state resident: part-time $537 per credit hour. Tuition, nonresident: part-time $1355 per credit hour. *Financial support:* Fellowships, research assistantships, teaching assistantships available. Financial award application deadline: 3/1. *Unit head:* Dr. Susan S. Wallace, Chairperson, 802-656-2164. *Application contact:* Dr. David Pederson, Coordinator, 802-656-2164.

University of Vermont, Graduate College, College of Agriculture and Life Sciences and College of Medicine, Department of Microbiology and Molecular Genetics, Burlington, VT 05405. Offers MS, PhD, MD/MS, MD/PhD. *Faculty:* 18 full-time (5 women). *Degree requirements:* For master's, thesis; for doctorate, thesis/dissertation. *Entrance requirements:* For master's and doctorate, GRE General Test. Additional exam requirements/recommendations for international students: Required—TOEFL (minimum score 550 paper-based; 213 computer-based; 80 iBT). *Application deadline:* For fall admission, 2/1 priority date for domestic students. Applications are processed on a rolling basis. Application fee: $40. Electronic applications accepted. *Expenses:* Tuition, state resident: part-time $537 per credit hour. Tuition, nonresident: part-time $1355 per credit hour. *Financial support:* Fellowships, research assistantships, teaching assistantships available. Financial award application deadline: 3/1. *Unit head:* Dr. Susan S. Wallace, Chairperson, 802-656-2164. *Application contact:* Dr. S. Doublie, Coordinator, 802-656-2164.

University of Virginia, School of Medicine, Department of Biochemistry and Molecular Genetics, Charlottesville, VA 22903. Offers biochemistry (PhD); MD/PhD. *Faculty:* 26 full-time (5 women), 1 (woman) part-time/adjunct. *Students:* 36 full-time (15 women); includes 1 Black or African American, non-Hispanic/Latino, 11 international. Average age 27. In 2010, 7 doctorates awarded. *Degree requirements:* For doctorate, thesis/dissertation, written research proposal and defense. *Entrance requirements:* For doctorate, GRE General Test, 3 letters of recommendation. Additional exam requirements/recommendations for international students: Recommended—TOEFL (minimum score 630 paper-based; 250 computer-based; 90 iBT). Application fee: $60. Electronic applications accepted. *Financial support:* Fellowships, health care benefits and tuition waivers (full) available. Financial award applicants required to submit FAFSA. *Unit head:* Joyce L. Hamlin, Chair, 434-924-1940, Fax: 434-924-5069. *Application contact:* Associate Dean for Graduate Programs and Research.

Wake Forest University, School of Medicine and Graduate School of Arts and Sciences, Graduate Programs in Medicine, Molecular Genetics and Genomics Program, Winston-Salem, NC 27109. Offers PhD, MD/PhD. *Degree requirements:* For doctorate, thesis/dissertation. *Entrance requirements:* For doctorate, GRE General Test. Additional exam requirements/recommendations for international students: Required—TOEFL. Electronic applications accepted. *Faculty research:* Control of gene expression, molecular pathogenesis, protein biosynthesis, cell development, clinical cytogenetics.

Washington University in St. Louis, Graduate School of Arts and Sciences, Division of Biology and Biomedical Sciences, Program in Molecular Genetics, St. Louis, MO 63130-4899. Offers PhD. *Degree requirements:* For doctorate, thesis/dissertation. *Entrance requirements:* For doctorate, GRE General Test, GRE Subject Test. Electronic applications accepted.

Reproductive Biology

Cornell University, Graduate School, Graduate Fields of Comparative Biomedical Sciences, Field of Comparative Biomedical Sciences, Ithaca, NY 14853-0001. Offers cellular and molecular medicine (MS, PhD); developmental and reproductive biology (MS, PhD); infectious diseases (MS, PhD); population medicine and epidemiology (MS, PhD); structural and functional biology (MS, PhD). *Faculty:* 94 full-time (27 women). *Students:* 47 full-time (33 women); includes 2 Black or African American, non-Hispanic/Latino; 1 Asian, non-Hispanic/Latino, 23 international. Average age 30. 31 applicants, 48% accepted, 14 enrolled. In 2010, 11 doctorates awarded. *Degree requirements:* For master's, thesis; for doctorate, comprehensive exam, thesis/dissertation. *Entrance requirements:* For master's and doctorate, GRE General Test, 2 letters of recommendation. Additional exam requirements/recommendations for international students: Required—TOEFL (minimum score 550 paper-based; 213 computer-based; 77 iBT). *Application deadline:* For fall admission, 12/15 for domestic students. Application fee: $70. Electronic applications accepted. *Expenses:* Tuition: Full-time $29,500. Required fees: $76. Tuition and fees vary according to degree level and program. *Financial support:* In 2010–11, 18 fellowships with full tuition reimbursements, 25 research assistantships with full tuition reimbursements were awarded; teaching assistantships with full tuition reimbursements, institutionally sponsored loans, scholarships/grants, health care benefits, tuition waivers (full and partial), and unspecified assistantships also available. Financial award applicants required to submit FAFSA. *Faculty research:* Receptors and signal transduction, viral and bacterial infectious diseases, tumor metastasis, clinical sciences/nutritional disease, developmental/neurological disorders. *Unit head:* Director of Graduate Studies, 607-253-3276, Fax: 607-253-3756. *Application contact:* Graduate Field Assistant, 607-253-3276, Fax: 607-253-3756, E-mail: graduate_edcvm@cornell.edu.

Eastern Virginia Medical School, Master's Program in Clinical Embryology and Andrology, Norfolk, VA 23501-1980. Offers MS. Postbaccalaureate distance learning degree programs offered (minimal on-campus study). *Faculty:* 12 full-time, 8 part-time/adjunct. *Students:* 66 full-time (44 women); includes 6 Black or African American, non-Hispanic/Latino; 10 Asian, non-Hispanic/Latino; 10 Hispanic/Latino. 35 applicants, 69% accepted, 23 enrolled. In 2010, 14 master's awarded. *Entrance requirements:* Additional exam requirements/recommendations for international students: Required—TOEFL (minimum score 550 paper-based; 213 computer-based; 80 iBT). *Application deadline:* For fall admission, 1/14 for domestic and international students. Applications are processed on a rolling basis. Application fee: $60. Electronic applications accepted. *Expenses:* Contact institution. *Unit head:* Dr. Jacob Mayer, Director, 757-446-5049, Fax: 757-446-5905. *Application contact:* Nancy Garcia, Administrator, 757-446-8935, Fax: 757-446-5905, E-mail: garcianw@evms.edu.

Northwestern University, The Graduate School, Interdepartmental Biological Sciences Program (IBiS), Evanston, IL 60208. Offers biochemistry, molecular biology, and cell biology (PhD), including biochemistry, cell and molecular biology, molecular biophysics, structural biology; biotechnology (PhD); cell and molecular biology (PhD); developmental biology and genetics (PhD); hormone action and signal transduction (PhD); neuroscience (PhD); structural biology, biochemistry, and biophysics (PhD). Program participants include the Departments of Biochemistry, Molecular Biology, and Cell Biology; Chemistry; Neurobiology and Physiology; Chemical Engineering; Civil Engineering; and Evanston Hospital. *Degree requirements:* For doctorate, thesis/dissertation, qualifying exam. *Entrance requirements:* For doctorate, GRE General Test. Additional exam requirements/recommendations for international students: Required—TOEFL (minimum score 600 paper-based). Electronic applications accepted. *Faculty research:* Developmental genetics, gene regulation, DNA-protein interactions, biological clocks, bioremediation.

Queen's University at Kingston, School of Graduate Studies and Research, Faculty of Health Sciences, Department of Anatomy and Cell Biology, Kingston, ON K7L 3N6, Canada.

Offers biology of reproduction (M Sc, PhD); cancer (M Sc, PhD); cardiovascular pathophysiology (M Sc, PhD); cell and molecular biology (M Sc, PhD); drug metabolism (M Sc, PhD); endocrinology (M Sc, PhD); motor control (M Sc, PhD); neural regeneration (M Sc, PhD); neurophysiology (M Sc, PhD). Part-time programs available. *Degree requirements:* For master's, thesis; for doctorate, one foreign language, comprehensive exam, thesis/dissertation. *Entrance requirements:* Additional exam requirements/recommendations for international students: Required—TOEFL. Electronic applications accepted. *Faculty research:* Human kinetics, neuroscience, reproductive biology, cardiovascular.

Rutgers, The State University of New Jersey, New Brunswick, Graduate School-New Brunswick, Program in Endocrinology and Animal Biosciences, Piscataway, NJ 08854-8097. Offers MS, PhD. Terminal master's awarded for partial completion of doctoral program. *Degree requirements:* For master's, thesis; for doctorate, comprehensive exam, thesis/dissertation. *Entrance requirements:* For master's and doctorate, GRE General Test. Additional exam requirements/recommendations for international students: Required—TOEFL. Electronic applications accepted. *Expenses:* Tuition, state resident: full-time $7200; part-time $600 per credit. Tuition, nonresident: full-time $11,124; part-time $927 per credit. *Faculty research:* Comparative and behavioral endocrinology, epigenetic regulation of the endocrine system, exercise physiology and immunology, fetal and neonatal developmental programming, mammary gland biology and breast cancer, neuroendocrinology and alcohol studies, reproductive and developmental toxicology.

The University of British Columbia, Faculty of Medicine, Department of Obstetrics and Gynecology, Program in Reproductive and Developmental Sciences, Vancouver, BC V6H 3N1, Canada. Offers M Sc, PhD. Part-time programs available. *Faculty:* 21 full-time (7 women). *Students:* 24 full-time (12 women); includes 16 Asian, non-Hispanic/Latino. Average age 27. 6 applicants, 67% accepted, 4 enrolled. In 2010, 1 master's, 7 doctorates awarded. Terminal master's awarded for partial completion of doctoral program. *Degree requirements:* For master's, thesis; for doctorate, thesis/dissertation. *Entrance requirements:* For master's, B Sc or equivalent, MD, DVM, DDS; for doctorate, B Sc with first class honors, M Sc, MD, DVM, DDS. Additional exam requirements/recommendations for international students: Required—TOEFL (minimum score 580 paper-based; 213 computer-based; 80 iBT), IELTS (minimum score 7). *Application deadline:* For fall admission, 4/1 for domestic students, 3/31 for international students; for winter admission, 9/15 for domestic students, 8/15 for international students; for spring admission, 1/31 for domestic students, 12/31 for international students. Application fee: $90 ($150 for international students). Electronic applications accepted. Tuition charges are reported in Canadian dollars. *Expenses:* Tuition, area resident: Full-time $4179 Canadian dollars. International tuition: $7344 Canadian dollars full-time. *Financial support:* In 2010–11, 4 students received support, including 10 fellowships with partial tuition reimbursements available (averaging $16,000 per year), 15 research assistantships with partial tuition reimbursements available (averaging $17,500 per year); tuition waivers (partial) also available. *Faculty research:* Reproductive and placental endocrinology; immunology of reproductive, fertilization, and embryonic development; perinatal metabolism; neonatal development. *Unit head:* Dr. Geoff Hammond, Program Director, 604-875-3108, Fax: 604-875-2725, E-mail: ghammond@cw.bc.ca. *Application contact:* Roshni D. Nair, Program Assistant, 604-875-3108, Fax: 604-875-2725, E-mail: rnair@cw.bc.ca.

University of Hawaii at Manoa, John A. Burns School of Medicine, Program in Developmental and Reproductive Biology, Honolulu, HI 96813. Offers MS, PhD. Part-time programs available. *Faculty:* 24 full-time (7 women). *Students:* 12 full-time (7 women), 8 part-time (3 women); includes 12 minority (8 Asian, non-Hispanic/Latino; 3 Native Hawaiian or other Pacific Islander, non-Hispanic/Latino; 1 Two or more races, non-Hispanic/Latino), 3 international. Average age

29. 22 applicants, 68% accepted, 11 enrolled. In 2010, 1 master's, 1 doctorate awarded. *Degree requirements:* For doctorate, thesis/dissertation. *Entrance requirements:* For doctorate, GRE General Test, GRE Subject Test. Additional exam requirements/recommendations for international students: Recommended—TOEFL (minimum score 560 paper-based; 83 computer-based), IELTS (minimum score 5). *Application deadline:* For fall admission, 3/1 for domestic and international students. Application fee: $50. *Financial support:* In 2010–11, 2 fellowships (averaging $4,577 per year), 10 research assistantships (averaging $16,328 per year) were awarded; teaching assistantships. *Faculty research:* Biology of gametes and fertilization, reproductive endocrinology. Total annual research expenditures: $5.4 million. *Application contact:* Steve Ward, Graduate Chair, 808-956-1412, Fax: 808-956-9722, E-mail: wward@hawaii.edu.

University of Saskatchewan, College of Medicine, Department of Obstetrics, Gynecology and Reproductive Services, Saskatoon, SK S7N 5A2, Canada. Offers M Sc, PhD. *Degree requirements:* For master's, thesis; for doctorate, thesis/dissertation. *Entrance requirements:* Additional exam requirements/recommendations for international students: Required—TOEFL.

University of Wyoming, College of Agriculture and Natural Resources, Department of Animal Sciences, Program in Reproductive Biology, Laramie, WY 82070. Offers MS, PhD. *Degree requirements:* For master's, thesis; for doctorate, thesis/dissertation. *Entrance requirements:* For master's, GRE General Test, minimum GPA of 3.0; for doctorate, GRE General Test, minimum GPA of 3,0 or MS degree. Additional exam requirements/recommendations for international students: Required—TOEFL. *Faculty research:* Fetal programming, chemical suppression, ovaria function, genetics.

West Virginia University, Davis College of Agriculture, Forestry and Consumer Sciences, Interdisciplinary Program in Genetics and Developmental Biology, Morgantown, WV 26506. Offers animal breeding (MS, PhD); biochemical and molecular genetics (MS, PhD); cytogenetics (MS, PhD); descriptive embryology (MS, PhD); developmental genetics (MS); experimental morphogenesis/teratology (MS); human genetics (MS, PhD); immunogenetics (MS, PhD); life cycles of animals and plants (MS, PhD); molecular aspects of development (MS, PhD); mutagenesis (MS, PhD); oncology (MS, PhD); plant genetics (MS, PhD); population and quantitative genetics (MS, PhD); regeneration (MS, PhD); teratology (PhD); toxicology (MS, PhD). *Degree requirements:* For master's, thesis; for doctorate, comprehensive exam, thesis/dissertation. *Entrance requirements:* For master's, GRE or MCAT, minimum GPA of 2.75. Additional exam requirements/recommendations for international students: Required—TOEFL.

Teratology

West Virginia University, Davis College of Agriculture, Forestry and Consumer Sciences, Interdisciplinary Program in Genetics and Developmental Biology, Morgantown, WV 26506. Offers animal breeding (MS, PhD); biochemical and molecular genetics (MS, PhD); cytogenetics (MS, PhD); descriptive embryology (MS, PhD); developmental genetics (MS); experimental morphogenesis/teratology (MS); human genetics (MS, PhD); immunogenetics (MS, PhD); life cycles of animals and plants (MS, PhD); molecular aspects of development (MS, PhD); mutagenesis (MS, PhD); oncology (MS, PhD); plant genetics (MS, PhD); population and quantitative genetics (MS, PhD); regeneration (MS, PhD); teratology (PhD); toxicology (MS, PhD). *Degree requirements:* For master's, thesis; for doctorate, comprehensive exam, thesis/dissertation. *Entrance requirements:* For master's, GRE or MCAT, minimum GPA of 2.75. Additional exam requirements/recommendations for international students: Required—TOEFL.

BAYLOR COLLEGE OF MEDICINE

Department of Molecular and Human Genetics

Programs of Study

The Department of Molecular and Human Genetics offers an NIGMS-supported training program leading to the Ph.D. degree. The Department also cooperates in the Medical Scientist Training Program that leads to a combined M.D./Ph.D. degree.

The research interests of the Department span a broad range, including the principles of DNA replication and repair, DNA recombination, cell division, aging, cancer, development, learning, memory, and social behavior. A variety of model organisms are used, from *E. coli* to yeast and *Dictyostelium* to flies and mice, and there is a strong research program in bioinformatics and genomics as well. Studies in model organisms are tightly integrated with studies on the genetic basis of the human condition. The research program addresses a variety of genetic diseases, and the unique environment of a large medical center allows students to obtain experience in aspects of both basic and clinical research.

The Graduate Program in Molecular and Human Genetics provides outstanding educational opportunities for students who wish to pursue a career in the broad field of genetics. Students in the program obtain rigorous training in modern biology, with an emphasis on genetics. They participate in cutting-edge research on a variety of topics and publish their work in the some of the best peer-reviewed journals in the world. Students are expected to devote full-time to this course of study. In the first year, they concentrate on course work and laboratory rotations designed to provide a firm basis in fundamental genetic concepts and cover recent developments in molecular biology. The program design permits students to move quickly into their thesis research project. The second year and subsequent years are devoted to independent thesis research and elective course work. Seminar programs, literature review meetings, and research presentations enable students to learn about faculty research programs and the current status of various fields of study in the larger scientific community. An annual two-day Departmental research retreat provides an excellent opportunity for students and faculty members to share information in an informal setting.

Students first enrolled in the program in 1987. To date, 153 degrees have been awarded, and the 2011–12 academic year began with 77 students in training. The Department continues to rank first, by a wide margin, in the number of NIH grants and first in total NIH funding among genetics departments at U.S. medical schools.

The Department of Molecular and Human Genetics interacts closely with other departments at Baylor and with other institutions in the Texas Medical Center. Course credit reciprocity among Baylor, Rice University, Texas A&M University, the University of Houston, and the University of Texas Health Science Center expands the scholastic horizon of Baylor students.

Research Facilities

Faculty members in the Department occupy research laboratories furnished with state-of-the-art equipment. The arrangement of laboratories consists of centralized core facilities in which instrumentation serves several investigators. Cooperative and collaborative interactions among Department faculty members and between the Department of Molecular and Human Genetics and other departments and organizations enable students to take full advantage of the facilities at the Texas Medical Center.

Financial Aid

A stipend and fringe-benefits package is awarded to all graduate students enrolled at Baylor College of Medicine. The current stipend is $29,000 per year and health insurance is provided at no cost. Tuition scholarships are awarded to students who are admitted to the program. Following admission to candidacy, students receive a $1000 travel grant from the Department to initiate participation in national meetings.

Cost of Study

Tuition costs are covered in full by tuition scholarships or training grants.

Living and Housing Costs

Most students and faculty members live within a few miles of the Texas Medical Center. Numerous housing options are available. The cost of living in Houston is lower than most major cities. Excellent job opportunities for spouses are available in the many institutions of the Texas Medical Center and throughout the city of Houston.

Student Group

Students in the Department of Molecular and Human Genetics may seek either the Ph.D. degree or the combined M.D./Ph.D. degree. In the past three years, about 15 students per year on average have joined the program. There are approximately 580 students enrolled in the Graduate School; the Medical School has about 680 students. Admission policies at Baylor offer equal opportunity to all, without regard to race, sex, age, religion, country of origin, or handicap.

Location

Baylor College of Medicine is located within the Texas Medical Center, a large and vigorous professional community that also includes the University of Texas Health Science Center, eight teaching hospitals, and the M. D. Anderson Cancer Center. Rice University is nearby. Houston is also the home of Houston Baptist University and the University of Houston. The fourth-largest city in the nation, Houston is an exciting cultural and metropolitan center. Ballet, opera, symphony, and theater are excellent and accessible to the general population. Many fine museums and parks enhance city life. Professional and amateur sports are very popular. The climate permits participation in a wide variety of outdoor activities, and Gulf Coast beaches are a short drive from the city.

The College

Baylor College of Medicine is an independent, private institution dedicated to training in basic and medical sciences. It has promoted the development of interdisciplinary research programs and has consistently identified and encouraged outstanding investigators and medical practitioners. The climate of interaction benefits the graduate student body by expanding its learning opportunities.

Applying

Applicants must have earned a bachelor's degree and have a strong background in biology and biochemistry. Candidates for admission must complete the application form of the Graduate School. The application should contain Graduate Record Examinations scores (less than three years old), three letters of recommendation, and official undergraduate transcripts. Applications receive two reviews, one by a faculty committee of the Department and a second by the Admissions Committee of the Graduate School. The application deadline for admission is January 1. Applications can be obtained through the Graduate School Web site listed in the Costs/Admission Information section.

Correspondence and Information

For an application:
Admissions Office
Graduate School
Baylor College of Medicine
Houston, Texas 77030
Phone: 713-798-4060
Web site: http://www.bcm.edu/gradschool/

For information:
Director of Graduate Studies
Department of Molecular and Human Genetics
Baylor College of Medicine
One Baylor Plaza
Houston, Texas 77030
Phone: 713-798-5056
E-mail: genetics-gradprgm@bcm.tmc.edu
Web site: http://www.bcm.edu/genetics/

Baylor College of Medicine

THE FACULTY AND THEIR RESEARCH

Benjamin R. Arenkiel, Assistant Professor; Ph.D. Utah, 2004. Molecular genetic studies to investigate mechanisms of neural circuit formation, function, and maintenance.

David Bates, Assistant Professor; Ph.D., New Mexico, 1998. Chromosome dynamics, molecular mechanisms of DNA replication, and cell-cycle control in *E. coli*.

Arthur L. Beaudet, Professor and Chair; M.D., Yale, 1967. Role of epigenetics and genomic imprinting in evolution and disease, including Prader-Willi and Angelman syndromes and autism; hepatocyte gene therapy.

Hugo J. Bellen, Professor; D.V.M./Ph.D., California, Davis, 1986. Genetic and molecular analysis of neurotransmitter release and neural development and neuronal degeneration in *Drosophila*.

John W. Belmont, Professor; M.D./Ph.D., Baylor College of Medicine, 1981. Structural congenital heart defects including abnormalities in laterality and hypoplastic left heart syndrome; functional studies of Zic3; genetics of human immune responses; medical population genetics.

Alison A. Bertuch, Assistant Professor; M.D./Ph.D., Rochester, 1993. Basic mechanisms of telomere maintenance, structure, and function and DNA repair in the yeast model organism and human cells; the role of telomere biology in tumorigenesis and bone marrow failure.

Penelope M. Bonnen, Assistant Professor; Ph.D., Baylor College of Medicine, 2002. Genomics; population genetics; genetics of mitochondrial and metabolic disease.

Juan Botas, Professor; Ph.D., Madrid, 1986. Comparative analysis of pathogenic mechanisms in neurodegenerative disorders; screens for common drugable targets.

Malcolm K. Brenner, Professor; M.D./Ph.D., Cambridge, 1981. Use of gene therapy to improve responses to cancer.

Chester W. Brown, Associate Professor; M.D./Ph.D., Cincinnati, 1993. Genetic and genomic contributions to obesity and nutrient metabolism.

Rui Chen, Associate Professor; Ph.D., Baylor, 1999. Functional genomics of visual system development and diseases; high throughput technology; bioinformatics.

William J. Craigen, Professor; M.D./Ph.D., Baylor College of Medicine, 1988. Regulation of cellular energy metabolism; mouse models of metabolic diseases.

Gretchen J. Darlington, Professor; Ph.D., Michigan, 1970. Molecular mechanisms of cellular and organismic aging.

Herman A. Dierick, Assistant Professor; M.D., Catholic University of Louvain (Belgium), 1991. Genetic and neurobiological mechanisms of *Drosophila* aggression.

Richard A. Gibbs, Professor; Ph.D., Melbourne (Australia), 1985. Genome science, human molecular evolution, and molecular basis of inherited disease.

Margaret A. Goodell, Professor; Ph.D., Cambridge, 1991. Murine and human hematopoietic stem cells; genetic and epigenetic regulation and development.

Brett H. Graham, Assistant Professor; M.D./Ph.D., Emory, 1998. Genetics of inborn errors of metabolism; genetic models of mitochondrial disease in *Drosophila* and mice.

Andrew Groves, Associate Professor; Ph.D., Ludwig Institute for Cancer Research (London), 1992. Development, evolution, and regeneration of the inner ear.

Philip Hastings, Professor; Ph.D., Cambridge, 1965. Mechanism of amplification and genome instability in *Escherichia coli*.

Xiangwei He, Assistant Professor; Ph.D., Baylor College of Medicine, 1997. Mechanisms of chromosome segregation: centromere, kinetochore, fission yeast.

Christophe Herman, Associate Professor; Ph.D., Bruxelles (Belgium), 1996. Epigenetics; stress response; membrane quality control mechanism.

Kendal D. Hirschi, Professor; Ph.D., Arizona, 1993. Analysis of nutrient and metal transporters in *Arabidopsis* and agriculturally important crops.

Grzegorz Ira, Associate Professor, Ph.D., Copernicus, 1999. DNA repair, recombination, and genome instability; molecular mechanisms of mitotic DNA recombination.

Milan Jamrich, Professor; Ph.D., Heidelberg, 1978. Pattern formation in vertebrate embryos; ocular development; gene therapy.

Monica J. Justice, Professor; Ph.D., Kansas State, 1987. Molecular genetic analysis of hematopoiesis; cancer genetics; mouse models of human disease; suppressors of disease for therapeutics.

Richard L. Kelley, Associate Professor; Ph.D., Stanford, 1984. Dosage compensation in *Drosophila*; targeting chromatin modifications with noncoding RNAs.

Adam Kuspa, Professor and Chair of Biochemistry and Molecular Biology; Ph.D., Stanford, 1989. Studies of cell signaling in bacterial recognition and development in the social amoeba *Dictyostelium*.

Suzanne M. Leal, Professor; Ph.D., Columbia, 1994. Statistical genetics; genetic epidemiology; method development; gene mapping and identification; nonsyndromic hearing loss.

Brendan Lee, Professor; M.D./Ph.D., SUNY Downstate Medical Center, 1993. Developmental genetics of the skeleton and human skeletal dysplasias; development of helper-dependent adenoviral gene therapy for immune modulation, inborn errors of metabolism, and skeletal diseases; clinical research into the diagnosis, intervention, and treatment of metabolic and skeletal diseases.

Olivier Lichtarge, Professor; M.D./Ph.D., Stanford, 1990. Structural bioinformatics studies of proteins to study and engineer pathway perturbations.

James R. Lupski, Professor and Vice Chair; M.D./Ph.D., NYU, 1985. Molecular genetics of Charcot-Marie-Tooth disease and related inherited neuropathies; molecular mechanisms for human DNA rearrangements; genomic disorders; copy number variation (CNV) and disease.

Graeme Mardon, Professor; Ph.D., MIT, 1990. Retinal cell fate determination, development, and function in *Drosophila*, and vertebrates.

Martin M. Matzuk, Professor; M.D./Ph.D., Washington (St. Louis), 1989. Mammalian reproduction and development.

Michael L. Metzker, Associate Professor; Ph.D., Baylor College of Medicine, 1996. Next-generation sequencing technology development; genetic variation studies associated with ketosis-prone diabetes; methods development in HIV forensics.

Aleksandar Milosavljevic, Associate Professor; Ph.D., California, Santa Cruz, 1990. Genomics; cancer genomics; epigenomics; bioinformatics.

David D. Moore, Professor; Ph.D., Wisconsin–Madison, 1980. Functions of members of the nuclear hormone receptor superfamily.

Paolo M. Moretti, Assistant Professor; M.D., Padua, 1990. Genetic and molecular studies in Parkinson's diseases, Rett syndrome, and traumatic brain injury.

David L. Nelson, Professor; Ph.D., MIT, 1984. Human genome and disease gene analysis; fragile X syndrome; incontinentia pigmenti; complex genetics.

Jeffrey L. Neul, Assistant Professor; M.D./Ph.D., Chicago, 2000. Determination of neuroanatomical, cellular, and molecular pathogenic mechanisms of clinical abnormalities in Rett syndrome.

Philip Ng, Associate Professor; Ph.D., Guelph, 1999. Liver and lung gene therapy.

Jeffrey L. Noebels, Professor; Ph.D., Stanford, 1977; M.D., Yale, 1981. Gene control of neuronal excitability within the developing mammalian CNS.

William E. O'Brien, Professor; Ph.D., Georgia, 1971. Inborn errors of metabolism; arginine metabolism; using genetic models to understand the role(s) of nitric oxide.

Paul A. Overbeek, Professor; Ph.D., Michigan, 1980. Gene regulation in transgenic mice; ocular development; growth factors; insertional mutagenesis.

Xuewen Pan, Assistant Professor; Ph.D., Duke, 2001. Elucidation of drug/chemical mechanisms of actions and resistance.

Donald W. Parsons, Assistant Professor; M.D./Ph.D., Ohio State, 2001. Genomic analysis of pediatric cancers for identification of biologically and clinically-relevant molecular targets.

Richard E. Paylor, Professor; Ph.D., Colorado, 1991. Behavioral analyses of mutant mouse models of developmental and neurodegenerative disorders.

Sharon E. Plon, Professor; M.D./Ph.D., Harvard, 1987. Cancer predisposition syndromes; the molecular basis of genomic instability in cancers.

Frank Probst, Assistant Professor, M.D./Ph.D., Michigan, 2001. Generation and characterization of mouse models of human diseases; mouse models of hearing impairment; detection of small genomic inversions; familial multiple lipomatosis.

Antony Rodriguez, Assistant Professor; Ph.D., Texas Southwestern Medical Center at Dallas, 2002. Molecular genetics of mammalian microRNAs.

Susan M. Rosenberg, Professor; Ph.D., Oregon, 1986. Molecular mechanisms of genome instability in evolution, antibiotic resistance, and cancer.

Marco Sardiello, Assistant Professor; Ph.D., Bari (Italy), 2003. Lysosomal enhancement as a therapeutic strategy for treating neuronal ceroid lipofuscinoses.

Daryl Scott, Assistant Professor; M.D./Ph.D., Iowa, 2000. Identifying and characterizing genes responsible for common birth defects.

Kenneth L. Scott, Assistant Professor; Ph.D. Baylor College of Medicine, 2005. Cancer gene discovery; pathways governing tumor metastasis and animal models for cancer.

Gad Shaulsky, Professor; Ph.D., Weizmann (Israel), 1991. Allorecognition; evolution of sociality and functional genomics in *Dictyostelium*.

Pawel Stankiewicz, Assistant Professor; M.D., Warsaw, 1991; Ph.D., 1999, Dr.Habil. (D.Sc.), 2006, Institute of Mother and Child (Poland). Molecular mechanisms and clinical consequences of genomic rearrangements.

Ignatia B. Van den Veyver, Associate Professor; M.D., Antwerp (Belgium), 1986. Genetics of X-linked disorders (Aicardi, Goltz, and MLS syndrome); epigenetics; DNA methylation in development; imprinting in hydatidiform moles.

James Versalovic, Professor; M.D./Ph.D., Baylor College of Medicine, 1995. Genomics of beneficial bacteria; molecular mechanisms of probiotic:intestinal interactions; human microbiome and metagenomics.

Jue D. (Jade) Wang, Assistant Professor; Ph.D., California, San Francisco, 2002. Regulation of DNA replication and maintenance of genomic stability in bacteria.

Meng Wang, Assistant Professor; Ph.D., Rochester, 2005. Systemic studies of endocrine and metabolic signaling in promoting healthy aging.

Robert A. Waterland, Assistant Professor; Ph.D., Cornell, 2000. Environmental influences on mammalian developmental epigenetics.

Thomas Westbrook, Assistant Professor; Ph.D., Rochester, 2003. RNAi-based strategies to cancer gene discovery; REST tumor suppressor pathway.

John H. Wilson, Professor; Ph.D., Caltech, 1971. Instability of trinucleotide repeat sequences in human cells and mouse models; gene-based therapy of retinitis pigmentosa in mouse models.

Lee-Jun C. Wong, Professor; Ph.D., Ohio State, 1975. Mitochondrial genetics and function in human diseases, cancer, and aging.

Hui Zheng, Professor; Ph.D., Baylor, 1990. Pathophysiological studies of Alzheimer's disease pathways using mouse models.

Huda Zoghbi, Professor; M.D., Meharry Medical College, 1979. Molecular basis of neurodegenerative and neurodevelopmental disorders; nervous system development.

Thomas P. Zwaka, Associate Professor; M.D./Ph.D., Ulm (Germany), 2000. The nature of embryonic stem cell pluripotency.

BAYLOR COLLEGE OF MEDICINE

Graduate Program in Developmental Biology

Program of Study	The Graduate Program in Developmental Biology (DB Program) awards a Ph.D. degree and is designed to prepare students both intellectually and technologically to pursue a successful career in biological and/or biomedical research. The program also participates in the Medical Scientist Training Program, which leads to a combined M.D./Ph.D. degree.
	The DB Program provides a wide spectrum of exciting research possibilities and a broad cross-disciplinary training. In order to understand how a single cell develops into a complex organism, the program laboratories use molecular biology, cell biology, biochemistry, imaging, physiology, genetics, and genomics. Studies of organisms as diverse as social molds, worms, flies, frogs, chickens, fish, mice, and humans are conducted using a wide variety of approaches, instruments, and techniques of modern biological research. Members of the DB Program study basic biological mechanisms of direct and fundamental relevance to human development, disease, and stem cell therapy. This allows students to unravel the principles and mechanisms that guide embryonic development, the maintenance and differentiation of stem cells, the differentiation of adult cell types, regeneration of organs and tissues, and the mechanisms underlying aging and neurodegeneration. The major research interests are neurobiology; cancer biology; cell death; aging; neurodegenerative and other human diseases; stem cell biology; gene therapy; reproductive development; oogenesis; skin, muscle, heart, blood, kidney, bone, limb, and eye development; cell lineage specification; X chromosome dosage compensation; and plant differentiation.
	During their first year, students take core courses in classical and molecular genetics, cell biology, molecular biology, and biochemistry, as well as several courses and seminars in developmental biology. They also sample several areas of research by doing rotations in the program's laboratories. Before the end of the first year, students take a qualifying exam and select a laboratory in which they carry out their dissertation research. Subsequently, students meet every six months with their thesis committee to evaluate the research accomplished and redefine goals necessary to complete the thesis project. In the final year, students defend their theses in a public seminar. Study for the Ph.D. degree generally requires five years of graduate work, most of which is spent on the dissertation research. The program is supported by a competitive NIH training grant, the local chapter of the March of Dimes, Texas Children's Hospital, and the College.
Research Facilities	DB Program faculty members are well-funded and drawn from eleven departments and four institutions, including Baylor College of Medicine (BCM), the University of Texas M. D. Anderson Cancer Center, the University of Texas Health Science Center, and Rice University, all within easy walking distance of the Texas Medical Center. They occupy extensive research space with state-of-the-art instrumentation and computing equipment. Cooperative and collaborative interactions among program laboratories and institutions enable students to take full advantage of the facilities of the Texas Medical Center.
Financial Aid	Students enrolled in the program receive a competitive stipend of $29,000 per year plus health insurance at no extra cost. Tuition scholarships are awarded to all students admitted to the program. Separate offices provide assistance to international students and students with financial hardships.
Cost of Study	Tuition is fully covered by the program, the College, or training grants.
Living and Housing Costs	Numerous affordable housing options are available within a few miles of the medical center. Some students rent a nearby house while others rent or buy their own apartment, condo, or townhome. The cost of living in Houston is below that of most large U.S. cities, and there are ample opportunities for employment of spouses in the Texas Medical Center and the greater Houston area.
Student Group	The DB Program currently has 56 full-time graduate students, including 29 women and 35 international students. Each year, 8–10 students join the program. Because of the program's commitment to excellence, it favors a low student-faculty ratio. In addition to the laboratories in the program, students have contact with students, postdoctoral fellows, and faculty members in other programs and departments throughout the school and the medical center. The BCM graduate school has approximately 550 students, the medical school about 700 students.
Student Outcomes	The Career Resource Center of the graduate school provides career information and counseling for all BCM graduate and postdoctoral students in biomedical sciences. DB students typically graduate with an excellent-to-outstanding publication record and go on to successful careers. The average number of publications per graduate student is above 4.5, with an average of more than 2.5 first-author papers. The average impact factor per graduate student publication is more than 10. The DB graduates have subsequently pursued postdoctoral training in excellent laboratories and high-quality institutions. A substantial number of former graduate students are now faculty members at universities and teaching colleges around the world.
Location	Houston is a dynamic city with an exciting cultural and metropolitan center. Ballet, opera, symphony, theater, and art museums are excellent and accessible to the general population. In addition, there are more than a thousand bars and restaurants, which are moderately priced. Recreation opportunities abound, with facilities for a wide range of professional and amateur sports. The climate offers very pleasant weather from fall through spring and permits participation in a wide variety of outdoor activities. Gulf Coast beaches are a short drive from the city.
The College	Baylor College of Medicine is an independent, private institution dedicated to training in basic and medical sciences. It is located in the heart of the Texas Medical Center, one of the largest medical centers in the world. It has promoted the development of interdisciplinary, interdepartmental, and interinstitutional programs and has consistently identified and encouraged outstanding investigators. Considered one of the top research institutions in the nation, the College continues to develop programs and services that meet new needs and trends, making higher education one of the most exciting and rewarding of human experiences.
Applying	Applicants must have a bachelor's degree, preferably with course work in biology and genetics. GRE General Test scores less than three years old at the time of application must be provided. Applications should be accompanied by transcripts, three letters of recommendation, and a statement of research interest and career goals; they must be complete by January 1, with a preferred deadline of December 15. Successful candidates are invited to meet with the participating faculty members and students to have a firsthand look at the DB Program. Expenses for travel and accommodations during the visit are provided for domestic and international students. Admission policies at BCM offer equal opportunity to all, without regard to race, sex, age, religion, country of origin, or handicap. Questions regarding the application process can be directed to cat@bcm.edu.
Correspondence and Information	Graduate Program in Developmental Biology Baylor College of Medicine, BCM 225 One Baylor Plaza Houston, Texas 77030 Phone: 713-798-7696 E-mail: cat@bcm.edu Web site: http://www.bcm.edu/db/

Baylor College of Medicine

THE FACULTY AND THEIR RESEARCH

Benjamin R. Arenkiel, Assistant Professor of Molecular and Human Genetics and Neuroscience, Neurological Research Institute; Ph.D., Utah, 2004. Molecular genetic studies to investigate mechanisms of neural circuit formation, function, and maintenance during development and adulthood.

Richard R. Behringer, Professor of Genetics, University of Texas M. D. Anderson Cancer Center; Ph.D., South Carolina, 1986. Mammalian embryogenesis; reproductive biology and disease; stem cell biology, evolution, and development.

Hugo J. Bellen, Professor of Molecular and Human Genetics and Neuroscience, Neurological Research Institute; Director, Program in Developmental Biology; and Investigator, Howard Hughes Medical Institute; D.V.M./Ph.D., California, Davis, 1986. Genetic and molecular analysis of nervous system development, neurotransmitter release, and neuronal degeneration in *Drosophila.*

John W. Belmont, Professor of Molecular and Human Genetics and Pathology and Immunology; M.D./Ph.D., Baylor College of Medicine, 1981. Cardiovascular genetics; vaccine response as a complex trait.

Janet Braam, Professor and Chair of Biochemistry and Cell Biology, Rice University; Ph.D., Cornell, 1985. Molecular and developmental responses of plants to environmental stresses.

Rui Chen, Associate Professor of Molecular and Human Genetics, Human Genome Sequencing Center; Ph.D., Baylor College of Medicine, 1999. Functional genomics of visual development and diseases; high throughput technology; bioinformatics.

Thomas A. Cooper, Professor of Pathology and Immunology and Molecular and Cellular Biology; M.D., Temple, 1982. Alternative splicing regulation in development and disease.

Mauro Costa-Mattioli, Assistant Professor of Neuroscience and Molecular and Cellular Biology; Ph.D., Nantes (France), 2002. Cellular and molecular mechanism of memory storage.

Francesco J. DeMayo, Professor of Molecular and Cellular Biology; Ph.D., Michigan, 1983. Molecular and developmental biology of the lung and uterus; cancer; reproductive biology.

Benjamin Deneen, Assistant Professor of Neuroscience, Center for Cell and Gene Therapy and Stem Cells and Regenerative Medicine Center; Ph.D., UCLA, 2002. Glial cell development and disease.

Mary E. Dickinson, Associate Professor of Molecular Physiology and Biophysics; Ph.D., Columbia, 1996. Vascular remodeling and heart morphogenesis in early vertebrate embryos.

Herman A. Dierick, Assistant Professor of Molecular and Human Genetics and Neuroscience; M.D., Leuven (Belgium), 1991. Genetic and neurobiological mechanism of *Drosophila* aggression.

Ido Golding, Assistant Professor of Biochemistry and Molecular Biology; Ph.D., Tel Aviv (Israel), 2001. Physical principles to understand living systems.

Margaret A. Goodell, Professor of Pediatrics and Molecular and Human Genetics; Director, Center for Cell and Gene Therapy and Stem Cells and Regenerative Medicine Center; Ph.D., Cambridge (United Kingdom), 1991. Murine and human hematopoietic stem cells; genetic and epigenetic regulation and development.

Brett H. Graham, Assistant Professor of Molecular and Human Genetics; M.D./Ph.D., Emory, 1998. Genetics of inborn errors of metabolism; genetic models of mitochondrial disease in *Drosophila* and mice.

Andy K. Groves, Associate Professor of Neuroscience and Molecular and Human Genetics; Ph.D., Ludwig Institute for Cancer Research (United Kingdom), 1992. The development, evolution, and regeneration of the inner ear.

Georg Halder, Associate Professor of Biochemistry and Molecular Biology, University of Texas M. D. Anderson Cancer Center; Ph.D., Basel (Switzerland), 1996. Growth control; regeneration; tumor suppressor genes; *Drosophila* genetics.

Hamed Jafar-Nejad, Assistant Professor of Molecular Medicine, University of Texas Health Science Center; M.D., Tehran (Iran), 1994. Developmental glycobiology; cell biological regulation of developmental signaling pathways.

Milan Jamrich, Professor of Molecular and Human Genetics and Molecular and Cellular Biology; Ph.D., Heidelberg (Germany), 1978. Molecular basis of embryonic pattern formation; ocular development; gene therapy.

Joanna L. Jankowsky, Assistant Professor of Neuroscience; Ph.D., Caltech, 1999. Functional consequences of Aβ accumulation in Alzheimer's disease on hippocampal neurogenesis, synaptic plasticity, and cognitive behavior.

Randy L. Johnson, Associate Professor of Biochemistry and Molecular Biology, University of Texas M. D. Anderson Cancer Center; Ph.D., Columbia, 1991. Modeling human disease and development in the mouse.

Monica J. Justice, Professor of Molecular and Human Genetics and Molecular Physiology and Biophysics; Ph.D., Kansas, 1987. Molecular genetic analysis of hematopoiesis; cancer genetics; mouse models of human disease.

Richard L. Kelley, Associate Professor of Molecular and Human Genetics; Ph.D., Stanford, 1984. Noncoding RNAs and chromatin structure.

Adam Kuspa, Professor of Biochemistry and Molecular Biology, Molecular and Human Genetics, and Pharmacology; Vice President of Research; Ph.D., Stanford, 1989. Genomic studies of cell signaling and development in *Dictyostelium.*

Brendan Lee, Professor of Molecular and Human Genetics and Investigator, Howard Hughes Medical Institute; M.D./Ph.D., SUNY Health Science Center at Brooklyn, 1993. Genetic pathways that specify development and homeostasis: translational studies of skeletal development and urea cycle disorders; therapy for metabolic diseases.

Michael T. Lewis, Associate Professor of Molecular and Cellular Biology, Lester and Sue Smith Breast Center; Ph.D., California, Santa Cruz, 1995. Genetic regulation of mammary gland development and early-stage breast cancer.

Olivier Lichtarge, Professor of Molecular and Human Genetics and Biochemistry and Molecular Biology; M.D./Ph.D., Stanford, 1990. Evolutionary studies of sequence; structural bioinformatics studies of proteins to study and engineer pathway perturbations.

Hui-Chen Lu, Assistant Professor of Pediatrics–Neurology and Neuroscience, Neurological Research Institute; Ph.D., Baylor College of Medicine, 1997. Molecular mechanisms of cortical development.

Peter Y. Lwigale, Assistant Professor of Biochemistry and Cell Biology, Rice University; Ph.D., Kansas, 2001. Eye development; cellular interactions and molecular regulation of neural crest cells during corneal development.

Mirjana Maletic-Savatic, Assistant Professor of Pediatrics, Neurological Research Institute; M.D./Ph.D., Belgrade (Serbia), 1996. Neurogenesis; computational modeling; systems biology of early developmental disorders and autism.

Graeme Mardon, Professor of Pathology and Immunology, Molecular and Human Genetics, and Neuroscience; Ph.D., MIT, 1990. Retinal cell-fate determination, development, and function in *Drosophila* and vertebrates.

James F. Martin, Professor of Molecular Physiology and Biophysics; M.D./Ph.D., Texas at Houston, 1995. Molecular mechanisms controlling cell growth and differentiation in the context of vertebrate embryogenesis.

Martin M. Matzuk, Professor of Pathology, Molecular and Human Genetics, and Molecular and Cellular Biology; M.D./Ph.D., Washington (St. Louis), 1989. Mammalian reproduction, oncogenesis, and development.

David D. Moore, Professor of Molecular and Cellular Biology and Molecular and Human Genetics; Ph.D., Wisconsin–Madison, 1979. Nuclear hormone receptors regulate metabolism and cancer.

Jeffrey L. Neul, Associate Professor of Pediatrics, Neurological Research Institute; M.D./Ph.D., Chicago, 1998. Determination of neuroanatomical, cellular, and molecular pathogenic mechanisms of clinical abnormalities in Rett Syndrome.

Hoang Nguyen, Assistant Professor of Molecular and Cellular Biology, Center for Cell and Gene Therapy and Stem Cells and Regenerative Medicine Center; Ph.D., Cornell/Sloan-Kettering, 2002. Skin epithelial stem cell fate maintenance and lineage determination.

Paul A. Overbeek, Professor of Molecular and Cellular Biology, Molecular and Human Genetics, and Neuroscience; Ph.D., Michigan, 1980. Gene regulation in transgenic mice; ocular development; growth factors; insertional mutagenesis in mice.

Matthew N. Rasband, Associate Professor of Neuroscience; Ph.D., Rochester, 1999. Role of neuronal-glial signaling in brain development, function, injury, and disease.

Antony Rodriguez, Assistant Professor of Molecular and Human Genetics; Ph.D., Texas Southwestern Medical Center at Dallas, 2002. Molecular genetics of mammalian microRNAs.

Jeffrey M. Rosen, Professor of Molecular and Cellular Biology; Ph.D., SUNY at Buffalo, 1971. Mammary gland development, stem cells, and breast cancer.

Marco Sardiello, Assistant Professor of Molecular and Human Genetics, Neurological Research Institute; Ph.D., Bari (Italy), 2003. Lysosomal enhancement as a therapeutic strategy for treating neuronal ceroid lipofuscinoses.

Gad Shaulsky, Professor of Molecular and Human Genetics; Ph.D., Weizmann (Israel), 1991. Developmental genetics in *Dictyostelium;* allorecognition; evolution of sociality; functional genomics.

Anna Marie Sokac, Assistant Professor of Biochemistry and Molecular Biology; Ph.D., Wisconsin–Madison, 2001. Shaping cells, shaping embryos: coordinated actin and membrane dynamics in flies and frogs.

Kimberly R. Tolias, Assistant Professor of Neuroscience; Ph.D., Harvard, 1998. Molecular signaling pathways in structural development and plasticity of dendrites and synapses.

Ming-Jer Tsai, Professor of Molecular and Cellular Biology; Ph.D., California, Davis, 1971. Pancreas islet and neural development; organogenesis steroid hormone action; prostate cancer.

Sophia Y. Tsai, Professor of Molecular and Cellular Biology; Ph.D., California, Davis, 1969. COUP-TFII and vein identity; angiogenesis; diabetes; obesity; kidney disease.

Meng Wang, Assistant Professor of Molecular and Human Genetics, and Huffington Center on Aging; Ph.D., Rochester, 2005. Systemic studies of endocrine and metabolic signaling in promoting healthy aging.

Thomas F. Westbrook, Assistant Professor of Biochemistry and Molecular Biology and Molecular and Human Genetics; Ph.D., Rochester, 2003. RNAi-based strategies to cancer gene discovery; REST tumor suppressor pathway.

Hui Zheng, Professor of Molecular and Human Genetics, Molecular and Cellular Biology, and Neuroscience; Director, Huffington Center on Aging; Ph.D., Baylor College of Medicine, 1990. Pathophysiological studies of Alzheimer's disease pathways using mouse models.

Zheng Zhou, Associate Professor of Biochemistry and Molecular Biology; Ph.D., Baylor College of Medicine, 1994. Molecular genetic studies of clearance of apoptotic cells in *C. elegans.*

Huda Y. Zoghbi, Professor of Pediatrics, Molecular and Human Genetics, and Neuroscience; Director, Neurological Research Institute; and Investigator, Howard Hughes Medical Institute; M.D., Meharry Medical College, 1979. Pathogenesis of polyglutamine neurodegenerative diseases and Rett syndrome; genes essential for neurodevelopment.

Thomas P. Zwaka, Associate Professor of Molecular and Cellular Biology and Molecular and Human Genetics, Center for Cell and Gene Therapy and Stem Cells and Regenerative Medicine Center; M.D./Ph.D., Ulm (Germany), 2000. The nature of embryonic stem cell pluripotency.

UNIVERSITY OF CONNECTICUT HEALTH CENTER

Graduate Program in Genetics and Developmental Biology

Program of Study

The genetics and developmental biology graduate program provides students with fundamental interdisciplinary training in modern molecular genetics and developmental biology, emphasizing cellular and molecular aspects as well as tissue interactions. The program is intended for students pursuing a Ph.D. degree and prepares students to compete for job opportunities in traditional medical and dental school departments as well as a productive research career in either academia or industry. Combined M.D./Ph.D. and D.M.D/Ph.D. programs are also available. Students are encouraged to obtain in-depth training through research and courses in biochemistry, molecular biology, cell biology, developmental biology, and genetics. Faculty members are from several basic science and clinical departments and study a wide range of organisms including yeast, worms, fruit flies, mice, and humans. Areas of research include the biology of human embryonic stem cells, mapping and cloning of genes responsible for human disease, RNA processing (including RNA editing, alternative splicing, antisense regulation, and RNA interference), the molecular mechanisms of aging, signal transduction pathways, microbial pathogenesis, developmental neurobiology, cell differentiation, musculoskeletal development, morphogenesis and pattern formation, reproductive biology, and endocrinology.

Research Facilities

The Department of Genetics and Developmental Biology is the academic home of the genetics and developmental biology graduate program. The Department of Genetics and Developmental Biology occupies three floors of the state-of-the-art Academic Research Building, which opened in 1999, as well as laboratory space in adjacent buildings. The department houses equipment and facilities for mouse transgenics, ES cell manipulation, DNA microarrays, nucleic acid sequencing, fluorescence microscopy, and digital imaging. Students also have ready access to first-rate flow cytometry and confocal microscopy facilities. Other institutional resources include a computer center and a library containing approximately 200,000 volumes and subscribing to more than 1,400 current periodicals. Students of the program therefore have an excellent opportunity for research and training in cutting-edge areas of genetics and developmental biology.

Financial Aid

Support for doctoral students engaged in full-time degree programs at the Health Center is provided on a competitive basis. Graduate research assistantships for 2011–12 provide a stipend of $28,000 per year, which includes a waiver of tuition/University fees for the fall and spring semesters and a student health insurance plan. While financial aid is offered competitively, the Health Center makes every possible effort to address the financial needs of all students during their period of training.

Cost of Study

For 2011–12, tuition is $10,224 per year for full-time students who are Connecticut residents and $26,532 per year for full-time out-of-state residents. General University fees are added to the cost of tuition for students who do not receive a tuition waiver. These costs are usually met by traineeships or research assistantships for doctoral students.

Living and Housing Costs

There is a wide range of affordable housing options in the greater Hartford area within easy commuting distance of the campus, including an extensive complex that is adjacent to the Health Center. Costs range from $600 to $900 per month for a one-bedroom unit; 2 or more students sharing an apartment usually pay less. University housing is not available at the Health Center.

Student Group

At UCHC, there are about 500 students in the Schools of Medicine and Dental Medicine, 150 Ph.D. students, and 50 postdoctoral fellows. There are no restrictions on the admission of out-of-state graduate students.

Location

The Health Center is located in the historic town of Farmington, Connecticut. Set in the beautiful New England countryside on a hill overlooking the Farmington Valley, it is close to ski areas, hiking trails, and facilities for boating, fishing, and swimming. Connecticut's capital city of Hartford, 7 miles east of Farmington, is the center of an urban region of approximately 800,000 people. The beaches of the Long Island Sound are about 50 minutes away to the south, and the beautiful Berkshires are a short drive to the northwest. New York City and Boston can be reached within 2½ hours by car. Hartford is the home of the acclaimed Hartford Stage Company, TheatreWorks, the Hartford Symphony and Chamber orchestras, two ballet companies, an opera company, the Wadsworth Athenaeum (the oldest public art museum in the nation), the Mark Twain house, the Hartford Civic Center, and many other interesting cultural and recreational facilities. The area is also home to several branches of the University of Connecticut, Trinity College, and the University of Hartford, which includes the Hartt School of Music. Bradley International Airport (about 30 minutes from campus) serves the Hartford/Springfield area with frequent airline connections to major cities in this country and abroad. Frequent bus and rail service is also available from Hartford.

The Health Center

The 200-acre Health Center campus at Farmington houses a division of the University of Connecticut Graduate School, as well as the School of Medicine and Dental Medicine. The campus also includes the John Dempsey Hospital, associated clinics, and extensive medical research facilities, all in a centralized facility with more than 1 million square feet of floor space. The Health Center's newest research addition, the Academic Research Building, was opened in 1999. This impressive eleven-story structure provides 170,000 square feet of state-of-the-art laboratory space. The faculty at the center includes more than 260 full-time members. The institution has a strong commitment to graduate study within an environment that promotes social and intellectual interaction among the various educational programs. Graduate students are represented on various administrative committees concerned with curricular affairs, and the Graduate Student Organization (GSO) represents graduate students' needs and concerns to the faculty and administration, in addition to fostering social contact among graduate students in the Health Center.

Applying

Applications for admission should be submitted on standard forms obtained from the Graduate Admissions Office at the UConn Health Center or the Web site. The application should be filed together with transcripts, three letters of recommendation, a personal statement, and recent results from the General Test of the Graduate Record Examinations. International students must take the Test of English as a Foreign Language (TOEFL) to satisfy Graduate School requirements. The deadline for completed applications and receipt of all supplemental materials is December 15. In accordance with the laws of the state of Connecticut and of the United States, the University of Connecticut Health Center does not discriminate against any person in its educational and employment activities on the grounds of race, color, creed, national origin, sex, age, or physical disability.

Correspondence and Information

Dr. William Mohler
Program Director
Department of Genetics and Developmental Biology
University of Connecticut Health Center
Farmington, Connecticut 06030-3301
Phone: 860-679-7947
E-mail: wmohler@neuron.uchc.edu
Web site: http://grad.uchc.edu

University of Connecticut Health Center

THE FACULTY AND THEIR RESEARCH

Hector Leonardo Aguila, Ph.D., Associate Professor of Immunology. Hematopoiesis and bone marrow microenvironment; lymphoid cell development; stem cell biology.

Alexander Amerik, Ph.D., Assistant Professor of Genetics and Developmental Biology. Deubiquitinating enzymes and ubiquitin homeostasis in the yeast *Saccharomyces cerevisiae*.

Andrew Arnold, M.D., Professor of Medicine and Murray-Heilig Chair in Molecular Medicine. Molecular genetic underpinnings of tumors of the endocrine glands; role of the cyclin D1 oncogene.

Peter Benn, Ph.D., Director, Diagnostic Human Genetics Laboratories. Clinical cytogenetics, molecular cytogenetics, and molecular genetics services; prenatal risk evaluation through maternal serum screening.

Michael Blinov, Ph.D., Assistant Professor of Genetics and Developmental Biology, Modeling of signal transcription systems and protein-DNA interactions; bioinformatics: data mining and visualization; developing software tools and mathematical methods for rule-based modeling of signal transduction systems.

Gordon Carmichael, Ph.D., Professor of Genetics and Developmental Biology. Regulation of gene expression in eukaryotes.

Stormy J. Chamberlain, Ph.D., Assistant Professor of Genetics and Developmental Biology. Human induced pluripotent stem (iPS) cell models to study 15q11-q13 imprinting disorders.

Kevin Claffey, Ph.D., Assistant Professor of Cell Biology. Angiogenesis in cancer progression and metastasis; vascular endothelial growth factor (VEGF) expression; hypoxia-mediated gene regulation.

Stephen Clark, Ph.D., Associate Professor of Medicine. Characterization of mutations affecting connective tissues; molecular genetic mapping; generation and analysis of transgenic mice.

Soheil (Sam) Dadras, M.D., Ph.D., Assistant Professor of Dermatology, and Genetics and Developmental Biology, Discovery of small RNAs (including microRNA) as novel biomarkers in human melanoma progression and metastasis using next generation sequencing.

Asis Das, Ph.D., Professor of Microbiology. Basic genetic and biomechanical mechanisms that govern the elongation-termination and decision in transcription.

Caroline N. Dealy, Ph.D., Assistant Professor of Anatomy. Roles of various growth factors and signaling molecules, particularly IGF-I and insulin, in the regulation of chick limb development.

Paul Epstein, Ph.D., Associate Professor of Pharmacology. Receptor signal transduction, second messengers, and protein phosphorylation in control of cell growth and regulation; purification and regulation of cyclic nucleotide phosphodiesterases; role of calmodulin in mediating Ca^{2+}-dependent cell processes.

Guo-Hua Fong, Ph.D., Assistant Professor of Cell Biology. Developmental biology of the vascular system, VEGF-A receptor signal transduction, embryonic stem cells, and gene knock-out in mice.

Brenton R. Graveley, Ph.D., Associate Professor of Genetics and Developmental Biology. Regulation of alternative splicing in the mammalian nervous system and mechanisms of alternative splicing.

Arthur Günzl, Ph.D., Associate Professor, Center for Microbial Pathogenesis. Transcription and antigenic variation in the mammalian parasite *Trypanosoma brucei*.

Marc Hansen, Ph.D., Professor of Medicine. Molecular genetics of osteosarcoma and related bone diseases.

Laurinda Jaffe, Ph.D., Professor of Cell Biology. Physiology of fertilization.

Robert A. Kosher, Ph.D., Professor of Anatomy. Limb development; role of extracellular matrix, cytoskeleton, and cyclic nucleotides in chondrogenesis; molecular regulation of gene activity during cartilage differentiation.

Barbara Kream, Ph.D., Professor of Medicine. Hormonal regulation of collagen gene expression in bone.

George Kuchel, M.D., Professor of Medicine. Role of hormones and cytokines in geriatric disability. Pathogenesis of impaired detrusor contractility and urinary retention. Molecular mechanisms of bladder muscle survival.

Marc Lalande, Ph.D., Professor of Genetics and Developmental Biology. Genomic imprinting; Angelman syndrome; mechanism of tissue-specific silencing of the Angelman ubiquitin ligase in mouse and human.

James Li, Ph.D., Assistant Professor of Genetics and Developmental Biology. Identifying the molecular mechanisms underlying formation of the mammalian cerebellum.

Alexander Lichtler, Ph.D., Associate Professor of Pediatrics. Regulation of collagen gene transcription; retrovirus vectors; role of homeobox genes in limb development.

Bruce Mayer, Ph.D., Associate Professor of Genetics and Developmental Biology. Biologically relevant Nck-interacting proteins.

Mina Mina, D.M.D., Ph.D., Associate Professor of Pediatric Dentistry. Characterization of genetic and epigenetic influences involved in pattern formation and skeletogenesis of the chick mandible and mouse tooth germ.

William Mohler, Ph.D., Assistant Professor of Genetics and Developmental Biology. Molecular and cellular mechanisms of cell fusion.

D. Kent Morest, M.D., Professor of Neuroscience. Role of cell and tissue interactions in the migration and differentiation of neurons; structure and function of neurons during development and synapse formation.

John Peluso, Ph.D., Professor of Cell Biology. Control of ovarian follicle growth steroidogenesis in vitro; proto-oncogene expression and ovarian follicular growth.

Carol C. Pilbeam, Ph.D., M.D., Professor of Medicine; Mechanisms of regulation of bone formation and resorption.

Justin D. Radolf, M.D., Professor of Medicine and Genetics and Developmental Biology. Molecular pathogenesis and immunobiology of spirochetal infections.

Blanka Rogina, Ph.D., Assistant Professor of Genetics and Developmental Biology. Molecular mechanism underlying aging process in *Drosophila melanogaster*.

Daniel W. Rosenberg, Ph.D., Professor of Medicine. Molecular genetics of colorectal cancer; signaling pathways in the development of tumors; toxicogenomics.

Edward F. Rossomando, D.D.S., Ph.D., Professor of BioStructure and Function. Control of gene expression in tumor and nontumor cell lines in response to stimulation by monokines; coding, transmission, and processing of environmental signals in normal and abnormal development.

Mansoor Sarfarazi, Ph.D., Associate Professor of Surgery. Positional mapping and mutation analysis of human genetic disorders; primary open angle glaucoma; primary congenital glaucoma; synpolydactyly; dyslexia; mitral valve prolapse and ascending aortic aneurysm.

Petros Tsipouras, M.D., Professor of Pediatrics. Heritable disorders of connective tissue, nosology, and genetics; genetic linkage studies; molecular mechanisms of mutations in human collagen genes.

William B. Upholt, Ph.D., Professor of BioStructure and Function. Regulation of gene expression during embryonic development; procollagen gene expression and regulation in limb chondrogenesis and skeletogenesis; pattern formation; homeobox genes.

Bruce White, Ph.D., Professor of Physiology. Control of prolactin gene expression at pretranslational level in GH3 cells; control of aromatase gene expression in ovarian and testicular tissues.

Ren-He Xu, Ph.D., Associate Professor of Genetics and Developmental Biology. Biology of human embryonic stem cells.

Ji Yu, Ph.D., Assistant Professor of Genetics and Developmental Biology; Optical imaging technology; regulation mechanisms in dendritic RNA translation; cytoskeletal dynamics.

Section 11
Marine Biology

This section contains a directory of institutions offering graduate work in marine biology. Additional information about programs listed in the directory may be obtained by writing directly to the dean of a graduate school or chair of a department at the address given in the directory.

For programs offering related work, see also in this book *Biological and Biomedical Sciences* and *Zoology*. In another guide in this series: **Graduate Programs in the Physical Sciences, Mathematics, Agricultural Sciences, the Environment & Natural Resources**
See *Marine Sciences and Oceanography*

CONTENTS

Program Directory

Marine Biology

College of Charleston, Graduate School, School of Sciences and Mathematics, Program in Marine Biology, Charleston, SC 29412. Offers MS. *Faculty:* 38 full-time (13 women), 8 part-time/adjunct (4 women). *Students:* 17 full-time (12 women), 28 part-time (14 women); includes 1 minority (Hispanic/Latino). Average age 25. 86 applicants, 24% accepted, 16 enrolled. In 2010, 18 master's awarded. *Degree requirements:* For master's, comprehensive exam, thesis. *Entrance requirements:* For master's, GRE General Test, 3 letters of recommendation. Additional exam requirements/recommendations for international students: Required—TOEFL (minimum score 81 iBT). *Application deadline:* For fall admission, 2/1 for domestic and international students; for spring admission, 11/1 for domestic and international students. Application fee: $45. Electronic applications accepted. *Financial support:* In 2010–11, 4 fellowships (averaging $22,000 per year), 22 research assistantships (averaging $19,000 per year), 19 teaching assistantships (averaging $16,000 per year) were awarded; career-related internships or fieldwork, Federal Work-Study, institutionally sponsored loans, scholarships/grants, and unspecified assistantships also available. Support available to part-time students. Financial award application deadline: 4/1; financial award applicants required to submit FAFSA. *Faculty research:* Ecology, environmental physiology, marine genomics, bioinformatics, toxicology, cell biology, population biology, fisheries science, animal physiology, biodiversity, estuarine ecology, evolution and systematics, microbial processes, plant physiology, immunology. *Unit head:* Dr. Craig J. Plante, Director, 843-953-9187, Fax: 843-953-9199, E-mail: plantec@cofc.edu. *Application contact:* Susan Hallatt, Director of Graduate Admissions, 843-953-5614, Fax: 843-953-1434, E-mail: hallatts@cofc.edu.

Florida Institute of Technology, Graduate Programs, College of Science, Department of Biological Sciences, Programs in Ecology and Marine Biology, Melbourne, FL 32901-6975. Offers ecology (MS); marine biology (MS). Part-time programs available. *Faculty:* 15 full-time (2 women), 1 part-time/adjunct (0 women). *Students:* 24 full-time (17 women), 3 part-time (all women); includes 1 American Indian or Alaska Native, non-Hispanic/Latino; 1 Asian, non-Hispanic/Latino; 2 Hispanic/Latino, 1 international. Average age 25. 52 applicants, 23% accepted, 11 enrolled. In 2010, 4 master's awarded. *Degree requirements:* For master's, thesis, research, seminar, internship or summer lab. *Entrance requirements:* For master's, GRE General Test, minimum GPA of 3.0, 3 letters of recommendation, statement of objectives. Additional exam requirements/recommendations for international students: Required—TOEFL (minimum score 550 paper-based; 213 computer-based; 79 iBT). *Application deadline:* For fall admission, 3/15 for domestic students; for spring admission, 10/1 for domestic students. Applications are processed on a rolling basis. Application fee: $50. Electronic applications accepted. *Expenses:* Tuition: Part-time $1040 per credit hour. Tuition and fees vary according to campus/location. *Financial support:* In 2010–11, 6 fellowships (averaging $20,737 per year), 15 research assistantships with full and partial tuition reimbursements (averaging $13,455 per year), 22 teaching assistantships with full and partial tuition reimbursements (averaging $13,353 per year) were awarded; career-related internships or fieldwork, institutionally sponsored loans, tuition waivers (partial), unspecified assistantships, and tuition remissions also available. Support available to part-time students. Financial award application deadline: 3/1; financial award applicants required to submit FAFSA. *Faculty research:* Endangered or threatened avian and mammalian species, hydroacoustics and feeding preference of the West Indian manatee, habitat preference of the Florida scrub jay. Total annual research expenditures: $1.3 million. *Unit head:* Dr. Richard B. Aronson, Department Head, 321-674-8034, Fax: 321-674-7238, E-mail: raronson@fit.edu. *Application contact:* Cheryl A. Brown, Associate Director of Graduate Admission, 321-674-7581, Fax: 321-723-9468, E-mail: cbrown@fit.edu.

Memorial University of Newfoundland, School of Graduate Studies, Department of Biology, St. John's, NL A1C 5S7, Canada. Offers biology (M Sc, PhD); marine biology (M Sc, PhD). Part-time programs available. *Degree requirements:* For master's, thesis; for doctorate, comprehensive exam, thesis/dissertation, oral defense of thesis. *Entrance requirements:* For master's, honors degree (minimum 2nd class standing) in related field. Electronic applications accepted. *Faculty research:* Northern flora and fauna, especially cold ocean and boreal environments.

Nicholls State University, Graduate Studies, College of Arts and Sciences, Department of Biological Sciences, Thibodaux, LA 70310. Offers marine and environmental biology (MS). Part-time programs available. *Degree requirements:* For master's, comprehensive exam, thesis. *Entrance requirements:* For master's, GRE. Additional exam requirements/recommendations for international students: Required—TOEFL (minimum score 600 paper-based). *Faculty research:* Bioremediation, ecology, public health, biotechnology, physiology.

Northeastern University, College of Science, Department of Biology, Boston, MA 02115-5096. Offers bioinformatics (PMS); biology (MS, PhD); biotechnology (MS, PSM); marine biology (MS). Part-time programs available. *Faculty:* 27 full-time (10 women), 5 part-time/adjunct (all women). *Students:* 112 full-time (74 women), 4 part-time (2 women). 255 applicants, 73% accepted. In 2010, 21 master's, 5 doctorates awarded. Terminal master's awarded for partial completion of doctoral program. *Degree requirements:* For master's, thesis (for some programs); for doctorate, thesis/dissertation, qualifying exam. *Entrance requirements:* For master's and doctorate, GRE General Test. Additional exam requirements/recommendations for international students: Required—TOEFL (minimum score 250 computer-based). *Application deadline:* For fall admission, 1/1 priority date for domestic and international students. Applications are processed on a rolling basis. Application fee: $50. Electronic applications accepted. *Financial support:* In 2010–11, 19 research assistantships with tuition reimbursements (averaging $18,285 per year), 41 teaching assistantships with tuition reimbursements (averaging $18,285 per year) were awarded; fellowships with tuition reimbursements, career-related internships or fieldwork, Federal Work-Study, tuition waivers (full and partial), and unspecified assistantships also available. Financial award application deadline: 3/1; financial award applicants required to submit FAFSA. *Faculty research:* Biochemistry, marine sciences, molecular biology, microbiology and immunology neurobiology, cellular and molecular biology, biochemistry, marine biochemistry and ecology, microbiology, neurobiology, biotechnology. *Unit head:* Dr. Wendy Smith, Graduate Coordinator, 617-373-2260, Fax: 617-373-3724, E-mail: gradbio@neu.edu. *Application contact:* Jo-Anne Dickinson, Admissions Assistant, 617-373-5990, Fax: 617-373-7281, E-mail: gsas@neu.edu.

Nova Southeastern University, Oceanographic Center, Program in Marine Biology, Fort Lauderdale, FL 33314-7796. Offers MS. *Faculty:* 15 full-time (1 woman), 5 part-time/adjunct (0 women). *Students:* 86 full-time (55 women), 50 part-time (35 women); includes 2 Asian, non-Hispanic/Latino; 11 Hispanic/Latino, 3 international. Average age 27. 80 applicants, 89% accepted, 59 enrolled. In 2010, 26 master's awarded. *Degree requirements:* For master's, thesis. *Entrance requirements:* For master's, GRE. Additional exam requirements/recommendations for international students: Required—TOEFL (minimum score 550 paper-based). *Application deadline:* Applications are processed on a rolling basis. Application fee: $50. *Expenses:* Contact institution. *Financial support:* In 2010–11, 6 research assistantships (averaging $4,000 per year), 3 teaching assistantships (averaging $3,500 per year) were awarded; career-related internships or fieldwork, Federal Work-Study, scholarships/grants, and unspecified assistantships also available. Support available to part-time students. Financial award applicants required to submit FAFSA. *Unit head:* Dr. Richard Spieler, Director of Academic Programs, 954-262-3600, Fax: 954-262-4020, E-mail: spieler@nova.edu. *Application contact:* Dr. Richard Spieler, Director of Academic Programs, 954-262-3600, Fax: 954-262-4020, E-mail: spieler@nova.edu.

Nova Southeastern University, Oceanographic Center, Program in Marine Biology and Oceanography, Fort Lauderdale, FL 33314-7796. Offers marine biology (PhD); oceanography (PhD). *Faculty:* 15 full-time (1 woman), 5 part-time/adjunct (0 women). *Students:* 10 full-time (6 women), 3 part-time (2 women); includes 1 Black or African American, non-Hispanic/Latino, 1 international. Average age 37. 3 applicants, 67% accepted, 1 enrolled. In 2010, 3 doctorates awarded. *Degree requirements:* For doctorate, comprehensive exam, thesis/dissertation. *Entrance requirements:* For doctorate, GRE, master's degree. Additional exam requirements/recommendations for international students: Required—TOEFL (minimum score 550 paper-based). Application fee: $50. *Financial support:* In 2010–11, 3 research assistantships (averaging $20,000 per year) were awarded; Federal Work-Study, scholarships/grants, tuition waivers (partial), and unspecified assistantships also available. Support available to part-time students. *Unit head:* Dr. Richard Dodge, Dean, 954-262-3600, Fax: 954-262-4020, E-mail: dodge@nsu.nova.edu. *Application contact:* Dr. Richard Spieler, Director of Academic Programs, 954-262-3600, Fax: 954-262-4020, E-mail: spieler@nova.edu.

Princeton University, Graduate School, Department of Geosciences, Princeton, NJ 08544-1019. Offers atmospheric and oceanic sciences (PhD); geosciences (PhD); ocean sciences and marine biology (PhD). *Degree requirements:* For doctorate, one foreign language, thesis/dissertation. *Entrance requirements:* For doctorate, GRE General Test. Additional exam requirements/recommendations for international students: Required—TOEFL (minimum score 600 paper-based; 250 computer-based). Electronic applications accepted. *Faculty research:* Biogeochemistry, climate science, earth history, regional geology and tectonics, solid–earth geophysics.

Rutgers, The State University of New Jersey, New Brunswick, Graduate School-New Brunswick, Department of Environmental Sciences, Piscataway, NJ 08854-8097. Offers air pollution and resources (MS, PhD); aquatic biology (MS, PhD); aquatic chemistry (MS, PhD); atmospheric science (MS, PhD); chemistry and physics of aerosol and hydrosol systems (MS, PhD); environmental chemistry (MS, PhD); environmental microbiology (MS, PhD); environmental toxicology (PhD); exposure assessment (PhD); fate and effects of pollutants (MS, PhD); pollution prevention and control (MS, PhD); water and wastewater treatment (MS, PhD); water resources (MS, PhD). Terminal master's awarded for partial completion of doctoral program. *Degree requirements:* For master's, comprehensive exam, thesis or alternative, oral final exam; for doctorate, comprehensive exam, thesis/dissertation, thesis defense, qualifying exam. *Entrance requirements:* For master's and doctorate, GRE General Test. Additional exam requirements/recommendations for international students: Required—TOEFL. Electronic applications accepted. *Expenses:* Tuition, state resident: full-time $7200; part-time $600 per credit. Tuition, nonresident: full-time $11,124; part-time $927 per credit. *Faculty research:* Biological waste treatment; contaminant fate and transport; air, soil and water quality.

San Francisco State University, Division of Graduate Studies, College of Science and Engineering, Department of Biology, Program in Marine Biology, San Francisco, CA 94132-1722. Offers MS. *Unit head:* Dr. Frances Wilkerson, Program Coordinator, 415-338-3519. *Application contact:* Dr. Robert Patterson, Graduate Coordinator, 415-338-1100, E-mail: patters@sfsu.edu.

San Francisco State University, Division of Graduate Studies, College of Science and Engineering, Department of Biology, Program in Marine Science, San Francisco, CA 94132-1722. Offers MS. Program offered through the Moss Landing Marine Laboratories. *Application deadline:* Applications are processed on a rolling basis. *Unit head:* Drew Seals, Coordinator, 831-771-4401, E-mail: dseals@mlml.calstate.edu. *Application contact:* Drew Seals, Coordinator, 831-771-4401, E-mail: dseals@mlml.calstate.edu.

Texas A&M University at Galveston, Department of Marine Biology, Galveston, TX 77553-1675. Offers MS, PhD. *Faculty:* 33 full-time (7 women). *Students:* 16 full-time (10 women), 2 part-time (both women); includes 5 minority (1 Asian, non-Hispanic/Latino; 2 Hispanic/Latino; 2 Two or more races, non-Hispanic/Latino), 1 international. Average age 23. 17 applicants, 35% accepted, 5 enrolled. *Degree requirements:* For master's, comprehensive exam (for some programs), thesis (for some programs); for doctorate, comprehensive exam, thesis/dissertation. *Entrance requirements:* For master's and doctorate, GRE. Additional exam requirements/recommendations for international students: Required—TOEFL (minimum score 550 paper-based; 213 computer-based). *Application deadline:* For fall admission, 12/15 priority date for domestic students; for spring admission, 5/15 priority date for domestic students. Applications are processed on a rolling basis. Application fee: $50 ($75 for international students). Electronic applications accepted. *Financial support:* In 2010–11, 16 students received support, including 4 research assistantships, 12 teaching assistantships; scholarships/grants, health care benefits, and unspecified assistantships also available. Financial award applicants required to submit FAFSA. *Faculty research:* Fisheries, coastal and wetland ecologies, phytoplankton, marine mammals, seafood safety, marine invertebrates and marine biospeleology. Total annual research expenditures: $2 million. *Unit head:* Dr. Christopher D. Marshall, Associate Professor/Chair of Marine Biology Interdisciplinary Program, 409-740-4884, E-mail: marshalc@tamug.edu. *Application contact:* Nicole Wilkins, Administrative Coordinator for Graduate Studies, 409-740-4937, Fax: 409-740-4754, E-mail: wilkinsn@tamug.edu.

Texas State University–San Marcos, Graduate School, College of Science, Department of Biology, Program in Aquatic Resources, San Marcos, TX 78666. Offers MS, PhD. *Faculty:* 21 full-time (5 women). *Students:* 41 full-time (21 women), 18 part-time (9 women); includes 6 minority (5 Hispanic/Latino; 1 Two or more races, non-Hispanic/Latino), 7 international. Average age 33. 14 applicants, 93% accepted, 12 enrolled. In 2010, 8 master's, 4 doctorates awarded. *Degree requirements:* For master's, comprehensive exam, thesis, 3 seminars. *Entrance requirements:* For master's, GRE General Test, previous course work in biology, minimum GPA of 2.75 in last 60 hours of course work. Additional exam requirements/recommendations for international students: Required—TOEFL (minimum score 550 paper-based; 213 computer-based; 78 iBT). *Application deadline:* For fall admission, 6/15 priority date for domestic students, 6/1 priority date for international students; for spring admission, 10/15 priority date for domestic students, 10/1 priority date for international students. Applications are processed on a rolling basis. Application fee: $40 ($90 for international students). Electronic applications accepted. *Expenses:* Tuition, state resident: full-time $6024; part-time $251 per credit hour. Tuition, nonresident: full-time $13,536; part-time $564 per credit hour. Required fees: $1776; $50 per credit hour. $306 per semester. *Financial support:* In 2010–11, 28 students received support, including 18 research assistantships (averaging $2,986 per year), 27 teaching assistantships (averaging $3,661 per year); Federal Work-Study, institutionally sponsored loans, scholarships/grants, health care benefits, and unspecified assistantships also available. Support available to part-time students. Financial award application deadline: 4/1; financial award applicants required to submit FAFSA. *Faculty research:* Projected water flow impact, Louisiana Irises, Texas Blind Salamander, Devils River Minnows, Endangered Aquatic Taxa. Total annual research expenditures: $814,666. *Unit head:* Dr. Tim Bonner, Advisor, 512-245-1616, Fax: 512-245-8713, E-mail: tb14@txstate.edu. *Application contact:* Dr. J. Michael Willoughby, Dean of the Graduate School, 512-245-2581, Fax: 512-245-8365, E-mail: jw02@swt.edu.

University of Alaska Fairbanks, School of Fisheries and Ocean Sciences, Program in Marine Sciences and Limnology, Fairbanks, AK 99775-7220. Offers marine biology (MS, PhD); oceanography (PhD), including biological oceanography, chemical oceanography, fisheries, geological oceanography, physical oceanography. Part-time programs available. *Faculty:* 8 full-time (4 women). *Students:* 40 full-time (26 women), 12 part-time (7 women); includes 3 minority (2 Asian, non-Hispanic/Latino; 1 Hispanic/Latino), 3 international. Average age 31. 54 applicants, 26% accepted, 14 enrolled. In 2010, 6 master's, 1 doctorate awarded. *Degree requirements:* For master's, comprehensive exam, thesis, oral defense; for doctorate, comprehensive exam, thesis/dissertation, oral defense. *Entrance requirements:* For master's and doctorate, GRE General Test. Additional exam requirements/recommendations for international students: Required—TOEFL (minimum score 550 paper-based; 213 computer-based; 80 iBT). *Application deadline:* For fall admission, 6/1 for domestic students, 3/1 for international students; for spring admission, 10/15 for domestic students, 8/1 for international students. Applications are processed on a rolling basis. Application fee: $60. Electronic applications accepted. *Expenses:* Tuition, state resident: full-time $5688; part-time $316 per credit. Tuition, nonresident: full-time $11,628; part-time $646 per credit. Required fees: $289 per semester. Tuition and fees vary according to course load and reciprocity agreements. *Financial support:* In 2010–11, 24 research assistantships with tuition reimbursements (averaging $11,704 per year), 9 teaching assistantships with tuition reimbursements (averaging $11,008 per year) were awarded; fellowships with tuition reimbursements, career-related internships or fieldwork, Federal Work-Study, scholarships/grants, health care benefits, and unspecified assistantships also available. Support available to part-time students. Financial award application deadline: 7/1; financial award applicants required to submit FAFSA. *Unit head:* Katrin Iken, Co-Chair, 907-474-7289, Fax: 907-474-5863, E-mail: academics@sfos.uaf.edu. *Application contact:* Christina Neumann, Academic Manager, 907-474-7289, Fax: 907-474-5863, E-mail: clneumann@alaska.edu.

University of California, San Diego, Office of Graduate Studies, Scripps Institution of Oceanography, La Jolla, CA 92093. Offers earth sciences (PhD); marine biology (PhD); oceanography (PhD). *Faculty:* 98. *Students:* 241 (115 women); includes 3 Black or African American, non-Hispanic/Latino; 4 American Indian or Alaska Native, non-Hispanic/Latino; 13 Asian, non-Hispanic/Latino, 52 international. 392 applicants, 19% accepted, 35 enrolled. *Degree requirements:* For doctorate, comprehensive exam, thesis/dissertation. *Entrance requirements:* For doctorate, GRE General Test. Additional exam requirements/recommendations for international students: Required—TOEFL (minimum score 550 paper-based; 213 computer-based; 80 iBT). *Application deadline:* For fall admission, 1/2 for domestic and international students. Application fee: $80 ($100 for international students). Electronic applications accepted. *Financial support:* Fellowships with full and partial tuition reimbursements, research assistantships with tuition reimbursements, teaching assistantships with tuition reimbursements, health care benefits available. *Unit head:* Dr. Douglas H. Bartlett, Chair, 858-534-3206, E-mail: siodept@sio.ucsd.edu. *Application contact:* Krystle Shertz, Graduate Coordinator, 858-534-3206, E-mail: kshertz@ucsd.edu.

University of California, Santa Barbara, Graduate Division, College of Letters and Sciences, Division of Mathematics, Life, and Physical Sciences, Department of Ecology, Evolution, and Marine Biology, Santa Barbara, CA 93106-9620. Offers computational science and engineering (MA); computational sciences and engineering (PhD); ecology, evolution, and marine biology (MA, PhD); MA/PhD. *Faculty:* 27 full-time (7 women). *Students:* 59 full-time (38 women); includes 2 Black or African American, non-Hispanic/Latino; 5 Asian, non-Hispanic/Latino; 2 Hispanic/Latino. Average age 29. 119 applicants, 11% accepted, 8 enrolled. In 2010, 5 master's, 3 doctorates awarded. *Degree requirements:* For master's, comprehensive exam (for some programs), thesis (for some programs); for doctorate, comprehensive exam, thesis/dissertation. *Entrance requirements:* For master's and doctorate, GRE General Test. Additional exam requirements/recommendations for international students: Required—TOEFL (minimum score 550 paper-based; 80 iBT), IELTS. *Application deadline:* For fall admission, 12/15 for domestic and international students. Application fee: $70 ($90 for international students). Electronic applications accepted. *Financial support:* In 2010–11, 54 students received support, including 35 fellowships with full and partial tuition reimbursements available (averaging $10,812 per year), 21 research assistantships with full and partial tuition reimbursements available (averaging $8,441 per year), 43 teaching assistantships with partial tuition reimbursements available (averaging $9,346 per year); Federal Work-Study, scholarships/grants, traineeships, health care benefits, and tuition waivers (full and partial) also available. Financial award application deadline: 12/15; financial award applicants required to submit FAFSA. *Faculty research:* Community ecology, evolution, marine biology, population genetics, stream ecology. *Unit head:* Dr. Cheryl Briggs, Chair, 805-893-2415, Fax: 805-893-5885. *Application contact:* Melanie Fujii, Staff Graduate Advisor, 805-893-2979, Fax: 805-893-5885, E-mail: eemb-info@lifesci.ucsb.edu.

University of Colorado Boulder, Graduate School, College of Arts and Sciences, Department of Ecology and Evolutionary Biology, Boulder, CO 80309. Offers animal behavior (MA); biology (MA, PhD); environmental biology (MA, PhD); evolutionary biology (MA, PhD); neurobiology (MA); population biology (MA); population genetics (PhD). *Faculty:* 32 full-time (10 women). *Students:* 71 full-time (36 women), 17 part-time (11 women); includes 10 minority (1 American Indian or Alaska Native, non-Hispanic/Latino; 2 Asian, non-Hispanic/Latino; 7 Hispanic/Latino), 4 international. Average age 30. 176 applicants, 20 enrolled. In 2010, 11 master's, 8 doctorates awarded. Terminal master's awarded for partial completion of doctoral program. *Degree requirements:* For master's, comprehensive exam, thesis or alternative; for doctorate, comprehensive exam, thesis/dissertation. *Entrance requirements:* For master's, GRE General Test, GRE Subject Test, minimum undergraduate GPA of 3.0; for doctorate, GRE General Test, GRE Subject Test. *Application deadline:* For fall admission, 12/30 priority date for domestic students, 12/1 for international students. Application fee: $50 ($60 for international students). *Financial support:* In 2010–11, 25 fellowships (averaging $17,876 per year), 27 research assistantships (averaging $15,070 per year) were awarded; Federal Work-Study, institutionally sponsored loans, and tuition waivers (full) also available. *Faculty research:* Behavior, ecology, genetics, morphology, endocrinology, physiology, systematics. Total annual research expenditures: $3.5 million.

University of Guam, Office of Graduate Studies, College of Natural and Applied Sciences, Program in Biology, Mangilao, GU 96923. Offers tropical marine biology (MS). *Degree requirements:* For master's, comprehensive exam, thesis. *Entrance requirements:* For master's, GRE General Test, GRE Subject Test. Additional exam requirements/recommendations for international students: Required—TOEFL. *Faculty research:* Maintenance and ecology of coral reefs.

University of Hawaii at Hilo, Program in Tropical Conservation Biology and Environmental Science, Hilo, HI 96720-4091. Offers MS.

University of Hawaii at Manoa, Graduate Division, School of Ocean and Earth Science and Technology, Interdisciplinary Program in Marine Biology, Honolulu, HI 96822. Offers MS, PhD. *Degree requirements:* For master's, thesis, research project; for doctorate, thesis/dissertation, research project. *Entrance requirements:* For master's and doctorate, GRE. Additional exam requirements/recommendations for international students: Required—TOEFL. Application fee: $50. *Expenses:* Contact institution. *Financial support:* Research assistantships, teaching assistantships, tuition waivers and unspecified assistantships available. *Faculty research:* Ecology, ichthyology, behavior of marine animals, developmental biology.

University of Maine, Graduate School, College of Natural Sciences, Forestry, and Agriculture, School of Marine Sciences, Program in Marine Biology, Orono, ME 04469. Offers MS, PhD. *Students:* 27 full-time (15 women), 6 part-time (2 women), 4 international. Average age 30. 56 applicants, 11% accepted, 6 enrolled. In 2010, 4 master's, 2 doctorates awarded. *Degree requirements:* For master's, thesis; for doctorate, thesis/dissertation. *Entrance requirements:* For master's and doctorate, GRE General Test. Additional exam requirements/recommendations for international students: Required—TOEFL. *Application deadline:* For fall admission, 2/1 priority date for domestic students. Applications are processed on a rolling basis. Application fee: $65. Electronic applications accepted. *Expenses:* Tuition, state resident: full-time $400. Tuition, nonresident: full-time $1050. *Financial support:* Career-related internships or fieldwork, Federal Work-Study, and tuition waivers (full and partial) available. Support available to part-time students. Financial award application deadline: 3/1. *Unit head:* Dr. Susan Brawley, Coordinator, 207-581-2973. *Application contact:* Scott G. Delcourt, Associate Dean of the Graduate School, 207-581-3291, Fax: 207-581-3232, E-mail: graduate@maine.edu.

University of Massachusetts Dartmouth, Graduate School, College of Arts and Sciences, Department of Biology, North Dartmouth, MA 02747-2300. Offers biology (MS); marine biology (MS). Part-time programs available. *Faculty:* 17 full-time (7 women), 4 part-time/adjunct (1 woman). *Students:* 12 full-time (9 women), 8 part-time (4 women); includes 1 Asian, non-Hispanic/Latino; 1 Hispanic/Latino. Average age 27. 35 applicants, 29% accepted, 9 enrolled. In 2010, 6 master's awarded. *Degree requirements:* For master's, thesis. *Entrance requirements:* For master's, GRE General Test, GRE Subject Test, 3 letters of recommendation. Additional exam requirements/recommendations for international students: Required—TOEFL (minimum score 500 paper-based). *Application deadline:* For fall admission, 3/15 for domestic students, 1/15 for international students; for spring admission, 11/15 priority date for domestic students, 9/15 priority date for international students. Application fee: $40 ($60 for international students). Electronic applications accepted. *Expenses:* Tuition, state resident: full-time $2071; part-time $86 per credit. Tuition, nonresident: full-time $8099; part-time $337 per credit. Required fees: $9446; $394 per credit. One-time fee: $75. Part-time tuition and fees vary according to class time, course load, degree level and reciprocity agreements. *Financial support:* In 2010–11, 6 research assistantships with full tuition reimbursements (averaging $12,577 per year), 7 teaching assistantships with full tuition reimbursements (averaging $10,340 per year) were awarded; Federal Work-Study and unspecified assistantships also available. Support available to part-time students. Financial award application deadline: 3/1; financial award applicants required to submit FAFSA. *Faculty research:* Fish biology, antibody-mediated protection, bottlenose dolphins, adaptations in fish via genetics, evolutionary biology. Total annual research expenditures: $1.4 million. *Unit head:* Dr. Diego Bernal, Director, 508-999-8307, Fax: 508-999-8196, E-mail: dbernal@umassd.edu. *Application contact:* Elan Turcotte-Shamski, Graduate Admissions Officer, 508-999-8604, Fax: 508-999-8183, E-mail: graduate@umassd.edu.

University of Miami, Graduate School, Rosenstiel School of Marine and Atmospheric Science, Division of Marine Biology and Fisheries, Coral Gables, FL 33124. Offers MA, MS, PhD. Terminal master's awarded for partial completion of doctoral program. *Degree requirements:* For master's, comprehensive exam, thesis; for doctorate, comprehensive exam, thesis/dissertation. *Entrance requirements:* For master's and doctorate, GRE General Test. Additional exam requirements/recommendations for international students: Required—TOEFL (minimum score 550 paper-based; 213 computer-based). Electronic applications accepted. *Faculty research:* Biochemistry, physiology, plankton, coral, biology.

The University of North Carolina Wilmington, Center for Marine Science, Wilmington, NC 28403-3297. Offers MS. Part-time programs available. *Faculty:* 66 full-time (16 women). *Students:* 8 full-time (6 women), 20 part-time (11 women); includes 1 Hispanic/Latino; 1 Two or more races, non-Hispanic/Latino. Average age 27. 28 applicants, 46% accepted, 7 enrolled. In 2010, 10 master's awarded. *Degree requirements:* For master's, comprehensive exam, thesis. *Entrance requirements:* For master's, GRE, minimum undergraduate B average. Additional exam requirements/recommendations for international students: Required—TOEFL (minimum score 550 paper-based; 217 computer-based; 79 iBT), IELTS (minimum score 6.5). *Application deadline:* For fall admission, 3/15 for domestic students. Application fee: $60. *Financial support:* In 2010–11, research assistantships with full and partial tuition reimbursements (averaging $10,000 per year), 11 teaching assistantships with full and partial tuition reimbursements (averaging $10,000 per year) were awarded; scholarships/grants and unspecified assistantships also available. Support available to part-time students. Total annual research expenditures: $12.9 million. *Unit head:* Dr. Daniel Baden, Director, 910-962-2301, E-mail: badend@uncw.edu. *Application contact:* Dr. Joan Willey, Graduate Coordinator, 910-962-3459, E-mail: willeyj@uncw.edu.

The University of North Carolina Wilmington, College of Arts and Sciences, Department of Biology and Marine Biology, Wilmington, NC 28403-3297. Offers biology (MS); marine biology (MS, PhD). Part-time programs available. *Faculty:* 34 full-time (7 women). *Students:* 39 part-time (21 women); includes 1 minority (Hispanic/Latino), 1 international. Average age 28. 96 applicants, 27% accepted, 21 enrolled. In 2010, 15 master's awarded. *Degree requirements:* For master's, comprehensive exam, thesis; for doctorate, comprehensive exam, thesis/dissertation. *Entrance requirements:* For master's, GRE General Test, GRE Subject Test, minimum B average in undergraduate major; for doctorate, GRE General Test, minimum B average in undergraduate major and graduate courses. Additional exam requirements/recommendations for international students: Required—TOEFL (minimum score 550 paper-based; 217 computer-based; 79 iBT), IELTS (minimum score 6.5). *Application deadline:* For fall admission, 3/15 for domestic students. Applications are processed on a rolling basis. Application fee: $60. Electronic applications accepted. *Financial support:* In 2010–11, 24 research assistantships with full and partial tuition reimbursements (averaging $14,000 per year), 36 teaching assistantships with full and partial tuition reimbursements (averaging $14,000 per year) were awarded; career-related internships or fieldwork and Federal Work-Study also available. Support available to part-time students. Financial award application deadline: 3/15. *Faculty research:* Ecology, physiology, cell and molecular biology, systematics, biomechanics. Total annual research expenditures: $3.1 million. *Unit head:* Dr. Martin H. Posey, Chairman, 910-962-3487, E-mail: poseym@uncw.edu. *Application contact:* Dr. D. Ann Pabst, Graduate Coordinator, 910-962-7266, Fax: 910-962-4066, E-mail: pabsta@uncw.edu.

University of Oregon, Graduate School, College of Arts and Sciences, Department of Biology, Eugene, OR 97403. Offers ecology and evolution (MA, MS, PhD); marine biology (MA, MS, PhD); molecular, cellular and genetic biology (PhD); neuroscience and development (PhD). Terminal master's awarded for partial completion of doctoral program. *Degree requirements:* For master's, thesis (for some programs); for doctorate, thesis/dissertation. *Entrance requirements:* For master's and doctorate, GRE General Test, minimum GPA of 3.2. Additional exam requirements/recommendations for international students: Required—TOEFL. *Faculty research:* Developmental neurobiology; evolution, population biology, and quantitative genetics; regulation of gene expression; biochemistry of marine organisms.

University of Southern California, Graduate School, Dana and David Dornsife College of Letters, Arts and Sciences, Department of Biological Sciences, Program in Marine Biology and Biological Oceanography, Los Angeles, CA 90089. Offers marine and environmental biology (MS); marine biology and biological oceanography (PhD). *Faculty:* 21 full-time (6 women), 11 part-time/adjunct (4 women). *Students:* 10 full-time (7 women); includes 6 minority (1 Black or African American, non-Hispanic/Latino; 3 Asian, non-Hispanic/Latino; 1 Hispanic/Latino; 1 Two or more races, non-Hispanic/Latino), 1 international. 35 applicants, 37% accepted, 10 enrolled. In 2010, 1 master's awarded. Terminal master's awarded for partial completion of doctoral program. *Degree requirements:* For master's, research paper; for doctorate, comprehensive exam, thesis/dissertation, qualifying examination, dissertation defense. *Entrance requirements:* For master's and doctorate, GRE, 3 letters of recommendation, personal statement, resume, minimum GPA of 3.0. Additional exam requirements/recommendations for international students: Required—TOEFL (minimum score 600 paper-based; 250 computer-based; 100 iBT). *Application deadline:* For fall admission, 12/1 priority date for domestic and international students. Application fee: $85. Electronic applications accepted. *Expenses:* Tuition: Full-time $31,240; part-time $1420 per unit. Required fees: $600. One-time fee: $35 full-time. Full-time tuition and fees vary according to degree level and program. *Financial support:* In 2010–11, 49 students received support, including 15 fellowships with full tuition reimbursements available (averaging $28,500 per year), 14 research assistantships with full tuition reimbursements available (averaging $26,700 per year), 13 teaching assistantships with full tuition reimbursements available (averaging $26,700 per year); scholarships/grants, traineeships, health care benefits, and tuition waivers also available. *Faculty research:* Microbial ecology, biogeochemistry, and geobiology; biodiversity and molecular ecology; integrative organismal biology; conservation biology; marine genomics. *Unit head:* Dr. David A. Caron, Professor of Biological Sciences/Director, 213-740-0203, E-mail: dcaron@usc.edu. *Application contact:* Adolfo dela Rosa, Student Services Advisor I, 213-821-3164, Fax: 213-740-1380, E-mail: adolfode@usc.edu.

University of Southern Mississippi, Graduate School, College of Science and Technology, Department of Biological Sciences, Hattiesburg, MS 39406-0001. Offers environmental biology (MS, PhD); marine biology (MS, PhD); microbiology (MS, PhD); molecular biology (MS, PhD). *Faculty:* 27 full-time (6 women). *Students:* 54 full-time (29 women), 5 part-time (4 women); includes 2 Black or African American, non-Hispanic/Latino; 4 Two or more races, non-Hispanic/Latino, 17 international. Average age 32. 54 applicants, 48% accepted, 13 enrolled. In 2010, 4 master's, 4 doctorates awarded. Terminal master's awarded for partial completion of doctoral program. *Degree requirements:* For master's, comprehensive exam, thesis; for doctorate, comprehensive exam, thesis/dissertation. *Entrance requirements:* For master's, GRE General Test, minimum GPA of 3.0 on last 60 hours; for doctorate, GRE General Test, minimum GPA of 3.5. Additional exam requirements/recommendations for international students: Required—TOEFL, IELTS. *Application deadline:* For fall admission, 3/1 priority date for domestic students,

Marine Biology

University of Southern Mississippi (continued)

3/1 for international students; for spring admission, 1/10 priority date for domestic and international students. Applications are processed on a rolling basis. Application fee: $50. *Financial support:* In 2010–11, 25 research assistantships with full tuition reimbursements (averaging $9,700 per year), 33 teaching assistantships with full tuition reimbursements (averaging $10,600 per year) were awarded; Federal Work-Study, scholarships/grants, health care benefits, and unspecified assistantships also available. Financial award application deadline: 3/15; financial award applicants required to submit FAFSA. *Unit head:* Dr. Glenmore Shearer, Chair, 601-266-4748, Fax: 601-266-5797. *Application contact:* Dr. Jake Schaefer, Director of Graduate Studies, 601-266-4748, Fax: 601-266-5797.

University of South Florida, Graduate School, College of Arts and Sciences, Department of Biology, Tampa, FL 33620-9951. Offers cell biology and molecular biology (MS); coastal marine biology (MS); coastal marine biology and ecology (PhD); conservation biology (MS, PhD); molecular and cell biology (PhD). Part-time programs available. *Faculty:* 8 full-time (4 women). *Students:* 85 full-time (50 women), 8 part-time (all women); includes 1 Black or African American, non-Hispanic/Latino; 3 Asian, non-Hispanic/Latino; 7 Hispanic/Latino, 12 international. Average age 27. 122 applicants, 30% accepted, 34 enrolled. In 2010, 10 master's, 9 doctorates awarded. *Degree requirements:* For master's, comprehensive exam, thesis (for some programs); for doctorate, comprehensive exam, thesis/dissertation. *Entrance requirements:* For master's and doctorate, GRE General Test, minimum GPA of 3.0. Additional exam requirements/recommendations for international students: Required—TOEFL (minimum score 570 paper-based; 213 computer-based). *Application deadline:* For fall admission, 2/15 priority date for domestic students, 1/2 for international students; for spring admission, 8/1 for domestic students, 6/1 for international students. Application fee: $30. Electronic applications accepted. *Financial support:* In 2010–11, 35 research assistantships (averaging $17,940 per year), 38 teaching assistantships with tuition reimbursements (averaging $16,621 per year) were awarded; unspecified assistantships also available. Financial award application deadline: 6/30; financial award applicants required to submit FAFSA. Total annual research expenditures: $4.5 million. *Unit head:* Susan Bell, Co-Chairperson, 813-974-6210, Fax: 813-974-2876, E-mail: sbell@cas. usf.edu. *Application contact:* James Garey, Graduate Advisor, 813-974-8434, Fax: 813-974-3263, E-mail: grarey@cas.usf.edu.

Western Illinois University, School of Graduate Studies, College of Arts and Sciences, Department of Biological Sciences, Macomb, IL 61455-1390. Offers biological sciences (MS); environmental geographic information systems (Certificate); zoo and aquarium studies (Certificate). Part-time programs available. *Students:* 64 full-time (41 women), 31 part-time (22 women); includes 10 minority (4 Black or African American, non-Hispanic/Latino; 1 Asian, non-Hispanic/Latino; 4 Hispanic/Latino; 1 Two or more races, non-Hispanic/Latino), 7 international. Average age 26. 60 applicants, 67% accepted. In 2010, 23 master's, 15 other advanced degrees awarded. *Degree requirements:* For master's, thesis or alternative. *Entrance requirements:* Additional exam requirements/recommendations for international students: Required—TOEFL (minimum score 550 paper-based; 213 computer-based; 80 iBT); Recommended—IELTS. *Application deadline:* Applications are processed on a rolling basis. Application fee: $30. Electronic applications accepted. *Expenses:* Tuition, state resident: full-time $6370; part-time $265.40 per credit hour. Tuition, nonresident: full-time $12,740; part-time $530.80 per credit hour. Required fees: $75.67 per credit hour. *Financial support:* In 2010–11, 28 students received support, including 10 research assistantships with full tuition reimbursements available (averaging $7,280 per year), 18 teaching assistantships with full tuition reimbursements available (averaging $8,400 per year). Financial award applicants required to submit FAFSA. *Unit head:* Dr. Michael Romano, Chairperson, 309-298-1546. *Application contact:* Evelyn Hoing, Assistant Director of Graduate Studies, 309-298-1806, Fax: 309-298-2345, E-mail: grad-office@wiu.edu.

Woods Hole Oceanographic Institution, MIT/WHOI Joint Program in Oceanography/Applied Ocean Science and Engineering, Woods Hole, MA 02543-1541. Offers applied ocean science and engineering (PhD); biological oceanography (PhD); chemical oceanography (PhD); marine geology and geophysics (PhD); physical oceanography (PhD). Program offered jointly with Massachusetts Institute of Technology. *Degree requirements:* For doctorate, thesis/dissertation. *Entrance requirements:* For doctorate, GRE General Test, GRE Subject Test. Additional exam requirements/recommendations for international students: Required—TOEFL. Electronic applications accepted.

Section 12
Microbiological Sciences

This section contains a directory of institutions offering graduate work in microbiological sciences, followed by in-depth entries submitted by institutions that chose to prepare detailed program descriptions. Additional information about programs listed in the directory but not augmented by an in-depth entry may be obtained by writing directly to the dean of a graduate school or chair of a department at the address given in the directory.

For programs offering related work, see also in this book *Biochemistry; Biological and Biomedical Sciences; Botany and Plant Biology; Cell, Molecular, and Structural Biology; Ecology, Environmental Biology, and Evolutionary Biology; Entomology; Genetics, Developmental Biology, and Reproductive Biology; Parasitology; Pathology and Pathobiology; Physiology;* and *Zoology.* In the other guides in this series:

Graduate Programs in the Physical Sciences, Mathematics, Agricultural Sciences, the Environment & Natural Resources

See *Agricultural and Food Sciences* and *Chemistry*

Graduate Programs in Engineering & Applied Sciences

See *Agricultural Engineering and Bioengineering* and *Biomedical Engineering and Biotechnology*

Graduate Programs in Business, Education, Health, Information Studies, Law & Social Work

See *Allied Health, Dentistry and Dental Sciences, Pharmacy and Pharmaceutical Sciences, Public Health,* and *Veterinary Medicine and Sciences*

CONTENTS

Bacteriology

Illinois State University, Graduate School, College of Arts and Sciences, Department of Biological Sciences, Normal, IL 61790-2200. Offers animal behavior (MS); bacteriology (MS); biochemistry (MS); biological sciences (MS); biology (PhD); biophysics (MS); biotechnology (MS); botany (MS, PhD); cell biology (MS); conservation biology (MS); developmental biology (MS); ecology (MS, PhD); entomology (MS); evolutionary biology (MS); genetics (MS, PhD); immunology (MS); microbiology (MS, PhD); molecular biology (MS); molecular genetics (MS); neurobiology (MS); neuroscience (MS); parasitology (MS); physiology (MS, PhD); plant biology (MS); plant molecular biology (MS); plant sciences (MS); structural biology (MS); zoology (MS, PhD). Part-time programs available. *Degree requirements:* For master's, thesis or alternative; for doctorate, variable foreign language requirement, thesis/dissertation, 2 terms of residency. *Entrance requirements:* For master's, GRE General Test, minimum GPA of 2.6 in last 60 hours of course work; for doctorate, GRE General Test. *Faculty research:* Redoc balance and drug development in schistosoma mansoni, control of the growth of listeria monocytogenes at low temperature, regulation of cell expansion and microtubule function by SPRI, CRUI: physiology and fitness consequences of different life history phenotypes.

The University of Iowa, Roy J. and Lucille A. Carver College of Medicine and Graduate College, Graduate Programs in Medicine, Department of Microbiology, Iowa City, IA 52242-1316. Offers general microbiology and microbial physiology (MS, PhD); immunology (MS, PhD); microbial genetics (MS, PhD); pathogenic bacteriology (MS, PhD); virology (MS, PhD). *Faculty:* 23 full-time (4 women), 11 part-time/adjunct (5 women). *Students:* 35 full-time (20 women); includes 2 American Indian or Alaska Native, non-Hispanic/Latino; 1 Hispanic/Latino, 5 international. Average age 25. 71 applicants, 20% accepted, 8 enrolled. In 2010, 1 master's, 5 doctorates awarded. *Degree requirements:* For master's, thesis; for doctorate, comprehensive exam, thesis/dissertation. *Entrance requirements:* For master's and doctorate, GRE General Test. Additional exam requirements/recommendations for international students: Required—TOEFL (minimum score 600 paper-based; 250 computer-based). *Application deadline:* For fall admission, 2/1 for domestic and international students. Application fee: $60 ($85 for international students). Electronic applications accepted. *Financial support:* In 2010–11, 4 fellowships with full tuition reimbursements (averaging $25,000 per year), 31 research assistantships with full tuition reimbursements (averaging $25,000 per year) were awarded; institutionally sponsored loans, scholarships/grants, traineeships, and health care benefits also available. *Faculty research:* Gene regulation, processing and transport of HIV, retroviral pathogenesis, biodegradation, biofilm. Total annual research expenditures: $12.6 million. *Unit head:* Dr. Michael A. Apicella, Head, 319-335-7810, E-mail: grad-micro-info@uiowa.edu. *Application contact:* Dr. Michael A. Apicella, Head, 319-335-7810, E-mail: grad-micro-info@uiowa.edu.

University of Prince Edward Island, Atlantic Veterinary College, Graduate Program in Veterinary Medicine, Charlottetown, PE C1A 4P3, Canada. Offers anatomy (M Sc, PhD); bacteriology (M Sc, PhD); clinical pharmacology (M Sc, PhD); clinical sciences (M Sc, PhD); epidemiology (M Sc, PhD), including reproduction; fish health (M Sc, PhD); food animal nutrition (M Sc, PhD); immunology (M Sc, PhD); microanatomy (M Sc, PhD); parasitology (M Sc, PhD); pathology (M Sc, PhD); pharmacology (M Sc, PhD); physiology (M Sc, PhD); toxicology (M Sc, PhD); veterinary science (M Vet Sc); virology (M Sc, PhD). Part-time programs available.

Degree requirements: For master's, thesis; for doctorate, thesis/dissertation. *Entrance requirements:* For master's, DVM, B Sc honors degree, or equivalent; for doctorate, M Sc. Additional exam requirements/recommendations for international students: Required—TOEFL (minimum score 550 paper-based; 213 computer-based; 80 iBT). *Expenses:* Contact institution. *Faculty research:* Animal health management, infectious diseases, fin fish and shellfish health, basic biomedical sciences, ecosystem health.

The University of Texas Medical Branch, Graduate School of Biomedical Sciences, Center for Biodefense and Emerging Infectious Diseases, Galveston, TX 77555. Offers biodefense training (PhD). *Entrance requirements:* For doctorate, GRE, minimum overall GPA of 3.0.

The University of Texas Medical Branch, Graduate School of Biomedical Sciences, Program in Emerging and Tropical Infectious Diseases, Galveston, TX 77555. Offers PhD, MD/PhD. *Degree requirements:* For doctorate, thesis/dissertation. *Entrance requirements:* For doctorate, GRE General Test. *Faculty research:* Emerging diseases, tropical diseases, parasitology, vitology and bacteriology.

University of Washington, Graduate School, School of Public Health, Department of Global Health, Graduate Program in Pathobiology, Seattle, WA 98195. Offers PhD. *Students:* 34 full-time (27 women), 1 part-time (0 women); includes 2 Black or African American, non-Hispanic/Latino; 3 Asian, non-Hispanic/Latino; 2 Hispanic/Latino, 6 international. Average age 29. 59 applicants, 24% accepted, 6 enrolled. In 2010, 3 doctorates awarded. *Degree requirements:* For doctorate, comprehensive exam, thesis/dissertation, published paper from thesis work. *Entrance requirements:* For doctorate, GRE General Test, minimum GPA of 3.0. *Application deadline:* For fall admission, 12/1 for domestic students, 11/1 for international students. Application fee: $75. Electronic applications accepted. *Financial support:* In 2010–11, 32 students received support, including 2 fellowships with full tuition reimbursements available (averaging $27,348 per year), 30 research assistantships with full tuition reimbursements available (averaging $27,348 per year); career-related internships or fieldwork, institutionally sponsored loans, scholarships/grants, traineeships, and unspecified assistantships also available. *Faculty research:* Malaria, immunological response to mycobacteria infections, HIV-cell interaction and the development of an anti-HIV vaccine, regulation of intercellular communication via gap junctions, genetic and nutritional regulation of proteins involved in lipid transport. *Unit head:* Dr. King Holmes, Chair, 206-744-3620, Fax: 206-744-3694. *Application contact:* Rachel Reichert, Program Manager, 206-543-4338, Fax: 206-543-3873, E-mail: pabio@u.washington.edu.

University of Wisconsin–Madison, Graduate School, College of Agricultural and Life Sciences, Department of Bacteriology, Madison, WI 53706-1380. Offers MS. Part-time programs available. *Entrance requirements:* Additional exam requirements/recommendations for international students: Required—TOEFL. Electronic applications accepted. *Expenses:* Tuition, state resident: full-time $9887; part-time $617.96 per credit. Tuition, nonresident: full-time $24,054; part-time $1503.40 per credit. Required fees: $67.63 per credit. Tuition and fees vary according to reciprocity agreements. *Faculty research:* Microbial physiology, gene regulation, microbial ecology, plant-microbe interactions, symbiosis.

Immunology

Albany Medical College, Center for Immunology and Microbial Disease, Albany, NY 12208-3479. Offers MS, PhD. Part-time programs available. *Faculty:* 19 full-time (4 women), 11 part-time/adjunct (6 women). *Students:* 18 full-time (10 women); includes 1 Asian, non-Hispanic/Latino. Average age 25. 20 applicants, 45% accepted, 6 enrolled. In 2010, 1 doctorate awarded. Terminal master's awarded for partial completion of doctoral program. *Degree requirements:* For master's, thesis; for doctorate, comprehensive exam, thesis/dissertation, oral qualifying exam, written preliminary exam, 1 published paper-peer review. *Entrance requirements:* For master's, GRE General Test, all transcripts, letters of recommendation; for doctorate, GRE General Test, letters of recommendation. Additional exam requirements/recommendations for international students: Required—TOEFL. *Application deadline:* For fall admission, 3/15 priority date for domestic and international students. Applications are processed on a rolling basis. Application fee: $0 ($60 for international students). *Financial support:* In 2010–11, 10 research assistantships (averaging $24,000 per year) were awarded; Federal Work-Study, scholarships/grants, and tuition waivers (full) also available. Financial award applicants required to submit FAFSA. *Faculty research:* Microbial and viral pathogenesis, cancer development and cell transformation, biochemical and genetic mechanisms responsible for human disease. *Unit head:* Dr. Thomas D. Friedrich, Graduate Director, 518-262-6750, Fax: 518-262-6161, E-mail: dgs_cimd@mail.amc.edu. *Application contact:* Dr. Thomas D. Friedrich, Graduate Director, 518-262-6750, Fax: 518-262-6161, E-mail: dgs_cimd@mail.amc.edu.

Albert Einstein College of Medicine, Graduate Division of Biomedical Sciences, Department of Microbiology and Immunology, Bronx, NY 10461. Offers PhD, MD/PhD. *Degree requirements:* For doctorate, thesis/dissertation. *Entrance requirements:* For doctorate, GRE General Test. Additional exam requirements/recommendations for international students: Required—TOEFL. *Faculty research:* Nature of histocompatibility antigens, lymphoid cell receptors, regulation of immune responses and mechanisms of resistance to infection.

Baylor College of Medicine, Graduate School of Biomedical Sciences, Department of Immunology, Houston, TX 77030-3498. Offers PhD, MD/PhD. *Faculty:* 40 full-time (13 women). *Students:* 30 full-time (17 women); includes 3 Black or African American, non-Hispanic/Latino; 6 Asian, non-Hispanic/Latino; 3 Hispanic/Latino, 15 international. Average age 29. 70 applicants, 14% accepted, 4 enrolled. In 2010, 1 doctorate awarded. *Degree requirements:* For doctorate, thesis/dissertation, public defense. *Entrance requirements:* For doctorate, GRE General Test, GRE Subject Test (strongly recommended), minimum GPA of 3.0. Additional exam requirements/recommendations for international students: Required—TOEFL. *Application deadline:* For fall admission, 1/1 priority date for domestic students. Application fee: $0. Electronic applications accepted. *Expenses:* Tuition: Full-time $11,000. Required fees: $4900. *Financial support:* In 2010–11, 11 fellowships with full tuition reimbursements (averaging $26,000 per year), 19 research assistantships with full tuition reimbursements (averaging $26,000 per year) were awarded; teaching assistantships, career-related internships or fieldwork, Federal Work-Study, institutionally sponsored loans, health care benefits, and students receive a scholarship unless there are grant funds available to pay tuition also available. Financial award applicants required to submit FAFSA. *Faculty research:* MHC expression, inflammation and allergy, germinal center biology, HIV pathogenesis, immune responses to gene therapy. *Unit head:* Dr. John Rodgers, Director, 713-798-3903, Fax: 713-798-3700, E-mail: jrodgers@bcm.edu. *Application contact:* Shannon Robertson, Graduate Program Administrator, 713-798-3921, Fax: 713-798-3900, E-mail: sdrobert@bcm.edu.

Baylor College of Medicine, Graduate School of Biomedical Sciences, Interdepartmental Program in Cell and Molecular Biology, Houston, TX 77030-3498. Offers biochemistry (PhD); cell and molecular biology (PhD); genetics (PhD); human genetics (PhD); immunology (PhD); microbiology (PhD); virology (PhD); MD/PhD. *Faculty:* 100 full-time (31 women). *Students:* 67 full-time (41 women); includes 4 Black or African American, non-Hispanic/Latino; 2 American

Indian or Alaska Native, non-Hispanic/Latino; 9 Asian, non-Hispanic/Latino; 9 Hispanic/Latino, 9 international. Average age 27. 120 applicants, 27% accepted, 15 enrolled. In 2010, 7 doctorates awarded. *Degree requirements:* For doctorate, thesis/dissertation, public defense. *Entrance requirements:* For doctorate, GRE General Test, GRE Subject Test (strongly recommended), minimum GPA of 3.0. Additional exam requirements/recommendations for international students: Required—TOEFL. *Application deadline:* For fall admission, 1/1 priority date for domestic students. Applications are processed on a rolling basis. Application fee: $0. Electronic applications accepted. *Expenses:* Tuition: Full-time $11,000. Required fees: $4900. *Financial support:* In 2010–11, 67 students received support, including 24 fellowships with full tuition reimbursements available (averaging $26,000 per year), 43 research assistantships with full tuition reimbursements available (averaging $26,000 per year); teaching assistantships, Federal Work-Study, institutionally sponsored loans, health care benefits, and tuition waivers (full) also available. Financial award applicants required to submit FAFSA. *Faculty research:* Molecular and cellular biology; cancer, aging and stem cells; genomics and proteomics; microbiome, molecular microbiology; infectious disease, immunology and translational research. *Unit head:* Dr. Susan Marriott, Director, 713-798-6557. *Application contact:* Lourdes Fernandez, Graduate Program Administrator, 713-798-6557, Fax: 713-798-6325, E-mail: cmbprog@bcm.edu.

See Close-Up on page 223.

Boston University, School of Medicine, Division of Graduate Medical Sciences, Department of Microbiology, Boston, MA 02118. Offers immunology (PhD); microbiology (MA); MD/PhD. *Faculty:* 14 full-time (7 women), 2 part-time/adjunct (1 woman). *Students:* 8 full-time (5 women); includes 1 Black or African American, non-Hispanic/Latino, 1 international. 52 applicants, 10% accepted, 0 enrolled. In 2010, 3 doctorates awarded. Terminal master's awarded for partial completion of doctoral program. *Degree requirements:* For master's, thesis; for doctorate, comprehensive exam, thesis/dissertation. *Entrance requirements:* For master's and doctorate, GRE General Test, GRE Subject Test. Additional exam requirements/recommendations for international students: Required—TOEFL. *Application deadline:* For fall admission, 1/15 priority date for domestic students; for spring admission, 10/15 priority date for domestic students. Application fee: $75. Electronic applications accepted. *Expenses:* Tuition: Full-time $39,314; part-time $1228 per credit. Required fees: $40 per semester. *Financial support:* In 2010–11, 5 research assistantships (averaging $30,500 per year) were awarded; fellowships, Federal Work-Study, scholarships/grants, and traineeships also available. Financial award applicants required to submit FAFSA. *Faculty research:* Eukaryotic cell biology, tumor cell biology, nutrition and cancer, experimental tumor therapy, photobiology. *Unit head:* Dr. Ronald B. Corley, Chairman, 617-638-4284, Fax: 617-638-4286, E-mail: rbcorley@bu.edu. *Application contact:* Dr. Gregory Viglianti, Graduate Director, 617-638-7790, Fax: 617-638-4286, E-mail: gviglian@bu.edu.

Boston University, School of Medicine, Division of Graduate Medical Sciences, Immunology Training Program, Boston, MA 02215. Offers PhD, MD/PhD. *Faculty:* 27 full-time (8 women). *Students:* 15 full-time (9 women); includes 2 Black or African American, non-Hispanic/Latino; 2 Asian, non-Hispanic/Latino; 1 Hispanic/Latino, 1 international. 112 applicants, 9% accepted, 6 enrolled. In 2010, 1 doctorate awarded. *Degree requirements:* For doctorate, thesis/dissertation, qualifying exam. *Entrance requirements:* For doctorate, GRE General Test, GRE Subject Test. Additional exam requirements/recommendations for international students: Required—TOEFL. *Application deadline:* For fall admission, 1/15 priority date for domestic students; for spring admission, 10/15 priority date for domestic students. Application fee: $75. Electronic applications accepted. *Expenses:* Tuition: Full-time $39,314; part-time $1228 per credit. Required fees: $40 per semester. *Financial support:* In 2010–11, 1 fellowship with tuition reimbursement (averaging $30,500 per year), 9 research assistantships with tuition reimbursements (averaging $30,500 per year) were awarded; Federal Work-Study, scholarships/grants, and traineeships also available. Financial award applicants required to submit FAFSA. *Unit head:* Dr. David

Sherr, Director, 617-638-6464, E-mail: itp@bu.edu. *Application contact:* Michelle Hall, Assistant Director of Admissions, 617-638-5121, Fax: 617-638-5740, E-mail: natashah@bu.edu.

Brown University, Graduate School, Division of Biology and Medicine, Program in Molecular Biology, Cell Biology, and Biochemistry, Providence, RI 02912. Offers biochemistry (M Med Sc, Sc M, PhD), including biochemistry (Sc M, PhD), biology (Sc M, PhD), medical science (M Med Sc, PhD); biology (MA); cell biology (M Med Sc, Sc M, PhD), including biochemistry (Sc M, PhD), biology (Sc M, PhD), medical science (M Med Sc, PhD); developmental biology (M Med Sc, Sc M, PhD), including biochemistry (Sc M, PhD), biology (Sc M, PhD), medical science (M Med Sc, PhD); immunology (M Med Sc, Sc M, PhD), including biochemistry (Sc M, PhD), biology (Sc M, PhD), medical science (M Med Sc, PhD); molecular microbiology (M Med Sc, Sc M, PhD), including biochemistry (Sc M, PhD), biology (Sc M, PhD), medical science (M Med Sc, PhD); MD/PhD. Part-time programs available. Terminal master's awarded for partial completion of doctoral program. *Degree requirements:* For master's, thesis (for some programs); for doctorate, one foreign language, thesis/dissertation, preliminary exam. *Entrance requirements:* For master's and doctorate, GRE General Test, GRE Subject Test. Additional exam requirements/recommendations for international students: Required—TOEFL. Electronic applications accepted. *Faculty research:* Molecular genetics, gene regulation.

Brown University, Graduate School, Division of Biology and Medicine, Program in Pathology and Laboratory Medicine, Providence, RI 02912. Offers biology (PhD); cancer biology (PhD); immunology and infection (PhD); medical science (PhD); pathobiology (Sc M); toxicology and environmental pathology (PhD). Terminal master's awarded for partial completion of doctoral program. *Degree requirements:* For doctorate, thesis/dissertation, preliminary exam. *Entrance requirements:* For master's and doctorate, GRE General Test, GRE Subject Test. Additional exam requirements/recommendations for international students: Required—TOEFL. Electronic applications accepted. *Faculty research:* Environmental pathology, carcinogenesis, immunopathology, signal transduction, innate immunity.

California Institute of Technology, Division of Biology, Program in Immunology, Pasadena, CA 91125-0001. Offers PhD. *Degree requirements:* For doctorate, thesis/dissertation, qualifying exam. *Entrance requirements:* For doctorate, GRE General Test.

Case Western Reserve University, School of Medicine and School of Graduate Studies, Graduate Programs in Medicine, Programs in Molecular and Cellular Basis of Disease/Pathology, Immunology Training Program, Cleveland, OH 44106. Offers MS, PhD, MD/PhD. *Degree requirements:* For doctorate, comprehensive exam, thesis/dissertation. *Entrance requirements:* For doctorate, GRE General Test, GRE Subject Test. Additional exam requirements/recommendations for international students: Required—TOEFL (minimum score 550 paper-based; 213 computer-based). Electronic applications accepted. *Faculty research:* Immunology, immunopathology, immunochemistry, infectious diseases.

Colorado State University, College of Veterinary Medicine and Biomedical Sciences, Department of Microbiology, Immunology and Pathology, Fort Collins, CO 80523-0015. Offers microbiology (MS, PhD); pathology (PhD). *Faculty:* 40 full-time (17 women), 2 part-time/adjunct (0 women). *Students:* 56 full-time (44 women), 39 part-time (25 women); includes 4 Asian, non-Hispanic/Latino; 6 Hispanic/Latino, 9 international. Average age 31. 107 applicants, 17% accepted, 18 enrolled. In 2010, 5 master's, 11 doctorates awarded. *Degree requirements:* For master's, thesis; for doctorate, comprehensive exam, thesis/dissertation. *Entrance requirements:* For master's, GRE General Test, minimum GPA of 3.0, BA/BS in biomedical field, reviewer evaluation forms, resume; for doctorate, GRE General Test, minimum GPA of 3.0, BA/BS in biomedical field, reviewer evaluation forms, resume, statement of interest. Additional exam requirements/recommendations for international students: Required—TOEFL (minimum score 550 paper-based). *Application deadline:* For fall admission, 1/1 priority date for domestic students; for spring admission, 10/1 priority date for domestic students. Applications are processed on a rolling basis. Application fee: $50. Electronic applications accepted. *Expenses:* Tuition, state resident: full-time $7434; part-time $413 per credit. Tuition, nonresident: full-time $19,022; part-time $1057 per credit. Required fees: $1729; $88 per credit. *Financial support:* In 2010–11, 74 students received support, including 27 fellowships with tuition reimbursements available (averaging $32,882 per year), 41 research assistantships with tuition reimbursements available (averaging $23,930 per year), 6 teaching assistantships with tuition reimbursements available (averaging $15,885 per year); Federal Work-Study, scholarships/grants, traineeships, and unspecified assistantships also available. Financial award applicants required to submit FAFSA. *Faculty research:* Medical and veterinary bacteriology, immunology, microbial physiology, pathology, vector-borne disease. Total annual research expenditures: $33.1 million. *Unit head:* Dr. Edward A. Hoover, Head, 970-491-7587, Fax: 970-491-0603, E-mail: edward.hoover@colostate.edu. *Application contact:* Lisa McCann, Academic Programs Coordinator, 970-491-6118, Fax: 970-491-1815, E-mail: lisa.mccann@colostate.edu.

Cornell University, Graduate School, Graduate Fields of Comparative Biomedical Sciences, Field of Immunology, Ithaca, NY 14853-0001. Offers cellular immunology (MS, PhD); immunochemistry (MS, PhD); immunogenetics (MS, PhD); immunopathology (MS, PhD); infection and immunity (MS, PhD). *Faculty:* 18 full-time (7 women). *Students:* 19 full-time (12 women); includes 3 Black or African American, non-Hispanic/Latino; 1 Asian, non-Hispanic/Latino, 6 international. Average age 29. 40 applicants, 25% accepted, 6 enrolled. In 2010, 3 doctorates awarded. Terminal master's awarded for partial completion of doctoral program. *Degree requirements:* For master's, thesis; for doctorate, comprehensive exam, thesis/dissertation. *Entrance requirements:* For master's and doctorate, GRE General Test, 2 letters of recommendation. Additional exam requirements/recommendations for international students: Required—TOEFL (minimum score 550 paper-based; 213 computer-based; 77 iBT). *Application deadline:* For fall admission, 12/15 for domestic students. Application fee: $70. Electronic applications accepted. *Expenses:* Tuition: Full-time $29,500. Required fees: $76. Tuition and fees vary according to degree level and program. *Financial support:* In 2010–11, 5 fellowships with full tuition reimbursements, 14 research assistantships with full tuition reimbursements were awarded; teaching assistantships with full tuition reimbursements, institutionally sponsored loans, scholarships/grants, health care benefits, tuition waivers (full and partial), and unspecified assistantships also available. Financial award applicants required to submit FAFSA. *Faculty research:* Avian immunology, mucosal immunity, anti-parasite and anti-viral immunity, neutrophil function, reproductive immunology. *Unit head:* Director of Graduate Studies, 607-253-3276, Fax: 607-253-3756. *Application contact:* Graduate Field Assistant, 607-253-3276, Fax: 607-253-3756, E-mail: graduate_edcvm@cornell.edu.

Cornell University, Joan and Sanford I. Weill Medical College and Graduate School of Medical Sciences, Weill Cornell Graduate School of Medical Sciences, Immunology and Microbial Pathogenesis Program, New York, NY 10065. Offers immunology (MS, PhD), including immunology, microbiology, pathology. *Faculty:* 37 full-time (12 women). *Students:* 50 full-time (36 women); includes 5 Asian, non-Hispanic/Latino; 2 Hispanic/Latino, 30 international. Average age 23. 129 applicants, 12% accepted, 7 enrolled. In 2010, 1 master's, 8 doctorates awarded. Terminal master's awarded for partial completion of doctoral program. *Degree requirements:* For master's, comprehensive exam; for doctorate, thesis/dissertation, final exam. *Entrance requirements:* For doctorate, GRE General Test, laboratory research experience, course work in biological sciences. Additional exam requirements/recommendations for international students: Required—TOEFL. *Application deadline:* For fall admission, 12/1 for domestic students. Application fee: $60. Electronic applications accepted. *Expenses:* Tuition: Full-time $45,545. Required fees: $2805. *Financial support:* In 2010–11, 7 fellowships (averaging $23,000 per year) were awarded; scholarships/grants, health care benefits, and stipends (given to all students) also available. *Faculty research:* Microbial immunity, tumor immunology, lymphoylte and leukocyte biology, auto immunity, stem cell/bone marrow transplantation. *Unit head:* Dr. Ulrich Hammerling, Director, 646-888-2303, E-mail: u-hammerling@ski.mskcc.org. *Application contact:* Stephen Nesbit, Assistant Dean of Admissions, 212-746-6565, Fax: 212-746-8906, E-mail: sjn2001@med.cornell.edu.

Creighton University, School of Medicine and Graduate School, Graduate Programs in Medicine, Department of Medical Microbiology and Immunology, Omaha, NE 68178-0001. Offers MS, PhD. Terminal master's awarded for partial completion of doctoral program. *Degree requirements:* For master's, comprehensive exam, thesis; for doctorate, thesis/dissertation, preliminary exams. *Entrance requirements:* For master's and doctorate, GRE General Test. Additional exam requirements/recommendations for international students: Required—TOEFL. *Expenses:* Tuition: Full-time $12,168; part-time $676 per credit hour. Required fees: $131 per semester. Tuition and fees vary according to program. *Faculty research:* Infectious diseases, molecular biology, genetics, antimicrobial agents and chemotherapy, virology.

Dalhousie University, Faculty of Medicine, Department of Microbiology and Immunology, Halifax, NS B3H 1X5, Canada. Offers M Sc, PhD. *Degree requirements:* For master's, thesis; for doctorate, comprehensive exam, thesis/dissertation. *Entrance requirements:* For master's, GRE General Test, honors B Sc; for doctorate, GRE General Test, honors B Sc in microbiology, M Sc in discipline or transfer after 1 year in master's program. Additional exam requirements/recommendations for international students: Required—TOEFL, IELTS, 1 of the following 5 approved tests: TOEFL, IELTS, CAEL, CANTEST, Michigan English Language Assessment Battery. Electronic applications accepted. *Faculty research:* Virology, molecular genetics, pathogenesis, bacteriology, immunology.

Dartmouth College, Graduate Program in Molecular and Cellular Biology, Department of Microbiology and Immunology, Program in Immunology, Hanover, NH 03755. Offers MD/PhD. *Faculty research:* Tumor immunotherapy, cell and molecular biology of connective tissue degradation in rheumatoid arthritis and cancer, immunology and immunotherapy of tumors of the central nervous system, transcriptional regulation of hematopoiesis and leukemia, bacterial pathogenesis.

Drexel University, College of Medicine, Biomedical Graduate Programs, Program in Microbiology and Immunology, Philadelphia, PA 19104-2875. Offers MS, PhD, MD/PhD. Terminal master's awarded for partial completion of doctoral program. *Degree requirements:* For master's, comprehensive exam, thesis; for doctorate, thesis/dissertation, qualifying exam. *Entrance requirements:* For master's, GRE General Test, minimum GPA of 2.75; for doctorate, GRE General Test, minimum GPA of 3.0. Additional exam requirements/recommendations for international students: Required—TOEFL. Electronic applications accepted. *Faculty research:* Immunology of malarial parasites, virology, bacteriology, molecular biology, parasitology.

Duke University, Graduate School, Department of Immunology, Durham, NC 27710. Offers PhD. *Faculty:* 48 full-time. *Students:* 39 full-time (23 women); includes 2 Black or African American, non-Hispanic/Latino; 1 Asian, non-Hispanic/Latino; 1 Hispanic/Latino, 15 international. 69 applicants, 23% accepted, 10 enrolled. In 2010, 3 doctorates awarded. *Degree requirements:* For doctorate, thesis/dissertation. *Entrance requirements:* For doctorate, GRE General Test, GRE Subject Test in biology or biochemistry, cell and molecular biology (strongly recommended). Additional exam requirements/recommendations for international students: Required—TOEFL (minimum score 550 paper-based; 213 computer-based; 83 iBT), IELTS (minimum score 7). *Application deadline:* For fall admission, 12/8 priority date for domestic and international students. Application fee: $75. Electronic applications accepted. *Financial support:* Fellowships, research assistantships available. Financial award application deadline: 12/8. *Unit head:* Yuan Zhuang, Director of Graduate Studies, 909-613-3578, Fax: 919-684-8982, E-mail: immunologydept@mc.duke.edu. *Application contact:* Elizabeth Hutton, Director of Admissions, 919-684-3913, Fax: 919-684-2277, E-mail: grad-admissions@duke.edu.

East Carolina University, Brody School of Medicine, Department of Microbiology and Immunology, Greenville, NC 27858-4353. Offers PhD. *Degree requirements:* For doctorate, comprehensive exam, thesis/dissertation. *Entrance requirements:* For doctorate, GRE General Test. Additional exam requirements/recommendations for international students: Required—TOEFL. *Expenses:* Tuition, state resident: full-time $3130; part-time $391.25 per credit hour. Tuition, nonresident: full-time $13,817; part-time $1727.13 per credit hour. Required fees: $1916; $239.50 per credit hour. Tuition and fees vary according to campus/location and program. *Faculty research:* Molecular virology, genetics of bacteria, yeast and somatic cells, bacterial physiology and metabolism, bioterrorism.

Emory University, Laney Graduate School, Division of Biological and Biomedical Sciences, Program in Immunology and Molecular Pathogenesis, Atlanta, GA 30322-1100. Offers PhD. *Faculty:* 52 full-time (8 women). *Students:* 73 full-time (42 women); includes 1 American Indian or Alaska Native, non-Hispanic/Latino; 12 Asian, non-Hispanic/Latino; 3 Hispanic/Latino; 1 Native Hawaiian or other Pacific Islander, non-Hispanic/Latino, 9 international. Average age 27. 179 applicants, 15% accepted, 11 enrolled. In 2010, 14 doctorates awarded. *Degree requirements:* For doctorate, comprehensive exam, thesis/dissertation. *Entrance requirements:* For doctorate, GRE General Test, minimum GPA of 3.0 in science course work (recommended). Additional exam requirements/recommendations for international students: Required—TOEFL. *Application deadline:* For fall admission, 12/1 for domestic and international students. Application fee: $75. Electronic applications accepted. *Expenses:* Tuition: Full-time $33,800. Required fees: $1300. *Financial support:* In 2010–11, 21 students received support, including 21 fellowships with full tuition reimbursements available (averaging $25,000 per year); institutionally sponsored loans, scholarships/grants, health care benefits, and tuition waivers (full) also available. *Faculty research:* Transplantation immunology, autoimmunity, microbial pathogenesis. *Unit head:* Dr. Brian Evavold, Director, 404-727-3393, Fax: 404-727-3659, E-mail: evavold@microbio.emory.edu. *Application contact:* Kathy Smith, Director of Recruitment and Admissions, 404-727-2547, Fax: 404-727-3322, E-mail: kathy.smith@emory.edu.

Georgetown University, Graduate School of Arts and Sciences, Programs in Biomedical Sciences, Department of Microbiology and Immunology, Washington, DC 20057. Offers biohazardous threat agents and emerging infectious diseases (MS); general microbiology and immunology (MS); global infectious diseases (PhD); microbiology and immunology research (PhD); science policy and advocacy (MS). Part-time programs available. *Degree requirements:* For master's, 30 credit hours of coursework; for doctorate, comprehensive exam, thesis/dissertation. *Entrance requirements:* For master's, GRE General Test, 3 letters of reference, bachelor's degree in related field; for doctorate, GRE General Test, 3 letters of reference, MS/BS in related field. Additional exam requirements/recommendations for international students: Required—TOEFL (minimum score 505 paper-based; 213 computer-based). Electronic applications accepted. *Faculty research:* Pathogenesis and basic biology of the fungus Candida albicans, molecular biology of viral immunopathological mechanisms in Multiple Sclerosis.

The George Washington University, Columbian College of Arts and Sciences, Institute for Biomedical Sciences, Program in Microbiology and Immunology, Washington, DC 20037. Offers PhD. *Students:* 6 full-time (5 women), 13 part-time (8 women); includes 1 American Indian or Alaska Native, non-Hispanic/Latino; 1 Asian, non-Hispanic/Latino; 1 Hispanic/Latino, 2 international. Average age 30. In 2010, 2 doctorates awarded. *Degree requirements:* For doctorate, thesis/dissertation. *Entrance requirements:* For doctorate, GRE General Test, minimum GPA of 3.0. Additional exam requirements/recommendations for international students: Required—TOEFL (minimum score 600 paper-based; 250 computer-based). *Application deadline:* For fall admission, 12/15 priority date for domestic and international students. Applications are processed on a rolling basis. Application fee: $75. Electronic applications accepted. *Financial support:* In 2010–11, 10 students received support; fellowships with tuition reimbursements available, tuition waivers available. *Unit head:* Dr. David Leitenberg, Director, 202-994-9475, Fax: 202-994-2913, E-mail: dleit@gwu.edu. *Application contact:* Information Contact, 202-994-3532, Fax: 202-994-2913, E-mail: mtmjxl@gwumc.edu.

Harvard University, Harvard School of Public Health, Department of Immunology and Infectious Diseases, Boston, MA 02115-6096. Offers PhD, SD. Part-time programs available. *Faculty:* 31 full-time (9 women), 5 part-time/adjunct (0 women). *Students:* 8 applicants, 0% accepted, 0 enrolled. *Degree requirements:* For doctorate, thesis/dissertation, qualifying exam. *Entrance requirements:* For doctorate, GRE. Additional exam requirements/recommendations for international students: Required—TOEFL (minimum score 600 paper-based; 240 computer-based; 100 iBT); Recommended—IELTS (minimum score 7). *Application deadline:* For fall admission, 12/15 for domestic and international students. Application fee: $115. Electronic

Immunology

Harvard University (continued)
applications accepted. *Expenses:* Tuition: Full-time $34,976. Required fees: $1166. Full-time tuition and fees vary according to program. *Financial support:* Fellowships, research assistantships, Federal Work-Study, scholarships/grants, traineeships, tuition waivers (partial), and unspecified assistantships available. Financial award application deadline: 2/8; financial award applicants required to submit FAFSA. *Faculty research:* Infectious disease epidemiology and tropical public health, vector biology, ecology and control, virology. *Unit head:* Dr. Dyann F. Wirth, Chair, 617-432-2234, Fax: 617-739-8348, E-mail: rkenwort@hsph.harvard.edu. *Application contact:* Vincent W. James, Director of Admissions, 617-432-1031, Fax: 617-432-7080, E-mail: admissions@hsph.harvard.edu.

Hood College, Graduate School, Program in Biomedical Science, Frederick, MD 21701-8575. Offers biomedical science (MS), including biotechnology/molecular biology, microbiology/immunology/virology, regulatory compliance; regulatory compliance (Certificate). Part-time and evening/weekend programs available. *Faculty:* 3 full-time (1 woman), 7 part-time/adjunct (4 women). *Students:* 9 full-time (2 women), 87 part-time (55 women); includes 16 Black or African American, non-Hispanic/Latino; 9 Asian, non-Hispanic/Latino; 3 Hispanic/Latino; 1 Two or more races, non-Hispanic/Latino, 7 international. Average age 29. 61 applicants, 64% accepted, 21 enrolled. In 2010, 9 master's, 3 other advanced degrees awarded. *Degree requirements:* For master's, comprehensive exam, thesis or alternative. *Entrance requirements:* For master's, bachelor's degree in biology; minimum GPA of 2.75; undergraduate course work in cell biology, chemistry, organic chemistry, and genetics. Additional exam requirements/recommendations for international students: Required—TOEFL (minimum score 575 paper-based; 231 computer-based; 89 iBT). *Application deadline:* For fall admission, 7/15 for domestic and international students; for spring admission, 12/15 for domestic and international students. Applications are processed on a rolling basis. Application fee: $35. Electronic applications accepted. *Expenses:* Tuition: Full-time $6480; part-time $360 per credit. Required fees: $100; $50 per term. *Financial support:* In 2010–11, 3 research assistantships with full tuition reimbursements (averaging $10,609 per year) were awarded. Financial award applicants required to submit FAFSA. *Unit head:* Dr. Oney Smith, Director, 301-696-3653, Fax: 301-696-3597, E-mail: osmith@hood.edu. *Application contact:* Dr. Allen P. Flora, Dean of Graduate School, 301-696-3811, Fax: 301-696-3597, E-mail: gofurther@hood.edu.

Illinois State University, Graduate School, College of Arts and Sciences, Department of Biological Sciences, Normal, IL 61790-2200. Offers animal behavior (MS); bacteriology (MS); biochemistry (MS); biological sciences (MS); biology (PhD); biophysics (MS); biotechnology (MS); botany (MS, PhD); cell biology (MS); conservation biology (MS); developmental biology (MS); ecology (MS, PhD); entomology (MS); evolutionary biology (MS); genetics (MS, PhD); immunology (MS); microbiology (MS, PhD); molecular biology (MS); molecular genetics (MS); neurobiology (MS); neuroscience (MS); parasitology (MS); physiology (MS, PhD); plant biology (MS); plant molecular biology (MS); plant sciences (MS); structural biology (MS); zoology (MS, PhD). Part-time programs available. *Degree requirements:* For master's, thesis or alternative; for doctorate, variable foreign language requirement, thesis/dissertation, 2 terms of residency. *Entrance requirements:* For master's, GRE General Test, minimum GPA of 2.6 in last 60 hours of course work; for doctorate, GRE General Test. *Faculty research:* Redoc balance and drug development in schistosoma mansoni, control of the growth of listeria monocytogenes at low temperature, regulation of cell expansion and microtubule function by SPRI, CRUI: physiology and fitness consequences of different life history phenotypes.

Indiana University–Purdue University Indianapolis, Indiana University School of Medicine, Department of Microbiology and Immunology, Indianapolis, IN 46202-2896. Offers MS, PhD, MD/MS, MD/PhD. *Faculty:* 20 full-time (2 women). *Students:* 31 full-time (22 women); includes 7 minority (2 Black or African American, non-Hispanic/Latino; 3 Asian, non-Hispanic/Latino; 1 Hispanic/Latino; 1 Two or more races, non-Hispanic/Latino), 10 international. Average age 27. 7 applicants, 86% accepted, 6 enrolled. In 2010, 1 master's, 10 doctorates awarded. Terminal master's awarded for partial completion of doctoral program. *Degree requirements:* For master's, thesis; for doctorate, thesis/dissertation. *Entrance requirements:* For master's and doctorate, GRE General Test, previous course work in calculus, cell biology, chemistry, genetics, physics, and biochemistry. *Application deadline:* For fall admission, 3/1 for domestic students. Applications are processed on a rolling basis. Application fee: $55 ($65 for international students). *Financial support:* In 2010–11, 2 fellowships with full tuition reimbursements (averaging $8,313 per year), 6 teaching assistantships with full tuition reimbursements (averaging $18,391 per year) were awarded; research assistantships with full tuition reimbursements, Federal Work-Study, institutionally sponsored loans, scholarships/grants, traineeships, and tuition waivers (partial) also available. Financial award application deadline: 2/1. *Faculty research:* Host-parasite interactions, molecular biology, cellular and molecular immunology and hematology, viral and bacterial pathogenesis, cancer research. Total annual research expenditures: $4.2 million. *Unit head:* Dr. Hal E. Broxmeyer, Chairman, 317-274-7672, Fax: 317-274-4090, E-mail: hbroxmey@iupui.edu. *Application contact:* 317-274-7671, Fax: 317-274-4090.

Iowa State University of Science and Technology, Graduate College, Interdisciplinary Programs, Program in Immunobiology, Ames, IA 50011. Offers MS, PhD. *Students:* 17 full-time (7 women), 7 part-time (4 women); includes 2 Black or African American, non-Hispanic/Latino, 5 international. In 2010, 1 master's, 1 doctorate awarded. *Degree requirements:* For master's, one foreign language, thesis; for doctorate, one foreign language, thesis/dissertation. *Entrance requirements:* For master's and doctorate, GRE General Test, resume. Additional exam requirements/recommendations for international students: Required—TOEFL (minimum score 600 paper-based; 85 iBT), IELTS (minimum score 7). *Application deadline:* For fall admission, 1/15 priority date for domestic and international students. Applications are processed on a rolling basis. Application fee: $40 ($90 for international students). Electronic applications accepted. *Financial support:* In 2010–11, 14 research assistantships with full and partial tuition reimbursements (averaging $18,135 per year) were awarded; fellowships, teaching assistantships, scholarships/grants, health care benefits, and unspecified assistantships also available. *Faculty research:* Immunogenetics, cellular and molecular immunology, infectious disease, neuroimmunology. *Unit head:* Dr. Marian Kohut, Supervisory Committee Chair, 515-294-7252, E-mail: idgp@iastate.edu. *Application contact:* Katie Blair, Information Contact, 515-294-7252, Fax: 515-924-6790, E-mail: idgp@iastate.edu.

The Johns Hopkins University, Bloomberg School of Public Health, W. Harry Feinstone Department of Molecular Microbiology and Immunology, Baltimore, MD 21218-2699. Offers MHS, Sc M, PhD. *Faculty:* 41 full-time (10 women), 10 part-time/adjunct (1 woman). *Students:* 91 full-time (58 women), 3 part-time (2 women); includes 33 minority (8 Black or African American, non-Hispanic/Latino; 13 Asian, non-Hispanic/Latino; 9 Hispanic/Latino; 3 Two or more races, non-Hispanic/Latino), 24 international. Average age 25. 184 applicants, 53% accepted, 38 enrolled. In 2010, 25 master's, 8 doctorates awarded. Terminal master's awarded for partial completion of doctoral program. *Degree requirements:* For master's, comprehensive exam, thesis (for some programs), essay, written exams; for doctorate, comprehensive exam, thesis/dissertation, 1 year full-time residency, oral and written exams. *Entrance requirements:* For master's, GRE General Test or MCAT, 3 letters of recommendation, curriculum vitae; for doctorate, GRE General Test, 3 letters of recommendation, transcripts, curriculum vitae. Additional exam requirements/recommendations for international students: Required—TOEFL (minimum score 600 paper-based; 250 computer-based). *Application deadline:* For fall admission, 1/2 priority date for domestic and international students. Applications are processed on a rolling basis. Application fee: $45. Electronic applications accepted. *Financial support:* In 2010–11, 37 fellowships with full and partial tuition reimbursements, 28 research assistantships with tuition reimbursements were awarded; Federal Work-Study, institutionally sponsored loans, scholarships/grants, and stipends also available. Financial award application deadline: 3/15; financial award applicants required to submit FAFSA. *Faculty research:* Immunology, virology, bacteriology, parasitology, vector biology, disease ecology, pathogenesis of infectious disease, immune responses to infectious agents, vector-borne and tropical diseases, biochemistry and molecular biology of infectious agents, population genetics of insect vectors, genetic regulation and immune responses in insect vectors, vaccine development, hormonal effects on pathogenesis and immune responses. Total annual research expenditures: $14.5 million. *Unit head:* Dr. Diane E. Griffin, Chair, 410-955-3459, Fax: 410-955-0105, E-mail: dgriffin@jhsph.edu. *Application contact:* Gail O'Connor, Senior Academic Program Coordinator, 410-614-4232, Fax: 410-955-0105, E-mail: goconnor@jhsph.edu.

The Johns Hopkins University, School of Medicine, Graduate Programs in Medicine, Immunology Training Program, Baltimore, MD 21218-2699. Offers PhD. *Faculty:* 34 full-time (8 women). *Students:* 38 full-time (22 women); includes 12 minority (2 Black or African American, non-Hispanic/Latino; 8 Asian, non-Hispanic/Latino; 1 Hispanic/Latino; 1 Two or more races, non-Hispanic/Latino), 4 international. Average age 23. 126 applicants, 11% accepted, 5 enrolled. In 2010, 8 doctorates awarded. *Degree requirements:* For doctorate, comprehensive exam, thesis/dissertation, oral exam, final thesis seminar. *Entrance requirements:* For doctorate, GRE General Test, 2 letters of recommendation. Additional exam requirements/recommendations for international students: Required—TOEFL (minimum score 550 paper-based). *Application deadline:* For fall admission, 1/10 for domestic students. Application fee: $85. Electronic applications accepted. *Financial support:* In 2010–11, 9 fellowships with full tuition reimbursements (averaging $20,976 per year), 31 research assistantships with full tuition reimbursements (averaging $27,125 per year) were awarded; scholarships/grants, traineeships, health care benefits, tuition waivers (full), unspecified assistantships, and institutional funds also available. Financial award application deadline: 1/10. *Faculty research:* HIV immunity, tumor immunity, major histocompatibility complex, transplantation, genetics of antibodies and T-cell receptors; immune response to infectious agents; antigen recognition; immune regulation; autoimmune diseases; immune cell signaling. Total annual research expenditures: $22.9 million. *Unit head:* Dr. Mark J. Soloski, Director, 410-550-8493, Fax: 410-550-2072, E-mail: mski@jhmi.edu. *Application contact:* Angela James, Academic Program Coordinator II, 410-955-2709, Fax: 410-955-0964, E-mail: ajames@jhmi.edu.

Long Island University, C.W. Post Campus, School of Health Professions and Nursing, Department of Biomedical Sciences, Brookville, NY 11548-1300. Offers cardiovascular perfusion (MS); clinical laboratory management (MS); medical biology (MS), including hematology, immunology, medical biology, medical chemistry, medical microbiology. Part-time and evening/weekend programs available. Postbaccalaureate distance learning degree programs offered. *Degree requirements:* For master's, thesis. *Entrance requirements:* For master's, minimum GPA of 2.75 in major. Electronic applications accepted.

Louisiana State University Health Sciences Center, School of Graduate Studies in New Orleans, Department of Microbiology, Immunology, and Parasitology, New Orleans, LA 70112-1393. Offers microbiology and immunology (MS, PhD); MD/PhD. Terminal master's awarded for partial completion of doctoral program. *Degree requirements:* For master's, comprehensive exam, thesis; for doctorate, comprehensive exam, thesis/dissertation, preliminary exam, qualifying exam. *Entrance requirements:* For master's and doctorate, GRE General Test. Additional exam requirements/recommendations for international students: Required—TOEFL. *Faculty research:* Microbial physiology, animal virology, vaccine development, AIDS drug studies, pathogenic mechanisms, molecular immunology.

Louisiana State University Health Sciences Center at Shreveport, Department of Microbiology and Immunology, Shreveport, LA 71130-3932. Offers MS, PhD, MD/PhD. Terminal master's awarded for partial completion of doctoral program. *Degree requirements:* For master's, thesis; for doctorate, thesis/dissertation. *Entrance requirements:* For master's and doctorate, GRE General Test. Additional exam requirements/recommendations for international students: Required—TOEFL. *Faculty research:* Infectious disease, pathogenesis, molecular virology and biology.

Loyola University Chicago, Graduate School, Department of Microbiology and Immunology, Maywood, IL 60153. Offers immunology (PhD); microbiology (MS); MD/PhD. *Faculty:* 15 full-time (4 women). *Students:* 34 full-time (22 women); includes 3 minority (2 Asian, non-Hispanic/Latino; 1 Hispanic/Latino), 8 international. Average age 27. 69 applicants, 23% accepted, 7 enrolled. In 2010, 1 doctorate awarded. Terminal master's awarded for partial completion of doctoral program. *Degree requirements:* For master's, thesis; for doctorate, comprehensive exam, thesis/dissertation. *Entrance requirements:* For master's and doctorate, GRE General Test. Additional exam requirements/recommendations for international students: Required—TOEFL. *Application deadline:* Applications are processed on a rolling basis. Application fee: $0. Electronic applications accepted. *Expenses:* Tuition: Full-time $14,940; part-time $830 per credit hour. Required fees: $87 per semester. Part-time tuition and fees vary according to course load and program. *Financial support:* In 2010–11, 5 fellowships with tuition reimbursements (averaging $25,000 per year), 24 research assistantships with tuition reimbursements (averaging $25,000 per year) were awarded; institutionally sponsored loans and scholarships/grants also available. Financial award application deadline: 2/15. *Faculty research:* Virology, microbial physiology and genetics, immune system development and regulation, signal transduction and host-pathogen interactions, biofilms. Total annual research expenditures: $2.2 million. *Unit head:* Dr. Katherine L. Knight, Chair, 708-216-3385, Fax: 708-216-9574, E-mail: kknight@lumc.edu. *Application contact:* Dr. Karen Visick, Graduate Program Director, 708-216-0869, Fax: 708-216-9574, E-mail: kvisick@lumc.edu.

Loyola University Chicago, Graduate School, Program in Infectious Disease and Immunology, Chicago, IL 60660. Offers MS. *Faculty:* 31 full-time (7 women). *Students:* 4 full-time (3 women). Average age 22. 13 applicants, 54% accepted, 4 enrolled. *Degree requirements:* For master's, thesis. *Entrance requirements:* For master's, GRE. Additional exam requirements/recommendations for international students: Required—TOEFL. *Application deadline:* Applications are processed on a rolling basis. Application fee: $0. *Expenses:* Tuition: Full-time $14,940; part-time $830 per credit hour. Required fees: $87 per semester. Part-time tuition and fees vary according to course load and program. *Faculty research:* Immunological tolerance and memory, molecular analysis of virus assembly and entry, biofilm mediated interactions, molecular analysis of clinical isolates of C. difficile, immune system development and regulation. *Unit head:* Dr. Katherine L. Knight, Co-Director, 708-216-3385, Fax: 708-216-9574, E-mail: kknight@lumc.edu. *Application contact:* Dr. Paul O'Keefe, Director of Admissions Committee, 708-216-6667, Fax: 707-216-9574, E-mail: pokeefe@lumc.edu.

Massachusetts Institute of Technology, School of Science, Department of Biology, Cambridge, MA 02139-4307. Offers biochemistry (PhD); biological oceanography (PhD); biology (PhD); biophysical chemistry and molecular structure (PhD); cell biology (PhD); computational and systems biology (PhD); developmental biology (PhD); genetics (PhD); immunology (PhD); microbiology (PhD); molecular biology (PhD); neurobiology (PhD). *Faculty:* 56 full-time (14 women). *Students:* 251 full-time (135 women); includes 74 minority (4 Black or African American, non-Hispanic/Latino; 1 American Indian or Alaska Native, non-Hispanic/Latino; 29 Asian, non-Hispanic/Latino; 33 Hispanic/Latino; 7 Two or more races, non-Hispanic/Latino), 29 international. Average age 26. 652 applicants, 18% accepted, 58 enrolled. In 2010, 41 doctorates awarded. *Degree requirements:* For doctorate, comprehensive exam, thesis/dissertation. *Entrance requirements:* For doctorate, GRE General Test. Additional exam requirements/recommendations for international students: Required—TOEFL (minimum score 577 paper-based; 233 computer-based), IELTS (minimum score 6.5). *Application deadline:* For fall admission, 12/1 for domestic and international students. Application fee: $75. Electronic applications accepted. *Expenses:* Tuition: Full-time $38,940; part-time $605 per unit. Required fees: $272. *Financial support:* In 2010–11, 215 students received support, including 115 fellowships with tuition reimbursements available (averaging $33,090 per year), 132 research assistantships with tuition reimbursements available (averaging $31,846 per year); teaching assistantships with tuition reimbursements available, Federal Work-Study, institutionally sponsored loans, scholarships/grants, traineeships, health care benefits, and unspecified assistantships also available. *Faculty research:* DNA recombination, replication and repair; transcription and gene regulation; signal transduction; cell cycle; neuronal cell fate. Total annual research expenditures: $60.6 million. *Unit head:* Prof. Chris Kaiser, Head, 617-253-4701, E-mail: mitbio@mit.edu. *Application contact:* Biology Education Office, 617-253-3717, Fax: 617-258-9329, E-mail: gradbio@mit.edu.

Mayo Graduate School, Graduate Programs in Biomedical Sciences, Program in Immunology, Rochester, MN 55905. Offers PhD. *Degree requirements:* For doctorate, oral defense of dissertation, qualifying oral and written exam. *Entrance requirements:* For doctorate, GRE, 1 year of chemistry, biology, calculus, and physics. Additional exam requirements/recommendations for international students: Required—TOEFL. Electronic applications accepted. *Faculty research:* Immunogenetics, autoimmunity, receptor signal transduction, T lymphocyte activation, transplantation.

McGill University, Faculty of Graduate and Postdoctoral Studies, Faculty of Medicine, Department of Microbiology and Immunology, Montréal, QC H3A 2T5, Canada. Offers M Sc, M Sc A, PhD.

McMaster University, Faculty of Health Sciences and School of Graduate Studies, Program in Medical Sciences, Immunity and Infection Area, Hamilton, ON L8S 4M2, Canada. Offers M Sc, PhD, MD/PhD. *Degree requirements:* For master's, thesis; for doctorate, comprehensive exam, thesis/dissertation. *Entrance requirements:* For master's, honors B Sc, B+ average in related field; for doctorate, M Sc, minimum B+ average, students with proven research experience and an A average may be admitted with a B Sc degree. Additional exam requirements/recommendations for international students: Required—TOEFL (minimum score 580 paper-based; 237 computer-based; 92 iBT).

Medical University of South Carolina, College of Graduate Studies, Department of Microbiology and Immunology, Charleston, SC 29425. Offers MS, PhD, DMD/PhD, MD/PhD. *Faculty:* 15 full-time (6 women), 30 part-time/adjunct (9 women). *Students:* 15 full-time (9 women), 2 part-time (0 women); includes 2 Black or African American, non-Hispanic/Latino; 1 Hispanic/Latino, 1 international. Average age 26. 8 applicants, 75% accepted, 4 enrolled. In 2010, 4 master's, 3 doctorates awarded. Terminal master's awarded for partial completion of doctoral program. *Degree requirements:* For master's, thesis; for doctorate, thesis/dissertation, oral and written exams. *Entrance requirements:* For master's, GRE General Test, MCAT, or DAT, minimum GPA of 3.0; for doctorate, GRE General Test, interview, minimum GPA of 3.0, research experience. Additional exam requirements/recommendations for international students: Required—TOEFL (minimum score 600 paper-based; 250 computer-based; 100 iBT). *Application deadline:* For fall admission, 1/15 priority date for domestic and international students. Applications are processed on a rolling basis. Application fee: $0 ($95 for international students). Electronic applications accepted. *Financial support:* In 2010–11, 10 research assistantships with partial tuition reimbursements (averaging $23,000 per year) were awarded; Federal Work-Study and scholarships/grants also available. Support available to part-time students. Financial award application deadline: 3/10; financial award applicants required to submit FAFSA. *Faculty research:* Inmate and adaptive immunology, gene therapy/vector development, vaccinology, proteomics of biowarfare agents, bacterial and fungal pathogenesis. *Unit head:* Dr. Zihai Li, Chair, 843-792-7915, Fax: 843-792-6590. *Application contact:* Dr. Laura Kasman, Assistant Professor, 843-792-8117, Fax: 843-792-2464, E-mail: kasmanl@musc.edu.

Meharry Medical College, School of Graduate Studies, Program in Biomedical Sciences, Microbiology and Immunology Emphasis, Nashville, TN 37208-9989. Offers PhD, MD/PhD. *Degree requirements:* For doctorate, comprehensive exam, thesis/dissertation. *Entrance requirements:* For doctorate, GRE General Test, GRE Subject Test, undergraduate degree in related science. *Faculty research:* Microbial and bacterial pathogenesis, viral transcription, immune response to viruses and parasites.

Memorial University of Newfoundland, Faculty of Medicine and School of Graduate Studies, Graduate Programs in Medicine, Division of Biomedical Sciences, St. John's, NL A1C 5S7, Canada. Offers cancer (M Sc, PhD); cardiovascular (M Sc, PhD); immunology (M Sc, PhD); neuroscience (M Sc, PhD). Part-time programs available. *Degree requirements:* For master's, thesis; for doctorate, comprehensive exam, thesis/dissertation, oral defense of thesis. *Entrance requirements:* For master's, MD or B Sc; for doctorate, MD or M Sc. Additional exam requirements/recommendations for international students: Required—TOEFL. *Faculty research:* Neuroscience, immunology, cardiovascular, and cancer.

Montana State University, College of Graduate Studies, College of Agriculture, Department of Immunology and Infectious Diseases, Bozeman, MT 59717. Offers MS, PhD. Part-time programs available. *Faculty:* 12 full-time (2 women), 1 (woman) part-time/adjunct. *Students:* 1 (woman) full-time, 13 part-time (8 women); includes 2 minority (1 American Indian or Alaska Native, non-Hispanic/Latino; 1 Hispanic/Latino), 2 international. Average age 29. 3 applicants, 67% accepted, 2 enrolled. In 2010, 1 doctorate awarded. *Degree requirements:* For master's, comprehensive exam; for doctorate, comprehensive exam, thesis/dissertation. *Entrance requirements:* For master's and doctorate, GRE General Test. Additional exam requirements/recommendations for international students: Required—TOEFL (minimum score 550 paper-based; 213 computer-based). *Application deadline:* For fall admission, 7/15 priority date for domestic students, 5/15 for international students; for spring admission, 12/1 priority date for domestic students, 10/1 priority date for international students. Applications are processed on a rolling basis. Application fee: $30. Electronic applications accepted. *Expenses:* Tuition, state resident: full-time $5554. Tuition, nonresident: full-time $14,646. Required fees: $1233. *Financial support:* In 2010–11, 13 students received support, including 2 fellowships with tuition reimbursements available (averaging $24,000 per year), 13 research assistantships with tuition reimbursements available (averaging $22,000 per year), 5 teaching assistantships with tuition reimbursements available (averaging $7,000 per year); health care benefits and unspecified assistantships also available. Financial award application deadline: 3/1; financial award applicants required to submit FAFSA. *Faculty research:* Immunology, mechanisms of infectious disease pathogenesis, mechanisms of host defense, lymphocyte development, host-pathogen interactions. Total annual research expenditures: $9.5 million. *Unit head:* Dr. Mark G. Quinn, Head, 406-994-5721, Fax: 406-994-4303, E-mail: mquinn@montana.edu. *Application contact:* Dr. Carl A. Fox, Vice Provost for Graduate Education, 406-994-4145, Fax: 406-994-7433, E-mail: gradstudy@montana.edu.

New York Medical College, Graduate School of Basic Medical Sciences, Microbiology and Immunology Department, Valhalla, NY 10595-1691. Offers MS, PhD, MD/PhD. Part-time and evening/weekend programs available. *Faculty:* 13 full-time (4 women), 1 part-time/adjunct (0 women). *Students:* 18 full-time (14 women), 5 part-time (4 women); includes 2 Black or African American, non-Hispanic/Latino; 1 Asian, non-Hispanic/Latino, 7 international. Average age 27. 8 applicants, 100% accepted, 5 enrolled. In 2010, 3 master's, 2 doctorates awarded. Terminal master's awarded for partial completion of doctoral program. *Degree requirements:* For master's, thesis; for doctorate, comprehensive exam, thesis/dissertation. *Entrance requirements:* For master's and doctorate, GRE General Test. Additional exam requirements/recommendations for international students: Required—TOEFL. *Application deadline:* For fall admission, 7/1 priority date for domestic students, 5/1 priority date for international students; for spring admission, 12/1 priority date for domestic students, 10/1 priority date for international students. Applications are processed on a rolling basis. Application fee: $50 ($75 for international students). Electronic applications accepted. *Financial support:* In 2010–11, 4 fellowships, 7 research assistantships with full tuition reimbursements (averaging $24,000 per year) were awarded; career-related internships or fieldwork, Federal Work-Study, institutionally sponsored loans, scholarships/grants, traineeships, tuition waivers (full), unspecified assistantships, and health benefits (for PhD candidates only) also available. Financial award applicants required to submit FAFSA. *Faculty research:* Tumor and transplantation immunology, molecular mechanisms of DNA repair, virus-host interactions. *Unit head:* Dr. Raj Tiwari, Director, 914-594-4870. *Application contact:* Valerie Romeo-Messana, Admission Coordinator, 914-594-4110, Fax: 914-594-4944, E-mail: v_romeomessana@nymc.edu.

New York University, Graduate School of Arts and Science, Department of Biology, New York, NY 10012-1019. Offers biology (PhD); biomedical journalism (MS); cancer and molecular biology (PhD); computational biology (PhD); computers in biological research (MS); developmental genetics (PhD); general biology (MS); immunology and microbiology (PhD); molecular genetics (PhD); neurobiology (PhD); oral biology (MS); plant biology (PhD); recombinant DNA technology (MS); MS/MBA. Part-time programs available. *Faculty:* 24 full-time (5 women). *Students:* 155 full-time (89 women), 38 part-time (24 women); includes 29 Asian, non-Hispanic/Latino; 7 Hispanic/Latino, 88 international. Average age 27. 324 applicants, 69% accepted, 63 enrolled. In 2010, 55 master's, 4 doctorates awarded. Terminal master's awarded for partial completion of doctoral program. *Degree requirements:* For master's, thesis or alternative, qualifying paper; for doctorate, comprehensive exam, thesis/dissertation. *Entrance requirements:* For master's, GRE General Test; for doctorate, GRE General Test, GRE Subject Test. Additional exam requirements/recommendations for international students: Required—TOEFL. *Application deadline:* For fall admission, 12/15 priority date for domestic students. Application fee: $90. *Financial support:* Fellowships with tuition reimbursements, research assistantships with tuition reimbursements, teaching assistantships with tuition reimbursements, career-related internships or fieldwork, Federal Work-Study, institutionally sponsored loans, scholarships/grants, health care benefits, and unspecified assistantships available. Financial award application deadline: 12/15; financial award applicants required to submit FAFSA. *Faculty research:* Genomics, molecular and cell biology, development and molecular genetics, molecular evolution of plants and animals. *Unit head:* Gloria Coruzzi, Chair, 212-998-8200, Fax: 212-995-4015, E-mail: biology@nyu.edu. *Application contact:* Justin Blau, Director of Graduate Studies, 212-998-8200, Fax: 212-995-4015, E-mail: biology@nyu.edu.

New York University, School of Medicine, New York, NY 10012-1019. Offers biomedical sciences (PhD), including biomedical imaging, cellular and molecular biology, computational biology, developmental genetics, medical and molecular parasitology, microbiology, molecular oncobiology and immunology, neuroscience and physiology, pathobiology, pharmacology, structural biology; clinical investigation (MS); medicine (MD); MD/MA; MD/MPA; MD/MS; MD/PhD. *Accreditation:* LCME/AMA (one or more programs are accredited). *Degree requirements:* For master's, comprehensive exam, thesis; for doctorate, comprehensive exam, thesis/dissertation. *Entrance requirements:* MCAT. Additional exam requirements/recommendations for international students: Required—TOEFL. *Expenses:* Contact institution. *Faculty research:* AIDS, cancer, neuroscience, molecular biology, neuroscience, cell biology and molecular genetics, structural biology, microbial pathogenesis and host defense, pharmacology, molecular oncology and immunology.

New York University, School of Medicine and Graduate School of Arts and Science, Sackler Institute of Graduate Biomedical Sciences, Programs in Molecular Oncology and Immunology, New York, NY 10012-1019. Offers immunology (PhD); molecular oncology (PhD); MD/PhD. *Degree requirements:* For doctorate, one foreign language, thesis/dissertation, qualifying exam. *Entrance requirements:* For doctorate, GRE General Test, GRE Subject Test. Additional exam requirements/recommendations for international students: Required—TOEFL. Electronic applications accepted. *Faculty research:* Stem cells, immunology, genome instability, DNA damage checkpoints.

North Carolina State University, Graduate School, College of Agriculture and Life Sciences and College of Veterinary Medicine, Program in Immunology, Raleigh, NC 27695. Offers MS, PhD. *Degree requirements:* For master's, thesis; for doctorate, thesis/dissertation. *Entrance requirements:* For master's and doctorate, GRE General Test. Additional exam requirements/recommendations for international students: Required—TOEFL (minimum score 550 paper-based; 213 computer-based). Electronic applications accepted. *Faculty research:* Immunogenetics, immunopathology, immunotoxicology, immunoparasitology, molecular and infectious disease immunology.

Northwestern University, Northwestern University Feinberg School of Medicine and Interdepartmental Programs, Integrated Graduate Programs in the Life Sciences, Chicago, IL 60611. Offers cancer biology (PhD); cell biology (PhD); developmental biology (PhD); evolutionary biology (PhD); immunology and microbial pathogenesis (PhD); molecular biology and genetics (PhD); neurobiology (PhD); pharmacology and toxicology (PhD); structural biology and biochemistry (PhD). *Degree requirements:* For doctorate, comprehensive exam, thesis/dissertation, written and oral qualifying exams. *Entrance requirements:* For doctorate, GRE General Test. Additional exam requirements/recommendations for international students: Required—TOEFL (minimum score 600 paper-based; 250 computer-based). Electronic applications accepted.

The Ohio State University, College of Medicine, School of Biomedical Science, Integrated Biomedical Science Graduate Program, Columbus, OH 43210. Offers immunology (PhD); medical genetics (PhD); molecular virology (PhD); pharmacology (PhD). *Degree requirements:* For doctorate, thesis/dissertation. *Entrance requirements:* For doctorate, GRE, GRE Subject Test in biochemistry, cell and molecular biology (recommended for some). Additional exam requirements/recommendations for international students: Required—TOEFL (minimum score 600 paper-based; 250 computer-based). Electronic applications accepted. *Expenses:* Tuition, state resident: full-time $10,605. Tuition, nonresident: full-time $26,535. Tuition and fees vary according to course load and program.

Oregon Health & Science University, School of Medicine, Graduate Programs in Medicine, Program in Molecular and Cellular Biosciences, Department of Molecular Microbiology and Immunology, Portland, OR 97239-3098. Offers PhD. *Faculty:* 10 full-time (3 women). *Students:* 29 full-time (18 women); includes 1 Asian, non-Hispanic/Latino; 4 Hispanic/Latino, 1 international. Average age 29. In 2010, 3 doctorates awarded. Terminal master's awarded for partial completion of doctoral program. *Degree requirements:* For doctorate, comprehensive exam, thesis/dissertation. *Entrance requirements:* For doctorate, GRE General Test (minimum scores: 500 Verbal/600 Quantitative/4.5 Analytical) or MCAT (for some programs). Additional exam requirements/recommendations for international students: Required—TOEFL. Electronic applications accepted. *Financial support:* Health care benefits and full tuition and stipends available. *Faculty research:* Molecular biology of bacterial and viral pathogens, cellular and humoral immunology, molecular biology of microbes. *Unit head:* Dr. Eric Barklis, Program Director, 503-494-7768, E-mail: mmi@ohsu.edu. *Application contact:* Kathy Shinall, Program Coordinator, 503-494-7768, E-mail: mmi@ohsu.edu.

Penn State Hershey Medical Center, College of Medicine, Graduate School Programs in the Biomedical Sciences, Graduate Program in Microbiology and Immunology, Hershey, PA 17033. Offers genetics (PhD); immunology (MS, PhD); microbiology (MS); microbiology/virology (PhD); molecular biology (PhD); MD/PhD. *Students:* 12 applicants, 75% accepted, 3 enrolled. In 2010, 1 doctorate awarded. Terminal master's awarded for partial completion of doctoral program. *Degree requirements:* For master's, thesis or alternative; for doctorate, comprehensive exam, thesis/dissertation, oral exam. *Entrance requirements:* For doctorate, GRE General Test, minimum GPA of 3.0. Additional exam requirements/recommendations for international students: Required—TOEFL. *Application deadline:* For fall admission, 1/31 priority date for domestic students, 2/1 priority date for international students. Applications are processed on a rolling basis. Application fee: $45. Electronic applications accepted. *Financial support:* In 2010–11, research assistantships with full tuition reimbursements (averaging $22,260 per year); fellowships with full tuition reimbursements, scholarships/grants, health care benefits, and unspecified assistantships also available. Financial award applicants required to submit FAFSA. *Faculty research:* Virus replication and assembly, oncogenesis, interactions of viruses with host cells and animal model systems. *Unit head:* Dr. Richard J. Courtney, Chair, 717-531-7659, Fax: 717-531-6522, E-mail: micro-grad-hmc@psu.edu. *Application contact:* Billie Burns, Secretary, 717-531-7659, Fax: 717-531-6522, E-mail: micro-grad-hmc@psu.edu.

Purdue University, School of Veterinary Medicine and Graduate School, Graduate Programs in Veterinary Medicine, Department of Comparative Pathobiology, West Lafayette, IN 47907-2027. Offers comparative epidemiology and public health (MS); comparative epidemiology and public heath (PhD); comparative microbiology and immunology (MS, PhD); comparative pathobiology (MS, PhD); interdisciplinary studies (PhD), including microbial pathogenesis, molecular signaling and cancer biology, molecular virology; lab animal medicine (MS); veterinary anatomic pathology (MS); veterinary clinical pathology (MS). Terminal master's awarded for partial completion of doctoral program. *Degree requirements:* For master's, thesis (for some programs); for doctorate, thesis/dissertation. *Entrance requirements:* For master's and doctorate, GRE General Test. Additional exam requirements/recommendations for international students:

Immunology

Purdue University (continued)
Required—TOEFL (minimum score 575 paper-based; 232 computer-based), IELTS (minimum score 6.5), TWE (minimum score 4). Electronic applications accepted.

Queen's University at Kingston, School of Graduate Studies and Research, Faculty of Health Sciences, Department of Microbiology and Immunology, Kingston, ON K7L 3N6, Canada. Offers M Sc, PhD. Part-time programs available. *Degree requirements:* For master's, thesis; for doctorate, comprehensive exam, thesis/dissertation. *Entrance requirements:* For master's and doctorate, minimum B+ average. Additional exam requirements/recommendations for international students: Required—TOEFL (minimum score 600 paper-based; 250 computer-based). Electronic applications accepted. *Faculty research:* Bacteriology, virology, immunology, education in microbiology and immunology, microbial pathogenesis.

Rosalind Franklin University of Medicine and Science, School of Graduate and Postdoctoral Studies—Interdisciplinary Graduate Program in Biomedical Sciences, Department of Microbiology and Immunology, North Chicago, IL 60064-3095. Offers MS, PhD, MD/PhD. Terminal master's awarded for partial completion of doctoral program. *Degree requirements:* For master's, comprehensive exam, thesis; for doctorate, comprehensive exam, thesis/dissertation. *Entrance requirements:* For master's and doctorate, GRE General Test. Additional exam requirements/recommendations for international students: Required—TOEFL, TWE. *Faculty research:* Molecular biology, parasitology, virology.

Rush University, Graduate College, Division of Immunology and Microbiology, Program in Immunology/Microbiology, Chicago, IL 60612-3832. Offers immunology (MS, PhD); virology (MS, PhD); MD/PhD. Part-time programs available. Terminal master's awarded for partial completion of doctoral program. *Degree requirements:* For master's, thesis; for doctorate, thesis/dissertation, comprehensive preliminary exam. *Entrance requirements:* For master's, GRE General Test; for doctorate, GRE General Test, interview, minimum GPA of 3.0. Additional exam requirements/recommendations for international students: Required—TOEFL. Electronic applications accepted. *Faculty research:* Human genetics, autoimmunity, tumor biology, complement, HIV immunopathology genesis.

Rutgers, The State University of New Jersey, New Brunswick, Graduate School-New Brunswick, Programs in the Molecular Biosciences, Program in Microbiology and Molecular Genetics, Piscataway, NJ 08854-8097. Offers applied microbiology (MS, PhD); clinical microbiology (MS, PhD); computational molecular biology (PhD); immunology (MS, PhD); microbial biochemistry (MS, PhD); molecular genetics (MS, PhD); virology (MS, PhD). MS, PhD offered jointly with University of Medicine and Dentistry of New Jersey. Part-time programs available. Terminal master's awarded for partial completion of doctoral program. *Degree requirements:* For master's, comprehensive exam, thesis or alternative; for doctorate, comprehensive exam, thesis/dissertation, written qualifying exam. *Entrance requirements:* For master's, GRE General Test, minimum GPA of 3.0; for doctorate, GRE General Test, GRE Subject Test (recommended), minimum GPA of 3.0. Additional exam requirements/recommendations for international students: Required—TOEFL. Electronic applications accepted. *Expenses:* Tuition, state resident: full-time $7200; part-time $600 per credit. Tuition, nonresident: full-time $11,124; part-time $927 per credit. *Faculty research:* Molecular genetics and microbial physiology; virology and pathogenic microbiology; applied, environmental and industrial microbiology; computers in molecular biology.

Saint Louis University, Graduate Education and School of Medicine, Graduate Program in Biomedical Sciences, Department of Molecular Microbiology and Immunology, St. Louis, MO 63103-2097. Offers PhD. *Degree requirements:* For doctorate, comprehensive exam, thesis/dissertation, qualifying exams. *Entrance requirements:* For doctorate, GRE General Test (GRE Subject Test optional), letters of recommendation, resume, interview. Additional exam requirements/recommendations for international students: Required—TOEFL (minimum score 525 paper-based; 194 computer-based). Electronic applications accepted. *Faculty research:* Pathogenesis of hepatitis C virus, herperviruses, pox viruses, rheumatoid arthritis, antiviral drugs and vaccines in biodefense, cancer gene therapy, virology and immunology.

Stanford University, School of Medicine, Graduate Programs in Medicine, Department of Microbiology and Immunology, Stanford, CA 94305-9991. Offers PhD. *Degree requirements:* For doctorate, comprehensive exam, thesis/dissertation, 2 quarters teaching assistantship. *Entrance requirements:* For doctorate, GRE General Test, GRE Subject Test (biology or biochemistry). Additional exam requirements/recommendations for international students: Required—TOEFL. Electronic applications accepted. *Expenses:* Tuition: Full-time $38,700; part-time $860 per unit. One-time fee: $200 full-time. *Faculty research:* Molecular pathogenesis of bacteria viruses and parasites, immune system function, autoimmunity, molecular biology.

Stanford University, School of Medicine, Graduate Programs in Medicine, Program in Immunology, Stanford, CA 94305-9991. Offers PhD. *Degree requirements:* For doctorate, thesis/dissertation, qualifying examination. *Entrance requirements:* For doctorate, GRE General Test, GRE Subject Test. Additional exam requirements/recommendations for international students: Required—TOEFL. Electronic applications accepted. *Expenses:* Tuition: Full-time $38,700; part-time $860 per unit. One-time fee: $200 full-time.

State University of New York Upstate Medical University, College of Graduate Studies, Program in Microbiology and Immunology, Syracuse, NY 13210-2334. Offers microbiology (MS); microbiology and immunology (PhD); MD/PhD. Terminal master's awarded for partial completion of doctoral program. *Degree requirements:* For master's, thesis; for doctorate, comprehensive exam, thesis/dissertation. *Entrance requirements:* For master's, GRE General Test, interview; for doctorate, GRE General Test, telephone interview. Additional exam requirements/recommendations for international students: Required—TOEFL. Electronic applications accepted. *Faculty research:* Cancer, disorders of the nervous system, infectious diseases, diabetes/metabolic disorders/cardiovascular diseases.

Stony Brook University, State University of New York, Graduate School, College of Arts and Sciences, Department of Biochemistry and Cell Biology, Molecular and Cellular Biology Program, Stony Brook, NY 11794. Offers biochemistry and molecular biology (PhD); biological sciences (MA); cellular and developmental biology (PhD); immunology and pathology (PhD); molecular and cellular biology (PhD). *Faculty:* 22 full-time (7 women). *Students:* 106 full-time (65 women); includes 2 Black or African American, non-Hispanic/Latino; 9 Asian, non-Hispanic/Latino; 1 Hispanic/Latino, 58 international. Average age 30. 320 applicants, 16% accepted, 26 enrolled. In 2010, 5 master's, 16 doctorates awarded. *Degree requirements:* For doctorate, comprehensive exam, thesis/dissertation, teaching experience. *Entrance requirements:* For doctorate, GRE General Test, GRE Subject Test. Additional exam requirements/recommendations for international students: Required—TOEFL. *Application deadline:* For fall admission, 1/15 for domestic students. Application fee: $100. *Expenses:* Tuition, state resident: full-time $8370; part-time $349 per credit. Tuition, nonresident: full-time $13,780; part-time $574 per credit. Required fees: $994. *Financial support:* In 2010–11, 42 research assistantships, 19 teaching assistantships were awarded; fellowships, Federal Work-Study also available. *Unit head:* Prof. Robert Haltiwanger, Chair, 631-632-8560. *Application contact:* Prof. Robert Haltiwanger, Chair, 631-632-8560.

Temple University, Health Sciences Center, School of Medicine and Graduate School, Doctor of Medicine Program, Department of Microbiology and Immunology, Philadelphia, PA 19140-5104. Offers MS, PhD, MD/PhD. *Degree requirements:* For master's, thesis; for doctorate, thesis/dissertation, research seminars. *Entrance requirements:* For master's and doctorate, GRE General Test, GRE Subject Test, minimum GPA of 3.0. Additional exam requirements/recommendations for international students: Required—TOEFL (minimum score 600 paper-based; 250 computer-based). Electronic applications accepted. *Faculty research:* Molecular and cellular immunology, molecular and biochemical microbiology, molecular genetics.

Texas A&M Health Science Center, Graduate School of Biomedical Sciences, Department of Microbial and Molecular Pathogenesis, College Station, TX 77840. Offers immunology (PhD); microbiology (PhD); molecular biology (PhD); virology (PhD). *Degree requirements:* For doctorate, thesis/dissertation. *Entrance requirements:* For doctorate, GRE General Test, minimum GPA of 3.0. *Faculty research:* Molecular pathogenesis, microbial therapeutics.

Thomas Jefferson University, Jefferson College of Graduate Studies, Graduate Program in Immunology and Microbial Pathogenesis, Philadelphia, PA 19107. Offers PhD. *Faculty:* 88 full-time (5 women), 2 part-time/adjunct (0 women). *Students:* 24 full-time (14 women); includes 3 minority (1 Black or African American, non-Hispanic/Latino; 2 Asian, non-Hispanic/Latino), 3 international. 50 applicants, 10% accepted, 3 enrolled. In 2010, 3 doctorates awarded. *Degree requirements:* For doctorate, comprehensive exam, thesis/dissertation. *Entrance requirements:* For doctorate, GRE General Test, minimum GPA of 3.2. Additional exam requirements/recommendations for international students: Required—TOEFL (minimum score 250 computer-based; 100 iBT) or IELTS. *Application deadline:* For fall admission, 1/5 priority date for domestic and international students. Applications are processed on a rolling basis. Application fee: $50. Electronic applications accepted. *Financial support:* In 2010–11, 24 students received support, including 24 fellowships with full tuition reimbursements available (averaging $54,723 per year); Federal Work-Study, institutionally sponsored loans, scholarships/grants, traineeships, and stipends also available. Support available to part-time students. Financial award application deadline: 5/1; financial award applicants required to submit FAFSA. Total annual research expenditures: $36.3 million. *Unit head:* Dr. Kishore Alugupalli, Program Director, 215-503-4550, Fax: 215-923-4153, E-mail: kishore.alugupalli@jefferson.edu. *Application contact:* Marc E. Stearns, Director of Admissions, 215-503-0155, Fax: 215-503-9920, E-mail: jcgs-info@jefferson.edu.

Tufts University, Sackler School of Graduate Biomedical Sciences, Program in Immunology, Medford, MA 02155. Offers PhD. *Faculty:* 24 full-time (8 women). *Students:* 29 full-time (15 women); includes 1 Black or African American, non-Hispanic/Latino; 3 Asian, non-Hispanic/Latino; 1 Hispanic/Latino, 3 international. Average age 27. 105 applicants, 7% accepted, 4 enrolled. In 2010, 10 doctorates awarded. Terminal master's awarded for partial completion of doctoral program. *Degree requirements:* For doctorate, thesis/dissertation. *Entrance requirements:* For doctorate, GRE General Test, 3 letters of reference. Additional exam requirements/recommendations for international students: Required—TOEFL. *Application deadline:* For fall admission, 12/15 for domestic and international students. Applications are processed on a rolling basis. Application fee: $70. Electronic applications accepted. *Expenses:* Tuition: Full-time $39,624; part-time $3962 per course. Required fees: $40 per year. Full-time tuition and fees vary according to degree level, program and student level. Part-time tuition and fees vary according to course load. *Financial support:* In 2010–11, 29 students received support, including 29 research assistantships with full tuition reimbursements available (averaging $28,250 per year); scholarships/grants and tuition waivers (full) also available. *Faculty research:* Genetic analysis of lymphocyte function, ontogeny and activation, transformation of hematopoietic cells, autoimmunity, the immune response to infection. *Unit head:* Dr. Henry H. Wortis, Director, 617-636-6836, Fax: 617-636-2990, E-mail: henry.wortis@tufts.edu. *Application contact:* Kellie Johnston, Associate Director of Admissions, 617-636-6767, Fax: 617-636-0375, E-mail: sackler-school@tufts.edu.

Tulane University, School of Medicine and School of Liberal Arts, Graduate Programs in Biomedical Sciences, Department of Microbiology and Immunology, New Orleans, LA 70118-5669. Offers MS, PhD, MD/PhD. MS and PhD offered through the Graduate School. *Degree requirements:* For master's, thesis; for doctorate, 2 foreign languages, thesis/dissertation. *Entrance requirements:* For master's, GRE General Test, minimum B average in undergraduate course work; for doctorate, GRE General Test, GRE Subject Test. Additional exam requirements/recommendations for international students: Required—TOEFL. Electronic applications accepted. *Faculty research:* Vaccine development, viral pathogenesis, molecular virology, bacterial pathogenesis, fungal pathogenesis.

Uniformed Services University of the Health Sciences, School of Medicine, Graduate Programs in the Biomedical Sciences and Public Health, Graduate Program in Emerging Infectious Diseases, Bethesda, MD 20814-4799. Offers PhD. *Faculty:* 35 full-time (5 women), 17 part-time/adjunct (6 women). *Students:* 37 full-time (24 women); includes 1 Black or African American, non-Hispanic/Latino; 3 Asian, non-Hispanic/Latino; 1 Hispanic/Latino, 3 international. Average age 26. 43 applicants, 44% accepted, 11 enrolled. In 2010, 7 doctorates awarded. *Degree requirements:* For doctorate, comprehensive exam, thesis/dissertation, qualifying exam. *Entrance requirements:* For doctorate, GRE General Test. Additional exam requirements/recommendations for international students: Required—TOEFL. *Application deadline:* For fall admission, 1/1 priority date for domestic and international students. Applications are processed on a rolling basis. Application fee: $0. Electronic applications accepted. *Financial support:* In 2010–11, fellowships with full tuition reimbursements (averaging $27,000 per year); scholarships/grants, health care benefits, and tuition waivers (full) also available. *Unit head:* Dr. Christopher Broder, Graduate Program Director, 301-295-3401, E-mail: cbroder@usuhs.mil. *Application contact:* Patricia Sinclair, Program Coordinator, 301-295-3400, Fax: 301-295-6772, E-mail: psinclair@usuhs.mil.

See Display on page 327 and Close-Up on page 345.

Universidad Central del Caribe, School of Medicine, Program in Biomedical Sciences, Bayamón, PR 00960-6032. Offers anatomy and cell biology (MA, MS); biochemistry (MS); biomedical sciences (MA); cellular and molecular biology (PhD); microbiology and immunology (MA, MS); pharmacology (MS); physiology (MS).

Université de Montréal, Faculty of Medicine, Department of Microbiology and Immunology, Montréal, QC H3C 3J7, Canada. Offers M Sc, PhD. Programs offered jointly with Faculty of Veterinary Medicine and Université du Québec, Institut Armand-Frappier. Terminal master's awarded for partial completion of doctoral program. *Degree requirements:* For master's, thesis; for doctorate, thesis/dissertation, general exam. *Entrance requirements:* For master's and doctorate, proficiency in French, knowledge of English. Electronic applications accepted.

Université de Montréal, Faculty of Veterinary Medicine, Program in Virology and Immunology, Montréal, QC H3C 3J7, Canada. Offers PhD. Program offered jointly with Université du Québec, Institut Armand-Frappier. *Degree requirements:* For doctorate, thesis/dissertation, general exam. *Entrance requirements:* For doctorate, proficiency in French, knowledge of English. Electronic applications accepted.

Université de Sherbrooke, Faculty of Medicine and Health Sciences, Graduate Programs in Medicine, Program in Immunology, Sherbrooke, QC J1H 5N4, Canada. Offers M Sc, PhD. Electronic applications accepted. *Faculty research:* Cytokine receptor signal transduction, lipid mediators and inflammation, TGFbeta convertases.

Université du Québec, Institut National de la Recherche Scientifique, Graduate Programs, Research Center—INRS—Institut Armand-Frappier—Human Health, Québec, QC G1K 9A9, Canada. Offers applied microbiology (M Sc); biology (PhD); experimental health sciences (M Sc); virology and immunology (M Sc, PhD). Programs given in French. Part-time programs available. *Faculty:* 36. *Students:* 157 full-time (92 women), 6 part-time (4 women), 54 international. Average age 30. In 2010, 20 master's, 13 doctorates awarded. *Degree requirements:* For master's, thesis optional; for doctorate, thesis/dissertation. *Entrance requirements:* For master's and doctorate, appropriate bachelor's degree, proficiency in French. *Application deadline:* For fall admission, 3/30 for domestic and international students; for winter admission, 11/1 for domestic and international students; for spring admission, 3/1 for domestic and international students. Application fee: $30 Canadian dollars. *Financial support:* Fellowships, research assistantships, teaching assistantships available. *Faculty research:* Immunity, infection and cancer; toxicology and environmental biotechnology; molecular pharmacochemistry. *Unit head:* Charles Dozois, Director, 450-687-5010, Fax: 450-686-5501, E-mail: charles.dozois@iaf.inrs.ca. *Application contact:* Yvonne Boisvert, Registrar, 418-654-3861, Fax: 418-654-3858, E-mail: registrariat@adm.inrs.ca.

Université Laval, Faculty of Medicine, Graduate Programs in Medicine, Programs in Microbiology-Immunology, Québec, QC G1K 7P4, Canada. Offers M Sc, PhD. Terminal master's awarded for partial completion of doctoral program. *Degree requirements:* For master's, thesis; for doctorate, comprehensive exam, thesis/dissertation. *Entrance requirements:* For master's and doctorate, knowledge of French, comprehension of written English. Electronic applications accepted.

University at Albany, State University of New York, School of Public Health, Department of Biomedical Sciences, Program in Immunobiology and Immunochemistry, Albany, NY 12222-0001. Offers MS, PhD. *Degree requirements:* For master's, thesis; for doctorate, thesis/dissertation. *Entrance requirements:* For master's and doctorate, GRE General Test, GRE Subject Test.

University at Buffalo, the State University of New York, Graduate School, Graduate Programs in Cancer Research and Biomedical Sciences at Roswell Park Cancer Institute, Department of Immunology at Roswell Park Cancer Institute, Buffalo, NY 14260. Offers cancer immunology (PhD). *Faculty:* 17 full-time (7 women). *Students:* 20 full-time (12 women), 7 part-time (1 woman); includes 1 Asian, non-Hispanic/Latino, 13 international. Average age 27. 32 applicants, 28% accepted, 6 enrolled. In 2010, 5 doctorates awarded. *Degree requirements:* For doctorate, comprehensive exam, thesis/dissertation. *Entrance requirements:* For doctorate, GRE. Additional exam requirements/recommendations for international students: Required—TOEFL (minimum score 600 paper-based; 250 computer-based; 100 iBT) or IELTS. *Application deadline:* For fall admission, 2/1 priority date for domestic students, 2/1 for international students. Applications are processed on a rolling basis. Application fee: $50. Electronic applications accepted. *Financial support:* In 2010–11, 10 students received support, including 4 fellowships with full tuition reimbursements available (averaging $24,000 per year), 6 research assistantships with full tuition reimbursements available (averaging $24,000 per year); Federal Work-Study also available. Financial award application deadline: 2/1; financial award applicants required to submit FAFSA. *Faculty research:* Immunochemistry, immunobiology, molecular immunology, hybridoma studies, recombinant DNA studies. Total annual research expenditures: $4 million. *Unit head:* Dr. Kelvin Lee, Chair, 716-845-4106, Fax: 716-845-2993, E-mail: kelvin.lee@roswellpark.org. *Application contact:* Craig R. Johnson, Director of Admissions, 716-845-2339, Fax: 716-845-8178, E-mail: craig.johnson@roswellpark.org.

University at Buffalo, the State University of New York, Graduate School, School of Medicine and Biomedical Sciences, Graduate Programs in Medicine and Biomedical Sciences, Department of Microbiology and Immunology, Buffalo, NY 14260. Offers MA, PhD. *Faculty:* 15 full-time (4 women), 4 part-time/adjunct (1 woman). *Students:* 23 full-time (15 women), 8 international. Average age 29. 6 applicants, 50% accepted, 1 enrolled. In 2010, 1 master's, 6 doctorates awarded. *Degree requirements:* For master's, comprehensive exam; for doctorate, thesis/dissertation, departmental qualifying exam. *Entrance requirements:* For master's and doctorate, GRE General Test, 3 letters of recommendation. Additional exam requirements/recommendations for international students: Required—TOEFL (minimum score 100 iBT). *Application deadline:* For fall admission, 2/1 priority date for domestic and international students. Applications are processed on a rolling basis. Application fee: $50. Electronic applications accepted. *Financial support:* In 2010–11, 1 student received support, including 5 fellowships with tuition reimbursements available (averaging $21,000 per year), 14 research assistantships with tuition reimbursements available (averaging $24,000 per year); Federal Work-Study, institutionally sponsored loans, traineeships, health care benefits, and unspecified assistantships also available. Financial award application deadline: 2/1; financial award applicants required to submit FAFSA. *Faculty research:* Bacteriology, immunology, parasitology, virology, mycology. Total annual research expenditures: $9.8 million. *Unit head:* Dr. John Hay, Interim Chairman, 716-829-2907, Fax: 716-829-2158. *Application contact:* Dr. Nejat Egilmez, Director of Graduate Studies, 716-829-2176, Fax: 716-829-2158.

University of Alberta, Faculty of Medicine and Dentistry and Faculty of Graduate Studies and Research, Graduate Programs in Medicine, Department of Medical Microbiology and Immunology, Edmonton, AB T6G 2E1, Canada. Offers M Sc, PhD. Terminal master's awarded for partial completion of doctoral program. *Degree requirements:* For master's, thesis; for doctorate, thesis/dissertation. *Entrance requirements:* For master's and doctorate, minimum GPA of 3.3. Additional exam requirements/recommendations for international students: Required—TOEFL (minimum score 600 paper-based; 232 computer-based; 96 iBT). *Faculty research:* Cellular and reproductive immunology, microbial pathogenesis, mechanisms of antibiotic resistance, molecular biology of mammalian viruses, antiviral chemotherapy.

The University of Arizona, College of Medicine, Department of Immunobiology, Tucson, AZ 85721. Offers MS, PhD. *Faculty:* 12 full-time (4 women), 1 part-time/adjunct (0 women). *Students:* 4 full-time (2 women), 9 part-time (7 women); includes 1 minority (Two or more races, non-Hispanic/Latino), 3 international. Average age 27. 91 applicants, 66% accepted. In 2010, 1 master's, 5 doctorates awarded. *Degree requirements:* For master's, thesis; for doctorate, thesis/dissertation. *Entrance requirements:* For master's and doctorate, GRE General Test, minimum GPA of 3.0. *Application deadline:* For fall admission, 3/1 priority date for domestic students; for spring admission, 9/1 for domestic students. Application fee: $45. *Expenses:* Tuition, state resident: full-time $7692. *Financial support:* In 2010–11, 11 research assistantships with full tuition reimbursements (averaging $21,388 per year) were awarded; fellowships with full tuition reimbursements, teaching assistantships with full tuition reimbursements, institutionally sponsored loans and tuition waivers (full) also available. Financial award application deadline: 4/30. *Faculty research:* Environmental and pathogenic microbiology, molecular biology. Total annual research expenditures: $1.4 million. *Unit head:* Dr. Emmanuel T. Akporiaye, Interim Head, 520-626-6409, Fax: 520-626-2100, E-mail: akporiay@u.arizona.edu. *Application contact:* Dr. Richard J. Ablin, Graduate Program Chairman, 520-626-7755, E-mail: ablinrj@email.arizona.edu.

University of Arkansas for Medical Sciences, Graduate School, Graduate Programs in Biomedical Sciences, Department of Microbiology and Immunology, Little Rock, AR 72205-7199. Offers MS, PhD, MD/PhD. *Degree requirements:* For master's, thesis; for doctorate, thesis/dissertation. *Entrance requirements:* For master's and doctorate, GRE General Test. Additional exam requirements/recommendations for international students: Required—TOEFL. *Faculty research:* Tumor immunology and immunotherapy, microbial pathogenesis and genetics, allergy, immune response in infectious diseases.

The University of British Columbia, Faculty of Science, Department of Microbiology and Immunology, Vancouver, BC V6T 1Z1, Canada. Offers M Sc, PhD. *Degree requirements:* For master's, thesis; for doctorate, comprehensive exam, thesis/dissertation. *Entrance requirements:* For master's and doctorate, GRE General Test. Additional exam requirements/recommendations for international students: Required—TOEFL (minimum score 590 paper-based; 243 computer-based). Electronic applications accepted. Tuition charges are reported in Canadian dollars. *Expenses:* Tuition, area resident: Full-time $4179 Canadian dollars. International tuition: $7344 Canadian dollars full-time. *Faculty research:* Bacterial genetics, metabolism, pathogenic bacteriology, virology.

University of Calgary, Faculty of Medicine and Faculty of Graduate Studies, Department of Medical Science, Calgary, AB T2N 1N4, Canada. Offers cancer biology (M Sc, PhD); immunology (M Sc, PhD); joint injury and arthritis research (M Sc, PhD); medical education (M Sc, PhD); medical science (M Sc, PhD); mountain medicine and high altitude physiology (M Sc). *Degree requirements:* For master's, thesis; for doctorate, thesis/dissertation, candidacy exam. *Entrance requirements:* For master's, minimum undergraduate GPA of 3.2; for doctorate, minimum graduate GPA of 3.2. Additional exam requirements/recommendations for international students: Required—TOEFL (minimum score 600 paper-based; 250 computer-based). Electronic applications accepted. *Faculty research:* Cancer biology, immunology, joint injury and arthritis, medical education, population genomics.

University of California, Berkeley, Graduate Division, School of Public Health, Group in Infectious Diseases and Immunity, Berkeley, CA 94720-1500. Offers PhD. *Entrance requirements:* For doctorate, GRE General Test, minimum GPA of 3.0, 3 letters of recommendation.

University of California, Davis, Graduate Studies, Graduate Group in Immunology, Davis, CA 95616. Offers MS, PhD. Terminal master's awarded for partial completion of doctoral program. *Degree requirements:* For master's, comprehensive exam (for some programs), thesis (for some programs); for doctorate, thesis/dissertation. *Entrance requirements:* For master's and doctorate, GRE General Test. Additional exam requirements/recommendations for international students: Required—TOEFL (minimum score 550 paper-based; 213 computer-based). Electronic applications accepted. *Faculty research:* Immune regulation in autoimmunity, immunopathology, immunotoxicology, tumor immunology, avian immunology.

University of California, Los Angeles, David Geffen School of Medicine and Graduate Division, Graduate Programs in Medicine, Department of Microbiology, Immunology and Molecular Genetics, Los Angeles, CA 90095. Offers MS, PhD. *Faculty:* 31 full-time (6 women). *Students:* 51 full-time (19 women); includes 19 minority (1 Black or African American, non-Hispanic/Latino; 9 Asian, non-Hispanic/Latino; 9 Hispanic/Latino), 6 international. Average age 28. 5 applicants, 100% accepted, 4 enrolled. In 2010, 4 master's, 14 doctorates awarded. *Degree requirements:* For doctorate, thesis/dissertation, oral and written qualifying exams. *Entrance requirements:* For doctorate, GRE General Test, GRE Subject Test. Additional exam requirements/recommendations for international students: Required—TOEFL. Application fee: $70 ($90 for international students). Electronic applications accepted. *Financial support:* In 2010–11, 50 fellowships, 47 research assistantships, 20 teaching assistantships were awarded; Federal Work-Study, institutionally sponsored loans, and tuition waivers (full and partial) also available. Financial award application deadline: 3/1. *Unit head:* Dr. Jeff F. Miller, Chair, 310-206-7926, Fax: 310-267-2774, E-mail: jfmiller@ucla.edu. *Application contact:* Bridget Wolfgang, Graduate Student Affairs, 310-825-8482, Fax: 310-206-5231, E-mail: bridgetw@microbio.ucla.edu.

University of California, Los Angeles, Graduate Division, College of Letters and Science and David Geffen School of Medicine, UCLA ACCESS to Programs in the Molecular, Cellular and Integrative Life Sciences, Los Angeles, CA 90095. Offers biochemistry and molecular biology (PhD); biological chemistry (PhD); cellular and molecular pathology (PhD); human genetics (PhD); microbiology, immunology, and molecular genetics (PhD); molecular biology (PhD); molecular toxicology (PhD); molecular, cellular and integrative physiology (PhD); neurobiology (PhD); oral biology (PhD); physiology (PhD). ACCESS is an umbrella program for first-year coursework in 12 PhD programs. *Students:* 48 full-time (28 women), 6 international. Average age 24. 388 applicants, 27% accepted, 48 enrolled. *Degree requirements:* For doctorate, thesis/dissertation, oral and written qualifying exams. *Entrance requirements:* For doctorate, GRE General Test, minimum undergraduate GPA of 3.0. Additional exam requirements/recommendations for international students: Required—TOEFL. *Application deadline:* For fall admission, 12/15 for domestic and international students. Application fee: $70 ($90 for international students). Electronic applications accepted. *Financial support:* In 2010–11, 31 fellowships with full and partial tuition reimbursements, 13 research assistantships with full and partial tuition reimbursements, 2 teaching assistantships with full and partial tuition reimbursements were awarded; Federal Work-Study, institutionally sponsored loans, scholarships/grants, health care benefits, tuition waivers (full and partial), and unspecified assistantships also available. Financial award application deadline: 3/1; financial award applicants required to submit FAFSA. *Faculty research:* Molecular, cellular, and developmental biology; immunology; microbiology; integrative biology. *Unit head:* Jody Spillane, Project Coordinator, 310-206-1845, E-mail: jspillane@mednet.ucla.edu. *Application contact:* UCLA Access Admissions, 310-206-1845, E-mail: uclaaccess@mednet.ucla.edu.

University of California, San Diego, Office of Graduate Studies, Division of Biological Sciences, Program in Immunology, Virology, and Cancer Biology, La Jolla, CA 92093. Offers PhD. Offered in association with the Salk Institute. *Degree requirements:* For doctorate, thesis/dissertation, qualifying exam. Electronic applications accepted.

University of California, San Francisco, Graduate Division, Department of Microbiology and Immunology, San Francisco, CA 94143. Offers PhD. *Degree requirements:* For doctorate, thesis/dissertation. *Entrance requirements:* For doctorate, GRE General Test.

University of Chicago, Division of Biological Sciences, Biomedical Sciences Cluster: Cancer Biology, Immunology, Molecular Metabolism and Nutrition, Pathology, and Microbiology, Committee on Immunology, Chicago, IL 60637-1513. Offers PhD. *Degree requirements:* For doctorate, thesis/dissertation, ethics class, 2 teaching assistantships. *Entrance requirements:* For doctorate, GRE General Test. Additional exam requirements/recommendations for international students: Required—TOEFL (minimum score 600 paper-based; 250 computer-based; 104 iBT), IELTS (minimum score 7). Electronic applications accepted. *Faculty research:* Molecular immunology, transplantation, autoimmunology, neuroimmunology, tumor immunology.

University of Cincinnati, Graduate School, College of Medicine, Graduate Programs in Biomedical Sciences, Department of Pediatrics, Cincinnati, OH 45221. Offers immunobiology (PhD); molecular and developmental biology (PhD). *Degree requirements:* For doctorate, thesis/dissertation, qualifying exam. *Entrance requirements:* For doctorate, GRE General Test, minimum GPA of 3.0. Additional exam requirements/recommendations for international students: Required—TOEFL (minimum score 600 paper-based; 250 computer-based; 100 iBT). Electronic applications accepted. *Faculty research:* Pulmonary biology, molecular cardiovascular, developmental biology, cancer biology, genetics.

University of Cincinnati, Graduate School, College of Medicine, Graduate Programs in Biomedical Sciences, Immunobiology Training Program, Cincinnati, OH 45221. Offers MS, PhD. *Degree requirements:* For master's, seminar, thesis with oral defense; for doctorate, seminar, dissertation with oral defense, written and oral candidacy exams.

University of Colorado Denver, School of Medicine, Integrated Department of Immunology, Denver, CO 80206. Offers PhD. *Students:* 43 full-time (29 women); includes 1 American Indian or Alaska Native, non-Hispanic/Latino; 1 Asian, non-Hispanic/Latino; 2 Hispanic/Latino, 2 international. Average age 28. 52 applicants, 8% accepted, 4 enrolled. In 2010, 13 doctorates awarded. *Degree requirements:* For doctorate, thesis/dissertation, 30 credit hours of formal course work, three laboratory rotations, oral comprehensive examination, 30 credit hours of dissertation research, final defense of the dissertation. *Entrance requirements:* For doctorate, GRE, letters of recommendation, statement of purpose, interview. Additional exam requirements/recommendations for international students: Required—TOEFL (minimum score 550 paper-based; 213 computer-based). *Application deadline:* For fall admission, 1/1 for domestic students. Application fee: $50 ($75 for international students). Electronic applications accepted. *Expenses:* Contact institution. *Financial support:* Fellowships with full tuition reimbursements, health care benefits, tuition waivers (full), and stipend available. Financial award application deadline: 3/15; financial award applicants required to submit FAFSA. *Faculty research:* Gene regulation, immune signaling, apoptosis, stem cells, vaccines. Total annual research expenditures: $5.1 million. *Unit head:* Dr. John C. Cambier, Professor/Chairman, 303-398-1325, E-mail: cambierj@njhealth.org. *Application contact:* Amy Scoby, Graduate Program Contact, 303-270-2593, E-mail: scobya@njhealth.org.

University of Connecticut Health Center, Graduate School, Programs in Biomedical Sciences, Graduate Program in Immunology, Farmington, CT 06030. Offers PhD, DMD/PhD, MD/PhD. *Faculty:* 158. *Students:* 21 full-time (12 women); includes 3 minority (2 Asian, non-Hispanic/Latino; 1 Hispanic/Latino), 11 international. Average age 29. 216 applicants, 22% accepted. In 2010, 7 doctorates awarded. *Degree requirements:* For doctorate, comprehensive exam, thesis/dissertation. *Entrance requirements:* For doctorate, GRE General Test. Additional exam requirements/recommendations for international students: Required—TOEFL (minimum score 600 paper-based; 250 computer-based). *Application deadline:* For fall admission, 12/15 for domestic students. Application fee: $55. Electronic applications accepted. *Financial support:* In 2010–11, 20 research assistantships with full tuition reimbursements (averaging $27,000 per year) were awarded; fellowships also available. *Faculty research:* Developmental immunology, T-cell immunity, lymphoid cell development, tolerance and tumor immunity, leukocyte chemotaxis. *Unit head:* Dr. Adam Adler, Program Director, 860-679-3935,

Immunology

University of Connecticut Health Center (continued)
Fax: 860-679-1868, E-mail: aadler@up.uchc.edu. *Application contact:* Tricia Avolt, Graduate Admissions Coordinator, 860-679-2175, Fax: 860-679-1899, E-mail: robertson@nso2.uchc.edu.
See Display below and Close-Up on page 347.

University of Florida, College of Medicine, Department of Pathology, Immunology and Laboratory Medicine, Gainesville, FL 32611. Offers immunology and molecular pathology (PhD). *Degree requirements:* For doctorate, thesis/dissertation. *Entrance requirements:* For doctorate, GRE General Test, minimum GPA of 3.0. Additional exam requirements/recommendations for international students: Required—TOEFL. Electronic applications accepted. *Expenses:* Tuition, state resident: full-time $10,916. Tuition, nonresident: full-time $28,309. *Faculty research:* Molecular immunology, autoimmunity and transplantation, tumor biology, oncogenic viruses, human immunodeficiency viruses.

University of Florida, College of Medicine and Graduate School, Interdisciplinary Program in Biomedical Sciences, Concentration in Immunology and Microbiology, Gainesville, FL 32611. Offers PhD. *Degree requirements:* For doctorate, thesis/dissertation. *Entrance requirements:* For doctorate, GRE General Test, minimum GPA of 3.0. Additional exam requirements/recommendations for international students: Required—TOEFL. Electronic applications accepted. *Expenses:* Tuition, state resident: full-time $10,916. Tuition, nonresident: full-time $28,309.

University of Guelph, Ontario Veterinary College and Graduate Studies, Graduate Programs in Veterinary Sciences, Department of Pathobiology, Guelph, ON N1G 2W1, Canada. Offers anatomic pathology (DV Sc, Diploma); clinical pathology (Diploma); comparative pathology (M Sc, PhD); immunology (M Sc, PhD); laboratory animal science (DV Sc); pathology (M Sc, PhD, Diploma); veterinary infectious diseases (M Sc, PhD); zoo animal/wildlife medicine (DV Sc). *Degree requirements:* For master's, thesis; for doctorate, thesis/dissertation. *Entrance requirements:* For master's, DVM with B average or an honours degree in biological sciences; for doctorate, DVM or MSC degree, minimum B+ average. Additional exam requirements/recommendations for international students: Required—TOEFL (minimum score 550 paper-based; 213 computer-based). *Faculty research:* Pathogenesis; diseases of animals, wildlife, fish, and laboratory animals; parasitology; immunology; veterinary infectious diseases; laboratory animal science.

University of Illinois at Chicago, College of Medicine and Graduate College, Graduate Programs in Medicine, Department of Microbiology and Immunology, Chicago, IL 60607-7128. Offers PhD, MD/PhD. *Degree requirements:* For doctorate, thesis/dissertation. *Entrance requirements:* For doctorate, GRE General Test, minimum GPA of 2.75. Additional exam requirements/recommendations for international students: Required—TOEFL.

The University of Iowa, Graduate College, Program in Immunology, Iowa City, IA 52242-1316. Offers PhD, MD/PhD. *Degree requirements:* For doctorate, comprehensive exam, thesis/dissertation. *Entrance requirements:* For doctorate, GRE General Test, minimum GPA of 3.0. Additional exam requirements/recommendations for international students: Required—TOEFL (minimum score 600 paper-based; 250 computer-based; 100 iBT). Electronic applications accepted.

The University of Iowa, Roy J. and Lucille A. Carver College of Medicine and Graduate College, Graduate Programs in Medicine, Department of Microbiology, Iowa City, IA 52242-1316. Offers general microbiology and microbial physiology (MS, PhD); immunology (MS, PhD); microbial genetics (MS, PhD); pathogenic bacteriology (MS, PhD); virology (MS, PhD). *Faculty:* 23 full-time (4 women), 11 part-time/adjunct (5 women). *Students:* 35 full-time (20 women); includes 2 American Indian or Alaska Native, non-Hispanic/Latino; 1 Hispanic/Latino, 5 international. Average age 25. 71 applicants, 20% accepted, 8 enrolled. In 2010, 1 master's, 5 doctorates awarded. *Degree requirements:* For master's, thesis; for doctorate, comprehensive exam, thesis/dissertation. *Entrance requirements:* For master's and doctorate, GRE General

Test. Additional exam requirements/recommendations for international students: Required—TOEFL (minimum score 600 paper-based; 250 computer-based). *Application deadline:* For fall admission, 2/1 for domestic and international students. Application fee: $60 ($85 for international students). Electronic applications accepted. *Financial support:* In 2010–11, 4 fellowships with full tuition reimbursements (averaging $25,000 per year), 31 research assistantships with full tuition reimbursements (averaging $25,000 per year) were awarded; institutionally sponsored loans, scholarships/grants, traineeships, and health care benefits also available. *Faculty research:* Gene regulation, processing and transport of HIV, retroviral pathogenesis, biodegradation, biofilm. Total annual research expenditures: $12.6 million. *Unit head:* Dr. Michael A. Apicella, Head, 319-335-7810, E-mail: grad-micro-info@uiowa.edu. *Application contact:* Dr. Michael A. Apicella, Head, 319-335-7810, E-mail: grad-micro-info@uiowa.edu.

University of Louisville, School of Medicine, Department of Microbiology and Immunology, Louisville, KY 40292-0001. Offers MS, PhD, MD/PhD. *Faculty:* 22 full-time (6 women). *Students:* 36 full-time (25 women); includes 4 Black or African American, non-Hispanic/Latino; 1 Asian, non-Hispanic/Latino, 14 international. Average age 29. 36 applicants, 39% accepted, 10 enrolled. In 2010, 6 doctorates awarded. Terminal master's awarded for partial completion of doctoral program. *Degree requirements:* For master's, thesis; for doctorate, comprehensive exam, thesis/dissertation. *Entrance requirements:* For master's and doctorate, GRE General Test (minimum score of 1000 verbal and quantitative), minimum GPA of 3.0; 1 year of course work in biology, organic chemistry, physics; 1 semester of course work in calculus and quantitative analysis, biochemistry, or molecular biology. Additional exam requirements/recommendations for international students: Required—TOEFL. *Application deadline:* For fall admission, 2/1 priority date for domestic and international students. Applications are processed on a rolling basis. Application fee: $50. Electronic applications accepted. *Expenses:* Tuition, state resident: full-time $9144; part-time $508 per credit hour. Tuition, nonresident: full-time $19,026; part-time $1057 per credit hour. Tuition and fees vary according to program and reciprocity agreements. *Financial support:* Fellowships with full tuition reimbursements, research assistantships with full tuition reimbursements available. Financial award application deadline: 4/15. *Faculty research:* Opportunistic and emerging infections; biology and regulation of the immune system; cellular and molecular bases of chronic inflammatory response; role of cytokines and chemokines in cancer, autoimmune and infectious disease; host defense and pathogenesis of viral infections. *Unit head:* Dr. Robert D. Stout, Chair, 502-852-5351, Fax: 502-852-7531, E-mail: bobstout@louisville.edu. *Application contact:* Carolyn M. Burton, Academic Coordinator, 502-852-6208, Fax: 502-852-7531, E-mail: cmburt01@gwise.louisville.edu.

The University of Manchester, Faculty of Life Sciences, Manchester, United Kingdom. Offers adaptive organismal biology (M Phil, PhD); animal biology (M Phil, PhD); biochemistry (M Phil, PhD); bioinformatics (M Phil, PhD); biomolecular sciences (M Phil, PhD); biotechnology (M Phil, PhD); cell biology (M Phil, PhD); cell matrix research (M Phil, PhD); channels and transporters (M Phil, PhD); developmental biology (M Phil, PhD); Egyptology (M Phil, PhD); environmental biology (M Phil, PhD); evolutionary biology (M Phil, PhD); gene expression (M Phil, PhD); genetics (M Phil, PhD); history of science, technology and medicine (M Phil, PhD); immunology (M Phil, PhD); integrative neurobiology and behavior (M Phil, PhD); membrane trafficking (M Phil, PhD); microbiology (M Phil, PhD); molecular and cellular neuroscience (M Phil, PhD); molecular biology (M Phil, PhD); molecular cancer studies (M Phil, PhD); neuroscience (M Phil, PhD); ophthalmology (M Phil, PhD); optometry (M Phil, PhD); organelle function (M Phil, PhD); pharmacology (M Phil, PhD); physiology (M Phil, PhD); plant sciences (M Phil, PhD); stem cell research (M Phil, PhD); structural biology (M Phil, PhD); systems neuroscience (M Phil, PhD); toxicology (M Phil, PhD).

University of Manitoba, Faculty of Medicine and Faculty of Graduate Studies, Graduate Programs in Medicine, Department of Immunology, Winnipeg, MB R3T 2N2, Canada. Offers M Sc, PhD. Terminal master's awarded for partial completion of doctoral program. *Degree requirements:* For master's, thesis; for doctorate, one foreign language, thesis/dissertation.

Faculty research: Immediate hypersensitivity, regulation of the immune response, natural immunity, cytokines, inflammation.

University of Maryland, Baltimore, Graduate School, Graduate Program in Life Sciences, Program in Molecular Microbiology and Immunology, Baltimore, MD 21201. Offers PhD, MD/PhD. *Entrance requirements:* For doctorate, GRE. Additional exam requirements/recommendations for international students: Required—TOEFL (minimum score 550 paper-based; 80 iBT); Recommended—IELTS (minimum score 7). Electronic applications accepted. Part-time tuition and fees vary according to course load, degree level and program.

University of Massachusetts Worcester, Graduate School of Biomedical Sciences, Worcester, MA 01655-0115. Offers biochemistry and molecular pharmacology (PhD); bioinformatics and computational biology (PhD); cancer biology (PhD); cell biology (PhD); clinical and population health research (PhD); clinical investigation (MS); immunology and virology (PhD); interdisciplinary graduate program (PhD); molecular genetics and microbiology (PhD); neuroscience (PhD); DVM/PhD; MD/PhD. *Faculty:* 1,059 full-time (357 women), 145 part-time/adjunct (100 women). *Students:* 438 full-time (239 women), 1 (woman) part-time; includes 44 minority (9 Black or African American, non-Hispanic/Latino; 31 Asian, non-Hispanic/Latino; 4 Hispanic/Latino), 148 international. Average age 29. 687 applicants, 28% accepted, 116 enrolled. In 2010, 6 master's, 45 doctorates awarded. Terminal master's awarded for partial completion of doctoral program. *Degree requirements:* For master's, thesis; for doctorate, thesis/dissertation. *Entrance requirements:* For master's, bachelor's degree; for doctorate, GRE General Test, MS, MA, or MPH (for some programs). Additional exam requirements/recommendations for international students: Required—TOEFL (minimum score 600 paper-based; 250 computer-based). *Application deadline:* For fall admission, 12/15 for domestic and international students; for winter admission, 1/15 for domestic students; for spring admission, 5/15 for domestic students. Application fee: $35. Electronic applications accepted. *Expenses:* Contact institution. *Financial support:* In 2010–11, 439 students received support, including 439 research assistantships with full tuition reimbursements available (averaging $28,350 per year); scholarships/grants, health care benefits, tuition waivers (full), and unspecified assistantships also available. Financial award application deadline: 4/20. *Faculty research:* RNA interference, gene therapy, cell biology, bioinformatics, clinical research. Total annual research expenditures: $232 million. *Unit head:* Dr. Anthony Carruthers, Dean, 508-856-4135, E-mail: anthony.carruthers@umassmed.edu. *Application contact:* Dr. Kendall Knight, Associate Dean and Interim Director of Admissions and Recruitment, 508-856-5628, Fax: 508-856-3659, E-mail: kendall.knight@umassmed.edu.

University of Medicine and Dentistry of New Jersey, Graduate School of Biomedical Sciences, Graduate Programs in Biomedical Sciences–Newark, Program in Molecular Pathology and Immunology, Newark, NJ 07107. Offers PhD. *Entrance requirements:* Additional exam requirements/recommendations for international students: Required—TOEFL. Electronic applications accepted.

University of Medicine and Dentistry of New Jersey, Graduate School of Biomedical Sciences, Graduate Programs in Biomedical Sciences–Piscataway, Program in Molecular Genetics, Microbiology and Immunology, Piscataway, NJ 08854-5635. Offers MS, PhD, MD/PhD. Terminal master's awarded for partial completion of doctoral program. *Degree requirements:* For master's, thesis, qualifying exam; for doctorate, thesis/dissertation, qualifying exam. *Entrance requirements:* For master's and doctorate, GRE General Test. Additional exam requirements/recommendations for international students: Required—TOEFL. *Application deadline:* For fall admission, 1/5 for domestic students. Applications are processed on a rolling basis. Application fee: $40. Electronic applications accepted. *Financial support:* Fellowships, research assistantships, teaching assistantships available. Financial award application deadline: 5/1. *Faculty research:* Interferon, receptors, retrovirus evolution, Arbo virus/host cell interactions. *Unit head:* Dr. Michael J. Leibowitz, Director, 732-235-4795, Fax: 732-235-5223, E-mail: leibowit@umdnj.edu. *Application contact:* Johanna Sierra, University Registrar, 732-235-5016, Fax: 732-235-4720.

University of Medicine and Dentistry of New Jersey, Graduate School of Biomedical Sciences, Graduate Programs in Biomedical Sciences–Stratford, Stratford, NJ 08084-5634. Offers biomedical sciences (MBS, MS); cell and molecular biology (MS, PhD); molecular pathology and immunology (MS); DO/MS; DO/PhD; MS/MPH. Part-time and evening/weekend programs available. *Students:* 79 full-time (43 women), 19 part-time (14 women); includes 21 Black or African American, non-Hispanic/Latino; 16 Asian, non-Hispanic/Latino; 7 Hispanic/Latino, 11 international. Average age 25. 128 applicants, 74% accepted, 64 enrolled. In 2010, 46 master's, 3 doctorates awarded. Terminal master's awarded for partial completion of doctoral program. *Degree requirements:* For master's, thesis (for some programs); for doctorate, thesis/dissertation, qualifying exam. *Entrance requirements:* For master's, GRE General Test, MCAT or DAT; for doctorate, GRE General Test. Additional exam requirements/recommendations for international students: Required—TOEFL. *Application deadline:* For fall admission, 2/1 for domestic and international students; for spring admission, 11/1 for domestic students. Applications are processed on a rolling basis. Application fee: $65. Electronic applications accepted. *Financial support:* Fellowships, Federal Work-Study available. Financial award application deadline: 5/1. *Unit head:* Dr. Carl E. Hock, Senior Associate Dean, Graduate School, 856-566-6282, Fax: 856-566-6232, E-mail: hock@umdnj.edu. *Application contact:* University Registrar, 973-972-5338.

University of Miami, Graduate School, Miller School of Medicine, Graduate Programs in Medicine, Department of Microbiology and Immunology, Coral Gables, FL 33124. Offers PhD, MD/PhD. *Degree requirements:* For doctorate, thesis/dissertation, oral and written qualifying exams. *Entrance requirements:* For doctorate, GRE General Test. Additional exam requirements/recommendations for international students: Required—TOEFL. Electronic applications accepted. *Faculty research:* Cellular and molecular immunology, molecular and pathogenic virology, pathogenic bacteriology and gene therapy of cancer.

University of Michigan, Rackham Graduate School, Program in Biomedical Sciences (PIBS), Department of Microbiology and Immunology, Ann Arbor, MI 48109. Offers PhD. *Faculty:* 22 full-time (11 women), 16 part-time/adjunct (6 women). *Students:* 40 full-time (25 women); includes 3 minority (all Asian, non-Hispanic/Latino), 2 international. Average age 28. 64 applicants, 27% accepted, 4 enrolled. In 2010, 8 doctorates awarded. *Degree requirements:* For doctorate, thesis/dissertation, oral defense of dissertation, preliminary exam. *Entrance requirements:* For doctorate, GRE General Test. Additional exam requirements/recommendations for international students: Required—TOEFL (minimum score 600 paper-based; 220 computer-based; 84 iBT), TWE. *Application deadline:* For fall admission, 12/15 for domestic students, 11/1 for international students. Application fee: $60 ($75 for international students). Electronic applications accepted. *Expenses:* Tuition, state resident: full-time $17,784; part-time $1116 per credit hour. Tuition, nonresident: full-time $35,944; part-time $2125 per credit hour. International tuition: $35,994 full-time. Required fees: $95 per semester. Tuition and fees vary according to course load, degree level and program. *Financial support:* In 2010–11, 17 students received support, including 15 fellowships with full tuition reimbursements available (averaging $24,500 per year), 20 research assistantships with full tuition reimbursements available (averaging $24,500 per year); teaching assistantships, health care benefits and tuition waivers (full) also available. Financial award application deadline: 2/1. *Faculty research:* Gene regulation, molecular biology of animal and bacterial viruses, molecular and cellular networks, pathogenesis and microbial genetics. Total annual research expenditures: $7.3 million. *Unit head:* Dr. Harry L. T. Mobley, Chair, 734-764-1466, Fax: 734-764-3562, E-mail: hmobley@umich.edu. *Application contact:* Heidi Thompson, Senior Student Administrative Assistant, 734-763-3532, Fax: 734-764-3562, E-mail: heiditho@umich.edu.

University of Michigan, Rackham Graduate School, Program in Biomedical Sciences (PIBS), Program in Immunology, Ann Arbor, MI 48109-0619. Offers PhD. *Faculty:* 53 full-time (13 women). *Students:* 22 full-time (15 women); includes 10 minority (1 Black or African American, non-Hispanic/Latino; 5 Asian, non-Hispanic/Latino; 4 Hispanic/Latino). Average age 27. 24 applicants, 50% accepted, 5 enrolled. In 2010, 7 doctorates awarded. *Degree requirements:*

For doctorate, thesis/dissertation, oral defense of dissertation, preliminary exam. *Entrance requirements:* For doctorate, GRE General Test, 3 letters of recommendation, research experience. Additional exam requirements/recommendations for international students: Required—TOEFL (minimum score 84 iBT). *Application deadline:* For fall admission, 12/1 for domestic and international students. Application fee: $65 ($75 for international students). Electronic applications accepted. *Expenses:* Tuition, state resident: full-time $17,784; part-time $1116 per credit hour. Tuition, nonresident: full-time $35,944; part-time $2125 per credit hour. International tuition: $35,994 full-time. Required fees: $95 per semester. Tuition and fees vary according to course load, degree level and program. *Financial support:* In 2010–11, 22 students received support, including 9 fellowships (averaging $26,500 per year), 13 research assistantships with tuition reimbursements available (averaging $26,500 per year); scholarships/grants, health care benefits, tuition waivers, and unspecified assistantships also available. Financial award application deadline: 12/1. *Faculty research:* Cytokine networks, T and B cell activation, autoimmunity, antigen processing/ presentation, cell signaling. Total annual research expenditures: $20 million. *Unit head:* Dr. D. Keith Bishop, Director, 734-763-0326, Fax: 734-936-9715, E-mail: kbishop@umich.edu. *Application contact:* Michelle S. Melis, Director of Student Life, 734-615-6538, Fax: 734-647-7022, E-mail: msmtegan@umich.edu.

University of Minnesota, Duluth, Medical School, Microbiology, Immunology and Molecular Pathobiology Section, Duluth, MN 55812-2496. Offers MS, PhD. MS, PhD offered jointly with University of Minnesota, Twin Cities Campus. Terminal master's awarded for partial completion of doctoral program. *Degree requirements:* For master's, thesis, final oral exam; for doctorate, thesis/dissertation, final exam, oral and written preliminary exams. *Entrance requirements:* For master's and doctorate, GRE General Test. Additional exam requirements/recommendations for international students: Required—TOEFL. *Faculty research:* Immunomodulation, molecular diagnosis of rabies, cytokines, cancer immunology, cytomegalovirus infection.

University of Minnesota, Twin Cities Campus, Graduate School, PhD Program in Microbiology, Immunology and Cancer Biology, Minneapolis, MN 55455-0213. Offers PhD. *Degree requirements:* For doctorate, thesis/dissertation. *Entrance requirements:* For doctorate, GRE General Test. Additional exam requirements/recommendations for international students: Required—TOEFL (minimum score 600 paper-based; 250 computer-based). Electronic applications accepted. *Faculty research:* Virology, microbiology, cancer biology, immunology.

University of Missouri, School of Medicine and Graduate School, Graduate Programs in Medicine, Department of Molecular Microbiology and Immunology, Columbia, MO 65211. Offers MS, PhD. Terminal master's awarded for partial completion of doctoral program. *Degree requirements:* For master's, thesis; for doctorate, thesis/dissertation. *Entrance requirements:* For master's and doctorate, GRE General Test, minimum GPA of 3.0. Additional exam requirements/recommendations for international students: Required—TOEFL (minimum score 580 paper-based; 237 computer-based; 92 iBT). *Faculty research:* Molecular biology, host-parasite interactions.

The University of North Carolina at Chapel Hill, School of Medicine and Graduate School, Graduate Programs in Medicine, Department of Microbiology and Immunology, Chapel Hill, NC 27599-7290. Offers immunology (MS, PhD); microbiology (MS, PhD). *Faculty:* 65 full-time (20 women). *Students:* 73 full-time (53 women); includes 6 Black or African American, non-Hispanic/Latino; 5 Asian, non-Hispanic/Latino; 2 Hispanic/Latino, 6 international. Average age 28. In 2010, 16 doctorates awarded. Terminal master's awarded for partial completion of doctoral program. *Degree requirements:* For master's, comprehensive exam, thesis; for doctorate, comprehensive exam, thesis/dissertation. *Entrance requirements:* For master's and doctorate, GRE General Test, minimum GPA of 3.0. *Application deadline:* Applications are processed on a rolling basis. Electronic applications accepted. *Financial support:* In 2010–11, 3 fellowships with full tuition reimbursements (averaging $26,000 per year), 69 research assistantships with full tuition reimbursements (averaging $26,000 per year) were awarded; scholarships/grants, traineeships, health care benefits, and unspecified assistantships also available. Financial award application deadline: 3/1; financial award applicants required to submit FAFSA. *Faculty research:* HIV pathogenesis, immune response, t-cell mediated autoimmunity, alpha-viruses, bacterial chemotaxis, francisella tularensis, pertussis, Mycobacterium tuberculosis, Burkholderia, Dengue virus. Total annual research expenditures: $11.3 million. *Unit head:* Dr. William Goldman, Chairman, 919-966-1191, Fax: 919-962-8103, E-mail: goldman@med.unc.edu. *Application contact:* Dixie Flannery, Student Services Specialist, 919-966-9005, Fax: 919-962-8103, E-mail: microimm@med.unc.edu.

University of North Dakota, Graduate School and Graduate School, Graduate Programs in Medicine, Department of Microbiology and Immunology, Grand Forks, ND 58202. Offers MS, PhD. *Faculty:* 6 full-time (2 women). *Students:* 10 full-time (7 women); includes 2 minority (1 American Indian or Alaska Native, non-Hispanic/Latino; 1 Asian, non-Hispanic/Latino), 2 international. Average age 27. 13 applicants, 23% accepted, 3 enrolled. In 2010, 2 master's, 1 doctorate awarded. *Degree requirements:* For master's, comprehensive exam, thesis or alternative; for doctorate, comprehensive exam, thesis/dissertation, final examination. *Entrance requirements:* For master's and doctorate, GRE General Test, minimum GPA of 3.0. Additional exam requirements/recommendations for international students: Required—TOEFL (minimum score 550 paper-based; 213 computer-based; 79 iBT), IELTS (minimum score 6.5). *Application deadline:* For fall admission, 8/1 priority date for domestic students, 5/1 priority date for international students; for spring admission, 12/1 priority date for domestic students, 9/1 priority date for international students. Applications are processed on a rolling basis. Application fee: $35. Electronic applications accepted. *Expenses:* Tuition, state resident: full-time $5857; part-time $306.74 per credit. Tuition, nonresident: full-time $15,666; part-time $729.77 per credit. Required fees: $53.42 per credit. Tuition and fees vary according to course load, program and reciprocity agreements. *Financial support:* In 2010–11, 10 students received support, including 5 research assistantships with full and partial tuition reimbursements available (averaging $13,997 per year), 5 teaching assistantships with full and partial tuition reimbursements available (averaging $13,997 per year); fellowships with full and partial tuition reimbursements available, Federal Work-Study, institutionally sponsored loans, scholarships/grants, health care benefits, tuition waivers (full and partial), and unspecified assistantships also available. Support available to part-time students. Financial award application deadline: 3/15; financial award applicants required to submit FAFSA. *Faculty research:* Genetic and immunological aspects of a murine model of human multiple sclerosis, termination of DNA replication, cell division in bacteria, yersinia pestis. Total annual research expenditures: $423,552. *Unit head:* Dr. Ann Flower, Graduate Director, 701-777-2214, Fax: 701-777-3527, E-mail: aflower@medicine.nodak.edu. *Application contact:* Matt Anderson, Admissions Specialist, 701-777-2947, Fax: 701-777-3619, E-mail: matthew.anderson@gradschool.und.edu.

University of North Texas Health Science Center at Fort Worth, Graduate School of Biomedical Sciences, Fort Worth, TX 76107-2699. Offers anatomy and cell biology (MS, PhD); biochemistry and molecular biology (MS, PhD); biomedical sciences (MS, PhD); biotechnology (MS); forensic genetics (MS); integrative physiology (MS, PhD); medical science (MS); microbiology and immunology (MS, PhD); pharmacology (MS, PhD); science education (MS); DO/MS; DO/PhD. Terminal master's awarded for partial completion of doctoral program. *Degree requirements:* For master's, thesis; for doctorate, thesis/dissertation. *Entrance requirements:* For master's and doctorate, GRE General Test. Additional exam requirements/recommendations for international students: Required—TOEFL. *Expenses:* Contact institution. *Faculty research:* Alzheimer's disease, aging, eye diseases, cancer, cardiovascular disease.

University of Oklahoma Health Sciences Center, College of Medicine and Graduate College, Graduate Programs in Medicine, Department of Microbiology and Immunology, Oklahoma City, OK 73190. Offers immunology (MS, PhD); microbiology (MS, PhD). Part-time programs available. Terminal master's awarded for partial completion of doctoral program. *Degree requirements:* For master's, thesis or alternative; for doctorate, one foreign language, thesis/dissertation. *Entrance requirements:* For doctorate, GRE General Test, 3 letters of recommendation. Additional exam requirements/recommendations for international students: Required—TOEFL.

Immunology

University of Oklahoma Health Sciences Center *(continued)*
Faculty research: Molecular genetics, pathogenesis, streptococcal infections, gram-positive virulence, monoclonal antibodies.

University of Ottawa, Faculty of Graduate and Postdoctoral Studies, Faculty of Medicine, Department of Biochemistry, Microbiology and Immunology, Ottawa, ON K1N 6N5, Canada. Offers biochemistry (M Sc, PhD); microbiology and immunology (M Sc, PhD). *Degree requirements:* For master's, thesis; for doctorate, comprehensive exam, thesis/dissertation, seminar. *Entrance requirements:* For master's, honors degree or equivalent, minimum B average; for doctorate, master's degree, minimum B+ average. Electronic applications accepted. *Faculty research:* General biochemistry, molecular biology, microbiology, host biology, nutrition and metabolism.

University of Pennsylvania, Perelman School of Medicine, Biomedical Graduate Studies, Graduate Group in Immunology, Philadelphia, PA 19104. Offers PhD, MD/PhD, VMD/PhD. *Faculty:* 108. *Students:* 71 full-time (44 women); includes 3 Black or African American, non-Hispanic/Latino; 1 American Indian or Alaska Native, non-Hispanic/Latino; 12 Asian, non-Hispanic/Latino; 2 Hispanic/Latino, 4 international. 133 applicants, 20% accepted, 9 enrolled. In 2010, 13 doctorates awarded. *Degree requirements:* For doctorate, thesis/dissertation, 2 preliminary exams. *Entrance requirements:* For doctorate, GRE General Test, undergraduate major in natural or physical science. Additional exam requirements/recommendations for international students: Required—TOEFL. *Application deadline:* For fall admission, 12/8 priority date for domestic students, 12/8 for international students. Applications are processed on a rolling basis. Application fee: $70. Electronic applications accepted. *Expenses:* Tuition: Full-time $25,660; part-time $4758 per course. Required fees: $2152; $270 per course. Tuition and fees vary according to course load, degree level and program. *Financial support:* In 2010–11, 71 students received support; fellowships, research assistantships, scholarships/grants, traineeships, and unspecified assistantships available. *Faculty research:* Immunoglobulin structure and function, cell surface receptors, lymphocyte functional transplantation immunology, cellular immunology, molecular biology of immunoglobulins. *Unit head:* Dr. Steven L. Reiner, Chairman. *Application contact:* Timothy Johnson, Graduate Coordinator, 215-573-4394, E-mail: timjohns@mail.med.upenn.edu.

University of Pittsburgh, School of Medicine, Graduate Programs in Medicine, Program in Immunology, Pittsburgh, PA 15260. Offers MS, PhD. *Faculty:* 52 full-time (17 women). *Students:* 45 full-time (26 women); includes 2 Black or African American, non-Hispanic/Latino; 4 Asian, non-Hispanic/Latino; 1 Hispanic/Latino, 18 international. Average age 27. 486 applicants, 14% accepted, 28 enrolled. In 2010, 8 doctorates awarded. *Degree requirements:* For doctorate, comprehensive exam, thesis/dissertation. *Entrance requirements:* For doctorate, GRE General Test, GRE Subject Test, minimum QPA of 3.0. Additional exam requirements/recommendations for international students: Required—TOEFL (minimum score 600 paper-based; 100 iBT), IELTS (minimum score 7). *Application deadline:* For fall admission, 12/15 priority date for domestic and international students. Application fee: $50. Electronic applications accepted. *Expenses:* Tuition, state resident: full-time $17,304; part-time $701 per credit. Tuition, nonresident: full-time $29,554; part-time $1210 per credit. Required fees: $740; $214 per term. Tuition and fees vary according to program. *Financial support:* In 2010–11, 45 research assistantships with full tuition reimbursements (averaging $25,500 per year) were awarded; institutionally sponsored loans, scholarships/grants, traineeships, health care benefits, and unspecified assistantships also available. *Faculty research:* Human T-cell biology, opportunistic infections associated with AIDS, autoimmunity, immunoglobin gene expression, tumor immunology. *Unit head:* Dr. Lawrence Kane, Graduate Program Director, 412-648-8947, Fax: 412-383-8096, E-mail: lkane@pitt.edu. *Application contact:* Graduate Studies Administrator, 412-648-8957, Fax: 412-648-1007, E-mail: gradstudies@medschool.pitt.edu.

University of Prince Edward Island, Atlantic Veterinary College, Graduate Program in Veterinary Medicine, Charlottetown, PE C1A 4P3, Canada. Offers anatomy (M Sc, PhD); bacteriology (M Sc, PhD); clinical pharmacology (M Sc, PhD); clinical sciences (M Sc, PhD); epidemiology (M Sc, PhD), including reproduction; fish health (M Sc, PhD); food animal nutrition (M Sc, PhD); immunology (M Sc, PhD); microanatomy (M Sc, PhD); parasitology (M Sc, PhD); pathology (M Sc, PhD); pharmacology (M Sc, PhD); physiology (M Sc, PhD); toxicology (M Sc, PhD); veterinary science (M Vet Sc); virology (M Sc, PhD). Part-time programs available. *Degree requirements:* For master's, thesis; for doctorate, thesis/dissertation. *Entrance requirements:* For master's, DVM, B Sc honors degree, or equivalent; for doctorate, M Sc. Additional exam requirements/recommendations for international students: Required—TOEFL (minimum score 550 paper-based; 213 computer-based; 80 iBT). *Expenses:* Contact institution. *Faculty research:* Animal health management, infectious diseases, fin fish and shellfish health, basic biomedical sciences, ecosystem health.

University of Rochester, School of Medicine and Dentistry, Graduate Programs in Medicine and Dentistry, Department of Microbiology and Immunology, Program in Microbiology and Immunology, Rochester, NY 14627.

University of Saskatchewan, College of Medicine, Department of Microbiology and Immunology, Saskatoon, SK S7N 5A2, Canada. Offers M Sc, PhD. *Degree requirements:* For master's, thesis; for doctorate, thesis/dissertation. *Entrance requirements:* Additional exam requirements/recommendations for international students: Required—TOEFL.

The University of South Dakota, School of Medicine and Health Sciences and Graduate School, Biomedical Sciences Graduate Program, Molecular Microbiology and Immunology Group, Vermillion, SD 57069-2390. Offers MS, PhD. Terminal master's awarded for partial completion of doctoral program. *Degree requirements:* For master's, thesis; for doctorate, comprehensive exam, thesis/dissertation. *Entrance requirements:* For master's and doctorate, GRE General Test, minimum GPA of 3.0. Additional exam requirements/recommendations for international students: Required—TOEFL (minimum score 550 paper-based; 213 computer-based; 80 iBT), IELTS (minimum score 6). Electronic applications accepted. *Expenses:* Contact institution. *Faculty research:* Structure-function membranes, plasmids, immunology, virology, pathogenesis.

University of Southern California, Keck School of Medicine and Graduate School, Graduate Programs in Medicine, Department of Molecular Microbiology and Immunology, Los Angeles, CA 90089. Offers MS, PhD. Part-time programs available. *Faculty:* 16 full-time (4 women), 1 (woman) part-time/adjunct. *Students:* 20 full-time (11 women); includes 3 Asian, non-Hispanic/Latino, 11 international. Average age 25. 24 applicants, 67% accepted, 10 enrolled. In 2010, 7 master's, 1 doctorate awarded. Terminal master's awarded for partial completion of doctoral program. *Degree requirements:* For master's, comprehensive exam (for some programs), thesis optional; for doctorate, comprehensive exam, thesis/dissertation. *Entrance requirements:* For master's, GRE General Test, minimum GPA of 3.0; for doctorate, GRE General Test, GRE Subject Test, minimum GPA of 3.0. Additional exam requirements/recommendations for international students: Required—TOEFL (minimum score 100 iBT). *Application deadline:* Applications are processed on a rolling basis. Application fee: $85. Electronic applications accepted. *Expenses:* Tuition: Full-time $31,240; part-time $1420 per unit. Required fees: $600. One-time fee: $35 full-time. Full-time tuition and fees vary according to degree level and program. *Financial support:* In 2010–11, 3 students received support, including 1 fellowship with full tuition reimbursement available (averaging $27,600 per year), 6 research assistantships with full tuition reimbursements available (averaging $27,600 per year), 1 teaching assistantship with full tuition reimbursement available (averaging $27,600 per year); Federal Work-Study, institutionally sponsored loans, scholarships/grants, health care benefits, and unspecified assistantships also available. Financial award application deadline: 5/3; financial award applicants required to submit FAFSA. *Faculty research:* Animal virology, microbial genetics, molecular and cellular immunology, cellular differentiation control of protein synthesis. *Unit head:* Dr. Jae U. Jung, Professor and Chair, 323-442-1713, Fax: 323-442-1721, E-mail: jaeujung@usc.edu. *Application contact:* Silvina V. Campos, Administrative Assistant II, 323-442-1713, Fax: 323-442-1721, E-mail: scampos@usc.edu.

University of Southern Maine, School of Applied Science, Engineering, and Technology, Program in Applied Medical Sciences, Portland, ME 04104-9300. Offers MS. Part-time programs available. *Degree requirements:* For master's, thesis. *Entrance requirements:* For master's, GRE General Test, minimum GPA of 3.0. Additional exam requirements/recommendations for international students: Required—TOEFL. Electronic applications accepted. *Faculty research:* Flow cytometry, cancer, epidemiology, monoclonal antibodies, DNA diagnostics.

The University of Texas Health Science Center at Houston, Graduate School of Biomedical Sciences, Program in Immunology, Houston, TX 77225-0036. Offers MS, PhD, MD/PhD. Terminal master's awarded for partial completion of doctoral program. *Degree requirements:* For master's, thesis; for doctorate, thesis/dissertation. *Entrance requirements:* For master's and doctorate, GRE General Test. Additional exam requirements/recommendations for international students: Required—TOEFL. Electronic applications accepted. *Faculty research:* Cancer immunology, molecular immunology, immune cell signaling, immune disease, immune system development.

The University of Texas Health Science Center at San Antonio, Graduate School of Biomedical Sciences, Department of Microbiology and Immunology, San Antonio, TX 78229-3900. Offers PhD. *Faculty:* 19 full-time (5 women). *Students:* 38 full-time (22 women); includes 3 Black or African American, non-Hispanic/Latino; 10 Hispanic/Latino, 7 international. Average age 30. In 2010, 10 doctorates awarded. *Degree requirements:* For doctorate, comprehensive exam, thesis/dissertation. *Entrance requirements:* For doctorate, GRE General Test. Additional exam requirements/recommendations for international students: Required—TOEFL (minimum score 560 paper-based; 220 computer-based; 68 iBT). *Application deadline:* For fall admission, 1/15 priority date for domestic and international students. Applications are processed on a rolling basis. Electronic applications accepted. *Expenses:* Tuition, state resident: full-time $3072; part-time $128 per credit hour. Tuition, nonresident: full-time $11,928; part-time $497 per credit hour. Required fees: $1078; $1078 per year. One-time fee: $60. *Financial support:* In 2010–11, 38 teaching assistantships (averaging $26,000 per year) were awarded; fellowships, research assistantships also available. Financial award application deadline: 6/30; financial award applicants required to submit FAFSA. *Faculty research:* Molecular immunology, mechanisms of microbial pathogenesis, molecular genetics, vaccine and immunodiagnostic development. Total annual research expenditures: $6.8 million. *Unit head:* Joel B. Baseman, Chairman, 210-567-3939, Fax: 210-567-6491, E-mail: baseman@uthscsa.edu. *Application contact:* Sophia Pina, Assistant Dean, 210-567-3984, Fax: 210-567-3719, E-mail: pina@uthscsa.edu.

The University of Texas Medical Branch, Graduate School of Biomedical Sciences, Program in Microbiology and Immunology, Galveston, TX 77555. Offers MS, PhD. Terminal master's awarded for partial completion of doctoral program. *Degree requirements:* For master's, thesis or alternative; for doctorate, thesis/dissertation. *Entrance requirements:* For doctorate, GRE General Test, minimum GPA of 3.0. Additional exam requirements/recommendations for international students: Required—TOEFL (minimum score 550 paper-based; 213 computer-based). Electronic applications accepted.

The University of Texas Southwestern Medical Center at Dallas, Southwestern Graduate School of Biomedical Sciences, Division of Basic Science, Program in Immunology, Dallas, TX 75390. Offers PhD. *Faculty:* 47 full-time (12 women), 2 part-time/adjunct (0 women). *Students:* 29 full-time (14 women), 1 part-time (0 women); includes 9 minority (1 American Indian or Alaska Native, non-Hispanic/Latino; 4 Asian, non-Hispanic/Latino; 4 Hispanic/Latino), 3 international. Average age 26. In 2010, 6 doctorates awarded. *Degree requirements:* For doctorate, thesis/dissertation, qualifying exam. *Entrance requirements:* For doctorate, GRE General Test, minimum GPA of 3.0. Additional exam requirements/recommendations for international students: Required—TOEFL. *Application deadline:* For fall admission, 12/15 priority date for domestic students. Applications are processed on a rolling basis. Application fee: $0. Electronic applications accepted. *Financial support:* Fellowships, research assistantships available. *Faculty research:* Antibody diversity and idiotype, cytotoxic effector mechanisms, natural killer cells, biology of immunoglobulins, oncogenes. *Unit head:* Dr. Nicolai Van Oers, Chair, 214-648-1236, Fax: 214-648-1902, E-mail: nicolai.vanoers@utsouthwestern.edu. *Application contact:* Dr. Nancy E. Street, Associate Dean, 214-648-6708, Fax: 214-648-2102, E-mail: nancy.street@utsouthwestern.edu.

The University of Toledo, College of Graduate Studies, College of Medicine and Life Sciences, Department of Medical Microbiology and Immunology, Toledo, OH 43606-3390. Offers infection, immunity, and transplantation (MSBS, PhD); MD/PhD. *Faculty:* 13. *Students:* 19 full-time (10 women), 1 part-time (0 women); includes 2 Asian, non-Hispanic/Latino, 12 international. Average age 27. 18 applicants, 67% accepted, 7 enrolled. In 2010, 1 master's, 3 doctorates awarded. Terminal master's awarded for partial completion of doctoral program. *Degree requirements:* For master's, thesis, qualifying exam; for doctorate, thesis/dissertation, qualifying exam. *Entrance requirements:* For master's and doctorate, GRE/MCAT, minimum undergraduate GPA of 3.0, three letters of recommendation, statement of purpose, transcripts from all prior institutions attended. Additional exam requirements/recommendations for international students: Required—TOEFL (minimum score 550 paper-based; 213 computer-based; 80 iBT), IELTS (minimum score 6.5). *Application deadline:* For fall admission, 5/1 priority date for domestic and international students. Applications are processed on a rolling basis. Application fee: $45 ($75 for international students). Electronic applications accepted. *Expenses:* Tuition, state resident: full-time $11,426; part-time $476 per credit hour. Tuition, nonresident: full-time $21,660; part-time $903 per credit hour. One-time fee: $62. *Financial support:* In 2010–11, research assistantships with full tuition reimbursements (averaging $21,180 per year); Federal Work-Study, institutionally sponsored loans, scholarships/grants, tuition waivers (full), and unspecified assistantships also available. *Unit head:* Dr. Akira Takashima, Chair, 419-383-5423, E-mail: akira.takashima@utoledo.edu. *Application contact:* Christine Wile, Admissions Analyst, 419-383-4116, Fax: 419-383-6140, E-mail: christine.wile@utoledo.edu.

University of Toronto, School of Graduate Studies, Life Sciences Division, Department of Immunology, Toronto, ON M5S 1A1, Canada. Offers M Sc, PhD. *Degree requirements:* For master's, thesis, thesis defense; for doctorate, thesis/dissertation, thesis defense. *Entrance requirements:* For master's, resume, 3 letters of reference. Additional exam requirements/recommendations for international students: Required—TOEFL, TWE, GRE.

University of Washington, Graduate School, School of Medicine, Graduate Programs in Medicine, Department of Immunology, Seattle, WA 98195. Offers PhD. *Faculty:* 24 full-time (7 women). *Students:* 39 full-time (19 women); includes 2 Black or African American, non-Hispanic/Latino; 3 Hispanic/Latino, 2 international. Average age 28. 87 applicants, 21% accepted, 8 enrolled. In 2010, 14 doctorates awarded. *Degree requirements:* For doctorate, thesis/dissertation. *Entrance requirements:* For doctorate, GRE General Test, BA or BS in related field. Additional exam requirements/recommendations for international students: Required—TOEFL (minimum score 600 paper-based; 250 computer-based; 100 iBT). *Application deadline:* For fall admission, 12/7 for domestic students, 12/1 for international students. Application fee: $50. Electronic applications accepted. *Financial support:* In 2010–11, 1 student received support, including 15 fellowships with full tuition reimbursements available (averaging $27,348 per year), 24 research assistantships with full tuition reimbursements available (averaging $27,348 per year); scholarships/grants, traineeships, health care benefits, tuition waivers (full), and stipends also available. *Faculty research:* Molecular and cellular immunology, regulation of lymphocyte differentiation and responses, genetics of immune recognition genetics and pathogenesis of autoimmune diseases, signal transduction. Total annual research expenditures: $10.8 million. *Unit head:* Dr. Joan M. Goverman, Professor and Interim Chair, 206-543-1010, Fax: 206-543-1013. *Application contact:* Peggy A. McCune, Training Program Manager, 206-685-3955, Fax: 206-543-1013, E-mail: immgrad@u.washington.edu.

The University of Western Ontario, Faculty of Graduate Studies, Biosciences Division, Department of Microbiology and Immunology, London, ON N6A 5B8, Canada. Offers M Sc, PhD. *Degree requirements:* For master's, thesis, oral and written exam; for doctorate, thesis/dissertation, oral and written exam. *Entrance requirements:* For master's, honors degree or equivalent in microbiology, immunology, or other biological science; minimum B average; for doctorate, M Sc in microbiology and immunology. Additional exam requirements/recommendations for international students: Required—TOEFL. *Faculty research:* Virology, molecular pathogenesis, cellular immunology, molecular biology.

Vanderbilt University, Graduate School and School of Medicine, Department of Microbiology and Immunology, Nashville, TN 37240-1001. Offers MS, PhD, MD/PhD. *Faculty:* 12 full-time (2 women). *Students:* 39 full-time (18 women); includes 3 Black or African American, non-Hispanic/Latino; 2 Asian, non-Hispanic/Latino; 2 Hispanic/Latino. Average age 28. In 2010, 1 master's, 4 doctorates awarded. Terminal master's awarded for partial completion of doctoral program. *Degree requirements:* For master's, thesis; for doctorate, thesis/dissertation, final and qualifying exams. *Entrance requirements:* For master's and doctorate, GRE General Test, GRE Subject Test (recommended). Additional exam requirements/recommendations for international students: Required—TOEFL (minimum score 570 paper-based; 230 computer-based; 88 iBT). *Application deadline:* For fall admission, 1/15 for domestic and international students. Application fee: $0. Electronic applications accepted. *Financial support:* Fellowships with full tuition reimbursements, research assistantships with full tuition reimbursements, Federal Work-Study, institutionally sponsored loans, scholarships/grants, traineeships, health care benefits, and tuition waivers (partial) available. Financial award application deadline: 1/15; financial award applicants required to submit CSS PROFILE or FAFSA. *Faculty research:* Cellular and molecular microbiology, viruses, genes, cancer, molecular pathogenesis of microbial diseases, immunobiology. *Unit head:* Dr. Jacek Hawiger, Chair, 615-343-8280, E-mail: jacek.hawiger@vanderbilt.edu. *Application contact:* Dr. Christopher R. Aiken, Director of Graduate Studies, 615-322-2087, E-mail: chris.aiken@vanderbilt.edu.

Virginia Commonwealth University, Medical College of Virginia-Professional Programs, School of Medicine, School of Medicine Graduate Programs, Department of Microbiology and Immunology, Richmond, VA 23284-9005. Offers microbiology and immunology (MS, PhD); MD/PhD. *Faculty:* 35 full-time (7 women). *Students:* 54 full-time (39 women), 5 part-time (3 women); includes 13 minority (3 Black or African American, non-Hispanic/Latino; 1 American Indian or Alaska Native, non-Hispanic/Latino; 5 Asian, non-Hispanic/Latino; 3 Hispanic/Latino; 1 Two or more races, non-Hispanic/Latino), 11 international. 103 applicants, 31% accepted, 16 enrolled. In 2010, 3 master's, 8 doctorates awarded. *Degree requirements:* For master's, thesis; for doctorate, thesis/dissertation, comprehensive oral and written exams. *Entrance requirements:* For master's and doctorate, GRE General Test or MCAT. Additional exam requirements/recommendations for international students: Required—TOEFL (minimum score 600 paper-based; 250 computer-based; 100 iBT). *Application deadline:* For fall admission, 12/15 priority date for domestic students. Application fee: $50. Electronic applications accepted. *Expenses:* Tuition, state resident: full-time $4308; part-time $479 per credit hour. Tuition, nonresident: full-time $8942; part-time $994 per credit hour. Required fees: $2000; $85 per credit hour. Tuition and fees vary according to course level, course load, degree level, campus/location and program. *Financial support:* Fellowships, research assistantships, teaching assistantships available. *Faculty research:* Microbial physiology and genetics, molecular biology, crystallography of biological molecules, antibiotics and chemotherapy, membrane transport. *Unit head:* Dr. Dennis E. Ohman, Chair, 804-828-9728, Fax: 804-828-9946, E-mail: deohman@vcu.edu. *Application contact:* Dr. Guy A. Cabral, Chair, Graduate Program Committee, 804-828-2306, E-mail: gacabral@vcu.edu.

Wake Forest University, School of Medicine and Graduate School of Arts and Sciences, Graduate Programs in Medicine, Department of Microbiology and Immunology, Winston-Salem, NC 27109. Offers PhD, MD/PhD. *Degree requirements:* For doctorate, thesis/dissertation. *Entrance requirements:* For doctorate, GRE General Test. Additional exam requirements/recommendations for international students: Required—TOEFL. Electronic applications accepted. *Faculty research:* Molecular immunology, bacterial pathogenesis and molecular genetics, viral pathogenesis, regulation of mRNA metabolism, leukocyte biology.

Washington University in St. Louis, Graduate School of Arts and Sciences, Division of Biology and Biomedical Sciences, Program in Immunology, St. Louis, MO 63130-4899. Offers PhD. *Degree requirements:* For doctorate, thesis/dissertation. *Entrance requirements:* For doctorate, GRE General Test, GRE Subject Test. Electronic applications accepted.

Wayne State University, School of Medicine, Department of Immunology and Microbiology, Detroit, MI 48202. Offers MS, PhD, MD/PhD. *Faculty:* 4 full-time (1 woman). *Students:* 15 full-time (6 women), 2 part-time (both women); includes 1 minority (Hispanic/Latino), 4 international. Average age 26. 17 applicants, 24% accepted, 3 enrolled. In 2010, 1 doctorate awarded. Terminal master's awarded for partial completion of doctoral program. *Degree requirements:* For master's, thesis; for doctorate, thesis/dissertation. *Entrance requirements:* For master's, GRE, minimum GPA of 2.5; for doctorate, GRE, minimum GPA of 3.0. Additional exam requirements/recommendations for international students: Required—TOEFL (minimum score 550 paper-based; 213 computer-based); Recommended—TWE (minimum score 6). *Application deadline:* For fall admission, 7/15 for domestic students, 6/1 for international students; for winter admission, 10/1 for international students; for spring admission, 2/1 for international students. Applications are processed on a rolling basis. Application fee: $30 ($50 for international students). Electronic applications accepted. *Expenses:* Tuition, state resident: full-time $7662; part-time $478.85 per credit hour. Tuition, nonresident: full-time $16,920; part-time $1057.55 per credit hour. Required fees: $571; $35.70 per credit hour. $188.05 per semester. Tuition and fees vary according to course load and program. *Financial support:* In 2010–11, 1 fellowship with tuition reimbursement (averaging $20,000 per year), 15 research assistantships with tuition reimbursements (averaging $21,454 per year) were awarded; teaching assistantships, career-related internships or fieldwork and Federal Work-Study also available. *Faculty research:* Immune regulation, bacterial pathophysiology, molecular biology/viruses/bacteria, cellular and molecular immunology, microbial pathogenesis. *Unit head:* Dr. Paul Montgomery, Chair, 313-577-1591, Fax: 313-577-1155, E-mail: aa2411@wayne.edu. *Application contact:* Harley Tse, Associate Professor, 313-577-1564, Fax: 313-577-1155, E-mail: ad6056@wayne.edu.

West Virginia University, Davis College of Agriculture, Forestry and Consumer Sciences, Interdisciplinary Program in Genetics and Developmental Biology, Morgantown, WV 26506. Offers animal breeding (MS, PhD); biochemical and molecular genetics (MS, PhD); cytogenetics (MS, PhD); descriptive embryology (MS, PhD); developmental genetics (MS); experimental morphogenesis/teratology (MS); human genetics (MS, PhD); immunogenetics (MS, PhD); life cycles of animals and plants (MS, PhD); molecular aspects of development (MS, PhD); mutagenesis (MS, PhD); oncology (MS, PhD); plant genetics (MS, PhD); population and quantitative genetics (MS, PhD); regeneration (MS, PhD); teratology (PhD); toxicology (MS, PhD). *Degree requirements:* For master's, thesis; for doctorate, comprehensive exam, thesis/dissertation. *Entrance requirements:* For master's, GRE or MCAT, minimum GPA of 2.75. Additional exam requirements/recommendations for international students: Required—TOEFL.

West Virginia University, School of Medicine, Graduate Programs at the Health Sciences Center, Interdisciplinary Graduate Programs in Biomedical Sciences, Program in Immunology and Microbial Pathogenesis, Morgantown, WV 26506. Offers MS, PhD, MD/PhD. *Degree requirements:* For doctorate, comprehensive exam, thesis/dissertation. *Entrance requirements:* For doctorate, GRE General Test, minimum GPA of 3.0. Additional exam requirements/recommendations for international students: Required—TOEFL. Electronic applications accepted. *Faculty research:* Regulation of signal transduction in immune responses, immune responses in bacterial and viral diseases, peptide and DNA vaccines for contraception, inflammatory bowel disease, physiology of pathogenic microbes.

Wright State University, School of Graduate Studies, College of Science and Mathematics, Program in Microbiology and Immunology, Dayton, OH 45435. Offers MS. Part-time programs available. *Degree requirements:* For master's, thesis. *Entrance requirements:* Additional exam requirements/recommendations for international students: Required—TOEFL. *Faculty research:* Reproductive immunology, viral pathogenesis, virus-host cell interactions.

Yale University, Graduate School of Arts and Sciences, Department of Immunobiology, New Haven, CT 06520. Offers PhD. *Degree requirements:* For doctorate, thesis/dissertation. *Entrance requirements:* For doctorate, GRE General Test.

Yale University, School of Medicine and Graduate School of Arts and Sciences, Combined Program in Biological and Biomedical Sciences (BBS), Immunology Track, New Haven, CT 06520. Offers PhD, MD/PhD. *Degree requirements:* For doctorate, thesis/dissertation. *Entrance requirements:* For doctorate, GRE General Test. Additional exam requirements/recommendations for international students: Required—TOEFL. Electronic applications accepted.

Infectious Diseases

Cornell University, Graduate School, Graduate Fields of Comparative Biomedical Sciences, Field of Comparative Biomedical Sciences, Ithaca, NY 14853-0001. Offers cellular and molecular medicine (MS, PhD); developmental and reproductive biology (MS, PhD); infectious diseases (MS, PhD); population medicine and epidemiology (MS, PhD); structural and functional biology (MS, PhD). *Faculty:* 94 full-time (27 women). *Students:* 47 full-time (33 women); includes 2 Black or African American, non-Hispanic/Latino; 1 Asian, non-Hispanic/Latino, 23 international. Average age 30. 31 applicants, 48% accepted, 14 enrolled. In 2010, 11 doctorates awarded. *Degree requirements:* For master's, thesis; for doctorate, comprehensive exam, thesis/dissertation. *Entrance requirements:* For master's and doctorate, GRE General Test, 2 letters of recommendation. Additional exam requirements/recommendations for international students: Required—TOEFL (minimum score 550 paper-based; 213 computer-based; 77 iBT). *Application deadline:* For fall admission, 12/15 for domestic students. Application fee: $70. Electronic applications accepted. *Expenses:* Tuition: Full-time $29,500. Required fees: $76. Tuition and fees vary according to degree level and program. *Financial support:* In 2010–11, 18 fellowships with full tuition reimbursements, 25 research assistantships with full tuition reimbursements were awarded; teaching assistantships with full tuition reimbursements, institutionally sponsored loans, scholarships/grants, health care benefits, tuition waivers (full and partial), and unspecified assistantships also available. Financial award applicants required to submit FAFSA. *Faculty research:* Receptors and signal transduction, viral and bacterial infectious diseases, tumor metastasis, clinical sciences/nutritional disease, developmental/neurological disorders. *Unit head:* Director of Graduate Studies, 607-253-3276, Fax: 607-253-3756. *Application contact:* Graduate Field Assistant, 607-253-3276, Fax: 607-253-3756, E-mail: graduate_edcvm@cornell.edu.

George Mason University, College of Science, Department of Molecular and Microbiology, Fairfax, VA 22030. Offers biology (MS), including bioinformatics and computational biology, general biology, microbiology and infectious disease, molecular biology, systematics and evolutionary biology; biosciences (PhD). *Faculty:* 10 full-time (5 women). *Students:* 12 full-time (6 women), 63 part-time (36 women); includes 2 Black or African American, non-Hispanic/Latino; 1 American Indian or Alaska Native, non-Hispanic/Latino; 8 Asian, non-Hispanic/Latino; 1 Hispanic/Latino, 16 international. Average age 31. 98 applicants, 37% accepted, 19 enrolled. In 2010, 7 master's, 7 doctorates awarded. *Entrance requirements:* Additional exam requirements/recommendations for international students: Required—TOEFL (minimum score 570 paper-based; 230 computer-based; 88 iBT). Application fee: $100. *Expenses:* Tuition, state resident: full-time $8192; part-time $440 per credit hour. Tuition, nonresident: full-time $22,952; part-time $1055 per credit hour. Required fees: $2364; $99 per credit hour. *Financial support:* In 2010–11, 32 students received support, including 3 fellowships (averaging $18,000 per year), 6 research assistantships (averaging $14,073 per year), 23 teaching assistantships (averaging $12,194 per year); career-related internships or fieldwork, Federal Work-Study, scholarships/grants, unspecified assistantships, and health care benefits (full-time research or teaching assistantship recipients) also available. Financial award applicants required to submit FAFSA. Total annual research expenditures: $457,760. *Unit head:* Dr. James Willett, Director, 703-993-8311, Fax: 703-993-8976, E-mail: jwillett@gmu.edu. *Application contact:* Daniel Cox, Associate Dean for Graduate Programs, 703-993-4971, Fax: 703-993-4325, E-mail: dcox5@gmu.edu.

Georgetown University, Graduate School of Arts and Sciences, Programs in Biomedical Sciences, Department of Microbiology and Immunology, Washington, DC 20057. Offers biohazardous threat agents and emerging infectious diseases (MS); general microbiology and immunology (MS); global infectious diseases (PhD); microbiology and immunology research (PhD); science policy and advocacy (MS). Part-time programs available. *Degree requirements:* For master's, 30 credit hours of coursework; for doctorate, comprehensive exam, thesis/dissertation. *Entrance requirements:* For master's, GRE General Test, 3 letters of reference, bachelor's degree in related field; for doctorate, GRE General Test, 3 letters of reference, MS/BS in related field. Additional exam requirements/recommendations for international students: Required—TOEFL (minimum score 505 paper-based; 213 computer-based). Electronic applications accepted. *Faculty research:* Pathogenesis and basic biology of the fungus Candida albicans, molecular biology of viral immunopathological mechanisms in Multiple Sclerosis.

The George Washington University, School of Public Health and Health Services, Department of Epidemiology and Biostatistics, Washington, DC 20052. Offers biostatistics (MPH); epidemiology (MPH); microbiology and emerging infectious diseases (MSPH). *Faculty:* 19 full-time (11 women), 28 part-time/adjunct (17 women). *Students:* 59 full-time (51 women), 49 part-time (34 women); includes 16 Black or African American, non-Hispanic/Latino; 1 American Indian or Alaska Native, non-Hispanic/Latino; 25 Asian, non-Hispanic/Latino; 6 Hispanic/Latino; 3 Two or more races, non-Hispanic/Latino, 9 international. Average age 28. 193 applicants, 74% accepted, 39 enrolled. In 2010, 43 master's awarded. *Degree requirements:* For master's, case study or special project. *Entrance requirements:* For master's, GMAT, GRE General Test, or MCAT. Additional exam requirements/recommendations for international students: Required—TOEFL. *Application deadline:* For fall admission, 4/15 priority date for domestic students, 4/15 for international students; for spring admission, 11/1 for domestic and international students. Applications are processed on a rolling basis. Application fee: $75. *Financial support:* In 2010–11, 6 students received support. Tuition waivers available. Financial award application deadline: 2/15. *Unit head:* Dr. Alan E. Greenberg, Chair, 202-994-0612, E-mail: aeg1@gwu.edu. *Application contact:* Jane Smith, Director of Admissions, 202-994-0248, Fax: 202-994-1860, E-mail: sphhsinfo@gwumc.edu.

Harvard University, Harvard School of Public Health, Department of Immunology and Infectious Diseases, Boston, MA 02115-6096. Offers PhD, SD. Part-time programs available.

Infectious Diseases

Harvard University (continued)

Faculty: 31 full-time (9 women), 5 part-time/adjunct (0 women). *Students:* 8 applicants, 0% accepted, 0 enrolled. *Degree requirements:* For doctorate, thesis/dissertation, qualifying exam. *Entrance requirements:* For doctorate, GRE. Additional exam requirements/recommendations for international students: Required—TOEFL (minimum score 600 paper-based; 240 computer-based; 100 iBT); Recommended—IELTS (minimum score 7). *Application deadline:* For fall admission, 12/15 for domestic and international students. Application fee: $115. Electronic applications accepted. *Expenses:* Tuition: Full-time $34,976. Required fees: $1166. Full-time tuition and fees vary according to program. *Financial support:* Fellowships, research assistantships, Federal Work-Study, scholarships/grants, traineeships, tuition waivers (partial), and unspecified assistantships available. Financial award application deadline: 2/8; financial award applicants required to submit FAFSA. *Faculty research:* Infectious disease epidemiology and tropical public health, vector biology, ecology and control, virology. *Unit head:* Dr. Dyann F. Wirth, Chair, 617-432-2234, Fax: 617-739-8348, E-mail: rkenwort@hsph.harvard.edu. *Application contact:* Vincent W. James, Director of Admissions, 617-432-1031, Fax: 617-432-7080, E-mail: admissions@hsph.harvard.edu.

The Johns Hopkins University, Bloomberg School of Public Health, Department of Epidemiology, Baltimore, MD 21205. Offers cancer epidemiology (MHS, Sc M, PhD, Sc D); cardiovascular disease epidemiology (MHS, Sc M, PhD, Sc D); clinical epidemiology (MHS, Sc M, PhD, Sc D); clinical trials (PhD, Sc D); epidemiology (Dr PH); epidemiology (general) (MHS, Sc M, PhD, Sc D); epidemiology of aging (MHS, Sc M, PhD, Sc D); human genetics/genetic epidemiology (MHS, Sc M, PhD, Sc D); infectious disease epidemiology (MHS, Sc M, PhD, Sc D); occupational/environmental epidemiology (MHS, Sc M, PhD, Sc D). Part-time programs available. *Faculty:* 80 full-time (44 women), 82 part-time/adjunct (36 women). *Students:* 143 full-time (108 women), 24 part-time (17 women); includes 43 minority (14 Black or African American, non-Hispanic/Latino; 1 American Indian or Alaska Native, non-Hispanic/Latino; 19 Asian, non-Hispanic/Latino; 3 Hispanic/Latino; 6 Two or more races, non-Hispanic/Latino), 36 international. Average age 30. 263 applicants, 41% accepted, 52 enrolled. In 2010, 30 master's, 33 doctorates awarded. *Degree requirements:* For master's, comprehensive exam, thesis, 1 year full-time residency; for doctorate, comprehensive exam, thesis/dissertation, 2 years full-time residency, oral and written exams, student teaching. *Entrance requirements:* For master's, GRE General Test or MCAT, 3 letters of recommendation, curriculum vitae; for doctorate, GRE General Test, minimum 1 year of work experience, 3 letters of recommendation, curriculum vitae, academic records from all schools. Additional exam requirements/recommendations for international students: Required—TOEFL (minimum score 600 paper-based; 250 computer-based; 100 iBT); Recommended—IELTS (minimum score 7.5), TWE. *Application deadline:* For fall admission, 12/1 priority date for domestic students. Applications are processed on a rolling basis. Application fee: $45. Electronic applications accepted. *Financial support:* In 2010–11, 2 fellowships (averaging $28,859 per year) were awarded; Federal Work-Study, institutionally sponsored loans, scholarships/grants, traineeships, tuition waivers (partial), and stipends also available. Support available to part-time students. Financial award application deadline: 3/15; financial award applicants required to submit FAFSA. *Faculty research:* Cancer and congenital malformations, nutritional epidemiology, AIDS, tuberculosis, cardiovascular disease, risk assessment. Total annual research expenditures: $70.1 million. *Unit head:* Dr. David D. Celentano, Chair, 410-955-3286, Fax: 410-955-0863, E-mail: dcelenta@jhsph.edu. *Application contact:* Frances S. Burman, Academic Program Manager, 410-955-3926, Fax: 410-955-0863, E-mail: fburman@jhsph.edu.

Loyola University Chicago, Graduate School, Marcella Niehoff School of Nursing, Population-Based Infection Control and Environmental Safety Program, Chicago, IL 60660. Offers population based infection control (MSN, Certificate). Part-time and evening/weekend programs available. *Students:* 20 part-time (19 women); includes 3 minority (2 Black or African American, non-Hispanic/Latino; 1 Hispanic/Latino). Average age 42. 5 applicants, 100% accepted, 3 enrolled. In 2010, 2 master's awarded. *Entrance requirements:* For master's, Illinois nursing license, 3 letters of recommendation, minimum nursing GPA of 3.0, 1000 hours experience before starting clinical. Application fee: $50. *Expenses:* Tuition: Full-time $14,940; part-time $830 per credit hour. Required fees: $87 per semester. Part-time tuition and fees vary according to course load and program. *Financial support:* Traineeships available. *Unit head:* Dr. Ida Androwich, Professor, 708-216-9276, Fax: 708-216-9555, E-mail: iandrow@luc.edu. *Application contact:* Amy Weatherford, Enrollment Advisor—School of Nursing, 773-508-3249, Fax: 773-508-3241, E-mail: aweatherford@luc.edu.

Loyola University Chicago, Graduate School, Program in Infectious Disease and Immunology, Chicago, IL 60660. Offers MS. *Faculty:* 31 full-time (7 women). *Students:* 4 full-time (3 women). Average age 22. 13 applicants, 54% accepted, 4 enrolled. *Degree requirements:* For master's, thesis. *Entrance requirements:* For master's, GRE. Additional exam requirements/recommendations for international students: Required—TOEFL. *Application deadline:* Applications are processed on a rolling basis. Application fee: $0. *Expenses:* Tuition: Full-time $14,940; part-time $830 per credit hour. Required fees: $87 per semester. Part-time tuition and fees vary according to course load and program. *Faculty research:* Immunological tolerance and memory, molecular analysis of virus assembly and entry, biofilm mediated interactions, molecular analysis of clinical isolates of C. difficile, immune system development and regulation. *Unit head:* Dr. Katherine L. Knight, Co-Director, 708-216-3385, Fax: 708-216-9574, E-mail: kknight@lumc.edu. *Application contact:* Dr. Paul O'Keefe, Director of Admissions Committee, 708-216-6667, Fax: 707-216-9574, E-mail: pokeefe@lumc.edu.

Montana State University, College of Graduate Studies, College of Agriculture, Department of Immunology and Infectious Diseases, Bozeman, MT 59717. Offers MS, PhD. Part-time programs available. *Faculty:* 12 full-time (2 women), 1 (woman) part-time/adjunct. *Students:* 1 (woman) full-time, 13 part-time (8 women); includes 2 minority (1 American Indian or Alaska Native, non-Hispanic/Latino; 1 Hispanic/Latino), 2 international. Average age 29. 3 applicants, 67% accepted, 2 enrolled. In 2010, 1 doctorate awarded. *Degree requirements:* For master's, comprehensive exam; for doctorate, comprehensive exam, thesis/dissertation. *Entrance requirements:* For master's and doctorate, GRE General Test. Additional exam requirements/recommendations for international students: Required—TOEFL (minimum score 550 paper-based; 213 computer-based). *Application deadline:* For fall admission, 7/15 priority date for domestic students, 5/15 for international students; for spring admission, 12/1 priority date for domestic students, 10/1 priority date for international students. Applications are processed on a rolling basis. Application fee: $30. Electronic applications accepted. *Expenses:* Tuition, state resident: full-time $5554. Tuition, nonresident: full-time $14,646. Required fees: $1233. *Financial support:* In 2010–11, 13 students received support, including 2 fellowships with tuition reimbursements available (averaging $24,000 per year), 13 research assistantships with tuition reimbursements available (averaging $22,000 per year), 5 teaching assistantships with tuition reimbursements available (averaging $7,000 per year); health care benefits and unspecified assistantships also available. Financial award application deadline: 3/1; financial award applicants required to submit FAFSA. *Faculty research:* Immunology, mechanisms of infectious disease pathogenesis, mechanisms of host defense, lymphocyte development, host-pathogen interactions. Total annual research expenditures: $9.5 million. *Unit head:* Dr. Mark G. Quinn, Head, 406-994-5721, Fax: 406-994-4303, E-mail: mquinn@montana.edu. *Application contact:* Dr. Carl A. Fox, Vice Provost for Graduate Education, 406-994-4145, Fax: 406-994-7433, E-mail: gradstudy@montana.edu.

North Carolina State University, College of Veterinary Medicine, Program in Comparative Biomedical Sciences, Raleigh, NC 27695. Offers cell biology (MS, PhD); infectious disease (MS, PhD); pathology (MS, PhD); pharmacology (MS, PhD); population medicine (MS, PhD). Part-time programs available. *Degree requirements:* For master's, thesis; for doctorate, thesis/dissertation. *Entrance requirements:* For master's and doctorate, GRE General Test. Additional exam requirements/recommendations for international students: Required—TOEFL (minimum score 550 paper-based; 213 computer-based). Electronic applications accepted. *Expenses:* Contact institution. *Faculty research:* Infectious diseases, cell biology, pharmacology and toxicology, genomics, pathology and population medicine.

State University of New York Upstate Medical University, College of Graduate Studies, Major Research Areas of the College of Graduate Studies, Syracuse, NY 13210-2334.

Tulane University, School of Public Health and Tropical Medicine, Department of Tropical Medicine, New Orleans, LA 70118-5669. Offers clinical tropical medicine and travelers health (Diploma); parasitology (MSPH, PhD); public health and tropical medicine (MPHTM); vector borne infectious diseases (MS, PhD); MD/PhD. MS and PhD offered through the Graduate School. *Degree requirements:* For master's, thesis; for doctorate, comprehensive exam, thesis/dissertation. *Entrance requirements:* For master's, GRE General Test, minimum B average in undergraduate course work; for doctorate, GRE General Test. Additional exam requirements/recommendations for international students: Required—TOEFL.

Uniformed Services University of the Health Sciences, School of Medicine, Graduate Programs in the Biomedical Sciences and Public Health, Graduate Program in Emerging Infectious Diseases, Bethesda, MD 20814-4799. Offers PhD. *Faculty:* 35 full-time (5 women), 17 part-time/adjunct (6 women). *Students:* 37 full-time (24 women); includes 1 Black or African American, non-Hispanic/Latino; 3 Asian, non-Hispanic/Latino; 1 Hispanic/Latino, 3 international. Average age 26. 43 applicants, 44% accepted, 11 enrolled. In 2010, 7 doctorates awarded. *Degree requirements:* For doctorate, comprehensive exam, thesis/dissertation, qualifying exam. *Entrance requirements:* For doctorate, GRE General Test. Additional exam requirements/recommendations for international students: Required—TOEFL. *Application deadline:* For fall admission, 1/1 priority date for domestic and international students. Applications are processed on a rolling basis. Application fee: $0. Electronic applications accepted. *Financial support:* In 2010–11, fellowships with full tuition reimbursements (averaging $27,000 per year); scholarships/grants, health care benefits, and tuition waivers (full) also available. *Unit head:* Dr. Christopher Broder, Graduate Program Director, 301-295-3401, E-mail: cbroder@usuhs.mil. *Application contact:* Patricia Sinclair, Program Coordinator, 301-295-3400, Fax: 301-295-6772, E-mail: psinclair@usuhs.mil.

See Display on next page and Close-Up on page 345.

Université Laval, Faculty of Medicine, Post-Professional Programs in Medical Studies, Québec, QC G1K 7P4, Canada. Offers anatomy–pathology (DESS); anesthesiology (DESS); cardiology (DESS); care of older people (Diploma); clinical research (DESS); community health (DESS); dermatology (DESS); diagnostic radiology (DESS); emergency medicine (Diploma); family medicine (DESS); general surgery (DESS); geriatrics (DESS); hematology (DESS); internal medicine (DESS); maternal and fetal medicine (Diploma); medical biochemistry (DESS); medical microbiology and infectious diseases (DESS); medical oncology (DESS); nephrology (DESS); neurology (DESS); neurosurgery (DESS); obstetrics and gynecology (DESS); ophthalmology (DESS); orthopedic surgery (DESS); oto-rhino-laryngology (DESS); palliative medicine (Diploma); pediatrics (DESS); plastic surgery (DESS); psychiatry (DESS); pulmonary medicine (DESS); radiology–oncology (DESS); thoracic surgery (DESS); urology (DESS). *Degree requirements:* For other advanced degree, comprehensive exam. *Entrance requirements:* For degree, knowledge of French. Electronic applications accepted.

University of Calgary, Faculty of Medicine and Faculty of Graduate Studies, Department of Microbiology and Infectious Diseases, Calgary, AB T2N 1N4, Canada. Offers M Sc, PhD. *Degree requirements:* For master's, thesis, oral thesis exam; for doctorate, thesis/dissertation, candidacy exam, oral thesis exam. *Entrance requirements:* For master's and doctorate, minimum GPA of 3.2. Additional exam requirements/recommendations for international students: Required—TOEFL (minimum score 580 paper-based; 237 computer-based). Electronic applications accepted. *Faculty research:* Bacteriology, virology, parasitology, immunology.

University of California, Berkeley, Graduate Division, School of Public Health, Group in Epidemiology, Berkeley, CA 94720-1500. Offers epidemiology (MS, PhD); infectious diseases (MPH, PhD). *Accreditation:* CEPH (one or more programs are accredited). *Degree requirements:* For master's, comprehensive exam; for doctorate, thesis/dissertation, oral and written exam. *Entrance requirements:* For master's, GRE General Test, minimum GPA of 3.0; MD, DDS, DVM, or PhD in biomedical science (MPH); for doctorate, GRE General Test, minimum GPA of 3.0.

University of California, Berkeley, Graduate Division, School of Public Health, Group in Infectious Diseases and Immunity, Berkeley, CA 94720-1500. Offers PhD. *Entrance requirements:* For doctorate, GRE General Test, minimum GPA of 3.0, 3 letters of recommendation.

University of Georgia, College of Veterinary Medicine and Graduate School, Graduate Programs in Veterinary Medicine, Department of Infectious Diseases, Athens, GA 30602. Offers MS, PhD. *Faculty:* 24 full-time (8 women), 2 part-time/adjunct (0 women). *Students:* 37 full-time (20 women), 2 part-time (1 woman); includes 2 Black or African American, non-Hispanic/Latino; 1 Asian, non-Hispanic/Latino, 12 international. 36 applicants, 25% accepted, 7 enrolled. In 2010, 1 master's, 2 doctorates awarded. *Degree requirements:* For master's, thesis; for doctorate, one foreign language, thesis/dissertation. *Entrance requirements:* For master's and doctorate, GRE General Test. *Application deadline:* For fall admission, 7/1 priority date for domestic students; for spring admission, 11/15 for domestic students. Application fee: $50. Electronic applications accepted. *Expenses:* Tuition, state resident: full-time $7200; part-time $344 per credit hour. Tuition, nonresident: full-time $21,900; part-time $944 per credit hour. Tuition and fees vary according to course load and program. *Financial support:* Fellowships, research assistantships, teaching assistantships, unspecified assistantships available. *Unit head:* Dr. Frederick Quinn, Head, 706-542-5790, Fax: 706-542-5771, E-mail: fquinn@uga.edu. *Application contact:* Dr. David S. Peterson, Graduate Coordinator, 706-542-5242, Fax: 706-542-5771, E-mail: dspete@uga.edu.

University of Guelph, Ontario Veterinary College and Graduate Studies, Graduate Programs in Veterinary Sciences, Department of Pathobiology, Guelph, ON N1G 2W1, Canada. Offers anatomic pathology (DV Sc, Diploma); clinical pathology (Diploma); comparative pathology (M Sc, PhD); immunology (M Sc, PhD); laboratory animal science (DV Sc); pathology (M Sc, PhD, Diploma); veterinary infectious diseases (M Sc, PhD); zoo animal/wildlife medicine (DV Sc). *Degree requirements:* For master's, thesis; for doctorate, thesis/dissertation. *Entrance requirements:* For master's, DVM with B average or an honours degree in biological sciences; for doctorate, DVM or MSC degree, minimum B+ average. Additional exam requirements/recommendations for international students: Required—TOEFL (minimum score 550 paper-based; 213 computer-based). *Faculty research:* Pathogenesis; diseases of animals, wildlife, fish, and laboratory animals; parasitology; immunology; veterinary infectious diseases; laboratory animal science.

University of Medicine and Dentistry of New Jersey, Graduate School of Biomedical Sciences, Graduate Programs in Biomedical Sciences–Newark, Newark, NJ 07107. Offers biodefense (Certificate); biomedical engineering (PhD); biomedical sciences (multidisciplinary) (PhD); cellular biology, neuroscience and physiology (PhD), including neuroscience, physiology, biophysics, cardiovascular biology, molecular pharmacology, stem cell biology; infection, immunity and inflammation (PhD), including immunology, infectious disease, microbiology, oral biology; molecular biology, genetics and cancer (PhD), including biochemistry, molecular genetics, cancer biology, radiation biology, bioinformatics; neuroscience (Certificate); pharmacological sciences (Certificate); stem cell (Certificate); DMD/PhD; MD/PhD. PhD in biomedical engineering offered jointly with New Jersey Institute of Technology. Part-time and evening/weekend programs available. *Students:* 330 full-time (199 women), 75 part-time (47 women); includes 32 Black or African American, non-Hispanic/Latino; 1 American Indian or Alaska Native, non-Hispanic/Latino; 109 Asian, non-Hispanic/Latino; 16 Hispanic/Latino, 83 international. Average age 28. 611 applicants, 52% accepted, 181 enrolled. In 2010, 24 doctorates, 2 other advanced degrees awarded. Terminal master's awarded for partial completion of doctoral program. *Degree requirements:* For doctorate, thesis/dissertation, qualifying exam. *Entrance requirements:* For doctorate, GRE General Test. Additional exam requirements/recommendations for international students: Required—TOEFL. *Application deadline:* For fall admission, 1/15 for domestic students. Applications are processed on a rolling basis. Application fee: $65. Electronic applica-

---

UNIFORMED SERVICES UNIVERSITY OF THE HEALTH SCIENCES
Graduate Program in Emerging & Infectious Diseases

The **Graduate Program in Emerging & Infectious Diseases (EID)** is designed for applicants who wish to pursue an interdisciplinary program of study leading to the Ph.D. degree and was created for students who are primarily interested in the pathogenesis, host response, and epidemiology of infectious diseases.

Courses are taught by an interdisciplinary EID faculty who hold primary appointments in the Departments of Microbiology and Immunology, Pathology, Preventive Medicine and Biometrics, Pediatrics, and Medicine. Research training emphasizes modern methods in molecular biology and cell biology, as well as interdisciplinary approaches.

Laboratories are available in most areas of study that encompass the interdisciplinary field of emerging infectious diseases, including both basic and medical aspects of bacteriology, bacterial genetics, virology, cellular and molecular immunology, parasitology, pathogenic mechanisms of disease, pathology of infectious disease, and epidemiology of infectious diseases.

Applications are accepted throughout the year. However, for full consideration and evaluation for stipend support, completed applications should be received by January 15 for matriculation in August. Students may be able to transfer into the EID program from other institutions. The maximum number of quarter credit hours is 24. **There is no application fee.**

For more information, contact:
Patricia Sinclair
USUHS, EID Program
4301 Jones Bridge Road
Bethesda, Maryland 20814-4799
301-295-3400
psinclair@usuhs.mil

http://www.usuhs.mil/eid/index.html

---

tions accepted. *Financial support:* In 2010–11, 28 fellowships (averaging $26,000 per year) were awarded; research assistantships, teaching assistantships, career-related internships or fieldwork, Federal Work-Study, institutionally sponsored loans, and tuition waivers (full and partial) also available. Financial award application deadline: 5/1. *Unit head:* Dr. Andrew Thomas, Senior Associate Dean, Graduate School of Biomedical Sciences, 973-972-4511, Fax: 973-972-7148, E-mail: thomas@umdnj.edu. *Application contact:* Dr. B. J. Wagner, 973-972-5335, Fax: 973-972-7148, E-mail: wagner@umdnj.edu.

University of Minnesota, Twin Cities Campus, School of Public Health, Division of Environmental Health Sciences, Area in Environmental Infectious Diseases, Minneapolis, MN 55455-0213. Offers MPH, MS, PhD. *Degree requirements:* For doctorate, thesis/dissertation. *Entrance requirements:* For master's and doctorate, GRE General Test. Electronic applications accepted.

The University of Montana, Graduate School, College of Arts and Sciences, Division of Biological Sciences, Program in Ecology of Infectious Disease, Missoula, MT 59812-0002. Offers PhD.

University of Pittsburgh, Graduate School of Public Health, Department of Infectious Diseases and Microbiology, Pittsburgh, PA 15260. Offers bioscience of infectious diseases (MPH); community and behavioral intervention of infectious diseases (MPH); infectious diseases and microbiology (MS, Dr PH, PhD); LGBT health and wellness (Certificate). Part-time programs available. *Faculty:* 21 full-time (7 women), 3 part-time/adjunct (1 woman). *Students:* 47 full-time (36 women), 12 part-time (5 women); includes 3 Black or African American, non-Hispanic/Latino; 5 Asian, non-Hispanic/Latino; 1 Hispanic/Latino, 8 international. Average age 28. 188 applicants, 58% accepted, 25 enrolled. In 2010, 16 master's, 4 doctorates awarded. Terminal master's awarded for partial completion of doctoral program. *Degree requirements:* For master's, one foreign language, comprehensive exam (for some programs), thesis; for doctorate, one foreign language, comprehensive exam, thesis/dissertation. *Entrance requirements:* For master's and doctorate, GRE General Test, MCAT, or DAT. Additional exam requirements/

recommendations for international students: Required—TOEFL (minimum score 550 paper-based; 213 computer-based; 80 iBT). *Application deadline:* For fall admission, 1/4 priority date for domestic and international students. Applications are processed on a rolling basis. Application fee: $115. Electronic applications accepted. *Expenses:* Tuition, state resident: full-time $17,304; part-time $701 per credit. Tuition, nonresident: full-time $29,554; part-time $1210 per credit. Required fees: $740; $214 per term. Tuition and fees vary according to program. *Financial support:* In 2010–11, 14 students received support, including 1 fellowship (averaging $6,000 per year), 13 research assistantships with full and partial tuition reimbursements available (averaging $8,675 per year). Financial award applicants required to submit FAFSA. *Faculty research:* HIV, Epstein-Barr virus, virology, immunology, malaria. Total annual research expenditures: $14.2 million. *Unit head:* Dr. Charles R. Rinaldo, Chairman, 412-624-3928, Fax: 412-624-4953, E-mail: rinaldo@pitt.edu. *Application contact:* Dr. Jeremy Martinson, Assistant Professor, 412-624-5646, Fax: 412-383-8926, E-mail: jmartins@pitt.edu.

The University of Texas Medical Branch, Graduate School of Biomedical Sciences, Center for Biodefense and Emerging Infectious Diseases, Galveston, TX 77555. Offers biodefense training (PhD). *Entrance requirements:* For doctorate, GRE, minimum overall GPA of 3.0.

The University of Texas Medical Branch, Graduate School of Biomedical Sciences, Program in Emerging and Tropical Infectious Diseases, Galveston, TX 77555. Offers PhD, MD/PhD. *Degree requirements:* For doctorate, thesis/dissertation. *Entrance requirements:* For doctorate, GRE General Test. *Faculty research:* Emerging diseases, tropical diseases, parasitology, vitology and bacteriology.

Yale University, School of Medicine and Graduate School of Arts and Sciences, Combined Program in Biological and Biomedical Sciences (BBS), Microbiology Track, New Haven, CT 06520. Offers PhD, MD/PhD. *Degree requirements:* For doctorate, thesis/dissertation. *Entrance requirements:* For doctorate, GRE General Test, GRE Subject Test. Additional exam requirements/recommendations for international students: Required—TOEFL. Electronic applications accepted.

Medical Microbiology

Creighton University, School of Medicine and Graduate School, Graduate Programs in Medicine, Department of Medical Microbiology and Immunology, Omaha, NE 68178-0001. Offers MS, PhD. Terminal master's awarded for partial completion of doctoral program. *Degree requirements:* For master's, comprehensive exam, thesis; for doctorate, thesis/dissertation, preliminary exams. *Entrance requirements:* For master's and doctorate, GRE General Test. Additional exam requirements/recommendations for international students: Required—TOEFL. *Expenses:* Tuition: Full-time $12,168; part-time $676 per credit hour. Required fees: $131 per semester. Tuition and fees vary according to program. *Faculty research:* Infectious diseases, molecular biology, genetics, antimicrobial agents and chemotherapy, virology.

Idaho State University, Office of Graduate Studies, College of Arts and Sciences, Department of Biological Sciences, Pocatello, ID 83209-8007. Offers biology (MNS, MS, DA, PhD); clinical laboratory science (MS); microbiology (MS). *Accreditation:* NAACLS. Part-time programs available. *Degree requirements:* For master's, comprehensive exam, thesis; for doctorate, comprehensive exam, thesis/dissertation, 9 credits of internship (for DA). *Entrance requirements:* For master's, GRE General Test, minimum GPA of 3.0 in all upper division classes; for

doctorate, GRE General Test, GRE Subject Test (biology), diagnostic exam (DA), minimum GPA of 3.0 in all upper division classes. Additional exam requirements/recommendations for international students: Required—TOEFL (minimum score 550 paper-based; 213 computer-based; 80 iBT). Electronic applications accepted. *Faculty research:* Ecology, plant and animal physiology, plant and animal developmental biology, immunology, molecular biology, bioinfomatics.

Rutgers, The State University of New Jersey, New Brunswick, Graduate School-New Brunswick, Programs in the Molecular Biosciences, Program in Microbiology and Molecular Genetics, Piscataway, NJ 08854-8097. Offers applied microbiology (MS, PhD); clinical microbiology (MS, PhD); computational molecular biology (PhD); immunology (MS, PhD); microbial biochemistry (MS, PhD); molecular genetics (MS, PhD); virology (MS, PhD). MS, PhD offered jointly with University of Medicine and Dentistry of New Jersey. Part-time programs available. Terminal master's awarded for partial completion of doctoral program. *Degree requirements:* For master's, comprehensive exam, thesis or alternative; for doctorate, comprehensive exam, thesis/dissertation, written qualifying exam. *Entrance requirements:* For master's, GRE General Test, minimum GPA of 3.0; for doctorate, GRE General Test, GRE Subject Test (recom-

Medical Microbiology

Rutgers, The State University of New Jersey, New Brunswick (continued)
mended), minimum GPA of 3.0. Additional exam requirements/recommendations for international students: Required—TOEFL. Electronic applications accepted. *Expenses:* Tuition, state resident: full-time $7200; part-time $600 per credit. Tuition, nonresident: full-time $11,124; part-time $927 per credit. *Faculty research:* Molecular genetics and microbial physiology; virology and pathogenic microbiology; applied, environmental and industrial microbiology; computers in molecular biology.

Texas Tech University Health Sciences Center, Graduate School of Biomedical Sciences, Department of Microbiology and Immunology, Lubbock, TX 79430. Offers medical microbiology (MS, PhD); MD/PhD; MS/PhD. Terminal master's awarded for partial completion of doctoral program. *Degree requirements:* For master's, thesis; for doctorate, thesis/dissertation. *Entrance requirements:* For master's and doctorate, GRE General Test, minimum GPA of 3.0. Additional exam requirements/recommendations for international students: Required—TOEFL (minimum score 550 paper-based; 213 computer-based). Electronic applications accepted. *Faculty research:* Genetics, pathogenic bacteriology, molecular biology, virology, medical mycology.

Université du Québec, Institut National de la Recherche Scientifique, Graduate Programs, Research Center—INRS—Institut Armand-Frappier—Human Health, Québec, QC G1K 9A9, Canada. Offers applied microbiology (M Sc); biology (PhD); experimental health sciences (M Sc); virology and immunology (M Sc, PhD). Programs given in French. Part-time programs available. *Faculty:* 36. *Students:* 157 full-time (92 women), 6 part-time (4 women), 54 international. Average age 30. In 2010, 20 master's, 13 doctorates awarded. *Degree requirements:* For master's, thesis optional; for doctorate, thesis/dissertation. *Entrance requirements:* For master's and doctorate, appropriate bachelor's degree, proficiency in French. *Application deadline:* For fall admission, 3/30 for domestic and international students; for winter admission, 11/1 for domestic and international students; for spring admission, 3/1 for domestic and international students. Application fee: $30 Canadian dollars. *Financial support:* Fellowships, research assistantships, teaching assistantships available. *Faculty research:* Immunity, infection and cancer; toxicology and environmental biotechnology; molecular pharmacochemistry. *Unit head:* Charles Dozois, Director, 450-687-5010, Fax: 450-686-5501, E-mail: charles.dozois@iaf.inrs.ca. *Application contact:* Yvonne Boisvert, Registrar, 418-654-3861, Fax: 418-654-3858, E-mail: registrariat@adm.inrs.ca.

University of Alberta, Faculty of Medicine and Dentistry and Faculty of Graduate Studies and Research, Graduate Programs in Medicine, Department of Medical Microbiology and Immunology, Edmonton, AB T6G 2E1, Canada. Offers M Sc, PhD. Terminal master's awarded for partial completion of doctoral program. *Degree requirements:* For master's, thesis; for doctorate, thesis/dissertation. *Entrance requirements:* For master's and doctorate, minimum GPA of 3.3. Additional exam requirements/recommendations for international students: Required—TOEFL (minimum score 600 paper-based; 232 computer-based; 96 iBT). *Faculty research:* Cellular and reproductive immunology, microbial pathogenesis, mechanisms of antibiotic resistance, molecular biology of mammalian viruses, antiviral chemotherapy.

University of Hawaii at Manoa, John A. Burns School of Medicine and Graduate Division, Graduate Programs in Biomedical Sciences, Department of Tropical Medicine, Medical Microbiology and Pharmacology, Honolulu, HI 96822. Offers tropical medicine (MS, PhD). Part-time programs available. *Faculty:* 27 full-time (11 women), 1 part-time/adjunct (0 women). *Students:* 16 full-time (10 women), 2 part-time (both women); includes 5 minority (3 Asian, non-Hispanic/Latino; 2 Two or more races, non-Hispanic/Latino), 7 international. Average age 33. 34 applicants, 26% accepted, 7 enrolled. In 2010, 2 master's, 1 doctorate awarded. Terminal master's awarded for partial completion of doctoral program. *Degree requirements:* For master's, thesis optional; for doctorate, comprehensive exam, thesis/dissertation. *Entrance requirements:* For master's and doctorate, GRE General Test. Additional exam requirements/recommendations for international students: Required—TOEFL (minimum score 580 paper-based; 237 computer-based; 92 iBT), IELTS (minimum score 5). *Application deadline:* For fall admission, 1/15 for domestic and international students; for spring admission, 9/1 for domestic and international students. Application fee: $60. *Financial support:* In 2010–11, 6 fellowships (averaging $1,583 per year), 15 research assistantships (averaging $20,967 per year) were awarded; teaching assistantships, tuition waivers (full) also available. *Faculty research:* Immunological studies of dengue, malaria, Kawasaki's disease, lupus erythematosus, rheumatoid disease. Total annual research expenditures: $2.4 million. *Application contact:* Sandra Chang, Graduate Chair, 808-692-1617, Fax: 808-692-1979, E-mail: sandrac@hawaii.edu.

University of Manitoba, Faculty of Medicine and Faculty of Graduate Studies, Graduate Programs in Medicine, Department of Medical Microbiology, Winnipeg, MB R3T 2N2, Canada. Offers M Sc, PhD. Part-time programs available. Terminal master's awarded for partial completion of doctoral program. *Degree requirements:* For master's, thesis; for doctorate, one foreign language, thesis/dissertation. *Entrance requirements:* For master's and doctorate, minimum GPA of 3.0. Electronic applications accepted. *Faculty research:* HIV, bacterial adhesion, sexually transmitted diseases, virus structure/function and assembly.

University of Minnesota, Duluth, Medical School, Microbiology, Immunology and Molecular Pathobiology Section, Duluth, MN 55812-2496. Offers MS, PhD. MS, PhD offered jointly with University of Minnesota, Twin Cities Campus. Terminal master's awarded for partial completion of doctoral program. *Degree requirements:* For master's, thesis, final oral exam; for doctorate, thesis/dissertation, final exam, oral and written preliminary exams. *Entrance requirements:* For master's and doctorate, GRE General Test. Additional exam requirements/recommendations for international students: Required—TOEFL. *Faculty research:* Immunomodulation, molecular diagnosis of rabies, cytokines, cancer immunology, cytomegalovirus infection.

University of Wisconsin–La Crosse, Office of University Graduate Studies, College of Science and Health, Department of Biology, Program in Clinical Microbiology, La Crosse, WI 54601-3742. Offers MS. Part-time programs available. *Faculty:* 13 full-time (3 women), 12 part-time/adjunct (4 women). *Students:* 5 full-time (all women), 11 part-time (9 women); includes 3 minority (1 Asian, non-Hispanic/Latino; 2 Hispanic/Latino), 1 international. Average age 28. 9 applicants, 56% accepted, 5 enrolled. In 2010, 2 master's awarded. *Degree requirements:* For master's, comprehensive exam, thesis. *Entrance requirements:* For master's, GRE General Test, minimum GPA of 2.85, three letters of recommendation. Additional exam requirements/recommendations for international students: Required—TOEFL (minimum score 550 paper-based; 213 computer-based; 79 iBT). *Application deadline:* For fall admission, 1/20 priority date for domestic and international students. Applications are processed on a rolling basis. Application fee: $56. Electronic applications accepted. *Expenses:* Tuition, state resident: full-time $7121; part-time $395.61 per credit. Tuition, nonresident: full-time $16,891; part-time $938.41 per credit. Part-time tuition and fees vary according to course load, program and reciprocity agreements. *Financial support:* In 2010–11, 9 research assistantships with partial tuition reimbursements (averaging $10,124 per year) were awarded; Federal Work-Study, scholarships/grants, health care benefits, and tuition waivers also available. Support available to part-time students. Financial award application deadline: 3/15; financial award applicants required to submit FAFSA. *Faculty research:* Pathogenic bacteriology, mycology, virology, parasitology, immunology. *Unit head:* Dr. Michael Hoffman, Program Director, 608-785-6984, E-mail: hoffman.mic2@uwlax.edu. *Application contact:* Kathryn Kiefer, Director of Admissions, 608-785-8939, E-mail: admissions@uwlax.edu.

University of Wisconsin–Madison, School of Medicine and Public Health and Graduate School, Graduate Programs in Medicine and College of Agricultural and Life Sciences, Microbiology Doctoral Training Program, Madison, WI 53706. Offers PhD. *Faculty:* 90 full-time (28 women). *Students:* 74 full-time (43 women); includes 3 Black or African American, non-Hispanic/Latino; 6 Hispanic/Latino, 3 international. Average age 24. 261 applicants, 16% accepted, 14 enrolled. In 2010, 18 doctorates awarded. *Degree requirements:* For doctorate, thesis/dissertation, preliminary exam, 2 semesters of teaching. *Entrance requirements:* For doctorate, GRE. Additional exam requirements/recommendations for international students: Required—TOEFL (minimum score 580 paper-based; 237 computer-based). *Application deadline:* For fall admission, 12/1 for domestic and international students. Application fee: $56. Electronic applications accepted. *Expenses:* Tuition, state resident: full-time $9887; part-time $617.96 per credit. Tuition, nonresident: full-time $24,054; part-time $1503.40 per credit. Required fees: $67.63 per credit. Tuition and fees vary according to reciprocity agreements. *Financial support:* In 2010–11, 88 students received support, including 26 fellowships with tuition reimbursements available (averaging $24,500 per year), 48 research assistantships with tuition reimbursements available (averaging $24,500 per year); career-related internships or fieldwork, scholarships/grants, traineeships, health care benefits, and tuition waivers (full) also available. Financial award application deadline: 12/1. *Faculty research:* Microbial pathogenesis, gene regulation, immunology, virology, cell biology. Total annual research expenditures: $15.1 million. *Unit head:* Dr. Joseph Dillard, Director, 608-265-2837, Fax: 608-262-8418, E-mail: jpdillard@wisc.edu. *Application contact:* Cathy Davis Gray, Coordinator, 608-265-0689, Fax: 608-262-8418, E-mail: cdg@bact.wisc.edu.

Microbiology

Albany Medical College, Center for Immunology and Microbial Disease, Albany, NY 12208-3479. Offers MS, PhD. Part-time programs available. *Faculty:* 19 full-time (4 women), 11 part-time/adjunct (6 women). *Students:* 18 full-time (10 women); includes 1 Asian, non-Hispanic/Latino. Average age 25. 20 applicants, 45% accepted, 6 enrolled. In 2010, 1 doctorate awarded. Terminal master's awarded for partial completion of doctoral program. *Degree requirements:* For master's, thesis; for doctorate, comprehensive exam, thesis/dissertation, oral qualifying exam, written preliminary exam, 1 published paper-peer review. *Entrance requirements:* For master's, GRE General Test, all transcripts, letters of recommendation; for doctorate, GRE General Test, letters of recommendation. Additional exam requirements/recommendations for international students: Required—TOEFL. *Application deadline:* For fall admission, 3/15 priority date for domestic and international students. Applications are processed on a rolling basis. Application fee: $0 ($60 for international students). *Financial support:* In 2010–11, 10 research assistantships (averaging $24,000 per year) were awarded; Federal Work-Study, scholarships/grants, and tuition waivers (full) also available. Financial award applicants required to submit FAFSA. *Faculty research:* Microbial and viral pathogenesis, cancer development and cell transformation, biochemical and genetic mechanisms responsible for human disease. *Unit head:* Dr. Thomas D. Friedrich, Graduate Director, 518-262-6750, Fax: 518-262-6161, E-mail: dgs_cimd@mail.amc.edu. *Application contact:* Dr. Thomas D. Friedrich, Graduate Director, 518-262-6750, Fax: 518-262-6161, E-mail: dgs_cimd@mail.amc.edu.

Albert Einstein College of Medicine, Graduate Division of Biomedical Sciences, Department of Microbiology and Immunology, Bronx, NY 10461. Offers PhD, MD/PhD. *Degree requirements:* For doctorate, thesis/dissertation. *Entrance requirements:* For doctorate, GRE General Test. Additional exam requirements/recommendations for international students: Required—TOEFL. *Faculty research:* Nature of histocompatibility antigens, lymphoid cell receptors, regulation of immune responses and mechanisms of resistance to infection.

American University of Beirut, Graduate Programs, Faculty of Medicine, Beirut, Lebanon. Offers biochemistry (MS); human morphology (MS); medicine (MD); microbiology and immunology (MS); neuroscience (MS); pharmacology and therapeutics (MS); physiology (MS). Part-time programs available. *Faculty:* 222 full-time (56 women), 58 part-time/adjunct (4 women). *Students:* 346 full-time (135 women), 69 part-time (57 women). Average age 23. In 2010, 81 first professional degrees, 19 master's awarded. *Degree requirements:* For master's, one foreign language, comprehensive exam, thesis (for some programs). *Entrance requirements:* For MD, MCAT, bachelor's degree; for master's, letter of recommendation. Additional exam requirements/recommendations for international students: Required—TOEFL (minimum score 600 paper-based; 250 computer-based; 100 iBT), IELTS (minimum score 7.5). *Application deadline:* For fall admission, 4/30 for domestic and international students; for spring admission, 11/1 for domestic and international students. Application fee: $50. *Expenses:* Tuition: Full-time $12,294; part-time $683 per credit. Required fees: $499; $499 per credit. Tuition and fees vary according to course load and program. *Financial support:* In 2010–11, 4 students received support. Career-related internships or fieldwork, institutionally sponsored loans, scholarships/grants, health care benefits, and unspecified assistantships available. Financial award application deadline: 2/2. *Faculty research:* Cancer research (targeted therapy, mechanisms of leukemogenesis, tumor cell extravasation and metastasis, cancer stem cells); stem cell research (regenerative medicine, drug discovery); genetic research (neurogenetics, hereditary cardiomyopathy, hemoglobinopathies, pharmacogenomics); neuroscience research (pain, neurodegenerative disorder); metabolism (inflammation and metabolism, metabolic disorder, diabetes mellitus). Total annual research expenditures: $1.2 million. *Unit head:* Dr. Mohamed Sayegh, Dean, 961-135-0000 Ext. 4700, Fax: 961-174-4464, E-mail: msayegh@aub.edu.lb. *Application contact:* Dr. Salim Kanaan, Director, Admissions Office, 961-135-0000 Ext. 2594, Fax: 961-175-0775, E-mail: sk00@aub.edu.lb.

Arizona State University, College of Liberal Arts and Sciences, School of Life Sciences, Tempe, AZ 85287-4601. Offers animal behavior (PhD); applied ethics (biomedical and health ethics) (MA); biological design (PhD); biology (MS, PhD); biology (biology and society) (MS, PhD); environmental life sciences (PhD); evolutionary biology (PhD); human and social dimensions of science and technology (PhD); microbiology (PhD); molecular and cellular biology (PhD); neuroscience (PhD); philosophy (history and philosophy of science) (MA); sustainability (PhD). *Faculty:* 102 full-time (26 women), 4 part-time/adjunct (1 woman). *Students:* 188 full-time (95 women), 45 part-time (29 women); includes 31 minority (3 Black or African American, non-Hispanic/Latino; 2 American Indian or Alaska Native, non-Hispanic/Latino; 12 Asian, non-Hispanic/Latino; 12 Hispanic/Latino; 2 Two or more races, non-Hispanic/Latino), 39 international. Average age 30. 203 applicants, 41% accepted, 60 enrolled. In 2010, 17 master's, 21 doctorates awarded. Terminal master's awarded for partial completion of doctoral program. *Degree requirements:* For master's, thesis (for some programs), interactive Program of Study (iPOS) submitted before completing 50 percent of required credit hours; for doctorate, variable foreign language requirement, comprehensive exam, thesis/dissertation, interactive Program of Study (iPOS) submitted before completing 50 percent of required credit hours. *Entrance requirements:* For master's and doctorate, GRE, minimum GPA of 3.0 or equivalent in last 2 years of work leading to bachelor's degree. Additional exam requirements/recommendations for international students: Required—TOEFL (minimum score 600 paper-based; 250 computer-based; 100 iBT). *Application deadline:* For fall admission, 12/15 for domestic and international students. Application fee: $70 ($90 for international students). Electronic applications accepted.

Expenses: Tuition, state resident: full-time $8510; part-time $608 per credit. Tuition, nonresident: full-time $16,542; part-time $919 per credit. Required fees: $339; $110 per credit. Part-time tuition and fees vary according to course load. *Financial support:* In 2010–11, 80 research assistantships with full and partial tuition reimbursements (averaging $17,888 per year), 101 teaching assistantships with full and partial tuition reimbursements (averaging $17,327 per year) were awarded; fellowships with full tuition reimbursements, career-related internships or fieldwork, Federal Work-Study, institutionally sponsored loans, scholarships/grants, and tuition waivers (full and partial) also available. Financial award application deadline: 3/1; financial award applicants required to submit FAFSA. Total annual research expenditures: $29.3 million. *Unit head:* Dr. Robert E. Page, Director, 480-965-0803, E-mail: robert.page@asu.edu. *Application contact:* Graduate Admissions, 480-965-6113.

Auburn University, Graduate School, College of Sciences and Mathematics, Department of Biological Sciences, Auburn University, AL 36849. Offers botany (MS, PhD); microbiology (MS, PhD); zoology (MS, PhD). *Faculty:* 33 full-time (8 women), 1 (woman) part-time/adjunct. *Students:* 42 full-time (17 women), 60 part-time (36 women); includes 4 Black or African American, non-Hispanic/Latino; 1 American Indian or Alaska Native, non-Hispanic/Latino; 3 Asian, non-Hispanic/Latino; 1 Hispanic/Latino, 21 international. Average age 28. 134 applicants, 20% accepted, 18 enrolled. In 2010, 22 master's, 11 doctorates awarded. *Entrance requirements:* For master's and doctorate, GRE General Test. Additional exam requirements/recommendations for international students: Required—TOEFL. *Application deadline:* For fall admission, 7/7 for domestic students; for spring admission, 11/24 for domestic students. Application fee: $50 ($60 for international students). Electronic applications accepted. *Expenses:* Tuition, state resident: full-time $7002. Tuition, nonresident: full-time $21,898. International tuition: $22,116 full-time. Required fees: $892. Tuition and fees vary according to course load and program. *Financial support:* Research assistantships, teaching assistantships available. Financial award applicants required to submit FAFSA. *Unit head:* Dr. James M. Barbaree, Chair, 334-844-7511, Fax: 334-844-1645. *Application contact:* Dr. George Flowers, Dean of the Graduate School, 334-844-2125.

Baylor College of Medicine, Graduate School of Biomedical Sciences, Department of Molecular Virology and Microbiology, Houston, TX 77030-3498. Offers PhD, MD/PhD. *Faculty:* 43 full-time (13 women). *Students:* 37 full-time (20 women); includes 1 Black or African American, non-Hispanic/Latino; 4 Asian, non-Hispanic/Latino; 5 Hispanic/Latino, 9 international. Average age 28. 74 applicants, 20% accepted, 4 enrolled. In 2010, 3 doctorates awarded. *Degree requirements:* For doctorate, thesis/dissertation, public defense. *Entrance requirements:* For doctorate, GRE General Test, GRE Subject Test (strongly recommended), minimum GPA of 3.0. Additional exam requirements/recommendations for international students: Required—TOEFL. *Application deadline:* For fall admission, 1/1 priority date for domestic students. Applications are processed on a rolling basis. Application fee: $0. Electronic applications accepted. *Expenses:* Tuition: Full-time $11,000. Required fees: $4900. *Financial support:* In 2010–11, 13 fellowships with full tuition reimbursements (averaging $26,000 per year), 24 research assistantships with full tuition reimbursements (averaging $26,000 per year) were awarded; career-related internships or fieldwork, Federal Work-Study, institutionally sponsored loans, health care benefits, and tuition waivers (full) also available. Financial award applicants required to submit FAFSA. *Faculty research:* Microbiology, viral molecular biology, bacterial molecular biology, microbial pathogenesis, microbial genomics. *Unit head:* Dr. Frank Ramig, Director, 713-798-4830, Fax: 713-798-5075, E-mail: rramig@bcm.edu. *Application contact:* Rosa Banegas, Graduate Program Administrator, 713-798-4472, Fax: 713-798-5075, E-mail: rbanegas@bcm.edu.

Baylor College of Medicine, Graduate School of Biomedical Sciences, Interdepartmental Program in Cell and Molecular Biology, Houston, TX 77030-3498. Offers biochemistry (PhD); cell and molecular biology (PhD); genetics (PhD); human genetics (PhD); immunology (PhD); microbiology (PhD); virology (PhD); MD/PhD. *Faculty:* 100 full-time (31 women). *Students:* 67 full-time (41 women); includes 4 Black or African American, non-Hispanic/Latino; 2 American Indian or Alaska Native, non-Hispanic/Latino; 9 Asian, non-Hispanic/Latino; 9 Hispanic/Latino, 9 international. Average age 27. 120 applicants, 27% accepted, 15 enrolled. In 2010, 7 doctorates awarded. *Degree requirements:* For doctorate, thesis/dissertation, public defense. *Entrance requirements:* For doctorate, GRE General Test, GRE Subject Test (strongly recommended), minimum GPA of 3.0. Additional exam requirements/recommendations for international students: Required—TOEFL. *Application deadline:* For fall admission, 1/1 priority date for domestic students. Applications are processed on a rolling basis. Application fee: $0. Electronic applications accepted. *Expenses:* Tuition: Full-time $11,000. Required fees: $4900. *Financial support:* In 2010–11, 67 students received support, including 24 fellowships with full tuition reimbursements available (averaging $26,000 per year), 43 research assistantships with full tuition reimbursements available (averaging $26,000 per year); teaching assistantships, Federal Work-Study, institutionally sponsored loans, health care benefits, and tuition waivers (full) also available. Financial award applicants required to submit FAFSA. *Faculty research:* Molecular and cellular biology; cancer, aging and stem cells; genomics and proteomics; microbiome, molecular microbiology; infectious disease, immunology and translational research. *Unit head:* Dr. Susan Marriott, Director, 713-798-6557. *Application contact:* Lourdes Fernandez, Graduate Program Administrator, 713-798-6557, Fax: 713-798-6325, E-mail: cmbprog@bcm.edu.

See Close-Up on page 223.

Boston University, School of Medicine, Division of Graduate Medical Sciences, Department of Microbiology, Boston, MA 02118. Offers immunology (PhD); microbiology (MA); MD/PhD. *Faculty:* 14 full-time (7 women), 2 part-time/adjunct (1 woman). *Students:* 8 full-time (5 women); includes 1 Black or African American, non-Hispanic/Latino, 1 international. 52 applicants, 10% accepted, 0 enrolled. In 2010, 3 doctorates awarded. Terminal master's awarded for partial completion of doctoral program. *Degree requirements:* For master's, thesis; for doctorate, comprehensive exam, thesis/dissertation. *Entrance requirements:* For master's and doctorate, GRE General Test, GRE Subject Test. Additional exam requirements/recommendations for international students: Required—TOEFL. *Application deadline:* For fall admission, 1/15 priority date for domestic students; for spring admission, 10/15 priority date for domestic students. Application fee: $75. Electronic applications accepted. *Expenses:* Tuition: Full-time $39,314; part-time $1228 per credit. Required fees: $40 per semester. *Financial support:* In 2010–11, 5 research assistantships (averaging $30,500 per year) were awarded; fellowships, Federal Work-Study, scholarships/grants, and traineeships also available. Financial award applicants required to submit FAFSA. *Faculty research:* Eukaryotic cell biology, tumor cell biology, nutrition and cancer, experimental tumor therapy, photobiology. *Unit head:* Dr. Ronald B. Corley, Chairman, 617-638-4284, Fax: 617-638-4286, E-mail: rbcorley@bu.edu. *Application contact:* Dr. Gregory Viglianti, Graduate Director, 617-638-7790, Fax: 617-638-4286, E-mail: gviglian@bu.edu.

Brandeis University, Graduate School of Arts and Sciences, Program in Molecular and Cell Biology, Waltham, MA 02454-9110. Offers genetics (PhD); microbiology (PhD); molecular and cell biology (MS, PhD); molecular biology (PhD); neurobiology (PhD). *Faculty:* 30 full-time (13 women), 1 (woman) part-time/adjunct. *Students:* 55 full-time (31 women); includes 1 Black or African American, non-Hispanic/Latino; 1 American Indian or Alaska Native, non-Hispanic/Latino; 1 Asian, non-Hispanic/Latino; 2 Hispanic/Latino, 12 international. 138 applicants, 32% accepted, 17 enrolled. In 2010, 3 master's, 3 doctorates awarded. Terminal master's awarded for partial completion of doctoral program. *Degree requirements:* For master's, thesis optional, research project; for doctorate, comprehensive exam, thesis/dissertation, teaching assistant experience. *Entrance requirements:* For master's and doctorate, GRE General Test, official transcript(s), resume, 3 letters of recommendation, statement of purpose. Additional exam requirements/recommendations for international students: Required—TOEFL (minimum score 600 paper-based; 250 computer-based; 100 iBT); Recommended—IELTS (minimum score 7). *Application deadline:* For fall admission, 1/15 priority date for domestic students. Applications are processed on a rolling basis. Application fee: $75. Electronic applications accepted. *Financial support:* In 2010–11, 41 students received support, including 13 fellowships with full tuition reimbursements available (averaging $27,500 per year), 27 research assistantships with full tuition reimbursements available (averaging $27,500 per year), 1 teaching assistantship with partial tuition reimbursement available (averaging $3,200 per year); scholarships/grants, traineeships, health care benefits, and tuition waivers (full and partial) also available. Financial award application deadline: 4/15; financial award applicants required to submit FAFSA. *Faculty research:* Molecular biology, cell biology, biology, structural biology, immunology, developmental biology, neurobiology, DNA, RNA. *Unit head:* Dr. Piali Sengupta, Chair, 781-736-2686, Fax: 781-736-3107, E-mail: piali@brandeis.edu. *Application contact:* Marcia Cabral, Department Administrator, 781-736-3100, Fax: 781-736-3107, E-mail: cabral@brandeis.edu.

Brigham Young University, Graduate Studies, College of Life Sciences, Department of Microbiology and Molecular Biology, Provo, UT 84602-1001. Offers microbiology (MS, PhD); molecular biology (MS, PhD). *Faculty:* 17 full-time (3 women), 2 part-time/adjunct (1 woman). *Students:* 21 full-time (9 women); includes 3 Asian, non-Hispanic/Latino; 3 Hispanic/Latino, 1 international. Average age 28. 17 applicants, 47% accepted, 7 enrolled. In 2010, 3 master's, 1 doctorate awarded. Terminal master's awarded for partial completion of doctoral program. *Degree requirements:* For master's, comprehensive exam, thesis; for doctorate, comprehensive exam, thesis/dissertation. *Entrance requirements:* For master's, GRE General Test, minimum GPA of 3.0 during previous 2 years; for doctorate, GRE General Test, minimum GPA of 3.0. Additional exam requirements/recommendations for international students: Required—TOEFL (minimum score 580 paper-based; 85 iBT), IELTS (minimum score 7). *Application deadline:* For fall admission, 12/15 priority date for domestic and international students. Application fee: $50. Electronic applications accepted. *Expenses:* Tuition: Full-time $5580; part-time $310 per credit hour. Tuition and fees vary according to program and student's religious affiliation. *Financial support:* In 2010–11, 17 students received support, including 8 research assistantships with full and partial tuition reimbursements available (averaging $18,000 per year), 7 teaching assistantships with full and partial tuition reimbursements available (averaging $18,000 per year); institutionally sponsored loans, scholarships/grants, health care benefits, and unspecified assistantships also available. Financial award application deadline: 2/1. *Faculty research:* Immunobiology, molecular genetics, molecular virology, cancer biology, pathogenic and environmental microbiology. Total annual research expenditures: $414,278. *Unit head:* Dr. Brent L. Nielsen, Chair, 801-422-1102, Fax: 801-422-0519, E-mail: brent_nielsen@byu.edu. *Application contact:* Dr. Richard A. Robison, Graduate Coordinator, 801-422-2416, Fax: 801-422-0519, E-mail: richard_robison@byu.edu.

Brown University, Graduate School, Division of Biology and Medicine, Program in Molecular Biology, Cell Biology, and Biochemistry, Providence, RI 02912. Offers biochemistry (M Med Sc, Sc M, PhD), including biochemistry (Sc M, PhD), biology (Sc M, PhD), medical science (M Med Sc, PhD); biology (MA); cell biology (M Med Sc, Sc M, PhD), including biochemistry (Sc M, PhD), biology (Sc M, PhD), medical science (M Med Sc, PhD); developmental biology (M Med Sc, Sc M, PhD), including biochemistry (Sc M, PhD), biology (Sc M, PhD), medical science (M Med Sc, PhD); immunology (M Med Sc, Sc M, PhD), including biochemistry (Sc M, PhD), biology (Sc M, PhD), medical science (M Med Sc, PhD); molecular microbiology (M Med Sc, Sc M, PhD), including biochemistry (Sc M, PhD), biology (Sc M, PhD), medical science (M Med Sc, PhD); MD/PhD. Part-time programs available. Terminal master's awarded for partial completion of doctoral program. *Degree requirements:* For master's, thesis (for some programs); for doctorate, one foreign language, thesis/dissertation, preliminary exam. *Entrance requirements:* For master's and doctorate, GRE General Test, GRE Subject Test. Additional exam requirements/recommendations for international students: Required—TOEFL. Electronic applications accepted. *Faculty research:* Molecular genetics, gene regulation.

California State University, Long Beach, Graduate Studies, College of Natural Sciences and Mathematics, Department of Biological Sciences, Long Beach, CA 90840. Offers biology (MS); microbiology (MS). Part-time programs available. *Faculty:* 26 full-time (10 women), 1 (woman) part-time/adjunct. *Students:* 16 full-time (9 women), 45 part-time (28 women); includes 2 Black or African American, non-Hispanic/Latino; 9 Asian, non-Hispanic/Latino; 8 Hispanic/Latino, 6 international. Average age 27. 102 applicants, 25% accepted, 12 enrolled. In 2010, 16 master's awarded. *Entrance requirements:* For master's, GRE Subject Test, minimum GPA of 3.0. *Application deadline:* For fall admission, 3/15 for domestic students. Applications are processed on a rolling basis. Application fee: $55. Electronic applications accepted. *Financial support:* Teaching assistantships, Federal Work-Study, institutionally sponsored loans, scholarships/grants, traineeships, and unspecified assistantships available. Financial award application deadline: 3/2. *Unit head:* Dr. Brian Livingston, Chair, 562-985-4807, Fax: 562-985-8878, E-mail: blivings@csulb.edu. *Application contact:* Dr. Christopher Lowe, Graduate Advisor, 562-985-4918, Fax: 562-985-8878, E-mail: clowe@csulb.edu.

Case Western Reserve University, School of Medicine and School of Graduate Studies, Graduate Programs in Medicine, Department of Molecular Biology and Microbiology, Cleveland, OH 44106-4960. Offers cellular biology (PhD); microbiology (PhD); molecular biology (PhD); molecular virology (PhD); MD/PhD. Students are admitted to an integrated Biomedical Sciences Training Program involving 11 basic science programs at Case Western Reserve University. *Degree requirements:* For doctorate, thesis/dissertation. *Entrance requirements:* For doctorate, GRE General Test, GRE Subject Test. Additional exam requirements/recommendations for international students: Required—TOEFL. Electronic applications accepted. *Faculty research:* Gene expression in eukaryotic and prokaryotic systems; microbial physiology; intracellular transport and signaling; mechanisms of oncogenesis; molecular mechanisms of RNA processing, editing, and catalysis.

The Catholic University of America, School of Arts and Sciences, Department of Biology, Washington, DC 20064. Offers cell and microbial biology (MS, PhD), including cell biology, microbiology; clinical laboratory science (MS, PhD); MSLS/MS. Part-time programs available. *Faculty:* 8 full-time (4 women), 2 part-time/adjunct (both women). *Students:* 10 full-time (7 women), 27 part-time (18 women); includes 2 Black or African American, non-Hispanic/Latino; 4 Asian, non-Hispanic/Latino; 3 Hispanic/Latino, 15 international. Average age 29. 39 applicants, 56% accepted, 13 enrolled. In 2010, 4 doctorates awarded. *Degree requirements:* For master's, comprehensive exam, thesis or alternative; for doctorate, comprehensive exam, thesis/dissertation. *Entrance requirements:* For master's and doctorate, GRE General Test, GRE Subject Test, statement of purpose, official copies of academic transcripts, three letters of recommendation. Additional exam requirements/recommendations for international students: Required—TOEFL (minimum score 580 paper-based; 237 computer-based). *Application deadline:* For fall admission, 8/1 priority date for domestic students, 7/15 for international students; for spring admission, 12/1 priority date for domestic students, 10/15 for international students. Applications are processed on a rolling basis. Application fee: $55. Electronic applications accepted. *Expenses:* Tuition: Full-time $33,580; part-time $1315 per credit hour. Required fees: $80; $40 per semester hour. One-time fee: $425. *Financial support:* Fellowships, research assistantships, teaching assistantships, Federal Work-Study, scholarships/grants, tuition waivers (full and partial), and unspecified assistantships available. Financial award application deadline: 2/1; financial award applicants required to submit FAFSA. *Faculty research:* Cell and microbiology, microbial pathogenesis, molecular biology of cell proliferation, cellular effects of electromagnetic radiation, biotechnology. Total annual research expenditures: $853,913. *Unit head:* Dr. Venigalla Rao, Chair, 202-319-5271, Fax: 202-319-5721, E-mail: rao@cua.edu. *Application contact:* Andrew Woodall, Director of Graduate Admissions, 202-319-5057, Fax: 202-319-6533, E-mail: cua-admissions@cua.edu.

Clemson University, Graduate School, College of Agriculture, Forestry and Life Sciences, Department of Biological Sciences, Program in Microbiology, Clemson, SC 29634. Offers MS, PhD. *Students:* 19 full-time (10 women), 6 part-time (5 women); includes 1 Black or African American, non-Hispanic/Latino, 10 international. Average age 30. 38 applicants, 21% accepted, 7 enrolled. In 2010, 6 master's, 4 doctorates awarded. *Degree requirements:* For master's, thesis; for doctorate, thesis/dissertation. *Entrance requirements:* For master's and doctorate, GRE General Test. Additional exam requirements/recommendations for international students: Required—TOEFL, IELTS. *Application deadline:* For fall admission, 1/15 for domestic students, 4/15 for international students. Applications are processed on a rolling basis. Application fee:

Microbiology

Clemson University (continued)
$70 ($80 for international students). Electronic applications accepted. *Expenses:* Contact institution. *Financial support:* In 2010–11, 19 students received support, including 2 fellowships with full and partial tuition reimbursements available (averaging $12,000 per year), 7 research assistantships with partial tuition reimbursements available (averaging $10,429 per year), 20 teaching assistantships with partial tuition reimbursements available (averaging $12,695 per year); career-related internships or fieldwork, institutionally sponsored loans, scholarships/grants, health care benefits, and unspecified assistantships also available. Support available to part-time students. Financial award application deadline: 3/1; financial award applicants required to submit FAFSA. *Faculty research:* Anaerobic microbiology, microbiology and ecology of soil and aquatic systems, genetic engineering, monoclonal antibodies and immunomodulation. *Unit head:* Dr. Alfred Wheeler, Department Chair, 864-656-1415, Fax: 864-656-0435, E-mail: wheeler@clemson.edu. *Application contact:* Jay Lyn Martin, Coordinator for Graduate Program, 864-656-3587, Fax: 864-656-0435, E-mail: gradbio@clemson.edu.

Colorado State University, College of Veterinary Medicine and Biomedical Sciences, Department of Microbiology, Immunology and Pathology, Fort Collins, CO 80523-0015. Offers microbiology (MS, PhD); pathology (PhD). *Faculty:* 40 full-time (17 women), 2 part-time/adjunct (0 women). *Students:* 56 full-time (44 women), 39 part-time (25 women); includes 4 Asian, non-Hispanic/Latino; 6 Hispanic/Latino, 9 international. Average age 31. 107 applicants, 17% accepted, 18 enrolled. In 2010, 5 master's, 11 doctorates awarded. *Degree requirements:* For master's, thesis; for doctorate, comprehensive exam, thesis/dissertation. *Entrance requirements:* For master's, GRE General Test, minimum GPA of 3.0, BA/BS in biomedical field, reviewer evaluation forms, resume; for doctorate, GRE General Test, minimum GPA of 3.0, BA/BS in biomedical field, reviewer evaluation forms, resume, statement of interest. Additional exam requirements/recommendations for international students: Required—TOEFL (minimum score 550 paper-based). *Application deadline:* For fall admission, 1/1 priority date for domestic students; for spring admission, 10/1 priority date for domestic students. Applications are processed on a rolling basis. Application fee: $50. Electronic applications accepted. *Expenses:* Tuition, state resident: full-time $7434; part-time $413 per credit. Tuition, nonresident: full-time $19,022; part-time $1057 per credit. Required fees: $1729; $88 per credit. *Financial support:* In 2010–11, 74 students received support, including 27 fellowships with tuition reimbursements available (averaging $32,882 per year), 41 research assistantships with tuition reimbursements available (averaging $23,930 per year), 6 teaching assistantships with tuition reimbursements available (averaging $15,885 per year); Federal Work-Study, scholarships/grants, traineeships, and unspecified assistantships also available. Financial award applicants required to submit FAFSA. *Faculty research:* Medical and veterinary bacteriology, immunology, microbial physiology, pathology, vector-borne disease. Total annual research expenditures: $33.1 million. *Unit head:* Dr. Edward A. Hoover, Head, 970-491-7587, Fax: 970-491-0603, E-mail: edward.hoover@colostate.edu. *Application contact:* Lisa McCann, Academic Programs Coordinator, 970-491-6118, Fax: 970-491-1815, E-mail: lisa.mccann@colostate.edu.

Columbia University, College of Physicians and Surgeons, Department of Microbiology, New York, NY 10032. Offers biomedical sciences (M Phil, MA, PhD); MD/PhD. Only candidates for the PhD are admitted. Terminal master's awarded for partial completion of doctoral program. *Degree requirements:* For doctorate, thesis/dissertation. *Entrance requirements:* For master's, GRE General Test; for doctorate, GRE. Additional exam requirements/recommendations for international students: Required—TOEFL. *Faculty research:* Prokaryotic molecular biology, immunology, virology, yeast molecular genetics, regulation of gene expression.

Cornell University, Graduate School, Graduate Fields of Agriculture and Life Sciences, Field of Microbiology, Ithaca, NY 14853-0001. Offers PhD. *Faculty:* 42 full-time (12 women). *Students:* 42 full-time (22 women); includes 1 Black or African American, non-Hispanic/Latino; 1 Asian, non-Hispanic/Latino; 1 Hispanic/Latino, 13 international. Average age 27. 73 applicants, 32% accepted, 9 enrolled. In 2010, 8 doctorates awarded. *Degree requirements:* For doctorate, comprehensive exam, thesis/dissertation, 2 semesters of teaching experience. *Entrance requirements:* For doctorate, GRE General Test, 3 letters of recommendation. Additional exam requirements/recommendations for international students: Required—TOEFL (minimum score 550 paper-based; 213 computer-based; 77 iBT). *Application deadline:* For fall admission, 1/15 for domestic students. Application fee: $70. Electronic applications accepted. *Expenses:* Tuition: Full-time $29,500. Required fees: $76. Tuition and fees vary according to degree level and program. *Financial support:* In 2010–11, 6 fellowships with full tuition reimbursements, 29 research assistantships with full tuition reimbursements, 7 teaching assistantships with full tuition reimbursements were awarded; institutionally sponsored loans, scholarships/grants, health care benefits, tuition waivers (full and partial), and unspecified assistantships also available. Financial award applicants required to submit FAFSA. *Faculty research:* Microbial diversity, molecular biology, biotechnology, microbial ecology, phytobacteriology. *Unit head:* Director of Graduate Studies, 607-255-3088. *Application contact:* Graduate Field Assistant, 607-255-3088, E-mail: microfield@cornell.edu.

Dalhousie University, Faculty of Medicine, Department of Microbiology and Immunology, Halifax, NS B3H 1X5, Canada. Offers M Sc, PhD. *Degree requirements:* For master's, thesis; for doctorate, comprehensive exam, thesis/dissertation. *Entrance requirements:* For master's, GRE General Test, honors B Sc; for doctorate, GRE General Test, honors B Sc in microbiology, M Sc in discipline or transfer after 1 year in master's program. Additional exam requirements/recommendations for international students: Required—TOEFL, IELTS, 1 of the following 5 approved tests: TOEFL, IELTS, CAEL, CANTEST, Michigan English Language Assessment Battery. Electronic applications accepted. *Faculty research:* Virology, molecular genetics, pathogenesis, bacteriology, immunology.

Dartmouth College, Graduate Program in Molecular and Cellular Biology, Department of Microbiology and Immunology, Program in Immunology, Hanover, NH 03755. Offers MD/PhD. *Faculty research:* Tumor immunotherapy, cell and molecular biology of connective tissue degradation in rheumatoid arthritis and cancer, immunology and immunotherapy of tumors of the central nervous system, transcriptional regulation of hematopoiesis and leukemia, bacterial pathogenesis.

Dartmouth College, Graduate Program in Molecular and Cellular Biology, Department of Microbiology and Immunology, Program in Molecular Pathogenesis, Hanover, NH 03755. Offers microbiology and immunology (PhD).

Drexel University, College of Medicine, Biomedical Graduate Programs, Program in Microbiology and Immunology, Philadelphia, PA 19104-2875. Offers MS, PhD, MD/PhD. Terminal master's awarded for partial completion of doctoral program. *Degree requirements:* For master's, comprehensive exam, thesis; for doctorate, thesis/dissertation, qualifying exam. *Entrance requirements:* For master's, GRE General Test, minimum GPA of 2.75; for doctorate, GRE General Test, minimum GPA of 3.0. Additional exam requirements/recommendations for international students: Required—TOEFL. Electronic applications accepted. *Faculty research:* Immunology of malarial parasites, virology, bacteriology, molecular biology, parasitology.

Duke University, Graduate School, Department of Molecular Genetics and Microbiology, Durham, NC 27710. Offers PhD. *Faculty:* 25 full-time. *Students:* 41 full-time (23 women); includes 2 Black or African American, non-Hispanic/Latino; 1 American Indian or Alaska Native, non-Hispanic/Latino; 2 Asian, non-Hispanic/Latino, 11 international. 73 applicants, 29% accepted, 15 enrolled. In 2010, 11 doctorates awarded. *Degree requirements:* For doctorate, thesis/dissertation. *Entrance requirements:* For doctorate, GRE General Test, GRE Subject Test in biology, chemistry, or biochemistry, cell and molecular biology (recommended). Additional exam requirements/recommendations for international students: Required—TOEFL (minimum score 550 paper-based; 213 computer-based; 83 iBT), IELTS (minimum score 7). *Application deadline:* For fall admission, 12/8 priority date for domestic and international students. Application fee: $75. Electronic applications accepted. *Financial support:* Fellowships with full tuition reimbursements, research assistantships with full tuition reimbursements, Federal Work-Study available. Financial award application deadline: 12/31. *Unit head:* Dr. Raphael Valdivia, Director of Graduate Studies, 919-684-6629, Fax: 919-684-8346, E-mail: andrea.lanahan@duke.edu. *Application contact:* Elizabeth Hutton, Director of Admissions, 919-684-3913, Fax: 919-684-2277, E-mail: grad-admissions@duke.edu.

East Carolina University, Brody School of Medicine, Department of Microbiology and Immunology, Greenville, NC 27858-4353. Offers PhD. *Degree requirements:* For doctorate, comprehensive exam, thesis/dissertation. *Entrance requirements:* For doctorate, GRE General Test. Additional exam requirements/recommendations for international students: Required—TOEFL. *Expenses:* Tuition, state resident: full-time $3130; part-time $391.25 per credit hour. Tuition, nonresident: full-time $13,817; part-time $1727.13 per credit hour. Required fees: $1916; $239.50 per credit hour. Tuition and fees vary according to campus/location and program. *Faculty research:* Molecular virology, genetics of bacteria, yeast and somatic cells, bacterial physiology and metabolism, bioterrorism.

Eastern New Mexico University, Graduate School, College of Liberal Arts and Sciences, Department of Biology, Portales, NM 88130. Offers applied ecology (MS); cell, molecular biology and biotechnology (MS); education (non-thesis) (MS); microbiology (MS); plant biology (MS); zoology (MS). Part-time programs available. *Faculty:* 8 full-time (0 women). *Students:* 11 full-time (8 women), 7 part-time (4 women); includes 7 minority (5 Hispanic/Latino; 2 Two or more races, non-Hispanic/Latino), 4 international. Average age 25. 21 applicants, 14% accepted, 3 enrolled. In 2010, 4 master's awarded. *Degree requirements:* For master's, comprehensive exam, thesis optional. *Entrance requirements:* For master's, GRE, minimum GPA of 3.0, 2 letters of recommendation, statement of research interest, bachelor's degree related to field of study or proof of common knowledge. Additional exam requirements/recommendations for international students: Required—TOEFL (minimum score 550 paper-based; 213 computer-based; 79 iBT), IELTS (minimum score 6). *Application deadline:* For fall admission, 7/20 priority date for domestic students, 6/20 priority date for international students; for spring admission, 12/15 priority date for domestic students, 11/15 priority date for international students. Applications are processed on a rolling basis. Application fee: $10. Electronic applications accepted. *Expenses:* Tuition, state resident: full-time $3210; part-time $130 per credit hour. Tuition, nonresident: full-time $8652; part-time $360.50 per credit hour. Required fees: $1212; $50.50 per credit hour. Tuition and fees vary according to course load. *Financial support:* In 2010–11, 11 teaching assistantships with partial tuition reimbursements (averaging $8,500 per year) were awarded; unspecified assistantships also available. Support available to part-time students. Financial award applicants required to submit FAFSA. *Unit head:* Dr. Zach Jones, Graduate Coordinator, 575-562-2723, Fax: 575-562-2192, E-mail: zach.jones@enmu.edu. *Application contact:* Sharon Potter, Department Secretary, Biology/Physical Sciences, 575-562-2174, Fax: 575-562-2192, E-mail: sharon.potter@enmu.edu.

East Tennessee State University, James H. Quillen College of Medicine, Biomedical Science Graduate Program, Johnson City, TN 37614. Offers anatomy (PhD); biochemistry (PhD); microbiology (PhD); pharmacology (PhD); physiology (PhD). Part-time programs available. *Faculty:* 49 full-time (12 women), 1 (woman) part-time/adjunct. *Students:* 27 full-time (14 women), 4 part-time (2 women); includes 4 minority (1 Black or African American, non-Hispanic/Latino; 1 Asian, non-Hispanic/Latino; 2 Hispanic/Latino), 5 international. Average age 32. 62 applicants, 11% accepted, 7 enrolled. In 2010, 2 doctorates awarded. Terminal master's awarded for partial completion of doctoral program. *Degree requirements:* For doctorate, thesis/dissertation, comprehensive qualifying exam. *Entrance requirements:* For doctorate, GRE General Test, GRE Subject Test. Additional exam requirements/recommendations for international students: Required—TOEFL (minimum score 550 paper-based; 213 computer-based; 79 iBT). *Application deadline:* For fall admission, 3/15 priority date for domestic students, 3/1 priority date for international students. Application fee: $25 ($35 for international students). Electronic applications accepted. *Expenses:* Contact institution. *Financial support:* In 2010–11, 7 research assistantships with full tuition reimbursements (averaging $15,000 per year) were awarded; teaching assistantships with full tuition reimbursements, career-related internships or fieldwork, institutionally sponsored loans, scholarships/grants, and unspecified assistantships also available. Financial award application deadline: 7/1; financial award applicants required to submit FAFSA. Total annual research expenditures: $2.1 million. *Unit head:* Dr. Mitchell E. Robinson, Assistant Dean/Director, 423-439-4658, E-mail: robinson@etsu.edu. *Application contact:* Edwin D. Taylor, Assistant Dean for Admissions and Records, 423-439-4753, Fax: 423-439-8206.

East Tennessee State University, School of Graduate Studies, College of Arts and Sciences, Department of Biological Sciences, Johnson City, TN 37614. Offers biology (MS); microbiology (MS); paleontology (MS). *Faculty:* 12 full-time (0 women). *Students:* 43 full-time (20 women), 9 part-time (5 women); includes 3 minority (2 Hispanic/Latino; 1 Two or more races, non-Hispanic/Latino), 17 international. Average age 26. 53 applicants, 43% accepted, 19 enrolled. In 2010, 20 master's awarded. *Degree requirements:* For master's, comprehensive exam, thesis optional. *Entrance requirements:* For master's, GRE General Test or GRE Subject Test, minimum GPA of 3.0. Additional exam requirements/recommendations for international students: Required—TOEFL (minimum score 550 paper-based; 213 computer-based; 79 iBT). *Application deadline:* For fall admission, 4/1 priority date for domestic students, 2/1 for international students; for spring admission, 9/1 for domestic students, 7/1 for international students. Application fee: $25 ($35 for international students). Electronic applications accepted. *Financial support:* In 2010–11, 1 research assistantship with full tuition reimbursement (averaging $6,000 per year), 15 teaching assistantships with full tuition reimbursements (averaging $6,000 per year) were awarded; institutionally sponsored loans, scholarships/grants, and unspecified assistantships also available. Financial award application deadline: 7/1; financial award applicants required to submit FAFSA. *Faculty research:* Vertebrate natural history, mutation rates in fruit flies, regulation of plant secondary metabolism, plant biochemistry, timekeeping in honeybees, gene expression in diapausing flies. Total annual research expenditures: $226,807. *Unit head:* Dr. Dan M. Johnson, Chair, 423-439-4329, Fax: 423-439-5958, E-mail: johnsodm@etsu.edu. *Application contact:* Admissions and Records Clerk, 423-439-4221, Fax: 423-439-5624, E-mail: gradsch@etsu.edu.

Emory University, Laney Graduate School, Division of Biological and Biomedical Sciences, Program in Microbiology and Molecular Genetics, Atlanta, GA 30322-1100. Offers PhD. *Faculty:* 36 full-time (7 women). *Students:* 44 full-time (31 women); includes 3 Black or African American, non-Hispanic/Latino; 2 Hispanic/Latino, 5 international. Average age 27. 104 applicants, 19% accepted, 7 enrolled. In 2010, 7 doctorates awarded. *Degree requirements:* For doctorate, comprehensive exam, thesis/dissertation. *Entrance requirements:* For doctorate, GRE General Test, minimum GPA of 3.0 in science course work (recommended). Additional exam requirements/recommendations for international students: Required—TOEFL. *Application deadline:* For fall admission, 12/1 for domestic and international students. Application fee: $75. Electronic applications accepted. *Expenses:* Tuition: Full-time $33,800. Required fees: $1300. *Financial support:* In 2010–11, 12 students received support, including 12 fellowships with full tuition reimbursements available (averaging $25,000 per year); institutionally sponsored loans, scholarships/grants, health care benefits, and tuition waivers (full) also available. *Faculty research:* Bacterial genetics and physiology, microbial development, molecular biology of viruses and bacterial pathogens, DNA recombination. *Unit head:* Dr. Phil Rather, Program Director, 404-728-5079, Fax: 404-728-7780, E-mail: prather@emory.edu. *Application contact:* Kathy Smith, Director of Recruitment and Admissions, 404-727-2547, Fax: 404-727-3322, E-mail: kathy.smith@emory.edu.

Emporia State University, Graduate School, College of Liberal Arts and Sciences, Department of Biological Sciences, Emporia, KS 66801-5087. Offers botany (MS); environmental biology (MS); general biology (MS); microbial and cellular biology (MS); zoology (MS). Part-time programs available. *Faculty:* 13 full-time (3 women). *Students:* 14 full-time (8 women), 19 part-time (9 women); includes 2 minority (1 Black or African American, non-Hispanic/Latino; 1 Hispanic/Latino), 6 international. 9 applicants, 100% accepted, 9 enrolled. In 2010, 4 master's awarded. *Degree requirements:* For master's, comprehensive exam or thesis. *Entrance requirements:* For master's, GRE, appropriate undergraduate degree, interview, letters of reference. Additional exam requirements/recommendations for international students: Required—

TOEFL (minimum score 520 paper-based; 133 computer-based; 68 iBT). *Application deadline:* For fall admission, 8/15 priority date for domestic students. Applications are processed on a rolling basis. Application fee: $30 ($75 for international students). Electronic applications accepted. *Expenses:* Tuition, state resident: full-time $4382; part-time $183 per credit hour. Tuition, nonresident: full-time $13,572; part-time $566 per credit hour. Required fees: $1022; $62 per credit hour. Tuition and fees vary according to course level, course load and campus/location. *Financial support:* In 2010–11, 10 research assistantships with full tuition reimbursements (averaging $7,353 per year), 9 teaching assistantships with full tuition reimbursements (averaging $7,809 per year) were awarded; career-related internships or fieldwork, Federal Work-Study, institutionally sponsored loans, health care benefits, and unspecified assistantships also available. Financial award application deadline: 3/15; financial award applicants required to submit FAFSA. *Faculty research:* Fisheries, range, and wildlife management; aquatic, plant, grassland, vertebrate, and invertebrate ecology; mammalian and plant systematics, taxonomy, and evolution; immunology, virology, and molecular biology. *Unit head:* Dr. R. Brent Thomas, Chair, 620-341-5311, Fax: 620-341-5608, E-mail: rthomas2@emporia.edu. *Application contact:* Dr. Scott Crupper, Graduate Coordinator, 620-341-5621, Fax: 620-341-5607, E-mail: scrupper@emporia.edu.

George Mason University, College of Science, Department of Molecular and Microbiology, Fairfax, VA 22030. Offers biology (MS), including bioinformatics and computational biology, general biology, microbiology and infectious disease, molecular biology, systematics and evolutionary biology; biosciences (PhD). *Faculty:* 10 full-time (5 women). *Students:* 12 full-time (6 women), 63 part-time (36 women); includes 2 Black or African American, non-Hispanic/Latino; 1 American Indian or Alaska Native, non-Hispanic/Latino; 8 Asian, non-Hispanic/Latino; 1 Hispanic/Latino, 16 international. Average age 31. 98 applicants, 37% accepted, 19 enrolled. In 2010, 7 master's, 7 doctorates awarded. *Entrance requirements:* Additional exam requirements/recommendations for international students: Required—TOEFL (minimum score 570 paper-based; 230 computer-based; 88 iBT). Application fee: $100. *Expenses:* Tuition, state resident: full-time $8192; part-time $440 per credit hour. Tuition, nonresident: full-time $22,952; part-time $1055 per credit hour. Required fees: $2364; $99 per credit hour. *Financial support:* In 2010–11, 32 students received support, including 3 fellowships (averaging $18,000 per year), 6 research assistantships (averaging $14,073 per year), 23 teaching assistantships (averaging $12,194 per year); career-related internships or fieldwork, Federal Work-Study, scholarships/grants, unspecified assistantships, and health care benefits (full-time research or teaching assistantship recipients) also available. Financial award applicants required to submit FAFSA. Total annual research expenditures: $457,760. *Unit head:* Dr. James Willett, Director, 703-993-8311, Fax: 703-993-8976, E-mail: jwillett@gmu.edu. *Application contact:* Daniel Cox, Associate Dean for Graduate Programs, 703-993-4971, Fax: 703-993-4325, E-mail: dcox5@gmu.edu.

Georgetown University, Graduate School of Arts and Sciences, Programs in Biomedical Sciences, Department of Microbiology and Immunology, Washington, DC 20057. Offers biohazardous threat agents and emerging infectious diseases (MS); general microbiology and immunology (MS); global infectious diseases (PhD); microbiology and immunology research (PhD); science policy and advocacy (MS). Part-time programs available. *Degree requirements:* For master's, 30 credit hours of coursework; for doctorate, comprehensive exam, thesis/dissertation. *Entrance requirements:* For master's, GRE General Test, 3 letters of reference, bachelor's degree in related field; for doctorate, GRE General Test, 3 letters of reference, MS/BS in related field. Additional exam requirements/recommendations for international students: Required—TOEFL (minimum score 505 paper-based; 213 computer-based). Electronic applications accepted. *Faculty research:* Pathogenesis and basic biology of the fungus Candida albicans, molecular biology of viral immunopathological mechanisms in Multiple Sclerosis.

The George Washington University, Columbian College of Arts and Sciences, Institute for Biomedical Sciences, Program in Microbiology and Immunology, Washington, DC 20037. Offers PhD. *Students:* 6 full-time (5 women), 13 part-time (8 women); includes 1 American Indian or Alaska Native, non-Hispanic/Latino; 1 Asian, non-Hispanic/Latino; 1 Hispanic/Latino, 2 international. Average age 30. In 2010, 2 doctorates awarded. *Degree requirements:* For doctorate, thesis/dissertation. *Entrance requirements:* For doctorate, GRE General Test, minimum GPA of 3.0. Additional exam requirements/recommendations for international students: Required—TOEFL (minimum score 600 paper-based; 250 computer-based). *Application deadline:* For fall admission, 12/15 priority date for domestic and international students. Applications are processed on a rolling basis. Application fee: $75. Electronic applications accepted. *Financial support:* In 2010–11, 10 students received support; fellowships with tuition reimbursements available, tuition waivers available. *Unit head:* Dr. David Leitenberg, Director, 202-994-9475, Fax: 202-994-2913, E-mail: dleit@gwu.edu. *Application contact:* Information Contact, 202-994-3532, Fax: 202-994-2913, E-mail: mtmjxl@gwumc.edu.

The George Washington University, School of Medicine and Health Sciences, Health Sciences Programs, Washington, DC 20052. Offers adult nurse practitioner (MSN, Post Master's Certificate); clinical practice management (MSHS); clinical research administration (MSHS); clinical research administration for nurses (MSN); emergency services management (MSHS); end-of-life care (MSHS, MSN); family nurse practitioner (MSN, Post Master's Certificate); immunohematology (MSHS); nursing (DNP); nursing leadership and management (MSN); physical therapy (DPT); physician assistant (MSHS); MSHS/MPH. Postbaccalaureate distance learning degree programs offered (no on-campus study). *Students:* 252 full-time (194 women), 328 part-time (238 women); includes 66 Black or African American, non-Hispanic/Latino; 4 American Indian or Alaska Native, non-Hispanic/Latino; 42 Asian, non-Hispanic/Latino; 24 Hispanic/Latino; 6 Native Hawaiian or other Pacific Islander, non-Hispanic/Latino, 38 international. Average age 32. 1,127 applicants, 49% accepted, 218 enrolled. In 2010, 171 master's, 52 doctorates, 71 other advanced degrees awarded. *Entrance requirements:* Additional exam requirements/recommendations for international students: Required—TOEFL (minimum score 550 paper-based; 213 computer-based). *Application deadline:* Applications are processed on a rolling basis. Application fee: $75. *Expenses:* Contact institution. *Unit head:* Jean E. Johnson, Senior Associate Dean, 202-994-3725, E-mail: jejohns@gwu.edu. *Application contact:* Joke Ogundiran, Director of Admission, 202-994-1668, Fax: 202-994-0870, E-mail: jokeogun@gwu.edu.

The George Washington University, School of Public Health and Health Services, Department of Epidemiology and Biostatistics, Washington, DC 20052. Offers biostatistics (MPH); epidemiology (MPH); microbiology and emerging infectious diseases (MSPH). *Faculty:* 19 full-time (11 women), 28 part-time/adjunct (17 women). *Students:* 59 full-time (51 women), 49 part-time (34 women); includes 16 Black or African American, non-Hispanic/Latino; 1 American Indian or Alaska Native, non-Hispanic/Latino; 25 Asian, non-Hispanic/Latino; 6 Hispanic/Latino; 3 Two or more races, non-Hispanic/Latino, 9 international. Average age 28. 193 applicants, 74% accepted, 39 enrolled. In 2010, 43 master's awarded. *Degree requirements:* For master's, case study or special project. *Entrance requirements:* For master's, GMAT, GRE General Test, or MCAT. Additional exam requirements/recommendations for international students: Required—TOEFL. *Application deadline:* For fall admission, 4/15 priority date for domestic students, 4/15 for international students; for spring admission, 11/1 for domestic and international students. Applications are processed on a rolling basis. Application fee: $75. *Financial support:* In 2010–11, 6 students received support. Tuition waivers available. Financial award application deadline: 2/15. *Unit head:* Dr. Alan E. Greenberg, Chair, 202-994-0612, E-mail: aeg1@gwu.edu. *Application contact:* Jane Smith, Director of Admissions, 202-994-0248, Fax: 202-994-1860, E-mail: sphhsinfo@gwumc.edu.

Georgia State University, College of Arts and Sciences, Department of Biology, Program in Applied and Environmental Microbiology, Atlanta, GA 30302-3083. Offers MS, PhD. Part-time programs available. Terminal master's awarded for partial completion of doctoral program. *Degree requirements:* For master's, thesis or alternative; for doctorate, thesis/dissertation, exam. *Entrance requirements:* For master's and doctorate, GRE General Test. Additional exam requirements/recommendations for international students: Required—TOEFL. Electronic applications accepted.

Harvard University, Graduate School of Arts and Sciences, Division of Medical Sciences, Boston, MA 02115. Offers biological chemistry and molecular pharmacology (PhD); cell biology (PhD); genetics (PhD); microbiology and molecular genetics (PhD); pathology (PhD), including experimental pathology. *Degree requirements:* For doctorate, thesis/dissertation. *Entrance requirements:* For doctorate, GRE General Test, GRE Subject Test. Additional exam requirements/recommendations for international students: Required—TOEFL. *Expenses:* Tuition: Full-time $34,976. Required fees: $1166. Full-time tuition and fees vary according to program.

Hood College, Graduate School, Program in Biomedical Science, Frederick, MD 21701-8575. Offers biomedical science (MS), including biotechnology/molecular biology, microbiology/immunology/virology, regulatory compliance; regulatory compliance (Certificate). Part-time and evening/weekend programs available. *Faculty:* 3 full-time (1 woman), 7 part-time/adjunct (4 women). *Students:* 9 full-time (2 women), 87 part-time (55 women); includes 16 Black or African American, non-Hispanic/Latino; 9 Asian, non-Hispanic/Latino; 3 Hispanic/Latino; 1 Two or more races, non-Hispanic/Latino, 7 international. Average age 29. 61 applicants, 64% accepted, 21 enrolled. In 2010, 9 master's, 3 other advanced degrees awarded. *Degree requirements:* For master's, comprehensive exam, thesis or alternative. *Entrance requirements:* For master's, bachelor's degree in biology; minimum GPA of 2.75; undergraduate course work in cell biology, chemistry, organic chemistry, and genetics. Additional exam requirements/recommendations for international students: Required—TOEFL (minimum score 575 paper-based; 231 computer-based; 89 iBT). *Application deadline:* For fall admission, 7/15 for domestic and international students; for spring admission, 12/15 for domestic and international students. Applications are processed on a rolling basis. Application fee: $35. Electronic applications accepted. *Expenses:* Tuition: Full-time $6480; part-time $360 per credit. Required fees: $100; $50 per term. *Financial support:* In 2010–11, 3 research assistantships with full tuition reimbursements (averaging $10,609 per year) were awarded. Financial award applicants required to submit FAFSA. *Unit head:* Dr. Oney Smith, Director, 301-696-3653, Fax: 301-696-3597, E-mail: osmith@hood.edu. *Application contact:* Dr. Allen P. Flora, Dean of Graduate School, 301-696-3811, Fax: 301-696-3597, E-mail: gofurther@hood.edu.

Howard University, College of Medicine, Department of Microbiology, Washington, DC 20059-0002. Offers PhD. *Degree requirements:* For doctorate, one foreign language, comprehensive exam, thesis/dissertation, qualifying exam, teaching experience. *Entrance requirements:* For doctorate, GRE General Test, minimum GPA of 3.0 in sciences. Additional exam requirements/recommendations for international students: Required—TOEFL. *Faculty research:* Immunology, molecular and cellular microbiology, microbial genetics, microbial physiology, pathogenic bacteriology, medical mycology, medical parasitology, virology.

Idaho State University, Office of Graduate Studies, College of Arts and Sciences, Department of Biological Sciences, Pocatello, ID 83209-8007. Offers biology (MNS, MS, DA, PhD); clinical laboratory science (MS); microbiology (MS). *Accreditation:* NAACLS. Part-time programs available. *Degree requirements:* For master's, comprehensive exam, thesis; for doctorate, comprehensive exam, thesis/dissertation, 9 credits of internship (for DA). *Entrance requirements:* For master's, GRE General Test, minimum GPA of 3.0 in all upper division classes; for doctorate, GRE General Test, GRE Subject Test (biology), diagnostic exam (DA), minimum GPA of 3.0 in all upper division classes. Additional exam requirements/recommendations for international students: Required—TOEFL (minimum score 550 paper-based; 213 computer-based; 80 iBT). Electronic applications accepted. *Faculty research:* Ecology, plant and animal physiology, plant and animal developmental biology, immunology, molecular biology, bioinfomatics.

Illinois Institute of Technology, Graduate College, College of Science and Letters, Department of Biological, Chemical and Physical Sciences, Biology Division, Chicago, IL 60616. Offers biochemistry (MBS, MS); biology (PhD); biotechnology (MBS, MS); cell and molecular biology (MBS, MS); microbiology (MB, MS); molecular biochemistry and biophysics (PhD); molecular biology and biophysics (MS). Part-time and evening/weekend programs available. Postbaccalaureate distance learning degree programs offered (minimal on-campus study). *Faculty:* 13 full-time (5 women), 5 part-time/adjunct (2 women). *Students:* 121 full-time (75 women), 56 part-time (37 women); includes 16 minority (5 Black or African American, non-Hispanic/Latino; 5 Asian, non-Hispanic/Latino; 5 Hispanic/Latino; 1 Two or more races, non-Hispanic/Latino), 104 international. Average age 27. 268 applicants, 76% accepted, 62 enrolled. In 2010, 74 master's, 4 doctorates awarded. Terminal master's awarded for partial completion of doctoral program. *Degree requirements:* For master's, comprehensive exam, thesis (for some programs); for doctorate, comprehensive exam, thesis/dissertation. *Entrance requirements:* For master's, GRE General Test (minimum score 1000 Quantitative and Verbal, 2.5 Analytical Writing), minimum undergraduate GPA of 3.0; for doctorate, GRE General Test (minimum score 1200 Quantitative and Verbal, 3.0 Analytical Writing), minimum undergraduate GPA of 3.0. Additional exam requirements/recommendations for international students: Required—TOEFL (minimum score 523 paper-based; 213 computer-based; 70 iBT); Recommended—IELTS (minimum score 5.5). *Application deadline:* For fall admission, 5/1 for domestic and international students; for spring admission, 10/15 for domestic and international students. Applications are processed on a rolling basis. Application fee: $40. Electronic applications accepted. *Expenses:* Tuition: Full-time $18,576; part-time $1032 per credit hour. Required fees: $583 per semester. One-time fee: $150. Tuition and fees vary according to program and student level. *Financial support:* In 2010–11, 15 research assistantships with full and partial tuition reimbursements (averaging $6,379 per year), 14 teaching assistantships with partial tuition reimbursements (averaging $6,296 per year) were awarded; fellowships with full and partial tuition reimbursements, career-related internships or fieldwork, Federal Work-Study, institutionally sponsored loans, scholarships/grants, traineeships, health care benefits, tuition waivers (partial), and unspecified assistantships also available. Support available to part-time students. Financial award applicants required to submit FAFSA. *Faculty research:* Structure and biophysics of macromolecular systems; efficacy and mechanism of action of chemopreventive agents in experimental carcinogenesis of breast, colon, lung and prostate; study of fundamental structural biochemistry problems that have direct links to the understanding and treatment of disease; spectroscopic techniques for the study of multi-domain proteins; molecular mechanisms of cancer and cancer gene therapy. Total annual research expenditures: $2.6 million. *Unit head:* Dr. Benjamin C. Stark, Professor and Associate Chair, 312-567-3488, Fax: 312-567-3494, E-mail: starkb@iit.edu. *Application contact:* Deborah Gibson, Director, Graduate Admissions, 866-472-3448, Fax: 312-567-3138, E-mail: inquiry.grad@iit.edu.

Illinois State University, Graduate School, College of Arts and Sciences, Department of Biological Sciences, Normal, IL 61790-2200. Offers animal behavior (MS); bacteriology (MS); biochemistry (MS); biological sciences (MS); biology (PhD); biophysics (MS); biotechnology (MS); botany (MS, PhD); cell biology (MS); conservation biology (MS); developmental biology (MS); ecology (MS, PhD); entomology (MS); evolutionary biology (MS); genetics (MS, PhD); immunology (MS); microbiology (MS, PhD); molecular biology (MS); molecular genetics (MS); neurobiology (MS); neuroscience (MS); parasitology (MS); physiology (MS, PhD); plant biology (MS); plant molecular biology (MS); plant sciences (MS); structural biology (MS); zoology (MS, PhD). Part-time programs available. *Degree requirements:* For master's, thesis or alternative; for doctorate, variable foreign language requirement, thesis/dissertation, 2 terms of residency. *Entrance requirements:* For master's, GRE General Test, minimum GPA of 2.6 in last 60 hours of course work; for doctorate, GRE General Test. *Faculty research:* Redoc balance and drug development in schistosoma mansoni, control of the growth of listeria monocytogenes at low temperature, regulation of cell expansion and microtubule function by SPRI, CRUI: physiology and fitness consequences of different life history phenotypes.

Indiana State University, College of Graduate and Professional Studies, College of Arts and Sciences, Department of Biology, Terre Haute, IN 47809. Offers ecology (PhD); life sciences (MS); microbiology (PhD); physiology (PhD); science education (MS). *Degree requirements:* For master's, thesis (for some programs); for doctorate, comprehensive exam, thesis/dissertation. *Entrance requirements:* For master's and doctorate, GRE General Test. Electronic applications accepted.

Indiana University Bloomington, University Graduate School, College of Arts and Sciences, Department of Biology, Bloomington, IN 47405. Offers biology teaching (MAT); biotechnology

Microbiology

Indiana University Bloomington (continued)

(MA); evolution, ecology, and behavior (MA, PhD); genetics (PhD); microbiology (MA, PhD); molecular, cellular, and developmental biology (PhD); plant sciences (MA, PhD); zoology (MA, PhD). *Faculty:* 58 full-time (15 women), 21 part-time/adjunct (6 women). *Students:* 163 full-time (98 women), 7 part-time (2 women); includes 17 minority (3 Black or African American, non-Hispanic/Latino; 1 American Indian or Alaska Native, non-Hispanic/Latino; 7 Asian, non-Hispanic/Latino; 5 Hispanic/Latino; 1 Native Hawaiian or other Pacific Islander, non-Hispanic/Latino), 52 international. Average age 27. 346 applicants, 15% accepted, 24 enrolled. In 2010, 17 master's, 24 doctorates awarded. Terminal master's awarded for partial completion of doctoral program. *Degree requirements:* For master's, thesis, oral defense; for doctorate, thesis/dissertation, oral defense. *Entrance requirements:* For master's and doctorate, GRE General Test. Additional exam requirements/recommendations for international students: Required—TOEFL (minimum score 100 iBT). *Application deadline:* For fall admission, 1/5 priority date for domestic students, 12/1 priority date for international students. Application fee: $55 ($65 for international students). Electronic applications accepted. *Financial support:* In 2010–11, 170 students received support, including 64 fellowships with tuition reimbursements available (averaging $19,484 per year), 44 research assistantships with tuition reimbursements available (averaging $20,300 per year), 62 teaching assistantships with tuition reimbursements available (averaging $20,521 per year); scholarships/grants, traineeships, health care benefits, and unspecified assistantships also available. Financial award application deadline: 1/5. *Faculty research:* Evolution, ecology and behavior; microbiology; molecular biology and genetics; plant biology. *Unit head:* Dr. Roger Innes, Chair, 812-855-2219, Fax: 812-855-6082, E-mail: rinnes@indiana.edu. *Application contact:* Tracey D. Stohr, Graduate Student Recruitment Coordinator, 812-856-6303, Fax: 812-855-6082, E-mail: gradbio@indiana.edu.

Indiana University–Purdue University Indianapolis, Indiana University School of Medicine, Department of Microbiology and Immunology, Indianapolis, IN 46202-2896. Offers MS, PhD, MD/MS, MD/PhD. *Faculty:* 20 full-time (2 women). *Students:* 31 full-time (22 women); includes 7 minority (2 Black or African American, non-Hispanic/Latino; 3 Asian, non-Hispanic/Latino; 1 Hispanic/Latino; 1 Two or more races, non-Hispanic/Latino), 10 international. Average age 27. 7 applicants, 86% accepted, 6 enrolled. In 2010, 1 master's, 10 doctorates awarded. Terminal master's awarded for partial completion of doctoral program. *Degree requirements:* For master's, thesis; for doctorate, thesis/dissertation. *Entrance requirements:* For master's and doctorate, GRE General Test, previous course work in calculus, cell biology, chemistry, genetics, physics, and biochemistry. *Application deadline:* For fall admission, 3/1 for domestic students. Applications are processed on a rolling basis. Application fee: $55 ($65 for international students). *Financial support:* In 2010–11, 2 fellowships with full tuition reimbursements (averaging $8,313 per year), 6 teaching assistantships with full tuition reimbursements (averaging $18,391 per year) were awarded; research assistantships with full tuition reimbursements, Federal Work-Study, institutionally sponsored loans, scholarships/grants, traineeships, and tuition waivers (partial) also available. Financial award application deadline: 2/1. *Faculty research:* Host-parasite interactions, molecular biology, cellular and molecular immunology and hematology, viral and bacterial pathogenesis, cancer research. Total annual research expenditures: $4.2 million. *Unit head:* Dr. Hal E. Broxmeyer, Chairman, 317-274-7672, Fax: 317-274-4090, E-mail: hbroxmey@iupui.edu. *Application contact:* 317-274-7671, Fax: 317-274-4090.

Inter American University of Puerto Rico, Metropolitan Campus, Graduate Programs, Program in Medical Technology, San Juan, PR 00919-1293. Offers administration of clinical laboratories (MS); molecular microbiology (MS). *Accreditation:* NAACLS. Part-time programs available. *Degree requirements:* For master's, comprehensive exam. *Entrance requirements:* For master's, BS in medical technology, minimum GPA of 2.5. Electronic applications accepted.

Iowa State University of Science and Technology, College of Veterinary Medicine and Graduate College, Graduate Programs in Veterinary Medicine, Department of Veterinary Microbiology and Preventive Medicine, Ames, IA 50011. Offers veterinary microbiology (MS, PhD). *Faculty:* 27 full-time (6 women), 9 part-time/adjunct (4 women). *Students:* 35 full-time (15 women), 30 part-time (17 women); includes 3 Black or African American, non-Hispanic/Latino; 4 Asian, non-Hispanic/Latino; 2 Hispanic/Latino, 16 international. 23 applicants, 57% accepted, 10 enrolled. In 2010, 4 master's, 7 doctorates awarded. *Degree requirements:* For master's, thesis or alternative; for doctorate, thesis/dissertation. *Entrance requirements:* For master's and doctorate, GRE General Test. Additional exam requirements/recommendations for international students: Required—TOEFL (minimum score 550 paper-based; 79 iBT), IELTS (minimum score 6.5). *Application deadline:* For fall admission, 2/1 priority date for domestic and international students. Applications are processed on a rolling basis. Application fee: $40 ($90 for international students). Electronic applications accepted. *Financial support:* In 2010–11, 21 research assistantships with full and partial tuition reimbursements (averaging $18,313 per year) were awarded; fellowships, teaching assistantships with full and partial tuition reimbursements, scholarships/grants, health care benefits, and unspecified assistantships also available. *Faculty research:* Bacteriology, immunology, virology, public health and food safety. *Unit head:* Dr. Michael Wannemuehler, Chair, 515-294-5776, E-mail: vetmicro@iastate.edu. *Application contact:* Dr. Michael Wannemuehler, Chair, 515-294-5776, E-mail: vetmicro@iastate.edu.

Iowa State University of Science and Technology, Graduate College, Interdisciplinary Programs, Program in Microbiology, Ames, IA 50011. Offers MS, PhD. *Students:* 16 full-time (10 women), 8 part-time (4 women); includes 1 Black or African American, non-Hispanic/Latino; 4 Asian, non-Hispanic/Latino, 4 international. In 2010, 5 master's, 3 doctorates awarded. *Degree requirements:* For master's, thesis or alternative; for doctorate, thesis/dissertation. *Entrance requirements:* For master's and doctorate, GRE General Test. Additional exam requirements/recommendations for international students: Required—TOEFL (minimum score 550 paper-based; 79 iBT), IELTS (minimum score 6.5). *Application deadline:* For fall admission, 2/1 priority date for domestic and international students. Application fee: $40 ($90 for international students). Electronic applications accepted. *Financial support:* In 2010–11, 15 research assistantships with partial tuition reimbursements (averaging $17,636 per year), 2 teaching assistantships with partial tuition reimbursements (averaging $16,250 per year) were awarded; scholarships/grants, health care benefits, and unspecified assistantships also available. *Unit head:* Dr. Adam Bogdanove, Chair, Supervising Committee, 515-294-9052. *Application contact:* Information Contact, 515-294-5836, Fax: 515-294-2592, E-mail: grad_admissions@iastate.edu.

The Johns Hopkins University, Bloomberg School of Public Health, W. Harry Feinstone Department of Molecular Microbiology and Immunology, Baltimore, MD 21218-2699. Offers MHS, Sc M, PhD. *Faculty:* 41 full-time (10 women), 10 part-time/adjunct (1 woman). *Students:* 91 full-time (58 women), 3 part-time (2 women); includes 33 minority (8 Black or African American, non-Hispanic/Latino; 13 Asian, non-Hispanic/Latino; 9 Hispanic/Latino; 3 Two or more races, non-Hispanic/Latino), 24 international. Average age 25. 184 applicants, 53% accepted, 38 enrolled. In 2010, 25 master's, 8 doctorates awarded. Terminal master's awarded for partial completion of doctoral program. *Degree requirements:* For master's, comprehensive exam, thesis (for some programs), essay, written exams; for doctorate, comprehensive exam, thesis/dissertation, 1 year full-time residency, oral and written exams. *Entrance requirements:* For master's, GRE General Test or MCAT, 3 letters of recommendation, curriculum vitae; for doctorate, GRE General Test, 3 letters of recommendation, transcripts, curriculum vitae. Additional exam requirements/recommendations for international students: Required—TOEFL (minimum score 600 paper-based; 250 computer-based). *Application deadline:* For fall admission, 1/2 priority date for domestic and international students. Applications are processed on a rolling basis. Application fee: $45. Electronic applications accepted. *Financial support:* In 2010–11, 37 fellowships with full and partial tuition reimbursements, 28 research assistantships with tuition reimbursements were awarded; Federal Work-Study, institutionally sponsored loans, scholarships/grants, and stipends also available. Financial award application deadline: 3/15; financial award applicants required to submit FAFSA. *Faculty research:* Immunology, virology, bacteriology, parasitology, vector biology, disease ecology, pathogenesis of infectious disease, immune responses to infectious agents, vector-borne and tropical diseases, biochemistry and molecular biology of infectious agents, population genetics of insect vectors, genetic regulation and immune responses in insect vectors, vaccine development, hormonal effects on pathogenesis and immune responses. Total annual research expenditures: $14.5 million. *Unit head:* Dr. Diane E. Griffin, Chair, 410-955-3459, Fax: 410-955-0105, E-mail: dgriffin@jhsph.edu. *Application contact:* Gail O'Connor, Senior Academic Program Coordinator, 410-614-4232, Fax: 410-955-0105, E-mail: goconnor@jhsph.edu.

Kansas State University, Graduate School, College of Arts and Sciences, Division of Biology, Manhattan, KS 66506. Offers biology (MS, PhD); microbiology (PhD). Terminal master's awarded for partial completion of doctoral program. *Degree requirements:* For master's, thesis; for doctorate, thesis/dissertation. *Entrance requirements:* For master's, GRE General Test, minimum undergraduate GPA of 3.0; for doctorate, GRE General Test, minimum GPA of 3.0. Additional exam requirements/recommendations for international students: Required—TOEFL (minimum score 550 paper-based; 213 computer-based). Electronic applications accepted. *Faculty research:* Ecology, genetics, developmental biology, microbiology, cell biology.

Loma Linda University, School of Medicine, Department of Biochemistry/Microbiology, Loma Linda, CA 92350. Offers MS, PhD. Part-time programs available. *Degree requirements:* For master's, thesis or alternative; for doctorate, thesis/dissertation. *Entrance requirements:* For master's and doctorate, GRE General Test. Additional exam requirements/recommendations for international students: Required—TOEFL (minimum score 550 paper-based; 213 computer-based). *Faculty research:* Physical chemistry of macromolecules, biochemistry of endocrine system, biochemical mechanism of bone volume regulation.

Long Island University, C.W. Post Campus, School of Health Professions and Nursing, Department of Biomedical Sciences, Brookville, NY 11548-1300. Offers cardiovascular perfusion (MS); clinical laboratory management (MS); medical biology (MS), including hematology, immunology, medical biology, medical chemistry, medical microbiology. Part-time and evening/weekend programs available. Postbaccalaureate distance learning degree programs offered. *Degree requirements:* For master's, thesis. *Entrance requirements:* For master's, minimum GPA of 2.75 in major. Electronic applications accepted.

Louisiana State University Health Sciences Center, School of Graduate Studies in New Orleans, Department of Microbiology, Immunology, and Parasitology, New Orleans, LA 70112-1393. Offers microbiology and immunology (MS, PhD); MD/PhD. Terminal master's awarded for partial completion of doctoral program. *Degree requirements:* For master's, comprehensive exam, thesis; for doctorate, comprehensive exam, thesis/dissertation, preliminary exam, qualifying exam. *Entrance requirements:* For master's and doctorate, GRE General Test. Additional exam requirements/recommendations for international students: Required—TOEFL. *Faculty research:* Microbial physiology, animal virology, vaccine development, AIDS drug studies, pathogenic mechanisms, molecular immunology.

Louisiana State University Health Sciences Center at Shreveport, Department of Microbiology and Immunology, Shreveport, LA 71130-3932. Offers MS, PhD, MD/PhD. Terminal master's awarded for partial completion of doctoral program. *Degree requirements:* For master's, thesis; for doctorate, thesis/dissertation. *Entrance requirements:* For master's and doctorate, GRE General Test. Additional exam requirements/recommendations for international students: Required—TOEFL. *Faculty research:* Infectious disease, pathogenesis, molecular virology and biology.

Loyola University Chicago, Graduate School, Department of Microbiology and Immunology, Maywood, IL 60153. Offers immunology (PhD); microbiology (MS); MD/PhD. *Faculty:* 15 full-time (4 women). *Students:* 34 full-time (22 women); includes 3 minority (2 Asian, non-Hispanic/Latino; 1 Hispanic/Latino), 8 international. Average age 27. 69 applicants, 23% accepted, 7 enrolled. In 2010, 1 doctorate awarded. Terminal master's awarded for partial completion of doctoral program. *Degree requirements:* For master's, thesis; for doctorate, comprehensive exam, thesis/dissertation. *Entrance requirements:* For master's and doctorate, GRE General Test. Additional exam requirements/recommendations for international students: Required—TOEFL. *Application deadline:* Applications are processed on a rolling basis. Application fee: $0. Electronic applications accepted. *Expenses:* Tuition: Full-time $14,940; part-time $830 per credit hour. Required fees: $87 per semester. Part-time tuition and fees vary according to course load and program. *Financial support:* In 2010–11, 5 fellowships with tuition reimbursements (averaging $25,000 per year), 24 research assistantships with tuition reimbursements (averaging $25,000 per year) were awarded; institutionally sponsored loans and scholarships/grants also available. Financial award application deadline: 2/15. *Faculty research:* Virology, microbial physiology and genetics, immune system development and regulation, signal transduction and host-pathogen interactions, biofilms. Total annual research expenditures: $2.2 million. *Unit head:* Dr. Katherine L. Knight, Chair, 708-216-3385, Fax: 708-216-9574, E-mail: kknight@lumc.edu. *Application contact:* Dr. Karen Visick, Graduate Program Director, 708-216-0869, Fax: 708-216-9574, E-mail: kvisick@lumc.edu.

Marquette University, Graduate School, College of Arts and Sciences, Department of Biology, Milwaukee, WI 53201-1881. Offers cell biology (MS, PhD); developmental biology (MS, PhD); ecology (MS, PhD); epithelial physiology (MS, PhD); genetics (MS, PhD); microbiology (MS, PhD); molecular biology (MS, PhD); muscle and exercise physiology (MS, PhD); neuroscience (PhD). *Faculty:* 25 full-time (12 women), 2 part-time/adjunct (1 woman). *Students:* 23 full-time (9 women), 12 part-time (8 women); includes 1 minority (Asian, non-Hispanic/Latino), 15 international. Average age 26. 82 applicants, 15% accepted, 5 enrolled. In 2010, 3 master's, 2 doctorates awarded. Terminal master's awarded for partial completion of doctoral program. *Degree requirements:* For master's, comprehensive exam, thesis, 1 year of teaching experience or equivalent; for doctorate, thesis/dissertation, 1 year of teaching experience or equivalent, qualifying exam. *Entrance requirements:* For master's and doctorate, GRE General Test, GRE Subject Test, official transcripts from all current and previous colleges/universities except Marquette, statement of professional goals and aspirations, three letters of recommendation. Additional exam requirements/recommendations for international students: Required—TOEFL (minimum score 530 paper-based; 78 computer-based). *Application deadline:* For fall admission, 12/15 for domestic and international students. Application fee: $50. Electronic applications accepted. *Expenses:* Tuition: Full-time $16,290; part-time $905 per credit hour. Tuition and fees vary according to program. *Financial support:* In 2010–11, 2 research assistantships, 34 teaching assistantships were awarded; fellowships, Federal Work-Study, institutionally sponsored loans, scholarships/grants, and tuition waivers (full and partial) also available. Support available to part-time students. Financial award application deadline: 2/15. *Faculty research:* Neurobiology, neuroendocrinology, epithelial physiology, neuropeptide interactions, synaptic transmission. Total annual research expenditures: $1.3 million. *Unit head:* Dr. Robert Fitts, Chair, 414-288-1748, Fax: 414-288-7357. *Application contact:* Debbie Weaver, Administrative Assistant, 414-288-7355, Fax: 414-288-7357.

Massachusetts Institute of Technology, School of Science, Department of Biology, Cambridge, MA 02139-4307. Offers biochemistry (PhD); biological oceanography (PhD); biology (PhD); biophysical chemistry and molecular structure (PhD); cell biology (PhD); computational and systems biology (PhD); developmental biology (PhD); genetics (PhD); immunology (PhD); microbiology (PhD); molecular biology (PhD); neurobiology (PhD). *Faculty:* 56 full-time (14 women). *Students:* 251 full-time (135 women); includes 74 minority (4 Black or African American, non-Hispanic/Latino; 1 American Indian or Alaska Native, non-Hispanic/Latino; 29 Asian, non-Hispanic/Latino; 33 Hispanic/Latino; 7 Two or more races, non-Hispanic/Latino), 29 international. Average age 26. 652 applicants, 18% accepted, 58 enrolled. In 2010, 41 doctorates awarded. *Degree requirements:* For doctorate, comprehensive exam, thesis/dissertation. *Entrance requirements:* For doctorate, GRE General Test. Additional exam requirements/recommendations for international students: Required—TOEFL (minimum score 577 paper-based; 233 computer-based), IELTS (minimum score 6.5). *Application deadline:* For fall admission, 12/1 for domestic and international students. Application fee: $75. Electronic applications accepted. *Expenses:* Tuition: Full-time $38,940; part-time $605 per unit. Required fees: $272. *Financial support:* In 2010–11, 215 students received support, including 115 fellowships with tuition reimbursements available (averaging $33,090 per year), 132 research assistantships with tuition reimbursements available (averaging $31,846 per year); teaching assistantships with tuition reimbursements available, Federal Work-Study, institutionally sponsored loans, scholarships/grants, traineeships, health care benefits, and unspecified assistantships also available. *Faculty research:* DNA recombination, replication and repair; transcription and gene regulation; signal transduction; cell cycle; neuronal cell fate. Total annual research expenditures: $60.6 million. *Unit head:* Prof. Chris Kaiser, Head, 617-253-4701, E-mail: mitbio@mit.edu. *Application contact:* Biology Education Office, 617-253-3717, Fax: 617-258-9329, E-mail: gradbio@mit.edu.

McGill University, Faculty of Graduate and Postdoctoral Studies, Faculty of Agricultural and Environmental Sciences, Department of Natural Resource Sciences, Montréal, QC H3A 2T5, Canada. Offers entomology (M Sc, PhD); environmental assessment (M Sc); forest science (M Sc, PhD); microbiology (M Sc, PhD); micrometeorology (M Sc, PhD); neotropical environment (M Sc, PhD); soil science (M Sc, PhD); wildlife biology (M Sc, PhD).

McGill University, Faculty of Graduate and Postdoctoral Studies, Faculty of Medicine, Department of Microbiology and Immunology, Montréal, QC H3A 2T5, Canada. Offers M Sc, M Sc A, PhD.

Medical College of Wisconsin, Graduate School of Biomedical Sciences, Department of Microbiology and Molecular Genetics, Milwaukee, WI 53226-0509. Offers MS, PhD, MD/PhD. *Degree requirements:* For doctorate, comprehensive exam, thesis/dissertation. *Entrance requirements:* For doctorate, GRE General Test. Additional exam requirements/recommendations for international students: Required—TOEFL. *Expenses:* Tuition: Full-time $30,000; part-time $710 per credit. Required fees: $150. *Faculty research:* Virology, immunology, bacterial toxins, regulation of gene expression.

Medical University of South Carolina, College of Graduate Studies, Department of Microbiology and Immunology, Charleston, SC 29425. Offers MS, PhD, DMD/PhD, MD/PhD. *Faculty:* 15 full-time (6 women), 30 part-time/adjunct (9 women). *Students:* 15 full-time (9 women), 2 part-time (0 women); includes 2 Black or African American, non-Hispanic/Latino; 1 Hispanic/Latino, 1 international. Average age 26. 8 applicants, 75% accepted, 4 enrolled. In 2010, 4 master's, 3 doctorates awarded. Terminal master's awarded for partial completion of doctoral program. *Degree requirements:* For master's, thesis; for doctorate, thesis/dissertation, oral and written exams. *Entrance requirements:* For master's, GRE General Test, MCAT, or DAT, minimum GPA of 3.0; for doctorate, GRE General Test, interview, minimum GPA of 3.0, research experience. Additional exam requirements/recommendations for international students: Required—TOEFL (minimum score 600 paper-based; 250 computer-based; 100 iBT). *Application deadline:* For fall admission, 1/15 priority date for domestic and international students. Applications are processed on a rolling basis. Application fee: $0 ($95 for international students). Electronic applications accepted. *Financial support:* In 2010–11, 10 research assistantships with partial tuition reimbursements (averaging $23,000 per year) were awarded; Federal Work-Study and scholarships/grants also available. Support available to part-time students. Financial award application deadline: 3/10; financial award applicants required to submit FAFSA. *Faculty research:* Inmate and adaptive immunology, gene therapy/vector development, vaccinology, proteomics of biowarfare agents, bacterial and fungal pathogenesis. *Unit head:* Dr. Zihai Li, Chair, 843-792-7915, Fax: 843-792-6590. *Application contact:* Dr. Laura Kasman, Assistant Professor, 843-792-8117, Fax: 843-792-2464, E-mail: kasmanl@musc.edu.

Meharry Medical College, School of Graduate Studies, Program in Biomedical Sciences, Microbiology and Immunology Emphasis, Nashville, TN 37208-9989. Offers PhD, MD/PhD. *Degree requirements:* For doctorate, comprehensive exam, thesis/dissertation. *Entrance requirements:* For doctorate, GRE General Test, GRE Subject Test, undergraduate degree in related science. *Faculty research:* Microbial and bacterial pathogenesis, viral transcription, immune response to viruses and parasites.

Miami University, Graduate School, College of Arts and Science, Department of Microbiology, Oxford, OH 45056. Offers MS, PhD. Part-time programs available. *Students:* 24 full-time (12 women); includes 3 minority (1 Black or African American, non-Hispanic/Latino; 2 Asian, non-Hispanic/Latino), 4 international. Average age 27. In 2010, 1 doctorate awarded. *Entrance requirements:* For master's, GRE General Test, minimum undergraduate GPA of 3.0 during previous 2 years or 2.75 overall; for doctorate, GRE General Test, minimum undergraduate GPA of 2.75, 3.0 graduate. Additional exam requirements/recommendations for international students: Required—TOEFL. Application fee: $50. *Expenses:* Tuition, state resident: full-time $11,616; part-time $484 per credit hour. Tuition, nonresident: full-time $25,656; part-time $1069 per credit hour. Required fees: $528. *Financial support:* Fellowships with full tuition reimbursements, research assistantships with full tuition reimbursements, teaching assistantships with full tuition reimbursements, Federal Work-Study, institutionally sponsored loans, scholarships/grants, health care benefits, tuition waivers (full), and unspecified assistantships available. Financial award application deadline: 3/1; financial award applicants required to submit FAFSA. *Unit head:* Dr. Louis A. Actis, Chair, 513-529-5421, Fax: 513-529-2431, E-mail: actisla@muohio.edu. *Application contact:* Graduate Admissions Chair, 513-529-5422, E-mail: microbiology@muohio.edu.

Michigan State University, College of Human Medicine and The Graduate School, Graduate Programs in Human Medicine, East Lansing, MI 48824. Offers biochemistry and molecular biology (MS, PhD); epidemiology (MS, PhD); microbiology (MS); microbiology and molecular genetics (PhD); pharmacology and toxicology (MS, PhD); physiology (MS, PhD); public health (MPH). *Entrance requirements:* Additional exam requirements/recommendations for international students: Required—TOEFL.

Michigan State University, College of Osteopathic Medicine and The Graduate School, Graduate Studies in Osteopathic Medicine, East Lansing, MI 48824. Offers biochemistry and molecular biology (MS, PhD); microbiology (MS); microbiology and molecular genetics (PhD); pharmacology and toxicology (MS, PhD), including integrative pharmacology (MS), pharmacology and toxicology, pharmacology and toxicology-environmental toxicology (PhD); physiology (MS, PhD).

Michigan State University, College of Veterinary Medicine and The Graduate School, Graduate Programs in Veterinary Medicine and College of Natural Science and Graduate Programs in Human Medicine, Department of Microbiology and Molecular Genetics, East Lansing, MI 48824. Offers industrial microbiology (MS, PhD); microbiology (MS, PhD); microbiology and molecular genetics (MS, PhD); microbiology–environmental toxicology (PhD). *Entrance requirements:* For master's, GRE General Test. Additional exam requirements/recommendations for international students: Required—TOEFL (minimum score 550 paper-based; 213 computer-based), Michigan State University ELT (minimum score 85), Michigan English Language Assessment Battery (minimum score 83). Electronic applications accepted.

Michigan State University, The Graduate School, College of Agriculture and Natural Resources, MSU-DOE Plant Research Laboratory, East Lansing, MI 48824. Offers biochemistry and molecular biology (PhD); cellular and molecular biology (PhD); crop and soil sciences (PhD); genetics (PhD); microbiology and molecular genetics (PhD); plant biology (PhD); plant physiology (PhD). Offered jointly with the Department of Energy. *Degree requirements:* For doctorate, comprehensive exam, thesis/dissertation, laboratory rotation, defense of dissertation. *Entrance requirements:* For doctorate, GRE General Test, acceptance into one of the affiliated department programs; 3 letters of recommendation; bachelor's degree or equivalent in life sciences, chemistry, biochemistry, or biophysics; research experience. Electronic applications accepted. *Faculty research:* Role of hormones in the regulation of plant development and physiology, molecular mechanisms associated with signal recognition, development and application of genetic methods and materials, protein routing and function.

Montana State University, College of Graduate Studies, College of Letters and Science, Department of Microbiology, Bozeman, MT 59717. Offers MS, PhD. Part-time programs available. *Faculty:* 7 full-time (2 women), 3 part-time/adjunct (all women). *Students:* 3 full-time (1 woman), 22 part-time (18 women); includes 1 minority (Hispanic/Latino), 5 international. Average age 31. 28 applicants, 18% accepted, 3 enrolled. In 2010, 1 master's awarded. *Degree requirements:* For master's, comprehensive exam; for doctorate, comprehensive exam, thesis/dissertation. *Entrance requirements:* For master's and doctorate, GRE General Test. Additional exam requirements/recommendations for international students: Required—TOEFL (minimum score 550 paper-based; 213 computer-based). *Application deadline:* For fall admission, 2/1 priority date for domestic students, 5/15 priority date for international students; for spring admission, 12/1 priority date for domestic students, 10/1 priority date for international students. Applications are processed on a rolling basis. Application fee: $30. Electronic applications accepted. *Expenses:* Tuition, state resident: full-time $5554. Tuition, nonresident: full-time $14,646. Required fees: $1233. *Financial support:* In 2010–11, 25 students received support, including 4 fellowships with full tuition reimbursements available (averaging $28,000 per year), 15 research assistantships with full tuition reimbursements available (averaging $22,000 per year), 4 teaching assistantships with full tuition reimbursements available (averaging $12,000 per year); traineeships and unspecified assistantships also available. Financial award application deadline: 3/1; financial award applicants required to submit FAFSA. *Faculty research:* Medical microbiology, environmental microbiology, biofilms, immunology, molecular biology and bioinformatics. Total annual research expenditures: $1.3 million. *Unit head:* Dr. Mark Jutila, Head, 406-994-4540, Fax: 406-994-4926. *Application contact:* Dr. Carl A. Fox, Vice Provost for Graduate Education, 406-994-4145, Fax: 406-994-7433, E-mail: gradstudy@montana.edu.

New York Medical College, Graduate School of Basic Medical Sciences, Microbiology and Immunology Department, Valhalla, NY 10595-1691. Offers MS, PhD, MD/PhD. Part-time and evening/weekend programs available. *Faculty:* 13 full-time (4 women), 1 part-time/adjunct (0 women). *Students:* 18 full-time (14 women), 5 part-time (4 women); includes 2 Black or African American, non-Hispanic/Latino; 1 Asian, non-Hispanic/Latino, 7 international. Average age 27. 8 applicants, 100% accepted, 5 enrolled. In 2010, 3 master's, 2 doctorates awarded. Terminal master's awarded for partial completion of doctoral program. *Degree requirements:* For master's, thesis; for doctorate, comprehensive exam, thesis/dissertation. *Entrance requirements:* For master's and doctorate, GRE General Test. Additional exam requirements/recommendations for international students: Required—TOEFL. *Application deadline:* For fall admission, 7/1 priority date for domestic students, 5/1 priority date for international students; for spring admission, 12/1 priority date for domestic students, 10/1 priority date for international students. Applications are processed on a rolling basis. Application fee: $50 ($75 for international students). Electronic applications accepted. *Financial support:* In 2010–11, 4 fellowships, 7 research assistantships with full tuition reimbursements (averaging $24,000 per year) were awarded; career-related internships or fieldwork, Federal Work-Study, institutionally sponsored loans, scholarships/grants, traineeships, tuition waivers (full), unspecified assistantships, and health benefits (for PhD candidates only) also available. Financial award applicants required to submit FAFSA. *Faculty research:* Tumor and transplantation immunology, molecular mechanisms of DNA repair, virus-host interactions. *Unit head:* Dr. Raj Tiwari, Director, 914-594-4870. *Application contact:* Valerie Romeo-Messana, Admission Coordinator, 914-594-4110, Fax: 914-594-4944, E-mail: v_romeomessana@nymc.edu.

New York University, Graduate School of Arts and Science, Department of Biology, New York, NY 10012-1019. Offers biology (PhD); biomedical journalism (MS); cancer and molecular biology (PhD); computational biology (PhD); computers in biological research (MS); developmental genetics (PhD); general biology (MS); immunology and microbiology (PhD); molecular genetics (PhD); neurobiology (PhD); oral biology (MS); plant biology (PhD); recombinant DNA technology (MS); MS/MBA. Part-time programs available. *Faculty:* 24 full-time (5 women). *Students:* 155 full-time (89 women), 38 part-time (24 women); includes 29 Asian, non-Hispanic/Latino; 7 Hispanic/Latino, 88 international. Average age 27. 324 applicants, 69% accepted, 63 enrolled. In 2010, 55 master's, 4 doctorates awarded. Terminal master's awarded for partial completion of doctoral program. *Degree requirements:* For master's, thesis or alternative, qualifying paper; for doctorate, comprehensive exam, thesis/dissertation. *Entrance requirements:* For master's, GRE General Test; for doctorate, GRE General Test, GRE Subject Test. Additional exam requirements/recommendations for international students: Required—TOEFL. *Application deadline:* For fall admission, 12/15 priority date for domestic students. Application fee: $90. *Financial support:* Fellowships with tuition reimbursements, research assistantships with tuition reimbursements, teaching assistantships with tuition reimbursements, career-related internships or fieldwork, Federal Work-Study, institutionally sponsored loans, scholarships/grants, health care benefits, and unspecified assistantships available. Financial award application deadline: 12/15; financial award applicants required to submit FAFSA. *Faculty research:* Genomics, molecular and cell biology, development and molecular genetics, molecular evolution of plants and animals. *Unit head:* Gloria Coruzzi, Chair, 212-998-8200, Fax: 212-995-4015, E-mail: biology@nyu.edu. *Application contact:* Justin Blau, Director of Graduate Studies, 212-998-8200, Fax: 212-995-4015, E-mail: biology@nyu.edu.

New York University, School of Medicine, New York, NY 10012-1019. Offers biomedical sciences (PhD), including biomedical imaging, cellular and molecular biology, computational biology, developmental genetics, medical and molecular parasitology, microbiology, molecular oncobiology and immunology, neuroscience and physiology, pathobiology, pharmacology, structural biology; clinical investigation (MS); medicine (MD); MD/MA; MD/MPA; MD/MS; MD/PhD. *Accreditation:* LCME/AMA (one or more programs are accredited). *Degree requirements:* For master's, comprehensive exam, thesis; for doctorate, comprehensive exam, thesis/dissertation. *Entrance requirements:* MCAT. Additional exam requirements/recommendations for international students: Required—TOEFL. *Expenses:* Contact institution. *Faculty research:* AIDS, cancer, neuroscience, molecular biology, neuroscience, cell biology and molecular genetics, structural biology, microbial pathogenesis and host defense, pharmacology, molecular oncology and immunology.

New York University, School of Medicine and Graduate School of Arts and Science, Sackler Institute of Graduate Biomedical Sciences, Department of Microbiology, New York, NY 10012-1019. Offers PhD, MD/PhD. *Degree requirements:* For doctorate, one foreign language, comprehensive exam, thesis/dissertation, qualifying exam. *Entrance requirements:* For doctorate, GRE General Test, GRE Subject Test. Additional exam requirements/recommendations for international students: Required—TOEFL. *Faculty research:* Aspects of microbiology, parasitology, and genetics; virology.

North Carolina State University, Graduate School, College of Agriculture and Life Sciences, Department of Microbiology, Program in Microbiology, Raleigh, NC 27695. Offers MS, PhD. *Degree requirements:* For master's, thesis (for some programs); for doctorate, thesis/dissertation. *Entrance requirements:* For master's and doctorate, GRE. Electronic applications accepted.

North Dakota State University, College of Graduate and Interdisciplinary Studies, College of Agriculture, Food Systems, and Natural Resources, Department of Veterinary and Microbiological Sciences, Fargo, ND 58108. Offers food safety (MS); microbiology (MS); molecular pathogenesis (PhD). Part-time programs available. *Students:* 12 full-time (7 women), 5 part-time (all women). 18 applicants, 17% accepted. In 2010, 1 master's awarded. *Degree requirements:* For master's, thesis; for doctorate, thesis/dissertation, oral and written preliminary exams. *Entrance requirements:* For master's and doctorate, GRE. Additional exam requirements/recommendations for international students: Required—TOEFL (minimum score 525 paper-based; 197 computer-based; 71 iBT). *Application deadline:* For fall admission, 3/15 priority date for domestic students. Applications are processed on a rolling basis. Application fee: $25. *Financial support:* Fellowships with full tuition reimbursements, research assistantships with full tuition reimbursements, teaching assistantships with full tuition reimbursements, Federal Work-Study and institutionally sponsored loans available. Financial award application deadline: 4/15. *Faculty research:* Bacterial gene regulation, antibiotic resistance, molecular virology, mechanisms of bacterial pathogenesis, immunology of animals. *Unit head:* Dr. Doug Freeman, Head, 701-231-7511, E-mail: douglas.freeman@ndsu.nodak.edu. *Application contact:* Dr. Eugene S. Berry, Associate Professor, 701-231-7520, Fax: 701-231-7514, E-mail: eugene.berry@ndsu.edu.

Northwestern University, Northwestern University Feinberg School of Medicine and Interdepartmental Programs, Integrated Graduate Programs in the Life Sciences, Chicago, IL

Microbiology

Northwestern University (continued)
60611. Offers cancer biology (PhD); cell biology (PhD); developmental biology (PhD); evolutionary biology (PhD); immunology and microbial pathogenesis (PhD); molecular biology and genetics (PhD); neurobiology (PhD); pharmacology and toxicology (PhD); structural biology and biochemistry (PhD). *Degree requirements:* For doctorate, comprehensive exam, thesis/dissertation, written and oral qualifying exams. *Entrance requirements:* For doctorate, GRE General Test. Additional exam requirements/recommendations for international students: Required—TOEFL (minimum score 600 paper-based; 250 computer-based). Electronic applications accepted.

The Ohio State University, Graduate School, College of Arts and Sciences, Division of Natural and Mathematical Sciences, Department of Microbiology, Columbus, OH 43210. Offers MS, PhD. *Faculty:* 24. *Students:* 22 full-time (10 women), 32 part-time (18 women); includes 1 Black or African American, non-Hispanic/Latino; 2 Asian, non-Hispanic/Latino, 19 international. Average age 27. In 2010, 3 master's, 8 doctorates awarded. *Degree requirements:* For master's, thesis optional; for doctorate, thesis/dissertation. *Entrance requirements:* For master's, GRE General Test, GRE Subject Test in biology, biochemistry or chemistry (recommended); for doctorate, GRE General Test; GRE Subject Test in biology, biochemistry or chemistry (recommended). Additional exam requirements/recommendations for international students: Required—TOEFL (minimum score 600 paper-based; 250 computer-based). *Application deadline:* For fall admission, 8/15 priority date for domestic students, 7/1 priority date for international students; for winter admission, 12/1 priority date for domestic students, 11/1 priority date for international students; for spring admission, 3/1 priority date for domestic students, 2/1 priority date for international students. Applications are processed on a rolling basis. Application fee: $40 ($50 for international students). Electronic applications accepted. *Expenses:* Tuition, state resident: full-time $10,605. Tuition, nonresident: full-time $26,535. Tuition and fees vary according to course load and program. *Financial support:* Fellowships, research assistantships, teaching assistantships, Federal Work-Study and institutionally sponsored loans available. Support available to part-time students. *Unit head:* Tina M. Henkin, Chair, 614-292-2301, Fax: 614-292-8120, E-mail: henkin.3@osu.edu. *Application contact:* 614-292-9444, Fax: 614-292-3895, E-mail: domestic.grad@osu.edu.

Ohio University, Graduate College, College of Arts and Sciences, Department of Biological Sciences, Athens, OH 45701-2979. Offers biological sciences (MS, PhD); cell biology and physiology (MS, PhD); ecology and evolutionary biology (MS, PhD); exercise physiology and muscle biology (MS, PhD); microbiology (MS, PhD); neuroscience (MS, PhD). *Students:* 32 full-time (9 women), 5 part-time (2 women); includes 2 minority (1 Black or African American, non-Hispanic/Latino; 1 Hispanic/Latino), 9 international. 51 applicants, 37% accepted, 7 enrolled. In 2010, 2 master's, 9 doctorates awarded. Terminal master's awarded for partial completion of doctoral program. *Degree requirements:* For master's, comprehensive exam, thesis, 1 quarter of teaching experience; for doctorate, comprehensive exam, thesis/dissertation, 2 quarters of teaching experience. *Entrance requirements:* For master's, GRE General Test, names of three faculty members whose research interests most closely match the applicant's interest; for doctorate, GRE General Test, essay concerning prior training, research interest and career goals, plus names of three faculty members whose research interests most closely match the applicant's interest. Additional exam requirements/recommendations for international students: Required—TOEFL (minimum score 620 paper-based; 105 iBT) or IELTS (minimum score 7.5). *Application deadline:* For fall admission, 1/15 for domestic and international students. Application fee: $50 ($55 for international students). Electronic applications accepted. *Financial support:* In 2010–11, 1 fellowship with full tuition reimbursement (averaging $18,957 per year), 10 research assistantships with full tuition reimbursements (averaging $18,957 per year), 42 teaching assistantships with full tuition reimbursements (averaging $18,957 per year) were awarded; Federal Work-Study and institutionally sponsored loans also available. Financial award application deadline: 1/15. *Faculty research:* Ecology and evolutionary biology, exercise physiology and muscle biology, neurobiology, cell biology, physiology. Total annual research expenditures: $2.8 million. *Unit head:* Dr. Ralph DiCaprio, Chair, 740-593-2290, Fax: 740-593-0300, E-mail: dicaprir@ohio.edu. *Application contact:* Dr. Patrick Hassett, Graduate Chair, 740-593-4793, Fax: 740-593-0300, E-mail: hassett@ohio.edu.

Oklahoma State University, College of Arts and Sciences, Department of Microbiology and Molecular Genetics, Stillwater, OK 74078. Offers MS, PhD. *Faculty:* 22 full-time (4 women). *Students:* 7 full-time (4 women), 20 part-time (10 women); includes 1 American Indian or Alaska Native, non-Hispanic/Latino; 1 Asian, non-Hispanic/Latino, 14 international. Average age 28. 81 applicants, 9% accepted, 3 enrolled. In 2010, 1 master's, 2 doctorates awarded. *Degree requirements:* For master's, thesis; for doctorate, comprehensive exam, thesis/dissertation. *Entrance requirements:* For master's, GRE General Test; for doctorate, GRE General Test. Additional exam requirements/recommendations for international students: Required—TOEFL (minimum score 550 paper-based; 79 iBT). *Application deadline:* For fall admission, 3/1 priority date for international students; for spring admission, 8/1 priority date for international students. Applications are processed on a rolling basis. Application fee: $40 ($75 for international students). Electronic applications accepted. *Expenses:* Tuition, state resident: full-time $3716; part-time $154.85 per credit hour. Tuition, nonresident: full-time $14,892; part-time $621 per credit hour. Required fees: $2044; $85.20 per credit hour. One-time fee: $50. Tuition and fees vary according to course load and campus/location. *Financial support:* In 2010–11, 16 research assistantships (averaging $17,685 per year), 11 teaching assistantships (averaging $17,044 per year) were awarded; career-related internships or fieldwork, Federal Work-Study, scholarships/grants, health care benefits, tuition waivers (partial), and unspecified assistantships also available. Support available to part-time students. Financial award application deadline: 3/1; financial award applicants required to submit FAFSA. *Faculty research:* Bioinformatics, genomics-genetics, virology, environmental microbiology, development-molecular mechanisms. *Unit head:* Dr. Bill Picking, Head, 405-744-7180, Fax: 405-744-6790. *Application contact:* Dr. Gordon Emslie, Dean, 405-744-6368, Fax: 405-744-0355, E-mail: grad-i@okstate.edu.

Oregon Health & Science University, School of Medicine, Graduate Programs in Medicine, Program in Molecular and Cellular Biosciences, Department of Molecular Microbiology and Immunology, Portland, OR 97239-3098. Offers PhD. *Faculty:* 10 full-time (3 women). *Students:* 29 full-time (18 women); includes 1 Asian, non-Hispanic/Latino; 4 Hispanic/Latino, 1 international. Average age 29. In 2010, 3 doctorates awarded. Terminal master's awarded for partial completion of doctoral program. *Degree requirements:* For doctorate, comprehensive exam, thesis/dissertation. *Entrance requirements:* For doctorate, GRE General Test (minimum scores: 500 Verbal/600 Quantitative/4.5 Analytical) or MCAT (for some programs). Additional exam requirements/recommendations for international students: Required—TOEFL. Electronic applications accepted. *Financial support:* Health care benefits and full tuition and stipends available. *Faculty research:* Molecular biology of bacterial and viral pathogens, cellular and humoral immunology, molecular biology of microbes. *Unit head:* Dr. Eric Barklis, Program Director, 503-494-7768, E-mail: mmi@ohsu.edu. *Application contact:* Kathy Shinall, Program Coordinator, 503-494-7768, E-mail: mmi@ohsu.edu.

Oregon State University, Graduate School, College of Science, Department of Microbiology, Corvallis, OR 97331. Offers MA, MAIS, MS, PhD. Part-time programs available. Terminal master's awarded for partial completion of doctoral program. *Degree requirements:* For master's, thesis; for doctorate, one foreign language, thesis/dissertation. *Entrance requirements:* For master's and doctorate, GRE General Test, minimum GPA of 3.0 in last 90 hours. Additional exam requirements/recommendations for international students: Required—TOEFL. *Faculty research:* Genetics, physiology, biotechnology, pathogenic microbiology, plant virology.

Penn State Hershey Medical Center, College of Medicine, Graduate School Programs in the Biomedical Sciences, Graduate Program in Microbiology and Immunology, Hershey, PA 17033. Offers genetics (PhD); immunology (MS, PhD); microbiology (MS); microbiology/virology (PhD); molecular biology (PhD); MD/PhD. *Students:* 12 applicants, 75% accepted, 3 enrolled. In 2010, 1 doctorate awarded. Terminal master's awarded for partial completion of doctoral program. *Degree requirements:* For master's, thesis or alternative; for doctorate, comprehensive exam, thesis/dissertation, oral exam. *Entrance requirements:* For doctorate, GRE General Test, minimum GPA of 3.0. Additional exam requirements/recommendations for international students: Required—TOEFL. *Application deadline:* For fall admission, 1/31 priority date for domestic students, 2/1 priority date for international students. Applications are processed on a rolling basis. Application fee: $45. Electronic applications accepted. *Financial support:* In 2010–11, research assistantships with full tuition reimbursements (averaging $22,260 per year); fellowships with full tuition reimbursements, scholarships/grants, health care benefits, and unspecified assistantships also available. Financial award applicants required to submit FAFSA. *Faculty research:* Virus replication and assembly, oncogenesis, interactions of viruses with host cells and animal model systems. *Unit head:* Dr. Richard J. Courtney, Chair, 717-531-7659, Fax: 717-531-6522, E-mail: micro-grad-hmc@psu.edu. *Application contact:* Billie Burns, Secretary, 717-531-7659, Fax: 717-531-6522, E-mail: micro-grad-hmc@psu.edu.

Penn State University Park, Graduate School, Eberly College of Science, Department of Biochemistry and Molecular Biology, Program in Biochemistry, Microbiology, and Molecular Biology, State College, University Park, PA 16802-1503. Offers MS, PhD. *Unit head:* Dr. Ronald Porter, Director of Graduate Studies, 814-863-4903, E-mail: rdp1@psu.edu. *Application contact:* Dr. Ronald Porter, Director of Graduate Studies, 814-863-4903, E-mail: rdp1@psu.edu.

Purdue University, Graduate School, College of Science, Department of Biological Sciences, West Lafayette, IN 47907. Offers biochemistry (PhD); biophysics (PhD); cell and developmental biology (PhD); ecology, evolutionary and population biology (MS, PhD), including ecology, evolutionary biology, population biology; genetics (MS, PhD); microbiology (MS, PhD); molecular biology (PhD); neurobiology (MS, PhD); plant physiology (PhD). Terminal master's awarded for partial completion of doctoral program. *Degree requirements:* For master's, thesis (for some programs); for doctorate, thesis/dissertation, seminars, teaching experience. *Entrance requirements:* For master's and doctorate, GRE General Test. Additional exam requirements/recommendations for international students: Required—TOEFL. Electronic applications accepted.

Purdue University, School of Veterinary Medicine and Graduate School, Graduate Programs in Veterinary Medicine, Department of Comparative Pathobiology, West Lafayette, IN 47907-2027. Offers comparative epidemiology and public health (MS); comparative epidemiology and public heath (PhD); comparative microbiology and immunology (MS, PhD); comparative pathobiology (MS, PhD); interdisciplinary studies (PhD), including microbial pathogenesis, molecular signaling and cancer biology, molecular virology; lab animal medicine (MS); veterinary anatomic pathology (MS); veterinary clinical pathology (MS). Terminal master's awarded for partial completion of doctoral program. *Degree requirements:* For master's, thesis (for some programs); for doctorate, thesis/dissertation. *Entrance requirements:* For master's and doctorate, GRE General Test. Additional exam requirements/recommendations for international students: Required—TOEFL (minimum score 575 paper-based; 232 computer-based), IELTS (minimum score 6.5), TWE (minimum score 4). Electronic applications accepted.

Queen's University at Kingston, School of Graduate Studies and Research, Faculty of Health Sciences, Department of Microbiology and Immunology, Kingston, ON K7L 3N6, Canada. Offers M Sc, PhD. Part-time programs available. *Degree requirements:* For master's, thesis; for doctorate, comprehensive exam, thesis/dissertation. *Entrance requirements:* For master's and doctorate, minimum B+ average. Additional exam requirements/recommendations for international students: Required—TOEFL (minimum score 600 paper-based; 250 computer-based). Electronic applications accepted. *Faculty research:* Bacteriology, virology, immunology, education in microbiology and immunology, microbial pathogenesis.

Quinnipiac University, School of Health Sciences, Program in Medical Laboratory Sciences, Hamden, CT 06518-1940. Offers biomedical sciences (MHS); laboratory management (MHS); microbiology (MHS). Part-time programs available. *Faculty:* 11 full-time (5 women), 15 part-time/adjunct (7 women). *Students:* 44 full-time (21 women), 32 part-time (15 women); includes 13 minority (5 Black or African American, non-Hispanic/Latino; 6 Asian, non-Hispanic/Latino; 2 Hispanic/Latino), 25 international. 54 applicants, 70% accepted, 27 enrolled. In 2010, 17 master's awarded. *Degree requirements:* For master's, comprehensive exam, thesis optional. *Entrance requirements:* For master's, minimum GPA of 2.75; bachelor's degree in biological, medical, or health sciences. Additional exam requirements/recommendations for international students: Required—TOEFL (minimum score 575 paper-based; 233 computer-based; 90 iBT), IELTS (minimum score 6.5). *Application deadline:* For fall admission, 7/30 priority date for domestic students, 4/30 priority date for international students; for spring admission, 12/15 priority date for domestic students, 9/15 priority date for international students. Applications are processed on a rolling basis. Application fee: $45. Electronic applications accepted. *Expenses:* Tuition: Part-time $810 per credit. Required fees: $35 per credit. *Financial support:* Federal Work-Study, tuition waivers (partial), and unspecified assistantships available. Support available to part-time students. Financial award application deadline: 4/15; financial award applicants required to submit FAFSA. *Faculty research:* Microbial physiology, fermentation technology. *Unit head:* Dr. Kenneth Kaloustian, Director, 203-582-8676, Fax: 203-582-3443, E-mail: ken.kaloustian@quinnipiac.edu. *Application contact:* Kristin Parent, Assistant Director of Graduate Health Sciences Admissions, 800-462-1944, Fax: 203-582-3443, E-mail: kristin.parent@quinnipiac.edu.

Rosalind Franklin University of Medicine and Science, School of Graduate and Post-doctoral Studies—Interdisciplinary Graduate Program in Biomedical Sciences, Department of Microbiology and Immunology, North Chicago, IL 60064-3095. Offers MS, PhD, MD/PhD. Terminal master's awarded for partial completion of doctoral program. *Degree requirements:* For master's, comprehensive exam, thesis; for doctorate, comprehensive exam, thesis/dissertation. *Entrance requirements:* For master's and doctorate, GRE General Test. Additional exam requirements/recommendations for international students: Required—TOEFL, TWE. *Faculty research:* Molecular biology, parasitology, virology.

Rush University, Graduate College, Division of Immunology and Microbiology, Chicago, IL 60612-3832. Offers microbiology (PhD); virology (MS, PhD), including immunology, virology; MD/PhD. *Degree requirements:* For doctorate, thesis/dissertation, comprehensive preliminary exam. *Entrance requirements:* For doctorate, GRE General Test, interview, minimum GPA of 3.0. Additional exam requirements/recommendations for international students: Required—TOEFL. *Faculty research:* Immune interactions of cells and membranes, HIV immunopathogenesis, autoimmunity, tumor biology.

Rutgers, The State University of New Jersey, New Brunswick, Graduate School-New Brunswick, Programs in the Molecular Biosciences, Program in Microbiology and Molecular Genetics, Piscataway, NJ 08854-8097. Offers applied microbiology (MS, PhD); clinical microbiology (MS, PhD); computational molecular biology (PhD); immunology (MS, PhD); microbial biochemistry (MS, PhD); molecular genetics (MS, PhD); virology (MS, PhD). MS, PhD offered jointly with University of Medicine and Dentistry of New Jersey. Part-time programs available. Terminal master's awarded for partial completion of doctoral program. *Degree requirements:* For master's, comprehensive exam, thesis or alternative; for doctorate, comprehensive exam, thesis/dissertation, written qualifying exam. *Entrance requirements:* For master's, GRE General Test, minimum GPA of 3.0; for doctorate, GRE General Test, GRE Subject Test (recommended), minimum GPA of 3.0. Additional exam requirements/recommendations for international students: Required—TOEFL. Electronic applications accepted. *Expenses:* Tuition, state resident: full-time $7200; part-time $600 per credit. Tuition, nonresident: full-time $11,124; part-time $927 per credit. *Faculty research:* Molecular genetics and microbial physiology; virology and pathogenic microbiology; applied, environmental and industrial microbiology; computers in molecular biology.

Saint Louis University, Graduate Education and School of Medicine, Graduate Program in Biomedical Sciences, Department of Molecular Microbiology and Immunology, St. Louis, MO 63103-2097. Offers PhD. *Degree requirements:* For doctorate, comprehensive exam, thesis/dissertation, qualifying exams. *Entrance requirements:* For doctorate, GRE General Test (GRE

Subject Test optional), letters of recommendation, resume, interview. Additional exam requirements/recommendations for international students: Required—TOEFL (minimum score 525 paper-based; 194 computer-based). Electronic applications accepted. *Faculty research:* Pathogenesis of hepatitis C virus, herperviruses, pox viruses, rheumatoid arthritis, antiviral drugs and vaccines in biodefense, cancer gene therapy, virology and immunology.

San Diego State University, Graduate and Research Affairs, College of Sciences, Department of Biology, Program in Microbiology, San Diego, CA 92182. Offers MS. *Degree requirements:* For master's, thesis, oral exam. *Entrance requirements:* For master's, GRE General Test, GRE Subject Test, resume or curriculum vitae, 2 letters of recommendation. Additional exam requirements/recommendations for international students: Required—TOEFL. Electronic applications accepted.

San Francisco State University, Division of Graduate Studies, College of Science and Engineering, Department of Biology, Program in Microbiology, San Francisco, CA 94132-1722. Offers MS. *Application deadline:* Applications are processed on a rolling basis. *Unit head:* Dr. Diana Chu, Program Coordinator, 415-405-3487, E-mail: chud@sfsu.edu. *Application contact:* Dr. Robert Patterson, Graduate Coordinator, 415-338-1100, E-mail: patters@sfsu.edu.

San Jose State University, Graduate Studies and Research, College of Science, Department of Biological Sciences, San Jose, CA 95192-0001. Offers biological sciences (MA, MS); molecular biology and microbiology (MS); organismal biology, conservation and ecology (MS); physiology (MS). Part-time programs available. *Entrance requirements:* For master's, GRE. Electronic applications accepted. *Faculty research:* Systemic physiology, molecular genetics, SEM studies, toxicology, large mammal ecology.

Seton Hall University, College of Arts and Sciences, Department of Biological Sciences, South Orange, NJ 07079-2697. Offers biology (MS); biology/business administration (MS); microbiology (MS); molecular bioscience (PhD); molecular bioscience/neuroscience (PhD). Part-time and evening/weekend programs available. *Degree requirements:* For master's, thesis optional; for doctorate, comprehensive exam, thesis/dissertation. *Entrance requirements:* For master's and doctorate, GRE or MS from accredited university in the U.S. Additional exam requirements/recommendations for international students: Required—TOEFL. Electronic applications accepted. *Faculty research:* Neurobiology, genetics, immunology, molecular biology, cellular physiology, toxicology, microbiology, bioinformatics.

South Dakota State University, Graduate School, College of Agriculture and Biological Sciences, Department of Biology and Microbiology, Brookings, SD 57007. Offers biological sciences (MS, PhD). Part-time programs available. *Degree requirements:* For master's, thesis (for some programs), oral exam; for doctorate, comprehensive exam, thesis/dissertation, oral exam. *Entrance requirements:* For master's and doctorate, GRE General Test. Additional exam requirements/recommendations for international students: Required—TOEFL (minimum score 600 paper-based; 250 computer-based; 100 iBT). *Faculty research:* Ecosystem ecology; plant, animal and microbial genomics; animal infectious disease, microbial bioproducts.

Southern Illinois University Carbondale, Graduate School, College of Science, Program in Molecular Biology, Microbiology, and Biochemistry, Carbondale, IL 62901-4701. Offers MS, PhD. *Degree requirements:* For master's, thesis; for doctorate, thesis/dissertation. *Entrance requirements:* For master's, GRE, minimum GPA of 2.7; for doctorate, GRE, minimum GPA of 3.25. Additional exam requirements/recommendations for international students: Required—TOEFL. *Faculty research:* Prokaryotic gene regulation and expression; eukaryotic gene regulation; microbial, phylogenetic, and metabolic diversity; immune responses to tumors, pathogens, and autoantigens; protein folding and structure.

Southwestern Oklahoma State University, College of Professional and Graduate Studies, School of Behavioral Sciences and Education, Specialization in Health Sciences and Microbiology, Weatherford, OK 73096-3098. Offers M Ed.

Stanford University, School of Medicine, Graduate Programs in Medicine, Department of Microbiology and Immunology, Stanford, CA 94305-9991. Offers PhD. *Degree requirements:* For doctorate, comprehensive exam, thesis/dissertation, 2 quarters teaching assistantship. *Entrance requirements:* For doctorate, GRE General Test, GRE Subject Test (biology or biochemistry). Additional exam requirements/recommendations for international students: Required—TOEFL. Electronic applications accepted. *Expenses:* Tuition: Full-time $38,700; part-time $860 per unit. One-time fee: $200 full-time. *Faculty research:* Molecular pathogenesis of bacteria viruses and parasites, immune system function, autoimmunity, molecular biology.

State University of New York Upstate Medical University, College of Graduate Studies, Program in Microbiology and Immunology, Syracuse, NY 13210-2334. Offers microbiology (MS); microbiology and immunology (PhD); MD/PhD. Terminal master's awarded for partial completion of doctoral program. *Degree requirements:* For master's, thesis; for doctorate, comprehensive exam, thesis/dissertation. *Entrance requirements:* For master's, GRE General Test, interview; for doctorate, GRE General Test, telephone interview. Additional exam requirements/recommendations for international students: Required—TOEFL. Electronic applications accepted. *Faculty research:* Cancer, disorders of the nervous system, infectious diseases, diabetes/metabolic disorders/cardiovascular diseases.

Stony Brook University, State University of New York, Stony Brook University Medical Center, School of Medicine and Graduate School, Graduate Programs in Medicine, Department of Molecular Genetics and Microbiology, Stony Brook, NY 11794. Offers molecular microbiology (PhD). *Faculty:* 18 full-time (6 women). *Students:* 26 full-time (16 women); includes 2 Asian, non-Hispanic/Latino; 1 Hispanic/Latino, 9 international. Average age 27. 85 applicants, 20% accepted, 5 enrolled. In 2010, 9 doctorates awarded. *Degree requirements:* For doctorate, comprehensive exam, thesis/dissertation. *Entrance requirements:* For doctorate, GRE General Test, GRE Subject Test. Additional exam requirements/recommendations for international students: Required—TOEFL. *Application deadline:* For fall admission, 1/15 for domestic students. Application fee: $100. *Expenses:* Tuition, state resident: full-time $8370; part-time $349 per credit. Tuition, nonresident: full-time $13,780; part-time $574 per credit. Required fees: $994. *Financial support:* In 2010–11, 19 research assistantships were awarded; fellowships, teaching assistantships, Federal Work-Study also available. Financial award application deadline: 3/15. *Faculty research:* Adenovirus molecular genetics, molecular biology of tumors, virus SV40, mechanism of tumor infection by SAV virus. Total annual research expenditures: $9.8 million. *Unit head:* Dr. Jorge Benach, Interim Chair, 631-632-8800, Fax: 631-632-9797. *Application contact:* Dr. Janet Hearing, Director, 631-632-8778, Fax: 631-632-9797, E-mail: jhearing@ms.cc.sunysb.edu.

Temple University, Health Sciences Center, School of Medicine and Graduate School, Doctor of Medicine Program, Department of Microbiology and Immunology, Philadelphia, PA 19140-5104. Offers MS, PhD, MD/PhD. *Degree requirements:* For master's, thesis; for doctorate, thesis/dissertation, research seminars. *Entrance requirements:* For master's and doctorate, GRE General Test, GRE Subject Test, minimum GPA of 3.0. Additional exam requirements/recommendations for international students: Required—TOEFL (minimum score 600 paper-based; 250 computer-based). Electronic applications accepted. *Faculty research:* Molecular and cellular immunology, molecular and biochemical microbiology, molecular genetics.

Texas A&M Health Science Center, Graduate School of Biomedical Sciences, Department of Microbial and Molecular Pathogenesis, College Station, TX 77840. Offers immunology (PhD); microbiology (PhD); molecular biology (PhD); virology (PhD). *Degree requirements:* For doctorate, thesis/dissertation. *Entrance requirements:* For doctorate, GRE General Test, minimum GPA of 3.0. *Faculty research:* Molecular pathogenesis, microbial therapeutics.

Texas A&M University, College of Science, Department of Biology, College Station, TX 77843. Offers biology (MS, PhD); botany (MS, PhD); microbiology (MS, PhD); molecular and cell biology (PhD); neuroscience (MS, PhD); zoology (MS, PhD). *Faculty:* 39. *Students:* 107 full-time (60 women), 4 part-time (3 women); includes 1 Black or African American, non-Hispanic/

Latino; 5 Asian, non-Hispanic/Latino; 5 Hispanic/Latino, 47 international. Average age 28. In 2010, 3 master's, 6 doctorates awarded. *Degree requirements:* For master's, thesis or alternative; for doctorate, comprehensive exam, thesis/dissertation. *Entrance requirements:* For master's and doctorate, GRE General Test. Additional exam requirements/recommendations for international students: Required—TOEFL. *Application deadline:* For fall admission, 1/15 for domestic students. Applications are processed on a rolling basis. Application fee: $50 ($75 for international students). Electronic applications accepted. *Financial support:* Fellowships, research assistantships, teaching assistantships available. Financial award application deadline: 4/1; financial award applicants required to submit FAFSA. *Unit head:* Dr. Jack McMahan, Department Head, 979-845-2301, E-mail: granster@mail.bio.tamu.edu. *Application contact:* Dr. Jack McMahan, Department Head, 979-845-2301, E-mail: granster@mail.bio.tamu.edu.

Texas A&M University, College of Veterinary Medicine and Biomedical Sciences, Department of Veterinary Pathobiology, College Station, TX 77843. Offers genetics (MS, PhD); veterinary microbiology (MS, PhD); veterinary parasitology (MS, PhD); veterinary pathology (MS, PhD). Part-time programs available. Postbaccalaureate distance learning degree programs offered. *Faculty:* 26. *Students:* 25 full-time (17 women), 18 part-time (14 women); includes 1 Black or African American, non-Hispanic/Latino; 3 Asian, non-Hispanic/Latino; 2 Hispanic/Latino, 10 international. Average age 33. In 2010, 1 master's, 5 doctorates awarded. Terminal master's awarded for partial completion of doctoral program. *Degree requirements:* For master's, thesis, seminars; for doctorate, thesis/dissertation, seminars. *Entrance requirements:* For master's and doctorate, GRE General Test, minimum GPA of 3.0 in last 60 hours. Additional exam requirements/recommendations for international students: Required—TOEFL. *Application deadline:* For fall admission, 3/1 priority date for domestic students; for spring admission, 8/1 priority date for domestic students. Applications are processed on a rolling basis. Application fee: $50 ($75 for international students). Electronic applications accepted. *Financial support:* In 2010–11, fellowships with partial tuition reimbursements (averaging $16,000 per year), research assistantships with partial tuition reimbursements (averaging $15,400 per year), teaching assistantships with partial tuition reimbursements (averaging $16,000 per year) were awarded; Federal Work-Study, institutionally sponsored loans, scholarships/grants, traineeships, health care benefits, and unspecified assistantships also available. Support available to part-time students. Financial award applicants required to submit FAFSA. *Faculty research:* Infectious and noninfectious diseases of animals and birds, animal genetics, molecular biology, immunology, virology. *Unit head:* Dr. Linda Logan, Head, 979-862-6559, Fax: 979-845-9231, E-mail: llogan@cvm.tamu.edu. *Application contact:* Dr. Patricia Holman, Graduate Advisor, 979-845-4202, Fax: 979-862-1147, E-mail: pholman@cvm.tamu.edu.

Texas Tech University, Graduate School, College of Arts and Sciences, Department of Biological Sciences, Lubbock, TX 79409-3131. Offers biology (MS, PhD); microbiology (MS); zoology (MS, PhD). Part-time programs available. *Faculty:* 28 full-time (6 women). *Students:* 115 full-time (63 women), 12 part-time (5 women); includes 1 Asian, non-Hispanic/Latino; 6 Hispanic/Latino; 2 Two or more races, non-Hispanic/Latino, 66 international. Average age 28. 79 applicants, 32% accepted, 20 enrolled. In 2010, 14 master's, 6 doctorates awarded. *Degree requirements:* For master's, thesis or alternative; for doctorate, thesis/dissertation. *Entrance requirements:* For master's and doctorate, GRE General Test. Additional exam requirements/recommendations for international students: Required—TOEFL (minimum score 550 paper-based; 213 computer-based; 79 iBT). *Application deadline:* For fall admission, 6/1 priority date for domestic students, 1/15 priority date for international students; for spring admission, 9/1 priority date for domestic students, 6/15 priority date for international students. Applications are processed on a rolling basis. Application fee: $50 ($75 for international students). Electronic applications accepted. *Expenses:* Tuition, state resident: full-time $5496; part-time $228.99 per credit hour. Tuition, nonresident: full-time $12,936; part-time $538.99 per credit hour. Required fees: $2674; $36 per credit hour. $905 per semester. *Financial support:* In 2010–11, 123 students received support, including 14 research assistantships with partial tuition reimbursements available (averaging $6,332 per year), 49 teaching assistantships with partial tuition reimbursements available (averaging $7,121 per year). Financial award application deadline: 4/15; financial award applicants required to submit FAFSA. *Faculty research:* Biodiversity and evolution, climate change in arid ecosystems, plant biology and biotechnology, animal communication and behavior, zoonotic and emerging diseases. Total annual research expenditures: $2.3 million. *Unit head:* Dr. Llewellyn D. Densmore, Chair, 806-742-2715, Fax: 806-742-2963, E-mail: lou.densmore@ttu.edu. *Application contact:* Dr. Randall M. Jeter, Graduate Adviser, 806-742-2710 Ext. 270, Fax: 806-742-2963, E-mail: randall.jeter@ttu.edu.

Thomas Jefferson University, Jefferson College of Graduate Studies, Graduate Program in Immunology and Microbial Pathogenesis, Philadelphia, PA 19107. Offers PhD. *Faculty:* 38 full-time (5 women), 2 part-time/adjunct (0 women). *Students:* 24 full-time (14 women); includes 3 minority (1 Black or African American, non-Hispanic/Latino; 2 Asian, non-Hispanic/Latino), 3 international. 50 applicants, 10% accepted, 3 enrolled. In 2010, 3 doctorates awarded. *Degree requirements:* For doctorate, comprehensive exam, thesis/dissertation. *Entrance requirements:* For doctorate, GRE General Test, minimum GPA of 3.2. Additional exam requirements/recommendations for international students: Required—TOEFL (minimum score 250 computer-based; 100 iBT) or IELTS. *Application deadline:* For fall admission, 1/5 priority date for domestic and international students. Applications are processed on a rolling basis. Application fee: $50. Electronic applications accepted. *Financial support:* In 2010–11, 24 students received support, including 24 fellowships with full tuition reimbursements available (averaging $54,723 per year); Federal Work-Study, institutionally sponsored loans, scholarships/grants, traineeships, and stipends also available. Support available to part-time students. Financial award application deadline: 5/1; financial award applicants required to submit FAFSA. Total annual research expenditures: $36.3 million. *Unit head:* Dr. Kishore Alugupalli, Program Director, 215-503-4550, Fax: 215-923-4153, E-mail: kishore.alugupalli@jefferson.edu. *Application contact:* Marc E. Stearns, Director of Admissions, 215-503-0155, Fax: 215-503-9920, E-mail: jcgs-info@jefferson.edu.

Thomas Jefferson University, Jefferson College of Graduate Studies, MS Program in Microbiology, Philadelphia, PA 19107. Offers MS. Part-time and evening/weekend programs available. *Faculty:* 15 full-time (4 women), 9 part-time/adjunct (5 women). *Students:* 36 part-time (19 women); includes 6 minority (4 Black or African American, non-Hispanic/Latino; 2 Asian, non-Hispanic/Latino), 3 international. 37 applicants, 70% accepted, 22 enrolled. In 2010, 8 master's awarded. *Degree requirements:* For master's, thesis, clerkship. *Entrance requirements:* For master's, GRE General Test or MCAT, minimum GPA of 3.0. Additional exam requirements/recommendations for international students: Required—TOEFL (minimum score 250 computer-based; 100 iBT) or IELTS. *Application deadline:* For fall admission, 8/1 priority date for domestic students, 3/1 priority date for international students; for winter admission, 12/1 priority date for domestic students, 6/1 priority date for international students; for spring admission, 4/1 priority date for domestic students. Applications are processed on a rolling basis. Application fee: $50. Electronic applications accepted. *Expenses:* Contact institution. *Financial support:* In 2010–11, 18 students received support. Federal Work-Study and institutionally sponsored loans available. Support available to part-time students. Financial award application deadline: 5/1; financial award applicants required to submit FAFSA. *Unit head:* Dr. Jerome G. Buescher, Program Director, 215-503-0159, Fax: 215-503-3433, E-mail: jerome.buescher@jefferson.edu. *Application contact:* Eleanor M. Gorman, Assistant Coordinator, Graduate Center Programs, 215-503-5799, Fax: 215-503-3433, E-mail: eleanor.gorman@jefferson.edu.

Tufts University, Sackler School of Graduate Biomedical Sciences, Department of Molecular Biology and Microbiology, Medford, MA 02155. Offers molecular microbiology (PhD), including microbiology, molecular biology, molecular microbiology. *Faculty:* 18 full-time (7 women). *Students:* 29 full-time (21 women); includes 2 Black or African American, non-Hispanic/Latino; 4 Asian, non-Hispanic/Latino; 2 Hispanic/Latino, 1 international. Average age 27. 80 applicants, 18% accepted, 5 enrolled. In 2010, 4 doctorates awarded. Terminal master's awarded for partial completion of doctoral program. *Degree requirements:* For doctorate, comprehensive exam, thesis/dissertation. *Entrance requirements:* For doctorate, GRE General Test, 3 letters

Microbiology

Tufts University (continued)

of reference. Additional exam requirements/recommendations for international students: Required—TOEFL. *Application deadline:* For fall admission, 12/15 priority date for domestic and international students. Applications are processed on a rolling basis. Application fee: $70. Electronic applications accepted. *Expenses:* Tuition: Full-time $39,624; part-time $3962 per course. Required fees: $40 per year. Full-time tuition and fees vary according to degree level, program and student level. Part-time tuition and fees vary according to course load. *Financial support:* In 2010–11, 29 students received support, including 29 research assistantships with full tuition reimbursements available (averaging $28,500 per year); scholarships/grants, health care benefits, and tuition waivers (full) also available. Financial award application deadline: 12/15. *Faculty research:* Fundamental problems of molecular biology of prokaryotes, eukaryotes and their viruses. *Unit head:* Dr. Michael Malamy, Director, 617-636-6750, Fax: 617-636-0337, E-mail: michael.malamy@tufts.edu. *Application contact:* Kellie Johnston, Associate Director of Admissions, 617-636-6767, Fax: 617-633-0375, E-mail: sackler-school@tufts.edu.

Tulane University, School of Medicine and School of Liberal Arts, Graduate Programs in Biomedical Sciences, Department of Microbiology and Immunology, New Orleans, LA 70118-5669. Offers MS, PhD, MD/PhD. MS and PhD offered through the Graduate School. *Degree requirements:* For master's, thesis; for doctorate, 2 foreign languages, thesis/dissertation. *Entrance requirements:* For master's, GRE General Test, minimum B average in undergraduate course work; for doctorate, GRE General Test, GRE Subject Test. Additional exam requirements/recommendations for international students: Required—TOEFL. Electronic applications accepted. *Faculty research:* Vaccine development, viral pathogenesis, molecular virology, bacterial pathogenesis, fungal pathogenesis.

Universidad Central del Caribe, School of Medicine, Program in Biomedical Sciences, Bayamón, PR 00960-6032. Offers anatomy and cell biology (MA, MS); biochemistry (MS); biomedical sciences (MA); cellular and molecular biology (PhD); microbiology and immunology (MA, MS); pharmacology (MS); physiology (MS).

Université de Montréal, Faculty of Medicine, Department of Microbiology and Immunology, Montréal, QC H3C 3J7, Canada. Offers M Sc, PhD. Programs offered jointly with Faculty of Veterinary Medicine and Université du Québec, Institut Armand-Frappier. Terminal master's awarded for partial completion of doctoral program. *Degree requirements:* For master's, thesis; for doctorate, thesis/dissertation, general exam. *Entrance requirements:* For master's and doctorate, proficiency in French, knowledge of English. Electronic applications accepted.

Université de Sherbrooke, Faculty of Medicine and Health Sciences, Graduate Programs in Medicine, Program in Microbiology, Sherbrooke, QC J1H 5N4, Canada. Offers M Sc, PhD. Terminal master's awarded for partial completion of doctoral program. *Degree requirements:* For master's, thesis; for doctorate, thesis/dissertation. Electronic applications accepted. *Faculty research:* Oncogenes, alternative splicing mechanisms, genomics, telomerase, DNA repair, Clostridium difficile, Campylobacter jejuni.

Université du Québec, Institut National de la Recherche Scientifique, Graduate Programs, Research Center—INRS—Institut Armand-Frappier—Human Health, Québec, QC G1K 9A9, Canada. Offers applied microbiology (M Sc); biology (PhD); experimental health sciences (M Sc); virology and immunology (M Sc, PhD). Programs given in French. Part-time programs available. *Faculty:* 36. *Students:* 157 full-time (92 women), 6 part-time (4 women), 54 international. Average age 30. In 2010, 20 master's, 13 doctorates awarded. *Degree requirements:* For master's, thesis optional; for doctorate, thesis/dissertation. *Entrance requirements:* For master's and doctorate, appropriate bachelor's degree, proficiency in French. *Application deadline:* For fall admission, 3/30 for domestic and international students; for winter admission, 11/1 for domestic and international students; for spring admission, 3/1 for domestic and international students. Application fee: $30 Canadian dollars. *Financial support:* Fellowships, research assistantships, teaching assistantships available. *Faculty research:* Immunity, infection and cancer; toxicology and environmental biotechnology; molecular pharmacochemistry. *Unit head:* Charles Dozois, Director, 450-687-5010, Fax: 450-686-5501, E-mail: charles.dozois@iaf.inrs.ca. *Application contact:* Yvonne Boisvert, Registrar, 418-654-3861, Fax: 418-654-3858, E-mail: registrariat@adm.inrs.ca.

Université Laval, Faculty of Agricultural and Food Sciences, Program in Agricultural Microbiology, Québec, QC G1K 7P4, Canada. Offers agricultural microbiology (M Sc); agro-food microbiology (PhD). Terminal master's awarded for partial completion of doctoral program. *Degree requirements:* For master's, thesis; for doctorate, comprehensive exam, thesis/dissertation. *Entrance requirements:* For master's and doctorate, knowledge of French and English. Electronic applications accepted.

Université Laval, Faculty of Medicine, Graduate Programs in Medicine, Programs in Microbiology-Immunology, Québec, QC G1K 7P4, Canada. Offers M Sc, PhD. Terminal master's awarded for partial completion of doctoral program. *Degree requirements:* For master's, thesis; for doctorate, comprehensive exam, thesis/dissertation. *Entrance requirements:* For master's and doctorate, knowledge of French, comprehension of written English. Electronic applications accepted.

Université Laval, Faculty of Sciences and Engineering, Department of Biochemistry and Microbiology, Programs in Microbiology, Québec, QC G1K 7P4, Canada. Offers M Sc, PhD. Terminal master's awarded for partial completion of doctoral program. *Degree requirements:* For master's, thesis; for doctorate, comprehensive exam, thesis/dissertation. *Entrance requirements:* For master's and doctorate, knowledge of French, comprehension of written English. Electronic applications accepted.

University at Buffalo, the State University of New York, Graduate School, School of Medicine and Biomedical Sciences, Graduate Programs in Medicine and Biomedical Sciences, Department of Microbiology and Immunology, Buffalo, NY 14260. Offers MA, PhD. *Faculty:* 15 full-time (4 women), 4 part-time/adjunct (1 woman). *Students:* 23 full-time (15 women), 8 international. Average age 29. 6 applicants, 50% accepted, 1 enrolled. In 2010, 1 master's, 6 doctorates awarded. *Degree requirements:* For master's, comprehensive exam; for doctorate, thesis/dissertation, departmental qualifying exam. *Entrance requirements:* For master's and doctorate, GRE General Test, 3 letters of recommendation. Additional exam requirements/recommendations for international students: Required—TOEFL (minimum score 100 iBT). *Application deadline:* For fall admission, 2/1 priority date for domestic and international students. Applications are processed on a rolling basis. Application fee: $50. Electronic applications accepted. *Financial support:* In 2010–11, 1 student received support, including 5 fellowships with tuition reimbursements available (averaging $21,000 per year), 14 research assistantships with tuition reimbursements available (averaging $24,000 per year); Federal Work-Study, institutionally sponsored loans, traineeships, health care benefits, and unspecified assistantships also available. Financial award application deadline: 2/1; financial award applicants required to submit FAFSA. *Faculty research:* Bacteriology, immunology, parasitology, virology, mycology. Total annual research expenditures: $9.8 million. *Unit head:* Dr. John Hay, Interim Chairman, 716-829-2907, Fax: 716-829-2158. *Application contact:* Dr. Nejat Egilmez, Director of Graduate Studies, 716-829-2176, Fax: 716-829-2158.

The University of Alabama at Birmingham, Graduate Programs in Joint Health Sciences, Program in Microbiology, Birmingham, AL 35294. Offers PhD. *Students:* 69 full-time (35 women), 2 part-time (1 woman); includes 12 minority (6 Black or African American, non-Hispanic/Latino; 1 American Indian or Alaska Native, non-Hispanic/Latino; 3 Asian, non-Hispanic/Latino; 2 Hispanic/Latino), 9 international. Average age 28. In 2010, 20 doctorates awarded. *Degree requirements:* For doctorate, thesis/dissertation. *Entrance requirements:* For doctorate, GRE General Test, interview. *Application deadline:* Applications are processed on a rolling basis. Electronic applications accepted. *Expenses:* Tuition, state resident: full-time $5482. Tuition, nonresident: full-time $12,430. Tuition and fees vary according to program. *Financial support:* Fellowships available. *Unit head:* Dr. David D. Chaplin, Chair, 205-934-3470, Fax: 205-934-1426. *Application contact:* Information Contact, 205-934-0621, Fax: 205-975-2536.

University of Alberta, Faculty of Graduate Studies and Research, Department of Biological Sciences, Edmonton, AB T6G 2E1, Canada. Offers environmental biology and ecology (M Sc, PhD); microbiology and biotechnology (M Sc, PhD); molecular biology and genetics (M Sc, PhD); physiology and cell biology (M Sc, PhD); plant biology (M Sc, PhD); systematics and evolution (M Sc, PhD). Terminal master's awarded for partial completion of doctoral program. *Degree requirements:* For master's, thesis; for doctorate, thesis/dissertation. *Entrance requirements:* Additional exam requirements/recommendations for international students: Required—TOEFL.

The University of Arizona, College of Agriculture and Life Sciences, Department of Veterinary Science and Microbiology, Program in Microbiology and Pathobiology, Tucson, AZ 85721. Offers MS, PhD. *Students:* 42 full-time (23 women), 43 part-time (22 women); includes 2 American Indian or Alaska Native, non-Hispanic/Latino; 2 Asian, non-Hispanic/Latino; 4 Hispanic/Latino, 16 international. Average age 31.Terminal master's awarded for partial completion of doctoral program. *Degree requirements:* For master's, thesis; for doctorate, comprehensive exam, thesis/dissertation. *Entrance requirements:* For master's and doctorate, GRE, minimum GPA of 3.0, 3 letters of recommendation, letter of intent. Additional exam requirements/recommendations for international students: Required—TOEFL (minimum score 550 paper-based; 213 computer-based; 80 iBT); Recommended—IELTS (minimum score 7). *Application deadline:* For fall admission, 2/28 for domestic students, 12/1 for international students. Applications are processed on a rolling basis. Application fee: $75. *Expenses:* Tuition, state resident: full-time $7692. *Financial support:* Research assistantships with tuition reimbursements, teaching assistantships with tuition reimbursements, scholarships/grants available. Financial award application deadline: 3/22. *Faculty research:* Antibiotic resistance, molecular pathogenesis of bacteria, food safety, diagnosis of animal disease, parasitology.

The University of Arizona, College of Agriculture and Life Sciences, Program in Microbiology, Tucson, AZ 85721. Offers MS, PhD. *Faculty:* 7. *Students:* 14 full-time (9 women), 5 part-time (2 women); includes 2 Black or African American, non-Hispanic/Latino; 1 Hispanic/Latino, 4 international. Average age 32. 31 applicants, 23% accepted, 2 enrolled. In 2010, 1 master's, 3 doctorates awarded. *Degree requirements:* For master's, thesis; for doctorate, comprehensive exam, thesis/dissertation. *Entrance requirements:* For master's and doctorate, GRE, minimum GPA of 3.0, 3 letters of recommendation, letter of intent. Additional exam requirements/recommendations for international students: Required—TOEFL (minimum score 550 paper-based; 213 computer-based). *Application deadline:* For fall admission, 2/28 for domestic students, 12/1 for international students. Application fee: $75. *Expenses:* Tuition, state resident: full-time $7692. *Financial support:* In 2010–11, 5 research assistantships (averaging $17,293 per year), 4 teaching assistantships (averaging $15,210 per year) were awarded. Financial award application deadline: 3/22. Total annual research expenditures: $2.7 million. *Unit head:* Dr. Jack Schmitz, Head, 520-626-5482, E-mail: jschmitz@u.arizona.edu. *Application contact:* Elaine Mattes, 520-621-4466, E-mail: emattes@email.arizona.edu.

The University of Arizona, College of Medicine, Department of Immunobiology, Tucson, AZ 85721. Offers MS, PhD. *Faculty:* 12 full-time (4 women), 1 part-time/adjunct (0 women). *Students:* 4 full-time (2 women), 9 part-time (7 women); includes 1 minority (Two or more races, non-Hispanic/Latino), 3 international. Average age 27. 91 applicants, 66% accepted. In 2010, 1 master's, 5 doctorates awarded. *Degree requirements:* For master's, thesis; for doctorate, thesis/dissertation. *Entrance requirements:* For master's and doctorate, GRE General Test, minimum GPA of 3.0. *Application deadline:* For fall admission, 3/1 priority date for domestic students; for spring admission, 9/1 for domestic students. Application fee: $45. *Expenses:* Tuition, state resident: full-time $7692. *Financial support:* In 2010–11, 11 research assistantships with full tuition reimbursements (averaging $21,388 per year) were awarded; fellowships with full tuition reimbursements, teaching assistantships with full tuition reimbursements, institutionally sponsored loans and tuition waivers (full) also available. Financial award application deadline: 4/30. *Faculty research:* Environmental and pathogenic microbiology, molecular biology. Total annual research expenditures: $1.4 million. *Unit head:* Dr. Emmanuel T. Akporiaye, Interim Head, 520-626-6409, Fax: 520-626-2100, E-mail: akporiay@u.arizona.edu. *Application contact:* Dr. Richard J. Ablin, Graduate Program Chairman, 520-626-7755, E-mail: ablinrj@email.arizona.edu.

University of Arkansas for Medical Sciences, Graduate School, Graduate Programs in Biomedical Sciences, Department of Microbiology and Immunology, Little Rock, AR 72205-7199. Offers MS, PhD, MD/PhD. *Degree requirements:* For master's, thesis; for doctorate, thesis/dissertation. *Entrance requirements:* For master's and doctorate, GRE General Test. Additional exam requirements/recommendations for international students: Required—TOEFL. *Faculty research:* Tumor immunology and immunotherapy, microbial pathogenesis and genetics, allergy, immune response in infectious diseases.

The University of British Columbia, Faculty of Science, Department of Microbiology and Immunology, Vancouver, BC V6T 1Z1, Canada. Offers M Sc, PhD. *Degree requirements:* For master's, thesis; for doctorate, comprehensive exam, thesis/dissertation. *Entrance requirements:* For master's and doctorate, GRE General Test. Additional exam requirements/recommendations for international students: Required—TOEFL (minimum score 590 paper-based; 243 computer-based). Electronic applications accepted. Tuition charges are reported in Canadian dollars. *Expenses:* Tuition, area resident: Full-time $4179 Canadian dollars. International tuition: $7344 Canadian dollars full-time. *Faculty research:* Bacterial genetics, metabolism, pathogenic bacteriology, virology.

University of Calgary, Faculty of Medicine and Faculty of Graduate Studies, Department of Microbiology and Infectious Diseases, Calgary, AB T2N 1N4, Canada. Offers M Sc, PhD. *Degree requirements:* For master's, thesis, oral thesis exam; for doctorate, thesis/dissertation, candidacy exam, oral thesis exam. *Entrance requirements:* For master's and doctorate, minimum GPA of 3.2. Additional exam requirements/recommendations for international students: Required—TOEFL (minimum score 580 paper-based; 237 computer-based). Electronic applications accepted. *Faculty research:* Bacteriology, virology, parasitology, immunology.

University of California, Berkeley, Graduate Division, College of Natural Resources, Group in Microbiology, Berkeley, CA 94720-1500. Offers PhD. *Degree requirements:* For doctorate, thesis/dissertation. *Entrance requirements:* For doctorate, GRE General Test, minimum GPA of 3.0, 3 letters of recommendation.

University of California, Davis, Graduate Studies, Graduate Group in Microbiology, Davis, CA 95616. Offers MS, PhD. Terminal master's awarded for partial completion of doctoral program. *Degree requirements:* For master's, thesis; for doctorate, thesis/dissertation. *Entrance requirements:* For master's and doctorate, GRE General Test, minimum GPA of 3.0. Additional exam requirements/recommendations for international students: Required—TOEFL (minimum score 550 paper-based; 213 computer-based). Electronic applications accepted. *Faculty research:* Microbial physiology and genetics, microbial molecular and cellular biology, microbial ecology, microbial pathogenesis and immunology, urology.

University of California, Irvine, School of Medicine and School of Biological Sciences, Department of Microbiology and Molecular Genetics, Irvine, CA 92697. Offers biological sciences (MS, PhD); MD/PhD. Students apply through the Graduate Program in Molecular Biology, Genetics, and Biochemistry. *Students:* 31 full-time (18 women); includes 16 minority (1 Black or African American, non-Hispanic/Latino; 9 Asian, non-Hispanic/Latino; 6 Hispanic/Latino). Average age 28. In 2010, 1 master's, 10 doctorates awarded. *Degree requirements:* For doctorate, thesis/dissertation. *Entrance requirements:* For doctorate, GRE General Test, GRE Subject Test, minimum GPA of 3.0. Additional exam requirements/recommendations for international students: Required—TOEFL (minimum score 550 paper-based; 213 computer-based). *Application deadline:* For fall admission, 12/15 priority date for domestic students, 12/15 for international students. Application fee: $80 ($100 for international students). Electronic applications accepted. *Financial support:* Fellowships, research assistantships with full tuition reimbursements, teaching assistantships, institutionally sponsored loans, traineeships, health care benefits, and unspecified assistantships available. Financial award applicants required to submit FAFSA. *Faculty research:* Molecular biology and genetics of viruses, bacteria, and yeast; immune response; molecular biology of cultured animal cells; genetic basis of cancer; genetics and physiology of infectious agents. *Unit head:* Rozanne M. Sandri-Goldin, Chair, 949-824-7570, Fax: 949-824-8598, E-mail: rmsandri@uci.edu. *Application contact:* Renee Marie Frigo, Program Manager, 949-824-8145, Fax: 949-824-1965, E-mail: rfrigo@uci.edu.

University of California, Los Angeles, David Geffen School of Medicine and Graduate Division, Graduate Programs in Medicine, Department of Microbiology, Immunology and Molecular Genetics, Los Angeles, CA 90095. Offers MS, PhD. *Faculty:* 31 full-time (6 women). *Students:* 51 full-time (19 women); includes 19 minority (1 Black or African American, non-Hispanic/Latino; 9 Asian, non-Hispanic/Latino; 9 Hispanic/Latino), 6 international. Average age 28. 5 applicants, 100% accepted, 4 enrolled. In 2010, 4 master's, 14 doctorates awarded. *Degree requirements:* For doctorate, thesis/dissertation, oral and written qualifying exams. *Entrance requirements:* For doctorate, GRE General Test, GRE Subject Test. Additional exam requirements/recommendations for international students: Required—TOEFL. Application fee: $70 ($90 for international students). Electronic applications accepted. *Financial support:* In 2010–11, 50 fellowships, 47 research assistantships, 20 teaching assistantships were awarded; Federal Work-Study, institutionally sponsored loans, and tuition waivers (full and partial) also available. Financial award application deadline: 3/1. *Unit head:* Dr. Jeff F. Miller, Chair, 310-206-7926, Fax: 310-267-2774, E-mail: jfmiller@ucla.edu. *Application contact:* Bridget Wolfgang, Graduate Student Affairs, 310-825-8482, Fax: 310-206-5231, E-mail: bridgetw@microbio.ucla.edu.

University of California, Riverside, Graduate Division, Program in Microbiology, Riverside, CA 92521-0102. Offers MS, PhD. Part-time programs available. Terminal master's awarded for partial completion of doctoral program. *Degree requirements:* For master's, thesis; for doctorate, thesis/dissertation, qualifying exams. *Entrance requirements:* For master's and doctorate, GRE General Test, minimum GPA of 3.2. Additional exam requirements/recommendations for international students: Required—TOEFL (minimum score 550 paper-based; 213 computer-based; 80 iBT). Electronic applications accepted. *Faculty research:* Host-pathogen interactions; environmental microbiology; bioremediation; molecular microbiology; microbial genetics, physiology, and pathogenesis.

University of California, San Diego, School of Medicine and Office of Graduate Studies, Molecular Pathology Program, La Jolla, CA 92093. Offers bioinformatics (PhD); cancer biology/oncology (PhD); cardiovascular sciences and disease (PhD); microbiology (PhD); molecular pathology (PhD); neurological disease (PhD); stem cell and developmental biology (PhD); structural biology/drug design (PhD). *Entrance requirements:* For doctorate, GRE General Test, GRE Subject Test. Additional exam requirements/recommendations for international students: Required—TOEFL. Electronic applications accepted.

University of California, San Francisco, Graduate Division, Department of Microbiology and Immunology, San Francisco, CA 94143. Offers PhD. *Degree requirements:* For doctorate, thesis/dissertation. *Entrance requirements:* For doctorate, GRE General Test.

University of Chicago, Division of Biological Sciences, Biomedical Sciences Cluster: Cancer Biology, Immunology, Molecular Metabolism and Nutrition, Pathology, and Microbiology, Committee on Microbiology, Chicago, IL 60637-1513. Offers PhD. *Degree requirements:* For doctorate, thesis/dissertation, ethics class, 2 teaching assistantships. *Entrance requirements:* For doctorate, GRE General Test. Additional exam requirements/recommendations for international students: Required—TOEFL (minimum score 600 paper-based; 250 computer-based; 104 iBT), IELTS (minimum score 7). Electronic applications accepted. *Faculty research:* Molecular genetics, herpes virus, adipoviruses, Picarna viruses, ENS viruses.

University of Cincinnati, Graduate School, College of Medicine, Graduate Programs in Biomedical Sciences, Department of Molecular Genetics, Biochemistry and Microbiology, Cincinnati, OH 45221. Offers MS, PhD. Terminal master's awarded for partial completion of doctoral program. *Degree requirements:* For master's, thesis or alternative; for doctorate, thesis/dissertation, qualifying exam. *Entrance requirements:* For master's and doctorate, GRE General Test. Additional exam requirements/recommendations for international students: Required—TOEFL (minimum score 600 paper-based; 250 computer-based; 100 iBT), TWE. Electronic applications accepted. *Faculty research:* Cancer biology and developmental genetics, gene regulation and chromosome structure, microbiology and pathogenic mechanisms, structural biology, membrane biochemistry and signal transduction.

University of Colorado Boulder, Graduate School, College of Arts and Sciences, Department of Ecology and Evolutionary Biology, Boulder, CO 80309. Offers animal behavior (MA); biology (MA, PhD); environmental biology (MA, PhD); evolutionary biology (MA, PhD); neurobiology (MA); population biology (MA); population genetics (PhD). *Faculty:* 32 full-time (10 women). *Students:* 71 full-time (36 women), 17 part-time (11 women); includes 10 minority (1 American Indian or Alaska Native, non-Hispanic/Latino; 2 Asian, non-Hispanic/Latino; 7 Hispanic/Latino), 4 international. Average age 30. 176 applicants, 20 enrolled. In 2010, 11 master's, 8 doctorates awarded. Terminal master's awarded for partial completion of doctoral program. *Degree requirements:* For master's, comprehensive exam, thesis or alternative; for doctorate, comprehensive exam, thesis/dissertation. *Entrance requirements:* For master's, GRE General Test, GRE Subject Test, minimum undergraduate GPA of 3.0; for doctorate, GRE General Test, GRE Subject Test. *Application deadline:* For fall admission, 12/30 priority date for domestic students, 12/1 for international students. Application fee: $50 ($60 for international students). *Financial support:* In 2010–11, 25 fellowships (averaging $17,876 per year), 27 research assistantships (averaging $15,070 per year) were awarded; Federal Work-Study, institutionally sponsored loans, and tuition waivers (full) also available. *Faculty research:* Behavior, ecology, genetics, morphology, endocrinology, physiology, systematics. Total annual research expenditures: $3.5 million.

University of Colorado Denver, School of Medicine, Program in Microbiology, Denver, CO 80217-3364. Offers PhD. *Students:* 19 full-time (11 women); includes 1 Asian, non-Hispanic/Latino; 1 Hispanic/Latino. Average age 27. 3 applicants, 100% accepted, 3 enrolled. In 2010, 3 doctorates awarded. *Degree requirements:* For doctorate, comprehensive exam, thesis/dissertation, 3 lab rotations; 30 credit hours coursework. *Entrance requirements:* For doctorate, GRE, three letters of reference, two copies of official transcripts, minimum GPA of 3.0. Additional exam requirements/recommendations for international students: Required—TOEFL (minimum score 550 paper-based; 213 computer-based). *Application deadline:* For fall admission, 1/1 for domestic students. Application fee: $65. Electronic applications accepted. *Expenses:* Contact institution. *Financial support:* In 2010–11, 3 students received support, including 3 fellowships with full tuition reimbursements available (averaging $25,000 per year); health care benefits, tuition waivers (full), and stipend also available. Financial award application deadline: 3/15; financial award applicants required to submit FAFSA. *Faculty research:* Molecular mechanisms of picornavirus replication, mechanisms of papovavirus assembly, human immune response in multiple sclerosis. Total annual research expenditures: $5.9 million. *Unit head:* Dr. Randall K. Holmes, Chair, 303-724-4223, E-mail: randall.holmes@ucdenver.edu. *Application contact:* Dr. Randall K. Holmes, Chair, 303-724-4223, E-mail: randall.holmes@ucdenver.edu.

University of Connecticut, Graduate School, College of Liberal Arts and Sciences, Department of Molecular and Cell Biology, Field of Microbiology, Storrs, CT 06269. Offers MS, PhD. Terminal master's awarded for partial completion of doctoral program. *Degree requirements:* For master's, comprehensive exam; for doctorate, thesis/dissertation. *Entrance requirements:* For master's and doctorate, GRE General Test, GRE Subject Test. Additional exam requirements/recommendations for international students: Required—TOEFL (minimum score 550 paper-based; 213 computer-based). Electronic applications accepted.

University of Delaware, College of Arts and Sciences, Department of Biological Sciences, Newark, DE 19716. Offers biotechnology (MS); cancer biology (MS, PhD); cell and extracellular matrix biology (MS, PhD); cell and systems physiology (MS, PhD); developmental biology (MS, PhD); ecology and evolution (MS, PhD); microbiology (MS, PhD); molecular biology and genetics (MS, PhD). Terminal master's awarded for partial completion of doctoral program. *Degree requirements:* For master's, thesis, preliminary exam; for doctorate, comprehensive exam, thesis/dissertation, preliminary exam. *Entrance requirements:* For master's and doctorate, GRE General Test. Additional exam requirements/recommendations for international students: Required—TOEFL (minimum score 600 paper-based; 250 computer-based); Recommended—TWE. Electronic applications accepted. *Faculty research:* Microorganisms, bone, cancer metastasis, developmental biology, cell biology, DNA.

University of Florida, College of Medicine, Department of Molecular Genetics and Microbiology, Gainesville, FL 32611. Offers MS, PhD. Terminal master's awarded for partial completion of doctoral program. *Degree requirements:* For master's, thesis; for doctorate, thesis/dissertation. *Entrance requirements:* For master's and doctorate, GRE General Test, minimum GPA of 3.0. Additional exam requirements/recommendations for international students: Required—TOEFL. Electronic applications accepted. *Expenses:* Tuition, state resident: full-time $10,916. Tuition, nonresident: full-time $28,309.

University of Florida, College of Medicine and Graduate School, Interdisciplinary Program in Biomedical Sciences, Concentration in Immunology and Microbiology, Gainesville, FL 32611. Offers PhD. *Degree requirements:* For doctorate, thesis/dissertation. *Entrance requirements:* For doctorate, GRE General Test, minimum GPA of 3.0. Additional exam requirements/recommendations for international students: Required—TOEFL. Electronic applications accepted. *Expenses:* Tuition, state resident: full-time $10,916. Tuition, nonresident: full-time $28,309.

University of Florida, Graduate School, College of Agricultural and Life Sciences, Department of Microbiology and Cell Science, Gainesville, FL 32611. Offers biochemistry and molecular biology (MS, PhD); microbiology and cell science (MS, PhD). *Faculty:* 22 full-time (7 women), 1 part-time/adjunct (0 women). *Students:* 45 full-time (21 women), 1 part-time (0 women); includes 2 Black or African American, non-Hispanic/Latino; 6 Asian, non-Hispanic/Latino; 4 Hispanic/Latino, 13 international. Average age 26. 67 applicants, 27% accepted, 10 enrolled. In 2010, 2 master's, 6 doctorates awarded. *Degree requirements:* For master's, comprehensive exam, thesis (for some programs); for doctorate, comprehensive exam, thesis/dissertation. *Entrance requirements:* For master's and doctorate, GRE General Test (minimum score 1000), minimum GPA of 3.0. Additional exam requirements/recommendations for international students: Required—TOEFL (minimum score 550 paper-based; 213 computer-based; 80 iBT), IELTS (minimum score 6). *Application deadline:* For fall admission, 6/1 priority date for domestic students. Applications are processed on a rolling basis. Application fee: $30. Electronic applications accepted. *Expenses:* Tuition, state resident: full-time $10,916. Tuition, nonresident: full-time $28,309. *Financial support:* In 2010–11, 49 students received support, including 13 fellowships, 27 research assistantships (averaging $22,767 per year), 9 teaching assistantships (averaging $23,678 per year). Financial award applicants required to submit FAFSA. *Faculty research:* Biomass conversion, membrane and cell wall chemistry, plant biochemistry and genetics. *Unit head:* Dr. Eric Triplett, Chair, 352-392-1906, Fax: 352-392-5922, E-mail: ewt@ufl.edu. *Application contact:* Dr. Tony Romeo, Graduate Coordinator, 352-392-2400, Fax: 352-392-5922, E-mail: tromeo@ufl.edu.

University of Georgia, College of Arts and Sciences, Department of Microbiology, Athens, GA 30602. Offers MS, PhD. *Faculty:* 15 full-time (4 women). *Students:* 47 full-time (26 women); includes 3 Black or African American, non-Hispanic/Latino; 2 Asian, non-Hispanic/Latino; 3 Hispanic/Latino, 6 international. 81 applicants, 25% accepted, 7 enrolled. In 2010, 2 master's, 4 doctorates awarded. *Degree requirements:* For master's, thesis; for doctorate, one foreign language, thesis/dissertation. *Entrance requirements:* For master's and doctorate, GRE General Test. Additional exam requirements/recommendations for international students: Required—TOEFL (minimum score 550 paper-based; 213 computer-based). *Application deadline:* For fall admission, 7/1 priority date for domestic students; for spring admission, 11/15 for domestic students. Application fee: $50. Electronic applications accepted. *Expenses:* Tuition, state resident: full-time $7200; part-time $344 per credit hour. Tuition, nonresident: full-time $21,900; part-time $944 per credit hour. Tuition and fees vary according to course load and program. *Financial support:* In 2010–11, 9 fellowships (averaging $20,000 per year), 20 research assistantships (averaging $18,461 per year), 12 teaching assistantships (averaging $18,461 per year) were awarded; unspecified assistantships also available. Financial award application deadline: 12/15. *Unit head:* Dr. William B. Whitman, Head, 706-542-4219, E-mail: whitman@uga.edu. *Application contact:* Dr. Anna C. Karls, Graduate Coordinator, 706-543-0822, Fax: 706-542-2674, E-mail: akarls@uga.edu.

University of Guelph, Graduate Studies, College of Biological Science, Department of Molecular and Cellular Biology, Guelph, ON N1G 2W1, Canada. Offers biochemistry (M Sc, PhD); biophysics (M Sc, PhD); botany (M Sc, PhD); microbiology (M Sc, PhD); molecular biology and genetics (M Sc, PhD). *Degree requirements:* For master's, thesis, research proposal; for doctorate, comprehensive exam, thesis/dissertation, research proposal. *Entrance requirements:* For master's, minimum B-average during previous 2 years of coursework; for doctorate, minimum A-average. Additional exam requirements/recommendations for international students: Required—TOEFL (minimum score 550 paper-based; 213 computer-based), IELTS (minimum score 6.5). Electronic applications accepted. *Faculty research:* Physiology, structure, genetics, and ecology of microbes; virology and microbial technology.

University of Hawaii at Manoa, Graduate Division, College of Natural Sciences, Department of Microbiology, Honolulu, HI 96822. Offers MS, PhD. Part-time programs available. *Faculty:* 25 full-time (6 women), 2 part-time/adjunct (1 woman). *Students:* 28 full-time (12 women), 2 part-time (both women); includes 8 minority (4 Asian, non-Hispanic/Latino; 4 Two or more races, non-Hispanic/Latino), 10 international. Average age 30. 37 applicants, 38% accepted, 13 enrolled. In 2010, 4 master's, 5 doctorates awarded. *Degree requirements:* For master's, thesis optional; for doctorate, comprehensive exam, thesis/dissertation. *Entrance requirements:* For master's and doctorate, GRE General Test. Additional exam requirements/recommendations for international students: Required—TOEFL (minimum score 580 paper-based; 237 computer-based; 92 iBT), IELTS (minimum score 5). *Application deadline:* For fall admission, 2/1 for domestic and international students; for spring admission, 8/1 for domestic and international students. Application fee: $60. *Financial support:* In 2010–11, 1 fellowship (averaging $2,000 per year), 15 research assistantships (averaging $18,180 per year), 12 teaching assistantships (averaging $16,086 per year) were awarded. *Faculty research:* Virology, immunology, microbial physiology, medical microbiology, bacterial genetics. Total annual research expenditures: $852,000. *Application contact:* Dr. Paul Q. Patek, Chairperson, 808-956-7025, Fax: 808-956-5339, E-mail: patek@hawaii.edu.

University of Idaho, College of Graduate Studies, College of Agricultural and Life Sciences, Department of Microbiology, Molecular Biology and Biochemistry, Moscow, ID 83844-2282. Offers MS, PhD. *Faculty:* 16 full-time. *Students:* 13 full-time, 6 part-time. Average age 30. In 2010, 4 master's, 3 doctorates awarded. *Degree requirements:* For master's, thesis; for doctorate, one foreign language, thesis/dissertation. *Entrance requirements:* For master's, minimum GPA of 2.8; for doctorate, minimum undergraduate GPA of 2.8, 3.0 graduate. *Application deadline:* For fall admission, 8/1 for domestic students; for spring admission, 12/15 for domestic students. Applications are processed on a rolling basis. Application fee: $60. Electronic applications accepted. *Expenses:* Tuition, nonresident: part-time $580 per credit. Required fees: $306 per credit. *Financial support:* Research assistantships, teaching assistantships available. Financial award applicants required to submit FAFSA. *Unit head:* Bruce L. Miller, Interim Chair, 208-885-7247, Fax: 208-885-6518, E-mail: mmbb@uidaho.edu. *Application contact:* Bruce L. Miller, Interim Chair, 208-885-7247, Fax: 208-885-6518, E-mail: mmbb@uidaho.edu.

University of Illinois at Chicago, College of Medicine and Graduate College, Graduate Programs in Medicine, Department of Microbiology and Immunology, Chicago, IL 60607-7128. Offers PhD, MD/PhD. *Degree requirements:* For doctorate, thesis/dissertation. *Entrance requirements:* For doctorate, GRE General Test, minimum GPA of 2.75. Additional exam requirements/recommendations for international students: Required—TOEFL.

Microbiology

University of Illinois at Urbana–Champaign, Graduate College, College of Liberal Arts and Sciences, School of Molecular and Cellular Biology, Department of Microbiology, Champaign, IL 61820. Offers MS, PhD. *Faculty:* 14 full-time (3 women). *Students:* 70 full-time (44 women); includes 2 Black or African American, non-Hispanic/Latino; 1 American Indian or Alaska Native, non-Hispanic/Latino; 5 Asian, non-Hispanic/Latino; 5 Hispanic/Latino; 1 Two or more races, non-Hispanic/Latino, 21 international. In 2010, 9 master's, 12 doctorates awarded. *Entrance requirements:* For master's and doctorate, GRE, minimum GPA of 3.0. Additional exam requirements/recommendations for international students: Required—TOEFL (minimum score 590 paper-based; 243 computer-based; 96 iBT). *Application deadline:* Applications are processed on a rolling basis. Application fee: $75 ($90 for international students). Electronic applications accepted. *Financial support:* In 2010–11, 23 fellowships, 49 research assistantships, 38 teaching assistantships were awarded; tuition waivers (full and partial) also available. *Faculty research:* Bacterial physiology and genetics, bacterial pathogenesis, host-pathogen interaction, molecular immunology. *Unit head:* John E. Cronan, Head, 217-333-7919, Fax: 217-244-6697, E-mail: jecronan@illinois.edu. *Application contact:* Deb LeBaugh, Office Manager, 217-333-9765, E-mail: lebaugh@illinois.edu.

The University of Iowa, Roy J. and Lucille A. Carver College of Medicine and Graduate College, Graduate Programs in Medicine, Department of Microbiology, Iowa City, IA 52242-1316. Offers general microbiology and microbial physiology (MS, PhD); immunology (MS, PhD); microbial genetics (MS, PhD); pathogenic bacteriology (MS, PhD); virology (MS, PhD). *Faculty:* 23 full-time (4 women), 11 part-time/adjunct (5 women). *Students:* 35 full-time (20 women); includes 2 American Indian or Alaska Native, non-Hispanic/Latino; 1 Hispanic/Latino, 5 international. Average age 25. 71 applicants, 20% accepted, 8 enrolled. In 2010, 1 master's, 5 doctorates awarded. *Degree requirements:* For master's, thesis; for doctorate, comprehensive exam, thesis/dissertation. *Entrance requirements:* For master's and doctorate, GRE General Test. Additional exam requirements/recommendations for international students: Required—TOEFL (minimum score 600 paper-based; 250 computer-based). *Application deadline:* For fall admission, 2/1 for domestic and international students. Application fee: $60 ($85 for international students). Electronic applications accepted. *Financial support:* In 2010–11, 4 fellowships with full tuition reimbursements (averaging $25,000 per year), 31 research assistantships with full tuition reimbursements (averaging $25,000 per year) were awarded; institutionally sponsored loans, scholarships/grants, traineeships, and health care benefits also available. *Faculty research:* Gene regulation, processing and transport of HIV, retroviral pathogenesis, biodegradation, biofilm. Total annual research expenditures: $12.6 million. *Unit head:* Dr. Michael A. Apicella, Head, 319-335-7810, E-mail: grad-micro-info@uiowa.edu. *Application contact:* Dr. Michael A. Apicella, Head, 319-335-7810, E-mail: grad-micro-info@uiowa.edu.

The University of Kansas, Graduate Studies, College of Liberal Arts and Sciences, Department of Molecular Biosciences, Lawrence, KS 66044. Offers biochemistry and biophysics (MA, PhD); microbiology (MA, PhD); molecular, cellular, and developmental biology (MA, PhD). *Faculty:* 34. *Students:* 65 full-time (31 women), 1 part-time (0 women); includes 7 minority (2 Asian, non-Hispanic/Latino; 4 Hispanic/Latino; 1 Two or more races, non-Hispanic/Latino), 24 international. Average age 27. 34 applicants, 47% accepted, 10 enrolled. In 2010, 1 master's, 5 doctorates awarded. Terminal master's awarded for partial completion of doctoral program. *Degree requirements:* For master's, comprehensive exam, thesis; for doctorate, comprehensive exam, thesis/dissertation. *Entrance requirements:* For master's and doctorate, GRE General Test. Additional exam requirements/recommendations for international students: Required—TOEFL (minimum score 24 iBT), OR IELTS Speaking: 8. *Application deadline:* For fall admission, 12/15 for domestic and international students. Application fee: $55 ($65 for international students). Electronic applications accepted. *Expenses:* Tuition, state resident: full-time $7092; part-time $295.50 per credit hour. Tuition, nonresident: full-time $16,590; part-time $691.25 per credit hour. Required fees: $858; $71.49 per credit hour. Tuition and fees vary according to course load, campus/location and program. *Financial support:* Fellowships with tuition reimbursements, research assistantships with tuition reimbursements, teaching assistantships with tuition reimbursements, health care benefits and unspecified assistantships available. Financial award application deadline: 3/1. *Faculty research:* Structure and function of proteins, genetics of organism development, molecular genetics, neurophysiology, molecular virology and pathogenics, developmental biology, cell biology. *Unit head:* Dr. Mark Richter, Chair, 785-864-3334, Fax: 785-864-5294, E-mail: richter@ku.edu. *Application contact:* John P. Connolly, Graduate Program Assistant, 785-864-4311, Fax: 785-864-5294, E-mail: jconnolly@ku.edu.

The University of Kansas, University of Kansas Medical Center, School of Medicine, Department of Microbiology, Molecular Genetics and Immunology, Kansas City, KS 66160. Offers microbiology (PhD); MD/PhD. *Faculty:* 14. *Students:* 15 full-time (7 women), 1 (woman) part-time; includes 2 minority (1 Asian, non-Hispanic/Latino; 1 Two or more races, non-Hispanic/Latino), 9 international. Average age 29. 2 applicants, 100% accepted, 2 enrolled. *Degree requirements:* For doctorate, comprehensive exam, thesis/dissertation, research skills. *Entrance requirements:* For doctorate, GRE General Test, B Sc. Additional exam requirements/recommendations for international students: Required—TOEFL. *Application deadline:* For fall admission, 1/15 priority date for international students. *Expenses:* Tuition, state resident: full-time $7092; part-time $295.50 per credit hour. Tuition, nonresident: full-time $16,590; part-time $691.25 per credit hour. Required fees: $858; $71.49 per credit hour. Tuition and fees vary according to course load, campus/location and program. *Financial support:* Fellowships with tuition reimbursements, research assistantships with partial tuition reimbursements, teaching assistantships with full and partial tuition reimbursements, scholarships/grants and unspecified assistantships available. Financial award application deadline: 2/15; financial award applicants required to submit FAFSA. *Faculty research:* Immunology, infectious disease, virology, molecular genetics, bacteriology. Total annual research expenditures: $4.5 million. *Unit head:* Dr. Michael Parmely, Interim Chair, 913-588-7010, Fax: 913-588-7295, E-mail: mparmely@kumc.edu. *Application contact:* Dr. Indranil Biswas, Microbiology Graduate Studies Director, 913-588-7019, Fax: 913-588-7295, E-mail: ibiswas@kumc.edu.

University of Kentucky, Graduate School, Graduate School Programs from the College of Medicine, Program in Microbiology and Immunology, Lexington, KY 40506-0032. Offers microbiology (PhD). *Degree requirements:* For doctorate, comprehensive exam, thesis/dissertation. *Entrance requirements:* For doctorate, GRE General Test, minimum undergraduate GPA of 2.75. Additional exam requirements/recommendations for international students: Required—TOEFL (minimum score 550 paper-based; 213 computer-based). Electronic applications accepted.

University of Louisville, School of Medicine, Department of Microbiology and Immunology, Louisville, KY 40292-0001. Offers MS, PhD, MD/PhD. *Faculty:* 22 full-time (6 women). *Students:* 36 full-time (25 women); includes 4 Black or African American, non-Hispanic/Latino; 1 Asian, non-Hispanic/Latino, 14 international. Average age 29. 36 applicants, 39% accepted, 10 enrolled. In 2010, 6 doctorates awarded. Terminal master's awarded for partial completion of doctoral program. *Degree requirements:* For master's, thesis; for doctorate, comprehensive exam, thesis/dissertation. *Entrance requirements:* For master's and doctorate, GRE General Test (minimum score of 1000 verbal and quantitative), minimum GPA of 3.0; 1 year of course work in biology, organic chemistry, physics; 1 semester of course work in calculus and quantitative analysis, biochemistry, or molecular biology. Additional exam requirements/recommendations for international students: Required—TOEFL. *Application deadline:* For fall admission, 2/1 priority date for domestic and international students. Applications are processed on a rolling basis. Application fee: $50. Electronic applications accepted. *Expenses:* Tuition, state resident: full-time $9144; part-time $508 per credit hour. Tuition, nonresident: full-time $19,026; part-time $1057 per credit hour. Tuition and fees vary according to program and reciprocity agreements. *Financial support:* Fellowships with full tuition reimbursements, research assistantships with full tuition reimbursements available. Financial award application deadline: 4/15. *Faculty research:* Opportunistic and emerging infections; biology and regulation of the immune system; cellular and molecular bases of chronic inflammatory response; role of cytokines and chemokines in cancer, autoimmune and infectious disease; host defense and pathogenesis of viral infections. *Unit head:* Dr. Robert D. Stout, Chair, 502-852-5351, Fax: 502-852-7531, E-mail: bobstout@louisville.edu. *Application contact:* Carolyn M. Burton, Academic Coordinator, 502-852-6208, Fax: 502-852-7531, E-mail: cmburt01@gwise.louisville.edu.

University of Maine, Graduate School, College of Natural Sciences, Forestry, and Agriculture, Department of Biochemistry, Molecular Biology, and Microbiology, Orono, ME 04469. Offers biochemistry (MPS, MS); biochemistry and molecular biology (PhD); microbiology (MPS, MS, PhD). *Faculty:* 9 full-time (5 women), 3 part-time/adjunct (2 women). *Students:* 19 full-time (12 women), 21 part-time (15 women); includes 5 minority (1 American Indian or Alaska Native, non-Hispanic/Latino; 2 Asian, non-Hispanic/Latino; 1 Hispanic/Latino; 1 Two or more races, non-Hispanic/Latino), 6 international. Average age 30. 39 applicants, 26% accepted, 9 enrolled. In 2010, 6 master's, 3 doctorates awarded. *Degree requirements:* For doctorate, thesis/dissertation. *Entrance requirements:* For master's and doctorate, GRE General Test. Additional exam requirements/recommendations for international students: Required—TOEFL. *Application deadline:* For fall admission, 2/1 priority date for domestic students. Applications are processed on a rolling basis. Application fee: $65. Electronic applications accepted. *Expenses:* Tuition, state resident: full-time $400. Tuition, nonresident: full-time $1050. *Financial support:* In 2010–11, 5 research assistantships with tuition reimbursements (averaging $20,893 per year), 12 teaching assistantships with tuition reimbursements (averaging $19,296 per year) were awarded; tuition waivers (full and partial) also available. Financial award application deadline: 3/1. *Unit head:* Dr. Robert Gundersen, Chair, 207-581-2802, Fax: 207-581-2801. *Application contact:* Scott G. Delcourt, Associate Dean of the Graduate School, 207-581-3291, Fax: 207-581-3232, E-mail: graduate@maine.edu.

The University of Manchester, Faculty of Life Sciences, Manchester, United Kingdom. Offers adaptive organismal biology (M Phil, PhD); animal biology (M Phil, PhD); biochemistry (M Phil, PhD); bioinformatics (M Phil, PhD); biomolecular sciences (M Phil, PhD); biotechnology (M Phil, PhD); cell biology (M Phil, PhD); cell matrix research (M Phil, PhD); channels and transporters (M Phil, PhD); developmental biology (M Phil, PhD); Egyptology (M Phil, PhD); environmental biology (M Phil, PhD); evolutionary biology (M Phil, PhD); gene expression (M Phil, PhD); genetics (M Phil, PhD); history of science, technology and medicine (M Phil, PhD); immunology (M Phil, PhD); integrative neurobiology and behavior (M Phil, PhD); membrane trafficking (M Phil, PhD); microbiology (M Phil, PhD); molecular and cellular neuroscience (M Phil, PhD); molecular biology (M Phil, PhD); molecular cancer studies (M Phil, PhD); neuroscience (M Phil, PhD); ophthalmology (M Phil, PhD); optometry (M Phil, PhD); organelle function (M Phil, PhD); pharmacology (M Phil, PhD); physiology (M Phil, PhD); plant sciences (M Phil, PhD); stem cell research (M Phil, PhD); structural biology (M Phil, PhD); systems neuroscience (M Phil, PhD); toxicology (M Phil, PhD).

University of Manitoba, Faculty of Graduate Studies, Faculty of Science, Department of Microbiology, Winnipeg, MB R3T 2N2, Canada. Offers M Sc, PhD. *Degree requirements:* For master's, thesis; for doctorate, one foreign language, thesis/dissertation.

University of Maryland, Baltimore, Graduate School, Graduate Program in Life Sciences, Program in Molecular Microbiology and Immunology, Baltimore, MD 21201. Offers PhD, MD/PhD. *Entrance requirements:* For doctorate, GRE. Additional exam requirements/recommendations for international students: Required—TOEFL (minimum score 550 paper-based; 80 iBT); Recommended—IELTS (minimum score 7). Electronic applications accepted. Part-time tuition and fees vary according to course load, degree level and program.

University of Massachusetts Amherst, Graduate School, College of Natural Sciences, Department of Microbiology, Amherst, MA 01003. Offers MS, PhD. Part-time programs available. *Faculty:* 15 full-time (4 women). *Students:* 32 full-time (22 women), 4 part-time (2 women); includes 11 minority (2 Black or African American, non-Hispanic/Latino; 4 Asian, non-Hispanic/Latino; 4 Hispanic/Latino; 1 Two or more races, non-Hispanic/Latino), 12 international. Average age 28. 80 applicants, 25% accepted, 13 enrolled. In 2010, 6 master's, 1 doctorate awarded. Terminal master's awarded for partial completion of doctoral program. *Degree requirements:* For master's, thesis or alternative; for doctorate, comprehensive exam, thesis/dissertation. *Entrance requirements:* For master's and doctorate, GRE General Test. Additional exam requirements/recommendations for international students: Required—TOEFL (minimum score 550 paper-based; 213 computer-based; 80 iBT), IELTS (minimum score 6.5). *Application deadline:* For fall admission, 12/1 for domestic and international students; for spring admission, 10/1 for domestic and international students. Applications are processed on a rolling basis. Application fee: $50 ($65 for international students). Electronic applications accepted. *Expenses:* Tuition, state resident: full-time $2640. Required fees: $8282. One-time fee: $357 full-time. *Financial support:* In 2010–11, 27 research assistantships with full tuition reimbursements (averaging $12,530 per year), 17 teaching assistantships with full tuition reimbursements (averaging $9,711 per year) were awarded; fellowships, career-related internships or fieldwork, Federal Work-Study, scholarships/grants, traineeships, health care benefits, tuition waivers (full), and unspecified assistantships also available. Support available to part-time students. Financial award application deadline: 12/1; financial award applicants required to submit FAFSA. *Unit head:* Dr. Klaus Nusslein, Graduate Program Director, 413-545-6675, Fax: 413-545-1578. *Application contact:* Jean M. Ames, Supervisor of Admissions, 413-545-0722, Fax: 413-577-0010, E-mail: gradadm@grad.umass.edu.

See Close-Up on page 349.

University of Massachusetts Worcester, Graduate School of Biomedical Sciences, Worcester, MA 01655-0115. Offers biochemistry and molecular pharmacology (PhD); bioinformatics and computational biology (PhD); cancer biology (PhD); cell biology (PhD); clinical and population health research (PhD); clinical investigation (MS); immunology and virology (PhD); interdisciplinary graduate program (PhD); molecular genetics and microbiology (PhD); neuroscience (PhD); DVM/PhD; MD/PhD. *Faculty:* 1,059 full-time (357 women), 145 part-time/adjunct (100 women). *Students:* 438 full-time (239 women), 1 (woman) part-time; includes 44 minority (9 Black or African American, non-Hispanic/Latino; 31 Asian, non-Hispanic/Latino; 4 Hispanic/Latino), 148 international. Average age 29. 687 applicants, 28% accepted, 116 enrolled. In 2010, 6 master's, 45 doctorates awarded. Terminal master's awarded for partial completion of doctoral program. *Degree requirements:* For master's, thesis; for doctorate, thesis/dissertation. *Entrance requirements:* For master's, bachelor's degree; for doctorate, GRE General Test, MS, MA, or MPH (for some programs). Additional exam requirements/recommendations for international students: Required—TOEFL (minimum score 600 paper-based; 250 computer-based). *Application deadline:* For fall admission, 12/15 for domestic and international students; for winter admission, 1/15 for domestic students; for spring admission, 5/15 for domestic students. Application fee: $35. Electronic applications accepted. *Expenses:* Contact institution. *Financial support:* In 2010–11, 439 students received support, including 439 research assistantships with full tuition reimbursements available (averaging $28,350 per year); scholarships/grants, health care benefits, tuition waivers (full), and unspecified assistantships also available. Financial award application deadline: 4/20. *Faculty research:* RNA interference, gene therapy, cell biology, bioinformatics, clinical research. Total annual research expenditures: $232 million. *Unit head:* Dr. Anthony Carruthers, Dean, 508-856-4135, E-mail: anthony.carruthers@umassmed.edu. *Application contact:* Dr. Kendall Knight, Associate Dean and Interim Director of Admissions and Recruitment, 508-856-5628, Fax: 508-856-3659, E-mail: kendall.knight@umassmed.edu.

University of Medicine and Dentistry of New Jersey, Graduate School of Biomedical Sciences, Graduate Programs in Biomedical Sciences–Newark, Department of Microbiology and Molecular Genetics, Newark, NJ 07107. Offers PhD. *Degree requirements:* For doctorate, thesis/dissertation, qualifying exam. *Entrance requirements:* For doctorate, GRE General Test. Additional exam requirements/recommendations for international students: Required—TOEFL. Electronic applications accepted. *Faculty research:* Molecular genetics of yeast, mutagenesis and carcinogenesis of DNA, bacterial protein synthesis, mammalian cell genetics, adenovirus gene expression.

University of Medicine and Dentistry of New Jersey, Graduate School of Biomedical Sciences, Graduate Programs in Biomedical Sciences–Piscataway, Program in Molecular Genetics, Microbiology and Immunology, Piscataway, NJ 08854-5635. Offers MS, PhD, MD/PhD. Terminal master's awarded for partial completion of doctoral program. *Degree requirements:* For master's, thesis, qualifying exam; for doctorate, thesis/dissertation, qualifying exam. *Entrance requirements:* For master's and doctorate, GRE General Test. Additional exam requirements/recommendations for international students: Required—TOEFL. *Application deadline:* For fall admission, 1/5 for domestic students. Applications are processed on a rolling basis. Application fee: $40. Electronic applications accepted. *Financial support:* Fellowships, research assistantships, teaching assistantships available. Financial award application deadline: 5/1. *Faculty research:* Interferon, receptors, retrovirus evolution, Arbo virus/host cell interactions. *Unit head:* Dr. Michael J. Leibowitz, Director, 732-235-4795, Fax: 732-235-5223, E-mail: leibowit@umdnj.edu. *Application contact:* Johanna Sierra, University Registrar, 732-235-5016, Fax: 732-235-4720.

University of Miami, Graduate School, Miller School of Medicine, Graduate Programs in Medicine, Department of Microbiology and Immunology, Coral Gables, FL 33124. Offers PhD, MD/PhD. *Degree requirements:* For doctorate, thesis/dissertation, oral and written qualifying exams. *Entrance requirements:* For doctorate, GRE General Test. Additional exam requirements/recommendations for international students: Required—TOEFL. Electronic applications accepted. *Faculty research:* Cellular and molecular immunology, molecular and pathogenic virology, pathogenic bacteriology and gene therapy of cancer.

University of Michigan, Rackham Graduate School, Program in Biomedical Sciences (PIBS), Department of Microbiology and Immunology, Ann Arbor, MI 48109. Offers PhD. *Faculty:* 22 full-time (11 women), 16 part-time/adjunct (6 women). *Students:* 40 full-time (25 women); includes 3 minority (all Asian, non-Hispanic/Latino), 2 international. Average age 28. 64 applicants, 27% accepted, 4 enrolled. In 2010, 8 doctorates awarded. *Degree requirements:* For doctorate, thesis/dissertation, oral defense of dissertation, preliminary exam. *Entrance requirements:* For doctorate, GRE General Test. Additional exam requirements/recommendations for international students: Required—TOEFL (minimum score 600 paper-based; 220 computer-based; 84 iBT), TWE. *Application deadline:* For fall admission, 12/15 for domestic students, 11/1 for international students. Application fee: $60 ($75 for international students). Electronic applications accepted. *Expenses:* Tuition, state resident: full-time $17,784; part-time $1116 per credit hour. Tuition, nonresident: full-time $35,944; part-time $2125 per credit hour. International tuition: $35,994 full-time. Required fees: $95 per semester. Tuition and fees vary according to course load, degree level and program. *Financial support:* In 2010–11, 17 students received support, including 15 fellowships with full tuition reimbursements available (averaging $24,500 per year), 20 research assistantships with full tuition reimbursements available (averaging $24,500 per year); teaching assistantships, health care benefits and tuition waivers (full) also available. Financial award application deadline: 2/1. *Faculty research:* Gene regulation, molecular biology of animal and bacterial viruses, molecular and cellular networks, pathogenesis and microbial genetics. Total annual research expenditures: $7.3 million. *Unit head:* Dr. Harry L. T. Mobley, Chair, 734-764-1466, Fax: 734-764-3562, E-mail: hmobley@umich.edu. *Application contact:* Heidi Thompson, Senior Student Administrative Assistant, 734-763-3532, Fax: 734-764-3562, E-mail: heiditho@umich.edu.

University of Minnesota, Twin Cities Campus, Graduate School, PhD Program in Microbiology, Immunology and Cancer Biology, Minneapolis, MN 55455-0213. Offers PhD. *Degree requirements:* For doctorate, thesis/dissertation. *Entrance requirements:* For doctorate, GRE General Test. Additional exam requirements/recommendations for international students: Required—TOEFL (minimum score 600 paper-based; 250 computer-based). Electronic applications accepted. *Faculty research:* Virology, microbiology, cancer biology, immunology.

University of Mississippi Medical Center, School of Graduate Studies in the Health Sciences, Department of Microbiology, Jackson, MS 39216-4505. Offers MS, PhD, MD/PhD. Terminal master's awarded for partial completion of doctoral program. *Degree requirements:* For master's, thesis; for doctorate, thesis/dissertation, first authored publication. *Entrance requirements:* For master's and doctorate, GRE General Test, minimum GPA of 3.0. *Faculty research:* Immunology, virology, microbial physiology/genetics, parasitology.

University of Missouri, School of Medicine and Graduate School, Graduate Programs in Medicine, Department of Molecular Microbiology and Immunology, Columbia, MO 65211. Offers MS, PhD. Terminal master's awarded for partial completion of doctoral program. *Degree requirements:* For master's, thesis; for doctorate, thesis/dissertation. *Entrance requirements:* For master's and doctorate, GRE General Test, minimum GPA of 3.0. Additional exam requirements/recommendations for international students: Required—TOEFL (minimum score 580 paper-based; 237 computer-based; 92 iBT). *Faculty research:* Molecular biology, host-parasite interactions.

The University of Montana, Graduate School, College of Arts and Sciences, Division of Biological Sciences, Program in Biochemistry and Microbiology, Missoula, MT 59812-0002. Offers biochemistry (MS); integrative microbiology and biochemistry (PhD); microbial ecology (MS, PhD); microbiology (MS). Terminal master's awarded for partial completion of doctoral program. *Degree requirements:* For master's, thesis; for doctorate, variable foreign language requirement, thesis/dissertation. *Entrance requirements:* For master's and doctorate, GRE General Test. *Faculty research:* Ribosome structure, medical microbiology/pathogenesis, microbial ecology/environmental microbiology.

University of Nebraska Medical Center, Graduate Studies, Department of Pathology and Microbiology, Omaha, NE 68198. Offers MS, PhD. Part-time programs available. *Faculty:* 36 full-time (7 women), 57 part-time/adjunct (8 women). *Students:* 35 full-time (19 women), 13 part-time (9 women); includes 1 Black or African American, non-Hispanic/Latino; 7 Asian, non-Hispanic/Latino; 1 Hispanic/Latino, 13 international. Average age 28. 40 applicants, 43% accepted, 16 enrolled. In 2010, 2 master's, 5 doctorates awarded. Terminal master's awarded for partial completion of doctoral program. *Degree requirements:* For master's, comprehensive exam, thesis; for doctorate, comprehensive exam, thesis/dissertation. *Entrance requirements:* For master's, previous course work in biology, chemistry, mathematics, and physics; for doctorate, GRE General Test, previous course work in biology, chemistry, mathematics, and physics. Additional exam requirements/recommendations for international students: Required—TOEFL (minimum score 550 paper-based; 213 computer-based). *Application deadline:* For fall admission, 6/1 for domestic students, 4/1 for international students; for spring admission, 10/1 for domestic students, 8/1 for international students. Applications are processed on a rolling basis. Application fee: $45. Electronic applications accepted. *Expenses:* Tuition, state resident: part-time $198.25 per semester hour. Required fees: $63 per semester. *Financial support:* In 2010–11, 9 fellowships with tuition reimbursements (averaging $21,000 per year), 18 research assistantships with tuition reimbursements (averaging $21,000 per year) were awarded; institutionally sponsored loans and tuition waivers (full) also available. Support available to part-time students. Financial award application deadline: 3/1. *Faculty research:* Carcinogenesis, cancer biology, immunobiology, molecular virology, molecular genetics. *Unit head:* Dr. Rakesh K. Singh, Chair, Graduate Committee, 402-559-9948, Fax: 402-559-4077, E-mail: rsingh@unmc.edu. *Application contact:* Marjorie Boyden, Office Associate, 402-559-4042, E-mail: mboyden@unmc.edu.

University of New Hampshire, Graduate School, College of Life Sciences and Agriculture, Department of Molecular, Cellular and Biomedical Sciences, Program in Microbiology, Durham, NH 03824. Offers MS, PhD. Part-time programs available. *Faculty:* 7 full-time. *Students:* 7 full-time (5 women), 13 part-time (5 women); includes 1 Black or African American, non-Hispanic/Latino; 2 Asian, non-Hispanic/Latino; 1 Hispanic/Latino, 2 international. Average age 28. 37 applicants, 24% accepted, 5 enrolled. In 2010, 3 master's, 2 doctorates awarded. Terminal master's awarded for partial completion of doctoral program. *Degree requirements:* For master's, thesis; for doctorate, thesis/dissertation. *Entrance requirements:* For master's and doctorate, GRE General Test. Additional exam requirements/recommendations for international students: Required—TOEFL (minimum score 550 paper-based; 213 computer-based; 80 iBT). *Application*

deadline: For fall admission, 1/15 priority date for domestic students, 1/15 for international students; for spring admission, 11/1 for domestic students. Applications are processed on a rolling basis. Application fee: $65. Electronic applications accepted. *Financial support:* In 2010–11, 17 students received support, including 3 fellowships, 4 research assistantships, 10 teaching assistantships; career-related internships or fieldwork, Federal Work-Study, scholarships/grants, and tuition waivers (full and partial) also available. Support available to part-time students. Financial award application deadline: 2/15. *Faculty research:* Bacterial host-parasite interactions, immunology, microbial structures, bacterial and bacteriophage genetics, virology. *Unit head:* Dr. Rick Cote, Chairperson, 603-862-0211. *Application contact:* Flora Joyal, Administrative Assistant, 603-862-4095, E-mail: flora.joyal@unh.edu.

University of New Mexico, School of Medicine, Biomedical Sciences Graduate Program, Albuquerque, NM 87131-5196. Offers biochemistry and molecular biology (MS, PhD); cell biology and physiology (MS, PhD); clinical and translational science (Certificate); molecular genetics and microbiology (MS, PhD); neuroscience (MS, PhD); pathology (MS, PhD); toxicology (MS, PhD); university science teaching (Certificate). Part-time programs available. *Faculty:* 33 full-time (14 women), 3 part-time/adjunct (1 woman). *Students:* 94 full-time (57 women), 14 part-time (8 women); includes 24 minority (3 Black or African American, non-Hispanic/Latino; 1 American Indian or Alaska Native, non-Hispanic/Latino; 6 Asian, non-Hispanic/Latino; 13 Hispanic/Latino; 1 Two or more races, non-Hispanic/Latino), 20 international. Average age 30. 135 applicants, 14% accepted, 19 enrolled. In 2010, 2 master's, 19 doctorates, 3 other advanced degrees awarded. Terminal master's awarded for partial completion of doctoral program. *Degree requirements:* For master's, thesis; for doctorate, comprehensive exam, thesis/dissertation. *Entrance requirements:* For master's and doctorate, GRE General Test, minimum undergraduate GPA of 3.0. Additional exam requirements/recommendations for international students: Required—TOEFL. *Application deadline:* For fall admission, 1/1 priority date for domestic students. Applications are processed on a rolling basis. Application fee: $50. Electronic applications accepted. *Expenses:* Tuition, state resident: full-time $5991; part-time $251 per credit hour. Tuition, nonresident: full-time $14,405; part-time $800.20 per credit hour. Tuition and fees vary according to course level, course load, program and reciprocity agreements. *Financial support:* In 2010–11, 99 students received support, including 5 fellowships (averaging $75 per year), 96 research assistantships with full tuition reimbursements available (averaging $17,401 per year), 2 teaching assistantships with full tuition reimbursements available (averaging $2,415 per year); career-related internships or fieldwork, Federal Work-Study, institutionally sponsored loans, scholarships/grants, traineeships, health care benefits, and unspecified assistantships also available. Financial award application deadline: 1/1; financial award applicants required to submit FAFSA. *Faculty research:* Signal transduction, infectious disease, biology of cancer, structural biology, neuroscience. *Unit head:* Laurie G. Hudson, Director, 505-272-1887, Fax: 505-272-8738, E-mail: lhudson@salud.unm.edu. *Application contact:* Angel Cooke-Jackson, Coordinator, 505-272-1887, Fax: 505-272-8738, E-mail: acooke-jackson@salud.unm.edu.

The University of North Carolina at Chapel Hill, School of Medicine and Graduate School, Graduate Programs in Medicine, Department of Microbiology and Immunology, Chapel Hill, NC 27599-7290. Offers immunology (MS, PhD); microbiology (MS, PhD). *Faculty:* 65 full-time (20 women). *Students:* 73 full-time (53 women); includes 6 Black or African American, non-Hispanic/Latino; 5 Asian, non-Hispanic/Latino; 2 Hispanic/Latino, 6 international. Average age 28. In 2010, 16 doctorates awarded. Terminal master's awarded for partial completion of doctoral program. *Degree requirements:* For master's, comprehensive exam, thesis; for doctorate, comprehensive exam, thesis/dissertation. *Entrance requirements:* For master's and doctorate, GRE General Test, minimum GPA of 3.0. *Application deadline:* Applications are processed on a rolling basis. Electronic applications accepted. *Financial support:* In 2010–11, 3 fellowships with full tuition reimbursements (averaging $26,000 per year), 69 research assistantships with full tuition reimbursements (averaging $26,000 per year) were awarded; scholarships/grants, traineeships, health care benefits, and unspecified assistantships also available. Financial award application deadline: 3/1; financial award applicants required to submit FAFSA. *Faculty research:* HIV pathogenesis, immune response, t-cell mediated autoimmunity, alpha-viruses, bacterial chemotaxis, francisella tularensis, pertussis, Mycobacterium tuberculosis, Burkholderia, Dengue virus. Total annual research expenditures: $11.3 million. *Unit head:* Dr. William Goldman, Chairman, 919-966-1191, Fax: 919-962-8103, E-mail: goldman@med.unc.edu. *Application contact:* Dixie Flannery, Student Services Specialist, 919-966-9005, Fax: 919-962-8103, E-mail: microimm@med.unc.edu.

University of North Dakota, Graduate School and Graduate School, Graduate Programs in Medicine, Department of Microbiology and Immunology, Grand Forks, ND 58202. Offers MS, PhD. *Faculty:* 6 full-time (2 women). *Students:* 10 full-time (7 women); includes 2 minority (1 American Indian or Alaska Native, non-Hispanic/Latino; 1 Asian, non-Hispanic/Latino), 2 international. Average age 27. 13 applicants, 23% accepted, 3 enrolled. In 2010, 2 master's, 1 doctorate awarded. *Degree requirements:* For master's, comprehensive exam, thesis or alternative; for doctorate, comprehensive exam, thesis/dissertation, final examination. *Entrance requirements:* For master's and doctorate, GRE General Test, minimum GPA of 3.0. Additional exam requirements/recommendations for international students: Required—TOEFL (minimum score 550 paper-based; 213 computer-based; 79 iBT), IELTS (minimum score 6.5). *Application deadline:* For fall admission, 8/1 priority date for domestic students, 5/1 priority date for international students; for spring admission, 12/1 priority date for domestic students, 9/1 priority date for international students. Applications are processed on a rolling basis. Application fee: $35. Electronic applications accepted. *Expenses:* Tuition, state resident: full-time $5857; part-time $306.74 per credit. Tuition, nonresident: full-time $15,666; part-time $729.77 per credit. Required fees: $53.42 per credit. Tuition and fees vary according to course load, program and reciprocity agreements. *Financial support:* In 2010–11, 10 students received support, including 5 research assistantships with full and partial tuition reimbursements available (averaging $13,997 per year), 5 teaching assistantships with full and partial tuition reimbursements available (averaging $13,997 per year); fellowships with full and partial tuition reimbursements available, Federal Work-Study, institutionally sponsored loans, scholarships/grants, health care benefits, tuition waivers (full and partial), and unspecified assistantships also available. Support available to part-time students. Financial award application deadline: 3/15; financial award applicants required to submit FAFSA. *Faculty research:* Genetic and immunological aspects of a murine model of human multiple sclerosis, termination of DNA replication, cell division in bacteria, yersinia pestis. Total annual research expenditures: $423,552. *Unit head:* Dr. Ann Flower, Graduate Director, 701-777-2214, Fax: 701-777-3527, E-mail: aflower@medicine.nodak.edu. *Application contact:* Matt Anderson, Admissions Specialist, 701-777-2947, Fax: 701-777-3619, E-mail: matthew.anderson@gradschool.und.edu.

University of North Texas Health Science Center at Fort Worth, Graduate School of Biomedical Sciences, Fort Worth, TX 76107-2699. Offers anatomy and cell biology (MS, PhD); biochemistry and molecular biology (MS, PhD); biomedical sciences (MS, PhD); biotechnology (MS); forensic genetics (MS); integrative physiology (MS, PhD); medical science (MS); microbiology and immunology (MS, PhD); pharmacology (MS, PhD); science education (MS); DO/MS; DO/PhD. Terminal master's awarded for partial completion of doctoral program. *Degree requirements:* For master's, thesis; for doctorate, thesis/dissertation. *Entrance requirements:* For master's and doctorate, GRE General Test. Additional exam requirements/recommendations for international students: Required—TOEFL. *Expenses:* Contact institution. *Faculty research:* Alzheimer's disease, aging, eye diseases, cancer, cardiovascular disease.

University of Oklahoma, College of Arts and Sciences, Department of Botany and Microbiology, Program in Microbiology, Norman, OK 73019. Offers MS, PhD. *Students:* 39 full-time (18 women), 7 part-time (2 women); includes 8 minority (2 Black or African American, non-Hispanic/Latino; 2 American Indian or Alaska Native, non-Hispanic/Latino; 2 Asian, non-Hispanic/Latino; 2 Two or more races, non-Hispanic/Latino), 15 international. Average age 27. 25 applicants, 40% accepted, 8 enrolled. In 2010, 3 master's, 2 doctorates awarded. Terminal master's awarded for partial completion of doctoral program. *Degree requirements:* For master's, thesis, oral exam; for doctorate, one foreign language, thesis/dissertation, general exam. *Entrance requirements:* For master's and doctorate, GRE. Additional exam requirements/

Microbiology

University of Oklahoma (continued)

recommendations for international students: Required—TOEFL (minimum score 550 paper-based; 213 computer-based; 79 iBT). *Application deadline:* For fall admission, 2/1 for domestic students, 4/1 for international students; for spring admission, 11/1 for domestic students, 9/1 for international students. Applications are processed on a rolling basis. Application fee: $40 ($90 for international students). Electronic applications accepted. *Expenses:* Tuition, state resident: full-time $3893; part-time $162.20 per credit hour. Tuition, nonresident: full-time $14,167; part-time $590.30 per credit hour. Required fees: $2523; $94.60 per credit hour. Tuition and fees vary according to course load and degree level. *Financial support:* Federal Work-Study, institutionally sponsored loans, scholarships/grants, health care benefits, and unspecified assistantships available. Support available to part-time students. Financial award applicants required to submit FAFSA. *Faculty research:* Anaerobic microbiology, bioremediation, microbial ecology, pathogen-host interactions, microbial systematics. *Unit head:* Dr. Gordon Uno, Chair, 405-325-4321, Fax: 405-325-7619, E-mail: guno@ou.edu. *Application contact:* Adell Hopper, Staff Assistant, 405-325-4322, Fax: 405-325-7619, E-mail: ahopper@ou.edu.

University of Oklahoma Health Sciences Center, College of Medicine and Graduate College, Graduate Programs in Medicine, Department of Microbiology and Immunology, Oklahoma City, OK 73190. Offers immunology (MS, PhD); microbiology (MS, PhD). Part-time programs available. Terminal master's awarded for partial completion of doctoral program. *Degree requirements:* For master's, thesis or alternative; for doctorate, one foreign language, thesis/dissertation. *Entrance requirements:* For doctorate, GRE General Test, 3 letters of recommendation. Additional exam requirements/recommendations for international students: Required—TOEFL. *Faculty research:* Molecular genetics, pathogenesis, streptococcal infections, gram-positive virulence, monoclonal antibodies.

University of Ottawa, Faculty of Graduate and Postdoctoral Studies, Faculty of Medicine, Department of Biochemistry, Microbiology and Immunology, Ottawa, ON K1N 6N5, Canada. Offers biochemistry (M Sc, PhD); microbiology and immunology (M Sc, PhD). *Degree requirements:* For master's, thesis; for doctorate, comprehensive exam, thesis/dissertation, seminar. *Entrance requirements:* For master's, honors degree or equivalent, minimum B average; for doctorate, master's degree, minimum B+ average. Electronic applications accepted. *Faculty research:* General biochemistry, molecular biology, microbiology, host biology, nutrition and metabolism.

University of Pennsylvania, Perelman School of Medicine, Biomedical Graduate Studies, Graduate Group in Cell and Molecular Biology, Philadelphia, PA 19104. Offers cancer biology (PhD); cell biology and physiology (PhD); developmental stem cell regenerative biology (PhD); gene therapy and vaccines (PhD); genetics and gene regulation (PhD); microbiology, virology, and parasitology (PhD); MD/PhD; VMD/PhD. *Faculty:* 299. *Students:* 315 full-time (166 women); includes 13 Black or African American, non-Hispanic/Latino; 1 American Indian or Alaska Native, non-Hispanic/Latino; 44 Asian, non-Hispanic/Latino; 18 Hispanic/Latino, 37 international. 579 applicants, 21% accepted, 49 enrolled. In 2010, 53 doctorates awarded. *Degree requirements:* For doctorate, thesis/dissertation. *Entrance requirements:* For doctorate, GRE General Test. Additional exam requirements/recommendations for international students: Required—TOEFL. *Application deadline:* For fall admission, 12/8 priority date for domestic and international students. Applications are processed on a rolling basis. Application fee: $70. Electronic applications accepted. *Expenses:* Tuition: Full-time $25,660; part-time $4758 per course. Required fees: $2152; $270 per course. Tuition and fees vary according to course load, degree level and program. *Financial support:* In 2010–11, 315 students received support; fellowships, research assistantships, scholarships/grants, traineeships, and unspecified assistantships available. Financial award application deadline: 12/8. *Unit head:* Dr. Daniel Kessler, Graduate Group Chair, 215-898-2180, E-mail: raperj@mail.med.upenn.edu. *Application contact:* Meagan Schofer, Coordinator, 215-898-9536, Fax: 215-573-2104, E-mail: camb@mailmed.upenn.edu.

University of Pittsburgh, Graduate School of Public Health, Department of Infectious Diseases and Microbiology, Pittsburgh, PA 15260. Offers bioscience of infectious diseases (MPH); community and behavioral intervention of infectious diseases (MPH); infectious diseases and microbiology (MS, Dr PH, PhD); LGBT health and wellness (Certificate). Part-time programs available. *Faculty:* 21 full-time (7 women), 3 part-time/adjunct (1 woman). *Students:* 47 full-time (36 women), 12 part-time (5 women); includes 3 Black or African American, non-Hispanic/Latino; 5 Asian, non-Hispanic/Latino; 1 Hispanic/Latino, 8 international. Average age 28. 188 applicants, 58% accepted, 25 enrolled. In 2010, 16 master's, 4 doctorates awarded. Terminal master's awarded for partial completion of doctoral program. *Degree requirements:* For master's, one foreign language, comprehensive exam (for some programs), thesis; for doctorate, one foreign language, comprehensive exam, thesis/dissertation. *Entrance requirements:* For master's and doctorate, GRE General Test, MCAT, or DAT. Additional exam requirements/recommendations for international students: Required—TOEFL (minimum score 550 paper-based; 213 computer-based; 80 iBT). *Application deadline:* For fall admission, 1/4 priority date for domestic and international students. Applications are processed on a rolling basis. Application fee: $115. Electronic applications accepted. *Expenses:* Tuition, state resident: full-time $17,304; part-time $701 per credit. Tuition, nonresident: full-time $29,554; part-time $1210 per credit. Required fees: $740; $214 per term. Tuition and fees vary according to program. *Financial support:* In 2010–11, 14 students received support, including 1 fellowship (averaging $6,000 per year), 13 research assistantships with full and partial tuition reimbursements available (averaging $8,675 per year). Financial award applicants required to submit FAFSA. *Faculty research:* HIV, Epstein-Barr virus, virology, immunology, malaria. Total annual research expenditures: $14.2 million. *Unit head:* Dr. Charles R. Rinaldo, Chairman, 412-624-3928, Fax: 412-624-4953, E-mail: rinaldo@pitt.edu. *Application contact:* Dr. Jeremy Martinson, Assistant Professor, 412-624-5646, Fax: 412-383-8926, E-mail: jmartins@pitt.edu.

University of Pittsburgh, School of Medicine, Graduate Programs in Medicine, Program in Molecular Virology and Microbiology, Pittsburgh, PA 15260. Offers MS, PhD. *Faculty:* 47 full-time (10 women). *Students:* 21 full-time (11 women); includes 2 Asian, non-Hispanic/Latino; 1 Hispanic/Latino, 3 international. Average age 27. 486 applicants, 14% accepted. In 2010, 5 doctorates awarded. *Degree requirements:* For doctorate, comprehensive exam, thesis/dissertation. *Entrance requirements:* For doctorate, GRE General Test, GRE Subject Test, minimum QPA of 3.0. Additional exam requirements/recommendations for international students: Required—TOEFL (minimum score 600 paper-based; 100 iBT), IELTS (minimum score 7). *Application deadline:* For fall admission, 12/15 priority date for domestic and international students. Application fee: $50. Electronic applications accepted. *Expenses:* Tuition, state resident: full-time $17,304; part-time $701 per credit. Tuition, nonresident: full-time $29,554; part-time $1210 per credit. Required fees: $740; $214 per term. Tuition and fees vary according to program. *Financial support:* In 2010–11, 21 research assistantships with full tuition reimbursements (averaging $25,500 per year) were awarded; institutionally sponsored loans, scholarships/grants, traineeships, health care benefits, and unspecified assistantships also available. *Faculty research:* Host-pathogen interactions, persistent microbial infections, microbial genetics and gene expression, microbial pathogenesis, anti-bacterial therapeutics. *Unit head:* Dr. Neal A. DeLuca, Graduate Program Director, 412-648-9947, Fax: 412-624-0298, E-mail: ndeluca@pitt.edu. *Application contact:* Graduate Studies Administrator, 412-648-8957, Fax: 412-648-1077, E-mail: gradstudies@medschool.pitt.edu.

University of Puerto Rico, Medical Sciences Campus, School of Medicine, Division of Graduate Studies, Department of Microbiology and Medical Zoology, San Juan, PR 00936-5067. Offers MS, PhD. *Degree requirements:* For master's, one foreign language, thesis; for doctorate, one foreign language, comprehensive exam, thesis/dissertation. *Entrance requirements:* For master's and doctorate, GRE General Test, GRE Subject Test, interview, minimum GPA of 3.0, 3 letters of recommendation. *Faculty research:* Molecular and general parasitology, immunology, development of viral vaccines and antiviral agents, antibiotic resistance, bacteriology.

University of Rhode Island, Graduate School, College of the Environment and Life Sciences, Department of Cell and Molecular Biology, Kingston, RI 02881. Offers biochemistry (MS, PhD); clinical laboratory sciences (MS), including biotechnology, clinical laboratory science, cytopathology; microbiology (MS, PhD); molecular genetics (MS, PhD). Part-time programs available. *Faculty:* 13 full-time (5 women), 2 part-time/adjunct (1 woman). *Students:* 32 full-time (15 women), 37 part-time (23 women); includes 10 minority (5 Black or African American, non-Hispanic/Latino; 2 Asian, non-Hispanic/Latino; 3 Hispanic/Latino), 4 international. In 2010, 29 master's, 3 doctorates awarded. *Degree requirements:* For master's, comprehensive exam (for some programs); for doctorate, comprehensive exam. *Entrance requirements:* For master's and doctorate, GRE, 2 letters of recommendation. Additional exam requirements/recommendations for international students: Required—TOEFL (minimum score 550 paper-based; 213 computer-based). *Application deadline:* For fall admission, 7/15 for domestic students, 2/1 for international students; for spring admission, 11/15 for domestic students, 7/15 for international students. Application fee: $65. Electronic applications accepted. *Expenses:* Tuition, state resident: full-time $9588; part-time $533 per credit hour. Tuition, nonresident: full-time $22,968; part-time $1276 per credit hour. Required fees: $1282; $68 per semester. Tuition and fees vary according to program. *Financial support:* In 2010–11, 3 research assistantships with full and partial tuition reimbursements (averaging $11,653 per year), 12 teaching assistantships with full and partial tuition reimbursements (averaging $12,379 per year) were awarded. Financial award application deadline: 7/15; financial award applicants required to submit FAFSA. *Faculty research:* Genomics and Sequencing Center: an interdisciplinary genomics research and undergraduate and graduate student training program which provides researchers access to cutting-edge technologies in the field of genomics. Total annual research expenditures: $3.5 million. *Unit head:* Dr. Jay Sperry, Chairperson, 401-874-2201, Fax: 401-874-2202, E-mail: jsperry@mail.uri.edu. *Application contact:* Dr. Jay Sperry, Chairperson, 401-874-2201, Fax: 401-874-2202, E-mail: jsperry@mail.uri.edu.

University of Rochester, School of Medicine and Dentistry, Graduate Programs in Medicine and Dentistry, Department of Microbiology and Immunology, Program in Medical Microbiology, Rochester, NY 14627.

University of Rochester, School of Medicine and Dentistry, Graduate Programs in Medicine and Dentistry, Department of Microbiology and Immunology, Program in Microbiology and Immunology, Rochester, NY 14627.

University of Saskatchewan, College of Medicine, Department of Microbiology and Immunology, Saskatoon, SK S7N 5A2, Canada. Offers M Sc, PhD. *Degree requirements:* For master's, thesis; for doctorate, thesis/dissertation. *Entrance requirements:* Additional exam requirements/recommendations for international students: Required—TOEFL.

University of Saskatchewan, Western College of Veterinary Medicine and College of Graduate Studies and Research, Graduate Programs in Veterinary Medicine, Department of Veterinary Microbiology, Saskatoon, SK S7N 5A2, Canada. Offers M Sc, M Vet Sc, PhD. *Faculty:* 5 full-time (2 women), 7 part-time/adjunct (0 women). *Students:* 29 full-time (19 women); includes 1 Black or African American, non-Hispanic/Latino. In 2010, 1 master's, 5 doctorates awarded. *Degree requirements:* For master's, thesis; for doctorate, comprehensive exam (for some programs), thesis/dissertation. *Entrance requirements:* Additional exam requirements/recommendations for international students: Required—TOEFL (minimum score 80 iBT) or IELTS (minimum score 6.5). *Application deadline:* For fall admission, 7/1 priority date for domestic students. Applications are processed on a rolling basis. Electronic applications accepted. *Financial support:* Fellowships, teaching assistantships available. Financial award application deadline: 1/31. *Faculty research:* Immunology, vaccinology, epidemiology, virology, parasitology. *Unit head:* Dr. Vikram Misra, Head, 306-966-7210, Fax: 306-966-4311, E-mail: vikram.misra@usask.ca. *Application contact:* Dr. Vikram Misra, Graduate Chair, 306-966-7210, E-mail: vikram.misra@usask.ca.

The University of South Dakota, School of Medicine and Health Sciences and Graduate School, Biomedical Sciences Graduate Program, Molecular Microbiology and Immunology Group, Vermillion, SD 57069-2390. Offers MS, PhD. Terminal master's awarded for partial completion of doctoral program. *Degree requirements:* For master's, thesis; for doctorate, comprehensive exam, thesis/dissertation. *Entrance requirements:* For master's and doctorate, GRE General Test, minimum GPA of 3.0. Additional exam requirements/recommendations for international students: Required—TOEFL (minimum score 550 paper-based; 213 computer-based; 80 iBT), IELTS (minimum score 6). Electronic applications accepted. *Expenses:* Contact institution. *Faculty research:* Structure-function membranes, plasmids, immunology, virology, pathogenesis.

University of Southern California, Keck School of Medicine and Graduate School, Graduate Programs in Medicine, Department of Molecular Microbiology and Immunology, Los Angeles, CA 90089. Offers MS, PhD. Part-time programs available. *Faculty:* 16 full-time (4 women), 1 (woman) part-time/adjunct. *Students:* 20 full-time (11 women); includes 3 Asian, non-Hispanic/Latino, 11 international. Average age 25. 24 applicants, 67% accepted, 10 enrolled. In 2010, 7 master's, 1 doctorate awarded. Terminal master's awarded for partial completion of doctoral program. *Degree requirements:* For master's, comprehensive exam (for some programs), thesis optional; for doctorate, comprehensive exam, thesis/dissertation. *Entrance requirements:* For master's, GRE General Test, minimum GPA of 3.0; for doctorate, GRE General Test, GRE Subject Test, minimum GPA of 3.0. Additional exam requirements/recommendations for international students: Required—TOEFL (minimum score 100 iBT). *Application deadline:* Applications are processed on a rolling basis. Application fee: $85. Electronic applications accepted. *Expenses:* Tuition: Full-time $31,240; part-time $1420 per unit. Required fees: $600. One-time fee: $35 full-time. Full-time tuition and fees vary according to degree level and program. *Financial support:* In 2010–11, 3 students received support, including 1 fellowship with full tuition reimbursement available (averaging $27,600 per year), 6 research assistantships with full tuition reimbursements available (averaging $27,600 per year), 1 teaching assistantship with full tuition reimbursement available (averaging $27,600 per year); Federal Work-Study, institutionally sponsored loans, scholarships/grants, health care benefits, and unspecified assistantships also available. Financial award application deadline: 5/3; financial award applicants required to submit FAFSA. *Faculty research:* Animal virology, microbial genetics, molecular and cellular immunology, cellular differentiation control of protein synthesis. *Unit head:* Dr. Jae U. Jung, Professor and Chair, 323-442-1713, Fax: 323-442-1721, E-mail: jaeujung@usc.edu. *Application contact:* Silvina V. Campos, Administrative Assistant II, 323-442-1713, Fax: 323-442-1721, E-mail: scampos@usc.edu.

University of Southern Mississippi, Graduate School, College of Science and Technology, Department of Biological Sciences, Hattiesburg, MS 39406-0001. Offers environmental biology (MS, PhD); marine biology (MS, PhD); microbiology (MS, PhD); molecular biology (MS, PhD). *Faculty:* 27 full-time (6 women). *Students:* 54 full-time (29 women), 5 part-time (4 women); includes 2 Black or African American, non-Hispanic/Latino; 4 Two or more races, non-Hispanic/Latino, 17 international. Average age 32. 54 applicants, 48% accepted, 13 enrolled. In 2010, 4 master's, 4 doctorates awarded. Terminal master's awarded for partial completion of doctoral program. *Degree requirements:* For master's, comprehensive exam, thesis; for doctorate, comprehensive exam, thesis/dissertation. *Entrance requirements:* For master's, GRE General Test, minimum GPA of 3.0 on last 60 hours; for doctorate, GRE General Test, minimum GPA of 3.5. Additional exam requirements/recommendations for international students: Required—TOEFL, IELTS. *Application deadline:* For fall admission, 3/1 priority date for domestic students, 3/1 for international students; for spring admission, 1/10 priority date for domestic and international students. Applications are processed on a rolling basis. Application fee: $50. *Financial support:* In 2010–11, 25 research assistantships with full tuition reimbursements (averaging $9,700 per year), 33 teaching assistantships with full tuition reimbursements (averaging $10,600 per year) were awarded; Federal Work-Study, scholarships/grants, health care benefits, and unspecified assistantships also available. Financial award application deadline: 3/15; financial award applicants required to submit FAFSA. *Unit head:* Dr. Glenmore Shearer, Chair, 601-266-

4748, Fax: 601-266-5797. *Application contact:* Dr. Jake Schaefer, Director of Graduate Studies, 601-266-4748, Fax: 601-266-5797.

The University of Tennessee, Graduate School, College of Arts and Sciences, Department of Microbiology, Knoxville, TN 37996. Offers MS, PhD. Part-time programs available. *Degree requirements:* For master's, thesis; for doctorate, thesis/dissertation. *Entrance requirements:* For master's and doctorate, GRE General Test, minimum GPA of 2.7. Additional exam requirements/recommendations for international students: Required—TOEFL. Electronic applications accepted. *Expenses:* Tuition, state resident: full-time $7440; part-time $414 per credit hour. Tuition, nonresident: full-time $22,478; part-time $1250 per credit hour. Required fees: $922; $43 per credit hour. Tuition and fees vary according to program.

The University of Texas at Austin, Graduate School, College of Natural Sciences, School of Biological Sciences, Program in Microbiology, Austin, TX 78712-1111. Offers PhD. *Entrance requirements:* For doctorate, GRE General Test. Electronic applications accepted.

The University of Texas Health Science Center at Houston, Graduate School of Biomedical Sciences, Program in Microbiology and Molecular Genetics, Houston, TX 77225-0036. Offers MS, PhD, MD/PhD. Terminal master's awarded for partial completion of doctoral program. *Degree requirements:* For master's, thesis; for doctorate, thesis/dissertation. *Entrance requirements:* For master's and doctorate, GRE General Test. Additional exam requirements/recommendations for international students: Required—TOEFL. Electronic applications accepted. *Faculty research:* Disease causation, environmental signaling, gene regulation, cell growth and division, cell structure and architecture.

The University of Texas Health Science Center at San Antonio, Graduate School of Biomedical Sciences, Department of Microbiology and Immunology, San Antonio, TX 78229-3900. Offers PhD. *Faculty:* 19 full-time (5 women). *Students:* 38 full-time (22 women); includes 3 Black or African American, non-Hispanic/Latino; 10 Hispanic/Latino, 7 international. Average age 30. In 2010, 10 doctorates awarded. *Degree requirements:* For doctorate, comprehensive exam, thesis/dissertation. *Entrance requirements:* For doctorate, GRE General Test. Additional exam requirements/recommendations for international students: Required—TOEFL (minimum score 560 paper-based; 220 computer-based; 68 iBT). *Application deadline:* For fall admission, 1/15 priority date for domestic and international students. Applications are processed on a rolling basis. Electronic applications accepted. *Expenses:* Tuition, state resident: full-time $3072; part-time $128 per credit hour. Tuition, nonresident: full-time $11,928; part-time $497 per credit hour. Required fees: $1078; $1078 per year. One-time fee: $60. *Financial support:* In 2010–11, 38 teaching assistantships (averaging $26,000 per year) were awarded; fellowships, research assistantships also available. Financial award application deadline: 6/30; financial award applicants required to submit FAFSA. *Faculty research:* Molecular immunology, mechanisms of microbial pathogenesis, molecular genetics, vaccine and immunodiagnostic development. Total annual research expenditures: $6.8 million. *Unit head:* Joel B. Baseman, Chairman, 210-567-3939, Fax: 210-567-6491, E-mail: baseman@uthscsa.edu. *Application contact:* Sophia Pina, Assistant Dean, 210-567-3984, Fax: 210-567-3719, E-mail: pina@uthscsa.edu.

The University of Texas Medical Branch, Graduate School of Biomedical Sciences, Program in Microbiology and Immunology, Galveston, TX 77555. Offers MS, PhD. Terminal master's awarded for partial completion of doctoral program. *Degree requirements:* For master's, thesis or alternative; for doctorate, thesis/dissertation. *Entrance requirements:* For doctorate, GRE General Test, minimum GPA of 3.0. Additional exam requirements/recommendations for international students: Required—TOEFL (minimum score 550 paper-based; 213 computer-based). Electronic applications accepted.

The University of Texas Southwestern Medical Center at Dallas, Southwestern Graduate School of Biomedical Sciences, Division of Basic Science, Program in Molecular Microbiology, Dallas, TX 75390. Offers PhD. *Faculty:* 34 full-time (10 women), 2 part-time/adjunct (0 women). *Students:* 23 full-time (13 women), 1 part-time (0 women); includes 7 minority (1 Black or African American, non-Hispanic/Latino; 3 Asian, non-Hispanic/Latino; 3 Hispanic/Latino), 5 international. Average age 26. In 2010, 5 doctorates awarded. *Degree requirements:* For doctorate, thesis/dissertation, oral and written exams. *Entrance requirements:* For doctorate, GRE General Test, minimum GPA of 3.0. Additional exam requirements/recommendations for international students: Required—TOEFL. *Application deadline:* For fall admission, 12/15 priority date for domestic students. Applications are processed on a rolling basis. Application fee: $0. Electronic applications accepted. *Financial support:* Fellowships, research assistantships, institutionally sponsored loans available. *Faculty research:* Cell and molecular immunology, molecular pathogenesis of infectious disease, virology. *Unit head:* Dr. Vanessa Speraudio, Chair, 214-648-1603, Fax: 214-648-1899, E-mail: vanessa.speraudio@utsouthwestern.edu. *Application contact:* Dr. Nancy E. Street, Associate Dean, 214-648-6708, Fax: 214-648-2102, E-mail: nancy.street@utsouthwestern.edu.

University of Vermont, College of Medicine and Graduate College, Graduate Programs in Medicine, Department of Microbiology and Molecular Genetics, Burlington, VT 05405. Offers MS, PhD, MD/MS, MD/PhD. *Faculty:* 18 full-time (5 women). *Students:* 26 (15 women); includes 1 Hispanic/Latino, 10 international. 47 applicants, 30% accepted, 5 enrolled. In 2010, 2 doctorates awarded. *Degree requirements:* For master's, thesis; for doctorate, thesis/dissertation. *Entrance requirements:* For master's and doctorate, GRE General Test. Additional exam requirements/recommendations for international students: Required—TOEFL (minimum score 550 paper-based; 213 computer-based; 80 iBT). *Application deadline:* For fall admission, 1/16 priority date for domestic students, 1/16 for international students. Applications are processed on a rolling basis. Application fee: $40. Electronic applications accepted. *Expenses:* Tuition, state resident: part-time $537 per credit hour. Tuition, nonresident: part-time $1355 per credit hour. *Financial support:* Fellowships, research assistantships, teaching assistantships available. Financial award application deadline: 3/1. *Unit head:* Dr. Susan S. Wallace, Chairperson, 802-656-2164. *Application contact:* Dr. David Pederson, Coordinator, 802-656-2164.

University of Vermont, Graduate College, College of Agriculture and Life Sciences and College of Medicine, Department of Microbiology and Molecular Genetics, Burlington, VT 05405. Offers MS, PhD, MD/MS, MD/PhD. *Faculty:* 18 full-time (5 women). *Degree requirements:* For master's, thesis; for doctorate, thesis/dissertation. *Entrance requirements:* For master's and doctorate, GRE General Test. Additional exam requirements/recommendations for international students: Required—TOEFL (minimum score 550 paper-based; 213 computer-based; 80 iBT). *Application deadline:* For fall admission, 2/1 priority date for domestic students. Applications are processed on a rolling basis. Application fee: $40. Electronic applications accepted. *Expenses:* Tuition, state resident: part-time $537 per credit hour. Tuition, nonresident: part-time $1355 per credit hour. *Financial support:* Fellowships, research assistantships, teaching assistantships available. Financial award application deadline: 3/1. *Unit head:* Dr. Susan S. Wallace, Chairperson, 802-656-2164. *Application contact:* Dr. S. Doublie, Coordinator, 802-656-2164.

University of Victoria, Faculty of Graduate Studies, Faculty of Science, Department of Biochemistry and Microbiology, Victoria, BC V8W 2Y2, Canada. Offers biochemistry (M Sc, PhD); microbiology (M Sc, PhD). *Degree requirements:* For master's, thesis, seminar; for doctorate, thesis/dissertation, seminar, candidacy exam. *Entrance requirements:* For master's, GRE General Test, minimum B+ average; for doctorate, GRE General Test, minimum B+ average, M Sc. Additional exam requirements/recommendations for international students: Required—TOEFL (minimum score 600 paper-based; 250 computer-based). Electronic applications accepted. *Faculty research:* Molecular pathogenesis, prokaryotic, eukaryotic, macromolecular interactions, microbial surfaces, virology, molecular genetics.

University of Virginia, School of Medicine, Department of Microbiology, Charlottesville, VA 22903. Offers PhD, MD/PhD. *Faculty:* 37 full-time (14 women). *Students:* 70 full-time (40 women); includes 5 Black or African American, non-Hispanic/Latino; 4 Asian, non-Hispanic/Latino; 2 Hispanic/Latino, 5 international. Average age 28. In 2010, 21 doctorates awarded. *Degree requirements:* For doctorate, thesis/dissertation. *Entrance requirements:* For doctorate, GRE General Test, 2 or more letters of recommendation. Additional exam requirements/recommendations for international students: Required—TOEFL (minimum score 600 paper-based; 250 computer-based; 90 iBT). *Application deadline:* For fall admission, 2/1 for domestic and international students. Applications are processed on a rolling basis. Application fee: $60. Electronic applications accepted. *Financial support:* Fellowships, traineeships and unspecified assistantships available. Financial award applicants required to submit FAFSA. *Faculty research:* Virology, membrane biology and molecular genetics. *Unit head:* Kodi S. Ravichandran, Chair, 434-924-1948, Fax: 434-982-1071. *Application contact:* Kodi S. Ravichandran, Chair, 434-924-1948, Fax: 434-982-1071.

University of Washington, Graduate School, School of Medicine, Graduate Programs in Medicine, Department of Microbiology, Seattle, WA 98195. Offers PhD. *Degree requirements:* For doctorate, thesis/dissertation. *Entrance requirements:* For doctorate, GRE General Test, GRE Subject Test (recommended). Electronic applications accepted. *Faculty research:* Bacterial genetics and physiology, mechanisms of bacterial and viral pathogenesis, bacterial-plant interaction.

The University of Western Ontario, Faculty of Graduate Studies, Biosciences Division, Department of Microbiology and Immunology, London, ON N6A 5B8, Canada. Offers M Sc, PhD. *Degree requirements:* For master's, thesis, oral and written exam; for doctorate, thesis/dissertation, oral and written exam. *Entrance requirements:* For master's, honors degree or equivalent in microbiology, immunology, or other biological science; minimum B average; for doctorate, M Sc in microbiology and immunology. Additional exam requirements/recommendations for international students: Required—TOEFL. *Faculty research:* Virology, molecular pathogenesis, cellular immunology, molecular biology.

University of Wisconsin–La Crosse, Office of University Graduate Studies, College of Science and Health, Department of Biology, La Crosse, WI 54601-3742. Offers aquatic sciences (MS); biology (MS); cellular and molecular biology (MS); clinical microbiology (MS); microbiology (MS); nurse anesthesia (MS); physiology (MS). Part-time programs available. *Faculty:* 31. *Students:* 23 full-time (14 women), 42 part-time (25 women); includes 4 minority (1 Asian, non-Hispanic/Latino; 3 Hispanic/Latino), 1 international. Average age 28. 100 applicants, 34% accepted, 29 enrolled. In 2010, 20 master's awarded. *Degree requirements:* For master's, comprehensive exam, thesis. *Entrance requirements:* For master's, GRE General Test, minimum GPA of 2.85. Additional exam requirements/recommendations for international students: Required—TOEFL (minimum score 550 paper-based; 213 computer-based; 79 iBT). *Application deadline:* For fall admission, 2/1 priority date for domestic and international students; for spring admission, 1/4 priority date for domestic and international students. Applications are processed on a rolling basis. Application fee: $56. Electronic applications accepted. *Expenses:* Tuition, state resident: full-time $7121; part-time $395.61 per credit. Tuition, nonresident: full-time $16,891; part-time $938.41 per credit. Part-time tuition and fees vary according to course load, program and reciprocity agreements. *Financial support:* In 2010–11, 14 research assistantships with partial tuition reimbursements (averaging $10,124 per year) were awarded; Federal Work-Study, scholarships/grants, health care benefits, and tuition waivers (partial) also available. Support available to part-time students. Financial award application deadline: 3/15; financial award applicants required to submit FAFSA. *Unit head:* Dr. Thomas Volk, Coordinator of Graduate Studies, 608-785-6972, Fax: 608-785-6959, E-mail: volk.thom@uwlax.edu. *Application contact:* Kathryn Kiefer, Director of Admissions, 608-785-8939, E-mail: admissions@uwlax.edu.

University of Wisconsin–Madison, School of Medicine and Public Health and Graduate School, Graduate Programs in Medicine and College of Agricultural and Life Sciences, Microbiology Doctoral Training Program, Madison, WI 53706. Offers PhD. *Faculty:* 90 full-time (28 women). *Students:* 74 full-time (43 women); includes 3 Black or African American, non-Hispanic/Latino; 6 Hispanic/Latino, 3 international. Average age 24. 261 applicants, 16% accepted, 14 enrolled. In 2010, 18 doctorates awarded. *Degree requirements:* For doctorate, thesis/dissertation, preliminary exam, 2 semesters of teaching. *Entrance requirements:* For doctorate, GRE. Additional exam requirements/recommendations for international students: Required—TOEFL (minimum score 580 paper-based; 237 computer-based). *Application deadline:* For fall admission, 12/1 for domestic and international students. Application fee: $56. Electronic applications accepted. *Expenses:* Tuition, state resident: full-time $9887; part-time $617.96 per credit. Tuition, nonresident: full-time $24,054; part-time $1503.40 per credit. Required fees: $67.63 per credit. Tuition and fees vary according to reciprocity agreements. *Financial support:* In 2010–11, 88 students received support, including 26 fellowships with tuition reimbursements available (averaging $24,500 per year), 48 research assistantships with tuition reimbursements available (averaging $24,500 per year); career-related internships or fieldwork, scholarships/grants, traineeships, health care benefits, and tuition waivers (full) also available. Financial award application deadline: 12/1. *Faculty research:* Microbial pathogenesis, gene regulation, immunology, virology, cell biology. Total annual research expenditures: $15.1 million. *Unit head:* Dr. Joseph Dillard, Director, 608-265-2837, Fax: 608-262-8418, E-mail: jpdillard@wisc.edu. *Application contact:* Cathy Davis Gray, Coordinator, 608-265-0689, Fax: 608-262-8418, E-mail: cdg@bact.wisc.edu.

University of Wisconsin–Oshkosh, The Office of Graduate Studies, College of Letters and Science, Department of Biology and Microbiology, Oshkosh, WI 54901. Offers biology (MS), including botany, microbiology, zoology. *Degree requirements:* For master's, comprehensive exam, thesis. *Entrance requirements:* For master's, GRE General Test, minimum GPA of 3.0, BS in biology. Additional exam requirements/recommendations for international students: Required—TOEFL (minimum score 550 paper-based; 213 computer-based; 79 iBT). Electronic applications accepted.

University of Wyoming, Graduate Program in Molecular and Cellular Life Sciences, Laramie, WY 82070. Offers PhD. *Degree requirements:* For doctorate, thesis/dissertation, four eight-week laboratory rotations, comprehensive basic practical exam, two-part qualifying exam, seminars, symposium.

Utah State University, School of Graduate Studies, College of Agriculture, Department of Nutrition and Food Sciences, Logan, UT 84322. Offers dietetic administration (MDA); food microbiology and safety (MFMS); nutrition and food sciences (MS, PhD); nutrition science (MS, PhD), including molecular biology. Postbaccalaureate distance learning degree programs offered. *Degree requirements:* For master's, thesis; for doctorate, comprehensive exam, thesis/dissertation, teaching experience. *Entrance requirements:* For master's, GRE General Test, minimum GPA of 3.0, course work in chemistry, biochemistry, physics, math, bacteriology, physiology; for doctorate, GRE General Test, minimum GPA of 3.2, course work in chemistry, MS or manuscript in referred journal. Additional exam requirements/recommendations for international students: Required—TOEFL (minimum score 550 paper-based). Electronic applications accepted. *Faculty research:* Mineral balance, meat microbiology and nitrate interactions, milk ultrafiltration, lactic culture, milk coagulation.

Vanderbilt University, Graduate School and School of Medicine, Department of Microbiology and Immunology, Nashville, TN 37240-1001. Offers MS, PhD, MD/PhD. *Faculty:* 12 full-time (2 women). *Students:* 39 full-time (18 women); includes 3 Black or African American, non-Hispanic/Latino; 2 Asian, non-Hispanic/Latino; 2 Hispanic/Latino. Average age 28. In 2010, 1 master's, 4 doctorates awarded. Terminal master's awarded for partial completion of doctoral program. *Degree requirements:* For master's, thesis; for doctorate, thesis/dissertation, final and qualifying exams. *Entrance requirements:* For master's and doctorate, GRE General Test, GRE Subject Test (recommended). Additional exam requirements/recommendations for international students: Required—TOEFL (minimum score 570 paper-based; 230 computer-based; 88 iBT). *Application deadline:* For fall admission, 1/15 for domestic and international students. Application fee: $0. Electronic applications accepted. *Financial support:* Fellowships with full tuition reimbursements, research assistantships with full tuition reimbursements, Federal Work-Study, institutionally sponsored loans, scholarships/grants, traineeships, health care benefits, and tuition waivers (partial) available. Financial award application deadline: 1/15; financial award

Microbiology

Vanderbilt University (continued)
applicants required to submit CSS PROFILE or FAFSA. *Faculty research:* Cellular and molecular microbiology, viruses, genes, cancer, molecular pathogenesis of microbial diseases, immunobiology. *Unit head:* Dr. Jacek Hawiger, Chair, 615-343-8280, E-mail: jacek.hawiger@vanderbilt.edu. *Application contact:* Dr. Christopher R. Aiken, Director of Graduate Studies, 615-322-2087, E-mail: chris.aiken@vanderbilt.edu.

Virginia Commonwealth University, Medical College of Virginia-Professional Programs, School of Medicine, School of Medicine Graduate Programs, Department of Microbiology and Immunology, Richmond, VA 23284-9005. Offers microbiology and immunology (MS, PhD); MD/PhD. *Faculty:* 35 full-time (7 women). *Students:* 54 full-time (39 women), 5 part-time (3 women); includes 13 minority (3 Black or African American, non-Hispanic/Latino; 1 American Indian or Alaska Native, non-Hispanic/Latino; 5 Asian, non-Hispanic/Latino; 3 Hispanic/Latino; 1 Two or more races, non-Hispanic/Latino), 11 international. 103 applicants, 31% accepted, 16 enrolled. In 2010, 3 master's, 8 doctorates awarded. *Degree requirements:* For master's, thesis; for doctorate, thesis/dissertation, comprehensive oral and written exams. *Entrance requirements:* For master's and doctorate, GRE General Test or MCAT. Additional exam requirements/recommendations for international students: Required—TOEFL (minimum score 600 paper-based; 250 computer-based; 100 iBT). *Application deadline:* For fall admission, 12/15 priority date for domestic students. Application fee: $50. Electronic applications accepted. *Expenses:* Tuition, state resident: full-time $4308; part-time $479 per credit hour. Tuition, nonresident: full-time $8942; part-time $994 per credit hour. Required fees: $2000; $85 per credit hour. Tuition and fees vary according to course level, course load, degree level, campus/location and program. *Financial support:* Fellowships, research assistantships, teaching assistantships available. *Faculty research:* Microbial physiology and genetics, molecular biology, crystallography of biological molecules, antibiotics and chemotherapy, membrane transport. *Unit head:* Dr. Dennis E. Ohman, Chair, 804-828-9728, Fax: 804-828-9946, E-mail: deohman@vcu.edu. *Application contact:* Dr. Guy A. Cabral, Chair, Graduate Program Committee, 804-828-2306, E-mail: gacabral@vcu.edu.

Virginia Commonwealth University, Program in Pre-Medical Basic Health Sciences, Richmond, VA 23284-9005. Offers anatomy (CBHS); biochemistry (CBHS); human genetics (CBHS); microbiology (CBHS); pharmacology (CBHS); physiology (CBHS). *Students:* 86 full-time (43 women), 2 part-time (1 woman); includes 42 minority (5 Black or African American, non-Hispanic/Latino; 29 Asian, non-Hispanic/Latino; 5 Hispanic/Latino; 3 Two or more races, non-Hispanic/Latino). 314 applicants, 64% accepted. In 2010, 70 CBHSs awarded. *Entrance requirements:* For degree, GRE, MCAT or DAT, course work in organic chemistry, minimum undergraduate GPA of 2.8. Additional exam requirements/recommendations for international students: Required—TOEFL (minimum score 600 paper-based). *Application deadline:* For fall admission, 6/1 for domestic students. Application fee: $50. Electronic applications accepted. *Expenses:* Tuition, state resident: full-time $4308; part-time $479 per credit hour. Tuition, nonresident: full-time $8942; part-time $994 per credit hour. Required fees: $2000; $85 per credit hour. Tuition and fees vary according to course level, course load, degree level, campus/location and program. *Unit head:* Dr. Louis J. De Felice, Director, 804-828-9501, E-mail: premedcert@vcu.edu. *Application contact:* Zack McDowell, Administrator, 804-828-9501, E-mail: premedcert@vcu.edu.

Virginia Polytechnic Institute and State University, Graduate School, Intercollege, Program in Microbiology, Blacksburg, VA 24061. Offers PhD. *Expenses:* Tuition, state resident: full-time $9399; part-time $488 per credit hour. Tuition, nonresident: full-time $17,854; part-time $957.75 per credit hour. Required fees: $1534. Full-time tuition and fees vary according to program.

Wagner College, Division of Graduate Studies, Department of Biological Sciences, Program in Microbiology, Staten Island, NY 10301-4495. Offers MS. Part-time and evening/weekend programs available. *Faculty:* 6 full-time (2 women), 4 part-time/adjunct (3 women). *Students:* 8 full-time (4 women), 3 part-time (0 women); includes 3 minority (2 Asian, non-Hispanic/Latino; 1 Hispanic/Latino). Average age 24. 10 applicants, 90% accepted, 7 enrolled. In 2010, 7 master's awarded. *Degree requirements:* For master's, comprehensive exam or thesis. *Entrance requirements:* For master's, minimum GPA of 2.6, proficiency in statistics, undergraduate major in biological science or chemistry, successful completion of an undergraduate microbiology course and 16 credits of chemistry including organic chemistry with lab. Additional exam requirements/recommendations for international students: Required—TOEFL (minimum score 550 paper-based; 217 computer-based; 79 iBT). *Application deadline:* For fall admission, 5/1 priority date for domestic students, 3/1 priority date for international students; for spring admission, 12/1 for domestic students, 10/1 for international students. Applications are processed on a rolling basis. Application fee: $50 ($85 for international students). *Expenses:* Tuition: Full-time $15,570; part-time $865 per credit. *Financial support:* Career-related internships or fieldwork, unspecified assistantships, and alumni fellowship grant available. Financial award applicants required to submit FAFSA. *Unit head:* Dr. Roy Mosher, Director, 718-420-4072, E-mail: rmosher@wagner.edu. *Application contact:* Patricia Clancy, Administrative Assistant, 718-420-4464, Fax: 718-390-3105, E-mail: patricia.clancy@wagner.edu.

Wake Forest University, School of Medicine and Graduate School of Arts and Sciences, Graduate Programs in Medicine, Department of Microbiology and Immunology, Winston-Salem, NC 27109. Offers PhD, MD/PhD. *Degree requirements:* For doctorate, thesis/dissertation. *Entrance requirements:* For doctorate, GRE General Test. Additional exam requirements/recommendations for international students: Required—TOEFL. Electronic applications accepted. *Faculty research:* Molecular immunology, bacterial pathogenesis and molecular genetics, viral pathogenesis, regulation of mRNA metabolism, leukocyte biology.

Washington State University, Graduate School, College of Sciences, School of Molecular Biosciences, Program in Microbiology, Pullman, WA 99164. Offers MS, PhD. *Faculty:* 23 full-time (5 women), 21 part-time/adjunct (4 women). *Students:* 12 full-time (9 women); includes 2 Hispanic/Latino, 4 international. Average age 25. 231 applicants, 18% accepted, 12 enrolled. In 2010, 1 master's, 1 doctorate awarded. Terminal master's awarded for partial completion of doctoral program. *Degree requirements:* For master's, thesis, oral exam; for doctorate, comprehensive exam, thesis/dissertation, oral exam. *Entrance requirements:* For master's and doctorate, GRE General Test, minimum GPA of 3.0. Additional exam requirements/recommendations for international students: Required—TOEFL (minimum score 550 paper-based; 213 computer-based). *Application deadline:* For fall admission, 12/15 for domestic and international students. Application fee: $50. Electronic applications accepted. *Expenses:* Tuition, state resident: full-time $8552; part-time $443 per credit. Tuition, nonresident: full-time $21,650; part-time $1083 per credit. Required fees: $846. *Financial support:* In 2010–11, fellowships with full tuition reimbursements (averaging $18,852 per year), 2 research assistantships with full and partial tuition reimbursements (averaging $18,852 per year), 10 teaching assistantships with full and partial tuition reimbursements (averaging $18,852 per year) were awarded; Federal Work-Study, institutionally sponsored loans, health care benefits, and unspecified assistantships also available. Financial award application deadline: 4/1; financial award applicants required to submit FAFSA. *Faculty research:* Viral-host interaction, bacterial-host interaction, microbial medicine, microbial pathogenesis, cancer biology. Total annual research expenditures: $5.8 million. *Unit head:* Dr. John H. Nilson, Director, 509-335-8724, Fax: 509-335-9688, E-mail: jhn@wsu.edu. *Application contact:* Kelly G. McGovern, Academic Coordinator, 509-335-4566, Fax: 509-335-1907, E-mail: smbgrad@wsu.edu.

Washington University in St. Louis, Graduate School of Arts and Sciences, Division of Biology and Biomedical Sciences, Program in Molecular Microbiology and Microbial Pathogenesis, St. Louis, MO 63130-4899. Offers PhD. *Degree requirements:* For doctorate, thesis/dissertation. *Entrance requirements:* For doctorate, GRE General Test, GRE Subject Test. Electronic applications accepted.

Wayne State University, School of Medicine, Department of Immunology and Microbiology, Detroit, MI 48202. Offers MS, PhD, MD/PhD. *Faculty:* 4 full-time (1 woman). *Students:* 15 full-time (6 women), 2 part-time (both women); includes 1 minority (Hispanic/Latino), 4 international. Average age 26. 17 applicants, 24% accepted, 3 enrolled. In 2010, 1 doctorate awarded. Terminal master's awarded for partial completion of doctoral program. *Degree requirements:* For master's, thesis; for doctorate, thesis/dissertation. *Entrance requirements:* For master's, GRE, minimum GPA of 2.5; for doctorate, GRE, minimum GPA of 3.0. Additional exam requirements/recommendations for international students: Required—TOEFL (minimum score 550 paper-based; 213 computer-based); Recommended—TWE (minimum score 6). *Application deadline:* For fall admission, 7/15 for domestic students, 6/1 for international students; for winter admission, 10/1 for international students; for spring admission, 2/1 for international students. Applications are processed on a rolling basis. Application fee: $30 ($50 for international students). Electronic applications accepted. *Expenses:* Tuition, state resident: full-time $7662; part-time $478.85 per credit hour. Tuition, nonresident: full-time $16,920; part-time $1057.55 per credit hour. Required fees: $571; $35.70 per credit hour. $188.05 per semester. Tuition and fees vary according to course load and program. *Financial support:* In 2010–11, 1 fellowship with tuition reimbursement (averaging $20,000 per year), 15 research assistantships with tuition reimbursements (averaging $21,454 per year) were awarded; teaching assistantships, career-related internships or fieldwork and Federal Work-Study also available. *Faculty research:* Immune regulation, bacterial pathophysiology, molecular biology/viruses/bacteria, cellular and molecular immunology, microbial pathogenesis. *Unit head:* Dr. Paul Montgomery, Chair, 313-577-1591, Fax: 313-577-1155, E-mail: aa2411@wayne.edu. *Application contact:* Harley Tse, Associate Professor, 313-577-1564, Fax: 313-577-1155, E-mail: ad6056@wayne.edu.

West Virginia University, School of Medicine, Graduate Programs at the Health Sciences Center, Interdisciplinary Graduate Programs in Biomedical Sciences, Program in Immunology and Microbial Pathogenesis, Morgantown, WV 26506. Offers MS, PhD, MD/PhD. *Degree requirements:* For doctorate, comprehensive exam, thesis/dissertation. *Entrance requirements:* For doctorate, GRE General Test, minimum GPA of 3.0. Additional exam requirements/recommendations for international students: Required—TOEFL. Electronic applications accepted. *Faculty research:* Regulation of signal transduction in immune responses, immune responses in bacterial and viral diseases, peptide and DNA vaccines for contraception, inflammatory bowel disease, physiology of pathogenic microbes.

Wright State University, School of Graduate Studies, College of Science and Mathematics, Program in Microbiology and Immunology, Dayton, OH 45435. Offers MS. Part-time programs available. *Degree requirements:* For master's, thesis. *Entrance requirements:* Additional exam requirements/recommendations for international students: Required—TOEFL. *Faculty research:* Reproductive immunology, viral pathogenesis, virus-host cell interactions.

Yale University, School of Medicine and Graduate School of Arts and Sciences, Combined Program in Biological and Biomedical Sciences (BBS), Microbiology Track, New Haven, CT 06520. Offers PhD, MD/PhD. *Degree requirements:* For doctorate, thesis/dissertation. *Entrance requirements:* For doctorate, GRE General Test, GRE Subject Test. Additional exam requirements/recommendations for international students: Required—TOEFL. Electronic applications accepted.

Youngstown State University, Graduate School, College of Science, Technology, Engineering and Mathematics, Department of Biological Sciences, Youngstown, OH 44555-0001. Offers environmental biology (MS); molecular biology, microbiology, and genetic (MS); physiology and anatomy (MS). Part-time programs available. *Degree requirements:* For master's, comprehensive exam, thesis, oral review. *Entrance requirements:* For master's, GRE General Test, minimum GPA of 2.7. Additional exam requirements/recommendations for international students: Required—TOEFL. *Faculty research:* Cell biology, neurophysiology, molecular biology, neurobiology, gene regulation.

Virology

Baylor College of Medicine, Graduate School of Biomedical Sciences, Department of Molecular Virology and Microbiology, Houston, TX 77030-3498. Offers PhD, MD/PhD. *Faculty:* 43 full-time (13 women). *Students:* 37 full-time (20 women); includes 1 Black or African American, non-Hispanic/Latino; 4 Asian, non-Hispanic/Latino; 5 Hispanic/Latino, 9 international. Average age 28. 74 applicants, 20% accepted, 4 enrolled. In 2010, 3 doctorates awarded. *Degree requirements:* For doctorate, thesis/dissertation, public defense. *Entrance requirements:* For doctorate, GRE General Test, GRE Subject Test (strongly recommended), minimum GPA of 3.0. Additional exam requirements/recommendations for international students: Required—TOEFL. *Application deadline:* For fall admission, 1/1 priority date for domestic students. Applications are processed on a rolling basis. Application fee: $0. Electronic applications accepted. *Expenses:* Tuition: Full-time $11,000. Required fees: $4900. *Financial support:* In 2010–11, 13 fellowships with full tuition reimbursements (averaging $26,000 per year), 24 research assistantships with full tuition reimbursements (averaging $26,000 per year) were awarded; career-related internships or fieldwork, Federal Work-Study, institutionally sponsored loans, health care benefits, and tuition waivers (full) also available. Financial award applicants required to submit FAFSA. *Faculty research:* Microbiology, viral molecular biology, bacterial molecular biology, microbial pathogenesis, microbial genomics. *Unit head:* Dr. Frank Ramig, Director, 713-798-4830, Fax: 713-798-5075, E-mail: rramig@bcm.edu. *Application contact:* Rosa Banegas, Graduate Program Administrator, 713-798-4472, Fax: 713-798-5075, E-mail: rbanegas@bcm.edu.

Baylor College of Medicine, Graduate School of Biomedical Sciences, Interdepartmental Program in Cell and Molecular Biology, Houston, TX 77030-3498. Offers biochemistry (PhD); cell and molecular biology (PhD); genetics (PhD); human genetics (PhD); immunology (PhD); microbiology (PhD); virology (PhD); MD/PhD. *Faculty:* 100 full-time (31 women). *Students:* 67 full-time (41 women); includes 4 Black or African American, non-Hispanic/Latino; 2 American Indian or Alaska Native, non-Hispanic/Latino; 9 Asian, non-Hispanic/Latino; 9 Hispanic/Latino, 9 international. Average age 27. 120 applicants, 27% accepted, 15 enrolled. In 2010, 7 doctorates awarded. *Degree requirements:* For doctorate, thesis/dissertation, public defense. *Entrance requirements:* For doctorate, GRE General Test, GRE Subject Test (strongly recommended), minimum GPA of 3.0. Additional exam requirements/recommendations for international students: Required—TOEFL. *Application deadline:* For fall admission, 1/1 priority date for domestic students. Applications are processed on a rolling basis. Application fee: $0. Electronic applications accepted. *Expenses:* Tuition: Full-time $11,000. Required fees: $4900. *Financial support:* In 2010–11, 67 students received support, including 24 fellowships with full tuition reimbursements available (averaging $26,000 per year), 43 research assistantships with full tuition reimbursements available (averaging $26,000 per year); teaching assistantships, Federal Work-Study, institutionally sponsored loans, health care benefits, and tuition waivers (full) also available. Financial award applicants required to submit FAFSA. *Faculty research:* Molecular and cellular biology; cancer, aging and stem cells; genomics and proteomics; microbiome, molecular microbiology; infectious disease, immunology and translational research. *Unit head:* Dr. Susan Marriott, Director, 713-798-6557. *Application contact:* Lourdes Fernandez, Graduate Program Administrator, 713-798-6557, Fax: 713-798-6325, E-mail: cmbprog@bcm.edu.

See Close-Up on page 223.

Case Western Reserve University, School of Medicine and School of Graduate Studies, Graduate Programs in Medicine, Department of Molecular Biology and Microbiology, Program in Molecular Virology, Cleveland, OH 44106. Offers PhD. *Entrance requirements:* Additional exam requirements/recommendations for international students: Required—TOEFL (minimum score 550 paper-based; 213 computer-based).

Mayo Graduate School, Graduate Programs in Biomedical Sciences, Program in Virology and Gene Therapy, Rochester, MN 55905. Offers PhD.

McMaster University, Faculty of Health Sciences and School of Graduate Studies, Program in Medical Sciences, Hamilton, ON L8S 4M2, Canada. Offers blood and vascular (M Sc, PhD); genetics and cancer (M Sc, PhD); immunity and infection (M Sc, PhD); metabolism and nutrition (M Sc, PhD); neurosciences and behavioral sciences (M Sc, PhD); physiology/pharmacology (M Sc, PhD); MD/PhD. *Degree requirements:* For master's, thesis; for doctorate, comprehensive exam, thesis/dissertation. *Entrance requirements:* For master's, honors B Sc, B+ average in related field; for doctorate, M Sc, minimum B+ average. Additional exam requirements/recommendations for international students: Required—TOEFL (minimum score 580 paper-based; 237 computer-based; 92 iBT).

The Ohio State University, College of Medicine, School of Biomedical Science, Integrated Biomedical Science Graduate Program, Columbus, OH 43210. Offers immunology (PhD); medical genetics (PhD); molecular virology (PhD); pharmacology (PhD). *Degree requirements:* For doctorate, thesis/dissertation. *Entrance requirements:* For doctorate, GRE, GRE Subject Test in biochemistry, cell and molecular biology (recommended for some). Additional exam requirements/recommendations for international students: Required—TOEFL (minimum score 600 paper-based; 250 computer-based). Electronic applications accepted. *Expenses:* Tuition, state resident: full-time $10,605. Tuition, nonresident: full-time $26,535. Tuition and fees vary according to course load and program.

Penn State Hershey Medical Center, College of Medicine, Graduate School Programs in the Biomedical Sciences, Graduate Program in Microbiology and Immunology, Hershey, PA 17033. Offers genetics (PhD); immunology (MS, PhD); microbiology (MS); microbiology/virology (PhD); molecular biology (PhD); MD/PhD. *Students:* 12 applicants, 75% accepted, 3 enrolled. In 2010, 1 doctorate awarded. Terminal master's awarded for partial completion of doctoral program. *Degree requirements:* For master's, thesis or alternative; for doctorate, comprehensive exam, thesis/dissertation, oral exam. *Entrance requirements:* For doctorate, GRE General Test, minimum GPA of 3.0. Additional exam requirements/recommendations for international students: Required—TOEFL. *Application deadline:* For fall admission, 1/31 priority date for domestic students, 2/1 priority date for international students. Applications are processed on a rolling basis. Application fee: $45. Electronic applications accepted. *Financial support:* In 2010–11, research assistantships with full tuition reimbursements (averaging $22,260 per year); fellowships with full tuition reimbursements, scholarships/grants, health care benefits, and unspecified assistantships also available. Financial award applicants required to submit FAFSA. *Faculty research:* Virus replication and assembly, oncogenesis, interactions of viruses with host cells and animal model systems. *Unit head:* Dr. Richard J. Courtney, Chair, 717-531-7659, Fax: 717-531-6522, E-mail: micro-grad-hmc@psu.edu. *Application contact:* Billie Burns, Secretary, 717-531-7659, Fax: 717-531-6522, E-mail: micro-grad-hmc@psu.edu.

Purdue University, School of Veterinary Medicine and Graduate School, Graduate Programs in Veterinary Medicine, Department of Comparative Pathobiology, West Lafayette, IN 47907-2027. Offers comparative epidemiology and public health (MS); comparative epidemiology and public heath (PhD); comparative microbiology and immunology (MS, PhD); comparative pathobiology (MS, PhD); interdisciplinary studies (PhD), including microbial pathogenesis, molecular signaling and cancer biology, molecular virology; lab animal medicine (MS); veterinary anatomic pathology (MS); veterinary clinical pathology (MS). Terminal master's awarded for partial completion of doctoral program. *Degree requirements:* For master's, thesis (for some programs); for doctorate, thesis/dissertation. *Entrance requirements:* For master's and doctorate, GRE General Test. Additional exam requirements/recommendations for international students: Required—TOEFL (minimum score 575 paper-based; 232 computer-based), IELTS (minimum score 6.5), TWE (minimum score 4). Electronic applications accepted.

Rush University, Graduate College, Division of Immunology and Microbiology, Program in Immunology/Microbiology, Chicago, IL 60612-3832. Offers immunology (MS, PhD); virology (MS, PhD); MD/PhD. Part-time programs available. Terminal master's awarded for partial completion of doctoral program. *Degree requirements:* For master's, thesis; for doctorate, thesis/dissertation, comprehensive preliminary exam. *Entrance requirements:* For master's, GRE General Test; for doctorate, GRE General Test, interview, minimum GPA of 3.0. Additional exam requirements/recommendations for international students: Required—TOEFL. Electronic applications accepted. *Faculty research:* Human genetics, autoimmunity, tumor biology, complement, HIV immunopathology genesis.

Rutgers, The State University of New Jersey, New Brunswick, Graduate School-New Brunswick, Programs in the Molecular Biosciences, Program in Microbiology and Molecular Genetics, Piscataway, NJ 08854-8097. Offers applied microbiology (MS, PhD); clinical microbiology (MS, PhD); computational molecular biology (PhD); immunology (MS, PhD); microbial biochemistry (MS, PhD); molecular genetics (MS, PhD); virology (MS, PhD). MS, PhD offered jointly with University of Medicine and Dentistry of New Jersey. Part-time programs available. Terminal master's awarded for partial completion of doctoral program. *Degree requirements:* For master's, comprehensive exam, thesis or alternative; for doctorate, comprehensive exam, thesis/dissertation, written qualifying exam. *Entrance requirements:* For master's, GRE General Test, minimum GPA of 3.0; for doctorate, GRE General Test, GRE Subject Test (recommended), minimum GPA of 3.0. Additional exam requirements/recommendations for international students: Required—TOEFL. Electronic applications accepted. *Expenses:* Tuition, state resident: full-time $7200; part-time $600 per credit. Tuition, nonresident: full-time $11,124; part-time $927 per credit. *Faculty research:* Molecular genetics and microbial physiology; virology and pathogenic microbiology; applied, environmental and industrial microbiology; computers in molecular biology.

Texas A&M Health Science Center, Graduate School of Biomedical Sciences, Department of Microbial and Molecular Pathogenesis, College Station, TX 77840. Offers immunology (PhD); microbiology (PhD); molecular biology (PhD); virology (PhD). *Degree requirements:* For doctorate, thesis/dissertation. *Entrance requirements:* For doctorate, GRE General Test, minimum GPA of 3.0. *Faculty research:* Molecular pathogenesis, microbial therapeutics.

Université de Montréal, Faculty of Veterinary Medicine, Program in Virology and Immunology, Montréal, QC H3C 3J7, Canada. Offers PhD. Program offered jointly with Université du Québec, Institut Armand-Frappier. *Degree requirements:* For doctorate, thesis/dissertation, general exam. *Entrance requirements:* For doctorate, proficiency in French, knowledge of English. Electronic applications accepted.

Université du Québec, Institut National de la Recherche Scientifique, Graduate Programs, Research Center—INRS—Institut Armand-Frappier—Human Health, Québec, QC G1K 9A9, Canada. Offers applied microbiology (M Sc); biology (PhD); experimental health sciences (M Sc); virology and immunology (M Sc, PhD). Programs given in French. Part-time programs available. *Faculty:* 36. *Students:* 157 full-time (92 women), 6 part-time (4 women), 54 international. Average age 30. In 2010, 20 master's, 13 doctorates awarded. *Degree requirements:* For master's, thesis optional; for doctorate, thesis/dissertation. *Entrance requirements:* For master's and doctorate, appropriate bachelor's degree, proficiency in French. *Application deadline:* For fall admission, 3/30 for domestic and international students; for winter admission, 11/1 for domestic and international students; for spring admission, 3/1 for domestic and international students. Application fee: $30 Canadian dollars. *Financial support:* Fellowships, research assistantships, teaching assistantships available. *Faculty research:* Immunity, infection and cancer; toxicology and environmental biotechnology; molecular pharmacochemistry. *Unit head:* Charles Dozois, Director, 450-687-5010, Fax: 450-686-5501, E-mail: charles.dozois@iaf.inrs.ca. *Application contact:* Yvonne Boisvert, Registrar, 418-654-3861, Fax: 418-654-3858, E-mail: registrariat@adm.inrs.ca.

University of California, San Diego, Office of Graduate Studies, Division of Biological Sciences, Program in Immunology, Virology, and Cancer Biology, La Jolla, CA 92093. Offers PhD. Offered in association with the Salk Institute. *Degree requirements:* For doctorate, thesis/dissertation, qualifying exam. Electronic applications accepted.

The University of Iowa, Roy J. and Lucille A. Carver College of Medicine and Graduate College, Graduate Programs in Medicine, Department of Microbiology, Iowa City, IA 52242-1316. Offers general microbiology and microbial physiology (MS, PhD); immunology (MS, PhD); microbial genetics (MS, PhD); pathogenic bacteriology (MS, PhD); virology (MS, PhD). *Faculty:* 23 full-time (4 women), 11 part-time/adjunct (5 women). *Students:* 35 full-time (20 women); includes 2 American Indian or Alaska Native, non-Hispanic/Latino; 1 Hispanic/Latino, 5 international. Average age 25. 71 applicants, 20% accepted, 8 enrolled. In 2010, 1 master's, 5 doctorates awarded. *Degree requirements:* For master's, thesis; for doctorate, comprehensive exam, thesis/dissertation. *Entrance requirements:* For master's and doctorate, GRE General Test. Additional exam requirements/recommendations for international students: Required—TOEFL (minimum score 600 paper-based; 250 computer-based). *Application deadline:* For fall admission, 2/1 for domestic and international students. Application fee: $60 ($85 for international students). Electronic applications accepted. *Financial support:* In 2010–11, 4 fellowships with full tuition reimbursements (averaging $25,000 per year), 31 research assistantships with full tuition reimbursements (averaging $25,000 per year) were awarded; institutionally sponsored loans, scholarships/grants, traineeships, and health care benefits also available. *Faculty research:* Gene regulation, processing and transport of HIV, retroviral pathogenesis, biodegradation, biofilm. Total annual research expenditures: $12.6 million. *Unit head:* Dr. Michael A. Apicella, Head, 319-335-7810, E-mail: grad-micro-info@uiowa.edu. *Application contact:* Dr. Michael A. Apicella, Head, 319-335-7810, E-mail: grad-micro-info@uiowa.edu.

University of Massachusetts Worcester, Graduate School of Biomedical Sciences, Worcester, MA 01655-0115. Offers biochemistry and molecular pharmacology (PhD); bioinformatics and computational biology (PhD); cancer biology (PhD); cell biology (PhD); clinical and population health research (PhD); clinical investigation (MS); immunology and virology (PhD); interdisciplinary graduate program (PhD); molecular genetics and microbiology (PhD); neuroscience (PhD); DVM/PhD; MD/PhD. *Faculty:* 1,059 full-time (357 women), 145 part-time/adjunct (100 women). *Students:* 438 full-time (239 women), 1 (woman) part-time; includes 44 minority (9 Black or African American, non-Hispanic/Latino; 31 Asian, non-Hispanic/Latino; 4 Hispanic/Latino), 148 international. Average age 29. 687 applicants, 28% accepted, 116 enrolled. In 2010, 6 master's, 45 doctorates awarded. Terminal master's awarded for partial completion of doctoral program. *Degree requirements:* For master's, thesis; for doctorate, thesis/dissertation. *Entrance requirements:* For master's, bachelor's degree; for doctorate, GRE General Test, MS, MA, or MPH (for some programs). Additional exam requirements/recommendations for international students: Required—TOEFL (minimum score 600 paper-based; 250 computer-based). *Application deadline:* For fall admission, 12/15 for domestic and international students; for winter admission, 1/15 for domestic students; for spring admission, 5/15 for domestic students. Application fee: $35. Electronic applications accepted. *Expenses:* Contact institution. *Financial support:* In 2010–11, 439 students received support, including 439 research assistantships with full tuition reimbursements available (averaging $28,350 per year); scholarships/grants, health care benefits, tuition waivers (full), and unspecified assistantships also available. Financial award application deadline: 4/20. *Faculty research:* RNA interference, gene therapy, cell biology, bioinformatics, clinical research. Total annual research expenditures: $232 million. *Unit head:* Dr. Anthony Carruthers, Dean, 508-856-4135, E-mail: anthony.carruthers@umassmed.edu. *Application contact:* Dr. Kendall Knight, Associate Dean and Interim Director of Admissions and Recruitment, 508-856-5628, Fax: 508-856-3659, E-mail: kendall.knight@umassmed.edu.

University of Minnesota, Twin Cities Campus, Graduate School, PhD Program in Microbiology, Immunology and Cancer Biology, Minneapolis, MN 55455-0213. Offers PhD. *Degree requirements:* For doctorate, thesis/dissertation. *Entrance requirements:* For doctorate, GRE General Test. Additional exam requirements/recommendations for international students: Required—TOEFL (minimum score 600 paper-based; 250 computer-based). Electronic applications accepted. *Faculty research:* Virology, microbiology, cancer biology, immunology.

University of Pennsylvania, Perelman School of Medicine, Biomedical Graduate Studies, Graduate Group in Cell and Molecular Biology, Philadelphia, PA 19104. Offers cancer biology (PhD); cell biology and physiology (PhD); developmental stem cell regenerative biology (PhD); gene therapy and vaccines (PhD); genetics and gene regulation (PhD); microbiology, virology, and parasitology (PhD); MD/PhD; VMD/PhD. *Faculty:* 299. *Students:* 315 full-time (166 women); includes 13 Black or African American, non-Hispanic/Latino; 1 American Indian or Alaska Native, non-Hispanic/Latino; 44 Asian, non-Hispanic/Latino; 18 Hispanic/Latino, 37 international. 579 applicants, 21% accepted, 49 enrolled. In 2010, 53 doctorates awarded. *Degree requirements:* For doctorate, thesis/dissertation. *Entrance requirements:* For doctorate, GRE General Test. Additional exam requirements/recommendations for international students: Required—TOEFL. *Application deadline:* For fall admission, 12/8 priority date for domestic and international students. Applications are processed on a rolling basis. Application fee: $70. Electronic applications accepted. *Expenses:* Tuition: Full-time $25,660; part-time $4758 per course. Required fees: $2152; $270 per course. Tuition and fees vary according to course load, degree level and program. *Financial support:* In 2010–11, 315 students received support; fellowships, research assistantships, scholarships/grants, traineeships, and unspecified assistantships available. Financial award application deadline: 12/8. *Unit head:* Dr. Daniel Kessler, Graduate Group Chair, 215-898-2180, E-mail: raperj@mail.med.upenn.edu. *Application contact:* Meagan Schofer, Coordinator, 215-898-9536, Fax: 215-573-2104, E-mail: camb@mailmed.upenn.edu.

University of Pittsburgh, School of Medicine, Graduate Programs in Medicine, Program in Molecular Virology and Microbiology, Pittsburgh, PA 15260. Offers MS, PhD. *Faculty:* 47 full-time (10 women). *Students:* 21 full-time (11 women); includes 2 Asian, non-Hispanic/Latino; 1 Hispanic/Latino, 3 international. Average age 27. 486 applicants, 14% accepted. In 2010, 5 doctorates awarded. *Degree requirements:* For doctorate, comprehensive exam, thesis/dissertation. *Entrance requirements:* For doctorate, GRE General Test, GRE Subject Test, minimum QPA of 3.0. Additional exam requirements/recommendations for international students: Required—TOEFL (minimum score 600 paper-based; 100 iBT), IELTS (minimum score 7). *Application deadline:* For fall admission, 12/15 priority date for domestic and international students. Application fee: $50. Electronic applications accepted. *Expenses:* Tuition, state resident: full-time $17,304; part-time $701 per credit. Tuition, nonresident: full-time $29,554; part-time $1210 per credit. Required fees: $740; $214 per term. Tuition and fees vary according to program. *Financial support:* In 2010–11, 21 research assistantships with full tuition reimbursements (averaging $25,500 per year) were awarded; institutionally sponsored loans, scholarships/grants, traineeships, health care benefits, and unspecified assistantships also available. *Faculty research:* Host-pathogen interactions, persistent microbial infections, microbial genetics and gene expression, microbial pathogenesis, anti-bacterial therapeutics. *Unit head:* Dr. Neal A. DeLuca, Graduate Program Director, 412-648-9947, Fax: 412-624-0298, E-mail: ndeluca@pitt.edu. *Application contact:* Graduate Studies Administrator, 412-648-8957, Fax: 412-648-1077, E-mail: gradstudies@medschool.pitt.edu.

Virology

University of Prince Edward Island, Atlantic Veterinary College, Graduate Program in Veterinary Medicine, Charlottetown, PE C1A 4P3, Canada. Offers anatomy (M Sc, PhD); bacteriology (M Sc, PhD); clinical pharmacology (M Sc, PhD); clinical sciences (M Sc, PhD); epidemiology (M Sc, PhD), including reproduction; fish health (M Sc, PhD); food animal nutrition (M Sc, PhD); immunology (M Sc, PhD); microanatomy (M Sc, PhD); parasitology (M Sc, PhD); pathology (M Sc, PhD); pharmacology (M Sc, PhD); physiology (M Sc, PhD); toxicology (M Sc, PhD); veterinary science (M Vet Sc); virology (M Sc, PhD). Part-time programs available. *Degree requirements:* For master's, thesis; for doctorate, thesis/dissertation. *Entrance requirements:* For master's, DVM, B Sc honors degree, or equivalent; for doctorate, M Sc. Additional exam requirements/recommendations for international students: Required—TOEFL (minimum score 550 paper-based; 213 computer-based; 80 iBT). *Expenses:* Contact institution. *Faculty research:* Animal health management, infectious diseases, fin fish and shellfish health, basic biomedical sciences, ecosystem health.

The University of Texas Health Science Center at Houston, Graduate School of Biomedical Sciences, Program in Virology and Gene Therapy, Houston, TX 77225-0036. Offers MS, PhD, MD/PhD. Terminal master's awarded for partial completion of doctoral program. *Degree requirements:* For master's, thesis; for doctorate, thesis/dissertation. *Entrance requirements:* For master's and doctorate, GRE General Test. Additional exam requirements/recommendations for international students: Required—TOEFL. Electronic applications accepted. *Faculty research:* Viruses, infectious diseases, vaccines, gene therapy, cancer.

The University of Texas Medical Branch, Graduate School of Biomedical Sciences, Center for Biodefense and Emerging Infectious Diseases, Galveston, TX 77555. Offers biodefense training (PhD). *Entrance requirements:* For doctorate, GRE, minimum overall GPA of 3.0.

The University of Texas Medical Branch, Graduate School of Biomedical Sciences, Program in Emerging and Tropical Infectious Diseases, Galveston, TX 77555. Offers PhD, MD/PhD. *Degree requirements:* For doctorate, thesis/dissertation. *Entrance requirements:* For doctorate, GRE General Test. *Faculty research:* Emerging diseases, tropical diseases, parasitology, vitology and bacteriology.

Yale University, School of Medicine and Graduate School of Arts and Sciences, Combined Program in Biological and Biomedical Sciences (BBS), Microbiology Track, New Haven, CT 06520. Offers PhD, MD/PhD. *Degree requirements:* For doctorate, thesis/dissertation. *Entrance requirements:* For doctorate, GRE General Test, GRE Subject Test. Additional exam requirements/recommendations for international students: Required—TOEFL. Electronic applications accepted.

UNIFORMED SERVICES UNIVERSITY OF THE HEALTH SCIENCES

F. Edward Hébert School of Medicine
Graduate Program in Emerging Infectious Diseases

Program of Study

One of the missions of the Uniformed Services University (USU) is to provide both civilians and military students with high-quality training leading to advanced degrees in the biomedical sciences. The Graduate Program in Emerging Infectious Diseases (EID) is designed for applicants who wish to pursue an interdisciplinary program of study leading to the Ph.D. degree and was created for students who are primarily interested in the pathogenesis, host response, and epidemiology of infectious diseases. No M.S. degree program is currently offered. A broadly based core program of formal training is combined with an intensive laboratory research experience in the different disciplines encompassed by the field of infectious diseases. Courses are taught by an interdisciplinary EID faculty who hold primary appointments in the Departments of Microbiology and Immunology, Pathology, Preventive Medicine and Biometrics, Pediatrics, and Medicine. Research training emphasizes modern methods in molecular biology and cell biology, as well as interdisciplinary approaches.

During the first two years, all students are required to complete a series of broadly based core courses and laboratory rotations. Students also select one of three academic tracks in which to focus the remainder of their course work. The three tracks are microbiology and immunology, pathology, and preventive medicine/parasitology. Advanced course work is required in each academic track. In addition, each student selects a faculty member with whom he or she would like to carry out a thesis research project. By the end of the second year, the student must complete all requirements for advancement to candidacy for the Ph.D. degree, which includes satisfactory completion of formal course work and passage of the qualifying examination. After advancement to candidacy, the student must complete an original research project and prepare and defend a written dissertation under the supervision of his or her faculty adviser and an advisory committee.

Research Facilities

Each academic department of the University is provided with laboratories for the support of a variety of research projects. Laboratories are available in most areas of study that encompass the interdisciplinary field of emerging infectious diseases, including both basic and medical aspects of bacteriology, bacterial genetics, virology, cellular and molecular immunology, parasitology, pathogenic mechanisms of disease, pathology of infectious disease, and epidemiology of infectious diseases. Resources available to students within the University include real-time PCR, microarray spotters and readers, EPICS, FACSAria and LSRII cell sorters and analyzers, Luminex 100 analyzer, automated oligonucleotide and peptide synthesizers and sequencing, MALDI-TOF Mass Spectrometer, high-resolution electron microscopes, confocal microscopes, a certified central animal facility, and state-of-the-art computer facilities. In addition, a BSL-3 biohazard containment laboratory suite is available. The library/learning resources center houses more than 521,000 bound volumes, subscribes to nearly 3,000 journals (print and online), and maintains 100 IBM and Macintosh personal computers for use by students, faculty members, and staff members. Biostatisticians serve as a resource for students and faculty members.

Financial Aid

Stipends are available for civilian applicants. Awards of stipends are competitive, are for one-year periods, and may be renewed. The 2011–12 stipend level begins at $27,000 per year. Special fellowships are also available.

Cost of Study

Graduate students in the Emerging Infectious Diseases Program are not required to pay tuition or fees. Civilian students do not incur obligations to the United States government for service after completion of their graduate training programs.

Living and Housing Costs

There is a reasonable supply of affordable rental housing in the area. The University does not have housing for graduate students. Living costs in the greater Washington, D.C., area are comparable to those of other East Coast metropolitan areas.

Student Group

The first full-time graduate students were admitted to the EID program in 2000. There are currently 41 full-time students enrolled in the EID graduate program. The University also has Ph.D. programs in departmentally based basic biomedical sciences, as well as interdisciplinary graduate programs in molecular and cell biology and in neurosciences.

Location

The greater Washington metropolitan area has a population of about 3 million that includes the District of Columbia and the surrounding areas of Maryland and Virginia. The region is a center of education and research and is home to five major universities, four medical schools, and numerous other internationally recognized private and government research centers. In addition, multiple cultural advantages exist in the area and include theaters, a major symphony orchestra, major-league sports, and world-famous museums. The Metro subway system has a station adjacent to the campus and provides a convenient connection from the University to cultural attractions and activities in downtown Washington. The international community in Washington is the source of many diverse cuisines and international cultural events. For a wide variety of outdoor activities, the Blue Ridge Mountains, Chesapeake Bay, and Atlantic coast beaches are all within a 1- to 3-hour drive. Many national and local parks serve the area for weekend hikes, bicycling, and picnics.

The University

USU is located just outside Washington, D.C., in Bethesda, Maryland. The campus is situated in an attractive, park-like setting on the grounds of the National Naval Medical Center (NNMC) and across the street from the National Institutes of Health (NIH). Wooded areas with jogging and biking trails surround the University. NIH, NNMC, and other research institutes in the area provide additional resources to enhance the education experience of graduate students at USU. Students can visit the USUHS Web site at http://www.usuhs.mil/eid.

Applying

The Admissions Committee, in consultation with other faculty members, evaluates applications to the program. Each applicant must submit an application form, complete academic transcripts of postsecondary education, and results of the Graduate Record Examinations. No GRE Subject Test is required. In addition, three letters of recommendation from individuals familiar with the academic achievements and/or research experience of the applicant are required, as well as a personal statement that expresses the applicant's career objectives. USU subscribes fully to the policy of equal educational opportunity and selects students on a competitive basis without regard to race, color, gender, creed, or national origin. Application forms may be obtained from the University Web site (available at http://ieb.usuhs.mil/gapp/). Completed applications should be received on or before January 1.

Both civilians and military personnel are eligible to apply. Prior to acceptance, each applicant must complete a baccalaureate degree that includes required courses in mathematics, biology, physics, and chemistry (inorganic, organic, and biochemistry). Advanced-level courses in microbiology, molecular biology, genetics, and cell biology are very strongly recommended. All students are expected to have a reasonable level of computer literacy. Active-duty military applicants must obtain the approval and sponsorship of their parent military service, in addition to acceptance into the EID graduate program.

Correspondence and Information

Dr. Eleanor S. Metcalf
Associate Dean for Graduate Education
Uniformed Services University
4301 Jones Bridge Road
Bethesda, Maryland 20814-4755
Phone: 800-772-1747 (toll-free)
Web site: http://www.usuhs.mil

Dr. Christopher C. Broder, Director
Graduate Program in Emerging Infectious Diseases
Uniformed Services University
4301 Jones Bridge Road
Bethesda, Maryland 20814-4755
Phone: 301-295-5749
Fax: 301-295-9861
E-mail: cbroder@usuhs.mil
Web site: http://www.usuhs.mil/eid

Uniformed Services University of the Health Sciences

THE FACULTY

The interdisciplinary graduate programs at USU are superimposed on the departmental structure. Therefore, all faculty members in the interdisciplinary Graduate Program in Emerging Infectious Diseases (EID) have primary appointments in either a basic science or a clinical department and secondary appointments in EID. The faculty is derived primarily from the Departments of Microbiology and Immunology, Pathology, Preventive Medicine and Biometrics, Pediatrics, and Medicine. Thus, the faculty in EID includes the experts in infectious diseases, regardless of department. For additional information, students should visit the USU Academic Department Web site at http://www.usuhs.mil/academic.html. To address e-mail to specific faculty members at USU, students should use the first letter of their first name plus the last name and @usuhs.mil as the address; for example, to send e-mail to John Doe, the address would be jdoe@usuhs.mil.

Nicole L. Achee, Ph.D.; Research Assistant Professor, Preventive Medicine and Biometrics.
Richard G. Andre, Ph.D.; Professor, Preventive Medicine and Biometrics.
Naomi E. Aronson, M.D.; Professor, Medicine.
Christopher C. Broder, Ph.D.; Professor, Microbiology and Immunology.
Timothy Burgess, M.D., M.P.H.; Assistant Professor, Medicine.
Drusilla L. Burns, Ph.D.; Adjunct Assistant Professor, CBER, FDA.
Richard M. Conran, M.D., Ph.D.; Professor, Pathology.
David F. Cruess, Ph.D.; Professor, Preventive Medicine and Biometrics.
Stephen J. Davies, Ph.D.; Associate Professor, Microbiology and Immunology.
Saibal Dey, Ph.D.; Adjunct Assistant Professor, Biochemistry.
Andre T. Dubois, M.D., Ph.D.; Professor, Medicine.
Michael W. Ellis, M.D.; Assistant Professor, Medicine.
Chou-Zen Giam, Ph.D.; Professor, Microbiology and Immunology.
Scott W. Gordon, Ph.D.; Adjunct Assistant Professor, Preventive Medicine and Biometrics.
John Grieco, Ph.D.; Assistant Professor, Preventive Medicine and Biometrics.
Patricia Guerry, Ph.D.; Assistant Professor, Immunology, NMRC.
Val G. Hemming, M.D.; Professor, Pediatrics.
John W. Huggins, Ph.D.; Adjunct Assistant Professor, Virology, USAMRIID.
Ann E. Jerse, Ph.D.; Professor, Microbiology and Immunology.
Elliott Kagan, M.D.; Professor, Pathology.
Johnan Kaleeba, Ph.D.; Assistant Professor, Microbiology and Immunology.
Barbara Knollman-Ritschel, M.D.; Associate Professor, Pathology.
Tadeusz J. Kochel, Ph.D.; Adjunct Assistant Professor, Immunology, NMRC.
Philip R. Krause, M.D.; Assistant Professor, CBER, FDA.
Larry W. Laughlin, M.D., Ph.D.; Professor, Preventive Medicine and Biometrics.
Radha K. Maheshwari, Ph.D.; Professor, Pathology.
Joseph Mattapallil, Ph.D.; Assistant Professor, Microbiology and Immunology.
Anthony T. Maurelli, Ph.D.; Professor, Microbiology and Immunology.
Ernest L. Maynard, Ph.D.; Assistant Professor, Biochemistry and Molecular Biology.
D. Scotty Merrell, Ph.D.; Associate Professor, Microbiology and Immunology.
Eleanor S. Metcalf, Ph.D.; Professor, Microbiology and Immunology.
Nelson L. Michael, M.D., Ph.D.; Adjunct Assistant Professor, Medicine.
Edward Mitre, M.D.; Assistant Professor, Microbiology and Immunology.
Alison D. O'Brien, Ph.D.; Professor, Microbiology and Immunology.
Christian F. Ockenhouse, M.D., Ph.D.; Adjunct Assistant Professor, Infectious Diseases, WRAIR.
Martin G. Ottolini, M.D.; Associate Professor, Pediatrics.
Gerald V. Quinnan Jr., M.D.; Professor, Preventive Medicine and Biometrics.
Allen L. Richards, Ph.D.; Associate Professor, Preventive Medicine and Biometrics.
Capt. Stephen J. Savarino, MC, USN; Adjunct Assistant Professor, Infectious Diseases, NMRC.
Brian C. Schaefer, Ph.D.; Associate Professor, Microbiology and Immunology.
Connie S. Schmaljohn, Ph.D.; Adjunct Assistant Professor, USAMRIID.
Frank P. Shewmaker, Ph.D.; Assistant Professor, Pharmacology.
Clifford M. Snapper, M.D.; Professor, Pathology.
Andrew L. Snow, Ph.D.; Assistant Professor, Pharmacology.
Shanmuga Sozhamannan, Ph.D.; Adjunct Assistant Professor, Biological Defense Research, NMRC.
V. Ann Stewart, D.V.M., Ph.D.; Assistant Professor, Preventive Medicine and Biometrics.
J. Thomas Stocker, M.D.; Professor, Pathology.
Charles Via, M.D.; Assistant Professor, Pathology.
Shuishu Wang, Ph.D.; Assistant Professor, Biochemistry.
Lt. Col. Glenn W. Wortmann, MC, USA; Adjunct Assistant Professor. Infectious Diseases, WRAIR.
Shuenn-Jue L. Wu, Ph.D.; Adjunct Associate Professor, Immunology, NMRC.
Pengfei Zhang, Ph.D.; Research Associate Professor, Preventive Medicine and Biometrics.

UNIVERSITY OF CONNECTICUT HEALTH CENTER
Graduate Program in Immunology

Program of Study

A Ph.D. in immunology is offered through an interdepartmental program consisting of 21 faculty members. The immunology faculty members also participate in training students in the combined M.D./Ph.D. and D.M.D./Ph.D. programs. The central focus of the program is to train students to become independent investigators who will provide meaningful research and educational contributions to the areas of basic, applied, or clinical immunology. This goal is achieved by lectures, seminars, laboratory rotations, research presentations, and a concentration on laboratory research. In addition to basic and advanced immunology courses, students are given a strong foundation in biomedical sciences through the core curriculum in biochemistry, genetics, molecular biology, and cell biology. Research laboratory training aims to provide a foundation in modern laboratory techniques and concentrates on hypothesis-based analysis of problems. Research in the program is focused on the cellular and molecular aspects of immune system structure and function in animal models and in humans. Areas of emphasis include molecular immunology (mechanisms of antigen presentation, major histocompatibility complex genetics and function, cytokines and cytokine receptors, and tumor antigens), cellular immunology (biochemical mechanisms and biological aspects of signal transduction of lymphocytes and granulocytes; cellular and molecular requirements for thymic T-lymphocyte development, selection, and activation; cytokines in B- and T-cell development; regulation of antitumor immunity; immunoparasitology, including parasite genetics and immune recognition of parasite antigens; and mechanisms of inflammation), organ-based immunology (immune effector mechanisms of the intestine, lymphocyte interactions in the lung, and immune regulation of the eye), immunity to infectious agents (viruses, bacteria, parasites, including vector-borne organisms), and autoimmunity (animal models of autoimmune disease and effector mechanisms in human autoimmunity).

Research Facilities

The Graduate Program in Immunology is interdepartmental, and therefore provides a broad base of training possibilities as well as ample shared facilities. State-of-the-art equipment is available in individual laboratories for analysis of molecular and cellular parameters of immune system structure and function. In addition, Health Center–supported facilities provide equipment and expertise in areas of advanced data acquisition and analysis. These facilities include the Center for Cell Analysis and Modeling, the Fluorescence Flow Cytometry Facility, the Gene Targeting and Transgenic Facility, the Molecular Core Facility, the Microarray Facility, the Gregory P. Mullen Structural Biology Facility, and the Electron Microscopy Facility. The Health Center Library is well equipped with extensive journal and book holdings and rapid electronic access to database searching, the World Wide Web, and library holdings. A computer center is also housed in the library for student use and training.

Financial Aid

Support for doctoral students engaged in full-time degree programs at the Health Center is provided on a competitive basis. Graduate research assistantships for 2011–12 provide a stipend of $28,000 per year, which includes a waiver of tuition/University fees for the fall and spring semesters and a student health insurance plan. While financial aid is offered competitively, the Health Center makes every possible effort to address the financial needs of all students.

Cost of Study

For 2011–12, tuition is $10,224 per year for full-time students who are Connecticut residents and $26,532 per year for full-time out-of-state residents. General University fees are added to the cost of tuition for students who do not receive a tuition waiver. These costs are usually met by traineeships or research assistantships for doctoral students.

Living and Housing Costs

There is a wide range of affordable housing options in the greater Hartford area within easy commuting distance of the campus, including an extensive complex that is adjacent to the Health Center. Costs range from $600 to $900 per month for a one-bedroom unit; 2 or more students sharing an apartment usually pay less. University housing is not available.

Student Group

At present, there are 30 students in the Graduate Program in Immunology. There are 150 students in the various Ph.D. programs on the Health Center campus.

Student Outcomes

Graduates have traditionally been accepted into high-quality laboratories for postdoctoral training. Following their training, graduates have accepted a wide range of positions in research in universities, colleges, research institutes, and industry, including the biotechnology sector.

Location

The Health Center is located in the historic town of Farmington, Connecticut. Set in the beautiful New England countryside on a hill overlooking the Farmington Valley, it is close to ski areas, hiking trails, and facilities for boating, fishing, and swimming. Connecticut's capital city of Hartford, 7 miles east of Farmington, is the center of an urban region of approximately 800,000 people. The beaches of the Long Island Sound are about 50 minutes away to the south, and the beautiful Berkshires are a short drive to the northwest. New York City and Boston can be reached within 2½ hours by car. Hartford is the home of the acclaimed Hartford Stage Company, TheatreWorks, the Hartford Symphony and Chamber orchestras, two ballet companies, an opera company, the Wadsworth Atheneaum (the oldest public art museum in the nation), the Mark Twain house, the Hartford Civic Center, and many other interesting cultural and recreational facilities. The area is also home to several branches of the University of Connecticut, Trinity College, and the University of Hartford, which includes the Hartt School of Music. Bradley International Airport (about 30 minutes from campus) serves the Hartford/Springfield area with frequent airline connections to major cities in this country and abroad. Frequent bus and rail service is also available from Hartford.

The Health Center

The 200-acre Health Center campus at Farmington houses a division of the University of Connecticut Graduate School, as well as the School of Medicine and Dental Medicine. The campus also includes the John Dempsey Hospital, associated clinics, and extensive medical research facilities, all in a centralized facility with more than 1 million square feet of floor space. The Health Center's newest research addition, the Academic Research Building, was opened in 1999. This impressive eleven-story structure provides 170,000 square feet of state-of-the-art laboratory space. The faculty at the center includes more than 260 full-time members. The institution has a strong commitment to graduate study within an environment that promotes social and intellectual interaction among the various educational programs. Graduate students are represented on various administrative committees concerned with curricular affairs, and the Graduate Student Organization (GSO) represents graduate students' needs and concerns to the faculty and administration, in addition to fostering social contact among graduate students in the Health Center.

Applying

Applications for admission should be submitted on standard forms obtained from the Graduate Admissions Office at the UConn Health Center or on the Web site. The application should be filed together with transcripts, three letters of recommendation, a personal statement, and recent results from the General Test of the Graduate Record Examinations. International students must take the Test of English as a Foreign Language (TOEFL) to satisfy Graduate School requirements. The deadline for completed applications and receipt of all supplemental materials is December 15. In accordance with the laws of the state of Connecticut and of the United States, the University of Connecticut Health Center does not discriminate against any person in its educational and employment activities on the grounds of race, color, creed, national origin, sex, age, or physical disability.

Correspondence and Information

Dr. Adam Adler, Program Director
Graduate Program in Immunology
Department of Immunology
MC 1601
University of Connecticut Health Center
Farmington, Connecticut 06030-1601
Phone: 860-679-7992
Fax: 860-679-1868
E-mail: aadler@uchc.edu
Web site: http://www.grad.uchc.edu

University of Connecticut Health Center

THE FACULTY AND THEIR RESEARCH

Adam J. Adler, Associate Professor of Immunology; Ph.D., Columbia. Mechanisms of T-cell tolerance induction to peripheral self- and tumor-antigens; immunological properties of prostate cancer.

Hector L. Aguila, Assistant Professor of Immunology; Ph.D., Yeshiva (Einstein). Hematopoiesis and bone marrow microenvironment; lymphoid cell development; stem cell biology.

Linda Cauley, Assistant Professor of Immunology; D.Phil., Oxford. T-cell memory and respiratory virus infections.

Robert B. Clark, Associate Professor of Immunology; M.D., Stanford. Autoimmunity; immune regulation; regulatory T cells.

Robert Cone, Professor Emeritus of Immunology; Ph.D., Michigan. Ocular immunology; regulatory T cells; neuroimmunology.

Irving Goldschneider, Professor of Immunology; M.D., Pennsylvania. T- and B-cell development; acquired thymic tolerance; cytokines.

Chi-Kuang Huang, Associate Professor of Immunology; Ph.D., Connecticut. Signal transduction in stimulated neutrophil and lymphocytes; roles of protein kinase and phosphoproteins in cell activation; chemotaxis.

Kamal Khanna, Assistant Professor of Immunology; Ph.D., Pittsburgh. Identifying the factors and the role they play in controlling the anatomy of a primary and secondary immune response in the hopes of explicating the underlying mechanisms that guide the complex movement of T cells during infection and recall responses in lymphoid and non-lymphoid tissues.

Leo Lefrancois, Professor of Immunology; Ph.D., Wake Forest. T-cell memory; immune response to infection; tolerance; vaccines.

Joseph A. Lorenzo, Professor of Medicine; M.D., SUNY Downstate Medical Center. Relationships between bone-absorbing osteoclasts and immune cells.

Bijay Mukherji, Professor of Medicine; M.D., Calcutta (India). Tumor immunology and cancer vaccines; tumor-specific antigens.

James O'Rourke, Professor Emeritus of Immunology and Surgery; M.D., Georgetown. Vascular biology; tissue plasminogen activator synthesis, transport, and release.

Lynn Puddington, Associate Professor of Immunology; Ph.D., Wake Forest. Allergic asthma; neonatal immunity and tolerance; developmental immunology.

Justin D. Radolf, Professor of Medicine and Center for Microbial Pathogenesis; M.D., California, San Francisco. Molecular pathogenesis and immunobiology of spirochetal infections.

Pramod K. Srivastava, Professor of Medicine; Ph.D., Hyderabad (India). Heat shock proteins as peptide chaperones; roles in antigen presentation and applications in immunotherapy of cancer, infectious diseases, and autoimmune disorders.

Roger S. Thrall, Professor of Immunology and Surgery; Ph.D., Marquette. Immune cells; pulmonary inflammation.

Anthony T. Vella, Associate Professor of Immunology; Ph.D., Cornell. T-cell immunity; costimulation; adjuvants and cytokines.

Richard A. Zeff, Associate Professor of Immunology; Ph.D., Rush. Major histocompatibility complex; antigen processing and presentation.

UNIVERSITY OF MASSACHUSETTS AMHERST

Department of Microbiology

Programs of Study

The Department of Microbiology at the University of Massachusetts Amherst offers programs of graduate study leading to the M.S. and Ph.D. degrees in microbiology. Postdoctoral training is also available. Courses covering various areas in the field of microbiology are offered by the Departmental faculty members, listed in the Faculty and Their Research section.

In the Ph.D. program, formal course work is generally completed during the first two years. After the first year, an increasing proportion of time is dedicated to research. Students select dissertation problems from a wide spectrum of research areas pursued by the faculty. The following research fields are represented: bioinformatics, physiology, genetics, immunology, parasitology, pathogenic bacteriology, molecular biology, microbial ecology, and environmental microbiology. In addition, close ties are maintained with the Departments of Biochemistry, Biology, and Chemistry through the interdepartmental program for doctoral training in molecular and cellular biology. In the second year, Ph.D. candidates must pass a comprehensive preliminary examination. Degree requirements are completed by submission and defense of a dissertation. There is no foreign language requirement. Completion of the Ph.D. program generally takes four years beyond the bachelor's degree.

Research Facilities

The Department of Microbiology occupies space in the Morrill Science Center. Air-conditioned laboratories are spacious and well equipped for research and teaching. The modern apparatus necessary for investigation into all aspects of microbiology is available within Departmental space. The Department's facilities include tissue- and cell-culture laboratories, animal quarters, and various instrument rooms containing preparative and analytical ultracentrifuges, scintillation counters, fermentors, anaerobic chambers, equipment for DNA sequence analysis and chromatographic and electrophoretic procedures, photography, and other standard laboratory procedures. Centralized facilities provide state-of-the-art equipment and expertise to support research projects, such as the Central Microscopy Facility; Phosphorimager, Genomics and Bioinformatics Facility; High Field NMR Facility; and Mass Spectrometry Facility.

Financial Aid

Financial aid is available in the form of University fellowships and teaching assistantships. Research assistantships are available for advanced graduate students. All assistantships include a waiver of tuition.

Cost of Study

In academic year 2011–12, annual tuition for in-state residents is $110 per credit; nonresident tuition is $414 per credit. Full-time students register for at least 9 credits per semester. The mandatory fees assessed for full-time graduate students is $4798 per semester for in-state residents and $7224 for nonresidents. Fees are subject to change. For more information on fees refer to the Bursar's Office fee schedule online at http://www.umass.edu/bursar/fee_schedule.htm.

Living and Housing Costs

Graduate student housing is available in several twelve-month campus residence halls through University Housing Services. The University owns and manages unfurnished apartments of various sizes for family housing on or near the campus. Off-campus housing is available; rents vary widely and depend on factors such as size and location.

Student Group

The Department has approximately 35 graduate and 150 undergraduate students as well as 35 postdoctoral fellows. Enrollment at the Amherst campus is about 26,000, including 5,000 graduate students.

Location

The 1,450-acre campus of the University provides a rich cultural environment in a rural setting. Amherst is situated in the picturesque Pioneer Valley in historic western Massachusetts. The area is renowned for its natural beauty. Green open land framed by the outline of the Holyoke Range, clear streams, country roads, forests, grazing cattle, and shade trees are characteristic of the region. A broad spectrum of cultural activities and extensive recreational facilities are available within the University and at four neighboring colleges—Smith, Amherst, Mount Holyoke, and Hampshire. Opportunities for outdoor winter sports are exceptional. Amherst is 90 miles west of Boston and 175 miles north of New York City, and Cape Cod is a 3½-hour drive away.

The University

The University of Massachusetts is the state university of the Commonwealth of Massachusetts and is the flagship campus of the five-campus UMass system. Departments affiliated with the ten colleges and schools of the University offer a variety of graduate degrees through the Graduate School. The Amherst campus consists of approximately 150 buildings, including the twenty-eight-story W. E. B. DuBois Library, which is the largest at a state-supported institution in New England. The library features more than 5.8 million items and is home to a state-of-the-art learning commons equipped with PC and Mac workstations and laptop network access.

Applying

Application forms may be obtained from the Graduate Admissions Office, 530 Goodell Building, University of Massachusetts, 140 Hicks Way, Amherst, Massachusetts 01003-9333, or online at http://www.umass.edu/gradschool. Prospective students are required to take the Graduate Record Examinations. Applications for admission should be received by the Graduate Admissions Office by December 20 for September enrollment and by October 1 for January enrollment. Applications received after these dates are considered only if space is available.

Correspondence and Information

Graduate Program Director
Department of Microbiology
Morrill IV, N203
639 North Pleasant Street
University of Massachusetts Amherst
Amherst, Massachusetts 01003-9298

Phone: 413-545-2051
Fax: 413-545-1578
E-mail: microbio-dept@microbio.umass.edu
Web site: http://www.bio.umass.edu/micro/

University of Massachusetts Amherst

THE FACULTY AND THEIR RESEARCH

J. M. Lopes, Professor and Department Head; Ph.D., South Carolina. Regulation of gene expression in eukaryotes. *Eukaryot. Cell* 9:1845, 2010. *Mol. Microbiol.* 70:1529, 2008. *Genetics* 173:621, 2006.

C. L. Baldwin, Adjunct Professor; Ph.D., Cornell. Cellular immunity to intracellular microbial parasites, including *Brucella abortus*, with particular interest in the interaction of the microbe with macrophages and the control of infection by T-cell cytokines; stimulation and control of gamma/delta T-cell responses to bacterial pathogens. *BMC Evol. Biol.*10:181, 2010. *Science* 324:522–8, 2009. *BMC Genom.* 10:191, 2009. *Crit. Rev. Immunol.* 26:407–42, 2006.

J. Blanchard, Associate Professor; Ph.D., Georgia. Biofuels; genomics; bioinformatics; metagenomics. *Mol. Biol. Evol.* 26:5–13, 2009. *PLoS ONE* 11:e1186, 2007.

J. P. Burand, Adjunct Associate Professor; Ph.D., Washington State. Biology and molecular biology of insect pathogenic viruses, particularly nonoccluded insect viruses and bee viruses, with emphasis on virus-host interactions that affect the virulence and persistence of these viruses in insects. *Virol. Sin.* 24:428–35, 2009. *Arch. Virol.* 154:909–18, 2009. *Virol. Sin.* 22:128–36, 2007. *Ann. Entomol. Soc. Am.* 99:967, 2006. *J. Insect Sci.* 5:6, 2005.

P. Chien, Adjunct Assistant Professor; Ph.D., California, San Francisco. Protein degradation during bacterial cell-cycle progression. *Protein Sci.* 19(2):242–54, 2010. *Mol. Microbiol.* 73(4):586–600, 2009. *Structure* 15(10):1296–305, 2007. *Proc. Natl. Acad. Sci. U.S.A.* 104(16):6590–5, 2007.

D. R. Cooley, Adjunct Associate Professor; Ph.D., Massachusetts. Ecology of diseases; plant pathogenic fungi and bacteria; plant disease management; integrated pest management; development of sustainable agricultural systems.

S. Goodwin, Dean, College of Natural Sciences; Ph.D., Wisconsin.

K. L. Griffith, Assistant Professor; Ph.D., Maryland. Cell-cell signaling in bacteria; development of tools for studying regulatory networks. *J. Mol. Bio.* 381:261–75, 2008. *Mol. Microbiol.* 70:1012–25, 2008.

J. F. Holden, Associate Professor; Ph.D., Washington (Seattle). Physiology of hyperthermophilic archaea; geomicrobiology of geothermal environments. *Appl. Environ. Microbiol.* 75:242–5, 2009. *Appl. Environ. Microbiol.* 74:396–402, 2008. *Extremophiles* 11:741–6, 2007.

M. M. Klingbeil, Associate Professor; Ph.D., Toledo. Molecular and biochemical parasitology, replication and repair of mitochondrial DNA (kinetoplast DNA) and nuclear DNA replication initiation in African trypanosomes. *Mol. Cell* 5:398–400, 2009. *Eukaryot. Cell* 7:2141–6, 2008. *Science* 309:409–15, 2005. *Proc. Natl. Acad. Sci. U.S.A.* 101:4333–4, 2004. *J. Biol. Chem.* 278:49095–101, 2003. *Mol. Cell* 10:175–86, 2002. *Protist* 152:255–62, 2001.

S. B. Leschine, Professor; Ph.D., Pittsburgh. Harnessing the diversity of the microbial world and the power of genomics for energy solutions. *Bergey's Manual of Systemic Bacteriology*, 2nd ed. 4:159–70, Springer, 2010 (with Paster), ed. N. R. Krieg et al. *Biofuels Technology* 1:37–44, 2008 (with Gorham et al.). *Biofilms*, 2008: doi:10.1017/S1479050508002238 (with Alonso and Pomposiello). *Handbook on Clostridia*, pp. 101–31, ed. P. Durre, CRC Press, 2005. *Arch. Microbiol.* 180:434–43, 2003 (with Reguera). *Int. J. Syst. Evol. Microbiol.* 52:1155–60, 2002 (with Warnick).

D. R. Lovley, Distinguished University Professor; Ph.D., Michigan State. Genome-enabled study of the physiology, ecology, and evolution of novel anaerobic microorganisms; microbe-electrode interactions with focus on novel bioenergy solutions; direct electron exchange between microorganisms; bioremediation of metal and organic contamination; life in extreme environments. *Science* 330:1413–5, 2010. *Nature Rev. Microbiol.* 4:497–508, 2006. *Nature* 435:1098–101, 2005. *Nature Rev. Microbiol.* 1:35–44, 2003. *Science* 301:934, 2003. *Nature* 416:767–9, 2002. *Science* 295:483–5, 2002. *Nature* 415:312–6, 2002.

L. Ma, Adjunct Assistant Professor; Ph.D., SUNY College of Environmental Science and Forestry. Comparative fungal genomics: A gateway toward understanding genome innovation and adaptation. *Nature* 465:367–73, 2010. *BMC Genom.* 11:208, 2010. *PLoS Genetics* 5(7):e1000549, 2009.

W. J. Manning, Adjunct Professor; Ph.D., Delaware. Effects of ozone on plants and associated mycoflora; plants as bioindicators of ozone; effects of ozone and other air pollutants on plants in urban environments; managing invasive plants with fungal pathogens. *Environ. Pollut.* 126:73–81, 2003.

L. Margulis, Adjunct Professor and Distinguished University Professor in the Department of Geosciences. Evolution of microbes; symbiogenesis and the origin of the nucleus; evolution of cells. *Handbook of Protoctista: The Structure, Cultivation, Habitats and Life Histories of the Eukaryotic, Microorganisms and Their Descendants Exclusive of Animals, Plants and Fungi.* Sudbury, MA: Jones and Bartlett, in press. *Kingdoms and Domains: Illustrated Phyla of Life in Color.* Amsterdam: Elsevier, 2010 (with M. J. Chapman). *Dazzle Gradually: Reflections on the Nature of Nature.* White River Junction, VT: Chelsea Green, 2007 (with D. Sagan). *Acquiring Genomes: A Theory of the Origins of Species,* New York: Basic Books, 2002. *Symbiosis in Cell Evolution: Microbial Communities in the Archean and Proterozoic Eons*, 4th ed. W. H. Freeman & Company, in press. *Proc. Natl. Acad. Sci. U.S.A.* 103:13080–5, 2006. *Proc. Natl. Acad. Sci. U.S.A.* 31:775–91, 2005. *Proc. Natl. Acad. Sci. U.S.A.* 106:18656–61. *Symbiosis* 47:51–8, 2009.

S. Nugen, Adjunct Assistant Professor; Ph.D., Cornell. Food and water pathogen detection; rapid biosensor technology; microfluidic assay development; nanofabrication; food processing. *J. Vet. Sci.* 10(1):35–42, 2009. *Biosens. Bioelectron.* 24(8):2428–33, 2009. *Microsystem Technologies* 15(3):477–83, 2008.

K. Nüsslein, Associate Professor; Ph.D., Michigan State. Microbial ecology of terrestrial and aquatic environments; relating the stress of environmental influences to community structure and function, with emphasis on understanding interactions among bacterial communities. *Water Res.* 44:4970–9, 2010. *Curr. Opin. Biotechnol.* 21:339–45, 2010. *Geomicrobiology* 26:9–20, 2009. *Geology* 36:139–42, 2008. *Chemosphere* 70:329–36. 2007. *Appl. Environ. Microbiol.* 73:4171–9, 2007. *FEMS Microb. Ecol.* 60:60–73, 2006. *Microb. Ecol.* 51:441–52, 2006.

S. T. Petsch, Adjunct Assistant Professor; Ph.D., Yale. Transport, transformation, and biodegradation of natural organic matter in sediments, soils, and sedimentary rocks. *Geology*, in press. *Appl. Environ. Microbiol.* 73:4171–9, 2007. *Geochim. Cosmochim. Acta* 71:4233–50, 2007. *SEPM* 5:5–9, 2007. *Am. J. Sci.* 306:575–615, 2006. *Palaeogeogr. Palaeoclim. Palaeoecol.* 219:157–70, 2005. *Gas Technol. Inst.* GRI-05/0023, 2004. *Am. J. Sci.* 304:234–49, 2004. *Org. Geochem.* 34:731–43, 2003.

S. M. Rich, Adjunct Associate Professor; Ph.D. California, Irvine. Evolutionary dynamics of pathogen and host populations.

M. A. Riley, Adjunct Professor; Ph.D., Harvard. Microbial ecology and evolution and genome evolution. *Microbiology* 156:2058–67, 2010. Competitive interactions in Escherichia coli populations: the role of bacteriocins. *ISME* 1–11, 2010. *BMC Microbial.* 2009, 9:165. *Genome Biol. Evol.* 400–8, 2009. Population and comparative genomics inform our understanding of bacterial species diversity in the soil. In *Biocommunication in Soil Microorganisms*, ed. Witzany. Berlin: Springer, 2010.

S. J. Sandler, Professor; Ph.D., Berkeley. Molecular genetics of recombination; DNA replication and DNA repair in bacteria. *Mol. Microbiol.* 57:1074, 2005. *Mol. Microbiol.* 53:1343, 2004.

E. Stuart, Associate Professor; Ph.D., Chicago. Infection, immunity, and pathogenesis, with special interest in processes used by chlamydial species for entry into host cells and replication, prevalence of blood cell-borne *Chlamydia*, and susceptibility of blood cells to infection by *Chlamydia*; vaccine components for use with *Chlamydia*; generation, display, and utility of recombinant vaccine components targeting viral or bacterial peptides. *BMC Microbiol.* 8:213, 2008. *Tocotrienols: Vitamin E beyond Tocopherols*, ch. 25 "Tocotrienol in the potential treatment of infectious disease," CRC Press, 2008;. *BMC Biotechnol.* 8:9, 2008. *J. Clin. Apheresis* 21(3):195–201, 2006. *BMC Infect. Dis.* 6:23, 2006. *Am. J. Respir. Crit. Care Med.* 171(10):1083–8, 2005. *BMC Infect. Dis.* 4(1):23, 2004. *Curr. Microbiol.* 49(1):13–21, 2004. *J. Biotechnol.* 114:225–37, 2004. *Exp. Cell Res.* 287(1):67–7, 2003. *J. Biotechnol.* 88(2):119–28, 2001.

W. Webley, Assistant Professor; Ph.D., Massachusetts. Immunology and pathogenic bacteriology; elucidating the role of *Chlamydia* in the initiation and exacerbation of neonatal asthma; evaluation of chlamydial survival and host range; development of novel antigen display and vaccine delivery systems for *Chlamydia* and other pathogenic bacteria of interest to community health; elucidating the role of *Chlamydia* in thromboembolitic diseases. *Pediatr. Infect. Dis. J.* 29(12):1093–8. *Eur. Respir. J.*, 33:1–8, 2009. *Biology of AIDS*, 2nd ed., Dubuque, Iowa: Kendall/Hunt Publishing Company, 2008. *CHEST* 134(suppl.), 2008. *CHEST* 132(4):607, 2007. *J. Clin. Apheresis* 3, 2006. *BMC Infect. Dis.* 6:23, 2006. *Am. J. Respir. Crit. Care Med.* 171(10):1083–8, 2005. *BMC Infect. Dis.* 4(1):23, 2004 (with Stuart and Norkin). *Curr. Microbiol.* 49(1):13–21, 2004. *Am. J. Respir. Crit. Care Med.* 169(7):A586, 2004. *J. Clin. Apheresis* 18(2), 2003. *Exp. Cell Res.* 287(1):67–78, 2003.

R. M. Weis, Adjunct Professor; Ph.D., Stanford. Signal transduction in chemotaxis system and chemotaxis-like pathways. *BMC Genom.* 9:471, 2008. *Proc. Natl. Acad. Sci. USA* 105:12289–94, 2008. *Methods Enzymol.* 423:267–98, 2007. *J. Biol. Chem.* 281:30512–23, 2006.

H. Xiao, Adjunct Assistant Professor; Ph.D., Wisconsin–Madison. Cancer preventive dietary components, diet-based strategy for cancer prevention, enhancement of biological activity of dietary components by combination regimen, food processing, and nanotechnology.

Section 13
Neuroscience and Neurobiology

This section contains a directory of institutions offering graduate work in neuroscience and neurobiology, followed by in-depth entries submitted by institutions that chose to prepare detailed program descriptions. Additional information about programs listed in the directory but not augmented by an in-depth entry may be obtained by writing directly to the dean of a graduate school or chair of a department at the address given in the directory.

For programs offering related work, see also in this book *Anatomy; Biochemistry; Biological and Biomedical Sciences; Biophysics; Cell, Molecular, and Structural Biology; Genetics, Developmental Biology, and Reproductive Biology; Pathology and Pathobiology; Pharmacology and Toxicology; Physiology;* and *Zoology.* In the other guides in this series:

Graduate Programs in the Humanities, Arts & Social Sciences
See *Psychology and Counseling*

Graduate Programs in Business, Education, Health, Information Studies, Law & Social Work
See *Optometry and Vision Sciences*

CONTENTS

Program Directories

Close-Ups and Displays

See also:

Biopsychology

Adler School of Professional Psychology, Programs in Psychology, Chicago, IL 60602. Offers advanced Adlerian psychotherapy (Certificate); art therapy (MA); clinical neuropsychology (Certificate); clinical psychology (Psy D); community psychology (MA); counseling and organizational psychology (MA); counseling psychology (MA); forensic psychology (MA); gerontological counseling (MA); marriage and family counseling (MA); marriage and family therapy (Certificate); organizational psychology (MA); police psychology (MA); rehabilitation counseling (MA); sport and health psychology (MA); substance abuse counseling (Certificate); Psy D/Certificate; Psy D/MACAT; Psy D/MACP; Psy D/MAMFC; Psy D/MASAC. *Accreditation:* APA. Part-time and evening/weekend programs available. Postbaccalaureate distance learning degree programs offered (minimal on-campus study). *Faculty:* 40 full-time (18 women), 61 part-time/adjunct (31 women). *Students:* 688 full-time (532 women), 142 part-time (110 women). Average age 27.Terminal master's awarded for partial completion of doctoral program. *Degree requirements:* For master's, thesis or alternative, oral exam, practicum; for doctorate, thesis/dissertation, clinical exam, internship, oral exam, practicum, written qualifying exam. *Entrance requirements:* For master's, 12 semester hours in psychology, minimum GPA of 3.0; for doctorate, 18 semester hours in psychology, minimum GPA of 3.25; for Certificate, appropriate master's or doctoral degree. Additional exam requirements/recommendations for international students: Required—TOEFL (minimum score 550 paper-based; 213 computer-based; 79 iBT). *Application deadline:* For fall admission, 2/15 priority date for domestic students, 12/1 priority date for international students. Applications are processed on a rolling basis. Application fee: $50. Electronic applications accepted. *Financial support:* Career-related internships or fieldwork, Federal Work-Study, scholarships/grants, and tuition waivers (full and partial) available. Support available to part-time students. Financial award application deadline: 5/15; financial award applicants required to submit FAFSA. *Application contact:* Michelle Brice, Director of Admissions, 312-662-4113, Fax: 312-662-4199, E-mail: admissions@adler.edu.

American University, College of Arts and Sciences, Department of Psychology, Washington, DC 22016-8062. Offers behavior, cognition, and neuroscience (PhD), including psychology; clinical psychology (PhD), including psychology; psychology (MA), including experimental/biological psychology, general psychology, personality/social psychology. *Accreditation:* APA. Part-time programs available. *Faculty:* 19 full-time (7 women), 6 part-time/adjunct (4 women). *Students:* 65 full-time (51 women), 47 part-time (41 women); includes 16 minority (4 Black or African American, non-Hispanic/Latino; 3 Asian, non-Hispanic/Latino; 9 Hispanic/Latino), 3 international. Average age 28. 445 applicants, 19% accepted, 36 enrolled. In 2010, 35 master's, 11 doctorates awarded. *Degree requirements:* For master's, comprehensive exam, thesis or alternative; for doctorate, comprehensive exam, thesis/dissertation, tools of research. *Entrance requirements:* For master's, GRE General Test, GRE Subject Test, recommendations; for doctorate, GRE General Test, GRE Subject Test. Additional exam requirements/recommendations for international students: Required—TOEFL. Application fee: $80. *Financial support:* Fellowships, research assistantships, teaching assistantships, career-related internships or fieldwork, Federal Work-Study, institutionally sponsored loans, tuition waivers (full and partial), and unspecified assistantships available. Support available to part-time students. Financial award application deadline: 2/1. *Faculty research:* Anxiety disorders, cognitive assessment, neuropsychology, conditioning and learning, psychopharmacology. *Unit head:* Dr. Anthony Riley, Chair, 202-885-1720, E-mail: alriley@american.edu. *Application contact:* Sara Holland, Senior Administrative Assistant, 202-885-1717, Fax: 202-885-1023, E-mail: holland@american.edu.

Argosy University, Atlanta, College of Psychology and Behavioral Sciences, Atlanta, GA 30328. Offers clinical psychology (MA, Psy D, Postdoctoral Respecialization Certificate), including child and family psychology (Psy D), general adult clinical (Psy D), health psychology (Psy D), neuropsychology/geropsychology (Psy D); community counseling (MA), including marriage and family therapy; counselor education and supervision (Ed D); forensic psychology (MA); industrial organizational psychology (MA); marriage and family therapy (Certificate); sport-exercise psychology (MA). *Accreditation:* APA.

Argosy University, Twin Cities, College of Psychology and Behavioral Sciences, Eagan, MN 55121. Offers clinical psychology (MA, Psy D), including child and family psychology (Psy D), forensic psychology (Psy D), health and neuropsychology (Psy D), trauma (Psy D); forensic counseling (Post-Graduate Certificate); forensic psychology (MA); industrial organizational psychology (MA); marriage and family therapy (MA, DMFT), including forensic counseling (MA). *Accreditation:* AAMFT; AAMFT/COAMFTE; APA.

Brown University, Graduate School, Department of Psychology, Providence, RI 02912. Offers behavioral neuroscience (PhD); cognitive processes (PhD); sensation and perception (PhD); social/developmental (PhD); MS/PhD. *Degree requirements:* For doctorate, thesis/dissertation. *Entrance requirements:* For doctorate, GRE General Test, GRE Subject Test.

Carnegie Mellon University, College of Humanities and Social Sciences, Department of Psychology, Area of Cognitive Neuroscience, Pittsburgh, PA 15213-3891. Offers PhD. *Degree requirements:* For doctorate, comprehensive exam, thesis/dissertation. *Entrance requirements:* For doctorate, GRE General Test. Additional exam requirements/recommendations for international students: Required—TOEFL.

Columbia University, Graduate School of Arts and Sciences, Division of Natural Sciences, Department of Psychology, New York, NY 10027. Offers experimental psychology (M Phil, MA, PhD); psychobiology (M Phil, MA, PhD); social psychology (M Phil, MA, PhD); JD/MA; JD/PhD; MD/PhD. *Degree requirements:* For master's, thesis; for doctorate, thesis/dissertation. *Entrance requirements:* For master's and doctorate, GRE General Test. Additional exam requirements/recommendations for international students: Required—TOEFL.

Cornell University, Graduate School, Graduate Fields of Arts and Sciences, Field of Psychology, Ithaca, NY 14853-0001. Offers biopsychology (PhD); human experimental psychology (PhD); personality and social psychology (PhD). *Faculty:* 40 full-time (15 women). *Students:* 39 full-time (25 women); includes 1 Black or African American, non-Hispanic/Latino; 4 Asian, non-Hispanic/Latino; 2 Hispanic/Latino, 13 international. Average age 27. 273 applicants, 5% accepted, 10 enrolled. In 2010, 4 doctorates awarded. *Degree requirements:* For doctorate, comprehensive exam, thesis/dissertation, 2 semesters of teaching experience. *Entrance requirements:* For doctorate, GRE General Test, 3 letters of recommendation. Additional exam requirements/recommendations for international students: Required—TOEFL (minimum score 550 paper-based; 213 computer-based; 77 iBT). *Application deadline:* For fall admission, 12/15 for domestic students. Application fee: $80. Electronic applications accepted. *Expenses:* Tuition: Full-time $29,500. Required fees: $76. Tuition and fees vary according to degree level and program. *Financial support:* In 2010–11, 12 fellowships with full tuition reimbursements, 2 research assistantships with full tuition reimbursements, 23 teaching assistantships with full tuition reimbursements were awarded; institutionally sponsored loans, scholarships/grants, health care benefits, tuition waivers (full and partial), and unspecified assistantships also available. Financial award applicants required to submit FAFSA. *Faculty research:* Sensory and perceptual systems, social cognition, cognitive development, quantitative and computational modeling, behavioral neuroscience. *Unit head:* Director of Graduate Studies, 607-255-6364, Fax: 607-255-8433. *Application contact:* Graduate Field Assistant, 607-255-3834, Fax: 607-255-8433, E-mail: psychapp@cornell.edu.

Drexel University, College of Arts and Sciences, Department of Psychology, Philadelphia, PA 19104-2875. Offers clinical psychology (PhD), including clinical psychology, forensic psychology, health psychology, neuropsychology; law-psychology (PhD); psychology (MS); JD/PhD. *Accreditation:* APA (one or more programs are accredited). *Degree requirements:* For doctorate, thesis/dissertation, internship. *Entrance requirements:* For doctorate, GRE General Test. Additional exam requirements/recommendations for international students: Required—TOEFL. Electronic applications accepted. *Expenses:* Contact institution. *Faculty research:* Neurosciences, rehabilitation psychology, cognitive science, neurological assessment.

Duke University, Graduate School, Department of Psychology and Neuroscience, Durham, NC 27708. Offers biological psychology (PhD); clinical psychology (PhD); cognitive psychology (PhD); developmental psychology (PhD); experimental psychology (PhD); health psychology (PhD); human social development (PhD); JD/MA. *Accreditation:* APA (one or more programs are accredited). *Faculty:* 40 full-time. *Students:* 92 full-time (67 women); includes 6 Black or African American, non-Hispanic/Latino; 2 Asian, non-Hispanic/Latino; 7 Hispanic/Latino, 13 international. 483 applicants, 8% accepted, 23 enrolled. In 2010, 24 doctorates awarded. *Degree requirements:* For doctorate, thesis/dissertation. *Entrance requirements:* For doctorate, GRE General Test. Additional exam requirements/recommendations for international students: Required—TOEFL (minimum score 550 paper-based; 213 computer-based; 83 iBT), IELTS (minimum score 7). *Application deadline:* For fall admission, 12/8 priority date for domestic and international students. Application fee: $75. Electronic applications accepted. *Financial support:* Fellowships, research assistantships, teaching assistantships, career-related internships or fieldwork and Federal Work-Study available. Financial award application deadline: 12/8. *Unit head:* Melanie Bonner, Director of Graduate Studies, 919-660-5715, Fax: 919-660-5726, E-mail: morrell@duke.edu. *Application contact:* Elizabeth Hutton, Director of Admissions, 919-684-3913, Fax: 919-684-2277, E-mail: grad-admissions@duke.edu.

Graduate School and University Center of the City University of New York, Graduate Studies, Program in Psychology, New York, NY 10016-4039. Offers basic applied neurocognition (PhD); biopsychology (PhD); clinical psychology (PhD); developmental psychology (PhD); environmental psychology (PhD); experimental psychology (PhD); industrial psychology (PhD); learning processes (PhD); neuropsychology (PhD); psychology (PhD); social personality (PhD). *Degree requirements:* For doctorate, one foreign language, thesis/dissertation. *Entrance requirements:* For doctorate, GRE General Test. Additional exam requirements/recommendations for international students: Required—TOEFL. Electronic applications accepted.

Harvard University, Graduate School of Arts and Sciences, Department of Psychology, Cambridge, MA 02138. Offers psychology (PhD), including behavior and decision analysis, cognition, developmental psychology, experimental psychology, personality, psychobiology, psychopathology; social psychology (PhD). *Accreditation:* APA. *Degree requirements:* For doctorate, thesis/dissertation, general exams. *Entrance requirements:* For doctorate, GRE General Test. Additional exam requirements/recommendations for international students: Required—TOEFL. *Expenses:* Tuition: Full-time $34,976. Required fees: $1166. Full-time tuition and fees vary according to program.

Howard University, Graduate School, Department of Psychology, Washington, DC 20059-0002. Offers clinical psychology (PhD); developmental psychology (PhD); experimental psychology (PhD); neuropsychology (PhD); personality psychology (PhD); psychology (MS); social psychology (PhD). *Accreditation:* APA (one or more programs are accredited). Part-time programs available. *Degree requirements:* For master's, thesis; for doctorate, comprehensive exam, thesis/dissertation, qualifying exam. *Entrance requirements:* For master's, GRE General Test, minimum GPA of 2.5, bachelor's degree in psychology or related field; for doctorate, GRE General Test, minimum GPA of 3.0. *Faculty research:* Personality and psychophysiology, educational and social development of African-American children, child and adult psychopathology.

Hunter College of the City University of New York, Graduate School, School of Arts and Sciences, Department of Psychology, New York, NY 10021-5085. Offers animal behavior and conservation (MA); applied and evaluative psychology (MA); biopsychology and behavioral neuroscience (PhD); biopsychology and comparative psychology (MA); social, cognitive, and developmental psychology (MA). Part-time and evening/weekend programs available. *Faculty:* 9 full-time (1 woman), 1 part-time/adjunct (0 women). *Students:* 10 full-time (7 women), 79 part-time (61 women); includes 3 Black or African American, non-Hispanic/Latino; 7 Asian, non-Hispanic/Latino; 9 Hispanic/Latino, 2 international. Average age 27. 151 applicants, 34% accepted, 21 enrolled. In 2010, 13 master's awarded. *Degree requirements:* For master's, comprehensive exam, thesis. *Entrance requirements:* For master's, GRE General Test, minimum 12 credits of course work in psychology, including statistics and experimental psychology; 2 letters of recommendation. Additional exam requirements/recommendations for international students: Required—TOEFL. *Application deadline:* For fall admission, 4/1 for domestic students, 2/1 for international students; for spring admission, 11/1 for domestic students, 9/1 for international students. Applications are processed on a rolling basis. Application fee: $125. *Financial support:* Federal Work-Study, scholarships/grants, and tuition waivers (partial) available. Support available to part-time students. *Faculty research:* Personality, cognitive and linguistic development, hormonal and neural control of behavior, gender and culture, social cognition of health and attitudes. *Unit head:* Dr. Jeffrey Parsons, Chairperson, 212-772-5550, Fax: 212-772-5620, E-mail: jeffrey.parsons@hunter.cuny.edu. *Application contact:* Martin Braun, Acting Program Director, 212-772-4482, Fax: 212-650-3336, E-mail: cbraun@hunter.cuny.edu.

Indiana University–Purdue University Indianapolis, School of Science, Department of Psychology, Psychobiology of Addictions Program, Indianapolis, IN 46202-2896. Offers MS, PhD. *Faculty:* 7 full-time (3 women). *Students:* 13 full-time (9 women), 5 part-time (4 women); includes 1 minority (Black or African American, non-Hispanic/Latino). Average age 29. 14 applicants, 36% accepted, 4 enrolled. *Entrance requirements:* For master's, GRE General Test, minimum undergraduate GPA of 3.2. *Application deadline:* For fall admission, 1/1 for domestic students. Application fee: $55 ($65 for international students). *Financial support:* Fellowships with partial tuition reimbursements, research assistantships with partial tuition reimbursements, teaching assistantships with partial tuition reimbursements, career-related internships or fieldwork and Federal Work-Study available. Financial award application deadline: 3/1; financial award applicants required to submit FAFSA. *Faculty research:* Behavioral genetics, behavior pharmacology, animal models, developmental psychology, neurobehavioral toxicology, neuropsychology of learning and memory, animal models of fetal alcohol syndrome. *Unit head:* Dr. J. Gregor Fetterman, Chairman, 317-274-6945, Fax: 317-274-6756, E-mail: gfetter@iupui.edu. *Application contact:* Dr. J. Gregor Fetterman, Chairman, 317-274-6945, Fax: 317-274-6756, E-mail: gfetter@iupui.edu.

Louisiana State University and Agricultural and Mechanical College, Graduate School, College of Humanities and Social Sciences, Department of Psychology, Baton Rouge, LA 70803. Offers biological psychology (MA, PhD); clinical psychology (MA, PhD); cognitive psychology (MA, PhD); developmental psychology (MA, PhD); industrial/organizational psychology (MA, PhD); school psychology (MA, PhD). PhD programs offered jointly with Southeastern Louisiana University. *Accreditation:* APA (one or more programs are accredited). *Faculty:* 26 full-time (10 women). *Students:* 96 full-time (68 women), 24 part-time (19 women); includes 7 Black or African American, non-Hispanic/Latino; 2 American Indian or Alaska Native, non-Hispanic/Latino; 1 Asian, non-Hispanic/Latino; 5 Hispanic/Latino, 2 international. Average age 27. 289 applicants, 11% accepted, 17 enrolled. In 2010, 16 master's, 11 doctorates awarded. Terminal master's awarded for partial completion of doctoral program. *Degree requirements:* For master's, thesis; for doctorate, thesis/dissertation, 1 year internship. *Entrance requirements:* For master's and doctorate, GRE General Test, minimum GPA of 3.0. Additional exam requirements/recommendations for international students: Required—TOEFL (minimum score 550 paper-based; 213 computer-based; 79 iBT) or IELTS (minimum score 6.5). *Application deadline:* For fall admission, 1/15 for domestic and international students. Applications are processed on a rolling basis. Application fee: $50 ($70 for international students). Electronic applications accepted. *Financial support:* In 2010–11, 115 students received support, including 5 fellowships (averaging $25,207 per year), 25 research assistantships with partial tuition reimbursements available (averaging $18,083 per year), 48 teaching assistantships with partial tuition reimbursements available (averaging $13,043 per year); career-related internships or fieldwork, Federal Work-Study, institutionally sponsored loans, scholarships/grants, health care benefits, and tuition waivers (full and partial) also available. Financial award applicants required to submit FAFSA. *Faculty research:* Clinical psychology, autism, anxiety, addition, neuropsychology, school psychology, cognitive psychology, experimental psychology. Total annual research expenditures: $1.3 million. *Unit head:* Dr. Robert Matthews, Chair, 225-578-8745, Fax: 225-578-4125, E-mail: psmath@lsu.edu. *Application contact:* Dr. Jason Hicks, Coordinator of Graduate Studies, 225-578-4109, Fax: 225-578-4125, E-mail: jhicks@lsu.edu.

Memorial University of Newfoundland, School of Graduate Studies, Interdisciplinary Program in Cognitive and Behavioral Ecology, St. John's, NL A1C 5S7, Canada. Offers M Sc, PhD. *Degree requirements:* For master's, thesis, public lecture; for doctorate, comprehensive exam, thesis/dissertation, oral defense of dissertation. *Entrance requirements:* For master's, honors degree (minimum 2nd class standing) in related field; for doctorate, master's degree. Electronic applications accepted. *Faculty research:* Seabird feeding ecology, marine mammal and seabird energetics, systems of fish, seabird/seal/fisheries interaction.

Northwestern University, The Graduate School, Judd A. and Marjorie Weinberg College of Arts and Sciences, Department of Psychology, Evanston, IL 60208. Offers brain, behavior and cognition (PhD); clinical psychology (PhD); cognitive psychology (PhD); personality (PhD); social psychology (PhD); JD/PhD. Admissions and degrees offered through The Graduate School. *Accreditation:* APA (one or more programs are accredited). Part-time programs available. *Degree requirements:* For doctorate, thesis/dissertation. *Entrance requirements:* For doctorate, GRE General Test, GRE Subject Test. Additional exam requirements/recommendations for international students: Required—TOEFL. Electronic applications accepted. *Faculty research:* Memory and higher order cognition, anxiety and depression, effectiveness of psychotherapy, social cognition, molecular basis of memory.

Northwestern University, The Graduate School and Northwestern University Feinberg School of Medicine, Program in Clinical Psychology, Evanston, IL 60208. Offers clinical psychology (PhD), including clinical neuropsychology, general clinical. PhD admissions and degree offered through The Graduate School. *Accreditation:* APA. *Degree requirements:* For doctorate, thesis/dissertation, clinical internship. *Entrance requirements:* For doctorate, GRE General Test, GRE Subject Test, minimum GPA of 3.2, course work in psychology. Additional exam requirements/recommendations for international students: Required—TOEFL. *Faculty research:* Cancer and cardiovascular risk reduction, evaluation of mental health services and policy, neuropsychological assessment, outcome of psychotherapy, cognitive therapy, pediatric and clinical child psychology.

Oregon Health & Science University, School of Medicine, Graduate Programs in Medicine, Department of Behavioral Neuroscience, Portland, OR 97239-3098. Offers PhD. *Faculty:* 14 full-time (4 women), 6 part-time/adjunct (3 women). *Students:* 32 full-time (19 women); includes 1 Black or African American, non-Hispanic/Latino; 1 Hispanic/Latino. Average age 27. 57 applicants, 14% accepted, 8 enrolled. In 2010, 4 doctorates awarded. Terminal master's awarded for partial completion of doctoral program. *Degree requirements:* For doctorate, comprehensive exam, thesis/dissertation, written exam. *Entrance requirements:* For doctorate, GRE General Test (minimum scores: 500 Verbal/600 Quantitative/4.5 Analytical), undergraduate coursework in biopsychology and other basic science areas. Additional exam requirements/recommendations for international students: Required—TOEFL. *Application deadline:* For fall admission, 12/1 for domestic students. Application fee: $65. Electronic applications accepted. *Financial support:* Health care benefits, tuition waivers (full), and stipends available. *Faculty research:* Neural basis of behavior, behavioral pharmacology, behavioral genetics, neuro-pharmacology and neuroendocrinology, biological basis of drug seeking and addiction. *Unit head:* Dr. Suzanne Mitchell, Program Director, 503-494-1650, E-mail: mitchesu@ohsu.edu. *Application contact:* Kris Thomason, Graduate Program Manager, 503-494-8464, E-mail: thomason@ohsu.edu.

Palo Alto University, PGSP-Stanford Psy D Consortium Program, Palo Alto, CA 94303-4232. Offers Psy D. Program offered jointly with Stanford University. *Accreditation:* APA. *Degree requirements:* For doctorate, thesis/dissertation. *Entrance requirements:* For doctorate, GRE, BA or MA in psychology or related area, minimum undergraduate GPA of 3.0, minimum graduate GPA of 3.3. Additional exam requirements/recommendations for international students: Required—TOEFL. Electronic applications accepted. *Faculty research:* Biopsychosocial research, neurobiology, psychopharmacology.

Penn State University Park, Graduate School, College of Health and Human Development, Department of Biobehavioral Health, State College, University Park, PA 16802-1503. Offers PhD.

Rutgers, The State University of New Jersey, Newark, Graduate School, Program in Integrative Neuroscience, Newark, NJ 07102. Offers PhD. Part-time programs available. *Faculty:* 18 full-time (4 women). *Students:* 24 full-time (12 women), 15 part-time (8 women); includes 6 Asian, non-Hispanic/Latino; 3 Hispanic/Latino. 60 applicants, 13% accepted, 7 enrolled. In 2010, 3 doctorates awarded. *Degree requirements:* For doctorate, thesis/dissertation. *Entrance requirements:* For doctorate, GRE, minimum GPA of 3.0. *Application deadline:* For fall admission, 2/1 priority date for domestic students. Applications are processed on a rolling basis. Application fee: $60. Electronic applications accepted. *Expenses:* Tuition, state resident: part-time $600 per credit. Tuition, nonresident: full-time $10,694. *Financial support:* In 2010–11, 21 teaching assistantships with full and partial tuition reimbursements (averaging $26,348 per year) were awarded. Financial award application deadline: 3/1. *Faculty research:* Systems neuroscience, cognitive neuroscience, molecular neuroscience, behavioral neuroscience. Total annual research expenditures: $3 million. *Unit head:* Dr. Ian Creese, Director, 973-353-1080 Ext. 3300, Fax: 973-353-1272, E-mail: creese@axon.rutgers.edu. *Application contact:* Dr. Ian Creese, Director, 973-353-1080 Ext. 3300, Fax: 973-353-1272, E-mail: creese@axon.rutgers.edu.

Rutgers, The State University of New Jersey, Newark, Graduate School, Program in Psychology, Newark, NJ 07102. Offers cognitive neuroscience (PhD); cognitive science (PhD); perception (PhD); psychobiology (PhD); social cognition (PhD). *Faculty:* 15 full-time (5 women), 6 part-time/adjunct (all women). *Students:* 23 full-time (19 women), 2 part-time (1 woman); includes 3 Black or African American, non-Hispanic/Latino; 1 Asian, non-Hispanic/Latino; 2 Hispanic/Latino. 48 applicants, 17% accepted, 6 enrolled. In 2010, 4 doctorates awarded. *Degree requirements:* For doctorate, comprehensive exam, thesis/dissertation. *Entrance requirements:* For doctorate, GRE General Test, GRE Subject Test, minimum undergraduate B average. *Application deadline:* For fall admission, 2/1 for domestic students; for spring admission, 11/1 for domestic students. Application fee: $60. Electronic applications accepted. *Expenses:* Tuition, state resident: part-time $600 per credit. Tuition, nonresident: full-time $10,694. *Financial support:* In 2010–11, 16 students received support, including 9 fellowships with full and partial tuition reimbursements available (averaging $18,000 per year), 8 teaching assistantships with full and partial tuition reimbursements available (averaging $23,112 per year); career-related internships or fieldwork, health care benefits, and minority scholarships also available. Financial award application deadline: 2/1. *Faculty research:* Visual perception (luminance, motion), neuroendocrine mechanisms in behavior (reproduction, pain), attachment theory, connectionist modeling of cognition. *Unit head:* Dr. Kenneth Kressel, Director, 973-353-5440 Ext. 232, Fax: 973-353-1171, E-mail: kkressel@andromeda.rutgers.edu. *Application contact:* Jason Hand, Director of Admissions, 973-353-5205, Fax: 973-353-1440.

Rutgers, The State University of New Jersey, New Brunswick, Graduate School-New Brunswick, Program in Psychology, Piscataway, NJ 08854-8097. Offers behavioral neuroscience (PhD); clinical psychology (PhD); cognitive psychology (PhD); interdisciplinary health psychology (PhD); social psychology (PhD). *Accreditation:* APA. *Degree requirements:* For doctorate, comprehensive exam, thesis/dissertation. *Entrance requirements:* For doctorate, GRE General Test, 3 letters of recommendation. Additional exam requirements/recommendations for international students: Required—TOEFL (minimum score 577 paper-based; 233 computer-based). Electronic applications accepted. *Expenses:* Tuition, state resident: full-time $7200; part-time $600 per credit. Tuition, nonresident: full-time $11,124; part-time $927 per credit. *Faculty research:* Learning and memory, behavioral ecology, hormones and behavior, psycho-pharmacology, anxiety disorders.

State University of New York at Binghamton, Graduate School, School of Arts and Sciences, Department of Psychology, Specialization in Behavioral Neuroscience, Binghamton, NY 13902-6000. Offers MA, PhD. *Students:* 18 full-time (12 women), 11 part-time (8 women); includes 3 Hispanic/Latino. Average age 26. 27 applicants, 37% accepted, 8 enrolled. In 2010, 2 doctorates awarded. *Degree requirements:* For master's, thesis; for doctorate, thesis/dissertation, departmental qualifying exam. *Entrance requirements:* For master's and doctorate, GRE General Test, GRE Subject Test. Additional exam requirements/recommendations for international students: Required—TOEFL (minimum score 550 paper-based; 213 computer-based; 80 iBT). *Application deadline:* For fall admission, 1/15 priority date for domestic and international students. Applications are processed on a rolling basis. Application fee: $60. Electronic applications accepted. *Financial support:* In 2010–11, 21 students received support, including 3 fellowships with full tuition reimbursements available (averaging $17,500 per year), 4 research assistantships with full tuition reimbursements available (averaging $17,500 per year), 12 teaching assistantships with full tuition reimbursements available (averaging $17,500 per year); career-related internships or fieldwork, Federal Work-Study, institutionally sponsored loans, scholarships/grants, health care benefits, tuition waivers (full and partial), and unspecified assistantships also available. Financial award application deadline: 2/15; financial award applicants required to submit FAFSA. *Unit head:* Dr. Lisa Savage, Graduate Coordinator, 607-777-4383, E-mail: lsavage@binghamton.edu. *Application contact:* Catherine Smith, Recruiting and Admissions Coordinator, 607-777-2151, Fax: 607-777-2501, E-mail: cmsmith@binghamton.edu.

Stony Brook University, State University of New York, Graduate School, College of Arts and Sciences, Department of Psychology, Program in Biopsychology, Stony Brook, NY 11794. Offers PhD. *Students:* 12 full-time (9 women); includes 1 Black or African American, non-Hispanic/Latino; 3 Asian, non-Hispanic/Latino, 4 international. Average age 28. 32 applicants, 9% accepted, 2 enrolled. In 2010, 5 doctorates awarded. *Degree requirements:* For doctorate, thesis/dissertation. *Entrance requirements:* For doctorate, GRE General Test, GRE Subject Test. Additional exam requirements/recommendations for international students: Required—TOEFL. *Application deadline:* For fall admission, 1/15 for domestic students. Application fee: $100. *Expenses:* Tuition, state resident: full-time $8370; part-time $349 per credit. Tuition, nonresident: full-time $13,780; part-time $574 per credit. Required fees: $994. *Unit head:* Dr. Daniel Klein, Head, 631-632-7855, E-mail: daniel.klein@stonybrook.edu. *Application contact:* Graduate Director, 631-632-7855, Fax: 631-632-7876.

Texas A&M University, College of Liberal Arts, Department of Psychology, College Station, TX 77843. Offers behavioral and cellular neuroscience (PhD); clinical psychology (PhD); cognitive psychology (PhD); developmental psychology (PhD); industrial/organizational psychology (PhD); social psychology (PhD). *Accreditation:* APA. *Faculty:* 39. *Students:* 91 full-time (57 women), 14 part-time (11 women); includes 7 Black or African American, non-Hispanic/Latino; 8 Asian, non-Hispanic/Latino; 17 Hispanic/Latino, 7 international. In 2010, 12 doctorates awarded. *Degree requirements:* For doctorate, comprehensive exam (for some programs), thesis/dissertation. *Entrance requirements:* For doctorate, GRE General Test. Additional exam requirements/recommendations for international students: Required—TOEFL. *Application deadline:* For fall admission, 1/5 for domestic and international students. Application fee: $50 ($75 for international students). Electronic applications accepted. *Financial support:* Fellowships with partial tuition reimbursements, research assistantships with partial tuition reimbursements, teaching assistantships with partial tuition reimbursements, career-related internships or fieldwork, institutionally sponsored loans, health care benefits, and unspecified assistantships available. Financial award application deadline: 1/5; financial award applicants required to submit FAFSA. *Unit head:* Ludy T. Benjamin, Head, 979-845-2540, Fax: 979-845-4727, E-mail: lbenjamin@tamu.edu. *Application contact:* Julie Austin, Graduate Admissions Supervisor, 979-458-1710, Fax: 979-845-4727, E-mail: gradadv@psyc.tamu.edu.

University at Albany, State University of New York, College of Arts and Sciences, Department of Psychology, Albany, NY 12222-0001. Offers autism (Certificate); biopsychology (PhD); clinical psychology (PhD); general/experimental psychology (PhD); industrial/organizational psychology (PhD); psychology (MA); social/personality psychology (PhD). *Accreditation:* APA (one or more programs are accredited). *Degree requirements:* For doctorate, thesis/dissertation. *Entrance requirements:* For doctorate, GRE General Test, GRE Subject Test. Additional exam requirements/recommendations for international students: Required—TOEFL (minimum score 550 paper-based; 213 computer-based). Electronic applications accepted.

The University of British Columbia, Faculty of Arts and Faculty of Graduate Studies, Department of Psychology, Vancouver, BC V6T 1Z4, Canada. Offers behavioral neuroscience (MA, PhD); clinical psychology (MA, PhD); cognitive science (MA, PhD); developmental psychology (MA, PhD); health psychology (MA, PhD); quantitative methods (MA, PhD); social/personality psychology (MA, PhD). *Accreditation:* APA (one or more programs are accredited). Terminal master's awarded for partial completion of doctoral program. *Degree requirements:* For master's, thesis; for doctorate, comprehensive exam, thesis/dissertation. *Entrance requirements:* For master's and doctorate, GRE General Test. Additional exam requirements/recommendations for international students: Required—TOEFL (minimum score 550 paper-based; 230 computer-based; 80 iBT). Electronic applications accepted. Tuition charges are reported in Canadian dollars. *Expenses:* Tuition, area resident: Full-time $4179 Canadian dollars. International tuition: $7344 Canadian dollars full-time. *Faculty research:* Clinical, developmental, social/personality, cognition, behavioral neuroscience.

University of Connecticut, Graduate School, College of Liberal Arts and Sciences, Department of Psychology, Storrs, CT 06269. Offers behavioral neuroscience (PhD); biopsychology (PhD); clinical psychology (MA, PhD); cognition and instruction (PhD); developmental psychology (MA, PhD); ecological psychology (PhD); experimental psychology (PhD); general psychology (MA, PhD); health psychology (Graduate Certificate); industrial/organizational psychology (PhD); language and cognition (PhD); neuroscience (PhD); occupational health psychology (Graduate Certificate); social psychology (MA, PhD). *Accreditation:* APA. Terminal master's awarded for partial completion of doctoral program. *Degree requirements:* For master's, comprehensive exam; for doctorate, thesis/dissertation. *Entrance requirements:* For master's and doctorate, GRE General Test, GRE Subject Test. Additional exam requirements/recommendations for international students: Required—TOEFL (minimum score 550 paper-based; 213 computer-based). Electronic applications accepted.

University of Michigan, Rackham Graduate School, College of Literature, Science, and the Arts, Department of Psychology, Ann Arbor, MI 48109. Offers biopsychology (PhD); clinical psychology (PhD); cognition and perception (PhD); developmental psychology (PhD); personality and social contexts (PhD); social psychology (PhD). *Accreditation:* APA. *Faculty:* 83 full-time (39 women), 30 part-time/adjunct (14 women). *Students:* 132 full-time (92 women); includes 13 Black or African American, non-Hispanic/Latino; 2 American Indian or Alaska Native, non-Hispanic/Latino; 18 Asian, non-Hispanic/Latino; 7 Hispanic/Latino; 2 Two or more races, non-Hispanic/Latino, 20 international. Average age 27. 608 applicants, 6% accepted; 24 enrolled. In 2010, 28 doctorates awarded. *Degree requirements:* For doctorate, comprehensive exam, thesis/dissertation, oral defense of dissertation, preliminary exam. *Entrance requirements:* For doctorate, GRE General Test. Additional exam requirements/recommendations for international students: Required—TOEFL. *Application deadline:* For fall admission, 12/1 for domestic and international students. Application fee: $65 ($75 for international students). Electronic applications accepted. *Expenses:* Tuition, state resident: full-time $17,784; part-time $1116 per credit hour. Tuition, nonresident: full-time $35,944; part-time $2125 per credit hour. International tuition: $35,994 full-time. Required fees: $95 per semester. Tuition and fees vary according to course load, degree level and program. *Financial support:* In 2010–11, 118 students received support, including 55 fellowships with full tuition reimbursements available (averaging $20,900 per year), 15 research assistantships with full tuition reimbursements available (averaging $25,950 per year), 52 teaching assistantships with full tuition reimbursements available (averaging $22,670 per year); career-related internships or fieldwork also available. Financial award application deadline: 4/15. Total annual research expenditures: $7.4

Biopsychology

University of Michigan (continued)
million. *Unit head:* Prof. Theresa Lee, Chair, 734-764-7429. *Application contact:* Laurie Brannan, Psychology Student Academic Affairs, 731-764-2580, Fax: 734-615-7584, E-mail: psych.saa@umich.edu.

University of Minnesota, Twin Cities Campus, Graduate School, College of Liberal Arts, Department of Psychology, Program in Cognitive and Biological Psychology, Minneapolis, MN 55455-0213. Offers PhD. *Degree requirements:* For doctorate, comprehensive exam, thesis/dissertation. *Entrance requirements:* For doctorate, GRE General Test, GRE Subject Test (recommended), 12 credits of upper-level psychology courses, including a course in statistics or psychological measurement. Additional exam requirements/recommendations for international students: Required—TOEFL (minimum score 550 paper-based; 213 computer-based; 79 iBT).

University of Nebraska at Omaha, Graduate Studies, College of Arts and Sciences, Department of Psychology, Omaha, NE 68182. Offers developmental psychology (PhD); industrial/organizational psychology (MS, PhD); psychobiology (PhD); psychology (MA); school psychology (MS, Ed S). Part-time programs available. *Faculty:* 18 full-time (8 women). *Students:* 50 full-time (38 women), 41 part-time (32 women); includes 9 minority (2 Black or African American, non-Hispanic/Latino; 1 American Indian or Alaska Native, non-Hispanic/Latino; 1 Asian, non-Hispanic/Latino; 5 Hispanic/Latino), 2 international. Average age 26. 92 applicants, 39% accepted, 34 enrolled. In 2010, 17 master's, 2 doctorates, 6 other advanced degrees awarded. *Degree requirements:* For master's, comprehensive exam, thesis (for some programs). *Entrance requirements:* For master's, GRE General Test, GRE Subject Test, previous course work in psychology, including statistics and a laboratory course; minimum GPA of 3.0, 3 letters of recommendation; for doctorate, GRE General Test. Additional exam requirements/recommendations for international students: Required—TOEFL (minimum score 500 paper-based; 173 computer-based; 61 iBT). *Application deadline:* For fall admission, 1/5 for domestic students. Application fee: $45. Electronic applications accepted. *Financial support:* In 2010–11, 66 students received support; fellowships, research assistantships with tuition reimbursements available, teaching assistantships with tuition reimbursements available, career-related internships or fieldwork, Federal Work-Study, institutionally sponsored loans, scholarships/grants, tuition waivers (partial), and unspecified assistantships available. Support available to part-time students. Financial award application deadline: 3/1; financial award applicants required to submit FAFSA. *Unit head:* Dr. Brigette Ryalls, Chairperson, 402-554-2592. *Application contact:* Dr. Joseph Brown, Student Contact, 402-554-2592.

University of Nebraska–Lincoln, Graduate College, College of Arts and Sciences, Department of Psychology, Lincoln, NE 68588. Offers biopsychology (PhD); clinical psychology (PhD); cognitive psychology (PhD); developmental psychology (PhD); psychology (MA); social/personality psychology (PhD); JD/MA; JD/PhD. *Accreditation:* APA (one or more programs are accredited). *Degree requirements:* For master's, thesis optional; for doctorate, comprehensive exam, thesis/dissertation. *Entrance requirements:* For master's and doctorate, GRE General Test. Additional exam requirements/recommendations for international students: Required—TOEFL (minimum score 550 paper-based; 213 computer-based). Electronic applications accepted. *Faculty research:* Law and psychology, rural mental health, chronic mental illness, neuropsychology, child clinical psychology.

University of Oklahoma Health Sciences Center, College of Medicine and Graduate College, Graduate Programs in Medicine, Department of Psychiatry and Behavioral Sciences, Oklahoma City, OK 73190. Offers biological psychology (MS, PhD). *Degree requirements:* For master's, thesis; for doctorate, thesis/dissertation. *Entrance requirements:* For doctorate, GRE General Test, 3 letters of recommendation. Additional exam requirements/recommendations for international students: Required—TOEFL. *Faculty research:* Behavioral neuroscience, human neuropsychology, psychophysiology, behavioral medicine, health psychology.

University of Oregon, Graduate School, College of Arts and Sciences, Department of Psychology, Eugene, OR 97403. Offers clinical psychology (PhD); cognitive psychology (MA, MS, PhD); developmental psychology (MA, MS, PhD); physiological psychology (MA, MS, PhD); psychology (MA, MS, PhD); social/personality psychology (MA, MS, PhD). *Accreditation:* APA (one or more programs are accredited). Terminal master's awarded for partial completion of doctoral program. *Degree requirements:* For doctorate, thesis/dissertation. *Entrance requirements:* For master's, GRE General Test, minimum GPA of 3.0; for doctorate, GRE General Test. Additional exam requirements/recommendations for international students: Required—TOEFL.

The University of Texas at Austin, Graduate School, The Institute for Neuroscience, Austin, TX 78712-1111. Offers PhD, MD/PhD. Terminal master's awarded for partial completion of doctoral program. *Degree requirements:* For doctorate, thesis/dissertation. *Entrance requirements:* For doctorate, GRE. Electronic applications accepted. *Faculty research:* Cellular/molecular biology, neurobiology, pharmacology, behavioral neuroscience.

University of Windsor, Faculty of Graduate Studies, Faculty of Arts and Social Sciences, Department of Psychology, Windsor, ON N9B 3P4, Canada. Offers adult clinical (MA, PhD); applied social psychology (MA, PhD); child clinical (MA, PhD); clinical neuropsychology (MA, PhD). *Accreditation:* APA (one or more programs are accredited). *Degree requirements:* For master's, thesis; for doctorate, comprehensive exam, thesis/dissertation. *Entrance requirements:* For master's, GRE General Test, GRE Subject Test in psychology, minimum B average; for doctorate, GRE General Test, GRE Subject Test in psychology, master's degree. Additional exam requirements/recommendations for international students: Required—TOEFL (minimum score 600 paper-based; 250 computer-based). Electronic applications accepted. *Faculty research:* Gambling, suicidology, emotional competence, psychotherapy and trauma.

University of Wisconsin–Madison, Graduate School, College of Letters and Science, Department of Psychology, Program in Biology of Brain and Behavior, Madison, WI 53706-1380. Offers PhD. *Degree requirements:* For doctorate, comprehensive exam, thesis/dissertation. *Entrance requirements:* For doctorate, GRE General Test, minimum undergraduate GPA of 3.0. Additional exam requirements/recommendations for international students: Required—TOEFL. Electronic applications accepted. *Expenses:* Tuition, state resident: full-time $9887; part-time $617.96 per credit. Tuition, nonresident: full-time $24,054; part-time $1503.40 per credit. Required fees: $67.63 per credit. Tuition and fees vary according to reciprocity agreements.

Virginia Commonwealth University, Graduate School, College of Humanities and Sciences, Department of Psychology, Program in General Psychology, Richmond, VA 23284-9005. Offers biopsychology (PhD); developmental psychology (PhD); social psychology (PhD). *Students:* 22 full-time (16 women), 9 part-time (4 women); includes 6 minority (4 Black or African American, non-Hispanic/Latino; 1 Asian, non-Hispanic/Latino; 1 Hispanic/Latino), 1 international. 68 applicants, 6% accepted, 1 enrolled. In 2010, 3 doctorates awarded. *Degree requirements:* For doctorate, thesis/dissertation. *Entrance requirements:* For doctorate, GRE General Test. Additional exam requirements/recommendations for international students: Required—TOEFL (minimum score 600 paper-based; 250 computer-based; 100 iBT); Recommended—IELTS (minimum score 6.5). *Application deadline:* For fall admission, 12/15 for domestic students. Application fee: $50. Electronic applications accepted. *Expenses:* Tuition, state resident: full-time $4308; part-time $479 per credit hour. Tuition, nonresident: full-time $8942; part-time $994 per credit hour. Required fees: $2000; $85 per credit hour. Tuition and fees vary according to course level, course load, degree level, campus/location and program. *Financial support:* Fellowships, research assistantships, teaching assistantships, Federal Work-Study, institutionally sponsored loans, and scholarships/grants available. Support available to part-time students. *Faculty research:* Biopsychology, developmental and social psychology. *Unit head:* Dr. Michael Southam-Gerow, Director, Graduate Programs in Psychology, 804-828-1193, Fax: 804-828-2237, E-mail: masouthamger@vcu.edu. *Application contact:* Dr. Joseph Porter, Director, Biopsychology Division, 804-828-0096, Fax: 804-828-2237, E-mail: jporter@vcu.edu.

Wayne State University, School of Medicine, Department of Psychiatry and Behavioral Neurosciences, Detroit, MI 48202. Offers psychiatry (MS); translational neuroscience (PhD). *Faculty:* 1 full-time (0 women). *Students:* 5 full-time (2 women), 2 international. Average age 28. 11 applicants, 27% accepted, 2 enrolled. *Expenses:* Tuition, state resident: full-time $7662; part-time $478.85 per credit hour. Tuition, nonresident: full-time $16,920; part-time $1057.55 per credit hour. Required fees: $571; $35.70 per credit hour. $188.05 per semester. Tuition and fees vary according to course load and program. *Financial support:* In 2010–11, 1 fellowship (averaging $25,799 per year), 4 research assistantships with tuition reimbursements (averaging $23,975 per year) were awarded. *Faculty research:* Substance abuse, brain imaging, schizophrenia, child psychopathy, child development, neurobiology of monoamine systems. *Unit head:* Manuel Tancer, Chair, 313-577-1673, E-mail: aa2656@wayne.edu. *Application contact:* Dr. Michael J. Bannon, Director, 313-577-4271, Fax: 313-993-4269, E-mail: mbannon@med.wayne.edu.

Neurobiology

Albert Einstein College of Medicine, Graduate Division of Biomedical Sciences, Department of Neuroscience, Bronx, NY 10461. Offers PhD, MD/PhD. *Degree requirements:* For doctorate, thesis/dissertation. *Entrance requirements:* For doctorate, GRE General Test. Additional exam requirements/recommendations for international students: Required—TOEFL. *Faculty research:* Structure-function relations at chemical and electrical synapses, mechanisms of electrogenesis, analysis of neuronal subsystems.

Brandeis University, Graduate School of Arts and Sciences, Program in Molecular and Cell Biology, Waltham, MA 02454-9110. Offers genetics (PhD); microbiology (PhD); molecular and cell biology (MS, PhD); molecular biology (PhD); neurobiology (PhD). *Faculty:* 30 full-time (13 women), 1 (woman) part-time/adjunct. *Students:* 55 full-time (31 women); includes 1 Black or African American, non-Hispanic/Latino; 1 American Indian or Alaska Native, non-Hispanic/Latino; 1 Asian, non-Hispanic/Latino; 2 Hispanic/Latino, 12 international. 138 applicants, 32% accepted, 17 enrolled. In 2010, 3 master's, 3 doctorates awarded. Terminal master's awarded for partial completion of doctoral program. *Degree requirements:* For master's, thesis optional, research project; for doctorate, comprehensive exam, thesis/dissertation, teaching assistant experience. *Entrance requirements:* For master's and doctorate, GRE General Test, official transcript(s), resume, 3 letters of recommendation, statement of purpose. Additional exam requirements/recommendations for international students: Required—TOEFL (minimum score 600 paper-based; 250 computer-based; 100 iBT); Recommended—IELTS (minimum score 7). *Application deadline:* For fall admission, 1/15 priority date for domestic students. Applications are processed on a rolling basis. Application fee: $75. Electronic applications accepted. *Financial support:* In 2010–11, 41 students received support, including 13 fellowships with full tuition reimbursements available (averaging $27,500 per year), 27 research assistantships with full tuition reimbursements available (averaging $27,500 per year), 1 teaching assistantship with partial tuition reimbursement available (averaging $3,200 per year); scholarships/grants, traineeships, health care benefits, and tuition waivers (full and partial) also available. Financial award application deadline: 4/15; financial award applicants required to submit FAFSA. *Faculty research:* Molecular biology, cell biology, biology, structural biology, immunology, developmental biology, neurobiology, DNA, RNA. *Unit head:* Dr. Piali Sengupta, Chair, 781-736-2686, Fax: 781-736-3107, E-mail: piali@brandeis.edu. *Application contact:* Marcia Cabral, Department Administrator, 781-736-3100, Fax: 781-736-3107, E-mail: cabral@brandeis.edu.

California Institute of Technology, Division of Biology, Program in Neurobiology, Pasadena, CA 91125-0001. Offers PhD. *Degree requirements:* For doctorate, thesis/dissertation, qualifying exam. *Entrance requirements:* For doctorate, GRE General Test.

Carnegie Mellon University, Mellon College of Science, Department of Biological Sciences, Pittsburgh, PA 15213-3891. Offers biochemistry (PhD); biophysics (PhD); cell biology (PhD); computational biology (MS, PhD); developmental biology (PhD); genetics (PhD); molecular biology (PhD); neuroscience (PhD). *Degree requirements:* For doctorate, comprehensive exam, thesis/dissertation. *Entrance requirements:* For doctorate, GRE General Test, GRE Subject Test, interview. Electronic applications accepted. *Faculty research:* Genetic structure, function, and regulation; protein structure and function; biological membranes; biological spectroscopy.

Case Western Reserve University, School of Medicine and School of Graduate Studies, Graduate Programs in Medicine, Department of Neurosciences, Cleveland, OH 44106. Offers neurobiology (PhD); neuroscience (PhD); MD/PhD. *Degree requirements:* For doctorate, thesis/dissertation. *Entrance requirements:* For doctorate, GRE General Test, 3 letters of recommendation. Additional exam requirements/recommendations for international students: Required—TOEFL. Electronic applications accepted. *Faculty research:* Neurotropic factors, synapse formation, regeneration, determination of cell fate, cellular neuroscience.

Columbia University, College of Physicians and Surgeons, Program in Neurobiology and Behavior, New York, NY 10032. Offers PhD. Only candidates for the PhD are admitted. *Degree requirements:* For doctorate, thesis/dissertation. *Entrance requirements:* For doctorate, GRE General Test. Additional exam requirements/recommendations for international students: Required—TOEFL. *Expenses:* Contact institution. *Faculty research:* Cellular and molecular mechanisms of neural development, neuropathology, neuropharmacology.

Cornell University, Graduate School, Graduate Fields of Agriculture and Life Sciences, Field of Neurobiology and Behavior, Ithaca, NY 14853-0001. Offers behavioral biology (PhD), including behavioral ecology, chemical ecology, ethology, neuroethology, sociobiology; neurobiology (PhD), including cellular and molecular neurobiology, neuroanatomy, neurochemistry, neuropharmacology, neurophysiology, sensory physiology. *Faculty:* 46 full-time (8 women). *Students:* 31 full-time (15 women); includes 1 Black or African American, non-Hispanic/Latino; 1 Asian, non-Hispanic/Latino; 1 Hispanic/Latino, 2 international. Average age 27. 52 applicants, 27% accepted, 5 enrolled. In 2010, 7 doctorates awarded. *Degree requirements:* For doctorate, comprehensive exam, thesis/dissertation, 1 year of teaching experience, seminar presentation. *Entrance requirements:* For doctorate, GRE General Test, GRE Subject Test (biology), 3 letters of recommendation. Additional exam requirements/recommendations for international students: Required—TOEFL (minimum score 550 paper-based; 213 computer-based; 77 iBT). *Application deadline:* For fall admission, 12/1 for domestic students. Application fee: $70. Electronic applications accepted. *Expenses:* Tuition: Full-time $29,500. Required fees: $76. Tuition and fees vary according to degree level and program. *Financial support:* In 2010–11, 11 fellowships with full tuition reimbursements, 8 research assistantships with full tuition reimbursements, 10 teaching assistantships with full tuition reimbursements were awarded; institutionally sponsored loans, scholarships/grants, health care benefits, tuition waivers (full and partial), and unspecified assistantships also available. Financial award applicants required to submit FAFSA. *Faculty research:* Cellular neurobiology and neuropharmacology, integrative neurobiology, social behavior, chemical ecology, neuroethology. *Unit head:* Director of Graduate Studies, 607-254-4340, Fax: 607-254-4340. *Application contact:* Graduate Field Assistant, 607-254-4340, Fax: 607-254-4340, E-mail: nbb_field@cornell.edu.

Dalhousie University, Faculty of Graduate Studies and Faculty of Medicine, Graduate Programs in Medicine, Department of Anatomy and Neurobiology, Halifax, NS B3H 4R2, Canada. Offers M Sc, PhD. *Degree requirements:* For master's, thesis; for doctorate, thesis/dissertation. *Entrance requirements:* For master's and doctorate, GRE (recommended), minimum A- average. Additional exam requirements/recommendations for international students: Required—TOEFL, IELTS, 1 of the following 5 approved tests: TOELF, IELTS, CANTEST, CAEL, Michigan English Language Assessment Battery. Electronic applications accepted. *Faculty research:* Neuroscience histology, cell biology, neuroendocrinology, evolutionary biology.

Duke University, Graduate School, Department of Biological Anthropology and Anatomy, Durham, NC 27710. Offers cellular and molecular biology (PhD); gross anatomy and physical anthropology (PhD), including comparative morphology of human and non-human primates, primate social behavior, vertebrate paleontology; neuroanatomy (PhD). *Faculty:* 9 full-time. *Students:* 13 full-time (9 women); includes 1 Black or African American, non-Hispanic/Latino; 2 Hispanic/Latino, 1 international. 54 applicants, 9% accepted, 2 enrolled. In 2010, 2 doctorates awarded. *Degree requirements:* For doctorate, one foreign language, thesis/dissertation. *Entrance requirements:* For doctorate, GRE General Test. Additional exam requirements/recommendations for international students: Required—TOEFL (minimum score 550 paper-based; 213 computer-based; 83 iBT), IELTS (minimum score 7). *Application deadline:* For fall admission, 12/8 priority date for domestic and international students. Application fee: $75. Electronic applications accepted. *Financial support:* Fellowships, teaching assistantships, Federal Work-Study available. Financial award application deadline: 12/31. *Unit head:* Daniel Schmitt, Director of Graduate Studies, 919-684-4124, Fax: 919-684-8542, E-mail: mlsquire@duke.edu. *Application contact:* Elizabeth Hutton, Director of Admissions, 919-684-3913, Fax: 919-684-2277, E-mail: grad-admissions@duke.edu.

Duke University, Graduate School, Department of Neurobiology, Durham, NC 27708-0586. Offers PhD. *Faculty:* 62 full-time. *Students:* 49 full-time (22 women); includes 6 Asian, non-Hispanic/Latino; 4 Hispanic/Latino, 14 international. 122 applicants, 9% accepted, 6 enrolled. In 2010, 10 doctorates awarded. *Degree requirements:* For doctorate, variable foreign language requirement, thesis/dissertation. *Entrance requirements:* For doctorate, GRE General Test. Additional exam requirements/recommendations for international students: Required—TOEFL (minimum score 550 paper-based; 213 computer-based; 83 iBT), IELTS (minimum score 7). *Application deadline:* For fall admission, 12/8 priority date for domestic and international students. Application fee: $75. Electronic applications accepted. *Financial support:* Fellowships, research assistantships, teaching assistantships, Federal Work-Study available. Financial award application deadline: 12/8. *Unit head:* Richard Mooney, Director, 919-681-4243, Fax: 919-684-4431, E-mail: beth.peloquin@duke.edu. *Application contact:* Elizabeth Hutton, Director of Admissions, 919-684-3913, Fax: 919-684-2277, E-mail: grad-admissions@duke.edu.

Georgia State University, College of Arts and Sciences, Department of Biology, Program in Neurobiology and Behavior, Atlanta, GA 30302-3083. Offers MS, PhD. Part-time programs available. Terminal master's awarded for partial completion of doctoral program. *Degree requirements:* For master's, thesis or alternative; for doctorate, thesis/dissertation, exam. *Entrance requirements:* For master's and doctorate, GRE General Test. Additional exam requirements/recommendations for international students: Required—TOEFL. Electronic applications accepted.

Harvard University, Graduate School of Arts and Sciences, Program in Neuroscience, Boston, MA 02115. Offers neurobiology (PhD). *Degree requirements:* For doctorate, thesis/dissertation, qualifying exam. *Entrance requirements:* For doctorate, GRE General Test, GRE Subject Test. Additional exam requirements/recommendations for international students: Required—TOEFL. *Expenses:* Tuition: Full-time $34,976. Required fees: $1166. Full-time tuition and fees vary according to program. *Faculty research:* Relationship between diseases of the nervous system and basic science.

Illinois State University, Graduate School, College of Arts and Sciences, Department of Biological Sciences, Normal, IL 61790-2200. Offers animal behavior (MS); bacteriology (MS); biochemistry (MS); biological sciences (MS); biology (PhD); biophysics (MS); biotechnology (MS); botany (MS, PhD); cell biology (MS); conservation biology (MS); developmental biology (MS); ecology (MS, PhD); entomology (MS); evolutionary biology (MS); genetics (MS, PhD); immunology (MS); microbiology (MS, PhD); molecular biology (MS); molecular genetics (MS); neurobiology (MS); neuroscience (MS); parasitology (MS); physiology (MS, PhD); plant biology (MS); plant molecular biology (MS); plant sciences (MS); structural biology (MS); zoology (MS, PhD). Part-time programs available. *Degree requirements:* For master's, thesis or alternative; for doctorate, variable foreign language requirement, thesis/dissertation, 2 terms of residency. *Entrance requirements:* For master's, GRE General Test, minimum GPA of 2.6 in last 60 hours of course work; for doctorate, GRE General Test. *Faculty research:* Redoc balance and drug development in schistosoma mansoni, control of the growth of listeria monocytogenes at low temperature, regulation of cell expansion and microtubule function by SPRI, CRUI: physiology and fitness consequences of different life history phenotypes.

Louisiana State University Health Sciences Center, School of Graduate Studies in New Orleans, Department of Cell Biology and Anatomy, New Orleans, LA 70112-2223. Offers cell biology and anatomy (MS, PhD), including cell biology, developmental biology, neurobiology and anatomy; MD/PhD. *Degree requirements:* For master's, comprehensive exam, thesis; for doctorate, comprehensive exam, thesis/dissertation. *Entrance requirements:* For master's and doctorate, GRE General Test, GRE Subject Test, minimum undergraduate GPA of 3.0. Additional exam requirements/recommendations for international students: Required—TOEFL. *Faculty research:* Visual system organization, neural development, plasticity of sensory systems, information processing through the nervous system, visuomotor integration.

Loyola University Chicago, Graduate School, Department of Cell Biology, Neurobiology and Anatomy, Chicago, IL 60660. Offers MS, PhD. Part-time programs available. *Faculty:* 16 full-time (6 women), 9 part-time/adjunct (4 women). *Students:* 21 full-time (12 women), 2 part-time (1 woman); includes 3 minority (2 Hispanic/Latino; 1 Two or more races, non-Hispanic/Latino), 1 international. Average age 26. 25 applicants, 24% accepted, 6 enrolled. In 2010, 3 master's, 4 doctorates awarded. Terminal master's awarded for partial completion of doctoral program. *Degree requirements:* For master's, thesis; for doctorate, comprehensive exam, thesis/dissertation. *Entrance requirements:* For master's, GRE General Test, minimum GPA of 3.0; for doctorate, GRE General Test, GRE Subject Test (biology), minimum GPA of 3.0. Additional exam requirements/recommendations for international students: Required—TOEFL (minimum score 600 paper-based; 250 computer-based). *Application deadline:* For fall admission, 5/1 priority date for domestic and international students. Applications are processed on a rolling basis. Application fee: $50. Electronic applications accepted. *Expenses:* Tuition: Full-time $14,940; part-time $830 per credit hour. Required fees: $87 per semester. Part-time tuition and fees vary according to course load and program. *Financial support:* In 2010–11, 5 fellowships with full tuition reimbursements (averaging $23,000 per year), 5 research assistantships with full tuition reimbursements (averaging $23,000 per year) were awarded; Federal Work-Study and unspecified assistantships also available. Financial award application deadline: 5/1; financial award applicants required to submit FAFSA. *Faculty research:* Brain steroids, immunology, neuroregeneration, cytokines. Total annual research expenditures: $1 million. *Unit head:* Dr. Phong Le, Head, 708-216-3603, Fax: 708-216-3913, E-mail: ple@lumc.edu. *Application contact:* Ginny Hayes, Graduate Program Secretary, 708-216-3353, Fax: 708-216-3913, E-mail: vhayes@lumc.edu.

Massachusetts Institute of Technology, School of Science, Department of Biology, Cambridge, MA 02139-4307. Offers biochemistry (PhD); biological oceanography (PhD); biology (PhD); biophysical chemistry and molecular structure (PhD); cell biology (PhD); computational and systems biology (PhD); developmental biology (PhD); genetics (PhD); immunology (PhD); microbiology (PhD); molecular biology (PhD); neurobiology (PhD). *Faculty:* 56 full-time (14 women). *Students:* 251 full-time (135 women); includes 74 minority (4 Black or African American, non-Hispanic/Latino; 1 American Indian or Alaska Native, non-Hispanic/Latino; 29 Asian, non-Hispanic/Latino; 33 Hispanic/Latino; 7 Two or more races, non-Hispanic/Latino), 29 international. Average age 26. 652 applicants, 18% accepted, 58 enrolled. In 2010, 41 doctorates awarded. *Degree requirements:* For doctorate, comprehensive exam, thesis/dissertation. *Entrance requirements:* For doctorate, GRE General Test. Additional exam requirements/recommendations for international students: Required—TOEFL (minimum score 577 paper-based; 233 computer-based), IELTS (minimum score 6.5). *Application deadline:* For fall admission, 12/1 for domestic and international students. Application fee: $75. Electronic applications accepted. *Expenses:* Tuition: Full-time $38,940; part-time $605 per unit. Required fees: $272. *Financial support:* In 2010–11, 215 students received support, including 115 fellowships with tuition reimbursements available (averaging $33,090 per year), 132 research assistantships with tuition reimbursements available (averaging $31,846 per year); teaching assistantships with tuition reimbursements available, Federal Work-Study, institutionally sponsored loans, scholarships/grants, traineeships, health care benefits, and unspecified assistantships also available. *Faculty research:* DNA recombination, replication and repair; transcription and gene regulation; signal transduction; cell cycle; neuronal cell fate. Total annual research expenditures: $60.6 million. *Unit head:* Prof. Chris Kaiser, Head, 617-253-4701, E-mail: mitbio@mit.edu. *Application contact:* Biology Education Office, 617-253-3717, Fax: 617-258-9329, E-mail: gradbio@mit.edu.

New York University, Graduate School of Arts and Science, Department of Biology, New York, NY 10012-1019. Offers biology (PhD); biomedical journalism (MS); cancer and molecular biology (PhD); computational biology (PhD); computers in biological research (MS); developmental genetics (PhD); general biology (MS); immunology and microbiology (PhD); molecular genetics (PhD); neurobiology (PhD); oral biology (MS); plant biology (PhD); recombinant DNA technology (MS); MS/MBA. Part-time programs available. *Faculty:* 24 full-time (5 women). *Students:* 155 full-time (89 women), 38 part-time (24 women); includes 29 Asian, non-Hispanic/Latino; 7 Hispanic/Latino, 88 international. Average age 27. 324 applicants, 69% accepted, 63 enrolled. In 2010, 55 master's, 4 doctorates awarded. Terminal master's awarded for partial completion of doctoral program. *Degree requirements:* For master's, thesis or alternative, qualifying paper; for doctorate, comprehensive exam, thesis/dissertation. *Entrance requirements:* For master's, GRE General Test; for doctorate, GRE General Test, GRE Subject Test. Additional exam requirements/recommendations for international students: Required—TOEFL. *Application deadline:* For fall admission, 12/15 priority date for domestic students. Application fee: $90. *Financial support:* Fellowships with tuition reimbursements, research assistantships with tuition reimbursements, teaching assistantships with tuition reimbursements, career-related internships or fieldwork, Federal Work-Study, institutionally sponsored loans, scholarships/grants, health care benefits, and unspecified assistantships available. Financial award application deadline: 12/15; financial award applicants required to submit FAFSA. *Faculty research:* Genomics, molecular and cell biology, development and molecular genetics, molecular evolution of plants and animals. *Unit head:* Gloria Coruzzi, Chair, 212-998-8200, Fax: 212-995-4015, E-mail: biology@nyu.edu. *Application contact:* Justin Blau, Director of Graduate Studies, 212-998-8200, Fax: 212-995-4015, E-mail: biology@nyu.edu.

Northwestern University, The Graduate School, Judd A. and Marjorie Weinberg College of Arts and Sciences, Department of Neurobiology and Physiology, Evanston, IL 60208. Offers MS. Admissions and degrees offered through The Graduate School. Part-time programs available. *Degree requirements:* For master's, thesis. *Entrance requirements:* For master's, GRE General Test and MCAT (strongly recommended). Additional exam requirements/recommendations for international students: Required—TOEFL. Electronic applications accepted. *Expenses:* Contact institution. *Faculty research:* Sensory neurobiology and neuroendocrinology, reproductive biology, vision physiology and psychophysics, cell and developmental biology.

Northwestern University, Northwestern University Feinberg School of Medicine and Interdepartmental Programs, Integrated Graduate Programs in the Life Sciences, Chicago, IL 60611. Offers cancer biology (PhD); cell biology (PhD); developmental biology (PhD); evolutionary biology (PhD); immunology and microbial pathogenesis (PhD); molecular biology and genetics (PhD); neurobiology (PhD); pharmacology and toxicology (PhD); structural biology and biochemistry (PhD). *Degree requirements:* For doctorate, comprehensive exam, thesis/dissertation, written and oral qualifying exams. *Entrance requirements:* For doctorate, GRE General Test. Additional exam requirements/recommendations for international students: Required—TOEFL (minimum score 600 paper-based; 250 computer-based). Electronic applications accepted.

Purdue University, Graduate School, College of Science, Department of Biological Sciences, West Lafayette, IN 47907. Offers biochemistry (PhD); biophysics (PhD); cell and developmental biology (PhD); ecology, evolutionary and population biology (MS, PhD), including ecology, evolutionary biology, population biology; genetics (MS, PhD); microbiology (MS, PhD); molecular biology (PhD); neurobiology (MS, PhD); plant physiology (PhD). Terminal master's awarded for partial completion of doctoral program. *Degree requirements:* For master's, thesis (for some programs); for doctorate, thesis/dissertation, seminars, teaching experience. *Entrance requirements:* For master's and doctorate, GRE General Test. Additional exam requirements/recommendations for international students: Required—TOEFL. Electronic applications accepted.

Queen's University at Kingston, School of Graduate Studies and Research, Faculty of Health Sciences, Department of Anatomy and Cell Biology, Kingston, ON K7L 3N6, Canada. Offers biology of reproduction (M Sc, PhD); cancer (M Sc, PhD); cardiovascular pathophysiology (M Sc, PhD); cell and molecular biology (M Sc, PhD); drug metabolism (M Sc, PhD); endocrinology (M Sc, PhD); motor control (M Sc, PhD); neural regeneration (M Sc, PhD); neurophysiology (M Sc, PhD). Part-time programs available. *Degree requirements:* For master's, thesis; for doctorate, one foreign language, comprehensive exam, thesis/dissertation. *Entrance requirements:* Additional exam requirements/recommendations for international students: Required—TOEFL. Electronic applications accepted. *Faculty research:* Human kinetics, neuroscience, reproductive biology, cardiovascular.

Université Laval, Faculty of Medicine, Graduate Programs in Medicine, Programs in Neurobiology, Québec, QC G1K 7P4, Canada. Offers M Sc, PhD. Terminal master's awarded for partial completion of doctoral program. *Degree requirements:* For master's, thesis; for doctorate, comprehensive exam, thesis/dissertation. *Entrance requirements:* For master's and doctorate, knowledge of French and English. Electronic applications accepted.

University at Albany, State University of New York, College of Arts and Sciences, Department of Biological Sciences, Specialization in Molecular, Cellular, Developmental, and Neural Biology, Albany, NY 12222-0001. Offers MS, PhD. *Degree requirements:* For master's, one foreign language; for doctorate, one foreign language, thesis/dissertation. *Entrance requirements:* For master's and doctorate, GRE General Test.

The University of Alabama at Birmingham, Graduate Programs in Joint Health Sciences, Program in Neurobiology, Birmingham, AL 35294. Offers PhD. *Students:* 53 full-time (24 women), 1 part-time (0 women); includes 7 Black or African American, non-Hispanic/Latino; 5 Asian, non-Hispanic/Latino; 1 Hispanic/Latino, 4 international. Average age 28. In 2010, 3 doctorates awarded. *Degree requirements:* For doctorate, thesis/dissertation. *Entrance requirements:* For doctorate, GRE, interview. *Application deadline:* Applications are processed on a rolling basis. Electronic applications accepted. *Expenses:* Tuition, state resident: full-time $5482. Tuition, nonresident: full-time $12,430. Tuition and fees vary according to program. *Unit head:* Dr. J. David Sweatt, Chair, 205-975-5196, Fax: 205-934-6571. *Application contact:* Information Contact, 205-975-5573, Fax: 205-934-6571.

Neurobiology

University of Arkansas for Medical Sciences, Graduate School, Graduate Programs in Biomedical Sciences, Department of Neurobiology and Developmental Sciences, Little Rock, AR 72205-7199. Offers MS, PhD, MD/PhD. *Degree requirements:* For master's, thesis; for doctorate, thesis/dissertation. *Entrance requirements:* For master's, GRE General Test; for doctorate, GRE General Test, GRE Subject Test. Additional exam requirements/recommendations for international students: Required—TOEFL. *Faculty research:* Cellular and molecular neuroscience, translation neuroscience.

University of California, Irvine, School of Biological Sciences, Department of Neurobiology and Behavior, Irvine, CA 92697. Offers biological sciences (MS, PhD); MD/PhD. *Students:* 45 full-time (27 women), 1 (woman) part-time; includes 12 minority (6 Asian, non-Hispanic/Latino; 6 Hispanic/Latino), 1 international. Average age 28. 48 applicants, 15% accepted, 4 enrolled. In 2010, 1 master's, 13 doctorates awarded. *Degree requirements:* For doctorate, thesis/dissertation. *Entrance requirements:* For master's and doctorate, GRE General Test, GRE Subject Test, minimum GPA of 3.0. Additional exam requirements/recommendations for international students: Required—TOEFL (minimum score 550 paper-based; 213 computer-based). *Application deadline:* For fall admission, 1/15 priority date for domestic students, 1/15 for international students. Applications are processed on a rolling basis. Application fee: $80 ($100 for international students). Electronic applications accepted. *Financial support:* Fellowships, research assistantships with full tuition reimbursements, teaching assistantships, institutionally sponsored loans, traineeships, health care benefits, and unspecified assistantships available. Financial award application deadline: 3/1; financial award applicants required to submit FAFSA. *Faculty research:* Synaptic processes, neurophysiology, neuroendocrinology, neuroanatomy, molecular neurobiology. *Unit head:* Prof. Thomas J. Carew, Chair, 949-824-6114, Fax: 949-824-2447, E-mail: tcarew@uci.edu. *Application contact:* Naima Louridi, Student Affairs Officer, 949-824-8519, Fax: 949-824-2447, E-mail: nlouridi@uci.edu.

University of California, Irvine, School of Medicine and School of Biological Sciences, Department of Anatomy and Neurobiology, Irvine, CA 92697. Offers biological sciences (MS, PhD); MD/PhD. *Students:* 28 full-time (17 women); includes 8 minority (3 Asian, non-Hispanic/Latino; 5 Hispanic/Latino), 2 international. Average age 28. In 2010, 1 master's, 10 doctorates awarded. *Degree requirements:* For doctorate, thesis/dissertation. *Entrance requirements:* For master's and doctorate, GRE General Test, GRE Subject Test. Additional exam requirements/recommendations for international students: Required—TOEFL (minimum score 550 paper-based; 213 computer-based). *Application deadline:* For fall admission, 1/15 priority date for domestic students, 1/15 for international students. Applications are processed on a rolling basis. Application fee: $80 ($100 for international students). Electronic applications accepted. *Financial support:* Fellowships, research assistantships with full tuition reimbursements, teaching assistantships, institutionally sponsored loans, traineeships, health care benefits, and unspecified assistantships available. Financial award application deadline: 3/1; financial award applicants required to submit FAFSA. *Faculty research:* Neurotransmitter immunocytochemistry, intracellular physiology, molecular neurobiology, forebrain organization and development, structure and function of sensory and motor systems. *Unit head:* Prof. Ivan Soltesz, Professor and Chair, 949-824-3957, Fax: 949-824-9860, E-mail: isoltesz@uci.edu. *Application contact:* Debra S. Caputo, Chief Administrative Officer, 949-824-6340, Fax: 949-824-8549, E-mail: dscaputo@uci.edu.

University of California, Los Angeles, David Geffen School of Medicine and Graduate Division, Graduate Programs in Medicine, Department of Neurobiology, Los Angeles, CA 90095. Offers anatomy and cell biology (PhD). *Faculty:* 21 full-time (0 women). *Students:* 14 full-time (7 women); includes 4 minority (2 Asian, non-Hispanic/Latino; 2 Hispanic/Latino), 1 international. Average age 28. In 2010, 1 doctorate awarded. *Degree requirements:* For doctorate, thesis/dissertation, oral and written qualifying exams. *Entrance requirements:* For doctorate, GRE General Test, GRE Subject Test, bachelor's degree in physical or biological science. Application fee: $70 ($90 for international students). Electronic applications accepted. *Financial support:* In 2010–11, 15 fellowships, 10 research assistantships, 8 teaching assistantships were awarded; Federal Work-Study, institutionally sponsored loans, scholarships/grants, and tuition waivers (full and partial) also available. Financial award application deadline: 3/1. *Faculty research:* Neuroendocrinology, neurophysiology. *Unit head:* Dr. Marie-Francoise Chesselet, Chair, 310-267-1781, Fax: 310-267-1786, E-mail: mchesselet@mednet.ucla.edu. *Application contact:* UCLA Access Coordinator, 310-206-1845, Fax: 310-206-1636, E-mail: uclaaccess@mednet.ucla.edu.

University of California, Los Angeles, Graduate Division, College of Letters and Science and David Geffen School of Medicine, UCLA ACCESS to Programs in the Molecular, Cellular and Integrative Life Sciences, Los Angeles, CA 90095. Offers biochemistry and molecular biology (PhD); biological chemistry (PhD); cellular and molecular pathology (PhD); human genetics (PhD); microbiology, immunology, and molecular genetics (PhD); molecular biology (PhD); molecular toxicology (PhD); molecular, cellular and integrative physiology (PhD); neurobiology (PhD); oral biology (PhD); physiology (PhD). ACCESS is an umbrella program for first-year coursework in 12 PhD programs. *Students:* 48 full-time (28 women), 6 international. Average age 24. 388 applicants, 27% accepted, 48 enrolled. *Degree requirements:* For doctorate, thesis/dissertation, oral and written qualifying exams. *Entrance requirements:* For doctorate, GRE General Test, minimum undergraduate GPA of 3.0. Additional exam requirements/recommendations for international students: Required—TOEFL. *Application deadline:* For fall admission, 12/15 for domestic and international students. Application fee: $70 ($90 for international students). Electronic applications accepted. *Financial support:* In 2010–11, 31 fellowships with full and partial tuition reimbursements, 13 research assistantships with full and partial tuition reimbursements, 2 teaching assistantships with full and partial tuition reimbursements were awarded; Federal Work-Study, institutionally sponsored loans, scholarships/grants, health care benefits, tuition waivers (full and partial), and unspecified assistantships also available. Financial award application deadline: 3/1; financial award applicants required to submit FAFSA. *Faculty research:* Molecular, cellular, and developmental biology; immunology; microbiology; integrative biology. *Unit head:* Jody Spillane, Project Coordinator, 310-206-1845, E-mail: jspillane@mednet.ucla.edu. *Application contact:* UCLA Access Admissions, 310-206-1845, E-mail: uclaaccess@mednet.ucla.edu.

University of California, San Diego, Office of Graduate Studies, Division of Biological Sciences, Program in Neurobiology, La Jolla, CA 92093. Offers PhD. Offered in association with the Salk Institute. *Degree requirements:* For doctorate, thesis/dissertation, qualifying exam. Electronic applications accepted.

University of Chicago, Division of Biological Sciences, Neuroscience Graduate Programs, Committee on Neurobiology, Chicago, IL 60637-1513. Offers PhD. *Degree requirements:* For doctorate, thesis/dissertation, ethics class, 2 teaching assistantships. *Entrance requirements:* For doctorate, GRE General Test. Additional exam requirements/recommendations for international students: Required—TOEFL (minimum score 600 paper-based; 250 computer-based; 104 iBT), IELTS (minimum score 7). Electronic applications accepted. *Faculty research:* Immunogenetic aspects of neurologic disease.

University of Colorado Boulder, Graduate School, College of Arts and Sciences, Department of Ecology and Evolutionary Biology, Boulder, CO 80309. Offers animal behavior (MA); biology (MA, PhD); environmental biology (MA, PhD); evolutionary biology (MA, PhD); neurobiology (MA); population biology (MA); population genetics (PhD). *Faculty:* 32 full-time (10 women). *Students:* 71 full-time (36 women), 17 part-time (11 women); includes 10 minority (1 American Indian or Alaska Native, non-Hispanic/Latino; 2 Asian, non-Hispanic/Latino; 7 Hispanic/Latino), 4 international. Average age 30. 176 applicants, 20 enrolled. In 2010, 11 master's, 8 doctorates awarded. Terminal master's awarded for partial completion of doctoral program. *Degree requirements:* For master's, comprehensive exam, thesis or alternative; for doctorate, comprehensive exam, thesis/dissertation. *Entrance requirements:* For master's, GRE General Test, GRE Subject Test, minimum undergraduate GPA of 3.0; for doctorate, GRE General Test, GRE Subject Test. *Application deadline:* For fall admission, 12/30 priority date for domestic students, 12/1 for international students. Application fee: $50 ($60 for international students). *Financial support:* In 2010–11, 25 fellowships (averaging $17,876 per year), 27 research assistantships (averaging $15,070 per year) were awarded; Federal Work-Study, institutionally sponsored loans, and tuition waivers (full) also available. *Faculty research:* Behavior, ecology, genetics, morphology, endocrinology, physiology, systematics. Total annual research expenditures: $3.5 million.

University of Connecticut, Graduate School, College of Liberal Arts and Sciences, Department of Physiology and Neurobiology, Storrs, CT 06269. Offers comparative physiology (MS, PhD); endocrinology (MS, PhD), including comparative physiology (MS), neurobiology (MS); neurobiology (MS, PhD). Terminal master's awarded for partial completion of doctoral program. *Degree requirements:* For master's, comprehensive exam; for doctorate, thesis/dissertation. *Entrance requirements:* For master's and doctorate, GRE General Test, GRE Subject Test. Additional exam requirements/recommendations for international students: Required—TOEFL (minimum score 550 paper-based; 213 computer-based). Electronic applications accepted.

See Close-Up on page 455.

University of Illinois at Chicago, Graduate College, Graduate Program in Neuroscience, Chicago, IL 60607-7128. Offers PhD, MD/PhD. Admissions and degrees offered through participating Departments of Anatomy and Cell Biology, Biochemistry, Bioengineering, Biological Sciences, Chemistry, Pathology, Pharmacology, Physiology and Biophysics, and Psychology. *Degree requirements:* For doctorate, thesis/dissertation. *Entrance requirements:* For doctorate, GRE General Test, minimum GPA of 3.75 on a 5.0 scale. Additional exam requirements/recommendations for international students: Required—TOEFL. *Faculty research:* Neurobiology and behavior.

The University of Iowa, Graduate College, College of Liberal Arts and Sciences, Department of Biology, Iowa City, IA 52242-1324. Offers biology (MS, PhD); cell and developmental biology (MS, PhD); evolution (MS, PhD); genetics (MS, PhD); neurobiology (MS, PhD). Terminal master's awarded for partial completion of doctoral program. *Degree requirements:* For master's, thesis optional, exam; for doctorate, comprehensive exam, thesis/dissertation. *Entrance requirements:* For master's and doctorate, GRE General Test, minimum GPA of 3.0. Additional exam requirements/recommendations for international students: Required—TOEFL (minimum score 600 paper-based; 250 computer-based; 100 iBT). Electronic applications accepted. *Faculty research:* Neurobiology, evolutionary biology, genetics, cell and developmental biology.

The University of Iowa, Graduate College, College of Liberal Arts and Sciences, Department of Psychology, Iowa City, IA 52242-1316. Offers neural and behavioral sciences (PhD); psychology (MA, PhD). *Degree requirements:* For master's, thesis optional, exam; for doctorate, comprehensive exam, thesis/dissertation. *Entrance requirements:* For master's and doctorate, GRE General Test, minimum GPA of 3.0. Additional exam requirements/recommendations for international students: Required—TOEFL (minimum score 550 paper-based; 213 computer-based; 81 iBT). Electronic applications accepted.

University of Kentucky, Graduate School, Graduate School Programs from the College of Medicine, Program in Anatomy and Neurobiology, Lexington, KY 40506-0032. Offers anatomy (PhD). *Degree requirements:* For doctorate, comprehensive exam, thesis/dissertation. *Entrance requirements:* For doctorate, GRE General Test, minimum undergraduate GPA of 2.75. Additional exam requirements/recommendations for international students: Required—TOEFL (minimum score 550 paper-based; 213 computer-based). Electronic applications accepted. *Faculty research:* Neuroendocrinology, developmental neurobiology, neurotrophic substances, neural plasticity and trauma, neurobiology of aging.

University of Louisville, School of Medicine, Department of Anatomical Sciences and Neurobiology, Louisville, KY 40292-0001. Offers MS, PhD, MD/PhD. *Faculty:* 20 full-time (3 women), 12 part-time/adjunct (1 woman). *Students:* 40 full-time (22 women), 3 part-time (1 woman); includes 1 Asian, non-Hispanic/Latino; 1 Hispanic/Latino; 1 Two or more races, non-Hispanic/Latino, 14 international. Average age 28. 32 applicants, 38% accepted, 12 enrolled. In 2010, 10 master's, 6 doctorates awarded. Terminal master's awarded for partial completion of doctoral program. *Degree requirements:* For master's, thesis; for doctorate, comprehensive exam, thesis/dissertation. *Entrance requirements:* For master's and doctorate, GRE General Test (minimum score of 1000 verbal and quantitative), minimum GPA of 3.0. Additional exam requirements/recommendations for international students: Required—TOEFL. *Application deadline:* For fall admission, 1/15 priority date for domestic students; for spring admission, 4/15 priority date for domestic and international students. Applications are processed on a rolling basis. Application fee: $50. Electronic applications accepted. *Expenses:* Tuition, state resident: full-time $9144; part-time $508 per credit hour. Tuition, nonresident: full-time $19,026; part-time $1057 per credit hour. Tuition and fees vary according to program and reciprocity agreements. *Financial support:* Fellowships with full tuition reimbursements, research assistantships with full tuition reimbursements, health care benefits and unspecified assistantships available. Financial award application deadline: 4/15. *Faculty research:* Human adult neural stem cells, development and plasticity of the nervous system, organization of the dorsal thalamus, electrophysiology/neuroanatomy of central neurons mediating control of reproductive and pelvic organs, normal neural mechanisms and plasticity following injury and/or chronic pain, differentiation and regeneration of motor neurons and oligodendrocytes. Total annual research expenditures: $4 million. *Unit head:* Dr. Fred J. Roisen, Chair, 502-852-5165, Fax: 502-852-6228, E-mail: fjrois01@gwise.louisville.edu. *Application contact:* Dr. Charles Hubscher, Director of Graduate Studies, 502-852-3058, Fax: 502-852-6228, E-mail: chhub01@louisville.edu.

The University of Manchester, Faculty of Life Sciences, Manchester, United Kingdom. Offers adaptive organismal biology (M Phil, PhD); animal biology (M Phil, PhD); biochemistry (M Phil, PhD); bioinformatics (M Phil, PhD); biomolecular sciences (M Phil, PhD); biotechnology (M Phil, PhD); cell biology (M Phil, PhD); cell matrix research (M Phil, PhD); channels and transporters (M Phil, PhD); developmental biology (M Phil, PhD); Egyptology (M Phil, PhD); environmental biology (M Phil, PhD); evolutionary biology (M Phil, PhD); gene expression (M Phil, PhD); genetics (M Phil, PhD); history of science, technology and medicine (M Phil, PhD); immunology (M Phil, PhD); integrative neurobiology and behavior (M Phil, PhD); membrane trafficking (M Phil, PhD); microbiology (M Phil, PhD); molecular and cellular neuroscience (M Phil, PhD); molecular biology (M Phil, PhD); molecular cancer studies (M Phil, PhD); neuroscience (M Phil, PhD); ophthalmology (M Phil, PhD); optometry (M Phil, PhD); organelle function (M Phil, PhD); pharmacology (M Phil, PhD); physiology (M Phil, PhD); plant sciences (M Phil, PhD); stem cell research (M Phil, PhD); structural biology (M Phil, PhD); systems neuroscience (M Phil, PhD); toxicology (M Phil, PhD).

University of Maryland, Baltimore, Graduate School, Graduate Program in Life Sciences, Program in Neuroscience, Baltimore, MD 21201. Offers PhD, MD/PhD. Part-time programs available. *Entrance requirements:* For doctorate, GRE General Test, minimum GPA of 3.0. Additional exam requirements/recommendations for international students: Required—TOEFL (minimum score 550 paper-based; 80 iBT); Recommended—IELTS (minimum score 7). Electronic applications accepted. Part-time tuition and fees vary according to course load, degree level and program. *Faculty research:* Molecular, biochemical, and cellular pharmacology; membrane biophysics; synaptology; developmental neurobiology.

University of Minnesota, Twin Cities Campus, Graduate School, Graduate Program in Neuroscience, Minneapolis, MN 55455-0213. Offers MS, PhD. Terminal master's awarded for partial completion of doctoral program. *Degree requirements:* For master's, thesis; for doctorate, thesis/dissertation. *Entrance requirements:* For doctorate, GRE. Additional exam requirements/recommendations for international students: Required—TOEFL. Electronic applications accepted. *Faculty research:* Cellular and molecular neuroscience, behavioral neuroscience, developmental neuroscience, neurodegenerative diseases, pain, addiction, motor control.

University of Missouri, Graduate School, College of Arts and Sciences, Division of Biological Sciences, Program in Neurobiology and Behavior, Columbia, MO 65211. Offers MA, PhD.

The University of North Carolina at Chapel Hill, School of Medicine and Graduate School, Graduate Programs in Medicine, Curriculum in Neurobiology, Chapel Hill, NC 27599. Offers PhD. *Degree requirements:* For doctorate, comprehensive exam, thesis/dissertation. *Entrance requirements:* For doctorate, GRE General Test, minimum GPA of 3.0. Electronic applications accepted.

University of Oklahoma, College of Arts and Sciences, Department of Chemistry and Biochemistry, Norman, OK 73019. Offers chemistry and biochemistry (MS, PhD), including bioinformatics, cellular and behavioral neurobiology (PhD), chemistry. Part-time programs available. *Faculty:* 27 full-time (6 women). *Students:* 72 full-time (27 women), 26 part-time (11 women); includes 12 minority (6 Black or African American, non-Hispanic/Latino; 1 American Indian or Alaska Native, non-Hispanic/Latino; 2 Asian, non-Hispanic/Latino; 1 Hispanic/Latino; 2 Two or more races, non-Hispanic/Latino), 50 international. Average age 28. 31 applicants, 61% accepted, 16 enrolled. In 2010, 17 master's, 17 doctorates awarded. Terminal master's awarded for partial completion of doctoral program. *Degree requirements:* For master's, thesis optional; for doctorate, thesis/dissertation. *Entrance requirements:* For master's, GRE, BS in chemistry; for doctorate, GRE. Additional exam requirements/recommendations for international students: Required—TOEFL (minimum score 550 paper-based; 213 computer-based; 79 iBT). *Application deadline:* For fall admission, 4/1 priority date for domestic students, 4/1 for international students; for spring admission, 9/1 priority date for domestic students, 9/1 for international students. Applications are processed on a rolling basis. Application fee: $40 ($90 for international students). Electronic applications accepted. *Expenses:* Tuition, state resident: full-time $3893; part-time $162.20 per credit hour. Tuition, nonresident: full-time $14,167; part-time $590.30 per credit hour. Required fees: $2523; $94.60 per credit hour. Tuition and fees vary according to course load and degree level. *Financial support:* In 2010–11, 1 fellowship with full tuition reimbursement (averaging $5,000 per year), 24 research assistantships with partial tuition reimbursements (averaging $14,788 per year), 62 teaching assistantships with partial tuition reimbursements (averaging $16,444 per year) were awarded; scholarships/grants and unspecified assistantships also available. Financial award application deadline: 4/1; financial award applicants required to submit FAFSA. *Faculty research:* Structural biology, synthesis and catalysis, biomaterials, membrane biochemistry, genomics. Total annual research expenditures: $6.8 million. *Unit head:* Dr. George Richter-Addo, Chair, 405-325-4811, Fax: 405-325-6111, E-mail: grichteraddo@ou.edu. *Application contact:* Angela Link-Perez, Graduate Program Assistant, 405-325-4811 Ext. 62946, Fax: 405-325-6111, E-mail: alperez@ou.edu.

University of Oklahoma, College of Arts and Sciences, Department of Zoology and School of Aerospace and Mechanical Engineering and Department of Chemistry and Biochemistry, Program in Cellular and Behavioral Neurobiology, Norman, OK 73019. Offers PhD. *Students:* 3 full-time (all women), 2 part-time (0 women), all international. Average age 27. 3 applicants, 33% accepted, 1 enrolled. In 2010, 1 doctorate awarded. *Entrance requirements:* Additional exam requirements/recommendations for international students: Required—TOEFL (minimum score 550 paper-based; 213 computer-based; 79 iBT). *Application deadline:* For fall admission, 4/1 for domestic and international students; for spring admission, 11/1 for domestic students, 9/1 for international students. Applications are processed on a rolling basis. Application fee: $40 ($90 for international students). Electronic applications accepted. *Expenses:* Tuition, state resident: full-time $3893; part-time $162.20 per credit hour. Tuition, nonresident: full-time $14,167; part-time $590.30 per credit hour. Required fees: $2523; $94.60 per credit hour. Tuition and fees vary according to course load and degree level. *Financial support:* In 2010–11, 5 students received support. Scholarships/grants, health care benefits, and unspecified assistantships available. *Faculty research:* Behavioral neurobiology, cellular neurobiology, molecular neurobiology, developmental neurobiology, cell signaling. *Unit head:* Bill Matthews, Academic Chair, 405-325-4712, Fax: 405-325-6202, E-mail: wmatthews@ou.edu. *Application contact:* Dr. Ari Berkowitz, Director, 405-325-3492, Fax: 405-325-6202, E-mail: ari@ou.edu.

University of Rochester, School of Medicine and Dentistry, Graduate Programs in Medicine and Dentistry, Department of Neurobiology and Anatomy, Programs in Neurobiology and Anatomy, Rochester, NY 14627. Offers MS, PhD. *Degree requirements:* For doctorate, thesis/dissertation, qualifying exam. *Entrance requirements:* For master's and doctorate, GRE General Test.

University of Southern California, Graduate School, Dana and David Dornsife College of Letters, Arts and Sciences, Department of Biological Sciences, Program in Neurobiology, Los Angeles, CA 90089. Offers PhD. M.S. is terminal degree only. *Faculty:* 16 full-time (5 women). *Students:* 10 full-time (7 women); includes 3 minority (2 Asian, non-Hispanic/Latino; 1 Hispanic/Latino), 4 international. 7 applicants, 71% accepted, 5 enrolled.Terminal master's awarded for partial completion of doctoral program. *Degree requirements:* For doctorate, comprehensive exam, thesis/dissertation, qualifying examination, dissertation defense. *Entrance requirements:* For doctorate, GRE, 3 letters of recommendation, personal statement, resume, minimum GPA of 3.0. Additional exam requirements/recommendations for international students: Required—TOEFL (minimum score 600 paper-based; 250 computer-based; 100 iBT). *Application deadline:* For fall admission, 12/1 priority date for domestic and international students. Application fee: $85. Electronic applications accepted. *Expenses:* Tuition: Full-time $31,240; part-time $1420 per unit. Required fees: $600. One-time fee: $35 full-time. Full-time tuition and fees vary according to degree level and program. *Financial support:* In 2010–11, 5 students received support, including 6 fellowships with full tuition reimbursements available (averaging $28,000 per year), 3 research assistantships with full tuition reimbursements available (averaging $28,000 per year), 1 teaching assistantship with full tuition reimbursement available (averaging $28,000 per year). *Faculty research:* Neural basis of emotion and motivation, learning and memory, cell biology and physiology of neuronal signaling, sensory processing, development and aging. *Unit head:* Dr. Chien-Ping Ko, Professor of Biological Sciences/Director, 213-740-9182, Fax: 213-740-5687, E-mail: cko@college.usc.edu. *Application contact:* Beatriz Gil, Administrative Assistant II, 213-740-9176, E-mail: bgil@usc.edu.

University of Southern California, Keck School of Medicine and Graduate School, Graduate Programs in Medicine, Department of Cell and Neurobiology, Los Angeles, CA 90089. Offers MS, PhD. *Faculty:* 29 full-time (11 women), 3 part-time/adjunct (1 woman). *Students:* 3 full-time (2 women); includes 1 Asian, non-Hispanic/Latino. Average age 24. 3 applicants, 0% accepted, 0 enrolled.Terminal master's awarded for partial completion of doctoral program. *Degree requirements:* For master's, thesis or alternative; for doctorate, thesis/dissertation. *Entrance requirements:* For master's, GRE General Test, minimum GPA of 3.0; for doctorate, GRE General Test. *Application deadline:* For fall admission, 3/1 priority date for domestic and international students. Application fee: $85. Electronic applications accepted. *Expenses:* Tuition: Full-time $31,240; part-time $1420 per unit. Required fees: $600. One-time fee: $35 full-time. Full-time tuition and fees vary according to degree level and program. *Financial support:* In 2010–11, 1 student received support, including 1 fellowship (averaging $27,060 per year), 4 research assistantships (averaging $27,060 per year); teaching assistantships, Federal Work-Study and institutionally sponsored loans also available. Support available to part-time students. *Faculty research:* Neurobiology and development, gene therapy in vision, lachrymal glands, neuroendocrinology, signal transduction mechanisms. *Unit head:* Dr. Mikel Henry Snow, Vice-Chair, 323-442-1881, Fax: 323-442-3466. *Application contact:* Darlene Marie Campbell, Project Specialist, 323-442-2843, Fax: 323-442-0466, E-mail: dmc@usc.edu.

The University of Texas at Austin, Graduate School, The Institute for Neuroscience, Austin, TX 78712-1111. Offers PhD, MD/PhD. Terminal master's awarded for partial completion of doctoral program. *Degree requirements:* For doctorate, thesis/dissertation. *Entrance requirements:* For doctorate, GRE. Electronic applications accepted. *Faculty research:* Cellular/molecular biology, neurobiology, pharmacology, behavioral neuroscience.

The University of Texas at San Antonio, College of Sciences, Department of Biology, San Antonio, TX 78249-0617. Offers biology (MS, PhD); biotechnology (MS); neurobiology (PhD). Part-time programs available. *Faculty:* 36 full-time (3 women), 7 part-time/adjunct (3 women). *Students:* 143 full-time (76 women), 65 part-time (37 women); includes 73 minority (10 Black or African American, non-Hispanic/Latino; 10 Asian, non-Hispanic/Latino; 40 Hispanic/Latino; 13 Two or more races, non-Hispanic/Latino), 73 international. Average age 27. 252 applicants, 50% accepted, 69 enrolled. In 2010, 42 master's, 17 doctorates awarded. *Degree requirements:* For master's, comprehensive exam, thesis; for doctorate, comprehensive exam, thesis/dissertation. *Entrance requirements:* For master's, GRE General Test, minimum GPA of 3.0; for doctorate, GRE General Test, minimum GPA of 3.3. Additional exam requirements/recommendations for international students: Required—TOEFL (minimum score 500 paper-based; 173 computer-based; 61 iBT), IELTS (minimum score 5). *Application deadline:* For fall admission, 7/1 for domestic students, 4/1 for international students; for spring admission, 11/1 for domestic students, 9/1 for international students. Applications are processed on a rolling basis. Application fee: $45 ($80 for international students). Electronic applications accepted. *Expenses:* Tuition, state resident: full-time $4172; part-time $231.75 per credit hour. Tuition, nonresident: full-time $15,332; part-time $851.75 per credit hour. *Financial support:* In 2010–11, 66 students received support, including 25 fellowships (averaging $24,632 per year), 162 research assistantships (averaging $19,317 per year), 73 teaching assistantships (averaging $10,841 per year); career-related internships or fieldwork, scholarships/grants, and unspecified assistantships also available. Support available to part-time students. *Faculty research:* Cell and molecular biology, neurobiology, microbiology, integrative biology, environmental science. Total annual research expenditures: $1.7 million. *Unit head:* Dr. Edwin J. Barea-Rodriguez, Interim Chair, 210-458-4511, Fax: 210-458-5658, E-mail: edwin.barea@utsa.edu. *Application contact:* Veronica Ramirez, Assistant Dean of the Graduate School, 210-458-4330, Fax: 210-458-4332, E-mail: graduatestudies@utsa.edu.

See Display on page 81 and Close-Up on page 115.

University of Utah, School of Medicine and Graduate School, Graduate Programs in Medicine, Department of Neurobiology and Anatomy, Salt Lake City, UT 84112-1107. Offers PhD. Part-time programs available. Terminal master's awarded for partial completion of doctoral program. *Degree requirements:* For doctorate, comprehensive exam, thesis/dissertation. *Entrance requirements:* For doctorate, GRE General Test. Additional exam requirements/recommendations for international students: Required—TOEFL. *Expenses:* Tuition, area resident: Part-time $179.19 per credit hour. Tuition, state resident: full-time $4384. Tuition, nonresident: full-time $16,684; part-time $630.67 per credit hour. Required fees: $350 per semester. Tuition and fees vary according to course load, degree level and program. *Faculty research:* Neuroscience, neuroanatomy, developmental neurobiology, neurogenetics.

University of Washington, Graduate School, School of Medicine, Graduate Programs in Medicine, Graduate Program in Neurobiology and Behavior, Seattle, WA 98195. Offers PhD. *Degree requirements:* For doctorate, thesis/dissertation. *Entrance requirements:* For doctorate, GRE. Additional exam requirements/recommendations for international students: Required—TOEFL. Electronic applications accepted. *Faculty research:* Motor, sensory systems, neuroplasticity, animal behavior, neuroendocrinology, computational neuroscience.

University of Wisconsin–Madison, School of Medicine and Public Health and Graduate School, Graduate Programs in Medicine, Department of Physiology, Madison, WI 53706-1380. Offers PhD. *Faculty:* 18 full-time (5 women). *Students:* 11 full-time (0 women); includes 1 Black or African American, non-Hispanic/Latino; 6 Asian, non-Hispanic/Latino; 2 Hispanic/Latino. Average age 22. 40 applicants, 8% accepted, 2 enrolled. In 2010, 7 doctorates awarded. *Degree requirements:* For doctorate, thesis/dissertation, written exams. *Entrance requirements:* For doctorate, GRE, minimum GPA of 3.0. Additional exam requirements/recommendations for international students: Required—TOEFL (minimum score 580 paper-based; 237 computer-based). *Application deadline:* For fall admission, 1/15 priority date for domestic and international students. Applications are processed on a rolling basis. Application fee: $45. Electronic applications accepted. *Expenses:* Tuition, state resident: full-time $9887; part-time $617.96 per credit. Tuition, nonresident: full-time $24,054; part-time $1503.40 per credit. Required fees: $67.63 per credit. Tuition and fees vary according to reciprocity agreements. *Financial support:* In 2010–11, fellowships with tuition reimbursements (averaging $24,000 per year), research assistantships with tuition reimbursements (averaging $24,000 per year), teaching assistantships with tuition reimbursements (averaging $24,000 per year) were awarded. *Faculty research:* Studies in molecular cellular systems, cardiovascular, neuroscience. *Unit head:* Dr. Tom C. T. Yin, Interim Chair, 608-262-0368, Fax: 608-265-5512, E-mail: tcyin@wisc.edu. *Application contact:* Sue S. Krey, Program Assistant 4, 608-262-9114, Fax: 608-265-5512, E-mail: sskrey@wisc.edu.

Virginia Commonwealth University, Medical College of Virginia-Professional Programs, School of Medicine, School of Medicine Graduate Programs, Department of Anatomy and Neurobiology, Program in Anatomy and Neurobiology, Richmond, VA 23284-9005. Offers PhD. *Accreditation:* APTA. *Faculty:* 26 full-time (5 women). *Students:* 7 full-time (1 woman); includes 1 minority (Asian, non-Hispanic/Latino), 3 international. 27 applicants, 26% accepted, 2 enrolled. In 2010, 5 doctorates awarded. *Degree requirements:* For doctorate, thesis/dissertation. *Entrance requirements:* For doctorate, GRE, MCAT or DAT. *Application deadline:* For fall admission, 1/7 priority date for domestic students. Application fee: $50. Electronic applications accepted. *Expenses:* Tuition, state resident: full-time $4308; part-time $479 per credit hour. Tuition, nonresident: full-time $8942; part-time $994 per credit hour. Required fees: $2000; $85 per credit hour. Tuition and fees vary according to course level, course load, degree level, campus/location and program. *Unit head:* Dr. William Guido, Graduate Program Director and Recruitment Contact, 804-828-0952, E-mail: wguido@vcu.edu. *Application contact:* Dr. William Guido, Graduate Program Director and Recruitment Contact, 804-828-0952, E-mail: wguido@vcu.edu.

Wake Forest University, School of Medicine and Graduate School of Arts and Sciences, Graduate Programs in Medicine, Department of Neurobiology and Anatomy, Winston-Salem, NC 27109. Offers PhD, MD/PhD. *Degree requirements:* For doctorate, thesis/dissertation. *Entrance requirements:* For doctorate, GRE General Test. Additional exam requirements/recommendations for international students: Required—TOEFL. Electronic applications accepted. *Faculty research:* Sensory neurobiology, reproductive endocrinology, regulatory processes in cell biology.

Wesleyan University, Graduate Programs, Department of Biology, Middletown, CT 06459. Offers animal behavior (PhD); bioformatics/genomics (PhD); cell biology (PhD); developmental biology (PhD); evolution/ecology (PhD); genetics (PhD); neurobiology (PhD); population biology (PhD). *Faculty:* 12 full-time (4 women). *Students:* 20 full-time (12 women); includes 1 Black or African American, non-Hispanic/Latino; 3 Asian, non-Hispanic/Latino. Average age 26. 24 applicants, 29% accepted, 2 enrolled. *Degree requirements:* For doctorate, variable foreign language requirement, thesis/dissertation. *Entrance requirements:* For doctorate, GRE. Additional exam requirements/recommendations for international students: Required—TOEFL. *Application deadline:* For fall admission, 1/15 for domestic and international students. Applications are processed on a rolling basis. Application fee: $0. *Expenses:* Tuition: Full-time $43,404. Required fees: $830. *Financial support:* In 2010–11, 5 research assistantships with full tuition reimbursements, 16 teaching assistantships with full tuition reimbursements were awarded; stipends also available. Financial award application deadline: 4/15; financial award applicants required to submit FAFSA. *Faculty research:* Microbial population genetics, genetic basis of evolutionary adaptation, genetic regulation of differentiation and pattern formation in *drosophila*. *Unit head:* Dr. Sonia E. Sultan, Chair/Professor, 860-685-3493, E-mail: jnaegele@wesleyan.edu. *Application contact:* Marjorie Fitzgibbons, Information Contact, 860-685-2140, E-mail: mfitzgibbons@wesleyan.edu.

West Virginia University, Eberly College of Arts and Sciences, Department of Biology, Morgantown, WV 26506. Offers cell and molecular biology (MS, PhD); environmental and evolutionary biology (MS, PhD); forensic biology (MS, PhD); genomic biology (MS, PhD); neurobiology (MS, PhD). Terminal master's awarded for partial completion of doctoral program. *Degree requirements:* For master's, thesis, final exam; for doctorate, thesis/dissertation, preliminary and final exams. *Entrance requirements:* For master's, GRE General Test, GRE

Neurobiology

West Virginia University (continued)

Subject Test, minimum GPA of 3.0; for doctorate, GRE General Test, minimum GPA of 3.0. Additional exam requirements/recommendations for international students: Required—TOEFL. *Faculty research:* Environmental biology, genetic engineering, developmental biology, global change, biodiversity.

Yale University, Graduate School of Arts and Sciences, Department of Molecular, Cellular, and Developmental Biology, Program in Neurobiology, New Haven, CT 06520. Offers PhD. *Degree requirements:* For doctorate, thesis/dissertation. *Entrance requirements:* For doctorate, GRE General Test, GRE Subject Test.

Yale University, School of Medicine and Graduate School of Arts and Sciences, Combined Program in Biological and Biomedical Sciences (BBS), Department of Neurobiology, New Haven, CT 06520. Offers PhD. *Degree requirements:* For doctorate, thesis/dissertation. *Entrance requirements:* For doctorate, GRE General Test, GRE Subject Test.

Neuroscience

Albany Medical College, Center for Neuropharmacology and Neuroscience, Albany, NY 12208-3479. Offers MS, PhD. *Faculty:* 19 full-time (6 women), 8 part-time/adjunct (2 women). *Students:* 16 full-time (5 women); includes 1 minority (Black or African American, non-Hispanic/Latino), 3 international. Average age 24. 31 applicants, 19% accepted, 6 enrolled. In 2010, 1 master's, 3 doctorates awarded. Terminal master's awarded for partial completion of doctoral program. *Degree requirements:* For master's, thesis; for doctorate, comprehensive exam, thesis/dissertation. *Entrance requirements:* For master's, GRE General Test, all transcripts, letters of recommendation; for doctorate, GRE General Test, letters of recommendation. Additional exam requirements/recommendations for international students: Required—TOEFL. *Application deadline:* For fall admission, 3/15 priority date for domestic and international students. Applications are processed on a rolling basis. Application fee: $0 ($60 for international students). *Financial support:* In 2010–11, 3 fellowships with partial tuition reimbursements (averaging $20,772 per year), 18 research assistantships with full tuition reimbursements (averaging $24,000 per year) were awarded; Federal Work-Study, scholarships/grants, and tuition waivers (full) also available. Financial award applicants required to submit FAFSA. *Faculty research:* Molecular and cellular neuroscience, neuronal development, addiction. *Unit head:* Dr. Stanley D. Glick, Director, 518-262-5303, Fax: 518-262-5799, E-mail: cnninfo@mail.amc.edu. *Application contact:* Dr. Mark Fleck, Graduate Director, 518-262-5303, Fax: 518-262-5799, E-mail: cnninfo@mail.amc.edu.

American University, College of Arts and Sciences, Department of Psychology, Washington, DC 22016-8062. Offers behavior, cognition, and neuroscience (PhD), including psychology; clinical psychology (PhD), including psychology; psychology (MA), including experimental/biological psychology, general psychology, personality/social psychology. *Accreditation:* APA. Part-time programs available. *Faculty:* 19 full-time (7 women), 6 part-time/adjunct (4 women). *Students:* 65 full-time (51 women), 47 part-time (41 women); includes 16 minority (4 Black or African American, non-Hispanic/Latino; 3 Asian, non-Hispanic/Latino; 9 Hispanic/Latino), 3 international. Average age 28. 445 applicants, 19% accepted, 36 enrolled. In 2010, 35 master's, 11 doctorates awarded. *Degree requirements:* For master's, comprehensive exam, thesis or alternative; for doctorate, comprehensive exam, thesis/dissertation, tools of research. *Entrance requirements:* For master's, GRE General Test, GRE Subject Test, recommendations; for doctorate, GRE General Test, GRE Subject Test. Additional exam requirements/recommendations for international students: Required—TOEFL. Application fee: $80. *Financial support:* Fellowships, research assistantships, teaching assistantships, career-related internships or fieldwork, Federal Work-Study, institutionally sponsored loans, tuition waivers (full and partial), and unspecified assistantships available. Support available to part-time students. Financial award application deadline: 2/1. *Faculty research:* Anxiety disorders, cognitive assessment, neuropsychology, conditioning and learning, psychopharmacology. *Unit head:* Dr. Anthony Riley, Chair, 202-885-1720, E-mail: alriley@american.edu. *Application contact:* Sara Holland, Senior Administrative Assistant, 202-885-1717, Fax: 202-885-1023, E-mail: holland@american.edu.

American University of Beirut, Graduate Programs, Faculty of Medicine, Beirut, Lebanon. Offers biochemistry (MS); human morphology (MS); medicine (MD); microbiology and immunology (MS); neuroscience (MS); pharmacology and therapeutics (MS); physiology (MS). Part-time programs available. *Faculty:* 222 full-time (56 women), 58 part-time/adjunct (4 women). *Students:* 346 full-time (135 women), 69 part-time (57 women). Average age 23. In 2010, 81 first professional degrees, 19 master's awarded. *Degree requirements:* For master's, one foreign language, comprehensive exam, thesis (for some programs). *Entrance requirements:* For MD, MCAT, bachelor's degree; for master's, letter of recommendation. Additional exam requirements/recommendations for international students: Required—TOEFL (minimum score 600 paper-based; 250 computer-based; 100 iBT), IELTS (minimum score 7.5). *Application deadline:* For fall admission, 4/30 for domestic and international students; for spring admission, 11/1 for domestic and international students. Application fee: $50. *Expenses:* Tuition: Full-time $12,294; part-time $683 per credit. Required fees: $499; $499 per credit. Tuition and fees vary according to course load and program. *Financial support:* In 2010–11, 4 students received support. Career-related internships or fieldwork, institutionally sponsored loans, scholarships/grants, health care benefits, and unspecified assistantships available. Financial award application deadline: 2/2. *Faculty research:* Cancer research (targeted therapy, mechanisms of leukemogenesis, tumor cell extravasation and metastasis, cancer stem cells); stem cell research (regenerative medicine, drug discovery); genetic research (neurogenetics, hereditary cardiomyopathy, hemoglobinopathies, pharmacogenomics); neuroscience research (pain, neurodegenerative disorder); metabolism (inflammation and metabolism, metabolic disorder, diabetes mellitus). Total annual research expenditures: $1.2 million. *Unit head:* Dr. Mohamed Sayegh, Dean, 961-135-0000 Ext. 4700, Fax: 961-174-4464, E-mail: msayegh@aub.edu.lb. *Application contact:* Dr. Salim Kanaan, Director, Admissions Office, 961-135-0000 Ext. 2594, Fax: 961-175-0775, E-mail: sk00@aub.edu.lb.

Argosy University, Chicago, College of Psychology and Behavioral Sciences, Doctoral Program in Clinical Psychology, Chicago, IL 60601. Offers child and adolescent psychology (Psy D); client-centered and experiential psychotherapies (Psy D); diversity and multicultural psychology (Psy D); family psychology (Psy D); forensic psychology (Psy D); health psychology (Psy D); neuropsychology (Psy D); organizational consulting (Psy D); psychoanalytic psychology (Psy D); psychology and spirituality (Psy D). *Accreditation:* APA.

Argosy University, Phoenix, College of Psychology and Behavioral Sciences, Program in Clinical Psychology, Phoenix, AZ 85021. Offers clinical psychology (MA); neuropsychology (Psy D); sports-exercise psychology (Psy D). *Accreditation:* APA (one or more programs are accredited).

Argosy University, Phoenix, College of Psychology and Behavioral Sciences, Program in Neuropsychology, Phoenix, AZ 85021. Offers Psy D.

Argosy University, Schaumburg, College of Psychology and Behavioral Sciences, Schaumburg, IL 60173-5403. Offers clinical health psychology (Post-Graduate Certificate); clinical psychology (MA, Psy D), including child and family psychology (Psy D), clinical health psychology (Psy D), diversity and multicultural psychology (Psy D), forensic psychology (Psy D), neuropsychology (Psy D); community counseling (MA); counseling psychology (Ed D), including counselor education and supervision; counselor education and supervision (Ed D); forensic psychology (Post-Graduate Certificate); industrial organizational psychology (MA). *Accreditation:* ACA; APA.

Argosy University, Tampa, College of Psychology and Behavioral Sciences, Program in Clinical Psychology, Tampa, FL 33607. Offers clinical psychology (MA, Psy D), including child and adolescent psychology (Psy D), geropsychology (Psy D), marriage/couples and family therapy (Psy D), neuropsychology (Psy D). *Accreditation:* APA.

Arizona State University, College of Liberal Arts and Sciences, Department of Psychology, Tempe, AZ 85287-1104. Offers behavioral neuroscience (PhD); clinical psychology (PhD); cognition, action and perception (PhD); developmental psychology (PhD); quantitative psychology (PhD); social psychology (PhD). *Accreditation:* APA. *Faculty:* 72 full-time (36 women), 9 part-time/adjunct (6 women). *Students:* 113 full-time (79 women), 17 part-time (12 women); includes 24 minority (2 Black or African American, non-Hispanic/Latino; 10 Asian, non-Hispanic/Latino; 10 Hispanic/Latino; 2 Two or more races, non-Hispanic/Latino), 9 international. Average age 28. 519 applicants, 8% accepted, 30 enrolled. In 2010, 19 doctorates awarded. *Degree requirements:* For doctorate, comprehensive exam, thesis/dissertation, interactive Program of Study (iPOS) submitted before completing 50 percent of required credit hours. *Entrance requirements:* For doctorate, GRE General Test, GRE Subject Test, minimum GPA of 3.0 or equivalent in last 2 years of work leading to bachelor's degree. Additional exam requirements/recommendations for international students: Required—TOEFL, IELTS, or Pearson Test of English. *Application deadline:* For fall admission, 12/15 for domestic and international students. Application fee: $70 ($90 for international students). Electronic applications accepted. *Expenses:* Tuition, state resident: full-time $8510; part-time $608 per credit. Tuition, nonresident: full-time $16,542; part-time $919 per credit. Required fees: $339; $110 per credit. Part-time tuition and fees vary according to course load. *Financial support:* In 2010–11, 58 research assistantships with tuition reimbursements (averaging $15,281 per year), 48 teaching assistantships with tuition reimbursements (averaging $15,062 per year) were awarded; fellowships with full tuition reimbursements, career-related internships or fieldwork, Federal Work-Study, institutionally sponsored loans, scholarships/grants, and tuition waivers (full and partial) also available. Financial award application deadline: 3/1; financial award applicants required to submit FAFSA. Total annual research expenditures: $9.4 million. *Unit head:* Dr. Keith Crnic, Chair, 480-965-3061, E-mail: keith.crnic@asu.edu. *Application contact:* Graduate Admissions, 480-965-6113.

Arizona State University, College of Liberal Arts and Sciences, School of Life Sciences, Tempe, AZ 85287-4601. Offers animal behavior (PhD); applied ethics (biomedical and health ethics) (MA); biological design (PhD); biology (MS, PhD); biology (biology and society) (MS, PhD); environmental life sciences (PhD); evolutionary biology (PhD); human and social dimensions of science and technology (PhD); microbiology (PhD); molecular and cellular biology (PhD); neuroscience (PhD); philosophy (history and philosophy of science) (MA); sustainability (PhD). *Faculty:* 102 full-time (26 women), 4 part-time/adjunct (1 woman). *Students:* 188 full-time (95 women), 45 part-time (29 women); includes 31 minority (3 Black or African American, non-Hispanic/Latino; 2 American Indian or Alaska Native, non-Hispanic/Latino; 12 Asian, non-Hispanic/Latino; 12 Hispanic/Latino; 2 Two or more races, non-Hispanic/Latino), 39 international. Average age 30. 203 applicants, 41% accepted, 60 enrolled. In 2010, 17 master's, 21 doctorates awarded. Terminal master's awarded for partial completion of doctoral program. *Degree requirements:* For master's, thesis (for some programs), interactive Program of Study (iPOS) submitted before completing 50 percent of required credit hours; for doctorate, variable foreign language requirement, comprehensive exam, thesis/dissertation, interactive Program of Study (iPOS) submitted before completing 50 percent of required credit hours. *Entrance requirements:* For master's and doctorate, GRE, minimum GPA of 3.0 or equivalent in last 2 years of work leading to bachelor's degree. Additional exam requirements/recommendations for international students: Required—TOEFL (minimum score 600 paper-based; 250 computer-based; 100 iBT). *Application deadline:* For fall admission, 12/15 for domestic and international students. Application fee: $70 ($90 for international students). Electronic applications accepted. *Expenses:* Tuition, state resident: full-time $8510; part-time $608 per credit. Tuition, nonresident: full-time $16,542; part-time $919 per credit. Required fees: $339; $110 per credit. Part-time tuition and fees vary according to course load. *Financial support:* In 2010–11, 80 research assistantships with full and partial tuition reimbursements (averaging $17,888 per year), 101 teaching assistantships with full and partial tuition reimbursements (averaging $17,327 per year) were awarded; fellowships with full tuition reimbursements, career-related internships or fieldwork, Federal Work-Study, institutionally sponsored loans, scholarships/grants, and tuition waivers (full and partial) also available. Financial award application deadline: 3/1; financial award applicants required to submit FAFSA. Total annual research expenditures: $29.3 million. *Unit head:* Dr. Robert E. Page, Director, 480-965-0803, E-mail: robert.page@asu.edu. *Application contact:* Graduate Admissions, 480-965-6113.

Baylor College of Medicine, Graduate School of Biomedical Sciences, Department of Neuroscience, Houston, TX 77030-3498. Offers PhD, MD/PhD. *Faculty:* 47 full-time (11 women). *Students:* 55 full-time (27 women); includes 2 Black or African American, non-Hispanic/Latino; 5 Asian, non-Hispanic/Latino; 8 Hispanic/Latino, 10 international. Average age 27. 161 applicants, 14% accepted, 11 enrolled. In 2010, 8 doctorates awarded. *Degree requirements:* For doctorate, thesis/dissertation, public defense. *Entrance requirements:* For doctorate, GRE General Test, GRE Subject Test (strongly recommended), minimum GPA of 3.0. Additional exam requirements/recommendations for international students: Required—TOEFL. *Application deadline:* For fall admission, 1/1 priority date for domestic students. Application fee: $0. Electronic applications accepted. *Expenses:* Tuition: Full-time $11,000. Required fees: $4900. *Financial support:* In 2010–11, 55 students received support, including 19 fellowships with full tuition reimbursements available (averaging $26,000 per year), 36 research assistantships with full tuition reimbursements available (averaging $26,000 per year); Federal Work-Study, institutionally sponsored loans, health care benefits, and students receive a scholarship unless there are grant funds available to pay tuition also available. Financial award applicants required to submit FAFSA. *Faculty research:* Neurodegenerative, neurodevelopment, neurophysiology, addiction, learning and memory. *Unit head:* Dr. Mariella DeBiasi, Director, 713-798-7270. *Application contact:* Krista Defalco, Graduate Program Administrator, 713-798-7270, Fax: 713-798-3946, E-mail: kdefalco@bcm.edu.

Baylor College of Medicine, Graduate School of Biomedical Sciences, Program in Developmental Biology, Houston, TX 77030-3498. Offers PhD, MD/PhD. *Faculty:* 63 full-time (19 women). *Students:* 55 full-time (26 women); includes 5 Asian, non-Hispanic/Latino; 3 Hispanic/Latino, 35 international. Average age 28. 73 applicants, 18% accepted, 10 enrolled. In 2010, 5 doctorates awarded. *Degree requirements:* For doctorate, thesis/dissertation, public defense. *Entrance requirements:* For doctorate, GRE General Test, GRE Subject Test (strongly recommended), minimum GPA of 3.0. Additional exam requirements/recommendations for international students: Required—TOEFL. *Application deadline:* For fall admission, 1/1 priority date for domestic students. Application fee: $0. Electronic applications accepted. *Expenses:* Tuition: Full-time $11,000. Required fees: $4900. *Financial support:* In 2010–11, 55 students received support, including 15 fellowships with full tuition reimbursements available (averaging

$26,000 per year), 40 research assistantships with full tuition reimbursements available (averaging $26,000 per year); career-related internships or fieldwork, Federal Work-Study, institutionally sponsored loans, health care benefits, tuition waivers (full), and stipends also available. *Faculty research:* Stem cells, cancer, neurobiology, organogenesis, genetics of model organisms. *Unit head:* Dr. Hugo Bellen, Director, 713-798-6410. *Application contact:* Catherine Tasnier, Graduate Program Administrator, 713-798-6410, Fax: 713-798-5386, E-mail: cat@bcm.edu.

See Display on page 282 and Close-Up on page 307.

Boston University, Graduate School of Arts and Sciences, Department of Cognitive and Neural Systems, Boston, MA 02215. Offers MA, PhD. *Students:* 46 full-time (9 women), 7 part-time (2 women); includes 6 minority (4 Asian, non-Hispanic/Latino; 1 Hispanic/Latino; 1 Two or more races, non-Hispanic/Latino), 15 international. Average age 30. 61 applicants, 31% accepted, 8 enrolled.Terminal master's awarded for partial completion of doctoral program. *Degree requirements:* For master's, one foreign language, comprehensive exam; for doctorate, one foreign language, comprehensive exam, thesis/dissertation. *Entrance requirements:* For master's and doctorate, GRE General Test, GRE Subject Test (recommended), 3 letters of recommendation. Additional exam requirements/recommendations for international students: Required—TOEFL (minimum score 550 paper-based; 213 computer-based). *Application deadline:* For fall admission, 1/15 for domestic and international students; for spring admission, 10/15 for domestic and international students. Application fee: $70. Electronic applications accepted. *Expenses:* Tuition: Full-time $39,314; part-time $1228 per credit. Required fees: $40 per semester. *Financial support:* In 2010–11, 2 fellowships with full tuition reimbursements (averaging $19,300 per year), 35 research assistantships with full tuition reimbursements (averaging $18,800 per year), 2 teaching assistantships with full tuition reimbursements were awarded; Federal Work-Study and unspecified assistantships also available. Support available to part-time students. Financial award application deadline: 1/15; financial award applicants required to submit FAFSA. *Unit head:* Ennio Mingolla, Chairman, 617-353-9485, Fax: 617-353-7755, E-mail: ennio@bu.edu. *Application contact:* Carol Y. Jefferson, Administrative Assistant, 617-353-7676, Fax: 617-353-7755, E-mail: caroly@bu.edu.

Boston University, School of Medicine, Division of Graduate Medical Sciences, Graduate Program for Neuroscience, Boston, MA 02215. Offers PhD. *Faculty:* 57 full-time (17 women). *Students:* 8 full-time (5 women), 1 (woman) part-time. 114 applicants, 11% accepted, 9 enrolled. *Degree requirements:* For doctorate, thesis/dissertation. *Entrance requirements:* For doctorate, GRE. Additional exam requirements/recommendations for international students: Required—TOEFL. Application fee: $75. Electronic applications accepted. *Expenses:* Tuition: Full-time $39,314; part-time $1228 per credit. Required fees: $40 per semester. *Financial support:* Fellowships, research assistantships available. Financial award applicants required to submit FAFSA. *Unit head:* Dr. Shelley Russek, Director, 617-638-4319, E-mail: srussek@bu.edu. *Application contact:* Michelle Hall, Associate Director of Admissions, 617-638-5121, Fax: 617-638-5740, E-mail: natashah@bu.edu.

Boston University, School of Medicine, Division of Graduate Medical Sciences, Interdepartmental Program in Neuroscience, Boston, MA 02215. Offers MA, PhD. *Students:* 26 full-time (13 women); includes 5 minority (1 Black or African American, non-Hispanic/Latino; 3 Asian, non-Hispanic/Latino; 1 Hispanic/Latino). Average age 26. 110 applicants, 12% accepted, 6 enrolled. In 2010, 10 doctorates awarded. Terminal master's awarded for partial completion of doctoral program. *Degree requirements:* For master's, one foreign language, thesis; for doctorate, one foreign language, comprehensive exam, thesis/dissertation. *Entrance requirements:* For master's and doctorate, GRE General Test, 3 letters of recommendation. Additional exam requirements/recommendations for international students: Required—TOEFL (minimum score 550 paper-based; 213 computer-based). *Application deadline:* For fall admission, 12/15 for domestic and international students. Application fee: $70. Electronic applications accepted. *Expenses:* Tuition: Full-time $39,314; part-time $1228 per credit. Required fees: $40 per semester. *Financial support:* In 2010–11, 12 students received support, including 1 fellowship with full tuition reimbursement available (averaging $18,900 per year), 7 research assistantships with full tuition reimbursements available (averaging $18,400 per year), 4 teaching assistantships with full tuition reimbursements available (averaging $18,400 per year); Federal Work-Study, scholarships/grants, and traineeships also available. Financial award application deadline: 12/15; financial award applicants required to submit FAFSA. *Unit head:* Dr. William Eldred, Director, 617-353-2439, Fax: 617-358-1857, E-mail: eldred@bu.edu. *Application contact:* Sandi Grasso, Program Administrator, 617-358-1123, Fax: 617-358-1857, E-mail: neurosci@bu.edu.

Brandeis University, Graduate School of Arts and Sciences, Department of Psychology, Waltham, MA 02454-9110. Offers brain, body and behavior (PhD); cognitive neuroscience (PhD); general psychology (MA); social/developmental psychology (PhD). Part-time programs available. *Faculty:* 17 full-time (4 women), 2 part-time/adjunct (1 woman). *Students:* 47 full-time (32 women); includes 2 Asian, non-Hispanic/Latino, 12 international. 164 applicants, 27% accepted, 24 enrolled. In 2010, 8 master's, 4 doctorates awarded. Terminal master's awarded for partial completion of doctoral program. *Degree requirements:* For master's, thesis; for doctorate, comprehensive exam, thesis/dissertation. *Entrance requirements:* For master's and doctorate, GRE General Test, GRE Subject Test (recommended), 3 letters of recommendation, statement of purpose. Additional exam requirements/recommendations for international students: Required—TOEFL (minimum score 600 paper-based; 250 computer-based; 100 iBT); Recommended—IELTS (minimum score 7). *Application deadline:* For fall admission, 1/15 priority date for domestic and international students. Applications are processed on a rolling basis. Application fee: $75. Electronic applications accepted. *Financial support:* In 2010–11, 16 fellowships with full tuition reimbursements (averaging $20,000 per year), 3 research assistantships with full tuition reimbursements (averaging $20,000 per year), 9 teaching assistantships with partial tuition reimbursements (averaging $3,200 per year) were awarded; institutionally sponsored loans, scholarships/grants, health care benefits, tuition waivers (full and partial), and unspecified assistantships also available. Support available to part-time students. Financial award application deadline: 4/15; financial award applicants required to submit FAFSA. *Faculty research:* Cognitive neuroscience, social developmental psychology, brain body and behavior. *Unit head:* Prof. Paul DiZio, Director of Graduate Studies, 781-736-3300, Fax: 781-736-3291, E-mail: dizio@brandeis.edu. *Application contact:* Phil Gnatowski, Department Administrator, 781-736-3303, Fax: 781-736-3291, E-mail: gnat@brandeis.edu.

Brandeis University, Graduate School of Arts and Sciences, Program in Neuroscience, Waltham, MA 02454-9110. Offers MS, PhD. *Faculty:* 22 full-time (9 women), 2 part-time/adjunct (1 woman). *Students:* 54 full-time (30 women); includes 3 Black or African American, non-Hispanic/Latino; 3 Asian, non-Hispanic/Latino; 4 Hispanic/Latino, 4 international. 115 applicants, 31% accepted, 18 enrolled. In 2010, 14 master's, 3 doctorates awarded. Terminal master's awarded for partial completion of doctoral program. *Degree requirements:* For master's, thesis optional, research project; for doctorate, comprehensive exam, thesis/dissertation, qualifying exams, teaching experience, journal club. *Entrance requirements:* For master's and doctorate, GRE General Test, official transcript(s), statement of purpose, resume, 3 letters of recommendation. Additional exam requirements/recommendations for international students: Required—TOEFL (minimum score 600 paper-based; 250 computer-based; 100 iBT); Recommended—IELTS (minimum score 7). *Application deadline:* For fall admission, 1/15 priority date for domestic students. Applications are processed on a rolling basis. Application fee: $75. Electronic applications accepted. *Financial support:* In 2010–11, 37 students received support, including 5 fellowships with full tuition reimbursements available (averaging $27,500 per year), 32 research assistantships with full tuition reimbursements available (averaging $27,500 per year), teaching assistantships with partial tuition reimbursements available (averaging $3,200 per year); scholarships/grants, traineeships, health care benefits, and tuition waivers (full and partial) also available. Support available to part-time students. Financial award application deadline: 4/15; financial award applicants required to submit FAFSA. *Faculty research:* Behavioral neuroscience, cellular and molecular neuroscience, computational and integrative neuroscience. *Unit head:* Dr. Don Katz, Director of Graduate Studies, 781-736-3100, Fax: 781-736-3107, E-mail: dbkatz@brandeis.edu. *Application contact:* Marcia Cabral, Department Administrator, 781-736-3100, Fax: 781-736-3107, E-mail: cabral@brandeis.edu.

Brigham Young University, Graduate Studies, College of Family, Home, and Social Sciences, Department of Psychology, Provo, UT 84602. Offers clinical psychology (PhD); general psychology (MS); psychology (PhD), including applied social psychology, behavioral neuroscience. *Accreditation:* APA (one or more programs are accredited). *Faculty:* 32 full-time (6 women), 4 part-time/adjunct (2 women). *Students:* 82 full-time (27 women); includes 3 Black or African American, non-Hispanic/Latino; 1 American Indian or Alaska Native, non-Hispanic/Latino; 6 Asian, non-Hispanic/Latino; 5 Hispanic/Latino; 68 Native Hawaiian or other Pacific Islander, non-Hispanic/Latino, 8 international. Average age 26. 91 applicants, 25% accepted, 18 enrolled. In 2010, 12 master's, 18 doctorates awarded. *Degree requirements:* For master's, thesis; for doctorate, comprehensive exam, thesis/dissertation, publishable paper. *Entrance requirements:* For master's and doctorate, GRE General Test, minimum GPA of 3.0 in last 60 hours of upper division course work. Additional exam requirements/recommendations for international students: Required—TOEFL. *Application deadline:* For fall admission, 1/5 for domestic students. Application fee: $50. Electronic applications accepted. *Expenses:* Tuition: Full-time $5580; part-time $310 per credit hour. Tuition and fees vary according to program and student's religious affiliation. *Financial support:* In 2010–11, 82 students received support, including 20 research assistantships with partial tuition reimbursements available (averaging $10,000 per year), 30 teaching assistantships with partial tuition reimbursements available (averaging $10,000 per year); fellowships, career-related internships or fieldwork, scholarships/grants, tuition waivers (partial), and unspecified assistantships also available. Financial award application deadline: 5/31. *Faculty research:* Psychotherapy process, Alzheimer's disease/dementia, psychology and law, health, psychology, developmental. Total annual research expenditures: $1 million. *Unit head:* Dr. Ramona Hopkins, Chair, 801-422-1170, Fax: 801-422-0602, E-mail: ramona_hopkins@byu.edu. *Application contact:* Karen A. Christensen, Coordinator of Student Programs, 801-422-4560, Fax: 801-422-0602, E-mail: karen@byu.edu.

Brigham Young University, Graduate Studies, College of Life Sciences, Department of Physiology and Developmental Biology, Provo, UT 84602. Offers neuroscience (MS, PhD); physiology and developmental biology (MS, PhD). Part-time programs available. *Faculty:* 19 full-time (0 women). *Students:* 25 full-time (11 women); includes 6 minority (1 American Indian or Alaska Native, non-Hispanic/Latino; 3 Asian, non-Hispanic/Latino; 2 Hispanic/Latino). Average age 29. 17 applicants, 47% accepted, 7 enrolled. In 2010, 5 master's, 2 doctorates awarded. Terminal master's awarded for partial completion of doctoral program. *Degree requirements:* For master's, thesis; for doctorate, thesis/dissertation. *Entrance requirements:* For master's, GRE General Test, minimum GPA of 3.0 during previous 2 years; for doctorate, GRE General Test, minimum GPA of 3.0 overall. Additional exam requirements/recommendations for international students: Required—TOEFL. *Application deadline:* For fall admission, 2/1 priority date for domestic and international students; for winter admission, 9/10 priority date for domestic and international students. Application fee: $50. Electronic applications accepted. *Expenses:* Tuition: Full-time $5580; part-time $310 per credit hour. Tuition and fees vary according to program and student's religious affiliation. *Financial support:* In 2010–11, 25 students received support, including 1 fellowship with partial tuition reimbursement available (averaging $7,100 per year), 12 research assistantships with full tuition reimbursements available (averaging $15,500 per year), 13 teaching assistantships with partial tuition reimbursements available (averaging $14,900 per year); career-related internships or fieldwork, institutionally sponsored loans, scholarships/grants, tuition waivers (full and partial), unspecified assistantships, and tuition awards also available. Financial award application deadline: 2/1. *Faculty research:* Sex differentiation of the brain, exercise physiology, developmental biology, membrane biophysics, neuroscience. Total annual research expenditures: $827,031. *Unit head:* Dr. William W. Winder, Chair, 801-422-3093, Fax: 801-422-0700, E-mail: william_winder@byu.edu. *Application contact:* Dr. Dixon J. Woodbury, Graduate Coordinator, 801-422-7562, Fax: 801-422-0700, E-mail: dixon_woodbury@byu.edu.

Brock University, Faculty of Graduate Studies, Faculty of Social Sciences, Program in Psychology, St. Catharines, ON L2S 3A1, Canada. Offers behavioral neuroscience (MA, PhD); life span development (MA, PhD); social personality (MA, PhD). Part-time programs available. *Degree requirements:* For master's, thesis; for doctorate, thesis/dissertation. *Entrance requirements:* For master's, GRE, honors degree; for doctorate, GRE, master's degree. Additional exam requirements/recommendations for international students: Required—TOEFL (minimum score 550 paper-based; 213 computer-based; 80 iBT), IELTS (minimum score 6.5), TWE (minimum score 4). Electronic applications accepted. *Faculty research:* Social personality, behavioral neuroscience, life-span development.

Brown University, Graduate School, Department of Neuroscience, Providence, RI 02912. Offers PhD. *Degree requirements:* For doctorate, comprehensive exam, thesis/dissertation. *Entrance requirements:* For doctorate, GRE.

Brown University, Graduate School, Department of Psychology, Providence, RI 02912. Offers behavioral neuroscience (PhD); cognitive processes (PhD); sensation and perception (PhD); social/developmental (PhD); MS/PhD. *Degree requirements:* For doctorate, thesis/dissertation. *Entrance requirements:* For doctorate, GRE General Test, GRE Subject Test.

Brown University, Graduate School, Division of Biology and Medicine, Department of Neuroscience, Providence, RI 02912. Offers PhD. *Degree requirements:* For doctorate, thesis/dissertation, preliminary exam. *Entrance requirements:* For doctorate, GRE General Test, GRE Subject Test. Additional exam requirements/recommendations for international students: Required—TOEFL. Electronic applications accepted. *Faculty research:* Neurophysiology, systems neuroscience, membrane biophysics, neuropharmacology, sensory systems.

Brown University, National Institutes of Health Sponsored Programs, Department of Neuroscience, Providence, RI 02912. Offers PhD. *Degree requirements:* For doctorate, comprehensive exam, thesis/dissertation.

California Institute of Technology, Division of Engineering and Applied Science, Option in Computation and Neural Systems, Pasadena, CA 91125-0001. Offers MS, PhD. *Faculty:* 3 full-time (0 women). *Students:* 41 full-time (12 women). 122 applicants, 11% accepted, 5 enrolled. In 2010, 6 doctorates awarded. Terminal master's awarded for partial completion of doctoral program. *Degree requirements:* For doctorate, thesis/dissertation, qualifying exam. *Entrance requirements:* For doctorate, GRE General Test. *Application deadline:* For fall admission, 1/1 for domestic students. Application fee: $0. *Financial support:* In 2010–11, 3 fellowships, 34 research assistantships, 5 teaching assistantships were awarded; Federal Work-Study and institutionally sponsored loans also available. Financial award application deadline: 1/15. *Faculty research:* Biological and artificial computational devices, modeling of sensory processes and learning, theory of collective computation. *Unit head:* Dr. Ali Hajimiri, Academic Officer, 626-395-2312, E-mail: hajimiri@caltech.edu. *Application contact:* Natalie Gilmore, Assistant Dean of Graduate Studies, 626-395-3812, Fax: 626-577-9246, E-mail: ngilmore@caltech.edu.

Carleton University, Faculty of Graduate Studies, Faculty of Arts and Social Sciences, Department of Psychology, Ottawa, ON K1S 5B6, Canada. Offers neuroscience (M Sc); psychology (MA, PhD). Part-time programs available. *Degree requirements:* For master's, thesis; for doctorate, comprehensive exam, thesis/dissertation. *Entrance requirements:* For master's, honors degree; for doctorate, GRE, master's degree. Additional exam requirements/recommendations for international students: Required—TOEFL. *Faculty research:* Behavioral neuroscience, social and personality psychology, cognitive/perception, developmental psychology, computer user research and evaluation, forensic psychology, health psychology.

Carnegie Mellon University, Center for the Neural Basis of Cognition, Pittsburgh, PA 15213-3891. Offers PhD.

Case Western Reserve University, School of Medicine and School of Graduate Studies, Graduate Programs in Medicine, Department of Neurosciences, Cleveland, OH 44106. Offers

Neuroscience

Case Western Reserve University (continued)
neurobiology (PhD); neuroscience (PhD); MD/PhD. *Degree requirements:* For doctorate, thesis/dissertation. *Entrance requirements:* For doctorate, GRE General Test, 3 letters of recommendation. Additional exam requirements/recommendations for international students: Required—TOEFL. Electronic applications accepted. *Faculty research:* Neurotropic factors, synapse formation, regeneration, determination of cell fate, cellular neuroscience.

Central Michigan University, College of Graduate Studies, College of Humanities and Social and Behavioral Sciences, Department of Psychology, Program in Neuroscience, Mount Pleasant, MI 48859. Offers MS, PhD. *Students:* 3 full-time (2 women), 3 part-time (0 women); includes 1 Asian, non-Hispanic/Latino, 1 international. *Degree requirements:* For master's, comprehensive exam, thesis or alternative; for doctorate, thesis/dissertation. *Entrance requirements:* For master's and doctorate, GRE. *Application deadline:* For fall admission, 2/1 for domestic students, 3/1 for international students. Electronic applications accepted. *Expenses:* Tuition, state resident: full-time $8208; part-time $456 per credit hour. Tuition, nonresident: full-time $13,788; part-time $766 per credit hour. One-time fee: $25. *Financial support:* Fellowships with tuition reimbursements, research assistantships with tuition reimbursements, career-related internships or fieldwork, Federal Work-Study, unspecified assistantships, and out-of-state merit awards, non-resident graduate awards available. *Unit head:* Hajime Otani, Chairperson, 989-774-6494, Fax: 989-774-2553, E-mail: otani1h@cmich.edu. *Application contact:* Gary Dunbar, Director, Neuroscience, 989-774-3282, Fax: 989-774-2553, E-mail: dunba1g@cmich.edu.

College of Staten Island of the City University of New York, Graduate Programs, Center for Developmental Neuroscience and Developmental Disabilities, Staten Island, NY 10314-6600. Offers neuroscience, mental retardation and developmental disabilities (MS). Part-time and evening/weekend programs available. *Faculty:* 7 full-time (1 woman), 3 part-time/adjunct (1 woman). *Students:* 1 (woman) full-time, 32 part-time (18 women); includes 1 Black or African American, non-Hispanic/Latino; 4 Asian, non-Hispanic/Latino; 2 Hispanic/Latino, 2 international. Average age 27. 26 applicants, 58% accepted, 10 enrolled. In 2010, 2 master's awarded. Terminal master's awarded for partial completion of doctoral program. *Degree requirements:* For master's, thesis, oral preliminary exam, thesis defense. *Entrance requirements:* For master's, 3 letters of recommendation; minimum GPA of 3.0 in undergraduate biology, mathematics, psychology or other science courses; 2 semesters of course work in biology, chemistry and psychology; 1 semester of course work in calculus and statistics. Additional exam requirements/recommendations for international students: Required—TOEFL (minimum score 550 paper-based; 213 computer-based; 79 iBT), IELTS (minimum score 6.5). *Application deadline:* Applications are processed on a rolling basis. Application fee: $125. Electronic applications accepted. *Expenses:* Tuition, state resident: full-time $7730; part-time $325 per credit. Tuition, nonresident: full-time $14,520; part-time $605 per credit. Required fees: $378. *Financial support:* In 2010–11, 1 student received support. Career-related internships or fieldwork and Federal Work-Study available. Financial award applicants required to submit FAFSA. *Unit head:* Dr. Probal Banerjee, Coordinator, 718-982-3950, Fax: 718-982-3953, E-mail: banerjee@mail.csi.cuny.edu. *Application contact:* Sasha Spence, Assistant Director of Graduate Recruitment and Admissions, 718-982-2699, Fax: 718-982-2500, E-mail: sasha.spence@csi.cuny.edu.

Colorado State University, Graduate School, Program in Molecular, Cellular and Integrative Neurosciences, Fort Collins, CO 80523-1617. Offers PhD. *Students:* 3 full-time (0 women); includes 1 minority (Two or more races, non-Hispanic/Latino). Average age 25. 14 applicants, 21% accepted, 3 enrolled. *Entrance requirements:* For doctorate, GRE, minimum GPA of 3.0, letter of recommendation. Additional exam requirements/recommendations for international students: Required—TOEFL (minimum score 650 paper-based; 267 computer-based; 109 iBT). *Application deadline:* For fall admission, 12/15 priority date for domestic and international students. Application fee: $50. Electronic applications accepted. *Expenses:* Tuition, state resident: full-time $7434; part-time $413 per credit. Tuition, nonresident: full-time $19,022; part-time $1057 per credit. Required fees: $1729; $88 per credit. *Financial support:* In 2010–11, 3 students received support, including 3 research assistantships with partial tuition reimbursements available (averaging $13,286 per year); fellowships, teaching assistantships with partial tuition reimbursements available, scholarships/grants, health care benefits, and unspecified assistantships also available. Financial award application deadline: 1/1; financial award applicants required to submit FAFSA. *Faculty research:* Ion channels, synaptic mechanisms, neuronal circuitry, degeneration and regeneration, artificial neural networks. *Unit head:* Dr. Kathryn Partin, Professor and Director, 970-491-2263, Fax: 970-491-7907, E-mail: kathy.partin@colostate.edu. *Application contact:* Nancy Graham, Administrative Assistant, 970-491-0425, Fax: 970-491-7907, E-mail: njgraham@colostate.edu.

Cornell University, Joan and Sanford I. Weill Medical College and Graduate School of Medical Sciences, Weill Cornell Graduate School of Medical Sciences, Neuroscience Program, New York, NY 10065. Offers MS, PhD. *Faculty:* 33 full-time (9 women). *Students:* 41 full-time (27 women); includes 3 Black or African American, non-Hispanic/Latino; 4 Asian, non-Hispanic/Latino; 1 Hispanic/Latino, 9 international. Average age 22. 111 applicants, 15% accepted, 9 enrolled. In 2010, 2 master's, 10 doctorates awarded. Terminal master's awarded for partial completion of doctoral program. *Degree requirements:* For master's, comprehensive exam; for doctorate, thesis/dissertation, final exam. *Entrance requirements:* For doctorate, GRE General Test, undergraduate training in biology, organic chemistry, physics, and mathematics. Additional exam requirements/recommendations for international students: Required—TOEFL. *Application deadline:* For fall admission, 12/1 for domestic students. Application fee: $60. Electronic applications accepted. *Expenses:* Tuition: Full-time $45,545. Required fees: $2805. *Financial support:* In 2010–11, 6 fellowships (averaging $21,180 per year) were awarded; scholarships/grants, health care benefits, and stipends (given to all students) also available. *Faculty research:* Regulation of neuronal development, neuronal stem cells, information processing, behavior, neuronal plasticity. *Unit head:* Dr. Betty Jo Casey, Director, 212-746-5832, E-mail: bjc2002@med.cornell.edu. *Application contact:* Alime Lukaj, Program Coordinator, 212-746-6582, E-mail: alukaj@med.cornell.edu.

Dalhousie University, Faculty of Graduate Studies, Neuroscience Institute, Halifax, NS B3H 4H7, Canada. Offers M Sc, PhD. *Degree requirements:* For doctorate, thesis/dissertation. *Entrance requirements:* For master's and doctorate, 4 year honors degree or equivalent, minimum A- average. Additional exam requirements/recommendations for international students: Required—TOEFL, IELTS, 1 of the following 5 approved tests: TOEFL, IELTS, CANTEST, CAEL, Michigan English Language Assessment Battery. Electronic applications accepted. *Faculty research:* Molecular, cellular, systems, behavioral and clinical neuroscience.

Dalhousie University, Faculty of Science, Department of Psychology, Halifax, NS B3H 4R2, Canada. Offers clinical psychology (PhD); psychology (M Sc, PhD); psychology/neuroscience (M Sc, PhD). *Accreditation:* APA (one or more programs are accredited). *Degree requirements:* For master's, thesis; for doctorate, thesis/dissertation. *Entrance requirements:* For doctorate, GRE General Test. Additional exam requirements/recommendations for international students: Required—TOEFL, IELTS, CANTEST, CAEL, or Michigan English Language Assessment Battery. Electronic applications accepted. *Faculty research:* Physiological psychology, psychology of learning, learning and behavior, forensic clinical health psychology, development perception and cognition.

Dartmouth College, Arts and Sciences Graduate Programs, Department of Psychological and Brain Sciences, Hanover, NH 03755. Offers cognitive neuroscience (PhD); psychology (PhD). *Degree requirements:* For doctorate, thesis/dissertation. *Entrance requirements:* For doctorate, GRE General Test, GRE Subject Test. Additional exam requirements/recommendations for international students: Required—TOEFL. *Faculty research:* Behavioral neuroscience, cognitive neuroscience, cognitive science, social/personality psychology.

Dartmouth College, Arts and Sciences Graduate Programs, Program in Experimental and Molecular Medicine, The Neuroscience Center, Hanover, NH 03755. Offers PhD, MD/PhD.

Degrees awarded through participating programs. *Entrance requirements:* Additional exam requirements/recommendations for international students: Required—TOEFL (minimum score 620 paper-based; 260 computer-based; 105 iBT). Electronic applications accepted.

Dartmouth College, Program in Experimental and Molecular Medicine, Neuroscience Track, Hanover, NH 03755. Offers PhD.

Delaware State University, Graduate Programs, Department of Biology, Dover, DE 19901-2277. Offers biological sciences (MA, MS); biology education (MS); molecular and cellular neuroscience (MS); neuroscience (PhD). Part-time and evening/weekend programs available. *Degree requirements:* For master's, thesis (for some programs). *Entrance requirements:* For master's, GRE, minimum GPA of 3.0 in major, 2.75 overall. Additional exam requirements/recommendations for international students: Required—TOEFL (minimum score 550 paper-based). Electronic applications accepted. *Faculty research:* Cell biology, immunology, microbiology, genetics, ecology.

Drexel University, College of Arts and Sciences, Department of Psychology, Clinical Psychology Program, Philadelphia, PA 19104-2875. Offers clinical psychology (PhD); forensic psychology (PhD); health psychology (PhD); neuropsychology (PhD). *Accreditation:* APA. Terminal master's awarded for partial completion of doctoral program. *Degree requirements:* For doctorate, thesis/dissertation, qualifying exam. *Entrance requirements:* For doctorate, GRE General Test, GRE Subject Test, minimum GPA of 3.0. Electronic applications accepted. *Expenses:* Contact institution. *Faculty research:* Cognitive behavioral therapy, stress and coping, eating disorders, substance abuse, developmental disabilities.

Drexel University, College of Medicine, Biomedical Graduate Programs, Program in Neuroscience, Philadelphia, PA 19104-2875. Offers MS, PhD, MD/PhD. *Degree requirements:* For doctorate, thesis/dissertation, qualifying exam. *Entrance requirements:* For doctorate, GRE General Test, or MCAT, minimum GPA of 2.75. Additional exam requirements/recommendations for international students: Required—TOEFL. Electronic applications accepted. *Faculty research:* Central monoamine systems, drugs of abuse, anatomy/physiology of sensory systems, neurodegenerative disorders and recovery of function, neuromodulation and synaptic plasticity.

Duke University, Graduate School, Department of Cognitive Neuroscience, Durham, NC 27708-0586. Offers PhD, Certificate. *Faculty:* 39 full-time. *Students:* 10 full-time (6 women); includes 1 Black or African American, non-Hispanic/Latino, 3 international. 59 applicants, 19% accepted, 5 enrolled. *Degree requirements:* For doctorate, thesis/dissertation. *Entrance requirements:* For doctorate, GRE General Test. Additional exam requirements/recommendations for international students: Required—TOEFL (minimum score 550 paper-based; 213 computer-based; 83 iBT), IELTS (minimum score 7). *Application deadline:* For fall admission, 12/8 priority date for domestic and international students. Application fee: $75. Electronic applications accepted. *Financial support:* Fellowships, research assistantships, teaching assistantships available. Financial award application deadline: 12/8. *Unit head:* Elizabeth Brannon, Director of Graduate Studies, 919-684-3422, Fax: 919-684-3475, E-mail: emily.clark@duke.edu. *Application contact:* Elizabeth Hutton, Director of Admissions, 919-684-3913, Fax: 919-684-2277, E-mail: grad-admissions@duke.edu.

Emory University, Laney Graduate School, Department of Psychology, Atlanta, GA 30322-1100. Offers clinical psychology (PhD); cognition and development (PhD); neuroscience and animal behavior (PhD). *Accreditation:* APA. *Degree requirements:* For doctorate, comprehensive exam, thesis/dissertation. *Entrance requirements:* For doctorate, GRE General Test, minimum GPA of 3.25. Additional exam requirements/recommendations for international students: Required—TOEFL. Electronic applications accepted. *Expenses:* Tuition: Full-time $33,800. Required fees: $1300. *Faculty research:* Neuroscience and animal behavior; adult and child psychopathology, cognition development assessment.

Emory University, Laney Graduate School, Division of Biological and Biomedical Sciences, Program in Neuroscience, Atlanta, GA 30322-1100. Offers PhD. *Faculty:* 109 full-time (26 women). *Students:* 102 full-time (65 women); includes 4 Black or African American, non-Hispanic/Latino; 3 Asian, non-Hispanic/Latino; 8 Hispanic/Latino, 6 international. Average age 27. 209 applicants, 16% accepted, 19 enrolled. In 2010, 7 doctorates awarded. *Median time to degree:* Of those who began their doctoral program in fall 2002, 94% received their degree in 8 years or less. *Degree requirements:* For doctorate, comprehensive exam, thesis/dissertation. *Entrance requirements:* For doctorate, GRE General Test, minimum GPA of 3.0 in science course work (recommended). Additional exam requirements/recommendations for international students: Required—TOEFL. *Application deadline:* For fall admission, 12/1 for domestic and international students. Application fee: $75. Electronic applications accepted. *Expenses:* Tuition: Full-time $33,800. Required fees: $1300. *Financial support:* In 2010–11, 34 students received support, including 34 fellowships with full tuition reimbursements available (averaging $25,000 per year); institutionally sponsored loans, scholarships/grants, health care benefits, and tuition waivers (full) also available. *Faculty research:* Cell and molecular biology, development, behavior, neurodegenerative disease. *Unit head:* Dr. Yoland Smith, Director, 404-727-7519, Fax: 404-727-3278, E-mail: yolands@rmy.emory.edu. *Application contact:* Kathy Smith, Director of Recruitment and Admissions, 404-727-2547, Fax: 404-727-3322, E-mail: kathy.smith@emory.edu.

Florida Atlantic University, Charles E. Schmidt College of Science, Center for Complex Systems and Brain Sciences, Boca Raton, FL 33431-0991. Offers PhD. *Faculty:* 6 full-time (3 women), 1 part-time/adjunct (0 women). *Students:* 39 full-time (25 women), 10 part-time (7 women); includes 8 minority (2 Black or African American, non-Hispanic/Latino; 3 Asian, non-Hispanic/Latino; 3 Hispanic/Latino), 4 international. Average age 34. 16 applicants, 25% accepted, 4 enrolled. In 2010, 5 doctorates awarded. *Degree requirements:* For doctorate, thesis/dissertation. *Entrance requirements:* For doctorate, GRE General Test, minimum GPA of 3.0 in last 60 hours of undergraduate course work. Additional exam requirements/recommendations for international students: Required—TOEFL. *Application deadline:* For fall admission, 1/15 priority date for domestic and international students. Application fee: $30. *Expenses:* Tuition, state resident: part-time $319.96 per credit. Tuition, nonresident: part-time $926.42 per credit. *Financial support:* Fellowships with full tuition reimbursements, research assistantships with partial tuition reimbursements, teaching assistantships with partial tuition reimbursements, Federal Work-Study, traineeships, and unspecified assistantships available. *Faculty research:* Motor behavior, speech perception, nonlinear dynamics and fractals, behavioral neuroscience, cellular and molecular neuroscience. *Unit head:* Dr. Janet Blanks, Director, 561-297-2229, Fax: 561-297-3634, E-mail: blanks@ccs.fau.edu. *Application contact:* Rhona Frankel, Associate Director, 561-297-2230, E-mail: frankel@fau.edu.

Florida State University, College of Medicine, Department of Biomedical Sciences, Tallahassee, FL 32306-4300. Offers biomedical sciences (PhD); neuroscience (PhD). *Faculty:* 20 full-time (5 women). *Students:* 32 full-time (16 women); includes 1 Black or African American, non-Hispanic/Latino; 2 Hispanic/Latino, 11 international. Average age 27. 34 applicants, 32% accepted, 6 enrolled. In 2010, 3 doctorates awarded. *Degree requirements:* For doctorate, thesis/dissertation. *Entrance requirements:* For doctorate, GRE (minimum score: 1000). Additional exam requirements/recommendations for international students: Required—TOEFL (minimum score 550 paper-based; 80 iBT). *Application deadline:* For fall admission, 2/1 for domestic and international students. Application fee: $30. *Expenses:* Tuition, state resident: full-time $8238. *Financial support:* In 2010–11, 32 students received support, including 32 research assistantships with full tuition reimbursements available (averaging $21,500 per year). Financial award applicants required to submit FAFSA. *Unit head:* Dr. Richard S. Nowakowski, Professor/Chair, 850-644-2013, Fax: 850-645-7153, E-mail: richard.nowakowski@med.fsu.edu. *Application contact:* Lilly Lewis, Academic Program Specialist, 850-645-6420, Fax: 850-645-7153, E-mail: lilly.lewis@med.fsu.edu.

Florida State University, The Graduate School, College of Arts and Sciences, Department of Biological Science, Tallahassee, FL 32306-4295. Offers cell and molecular biology and genetics (MS, PhD); ecology and evolutionary biology (MS, PhD); neuroscience (PhD); plant biology

(MS, PhD); science teaching (MST); structural biology (MS, PhD). *Faculty:* 53 full-time (16 women). *Students:* 110 full-time (51 women); includes 2 Black or African American, non-Hispanic/Latino; 2 Asian, non-Hispanic/Latino; 10 Hispanic/Latino, 13 international. 323 applicants, 12% accepted, 26 enrolled. In 2010, 5 master's, 13 doctorates awarded. Terminal master's awarded for partial completion of doctoral program. *Degree requirements:* For master's, comprehensive exam, thesis, teaching experience, seminar presentations; for doctorate, comprehensive exam, thesis/dissertation, teaching experience; seminar presentations. *Entrance requirements:* For master's, GRE General Test (minimum combined score 1100, 500 verbal, 500 quantitative), minimum upper-division GPA of 3.0; for doctorate, GRE General Test (minimum combined score 1100, Verbal 500, Quantitative 500), minimum upper-division GPA of 3.0. Additional exam requirements/recommendations for international students: Required—TOEFL (minimum score 600 paper-based; 250 computer-based; 92 iBT). *Application deadline:* For fall admission, 12/15 for domestic and international students. Application fee: $30. Electronic applications accepted. *Expenses:* Tuition, state resident: full-time $8238. *Financial support:* In 2010–11, 108 students received support, including 7 fellowships with full tuition reimbursements available (averaging $24,000 per year), 41 research assistantships with full tuition reimbursements available (averaging $21,000 per year), 56 teaching assistantships with full tuition reimbursements available (averaging $21,000 per year); traineeships also available. Financial award application deadline: 12/15; financial award applicants required to submit FAFSA. *Faculty research:* Cell and molecular biology and genetics, ecology and evolutionary biology, plant science, structural biology. *Unit head:* Dr. George W. Bates, Professor and Associate Chairman, 850-644-5749, Fax: 850-644-9829, E-mail: bates@bio.fsu.edu. *Application contact:* Judy Bowers, Coordinator, Graduate Affairs, 850-644-3023, Fax: 850-644-9829, E-mail: gradinfo@bio.fsu.edu.

Florida State University, The Graduate School, College of Arts and Sciences, Department of Psychology, Interdisciplinary Program in Neuroscience, Tallahassee, FL 32306. Offers PhD. *Faculty:* 11 full-time (4 women). *Students:* 25 full-time (14 women), 1 (woman) part-time; includes 2 Black or African American, non-Hispanic/Latino; 1 Asian, non-Hispanic/Latino; 2 Hispanic/Latino, 1 international. Average age 26. 49 applicants, 12% accepted, 3 enrolled. In 2010, 6 doctorates awarded. *Degree requirements:* For doctorate, thesis/dissertation, preliminary exam. *Entrance requirements:* For doctorate, GRE General Test (suggested minimum total score of 1100), minimum GPA of 3.0, research experience, letters of recommendation. Additional exam requirements/recommendations for international students: Required—TOEFL (minimum score 550 paper-based; 213 computer-based; 80 iBT). *Application deadline:* For fall admission, 12/1 for domestic and international students. Application fee: $30. Electronic applications accepted. *Expenses:* Tuition, state resident: full-time $8238. *Financial support:* In 2010–11, 25 students received support, including 5 fellowships with full tuition reimbursements available (averaging $22,000 per year), 11 research assistantships with full tuition reimbursements available (averaging $21,000 per year), 9 teaching assistantships with full tuition reimbursements available (averaging $21,000 per year); Federal Work-Study, institutionally sponsored loans, scholarships/grants, traineeships, health care benefits, and unspecified assistantships also available. Financial award applicants required to submit FAFSA. *Faculty research:* Sensory processes, neural development and plasticity, circadian rhythms, behavioral and molecular genetics, hormonal control of behavior. Total annual research expenditures: $3.4 million. *Unit head:* Dr. Richard Hyson, Director, 850-644-3076, Fax: 850-645-0349, E-mail: hyson@psy.fsu.edu. *Application contact:* Cherie P. Miller, Graduate Program Assistant, 850-644-2499, Fax: 850-644-7739, E-mail: grad-info@psy.fsu.edu.

George Mason University, College of Science, Fairfax, VA 22030. Offers advanced biomedical sciences (Certificate); bioinformatics and computational biology (MS, PhD, Certificate); biosciences (PhD); chemistry and biochemistry (MS, PhD), including chemistry (MS), chemistry and biochemistry (PhD); climate dynamics (PhD); computational and data sciences (MS, PhD, Certificate), including computational sciences (MS), computational sciences and informatics (PhD), computational techniques and applications (Certificate); environmental science and policy (MS, PhD, Certificate), including environmental management (Certificate), environmental science and policy (MS), environmental science and public policy (PhD); forensic science (MS); forensics (Certificate); geography and geoinformation science (MS, PhD, Certificate), including earth system science (MS), earth systems and geoinformation sciences (PhD), geographic and cartographic sciences (MS), geographic information sciences (Certificate), geoinformatics and geospatial intelligence (MS), geospatial intelligence (Certificate), remote sensing (Certificate); mathematical sciences (MS, PhD, Certificate), including actuarial sciences (Certificate), mathematics (MS, PhD); molecular and microbiology (MS, PhD), including biology (MS), biosciences (PhD); neuroscience (PhD); physical sciences (PhD); physics and astronomy (MS, PhD), including applied and engineering physics (MS), physics (PhD). Part-time and evening/weekend programs available. *Faculty:* 262 full-time (73 women), 62 part-time/adjunct (23 women). *Students:* 223 full-time (97 women), 716 part-time (305 women); includes 180 minority (36 Black or African American, non-Hispanic/Latino; 2 American Indian or Alaska Native, non-Hispanic/Latino; 90 Asian, non-Hispanic/Latino; 47 Hispanic/Latino; 1 Native Hawaiian or other Pacific Islander, non-Hispanic/Latino; 4 Two or more races, non-Hispanic/Latino), 144 international. Average age 33. 894 applicants, 59% accepted, 315 enrolled. In 2010, 95 master's, 32 doctorates, 27 other advanced degrees awarded. *Degree requirements:* For doctorate, comprehensive exam, thesis/dissertation. *Entrance requirements:* For master's and doctorate, GRE General Test, minimum GPA of 3.0 in last 60 hours. Additional exam requirements/recommendations for international students: Required—TOEFL (minimum score 570 paper-based; 230 computer-based; 88 iBT). *Application deadline:* For fall admission, 3/1 priority date for domestic students, 2/1 for international students; for spring admission, 11/1 priority date for domestic students. Applications are processed on a rolling basis. Application fee: $100. Electronic applications accepted. *Expenses:* Tuition, state resident: full-time $8192; part-time $440 per credit hour. Tuition, nonresident: full-time $22,952; part-time $1055 per credit hour. Required fees: $2364; $99 per credit hour. *Financial support:* In 2010–11, 233 students received support, including 26 fellowships with tuition reimbursements available (averaging $18,000 per year), 104 research assistantships with full tuition reimbursements available (averaging $15,616 per year), 107 teaching assistantships (averaging $12,215 per year); career-related internships or fieldwork, Federal Work-Study, scholarships/grants, and health care benefits (full time research or teaching assistantship recipients) also available. Support available to part-time students. Financial award application deadline: 2/1; financial award applicants required to submit FAFSA. *Faculty research:* Space sciences and astrophysics, fluid dynamics, materials modeling and simulation, bioinformatics, global changes and statistics. *Unit head:* Dr. Vikas E. Chandhoke, Director, 703-993-3622, Fax: 703-993-1993, E-mail: cosinfo@gmu.edu. *Application contact:* Dr. Tim Born, Associate Dean for Graduate Programs, 703-993-4171, Fax: 703-993-9034, E-mail: tborn@gmu.edu.

Georgetown University, Graduate School of Arts and Sciences, Programs in Biomedical Sciences, Program in Neuroscience, Washington, DC 20057. Offers PhD, MD/PhD. *Degree requirements:* For doctorate, thesis/dissertation. *Entrance requirements:* For doctorate, GRE General Test. Additional exam requirements/recommendations for international students: Required—TOEFL.

Georgia Health Sciences University, College of Graduate Studies, Program in Neuroscience, Augusta, GA 30912. Offers MS, PhD. *Students:* 19 full-time (10 women); includes 1 Asian, non-Hispanic/Latino; 2 Two or more races, non-Hispanic/Latino, 7 international. Average age 29. In 2010, 1 doctorate awarded. *Degree requirements:* For doctorate, comprehensive exam, thesis/dissertation. *Entrance requirements:* For doctorate, GRE General Test. Additional exam requirements/recommendations for international students: Required—TOEFL (minimum score 550 paper-based; 213 computer-based; 79 iBT). *Application deadline:* For fall admission, 1/15 for domestic and international students. Application fee: $30. Electronic applications accepted. *Expenses:* Tuition, state resident: full-time $7500; part-time $313 per semester hour. Tuition, nonresident: full-time $24,772; part-time $1033 per semester hour. Required fees: $1112. *Financial support:* In 2010–11, 2 students received support, including 13 research assistantships with partial tuition reimbursements available (averaging $23,000 per year); Federal Work-Study also available. Support available to part-time students. Financial award application deadline: 5/31. *Faculty research:* Learning and memory, neuronal migration, synapse formation, regeneration, developmental neurobiology, neurodegeneration and neural repair. Total annual research expenditures: $1.8 million. *Unit head:* Dr. Lin Mei, Director of Institute of Molecular Medicine and Genetics, 706-721-8775, Fax: 706-721-7915, E-mail: lmei@georgiahealth.edu. *Application contact:* Dr. Patricia L. Cameron, Acting Vice Dean, 706-721-3279, E-mail: pcameron@georgiahealth.edu.

Graduate School and University Center of the City University of New York, Graduate Studies, Program in Psychology, New York, NY 10016-4039. Offers basic applied neurocognition (PhD); biopsychology (PhD); clinical psychology (PhD); developmental psychology (PhD); environmental psychology (PhD); experimental psychology (PhD); industrial psychology (PhD); learning processes (PhD); neuropsychology (PhD); psychology (PhD); social personality (PhD). *Degree requirements:* For doctorate, one foreign language, thesis/dissertation. *Entrance requirements:* For doctorate, GRE General Test. Additional exam requirements/recommendations for international students: Required—TOEFL. Electronic applications accepted.

Harvard University, Graduate School of Arts and Sciences, Program in Neuroscience, Boston, MA 02115. Offers neurobiology (PhD). *Degree requirements:* For doctorate, thesis/dissertation, qualifying exam. *Entrance requirements:* For doctorate, GRE General Test, GRE Subject Test. Additional exam requirements/recommendations for international students: Required—TOEFL. *Expenses:* Tuition: Full-time $34,976. Required fees: $1166. Full-time tuition and fees vary according to program. *Faculty research:* Relationship between diseases of the nervous system and basic science.

Hunter College of the City University of New York, Graduate School, School of Arts and Sciences, Department of Psychology, New York, NY 10021-5085. Offers animal behavior and conservation (MA); applied and evaluative psychology (MA); biopsychology and behavioral neuroscience (PhD); biopsychology and comparative psychology (MA); social, cognitive, and developmental psychology (MA). Part-time and evening/weekend programs available. *Faculty:* 9 full-time (1 woman), 1 part-time/adjunct (0 women). *Students:* 10 full-time (7 women), 79 part-time (61 women); includes 3 Black or African American, non-Hispanic/Latino; 7 Asian, non-Hispanic/Latino; 9 Hispanic/Latino, 2 international. Average age 27. 151 applicants, 34% accepted, 21 enrolled. In 2010, 13 master's awarded. *Degree requirements:* For master's, comprehensive exam, thesis. *Entrance requirements:* For master's, GRE General Test, minimum 12 credits of course work in psychology, including statistics and experimental psychology; 2 letters of recommendation. Additional exam requirements/recommendations for international students: Required—TOEFL. *Application deadline:* For fall admission, 4/1 for domestic students, 2/1 for international students; for spring admission, 11/1 for domestic students, 9/1 for international students. Applications are processed on a rolling basis. Application fee: $125. *Financial support:* Federal Work-Study, scholarships/grants, and tuition waivers (partial) available. Support available to part-time students. *Faculty research:* Personality, cognitive and linguistic development, hormonal and neural control of behavior, gender and culture, social cognition of health and attitudes. *Unit head:* Dr. Jeffrey Parsons, Chairperson, 212-772-5550, Fax: 212-772-5620, E-mail: jeffrey.parsons@hunter.cuny.edu. *Application contact:* Martin Braun, Acting Program Director, 212-772-4482, Fax: 212-650-3336, E-mail: cbraun@hunter.cuny.edu.

Illinois State University, Graduate School, College of Arts and Sciences, Department of Biological Sciences, Normal, IL 61790-2200. Offers animal behavior (MS); bacteriology (MS); biochemistry (MS); biological sciences (MS); biology (PhD); biophysics (MS); biotechnology (MS); botany (MS, PhD); cell biology (MS); conservation biology (MS); developmental biology (MS); ecology (MS, PhD); entomology (MS); evolutionary biology (MS); genetics (MS, PhD); immunology (MS); microbiology (MS, PhD); molecular biology (MS); molecular genetics (MS); neurobiology (MS); neuroscience (MS); parasitology (MS); physiology (MS, PhD); plant biology (MS); plant molecular biology (MS); plant sciences (MS); structural biology (MS); zoology (MS, PhD). Part-time programs available. *Degree requirements:* For master's, thesis or alternative; for doctorate, variable foreign language requirement, thesis/dissertation, 2 terms of residency. *Entrance requirements:* For master's, GRE General Test, minimum GPA of 2.6 in last 60 hours of course work; for doctorate, GRE General Test. *Faculty research:* Redoc balance and drug development in schistosoma mansoni, control of the growth of listeria monocytogenes at low temperature, regulation of cell expansion and microtubule function by SPRI, CRUI: physiology and fitness consequences of different life history phenotypes.

Indiana University Bloomington, University Graduate School, College of Arts and Sciences, Program in Neuroscience, Bloomington, IN 47405-7000. Offers PhD. *Students:* 15 full-time (8 women); includes 1 minority (Black or African American, non-Hispanic/Latino), 5 international. Average age 29. 63 applicants, 11% accepted, 4 enrolled. In 2010, 8 doctorates awarded. Application fee: $55 ($65 for international students). *Financial support:* In 2010–11, 6 fellowships with tuition reimbursements (averaging $20,000 per year), 3 research assistantships with tuition reimbursements (averaging $17,900 per year), 6 teaching assistantships with tuition reimbursements (averaging $18,275 per year) were awarded. *Unit head:* George Rebec, Director of Graduate Studies, 812-855-4832, E-mail: rebec@indiana.edu. *Application contact:* Faye Caylor, Administrative Assistant, 812-855-7756, E-mail: fcaylor@indiana.edu.

Iowa State University of Science and Technology, Graduate College, Interdisciplinary Programs, Program in Neuroscience, Ames, IA 50011. Offers MS, PhD. *Students:* 13 full-time (7 women); includes 3 Asian, non-Hispanic/Latino, 4 international. In 2010, 1 doctorate awarded. Terminal master's awarded for partial completion of doctoral program. *Degree requirements:* For master's, thesis; for doctorate, thesis/dissertation. *Entrance requirements:* For master's and doctorate, GRE General Test, resume. Additional exam requirements/recommendations for international students: Required—TOEFL (minimum score 580 paper-based; 85 iBT), IELTS (minimum score 7). *Application deadline:* For fall admission, 2/1 priority date for domestic students, 2/1 for international students. Application fee: $40 ($90 for international students). *Financial support:* In 2010–11, 9 research assistantships with full and partial tuition reimbursements (averaging $16,062 per year), 2 teaching assistantships with full and partial tuition reimbursements (averaging $10,896 per year) were awarded; scholarships/grants, health care benefits, and unspecified assistantships also available. *Faculty research:* Behavioral pharmacology and immunology, developmental neurobiology, neuroendocrinology, neuroregulatory mechanisms at the cellular level, signal transduction in neurons. *Unit head:* Dr. Donald Sakaguchi, Chair, Supervising Committee, 515-294-7252, E-mail: idgp@iastate.edu. *Application contact:* Katie Blair, Information Contact, 515-294-7252, Fax: 515-924-6790, E-mail: idgp@iastate.edu.

The Johns Hopkins University, School of Medicine, Graduate Programs in Medicine, Neuroscience Training Program, Baltimore, MD 21218-2699. Offers PhD. *Faculty:* 66 full-time (10 women). *Students:* 94 full-time (51 women); includes 17 minority (2 Black or African American, non-Hispanic/Latino; 8 Asian, non-Hispanic/Latino; 6 Hispanic/Latino; 1 Two or more races, non-Hispanic/Latino), 42 international. Average age 28. 239 applicants, 12% accepted, 13 enrolled. In 2010, 12 doctorates awarded. *Degree requirements:* For doctorate, comprehensive exam, thesis/dissertation, thesis defense. *Entrance requirements:* For doctorate, GRE General Test, bachelor's degree in science or mathematics. Additional exam requirements/recommendations for international students: Required—TOEFL. *Application deadline:* For winter admission, 12/7 for domestic and international students. Application fee: $85. Electronic applications accepted. *Financial support:* In 2010–11, 94 fellowships (averaging $27,125 per year) were awarded; scholarships/grants and tuition waivers (full and partial) also available. Financial award application deadline: 1/1. *Faculty research:* Neurophysiology, neurochemistry, neuroanatomy, pharmacology, development. Total annual research expenditures: $15.5 million. *Unit head:* Dr. David D. Ginty, Professor and Director of Graduate Studies, 410-614-9494, Fax: 410-614-6249, E-mail: dginty@jhmi.edu. *Application contact:* Rita G. Ragan, Graduate Program Manager, 410-955-7947, Fax: 410-614-6249, E-mail: rgragan@jhmi.edu.

Kent State University, School of Biomedical Sciences, Program in Neuroscience, Kent, OH 44242-0001. Offers MS, PhD. Offered in cooperation with Northeastern Ohio Universities College of Medicine. Terminal master's awarded for partial completion of doctoral program. *Degree requirements:* For master's, thesis; for doctorate, thesis/dissertation. *Entrance*

Neuroscience

Kent State University *(continued)*
requirements: For master's and doctorate, GRE General Test, minimum GPA of 3.0. Additional exam requirements/recommendations for international students: Required—TOEFL. Electronic applications accepted. *Expenses:* Tuition, state resident: full-time $7866; part-time $437 per credit hour. Tuition, nonresident: full-time $14,022; part-time $779 per credit hour. *Faculty research:* Plasticity of the nervous system, learning and memory processes–neural correlates, neuroendocrinology of cyclic behavior, synaptic neurochemistry.

Lehigh University, College of Arts and Sciences, Department of Biological Sciences, Bethlehem, PA 18015. Offers biochemistry (PhD); integrative biology and neuroscience (PhD); molecular biology (MS, PhD). Part-time programs available. Postbaccalaureate distance learning degree programs offered (no on-campus study). *Faculty:* 17 full-time (7 women). *Students:* 30 full-time (14 women), 30 part-time (18 women); includes 6 minority (1 Black or African American, non-Hispanic/Latino; 1 Asian, non-Hispanic/Latino; 3 Hispanic/Latino; 1 Native Hawaiian or other Pacific Islander, non-Hispanic/Latino), 7 international. Average age 29. 79 applicants, 25% accepted, 19 enrolled. In 2010, 9 master's, 3 doctorates awarded. Terminal master's awarded for partial completion of doctoral program. *Degree requirements:* For master's, research report; for doctorate, comprehensive exam, thesis/dissertation. *Entrance requirements:* For doctorate, GRE General Test. Additional exam requirements/recommendations for international students: Required—TOEFL. *Application deadline:* For fall admission, 12/15 for domestic and international students. Applications are processed on a rolling basis. Application fee: $65. Electronic applications accepted. *Financial support:* In 2010–11, 31 students received support, including 4 fellowships with full tuition reimbursements available (averaging $24,500 per year), 6 research assistantships with full tuition reimbursements available (averaging $23,750 per year), 16 teaching assistantships with full tuition reimbursements available (averaging $23,750 per year); scholarships/grants and unspecified assistantships also available. Financial award application deadline: 12/15. *Faculty research:* Gene expression, cytoskeleton and cell structure, cell cycle and growth regulation, neuroscience, animal behavior, microbiology. Total annual research expenditures: $2.4 million. *Unit head:* Dr. Murray Itzkowitz, Chairperson, 610-758-3680, Fax: 610-758-4004, E-mail: mi00@lehigh.edu. *Application contact:* Dr. Jennifer M. Swann, Graduate Coordinator, 610-758-5484, Fax: 610-758-4004, E-mail: jms5@lehigh.edu.

Louisiana State University Health Sciences Center, School of Graduate Studies in New Orleans, Interdisciplinary Neuroscience Graduate Program, New Orleans, LA 70112-2223. Offers MS, PhD, MD/PhD. *Degree requirements:* For master's, comprehensive exam, thesis; for doctorate, comprehensive exam, thesis/dissertation. *Entrance requirements:* For master's, GRE; for doctorate, GRE General Test, GRE Subject Test, previous course work in chemistry, mathematics, physics, and computer science. Additional exam requirements/recommendations for international students: Required—TOEFL. *Faculty research:* Visual system, second messengers, drugs and behavior, signal transduction, plasticity and development.

Loyola University Chicago, Graduate School, Program in Neuroscience, Maywood, IL 60153. Offers MS, PhD, MD/PhD. *Faculty:* 22 full-time (9 women). *Students:* 13 full-time (10 women), 2 part-time (both women), 1 international. Average age 27. 32 applicants, 22% accepted, 4 enrolled. In 2010, 1 master's, 5 doctorates awarded. Terminal master's awarded for partial completion of doctoral program. *Degree requirements:* For master's, comprehensive exam, thesis; for doctorate, comprehensive exam, thesis/dissertation. *Entrance requirements:* For master's, GRE or MCAT; for doctorate, GRE General Test. Additional exam requirements/recommendations for international students: Required—TOEFL (minimum score 600 paper-based; 220 computer-based). *Application deadline:* For fall admission, 3/15 priority date for domestic and international students. Applications are processed on a rolling basis. Application fee: $50. Electronic applications accepted. *Expenses:* Tuition: Full-time $14,940; part-time $830 per credit hour. Required fees: $87 per semester. Part-time tuition and fees vary according to course load and program. *Financial support:* In 2010–11, 3 fellowships with full tuition reimbursements (averaging $25,000 per year) were awarded; Federal Work-Study, scholarships/grants, and health care benefits also available. Financial award application deadline: 3/15; financial award applicants required to submit FAFSA. *Faculty research:* Parkinson's disease, drugs of abuse, neuroendocrinology, neuroimmunology, neurotoxicity. Total annual research expenditures: $3.5 million. *Unit head:* Dr. Edward J. Neafsey, Director, 708-216-3355, Fax: 708-216-6823, E-mail: eneafse@lumc.edu. *Application contact:* Kim Stubbs, Administrative Secretary, 708-216-3361, Fax: 708-216-3913, E-mail: kstubbs@lumc.edu.

Marquette University, Graduate School, College of Arts and Sciences, Department of Biology, Milwaukee, WI 53201-1881. Offers cell biology (MS, PhD); developmental biology (MS, PhD); ecology (MS, PhD); epithelial physiology (MS, PhD); genetics (MS, PhD); microbiology (MS, PhD); molecular biology (MS, PhD); muscle and exercise physiology (MS, PhD); neuroscience (PhD). *Faculty:* 25 full-time (12 women), 2 part-time/adjunct (1 woman). *Students:* 23 full-time (9 women), 12 part-time (8 women); includes 1 minority (Asian, non-Hispanic/Latino), 15 international. Average age 26. 82 applicants, 15% accepted, 5 enrolled. In 2010, 3 master's, 2 doctorates awarded. Terminal master's awarded for partial completion of doctoral program. *Degree requirements:* For master's, comprehensive exam, thesis, 1 year of teaching experience or equivalent; for doctorate, thesis/dissertation, 1 year of teaching experience or equivalent, qualifying exam. *Entrance requirements:* For master's and doctorate, GRE General Test, GRE Subject Test, official transcripts from all current and previous colleges/universities except Marquette, statement of professional goals and aspirations, three letters of recommendation. Additional exam requirements/recommendations for international students: Required—TOEFL (minimum score 530 paper-based; 78 computer-based). *Application deadline:* For fall admission, 12/15 for domestic and international students. Application fee: $50. Electronic applications accepted. *Expenses:* Tuition: Full-time $16,290; part-time $905 per credit hour. Tuition and fees vary according to program. *Financial support:* In 2010–11, 2 research assistantships, 34 teaching assistantships were awarded; fellowships, Federal Work-Study, institutionally sponsored loans, scholarships/grants, and tuition waivers (full and partial) also available. Support available to part-time students. Financial award application deadline: 2/15. *Faculty research:* Neurobiology, neuroendocrinology, epithelial physiology, neuropeptide interactions, synaptic transmission. Total annual research expenditures: $1.3 million. *Unit head:* Dr. Robert Fitts, Chair, 414-288-1748, Fax: 414-288-7357. *Application contact:* Debbie Weaver, Administrative Assistant, 414-288-7355, Fax: 414-288-7357.

Massachusetts Institute of Technology, School of Science, Department of Brain and Cognitive Sciences, Cambridge, MA 02139-4307. Offers cognitive science (PhD); neuroscience (PhD). *Faculty:* 37 full-time (14 women). *Students:* 96 full-time (33 women); includes 24 minority (2 Black or African American, non-Hispanic/Latino; 1 American Indian or Alaska Native, non-Hispanic/Latino; 9 Asian, non-Hispanic/Latino; 10 Hispanic/Latino; 2 Two or more races, non-Hispanic/Latino), 16 international. Average age 27. 415 applicants, 8% accepted, 16 enrolled. In 2010, 13 doctorates awarded. *Degree requirements:* For doctorate, comprehensive exam, thesis/dissertation. *Entrance requirements:* For doctorate, GRE General Test. Additional exam requirements/recommendations for international students: Required—TOEFL (minimum score 577 paper-based; 233 computer-based; 90 iBT), IELTS (minimum score 7). *Application deadline:* For fall admission, 12/1 for domestic and international students. Application fee: $75. Electronic applications accepted. *Expenses:* Tuition: Full-time $38,940; part-time $605 per unit. Required fees: $272. *Financial support:* In 2010–11, 83 students received support, including 72 fellowships with tuition reimbursements available (averaging $28,951 per year), 18 research assistantships with tuition reimbursements available (averaging $30,165 per year), 6 teaching assistantships with tuition reimbursements available (averaging $31,586 per year); Federal Work-Study, institutionally sponsored loans, scholarships/grants, traineeships, health care benefits, and unspecified assistantships also available. *Faculty research:* Vision—perception and physiology; learning, memory, and executive control—molecular and systems approaches; sensorimotor systems—physiology and computation; neural and cognitive development and plasticity; language and high-level cognition—learning, acquisition, and computation. Total annual research expenditures: $28.3 million. *Unit head:* Prof. Mriganka Sur, Department Head, 617-253-5748, E-mail: bcs-info@mit.edu. *Application contact:* Academic Office, 617-253-7403, Fax: 617-253-9216, E-mail: bcs-admissions@mit.edu.

Mayo Graduate School, Graduate Programs in Biomedical Sciences, Program in Molecular Neuroscience, Rochester, MN 55905. Offers PhD. Program also offered in Jacksonville, FL. *Degree requirements:* For doctorate, oral defense of dissertation, qualifying oral and written exam. *Entrance requirements:* For doctorate, GRE, 1 year of chemistry, biology, calculus, and physics. Additional exam requirements/recommendations for international students: Required—TOEFL. Electronic applications accepted. *Faculty research:* Cholinergic receptor/Alzheimer's; molecular biology, channels, receptors, and mental disease; neuronal cytoskeleton; growth factors; gene regulation.

McGill University, Faculty of Graduate and Postdoctoral Studies, Faculty of Medicine, Department of Neurology and Neurosurgery, Montréal, QC H3A 2T5, Canada. Offers M Sc, PhD.

McMaster University, Faculty of Health Sciences and School of Graduate Studies, Program in Medical Sciences, Neurosciences and Behavioral Sciences Area, Hamilton, ON L8S 4M2, Canada. Offers M Sc, PhD, MD/PhD. *Degree requirements:* For master's, thesis; for doctorate, comprehensive exam, thesis/dissertation. *Entrance requirements:* For master's, honors B Sc, B+ average in related field; for doctorate, M Sc, minimum B+ average, students with proven research experience and an A average may be admitted with a B Sc degree. Additional exam requirements/recommendations for international students: Required—TOEFL (minimum score 580 paper-based; 237 computer-based).

Medical College of Wisconsin, Graduate School of Biomedical Sciences, Neuroscience Doctoral Program, Milwaukee, WI 53226-0509. Offers PhD, MD/PhD. Terminal master's awarded for partial completion of doctoral program. *Degree requirements:* For doctorate, comprehensive exam, thesis/dissertation. *Entrance requirements:* For doctorate, GRE General Test. Additional exam requirements/recommendations for international students: Required—TOEFL. *Expenses:* Tuition: Full-time $30,000; part-time $710 per credit. Required fees: $150. *Faculty research:* Neurobiology, development, neuroscience, teratology.

Medical University of South Carolina, College of Graduate Studies, Department of Neurosciences, Charleston, SC 29425. Offers MS, PhD, DMD/PhD, MD/PhD. *Faculty:* 22 full-time (6 women). *Students:* 25 full-time (11 women); includes 1 Black or African American, non-Hispanic/Latino, 4 international. Average age 27. 6 applicants, 0% accepted, 0 enrolled. Terminal master's awarded for partial completion of doctoral program. *Degree requirements:* For master's, thesis; for doctorate, thesis/dissertation, oral and written exams. *Entrance requirements:* For master's, GRE General Test; for doctorate, GRE General Test, interview, minimum GPA of 3.0. Additional exam requirements/recommendations for international students: Required—TOEFL (minimum score 600 paper-based; 250 computer-based; 100 iBT). *Application deadline:* For fall admission, 1/15 priority date for domestic and international students. Applications are processed on a rolling basis. Application fee: $0 ($85 for international students). Electronic applications accepted. *Financial support:* In 2010–11, 13 research assistantships with partial tuition reimbursements (averaging $23,000 per year) were awarded; Federal Work-Study and scholarships/grants also available. Support available to part-time students. Financial award application deadline: 3/10; financial award applicants required to submit FAFSA. *Faculty research:* Addiction, aging, movement disorders, membrane physiology, neurotransmission and behavior. *Unit head:* Dr. Peter Kalivas, Chair, 843-792-4400, Fax: 843-792-6590, E-mail: kalivasp@musc.edu. *Application contact:* Dr. L. Judson Chandler, Associate Professor, 843-792-5224, Fax: 843-792-6590, E-mail: chandj@musc.edu.

Meharry Medical College, School of Graduate Studies, Program in Biomedical Sciences, Neuroscience Emphasis, Nashville, TN 37208-9989. Offers PhD, MD/PhD. *Degree requirements:* For doctorate, comprehensive exam, thesis/dissertation. *Entrance requirements:* For doctorate, GRE. *Faculty research:* Neurochemistry, pain, smooth muscle tone, HP axis and peptides neural plasticity.

Memorial University of Newfoundland, Faculty of Medicine and School of Graduate Studies, Graduate Programs in Medicine, Division of Biomedical Sciences, St. John's, NL A1C 5S7, Canada. Offers cancer (M Sc, PhD); cardiovascular (M Sc, PhD); immunology (M Sc, PhD); neuroscience (M Sc, PhD). Part-time programs available. *Degree requirements:* For master's, thesis; for doctorate, comprehensive exam, thesis/dissertation, oral defense of thesis. *Entrance requirements:* For master's, MD or B Sc; for doctorate, MD or M Sc. Additional exam requirements/recommendations for international students: Required—TOEFL. *Faculty research:* Neuroscience, immunology, cardiovascular, and cancer.

Michigan State University, The Graduate School, College of Natural Science, Program in Neuroscience, East Lansing, MI 48824. Offers MS, PhD. *Entrance requirements:* Additional exam requirements/recommendations for international students: Required—TOEFL. Electronic applications accepted.

Montana State University, College of Graduate Studies, College of Letters and Science, Department of Cell Biology and Neuroscience, Bozeman, MT 59717. Offers biological sciences (PhD); neuroscience (MS, PhD). Part-time programs available. *Faculty:* 7 full-time (2 women), 2 part-time/adjunct (1 woman). *Students:* 4 part-time (1 woman). Average age 28. 3 applicants, 0% accepted, 0 enrolled. *Degree requirements:* For master's, comprehensive exam; for doctorate, comprehensive exam, thesis/dissertation. *Entrance requirements:* For master's and doctorate, GRE General Test. Additional exam requirements/recommendations for international students: Required—TOEFL (minimum score 550 paper-based; 213 computer-based). *Application deadline:* For fall admission, 7/15 priority date for domestic students, 5/15 priority date for international students; for spring admission, 12/1 priority date for domestic students, 10/1 priority date for international students. Applications are processed on a rolling basis. Application fee: $30. Electronic applications accepted. *Expenses:* Tuition, state resident: full-time $5554. Tuition, nonresident: full-time $14,646. Required fees: $1233. *Financial support:* In 2010–11, 8 teaching assistantships (averaging $10,500 per year) were awarded; health care benefits and unspecified assistantships also available. Financial award application deadline: 3/1; financial award applicants required to submit FAFSA. *Faculty research:* Development of the nervous system, neuronal mechanisms of visual perception, ion channel biophysics, mechanisms of sensory coding, neuroinformatics. Total annual research expenditures: $3.4 million. *Unit head:* Dr. Thomas Hughes, Head, 406-994-5395, Fax: 406-994-7077, E-mail: thughes@montana.edu. *Application contact:* Dr. Carl A. Fox, Vice Provost for Graduate Education, 406-994-4145, Fax: 406-994-7433, E-mail: gradstudy@montana.edu.

Mount Sinai School of Medicine, Graduate School of Biological Sciences, New York, NY 10029-6504. Offers biomedical sciences (MS, PhD); clinical research education (MS, PhD); community medicine (MPH); genetic counseling (MS); neurosciences (PhD); MD/PhD. *Faculty:* 126 full-time (40 women). *Students:* 438 full-time (260 women); includes 29 Black or African American, non-Hispanic/Latino; 3 American Indian or Alaska Native, non-Hispanic/Latino; 86 Asian, non-Hispanic/Latino; 18 Hispanic/Latino, 99 international. 924 applicants, 29% accepted, 104 enrolled. In 2010, 58 master's, 36 doctorates awarded. Terminal master's awarded for partial completion of doctoral program. *Degree requirements:* For master's, thesis; for doctorate, comprehensive exam, thesis/dissertation. *Entrance requirements:* For master's, GRE General Test; for doctorate, GRE General Test, GRE Subject Test, 3 years of college pre-med course work. Additional exam requirements/recommendations for international students: Required—TOEFL. *Application deadline:* For fall admission, 12/15 for domestic and international students. Applications are processed on a rolling basis. Application fee: $80. Electronic applications accepted. *Expenses:* Tuition: Full-time $25,600; part-time $800 per credit hour. Required fees: $1600. Full-time tuition and fees vary according to program. *Financial support:* In 2010–11, fellowships with full tuition reimbursements (averaging $32,000 per year), research assistantships with full tuition reimbursements (averaging $32,000 per year) were awarded; Federal Work-Study, institutionally sponsored loans, scholarships/grants, health care benefits, and unspecified assistantships also available. Financial award application deadline: 4/30; financial award applicants required to submit FAFSA. *Faculty research:* Cancer, genetics and genomics, immunology, neuroscience, developmental and stem cell biology, translational research. Total annual research expenditures: $264.9 million. *Unit head:* Dr. John Morrison, Dean, 212-241-

6546, Fax: 212-241-0651, E-mail: john.morrison@mssm.edu. *Application contact:* Lily Recanati, Manager, 212-241-2793, Fax: 212-241-0651, E-mail: lily.recantati@mssm.edu.

New York Medical College, Graduate School of Basic Medical Sciences, Department of Cell Biology, Valhalla, NY 10595-1691. Offers cell biology and neuroscience (MS, PhD); MD/PhD. Part-time and evening/weekend programs available. *Faculty:* 13 full-time (2 women), 2 part-time/adjunct (both women). *Students:* 6 full-time (1 woman), 3 part-time (all women); includes 1 Asian, non-Hispanic/Latino, 2 international. Average age 26. In 2010, 2 master's, 1 doctorate awarded. Terminal master's awarded for partial completion of doctoral program. *Degree requirements:* For master's, thesis; for doctorate, comprehensive exam, thesis/dissertation. *Entrance requirements:* For master's and doctorate, GRE General Test. Additional exam requirements/recommendations for international students: Required—TOEFL. *Application deadline:* For fall admission, 7/1 priority date for domestic students, 5/1 priority date for international students; for spring admission, 12/1 priority date for domestic students, 10/1 priority date for international students. Applications are processed on a rolling basis. Application fee: $50 ($75 for international students). Electronic applications accepted. *Financial support:* In 2010–11, 4 research assistantships with full tuition reimbursements (averaging $24,000 per year) were awarded; Federal Work-Study, institutionally sponsored loans, scholarships/grants, traineeships, tuition waivers (full), unspecified assistantships, and health benefits (for PhD candidates only) also available. Financial award applicants required to submit FAFSA. *Faculty research:* Mechanisms of growth control in skeletal muscle, cartilage differentiation, cytoskeletal functions, signal transduction pathways, neuronal development and plasticity. *Unit head:* Dr. Victor Fried, Director, 914-594-4036. *Application contact:* Valerie Romeo-Messana, Admission Coordinator, 914-594-4110, Fax: 914-594-4944, E-mail: v_romeomessana@nymc.edu.

New York University, Graduate School of Arts and Science, Center for Neural Science, New York, NY 10012-1019. Offers PhD. *Faculty:* 15 full-time (3 women). *Students:* 40 full-time (23 women); includes 2 Black or African American, non-Hispanic/Latino; 7 Asian, non-Hispanic/Latino; 2 Hispanic/Latino, 6 international. Average age 27. 162 applicants, 15% accepted, 12 enrolled. In 2010, 5 doctorates awarded. *Degree requirements:* For doctorate, one foreign language, thesis/dissertation. *Entrance requirements:* For doctorate, GRE, interview. Additional exam requirements/recommendations for international students: Required—TOEFL. *Application deadline:* For fall admission, 12/12 for domestic students. Application fee: $90. *Financial support:* Fellowships with tuition reimbursements, research assistantships with tuition reimbursements, career-related internships or fieldwork, Federal Work-Study, institutionally sponsored loans, scholarships/grants, health care benefits, and unspecified assistantships available. Financial award application deadline: 12/15; financial award applicants required to submit FAFSA. *Faculty research:* Systems and integrative neuroscience; combining biology, cognition, computation, and theory. *Unit head:* J. Anthony Movshon, Chair, 212-998-7780, Fax: 212-995-4011, E-mail: cns@nyu.edu. *Application contact:* Alex Reyes, Director of Graduate Studies, 212-998-7780, Fax: 212-995-4011, E-mail: cns@nyu.edu.

New York University, School of Medicine, New York, NY 10012-1019. Offers biomedical sciences (PhD), including biomedical imaging, cellular and molecular biology, computational biology, developmental genetics, medical and molecular parasitology, microbiology, molecular oncobiology and immunology, neuroscience and physiology, pathobiology, pharmacology, structural biology; clinical investigation (MS); medicine (MD); MD/MA; MD/MPA; MD/MS; MD/PhD. *Accreditation:* LCME/AMA (one or more programs are accredited). *Degree requirements:* For master's, comprehensive exam, thesis; for doctorate, comprehensive exam, thesis/dissertation. *Entrance requirements:* MCAT. Additional exam requirements/recommendations for international students: Required—TOEFL. *Expenses:* Contact institution. *Faculty research:* AIDS, cancer, neuroscience, molecular biology, neuroscience, cell biology and molecular genetics, structural biology, microbial pathogenesis and host defense, pharmacology, molecular oncology and immunology.

New York University, School of Medicine and Graduate School of Arts and Science, Sackler Institute of Graduate Biomedical Sciences, Department of Neuroscience and Physiology, New York, NY 10012-1019. Offers PhD, MD/PhD. *Degree requirements:* For doctorate, one foreign language, comprehensive exam, thesis/dissertation, qualifying exam. *Entrance requirements:* For doctorate, GRE General Test. Additional exam requirements/recommendations for international students: Required—TOEFL. *Faculty research:* Synaptic transmission, retinal physiology, signal transduction, CNS intrinsic properties, cerebellar function.

Northwestern University, The Graduate School, Institute for Neuroscience, Evanston, IL 60208. Offers PhD. Admissions and degree offered through The Graduate School. *Degree requirements:* For doctorate, thesis/dissertation. *Entrance requirements:* For doctorate, GRE General Test. Additional exam requirements/recommendations for international students: Required—TOEFL. *Faculty research:* Circadian rhythms, synaptic neurotransmissions, cognitive neuroscience, sensory/motor systems, cell biology and structure/function, neurobiology of disease.

Northwestern University, The Graduate School, Interdepartmental Biological Sciences Program (IBiS), Evanston, IL 60208. Offers biochemistry, molecular biology, and cell biology (PhD), including biochemistry, cell and molecular biology, molecular biophysics, structural biology; biotechnology (PhD); cell and molecular biology (PhD); developmental biology and genetics (PhD); hormone action and signal transduction (PhD); neuroscience (PhD); structural biology, biochemistry, and biophysics (PhD). Program participants include the Departments of Biochemistry, Molecular Biology, and Cell Biology; Chemistry; Neurobiology and Physiology; Chemical Engineering; Civil Engineering; and Evanston Hospital. *Degree requirements:* For doctorate, thesis/dissertation, qualifying exam. *Entrance requirements:* For doctorate, GRE General Test. Additional exam requirements/recommendations for international students: Required—TOEFL (minimum score 600 paper-based). Electronic applications accepted. *Faculty research:* Developmental genetics, gene regulation, DNA-protein interactions, biological clocks, bioremediation.

The Ohio State University, Graduate School, College of Arts and Sciences, Division of Natural and Mathematical Sciences, Neuroscience Graduate Studies Program, Columbus, OH 43210. Offers PhD. *Faculty:* 37 full-time (10 women). *Students:* 20 full-time (9 women), 17 part-time (10 women); includes 1 Black or African American, non-Hispanic/Latino; 1 Asian, non-Hispanic/Latino; 2 Two or more races, non-Hispanic/Latino, 6 international. Average age 27. In 2010, 5 doctorates awarded. *Degree requirements:* For doctorate, comprehensive exam, thesis/dissertation. *Entrance requirements:* For doctorate, GRE General Test, GRE Subject Test. Additional exam requirements/recommendations for international students: Required—TOEFL (minimum score 600 paper-based; 250 computer-based). *Application deadline:* For fall admission, 1/31 for domestic students, 11/30 for international students. Applications are processed on a rolling basis. Application fee: $40 ($50 for international students). Electronic applications accepted. *Expenses:* Tuition, state resident: full-time $10,605. Tuition, nonresident: full-time $26,535. Tuition and fees vary according to course load and program. *Financial support:* In 2010–11, 10 students received support, including 1 fellowship with tuition reimbursement available (averaging $21,000 per year), 9 research assistantships with tuition reimbursements available (averaging $21,000 per year); unspecified assistantships also available. *Faculty research:* Neurotrauma and disease, behavioral neuroscience, systems neuroscience, stress and neuroimmunology, molecular and cellular neuroscience. *Unit head:* Dr. Dana Mctigue, Co-Director, 614-292-5523, Fax: 614-292-7544, E-mail: mctigue.2@osu.edu. *Application contact:* Graduate Admissions, 614-292-9444, Fax: 614-292-3895, E-mail: domestic.grad@osu.edu.

The Ohio State University, Graduate School, College of Arts and Sciences, Division of Social and Behavioral Sciences, Department of Psychology, Columbus, OH 43210. Offers behavioral neuroscience (PhD); clinical psychology (PhD); cognitive psychology (PhD); developmental psychology (PhD); mental retardation and developmental disabilities (PhD); psychology (MA); quantitative psychology (PhD); social psychology (PhD). *Accreditation:* APA (one or more programs are accredited). *Faculty:* 60. *Students:* 106 full-time (65 women), 42 part-time (31 women); includes 5 Black or African American, non-Hispanic/Latino; 1 American Indian or Alaska Native, non-Hispanic/Latino; 5 Asian, non-Hispanic/Latino; 10 Hispanic/Latino; 3 Two or more races, non-Hispanic/Latino, 23 international. Average age 27. In 2010, 21 master's, 22 doctorates awarded. *Degree requirements:* For doctorate, thesis/dissertation. *Entrance requirements:* For master's and doctorate, GRE General Test. Additional exam requirements/recommendations for international students: Required—TOEFL (minimum score 600 paper-based; 250 computer-based). *Application deadline:* For fall admission, 12/31 for domestic students, 11/30 for international students. Applications are processed on a rolling basis. Application fee: $40 ($50 for international students). Electronic applications accepted. *Expenses:* Tuition, state resident: full-time $10,605. Tuition, nonresident: full-time $26,535. Tuition and fees vary according to course load and program. *Financial support:* Fellowships, research assistantships, teaching assistantships available. *Unit head:* Dr. Richard Petty, Chair, 614-292-1640, E-mail: petty.1@osu.edu. *Application contact:* 614-292-9444, Fax: 614-292-3895, E-mail: domestic.grad@osu.edu.

Ohio University, Graduate College, College of Arts and Sciences, Department of Biological Sciences, Athens, OH 45701-2979. Offers biological sciences (MS, PhD); cell biology and physiology (MS, PhD); ecology and evolutionary biology (MS, PhD); exercise physiology and muscle biology (MS, PhD); microbiology (MS, PhD); neuroscience (MS, PhD). *Students:* 32 full-time (9 women), 5 part-time (2 women); includes 2 minority (1 Black or African American, non-Hispanic/Latino; 1 Hispanic/Latino), 9 international. 51 applicants, 37% accepted, 7 enrolled. In 2010, 2 master's, 9 doctorates awarded. Terminal master's awarded for partial completion of doctoral program. *Degree requirements:* For master's, comprehensive exam, thesis, 1 quarter of teaching experience; for doctorate, comprehensive exam, thesis/dissertation, 2 quarters of teaching experience. *Entrance requirements:* For master's, GRE General Test, names of three faculty members whose research interests most closely match the applicant's interest; for doctorate, GRE General Test, essay concerning prior training, research interest and career goals, plus names of three faculty members whose research interests most closely match the applicant's interest. Additional exam requirements/recommendations for international students: Required—TOEFL (minimum score 620 paper-based; 105 iBT) or IELTS (minimum score 7.5). *Application deadline:* For fall admission, 1/15 for domestic and international students. Application fee: $50 ($55 for international students). Electronic applications accepted. *Financial support:* In 2010–11, 1 fellowship with full tuition reimbursement (averaging $18,957 per year), 10 research assistantships with full tuition reimbursements (averaging $18,957 per year), 42 teaching assistantships with full tuition reimbursements (averaging $18,957 per year) were awarded; Federal Work-Study and institutionally sponsored loans also available. Financial award application deadline: 1/15. *Faculty research:* Ecology and evolutionary biology, exercise physiology and muscle biology, neurobiology, cell biology, physiology. Total annual research expenditures: $2.8 million. *Unit head:* Dr. Ralph DiCaprio, Chair, 740-593-2290, Fax: 740-593-0300, E-mail: dicaprir@ohio.edu. *Application contact:* Dr. Patrick Hassett, Graduate Chair, 740-593-4793, Fax: 740-593-0300, E-mail: hassett@ohio.edu.

Oregon Health & Science University, School of Medicine, Graduate Programs in Medicine, Department of Behavioral Neuroscience, Portland, OR 97239-3098. Offers PhD. *Faculty:* 14 full-time (4 women), 6 part-time/adjunct (3 women). *Students:* 32 full-time (19 women); includes 1 Black or African American, non-Hispanic/Latino; 1 Hispanic/Latino. Average age 27. 57 applicants, 14% accepted, 8 enrolled. In 2010, 4 doctorates awarded. Terminal master's awarded for partial completion of doctoral program. *Degree requirements:* For doctorate, comprehensive exam, thesis/dissertation, written exam. *Entrance requirements:* For doctorate, GRE General Test (minimum scores: 500 Verbal/600 Quantitative/4.5 Analytical), undergraduate coursework in biopsychology and other basic science areas. Additional exam requirements/recommendations for international students: Required—TOEFL. *Application deadline:* For fall admission, 12/1 for domestic students. Application fee: $65. Electronic applications accepted. *Financial support:* Health care benefits, tuition waivers (full), and stipends available. *Faculty research:* Neural basis of behavior, behavioral pharmacology, behavioral genetics, neuropharmacology and neuroendocrinology, biological basis of drug seeking and addiction. *Unit head:* Dr. Suzanne Mitchell, Program Director, 503-494-1650, E-mail: mitchesu@ohsu.edu. *Application contact:* Kris Thomason, Graduate Program Manager, 503-494-8464, E-mail: thomason@ohsu.edu.

Oregon Health & Science University, School of Medicine, Graduate Programs in Medicine, Neuroscience Graduate Program, Portland, OR 97239-3098. Offers PhD. *Faculty:* 146. *Students:* 61 full-time (30 women); includes 4 Asian, non-Hispanic/Latino; 4 Hispanic/Latino; 1 Native Hawaiian or other Pacific Islander, non-Hispanic/Latino, 7 international. Average age 29. 121 applicants, 11% accepted, 12 enrolled. In 2010, 4 doctorates awarded. Terminal master's awarded for partial completion of doctoral program. *Degree requirements:* For doctorate, comprehensive exam, thesis/dissertation. *Entrance requirements:* For doctorate, GRE General Test (minimum scores: 500 Verbal/600 Quantitative/4.5 Analytical) or MCAT (for some programs). Additional exam requirements/recommendations for international students: Required—TOEFL. *Application deadline:* For fall admission, 12/15 for domestic students. Application fee: $65. Electronic applications accepted. *Financial support:* Health care benefits and full tuition and stipends available. *Faculty research:* Signal transduction, receptors and ion channels, transcriptional regulation, drug abuse, systems, behavioral neuroscience. *Unit head:* Dr. Gary Westbrook, Program Director, 503-494-6932, E-mail: ngp@ohsu.edu. *Application contact:* Liz Lawson-Weber, Program Coordinator, 503-494-6932, E-mail: ngp@ohsu.edu.

See Close-Up on page 373.

Penn State Hershey Medical Center, College of Medicine, Graduate School Programs in the Biomedical Sciences, The Huck Institutes of the Life Sciences, Intercollege Graduate Program in Neuroscience, Hershey, PA 17033. Offers MS, PhD, MD/PhD. *Students:* 96 applicants, 4% accepted, 2 enrolled. In 2010, 2 master's, 4 doctorates awarded. Terminal master's awarded for partial completion of doctoral program. *Degree requirements:* For master's, thesis or alternative; for doctorate, comprehensive exam, thesis/dissertation, oral exam. *Entrance requirements:* For master's, GRE General Test; for doctorate, GRE General Test, minimum GPA of 3.0. Additional exam requirements/recommendations for international students: Required—TOEFL (minimum score 500 paper-based; 213 computer-based). *Application deadline:* For fall admission, 1/31 priority date for domestic students, 2/1 priority date for international students. Applications are processed on a rolling basis. Application fee: $65. Electronic applications accepted. *Financial support:* In 2010–11, research assistantships with full tuition reimbursements (averaging $22,260 per year); fellowships with full tuition reimbursements, career-related internships or fieldwork, institutionally sponsored loans, scholarships/grants, health care benefits, and unspecified assistantships also available. Financial award applicants required to submit FAFSA. *Faculty research:* Behavioral neuroscience, growth factors and neuropeptides, molecular neurobiology and neurogenetics, neuronal aging and brain metabolism, neuronal and glial development. *Unit head:* Dr. Patricia Grigson, Program Director, 717-531-1045, Fax: 717-531-0786, E-mail: neuro-grad-hmc@psu.edu. *Application contact:* Lori Coover, Program Assistant, 717-531-1045, Fax: 717-531-0786, E-mail: neuro-grad-hmc@psu.edu.

Princeton University, Graduate School, Department of Psychology, Princeton, NJ 08544-1019. Offers neuroscience (PhD); psychology (PhD). *Degree requirements:* For doctorate, thesis/dissertation. *Entrance requirements:* For doctorate, GRE General Test, GRE Subject Test. Additional exam requirements/recommendations for international students: Required—TOEFL (minimum score 550 paper-based). Electronic applications accepted.

Princeton University, Princeton Neuroscience Institute, Princeton, NJ 08544-1019. Offers PhD. Electronic applications accepted.

Queen's University at Kingston, School of Graduate Studies and Research, Faculty of Health Sciences, Department of Anatomy and Cell Biology, Kingston, ON K7L 3N6, Canada. Offers biology of reproduction (M Sc, PhD); cancer (M Sc, PhD); cardiovascular pathophysiology (M Sc, PhD); cell and molecular biology (M Sc, PhD); drug metabolism (M Sc, PhD); endocrinology (M Sc, PhD); motor control (M Sc, PhD); neural regeneration (M Sc, PhD); neurophysiology (M Sc, PhD). Part-time programs available. *Degree requirements:* For

Neuroscience

Queen's University at Kingston (continued)

master's, thesis; for doctorate, one foreign language, comprehensive exam, thesis/dissertation. *Entrance requirements:* Additional exam requirements/recommendations for international students: Required—TOEFL. Electronic applications accepted. *Faculty research:* Human kinetics, neuroscience, reproductive biology, cardiovascular.

Rosalind Franklin University of Medicine and Science, School of Graduate and Post-doctoral Studies—Interdisciplinary Graduate Program in Biomedical Sciences, Department of Neuroscience, North Chicago, IL 60064-3095. Offers PhD, MD/PhD. *Degree requirements:* For doctorate, comprehensive exam, thesis/dissertation, original research project. *Entrance requirements:* For doctorate, GRE General Test. Additional exam requirements/recommendations for international students: Required—TOEFL, TWE.

Rush University, Graduate College, Division of Neuroscience, Chicago, IL 60612-3832. Offers MS, PhD. Terminal master's awarded for partial completion of doctoral program. *Degree requirements:* For master's, thesis; for doctorate, thesis/dissertation. *Entrance requirements:* For master's and doctorate, GRE General Test. Additional exam requirements/recommendations for international students: Required—TOEFL. Electronic applications accepted. *Faculty research:* Neurodegenerative disorders, neurobiology of memory, aging, pathology and genetics of Alzheimer's disease.

Rutgers, The State University of New Jersey, Newark, Graduate School, Program in Integrative Neuroscience, Newark, NJ 07102. Offers PhD. Part-time programs available. *Faculty:* 18 full-time (4 women). *Students:* 24 full-time (12 women), 15 part-time (8 women); includes 6 Asian, non-Hispanic/Latino; 3 Hispanic/Latino. 60 applicants, 13% accepted, 7 enrolled. In 2010, 3 doctorates awarded. *Degree requirements:* For doctorate, thesis/dissertation. *Entrance requirements:* For doctorate, GRE, minimum GPA of 3.0. *Application deadline:* For fall admission, 2/1 priority date for domestic students. Applications are processed on a rolling basis. Application fee: $60. Electronic applications accepted. *Expenses:* Tuition, state resident: part-time $600 per credit. Tuition, nonresident: full-time $10,694. *Financial support:* In 2010–11, 21 teaching assistantships with full and partial tuition reimbursements (averaging $26,348 per year) were awarded. Financial award application deadline: 3/1. *Faculty research:* Systems neuroscience, cognitive neuroscience, molecular neuroscience, behavioral neuroscience. Total annual research expenditures: $3 million. *Unit head:* Dr. Ian Creese, Director, 973-353-1080 Ext. 3300, Fax: 973-353-1272, E-mail: creese@axon.rutgers.edu. *Application contact:* Dr. Ian Creese, Director, 973-353-1080 Ext. 3300, Fax: 973-353-1272, E-mail: creese@axon.rutgers.edu.

Rutgers, The State University of New Jersey, Newark, Graduate School, Program in Psychology, Newark, NJ 07102. Offers cognitive neuroscience (PhD); cognitive science (PhD); perception (PhD); psychobiology (PhD); social cognition (PhD). *Faculty:* 15 full-time (5 women), 6 part-time/adjunct (all women). *Students:* 23 full-time (19 women), 2 part-time (1 woman); includes 3 Black or African American, non-Hispanic/Latino; 1 Asian, non-Hispanic/Latino; 2 Hispanic/Latino. 48 applicants, 17% accepted, 6 enrolled. In 2010, 4 doctorates awarded. *Degree requirements:* For doctorate, comprehensive exam, thesis/dissertation. *Entrance requirements:* For doctorate, GRE General Test, GRE Subject Test, minimum undergraduate B average. *Application deadline:* For fall admission, 2/1 for domestic students; for spring admission, 11/1 for domestic students. Application fee: $60. Electronic applications accepted. *Expenses:* Tuition, state resident: part-time $600 per credit. Tuition, nonresident: full-time $10,694. *Financial support:* In 2010–11, 16 students received support, including 9 fellowships with full and partial tuition reimbursements available (averaging $18,000 per year), 8 teaching assistantships with full and partial tuition reimbursements available (averaging $23,112 per year); career-related internships or fieldwork, health care benefits, and minority scholarships also available. Financial award application deadline: 2/1. *Faculty research:* Visual perception (luminance, motion), neuroendocrine mechanisms in behavior (reproduction, pain), attachment theory, connectionist modeling of cognition. *Unit head:* Dr. Kenneth Kressel, Director, 973-353-5440 Ext. 232, Fax: 973-353-1171, E-mail: kkressel@andromeda.rutgers.edu. *Application contact:* Jason Hand, Director of Admissions, 973-353-5205, Fax: 973-353-1440.

Rutgers, The State University of New Jersey, New Brunswick, Graduate School-New Brunswick, Program in Endocrinology and Animal Biosciences, Piscataway, NJ 08854-8097. Offers MS, PhD. Terminal master's awarded for partial completion of doctoral program. *Degree requirements:* For master's, thesis; for doctorate, comprehensive exam, thesis/dissertation. *Entrance requirements:* For master's and doctorate, GRE General Test. Additional exam requirements/recommendations for international students: Required—TOEFL. Electronic applications accepted. *Expenses:* Tuition, state resident: full-time $7200; part-time $600 per credit. Tuition, nonresident: full-time $11,124; part-time $927 per credit. *Faculty research:* Comparative and behavioral endocrinology, epigenetic regulation of the endocrine system, exercise physiology and immunology, fetal and neonatal developmental programming, mammary gland biology and breast cancer, neuroendocrinology and alcohol studies, reproductive and developmental toxicology.

Rutgers, The State University of New Jersey, New Brunswick, Graduate School-New Brunswick, Program in Neuroscience, Piscataway, NJ 08854-8097. Offers PhD. Program offered jointly with University of Medicine and Dentistry of New Jersey. *Degree requirements:* For doctorate, thesis/dissertation, qualifying exam, research project. *Entrance requirements:* For doctorate, GRE General Test, 3 letters of recommendation. Additional exam requirements/recommendations for international students: Required—TOEFL. Electronic applications accepted. *Expenses:* Tuition, state resident: full-time $7200; part-time $600 per credit. Tuition, nonresident: full-time $11,124; part-time $927 per credit. *Faculty research:* Neural patterning, neurogenesis, neurogenetics, cell population behavior, regeneration.

Seton Hall University, College of Arts and Sciences, Department of Biological Sciences, South Orange, NJ 07079-2697. Offers biology (MS); biology/business administration (MS); microbiology (MS); molecular bioscience (PhD); molecular bioscience/neuroscience (PhD). Part-time and evening/weekend programs available. *Degree requirements:* For master's, thesis optional; for doctorate, comprehensive exam, thesis/dissertation. *Entrance requirements:* For master's and doctorate, GRE or MS from accredited university in the U.S. Additional exam requirements/recommendations for international students: Required—TOEFL. Electronic applications accepted. *Faculty research:* Neurobiology, genetics, immunology, molecular biology, cellular physiology, toxicology, microbiology, bioinformatics.

Seton Hall University, College of Arts and Sciences, Department of Psychology, South Orange, NJ 07079-2697. Offers experimental psychology (MS), including behavioral neuroscience. Part-time and evening/weekend programs available. *Entrance requirements:* For master's, GRE. Additional exam requirements/recommendations for international students: Required—TOEFL. Electronic applications accepted. *Faculty research:* Behavioral neuroscience, cognitive psychology, social psychology, perception/motor skills, memory, depression, anxiety.

Stanford University, School of Medicine, Graduate Programs in Medicine, Neurosciences Program, Stanford, CA 94305-9991. Offers PhD. *Degree requirements:* For doctorate, thesis/dissertation. *Entrance requirements:* For doctorate, GRE General Test, GRE Subject Test. Additional exam requirements/recommendations for international students: Required—TOEFL. Electronic applications accepted. *Expenses:* Tuition: Full-time $38,700; part-time $860 per unit. One-time fee: $200 full-time.

State University of New York Downstate Medical Center, School of Graduate Studies, Program in Neural and Behavioral Science, Brooklyn, NY 11203-2098. Offers PhD, MD/PhD. *Degree requirements:* For doctorate, comprehensive exam, thesis/dissertation. *Entrance requirements:* For doctorate, GRE. *Faculty research:* Molecular neuroscience, cellular neuroscience, systems neuroscience, behavioral neuroscience, behavior.

State University of New York Upstate Medical University, College of Graduate Studies, Program in Neuroscience, Syracuse, NY 13210-2334. Offers PhD. *Degree requirements:* For doctorate, comprehensive exam, thesis/dissertation. *Entrance requirements:* For doctorate, GRE General Test, telephone interview. Additional exam requirements/recommendations for international students: Required—TOEFL. Electronic applications accepted. *Faculty research:* Cancer, disorders of the nervous system, infectious diseases, diabetes/metabolic disorders/cardiovascular diseases.

Stony Brook University, State University of New York, Graduate School, College of Arts and Sciences, Department of Neurobiology and Behavior, Stony Brook, NY 11794. Offers neuroscience (PhD). *Faculty:* 18 full-time (4 women), 1 part-time/adjunct (0 women). *Students:* 35 full-time (15 women); includes 3 Asian, non-Hispanic/Latino; 3 Hispanic/Latino, 12 international. Average age 27. 97 applicants, 18% accepted, 8 enrolled. In 2010, 8 doctorates awarded. *Degree requirements:* For doctorate, comprehensive exam, thesis/dissertation, teaching experience. *Entrance requirements:* For doctorate, GRE General Test, GRE Subject Test, minimum GPA of 3.0. Additional exam requirements/recommendations for international students: Required—TOEFL. *Application deadline:* For fall admission, 1/15 for domestic students. Application fee: $100. *Expenses:* Tuition, state resident: full-time $8370; part-time $349 per credit. Tuition, nonresident: full-time $13,780; part-time $574 per credit. Required fees: $994. *Financial support:* In 2010–11, 18 research assistantships, 10 teaching assistantships were awarded; fellowships, Federal Work-Study also available. *Faculty research:* Biophysics; neurochemistry; cellular, developmental, and integrative neurobiology. Total annual research expenditures: $5.3 million. *Unit head:* Dr. Lorna Role, Interim Chair, 631-632-8616, Fax: 631-632-6661. *Application contact:* Dr. Gary G. Matthews, Director, 631-632-8616, Fax: 631-632-6661, E-mail: ggmatthews@notes.cc.sunysb.edu.

Teachers College, Columbia University, Graduate Faculty of Education, Department of Biobehavioral Studies, Program in Neuroscience and Education, New York, NY 10027. Offers MA. *Faculty:* 6 full-time (3 women), 2 part-time/adjunct (1 woman). *Students:* 11 full-time (7 women), 19 part-time (17 women); includes 9 minority (3 Black or African American, non-Hispanic/Latino; 3 Asian, non-Hispanic/Latino; 2 Hispanic/Latino; 1 Two or more races, non-Hispanic/Latino), 2 international. Average age 28. 24 applicants, 83% accepted, 7 enrolled. In 2010, 13 master's awarded. *Degree requirements:* For master's, integrative project, practicum, research experience. *Application deadline:* For fall admission, 1/15 priority date for domestic students. Applications are processed on a rolling basis. Application fee: $65. Electronic applications accepted. *Expenses:* Tuition: Full-time $28,272; part-time $1178 per credit. Required fees: $756; $378 per semester. *Financial support:* Career-related internships or fieldwork, Federal Work-Study, institutionally sponsored loans, and tuition waivers (full and partial) available. Support available to part-time students. Financial award application deadline: 2/1. *Faculty research:* Neuropsychological diagnosis and intervention. *Unit head:* Prof. Peter Gordon, Program Coordinator, 212-678-8162, E-mail: pgordon@tc.edu. *Application contact:* Prof. Peter Gordon, Program Coordinator, 212-678-8162, E-mail: pgordon@tc.edu.

Temple University, Health Sciences Center, School of Medicine and Graduate School, Doctor of Medicine Program, Department of Neuroscience, Philadelphia, PA 19122-6096. Offers MS, PhD. *Faculty:* 8 full-time (3 women). *Students:* 9 full-time (2 women), 1 international. 32 applicants, 22% accepted, 3 enrolled. *Entrance requirements:* For master's and doctorate, GRE or MCAT, minimum GPA of 3.0. Additional exam requirements/recommendations for international students: Required—TOEFL. *Application deadline:* For fall admission, 7/15 for domestic students, 12/15 for international students; for spring admission, 1/1 for domestic students, 8/1 for international students. Applications are processed on a rolling basis. Application fee: $50. Electronic applications accepted. *Financial support:* Application deadline: 1/15. *Unit head:* Dr. Kamel Khalili, Chair, 215-204-4500, Fax: 215-204-4888, E-mail: kamel.khalili@temple.edu. *Application contact:* Dr. Kamel Khalili, Chair, 215-204-4500, Fax: 215-204-4888, E-mail: kamel.khalili@temple.edu.

Texas A&M Health Science Center, Graduate School of Biomedical Sciences, Department of Neuroscience and Experimental Therapeutics, College Station, TX 77840. Offers PhD.

Texas A&M University, College of Liberal Arts, Department of Psychology, College Station, TX 77843. Offers behavioral and cellular neuroscience (PhD); clinical psychology (PhD); cognitive psychology (PhD); developmental psychology (PhD); industrial/organizational psychology (PhD); social psychology (PhD). *Accreditation:* APA. *Faculty:* 39. *Students:* 91 full-time (57 women), 14 part-time (11 women); includes 7 Black or African American, non-Hispanic/Latino; 8 Asian, non-Hispanic/Latino; 17 Hispanic/Latino, 7 international. In 2010, 12 doctorates awarded. *Degree requirements:* For doctorate, comprehensive exam (for some programs), thesis/dissertation. *Entrance requirements:* For doctorate, GRE General Test. Additional exam requirements/recommendations for international students: Required—TOEFL. *Application deadline:* For fall admission, 1/5 for domestic and international students. Application fee: $50 ($75 for international students). Electronic applications accepted. *Financial support:* Fellowships with partial tuition reimbursements, research assistantships with partial tuition reimbursements, teaching assistantships with partial tuition reimbursements, career-related internships or fieldwork, institutionally sponsored loans, health care benefits, and unspecified assistantships available. Financial award application deadline: 1/5; financial award applicants required to submit FAFSA. *Unit head:* Ludy T. Benjamin, Head, 979-845-2540, Fax: 979-845-4727, E-mail: lbenjamin@tamu.edu. *Application contact:* Julie Austin, Graduate Admissions Supervisor, 979-458-1710, Fax: 979-845-4727, E-mail: gradadv@psyc.tamu.edu.

Texas A&M University, College of Science, Department of Biology, College Station, TX 77843. Offers biology (MS, PhD); botany (MS, PhD); microbiology (MS, PhD); molecular and cell biology (PhD); neuroscience (MS, PhD); zoology (MS, PhD). *Faculty:* 39. *Students:* 107 full-time (60 women), 4 part-time (3 women); includes 1 Black or African American, non-Hispanic/Latino; 5 Asian, non-Hispanic/Latino; 5 Hispanic/Latino, 47 international. Average age 28. In 2010, 3 master's, 6 doctorates awarded. *Degree requirements:* For master's, thesis or alternative; for doctorate, comprehensive exam, thesis/dissertation. *Entrance requirements:* For master's and doctorate, GRE General Test. Additional exam requirements/recommendations for international students: Required—TOEFL. *Application deadline:* For fall admission, 1/15 for domestic students. Applications are processed on a rolling basis. Application fee: $50 ($75 for international students). Electronic applications accepted. *Financial support:* Fellowships, research assistantships, teaching assistantships available. Financial award application deadline: 4/1; financial award applicants required to submit FAFSA. *Unit head:* Dr. Jack McMahan, Department Head, 979-845-2301, E-mail: granster@mail.bio.tamu.edu. *Application contact:* Dr. Jack McMahan, Department Head, 979-845-2301, E-mail: granster@mail.bio.tamu.edu.

Texas Christian University, College of Science and Engineering, Department of Psychology, Fort Worth, TX 76129-0002. Offers experimental psychology (PhD), including cognitive psychology, learning, neuropsychology, social psychology; psychology (MA, MS). In 2010, 7 master's, 3 doctorates awarded. Terminal master's awarded for partial completion of doctoral program. *Degree requirements:* For master's, thesis; for doctorate, thesis/dissertation. *Entrance requirements:* For master's and doctorate, GRE General Test. Additional exam requirements/recommendations for international students: Required—TOEFL. *Application deadline:* For fall admission, 3/1 for domestic and international students; for spring admission, 12/1 for domestic students. Applications are processed on a rolling basis. Application fee: $50. Electronic applications accepted. *Expenses:* Tuition: Full-time $18,720; part-time $1040 per credit hour. Tuition and fees vary according to course load and program. *Financial support:* In 2010–11, 20 students received support; teaching assistantships with full tuition reimbursements available, unspecified assistantships available. Financial award application deadline: 3/1. *Unit head:* Dr. Charles Lord, Coordinator of Graduate Studies, 817-257-7410, Fax: 817-257-7681, E-mail: c.lord@tcu.edu. *Application contact:* Tami Joyce, Department Manager, 817-257-7410, Fax: 817-257-7681, E-mail: t.joyce@tcu.edu.

Texas Tech University Health Sciences Center, Graduate School of Biomedical Sciences, Department of Pharmacology and Neuroscience, Lubbock, TX 79430. Offers MS, PhD, MD/PhD, MS/PhD. Terminal master's awarded for partial completion of doctoral program. *Degree requirements:* For master's, thesis; for doctorate, thesis/dissertation. *Entrance requirements:* For master's and doctorate, GRE General Test, minimum GPA of 3.0. Additional exam requirements/recommendations for international students: Required—TOEFL. Electronic applications accepted. *Faculty research:* Neuroscience, neuropsychopharmacology, autonomic pharmacology, cardiovascular pharmacology, molecular pharmacology.

Thomas Jefferson University, Jefferson College of Graduate Studies, PhD Program in Neuroscience, Philadelphia, PA 19107. Offers PhD. Offered jointly with the Farber Institute for Neuroscience. *Faculty:* 34 full-time (12 women). *Students:* 18 full-time (12 women); includes 2 minority (1 Asian, non-Hispanic/Latino; 1 Native Hawaiian or other Pacific Islander, non-Hispanic/Latino), 2 international. 30 applicants, 23% accepted, 3 enrolled. In 2010, 1 doctorate awarded. *Degree requirements:* For doctorate, comprehensive exam, thesis/dissertation. *Entrance requirements:* For doctorate, GRE General Test, strong background in the sciences, interview, previous research experience. Additional exam requirements/recommendations for international students: Required—TOEFL (minimum score 250 computer-based; 100 iBT) or IELTS. *Application deadline:* For fall admission, 1/5 priority date for domestic and international students. Application fee: $50. *Financial support:* In 2010–11, 18 students received support, including 18 fellowships with full tuition reimbursements available (averaging $54,723 per year); institutionally sponsored loans, scholarships/grants, and stipends also available. Financial award application deadline: 5/1. Total annual research expenditures: $19.6 million. *Unit head:* Dr. Elisabeth J. Van Bockstaele, Program Director, 215-503-1245, Fax: 215-503-9238, E-mail: elisabeth.vanbockstaele@jefferson.edu. *Application contact:* Marc E. Stearns, Director of Admissions and Recruitment, 215-503-4400, Fax: 215-503-9920, E-mail: jcgs-info@jefferson.edu.

Tufts University, Sackler School of Graduate Biomedical Sciences, Program in Neuroscience, Medford, MA 02155. Offers PhD. *Faculty:* 29 full-time (8 women). *Students:* 12 full-time (10 women); includes 1 Hispanic/Latino, 1 international. Average age 26. In 2010, 3 doctorates awarded. *Degree requirements:* For doctorate, thesis/dissertation. *Entrance requirements:* For doctorate, GRE General Test, 3 letters of reference. Additional exam requirements/recommendations for international students: Required—TOEFL. *Application deadline:* For fall admission, 12/15 for domestic students, 12/15 priority date for international students. Applications are processed on a rolling basis. *Expenses:* Tuition: Full-time $39,624; part-time $3962 per course. Required fees: $40 per year. Full-time tuition and fees vary according to degree level, program and student level. Part-time tuition and fees vary according to course load. *Financial support:* In 2010–11, 12 students received support, including 12 research assistantships with full tuition reimbursements available (averaging $28,250 per year); fellowships, scholarships/grants, health care benefits, and tuition waivers (full) also available. *Faculty research:* Electrophysiology, molecular neurobiology, structure and function of sensory systems, neural regulation of development. *Unit head:* Dr. Kathleen Dunlap, Director, 617-636-4942. *Application contact:* Kellie Johnston, Associate Director of Admissions, 617-636-6767, Fax: 617-636-0375, E-mail: sackler-school@tufts.edu.

Tulane University, School of Medicine and School of Liberal Arts, Graduate Programs in Biomedical Sciences, Program in Neuroscience, New Orleans, LA 70118-5669. Offers MS, PhD, MD/PhD. MS and PhD offered through the Graduate School. *Degree requirements:* For doctorate, thesis/dissertation, qualifying exam. *Entrance requirements:* For doctorate, GRE General Test. Additional exam requirements/recommendations for international students: Required—TOEFL. Electronic applications accepted. *Faculty research:* Neuroendocrinology, ion channels, neuropeptides.

Tulane University, School of Science and Engineering, Neuroscience Program, New Orleans, LA 70118-5669. Offers MS, PhD.

Uniformed Services University of the Health Sciences, School of Medicine, Graduate Programs in the Biomedical Sciences and Public Health, Graduate Program in Neuroscience, Bethesda, MD 20814-4799. Offers PhD. *Faculty:* 35 full-time (13 women), 6 part-time/adjunct (2 women). *Students:* 21 full-time (8 women); includes 2 Black or African American, non-Hispanic/Latino, 3 international. Average age 26. 22 applicants, 32% accepted, 5 enrolled. In 2010, 6 doctorates awarded. *Degree requirements:* For doctorate, comprehensive exam, thesis/dissertation, qualifying exams. *Entrance requirements:* For doctorate, GRE General Test, minimum GPA of 3.0; course work in biology, general chemistry, organic chemistry. Additional exam requirements/recommendations for international students: Required—TOEFL. *Application deadline:* For fall admission, 1/1 priority date for domestic and international students. Applications are processed on a rolling basis. Application fee: $0. Electronic applications accepted. *Financial support:* In 2010–11, fellowships with full tuition reimbursements (averaging $27,000 per year); scholarships/grants, health care benefits, and tuition waivers (full) also available. *Faculty research:* Neuronal development and plasticity, molecular neurobiology, environmental adaptations, stress and injury. *Unit head:* Dr. Sharon Juliano, Graduate Program Director, 301-295-3673, Fax: 301-295-1996, E-mail: sjuliano@usuhs.mil. *Application contact:* Tina Finley, Graduate Program Coordinator, 301-295-3642, Fax: 301-295-1996, E-mail: nfinley@usuhs.mil.

See Display below and Close-Up on page 375.

Universidad de Iberoamerica, Graduate School, San Jose, Costa Rica. Offers clinical neuropsychology (PhD); clinical psychology (M Psych); educational psychology (M Psych); forensic psychology (M Psych); hospital management (MHA); intensive care nursing (MN); medicine (MD). *Entrance requirements:* For master's, 2 letters of recommendation, interview.

Université de Montréal, Faculty of Medicine, Department of Physiology, Program in Neurological Sciences, Montréal, QC H3C 3J7, Canada. Offers M Sc, PhD. Terminal master's awarded for partial completion of doctoral program. *Degree requirements:* For master's, thesis; for doctorate, thesis/dissertation, general exam. *Entrance requirements:* For master's and doctorate, proficiency in French, knowledge of English. Electronic applications accepted.

University at Albany, State University of New York, School of Public Health, Department of Biomedical Sciences, Program in Neuroscience, Albany, NY 12222-0001. Offers MS, PhD. *Degree requirements:* For master's, thesis; for doctorate, thesis/dissertation. *Entrance requirements:* For master's and doctorate, GRE General Test, GRE Subject Test.

University at Buffalo, the State University of New York, Graduate School, College of Arts and Sciences, Department of Psychology, Buffalo, NY 14260. Offers behavioral neuroscience (PhD); clinical psychology (PhD); cognitive psychology (PhD); general psychology (MA); social-personality psychology (PhD). *Accreditation:* APA (one or more programs are accredited). *Faculty:* 26 full-time (8 women), 10 part-time/adjunct (5 women). *Students:* 88 full-time (60 women), 6 part-time (4 women); includes 21 minority (2 Black or African American, non-Hispanic/Latino; 2 American Indian or Alaska Native, non-Hispanic/Latino; 7 Asian, non-Hispanic/Latino; 9 Hispanic/Latino; 1 Two or more races, non-Hispanic/Latino), 11 international. Average age 27. 367 applicants, 12% accepted, 21 enrolled. In 2010, 14 master's, 6 doctorates awarded. Terminal master's awarded for partial completion of doctoral program. *Degree requirements:* For master's, project; for doctorate, thesis/dissertation. *Entrance requirements:* For master's and doctorate, GRE General Test. Additional exam requirements/recommendations for international students: Required—TOEFL (minimum score 550 paper-based; 79 iBT). *Application deadline:* For fall admission, 12/1 for domestic and international students. Application fee: $75. Electronic applications accepted. *Financial support:* In 2010–11, 65 students received support, including 8 fellowships with full tuition reimbursements available (averaging $13,700 per year), 16 research assistantships with full tuition reimbursements available (averaging $13,700 per year), 38 teaching assistantships with full tuition reimbursements available (averaging $13,700 per year); career-related internships or fieldwork, Federal Work-Study, institutionally sponsored loans, scholarships/grants, and tuition waivers (partial) also available. Financial award application deadline: 12/1; financial award applicants required to submit FAFSA. *Faculty research:* Neural, endocrine, and molecular bases of behavior; adult mood and anxiety disorders; relationship dysfunction; attention deficit/hyperactivity disorder; psycho-linguistics. Total annual research expenditures: $7.9 million. *Unit head:* Dr. Paul A. Luce, Chair, 716-645-3650 Ext. 203, Fax: 716-645-3801, E-mail: psychair@acsu.buffalo.edu.

Neuroscience

University at Buffalo, the State University of New York (continued)
Application contact: Mary Claire Schnepf, Coordinator of Admissions, 716-645-3660, Fax: 716-645-3801, E-mail: psych@abuffalo.edu.

University at Buffalo, the State University of New York, Graduate School, School of Medicine and Biomedical Sciences, Graduate Programs in Medicine and Biomedical Sciences, Program in Neuroscience, Buffalo, NY 14260. Offers MS, PhD. Part-time programs available. *Students:* 24 full-time (10 women), 6 international. Average age 25. 13 applicants, 46% accepted. In 2010, 3 master's, 2 doctorates awarded. Terminal master's awarded for partial completion of doctoral program. *Degree requirements:* For master's, thesis or alternative; for doctorate, comprehensive exam, thesis/dissertation. *Entrance requirements:* For master's, GRE General Test; for doctorate, GRE General Test, 3 letters of recommendation. Additional exam requirements/recommendations for international students: Required—TOEFL (minimum score 79 iBT). *Application deadline:* For fall admission, 2/1 priority date for domestic and international students. Application fee: $50. *Financial support:* In 2010–11, 17 students received support, including 17 research assistantships with full tuition reimbursements available (averaging $21,000 per year). *Faculty research:* Neural plasticity, development, synapse, neurodisease, genetics of neuropathology. Total annual research expenditures: $6 million. *Unit head:* Dr. Malcolm Slaughter, Professor, 716-829-3240, Fax: 716-829-2364, E-mail: mslaught@buffalo.edu. *Application contact:* Kristen Kahi, Program Administrator, 716-829-2419, Fax: 716-829-3849, E-mail: kkms@buffalo.edu.

University of Alberta, Faculty of Medicine and Dentistry and Faculty of Graduate Studies and Research, Graduate Programs in Medicine, Centre for Neuroscience, Edmonton, AB T6G 2E1, Canada. Offers M Sc, PhD. Terminal master's awarded for partial completion of doctoral program. *Degree requirements:* For master's, thesis; for doctorate, thesis/dissertation. *Entrance requirements:* For master's and doctorate, minimum GPA of 3.3. Additional exam requirements/recommendations for international students: Required—TOEFL (minimum score 600 paper-based; 250 computer-based). Electronic applications accepted. *Faculty research:* Sensory and motor mechanisms, neural growth and regeneration, molecular neurobiology, synaptic mechanisms, behavioral and psychiatric neuroscience.

The University of Arizona, Graduate Interdisciplinary Programs, Graduate Interdisciplinary Program in Neuroscience, Tucson, AZ 85719. Offers PhD. *Faculty:* 6 full-time (1 woman). *Students:* 24 full-time (15 women), 1 (woman) part-time; includes 1 Asian, non-Hispanic/Latino; 2 Hispanic/Latino, 4 international. Average age 27. 49 applicants, 12% accepted, 4 enrolled. In 2010, 6 doctorates awarded. *Degree requirements:* For doctorate, thesis/dissertation. *Entrance requirements:* For doctorate, GRE (minimum score 1100), minimum GPA of 3.5, 3 letters of recommendation. Additional exam requirements/recommendations for international students: Required—TOEFL (minimum score 550 paper-based; 213 computer-based; 79 iBT). *Application deadline:* For fall admission, 12/1 for domestic and international students. Application fee: $65. Electronic applications accepted. *Expenses:* Tuition, state resident: full-time $7692. *Financial support:* In 2010–11, 10 research assistantships with full tuition reimbursements (averaging $44,615 per year) were awarded; health care benefits, tuition waivers (full), and unspecified assistantships also available. Financial award application deadline: 12/1. *Faculty research:* Cognitive neuroscience, developmental neurobiology, speech and hearing, motor control, insect neurobiology. Total annual research expenditures: $1.8 million. *Unit head:* Dr. Konrad E. Zinsmaier, Chairman, 520-621-1343, Fax: 520-621-8282, E-mail: kez@neurobio.arizona.edu. *Application contact:* Erin Wolfe, Graduate Coordinator, 520-621-8380, Fax: 520-626-2618, E-mail: nrsc@u.arizona.edu.

The University of British Columbia, Faculty of Arts and Faculty of Graduate Studies, Department of Psychology, Vancouver, BC V6T 1Z4, Canada. Offers behavioral neuroscience (MA, PhD); clinical psychology (MA, PhD); cognitive science (MA, PhD); developmental psychology (MA, PhD); health psychology (MA, PhD); quantitative methods (MA, PhD); social/personality psychology (MA, PhD). *Accreditation:* APA (one or more programs are accredited). Terminal master's awarded for partial completion of doctoral program. *Degree requirements:* For master's, thesis; for doctorate, comprehensive exam, thesis/dissertation. *Entrance requirements:* For master's and doctorate, GRE General Test. Additional exam requirements/recommendations for international students: Required—TOEFL (minimum score 550 paper-based; 230 computer-based; 80 iBT). Electronic applications accepted. Tuition charges are reported in Canadian dollars. *Expenses:* Tuition, area resident: Full-time $4179 Canadian dollars. International tuition: $7344 Canadian dollars full-time. *Faculty research:* Clinical, developmental, social/personality, cognition, behavioral neuroscience.

University of Calgary, Faculty of Medicine and Faculty of Graduate Studies, Department of Neuroscience, Calgary, AB T2N 1N4, Canada. Offers M Sc, PhD. *Degree requirements:* For master's, thesis, oral thesis exam; for doctorate, thesis/dissertation, candidacy exam, oral thesis exam. *Entrance requirements:* For master's and doctorate, minimum GPA of 3.2 during previous 2 years. Additional exam requirements/recommendations for international students: Required—TOEFL (minimum score 580 paper-based; 237 computer-based). Electronic applications accepted. *Faculty research:* Cellular pharmacology and neurotoxicology, developmental neurobiology, molecular basis of neurodegenerative diseases, neural systems, ion channels.

University of California, Berkeley, Graduate Division, Group in Neuroscience, Berkeley, CA 94720-3200. Offers PhD. *Degree requirements:* For doctorate, qualifying exam, teaching, research thesis/dissertation. *Entrance requirements:* For doctorate, GRE General Test, minimum GPA of 3.0, 3 letters of recommendation, at least one year of laboratory experience. Additional exam requirements/recommendations for international students: Required—TOEFL or IELTS. Electronic applications accepted. *Faculty research:* Analysis of ion channels, signal transduction mechanisms, and gene regulation; development of neurons, synapses, and circuits; synapse function and plasticity; mechanisms of sensory processing; principles of function of cerebral cortex; neural basis for learning, attention, and sleep; neural basis for human emotion, language, motor control, and other high-level cognitive processes.

See Close-Up on page 377.

University of California, Davis, Graduate Studies, Graduate Group in Neuroscience, Davis, CA 95616. Offers PhD. *Degree requirements:* For doctorate, thesis/dissertation. *Entrance requirements:* For doctorate, GRE General Test, GRE Subject Test. Additional exam requirements/recommendations for international students: Required—TOEFL (minimum score 550 paper-based; 213 computer-based). Electronic applications accepted. *Faculty research:* Neuroethology, cognitive neurosciences, cortical neurophysics, cellular and molecular neurobiology.

University of California, Irvine, School of Biological Sciences, Interdepartmental Neuroscience Program, Irvine, CA 92697. Offers PhD. *Students:* 9 full-time (5 women); includes 5 minority (3 Asian, non-Hispanic/Latino; 2 Hispanic/Latino). Average age 28. 102 applicants, 21% accepted, 8 enrolled. *Application deadline:* For fall admission, 12/2 for domestic students. Application fee: $80 ($100 for international students). Electronic applications accepted. *Application contact:* Gary R. Roman, Program Administrator, 949-824-6226, Fax: 949-824-4150, E-mail: groman@uci.edu.

University of California, Los Angeles, David Geffen School of Medicine and Graduate Division, Graduate Programs in Medicine, Interdepartmental Program in Neuroscience, Los Angeles, CA 90095. Offers PhD. *Students:* 92 full-time (41 women); includes 19 minority (2 Black or African American, non-Hispanic/Latino; 11 Asian, non-Hispanic/Latino; 5 Hispanic/Latino; 1 Two or more races, non-Hispanic/Latino), 7 international. Average age 28. 191 applicants, 18% accepted, 15 enrolled. In 2010, 14 doctorates awarded. *Degree requirements:* For doctorate, thesis/dissertation, oral and written qualifying exams. *Entrance requirements:* For doctorate, GRE General Test. *Application deadline:* For fall admission, 12/15 for domestic students. Application fee: $70 ($90 for international students). Electronic applications accepted. *Financial support:* In 2010–11, 84 fellowships, 62 research assistantships, 13 teaching assistantships were awarded; Federal Work-Study, institutionally sponsored loans, scholarships/grants,

and tuition waivers (full and partial) also available. Financial award application deadline: 3/1. *Unit head:* Dr. Michael Levine, Chair, 310-825-7595, E-mail: mlevine@mednet.ucla.edu. *Application contact:* Program Information, 310-206-2349, E-mail: neurophd@mednet.ucla.edu.

University of California, Riverside, Graduate Division, Program in Neuroscience, Riverside, CA 92521-0102. Offers PhD. *Degree requirements:* For doctorate, comprehensive exam, thesis/dissertation, 2 quarters of teaching experience, qualifying exams. *Entrance requirements:* For doctorate, GRE General Test, minimum GPA of 3.2. Additional exam requirements/recommendations for international students: Required—TOEFL (minimum score 550 paper-based; 213 computer-based; 80 iBT). Electronic applications accepted. *Faculty research:* Cellular and molecular neuroscience, development and plasticity, systems neuroscience and behavior, computational neuroscience, cognitive neuroscience, medical neuroscience.

University of California, San Diego, Office of Graduate Studies, Interdisciplinary Program in Cognitive Science, La Jolla, CA 92093. Offers cognitive science/anthropology (PhD); cognitive science/communication (PhD); cognitive science/computer science and engineering (PhD); cognitive science/linguistics (PhD); cognitive science/neuroscience (PhD); cognitive science/philosophy (PhD); cognitive science/psychology (PhD); cognitive science/sociology (PhD). Admissions offered through affiliated departments. *Degree requirements:* For doctorate, thesis/dissertation. *Entrance requirements:* For doctorate, GRE General Test, acceptance into one of the eight participating departments. *Faculty research:* Language and cognition, philosophy of mind, visual perception, biological anthropology, sociolinguistics.

University of California, San Diego, School of Medicine and Office of Graduate Studies, Molecular Pathology Program, La Jolla, CA 92093. Offers bioinformatics (PhD); cancer biology/oncology (PhD); cardiovascular sciences and disease (PhD); microbiology (PhD); molecular pathology (PhD); neurological disease (PhD); stem cell and developmental biology (PhD); structural biology/drug design (PhD). *Entrance requirements:* For doctorate, GRE General Test, GRE Subject Test. Additional exam requirements/recommendations for international students: Required—TOEFL. Electronic applications accepted.

University of California, San Diego, School of Medicine and Office of Graduate Studies, Neurosciences Program, La Jolla, CA 92093. Offers PhD. *Degree requirements:* For doctorate, thesis/dissertation, qualifying exam. *Entrance requirements:* For doctorate, GRE General Test, GRE Subject Test. Additional exam requirements/recommendations for international students: Required—TOEFL. Electronic applications accepted. *Faculty research:* Neurophysiology, neuropharmacology, neurochemistry.

University of California, San Francisco, Graduate Division, Program in Neuroscience, San Francisco, CA 94143. Offers PhD. *Degree requirements:* For doctorate, thesis/dissertation. *Entrance requirements:* For doctorate, GRE General Test, GRE Subject Test. *Faculty research:* Molecular neurobiology, synaptic plasticity, mechanisms of motor learning.

University of Chicago, Division of Biological Sciences, Neuroscience Graduate Programs, Committee on Computational Neuroscience, Chicago, IL 60637-1513. Offers PhD. *Degree requirements:* For doctorate, thesis/dissertation, ethics class, 2 teaching assistantships. *Entrance requirements:* For doctorate, GRE General Test. Additional exam requirements/recommendations for international students: Required—TOEFL (minimum score 600 paper-based; 250 computer-based; 104 iBT), IELTS (minimum score 7). Electronic applications accepted.

University of Chicago, Division of Biological Sciences, Neuroscience Graduate Programs, Department of Integrative Neuroscience, Chicago, IL 60637-1513. Offers cell physiology (PhD); pharmacological and physiological sciences (PhD). *Degree requirements:* For doctorate, thesis/dissertation, preliminary exam. *Entrance requirements:* For doctorate, GRE General Test. Additional exam requirements/recommendations for international students: Required—TOEFL. Electronic applications accepted. *Faculty research:* Psychopharmacology, neuropharmacology.

University of Cincinnati, Graduate School, Interdisciplinary PhD Study Program in Neuroscience, Cincinnati, OH 45221. Offers PhD. *Degree requirements:* For doctorate, thesis/dissertation, qualifying exam. *Entrance requirements:* For doctorate, GRE General Test. Additional exam requirements/recommendations for international students: Required—TOEFL. Electronic applications accepted. *Faculty research:* Developmental neurobiology, membrane and channel biophysics, molecular neurobiology, neuroendocrinology, neuronal cell biology.

University of Colorado Denver, School of Medicine, Program in Neuroscience, Denver, CO 80217-3364. Offers PhD. *Students:* 31 full-time (19 women); includes 2 Asian, non-Hispanic/Latino; 2 Hispanic/Latino; 1 Two or more races, non-Hispanic/Latino, 1 international. Average age 29. 33 applicants, 15% accepted, 5 enrolled. In 2010, 4 doctorates awarded. *Degree requirements:* For doctorate, comprehensive exam, thesis/dissertation, lab rotations. *Entrance requirements:* For doctorate, GRE, baccalaureate degree in a biological science, chemistry, physics or engineering (recommended); minimum GPA of 3.2. Additional exam requirements/recommendations for international students: Required—TOEFL (minimum score 550 paper-based). *Application deadline:* For fall admission, 1/1 for domestic students. Application fee: $65. Electronic applications accepted. *Expenses:* Contact institution. *Financial support:* In 2010–11, 5 students received support; fellowships, health care benefits, tuition waivers (full), and stipend available. Financial award application deadline: 3/15; financial award applicants required to submit FAFSA. *Faculty research:* Neurobiology of olfaction, ion channels, schizophrenia, spinal cord regeneration, neurotransplantation. *Unit head:* Dr. Diego Restrepo, Director, 303-724-3405, Fax: 303-724-3420, E-mail: diego.restrepo@ucdenver.edu. *Application contact:* Mellodee Phillips, Program Administrator, 303-724-3120, Fax: 303-724-3121, E-mail: mellodee.phillips@ucdenver.edu.

University of Connecticut, Graduate School, College of Liberal Arts and Sciences, Department of Psychology, Storrs, CT 06269. Offers behavioral neuroscience (PhD); biopsychology (PhD); clinical psychology (MA, PhD); cognition and instruction (PhD); developmental psychology (MA, PhD); ecological psychology (PhD); experimental psychology (PhD); general psychology (MA, PhD); health psychology (Graduate Certificate); industrial/organizational psychology (PhD); language and cognition (PhD); neuroscience (PhD); occupational health psychology (Graduate Certificate); social psychology (MA, PhD). *Accreditation:* APA. Terminal master's awarded for partial completion of doctoral program. *Degree requirements:* For master's, comprehensive exam; for doctorate, thesis/dissertation. *Entrance requirements:* For master's and doctorate, GRE General Test, GRE Subject Test. Additional exam requirements/recommendations for international students: Required—TOEFL (minimum score 550 paper-based; 213 computer-based). Electronic applications accepted.

University of Connecticut Health Center, Graduate School, Programs in Biomedical Sciences, Program in Neuroscience, Farmington, CT 06030. Offers PhD, DMD/PhD, MD/PhD. *Faculty:* 158. *Students:* 18 full-time (9 women); includes 3 minority (2 Black or African American, non-Hispanic/Latino; 1 Asian, non-Hispanic/Latino), 7 international. Average age 29. 216 applicants, 22% accepted. In 2010, 3 doctorates awarded. *Degree requirements:* For doctorate, comprehensive exam, thesis/dissertation. *Entrance requirements:* For doctorate, GRE General Test, interview (recommended). Additional exam requirements/recommendations for international students: Required—TOEFL (minimum score 600 paper-based; 250 computer-based). *Application deadline:* For fall admission, 12/15 for domestic students. Application fee: $55. Electronic applications accepted. *Financial support:* In 2010–11, 18 research assistantships with full tuition reimbursements (averaging $27,000 per year) were awarded; health care benefits also available. *Faculty research:* Molecular and systems neuroscience, neuroanatomy, neurophysiology, neurochemistry, neuropathology. *Unit head:* Dr. James Hewett, Director, 860-679-4131, Fax: 860-679-1885, E-mail: jhewett@nso1.uchc.edu. *Application contact:* Tricia Avolt, Graduate Admissions Coordinator, 860-679-2175, Fax: 860-679-1899, E-mail: robertson@nso2.uchc.edu.

See Display on next page and Close-Up on page 379.

Neuroscience

University of Delaware, College of Arts and Sciences, Department of Psychology, Newark, DE 19716. Offers behavioral neuroscience (PhD); clinical psychology (PhD); cognitive psychology (PhD); social psychology (PhD). *Accreditation:* APA. *Degree requirements:* For doctorate, thesis/dissertation. *Entrance requirements:* For doctorate, GRE General Test. Additional exam requirements/recommendations for international students: Required—TOEFL (minimum score 600 paper-based; 250 computer-based). Electronic applications accepted. *Faculty research:* Emotion development, neural and cognitive aspects of memory, neural control of feeding, intergroup relations, social cognition and communication.

University of Denver, Division of Arts, Humanities and Social Sciences, Department of Psychology, Denver, CO 80208. Offers affective science (PhD); affective/social psychology (PhD); clinical child psychology (PhD); developmental cognitive neuroscience (PhD); developmental psychology (PhD). Incidental Master's program available. *Accreditation:* APA. *Faculty:* 18 full-time (8 women), 5 part-time/adjunct (4 women). *Students:* 32 full-time (31 women), 2 part-time (1 woman); includes 6 minority (3 Asian, non-Hispanic/Latino; 2 Hispanic/Latino; 1 Two or more races, non-Hispanic/Latino), 2 international. Average age 26. 320 applicants, 5% accepted, 13 enrolled. In 2010, 6 doctorates awarded. Terminal master's awarded for partial completion of doctoral program. *Degree requirements:* For doctorate, one foreign language, comprehensive exam (for some programs), thesis/dissertation. *Entrance requirements:* For doctorate, GRE General Test. Additional exam requirements/recommendations for international students: Required—TOEFL (minimum score 550 paper-based; 80 iBT). *Application deadline:* For fall admission, 12/1 for domestic students. Applications are processed on a rolling basis. Application fee: $60. Electronic applications accepted. *Expenses:* Tuition: Full-time $35,604; part-time $29,670 per year. Required fees: $687 per year. Tuition and fees vary according to program. *Financial support:* In 2010–11, 12 research assistantships with full and partial tuition reimbursements (averaging $15,500 per year), 22 teaching assistantships with full and partial tuition reimbursements (averaging $16,773 per year) were awarded; career-related internships or fieldwork, Federal Work-Study, institutionally sponsored loans, scholarships/grants, and unspecified assistantships also available. Support available to part-time students. Financial award application deadline: 1/1; financial award applicants required to submit FAFSA. *Faculty research:* Developmental neuropsychology, self-esteem and peer relationships, child abuse and neglect, marital and family interactions, adolescent peer and romantic relationships. *Unit head:* Dr. Rob Roberts, Chair, 303-871-3792, Fax: 303-871-4747. *Application contact:* Paula Plank-Houghtaling, Graduate Secretary, 303-871-3803, Fax: 303-871-4747, E-mail: info@psy.du.edu.

University of Florida, College of Medicine, Department of Neuroscience, Gainesville, FL 32611. Offers MS, PhD. Terminal master's awarded for partial completion of doctoral program. *Degree requirements:* For master's, thesis; for doctorate, thesis/dissertation. *Entrance requirements:* For master's and doctorate, GRE General Test, minimum GPA of 3.0. Additional exam requirements/recommendations for international students: Required—TOEFL. Electronic applications accepted. *Expenses:* Tuition, state resident: full-time $10,916. Tuition, nonresident: full-time $28,309. *Faculty research:* Neural injury and repair, neuroimmunology and endocrinology, neurophysiology, neurotoxicology, cellular and molecular neurobiology.

University of Florida, College of Medicine and Graduate School, Interdisciplinary Program in Biomedical Sciences, Concentration in Neuroscience, Gainesville, FL 32611. Offers PhD. *Degree requirements:* For doctorate, thesis/dissertation. *Entrance requirements:* For doctorate, GRE General Test, minimum GPA of 3.0. Additional exam requirements/recommendations for international students: Required—TOEFL. Electronic applications accepted. *Expenses:* Tuition, state resident: full-time $10,916. Tuition, nonresident: full-time $28,309. *Faculty research:* Neural injury and repair, neurophysiology, neurotoxicology, cellular and molecular neurobiology, neuroimmunology and endocrinology.

University of Florida, Graduate School, College of Liberal Arts and Sciences, Department of Psychology, Gainesville, FL 32611. Offers behavior analysis (PhD); behavioral neuroscience

(MS, PhD); cognitive and sensory processes (PhD); counseling psychology (PhD); developmental psychology (PhD); social psychology (MS, PhD); JD/PhD. *Faculty:* 29 full-time (10 women). *Students:* 106 full-time (82 women), 14 part-time (7 women); includes 3 Black or African American, non-Hispanic/Latino; 2 American Indian or Alaska Native, non-Hispanic/Latino; 7 Asian, non-Hispanic/Latino; 12 Hispanic/Latino, 11 international. Average age 27. 614 applicants, 7% accepted. In 2010, 25 master's, 13 doctorates awarded. *Degree requirements:* For master's, comprehensive exam, thesis or alternative; for doctorate, comprehensive exam, thesis/dissertation. *Entrance requirements:* For master's and doctorate, GRE General Test, minimum GPA of 3.0. Additional exam requirements/recommendations for international students: Required—TOEFL (minimum score 550 paper-based; 213 computer-based; 80 iBT), IELTS (minimum score 6). *Application deadline:* For fall admission, 12/9 priority date for domestic students, 12/9 for international students. Applications are processed on a rolling basis. Application fee: $30. Electronic applications accepted. *Expenses:* Tuition, state resident: full-time $10,916. Tuition, nonresident: full-time $28,309. *Financial support:* In 2010–11, 105 students received support, including 19 fellowships, 24 research assistantships (averaging $18,742 per year), 62 teaching assistantships (averaging $19,797 per year); career-related internships or fieldwork and unspecified assistantships also available. Financial award application deadline: 12/9; financial award applicants required to submit FAFSA. *Faculty research:* Behavior analysis, behavioral and cognitive neuroscience, counseling, developmental psychology, social psychology. Total annual research expenditures: $2.7 million. *Unit head:* Dr. Neil E. Rowland, Chair, 352-273-2128, Fax: 352-392-7985, E-mail: nrowland@ufl.edu. *Application contact:* Dr. Clive D. Wynne, Graduate Coordinator, 352-392-0601, Fax: 352-392-7985, E-mail: wynne@ufl.edu.

University of Georgia, Biomedical and Health Sciences Institute, Athens, GA 30602. Offers neuroscience (PhD). *Students:* 13 full-time (9 women), 1 (woman) part-time; includes 1 Black or African American, non-Hispanic/Latino; 1 Asian, non-Hispanic/Latino; 1 Hispanic/Latino, 4 international. 23 applicants, 13% accepted, 2 enrolled. In 2010, 6 doctorates awarded. *Entrance requirements:* For doctorate, GRE, official transcripts, 3 letters of recommendation, statement of interest. Additional exam requirements/recommendations for international students: Required—TOEFL. *Expenses:* Tuition, state resident: full-time $10,916. Tuition, nonresident: full-time $21,900; part-time $944 per credit hour. Tuition and fees vary according to course load and program. *Financial support:* Unspecified assistantships available. Financial award application deadline: 12/31. *Unit head:* Dr. Gaylen Edwards, Chair, 706-542-5922, Fax: 706-542-5285, E-mail: gedwards@uga.edu. *Application contact:* Philip V. Holmes, Graduate Coordinator, 706-542-5922, Fax: 706-542-5285, E-mail: pvholmes@uga.edu.

University of Guelph, Ontario Veterinary College and Graduate Studies, Graduate Programs in Veterinary Sciences, Department of Biomedical Sciences, Guelph, ON N1G 2W1, Canada. Offers morphology (M Sc, DV Sc, PhD); neuroscience (M Sc, DV Sc, PhD); pharmacology (M Sc, DV Sc, PhD); physiology (M Sc, DV Sc, PhD); toxicology (M Sc, DV Sc, PhD). Part-time programs available. *Degree requirements:* For master's, thesis; for doctorate, comprehensive exam, thesis/dissertation. *Entrance requirements:* For master's, honors B Sc, minimum 75% average in last 20 courses; for doctorate, M Sc with thesis from accredited institution. Additional exam requirements/recommendations for international students: Required—TOEFL (minimum score 550 paper-based; 213 computer-based; 89 iBT). Electronic applications accepted. *Faculty research:* Cellular morphology; endocrine, vascular and reproductive physiology; clinical pharmacology; veterinary toxicology; developmental biology, neuroscience.

University of Guelph, Ontario Veterinary College and Graduate Studies, Graduate Programs in Veterinary Sciences, Department of Clinical Studies, Guelph, ON N1G 2W1, Canada. Offers anesthesiology (M Sc, DV Sc); cardiology (DV Sc, Diploma); clinical studies (Diploma); dermatology (M Sc, DV Sc); diagnostic imaging (M Sc, DV Sc); emergency/critical care (M Sc, DV Sc, Diploma); medicine (M Sc, DV Sc); neurology (M Sc, DV Sc); ophthalmology (M Sc, DV Sc); surgery (M Sc, DV Sc). *Degree requirements:* For master's, thesis; for doctorate, comprehensive

University of Connecticut Health Center

UCHC offers you exceptional research opportunities spanning **Cell Analysis and Modeling; Cell Biology; Genetics and Developmental Biology; Immunology; Molecular Biology and Biochemistry; Neuroscience;** and **Skeletal, Craniofacial and Oral Biology**.

Key features of our program include:

❖ Integrated admissions with access to more than 100 laboratories.

❖ Flexible educational program tailored to the interests of each student.

❖ Excellent education in a stimulating, cutting edge research environment.

❖ Competitive stipend ($28,000 for 2011–12 year), tuition waiver, and availability of student health plan.

❖ State-of-the-art research facilities, including the new Cell and Genome Sciences Building, which houses the UConn Stem Cell Institute, the Center for Cell Analysis and Modeling, and the Department of Genetics and Developmental Biology.

For more information, please contact:
Stephanie Rauch, Biomedical Science Admissions Coordinator
University of Connecticut Health Center
Farmington, CT 06030
BiomedSciAdmissions@uchc.edu
http://grad.uchc.edu/prospective/programs/phd_biosci/index.html

Neuroscience

University of Guelph (continued)
exam, thesis/dissertation. *Entrance requirements:* Additional exam requirements/recommendations for international students: Required—TOEFL (minimum score 550 paper-based; 213 computer-based), IELTS (minimum score 6.5). Electronic applications accepted. *Faculty research:* Orthopedics, respirology, oncology, exercise physiology, cardiology.

University of Hartford, College of Arts and Sciences, Department of Biology, Program in Neuroscience, West Hartford, CT 06117-1599. Offers MS. Part-time and evening/weekend programs available. *Degree requirements:* For master's, comprehensive exam, thesis optional, oral exams. *Entrance requirements:* For master's, GRE General Test, GRE Subject Test, MCAT. Additional exam requirements/recommendations for international students: Required—TOEFL (minimum score 550 paper-based; 213 computer-based). Electronic applications accepted. *Faculty research:* Neurobiology of aging, central actions of neural steroids, neuroendocrine control of reproduction, retinopathies in sharks, plasticity in the central nervous system.

University of Idaho, College of Graduate Studies, Program in Neuroscience, Moscow, ID 83844-2282. Offers MS, PhD. *Faculty:* 6 full-time. *Students:* 5 full-time, 3 part-time. Average age 34. In 2010, 1 master's, 1 doctorate awarded. *Application deadline:* For fall admission, 2/15 for domestic students. Applications are processed on a rolling basis. Application fee: $60. Electronic applications accepted. *Expenses:* Tuition, nonresident: part-time $580 per credit. Required fees: $306 per credit. *Financial support:* Applicants required to submit FAFSA. *Unit head:* Dr. Nilsa Bosque-Perez, Interim Dean of the College of Graduate Studies, 208-885-6243, Fax: 208-885-6198, E-mail: uigrad@uidaho.edu. *Application contact:* Dr. Nilsa Bosque-Perez, Interim Dean of the College of Graduate Studies, 208-885-6243, Fax: 208-885-6198, E-mail: uigrad@uidaho.edu.

University of Illinois at Chicago, College of Medicine and Graduate College, Graduate Programs in Medicine, Department of Anatomy and Cell Biology, Program in Neuroscience, Chicago, IL 60607-7128. Offers cellular and systems neuroscience and cell biology (PhD).

University of Illinois at Urbana–Champaign, Graduate College, College of Liberal Arts and Sciences, School of Molecular and Cellular Biology, Neuroscience Program, Champaign, IL 61820. Offers PhD. *Students:* 61 full-time (35 women), 2 part-time (both women); includes 24 minority (2 Black or African American, non-Hispanic/Latino; 14 Asian, non-Hispanic/Latino; 6 Hispanic/Latino; 1 Native Hawaiian or other Pacific Islander, non-Hispanic/Latino; 1 Two or more races, non-Hispanic/Latino), 10 international. 126 applicants, 14% accepted, 13 enrolled. In 2010, 6 doctorates awarded. *Entrance requirements:* For doctorate, GRE, minimum GPA of 3.0. Additional exam requirements/recommendations for international students: Required—TOEFL (minimum score 570 paper-based; 230 computer-based). *Application deadline:* Applications are processed on a rolling basis. Application fee: $75 ($90 for international students). Electronic applications accepted. *Financial support:* In 2010–11, 23 fellowships, 29 research assistantships, 19 teaching assistantships were awarded; tuition waivers (full and partial) also available. *Unit head:* Gene Robinson, Director, 217-333-4971, Fax: 217-244-3499, E-mail: generobi@illinois.edu. *Application contact:* Sam Beshers, Program Coordinator, 217-333-4971, Fax: 217-244-3499, E-mail: beshers@illinois.edu.

The University of Iowa, Graduate College, Program in Neuroscience, Iowa City, IA 52242-1316. Offers PhD, MD/PhD. *Degree requirements:* For doctorate, comprehensive exam, thesis/dissertation. *Entrance requirements:* For doctorate, GRE General Test, minimum GPA of 3.0. Additional exam requirements/recommendations for international students: Required—TOEFL (minimum score 600 paper-based; 250 computer-based; 100 iBT). Electronic applications accepted. *Faculty research:* Molecular, cellular, and developmental systems; behavioral neurosciences.

The University of Kansas, Graduate Studies, School of Pharmacy, Program in Neurosciences, Lawrence, KS 66045. Offers MS, PhD. *Students:* 7 full-time (4 women); includes 2 Asian, non-Hispanic/Latino, 1 international. Average age 27. 27 applicants, 7% accepted, 1 enrolled. In 2010, 2 master's, 2 doctorates awarded. *Degree requirements:* For doctorate, comprehensive exam, thesis/dissertation. *Entrance requirements:* For master's and doctorate, GRE. Additional exam requirements/recommendations for international students: Required—TOEFL. *Application deadline:* For fall admission, 1/5 priority date for domestic and international students. Applications are processed on a rolling basis. Application fee: $55 ($65 for international students). Electronic applications accepted. *Expenses:* Tuition, state resident: full-time $7092; part-time $295.50 per credit hour. Tuition, nonresident: full-time $16,590; part-time $691.25 per credit hour. Required fees: $858; $71.49 per credit hour. Tuition and fees vary according to course load, campus/location and program. *Financial support:* Fellowships, research assistantships with full tuition reimbursements available. Financial award application deadline: 1/15. *Unit head:* Prof. Elias Michaelis, 785-864-4001, Fax: 785-864-5219, E-mail: emichaelis@ku.edu. *Application contact:* Prof. Elias K. Michaelis, 785-864-4001, E-mail: emichaelis@ku.edu.

The University of Kansas, University of Kansas Medical Center, School of Medicine, Department of Molecular and Integrative Physiology, Neuroscience Graduate Program, Lawrence, KS 66045-7582. Offers MS, PhD. *Entrance requirements:* Additional exam requirements/recommendations for international students: Required—TOEFL. *Expenses:* Tuition, state resident: full-time $7092; part-time $295.50 per credit hour. Tuition, nonresident: full-time $16,590; part-time $691.25 per credit hour. Required fees: $858; $71.49 per credit hour. Tuition and fees vary according to course load, campus/location and program. *Unit head:* Dr. Paul D. Cheney, Chair of Molecular and Integrative Physiology, 913-588-7400, Fax: 913-588-7430, E-mail: pcheney@kumc.edu. *Application contact:* Marcia Jones, Director of Graduate Studies, 913-588-1238, Fax: 913-588-5242, E-mail: mjones@kumc.edu.

University of Lethbridge, School of Graduate Studies, Lethbridge, AB T1K 3M4, Canada. Offers accounting (MScM); addictions counseling (M Sc); agricultural biotechnology (M Sc); agricultural studies (M Sc, MA); anthropology (MA); archaeology (MA); art (MA, MFA); biochemistry (M Sc); biological sciences (M Sc); biomolecular science (PhD); biosystems and biodiversity (PhD); Canadian studies (MA); chemistry (M Sc); computer science (M Sc); computer science and geographical information science (M Sc); counseling psychology (M Ed); dramatic arts (MA); earth, space, and physical science (PhD); economics (MA); educational leadership (M Ed); English (MA); environmental science (M Sc); evolution and behavior (PhD); exercise science (M Sc); finance (MScM); French (MA); French/German (MA); French/Spanish (MA); general education (M Ed); general management (MScM); geography (M Sc, MA); German (MA); health science (M Sc); history (MA); human resource management and labour relations (MScM); individualized multidisciplinary (M Sc, MA); information systems (MScM); international management (MScM); kinesiology (M Sc, MA); management (M Sc, MA); marketing (MScM); mathematics (M Sc); music (M Mus, MA); Native American studies (MA); neuroscience (M Sc, PhD); new media (MA); nursing (M Sc); philosophy (MA); physics (M Sc); policy and strategy (MScM); political science (MA); psychology (M Sc, MA); religious studies (MA); social sciences (MA); sociology (MA); theatre and dramatic arts (MFA); theoretical and computational science (PhD); urban and regional studies (MA); women's studies (MA). Part-time and evening/weekend programs available. *Degree requirements:* For doctorate, comprehensive exam, thesis/dissertation. *Entrance requirements:* For master's, GMAT (M Sc in management), bachelor's degree in related field, minimum GPA of 3.0 during previous 20 graded semester courses, 2 years teaching or related experience (M Ed); for doctorate, master's degree, minimum graduate GPA of 3.5. Additional exam requirements/recommendations for international students: Required—TOEFL. *Faculty research:* Movement and brain plasticity, gibberellin physiology, photosynthesis, carbon cycling, molecular properties of main-group ring components.

University of Maine, Graduate School, Program in Biomedical Sciences, Orono, ME 04469. Offers biomedical engineering (PhD); cell and molecular biology (PhD); neuroscience (PhD); toxicology (PhD). *Students:* 11 full-time (8 women), 13 part-time (6 women); includes 1 American Indian or Alaska Native, non-Hispanic/Latino, 5 international. Average age 29. 32 applicants, 19% accepted, 6 enrolled. Application fee: $60. *Expenses:* Tuition, state resident: full-time $400. Tuition, nonresident: full-time $1050. *Financial support:* In 2010–11, 8 research assistantships (averaging $25,625 per year) were awarded. *Unit head:* Dr. Carol Kim, Unit Head, 207-581-2803. *Application contact:* Dr. Carol Kim, Unit Head, 207-581-2803.

The University of Manchester, Faculty of Life Sciences, Manchester, United Kingdom. Offers adaptive organismal biology (M Phil, PhD); animal biology (M Phil, PhD); biochemistry (M Phil, PhD); bioinformatics (M Phil, PhD); biomolecular sciences (M Phil, PhD); biotechnology (M Phil, PhD); cell biology (M Phil, PhD); cell matrix research (M Phil, PhD); channels and transporters (M Phil, PhD); developmental biology (M Phil, PhD); Egyptology (M Phil, PhD); environmental biology (M Phil, PhD); evolutionary biology (M Phil, PhD); gene expression (M Phil, PhD); genetics (M Phil, PhD); history of science, technology and medicine (M Phil, PhD); immunology (M Phil, PhD); integrative neurobiology and behavior (M Phil, PhD); membrane trafficking (M Phil, PhD); microbiology (M Phil, PhD); molecular and cellular neuroscience (M Phil, PhD); molecular biology (M Phil, PhD); molecular cancer studies (M Phil, PhD); neuroscience (M Phil, PhD); ophthalmology (M Phil, PhD); optometry (M Phil, PhD); organelle function (M Phil, PhD); pharmacology (M Phil, PhD); physiology (M Phil, PhD); plant sciences (M Phil, PhD); stem cell research (M Phil, PhD); structural biology (M Phil, PhD); systems neuroscience (M Phil, PhD); toxicology (M Phil, PhD).

University of Maryland, Baltimore, Graduate School, Graduate Program in Life Sciences, Program in Neuroscience, Baltimore, MD 21201. Offers PhD, MD/PhD. Part-time programs available. *Entrance requirements:* For doctorate, GRE General Test, minimum GPA of 3.0. Additional exam requirements/recommendations for international students: Required—TOEFL (minimum score 550 paper-based; 80 iBT); Recommended—IELTS (minimum score 7). Electronic applications accepted. Part-time tuition and fees vary according to course load, degree level and program. *Faculty research:* Molecular, biochemical, and cellular pharmacology; membrane biophysics; synaptology; developmental neurobiology.

University of Maryland, Baltimore County, Graduate School, College of Natural and Mathematical Sciences, Department of Biological Sciences and Department of Psychology, Program in Neurosciences and Cognitive Sciences, Baltimore, MD 21250. Offers PhD. *Faculty:* 4 full-time (3 women). *Students:* 2 full-time (0 women); includes 1 Asian, non-Hispanic/Latino; 1 Hispanic/Latino. Average age 30. 7 applicants, 0% accepted, 0 enrolled. *Degree requirements:* For doctorate, comprehensive exam (for some programs), thesis/dissertation. *Entrance requirements:* For doctorate, GRE General Test, minimum GPA of 3.0. Additional exam requirements/recommendations for international students: Required—TOEFL. *Application deadline:* For fall admission, 1/15 for domestic students, 12/15 for international students. Applications are processed on a rolling basis. Application fee: $50. Electronic applications accepted. *Financial support:* In 2010–11, 5 students received support, including 3 research assistantships with full tuition reimbursements available (averaging $22,300 per year), 2 teaching assistantships with full tuition reimbursements available (averaging $21,300 per year). *Unit head:* Dr. Jeff Leips, Director, 410-455-3669, Fax: 410-455-3875, E-mail: biograd@umbc.edu. *Application contact:* Dr. Jeff Leips, Director, 410-455-3669, Fax: 410-455-3875, E-mail: biograd@umbc.edu.

University of Maryland, College Park, Academic Affairs, College of Behavioral and Social Sciences, Department of Hearing and Speech Sciences, College Park, MD 20742. Offers audiology (MA, PhD); hearing and speech sciences (Au D); language pathology (MA, PhD); neuroscience (PhD); speech (MA, PhD). *Accreditation:* ASHA (one or more programs are accredited). *Faculty:* 22 full-time (20 women), 12 part-time/adjunct (9 women). *Students:* 68 full-time (62 women), 22 part-time (21 women); includes 19 minority (8 Black or African American, non-Hispanic/Latino; 5 Asian, non-Hispanic/Latino; 4 Hispanic/Latino; 1 Native Hawaiian or other Pacific Islander, non-Hispanic/Latino; 1 Two or more races, non-Hispanic/Latino), 2 international. 291 applicants, 32% accepted, 28 enrolled. In 2010, 20 master's, 11 doctorates awarded. *Degree requirements:* For master's, thesis optional; for doctorate, thesis/dissertation, written and oral exams. *Entrance requirements:* For master's, GRE General Test, minimum GPA of 3.5, 3 letters of recommendation; for doctorate, GRE General Test, minimum GPA of 3.5. Additional exam requirements/recommendations for international students: Required—TOEFL. *Application deadline:* For fall admission, 1/15 for domestic and international students. Applications are processed on a rolling basis. Application fee: $75. Electronic applications accepted. *Expenses:* Tuition, state resident: part-time $471 per credit hour. Tuition, nonresident: part-time $1016 per credit hour. Required fees: $337 per term. *Financial support:* In 2010–11, 5 fellowships with full and partial tuition reimbursements (averaging $14,722 per year), 22 research assistantships (averaging $15,396 per year), 16 teaching assistantships (averaging $14,171 per year) were awarded; career-related internships or fieldwork, Federal Work-Study, scholarships/grants, and health care benefits also available. Support available to part-time students. Financial award applicants required to submit FAFSA. *Faculty research:* Speech perception, language acquisition, bilingualism, hearing loss. Total annual research expenditures: $906,503. *Unit head:* Dr. Nan B. Bernstein-Ratner, Chair, 301-405-4217, Fax: 301-314-2023, E-mail: nratner@umd.edu. *Application contact:* Dean of Graduate School, 301-405-0358, Fax: 301-314-9305.

University of Maryland, College Park, Academic Affairs, College of Behavioral and Social Sciences, Program in Neurosciences and Cognitive Sciences, College Park, MD 20742. Offers PhD. *Students:* 49 full-time (28 women), 3 part-time (2 women); includes 3 Black or African American, non-Hispanic/Latino; 1 Asian, non-Hispanic/Latino, 13 international. 105 applicants, 17% accepted, 7 enrolled. In 2010, 7 doctorates awarded. *Degree requirements:* For doctorate, comprehensive exam, thesis/dissertation. *Entrance requirements:* For doctorate, GRE General Test, 3 letters of recommendation. Additional exam requirements/recommendations for international students: Required—TOEFL. *Application deadline:* For fall admission, 12/15 for domestic and international students. Applications are processed on a rolling basis. Application fee: $75. Electronic applications accepted. *Expenses:* Tuition, state resident: part-time $471 per credit hour. Tuition, nonresident: part-time $1016 per credit hour. Required fees: $337 per term. *Financial support:* In 2010–11, 11 fellowships with full and partial tuition reimbursements (averaging $17,924 per year), 12 research assistantships (averaging $18,643 per year), 26 teaching assistantships (averaging $17,870 per year) were awarded; Federal Work-Study and scholarships/grants also available. Support available to part-time students. Financial award applicants required to submit FAFSA. *Faculty research:* Molecular neurobiology, cognition, neural and behavioral systems language, memory, human development. *Unit head:* Dr. Cynthia F. Moss, Director, 301-405-0353, Fax: 301-405-7104, E-mail: moss@umd.edu. *Application contact:* Dean of Graduate School, 301-405-0358, Fax: 301-314-9305.

University of Massachusetts Amherst, Graduate School, Interdisciplinary Programs, Program in Neuroscience and Behavior, Amherst, MA 01003. Offers animal behavior and learning (PhD); molecular and cellular neuroscience (PhD); neural and behavioral development (PhD); neuroendocrinology (PhD); neuroscience and behavior (MS); sensorimotor, cognitive, and computational neuroscience (PhD). *Students:* 31 full-time (19 women); includes 5 minority (2 Asian, non-Hispanic/Latino; 3 Hispanic/Latino), 2 international. Average age 26. 77 applicants, 30% accepted, 10 enrolled. In 2010, 2 master's, 4 doctorates awarded. Terminal master's awarded for partial completion of doctoral program. *Degree requirements:* For master's, thesis or alternative; for doctorate, comprehensive exam, thesis/dissertation. *Entrance requirements:* For master's and doctorate, GRE General Test. Additional exam requirements/recommendations for international students: Required—TOEFL (minimum score 550 paper-based; 213 computer-based; 80 iBT), IELTS (minimum score 6.5). *Application deadline:* For fall admission, 1/2 for domestic and international students. Applications are processed on a rolling basis. Application fee: $50 ($65 for international students). Electronic applications accepted. *Expenses:* Tuition, state resident: full-time $2640. Required fees: $8282. One-time fee: $357 full-time. *Financial support:* In 2010–11, 8 fellowships with full tuition reimbursements (averaging $11,100 per year), 3 research assistantships with full tuition reimbursements (averaging $1,529 per year) were awarded; teaching assistantships, career-related internships or fieldwork, Federal Work-Study, scholarships/grants, traineeships, health care benefits, tuition waivers (full), and unspecified assistantships also available. Support available to part-time students. Financial award application deadline: 1/2; financial award applicants required to submit FAFSA. *Unit head:* Dr. Neil Berthier, Graduate Program Director, 413-545-2046, Fax: 413-545-3243. *Application contact:* Jean M. Ames, Supervisor of Admissions, 413-545-0722, Fax: 413-577-0010, E-mail: gradadm@grad.umass.edu.

University of Massachusetts Worcester, Graduate School of Biomedical Sciences, Worcester, MA 01655-0115. Offers biochemistry and molecular pharmacology (PhD); bioinformatics and computational biology (PhD); cancer biology (PhD); cell biology (PhD); clinical and population health research (PhD); clinical investigation (MS); immunology and virology (PhD); interdisciplinary graduate program (PhD); molecular genetics and microbiology (PhD); neuroscience (PhD); DVM/PhD; MD/PhD. *Faculty:* 1,059 full-time (357 women), 145 part-time/adjunct (100 women). *Students:* 438 full-time (239 women), 1 (woman) part-time; includes 44 minority (9 Black or African American, non-Hispanic/Latino; 31 Asian, non-Hispanic/Latino; 4 Hispanic/Latino), 148 international. Average age 29. 687 applicants, 28% accepted, 116 enrolled. In 2010, 6 master's, 45 doctorates awarded. Terminal master's awarded for partial completion of doctoral program. *Degree requirements:* For master's, thesis; for doctorate, thesis/dissertation. *Entrance requirements:* For master's, bachelor's degree; for doctorate, GRE General Test, MS, MA, or MPH (for some programs). Additional exam requirements/recommendations for international students: Required—TOEFL (minimum score 600 paper-based; 250 computer-based). *Application deadline:* For fall admission, 12/15 for domestic and international students; for winter admission, 1/15 for domestic students; for spring admission, 5/15 for domestic students. Application fee: $35. Electronic applications accepted. *Expenses:* Contact institution. *Financial support:* In 2010–11, 439 students received support, including 439 research assistantships with full tuition reimbursements available (averaging $28,350 per year); scholarships/grants, health care benefits, tuition waivers (full), and unspecified assistantships also available. Financial award application deadline: 4/20. *Faculty research:* RNA interference, gene therapy, cell biology, bioinformatics, clinical research. Total annual research expenditures: $232 million. *Unit head:* Dr. Anthony Carruthers, Dean, 508-856-4135, E-mail: anthony.carruthers@umassmed.edu. *Application contact:* Dr. Kendall Knight, Associate Dean and Interim Director of Admissions and Recruitment, 508-856-5628, Fax: 508-856-3659, E-mail: kendall.knight@umassmed.edu.

University of Medicine and Dentistry of New Jersey, Graduate School of Biomedical Sciences, Graduate Programs in Biomedical Sciences–Newark, Program in Integrative Neuroscience, Newark, NJ 07107. Offers PhD. Program offered jointly with Rutgers, The State University of New Jersey, New Brunswick. *Degree requirements:* For doctorate, thesis/dissertation, qualifying exam. *Entrance requirements:* For doctorate, GRE General Test, minimum GPA of 3.5. Additional exam requirements/recommendations for international students: Required—TOEFL. Electronic applications accepted.

University of Medicine and Dentistry of New Jersey, Graduate School of Biomedical Sciences, Graduate Programs in Biomedical Sciences–Piscataway, Program in Neuroscience, Piscataway, NJ 08854-5635. Offers MS, PhD, MD/PhD. *Degree requirements:* For master's, thesis, qualifying exam; for doctorate, thesis/dissertation, qualifying exam. *Entrance requirements:* Additional exam requirements/recommendations for international students: Required—TOEFL. Electronic applications accepted.

University of Miami, Graduate School, College of Arts and Sciences, Department of Psychology, Coral Gables, FL 33124. Offers adult clinical (PhD); behavioral neuroscience (PhD); child clinical (PhD); developmental psychology (PhD); health clinical (PhD); psychology (MS). *Accreditation:* APA (one or more programs are accredited). *Degree requirements:* For doctorate, comprehensive exam, thesis/dissertation. *Entrance requirements:* For doctorate, GRE General Test, minimum GPA of 3.5. Additional exam requirements/recommendations for international students: Required—TOEFL. Electronic applications accepted. *Faculty research:* Behavioral factors in cardiovascular disease and cancer adult psychopathology, developmental disabilities, social and emotional development, mechanisms of coping.

University of Miami, Graduate School, Miller School of Medicine, Graduate Programs in Medicine, Neuroscience Program, Coral Gables, FL 33124. Offers PhD, MD/PhD. *Degree requirements:* For doctorate, thesis/dissertation, qualifying exam. *Entrance requirements:* For doctorate, GRE General Test. Additional exam requirements/recommendations for international students: Required—TOEFL (minimum score 550 paper-based; 213 computer-based). Electronic applications accepted. *Faculty research:* Cellular and molecular biology, transduction, nerve regeneration and embryonic development, membrane biophysics.

University of Michigan, Rackham Graduate School, Program in Biomedical Sciences (PIBS), Neuroscience Graduate Program, Ann Arbor, MI 48072-2215. Offers PhD. *Faculty:* 122 full-time (35 women). *Students:* 51 full-time (28 women); includes 17 minority (2 Black or African American, non-Hispanic/Latino; 6 Asian, non-Hispanic/Latino; 9 Hispanic/Latino), 2 international. Average age 28. 88 applicants, 9% accepted, 3 enrolled. In 2010, 15 doctorates awarded. *Degree requirements:* For doctorate, thesis/dissertation, oral defense of dissertation, preliminary exam. *Entrance requirements:* For doctorate, GRE General Test, 3 letters of recommendation, research experience. Additional exam requirements/recommendations for international students: Required—TOEFL (minimum score 84 iBT). *Application deadline:* For fall admission, 12/1 for domestic and international students. Application fee: $65 ($75 for international students). Electronic applications accepted. *Expenses:* Tuition, state resident: full-time $17,784; part-time $1116 per credit hour. Tuition, nonresident: full-time $35,944; part-time $2125 per credit hour. International tuition: $35,994 full-time. Required fees: $95 per semester. Tuition and fees vary according to course load, degree level and program. *Financial support:* In 2010–11, 51 students received support, including 51 fellowships with full tuition reimbursements available (averaging $26,500 per year); scholarships/grants, health care benefits, tuition waivers (full), and unspecified assistantships also available. Financial award application deadline: 12/1. *Faculty research:* Developmental neurobiology, cellular and molecular neurobiology, cognitive neuroscience, sensory neuroscience, behavioral neuroscience. *Unit head:* Dr. Stephen Maren, Director, 734-763-9638, Fax: 734-647-0717, E-mail: maren@umich.edu. *Application contact:* Rachel F. Flaten, Student Services Administrator, 734-763-9638, Fax: 734-647-0717, E-mail: rachelfk@umich.edu.

University of Minnesota, Twin Cities Campus, Graduate School, Graduate Program in Neuroscience, Minneapolis, MN 55455-0213. Offers MS, PhD. Terminal master's awarded for partial completion of doctoral program. *Degree requirements:* For master's, thesis; for doctorate, thesis/dissertation. *Entrance requirements:* For doctorate, GRE. Additional exam requirements/recommendations for international students: Required—TOEFL. Electronic applications accepted. *Faculty research:* Cellular and molecular neuroscience, behavioral neuroscience, developmental neuroscience, neurodegenerative diseases, pain, addiction, motor control.

University of Missouri, Graduate School, Neuroscience Interdisciplinary Program, Columbia, MO 65211. Offers MS, PhD. *Entrance requirements:* Additional exam requirements/recommendations for international students: Required—TOEFL (minimum score 600 paper-based; 250 computer-based; 100 iBT).

University of Missouri–St. Louis, College of Arts and Sciences, Department of Psychology, St. Louis, MO 63121. Offers behavioral neuroscience (PhD); clinical community psychology (PhD); clinical psychology respecialization (Certificate); general psychology (MA); industrial/organizational psychology (PhD); trauma studies (Certificate). *Accreditation:* APA (one or more programs are accredited). Evening/weekend programs available. *Faculty:* 19 full-time (9 women), 5 part-time/adjunct (3 women). *Students:* 44 full-time (34 women), 35 part-time (25 women); includes 7 minority (1 Black or African American, non-Hispanic/Latino; 1 American Indian or Alaska Native, non-Hispanic/Latino; 3 Asian, non-Hispanic/Latino; 2 Hispanic/Latino). Average age 27. 220 applicants, 10% accepted, 18 enrolled. In 2010, 10 master's, 6 doctorates awarded. Terminal master's awarded for partial completion of doctoral program. *Degree requirements:* For master's, thesis; for doctorate, thesis/dissertation. *Entrance requirements:* For master's, GRE General Test, 3 letters of recommendation; for doctorate, GRE General Test, GRE Subject Test, 3 letters of recommendation. Additional exam requirements/recommendations for international students: Required—TOEFL (minimum score 550 paper-based; 213 computer-based). *Application deadline:* For fall admission, 1/15 for domestic and international students. Application fee: $35 ($40 for international students). Electronic applications accepted. *Expenses:* Tuition, state resident: full-time $5522; part-time $306.80 per credit hour. Tuition, nonresident: full-time $14,253; part-time $792.10 per credit hour. Required fees: $658; $49 per credit hour. One-time fee: $12. Tuition and fees vary according to program. *Financial support:* In 2010–11, 5 research assistantships with full and partial tuition reimbursements (averaging $13,352 per year), 26 teaching assistantships with full and partial tuition reimbursements (averaging $11,000 per year) were awarded; fellowships with full tuition reimbursements also available. Financial award applicants required to submit FAFSA. *Faculty research:* Bereavement and loss, neuroscience, post-traumatic stress disorder, conflict and negotiation, social psychology. *Unit head:* Dr. George Taylor, Chair, 314-516-5391, Fax: 314-516-5392, E-mail: umslpsychology@msx.umsl.edu. *Application contact:* 314-516-5458, Fax: 314-516-6996, E-mail: gradadm@umsl.edu.

The University of Montana, Graduate School, College of Health Professions and Biomedical Sciences, Skaggs School of Pharmacy, Department of Biomedical and Pharmaceutical Sciences, Missoula, MT 59812-0002. Offers biomedical sciences (PhD); neuroscience (MS, PhD); pharmaceutical sciences (MS); toxicology (MS, PhD). *Accreditation:* ACPE. *Degree requirements:* For master's, oral defense of thesis; for doctorate, research dissertation defense. *Entrance requirements:* For master's and doctorate, GRE General Test. Additional exam requirements/recommendations for international students: Required—TOEFL (minimum score 540 paper-based; 210 computer-based). Electronic applications accepted. *Faculty research:* Cardiovascular pharmacology, medicinal chemistry, neurosciences, environmental toxicology, pharmacogenetics, cancer.

University of Nebraska Medical Center, Graduate Studies, Department of Pharmacology and Experimental Neuroscience, Omaha, NE 68198. Offers neuroscience (MS, PhD); pharmacology (MS, PhD). *Faculty:* 25 full-time, 9 part-time/adjunct. *Students:* 26 full-time (15 women), 3 part-time (2 women); includes 3 Asian, non-Hispanic/Latino; 1 Hispanic/Latino, 9 international. Average age 25. 31 applicants, 42% accepted, 12 enrolled. In 2010, 4 doctorates awarded. Terminal master's awarded for partial completion of doctoral program. *Degree requirements:* For master's, comprehensive exam, thesis; for doctorate, comprehensive exam, thesis/dissertation. *Entrance requirements:* For master's and doctorate, GRE General Test. Additional exam requirements/recommendations for international students: Required—TOEFL (minimum score 600 paper-based; 250 computer-based). *Application deadline:* For fall admission, 2/1 for domestic and international students. Applications are processed on a rolling basis. Application fee: $45. Electronic applications accepted. *Expenses:* Tuition, state resident: part-time $198.25 per semester hour. Required fees: $63 per semester. *Financial support:* In 2010–11, 3 students received support, including fellowships with full tuition reimbursements available (averaging $21,000 per year), research assistantships with full tuition reimbursements available (averaging $21,000 per year); career-related internships or fieldwork, institutionally sponsored loans, scholarships/grants, traineeships, health care benefits, and unspecified assistantships also available. Financial award application deadline: 2/15. *Faculty research:* Neuropharmacology, molecular pharmacology, toxicology, molecular biology, neuroscience. Total annual research expenditures: $1.8 million. *Unit head:* Dr. Keshore Bidasee, Chair, Graduate Studies, 402-559-9018, Fax: 402-559-7495, E-mail: kbidasee@unmc.edu. *Application contact:* Connie Curro, Office Assistant, 402-559-4044, E-mail: ccurro@unmc.edu.

University of New Mexico, School of Medicine, Biomedical Sciences Graduate Program, Albuquerque, NM 87131-5196. Offers biochemistry and molecular biology (MS, PhD); cell biology and physiology (MS, PhD); clinical and translational science (Certificate); molecular genetics and microbiology (MS, PhD); neuroscience (MS, PhD); pathology (MS, PhD); toxicology (MS, PhD); university science teaching (Certificate). Part-time programs available. *Faculty:* 33 full-time (14 women), 3 part-time/adjunct (1 woman). *Students:* 94 full-time (57 women), 14 part-time (8 women); includes 24 minority (3 Black or African American, non-Hispanic/Latino; 1 American Indian or Alaska Native, non-Hispanic/Latino; 6 Asian, non-Hispanic/Latino; 13 Hispanic/Latino; 1 Two or more races, non-Hispanic/Latino), 20 international. Average age 30. 135 applicants, 14% accepted, 19 enrolled. In 2010, 2 master's, 19 doctorates, 3 other advanced degrees awarded. Terminal master's awarded for partial completion of doctoral program. *Degree requirements:* For master's, thesis; for doctorate, comprehensive exam, thesis/dissertation. *Entrance requirements:* For master's and doctorate, GRE General Test, minimum undergraduate GPA of 3.0. Additional exam requirements/recommendations for international students: Required—TOEFL. *Application deadline:* For fall admission, 1/1 priority date for domestic students. Applications are processed on a rolling basis. Application fee: $50. Electronic applications accepted. *Expenses:* Tuition, state resident: full-time $5991; part-time $251 per credit hour. Tuition, nonresident: full-time $14,405; part-time $800.20 per credit hour. Tuition and fees vary according to course level, course load, program and reciprocity agreements. *Financial support:* In 2010–11, 99 students received support, including 5 fellowships (averaging $75 per year), 96 research assistantships with full tuition reimbursements available (averaging $17,401 per year), 2 teaching assistantships with full tuition reimbursements available (averaging $2,415 per year); career-related internships or fieldwork, Federal Work-Study, institutionally sponsored loans, scholarships/grants, traineeships, health care benefits, and unspecified assistantships also available. Financial award application deadline: 1/1; financial award applicants required to submit FAFSA. *Faculty research:* Signal transduction, infectious disease, biology of cancer, structural biology, neuroscience. *Unit head:* Laurie G. Hudson, Director, 505-272-1887, Fax: 505-272-8738, E-mail: lhudson@salud.unm.edu. *Application contact:* Angel Cooke-Jackson, Coordinator, 505-272-1887, Fax: 505-272-8738, E-mail: acooke-jackson@salud.unm.edu.

University of Oklahoma Health Sciences Center, College of Medicine and Graduate College, Graduate Programs in Medicine, Department of Neuroscience, Oklahoma City, OK 73190. Offers MS, PhD. *Degree requirements:* For doctorate, thesis/dissertation. *Entrance requirements:* For master's and doctorate, GRE General Test, 3 letters of recommendation. Additional exam requirements/recommendations for international students: Required—TOEFL.

University of Oregon, Graduate School, College of Arts and Sciences, Department of Biology, Eugene, OR 97403. Offers ecology and evolution (MA, MS, PhD); marine biology (MA, MS, PhD); molecular, cellular and genetic biology (PhD); neuroscience and development (PhD). Terminal master's awarded for partial completion of doctoral program. *Degree requirements:* For master's, thesis (for some programs); for doctorate, thesis/dissertation. *Entrance requirements:* For master's and doctorate, GRE General Test, minimum GPA of 3.2. Additional exam requirements/recommendations for international students: Required—TOEFL. *Faculty research:* Developmental neurobiology; evolution, population biology, and quantitative genetics; regulation of gene expression; biochemistry of marine organisms.

University of Pennsylvania, Perelman School of Medicine, Biomedical Graduate Studies, Graduate Group in Neuroscience, Philadelphia, PA 19104. Offers PhD, MD/PhD. *Faculty:* 127. *Students:* 128 full-time (66 women); includes 2 Black or African American, non-Hispanic/Latino; 3 American Indian or Alaska Native, non-Hispanic/Latino; 18 Asian, non-Hispanic/Latino; 7 Hispanic/Latino, 8 international. 228 applicants, 19% accepted, 16 enrolled. In 2010, 13 doctorates awarded. *Degree requirements:* For doctorate, thesis/dissertation, research project. *Entrance requirements:* For doctorate, GRE General Test. Additional exam requirements/recommendations for international students: Required—TOEFL. *Application deadline:* For fall admission, 12/8 priority date for domestic and international students. Applications are processed on a rolling basis. Application fee: $70. Electronic applications accepted. *Expenses:* Tuition: Full-time $25,660; part-time $4758 per course. Required fees: $2152; $270 per course. Tuition and fees vary according to course load, degree level and program. *Financial support:* In 2010–11, 128 students received support; fellowships, research assistantships, teaching assistantships, scholarships/grants, traineeships, and unspecified assistantships available. *Faculty research:* Molecular and cellular neuroscience, behavioral neuroscience, developmental neurobiology, systems neuroscience and neurophysiology, neurochemistry. *Unit head:* Dr. Rita

Neuroscience

University of Pennsylvania (continued)
Balice-Gordon, Chairperson. *Application contact:* Jane Hoshi, Coordinator, 215-898-8048, Fax: 215-573-2248.

University of Pittsburgh, School of Arts and Sciences and School of Medicine, Center for Neuroscience, Pittsburgh, PA 15260. Offers neurobiology (PhD); neuroscience (PhD). *Faculty:* 95 full-time (25 women). *Students:* 77 full-time (37 women); includes 2 Black or African American, non-Hispanic/Latino; 8 Asian, non-Hispanic/Latino; 1 Hispanic/Latino, 14 international. Average age 25. 138 applicants, 22% accepted, 14 enrolled. In 2010, 9 doctorates awarded. *Degree requirements:* For doctorate, comprehensive exam, thesis/dissertation. *Entrance requirements:* For doctorate, GRE, interview. Additional exam requirements/recommendations for international students: Required—TOEFL (minimum score 600 paper-based; 250 computer-based; 100 iBT). *Application deadline:* For fall admission, 12/1 priority date for domestic and international students. Application fee: $50. Electronic applications accepted. *Expenses:* Contact institution. *Financial support:* In 2010–11, 77 students received support, including 35 fellowships with full tuition reimbursements available (averaging $25,550 per year), 40 research assistantships with full tuition reimbursements available (averaging $25,550 per year), 2 teaching assistantships with full tuition reimbursements available (averaging $25,550 per year). Financial award application deadline: 12/1. *Faculty research:* Behavioral/systems/cognitive, cell and molecular, development/plasticity/repair, neurobiology of disease. *Unit head:* Dr. Alan Sved, Co-Director, 412-624-6996, Fax: 412-624-9188. *Application contact:* Joan M. Blaney, Administrator, 412-624-5043, Fax: 412-624-9198, E-mail: jblaney@pitt.edu.

University of Puerto Rico, Río Piedras, College of Natural Sciences, Department of Biology, San Juan, PR 00931-3300. Offers ecology/systematics (MS, PhD); evolution/genetics (MS, PhD); molecular/cellular biology (MS, PhD); neuroscience (MS, PhD). Part-time programs available. *Degree requirements:* For master's, one foreign language, comprehensive exam, thesis; for doctorate, one foreign language, comprehensive exam, thesis/dissertation. *Entrance requirements:* For master's, GRE Subject Test, interview, minimum GPA of 3.0, letter of recommendation; for doctorate, GRE Subject Test, interview, master's degree, minimum GPA of 3.0, letter of recommendation. *Faculty research:* Environmental, poblational and systematic biology.

University of Rochester, School of Medicine and Dentistry, Graduate Programs in Medicine and Dentistry, Department of Neurobiology and Anatomy, Interdepartmental Programs in Neuroscience, Rochester, NY 14627. Offers MS, PhD. Terminal master's awarded for partial completion of doctoral program. *Degree requirements:* For doctorate, one foreign language, thesis/dissertation, qualifying exam. *Entrance requirements:* For master's and doctorate, GRE General Test.

The University of South Dakota, School of Medicine and Health Sciences and Graduate School, Biomedical Sciences Graduate Program, Program in Neuroscience, Vermillion, SD 57069-2390. Offers MS, PhD. Terminal master's awarded for partial completion of doctoral program. *Degree requirements:* For master's, thesis; for doctorate, comprehensive exam, thesis/dissertation. *Entrance requirements:* For master's and doctorate, GRE General Test, minimum GPA of 3.0. Additional exam requirements/recommendations for international students: Required—TOEFL (minimum score 550 paper-based; 213 computer-based; 80 iBT), IELTS (minimum score 6). Electronic applications accepted. *Expenses:* Contact institution. *Faculty research:* Central nervous system learning, neural plasticity, respiratory control.

University of Southern California, Graduate School, Dana and David Dornsife College of Letters, Arts and Sciences, Program in Neuroscience, Los Angeles, CA 90089. Offers MS, PhD. M.S. degree is terminal degree only. *Faculty:* 74 full-time (25 women), 12 part-time/adjunct (4 women). *Students:* 91 full-time (43 women); includes 12 minority (8 Asian, non-Hispanic/Latino; 4 Hispanic/Latino), 44 international. 191 applicants, 19% accepted, 19 enrolled. In 2010, 1 master's, 16 doctorates awarded. Terminal master's awarded for partial completion of doctoral program. *Degree requirements:* For master's, research paper; for doctorate, comprehensive exam, thesis/dissertation, qualifying examination, dissertation defense. *Entrance requirements:* For doctorate, GRE, 3 letters of recommendation, personal statement, resume. Additional exam requirements/recommendations for international students: Required—TOEFL (minimum score 600 paper-based; 250 computer-based; 100 iBT). *Application deadline:* For fall admission, 12/1 priority date for domestic and international students. Application fee: $85. Electronic applications accepted. *Expenses:* Tuition: Full-time $31,240; part-time $1420 per unit. Required fees: $600. One-time fee: $35 full-time. Full-time tuition and fees vary according to degree level and program. *Financial support:* In 2010–11, 91 students received support, including 17 fellowships with full tuition reimbursements available (averaging $27,500 per year), 54 research assistantships with full tuition reimbursements available (averaging $27,500 per year), 14 teaching assistantships with full tuition reimbursements available (averaging $27,500 per year); traineeships, health care benefits, and tuition waivers also available. *Faculty research:* Cellular and molecular neurobiology, behavioral and systems neurobiology, cognitive neuroscience, computation neuroscience and neural engineering, neuroscience of aging. *Unit head:* Dr. Pat Levitt, Provost/Professor of Neuroscience, Psychiatry and Pharmacy/Chair, Department of Cell and Neurobiology/Director, 323-442-1509, Fax: 213-442-2145, E-mail: plevitt@usc.edu. *Application contact:* Vanessa Clark, Student Services Advisor I, 213-740-2245, Fax: 213-740-6980, E-mail: saydacla@dornsife.usc.edu.

University of South Florida, Graduate School, College of Arts and Sciences, Department of Psychology, Tampa, FL 33620-9951. Offers clinical psychology (PhD); cognitive and neural sciences (PhD); industrial-organizational psychology (PhD). *Accreditation:* APA. *Faculty:* 17 full-time (4 women). *Students:* 101 full-time (55 women), 24 part-time (16 women); includes 3 Black or African American, non-Hispanic/Latino; 9 Asian, non-Hispanic/Latino; 8 Hispanic/Latino; 1 Two or more races, non-Hispanic/Latino, 12 international. Average age 28. 452 applicants, 8% accepted, 22 enrolled. In 2010, 11 doctorates awarded. *Degree requirements:* For doctorate, comprehensive exam, thesis/dissertation, internship. *Entrance requirements:* For doctorate, GRE General Test, minimum GPA of 3.0 in last 60 hours of course work. Additional exam requirements/recommendations for international students: Required—TOEFL (minimum score 550 paper-based; 213 computer-based). *Application deadline:* For fall admission, 12/1 for domestic and international students. Application fee: $30. Electronic applications accepted. *Expenses:* Contact institution. *Financial support:* In 2010–11, 18 research assistantships (averaging $13,719 per year), 63 teaching assistantships with tuition reimbursements (averaging $13,724 per year) were awarded; tuition waivers (partial) and unspecified assistantships also available. Financial award applicants required to submit FAFSA. *Faculty research:* Clinical, cognitive, neuroscience, social, industrial/organizational. Total annual research expenditures: $3.5 million. *Unit head:* Michael Brannick, Chairperson, 813-974-0478, Fax: 813-974-4617, E-mail: mbrannick@usf.edu. *Application contact:* William Sacco, Program Director, 813-974-0375, Fax: 813-974-4617, E-mail: sacco@cas.usf.edu.

The University of Texas at Austin, Graduate School, The Institute for Neuroscience, Austin, TX 78712-1111. Offers PhD, MD/PhD. Terminal master's awarded for partial completion of doctoral program. *Degree requirements:* For doctorate, thesis/dissertation. *Entrance requirements:* For doctorate, GRE. Electronic applications accepted. *Faculty research:* Cellular/molecular biology, neurobiology, pharmacology, behavioral neuroscience.

The University of Texas at Dallas, School of Behavioral and Brain Sciences, Program in Cognition and Neuroscience, Richardson, TX 75080. Offers applied cognition and neuroscience (MS); cognition and neuroscience (PhD). Part-time and evening/weekend programs available. *Faculty:* 25 full-time (8 women). *Students:* 85 full-time (48 women), 35 part-time (20 women); includes 25 minority (3 Black or African American, non-Hispanic/Latino; 14 Asian, non-Hispanic/Latino; 8 Hispanic/Latino), 16 international. Average age 30. 88 applicants, 51% accepted, 17 enrolled. In 2010, 33 master's, 2 doctorates awarded. *Degree requirements:* For master's, internship; for doctorate, thesis/dissertation. *Entrance requirements:* For master's and doctorate, GRE General Test, minimum GPA of 3.0 in upper-level coursework in field. Additional exam requirements/recommendations for international students: Required—TOEFL (minimum score 550 paper-based; 215 computer-based). *Application deadline:* For fall admission, 7/15 for domestic students, 5/1 priority date for international students; for spring admission, 11/15 for domestic students, 9/1 priority date for international students. Applications are processed on a rolling basis. Application fee: $50 ($100 for international students). Electronic applications accepted. *Expenses:* Tuition, state resident: full-time $10,248; part-time $569 per credit hour. Tuition, nonresident: full-time $18,544; part-time $1030 per credit hour. Tuition and fees vary according to course load. *Financial support:* In 2010–11, 75 students received support, including 17 research assistantships with partial tuition reimbursements available (averaging $14,189 per year), 26 teaching assistantships with partial tuition reimbursements available (averaging $13,259 per year); career-related internships or fieldwork, Federal Work-Study, institutionally sponsored loans, scholarships/grants, and unspecified assistantships also available. Support available to part-time students. Financial award application deadline: 4/30; financial award applicants required to submit FAFSA. *Faculty research:* Neural plasticity, neuroimaging, face recognition, cognitive and neurobiological mechanisms of human memory, treatment interventions for semantic memory retrieval problems. *Unit head:* Dr. James C. Bartlett, Program Head, 972-883-2079, Fax: 972-883-2491, E-mail: jbartlet@utdallas.edu. *Application contact:* Mary Felipe, Program Assistant, 972-883-2358, Fax: 972-883-2491, E-mail: mary.felipe@utdallas.edu.

The University of Texas Health Science Center at Houston, Graduate School of Biomedical Sciences, Program in Neuroscience, Houston, TX 77225-0036. Offers MS, PhD, MD/PhD. Terminal master's awarded for partial completion of doctoral program. *Degree requirements:* For master's, thesis; for doctorate, thesis/dissertation. *Entrance requirements:* For master's and doctorate, GRE General Test. Additional exam requirements/recommendations for international students: Required—TOEFL. Electronic applications accepted. *Faculty research:* Behavior, cognitive, computational, neuroimaging, substance abuse.

The University of Texas Health Science Center at San Antonio, Graduate School of Biomedical Sciences, Department of Pharmacology, San Antonio, TX 78229-3900. Offers neuroscience (PhD). *Faculty:* 20 full-time (3 women), 7 part-time/adjunct (1 woman). *Students:* 23 full-time (15 women), 1 (woman) part-time; includes 1 American Indian or Alaska Native, non-Hispanic/Latino; 5 Asian, non-Hispanic/Latino; 5 Hispanic/Latino, 2 international. Average age 24. In 2010, 1 doctorate awarded. *Degree requirements:* For doctorate, comprehensive exam, thesis/dissertation. *Entrance requirements:* For doctorate, GRE General Test, minimum GPA of 3.0. Additional exam requirements/recommendations for international students: Required—TOEFL (minimum score 560 paper-based; 220 computer-based; 68 iBT). *Application deadline:* For fall admission, 1/15 priority date for domestic and international students. Applications are processed on a rolling basis. Application fee: $0. Electronic applications accepted. *Expenses:* Tuition, state resident: full-time $3072; part-time $128 per credit hour. Tuition, nonresident: full-time $11,928; part-time $497 per credit hour. Required fees: $1078; $1078 per year. One-time fee: $60. *Financial support:* In 2010–11, 1 fellowship (averaging $26,000 per year), 23 teaching assistantships (averaging $26,000 per year) were awarded; institutionally sponsored loans, scholarships/grants, and health care benefits also available. Financial award application deadline: 6/30; financial award applicants required to submit FAFSA. *Faculty research:* Neuropharmacology, autonomic and endocrine homeostasis, aging, cancer biology. Total annual research expenditures: $11.1 million. *Unit head:* Alan Frazer, Chairman, 210-567-4205, Fax: 210-567-4300, E-mail: frazer@uthscsa.edu. *Application contact:* Nakia Scott, Academic Program Coordinator, 210-567-4220, Fax: 210-567-4303, E-mail: scottn3@uthscsa.edu.

The University of Texas Medical Branch, Graduate School of Biomedical Sciences, Program in Neuroscience, Galveston, TX 77555. Offers PhD. *Degree requirements:* For doctorate, thesis/dissertation. *Entrance requirements:* For doctorate, GRE General Test. Additional exam requirements/recommendations for international students: Required—TOEFL (minimum score 550 paper-based; 213 computer-based). Electronic applications accepted.

The University of Texas Southwestern Medical Center at Dallas, Southwestern Graduate School of Biomedical Sciences, Division of Basic Science, Program in Neuroscience, Dallas, TX 75390. Offers PhD. *Faculty:* 35 full-time (5 women). *Students:* 49 full-time (24 women), 1 (woman) part-time; includes 14 minority (3 Black or African American, non-Hispanic/Latino; 1 American Indian or Alaska Native, non-Hispanic/Latino; 5 Asian, non-Hispanic/Latino; 5 Hispanic/Latino), 8 international. Average age 28. In 2010, 12 doctorates awarded. *Degree requirements:* For doctorate, thesis/dissertation, qualifying exam. *Entrance requirements:* For doctorate, GRE General Test, minimum GPA of 3.0. Additional exam requirements/recommendations for international students: Required—TOEFL. *Application deadline:* For fall admission, 12/15 priority date for domestic students. Applications are processed on a rolling basis. Application fee: $0. Electronic applications accepted. *Financial support:* Fellowships, research assistantships available. *Faculty research:* Ion channels, sensory transduction, membrane excitability and biophysics, synaptic transmission, developmental neurogenetics. *Unit head:* Dr. Nancy E. Street, Associate Dean, 214-648-6708, Fax: 214-648-2102, E-mail: nancy.street@utsouthwestern.edu. *Application contact:* Dr. Nancy E. Street, Associate Dean, 214-648-6708, Fax: 214-648-2102, E-mail: nancy.street@utsouthwestern.edu.

The University of Toledo, College of Graduate Studies, College of Medicine and Life Sciences, Department of Neurosciences, Toledo, OH 43606-3390. Offers MSBS, PhD, MD/PhD. *Faculty:* 11. *Students:* 8 full-time (3 women); includes 1 Hispanic/Latino, 3 international. Average age 25. 21 applicants, 38% accepted, 4 enrolled. In 2010, 2 doctorates awarded. Terminal master's awarded for partial completion of doctoral program. *Degree requirements:* For master's, thesis, qualifying exam; for doctorate, thesis/dissertation, qualifying exam. *Entrance requirements:* For master's and doctorate, GRE/MCAT, minimum undergraduate GPA of 3.0, three letters of recommendation, statement of purpose, transcripts from all prior institutions attended. Additional exam requirements/recommendations for international students: Required—TOEFL (minimum score 550 paper-based; 213 computer-based; 80 iBT), IELTS (minimum score 6.5). *Application deadline:* For fall admission, 5/1 priority date for domestic and international students. Applications are processed on a rolling basis. Application fee: $45 ($75 for international students). Electronic applications accepted. *Expenses:* Tuition, state resident: full-time $11,426; part-time $476 per credit hour. Tuition, nonresident: full-time $21,660; part-time $903 per credit hour. One-time fee: $62. *Financial support:* In 2010–11, research assistantships with full tuition reimbursements (averaging $21,180 per year); Federal Work-Study, institutionally sponsored loans, scholarships/grants, tuition waivers (full), and unspecified assistantships also available. *Unit head:* Dr. Bryan Yamamoto, Chair, 419-383-3346, E-mail: bryan.yamamoto@utoledo.edu. *Application contact:* Christine Wile, Admissions Analyst, 419-383-4116, Fax: 419-383-6140, E-mail: christine.wile@utoledo.edu.

University of Utah, School of Medicine and Graduate School, Graduate Programs in Medicine, Program in Neuroscience, Salt Lake City, UT 84112-1107. Offers PhD. *Degree requirements:* For doctorate, thesis/dissertation. *Entrance requirements:* For doctorate, GRE General Test, minimum GPA of 3.0. Additional exam requirements/recommendations for international students: Required—TOEFL (minimum score 500 paper-based; 173 computer-based); Recommended—TWE (minimum score 6). Electronic applications accepted. *Expenses:* Tuition, area resident: Part-time $179.19 per credit hour. Tuition, state resident: full-time $4384. Tuition, nonresident: full-time $16,684; part-time $630.67 per credit hour. Required fees: $350 per semester. Tuition and fees vary according to course load, degree level and program. *Faculty research:* Brain and behavioral neuroscience, cellular neuroscience, molecular neuroscience, neurobiology of disease, developmental neuroscience.

University of Vermont, College of Medicine and Graduate College, Graduate Programs in Medicine, Graduate Program in Neuroscience, Burlington, VT 05405. Offers PhD. *Students:* 25 (14 women); includes 1 Asian, non-Hispanic/Latino; 3 Hispanic/Latino. 27 applicants, 56% accepted, 8 enrolled. *Degree requirements:* For doctorate, thesis/dissertation. *Entrance requirements:* For doctorate, GRE General Test. Additional exam requirements/recommendations for international students: Required—TOEFL (minimum score 550 paper-based; 213 computer-based; 80 iBT). *Application deadline:* For fall admission, 12/15 priority date for domestic students, 12/15 for international students. Application fee: $40. Electronic applications accepted. *Expenses:* Tuition, state resident: part-time $537 per credit hour. Tuition, nonresident: part-time $1355 per credit hour. *Financial support:* Research assistantships, teaching assistantships available. Financial award application deadline: 3/1. *Unit head:* Dr. Rae Nishi, Director, 802-656-1178, E-mail: rae.nishi@uvm.edu. *Application contact:* Dr. Rae Nishi, Director, 802-656-1178, E-mail: rae.nishi@uvm.edu.

University of Virginia, School of Medicine, Department of Neuroscience, Charlottesville, VA 22903. Offers PhD, MD/PhD. *Faculty:* 12 full-time (5 women). *Students:* 29 full-time (18 women); includes 2 Black or African American, non-Hispanic/Latino; 4 Hispanic/Latino, 3 international. Average age 29. In 2010, 4 doctorates awarded. *Degree requirements:* For doctorate, thesis/dissertation. *Entrance requirements:* For doctorate, GRE General Test, 2 letters of recommendation. Additional exam requirements/recommendations for international students: Required—TOEFL. *Application deadline:* For fall admission, 4/15 for domestic and international students. Applications are processed on a rolling basis. Application fee: $60. Electronic applications accepted. *Financial support:* Application deadline: 1/15. *Unit head:* Dr. Kevin Lee, Chair, 434-982-2927, Fax: 434-982-4380, E-mail: neurograd@virginia.edu. *Application contact:* Tracy Mourton, Program Coordinator, 434-982-4285, Fax: 434-982-4380, E-mail: neurograd@virginia.edu.

The University of Western Ontario, Faculty of Graduate Studies, Biosciences Division, Department of Clinical Neurological Sciences, London, ON N6A 5B8, Canada. Offers M Sc, PhD. Terminal master's awarded for partial completion of doctoral program. *Degree requirements:* For master's, thesis; for doctorate, thesis/dissertation. *Entrance requirements:* For master's, honors degree or equivalent, minimum B+ average; for doctorate, master's degree, minimum B+ average. *Faculty research:* Behavioral neuroscience, neural regeneration and degeneration, visual development, human motor function.

University of Wisconsin–Madison, Graduate School, College of Letters and Science, Department of Psychology, Program in Cognitive Neurosciences, Madison, WI 53706-1380. Offers PhD. *Degree requirements:* For doctorate, comprehensive exam, thesis/dissertation. *Entrance requirements:* For doctorate, GRE General Test, minimum undergraduate GPA of 3.0. Additional exam requirements/recommendations for international students: Required—TOEFL. Electronic applications accepted. *Expenses:* Tuition, state resident: full-time $9887; part-time $617.96 per credit. Tuition, nonresident: full-time $24,054; part-time $1503.40 per credit. Required fees: $67.63 per credit. Tuition and fees vary according to reciprocity agreements.

University of Wisconsin–Madison, Graduate School, Neuroscience Training Program, Madison, WI 53706. Offers PhD. *Faculty:* 102 full-time (30 women). *Students:* 63 full-time (35 women); includes 1 Black or African American, non-Hispanic/Latino; 4 Asian, non-Hispanic/Latino; 4 Hispanic/Latino, 10 international. Average age 27. 191 applicants, 14% accepted, 12 enrolled. In 2010, 10 doctorates awarded. *Degree requirements:* For doctorate, thesis/dissertation. *Entrance requirements:* For doctorate, GRE General Test. Additional exam requirements/recommendations for international students: Required—TOEFL. *Application deadline:* For fall admission, 12/15 for domestic and international students. Application fee: $56. Electronic applications accepted. *Expenses:* Tuition, state resident: full-time $9887; part-time $617.96 per credit. Tuition, nonresident: full-time $24,054; part-time $1503.40 per credit. Required fees: $67.63 per credit. Tuition and fees vary according to reciprocity agreements. *Financial support:* In 2010–11, 63 students received support, including 19 fellowships with full tuition reimbursements available (averaging $24,000 per year), 44 research assistantships with full tuition reimbursements available (averaging $24,000 per year); traineeships, health care benefits, unspecified assistantships, and training grant, fellowships, research assistantships also available. Financial award application deadline: 12/15. *Faculty research:* Behavior, cognition and emotion; development, plasticity and repair; membrane excitability and synaptic transmission; molecular neuroscience; neuronal circuits; neurobiology of disease; perception and movement. *Unit head:* Dr. Tom C. Yin, Director, 608-262-0368, Fax: 608-265-2267, E-mail: tcyin@wisc.edu. *Application contact:* Jenny M. Dahlberg, Program Administrator, 608-262-4932, Fax: 608-265-2267, E-mail: ntp@mhub.neuroscience.wisc.edu.

Virginia Commonwealth University, Medical College of Virginia-Professional Programs, School of Medicine, Graduate Program in Neuroscience, Richmond, VA 23284-9005. Offers PhD. Program offered with Departments of Anatomy, Biochemistry and Molecular Biophysics, Pharmacology and Toxicology, and Physiology. *Students:* 15 full-time (9 women); includes 2 minority (1 Asian, non-Hispanic/Latino; 1 Hispanic/Latino), 3 international. 3 applicants, 67% accepted, 2 enrolled. In 2010, 2 doctorates awarded. *Entrance requirements:* For doctorate, GRE or MCAT. Additional exam requirements/recommendations for international students: Required—TOEFL (minimum score 600 paper-based; 250 computer-based; 100 iBT). *Application deadline:* For fall admission, 12/15 priority date for domestic students. Application fee: $50. Electronic applications accepted. *Expenses:* Tuition, state resident: full-time $4308; part-time $479 per credit hour. Tuition, nonresident: full-time $8942; part-time $994 per credit hour. Required fees: $2000; $85 per credit hour. Tuition and fees vary according to course level, course load, degree level, campus/location and program. *Unit head:* Dr. John W. Bigbee, Director, Interdisciplinary Neuroscience Curriculum, 804-828-0948, Fax: 804-828-9477, E-mail: jbigbee@vcu.edu. *Application contact:* Dr. Gail E. Christie, Graduate Program Director and Recruitment Contact, 804-828-9093, E-mail: christie@vcu.edu.

Virginia Commonwealth University, Medical College of Virginia-Professional Programs, School of Medicine, School of Medicine Graduate Programs, Department of Anatomy and Neurobiology, Richmond, VA 23284-9005. Offers anatomy (MS); anatomy and neurobiology (PhD); neurobiology (MS); neuroscience (MS); MD/PhD. *Faculty:* 29 full-time (5 women). *Students:* 15 full-time (2 women), 1 part-time (0 women); includes 4 minority (1 Black or African American, non-Hispanic/Latino; 3 Asian, non-Hispanic/Latino), 3 international. 31 applicants, 26% accepted, 2 enrolled. In 2010, 8 master's, 5 doctorates awarded. *Degree requirements:* For master's, thesis; for doctorate, thesis/dissertation, comprehensive oral and written exams. *Entrance requirements:* For master's and doctorate, GRE, MCAT or DAT. *Application deadline:* For fall admission, 12/15 priority date for domestic students. Application fee: $50. Electronic applications accepted. *Expenses:* Tuition, state resident: full-time $4308; part-time $479 per credit hour. Tuition, nonresident: full-time $8942; part-time $994 per credit hour. Required fees: $2000; $85 per credit hour. Tuition and fees vary according to course level, course load, degree level, campus/location and program. *Financial support:* Fellowships available. *Unit head:* Dr. William Guido, Graduate Program Director and Recruitment Contact, 804-828-0952, E-mail: wguido@vcu.edu. *Application contact:* Dr. Gail E. Christie, Graduate Program Director and Recruitment Contact, 804-828-9093, E-mail: christie@vcu.edu.

Virginia Commonwealth University, Medical College of Virginia-Professional Programs, School of Medicine, School of Medicine Graduate Programs, Department of Pharmacology and Toxicology, Richmond, VA 23284-9005. Offers neuroscience (PhD); pharmacology (Certificate); pharmacology and toxicology (MS, PhD); MD/PhD. *Faculty:* 35 full-time (9 women). *Students:* 47 full-time (27 women), 4 part-time (2 women); includes 13 minority (5 Black or African American, non-Hispanic/Latino; 6 Asian, non-Hispanic/Latino; 1 Hispanic/Latino; 1 Two or more races, non-Hispanic/Latino), 13 international. 66 applicants, 27% accepted, 10 enrolled. In 2010, 2 master's, 4 doctorates awarded. Terminal master's awarded for partial completion of doctoral program. *Degree requirements:* For master's, thesis; for doctorate, thesis/dissertation, comprehensive oral and written exams. *Entrance requirements:* For master's and doctorate, GRE or MCAT. Additional exam requirements/recommendations for international students: Required—TOEFL (minimum score 600 paper-based; 250 computer-based; 100 iBT). *Application deadline:* For fall admission, 4/15 for domestic students. Application fee: $50. Electronic applications accepted. *Expenses:* Tuition, state resident: full-time $4308; part-time $479 per credit hour. Tuition, nonresident: full-time $8942; part-time $994 per credit hour. Required fees: $2000; $85 per credit hour. Tuition and fees vary according to course level, course load, degree level, campus/location and program. *Financial support:* Fellowships, teaching assistantships available. *Faculty research:* Drug abuse, drug metabolism, pharmacodynamics, peptide synthesis, receptor mechanisms. *Unit head:* Dr. William L. Dewey, Chair, 804-827-0375, Fax: 804-827-1548, E-mail: wdewey@vcu.edu. *Application contact:* Dr. Stephen T. Sawyer, Graduate Program Coordinator, 804-828-7918, Fax: 804-827-1548, E-mail: ssawyer@vcu.edu.

Wake Forest University, School of Medicine and Graduate School of Arts and Sciences, Graduate Programs in Medicine, Interdisciplinary Program in Neuroscience, Winston-Salem, NC 27109. Offers PhD, MD/PhD. *Degree requirements:* For doctorate, thesis/dissertation. *Entrance requirements:* For doctorate, GRE General Test. Additional exam requirements/recommendations for international students: Required—TOEFL. Electronic applications accepted. *Faculty research:* Neurobiology of substance abuse, learning and memory, aging, sensory neurobiology, nervous system development.

Washington State University, College of Veterinary Medicine and Graduate School, Graduate Programs in Veterinary Science, Pullman, WA 99164. Offers veterinary and comparative anatomy, pharmacology, and physiology (MS, PhD), including neuroscience, veterinary science; veterinary clinical sciences (MS); veterinary microbiology and pathology (MS, PhD), including veterinary science; DVM/MS; PhD/Certificate. Part-time programs available. *Faculty:* 39 full-time (6 women), 21 part-time/adjunct (6 women). *Students:* 104 full-time (58 women), 1 part-time (0 women); includes 1 Black or African American, non-Hispanic/Latino; 1 Asian, non-Hispanic/Latino; 2 Hispanic/Latino, 39 international. Average age 33. 87 applicants, 37% accepted, 30 enrolled. In 2010, 15 master's, 10 doctorates awarded. Terminal master's awarded for partial completion of doctoral program. *Degree requirements:* For master's, thesis, oral exam; for doctorate, thesis/dissertation, oral exam, written exam. *Entrance requirements:* For master's and doctorate, GRE General Test, minimum GPA of 3.0. Additional exam requirements/recommendations for international students: Required—TOEFL (minimum score 550 paper-based; 213 computer-based; 80 iBT). *Application deadline:* For fall admission, 12/31 priority date for domestic and international students; for spring admission, 8/1 for domestic and international students. Applications are processed on a rolling basis. Application fee: $60. Electronic applications accepted. *Expenses:* Contact institution. *Financial support:* In 2010–11, 24 students received support, including 4 fellowships with partial tuition reimbursements available (averaging $28,000 per year), 49 research assistantships with partial tuition reimbursements available (averaging $21,558 per year), 9 teaching assistantships with partial tuition reimbursements available (averaging $21,558 per year); institutionally sponsored loans, scholarships/grants, traineeships, health care benefits, and unspecified assistantships also available. Financial award application deadline: 3/1; financial award applicants required to submit FAFSA. *Unit head:* Dr. Bryan K. Slinker, Dean, 509-335-9515, Fax: 509-335-0160, E-mail: vetmed-dean@vetmed.wsu.edu. *Application contact:* Julie K. Smith, Principal Assistant, 509-335-3164, E-mail: jksmith@vetmed.wsu.edu.

Washington State University, College of Veterinary Medicine and Graduate School, Graduate Programs in Veterinary Science, Department of Veterinary and Comparative Anatomy, Pharmacology, and Physiology, Program in Neuroscience, Pullman, WA 99164-6520. Offers MS, PhD. Part-time programs available. *Faculty:* 24 full-time (8 women), 13 part-time/adjunct (5 women). *Students:* 28 full-time (11 women); includes 1 Asian, non-Hispanic/Latino; 2 Hispanic/Latino, 7 international. Average age 28. 40 applicants, 20% accepted, 7 enrolled. In 2010, 1 doctorate awarded. Terminal master's awarded for partial completion of doctoral program. *Degree requirements:* For master's, thesis, written exam; for doctorate, thesis/dissertation, written exam, oral exam. *Entrance requirements:* For master's and doctorate, GRE General Test, MCAT, minimum GPA of 3.0. Additional exam requirements/recommendations for international students: Required—TOEFL (minimum score 550 paper-based; 213 computer-based; 80 iBT). *Application deadline:* For fall admission, 12/31 for domestic and international students; for spring admission, 8/1 for domestic and international students. Applications are processed on a rolling basis. Application fee: $50. Electronic applications accepted. *Expenses:* Tuition, state resident: full-time $8552; part-time $443 per credit. Tuition, nonresident: full-time $21,650; part-time $1083 per credit. Required fees: $846. *Financial support:* In 2010–11, 22 students received support, including 4 fellowships with full tuition reimbursements available (averaging $28,000 per year), 14 research assistantships with full tuition reimbursements available (averaging $21,558 per year), 9 teaching assistantships with full tuition reimbursements available (averaging $21,558 per year); scholarships/grants, health care benefits, and unspecified assistantships also available. Financial award application deadline: 4/15. *Faculty research:* Addiction, sleep and performance, body weight and energy balance, emotion and well being, learning and memory, reproduction, vision, movement. Total annual research expenditures: $5.5 million. *Unit head:* Dr. Steve Simasko, Chairman, 509-335-6624, Fax: 509-335-4650, E-mail: simasko@vetmed.wsu.edu. *Application contact:* Bobbi Sauer, Office Assistant II, 509-335-7675, Fax: 509-335-4650, E-mail: grad.neuro@vetmed.wsu.edu.

Washington University in St. Louis, Graduate School of Arts and Sciences, Department of Philosophy, Program in Philosophy/Neuroscience/Psychology, St. Louis, MO 63130-4899. Offers PhD. *Degree requirements:* For doctorate, thesis/dissertation. *Entrance requirements:* For doctorate, GRE General Test, sample of written work. Electronic applications accepted.

Washington University in St. Louis, Graduate School of Arts and Sciences, Division of Biology and Biomedical Sciences, Program in Neurosciences, St. Louis, MO 63130-4899. Offers PhD. *Degree requirements:* For doctorate, thesis/dissertation. *Entrance requirements:* For doctorate, GRE General Test, GRE Subject Test. Electronic applications accepted.

Wayne State University, School of Medicine, Department of Psychiatry and Behavioral Neurosciences, Detroit, MI 48202. Offers psychiatry (MS); translational neuroscience (PhD). *Faculty:* 1 full-time (0 women). *Students:* 5 full-time (2 women), 2 international. Average age 28. 11 applicants, 27% accepted, 2 enrolled. *Expenses:* Tuition, state resident: full-time $7662; part-time $478.85 per credit hour. Tuition, nonresident: full-time $16,920; part-time $1057.55 per credit hour. Required fees: $571; $35.70 per credit hour. $188.05 per semester. Tuition and fees vary according to course load and program. *Financial support:* In 2010–11, 1 fellowship (averaging $25,799 per year), 4 research assistantships with tuition reimbursements (averaging $23,975 per year) were awarded. *Faculty research:* Substance abuse, brain imaging, schizophrenia, child psychopathy, child development, neurobiology of monoamine systems. *Unit head:* Manuel Tancer, Chair, 313-577-1673, E-mail: aa2656@wayne.edu. *Application contact:* Dr. Michael J. Bannon, Director, 313-577-4271, Fax: 313-993-4269, E-mail: mbannon@med.wayne.edu.

West Virginia University, School of Medicine, Graduate Programs at the Health Sciences Center, Interdisciplinary Graduate Programs in Biomedical Sciences, Program in Neuroscience, Morgantown, WV 26506. Offers PhD, MD/PhD. *Degree requirements:* For doctorate, comprehensive exam, thesis/dissertation. *Entrance requirements:* For doctorate, GRE General Test, minimum GPA of 3.0. Additional exam requirements/recommendations for international students: Required—TOEFL. Electronic applications accepted. *Faculty research:* Sensory neuroscience, cognitive neuroscience, neural injury, homeostasis, behavioral neuroscience.

Wilfrid Laurier University, Faculty of Graduate and Postdoctoral Studies, Faculty of Science, Department of Psychology, Waterloo, ON N2L 3C5, Canada. Offers behavioral neuroscience (M Sc, PhD); cognitive neuroscience (M Sc, PhD); community psychology (MA, PhD); social and developmental psychology (MA, PhD). Part-time programs available. *Faculty:* 32 full-time (12 women), 8 part-time/adjunct (1 woman). *Students:* 68 full-time (49 women), 4 part-time (3 women), 2 international. 94 applicants, 51% accepted, 27 enrolled. In 2010, 27 master's, 5 doctorates awarded. *Degree requirements:* For master's, thesis; for doctorate, thesis/dissertation. *Entrance requirements:* For master's, GRE General Test, honors BA or the equivalent in psychology, minimum B average in undergraduate course work; for doctorate, GRE General Test, master's degree, minimum A- average. Additional exam requirements/recommendations for international students: Required—TOEFL (minimum score 89 iBT). *Application deadline:* For fall admission, 1/15 priority date for domestic and international students. Application fee: $100. Electronic applications accepted. Tuition and fees charges are reported in Canadian dollars. *Expenses:* Tuition, area resident: Full-time $15,300 Canadian dollars; part-time $1200 Canadian dollars per credit. International tuition: $21,300 Canadian dollars full-time. Required fees: $650 Canadian dollars; $100 Canadian dollars per credit. Tuition and fees vary according

Neuroscience

Wilfrid Laurier University *(continued)*
to course load, degree level, campus/location and program. *Financial support:* In 2010–11, 116 fellowships, 116 teaching assistantships were awarded; career-related internships or fieldwork, scholarships/grants, health care benefits, and unspecified assistantships also available. *Faculty research:* Brain and cognition, community psychology, social and developmental psychology. *Unit head:* Dr. Alexandra Gottardo, Graduate Coordinator, 519-884-0710 Ext. 2169, Fax: 519-746-7605, E-mail: agottard@wlu.ca. *Application contact:* Rosemary Springett, Graduate Admissions and Records Officer, 519-884-0710 Ext. 3078, Fax: 519-884-1020, E-mail: gradstudies@wlu.ca.

Yale University, Graduate School of Arts and Sciences, Department of Psychology, New Haven, CT 06520. Offers behavioral neuroscience (PhD); clinical psychology (PhD); cognitive psychology (PhD); developmental psychology (PhD); social/personality psychology (PhD).

Accreditation: APA. *Degree requirements:* For doctorate, thesis/dissertation. *Entrance requirements:* For doctorate, GRE General Test.

Yale University, Graduate School of Arts and Sciences, Interdepartmental Neuroscience Program, New Haven, CT 06520. Offers PhD. *Degree requirements:* For doctorate, thesis/dissertation. *Entrance requirements:* For doctorate, GRE General Test. *Expenses:* Contact institution.

Yale University, School of Medicine and Graduate School of Arts and Sciences, Combined Program in Biological and Biomedical Sciences (BBS), Neuroscience Track, New Haven, CT 06520. Offers PhD, MD/PhD. *Degree requirements:* For doctorate, thesis/dissertation. *Entrance requirements:* For doctorate, GRE General Test. Additional exam requirements/recommendations for international students: Required—TOEFL. Electronic applications accepted.

OREGON HEALTH & SCIENCE UNIVERSITY

Neuroscience Graduate Program

Program of Study

The Neuroscience Graduate Program (NGP) at Oregon Health & Science University (OHSU) offers training leading to the Doctor of Philosophy (Ph.D.) degree. The program is most appropriate for students intending to pursue a professional career in research and teaching, but the University encourages students to pursue the career path that best matches their interests and skills. Students admitted to the M.D./Ph.D. program at OHSU also can pursue their Ph.D. in the program. Highly qualified students admitted to the M.D. program may apply for concurrent admission to the NGP to pursue a Ph.D. in neuroscience. For further information visit http://www.ohsu.edu/ngp.

The interdepartmental program is broad and diverse, comprised of over 140 faculty members and including members of the National Academy of Sciences, the Institute of Medicine, and investigators of the Howard Hughes Medical Institute. The program offers opportunities for advanced study and research in all areas of modern neuroscience including molecular, cellular, developmental, endocrine, behavioral, and systems neuroscience. As a medical campus, there are numerous opportunities for translational projects as well. The faculty represents basic and clinical departments as well as the Vollum Institute, the Center for Research on Occupational and Environmental Toxicology, the Jungers Center, the Oregon National Primate Research Center, the School of Dentistry, and, the Veterans Administration Medical Center.

The first year includes required course work as well as laboratory rotations. Course work includes a four-course series that provides a broad foundation for a career in neuroscience (cellular neuroscience; neuronal cell biology, signaling and development; systems neuroscience; and neurobiology of disease). Students also rotate in at least three laboratories and participate in special topics and seminar courses. Four elective courses selected from biochemistry, molecular biology, genetics, cell biology, statistics, or advanced neuroscience topics make up the remainder of the course work, typically completed in the first two years. Students identify their dissertation mentor at the end of the first year and spend most of their time in the laboratory during the second year defining their dissertation project. An oral qualifying exam, which incorporates a written thesis proposal, is taken after the second year. Students require an average of five years to complete the Ph.D.

Research Facilities

The faculty is well funded by extramural research grants and maintains modern laboratories for state-of-the-art biomedical research. Students of the program also have access to specialized resources within OHSU through their individual mentors.

Financial Aid

In 2011–12, incoming full-time Ph.D. students receive stipends of $27,000 per year with several fellowships available to supplement stipends. After passing the oral exam at the end of the second year, the stipend increases. Fees such as health care and hospitalization insurance are paid for students on stipends. After the first year of study, students are supported by funds provided by their thesis adviser or training grants. Many students in the NGP apply for and receive extramural fellowships from NIH or private foundations. Several fellowship programs at OHSU offer stipends for projects in translational neuroscience.

Cost of Study

Graduate students are enrolled as graduate research assistants and thus receive a full tuition waiver.

Living and Housing Costs

Many apartments are within walking distance of the campus or on a campus bus route and rent for $600 to $800 per month.

Student Group

The Oregon Health & Science University has approximately 1,000 students in professional schools and 300 students in graduate programs. The Neuroscience Graduate Program admits about 10 students per year with approximately 60 currently in the program. NGP students also benefit from interactions with students in the molecular and cellular biology program, the M.D./Ph.D. program and the behavioral neuroscience program.

Student Outcomes

Since its inception in 1992, more than 75 students have graduated from the program. Nearly all have pursued biomedical research and a number hold tenure-track faculty positions in the U.S. and Europe. Others hold positions in industry, government, or non-profit agencies.

Location

OHSU is located on Marquam Hill near the center of Portland. The site allows sweeping views of the downtown, the Willamette River and the Cascades, including Mount Hood and Mount St. Helens. An overhead tram connects the main campus to a new clinical/translational campus at the South Waterfront and provides easy public transportation access to OHSU from across Portland. The greater Portland area is a major cultural center with a population of two million, and a reputation for great neighborhoods, sustainable living, bicycle commuting, and all forms of outdoor activities within easy driving. The Willamette River and Columbia River gorge are popular areas for water sports including windsurfing. The high desert of Central Oregon offers rock climbing, whitewater rafting, and great sunny weather. The driving time from Portland to the mountains or high desert (to the east) and ocean beaches (to the west) is just over an hour. Portland's climate is mild, with summer high temperatures in the 70s and 80s and winter temperatures between 40 and 50 degrees. Other colleges and universities located in Portland include Reed College, Lewis and Clark College, Portland State University, and the University of Portland.

The University

The Oregon Health & Science University is the only academic health center in the state of Oregon. It houses the Schools of Medicine, Dentistry, Nursing, and Engineering; the Vollum Institute; the Oregon National Primate Research Center; the University Hospital and Clinics; and Doernbecher Children's Hospital. Affiliations exist with many other institutions, including Portland State University, the Veterans Administration Medical Center, and the Shriners Hospital for Crippled Children.

Applying

Students with a bachelor's degree in the biological or physical sciences and with a strong commitment to research are encouraged to apply. The deadline is December 15. Applicants must submit scores on the Graduate Record Examinations, and international applicants whose native language is not English must submit scores from the Test of English as a Foreign Language (TOEFL). Successful applicants generally have significant research experience. Applicants are notified of acceptance no later than April 1, and accepted students are strongly encouraged to begin research rotations on July 1.

Correspondence and Information

Neuroscience Graduate Program
Oregon Health & Science University
Vollum Institute, L-474
3181 Southwest Sam Jackson Park Road
Portland, Oregon 97239
Phone: 503-494-6932
Fax: 503-494-5518
E-mail: ngp@ohsu.edu
Web site: http://www.ohsu.edu/ngp

Oregon Health & Science University

THE FACULTY

Neuroscience is multidisciplinary and becoming even more so, despite increasing technology. Thus most faculty members and most projects in neuroscience no longer fit a single subdiscipline within neuroscience. That is certainly true of the over 140 NGP faculty members at OHSU. On the University's Web site at http://www.ohsu.edu/academic/som/ngp/faculty.cfm, faculty members have been listed by traditional subdisciplines in neuroscience as well as areas of particular strength.

UNIFORMED SERVICES UNIVERSITY OF THE HEALTH SCIENCES

F. Edward Hébert School of Medicine
Graduate Program in Neuroscience

Program of Study

The Uniformed Services University of the Health Sciences (USUHS) offers the Graduate Program in Neuroscience, a broadly based interdisciplinary program leading to the Ph.D. degree in neuroscience. Courses and research training are provided by the neuroscience faculty members, who hold primary appointments in the Departments of Anatomy, Physiology, and Genetics; Biochemistry; Medical and Clinical Psychology; Microbiology and Immunology; Neurology; Pathology; Pediatrics; Pharmacology; and Psychiatry at the University. The program permits considerable flexibility in the choice of courses and research areas; training programs are tailored to meet the individual requirements of each student. The program is designed for students with strong undergraduate training in the physical sciences, biology, or psychology who wish to pursue a professional career in neuroscience research. Integrated instruction in the development, structure, function, and pathology of the nervous system and its interaction with the environment is provided. Students in the program conduct their research under the direction of neuroscience faculty members in laboratories that are located in the medical school. During the first year of study, students begin formal course work. Each student is required to take laboratory training rotations in the research laboratories of program faculty members. By the end of the first year, students select a research area and a faculty thesis adviser. During the second year, students complete requirements for advancement to candidacy, including required course work and passage of the qualifying examination. After advancement to candidacy, each student develops an original research project and prepares and defends a written dissertation under the guidance of his or her faculty adviser and advisory committee.

Research Facilities

Each academic department at the University is provided with laboratories for the support of a variety of research projects. Neuroscience research laboratories available to students are suitable for research in most areas of neuroscience, including behavioral studies, electrophysiology, molecular and cellular neurobiology, neuroanatomy, neurochemistry, neuropathology, neuropharmacology, and neurophysiology. High-resolution electron microscopes, confocal microscopes, two photon microscopes, deconvolution wide-field fluorescence microscopes, a central resource facility providing custom synthesis of oligonucleotides and peptides and DNA sequencing, centralized animal facilities, computer support, a medical library, and a learning resources center are available within the University.

Financial Aid

Stipends are available on a competitive basis. Awards are made on a yearly basis and are renewable. For the 2011–12 academic year, stipends for entering students begin at $27,000. Outstanding students may be nominated for the Dean's Special Fellowship or other special fellowships, which support a stipend of $32,000.

Cost of Study

Graduate students in the neuroscience program are not required to pay tuition or fees. Civilian students incur no obligation to the United States government for service after completion of their graduate training program. Students are required to carry health insurance.

Living and Housing Costs

There is a reasonable supply of affordable rental housing in the area. The University does not have housing for graduate students. Students are responsible for making their own arrangements for accommodations. Costs in the Washington, D.C., area are comparable to those in other major metropolitan areas.

Student Group

The neuroscience graduate program is an active and growing graduate program; approximately 21 students are enrolled. The Uniformed Services University (USU) also has Ph.D. programs in departmentally based basic biomedical sciences, as well as interdisciplinary graduate programs in molecular and cell biology and in emerging infectious diseases. In addition to the graduate and medical programs in the medical school, the nursing school has graduate programs for nurse practitioners and nurse anesthetists.

Student Outcomes

Graduates hold faculty, research associate, postdoctoral, science policy, and other positions in universities, medical schools, government, and industrial research institutions.

Location

USU is located in Bethesda, Maryland, an immediately adjacent northern suburb of Washington, D.C. The University is located in a parklike setting at the National Naval Medical Center, which is across the street from the National Institutes of Health and the National Library of Medicine. A nearby Metro subway and bus station provides convenient access to downtown Washington and surrounding areas. The D.C. metropolitan area has about 3 million people and offers seven major universities (including three other medical schools), numerous colleges, and internationally renowned research facilities. Wooded areas and jogging and biking trails surround the University. Cultural and recreational activities are plentiful, with a major park system, recreation facilities, museums, theaters, symphonies, opera, and major-league sports teams. The Chesapeake Bay, Atlantic Ocean, and Shenandoah Mountains are easily accessible.

The University

The University was established by Congress in 1972 to provide a comprehensive education in medicine to those who demonstrate potential for careers as Medical Corps officers in the uniformed services. Graduate programs in the basic medical sciences are offered to both civilian and military students and are an essential part of the academic environment at the University. The University is located in proximity to major research facilities, including the National Institutes of Health (NIH), the National Library of Medicine, Walter Reed Army Medical Center at the National Naval Medical Center, the Armed Forces Institute of Pathology, the National Institute of Standards and Technology, and numerous biotechnology companies.

Uniformed Services University subscribes fully to the policy of equal educational opportunity and accepts students on a competitive basis without regard to race, color, sex, age, or creed.

Applying

Civilian applicants are accepted as full-time students only. Each applicant must have a bachelor's degree from an accredited academic institution. A strong background in science with courses in several of the following disciplines—biochemistry, biology, chemistry, mathematics, physics, physiology, and psychology—is desirable. Applicants must arrange for official transcripts of all prior college-level courses taken and their GRE scores (taken within the last two years) to be sent to the Office of Graduate Education. Students may elect to submit scores obtained in one or more GRE Subject Tests (from the subject areas listed above) in support of their application. Applicants must also arrange for letters of recommendation from 3 people who are familiar with their academic work to be sent to the University. For full consideration and evaluation for stipend support, completed applications should be received before January 1 for matriculation in late August. Late applications are evaluated on a space-available basis. There is no application fee. Application forms may be obtained from the Web site at http://www.usuhs.mil/nes/progdescription.html#app.

Correspondence and Information

For applications:
Associate Dean for Graduate Education
Uniformed Services University
4301 Jones Bridge Road
Bethesda, Maryland 20814-4799
Phone: 301-295-3913
      800-772-1747 (toll-free)
E-mail: nfinley@usuhs.mil
Web site: http://www.usuhs.mil/graded/

For information about the neuroscience program:
Sharon Juliano, Ph.D.
Director, Graduate Program in Neuroscience
Uniformed Services University
4301 Jones Bridge Road
Bethesda, Maryland 20814-4799
Phone: 301-295-3642
Fax: 301-295-1996
E-mail: nfinley@usuhs.mil
Web site: http://www.usuhs.mil/nes/index.html

Uniformed Services University of the Health Sciences

THE FACULTY AND THEIR RESEARCH

Denes V. Agoston, M.D., Ph.D., Associate Professor, Department of Anatomy, Physiology, and Genetics. Molecular and cellular mechanisms of functional recovery after traumatic brain injury.

Juanita Anders, Ph.D., Professor, Department of Anatomy, Physiology, and Genetics. Innovative therapies for neuronal regeneration of injured central and peripheral nervous systems, light-cellular interaction.

Regina Armstrong, Ph.D., Professor, Department of Anatomy, Physiology, and Genetics, and Director, Center for Neuroscience and Regenerative Medicine. Cellular and molecular mechanisms of neural stem/progenitor cell development and regeneration in demyelinating diseases and brain injury models.

Suzanne B. Bausch, Ph.D., Associate Professor, Department of Pharmacology. Synaptic plasticity in traumatic brain injury and epileptogenesis; NMDAR-regulated plasticity in neuronal circuits.

David Benedek, M.D., Professor, Department of Psychiatry.

Rosemary C. Borke, Ph.D., Professor Emerita, Department of Anatomy, Physiology, and Genetics. Neuronal plasticity in development and regeneration.

Diane E. Borst, Ph.D., Research Assistant Professor, Department of Anatomy, Physiology, and Genetics. Molecular mechanisms of retinal gene regulation and function.

Maria F. Braga, D.D.S., Ph.D., Assistant Professor, Department of Anatomy, Physiology, and Genetics. Cellular and molecular mechanisms regulating neuronal excitability in the amygdala; pathophysiology of anxiety disorders and epilepsy.

Howard Bryant, Ph.D., Associate Professor, Department of Anatomy, Physiology, and Genetics. Electrophysiology of vascular smooth muscle.

Kimberly Byrnes, Ph.D., Assistant Professor, Department of Anatomy, Physiology, and Genetics. Microglial and macrophage-based chronic inflammation after traumatic brain and spinal cord injury; noninvasive imaging of post-injury metabolic and inflammatory events.

Col. William W. Campbell, USA, MC; M.D., M.S.H.A.; Professor and Chair, Department of Neurology, and Professor, Department of Neuroscience. Neuromuscular disease and clinical neurophysiology.

Kwang Choi, Ph.D., Research Assistant Professor, Department of Psychiatry. Translational research on psychiatric disorders using genetic, behavioral, and bioinformatic approaches.

Jeffrey Cole, Ph.D., Assistant Professor, Department of Neurology.

De-Maw Chuang, Ph.D., Adjunct Professor, Department of Psychiatry. Molecular and cellular of actions of mood stabilizers: neuroprotection against excitotoxicity-related neurodegeneration.

Thomas Côté, Ph.D., Associate Professor, Department of Pharmacology. Mu opioid receptor interaction with GTP-binding proteins and RGS proteins.

Brian Cox, Ph.D., Professor, Department of Pharmacology. Opiate drugs, endogenous opioids, neuropeptides, and their roles in responses of the brain to pain, stress, and injury.

Clifton Dalgard, Ph.D., Assistant Professor, Department of Anatomy, Physiology, and Genetics. Molecular mechanisms of damage-associated inflammation.

Patricia A. Deuster, Ph.D., M.P.H., Professor, Department of Military and Emergency Medicine. Mechanisms of neuroendocrine and immune activation with stress.

Martin Doughty, Ph.D., Assistant Professor, Department of Anatomy, Physiology, and Genetics.

Ying-Hong Feng, Associate Professor, M.D., Ph.D. Angiotensin receptor and signal transduction.

Zygmunt Galdzicki, Ph.D., Associate Professor, Department of Anatomy, Physiology, and Genetics. Molecular and electrophysiological approach to understand mental retardation in Down syndrome; role of glutamate receptors in neurodegenerative disorders.

Neil Grunberg, Ph.D., Professor, Department of Medical and Clinical Psychology. Nicotine and tobacco; drug abuse; stress; traumatic brain injury; PTSD.

Carl Gunderson, M.D., Professor, Department of Neurology. Education of medical students; history of military neurology.

Harry Holloway, M.D., Professor, Department of Psychiatry. Clinical psychiatry; alcohol and drug misuse; posttraumatic stress; neurobiology of psychiatric disorders; clinical psychopharmacology.

Christopher J. Hough, Ph.D., Assistant Professor, Department of Psychiatry. Affective and anxiety disorders; the mechanisms of action and mood stabilizers, including lithium and zinc.

David Jacobowitz, Ph.D., Professor, Department of Anatomy, Physiology, and Genetics. Gene and protein discovery in the diseased and developing brain.

Luke Johnson, Ph.D., Assistant Professor, Department of Psychiatry and Program in Neuroscience. Microanatomy of fear and stress.

Martha Johnson, Ph.D., Associate Professor, Department of Anatomy, Physiology, and Genetics. Education of first-year medical and graduate students in the anatomical and physiological sciences.

Sharon Juliano, Ph.D., Professor, Department of Anatomy, Physiology, and Genetics. Mechanisms of development and plasticity in the cerebral cortex, with particular emphasis on the migration of neurons into the cortical plate and factors maintaining the function and morphology of radial glia and Cajal-Retzius cells.

Fabio Leonessa, M.D., Research Assistant Professor, Department of Neurology. Pathobiology and biomarkers of traumatic brain injury and posttraumatic stress disorder.

He Li, M.D., Ph.D., Associate Professor, Department of Psychiatry. Neurobiological basis of post-traumatic stress disorder: synaptic plasticity and neuronal signaling in the amygdala circuitry.

Geoffrey Ling, M.D., Ph.D., Professor, Departments of Anesthesiology, Neurology, and Surgery. Novel therapeutics and diagnostic tools for traumatic brain injury and hemorrhagic shock; mechanisms of cellular injury and edema formation in traumatic brain injury.

Ann M. Marini, Ph.D., M.D., Professor, Department of Neurology. Molecular and cellular mechanisms of intrinsic survival pathways through glutamate receptors to protect against neurodegenerative disorders.

Joseph McCabe, Ph.D., Professor and Vice Chair, Department of Anatomy, Physiology, and Genetics. Traumatic brain injury, hemorrhagic shock, and gene expression of neuroendocrine-related gene products.

Debra McLaughlin, Ph.D., Research Assistant Professor, Department of Anatomy, Physiology, and Genetics. Sensory processing and cortical neurophysiology.

David Mears, Ph.D., Associate Professor, Department of Anatomy, Physiology, and Genetics. Electrophysiology and calcium signaling in neuroendocrine cells.

Chantal Moratz, Ph.D, Assistant Professor, Department of Medicine. Regulation mechanisms of inflammation; autoimmune diseases, traumatic brain injury, and complement activation.

Gregory Mueller, Ph.D., Professor, Department of Anatomy, Physiology, and Genetics. Neuroendocrine regulation; neuropeptide gene expression; regulation of peptide biosynthesis and the proteomics of neuropeptide secretion.

Aryan Namboodiri, Ph.D., Associate Professor, Department of Anatomy, Physiology, and Genetics. Neurobiology of N-acetylaspartate (NAA), and pathogenesis and treatment of Canavan disease.

Feresh Nugent, Ph.D., Assistant Professor, Department of Pharmacology. Synaptic plasticity and drug addiction.

J. Timothy O'Neill, Ph.D., Assistant Professor, Departments of Pediatrics and Anatomy, Physiology, and Genetics. Mechanisms of control of newborn and developmental cerebral blood and oxygen supply.

Harvey B. Pollard, M.D., Ph.D., Professor and Chair, Department of Anatomy, Physiology, and Genetics. Molecular biology of secretory processes.

Sylvie Poluch, Ph.D., Research Assistant Professor, Department of Anatomy, Physiology, and Genetics. Development of the cerebral cortex.

Brian Schaefer, Ph.D., Associate Professor, Department of Microbiology and Immunology. Biology of lymphocyte activation, particularly the antigen-regulated NF-kappaB pathway; role of inflammation in traumatic brain injury; imaging, biochemical, and cellular approaches to elucidate signal transduction mechanisms.

Michael Schell, Ph.D., Assistant Professor, Department of Pharmacology. Synaptic mechanisms regulating the actin cytoskeleton in dendritic spines.

Jennifer Schiltz, Ph.D., Assistant Professor, Department of Anatomy, Physiology, and Genetics.

Aviva Symes, Ph.D., Associate Professor, Department of Pharmacology. Glial response to traumatic brain and spinal cord injury; mechanism of cytokine action in the CNS after injury.

E. Fuller Torrey, M.D., Professor, Department of Psychiatry. Infectious agents as causes of schizophrenia and bipolar disorder.

Jack W. Tsao, M.D., Ph.D., Associate Professor, Department of Neurology and Neuroscience. Clinical studies on phantom limb pain, traumatic brain injury, and low back pain; basic science studies on cellular and developmental mechanisms governing nerve degeneration.

Robert J. Ursano, M.D., Professor and Chairman, Department of Psychiatry, and Director, Center for the Study of Traumatic Stress. Posttraumatic stress disorder.

Maree J. Webster, Ph.D., Assistant Professor, Department of Psychiatry. Neuropathology of severe mental illness; schizophrenia and bipolar disorder.

T. John Wu, Ph.D., Associate Professor, Department of Obstetrics and Gynecology. Neuroendocrine regulation of reproduction and stress.

Xiang-Lan Yao, Ph.D., Research Assistant Professor, Department of Anatomy, Physiology, and Genetics.

Lei Zhang, M.D., Associate Professor, Department of Psychiatry. PTSD and biomarkers.

Yumin Zhang, M.D., Ph.D., Assistant Professor, Department of Anatomy, Physiology, and Genetics.

UNIVERSITY OF CALIFORNIA, BERKELEY

Neuroscience Graduate Program

Program of Study

The Neuroscience Graduate Program is a campuswide interdisciplinary organization that includes more than 40 faculty members with state-of-the-art laboratories from the Departments of Molecular and Cell Biology, Psychology, Physics, and Integrative Biology in the College of Letters and Sciences; the Department of Chemical and Biomolecular Engineering in the College of Chemistry; the Department of Environmental Science Policy and Management in the College of Natural Resources; the Helen Wills Neuroscience Institute; the School of Public Health; the Department of Electrical Engineering in the College of Engineering; and the School of Optometry's Program in Vision Sciences. Faculty members participate in neuroscience graduate training and research from the molecular and genetic levels to the cognitive and computational levels. Areas of training and research include analysis of ion channels, receptors, and signal transduction mechanisms; formation, function, and plasticity of synapses; control of neural cell fate and pattern formation; neuronal growth cone guidance and target recognition; mechanisms of sensory processing in the visual, auditory, and olfactory systems; development and function of neural networks; motor control; and the neural basis of cognition. The preparations in use range from reductionist models to complex neural systems and include cells in culture, simple invertebrate and vertebrate organisms, model genetic systems, the mammalian cerebral cortex, and human brain imaging.

The graduate training includes a series of graduate-level courses, three laboratory rotations during the first year, placement in a thesis laboratory starting with the second year, a qualifying examination that includes a thesis proposal at the end of the second year, two semesters of teaching assistantship, and approximately three years of in-candidacy, full-time research ending with the thesis presentation and filing.

Research Facilities

In addition to the neuroscience faculty members' research laboratories, the Neuroscience Institute has four technology centers: the Brain Imaging Center, with a 4-Tesla fMRI and a 3-Tesla fMRI, as well as a networked computer system; the Redwood Center for Theoretical Neuroscience; the Functional Genomics Laboratory; and the Molecular Imaging Center. All facilities are used for research and training purposes. Faculty laboratories and the technology centers are housed in various buildings on the UC Berkeley main campus.

Financial Aid

All graduate students are fully supported by the program during their training. Financial aid packages include scholarships, teaching assistantships, and research assistantships. Applicants are strongly encouraged to apply for National Science Foundation fellowships in November during their senior year. University fellowships are also available. The 2011–12 minimum stipend level is set at $29,500 for twelve months.

Cost of Study

In 2011–12 University registration fees for legal California residents amount to $13,916.50 for the academic year, or two semesters. For nonresidents, tuition and fees for the same period of study amount to $29,018.50. All admitted students have fees and tuition, as well as health and dental insurance, paid in full by the program.

Living and Housing Costs

Most graduate students live in apartments or houses in the vicinity of the campus. Rents for shared housing range from $800 to $1200 per month. The University maintains a family student housing complex for married couples and single-parent families. The Student Housing Office has its own Web site (http://www.housing.berkeley.edu/) and assists students in locating housing both on and off campus.

Student Group

The Berkeley campus has approximately 35,000 students, including more than 10,000 graduate students. Around 3,000 international students from more than 100 countries add to the cosmopolitan flavor of the campus. The Neuroscience Graduate Program, with more than 100 graduate student affiliates from widely varied backgrounds and with wide-ranging interests and pursuits, is a vigorous, stimulating group within Berkeley's outstanding scientific community. Cohesion within this group is enhanced by weekly seminars, Journal Club activities, and annual off-site neuroscience retreats.

Student Outcomes

Neuroscience graduates find employment as postdoctoral fellows at peer institutions such as Caltech, Columbia, Harvard, MIT, Stanford, the University of California at San Francisco, the University of California at San Diego, and the NIH; as faculty members in academia; and as researchers in both private and public institutions. Some graduates work in biotechnology firms or choose to continue their studies at medical, veterinary, or law schools.

Location

The campus, at the foot of the Berkeley Hills and in the center of the city of Berkeley, is surrounded by business and residential districts. The setting retains a park atmosphere, with wooded glens, spacious plazas, and the picturesque Strawberry Creek running the length of the campus. Many areas and buildings on campus provide panoramic views of San Francisco and the entire nine-county Bay Area, a region renowned for its cultural and recreational activities, including public lectures, concerts, theater and other dramatic presentations, museums, galleries, exhibits, and a wide variety of restaurants, eateries, and cafés. Hiking and biking trails are in abundance, and sailing on the bay is nearby.

The University

The Berkeley campus, which was founded in 1868, is the oldest of the ten University of California campuses. Just to name a few of its outstanding and diverse faculty members, there are 8 out of a total of 20 Nobel laureates who are still active faculty members. The University is home to 216 American Association for the Advancement of Science Fellows, 224 American Academy of Arts and Sciences Fellows, 32 MacArthur Fellows, 135 National Academy of Sciences members (including Mu-ming Poo of the Neuroscience Graduate Program), 12 recipients of the National Medal of Science, 1 poet laureate, 14 Howard Hughes Medical Institute Investigators including Yang Dan from the Neuroscience Graduate Program (Kristin Scott is the recipient of the HHMI Early Career Scientist Award), and 4 Pulitzer Prize winners. Generally considered the leading public university in the nation, with its graduate programs ranked among first in the nation in both number and scholarship according to the National Research Council, Berkeley is continually developing new programs and redefining existing ones, such as the integrated Neuroscience Graduate Program (ranked 5–13 according to the newest 2010 NRC report), in an attempt to meet each new challenge and forge new paths.

Applying

The Neuroscience Graduate Program admits students starting in the fall semester only for a Ph.D. course of study exclusively. Inquiries regarding application procedures should be directed to the Graduate Affairs Office. Applicants must use the online application method at https://gradadm.berkeley.edu/grdappl/welcome. The application deadline is December 1 each year, but students can apply as early as September. Graduate Record Examinations scores (Institute Code 4833; Department Code 0213) for the General Test, mandatory, and one Subject Test, highly recommended (same codes; tests in biochemistry and cell biology, chemistry, biology, psychology, computer science, mathematics, or physics), a TOEFL (Institute Code 4833) for international applicants whose first language is not English (with a minimum score of 230 on the CBT or 68 on the iBT), and a minimum GPA of 3.0 are required. At least one year of proven laboratory experience is likewise required. Admitted students have historically scored above the high 80th percentile on the tests and have higher average GPAs. The Neuroscience Graduate Program actively solicits applications from underrepresented groups.

Correspondence and Information

Graduate Affairs Office
Neuroscience Graduate Program
3210F Tolman Hall, MC#3192
University of California, Berkeley
Berkeley, California 94720

Phone: 510-642-8915
Fax: 510-643-4966
E-mail: neurosci@berkeley.edu
Web site: http://neuroscience.berkeley.edu/grad/home/

University of California, Berkeley

THE FACULTY AND THEIR RESEARCH

Faculty members in the Neuroscience Graduate Program are divided into four broad research areas: cellular, molecular, and developmental neuroscience; systems and animal behavior; computational and theoretical neuroscience; and human cognitive neuroscience. Individual faculty members may be involved in more than one research area.

Martin S. Banks, Professor. Visual space perception; psychophysics; modeling of vision; virtual reality.

Shaowen Bao, Adjunct Associate Professor. Sensory processing.

Diana Bautista, Assistant Professor (McKnight and Pew Scholar). Molecular mechanisms of transduction in touch and pain receptors.

George Bentley, Associate Professor. Neural integration and transduction of environmental cues into endocrine signals.

Sonia Bishop, Assistant Professor (National Institute of Mental Health BRAINS Award). Affective cognitive neuroscience; individual (including genetic) differences in cognitive control.

Silvia Bunge, Associate Professor. Cognitive neuroscience and developmental cognitive neuroscience; cognitive control and prefrontal function.

Jose Carmena, Associate Professor (NSF Faculty Early Career Development Award; 2011 IEEE Engineering in Medicine and Biology Society Early Career Achievement Award). Brain-machine interfaces; neural mechanisms of sensorimotor control and learning; neural ensemble computation; neuroprosthetics.

Yang Dan, Professor (HHMI Investigator). Processing and computation of visual information in the thalamus and cortex.

Mark D'Esposito, Professor. Neural basis of working memory in humans; functions of human prefrontal cortex; fMRI.

Michael DeWeese, Assistant Professor. Auditory sensory processing in cortex; cortical mechanisms of selective attention.

Dan Feldman, Associate Professor. Synaptic mechanisms for cortical map plasticity; mechanisms and function of spike timing-dependant synaptic plasticity; sensory coding in the whisker system.

Marla Feller, Associate Professor. Neural activity in assembly of neural circuits; cellular mechanisms that underlie the spontaneous generation of retinal waves; role of retinal waves in the maturation of retinal projection to its primary targets in the CNS; role of retinal waves in the development of receptive fields of retinal ganglion cells.

John Flannery, Professor. Molecular genetics of transduction and retinal degeneration; gene therapy for retinal diseases.

Darlene Francis, Associate Professor. Behavioral neuroscience; developmental psychobiology; animal models; stress; maternal care; gene-environment interaction.

Jack Gallant, Professor. Neural mechanisms of visual form perception and attention.

Gian Garriga, Professor. Neuronal migration and axonal pathfinding in *C. elegans*.

Donald Glaser, Professor and Nobel Laureate. Computational modeling of human vision.

Xiaohua Gong, Associate Professor. Eye development and disease; cell-to-cell communication; intracellular signaling pathways in the lens.

Thomas Griffiths, Associate Professor. Computational models of cognition, including causality, categorization, inductive inference, probabilistic reasoning, language learning, and language evolution; machine learning; Bayesian statistics.

Ehud Isacoff, Professor. Biophysical properties of ion channels; advanced optical methods.

Richard Ivry, Professor. Neural basis of motor control and motor learning in humans.

Lucia Jacobs, Associate Professor. Neural mechanisms of complex behaviors.

William Jagust, Professor. Structural and functional imaging of aging and dementia.

Daniela Kaufer, Associate Professor (National Institute of Mental Health BRAINS Award). Molecular mechanisms underlying stress responses in the brain.

Stanley Klein, Professor. Modeling of spatial vision and its application in image compression.

Robert Knight, Professor. Role of human prefrontal cortex in attention and memory control.

Richard Kramer, Professor. Mechanisms of cell signaling mediated by cyclic nucleotides.

Lance Kriegsfeld, Associate Professor. Genetic, cellular, and hormonal mechanisms responsible for the temporal control of motivated behaviors.

Dennis Levi, Professor. Peripheral and central mechanisms of amblyopia.

John Ngai, Professor. Cellular and molecular mechanisms of olfaction; functional genomics.

Bruno Olshausen, Professor. Computational models of perception.

Mu-ming Poo, Professor (Academy of Science member). Mechanisms of axon guidance; synaptic plasticity.

Lynn Robertson, Adjunct Professor. Neural basis of human perception and attention.

David Schaffer, Professor. Mechanisms of stem cell differentiation.

Kristin Scott, Associate Professor (HHMI Early Career Scientist, Merck Fellow). Taste recognition in *Drosophila*.

Arthur Shimamura, Professor (Guggenheim Fellow). Biological basis of memory and cognitive functions in humans.

Michael Silver, Associate Professor. Neural correlates of human visual perception and attention.

Friedrich Sommer, Associate Adjunct Professor. Models of associative memory; sensory processing.

Mark Tanouye, Professor. Molecular genetics and physiology of behavior in *Drosophila*.

Frédéric Theunissen, Professor. Neural mechanisms underlying complex sound recognition.

Matthew Walker, Associate Professor. Cognitive neuroscience of the sleeping brain.

Jonathan Wallis, Associate Professor. Neuronal mechanisms of goal-directed behavior.

David Whitney, Associate Professor. Visual and visuomotor localization.

Andrew Wurmser, Assistant Professor. Differentiation of neural stem cells.

Robert Zucker, Professor. Role of calcium in transmitter release, synaptic transmission, and plasticity.

UNIVERSITY OF CONNECTICUT HEALTH CENTER

Graduate Program in Neuroscience

Program of Study

The neuroscience graduate program at the University of Connecticut Health Center offers an interdisciplinary training environment that is committed to preparing students for research and teaching careers in both academic and industrial settings. The curriculum and research are dedicated to understanding the normal function and disorders of the nervous system.

All course requirements are fulfilled within the first two years of the program. Introductory core courses establish a strong foundation in molecular, cellular, and systems-level neurobiology.

A wide selection of advanced elective courses on such topics as physiology of excitable tissue, computational neuroscience, neuropharmacology, neuroimmunology, neurobiology of disease, microscopy, biochemistry, immunology, genetics, and cell biology allows tailoring of the curriculum to accommodate the specific needs and diverse interests of students. Participation in weekly journal clubs provides a broad perspective of cutting-edge research in the field.

During the first year of the program, three research rotation projects are performed in laboratories of the student's choice and a laboratory is identified for the dissertation research project by the beginning of the second year. Experimental training opportunities ranging from recombinant DNA to human studies are available. The breadth of these opportunities is shown in a survey of the areas of faculty research, which include regulation of gene expression, signal transduction, and intracellular trafficking in neurons and glia; function of voltage-sensitive ion channels and neurotransmitter receptors; biology of neuropeptides; synaptic transmission and neuroplasticity; development of neurons and glia; synaptic organization and stimulus coding; and sensory perception, behavior, and human psychophysics. Research pertaining to specific maladies of the nervous system includes neuroinflammation, autoimmunity, and neurodegeneration; substance abuse; stroke; epilepsy; multiple sclerosis; and deafness. Approaches employed include genetic engineering; cell and brain slice cultures; stem cells; electrophysiology; confocal microscopy and other imaging; neuroanatomical, virtual cell and mathematical modeling; and behavioral and transgenic animal models.

Research Facilities

Because of the interdepartmental format, the students have access to all of the facilities of modern biomedical research at the University of Connecticut Health Center, including those in clinical and basic science departments. Most of the neuroscience faculty members are housed in the same building on adjoining floors, providing for a congenial atmosphere of informal scientific exchange and collaborations between laboratories. The Center for Cell Analysis and Modeling (CCAM) has state-of-the-art facilities for confocal and two-photon microscopy and image analysis and is available to members of the Program in Neuroscience. The Lyman Maynard Stowe Library has an extensive collection of periodicals and monographs as well as subscriptions to journals of current interest in the field of neuroscience.

Financial Aid

Support for doctoral students engaged in full-time degree programs at the Health Center is provided on a competitive basis. Graduate research assistantships for 2011–12 provide a stipend of $28,000 per year, which includes a waiver of tuition/University fees for the fall and spring semesters and a student health insurance plan. While financial aid is offered competitively, the Health Center makes every possible effort to address the financial needs of all students.

Cost of Study

For 2011–12, tuition is $10,224 per year for full-time students who are Connecticut residents and $26,532 per year for full-time students who are out-of-state residents. General University fees are added to the cost of tuition for students who do not receive a tuition waiver. These costs are usually met by traineeships or research assistantships for doctoral students.

Living and Housing Costs

There is a wide range of affordable housing options in the greater Hartford area within easy commuting distance of the campus, including an extensive complex that is adjacent to the Health Center. Costs range from $600 to $900 per month for a one-bedroom unit; 2 or more students sharing an apartment usually pay less. University housing is not available.

Student Group

Twenty-two students are registered in the Ph.D. program (including combined-degree students). The total number of master's and Ph.D. students at the Health Center is approximately 400, and there are about 125 medical and dental students per class.

Location

The Health Center is located in the historic town of Farmington, Connecticut. Set in the beautiful New England countryside on a hill overlooking the Farmington Valley, it is close to ski areas, hiking trails, and facilities for boating, fishing, and swimming. Connecticut's capital city of Hartford, 7 miles east of Farmington, is the center of an urban region of approximately 800,000 people. The beaches of the Long Island Sound are about 50 minutes away to the south, and the beautiful Berkshires are a short drive to the northwest. New York City and Boston can be reached within 2½ hours by car. Hartford is the home of the acclaimed Hartford Stage Company, TheatreWorks, the Hartford Symphony and Chamber orchestras, two ballet companies, an opera company, the Wadsworth Athenaeum (the oldest public art museum in the nation), the Mark Twain house, the Hartford Civic Center, and many other interesting cultural and recreational facilities. The area is also home to several branches of the University of Connecticut, Trinity College, and the University of Hartford, which includes the Hartt School of Music. Bradley International Airport (about 30 minutes from campus) serves the Hartford/Springfield area with frequent airline connections to major cities in this country and abroad. Frequent bus and rail service is also available from Hartford.

The Health Center

The 200-acre Health Center campus at Farmington houses a division of the University of Connecticut Graduate School, as well as the School of Medicine and Dental Medicine. The campus also includes the John Dempsey Hospital, associated clinics, and extensive medical research facilities, all in a centralized facility with more than 1 million square feet of floor space. The Health Center's newest research addition, the Academic Research Building, was opened in 1999. This impressive eleven-story structure provides 170,000 square feet of state-of-the-art laboratory space. The faculty at the center includes more than 260 full-time members. The institution has a strong commitment to graduate study within an environment that promotes social and intellectual interaction among the various educational programs. Graduate students are represented on various administrative committees concerned with curricular affairs, and the Graduate Student Organization (GSO) represents graduate students' needs and concerns to the faculty and administration, in addition to fostering social contact among graduate students in the Health Center.

Applying

Applications for admission should be submitted on standard forms obtained from the Graduate Admissions Office at the UConn Health Center or on the Web site. The application should be filed together with transcripts, three letters of recommendation, a personal statement, and recent results from the General Test of the Graduate Record Examinations. International students must take the Test of English as a Foreign Language (TOEFL) to satisfy Graduate School requirements. The deadline for completed applications and receipt of all supplemental materials is December 15. Earlier submission of applications is recommended, and interviews are considered highly desirable. Applicants should have had undergraduate instruction in chemistry and biology. In accordance with the laws of the state of Connecticut and of the United States, the University of Connecticut Health Center does not discriminate against any person in its educational and employment activities on the grounds of race, color, creed, national origin, sex, age, or physical disability.

Correspondence and Information

Dr. Richard Mains, Neuroscience Program Director
Lori Capozzi, Neuroscience Graduate Program Coordinator
University of Connecticut Health Center, E-4056
Farmington, Connecticut 06030-3401

Phone: 860-679-2658
Fax: 860-679-8766
E-mail: capozzi@uchc.edu
Web site: http://grad.uchc.edu
http://grad.uchc.edu/neuroscience/neuroscience_intro.html

University of Connecticut Health Center

THE FACULTY AND THEIR RESEARCH

Srdjan Antic, Assistant Professor of Neuroscience; M.D., Belgrade. Dendritic integration of synaptic inputs; dopaminergic modulation of dendritic excitability.

Rashmi Bansal, Associate Professor of Neuroscience; Ph.D., Central Drug Research Institute, 1976. Developmental, cellular, and molecular biology of oligodendrocytes; growth-factor regulation of development and function and its relationship to neurodegenerative disease, including multiple sclerosis.

Elisa Barbarese, Professor of Neuroscience and Neurology; Ph.D. McGill, 1978. Molecular and cellular biology of neural cells, with emphasis on RNA trafficking.

Leslie R. Bernstein, Associate Professor of Neuroscience; Ph.D., Illinois, 1984. Behavioral neuroscience: psychoacoustics, binaural hearing.

John H. Carson, Professor of Molecular, Microbial, and Structural Biology; Ph.D., MIT, 1972. Molecular and developmental neurobiology; myelination; intracellular RNA trafficking.

Lisa Conti, Assistant Professor of Psychiatry; Ph.D., Vermont, 1986. Behavioral neuroscience: roles of stress and neuropeptides in animal models of psychiatric disorders.

Jonathan Covault, Associate Professor of Psychiatry; M.D., Ph.D., Iowa, 1982. Genetic correlates of alcohol use disorders; role of neuroactive steroids in the effects of alcohol.

Stephen Crocker, Assistant Professor of Neuroscience; Ph.D., Ottawa. Brain injury and repair in neurodegenerative diseases, with a focus on neuroinflammation; myelin injury; neural stem cell differentiation; signal transduction; glia; matrix metalloproteinases and their tissue inhibitors.

Betty Eipper, Professor of Neuroscience; Ph.D., Harvard, 1973. Cell biology, biochemistry, and physiology of peptide synthesis, storage, and secretion in neurons and endocrine cells.

Marion E. Frank, Professor of BioStructure and Function and Director, Connecticut Chemosensory Clinical Research Center; Ph.D., Brown, 1968. Gustatory neurophysiology, neuroanatomy, behavior, and disorders; chemosensory information processing; clinical testing of oral chemosensory function in humans.

Duck O. Kim, Professor of Neuroscience and Biological Engineering Program; D.Sc., Washington (St. Louis), 1972. Neurobiology and biophysics of the auditory system; computational neuroscience of single neurons and neural systems; experimental otolaryngology; biomedical engineering.

Shigeyuki Kuwada, Professor of Neuroscience; Ph.D., Cincinnati, 1973. Neurophysiology and anatomy of mammalian auditory system; principles of binaural signal processing, electrical audiometry in infants.

Eric S. Levine, Associate Professor of Neuroscience; Ph.D., Princeton, 1992. Synapse plasticity and role of neuromodulators in brain development and learning, focusing on neurotrophins and endocannabinoids.

James Li, Professor of Genetics and Developmental Biology; Ph.D., Texas. Development of the central nervous system, with an emphasis on the cellular and molecular mechanisms underlying formation of the mammalian cerebellum.

Xue-Jun Li, Assistant Professor of Neuroscience; Ph.D., Fudan (China). Stem cell biology: mechanisms and pathways underlying the development and degeneration of human motor neurons, using human stem cells as an experimental system.

Leslie Loew, Professor of Cell Biology; Ph.D., Cornell, 1974. Morphological determinants of cell physiology; image-based computational models of cellular biology; spatial variations of cell membrane electrophysiology; new optical methods for probing living cells.

Xin-Ming Ma, Assistant Professor of Neuroscience; Ph.D., Beijing. Synaptogenesis and spine plasticity in hippocampal neurons; estrogen hormones and synaptic plasticity; stress and neuronal plasticity.

Richard Mains, Professor and Chair of Neuroscience; Ph.D., Harvard, 1973. Pituitary; neuronal tissue culture; peptides, vesicles; enzymes; drug abuse; development.

Louise McCullough, Associate Professor of Neurology and Neuroscience; M.D., Ph.D., Connecticut. Effects of estrogens on stroke.

D. Kent Morest, Professor of Neuroscience and Communication Sciences and Director of the Center for Neurological Sciences; M.D., Yale, 1960. Synaptic organization and fine structure of nervous system: plastic changes following activity changes; noise-induced hearing loss; development of synapses; tissue culture; neuronal transplantation.

Douglas L. Oliver, Professor of Neuroscience and Biomedical Engineering; Ph.D., Duke, 1977. Synaptic organization; parallel information processing in CNS; role of ionic currents, channel expression in information processing; neurocytology, morphology, cellular physiology of CNS sensory systems; biology of hearing and deafness.

Joel S. Pachter, Professor of Cell Biology; Ph.D., NYU, 1983. Mechanisms regulating pathogenesis of CNS infectious/inflammatory disease.

Patrick B. Senatus, Assistant Professor of Surgery, Orthopedic Surgery, and Neuroscience; Director of Functional and Restorative Neurosurgery; M.D., Ph.D., Harvard. Deep-brain stimulation and neuromodulation for the treatment of movement and psychological disorders.

Henry Smilowitz, Professor of Radiology, Ph.D., MIT. Development of novel therapies for experimental advanced, imminently lethal, malignant brain tumors in rats and mice; use of gold nanoparticles to develop a new form of radiation therapy (gold-enhanced radiation therapy) and novel approaches to both tumor and vascular imaging.

David M. Waitzman, Associate Professor of Neurology; M.D./Ph.D., CUNY, Mount Sinai, 1982. Neurophysiology; oculomotor system; gaze control system; modeling of CNS.

Zhaowen Wang, Assistant Professor of Neuroscience; Ph.D., Michigan State, 1993. Molecular mechanisms of synaptic transmission, focusing on neurotransmitter release and mechanisms of potassium channel localization, using *C. elegans* as a model organism.

Ji Yu, Assistant Professor of Genetics and Developmental Biology; Ph.D., Texas, 2002. Optical imaging technology; regulatory mechanisms in dendritic RNA translation; cytoskeletal dynamics.

Nada Zecevic, Assistant Professor of Neuroscience; M.D., 1970, Ph.D., 1978, Belgrade. Cellular and molecular aspects of CNS development; primate cerebral cortex; oligodendrocyte progenitors, stem cells, microglia; multiple sclerosis.

Section 14
Nutrition

This section contains a directory of institutions offering graduate work in nutrition, followed by an in-depth entry submitted by an institution that chose to prepare a detailed program description. Additional information about programs listed in the directory but not augmented by an in-depth entry may be obtained by writing directly to the dean of a graduate school or chair of a department at the address given in the directory.

For programs offering related work, see also in this book *Biochemistry, Biological and Biomedical Sciences, Botany and Plant Biology, Microbiological Sciences, Pathology and Pathobiology, Pharmacology and Toxicology,* and *Physiology.* In the other guides in this series:

Graduate Programs in the Humanities, Arts & Social Sciences
See *Economics (Agricultural Economics and Agribusiness)* and *Family and Consumer Sciences*

Graduate Programs in the Physical Sciences, Mathematics, Agricultural Sciences, the Environment & Natural Resources
See *Agricultural and Food Sciences* and *Chemistry*

Graduate Programs in Engineering & Applied Sciences
See *Agricultural Engineering and Bioengineering* and *Biomedical Engineering and Biotechnology*

Graduate Programs in Business, Education, Health, Information Studies, Law & Social Work
See *Allied Health, Public Health,* and *Veterinary Medicine and Sciences*

CONTENTS

Nutrition

American University of Beirut, Graduate Programs, Faculty of Agricultural and Food Sciences, Beirut, Lebanon. Offers agricultural economics (MS); animal sciences (MS); ecosystem management (MSES); food technology (MS); irrigation (MS); mechanization (MS); nutrition (MS); plant protection (MS); plant science (MS); poultry science (MS); soils (MS). Part-time programs available. *Faculty:* 22 full-time (6 women). *Students:* 6 full-time (3 women), 86 part-time (77 women). Average age 24. 94 applicants, 60% accepted, 15 enrolled. In 2010, 28 master's awarded. *Degree requirements:* For master's, one foreign language, comprehensive exam, thesis (for some programs). *Entrance requirements:* Additional exam requirements/recommendations for international students: Required—TOEFL (minimum score 600 paper-based; 250 computer-based; 100 iBT), IELTS (minimum score 7.5). *Application deadline:* For fall admission, 4/30 for domestic and international students; for spring admission, 11/1 for domestic and international students. Applications are processed on a rolling basis. Application fee: $50. Electronic applications accepted. *Expenses:* Tuition: Full-time $12,294; part-time $683 per credit. Required fees: $499; $499 per credit. Tuition and fees vary according to course load and program. *Financial support:* In 2010–11, 18 research assistantships with partial tuition reimbursements (averaging $13,132 per year), 42 teaching assistantships with full and partial tuition reimbursements (averaging $1,000 per year) were awarded; scholarships/grants, health care benefits, and unspecified assistantships also available. Financial award application deadline: 2/2. *Faculty research:* Community and therapeutic nutrition; food safety and food microbiology; landscape planning, nature and rural heritage conservation; pathology, immunology and control of poultry and animal diseases; agricultural economics and development. Total annual research expenditures: $900,000. *Unit head:* Prof. Nahla Hwalla, Dean, 961-134-3002 Ext. 4400, Fax: 961-174-4460, E-mail: nahla@aub.edu.lb. *Application contact:* Dr. Salim Kanaan, Director, Admissions Office, 961-135-0000 Ext. 2594, Fax: 961-175-0775, E-mail: sk00@aub.edu.lb.

Andrews University, School of Graduate Studies, College of Arts and Sciences, Department of Nutrition, Berrien Springs, MI 49104. Offers MS. Part-time programs available. *Entrance requirements:* For master's, GRE. Additional exam requirements/recommendations for international students: Required—TOEFL (minimum score 550 paper-based).

Appalachian State University, Cratis D. Williams Graduate School, Department of Nutrition and Health Care Management, Boone, NC 28608. Offers nutrition (MS). Part-time programs available. *Faculty:* 5 full-time (4 women), 1 part-time/adjunct (0 women). *Students:* 17 full-time (16 women). 16 applicants, 63% accepted, 9 enrolled. In 2010, 5 master's awarded. *Application deadline:* For fall admission, 3/1 for domestic students, 2/1 for international students; for spring admission, 11/1 for domestic students, 7/1 for international students. Applications are processed on a rolling basis. Application fee: $55. Electronic applications accepted. *Expenses:* Tuition, state resident: full-time $3428; part-time $428 per unit. Tuition, nonresident: full-time $14,518; part-time $1814 per unit. Required fees: $2320; $344 per unit. Tuition and fees vary according to campus/location. *Financial support:* In 2010–11, 5 research assistantships (averaging $8,000 per year) were awarded; career-related internships or fieldwork, scholarships/grants, and unspecified assistantships also available. Financial award application deadline: 7/1; financial award applicants required to submit FAFSA. *Faculty research:* Food antioxidants and nutrition. *Unit head:* Dr. Sarah Jordan. *Application contact:* Sandy Krause, Director of Admissions and Recruiting, 828-262-2130, Fax: 828-262-2709, E-mail: krausesl@appstate.edu.

Arizona State University, College of Nursing and Health Innovation, Phoenix, AZ 85004. Offers advanced nursing practice (DNP); child/family mental health nurse practitioner (Graduate Certificate); clinical research management (MS); community and public health practice (Graduate Certificate); community health (MS); exercise and wellness (MS), including exercise and wellness; family nurse practitioner (Graduate Certificate); healthcare innovation (MHI); international health for healthcare (Graduate Certificate); kinesiology (MS, PhD); nursing (MS, Graduate Certificate); nursing and healthcare innovation (PhD); nutrition (MS); physical activity nutrition and wellness (PhD), including physical activity, nutrition and wellness; public health (MPH); regulatory science and health safety (MS). *Accreditation:* AACN. Postbaccalaureate distance learning degree programs offered (minimal on-campus study). *Faculty:* 111 full-time (95 women), 37 part-time/adjunct (34 women). *Students:* 269 full-time (227 women), 163 part-time (148 women); includes 94 minority (22 Black or African American, non-Hispanic/Latino; 11 American Indian or Alaska Native, non-Hispanic/Latino; 20 Asian, non-Hispanic/Latino; 34 Hispanic/Latino; 7 Two or more races, non-Hispanic/Latino), 22 international. Average age 36. 410 applicants, 62% accepted, 173 enrolled. In 2010, 114 master's, 30 doctorates, 24 other advanced degrees awarded. *Degree requirements:* For master's, comprehensive exam (for some programs), thesis (for some programs), interactive Program of Study (iPOS) submitted before completing 50 percent of required credit hours; for doctorate, comprehensive exam, thesis/dissertation, interactive Program of Study (iPOS) submitted before completing 50 percent of required credit hours. *Entrance requirements:* For master's and doctorate, GRE, minimum GPA of 3.0 or equivalent in last 2 years of work leading to bachelor's degree. Additional exam requirements/recommendations for international students: Required—TOEFL, IELTS, or Pearson Test of English. *Application deadline:* For fall admission, 7/1 for domestic and international students; for spring admission, 12/1 for domestic and international students. Applications are processed on a rolling basis. Application fee: $70 ($90 for international students). Electronic applications accepted. *Expenses:* Contact institution. *Financial support:* In 2010–11, 32 research assistantships with full and partial tuition reimbursements (averaging $10,566 per year), 39 teaching assistantships with full and partial tuition reimbursements (averaging $11,266 per year) were awarded; fellowships with full tuition reimbursements, career-related internships or fieldwork, Federal Work-Study, institutionally sponsored loans, scholarships/grants, and tuition waivers (full and partial) also available. Financial award application deadline: 3/1; financial award applicants required to submit FAFSA. Total annual research expenditures: $7.7 million. *Unit head:* Dr. Bernadette Melnyk, Dean, 602-496-2200, E-mail: bernadette.melnyk@asu.edu. *Application contact:* Graduate Admissions, 480-965-6113.

Auburn University, Graduate School, College of Human Sciences, Department of Nutrition and Food Science, Auburn University, AL 36849. Offers MS, PhD. Part-time programs available. *Faculty:* 16 full-time (7 women). *Students:* 16 full-time (11 women), 13 part-time (6 women); includes 4 Black or African American, non-Hispanic/Latino, 7 international. Average age 31. 79 applicants, 37% accepted, 9 enrolled. In 2010, 10 master's, 5 doctorates awarded. *Degree requirements:* For master's, thesis (for some programs); for doctorate, thesis/dissertation. *Entrance requirements:* For master's and doctorate, GRE General Test. *Application deadline:* For fall admission, 7/7 for domestic students; for spring admission, 11/24 for domestic students. Applications are processed on a rolling basis. Application fee: $50 ($60 for international students). Electronic applications accepted. *Expenses:* Tuition, state resident: full-time $7002. Tuition, nonresident: full-time $21,898. International tuition: $22,116 full-time. Required fees: $892. Tuition and fees vary according to course load and program. *Financial support:* Research assistantships, teaching assistantships, career-related internships or fieldwork and Federal Work-Study available. Support available to part-time students. Financial award application deadline: 3/15; financial award applicants required to submit FAFSA. *Faculty research:* Food quality and safety, diet, food supply, physical activity in maintenance of health, prevention of selected chronic disease states. *Unit head:* Dr. Douglas B. White, Head, 334-844-3266. *Application contact:* Dr. George Flowers, Dean of the Graduate School, 334-844-2125.

Bastyr University, School of Nutrition and Exercise Science, Kenmore, WA 98028-4966. Offers nutrition (MS); nutrition and clinical health psychology (MS). *Accreditation:* ADtA. Part-time programs available. *Students:* 91 full-time (88 women), 26 part-time (25 women). Average age 31. In 2010, 36 master's awarded. *Degree requirements:* For master's, thesis optional. *Entrance requirements:* For master's, 1 year of course work in chemistry, biochemistry, physiology and nutrition. Additional exam requirements/recommendations for international students: Required—TOEFL (minimum score 550 paper-based; 213 computer-based; 79 iBT). *Application deadline:* For fall admission, 3/15 priority date for domestic and international students. Applications are processed on a rolling basis. Application fee: $75. *Expenses:* Tuition: Full-time $19,995;

part-time $528 per credit hour. *Financial support:* Career-related internships or fieldwork, Federal Work-Study, and scholarships/grants available. Support available to part-time students. Financial award application deadline: 4/15; financial award applicants required to submit FAFSA. *Unit head:* Debra Boutin, Chair, 425-823-1300, Fax: 425-823-6222. *Application contact:* Admissions Office, 425-602-3330, Fax: 425-602-3090, E-mail: admissions@bastyr.edu.

Baylor University, Graduate School, Military Programs, Program in Nutrition, Waco, TX 76798. Offers MS. *Students:* 22 full-time (14 women); includes 3 minority (1 Asian, non-Hispanic/Latino; 2 Hispanic/Latino). In 2010, 9 master's awarded. *Unit head:* Lt. Col. Lori Sigrist, Graduate Program Director, 210-221-6274, Fax: 210-221-7306, E-mail: lori.sigrist@us.army.mil. *Application contact:* S. Sgt. Janean Ortega, Administrative Assistant, 210-221-6274, E-mail: janean.ortega@us.army.mil.

Baylor University, Graduate School, School of Education, Department of Health, Human Performance and Recreation, Waco, TX 76798. Offers exercise, nutrition and preventive health (PhD); health, human performance and recreation (MS Ed). *Accreditation:* NCATE. Part-time programs available. *Faculty:* 13 full-time (5 women), 3 part-time/adjunct (1 woman). *Students:* 52 full-time (29 women), 34 part-time (8 women); includes 11 minority (5 Black or African American, non-Hispanic/Latino; 1 Asian, non-Hispanic/Latino; 3 Hispanic/Latino; 2 Two or more races, non-Hispanic/Latino), 3 international. 30 applicants, 87% accepted. In 2010, 48 master's, 4 doctorates awarded. *Degree requirements:* For master's, thesis optional. *Entrance requirements:* For master's, GRE General Test. *Application deadline:* For fall admission, 4/1 priority date for domestic students; for spring admission, 10/1 for domestic students. Applications are processed on a rolling basis. Application fee: $25. Electronic applications accepted. *Financial support:* In 2010–11, 35 students received support, including 22 teaching assistantships; career-related internships or fieldwork, Federal Work-Study, institutionally sponsored loans, tuition waivers (partial), and recreation supplements also available. *Faculty research:* Behavior change theory, pedagogy, nutrition and enzyme therapy, exercise testing, health planning. *Unit head:* Dr. Glenn Miller, Graduate Program Director, 254-710-4001, Fax: 254-710-3527, E-mail: glenn_miller@baylor.edu. *Application contact:* Eva Berger-Rhodes, Administrative Assistant, 254-710-4945, Fax: 254-710-3870, E-mail: eva_rhodes@baylor.edu.

Benedictine University, Graduate Programs, Program in Nutrition and Wellness, Lisle, IL 60532-0900. Offers MS. *Students:* 17 full-time (all women), 17 part-time (all women). 48 applicants, 77% accepted, 11 enrolled. In 2010, 20 master's awarded. *Entrance requirements:* Additional exam requirements/recommendations for international students: Required—TOEFL (minimum score 550 paper-based; 213 computer-based). *Application deadline:* For fall admission, 9/1 for domestic students; for winter admission, 12/1 for domestic students; for spring admission, 2/15 for domestic students. Applications are processed on a rolling basis. Application fee: $40. Electronic applications accepted. *Financial support:* Career-related internships or fieldwork and health care benefits available. Support available to part-time students. *Faculty research:* Community and corporate wellness risk assessment, health behavior change, self-efficacy, evaluation of health program impact and effectiveness. Total annual research expenditures: $8,335. *Unit head:* Catherine Arnold, Director, 630-829-6534, E-mail: carnold@ben.edu. *Application contact:* Kari Gibbons, Director, Admissions, 630-829-6200, Fax: 630-829-6584, E-mail: kgibbons@ben.edu.

Benedictine University, Graduate Programs, Program in Public Health, Lisle, IL 60532-0900. Offers administration of health care institutions (MPH); dietetics (MPH); disaster management (MPH); health education (MPH); health information systems (MPH); MBA/MPH; MPH/MS. Part-time and evening/weekend programs available. Postbaccalaureate distance learning degree programs offered. *Faculty:* 2 full-time (0 women), 8 part-time/adjunct (3 women). *Students:* 105 full-time (80 women), 401 part-time (313 women); includes 192 minority (121 Black or African American, non-Hispanic/Latino; 1 American Indian or Alaska Native, non-Hispanic/Latino; 48 Asian, non-Hispanic/Latino; 21 Hispanic/Latino; 1 Native Hawaiian or other Pacific Islander, non-Hispanic/Latino), 10 international. Average age 33. 293 applicants, 89% accepted, 145 enrolled. In 2010, 106 master's awarded. *Entrance requirements:* For master's, MAT, GRE, or GMAT. Additional exam requirements/recommendations for international students: Required—TOEFL (minimum score 550 paper-based; 213 computer-based). *Application deadline:* For fall admission, 9/1 for domestic students; for winter admission, 12/1 for domestic students; for spring admission, 2/15 for domestic students. Application fee: $40. *Financial support:* Career-related internships or fieldwork and health care benefits available. Support available to part-time students. *Unit head:* Dr. Alan Gorr, Director, 630-829-6566, Fax: 630-960-1126, E-mail: agorr@ben.edu. *Application contact:* Kari Gibbons, Director, Admissions, 630-829-6200, Fax: 630-829-6584, E-mail: kgibbons@ben.edu.

Boston University, College of Health and Rehabilitation Sciences: Sargent College, Department of Health Sciences, Program in Nutrition, Boston, MA 02215. Offers MS. *Faculty:* 10 full-time (9 women), 5 part-time/adjunct (3 women). *Students:* 50 full-time (49 women), 5 part-time (all women); includes 1 Asian, non-Hispanic/Latino; 3 Hispanic/Latino, 3 international. Average age 25. 131 applicants, 23% accepted, 23 enrolled. In 2010, 23 master's awarded. *Entrance requirements:* For master's, GRE General Test, minimum GPA of 3.0. Additional exam requirements/recommendations for international students: Required—TOEFL (minimum score 550 paper-based; 84 iBT). *Application deadline:* For fall admission, 2/15 priority date for domestic students; for spring admission, 10/1 for domestic students. Applications are processed on a rolling basis. Application fee: $70. Electronic applications accepted. *Expenses:* Tuition: Full-time $39,314; part-time $1228 per credit. Required fees: $40 per semester. *Financial support:* In 2010–11, 39 students received support, including 20 fellowships (averaging $14,250 per year); career-related internships or fieldwork, Federal Work-Study, institutionally sponsored loans, scholarships/grants, and tuition waivers (partial) also available. Support available to part-time students. Financial award application deadline: 4/15; financial award applicants required to submit FAFSA. *Faculty research:* Metabolism, health promotion, obesity, epidemiology. *Unit head:* Dr. Kathleen Morgan, Chair, 617-353-2717, E-mail: kmorgan@bu.edu. *Application contact:* Sharon Sankey, Director, Student Services, 617-353-2713, Fax: 617-353-7500, E-mail: ssankey@bu.edu.

Bowling Green State University, Graduate College, College of Education and Human Development, School of Family and Consumer Sciences, Bowling Green, OH 43403. Offers food and nutrition (MFCS); human development and family studies (MFCS). Part-time programs available. *Degree requirements:* For master's, thesis. *Entrance requirements:* For master's, GRE General Test, minimum GPA of 3.0. Additional exam requirements/recommendations for international students: Required—TOEFL. Electronic applications accepted. *Faculty research:* Public health, wellness, social issues and policies, ethnic foods, nutrition and aging.

Brigham Young University, Graduate Studies, College of Life Sciences, Department of Nutrition, Dietetics and Food Science, Provo, UT 84602-1001. Offers food science (MS); nutrition (MS). *Faculty:* 13 full-time (5 women). *Students:* 14 full-time (9 women), 2 part-time (both women); includes 1 Black or African American, non-Hispanic/Latino; 1 Asian, non-Hispanic/Latino. Average age 24. 5 applicants, 60% accepted, 1 enrolled. In 2010, 6 master's awarded. *Degree requirements:* For master's, comprehensive exam, thesis. *Entrance requirements:* For master's, GRE General Test. Additional exam requirements/recommendations for international students: Required—TOEFL (minimum score 550 paper-based; 213 computer-based). *Application deadline:* For fall admission, 2/1 for domestic students, 2/1 priority date for international students; for winter admission, 6/30 for domestic students, 6/30 priority date for international students. Application fee: $50. Electronic applications accepted. *Expenses:* Tuition: Full-time $5580; part-time $310 per credit hour. Tuition and fees vary according to program and student's religious affiliation. *Financial support:* In 2010–11, 9 students received support, including 4 research assistantships (averaging $20,325 per year), 3 teaching assistantships (averaging $20,325 per year); career-related internships or fieldwork, institutionally sponsored loans, and scholarships/grants also available. Financial award application deadline: 4/1. *Faculty*

Nutrition

research: Dairy foods, lipid oxidation, food processes, magnesium and selenium nutrition, nutrient effect on gene expression. Total annual research expenditures: $312,604. *Unit head:* Dr. Michael L. Dunn, Chair, 801-422-6670, Fax: 801-422-0258, E-mail: michael_dunn@byu.edu. *Application contact:* Dr. Susan Fullmer, Graduate Coordinator, 801-422-3349, Fax: 801-422-0258, E-mail: susan_fullmer@byu.edu.

Brooklyn College of the City University of New York, Division of Graduate Studies, Department of Health and Nutrition Science, Program in Nutrition, Brooklyn, NY 11210-2889. Offers MS. Part-time programs available. *Students:* 6 full-time (all women), 61 part-time (55 women); includes 20 minority (10 Black or African American, non-Hispanic/Latino; 8 Asian, non-Hispanic/Latino; 2 Hispanic/Latino), 8 international. Average age 34. 31 applicants, 52% accepted, 7 enrolled. In 2010, 18 master's awarded. *Degree requirements:* For master's, thesis or alternative. *Entrance requirements:* For master's, 18 credits in health-related areas, 2 letters of recommendation, essay. Additional exam requirements/recommendations for international students: Required—TOEFL. *Application deadline:* For fall admission, 3/1 priority date for domestic students, 2/1 priority date for international students; for spring admission, 11/1 priority date for domestic students, 10/1 priority date for international students. Applications are processed on a rolling basis. Application fee: $125. Electronic applications accepted. *Expenses:* Tuition, state resident: full-time $7360; part-time $310 per credit hour. Tuition, nonresident: full-time $13,800; part-time $575 per credit hour. Required fees: $190 per semester. *Financial support:* Federal Work-Study, institutionally sponsored loans, and scholarships/grants available. Support available to part-time students. Financial award application deadline: 5/1; financial award applicants required to submit FAFSA. *Faculty research:* Medical ethics, AIDS, history of public health, diet restriction, palliative care, risk reduction/disease prevention, metabolism, diabetes. *Unit head:* Dr. Kathleen Axen, Graduate Deputy Chairperson, 718-951-5909, Fax: 718-951-4670, E-mail: kaxen@brooklyn.cuny.edu. *Application contact:* Hernan Sierra, Graduate Admissions Coordinator, 718-951-4536, Fax: 718-951-4506, E-mail: grads@brooklyn.cuny.edu.

California State University, Chico, Graduate School, College of Natural Sciences, Department of Biological Sciences, Program in Nutritional Sciences, Chico, CA 95929-0722. Offers nutrition education (MS). Part-time programs available. *Students:* 15 full-time (all women), 3 part-time (all women); includes 1 Black or African American, non-Hispanic/Latino; 2 Asian, non-Hispanic/Latino; 4 Hispanic/Latino, 3 international. Average age 28. 50 applicants, 44% accepted, 10 enrolled. In 2010, 6 master's awarded. *Degree requirements:* For master's, thesis, seminar presentation. *Entrance requirements:* For master's, GRE General Test, 2 letters of recommendation. Additional exam requirements/recommendations for international students: Required—TOEFL (minimum score 550 paper-based; 213 computer-based; 80 iBT), IELTS (minimum score 6.5). *Application deadline:* For fall admission, 3/1 priority date for domestic students, 3/1 for international students; for spring admission, 9/15 priority date for domestic students, 9/15 for international students. Applications are processed on a rolling basis. Application fee: $55. Electronic applications accepted. *Financial support:* Teaching assistantships available. *Unit head:* Dr. Kathryn Silliman, Graduate Coordinator, 530-898-6805. *Application contact:* Larry Hanne, Graduate Coordinator, 530-898-5356.

California State University, Long Beach, Graduate Studies, College of Health and Human Services, Department of Family and Consumer Sciences, Master of Science in Nutritional Science Program, Long Beach, CA 90840. Offers food science (MS); hospitality foodservice and hotel management (MS); nutritional science (MS). Part-time programs available. *Students:* 30 full-time (all women), 19 part-time (18 women); includes 1 Black or African American, non-Hispanic/Latino; 7 Asian, non-Hispanic/Latino; 4 Hispanic/Latino. Average age 26. 119 applicants, 39% accepted, 23 enrolled. In 2010, 11 master's awarded. *Degree requirements:* For master's, thesis, oral presentation of thesis or directed project. *Entrance requirements:* For master's, GRE, minimum GPA of 2.5 in last 60 units. *Application deadline:* For fall admission, 5/1 for domestic students. Applications are processed on a rolling basis. Application fee: $55. Electronic applications accepted. *Financial support:* Federal Work-Study, institutionally sponsored loans, and scholarships/grants available. Financial award application deadline: 3/2. *Faculty*

research: Protein and water-soluble vitamins, sensory evaluation of foods, mineral deficiencies in humans, child nutrition, minerals and blood pressure. *Unit head:* Dr. M. Sue Stanley, Chair, 562-985-4484, Fax: 562-985-4414, E-mail: stanleym@csulb.edu. *Application contact:* Dr. Mary Jacob, Graduate Coordinator, 562-985-4484, Fax: 562-985-4414, E-mail: marjacob@csulb.edu.

California State University, Long Beach, Graduate Studies, College of Health and Human Services, Department of Kinesiology, Long Beach, CA 90840. Offers adapted physical education (MA); coaching and student athlete development (MA); exercise physiology and nutrition (MS); exercise science (MS); individualized studies (MA); kinesiology (MA); pedagogical studies (MA); sport and exercise psychology (MS); sport management (MA); sports medicine and injury studies (MS). Part-time programs available. *Faculty:* 11 full-time (4 women), 5 part-time/adjunct (all women). *Students:* 38 full-time (18 women), 23 part-time (14 women); includes 5 Black or African American, non-Hispanic/Latino; 1 American Indian or Alaska Native, non-Hispanic/Latino; 9 Asian, non-Hispanic/Latino; 7 Hispanic/Latino, 9 international. Average age 27. 209 applicants, 45% accepted, 30 enrolled. In 2010, 89 master's awarded. *Degree requirements:* For master's, oral and written comprehensive exams or thesis. *Entrance requirements:* For master's, GRE General Test, minimum GPA of 2.75 during previous 2 years of course work. *Application deadline:* For fall admission, 6/1 for domestic students. Applications are processed on a rolling basis. Application fee: $55. Electronic applications accepted. *Financial support:* Federal Work-Study, institutionally sponsored loans, and scholarships/grants available. Financial award application deadline: 3/2. *Faculty research:* Pulmonary functioning, feedback and practice structure, strength training, history and politics of sports, special population research issues. *Unit head:* Dr. Sharon R. Guthrie, Chair, 562-985-7487, Fax: 562-985-8067, E-mail: guthrie@csulb.edu. *Application contact:* Dr. Grant Hill, Graduate Advisor, 562-985-8856, Fax: 562-985-8067, E-mail: ghill@csulb.edu.

California State University, Los Angeles, Graduate Studies, College of Health and Human Services, Department of Kinesiology and Nutritional Sciences, Los Angeles, CA 90032-8530. Offers nutritional science (MS); physical education and kinesiology (MA, MS). *Accreditation:* ADtA. Part-time and evening/weekend programs available. *Faculty:* 2 full-time (1 woman), 2 part-time/adjunct (1 woman). *Students:* 4 full-time (1 woman), 13 part-time (9 women); includes 9 minority (1 Black or African American, non-Hispanic/Latino; 2 Asian, non-Hispanic/Latino; 5 Hispanic/Latino; 1 Two or more races, non-Hispanic/Latino), 5 international. Average age 30. 28 applicants, 100% accepted, 6 enrolled. In 2010, 4 master's awarded. *Degree requirements:* For master's, comprehensive exam, project or thesis. *Entrance requirements:* For master's, minimum GPA of 2.75. Additional exam requirements/recommendations for international students: Required—TOEFL (minimum score 500 paper-based; 173 computer-based). *Application deadline:* For fall admission, 5/1 for domestic and international students. Applications are processed on a rolling basis. Application fee: $55. *Financial support:* Federal Work-Study available. Support available to part-time students. Financial award application deadline: 3/1. *Unit head:* Dr. Nazareth Khodiguian, Chair, 323-343-4650, Fax: 323-343-6482, E-mail: nkhodig@calstatela.edu. *Application contact:* Dr. Alan Muchlinski, Dean of Graduate Studies, 323-343-3820, Fax: 323-343-5653, E-mail: amuchli@exchange.calstatela.edu.

Case Western Reserve University, School of Medicine and School of Graduate Studies, Graduate Programs in Medicine, Department of Nutrition, Cleveland, OH 44106. Offers dietetics (MS); nutrition (MS, PhD), including molecular nutrition (PhD), nutrition and biochemistry (PhD); public health nutrition (MS). Part-time programs available. Terminal master's awarded for partial completion of doctoral program. *Degree requirements:* For master's, thesis (for some programs); for doctorate, thesis/dissertation. *Entrance requirements:* For master's, GRE General Test; for doctorate, GRE General Test, GRE Subject Test. Additional exam requirements/recommendations for international students: Required—TOEFL. *Faculty research:* Fatty acid metabolism, application of gene therapy to nutritional problems, dietary intake methodology, nutrition and physical fitness, metabolism during infancy and pregnancy.

See Display below and Close-Up on page 399.

Nutrition

Central Michigan University, Central Michigan University Off-Campus Programs, Program in Health Administration, Mount Pleasant, MI 48859. Offers health administration (DHA); international health (Certificate); nutrition and dietetics (MS). Part-time and evening/weekend programs available. Postbaccalaureate distance learning degree programs offered (minimal on-campus study). Electronic applications accepted. *Expenses:* Tuition, state resident: full-time $8208; part-time $456 per credit hour. Tuition, nonresident: full-time $13,788; part-time $766 per credit hour. One-time fee: $25. *Financial support:* Scholarships/grants available. Support available to part-time students. Financial award applicants required to submit FAFSA. *Unit head:* Steven D. Berkshire, Director, 989-774-1640, E-mail: berks1sd@cmich.edu. *Application contact:* Off-Campus Programs Call Center, 877-268-4636, E-mail: cmuoffcampus@cmich.edu.

Central Michigan University, College of Graduate Studies, College of Education and Human Services, Department of Human Environmental Studies, Mount Pleasant, MI 48859. Offers apparel product development and merchandising technology (MS); gerontology (Graduate Certificate); human development and family studies (MA); nutrition and dietetics (MS). Part-time and evening/weekend programs available. *Faculty:* 15 full-time (11 women), 1 (woman) part-time/adjunct. *Students:* 6 full-time (4 women), 24 part-time (22 women); includes 2 Black or African American, non-Hispanic/Latino, 4 international. *Degree requirements:* For master's, thesis or alternative. *Application deadline:* Applications are processed on a rolling basis. Application fee: $35 ($45 for international students). Electronic applications accepted. *Expenses:* Tuition, state resident: full-time $8208; part-time $456 per credit hour. Tuition, nonresident: full-time $13,788; part-time $766 per credit hour. One-time fee: $25. *Financial support:* Fellowships with tuition reimbursements, research assistantships, career-related internships or fieldwork, Federal Work-Study, unspecified assistantships, and out-of-state merit awards, non-resident graduate awards available. *Faculty research:* Human growth and development, family studies and human sexuality, human nutrition and dietetics, apparel and textile retailing, computer-aided design for apparel. *Unit head:* Dr. Megan P. Goodwin, Chairperson, 989-774-3218, Fax: 989-774-2435, E-mail: goodw1mp@cmich.edu. *Application contact:* Dr. Candace Maylee, Assistant Coordinator of Graduate Programs, 989-774-2613, Fax: 989-774-2435, E-mail: mayle1ce@cmich.edu.

Central Washington University, Graduate Studies and Research, College of Education and Professional Studies, Department of Nutrition, Exercise and Health Services, Ellensburg, WA 98926. Offers exercise science (MS); nutrition (MS). Part-time programs available. *Degree requirements:* For master's, thesis or alternative. *Entrance requirements:* For master's, GRE (nutrition), minimum GPA of 3.0. Additional exam requirements/recommendations for international students: Required—TOEFL (minimum score 550 paper-based; 213 computer-based; 79 iBT). Electronic applications accepted.

Chapman University, Graduate Studies, Schmid College of Science, Food Science Program, Orange, CA 92866. Offers MS, MBA/MS. Part-time and evening/weekend programs available. *Faculty:* 3 full-time (2 women), 4 part-time/adjunct (3 women). *Students:* 9 full-time (7 women), 34 part-time (27 women); includes 15 minority (1 Black or African American, non-Hispanic/Latino; 12 Asian, non-Hispanic/Latino; 2 Hispanic/Latino), 13 international. Average age 27. 45 applicants, 69% accepted, 19 enrolled. In 2010, 14 master's awarded. *Degree requirements:* For master's, comprehensive exam, thesis optional. *Entrance requirements:* For master's, GRE or GMAT, minimum undergraduate GPA of 3.0. Additional exam requirements/recommendations for international students: Required—TOEFL (minimum score 550 paper-based; 213 computer-based; 80 iBT). *Application deadline:* For fall admission, 5/2 priority date for domestic students; for spring admission, 11/1 priority date for domestic students. Application fee: $60. Electronic applications accepted. *Financial support:* Fellowships, Federal Work-Study and scholarships/grants available. Financial award applicants required to submit FAFSA. *Unit head:* Dr. Anuradha Prakash, Program Director, 714-744-7895, E-mail: prakash@chapman.edu. *Application contact:* Gianne Diosomito, Graduate Admission Counselor, 714-997-6711, E-mail: diosomit@chapman.edu.

Clemson University, Graduate School, College of Agriculture, Forestry and Life Sciences, Department of Food, Nutrition and Packaging Sciences, Program in Food, Nutrition, and Culinary Science, Clemson, SC 29634. Offers MS. *Students:* 27 full-time (18 women), 5 part-time (2 women); includes 2 Hispanic/Latino, 14 international. Average age 29. 54 applicants, 28% accepted, 12 enrolled. In 2010, 8 master's awarded. *Degree requirements:* For master's, thesis. *Entrance requirements:* For master's, GRE General Test. Additional exam requirements/recommendations for international students: Required—TOEFL, IELTS. *Application deadline:* For fall admission, 6/1 for domestic students, 4/15 for international students; for spring admission, 9/15 for international students. Applications are processed on a rolling basis. Application fee: $70 ($80 for international students). Electronic applications accepted. *Expenses:* Contact institution. *Financial support:* In 2010–11, 18 students received support, including 11 research assistantships with partial tuition reimbursements available (averaging $9,871 per year), 13 teaching assistantships with partial tuition reimbursements available (averaging $6,692 per year); fellowships with full and partial tuition reimbursements available, career-related internships or fieldwork, institutionally sponsored loans, scholarships/grants, health care benefits, and unspecified assistantships also available. Support available to part-time students. Financial award applicants required to submit FAFSA. *Unit head:* Dr. Anthony L. Pometto, Chair, 864-656-4382, Fax: 864-656-3131, E-mail: pometto@clemson.edu. *Application contact:* Dr. Paul Dawson, Coordinator, 864-656-1138, Fax: 864-656-3131, E-mail: pdawson@clemson.edu.

College of Saint Elizabeth, Department of Foods and Nutrition, Morristown, NJ 07960-6989. Offers dietetic internship (Certificate); nutrition (MS). Part-time and evening/weekend programs available. *Faculty:* 2 full-time (both women), 2 part-time/adjunct (both women). *Students:* 8 full-time (all women), 17 part-time (16 women); includes 2 Black or African American, non-Hispanic/Latino; 2 Asian, non-Hispanic/Latino, 1 international. Average age 31. 38 applicants, 84% accepted, 24 enrolled. In 2010, 10 master's, 18 other advanced degrees awarded. *Entrance requirements:* Additional exam requirements/recommendations for international students: Required—TOEFL (minimum score 550 paper-based). *Application deadline:* Applications are processed on a rolling basis. Application fee: $35. Electronic applications accepted. *Expenses:* Tuition: Part-time $857 per credit. Required fees: $70 per credit. *Financial support:* Tuition waivers (partial) and unspecified assistantships available. Support available to part-time students. Financial award application deadline: 3/15; financial award applicants required to submit FAFSA. *Faculty research:* Medical nutrition intervention, public policy, obesity, hunger and food security, osteoporosis, nutrition and exercise. *Unit head:* Dr. Jean C. Burge, Director of the Graduate Program in Nutrition, 973-290-4127, Fax: 973-290-4167, E-mail: nutrition@cse.edu. *Application contact:* Donna Tatarka, Dean of Admission, 973-290-4705, Fax: 973-290-4710, E-mail: dtatarka@cse.edu.

Colorado State University, Graduate School, College of Applied Human Sciences, Department of Food Science and Human Nutrition, Fort Collins, CO 80523-1571. Offers MS, PhD. *Accreditation:* ADtA. Part-time programs available. *Faculty:* 16 full-time (7 women), 2 part-time/adjunct (1 woman). *Students:* 54 full-time (45 women), 33 part-time (22 women); includes 7 minority (3 Asian, non-Hispanic/Latino; 3 Hispanic/Latino; 1 Two or more races, non-Hispanic/Latino), 5 international. Average age 29. 142 applicants, 39% accepted, 24 enrolled. In 2010, 30 master's, 2 doctorates awarded. *Degree requirements:* For master's, thesis; for doctorate, thesis/dissertation. *Entrance requirements:* For master's and doctorate, GRE General Test, minimum GPA of 3.0, resume, 3 letters of recommendation. Additional exam requirements/recommendations for international students: Required—TOEFL (minimum score 550 paper-based; 213 computer-based; 80 iBT). *Application deadline:* For fall admission, 2/15 priority date for domestic and international students; for spring admission, 7/15 priority date for domestic and international students. Application fee: $50. Electronic applications accepted. *Expenses:* Tuition, state resident: full-time $7434; part-time $413 per credit. Tuition, nonresident: full-time $19,022; part-time $1057 per credit. Required fees: $1729; $88 per credit. *Financial support:* In 2010–11, 18 students received support, including 9 research assistantships with full and partial tuition reimbursements available (averaging $9,201 per year), 9 teaching assistantships with full and partial tuition reimbursements available (averaging $7,533 per year); fellowships, Federal Work-Study, scholarships/grants, and unspecified assistantships also available. Financial award application deadline: 3/1; financial award applicants required to submit FAFSA. *Faculty research:* Metabolic regulation, nutrition education, food safety, obesity and diabetes, metabolism. Total annual research expenditures: $5 million. *Unit head:* Dr. Christopher Melby, Head, 970-491-6736, Fax: 970-491-7252, E-mail: christopher.melby@colostate.edu. *Application contact:* Paula Coleman, Graduate Coordinator, 970-491-3819, Fax: 970-491-3875, E-mail: pcoleman@cahs.colostate.edu.

Colorado State University, Graduate School, College of Applied Human Sciences, Department of Health and Exercise Science, Fort Collins, CO 80523-1582. Offers exercise science and nutrition (MS); health and exercise science (MS); human bioenergetics (PhD). Part-time programs available. *Faculty:* 15 full-time (3 women). *Students:* 35 full-time (17 women), 4 part-time (2 women); includes 1 minority (Hispanic/Latino), 2 international. Average age 29. 35 applicants, 43% accepted, 11 enrolled. In 2010, 11 master's awarded. *Degree requirements:* For master's, thesis; for doctorate, comprehensive exam, thesis/dissertation, mentored teaching. *Entrance requirements:* For master's, GRE General Test, minimum GPA of 3.0; for doctorate, bachelor's or master's degree. Additional exam requirements/recommendations for international students: Required—TOEFL (minimum score 550 paper-based; 213 computer-based; 80 iBT). *Application deadline:* For fall admission, 1/31 priority date for domestic and international students; for spring admission, 9/30 priority date for domestic and international students. Application fee: $50. Electronic applications accepted. *Expenses:* Tuition, state resident: full-time $7434; part-time $413 per credit. Tuition, nonresident: full-time $19,022; part-time $1057 per credit. Required fees: $1729; $88 per credit. *Financial support:* In 2010–11, 35 students received support, including 17 research assistantships with full tuition reimbursements available (averaging $14,219 per year), 18 teaching assistantships with full tuition reimbursements available (averaging $13,670 per year); fellowships, unspecified assistantships also available. Financial award application deadline: 1/31; financial award applicants required to submit FAFSA. *Faculty research:* Metabolism and metabolic disease, obesity, diabetes, hypertension, physical activity and health across the lifespan, bioenergetics. Total annual research expenditures: $1.1 million. *Unit head:* Dr. Richard Gay Israel, Head, 970-491-3785, Fax: 970-491-0216, E-mail: richard.israel@colostate.edu. *Application contact:* Robin Noehl, Department Operations, 970-491-7161, Fax: 970-491-0445, E-mail: robin.noehl@colostate.edu.

Columbia University, College of Physicians and Surgeons, Institute of Human Nutrition, MS Program in Nutrition, New York, NY 10032. Offers MS, MPH/MS. Part-time and evening/weekend programs available. *Degree requirements:* For master's, thesis. *Entrance requirements:* For master's, GRE General Test, TOEFL, MCAT. Additional exam requirements/recommendations for international students: Required—TOEFL.

Columbia University, College of Physicians and Surgeons, Institute of Human Nutrition and Graduate School of Arts and Sciences at the College of Physicians and Surgeons, PhD Program in Nutrition, New York, NY 10032. Offers PhD. *Degree requirements:* For doctorate, thesis/dissertation. *Entrance requirements:* For doctorate, GRE General Test. Additional exam requirements/recommendations for international students: Required—TOEFL. *Faculty research:* Growth and development, nutrition and metabolism.

Cornell University, Graduate School, Graduate Fields of Agriculture and Life Sciences and Graduate Fields of Human Ecology, Field of Nutrition, Ithaca, NY 14853-0001. Offers animal nutrition (MPS, MS, PhD); community nutrition (MPS, MS, PhD); human nutrition (MPS, MS, PhD); international nutrition (MPS, MS, PhD); nutritional biochemistry (MPS, MS, PhD). *Faculty:* 44 full-time (21 women). *Students:* 72 full-time (61 women); includes 1 Black or African American, non-Hispanic/Latino; 2 Asian, non-Hispanic/Latino; 3 Hispanic/Latino, 17 international. Average age 27. 111 applicants, 31% accepted, 30 enrolled. In 2010, 6 doctorates awarded. *Degree requirements:* For master's, thesis (MS), project papers (MPS); for doctorate, comprehensive exam, thesis/dissertation. *Entrance requirements:* For master's and doctorate, GRE General Test, previous course work in organic chemistry (with laboratory) and biochemistry; 2 letters of recommendation. Additional exam requirements/recommendations for international students: Required—TOEFL (minimum score 550 paper-based; 213 computer-based; 77 iBT). *Application deadline:* For fall admission, 1/10 priority date for domestic students; for spring admission, 10/1 for domestic students. Application fee: $70. Electronic applications accepted. *Expenses:* Tuition: Full-time $29,500. Required fees: $76. Tuition and fees vary according to degree level and program. *Financial support:* In 2010–11, 25 fellowships with full tuition reimbursements, 9 research assistantships with full tuition reimbursements, 23 teaching assistantships with full tuition reimbursements were awarded; institutionally sponsored loans, scholarships/grants, health care benefits, tuition waivers (full and partial), and unspecified assistantships also available. Financial award applicants required to submit FAFSA. *Faculty research:* Nutritional biochemistry, experimental human and animal nutrition, international nutrition, community nutrition. *Unit head:* Director of Graduate Studies, 607-255-2528, Fax: 607-255-0178. *Application contact:* Graduate Field Assistant, 607-255-2628, Fax: 607-225-0178, E-mail: nutrition_gfr@cornell.edu.

Cornell University, Graduate School, Graduate Fields of Arts and Sciences, Field of International Development, Ithaca, NY 14853-0001. Offers development policy (MPS); international nutrition (MPS); international planning (MPS); international population (MPS); science and technology policy (MPS). *Faculty:* 41 full-time (14 women). *Students:* 7 full-time (3 women), 5 international. Average age 28. 36 applicants, 22% accepted, 4 enrolled. In 2010, 7 master's awarded. *Degree requirements:* For master's, project paper. *Entrance requirements:* For master's, GRE General Test (recommended), 2 academic recommendations, 2 years of development experience. Additional exam requirements/recommendations for international students: Required—TOEFL (minimum score 77 iBT). *Application deadline:* Applications are processed on a rolling basis. Application fee: $80. Electronic applications accepted. *Expenses:* Tuition: Full-time $29,500. Required fees: $76. Tuition and fees vary according to degree level and program. *Financial support:* In 2010–11, 1 fellowship with full tuition reimbursement was awarded; research assistantships with full tuition reimbursements, teaching assistantships with full tuition reimbursements, institutionally sponsored loans, scholarships/grants, health care benefits, tuition waivers (full and partial), and unspecified assistantships also available. Financial award applicants required to submit FAFSA. *Faculty research:* Development policy, international nutrition, international planning, science and technology policy, international population. *Unit head:* Director of Graduate Studies, 607-255-3037, Fax: 607-255-1005. *Application contact:* Graduate Field Assistant, 607-255-0831, Fax: 607-255-1005, E-mail: mpsid@cornell.edu.

Drexel University, College of Arts and Sciences, Department of Biology, Program in Human Nutrition, Philadelphia, PA 19104-2875. Offers MS. *Accreditation:* ADtA. Part-time programs available. Terminal master's awarded for partial completion of doctoral program. *Degree requirements:* For master's, thesis. *Entrance requirements:* For master's, GRE General Test. Additional exam requirements/recommendations for international students: Required—TOEFL. Electronic applications accepted. *Faculty research:* Metabolism of lipids, W-3 fatty acids, obesity, diabetes and heart disease, mineral metabolism.

D'Youville College, Department of Dietetics, Buffalo, NY 14201-1084. Offers MS. Five-year program begins at freshman entry. *Accreditation:* ADtA. *Faculty:* 2 full-time (1 woman), 3 part-time/adjunct (all women). *Students:* 64 full-time (60 women), 9 part-time (all women); includes 4 minority (1 Black or African American, non-Hispanic/Latino; 1 American Indian or Alaska Native, non-Hispanic/Latino; 1 Asian, non-Hispanic/Latino; 1 Two or more races, non-Hispanic/Latino), 4 international. Average age 24. 106 applicants, 61% accepted, 18 enrolled. In 2010, 10 master's awarded. *Degree requirements:* For master's, thesis. *Entrance requirements:* Additional exam requirements/recommendations for international students: Required—TOEFL (minimum score 500 paper-based; 173 computer-based). *Application deadline:* For fall admission, 5/1 priority date for international students; for spring admission, 9/1 priority date for international students. Applications are processed on a rolling basis. Application fee: $25. Electronic applications accepted. *Expenses:* Tuition: Part-time $790 per credit hour. Part-time tuition and fees vary according to degree level. *Faculty research:*

Nutrition education, clinical nutrition, herbal supplements, obesity. *Unit head:* Dr. Charlotte Baumgart, Chair, 716-829-7752, Fax: 716-829-8137. *Application contact:* Dr. Steven Smith, Director of Admissions, 716-829-7600, Fax: 716-829-7900, E-mail: admiss@dyc.edu.

East Carolina University, Graduate School, College of Human Ecology, Department of Nutrition and Hospitality Management, Greenville, NC 27858-4353. Offers nutrition (MS). Part-time programs available. *Degree requirements:* For master's, comprehensive exam, thesis optional. *Entrance requirements:* For master's, GRE. Additional exam requirements/recommendations for international students: Required—TOEFL. *Expenses:* Tuition, state resident: full-time $3130; part-time $391.25 per credit hour. Tuition, nonresident: full-time $13,817; part-time $1727.13 per credit hour. Required fees: $1916; $239.50 per credit hour. Tuition and fees vary according to campus/location and program. *Faculty research:* Lifecycle nutrition, nutrition and disease, nutrition for fish species, food service management.

Eastern Illinois University, Graduate School, Lumpkin College of Business and Applied Sciences, School of Family and Consumer Sciences, Charleston, IL 61920-3099. Offers dietetics (MS); family and consumer sciences (MS). Part-time programs available. *Degree requirements:* For master's, comprehensive exam.

Eastern Kentucky University, The Graduate School, College of Health Sciences, Department of Family and Consumer Sciences, Richmond, KY 40475-3102. Offers community nutrition (MS). Part-time programs available. *Entrance requirements:* For master's, GRE General Test, minimum GPA of 2.5.

Eastern Michigan University, Graduate School, College of Health and Human Services, School of Health Sciences, Programs in Dietetics and Nutrition, Ypsilanti, MI 48197. Offers human nutrition (MS); human nutrition-coordinated track in dietetics (MS). *Accreditation:* ADtA. Part-time and evening/weekend programs available. Postbaccalaureate distance learning degree programs offered (minimal on-campus study). *Students:* 14 full-time (all women), 50 part-time (48 women); includes 10 minority (5 Black or African American, non-Hispanic/Latino; 2 Asian, non-Hispanic/Latino; 3 Hispanic/Latino). Average age 34. In 2010, 28 master's awarded. *Entrance requirements:* Additional exam requirements/recommendations for international students: Required—TOEFL. *Application deadline:* Applications are processed on a rolling basis. Application fee: $35. *Financial support:* Fellowships, research assistantships with full tuition reimbursements, teaching assistantships with full tuition reimbursements, career-related internships or fieldwork, Federal Work-Study, institutionally sponsored loans, scholarships/grants, tuition waivers (partial), and unspecified assistantships available. Support available to part-time students. Financial award applicants required to submit FAFSA. *Unit head:* Lydia Kret, Interim Program Director, 734-487-7862, Fax: 734-487-4095, E-mail: lydia.kret@emich.edu. *Application contact:* Lydia Kret, Interim Program Director, 734-487-7862, Fax: 734-487-4095, E-mail: lydia.kret@emich.edu.

East Tennessee State University, School of Graduate Studies, College of Clinical and Rehabilitative Health Sciences, Department of Family and Consumer Sciences, Johnson City, TN 37614. Offers clinical nutrition (MS). *Faculty:* 6 full-time (all women). *Students:* 22 applicants, 41% accepted, 9 enrolled. In 2010, 15 master's awarded. *Degree requirements:* For master's, comprehensive exam, thesis optional, internship/practicum (for non-thesis option). *Entrance requirements:* For master's, GRE General Test, ADA-approved undergraduate didactic program in dietetics, minimum GPA of 3.0. Additional exam requirements/recommendations for international students: Required—TOEFL (minimum score 550 paper-based; 213 computer-based; 79 iBT). *Application deadline:* For fall admission, 2/15 for domestic and international students. Application fee: $25 ($35 for international students). Electronic applications accepted. *Financial support:* In 2010–11, 4 research assistantships with full tuition reimbursements (averaging $5,500 per year), 2 teaching assistantships with full tuition reimbursements (averaging $5,500 per year) were awarded; career-related internships or fieldwork, institutionally sponsored loans, scholarships/grants, and unspecified assistantships also available. Financial award application deadline: 7/1; financial award applicants required to submit FAFSA. *Faculty research:* Kindergarten students, measures of percent body fat during pregnancy, writing to read in preschool children, computer research in food systems management, students' knowledge of aging. Total annual research expenditures: $26,794. *Unit head:* Dr. Elizabeth Lowe, Program Director, 423-439-7537, Fax: 423-439-4030, E-mail: lowee@etsu.edu. *Application contact:* Dr. Elizabeth Lowe, Program Director, 423-439-7537, Fax: 423-439-4030, E-mail: lowee@etsu.edu.

Emory University, Laney Graduate School, Division of Biological and Biomedical Sciences, Program in Nutrition and Health Sciences, Atlanta, GA 30322-1100. Offers PhD. *Faculty:* 49 full-time (23 women). *Students:* 31 full-time (27 women); includes 1 Black or African American, non-Hispanic/Latino; 1 Asian, non-Hispanic/Latino; 1 Hispanic/Latino, 5 international. Average age 27. 57 applicants, 18% accepted, 4 enrolled. In 2010, 3 doctorates awarded. *Degree requirements:* For doctorate, comprehensive exam, thesis/dissertation. *Entrance requirements:* For doctorate, GRE General Test, minimum GPA of 3.0 in science course work (recommended). Additional exam requirements/recommendations for international students: Required—TOEFL. *Application deadline:* For fall admission, 12/1 for domestic and international students. Application fee: $75. Electronic applications accepted. *Expenses:* Tuition: Full-time $33,800. Required fees: $1300. *Financial support:* In 2010–11, 12 students received support, including 12 fellowships with full tuition reimbursements available (averaging $25,000 per year); institutionally sponsored loans, scholarships/grants, health care benefits, and tuition waivers (full) also available. *Faculty research:* Biochemistry, molecular and cell biology, clinical nutrition, community and preventive health, nutritional epidemiology. *Unit head:* Dr. Usha Ramakrishnan, Director, 404-727-1092, Fax: 404-727-1278, E-mail: uramakr@sph.emory.edu. *Application contact:* Kathy Smith, Director of Recruitment and Admissions, 404-727-2547, Fax: 404-727-3322, E-mail: kathy.smith@emory.edu.

Emory University, Rollins School of Public Health, Hubert Department of Global Health, Atlanta, GA 30322-1100. Offers global demography (MSPH); global environmental health (MPH); public nutrition (MSPH). *Accreditation:* CEPH. Part-time programs available. *Degree requirements:* For master's, thesis, practicum. *Entrance requirements:* For master's, GRE General Test. Additional exam requirements/recommendations for international students: Required—TOEFL (minimum score 550 paper-based; 213 computer-based; 80 iBT). Electronic applications accepted. *Expenses:* Tuition: Full-time $33,800. Required fees: $1300.

Florida International University, Stempel College of Public Health and Social Work, Department of Dietetics and Nutrition, Miami, FL 33199. Offers MS, PhD. Part-time programs available. *Faculty:* 12 full-time (11 women), 4 part-time/adjunct (3 women). *Students:* 85 full-time (73 women), 52 part-time (44 women); includes 7 Black or African American, non-Hispanic/Latino; 7 Asian, non-Hispanic/Latino; 52 Hispanic/Latino, 21 international. Average age 29. 205 applicants, 36% accepted, 58 enrolled. In 2010, 27 master's, 2 doctorates awarded. *Degree requirements:* For master's, thesis; for doctorate, comprehensive exam, thesis/dissertation. *Entrance requirements:* For master's, minimum GPA of 3.0; for doctorate, GRE General Test, minimum GPA of 3.0, resume, letters of recommendation, faculty sponsor. Additional exam requirements/recommendations for international students: Required—TOEFL (minimum score 550 paper-based; 80 iBT). *Application deadline:* For fall admission, 6/1 for domestic students, 4/1 for international students; for spring admission, 10/1 for domestic students, 9/1 for international students. Applications are processed on a rolling basis. Application fee: $30. Electronic applications accepted. *Financial support:* Career-related internships or fieldwork, Federal Work-Study, institutionally sponsored loans, and scholarships/grants available. Financial award application deadline: 3/1; financial award applicants required to submit FAFSA. *Faculty research:* Clinical nutrition, cultural food habits, pediatric nutrition, diabetes, dietetic education. *Unit head:* Dr. Fatma Huffman, Chair, 305-348-3788, Fax: 305-348-1996, E-mail: fatma.ercanli-huffman@fiu.edu. *Application contact:* Nanett Rojas, Assistant Director of Graduate Admissions, 305-348-7442, Fax: 305-348-7441, E-mail: gradadm@fiu.edu.

Florida State University, The Graduate School, College of Human Sciences, Department of Nutrition, Food, and Exercise Sciences, Tallahassee, FL 32306-1493. Offers exercise science (MS, PhD), including exercise physiology, sports sciences (MS); nutrition and food sciences (MS, PhD), including clinical nutrition (MS), food science, human nutrition (PhD), nutrition and sport (MS), nutrition science (MS), nutrition, education and health promotion (MS). Part-time programs available. *Faculty:* 19 full-time (11 women). *Students:* 135 full-time (87 women), 34 part-time (26 women); includes 18 minority (7 Black or African American, non-Hispanic/Latino; 4 Asian, non-Hispanic/Latino; 6 Hispanic/Latino; 1 Two or more races, non-Hispanic/Latino), 28 international. 155 applicants, 37% accepted, 34 enrolled. In 2010, 30 master's, 7 doctorates awarded. *Degree requirements:* For master's, comprehensive exam (for some programs), thesis optional; for doctorate, thesis/dissertation. *Entrance requirements:* For master's, GRE General Test, minimum upper-division GPA of 3.0; for doctorate, GRE General Test, minimum upper-division GPA of 3.0, MS. Additional exam requirements/recommendations for international students: Required—TOEFL (minimum score 550 paper-based; 80 iBT). *Application deadline:* For fall admission, 7/1 for domestic students, 3/1 for international students; for spring admission, 11/1 for domestic students, 5/1 for international students. Applications are processed on a rolling basis. Application fee: $30. Electronic applications accepted. *Expenses:* Tuition, state resident: full-time $8238. *Financial support:* In 2010–11, 62 students received support, including 1 fellowship with partial tuition reimbursement available (averaging $10,000 per year), 13 research assistantships with partial tuition reimbursements available (averaging $8,000 per year), 42 teaching assistantships with partial tuition reimbursements available (averaging $8,000 per year); career-related internships or fieldwork, Federal Work-Study, institutionally sponsored loans, scholarships/grants, and unspecified assistantships also available. Financial award application deadline: 1/15; financial award applicants required to submit FAFSA. *Faculty research:* Body composition, functional food, chronic disease and aging response; food safety, food allergy, and safety/quality detection methods; sports nutrition, energy and human performance; strength training, functional performance, cardiovascular physiology, sarcopenia. *Unit head:* Dr. Bahram H. Arjmandi, Professor/Chair, 850-645-1517, Fax: 850-645-5000, E-mail: barjmandi@fsu.edu. *Application contact:* Joseph J. Carroll, Administrative Support Assistant, 850-644-4800, Fax: 850-645-5000, E-mail: jjcarroll@admin.fsu.edu.

Framingham State University, Division of Graduate and Continuing Education, Programs in Food and Nutrition, Coordinated Program in Dietetics, Framingham, MA 01701-9101. Offers MS.

Framingham State University, Division of Graduate and Continuing Education, Programs in Food and Nutrition, Food Science and Nutrition Science Program, Framingham, MA 01701-9101. Offers MS. Part-time and evening/weekend programs available. *Entrance requirements:* For master's, GRE General Test.

Framingham State University, Division of Graduate and Continuing Education, Programs in Food and Nutrition, Program in Human Nutrition: Education and Media Technologies, Framingham, MA 01701-9101. Offers MS.

George Mason University, College of Health and Human Services, Department of Global and Community Health, Fairfax, VA 22030. Offers biostatistics (Certificate); epidemiology (Certificate); epidemiology and biostatistics (MS); gerontology (Certificate); global health (MS, Certificate); nutrition (Certificate); public health (MPH, Certificate); rehabilitation science (Certificate). *Faculty:* 15 full-time (10 women), 21 part-time/adjunct (17 women). *Students:* 99 full-time (80 women), 158 part-time (126 women); includes 110 minority (66 Black or African American, non-Hispanic/Latino; 1 American Indian or Alaska Native, non-Hispanic/Latino; 30 Asian, non-Hispanic/Latino; 11 Hispanic/Latino; 2 Two or more races, non-Hispanic/Latino), 23 international. Average age 32. 202 applicants, 41% accepted, 41 enrolled. In 2010, 29 master's, 11 other advanced degrees awarded. *Degree requirements:* For master's, comprehensive exam (for some programs), thesis or practicum. *Entrance requirements:* For master's, GRE, BA with minimum GPA of 3.0, 2 letters of recommendation. Additional exam requirements/recommendations for international students: Required—TOEFL (minimum score 570 paper-based; 230 computer-based; 88 iBT). *Application deadline:* For fall admission, 4/1 priority date for domestic students, 4/1 for international students; for spring admission, 11/1 for domestic and international students. Applications are processed on a rolling basis. Application fee: $100. Electronic applications accepted. *Expenses:* Tuition, state resident: full-time $8192; part-time $440 per credit hour. Tuition, nonresident: full-time $22,952; part-time $1055 per credit hour. Required fees: $2364; $99 per credit hour. *Financial support:* In 2010–11, 15 students received support, including 13 research assistantships with full and partial tuition reimbursements available (averaging $13,006 per year), 3 teaching assistantships with full and partial tuition reimbursements available (averaging $15,000 per year); career-related internships or fieldwork, Federal Work-Study, scholarships/grants, health care benefits, unspecified assistantships, and research awards also available. Financial award application deadline: 3/1; financial award applicants required to submit FAFSA. *Faculty research:* Providing introductory and advanced degrees in health-related disciplines centered in global and community issues, health issues and the needs of affected populations at the regional and global level. Total annual research expenditures: $13,285. *Unit head:* Dr. Shirley S. Travis, Dean, 703-993-1918. *Application contact:* Allan Weiss, Office Manager, 703-993-3126, E-mail: aweiss2@gmu.edu.

Georgia State University, College of Health and Human Sciences, School of Health Professions, Division of Nutrition, Atlanta, GA 30302-3083. Offers MS. *Accreditation:* ADtA. Part-time and evening/weekend programs available. *Degree requirements:* For master's, thesis optional. *Entrance requirements:* For master's, GRE or MAT. Additional exam requirements/recommendations for international students: Required—TOEFL (minimum score 550 paper-based; 213 computer-based). Electronic applications accepted. *Faculty research:* Food safety, sports nutrition, obesity, food fortification, nutrition interventions.

Harvard University, Harvard School of Public Health, Department of Nutrition, Boston, MA 02115-6096. Offers nutrition (DPH, PhD, SD); nutritional epidemiology (DPH, SD); public health nutrition (DPH, SD). *Faculty:* 21 full-time (4 women), 7 part-time/adjunct (2 women). *Students:* 30 full-time, 1 part-time; includes 5 minority (1 Black or African American, non-Hispanic/Latino; 1 American Indian or Alaska Native, non-Hispanic/Latino; 1 Asian, non-Hispanic/Latino; 1 Hispanic/Latino; 1 Two or more races, non-Hispanic/Latino), 14 international. Average age 31. 39 applicants, 28% accepted, 8 enrolled. In 2010, 9 doctorates awarded. *Degree requirements:* For doctorate, thesis/dissertation, qualifying exam. *Entrance requirements:* For doctorate, GRE. Additional exam requirements/recommendations for international students: Required—TOEFL (minimum score 595 paper-based; 240 computer-based; 95 iBT); Recommended—IELTS (minimum score 7). *Application deadline:* For fall admission, 12/15 for domestic and international students. Application fee: $115. Electronic applications accepted. *Expenses:* Tuition: Full-time $34,976. Required fees: $1166. Full-time tuition and fees vary according to program. *Financial support:* Fellowships, research assistantships, teaching assistantships, Federal Work-Study, scholarships/grants, traineeships, tuition waivers (partial), and unspecified assistantships available. Support available to part-time students. Financial award application deadline: 2/8; financial award applicants required to submit FAFSA. *Faculty research:* Dietary and genetic factors affecting heart diseases in humans; interactions among nutrition, immunity, and infection; role of diet and lifestyle in preventing macrovascular complications in diabetics. *Unit head:* Dr. Walter Willett, Chair, 617-432-1333, Fax: 617-432-2435, E-mail: walter.willett@channing.harvard.edu. *Application contact:* Vincent W. James, Director of Admissions, 617-432-1031, Fax: 617-432-7080, E-mail: admissions@hsph.harvard.edu.

Howard University, Graduate School, Department of Nutritional Sciences, Washington, DC 20059-0002. Offers nutrition (MS, PhD). Part-time and evening/weekend programs available. *Degree requirements:* For master's, comprehensive exam, thesis; for doctorate, comprehensive exam, thesis/dissertation. *Entrance requirements:* For master's and doctorate, minimum GPA of 3.0, general chemistry, organic chemistry, biochemistry, nutrition. Additional exam requirements/recommendations for international students: Required—TOEFL (minimum score 213 computer-based). Electronic applications accepted. *Faculty research:* Dietary fiber, phytate, trace minerals, cardio-vascular diseases, overweight/obesity.

Nutrition

Hunter College of the City University of New York, Graduate School, Schools of the Health Professions, School of Health Sciences, Programs in Urban Public Health, Program in Nutrition and Public Health, New York, NY 10021-5085. Offers MPH. *Accreditation:* ADtA. Part-time and evening/weekend programs available. *Faculty:* 26 full-time (17 women), 21 part-time/adjunct (16 women). *Students:* 19 full-time (17 women), 5 part-time (4 women); includes 2 Black or African American, non-Hispanic/Latino; 4 Asian, non-Hispanic/Latino, 1 international. Average age 30. 29 applicants, 86% accepted, 14 enrolled. *Degree requirements:* For master's, comprehensive exam, thesis optional, internship. *Entrance requirements:* For master's, GRE General Test, previous course work in calculus and statistics. Additional exam requirements/recommendations for international students: Required—TOEFL. *Application deadline:* For fall admission, 4/1 for domestic students; for spring admission, 11/1 for domestic students. Application fee: $125. *Financial support:* In 2010–11, 6 fellowships were awarded; career-related internships or fieldwork, Federal Work-Study, institutionally sponsored loans, and tuition waivers (partial) also available. Support available to part-time students. *Unit head:* Arlene Spark, Coordinator, 212-481-7950, Fax: 212-481-5260, E-mail: aspark@hunter.cuny.edu. *Application contact:* Milena Solo, Assistant Director for Graduate Admissions, 212-772-4288, Fax: 212-650-3336, E-mail: milena.solo@hunter.cuny.edu.

Huntington College of Health Sciences, Program in Nutrition, Knoxville, TN 37919-7736. Offers MS. Part-time and evening/weekend programs available. Postbaccalaureate distance learning degree programs offered (no on-campus study). *Entrance requirements:* For master's, high school diploma/bachelor's degree.

Idaho State University, Office of Graduate Studies, Kasiska College of Health Professions, Department of Health and Nutrition Sciences, Pocatello, ID 83209-8109. Offers dietetics (Certificate); health education (MHE); public health (MPH). Part-time programs available. *Degree requirements:* For master's, comprehensive exam, internship, thesis or project. *Entrance requirements:* For master's, GRE General Test or GPA greater than 3.5, minimum GPA of 3.0 for upper division classes, 2 letters of recommendation. Additional exam requirements/recommendations for international students: Required—TOEFL (minimum score 600 paper-based; 213 computer-based). Electronic applications accepted. *Faculty research:* Epidemiology, environmental health, nutrition and aging, dietetics.

Immaculata University, College of Graduate Studies, Program in Nutrition Education, Immaculata, PA 19345. Offers nutrition education (MA); nutrition education/approved pre-professional practice program (MA). Part-time and evening/weekend programs available. *Students:* 17 full-time (all women), 47 part-time (44 women). Average age 34. 17 applicants, 71% accepted, 12 enrolled. In 2010, 9 master's awarded. *Degree requirements:* For master's, comprehensive exam, thesis optional. *Entrance requirements:* For master's, GRE or MAT, minimum GPA of 3.0. Additional exam requirements/recommendations for international students: Required—TOEFL. *Application deadline:* Applications are processed on a rolling basis. Application fee: $50. Electronic applications accepted. *Financial support:* Application deadline: 5/1. *Faculty research:* Sports nutrition, pediatric nutrition, changes in food consumption patterns in weight loss, nutritional counseling. *Unit head:* Dr. Laura Frank, Chair, 610-647-4400 Ext. 3482, E-mail: lfrank@immaculata.edu. *Application contact:* 610-647-4400 Ext. 3211, Fax: 610-993-8550, E-mail: graduate@immaculata.edu.

Indiana State University, College of Graduate and Professional Studies, College of Arts and Sciences, Department of Family and Consumer Sciences, Terre Haute, IN 47809. Offers dietetics (MS); family and consumer sciences education (MS); inter-area option (MS). *Accreditation:* ADtA. Part-time programs available. *Degree requirements:* For master's, thesis optional. Electronic applications accepted.

Indiana University Bloomington, School of Health, Physical Education and Recreation, Department of Applied Health Science, Bloomington, IN 47405-7000. Offers health behavior (PhD); health promotion (MS); human development/family studies (MS); nutrition science (MS); public health (MPH); safety management (MS); school and college health programs (MS). *Accreditation:* CEPH (one or more programs are accredited). *Faculty:* 24 full-time (12 women). *Students:* 143 full-time (105 women), 32 part-time (20 women); includes 36 Black or African American, non-Hispanic/Latino; 2 American Indian or Alaska Native, non-Hispanic/Latino; 2 Asian, non-Hispanic/Latino; 7 Hispanic/Latino; 1 Two or more races, non-Hispanic/Latino, 28 international. Average age 30. 135 applicants, 80% accepted, 73 enrolled. In 2010, 49 master's, 7 doctorates awarded. *Degree requirements:* For master's, thesis optional; for doctorate, thesis/dissertation. *Entrance requirements:* For master's, GRE (MS in nutrition science), 3 recommendations; for doctorate, GRE, 3 recommendations. Additional exam requirements/recommendations for international students: Required—TOEFL (minimum score 550 paper-based; 213 computer-based; 79 iBT). *Application deadline:* For fall admission, 4/30 priority date for domestic students, 12/1 priority date for international students; for spring admission, 11/15 priority date for domestic students, 9/1 priority date for international students. Application fee: $55 ($65 for international students). *Financial support:* Fellowships, research assistantships with full and partial tuition reimbursements, teaching assistantships with full and partial tuition reimbursements, career-related internships or fieldwork, Federal Work-Study, institutionally sponsored loans, scholarships/grants, tuition waivers (partial), and fee remissions available. Financial award application deadline: 3/1. *Faculty research:* Cancer education, HIV/AIDS and drug education, public health, parent-child interactions, safety education. Total annual research expenditures: $2.8 million. *Unit head:* Dr. Mohammad R. Torabi, Chair, 812-855-4808, Fax: 812-855-3936, E-mail: torabi@indiana.edu. *Application contact:* Dr. Mohammad R. Torabi, Chair, 812-855-4808, Fax: 812-855-3936, E-mail: torabi@indiana.edu.

Indiana University of Pennsylvania, School of Graduate Studies and Research, College of Health and Human Services, Department of Food and Nutrition, Program in Food and Nutrition, Indiana, PA 15705-1087. Offers MS. Part-time programs available. *Faculty:* 6 full-time (all women). *Students:* 9 full-time (all women), 15 part-time (13 women); includes 2 minority (1 American Indian or Alaska Native, non-Hispanic/Latino; 1 Asian, non-Hispanic/Latino), 3 international. Average age 24. 47 applicants, 32% accepted, 12 enrolled. In 2010, 10 master's awarded. *Degree requirements:* For master's, thesis optional. *Entrance requirements:* For master's, GRE General Test, 2 letters of recommendation. Additional exam requirements/recommendations for international students: Required—TOEFL. *Application deadline:* For fall admission, 7/1 priority date for domestic students; for spring admission, 11/1 for domestic students. Applications are processed on a rolling basis. Application fee: $40. *Financial support:* In 2010–11, 5 research assistantships with full and partial tuition reimbursements (averaging $3,904 per year) were awarded. Financial award applicants required to submit FAFSA. *Unit head:* Dr. Stephanie Taylor-Davis, Graduate Coordinator, 724-357-7733, E-mail: stdavis@iup.edu. *Application contact:* Dr. Stephanie Taylor-Davis, Graduate Coordinator, 724-357-7733, E-mail: stdavis@iup.edu.

Indiana University–Purdue University Indianapolis, School of Health and Rehabilitation Sciences, Indianapolis, IN 46202-2896. Offers health sciences education (MS); nutrition and dietetics (MS); occupational therapy (MS); physical therapy (DPT). Part-time and evening/weekend programs available. *Faculty:* 8 full-time (5 women). *Students:* 196 full-time (156 women), 8 part-time (7 women); includes 11 minority (4 Asian, non-Hispanic/Latino; 5 Hispanic/Latino; 2 Two or more races, non-Hispanic/Latino), 1 international. Average age 26. 233 applicants, 29% accepted, 61 enrolled. In 2010, 36 master's awarded. *Degree requirements:* For master's, thesis (for some programs). *Entrance requirements:* For master's, GRE General Test, minimum GPA of 3.0. Additional exam requirements/recommendations for international students: Required—TOEFL. *Application deadline:* For fall admission, 1/15 priority date for domestic students; for spring admission, 10/15 for domestic students. Application fee: $55 ($65 for international students). *Financial support:* In 2010–11, 10 fellowships (averaging $2,485 per year), 1 teaching assistantship (averaging $3,600 per year) were awarded; research assistantships, Federal Work-Study, institutionally sponsored loans and scholarships/grants also available. Support available to part-time students. Financial award applicants required to submit FAFSA. *Unit head:* Dr. Augustine Agho, Dean, 317-274-4704, E-mail: aagho@iupui.edu. *Application contact:* Dr. Augustine Agho, Dean, 317-274-4704, E-mail: aagho@iupui.edu.

Instituto Tecnologico de Santo Domingo, Graduate School, Area of Health Sciences, Santo Domingo, Dominican Republic. Offers bioethics (M Bioethics); clinical bioethics (Certificate); clinical nutrition (Certificate); comprehensive health and the adolescent (Certificate); comrehensive adloescent health (MS); health and social security (M Mgmt).

Iowa State University of Science and Technology, Graduate College, College of Human Sciences and College of Agriculture, Department of Food Science and Human Nutrition, Ames, IA 50011. Offers food science and technology (MS, PhD); nutrition (MS, PhD). *Faculty:* 49 full-time (27 women), 3 part-time/adjunct (2 women). *Students:* 39 full-time (25 women), 11 part-time (10 women); includes 4 Black or African American, non-Hispanic/Latino; 2 Asian, non-Hispanic/Latino; 1 Hispanic/Latino, 21 international. 58 applicants, 16% accepted, 6 enrolled. In 2010, 9 master's, 4 doctorates awarded. *Degree requirements:* For master's, thesis; for doctorate, thesis/dissertation. *Entrance requirements:* For master's and doctorate, GRE General Test. Additional exam requirements/recommendations for international students: Required—TOEFL (minimum score 550 paper-based; 79 iBT), IELTS (minimum score 6.5). *Application deadline:* For fall admission, 1/15 priority date for domestic and international students. Applications are processed on a rolling basis. Application fee: $40 ($90 for international students). Electronic applications accepted. *Financial support:* In 2010–11, 47 research assistantships with full and partial tuition reimbursements (averaging $15,342 per year), 1 teaching assistantship with full and partial tuition reimbursement (averaging $9,111 per year) were awarded; fellowships, scholarships/grants also available. *Unit head:* Dr. Ruth S. MacDonald, Chair, 515-294-5991, Fax: 515-294-8181, E-mail: ruthmacd@iastate.edu. *Application contact:* Dr. Patricia Murphy, Director of Graduate Education, 515-294-6442, E-mail: gradsecretary@iastate.edu.

Iowa State University of Science and Technology, Graduate College, Interdisciplinary Programs, Program in Nutritional Sciences, Ames, IA 50011. Offers MS, PhD. *Students:* 28 full-time (19 women), 7 part-time (3 women); includes 1 Black or African American, non-Hispanic/Latino; 1 Asian, non-Hispanic/Latino, 11 international. In 2010, 9 master's, 2 doctorates awarded. *Degree requirements:* For master's, thesis; for doctorate, thesis/dissertation. *Entrance requirements:* For master's and doctorate, GRE General Test. Additional exam requirements/recommendations for international students: Required—TOEFL (minimum score 550 paper-based; 79 iBT), IELTS (minimum score 6.5). *Application deadline:* For fall admission, 1/15 priority date for domestic and international students. Applications are processed on a rolling basis. Application fee: $40 ($90 for international students). Electronic applications accepted. *Financial support:* In 2010–11, 27 research assistantships with full and partial tuition reimbursements (averaging $15,410 per year), 1 teaching assistantship with full and partial tuition reimbursement (averaging $9,111 per year) were awarded. *Unit head:* Dr. Kevin Schalinske, Chair, Supervising Committee, 515-294-8442, E-mail: gradsecretary@iastate.edu. *Application contact:* Dr. Wendy White, Professor, 515-294-6442, E-mail: gradsecretary@iastate.edu.

The Johns Hopkins University, Bloomberg School of Public Health, Department of International Health, Baltimore, MD 21205. Offers global disease epidemiology and control (MHS, PhD); health systems (MHS, PhD); human nutrition (MHS, PhD); international health (Dr PH); social and behavioral interventions (MHS, PhD). *Faculty:* 137 full-time (82 women), 185 part-time/adjunct (63 women). *Students:* 290 full-time (228 women); includes 9 Black or African American, non-Hispanic/Latino; 83 Asian, non-Hispanic/Latino; 8 Hispanic/Latino, 87 international. Average age 28. 494 applicants, 48% accepted, 100 enrolled. In 2010, 66 master's, 15 doctorates awarded. *Degree requirements:* For master's, comprehensive exam, thesis (for some programs), 1 year full-time residency, 4-9 month internship; for doctorate, comprehensive exam, thesis/dissertation or alternative, 1.5 years full-time residency, oral and written exams. *Entrance requirements:* For master's, GRE General Test or MCAT, 3 letters of recommendation, resume; for doctorate, GRE General Test or MCAT, 3 letters of recommendation, resume, transcripts. Additional exam requirements/recommendations for international students: Required—TOEFL (minimum score 600 paper-based; 250 computer-based; 100 iBT). Recommended—IELTS (minimum score 7). *Application deadline:* For fall admission, 1/2 priority date for domestic and international students. Applications are processed on a rolling basis. Application fee: $45. Electronic applications accepted. *Financial support:* In 2010–11, 188 students received support, including 15 fellowships (averaging $50,000 per year); Federal Work-Study, institutionally sponsored loans, scholarships/grants, traineeships, and stipends also available. Financial award application deadline: 1/2. *Faculty research:* Nutrition, infectious diseases, health systems, health economics, humanitarian emergencies. Total annual research expenditures: $72 million. *Unit head:* Dr. Robert E. Black, Chairman, 410-955-3934, Fax: 410-955-7159, E-mail: rblack@jhsph.edu. *Application contact:* Cristina G. Salazar, Academic Program Manager, 410-955-3734, Fax: 410-955-7159, E-mail: csalazar@jhsph.edu.

Kansas State University, Graduate School, College of Human Ecology, Department of Human Nutrition, Manhattan, KS 66506. Offers MS, PhD. Part-time programs available. *Degree requirements:* For master's, thesis or alternative, residency; for doctorate, thesis/dissertation, residency. *Entrance requirements:* For master's, GRE General Test, minimum undergraduate GPA of 3.0; for doctorate, GRE General Test, minimum graduate GPA of 3.5, course work in biochemistry and statistics. Additional exam requirements/recommendations for international students: Required—TOEFL (minimum score 600 paper-based; 250 computer-based). Electronic applications accepted. *Faculty research:* Sensory analysis and consumer behavior, nutrition education and communication, human metabolism and performance, molecular and biochemical nutrition, public health nutrition.

Kent State University, Graduate School of Education, Health, and Human Services, School of Health Sciences, Program in Nutrition, Kent, OH 44242-0001. Offers dietetic (MS). *Faculty:* 6 full-time (all women), 1 (woman) part-time/adjunct. *Students:* 35 full-time (33 women), 9 part-time (all women). 41 applicants, 78% accepted. In 2010, 18 master's awarded. Application fee: $30 ($60 for international students). *Expenses:* Tuition, state resident: full-time $7866; part-time $437 per credit hour. Tuition, nonresident: full-time $14,022; part-time $779 per credit hour. *Financial support:* In 2010–11, 2 research assistantships (averaging $8,313 per year) were awarded; Federal Work-Study and 1 administrative assistantship (averaging $8,313 per year) also available. *Unit head:* Karen Gordon, Coordinator, 330-672-2248, E-mail: klowry@kent.edu. *Application contact:* Nancy Miller, Academic Program Coordinator, Office of Graduate Student Services, 330-672-2576, Fax: 330-672-9162.

Lehman College of the City University of New York, Division of Natural and Social Sciences, Department of Health Sciences, Program in Nutrition, Bronx, NY 10468-1589. Offers clinical nutrition (MS); community nutrition (MS); dietetic internship (MS). *Degree requirements:* For master's, thesis or alternative.

Lipscomb University, Program in Exercise and Nutrition Science, Nashville, TN 37204-3951. Offers MS. *Faculty:* 6 full-time (5 women), 4 part-time/adjunct (2 women). *Students:* 18 full-time (13 women), 22 part-time (18 women); includes 4 Black or African American, non-Hispanic/Latino; 1 Asian, non-Hispanic/Latino, 1 international. Average age 26. 33 applicants, 67% accepted, 11 enrolled. In 2010, 3 master's awarded. *Entrance requirements:* For master's, GRE (minimum score of 800), BS in exercise science or nutrition; official transcripts; minimum GPA of 2.75 on all undergraduate work; 2 letters of recommendation; resume. *Application deadline:* For fall admission, 6/1 for domestic students; for spring admission, 12/1 for domestic students. *Expenses:* Tuition: Full-time $18,149; part-time $943 per hour. Tuition and fees vary according to program. *Unit head:* Dr. Autumn Marshall, Chair, Department of Family and Consumer Sciences, 615-966-6106, E-mail: autumn.marshall@lipscomb.edu. *Application contact:* Dr. Autumn Marshall, Chair, Department of Family and Consumer Sciences, 615-966-6106, E-mail: autumn.marshall@lipscomb.edu.

Logan University–College of Chiropractic, University Programs, Chesterfield, MO 63006-1065. Offers nutrition and human performance (MS); sports science and rehabilitation (MS). *Faculty:* 12 full-time (7 women), 10 part-time/adjunct (4 women). *Students:* 15 full-time (7 women), 188 part-time (53 women); includes 7 Black or African American, non-Hispanic/Latino; 1 American Indian or Alaska Native, non-Hispanic/Latino; 7 Asian, non-Hispanic/Latino; 1 Hispanic/Latino, 2 international. Average age 26. 45 applicants, 98% accepted, 34 enrolled.

In 2010, 51 master's awarded. *Degree requirements:* For master's, comprehensive exam. *Entrance requirements:* For master's, GRE or National Board of Chiropractic Examiners test, minimum GPA of 2.5. Additional exam requirements/recommendations for international students: Required—TOEFL (minimum score 79 iBT). *Application deadline:* For fall admission, 7/15 priority date for domestic and international students; for winter admission, 11/15 priority date for domestic and international students; for spring admission, 3/15 priority date for domestic students, 3/15 for international students. Application fee: $50. *Expenses:* Contact institution. *Financial support:* Federal Work-Study available. Support available to part-time students. Financial award applicants required to submit FAFSA. *Faculty research:* Effects of exercise on physical conditioning in primary school children, low back pain in college football lineman, effects on lower extremity strength on knee injuries, short arc banding and low back pain, interventions to improve core stability. *Unit head:* Dr. Elizabeth A. Goodman, Dean, 636-227-2100, Fax: 636-207-2431, E-mail: elizabeth.goodman@logan.edu. *Application contact:* Steve Held, Director of Admissions, 636-227-2100 Ext. 1754, Fax: 636-207-2425, E-mail: loganadm@logan.edu.

Loma Linda University, School of Public Health, Department of Nutrition, Loma Linda, CA 92350. Offers public health nutrition (MPH, Dr PH). *Accreditation:* ADtA. *Degree requirements:* For doctorate, thesis/dissertation. *Entrance requirements:* For doctorate, GRE General Test. Additional exam requirements/recommendations for international students: Required—Michigan English Language Assessment Battery or TOEFL. *Faculty research:* Sports nutrition in minorities, dietary determinance of chronic disease, protein adequacy in vegetarian diets, relationship of dietary intake to hormone level.

Long Island University, C.W. Post Campus, School of Health Professions and Nursing, Department of Nutrition, Brookville, NY 11548-1300. Offers dietetic internship (Certificate); nutrition (MS). Part-time and evening/weekend programs available. *Degree requirements:* For master's, thesis. *Entrance requirements:* For master's, minimum GPA of 2.75 in major. Electronic applications accepted. *Faculty research:* Hematopoiesis, interleukins in allergy, growth factors effect in metastasis affecting behavioral change for nutrition.

Louisiana Tech University, Graduate School, College of Applied and Natural Sciences, School for Human Ecology, Ruston, LA 71272. Offers dietetics (MS); human ecology (MS). Part-time programs available. *Degree requirements:* For master's, thesis or alternative, Registered Dietician Exam eligibility. *Entrance requirements:* For master's, GRE General Test.

Loyola University Chicago, Graduate School, Marcella Niehoff School of Nursing, Dietetics Program, Chicago, IL 60660. Offers MS, Certificate. *Students:* 10 full-time (9 women), 13 part-time (12 women); includes 1 minority (Hispanic/Latino). Average age 27. 11 applicants, 100% accepted, 11 enrolled. In 2010, 4 master's, 1 other advanced degree awarded. *Expenses:* Tuition: Full-time $14,940; part-time $830 per credit hour. Required fees: $87 per semester. Part-time tuition and fees vary according to course load and program. *Unit head:* Dr. Joanna Kouba, Director, 708-216-4132, E-mail: jkouba@luc.edu. *Application contact:* Amy Weatherford, Enrollment Advisor, School of Nursing, 773-508-3249, Fax: 773-508-3241, E-mail: aweatherford@luc.edu.

Marshall University, Academic Affairs Division, College of Health Professions, Department of Dietetics, Huntington, WV 25755. Offers MS. *Faculty:* 2 full-time (both women). *Students:* 13 full-time (11 women), 2 part-time (both women), 1 international. Average age 25. In 2010, 13 master's awarded. *Unit head:* Dr. Kelli Williams, Chairperson, 304-696-4336, E-mail: williamsk@marshall.edu. *Application contact:* Information Contact, 304-746-1900, Fax: 304-746-1902, E-mail: services@marshall.edu.

Marywood University, Academic Affairs, College of Health and Human Services, Department of Nutrition and Dietetics, Program in Dietetic Internship, Scranton, PA 18509-1598. Offers Certificate. *Entrance requirements:* Additional exam requirements/recommendations for international students: Required—TOEFL (minimum score 550 paper-based; 213 computer-based; 79 iBT). Electronic applications accepted. *Expenses:* Tuition: Part-time $735 per credit. Required fees: $470 per semester. Tuition and fees vary according to degree level and campus/location.

Marywood University, Academic Affairs, College of Health and Human Services, Department of Nutrition and Dietetics, Program in Nutrition, Scranton, PA 18509-1598. Offers MS. *Entrance requirements:* Additional exam requirements/recommendations for international students: Required—TOEFL (minimum score 550 paper-based; 213 computer-based; 79 iBT). Electronic applications accepted. *Expenses:* Tuition: Part-time $735 per credit. Required fees: $470 per semester. Tuition and fees vary according to degree level and campus/location. *Faculty research:* Obesity and childhood nutrition, dietary supplements (Resveratrol).

Marywood University, Academic Affairs, College of Health and Human Services, Department of Nutrition and Dietetics, Program in Sports Nutrition and Exercise Science, Scranton, PA 18509-1598. Offers MS. *Entrance requirements:* Additional exam requirements/recommendations for international students: Required—TOEFL (minimum score 550 paper-based; 213 computer-based; 79 iBT). Electronic applications accepted. *Expenses:* Tuition: Part-time $735 per credit. Required fees: $470 per semester. Tuition and fees vary according to degree level and campus/location. *Faculty research:* Lung function studies (pulmonary diffusing capacity of nitric oxide).

McGill University, Faculty of Graduate and Postdoctoral Studies, Faculty of Agricultural and Environmental Sciences, School of Dietetics and Human Nutrition, Montréal, QC H3A 2T5, Canada. Offers dietetics (M Sc A, Graduate Diploma); human nutrition (M Sc, M Sc A, PhD).

McMaster University, Faculty of Health Sciences and School of Graduate Studies, Program in Medical Sciences, Metabolism and Nutrition Area, Hamilton, ON L8S 4M2, Canada. Offers M Sc, PhD, MD/PhD. *Degree requirements:* For master's, thesis; for doctorate, comprehensive exam, thesis/dissertation. *Entrance requirements:* For master's, honors B Sc, B+ average in related field; for doctorate, M Sc, minimum B+ average, students with proven research experience and an A average may be admitted with a B Sc degree. Additional exam requirements/recommendations for international students: Required—TOEFL (minimum score 580 paper-based; 237 computer-based; 92 iBT).

McNeese State University, Doré School of Graduate Studies, Burton College of Education, Department of Health and Human Performance, Lake Charles, LA 70609. Offers exercise physiology (MS); health promotion (MS); nutrition and wellness (MS). *Accreditation:* NCATE. Evening/weekend programs available. *Faculty:* 5 full-time (2 women). *Students:* 42 full-time (29 women), 6 part-time (3 women); includes 9 minority (7 Black or African American, non-Hispanic/Latino; 1 Asian, non-Hispanic/Latino; 1 Two or more races, non-Hispanic/Latino), 2 international. In 2010, 26 master's awarded. *Entrance requirements:* For master's, GRE, undergraduate major or minor in health and human performance or related field of study. *Application deadline:* For fall admission, 5/15 priority date for domestic and international students; for spring admission, 10/15 priority date for domestic and international students. Applications are processed on a rolling basis. Application fee: $20 ($30 for international students). Tuition and fees vary according to course load. *Financial support:* Application deadline: 5/1. *Unit head:* Dr. Michael Soileau, Head, 337-475-5374, Fax: 337-475-5947, E-mail: msoileau@mcneese.edu. *Application contact:* Dr. George F. Mead, Interim Dean of Dore' School of Graduate Studies, 337-475-5396, Fax: 337-475-5397, E-mail: admissions@mcneese.edu.

Meredith College, John E. Weems Graduate School, Department of Human Environmental Sciences, Raleigh, NC 27607-5298. Offers dietetic internship (Postbaccalaureate Certificate); nutrition (MS). *Faculty:* 3 full-time (2 women), 2 part-time/adjunct (both women). *Students:* 28 full-time (all women), 44 part-time (41 women); includes 5 Black or African American, non-Hispanic/Latino; 1 Hispanic/Latino; 2 Two or more races, non-Hispanic/Latino. Average age 30. 252 applicants, 23% accepted, 42 enrolled. In 2010, 13 master's, 13 other advanced degrees awarded. *Degree requirements:* For master's, thesis optional. *Entrance requirements:* For master's, GRE, recommendations, interview. Additional exam requirements/

recommendations for international students: Required—TOEFL. *Application deadline:* For fall admission, 7/1 priority date for domestic and international students; for spring admission, 11/1 priority date for domestic and international students. Applications are processed on a rolling basis. Application fee: $50. Electronic applications accepted. *Expenses:* Contact institution. *Financial support:* Application deadline: 2/15. *Unit head:* Dr. Deborah Tippett, Head, 919-760-2355, Fax: 919-760-2819, E-mail: tipettd@meredith.edu. *Application contact:* Dr. William H. Landis, Director, 919-760-2355, Fax: 919-760-2819, E-mail: landisb@meredith.edu.

Michigan State University, The Graduate School, College of Agriculture and Natural Resources and College of Natural Science, Department of Food Science and Human Nutrition, East Lansing, MI 48824. Offers food science (MS, PhD); food science—environmental toxicology (PhD); human nutrition (MS, PhD); human nutrition-environmental toxicology (PhD). *Entrance requirements:* Additional exam requirements/recommendations for international students: Required—TOEFL (minimum score 550 paper-based; 213 computer-based), Michigan State University ELT (minimum score 85), Michigan English Language Assessment Battery (minimum score 83). Electronic applications accepted.

Middle Tennessee State University, College of Graduate Studies, College of Behavioral and Health Sciences, Department of Human Sciences, Murfreesboro, TN 37132. Offers child development and family studies (MS); nutrition and food science (MS). Part-time and evening/weekend programs available. Postbaccalaureate distance learning degree programs offered. *Faculty:* 7 full-time (all women). *Students:* 24 part-time (23 women); includes 4 Black or African American, non-Hispanic/Latino; 2 Asian, non-Hispanic/Latino; 1 Hispanic/Latino. Average age 31. 22 applicants, 82% accepted, 18 enrolled. In 2010, 5 master's awarded. *Degree requirements:* For master's, comprehensive exam, thesis. *Entrance requirements:* For master's, GRE or MAT. Additional exam requirements/recommendations for international students: Required—TOEFL (minimum score 525 paper-based; 195 computer-based; 71 iBT) or IELTS (minimum score 6). *Application deadline:* For fall admission, 6/1 for domestic and international students. Applications are processed on a rolling basis. Application fee: $25 ($30 for international students). Electronic applications accepted. *Expenses:* Tuition, state resident: full-time $4632. Tuition, nonresident: full-time $11,520. *Financial support:* In 2010–11, 5 students received support. Application deadline: 5/1. *Faculty research:* Courtship relationships, feminist methodology and epistemology in family studies, school uniforms, body fat in elderly, asynchronous distance education. *Unit head:* Dr. Deborah G. Belcher, Interim Chair, 615-898-2884, Fax: 615-898-5130, E-mail: dbelcher@mtsu.edu. *Application contact:* Dr. Michael Allen, Dean and Vice Provost for Research, 615-898-2840, Fax: 615-904-8020, E-mail: mallen@mtsu.edu.

Mississippi State University, College of Agriculture and Life Sciences, Department of Food Science, Nutrition and Health Promotion, Mississippi State, MS 39762. Offers food science and technology (MS, PhD); health promotion (MS); nutrition (MS, PhD). Postbaccalaureate distance learning degree programs offered (no on-campus study). *Faculty:* 11 full-time (4 women), 1 part-time/adjunct (0 women). *Students:* 48 full-time (32 women), 37 part-time (28 women); includes 12 minority (10 Black or African American, non-Hispanic/Latino; 2 Hispanic/Latino), 16 international. Average age 29. 97 applicants, 53% accepted, 29 enrolled. In 2010, 23 master's, 7 doctorates awarded. *Degree requirements:* For master's, comprehensive exam, thesis; for doctorate, comprehensive exam, thesis/dissertation. *Entrance requirements:* For master's, GRE General Test, minimum GPA of 2.8; for doctorate, GRE General Test, minimum GPA of 3.0. Additional exam requirements/recommendations for international students: Required—TOEFL (minimum score 475 paper-based; 153 computer-based; 53 iBT); Recommended—IELTS (minimum score 4.5). *Application deadline:* For fall admission, 7/1 for domestic students, 5/1 for international students; for spring admission, 11/1 for domestic students, 9/1 for international students. Applications are processed on a rolling basis. Application fee: $40. Electronic applications accepted. *Expenses:* Tuition, state resident: full-time $2731; part-time $304 per credit hour. Tuition, nonresident: full-time $6901; part-time $767 per credit hour. *Financial support:* In 2010–11, 12 research assistantships with full tuition reimbursements (averaging $12,115 per year), 4 teaching assistantships with full tuition reimbursements (averaging $13,380 per year) were awarded; Federal Work-Study, institutionally sponsored loans, scholarships/grants, and unspecified assistantships also available. Financial award application deadline: 4/1; financial award applicants required to submit FAFSA. *Faculty research:* Food preservation, food chemistry, food safety, food processing, product development. *Unit head:* Dr. Benjy Mikel, Professor and Head, 662-325-3200, Fax: 662-325-8728, E-mail: wmikel@fsnhp.msstate.edu. *Application contact:* Dr. Juan Silva, Professor and Graduate Coordinator, 662-325-3200, Fax: 662-325-8728, E-mail: jls@ra.msstate.edu.

Montclair State University, The Graduate School, College of Education and Human Services, Department of Health and Nutrition Sciences, Montclair, NJ 07043-1624. Offers American Dietetic Association (Certificate); food safety instructor (Certificate); health education (MA); nutrition and exercise science (Certificate); nutrition and food science (MS); public health (MPH), including community health education. Part-time and evening/weekend programs available. *Faculty:* 16 full-time (11 women), 59 part-time/adjunct (46 women). *Students:* 62 full-time (52 women), 63 part-time (56 women); includes 15 Black or African American, non-Hispanic/Latino; 9 Asian, non-Hispanic/Latino; 9 Hispanic/Latino; 1 Native Hawaiian or other Pacific Islander, non-Hispanic/Latino, 5 international. Average age 31. 75 applicants, 56% accepted, 31 enrolled. In 2010, 32 master's, 12 other advanced degrees awarded. *Degree requirements:* For master's, comprehensive exam, thesis optional. *Entrance requirements:* For master's, GRE, 2 letters of recommendation. Additional exam requirements/recommendations for international students: Required—TOEFL (minimum iBT score of 83) or IELTS. *Application deadline:* For fall admission, 6/1 for international students; for spring admission, 10/1 for international students. Application fee: $60. *Expenses:* Tuition, state resident: part-time $501.34 per credit. Tuition, nonresident: part-time $773.88 per credit. Required fees: $71.15 per credit. *Financial support:* In 2010–11, 8 research assistantships with full tuition reimbursements (averaging $7,000 per year), 1 teaching assistantship with full tuition reimbursement (averaging $7,000 per year) were awarded; Federal Work-Study, scholarships/grants, and unspecified assistantships also available. Support available to part-time students. Financial award application deadline: 3/1; financial award applicants required to submit FAFSA. *Faculty research:* Improving health via improved nutrition, nutrition epidemiology: assessing health behaviors, mechanisms or pathways to reduce health disparities in underserved or nutritionally at-risk populations, dietary behaviors and theories, psychosocial determinants. Total annual research expenditures: $688,174. *Unit head:* Dr. Eva Goldfarb, Chairperson, 973-655-4154. *Application contact:* Amy Aiello, Director of Graduate Admissions and Operations, 973-655-5147, Fax: 973-655-7869, E-mail: graduate.school@montclair.edu.

Mount Mary College, Graduate Programs, Program in Dietetics, Milwaukee, WI 53222-4597. Offers administrative dietetics (MS); clinical dietetics (MS); nutrition education (MS). Part-time and evening/weekend programs available. *Degree requirements:* For master's, thesis. *Entrance requirements:* For master's, minimum GPA of 2.75, completion of ADA and DPD requirements. Additional exam requirements/recommendations for international students: Required—TOEFL (minimum score 500 paper-based; 173 computer-based).

Mount Saint Vincent University, Graduate Programs, Department of Applied Human Nutrition, Halifax, NS B3M 2J6, Canada. Offers M Sc AHN, MAHN. Part-time and evening/weekend programs available. *Degree requirements:* For master's, thesis (for some programs). *Entrance requirements:* For master's, bachelor's degree in related field, minimum GPA of 3.0, professional experience. Electronic applications accepted.

New York Chiropractic College, Program in Applied Clinical Nutrition, Seneca Falls, NY 13148-0800. Offers MS. Part-time and evening/weekend programs available. *Faculty:* 4 part-time/adjunct (2 women). *Students:* 59 part-time (40 women); includes 5 minority (4 Black or African American, non-Hispanic/Latino; 1 Hispanic/Latino), 5 international. Average age 34. 53 applicants, 87% accepted, 30 enrolled. In 2010, 34 master's awarded. *Entrance requirements:* For master's, minimum GPA of 2.5, transcripts, writing sample. *Application deadline:* Applications are processed on a rolling basis. Application fee: $60. Electronic applications accepted.

Nutrition

New York Chiropractic College (continued)

Expenses: Tuition: Full-time $19,050; part-time $443 per credit hour. Required fees: $680; $340 per term. Part-time tuition and fees vary according to program. *Financial support:* In 2010–11, 3 students received support. Federal Work-Study and scholarships/grants available. Financial award applicants required to submit FAFSA. *Unit head:* Dr. Anna R. Kelles, Director, 315-568-3310. *Application contact:* Michael Lynch, Director of Admissions, 315-568-3040, Fax: 315-568-3087, E-mail: mlynch@nycc.edu.

New York Institute of Technology, Graduate Division, School of Health Professions, Program in Clinical Nutrition, Old Westbury, NY 11568-8000. Offers MS, DO/MS. Part-time and evening/weekend programs available. *Students:* 10 full-time (all women), 34 part-time (29 women); includes 14 minority (4 Black or African American, non-Hispanic/Latino; 4 Asian, non-Hispanic/Latino; 6 Hispanic/Latino). Average age 30. In 2010, 10 master's awarded. *Degree requirements:* For master's, comprehensive exam, thesis (for some programs). *Entrance requirements:* For master's, minimum QPA of 2.85. Additional exam requirements/recommendations for international students: Required—TOEFL (minimum score 550 paper-based; 213 computer-based). *Application deadline:* For fall admission, 7/1 priority date for domestic students; for spring admission, 12/1 priority date for domestic students. Applications are processed on a rolling basis. Application fee: $50. Electronic applications accepted. *Expenses:* Tuition: Part-time $835 per credit. *Financial support:* Fellowships, research assistantships with partial tuition reimbursements, career-related internships or fieldwork, institutionally sponsored loans, tuition waivers (full and partial), and unspecified assistantships available. Support available to part-time students. Financial award applicants required to submit FAFSA. *Faculty research:* Medical nutrition training. *Unit head:* Mindy Haar, Chair, 516-686-3818, Fax: 516-686-3795, E-mail: mhaar@nyit.edu. *Application contact:* Dr. Jacquelyn Nealon, Vice President for Enrollment Services, 516-686-7925, Fax: 516-686-7597, E-mail: jnealon@nyit.edu.

New York University, Steinhardt School of Culture, Education, and Human Development, Department of Nutrition, Food Studies, and Public Health, Program in Nutrition and Dietetics, New York, NY 10012-1019. Offers nutrition and dietetics (MS), including clinical nutrition, food and nutrition. Part-time programs available. *Faculty:* 6 full-time (5 women). *Students:* 99 full-time (91 women), 111 part-time (105 women); includes 8 Black or African American, non-Hispanic/Latino; 18 Asian, non-Hispanic/Latino; 9 Hispanic/Latino, 9 international. Average age 27. 252 applicants, 21% accepted, 37 enrolled. In 2010, 41 master's, 1 doctorate awarded. *Degree requirements:* For master's, thesis (for some programs); for doctorate, thesis/dissertation. *Entrance requirements:* For doctorate, GRE General Test, interview. Additional exam requirements/recommendations for international students: Required—TOEFL. *Application deadline:* For fall admission, 12/1 priority date for domestic students, 12/15 for international students; for spring admission, 11/1 for domestic and international students. Applications are processed on a rolling basis. Application fee: $75. Electronic applications accepted. *Financial support:* Fellowships with full and partial tuition reimbursements, career-related internships or fieldwork, Federal Work-Study, institutionally sponsored loans, scholarships/grants, tuition waivers (partial), and unspecified assistantships available. Financial award application deadline: 2/1; financial award applicants required to submit FAFSA. *Faculty research:* Nutrition and race, childhood obesity and other eating disorders, nutritional epidemiology, nutrition policy, nutrition and health promotion. *Unit head:* Dr. Lisa Sasson, 212-998-5580, Fax: 212-995-4194. *Application contact:* 212-998-5030, Fax: 212-995-4328, E-mail: steinhardt.gradadmissions@nyu.edu.

North Carolina Agricultural and Technical State University, Graduate School, School of Agriculture and Environmental Sciences, Department of Family and Consumer Sciences, Greensboro, NC 27411. Offers food and nutrition (MS). Part-time and evening/weekend programs available. *Degree requirements:* For master's, comprehensive exam, thesis or alternative, qualifying exam. *Entrance requirements:* For master's, GRE General Test, minimum GPA of 2.6.

North Carolina State University, Graduate School, College of Agriculture and Life Sciences and College of Veterinary Medicine, Program in Nutrition, Raleigh, NC 27695. Offers MN, MS, PhD. Part-time programs available. *Degree requirements:* For master's, thesis (for some programs); for doctorate, thesis/dissertation. *Entrance requirements:* For master's and doctorate, GRE General Test. Additional exam requirements/recommendations for international students: Required—TOEFL (minimum score 550 paper-based; 213 computer-based). Electronic applications accepted. *Faculty research:* Effects of food/feed ingredients and components on health and growth, community nutrition, waste management and reduction, experimental animal nutrition.

North Dakota State University, College of Graduate and Interdisciplinary Studies, College of Human Development and Education, Department of Health, Nutrition, and Exercise Sciences, Fargo, ND 58108. Offers dietetics (MS); entry level athletic training (MS); exercise science (MS); nutrition science (MS); public health (MS); sport pedagogy (MS); sports recreation management (MS). Part-time and evening/weekend programs available. Postbaccalaureate distance learning degree programs offered (no on-campus study). *Faculty:* 12 full-time (6 women). *Students:* 23 full-time (14 women), 8 part-time (3 women); includes 1 Black or African American, non-Hispanic/Latino; 2 Two or more races, non-Hispanic/Latino, 1 international. 33 applicants, 67% accepted, 10 enrolled. In 2010, 21 master's awarded. *Degree requirements:* For master's, thesis (for some programs). *Entrance requirements:* For master's, minimum GPA of 3.0. Additional exam requirements/recommendations for international students: Required—TOEFL (minimum score 525 paper-based; 197 computer-based; 71 iBT). *Application deadline:* For fall admission, 3/1 priority date for domestic and international students. Application fee: $45 ($60 for international students). Electronic applications accepted. *Financial support:* In 2010–11, 28 students received support, including 18 teaching assistantships with full tuition reimbursements available (averaging $6,500 per year). Financial award application deadline: 3/31. *Faculty research:* Biomechanics, sport specialization, recreation, nutrition, athletic training. Total annual research expenditures: $10,000. *Unit head:* Brad Strand, Head, 701-231-7474, Fax: 701-231-8872, E-mail: bradford.strand@ndsu.edu. *Application contact:* Brad Strand, Head, 701-231-7474, Fax: 701-231-8872, E-mail: bradford.strand@ndsu.edu.

Northern Illinois University, Graduate School, College of Health and Human Sciences, School of Family, Consumer and Nutrition Sciences, De Kalb, IL 60115-2854. Offers applied family and child studies (MS); nutrition and dietetics (MS). *Accreditation:* AAMFT/COAMFTE. Part-time programs available. *Faculty:* 16 full-time (14 women), 2 part-time/adjunct (1 woman). *Students:* 56 full-time (42 women), 28 part-time (27 women); includes 8 Black or African American, non-Hispanic/Latino; 3 Asian, non-Hispanic/Latino; 3 Hispanic/Latino; 2 Two or more races, non-Hispanic/Latino, 5 international. Average age 27. In 2010, 35 master's awarded. *Degree requirements:* For master's, comprehensive exam, internship, thesis (nutrition and dietetics). *Entrance requirements:* For master's, GRE General Test, minimum GPA of 2.75. Additional exam requirements/recommendations for international students: Required—TOEFL (minimum score 550 paper-based; 213 computer-based). *Application deadline:* For fall admission, 6/1 for domestic students, 5/1 for international students; for spring admission, 11/1 for domestic students, 10/1 for international students. Applications are processed on a rolling basis. Application fee: $30. Electronic applications accepted. *Expenses:* Tuition, state resident: full-time $7200; part-time $300 per credit hour. Tuition, nonresident: full-time $14,400; part-time $600 per credit hour. Required fees: $79 per credit hour. *Financial support:* In 2010–11, 8 research assistantships with full tuition reimbursements, 30 teaching assistantships with full tuition reimbursements were awarded; fellowships with full tuition reimbursements, career-related internships or fieldwork, Federal Work-Study, scholarships/grants, tuition waivers (full), and staff assistantships also available. Support available to part-time students. Financial award applicants required to submit FAFSA. *Faculty research:* Preliminary child development, hospitality administration in Asia, sports nutrition, eating disorders. *Unit head:* Dr. Laura Smart, Acting Chair, 815-753-1960, Fax: 815-753-1321, E-mail: lsmart@niu.edu. *Application contact:* Dr. Laura Smart, Acting Chair, 815-753-1960, Fax: 815-753-1321, E-mail: lsmart@niu.edu.

The Ohio State University, Graduate School, College of Education and Human Ecology, Department of Human Nutrition, Ohio State University Nutrition Program, Columbus, OH 43210. Offers PhD. Offered jointly with College of Food, Agricultural, and Environmental Sciences; College of Medicine; and College of Veterinary Medicine. *Students:* 16 full-time (10 women), 9 part-time (8 women), 15 international. Average age 29. In 2010, 2 doctorates awarded. *Degree requirements:* For doctorate, thesis/dissertation. *Entrance requirements:* For doctorate, GRE. Additional exam requirements/recommendations for international students: Required—TOEFL. *Application deadline:* Applications are processed on a rolling basis. Application fee: $40 ($50 for international students). Electronic applications accepted. *Expenses:* Tuition, state resident: full-time $10,605. Tuition, nonresident: full-time $26,535. Tuition and fees vary according to course load and program. *Financial support:* Applicants required to submit FAFSA. *Unit head:* Dr. Jeff Firkins, Director, 614-292-9957, E-mail: osun@osu.edu. *Application contact:* Dr. Jeff Firkins, Director, 614-292-9957, E-mail: osun@osu.edu.

The Ohio State University, Graduate School, College of Food, Agricultural, and Environmental Sciences, Department of Food Science and Nutrition, Columbus, OH 43210. Offers food science (MS, PhD). *Accreditation:* ADtA. *Faculty:* 23. *Students:* 53 full-time (37 women), 22 part-time (8 women); includes 5 Black or African American, non-Hispanic/Latino; 6 Asian, non-Hispanic/Latino; 2 Hispanic/Latino, 34 international. Average age 28. In 2010, 14 master's, 9 doctorates awarded. *Degree requirements:* For master's, thesis optional; for doctorate, thesis/dissertation. *Entrance requirements:* For master's and doctorate, GRE General Test. Additional exam requirements/recommendations for international students: Required—TOEFL (minimum score 550 paper-based; 213 computer-based), IELTS (minimum score 7), or Michigan English Language Assessment Battery (minimum score 89). *Application deadline:* For fall admission, 8/15 priority date for domestic students, 7/1 priority date for international students; for winter admission, 12/1 priority date for domestic students, 11/1 priority date for international students; for spring admission, 3/1 priority date for domestic students, 2/1 priority date for international students. Applications are processed on a rolling basis. Application fee: $40 ($50 for international students). Electronic applications accepted. *Expenses:* Tuition, state resident: full-time $10,605. Tuition, nonresident: full-time $26,535. Tuition and fees vary according to course load and program. *Financial support:* Fellowships, research assistantships, Federal Work-Study and institutionally sponsored loans available. Support available to part-time students. *Unit head:* Mike Mangino, Interim Chair, 614-292-7769, E-mail: mangino.2@osu.edu. *Application contact:* Graduate Admissions, 614-292-9444, Fax: 614-292-3895, E-mail: domestic.grad@osu.edu.

Ohio University, Graduate College, College of Health Sciences and Professions, School of Applied Health Sciences and Wellness, Program in Food and Nutrition, Athens, OH 45701-2979. Offers MS. *Students:* 16 full-time (10 women), 1 (woman) part-time; includes 2 minority (both Hispanic/Latino), 9 international. 17 applicants, 82% accepted, 10 enrolled. *Unit head:* Dr. Robert G. Brannan, Director, 740-593-2879, E-mail: brannan@ohio.edu. *Application contact:* Dr. Robert G. Brannan, Director, 740-593-2879, E-mail: brannan@ohio.edu.

Oklahoma State University, College of Human Sciences, Department of Nutritional Sciences, Stillwater, OK 74078. Offers MS, PhD. Postbaccalaureate distance learning degree programs offered. *Faculty:* 19 full-time (16 women). *Students:* 42 full-time (40 women), 19 part-time (17 women); includes 4 Black or African American, non-Hispanic/Latino; 2 American Indian or Alaska Native, non-Hispanic/Latino; 1 Asian, non-Hispanic/Latino, 15 international. Average age 29. 38 applicants, 61% accepted, 17 enrolled. In 2010, 5 master's, 1 doctorate awarded. *Degree requirements:* For master's, thesis (for some programs); for doctorate, comprehensive exam, thesis/dissertation. *Entrance requirements:* For master's and doctorate, GRE or GMAT. Additional exam requirements/recommendations for international students: Required—TOEFL (minimum score 550 paper-based; 79 iBT). *Application deadline:* For fall admission, 3/1 priority date for international students; for spring admission, 8/1 priority date for international students. Applications are processed on a rolling basis. Application fee: $40 ($75 for international students). Electronic applications accepted. *Expenses:* Tuition, state resident: full-time $3716; part-time $154.85 per credit hour. Tuition, nonresident: full-time $14,892; part-time $621 per credit hour. Required fees: $2044; $85.20 per credit hour. One-time fee: $50. Tuition and fees vary according to course load and campus/location. *Financial support:* In 2010–11, 27 research assistantships (averaging $10,089 per year), 15 teaching assistantships (averaging $8,927 per year) were awarded; career-related internships or fieldwork, Federal Work-Study, scholarships/grants, health care benefits, tuition waivers (partial), and unspecified assistantships also available. Support available to part-time students. Financial award application deadline: 3/1; financial award applicants required to submit FAFSA. *Faculty research:* Nutritional sciences, micronutrients and chronic disease, phytochemicals, nutrition education, osteoporosis, food service administration. *Unit head:* Dr. Nancy M. Betts, Head, 405-744-5040, Fax: 405-744-1357. *Application contact:* Dr. Gordon Emslie, Dean, 405-744-6368, Fax: 405-744-0355, E-mail: grad-i@okstate.edu.

Oregon Health & Science University, School of Medicine, Graduate Programs in Medicine, Program in Clinical Nutrition, Portland, OR 97239-3098. Offers clinical dietetics (MS); clinical dietetics and nutrition (MSCNU); dietetic internship (Certificate). Part-time programs available. *Faculty:* 1 (woman) full-time, 3 part-time/adjunct (all women). *Students:* 7 full-time (all women), 1 international. Average age 25. 6 applicants, 67% accepted, 4 enrolled. In 2010, 5 master's awarded. *Degree requirements:* For master's, thesis optional. *Entrance requirements:* For master's, GRE. *Application deadline:* For fall admission, 1/1 for domestic students. Application fee: $120. *Financial support:* Health care benefits available. *Unit head:* Dr. Diane Stadler, Program Director. *Application contact:* Chandra Nautiyal, Administrative Coordinator, 503-494-7596, E-mail: nautiyal@ohsu.edu.

Oregon State University, Graduate School, College of Health and Human Sciences, Department of Nutrition and Exercise Sciences, Corvallis, OR 97331. Offers exercise and sport science (MS, PhD); movement studies in disabilities (MAIS, MS); nutrition and exercise sciences (MAIS); nutrition and food management (MS). Terminal master's awarded for partial completion of doctoral program. *Degree requirements:* For master's, thesis; for doctorate, thesis/dissertation. *Entrance requirements:* For master's and doctorate, minimum GPA of 3.0 in last 90 hours. Additional exam requirements/recommendations for international students: Required—TOEFL. *Faculty research:* Motor control, sports medicine, exercise physiology, sport psychology, biomechanics.

Penn State University Park, Graduate School, College of Health and Human Development, Department of Nutritional Sciences, State College, University Park, PA 16802-1503. Offers M Ed, MS, PhD.

Purdue University, Graduate School, College of Consumer and Family Sciences, Department of Foods and Nutrition, West Lafayette, IN 47907. Offers nutrition (MS, PhD). *Degree requirements:* For master's, thesis; for doctorate, thesis/dissertation. *Entrance requirements:* For master's and doctorate, GRE General Test. Additional exam requirements/recommendations for international students: Required—TOEFL (minimum score 600 paper-based). Electronic applications accepted. *Faculty research:* Nutrient requirements, nutrient metabolism, nutrition and disease prevention.

Rosalind Franklin University of Medicine and Science, College of Health Professions, Department of Nutrition, North Chicago, IL 60064-3095. Offers clinical nutrition (MS); nutrition education (MS). Part-time and evening/weekend programs available. Postbaccalaureate distance learning degree programs offered (no on-campus study). *Degree requirements:* For master's, thesis optional, portfolio. *Entrance requirements:* For master's, minimum GPA of 2.75, registered dietitian (RD), professional certificate or license. Additional exam requirements/recommendations for international students: Required—TOEFL. *Expenses:* Contact institution. *Faculty research:* Nutrition education, distance learning, computer-based graduate education, childhood obesity, nutrition medical education.

Rush University, College of Health Sciences, Department of Clinical Nutrition, Chicago, IL 60612. Offers MS. Part-time programs available. *Degree requirements:* For master's, thesis. *Entrance requirements:* For master's, GRE General Test, minimum GPA of 3.0, course work in statistics, undergraduate didactic program approved by the American Dietetic Association.

Additional exam requirements/recommendations for international students: Required—TOEFL. *Faculty research:* Food service management, chronic disease prevention/treatment, obesity, Alzheimer's.

Rutgers, The State University of New Jersey, New Brunswick, Graduate School-New Brunswick, Program in Nutritional Sciences, Piscataway, NJ 08854-8097. Offers MS, PhD. Part-time programs available. Terminal master's awarded for partial completion of doctoral program. *Degree requirements:* For master's, thesis; for doctorate, thesis/dissertation, written qualifying exam. *Entrance requirements:* For master's and doctorate, GRE General Test, 3 letters of recommendation. Additional exam requirements/recommendations for international students: Required—TOEFL (minimum score 560 paper-based; 220 computer-based; 83 iBT). Electronic applications accepted. *Expenses:* Tuition, state resident: full-time $7200; part-time $600 per credit. Tuition, nonresident: full-time $11,124; part-time $927 per credit. *Faculty research:* Nutrition and gene expression, nutrition and disease (obesity, diabetes, cancer, osteoporosis, alcohol), community nutrition and nutrition education, cellular lipid transport and metabolism.

Sacred Heart University, Graduate Programs, College of Education and Health Professions, Department of Physical Therapy and Human Movement and Sports Science, Fairfield, CT 06825-1000. Offers exercise science and nutrition (MS); physical therapy (DPT). *Accreditation:* APTA. *Entrance requirements:* Additional exam requirements/recommendations for international students: Required—TOEFL (minimum score 550 paper-based; 213 computer-based). Electronic applications accepted. *Expenses:* Contact institution.

Sage Graduate School, Graduate School, School of Health Sciences, Program in Nutrition, Troy, NY 12180-4115. Offers applied nutrition (MS); dietetic internship (Certificate). Part-time and evening/weekend programs available. *Faculty:* 2 full-time (both women), 6 part-time/adjunct (all women). *Students:* 40 full-time (all women), 17 part-time (all women); includes 2 minority (1 Asian, non-Hispanic/Latino; 1 Hispanic/Latino), 1 international. Average age 27. 96 applicants, 49% accepted, 33 enrolled. In 2010, 11 master's, 9 other advanced degrees awarded. *Entrance requirements:* For master's, minimum GPA of 2.75, resume, 2 letters of recommendation, interview with director. Additional exam requirements/recommendations for international students: Required—TOEFL (minimum score 550 paper-based; 213 computer-based). *Application deadline:* Applications are processed on a rolling basis. Application fee: $40. *Expenses:* Tuition: Full-time $10,980; part-time $610 per credit hour. Tuition and fees vary according to course load, degree level and program. *Financial support:* Fellowships, research assistantships, Federal Work-Study, scholarships/grants, and unspecified assistantships available. Support available to part-time students. *Unit head:* Dr. Esther Haskevitz, Interim Dean, School of Health Sciences, 518-244-2296, Fax: 518-244-4571, E-mail: haskve@sage.edu. *Application contact:* Rayane AbuSabha, Director of Didactic Program Dietetics, 518-244-2396, Fax: 518-244-4586, E-mail: abusar@sage.edu.

Sage Graduate School, Graduate School, School of Management, Program in Health Services Administration, Troy, NY 12180-4115. Offers dietetic internship (Certificate); gerontology (MS). Part-time and evening/weekend programs available. *Faculty:* 4 full-time (2 women), 8 part-time/adjunct (3 women). *Students:* 7 full-time (6 women), 24 part-time (18 women); includes 6 Black or African American, non-Hispanic/Latino; 1 Asian, non-Hispanic/Latino; 2 Hispanic/Latino. Average age 30. 18 applicants, 39% accepted, 3 enrolled. In 2010, 4 master's awarded. *Entrance requirements:* For master's, minimum GPA of 2.75, resume, 2 letters of recommendation. Additional exam requirements/recommendations for international students: Required—TOEFL (minimum score 550 paper-based; 213 computer-based). Application fee: $40. *Expenses:* Tuition: Full-time $10,980; part-time $610 per credit hour. Tuition and fees vary according to course load, degree level and program. *Financial support:* Fellowships, research assistantships, Federal Work-Study, scholarships/grants, and unspecified assistantships available. Support available to part-time students. Financial award application deadline: 3/1; financial award applicants required to submit FAFSA. *Unit head:* Dr. Kimberly Fredricks, Program Director, 518-292-1782, Fax: 518-292-1964, E-mail: fredek1@sage.edu. *Application contact:* Wendy D. Diefendorf, Director of Graduate and Adult Admission, 518-244-2443, Fax: 518-244-6880, E-mail: diefew@sage.edu.

Saint Joseph College, Department of Nutrition, West Hartford, CT 06117-2700. Offers MS. Part-time and evening/weekend programs available. Postbaccalaureate distance learning degree programs offered. *Students:* 18 full-time (all women), 59 part-time (56 women). *Entrance requirements:* For master's, 2 letters of recommendation. *Application deadline:* Applications are processed on a rolling basis. Application fee: $50. Electronic applications accepted. *Expenses:* Tuition: Full-time $11,340; part-time $630 per credit. Required fees: $540; $30 per credit. Tuition and fees vary according to course load, campus/location and program. *Financial support:* Career-related internships or fieldwork and unspecified assistantships available. Support available to part-time students. Financial award applicants required to submit FAFSA. *Application contact:* Graduate Admissions Office, 860-231-5261, E-mail: graduate@sjc.edu.

Saint Louis University, Graduate Education, Doisy College of Health Sciences and Graduate Education, Department of Nutrition and Dietetics, St. Louis, MO 63103-2097. Offers medical dietetics (MS); nutrition and physical performance (MS). Part-time programs available. *Degree requirements:* For master's, comprehensive exam (for some programs). *Entrance requirements:* For master's, GRE General Test, letters of recommendation, resume, interview. Additional exam requirements/recommendations for international students: Required—TOEFL (minimum score 525 paper-based; 194 computer-based). Electronic applications accepted. *Faculty research:* Sustainable food systems, nutrition education, public health nutrition, culinary nutrition and physical performance.

Sam Houston State University, College of Humanities and Social Sciences, Department of Family and Consumer Sciences, Huntsville, TX 77341. Offers dietetics (MS); family and consumer sciences (MS). Part-time and evening/weekend programs available. *Faculty:* 5 full-time (all women). *Students:* 20 full-time (18 women), 2 part-time (both women); includes 1 Hispanic/Latino. Average age 24. 15 applicants, 93% accepted, 12 enrolled. In 2010, 9 master's awarded. *Entrance requirements:* For master's, GRE General Test, minimum GPA of 2.5. Additional exam requirements/recommendations for international students: Required—TOEFL (minimum score 550 paper-based; 213 computer-based; 79 iBT). *Application deadline:* For fall admission, 8/1 for domestic students; for spring admission, 12/1 for domestic students. Application fee: $20. *Expenses:* Tuition, state resident: full-time $1363; part-time $163 per credit hour. Tuition, nonresident: full-time $3856; part-time $473 per credit hour. *Financial support:* Teaching assistantships available. Financial award application deadline: 5/31; financial award applicants required to submit FAFSA. *Unit head:* Dr. Janis White, Chair, 936-294-1242, Fax: 936-294-4204, E-mail: jwhite@shsu.edu. *Application contact:* Dr. Claudia Sealey-Potts, Advisor, 936-294-1250, E-mail: clapotts@shsu.edu.

San Diego State University, Graduate and Research Affairs, College of Professional Studies and Fine Arts, Department of Exercise and Nutritional Sciences, Program in Nutritional Science, San Diego, CA 92182. Offers nutritional sciences (MS); MS/MS. *Degree requirements:* For master's, thesis. *Entrance requirements:* For master's, GRE General Test, 2 letters of reference. Additional exam requirements/recommendations for international students: Required—TOEFL. Electronic applications accepted.

San Jose State University, Graduate Studies and Research, College of Applied Sciences and Arts, Department of Nutrition, Food Science, and Packaging, San Jose, CA 95192-0001. Offers nutritional science (MS). Electronic applications accepted.

Saybrook University, Graduate College of Mind-Body Medicine, San Francisco, CA 94111-1920. Offers MS, PhD, Certificate. *Entrance requirements:* Additional exam requirements/recommendations for international students: Required—TOEFL (minimum score 580 paper-based; 237 computer-based; 93 iBT). *Application deadline:* For fall admission, 5/1 priority date for domestic students, 5/1 for international students; for spring admission, 10/1 priority date for domestic students, 10/1 for international students. Applications are processed on a rolling basis. Electronic applications accepted. *Application contact:* Admissions Specialist, 800-825-4480, Fax: 415-433-9271, E-mail: admissions@saybrook.edu.

Simmons College, School of Health Sciences, Program in Nutrition and Health Promotion, Boston, MA 02115. Offers didactic program in dietetics (Certificate); nutrition (dietetic internship) (Certificate); nutrition and health promotion (MS); sports nutrition (Certificate). Part-time programs available. Postbaccalaureate distance learning degree programs offered (no on-campus study). *Degree requirements:* For master's, research project. *Entrance requirements:* For master's, GRE, courses in community nutrition, nutritional metabolism, introduction to nutrition, organic and inorganic chemistry, statistics, anatomy and physiology; for Certificate, 1 year of anatomy and physiology with lab, half-year of introductory nutrition, bachelor's degree. Additional exam requirements/recommendations for international students: Required—TOEFL (minimum score 570 paper-based; 230 computer-based; 88 iBT). *Expenses:* Contact institution. *Faculty research:* Good insecurity, chronic disease and nutrition, childhood obesity, dietary assessment, food safety.

South Carolina State University, School of Graduate Studies, Department of Family and Consumer Sciences, Orangeburg, SC 29117-0001. Offers individual and family development (MS); nutritional sciences (MS). Part-time and evening/weekend programs available. *Degree requirements:* For master's, comprehensive exam, thesis optional, departmental qualifying exam. *Entrance requirements:* For master's, GRE, MAT, or NTE, minimum GPA of 2.7. Electronic applications accepted. *Faculty research:* Societal competence, relationship of parent-child interaction to adult, quality of well-being of rural elders.

South Dakota State University, Graduate School, College of Education and Human Sciences, Department of Nutrition, Food Science and Hospitality, Brookings, SD 57007. Offers dietetics (MS); nutrition, food science and hospitality (MFCS); nutritional sciences (MS, PhD). Part-time programs available. *Degree requirements:* For master's, comprehensive exam (for some programs), thesis (for some programs), oral exam. *Entrance requirements:* Additional exam requirements/recommendations for international students: Required—TOEFL (minimum score 525 paper-based). *Faculty research:* Food chemistry, bone density, functional food, nutrition education, nutrition biochemistry.

Southeast Missouri State University, School of Graduate Studies, Department of Health, Human Performance and Recreation, Cape Girardeau, MO 63701-4799. Offers community wellness and leisure (MPA); nutrition and exercise science (MS). Part-time and evening/weekend programs available. *Faculty:* 7 full-time (1 woman), 2 part-time/adjunct (1 woman). *Students:* 9 full-time (5 women), 8 part-time (5 women); includes 1 minority (Black or African American, non-Hispanic/Latino), 4 international. Average age 24. 17 applicants, 82% accepted, 6 enrolled. In 2010, 2 master's awarded. *Degree requirements:* For master's, thesis or alternative, internship. *Entrance requirements:* For master's, GRE General Test (minimum combined score of 950), minimum undergraduate GPA of 3.0. Additional exam requirements/recommendations for international students: Required—TOEFL (minimum score 600 paper-based; 213 computer-based; 79 iBT); Recommended—IELTS (minimum score 6). *Application deadline:* For fall admission, 8/1 for domestic students, 6/1 for international students; for spring admission, 11/21 for domestic students, 10/1 for international students. Applications are processed on a rolling basis. Application fee: $25 ($35 for international students). Electronic applications accepted. *Expenses:* Tuition, state resident: full-time $4698; part-time $261 per credit hour. Tuition, nonresident: full-time $8379; part-time $465.50 per credit hour. *Financial support:* In 2010–11, 12 students received support, including 3 teaching assistantships with full tuition reimbursements available (averaging $7,600 per year); career-related internships or fieldwork, Federal Work-Study, institutionally sponsored loans, scholarships/grants, tuition waivers (full), and unspecified assistantships also available. Financial award application deadline: 6/30; financial award applicants required to submit FAFSA. *Faculty research:* Health issues of athletes, body composition assessment, exercise testing, exercise training, perceptual responses to physical activity. *Unit head:* Dr. Joe Pujol, Chairperson, 573-651-2664, Fax: 573-651-5150, E-mail: jpujol@semo.edu. *Application contact:* Gail Amick, Administrative Secretary, 573-651-2049, Fax: 573-651-2001, E-mail: gamick@semo.edu.

Southern Illinois University Carbondale, Graduate School, College of Agriculture, Department of Animal Science, Food and Nutrition, Program in Food and Nutrition, Carbondale, IL 62901-4701. Offers MS. *Degree requirements:* For master's, thesis or alternative. *Entrance requirements:* For master's, minimum GPA of 2.7. Additional exam requirements/recommendations for international students: Required—TOEFL. *Faculty research:* Public health nutrition, nutrition physiology, soybean utilization, nutrition education.

State University of New York College at Oneonta, Graduate Education, Department of Human Ecology, Oneonta, NY 13820-4015. Offers nutrition and dietetics (MS). Postbaccalaureate distance learning degree programs offered (no on-campus study). *Students:* 18 full-time (17 women), 2 part-time (both women). Average age 25. 61 applicants, 33% accepted, 20 enrolled. In 2010, 16 master's awarded. *Application deadline:* For fall admission, 2/15 for domestic students. Application fee: $50. *Expenses:* Tuition, state resident: full-time $8370; part-time $349 per credit hour. Tuition, nonresident: full-time $13,780; part-time $558 per credit hour. Required fees: $899; $22 per credit hour. *Unit head:* Dr. Katherine Angell, Chair, 607-436-2068, E-mail: angellkg@oneonta.edu. *Application contact:* Patrick J. Mente, Director of Graduate Studies, 607-436-2523, Fax: 607-436-3084, E-mail: gradstudies@oneonta.edu.

Syracuse University, College of Human Ecology, Program in Nutrition Science, Syracuse, NY 13244. Offers MA, MS. *Accreditation:* ADtA. Part-time programs available. *Students:* 11 full-time (10 women), 4 part-time (all women); includes 3 minority (all Asian, non-Hispanic/Latino), 5 international. Average age 26. 32 applicants, 47% accepted, 9 enrolled. In 2010, 10 master's awarded. *Degree requirements:* For master's, thesis (for some programs). *Entrance requirements:* For master's, GRE General Test. Additional exam requirements/recommendations for international students: Required—TOEFL (minimum score 100 iBT). *Application deadline:* For fall admission, 3/15 priority date for domestic and international students; for spring admission, 11/1 priority date for domestic and international students. Applications are processed on a rolling basis. Application fee: $75. Electronic applications accepted. *Expenses:* Tuition: Part-time $1162 per credit. *Financial support:* Fellowships with full tuition reimbursements, research assistantships with full and partial tuition reimbursements, teaching assistantships with full and partial tuition reimbursements, tuition waivers (partial) available. Financial award application deadline: 1/1; financial award applicants required to submit FAFSA. *Unit head:* Dr. Kay Bruening, Program Director, 315-443-9326, Fax: 315-443-2562, E-mail: inquire@hshp.syr.edu. *Application contact:* Kathy Pitts, Information Contact, 315-443-5555, E-mail: inquire@hshp.syr.edu.

Teachers College, Columbia University, Graduate Faculty of Education, Department of Health and Behavior Studies, Program in Nutrition and Education, New York, NY 10027. Offers nutrition education (Ed M, MS, Ed D); nutrition education and public health nutrition (Ed M, MS, Ed D), including community nutrition education (Ed M), nutrition and public health (MS, Ed D), nutrition education (MS, Ed D). Part-time and evening/weekend programs available. *Faculty:* 4 full-time (all women), 9 part-time/adjunct (7 women). *Students:* 36 full-time (34 women), 98 part-time (91 women); includes 38 minority (9 Black or African American, non-Hispanic/Latino; 1 American Indian or Alaska Native, non-Hispanic/Latino; 17 Asian, non-Hispanic/Latino; 7 Hispanic/Latino; 4 Two or more races, non-Hispanic/Latino), 14 international. Average age 29. 56 applicants, 66% accepted, 18 enrolled. In 2010, 33 master's, 2 doctorates awarded. Terminal master's awarded for partial completion of doctoral program. *Degree requirements:* For master's, thesis optional, integrative project; for doctorate, thesis/dissertation. *Entrance requirements:* For master's, GRE General Test; for doctorate, GRE General Test, sample of written work. *Application deadline:* For fall admission, 1/15 for domestic students; for spring admission, 11/1 for domestic students. Applications are processed on a rolling basis. Application fee: $65. Electronic applications accepted. *Expenses:* Tuition: Full-time $28,272; part-time $1178 per credit. Required fees: $756; $378 per semester. *Financial support:* Fellowships, research assistantships, career-related internships or fieldwork, Federal Work-Study, institutionally sponsored loans, and tuition waivers (full and partial) available. Support

Nutrition

Teachers College, Columbia University (continued)

available to part-time students. Financial award application deadline: 2/1; financial award applicants required to submit FAFSA. *Faculty research:* Psychosocial determinants of eating behavior, food supply and environmental education, development and evaluation of nutrition education. *Unit head:* Prof. Isobel R. Contento, Program Coordinator, 212-678-3950, E-mail: nutrition-tc@columbia.edu. *Application contact:* Prof. Isobel R. Contento, Program Coordinator, 212-678-3950, E-mail: nutrition-tc@columbia.edu.

Teachers College, Columbia University, Graduate Faculty of Education, Department of Health and Behavior Studies, Program in Nutrition and Public Health, New York, NY 10027-6696. Offers MS, Ed D. *Expenses:* Tuition: Full-time $28,272; part-time $1178 per credit. Required fees: $756; $378 per semester.

Texas A&M University, College of Agriculture and Life Sciences, Department of Nutrition and Food Science, College Station, TX 77843. Offers food science and technology (M Agr); nutrition (MS, PhD). *Faculty:* 17. *Students:* 74 full-time (52 women), 10 part-time (9 women); includes 11 minority (1 Black or African American, non-Hispanic/Latino; 5 Asian, non-Hispanic/Latino; 5 Hispanic/Latino), 30 international. *Degree requirements:* For master's, thesis; for doctorate, thesis/dissertation. *Entrance requirements:* For master's and doctorate, GRE General Test. Additional exam requirements/recommendations for international students: Required—TOEFL. *Application deadline:* For fall admission, 2/1 priority date for domestic students; for spring admission, 10/1 priority date for domestic students. Applications are processed on a rolling basis. Application fee: $50 ($75 for international students). *Financial support:* Fellowships, research assistantships, teaching assistantships, career-related internships or fieldwork and scholarships/grants available. *Faculty research:* Food safety, microbiology, product development. *Unit head:* Dr. Jimmy T. Keeton, Department Head, 979-458-3428, E-mail: jkeeton@tamu.edu. *Application contact:* Dr. Jimmy T. Keeton, Department Head, 979-458-3428, E-mail: jkeeton@tamu.edu.

Texas State University–San Marcos, Graduate School, College of Applied Arts, Department of Family and Consumer Science, San Marcos, TX 78666. Offers family and child studies (MS); human nutrition (MS). Part-time programs available. *Faculty:* 10 full-time (7 women), 2 part-time/adjunct (both women). *Students:* 38 full-time (34 women), 27 part-time (26 women); includes 2 Black or African American, non-Hispanic/Latino; 2 Asian, non-Hispanic/Latino; 9 Hispanic/Latino; 1 Two or more races, non-Hispanic/Latino. Average age 27. 55 applicants, 80% accepted, 23 enrolled. In 2010, 18 master's awarded. *Degree requirements:* For master's, comprehensive exam, thesis (for some programs). *Entrance requirements:* For master's, GRE General Test (preferred), minimum GPA of 3.0 in last 60 hours of course work. Additional exam requirements/recommendations for international students: Required—TOEFL (minimum score 550 paper-based; 213 computer-based; 78 iBT). *Application deadline:* For fall admission, 6/15 priority date for domestic students, 6/1 for international students; for spring admission, 10/15 priority date for domestic students, 10/1 for international students. Applications are processed on a rolling basis. Application fee: $40 ($90 for international students). Electronic applications accepted. *Expenses:* Tuition, state resident: full-time $6024; part-time $251 per credit hour. Tuition, nonresident: full-time $13,536; part-time $564 per credit hour. Required fees: $1776; $50 per credit hour. $306 per semester. *Financial support:* In 2010–11, 30 students received support, including 6 research assistantships (averaging $5,469 per year), 25 teaching assistantships (averaging $3,565 per year). Financial award application deadline: 4/1. *Faculty research:* Hair fiber products, retinol and cancer met, light/color assessment, interactive VITA, testing of ALKA-V6. Total annual research expenditures: $228,767. *Unit head:* Dr. Maria E. Canabal, Chair, 512-245-2155, Fax: 512-245-3829, E-mail: me57@txstate.edu. *Application contact:* Dr. Michelle Toews, Graduate Adviser, 512-245-2155, Fax: 512-245-3829, E-mail: mtoews@txstate.edu.

Texas Tech University, Graduate School, College of Human Sciences, Department of Nutrition, Hospitality, and Retailing, Program in Nutritional Sciences, Lubbock, TX 79409. Offers MS, PhD. Part-time programs available. *Students:* 38 full-time (37 women), 4 part-time (all women); includes 1 Black or African American, non-Hispanic/Latino; 1 Asian, non-Hispanic/Latino; 2 Hispanic/Latino, 11 international. Average age 24. 46 applicants, 74% accepted, 18 enrolled. In 2010, 11 master's awarded. *Degree requirements:* For master's, thesis or alternative; for doctorate, thesis/dissertation. *Entrance requirements:* For master's and doctorate, GRE General Test. Additional exam requirements/recommendations for international students: Required—TOEFL (minimum score 550 paper-based; 213 computer-based; 79 iBT). *Application deadline:* For fall admission, 6/1 priority date for domestic students, 1/15 priority date for international students; for spring admission, 9/1 priority date for domestic students, 6/15 priority date for international students. Applications are processed on a rolling basis. Application fee: $50 ($75 for international students). Electronic applications accepted. *Expenses:* Tuition, state resident: full-time $5496; part-time $228.99 per credit hour. Tuition, nonresident: full-time $12,936; part-time $538.99 per credit hour. Required fees: $2674; $36 per credit hour. $905 per semester. *Financial support:* Research assistantships with partial tuition reimbursements, teaching assistantships with partial tuition reimbursements available. Financial award application deadline: 4/15; financial award applicants required to submit FAFSA. *Faculty research:* Obesity prevention, fat metabolism, nutrition education for underserved populations, nanonutrition and chronic diseases, health effects of selenium. *Unit head:* Dr. Debra Reed, Graduate Advisor, 806-742-3068 Ext. 251, Fax: 806-742-3042, E-mail: debra.reed@ttu.edu. *Application contact:* Dr. Debra Reed, Graduate Advisor, 806-742-3068 Ext. 251, Fax: 806-742-3042; E-mail: debra.reed@ttu.edu.

Texas Woman's University, Graduate School, College of Health Sciences, Department of Nutrition and Food Sciences, Denton, TX 76201. Offers food science (MS); food systems administration (MS); nutrition (MS, PhD). Part-time and evening/weekend programs available. *Faculty:* 17 full-time (9 women). *Students:* 94 full-time (87 women), 97 part-time (89 women); includes 11 Black or African American, non-Hispanic/Latino; 21 Asian, non-Hispanic/Latino; 17 Hispanic/Latino, 24 international. Average age 28. 114 applicants, 73% accepted, 51 enrolled. In 2010, 72 master's, 6 doctorates awarded. *Degree requirements:* For master's, comprehensive exam; for doctorate, comprehensive exam, thesis/dissertation, qualifying exam. *Entrance requirements:* For master's, GRE General Test (preferred minimum score 350 Verbal, 450 Quantitative), minimum GPA of 3.25, resume; for doctorate, GRE General Test (preferred minimum score 450 Verbal, 550 Quantitative), minimum GPA of 3.5, 2 letters of reference, resume. Additional exam requirements/recommendations for international students: Required—TOEFL (minimum score 550 paper-based; 213 computer-based; 79 iBT). *Application deadline:* For fall admission, 7/1 priority date for domestic students, 3/1 for international students; for spring admission, 12/1 priority date for domestic students, 7/1 for international students. Applications are processed on a rolling basis. Application fee: $50 ($75 for international students). Electronic applications accepted. *Expenses:* Tuition, state resident: full-time $3834; part-time $213 per credit hour. Tuition, nonresident: full-time $9468; part-time $526 per credit hour. Required fees: $1247; $220 per credit hour. *Financial support:* In 2010–11, 64 students received support, including 33 research assistantships (averaging $12,942 per year), 1 teaching assistantship (averaging $12,942 per year); career-related internships or fieldwork, Federal Work-Study, institutionally sponsored loans, scholarships/grants, traineeships, health care benefits, and unspecified assistantships also available. Support available to part-time students. Financial award application deadline: 3/1; financial award applicants required to submit FAFSA. *Faculty research:* Bioactive food components and cancer, nutraceuticals and functional foods in diabetes, obesity and bone health, food safety, dietary modulation of dyslipidemia, childhood obesity prevention. Total annual research expenditures: $1.1 million. *Unit head:* Dr. Chandan Prasad, Chair, 940-898-2636, Fax: 940-898-2634, E-mail: nutrfdsci@twu.edu. *Application contact:* Dr. Samuel Wheeler, Assistant Director of Admissions, 940-898-3188, Fax: 940-898-3081, E-mail: wheelersr@twu.edu.

Tufts University, The Gerald J. and Dorothy R. Friedman School of Nutrition Science and Policy, Medford, MA 02155. Offers humanitarian assistance (MAHA); nutrition (MS, PhD). Part-time programs available. *Degree requirements:* For doctorate, comprehensive exam,

thesis/dissertation. *Entrance requirements:* For master's and doctorate, GRE General Test. Additional exam requirements/recommendations for international students: Required—TOEFL. Electronic applications accepted. *Expenses:* Contact institution. *Faculty research:* Nutritional biochemistry and metabolism, cell and molecular biochemistry, epidemiology, policy/planning, applied nutrition.

Tulane University, School of Public Health and Tropical Medicine, Department of Community Health Sciences, Program in Nutrition, New Orleans, LA 70118-5669. Offers MPH. *Degree requirements:* For master's, comprehensive exam. *Entrance requirements:* For master's, GRE General Test. Additional exam requirements/recommendations for international students: Required—TOEFL.

Tuskegee University, Graduate Programs, College of Agricultural, Environmental and Natural Sciences, Department of Food and Nutritional Sciences, Tuskegee, AL 36088. Offers MS. *Faculty:* 4 full-time (3 women). *Students:* 9 full-time (all women); includes 7 Black or African American, non-Hispanic/Latino, 1 international. Average age 28. In 2010, 6 master's awarded. *Degree requirements:* For master's, thesis. *Entrance requirements:* For master's, GRE General Test. Additional exam requirements/recommendations for international students: Required—TOEFL (minimum score 500 paper-based; 69 computer-based). *Application deadline:* For fall admission, 7/15 for domestic students. Applications are processed on a rolling basis. Application fee: $25 ($35 for international students). *Expenses:* Tuition: Full-time $16,100; part-time $665 per credit hour. Required fees: $650. *Financial support:* Application deadline: 4/15. *Unit head:* Dr. Ralphenia Pace, Head, 334-727-8162. *Application contact:* Dr. Robert L. Laney, Vice President/Director of Admissions and Enrollment Management, 334-727-8580, Fax: 334-727-5750, E-mail: planey@tuskegee.edu.

Université de Moncton, School of Food Science, Nutrition and Family Studies, Moncton, NB E1A 3E9, Canada. Offers foods/nutrition (M Sc). Part-time programs available. *Degree requirements:* For master's, one foreign language, thesis. *Entrance requirements:* For master's, previous course work in statistics. Electronic applications accepted. *Faculty research:* Clinic nutrition (anemia, elderly, osteoporosis), applied nutrition, metabolic activities of lactic bacteria, solubility of low density lipoproteins, bile acids.

Université de Montréal, Faculty of Medicine, Department of Nutrition, Montréal, QC H3C 3J7, Canada. Offers M Sc, PhD, DESS. Terminal master's awarded for partial completion of doctoral program. *Degree requirements:* For master's, thesis; for doctorate, thesis/dissertation, general exam. *Entrance requirements:* For master's, MD, B Sc in nutrition or equivalent, proficiency in French; for doctorate, M Sc in nutrition or equivalent, proficiency in French. Electronic applications accepted. *Faculty research:* Nutritional aspects of diabetes, obesity, anorexia nervosa, lipid metabolism, hepatic function.

Université Laval, Faculty of Agricultural and Food Sciences, Department of Food Sciences and Nutrition, Programs in Nutrition, Québec, QC G1K 7P4, Canada. Offers M Sc, PhD. Terminal master's awarded for partial completion of doctoral program. *Degree requirements:* For master's, thesis; for doctorate, comprehensive exam, thesis/dissertation. *Entrance requirements:* For master's and doctorate, knowledge of French and English. Electronic applications accepted.

University at Buffalo, the State University of New York, Graduate School, School of Public Health and Health Professions, Department of Exercise and Nutrition Sciences, Buffalo, NY 14260. Offers exercise science (MS, PhD); nutrition (MS). Part-time programs available. *Faculty:* 16 full-time (4 women), 14 part-time/adjunct (12 women). *Students:* 71 full-time (42 women), 19 part-time (17 women); includes 5 Black or African American, non-Hispanic/Latino; 8 Asian, non-Hispanic/Latino; 2 Hispanic/Latino, 17 international. Average age 24. 62 applicants, 60% accepted, 27 enrolled. In 2010, 18 master's, 1 doctorate awarded. *Degree requirements:* For master's, comprehensive exam or thesis; for doctorate, comprehensive exam, thesis/dissertation. *Entrance requirements:* For master's, GRE General Test (nutrition), minimum GPA of 3.0; for doctorate, GRE General Test, minimum GPA of 3.0 (PhD). Additional exam requirements/recommendations for international students: Required—TOEFL (minimum score 550 paper-based; 213 computer-based; 79 iBT), IELTS (minimum score 6.5). *Application deadline:* For fall admission, 4/1 for domestic students, 2/1 for international students; for spring admission, 8/15 for international students. Applications are processed on a rolling basis. Application fee: $50. Electronic applications accepted. *Financial support:* In 2010–11, 10 students received support, including 1 research assistantship with tuition reimbursement available (averaging $18,000 per year), 9 teaching assistantships with full and partial tuition reimbursements available (averaging $11,000 per year); career-related internships or fieldwork, Federal Work-Study, institutionally sponsored loans, scholarships/grants, health care benefits, tuition waivers (full and partial), unspecified assistantships, and stipends also available. Financial award application deadline: 3/15; financial award applicants required to submit FAFSA. *Faculty research:* Cardiovascular disease-diet and exercise, respiratory control and muscle function, plasticity of connective and neural tissue, exercise nutrition, diet and cancer. *Unit head:* Dr. Joan Dorn, Chair, 716-829-6795, Fax: 716-829-2979, E-mail: jdorn@buffalo.edu. *Application contact:* Dr. Gaspar Farkas, Director of Graduate Studies, 716-829-6756, Fax: 716-829-2428, E-mail: farkas@buffalo.edu.

The University of Akron, Graduate School, College of Health Sciences and Human Services, School of Family and Consumer Sciences, Program in Nutrition and Dietetics, Akron, OH 44325. Offers MS. *Students:* 6 full-time (5 women), 2 part-time (1 woman), 1 international. Average age 27. 13 applicants, 23% accepted, 3 enrolled. In 2010, 4 master's awarded. *Degree requirements:* For master's, comprehensive exam, thesis or project. *Entrance requirements:* For master's, GRE, minimum GPA of 2.75, three letters of recommendation, statement of purpose, resume. Additional exam requirements/recommendations for international students: Required—TOEFL (minimum score 550 paper-based; 213 computer-based; 79 iBT). *Application deadline:* For fall admission, 3/1 for domestic and international students; for spring admission, 10/1 for domestic and international students. Application fee: $30 ($40 for international students). Electronic applications accepted. *Expenses:* Tuition, state resident: full-time $6800; part-time $378 per credit hour. Tuition, nonresident: full-time $11,644; part-time $647 per credit hour. Required fees: $1265. One-time fee: $30 full-time. *Unit head:* Dr. Deborah Marino, Associate Professor, 330-972-6322, E-mail: debora7@uakron.edu. *Application contact:* Dr. Deborah Marino, Associate Professor, 330-972-6322, E-mail: debora7@uakron.edu.

The University of Alabama, Graduate School, College of Human Environmental Sciences, Department of Human Nutrition and Hospitality Management, Tuscaloosa, AL 35487. Offers MSHES. Part-time programs available. Postbaccalaureate distance learning degree programs offered (no on-campus study). *Faculty:* 7 full-time (5 women). *Students:* 25 full-time (21 women), 64 part-time (63 women); includes 12 minority (9 Black or African American, non-Hispanic/Latino; 2 Asian, non-Hispanic/Latino; 1 Hispanic/Latino), 2 international. Average age 31. 53 applicants, 70% accepted, 29 enrolled. In 2010, 29 master's awarded. *Degree requirements:* For master's, comprehensive exam, thesis optional. *Entrance requirements:* For master's, minimum GPA of 3.0. Additional exam requirements/recommendations for international students: Required—TOEFL. *Application deadline:* For fall admission, 7/6 for domestic students. Applications are processed on a rolling basis. Application fee: $50 ($60 for international students). Electronic applications accepted. *Expenses:* Tuition, state resident: full-time $7900. Tuition, nonresident: full-time $20,500. *Financial support:* In 2010–11, 4 students received support, including 2 research assistantships (averaging $8,100 per year), 2 teaching assistantships (averaging $8,100 per year); career-related internships or fieldwork also available. Financial award application deadline: 3/15. *Faculty research:* Maternal and child nutrition, childhood obesity, community nutrition interventions, geriatric nutrition, family eating patterns. Total annual research expenditures: $12,180. *Unit head:* Dr. Olivia W. Kendrick, Chair and Associate Professor, 205-348-6150, Fax: 205-348-3789, E-mail: okendric@ches.ua.edu. *Application contact:* Dr. Olivia W. Kendrick, Chair and Associate Professor, 205-348-6150, Fax: 205-348-3789, E-mail: okendric@ches.ua.edu.

The University of Alabama at Birmingham, School of Health Professions, Program in Clinical Nutrition and Dietetics, Birmingham, AL 35294. Offers MS. Part-time programs available. *Students:* 35 full-time (34 women), 6 part-time (all women); includes 2 minority (both Black or African American, non-Hispanic/Latino), 4 international. Average age 25. 49 applicants, 57% accepted, 27 enrolled. In 2010, 17 master's awarded. *Degree requirements:* For master's, thesis. *Entrance requirements:* For master's, GRE General Test or MAT, bachelor's degree in dietetics or related field. *Expenses:* Tuition, state resident: full-time $5482. Tuition, nonresident: full-time $12,430. Tuition and fees vary according to program. *Financial support:* In 2010–11, 5 students received support, including 5 research assistantships; career-related internships or fieldwork also available. *Faculty research:* Clinical assessment, folic acid, energy metabolism, nutrition and cancer, nutrition for children and adolescents with special health care needs. *Unit head:* Dr. Timothy Garvey, Director, 205-934-6103, Fax: 205-934-7049. *Application contact:* Julie Bryant, Director of Graduate Admissions, 205-934-8227, Fax: 205-934-8413, E-mail: jbryant@uab.edu.

The University of Alabama at Birmingham, School of Health Professions, Program in Nutrition Sciences, Birmingham, AL 35294. Offers PhD. *Students:* 15 full-time (9 women), 1 (woman) part-time; includes 3 minority (1 Asian, non-Hispanic/Latino; 2 Hispanic/Latino), 7 international. Average age 29. 12 applicants, 25% accepted, 2 enrolled. In 2010, 1 doctorate awarded. *Degree requirements:* For doctorate, thesis/dissertation. *Entrance requirements:* For doctorate, GRE General Test. *Expenses:* Tuition, state resident: full-time $5482. Tuition, nonresident: full-time $12,430. Tuition and fees vary according to program. *Financial support:* In 2010–11, 6 fellowships with tuition reimbursements, 1 research assistantship with tuition reimbursement were awarded; career-related internships or fieldwork also available. *Faculty research:* Energy metabolism, obesity, body composition, cancer prevention, bone metabolism. Total annual research expenditures: $2 million. *Unit head:* Dr. Timothy R. Garvey, Interim Chair, 205-934-6103. *Application contact:* Julie Bryant, Director of Graduate Admissions, 205-934-8227, Fax: 205-934-8413, E-mail: jbryant@uab.edu.

University of Alaska Fairbanks, School of Fisheries and Ocean Sciences, Fairbanks, AK 99775-7220. Offers fisheries (MS, PhD); marine sciences and limnology (MS, PhD), including marine biology, oceanography (PhD); seafood science and nutrition (MS, PhD). Part-time programs available. *Faculty:* 59 full-time (23 women), 5 part-time/adjunct (3 women). *Students:* 93 full-time (52 women), 43 part-time (23 women); includes 9 minority (1 American Indian or Alaska Native, non-Hispanic/Latino; 3 Asian, non-Hispanic/Latino; 4 Hispanic/Latino; 1 Two or more races, non-Hispanic/Latino), 9 international. Average age 31. 103 applicants, 37% accepted, 35 enrolled. In 2010, 22 master's, 3 doctorates awarded. Terminal master's awarded for partial completion of doctoral program. *Degree requirements:* For master's, comprehensive exam, thesis or alternative; for doctorate, comprehensive exam, thesis/dissertation, oral defense. *Entrance requirements:* For master's and doctorate, GRE General Test. Additional exam requirements/recommendations for international students: Required—TOEFL (minimum score 550 paper-based; 213 computer-based; 80 iBT). *Application deadline:* For fall admission, 6/1 for domestic students, 3/1 for international students; for spring admission, 10/15 for domestic students, 9/1 for international students. Applications are processed on a rolling basis. Application fee: $60. Electronic applications accepted. *Expenses:* Tuition, state resident: full-time $5688; part-time $316 per credit. Tuition, nonresident: full-time $11,628; part-time $646 per credit. Required fees: $289 per semester. Tuition and fees vary according to course load and reciprocity agreements. *Financial support:* In 2010–11, 65 research assistantships with tuition reimbursements (averaging $13,094 per year), 19 teaching assistantships with tuition reimbursements (averaging $9,396 per year) were awarded; fellowships with tuition reimbursements, career-related internships or fieldwork, Federal Work-Study, scholarships/grants, health care benefits, and unspecified assistantships also available. Support available to part-time students. Financial award application deadline: 2/15; financial award applicants required to submit FAFSA. *Faculty research:* Marine mammals, hydrology, sea ice, harmful algal blooms, polar ecology. Total annual research expenditures: $15.8 million. *Unit head:* Michael Castellini, Dean, 907-474-7824, Fax: 907-474-7204, E-mail: academics@sfos.uaf.edu. *Application contact:* Christina Neumann, Academic Manager, 907-474-7289, Fax: 907-474-5863, E-mail: clneumann@alaska.edu.

The University of Arizona, College of Agriculture and Life Sciences, Department of Nutritional Sciences, Tucson, AZ 85721. Offers MS, PhD. *Faculty:* 9 full-time (5 women). *Students:* 15 full-time (13 women), 2 part-time (both women); includes 1 Black or African American, non-Hispanic/Latino; 1 Two or more races, non-Hispanic/Latino, 2 international. Average age 30. 26 applicants, 23% accepted, 5 enrolled. In 2010, 2 master's, 3 doctorates awarded. *Entrance requirements:* For master's, GRE, minimum GPA of 3.0, 2 letters of recommendation; for doctorate, GRE, minimum GPA of 3.0, 2 letters of recommendation, statement of purpose. Additional exam requirements/recommendations for international students: Required—TOEFL. *Application deadline:* Applications are processed on a rolling basis. Application fee: $75. Electronic applications accepted. *Expenses:* Tuition, state resident: full-time $7692. *Financial support:* In 2010–11, 6 research assistantships with full and partial tuition reimbursements (averaging $20,010 per year), 6 teaching assistantships with full and partial tuition reimbursements (averaging $18,069 per year) were awarded; fellowships, scholarships/grants, health care benefits, tuition waivers (full and partial), and unspecified assistantships also available. *Faculty research:* Bioactive compounds, nutrients and lifestyle: relationships to cancer; metabolic and behavior factors Influencing body composition; diabetes, obesity, musculoskeletal and cardiovascular diseases. Total annual research expenditures: $3.6 million. *Unit head:* Dr. Cynthia Thomson, Head, 520-626-1565, E-mail: cthomson@u.arizona.edu. *Application contact:* Nancy Driscoll, Information Contact, 520-626-0970, Fax: 520-621-9446, E-mail: nancya@email.arizona.edu.

University of Arkansas for Medical Sciences, Graduate School, Program in Clinical Nutrition, Little Rock, AR 72205-7199. Offers MS. Part-time programs available. *Degree requirements:* For master's, thesis. *Entrance requirements:* For master's, GRE. Additional exam requirements/recommendations for international students: Required—TOEFL. *Faculty research:* Geriatric nutrition, pediatric nutrition, nutrition and health promotion wellness emphasis, community nutrition.

University of Bridgeport, Nutrition Institute, Bridgeport, CT 06604. Offers human nutrition (MS). Part-time and evening/weekend programs available. Postbaccalaureate distance learning degree programs offered (no on-campus study). *Degree requirements:* For master's, thesis, research project. *Entrance requirements:* For master's, previous course work in anatomy, biochemistry, organic chemistry, or physiology. Additional exam requirements/recommendations for international students: Recommended—TOEFL (minimum score 550 paper-based; 213 computer-based; 80 iBT), IELTS (minimum score 6.5). Electronic applications accepted. *Expenses:* Contact institution.

The University of British Columbia, Faculty of Land and Food Systems, Human Nutrition Program, Vancouver, BC V6T 1Z1, Canada. Offers M Sc, PhD. Part-time programs available. Terminal master's awarded for partial completion of doctoral program. *Degree requirements:* For master's, thesis; for doctorate, comprehensive exam, thesis/dissertation. *Entrance requirements:* Additional exam requirements/recommendations for international students: Required—TOEFL (minimum score 577 paper-based; 233 computer-based; 90 iBT), IELTS (minimum score 6.5). Electronic applications accepted. Tuition charges are reported in Canadian dollars. *Expenses:* Tuition, area resident: Full-time $4179 Canadian dollars. International tuition: $7344 Canadian dollars full-time. *Faculty research:* Basic nutrition, clinical nutrition, community nutrition, women's health, pediatric nutrition.

University of California, Berkeley, Graduate Division, College of Natural Resources, Group in Molecular and Biochemical Nutrition, Berkeley, CA 94720-1500. Offers PhD. *Degree requirements:* For doctorate, thesis/dissertation, qualifying exam. *Entrance requirements:* For doctorate, GRE General Test, minimum GPA of 3.0, 3 letters of recommendation. Additional exam requirements/recommendations for international students: Required—TOEFL. Electronic applications accepted. *Faculty research:* Regulation of metabolism; nutritional genomics and nutrient-gene interactions; transport, metabolism and function of minerals; carcinogenesis and dietary anti-carcinogens.

University of California, Davis, Graduate Studies, Graduate Group in Nutritional Biology, Davis, CA 95616. Offers MS, PhD. *Degree requirements:* For master's, thesis; for doctorate, thesis/dissertation. *Entrance requirements:* For master's and doctorate, GRE General Test, minimum GPA of 3.0. Additional exam requirements/recommendations for international students: Required—TOEFL (minimum score 550 paper-based; 213 computer-based). Electronic applications accepted. *Faculty research:* Human/animal nutrition.

University of California, Davis, Graduate Studies, Program in Maternal and Child Nutrition, Davis, CA 95616. Offers MAS. *Degree requirements:* For master's, comprehensive exam. *Entrance requirements:* Additional exam requirements/recommendations for international students: Required—TOEFL (minimum score 550 paper-based; 213 computer-based).

University of Central Oklahoma, College of Graduate Studies and Research, College of Education, Department of Human Environmental Sciences, Edmond, OK 73034-5209. Offers family and child studies (MS); family and consumer science education (MS); interior design (MS); nutrition-food management (MS). Part-time programs available. *Entrance requirements:* Additional exam requirements/recommendations for international students: Required—TOEFL (minimum score 550 paper-based; 213 computer-based). Electronic applications accepted. *Faculty research:* Dietetics and food science.

University of Chicago, Division of Biological Sciences, Biomedical Sciences Cluster: Cancer Biology, Immunology, Molecular Metabolism and Nutrition, Pathology, and Microbiology, Committee on Molecular Metabolism and Nutrition, Chicago, IL 60637-1513. Offers PhD. *Degree requirements:* For doctorate, thesis/dissertation, ethics class, 2 teaching assistantships. *Entrance requirements:* For doctorate, GRE General Test. Additional exam requirements/recommendations for international students: Required—TOEFL (minimum score 600 paper-based; 250 computer-based; 104 iBT), IELTS (minimum score 7). Electronic applications accepted. *Faculty research:* Regulation of lipoprotein metabolism, cellular vitamin metabolism, obesity and body composition, adipocyte differentiation.

University of Cincinnati, Graduate School, College of Allied Health Sciences, Department of Nutritional Science, Cincinnati, OH 45221. Offers MS. Part-time programs available. *Degree requirements:* For master's, thesis. *Entrance requirements:* For master's, GRE General Test. Additional exam requirements/recommendations for international students: Required—TOEFL (minimum score 550 paper-based; 230 computer-based). Electronic applications accepted. *Faculty research:* Phytochemicals-osteoarthritis, pediatric hypertension and hypercholesterol, cancer prevention/Type II diabetes.

University of Colorado at Colorado Springs, College of Letters, Arts and Sciences, Master of Sciences Program, Colorado Springs, CO 80933-7150. Offers applied science—bioscience (M Sc); applied science—physics (M Sc); biology (M Sc); chemistry (M Sc); health promotion (M Sc); mathematics (M Sc); physics (M Sc); sports medicine (M Sc); sports nutrition (M Sc). Part-time programs available. *Students:* 19 full-time (10 women), 11 part-time (4 women); includes 2 Asian, non-Hispanic/Latino; 3 Hispanic/Latino. Average age 34. 20 applicants, 55% accepted, 7 enrolled. In 2010, 14 master's awarded. *Degree requirements:* For master's, thesis or alternative. *Entrance requirements:* For master's, minimum GPA of 2.75. *Application deadline:* For fall admission, 6/1 priority date for domestic students; for spring admission, 12/1 for domestic students. Application fee: $60 ($75 for international students). *Expenses:* Contact institution. *Financial support:* Fellowships, research assistantships, teaching assistantships, career-related internships or fieldwork, Federal Work-Study, and scholarships/grants available. Support available to part-time students. Financial award application deadline: 3/1; financial award applicants required to submit FAFSA. *Faculty research:* Biomechanics and physiology of elite athletic training, genetic engineering in yeast and bacteria including phage display and DNA repair, immunology and cell biology, synthetic organic chemistry. *Application contact:* Michael Sanderson, Information Contact, 719-255-3417, Fax: 719-255-3037, E-mail: gradschl@uccs.edu.

University of Connecticut, Graduate School, College of Agriculture and Natural Resources, Department of Nutritional Sciences, Storrs, CT 06269. Offers MS, PhD. Terminal master's awarded for partial completion of doctoral program. *Degree requirements:* For master's, comprehensive exam, thesis; for doctorate, thesis/dissertation. *Entrance requirements:* For master's and doctorate, GRE General Test. Additional exam requirements/recommendations for international students: Required—TOEFL (minimum score 550 paper-based; 213 computer-based). Electronic applications accepted.

University of Delaware, College of Health Sciences, Department of Health, Nutrition, and Exercise Sciences, Newark, DE 19716. Offers exercise science (MS), including biomechanics, exercise physiology, motor control; health promotion (MS); human nutrition (MS). Part-time programs available. *Degree requirements:* For master's, thesis. *Entrance requirements:* For master's, GRE General Test, interview, minimum GPA of 3.0. Additional exam requirements/recommendations for international students: Required—TOEFL (minimum score 550 paper-based; 213 computer-based). Electronic applications accepted. *Faculty research:* Sport biomechanics, rehabilitation biomechanics, vascular dynamics.

University of Florida, Graduate School, College of Agricultural and Life Sciences, Department of Food Science and Human Nutrition, Gainesville, FL 32611. Offers food science (MS, PhD); nutritional sciences (MS, PhD). *Degree requirements:* For master's, thesis optional; for doctorate, thesis/dissertation. *Entrance requirements:* For master's and doctorate, GRE General Test, minimum GPA of 3.0. Additional exam requirements/recommendations for international students: Required—TOEFL. Electronic applications accepted. *Expenses:* Tuition, state resident: full-time $10,916. Tuition, nonresident: full-time $28,309. *Faculty research:* Pesticide research, nutritional biochemistry and microbiology, food safety and toxicology assessment and dietetics, food chemistry.

University of Georgia, College of Family and Consumer Sciences, Department of Foods and Nutrition, Athens, GA 30602. Offers MFCS, MS, PhD. *Faculty:* 13 full-time (9 women). *Students:* 33 full-time (29 women), 12 part-time (all women); includes 2 Black or African American, non-Hispanic/Latino; 1 Hispanic/Latino, 3 international. 63 applicants, 56% accepted, 15 enrolled. In 2010, 17 master's, 1 doctorate awarded. *Degree requirements:* For master's, thesis (MS); for doctorate, thesis/dissertation. *Entrance requirements:* For master's, GRE General Test, minimum GPA of 3.0, course work in biochemistry and physiology; for doctorate, GRE General Test, master's degree, minimum GPA of 3.0. *Application deadline:* For fall admission, 7/1 priority date for domestic students; for spring admission, 11/15 for domestic students. Application fee: $50. Electronic applications accepted. *Expenses:* Tuition, state resident: full-time $7200; part-time $344 per credit hour. Tuition, nonresident: full-time $21,900; part-time $944 per credit hour. Tuition and fees vary according to course load and program. *Financial support:* Fellowships, research assistantships, teaching assistantships, unspecified assistantships available. *Unit head:* Dr. Rebecca M. Mullis, Head, 706-542-4875, Fax: 706-542-5059, E-mail: rmm@fcs.uga.edu. *Application contact:* Dr. Mary Ann Johnson, Graduate Coordinator, 706-542-2292, E-mail: mjohnson@fcs.uga.edu.

University of Guelph, Graduate Studies, College of Biological Science, Department of Human Health and Nutritional Sciences, Guelph, ON N1G 2W1, Canada. Offers nutritional sciences (M Sc, PhD). Part-time programs available. *Degree requirements:* For master's, thesis (for some programs); for doctorate, comprehensive exam, thesis/dissertation. *Entrance requirements:* For master's, minimum B-average during previous 2 years of coursework; for doctorate, minimum A-average. Additional exam requirements/recommendations for international students: Required—TOEFL (minimum score 550 paper-based; 213 computer-based). Electronic applications accepted. *Faculty research:* Nutrition and biochemistry, exercise metabolism and physiology, toxicology, gene expression, biomechanics and ergonomics.

Nutrition

University of Guelph, Graduate Studies, College of Social and Applied Human Sciences, Department of Family Relations and Applied Nutrition, Guelph, ON N1G 2W1, Canada. Offers applied nutrition (MAN); family relations and human development (M Sc, PhD), including applied human nutrition, couple and family therapy (M Sc), family relations and human development. *Accreditation:* AAMFT/COAMFTE (one or more programs are accredited). Part-time programs available. *Degree requirements:* For master's, thesis (for some programs); for doctorate, comprehensive exam, thesis/dissertation. *Entrance requirements:* For master's, minimum B+ average; for doctorate, master's degree in family relations and human development or related field with a minimum B+ average or master's degree in applied human nutrition. Additional exam requirements/recommendations for international students: Required—TOEFL (minimum score 600 paper-based; 250 computer-based). Electronic applications accepted. *Faculty research:* Child and adolescent development, social gerontology, family roles and relations, couple and family therapy, applied human nutrition.

University of Hawaii at Manoa, Graduate Division, College of Tropical Agriculture and Human Resources, Department of Human Nutrition, Food and Animal Sciences, Program in Nutrition, Honolulu, HI 96822. Offers PhD. Part-time programs available. *Faculty:* 26 full-time (11 women), 2 part-time/adjunct (1 woman). *Students:* 1 full-time (0 women), 2 part-time (1 woman); includes 2 minority (1 Asian, non-Hispanic/Latino; 1 Two or more races, non-Hispanic/Latino). Average age 30. 12 applicants, 25% accepted, 1 enrolled. *Degree requirements:* For doctorate, comprehensive exam; thesis/dissertation. *Entrance requirements:* For doctorate, GRE General Test. Additional exam requirements/recommendations for international students: Required—TOEFL (minimum score 580 paper-based; 237 computer-based; 92 iBT), IELTS (minimum score 5). *Application deadline:* For fall admission, 2/1 for domestic and international students; for spring admission, 9/1 for domestic and international students. Application fee: $60. *Financial support:* In 2010–11, 3 students received support, including 1 fellowship (averaging $500 per year), 2 research assistantships (averaging $17,511 per year). *Application contact:* Dr. Michael Dunn, Graduate Chair, 808-956-8523, Fax: 808-956-4024, E-mail: mdunn@hawaii.edu.

University of Hawaii at Manoa, Graduate Division, College of Tropical Agriculture and Human Resources, Department of Human Nutrition, Food and Animal Sciences, Program in Nutritional Sciences, Honolulu, HI 96822. Offers MS, PhD. Part-time programs available. *Faculty:* 26 full-time (11 women), 2 part-time/adjunct (1 woman). *Students:* 9 full-time (6 women), 4 part-time (3 women); includes 8 minority (6 Asian, non-Hispanic/Latino; 1 Native Hawaiian or other Pacific Islander, non-Hispanic/Latino; 1 Two or more races, non-Hispanic/Latino), 4 international. Average age 30. 28 applicants, 32% accepted, 6 enrolled. In 2010, 3 master's awarded. *Degree requirements:* For master's, thesis optional; for doctorate, comprehensive exam, thesis/dissertation. *Entrance requirements:* For master's and doctorate, GRE General Test. Additional exam requirements/recommendations for international students: Required—TOEFL (minimum score 580 paper-based; 237 computer-based; 92 iBT), IELTS (minimum score 5). *Application deadline:* For fall admission, 2/1 for domestic and international students; for spring admission, 9/1 for domestic and international students. Application fee: $60. *Financial support:* In 2010–11, 4 fellowships (averaging $5,125 per year), 9 research assistantships (averaging $16,193 per year) were awarded; teaching assistantships, tuition waivers (full) also available. Financial award application deadline: 3/1. *Faculty research:* Nutritional biochemistry, human nutrition, nutrition education, international nutrition, nutritional epidemiology. Total annual research expenditures: $1 million. *Application contact:* Dr. Michael Dunn, Graduate Chairperson, 808-956-8523, Fax: 808-956-4024, E-mail: mdunn@hawaii.edu.

University of Houston, College of Liberal Arts and Social Sciences, Department of Health and Human Performance, Houston, TX 77204. Offers exercise science (MS); human nutrition (MS); human space exploration sciences (MS); kinesiology (PhD); physical education (M Ed). *Accreditation:* NCATE (one or more programs are accredited). Part-time and evening/weekend programs available. *Faculty:* 14 full-time (4 women), 4 part-time/adjunct (1 woman). *Students:* 47 full-time (25 women), 28 part-time (9 women); includes 9 Black or African American, non-Hispanic/Latino; 2 Asian, non-Hispanic/Latino; 5 Hispanic/Latino; 1 Two or more races, non-Hispanic/Latino, 9 international. Average age 27. 87 applicants, 49% accepted, 22 enrolled. In 2010, 32 master's, 2 doctorates awarded. *Degree requirements:* For master's, comprehensive exam (for some programs), thesis (for some programs); for doctorate, comprehensive exam, thesis/dissertation, qualifying exam, candidacy paper. *Entrance requirements:* For master's, GRE (minimum 35th percentile on each section), minimum cumulative GPA of 3.0; for doctorate, GRE (minimum 35th percentile on each section), minimum cumulative GPA of 3.3. Additional exam requirements/recommendations for international students: Required—TOEFL (minimum score 550 paper-based; 79 iBT). *Application deadline:* For fall admission, 4/1 for domestic and international students; for spring admission, 10/1 for domestic and international students. Applications are processed on a rolling basis. Application fee: $45 ($75 for international students). Electronic applications accepted. *Expenses:* Tuition, state resident: full-time $8592; part-time $358 per credit hour. Tuition, nonresident: full-time $16,032; part-time $668 per credit hour. Required fees: $2889. Tuition and fees vary according to course load and program. *Financial support:* In 2010–11, 4 research assistantships with full tuition reimbursements (averaging $8,640 per year), 29 teaching assistantships with full tuition reimbursements (averaging $8,518 per year) were awarded; career-related internships or fieldwork, Federal Work-Study, institutionally sponsored loans, scholarships/grants, health care benefits, and unspecified assistantships also available. Support available to part-time students. Financial award application deadline: 2/1. *Faculty research:* Biomechanics, exercise physiology, obesity, nutrition, space exploration science. *Unit head:* Dr. Charles Layne, Chairperson, 713-743-9868, Fax: 713-743-9860, E-mail: clayne2@uh.edu. *Application contact:* Todd Boutte, Graduate Admission Counselor, 713-743-0571, Fax: 713-743-0123, E-mail: tboutte@mail.coe.uh.edu.

University of Illinois at Chicago, Graduate College, College of Applied Health Sciences, Program in Nutrition, Chicago, IL 60607-7128. Offers MS, PhD. *Accreditation:* ADtA. *Degree requirements:* For master's, thesis; for doctorate, thesis/dissertation. *Entrance requirements:* For master's and doctorate, GRE General Test, minimum GPA of 2.75. Additional exam requirements/recommendations for international students: Required—TOEFL. Electronic applications accepted. *Faculty research:* Nutrition for the elderly, inborn errors of metabolism, nutrition and cancer, lipid metabolism, dietary fat markers.

University of Illinois at Urbana–Champaign, Graduate College, College of Agricultural, Consumer and Environmental Sciences, Department of Food Science and Human Nutrition, Champaign, IL 61820. Offers food science (MS); food science and human nutrition (MS, PhD), including professional science (MS); human nutrition (MS). Part-time programs available. Postbaccalaureate distance learning degree programs offered (minimal on-campus study). *Faculty:* 26 full-time (12 women), 1 (woman) part-time/adjunct. *Students:* 63 full-time (41 women), 18 part-time (10 women); includes 9 minority (2 Black or African American, non-Hispanic/Latino; 6 Asian, non-Hispanic/Latino; 1 Two or more races, non-Hispanic/Latino), 37 international. 153 applicants, 16% accepted, 18 enrolled. In 2010, 20 master's, 4 doctorates awarded. *Entrance requirements:* For master's and doctorate, GRE, minimum GPA of 3.0. Additional exam requirements/recommendations for international students: Required—TOEFL (minimum score 550 paper-based; 213 computer-based; 79 iBT) or IELTS (minimum score 6.5). *Application deadline:* Applications are processed on a rolling basis. Application fee: $75 ($90 for international students). Electronic applications accepted. *Financial support:* In 2010–11, 14 fellowships, 36 research assistantships, 16 teaching assistantships were awarded; tuition waivers (full and partial) also available. *Unit head:* Faye L. Dong, Head, 217-244-4498, Fax: 217-265-0925, E-mail: fayedong@illinois.edu. *Application contact:* Barb J. Vandeventer, Office Administrator, 217-333-1324, Fax: 217-265-0925, E-mail: vandvntr@illinois.edu.

University of Illinois at Urbana–Champaign, Graduate College, College of Agricultural, Consumer and Environmental Sciences, Division of Nutritional Sciences, Champaign, IL 61820. Offers MS, PhD. *Students:* 56 full-time (38 women), 5 part-time (4 women); includes 1 Black or African American, non-Hispanic/Latino; 7 Asian, non-Hispanic/Latino; 4 Hispanic/Latino; 1 Two or more races, non-Hispanic/Latino, 13 international. 73 applicants, 16% accepted, 11 enrolled. In 2010, 7 master's, 9 doctorates awarded. *Entrance requirements:* For master's and doctorate,

GRE, minimum GPA of 3.0. Additional exam requirements/recommendations for international students: Required—TOEFL (minimum score 560 paper-based; 220 computer-based; 83 iBT) or IELTS (minimum score 6.5). *Application deadline:* Applications are processed on a rolling basis. Application fee: $75 ($90 for international students). Electronic applications accepted. *Financial support:* In 2010–11, 20 fellowships, 38 research assistantships, 7 teaching assistantships were awarded; tuition waivers (full and partial) also available. *Unit head:* Rodney W. Johnson, Director, 217-333-2118, Fax: 217-333-9368, E-mail: rwjohn@illinois.edu. *Application contact:* Jessica L. Hartke, Visiting Program Coordinator, 217-333-4177, Fax: 217-333-9368, E-mail: jessh@illinois.edu.

The University of Kansas, University of Kansas Medical Center, School of Allied Health, Department of Dietetics and Nutrition, Lawrence, KS 66045. Offers dietetic internship (Certificate); dietetics and nutrition (MS); medical nutrition science (PhD). Part-time programs available. *Faculty:* 15. *Students:* 43 full-time (41 women), 16 part-time (all women); includes 5 minority (1 American Indian or Alaska Native, non-Hispanic/Latino; 2 Asian, non-Hispanic/Latino; 1 Hispanic/Latino; 1 Two or more races, non-Hispanic/Latino), 6 international. Average age 26. 60 applicants, 50% accepted, 30 enrolled. In 2010, 20 master's, 16 other advanced degrees awarded. *Degree requirements:* For master's, thesis, oral exam; for doctorate, thesis/dissertation, oral exam. *Entrance requirements:* For master's, GRE, prerequisite courses in nutrition, biochemistry, and physiology; for Certificate, GRE. Additional exam requirements/recommendations for international students: Required—TOEFL (minimum score 228 computer-based; 92 iBT). *Application deadline:* For fall admission, 8/1 for domestic students, 7/1 for international students; for winter admission, 12/1 for domestic students, 11/1 for international students; for spring admission, 5/1 for domestic students, 4/1 for international students. Applications are processed on a rolling basis. Application fee: $60. Electronic applications accepted. *Expenses:* Tuition, state resident: full-time $7092; part-time $295.50 per credit hour. Tuition, nonresident: full-time $16,590; part-time $691.25 per credit hour. Required fees: $858; $71.49 per credit hour. Tuition and fees vary according to course load, campus/location and program. *Financial support:* Fellowships, research assistantships with full tuition reimbursements, teaching assistantships with full tuition reimbursements, career-related internships or fieldwork, Federal Work-Study, institutionally sponsored loans, scholarships/grants, traineeships, tuition waivers, and unspecified assistantships available. Support available to part-time students. Financial award application deadline: 2/14; financial award applicants required to submit FAFSA. *Faculty research:* Obesity prevention and treatment, omega-3 fatty acids impact on infant development and immunity, iron status of infants, appetitive and endocrine responses to food intake, vitamin D and bone metabolism in osteosarcoma cells, food security in individuals with mental illness, cancer prevention and recovery, nutrigenomic. Total annual research expenditures: $1.3 million. *Unit head:* Dr. Debra Kay Sullivan, Chairperson, 913-588-5357, Fax: 913-588-8946, E-mail: dsulliva@kumc.edu. *Application contact:* Dr. Linda Dianne Griffith, Graduate Director, 913-588-7652, Fax: 913-588-8946, E-mail: lgriffith@kumc.edu.

University of Kentucky, Graduate School, College of Agriculture, Program in Hospitality and Dietetic Administration, Lexington, KY 40506-0032. Offers MS. *Degree requirements:* For master's, comprehensive exam, thesis optional. *Entrance requirements:* For master's, GRE General Test, minimum undergraduate GPA of 2.75. Additional exam requirements/recommendations for international students: Required—TOEFL (minimum score 550 paper-based; 213 computer-based). Electronic applications accepted.

University of Kentucky, Graduate School, Program in Nutritional Sciences, Lexington, KY 40506-0032. Offers MSNS, PhD. *Degree requirements:* For doctorate, comprehensive exam, thesis/dissertation. *Entrance requirements:* For master's, GRE General Test, minimum undergraduate GPA of 2.75; for doctorate, GRE General Test, minimum graduate GPA of 3.0. Additional exam requirements/recommendations for international students: Required—TOEFL (minimum score 550 paper-based; 213 computer-based). Electronic applications accepted. *Faculty research:* Nutrition and AIDS, nutrition and alcoholism, nutrition and cardiovascular disease, nutrition and cancer, nutrition and diabetes.

University of Maine, Graduate School, College of Natural Sciences, Forestry, and Agriculture, Department of Food Science and Human Nutrition, Orono, ME 04469. Offers food and nutritional sciences (PhD); food science and human nutrition (MS). Part-time programs available. *Faculty:* 7 full-time (6 women), 2 part-time/adjunct (1 woman). *Students:* 35 full-time (28 women), 3 part-time (all women); includes 1 American Indian or Alaska Native, non-Hispanic/Latino; 1 Asian, non-Hispanic/Latino, 4 international. Average age 27. 53 applicants, 34% accepted, 15 enrolled. In 2010, 17 master's awarded. *Degree requirements:* For master's, thesis; for doctorate, thesis/dissertation. *Entrance requirements:* For master's, GRE General Test, minimum GPA of 3.0; for doctorate, GRE General Test. Additional exam requirements/recommendations for international students: Required—TOEFL. *Application deadline:* For fall admission, 2/1 priority date for domestic students. Applications are processed on a rolling basis. Application fee: $65. Electronic applications accepted. *Expenses:* Tuition, state resident: full-time $400. Tuition, nonresident: full-time $1050. *Financial support:* In 2010–11, 9 research assistantships with tuition reimbursements (averaging $13,500 per year), 4 teaching assistantships with tuition reimbursements (averaging $12,000 per year) were awarded; scholarships/grants and tuition waivers (full and partial) also available. Financial award application deadline: 3/1. *Faculty research:* Product development of fruit and vegetables, lipid oxidation in fish and meat, analytical methods development, metabolism of potato glycoalkaloids, seafood quality. *Unit head:* Dr. Denise Skonberg, 207-581-1639. *Application contact:* Scott G. Delcourt, Associate Dean of the Graduate School, 207-581-3291, Fax: 207-581-3232, E-mail: graduate@maine.edu.

University of Manitoba, Faculty of Graduate Studies, Faculty of Agricultural and Food Sciences, Department of Food Science, Winnipeg, MB R3T 2N2, Canada. Offers food and nutritional sciences (PhD); food science (M Sc); foods and nutrition (M Sc). *Degree requirements:* For master's, thesis.

University of Manitoba, Faculty of Graduate Studies, Faculty of Human Ecology, Department of Human Nutritional Sciences, Winnipeg, MB R3T 2N2, Canada. Offers M Sc. *Degree requirements:* For master's, thesis.

University of Maryland, College Park, Academic Affairs, College of Agriculture and Natural Resources, Department of Nutrition and Food Science, Program in Nutrition, College Park, MD 20742. Offers MS, PhD. *Students:* 15 full-time (13 women), 2 part-time (both women); includes 1 Black or African American, non-Hispanic/Latino; 4 Asian, non-Hispanic/Latino, 6 international. 26 applicants, 12% accepted, 2 enrolled. In 2010, 5 master's, 3 doctorates awarded. *Degree requirements:* For master's, thesis; for doctorate, comprehensive exam, thesis/dissertation, candidacy exam. *Entrance requirements:* For master's, GRE General Test, minimum GPA of 3.0, 3 letters of recommendation; for doctorate, GRE General Test, minimum GPA of 3.0. Additional exam requirements/recommendations for international students: Required—TOEFL. *Application deadline:* For fall admission, 12/15 for domestic and international students; for spring admission, 6/1 for domestic and international students. Applications are processed on a rolling basis. Application fee: $75. Electronic applications accepted. *Expenses:* Tuition, state resident: part-time $471 per credit hour. Tuition, nonresident: part-time $1016 per credit hour. Required fees: $337 per term. *Financial support:* In 2010–11, 1 fellowship with partial tuition reimbursement (averaging $10,800 per year), 1 research assistantship (averaging $15,800 per year), 9 teaching assistantships with tuition reimbursements (averaging $15,783 per year) were awarded. Financial award applicants required to submit FAFSA. *Faculty research:* Nutrition education, carbohydrates and physical activity. *Unit head:* Lucy Yu, Acting Chair, 301-405-0773, E-mail: lyu5@umd.edu. *Application contact:* Dr. Charles A. Caramello, Dean of Graduate School, 301-405-0358, Fax: 301-314-9305, E-mail: ccaramel@umd.edu.

University of Massachusetts Amherst, Graduate School, School of Public Health and Health Sciences, Department of Nutrition, Amherst, MA 01003. Offers nutrition (MPH, MS); public health (PhD). Part-time and evening/weekend programs available. Postbaccalaureate distance learning degree programs offered (no on-campus study). *Faculty:* 13 full-time (8 women). *Students:* 10 full-time (all women), 3 part-time (all women); includes 1 minority (Asian, non-Hispanic/Latino), 3 international. Average age 30. 38 applicants, 39% accepted, 5 enrolled.Terminal master's awarded for partial completion of doctoral program. *Degree requirements:* For master's, thesis or alternative; for doctorate, comprehensive exam, thesis/dissertation. *Entrance requirements:* For master's and doctorate, GRE General Test. Additional exam requirements/recommendations for international students: Required—TOEFL (minimum score 550 paper-based; 213 computer-based; 80 iBT), IELTS (minimum score 6.5). *Application deadline:* For fall admission, 2/1 for domestic and international students; for spring admission, 10/1 for domestic and international students. Applications are processed on a rolling basis. Application fee: $50 ($65 for international students). Electronic applications accepted. *Expenses:* Tuition, state resident: full-time $2640. Required fees: $8282. One-time fee: $357 full-time. *Financial support:* In 2010–11, 7 research assistantships with full tuition reimbursements (averaging $3,996 per year), 13 teaching assistantships with full tuition reimbursements (averaging $7,280 per year) were awarded; fellowships, career-related internships or fieldwork, Federal Work-Study, scholarships/grants, traineeships, health care benefits, tuition waivers (full), and unspecified assistantships also available. Support available to part-time students. Financial award application deadline: 2/1; financial award applicants required to submit FAFSA. *Unit head:* Dr. Elena T. Carbone, Graduate Program Director, 413-545-0740, Fax: 413-545-1074. *Application contact:* Jean M. Ames, Supervisor of Admissions, 413-545-0722, Fax: 413-577-0010, E-mail: gradadm@grad.umass.edu.

University of Massachusetts Amherst, Graduate School, School of Public Health and Health Sciences, Department of Public Health, Amherst, MA 01003. Offers biostatistics (MPH, MS, PhD); community health education (MPH, MS, PhD); environmental health sciences (MPH, MS, PhD); epidemiology (MPH, MS, PhD); health policy and management (MPH, MS, PhD); nutrition (PhD); public health practice (MPH). *Accreditation:* CEPH (one or more programs are accredited). Part-time and evening/weekend programs available. Postbaccalaureate distance learning degree programs offered (no on-campus study). *Faculty:* 38 full-time (23 women). *Students:* 116 full-time (92 women), 215 part-time (153 women); includes 58 minority (19 Black or African American, non-Hispanic/Latino; 15 Asian, non-Hispanic/Latino; 16 Hispanic/Latino; 1 Native Hawaiian or other Pacific Islander, non-Hispanic/Latino; 7 Two or more races, non-Hispanic/Latino), 58 international. Average age 36. 311 applicants, 58% accepted, 85 enrolled. In 2010, 99 master's, 2 doctorates awarded. Terminal master's awarded for partial completion of doctoral program. *Degree requirements:* For master's, thesis (for some programs); for doctorate, comprehensive exam, thesis/dissertation. *Entrance requirements:* For master's and doctorate, GRE General Test. Additional exam requirements/recommendations for international students: Required—TOEFL (minimum score 550 paper-based; 213 computer-based; 80 iBT), IELTS (minimum score 6.5). *Application deadline:* For fall admission, 2/1 for domestic and international students. Applications are processed on a rolling basis. Application fee: $40 ($65 for international students). Electronic applications accepted. *Expenses:* Tuition, state resident: full-time $2640. Required fees: $8282. One-time fee: $357 full-time. *Financial support:* In 2010–11, 35 research assistantships with full tuition reimbursements (averaging $7,080 per year), 25 teaching assistantships with full tuition reimbursements (averaging $5,902 per year) were awarded; fellowships, career-related internships or fieldwork, Federal Work-Study, scholarships/grants, traineeships, health care benefits, tuition waivers (full), and unspecified assistantships also available. Support available to part-time students. Financial award application deadline: 2/1. *Unit head:* Dr. Paula Stamps, Graduate Program Director, 413-545-2861, Fax: 413-545-0964. *Application contact:* Jean M. Ames, Supervisor of Admissions, 413-545-0722, Fax: 413-577-0010, E-mail: gradadm@grad.umass.edu.

University of Massachusetts Lowell, School of Health and Environment, Department of Clinical Laboratory and Nutritional Sciences, Lowell, MA 01854-2881. Offers clinical laboratory sciences (MS); clinical pathology (Graduate Certificate); nutritional sciences (Graduate Certificate); public health laboratory sciences (Graduate Certificate). *Accreditation:* NAACLS. Part-time programs available. Postbaccalaureate distance learning degree programs offered. *Degree requirements:* For master's, thesis optional. *Entrance requirements:* For master's, GRE General Test, minimum GPA of 3.0, letters of recommendation. *Faculty research:* Cardiovascular disease, lipoprotein metabolism, micronutrient evaluation, alcohol metabolism, mycobacterial drug resistance.

University of Medicine and Dentistry of New Jersey, School of Health Related Professions, Department of Interdisciplinary Studies, Program in Health Sciences, Newark, NJ 07107-1709. Offers cardiopulmonary sciences (PhD); clinical laboratory sciences (PhD); health sciences (MS); interdisciplinary studies (PhD); nutrition (PhD); physical therapy/movement science (PhD). Part-time and evening/weekend programs available. Postbaccalaureate distance learning degree programs offered (no on-campus study). *Students:* 6 full-time (4 women), 125 part-time (94 women); includes 12 Black or African American, non-Hispanic/Latino; 5 Asian, non-Hispanic/Latino; 8 Hispanic/Latino, 5 international. Average age 40. 78 applicants, 46% accepted, 29 enrolled. In 2010, 14 master's, 2 doctorates awarded. *Degree requirements:* For doctorate, thesis/dissertation. *Entrance requirements:* For doctorate, interview, writing sample. Additional exam requirements/recommendations for international students: Required—TOEFL. *Application deadline:* For fall admission, 3/1 for domestic students. Applications are processed on a rolling basis. Application fee: $50. Electronic applications accepted. *Unit head:* Dr. Margaret Kildoff, Director, 973-972-4989, Fax: 973-972-7854, E-mail: ms-phd-hs@umdnj.edu. *Application contact:* Douglas Lomonaco, Assistant Dean, 973-972-5454, Fax: 973-972-7463, E-mail: shrpadm@umdnj.edu.

University of Medicine and Dentistry of New Jersey, School of Health Related Professions, Department of Nutritional Sciences, Dietetic Internship Program, Newark, NJ 07107-1709. Offers Certificate. Postbaccalaureate distance learning degree programs offered (minimal on-campus study). *Students:* 16 full-time (15 women), 1 (woman) part-time; includes 1 Black or African American, non-Hispanic/Latino; 1 Asian, non-Hispanic/Latino. Average age 23. In 2010, 2 Certificates awarded. *Entrance requirements:* For degree, bachelor's degree in dietetics, nutrition, or related field; interview; minimum GPA of 2.9. Additional exam requirements/recommendations for international students: Required—TOEFL (minimum score 500 paper-based; 79 iBT). *Application deadline:* For fall admission, 2/15 for domestic and international students. Applications are processed on a rolling basis. Application fee: $75. Electronic applications accepted. *Unit head:* Denise Langevin, Director, 908-889-2488, Fax: 908-889-2487, E-mail: langevdd@umdnj.edu. *Application contact:* Douglas Lomonaco, Assistant Dean, 973-972-5454, Fax: 973-972-7463, E-mail: shrpadm@umdnj.edu.

University of Medicine and Dentistry of New Jersey, School of Health Related Professions, Department of Nutritional Sciences, Program in Clinical Nutrition, Newark, NJ 07107-1709. Offers MS, DCN. Part-time and evening/weekend programs available. Postbaccalaureate distance learning degree programs offered (minimal on-campus study). *Students:* 1 (woman) full-time, 93 part-time (90 women); includes 1 Black or African American, non-Hispanic/Latino; 4 Asian, non-Hispanic/Latino; 1 Hispanic/Latino, 12 international. Average age 38. 22 applicants, 73% accepted, 13 enrolled. In 2010, 15 master's, 7 doctorates awarded. *Entrance requirements:* For master's, statement of career goals, minimum GPA of 3.2, proof of registered dietician status, interview, transcript of highest degree, bachelor's degree; for doctorate, minimum GPA of 3.4, transcript of highest degree, statement of career goals, interview, master's degree. Additional exam requirements/recommendations for international students: Required—TOEFL (minimum score 500 paper-based; 79 iBT). *Application deadline:* For fall admission, 4/1 for domestic students, 3/1 for international students; for spring admission, 10/15 for domestic students, 7/1 for international students. Applications are processed on a rolling basis. Application fee: $75. Electronic applications accepted. *Unit head:* Dr. Diane Rigassio, Program Director, 973-972-6731, Fax: 973-972-7403, E-mail: rigassdl@umdnj.edu. *Application contact:* Douglas Lomonaco, Assistant Professor, 973-972-5454, Fax: 973-972-7463, E-mail: shrpadm@umdnj.edu.

University of Memphis, Graduate School, College of Education, Department of Health and Sport Sciences, Memphis, TN 38152. Offers clinical nutrition (MS); exercise and sport science (MS); health promotion (MS); physical education teacher education (MS), including teacher education; sport and leisure commerce (MS). Part-time and evening/weekend programs available. *Faculty:* 18 full-time (9 women), 3 part-time/adjunct (1 woman). *Students:* 64 full-time (35 women), 36 part-time (23 women); includes 17 Black or African American, non-Hispanic/Latino; 1 Asian, non-Hispanic/Latino; 1 Hispanic/Latino, 4 international. Average age 27. 99 applicants, 72% accepted, 50 enrolled. In 2010, 35 master's awarded. *Degree requirements:* For master's, comprehensive exam, thesis. *Entrance requirements:* For master's, GRE General Test or GMAT (sport and leisure commerce). *Application deadline:* For fall admission, 5/1 priority date for domestic students; for spring admission, 11/1 for domestic students. Applications are processed on a rolling basis. Application fee: $35 ($60 for international students). *Financial support:* In 2010–11, 59 students received support; research assistantships with full tuition reimbursements available, teaching assistantships with full tuition reimbursements available, career-related internships or fieldwork, Federal Work-Study, scholarships/grants, tuition waivers (partial), and unspecified assistantships available. Financial award application deadline: 2/15; financial award applicants required to submit FAFSA. *Faculty research:* Sport marketing and consumer analysis, health psychology, smoking cessation, psychosocial aspects of cardiovascular disease, global health promotion. *Unit head:* Linda H. Clemens, Interim Chair, 901-678-2324, Fax: 901-678-3591, E-mail: lhclemns@memphis.edu. *Application contact:* Dr. Kenneth Ward, Graduate Studies Coordinator, 901-678-1714, E-mail: kdward@memphis.edu.

University of Michigan, School of Public Health, Department of Environmental Health Sciences, Ann Arbor, MI 48109. Offers environmental health sciences (MS, PhD); environmental quality and health (MPH); human nutrition (MPH); industrial hygiene (MPH, MS); nutritional sciences (MS); occupational and environmental epidemiology (MPH); toxicology (MPH, MS, PhD). *Accreditation:* CEPH (one or more programs are accredited). Part-time programs available. *Faculty:* 25 full-time (7 women), 23 part-time/adjunct (10 women). *Students:* 134 full-time (104 women), 37 part-time (23 women); includes 32 minority (10 Black or African American, non-Hispanic/Latino; 1 American Indian or Alaska Native, non-Hispanic/Latino; 14 Asian, non-Hispanic/Latino; 5 Hispanic/Latino; 2 Two or more races, non-Hispanic/Latino), 30 international. Average age 26. 254 applicants, 69% accepted, 68 enrolled. In 2010, 38 master's, 4 doctorates awarded. Terminal master's awarded for partial completion of doctoral program. *Degree requirements:* For master's, thesis (for some programs); for doctorate, thesis/dissertation, preliminary exam, oral defense of dissertation. *Entrance requirements:* For master's and doctorate, GRE General Test and/or MCAT. Additional exam requirements/recommendations for international students: Required—TOEFL (minimum score 560 paper-based; 220 computer-based; 100 iBT). *Application deadline:* For fall admission, 1/1 priority date for domestic and international students. Applications are processed on a rolling basis. Application fee: $65 ($75 for international students). Electronic applications accepted. *Expenses:* Tuition, state resident: full-time $17,784; part-time $1116 per credit hour. Tuition, nonresident: full-time $35,944; part-time $2125 per credit hour. International tuition: $35,994 full-time. Required fees: $95 per semester. Tuition and fees vary according to course load, degree level and program. *Financial support:* In 2010–11, 86 students received support, including 57 fellowships with full and partial tuition reimbursements available, 17 research assistantships with full tuition reimbursements available (averaging $21,000 per year), 12 teaching assistantships with full tuition reimbursements available (averaging $21,000 per year); Federal Work-Study, scholarships/grants, traineeships, and unspecified assistantships also available. Financial award application deadline: 3/1. *Faculty research:* Toxicology, occupational hygiene, nutrition, environmental exposure sciences, environmental epidemiology. Total annual research expenditures: $7.5 million. *Unit head:* Dr. Howard Hu, Chair, 734-764-3188, E-mail: howardhu@umich.edu. *Application contact:* Susan Crawford, Student Administrative Coordinator, 734-764-3018, E-mail: sph.inquiries@umich.edu.

University of Minnesota, Twin Cities Campus, Graduate School, College of Food, Agricultural and Natural Resource Sciences, Program in Nutrition, Minneapolis, MN 55455-0213. Offers MS, PhD. Part-time programs available. *Faculty:* 53 full-time (30 women). *Students:* 45 full-time (36 women), 4 part-time (all women); includes 5 minority (3 Asian, non-Hispanic/Latino; 2 Hispanic/Latino), 16 international. Average age 30. 77 applicants, 40% accepted, 17 enrolled. In 2010, 7 master's, 2 doctorates awarded. Terminal master's awarded for partial completion of doctoral program. *Degree requirements:* For master's, comprehensive exam, thesis; for doctorate, comprehensive exam, thesis/dissertation. *Entrance requirements:* For master's, GRE General Test, previous course work in general chemistry, organic chemistry, physiology, biology, biochemistry, statistics; minimum GPA of 3.0 (preferred); for doctorate, GRE General Test, previous course work in general chemistry, organic chemistry, calculus, biology, physics, physiology, biochemistry, statistics; minimum GPA of 3.0 (preferred). Additional exam requirements/recommendations for international students: Required—TOEFL (minimum score 550 paper-based; 213 computer-based; 79 iBT). *Application deadline:* For fall admission, 12/15 for domestic and international students; for spring admission, 10/15 for domestic and international students. Applications are processed on a rolling basis. Application fee: $75 ($95 for international students). Electronic applications accepted. *Financial support:* In 2010–11, fellowships with full tuition reimbursements (averaging $23,500 per year), research assistantships with partial tuition reimbursements (averaging $17,500 per year), teaching assistantships with partial tuition reimbursements (averaging $17,500 per year) were awarded; career-related internships or fieldwork, scholarships/grants, traineeships, health care benefits, and unspecified assistantships also available. Support available to part-time students. *Faculty research:* Diet and chronic disease: from basic biological and molecular biology approaches to a public health/intervention/epidemiology perspective. Total annual research expenditures: $2.1 million. *Unit head:* Dr. Marla Reicks, Director of Graduate Studies, 612-624-4735, Fax: 612-625-5272, E-mail: mreicks@umn.edu. *Application contact:* Nancy L. Toedt, Program Coordinator, 612-624-6753, Fax: 612-625-5272, E-mail: sviker@umn.edu.

University of Minnesota, Twin Cities Campus, School of Public Health, Major in Public Health Nutrition, Minneapolis, MN 55455-0213. Offers MPH. *Accreditation:* ADtA. Part-time programs available. *Degree requirements:* For master's, fieldwork, project. *Entrance requirements:* For master's, GRE General Test. Additional exam requirements/recommendations for international students: Required—TOEFL. Electronic applications accepted. *Expenses:* Contact institution. *Faculty research:* Nutrition and pregnancy outcomes, nutrition and women's health, child growth and nutrition, child and adolescent nutrition and eating behaviors, obesity and eating disorder prevention.

University of Missouri, Graduate School, College of Agriculture, Food and Natural Resources, Department of Food Science, Columbia, MO 65211. Offers food science (MS, PhD); foods and food systems management (MS); human nutrition (MS). *Faculty:* 17 full-time (4 women), 2 part-time/adjunct (0 women). *Students:* 28 full-time (12 women), 8 part-time (4 women); includes 1 minority (Hispanic/Latino), 19 international. Average age 27. 53 applicants, 40% accepted, 6 enrolled. In 2010, 9 master's, 2 doctorates awarded. Terminal master's awarded for partial completion of doctoral program. *Degree requirements:* For doctorate, comprehensive exam, thesis/dissertation. *Entrance requirements:* For master's, GRE General Test (minimum score: Verbal and Quantitative 1000 with neither section below 400, Analytical 3.5), minimum GPA of 3.0; BS in food science from accredited university; for doctorate, GRE General Test (minimum score: Verbal and Quantitative 1000 with neither section below 400, Analytical 3.5), minimum GPA of 3.0; BS and MS in food science from accredited university. Additional exam requirements/recommendations for international students: Required—TOEFL (minimum score 550 paper-based; 79 iBT). *Application deadline:* For fall admission, 4/1 priority date for domestic students; for winter admission, 10/1 priority date for domestic students. Applications are processed on a rolling basis. Application fee: $45 ($60 for international students). Electronic applications accepted. *Financial support:* Fellowships, research assistantships with tuition reimbursements, teaching assistantships with tuition reimbursements, institutionally sponsored loans, scholarships/grants, health care benefits, and unspecified assistantships available. Support available to part-time students. *Faculty research:* Food chemistry, food analysis, food microbiology, food engineering and process control, functional foods, meat science and processing technology. *Unit head:* Dr. Jinglu Tan, Department Chair, 573-882-2369, E-mail: tanj@missouri.edu. *Application contact:* JoAnn Lewis, 573-882-4113, E-mail: lewisj@missouri.edu.

University of Missouri, Graduate School, College of Human Environmental Science, Department of Nutritional Sciences, Columbia, MO 65211. Offers exercise physiology (MA,

Nutrition

University of Missouri (continued)

PhD); nutritional sciences (MS, PhD). *Degree requirements:* For doctorate, thesis/dissertation. *Entrance requirements:* For master's and doctorate, GRE General Test, minimum GPA of 3.0. Additional exam requirements/recommendations for international students: Required—TOEFL (minimum score 500 paper-based; 173 computer-based; 61 iBT).

University of Nebraska–Lincoln, Graduate College, College of Agricultural Sciences and Natural Resources, Department of Agricultural Leadership, Education and Communication, Lincoln, NE 68588. Offers distance education specialization (MS); leadership development (MS); leadership education (MS); nutrition outreach education specialization (MS); teaching and extension education specialization (MS). *Accreditation:* Teacher Education Accreditation Council. *Degree requirements:* For master's, thesis optional. *Entrance requirements:* For master's, resume. Additional exam requirements/recommendations for international students: Required—TOEFL (minimum score 550 paper-based; 213 computer-based). Electronic applications accepted. *Faculty research:* Teaching and instruction, extension education, leadership and human resource development, international agricultural education.

University of Nebraska–Lincoln, Graduate College, College of Agricultural Sciences and Natural Resources, Interdepartmental Area of Nutrition, Lincoln, NE 68588. Offers MS, PhD. *Degree requirements:* For master's, thesis optional; for doctorate, comprehensive exam, thesis/dissertation. *Entrance requirements:* For master's and doctorate, GRE General Test. Additional exam requirements/recommendations for international students: Required—TOEFL (minimum score 550 paper-based; 213 computer-based). Electronic applications accepted. *Faculty research:* Human nutrition and metabolism, animal nutrition and metabolism, biochemistry, community and clinical nutrition.

University of Nebraska–Lincoln, Graduate College, College of Education and Human Sciences, Department of Nutrition and Health Sciences, Lincoln, NE 68588. Offers community nutrition and health promotion (MS); nutrition (MS, PhD); nutrition and exercise (MS); nutrition and health sciences (MS, PhD). *Degree requirements:* For master's, thesis optional. *Entrance requirements:* For master's, GRE General Test. Additional exam requirements/recommendations for international students: Required—TOEFL (minimum score 550 paper-based; 213 computer-based). Electronic applications accepted. *Faculty research:* Foods/food service administration, community nutrition science, diet-health relationships.

University of Nebraska Medical Center, School of Allied Health Professions and College of Medicine, UNMC Dietetic Internship Program (Medical Nutrition Education Division), Omaha, NE 68198. Offers Certificate. *Entrance requirements:* Additional exam requirements/recommendations for international students: Required—TOEFL. *Expenses:* Tuition, state resident: part-time $198.25 per semester hour. Required fees: $63 per semester. *Faculty research:* Nutrition intervention outcomes.

University of Nevada, Reno, Graduate School, College of Agriculture, Biotechnology and Natural Resources, Department of Nutrition, Reno, NV 89557. Offers MS. *Degree requirements:* For master's, thesis optional. *Entrance requirements:* For master's, GRE, minimum GPA of 2.75. Additional exam requirements/recommendations for international students: Required—TOEFL (minimum score 500 paper-based; 173 computer-based; 61 iBT), IELTS (minimum score 6). Electronic applications accepted. *Expenses:* Tuition, state resident: full-time $2219; part-time $246 per credit. Tuition, nonresident: part-time $510 per credit. International tuition: $9009 full-time. Required fees: $59 per term. One-time fee: $101. Tuition and fees vary according to course load. *Faculty research:* Nutritional education, food technology, therapeutic human nutrition, human nutritional requirements, diet and disease.

University of New Hampshire, Graduate School, College of Life Sciences and Agriculture, Department of Molecular, Cellular and Biomedical Sciences, Program in Animal and Nutritional Sciences, Durham, NH 03824. Offers PhD. Part-time programs available. *Faculty:* 23 full-time. *Students:* 6 full-time (2 women), 1 (woman) part-time. Average age 39. 7 applicants, 29% accepted, 2 enrolled. *Entrance requirements:* For doctorate, GRE. Additional exam requirements/recommendations for international students: Required—TOEFL (minimum score 550 paper-based; 213 computer-based; 80 iBT). *Application deadline:* For fall admission, 6/1 priority date for domestic students, 4/1 priority date for international students; for spring admission, 12/1 for domestic students. Application fee: $65. Electronic applications accepted. *Financial support:* In 2010–11, 4 students received support, including 4 teaching assistantships; fellowships, research assistantships, scholarships/grants, traineeships, and unspecified assistantships also available. Support available to part-time students. *Unit head:* Dr. Rick Cote, Chairperson, 603-862-2458. *Application contact:* Flora Joyal, Administrative Assistant, 603-862-4095, E-mail: ansc.grad.program.info@unh.edu.

University of New Hampshire, Graduate School, College of Life Sciences and Agriculture, Department of Molecular, Cellular and Biomedical Sciences, Program in Nutritional Sciences, Durham, NH 03824. Offers MS. Part-time programs available. *Faculty:* 23 full-time. *Students:* 4 part-time (all women). Average age 33. 11 applicants, 9% accepted, 1 enrolled. In 2010, 2 master's awarded. *Degree requirements:* For master's, thesis. *Entrance requirements:* Additional exam requirements/recommendations for international students: Required—TOEFL (minimum score 550 paper-based; 213 computer-based; 80 iBT). *Application deadline:* For fall admission, 4/1 priority date for domestic students, 4/1 for international students; for spring admission, 12/1 for domestic students. Applications are processed on a rolling basis. Application fee: $65. Electronic applications accepted. *Financial support:* In 2010–11, 3 students received support, including 3 teaching assistantships; fellowships, research assistantships, career-related internships or fieldwork, Federal Work-Study, and scholarships/grants also available. Support available to part-time students. Financial award application deadline: 2/15. *Unit head:* Dr. Rick Cote, Chair, 603-862-2458. *Application contact:* Flora Joyal, Administrative Assistant, 603-862-4095.

University of New Haven, Graduate School, College of Arts and Sciences, Program in Human Nutrition, West Haven, CT 06516-1916. Offers MS. *Students:* 7 full-time (6 women), 18 part-time (15 women); includes 2 Asian, non-Hispanic/Latino; 1 Hispanic/Latino, 5 international. Average age 28. 24 applicants, 100% accepted, 10 enrolled. In 2010, 8 master's awarded. *Entrance requirements:* Additional exam requirements/recommendations for international students: Required—TOEFL (minimum score 520 paper-based; 190 computer-based; 70 iBT); Recommended—IELTS (minimum score 5.5). *Application deadline:* For fall admission, 5/31 for international students; for winter admission, 10/15 for international students; for spring admission, 1/15 for international students. Applications are processed on a rolling basis. Application fee: $50. Electronic applications accepted. *Financial support:* Research assistantships with partial tuition reimbursements, teaching assistantships with partial tuition reimbursements, career-related internships or fieldwork, Federal Work-Study, scholarships/grants, tuition waivers, and unspecified assistantships available. Support available to part-time students. Financial award applicants required to submit FAFSA. *Unit head:* Dr. Rosa A. Mo, Director, 203-932-7352. *Application contact:* Eloise Gormley, Director of Graduate Admissions, 203-932-7449, Fax: 203-932-7137, E-mail: gradinfo@newhaven.edu.

University of New Mexico, Graduate School, College of Education, Department of Individual, Family and Community Education, Program in Nutrition, Albuquerque, NM 87131-2039. Offers MS. Part-time programs available. *Students:* 10 full-time (9 women), 6 part-time (all women); includes 1 American Indian or Alaska Native, non-Hispanic/Latino; 1 Asian, non-Hispanic/Latino; 3 Hispanic/Latino. Average age 32. 20 applicants, 45% accepted, 7 enrolled. In 2010, 5 master's awarded. *Degree requirements:* For master's, comprehensive exam or thesis. *Entrance requirements:* For master's, GRE. *Application deadline:* For fall admission, 2/1 priority date for domestic students; for spring admission, 11/1 priority date for domestic students. Application fee: $50. Electronic applications accepted. *Expenses:* Tuition, state resident: full-time $5991; part-time $251 per credit hour. Tuition, nonresident: full-time $14,405; part-time $800.20 per credit hour. Tuition and fees vary according to course level, course load, program and reciprocity agreements. *Financial support:* In 2010–11, 12 students received support, including 2 fellowships (averaging $2,290 per year). Financial award application deadline: 3/1; financial award applicants required to submit FAFSA. *Faculty research:* Nutritional needs of children, obesity prevention, phytochemicals, international nutrition. *Unit head:* Dr. Carole Conn, Graduate Coordinator, 505-277-8185, Fax: 505-277-8361, E-mail: cconn@unm.edu. *Application contact:* Cynthia Salas, Program Office, 505-277-4535, Fax: 505-277-8361, E-mail: casalas@unm.edu.

The University of North Carolina at Chapel Hill, Graduate School, School of Public Health, Department of Nutrition, Chapel Hill, NC 27599. Offers nutrition (MPH, Dr PH, PhD); nutritional biochemistry (MS); professional practice program (MPH). *Accreditation:* ADtA. *Degree requirements:* For master's, comprehensive exam, thesis, major paper; for doctorate, comprehensive exam, thesis/dissertation. *Entrance requirements:* For master's and doctorate, GRE General Test, minimum GPA of 3.0. Additional exam requirements/recommendations for international students: Required—TOEFL. Electronic applications accepted. *Faculty research:* Nutrition policy, management and leadership development, lipid and carbohydrate metabolism, dietary trends and determinants, transmembrane signal transduction and carcinogenesis, maternal and child nutrition.

The University of North Carolina at Greensboro, Graduate School, School of Human Environmental Sciences, Department of Nutrition, Greensboro, NC 27412-5001. Offers MS, PhD. *Degree requirements:* For master's, thesis; for doctorate, thesis/dissertation. *Entrance requirements:* For master's and doctorate, GRE General Test. Additional exam requirements/recommendations for international students: Required—TOEFL. Electronic applications accepted.

University of North Florida, Brooks College of Health, Department of Nutrition and Dietetics, Jacksonville, FL 32224. Offers MSH. Part-time programs available. *Faculty:* 5 full-time (all women). *Students:* 30 full-time (27 women), 6 part-time (5 women); includes 3 Black or African American, non-Hispanic/Latino; 3 Hispanic/Latino. Average age 28. 62 applicants, 27% accepted, 16 enrolled. In 2010, 16 master's awarded. *Entrance requirements:* For master's, GRE General Test, minimum GPA of 3.0 in last 60 hours. Additional exam requirements/recommendations for international students: Required—TOEFL (minimum score 500 paper-based; 173 computer-based; 61 iBT). *Application deadline:* For fall admission, 7/1 for domestic students, 5/1 for international students; for spring admission, 11/1 for domestic students, 10/1 for international students. Applications are processed on a rolling basis. Application fee: $30. Electronic applications accepted. *Expenses:* Tuition, state resident: full-time $7646; part-time $318.60 per credit hour. Tuition, nonresident: full-time $23,502; part-time $979.24 per credit hour. Required fees: $1209; $50.37 per credit hour. Tuition and fees vary according to course load and program. *Financial support:* In 2010–11, 7 students received support, including 1 research assistantship (averaging $80 per year); career-related internships or fieldwork, Federal Work-Study, scholarships/grants, and tuition waivers (partial) also available. Financial award application deadline: 4/1; financial award applicants required to submit FAFSA. Total annual research expenditures: $42,149. *Application contact:* Dr. Catherine Christie, Program Director, 904-620-1423, Fax: 904-620-1942, E-mail: c.christie@unf.edu.

University of Oklahoma Health Sciences Center, Graduate College, College of Allied Health, Department of Nutritional Sciences, Oklahoma City, OK 73190. Offers MS. *Accreditation:* ADtA. *Degree requirements:* For master's, comprehensive exam, thesis optional. *Entrance requirements:* For master's, GRE General Test, interview, 3 letters of reference. Additional exam requirements/recommendations for international students: Required—TOEFL (minimum score 550 paper-based).

University of Pittsburgh, School of Health and Rehabilitation Sciences, Coordinated Master in Dietetics Program, Pittsburgh, PA 15260. Offers MS. *Accreditation:* ADtA. Part-time and evening/weekend programs available. *Students:* 31 full-time (29 women), 4 part-time (all women); includes 1 minority (Hispanic/Latino), 1 international. Average age 26. 34 applicants, 68% accepted, 17 enrolled. In 2010, 15 master's awarded. *Entrance requirements:* Additional exam requirements/recommendations for international students: Required—TOEFL (minimum score 550 paper-based; 213 computer-based; 80 iBT), IELTS (minimum score 6.5). *Application deadline:* For fall admission, 3/15 for domestic students, 1/31 for international students. Application fee: $50. Electronic applications accepted. *Expenses:* Contact institution. *Faculty research:* Targeted approaches to weight control, pediatric obesity treatment, effect of tart cherry juice on muscles. Total annual research expenditures: $40,979. *Unit head:* Dr. Scott Lephart, Department Chair and Associate Professor, 412-383-6530, Fax: 412-383-6527, E-mail: lephart@pitt.edu. *Application contact:* Shameem Gangjee, Director of Admissions, 412-383-6558, Fax: 412-383-6535, E-mail: admissions@shrs.pitt.edu.

University of Pittsburgh, School of Health and Rehabilitation Sciences, Master's Programs in Health and Rehabilitation Sciences, Pittsburgh, PA 15260. Offers health and rehabilitation sciences (MS), including clinical dietetics and nutrition, health care supervision and management, health information systems, occupational therapy, physical therapy, rehabilitation counseling, rehabilitation science and technology, sports medicine, wellness and human performance. *Accreditation:* APTA. Part-time and evening/weekend programs available. *Faculty:* 23 full-time (12 women), 4 part-time/adjunct (2 women). *Students:* 117 full-time (81 women), 41 part-time (27 women); includes 19 minority (8 Black or African American, non-Hispanic/Latino; 7 Asian, non-Hispanic/Latino; 1 Hispanic/Latino; 3 Two or more races, non-Hispanic/Latino), 67 international. Average age 28. 337 applicants, 64% accepted, 100 enrolled. In 2010, 110 master's awarded. *Degree requirements:* For master's, comprehensive exam (for some programs), thesis optional. *Entrance requirements:* For master's, minimum GPA of 3.0. Additional exam requirements/recommendations for international students: Required—TOEFL, IELTS. *Application deadline:* For fall admission, 1/31 for international students; for spring admission, 7/31 for international students. Applications are processed on a rolling basis. Application fee: $50. Electronic applications accepted. *Expenses:* Contact institution. *Financial support:* Research assistantships, teaching assistantships, Federal Work-Study, institutionally sponsored loans, traineeships, and unspecified assistantships available. Financial award applicants required to submit FAFSA. *Faculty research:* Assistive technology, seating and wheeled mobility, cellular neurophysiology, low back syndrome, augmentative communication. Total annual research expenditures: $7.8 million. *Unit head:* Dr. Clifford E. Brubaker, Dean, 412-383-6560, Fax: 412-383-6535, E-mail: cliffb@pitt.edu. *Application contact:* Shameem Gangjee, Director of Admissions, 412-383-6558, Fax: 412-383-6535, E-mail: admissions@shrs.pitt.edu.

University of Puerto Rico, Medical Sciences Campus, Graduate School of Public Health, Department of Human Development, Program in Nutrition, San Juan, PR 00936-5067. Offers MS. Part-time programs available. *Degree requirements:* For master's, thesis. *Entrance requirements:* For master's, GRE, previous course work in algebra, biochemistry, biology, chemistry, and social sciences.

University of Puerto Rico, Medical Sciences Campus, School of Health Professions, Program in Dietetics Internship, San Juan, PR 00936-5067. Offers Certificate. *Degree requirements:* For Certificate, one foreign language, clinical practice. *Entrance requirements:* For degree, minimum GPA of 2.5, interview, participation in the computer matching process by the American Dietetic Association.

University of Puerto Rico, Medical Sciences Campus, School of Medicine, Division of Graduate Studies, Department of Biochemistry, San Juan, PR 00936-5067. Offers MS, PhD. *Degree requirements:* For master's, thesis; for doctorate, comprehensive exam, thesis/dissertation. *Entrance requirements:* For master's and doctorate, GRE General Test, GRE Subject Test, interview, minimum GPA of 3.0. Electronic applications accepted. *Faculty research:* Genetics, cell and molecular biology, cancer biology, protein structure/function, glycosilation of proteins.

University of Puerto Rico, Río Piedras, College of Education, Program in Family Ecology and Nutrition, San Juan, PR 00931-3300. Offers M Ed. Part-time programs available. *Degree requirements:* For master's, thesis. *Entrance requirements:* For master's, PAEG or GRE, minimum GPA of 3.0, letter of recommendation.

University of Rhode Island, Graduate School, College of the Environment and Life Sciences, Department of Nutrition and Food Sciences, Kingston, RI 02881. Offers food science (MS, PhD); nutrition (MS, PhD). Part-time programs available. *Faculty:* 8 full-time (5 women), 1 (woman) part-time/adjunct. *Students:* 18 full-time (15 women), 10 part-time (all women); includes 1 minority (Asian, non-Hispanic/Latino), 1 international. In 2010, 11 master's awarded. *Degree requirements:* For master's, comprehensive exam (for some programs), thesis optional; for doctorate, thesis/dissertation. *Entrance requirements:* For master's and doctorate, GRE, 2 letters of recommendation. Additional exam requirements/recommendations for international students: Required—TOEFL (minimum score 550 paper-based; 213 computer-based). *Application deadline:* For fall admission, 7/15 for domestic students, 2/1 for international students; for spring admission, 11/15 for domestic students, 7/15 for international students. Application fee: $65. Electronic applications accepted. *Expenses:* Tuition, state resident: full-time $9588; part-time $533 per credit hour. Tuition, nonresident: full-time $22,968; part-time $1276 per credit hour. Required fees: $1282; $68 per semester. Tuition and fees vary according to program. *Financial support:* In 2010–11, 9 research assistantships with full and partial tuition reimbursements (averaging $13,122 per year), 5 teaching assistantships with full and partial tuition reimbursements (averaging $11,578 per year) were awarded. Financial award application deadline: 7/15; financial award applicants required to submit FAFSA. *Faculty research:* Food safety and quality, marine resource utilization, nutrition in underserved populations, eating behavior, lipid metabolism. Total annual research expenditures: $2.2 million. *Unit head:* Dr. Catherine English, Chair, 401-874-5869, Fax: 401-874-5974, E-mail: cathy@uri.edu. *Application contact:* Dr. Geoffrey Greene, Director of Graduate Studies, 401-874-4028, E-mail: gwg@uri.edu.

University of Southern Mississippi, Graduate School, College of Health, Department of Community Health Sciences, Hattiesburg, MS 39406-0001. Offers epidemiology and biostatistics (MPH); health education (MPH); health policy/administration (MPH); occupational/environmental health (MPH); public health nutrition (MPH). *Accreditation:* CEPH. Part-time and evening/weekend programs available. *Faculty:* 8 full-time (4 women), 1 part-time/adjunct (0 women). *Students:* 74 full-time (52 women), 19 part-time (15 women); includes 37 Black or African American, non-Hispanic/Latino; 2 Hispanic/Latino; 3 Two or more races, non-Hispanic/Latino, 6 international. Average age 32. 71 applicants, 63% accepted, 35 enrolled. In 2010, 46 master's awarded. *Degree requirements:* For master's, comprehensive exam, thesis (for some programs). *Entrance requirements:* For master's, GRE General Test, minimum GPA of 2.75 in last 60 hours. Additional exam requirements/recommendations for international students: Required—TOEFL, IELTS. *Application deadline:* For fall admission, 3/1 priority date for domestic and international students; for spring admission, 1/10 priority date for domestic and international students. Applications are processed on a rolling basis. Application fee: $50. Electronic applications accepted. *Financial support:* In 2010–11, 5 research assistantships with full tuition reimbursements (averaging $7,000 per year), 1 teaching assistantship with full tuition reimbursement (averaging $8,263 per year) were awarded; career-related internships or fieldwork, Federal Work-Study, institutionally sponsored loans, scholarships/grants, health care benefits, and unspecified assistantships also available. Financial award application deadline: 3/15; financial award applicants required to submit FAFSA. *Faculty research:* Rural health care delivery, school health, nutrition of pregnant teens, risk factor reduction, sexually transmitted diseases. *Unit head:* Dr. Emanual Ahua, Interim Chair, 601-266-5437, Fax: 601-266-5043. *Application contact:* Dr. Emanual Ahua, Interim Chair, 601-266-5437, Fax: 601-266-5043.

University of Southern Mississippi, Graduate School, College of Health, Department of Nutrition and Food Systems, Hattiesburg, MS 39406-0001. Offers nutrition (MS, PhD). Part-time programs available. *Faculty:* 6 full-time (5 women). *Students:* 15 full-time (all women), 37 part-time (36 women); includes 7 Black or African American, non-Hispanic/Latino; 1 Asian, non-Hispanic/Latino; 1 Hispanic/Latino; 1 Two or more races, non-Hispanic/Latino. Average age 30. 26 applicants, 38% accepted, 4 enrolled. In 2010, 7 master's, 1 doctorate awarded. *Degree requirements:* For master's, comprehensive exam, thesis (for some programs); for doctorate, comprehensive exam, thesis/dissertation. *Entrance requirements:* For master's, GRE General Test, minimum GPA of 2.75 on last 60 hours; for doctorate, GRE General Test, minimum GPA of 3.5. Additional exam requirements/recommendations for international students: Required—TOEFL, IELTS. *Application deadline:* For fall admission, 3/1 for domestic and international students; for spring admission, 1/10 priority date for domestic and international students. Application fee: $50. *Financial support:* In 2010–11, 2 research assistantships with full tuition reimbursements (averaging $12,069 per year), 6 teaching assistantships with full tuition reimbursements (averaging $7,676 per year) were awarded; career-related internships or fieldwork, Federal Work-Study, institutionally sponsored loans, scholarships/grants, traineeships, health care benefits, and unspecified assistantships also available. Financial award applicants required to submit FAFSA. *Unit head:* Dr. Kathleen Yadrick, Chair, 601-266-5377, Fax: 601-266-6343. *Application contact:* Belynda Brock, Graduate Admission Secretary, 601-266-5377, Fax: 601-266-5138.

The University of Tennessee, Graduate School, College of Education, Health and Human Sciences, Department of Nutrition, Knoxville, TN 37996. Offers nutrition (MS), including nutrition science, public health nutrition; MS/MPH. Part-time programs available. *Degree requirements:* For master's, thesis or alternative. *Entrance requirements:* For master's, GRE General Test, minimum GPA of 2.7. Additional exam requirements/recommendations for international students: Required—TOEFL. Electronic applications accepted. *Expenses:* Tuition, state resident: full-time $7440; part-time $414 per credit hour. Tuition, nonresident: full-time $22,478; part-time $1250 per credit hour. Required fees: $922; $43 per credit hour. Tuition and fees vary according to program.

The University of Tennessee at Martin, Graduate Programs, College of Agriculture and Applied Sciences, Department of Family and Consumer Sciences, Martin, TN 38238-1000. Offers dietetics (MSFCS); general family and consumer sciences (MSFCS). Part-time programs available. Postbaccalaureate distance learning degree programs offered (minimal on-campus study). *Faculty:* 8. *Students:* 40 (38 women); includes 6 Black or African American, non-Hispanic/Latino; 2 Hispanic/Latino; 1 Two or more races, non-Hispanic/Latino, 1 international. 45 applicants, 69% accepted, 12 enrolled. In 2010, 10 master's awarded. *Degree requirements:* For master's, comprehensive exam, thesis optional. *Entrance requirements:* For master's, GRE General Test, minimum GPA of 2.5. Additional exam requirements/recommendations for international students: Required—TOEFL (minimum score 525 paper-based; 197 computer-based; 71 iBT). *Application deadline:* For fall admission, 8/1 priority date for domestic students, 6/15 priority date for international students; for spring admission, 12/15 priority date for domestic students, 12/1 priority date for international students. Applications are processed on a rolling basis. Application fee: $30 ($130 for international students). Electronic applications accepted. *Expenses:* Tuition, state resident: full-time $7164; part-time $400 per credit hour. Tuition, nonresident: full-time $19,574; part-time $1090 per credit hour. Required fees: $1044; $60 per credit hour. *Financial support:* In 2010–11, 2 students received support, including 2 research assistantships with full tuition reimbursements available (averaging $7,893 per year); scholarships/grants and unspecified assistantships also available. Support available to part-time students. Financial award application deadline: 2/15; financial award applicants required to submit FAFSA. *Faculty research:* Children with developmental disabilities, regional food product development and marketing, parent education. *Unit head:* Dr. Lisa LeBleu, Coordinator, 731-881-7116, Fax: 731-881-7106, E-mail: llebleu@utm.edu. *Application contact:* Linda S. Arant, Student Services Specialist, 731-881-7012, Fax: 731-881-7499, E-mail: larant@utm.edu.

The University of Texas at Austin, Graduate School, College of Natural Sciences, School of Human Ecology, Program in Nutritional Sciences, Austin, TX 78712-1111. Offers nutrition (MA); nutritional sciences (PhD). *Degree requirements:* For master's, thesis; for doctorate, thesis/dissertation. *Entrance requirements:* For master's and doctorate, GRE General Test. Additional exam requirements/recommendations for international students: Required—TOEFL. Electronic applications accepted. *Faculty research:* Nutritional biochemistry, nutrient health assessment, obesity, nutrition education, molecular/cellular aspects of nutrient functions.

The University of Texas Southwestern Medical Center at Dallas, Southwestern School of Health Professions, Clinical Nutrition Program, Dallas, TX 75390. Offers MCN. *Accreditation:* ADtA. *Students:* 16 full-time (14 women), 1 (woman) part-time; includes 2 minority (both Black or African American, non-Hispanic/Latino). Average age 26. 43 applicants, 51% accepted, 17 enrolled. *Unit head:* Dr. Raul Caetano, Dean, 214-648-1500. *Application contact:* Anne Mclane, Associate Director of Admissions, 214-648-6708, Fax: 214-648-2102, E-mail: admissions@utsouthwestern.edu.

University of the District of Columbia, College of Arts and Sciences, Department of Biological and Environmental Sciences, Program in Nutrition and Dietetics, Washington, DC 20008-1175. Offers MS. *Degree requirements:* For master's, thesis. *Entrance requirements:* For master's, GRE, 3 letters of recommendation, personal interview. *Expenses:* Tuition, state resident: full-time $7580; part-time $421 per credit. Tuition, nonresident: full-time $14,580; part-time $810 per credit. Required fees: $620; $30 per credit. One-time fee: $100 part-time.

University of the Incarnate Word, School of Graduate Studies and Research, H-E-B School of Business and Administration, Programs in Administration, San Antonio, TX 78209-6397. Offers adult education (MAA); applied administration (MAA); communication arts (MAA); healthcare administration (MAA); instructional technology (MAA); international business (Certificate); nutrition (MAA); organizational development (MAA, Certificate); project management (Certificate); sports management (MAA). Part-time and evening/weekend programs available. Postbaccalaureate distance learning degree programs offered (no on-campus study). *Students:* 30 full-time (20 women), 64 part-time (37 women); includes 10 Black or African American, non-Hispanic/Latino; 1 Asian, non-Hispanic/Latino; 48 Hispanic/Latino, 8 international. Average age 35. In 2010, 68 master's awarded. *Degree requirements:* For master's, capstone. *Entrance requirements:* For master's, GRE, GMAT, undergraduate degree, minimum GPA of 2.5. Additional exam requirements/recommendations for international students: Required—TOEFL (minimum score 560 paper-based; 220 computer-based; 83 iBT). *Application deadline:* Applications are processed on a rolling basis. Application fee: $20. Electronic applications accepted. *Expenses:* Tuition: Part-time $725 per contact hour. Required fees: $890 per semester. *Financial support:* Federal Work-Study and scholarships/grants available. Financial award applicants required to submit FAFSA. *Unit head:* Dr. Daniel Dominguez, MAA Programs Director, 210-829-3180, Fax: 210-805-3564, E-mail: domingue@uiwtx.edu. *Application contact:* Andrea Cyterski-Acosta, Dean of Enrollment, 210-829-6005, Fax: 210-829-3921, E-mail: admis@uiwtx.edu.

University of the Incarnate Word, School of Graduate Studies and Research, School of Mathematics, Science, and Engineering, Program in Nutrition, San Antonio, TX 78209-6397. Offers administration (MS); medical nutrition therapy (MS); nutrition education and health promotion (MS); nutrition services administration (MS). Part-time and evening/weekend programs available. *Faculty:* 3 full-time (2 women), 2 part-time/adjunct (1 woman). *Students:* 12 full-time (11 women), 13 part-time (11 women); includes 1 Black or African American, non-Hispanic/Latino; 1 Asian, non-Hispanic/Latino; 7 Hispanic/Latino. Average age 27. In 2010, 5 master's awarded. *Degree requirements:* For master's, comprehensive exam, thesis or alternative. *Entrance requirements:* For master's, two letters of recommendation. Additional exam requirements/recommendations for international students: Required—TOEFL (minimum score 560 paper-based; 220 computer-based; 83 iBT). *Application deadline:* Applications are processed on a rolling basis. Application fee: $20. Electronic applications accepted. *Expenses:* Tuition: Part-time $725 per contact hour. Required fees: $890 per semester. *Financial support:* Federal Work-Study and scholarships/grants available. Financial award applicants required to submit FAFSA. *Faculty research:* Minority nutrition issues, child nutrition, diabetes prevention, international nutrition. Total annual research expenditures: $30,000. *Unit head:* Dr. Beth Senne-Duff, Associate Professor, 210-829-3165, Fax: 210-829-3153, E-mail: beths@uiwtx.edu. *Application contact:* Andrea Cyterski-Acosta, Dean of Enrollment, 210-829-6005, Fax: 210-829-3921, E-mail: admis@uiwtx.edu.

The University of Toledo, College of Graduate Studies, College of Medicine and Life Sciences, Department of Public Health and Preventative Medicine, Toledo, OH 43606-3390. Offers biostatistics and epidemiology (Certificate); contemporary gerontological practice (Certificate); environmental and occupational health and safety (MPH), including public health; epidemiology (MPH, Certificate); health administration (MPH); health promotion (MPH); nutrition (MPH); occupational health (MSOH, Certificate); MD/MPH. Part-time programs available. *Faculty:* 5. *Students:* 98 full-time (69 women), 42 part-time (28 women); includes 20 Black or African American, non-Hispanic/Latino; 8 Asian, non-Hispanic/Latino; 4 Hispanic/Latino, 3 international. Average age 29. 132 applicants, 75% accepted, 70 enrolled. In 2010, 44 master's, 28 other advanced degrees awarded. *Degree requirements:* For master's, thesis or alternative. *Entrance requirements:* For master's, minimum undergraduate GPA of 3.0, three letters of recommendation, statement of purpose, transcripts from all prior institutions attended; for Certificate, GRE, minimum undergraduate GPA of 3.0, three letters of recommendation, statement of purpose, transcripts from all prior institutions attended. Additional exam requirements/recommendations for international students: Required—TOEFL (minimum score 550 paper-based; 213 computer-based; 80 iBT), IELTS (minimum score 6.5), GRE. *Application deadline:* For fall admission, 6/15 for domestic students, 3/15 for international students; for spring admission, 10/15 for domestic students, 2/15 for international students. Applications are processed on a rolling basis. Application fee: $45 ($75 for international students). Electronic applications accepted. *Expenses:* Tuition, state resident: full-time $11,426; part-time $476 per credit hour. Tuition, nonresident: full-time $21,660; part-time $903 per credit hour. One-time fee: $62. *Financial support:* In 2010–11, 14 research assistantships with full tuition reimbursements (averaging $10,000 per year) were awarded; Federal Work-Study, institutionally sponsored loans, scholarships/grants, tuition waivers (full and partial), and unspecified assistantships also available. *Unit head:* Dr. Sheryl A. Milz, Chair, 419-383-3976, Fax: 419-383-6140, E-mail: sheryl.milz@utoledo.edu. *Application contact:* Joan Mulligan, Admissions Analyst, 419-383-4186, Fax: 419-383-6140, E-mail: joan.mulligan@utoledo.edu.

University of Toronto, School of Graduate Studies, Life Sciences Division, Department of Nutritional Sciences, Toronto, ON M5S 1A1, Canada. Offers M Sc, PhD. Part-time programs available. *Degree requirements:* For master's, thesis, oral thesis defense; for doctorate, comprehensive exam, thesis/dissertation, departmental examination, oral examination. *Entrance requirements:* For master's, minimum B average, background in nutrition or an area of biological or health sciences, 2 letters of reference; for doctorate, minimum B+ average in final 2 years, background in nutrition or an area of biological of health sciences, 2 letters of reference. Additional exam requirements/recommendations for international students: Required—TOEFL (580 paper-based; 237 computer-based), TWE (5), IELTS (7), Michigan English Language Assessment Battery (85), or COPE (4).

University of Utah, Graduate School, College of Health, Division of Nutrition, Salt Lake City, UT 84112. Offers MS. *Accreditation:* ADtA. *Faculty:* 7 full-time (5 women), 1 (woman) part-time/adjunct. *Students:* 29 full-time (26 women); includes 2 minority (1 Asian, non-Hispanic/Latino; 1 Hispanic/Latino), 2 international. Average age 28. 67 applicants, 31% accepted, 15 enrolled. In 2010, 16 master's awarded. *Degree requirements:* For master's, comprehensive exam, thesis. *Entrance requirements:* For master's, GRE General Test, minimum undergraduate GPA of 3.0. Additional exam requirements/recommendations for international students: Required—TOEFL (minimum score 500 paper-based; 173 computer-based). *Application deadline:* For fall admission, 1/3 for domestic and international students. Application fee: $55 ($65 for international students). Electronic applications accepted. *Expenses:* Contact institution. *Financial support:* In 2010–11, 21 students received support, including 4 fellowships, 1 research assistantship with partial tuition reimbursement available (averaging $5,750 per year), 11 teaching assistantships with partial tuition reimbursements available (averaging $5,750 per year); career-related internships or fieldwork, Federal Work-Study, and institutionally sponsored loans also available. Financial award application deadline: 1/3; financial award applicants required to submit FAFSA. *Faculty research:* Cholesterol metabolism, sport nutrition education, metabolic and critical care, cardiovascular nutrition, wilderness nutrition, pediatric nutrition. Total annual research expenditures: $29,452. *Unit head:* Dr. E. Wayne Askew, Director, 801-581-8240, Fax: 801-585-3874, E-mail: wayne.askew@health.utah.edu. *Application contact:* Jean Zancanella, Academic Adviser, 801-581-5280, Fax: 801-585-3874, E-mail: jean.zancanella@health.utah.edu.

Nutrition

University of Vermont, Graduate College, College of Agriculture and Life Sciences, Department of Nutrition and Food Sciences, Program in Dietetics, Burlington, VT 05405. Offers MSD. *Students:* 13 (all women). 16 applicants, 44% accepted, 7 enrolled. In 2010, 5 master's awarded. *Entrance requirements:* For master's, GRE General Test. Additional exam requirements/recommendations for international students: Required—TOEFL (minimum score 550 paper-based; 213 computer-based; 80 iBT). *Application deadline:* For fall admission, 12/15 priority date for domestic and international students. Application fee: $40. Electronic applications accepted. *Expenses:* Tuition, state resident: part-time $537 per credit hour. Tuition, nonresident: part-time $1355 per credit hour. *Unit head:* Dr. Jane Ross, Director, 802-656-3374. *Application contact:* Amy Nickerson, Coordinator, 802-656-3374.

University of Vermont, Graduate College, College of Agriculture and Life Sciences, Program in Animal, Nutrition and Food Sciences, Burlington, VT 05405. Offers PhD. *Students:* 18 (7 women); includes 2 Asian, non-Hispanic/Latino, 10 international. 18 applicants, 44% accepted, 5 enrolled. In 2010, 2 doctorates awarded. *Degree requirements:* For doctorate, one foreign language, thesis/dissertation. *Entrance requirements:* For doctorate, GRE General Test. Additional exam requirements/recommendations for international students: Required—TOEFL (minimum score 550 paper-based; 213 computer-based; 80 iBT). *Application deadline:* For fall admission, 4/1 priority date for domestic students. Applications are processed on a rolling basis. Application fee: $40. Electronic applications accepted. *Expenses:* Tuition, state resident: part-time $537 per credit hour. Tuition, nonresident: part-time $1355 per credit hour. *Financial support:* Application deadline: 3/1. *Unit head:* Dr. R. K. Johnson, Dean, 802-656-2070. *Application contact:* Dr. David Kerr, Coordinator, 802-656-2070.

University of Washington, Graduate School, School of Public Health, Department of Epidemiology, Interdisciplinary Graduate Program in Nutritional Sciences, Seattle, WA 98195. Offers MPH, MS, PhD. *Accreditation:* ADtA. Part-time programs available. *Students:* 33 full-time (29 women), 13 part-time (all women); includes 7 Asian, non-Hispanic/Latino; 1 Hispanic/Latino, 2 international. Average age 28. 142 applicants, 30% accepted, 17 enrolled. In 2010, 9 master's, 2 doctorates awarded. Terminal master's awarded for partial completion of doctoral program. *Degree requirements:* For master's, thesis, practicum (MPH); for doctorate, comprehensive exam, thesis/dissertation. *Entrance requirements:* For master's, GRE General Test, experience in health sciences (preferred); minimum GPA of 3.0; for doctorate, GRE General Test, master's degree, experience in health sciences (preferred), minimum GPA of 3.0. Additional exam requirements/recommendations for international students: Required—TOEFL (minimum score 580 paper-based; 237 computer-based; 92 iBT), IELTS (minimum score 7). *Application deadline:* For fall admission, 2/1 for domestic students, 11/1 for international students. Application fee: $75. Electronic applications accepted. *Financial support:* Scholarships/grants available. *Faculty research:* Dietary behavior, dietary supplements, obesity, clinical nutrition, addictive behaviors. *Unit head:* Dr. Adam Drewnowski, Chair, 206-543-1065. *Application contact:* Carey Purnell, Graduate Program Assistant, 206-543-1730, Fax: 206-685-1696, E-mail: nutr@u.washington.edu.

University of Wisconsin–Madison, Graduate School, College of Agricultural and Life Sciences, Department of Nutritional Sciences, Madison, WI 53706. Offers MS, PhD. *Faculty:* 12 full-time (5 women). *Students:* 28 full-time (18 women); includes 1 Black or African American, non-Hispanic/Latino; 2 Asian, non-Hispanic/Latino; 1 Hispanic/Latino, 3 international. Average age 27. 91 applicants, 14% accepted, 5 enrolled. In 2010, 2 master's, 5 doctorates awarded. Terminal master's awarded for partial completion of doctoral program. *Degree requirements:* For master's, thesis or research report; for doctorate, comprehensive exam, thesis/dissertation. *Entrance requirements:* For master's and doctorate, GRE General Test. Additional exam requirements/recommendations for international students: Required—TOEFL (minimum score 550 paper-based; 213 computer-based; 80 iBT). *Application deadline:* For fall admission, 1/1 priority date for domestic and international students. Application fee: $56. Electronic applications accepted. *Expenses:* Tuition, state resident: full-time $9887; part-time $617.96 per credit. Tuition, nonresident: full-time $24,054; part-time $1503.40 per credit. Required fees: $67.63 per credit. Tuition and fees vary according to reciprocity agreements. *Financial support:* In 2010–11, 28 research assistantships with partial tuition reimbursements (averaging $22,000 per year), 28 teaching assistantships with partial tuition reimbursements (averaging $22,000 per year) were awarded; traineeships and unspecified assistantships also available. *Faculty research:* Human and animal nutrition, nutrition epidemiology, nutrition education, biochemical and molecular nutrition. Total annual research expenditures: $3 million. *Unit head:* Dr. James M. Ntambi, Chair, 608-262-2727, Fax: 608-262-5860, E-mail: ntambi@biochem.wisc.edu. *Application contact:* Danielle L. Devereaux-Weber, Graduate Coordinator, 608-262-2513, Fax: 608-262-5860, E-mail: devereaux@nutrisci.wisc.edu.

University of Wisconsin–Stevens Point, College of Professional Studies, School of Health Promotion and Human Development, Program in Nutritional Sciences, Stevens Point, WI 54481-3897. Offers MS. Part-time programs available. *Degree requirements:* For master's, thesis or alternative. *Entrance requirements:* For master's, minimum GPA of 2.75.

University of Wisconsin–Stout, Graduate School, College of Human Development, Program in Food and Nutritional Sciences, Menomonie, WI 54751. Offers MS. Part-time programs available. *Degree requirements:* For master's, thesis. *Entrance requirements:* For master's, minimum GPA of 3.0. Additional exam requirements/recommendations for international students: Required—TOEFL (minimum score 500 paper-based; 173 computer-based; 61 iBT). Electronic applications accepted. *Faculty research:* Disease states and nutrition, childhood obesity, nutraceuticals, food safety, nanotechnology.

University of Wyoming, College of Agriculture and Natural Resources, Department of Animal Sciences, Program in Food Science and Human Nutrition, Laramie, WY 82070. Offers MS. *Degree requirements:* For master's, thesis. *Entrance requirements:* For master's, GRE General Test, minimum GPA of 3.0. Additional exam requirements/recommendations for international students: Required—TOEFL (minimum score 525 paper-based). Electronic applications accepted. *Faculty research:* Protein and lipid metabolism, food microbiology, food safety, meat science.

Utah State University, School of Graduate Studies, College of Agriculture, Department of Nutrition and Food Sciences, Logan, UT 84322. Offers dietetic administration (MDA); food microbiology and safety (MFMS); nutrition and food sciences (MS, PhD); nutrition science (MS, PhD), including molecular biology. Postbaccalaureate distance learning degree programs offered. *Degree requirements:* For master's, thesis; for doctorate, comprehensive exam, thesis/dissertation, teaching experience. *Entrance requirements:* For master's, GRE General Test, minimum GPA of 3.0, course work in chemistry, biochemistry, physics, math, bacteriology, physiology; for doctorate, GRE General Test, minimum GPA of 3.2, course work in chemistry, MS or manuscript in referred journal. Additional exam requirements/recommendations for international students: Required—TOEFL (minimum score 550 paper-based). Electronic applications accepted. *Faculty research:* Mineral balance, meat microbiology and nitrate interactions, milk ultrafiltration, lactic culture, milk coagulation.

Vanderbilt University, School of Nursing, Nashville, TN 37240. Offers adult acute care nurse practitioner (MSN); adult nurse practitioner/cardiovascular disease management and prevention (MSN); adult nurse practitioner/palliative care (MSN); clinical management (clinical nurse leader/specialist) (MSN); emergency nurse practitioner (MSN); family nurse practitioner (MSN); gerontology nurse practitioner (MSN); health systems management (MSN); neonatal nurse practitioner (MSN); nurse midwifery (MSN); nurse midwifery/family nurse practitioner (MSN); nursing informatics (MSN); nursing practice (DNP); nursing science (PhD); nutrition (MS); pediatric acute care nurse practitioner (MSN); pediatric primary care nurse practitioner (MSN); psychiatric-mental health nurse practitioner (MSN); women's health nurse practitioner (MSN); including urogynecology; women's health nurse practitioner/adult nurse practitioner (MSN); MSN/M Div; MSN/MTS. *Accreditation:* ACNM/DOA; NLN (one or more programs are accredited). Part-time programs available. Postbaccalaureate distance learning degree programs offered (minimal on-campus study). *Degree requirements:* For doctorate, comprehensive exam, thesis/dissertation. *Entrance requirements:* For master's, GRE General Test, minimum B average in

undergraduate course work, 3 letters of recommendation; for doctorate, GRE General Test, interview, 3 letters of recommendation from doctorally-prepared faculty, MSN, essay. Additional exam requirements/recommendations for international students: Required—TOEFL. *Expenses:* Contact institution. *Faculty research:* Lymphedema, palliative care and bereavement, health services research including workforce, safety and quality of care, gerontology, better birth outcomes including nutrition.

Virginia Polytechnic Institute and State University, Graduate School, College of Agriculture and Life Sciences, Department of Human Nutrition, Foods and Exercise, Blacksburg, VA 24061. Offers MS, PhD. *Faculty:* 23 full-time (16 women). *Students:* 47 full-time (33 women), 5 part-time (all women); includes 8 Black or African American, non-Hispanic/Latino; 2 Asian, non-Hispanic/Latino, 7 international. Average age 28. 61 applicants, 38% accepted, 18 enrolled. In 2010, 5 master's, 8 doctorates awarded. *Degree requirements:* For master's, comprehensive exam (for some programs), thesis (for some programs); for doctorate, comprehensive exam (for some programs), thesis/dissertation (for some programs). *Entrance requirements:* For master's and doctorate, GRE. Additional exam requirements/recommendations for international students: Required—TOEFL (minimum score 550 paper-based; 213 computer-based). *Application deadline:* For fall admission, 7/1 for domestic and international students; for spring admission, 12/1 for domestic and international students. Applications are processed on a rolling basis. Application fee: $65. Electronic applications accepted. *Expenses:* Tuition, state resident: full-time $9399; part-time $488 per credit hour. Tuition, nonresident: full-time $17,854; part-time $957.75 per credit hour. Required fees: $1534. Full-time tuition and fees vary according to program. *Financial support:* In 2010–11, 4 fellowships with full tuition reimbursements (averaging $2,000 per year), 18 research assistantships with full tuition reimbursements (averaging $16,817 per year), 23 teaching assistantships with full tuition reimbursements (averaging $13,691 per year) were awarded; career-related internships or fieldwork, Federal Work-Study, scholarships/grants, health care benefits, and unspecified assistantships also available. Financial award application deadline: 1/15. *Faculty research:* Nutrition and food science research. Total annual research expenditures: $6.8 million. *Unit head:* Dr. Susan M. Hutson, UNIT HEAD, 540-231-4672, Fax: 540-231-3916, E-mail: susanh5@vt.edu. *Application contact:* Robert Grange, Contact, 540-231-2725, Fax: 540-231-3916, E-mail: rgrange@vt.edu.

Washington State University, Graduate School, College of Pharmacy, Department of Nutrition and Dietetics, Program in Human Nutrition, Pullman, WA 99164. Offers MS. *Faculty:* 13. *Students:* 5 full-time (4 women); includes 1 American Indian or Alaska Native, non-Hispanic/Latino; 1 Asian, non-Hispanic/Latino, 2 international. Average age 29. 11 applicants, 9% accepted, 1 enrolled. In 2010, 4 master's awarded. *Degree requirements:* For master's, comprehensive exam (for some programs), thesis (for some programs), oral exam, written exam. *Entrance requirements:* For master's, GRE General Test, minimum GPA of 3.0, resume, 3 letters of recommendation, letter of interest. Additional exam requirements/recommendations for international students: Required—TOEFL (minimum score 550 paper-based; 213 computer-based). *Application deadline:* For fall admission, 2/1 priority date for domestic students, 2/1 for international students; for spring admission, 8/1 priority date for domestic students, 7/1 for international students. Applications are processed on a rolling basis. Application fee: $50. Electronic applications accepted. *Expenses:* Tuition, state resident: full-time $8552; part-time $443 per credit. Tuition, nonresident: full-time $21,650; part-time $1083 per credit. Required fees: $846. *Financial support:* In 2010–11, 3 students received support, including 1 research assistantship with full and partial tuition reimbursement available (averaging $13,917 per year), 2 teaching assistantships with full and partial tuition reimbursements available (averaging $13,056 per year); career-related internships or fieldwork, Federal Work-Study, scholarships/grants, tuition waivers (partial), and unspecified assistantships also available. Financial award application deadline: 2/1; financial award applicants required to submit FAFSA. *Faculty research:* Nutrition education programs, cultural issues in community nutrition programs. *Unit head:* Dr. Kathryn E. Meier, Chair, 509-335-3573, Fax: 509-335-5902. E-mail: kmeier@wsu.edu. *Application contact:* Graduate School Admissions, 800-GRADWSU, Fax: 509-335-1949, E-mail: gradsch@wsu.edu.

Washington State University, Graduate School, College of Pharmacy, Department of Nutrition and Dietetics, Program in Nutrition, Pullman, WA 99164. Offers PhD. *Faculty:* 10. *Students:* 2 full-time (both women), 1 (woman) part-time, 1 international. Average age 29. 11 applicants, 9% accepted, 1 enrolled. In 2010, 2 doctorates awarded. *Degree requirements:* For doctorate, comprehensive exam, thesis/dissertation, oral exam, written exam. *Entrance requirements:* For doctorate, GRE, minimum GPA of 3.0, resume, 3 letters of recommendation. Additional exam requirements/recommendations for international students: Required—TOEFL (minimum score 550 paper-based; 213 computer-based). *Application deadline:* For fall admission, 2/1 priority date for domestic and international students; for spring admission, 8/1 priority date for domestic students, 7/1 priority date for international students. Applications are processed on a rolling basis. Application fee: $50. Electronic applications accepted. *Expenses:* Tuition, state resident: full-time $8552; part-time $443 per credit. Tuition, nonresident: full-time $21,650; part-time $1083 per credit. Required fees: $846. *Financial support:* In 2010–11, 2 students received support, including 1 fellowship (averaging $3,250 per year), 1 research assistantship with full and partial tuition reimbursement available (averaging $13,917 per year), teaching assistantships with full and partial tuition reimbursements available (averaging $13,056 per year); career-related internships or fieldwork, Federal Work-Study, institutionally sponsored loans, scholarships/grants, health care benefits, tuition waivers (partial), and unspecified assistantships also available. Financial award application deadline: 2/1; financial award applicants required to submit FAFSA. *Faculty research:* Breastfeeding and lactation influence on maternal child wellbeing, sports anemia preschool nutrition. *Unit head:* Dr. Kathryn E. Meier, Chair, 509-335-3573, Fax: 509-335-5902, E-mail: kmeier@wsu.edu. *Application contact:* Graduate School Admissions, 800-GRADWSU, Fax: 509-335-1949, E-mail: gradsch@wsu.edu.

Wayne State University, College of Liberal Arts and Sciences, Department of Nutrition and Food Science, Detroit, MI 48202. Offers MA, MS, PhD. *Faculty:* 10 full-time (7 women). *Students:* 43 full-time (36 women), 14 part-time (13 women); includes 11 minority (3 Black or African American, non-Hispanic/Latino; 8 Asian, non-Hispanic/Latino), 19 international. Average age 30. 49 applicants, 65% accepted, 16 enrolled. In 2010, 5 master's, 2 doctorates awarded. Terminal master's awarded for partial completion of doctoral program. *Degree requirements:* For master's, thesis (for some programs); for doctorate, thesis/dissertation. *Entrance requirements:* For master's, GRE General Test, minimum GPA of 3.0; for doctorate, GRE General Test, minimum GPA of 3.0; letters of recommendation; personal statement. Additional exam requirements/recommendations for international students: Required—TOEFL (minimum score 550 paper-based; 213 computer-based); Recommended—TWE (minimum score 6). *Application deadline:* For fall admission, 7/1 for domestic students, 6/1 for international students; for winter admission, 10/1 for international students; for spring admission, 2/1 for international students. Applications are processed on a rolling basis. Application fee: $30 ($50 for international students). Electronic applications accepted. *Expenses:* Tuition, state resident: full-time $7662; part-time $478.85 per credit hour. Tuition, nonresident: full-time $16,920; part-time $1057.55 per credit hour. Required fees: $571; $35.70 per credit hour. $188.05 per semester. Tuition and fees vary according to course load and program. *Financial support:* In 2010–11, 10 students received support, including 2 fellowships with tuition reimbursements available (averaging $16,875 per year), 2 research assistantships (averaging $18,788 per year), 8 teaching assistantships (averaging $16,984 per year); career-related internships or fieldwork and Federal Work-Study also available. Financial award application deadline: 4/1. *Faculty research:* Nutrition, cancer and gene expression, food microbiology and food safety, lipids, lipoprotein and cholesterol metabolism, obesity and diabetes, metabolomics. *Unit head:* Dr. K. L. Catherine Jen, Chair, 313-577-2500, E-mail: cjen@sun.science.wayne.edu. *Application contact:* Pramod Khosla, Assistant Professor, 313-577-9055, Fax: 313-577-8616, E-mail: pkhosla@sun.science.wayne.edu.

West Chester University of Pennsylvania, Office of Graduate Studies, College of Health Sciences, Department of Health, West Chester, PA 19383. Offers emergency preparedness (Certificate); health care management (MPH, Certificate), including administration (MPH),

Nutrition

community (MPH), environment (MPH), health care management (Certificate), integrative (MPH), nutrition (MPH); integrative health (Certificate); school health (M Ed). *Accreditation:* CEPH. Part-time and evening/weekend programs available. *Students:* 84 full-time (61 women), 97 part-time (75 women); includes 66 minority (53 Black or African American, non-Hispanic/Latino; 2 American Indian or Alaska Native, non-Hispanic/Latino; 9 Asian, non-Hispanic/Latino; 2 Hispanic/Latino), 20 international. Average age 30. 114 applicants, 81% accepted, 48 enrolled. In 2010, 57 master's, 9 other advanced degrees awarded. *Degree requirements:* For master's, thesis (for some programs), minimum GPA of 3.0. *Entrance requirements:* For master's, one-page statement of career objectives, two letters of reference. Additional exam requirements/recommendations for international students: Required—TOEFL (minimum score 550 paper-based; 213 computer-based; 80 iBT). *Application deadline:* For fall admission, 4/15 priority date for domestic students, 3/15 for international students; for spring admission, 10/15 for domestic students, 9/1 for international students. Applications are processed on a rolling basis. Application fee: $35. Electronic applications accepted. *Expenses:* Tuition, state resident: full-time $6966; part-time $387 per credit. Tuition, nonresident: full-time $11,146; part-time $619 per credit. Required fees: $1614; $133.24 per credit. Part-time tuition and fees vary according to campus/location. *Financial support:* Unspecified assistantships available. Support available to part-time students. Financial award application deadline: 2/15; financial award applicants required to submit FAFSA. *Faculty research:* Health school communities, community health issues and evidence-based programs, environment and health, nutrition and health, integrative health. *Unit head:* Dr. Bethann Cinelli, Chair, 610-436-2267, E-mail: bcinelli@wcupa.edu. *Application contact:* Dr. Lynn Carson, Graduate Coordinator, 610-436-2138, E-mail: lcarson@wcupa.edu.

West Virginia University, Davis College of Agriculture, Forestry and Consumer Sciences, Division of Animal and Nutritional Sciences, Program in Animal and Nutritional Sciences, Morgantown, WV 26506. Offers breeding (MS); food sciences (MS); nutrition (MS); physiology (MS); production management (MS); reproduction (MS). Part-time programs available. *Degree requirements:* For master's, thesis, oral and written exams. *Entrance requirements:* For master's, GRE, minimum GPA of 2.5. Additional exam requirements/recommendations for international students: Required—TOEFL. *Faculty research:* Animal nutrition, reproductive physiology, food science.

Winthrop University, College of Arts and Sciences, Department of Human Nutrition, Rock Hill, SC 29733. Offers MS. Part-time programs available. *Degree requirements:* For master's, thesis optional. *Entrance requirements:* For master's, GRE General Test, PRAXIS, or MAT, interview, minimum GPA of 3.0. Electronic applications accepted.

CASE WESTERN RESERVE UNIVERSITY

Case School of Medicine
Department of Nutrition

Programs of Study	The Department of Nutrition offers programs that span the breadth of the discipline, from applied nutrition and dietetics to basic nutritional sciences. These include the Master of Science in Nutrition Program; the Master of Science in Public Health Nutrition Internship Program, with fieldwork experiences in public health and community-based agencies; and the Coordinated Dietetic Internship/Master's Program, with University Hospitals Case Medical Center and Veterans Affairs Medical Center. The Doctor of Philosophy degree is also offered.
	The master's degree programs require from one to two years of course work, depending upon the student's undergraduate preparation and the specific program. A thesis or nonthesis option may be selected.
	The Ph.D. program emphasizes nutritional biochemistry/metabolism, molecular nutrition, and human nutrition. It builds upon faculty expertise in the Departments of Nutrition, Biochemistry, Molecular Biology, Medicine, and Pediatrics. In recent years, investigators in nutritional biochemistry have used molecular biology techniques to enhance understanding of human metabolism. In the first year, nutrition students join graduate students from the other basic science departments in an integrated course that provides a broad introduction to cellular and molecular biology. The subsequent graduate program includes formal courses in human nutrition and nutritional biochemistry, seminars, and, most importantly, the performance of original research.
Research Facilities	Several well-equipped laboratories are housed in the Case School of Medicine Building. The Department has access to clinical research units at University Hospitals Case Medical Center and Cleveland Clinic Lerner College of Medicine for the conduct of human clinical nutrition and whole-body metabolism studies. The Department has all general equipment necessary for conducting studies in nutritional biochemistry, including three gas chromatographs and mass spectrometers used for human investigation with stable isotopes. Facilities for isolated organ perfusion and a comprehensive organic chemistry laboratory for synthesis of new nutrients are also available.
Financial Aid	The University sponsors a federally funded work-study program as well as loan assistance. Students in the Coordinated Dietetic Internship/Master's Program are paid a stipend by the hospital for the first twelve months of the program. Ph.D. students in nutritional biochemistry or molecular nutrition will receive an annual stipend of $25,000 in 2011–12.
Cost of Study	Tuition for 2011–12 is $1487 per credit hour. It is $17,845 per semester for 12 or more credit hours. Partial-tuition scholarships are available for some master's students. Full-tuition scholarships are provided by the Department for students in the Ph.D. nutritional biochemistry or molecular nutrition program.
Living and Housing Costs	Most graduate students find privately owned apartments near the campus. Costs are below average for large urban areas.
Student Group	The University has 9,228 students, of whom about 5,360 are enrolled in graduate and professional schools. About 305 students attend adjacent institutes of music and art. Approximately 85 graduate students are in residence in the Department.
Location	Cleveland is an industrial and financial center. The city is richly endowed with cultural facilities, nearly all of them located in a single area known as the University Circle. In this area are the University, the Cleveland Orchestra, the Museum of Art, the Museum of Natural History, and several excellent repertory theaters. The city is also the home of the Cleveland Indians and Cavaliers and the Rock and Roll Hall of Fame. The camping, sailing, and skiing areas of Ohio, western Pennsylvania, and western New York are readily accessible.
The University and The Department	The strength of its combined science departments places the University in the top rank of institutions in this country. The Department of Nutrition has a number of associate members in several departments in the Case School of Medicine and in the University and has strong ties with the Departments of Chemistry, Biology, and Biomedical Engineering. A major emphasis is on interdisciplinary training programs in biological and chemical sciences.
Applying	Prerequisites for entrance into the Ph.D. program are organic chemistry, biology, and mathematics through calculus. Applications should be submitted in late autumn or early winter for an anticipated entrance in the following autumn semester. Application forms may be obtained from the Department or online at http://www.applyweb.com/apply/cwrug/menu.html. Ph.D. applicants are required to take the Graduate Record Examinations, including the General Test and one Subject Test.
	Information concerning application and prerequisites for specific master's programs should be obtained directly from the Department.
Correspondence and Information	Graduate Admissions Committee Department of Nutrition (M.S. or Ph.D.) Case Western Reserve University 10900 Euclid Avenue Cleveland, Ohio 44106-4954 Phone: 216-368-2440 E-mail: paw5@cwru.edu Web site: http://www.cwru.edu/med/nutrition/home.html	Coordinator Biomedical Science Training Program (Ph.D. only) Case School of Medicine WG1 Case Western Reserve University Cleveland, Ohio 44106-4935 Phone: 216-368-3347

Case Western Reserve University

THE FACULTY AND THEIR RESEARCH

Hope Barkoukis, Associate Professor; Ph.D., Case Western Reserve, 1997. Clinical nutrition, diet and liver cirrhosis.

Henri Brunengraber, Professor and Chairman; M.D., 1968, Ph.D., 1976, Brussels. Metabolic regulation; control of flux through metabolic pathways; design and testing of artificial nutrients; noninvasive probes of liver metabolism; markers of alcoholism; mass spectrometry.

Colleen Croniger, Assistant Professor; Ph.D., Case Western Reserve, 1990. Metabolic regulation of carbohydrate and lipid metabolism using genetically altered animal models.

Paul Ernsberger, Associate Professor; Ph.D., Northwestern, 1984. Genetic obesity and the role of nutrition in cardiovascular disease; novel signaling pathways.

Maria Hatzoglou, Professor; Ph.D., Athens, 1985. Identification of retroviral receptors and their use in gene therapy.

Mary Beth Kavanagh, Senior Instructor; M.S., Case Western Reserve, 1992; RD, LD. Nutritional education for nursing and dentistry; nutrition and the media.

Jane Korsberg, Senior Instructor and Private Practice; M.S., Case Western Reserve, 1977; RD, LD.

Edith Lerner, Associate Professor and Vice-Chairman; Ph.D., Wisconsin, 1971. Assessment of nutritional status during pregnancy; trace-mineral metabolism during pregnancy; nutritional requirements for the preterm infant.

Danny Manor, Associate Professor; Ph.D., Yeshiva (Einstein), 1989. Molecular-level treatment and prevention of cancer.

Isabel Parraga, Associate Professor and Director, M.S. in Public Health Nutrition Internship Program; Ph.D., Case Western Reserve, 1992. Nutritional anthropology; maternal and child nutrition; public health nutrition; child growth and schistosomiasis.

Kay Sisk, Visiting Instructor; M.S., Case Western Reserve, 2011; RD, LD.

Alison Steiber, Associate Professor and Director, Coordinated Dietetic Internship/M.S. Degree Program; Ph.D., Michigan State, 2005; RD. General nutrition assessment of patients, with emphasis in chronic renal failure.

James Swain, Associate Professor and Director, Didactic Program in Dietetics; Ph.D., Iowa State, 2000; RD. Food chemistry; nutrition in management of chronic disease; absorption and efficacy in humans of different forms of iron used in food fortification.

Guofang Zhang, Assistant Professor, Metabolimics Center; Ph.D., Nanjing (China), 2001; Lipid metabolism in the heart.

Secondary Appointments

Catherine Demko, Assistant Professor in Dentistry; Ph.D., Case Western Reserve, 2002.

Saul Genuth, Professor in Medicine; M.D., Western Reserve, 1957. Diabetes mellitus; blood glucose control and complications.

Sharon Groh-Wargo, Assistant Professor in Pediatrics and Neonatal Nutritionist, MetroHealth Medical Center, Cleveland, Ohio; Ph.D.; Case Western Reserve, 2002. Tolerance of a nutrient-enriched post-discharge formula for preterm infants.

Sanjay Gupta, Associate Professor in Urology; Ph.D., Avadh (India), 1992. Mechanisms of prostate carcinogenesis, treatment and prevention of prostate cancer.

Richard Hanson, Professor in Biochemistry; Ph.D., Brown, 1963. Hormonal control of gene expression.

Janos Kerner, Assistant Professor; Ph.D., Hungarian Academy, 1986. Mitochondrial fatty acid oxidation and the regulation of the pathway by a malonyl-CoA.

Douglas Kerr, Associate Professor in Pediatrics; M.D./Ph.D., Western Reserve, 1965. Metabolic disorders in infants.

John Kirwan, Associate Professor in Reproductive Biology; Ph.D., Ball State, 1987. Aging; metabolism; endocrinology.

Laura Nagy, Professor in Pathobiology, Cleveland Clinic, Lerner College of Medicine; Ph.D., Berkeley, 1986. Effects of environmental factors such as diet and drugs on cellular signal transduction mechanisms.

Noa Noy, Professor in Pharmacology; Ph.D., Tel Aviv, 1981. Transcriptional regulations by nuclear hormone receptors.

Adjunct Faculty

Adjunct faculty members provide students with specialized clinical, research, and/or public health fieldwork experiences. Their current job position is listed directly after their name.

Victoria Adeleke, Wake County Human Services WIC Program, Raleigh, North Carolina; M.P.H., North Carolina at Chapel Hill, 1992; RD, LDN.

Phyllis Allen, Office of Public Health, Columbia, South Carolina; M.S., Case Western Reserve, 1989; RD.

Janet Anselmo, Diabetes Self Management Program, Louis Stokes VA Medical Center, Cleveland, Ohio; M.S., Case Western Reserve, 1988; RD, LD.

Anika Avery-Grant, Centers for Dialysis Care, Euclid, Ohio; M.S., Case Western Reserve, 1994; RD, LD.

Cynthia Bayerl, Massachusetts Department of Public Health; M.S., Boston University, 1976; RD, LDN.

Jennifer Bier, MetroHealth Center for Community Health; M.S., Case Western Reserve, 2002; RD, LD.

Mark Bindus, Twinsburg City School District; B.S., Akron, 1993, RD, LD.

Suzanne Bogert, Los Angeles County Department of Public Health, Los Angeles, California; M.S., Case Western Reserve; RD.

Josephine Anne Cialone, North Carolina Division of Maternal and Child Health; M.S., Case Western Reserve, 1980; RD.

Rachel Colchamiro, Massachusetts WIC Nutrition Program; M.S., Berkeley, 1999; RD, LDN.

Cheri Collier, Clement Center, MetroHealth Center for Community Health, Cleveland, Ohio; M.S. Case Western Reserve, 1998; RD, LD.

Janice Davis, Western Reserve Area on Aging, Cleveland, Ohio; M.S., Case Western Reserve, 1986; RD.

Helen Dumski, Diabetes Association of Greater Cleveland; B.S., Ohio State; RD, LD.

Maureen Faron, Hudson City School District, Hudson, Ohio; B.S., Case Western Reserve; RD, LD.

Marcie Fenton, Los Angeles County Department of Public Health, Los Angeles, California; M.S., Case Western Reserve, 1982; RD.

Denise Ferris, West Virginia Office of Nutrition Services; Ph.D., Pittsburgh, 1989; RD.

Karen Fiedler, Adjunct Associate Professor; Ph.D., Tennessee, Knoxville, 1977.

Cynthia Finohr, Orange City School District; B.S., Kent State, 1981; RD, LD.

Michelle Lundon Fox, Abbott Nutrition, Cleveland, Ohio; M.Ed., Vanderbilt; RD, LD.

Lorna Fuller, Sodexho Marriott Services, Huron Hospital; M.S., Kent State, 1995; RD, LD.

Deborah Gammell, MetroHealth Medical Center (WIC), Cleveland, Ohio; M.S., Miami (Ohio), 1980; RD, LD.

Diana Garrison, Regency Hospitals–Cleveland West, Cleveland, Ohio; B.S. Michigan State, 2001; RD, LD.

Brenda Garritson, Baylor University Medical Center, Dallas, Texas; M.S., Texas Woman's, 1993; RD, LD.

Melinda Gedeon, UH Bedford Medical Center; B.S., Ohio State; RD, LD.

Martha Halko, Cuyahoga County Board of Health; M.S., Akron, 2000; RD, LD.

Samia Hamdan, USDA, Food and Nutrition Service, Chicago; M.P.H., Minnesota, Twin Cities, 2003; RD.

Brigette Hires, Ohio Department of Education; Ph.D., Kentucky, 2005; RD.

Karen Horvath, UH Bedford Medical Center; B.S., Akron, 1986; RD, LD.

Claire Hughes, Hawaii State Department of Health; Dr.P.H., Hawaii, 1998; RD.

Deborah Hutsler, Children's Hospital Medical Center of Akron; Kent State, M.S., 1991; RD, LD.

Lisa Isham, Cuyahoga County Board of Health; M.S., Case Western Reserve, 1997; RD, LD.

Jennifer Kernc, Centers for Dialysis Care, Cleveland, Ohio; B.S., Akron; RD, LD.

Natalia Kliszczuk-Smolio, Mt. Alverna Home, Inc., Parma, Ohio; B.S., Cincinnati, 1982; RD, LD.

Katherine Koch, MetroHealth Center for Community Health, Cleveland, Ohio; M.S., Case Western Reserve, 1988; RD, LD.

Richard Koletsky, Adjunct Assistant Clinical Professor; M.D., Case Western Reserve, 1975.

Jennifer Kravec, MetroHealth Medical Center; B.S., Ohio State, 1997; RD, LD.

Perri Kushan, Menorah Park Center for Senior Living, Beachwood, Ohio; B.S., Akron, 1986; RD, LD.

Lois Lenard, Nutrition and Food Service, Louis Stokes Cleveland VA Medical Center, Cleveland, Ohio; B.S., Kent State, 1974; RD, LD.

Janelle L'Heureux, AIDS Project Los Angeles, Los Angeles,California; M.S., New Haven, Connecticut, 1998; RD.

Patricia Liang-Tong, Native Hawaiian Health Care System; B.S., Hawaii at Manoa, 1998; RD, CDE, CDM, CFPP.

Lauren Melnick, Expanded Food and Nutrition Education Program, OSU Extension, Cleveland, Ohio; M.S., Case Western Reserve, 2007; RD, LD.

Christine Munoz, Centers for Dialysis Care, Euclid, Ohio; B.S., Bowling Green State, 1995; RD, LD.

Linda Novak-Eedy, Menorah Park Center for Senior Living, Beachwood, Ohio; B.S., Bowling Green State, 1983; RD, LD.

Lisa Ogg, Nutrition Health Professional, Cuyahoga County WIC Program; B.S., Kent State, 1996; RD, LD.

Alison Patrick, Cuyahoga County Board of Health; M.P.H., Ohio State, 2006; RD, LD.

Valerie M. Poirier, Cuyahoga County Board of Health, Cleveland, Ohio; B.S., Kent State, 1983; RD, LD.

Stephen Previs, Ph.D., Merck Research Laboratories, Case Western Reserve, 1997.

Barbara Pryor, Ohio Department of Health; M.S., Ohio State, 1994; RD, LD.

Anne Raguso, Director, Dietetic Internship, VA Medical Center, Cleveland, Ohio; Ph.D., Case Western Reserve, 1985; RD, LD.

Tamara Kurtis Randall, Director of Education, Diabetes Association of Greater Cleveland; M.S. Case Western Reserve; RD, LD, CDE.

Jacqueline Rohr, Parma City School District; B.S., Case Western Reserve, 1973; RD, LD.

Anna Rostafinski, MetroHealth Medical Center (WIC); M.S., Case Western Reserve, 1988; RD, LD.

Maryanne Salsbury, Cuyahoga County WIC Program, Cleveland, Ohio; B.S., Seton Hill; RD, LD.

Joanne Samuels, Solon City School District; B.S., SUNY, 1992; RD, LD.

Sharon Sass, Arizona Department of Health Services, Bureau of Nutrition and Physical Activity; B.S., Nebraska–Lincoln, 1975; RD.

Najeeba Shine, Cuyahoga County Board of Health; M.S., Case Western Reserve, 1992; RD, LD.

Susan Shubrook, Southwest General Health Center, Middleburg Heights, Ohio; B.S., Rutgers, 1985; RD, LD.

Suzanne Silverstein, Virginia Department of Health; M.A., George Washington, 1999; RD.

Barbara Sipe, Summit County Health District, Ohio; M.A., Kent State, 1979.

Gil Sisneros, California Department of Health Services, Sacramento, California; M.P.H., California State, 1990.

Donna Skoda, Summit County General Health District, Stow, Ohio; M.S., Case Western Reserve, 1980; RD.

Mary Kay Solera, Centers for Disease Control and Prevention, Atlanta, Georgia; M.S., Whitworth, 1988; CHES.

Lura Elizabeth Spinks, Berea City Schools; M.S., Ohio State; RD.

Ann Stahlheber, Cuyahoga County Board of Health, Ohio; M.A., Simmons, 2004; RD, LD, CSN.

Denise Tabar, Olmsted Falls City School District, Ohio; M.S., Kent State, 1982; RD, LD.

Felicia Vatakis, UHCMS Department of Nutrition Services; M.S., NYIT; RD, LD.

Sarah Walden, DaVita Dialysis; M.S., Case Western Reserve, 2002; RD, LD.

Marisa Warrix, Family and Consumer Sciences, Cuyahoga County, Ohio State University Extension; M.A., Kent State, 1991.

Diane Ohama Yates, Medical Nutritional Representative, Ross Products Division, Abbott Laboratories, Cleveland, Ohio; B.S., Hawaii, 1978; RD, LD.

Wendy Youmans, Davita Dialysis; M.S., Case Western Reserve, 1996; RD, LD.

Siri Zimmerman, Diabetes Association of Greater Cleveland; M.S. Case Western Reserve, 2009; RD, LD.

Sharon Zwick-Hamilton, Harborside Health Care; M.S., Case Western Reserve, 1988; RD, LD, CDE, CSG.

Section 15
Parasitology

This section contains a directory of institutions offering graduate work in parasitology. Additional information about programs listed in the directory may be obtained by writing directly to the dean of a graduate school or chair of a department at the address given in the directory.

For programs offering related work, see also in this book *Biological and Biomedical Sciences* and *Microbiological Sciences.* In another guide in this series:

Graduate Programs in Business, Education, Health, Information Studies, Law & Social Work
See *Allied Health* and *Public Health*

CONTENTS

Program Directory

Parasitology

Illinois State University, Graduate School, College of Arts and Sciences, Department of Biological Sciences, Normal, IL 61790-2200. Offers animal behavior (MS); bacteriology (MS); biochemistry (MS); biological sciences (MS); biology (PhD); biophysics (MS); biotechnology (MS); botany (MS, PhD); cell biology (MS); conservation biology (MS); developmental biology (MS); ecology (MS, PhD); entomology (MS); evolutionary biology (MS); genetics (MS, PhD); immunology (MS); microbiology (MS, PhD); molecular biology (MS); molecular genetics (MS); neurobiology (MS); neuroscience (MS); parasitology (MS); physiology (MS, PhD); plant biology (MS); plant molecular biology (MS); plant sciences (MS); structural biology (MS); zoology (MS, PhD). Part-time programs available. *Degree requirements:* For master's, thesis or alternative; for doctorate, variable foreign language requirement, thesis/dissertation, 2 terms of residency. *Entrance requirements:* For master's, GRE General Test, minimum GPA of 2.6 in last 60 hours of course work; for doctorate, GRE General Test. *Faculty research:* Redoc balance and drug development in schistosoma mansoni, control of the growth of listeria monocytogenes at low temperature, regulation of cell expansion and microtubule function by SPRI, CRUI: physiology and fitness consequences of different life history phenotypes.

Louisiana State University Health Sciences Center, School of Graduate Studies in New Orleans, Department of Microbiology, Immunology, and Parasitology, New Orleans, LA 70112-1393. Offers microbiology and immunology (MS, PhD); MD/PhD. Terminal master's awarded for partial completion of doctoral program. *Degree requirements:* For master's, comprehensive exam, thesis; for doctorate, comprehensive exam, thesis/dissertation, preliminary exam, qualifying exam. *Entrance requirements:* For master's and doctorate, GRE General Test. Additional exam requirements/recommendations for international students: Required—TOEFL. *Faculty research:* Microbial physiology, animal virology, vaccine development, AIDS drug studies, pathogenic mechanisms, molecular immunology.

McGill University, Faculty of Graduate and Postdoctoral Studies, Faculty of Agricultural and Environmental Sciences, Institute of Parasitology, Montréal, QC H3A 2T5, Canada. Offers biotechnology (M Sc A, Certificate); parasitology (M Sc, PhD).

New York University, School of Medicine, New York, NY 10012-1019. Offers biomedical sciences (PhD), including biomedical imaging, cellular and molecular biology, computational biology, developmental genetics, medical and molecular parasitology, microbiology, molecular oncobiology and immunology, neuroscience and physiology, pathobiology, pharmacology, structural biology; clinical investigation (MS); medicine (MD); MD/MA; MD/MPA; MD/MS; MD/PhD. *Accreditation:* LCME/AMA (one or more programs are accredited). *Degree requirements:* For master's, comprehensive exam, thesis; for doctorate, comprehensive exam, thesis/dissertation. *Entrance requirements:* MCAT. Additional exam requirements/recommendations for international students: Required—TOEFL. *Expenses:* Contact institution. *Faculty research:* AIDS, cancer, neuroscience, molecular biology, neuroscience, cell biology and molecular genetics, structural biology, microbial pathogenesis and host defense, pharmacology, molecular oncology and immunology.

New York University, School of Medicine and Graduate School of Arts and Science, Sackler Institute of Graduate Biomedical Sciences, Department of Medical and Molecular Parasitology, New York, NY 10012-1019. Offers PhD, MD/PhD. *Degree requirements:* For doctorate, one foreign language, comprehensive exam, thesis/dissertation, qualifying exam. *Entrance requirements:* For doctorate, GRE General Test. Additional exam requirements/recommendations for international students: Required—TOEFL. *Faculty research:* Immunoparasitology, cell biology of parasites, genetics of parasites, mode of action of antiparasitic drugs.

Texas A&M University, College of Veterinary Medicine and Biomedical Sciences, Department of Veterinary Pathobiology, College Station, TX 77843. Offers genetics (MS, PhD); veterinary microbiology (MS, PhD); veterinary parasitology (MS, PhD); veterinary pathology (MS, PhD). Part-time programs available. Postbaccalaureate distance learning degree programs offered. *Faculty:* 26. *Students:* 25 full-time (17 women), 18 part-time (14 women); includes 1 Black or African American, non-Hispanic/Latino; 3 Asian, non-Hispanic/Latino; 2 Hispanic/Latino, 10 international. Average age 33. In 2010, 1 master's, 5 doctorates awarded. Terminal master's awarded for partial completion of doctoral program. *Degree requirements:* For master's, thesis, seminars; for doctorate, thesis/dissertation, seminars. *Entrance requirements:* For master's and doctorate, GRE General Test, minimum GPA of 3.0 in last 60 hours. Additional exam requirements/recommendations for international students: Required—TOEFL. *Application deadline:* For fall admission, 3/1 priority date for domestic students; for spring admission, 8/1 priority date for domestic students. Applications are processed on a rolling basis. Application fee: $50 ($75 for international students). Electronic applications accepted. *Financial support:* In 2010–11, fellowships with partial tuition reimbursements (averaging $16,000 per year), research assistantships with partial tuition reimbursements (averaging $15,400 per year), teaching assistantships with partial tuition reimbursements (averaging $16,000 per year) were awarded; Federal Work-Study, institutionally sponsored loans, scholarships/grants, traineeships, health care benefits, and unspecified assistantships also available. Support available to part-time students. Financial award applicants required to submit FAFSA. *Faculty research:* Infectious and noninfectious diseases of animals and birds, animal genetics, molecular biology, immunology, virology. *Unit head:* Dr. Linda Logan, Head, 979-862-6559, Fax: 979-845-9231, E-mail: llogan@cvm.tamu.edu. *Application contact:* Dr. Patricia Holman, Graduate Advisor, 979-845-4202, Fax: 979-862-1147, E-mail: pholman@cvm.tamu.edu.

Tulane University, School of Public Health and Tropical Medicine, Department of Tropical Medicine, New Orleans, LA 70118-5669. Offers clinical tropical medicine and travelers health (Diploma); parasitology (MSPH, PhD); public health and tropical medicine (MPHTM); vector borne infectious diseases (MS, PhD); MD/PhD. MS and PhD offered through the Graduate School. *Degree requirements:* For master's, thesis; for doctorate, comprehensive exam, thesis/dissertation. *Entrance requirements:* For master's, GRE General Test, minimum B average in undergraduate course work; for doctorate, GRE General Test. Additional exam requirements/recommendations for international students: Required—TOEFL.

University of Notre Dame, Graduate School, College of Science, Department of Biological Sciences, Notre Dame, IN 46556. Offers aquatic ecology, evolution and environmental biology (MS, PhD); cellular and molecular biology (MS, PhD); genetics (MS, PhD); physiology (MS, PhD); vector biology and parasitology (MS, PhD). Terminal master's awarded for partial completion of doctoral program. *Degree requirements:* For master's, comprehensive exam, thesis; for doctorate, comprehensive exam, thesis/dissertation, candidacy exam. *Entrance requirements:* For master's and doctorate, GRE General Test. Additional exam requirements/recommendations for international students: Required—TOEFL (minimum score 600 paper-based; 250 computer-based; 80 iBT). Electronic applications accepted. *Faculty research:* Tropical disease, molecular genetics, neurobiology, evolutionary biology, aquatic biology.

University of Prince Edward Island, Atlantic Veterinary College, Graduate Program in Veterinary Medicine, Charlottetown, PE C1A 4P3, Canada. Offers anatomy (M Sc, PhD); bacteriology (M Sc, PhD); clinical pharmacology (M Sc, PhD); clinical sciences (M Sc, PhD); epidemiology (M Sc, PhD), including reproduction; fish health (M Sc, PhD); food animal nutrition (M Sc, PhD); immunology (M Sc, PhD); microanatomy (M Sc, PhD); parasitology (M Sc, PhD); pathology (M Sc, PhD); pharmacology (M Sc, PhD); physiology (M Sc, PhD); toxicology (M Sc, PhD); veterinary science (M Vet Sc); virology (M Sc, PhD). Part-time programs available. *Degree requirements:* For master's, thesis; for doctorate, thesis/dissertation. *Entrance requirements:* For master's, DVM, B Sc honors degree, or equivalent; for doctorate, M Sc. Additional exam requirements/recommendations for international students: Required—TOEFL (minimum score 550 paper-based; 213 computer-based; 80 iBT). *Expenses:* Contact institution. *Faculty research:* Animal health management, infectious diseases, fin fish and shellfish health, basic biomedical sciences, ecosystem health.

University of Washington, Graduate School, School of Public Health, Department of Global Health, Graduate Program in Pathobiology, Seattle, WA 98195. Offers PhD. *Students:* 34 full-time (27 women), 1 part-time (0 women); includes 2 Black or African American, non-Hispanic/Latino; 3 Asian, non-Hispanic/Latino; 2 Hispanic/Latino, 6 international. Average age 29. 59 applicants, 24% accepted, 6 enrolled. In 2010, 3 doctorates awarded. *Degree requirements:* For doctorate, comprehensive exam, thesis/dissertation, published paper from thesis work. *Entrance requirements:* For doctorate, GRE General Test, minimum GPA of 3.0. *Application deadline:* For fall admission, 12/1 for domestic students, 11/1 for international students. Application fee: $75. Electronic applications accepted. *Financial support:* In 2010–11, 32 students received support, including 2 fellowships with full tuition reimbursements available (averaging $27,348 per year), 30 research assistantships with full tuition reimbursements available (averaging $27,348 per year); career-related internships or fieldwork, institutionally sponsored loans, scholarships/grants, traineeships, and unspecified assistantships also available. *Faculty research:* Malaria, immunological response to mycobacteria infections, HIV-cell interaction and the development of an anti-HIV vaccine, regulation of intercellular communication via gap junctions, genetic and nutritional regulation of proteins involved in lipid transport. *Unit head:* Dr. King Holmes, Chair, 206-744-3620, Fax: 206-744-3694. *Application contact:* Rachel Reichert, Program Manager, 206-543-4338, Fax: 206-543-3873, E-mail: pabio@u.washington.edu.

Section 16
Pathology and Pathobiology

This section contains a directory of institutions offering graduate work in pathology and pathobiology, followed by in-depth entries submitted by institutions that chose to prepare detailed program descriptions. Additional information about programs listed in the directory but not augmented by an in-depth entry may be obtained by writing directly to the dean of a graduate school or chair of a department at the address given in the directory.

For programs offering related work, see also in this book *Anatomy; Biochemistry; Biological and Biomedical Sciences; Cell, Molecular, and Structural Biology; Genetics, Developmental Biology, and Reproductive Biology; Microbiological Sciences; Pharmacology and Toxicology;* and *Physiology.* In another guide in this series:

Graduate Programs in Business, Education, Health, Information Studies, Law & Social Work

See *Allied Health, Public Health,* and *Veterinary Medicine and Sciences*

CONTENTS

Molecular Pathogenesis

Dartmouth College, Graduate Program in Molecular and Cellular Biology, Department of Microbiology and Immunology, Program in Molecular Pathogenesis, Hanover, NH 03755. Offers microbiology and immunology (PhD).

Emory University, Laney Graduate School, Division of Biological and Biomedical Sciences, Program in Immunology and Molecular Pathogenesis, Atlanta, GA 30322-1100. Offers PhD. *Faculty:* 52 full-time (8 women). *Students:* 73 full-time (42 women); includes 1 American Indian or Alaska Native, non-Hispanic/Latino; 12 Asian, non-Hispanic/Latino; 3 Hispanic/Latino; 1 Native Hawaiian or other Pacific Islander, non-Hispanic/Latino, 9 international. Average age 27. 179 applicants, 15% accepted, 11 enrolled. In 2010, 14 doctorates awarded. *Degree requirements:* For doctorate, comprehensive exam, thesis/dissertation. *Entrance requirements:* For doctorate, GRE General Test, minimum GPA of 3.0 in science course work (recommended). Additional exam requirements/recommendations for international students: Required—TOEFL. *Application deadline:* For fall admission, 12/1 for domestic and international students. Application fee: $75. Electronic applications accepted. *Expenses:* Tuition: Full-time $33,800. Required fees: $1300. *Financial support:* In 2010–11, 21 students received support, including 21 fellowships with full tuition reimbursements available (averaging $25,000 per year); institutionally sponsored loans, scholarships/grants, health care benefits, and tuition waivers (full) also available. *Faculty research:* Transplantation immunology, autoimmunity, microbial pathogenesis. *Unit head:* Dr. Brian Evavold, Director, 404-727-3393, Fax: 404-727-3659, E-mail: evavold@microbio.emory.edu. *Application contact:* Kathy Smith, Director of Recruitment and Admissions, 404-727-2547, Fax: 404-727-3322, E-mail: kathy.smith@emory.edu.

North Dakota State University, College of Graduate and Interdisciplinary Studies, College of Agriculture, Food Systems, and Natural Resources, Department of Veterinary and Microbiological Sciences, Fargo, ND 58108. Offers food safety (MS); microbiology (MS); molecular pathogenesis (PhD). Part-time programs available. *Students:* 12 full-time (7 women), 5 part-time (all women). 18 applicants, 17% accepted. In 2010, 1 master's awarded. *Degree requirements:* For master's, thesis; for doctorate, thesis/dissertation, oral and written preliminary exams. *Entrance requirements:* For master's and doctorate, GRE. Additional exam requirements/recommendations for international students: Required—TOEFL (minimum score 525 paper-based; 197 computer-based; 71 iBT). *Application deadline:* For fall admission, 3/15 priority date for domestic students. Applications are processed on a rolling basis. Application fee: $25. *Financial support:* Fellowships with full tuition reimbursements, research assistantships with full tuition reimbursements, teaching assistantships with full tuition reimbursements, Federal Work-Study and institutionally sponsored loans available. Financial award application deadline: 4/15. *Faculty research:* Bacterial gene regulation, antibiotic resistance, molecular virology, mechanisms of bacterial pathogenesis, immunology of animals. *Unit head:* Dr. Doug Freeman, Head, 701-231-7511, E-mail: douglas.freeman@ndsu.nodak.edu. *Application contact:* Dr. Eugene S. Berry, Associate Professor, 701-231-7520, Fax: 701-231-7514, E-mail: eugene.berry@ndsu.edu.

Texas A&M Health Science Center, Graduate School of Biomedical Sciences, Department of Microbial and Molecular Pathogenesis, College Station, TX 77840. Offers immunology (PhD); microbiology (PhD); molecular biology (PhD); virology (PhD). *Degree requirements:* For doctorate, thesis/dissertation. *Entrance requirements:* For doctorate, GRE General Test, minimum GPA of 3.0. *Faculty research:* Molecular pathogenesis, microbial therapeutics.

University at Albany, State University of New York, School of Public Health, Department of Biomedical Sciences, Program in Molecular Pathogenesis, Albany, NY 12222-0001. Offers MS, PhD. *Degree requirements:* For master's, thesis; for doctorate, thesis/dissertation. *Entrance requirements:* For master's and doctorate, GRE General Test, GRE Subject Test.

University of Chicago, Division of Biological Sciences, Biomedical Sciences Cluster: Cancer Biology, Immunology, Molecular Metabolism and Nutrition, Pathology, and Microbiology, Department of Pathology, Chicago, IL 60637-1513. Offers molecular pathogenesis and molecular medicine (PhD). *Degree requirements:* For doctorate, thesis/dissertation, ethics class, 2 teaching assistantships. *Entrance requirements:* For doctorate, GRE General Test. Additional exam requirements/recommendations for international students: Required—IELTS (minimum score 7); Recommended—TOEFL (minimum score 600 paper-based; 250 computer-based; 104 iBT). Electronic applications accepted. *Faculty research:* Vascular biology, apolipoproteins, cardiovascular disease, immunopathology.

Washington University in St. Louis, Graduate School of Arts and Sciences, Division of Biology and Biomedical Sciences, Program in Molecular Microbiology and Microbial Pathogenesis, St. Louis, MO 63130-4899. Offers PhD. *Degree requirements:* For doctorate, thesis/dissertation. *Entrance requirements:* For doctorate, GRE General Test, GRE Subject Test. Electronic applications accepted.

Molecular Pathology

Texas Tech University Health Sciences Center, School of Allied Health Sciences, Program in Molecular Pathology, Lubbock, TX 79430. Offers MS. *Faculty:* 10 full-time (8 women). *Students:* 20 full-time (13 women), 1 (woman) part-time; includes 1 Black or African American, non-Hispanic/Latino; 1 American Indian or Alaska Native, non-Hispanic/Latino; 4 Asian, non-Hispanic/Latino; 2 Hispanic/Latino. Average age 24. 35 applicants, 57% accepted, 20 enrolled. In 2010, 16 master's awarded. *Entrance requirements:* Additional exam requirements/recommendations for international students: Required—TOEFL, IELTS. *Application deadline:* For spring admission, 3/1 priority date for domestic students. Application fee: $35. Electronic applications accepted. *Financial support:* Career-related internships or fieldwork, institutionally sponsored loans, and scholarships/grants available. Financial award applicants required to submit FAFSA. *Unit head:* Dr. Hal Larsen, Chair, 806-743-3223, E-mail: hal.larsen@ttuhsc.edu. *Application contact:* Jeri Moravcik, Assistant Director of Admissions and Student Affairs, 806-743-3220, Fax: 806-743-2994, E-mail: jeri.moravcik@ttuhsc.edu.

University of California, San Diego, School of Medicine and Office of Graduate Studies, Molecular Pathology Program, La Jolla, CA 92093. Offers bioinformatics (PhD); cancer biology/oncology (PhD); cardiovascular sciences and disease (PhD); microbiology (PhD); molecular pathology (PhD); neurological disease (PhD); stem cell and developmental biology (PhD); structural biology/drug design (PhD). *Entrance requirements:* For doctorate, GRE General Test, GRE Subject Test. Additional exam requirements/recommendations for international students: Required—TOEFL. Electronic applications accepted.

University of Medicine and Dentistry of New Jersey, Graduate School of Biomedical Sciences, Graduate Programs in Biomedical Sciences–Newark, Program in Molecular Pathology and Immunology, Newark, NJ 07107. Offers PhD. *Entrance requirements:* Additional exam requirements/recommendations for international students: Required—TOEFL. Electronic applications accepted.

University of Medicine and Dentistry of New Jersey, Graduate School of Biomedical Sciences, Graduate Programs in Biomedical Sciences–Stratford, Stratford, NJ 08084-5634. Offers biomedical sciences (MBS, MS); cell and molecular biology (MS, PhD); molecular pathology and immunology (MS); DO/MS; DO/PhD; MS/MPH. Part-time and evening/weekend programs available. *Students:* 79 full-time (43 women), 19 part-time (14 women); includes 21 Black or African American, non-Hispanic/Latino; 16 Asian, non-Hispanic/Latino; 7 Hispanic/Latino, 11 international. Average age 25. 128 applicants, 74% accepted, 64 enrolled. In 2010, 46 master's, 3 doctorates awarded. Terminal master's awarded for partial completion of doctoral program. *Degree requirements:* For master's, thesis (for some programs); for doctorate, thesis/dissertation, qualifying exam. *Entrance requirements:* For master's, GRE General Test, MCAT or DAT; for doctorate, GRE General Test. Additional exam requirements/recommendations for international students: Required—TOEFL. *Application deadline:* For fall admission, 2/1 for domestic and international students; for spring admission, 11/1 for domestic students. Applications are processed on a rolling basis. Application fee: $65. Electronic applications accepted. *Financial support:* Fellowships, Federal Work-Study available. Financial award application deadline: 5/1. *Unit head:* Dr. Carl E. Hock, Senior Associate Dean, Graduate School, 856-566-6282, Fax: 856-566-6232, E-mail: hock@umdnj.edu. *Application contact:* University Registrar, 973-972-5338.

University of Michigan, Rackham Graduate School, Program in Biomedical Sciences (PIBS), Program in Molecular and Cellular Pathology, Ann Arbor, MI 48109. Offers PhD. *Faculty:* 37 full-time (10 women). *Students:* 20 full-time (9 women); includes 6 minority (1 Black or African American, non-Hispanic/Latino; 5 Asian, non-Hispanic/Latino). Average age 28. 52 applicants, 17% accepted, 6 enrolled. In 2010, 1 doctorate awarded. *Degree requirements:* For doctorate, comprehensive exam, thesis/dissertation. *Entrance requirements:* For doctorate, GRE General Test, 3 letters of recommendation, research experience. Additional exam requirements/recommendations for international students: Required—TOEFL (minimum score 84 iBT). *Application deadline:* For fall admission, 12/1 for domestic and international students. Application fee: $60 ($75 for international students). Electronic applications accepted. *Expenses:* Tuition, state resident: full-time $17,784; part-time $1116 per credit hour. Tuition, nonresident: full-time $35,944; part-time $2125 per credit hour. International tuition: $35,994 full-time. Required fees: $95 per semester. Tuition and fees vary according to course load, degree level and program. *Financial support:* In 2010–11, 1 student received support, including fellowships with full tuition reimbursements available (averaging $40,042 per year); scholarships/grants, traineeships, health care benefits, tuition waivers (full), and unspecified assistantships also available. *Faculty research:* Cancer biology, stem cell and developmental biology, immunopathology and inflammatory disease, epigenetics and gene regulation, cell death and regulation. *Unit head:* Dr. Nicholas W. Lukacs, Professor of Pathology/Director, 734-763-6454, Fax: 734-615-2331, E-mail: pathgradprog@med.umich.edu. *Application contact:* Laura L. Hessler, Administrative Specialist, 734-763-6454, Fax: 734-615-2331, E-mail: lauralh@med.umich.edu.

University of Pittsburgh, School of Medicine, Graduate Programs in Medicine, Program in Cellular and Molecular Pathology, Pittsburgh, PA 15260. Offers MS, PhD. *Faculty:* 64 full-time (18 women). *Students:* 37 full-time (22 women); includes 3 Black or African American, non-Hispanic/Latino; 6 American Indian or Alaska Native, non-Hispanic/Latino; 6 Asian, non-Hispanic/Latino; 2 Hispanic/Latino, 9 international. Average age 27. 486 applicants, 14% accepted, 28 enrolled. In 2010, 7 doctorates awarded. *Degree requirements:* For doctorate, comprehensive exam, thesis/dissertation. *Entrance requirements:* For doctorate, GRE General Test, GRE Subject Test, minimum QPA of 3.0. Additional exam requirements/recommendations for international students: Required—TOEFL (minimum score 600 paper-based; 100 iBT), IELTS (minimum score 7). *Application deadline:* For fall admission, 12/15 priority date for domestic and international students. Application fee: $50. Electronic applications accepted. *Expenses:* Tuition, state resident: full-time $17,304; part-time $701 per credit. Tuition, nonresident: full-time $29,554; part-time $1210 per credit. Required fees: $740; $214 per term. Tuition and fees vary according to program. *Financial support:* In 2010–11, 13 fellowships with full tuition reimbursements (averaging $25,500 per year), 24 research assistantships with full tuition reimbursements (averaging $25,500 per year) were awarded; teaching assistantships with full tuition reimbursements, institutionally sponsored loans, scholarships/grants, traineeships, health care benefits, and unspecified assistantships also available. *Faculty research:* Liver growth and differentiation, pathogenesis of neurodegeneration, cancer research. *Unit head:* Dr. Wendy Mars, Graduate Program Director, 412-648-9690, Fax: 412-648-9846, E-mail: wmars@pitt.edu. *Application contact:* Graduate Studies Administrator, 412-648-8957, Fax: 412-648-1077, E-mail: gradstudies@medschool.pitt.edu.

The University of Texas Health Science Center at Houston, Graduate School of Biomedical Sciences, Program in Molecular Pathology, Houston, TX 77225-0036. Offers MS, PhD, MD/PhD. Terminal master's awarded for partial completion of doctoral program. *Degree requirements:* For master's, thesis; for doctorate, thesis/dissertation. *Entrance requirements:* For master's and doctorate, GRE General Test. Additional exam requirements/recommendations for international students: Required—TOEFL. Electronic applications accepted. *Faculty research:* Infectious disease, carcinogenesis, structural biology, cell biology.

Yale University, School of Medicine and Graduate School of Arts and Sciences, Combined Program in Biological and Biomedical Sciences (BBS), Pharmacological Sciences and Molecular Medicine Track, New Haven, CT 06520. Offers PhD, MD/PhD. *Degree requirements:* For doctorate, thesis/dissertation. *Entrance requirements:* For doctorate, GRE General Test. Additional exam requirements/recommendations for international students: Required—TOEFL. Electronic applications accepted.

Pathobiology

Auburn University, College of Veterinary Medicine and Graduate School, Graduate Programs in Veterinary Medicine, Auburn University, AL 36849. Offers biomedical sciences (MS, PhD), including anatomy, physiology and pharmacology (MS), biomedical sciences (PhD), clinical sciences (MS), large animal surgery and medicine (MS), pathobiology (MS), radiology (MS), small animal surgery and medicine (MS); DVM/MS. Part-time programs available. *Faculty:* 100 full-time (40 women), 5 part-time/adjunct (1 woman). *Students:* 17 full-time (6 women), 51 part-time (35 women); includes 2 Black or African American, non-Hispanic/Latino; 1 American Indian or Alaska Native, non-Hispanic/Latino; 3 Asian, non-Hispanic/Latino; 2 Hispanic/Latino, 22 international. Average age 31. 70 applicants, 34% accepted, 10 enrolled. In 2010, 12 master's, 7 doctorates awarded. *Degree requirements:* For doctorate, thesis/dissertation. *Entrance requirements:* For master's, GRE General Test; for doctorate, GRE General Test, GRE Subject Test. *Application deadline:* For fall admission, 7/7 for domestic students; for spring admission, 11/24 for domestic students. Applications are processed on a rolling basis. Application fee: $50 ($60 for international students). Electronic applications accepted. *Expenses:* Tuition, state resident: full-time $7002. Tuition, nonresident: full-time $21,898. International tuition: $22,116 full-time. Required fees: $892. Tuition and fees vary according to course load and program. *Financial support:* Research assistantships, teaching assistantships, Federal Work-Study available. Support available to part-time students. Financial award application deadline: 3/15; financial award applicants required to submit FAFSA. *Unit head:* Dr. Timothy R. Boosinger, Dean, 334-844-4546. *Application contact:* Dr. George Flowers, Dean of the Graduate School, 334-844-2125.

Brown University, Graduate School, Division of Biology and Medicine, Program in Pathology and Laboratory Medicine, Providence, RI 02912. Offers biology (PhD); cancer biology (PhD); immunology and infection (PhD); medical science (PhD); pathobiology (Sc M); toxicology and environmental pathology (PhD). Terminal master's awarded for partial completion of doctoral program. *Degree requirements:* For doctorate, thesis/dissertation, preliminary exam. *Entrance requirements:* For master's and doctorate, GRE General Test, GRE Subject Test. Additional exam requirements/recommendations for international students: Required—TOEFL. Electronic applications accepted. *Faculty research:* Environmental pathology, carcinogenesis, immunopathology, signal transduction, innate immunity.

Columbia University, College of Physicians and Surgeons, Department of Pathology, New York, NY 10032. Offers pathobiology (M Phil, MA, PhD); MD/PhD. Only candidates for the PhD are admitted. Terminal master's awarded for partial completion of doctoral program. *Degree requirements:* For doctorate, thesis/dissertation. *Entrance requirements:* For master's and doctorate, GRE General Test. Additional exam requirements/recommendations for international students: Required—TOEFL. *Faculty research:* Virology, molecular biology, cell biology, neurobiology, immunology.

Drexel University, College of Medicine, Biomedical Graduate Programs, Interdisciplinary Program in Molecular Pathobiology, Philadelphia, PA 19104-2875. Offers MS, PhD, MD/PhD. *Degree requirements:* For doctorate, comprehensive exam, thesis/dissertation, qualifying exams. *Entrance requirements:* For doctorate, GRE General Test, minimum GPA of 3.0. Additional exam requirements/recommendations for international students: Required—TOEFL. Electronic applications accepted. *Faculty research:* Cell and molecular immunology, tumor immunology, molecular genetics, immunopathology, immunology of aging.

The Johns Hopkins University, School of Medicine, Graduate Programs in Medicine, Department of Pathology, Baltimore, MD 21218-2699. Offers pathobiology (PhD). *Faculty:* 68 full-time (14 women). *Students:* 48 full-time (29 women); includes 9 minority (3 Black or African American, non-Hispanic/Latino; 3 Asian, non-Hispanic/Latino; 2 Hispanic/Latino; 1 Two or more races, non-Hispanic/Latino), 22 international. Average age 29. 124 applicants, 6% accepted, 8 enrolled. In 2010, 6 doctorates awarded. *Degree requirements:* For doctorate, thesis/dissertation, qualifying oral exam. *Entrance requirements:* For doctorate, GRE General Test, previous course work with laboratory in organic and inorganic chemistry, general biology, calculus; interview. Additional exam requirements/recommendations for international students: Required—TOEFL. *Application deadline:* For winter admission, 1/10 for domestic students. Application fee: $85. Electronic applications accepted. *Financial support:* In 2010–11, 42 fellowships with full tuition reimbursements (averaging $26,855 per year) were awarded; scholarships/grants also available. *Faculty research:* Role of mutant proteins in Alzheimer's disease, nuclear protein function in breast and prostate cancer, medically important fungi, glycoproteins in HIV pathogenesis. Total annual research expenditures: $38.6 million. *Unit head:* Dr. J. Brooks Jackson, Chair, 410-955-9790, Fax: 410-955-0394. *Application contact:* Wilhelmena M. Braswell, Senior Academic Program Coordinator, 443-287-3163, Fax: 410-614-3548, E-mail: wbraswel@jhmi.edu.

Kansas State University, College of Veterinary Medicine, Department of Diagnostic Medicine/Pathobiology, Manhattan, KS 66506. Offers biomedical science (MS); diagnostic medicine/pathobiology (PhD). Terminal master's awarded for partial completion of doctoral program. *Degree requirements:* For doctorate, thesis/dissertation. *Entrance requirements:* For master's and doctorate, interviews. Additional exam requirements/recommendations for international students: Required—TOEFL (minimum score 550 paper-based; 213 computer-based). Electronic applications accepted. *Faculty research:* Infectious disease of animals, food safety and security, epidemiology and public health, toxicology, and pathology.

Medical University of South Carolina, College of Graduate Studies, Program in Molecular and Cellular Biology and Pathobiology, Charleston, SC 29425. Offers cancer biology (PhD); cardiovascular biology (PhD); cardiovascular imaging (PhD); cell regulation (PhD); craniofacial biology (PhD); genetics and development (PhD); marine biomedicine (PhD); DMD/PhD; MD/PhD. *Faculty:* 137 full-time (33 women). *Students:* 27 full-time (20 women); includes 3 Black or African American, non-Hispanic/Latino; 1 Hispanic/Latino, 6 international. Average age 30. In 2010, 16 doctorates awarded. *Degree requirements:* For doctorate, thesis/dissertation, oral and written exams. *Entrance requirements:* For doctorate, GRE General Test, interview, minimum GPA of 3.0. Additional exam requirements/recommendations for international students: Required—TOEFL (minimum score 600 paper-based; 250 computer-based; 100 iBT). *Application deadline:* For fall admission, 1/15 priority date for domestic and international students. Applications are processed on a rolling basis. Application fee: $0 ($85 for international students). Electronic applications accepted. *Financial support:* In 2010–11, 39 research assistantships with partial tuition reimbursements (averaging $23,000 per year) were awarded; Federal Work-Study and scholarships/grants also available. Support available to part-time students. Financial award application deadline: 3/10; financial award applicants required to submit FAFSA. *Unit head:* Dr. Donald R. Menick, Director, 843-876-5045, Fax: 843-792-6590, E-mail: menickd@musc.edu. *Application contact:* Dr. Cynthia F. Wright, Associate Dean for Admissions and Career Development, 843-792-2564, Fax: 843-792-6590, E-mail: wrightcf@musc.edu.

Michigan State University, College of Veterinary Medicine and The Graduate School, Graduate Programs in Veterinary Medicine, Department of Pathobiology and Diagnostic Investigation, East Lansing, MI 48824. Offers pathology (MS, PhD); pathology–environmental toxicology (PhD). *Entrance requirements:* Additional exam requirements/recommendations for international students: Required—TOEFL. Electronic applications accepted.

New York University, School of Medicine, New York, NY 10012-1019. Offers biomedical sciences (PhD), including biomedical imaging, cellular and molecular biology, computational biology, developmental genetics, medical and molecular parasitology, microbiology, molecular oncobiology and immunology, neuroscience and physiology, pathobiology, pharmacology, structural biology; clinical investigation (MS); medicine (MD); MD/MA; MD/MPA; MD/MS; MD/PhD. *Accreditation:* LCME/AMA (one or more programs are accredited). *Degree requirements:* For master's, comprehensive exam, thesis; for doctorate, comprehensive exam, thesis/dissertation. *Entrance requirements:* MCAT. Additional exam requirements/recommendations for international students: Required—TOEFL. *Expenses:* Contact institution. *Faculty research:* AIDS, cancer, neuroscience, molecular biology, neuroscience, cell biology and molecular genetics, structural biology, microbial pathogenesis and host defense, pharmacology, molecular oncology and immunology.

New York University, School of Medicine and Graduate School of Arts and Science, Sackler Institute of Graduate Biomedical Sciences, Program in Pathobiology, New York, NY 10012-1019. Offers PhD.

The Ohio State University, College of Medicine, Department of Pathology, Columbus, OH 43210. Offers experimental pathobiology (MS); pathology assistant (MS); MD/PhD. *Accreditation:* NAACLS. *Degree requirements:* For master's, comprehensive exam (for some programs), thesis. *Entrance requirements:* For master's, GRE General Test. Additional exam requirements/recommendations for international students: Required—TOEFL (minimum score 550 paper-based; 213 computer-based). Electronic applications accepted. *Expenses:* Tuition, state resident: full-time $10,605. Tuition, nonresident: full-time $26,535. Tuition and fees vary according to course load and program. *Faculty research:* Clinical pathology, transplantation pathology, cancer research, neuropathology, vascular pathology.

The Ohio State University, College of Veterinary Medicine, Department of Veterinary Biosciences, Columbus, OH 43210. Offers anatomy and cellular biology (MS, PhD); pathobiology (MS, PhD); pharmacology (MS, PhD); toxicology (MS, PhD); veterinary physiology (MS, PhD). *Faculty:* 45. *Students:* 4 full-time (all women), 7 part-time (5 women); includes 1 Black or African American, non-Hispanic/Latino, 3 international. Average age 30. In 2010, 2 master's, 7 doctorates awarded. *Entrance requirements:* For master's and doctorate, GRE General Test. Additional exam requirements/recommendations for international students: Required—TOEFL. *Application deadline:* Applications are processed on a rolling basis. Application fee: $40 ($50 for international students). Electronic applications accepted. *Expenses:* Tuition, state resident: full-time $10,605. Tuition, nonresident: full-time $26,535. Tuition and fees vary according to course load and program. *Faculty research:* Microvasculature, muscle biology, neonatal lung and bone development. *Unit head:* Dr. Michael J. Oglesbee, Graduate Studies Committee Chair, 614-292-5661, Fax: 614-292-6473, E-mail: oglesbee.1@osu.edu. *Application contact:* Graduate Admissions, 614-292-9444, Fax: 614-292-3895, E-mail: domestic.grad@osu.edu.

Penn State University Park, Graduate School, College of Agricultural Sciences, Department of Veterinary and Biomedical Sciences, State College, University Park, PA 16802-1503. Offers pathobiology (PhD).

Purdue University, School of Veterinary Medicine and Graduate School, Graduate Programs in Veterinary Medicine, Department of Comparative Pathobiology, West Lafayette, IN 47907-2027. Offers comparative epidemiology and public health (MS); comparative epidemiology and public heath (PhD); comparative microbiology and immunology (MS, PhD); comparative pathobiology (MS, PhD); interdisciplinary studies (PhD), including microbial pathogenesis, molecular signaling and cancer biology, molecular virology; lab animal medicine (MS); veterinary anatomic pathology (MS); veterinary clinical pathology (MS). Terminal master's awarded for partial completion of doctoral program. *Degree requirements:* For master's, thesis (for some programs); for doctorate, thesis/dissertation. *Entrance requirements:* For master's and doctorate, GRE General Test. Additional exam requirements/recommendations for international students: Required—TOEFL (minimum score 575 paper-based; 232 computer-based), IELTS (minimum score 6.5), TWE (minimum score 4). Electronic applications accepted.

Texas A&M University, College of Veterinary Medicine and Biomedical Sciences, Department of Veterinary Pathobiology, College Station, TX 77843. Offers genetics (MS, PhD); veterinary microbiology (MS, PhD); veterinary parasitology (MS, PhD); veterinary pathology (MS, PhD). Part-time programs available. Postbaccalaureate distance learning degree programs offered. *Faculty:* 26. *Students:* 25 full-time (17 women), 18 part-time (14 women); includes 1 Black or African American, non-Hispanic/Latino; 3 Asian, non-Hispanic/Latino; 2 Hispanic/Latino, 10 international. Average age 33. In 2010, 1 master's, 5 doctorates awarded. Terminal master's awarded for partial completion of doctoral program. *Degree requirements:* For master's, thesis, seminars; for doctorate, thesis/dissertation, seminars. *Entrance requirements:* For master's and doctorate, GRE General Test, minimum GPA of 3.0 in last 60 hours. Additional exam requirements/recommendations for international students: Required—TOEFL. *Application deadline:* For fall admission, 3/1 priority date for domestic students; for spring admission, 8/1 priority date for domestic students. Applications are processed on a rolling basis. Application fee: $50 ($75 for international students). Electronic applications accepted. *Financial support:* In 2010–11, fellowships with partial tuition reimbursements (averaging $16,000 per year), research assistantships with partial tuition reimbursements (averaging $15,400 per year), teaching assistantships with partial tuition reimbursements (averaging $16,000 per year) were awarded; Federal Work-Study, institutionally sponsored loans, scholarships/grants, traineeships, health care benefits, and unspecified assistantships also available. Support available to part-time students. Financial award applicants required to submit FAFSA. *Faculty research:* Infectious and noninfectious diseases of animals and birds, animal genetics, molecular biology, immunology, virology. *Unit head:* Dr. Linda Logan, Head, 979-862-6559, Fax: 979-845-9231, E-mail: llogan@cvm.tamu.edu. *Application contact:* Dr. Patricia Holman, Graduate Advisor, 979-845-4202, Fax: 979-862-1147, E-mail: pholman@cvm.tamu.edu.

The University of Arizona, College of Agriculture and Life Sciences, Department of Veterinary Science and Microbiology, Program in Microbiology and Pathobiology, Tucson, AZ 85721. Offers MS, PhD. *Students:* 42 full-time (23 women), 43 part-time (22 women); includes 2 American Indian or Alaska Native, non-Hispanic/Latino; 2 Asian, non-Hispanic/Latino; 4 Hispanic/Latino, 16 international. Average age 31.Terminal master's awarded for partial completion of doctoral program. *Degree requirements:* For master's, thesis; for doctorate, comprehensive exam, thesis/dissertation. *Entrance requirements:* For master's and doctorate, GRE, minimum GPA of 3.0, 3 letters of recommendation, letter of intent. Additional exam requirements/recommendations for international students: Required—TOEFL (minimum score 550 paper-based; 213 computer-based; 80 iBT); Recommended—IELTS (minimum score 7). *Application deadline:* For fall admission, 2/28 for domestic students, 12/1 for international students. Applications are processed on a rolling basis. Application fee: $75. *Expenses:* Tuition, state resident: full-time $7692. *Financial support:* Research assistantships with tuition reimbursements, teaching assistantships with tuition reimbursements, scholarships/grants available. Financial award application deadline: 3/22. *Faculty research:* Antibiotic resistance, molecular pathogenesis of bacteria, food safety, diagnosis of animal disease, parasitology.

University of Cincinnati, Graduate School, College of Medicine, Graduate Programs in Biomedical Sciences, Program in Pathobiology and Molecular Medicine, Cincinnati, OH 45221. Offers pathology (PhD), including anatomic pathology, laboratory medicine, pathobiology and molecular medicine. *Degree requirements:* For doctorate, thesis/dissertation, qualifying exam. *Entrance requirements:* For doctorate, GRE General Test. Additional exam requirements/recommendations for international students: Required—TOEFL (minimum score 620 paper-based; 260 computer-based). Electronic applications accepted. *Faculty research:* Cardiovascular and lipid disorders, digestive and kidney disease, endocrine and metabolic disorders, hematologic and oncogenic, immunology and infectious disease.

University of Connecticut, Graduate School, College of Agriculture and Natural Resources, Department of Pathobiology and Veterinary Science, Storrs, CT 06269. Offers pathobiology (MS, PhD). Terminal master's awarded for partial completion of doctoral program. *Degree requirements:* For master's, comprehensive exam; for doctorate, thesis/dissertation. *Entrance requirements:* For master's and doctorate, GRE General Test, GRE Subject Test. Additional exam requirements/recommendations for international students: Required—TOEFL (minimum score 550 paper-based; 213 computer-based). Electronic applications accepted.

Pathobiology

University of Illinois at Urbana–Champaign, College of Veterinary Medicine, Department of Pathobiology, Urbana, IL 61802. Offers MS, PhD, DVM/PhD. Part-time programs available. *Faculty:* 18 full-time (6 women). *Students:* 10 full-time (6 women), 7 part-time (2 women); includes 1 Black or African American, non-Hispanic/Latino; 1 Asian, non-Hispanic/Latino; 1 Hispanic/Latino, 7 international. 32 applicants, 13% accepted, 4 enrolled. In 2010, 1 doctorate awarded. Terminal master's awarded for partial completion of doctoral program. *Degree requirements:* For doctorate, thesis/dissertation. *Entrance requirements:* For master's and doctorate, GRE, minimum GPA of 3.0. Additional exam requirements/recommendations for international students: Required—TOEFL (minimum score 590 paper-based; 243 computer-based). *Application deadline:* Applications are processed on a rolling basis. Application fee: $75 ($90 for international students). Electronic applications accepted. *Financial support:* In 2010–11, 3 fellowships, 8 research assistantships, 1 teaching assistantship were awarded; tuition waivers (full and partial) also available. *Faculty research:* Epidemiology, immunology, microbiology, parasitology, clinical pathology. *Unit head:* Daniel L. Rock, Head, 217-333-2449, Fax: 217-244-7421, E-mail: dlrock@illinois.edu. *Application contact:* Paula Moxley, Administrative Aide, 217-244-8924, Fax: 217-244-7421, E-mail: pkm@illinois.edu.

University of Missouri, College of Veterinary Medicine and Graduate School, Graduate Programs in Veterinary Medicine, Department of Veterinary Pathobiology, Columbia, MO 65211. Offers laboratory animal medicine (MS); pathobiology (MS, PhD). *Degree requirements:* For master's, thesis; for doctorate, 2 foreign languages, thesis/dissertation. *Entrance requirements:* For master's and doctorate, GRE General Test, minimum GPA of 3.0. Additional exam requirements/recommendations for international students: Required—TOEFL (minimum score 500 paper-based; 61 iBT). Electronic applications accepted.

University of Southern California, Keck School of Medicine and Graduate School, Graduate Programs in Medicine, Department of Pathology, Los Angeles, CA 90089. Offers experimental and molecular pathology (MS); pathobiology (PhD). *Faculty:* 55 full-time (12 women), 5 part-time/adjunct (1 woman). *Students:* 40 full-time (23 women); includes 13 Asian, non-Hispanic/Latino; 6 Hispanic/Latino, 10 international. Average age 26. 26 applicants, 38% accepted, 9 enrolled. In 2010, 4 master's, 8 doctorates awarded. *Median time to degree:* Of those who began their doctoral program in fall 2002, 89% received their degree in 8 years or less. *Degree requirements:* For master's, thesis; for doctorate, thesis/dissertation. *Entrance requirements:* For master's, GRE General Test, minimum GPA of 3.0; for doctorate, GRE General Test, minimum GPA of 3.0, BS in natural sciences. Additional exam requirements/recommendations for international students: Required—TOEFL (minimum score 600 paper-based; 250 computer-based; 100 iBT). *Application deadline:* For fall admission, 12/1 priority date for domestic and international students. Application fee: $85. Electronic applications accepted. *Expenses:* Tuition: Full-time $31,240; part-time $1420 per unit. Required fees: $600. One-time fee: $35 full-time. Full-time tuition and fees vary according to degree level and program. *Financial support:* In 2010–11, 27 students received support, including 4 fellowships with tuition reimbursements available (averaging $27,600 per year), 22 research assistantships with tuition reimbursements available (averaging $27,600 per year), 1 teaching assistantship with tuition reimbursement available (averaging $27,600 per year); Federal Work-Study, institutionally sponsored loans, scholarships/grants, health care benefits, and unspecified assistantships also available. Financial award application deadline: 5/3. *Faculty research:* Immunology of lymphomas and leukemias, lung cancer, molecular basis of oncogenesis, central nervous system disease, organic chemical carcinogens and carcinogenic metal salts. *Unit head:* Dr. Michael E. Selsted, Chair, 323-442-1179, Fax: 323-442-3049,

E-mail: selsted@usc.edu. *Application contact:* Lisa A. Doumak, Student Services Assistant, 323-442-1168, Fax: 323-442-3049, E-mail: doumak@usc.edu.

See Display below and Close-Up on page 413.

University of Toronto, School of Graduate Studies, Life Sciences Division, Department of Laboratory Medicine and Pathobiology, Toronto, ON M5S 1A1, Canada. Offers M Sc, PhD, MD/PhD. *Degree requirements:* For master's, thesis; for doctorate, thesis/dissertation, oral defense of thesis. *Entrance requirements:* For master's, minimum B+ average in final 2 years, research experience, 2 letters of recommendation, resume, interview; for doctorate, minimum A– average, 2 letters of recommendation, research experience, resumé, interview. Additional exam requirements/recommendations for international students: Required—TOEFL (600 paper-based, 250 computer-based), TWE (5) or IELTS (7).

University of Washington, Graduate School, School of Public Health, Department of Global Health, Graduate Program in Pathobiology, Seattle, WA 98195. Offers PhD. *Students:* 34 full-time (27 women), 1 part-time (0 women); includes 2 Black or African American, non-Hispanic/Latino; 3 Asian, non-Hispanic/Latino; 2 Hispanic/Latino, 6 international. Average age 29. 59 applicants, 24% accepted, 6 enrolled. In 2010, 3 doctorates awarded. *Degree requirements:* For doctorate, comprehensive exam, thesis/dissertation, published paper from thesis work. *Entrance requirements:* For doctorate, GRE General Test, minimum GPA of 3.0. *Application deadline:* For fall admission, 12/1 for domestic students, 11/1 for international students. Application fee: $75. Electronic applications accepted. *Financial support:* In 2010–11, 32 students received support, including 2 fellowships with full tuition reimbursements available (averaging $27,348 per year), 30 research assistantships with full tuition reimbursements available (averaging $27,348 per year); career-related internships or fieldwork, institutionally sponsored loans, scholarships/grants, traineeships, and unspecified assistantships also available. *Faculty research:* Malaria, immunological response to mycobacteria infections, HIV-cell interaction and the development of an anti-HIV vaccine, regulation of intercellular communication via gap junctions, genetic and nutritional regulation of proteins involved in lipid transport. *Unit head:* Dr. King Holmes, Chair, 206-744-3620, Fax: 206-744-3694. *Application contact:* Rachel Reichert, Program Manager, 206-543-4338, Fax: 206-543-3873, E-mail: pabio@u.washington.edu.

University of Wyoming, College of Agriculture and Natural Resources, Department of Veterinary Sciences, Laramie, WY 82070. Offers pathobiology (MS). *Degree requirements:* For master's, thesis. *Entrance requirements:* For master's, GRE General Test, minimum GPA of 3.0. Additional exam requirements/recommendations for international students: Required—TOEFL. *Faculty research:* Infectious diseases, pathology, toxicology, immunology, microbiology.

Wake Forest University, School of Medicine and Graduate School of Arts and Sciences, Graduate Programs in Medicine, Program in Molecular and Cellular Pathobiology, Winston-Salem, NC 27109. Offers MS, PhD, MD/PhD. *Degree requirements:* For master's, thesis; for doctorate, thesis/dissertation. *Entrance requirements:* For master's and doctorate, GRE General Test. Additional exam requirements/recommendations for international students: Required—TOEFL. Electronic applications accepted. *Faculty research:* Atherosclerosis, lipoproteins, arterial wall metabolism.

Yale University, School of Medicine and Graduate School of Arts and Sciences, Combined Program in Biological and Biomedical Sciences (BBS), Pharmacological Sciences and Molecular Medicine Track, New Haven, CT 06520. Offers PhD, MD/PhD. *Degree requirements:* For doctorate, thesis/dissertation. *Entrance requirements:* For doctorate, GRE General Test. Additional exam requirements/recommendations for international students: Required—TOEFL. Electronic applications accepted.

USC
UNIVERSITY OF SOUTHERN CALIFORNIA

DEPARTMENT OF PATHOLOGY

The Department of Pathology offers a program for the Master of Science degree with a major in Experimental and Molecular Pathology. The primary objectives are to provide the necessary theoretical and practical training in experimental pathology that will culminate with the M.S. degree. Goals of the program are to train students for positions as senior research staff or senior technicians in academic or industrial situations, to enable students to continue toward their M.D. or Ph.D. degrees, to prepare graduates for multidisciplinary consulting positions or teaching positions in community colleges. For the master's program, students should complete the application form online using the following Web site: http://www.usc.edu/admission/graduate/applyonline/

The Ph.D. program is integrated with the Ph.D. Programs in Biomedical and Biological Sciences (PIBBS), an integrated Ph.D. admission program for students who want to study biomedical science at USC.

For further information on the PIBBS application, students should visit http://www.usc.edu/pibbs.

For more information, please contact:
Lisa Doumak, Staff Graduate Advisor
Department of Pathology
USC Keck School of Medicine
Los Angeles, CA 90089-9092
pathgrad@usc.edu
http://www.usc.edu/medicine/pathology

Pathology

Albert Einstein College of Medicine, Graduate Division of Biomedical Sciences, Department of Pathology, Bronx, NY 10467. Offers PhD, MD/PhD. *Degree requirements:* For doctorate, thesis/dissertation. *Entrance requirements:* For doctorate, GRE General Test. Additional exam requirements/recommendations for international students: Required—TOEFL. *Faculty research:* Clinical and disease-related research at tissue, cellular, and subcellular levels; biochemistry and morphology of enzyme and lysosome disorders.

Baylor College of Medicine, Graduate School of Biomedical Sciences, Program in Developmental Biology, Houston, TX 77030-3498. Offers PhD, MD/PhD. *Faculty:* 63 full-time (19 women). *Students:* 55 full-time (26 women); includes 5 Asian, non-Hispanic/Latino; 3 Hispanic/Latino, 35 international. Average age 28. 73 applicants, 18% accepted, 10 enrolled. In 2010, 5 doctorates awarded. *Degree requirements:* For doctorate, thesis/dissertation, public defense. *Entrance requirements:* For doctorate, GRE General Test, GRE Subject Test (strongly recommended), minimum GPA of 3.0. Additional exam requirements/recommendations for international students: Required—TOEFL. *Application deadline:* For fall admission, 1/1 priority date for domestic students. Application fee: $0. Electronic applications accepted. *Expenses:* Tuition: Full-time $11,000. Required fees: $4900. *Financial support:* In 2010–11, 55 students received support, including 15 fellowships with full tuition reimbursements available (averaging $26,000 per year), 40 research assistantships with full tuition reimbursements available (averaging $26,000 per year); career-related internships or fieldwork, Federal Work-Study, institutionally sponsored loans, health care benefits, tuition waivers (full), and stipends also available. *Faculty research:* Stem cells, cancer, neurobiology, organogenesis, genetics of model organisms. *Unit head:* Dr. Hugo Bellen, Director, 713-798-6410. *Application contact:* Catherine Tasnier, Graduate Program Administrator, 713-798-6410, Fax: 713-798-5386, E-mail: cat@bcm.edu.

See Display on page 282 and Close-Up on page 307.

Brown University, Graduate School, Division of Biology and Medicine, Program in Pathology and Laboratory Medicine, Providence, RI 02912. Offers biology (PhD); cancer biology (PhD); immunology and infection (PhD); medical science (PhD); pathobiology (Sc M); toxicology and environmental pathology (PhD). Terminal master's awarded for partial completion of doctoral program. *Degree requirements:* For doctorate, thesis/dissertation, preliminary exam. *Entrance requirements:* For master's and doctorate, GRE General Test, GRE Subject Test. Additional exam requirements/recommendations for international students: Required—TOEFL. Electronic applications accepted. *Faculty research:* Environmental pathology, carcinogenesis, immunopathology, signal transduction, innate immunity.

Case Western Reserve University, School of Medicine and School of Graduate Studies, Graduate Programs in Medicine, Programs in Molecular and Cellular Basis of Disease/Pathology, Cleveland, OH 44106. Offers cancer biology (PhD); cell biology (MS, PhD); immunology (MS, PhD); pathology (MS, PhD); MD/PhD. Terminal master's awarded for partial completion of doctoral program. *Degree requirements:* For master's, thesis; for doctorate, thesis/dissertation. *Entrance requirements:* For master's and doctorate, GRE General Test, GRE Subject Test. Additional exam requirements/recommendations for international students: Required—TOEFL (minimum score 550 paper-based; 213 computer-based). Electronic applications accepted. *Faculty research:* Neurobiology, molecular biology, cancer biology, biomaterials, biocompatibility.

Colorado State University, College of Veterinary Medicine and Biomedical Sciences, Department of Microbiology, Immunology and Pathology, Fort Collins, CO 80523-0015. Offers microbiology (MS, PhD); pathology (PhD). *Faculty:* 40 full-time (17 women), 2 part-time/adjunct (0 women). *Students:* 56 full-time (44 women), 39 part-time (25 women); includes 4 Asian, non-Hispanic/Latino; 6 Hispanic/Latino, 9 international. Average age 31. 107 applicants, 17% accepted, 18 enrolled. In 2010, 5 master's, 11 doctorates awarded. *Degree requirements:* For master's, thesis; for doctorate, comprehensive exam, thesis/dissertation. *Entrance requirements:* For master's, GRE General Test, minimum GPA of 3.0, BA/BS in biomedical field, reviewer evaluation forms, resume; for doctorate, GRE General Test, minimum GPA of 3.0, BA/BS in biomedical field, reviewer evaluation forms, resume, statement of interest. Additional exam requirements/recommendations for international students: Required—TOEFL (minimum score 550 paper-based). *Application deadline:* For fall admission, 1/1 priority date for domestic students; for spring admission, 10/1 priority date for domestic students. Applications are processed on a rolling basis. Application fee: $50. Electronic applications accepted. *Expenses:* Tuition, state resident: full-time $7434; part-time $413 per credit. Tuition, nonresident: full-time $19,022; part-time $1057 per credit. Required fees: $1729; $88 per credit. *Financial support:* In 2010–11, 74 students received support, including 27 fellowships with tuition reimbursements available (averaging $32,882 per year), 41 research assistantships with tuition reimbursements available (averaging $23,930 per year), 6 teaching assistantships with tuition reimbursements available (averaging $15,885 per year); Federal Work-Study, scholarships/grants, traineeships, and unspecified assistantships also available. Financial award applicants required to submit FAFSA. *Faculty research:* Medical and veterinary bacteriology, immunology, microbial physiology, pathology, vector-borne disease. Total annual research expenditures: $33.1 million. *Unit head:* Dr. Edward A. Hoover, Head, 970-491-7587, Fax: 970-491-0603, E-mail: edward.hoover@colostate.edu. *Application contact:* Lisa McCann, Academic Programs Coordinator, 970-491-6118, Fax: 970-491-1815, E-mail: lisa.mccann@colostate.edu.

Columbia University, College of Physicians and Surgeons, Department of Pathology, New York, NY 10032. Offers pathobiology (M Phil, MA, PhD); MD/PhD. Only candidates for the PhD are admitted. Terminal master's awarded for partial completion of doctoral program. *Degree requirements:* For doctorate, thesis/dissertation. *Entrance requirements:* For master's and doctorate, GRE General Test. Additional exam requirements/recommendations for international students: Required—TOEFL. *Faculty research:* Virology, molecular biology, cell biology, neurobiology, immunology.

Dalhousie University, Faculty of Graduate Studies and Faculty of Medicine, Graduate Programs in Medicine, Department of Pathology, Halifax, NS B3H 4R2, Canada. Offers M Sc, PhD. *Degree requirements:* For master's, oral defense of thesis. *Entrance requirements:* Additional exam requirements/recommendations for international students: Required—TOEFL, IELTS, 1 of the following 5 approved tests: TOEFL, IELTS, CAEL, CANTEST, Michigan English Language Assessment Battery. Electronic applications accepted. *Faculty research:* Tumor immunology, molecular oncology, clinical chemistry, hematology, molecular genetics/oncology.

Duke University, Graduate School, Department of Pathology, Durham, NC 27710. Offers PhD. *Accreditation:* NAACLS. *Faculty:* 31 full-time. *Students:* 35 full-time (21 women); includes 2 Black or African American, non-Hispanic/Latino; 1 Asian, non-Hispanic/Latino; 1 Hispanic/Latino, 13 international. 22 applicants, 23% accepted, 4 enrolled. In 2010, 5 doctorates awarded. *Degree requirements:* For doctorate, thesis/dissertation. *Entrance requirements:* For doctorate, GRE General Test, GRE Subject Test (recommended). Additional exam requirements/recommendations for international students: Required—TOEFL (minimum score 550 paper-based; 213 computer-based; 73 iBT), IELTS (minimum score 7). *Application deadline:* For fall admission, 12/8 priority date for domestic and international students. Application fee: $75. Electronic applications accepted. *Financial support:* Fellowships, research assistantships, Federal Work-Study available. Financial award application deadline: 12/8. *Unit head:* Soman Abraham, Director of Graduate Studies, 919-684-9929, Fax: 919-681-8868, E-mail: pamela.harris@duke.edu. *Application contact:* Elizabeth Hutton, Director of Admissions, 919-684-3913, Fax: 919-684-2277, E-mail: grad-admissions@duke.edu.

Duke University, School of Medicine, Pathologists' Assistant Program, Durham, NC 27708-0586. Offers MHS. *Accreditation:* NAACLS. *Faculty:* 1 (woman) full-time, 42 part-time/adjunct (21 women). *Students:* 16 full-time (14 women); includes 1 Black or African American, non-Hispanic/Latino; 2 Asian, non-Hispanic/Latino. Average age 26. 44 applicants, 18% accepted, 8 enrolled. In 2010, 8 master's awarded. *Degree requirements:* For master's, comprehensive exam. *Entrance requirements:* For master's, GRE. Additional exam requirements/recommendations for international students: Required—TOEFL, IELTS. *Application deadline:* For fall admission, 1/31 priority date for domestic students. Application fee: $55. *Expenses:* Contact institution. *Financial support:* In 2010–11, 15 students received support; fellowships, research assistantships, teaching assistantships, scholarships/grants available. Financial award application deadline: 5/1; financial award applicants required to submit FAFSA. *Unit head:* Dr. Rex C. Bentley, Program Director, 919-684-6423, Fax: 919-681-7799, E-mail: bentl003@mc.duke.edu. *Application contact:* Pamela Vollmer, Associate Director, 919-684-2159, E-mail: vollm003@mc.duke.edu.

East Carolina University, Brody School of Medicine, Department of Pathology, Greenville, NC 27858-4353. Offers PhD. *Degree requirements:* For doctorate, comprehensive exam, thesis/dissertation. *Entrance requirements:* For doctorate, GRE General Test, bachelor's degree in biological chemistry or physical science. *Expenses:* Tuition, state resident: full-time $3130; part-time $391.25 per credit hour. Tuition, nonresident: full-time $13,817; part-time $1727.13 per credit hour. Required fees: $1916; $239.50 per credit hour. Tuition and fees vary according to campus/location and program.

Georgetown University, Graduate School of Arts and Sciences, Programs in Biomedical Sciences, Department of Pathology, Washington, DC 20057. Offers MS, PhD, MD/PhD, MS/PhD. *Degree requirements:* For master's, thesis; for doctorate, comprehensive exam, thesis/dissertation. *Entrance requirements:* For master's and doctorate, GRE General Test. Additional exam requirements/recommendations for international students: Required—TOEFL. *Faculty research:* Virus-induced diabetes, viral oncology, renal pathophysiology.

Harvard University, Graduate School of Arts and Sciences, Division of Medical Sciences, Boston, MA 02115. Offers biological chemistry and molecular pharmacology (PhD); cell biology (PhD); genetics (PhD); microbiology and molecular genetics (PhD); pathology (PhD), including experimental pathology. *Degree requirements:* For doctorate, thesis/dissertation. *Entrance requirements:* For doctorate, GRE General Test, GRE Subject Test. Additional exam requirements/recommendations for international students: Required—TOEFL. *Expenses:* Tuition: Full-time $34,976. Required fees: $1166. Full-time tuition and fees vary according to program.

Indiana University–Purdue University Indianapolis, Indiana University School of Medicine, Department of Pathology and Laboratory Medicine, Indianapolis, IN 46202-2896. Offers MS, PhD, MD/PhD. *Faculty:* 27 full-time (4 women). *Students:* 6 full-time (4 women), 5 part-time (4 women); includes 1 minority (Hispanic/Latino), 1 international. Average age 26. 32 applicants, 19% accepted, 5 enrolled. In 2010, 3 master's awarded. *Degree requirements:* For master's, thesis; for doctorate, thesis/dissertation. *Entrance requirements:* For master's and doctorate, GRE General Test. Additional exam requirements/recommendations for international students: Required—TOEFL. *Application deadline:* For fall admission, 1/15 priority date for domestic students. Applications are processed on a rolling basis. Application fee: $55 ($65 for international students). *Financial support:* In 2010–11, 4 teaching assistantships with full tuition reimbursements (averaging $10,711 per year) were awarded; fellowships, research assistantships with full tuition reimbursements, institutionally sponsored loans also available. Financial award application deadline: 2/1. *Faculty research:* Intestinal microecology and anaerobes, molecular pathogenesis of infectious diseases, AIDS pneumocystis, sports medicine toxicology, neuropathology of aging. *Unit head:* Dr. John Eble, Chairman, 317-274-4806. *Application contact:* Dr. Diane S. Leland, Graduate Adviser, 317-274-0148.

Iowa State University of Science and Technology, College of Veterinary Medicine and Graduate College, Graduate Programs in Veterinary Medicine, Department of Veterinary Pathology, Ames, IA 50011. Offers MS, PhD. *Faculty:* 19 full-time (7 women), 5 part-time/adjunct (1 woman). *Students:* 3 full-time (1 woman), 6 part-time (3 women); includes 1 Hispanic/Latino, 1 international. 4 applicants, 25% accepted, 1 enrolled. In 2010, 5 doctorates awarded. *Degree requirements:* For master's, thesis or alternative; for doctorate, thesis/dissertation. *Entrance requirements:* For master's and doctorate, GRE General Test. Additional exam requirements/recommendations for international students: Recommended—TOEFL (minimum score 550 paper-based; 79 iBT), IELTS (minimum score 6.5). *Application deadline:* Applications are processed on a rolling basis. Application fee: $40 ($90 for international students). Electronic applications accepted. *Financial support:* In 2010–11, 5 research assistantships with full and partial tuition reimbursements (averaging $18,432 per year) were awarded; teaching assistantships with full and partial tuition reimbursements, scholarships/grants, health care benefits, and unspecified assistantships also available. *Unit head:* Dr. Claire B. Andreasen, Chair, 515-294-0877. *Application contact:* Dr. Claire B. Andreasen, Chair, 515-294-0877.

The Johns Hopkins University, School of Medicine, Graduate Programs in Medicine, Department of Pathology, Baltimore, MD 21218-2699. Offers pathobiology (PhD). *Faculty:* 68 full-time (14 women). *Students:* 48 full-time (29 women); includes 9 minority (3 Black or African American, non-Hispanic/Latino; 3 Asian, non-Hispanic/Latino; 2 Hispanic/Latino; 1 Two or more races, non-Hispanic/Latino), 22 international. Average age 29. 124 applicants, 6% accepted, 8 enrolled. In 2010, 6 doctorates awarded. *Degree requirements:* For doctorate, thesis/dissertation, qualifying oral exam. *Entrance requirements:* For doctorate, GRE General Test, previous course work with laboratory in organic and inorganic chemistry, general biology, calculus; interview. Additional exam requirements/recommendations for international students: Required—TOEFL. *Application deadline:* For winter admission, 1/10 for domestic students. Application fee: $85. Electronic applications accepted. *Financial support:* In 2010–11, 42 fellowships with full tuition reimbursements (averaging $26,855 per year) were awarded; scholarships/grants also available. *Faculty research:* Role of mutant proteins in Alzheimer's disease, nuclear protein function in breast and prostate cancer, medically important fungi, glycoproteins in HIV pathogenesis. Total annual research expenditures: $38.6 million. *Unit head:* Dr. J. Brooks Jackson, Chair, 410-955-9790, Fax: 410-955-0394. *Application contact:* Wilhelmena M. Braswell, Senior Academic Program Coordinator, 443-287-3163, Fax: 410-614-3548, E-mail: wbraswel@jhmi.edu.

Loma Linda University, School of Medicine, Department of Pathology and Human Anatomy, Loma Linda, CA 92350. Offers MS, PhD. Part-time programs available. Terminal master's awarded for partial completion of doctoral program. *Degree requirements:* For master's, thesis; for doctorate, 2 foreign languages, thesis/dissertation. *Entrance requirements:* For master's and doctorate, GRE General Test. Additional exam requirements/recommendations for international students: Required—TOEFL (minimum score 550 paper-based; 213 computer-based). *Faculty research:* Neuroendocrine system, histochemistry and image analysis, effect of age and diabetes on PNS, electron microscopy, histology.

Louisiana State University Health Sciences Center, School of Graduate Studies in New Orleans, Department of Pathology, New Orleans, LA 70112-2223. Offers MS, PhD, MD/PhD. Part-time programs available. *Degree requirements:* For master's, comprehensive exam, thesis; for doctorate, comprehensive exam, thesis/dissertation. *Entrance requirements:* For master's and doctorate, GRE General Test. Additional exam requirements/recommendations for international students: Required—TOEFL. *Faculty research:* Immunohematology, hematology, experimental and epidemiological studies in atherosclerosis, epidemiology of cancer.

McGill University, Faculty of Graduate and Postdoctoral Studies, Faculty of Medicine, Department of Pathology, Montréal, QC H3A 2T5, Canada. Offers M Sc, PhD.

Medical University of South Carolina, College of Graduate Studies, Department of Pathology and Laboratory Medicine, Charleston, SC 29425. Offers MS, PhD, DMD/PhD, MD/PhD. *Faculty:* 11 full-time (5 women). *Students:* 15 full-time (11 women), 1 (woman) part-time; includes 2 Black or African American, non-Hispanic/Latino; 1 Hispanic/Latino, 1 international. Average age 26. 7 applicants, 29% accepted, 1 enrolled. In 2010, 1 doctorate awarded. Terminal

Pathology

Medical University of South Carolina (continued)
master's awarded for partial completion of doctoral program. *Degree requirements:* For master's, thesis; for doctorate, thesis/dissertation, oral and written exams. *Entrance requirements:* For master's, GRE General Test; for doctorate, GRE General Test, interview, minimum GPA of 3.0. Additional exam requirements/recommendations for international students: Required—TOEFL (minimum score 600 paper-based; 250 computer-based; 100 iBT). *Application deadline:* For fall admission, 1/15 priority date for domestic and international students. Applications are processed on a rolling basis. Application fee: $0 ($85 for international students). Electronic applications accepted. *Financial support:* In 2010–11, 3 fellowships with full and partial tuition reimbursements (averaging $28,000 per year) were awarded; Federal Work-Study and scholarships/grants also available. Support available to part-time students. Financial award application deadline: 3/10; financial award applicants required to submit FAFSA. *Faculty research:* Neurobiology of hearing loss; inner ear ion homeostasis; cancer biology, genetics and stem cell biology; cellular defense mechanisms0. *Unit head:* Dr. Janice M. Lage, Chair, 843-792-3121, Fax: 843-792-6590, E-mail: lagejm@musc.edu. *Application contact:* Dr. Victoria Jane Findlay, Assistant Professor and Coordinator of Graduate Studies, 843-792-1889, Fax: 843-792-6590, E-mail: findlay@musc.edu.

Michigan State University, College of Veterinary Medicine and The Graduate School, Graduate Programs in Veterinary Medicine, Department of Pathobiology and Diagnostic Investigation, East Lansing, MI 48824. Offers pathology (MS, PhD); pathology–environmental toxicology (PhD). *Entrance requirements:* Additional exam requirements/recommendations for international students: Required—TOEFL. Electronic applications accepted.

New York Medical College, Graduate School of Basic Medical Sciences, Program in Experimental Pathology, Valhalla, NY 10595-1691. Offers MS, PhD, MD/PhD. Part-time and evening/weekend programs available. *Faculty:* 16 full-time (1 woman). *Students:* 6 full-time (2 women), 4 part-time (3 women); includes 1 Black or African American, non-Hispanic/Latino, 4 international. Average age 27. 6 applicants, 100% accepted, 4 enrolled. In 2010, 5 master's awarded. Terminal master's awarded for partial completion of doctoral program. *Degree requirements:* For master's, thesis; for doctorate, comprehensive exam, thesis/dissertation. *Entrance requirements:* For master's and doctorate, GRE General Test. Additional exam requirements/recommendations for international students: Required—TOEFL. *Application deadline:* For fall admission, 7/1 priority date for domestic students, 5/1 priority date for international students; for spring admission, 12/1 priority date for domestic students, 10/1 priority date for international students. Applications are processed on a rolling basis. Application fee: $50 ($75 for international students). Electronic applications accepted. *Financial support:* In 2010–11, 3 research assistantships with full tuition reimbursements (averaging $24,000 per year) were awarded; Federal Work-Study, institutionally sponsored loans, scholarships/grants, traineeships, tuition waivers (full), unspecified assistantships, and health benefits (for PhD candidates only) also available. Financial award applicants required to submit FAFSA. *Faculty research:* Atherogenesis and endothelial cell biology, immunology and inflammation, tumor biology and metastasis, mechanisms of chemical carcinogens, mechanisms of free radial tissue damage. *Unit head:* Dr. Henry P. Godfrey, Co-Director, 914-594-4160, Fax: 914-594-4944. *Application contact:* Valerie Romeo-Messana, Admission Coordinator, 914-594-4110, Fax: 914-594-4944, E-mail: v_romeomessana@nymc.edu.

North Carolina State University, College of Veterinary Medicine, Program in Comparative Biomedical Sciences, Raleigh, NC 27695. Offers cell biology (MS, PhD); infectious disease (MS, PhD); pathology (MS, PhD); pharmacology (MS, PhD); population medicine (MS, PhD). Part-time programs available. *Degree requirements:* For master's, thesis; for doctorate, thesis/dissertation. *Entrance requirements:* For master's and doctorate, GRE General Test. Additional exam requirements/recommendations for international students: Required—TOEFL (minimum score 550 paper-based; 213 computer-based). Electronic applications accepted. *Expenses:* Contact institution. *Faculty research:* Infectious diseases, cell biology, pharmacology and toxicology, genomics, pathology and population medicine.

North Dakota State University, College of Graduate and Interdisciplinary Studies, College of Agriculture, Food Systems, and Natural Resources, Department of Veterinary and Microbiological Sciences, Fargo, ND 58108. Offers food safety (MS); microbiology (MS); molecular pathogenesis (PhD). Part-time programs available. *Students:* 12 full-time (7 women), 5 part-time (all women). 18 applicants, 17% accepted. In 2010, 1 master's awarded. *Degree requirements:* For master's, thesis; for doctorate, thesis/dissertation, oral and written preliminary exams. *Entrance requirements:* For master's and doctorate, GRE. Additional exam requirements/recommendations for international students: Required—TOEFL (minimum score 525 paper-based; 197 computer-based; 71 iBT). *Application deadline:* For fall admission, 3/15 priority date for domestic students. Applications are processed on a rolling basis. Application fee: $25. *Financial support:* Fellowships with full tuition reimbursements, research assistantships with full tuition reimbursements, teaching assistantships with full tuition reimbursements, Federal Work-Study and institutionally sponsored loans available. Financial award application deadline: 4/15. *Faculty research:* Bacterial gene regulation, antibiotic resistance, molecular virology, mechanisms of bacterial pathogenesis, immunology of animals. *Unit head:* Dr. Doug Freeman, Head, 701-231-7511, E-mail: douglas.freeman@ndsu.nodak.edu. *Application contact:* Dr. Eugene S. Berry, Associate Professor, 701-231-7520, Fax: 701-231-7514, E-mail: eugene.berry@ndsu.edu.

The Ohio State University, College of Medicine, Department of Pathology, Columbus, OH 43210. Offers experimental pathobiology (MS); pathology assistant (MS); MD/PhD. *Accreditation:* NAACLS. *Degree requirements:* For master's, comprehensive exam (for some programs), thesis. *Entrance requirements:* For master's, GRE General Test. Additional exam requirements/recommendations for international students: Required—TOEFL (minimum score 550 paper-based; 213 computer-based). Electronic applications accepted. *Expenses:* Tuition, state resident: full-time $10,605. Tuition, nonresident: full-time $26,535. Tuition and fees vary according to course load and program. *Faculty research:* Clinical pathology, transplantation pathology, cancer research, neuropathology, vascular pathology.

Purdue University, School of Veterinary Medicine and Graduate School, Graduate Programs in Veterinary Medicine, Department of Comparative Pathobiology, West Lafayette, IN 47907-2027. Offers comparative epidemiology and public health (MS); comparative epidemiology and public heath (PhD); comparative microbiology and immunology (MS, PhD); comparative pathobiology (MS, PhD); interdisciplinary studies (PhD), including microbial pathogenesis, molecular signaling and cancer biology, molecular virology; lab animal medicine (MS); veterinary anatomic pathology (MS); veterinary clinical pathology (MS). Terminal master's awarded for partial completion of doctoral program. *Degree requirements:* For master's, thesis (for some programs); for doctorate, thesis/dissertation. *Entrance requirements:* For master's and doctorate, GRE General Test. Additional exam requirements/recommendations for international students: Required—TOEFL (minimum score 575 paper-based; 232 computer-based), IELTS (minimum score 6.5), TWE (minimum score 4). Electronic applications accepted.

Queen's University at Kingston, School of Graduate Studies and Research, Faculty of Health Sciences, Department of Pathology and Molecular Medicine, Kingston, ON K7L 3N6, Canada. Offers M Sc, PhD. Part-time programs available. *Degree requirements:* For master's, thesis; for doctorate, comprehensive exam, thesis/dissertation. *Entrance requirements:* Additional exam requirements/recommendations for international students: Required—TOEFL. *Faculty research:* Immunopathology, cancer biology, immunology and metastases, cell differentiation, blood coagulation.

Quinnipiac University, School of Health Sciences, Program for Pathologists' Assistant, Hamden, CT 06518-1940. Offers MHS. *Accreditation:* NAACLS. *Faculty:* 3 full-time (0 women), 5 part-time/adjunct (2 women). *Students:* 35 full-time (30 women); includes 3 minority (1 Black or African American, non-Hispanic/Latino; 1 Asian, non-Hispanic/Latino; 1 Hispanic/Latino). Average age 27. 100 applicants, 21% accepted, 18 enrolled. In 2010, 18 master's awarded. *Degree requirements:* For master's, residency. *Entrance requirements:* For master's, interview, coursework in biological and health sciences, minimum GPA of 2.8. Additional exam

requirements/recommendations for international students: Required—TOEFL (minimum score 575 paper-based; 233 computer-based; 90 iBT), IELTS (minimum score 6.5). *Application deadline:* For fall admission, 12/15 for domestic students. Applications are processed on a rolling basis. Application fee: $45. Electronic applications accepted. *Expenses:* Tuition: Part-time $810 per credit. Required fees: $35 per credit. *Financial support:* Career-related internships or fieldwork, tuition waivers (partial), and unspecified assistantships available. Financial award application deadline: 4/15; financial award applicants required to submit FAFSA. *Unit head:* Dr. Kenneth Kaloustian, Director, 203-582-8676, Fax: 203-582-3443, E-mail: ken.kaloustian@quinnipiac.edu. *Application contact:* Kristin Parent, Assistant Director of Graduate Health Sciences Admissions, 800-462-1944, Fax: 203-582-3443, E-mail: kristin.parent@quinnipiac.edu.

Rosalind Franklin University of Medicine and Science, College of Health Professions, Pathologists' Assistant Department, North Chicago, IL 60064-3095. Offers MS. *Entrance requirements:* For master's, bachelor's degree from an accredited college or university, minimum cumulative GPA of 3.0. Additional exam requirements/recommendations for international students: Required—TOEFL. *Faculty research:* Adaptation of ACGME/ADASP pathology resident training competencies to pathologists' assistant clinical education, utilization of structural portfolios in pathologists' assistant clinical education.

Saint Louis University, Graduate Education and School of Medicine, Graduate Program in Biomedical Sciences and Graduate Education, Department of Pathology, St. Louis, MO 63103-2097. Offers PhD. *Degree requirements:* For doctorate, comprehensive exam, thesis/dissertation, oral and written preliminary exams, oral defense of dissertation. *Entrance requirements:* For doctorate, GRE General Test (GRE Subject Test optional), letters of recommendation, resume, interview. Additional exam requirements/recommendations for international students: Required—TOEFL (minimum score 525 paper-based; 194 computer-based). Electronic applications accepted. *Faculty research:* Cancer research, hepatitis C virology, cell imaging, liver disease.

Stony Brook University, State University of New York, Graduate School, College of Arts and Sciences, Department of Biochemistry and Cell Biology, Molecular and Cellular Biology Program, Stony Brook, NY 11794. Offers biochemistry and molecular biology (PhD); biological sciences (MA); cellular and developmental biology (PhD); immunology and pathology (PhD); molecular and cellular biology (PhD). *Faculty:* 22 full-time (7 women). *Students:* 106 full-time (65 women); includes 2 Black or African American, non-Hispanic/Latino; 9 Asian, non-Hispanic/Latino; 1 Hispanic/Latino, 58 international. Average age 30. 320 applicants, 16% accepted, 26 enrolled. In 2010, 5 master's, 16 doctorates awarded. *Degree requirements:* For doctorate, comprehensive exam, thesis/dissertation, teaching experience. *Entrance requirements:* For doctorate, GRE General Test, GRE Subject Test. Additional exam requirements/recommendations for international students: Required—TOEFL. *Application deadline:* For fall admission, 1/15 for domestic students. Application fee: $100. *Expenses:* Tuition, state resident: full-time $8370; part-time $349 per credit. Tuition, nonresident: full-time $13,780; part-time $574 per credit. Required fees: $994. *Financial support:* In 2010–11, 42 research assistantships, 19 teaching assistantships were awarded; fellowships, Federal Work-Study also available. *Unit head:* Prof. Robert Haltiwanger, Chair, 631-632-8560. *Application contact:* Prof. Robert Haltiwanger, Chair, 631-632-8560.

Temple University, Health Sciences Center, School of Medicine and Graduate School, Doctor of Medicine Program, Department of Pathology and Laboratory Medicine, Philadelphia, PA 19122-6096. Offers PhD. *Faculty:* 6 full-time (0 women). *Students:* 1 (woman) full-time. 11 applicants, 18% accepted, 1 enrolled. In 2010, 1 doctorate awarded. *Degree requirements:* For doctorate, one foreign language, thesis/dissertation, research seminars. *Entrance requirements:* For doctorate, GRE General Test, GRE Subject Test, minimum GPA of 3.0. Additional exam requirements/recommendations for international students: Required—TOEFL (minimum score 550 paper-based; 213 computer-based; 79 iBT). *Application deadline:* For fall admission, 1/15 priority date for domestic students, 12/15 for international students; for spring admission, 11/1 priority date for domestic students, 8/1 for international students. Applications are processed on a rolling basis. Application fee: $50. Electronic applications accepted. *Financial support:* Fellowships, research assistantships available. Financial award application deadline: 1/15; financial award applicants required to submit FAFSA. *Faculty research:* Molecular cloning, cell proliferation, cell cycle regulation, DNA repair, cytogenetics. *Unit head:* Dr. Yuri Persidsky, Chair, 215-707-4353, Fax: 215-707-2781, E-mail: yuri.persidsky@temple.edu. *Application contact:* Dr. Yuri Persidsky, Chair, 215-707-4353, Fax: 215-707-2781, E-mail: yuri.persidsky@temple.edu.

Texas A&M University, College of Veterinary Medicine and Biomedical Sciences, Department of Veterinary Pathobiology, College Station, TX 77843. Offers genetics (MS, PhD); veterinary microbiology (MS, PhD); veterinary parasitology (MS, PhD); veterinary pathology (MS, PhD). Part-time programs available. Postbaccalaureate distance learning degree programs offered. *Faculty:* 26. *Students:* 25 full-time (17 women), 18 part-time (14 women); includes 1 Black or African American, non-Hispanic/Latino; 3 Asian, non-Hispanic/Latino; 2 Hispanic/Latino, 10 international. Average age 33. In 2010, 1 master's, 5 doctorates awarded. Terminal master's awarded for partial completion of doctoral program. *Degree requirements:* For master's, thesis, seminars; for doctorate, thesis/dissertation, seminars. *Entrance requirements:* For master's and doctorate, GRE General Test, minimum GPA of 3.0 in last 60 hours. Additional exam requirements/recommendations for international students: Required—TOEFL. *Application deadline:* For fall admission, 3/1 priority date for domestic students; for spring admission, 8/1 priority date for domestic students. Applications are processed on a rolling basis. Application fee: $50 ($75 for international students). Electronic applications accepted. *Financial support:* In 2010–11, fellowships with partial tuition reimbursements (averaging $16,000 per year), research assistantships with partial tuition reimbursements (averaging $15,400 per year), teaching assistantships with partial tuition reimbursements (averaging $16,000 per year) were awarded; Federal Work-Study, institutionally sponsored loans, scholarships/grants, traineeships, health care benefits, and unspecified assistantships also available. Support available to part-time students. Financial award applicants required to submit FAFSA. *Faculty research:* Infectious and noninfectious diseases of animals and birds, animal genetics, molecular biology, immunology, virology. *Unit head:* Dr. Linda Logan, Head, 979-862-6559, Fax: 979-845-9231, E-mail: llogan@cvm.tamu.edu. *Application contact:* Dr. Patricia Holman, Graduate Advisor, 979-845-4202, Fax: 979-862-1147, E-mail: pholman@cvm.tamu.edu.

Université de Montréal, Faculty of Medicine, Department of Pathology and Cellular Biology, Montréal, QC H3C 3J7, Canada. Offers M Sc, PhD. Terminal master's awarded for partial completion of doctoral program. *Degree requirements:* For master's, thesis; for doctorate, thesis/dissertation, general exam. *Entrance requirements:* For master's and doctorate, proficiency in French, knowledge of English. Electronic applications accepted. *Faculty research:* Immunopathology, cardiovascular pathology, oncogenetics, cellular neurocytology, muscular dystrophy.

Université Laval, Faculty of Medicine, Post-Professional Programs in Medical Studies, Québec, QC G1K 7P4, Canada. Offers anatomy–pathology (DESS); anesthesiology (DESS); cardiology (DESS); care of older people (Diploma); clinical research (DESS); community health (DESS); dermatology (DESS); diagnostic radiology (DESS); emergency medicine (Diploma); family medicine (DESS); general surgery (DESS); geriatrics (DESS); hematology (DESS); internal medicine (DESS); maternal and fetal medicine (Diploma); medical biochemistry (DESS); medical microbiology and infectious diseases (DESS); medical oncology (DESS); nephrology (DESS); neurology (DESS); neurosurgery (DESS); obstetrics and gynecology (DESS); ophthalmology (DESS); orthopedic surgery (DESS); oto-rhino-laryngology (DESS); palliative medicine (Diploma); pediatrics (DESS); plastic surgery (DESS); psychiatry (DESS); pulmonary medicine (DESS); radiology–oncology (DESS); thoracic surgery (DESS); urology (DESS). *Degree requirements:* For other advanced degree, comprehensive exam. *Entrance requirements:* For degree, knowledge of French. Electronic applications accepted.

University at Buffalo, the State University of New York, Graduate School, Graduate Programs in Cancer Research and Biomedical Sciences at Roswell Park Cancer Institute, Department of Cancer Pathology and Prevention at Roswell Park Cancer Institute, Buffalo, NY

14263-0001. Offers PhD. *Faculty:* 24 full-time (9 women). *Students:* 10 full-time (5 women); includes 1 Black or African American, non-Hispanic/Latino, 7 international. Average age 25. 14 applicants, 43% accepted, 4 enrolled. In 2010, 2 doctorates awarded. *Degree requirements:* For doctorate, comprehensive exam, thesis/dissertation, dissertation defense, project. *Entrance requirements:* For doctorate, GRE, minimum GPA of 3.0, 3 letters of recommendation. Additional exam requirements/recommendations for international students: Required—TOEFL (minimum score: paper-based 600, computer 250, iBT 100) or IELTS (minimum score 7). *Application deadline:* For fall admission, 2/1 priority date for domestic and international students. Applications are processed on a rolling basis. Application fee: $50. Electronic applications accepted. *Financial support:* In 2010–11, 10 students received support, including 4 fellowships with full tuition reimbursements available (averaging $24,000 per year), 5 research assistantships with full tuition reimbursements available (averaging $24,000 per year); Federal Work-Study and health care benefits also available. Financial award application deadline: 2/1; financial award applicants required to submit FAFSA. *Faculty research:* Molecular pathology of cancer, chemoprevention of cancer, genomic instability, molecular diagnosis and prognosis of cancer, molecular epidemiology. Total annual research expenditures: $3 million. *Unit head:* Dr. Kirsten Moysich, Chairman, 716-845-3082, Fax: 716-845-8178, E-mail: kirsten.moysich@roswellpark.org. *Application contact:* Craig R. Johnson, Director of Admissions, 716-845-2339, Fax: 716-845-8178, E-mail: craig.johnson@roswellpark.org.

University at Buffalo, the State University of New York, Graduate School, School of Medicine and Biomedical Sciences, Graduate Programs in Medicine and Biomedical Sciences, Department of Pathology and Anatomical Sciences, Buffalo, NY 14260. Offers anatomical sciences (MA, PhD); pathology (MA, PhD). *Degree requirements:* For master's, thesis; for doctorate, comprehensive exam, thesis/dissertation. *Entrance requirements:* For master's, GRE, MCAT, or DAT, 3 letters of recommendation; for doctorate, GRE, 3 letters of recommendation. Additional exam requirements/recommendations for international students: Required—TOEFL (minimum score 600 paper-based; 250 computer-based; 100 iBT). *Faculty research:* Immunopathology-immunobiology, experimental hypertension, neuromuscular disease, molecular pathology, cell motility and cytoskeleton.

The University of Alabama at Birmingham, Graduate Programs in Joint Health Sciences, Program in Pathology, Birmingham, AL 35294. Offers PhD. *Students:* 60 full-time (21 women), 1 part-time (0 women); includes 12 minority (7 Black or African American, non-Hispanic/Latino; 1 American Indian or Alaska Native, non-Hispanic/Latino; 2 Asian, non-Hispanic/Latino; 2 Hispanic/Latino), 11 international. Average age 28. In 2010, 11 doctorates awarded. *Degree requirements:* For doctorate, thesis/dissertation. *Entrance requirements:* For doctorate, GRE General Test, interview. *Application deadline:* Applications are processed on a rolling basis. Application fee: $35 ($60 for international students). Electronic applications accepted. *Expenses:* Tuition, state resident: full-time $5482. Tuition, nonresident: full-time $12,430. Tuition and fees vary according to program. *Financial support:* In 2010–11, 15 fellowships were awarded; career-related internships or fieldwork also available. *Unit head:* Dr. Kevin Roth, Chairman, 205-934-5802, Fax: 205-934-5499. *Application contact:* Julie Bryant, Director of Graduate Admissions, 205-934-8227, Fax: 205-934-8413, E-mail: jbryant@uab.edu.

University of Alberta, Faculty of Medicine and Dentistry and Faculty of Graduate Studies and Research, Graduate Programs in Medicine, Department of Laboratory Medicine and Pathology, Edmonton, AB T6G 2E1, Canada. Offers medical sciences (M Sc, PhD). Part-time programs available. Terminal master's awarded for partial completion of doctoral program. *Degree requirements:* For master's, thesis; for doctorate, thesis/dissertation, candidacy exam. *Entrance requirements:* For master's and doctorate, 3 letters of recommendation, minimum GPA of 3.0. Additional exam requirements/recommendations for international students: Required—TOEFL. *Faculty research:* Transplantation, renal pathology, molecular mechanisms of diseases, cryobiology, immunodiagnostics, informatics/cyber medicine, neuroimmunology, microbiology.

University of Arkansas for Medical Sciences, Graduate School, Graduate Programs in Biomedical Sciences, Department of Pathology, Little Rock, AR 72205-7199. Offers MS. *Degree requirements:* For master's, thesis. *Entrance requirements:* For master's, GRE General Test. Additional exam requirements/recommendations for international students: Required—TOEFL. *Faculty research:* Metastasis of cancer pediatric cancers, oxidative damage of DNA.

The University of British Columbia, Faculty of Medicine, Department of Pathology and Laboratory Medicine, Vancouver, BC V5Z 1M9, Canada. Offers experimental pathology (M Sc, PhD). *Faculty:* 139 full-time (47 women). *Students:* 71 full-time (41 women). Average age 25. 26 applicants, 65% accepted, 17 enrolled. In 2010, 3 master's, 14 doctorates awarded. *Degree requirements:* For master's, thesis; for doctorate, comprehensive exam, thesis/dissertation, internal oral defense. *Entrance requirements:* For master's, GRE, upper-level course work in biochemistry and physiology; for doctorate, GRE. Additional exam requirements/recommendations for international students: Required—TOEFL (minimum score 550 paper-based; 80 computer-based), IELTS (minimum score 6.5). *Application deadline:* For fall admission, 3/1 for domestic and international students; for winter admission, 7/1 for domestic students, 6/1 for international students; for spring admission, 11/1 for domestic students, 9/1 for international students. Applications are processed on a rolling basis. Application fee: $90 Canadian dollars ($150 Canadian dollars for international students). Electronic applications accepted. Tuition charges are reported in Canadian dollars. *Expenses:* Tuition, area resident: Full-time $4179 Canadian dollars. International tuition: $7344 Canadian dollars full-time. *Financial support:* In 2010–11, 23 students received support, including 71 research assistantships with full tuition reimbursements available (averaging $17,850 per year); teaching assistantships with partial tuition reimbursements available, institutionally sponsored loans, scholarships/grants, traineeships, health care benefits, tuition waivers, and unspecified assistantships also available. Financial award application deadline: 10/5. *Faculty research:* Molecular biology of disease processes, cancer, hematopathology, atherosclerosis, pulmonary and cardiovascular pathophysiology. Total annual research expenditures: $13.5 million Canadian dollars. *Unit head:* Dr. Mike Allard, Head, 604-822-7100, Fax: 604-822-7635, E-mail: mike.allard@pathology.ubc.ca. *Application contact:* Dr. Haydn Pritchard, Graduate Adviser, 604-675-3945 Ext. 21075, Fax: 604-875-3971, E-mail: hpritchard@pathology.ubc.ca.

University of California, Davis, Graduate Studies, Graduate Group in Comparative Pathology, Davis, CA 95616. Offers MS, PhD. *Accreditation:* NAACLS. Terminal master's awarded for partial completion of doctoral program. *Degree requirements:* For master's, comprehensive exam (for some programs), thesis (for some programs); for doctorate, thesis/dissertation. *Entrance requirements:* For master's and doctorate, GRE General Test. Additional exam requirements/recommendations for international students: Required—TOEFL (minimum score 550 paper-based; 213 computer-based). Electronic applications accepted. *Faculty research:* Immunopathology, toxicological and environmental pathology, reproductive pathology, pathology of infectious diseases.

University of California, Irvine, School of Medicine, Department of Pathology and Laboratory Medicine, Irvine, CA 92697. Offers experimental pathology (PhD). *Students:* 9 full-time (5 women), 1 (woman) part-time; includes 4 minority (2 Asian, non-Hispanic/Latino; 2 Hispanic/Latino), 1 international. Average age 28. In 2010, 4 doctorates awarded. *Unit head:* Dr. Fritz Lin, Interim Chairman, 714-456-6141, Fax: 714-456-5873, E-mail: flin@uci.edu. *Application contact:* Dr. Edwin Monuki, Director of Graduate Program, 949-824-6574, Fax: 949-824-2160, E-mail: emonuki@uci.edu.

University of California, Los Angeles, David Geffen School of Medicine and Graduate Division, Graduate Programs in Medicine, Program in Cellular and Molecular Pathology, Los Angeles, CA 90095. Offers MS, PhD. *Students:* 21 full-time (16 women); includes 9 minority (6 Asian, non-Hispanic/Latino; 3 Hispanic/Latino), 2 international. Average age 29. In 2010, 5 doctorates awarded. Application fee: $70 ($90 for international students). Electronic applications accepted. *Financial support:* In 2010–11, 22 fellowships, 16 research assistantships, 7 teaching assistantships were awarded. *Unit head:* Dr. Kenneth I. Dorshkind, Program Director, 310-206-9535, E-mail: kdorshki@mednet.ucla.edu. *Application contact:* UCLA ACCESS Information, 310-206-6051, E-mail: uclaaccess@mednet.ucla.edu.

University of California, Los Angeles, David Geffen School of Medicine and Graduate Division, Graduate Programs in Medicine, Program in Experimental Pathology, Los Angeles, CA 90095. Offers MS, PhD. In 2010, 2 master's, 3 doctorates awarded. *Degree requirements:* For doctorate, thesis/dissertation, oral and written qualifying exams. *Entrance requirements:* For master's, GRE General Test; for doctorate, GRE General Test, previous course work in physical chemistry and physics. Application fee: $70 ($90 for international students). *Financial support:* In 2010–11, 4 teaching assistantships were awarded; fellowships, research assistantships, Federal Work-Study, institutionally sponsored loans, scholarships/grants, and tuition waivers (full and partial) also available. Financial award application deadline: 3/1. *Unit head:* Dr. Jonathan Braun, Chair, 310-825-5719. *Application contact:* UCLA Access Coordinator, 800-284-8252, Fax: 310-206-5280, E-mail: uclaaccess@lbes.medsch.ucla.edu.

University of California, Los Angeles, Graduate Division, College of Letters and Science and David Geffen School of Medicine, UCLA ACCESS to Programs in the Molecular, Cellular and Integrative Life Sciences, Los Angeles, CA 90095. Offers biochemistry and molecular biology (PhD); biological chemistry (PhD); cellular and molecular pathology (PhD); human genetics (PhD); microbiology, immunology, and molecular genetics (PhD); molecular biology (PhD); molecular toxicology (PhD); molecular, cellular and integrative physiology (PhD); neurobiology (PhD); oral biology (PhD); physiology (PhD). ACCESS is an umbrella program for first-year coursework in 12 PhD programs. *Students:* 48 full-time (28 women), 6 international. Average age 24. 388 applicants, 27% accepted, 48 enrolled. *Degree requirements:* For doctorate, thesis/dissertation, oral and written qualifying exams. *Entrance requirements:* For doctorate, GRE General Test, minimum undergraduate GPA of 3.0. Additional exam requirements/recommendations for international students: Required—TOEFL. *Application deadline:* For fall admission, 12/15 for domestic and international students. Application fee: $70 ($90 for international students). Electronic applications accepted. *Financial support:* In 2010–11, 31 fellowships with full and partial tuition reimbursements, 13 research assistantships with full and partial tuition reimbursements, 2 teaching assistantships with full and partial tuition reimbursements were awarded; Federal Work-Study, institutionally sponsored loans, scholarships/grants, health care benefits, tuition waivers (full and partial), and unspecified assistantships also available. Financial award application deadline: 3/1; financial award applicants required to submit FAFSA. *Faculty research:* Molecular, cellular, and developmental biology; immunology; microbiology; integrative biology. *Unit head:* Jody Spillane, Project Coordinator, 310-206-1845, E-mail: jspillane@mednet.ucla.edu. *Application contact:* UCLA Access Admissions, 310-206-1845, E-mail: uclaaccess@mednet.ucla.edu.

University of California, San Francisco, Graduate Division, Biomedical Sciences Graduate Group, San Francisco, CA 94143. Offers anatomy (PhD); endocrinology (PhD); experimental pathology (PhD); physiology (PhD). *Degree requirements:* For doctorate, thesis/dissertation. *Entrance requirements:* For doctorate, GRE General Test.

University of Chicago, Division of Biological Sciences, Biomedical Sciences Cluster: Cancer Biology, Immunology, Molecular Metabolism and Nutrition, Pathology, and Microbiology, Department of Pathology, Chicago, IL 60637-1513. Offers molecular pathogenesis and molecular medicine (PhD). *Degree requirements:* For doctorate, thesis/dissertation, ethics class, 2 teaching assistantships. *Entrance requirements:* For doctorate, GRE General Test. Additional exam requirements/recommendations for international students: Required—IELTS (minimum score 7); Recommended—TOEFL (minimum score 600 paper-based; 250 computer-based; 104 iBT). Electronic applications accepted. *Faculty research:* Vascular biology, apolipoproteins, cardiovascular disease, immunopathology.

University of Cincinnati, Graduate School, College of Medicine, Graduate Programs in Biomedical Sciences, Program in Pathobiology and Molecular Medicine, Cincinnati, OH 45221. Offers pathology (PhD), including anatomic pathology, laboratory medicine, pathobiology and molecular medicine. *Degree requirements:* For doctorate, thesis/dissertation, qualifying exam. *Entrance requirements:* For doctorate, GRE General Test. Additional exam requirements/recommendations for international students: Required—TOEFL (minimum score 620 paper-based; 260 computer-based). Electronic applications accepted. *Faculty research:* Cardiovascular and lipid disorders, digestive and kidney disease, endocrine and metabolic disorders, hematologic and oncogenic, immunology and infectious disease.

University of Florida, College of Medicine, Department of Pathology, Immunology and Laboratory Medicine, Gainesville, FL 32611. Offers immunology and molecular pathology (PhD). *Degree requirements:* For doctorate, thesis/dissertation. *Entrance requirements:* For doctorate, GRE General Test, minimum GPA of 3.0. Additional exam requirements/recommendations for international students: Required—TOEFL. Electronic applications accepted. *Expenses:* Tuition, state resident: full-time $10,916. Tuition, nonresident: full-time $28,309. *Faculty research:* Molecular immunology, autoimmunity and transplantation, tumor biology, oncogenic viruses, human immunodeficiency viruses.

University of Georgia, College of Veterinary Medicine and Graduate School, Graduate Programs in Veterinary Medicine, Department of Pathology, Athens, GA 30602. Offers MS, PhD. *Faculty:* 20 full-time (13 women), 6 part-time/adjunct (2 women). *Students:* 20 full-time (12 women), 1 part-time (0 women); includes 1 Hispanic/Latino, 10 international. 13 applicants, 15% accepted, 2 enrolled. In 2010, 2 master's, 4 doctorates awarded. *Degree requirements:* For master's, thesis; for doctorate, one foreign language, thesis/dissertation. *Entrance requirements:* For master's and doctorate, GRE General Test. *Application deadline:* For fall admission, 7/1 priority date for domestic students; for spring admission, 11/15 for domestic students. Application fee: $50. Electronic applications accepted. *Expenses:* Tuition, state resident: full-time $7200; part-time $344 per credit hour. Tuition, nonresident: full-time $21,900; part-time $944 per credit hour. Tuition and fees vary according to course load and program. *Financial support:* Fellowships, research assistantships, teaching assistantships, unspecified assistantships available. *Unit head:* Dr. R. Keith Harris, Acting Head, 706-542-5831, Fax: 706-542-5828, E-mail: rkharris@uga.edu. *Application contact:* Dr. Jaroslava Halper, Graduate Coordinator, 706-542-5830, Fax: 706-542-5828, E-mail: jhalper@uga.edu.

University of Guelph, Ontario Veterinary College and Graduate Studies, Graduate Programs in Veterinary Sciences, Department of Pathobiology, Guelph, ON N1G 2W1, Canada. Offers anatomic pathology (DV Sc, Diploma); clinical pathology (Diploma); comparative pathology (M Sc, PhD); immunology (M Sc, PhD); laboratory animal science (DV Sc); pathology (M Sc, PhD, Diploma); veterinary infectious diseases (M Sc, PhD); zoo animal/wildlife medicine (DV Sc). *Degree requirements:* For master's, thesis; for doctorate, thesis/dissertation. *Entrance requirements:* For master's, DVM with B average or an honours degree in biological sciences; for doctorate, DVM or MSC degree, minimum B+ average. Additional exam requirements/recommendations for international students: Required—TOEFL (minimum score 550 paper-based; 213 computer-based). *Faculty research:* Pathogenesis; diseases of animals, wildlife, fish, and laboratory animals; parasitology; immunology; veterinary infectious diseases; laboratory animal science.

The University of Iowa, Roy J. and Lucille A. Carver College of Medicine and Graduate College, Graduate Programs in Medicine, Department of Pathology, Iowa City, IA 52242-1316. Offers MS. *Faculty:* 24 full-time (5 women). *Students:* 4 full-time (2 women), 1 international. Average age 25. 14 applicants, 14% accepted, 2 enrolled. In 2010, 3 master's awarded. *Degree requirements:* For master's, thesis. *Entrance requirements:* For master's, GRE, minimum GPA of 3.0. Additional exam requirements/recommendations for international students: Required—TOEFL. *Application deadline:* For fall admission, 2/15 priority date for domestic students, 1/15 priority date for international students. Applications are processed on a rolling basis. Application fee: $60 ($100 for international students). Electronic applications accepted. *Financial support:* In 2010–11, 4 students received support, including 4 research assistantships with full tuition reimbursements available (averaging $25,000 per year); health care benefits also available. *Faculty research:* Oncology, microbiology, vascular biology, immunology, neuroscience, stem cells, virology, signaling and cell death. Total annual research expenditures: $3.5 million. *Unit head:* Dr. Michael Cohen, Head, 319-335-8232, Fax: 319-335-8348, E-mail:

Pathology

The University of Iowa (continued)
michael-cohen@uiowa.edu. *Application contact:* Dr. Thomas J. Waldschmidt, Graduate Program Director, 319-335-8223, Fax: 319-335-8453, E-mail: thomas-waldschmidt@uiowa.edu.

The University of Kansas, University of Kansas Medical Center, School of Medicine, Department of Pathology and Laboratory Medicine, Kansas City, KS 66160. Offers MA, PhD, MD/PhD. *Faculty:* 28. *Students:* 10 full-time (5 women); includes 1 minority (Hispanic/Latino), 6 international. Average age 28. 2 applicants, 100% accepted, 2 enrolled.Terminal master's awarded for partial completion of doctoral program. *Degree requirements:* For master's, comprehensive exam (for some programs), thesis; for doctorate, comprehensive exam, thesis/dissertation. *Entrance requirements:* For master's, GRE, curriculum vitae, 3 reference letters; for doctorate, GRE, curriculum vitae, statement of research and career interests, official transcripts for all undergraduate and graduate coursework, 3 reference letters. Additional exam requirements/recommendations for international students: Required—TOEFL (preferred) or IELTS. *Application deadline:* For fall admission, 1/15 priority date for domestic and international students. Applications are processed on a rolling basis. Application fee: $60. *Expenses:* Tuition, state resident: full-time $7092; part-time $295.50 per credit hour. Tuition, nonresident: full-time $16,590; part-time $691.25 per credit hour. Required fees: $858; $71.49 per credit hour. Tuition and fees vary according to course load, campus/location and program. *Financial support:* Fellowships, research assistantships, teaching assistantships with full and partial tuition reimbursements, Federal Work-Study, scholarships/grants, traineeships, tuition waivers (full), and unspecified assistantships available. Financial award application deadline: 2/14; financial award applicants required to submit FAFSA. *Faculty research:* Cancer biology, developmental biology and cell differentiation, stem cell biology, microbial and viral pathogenesis. Total annual research expenditures: $4.7 million. *Unit head:* Dr. Soumen Paul, Director, Pathology Graduate Program, 913-588-4876, Fax: 913-588-5242, E-mail: spaul2@kumc.edu. *Application contact:* Dr. Soumen Paul, Director, Pathology Graduate Program, 913-588-4876, Fax: 913-588-5242, E-mail: spaul2@kumc.edu.

University of Manitoba, Faculty of Medicine and Faculty of Graduate Studies, Graduate Programs in Medicine, Department of Pathology, Winnipeg, MB R3E 3P5, Canada. Offers M Sc. *Degree requirements:* For master's, thesis. *Entrance requirements:* For master's, B Sc honours degree. Additional exam requirements/recommendations for international students: Required—TOEFL (minimum score 550 paper-based; 213 computer-based; 80 iBT), IELTS (minimum score 6.5). *Faculty research:* Experimental hydrocephalus; brain development; stroke; developmental neurobiology; myelination in Rett Syndrome; glial migration during cortical development; growth factors and breast cancer; transgenic models of breast cancer; molecular genetics and cancer diagnosis; graft-vs-host disease; biology of natural killer cells; transplantation immunology.

University of Maryland, Baltimore, School of Medicine, Department of Pathology, Baltimore, MD 21201. Offers pathologists' assistant (MS). *Accreditation:* NAACLS. *Students:* 19 full-time (16 women); includes 2 Asian, non-Hispanic/Latino; 1 Hispanic/Latino. Average age 28. In 2010, 6 master's awarded. *Entrance requirements:* For master's, GRE General Test. Additional exam requirements/recommendations for international students: Required—TOEFL (minimum score 600 paper-based; 250 computer-based; 100 iBT); Recommended—IELTS. *Application deadline:* For fall admission, 2/1 for domestic and international students. Electronic applications accepted. *Expenses:* Contact institution. *Financial support:* Application deadline: 3/1. *Unit head:* Dr. Rudy Castellani, Program Director, 410-328-5555, Fax: 410-706-8414, E-mail: rcastellani@som.umaryland.edu. *Application contact:* Carmen White, Program Coordinator, 410-706-6518, Fax: 410-706-8414, E-mail: cwhite@som.umaryland.edu.

University of Massachusetts Lowell, School of Health and Environment, Department of Clinical Laboratory and Nutritional Sciences, Lowell, MA 01854-2881. Offers clinical laboratory sciences (MS); clinical pathology (Graduate Certificate); nutritional sciences (Graduate Certificate); public health laboratory sciences (Graduate Certificate). *Accreditation:* NAACLS. Part-time programs available. Postbaccalaureate distance learning degree programs offered. *Degree requirements:* For master's, thesis optional. *Entrance requirements:* For master's, GRE General Test, minimum GPA of 3.0, letters of recommendation. *Faculty research:* Cardiovascular disease, lipoprotein metabolism, micronutrient evaluation, alcohol metabolism, mycobacterial drug resistance.

University of Medicine and Dentistry of New Jersey, Graduate School of Biomedical Sciences, Graduate Programs in Biomedical Sciences–Newark, Program in Molecular Pathology and Immunology, Newark, NJ 07107. Offers PhD. *Entrance requirements:* Additional exam requirements/recommendations for international students: Required—TOEFL. Electronic applications accepted.

University of Michigan, Rackham Graduate School, Program in Biomedical Sciences (PIBS), Program in Molecular and Cellular Pathology, Ann Arbor, MI 48109. Offers PhD. *Faculty:* 37 full-time (10 women). *Students:* 20 full-time (9 women); includes 6 minority (1 Black or African American, non-Hispanic/Latino; 5 Asian, non-Hispanic/Latino). Average age 28. 52 applicants, 17% accepted, 6 enrolled. In 2010, 1 doctorate awarded. *Degree requirements:* For doctorate, comprehensive exam, thesis/dissertation. *Entrance requirements:* For doctorate, GRE General Test, 3 letters of recommendation, research experience. Additional exam requirements/recommendations for international students: Required—TOEFL (minimum score 84 iBT). *Application deadline:* For fall admission, 12/1 for domestic and international students. Application fee: $60 ($75 for international students). Electronic applications accepted. *Expenses:* Tuition, state resident: full-time $17,784; part-time $1116 per credit hour. Tuition, nonresident: full-time $35,944; part-time $2125 per credit hour. International tuition: $35,994 full-time. Required fees: $95 per semester. Tuition and fees vary according to course load, degree level and program. *Financial support:* In 2010–11, 1 student received support, including fellowships with full tuition reimbursements available (averaging $40,042 per year); scholarships/grants, traineeships, health care benefits, tuition waivers (full), and unspecified assistantships also available. *Faculty research:* Cancer biology, stem cell and developmental biology, immunopathology and inflammatory disease, epigenetics and gene regulation, cell death and regulation. *Unit head:* Dr. Nicholas W. Lukacs, Professor of Pathology/Director, 734-763-6454, Fax: 734-615-2331, E-mail: pathgradprog@med.umich.edu. *Application contact:* Laura L. Hessler, Administrative Specialist, 734-763-6454, Fax: 734-615-2331, E-mail: lauralh@med.umich.edu.

University of Mississippi Medical Center, School of Graduate Studies in the Health Sciences, Department of Pathology, Jackson, MS 39216-4505. Offers MS, PhD, MD/PhD. Terminal master's awarded for partial completion of doctoral program. *Degree requirements:* For master's, thesis; for doctorate, thesis/dissertation, first authored publication in peer-reviewed journal. *Entrance requirements:* For master's, GRE General Test, minimum GPA of 3.0; for doctorate, GRE General Test, GRE Subject Test, minimum GPA of 3.0. *Faculty research:* Effects of rehabilitation therapy on immune system/hypothalamic/pituitary adrenal axis interaction; HLA, GC, CM, KM, and/or genetic factors in the pathogenesis of AIDS; stem cell research; renal disease.

University of Missouri, School of Medicine and Graduate School, Graduate Programs in Medicine, Department of Pathology and Anatomical Sciences, Columbia, MO 65211. Offers MS.

University of Nebraska Medical Center, Graduate Studies, Department of Pathology and Microbiology, Omaha, NE 68198. Offers MS, PhD. Part-time programs available. *Faculty:* 36 full-time (7 women), 57 part-time/adjunct (8 women). *Students:* 35 full-time (19 women), 13 part-time (9 women); includes 1 Black or African American, non-Hispanic/Latino; 7 Asian, non-Hispanic/Latino; 1 Hispanic/Latino, 13 international. Average age 28. 40 applicants, 43% accepted, 16 enrolled. In 2010, 2 master's, 5 doctorates awarded. Terminal master's awarded for partial completion of doctoral program. *Degree requirements:* For master's, comprehensive exam, thesis; for doctorate, comprehensive exam, thesis/dissertation. *Entrance requirements:* For master's, previous course work in biology, chemistry, mathematics, and physics; for

doctorate, GRE General Test, previous course work in biology, chemistry, mathematics, and physics. Additional exam requirements/recommendations for international students: Required—TOEFL (minimum score 550 paper-based; 213 computer-based). *Application deadline:* For fall admission, 6/1 for domestic students, 4/1 for international students; for spring admission, 10/1 for domestic students, 8/1 for international students. Applications are processed on a rolling basis. Application fee: $45. Electronic applications accepted. *Expenses:* Tuition, state resident: part-time $198.25 per semester hour. Required fees: $63 per semester. *Financial support:* In 2010–11, 9 fellowships with tuition reimbursements (averaging $21,000 per year), 18 research assistantships with tuition reimbursements (averaging $21,000 per year) were awarded; institutionally sponsored loans and tuition waivers (full) also available. Support available to part-time students. Financial award application deadline: 3/1. *Faculty research:* Carcinogenesis, cancer biology, immunobiology, molecular virology, molecular genetics. *Unit head:* Dr. Rakesh K. Singh, Chair, Graduate Committee, 402-559-9948, Fax: 402-559-4077, E-mail: rsingh@unmc.edu. *Application contact:* Marjorie Boyden, Office Associate, 402-559-4042, E-mail: mboyden@unmc.edu.

University of New Mexico, School of Medicine, Biomedical Sciences Graduate Program, Albuquerque, NM 87131-5196. Offers biochemistry and molecular biology (MS, PhD); cell biology and physiology (MS, PhD); clinical and translational science (Certificate); molecular genetics and microbiology (MS, PhD); neuroscience (MS, PhD); pathology (MS, PhD); toxicology (MS, PhD); university science teaching (Certificate). Part-time programs available. *Faculty:* 33 full-time (14 women), 3 part-time/adjunct (1 woman). *Students:* 94 full-time (57 women), 14 part-time (8 women); includes 24 minority (3 Black or African American, non-Hispanic/Latino; 1 American Indian or Alaska Native, non-Hispanic/Latino; 6 Asian, non-Hispanic/Latino; 13 Hispanic/Latino; 1 Two or more races, non-Hispanic/Latino), 20 international. Average age 30. 135 applicants, 14% accepted, 19 enrolled. In 2010, 2 master's, 19 doctorates, 3 other advanced degrees awarded. Terminal master's awarded for partial completion of doctoral program. *Degree requirements:* For master's, thesis; for doctorate, comprehensive exam, thesis/dissertation. *Entrance requirements:* For master's and doctorate, GRE General Test, minimum undergraduate GPA of 3.0. Additional exam requirements/recommendations for international students: Required—TOEFL. *Application deadline:* For fall admission, 1/1 priority date for domestic students. Applications are processed on a rolling basis. Application fee: $50. Electronic applications accepted. *Expenses:* Tuition, state resident: full-time $5991; part-time $251 per credit hour. Tuition, nonresident: full-time $14,405; part-time $800.20 per credit hour. Tuition and fees vary according to course level, course load, program and reciprocity agreements. *Financial support:* In 2010–11, 99 students received support, including 5 fellowships (averaging $75 per year), 96 research assistantships with full tuition reimbursements available (averaging $17,401 per year), 2 teaching assistantships with full tuition reimbursements available (averaging $2,415 per year); career-related internships or fieldwork, Federal Work-Study, institutionally sponsored loans, scholarships/grants, traineeships, health care benefits, and unspecified assistantships also available. Financial award application deadline: 1/1; financial award applicants required to submit FAFSA. *Faculty research:* Signal transduction, infectious disease, biology of cancer, structural biology, neuroscience. *Unit head:* Laurie G. Hudson, Director, 505-272-1887, Fax: 505-272-8738, E-mail: lhudson@salud.unm.edu. *Application contact:* Angel Cooke-Jackson, Coordinator, 505-272-1887, Fax: 505-272-8738, E-mail: acooke-jackson@salud.unm.edu.

The University of North Carolina at Chapel Hill, School of Medicine and Graduate School, Graduate Programs in Medicine, Department of Pathology and Laboratory Medicine, Chapel Hill, NC 27599-7525. Offers experimental pathology (PhD). *Accreditation:* NAACLS. *Faculty:* 69 full-time (26 women), 5 part-time/adjunct (0 women). *Students:* 25 full-time (16 women); includes 3 Black or African American, non-Hispanic/Latino; 3 Hispanic/Latino, 4 international. Average age 28. In 2010, 7 doctorates awarded. *Degree requirements:* For doctorate, comprehensive exam, thesis/dissertation, oral exam, proposal defense. *Entrance requirements:* For doctorate, GRE General Test. Additional exam requirements/recommendations for international students: Required—TOEFL (minimum score 550 paper-based; 213 computer-based). *Application deadline:* For fall admission, 12/7 priority date for domestic and international students. Applications are processed on a rolling basis. Application fee: $77. Electronic applications accepted. *Financial support:* In 2010–11, 24 students received support, including 15 fellowships with full and partial tuition reimbursements available (averaging $26,000 per year), 9 research assistantships with full and partial tuition reimbursements available (averaging $26,000 per year); Federal Work-Study, institutionally sponsored loans, scholarships/grants, traineeships, tuition waivers (full), and unspecified assistantships also available. Financial award application deadline: 12/7; financial award applicants required to submit FAFSA. *Faculty research:* Carcinogenesis, mutagenesis and cancer biology; molecular biology, genetics and animal models of human disease; cardiovascular biology, hemostasis, and thrombosis; immunology and infectious disease; progenitor cell research. Total annual research expenditures: $14.2 million. *Unit head:* Dr. J. Charles Jennette, Brinkhous Distinguished Professor and Chair, 919-966-4676, Fax: 919-966-6718, E-mail: charles.jennette@pathology.unc.edu. *Application contact:* Dr. William B. Coleman, Professor and Director of Graduate Studies, 919-966-2699, Fax: 919-966-6718, E-mail: william.coleman@pathology.unc.edu.

University of Oklahoma Health Sciences Center, College of Medicine and Graduate College, Graduate Programs in Medicine, Department of Pathology, Oklahoma City, OK 73190. Offers PhD. *Degree requirements:* For doctorate, thesis/dissertation. *Entrance requirements:* For doctorate, GRE General Test, 3 letters of recommendation. Additional exam requirements/recommendations for international students: Required—TOEFL. *Faculty research:* Molecular pathology, tissue response in disease, anatomic pathology, immunopathology, histocytochemistry.

University of Pittsburgh, School of Medicine, Graduate Programs in Medicine, Program in Cellular and Molecular Pathology, Pittsburgh, PA 15260. Offers MS, PhD. *Faculty:* 64 full-time (18 women). *Students:* 37 full-time (22 women); includes 3 Black or African American, non-Hispanic/Latino; 6 American Indian or Alaska Native, non-Hispanic/Latino; 6 Asian, non-Hispanic/Latino; 2 Hispanic/Latino, 9 international. Average age 27. 486 applicants, 14% accepted, 28 enrolled. In 2010, 7 doctorates awarded. *Degree requirements:* For doctorate, comprehensive exam, thesis/dissertation. *Entrance requirements:* For doctorate, GRE General Test, GRE Subject Test, minimum QPA of 3.0. Additional exam requirements/recommendations for international students: Required—TOEFL (minimum score 600 paper-based; 100 iBT), IELTS (minimum score 7). *Application deadline:* For fall admission, 12/15 priority date for domestic and international students. Application fee: $50. Electronic applications accepted. *Expenses:* Tuition, state resident: full-time $17,304; part-time $701 per credit. Tuition, nonresident: full-time $29,554; part-time $1210 per credit. Required fees: $740; $214 per term. Tuition and fees vary according to program. *Financial support:* In 2010–11, 13 fellowships with full tuition reimbursements (averaging $25,500 per year), 24 research assistantships with full tuition reimbursements (averaging $25,500 per year) were awarded; teaching assistantships with full tuition reimbursements, institutionally sponsored loans, scholarships/grants, traineeships, health care benefits, and unspecified assistantships also available. *Faculty research:* Liver growth and differentiation, pathogenesis of neurodegeneration, cancer research. *Unit head:* Dr. Wendy Mars, Graduate Program Director, 412-648-9690, Fax: 412-648-9846, E-mail: wmars@pitt.edu. *Application contact:* Graduate Studies Administrator, 412-648-8957, Fax: 412-648-1077, E-mail: gradstudies@medschool.pitt.edu.

University of Prince Edward Island, Atlantic Veterinary College, Graduate Program in Veterinary Medicine, Charlottetown, PE C1A 4P3, Canada. Offers anatomy (M Sc, PhD); bacteriology (M Sc, PhD); clinical pharmacology (M Sc, PhD); clinical sciences (M Sc, PhD); epidemiology (M Sc, PhD), including reproduction; fish health (M Sc, PhD); food animal nutrition (M Sc, PhD); immunology (M Sc, PhD); microanatomy (M Sc, PhD); parasitology (M Sc, PhD); pathology (M Sc, PhD); pharmacology (M Sc, PhD); physiology (M Sc, PhD); toxicology (M Sc, PhD); veterinary science (M Vet Sc); virology (M Sc, PhD). Part-time programs available. *Degree requirements:* For master's, thesis; for doctorate, thesis/dissertation. *Entrance requirements:* For master's, DVM, B Sc honors degree, or equivalent; for doctorate, M Sc. Additional exam requirements/recommendations for international students: Required—TOEFL (minimum score 550 paper-based; 213 computer-based; 80 iBT). *Expenses:* Contact institution.

Faculty research: Animal health management, infectious diseases, fin fish and shellfish health, basic biomedical sciences, ecosystem health.

University of Rochester, School of Medicine and Dentistry, Graduate Programs in Medicine and Dentistry, Department of Pathology and Laboratory Medicine, Rochester, NY 14627. Offers pathology (MS, PhD). *Degree requirements:* For doctorate, variable foreign language requirement, thesis/dissertation, qualifying exam. *Entrance requirements:* For doctorate, GRE General Test, GRE Subject Test.

University of Saskatchewan, College of Medicine, Department of Pathology, Saskatoon, SK S7N 5A2, Canada. Offers M Sc, PhD. *Degree requirements:* For master's, thesis; for doctorate, thesis/dissertation. *Entrance requirements:* Additional exam requirements/recommendations for international students: Required—TOEFL.

University of Saskatchewan, Western College of Veterinary Medicine and College of Graduate Studies and Research, Graduate Programs in Veterinary Medicine, Department of Veterinary Pathology, Saskatoon, SK S7N 5A2, Canada. Offers M Sc, M Vet Sc, PhD. *Faculty:* 6 full-time (0 women), 2 part-time/adjunct (1 woman). *Students:* 15 full-time (11 women); includes 1 Black or African American, non-Hispanic/Latino. In 2010, 3 master's awarded. *Degree requirements:* For master's, thesis; for doctorate, comprehensive exam (for some programs), thesis/dissertation. *Entrance requirements:* Additional exam requirements/recommendations for international students: Required—TOEFL or IELTS (minimum score 6.5). *Application deadline:* For fall admission, 7/1 priority date for domestic students. Applications are processed on a rolling basis. Electronic applications accepted. *Financial support:* Fellowships, teaching assistantships available. Financial award application deadline: 1/31. *Faculty research:* Thyroid, oncology, immunology/infectious diseases, vaccinology. *Unit head:* Dr. Marion Jackson, Head, 306-966-7332, Fax: 306-966-7439, E-mail: marion.jackson@usask.ca. *Application contact:* Dr. Beverly Kidney, Graduate Chair, 306-966-7304, Fax: 306-966-7439, E-mail: beverly.kidney@usask.ca.

University of Southern California, Keck School of Medicine and Graduate School, Graduate Programs in Medicine, Department of Pathology, Los Angeles, CA 90089. Offers experimental and molecular pathology (MS); pathobiology (PhD). *Faculty:* 55 full-time (12 women), 5 part-time/adjunct (1 woman). *Students:* 40 full-time (23 women); includes 13 Asian, non-Hispanic/Latino; 6 Hispanic/Latino, 10 international. Average age 26. 26 applicants, 38% accepted, 9 enrolled. In 2010, 4 master's, 8 doctorates awarded. *Median time to degree:* Of those who began their doctoral program in fall 2002, 89% received their degree in 8 years or less. *Degree requirements:* For master's, thesis; for doctorate, thesis/dissertation. *Entrance requirements:* For master's, GRE General Test, minimum GPA of 3.0; for doctorate, GRE General Test, minimum GPA of 3.0, BS in natural sciences. Additional exam requirements/recommendations for international students: Required—TOEFL (minimum score 600 paper-based; 250 computer-based; 100 iBT). *Application deadline:* For fall admission, 12/1 priority date for domestic and international students. Application fee: $85. Electronic applications accepted. *Expenses:* Tuition: Full-time $31,240; part-time $1420 per unit. Required fees: $600. One-time fee: $35 full-time. Full-time tuition and fees vary according to degree level and program. *Financial support:* In 2010–11, 27 students received support, including 4 fellowships with tuition reimbursements available (averaging $27,600 per year), 22 research assistantships with tuition reimbursements available (averaging $27,600 per year), 1 teaching assistantship with tuition reimbursement available (averaging $27,600 per year); Federal Work-Study, institutionally sponsored loans, scholarships/grants, health care benefits, and unspecified assistantships also available. Financial award application deadline: 5/3. *Faculty research:* Immunology of lymphomas and leukemias, lung cancer, molecular basis of oncogenesis, central nervous system disease, organic chemical carcinogens and carcinogenic metal salts. *Unit head:* Dr. Michael E. Selsted, Chair, 323-442-1179, Fax: 323-442-3049, E-mail: selsted@usc.edu. *Application contact:* Lisa A. Doumak, Student Services Assistant, 323-442-1168, Fax: 323-442-3049, E-mail: doumak@usc.edu.

See Display on page 406 and Close-Up on page 413.

The University of Texas Medical Branch, Graduate School of Biomedical Sciences, Program in Experimental Pathology, Galveston, TX 77555. Offers PhD. *Degree requirements:* For doctorate, thesis/dissertation. *Entrance requirements:* For doctorate, GRE General Test. Additional exam requirements/recommendations for international students: Required—TOEFL (minimum score 550 paper-based; 213 computer-based). Electronic applications accepted.

The University of Toledo, College of Graduate Studies, College of Medicine and Life Sciences, Department of Pathology, Toledo, OH 43606-3390. Offers Certificate. Part-time programs available. *Faculty:* 4. *Students:* 3 part-time (2 women). Average age 24. 3 applicants, 100% accepted, 3 enrolled. In 2010, 7 Certificates awarded. *Entrance requirements:* For degree, second-year medical student in good academic standing with recommendation by Medical School. Application fee: $45 ($75 for international students). Electronic applications accepted. *Expenses:* Tuition, state resident: full-time $11,426; part-time $476 per credit hour. Tuition, nonresident: full-time $21,660; part-time $903 per credit hour. One-time fee: $62. *Financial support:* Tuition waivers (full and partial) available. *Unit head:* Dr. Robert Mrak, Professor, Chairman, 419-383-3469, E-mail: robert.mrak@utoledo.edu. *Application contact:* Christine Wile, Admissions Analyst, 419-383-4116, Fax: 419-383-6140, E-mail: christine.wile@utoledo.edu.

University of Utah, School of Medicine and Graduate School, Graduate Programs in Medicine, Department of Pathology, Salt Lake City, UT 84112-1107. Offers experimental pathology (PhD); laboratory medicine and biomedical science (MS). PhD offered after acceptance into the combined Program in Molecular Biology. *Degree requirements:* For doctorate, comprehensive exam, thesis/dissertation. *Entrance requirements:* For doctorate, GRE, minimum GPA of 3.0. *Expenses:* Tuition, area resident: Part-time $179.19 per credit hour. Tuition, state resident: full-time $4384. Tuition, nonresident: full-time $16,684; part-time $630.67 per credit hour. Required fees: $350 per semester. Tuition and fees vary according to course load, degree level and program. *Faculty research:* Immunology, cell biology, signal transduction, gene regulation, receptor biology.

University of Vermont, College of Medicine and Graduate College, Graduate Programs in Medicine, Department of Pathology, Burlington, VT 05405. Offers MS, MD/MS. *Students:* 5 (2 women); includes 1 Asian, non-Hispanic/Latino; 1 Hispanic/Latino. 8 applicants, 0% accepted, 0 enrolled. In 2010, 1 master's awarded. *Degree requirements:* For master's, thesis. *Entrance requirements:* For master's, GRE General Test. Additional exam requirements/recommendations for international students: Required—TOEFL (minimum score 550 paper-based; 213 computer-based; 80 iBT). *Application deadline:* For fall admission, 4/1 priority date for domestic students, 4/1 for international students. Applications are processed on a rolling basis. Application fee: $40. Electronic applications accepted. *Expenses:* Tuition, state resident: part-time $537 per credit hour. Tuition, nonresident: part-time $1355 per credit hour. *Financial support:* Fellowships, research assistantships, traineeships available. Financial award application deadline: 3/1. *Unit head:* Dr. E. Bovill, Chairperson, 802-656-0397. *Application contact:* Dr. S. Huber, Coordinator, 802-656-0397.

University of Virginia, School of Medicine, Program in Experimental Pathology, Charlottesville, VA 22903. Offers PhD. *Students:* 12 full-time (10 women); includes 2 Black or African American, non-Hispanic/Latino; 1 Asian, non-Hispanic/Latino, 3 international. Average age 26. In 2010, 2 doctorates awarded. *Degree requirements:* For doctorate, thesis/dissertation, oral defense of thesis. *Entrance requirements:* For doctorate, GRE General Test; GRE Subject Test (recommended), 2 letters of recommendation. Additional exam requirements/recommendations for international students: Required—TOEFL. *Application deadline:* For fall admission, 1/15 for domestic and international students. *Financial support:* Application deadline: 1/15. *Unit head:* Janet V. Cross, Program Director, 434-924-7185, E-mail: molmed@virginia.edu. *Application contact:* Janet V. Cross, Program Director, 434-924-7185, E-mail: molmed@virginia.edu.

University of Washington, Graduate School, School of Medicine, Graduate Programs in Medicine, Department of Pathology, Seattle, WA 98195. Offers experimental and molecular pathology (PhD). *Degree requirements:* For doctorate, thesis/dissertation. *Entrance requirements:* For doctorate, GRE General Test. *Faculty research:* Viral oncogenesis, aging, mutagenesis and repair, extracellular matrix biology, vascular biology.

The University of Western Ontario, Faculty of Graduate Studies, Biosciences Division, Department of Pathology, London, ON N6A 5B8, Canada. Offers M Sc, PhD. *Degree requirements:* For master's, thesis; for doctorate, comprehensive exam, thesis/dissertation. *Entrance requirements:* For master's and doctorate, minimum B+ average, honors degree. Additional exam requirements/recommendations for international students: Required—TOEFL. *Faculty research:* Heavy metal toxicology, transplant pathology, immunopathology, immunological cancers, neurochemistry, aging and dementia, cancer pathology.

University of Wisconsin–Madison, School of Medicine and Public Health and Graduate School, Graduate Programs in Medicine, Department of Pathology and Laboratory Medicine, Madison, WI 53706-1380. Offers PhD. *Accreditation:* NAACLS. *Faculty:* 43 full-time (15 women). *Students:* 36 full-time (21 women); includes 4 Black or African American, non-Hispanic/Latino; 5 Asian, non-Hispanic/Latino; 3 Hispanic/Latino, 9 international. Average age 25. 164 applicants, 13% accepted, 12 enrolled. In 2010, 6 doctorates awarded. *Degree requirements:* For doctorate, thesis/dissertation. *Entrance requirements:* For doctorate, GRE, minimum GPA of 3.0. Additional exam requirements/recommendations for international students: Required—TOEFL (minimum score 580 paper-based; 237 computer-based; 92 iBT). *Application deadline:* For fall admission, 12/1 priority date for domestic and international students. Applications are processed on a rolling basis. Application fee: $76. Electronic applications accepted. *Expenses:* Tuition, state resident: full-time $9887; part-time $617.96 per credit. Tuition, nonresident: full-time $24,054; part-time $1503.40 per credit. Required fees: $67.63 per credit. Tuition and fees vary according to reciprocity agreements. *Financial support:* In 2010–11, 36 students received support, including 13 fellowships with full tuition reimbursements available (averaging $24,000 per year), 23 research assistantships with full tuition reimbursements available (averaging $24,000 per year); health care benefits also available. Financial award application deadline: 12/1. *Faculty research:* Cellular and molecular pathology: immunology/immunopathology, cancer biology, neuroscience/neuropathology, growth factor/matrix biology, developmental pathology. *Unit head:* Dr. Andreas Friedl, Chair, 608-265-3735, Fax: 608-265-3301, E-mail: gharvey@facstaff.wisc.edu. *Application contact:* Joanne Thornton, Student Services Coordinator, 608-262-2665, Fax: 608-265-3301, E-mail: gradinfo@pathology.wisc.edu.

See Close-Up on page 415.

Vanderbilt University, Graduate School and School of Medicine, Department of Pathology, Nashville, TN 37240-1001. Offers PhD, MD/PhD. *Faculty:* 31 full-time (9 women). *Students:* 21 full-time (13 women); includes 5 Black or African American, non-Hispanic/Latino; 2 Asian, non-Hispanic/Latino; 4 Hispanic/Latino. Average age 28. In 2010, 2 doctorates awarded. *Degree requirements:* For doctorate, thesis/dissertation, qualifying and final exams. *Entrance requirements:* For doctorate, GRE General Test. Additional exam requirements/recommendations for international students: Required—TOEFL (minimum score 570 paper-based; 230 computer-based; 88 iBT). *Application deadline:* For fall admission, 1/15 for domestic and international students. Application fee: $0. Electronic applications accepted. *Financial support:* Fellowships with full tuition reimbursements, research assistantships with full tuition reimbursements, Federal Work-Study, institutionally sponsored loans, traineeships, health care benefits, and tuition waivers (partial) available. Financial award application deadline: 1/15; financial award applicants required to submit CSS PROFILE or FAFSA. *Faculty research:* Vascular biology and biochemistry, tumor pathology, the immune response, inflammation and repair, the biology of the extracellular matrix in response to disease processes, the pathogenesis of infectious agents, the regulation of gene expression in disease. *Unit head:* Dr. Samuel A. Santoro, Chair, 615-322-3234, Fax: 615-343-7023, E-mail: samuel.a.santoro@vanderbilt.edu. *Application contact:* Dr. Sarki Abdulkadir, Director of Graduate Studies, 615-322-9668, Fax: 615-322-0576, E-mail: sarki.a.abdulkadir@vanderbilt.edu.

Virginia Commonwealth University, Medical College of Virginia-Professional Programs, School of Medicine, School of Medicine Graduate Programs, Department of Pathology, Richmond, VA 23284-9005. Offers PhD, MD/PhD. Part-time programs available. *Faculty:* 13 full-time (6 women). *Students:* 3 full-time (1 woman), 1 part-time (0 women); includes 1 minority (Hispanic/Latino), 2 international. 2 applicants, 0% accepted, 0 enrolled. In 2010, 2 doctorates awarded. Terminal master's awarded for partial completion of doctoral program. *Degree requirements:* For doctorate, thesis/dissertation, comprehensive oral and written exams. *Entrance requirements:* For doctorate, GRE General Test, MCAT. *Application deadline:* For fall admission, 2/15 priority date for domestic students. Application fee: $50. *Expenses:* Tuition, state resident: full-time $4308; part-time $479 per credit hour. Tuition, nonresident: full-time $8942; part-time $994 per credit hour. Required fees: $2000; $85 per credit hour. Tuition and fees vary according to course level, course load, degree level, campus/location and program. *Financial support:* Fellowships, teaching assistantships, tuition waivers (full) available. *Faculty research:* Biochemical and clinical applications of enzyme and protein immobilization, clinical enzymology. *Unit head:* Dr. David S. Wilkinson, Chair, 804-828-0183, Fax: 804-828-9749, E-mail: dswilkin@vcu.edu. *Application contact:* Dr. Shawn E. Holt, Director of Graduate Studies, 804-827-0458, Fax: 804-828-9749, E-mail: seholt@vcu.edu.

Wayne State University, School of Medicine, Graduate Programs in Medicine, Department of Pathology, Detroit, MI 48202. Offers MS, PhD. *Accreditation:* NAACLS. *Faculty:* 1 full-time (0 women). *Students:* 10 full-time (7 women), 5 international. Average age 30. 8 applicants, 75% accepted, 2 enrolled. In 2010, 3 doctorates awarded. *Degree requirements:* For doctorate, thesis/dissertation. *Entrance requirements:* For doctorate, GRE General Test. Additional exam requirements/recommendations for international students: Required—TOEFL (minimum score 550 paper-based; 213 computer-based); Recommended—TWE (minimum score 6). *Application deadline:* For fall admission, 4/1 for domestic students, 6/1 for international students; for winter admission, 10/1 for international students; for spring admission, 2/1 for international students. Applications are processed on a rolling basis. Application fee: $30 ($50 for international students). Electronic applications accepted. *Expenses:* Tuition, state resident: full-time $7662; part-time $478.85 per credit hour. Tuition, nonresident: full-time $16,920; part-time $1057.55 per credit hour. Required fees: $571; $35.70 per credit hour. $188.05 per semester. Tuition and fees vary according to course load and program. *Financial support:* In 2010–11, 2 fellowships with tuition reimbursements (averaging $24,368 per year), 7 research assistantships with tuition reimbursements (averaging $22,317 per year) were awarded; teaching assistantships, career-related internships or fieldwork and Federal Work-Study also available. Financial award application deadline: 4/30. *Faculty research:* Cardiovascular physiology, cancer biology, cellular and tissue proteases, cancer chemoprevention, lung development, diabetes. *Application contact:* Clement Diglio, Graduate Director, 313-577-1357, Fax: 313-577-0057, E-mail: cdiglio@med.wayne.edu.

Yale University, Graduate School of Arts and Sciences, Department of Experimental Pathology, New Haven, CT 06520. Offers MS, PhD. *Degree requirements:* For doctorate, thesis/dissertation, qualifying exam. *Entrance requirements:* For doctorate, GRE General Test.

Yale University, School of Medicine and Graduate School of Arts and Sciences, Combined Program in Biological and Biomedical Sciences (BBS), Pharmacological Sciences and Molecular Medicine Track, New Haven, CT 06520. Offers PhD, MD/PhD. *Degree requirements:* For doctorate, thesis/dissertation. *Entrance requirements:* For doctorate, GRE General Test. Additional exam requirements/recommendations for international students: Required—TOEFL. Electronic applications accepted.

UNIVERSITY OF SOUTHERN CALIFORNIA

Department of Pathology
Ph.D. Degree Program in Pathobiology
M.S. Degree Program in Experimental and Molecular Pathology

Programs of Study

The Department of Pathology offers a program leading to the M.S. or Ph.D. degree. The purpose of the program is to educate individuals who are interested in investigating mechanisms of disease and who will pursue careers in research, biotechnology, and teaching. Emphasis is placed on interdisciplinary approaches to the study of human disease. Areas currently under investigation include cellular and molecular biology of cancer, chemical carcinogenesis, virology, stem cell and developmental pathology, liver and pulmonary diseases, environmental pathology, and circulatory, endocrine, and neurodegenerative diseases.

Courses are offered in general pathology, viral oncology, and molecular bases of diseases as well as techniques in experimental pathology. Other graduate courses offered include biochemistry, physiology, histology, and microbiology. A wide range of courses geared to contribute to the individual's educational objectives are available.

The master's program in experimental and molecular pathology offers students the flexibility to prepare for a wide range of careers, including research, teaching, industry, or consulting. For University of Southern California (USC) undergraduates, it is possible to obtain a combined bachelor's and master's degree in pathology.

To obtain a Ph.D. in pathology, the potential student must first be admitted to the Programs in Biomedical and Biological Sciences (PIBBS), an integrated Ph.D. admission program for students who want to study biomedical science at USC. In the second year, students can choose to major in pathology under the Genetic, Molecular, and Cellular Biology (GMCB) track.

Postdoctoral positions are also available. Applicants for a postdoctoral position must first go directly to the faculty member of choice and make arrangements with that faculty member.

Research Facilities

The facilities of the Pathology Department include the latest equipment for research in cell biology, biochemistry, and molecular biology. Excellent facilities are also available in the neighboring Kenneth Norris Jr. Cancer Hospital Research Institute, Topping Research Tower, Broad Center of Regenerative Medicine and Stem Cell Research, and Children's Hospital of Los Angeles.

Financial Aid

Research assistantships are available for Ph.D. students through faculty research grants. Special fellowships are available for qualified students. Most students are financially supported beginning in the second year by their mentors. No financial aid is available for the master's program at this time.

Cost of Study

Research assistantships include tuition. Full tuition for both the M.S. and Ph.D. programs is $34,080 for the 2011–12 academic year, plus mandatory fees of $1937 per year.

Living and Housing Costs

Housing arrangements are the responsibility of the students. Housing costs vary greatly, depending on location and type of accommodations. There are ample housing facilities in the many communities surrounding the medical school.

Student Group

Of the 33,747 students enrolled at the University of Southern California, 16,213 are engaged in graduate or professional study. The student body includes undergraduates from all parts of the United States and many other countries. Currently, there are 21 students enrolled in the Ph.D. pathology program and 14 enrolled in the M.S. in experimental and molecular pathology program.

Student Outcomes

Job opportunities for graduates are available in academic, hospital, and government institutions and in industry.

Location

The Health Sciences Campus of the University of Southern California is located in the center of Los Angeles, close to other universities and medical schools and within an hour's drive of both beaches and mountains. The city's excellent climate makes it possible to participate the year round in outdoor sports: camping and hiking at nearby mountain parks, skiing during the winter months, and swimming, surfing, and water sports. This exciting seaside city is rich in cultural, athletic, and scholastic opportunities.

The University and The Program

The graduate program in pathobiology is based at the Health Sciences Campus, which is approximately 10 miles from the main University campus. The Health Sciences Campus comprises the School of Medicine, School of Pharmacy, LAC-USC Healthcare Network, Doheny Eye Foundation, Norris Cancer Research Institute, Topping Research Tower, Harlayne J. Norris Research Tower, Institute for Genetic Medicine, and USC University Hospital.

Applying

Admission to the graduate program requires an undergraduate degree in the natural sciences and demonstration of competence and achievement in these studies. Scores on the General Test of the Graduate Record Examinations are required of all students, with a combined score of 1100 or better for the verbal and quantitative sections. The GRE score is preferred over the MCAT score for the master's program; however, only the GRE score is acceptable for the Ph.D. program. A score of 600 or better on the Test of English as a Foreign Language (TOEFL) is required of international applicants. Applicants must have a minimum GPA of 3.0. The deadline for applying to the Ph.D. program is December 1. For the M.S. program, the deadline for applying for fall is July 15, and for the spring semester, it is December 1.

The Ph.D. program is integrated with the Ph.D. Programs in Biomedical and Biological Sciences (PIBBS), an integrated pan–Health Sciences Campus graduate program. For the PIBBS application, students can visit http://www.usc.edu/pibbs for directions on how to apply. For the master's program, students should complete the application form online using the following Web site: http://www.usc.edu/admission/graduate/applyonline/.

Correspondence and Information

Chairman, Graduate Committee
Department of Pathology
School of Medicine
University of Southern California
2011 Zonal Avenue
Los Angeles, California 90089-9092
Phone: 323-442-1168
Fax: 323-442-3049
E-mail: pathgrad@usc.edu
Web site: http://www.usc.edu/medicine/pathology

University of Southern California

THE FACULTY AND THEIR RESEARCH

Thomas C. Chen, Associate Professor and Director, Neuro-Oncology; M.D., California, San Francisco, 1988; Ph.D., USC, 1996. Translational research for brain tumors. *Vaccine* 26:1764, 2008. *Cancer Res.* 67(20):9809, 2007; 10920, 2007. *Mol. Cancer Ther.* 6(4):1262, 2007.

Cheng-Ming Chuong, Professor and Chairman, Graduate Committee; M.D., Taiwan, 1978; Ph.D., Rockefeller, 1983; Academician, Academia Sinica, 2008. Stell cells, regenerative biology, hair engineering, Evo-Devo integument. *Science* 332:586, 2011; 305:1465, 2004. *Cell Stem Cell* 4:100, 2009. *Nature* 451:340, 2008; 438:1026, 2005; 420:308, 2002. *Proc. Natl. Acad. Sci. U.S.A.* 103:951, 2006.

Thomas D. Coates, Professor; M.D., Michigan, 1975. Pathophysiology of vaso-occlusion in sickle cell disease; iron overload and inflammatory damage in chronically transfused sickle cell and thalassemia patients; computer image analysis of biologic systems; role of inflammation in vascular damage in sickle cell disease; abnormal autonomic cardiac response to transient hypoxia in sickle cell anemia. *Blood* 116:537, 2010; 103:1934, 2004; 78:1338, 1991. *Br. J. Haematol.* 141:891, 2008. *Conf. Proc. IEEE Eng. Med. Biol. Soc.* 2008:1996–99, 2008. *J. Cell. Biol.* 117:765, 1992.

Edward D. Crandall, Professor; Ph.D., Northwestern, 1964; M.D., Pennsylvania, 1972. Alveolar epithelial development, growth, differentiation, and pathobiology. *Am. J. Respir. Cell Mol. Biol.*,42(5):604, 2010. *Nanomedicine* 4:139, 2008. *Toxicol. Vitro* 21:1373–81, 2007. *Am. J. Pathol.* 168:1452, 2006; 166:1321, 2005. *J. Histochem. Cytochem.* 2:759, 2004. *Cell Tissue Res.* 312:313, 2003. *J. Virol.* 75:11747, 2001.

J. A. Louis Dubeau, Professor; M.D., 1979, Ph.D., 1981, McGill. Biology, molecular genetics, and animal modeling of ovarian cancer. *Cancer Res.* 70:221, 2010. *Lancet Oncol.* 9:1191, 2008. *Curr. Biol.* 15:561, 2005.

Alan L. Epstein, Professor; M.D./Ph.D., Stanford, 1978. Monoclonal antibody–based immunotherapy of cancer. *J. Immunology* 185:2273–84, 2010. *J. Immunother.* 31:235, 2008. *Clin. Cancer Res.* 13:4016, 2007; 11:8492, 2005; 11:3084, 2005; 5:51, 1999. *Blood* 101:4853, 2003. *Cancer Res.* 63:8384, 2003.

Parkash Gill, Professor; M.D., Punjabi (India), 1974. Molecular mechanisms of angiogenesis. *Blood* 115:887, 2010. *Nature*, in press. *Proc. Natl. Acad. Sci. U.S.A.* 94:978, 1997. *N. Engl. J. Med.* 335:1261, 1996.

John Groffen, Professor; Ph.D., Groningen (Netherlands), 1981. Genetics of Ph-positive leukemias and innate immune system regulation. *Cancer Res.* 70:4346, 2010. *J. Biol. Chem.* 284:35645, 2009. *Mol. Cell. Biol.* 29:5742, 2009. *J. Biol. Chem.* 283:3023, 2008. *Hum. Genet.* 123:321, 2008.

Yuan-Ping Han, Assistant Professor; Ph.D., CUNY, Mount Sinai, 1996. Tissue injury, repair, and fibrosis; MMPs. *Am. J. Pathol.* doi:10:2353, September 16, 2010; 176:2447, May 2010; *J. Invest. Dermatol.* 128(9):2344, September 2008. *J. Biol. Chem.* 282(17):12928, April 27, 2007.

Nora Heisterkamp, Professor; Ph.D., Groningen (Netherlands), 1981. Cell biology and innate immunity; signal transduction, drug resistance, and treatment of Bcr-Abl-positive leukemia. *BMC Biochem.* 11:48, 2010. *Cancer Res.* 70:4346, 2010. *Leukemia* 24:813, 2010. *Mol. Canc. Therapeut.* 9:1318, 2010. *Mol. Cell. Biol.* 29:5742, 2009.

David R. Hinton, Professor and Vice Chairman, Department of Pathology; M.D., Toronto, 1978. Age-related macular degeneration; retinal pigment epithelium; stem cell therapy for ocular disorders; demyelination. *Investig. Ophthalmol. Vis. Sci.* 52:1573–85, 2011. *PLoS One* 5(10):e12578, 2010.

Alan L. Hiti, Professor of Clinical; Ph.D., UCLA, 1981; M.D., Miami (Florida), 1983. Applications of flow cytometry to diagnostic hematopathology and HIV disease.

Florence M. Hofman, Professor and Director, Ph.D. Program; Ph.D., Weizmann (Israel), 1976. Antiangiogenic therapy for primary and metastatic brain tumors; signal transduction mechanisms in tumor-derived vasculature. *Mol. Canc. Ther.* 9:631–41, 2010. *Mol. Canc. Res.* 6(8):1268, 2008. *Am. J. Pathol.* 173(2):575, 2008.

Tingxin Jiang, Assistant Professor; M.D., Shanghai (China), 1978. Tissue engineering of hair formation; reconstitution of feather and hairs. *Int. J. Dev. Biol.* 48:117, 2004. *Development.* 126:4997, 1999.

Emil P. Kartalov, Assistant Professor; Ph.D., Caltech, 2004. Nanotechnology in biology and medicine; focus on elastomer microfluidics in biomedical diagnostics. *Electrophoresis* 29, 2008. *J. Appl. Phys.* 102, 2007; 101, 2007. *Proc. Natl. Acad. Sci. U.S.A.* 103:33, 2006; 100, 2003.

Anthony J. Keyser, Professor of Clinical; Ph.D., Emory, 1976. Connective tissue; clinical pathology; non-mucinous nature of the surface material of the bladder mucosa. *Clin. Biochem.* 30:613, 1997. *Am. J. Med. Sci.* 304:285, 1993.

Yong-Mi Kim, Assistant Professor of Pediatrics and Pathology; M.D./Ph.D., Düsseldorf (Germany), 1998; M.P.H., Harvard, 2003. Leukemia stem cells; survivin and integrins in acute lymphoblastic leukemia; preclinical leukemia models. *Canc. Res.* September 13, 2010 (Epub ahead of print); 70(11):4346, June 1, 2010. *Leukemia* 24(4):813, April 2010; 22(1):66, 2008. *Cancer Cell.* 16(3):232, September 8, 2009.

Krzysztof Kobielak, Assistant Professor of Pathology; M.D., 1996, Ph.D., 1999, Marcinkowski University of Medical Sciences (Poland). Regulation of hair follicle stem cell niche; morphogenesis of skin appendages; skin and hair follicle regeneration. *Proc. Natl. Acad. Sci. U.S.A.* 104:10063, 2007. *J. Cell Biol.* 163:609, 2003.

Robert D. Ladner, Assistant Professor; Ph.D., Rutgers, 1996. Regulation and posttranslational modification of enzymes involved in thymidylate nucleotide metabolism. *Nucleic Acids Res.* 37(1):78, 2009. *Mol. Canc. Therapeut.* 7(9):3029, 2008. *Mol. Pharmacol.* 66:620, 2004. *Pharmacogenetics* 14:319, 2004.

Joseph R. Landolph Jr., Associate Professor; Ph.D., Berkeley, 1976. Molecular biology of neoplastic transformation by carcinogenic Ni^{+2}/Cr^{+6} compounds; differential gene expression in transformed cell lines; oncogene activation/tumor suppressor gene inactivation. *Regul. Toxicol. Pharmacol.*, in press. *Metal Ions in Biology and Medicine* 10:63, 2008. *Toxicol. Appl. Pharmacol.* 206:138, 2005. *Mol. Cell. Biochem.* 255:203, 2004.

Michael R. Lieber, Professor; Ph.D., 1981, M.D., 1983, Chicago. DNA repair in human cancer, aging, and the immune system. *Cell* 135:1130, 2008; 109:807, 2002; 108:781, 2002. *Mol. Cell* 34:535, 2009; 31:485, 2008; 16:701, 2004; 2:477, 1998. *Mol. Cell. Biol.* 28:50, 2008; 27:5921, 2007. *Nature* 428:88, 2004; 388:495, 1997; 388:492, 1997. *Nat. Immunol.* 4:442, 2003. *Curr. Biol.* 12:397, 2002.

Carol A. Miller, Professor; M.D., Jefferson Medical, 1965. Molecular and cellular basis for degenerative and developmental neurologic diseases. *PLoS One,* 4(3):e4936, 2009. *Am. J. Path.* 172:6, 2008. *J. Mol. Neurosci.* 25(1):79, 2005. *Mol. Brain Res.* 134:282, 2005. *Proc. Natl. Acad. Sci. U.S.A.* 101(12):4210, 2004; 95:2586, 1998.

Kevin A. Nash, Assistant Professor; Ph.D., Aberdeen (UK), 1987. Impact of antibiotics on microbial physiology; molecular basis of drug resistance and drug susceptibility in bacteria, especially *Mycobacterium tuberculosis*. *Antimicrob. Agents Chemother.* 53:1367, 2009; 50:3476, 2006; 47:3053, 2003; 45:1982, 2001; 45:1607, 2001. *J. Antimicrob. Chemother.* 55:170, 2005.

André J. Ouellette, Professor, Department of Pathology and Laboratory Medicine; Ph.D., Indiana, 1972. Role of Paneth Cell alpha-defensins in innate mucosal immunity in the lower gastrointestinal tract; structural determinants of alpha-defensin bactericidal activity; mechanisms of pro-alpha-defensin conversion to active forms; Paneth cell homeostasis in health and disease. *J. Biol. Chem.* 284:6826, 2009; 284:27848, 2009. *Infect. Immun.* 77:5035, 2009.

Paul K. Pattengale, Professor; M.D., NYU, 1970. Structure and function of human M-CSF; minimal residual disease in ALL; molecular pathogenesis of lymphoid cell neoplasms (mouse and human). *Am. J. Pathol.* 151:647, 1997. *Blood* 90:2901, 1997. *J. Biol. Chem.* 271:16388, 1996.

Michael F. Press, Professor; Ph.D., 1975, M.D., 1977, Chicago. Pathobiology of breast and gynecologic cancer. *J. Clin. Oncol.* 29:859, 2011; 27:1323, 2009; 26(34):5544, 2008; 25:118, 2007. *Clin. Canc. Res.* 16:1281, 2010; 14(23):7861, 2008. *Br. J. Canc.* 100(1):89, 2009. *BMC Canc.* 9:43, 2009. *J. Natl. Canc. Inst.* 101:615, 2009.

Suraiya Rasheed, Professor and Director, Viral Oncology and Proteomics Research; Ph.D., Osmania (India), 1958; Ph.D., London, 1964. Biomarkers and protein-protein interaction pathways in cancer and viral (HIV) diseases (Melanoma/ neuronal stem cells and HIV-associated diseases). *J. Transl. Med.* 7:75, 2009. *PLoS One* 2008. doi: 10.1371. *Cancer Stem Cells, Identification and Targets,* Chapters 1 and 8, John Wiley & Sons Publisher, 2008. *Int. J. Bioinformatics Res. Appl.* 3(4):480, 2007. *Virol. J.* 3:101, 2006. *J. Transl. Med.* 5:14, 2005 (doi: 10.1186/1479-5876-3-14).

Pradip Roy-Burman, Professor; Ph.D., Calcutta, 1963. Modeling human prostate cancer in mice; mechanisms of prostate tumorigenesis and role of cancer stem cells and tissue microenvironment in disease progression. *Cancer Res.* 70:7294, 2010; 68:198, 2008. *Hormones and Cancer* 1:297, 2010. *Lab. Investig.* 90:222, 2010. *Proc. Natl. Acad. Sci. U.S.A.* 105:19444, 2008.

Michael E. Selsted, Professor and Chairman of the Department of Pathology; Ph.D., UCLA, 1980; M.D., UCLA, 1985. Role of host defense peptides in innate immunity and inflammation. *J. Biol. Chem.* 284:5602, 2009. *J. Virol.* 83:11385, 2009. *Science* 286:498, 1999.

Russell P. Sherwin, Professor; M.D., Boston University, 1948. Environmental, occupational, and oncologic pathology; COPD; image analysis; immunopathology. *Mol. Cancer Ther.* 3:499, 2004. *Virchows Arch.* 437:422, 2000; 433:341, 1998. *Inhal. Toxicol.* 9:405, 1997; 7:1183, 1995; 7:1173, 1995.

Darryl Shibata, Professor; M.D., USC, 1983. Molecular clocks; investigating stem cells in human colon by using methylation patterns. *Proc. Natl. Acad. Sci. U.S.A.* 98:10839, 2001.

Michael R. Stallcup, Professor; Ph.D., Berkeley, 1974. Regulation of gene transcription by steroid hormone receptors and transcriptional coactivator proteins. *Gene. Dev.* 25:176, 2011; 19:1466, 2005. *J. Biol. Chem.* 284:29298, 2009; 281:3389, 2006. *Nat. Struct. Mol. Biol.* 15:245, 2008. *Mol. Cell* 31:510, 2008. *Proc. Natl. Acad. Sci. U.S.A.* 102:3611, 2005. *Mol. Cell. Biol.* 24:2103, 2004. *Science* 284:2174, 1999.

Bangyan Stiles, Assistant Professor; Ph.D., Texas at Austin, 1998. Regeneration of pancreatic B cells; liver stem cells and liver cancer. *Stem Cell* 27(2):290, 2009. *Mol. Cell. Biol.* 26:2772, 2006; 25:2498, 2005; 22:3842, 2002. *J. Clin. Invest.* 116:1843, 2006. *Cancer Cell* 8:185, 2005. *Proc. Natl. Acad. Sci. U.S.A.* 101:2081, 2004; 98:10314, 2001.

Clive R. Taylor, Professor; D.Phil., Oxford, 1975; M.D.,Cambridge, 1980 . *Hum. Pathol.* 39:1555, 2008. *Applied Immunohistochemistry and Molecular Morphology* 17:366, 2009.

Prasad Tongaonkar; Assistant Professor of Research; Ph.D., University of Medicine and Dentistry of New Jersey, 1999. Expression and biosynthesis of mammalian antimicrobial peptides and their role in innate immnune and inflammatory processes. *J. Leukoc. Biol.* 89:283, 2010. *J. Biol. Chem.* 284:5602, 2009.

Timothy J. Triche, Professor; M.D./Ph.D., Tulane, 1971. Molecular characterization of chimeric tumor genes, control of gene expression, and relationship to tumor phenotype, biologic aggressiveness, and treatment responsiveness. *Nat. Genet.* 6:146, 1994. *Diagn. Mol. Pathol.* 2:147, 1993. *EMBO J.* 12:4481, 1993.

Hide Tsukamoto, Professor; D.V.M., Tokyo, 1975; Ph.D., Kobe (Japan), 1988. Cellular and molecular mechanisms of liver cirrhosis; adipogenic transcriptional programs that are molecular targets for potential treatment of cirrhosis; iron-mediated intracellular signaling for proinflammatory activation of NF-kappaB in macrophages; roles of mesenchyme-epithelial interactions in liver development and regeneration; TLR4-TGFbeta reciprocal interactions in the genesis of liver cancer stem cells. *J. Biol. Chem.* 285:30463, 2010; 282:5582, 2007; 280:4959, 2005; 279:11392, 2004. *Proc. Natl. Acad. Sci. U.S.A.* 106:1548, 2009.

Randall Widelitz, Associate Professor; Ph.D., Arizona, 1986. Growth control in tumorigenesis and embryonic development; focus on roles of sex hormones, adhesion molecules, Wnts, and beta-catenin. *Cell Stem Cell* 4:100, 2009. *Organogenesis* 4:123, 2008. *Am. J. Pathol.* 173:1339, 2008.

Ping Wu, Assistant Professor of Research; Ph.D., Nanjing (China), 1997. Regenerative biology; focus on reptile scale, teeth, and tail regeneration. *Dev. Dyn.* 235:1400, 2006. *Science* 305:1465, 2004. *Int. J. Dev. Biol.* 48:249, 2004.

Jun Xu, Assistant Professor, M.D., China, 1987; Ph.D., UCLA, 2004. Metabolism in liver function and disease. *Clin. Biochem.* 2010. *Cell Metab.* 5(5):371, 2007. *Diabetes* 55:3429, 2006; 55:3372, 2006. *J. Biol. Chem.* 277(52):50237, 2002.

Dan Hong Zhu, Assistant Professor; M.D., Jiao Tong (China), 1983; Ph.D., USC, 2004. Pathological mechanisms of age-related macular degeneration. Stem cell biology and its application in the treatment of age-related macular degeneration. *Vision Res.* 50(7):643-51, 2010. *J. Biol. Chem.* 281(30):21173–82. 2006. In *Eighth International Conference on the Chemistry and Biology of Mineralized Tissues,* pp. 99–102, eds. W. J. Landis and J. Sodek, University of Toronto Press Inc., Canada, 2005.

UNIVERSITY OF WISCONSIN–MADISON

Department of Pathology and Laboratory Medicine

Program of Study

The Cellular and Molecular Pathology (CMP) graduate training program originated more than fifty years ago as a program focused on general pathology research and education. Through the years, much of the training involved examination of pathological specimens, and graduates were highly valued for their skills by health institutions and industry. Seven years ago, the graduate program was restructured to emphasize the pathogenesis of human disease, and the program faculty was expanded. Today, the faculty of the CMP program includes 60 National Institutes of Health/National Science Foundation or similarly funded investigators focusing on research programs in immunology, cancer biology, neuropathology, and signal transduction. These investigators come from twenty different basic science, preclinical, and clinical departments. Of these trainers, 31 hold Ph.D. degrees and 29 hold M.D. or M.D./Ph.D. degrees, and carry out both patient care and basic research. The Department of Pathology serves as a core for the CMP graduate program, integrating these faculty and trainers from across campus into a unified, multidisciplinary graduate training program focused on the pathogenesis of human diseases.

The primary objective of the CMP program is to prepare graduates for productive careers in scientific research and education and to position them to make significant contributions toward the nation's health-related research needs.

The CMP program focuses on the integration of medical knowledge into graduate education, and the Department of Pathology offers a translational bridge between basic and clinical sciences by offering an interdisciplinary curriculum focused on the concepts of human disease pathogenesis and translational research.

Research Facilities

The Department is housed in the Medical School complex at the center of the Madison campus and at the Clinical Sciences Center on the west side of campus. The Department has modern research facilities including centralized support facilities. In addition, the Integrated Microscopy Resource on the Madison campus is a national microscopy center that provides equipment and support for scanning and transmission of electron microscopy and video-enhanced fluorescence microscopy. Extensive library facilities, including Departmental collections, the Medical School Library, and extensive holdings at other science libraries on the Madison campus, are available.

Financial Aid

It is the intention of the program that students receive stipend support during the duration of their graduate study. Support for students is offered through a variety of sources, including Department teaching and research assistantships, research assistantships from individual faculty research grants, project assistantships, fellowships, the thesis adviser's research funds, or other campus sources. In addition, students compete for University fellowships and research assistantships on several training grants on the Madison campus. For the 2011–12 school year, the stipend rate for graduate students in the Department of Pathology and Laboratory Medicine was $24,000, with an increase of approximately 4 percent annually. In addition, assistantship recipients qualify for full remission of nonresident and resident tuition and subsidized enrollment in the Graduate Assistant Health Insurance Program.

Cost of Study

As discussed in the Financial Aid section, students receive stipend support throughout their graduate study. In the fall of 2011, tuition and fees were $5687.56 per semester for Wisconsin residents and $12,566.68 per semester for nonresidents.

Living and Housing Costs

For single graduate students, the University maintains graduate student apartments that offer one- and two-bedroom units; rents ranged from $785 to $925 per month in 2010–11. University Student Apartments, better known as Eagle Heights, offers one- to three-bedroom unfurnished apartments; rents ranged from $670 to $1005 per month in 2010–11. There may be a waiting list for the Eagle Heights units, and priority is given to students with dependent children. For more details, students should visit the Division of University Housing Web site at http://www.housing.wisc.edu. Most students live off campus; costs for off-campus housing vary depending on size and location. Additional information about off-campus housing is available at the UW–Madison Campus Information, Assistance, and Orientation Web site at http://www.wisc.edu/cac/housing/.

Student Group

The Madison campus is the flagship of the University of Wisconsin, with an enrollment of more than 40,000 students, including 9,000 graduate students. In the sciences, the graduate students belong to individual department graduate programs or are members of interdepartmental training programs, such as the CMP program.

Student Outcomes

Students in this program have successfully pursued a number of options after obtaining their Ph.D. degrees. They have received postdoctoral training and obtained faculty positions in academic institutions, taken research positions in industry, or continued on to medical school and secured faculty positions in medical institutions.

Location

Madison, recently ranked as one of the top cities of America to live in, is the capital of the state, with a metropolitan population of approximately 215,000. The city, situated on four picturesque lakes, is approximately 150 miles northwest of Chicago. The city and the University offer a wide variety of educational, cultural, and recreational opportunities. Superb facilities are available for summer and winter sports, such as sailing, camping, hiking, ice-skating, skiing, and bicycling.

The University

The University, founded in 1848, is one of the Big Ten schools and has a rich tradition of excellence in research. The University System includes the main campus in Madison plus twelve other comprehensive universities, thirteen freshman/sophomore campuses (UW Colleges), and the UW–Extension Program.

Applying

Applicants should have a bachelor's degree and an undergraduate minimum grade point average of 3.0 (on a 4.0 scale). Applicants should have a strong background in organic and physical chemistry, biochemistry, biology (including genetics), and mathematics through calculus. Completed application forms, Graduate Record Examinations (GRE) scores, transcripts, a resume, statement of purpose, and a minimum of three letters of recommendation are required for an admission decision. The application submission deadline for fall admission is December 1.

Correspondence and Information

CMP Program Coordinator
Department of Pathology
3170-10K/L Medical Foundation Centennial Building
University of Wisconsin
1685 Highland Avenue
Madison, Wisconsin 53705
Phone: 608-262-2665
Fax: 608-265-3301
E-mail: gradinfo@pathology.wisc.edu
Web site: http://www.cmp.wisc.edu

University of Wisconsin–Madison

THE FACULTY AND THEIR RESEARCH

Caroline Alexander, Associate Professor, Oncology. Role of breast stem cells in tumor induction; multiple functions of Wnt signaling in the regulation of mammary epithelial cell growth; changes in tumor susceptibility that are effected by alterations of normal development.

Nihal Ahmed, Associate Professor, Dermatology. Cancer biology; prevention and experimental therapeutics of cancer.

Fotis Asimakopoulos, Assistant Professor, Medicine. Myeloma research; phase I experimental therapeutics.

B. Lynn Allen-Hoffmann, Professor, Pathology. Keratinocytes; cancer biology; extracellular matrices.

Craig S. Atwood, Associate Professor, Medicine. Hormonal regulation of aging and neurodegenerative diseases.

Emery H. Bresnick, Professor, Pharmacology. Regulation of transcription, hematopoiesis, and leukemogenesis.

William J. Burlingham, Professor, Surgery. Mechanisms of transplant tolerance and rejection.

Herbert Chen, Professor, Surgery. Development, progression, and treatment of endocrine tumors including gastrointestinal carcinoids, thyroid cancer, adrenal cancer, and pancreatic islet cell tumors.

Joshua Coon, Assistant Professor, Chemistry. Bioanalytical chemistry; mass spectrometry.

Loren Denlinger, Assistant Professor, Medicine. Host-pathogen interactions; the role of macrophages in immunity to intracellular pathogens.

Arjang Djamali, Assistant Professor, Medicine. The mechanisms of disease progression in kidney disease.

Karen Downs, Professor, Anatomy. Cellular, molecular, and genetic components of differentiation during placental morphogenesis.

Marina Emborg, Assistant Professor, Medical Physics. Solutions for neurodegenerative disorders, in particular Parkinson's disease.

Zsuzsa Fabry, Professor, Pathology. Immunopathology; neuroimmunology; multiple sclerosis.

John Fleming, Professor, Neurology. Multiple sclerosis.

Andreas Friedl, Professor, Pathology. Heparan sulfate proteoglycans as modulators of growth factors in human disease; tumor angiogenesis.

Daniel Greenspan, Professor, Pathology. Extracellular controls of cell behavior.

Jeff Hardin, Professor, Zoology. Morphogenesis and pattern formation during early development.

Peiman Hematti, Assistant Professor, Medicine. Characterization and study of mesenchymal stromal cells derived from human embryonic stem cells; development of a preclinical rhesus macaque model.

Anna Huttenlocher, Associate Professor, Medical Microbiology and Immunology. Cell migration and chemotaxis; adhesive mechanisms that regulate cell migration; the role of integrin signaling.

Nizar Jarjour, Professor, Medicine. Asthma; circadian rhythm; investigative bronchoscopy.

Juan Jaume, Assistant Professor, Medicine. Endocrine autoimmunity, type 1 diabetes, and thyroid diseases.

Shannon Kenney, Professor, Medicine. Epstein-Barr virus pathogenesis and treatment.

Bruce Klein, Professor, Pediatrics. Microbial immunology and pathogenesis.

Youngsook Lee, Associate Professor, Anatomy. Transcriptional control of cardiovascular development and mechanisms of cardiac-specific gene regulation.

Gary E. Lyons, Associate Professor, Anatomy. Developmental biology of the mammalian cardiovascular system.

Albee Messing, Professor, Pathobiological Sciences. Transgenic mice; developmental neuropathology; molecular neurobiology.

Deane F. Mosher, Professor, Medicine. Extracellular matrix and cell adhesion.

David O'Connor, Assistant Professor, Pathology. HIV/AIDS pathogenesis.

Julie Olson, Assistant Professor, Neurological Surgery. Role of resident immune cells and infiltrating peripheral immune cells in the response to virus infection in the CNS.

Donna P. Peters, Professor, Pathology. Cell-matrix signaling in the human eye; glaucoma.

Alan Rapraeger, Professor, Pathology. Mechanisms by which the syndecan family of cell-surface receptors regulate cell growth, adhesion, and migration.

Matyas Sandor, Professor, Pathology. Immune responses to infectious disease.

Christine M. Seroogy, Assistant Professor, Pediatrics. Biological role of a novel E3 ubiquitin ligase called GRAIL in T-cell function and hematopoietic tissue development.

John Sheehan, Associate Professor, Medicine. Blood coagulation; intrinsic tenase regulation; coagulation factor IX.

Nader Sheibani, Associate Professor, Ophthalmology and Visual Sciences. Cell adhesion and signaling in vascular cells; diabetic retinopathy.

Igor Slukvin, Assistant Professor, Pathology. Hematopoietic differentiation of human embryonic stem cells; immune-privileged properties of embryonic and fetal tissues.

Paul M. Sondel, Professor, Pediatrics. Immune-mediated recognition and destruction of neoplasms.

Dandan Sun, Professor, Neurosurgery. The role of Na^+, K^+, $2Cl^-$ cotransporter in ion homeostasis and cell volume regulation in the central nervous system.

M. Suresh, Associate Professor, Pathobiological Sciences. Molecular and cellular basis of T-cell memory; $CD8^+$ T-cell responses in chronic viral infections.

Adel Talaat, Assistant Professor, Pathobiological Sciences. Genomic and functional analyses of tuberculosis and paratuberculosis to understand pathogenesis and develop novel vaccines.

Robert Thorne, Assistant Professor, Pharmacy. Using biopharmaceuticals to treat neurological disorders (e.g., Alzheimer's disease, Parkinson's disease, and stroke); intranasal targeting of drugs to the brain, spinal cord, and cervical lymph nodes.

David I. Watkins, Professor, Pathology. HIV vaccine development; SIV pathogenesis.

Jon P. Woods, Associate Professor, Medical Microbiology and Immunology. *Histoplasma capsulatum* molecular pathogenesis and host interactions.

Xinyu Zhao, Neuroscience. Using molecular mechanisms that regulate neural stem cells and neurodevelopment to treat neurological disorders and injuries.

Weixiong Zhong, Assistant Professor, Pathology. Redox effects of selenium in human prostate cancer chemoprevention.

Section 17
Pharmacology and Toxicology

This section contains a directory of institutions offering graduate work in pharmacology and toxicology, followed by in-depth entries submitted by institutions that chose to prepare detailed program descriptions. Additional information about programs listed in the directory but not augmented by an in-depth entry may be obtained by writing directly to the dean of a graduate school or chair of a department at the address given in the directory.

For programs offering related work, see also in this book *Biochemistry; Biological and Biomedical Sciences; Cell, Molecular, and Structural Biology; Ecology, Environmental Biology, and Evolutionary Biology; Genetics, Developmental Biology, and Reproductive Biology; Neuroscience and Neurobiology; Nutrition; Pathology and Pathobiology;* and *Physiology.* In the other guides in this series:

Graduate Programs in the Humanities, Arts & Social Sciences
See *Psychology and Counseling*
Graduate Programs in the Physical Sciences, Mathematics, Agricultural Sciences, the Environment & Natural Resources
See *Chemistry* and *Environmental Sciences and Management*
Graduate Programs in Engineering & Applied Sciences
See *Chemical Engineering* and *Civil and Environmental Engineering*
Graduate Programs in Business, Education, Health, Information Studies, Law & Social Work
See *Pharmacy and Pharmaceutical Sciences, Public Health,* and *Veterinary Medicine and Sciences*

CONTENTS

Molecular Pharmacology

Albert Einstein College of Medicine, Graduate Division of Biomedical Sciences, Division of Biological Sciences, Department of Molecular Pharmacology, Bronx, NY 10461. Offers PhD, MD/PhD. *Degree requirements:* For doctorate, thesis/dissertation. *Entrance requirements:* For doctorate, GRE General Test. Additional exam requirements/recommendations for international students: Required—TOEFL. *Faculty research:* Effects of drugs on macromolecules, enzyme systems, cell morphology and function.

Brown University, Graduate School, Division of Biology and Medicine, Program in Molecular Pharmacology and Physiology, Providence, RI 02912. Offers MA, Sc M, PhD, MD/PhD. *Degree requirements:* For doctorate, thesis/dissertation, preliminary exam. *Entrance requirements:* For master's and doctorate, GRE General Test, GRE Subject Test. Additional exam requirements/recommendations for international students: Required—TOEFL. Electronic applications accepted. *Faculty research:* Structural biology, antiplatelet drugs, nicotinic receptor structure/function.

Dartmouth College, Program in Experimental and Molecular Medicine, Molecular Pharmacology, Toxicology and Experimental Therapeutics Track, Hanover, NH 03755. Offers PhD.

Harvard University, Graduate School of Arts and Sciences, Division of Medical Sciences, Boston, MA 02115. Offers biological chemistry and molecular pharmacology (PhD); cell biology (PhD); genetics (PhD); microbiology and molecular genetics (PhD); pathology (PhD), including experimental pathology. *Degree requirements:* For doctorate, thesis/dissertation. *Entrance requirements:* For doctorate, GRE General Test, GRE Subject Test. Additional exam requirements/recommendations for international students: Required—TOEFL. *Expenses:* Tuition: Full-time $34,976. Required fees: $1166. Full-time tuition and fees vary according to program.

Mayo Graduate School, Graduate Programs in Biomedical Sciences, Program in Molecular Pharmacology and Experimental Therapeutics, Rochester, MN 55905. Offers PhD. *Degree requirements:* For doctorate, oral defense of dissertation, qualifying oral and written exam. *Entrance requirements:* For doctorate, GRE, 1 year of chemistry, biology, calculus, and physics. Additional exam requirements/recommendations for international students: Required—TOEFL. Electronic applications accepted. *Faculty research:* Patch clamping, G-proteins, pharmacogenetics, receptor-induced transcriptional events, cholinesterase biology.

Medical University of South Carolina, College of Graduate Studies, Program in Cell and Molecular Pharmacology and Experimental Therapeutics, Charleston, SC 29425. Offers MS, PhD, DMD/PhD, MD/PhD. *Faculty:* 16 full-time (3 women). *Students:* 1 (woman) full-time. Average age 24. 5 applicants, 0% accepted. In 2010, 2 doctorates awarded. Terminal master's awarded for partial completion of doctoral program. *Degree requirements:* For master's, thesis; for doctorate, comprehensive exam, thesis/dissertation, oral and written exams. *Entrance requirements:* For master's, GRE General Test; for doctorate, GRE General Test, interview, minimum GPA of 3.0. Additional exam requirements/recommendations for international students: Required—TOEFL (minimum score 600 paper-based; 250 computer-based; 100 iBT). *Application deadline:* For fall admission, 1/15 priority date for domestic and international students. Applications are processed on a rolling basis. Application fee: $0 ($85 for international students). Electronic applications accepted. *Financial support:* In 2010–11, fellowships with partial tuition reimbursements (averaging $23,000 per year); Federal Work-Study and scholarships/grants also available. Support available to part-time students. Financial award application deadline: 3/10; financial award applicants required to submit FAFSA. *Faculty research:* Cancer drug discovery and development, growth factor receptor signaling, regulation of G-protein signaling, redox signal transduction, proteomics and mass spectrometry. *Unit head:* Dr. Kenneth D. Tew, Chair, 843-792-2514, Fax: 843-792-9588, E-mail: tewk@musc.edu. *Application contact:* Dr. Lauren Ball, Assistant Professor and Co-Director of the Graduate Training Program, 843-792-4513, Fax: 843-792-6590, E-mail: ballle@musc.edu.

New York University, School of Medicine and Graduate School of Arts and Science, Sackler Institute of Graduate Biomedical Sciences, Department of Pharmacology, New York, NY 10012-1019. Offers molecular pharmacology (PhD); MD/PhD. *Degree requirements:* For doctorate, comprehensive exam, thesis/dissertation, qualifying exam. *Entrance requirements:* For doctorate, GRE General Test. Additional exam requirements/recommendations for international students: Required—TOEFL. *Faculty research:* Pharmacology and neurobiology, neuropeptides, receptor biochemistry, cytoskeleton, endocrinology.

Purdue University, College of Pharmacy and Pharmacal Sciences and Graduate School, Graduate Programs in Pharmacy and Pharmacal Sciences, Department of Medicinal Chemistry and Molecular Pharmacology, West Lafayette, IN 47907. Offers analytical medicinal chemistry (PhD); computational and biophysical medicinal chemistry (PhD); medicinal and bioorganic chemistry (PhD); medicinal biochemistry and molecular biology (PhD); molecular pharmacology and toxicology (PhD); natural products and pharmacognosy (PhD); nuclear pharmacy (MS); radiopharmaceutical chemistry and nuclear pharmacy (PhD); MS/PhD. Terminal master's awarded for partial completion of doctoral program. *Degree requirements:* For master's, thesis; for doctorate, thesis/dissertation. *Entrance requirements:* For master's, GRE General Test, minimum B average; BS in biology, chemistry, or pharmacy; for doctorate, GRE General Test, minimum B average; BS in biology, chemistry, or pharmacology. Additional exam requirements/recommendations for international students: Required—TOEFL. Electronic applications accepted. *Faculty research:* Drug design and development, cancer research, drug synthesis and analysis, chemical pharmacology, environmental toxicology.

Rosalind Franklin University of Medicine and Science, School of Graduate and Postdoctoral Studies—Interdisciplinary Graduate Program in Biomedical Sciences, Department of Cellular and Molecular Pharmacology, North Chicago, IL 60064-3095. Offers MS, PhD, MD/PhD. Terminal master's awarded for partial completion of doctoral program. *Degree requirements:* For master's, comprehensive exam, thesis; for doctorate, comprehensive exam, thesis/dissertation. *Entrance requirements:* For master's and doctorate, GRE General Test. Additional exam requirements/recommendations for international students: Required—TOEFL, TWE. Electronic applications accepted. *Faculty research:* Control of gene expression in higher organisms, molecular mechanism of action of growth factors and hormones, hormonal regulation in brain neuropsychopharmacology.

Rutgers, The State University of New Jersey, New Brunswick, Graduate School-New Brunswick, Program in Cellular and Molecular Pharmacology, Piscataway, NJ 08854-8097. Offers PhD. Program offered jointly with University of Medicine and Dentistry of New Jersey. *Degree requirements:* For doctorate, thesis/dissertation, qualifying exam. *Entrance requirements:* For doctorate, GRE General Test, GRE Subject Test. Additional exam requirements/recommendations for international students: Required—TOEFL. *Expenses:* Tuition, state resident: full-time $7200; part-time $600 per credit. Tuition, nonresident: full-time $11,124; part-time $927 per credit. *Faculty research:* Molecular, cellular, and neuropharmacology; drug metabolism; intracellular signaling systems; protein synthesis and processing; carcinogenesis.

Stanford University, School of Medicine, Graduate Programs in Medicine, Department of Molecular Pharmacology, Stanford, CA 94305-9991. Offers PhD. *Degree requirements:* For doctorate, thesis/dissertation, qualifying examination. *Entrance requirements:* For doctorate, GRE General Test, GRE Subject Test. Additional exam requirements/recommendations for international students: Required—TOEFL. Electronic applications accepted. *Expenses:* Tuition: Full-time $38,700; part-time $860 per unit. One-time fee: $200 full-time. *Faculty research:* Action of such drugs as epinephrine, cell differentiation and development, microsomal enzymes, neuropeptide gene expression.

Thomas Jefferson University, Jefferson College of Graduate Studies, Graduate Program in Molecular Pharmacology and Structural Biology, Philadelphia, PA 19107. Offers PhD. *Faculty:* 37 full-time (7 women). *Students:* 15 full-time (6 women); includes 4 minority (all Asian, non-Hispanic/Latino), 3 international. 20 applicants, 35% accepted, 3 enrolled. In 2010, 4 doctorates awarded. *Degree requirements:* For doctorate, comprehensive exam, thesis/dissertation. *Entrance requirements:* For doctorate, GRE General Test, minimum GPA of 3.2. Additional exam requirements/recommendations for international students: Required—TOEFL (minimum score 250 computer-based; 100 iBT) or IELTS. *Application deadline:* For fall admission, 1/2 priority date for domestic and international students. Applications are processed on a rolling basis. Application fee: $50. Electronic applications accepted. *Financial support:* In 2010–11, 15 students received support, including 15 fellowships with full tuition reimbursements available (averaging $54,723 per year); Federal Work-Study, institutionally sponsored loans, scholarships/grants, traineeships, and stipends also available. Support available to part-time students. Financial award application deadline: 5/1; financial award applicants required to submit FAFSA. *Faculty research:* Biochemistry and cell, molecular and structural biology of cell-surface and intracellular receptors, molecular modeling, signal transduction. Total annual research expenditures: $36.7 million. *Unit head:* Dr. Philip Wedegaertner, Program Director, 215-503-3137, Fax: 215-923-2117, E-mail: philip.wedegaertner@mail.tju.edu. *Application contact:* Marc E. Stearns, Director of Admissions, 215-503-0155, Fax: 215-503-9920, E-mail: jcgs-info@jefferson.edu.

University at Buffalo, the State University of New York, Graduate School, Graduate Programs in Cancer Research and Biomedical Sciences at Roswell Park Cancer Institute, Department of Molecular Pharmacology and Cancer Therapeutics at Roswell Park Cancer Institute, Buffalo, NY 14260. Offers molecular pharmacology and cancer therapeutics (PhD). *Faculty:* 21 full-time (5 women). *Students:* 24 full-time (16 women), 1 part-time (0 women); includes 1 Black or African American, non-Hispanic/Latino; 1 Asian, non-Hispanic/Latino; 2 Hispanic/Latino, 13 international. Average age 26. 30 applicants, 33% accepted, 5 enrolled. In 2010, 3 doctorates awarded. *Degree requirements:* For doctorate, comprehensive exam, thesis/dissertation. *Entrance requirements:* For doctorate, GRE. Additional exam requirements/recommendations for international students: Required—TOEFL (minimum score 600 paper-based; 250 computer-based; 100 iBT), IELTS (minimum score 7), TWE (minimum score 4). *Application deadline:* For fall admission, 2/1 priority date for domestic and international students. Applications are processed on a rolling basis. Application fee: $50. Electronic applications accepted. *Financial support:* In 2010–11, 25 students received support, including 25 research assistantships with full tuition reimbursements available (averaging $24,000 per year); Federal Work-Study and health care benefits also available. Financial award application deadline: 2/1. *Faculty research:* Cell cycle regulation, apoptosis, signal transduction, k+s signaling pathway, drug development. Total annual research expenditures: $6.5 million. *Unit head:* Dr. David Goodrich, Chair, 716-845-8225, Fax: 716-845-3879, E-mail: david.goodrich@roswellpark.org. *Application contact:* Dr. Moray Campbell, Director of Graduate Studies, 716-845-8225, Fax: 716-845-8857, E-mail: theresa.skurzewski@roswellpark.org.

University of Massachusetts Worcester, Graduate School of Biomedical Sciences, Worcester, MA 01655-0115. Offers biochemistry and molecular pharmacology (PhD); bioinformatics and computational biology (PhD); cancer biology (PhD); cell biology (PhD); clinical and population health research (PhD); clinical investigation (MS); immunology and virology (PhD); interdisciplinary graduate program (PhD); molecular genetics and microbiology (PhD); neuroscience (PhD); DVM/PhD; MD/PhD. *Faculty:* 1,059 full-time (357 women), 145 part-time/adjunct (100 women). *Students:* 438 full-time (239 women), 1 (woman) part-time; includes 44 minority (9 Black or African American, non-Hispanic/Latino; 31 Asian, non-Hispanic/Latino; 4 Hispanic/Latino), 148 international. Average age 29. 687 applicants, 28% accepted, 116 enrolled. In 2010, 6 master's, 45 doctorates awarded. Terminal master's awarded for partial completion of doctoral program. *Degree requirements:* For master's, thesis; for doctorate, thesis/dissertation. *Entrance requirements:* For master's, bachelor's degree; for doctorate, GRE General Test, MS, MA, or MPH (for some programs). Additional exam requirements/recommendations for international students: Required—TOEFL (minimum score 600 paper-based; 250 computer-based). *Application deadline:* For fall admission, 12/15 for domestic and international students; for winter admission, 1/15 for domestic students; for spring admission, 5/15 for domestic students. Application fee: $35. Electronic applications accepted. *Expenses:* Contact institution. *Financial support:* In 2010–11, 439 students received support, including 439 research assistantships with full tuition reimbursements available (averaging $28,350 per year); scholarships/grants, health care benefits, tuition waivers (full), and unspecified assistantships also available. Financial award application deadline: 4/20. *Faculty research:* RNA interference, gene therapy, cell biology, bioinformatics, clinical research. Total annual research expenditures: $232 million. *Unit head:* Dr. Anthony Carruthers, Dean, 508-856-4135, E-mail: anthony.carruthers@umassmed.edu. *Application contact:* Dr. Kendall Knight, Associate Dean and Interim Director of Admissions and Recruitment, 508-856-5628, Fax: 508-856-3659, E-mail: kendall.knight@umassmed.edu.

University of Medicine and Dentistry of New Jersey, Graduate School of Biomedical Sciences, Graduate Programs in Biomedical Sciences–Piscataway, Program in Cellular and Molecular Pharmacology, Piscataway, NJ 08854-5635. Offers MS, PhD, MD/PhD. *Degree requirements:* For master's, thesis, qualifying exam; for doctorate, thesis/dissertation, qualifying exam. *Entrance requirements:* Additional exam requirements/recommendations for international students: Required—TOEFL. Electronic applications accepted.

University of Nevada, Reno, Graduate School, Interdisciplinary Program in Cellular and Molecular Pharmacology and Physiology, Reno, NV 89557. Offers PhD. *Degree requirements:* For doctorate, one foreign language, thesis/dissertation. *Entrance requirements:* For doctorate, GRE General Test or MCAT, minimum GPA of 3.0. Additional exam requirements/recommendations for international students: Required—TOEFL (minimum score 500 paper-based; 173 computer-based; 61 iBT), IELTS (minimum score 6). Electronic applications accepted. *Expenses:* Tuition, state resident: full-time $2219; part-time $246 per credit. Tuition, nonresident: part-time $510 per credit. International tuition: $9009 full-time. Required fees: $59 per term. One-time fee: $101. Tuition and fees vary according to course load. *Faculty research:* Neuropharmacology, toxicology, cardiovascular pharmacology, neuromuscular pharmacology.

University of Pittsburgh, School of Medicine, Graduate Programs in Medicine, Program in Molecular Pharmacology, Pittsburgh, PA 15260. Offers MS, PhD. *Faculty:* 60 full-time (11 women). *Students:* 27 full-time (18 women); includes 2 Asian, non-Hispanic/Latino; 1 Hispanic/Latino, 5 international. Average age 27. 486 applicants, 14% accepted, 27 enrolled. In 2010, 5 doctorates awarded. *Degree requirements:* For doctorate, comprehensive exam, thesis/dissertation. *Entrance requirements:* For doctorate, GRE General Test, GRE Subject Test, minimum QPA of 3.0. Additional exam requirements/recommendations for international students: Required—TOEFL (minimum score 600 paper-based; 100 iBT), IELTS (minimum score 7). *Application deadline:* For fall admission, 12/15 priority date for domestic and international students. Application fee: $50. Electronic applications accepted. *Expenses:* Tuition, state resident: full-time $17,304; part-time $701 per credit. Tuition, nonresident: full-time $29,554; part-time $1210 per credit. Required fees: $740; $214 per term. Tuition and fees vary according to program. *Financial support:* In 2010–11, 4 fellowships with full tuition reimbursements (averaging $25,500 per year), 23 research assistantships with full tuition reimbursements (averaging $25,500 per year) were awarded; institutionally sponsored loans, scholarships/grants, traineeships, health care benefits, tuition waivers (full), and unspecified assistantships also available. *Faculty research:* Drug discovery, signal transduction, cancer therapeutics, neurophramacology, cardiovascular and renal pharmacology. *Unit head:* Dr. Patrick Pagano, Graduate Program Director, 412-383-6505, Fax: 412-648-9009, E-mail: pagano@pitt.edu. *Application contact:* Graduate Studies Administrator, 412-648-8957, Fax: 412-648-1007, E-mail: gradstudies@medschool.pitt.edu.

University of Southern California, Graduate School, School of Pharmacy, Graduate Programs in Molecular Pharmacology and Toxicology, Los Angeles, CA 90033. Offers pharmacology and pharmaceutical sciences (MS, PhD). *Faculty:* 20 full-time (13 women). *Students:* 19 full-time (11 women); includes 5 minority (1 Black or African American, non-Hispanic/Latino; 1 Asian, non-Hispanic/Latino; 1 Hispanic/Latino; 2 Two or more races, non-Hispanic/Latino), 10 international. 60 applicants, 10% accepted, 3 enrolled. In 2010, 1 master's, 3 doctorates awarded. Terminal master's awarded for partial completion of doctoral program. *Degree requirements:* For master's, comprehensive exam, thesis, 24 units of formal course work, excluding research and seminar courses; for doctorate, comprehensive exam, thesis/dissertation, 24 units of formal course work, excluding research and seminar courses. *Entrance requirements:* For master's and doctorate, GRE. Additional exam requirements/recommendations for international students: Required—TOEFL (minimum score 603 paper-based; 250 computer-based; 100 iBT). *Application deadline:* For fall admission, 1/15 for domestic and international students; for spring admission, 10/15 for domestic and international students. Application fee: $75.

Electronic applications accepted. *Expenses:* Contact institution. *Financial support:* In 2010–11, 15 students received support, including 4 fellowships with full tuition reimbursements available (averaging $23,395 per year), 4 research assistantships with full tuition reimbursements available (averaging $23,395 per year), 7 teaching assistantships with full tuition reimbursements available (averaging $23,395 per year); health care benefits and tuition waivers also available. *Faculty research:* Degenerative diseases, toxicology of drugs. *Unit head:* Dr. Roger Duncan, Director of Graduate Affairs Committee, 323-442-1449, Fax: 323-442-2258, E-mail: rduncan@usc.edu. *Application contact:* Linda Jankins, Student Affairs Assistant, 323-442-1474, Fax: 323-442-2258, E-mail: pharmgrd@usc.edu.

Molecular Toxicology

Massachusetts Institute of Technology, School of Science, Department of Biology, Cambridge, MA 02139-4307. Offers biochemistry (PhD); biological oceanography (PhD); biology (PhD); biophysical chemistry and molecular structure (PhD); cell biology (PhD); computational and systems biology (PhD); developmental biology (PhD); genetics (PhD); immunology (PhD); microbiology (PhD); molecular biology (PhD); neurobiology (PhD). *Faculty:* 56 full-time (14 women). *Students:* 251 full-time (135 women); includes 74 minority (4 Black or African American, non-Hispanic/Latino; 1 American Indian or Alaska Native, non-Hispanic/Latino; 29 Asian, non-Hispanic/Latino; 33 Hispanic/Latino; 7 Two or more races, non-Hispanic/Latino), 29 international. Average age 26. 652 applicants, 18% accepted, 58 enrolled. In 2010, 41 doctorates awarded. *Degree requirements:* For doctorate, comprehensive exam, thesis/dissertation. *Entrance requirements:* For doctorate, GRE General Test. Additional exam requirements/recommendations for international students: Required—TOEFL (minimum score 577 paper-based; 233 computer-based), IELTS (minimum score 6.5). *Application deadline:* For fall admission, 12/1 for domestic and international students. Application fee: $75. Electronic applications accepted. *Expenses:* Tuition: Full-time $38,940; part-time $605 per unit. Required fees: $272. *Financial support:* In 2010–11, 215 students received support, including 115 fellowships with tuition reimbursements available (averaging $33,090 per year), 132 research assistantships with tuition reimbursements available (averaging $31,846 per year); teaching assistantships with tuition reimbursements available, Federal Work-Study, institutionally sponsored loans, scholarships/grants, traineeships, health care benefits, and unspecified assistantships also available. *Faculty research:* DNA recombination, replication and repair; transcription and gene regulation; signal transduction; cell cycle; neuronal cell fate. Total annual research expenditures: $60.6 million. *Unit head:* Prof. Chris Kaiser, Head, 617-253-4701, E-mail: mitbio@mit.edu. *Application contact:* Biology Education Office, 617-253-3717, Fax: 617-258-9329, E-mail: gradbio@mit.edu.

New York University, Graduate School of Arts and Science, Department of Environmental Medicine, New York, NY 10012-1019. Offers environmental health sciences (MS, PhD), including biostatistics (PhD), environmental hygiene (MS), epidemiology (PhD), ergonomics and biomechanics (PhD), exposure assessment and health effects (PhD), molecular toxicology/carcinogenesis (PhD), toxicology. Part-time programs available. *Faculty:* 26 full-time (7 women). *Students:* 53 full-time (38 women), 10 part-time (3 women); includes 3 Black or African American, non-Hispanic/Latino; 4 Asian, non-Hispanic/Latino; 5 Hispanic/Latino, 23 international. Average age 30. 60 applicants, 48% accepted, 14 enrolled. In 2010, 8 master's, 5 doctorates awarded. Terminal master's awarded for partial completion of doctoral program. *Degree requirements:* For master's, thesis or alternative; for doctorate, one foreign language, thesis/dissertation, oral and written exams. *Entrance requirements:* For master's and doctorate, GRE General Test, GRE Subject Test, minimum GPA of 3.0; bachelor's degree in biological, physical, or engineering science. Additional exam requirements/recommendations for international students: Required—TOEFL. *Application deadline:* For fall admission, 12/15 for domestic students. Application fee: $90. *Financial support:* Fellowships with tuition reimbursements, teaching assistantships with tuition reimbursements, career-related internships or fieldwork, Federal Work-Study, institutionally sponsored loans, and health care benefits available. Financial award application deadline: 12/15; financial award applicants required to submit FAFSA. *Unit head:* Dr. Max Costa, Chair, 845-731-3661, Fax: 845-351-4510, E-mail: ehs@env.med.

nyu.edu. *Application contact:* Dr. Jerome J. Solomon, Director of Graduate Studies, 845-731-3661, Fax: 845-351-4510, E-mail: ehs@env.med.nyu.edu.

North Carolina State University, Graduate School, College of Agriculture and Life Sciences and College of Veterinary Medicine, Department of Environmental and Molecular Toxicology, Raleigh, NC 27695. Offers M Tox, MS, PhD. Terminal master's awarded for partial completion of doctoral program. *Degree requirements:* For master's, thesis (for some programs); for doctorate, thesis/dissertation. *Entrance requirements:* For master's and doctorate, GRE General Test, minimum GPA of 3.0. Electronic applications accepted. *Faculty research:* Chemical fate, carcinogenesis, developmental and endocrine toxicity, xenobiotic metabolism, signal transduction.

Oregon State University, Graduate School, College of Agricultural Sciences, Department of Environmental and Molecular Toxicology, Corvallis, OR 97331. Offers toxicology (MS, PhD).

Penn State Hershey Medical Center, College of Medicine, Graduate School Programs in the Biomedical Sciences, The Huck Institutes of the Life Sciences, Intercollege Graduate Program in Molecular Toxicology, Hershey, PA 17033. Offers MS, PhD, MD/PhD. *Students:* 13 applicants, 8% accepted, 1 enrolled. *Degree requirements:* For doctorate, comprehensive exam, thesis/dissertation. *Entrance requirements:* For doctorate, GRE. Additional exam requirements/recommendations for international students: Required—TOEFL (minimum score 550 paper-based). *Application deadline:* For fall admission, 3/1 priority date for domestic students, 2/1 priority date for international students. Applications are processed on a rolling basis. Application fee: $65. Electronic applications accepted. *Financial support:* In 2010–11, research assistantships with full tuition reimbursements (averaging $22,260 per year); fellowships with full tuition reimbursements, career-related internships or fieldwork, scholarships/grants, and unspecified assistantships also available. *Unit head:* Dr. Jung Yun, Head, 717-531-8982, E-mail: grad-hmc@psu.edu. *Application contact:* Kathy Shuey, Administrative Assistant, 717-531-8982, Fax: 717-531-0786, E-mail: grad-hmc@psu.edu.

University of California, Berkeley, Graduate Division, College of Natural Resources, Group in Molecular Toxicology, Berkeley, CA 94720-1500. Offers PhD. *Entrance requirements:* For doctorate, GRE General Test, 3 letters of recommendation.

University of California, Los Angeles, Graduate Division, School of Public Health, Department of Environmental Health Sciences, Interdepartmental Program in Molecular Toxicology, Los Angeles, CA 90095. Offers PhD. *Degree requirements:* For doctorate, thesis/dissertation, oral and written qualifying exams. *Entrance requirements:* For doctorate, GRE General Test. Electronic applications accepted.

University of Cincinnati, Graduate School, College of Medicine, Graduate Programs in Biomedical Sciences, Department of Environmental Health, Programs in Environmental Genetics and Molecular Toxicology, Cincinnati, OH 45221. Offers MS, PhD. *Degree requirements:* For doctorate, thesis/dissertation. *Entrance requirements:* For master's, GRE, minimum GPA of 3.0, 3 letters of recommendation. Additional exam requirements/recommendations for international students: Required—TOEFL (minimum score 520 paper-based; 190 computer-based).

Pharmacology

Albany Medical College, Center for Neuropharmacology and Neuroscience, Albany, NY 12208-3479. Offers MS, PhD. *Faculty:* 19 full-time (6 women), 8 part-time/adjunct (2 women). *Students:* 16 full-time (5 women); includes 1 minority (Black or African American, non-Hispanic/Latino), 3 international. Average age 24. 31 applicants, 19% accepted, 6 enrolled. In 2010, 1 master's, 3 doctorates awarded. Terminal master's awarded for partial completion of doctoral program. *Degree requirements:* For master's, thesis; for doctorate, comprehensive exam, thesis/dissertation. *Entrance requirements:* For master's, GRE General Test, all transcripts, letters of recommendation; for doctorate, GRE General Test, letters of recommendation. Additional exam requirements/recommendations for international students: Required—TOEFL. *Application deadline:* For fall admission, 3/15 priority date for domestic and international students. Applications are processed on a rolling basis. Application fee: $0 ($60 for international students). *Financial support:* In 2010–11, 3 fellowships with partial tuition reimbursements (averaging $20,772 per year), 18 research assistantships with full tuition reimbursements (averaging $24,000 per year) were awarded; Federal Work-Study, scholarships/grants, and tuition waivers (full) also available. Financial award applicants required to submit FAFSA. *Faculty research:* Molecular and cellular neuroscience, neuronal development, addiction. *Unit head:* Dr. Stanley D. Glick, Director, 518-262-5303, Fax: 518-262-5799, E-mail: cnninfo@mail.amc.edu. *Application contact:* Dr. Mark Fleck, Graduate Director, 518-262-5303, Fax: 518-262-5799, E-mail: cnninfo@mail.amc.edu.

Alliant International University–San Francisco, California School of Professional Psychology, Program in Psychopharmacology, San Francisco, CA 94133-1221. Offers Post-Doctoral MS. Part-time programs available. Postbaccalaureate distance learning degree programs offered. *Entrance requirements:* For master's, doctorate in clinical psychology, minimum GPA of 3.0 in psychology and overall. Additional exam requirements/recommendations for international students: Required—TOEFL. Electronic applications accepted.

American University of Beirut, Graduate Programs, Faculty of Medicine, Beirut, Lebanon. Offers biochemistry (MS); human morphology (MS); medicine (MD); microbiology and immunology (MS); neuroscience (MS); pharmacology and therapeutics (MS); physiology (MS). Part-time programs available. *Faculty:* 222 full-time (56 women), 58 part-time/adjunct (4 women). *Students:* 346 full-time (135 women), 69 part-time (57 women). Average age 23. In 2010, 81 first professional degrees, 19 master's awarded. *Degree requirements:* For master's, one foreign language, comprehensive exam, thesis (for some programs). *Entrance requirements:* For MD, MCAT, bachelor's degree; for master's, letter of recommendation. Additional exam requirements/recommendations for international students: Required—TOEFL (minimum score

600 paper-based; 250 computer-based; 100 iBT), IELTS (minimum score 7.5). *Application deadline:* For fall admission, 4/30 for domestic and international students; for spring admission, 11/1 for domestic and international students. Application fee: $50. *Expenses:* Tuition: Full-time $12,294; part-time $683 per credit. Required fees: $499; $499 per credit. Tuition and fees vary according to course load and program. *Financial support:* In 2010–11, 4 students received support. Career-related internships or fieldwork, institutionally sponsored loans, scholarships/grants, health care benefits, and unspecified assistantships available. Financial award application deadline: 2/2. *Faculty research:* Cancer research (targeted therapy, mechanisms of leukemogenesis, tumor cell extravasation and metastasis, cancer stem cells); stem cell research (regenerative medicine, drug discovery); genetic research (neurogenetics, hereditary cardiomyopathy, hemoglobinopathies, pharmacogenomics); neuroscience research (pain, neurodegenerative disorder); metabolism (inflammation and metabolism, metabolic disorder, diabetes mellitus). Total annual research expenditures: $1.2 million. *Unit head:* Dr. Mohamed Sayegh, Dean, 961-135-0000 Ext. 4700, Fax: 961-174-4464, E-mail: msayegh@aub.edu.lb. *Application contact:* Dr. Salim Kanaan, Director, Admissions Office, 961-135-0000 Ext. 2594, Fax: 961-175-0775, E-mail: sk00@aub.edu.lb.

Argosy University, Hawai'i, College of Psychology and Behavioral Sciences, Program in Psychopharmacology, Honolulu, HI 96813. Offers MS, Certificate.

Auburn University, College of Veterinary Medicine and Graduate School, Graduate Programs in Veterinary Medicine, Auburn University, AL 36849. Offers biomedical sciences (MS, PhD), including anatomy, physiology and pharmacology (MS), biomedical sciences (PhD), clinical sciences (MS), large animal surgery and medicine (MS), pathobiology (MS), radiology (MS), small animal surgery and medicine (MS); DVM/MS. Part-time programs available. *Faculty:* 100 full-time (40 women), 5 part-time/adjunct (1 woman). *Students:* 17 full-time (6 women), 51 part-time (35 women); includes 2 Black or African American, non-Hispanic/Latino; 1 American Indian or Alaska Native, non-Hispanic/Latino; 3 Asian, non-Hispanic/Latino; 2 Hispanic/Latino, 22 international. Average age 31. 70 applicants, 34% accepted, 10 enrolled. In 2010, 12 master's, 7 doctorates awarded. *Degree requirements:* For doctorate, thesis/dissertation. *Entrance requirements:* For master's, GRE General Test; for doctorate, GRE General Test, GRE Subject Test. *Application deadline:* For fall admission, 7/7 for domestic students; for spring admission, 11/24 for domestic students. Applications are processed on a rolling basis. Application fee: $50 ($60 for international students). Electronic applications accepted. *Expenses:* Tuition, state resident: full-time $7002. Tuition, nonresident: full-time $21,898. International tuition: $22,116 full-time. Required fees: $892. Tuition and fees vary according to course load

Pharmacology

Auburn University (continued)

and program. *Financial support:* Research assistantships, teaching assistantships, Federal Work-Study available. Support available to part-time students. Financial award application deadline: 3/15; financial award applicants required to submit FAFSA. *Unit head:* Dr. Timothy R. Boosinger, Dean, 334-844-4546. *Application contact:* Dr. George Flowers, Dean of the Graduate School, 334-844-2125.

Baylor College of Medicine, Graduate School of Biomedical Sciences, Department of Pharmacology, Houston, TX 77030-3498. Offers PhD, MD/PhD. *Faculty:* 17 full-time (1 woman). *Students:* 5 full-time (1 woman); includes 2 Black or African American, non-Hispanic/Latino, 2 international. Average age 24. 38 applicants, 16% accepted, 2 enrolled. *Degree requirements:* For doctorate, thesis/dissertation, public defense. *Entrance requirements:* For doctorate, GRE General Test, GRE Subject Test (strongly recommended), minimum GPA of 3.0. Additional exam requirements/recommendations for international students: Required—TOEFL. *Application deadline:* For fall admission, 1/1 priority date for domestic students. Application fee: $0. Electronic applications accepted. *Expenses:* Tuition: Full-time $11,000. Required fees: $4900. *Financial support:* In 2010–11, 5 students received support, including 2 fellowships with full tuition reimbursements available (averaging $3 per year); research assistantships with tuition reimbursements available, career-related internships or fieldwork, Federal Work-Study, institutionally sponsored loans, health care benefits, and students receive a scholarship unless there are grant funds available to pay tuition also available. Financial award applicants required to submit FAFSA. *Faculty research:* Drug discovery, antibiotics, antitumor, computational drug design, signal transduction complex. *Unit head:* Dr. P. K. Chan, Director, 713-798-7915, E-mail: pchan@bcm.edu. *Application contact:* Tran Kim, Graduate Program Administrator, 713-798-4457, E-mail: kimt@bcm.edu.

Boston University, School of Medicine, Division of Graduate Medical Sciences, Department of Pharmacology and Experimental Therapeutics, Boston, MA 02118. Offers MA, PhD, MD/PhD. *Faculty:* 11 full-time (4 women), 16 part-time/adjunct (4 women). *Students:* 8 full-time (6 women), 7 part-time (6 women); includes 1 Black or African American, non-Hispanic/Latino; 2 Asian, non-Hispanic/Latino; 1 Hispanic/Latino. 76 applicants, 12% accepted, 5 enrolled. In 2010, 1 doctorate awarded. Terminal master's awarded for partial completion of doctoral program. *Degree requirements:* For master's, thesis; for doctorate, thesis/dissertation. *Entrance requirements:* For master's and doctorate, GRE General Test, GRE Subject Test. Additional exam requirements/recommendations for international students: Required—TOEFL. *Application deadline:* For fall admission, 1/15 priority date for domestic students; for spring admission, 10/15 priority date for domestic students. Application fee: $75. Electronic applications accepted. *Expenses:* Tuition: Full-time $39,314; part-time $1228 per credit. Required fees: $40 per semester. *Financial support:* In 2010–11, 1 fellowship with full tuition reimbursement (averaging $30,500 per year), 9 research assistantships with full and partial tuition reimbursements (averaging $30,500 per year) were awarded; Federal Work-Study, scholarships/grants, traineeships, tuition waivers, and research stipends also available. Financial award applicants required to submit FAFSA. *Faculty research:* Molecular pharmacology, neuropharmacology, peptide receptors, psychopharmacology. *Unit head:* Dr. David H. Farb, Chairman, 617-638-4300, Fax: 617-638-4329, E-mail: dfarb@bu.edu. *Application contact:* Dr. Carol T. Walsh, Graduate Director, 617-638-4326, Fax: 617-638-4329, E-mail: ctwalsh@bu.edu.

Case Western Reserve University, School of Medicine and School of Graduate Studies, Graduate Programs in Medicine, Department of Pharmacology, Cleveland, OH 44106. Offers PhD, MD/PhD. Terminal master's awarded for partial completion of doctoral program. *Degree requirements:* For doctorate, comprehensive exam, thesis/dissertation. *Entrance requirements:* For doctorate, GRE General Test, GRE Subject Test, or MCAT. Additional exam requirements/recommendations for international students: Required—TOEFL. Electronic applications accepted. *Faculty research:* Aspects of cellular, molecular, and clinical pharmacology; neuroendocrine pharmacology; drug metabolism.

Columbia University, College of Physicians and Surgeons, Department of Pharmacology, New York, NY 10032. Offers pharmacology (M Phil, MA, PhD); pharmacology-toxicology (M Phil, MA, PhD); MD/PhD. Only candidates for the PhD are admitted. Terminal master's awarded for partial completion of doctoral program. *Degree requirements:* For doctorate, thesis/dissertation. *Entrance requirements:* For master's and doctorate, GRE General Test. Additional exam requirements/recommendations for international students: Required—TOEFL. *Faculty research:* Cardiovascular pharmacology, receptor pharmacology, neuropharmacology, membrane biophysics, eicosanoids.

Cornell University, Graduate School, Graduate Fields of Comparative Biomedical Sciences, Field of Pharmacology, Ithaca, NY 14853-0001. Offers MS, PhD. *Faculty:* 29 full-time (7 women). *Students:* 16 full-time (10 women); includes 1 Black or African American, non-Hispanic/Latino; 2 Hispanic/Latino, 4 international. Average age 26. 22 applicants, 23% accepted, 4 enrolled. In 2010, 1 doctorate awarded. *Degree requirements:* For master's, thesis; for doctorate, comprehensive exam, thesis/dissertation. *Entrance requirements:* For master's and doctorate, GRE General Test, 3 letters of recommendation. Additional exam requirements/recommendations for international students: Required—TOEFL (minimum score 550 paper-based; 213 computer-based; 77 iBT). *Application deadline:* For fall admission, 12/5 for domestic students. Application fee: $70. Electronic applications accepted. *Expenses:* Tuition: Full-time $29,500. Required fees: $76. Tuition and fees vary according to degree level and program. *Financial support:* In 2010–11, 9 students received support, including 4 fellowships with full tuition reimbursements available, 9 research assistantships with full tuition reimbursements available, 2 teaching assistantships with full tuition reimbursements available; institutionally sponsored loans, scholarships/grants, health care benefits, tuition waivers (full and partial), and unspecified assistantships also available. Financial award applicants required to submit FAFSA. *Faculty research:* Signal transduction, ion channels, calcium signaling, G proteins, cancer cell biology. *Unit head:* Director of Graduate Studies, 607-253-3276, Fax: 607-253-3756. *Application contact:* Graduate Field Assistant, 607-253-3276, Fax: 607-253-3756, E-mail: graduate_edcvm@cornell.edu.

Cornell University, Joan and Sanford I. Weill Medical College and Graduate School of Medical Sciences, Weill Cornell Graduate School of Medical Sciences, Pharmacology Program, New York, NY 10065. Offers MS, PhD. *Faculty:* 31 full-time (6 women). *Students:* 66 full-time (41 women); includes 3 Black or African American, non-Hispanic/Latino; 8 Asian, non-Hispanic/Latino; 2 Hispanic/Latino, 15 international. 76 applicants, 25% accepted, 12 enrolled. In 2010, 1 master's, 6 doctorates awarded. Terminal master's awarded for partial completion of doctoral program. *Degree requirements:* For master's, comprehensive exam; for doctorate, thesis/dissertation, final exam. *Entrance requirements:* For doctorate, GRE General Test, previous course work in natural and/or health sciences. Additional exam requirements/recommendations for international students: Required—TOEFL. *Application deadline:* For fall admission, 12/1 for domestic students. Application fee: $60. *Expenses:* Tuition: Full-time $45,545. Required fees: $2805. *Financial support:* In 2010–11, 15 fellowships (averaging $24,189 per year) were awarded; scholarships/grants, health care benefits, and stipends (given to all students) also available. *Faculty research:* Modulation of gene expression by drugs, signal transduction, nitric oxide signaling RNA trafficking, neuropharmacology of opiates. *Unit head:* Dr. Geoffrey Abbott, Director, 212-746-6275, E-mail: gwa2001@med.cornell.edu. *Application contact:* Olga Willis, Program Coordinator, 212-746-6250, E-mail: orw2003@med.cornell.edu.

Creighton University, School of Medicine and Graduate School, Graduate Programs in Medicine, Department of Pharmacology, Omaha, NE 68178-0001. Offers pharmaceutical sciences (MS); pharmacology (MS, PhD); Pharm D/MS. Terminal master's awarded for partial completion of doctoral program. *Degree requirements:* For master's, comprehensive exam, thesis; for doctorate, comprehensive exam, thesis/dissertation, oral and written preliminary exams. *Entrance requirements:* For master's and doctorate, GRE General Test, minimum GPA of 3.0, undergraduate degree in sciences. Additional exam requirements/recommendations for international students: Required—TOEFL. Electronic applications accepted. *Expenses:* Tuition: Full-time $12,168; part-time $676 per credit hour. Required fees: $131 per semester. Tuition and fees vary according to program. *Faculty research:* Pharmacology secretion, cardiovascular-renal pharmacology, adrenergic receptors, signal transduction, genetic regulation of receptors.

Dalhousie University, Faculty of Graduate Studies and Faculty of Medicine, Graduate Programs in Medicine, Department of Pharmacology, Halifax, NS B3H 4R2, Canada. Offers M Sc, PhD. *Degree requirements:* For master's, thesis; for doctorate, comprehensive exam, thesis/dissertation. *Entrance requirements:* Additional exam requirements/recommendations for international students: Required—TOEFL, IELTS, 1 of the following 5 approved tests: TOEFL, IELTS, CAEL, CANTEST, Michigan English Language Assessment Battery. Electronic applications accepted. *Faculty research:* Electrophysiology and neurochemistry; endocrinology, immunology and cancer research; molecular biology; cardiovascular and autonomic; drug biotransformation and metabolism; ocular pharmacology.

Dartmouth College, Arts and Sciences Graduate Programs, Department of Pharmacology and Toxicology, Hanover, NH 03755. Offers PhD, MD/PhD. *Degree requirements:* For doctorate, thesis/dissertation. *Entrance requirements:* For doctorate, GRE General Test, GRE Subject Test, bachelor's degree in biological, chemical, or physical science. Additional exam requirements/recommendations for international students: Required—TOEFL. Electronic applications accepted. *Faculty research:* Molecular biology of carcinogenesis, DNA repair and gene expression, biochemical and environmental toxicology, protein receptor ligand interactions.

Drexel University, College of Medicine, Biomedical Graduate Programs, Pharmacology and Physiology Program, Philadelphia, PA 19104-2875. Offers MS, PhD, MD/PhD. Part-time programs available. Terminal master's awarded for partial completion of doctoral program. *Degree requirements:* For master's, comprehensive exam; for doctorate, thesis/dissertation, qualifying exam. *Entrance requirements:* For master's, GRE General Test, minimum GPA of 2.75; for doctorate, GRE General Test, minimum GPA of 3.0. Additional exam requirements/recommendations for international students: Required—TOEFL. Electronic applications accepted. *Faculty research:* Cardiovascular pharmacology, drugs of abuse, neurotransmitter mechanisms.

Duke University, Graduate School, Department of Pharmacology and Cancer Biology, Durham, NC 27710. Offers pharmacology (PhD). *Faculty:* 39 full-time. *Students:* 43 full-time (23 women). Average age 23. 81 applicants, 14% accepted, 7 enrolled. In 2010, 14 doctorates awarded. *Degree requirements:* For doctorate, thesis/dissertation. *Entrance requirements:* For doctorate, GRE General Test, minimum GPA of 2.8. Additional exam requirements/recommendations for international students: Required—TOEFL or IELTS (preferred). *Application deadline:* For fall admission, 12/8 priority date for domestic and international students. Application fee: $75. Electronic applications accepted. *Financial support:* In 2010–11, 11 fellowships with tuition reimbursements (averaging $27,000 per year), 8 research assistantships with tuition reimbursements (averaging $27,000 per year), 2 teaching assistantships with tuition reimbursements (averaging $27,000 per year) were awarded; Federal Work-Study, scholarships/grants, traineeships, health care benefits, and unspecified assistantships also available. Financial award application deadline: 12/31. *Faculty research:* Developmental pharmacology, neuropharmacology, molecular pharmacology, toxicology, cell growth. *Unit head:* Dr. Jeffrey Rathmell, Director of Graduate Studies, 919-681-1084, Fax: 919-684-8922, E-mail: jeff.rathmell@duke.edu. *Application contact:* Jamie Baize-Smith, Assistant to the Director of Graduate Studies, 919-613-8600, Fax: 919-681-7767, E-mail: baize@duke.edu.

Duquesne University, Mylan School of Pharmacy, Graduate School of Pharmaceutical Sciences, Program in Pharmacology, Pittsburgh, PA 15282-0001. Offers MS, PhD. *Faculty:* 6 full-time (4 women). *Students:* 15 full-time (11 women); includes 1 Black or African American, non-Hispanic/Latino, 4 international. 30 applicants, 10% accepted, 2 enrolled. In 2010, 1 doctorate awarded. *Degree requirements:* For master's, thesis; for doctorate, comprehensive exam, thesis/dissertation. *Entrance requirements:* For master's and doctorate, GRE General Test. Additional exam requirements/recommendations for international students: Required—TOEFL. *Application deadline:* For fall admission, 2/1 priority date for domestic and international students; for spring admission, 10/1 priority date for domestic and international students. Applications are processed on a rolling basis. Application fee: $50. Electronic applications accepted. *Expenses:* Tuition: Part-time $884 per credit. Required fees: $84 per credit. Tuition and fees vary according to course load. *Financial support:* In 2010–11, 15 students received support, including 15 teaching assistantships with full tuition reimbursements available; research assistantships with full tuition reimbursements available. *Unit head:* Dr. David A. Johnson, Head, 412-396-5952. *Application contact:* Information Contact, 412-396-1172, E-mail: gsps-adm@duq.edu.

East Carolina University, Brody School of Medicine, Department of Pharmacology, Greenville, NC 27858-4353. Offers PhD, MD/PhD. *Degree requirements:* For doctorate, comprehensive exam, thesis/dissertation. *Entrance requirements:* For doctorate, GRE General Test, GRE Subject Test. Additional exam requirements/recommendations for international students: Required—TOEFL. *Expenses:* Tuition, state resident: full-time $3130; part-time $391.25 per credit hour. Tuition, nonresident: full-time $13,817; part-time $1727.13 per credit hour. Required fees: $1916; $239.50 per credit hour. Tuition and fees vary according to campus/location and program. *Faculty research:* GNS/behavioral pharmacology, cardiovascular pharmacology, cell signaling and second messenger, effects of calcium channel blockers.

East Tennessee State University, James H. Quillen College of Medicine, Biomedical Science Graduate Program, Johnson City, TN 37614. Offers anatomy (PhD); biochemistry (PhD); microbiology (PhD); pharmacology (PhD); physiology (PhD). Part-time programs available. *Faculty:* 49 full-time (12 women), 1 (woman) part-time/adjunct. *Students:* 27 full-time (14 women), 4 part-time (2 women); includes 4 minority (1 Black or African American, non-Hispanic/Latino; 1 Asian, non-Hispanic/Latino; 2 Hispanic/Latino), 5 international. Average age 32. 62 applicants, 11% accepted, 7 enrolled. In 2010, 2 doctorates awarded. Terminal master's awarded for partial completion of doctoral program. *Degree requirements:* For doctorate, thesis/dissertation, comprehensive qualifying exam. *Entrance requirements:* For doctorate, GRE General Test, GRE Subject Test. Additional exam requirements/recommendations for international students: Required—TOEFL (minimum score 550 paper-based; 213 computer-based; 79 iBT). *Application deadline:* For fall admission, 3/15 priority date for domestic students, 3/1 priority date for international students. Application fee: $25 ($35 for international students). Electronic applications accepted. *Expenses:* Contact institution. *Financial support:* In 2010–11, 7 research assistantships with full tuition reimbursements (averaging $15,000 per year) were awarded; teaching assistantships with full tuition reimbursements, career-related internships or fieldwork, institutionally sponsored loans, scholarships/grants, and unspecified assistantships also available. Financial award application deadline: 7/1; financial award applicants required to submit FAFSA. Total annual research expenditures: $2.1 million. *Unit head:* Dr. Mitchell E. Robinson, Assistant Dean/Director, 423-439-4658, E-mail: robinson@etsu.edu. *Application contact:* Edwin D. Taylor, Assistant Dean for Admissions and Records, 423-439-4753, Fax: 423-439-8206.

Emory University, Laney Graduate School, Division of Biological and Biomedical Sciences, Program in Molecular and Systems Pharmacology, Atlanta, GA 30322-1100. Offers PhD. *Faculty:* 45 full-time (9 women). *Students:* 52 full-time (27 women); includes 10 Black or African American, non-Hispanic/Latino; 2 Asian, non-Hispanic/Latino, 4 international. Average age 27. 119 applicants, 15% accepted, 10 enrolled. In 2010, 8 doctorates awarded. *Degree requirements:* For doctorate, comprehensive exam, thesis/dissertation. *Entrance requirements:* For doctorate, GRE General Test, minimum GPA of 3.0 in science course work (recommended). Additional exam requirements/recommendations for international students: Required—TOEFL. *Application deadline:* For fall admission, 2/1 for domestic students, 12/1 for international students. Application fee: $75. Electronic applications accepted. *Expenses:* Tuition: Full-time $33,800. Required fees: $1300. *Financial support:* In 2010–11, 16 students received support, including 16 fellowships with full tuition reimbursements available (averaging $25,000 per year); institutionally sponsored loans, scholarships/grants, health care benefits, and tuition waivers (full) also available. *Faculty research:* Transmembrane signaling, neuropharmacology, neurophysiology and neurodegeneration, metabolism and molecular toxicology, cell and developmental biology. *Unit head:* Dr. Randy Hal, Program Director, 404-727-3699, Fax:

404-727-0365, E-mail: rhall3@emory.edu. *Application contact:* Kathy Smith, Director of Recruitment and Admissions, 404-727-2547, Fax: 404-727-3322, E-mail: kathy.smith@emory.edu.

Fairleigh Dickinson University, College at Florham, Silberman College of Business, Program in Pharmaceutical Studies, Madison, NJ 07940-1099. Offers MBA, Certificate. *Students:* 8 full-time (4 women), 12 part-time (5 women), 7 international. Average age 30. 10 applicants, 70% accepted, 2 enrolled. In 2010, 14 master's awarded. *Application deadline:* Applications are processed on a rolling basis. Application fee: $40.

Florida Agricultural and Mechanical University, Division of Graduate Studies, Research, and Continuing Education, College of Pharmacy and Pharmaceutical Sciences, Graduate Programs in Pharmaceutical Sciences, Tallahassee, FL 32307-3200. Offers environmental toxicology (PhD); medicinal chemistry (MS, PhD); pharmaceutics (MS, PhD); pharmacology/toxicology (MS, PhD); pharmacy administration (MS). *Accreditation:* CEPH. *Degree requirements:* For master's, comprehensive exam, thesis, publishable paper; for doctorate, comprehensive exam, thesis/dissertation, publishable paper. *Entrance requirements:* For master's and doctorate, GRE General Test, minimum GPA of 3.0 in last 60 hours. Additional exam requirements/recommendations for international students: Required—TOEFL. *Faculty research:* Anticancer agents, anti-inflammatory drugs, chronopharmacology, neuroendocrinology, microbiology.

Georgetown University, Graduate School of Arts and Sciences, Programs in Biomedical Sciences, Department of Pharmacology, Washington, DC 20057. Offers MS, PhD, MD/PhD, MS/PhD. *Degree requirements:* For doctorate, comprehensive exam, thesis/dissertation. *Entrance requirements:* For doctorate, GRE General Test, previous course work in biology and chemistry. Additional exam requirements/recommendations for international students: Required—TOEFL. *Faculty research:* Neuropharmacology, techniques in biochemistry and tissue culture.

Georgia Health Sciences University, College of Graduate Studies, Program in Pharmacology, Augusta, GA 30912. Offers MS, PhD. *Faculty:* 12 full-time (4 women), 2 part-time/adjunct (0 women). *Students:* 9 full-time (5 women); includes 1 Black or African American, non-Hispanic/Latino; 1 Asian, non-Hispanic/Latino; 1 Hispanic/Latino, 3 international. Average age 29. In 2010, 1 doctorate awarded. *Degree requirements:* For doctorate, comprehensive exam, thesis/dissertation. *Entrance requirements:* For doctorate, GRE General Test. Additional exam requirements/recommendations for international students: Required—TOEFL (minimum score 550 paper-based; 213 computer-based; 79 iBT). *Application deadline:* For fall admission, 1/15 for domestic and international students. Application fee: $30. Electronic applications accepted. *Expenses:* Tuition, state resident: full-time $7500; part-time $313 per semester hour. Tuition, nonresident: full-time $24,772; part-time $1033 per semester hour. Required fees: $1112. *Financial support:* In 2010–11, 3 students received support, including 8 research assistantships with partial tuition reimbursements available (averaging $23,000 per year); fellowships with partial tuition reimbursements available, Federal Work-Study, institutionally sponsored loans, and scholarships/grants also available. Support available to part-time students. Financial award application deadline: 5/31; financial award applicants required to submit FAFSA. *Faculty research:* Protein signaling, neural development, cardiovascular pharmacology, endothelial cell function, neuropharmacology. Total annual research expenditures: $3.6 million. *Unit head:* Dr. R. William Caldwell, Chair, 706-721-3383, Fax: 706-721-6059, E-mail: wcaldwell@georgiahealth.edu. *Application contact:* Dr. Patricia L. Cameron, Acting Vice Dean, 706-721-3279, E-mail: pcameron@georgiahealth.edu.

Howard University, College of Medicine, Department of Pharmacology, Washington, DC 20059-0002. Offers MS, PhD, MD/PhD. Part-time programs available. *Degree requirements:* For master's, comprehensive exam, thesis; for doctorate, one foreign language, comprehensive exam, thesis/dissertation, qualifying exam. *Entrance requirements:* For master's, GRE General Test, minimum GPA of 3.2, BS in chemistry, biology, pharmacy, psychology or related field; for doctorate, GRE General Test, minimum graduate GPA of 3.2. *Faculty research:* Biochemical pharmacology, molecular pharmacology, neuropharmacology, drug metabolism, cancer research.

Idaho State University, Office of Graduate Studies, College of Pharmacy, Department of Biomedical and Pharmaceutical Sciences, Pocatello, ID 83209-8334. Offers biopharmaceutical analysis (PhD); drug delivery (PhD); medicinal chemistry (PhD); pharmaceutical sciences (MS); pharmacology (PhD). Part-time programs available. *Degree requirements:* For master's, one foreign language, comprehensive exam, thesis, thesis research, classes in speech and technical writing; for doctorate, comprehensive exam, thesis/dissertation, written and oral exams, classes in speech and technical writing. *Entrance requirements:* For master's, GRE General Test, minimum GPA of 3.0, 3 letters of recommendation; for doctorate, GRE General Test, BS in pharmacy or related field, minimum GPA of 3.0, 3 letters of recommendation. Additional exam requirements/recommendations for international students: Required—TOEFL (minimum score 550 paper-based; 213 computer-based; 80 iBT). Electronic applications accepted. *Expenses:* Contact institution. *Faculty research:* Metabolic toxicity of heavy metals, neuroendocrine pharmacology, cardiovascular pharmacology, cancer biology, immunopharmacology.

Indiana University–Purdue University Indianapolis, Indiana University School of Medicine, Department of Pharmacology and Toxicology, Indianapolis, IN 46202-2896. Offers pharmacology (MS, PhD); toxicology (MS, PhD); MD/PhD. *Faculty:* 11 full-time (2 women). *Students:* 24 full-time (17 women); includes 2 minority (1 Asian, non-Hispanic/Latino; 1 Hispanic/Latino), 12 international. Average age 27. 18 applicants, 39% accepted, 7 enrolled. In 2010, 1 master's, 3 doctorates awarded. Terminal master's awarded for partial completion of doctoral program. *Degree requirements:* For master's, thesis; for doctorate, thesis/dissertation. *Entrance requirements:* For master's and doctorate, GRE General Test, GRE Subject Test, minimum GPA of 3.0. *Application deadline:* For fall admission, 1/15 priority date for domestic students. Applications are processed on a rolling basis. Application fee: $55 ($65 for international students). *Financial support:* In 2010–11, 14 students received support, including 7 teaching assistantships (averaging $20,940 per year); fellowships with partial tuition reimbursements available, research assistantships with partial tuition reimbursements available, Federal Work-Study, institutionally sponsored loans, and tuition waivers (partial) also available. Financial award application deadline: 1/15. *Faculty research:* Neuropharmacology, cardiovascular biopharmacology, chemotherapy, oncogenesis. *Unit head:* Dr. Michael Vasko, Chairman, 317-274-7844, Fax: 317-274-7714. *Application contact:* Director of Graduate Studies, 317-274-1564, Fax: 317-274-7714.

The Johns Hopkins University, School of Medicine, Graduate Programs in Medicine, Department of Pharmacology and Molecular Sciences, Baltimore, MD 21205. Offers PhD. *Faculty:* 42 full-time (8 women). *Students:* 60 full-time (28 women); includes 15 minority (5 Black or African American, non-Hispanic/Latino; 9 Asian, non-Hispanic/Latino; 1 Hispanic/Latino), 16 international. 180 applicants, 10% accepted, 9 enrolled. In 2010, 10 doctorates awarded. *Degree requirements:* For doctorate, comprehensive exam, thesis/dissertation, departmental seminar. *Entrance requirements:* For doctorate, GRE General Test. Additional exam requirements/recommendations for international students: Required—TOEFL. *Application deadline:* For fall admission, 1/10 for domestic and international students. Application fee: $85. Electronic applications accepted. *Unit head:* Dr. Philip A. Cole, Chairman, 410-614-0540, Fax: 410-614-7717, E-mail: pcole@jhmi.edu. *Application contact:* Dr. James T. Stivers, Director of Admissions, 410-955-7117, Fax: 410-955-3023, E-mail: jstivers@jhmi.edu.

Kent State University, School of Biomedical Sciences, Program in Pharmacology, Kent, OH 44242-0001. Offers MS, PhD. Offered in cooperation with Northeastern Ohio Universities College of Medicine. Terminal master's awarded for partial completion of doctoral program. *Degree requirements:* For master's, thesis; for doctorate, thesis/dissertation. *Entrance requirements:* For master's and doctorate, GRE General Test, minimum GPA of 3.0, 3 letters of recommendation. Additional exam requirements/recommendations for international students: Required—TOEFL. Electronic applications accepted. *Expenses:* Tuition, state resident: full-time $7866; part-time $437 per credit hour. Tuition, nonresident: full-time $14,022; part-time $779 per credit hour. *Faculty research:* Neuropharmacology, psychotherapeutics and substance abuse, molecular biology of substance abuse, toxicology.

Loma Linda University, School of Medicine, Department of Physiology/Pharmacology, Loma Linda, CA 92350. Offers MS, PhD. Part-time programs available. *Degree requirements:* For master's, thesis or alternative; for doctorate, 2 foreign languages, thesis/dissertation. *Entrance requirements:* For master's and doctorate, GRE General Test. *Faculty research:* Drug metabolism, biochemical pharmacology, structure and function of cell membranes, neuropharmacology.

Long Island University, Brooklyn Campus, Arnold and Marie Schwartz College of Pharmacy and Health Sciences, Graduate Programs in Pharmacy, Division of Pharmaceutical Sciences, Brooklyn, NY 11201-8423. Offers cosmetic science (MS); industrial pharmacy (MS); pharmaceutics (PhD); pharmacology/toxicology (MS). Part-time and evening/weekend programs available. Terminal master's awarded for partial completion of doctoral program. *Degree requirements:* For master's, thesis optional; for doctorate, thesis/dissertation, candidacy exam. *Entrance requirements:* For master's and doctorate, minimum GPA of 3.0.

Louisiana State University Health Sciences Center, School of Graduate Studies in New Orleans, Department of Pharmacology and Experimental Therapeutics, New Orleans, LA 70112-2223. Offers MS, PhD, MD/PhD. Terminal master's awarded for partial completion of doctoral program. *Degree requirements:* For master's, comprehensive exam, thesis; for doctorate, comprehensive exam, thesis/dissertation. *Entrance requirements:* For master's, GRE; for doctorate, GRE General Test. Additional exam requirements/recommendations for international students: Required—TOEFL. *Faculty research:* Neuropharmacology, gastrointestinal pharmacology, drug metabolism, behavioral pharmacology, cardiovascular pharmacology.

Louisiana State University Health Sciences Center at Shreveport, Department of Pharmacology, Toxicology and Neuroscience, Shreveport, LA 71130-3932. Offers pharmacology (PhD); MD/PhD. Terminal master's awarded for partial completion of doctoral program. *Degree requirements:* For doctorate, thesis/dissertation. *Entrance requirements:* For doctorate, GRE General Test, minimum GPA of 3.0. Additional exam requirements/recommendations for international students: Required—TOEFL. *Faculty research:* Behavioral, cardiovascular, clinical, and gastrointestinal pharmacology; neuropharmacology; psychopharmacology; drug abuse; pharmacokinetics; neuroendocrinology, psychoneuroimmunology, and stress; toxicology.

Loyola University Chicago, Graduate School, Department of Molecular Pharmacology and Therapeutics, Chicago, IL 60626. Offers MS, PhD, MD/PhD, MS/MBA. *Faculty:* 16 full-time (4 women), 10 part-time/adjunct (2 women). *Students:* 10 full-time (7 women), 3 international. Average age 27. 32 applicants, 9% accepted, 2 enrolled. In 2010, 1 master's, 3 doctorates awarded. Terminal master's awarded for partial completion of doctoral program. *Degree requirements:* For master's, comprehensive exam, thesis; for doctorate, comprehensive exam, thesis/dissertation. *Entrance requirements:* For master's and doctorate, GRE General Test, minimum GPA of 3.0. Additional exam requirements/recommendations for international students: Required—TOEFL. *Application deadline:* For fall admission, 2/1 for domestic and international students. Application fee: $50. Electronic applications accepted. *Expenses:* Tuition: Full-time $14,940; part-time $830 per credit hour. Required fees: $87 per semester. Part-time tuition and fees vary according to course load and program. *Financial support:* In 2010–11, 2 fellowships with full tuition reimbursements (averaging $32,165 per year), 7 research assistantships with full tuition reimbursements (averaging $25,000 per year), 1 teaching assistantship with full tuition reimbursement (averaging $36,000 per year) were awarded; career-related internships or fieldwork and Federal Work-Study also available. Financial award application deadline: 2/1; financial award applicants required to submit FAFSA. *Faculty research:* Neuropharmacology, molecular pharmacology, neuroendocrinology, hematopharmacology, neurodegeneration. *Unit head:* Dr. Tarun Patel, Chair, 708-216-5773, Fax: 708-216-6956. *Application contact:* Dr. Kenneth L. Byron, Graduate Program Director, 708-327-2819, Fax: 708-216-6596, E-mail: kbyron@luc.edu.

Massachusetts College of Pharmacy and Health Sciences, Graduate Studies, Program in Pharmacology, Boston, MA 02115-5896. Offers MS, PhD. *Accreditation:* ACPE (one or more programs are accredited). Terminal master's awarded for partial completion of doctoral program. *Degree requirements:* For master's, oral defense of thesis; for doctorate, one foreign language, oral defense of dissertation, qualifying exam. *Entrance requirements:* For master's and doctorate, GRE General Test, minimum QPA of 3.0. Additional exam requirements/recommendations for international students: Required—TOEFL (minimum score 550 paper-based; 213 computer-based; 79 iBT). *Faculty research:* Neuropharmacology, cardiovascular pharmacology, nutritional pharmacology, pulmonary physiology, drug metabolism.

McGill University, Faculty of Graduate and Postdoctoral Studies, Faculty of Medicine, Department of Pharmacology and Therapeutics, Montréal, QC H3A 2T5, Canada. Offers M Sc, PhD.

McMaster University, Faculty of Health Sciences and School of Graduate Studies, Program in Medical Sciences, Physiology/Pharmacology Area, Hamilton, ON L8S 4M2, Canada. Offers M Sc, PhD, MD/PhD. *Degree requirements:* For master's, thesis; for doctorate, comprehensive exam, thesis/dissertation. *Entrance requirements:* For master's, honors B Sc, B+ average in related field; for doctorate, M Sc, minimum B+ average, students with proven research experience and an A average may be admitted with a B Sc degree. Additional exam requirements/recommendations for international students: Required—TOEFL (minimum score 580 paper-based; 237 computer-based; 92 iBT).

Medical College of Wisconsin, Graduate School of Biomedical Sciences, Department of Pharmacology and Toxicology, Milwaukee, WI 53226-0509. Offers PhD, MD/PhD. Terminal master's awarded for partial completion of doctoral program. *Degree requirements:* For doctorate, comprehensive exam, thesis/dissertation, oral and written qualifying exams. *Entrance requirements:* For doctorate, GRE General Test, minimum B average. Additional exam requirements/recommendations for international students: Required—TOEFL. *Expenses:* Tuition: Full-time $30,000; part-time $710 per credit. Required fees: $150. *Faculty research:* Cardiovascular physiology and pharmacology, drugs of abuse, environmental and aquatic toxicology, central nervous system and biochemical pharmacology, signal transduction.

Meharry Medical College, School of Graduate Studies, Program in Biomedical Sciences, Pharmacology Emphasis, Nashville, TN 37208-9989. Offers PhD, MD/PhD. *Degree requirements:* For doctorate, comprehensive exam, thesis/dissertation. *Entrance requirements:* For doctorate, GRE. *Faculty research:* Neuropharmacology, cardiovascular pharmacology, behavioral pharmacology, molecular pharmacology, drug metabolism, anticancer.

Michigan State University, College of Human Medicine and The Graduate School, Graduate Programs in Human Medicine, East Lansing, MI 48824. Offers biochemistry and molecular biology (MS, PhD); epidemiology (MS, PhD); microbiology (MS); microbiology and molecular genetics (PhD); pharmacology and toxicology (MS, PhD); physiology (MS, PhD); public health (MPH). *Entrance requirements:* Additional exam requirements/recommendations for international students: Required—TOEFL.

Michigan State University, College of Osteopathic Medicine and The Graduate School, Graduate Studies in Osteopathic Medicine and Graduate Programs in Human Medicine and Graduate Programs in Veterinary Medicine, Department of Pharmacology and Toxicology, East Lansing, MI 48824. Offers integrative pharmacology (MS); pharmacology and toxicology (MS, PhD); pharmacology and toxicology–environmental toxicology (PhD). *Entrance requirements:* Additional exam requirements/recommendations for international students: Required—TOEFL (minimum score 600 paper-based; 220 computer-based). Electronic applications accepted.

Michigan State University, College of Veterinary Medicine and The Graduate School, Graduate Programs in Veterinary Medicine, East Lansing, MI 48824. Offers comparative medicine and integrative biology (MS, PhD), including comparative medicine and integrative biology, comparative medicine and integrative biology–environmental toxicology (PhD); food safety and toxicology (MS), including food safety; integrative toxicology (PhD), including animal science–environmental toxicology, biochemistry and molecular biology–environmental toxicology,

Pharmacology

Michigan State University (continued)
chemistry–environmental toxicology, crop and soil sciences–environmental toxicology, environmental engineering–environmental toxicology, environmental geosciences–environmental toxicology, fisheries and wildlife–environmental toxicology, food science–environmental toxicology, forestry–environmental toxicology, genetics–environmental toxicology, human nutrition–environmental toxicology, microbiology–environmental toxicology, pharmacology and toxicology–environmental toxicology, zoology–environmental toxicology; large animal clinical sciences (MS, PhD); microbiology and molecular genetics (MS, PhD), including industrial microbiology, microbiology, microbiology and molecular genetics, microbiology–environmental toxicology (PhD); pathobiology and diagnostic investigation (MS, PhD), including pathology, pathology–environmental toxicology (PhD); pharmacology and toxicology (MS, PhD); pharmacology and toxicology–environmental toxicology (PhD); physiology (MS, PhD); small animal clinical sciences (MS). Electronic applications accepted. *Faculty research:* Molecular genetics, food safety/toxicology, comparative orthopedics, airway disease, population medicine.

New York Medical College, Graduate School of Basic Medical Sciences, Program in Pharmacology, Valhalla, NY 10595-1691. Offers MS, PhD, MD/PhD. Part-time and evening/weekend programs available. *Faculty:* 11 full-time (2 women), 1 part-time/adjunct (0 women). *Students:* 7 full-time (5 women), 8 part-time (6 women); includes 4 minority (1 Black or African American, non-Hispanic/Latino; 3 Asian, non-Hispanic/Latino), 3 international. Average age 27. 11 applicants, 100% accepted, 5 enrolled. In 2010, 1 master's, 3 doctorates awarded. Terminal master's awarded for partial completion of doctoral program. *Degree requirements:* For master's, thesis; for doctorate, comprehensive exam, thesis/dissertation. *Entrance requirements:* For master's and doctorate, GRE General Test. Additional exam requirements/recommendations for international students: Required—TOEFL. *Application deadline:* For fall admission, 7/1 priority date for domestic students, 5/1 priority date for international students; for spring admission, 12/1 priority date for domestic students, 10/1 priority date for international students. Applications are processed on a rolling basis. Application fee: $50 ($75 for international students). Electronic applications accepted. *Financial support:* In 2010–11, 1 fellowship, 2 research assistantships with full tuition reimbursements (averaging $24,500 per year) were awarded; Federal Work-Study, institutionally sponsored loans, scholarships/grants, traineeships, health care benefits, tuition waivers, unspecified assistantships, and health benefits (for PhD applicants only) also available. Financial award applicants required to submit FAFSA. *Faculty research:* Eicosanoids in angiogenesis and cancer; hormonal, cytokine and inflammatory mediators in hypertension and target organ damage; ocular pharmacology; mechanisms of diabetes and prediabetes; potassium channel electrophysiology and regulations of kidney function. *Unit head:* Dr. Charles Steir, Program Director, 914-594-4138, Fax: 914-594-4944, E-mail: charles_stier@nymc.edu. *Application contact:* Valerie Romeo-Messana, Admission Coordinator, 914-594-4110, Fax: 914-594-4944, E-mail: v_romeomessana@nymc.edu.

New York University, School of Medicine, New York, NY 10012-1019. Offers biomedical sciences (PhD), including biomedical imaging, cellular and molecular biology, computational biology, developmental genetics, medical and molecular parasitology, microbiology, molecular oncobiology and immunology, neuroscience and physiology, pathobiology, pharmacology, structural biology; clinical investigation (MS); medicine (MD); MD/MA; MD/MPA; MD/MS; MD/PhD. *Accreditation:* LCME/AMA (one or more programs are accredited). *Degree requirements:* For master's, comprehensive exam, thesis; for doctorate, comprehensive exam, thesis/dissertation. *Entrance requirements:* MCAT. Additional exam requirements/recommendations for international students: Required—TOEFL. *Expenses:* Contact institution. *Faculty research:* AIDS, cancer, neuroscience, molecular biology, neuroscience, cell biology and molecular genetics, structural biology, microbial pathogenesis and host defense, pharmacology, molecular oncology and immunology.

New York University, School of Medicine and Graduate School of Arts and Science, Sackler Institute of Graduate Biomedical Sciences, Department of Pharmacology, New York, NY 10012-1019. Offers molecular pharmacology (PhD); MD/PhD. *Degree requirements:* For doctorate, comprehensive exam, thesis/dissertation, qualifying exam. *Entrance requirements:* For doctorate, GRE General Test. Additional exam requirements/recommendations for international students: Required—TOEFL. *Faculty research:* Pharmacology and neurobiology, neuropeptides, receptor biochemistry, cytoskeleton, endocrinology.

North Carolina State University, College of Veterinary Medicine, Program in Comparative Biomedical Sciences, Raleigh, NC 27695. Offers cell biology (MS, PhD); infectious disease (MS, PhD); pathology (MS, PhD); pharmacology (MS, PhD); population medicine (MS, PhD). Part-time programs available. *Degree requirements:* For master's, thesis; for doctorate, thesis/dissertation. *Entrance requirements:* For master's and doctorate, GRE General Test. Additional exam requirements/recommendations for international students: Required—TOEFL (minimum score 550 paper-based; 213 computer-based). Electronic applications accepted. *Expenses:* Contact institution. *Faculty research:* Infectious diseases, cell biology, pharmacology and toxicology, genomics, pathology and population medicine.

Northwestern University, Northwestern University Feinberg School of Medicine and Interdepartmental Programs, Integrated Graduate Programs in the Life Sciences, Chicago, IL 60611. Offers cancer biology (PhD); cell biology (PhD); developmental biology (PhD); evolutionary biology (PhD); immunology and microbial pathogenesis (PhD); molecular biology and genetics (PhD); neurobiology (PhD); pharmacology and toxicology (PhD); structural biology and biochemistry (PhD). *Degree requirements:* For doctorate, comprehensive exam, thesis/dissertation, written and oral qualifying exams. *Entrance requirements:* For doctorate, GRE General Test. Additional exam requirements/recommendations for international students: Required—TOEFL (minimum score 600 paper-based; 250 computer-based). Electronic applications accepted.

Nova Southeastern University, Center for Psychological Studies, Master's Programs in Counseling, Mental Health, School Guidance, and Clinical Pharmacology, Fort Lauderdale, FL 33314-7796. Offers clinical pharmacology (MS); mental health counseling (MS); school guidance and counseling (MS). Part-time and evening/weekend programs available. *Faculty:* 7 full-time (2 women), 27 part-time/adjunct (8 women). *Students:* 331 full-time (299 women), 706 part-time (637 women); includes 520 minority (219 Black or African American, non-Hispanic/Latino; 20 Asian, non-Hispanic/Latino; 264 Hispanic/Latino; 1 Native Hawaiian or other Pacific Islander, non-Hispanic/Latino; 16 Two or more races, non-Hispanic/Latino), 22 international. Average age 32. 562 applicants, 65% accepted, 262 enrolled. In 2010, 382 master's awarded. *Degree requirements:* For master's, comprehensive exam, 3 practica. *Entrance requirements:* Additional exam requirements/recommendations for international students: Required—TOEFL (minimum score 550 paper-based; 213 computer-based). *Application deadline:* For fall admission, 7/29 for domestic students; for winter admission, 11/29 for domestic students; for spring admission, 3/29 for domestic students. Applications are processed on a rolling basis. Application fee: $50. Electronic applications accepted. *Financial support:* Career-related internships or fieldwork, Federal Work-Study, and institutionally sponsored loans available. Financial award application deadline: 4/1. *Faculty research:* Clinical and child clinical psychology, geriatrics, interpersonal violence. *Unit head:* Karen S. Grosby, Dean, 954-262-5701, Fax: 954-262-3859. *Application contact:* Carlos Perez, Enrollment Management, 954-262-5790, Fax: 954-262-3893, E-mail: cpsinfo@cps.nova.edu.

The Ohio State University, College of Medicine, School of Biomedical Science, Integrated Biomedical Science Graduate Program, Columbus, OH 43210. Offers immunology (PhD); medical genetics (PhD); molecular virology (PhD); pharmacology (PhD). *Degree requirements:* For doctorate, thesis/dissertation. *Entrance requirements:* For doctorate, GRE, GRE Subject Test in biochemistry, cell and molecular biology (recommended for some). Additional exam requirements/recommendations for international students: Required—TOEFL (minimum score 600 paper-based; 250 computer-based). Electronic applications accepted. *Expenses:* Tuition, state resident: full-time $10,605. Tuition, nonresident: full-time $26,535. Tuition and fees vary according to course load and program.

The Ohio State University, College of Pharmacy, Columbus, OH 43210. Offers Pharm D, MS, PhD. *Accreditation:* ACPE (one or more programs are accredited). Part-time programs available. *Students:* 572 full-time (343 women), 27 part-time (11 women); includes 21 Black or African American, non-Hispanic/Latino; 1 American Indian or Alaska Native, non-Hispanic/Latino; 101 Asian, non-Hispanic/Latino; 13 Hispanic/Latino; 2 Two or more races, non-Hispanic/Latino, 59 international. Average age 28. In 2010, 131 first professional degrees, 9 master's, 11 doctorates awarded. Terminal master's awarded for partial completion of doctoral program. *Degree requirements:* For doctorate, thesis/dissertation. *Entrance requirements:* For Pharm D, PCAT; for master's and doctorate, GRE General Test, minimum GPA of 3.0. Additional exam requirements/recommendations for international students: Required—TOEFL. *Application deadline:* For fall admission, 1/1 priority date for domestic students. Application fee: $40 ($50 for international students). Electronic applications accepted. *Expenses:* Contact institution. *Financial support:* Fellowships with full tuition reimbursements, research assistantships with full tuition reimbursements, teaching assistantships with full tuition reimbursements, career-related internships or fieldwork, Federal Work-Study, institutionally sponsored loans, scholarships/grants, and traineeships available. *Unit head:* Dr. Robert W. Brueggemeier, Dean, 614-292-5711, Fax: 614-292-2435, E-mail: brueggemeier@pharmacy.ohio-state.edu. *Application contact:* Kathy I. Brooks, Graduate Program Coordinator, 614-292-6822, Fax: 614-292-2588, E-mail: brooks@pharmacy.ohio-state.edu.

The Ohio State University, College of Veterinary Medicine, Department of Veterinary Biosciences, Columbus, OH 43210. Offers anatomy and cellular biology (MS, PhD); pathobiology (MS, PhD); pharmacology (MS, PhD); toxicology (MS, PhD); veterinary physiology (MS, PhD). *Faculty:* 45. *Students:* 4 full-time (all women), 7 part-time (5 women); includes 1 Black or African American, non-Hispanic/Latino, 3 international. Average age 30. In 2010, 2 master's, 7 doctorates awarded. *Entrance requirements:* For master's and doctorate, GRE General Test. Additional exam requirements/recommendations for international students: Required—TOEFL. *Application deadline:* Applications are processed on a rolling basis. Application fee: $40 ($50 for international students). Electronic applications accepted. *Expenses:* Tuition, state resident: full-time $10,605. Tuition, nonresident: full-time $26,535. Tuition and fees vary according to course load and program. *Faculty research:* Microvasculature, muscle biology, neonatal lung and bone development. *Unit head:* Dr. Michael J. Oglesbee, Graduate Studies Committee Chair, 614-292-5661, Fax: 614-292-6473, E-mail: oglesbee.1@osu.edu. *Application contact:* Graduate Admissions, 614-292-9444, Fax: 614-292-3895, E-mail: domestic.grad@osu.edu.

Oregon Health & Science University, School of Medicine, Graduate Programs in Medicine, Program in Molecular and Cellular Biosciences, Department of Physiology and Pharmacology, Portland, OR 97239-3098. Offers PhD. *Faculty:* 18. *Students:* 11 full-time (7 women); includes 1 Black or African American, non-Hispanic/Latino; 1 American Indian or Alaska Native, non-Hispanic/Latino; 1 Asian, non-Hispanic/Latino, 2 international. Average age 28. In 2010, 3 doctorates awarded. *Degree requirements:* For doctorate, comprehensive exam, thesis/dissertation. *Entrance requirements:* For doctorate, GRE General Test (minimum scores: 500 Verbal/600 Quantitative/4.5 Analytical) or MCAT (for some programs). Additional exam requirements/recommendations for international students: Required—TOEFL. Electronic applications accepted. *Financial support:* Full tuition and stipends available. *Unit head:* Dr. Beth Habecker, Program Director, 503-494-6252, E-mail: habecker@ohsu.edu. *Application contact:* Julie Walvatne, Program Coordinator, 503-494-6252.

Penn State Hershey Medical Center, College of Medicine, Graduate School Programs in the Biomedical Sciences, Graduate Program in Pharmacology, Hershey, PA 17033. Offers MS, PhD, MD/PhD, PhD/MBA. PhD/MBA offered jointly with Penn State Harrisburg. *Students:* 419 applicants, 1% accepted, 3 enrolled.Terminal master's awarded for partial completion of doctoral program. *Degree requirements:* For master's, thesis or alternative; for doctorate, comprehensive exam, thesis/dissertation, oral exam. *Entrance requirements:* For master's, GRE General Test; for doctorate, GRE General Test, minimum GPA of 3.0. Additional exam requirements/recommendations for international students: Required—TOEFL (minimum score 550 paper-based; 213 computer-based). *Application deadline:* For fall admission, 1/31 priority date for domestic students, 2/1 priority date for international students. Applications are processed on a rolling basis. Application fee: $65. Electronic applications accepted. *Financial support:* In 2010–11, research assistantships with full tuition reimbursements (averaging $22,260 per year); fellowships with full tuition reimbursements, institutionally sponsored loans, scholarships/grants, health care benefits, and unspecified assistantships also available. Financial award applicants required to submit FAFSA. *Faculty research:* Ion pump structure and function, drug development and targeting, mechanisms of drug resistance, neuropharmacology and toxicology, breast cancer, identification of molecular targets for drug development in cancer and cardiovascular and neurological diseases. *Unit head:* Dr. Kent Vrana, Chair, 717-531-8285, Fax: 717-531-5013, E-mail: pharm-grad-hmc@psu.edu. *Application contact:* Elaine Neldigh, Program Secretary, 717-531-8285, Fax: 717-531-5013, E-mail: pharm-grad-hmc@psu.edu.

Purdue University, College of Pharmacy and Pharmacal Sciences and Graduate School, Graduate Programs in Pharmacy and Pharmacal Sciences, Department of Medicinal Chemistry and Molecular Pharmacology, West Lafayette, IN 47907. Offers analytical medicinal chemistry (PhD); computational and biophysical medicinal chemistry (PhD); medicinal and bioorganic chemistry (PhD); medicinal biochemistry and molecular biology (PhD); molecular pharmacology and toxicology (PhD); natural products and pharmacognosy (PhD); nuclear pharmacy (MS); radiopharmaceutical chemistry and nuclear pharmacy (PhD); MS/PhD. Terminal master's awarded for partial completion of doctoral program. *Degree requirements:* For master's, thesis; for doctorate, thesis/dissertation. *Entrance requirements:* For master's, GRE General Test, minimum B average; BS in biology, chemistry, or pharmacy; for doctorate, GRE General Test, minimum B average; BS in biology, chemistry, or pharmacology. Additional exam requirements/recommendations for international students: Required—TOEFL. Electronic applications accepted. *Faculty research:* Drug design and development, cancer research, drug synthesis and analysis, chemical pharmacology, environmental toxicology.

Purdue University, School of Veterinary Medicine and Graduate School, Graduate Programs in Veterinary Medicine, Department of Basic Medical Sciences, West Lafayette, IN 47907. Offers anatomy (MS, PhD); pharmacology (MS, PhD); physiology (MS, PhD). Part-time programs available. Terminal master's awarded for partial completion of doctoral program. *Degree requirements:* For master's, thesis; for doctorate, thesis/dissertation. *Entrance requirements:* For master's and doctorate, GRE General Test. Additional exam requirements/recommendations for international students: Required—TOEFL. Electronic applications accepted. *Faculty research:* Development and regeneration, tissue injury and shock, biomedical engineering, ovarian function, bone and cartilage biology, cell and molecular biology.

Queen's University at Kingston, School of Graduate Studies and Research, Faculty of Health Sciences, Department of Pharmacology and Toxicology, Kingston, ON K7L 3N6, Canada. Offers M Sc, PhD. *Degree requirements:* For master's, thesis; for doctorate, comprehensive exam, thesis/dissertation. *Entrance requirements:* For master's, minimum 2nd class standing, honors bachelor of science degree (life sciences, health sciences, or equivalent); for doctorate, masters of science degree or outstanding performance in honors bachelor of science program. Additional exam requirements/recommendations for international students: Required—TOEFL (minimum score 600 paper-based; 250 computer-based). Electronic applications accepted. *Faculty research:* Biochemical toxicology, cardiovascular pharmacology and neuropharmacology.

Rush University, Graduate College, Division of Pharmacology, Chicago, IL 60612-3832. Offers clinical research (MS); pharmacology (MS, PhD); MD/PhD. Terminal master's awarded for partial completion of doctoral program. *Degree requirements:* For master's, thesis; for doctorate, thesis/dissertation. *Entrance requirements:* For master's and doctorate, GRE General Test, interview. Additional exam requirements/recommendations for international students: Required—TOEFL (minimum score 550 paper-based; 213 computer-based). *Faculty research:* Dopamine neurobiology and Parkinson's disease; cardiac electrophysiology and clinical pharmacology; neutrophil motility, apoptosis, and adhesion; angiogenesis; pulmonary vascular physiology.

Saint Louis University, Graduate Education and School of Medicine, Graduate Program in Biomedical Sciences and Graduate Education, Department of Pharmacological and Physiological Science, St. Louis, MO 63103-2097. Offers PhD. *Degree requirements:* For doctorate, comprehensive exam, thesis/dissertation, departmental qualifying exams. *Entrance requirements:* For doctorate, GRE General Test (GRE Subject Test optional), letters of recommendation, resume, interview. Additional exam requirements/recommendations for international students: Required—TOEFL (minimum score 525 paper-based; 194 computer-based). Electronic applications accepted. *Faculty research:* Molecular endocrinology, neuropharmacology, cardiovascular science, drug abuse, neurotransmitter and hormonal signaling mechanisms.

Southern Illinois University Carbondale, Graduate School, Graduate Program in Medicine, Program in Pharmacology, Springfield, IL 62794-9629. Offers MS, PhD. *Degree requirements:* For master's, thesis; for doctorate, thesis/dissertation. *Entrance requirements:* For master's, minimum GPA of 3.0; for doctorate, minimum GPA of 3.25. Additional exam requirements/recommendations for international students: Required—TOEFL. *Faculty research:* Autonomic nervous system pharmacology, biochemical pharmacology, neuropharmacology, toxicology, cardiovascular pharmacology.

State University of New York Upstate Medical University, College of Graduate Studies, Program in Pharmacology, Syracuse, NY 13210-2334. Offers PhD, MD/PhD. Terminal master's awarded for partial completion of doctoral program. *Degree requirements:* For doctorate, comprehensive exam, thesis/dissertation. *Entrance requirements:* For doctorate, GRE General Test, telephone interview. Additional exam requirements/recommendations for international students: Required—TOEFL. Electronic applications accepted. *Faculty research:* Cancer, disorders of the nervous system, infectious diseases, diabetes/metabolic disorders/cardiovascular diseases.

Stony Brook University, State University of New York, Stony Brook University Medical Center, School of Medicine and Graduate School, Graduate Programs in Medicine, Department of Pharmacological Sciences, Graduate Program in Molecular and Cellular Pharmacology, Stony Brook, NY 11794. Offers PhD. *Faculty:* 17 full-time (3 women). *Students:* 33 full-time (19 women), 1 (woman) part-time; includes 2 Black or African American, non-Hispanic/Latino; 8 Asian, non-Hispanic/Latino; 5 Hispanic/Latino, 6 international. Average age 28. 48 applicants, 23% accepted, 7 enrolled. In 2010, 5 doctorates awarded. *Degree requirements:* For doctorate, thesis/dissertation, departmental qualifying exam. *Entrance requirements:* For doctorate, GRE General Test. Additional exam requirements/recommendations for international students: Required—TOEFL. *Application deadline:* For fall admission, 1/15 priority date for domestic students. Applications are processed on a rolling basis. Application fee: $100. Electronic applications accepted. *Expenses:* Tuition, state resident: full-time $8370; part-time $349 per credit. Tuition, nonresident: full-time $13,780; part-time $574 per credit. Required fees: $994. *Financial support:* In 2010–11, 16 research assistantships, 4 teaching assistantships were awarded; fellowships, Federal Work-Study also available. Financial award application deadline: 3/15; financial award applicants required to submit FAFSA. *Faculty research:* Toxicology, molecular and cellular biochemistry. Total annual research expenditures: $9.4 million. *Unit head:* Prof. Michael Frohman, Chair, 631-444-3050, Fax: 631-444-9749. *Application contact:* Dr. Stella Tsirka, Director, 631-444-3859, Fax: 631-444-9749, E-mail: stella.tsirka@stonybrook.edu.

Temple University, Health Sciences Center, School of Medicine and Graduate School, Doctor of Medicine Program, Department of Pharmacology, Philadelphia, PA 19122-6096. Offers PhD, MD/PhD. *Faculty:* 12 full-time (3 women). *Students:* 18 full-time (11 women), 1 part-time (0 women); includes 4 Asian, non-Hispanic/Latino, 10 international. 24 applicants, 38% accepted, 4 enrolled. In 2010, 2 doctorates awarded. Terminal master's awarded for partial completion of doctoral program. *Degree requirements:* For doctorate, one foreign language, thesis/dissertation, research seminars. *Entrance requirements:* For doctorate, GRE General Test, minimum GPA of 3.0. Additional exam requirements/recommendations for international students: Required—TOEFL (minimum score 620 paper-based; 260 computer-based). *Application deadline:* For fall admission, 1/15 priority date for domestic students, 12/15 for international students. Applications are processed on a rolling basis. Application fee: $50. Electronic applications accepted. *Financial support:* Fellowships, research assistantships, Federal Work-Study available. Financial award application deadline: 1/15; financial award applicants required to submit FAFSA. *Faculty research:* Cardiovascular and central nervous systems, biochemical pharmacology. *Unit head:* Dr. Nae Dun, Chair, 215-707-3236, Fax: 215-707-7068, E-mail: nae.dun@temple.edu. *Application contact:* Dr. Nae Dun, Chair, 215-707-3236, Fax: 215-707-7068, E-mail: nae.dun@temple.edu.

Texas Tech University Health Sciences Center, Graduate School of Biomedical Sciences, Department of Pharmacology and Neuroscience, Lubbock, TX 79430. Offers MS, PhD, MD/PhD, MS/PhD. Terminal master's awarded for partial completion of doctoral program. *Degree requirements:* For master's, thesis; for doctorate, thesis/dissertation. *Entrance requirements:* For master's and doctorate, GRE General Test, minimum GPA of 3.0. Additional exam requirements/recommendations for international students: Required—TOEFL. Electronic applications accepted. *Faculty research:* Neuroscience, neuropsychopharmacology, autonomic pharmacology, cardiovascular pharmacology, molecular pharmacology.

Thomas Jefferson University, Jefferson College of Graduate Studies, MS Program in Pharmacology, Philadelphia, PA 19107. Offers MS. Part-time and evening/weekend programs available. *Faculty:* 18 full-time (5 women), 11 part-time/adjunct (4 women). *Students:* 36 part-time (20 women); includes 5 minority (3 Black or African American, non-Hispanic/Latino; 2 Asian, non-Hispanic/Latino), 7 international. 32 applicants, 63% accepted, 19 enrolled. In 2010, 9 master's awarded. *Degree requirements:* For master's, thesis, clerkship. *Entrance requirements:* For master's, GRE General Test or MCAT, minimum GPA of 3.0. Additional exam requirements/recommendations for international students: Required—TOEFL (minimum score 250 computer-based; 100 iBT) or IELTS. *Application deadline:* For fall admission, 8/1 priority date for domestic students, 3/1 priority date for international students; for winter admission, 12/1 priority date for domestic students, 6/1 priority date for international students; for spring admission, 4/1 priority date for domestic students. Applications are processed on a rolling basis. Application fee: $50. Electronic applications accepted. *Expenses:* Contact institution. *Financial support:* In 2010–11, 9 students received support. Federal Work-Study and institutionally sponsored loans available. Support available to part-time students. Financial award application deadline: 5/1; financial award applicants required to submit FAFSA. *Unit head:* Dr. Carol L. Beck, Assistant Dean/Director, 215-503-6539, Fax: 215-503-3433, E-mail: carol.beck@jefferson.edu. *Application contact:* Eleanor M. Gorman, Assistant Coordinator, Graduate Center Programs, 215-503-5799, Fax: 215-503-3433, E-mail: eleanor.gorman@jefferson.edu.

Tufts University, Sackler School of Graduate Biomedical Sciences, Program in Pharmacology and Experimental Therapeutics, Medford, MA 02155. Offers PhD. *Faculty:* 16 full-time (6 women). *Students:* 9 full-time (7 women), 3 international. Average age 26. 72 applicants, 8% accepted, 5 enrolled. In 2010, 4 doctorates awarded. *Degree requirements:* For doctorate, thesis/dissertation, qualifying exam. *Entrance requirements:* For doctorate, GRE General Test, 3 letters of reference. Additional exam requirements/recommendations for international students: Required—TOEFL. *Application deadline:* For fall admission, 11/15 for domestic students, 12/15 priority date for international students. Applications are processed on a rolling basis. Application fee: $70. Electronic applications accepted. *Expenses:* Tuition: Full-time $39,624; part-time $3962 per course. Required fees: $40 per year. Full-time tuition and fees vary according to degree level, program and student level. Part-time tuition and fees vary according to course load. *Financial support:* In 2010–11, 9 research assistantships with full tuition reimbursements (averaging $28,250 per year) were awarded; scholarships/grants and health care benefits also available. Financial award application deadline: 1/15. *Faculty research:* Biochemical mechanisms of narcotic addiction, clinical psychopharmacology, pharmacokinetics, neurotransmitter receptors, neuropeptides. *Unit head:* Dr. Richard Shader, Director, 617-636-3856, Fax: 617-636-6738. *Application contact:* Kellie Johnston, Associate Director of Admissions, 617-636-6767, Fax: 617-636-0375, E-mail: sackler-school@tufts.edu.

Tulane University, School of Medicine and School of Liberal Arts, Graduate Programs in Biomedical Sciences, Department of Pharmacology, New Orleans, LA 70118-5669. Offers MS, PhD, MD/MS, MD/PhD. MS and PhD offered through the Graduate School. *Degree requirements:* For master's, one foreign language, thesis; for doctorate, 2 foreign languages, thesis/dissertation. *Entrance requirements:* For master's, GRE General Test, minimum B average in undergraduate course work; for doctorate, GRE General Test. Additional exam requirements/recommendations for international students: Required—TOEFL. Electronic applications accepted.

Universidad Central del Caribe, School of Medicine, Program in Biomedical Sciences, Bayamón, PR 00960-6032. Offers anatomy and cell biology (MA, MS); biochemistry (MS); biomedical sciences (MA); cellular and molecular biology (PhD); microbiology and immunology (MA, MS); pharmacology (MS); physiology (MS).

Université de Montréal, Faculty of Medicine, Department of Pharmacology, Montréal, QC H3C 3J7, Canada. Offers M Sc, PhD. Terminal master's awarded for partial completion of doctoral program. *Degree requirements:* For master's, thesis; for doctorate, thesis/dissertation, general exam. *Entrance requirements:* For master's, proficiency in French, knowledge of English; for doctorate, master's degree, proficiency in French. Electronic applications accepted. *Faculty research:* Molecular, clinical, and cardiovascular pharmacology; pharmacokinetics; mechanisms of drug interactions and toxicity; neuropharmacology and receptology.

Université de Sherbrooke, Faculty of Medicine and Health Sciences, Graduate Programs in Medicine, Department of Pharmacology, Sherbrooke, QC J1H 5N4, Canada. Offers M Sc, PhD. Terminal master's awarded for partial completion of doctoral program. *Degree requirements:* For master's, thesis; for doctorate, thesis/dissertation. Electronic applications accepted. *Faculty research:* Pharmacology of peptide hormones, pharmacology of lipid mediators, protein-protein interactions, medicinal pharmacology.

University at Buffalo, the State University of New York, Graduate School, School of Medicine and Biomedical Sciences, Graduate Programs in Medicine and Biomedical Sciences, Department of Pharmacology and Toxicology, Buffalo, NY 14260. Offers biochemical pharmacology (MS); pharmacology (MA, PhD); MD/PhD. Terminal master's awarded for partial completion of doctoral program. *Degree requirements:* For master's, thesis; for doctorate, thesis/dissertation. *Entrance requirements:* For master's and doctorate, GRE General Test, 3 letters of recommendation. Additional exam requirements/recommendations for international students: Required—TOEFL (minimum score 100 iBT). Electronic applications accepted. *Faculty research:* Neuropharmacology, toxicology, signal transduction, molecular pharmacology, behavioral pharmacology.

The University of Alabama at Birmingham, Graduate Programs in Joint Health Sciences, Program in Pharmacology and Toxicology, Birmingham, AL 35294. Offers PhD. *Students:* 13 full-time (5 women); includes 2 minority (1 Black or African American, non-Hispanic/Latino; 1 Hispanic/Latino), 3 international. Average age 27. In 2010, 4 doctorates awarded. *Degree requirements:* For doctorate, thesis/dissertation. *Entrance requirements:* For doctorate, GRE General Test, interview. *Application deadline:* Applications are processed on a rolling basis. Application fee: $35 ($60 for international students). Electronic applications accepted. *Expenses:* Contact institution. *Financial support:* In 2010–11, 6 fellowships were awarded. *Faculty research:* Biochemical pharmacology, neuropharmacology, endocrine pharmacology. *Unit head:* Dr. Mary-Ann Bjornsti, Interim Chair, 205-934-4579. *Application contact:* Graduate Coordinator, 205-934-4584, Fax: 205-934-4209.

University of Alberta, Faculty of Graduate Studies and Research, Department of Pharmacology, Edmonton, AB T6G 2E1, Canada. Offers M Sc, PhD. Terminal master's awarded for partial completion of doctoral program. *Degree requirements:* For master's, thesis; for doctorate, thesis/dissertation. *Entrance requirements:* For master's, B Sc, minimum GPA of 3.3; for doctorate, M Sc in pharmacology or closely related field, honors B Sc in pharmacology. *Faculty research:* Cardiovascular pharmacology, neuropharmacology, cancer pharmacology, molecular pharmacology, toxicology.

The University of Arizona, College of Pharmacy, Department of Pharmacology and Toxicology, Graduate Program in Medical Pharmacology, Tucson, AZ 85721. Offers medical pharmacology (PhD); perfusion science (MS). *Faculty:* 11 full-time (3 women). *Students:* 28 full-time (20 women); includes 2 Asian, non-Hispanic/Latino; 5 Hispanic/Latino; 2 Two or more races, non-Hispanic/Latino, 8 international. Average age 28. 40 applicants, 13% accepted, 5 enrolled. In 2010, 7 master's, 4 doctorates awarded. *Degree requirements:* For master's, thesis; for doctorate, comprehensive exam, thesis/dissertation. *Entrance requirements:* For master's, GRE General Test, 3 letters of recommendation; for doctorate, GRE General Test, personal statement, 3 letters of recommendation. Additional exam requirements/recommendations for international students: Required—TOEFL (minimum score 550 paper-based; 213 computer-based; 79 iBT). *Application deadline:* For fall admission, 1/1 for domestic and international students. Applications are processed on a rolling basis. Application fee: $65. Electronic applications accepted. *Expenses:* Tuition, state resident: full-time $7692. *Financial support:* In 2010–11, 17 research assistantships with full tuition reimbursements (averaging $23,929 per year) were awarded; institutionally sponsored loans and tuition waivers (partial) also available. Financial award applicants required to submit FAFSA. *Faculty research:* Immunopharmacology, pharmacogenetics, pharmacogenomics, clinical pharmacology, ocularpharmacology and neuropharmacology. *Unit head:* Dr. I. Glenn Sipes, Head, 520-626-7123, Fax: 520-626-2204, E-mail: sipes@email.arizona.edu. *Application contact:* Trisha Stanley, Coordinator, 520-626-7218, Fax: 520-626-2204, E-mail: stanley@email.arizona.edu.

University of Arkansas for Medical Sciences, Graduate School, Graduate Programs in Biomedical Sciences, Pharmacology Program, Little Rock, AR 72205-7199. Offers MS, PhD, MD/PhD. *Degree requirements:* For master's, thesis; for doctorate, thesis/dissertation. *Entrance requirements:* For master's and doctorate, GRE General Test. Additional exam requirements/recommendations for international students: Required—TOEFL. *Faculty research:* Neuroscience, behavior, pharmacokinetics, metabolism.

The University of British Columbia, Faculty of Medicine, Department of Anesthesiology, Pharmacology and Therapeutics, Vancouver, BC V6T 1Z3, Canada. Offers M Sc, PhD. *Faculty:* 20 full-time (4 women), 2 part-time/adjunct (0 women). *Students:* 29 full-time (12 women); includes 10 Asian, non-Hispanic/Latino; 1 Hispanic/Latino, 8 international. Average age 28. 29 applicants, 17% accepted, 5 enrolled. In 2010, 2 master's, 1 doctorate awarded. Terminal master's awarded for partial completion of doctoral program. *Degree requirements:* For master's, thesis; for doctorate, comprehensive exam, thesis/dissertation. *Entrance requirements:* For master's, MD or appropriate bachelor's degree; for doctorate, MD or M Sc. Additional exam requirements/recommendations for international students: Required—TOEFL (minimum score 600 paper-based; 250 computer-based; 100 iBT). *Application deadline:* For fall admission, 4/1 for domestic students, 3/1 for international students; for winter admission, 8/1 for domestic students, 7/1 for international students; for spring admission, 12/1 for domestic students, 11/1 for international students. Application fee: $90 Canadian dollars ($150 Canadian dollars for international students). Electronic applications accepted. Tuition charges are reported in Canadian dollars. *Expenses:* Tuition, area resident: Full-time $4179 Canadian dollars. International tuition: $7344 Canadian dollars full-time. *Financial support:* In 2010–11, 10 students received support, including 10 fellowships (averaging $21,409 per year), 16 research assistantships with full and partial tuition reimbursements available (averaging $20,576 per year); institutionally sponsored loans, scholarships/grants, and unspecified assistantships also available. Financial award application deadline: 10/15. *Faculty research:* Cellular, biochemical, autonomic, cardiovascular pharmacology; neuropharmacology and pulmonary pharmacology. Total annual research expenditures: $406,074 Canadian dollars. *Unit head:* Dr. C. B. Warriner, Head, 604-822-2575, Fax: 604-822-2281, E-mail: brian.warriner@vch.ca. *Application contact:* Wynne Leung, Graduate Secretary, 604-827-3289, Fax: 604-822-6012, E-mail: wynne.leung@ubc.ca.

Pharmacology

University of California, Davis, Graduate Studies, Graduate Group in Pharmacology and Toxicology, Davis, CA 95616. Offers MS, PhD. Terminal master's awarded for partial completion of doctoral program. *Degree requirements:* For master's, comprehensive exam or thesis; for doctorate, thesis/dissertation, qualifying exam. *Entrance requirements:* For master's and doctorate, GRE General Test, minimum GPA of 3.0, course work in biochemistry and/or physiology. Additional exam requirements/recommendations for international students: Required—TOEFL (minimum score 550 paper-based; 213 computer-based). Electronic applications accepted. *Faculty research:* Respiratory, neurochemical, molecular, genetic, and ecological toxicology.

University of California, Irvine, School of Medicine, Department of Pharmacology, Irvine, CA 92697. Offers pharmacology and toxicology (MS, PhD); MD/PhD. *Students:* 24 full-time (10 women); includes 10 minority (2 Black or African American, non-Hispanic/Latino; 6 Asian, non-Hispanic/Latino; 2 Hispanic/Latino), 3 international. Average age 28. 44 applicants, 20% accepted, 4 enrolled. In 2010, 4 master's, 6 doctorates awarded. *Degree requirements:* For doctorate, thesis/dissertation. *Entrance requirements:* For master's, GRE, minimum GPA of 3.0; for doctorate, GRE General Test, GRE Subject Test, minimum GPA of 3.0. Additional exam requirements/recommendations for international students: Required—TOEFL (minimum score 550 paper-based; 213 computer-based). *Application deadline:* For fall admission, 1/15 priority date for domestic students, 1/15 for international students. Applications are processed on a rolling basis. Application fee: $80 ($100 for international students). Electronic applications accepted. *Financial support:* Fellowships, research assistantships with full tuition reimbursements, teaching assistantships, institutionally sponsored loans, traineeships, health care benefits, and unspecified assistantships available. Financial award application deadline: 3/1; financial award applicants required to submit FAFSA. *Faculty research:* Mechanisms of action and effects of drugs on the nervous system, behavior, skeletal muscle, heart, and blood vessels; basic processes in the nervous system, skeletal muscle, heart, and blood vessels. *Unit head:* Paolo Sassone-Corsi, Chair, 949-824-4540, Fax: 949-824-2078, E-mail: psc@uci.edu. *Application contact:* Pamela J. Bhalla, Chief Administrative Officer, 949-824-6772, Fax: 949-824-4855, E-mail: pamela.bhalla@uci.edu.

See Display below and Close-Up on page 437.

University of California, Los Angeles, David Geffen School of Medicine and Graduate Division, Graduate Programs in Medicine, Department of Molecular and Medical Pharmacology, Los Angeles, CA 90095. Offers PhD. *Faculty:* 26 full-time (7 women). *Students:* 58 full-time (28 women); includes 17 minority (1 Black or African American, non-Hispanic/Latino; 11 Asian, non-Hispanic/Latino; 5 Hispanic/Latino), 18 international. Average age 27. 65 applicants, 18% accepted, 8 enrolled. In 2010, 9 doctorates awarded. *Degree requirements:* For doctorate, thesis/dissertation, qualifying exams. *Entrance requirements:* For doctorate, GRE General Test. Application fee: $70 ($90 for international students). Electronic applications accepted. *Financial support:* In 2010–11, 61 fellowships, 52 research assistantships, 11 teaching assistantships were awarded; scholarships/grants also available. Financial award application deadline: 3/1. *Faculty research:* Cardiovascular pharmacology, chemical pharmacology, neuropharmacology, clinical pharmacology, molecular pharmacology. *Unit head:* Dr. Michael Phelps, Chair, 310-825-6539, E-mail: mphelps@mednet.ucla.edu. *Application contact:* Sarah Starrett, Student Affairs Office, 310-825-0390, Fax: 310-794-1819, E-mail: sstarrett@mednet.ucla.edu.

University of California, San Diego, School of Medicine and Office of Graduate Studies, Graduate Studies in Biomedical Sciences, Department of Pharmacology, La Jolla, CA 92093-0685. Offers PhD. *Degree requirements:* For doctorate, thesis/dissertation, qualifying exam. *Entrance requirements:* For doctorate, GRE General Test. Additional exam requirements/recommendations for international students: Required—TOEFL. Electronic applications accepted.

Faculty research: Molecular and cellular pharmacology, cell and organ physiology, cellular and molecular biology.

University of California, San Francisco, School of Pharmacy and Graduate Division, Pharmaceutical Sciences and Pharmacogenomics Graduate Group, San Francisco, CA 94158-0775. Offers PhD. *Faculty:* 52 full-time (14 women). *Students:* 48 full-time (24 women); includes 15 Asian, non-Hispanic/Latino; 1 Hispanic/Latino. Average age 24. 92 applicants, 15% accepted, 8 enrolled. In 2010, 7 doctorates awarded. *Degree requirements:* For doctorate, comprehensive exam, thesis/dissertation. *Entrance requirements:* For doctorate, GRE General Test, minimum GPA of 3.0. Additional exam requirements/recommendations for international students: Required—TOEFL. *Application deadline:* For fall admission, 12/1 for domestic and international students. Application fee: $70 ($90 for international students). Electronic applications accepted. *Financial support:* In 2010–11, 6 fellowships with full tuition reimbursements (averaging $28,000 per year), 34 research assistantships with full tuition reimbursements (averaging $28,000 per year), 8 teaching assistantships with full tuition reimbursements (averaging $28,000 per year) were awarded; career-related internships or fieldwork, institutionally sponsored loans, scholarships/grants, traineeships, tuition waivers (full), and unspecified assistantships also available. Financial award application deadline: 4/6. *Faculty research:* Drug development, drug delivery, molecular pharmacology. *Unit head:* Deanna L. Kroetz, Program Director, 415-476-1153, Fax: 415-476-6022, E-mail: deanna.kroetz@ucsf.edu. *Application contact:* Debbie Acoba-Idlebi, Program Coordinator, 415-476-1947, Fax: 415-476-6022, E-mail: debbie.acoba@ucsf.edu.

University of Chicago, Division of Biological Sciences, Neuroscience Graduate Programs, Department of Integrative Neuroscience, Chicago, IL 60637-1513. Offers cell physiology (PhD); pharmacological and physiological sciences (PhD). *Degree requirements:* For doctorate, thesis/dissertation, preliminary exam. *Entrance requirements:* For doctorate, GRE General Test. Additional exam requirements/recommendations for international students: Required—TOEFL. Electronic applications accepted. *Faculty research:* Psychopharmacology, neuropharmacology.

University of Cincinnati, Graduate School, College of Medicine, Graduate Programs in Biomedical Sciences, Department of Pharmacology and Cell Biophysics, Cincinnati, OH 45221. Offers cell biophysics (PhD); pharmacology (PhD). *Degree requirements:* For doctorate, thesis/dissertation, qualifying exam. *Entrance requirements:* For doctorate, GRE General Test. Additional exam requirements/recommendations for international students: Required—TOEFL. Electronic applications accepted. *Faculty research:* Lipoprotein research, enzyme regulation, electrophysiology, gene actuation.

University of Colorado Denver, School of Medicine, Program in Pharmacology, Denver, CO 80217-3364. Offers bioinformatics (PhD); biomolecular structure (PhD); pharmacology (PhD). *Students:* 25 full-time (13 women); includes 1 Black or African American, non-Hispanic/Latino; 2 Asian, non-Hispanic/Latino; 1 Hispanic/Latino. Average age 28. 31 applicants, 16% accepted, 5 enrolled. In 2010, 3 doctorates awarded. *Degree requirements:* For doctorate, comprehensive exam, thesis/dissertation, major seminar, 3 research rotations, 30 hours each of course work and thesis. *Entrance requirements:* For doctorate, GRE General Test. Additional exam requirements/recommendations for international students: Required—TOEFL (minimum score 550 paper-based; 213 computer-based; 80 iBT). *Application deadline:* For fall admission, 1/1 priority date for domestic students. Application fee: $50 ($75 for international students). Electronic applications accepted. *Expenses:* Contact institution. *Financial support:* Fellowships, research assistantships, teaching assistantships, health care benefits, tuition waivers (full), and stipend available. Financial award application deadline: 3/15; financial award applicants required to submit FAFSA. *Faculty research:* Cancer biology, drugs of abuse, neuroscience, signal transduction, structural biology. Total annual research expenditures: $16.7 million. *Unit* *head:* Dr. Andrew Thorburn, Interim Chair, 303-724-3290, Fax: 303-724-3663, E-mail: andrew.thorburn@ucdenver.edu. *Application contact:* Graduate Training Coordinator, 303-724-3565, E-mail: grad.pharm@ucdenver.edu.

University of Connecticut, Graduate School, School of Pharmacy, Department of Pharmaceutical Sciences, Graduate Program in Pharmacology and Toxicology, Storrs, CT 06269. Offers pharmacology (MS, PhD); toxicology (MS, PhD). Terminal master's awarded for partial completion of doctoral program. *Degree requirements:* For master's, comprehensive exam, thesis; for doctorate, thesis/dissertation. *Entrance requirements:* For master's and doctorate, GRE General Test. Additional exam requirements/recommendations for international students: Required—TOEFL (minimum score 550 paper-based; 213 computer-based). Electronic applications accepted.

University of Florida, College of Medicine, Department of Pharmacology and Therapeutics, Gainesville, FL 32611. Offers PhD. *Degree requirements:* For doctorate, thesis/dissertation. *Entrance requirements:* For doctorate, GRE General Test, minimum GPA of 3.0. Additional exam requirements/recommendations for international students: Required—TOEFL. Electronic applications accepted. *Expenses:* Tuition, state resident: full-time $10,916. Tuition, nonresident: full-time $28,309. *Faculty research:* Receptor and membrane pharmacology, autonomics, tetralogy, enzymes, opioid peptides.

University of Florida, College of Medicine and Graduate School, Interdisciplinary Program in Biomedical Sciences, Concentration in Physiology and Pharmacology, Gainesville, FL 32611. Offers PhD. *Degree requirements:* For doctorate, thesis/dissertation. *Entrance requirements:* For doctorate, GRE General Test, minimum GPA of 3.0. Electronic applications accepted. *Expenses:* Tuition, state resident: full-time $10,916. Tuition, nonresident: full-time $28,309.

University of Florida, College of Pharmacy and Graduate School, Graduate Programs in Pharmacy, Department of Pharmacodynamics, Gainesville, FL 32611. Offers MSP, PhD, Pharm D/PhD. *Faculty:* 8 full-time (4 women). *Students:* 10 full-time (6 women), 6 international. Average age 29. 14 applicants, 0% accepted, 0 enrolled.Terminal master's awarded for partial completion of doctoral program. *Degree requirements:* For master's, thesis; for doctorate, comprehensive exam, thesis/dissertation. *Entrance requirements:* For master's and doctorate, GRE General Test, minimum GPA of 3.0. Additional exam requirements/recommendations for international students: Required—TOEFL (minimum score 550 paper-based; 213 computer-based; 80 iBT), IELTS (minimum score 6). *Application deadline:* For fall admission, 2/15 priority date for domestic students, 2/15 for international students. Applications are processed on a rolling basis. Application fee: $30. Electronic applications accepted. *Expenses:* Tuition, state resident: full-time $10,916. Tuition, nonresident: full-time $28,309. *Financial support:* In 2010–11, 10 students received support, including 3 fellowships, 7 teaching assistantships (averaging $20,967 per year); institutionally sponsored loans and unspecified assistantships also available. Support available to part-time students. Financial award application deadline: 2/15; financial award applicants required to submit FAFSA. *Faculty research:* Neurochemistry and neurologic pathways involved in addiction and stress; cellular and molecular neurobiology of epilepsy, dementia and Parkinson's; hypertension and cardiac hypertrophy; stress hormone effects on fetal and neonatal development; cellular mechanism of glaucoma. Total annual research expenditures: $1.1 million. *Unit head:* Dr. Maureen Keller-Wood, Chair, 352-273-7687, Fax: 352-392-9187, E-mail: kellerwd@cop.ufl.edu. *Application contact:* Michael J. Katovich, Graduate Coordinator, 352-273-7690, Fax: 352-392-9187, E-mail: katovich@cop.ufl.edu.

University of Georgia, College of Veterinary Medicine and Graduate School, Graduate Programs in Veterinary Medicine, Department of Physiology and Pharmacology, Athens, GA 30602. Offers pharmacology (MS, PhD); physiology (MS, PhD). *Faculty:* 12 full-time (4 women), 1 part-time/adjunct (0 women). *Students:* 19 full-time (9 women); includes 1 Asian, non-Hispanic/Latino; 1 Hispanic/Latino, 9 international. 19 applicants, 26% accepted, 3 enrolled. In 2010, 1 master's, 1 doctorate awarded. *Degree requirements:* For master's, thesis; for doctorate, one foreign language, thesis/dissertation. *Entrance requirements:* For master's and doctorate, GRE General Test. *Application deadline:* For fall admission, 7/1 priority date for domestic students; for spring admission, 11/15 for domestic students. Application fee: $50. Electronic applications accepted. *Expenses:* Tuition, state resident: full-time $7200; part-time $344 per credit hour. Tuition, nonresident: full-time $21,900; part-time $944 per credit hour. Tuition and fees vary according to course load and program. *Financial support:* Fellowships, research assistantships, teaching assistantships, unspecified assistantships available. *Unit head:* Dr. Gaylen L. Edwards, Acting Head, 706-542-3014, Fax: 706-542-3015, E-mail: gedwards@uga.edu. *Application contact:* Dr. John Wagner, Graduate Coordinator, 706-542-6428, Fax: 706-542-3015, E-mail: jwagner@uga.edu.

University of Guelph, Ontario Veterinary College and Graduate Studies, Graduate Programs in Veterinary Sciences, Department of Biomedical Sciences, Guelph, ON N1G 2W1, Canada. Offers morphology (M Sc, DV Sc, PhD); neuroscience (M Sc, DV Sc, PhD); pharmacology (M Sc, DV Sc, PhD); physiology (M Sc, DV Sc, PhD); toxicology (M Sc, DV Sc, PhD). Part-time programs available. *Degree requirements:* For master's, thesis; for doctorate, comprehensive exam, thesis/dissertation. *Entrance requirements:* For master's, honors B Sc, minimum 75% average in last 20 courses; for doctorate, M Sc with thesis from accredited institution. Additional exam requirements/recommendations for international students: Required—TOEFL (minimum score 550 paper-based; 213 computer-based; 89 iBT). Electronic applications accepted. *Faculty research:* Cellular morphology; endocrine, vascular and reproductive physiology; clinical pharmacology; veterinary toxicology; developmental biology, neuroscience.

University of Houston, College of Pharmacy, Houston, TX 77204. Offers pharmaceutics (MSPHR, PhD); pharmacology (MSPHR, PhD); pharmacy (Pharm D); pharmacy administration (MSPHR, PhD). *Accreditation:* ACPE. Part-time programs available. *Faculty:* 26 full-time (7 women), 13 part-time/adjunct (9 women). *Students:* 525 full-time (324 women), 43 part-time (24 women); includes 291 minority (25 Black or African American, non-Hispanic/Latino; 2 American Indian or Alaska Native, non-Hispanic/Latino; 219 Asian, non-Hispanic/Latino; 40 Hispanic/Latino; 1 Native Hawaiian or other Pacific Islander, non-Hispanic/Latino; 4 Two or more races, non-Hispanic/Latino), 78 international. Average age 25. 703 applicants, 28% accepted, 133 enrolled. In 2010, 115 first professional degrees, 18 master's, 7 doctorates awarded. Terminal master's awarded for partial completion of doctoral program. *Entrance requirements:* PCAT, community service, letter of recommendation. Additional exam requirements/recommendations for international students: Required—TOEFL. *Application deadline:* For fall admission, 1/15 for domestic and international students. Applications are processed on a rolling basis. Application fee: $150. Electronic applications accepted. *Expenses:* Tuition, state resident: full-time $8592; part-time $358 per credit hour. Tuition, nonresident: full-time $16,032; part-time $668 per credit hour. Required fees: $2889. Tuition and fees vary according to course load and program. *Financial support:* In 2010–11, 3 fellowships with partial tuition reimbursements (averaging $2,000 per year), 9 research assistantships with partial tuition reimbursements (averaging $13,101 per year), 27 teaching assistantships with partial tuition reimbursements (averaging $13,123 per year) were awarded; career-related internships or fieldwork, Federal Work-Study, institutionally sponsored loans, scholarships/grants, health care benefits, and unspecified assistantships also available. Support available to part-time students. Financial award application deadline: 2/1. *Faculty research:* Drug screening and design, cardiovascular pharmacology, infectious disease, asthma research, herbal medicine. *Unit head:* Dr. Lamar Pritchard, Dean, 713-743-1253, Fax: 713-743-1259, E-mail: flpritchard@uh.edu. *Application contact:* Barbara Lewis, Assistant Dean for Student and Professional Affairs, 713-743-1264, Fax: 713-743-1237, E-mail: pharmacyadmissions@uh.edu.

University of Illinois at Chicago, College of Medicine and Graduate College, Graduate Programs in Medicine, Department of Pharmacology, Chicago, IL 60612. Offers PhD, MD/PhD. *Degree requirements:* For doctorate, thesis/dissertation. *Entrance requirements:* For doctorate, GRE General Test. Additional exam requirements/recommendations for international students: Required—TOEFL. *Faculty research:* Cardiovascular and lung biology, cell signaling, molecular pharmacology of G-proteins, immunopharmcology, molecular and cellular basis of inflammation, neuroscience.

The University of Iowa, Roy J. and Lucille A. Carver College of Medicine and Graduate College, Graduate Programs in Medicine, Department of Pharmacology, Iowa City, IA 52242-1316. Offers MS, PhD. *Faculty:* 11 full-time (1 woman), 10 part-time/adjunct (4 women). *Students:* 23 full-time (9 women); includes 1 Black or African American, non-Hispanic/Latino; 1 Hispanic/Latino, 7 international. Average age 28. 33 applicants, 12% accepted, 2 enrolled. In 2010, 1 master's, 5 doctorates awarded. Terminal master's awarded for partial completion of doctoral program. *Degree requirements:* For master's, thesis; for doctorate, comprehensive exam, thesis/dissertation. *Entrance requirements:* For master's, GRE General Test; for doctorate, GRE General Test, minimum GPA of 3.0, undergraduate course work in biochemistry. Additional exam requirements/recommendations for international students: Required—TOEFL (minimum score 600 paper-based; 250 computer-based). *Application deadline:* For fall admission, 2/1 priority date for domestic and international students. Applications are processed on a rolling basis. Application fee: $60 ($85 for international students). Electronic applications accepted. *Financial support:* In 2010–11, 23 research assistantships with full tuition reimbursements (averaging $24,250 per year) were awarded; scholarships/grants, traineeships, and unspecified assistantships also available. *Faculty research:* Cancer and cell cycle, hormones and growth factors, nervous system function and dysfunction, receptors and signal transduction, stroke and hypertension. Total annual research expenditures: $2.7 million. *Unit head:* Dr. Donna L. Hammond, Interim Head, 319-335-7946, Fax: 319-335-8930, E-mail: donna-hammond@uiowa.edu. *Application contact:* Dr. Stefan Strack, Director, Graduate Admissions, 319-384-4439, Fax: 319-335-8930, E-mail: pharmacology-admissions@uiowa.edu.

The University of Kansas, Graduate Studies, School of Pharmacy, Department of Pharmacology and Toxicology, Program in Pharmacology and Toxicology, Lawrence, KS 66045. Offers MS, PhD. *Faculty:* 11 full-time (3 women). *Students:* 13 full-time (all women); includes 1 minority (Hispanic/Latino), 8 international. Average age 25. 58 applicants, 12% accepted, 4 enrolled. In 2010, 2 master's, 1 doctorate awarded. Terminal master's awarded for partial completion of doctoral program. *Degree requirements:* For master's, comprehensive exam, thesis; for doctorate, comprehensive exam, thesis/dissertation. *Entrance requirements:* For master's, GRE; for doctorate, GRE (minimum score: 600 verbal, 600 quantitative, 4.5 analytic). Additional exam requirements/recommendations for international students: Required—TOEFL (minimum score 600 paper-based; 250 computer-based; 100 iBT). *Application deadline:* For fall admission, 1/15 priority date for domestic students, 2/1 priority date for international students. Applications are processed on a rolling basis. Application fee: $55 ($65 for international students). Electronic applications accepted. *Expenses:* Tuition, state resident: full-time $7092; part-time $295.50 per credit hour. Tuition, nonresident: full-time $16,590; part-time $691.25 per credit hour. Required fees: $858; $71.49 per credit hour. Tuition and fees vary according to course load, campus/location and program. *Financial support:* Fellowships with full tuition reimbursements, research assistantships with full tuition reimbursements available. *Faculty research:* Neuropharmacology, neurodegeneration. *Unit head:* Dr. Nancy Muma, Chair, 785-864-4001, Fax: 785-864-5219, E-mail: nmuma@ku.edu. *Application contact:* Dr. R. Alexandar Moise, Assistant Professor/Director, 785-864-1010, Fax: 785-864-5219, E-mail: alexmoise@ku.edu.

The University of Kansas, University of Kansas Medical Center, School of Medicine, Department of Pharmacology, Toxicology and Therapeutics, Kansas City, KS 66160. Offers pharmacology (MS, PhD); toxicology (MS, PhD); MD/MS; MD/PhD. *Faculty:* 22 full-time (4 women). *Students:* 29 full-time (17 women); includes 1 minority (Hispanic/Latino), 11 international. Average age 28. 8 applicants, 100% accepted, 8 enrolled. In 2010, 4 doctorates awarded. Terminal master's awarded for partial completion of doctoral program. *Degree requirements:* For master's, comprehensive exam, thesis; for doctorate, one foreign language, comprehensive exam, thesis/dissertation. *Entrance requirements:* For master's and doctorate, GRE General Test. Additional exam requirements/recommendations for international students: Required—TOEFL. *Application deadline:* For fall admission, 1/15 priority date for domestic students. Applications are processed on a rolling basis. Application fee: $0. Electronic applications accepted. *Expenses:* Tuition, state resident: full-time $7092; part-time $295.50 per credit hour. Tuition, nonresident: full-time $16,590; part-time $691.25 per credit hour. Required fees: $858; $71.49 per credit hour. Tuition and fees vary according to course load, campus/location and program. *Financial support:* Fellowships with full tuition reimbursements, research assistantships with full tuition reimbursements, teaching assistantships with full tuition reimbursements, Federal Work-Study, scholarships/grants, traineeships, and unspecified assistantships available. Support available to part-time students. Financial award application deadline: 2/14; financial award applicants required to submit FAFSA. *Faculty research:* Liver nuclear receptors, hepatobiliary transporters, pharmacogenomics, estrogen-induced carcinogenesis, neuropharmacology of pain and depression. Total annual research expenditures: $7.9 million. *Unit head:* Dr. Gerald Carlson, Professor and Interim Chair, 913-588-7140, Fax: 913-588-7501, E-mail: gcarlson@kumc.edu. *Application contact:* Dr. Bruno Hagenbuch, Chair, Departmental Graduate Committee, 913-588-0028, Fax: 913-588-7501, E-mail: bhagenbuch@kumc.edu.

University of Kentucky, Graduate School, Graduate School Programs from the College of Medicine, Program in Molecular and Biomedical Pharmacology, Lexington, KY 40506-0032. Offers pharmacology (PhD); MD/PhD. *Degree requirements:* For doctorate, comprehensive exam, thesis/dissertation. *Entrance requirements:* For doctorate, GRE General Test, minimum undergraduate GPA of 2.75, graduate 3.0. Additional exam requirements/recommendations for international students: Required—TOEFL (minimum score 550 paper-based; 213 computer-based). Electronic applications accepted.

University of Louisville, School of Medicine, Department of Pharmacology and Toxicology, Louisville, KY 40292-0001. Offers MS, PhD, MD/PhD. *Faculty:* 59 full-time (9 women). *Students:* 34 full-time (19 women), 5 part-time (2 women); includes 5 Black or African American, non-Hispanic/Latino; 2 Asian, non-Hispanic/Latino; 1 Two or more races, non-Hispanic/Latino, 15 international. Average age 29. 52 applicants, 27% accepted, 10 enrolled. In 2010, 7 master's, 5 doctorates awarded. Terminal master's awarded for partial completion of doctoral program. *Degree requirements:* For master's, thesis; for doctorate, comprehensive exam, thesis/dissertation. *Entrance requirements:* For master's and doctorate, GRE General Test (minimum score of 1000 verbal and quantitative), minimum GPA of 3.0. Additional exam requirements/recommendations for international students: Required—TOEFL. *Application deadline:* For fall admission, 1/15 priority date for domestic and international students. Applications are processed on a rolling basis. Application fee: $50. Electronic applications accepted. *Expenses:* Tuition, state resident: full-time $9144; part-time $508 per credit hour. Tuition, nonresident: full-time $19,026; part-time $1057 per credit hour. Tuition and fees vary according to program and reciprocity agreements. *Financial support:* Fellowships with full tuition reimbursements, research assistantships with full tuition reimbursements available. Financial award application deadline: 4/15. *Faculty research:* Molecular pharmacogenetics; epidemiology; functional genomics; genetic predisposition to chemical carcinogenesis and drug toxicity; mechanisms of oxidative stress; alcohol-induced hepatitis, pancreatitis, and hepatocellular carcinoma; molecular and cardiac toxicology; molecular biology and genetics of DNA damage and repair in humans; mechanisms of chemoresistance; arsenic toxicity and cell cycle disruption; molecular pharmacology of novel G protein-coupled receptors. *Unit head:* Dr. David W. Hein, Chair, 502-852-5141, Fax: 502-852-7868, E-mail: dhein@louisville.edu. *Application contact:* Heddy R. Rubin, Information Contact, 502-852-5741, Fax: 502-852-7868, E-mail: hrrubi01@gwise.louisville.edu.

The University of Manchester, Faculty of Life Sciences, Manchester, United Kingdom. Offers adaptive organismal biology (M Phil, PhD); animal biology (M Phil, PhD); biochemistry (M Phil, PhD); bioinformatics (M Phil, PhD); biomolecular sciences (M Phil, PhD); biotechnology (M Phil, PhD); cell biology (M Phil, PhD); cell matrix research (M Phil, PhD); channels and transporters (M Phil, PhD); developmental biology (M Phil, PhD); Egyptology (M Phil, PhD); environmental biology (M Phil, PhD); evolutionary biology (M Phil, PhD); gene expression (M Phil, PhD); genetics (M Phil, PhD); history of science, technology and medicine (M Phil, PhD); immunology (M Phil, PhD); integrative neurobiology and behavior (M Phil, PhD); membrane trafficking (M Phil, PhD); microbiology (M Phil, PhD); molecular and cellular neuroscience (M Phil, PhD); molecular biology (M Phil, PhD); molecular cancer studies (M Phil, PhD); neuroscience (M Phil,

Pharmacology

The University of Manchester (continued)

PhD); ophthalmology (M Phil, PhD); optometry (M Phil, PhD); organelle function (M Phil, PhD); pharmacology (M Phil, PhD); physiology (M Phil, PhD); plant sciences (M Phil, PhD); stem cell research (M Phil, PhD); structural biology (M Phil, PhD); systems neuroscience (M Phil, PhD); toxicology (M Phil, PhD).

University of Manitoba, Faculty of Medicine and Faculty of Graduate Studies, Graduate Programs in Medicine, Department of Pharmacology and Therapeutics, Winnipeg, MB R3T 2N2, Canada. Offers M Sc, PhD. Part-time programs available. Terminal master's awarded for partial completion of doctoral program. *Degree requirements:* For master's, thesis; for doctorate, thesis/dissertation. *Entrance requirements:* For master's and doctorate, GRE. Additional exam requirements/recommendations for international students: Required—TOEFL. *Faculty research:* Clinical pharmacology; neuropharmacology; cardiac, hepatic, and renal pharmacology.

University of Maryland, Baltimore, Graduate School, Graduate Program in Life Sciences, Program in Molecular Medicine, Baltimore, MD 21201. Offers cancer biology (PhD); cell and molecular physiology (PhD); human genetics and genomic medicine (PhD); molecular medicine (MS); molecular toxicology and pharmacology (PhD); MD/PhD. *Entrance requirements:* Additional exam requirements/recommendations for international students: Required—TOEFL (minimum score 600 paper-based; 100 iBT); Recommended—IELTS (minimum score 7). Electronic applications accepted. Part-time tuition and fees vary according to course load, degree level and program.

University of Medicine and Dentistry of New Jersey, Graduate School of Biomedical Sciences, Graduate Programs in Biomedical Sciences–Newark, Department of Pharmacology and Physiology, Newark, NJ 07107. Offers PhD. *Degree requirements:* For doctorate, thesis/dissertation, qualifying exam. *Entrance requirements:* For doctorate, GRE General Test. Additional exam requirements/recommendations for international students: Required—TOEFL. Electronic applications accepted.

University of Miami, Graduate School, Miller School of Medicine, Graduate Programs in Medicine, Department of Molecular and Cellular Pharmacology, Coral Gables, FL 33124. Offers PhD, MD/PhD. *Degree requirements:* For doctorate, thesis/dissertation, dissertation defense, laboratory rotations, qualifying exam. *Entrance requirements:* For doctorate, GRE General Test. Additional exam requirements/recommendations for international students: Required—TOEFL (minimum score 550 paper-based; 213 computer-based). *Faculty research:* Membrane and cardiovascular pharmacology, muscle contraction, hormone action signal transduction, nuclear transport.

University of Michigan, Rackham Graduate School, Program in Biomedical Sciences (PIBS), Department of Pharmacology, Ann Arbor, MI 48109-5632. Offers MS, PhD. *Faculty:* 16 full-time (5 women), 6 part-time/adjunct (0 women). *Students:* 19 full-time (12 women); includes 5 minority (2 Black or African American, non-Hispanic/Latino; 3 Asian, non-Hispanic/Latino). Average age 26. 46 applicants, 15 enrolled. In 2010, 7 doctorates awarded. *Degree requirements:* For doctorate, thesis/dissertation, oral preliminary exam, oral defense of dissertation. *Entrance requirements:* For doctorate, GRE General Test, 3 letters of recommendation, research experience, all undergraduate transcripts. *Application deadline:* For fall admission, 12/1 for domestic students. Application fee: $65 ($75 for international students). Electronic applications accepted. *Expenses:* Tuition, state resident: full-time $17,784; part-time $1116 per credit hour. Tuition, nonresident: full-time $35,944; part-time $2125 per credit hour. International tuition: $35,994 full-time. Required fees: $95 per semester. Tuition and fees vary according to course load, degree level and program. *Financial support:* In 2010–11, 19 students received support, including 9 fellowships with full tuition reimbursements available (averaging $26,500 per year), 10 research assistantships with full tuition reimbursements available (averaging $26,500 per year); scholarships/grants, traineeships, health care benefits, and unspecified assistantships also available. Financial award application deadline: 12/1. *Faculty research:* Signal transduction, addiction research, cancer pharmacology, drug metabolism and pharmacogenetics. Total annual research expenditures: $7.2 million. *Unit head:* Dr. Paul F. Hollenberg, Professor/Chair, 734-764-8166, Fax: 734-763-5387, E-mail: phollen@umich.edu. *Application contact:* Michelle S. Melis, Director of Student Life, 734-615-6538, Fax: 734-647-7022, E-mail: msmtegan@umich.edu.

University of Minnesota, Duluth, Medical School, Program in Pharmacology, Duluth, MN 55812-2496. Offers MS, PhD. MS, PhD offered jointly with University of Minnesota, Twin Cities Campus. Terminal master's awarded for partial completion of doctoral program. *Degree requirements:* For master's, thesis, final oral exam; for doctorate, thesis/dissertation, final oral exam, oral and written preliminary exams. *Entrance requirements:* For master's and doctorate, GRE General Test. Additional exam requirements/recommendations for international students: Required—TOEFL. *Faculty research:* Drug addiction, alcohol and hypertension, neurotransmission, allergic airway disease, auditory neuroscience.

University of Minnesota, Twin Cities Campus, College of Pharmacy and Graduate School, Graduate Programs in Pharmacy, Graduate Program in Experimental and Clinical Pharmacology, Minneapolis, MN 55455-0213. Offers MS, PhD. *Degree requirements:* For doctorate, thesis/dissertation.

University of Minnesota, Twin Cities Campus, Medical School, Department of Pharmacology, Minneapolis, MN 55455. Offers MS, PhD. *Faculty:* 47 full-time (10 women). *Students:* 39 full-time (23 women); includes 4 Asian, non-Hispanic/Latino, 14 international. Average age 28. 57 applicants, 25% accepted, 5 enrolled. In 2010, 2 master's, 8 doctorates awarded. Terminal master's awarded for partial completion of doctoral program. *Degree requirements:* For master's, thesis (for some programs); for doctorate, thesis/dissertation. *Entrance requirements:* For master's and doctorate, GRE General Test. Additional exam requirements/recommendations for international students: Required—TOEFL (minimum score 603 paper-based; 250 computer-based; 100 iBT). *Application deadline:* For fall admission, 1/15 for domestic and international students. Applications are processed on a rolling basis. Application fee: $75 ($95 for international students). Electronic applications accepted. *Financial support:* In 2010–11, 39 students received support, including 13 fellowships with full tuition reimbursements available (averaging $24,500 per year), 38 research assistantships with full tuition reimbursements available (averaging $24,500 per year); institutionally sponsored loans, scholarships/grants, and traineeships also available. Financial award application deadline: 1/15. *Faculty research:* Molecular pharmacology, cancer chemotherapy, neuropharmacology, biochemical pharmacology, behavioral pharmacology. Total annual research expenditures: $7.6 million. *Unit head:* Dr. Horace Loh, Head, 612-625-9997, Fax: 612-625-8408, E-mail: lohxx001@umn.edu. *Application contact:* Graduate Program Assistant, 612-625-9997, Fax: 612-625-8408, E-mail: phclgrad@umn.edu.

University of Mississippi, Graduate School, School of Pharmacy, Graduate Programs in Pharmacy, Oxford, University, MS 38677. Offers medicinal chemistry (PhD); pharmaceutical sciences (MS); pharmaceutics (PhD); pharmacognosy (PhD); pharmacology (PhD); pharmacy administration (PhD). *Students:* 99 full-time (37 women), 10 part-time (5 women); includes 14 minority (5 Black or African American, non-Hispanic/Latino; 6 Asian, non-Hispanic/Latino; 2 Hispanic/Latino; 1 Two or more races, non-Hispanic/Latino), 71 international. In 2010, 8 master's, 10 doctorates awarded. *Unit head:* Dr. Barbara G. Wells, Dean, 662-915-7265, Fax: 662-915-5704, E-mail: pharmacy@olemiss.edu. *Application contact:* Dr. Christy M. Wyandt, Associate Dean, 662-915-7474, Fax: 662-915-7577, E-mail: cwyandt@olemiss.edu.

University of Mississippi Medical Center, School of Graduate Studies in the Health Sciences, Department of Pharmacology and Toxicology, Jackson, MS 39216-4505. Offers pharmacology (MS, PhD); toxicology (MS, PhD); MD/PhD. Terminal master's awarded for partial completion of doctoral program. *Degree requirements:* For master's, thesis; for doctorate, thesis/dissertation, first authored publication. *Entrance requirements:* For master's and doctorate, GRE General Test, minimum GPA of 3.0. *Faculty research:* Neuropharmacology, environmental toxicology, aging, immunopharmacology, cardiovascular pharmacology.

University of Missouri, School of Medicine and Graduate School, Graduate Programs in Medicine, Department of Medical Pharmacology and Physiology, Columbia, MO 65211. Offers pharmacology (MS, PhD); physiology (MS, PhD). *Degree requirements:* For master's, thesis; for doctorate, thesis/dissertation. *Entrance requirements:* For master's and doctorate, GRE General Test, minimum GPA of 3.0. Additional exam requirements/recommendations for international students: Required—TOEFL (minimum score 500 paper-based; 173 computer-based; 61 iBT). *Faculty research:* Endocrine and metabolic pharmacology, biochemical pharmacology, neuropharmacology, receptors and transmembrane signaling.

University of Nebraska Medical Center, Graduate Studies, Department of Pharmacology and Experimental Neuroscience, Omaha, NE 68198. Offers neuroscience (MS, PhD); pharmacology (MS, PhD). *Faculty:* 25 full-time, 9 part-time/adjunct. *Students:* 26 full-time (15 women), 3 part-time (2 women); includes 3 Asian, non-Hispanic/Latino; 1 Hispanic/Latino, 9 international. Average age 25. 31 applicants, 42% accepted, 12 enrolled. In 2010, 4 doctorates awarded. Terminal master's awarded for partial completion of doctoral program. *Degree requirements:* For master's, comprehensive exam, thesis; for doctorate, comprehensive exam, thesis/dissertation. *Entrance requirements:* For master's and doctorate, GRE General Test. Additional exam requirements/recommendations for international students: Required—TOEFL (minimum score 600 paper-based; 250 computer-based). *Application deadline:* For fall admission, 2/1 for domestic and international students. Applications are processed on a rolling basis. Application fee: $45. Electronic applications accepted. *Expenses:* Tuition, state resident: part-time $198.25 per semester hour. Required fees: $63 per semester. *Financial support:* In 2010–11, 3 students received support, including fellowships with full tuition reimbursements available (averaging $21,000 per year), research assistantships with full tuition reimbursements available (averaging $21,000 per year); career-related internships or fieldwork, institutionally sponsored loans, scholarships/grants, traineeships, health care benefits, and unspecified assistantships also available. Financial award application deadline: 2/15. *Faculty research:* Neuropharmacology, molecular pharmacology, toxicology, molecular biology, neuroscience. Total annual research expenditures: $1.8 million. *Unit head:* Dr. Keshore Bidasee, Chair, Graduate Studies, 402-559-9018, Fax: 402-559-7495, E-mail: kbidasee@unmc.edu. *Application contact:* Connie Curro, Office Assistant, 402-559-4044, E-mail: ccurro@unmc.edu.

The University of North Carolina at Chapel Hill, School of Medicine and Graduate School, Graduate Programs in Medicine, Department of Pharmacology, Chapel Hill, NC 27599-7365. Offers PhD. *Faculty:* 45 full-time (11 women), 8 part-time/adjunct (0 women). *Students:* 39 full-time (18 women); includes 2 Black or African American, non-Hispanic/Latino; 1 Hispanic/Latino, 3 international. Average age 25. In 2010, 6 doctorates awarded. *Degree requirements:* For doctorate, comprehensive exam, thesis/dissertation. *Entrance requirements:* For doctorate, GRE General Test, minimum GPA of 3.0. Additional exam requirements/recommendations for international students: Required—TOEFL. *Application deadline:* For fall admission, 1/1 priority date for domestic and international students. Applications are processed on a rolling basis. Application fee: $77. Electronic applications accepted. *Financial support:* In 2010–11, 17 fellowships with full tuition reimbursements (averaging $26,000 per year), 22 research assistantships with full tuition reimbursements (averaging $26,000 per year) were awarded. *Faculty research:* Signal transduction, cell adhesion, receptors, ion channels. Total annual research expenditures: $13.7 million. *Unit head:* Dr. Gary L. Johnson, Chair, 919-843-3107, Fax: 919-966-5640, E-mail: glj@med.unc.edu. *Application contact:* Kathy C. Justice, Student Services Manager, Pharmacology, 919-966-1153, Fax: 919-966-5640, E-mail: kcj@med.unc.edu.

University of North Dakota, Graduate School and Graduate School, Graduate Programs in Medicine, Department of Pharmacology, Physiology, and Therapeutics, Grand Forks, ND 58202. Offers pharmacology (MS, PhD); physiology (MS, PhD). *Faculty:* 14 full-time (2 women), 2 part-time/adjunct (0 women). *Students:* 14 full-time (5 women), 2 part-time (1 woman); includes 1 minority (Asian, non-Hispanic/Latino), 5 international. Average age 28. 23 applicants, 17% accepted, 4 enrolled. In 2010, 3 doctorates awarded. *Degree requirements:* For master's, comprehensive exam, thesis; for doctorate, thesis/dissertation, written and oral exams. *Entrance requirements:* For master's, GRE General Test or MCAT, minimum GPA of 3.0; for doctorate, GRE General Test, minimum GPA of 3.5. Additional exam requirements/recommendations for international students: Required—TOEFL (minimum score 550 paper-based; 213 computer-based; 79 iBT), IELTS (minimum score 6.5). *Application deadline:* For fall admission, 2/1 priority date for domestic and international students. Application fee: $35. Electronic applications accepted. *Expenses:* Tuition, state resident: full-time $5857; part-time $306.74 per credit. Tuition, nonresident: full-time $15,666; part-time $729.77 per credit. Required fees: $53.42 per credit. Tuition and fees vary according to course load, program and reciprocity agreements. *Financial support:* In 2010–11, 14 students received support, including 14 research assistantships with full tuition reimbursements available (averaging $13,997 per year); fellowships with full and partial tuition reimbursements available, teaching assistantships with full tuition reimbursements available, Federal Work-Study, institutionally sponsored loans, scholarships/grants, health care benefits, tuition waivers (full and partial), and unspecified assistantships also available. Support available to part-time students. Financial award application deadline: 3/15; financial award applicants required to submit FAFSA. Total annual research expenditures: $3.4 million. *Unit head:* Dr. James Hasselton, Graduate Director, 701-777-4683, Fax: 701-777-4490, E-mail: hasselton@medicine.nodak.edu. *Application contact:* Matt Anderson, Admissions Specialist, 701-777-2947, Fax: 701-777-3619, E-mail: matthew.anderson@gradschool.und.edu.

University of North Texas Health Science Center at Fort Worth, Graduate School of Biomedical Sciences, Fort Worth, TX 76107-2699. Offers anatomy and cell biology (MS, PhD); biochemistry and molecular biology (MS, PhD); biomedical sciences (MS, PhD); biotechnology (MS); forensic genetics (MS); integrative physiology (MS, PhD); medical science (MS); microbiology and immunology (MS, PhD); pharmacology (MS, PhD); science education (MS); DO/MS; DO/PhD. Terminal master's awarded for partial completion of doctoral program. *Degree requirements:* For master's, thesis; for doctorate, thesis/dissertation. *Entrance requirements:* For master's and doctorate, GRE General Test. Additional exam requirements/recommendations for international students: Required—TOEFL. *Expenses:* Contact institution. *Faculty research:* Alzheimer's disease, aging, eye diseases, cancer, cardiovascular disease.

University of Pennsylvania, Perelman School of Medicine, Biomedical Graduate Studies, Graduate Group in Pharmacological Sciences, Philadelphia, PA 19104. Offers pharmacology (PhD); MD/PhD; VMD/PhD. *Faculty:* 94. *Students:* 73 full-time (40 women); includes 2 Black or African American, non-Hispanic/Latino; 1 American Indian or Alaska Native, non-Hispanic/Latino; 12 Asian, non-Hispanic/Latino; 3 Hispanic/Latino, 7 international. 99 applicants, 23% accepted, 15 enrolled. In 2010, 13 doctorates awarded. *Degree requirements:* For doctorate, thesis/dissertation. *Entrance requirements:* For doctorate, GRE General Test, previous course work in physical or natural science. Additional exam requirements/recommendations for international students: Required—TOEFL. *Application deadline:* For fall admission, 12/8 priority date for domestic and international students. Applications are processed on a rolling basis. Application fee: $70. Electronic applications accepted. *Expenses:* Tuition: Full-time $25,660; part-time $4758 per course. Required fees: $2152; $270 per course. Tuition and fees vary according to course load, degree level and program. *Financial support:* In 2010–11, 73 students received support; fellowships, research assistantships, scholarships/grants, traineeships, and unspecified assistantships available. *Faculty research:* Properties and regulation of receptors for biogenic amines, molecular aspects of transduction, mechanisms of biosynthesis, biological mechanisms of depression, developmental events in the nervous system. *Unit head:* Dr. Vladimir Muzykantov, Chair, 215-898-9823, E-mail: coord@pharm.med.upenn.edu. *Application contact:* Sarah Squire, Coordinator, 215-898-1790, Fax: 215-573-2236, E-mail: sasquire@mail.med.upenn.edu.

University of Prince Edward Island, Atlantic Veterinary College, Graduate Program in Veterinary Medicine, Charlottetown, PE C1A 4P3, Canada. Offers anatomy (M Sc, PhD); bacteriology (M Sc, PhD); clinical pharmacology (M Sc, PhD); clinical sciences (M Sc, PhD); epidemiology (M Sc, PhD), including reproduction; fish health (M Sc, PhD); food animal nutrition (M Sc, PhD); immunology (M Sc, PhD); microanatomy (M Sc, PhD); parasitology (M Sc, PhD);

pathology (M Sc, PhD); pharmacology (M Sc, PhD); physiology (M Sc, PhD); toxicology (M Sc, PhD); veterinary science (M Vet Sc); virology (M Sc, PhD). Part-time programs available. *Degree requirements:* For master's, thesis; for doctorate, thesis/dissertation. *Entrance requirements:* For master's, DVM, B Sc honors degree, or equivalent; for doctorate, M Sc. Additional exam requirements/recommendations for international students: Required—TOEFL (minimum score 550 paper-based; 213 computer-based; 80 iBT). *Expenses:* Contact institution. *Faculty research:* Animal health management, infectious diseases, fin fish and shellfish health, basic biomedical sciences, ecosystem health.

University of Puerto Rico, Medical Sciences Campus, School of Medicine, Division of Graduate Studies, Department of Pharmacology and Toxicology, San Juan, PR 00936-5067. Offers MS, PhD. *Degree requirements:* For master's, one foreign language, thesis; for doctorate, one foreign language, comprehensive exam, thesis/dissertation. *Entrance requirements:* For master's and doctorate, GRE General Test, GRE Subject Test, interview, minimum GPA of 3.0, 3 letters of recommendation. Electronic applications accepted. *Faculty research:* Cardiovascular, central nervous system, and endocrine pharmacology; anti-cancer drugs; sodium pump; mitochondrial DNA repair; Huntington's disease.

University of Rhode Island, Graduate School, College of Pharmacy, Department of Biomedical and Pharmaceutical Sciences, Kingston, RI 02881. Offers medicinal chemistry and pharmacognosy (MS, PhD); pharmaceutics and pharmacokinetics (MS, PhD); pharmacology and toxicology (MS, PhD). Part-time programs available. *Faculty:* 20 full-time (6 women), 4 part-time/adjunct (1 woman). *Students:* 43 full-time (23 women), 15 part-time (4 women); includes 11 minority (2 Black or African American, non-Hispanic/Latino; 8 Asian, non-Hispanic/Latino; 1 Two or more races, non-Hispanic/Latino), 21 international. In 2010, 7 master's, 8 doctorates awarded. *Entrance requirements:* For master's and doctorate, GRE, 2 letters of recommendation. Additional exam requirements/recommendations for international students: Required—TOEFL (minimum score 550 paper-based; 213 computer-based). Application fee: $65. Electronic applications accepted. *Expenses:* Tuition, state resident: full-time $9588; part-time $533 per credit hour. Tuition, nonresident: full-time $22,968; part-time $1276 per credit hour. Required fees: $1282; $68 per semester. Tuition and fees vary according to program. *Financial support:* In 2010–11, 8 research assistantships with partial tuition reimbursements (averaging $8,572 per year), 15 teaching assistantships with full and partial tuition reimbursements (averaging $11,446 per year) were awarded. Financial award applicants required to submit FAFSA. *Faculty research:* Chemical carcinogenesis with a major emphasis on the structural and synthetic aspects of DNA-adduct formation, drug-drug/herb interaction, drug-genetic interaction, signaling of nuclear receptors, transcriptional regulation, oncogenesis. Total annual research expenditures: $6.1 million. *Unit head:* Dr. Clinton O. Chichester, Chair, 401-874-5034, Fax: 401-874-5787, E-mail: chichester@uri.edu. *Application contact:* Dr. David C. Rowley, Graduate Coordinator, 401-874-9228, Fax: 401-874-2516, E-mail: drowley@uri.edu.

University of Rochester, School of Medicine and Dentistry, Graduate Programs in Medicine and Dentistry, Department of Pharmacology and Physiology, Programs in Pharmacology, Rochester, NY 14627. Offers MS, PhD. Terminal master's awarded for partial completion of doctoral program. *Degree requirements:* For master's, thesis; for doctorate, thesis/dissertation, qualifying exam. *Entrance requirements:* For master's and doctorate, GRE General Test.

University of Saskatchewan, College of Medicine, Department of Pharmacology, Saskatoon, SK S7N 5A2, Canada. Offers M Sc, PhD. *Degree requirements:* For master's, thesis; for doctorate, thesis/dissertation. *Entrance requirements:* Additional exam requirements/recommendations for international students: Required—TOEFL. *Faculty research:* Neuropharmacology, mechanisms of action of anticancer drugs, clinical pharmacology, cardiovascular pharmacology, toxicology: alcohol-related changes in fetal brain development.

The University of South Dakota, School of Medicine and Health Sciences and Graduate School, Biomedical Sciences Graduate Program, Physiology and Pharmacology Group, Vermillion, SD 57069-2390. Offers MS, PhD. Terminal master's awarded for partial completion of doctoral program. *Degree requirements:* For master's, thesis; for doctorate, comprehensive exam, thesis/dissertation. *Entrance requirements:* For master's and doctorate, GRE General Test, minimum GPA of 3.0. Additional exam requirements/recommendations for international students: Required—TOEFL (minimum score 550 paper-based; 213 computer-based; 80 iBT), IELTS (minimum score 6). Electronic applications accepted. *Expenses:* Contact institution. *Faculty research:* Pulmonary physiology and pharmacology, drug abuse, reproduction, signal transduction, cardiovascular physiology and pharmacology.

The University of Texas Health Science Center at San Antonio, Graduate School of Biomedical Sciences, Department of Pharmacology, San Antonio, TX 78229-3900. Offers neuroscience (PhD). *Faculty:* 20 full-time (3 women), 7 part-time/adjunct (1 woman). *Students:* 23 full-time (15 women), 1 (woman) part-time; includes 1 American Indian or Alaska Native, non-Hispanic/Latino; 5 Asian, non-Hispanic/Latino; 5 Hispanic/Latino, 2 international. Average age 24. In 2010, 1 doctorate awarded. *Degree requirements:* For doctorate, comprehensive exam, thesis/dissertation. *Entrance requirements:* For doctorate, GRE General Test, minimum GPA of 3.0. Additional exam requirements/recommendations for international students: Required—TOEFL (minimum score 560 paper-based; 220 computer-based; 68 iBT). *Application deadline:* For fall admission, 1/15 priority date for domestic and international students. Applications are processed on a rolling basis. Application fee: $0. Electronic applications accepted. *Expenses:* Tuition, state resident: full-time $3072; part-time $128 per credit hour. Tuition, nonresident: full-time $11,928; part-time $497 per credit hour. Required fees: $1078; $1078 per year. One-time fee: $60. *Financial support:* In 2010–11, 1 fellowship (averaging $26,000 per year), 23 teaching assistantships (averaging $26,000 per year) were awarded; institutionally sponsored loans, scholarships/grants, and health care benefits also available. Financial award application deadline: 6/30; financial award applicants required to submit FAFSA. *Faculty research:* Neuropharmacology, autonomic and endocrine homeostasis, aging, cancer biology. Total annual research expenditures: $11.1 million. *Unit head:* Alan Frazer, Chairman, 210-567-4205, Fax: 210-567-4300, E-mail: frazer@uthscsa.edu. *Application contact:* Nakia Scott, Academic Program Coordinator, 210-567-4220, Fax: 210-567-4303, E-mail: scottn3@uthscsa.edu.

The University of Texas Medical Branch, Graduate School of Biomedical Sciences, Program in Pharmacology and Toxicology, Galveston, TX 77555. Offers pharmacology (MS); pharmacology and toxicology (PhD). *Degree requirements:* For master's, thesis or alternative; for doctorate, thesis/dissertation. *Entrance requirements:* For master's and doctorate, GRE General Test. Additional exam requirements/recommendations for international students: Required—TOEFL (minimum score 550 paper-based; 213 computer-based).

University of the Sciences in Philadelphia, College of Graduate Studies, Program in Chemistry, Biochemistry and Pharmacognosy, Philadelphia, PA 19104-4495. Offers biochemistry (MS, PhD); chemistry (MS, PhD); pharmacognosy (MS, PhD). Part-time programs available. *Degree requirements:* For master's, thesis, qualifying exams; for doctorate, comprehensive exam, thesis/dissertation, qualifying exams. *Entrance requirements:* For master's and doctorate, GRE General Test, GRE Subject Test. Additional exam requirements/recommendations for international students: Required—TOEFL, TWE. *Expenses:* Contact institution. *Faculty research:* Organic and medicinal synthesis, mass spectroscopy use in protein analysis, study of analogues of taxol, cholesteryl esters.

University of the Sciences in Philadelphia, College of Graduate Studies, Program in Pharmacology and Toxicology, Philadelphia, PA 19104-4495. Offers pharmacology (MS, PhD); toxicology (MS, PhD). Terminal master's awarded for partial completion of doctoral program. *Degree requirements:* For master's, thesis; for doctorate, comprehensive exam, thesis/dissertation. *Entrance requirements:* For master's and doctorate, GRE General Test. Additional exam requirements/recommendations for international students: Required—TOEFL, TWE. *Expenses:* Contact institution. *Faculty research:* Autonomic, cardiovascular, cellular, and molecular pharmacology; mechanisms of carcinogenesis; drug metabolism.

The University of Toledo, College of Graduate Studies, College of Pharmacy, Program in Pharmaceutical Sciences, Toledo, OH 43606-3390. Offers administrative pharmacy (MSPS); industrial pharmacy (MSPS); pharmacology toxicology (MSPS). *Degree requirements:* For master's, thesis. *Entrance requirements:* For master's, GRE General Test. Additional exam requirements/recommendations for international students: Required—TOEFL (minimum score 550 paper-based; 213 computer-based; 80 iBT). Electronic applications accepted. *Expenses:* Tuition, state resident: full-time $11,426; part-time $476 per credit hour. Tuition, nonresident: full-time $21,660; part-time $903 per credit hour. One-time fee: $62.

University of Toronto, School of Graduate Studies, Life Sciences Division, Department of Pharmacology and Toxicology, Toronto, ON M5S 1A1, Canada. Offers M Sc, PhD. Part-time programs available. *Degree requirements:* For master's, thesis; for doctorate, thesis/dissertation. *Entrance requirements:* For master's, B Sc or equivalent; background in pharmacology, biochemistry, and physiology; minimum B+ earned in at least 4 senior level classes; for doctorate, minimum B+ average.

University of Utah, Graduate School, College of Pharmacy, Department of Pharmacology and Toxicology, Salt Lake City, UT 84112. Offers PhD. *Faculty:* 19 full-time (5 women), 1 part-time/adjunct (0 women). *Students:* 16 full-time (9 women), 3 part-time (1 woman); includes 2 minority (both Hispanic/Latino), 1 international. Average age 28. 64 applicants, 9% accepted, 3 enrolled. In 2010, 5 doctorates awarded. Terminal master's awarded for partial completion of doctoral program. *Degree requirements:* For doctorate, comprehensive exam, thesis/dissertation, final exam. *Entrance requirements:* For doctorate, GRE Subject Test, BS in biology, chemistry, neuroscience. Additional exam requirements/recommendations for international students: Required—TOEFL (minimum score 600 paper-based; 250 computer-based; 100 iBT). *Application deadline:* For fall admission, 1/15 for domestic and international students. Application fee: $55 ($65 for international students). *Expenses:* Tuition, area resident: Part-time $179.19 per credit hour. Tuition, state resident: full-time $4384. Tuition, nonresident: full-time $16,684; part-time $630.67 per credit hour. Required fees: $350 per semester. Tuition and fees vary according to course load, degree level and program. *Financial support:* In 2010–11, 14 students received support, including 5 fellowships with partial tuition reimbursements available (averaging $11,000 per year), 17 research assistantships with full tuition reimbursements available (averaging $25,000 per year). Financial award application deadline: 1/15. *Faculty research:* Neuropharmacology, neurochemistry, biochemistry, molecular pharmacology, analytical chemistry. Total annual research expenditures: $4.8 million. *Unit head:* Dr. William R. Crowley, Chairman, 801-581-6287, Fax: 801-585-5111, E-mail: william.crowley@deans.pharm.utah.edu. *Application contact:* Sheila H. Merrill, Executive Secretary, 801-581-6287, Fax: 801-585-5111, E-mail: sheila.merrill@pharm.utah.edu.

University of Vermont, College of Medicine and Graduate College, Graduate Programs in Medicine, Department of Pharmacology, Burlington, VT 05405. Offers MS, PhD, MD/MS, MD/PhD. *Faculty:* 12 full-time (1 woman). *Students:* 6 (2 women); includes 1 Hispanic/Latino, 3 international. 24 applicants, 13% accepted, 2 enrolled. In 2010, 2 doctorates awarded. *Degree requirements:* For master's, thesis; for doctorate, thesis/dissertation. *Entrance requirements:* For master's and doctorate, GRE General Test. Additional exam requirements/recommendations for international students: Required—TOEFL (minimum score 550 paper-based; 213 computer-based; 80 iBT). *Application deadline:* For fall admission, 1/15 priority date for domestic students, 1/15 for international students. Applications are processed on a rolling basis. Application fee: $40. Electronic applications accepted. *Expenses:* Tuition, state resident: part-time $537 per credit hour. Tuition, nonresident: part-time $1355 per credit hour. *Financial support:* Fellowships, research assistantships, teaching assistantships available. Financial award application deadline: 3/1. *Faculty research:* Cardiovascular drugs, anticancer drugs. *Unit head:* Dr. M. Nelson, Chairperson, 802-656-2500. *Application contact:* Dr. Anthony Morielli, Director of Graduate Studies, 802-656-2500.

University of Virginia, School of Medicine, Department of Pharmacology, Charlottesville, VA 22903. Offers PhD, MD/PhD. *Faculty:* 22 full-time (5 women). *Students:* 14 full-time (10 women), 1 (woman) part-time; includes 1 Asian, non-Hispanic/Latino. Average age 27. In 2010, 4 doctorates awarded. *Degree requirements:* For doctorate, thesis/dissertation. *Entrance requirements:* For doctorate, GRE General Test, GRE Subject Test (recommended), 2 letters of recommendation. Additional exam requirements/recommendations for international students: Required—TOEFL. *Application deadline:* For fall admission, 1/15 for domestic and international students. Applications are processed on a rolling basis. Application fee: $60. Electronic applications accepted. *Financial support:* Fellowships, research assistantships, teaching assistantships available. Financial award applicants required to submit FAFSA. *Unit head:* Dr. Douglas A. Bayliss, Chairman, 434-924-1919, Fax: 434-982-3878. *Application contact:* Dr. Douglas A. Bayliss, Chairman, 434-924-1919, Fax: 434-982-3878.

University of Washington, Graduate School, School of Medicine, Graduate Programs in Medicine, Department of Pharmacology, Seattle, WA 98195. Offers PhD. *Degree requirements:* For doctorate, thesis/dissertation. *Entrance requirements:* For doctorate, GRE General Test, minimum GPA of 3.0. *Faculty research:* Neuroscience, cell physiology, molecular biology, regulation of metabolism, signal transduction.

University of Wisconsin–Madison, School of Medicine and Public Health and Graduate School, Graduate Programs in Medicine, Molecular and Cellular Pharmacology Program, Madison, WI 53706. Offers PhD. *Faculty:* 56 full-time (12 women). *Students:* 46 full-time (26 women); includes 1 Black or African American, non-Hispanic/Latino; 8 Asian, non-Hispanic/Latino; 3 Hispanic/Latino, 6 international. Average age 26. 86 applicants, 22% accepted, 12 enrolled. In 2010, 16 doctorates awarded. *Degree requirements:* For doctorate, comprehensive exam, thesis/dissertation. *Entrance requirements:* For doctorate, GRE. Additional exam requirements/recommendations for international students: Required—TOEFL (minimum score 550 paper-based; 213 computer-based). *Application deadline:* For fall admission, 12/15 priority date for domestic and international students. Applications are processed on a rolling basis. Application fee: $56. Electronic applications accepted. *Expenses:* Tuition, state resident: full-time $9887; part-time $617.96 per credit. Tuition, nonresident: full-time $24,054; part-time $1503.40 per credit. Required fees: $67.63 per credit. Tuition and fees vary according to reciprocity agreements. *Financial support:* In 2010–11, 46 students received support, including 13 fellowships with full tuition reimbursements available (averaging $24,000 per year), 33 research assistantships with full tuition reimbursements available (averaging $24,000 per year), teaching assistantships with full tuition reimbursements available (averaging $24,000 per year); scholarships/grants, traineeships, health care benefits, and unspecified assistantships also available. *Faculty research:* Protein kinases, signaling pathways, neurotransmitters, molecular recognition, receptors and transporters. *Unit head:* Dr. Patricia J. Keely, Director, 608-213-6820, Fax: 608-262-1257, E-mail: pjkeely@wisc.edu. *Application contact:* Lynn Louise Squire, Student Services Coordinator, 608-262-9826, Fax: 608-262-1257, E-mail: lsquire@wisc.edu.

Vanderbilt University, Graduate School and School of Medicine, Department of Pharmacology, Nashville, TN 37240-1001. Offers PhD, MD/PhD. *Faculty:* 22 full-time (5 women). *Students:* 56 full-time (25 women); includes 5 Black or African American, non-Hispanic/Latino; 3 Asian, non-Hispanic/Latino; 1 Hispanic/Latino; 2 Two or more races, non-Hispanic/Latino. Average age 28. In 2010, 14 doctorates awarded. *Degree requirements:* For doctorate, comprehensive exam, thesis/dissertation, preliminary, qualifying, and final exams. *Entrance requirements:* For doctorate, GRE General Test, GRE Subject Test (recommended). Additional exam requirements/recommendations for international students: Required—TOEFL (minimum score 570 paper-based; 230 computer-based; 88 iBT). *Application deadline:* For fall admission, 1/15 for domestic and international students. Application fee: $0. Electronic applications accepted. *Financial support:* Fellowships with full tuition reimbursements, research assistantships with full tuition reimbursements, Federal Work-Study, institutionally sponsored loans, scholarships/grants, traineeships, health care benefits, and tuition waivers (partial) available. Financial award application deadline: 1/15; financial award applicants required to submit CSS PROFILE or FAFSA. *Faculty research:* Molecular pharmacology, neuropharmacology, drug disposition

Pharmacology

Vanderbilt University *(continued)*
and toxicology, genetic mechanics, cell regulation. *Unit head:* Dr. Heidi E. Hamm, Chair, 615-343-3533, Fax: 615-343-1084, E-mail: heidi.hamm@vanderbilt.edu. *Application contact:* Dr. Joey V. Barnett, Director of Graduate Studies, 615-936-1722, Fax: 615-936-3910, E-mail: joey.barnett@vanderbilt.edu.

Virginia Commonwealth University, Medical College of Virginia-Professional Programs, School of Medicine, School of Medicine Graduate Programs, Department of Pharmacology and Toxicology, Richmond, VA 23284-9005. Offers neuroscience (PhD); pharmacology (Certificate); pharmacology and toxicology (MS, PhD); MD/PhD. *Faculty:* 35 full-time (9 women). *Students:* 47 full-time (27 women), 4 part-time (2 women); includes 13 minority (5 Black or African American, non-Hispanic/Latino; 6 Asian, non-Hispanic/Latino; 1 Hispanic/Latino; 1 Two or more races, non-Hispanic/Latino), 13 international. 66 applicants, 27% accepted, 10 enrolled. In 2010, 2 master's, 4 doctorates awarded. Terminal master's awarded for partial completion of doctoral program. *Degree requirements:* For master's, thesis; for doctorate, thesis/dissertation, comprehensive oral and written exams. *Entrance requirements:* For master's and doctorate, GRE or MCAT. Additional exam requirements/recommendations for international students: Required—TOEFL (minimum score 600 paper-based; 250 computer-based; 100 iBT). *Application deadline:* For fall admission, 4/15 for domestic students. Application fee: $50. Electronic applications accepted. *Expenses:* Tuition, state resident: full-time $4308; part-time $479 per credit hour. Tuition, nonresident: full-time $8942; part-time $994 per credit hour. Required fees: $2000; $85 per credit hour. Tuition and fees vary according to course level, course load, degree level, campus/location and program. *Financial support:* Fellowships, teaching assistantships available. *Faculty research:* Drug abuse, drug metabolism, pharmacodynamics, peptide synthesis, receptor mechanisms. *Unit head:* Dr. William L. Dewey, Chair, 804-827-0375, Fax: 804-827-1548, E-mail: wdewey@vcu.edu. *Application contact:* Dr. Stephen T. Sawyer, Graduate Program Coordinator, 804-828-7918, Fax: 804-827-1548, E-mail: ssawyer@vcu.edu.

Virginia Commonwealth University, Program in Pre-Medical Basic Health Sciences, Richmond, VA 23284-9005. Offers anatomy (CBHS); biochemistry (CBHS); human genetics (CBHS); microbiology (CBHS); pharmacology (CBHS); physiology (CBHS). *Students:* 86 full-time (43 women), 2 part-time (1 woman); includes 42 minority (5 Black or African American, non-Hispanic/Latino; 29 Asian, non-Hispanic/Latino; 5 Hispanic/Latino; 3 Two or more races, non-Hispanic/Latino). 314 applicants, 64% accepted. In 2010, 70 CBHSs awarded. *Entrance requirements:* For degree, GRE, MCAT or DAT, course work in organic chemistry, minimum undergraduate GPA of 2.8. Additional exam requirements/recommendations for international students: Required—TOEFL (minimum score 600 paper-based). *Application deadline:* For fall admission, 6/1 for domestic students. Application fee: $50. Electronic applications accepted. *Expenses:* Tuition, state resident: full-time $4308; part-time $479 per credit hour. Tuition, nonresident: full-time $8942; part-time $994 per credit hour. Required fees: $2000; $85 per credit hour. Tuition and fees vary according to course level, course load, degree level, campus/location and program. *Unit head:* Dr. Louis J. De Felice, Director, 804-828-9501, E-mail: premedcert@vcu.edu. *Application contact:* Zack McDowell, Administrator, 804-828-9501, E-mail: premedcert@vcu.edu.

Wake Forest University, School of Medicine and Graduate School of Arts and Sciences, Graduate Programs in Medicine, Program in Physiology and Pharmacology, Winston-Salem, NC 27109. Offers pharmacology (PhD); physiology (PhD); MD/PhD. *Degree requirements:* For doctorate, thesis/dissertation. *Entrance requirements:* For doctorate, GRE General Test. Additional exam requirements/recommendations for international students: Required—TOEFL. Electronic applications accepted. *Faculty research:* Aging, substance abuse, cardiovascular control, endocrine systems, toxicology.

Wayne State University, Eugene Applebaum College of Pharmacy and Health Sciences, Department of Pharmacy Practice, Detroit, MI 48202. Offers medicinal chemistry (MS, PhD); pharmaceutical sciences (MS, PhD); pharmaceutics (MS, PhD); pharmacology (MS, PhD); pharmacy (Pharm D). *Faculty:* 1 full-time (0 women). *Students:* 298 full-time (185 women), 42 part-time (26 women); includes 53 minority (8 Black or African American, non-Hispanic/Latino; 45 Asian, non-Hispanic/Latino), 39 international. Average age 25. 73 applicants, 53% accepted, 39 enrolled. In 2010, 77 doctorates awarded. Terminal master's awarded for partial completion of doctoral program. *Degree requirements:* For master's, thesis; for doctorate, thesis/dissertation. *Entrance requirements:* For master's, GRE General Test, minimum GPA of 2.6; for doctorate, GRE General Test, minimum GPA of 3.0. Additional exam requirements/

recommendations for international students: Required—TOEFL (minimum score 550 paper-based; 213 computer-based); Recommended—TWE (minimum score 6). *Application deadline:* For fall admission, 1/31 priority date for domestic students, 6/1 for international students; for winter admission, 10/1 for international students; for spring admission, 2/1 for international students. Applications are processed on a rolling basis. Application fee: $30 ($50 for international students). Electronic applications accepted. *Expenses:* Tuition, state resident: full-time $7662; part-time $478.85 per credit hour. Tuition, nonresident: full-time $16,920; part-time $1057.55 per credit hour. Required fees: $571; $35.70 per credit hour. $188.05 per semester. Tuition and fees vary according to course load and program. *Financial support:* Fellowships, research assistantships with tuition reimbursements, scholarships/grants available. Support available to part-time students. *Faculty research:* Pharmacodynamics and pharmacokinetics of anti-infective agents, efficacy of drug treatments for traumatic head injury and stroke, cultural difference in Arab-Americans related to diabetes treatment and prevention, drug disposition and effect in pediatrics, evaluation of anticoagulation regimens. *Unit head:* Dr. David J. Edwards, Chair, 313-577-0827, Fax: 313-577-5369. *Application contact:* William Lindblad, Associate Professor, 313-577-0513, E-mail: wlindbl@wayne.edu.

Wayne State University, School of Medicine, Department of Pharmacology, Detroit, MI 48202. Offers MS, PhD. *Faculty:* 3 full-time (0 women). *Students:* 7 full-time (all women), 1 (woman) part-time; includes 2 Asian, non-Hispanic/Latino; 1 Hispanic/Latino, 2 international. Average age 28. 23 applicants, 0% accepted, 0 enrolled. In 2010, 1 doctorate awarded. *Degree requirements:* For doctorate, thesis/dissertation. *Entrance requirements:* For master's and doctorate, GRE General Test. Additional exam requirements/recommendations for international students: Required—TOEFL (minimum score 550 paper-based; 213 computer-based); Recommended—TWE (minimum score 6). *Application deadline:* For fall admission, 4/30 for domestic students, 6/1 for international students; for winter admission, 10/1 for international students; for spring admission, 2/1 for international students. Applications are processed on a rolling basis. Application fee: $30 ($50 for international students). Electronic applications accepted. *Expenses:* Tuition, state resident: full-time $7662; part-time $478.85 per credit hour. Tuition, nonresident: full-time $16,920; part-time $1057.55 per credit hour. Required fees: $571; $35.70 per credit hour. $188.05 per semester. Tuition and fees vary according to course load and program. *Financial support:* In 2010–11, 1 fellowship with tuition reimbursement (averaging $20,867 per year), 7 research assistantships with tuition reimbursements (averaging $21,501 per year) were awarded; teaching assistantships. Financial award application deadline: 4/30. *Faculty research:* Molecular and cellular biology of cancer and anti-cancer therapies; molecular and cellular biology of protein trafficking, signal transduction and aging; environmental toxicology and drug metabolism; functional cellular and in vivo imaging; neuroscience. Total annual research expenditures: $2.6 million. *Unit head:* Dr. Bonnie Sloane, Chair, 313-577-1580, Fax: 313-577-6739, E-mail: aa3402@wayne.edu. *Application contact:* Ray Mattingly, Associate Professor, 313-577-6022, E-mail: r.mattingly@wayne.edu.

West Virginia University, School of Medicine, Graduate Programs at the Health Sciences Center, Interdisciplinary Graduate Programs in Biomedical Sciences, Program in Pharmaceutical and Pharmacological Sciences, Morgantown, WV 26506. Offers MS, PhD, MD/PhD. *Degree requirements:* For doctorate, comprehensive exam, thesis/dissertation. *Entrance requirements:* For doctorate, GRE General Test, minimum GPA of 3.0. Additional exam requirements/recommendations for international students: Required—TOEFL. Electronic applications accepted. *Faculty research:* Medicinal chemistry, pharmacokinetics, nano-pharmaceutics, polymer-based drug delivery, molecular therapeutics.

Wright State University, School of Medicine, Program in Pharmacology and Toxicology, Dayton, OH 45435. Offers MS. *Degree requirements:* For master's, thesis optional.

Yale University, School of Medicine and Graduate School of Arts and Sciences, Combined Program in Biological and Biomedical Sciences (BBS), Department of Pharmacology, New Haven, CT 06520. Offers PhD. *Degree requirements:* For doctorate, thesis/dissertation. *Entrance requirements:* For doctorate, GRE General Test. Additional exam requirements/recommendations for international students: Required—TOEFL. *Expenses:* Contact institution.

Yale University, School of Medicine and Graduate School of Arts and Sciences, Combined Program in Biological and Biomedical Sciences (BBS), Pharmacological Sciences and Molecular Medicine Track, New Haven, CT 06520. Offers PhD, MD/PhD. *Degree requirements:* For doctorate, thesis/dissertation. *Entrance requirements:* For doctorate, GRE General Test. Additional exam requirements/recommendations for international students: Required—TOEFL. Electronic applications accepted.

Toxicology

American University, College of Arts and Sciences, Department of Chemistry, Washington, DC 20016-8014. Offers chemistry (MS); pre-medical (Certificate); toxicology (MS, Certificate). Part-time and evening/weekend programs available. *Faculty:* 8 full-time (3 women), 2 part-time/adjunct (1 woman). *Students:* 7 full-time (3 women), 36 part-time (25 women); includes 4 minority (3 Black or African American, non-Hispanic/Latino; 1 Asian, non-Hispanic/Latino). Average age 25. 6 applicants, 67% accepted, 2 enrolled. In 2010, 2 degrees awarded. *Degree requirements:* For master's, comprehensive exam, thesis, tool of research in foreign language or statistics. *Entrance requirements:* For master's, GRE. Additional exam requirements/recommendations for international students: Required—TOEFL. *Application deadline:* For fall admission, 2/1 priority date for domestic students; for spring admission, 10/1 priority date for domestic students. Applications are processed on a rolling basis. Application fee: $80. *Financial support:* In 2010–11, 33 students received support; fellowships, research assistantships with full and partial tuition reimbursements available, teaching assistantships with full and partial tuition reimbursements available, career-related internships or fieldwork, Federal Work-Study, institutionally sponsored loans, scholarships/grants, traineeships, tuition waivers (full and partial), unspecified assistantships, and service awards available. Financial award application deadline: 2/1. *Faculty research:* AIDS, chemical damage to DNA, organic reaction mechanisms, chromatography in environmental samples. *Unit head:* Dr. James E. Girard, Chair, 202-885-1791, E-mail: jgirard@american.edu. *Application contact:* Kathleen Clowery, Director, Graduate Admissions, 202-885-3621, Fax: 202-885-1505.

Brown University, Graduate School, Division of Biology and Medicine, Program in Pathology and Laboratory Medicine, Providence, RI 02912. Offers biology (PhD); cancer biology (PhD); immunology and infection (PhD); medical science (PhD); pathobiology (Sc M); toxicology and environmental pathology (PhD). Terminal master's awarded for partial completion of doctoral program. *Degree requirements:* For doctorate, thesis/dissertation, preliminary exam. *Entrance requirements:* For master's and doctorate, GRE General Test, GRE Subject Test. Additional exam requirements/recommendations for international students: Required—TOEFL. Electronic applications accepted. *Faculty research:* Environmental pathology, carcinogenesis, immunopathology, signal transduction, innate immunity.

Columbia University, College of Physicians and Surgeons, Department of Pharmacology, New York, NY 10032. Offers pharmacology (M Phil, MA, PhD); pharmacology-toxicology (M Phil, MA, PhD); MD/PhD. Only candidates for the PhD are admitted. Terminal master's awarded for partial completion of doctoral program. *Degree requirements:* For doctorate, thesis/dissertation. *Entrance requirements:* For master's and doctorate, GRE General Test. Additional exam requirements/recommendations for international students: Required—TOEFL. *Faculty research:* Cardiovascular pharmacology, receptor pharmacology, neuropharmacology, membrane biophysics, eicosanoids.

Cornell University, Graduate School, Graduate Fields of Agriculture and Life Sciences, Field of Environmental Toxicology, Ithaca, NY 14853-0001. Offers cellular and molecular toxicology (MS, PhD); ecotoxicology and environmental chemistry (MS, PhD); nutritional and food toxicology (MS, PhD); risk assessment, management and public policy (MS, PhD). *Faculty:* 37 full-time (10 women). *Students:* 10 full-time (5 women); includes 1 American Indian or Alaska Native, non-Hispanic/Latino, 2 international. Average age 30. 26 applicants, 12% accepted, 2 enrolled. In 2010, 3 doctorates awarded. *Degree requirements:* For master's, thesis; for doctorate, comprehensive exam, thesis/dissertation. *Entrance requirements:* For master's and doctorate, GRE General Test, GRE Subject Test (biology or chemistry recommended), 2 letters of recommendation. Additional exam requirements/recommendations for international students: Required—TOEFL (minimum score 600 paper-based; 250 computer-based; 77 iBT). *Application deadline:* For fall admission, 1/15 for domestic students. Application fee: $70. Electronic applications accepted. *Expenses:* Tuition: Full-time $29,500. Required fees: $76. Tuition and fees vary according to degree level and program. *Financial support:* In 2010–11, 4 fellowships with full tuition reimbursements, 4 research assistantships with full tuition reimbursements, 2 teaching assistantships with full tuition reimbursements were awarded; institutionally sponsored loans, scholarships/grants, health care benefits, tuition waivers (full and partial), and unspecified assistantships also available. Financial award applicants required to submit FAFSA. *Faculty research:* Cellular and molecular toxicology, cancer toxicology, bioremediation, ecotoxicology, nutritional and food toxicology, reproductive toxicology. *Unit head:* Director of Graduate Studies, 607-255-8008, Fax: 607-755-0238. *Application contact:* Graduate Field Assistant, 607-255-8008, Fax: 607-255-0238, E-mail: envtox@cornell.edu.

Dartmouth College, Arts and Sciences Graduate Programs, Department of Pharmacology and Toxicology, Hanover, NH 03755. Offers PhD, MD/PhD. *Degree requirements:* For doctorate, thesis/dissertation. *Entrance requirements:* For doctorate, GRE General Test, GRE Subject Test, bachelor's degree in biological, chemical, or physical science. Additional exam requirements/recommendations for international students: Required—TOEFL. Electronic applications accepted. *Faculty research:* Molecular biology of carcinogenesis, DNA repair and gene expression, biochemical and environmental toxicology, protein receptor ligand interactions.

Dartmouth College, Program in Experimental and Molecular Medicine, Molecular Pharmacology, Toxicology and Experimental Therapeutics Track, Hanover, NH 03755. Offers PhD.

Duke University, Graduate School, Integrated Toxicology and Environmental Health Program, Durham, NC 27708. Offers PhD, Certificate. *Faculty:* 36 full-time. *Students:* 5 full-time (3 women). 27 applicants, 15% accepted, 3 enrolled. *Entrance requirements:* For doctorate, GRE General Test. Additional exam requirements/recommendations for international students:

Required—TOEFL (minimum score 550 paper-based; 213 computer-based; 83 iBT), IELTS (minimum score 7). *Application deadline:* For fall admission, 12/8 priority date for domestic and international students. Application fee: $75. Electronic applications accepted. *Financial support:* Fellowships available. Financial award application deadline: 12/8. *Unit head:* Cynthia Kuhn, Director, 919-613-8078, Fax: 919-668-1799, E-mail: emarion@duke.edu. *Application contact:* Elizabeth Hutton, Director of Admissions, 919-684-3913, Fax: 919-684-2277, E-mail: gradadmissions@duke.edu.

Florida Agricultural and Mechanical University, Division of Graduate Studies, Research, and Continuing Education, College of Pharmacy and Pharmaceutical Sciences, Graduate Programs in Pharmaceutical Sciences, Tallahassee, FL 32307-3200. Offers environmental toxicology (PhD); medicinal chemistry (MS, PhD); pharmaceutics (MS, PhD); pharmacology/ toxicology (MS, PhD); pharmacy administration (MS). *Accreditation:* CEPH. *Degree requirements:* For master's, comprehensive exam, thesis, publishable paper; for doctorate, comprehensive exam, thesis/dissertation, publishable paper. *Entrance requirements:* For master's and doctorate, GRE General Test, minimum GPA of 3.0 in last 60 hours. Additional exam requirements/ recommendations for international students: Required—TOEFL. *Faculty research:* Anticancer agents, anti-inflammatory drugs, chronopharmacology, neuroendocrinology, microbiology.

The George Washington University, Columbian College of Arts and Sciences, Department of Forensic Sciences, Washington, DC 20052. Offers crime scene investigation (MFS); forensic chemistry (MFS); forensic molecular biology (MFS); forensic toxicology (MFS); high-technology crime investigation (MFS); security management (MFS). High-technology crime investigation and security management programs offered in Arlington, VA. Part-time and evening/weekend programs available. *Faculty:* 6 full-time (1 woman), 22 part-time/adjunct (5 women). *Students:* 80 full-time (61 women), 60 part-time (37 women); includes 8 Black or African American, non-Hispanic/Latino; 2 American Indian or Alaska Native, non-Hispanic/Latino; 7 Asian, non-Hispanic/Latino; 8 Hispanic/Latino, 7 international. Average age 27. 149 applicants, 91% accepted, 58 enrolled. In 2010, 57 master's awarded. *Degree requirements:* For master's, comprehensive exam. *Entrance requirements:* For master's, GRE General Test, minimum GPA of 3.0. Additional exam requirements/recommendations for international students: Required—TOEFL (minimum score 550 paper-based; 213 computer-based; 80 iBT). *Application deadline:* For fall admission, 1/16 priority date for international students; for spring admission, 10/1 priority date for domestic students, 9/1 priority date for international students. Applications are processed on a rolling basis. Application fee: $75. Electronic applications accepted. *Financial support:* In 2010–11, 19 students received support; fellowships with partial tuition reimbursements available, Federal Work-Study and tuition waivers available. *Unit head:* Dr. Walter F. Rowe, Chair, 202-994-1469, E-mail: wfrowe@gwu.edu. *Application contact:* Dr. Walter F. Rowe, Chair, 202-994-1469, E-mail: wfrowe@gwu.edu.

Indiana University Bloomington, School of Public and Environmental Affairs, Environmental Science Programs, Bloomington, IN 47405-7000. Offers applied ecology (MSES); energy (MSES); environmental chemistry, toxicology, and risk assessment (MSES); environmental science (PhD); specialized environmental science (MSES); water resources (MSES); JD/MSES; MSES/MS. Part-time programs available. *Faculty:* 17 full-time, 8 part-time/adjunct. *Students:* 87 full-time (49 women), 2 part-time (1 woman); includes 1 Black or African American, non-Hispanic/Latino; 1 American Indian or Alaska Native, non-Hispanic/Latino; 10 Asian, non-Hispanic/Latino; 3 Hispanic/Latino, 11 international. Average age 26. 79 applicants, 29 enrolled. In 2010, 53 master's, 10 doctorates awarded. Terminal master's awarded for partial completion of doctoral program. *Degree requirements:* For master's, thesis optional; for doctorate, comprehensive exam, thesis/dissertation. *Entrance requirements:* For master's, GRE General Test or GMAT, official transcripts, 3 letters of recommendation, resume, personal statement, departmental questions; for doctorate, GRE General Test or LSAT, official transcripts, 3 letters of recommendation, resume or curriculum vitae, statement of purpose. Additional exam requirements/recommendations for international students: Required—TOEFL (minimum score 600 paper-based; 96 iBT); Recommended—IELTS (minimum score 7). *Application deadline:* For fall admission, 5/1 for domestic students, 12/1 for international students; for spring admission, 11/1 for domestic and international students. Applications are processed on a rolling basis. Application fee: $55 ($65 for international students). Electronic applications accepted. *Financial support:* Fellowships with partial tuition reimbursements, research assistantships with partial tuition reimbursements, teaching assistantships with partial tuition reimbursements, career-related internships or fieldwork, Federal Work-Study, scholarships/grants, health care benefits, and unspecified assistantships available. Financial award application deadline: 2/1; financial award applicants required to submit FAFSA. *Faculty research:* Applied ecology, bio-geo chemistry, toxicology, wetlands ecology, environmental microbiology, forest ecology, environmental chemistry. *Unit head:* Jennifer J. Forney, Director, Graduate Student Services, 812-855-9485, Fax: 812-856-3665, E-mail: speampo@indiana.edu. *Application contact:* Audrey Whittaker, Admissions Assistant, 812-855-2840, Fax: 812-856-3665, E-mail: speaapps@indiana.edu.

Indiana University–Purdue University Indianapolis, Indiana University School of Medicine, Department of Pharmacology and Toxicology, Indianapolis, IN 46202-2896. Offers pharmacology (MS, PhD); toxicology (MS, PhD); MD/PhD. *Faculty:* 11 full-time (2 women). *Students:* 24 full-time (17 women); includes 2 minority (1 Asian, non-Hispanic/Latino; 1 Hispanic/Latino), 12 international. Average age 27. 18 applicants, 39% accepted, 7 enrolled. In 2010, 1 master's, 3 doctorates awarded. Terminal master's awarded for partial completion of doctoral program. *Degree requirements:* For master's, thesis; for doctorate, thesis/dissertation. *Entrance requirements:* For master's and doctorate, GRE General Test, GRE Subject Test, minimum GPA of 3.0. *Application deadline:* For fall admission, 1/15 priority date for domestic students. Applications are processed on a rolling basis. Application fee: $55 ($65 for international students). *Financial support:* In 2010–11, 14 students received support, including 7 teaching assistantships (averaging $20,940 per year); fellowships with partial tuition reimbursements available, research assistantships with partial tuition reimbursements available, Federal Work-Study, institutionally sponsored loans, and tuition waivers (partial) also available. Financial award application deadline: 1/15. *Faculty research:* Neuropharmacology, cardiovascular biopharmacology, chemotherapy, oncogenesis. *Unit head:* Dr. Michael Vasko, Chairman, 317-274-7844, Fax: 317-274-7714. *Application contact:* Director of Graduate Studies, 317-274-1564, Fax: 317-274-7714.

Iowa State University of Science and Technology, Graduate College, College of Agriculture and College of Liberal Arts and Sciences, Department of Biochemistry, Biophysics, and Molecular Biology, Ames, IA 50011. Offers biochemistry (MS, PhD); biophysics (MS, PhD); genetics (MS, PhD); molecular, cellular, and developmental biology (MS, PhD); toxicology (MS, PhD). *Faculty:* 31 full-time (7 women), 1 (woman) part-time/adjunct. *Students:* 81 full-time (33 women), 11 part-time (6 women); includes 2 Black or African American, non-Hispanic/Latino; 2 Asian, non-Hispanic/Latino, 58 international. 38 applicants, 29% accepted, 8 enrolled. In 2010, 3 master's, 9 doctorates awarded. *Degree requirements:* For master's, thesis; for doctorate, thesis/dissertation. *Entrance requirements:* For master's and doctorate, GRE General Test. Additional exam requirements/recommendations for international students: Required—TOEFL (minimum score 550 paper-based; 79 iBT), IELTS (minimum score 6.5). *Application deadline:* For fall admission, 1/15 priority date for domestic and international students; for spring admission, 10/15 for domestic and international students. Application fee: $40 ($90 for international students). Electronic applications accepted. *Financial support:* In 2010–11, 67 research assistantships with full and partial tuition reimbursements (averaging $17,228 per year) were awarded; teaching assistantships with full and partial tuition reimbursements, scholarships/grants, health care benefits, and unspecified assistantships also available. *Unit head:* Dr. Guru Rao, Interim Chair, 515-294-6116, E-mail: biochem@iastate.edu. *Application contact:* Dr. Reuben Peters, Director of Graduate Education, 515-294-6116, E-mail: biochem@iastate.edu.

See Display on page 129 and Close-Up on page 147.

Iowa State University of Science and Technology, Graduate College, Interdisciplinary Programs, Program in Toxicology, Ames, IA 50011. Offers MS, PhD. *Students:* 23 full-time (7

women), 3 part-time (1 woman); includes 2 Black or African American, non-Hispanic/Latino; 1 Asian, non-Hispanic/Latino; 1 Hispanic/Latino, 13 international. In 2010, 2 master's awarded. *Degree requirements:* For master's, thesis; for doctorate, thesis/dissertation. *Entrance requirements:* For master's and doctorate, GRE General Test. Additional exam requirements/ recommendations for international students: Required—TOEFL (minimum score 550 paper-based; 79 iBT), IELTS (minimum score 6.5). *Application deadline:* For fall admission, 2/1 priority date for domestic and international students. Applications are processed on a rolling basis. Application fee: $40 ($90 for international students). Electronic applications accepted. *Financial support:* In 2010–11, 23 research assistantships with full and partial tuition reimbursements (averaging $16,588 per year) were awarded; teaching assistantships with full and partial tuition reimbursements, scholarships/grants, health care benefits, and unspecified assistantships also available. *Unit head:* Dr. Anumantha Kanthasamy, Supervisory Committee Chair, 515-294-7697, Fax: 515-294-6669, E-mail: toxmajor@iastate.edu. *Application contact:* Linda Wild, Information Contact, 800-499-1972, E-mail: toxmajor@iastate.edu.

The Johns Hopkins University, Bloomberg School of Public Health, Department of Environmental Health Sciences, Baltimore, MD 21218-2699. Offers environmental health engineering (PhD); environmental health sciences (MHS, Dr PH); occupational and environmental health (PhD); occupational and environmental hygiene (MHS, MHS); physiology (PhD); toxicology (PhD). Postbaccalaureate distance learning degree programs offered (minimal on-campus study). *Faculty:* 71 full-time (27 women), 58 part-time/adjunct (26 women). *Students:* 66 full-time (38 women), 19 part-time (12 women); includes 25 minority (3 Black or African American, non-Hispanic/Latino; 13 Asian, non-Hispanic/Latino; 4 Hispanic/Latino; 5 Two or more races, non-Hispanic/Latino), 11 international. Average age 30. 101 applicants, 49% accepted, 31 enrolled. In 2010, 21 master's, 14 doctorates awarded. *Degree requirements:* For master's, essay, presentation; for doctorate, comprehensive exam, thesis/dissertation, 1 year full-time residency, oral and written exams. *Entrance requirements:* For master's, GRE General Test or MCAT, 3 letters of recommendation, transcripts; for doctorate, GRE General Test or MCAT, 3 letters of recommendation. Additional exam requirements/recommendations for international students: Required—TOEFL (minimum score 600 paper-based; 250 computer-based). *Application deadline:* For fall admission, 12/15 priority date for domestic and international students. Applications are processed on a rolling basis. Application fee: $45. Electronic applications accepted. *Financial support:* In 2010–11, 5 fellowships with full tuition reimbursements (averaging $26,500 per year) were awarded; Federal Work-Study, institutionally sponsored loans, scholarships/grants, traineeships, health care benefits, and stipends also available. Support available to part-time students. Financial award application deadline: 3/15; financial award applicants required to submit FAFSA. *Faculty research:* Chemical carcinogenesis/ toxicology, lung disease, occupational and environmental health, nuclear imaging, molecular epidemiology. Total annual research expenditures: $23.7 million. *Unit head:* Dr. John Davis Groopman, Chair, 410-955-3720, Fax: 410-955-0617, E-mail: jgroopma@jhsph.edu. *Application contact:* Nina J. Kulacki, Academic Program Manager, 410-955-2212, Fax: 410-955-0617, E-mail: nkulacki@jhsph.edu.

Long Island University, Brooklyn Campus, Arnold and Marie Schwartz College of Pharmacy and Health Sciences, Graduate Programs in Pharmacy, Division of Pharmaceutical Sciences, Brooklyn, NY 11201-8423. Offers cosmetic science (MS); industrial pharmacy (MS); pharmaceutics (PhD); pharmacology/toxicology (MS). Part-time and evening/weekend programs available. Terminal master's awarded for partial completion of doctoral program. *Degree requirements:* For master's, thesis optional; for doctorate, thesis/dissertation, candidacy exam. *Entrance requirements:* For master's and doctorate, minimum GPA of 3.0.

Louisiana State University and Agricultural and Mechanical College, Graduate School, School of the Coast and Environment, Department of Environmental Sciences, Baton Rouge, LA 70803. Offers environmental planning and management (MS); environmental toxicology (MS). *Faculty:* 9 full-time (3 women). *Students:* 26 full-time (17 women), 7 part-time (2 women); includes 5 Black or African American, non-Hispanic/Latino; 2 Asian, non-Hispanic/ Latino, 6 international. Average age 26. 19 applicants, 84% accepted, 10 enrolled. In 2010, 6 master's awarded. *Degree requirements:* For master's, thesis (for some programs). *Entrance requirements:* For master's, GRE General Test, minimum GPA of 3.0. Additional exam requirements/recommendations for international students: Required—TOEFL (minimum score 550 paper-based; 213 computer-based; 79 iBT) or IELTS (minimum score 6.5). *Application deadline:* For fall admission, 1/25 priority date for domestic students, 5/15 for international students; for spring admission, 10/15 for international students. Applications are processed on a rolling basis. Application fee: $50 ($70 for international students). Electronic applications accepted. *Financial support:* In 2010–11, 27 students received support, including 1 fellowship with full and partial tuition reimbursement available (averaging $17,831 per year), 19 research assistantships with full and partial tuition reimbursements available (averaging $14,842 per year), 1 teaching assistantship with full and partial tuition reimbursement available (averaging $15,740 per year); career-related internships or fieldwork, Federal Work-Study, institutionally sponsored loans, scholarships/grants, health care benefits, and unspecified assistantships also available. Support available to part-time students. Financial award applicants required to submit FAFSA. *Faculty research:* Environmental toxicology, environmental policy and law, microbial ecology, bioremediation, genetic toxicology. Total annual research expenditures: $921,141. *Unit head:* Dr. Ed Laws, Chair, 225-578-8521, Fax: 225-578-4286, E-mail: edlaws@lsu.edu. *Application contact:* Charlotte G. St. Romain, Academic Coordinator, 225-578-8522, Fax: 225-578-4286, E-mail: cstrom4@lsu.edu.

Massachusetts Institute of Technology, School of Engineering, Department of Biological Engineering, Cambridge, MA 02139-4307. Offers applied biosciences (PhD, Sc D); bioengineering (PhD, Sc D); biological engineering (PhD, Sc D); biomedical engineering (M Eng); toxicology (SM); SM/MBA. *Faculty:* 30 full-time (5 women). *Students:* 112 full-time (56 women); includes 32 minority (2 Black or African American, non-Hispanic/Latino; 20 Asian, non-Hispanic/Latino; 8 Hispanic/Latino; 2 Two or more races, non-Hispanic/Latino), 31 international. Average age 26. 441 applicants, 9% accepted, 24 enrolled. In 2010, 3 master's, 16 doctorates awarded. Terminal master's awarded for partial completion of doctoral program. *Degree requirements:* For master's, thesis; for doctorate, comprehensive exam, thesis/dissertation. *Entrance requirements:* For master's and doctorate, GRE General Test. Additional exam requirements/ recommendations for international students: Required—TOEFL (minimum score 600 paper-based; 250 computer-based), IELTS (minimum score 7). *Application deadline:* For fall admission, 12/31 for domestic and international students. Application fee: $75. Electronic applications accepted. *Expenses:* Tuition: Full-time $38,940; part-time $605 per unit. Required fees: $272. *Financial support:* In 2010–11, 111 students received support, including 57 fellowships with tuition reimbursements available (averaging $35,847 per year), 51 research assistantships with tuition reimbursements available (averaging $32,873 per year), 3 teaching assistantships with tuition reimbursements available (averaging $31,681 per year); Federal Work-Study, institutionally sponsored loans, scholarships/grants, traineeships, health care benefits, and unspecified assistantships also available. *Faculty research:* Bioinformatics, computational, systems, and synthetic biology; biological materials, imaging, and transport phenomena; biomolecular and cell engineering; cancer initiation, progression, and therapeutics; genomics, proteomics, and glycomics; nanoscale engineering of biological systems; neurobiological systems; systems biology; macromolecular biochemistry and biophysics. Total annual research expenditures: $35.1 million. *Unit head:* Prof. Douglas A. Lauffenburger, Head, 617-253-1712, E-mail: be-acad@mit.edu. *Application contact:* Biological Engineering Academic Office, 617-253-1712, Fax: 617-258-8676, E-mail: be-acad@mit.edu.

Medical College of Wisconsin, Graduate School of Biomedical Sciences, Department of Pharmacology and Toxicology, Milwaukee, WI 53226-0509. Offers PhD, MD/PhD. Terminal master's awarded for partial completion of doctoral program. *Degree requirements:* For doctorate, comprehensive exam, thesis/dissertation, oral and written qualifying exams. *Entrance requirements:* For doctorate, GRE General Test, minimum B average. Additional exam requirements/recommendations for international students: Required—TOEFL. *Expenses:* Tuition: Full-time $30,000; part-time $710 per credit. Required fees: $150. *Faculty research:*

Toxicology

Medical College of Wisconsin (continued)
Cardiovascular physiology and pharmacology, drugs of abuse, environmental and aquatic toxicology, central nervous system and biochemical pharmacology, signal transduction.

Medical University of South Carolina, College of Graduate Studies, Department of Pharmaceutical and Biomedical Sciences, Charleston, SC 29425. Offers cell injury and repair (PhD); drug discovery (PhD); medicinal chemistry (PhD); toxicology (PhD); DMD/PhD; MD/PhD; Pharm D/PhD. *Faculty:* 8 full-time (1 woman), 1 part-time/adjunct (0 women). *Students:* 11 full-time (3 women); includes 1 Black or African American, non-Hispanic/Latino, 1 international. Average age 29. In 2010, 3 doctorates awarded. *Degree requirements:* For doctorate, thesis/dissertation, oral and written exams, teaching and research seminar. *Entrance requirements:* For doctorate, GRE General Test, interview, minimum GPA of 3.0. Additional exam requirements/recommendations for international students: Required—TOEFL (minimum score 600 paper-based; 250 computer-based; 100 iBT). *Application deadline:* For fall admission, 1/15 priority date for domestic and international students. Applications are processed on a rolling basis. Application fee: $0 ($85 for international students). Electronic applications accepted. *Financial support:* In 2010–11, 7 students received support, including 17 research assistantships with partial tuition reimbursements available (averaging $23,000 per year); Federal Work-Study, scholarships/grants, and traineeships also available. Support available to part-time students. Financial award application deadline: 3/10; financial award applicants required to submit FAFSA. *Faculty research:* Drug discovery, toxicology, metabolomics, cell stress and injury. *Unit head:* Dr. Rick Schnellmann, Eminent Scholar, Professor and Chair, 843-792-3754, Fax: 843-792-6590, E-mail: schnell@musc.edu. *Application contact:* Dr. Craig C. Beeson, Associate Professor, 843-876-5091, Fax: 843-792-6590, E-mail: beesonc@musc.edu.

Michigan State University, College of Human Medicine and The Graduate School, Graduate Programs in Human Medicine, East Lansing, MI 48824. Offers biochemistry and molecular biology (MS, PhD); epidemiology (MS, PhD); microbiology (MS); microbiology and molecular genetics (PhD); pharmacology and toxicology (MS, PhD); physiology (MS, PhD); public health (MPH). *Entrance requirements:* Additional exam requirements/recommendations for international students: Required—TOEFL.

Michigan State University, College of Osteopathic Medicine and The Graduate School, Graduate Studies in Osteopathic Medicine and Graduate Programs in Human Medicine and Graduate Programs in Veterinary Medicine, Department of Pharmacology and Toxicology, East Lansing, MI 48824. Offers integrative pharmacology (MS); pharmacology and toxicology (MS, PhD); pharmacology and toxicology-environmental toxicology (PhD). *Entrance requirements:* Additional exam requirements/recommendations for international students: Required—TOEFL (minimum score 600 paper-based; 220 computer-based). Electronic applications accepted.

Michigan State University, College of Veterinary Medicine and The Graduate School, Graduate Programs in Veterinary Medicine, Center for Integrative Toxicology, East Lansing, MI 48824. Offers animal science–environmental toxicology (PhD); biochemistry and molecular biology–environmental toxicology (PhD); chemistry–environmental toxicology (PhD); crop and soil sciences–environmental toxicology (PhD); environmental engineering–environmental toxicology (PhD); environmental geosciences–environmental toxicology (PhD); fisheries and wildlife–environmental toxicology (PhD); food science–environmental toxicology (PhD); forestry–environmental toxicology (PhD); genetics–environmental toxicology (PhD); human nutrition–environmental toxicology (PhD); microbiology–environmental toxicology (PhD); pharmacology and toxicology–environmental toxicology (PhD); zoology–environmental toxicology (PhD). *Entrance requirements:* Additional exam requirements/recommendations for international students: Required—TOEFL (minimum score 550 paper-based; 213 computer-based), Michigan State University ELT (minimum score 85), Michigan English Language Assessment Battery (minimum score 83). Electronic applications accepted. *Faculty research:* Environmental risk assessment, toxicogenomics, phytoremediation, storage and disposal of hazardous waste, environmental regulation.

Michigan State University, College of Veterinary Medicine and The Graduate School, Graduate Programs in Veterinary Medicine and College of Natural Science and Graduate Programs in Human Medicine, Department of Microbiology and Molecular Genetics, East Lansing, MI 48824. Offers industrial microbiology (MS, PhD); microbiology (MS, PhD); microbiology and molecular genetics (MS, PhD); microbiology–environmental toxicology (PhD). *Entrance requirements:* For master's, GRE General Test. Additional exam requirements/recommendations for international students: Required—TOEFL (minimum score 550 paper-based; 213 computer-based), Michigan State University ELT (minimum score 85), Michigan English Language Assessment Battery (minimum score 83). Electronic applications accepted.

Michigan State University, The Graduate School, College of Agriculture and Natural Resources, Department of Animal Science, East Lansing, MI 48824. Offers animal science (MS, PhD); animal science-environmental toxicology (PhD). *Entrance requirements:* Additional exam requirements/recommendations for international students: Required—TOEFL (minimum score 550 paper-based; 213 computer-based), Michigan State University ELT (minimum score 85), Michigan English Language Assessment Battery (minimum score 83). Electronic applications accepted.

Michigan State University, The Graduate School, College of Agriculture and Natural Resources, Department of Crop and Soil Sciences, East Lansing, MI 48824. Offers crop and soil sciences (MS, PhD); crop and soil sciences-environmental toxicology (PhD); plant breeding and genetics-crop and soil sciences (MS); plant breeding, genetics and biotechnology-crop and soil sciences (PhD). *Entrance requirements:* Additional exam requirements/recommendations for international students: Required—TOEFL (minimum score 550 paper-based; 213 computer-based), Michigan State University ELT (minimum score 85), Michigan Michigan English Language Assessment Battery (minimum score 83). Electronic applications accepted.

Michigan State University, The Graduate School, College of Agriculture and Natural Resources and College of Natural Science, Department of Food Science and Human Nutrition, East Lansing, MI 48824. Offers food science (MS, PhD); food science—environmental toxicology (PhD); human nutrition (MS, PhD); human nutrition-environmental toxicology (PhD). *Entrance requirements:* Additional exam requirements/recommendations for international students: Required—TOEFL (minimum score 550 paper-based; 213 computer-based), Michigan State University ELT (minimum score 85), Michigan English Language Assessment Battery (minimum score 83). Electronic applications accepted.

Michigan State University, The Graduate School, College of Engineering, Department of Civil and Environmental Engineering, East Lansing, MI 48824. Offers civil engineering (MS, PhD); environmental engineering (MS, PhD); environmental engineering-environmental toxicology (PhD). Part-time programs available. *Entrance requirements:* Additional exam requirements/recommendations for international students: Required—TOEFL. Electronic applications accepted.

Michigan State University, The Graduate School, College of Natural Science and Graduate Programs in Human Medicine and Graduate Studies in Osteopathic Medicine, Department of Biochemistry and Molecular Biology, East Lansing, MI 48824. Offers biochemistry and molecular biology (MS, PhD); biochemistry and molecular biology/environmental toxicology (PhD). *Entrance requirements:* Additional exam requirements/recommendations for international students: Required—TOEFL. Electronic applications accepted.

Michigan State University, The Graduate School, College of Natural Science, Department of Chemistry, East Lansing, MI 48824. Offers chemical physics (PhD); chemistry (MS, PhD); chemistry-environmental toxicology (PhD); computational chemistry (MS). *Entrance requirements:* Additional exam requirements/recommendations for international students: Required—TOEFL. Electronic applications accepted. *Faculty research:* Analytical chemistry, inorganic and organic chemistry, nuclear chemistry, physical chemistry, theoretical and computational chemistry.

Michigan State University, The Graduate School, College of Natural Science, Department of Geological Sciences, East Lansing, MI 48824. Offers environmental geosciences (MS, PhD); environmental geosciences-environmental toxicology (PhD); geological sciences (MS, PhD). *Degree requirements:* For master's, thesis (for those without prior thesis work); for doctorate, thesis/dissertation. *Entrance requirements:* For master's, GRE General Test, minimum GPA of 3.0, course work in geoscience, 3 letters of recommendation; for doctorate, GRE General Test, 3 letters of recommendation. Additional exam requirements/recommendations for international students: Required—TOEFL (minimum score 550 paper-based; 213 computer-based), Michigan State University ELT (minimum score 85), Michigan English Language Assessment Battery (minimum score 83). Electronic applications accepted. *Faculty research:* Water in the environment, global and biological change, crystal dynamics.

Michigan State University, The Graduate School, College of Natural Science, Program in Genetics, East Lansing, MI 48824. Offers genetics (MS, PhD); genetics–environmental toxicology (PhD). *Entrance requirements:* Additional exam requirements/recommendations for international students: Required—TOEFL. Electronic applications accepted.

New York University, Graduate School of Arts and Science, Department of Environmental Medicine, New York, NY 10012-1019. Offers environmental health sciences (MS, PhD), including biostatistics (PhD), environmental hygiene (MS), epidemiology (PhD), ergonomics and biomechanics (PhD), exposure assessment and health effects (PhD), molecular toxicology/carcinogenesis (PhD), toxicology. Part-time programs available. *Faculty:* 26 full-time (7 women). *Students:* 53 full-time (38 women), 10 part-time (3 women); includes 3 Black or African American, non-Hispanic/Latino; 4 Asian, non-Hispanic/Latino; 5 Hispanic/Latino, 23 international. Average age 30. 60 applicants, 48% accepted, 14 enrolled. In 2010, 8 master's, 5 doctorates awarded. Terminal master's awarded for partial completion of doctoral program. *Degree requirements:* For master's, thesis or alternative; for doctorate, one foreign language, thesis/dissertation, oral and written exams. *Entrance requirements:* For master's and doctorate, GRE General Test, GRE Subject Test, minimum GPA of 3.0; bachelor's degree in biological, physical, or engineering science. Additional exam requirements/recommendations for international students: Required—TOEFL. *Application deadline:* For fall admission, 12/15 for domestic students. Application fee: $90. *Financial support:* Fellowships with tuition reimbursements, teaching assistantships with tuition reimbursements, career-related internships or fieldwork, Federal Work-Study, institutionally sponsored loans, and health care benefits available. Financial award application deadline: 12/15; financial award applicants required to submit FAFSA. *Unit head:* Dr. Max Costa, Chair, 845-731-3661, Fax: 845-351-4510, E-mail: ehs@env.med.nyu.edu. *Application contact:* Dr. Jerome J. Solomon, Director of Graduate Studies, 845-731-3661, Fax: 845-351-4510, E-mail: ehs@env.med.nyu.edu.

North Carolina State University, Graduate School, College of Agriculture and Life Sciences and College of Veterinary Medicine, Department of Environmental and Molecular Toxicology, Raleigh, NC 27695. Offers M Tox, MS, PhD. Terminal master's awarded for partial completion of doctoral program. *Degree requirements:* For master's, thesis (for some programs); for doctorate, thesis/dissertation. *Entrance requirements:* For master's and doctorate, GRE General Test, minimum GPA of 3.0. Electronic applications accepted. *Faculty research:* Chemical fate, carcinogenesis, developmental and endocrine toxicity, xenobiotic metabolism, signal transduction.

Northwestern University, Northwestern University Feinberg School of Medicine and Interdepartmental Programs, Integrated Graduate Programs in the Life Sciences, Chicago, IL 60611. Offers cancer biology (PhD); cell biology (PhD); developmental biology (PhD); evolutionary biology (PhD); immunology and microbial pathogenesis (PhD); molecular biology and genetics (PhD); neurobiology (PhD); pharmacology and toxicology (PhD); structural biology and biochemistry (PhD). *Degree requirements:* For doctorate, comprehensive exam, thesis/dissertation, written and oral qualifying exams. *Entrance requirements:* For doctorate, GRE General Test. Additional exam requirements/recommendations for international students: Required—TOEFL (minimum score 600 paper-based; 250 computer-based). Electronic applications accepted.

The Ohio State University, College of Veterinary Medicine, Department of Veterinary Biosciences, Columbus, OH 43210. Offers anatomy and cellular biology (MS, PhD); pathobiology (MS, PhD); pharmacology (MS, PhD); toxicology (MS, PhD); veterinary physiology (MS, PhD). *Faculty:* 45. *Students:* 4 full-time (all women), 7 part-time (5 women); includes 1 Black or African American, non-Hispanic/Latino, 3 international. Average age 30. In 2010, 2 master's, 7 doctorates awarded. *Entrance requirements:* For master's and doctorate, GRE General Test. Additional exam requirements/recommendations for international students: Required—TOEFL. *Application deadline:* Applications are processed on a rolling basis. Application fee: $40 ($50 for international students). Electronic applications accepted. *Expenses:* Tuition, state resident: full-time $10,605. Tuition, nonresident: full-time $26,535. Tuition and fees vary according to course load and program. *Faculty research:* Microvasculature, muscle biology, neonatal lung and bone development. *Unit head:* Dr. Michael J. Oglesbee, Graduate Studies Committee Chair, 614-292-5661, Fax: 614-292-6473, E-mail: oglesbee.1@osu.edu. *Application contact:* Graduate Admissions, 614-292-9444, Fax: 614-292-3895, E-mail: domestic.grad@osu.edu.

Oklahoma State University Center for Health Sciences, Graduate Program in Forensic Sciences, Tulsa, OK 74107-1898. Offers forensic DNA/molecular biology (MS); forensic examination of questioned documents (Certificate); forensic pathology (MS); forensic psychology (MS); forensic toxicology (MS). Part-time and evening/weekend programs available. Post-baccalaureate distance learning degree programs offered (no on-campus study). *Faculty:* 2 full-time (0 women), 14 part-time/adjunct (5 women). *Students:* 7 full-time (6 women), 21 part-time (12 women); includes 5 minority (2 Black or African American, non-Hispanic/Latino; 2 Asian, non-Hispanic/Latino; 1 Hispanic/Latino). Average age 34. 21 applicants, 57% accepted, 7 enrolled. In 2010, 6 master's awarded. *Degree requirements:* For master's, comprehensive exam (for some programs), thesis (for some programs). *Entrance requirements:* For master's, MAT (MFSA) or GRE General Test, professional experience (MFSA). Additional exam requirements/recommendations for international students: Required—TOEFL (minimum score 600 paper-based; 250 computer-based), TWE (minimum score 5). *Application deadline:* For fall admission, 3/1 for domestic and international students; for spring admission, 10/1 for domestic and international students. Application fee: $40 ($75 for international students). *Financial support:* In 2010–11, 10 students received support, including 10 research assistantships (averaging $29,000 per year); career-related internships or fieldwork, Federal Work-Study, and tuition waivers (partial) also available. Support available to part-time students. Financial award application deadline: 4/1; financial award applicants required to submit FAFSA. *Faculty research:* DNA typing, DNA polymorphism, identification through DNA, disease transmission, forensic dentistry, neurotoxicity of HIV, forensic toxicology method development, toxin detection and characterization. Total annual research expenditures: $58,000. *Unit head:* Dr. Robert T. Allen, Director, 918-561-1108, Fax: 918-561-8414. *Application contact:* Cathy Newsome, Coordinator, 918-561-1108, Fax: 918-561-8414, E-mail: cathy.newsome@okstate.edu.

Oregon State University, Graduate School, College of Agricultural Sciences, Department of Environmental and Molecular Toxicology, Program in Toxicology, Corvallis, OR 97331. Offers MS, PhD. *Degree requirements:* For master's, thesis; for doctorate, thesis/dissertation. *Entrance requirements:* For master's and doctorate, GRE, bachelor's degree in chemistry or biological sciences, minimum GPA of 3.0 in last 90 hours of course work. Additional exam requirements/recommendations for international students: Required—TOEFL. *Faculty research:* Biochemical mechanisms for toxicology; analytical, comparative, aquatic, and food toxicology; aquaculture of salmonids; immunotoxicology; fish toxicology.

Prairie View A&M University, College of Arts and Sciences, Department of Biology, Prairie View, TX 77446-0519. Offers bio- environmental toxicology (MS); biology (MS). Part-time and evening/weekend programs available. *Faculty:* 5 full-time (2 women). *Students:* 6 full-time (4 women), 3 part-time (2 women); includes all Black or African American, non-Hispanic/Latino. Average age 25. 14 applicants, 86% accepted. In 2010, 1 master's awarded. *Degree requirements:* For master's, comprehensive exam, thesis optional. *Entrance requirements:* For master's, GRE General Test. Additional exam requirements/recommendations for international students: Required—TOEFL. *Application deadline:* For fall admission, 7/1 for domestic and international students; for spring admission, 11/1 for domestic and international students. Applications are processed on a rolling basis. *Expenses:* Tuition, state resident: part-time $119.06 per credit hour. Tuition, nonresident: part-time $511.23 per credit hour. *Financial support:* In 2010–11, 3 students received support, including 3 teaching assistantships (averaging $13,440 per year); Federal Work-Study and unspecified assistantships also available. Financial award application deadline: 4/1; financial award applicants required to submit FAFSA. *Faculty research:* Geonomics, hypertension, control of gene express, proteins, kigands that interact with hormone receptors, prostate cancer, renin-angiotensin yeast metabolism. *Unit head:* Dr. Harriette Howard-Lee-Block, Head, 936-261-3160, Fax: 936-261-3179, E-mail: hlblock@pvamu.edu. *Application contact:* Dr. Seab A. Smith, Associate Professor, 936-261-3169, Fax: 936-261-3179, E-mail: sasmith@pvamu.edu.

Purdue University, College of Pharmacy and Pharmacal Sciences and Graduate School, Graduate Programs in Pharmacy and Pharmacal Sciences, Department of Medicinal Chemistry and Molecular Pharmacology, West Lafayette, IN 47907. Offers analytical medicinal chemistry (PhD); computational and biophysical medicinal chemistry (PhD); medicinal and bioorganic chemistry (PhD); medicinal biochemistry and molecular biology (PhD); molecular pharmacology and toxicology (PhD); natural products and pharmacognosy (PhD); nuclear pharmacy (MS); radiopharmaceutical chemistry and nuclear pharmacy (PhD); MS/PhD. Terminal master's awarded for partial completion of doctoral program. *Degree requirements:* For master's, thesis; for doctorate, thesis/dissertation. *Entrance requirements:* For master's, GRE General Test, minimum B average; BS in biology, chemistry, or pharmacy; for doctorate, GRE General Test, minimum B average; BS in biology, chemistry, or pharmacology. Additional exam requirements/recommendations for international students: Required—TOEFL. Electronic applications accepted. *Faculty research:* Drug design and development, cancer research, drug synthesis and analysis, chemical pharmacology, environmental toxicology.

Queen's University at Kingston, School of Graduate Studies and Research, Faculty of Health Sciences, Department of Pharmacology and Toxicology, Kingston, ON K7L 3N6, Canada. Offers M Sc, PhD. *Degree requirements:* For master's, thesis; for doctorate, comprehensive exam, thesis/dissertation. *Entrance requirements:* For master's, minimum 2nd class standing, honors bachelor of science degree (life sciences, health sciences, or equivalent); for doctorate, masters of science degree or outstanding performance in honors bachelor of science program. Additional exam requirements/recommendations for international students: Required—TOEFL (minimum score 600 paper-based; 250 computer-based). Electronic applications accepted. *Faculty research:* Biochemical toxicology, cardiovascular pharmacology and neuropharmacology.

Rutgers, The State University of New Jersey, New Brunswick, Graduate School-New Brunswick, Department of Environmental Sciences, Piscataway, NJ 08854-8097. Offers air pollution and resources (MS, PhD); aquatic biology (MS, PhD); aquatic chemistry (MS, PhD); atmospheric science (MS, PhD); chemistry and physics of aerosol and hydrosol systems (MS, PhD); environmental chemistry (MS, PhD); environmental microbiology (MS, PhD); environmental toxicology (PhD); exposure assessment (PhD); fate and effects of pollutants (MS, PhD); pollution prevention and control (MS, PhD); water and wastewater treatment (MS, PhD); water resources (MS, PhD). Terminal master's awarded for partial completion of doctoral program. *Degree requirements:* For master's, comprehensive exam, thesis or alternative, oral final exam; for doctorate, comprehensive exam, thesis/dissertation, thesis defense, qualifying exam. *Entrance requirements:* For master's and doctorate, GRE General Test. Additional exam requirements/recommendations for international students: Required—TOEFL. Electronic applications accepted. *Expenses:* Tuition, state resident: full-time $7200; part-time $600 per credit. Tuition, nonresident: full-time $11,124; part-time $927 per credit. *Faculty research:* Biological waste treatment; contaminant fate and transport; air, soil and water quality.

Rutgers, The State University of New Jersey, New Brunswick, Graduate School-New Brunswick, Joint Program in Toxicology, Piscataway, NJ 08854-8097. Offers environmental toxicology (MS, PhD); industrial-occupational toxicology (MS, PhD); nutritional toxicology (MS, PhD); pharmaceutical toxicology (MS, PhD). MS, PhD offered jointly with University of Medicine and Dentistry of New Jersey. *Degree requirements:* For master's, thesis; for doctorate, comprehensive exam, thesis/dissertation, qualifying exams (written and oral). *Entrance requirements:* For master's and doctorate, GRE General Test. Additional exam requirements/recommendations for international students: Required—TOEFL. Electronic applications accepted. *Expenses:* Tuition, state resident: full-time $7200; part-time $600 per credit. Tuition, nonresident: full-time $11,124; part-time $927 per credit. *Faculty research:* Neurotoxicants, immunotoxicology, carcinogenesis and chemoprevention, molecular toxicology, xenobiotic metabolism.

St. John's University, College of Pharmacy and Allied Health Professions, Graduate Programs in Pharmacy, Program in Toxicology, Queens, NY 11439. Offers MS. Part-time and evening/weekend programs available. *Students:* 9 full-time (5 women), 19 part-time (13 women); includes 13 minority (2 Black or African American, non-Hispanic/Latino; 7 Asian, non-Hispanic/Latino; 4 Hispanic/Latino), 9 international. Average age 25. 19 applicants, 47% accepted, 4 enrolled. In 2010, 10 master's awarded. *Degree requirements:* For master's, comprehensive exam, thesis optional, one-year residency. *Entrance requirements:* For master's, GRE General Test, minimum GPA of 3.0; 2 letters of recommendation. Additional exam requirements/recommendations for international students: Required—TOEFL (minimum score 600 paper-based; 250 computer-based; 100 iBT), IELTS (minimum score 5.5). *Application deadline:* For fall admission, 3/1 priority date for domestic students, 5/1 priority date for international students; for spring admission, 11/1 priority date for domestic and international students. Applications are processed on a rolling basis. Application fee: $70. Electronic applications accepted. *Expenses:* Contact institution. *Financial support:* Fellowships, research assistantships, career-related internships or fieldwork and scholarships/grants available. Support available to part-time students. Financial award application deadline: 3/1; financial award applicants required to submit FAFSA. *Faculty research:* Neurotoxicology, renal toxicology, toxicology of metals, regulatory toxicology. *Unit head:* Dr. Louis Trombetta, Chair, 718-990-6025, E-mail: trombetl@stjohns.edu. *Application contact:* Kathleen Davis, Director of Graduate Admission, 718-990-1601, Fax: 718-990-5686, E-mail: gradhelp@stjohns.edu.

San Diego State University, Graduate and Research Affairs, College of Health and Human Services, Graduate School of Public Health, San Diego, CA 92182. Offers environmental health (MPH); epidemiology (MPH, PhD), including biostatistics (MPH); global emergency preparedness and response (MS); global health (PhD); health behavior (PhD); health promotion (MPH); health services administration (MPH); toxicology (MS); MPH/MA; MSW/MPH. *Accreditation:* ABET (one or more programs are accredited); CAHME (one or more programs are accredited); CEPH (one or more programs are accredited). Part-time programs available. *Degree requirements:* For master's, comprehensive exam (for some programs), thesis (for some programs); for doctorate, thesis/dissertation. *Entrance requirements:* For master's, GMAT (MPH in health services administration), GRE General Test; for doctorate, GRE General Test. Additional exam requirements/recommendations for international students: Required—TOEFL. *Faculty research:* Evaluation of tobacco, AIDS prevalence and prevention, mammography, infant death project, Alzheimer's in elderly Chinese.

Simon Fraser University, Graduate Studies, Faculty of Science, Department of Biological Sciences, Burnaby, BC V5A 1S6, Canada. Offers biological sciences (M Sc, PhD); environmental toxicology (MET); pest management (MPM). *Degree requirements:* For master's, thesis; for doctorate, thesis/dissertation. *Entrance requirements:* For master's, minimum GPA of 3.0; for doctorate, minimum GPA of 3.5. Additional exam requirements/recommendations for international students: Required—TOEFL or IELTS. Electronic applications accepted. *Faculty research:* Molecular biology, marine biology, ecology, wildlife biology, endocrinology.

Texas A&M University, College of Veterinary Medicine and Biomedical Sciences, Department of Veterinary Integrative Biosciences, College Station, TX 77843. Offers epidemiology (MS); food safety/toxicology/environmental health (MS); science and technology journalism (MS); veterinary public health (MS). *Faculty:* 22. *Students:* 35 full-time (20 women), 13 part-time (8 women); includes 1 Asian, non-Hispanic/Latino; 1 Hispanic/Latino, 21 international. Average age 30. In 2010, 1 master's awarded. Terminal master's awarded for partial completion of doctoral program. *Degree requirements:* For master's, comprehensive exam, thesis. *Entrance requirements:* For master's, GRE General Test, minimum undergraduate GPA of 3.0. Additional exam requirements/recommendations for international students: Required—TOEFL. *Application deadline:* For fall admission, 7/15 priority date for domestic students, 4/1 priority date for international students; for spring admission, 10/1 priority date for domestic students, 9/15 priority date for international students. Applications are processed on a rolling basis. Application fee: $50 ($75 for international students). Electronic applications accepted. *Financial support:* In 2010–11, fellowships (averaging $18,000 per year), research assistantships (averaging $15,600 per year), teaching assistantships (averaging $15,600 per year) were awarded; institutionally sponsored loans, unspecified assistantships, and clinical associateships also available. Financial award application deadline: 7/15; financial award applicants required to submit FAFSA. *Faculty research:* Metal toxicology, reproductive biology, genetics of neural development, developmental biology, environmental toxicology. *Unit head:* Dr. Evelyn Tiffany-Castiglioni, Head, 979-458-1077, E-mail: ecastiglioni@cvm.tamu.edu. *Application contact:* Dr. Evelyn Tiffany-Castiglioni, Head, 979-458-1077, E-mail: ecastiglioni@cvm.tamu.edu.

Texas A&M University, College of Veterinary Medicine and Biomedical Sciences, Department of Veterinary Physiology and Pharmacology, College Station, TX 77843. Offers biomedical science (MS, PhD); toxicology (PhD). *Faculty:* 17. *Students:* 25 full-time (15 women); includes 1 Black or African American, non-Hispanic/Latino; 2 Asian, non-Hispanic/Latino; 1 Hispanic/Latino, 10 international. Average age 30. In 2010, 1 doctorate awarded. *Entrance requirements:* For master's and doctorate, GRE General Test. Additional exam requirements/recommendations for international students: Required—TOEFL. Application fee: $50 ($75 for international students). *Financial support:* Fellowships, research assistantships, teaching assistantships available. Financial award application deadline: 4/1; financial award applicants required to submit FAFSA. *Faculty research:* Gamete and embryo physiology, endocrinology, equine laminitis. *Unit head:* Glen Laine, Head, 979-845-7261, E-mail: glaine@tamu.edu. *Application contact:* Graduate Admissions, 979-845-1044, E-mail: admissions@tamu.edu.

Texas Southern University, School of Science and Technology, Program in Environmental Toxicology, Houston, TX 77004-4584. Offers MS, PhD. Part-time programs available. *Students:* 28 full-time (17 women), 22 part-time (12 women); includes 36 Black or African American, non-Hispanic/Latino; 3 Asian, non-Hispanic/Latino; 3 Hispanic/Latino, 3 international. Average age 36. 14 applicants, 100% accepted, 12 enrolled. In 2010, 1 doctorate awarded. *Degree requirements:* For master's, thesis; for doctorate, thesis/dissertation. *Entrance requirements:* For master's, minimum GPA of 2.75; for doctorate, GRE, minimum GPA of 2.75. *Application deadline:* For fall admission, 7/1 for domestic and international students; for spring admission, 11/1 for domestic and international students. Applications are processed on a rolling basis. Application fee: $35 ($75 for international students). Electronic applications accepted. *Expenses:* Contact institution. *Financial support:* In 2010–11, 8 fellowships (averaging $28,000 per year), 2 research assistantships (averaging $7,667 per year), 14 teaching assistantships (averaging $5,405 per year) were awarded; institutionally sponsored loans, scholarships/grants, tuition waivers (partial), and unspecified assistantships also available. Financial award application deadline: 5/1; financial award applicants required to submit FAFSA. *Faculty research:* Air quality, water quality, soil remediation, computer modeling. *Unit head:* Dr. James DuMond, Associate Professor/Interim Associate Dean/Interim Chair, 713-313-7095, Fax: 713-313-4217, E-mail: dumond_jw@tsu.edu. *Application contact:* Chalotte Whaley, Administrative Assistant, 713-313-7009, E-mail: whaley_cs@tsu.edu.

Texas Tech University, Graduate School, College of Arts and Sciences, Department of Environmental Toxicology, Lubbock, TX 79409. Offers MS, PhD, JD/MS, MBA/MS, MS/MPA. Part-time programs available. *Faculty:* 10 full-time (1 woman), 1 part-time/adjunct (0 women). *Students:* 53 full-time (26 women), 2 part-time (1 woman); includes 1 Black or African American, non-Hispanic/Latino; 1 Asian, non-Hispanic/Latino; 1 Hispanic/Latino; 1 Two or more races, non-Hispanic/Latino, 23 international. Average age 26. 51 applicants, 45% accepted, 13 enrolled. In 2010, 4 master's, 4 doctorates awarded. *Degree requirements:* For master's, thesis; for doctorate, thesis/dissertation. *Entrance requirements:* For master's and doctorate, GRE General Test. Additional exam requirements/recommendations for international students: Required—TOEFL (minimum score 550 paper-based; 213 computer-based; 79 iBT). *Application deadline:* For fall admission, 6/1 priority date for domestic students, 1/15 priority date for international students; for spring admission, 9/1 priority date for domestic students, 6/15 priority date for international students. Applications are processed on a rolling basis. Application fee: $50 ($75 for international students). Electronic applications accepted. *Expenses:* Tuition, state resident: full-time $5496; part-time $228.99 per credit hour. Tuition, nonresident: full-time $12,936; part-time $538.99 per credit hour. Required fees: $2674; $36 per credit hour. $905 per semester. *Financial support:* In 2010–11, 50 students received support, including 19 research assistantships (averaging $7,129 per year), 5 teaching assistantships with partial tuition reimbursements available (averaging $5,581 per year). Financial award application deadline: 4/15; financial award applicants required to submit FAFSA. *Faculty research:* Terrestrial and aquatic toxicology, biochemical and developmental toxicology, advanced materials, countermeasures to biologic and chemical threats, molecular epidemiology and modeling. Total annual research expenditures: $1.9 million. *Unit head:* Dr. Ronald J. Kendall, Director and Chairman, 806-885-4567, Fax: 806-885-2132, E-mail: ron.kendall@tiehh.ttu.edu. *Application contact:* Ryan Bounds, Assistant Managing Director, 806-885-4567, Fax: 806-885-2132, E-mail: ryan.bounds@ttu.edu.

Université de Montréal, Faculty of Medicine, Program in Toxicology and Risk Analysis, Montréal, QC H3C 3J7, Canada. Offers DESS. Electronic applications accepted.

University at Albany, State University of New York, School of Public Health, Department of Environmental Health Sciences, Albany, NY 12222-0001. Offers environmental and analytical chemistry (MS, PhD); environmental and occupational health (MS, PhD); toxicology (MS, PhD). *Degree requirements:* For master's, thesis; for doctorate, comprehensive exam, thesis/dissertation. *Entrance requirements:* For master's and doctorate, GRE General Test, GRE Subject Test, 3 letters of reference. Additional exam requirements/recommendations for international students: Required—TOEFL (minimum score 600 paper-based; 213 computer-based). Electronic applications accepted. *Faculty research:* Xenobiotic metabolism, neurotoxicity of halogenated hydrocarbons, pharmac/toxicogenomics, environmental analytical chemistry.

University at Buffalo, the State University of New York, Graduate School, School of Medicine and Biomedical Sciences, Graduate Programs in Medicine and Biomedical Sciences, Department of Pharmacology and Toxicology, Buffalo, NY 14260. Offers biochemical pharmacology (MS); pharmacology (MA, PhD); MD/PhD. Terminal master's awarded for partial completion of doctoral program. *Degree requirements:* For master's, thesis; for doctorate, thesis/dissertation. *Entrance requirements:* For master's and doctorate, GRE General Test, 3 letters of recommendation. Additional exam requirements/recommendations for international students: Required—TOEFL (minimum score 100 iBT). Electronic applications accepted. *Faculty research:* Neuropharmacology, toxicology, signal transduction, molecular pharmacology, behavioral pharmacology.

The University of Alabama at Birmingham, Graduate Programs in Joint Health Sciences, Program in Pharmacology and Toxicology, Birmingham, AL 35294. Offers PhD. *Students:* 13 full-time (5 women); includes 2 minority (1 Black or African American, non-Hispanic/Latino; 1 Hispanic/Latino), 3 international. Average age 27. In 2010, 4 doctorates awarded. *Degree requirements:* For doctorate, thesis/dissertation. *Entrance requirements:* For doctorate, GRE General Test, interview. *Application deadline:* Applications are processed on a rolling basis. Application fee: $35 ($60 for international students). Electronic applications accepted. *Expenses:* Contact institution. *Financial support:* In 2010–11, 6 fellowships were awarded. *Faculty research:* Biochemical pharmacology, neuropharmacology, endocrine pharmacology. *Unit head:* Dr. Mary-Ann Bjornsti, Interim Chair, 205-934-4579. *Application contact:* Graduate Coordinator, 205-934-4584, Fax: 205-934-4209.

Toxicology

University of Arkansas for Medical Sciences, Graduate School, Graduate Programs in Biomedical Sciences, Interdisciplinary Toxicology Program, Little Rock, AR 72205-7199. Offers MS, PhD, MD/PhD. *Degree requirements:* For master's, thesis; for doctorate, thesis/dissertation. *Entrance requirements:* For master's and doctorate, GRE General Test. Additional exam requirements/recommendations for international students: Required—TOEFL.

University of California, Davis, Graduate Studies, Graduate Group in Pharmacology and Toxicology, Davis, CA 95616. Offers MS, PhD. Terminal master's awarded for partial completion of doctoral program. *Degree requirements:* For master's, comprehensive exam or thesis; for doctorate, thesis/dissertation, qualifying exam. *Entrance requirements:* For master's and doctorate, GRE General Test, minimum GPA of 3.0, course work in biochemistry and/or physiology. Additional exam requirements/recommendations for international students: Required—TOEFL (minimum score 550 paper-based; 213 computer-based). Electronic applications accepted. *Faculty research:* Respiratory, neurochemical, molecular, genetic, and ecological toxicology.

University of California, Irvine, School of Medicine, Department of Pharmacology, Program in Pharmacology and Toxicology, Irvine, CA 92697. Offers MS, PhD, MD/PhD. *Students:* 24 full-time (10 women); includes 10 minority (2 Black or African American, non-Hispanic/Latino; 6 Asian, non-Hispanic/Latino; 2 Hispanic/Latino), 3 international. Average age 28. 44 applicants, 20% accepted, 4 enrolled. In 2010, 4 master's, 6 doctorates awarded. *Degree requirements:* For doctorate, thesis/dissertation. *Entrance requirements:* For master's, GRE, minimum GPA of 3.0; for doctorate, GRE General Test, GRE Subject Test, minimum GPA of 3.0. Additional exam requirements/recommendations for international students: Required—TOEFL (minimum score 550 paper-based; 213 computer-based). *Application deadline:* For fall admission, 1/15 priority date for domestic students; 1/15 for international students. Applications are processed on a rolling basis. Application fee: $80 ($100 for international students). Electronic applications accepted. *Financial support:* Fellowships, research assistantships, teaching assistantships, institutionally sponsored loans, traineeships, and unspecified assistantships available. Financial award application deadline: 3/1; financial award applicants required to submit FAFSA. *Unit head:* Olivier Civelli, Acting Chair, 949-924-2522, Fax: 949-824-4855, E-mail: ocivelli@uci.edu. *Application contact:* Pamela J. Bhalla, Chief Administrative Officer, 949-824-6772, Fax: 949-824-4855, E-mail: pamela.bhalla@uci.edu.

University of California, Los Angeles, Graduate Division, College of Letters and Science and David Geffen School of Medicine, UCLA ACCESS to Programs in the Molecular, Cellular and Integrative Life Sciences, Los Angeles, CA 90095. Offers biochemistry and molecular biology (PhD); biological chemistry (PhD); cellular and molecular pathology (PhD); human genetics (PhD); microbiology, immunology, and molecular genetics (PhD); molecular biology (PhD); molecular toxicology (PhD); molecular, cellular and integrative physiology (PhD); neurobiology (PhD); oral biology (PhD); physiology (PhD). ACCESS is an umbrella program for first-year coursework in 12 PhD programs. *Students:* 48 full-time (28 women), 6 international. Average age 24. 388 applicants, 27% accepted, 48 enrolled. *Degree requirements:* For doctorate, thesis/dissertation, oral and written qualifying exams. *Entrance requirements:* For doctorate, GRE General Test, minimum undergraduate GPA of 3.0. Additional exam requirements/recommendations for international students: Required—TOEFL. *Application deadline:* For fall admission, 12/15 for domestic and international students. Application fee: $70 ($90 for international students). Electronic applications accepted. *Financial support:* In 2010–11, 31 fellowships with full and partial tuition reimbursements, 13 research assistantships with full and partial tuition reimbursements, 2 teaching assistantships with full and partial tuition reimbursements were awarded; Federal Work-Study, institutionally sponsored loans, scholarships/grants, health care benefits, tuition waivers (full and partial), and unspecified assistantships also available. Financial award application deadline: 3/1; financial award applicants required to submit FAFSA. *Faculty research:* Molecular, cellular, and developmental biology; immunology; microbiology; integrative biology. *Unit head:* Jody Spillane, Project Coordinator, 310-206-1845, E-mail: jspillane@mednet.ucla.edu. *Application contact:* UCLA Access Admissions, 310-206-1845, E-mail: uclaaccess@mednet.ucla.edu.

University of California, Riverside, Graduate Division, Program in Environmental Toxicology, Riverside, CA 92521-0102. Offers MS, PhD. Terminal master's awarded for partial completion of doctoral program. *Degree requirements:* For master's, thesis; for doctorate, comprehensive exam, thesis/dissertation, qualifying exams. *Entrance requirements:* For master's and doctorate, GRE General Test, minimum GPA of 3.25. Additional exam requirements/recommendations for international students: Required—TOEFL (minimum score 550 paper-based; 213 computer-based; 80 iBT). Electronic applications accepted. *Faculty research:* Cellular/molecular toxicology, atmospheric chemistry, bioremediation, carcinogenesis, mechanism of toxicity.

University of California, Santa Cruz, Division of Graduate Studies, Division of Physical and Biological Sciences, Environmental Toxicology Department, Santa Cruz, CA 95064. Offers MS, PhD. *Students:* 18 full-time (9 women); includes 8 minority (2 Black or African American, non-Hispanic/Latino; 2 Asian, non-Hispanic/Latino; 4 Hispanic/Latino), 1 international. Average age 27. 45 applicants, 18% accepted, 7 enrolled. In 2010, 3 doctorates awarded. Terminal master's awarded for partial completion of doctoral program. *Degree requirements:* For master's, comprehensive exam, thesis; for doctorate, thesis/dissertation, qualifying exams. *Entrance requirements:* For master's and doctorate, GRE. Additional exam requirements/recommendations for international students: Required—TOEFL (minimum score 550 paper-based; 220 computer-based; 83 iBT); Recommended—IELTS (minimum score 8). *Application deadline:* For fall admission, 12/3 for domestic and international students. Application fee: $70 ($90 for international students). Electronic applications accepted. *Financial support:* Fellowships, research assistantships, teaching assistantships, institutionally sponsored loans and tuition waivers available. Financial award applicants required to submit FAFSA. *Faculty research:* Molecular mechanisms of reactive DNA methylation toxicity, anthropogenic perturbations of biogeochemical cycles, anaerobic microbiology and biotransformation of pollutants and toxic metals, organismal responses and therapeutic treatment of toxins, microbiology, molecular genetics, genomics. *Unit head:* Claudia McClure, Graduate Program Coordinator, 831-459-4719, E-mail: clmcclur@ucsc.edu. *Application contact:* Claudia McClure, Graduate Program Coordinator, 831-459-4719, E-mail: clmcclur@ucsc.edu.

University of Colorado Denver, School of Pharmacy, Program in Toxicology, Denver, CO 80217-3364. Offers PhD. *Students:* 26 full-time (14 women); includes 1 Hispanic/Latino, 11 international. Average age 28. 14 applicants, 29% accepted, 4 enrolled. In 2010, 8 doctorates awarded. *Degree requirements:* For doctorate, comprehensive exam, thesis/dissertation. *Entrance requirements:* For doctorate, GRE, minimum undergraduate GPA of 3.0; prior coursework in general chemistry, organic chemistry, calculus, biology, and physics. Additional exam requirements/recommendations for international students: Required—TOEFL (minimum score 550 paper-based; 213 computer-based). Application fee: $50 ($75 for international students). Electronic applications accepted. *Expenses:* Contact institution. *Financial support:* Fellowships, research assistantships, teaching assistantships, Federal Work-Study, scholarships/grants, and unspecified assistantships available. Financial award application deadline: 3/15; financial award applicants required to submit FAFSA. *Faculty research:* Regulation of apoptotic cell death; cancer chemoprevention; innate immunity and hepatotoxicity; role of chronic inflammation in cancer; Parkinson's disease, epilepsy and oxidative stress. *Unit head:* Dr. Vasilis Vasiliou, Director, 303-724-3520, Fax: 303-724-7266, E-mail: vasilis.vasiliou@ucdenver.edu. *Application contact:* Jackie Milowski, Information Contact, 303-724-7263, E-mail: jackie.milowski@ucdenver.edu.

University of Connecticut, Graduate School, School of Pharmacy, Department of Pharmaceutical Sciences, Graduate Program in Pharmacology and Toxicology, Storrs, CT 06269. Offers pharmacology (MS, PhD); toxicology (MS, PhD). Terminal master's awarded for partial completion of doctoral program. *Degree requirements:* For master's, comprehensive exam, thesis; for doctorate, thesis/dissertation. *Entrance requirements:* For master's and doctorate, GRE General Test. Additional exam requirements/recommendations for international students: Required—TOEFL (minimum score 550 paper-based; 213 computer-based). Electronic applications accepted.

University of Florida, College of Pharmacy, Programs in Forensic Science, Gainesville, FL 32611. Offers clinical toxicology (Certificate); drug chemistry (Certificate); environmental forensics (Certificate); forensic death investigation (Certificate); forensic DNA and serology (MSP, Certificate); forensic drug chemistry (MSP); forensic science (MSP); forensic toxicology (Certificate). Postbaccalaureate distance learning degree programs offered (no on-campus study). *Faculty:* 7 full-time (2 women). *Students:* 35 full-time (24 women), 163 part-time (124 women); includes 14 Black or African American, non-Hispanic/Latino; 4 American Indian or Alaska Native, non-Hispanic/Latino; 5 Asian, non-Hispanic/Latino; 13 Hispanic/Latino, 6 international. Average age 28. In 2010, 88 master's awarded. *Degree requirements:* For master's, comprehensive exam. *Entrance requirements:* For master's, GRE General Test (minimum score 1000), minimum GPA of 3.0. Additional exam requirements/recommendations for international students: Required—TOEFL (minimum score 550 paper-based; 213 computer-based; 80 iBT), IELTS (minimum score 6). Application fee: $30. *Expenses:* Tuition, state resident: full-time $10,916. Tuition, nonresident: full-time $28,309. *Financial support:* In 2010–11, 2 students received support, including 2 research assistantships (averaging $14,076 per year). Financial award applicants required to submit FAFSA. *Unit head:* Dr. Ian Tibbett, Director, 352-273-6871, E-mail: itebbett@ufl.edu. *Application contact:* Dr. Ian Tibbett, Director, 352-273-6871, E-mail: itebbett@ufl.edu.

University of Florida, College of Veterinary Medicine, Graduate Program in Veterinary Medical Sciences, Gainesville, FL 32611. Offers forensic toxicology (Certificate); veterinary medical sciences (MS, PhD), including forensic toxicology (MS). Postbaccalaureate distance learning degree programs offered (no on-campus study). Terminal master's awarded for partial completion of doctoral program. *Degree requirements:* For master's, thesis; for doctorate, thesis/dissertation. *Entrance requirements:* For master's and doctorate, GRE General Test, minimum GPA of 3.0. Additional exam requirements/recommendations for international students: Required—TOEFL (minimum score 550 paper-based; 213 computer-based). Electronic applications accepted. *Expenses:* Contact institution.

University of Georgia, College of Veterinary Medicine and Graduate School, Graduate Programs in Veterinary Medicine, Interdisciplinary Graduate Program in Toxicology, Athens, GA 30602. Offers MS, PhD. Postbaccalaureate distance learning degree programs offered (minimal on-campus study). *Faculty:* 9 full-time (3 women), 1 part-time/adjunct (0 women). *Students:* 20 full-time (8 women); includes 1 Black or African American, non-Hispanic/Latino, 12 international. 39 applicants, 21% accepted, 4 enrolled. In 2010, 1 master's, 2 doctorates awarded. *Degree requirements:* For master's, thesis; for doctorate, one foreign language, thesis/dissertation. *Entrance requirements:* For master's and doctorate, GRE General Test. *Application deadline:* For fall admission, 7/1 priority date for domestic students; for spring admission, 11/15 for domestic students. Application fee: $50. Electronic applications accepted. *Expenses:* Tuition, state resident: full-time $7200; part-time $344 per credit hour. Tuition, nonresident: full-time $21,900; part-time $944 per credit hour. Tuition and fees vary according to course load and program. *Financial support:* In 2010–11, fellowships with full tuition reimbursements (averaging $14,600 per year), research assistantships with full tuition reimbursements (averaging $16,000 per year) were awarded; scholarships/grants and unspecified assistantships also available. Financial award application deadline: 5/1. *Faculty research:* Neurotoxicology, cell signal modulation, biological toxins, PBPK modeling, environmental risk assessment. Total annual research expenditures: $3 million. *Unit head:* Dr. Julie A. Coffield, Director, 706-542-5979, Fax: 706-542-7472, E-mail: coffield@uga.edu. *Application contact:* Dr. Brain Cummings, Graduate Coordinator, 706-542-3792, Fax: 706-542-7472, E-mail: bsc@rx.uga.edu.

University of Guelph, Graduate Studies, Ontario Agricultural College, Department of Environmental Biology, Guelph, ON N1G 2W1, Canada. Offers entomology (M Sc, PhD); environmental microbiology and biotechnology (M Sc, PhD); environmental toxicology (M Sc, PhD); plant and forest systems (M Sc, PhD); plant pathology (M Sc, PhD). Part-time programs available. *Degree requirements:* For master's, thesis; for doctorate, comprehensive exam, thesis/dissertation. *Entrance requirements:* For master's, minimum 75% average during previous 2 years of course work; for doctorate, minimum 75% average. Additional exam requirements/recommendations for international students: Required—TOEFL or IELTS. Electronic applications accepted. *Faculty research:* Entomology, environmental microbiology and biotechnology, environmental toxicology, forest ecology, plant pathology.

University of Guelph, Ontario Veterinary College and Graduate Studies, Graduate Programs in Veterinary Sciences, Department of Biomedical Sciences, Guelph, ON N1G 2W1, Canada. Offers morphology (M Sc, DV Sc, PhD); neuroscience (M Sc, DV Sc, PhD); pharmacology (M Sc, DV Sc, PhD); physiology (M Sc, DV Sc, PhD); toxicology (M Sc, DV Sc, PhD). Part-time programs available. *Degree requirements:* For master's, thesis; for doctorate, comprehensive exam, thesis/dissertation. *Entrance requirements:* For master's, honors B Sc, minimum 75% average in last 20 courses; for doctorate, M Sc with thesis from accredited institution. Additional exam requirements/recommendations for international students: Required—TOEFL (minimum score 550 paper-based; 213 computer-based; 89 iBT). Electronic applications accepted. *Faculty research:* Cellular morphology; endocrine, vascular and reproductive physiology; clinical pharmacology; veterinary toxicology; developmental biology, neuroscience.

University of Guelph, Ontario Veterinary College, Interdepartmental Program in Toxicology, Guelph, ON N1G 2W1, Canada. Offers M Sc, PhD. Part-time programs available. *Degree requirements:* For master's, thesis (for some programs); for doctorate, comprehensive exam, thesis/dissertation. *Entrance requirements:* For master's, B Sc; for doctorate, M Sc. Additional exam requirements/recommendations for international students: Required—TOEFL (minimum score 550 paper-based; 213 computer-based; 89 iBT).

The University of Iowa, Graduate College, Program in Human Toxicology, Iowa City, IA 52242-1316. Offers MS, PhD. *Degree requirements:* For master's, thesis; for doctorate, comprehensive exam, thesis/dissertation. *Entrance requirements:* For master's and doctorate, GRE General Test, minimum GPA of 3.0. Additional exam requirements/recommendations for international students: Required—TOEFL (minimum score 600 paper-based; 250 computer-based; 100 iBT). Electronic applications accepted.

The University of Kansas, Graduate Studies, School of Pharmacy, Department of Pharmacology and Toxicology, Program in Pharmacology and Toxicology, Lawrence, KS 66045. Offers MS, PhD. *Faculty:* 11 full-time (3 women). *Students:* 13 full-time (all women); includes 1 minority (Hispanic/Latino), 8 international. Average age 25. 58 applicants, 12% accepted, 4 enrolled. In 2010, 2 master's, 1 doctorate awarded. Terminal master's awarded for partial completion of doctoral program. *Degree requirements:* For master's, comprehensive exam, thesis; for doctorate, comprehensive exam, thesis/dissertation. *Entrance requirements:* For master's, GRE; for doctorate, GRE (minimum score: 600 verbal, 600 quantitative, 4.5 analytic). Additional exam requirements/recommendations for international students: Required—TOEFL (minimum score 600 paper-based; 250 computer-based; 100 iBT). *Application deadline:* For fall admission, 1/15 priority date for domestic students, 2/1 priority date for international students. Applications are processed on a rolling basis. Application fee: $55 ($65 for international students). Electronic applications accepted. *Expenses:* Tuition, state resident: full-time $7092; part-time $295.50 per credit hour. Tuition, nonresident: full-time $16,590; part-time $691.25 per credit hour. Required fees: $858; $71.49 per credit hour. Tuition and fees vary according to course load, campus/location and program. *Financial support:* Fellowships with full tuition reimbursements, research assistantships with full tuition reimbursements available. *Faculty research:* Neuropharmacology, neurodegeneration. *Unit head:* Dr. Nancy Muma, Chair, 785-864-4001, Fax: 785-864-5219, E-mail: nmuma@ku.edu. *Application contact:* Dr. R. Alexandar Moise, Assistant Professor/Director, 785-864-1010, Fax: 785-864-5219, E-mail: alexmoise@ku.edu.

The University of Kansas, University of Kansas Medical Center, School of Medicine, Department of Pharmacology, Toxicology and Therapeutics, Kansas City, KS 66160. Offers pharmacology (MS, PhD); toxicology (MS, PhD); MD/MS; MD/PhD. *Faculty:* 22 full-time (4 women). *Students:* 29 full-time (17 women); includes 1 minority (Hispanic/Latino), 11 international. Average age 28. 8 applicants, 100% accepted, 8 enrolled. In 2010, 4 doctorates awarded.

Terminal master's awarded for partial completion of doctoral program. *Degree requirements:* For master's, comprehensive exam, thesis; for doctorate, one foreign language, comprehensive exam, thesis/dissertation. *Entrance requirements:* For master's and doctorate, GRE General Test. Additional exam requirements/recommendations for international students: Required—TOEFL. *Application deadline:* For fall admission, 1/15 priority date for domestic students. Applications are processed on a rolling basis. Application fee: $0. Electronic applications accepted. *Expenses:* Tuition, state resident: full-time $7092; part-time $295.50 per credit hour. Tuition, nonresident: full-time $16,590; part-time $691.25 per credit hour. Required fees: $858; $71.49 per credit hour. Tuition and fees vary according to course load, campus/location and program. *Financial support:* Fellowships with full tuition reimbursements, research assistantships with full tuition reimbursements, teaching assistantships with full tuition reimbursements, Federal Work-Study, scholarships/grants, traineeships, and unspecified assistantships available. Support available to part-time students. Financial award application deadline: 2/14; financial award applicants required to submit FAFSA. *Faculty research:* Liver nuclear receptors, hepatobiliary transporters, pharmacogenomics, estrogen-induced carcinogenesis, neuropharmacology of pain and depression. Total annual research expenditures: $7.9 million. *Unit head:* Dr. Gerald Carlson, Professor and Interim Chair, 913-588-7140, Fax: 913-588-7501, E-mail: gcarlson@kumc.edu. *Application contact:* Dr. Bruno Hagenbuch, Chair, Departmental Graduate Committee, 913-588-0028, Fax: 913-588-7501, E-mail: bhagenbuch@kumc.edu.

University of Kentucky, Graduate School, Graduate School Programs from the College of Medicine, Program in Toxicology, Lexington, KY 40506-0032. Offers MS, PhD. Terminal master's awarded for partial completion of doctoral program. *Degree requirements:* For master's, comprehensive exam, thesis optional; for doctorate, comprehensive exam, thesis/dissertation. *Entrance requirements:* For master's, GRE General Test, minimum undergraduate GPA of 2.75; for doctorate, GRE General Test, minimum graduate GPA of 3.0. Additional exam requirements/recommendations for international students: Required—TOEFL (minimum score 550 paper-based; 213 computer-based). Electronic applications accepted. *Faculty research:* Chemical carcinogenesis, immunotoxicology, neurotoxicology, metabolism and disposition, gene regulation.

University of Louisville, School of Medicine, Department of Pharmacology and Toxicology, Louisville, KY 40292-0001. Offers MS, PhD, MD/PhD. *Faculty:* 59 full-time (9 women). *Students:* 34 full-time (19 women), 5 part-time (2 women); includes 5 Black or African American, non-Hispanic/Latino; 2 Asian, non-Hispanic/Latino; 1 Two or more races, non-Hispanic/Latino, 15 international. Average age 29. 52 applicants, 27% accepted, 10 enrolled. In 2010, 7 master's, 5 doctorates awarded. Terminal master's awarded for partial completion of doctoral program. *Degree requirements:* For master's, thesis; for doctorate, comprehensive exam, thesis/dissertation. *Entrance requirements:* For master's and doctorate, GRE General Test (minimum score of 1000 verbal and quantitative), minimum GPA of 3.0. Additional exam requirements/recommendations for international students: Required—TOEFL. *Application deadline:* For fall admission, 1/15 priority date for domestic and international students. Applications are processed on a rolling basis. Application fee: $50. Electronic applications accepted. *Expenses:* Tuition, state resident: full-time $9144; part-time $508 per credit hour. Tuition, nonresident: full-time $19,026; part-time $1057 per credit hour. Tuition and fees vary according to program and reciprocity agreements. *Financial support:* Fellowships with full tuition reimbursements, research assistantships with full tuition reimbursements available. Financial award application deadline: 4/15. *Faculty research:* Molecular pharmacogenetics; epidemiology; functional genomics; genetic predisposition to chemical carcinogenesis and drug toxicity; mechanisms of oxidative stress; alcohol-induced hepatitis, pancreatitis, and hepatocellular carcinoma; molecular and cardiac toxicology; molecular biology and genetics of DNA damage and repair in humans; mechanisms of chemoresistance; arsenic toxicity and cell cycle disruption; molecular pharmacology of novel G protein-coupled receptors. *Unit head:* Dr. David W. Hein, Chair, 502-852-5141, Fax: 502-852-7868, E-mail: dhein@louisville.edu. *Application contact:* Heddy R. Rubin, Information Contact, 502-852-5741, Fax: 502-852-7868, E-mail: hrrubi01@gwise.louisville.edu.

University of Maine, Graduate School, Program in Biomedical Sciences, Orono, ME 04469. Offers biomedical engineering (PhD); cell and molecular biology (PhD); neuroscience (PhD); toxicology (PhD). *Students:* 11 full-time (8 women), 13 part-time (6 women); includes 1 American Indian or Alaska Native, non-Hispanic/Latino, 5 international. Average age 29. 32 applicants, 19% accepted, 6 enrolled. Application fee: $60. *Expenses:* Tuition, state resident: full-time $400. Tuition, nonresident: full-time $1050. *Financial support:* In 2010–11, 8 research assistantships (averaging $25,625 per year) were awarded. *Unit head:* Dr. Carol Kim, Unit Head, 207-581-2803. *Application contact:* Dr. Carol Kim, Unit Head, 207-581-2803.

The University of Manchester, Faculty of Life Sciences, Manchester, United Kingdom. Offers adaptive organismal biology (M Phil, PhD); animal biology (M Phil, PhD); biochemistry (M Phil, PhD); bioinformatics (M Phil, PhD); biomolecular sciences (M Phil, PhD); biotechnology (M Phil, PhD); cell biology (M Phil, PhD); cell matrix research (M Phil, PhD); channels and transporters (M Phil, PhD); developmental biology (M Phil, PhD); Egyptology (M Phil, PhD); environmental biology (M Phil, PhD); evolutionary biology (M Phil, PhD); gene expression (M Phil, PhD); genetics (M Phil, PhD); history of science, technology and medicine (M Phil, PhD); immunology (M Phil, PhD); integrative neurobiology and behavior (M Phil, PhD); membrane trafficking (M Phil, PhD); microbiology (M Phil, PhD); molecular and cellular neuroscience (M Phil, PhD); molecular biology (M Phil, PhD); molecular cancer studies (M Phil, PhD); neuroscience (M Phil, PhD); ophthalmology (M Phil, PhD); optometry (M Phil, PhD); organelle function (M Phil, PhD); pharmacology (M Phil, PhD); physiology (M Phil, PhD); plant sciences (M Phil, PhD); stem cell research (M Phil, PhD); structural biology (M Phil, PhD); systems neuroscience (M Phil, PhD); toxicology (M Phil, PhD).

University of Maryland, Baltimore, Graduate School, Graduate Program in Life Sciences, Program in Toxicology, Baltimore, MD 21201. Offers MS, PhD, MD/MS, MD/PhD. Part-time programs available. *Degree requirements:* For doctorate, comprehensive exam, thesis/dissertation. *Entrance requirements:* For master's and doctorate, GRE General Test, GRE Subject Test, minimum GPA of 3.0. Additional exam requirements/recommendations for international students: Required—TOEFL (minimum score 550 paper-based; 80 iBT); Recommended—IELTS (minimum score 7). Electronic applications accepted. Part-time tuition and fees vary according to course load, degree level and program.

University of Maryland, Baltimore, School of Medicine, Department of Epidemiology and Preventive Medicine, Baltimore, MD 21201. Offers biostatistics (MS); clinical research (MS); epidemiology and preventative medicine (PhD); epidemiology and preventive medicine (MPH, MS); gerontology (PhD); human genetics and genomic (PhD); human genetics and genomic medicine (MS); molecular epidemiology (MS, PhD); toxicology (MS, PhD); JD/MS; MD/PhD; MS/PhD. *Accreditation:* CEPH. Part-time programs available. *Students:* 84 full-time (57 women), 64 part-time (46 women); includes 17 Black or African American, non-Hispanic/Latino; 23 Asian, non-Hispanic/Latino; 4 Hispanic/Latino, 18 international. Average age 32. In 2010, 21 master's, 10 doctorates awarded. *Entrance requirements:* For master's and doctorate, GRE General Test. Additional exam requirements/recommendations for international students: Required—TOEFL (minimum score 550 paper-based; 213 computer-based; 80 iBT); Recommended—IELTS. *Application deadline:* For fall admission, 1/15 for domestic and international students. Electronic applications accepted. *Expenses:* Contact institution. *Financial support:* In 2010–11, research assistantships with partial tuition reimbursements (averaging $25,000 per year); fellowships, Federal Work-Study, scholarships/grants, and unspecified assistantships also available. Financial award application deadline: 3/1; financial award applicants required to submit FAFSA. *Unit head:* Dr. Patricia Langenberg, Program Director, 410-706-3251, Fax: 410-706-8013. *Application contact:* Danielle Fitzpatrick, Program Coordinator, 410-706-8492, Fax: 410-706-4225, E-mail: dfitzpatrick@epi.umaryland.edu.

University of Maryland Eastern Shore, Graduate Programs, Department of Natural Sciences, Program in Toxicology, Princess Anne, MD 21853-1299. Offers MS, PhD.

University of Medicine and Dentistry of New Jersey, Graduate School of Biomedical Sciences, Graduate Programs in Biomedical Sciences–Piscataway, Piscataway, NJ 08854-5635. Offers biochemistry and molecular biology (MS, PhD); biomedical engineering (MS, PhD); biomedical science (MS); cellular and molecular pharmacology (MS, PhD); clinical and translational science (MS); environmental sciences/exposure assessment (PhD); molecular genetics, microbiology and immunology (MS, PhD); neuroscience (MS, PhD); physiology and integrative biology (MS, PhD); toxicology (PhD); MD/PhD. *Students:* 474 full-time (260 women), 22 part-time (7 women); includes 30 Black or African American, non-Hispanic/Latino; 89 Asian, non-Hispanic/Latino; 36 Hispanic/Latino, 158 international. Average age 28. 1,064 applicants, 18% accepted, 121 enrolled. In 2010, 32 master's, 70 doctorates awarded. Terminal master's awarded for partial completion of doctoral program. *Degree requirements:* For master's, thesis (for some programs), ethics training; for doctorate, comprehensive exam, thesis/dissertation, ethics training. *Entrance requirements:* For master's, GRE General Test, MCAT, DAT; for doctorate, GRE General Test. Additional exam requirements/recommendations for international students: Required—TOEFL. *Application deadline:* For fall admission, 1/5 for domestic students. Applications are processed on a rolling basis. Application fee: $65. Electronic applications accepted. *Financial support:* Fellowships, research assistantships, teaching assistantships, career-related internships or fieldwork, Federal Work-Study, traineeships, health care benefits, and unspecified assistantships available. *Unit head:* Dr. Terri Goss Kinzy, Senior Associate Dean, Graduate School, 732-235-5016, Fax: 732-235-4720, E-mail: gsbspisc@umdnj.edu. *Application contact:* Johanna Sierra, University Registrar, 732-235-5016, Fax: 732-235-4720.

University of Michigan, School of Public Health, Department of Environmental Health Sciences, Ann Arbor, MI 48109. Offers environmental health sciences (MS, PhD); environmental quality and health (MPH); human nutrition (MPH); industrial hygiene (MPH, MS); nutritional sciences (MS); occupational and environmental epidemiology (MPH); toxicology (MPH, MS, PhD). *Accreditation:* CEPH (one or more programs are accredited). Part-time programs available. *Faculty:* 25 full-time (7 women), 23 part-time/adjunct (10 women). *Students:* 134 full-time (104 women), 37 part-time (23 women); includes 32 minority (10 Black or African American, non-Hispanic/Latino; 1 American Indian or Alaska Native, non-Hispanic/Latino; 14 Asian, non-Hispanic/Latino; 5 Hispanic/Latino; 2 Two or more races, non-Hispanic/Latino), 30 international. Average age 26. 254 applicants, 69% accepted, 68 enrolled. In 2010, 38 master's, 4 doctorates awarded. Terminal master's awarded for partial completion of doctoral program. *Degree requirements:* For master's, thesis (for some programs); for doctorate, thesis/dissertation, preliminary exam, oral defense of dissertation. *Entrance requirements:* For master's and doctorate, GRE General Test and/or MCAT. Additional exam requirements/recommendations for international students: Required—TOEFL (minimum score 560 paper-based; 220 computer-based; 100 iBT). *Application deadline:* For fall admission, 1/1 priority date for domestic and international students. Applications are processed on a rolling basis. Application fee: $65 ($75 for international students). Electronic applications accepted. *Expenses:* Tuition, state resident: full-time $17,784; part-time $1116 per credit hour. Tuition, nonresident: full-time $35,944; part-time $2125 per credit hour. International tuition: $35,994 full-time. Required fees: $95 per semester. Tuition and fees vary according to course load, degree level and program. *Financial support:* In 2010–11, 86 students received support, including 57 fellowships with full and partial tuition reimbursements available, 17 research assistantships with full tuition reimbursements available (averaging $21,000 per year), 12 teaching assistantships with full tuition reimbursements available (averaging $21,000 per year); Federal Work-Study, scholarships/grants, traineeships, and unspecified assistantships also available. Financial award application deadline: 3/1. *Faculty research:* Toxicology, occupational hygiene, nutrition, environmental exposure sciences, environmental epidemiology. Total annual research expenditures: $7.5 million. *Unit head:* Dr. Howard Hu, Chair, 734-764-3188, E-mail: howardhu@umich.edu. *Application contact:* Susan Crawford, Student Administrative Coordinator, 734-764-3018, E-mail: sph.inquiries@umich.edu.

University of Minnesota, Duluth, Graduate School, Program in Toxicology, Duluth, MN 55812-2496. Offers MS, PhD. MS, PhD offered jointly with University of Minnesota, Twin Cities Campus. Terminal master's awarded for partial completion of doctoral program. *Degree requirements:* For master's, thesis; for doctorate, comprehensive exam, thesis/dissertation, written and oral preliminary and final exams. *Entrance requirements:* For master's and doctorate, GRE General Test, BS in basic science; full year each of biology, chemistry, and physics; mathematics coursework through calculus. Additional exam requirements/recommendations for international students: Required—TOEFL (minimum score 550 paper-based; 79 iBT). Electronic applications accepted. *Faculty research:* Structure activity correlations, neurotoxicity, aquatic toxicology, biochemical mechanisms, immunotoxicology.

University of Minnesota, Duluth, Medical School, Department of Biochemistry, Molecular Biology and Biophysics, Duluth, MN 55812-2496. Offers biochemistry, molecular biology and biophysics (MS); biology and biophysics (PhD); social, administrative, and clinical pharmacy (MS, PhD); toxicology (MS, PhD). *Faculty:* 10 full-time (3 women). *Students:* 16 full-time (5 women); includes 3 Asian, non-Hispanic/Latino. Average age 29. 7 applicants, 29% accepted, 2 enrolled. In 2010, 1 master's, 1 doctorate awarded. Terminal master's awarded for partial completion of doctoral program. *Degree requirements:* For master's, comprehensive exam, thesis; for doctorate, comprehensive exam, thesis/dissertation. *Entrance requirements:* For master's and doctorate, GRE General Test. Additional exam requirements/recommendations for international students: Required—TOEFL. *Application deadline:* For winter admission, 1/3 for domestic students, 1/2 for international students; for spring admission, 3/15 priority date for domestic and international students. Application fee: $75 ($95 for international students). Electronic applications accepted. *Financial support:* In 2010–11, 8 students received support, including research assistantships with full tuition reimbursements available (averaging $27,300 per year), teaching assistantships with full tuition reimbursements available (averaging $27,300 per year); career-related internships or fieldwork, scholarships/grants, health care benefits, and unspecified assistantships also available. Financial award application deadline: 9/1. *Faculty research:* Intestinal cancer biology; hepatotoxins and mitochondriopathies; toxicology; cell cycle regulation in stem cells; neurobiology of brain development, trace metal function and blood-brain barrier; hibernation biology. Total annual research expenditures: $1.5 million. *Unit head:* Dr. Lester R. Drewes, Professor/Head, 218-726-7925, Fax: 218-726-8014, E-mail: ldrewes@d.umn.edu. *Application contact:* Cheryl Beeman, Executive Office and Administrative Assistant, 218-726-6354, Fax: 218-726-8014, E-mail: ahcd@d.umn.edu.

University of Minnesota, Twin Cities Campus, School of Public Health, Division of Environmental Health Sciences, Area in Environmental Toxicology, Minneapolis, MN 55455-0213. Offers MPH, MS, PhD. *Degree requirements:* For doctorate, thesis/dissertation. *Entrance requirements:* For master's and doctorate, GRE General Test. Electronic applications accepted.

University of Mississippi Medical Center, School of Graduate Studies in the Health Sciences, Department of Pharmacology and Toxicology, Jackson, MS 39216-4505. Offers pharmacology (MS, PhD); toxicology (MS, PhD); MD/PhD. Terminal master's awarded for partial completion of doctoral program. *Degree requirements:* For master's, thesis; for doctorate, thesis/dissertation, first authored publication. *Entrance requirements:* For master's and doctorate, GRE General Test, minimum GPA of 3.0. *Faculty research:* Neuropharmacology, environmental toxicology, aging, immunopharmacology, cardiovascular pharmacology.

The University of Montana, Graduate School, College of Health Professions and Biomedical Sciences, Skaggs School of Pharmacy, Department of Biomedical and Pharmaceutical Sciences, Missoula, MT 59812-0002. Offers biomedical sciences (PhD); neuroscience (MS, PhD); pharmaceutical sciences (MS); toxicology (MS, PhD). *Accreditation:* ACPE. *Degree requirements:* For master's, oral defense of thesis; for doctorate, research dissertation defense. *Entrance requirements:* For master's and doctorate, GRE General Test. Additional exam requirements/recommendations for international students: Required—TOEFL (minimum score 540 paper-based; 210 computer-based). Electronic applications accepted. *Faculty research:* Cardiovascular pharmacology, medicinal chemistry, neurosciences, environmental toxicology, pharmacogenetics, cancer.

Toxicology

University of Nebraska–Lincoln, Graduate College, Interdepartmental Area of Environmental Health, Occupational Health and Toxicology, Lincoln, NE 68588. Offers MS, PhD. MS, PhD offered jointly with University of Nebraska Medical Center. *Entrance requirements:* Additional exam requirements/recommendations for international students: Required—TOEFL (minimum score 550 paper-based; 213 computer-based). Electronic applications accepted.

University of Nebraska Medical Center, Graduate Studies, Program in Environmental Health, Occupational Health and Toxicology, Omaha, NE 68198. Offers MS, PhD. *Faculty:* 55 full-time (10 women). *Students:* 15 full-time (7 women), 2 part-time (1 woman); includes 3 Asian, non-Hispanic/Latino, 6 international. Average age 29. 9 applicants, 56% accepted, 5 enrolled. In 2010, 1 doctorate awarded. Terminal master's awarded for partial completion of doctoral program. *Degree requirements:* For master's, comprehensive exam (for some programs), thesis; for doctorate, comprehensive exam (for some programs), thesis/dissertation. *Entrance requirements:* For master's, GRE General Test, bachelor's degree in chemistry, biology, biochemistry or related area; for doctorate, GRE General Test, BS in chemistry, biology, biochemistry or related area. Additional exam requirements/recommendations for international students: Required—TOEFL (minimum score 550 paper-based; 213 computer-based). *Application deadline:* For fall admission, 6/1 for domestic students, 4/1 for international students; for spring admission, 10/1 for domestic students, 8/1 for international students. Applications are processed on a rolling basis. Application fee: $45. Electronic applications accepted. *Expenses:* Tuition, state resident: part-time $198.25 per semester hour. Required fees: $63 per semester. *Financial support:* In 2010–11, 2 students received support, including 1 fellowship with full tuition reimbursement available (averaging $21,000 per year), 1 research assistantship with full tuition reimbursement available (averaging $21,000 per year); teaching assistantships, institutionally sponsored loans, traineeships, health care benefits, and tuition waivers (full) also available. *Faculty research:* Mechanisms of carcinogenesis, alcohol and metal toxicity, DNA damage, human molecular genetics, agrochemicals in soil and water. *Unit head:* Dr. Eleanor G. Rogan, Chair, Department of Environmental, Agricultural and Occupational Health, 402-559-4095, Fax: 402-559-8068, E-mail: uncetox@unmc.edu. *Application contact:* Sherry Cherek, Coordinator, 402-559-8924, Fax: 402-559-8068, E-mail: scherek@unmc.edu.

University of New Mexico, School of Medicine, Biomedical Sciences Graduate Program, Albuquerque, NM 87131-5196. Offers biochemistry and molecular biology (MS, PhD); cell biology and physiology (MS, PhD); clinical and translational science (Certificate); molecular genetics and microbiology (MS, PhD); neuroscience (MS, PhD); pathology (MS, PhD); toxicology (MS, PhD); university science teaching (Certificate). Part-time programs available. *Faculty:* 33 full-time (14 women), 3 part-time/adjunct (1 woman). *Students:* 94 full-time (57 women), 14 part-time (8 women); includes 24 minority (3 Black or African American, non-Hispanic/Latino; 1 American Indian or Alaska Native, non-Hispanic/Latino; 6 Asian, non-Hispanic/Latino; 13 Hispanic/Latino; 1 Two or more races, non-Hispanic/Latino), 20 international. Average age 30. 135 applicants, 14% accepted, 19 enrolled. In 2010, 2 master's, 19 doctorates, 3 other advanced degrees awarded. Terminal master's awarded for partial completion of doctoral program. *Degree requirements:* For master's, thesis; for doctorate, comprehensive exam, thesis/dissertation. *Entrance requirements:* For master's and doctorate, GRE General Test, minimum undergraduate GPA of 3.0. Additional exam requirements/recommendations for international students: Required—TOEFL. *Application deadline:* For fall admission, 1/1 priority date for domestic students. Applications are processed on a rolling basis. Application fee: $50. Electronic applications accepted. *Expenses:* Tuition, state resident: full-time $5991; part-time $251 per credit hour. Tuition, nonresident: full-time $14,405; part-time $800.20 per credit hour. Tuition and fees vary according to course level, course load, program and reciprocity agreements. *Financial support:* In 2010–11, 99 students received support, including 5 fellowships (averaging $75 per year), 96 research assistantships with full tuition reimbursements available (averaging $17,401 per year), 2 teaching assistantships with full tuition reimbursements available (averaging $2,415 per year); career-related internships or fieldwork, Federal Work-Study, institutionally sponsored loans, scholarships/grants, traineeships, health care benefits, and unspecified assistantships also available. Financial award application deadline: 1/1; financial award applicants required to submit FAFSA. *Faculty research:* Signal transduction, infectious disease, biology of cancer, structural biology, neuroscience. *Unit head:* Laurie G. Hudson, Director, 505-272-1887, Fax: 505-272-8738, E-mail: lhudson@salud.unm.edu. *Application contact:* Angel Cooke-Jackson, Coordinator, 505-272-1887, Fax: 505-272-8738, E-mail: acooke-jackson@salud.unm.edu.

The University of North Carolina at Chapel Hill, School of Medicine, Curriculum in Toxicology, Chapel Hill, NC 27599. Offers MS, PhD. Terminal master's awarded for partial completion of doctoral program. *Degree requirements:* For master's, comprehensive exam, thesis; for doctorate, comprehensive exam, thesis/dissertation. *Entrance requirements:* For doctorate, GRE General Test. Electronic applications accepted. *Faculty research:* Molecular and cellular toxicology, carcinogenesis, neurotoxicology, pulmonary toxicology, developmental toxicology.

University of Prince Edward Island, Atlantic Veterinary College, Graduate Program in Veterinary Medicine, Charlottetown, PE C1A 4P3, Canada. Offers anatomy (M Sc, PhD); bacteriology (M Sc, PhD); clinical pharmacology (M Sc, PhD); clinical sciences (M Sc, PhD); epidemiology (M Sc, PhD), including reproduction; fish health (M Sc, PhD); food animal nutrition (M Sc, PhD); immunology (M Sc, PhD); microanatomy (M Sc, PhD); parasitology (M Sc, PhD); pathology (M Sc, PhD); pharmacology (M Sc, PhD); physiology (M Sc, PhD); toxicology (M Sc, PhD); veterinary science (M Vet Sc); virology (M Sc, PhD). Part-time programs available. *Degree requirements:* For master's, thesis; for doctorate, thesis/dissertation. *Entrance requirements:* For master's, DVM, B Sc honors degree, or equivalent; for doctorate, M Sc. Additional exam requirements/recommendations for international students: Required—TOEFL (minimum score 550 paper-based; 213 computer-based; 80 iBT). *Expenses:* Contact institution. *Faculty research:* Animal health management, infectious diseases, fin fish and shellfish health, basic biomedical sciences, ecosystem health.

University of Puerto Rico, Medical Sciences Campus, School of Medicine, Division of Graduate Studies, Department of Pharmacology and Toxicology, San Juan, PR 00936-5067. Offers MS, PhD. *Degree requirements:* For master's, one foreign language, thesis; for doctorate, one foreign language, comprehensive exam, thesis/dissertation. *Entrance requirements:* For master's and doctorate, GRE General Test, GRE Subject Test, interview, minimum GPA of 3.0, 3 letters of recommendation. Electronic applications accepted. *Faculty research:* Cardiovascular, central nervous system, and endocrine pharmacology; anti-cancer drugs; sodium pump; mitochondrial DNA repair; Huntington's disease.

University of Rhode Island, Graduate School, College of Pharmacy, Department of Biomedical and Pharmaceutical Sciences, Kingston, RI 02881. Offers medicinal chemistry and pharmacognosy (MS, PhD); pharmaceutics and pharmacokinetics (MS, PhD); pharmacology and toxicology (MS, PhD). Part-time programs available. *Faculty:* 20 full-time (6 women), 4 part-time/adjunct (1 woman). *Students:* 43 full-time (23 women), 15 part-time (4 women); includes 11 minority (2 Black or African American, non-Hispanic/Latino; 8 Asian, non-Hispanic/Latino; 1 Two or more races, non-Hispanic/Latino), 21 international. In 2010, 7 master's, 8 doctorates awarded. *Entrance requirements:* For master's and doctorate, GRE, 2 letters of recommendation. Additional exam requirements/recommendations for international students: Required—TOEFL (minimum score 550 paper-based; 213 computer-based). Application fee: $65. Electronic applications accepted. *Expenses:* Tuition, state resident: full-time $9588; part-time $533 per credit hour. Tuition, nonresident: full-time $22,968; part-time $1276 per credit hour. Required fees: $1282; $68 per semester. Tuition and fees vary according to program. *Financial support:* In 2010–11, 8 research assistantships with partial tuition reimbursements (averaging $8,572 per year), 15 teaching assistantships with full and partial tuition reimbursements (averaging $11,446 per year) were awarded. Financial award applicants required to submit FAFSA. *Faculty research:* Chemical carcinogenesis with a major emphasis on the structural and synthetic aspects of DNA-adduct formation, drug-drug/herb interaction, drug-genetic interaction, signaling of nuclear receptors, transcriptional regulation, oncogenesis. Total annual research expenditures: $6.1 million. *Unit head:* Dr. Clinton O. Chichester, Chair, 401-874-5034, Fax: 401-874-5787, E-mail: chichester@uri.edu. *Application contact:* Dr. David C. Rowley, Graduate Coordinator, 401-874-9228, Fax: 401-874-2516, E-mail: drowley@uri.edu.

University of Rochester, School of Medicine and Dentistry, Graduate Programs in Medicine and Dentistry, Department of Environmental Medicine, Programs in Toxicology, Rochester, NY 14627. Offers MS, PhD. *Degree requirements:* For doctorate, thesis/dissertation, qualifying exam. *Entrance requirements:* For master's and doctorate, GRE General Test.

University of Saskatchewan, College of Graduate Studies and Research, Toxicology Centre, Saskatoon, SK S7N 5A2, Canada. Offers M Sc, PhD, Diploma. *Degree requirements:* For master's, thesis; for doctorate, thesis/dissertation. *Entrance requirements:* Additional exam requirements/recommendations for international students: Required—TOEFL.

University of South Alabama, Graduate School, Program in Environmental Toxicology, Mobile, AL 36688-0002. Offers MS. *Students:* 16 full-time (8 women), 4 international. 11 applicants, 55% accepted, 6 enrolled. In 2010, 1 master's awarded. *Degree requirements:* For master's, thesis. *Entrance requirements:* For master's, GRE. *Application deadline:* For fall admission, 7/15 for domestic students, 6/15 for international students; for spring admission, 12/1 for domestic students, 11/1 for international students. Application fee: $35. *Expenses:* Tuition, state resident: part-time $300 per credit hour. Tuition, nonresident: part-time $600 per credit hour. Required fees: $150 per semester. *Unit head:* Dr. Julio F. Turrens, Director of Graduate Studies, 251-380-2714. *Application contact:* Dr. B. Keith Harrison, Dean of the Graduate School, 251-460-6310, Fax: 251-461-1513, E-mail: kharriso@usouthal.edu.

University of Southern California, Graduate School, School of Pharmacy, Graduate Programs in Molecular Pharmacology and Toxicology, Los Angeles, CA 90033. Offers pharmacology and pharmaceutical sciences (MS, PhD). *Faculty:* 20 full-time (13 women). *Students:* 19 full-time (11 women); includes 5 minority (1 Black or African American, non-Hispanic/Latino; 1 Asian, non-Hispanic/Latino; 1 Hispanic/Latino; 2 Two or more races, non-Hispanic/Latino), 10 international. 60 applicants, 10% accepted, 3 enrolled. In 2010, 1 master's, 3 doctorates awarded. Terminal master's awarded for partial completion of doctoral program. *Degree requirements:* For master's, comprehensive exam, thesis, 24 units of formal course work, excluding research and seminar courses; for doctorate, comprehensive exam, thesis/dissertation, 24 units of formal course work, excluding research and seminar courses. *Entrance requirements:* For master's and doctorate, GRE. Additional exam requirements/recommendations for international students: Required—TOEFL (minimum score 603 paper-based; 250 computer-based; 100 iBT). *Application deadline:* For fall admission, 1/15 for domestic and international students; for spring admission, 10/15 for domestic and international students. Application fee: $75. Electronic applications accepted. *Expenses:* Contact institution. *Financial support:* In 2010–11, 15 students received support, including 4 fellowships with full tuition reimbursements available (averaging $23,395 per year), 4 research assistantships with full tuition reimbursements available (averaging $23,395 per year), 7 teaching assistantships with full tuition reimbursements available (averaging $23,395 per year); health care benefits and tuition waivers also available. *Faculty research:* Degenerative diseases, toxicology of drugs. *Unit head:* Dr. Roger Duncan, Director of Graduate Affairs Committee, 323-442-1449, Fax: 323-442-2258, E-mail: rduncan@usc.edu. *Application contact:* Linda Jankins, Student Affairs Assistant, 323-442-1474, Fax: 323-442-2258, E-mail: pharmgrd@usc.edu.

The University of Texas Medical Branch, Graduate School of Biomedical Sciences, Program in Pharmacology and Toxicology, Galveston, TX 77555. Offers pharmacology (MS); pharmacology and toxicology (PhD). *Degree requirements:* For master's, thesis or alternative; for doctorate, thesis/dissertation. *Entrance requirements:* For master's and doctorate, GRE General Test. Additional exam requirements/recommendations for international students: Required—TOEFL (minimum score 550 paper-based; 213 computer-based).

University of the Sciences in Philadelphia, College of Graduate Studies, Program in Pharmacology and Toxicology, Philadelphia, PA 19104-4495. Offers pharmacology (MS, PhD); toxicology (MS, PhD). Terminal master's awarded for partial completion of doctoral program. *Degree requirements:* For master's, thesis; for doctorate, comprehensive exam, thesis/dissertation. *Entrance requirements:* For master's and doctorate, GRE General Test. Additional exam requirements/recommendations for international students: Required—TOEFL, TWE. *Expenses:* Contact institution. *Faculty research:* Autonomic, cardiovascular, cellular, and molecular pharmacology; mechanisms of carcinogenesis; drug metabolism.

University of Toronto, School of Graduate Studies, Life Sciences Division, Department of Pharmacology and Toxicology, Toronto, ON M5S 1A1, Canada. Offers M Sc, PhD. Part-time programs available. *Degree requirements:* For master's, thesis; for doctorate, thesis/dissertation. *Entrance requirements:* For master's, B Sc or equivalent; background in pharmacology, biochemistry, and physiology; minimum B+ earned in at least 4 senior level classes; for doctorate, minimum B+ average.

University of Utah, Graduate School, College of Pharmacy, Department of Pharmacology and Toxicology, Salt Lake City, UT 84112. Offers PhD. *Faculty:* 19 full-time (5 women), 1 part-time/adjunct (0 women). *Students:* 16 full-time (9 women), 3 part-time (1 woman); includes 2 minority (both Hispanic/Latino), 1 international. Average age 28. 64 applicants, 9% accepted, 3 enrolled. In 2010, 5 doctorates awarded. Terminal master's awarded for partial completion of doctoral program. *Degree requirements:* For doctorate, comprehensive exam, thesis/dissertation, final exam. *Entrance requirements:* For doctorate, GRE Subject Test, BS in biology, chemistry, neuroscience. Additional exam requirements/recommendations for international students: Required—TOEFL (minimum score 600 paper-based; 250 computer-based; 100 iBT). *Application deadline:* For fall admission, 1/15 for domestic and international students. Application fee: $55 ($65 for international students). *Expenses:* Tuition, area resident: Part-time $179.19 per credit hour. Tuition, state resident: full-time $4384. Tuition, nonresident: full-time $16,684; part-time $630.67 per credit hour. Required fees: $350 per semester. Tuition and fees vary according to course load, degree level and program. *Financial support:* In 2010–11, 14 students received support, including 5 fellowships with partial tuition reimbursements available (averaging $11,000 per year), 17 research assistantships with full tuition reimbursements available (averaging $25,000 per year). Financial award application deadline: 1/15. *Faculty research:* Neuropharmacology, neurochemistry, biochemistry, molecular pharmacology, analytical chemistry. Total annual research expenditures: $4.8 million. *Unit head:* Dr. William R. Crowley, Chairman, 801-581-6287, Fax: 801-585-5111, E-mail: william.crowley@deans.pharm.utah.edu. *Application contact:* Sheila H. Merrill, Executive Secretary, 801-581-6287, Fax: 801-585-5111, E-mail: sheila.merrill@pharm.utah.edu.

University of Washington, Graduate School, School of Public Health, Department of Environmental and Occupational Health Sciences, Seattle, WA 98195. Offers environmental and occupational health (MPH); environmental and occupational hygiene (PhD); environmental health (MS); occupational and environmental exposure sciences (MS); occupational and environmental medicine (MPH); toxicology (MS, PhD). Part-time programs available. *Faculty:* 29 full-time (4 women), 9 part-time/adjunct (3 women). *Students:* 65 full-time (37 women), 5 part-time (2 women); includes 1 Black or African American, non-Hispanic/Latino; 2 American Indian or Alaska Native, non-Hispanic/Latino; 8 Asian, non-Hispanic/Latino; 3 Hispanic/Latino, 2 international. Average age 29. 129 applicants, 33% accepted, 23 enrolled. In 2010, 24 master's, 6 doctorates awarded. Terminal master's awarded for partial completion of doctoral program. *Degree requirements:* For master's, thesis (for some programs), project or portfolio (for some tracks); for doctorate, comprehensive exam, thesis/dissertation. *Entrance requirements:* For master's and doctorate, GRE General Test, minimum GPA of 3.0, prerequisite course work in biology, chemistry, physics, calculus. Additional exam requirements/recommendations for international students: Required—TOEFL (minimum score 580 paper-based; 237 computer-based; 92 iBT). *Application deadline:* For fall admission, 1/1 for domestic students, 11/1 for international students. Application fee: $75. Electronic applications accepted. *Financial support:* In 2010–11, 19 fellowships with full tuition reimbursements (averaging $21,180 per year), 30 research assistantships with full tuition reimbursements (averaging $21,324 per year), 7 teaching assistantships with full tuition reimbursements (averaging $21,324 per year) were awarded; career-related internships or fieldwork, institutionally sponsored loans, traineeships, health care benefits, and unspecified assistantships also available. Financial award application deadline: 1/1. *Faculty research:* Developmental and behavioral toxicology, biochemical toxicology, exposure assessment, hazardous waste, industrial chemistry. *Unit head:* Dr. David Kalman, Chair, 206-543-6991, Fax: 206-543-0477. *Application contact:* Rory A. Murphy, Manager, Student Services, 206-543-6991, Fax: 206-543-0477, E-mail: ehgrad@u.washington.edu.

University of Wisconsin–Madison, School of Medicine and Public Health, Molecular and Environmental Toxicology Center, Madison, WI 53706. Offers MS, PhD. *Faculty:* 77 full-time (25 women), 1 part-time/adjunct (0 women). *Students:* 34 full-time (20 women); includes 1 American Indian or Alaska Native, non-Hispanic/Latino; 1 Asian, non-Hispanic/Latino; 3 Hispanic/Latino; 2 Native Hawaiian or other Pacific Islander, non-Hispanic/Latino, 8 international. Average age 28. 51 applicants, 31% accepted, 5 enrolled. In 2010, 1 master's, 10 doctorates awarded. Terminal master's awarded for partial completion of doctoral program. *Degree requirements:* For master's, thesis; for doctorate, thesis/dissertation. *Entrance requirements:* For master's and doctorate, bachelor's degree in science-related field. Additional exam requirements/recommendations for international students: Required—TOEFL. *Application deadline:* For fall admission, 12/15 priority date for domestic and international students. Application fee: $56. Electronic applications accepted. *Expenses:* Tuition, state resident: full-time $9887; part-time $617.96 per credit. Tuition, nonresident: full-time $24,054; part-time $1503.40 per credit. Required fees: $67.63 per credit. Tuition and fees vary according to reciprocity agreements. *Financial support:* In 2010–11, 5 research assistantships with tuition reimbursements (averaging $23,500 per year) were awarded; fellowships with tuition reimbursements, traineeships, health care benefits, and unspecified assistantships also available. *Faculty research:* Toxicology cancer, genetics, cell cycle, xenobotic metabolism. *Unit head:* Dr. Christopher Bradfield, Director, 608-262-2024, E-mail: bradfield@oncology.wisc.edu. *Application contact:* Eileen M. Stevens, Program Administrator, 608-263-4580, Fax: 608-262-5245, E-mail: emstevens@wisc.edu.

Utah State University, School of Graduate Studies, College of Agriculture, Program in Toxicology, Logan, UT 84322. Offers MS, PhD. Terminal master's awarded for partial completion of doctoral program. *Degree requirements:* For master's, thesis; for doctorate, thesis/dissertation. *Entrance requirements:* For master's and doctorate, GRE General Test, minimum GPA of 3.0. Additional exam requirements/recommendations for international students: Required—TOEFL. *Faculty research:* Free-radical mechanisms, toxicity of iron, carcinogenesis of natural compounds, molecular mechanisms of retinoid toxicity, aflatoxins.

Virginia Commonwealth University, Graduate School, College of Humanities and Sciences, Department of Forensic Science, Richmond, VA 23284-9005. Offers forensic biology (MS); forensic chemistry/drugs and toxicology (MS); forensic chemistry/trace (MS); forensic physical evidence (MS). Part-time programs available. *Students:* 42 full-time (32 women), 3 part-time (all women); includes 8 minority (3 Black or African American, non-Hispanic/Latino; 1 American Indian or Alaska Native, non-Hispanic/Latino; 3 Asian, non-Hispanic/Latino; 1 Hispanic/Latino), 1 international. 95 applicants, 39% accepted, 23 enrolled. In 2010, 21 master's awarded. *Entrance requirements:* For master's, GRE General Test, bachelor's degree in a natural science discipline, including forensic science, or a degree with equivalent work. Additional exam requirements/recommendations for international students: Required—Either TOEFL (minimum score: paper-based 600, computer-based 250) or IELTS (6.5). *Application deadline:* For fall admission, 3/1 for domestic students. Application fee: $50. Electronic applications accepted. *Expenses:* Tuition, state resident: full-time $4308; part-time $479 per credit hour. Tuition, nonresident: full-time $8942; part-time $994 per credit hour. Required fees: $2000; $85 per credit hour. Tuition and fees vary according to course level, course load, degree level, campus/location and program. *Financial support:* Federal Work-Study, institutionally sponsored loans, and tuition waivers (full and partial) available. Support available to part-time students. Financial award applicants required to submit FAFSA. *Unit head:* Dr. Michelle R. Peace, Interim Chair, 804-828-8420, E-mail: mrpeace@vcu.edu. *Application contact:* Dr. Tracey Dawson Cruz, Graduate Director, 804-828-0642, E-mail: tcdawson@vcu.edu.

Virginia Commonwealth University, Medical College of Virginia-Professional Programs, School of Medicine, School of Medicine Graduate Programs, Department of Pharmacology and Toxicology, Richmond, VA 23284-9005. Offers neuroscience (PhD); pharmacology (Certificate); pharmacology and toxicology (MS, PhD); MD/PhD. *Faculty:* 35 full-time (9 women). *Students:* 47 full-time (27 women), 4 part-time (2 women); includes 13 minority (5 Black or African American, non-Hispanic/Latino; 6 Asian, non-Hispanic/Latino; 1 Hispanic/Latino; 1 Two or more races, non-Hispanic/Latino), 13 international. 66 applicants, 27% accepted, 10 enrolled. In 2010, 2 master's, 4 doctorates awarded. Terminal master's awarded for partial completion of

doctoral program. *Degree requirements:* For master's, thesis; for doctorate, thesis/dissertation, comprehensive oral and written exams. *Entrance requirements:* For master's and doctorate, GRE or MCAT. Additional exam requirements/recommendations for international students: Required—TOEFL (minimum score 600 paper-based; 250 computer-based; 100 iBT). *Application deadline:* For fall admission, 4/15 for domestic students. Application fee: $50. Electronic applications accepted. *Expenses:* Tuition, state resident: full-time $4308; part-time $479 per credit hour. Tuition, nonresident: full-time $8942; part-time $994 per credit hour. Required fees: $2000; $85 per credit hour. Tuition and fees vary according to course level, course load, degree level, campus/location and program. *Financial support:* Fellowships, teaching assistantships available. *Faculty research:* Drug abuse, drug metabolism, pharmacodynamics, peptide synthesis, receptor mechanisms. *Unit head:* Dr. William L. Dewey, Chair, 804-827-0375, Fax: 804-827-1548, E-mail: wdewey@vcu.edu. *Application contact:* Dr. Stephen T. Sawyer, Graduate Program Coordinator, 804-828-7918, Fax: 804-827-1548, E-mail: ssawyer@vcu.edu.

Wayne State University, Graduate School, Interdisciplinary Program in Molecular and Cellular Toxicology, Detroit, MI 48201-2427. Offers MS, PhD. *Faculty:* 2 full-time (0 women). *Students:* 5 full-time (3 women), 4 international. Average age 28. 7 applicants, 29% accepted, 1 enrolled. In 2010, 1 doctorate awarded. *Degree requirements:* For master's, thesis or alternative; for doctorate, thesis/dissertation. *Entrance requirements:* For master's, GRE General Test, GRE Subject Test, personal statement; for doctorate, GRE General Test, GRE Subject Test, minimum GPA of 3.0. Additional exam requirements/recommendations for international students: Required—TOEFL (minimum score 550 paper-based); 213 computer-based); Recommended—TWE (minimum score 6). *Application deadline:* For fall admission, 4/15 priority date for domestic students, 6/1 for international students; for winter admission, 10/1 for international students; for spring admission, 2/1 for international students. Applications are processed on a rolling basis. Application fee: $30 ($50 for international students). Electronic applications accepted. *Expenses:* Tuition, state resident: full-time $7662; part-time $478.85 per credit hour. Tuition, nonresident: full-time $16,920; part-time $1057.55 per credit hour. Required fees: $571; $35.70 per credit hour. $188.05 per semester. Tuition and fees vary according to course load and program. *Financial support:* In 2010–11, 1 fellowship (averaging $29,446 per year), 4 research assistantships (averaging $21,685 per year) were awarded; teaching assistantships, institutionally sponsored loans also available. Financial award application deadline: 4/15. *Faculty research:* Molecular and cellular mechanisms of chemically-induced cell injury and death; effect of xenobiotics on cell growth, proliferation, transformation and differentiation; regulation of gene expression; cell signaling; global gene expression profiling. *Unit head:* Dr. Paul M. Stemmer, Director, Admissions Committee, 313-577-0100, Fax: 313-577-0082, E-mail: ak5245@wayne.edu. *Application contact:* Dr. Dharam P. Chopra, Program Director, 313-577-5585, Fax: 313-577-0082, E-mail: d.chopra@wayne.edu.

West Virginia University, Davis College of Agriculture, Forestry and Consumer Sciences, Interdisciplinary Program in Genetics and Developmental Biology, Morgantown, WV 26506. Offers animal breeding (MS, PhD); biochemical and molecular genetics (MS, PhD); cytogenetics (MS, PhD); descriptive embryology (MS, PhD); developmental genetics (MS); experimental morphogenesis/teratology (MS); human genetics (MS, PhD); immunogenetics (MS, PhD); life cycles of animals and plants (MS, PhD); molecular aspects of development (MS, PhD); mutagenesis (MS, PhD); oncology (MS, PhD); plant genetics (MS, PhD); population and quantitative genetics (MS, PhD); regeneration (MS, PhD); teratology (PhD); toxicology (MS, PhD). *Degree requirements:* For master's, thesis; for doctorate, comprehensive exam, thesis/dissertation. *Entrance requirements:* For master's, GRE or MCAT, minimum GPA of 2.75. Additional exam requirements/recommendations for international students: Required—TOEFL.

West Virginia University, School of Pharmacy, Program in Pharmaceutical and Pharmacological Sciences, Morgantown, WV 26506. Offers administrative pharmacy (PhD); behavioral pharmacy (MS, PhD); biopharmaceutics/pharmacokinetics (MS, PhD); industrial pharmacy (MS); medicinal chemistry (MS, PhD); pharmaceutical chemistry (MS, PhD); pharmaceutics (MS, PhD); pharmacology and toxicology (MS); pharmacy (MS); pharmacy administration (MS). Part-time programs available. Terminal master's awarded for partial completion of doctoral program. *Degree requirements:* For master's, thesis; for doctorate, one foreign language, comprehensive exam, thesis/dissertation. *Entrance requirements:* For master's and doctorate, GRE General Test, minimum GPA of 2.75. Additional exam requirements/recommendations for international students: Required—TOEFL; Recommended—TWE. Electronic applications accepted. *Expenses:* Contact institution. *Faculty research:* Pharmaceutics, medicinal chemistry, biopharmaceutics/pharmacokinetics, health outcomes research.

Wright State University, School of Medicine, Program in Pharmacology and Toxicology, Dayton, OH 45435. Offers MS. *Degree requirements:* For master's, thesis optional.

UNIVERSITY OF CALIFORNIA, IRVINE

School of Medicine
Department of Pharmacology

Program of Study	The Ph.D. program prepares students for careers in academia, research institutions, biotechnology, and the pharmaceutical industry by providing a foundation in all aspects of pharmacology, from molecular mechanisms through behavior. Specific areas of study include molecular and cellular pharmacology, neurosciences, gene regulation, circadian rhythms, epigenetic modifications, neuropharmacology, psychopharmacology, and cardiovascular pharmacology. Emphasis is placed on providing an integrated understanding of drug receptors: their structure, location, and function; molecular aspects of drug action; receptor signaling mechanisms; structure–activity relationships and drug design; and the role of receptors and drugs in development and aging, plasticity, reinforcement and drug abuse, neural disorders, and cardiovascular physiology and disease. Students take three laboratory rotations in the first year, complete the required course work, and then take a comprehensive written exam. Students advance to candidacy in their third year by orally defending their research proposal; they generally complete the Ph.D. degree in their fifth year.
Research Facilities	The well-equipped laboratories of the Department of Pharmacology are housed in the Med Surge II Building and the Gillespie Neurosciences Research Facility, located in the School of Medicine adjacent to the main campus. The Science Library and animal-care facility are conveniently located nearby, and a large computing facility is available on the main campus.
Financial Aid	Students who maintain satisfactory academic progress receive full financial support, i.e., tuition, fees, health insurance, and a living stipend ($27,000 for 2011–12). Sources of support include University fellowships and NIH training and research grants.
Cost of Study	The cost of tuition for 2011–12 is $13,875.50 for state residents and $28,977.50 for nonresidents.
Living and Housing Costs	University housing is available, as is off-campus housing in nearby communities. For rates and more information, students should visit the University housing Web site at http://www.housing.uci.edu.
Student Group	The University's total enrollment in fall 2010 was 27,676 students, of whom 4,407 were graduate students. Pharmacology maintains approximately 20 graduate students in its program.
Student Outcomes	Recent graduates of the program are doing postdoctoral research at the University of California, Irvine (UCI); UC Los Angeles (UCLA); UC San Diego (UCSD); UC San Francisco (UCSF); Stanford; Scripps Research Institute; and the National Institute of Mental Health. Other graduates hold faculty positions (tenured or tenure track) at UCI, UCLA, UCSD, Yale, and the Universities of Colorado, Michigan, and Minnesota.
Location	UCI is located 5 miles from the Pacific Ocean and 40 miles south of Los Angeles. The surrounding hills and grazing lands give the campus an open feeling, though an estimated 2 million people live within a 20-mile radius. Concerts, repertory theater, and art galleries are available both on and off campus. Beaches, marinas, ski resorts, and mountain trails are within easy driving distance, and the mild climate permits a wide variety of year-round recreation.
The University	UCI is a young, dynamic campus that has rapidly become a full partner in the region's growing culture and economy. As a major research university, UCI offers excellent opportunities for graduate students in most traditional academic disciplines and in several interdisciplinary programs unique to the campus. Collaborations between departments in the School of Medicine and the School of Biological Sciences enhance the graduate program, providing students with access to all courses and the research expertise of all faculty members. Graduate students have access to the facilities of the entire nine-campus University of California system.
Applying	To be considered for entrance to the program in the fall quarter, students must submit applications no later than December 15 of the preceding calendar year. Applicants are required to submit an official online application, two sets of official transcripts, three letters of recommendation, GRE General and Subject test scores in biology or chemistry (highly recommended but not required), and pay the application fee. International students are required to submit TOEFL scores.
Correspondence and Information	Student Affairs Coordinator Department of Pharmacology 360 Med Surge II University of California, Irvine Irvine, California 92697-4625 Phone: 949-824-7651 Fax: 949-824-4855 E-mail: pharm@uci.edu Web site: http://www.pharmacology.uci.edu/

University of California, Irvine

THE FACULTY AND THEIR RESEARCH

Although diverse in their research specialties, the faculty members share a common interest in the molecular basis of drug-receptor interactions. They enjoy international recognition for their contributions to research and service on grant review committees and editorial boards. Graduate students are expected to be active researchers and to publish in major medical and biological journals.

The faculty research programs attract postdoctoral fellows and visiting scientists who provide additional resources for research and training. Strong programs in neuroscience, cell biology, physiology, and molecular biology in other departments of the School of Medicine and the School of Biological Sciences provide students with additional opportunities for interaction. The Department also has affiliations with scientists from other academic institutions and from the growing biopharmaceutical industry in Irvine. The latter especially provides the opportunity to experience pharmacology from a drug discovery standpoint.

Core Faculty

James D. Belluzzi, Adjunct Professor; Ph.D., Chicago, 1970. Brain substrates and pharmacology of reward; characterization of nicotine reinforcement; drug therapies for Parkinson's disease, anxiety, and drug abuse.

Olivier Civelli, Eric and Lila Nelson Professor of Neuropharmacology; Ph.D., Zurich (Switzerland), 1979. Molecular biology of G-protein–coupled receptors; diversity of the dopamine receptors; cloning and analyses of new receptors, in particular orphan receptors (receptors with unknown natural ligand); discovery and characterization of novel neurotransmitters and neuropeptides; determination of the pharmacological, biological, and behavioral activities of the novel neurotransmitters and neuropeptides.

Frederick J. Ehlert, Professor; Ph.D., California, Irvine, 1978. Subtypes of muscarinic receptors and their signaling mechanisms in brain, heart, smooth muscle, ocular tissue, and exocine glands; receptor G-protein interactions; interactions between the signaling pathways of specific neurotransmitter receptors; molecular basis of drug selectivity.

Kelvin W. Gee, Professor; Ph.D., California, Davis, 1981. Molecular characterization of a novel receptor site coupled to the GABAA receptor-ion channel complex; discovery of novel ligands that interact with these sites and their potential therapeutic application.

Naoto Hoshi, Assistant Professor; Ph.D., Kanazawa (Japan) 1999. Physiological role and regulation of the M-channel, molecular biology, electrophysiology, live cell FRET imaging.

Diana N. Krause, Adjunct Professor; Ph.D., UCLA, 1977. Characterization of the receptors for the circadian hormone melatonin; pharmacology, localization, and function in the brain and vascular system; vascular effects of estrogen.

Frances M. Leslie, Professor and Dean, Graduate Division; Ph.D., Aberdeen (Scotland), 1977. Cellular and molecular characterization of action of drugs of abuse, with particular reference to morphine and nicotine; analysis of the effects of drug abuse and stress on neural plasticity, particularly during brain development.

Daniele Piomelli, Professor and Louise Turner Arnold Chair in Neurosciences; Ph.D., Columbia, 1987. Various signaling pathways that involve lipids with particular interest in the endogenous cannabinoids; arachidonic acid derivatives that activate cannabinoid (marijuana) receptors in brain and other tissues; biochemical mechanisms involved in the formation and inactivation of these molecules; developing pharmacological tools to interfere with these pathways; wide range of molecular biological, pharmacological, and analytical techniques.

Paolo Sassone-Corsi, Donald Bren Professor and Chair; Ph.D., Naples (Italy), 1979. Cellular and molecular pathways regulating gene expression, epigenetic mechanisms, physiological functions, circadian clock, light signaling, metabolism, cancer, and male germ cells.

Qun-Yong Zhou, Professor; Ph.D., Oregon Health and Science, 1992. Physiology and neuropharmacology of prokineticins and prokineticin receptors, circadian rhythms and neurogenesis.

Joint Faculty

Emiliana Borrelli, Professor, Microbiology and Molecular Genetics; Ph.D., Naples (Italy), 1979. Mouse models for the study of brain disorders; dopamine system; molecular basis of addiction and neurodegeneration.

William E. Bunney Jr., Professor, Psychiatry and Human Behavior; M.D., Pennsylvania, 1956. Clinical psychobiological and neuropsychopharmacological studies of manic-depressive illness; schizophrenia and childhood mental illness.

Pietro R. Galassetti, Associate Professor in Residence, Pediatrics; M.D., Rome (Italy), 1986; Ph.D., Vanderbilt, 1998. Physiological and altered adaptive responses to stress in healthy and dysmetabolic children and adults; noninvasive monitoring of metabolic variables through analysis of exhaled gases.

Mahtab Jafari, Associate Professor and Director of Pharmaceutical Sciences undergraduate program; Pharm.D., California, San Francisco, 1994. Anti-aging effects of botanicals and pharmaceutical compounds; the impact of botanical extracts on mitochondrial bioenergetics, oxidative stress, and other pathways of aging using cell culture and *Drosophila*.

Arthur D. Lander, Professor, Developmental and Cell Biology; M.D., Ph.D., California, San Francisco, 1985. Molecular neurobiology; intracellular and extracellular signaling in the control of axon guidance and cell motility; functions of the extracellular matrix; transgenic animal approaches to neural development and function.

Wen-Hwa Lee, Donald Bren Professor of Biomedicine, Biological Chemistry; Ph.D., Berkeley, 1981. Tumor-suppressor genes and why repair mechanisms for DNA can fail and cause subsequent accumulations of cancer-promoting mutations.

Ellis R. Levin, Professor in Residence, Department of Medicine; M.D., Thomas Jefferson, 1975. Molecular and cellular biology of natriuretic peptides and endothelin and their receptors in the brain and the vasculature; regulation of astrocyte growth by these peptides.

John C. Longhurst, Professor, Department of Medicine; M.D., 1973, Ph.D., 1974, California, Davis. Regulation of the cardiovascular system and the nervous system's role in this regulation.

Z. David Luo, Associate Professor, Anesthesiology and Preoperative Care; M.D., Guangzhou Medical (China), 1984; Ph.D., SUNY at Buffalo, 1993. Study of gene regulation and signaling pathways in chronic pain processing using animal models and molecular biology techniques.

Rainer Reinscheid, Associate Professor, Pharmaceutical Sciences; Ph.D., Center for Molecular Neurobiology (Germany), 1993. Isolation of natural ligands for orphan G-protein-coupled receptors (GPCRs) and their physiological functions; the neurobiology of anxiety and stress behavior; neuropeptides involved in sleep and arousal.

Sandor Szabo, Professor in Residence, Pathology; M.D., Belgrade (Ireland), 1968; Ph.D., Montreal, 1973; Effects of growth factors (e.g., FGF, PDGF) on ulcer healing and prevention.

Section 18
Physiology

This section contains a directory of institutions offering graduate work in physiology, followed by in-depth entries submitted by institutions that chose to prepare detailed program descriptions. Additional information about programs listed in the directory but not augmented by an in-depth entry may be obtained by writing directly to the dean of a graduate school or chair of a department at the address given in the directory.

For programs offering related work, see also all other sections in this book. In the other guides in this series:

Graduate Programs in the Physical Sciences, Mathematics, Agricultural Sciences, the Environment & Natural Resources

See *Agricultural and Food Sciences, Chemistry,* and *Marine Sciences and Oceanography*

Graduate Programs in Engineering & Applied Sciences

See *Agricultural Engineering and Bioengineering, Biomedical Engineering and Biotechnology, Electrical and Computer Engineering,* and *Mechanical Engineering and Mechanics*

Graduate Programs in Business, Education, Health, Information Studies, Law & Social Work

See *Optometry and Vision Sciences, Physical Education and Kinesiology,* and *Veterinary Medicine and Sciences*

CONTENTS

Cardiovascular Sciences

Albany Medical College, Center for Cardiovascular Sciences, Albany, NY 12208-3479. Offers MS, PhD. Part-time programs available. *Faculty:* 18 full-time (3 women). *Students:* 18 full-time (10 women); includes 1 Black or African American, non-Hispanic/Latino; 7 Asian, non-Hispanic/Latino; 1 Hispanic/Latino. Average age 25. 8 applicants, 75% accepted, 4 enrolled. In 2010, 1 doctorate awarded. Terminal master's awarded for partial completion of doctoral program. *Degree requirements:* For master's, thesis; for doctorate, comprehensive exam, thesis/dissertation, candidacy exam, written preliminary exam, 1 published paper-peer review. *Entrance requirements:* For master's, GRE General Test, letters of recommendation; for doctorate, GRE General Test, all transcripts, letters of recommendation. Additional exam requirements/recommendations for international students: Required—TOEFL. *Application deadline:* For fall admission, 3/15 priority date for domestic and international students. Applications are processed on a rolling basis. Application fee: $60. *Financial support:* In 2010–11, 9 students received support, including 9 research assistantships (averaging $24,000 per year); Federal Work-Study, scholarships/grants, and tuition waivers (full) also available. Financial award applicants required to submit FAFSA. *Faculty research:* Vascular smooth muscle, endothelial cell biology, molecular and genetic bases underlying cardiac disease, reactive oxygen and nitrogen species biology, fatty acid trafficking and fatty acid mediated transcription control. *Unit head:* Dr. Peter A. Vincent, Graduate Director, 518-262-6296, Fax: 518-262-8101, E-mail: vincenp@mail.amc.edu. *Application contact:* Wendy M. Vienneau, Administrative Coordinator, 518-262-8102, Fax: 518-262-8101, E-mail: hobbw@mail.amc.edu.

Baylor College of Medicine, Graduate School of Biomedical Sciences, Program in Cardiovascular Sciences, Houston, TX 77030-3498. Offers PhD, MD/PhD. *Faculty:* 42 full-time (7 women). *Students:* 10 full-time (4 women); includes 2 Black or African American, non-Hispanic/Latino, 5 international. Average age 27. 18 applicants, 33% accepted, 3 enrolled. In 2010, 5 doctorates awarded. *Degree requirements:* For doctorate, thesis/dissertation, public defense. *Entrance requirements:* For doctorate, GRE General Test, GRE Subject Test (strongly recommended), minimum GPA of 3.0, strong background in biology and biochemistry. Additional exam requirements/recommendations for international students: Required—TOEFL. *Application deadline:* For fall admission, 1/1 priority date for domestic students. Applications are processed on a rolling basis. Application fee: $0. Electronic applications accepted. *Expenses:* Tuition: Full-time $11,000. Required fees: $4900. *Financial support:* In 2010–11, 10 students received support, including 2 fellowships with full tuition reimbursements available (averaging $26,000 per year), 8 research assistantships with full tuition reimbursements available (averaging $26,000 per year); career-related internships or fieldwork, Federal Work-Study, institutionally sponsored loans, health care benefits, and students receive a scholarship unless there are grant funds available to pay tuition also available. Financial award applicants required to submit FAFSA. *Faculty research:* Biophysics, cardiovascular biology, imaging, muscle physiology, ion channels. *Unit head:* Dr. Lloyd Michael, Head, 713-798-6825, Fax: 713-796-0015, E-mail: lmichael@bcm.edu. *Application contact:* Cherrie McGlory, Graduate Program Administrator, 713-798-5190, Fax: 713-798-3475, E-mail: cmcglory@bcm.edu.

Dartmouth College, Program in Experimental and Molecular Medicine, Cardiovascular Diseases Track, Hanover, NH 03755. Offers PhD.

Geneva College, Program in Cardiovascular Science, Beaver Falls, PA 15010-3599. Offers MS. *Degree requirements:* For master's, RCIS and RCES registry exams. *Entrance requirements:* Additional exam requirements/recommendations for international students: Required—TOEFL. Electronic applications accepted.

Georgia Health Sciences University, College of Graduate Studies, Program in Vascular Biology, Augusta, GA 30912. Offers MS, PhD. *Faculty:* 21 full-time (7 women), 2 part-time/adjunct (1 woman). *Students:* 16 full-time (11 women); includes 2 Black or African American, non-Hispanic/Latino; 1 American Indian or Alaska Native, non-Hispanic/Latino, 10 international. Average age 28. In 2010, 3 doctorates awarded. *Degree requirements:* For doctorate, comprehensive exam, thesis/dissertation. *Entrance requirements:* For doctorate, GRE General Test. Additional exam requirements/recommendations for international students: Required—TOEFL (minimum score 550 paper-based; 213 computer-based; 79 iBT). *Application deadline:* For fall admission, 1/15 for domestic and international students. Application fee: $30. Electronic applications accepted. *Expenses:* Tuition, state resident: full-time $7500; part-time $313 per semester hour. Tuition, nonresident: full-time $24,772; part-time $1033 per semester hour. Required fees: $1112. *Financial support:* In 2010–11, 5 fellowships with partial tuition reimbursements (averaging $26,000 per year), 19 research assistantships with partial tuition reimbursements (averaging $23,000 per year) were awarded; Federal Work-Study, institutionally sponsored loans, scholarships/grants, and traineeships also available. Support available to part-time students. Financial award application deadline: 5/31. *Faculty research:* Hypertension and renal disease, diabetes and obesity, peripheral vascular disease, acute lung injury, signal transduction. Total annual research expenditures: $7 million. *Unit head:* Dr. John D. Catravas, Professor/Director of Vascular Biology Center, 706-721-6338, Fax: 706-721-8545, E-mail: jcatrava@mail.mcg.edu. *Application contact:* Dr. Patricia L. Cameron, Acting Vice Dean, 706-721-3279, E-mail: pcameron@georgiahealth.edu.

Long Island University, C.W. Post Campus, School of Health Professions and Nursing, Department of Biomedical Sciences, Brookville, NY 11548-1300. Offers cardiovascular perfusion (MS); clinical laboratory management (MS); medical biology (MS), including hematology, immunology, medical biology, medical chemistry, medical microbiology. Part-time and evening/weekend programs available. Postbaccalaureate distance learning degree programs offered. *Degree requirements:* For master's, thesis. *Entrance requirements:* For master's, minimum GPA of 2.75 in major. Electronic applications accepted.

Loyola University Chicago, Graduate School, Marcella Niehoff School of Nursing, Adult Clinical Nurse Specialist Program, Chicago, IL 60660. Offers adult clinical nurse specialist (MSN, Certificate); cardiovascular health (Certificate); oncology nursing (Certificate). Part-time and evening/weekend programs available. Postbaccalaureate distance learning degree programs offered (minimal on-campus study). In 2010, 1 master's awarded. *Entrance requirements:* For master's, Illinois nursing license, BSN, minimum nursing GPA of 3.0, 3 letters of recommendation, 1,000 hours experience in area of specialty. *Expenses:* Tuition: Full-time $14,940; part-time $830 per credit hour. Required fees: $87 per semester. Part-time tuition and fees vary according to course load and program. *Unit head:* Dr. Meg Gulanick, Professor, 708-216-9687, Fax: 708-216-9555, E-mail: mgulani@luc.edu. *Application contact:* Amy Weatherford, Enrollment Advisor, School of Nursing, 773-508-3249, Fax: 773-508-3241, E-mail: aweatherford@luc.edu.

Loyola University Chicago, Graduate School, Marcella Niehoff School of Nursing, Adult Nurse Practitioner Program, Chicago, IL 60660. Offers cardiovascular health and disease management (Certificate). *Accreditation:* AACN. Part-time and evening/weekend programs available. *Students:* 4 full-time (all women), 72 part-time (71 women); includes 13 minority (2 Black or African American, non-Hispanic/Latino; 5 Asian, non-Hispanic/Latino; 4 Hispanic/Latino; 2 Two or more races, non-Hispanic/Latino). Average age 34. 18 applicants, 67% accepted, 12 enrolled. *Application deadline:* Applications are processed on a rolling basis. Application fee: $50. Electronic applications accepted. *Expenses:* Tuition: Full-time $14,940; part-time $830 per credit hour. Required fees: $87 per semester. Part-time tuition and fees vary according to course load and program. *Financial support:* Traineeships available. *Faculty research:* Menopause. *Unit head:* Dr. Marijo Letizia, Associate Professor, 708-216-9325, Fax: 708-216-9555, E-mail: mletizi@luc.edu. *Application contact:* Amy Weatherford, Enrollment Advisor, School of Nursing, 773-508-3249, Fax: 773-508-3241, E-mail: aweatherford@luc.edu.

McMaster University, Faculty of Health Sciences and School of Graduate Studies, Program in Medical Sciences, Blood and Vascular Area, Hamilton, ON L8S 4M2, Canada. Offers M Sc, PhD, MD/PhD. *Degree requirements:* For master's, thesis; for doctorate, comprehensive exam, thesis/dissertation. *Entrance requirements:* For master's, honors B Sc, B+ average in related field; for doctorate, M Sc, minimum B+ average, students with proven research experience and an A average may be admitted with a B Sc degree. Additional exam requirements/recommendations for international students: Required—TOEFL (minimum score 580 paper-based; 237 computer-based; 92 iBT).

Medical University of South Carolina, College of Graduate Studies, Program in Molecular and Cellular Biology and Pathobiology, Charleston, SC 29425. Offers cancer biology (PhD); cardiovascular biology (PhD); cardiovascular imaging (PhD); cell regulation (PhD); craniofacial biology (PhD); genetics and development (PhD); marine biomedicine (PhD); DMD/PhD; MD/PhD. *Faculty:* 137 full-time (33 women). *Students:* 27 full-time (20 women); includes 3 Black or African American, non-Hispanic/Latino; 1 Hispanic/Latino, 6 international. Average age 30. In 2010, 16 doctorates awarded. *Degree requirements:* For doctorate, thesis/dissertation, oral and written exams. *Entrance requirements:* For doctorate, GRE General Test, interview, minimum GPA of 3.0. Additional exam requirements/recommendations for international students: Required—TOEFL (minimum score 600 paper-based; 250 computer-based; 100 iBT). *Application deadline:* For fall admission, 1/15 priority date for domestic and international students. Applications are processed on a rolling basis. Application fee: $0 ($85 for international students). Electronic applications accepted. *Financial support:* In 2010–11, 39 research assistantships with partial tuition reimbursements (averaging $23,000 per year) were awarded; Federal Work-Study and scholarships/grants also available. Support available to part-time students. Financial award application deadline: 3/10; financial award applicants required to submit FAFSA. *Unit head:* Dr. Donald R. Menick, Director, 843-876-5045, Fax: 843-792-6590, E-mail: menickd@musc.edu. *Application contact:* Dr. Cynthia F. Wright, Associate Dean for Admissions and Career Development, 843-792-2564, Fax: 843-792-6590, E-mail: wrightcf@musc.edu.

Memorial University of Newfoundland, Faculty of Medicine and School of Graduate Studies, Graduate Programs in Medicine, Division of Biomedical Sciences, St. John's, NL A1C 5S7, Canada. Offers cancer (M Sc, PhD); cardiovascular (M Sc, PhD); immunology (M Sc, PhD); neuroscience (M Sc, PhD). Part-time programs available. *Degree requirements:* For master's, thesis; for doctorate, comprehensive exam, thesis/dissertation, oral defense of thesis. *Entrance requirements:* For master's, MD or B Sc; for doctorate, MD or M Sc. Additional exam requirements/recommendations for international students: Required—TOEFL. *Faculty research:* Neuroscience, immunology, cardiovascular, and cancer.

Midwestern University, Glendale Campus, College of Health Sciences, Arizona Campus, Program in Cardiovascular Science, Glendale, AZ 85308. Offers MCVS. *Faculty:* 4 full-time (1 woman). *Students:* 46 full-time (20 women); includes 3 Black or African American, non-Hispanic/Latino; 1 Asian, non-Hispanic/Latino; 3 Hispanic/Latino, 1 international. Average age 27. 55 applicants, 65% accepted, 24 enrolled. In 2010, 10 master's awarded. Application fee: $50. *Expenses:* Contact institution. *Unit head:* Dr. Jon Austin, Dean, 623-572-3616. *Application contact:* James Walter, Director of Admissions, 888-247-9277, Fax: 623-572-3229, E-mail: admissaz@midwestern.edu.

Milwaukee School of Engineering, Department of Electrical Engineering and Computer Science, Program in Cardiovascular Studies, Milwaukee, WI 53202-3109. Offers MS. *Faculty:* 1 full-time (0 women), 1 part-time/adjunct (0 women). *Students:* 2 applicants, 100% accepted, 2 enrolled. In 2010, 1 master's awarded. *Entrance requirements:* For master's, GRE General Test or GMAT. Additional exam requirements/recommendations for international students: Required—TOEFL (minimum score 79 iBT). *Application deadline:* Applications are processed on a rolling basis. Application fee: $30. Electronic applications accepted. *Expenses:* Tuition: Full-time $17,550; part-time $650 per credit. One-time fee: $75. *Financial support:* In 2010–11, 2 students received support. *Unit head:* Dr. Ronald Gerrits, Director, 414-277-7561, Fax: 414-277-7494, E-mail: gerrits@msoe.edu. *Application contact:* Sarah K. Winchowky, Graduate Admissions Director, 800-321-6763, Fax: 414-277-7475, E-mail: wp@msoe.edu.

Milwaukee School of Engineering, Department of Electrical Engineering and Computer Science, Program in Perfusion, Milwaukee, WI 53202-3109. Offers MS. Part-time and evening/weekend programs available. *Faculty:* 1 full-time (0 women), 4 part-time/adjunct (1 woman). *Students:* 12 full-time (4 women); includes 1 Black or African American, non-Hispanic/Latino; 2 Asian, non-Hispanic/Latino. Average age 33. 30 applicants, 33% accepted, 7 enrolled. In 2010, 1 master's awarded. *Degree requirements:* For master's, comprehensive exam, thesis. *Entrance requirements:* For master's, GRE General Test or GMAT, BS in appropriate discipline, undergraduate work in human physiology or anatomy, 3 letters of recommendation, interview, observation of 2 perfusion cases. Additional exam requirements/recommendations for international students: Required—TOEFL (minimum score 79 iBT). *Application deadline:* Applications are processed on a rolling basis. Application fee: $30. Electronic applications accepted. *Expenses:* Tuition: Full-time $17,550; part-time $650 per credit. One-time fee: $75. *Financial support:* In 2010–11, 8 students received support. Career-related internships or fieldwork available. Support available to part-time students. Financial award applicants required to submit FAFSA. *Faculty research:* Heart medicine. *Unit head:* Dr. Ronald Gerrits, Director, 414-277-7561, Fax: 414-277-7494, E-mail: gerrits@msoe.edu. *Application contact:* Sarah K. Winchowky, Graduate Admissions Director, 800-321-6763, Fax: 414-277-7475, E-mail: wp@msoe.edu.

Queen's University at Kingston, School of Graduate Studies and Research, Faculty of Health Sciences, Department of Anatomy and Cell Biology, Kingston, ON K7L 3N6, Canada. Offers biology of reproduction (M Sc, PhD); cancer (M Sc, PhD); cardiovascular pathophysiology (M Sc, PhD); cell and molecular biology (M Sc, PhD); drug metabolism (M Sc, PhD); endocrinology (M Sc, PhD); motor control (M Sc, PhD); neural regeneration (M Sc, PhD); neurophysiology (M Sc, PhD). Part-time programs available. *Degree requirements:* For master's, thesis; for doctorate, one foreign language, comprehensive exam, thesis/dissertation. *Entrance requirements:* Additional exam requirements/recommendations for international students: Required—TOEFL. Electronic applications accepted. *Faculty research:* Human kinetics, neuroscience, reproductive biology, cardiovascular.

Quinnipiac University, School of Health Sciences, Program in Cardiovascular Perfusion, Hamden, CT 06518-1940. Offers MHS. *Faculty:* 1 full-time (0 women), 4 part-time/adjunct (0 women). *Students:* 8 full-time (2 women), 19 part-time (3 women); includes 6 minority (2 Black or African American, non-Hispanic/Latino; 1 Asian, non-Hispanic/Latino; 3 Hispanic/Latino), 3 international. 23 applicants, 57% accepted, 9 enrolled. In 2010, 3 master's awarded. *Entrance requirements:* For master's, bachelor's degree in science or health-related discipline from an accredited American or Canadian college or university; 2 years health care work experience; interview. Additional exam requirements/recommendations for international students: Required—TOEFL (minimum score 575 paper-based; 233 computer-based; 90 iBT), IELTS (minimum score 6.5). *Application deadline:* For fall admission, 7/30 priority date for domestic students, 4/30 priority date for international students. Applications are processed on a rolling basis. Application fee: $45. Electronic applications accepted. *Expenses:* Tuition: Part-time $810 per credit. Required fees: $35 per credit. *Financial support:* Career-related internships or fieldwork, tuition waivers, and unspecified assistantships available. Financial award application deadline: 4/15; financial award applicants required to submit FAFSA. *Unit head:* Michael Smith, Director, 203-582-3427, Fax: 203-582-8706, E-mail: michael.smith@quinnipiac.edu. *Application contact:* Kristin Parent, Assistant Director of Graduate Health Sciences Admissions, 800-462-1944, Fax: 208-582-3443, E-mail: kristin.parent@quinnipiac.edu.

State University of New York Upstate Medical University, College of Graduate Studies, Major Research Areas of the College of Graduate Studies, Syracuse, NY 13210-2334.

Université Laval, Faculty of Medicine, Post-Professional Programs in Medical Studies, Québec, QC G1K 7P4, Canada. Offers anatomy–pathology (DESS); anesthesiology (DESS); cardiology (DESS); care of older people (Diploma); clinical research (DESS); community health (DESS);

dermatology (DESS); diagnostic radiology (DESS); emergency medicine (Diploma); family medicine (DESS); general surgery (DESS); geriatrics (DESS); hematology (DESS); internal medicine (DESS); maternal and fetal medicine (Diploma); medical biochemistry (DESS); medical microbiology and infectious diseases (DESS); medical oncology (DESS); nephrology (DESS); neurology (DESS); neurosurgery (DESS); obstetrics and gynecology (DESS); ophthalmology (DESS); orthopedic surgery (DESS); oto-rhino-laryngology (DESS); palliative medicine (Diploma); pediatrics (DESS); plastic surgery (DESS); psychiatry (DESS); pulmonary medicine (DESS); radiology–oncology (DESS); thoracic surgery (DESS); urology (DESS). *Degree requirements:* For other advanced degree, comprehensive exam. *Entrance requirements:* For degree, knowledge of French. Electronic applications accepted.

University of Calgary, Faculty of Medicine and Faculty of Graduate Studies, Department of Cardiovascular and Respiratory Sciences, Calgary, AB T2N 1N4, Canada. Offers M Sc, PhD. *Degree requirements:* For master's, thesis; for doctorate, thesis/dissertation, candidacy exam. *Entrance requirements:* For master's and doctorate, minimum GPA of 3.2. Additional exam requirements/recommendations for international students: Required—TOEFL (minimum score 600 paper-based; 250 computer-based). Electronic applications accepted. *Faculty research:* Cardiac mechanics, physiology and pharmacology; lung mechanics, physiology and pathophysiology; smooth muscle biochemistry; physiology and pharmacology.

University of California, San Diego, School of Medicine and Office of Graduate Studies, Molecular Pathology Program, La Jolla, CA 92093. Offers bioinformatics (PhD); cancer biology/oncology (PhD); cardiovascular sciences and disease (PhD); microbiology (PhD); molecular pathology (PhD); neurological disease (PhD); stem cell and developmental biology (PhD); structural biology/drug design (PhD). *Entrance requirements:* For doctorate, GRE General Test, GRE Subject Test. Additional exam requirements/recommendations for international students: Required—TOEFL. Electronic applications accepted.

University of Guelph, Ontario Veterinary College and Graduate Studies, Graduate Programs in Veterinary Sciences, Department of Clinical Studies, Guelph, ON N1G 2W1, Canada. Offers anesthesiology (M Sc, DV Sc); cardiology (DV Sc, Diploma); clinical studies (Diploma); dermatology (M Sc); diagnostic imaging (M Sc, DV Sc); emergency/critical care (M Sc, DV Sc, Diploma); medicine (M Sc, DV Sc); neurology (M Sc, DV Sc); ophthalmology (M Sc, DV Sc); surgery (M Sc, DV Sc). *Degree requirements:* For master's, thesis; for doctorate, comprehensive exam, thesis/dissertation. *Entrance requirements:* Additional exam requirements/recommendations for international students: Required—TOEFL (minimum score 550 paper-based; 213 computer-based), IELTS (minimum score 6.5). Electronic applications accepted. *Faculty research:* Orthopedics, respirology, oncology, exercise physiology, cardiology.

University of Mary, School of Health Sciences, Program in Respiratory Therapy, Bismarck, ND 58504-9652. Offers MS. *Faculty:* 4 full-time (2 women). *Entrance requirements:* For master's, minimum GPA of 3.0, 3 letters of reference, interview. Additional exam requirements/recommendations for international students: Required—TOEFL (minimum score 500 paper-based; 197 computer-based; 71 iBT). *Application deadline:* For fall admission, 2/15 priority date for domestic students. Application fee: $40. Electronic applications accepted. *Expenses:* Tuition: Full-time $10,800; part-time $450 per credit. Tuition and fees vary according to course load, degree level, program and student level. *Financial support:* Career-related internships or fieldwork available. Financial award application deadline: 8/1; financial award applicants required to submit FAFSA. *Unit head:* Dr. Will Beachey, Director, 701-530-7757, Fax: 701-255-7387, E-mail: wbeachey@primecare.org. *Application contact:* Dr. Kathy Perrin, Director of Graduate Studies, 701-355-8119, Fax: 701-255-7687, E-mail: kperrin@umary.edu.

University of Medicine and Dentistry of New Jersey, School of Health Related Professions, Department of Interdisciplinary Studies, Program in Health Sciences, Newark, NJ 07107-1709. Offers cardiopulmonary sciences (PhD); clinical laboratory sciences (PhD); health sciences (MS); interdisciplinary studies (PhD); nutrition (PhD); physical therapy/movement science (PhD). Part-time and evening/weekend programs available. Postbaccalaureate distance learning degree programs offered (no on-campus study). *Students:* 6 full-time (4 women), 125 part-time (94 women); includes 12 Black or African American, non-Hispanic/Latino; 5 Asian, non-Hispanic/Latino; 8 Hispanic/Latino, 5 international. Average age 40. 78 applicants, 46% accepted, 29 enrolled. In 2010, 14 master's, 2 doctorates awarded. *Degree requirements:* For doctorate, thesis/dissertation. *Entrance requirements:* For doctorate, interview, writing sample. Additional exam requirements/recommendations for international students: Required—TOEFL. *Application deadline:* For fall admission, 3/1 for domestic students. Applications are processed on a rolling basis. Application fee: $50. Electronic applications accepted. *Unit head:* Dr. Margaret Kildoff, Director, 973-972-4989, Fax: 973-972-7854, E-mail: ms-phd-hs@umdnj.edu. *Application contact:* Douglas Lomonaco, Assistant Dean, 973-972-5454, Fax: 973-972-7463, E-mail: shrpadm@umdnj.edu.

The University of South Dakota, School of Medicine and Health Sciences and Graduate School, Biomedical Sciences Graduate Program, Cardiovascular Research Program, Vermillion, SD 57069-2390. Offers MS, PhD. Terminal master's awarded for partial completion of doctoral program. *Degree requirements:* For master's, thesis; for doctorate, comprehensive exam, thesis/dissertation. *Entrance requirements:* For master's and doctorate, GRE General Test, minimum GPA of 3.0. Additional exam requirements/recommendations for international students: Required—TOEFL (minimum score 550 paper-based; 213 computer-based; 80 iBT), IELTS (minimum score 6). Electronic applications accepted. *Expenses:* Contact institution. *Faculty research:* Cardiovascular disease.

The University of Toledo, College of Graduate Studies, College of Medicine and Life Sciences, Department of Physiology and Pharmacology, Toledo, OH 43606-3390. Offers cardiovascular and metabolic diseases (MSBS, PhD); MD/PhD. *Faculty:* 21. *Students:* 22 full-time (8 women); includes 1 Asian, non-Hispanic/Latino, 13 international. Average age 27. 26 applicants, 38% accepted, 6 enrolled. In 2010, 1 master's, 12 doctorates awarded. Terminal master's awarded for partial completion of doctoral program. *Degree requirements:* For master's, thesis, qualifying exam; for doctorate, thesis/dissertation, qualifying exam. *Entrance requirements:* For master's and doctorate, GRE/MCAT, minimum undergraduate GPA of 3.0, three letters of recommendation, statement of purpose, transcripts from all prior institutions attended. Additional exam requirements/recommendations for international students: Required—TOEFL (minimum score 550 paper-based; 213 computer-based; 80 iBT), IELTS (minimum score 6.5). *Application deadline:* For fall admission, 5/1 priority date for domestic and international students. Applications are processed on a rolling basis. Application fee: $45 ($75 for international students). Electronic applications accepted. *Expenses:* Tuition, state resident: full-time $11,426; part-time $476 per credit hour. Tuition, nonresident: full-time $21,660; part-time $903 per credit hour. One-time fee: $62. *Financial support:* In 2010–11, research assistantships with full tuition reimbursements (averaging $21,180 per year); Federal Work-Study, institutionally sponsored loans, scholarships/grants, tuition waivers (full), and unspecified assistantships also available. *Unit head:* Dr. Nader Abraham, Chair, 419-383-4425, E-mail: nader.abraham@utoledo.edu. *Application contact:* Christine Wile, Admissions Analyst, 419-383-4116, Fax: 419-383-6140, E-mail: christine.wile@utoledo.edu.

Molecular Physiology

Baylor College of Medicine, Graduate School of Biomedical Sciences, Department of Molecular Physiology and Biophysics, Houston, TX 77030-3498. Offers PhD, MD/PhD. *Faculty:* 34 full-time (10 women). *Students:* 20 full-time (10 women); includes 1 Black or African American, non-Hispanic/Latino; 1 Asian, non-Hispanic/Latino; 1 Hispanic/Latino, 8 international. Average age 27. 22 applicants, 32% accepted, 5 enrolled. In 2010, 3 doctorates awarded. *Degree requirements:* For doctorate, thesis/dissertation, public defense. *Entrance requirements:* For doctorate, GRE General Test, GRE Subject Test (strongly recommended), minimum GPA of 3.0. Additional exam requirements/recommendations for international students: Required—TOEFL. *Application deadline:* For fall admission, 1/1 priority date for domestic students. Electronic applications accepted. *Expenses:* Tuition: Full-time $11,000. Required fees: $4900. *Financial support:* In 2010–11, 8 fellowships with full tuition reimbursements (averaging $26,000 per year), 12 research assistantships with full tuition reimbursements (averaging $26,000 per year) were awarded; career-related internships or fieldwork, Federal Work-Study, institutionally sponsored loans, health care benefits, and students receive a scholarship unless there are grant funds available to pay tuition also available. Financial award applicants required to submit FAFSA. *Faculty research:* Biophysics, cardiovascular biology, imaging, muscle physiology, ion channels. *Unit head:* Dr. Robia Pautler, Director, 713-798-5630, Fax: 713-798-3475. *Application contact:* Cherrie McGlory, Graduate Program Administrator, 713-798-5109, Fax: 713-798-3475, E-mail: molphysgrad@bcm.edu.

Case Western Reserve University, School of Medicine and School of Graduate Studies, Graduate Programs in Medicine, Department of Physiology and Biophysics, Cleveland, OH 44106. Offers cell and molecular physiology (MS); cell physiology (PhD); molecular/cellular biophysics (PhD); physiology and biophysics (PhD); systems physiology (PhD); MD/PhD. Terminal master's awarded for partial completion of doctoral program. *Degree requirements:* For master's, thesis; for doctorate, thesis/dissertation. *Entrance requirements:* For master's, GRE General Test, minimum GPA of 3.28; for doctorate, GRE General Test, minimum GPA of 3.6. Additional exam requirements/recommendations for international students: Required—TOEFL. Electronic applications accepted. *Faculty research:* Cardiovascular physiology, calcium metabolism, epithelial cell biology.

See Display on page 443 and Close-Up on page 453.

Loyola University Chicago, Graduate School, Programs in Cell and Molecular Physiology, Chicago, IL 60660. Offers MS, PhD. MS offered only to students enrolled in a first-professional degree program. *Faculty:* 17 full-time (4 women), 5 part-time/adjunct (1 woman). *Students:* 6 full-time (1 woman), 3 international. Average age 29. 6 applicants, 0% accepted, 0 enrolled. In 2010, 1 master's awarded. *Degree requirements:* For master's, thesis; for doctorate, comprehensive exam, thesis/dissertation. *Entrance requirements:* For master's, GRE General Test or MCAT; for doctorate, GRE General Test. Additional exam requirements/recommendations for international students: Required—TOEFL. *Application deadline:* For fall admission, 5/15 for domestic and international students. Application fee: $0. Electronic applications accepted. *Expenses:* Tuition: Full-time $14,940; part-time $830 per credit hour. Required fees: $87 per semester. Part-time tuition and fees vary according to course load and program. *Financial support:* In 2010–11, 5 fellowships with tuition reimbursements (averaging $23,000 per year), 9 research assistantships with tuition reimbursements (averaging $23,000 per year) were awarded. *Faculty research:* Cardiovascular system-emphasis in neural and metabolic control of circulation, ion channels, excitation contraction coupling, molecular cloning. *Unit head:* Dr. Pieter deTombe, Chair, 708-216-6305, Fax: 708-216-6308, E-mail: pdetombe@lumc.edu. *Application contact:* Dr. Ruben Mestril, Graduate Program Director, 708-327-2395, Fax: 708-216-6308, E-mail: rmestri@lumc.edu.

Rutgers, The State University of New Jersey, New Brunswick, Graduate School-New Brunswick, Program in Endocrinology and Animal Biosciences, Piscataway, NJ 08854-8097. Offers MS, PhD. Terminal master's awarded for partial completion of doctoral program. *Degree requirements:* For master's, thesis; for doctorate, comprehensive exam, thesis/dissertation. *Entrance requirements:* For master's and doctorate, GRE General Test. Additional exam requirements/recommendations for international students: Required—TOEFL. Electronic applications accepted. *Expenses:* Tuition, state resident: full-time $7200; part-time $600 per credit. Tuition, nonresident: full-time $11,124; part-time $927 per credit. *Faculty research:* Comparative and behavioral endocrinology, epigenetic regulation of the endocrine system, exercise physiology and immunology, fetal and neonatal developmental programming, mammary gland biology and breast cancer, neuroendocrinology and alcohol studies, reproductive and developmental toxicology.

Stony Brook University, State University of New York, Stony Brook University Medical Center, School of Medicine and Graduate School, Graduate Programs in Medicine, Department of Physiology and Biophysics, Stony Brook, NY 11794. Offers PhD. *Faculty:* 16 full-time (5 women). *Students:* 11 full-time (6 women); includes 1 Black or African American, non-Hispanic/Latino, 4 international. Average age 29. 46 applicants, 33% accepted. In 2010, 2 doctorates awarded. *Degree requirements:* For doctorate, comprehensive exam, thesis/dissertation. *Entrance requirements:* For doctorate, GRE General Test, GRE Subject Test, BS in related field, minimum GPA of 3.0. Additional exam requirements/recommendations for international students: Required—TOEFL. *Application deadline:* For fall admission, 1/15 for domestic students. Application fee: $100. *Expenses:* Tuition, state resident: full-time $8370; part-time $349 per credit. Tuition, nonresident: full-time $13,780; part-time $574 per credit. Required fees: $994. *Financial support:* In 2010–11, 10 research assistantships, 1 teaching assistantship were awarded; fellowships, Federal Work-Study also available. Financial award application deadline: 3/15. *Faculty research:* Cellular electrophysiology, membrane permeation and transport, metabolic endocrinology. Total annual research expenditures: $5.1 million. *Unit head:* Dr. Peter Brink, Chair, 631-444-2299, Fax: 631-444-3432, E-mail: peter.brink@stonybrook.edu. *Application contact:* Dr. Raafat El-Maghrabi, Graduate Program Director, 631-444-3049, Fax: 631-444-3432, E-mail: raafat.el-maghrabi@stonybrook.edu.

Texas Tech University Health Sciences Center, Graduate School of Biomedical Sciences, Department of Cell Physiology and Molecular Biophysics, Lubbock, TX 79430. Offers MS, PhD, MD/PhD. Terminal master's awarded for partial completion of doctoral program. *Degree requirements:* For master's, thesis; for doctorate, thesis/dissertation. *Entrance requirements:* For master's and doctorate, GRE General Test, minimum GPA of 3.4. Additional exam requirements/recommendations for international students: Required—TOEFL. Electronic applications accepted. *Faculty research:* Cardiovascular physiology, neurophysiology, renal physiology, respiratory physiology.

Thomas Jefferson University, Jefferson College of Graduate Studies, Program in Molecular Physiology and Biophysics, Philadelphia, PA 19107. Offers PhD. *Faculty:* 13 full-time (5 women). *Students:* 2 full-time (1 woman). 4 applicants, 0% accepted. *Degree requirements:* For doctorate, comprehensive exam, thesis/dissertation. *Entrance requirements:* For doctorate, GRE General Test, minimum GPA of 3.2. Additional exam requirements/recommendations for international students: Required—TOEFL (minimum score 250 computer-based; 100 iBT). *Application deadline:* For fall admission, 1/15 priority date for domestic and international students. Applications are processed on a rolling basis. Application fee: $50. Electronic applications accepted. *Financial support:* In 2010–11, 2 students received support, including 2 fellowships with full tuition reimbursements available (averaging $52,883 per year); Federal Work-Study, institutionally sponsored loans, scholarships/grants, traineeships, and stipends also

Molecular Physiology

Thomas Jefferson University (continued)
available. Support available to part-time students. Financial award application deadline: 5/1; financial award applicants required to submit FAFSA. *Faculty research:* Cardiovascular physiology, smooth muscle physiology, pathophysiology of myocardial ischemia, endothelial cell physiology, molecular biology of ion channel physiology. Total annual research expenditures: $3.2 million. *Unit head:* Dr. Thomas M. Butler, Program Director, 215-503-6583, E-mail: thomas.butler@jefferson.edu. *Application contact:* Marc E. Stearns, Director of Admissions, 215-503-0155, Fax: 215-503-9920, E-mail: jcgs-info@jefferson.edu.

Tufts University, Sackler School of Graduate Biomedical Sciences, Graduate Program in Cellular and Molecular Physiology, Medford, MA 02155. Offers PhD. *Faculty:* 23 full-time (8 women). *Students:* 11 full-time (7 women); includes 1 Asian, non-Hispanic/Latino, 2 international. Average age 28. In 2010, 1 doctorate awarded. *Degree requirements:* For doctorate, thesis/dissertation. *Expenses:* Tuition: Full-time $39,624; part-time $3962 per course. Required fees: $40 per year. Full-time tuition and fees vary according to degree level, program and student level. Part-time tuition and fees vary according to course load. *Financial support:* In 2010–11, 11 students received support, including 11 research assistantships with full tuition reimbursements available (averaging $28,250 per year); scholarships/grants, health care benefits, and tuition waivers (full) also available. *Unit head:* Dr. Laura Liscum, Head, 617-636-6945, Fax: 617-636-0445. *Application contact:* Kellie Johnston, Associate Director of Admissions, 617-636-6767, Fax: 617-636-0375, E-mail: sackler-school@tufts.edu.

The University of Alabama at Birmingham, Graduate Programs in Joint Health Sciences, Program in Cellular and Molecular Physiology, Birmingham, AL 35294. Offers PhD. *Students:* 15 full-time (3 women), 1 part-time (0 women); includes 2 minority (1 Black or African American, non-Hispanic/Latino; 1 Hispanic/Latino), 3 international. Average age 28. In 2010, 8 doctorates awarded. Application fee: $35 ($60 for international students). *Expenses:* Tuition, state resident: full-time $5482. Tuition, nonresident: full-time $12,430. Tuition and fees vary according to program. *Unit head:* Dr. Ray L. Watts, Vice President/Dean, School of Medicine, 205-934-1111, Fax: 205-943-0333. *Application contact:* Julie Bryant, Director of Graduate Admissions, 205-934-8227, Fax: 205-934-8413, E-mail: jbryant@uab.edu.

University of Chicago, Division of Biological Sciences, Neuroscience Graduate Programs, Chicago, IL 60637-1513. Offers cellular and molecular physiology (PhD); computational neuroscience (PhD); integrative neuroscience (PhD), including cell physiology, pharmacological and physiological sciences; neurobiology (PhD). *Degree requirements:* For doctorate, thesis/dissertation, ethics class, 2 teaching assistantships. *Entrance requirements:* For doctorate, GRE General Test. Additional exam requirements/recommendations for international students: Required—TOEFL (minimum score 600 paper-based; 250 computer-based; 104 iBT), IELTS (minimum score 7). Electronic applications accepted.

University of Chicago, Division of Biological Sciences, Program in Cellular and Molecular Physiology, Chicago, IL 60637-1513. Offers PhD. *Degree requirements:* For doctorate, thesis/dissertation, ethics class, 2 teaching assistantships. *Entrance requirements:* For doctorate, GRE General Test. Additional exam requirements/recommendations for international students: Required—TOEFL (minimum score 600 paper-based; 250 computer-based; 104 iBT), IELTS (minimum score 7). Electronic applications accepted. *Faculty research:* Molecular genetics, biochemical biological and physical approaches to cell physiology.

University of Illinois at Urbana–Champaign, Graduate College, College of Liberal Arts and Sciences, School of Molecular and Cellular Biology, Department of Molecular and Integrative Physiology, Champaign, IL 61820. Offers MS, PhD. *Faculty:* 13 full-time (5 women). *Students:* 39 full-time (21 women); includes 2 Black or African American, non-Hispanic/Latino; 2 Asian, non-Hispanic/Latino; 3 Hispanic/Latino; 1 Two or more races, non-Hispanic/Latino, 14 international. In 2010, 5 master's, 5 doctorates awarded. *Entrance requirements:* For master's and doctorate, GRE, minimum GPA of 3.0. Additional exam requirements/recommendations for international students: Required—TOEFL (minimum score 590 paper-based; 243 computer-based). *Application deadline:* Applications are processed on a rolling basis. Application fee: $75 ($90 for international students). Electronic applications accepted. *Financial support:* In 2010–11, 2 fellowships, 33 research assistantships, 20 teaching assistantships were awarded; tuition waivers (full and partial) also available. *Unit head:* Byron Kemper, Head, 217-333-1146, Fax: 217-333-1133, E-mail: byronkem@illinois.edu. *Application contact:* Penny Morman, Office Manager, 217-333-8275, Fax: 217-333-1133, E-mail: morman@illinois.edu.

The University of North Carolina at Chapel Hill, School of Medicine and Graduate School, Graduate Programs in Medicine, Department of Cell and Molecular Physiology, Chapel Hill, NC 27599. Offers PhD. *Faculty:* 27 full-time (9 women), 14 part-time/adjunct (4 women). *Students:* 22 full-time (12 women); includes 1 American Indian or Alaska Native, non-Hispanic/Latino; 3 Asian, non-Hispanic/Latino, 3 international. Average age 27. In 2010, 5 doctorates awarded. Terminal master's awarded for partial completion of doctoral program. *Degree requirements:* For doctorate, comprehensive exam, thesis/dissertation, ethics training. *Entrance requirements:* For doctorate, GRE General Test. *Application deadline:* For fall admission, 1/1 priority date for domestic and international students. Applications are processed on a rolling basis. Application fee: $77. Electronic applications accepted. *Financial support:* In 2010–11, 2 fellowships with full tuition reimbursements (averaging $24,000 per year), 16 research assistantships with full tuition reimbursements (averaging $24,000 per year) were awarded; Federal Work-Study, institutionally sponsored loans, scholarships/grants, traineeships, health care benefits, and unspecified assistantships also available. Support available to part-time students. Financial award applicants required to submit FAFSA. *Faculty research:* Signal transduction; growth factors; cardiovascular diseases; neurobiology; hormones, receptors, ion channels. Total annual research expenditures: $8.1 million. *Unit head:* Dr. Carol A. Otey, Interim Chair, 919-966-0273, Fax: 919-966-6927, E-mail: carol_otey@med.unc.edu. *Application contact:* Dr. Manzoor A. Bhat, Director of Graduate Studies, 919-966-1018, Fax: 919-966-6927, E-mail: manzoor_bhat@med.unc.edu.

University of Pittsburgh, School of Medicine, Graduate Programs in Medicine, Program in Cell Biology and Molecular Physiology, Pittsburgh, PA 15260. Offers MS, PhD. *Faculty:* 43 full-time (12 women). *Students:* 11 full-time (6 women); includes 1 Asian, non-Hispanic/Latino, 5 international. Average age 27. 486 applicants, 14% accepted. In 2010, 4 doctorates awarded. *Degree requirements:* For doctorate, comprehensive exam, thesis/dissertation. *Entrance requirements:* For doctorate, GRE General Test, GRE Subject Test, minimum QPA of 3.0. Additional exam requirements/recommendations for international students: Required—TOEFL (minimum score 600 paper-based; 100 iBT), IELTS (minimum score 7). *Application deadline:* For fall admission, 12/15 priority date for domestic and international students. Application fee: $50. Electronic applications accepted. *Expenses:* Tuition, state resident: full-time $17,304; part-time $701 per credit. Tuition, nonresident: full-time $29,554; part-time $1210 per credit. Required fees: $740; $214 per term. Tuition and fees vary according to program. *Financial support:* In 2010–11, 4 research assistantships with full tuition reimbursements (averaging $25,500 per year), 7 teaching assistantships with full tuition reimbursements (averaging $25,500 per year) were awarded; institutionally sponsored loans, scholarships/grants, traineeships, health care benefits, and unspecified assistantships also available. *Faculty research:* Genetic disorders of ion channels, regulation of gene expression/development, membrane traffic of proteins and lipids, reproductive biology, signal transduction in diabetes and metabolism. *Unit head:* Dr. William H. Walker, Graduate Program Director, 412-641-7672, Fax: 412-641-7676, E-mail: walkerw@pitt.edu. *Application contact:* Graduate Studies Administrator, 412-648-8957, Fax: 412-648-1077, E-mail: gradstudies@medschool.pitt.edu.

University of Vermont, College of Medicine and Graduate College, Graduate Programs in Medicine, Department of Molecular Physiology and Biophysics, Burlington, VT 05405. Offers MS, PhD, MD/MS, MD/PhD. *Students:* 4 (2 women), 1 international. 8 applicants, 38% accepted, 2 enrolled. *Degree requirements:* For master's, thesis; for doctorate, thesis/dissertation. *Entrance requirements:* For master's and doctorate, GRE General Test. Additional exam requirements/recommendations for international students: Required—TOEFL (minimum score 550 paper-based; 213 computer-based; 80 iBT). *Application deadline:* For fall admission, 4/1 priority date for domestic students, 4/1 for international students. Applications are processed on a rolling basis. Application fee: $40. Electronic applications accepted. *Expenses:* Tuition, state resident: part-time $537 per credit hour. Tuition, nonresident: part-time $1355 per credit hour. *Financial support:* Fellowships, research assistantships, teaching assistantships available. Financial award application deadline: 3/1. *Unit head:* Dr. D. Warshaw, Chairperson, 802-656-2540. *Application contact:* Dr. Terese Ruiz, Coordinator, 802-656-2540.

University of Virginia, School of Medicine, Department of Molecular Physiology and Biological Physics, Charlottesville, VA 22903. Offers biological and physical sciences (MS); physiology (PhD); MD/PhD. *Faculty:* 30 full-time (5 women), 1 part-time/adjunct (0 women). *Students:* 14 full-time (6 women), 1 part-time (0 women); includes 2 Black or African American, non-Hispanic/Latino. Average age 29. In 2010, 21 master's, 1 doctorate awarded. *Entrance requirements:* For doctorate, GRE General Test, GRE Subject Test. Additional exam requirements/recommendations for international students: Required—TOEFL. *Application deadline:* For fall admission, 2/15 for domestic and international students. Applications are processed on a rolling basis. Application fee: $60. Electronic applications accepted. *Financial support:* Fellowships, research assistantships, teaching assistantships available. Financial award applicants required to submit FAFSA. *Unit head:* Dr. Mark Yeager, Chair, 434-924-5108, Fax: 434-982-1616, E-mail: my3r@virginia.edu. *Application contact:* Dr. Mark Yeager, Chair, 434-924-5108, Fax: 434-982-1616, E-mail: my3r@virginia.edu.

Vanderbilt University, Graduate School and School of Medicine, Department of Molecular Physiology and Biophysics, Nashville, TN 37240-1001. Offers MS, PhD, MD/PhD. *Faculty:* 38 full-time (11 women). *Students:* 33 full-time (25 women), 9 part-time (3 women); includes 2 Black or African American, non-Hispanic/Latino; 1 American Indian or Alaska Native, non-Hispanic/Latino; 3 Hispanic/Latino; 2 Two or more races, non-Hispanic/Latino. Average age 28. In 2010, 8 doctorates awarded. *Degree requirements:* For doctorate, comprehensive exam, thesis/dissertation, preliminary, qualifying, and final exams. *Entrance requirements:* For doctorate, GRE General Test, GRE Subject Test (recommended). Additional exam requirements/recommendations for international students: Required—TOEFL (minimum score 570 paper-based; 230 computer-based; 88 iBT). *Application deadline:* For fall admission, 1/15 for domestic and international students. Application fee: $0. Electronic applications accepted. *Financial support:* Fellowships with full tuition reimbursements, research assistantships with full tuition reimbursements, Federal Work-Study, institutionally sponsored loans, scholarships/grants, traineeships, health care benefits, and tuition waivers (partial) available. Financial award application deadline: 1/15; financial award applicants required to submit CSS PROFILE or FAFSA. *Faculty research:* Biophysics, cell signaling and gene regulation, human genetics, diabetes and obesity, neuroscience. *Unit head:* Roger Cone, Chair, 615-322-7000, Fax: 615-343-0490. *Application contact:* Michelle Grundy, Assistant Director, 800-373-0675, E-mail: michelle.grundy@vanderbilt.edu.

Yale University, Graduate School of Arts and Sciences, Department of Cellular and Molecular Physiology, New Haven, CT 06520. Offers PhD. *Degree requirements:* For doctorate, thesis/dissertation. *Entrance requirements:* For doctorate, GRE General Test, GRE Subject Test.

Physiology

Albert Einstein College of Medicine, Graduate Division of Biomedical Sciences, Department of Physiology and Biophysics, Bronx, NY 10461. Offers PhD, MD/PhD. *Degree requirements:* For doctorate, thesis/dissertation. *Entrance requirements:* For doctorate, GRE General Test. Additional exam requirements/recommendations for international students: Required—TOEFL. *Faculty research:* Biophysical and biochemical basis of body function at the subcellular, cellular, organ, and whole-body level.

American University of Beirut, Graduate Programs, Faculty of Medicine, Beirut, Lebanon. Offers biochemistry (MS); human morphology (MS); medicine (MD); microbiology and immunology (MS); neuroscience (MS); pharmacology and therapeutics (MS); physiology (MS). Part-time programs available. *Faculty:* 222 full-time (56 women), 58 part-time/adjunct (4 women). *Students:* 346 full-time (135 women), 69 part-time (57 women). Average age 23. In 2010, 81 first professional degrees, 19 master's awarded. *Degree requirements:* For master's, one foreign language, comprehensive exam, thesis (for some programs). *Entrance requirements:* For MD, MCAT, bachelor's degree; for master's, letter of recommendation. Additional exam requirements/recommendations for international students: Required—TOEFL (minimum score 600 paper-based; 250 computer-based; 100 iBT), IELTS (minimum score 7.5). *Application deadline:* For fall admission, 4/30 for domestic and international students; for spring admission, 11/1 for domestic and international students. Application fee: $50. *Expenses:* Tuition: Full-time $12,294; part-time $683 per credit. Required fees: $499; $499 per credit. Tuition and fees vary according to course load and program. *Financial support:* In 2010–11, 4 students received support. Career-related internships or fieldwork, institutionally sponsored loans, scholarships/grants, health care benefits, and unspecified assistantships available. Financial award application deadline: 2/2. *Faculty research:* Cancer research (targeted therapy, mechanisms of leukemogenesis, tumor cell extravasation and metastasis, cancer stem cells); stem cell research (regenerative medicine, drug discovery); genetic research (neurogenetics, hereditary cardiomyopathy, hemoglobinopathies, pharmacogenomics); neuroscience research (pain, neurodegenerative disorder); metabolism (inflammation and metabolism, metabolic disorder, diabetes mellitus). Total annual research expenditures: $1.2 million. *Unit head:* Dr. Mohamed Sayegh, Dean, 961-135-0000 Ext. 4700, Fax: 961-174-4464, E-mail: msayegh@aub.edu.lb. *Application contact:* Dr. Salim Kanaan, Director, Admissions Office, 961-135-0000 Ext. 2594, Fax: 961-175-0775, E-mail: sk00@aub.edu.lb.

Ball State University, Graduate School, College of Sciences and Humanities, Department of Physiology and Health Science, Program in Physiology, Muncie, IN 47306-1099. Offers MA, MS. *Students:* 27 full-time (9 women), 9 part-time (4 women); includes 1 Two or more races, non-Hispanic/Latino, 13 international. Average age 22. 40 applicants, 73% accepted, 18 enrolled. In 2010, 9 master's awarded. Application fee: $50. *Expenses:* Tuition, state resident: full-time $6160; part-time $299 per credit hour. Tuition, nonresident: full-time $16,020; part-time $783 per credit hour. Required fees: $2278; $95 per credit hour. *Financial support:* In 2010–11, 8 teaching assistantships with full tuition reimbursements (averaging $9,482 per year) were awarded. Financial award application deadline: 3/1. *Unit head:* Dr. Jeffrey K. Clark, Director, 765-285-8360, Fax: 765-285-3210. *Application contact:* Dr. Marianna Tucker, Director of Graduate Programs, 765-285-5961, Fax: 765-285-3210, E-mail: jclark@bsu.edu.

Boston University, College of Health and Rehabilitation Sciences: Sargent College, Department of Health Sciences, Programs in Applied Anatomy and Physiology, Boston, MA 02215. Offers

MS, PhD. *Faculty:* 10 full-time (9 women), 5 part-time/adjunct (2 women). *Students:* 4 full-time (2 women), 4 part-time (all women), 1 international. Average age 27. 37 applicants, 41% accepted.Terminal master's awarded for partial completion of doctoral program. *Degree requirements:* For master's, thesis or alternative; for doctorate, comprehensive exam, thesis/dissertation. *Entrance requirements:* For master's, GRE General Test, minimum GPA of 3.0; for doctorate, GRE General Test. Additional exam requirements/recommendations for international students: Required—TOEFL (minimum score 550 paper-based; 84 iBT). *Application deadline:* For fall admission, 1/15 priority date for domestic students; for spring admission, 10/1 for domestic students. Applications are processed on a rolling basis. Application fee: $70. Electronic applications accepted. *Expenses:* Tuition: Full-time $39,314; part-time $1228 per credit. Required fees: $40 per semester. *Financial support:* In 2010–11, 2 fellowships (averaging $21,000 per year), 1 research assistantship with full tuition reimbursement (averaging $18,000 per year), 3 teaching assistantships with full and partial tuition reimbursements were awarded; career-related internships or fieldwork, Federal Work-Study, institutionally sponsored loans, and scholarships/grants also available. Support available to part-time students. Financial award application deadline: 4/15; financial award applicants required to submit FAFSA. *Faculty research:* Skeletal muscle, neural systems, smooth muscle, muscular dystrophy. *Unit head:* Dr. Kathleen Morgan, Chair, 617-353-2717, E-mail: kmorgan@bu.edu. *Application contact:* Sharon Sankey, Director, Student Services, 617-353-2713, Fax: 617-353-7500, E-mail: ssankey@bu.edu.

Brigham Young University, Graduate Studies, College of Life Sciences, Department of Physiology and Developmental Biology, Provo, UT 84602. Offers neuroscience (MS, PhD); physiology and developmental biology (MS, PhD). Part-time programs available. *Faculty:* 19 full-time (0 women). *Students:* 25 full-time (11 women); includes 6 minority (1 American Indian or Alaska Native, non-Hispanic/Latino; 3 Asian, non-Hispanic/Latino; 2 Hispanic/Latino). Average age 29. 17 applicants, 47% accepted, 7 enrolled. In 2010, 5 master's, 2 doctorates awarded. Terminal master's awarded for partial completion of doctoral program. *Degree requirements:* For master's, thesis; for doctorate, thesis/dissertation. *Entrance requirements:* For master's, GRE General Test, minimum GPA of 3.0 during previous 2 years; for doctorate, GRE General Test, minimum GPA of 3.0 overall. Additional exam requirements/recommendations for international students: Required—TOEFL. *Application deadline:* For fall admission, 2/1 priority date for domestic and international students; for winter admission, 9/10 priority date for domestic and international students. Application fee: $50. Electronic applications accepted. *Expenses:* Tuition: Full-time $5580; part-time $310 per credit hour. Tuition and fees vary according to program and student's religious affiliation. *Financial support:* In 2010–11, 25 students received support, including 1 fellowship with partial tuition reimbursement available (averaging $7,100 per year), 12 research assistantships with full tuition reimbursements available (averaging $15,500 per year), 13 teaching assistantships with partial tuition reimbursements available (averaging $14,900 per year); career-related internships or fieldwork, institutionally sponsored loans, scholarships/grants, tuition waivers (full and partial), unspecified assistantships, and tuition awards also available. Financial award application deadline: 2/1. *Faculty research:* Sex differentiation of the brain, exercise physiology, developmental biology, membrane biophysics, neuroscience. Total annual research expenditures: $827,031. *Unit head:* Dr. William W. Winder, Chair, 801-422-3093, Fax: 801-422-0700, E-mail: william_winder@byu.edu. *Application contact:* Dr. Dixon J. Woodbury, Graduate Coordinator, 801-422-7562, Fax: 801-422-0700, E-mail: dixon_woodbury@byu.edu.

Brown University, Graduate School, Division of Biology and Medicine, Program in Molecular Pharmacology and Physiology, Providence, RI 02912. Offers MA, Sc M, PhD, MD/PhD. *Degree requirements:* For doctorate, thesis/dissertation, preliminary exam. *Entrance requirements:* For master's and doctorate, GRE General Test, GRE Subject Test. Additional exam requirements/recommendations for international students: Required—TOEFL. Electronic applications accepted. *Faculty research:* Structural biology, antiplatelet drugs, nicotinic receptor structure/function.

Case Western Reserve University, School of Medicine and School of Graduate Studies, Graduate Programs in Medicine, Department of Physiology and Biophysics, Cleveland, OH 44106. Offers cell and molecular physiology (MS); cell physiology (PhD); molecular/cellular biophysics (PhD); physiology and biophysics (PhD); systems physiology (PhD); MD/PhD. Terminal master's awarded for partial completion of doctoral program. *Degree requirements:* For master's, thesis; for doctorate, thesis/dissertation. *Entrance requirements:* For master's, GRE General Test, minimum GPA of 3.28; for doctorate, GRE General Test, minimum GPA of 3.6. Additional exam requirements/recommendations for international students: Required—TOEFL. Electronic applications accepted. *Faculty research:* Cardiovascular physiology, calcium metabolism, epithelial cell biology.

See Display below and Close-Up on page 453.

Columbia University, College of Physicians and Surgeons, Department of Physiology and Cellular Biophysics, New York, NY 10032. Offers M Phil, MA, PhD, MD/PhD. Only candidates for the PhD are admitted. Terminal master's awarded for partial completion of doctoral program. *Degree requirements:* For doctorate, thesis/dissertation. *Entrance requirements:* For master's and doctorate, GRE General Test. Additional exam requirements/recommendations for international students: Required—TOEFL. *Faculty research:* Membrane physiology, cellular biology, cardiovascular physiology, neurophysiology.

Cornell University, Graduate School, Graduate Fields of Comparative Biomedical Sciences, Field of Molecular and Integrative Physiology, Ithaca, NY 14853-0001. Offers behavioral physiology (MS, PhD); cardiovascular and respiratory physiology (MS, PhD); endocrinology (MS, PhD); environmental and comparative physiology (MS, PhD); gastrointestinal and metabolic physiology (MS, PhD); membrane and epithelial physiology (MS, PhD); molecular and cellular physiology (MS, PhD); neural and sensory physiology (MS, PhD); physiological genomics (MS, PhD); reproductive physiology (MS, PhD). *Faculty:* 40 full-time (15 women). *Students:* 14 full-time (10 women); includes 1 Asian, non-Hispanic/Latino, 9 international. Average age 28. 6 applicants, 50% accepted, 2 enrolled. In 2010, 3 doctorates awarded. *Degree requirements:* For master's, thesis; for doctorate, comprehensive exam, thesis/dissertation, 1 semester of teaching experience, seminar presentation. *Entrance requirements:* For master's and doctorate, GRE General Test, GRE Subject Test (biochemistry, cell and molecular biology, biology, or chemistry), 2 letters of recommendation. Additional exam requirements/recommendations for international students: Required—TOEFL (minimum score 550 paper-based; 213 computer-based; 77 iBT). *Application deadline:* For fall admission, 12/15 for domestic students. Application fee: $70. Electronic applications accepted. *Expenses:* Tuition: Full-time $29,500. Required fees: $76. Tuition and fees vary according to degree level and program. *Financial support:* In 2010–11, 14 research assistantships with full tuition reimbursements were awarded; fellowships with full tuition reimbursements, teaching assistantships with full tuition reimbursements, institutionally sponsored loans, scholarships/grants, health care benefits, tuition waivers (full and partial), and unspecified assistantships also available. Financial award applicants required to submit FAFSA. *Faculty research:* Endocrinology and reproductive physiology, cardiovascular and respiratory physiology, gastrointestinal and metabolic physiology, molecular and cellular physiology, physiological genomics. *Unit head:* Director of Graduate Studies, 607-253-3276, Fax: 607-253-3756. *Application contact:* Graduate Field Assistant, 607-253-3276, Fax: 607-253-3756, E-mail: graduate_edcvm@cornell.edu.

Cornell University, Joan and Sanford I. Weill Medical College and Graduate School of Medical Sciences, Weill Cornell Graduate School of Medical Sciences, Physiology, Biophysics and Systems Biology Program, New York, NY 10065. Offers MS, PhD. *Faculty:* 35 full-time (9 women). *Students:* 51 full-time (20 women); includes 2 Black or African American, non-Hispanic/Latino; 5 Asian, non-Hispanic/Latino; 1 Hispanic/Latino, 24 international. Average age 23. 44 applicants, 59% accepted, 13 enrolled. In 2010, 5 doctorates awarded. Terminal master's awarded for partial completion of doctoral program. *Degree requirements:* For master's, comprehensive exam; for doctorate, thesis/dissertation, final exam. *Entrance requirements:*

Physiology

Cornell University, Joan and Sanford I. Weill Medical College and Graduate School of Medical Sciences (continued)

For doctorate, GRE General Test, introductory courses in biology, inorganic and organic chemistry, physics, and mathematics. Additional exam requirements/recommendations for international students: Required—TOEFL. *Application deadline:* For fall admission, 12/1 for domestic students. Application fee: $60. *Expenses:* Tuition: Full-time $45,545. Required fees: $2805. *Financial support:* In 2010–11, 4 fellowships (averaging $24,735 per year) were awarded; scholarships/grants, health care benefits, and stipends (given to all students) also available. *Faculty research:* Receptor-mediated regulation of cell function, molecular properties of channels or receptors, bioinformatics, mathematical modeling. *Unit head:* Dr. Emre Aksay, Co-Director, 212-746-6207, E-mail: ema2004@med.cornell.edu. *Application contact:* Audrey Rivera, Program Coordinator, 212-746-6361, E-mail: ajr2004@med.cornell.edu.

Dalhousie University, Faculty of Medicine, Department of Physiology and Biophysics, Halifax, NS B3H 1X5, Canada. Offers M Sc, PhD, M Sc/PhD. *Degree requirements:* For master's, thesis; for doctorate, thesis/dissertation. *Entrance requirements:* For master's and doctorate, GRE Subject Test (for international students). Additional exam requirements/recommendations for international students: Required—TOEFL, IELTS, 1 of the following 5 approved tests: TOEFL, IELTS, CANTEST, CAEL, Michigan English Language Assessment Battery. Electronic applications accepted. *Faculty research:* Computer modeling, reproductive and endocrine physiology, cardiovascular physiology, neurophysiology, membrane biophysics.

Dartmouth College, Arts and Sciences Graduate Programs, Department of Physiology, Lebanon, NH 03756. Offers PhD, MD/PhD. *Degree requirements:* For doctorate, thesis/dissertation. *Entrance requirements:* For doctorate, GRE General Test, GRE Subject Test. Additional exam requirements/recommendations for international students: Required—TOEFL. *Faculty research:* Respiratory control, endocrinology of reproduction and immunology, regulation of receptors and channels, electrophysiology of membranes, renal function.

East Carolina University, Brody School of Medicine, Department of Physiology, Greenville, NC 27858-4353. Offers PhD. *Degree requirements:* For doctorate, comprehensive exam, thesis/dissertation. *Entrance requirements:* For doctorate, GRE General Test. Additional exam requirements/recommendations for international students: Required—TOEFL. *Expenses:* Tuition, state resident: full-time $3130; part-time $391.25 per credit hour. Tuition, nonresident: full-time $13,817; part-time $1727.13 per credit hour. Required fees: $1916; $239.50 per credit hour. Tuition and fees vary according to campus/location and program. *Faculty research:* Cell and nerve biophysics; neurophysiology; cardiovascular, renal, endocrine, and gastrointestinal physiology; pulmonary/asthma.

Eastern Michigan University, Graduate School, College of Health and Human Services, School of Health Promotion and Human Performance, Programs in Exercise Physiology, Ypsilanti, MI 48197. Offers exercise physiology (MS); sports medicine-biomechanics (MS); sports medicine-corporate adult fitness (MS); sports medicine-exercise physiology (MS). Part-time and evening/weekend programs available. *Students:* 14 full-time (8 women), 41 part-time (16 women); includes 8 minority (2 Black or African American, non-Hispanic/Latino; 1 American Indian or Alaska Native, non-Hispanic/Latino; 4 Hispanic/Latino; 1 Two or more races, non-Hispanic/Latino), 3 international. Average age 29. In 2010, 10 master's awarded. *Degree requirements:* For master's, comprehensive exam, thesis or 450-hour internship. *Entrance requirements:* Additional exam requirements/recommendations for international students: Required—TOEFL. *Application deadline:* For fall admission, 8/1 for domestic students, 5/1 for international students; for winter admission, 12/1 for domestic students, 10/1 for international students; for spring admission, 3/15 for domestic students, 3/1 for international students. Application fee: $35. *Unit head:* Dr. Steve McGregor, Program Coordinator, 734-487-0090, Fax: 734-487-2024, E-mail: stephen.mcgregor@emich.edu. *Application contact:* Dr. Steve McGregor, Program Coordinator, 734-487-0090, Fax: 734-487-2024, E-mail: stephen.mcgregor@emich.edu.

East Tennessee State University, James H. Quillen College of Medicine, Biomedical Science Graduate Program, Johnson City, TN 37614. Offers anatomy (PhD); biochemistry (PhD); microbiology (PhD); pharmacology (PhD); physiology (PhD). Part-time programs available. *Faculty:* 49 full-time (12 women), 1 (woman) part-time/adjunct. *Students:* 27 full-time (14 women), 4 part-time (2 women); includes 4 minority (1 Black or African American, non-Hispanic/Latino; 1 Asian, non-Hispanic/Latino; 2 Hispanic/Latino), 5 international. Average age 32. 62 applicants, 11% accepted, 7 enrolled. In 2010, 2 doctorates awarded. Terminal master's awarded for partial completion of doctoral program. *Degree requirements:* For doctorate, thesis/dissertation, comprehensive qualifying exam. *Entrance requirements:* For doctorate, GRE General Test, GRE Subject Test. Additional exam requirements/recommendations for international students: Required—TOEFL (minimum score 550 paper-based; 213 computer-based; 79 iBT). *Application deadline:* For fall admission, 3/15 priority date for domestic students, 3/1 priority date for international students. Application fee: $25 ($35 for international students). Electronic applications accepted. *Expenses:* Contact institution. *Financial support:* In 2010–11, 7 research assistantships with full tuition reimbursements (averaging $15,000 per year) were awarded; teaching assistantships with full tuition reimbursements, career-related internships or fieldwork, institutionally sponsored loans, scholarships/grants, and unspecified assistantships also available. Financial award application deadline: 7/1; financial award applicants required to submit FAFSA. Total annual research expenditures: $2.1 million. *Unit head:* Dr. Mitchell E. Robinson, Assistant Dean/Director, 423-439-4658, E-mail: robinson@etsu.edu. *Application contact:* Edwin D. Taylor, Assistant Dean for Admissions and Records, 423-439-4753, Fax: 423-439-8206.

Georgetown University, Graduate School of Arts and Sciences, Programs in Biomedical Sciences, Department of Physiology and Biophysics, Washington, DC 20057. Offers MS, PhD, MD/PhD. *Degree requirements:* For doctorate, thesis/dissertation. *Entrance requirements:* For master's, GRE General Test, MCAT; for doctorate, GRE General Test. Additional exam requirements/recommendations for international students: Required—TOEFL.

Georgia Health Sciences University, College of Graduate Studies, Program in Physiology, Augusta, GA 30912. Offers MS, PhD. *Faculty:* 14 full-time (5 women). *Students:* 16 full-time (14 women), 1 part-time (0 women); includes 1 Black or African American, non-Hispanic/Latino, 11 international. Average age 28. In 2010, 5 doctorates awarded. *Degree requirements:* For doctorate, comprehensive exam, thesis/dissertation. *Entrance requirements:* For doctorate, GRE General Test. Additional exam requirements/recommendations for international students: Required—TOEFL (minimum score 550 paper-based; 213 computer-based; 79 iBT). *Application deadline:* For fall admission, 1/15 for domestic and international students. Application fee: $30. Electronic applications accepted. *Expenses:* Tuition, state resident: full-time $7500; part-time $313 per semester hour. Tuition, nonresident: full-time $24,772; part-time $1033 per semester hour. Required fees: $1112. *Financial support:* In 2010–11, 1 student received support, including 4 fellowships with partial tuition reimbursements available (averaging $26,000 per year), 7 research assistantships with partial tuition reimbursements available (averaging $23,000 per year); Federal Work-Study, institutionally sponsored loans, scholarships/grants, and traineeships also available. Support available to part-time students. Financial award application deadline: 5/31; financial award applicants required to submit FAFSA. *Faculty research:* Cardiovascular and renal physiology, behavioral neuroscience and genetics, neurophysiology, adrenal steroid endocrinology and genetics, inflammatory mediators and cardiovascular disease, hypertension, diabetes and stroke. Total annual research expenditures: $5.1 million. *Unit head:* Dr. Clinton Webb, Chair and Professor, 706-721-7742, Fax: 706-721-7299, E-mail: cwebb@georgiahealth.edu. *Application contact:* Dr. Patricia L. Cameron, Acting Vice Dean, 706-721-3279, E-mail: pcameron@georgiahealth.edu.

Georgia Institute of Technology, Graduate Studies and Research, College of Sciences, School of Applied Physiology, Program in Prosthetics and Orthotics, Atlanta, GA 30332-0001. Offers MS.

Georgia State University, College of Arts and Sciences, Department of Biology, Program in Cellular and Molecular Biology and Physiology, Atlanta, GA 30302-3083. Offers MS, PhD. Part-time programs available. Terminal master's awarded for partial completion of doctoral program. *Degree requirements:* For master's, thesis or alternative; for doctorate, thesis/dissertation, exam. *Entrance requirements:* For master's and doctorate, GRE General Test. Additional exam requirements/recommendations for international students: Required—TOEFL.

Harvard University, Graduate School of Arts and Sciences, Department of Systems Biology, Cambridge, MA 02138. Offers PhD. *Degree requirements:* For doctorate, thesis/dissertation, lab rotation, qualifying examination. *Entrance requirements:* For doctorate, GRE. Additional exam requirements/recommendations for international students: Required—TOEFL. Electronic applications accepted. *Expenses:* Tuition: Full-time $34,976. Required fees: $1166. Full-time tuition and fees vary according to program.

Harvard University, Harvard School of Public Health, Department of Environmental Health, Boston, MA 02115-6096. Offers environmental health (MOH, SM, DPH, PhD, SD); occupational health (MOH, SM, DPH, SD); physiology (PhD, SD). Part-time programs available. *Faculty:* 47 full-time (11 women), 20 part-time/adjunct (5 women). *Students:* 76 full-time, 5 part-time; includes 4 Black or African American, non-Hispanic/Latino; 7 Asian, non-Hispanic/Latino, 36 international. Average age 29. 76 applicants, 47% accepted, 22 enrolled. In 2010, 15 master's, 12 doctorates awarded. *Degree requirements:* For doctorate, thesis/dissertation, qualifying exam. *Entrance requirements:* For master's and doctorate, GRE. Additional exam requirements/recommendations for international students: Required—TOEFL (minimum score 595 paper-based; 240 computer-based; 95 iBT); Recommended—IELTS (minimum score 7). *Application deadline:* For fall admission, 12/15 for domestic and international students. Application fee: $115. Electronic applications accepted. *Expenses:* Tuition: Full-time $34,976. Required fees: $1166. Full-time tuition and fees vary according to program. *Financial support:* Fellowships, research assistantships, teaching assistantships, career-related internships or fieldwork, Federal Work-Study, scholarships/grants, traineeships, tuition waivers (partial), and unspecified assistantships available. Support available to part-time students. Financial award application deadline: 2/8; financial award applicants required to submit FAFSA. *Faculty research:* Industrial hygiene and occupational safety, population genetics, indoor and outdoor air pollution, cell and molecular biology of the lungs, infectious diseases. *Unit head:* Dr. Douglas Dockery, Chairman, 617-432-1270, Fax: 617-432-6913. *Application contact:* Vincent W. James, Director of Admissions, 617-432-1031, Fax: 617-432-7080, E-mail: admissions@hsph.harvard.edu.

Howard University, Graduate School, Department of Physiology and Biophysics, Washington, DC 20059-0002. Offers biophysics (PhD); physiology (PhD). *Degree requirements:* For doctorate, comprehensive exam, thesis/dissertation. *Entrance requirements:* For doctorate, GRE General Test, minimum B average in field. *Faculty research:* Cardiovascular physiology, pulmonary physiology, renal physiology, neurophysiology, endocrinology.

Illinois State University, Graduate School, College of Arts and Sciences, Department of Biological Sciences, Normal, IL 61790-2200. Offers animal behavior (MS); bacteriology (MS); biochemistry (MS); biological sciences (MS); biology (PhD); biophysics (MS); biotechnology (MS); botany (MS, PhD); cell biology (MS); conservation biology (MS); developmental biology (MS); ecology (MS, PhD); entomology (MS); evolutionary biology (MS); genetics (MS, PhD); immunology (MS); microbiology (MS, PhD); molecular biology (MS); molecular genetics (MS); neurobiology (MS); neuroscience (MS); parasitology (MS); physiology (MS, PhD); plant biology (MS); plant molecular biology (MS); plant sciences (MS); structural biology (MS); zoology (MS, PhD). Part-time programs available. *Degree requirements:* For master's, thesis or alternative; for doctorate, variable foreign language requirement, thesis/dissertation, 2 terms of residency. *Entrance requirements:* For master's, GRE General Test, minimum GPA of 2.6 in last 60 hours of course work; for doctorate, GRE General Test. *Faculty research:* Redoc balance and drug development in schistosoma mansoni, control of the growth of listeria monocytogenes at low temperature, regulation of cell expansion and microtubule function by SPRI, CRUI: physiology and fitness consequences of different life history phenotypes.

Indiana State University, College of Graduate and Professional Studies, College of Arts and Sciences, Department of Biology, Terre Haute, IN 47809. Offers ecology (PhD); life sciences (MS); microbiology (PhD); physiology (PhD); science education (MS). *Degree requirements:* For master's, thesis (for some programs); for doctorate, comprehensive exam, thesis/dissertation. *Entrance requirements:* For master's and doctorate, GRE General Test. Electronic applications accepted.

The Johns Hopkins University, Bloomberg School of Public Health, Department of Environmental Health Sciences, Baltimore, MD 21218-2699. Offers environmental health engineering (PhD); environmental health sciences (MHS, Dr PH); occupational and environmental health (PhD); occupational and environmental hygiene (MHS, MHS); physiology (PhD); toxicology (PhD). Postbaccalaureate distance learning degree programs offered (minimal on-campus study). *Faculty:* 71 full-time (27 women), 58 part-time/adjunct (26 women). *Students:* 66 full-time (38 women), 19 part-time (12 women); includes 25 minority (3 Black or African American, non-Hispanic/Latino; 13 Asian, non-Hispanic/Latino; 4 Hispanic/Latino; 5 Two or more races, non-Hispanic/Latino), 11 international. Average age 30. 101 applicants, 49% accepted, 31 enrolled. In 2010, 21 master's, 14 doctorates awarded. *Degree requirements:* For master's, essay, presentation; for doctorate, comprehensive exam, thesis/dissertation, 1 year full-time residency, oral and written exams. *Entrance requirements:* For master's, GRE General Test or MCAT, 3 letters of recommendation, transcripts; for doctorate, GRE General Test or MCAT, 3 letters of recommendation. Additional exam requirements/recommendations for international students: Required—TOEFL (minimum score 600 paper-based; 250 computer-based). *Application deadline:* For fall admission, 12/15 priority date for domestic and international students. Applications are processed on a rolling basis. Application fee: $45. Electronic applications accepted. *Financial support:* In 2010–11, 5 fellowships with full tuition reimbursements (averaging $26,500 per year) were awarded; Federal Work-Study, institutionally sponsored loans, scholarships/grants, traineeships, health care benefits, and stipends also available. Support available to part-time students. Financial award application deadline: 3/15; financial award applicants required to submit FAFSA. *Faculty research:* Chemical carcinogenesis/toxicology, lung disease, occupational and environmental health, nuclear imaging, molecular epidemiology. Total annual research expenditures: $23.7 million. *Unit head:* Dr. John Davis Groopman, Chair, 410-955-3720, Fax: 410-955-0617, E-mail: jgroopma@jhsph.edu. *Application contact:* Nina J. Kulacki, Academic Program Manager, 410-955-2212, Fax: 410-955-0617, E-mail: nkulacki@jhsph.edu.

The Johns Hopkins University, School of Medicine, Graduate Programs in Medicine, Department of Physiology, Baltimore, MD 21205. Offers cellular and molecular physiology (PhD); physiology (PhD). *Faculty:* 19 full-time (6 women). *Students:* 19 full-time (9 women); includes 2 minority (both Black or African American, non-Hispanic/Latino), 13 international. Average age 23. 50 applicants, 4% accepted, 2 enrolled. *Degree requirements:* For doctorate, thesis/dissertation, oral and qualifying exams. *Entrance requirements:* For doctorate, GRE General Test, previous course work in biology, calculus, chemistry, and physics. Additional exam requirements/recommendations for international students: Required—TOEFL. *Application deadline:* For fall admission, 1/10 for domestic and international students. Application fee: $85. Electronic applications accepted. *Financial support:* In 2010–11, 2 students received support, including 2 fellowships with full tuition reimbursements available (averaging $26,855 per year), research assistantships with full tuition reimbursements available (averaging $26,855 per year), teaching assistantships with full tuition reimbursements available (averaging $26,855 per year); scholarships/grants, traineeships, tuition waivers (full), unspecified assistantships, and stipends also available. Financial award application deadline: 1/10. *Faculty research:* Membrane biochemistry and biophysics; signal transduction; developmental genetics and physiology; physiology and biochemistry; transporters, carriers, and ion channels. *Unit head:* Dr. William B. Guggino, Director, 410-955-7166, Fax: 410-955-0461. *Application contact:* Madeline J. McLaughlin, Academic Program Manager, 410-955-8333, Fax: 410-955-0461, E-mail: mmclaugh@jhmi.edu.

Kansas State University, College of Veterinary Medicine, Department of Anatomy and Physiology, Manhattan, KS 66506. Offers physiology (PhD). Terminal master's awarded for partial completion of doctoral program. *Degree requirements:* For doctorate, one foreign language, thesis/dissertation. *Entrance requirements:* Additional exam requirements/recommendations for international students: Required—TOEFL (minimum score 550 paper-based; 213 computer-based). Electronic applications accepted. *Faculty research:* Cardiovascular and pulmonary, immunophysiology, neuroscience, pharmacology, epithelial.

Kent State University, College of Arts and Sciences, Department of Biological Sciences, Program in Physiology, Kent, OH 44242-0001. Offers MS, PhD. *Degree requirements:* For master's, thesis; for doctorate, thesis/dissertation. *Entrance requirements:* For master's, GRE General Test, minimum GPA of 3.0; for doctorate, GRE General Test, minimum GPA of 3.25. Additional exam requirements/recommendations for international students: Required—TOEFL (minimum score 600 paper-based; 257 computer-based). *Expenses:* Tuition, state resident: full-time $7866; part-time $437 per credit hour. Tuition, nonresident: full-time $14,022; part-time $779 per credit hour.

Kent State University, School of Biomedical Sciences, Program in Physiology, Kent, OH 44242-0001. Offers MS, PhD. *Degree requirements:* For master's, thesis; for doctorate, thesis/dissertation. *Entrance requirements:* For master's and doctorate, GRE General Test, minimum GPA of 3.0, 3 letters of recommendation. Additional exam requirements/recommendations for international students: Required—TOEFL (minimum score 600 paper-based; 287 computer-based). Electronic applications accepted. *Expenses:* Tuition, state resident: full-time $7866; part-time $437 per credit hour. Tuition, nonresident: full-time $14,022; part-time $779 per credit hour.

Loma Linda University, School of Medicine, Department of Physiology/Pharmacology, Loma Linda, CA 92350. Offers MS, PhD. Part-time programs available. *Degree requirements:* For master's, thesis or alternative; for doctorate, 2 foreign languages, thesis/dissertation. *Entrance requirements:* For master's and doctorate, GRE General Test. *Faculty research:* Drug metabolism, biochemical pharmacology, structure and function of cell membranes, neuropharmacology.

Louisiana State University Health Sciences Center, School of Graduate Studies in New Orleans, Department of Physiology, New Orleans, LA 70112-2223. Offers MS, PhD, MD/PhD. Terminal master's awarded for partial completion of doctoral program. *Degree requirements:* For master's, comprehensive exam, thesis; for doctorate, comprehensive exam, thesis/dissertation. *Entrance requirements:* For master's and doctorate, GRE General Test. Additional exam requirements/recommendations for international students: Required—TOEFL. *Faculty research:* Host defense, lipoprotein metabolism, regulation of cardiopulmonary function, alcohol and drug abuse, cell to cell communication, cytokinesis, physiologic functions of nitric oxide.

Louisiana State University Health Sciences Center at Shreveport, Department of Molecular and Cellular Physiology, Shreveport, LA 71130-3932. Offers physiology (MS, PhD); MD/PhD. *Degree requirements:* For master's, thesis; for doctorate, thesis/dissertation. *Entrance requirements:* For master's and doctorate, GRE General Test. Additional exam requirements/recommendations for international students: Required—TOEFL. *Faculty research:* Cardiovascular, gastrointestinal, renal, and neutrophil function; cellular detoxification systems; hypoxia and mitochondria function.

Loyola University Chicago, Graduate School, Programs in Cell and Molecular Physiology, Chicago, IL 60660. Offers MS, PhD. MS offered only to students enrolled in a first-professional degree program. *Faculty:* 17 full-time (4 women), 5 part-time/adjunct (1 woman). *Students:* 6 full-time (1 woman), 3 international. Average age 29. 6 applicants, 0% accepted, 0 enrolled. In 2010, 1 master's awarded. *Degree requirements:* For master's, thesis; for doctorate, comprehensive exam, thesis/dissertation. *Entrance requirements:* For master's, GRE General Test or MCAT; for doctorate, GRE General Test. Additional exam requirements/recommendations for international students: Required—TOEFL. *Application deadline:* For fall admission, 5/15 for domestic and international students. Application fee: $0. Electronic applications accepted. *Expenses:* Tuition: Full-time $14,940; part-time $830 per credit hour. Required fees: $87 per semester. Part-time tuition and fees vary according to course load and program. *Financial support:* In 2010–11, 5 fellowships with tuition reimbursements (averaging $23,000 per year), 9 research assistantships with tuition reimbursements (averaging $23,000 per year) were awarded. *Faculty research:* Cardiovascular system-emphasis in neural and metabolic control of circulation, ion channels, excitation contraction coupling, molecular cloning. *Unit head:* Dr. Pieter deTombe, Chair, 708-216-6305, Fax: 708-216-6308, E-mail: pdetombe@lumc.edu. *Application contact:* Dr. Ruben Mestril, Graduate Program Director, 708-327-2395, Fax: 708-216-6308, E-mail: rmestri@lumc.edu.

Marquette University, Graduate School, College of Arts and Sciences, Department of Biology, Milwaukee, WI 53201-1881. Offers cell biology (MS, PhD); developmental biology (MS, PhD); ecology (MS, PhD); epithelial physiology (MS, PhD); genetics (MS, PhD); microbiology (MS, PhD); molecular biology (MS, PhD); muscle and exercise physiology (MS, PhD); neuroscience (PhD). *Faculty:* 25 full-time (12 women), 2 part-time/adjunct (1 woman). *Students:* 23 full-time (9 women), 12 part-time (8 women); includes 1 minority (Asian, non-Hispanic/Latino), 15 international. Average age 26. 82 applicants, 15% accepted, 5 enrolled. In 2010, 3 master's, 2 doctorates awarded. Terminal master's awarded for partial completion of doctoral program. *Degree requirements:* For master's, comprehensive exam, thesis, 1 year of teaching experience or equivalent; for doctorate, thesis/dissertation, 1 year of teaching experience or equivalent, qualifying exam. *Entrance requirements:* For master's and doctorate, GRE General Test, GRE Subject Test, official transcripts from all current and previous colleges/universities except Marquette, statement of professional goals and aspirations, three letters of recommendation. Additional exam requirements/recommendations for international students: Required—TOEFL (minimum score 530 paper-based; 78 computer-based). *Application deadline:* For fall admission, 12/15 for domestic and international students. Application fee: $50. Electronic applications accepted. *Expenses:* Tuition: Full-time $16,290; part-time $905 per credit hour. Tuition and fees vary according to program. *Financial support:* In 2010–11, 2 research assistantships, 34 teaching assistantships were awarded; fellowships, Federal Work-Study, institutionally sponsored loans, scholarships/grants, and tuition waivers (full and partial) also available. Support available to part-time students. Financial award application deadline: 2/15. *Faculty research:* Neurobiology, neuroendocrinology, epithelial physiology, neuropeptide interactions, synaptic transmission. Total annual research expenditures: $1.3 million. *Unit head:* Dr. Robert Fitts, Chair, 414-288-1748, Fax: 414-288-7357. *Application contact:* Debbie Weaver, Administrative Assistant, 414-288-7355, Fax: 414-288-7357.

McGill University, Faculty of Graduate and Postdoctoral Studies, Faculty of Medicine, Department of Physiology, Montréal, QC H3A 2T5, Canada. Offers M Sc, PhD.

McMaster University, Faculty of Health Sciences and School of Graduate Studies, Program in Medical Sciences, Physiology/Pharmacology Area, Hamilton, ON L8S 4M2, Canada. Offers M Sc, PhD, MD/PhD. *Degree requirements:* For master's, thesis; for doctorate, comprehensive exam, thesis/dissertation. *Entrance requirements:* For master's, honors B Sc, B+ average in related field; for doctorate, M Sc, minimum B+ average, students with proven research experience and an A average may be admitted with a B Sc degree. Additional exam requirements/recommendations for international students: Required—TOEFL (minimum score 580 paper-based; 237 computer-based; 92 iBT).

Medical College of Wisconsin, Graduate School of Biomedical Sciences, Department of Physiology, Milwaukee, WI 53226-0509. Offers PhD, MD/PhD. *Degree requirements:* For doctorate, comprehensive exam, thesis/dissertation. *Entrance requirements:* For doctorate, GRE General Test. Additional exam requirements/recommendations for international students: Required—TOEFL. *Expenses:* Tuition: Full-time $30,000; part-time $710 per credit. Required fees: $150. *Faculty research:* Cardiovascular, respiratory, renal, and exercise physiology; mathematical modeling; molecular and cellular biology.

Michigan State University, College of Human Medicine and The Graduate School, Graduate Programs in Human Medicine, East Lansing, MI 48824. Offers biochemistry and molecular biology (MS, PhD); epidemiology (MS, PhD); microbiology (MS); microbiology and molecular genetics (PhD); pharmacology and toxicology (MS, PhD); physiology (MS, PhD); public health (MPH). *Entrance requirements:* Additional exam requirements/recommendations for international students: Required—TOEFL.

Michigan State University, College of Osteopathic Medicine and The Graduate School, Graduate Studies in Osteopathic Medicine, East Lansing, MI 48824. Offers biochemistry and molecular biology (MS, PhD); microbiology (MS); microbiology and molecular genetics (PhD); pharmacology and toxicology (MS, PhD), including integrative pharmacology (MS), pharmacology and toxicology, pharmacology and toxicology-environmental toxicology (PhD); physiology (MS, PhD).

Michigan State University, College of Veterinary Medicine and The Graduate School, Graduate Programs in Veterinary Medicine, East Lansing, MI 48824. Offers comparative medicine and integrative biology (MS, PhD), including comparative medicine and integrative biology, comparative medicine and integrative biology–environmental toxicology (PhD); food safety and toxicology (MS), including food safety; integrative toxicology (PhD), including animal science–environmental toxicology, biochemistry and molecular biology–environmental toxicology, chemistry–environmental toxicology, crop and soil sciences–environmental toxicology, environmental engineering–environmental toxicology, environmental geosciences–environmental toxicology, fisheries and wildlife–environmental toxicology, food science–environmental toxicology, forestry–environmental toxicology, genetics–environmental toxicology, human nutrition–environmental toxicology, microbiology–environmental toxicology, pharmacology and toxicology–environmental toxicology, zoology–environmental toxicology; large animal clinical sciences (MS, PhD); microbiology and molecular genetics (MS, PhD), including industrial microbiology, microbiology, microbiology and molecular genetics, microbiology–environmental toxicology (PhD); pathobiology and diagnostic investigation (MS, PhD), including pathology, pathology–environmental toxicology (PhD); pharmacology and toxicology (MS, PhD); pharmacology and toxicology–environmental toxicology (PhD); physiology (MS, PhD); small animal clinical sciences (MS). Electronic applications accepted. *Faculty research:* Molecular genetics, food safety/toxicology, comparative orthopedics, airway disease, population medicine.

Michigan State University, The Graduate School, College of Natural Science and Graduate Programs in Human Medicine and Graduate Studies in Osteopathic Medicine, Department of Physiology, East Lansing, MI 48824. Offers MS, PhD. *Entrance requirements:* Additional exam requirements/recommendations for international students: Required—TOEFL (minimum score 600 paper-based; 220 computer-based). Electronic applications accepted.

Montclair State University, The Graduate School, College of Science and Mathematics, Department of Biology and Molecular Biology, Montclair, NJ 07043-1624. Offers biological science (Certificate); biology (MS), including biology, biology science/education, ecology and evolution, physiology; molecular biology (MS, Certificate). Part-time and evening/weekend programs available. *Faculty:* 22 full-time (9 women), 26 part-time/adjunct (13 women). *Students:* 30 full-time (20 women), 73 part-time (55 women); includes 5 Black or African American, non-Hispanic/Latino; 6 Asian, non-Hispanic/Latino; 25 Hispanic/Latino, 3 international. Average age 28. 48 applicants, 71% accepted, 24 enrolled. In 2010, 21 master's, 2 other advanced degrees awarded. *Degree requirements:* For master's, comprehensive exam, thesis or alternative. *Entrance requirements:* For master's, GRE General Test, 24 credits of course work in undergraduate biology, 2 letters of recommendation, teaching certificate (biology sciences education concentration). Additional exam requirements/recommendations for international students: Required—TOEFL (minimum iBT score of 83) or IELTS. *Application deadline:* For fall admission, 6/1 for international students; for spring admission, 10/1 for international students. Applications are processed on a rolling basis. Application fee: $60. Electronic applications accepted. *Expenses:* Tuition, state resident: part-time $501.34 per credit. Tuition, nonresident: part-time $773.88 per credit. Required fees: $71.15 per credit. *Financial support:* In 2010–11, 12 research assistantships with full tuition reimbursements (averaging $7,000 per year) were awarded; Federal Work-Study, scholarships/grants, and unspecified assistantships also available. Support available to part-time students. Financial award application deadline: 3/1; financial award applicants required to submit FAFSA. *Faculty research:* Cells, algae blooms, scallops, New Jersey bays, Barnegat Bay. Total annual research expenditures: $1.3 million. *Unit head:* Dr. Quinn Vega, Chairperson, 973-655-7178. *Application contact:* Amy Aiello, Director of Graduate Admissions and Operations, 973-655-5147, Fax: 973-655-7869, E-mail: graduate.school@montclair.edu.

New York Medical College, Graduate School of Basic Medical Sciences, Program in Physiology, Valhalla, NY 10595-1691. Offers MS, PhD, MD/PhD. Part-time and evening/weekend programs available. *Faculty:* 24 full-time (4 women), 1 (woman) part-time/adjunct. *Students:* 17 full-time (10 women), 1 (woman) part-time; includes 4 minority (2 Black or African American, non-Hispanic/Latino; 2 Asian, non-Hispanic/Latino), 6 international. Average age 27. 5 applicants, 100% accepted, 2 enrolled. In 2010, 11 master's awarded. Terminal master's awarded for partial completion of doctoral program. *Degree requirements:* For master's, thesis; for doctorate, comprehensive exam, thesis/dissertation. *Entrance requirements:* For master's and doctorate, GRE General Test. Additional exam requirements/recommendations for international students: Required—TOEFL. *Application deadline:* For fall admission, 7/1 priority date for domestic students, 5/1 priority date for international students; for spring admission, 12/1 priority date for domestic students, 10/1 priority date for international students. Applications are processed on a rolling basis. Application fee: $50 ($75 for international students). Electronic applications accepted. *Financial support:* In 2010–11, 1 fellowship, 8 research assistantships with full tuition reimbursements (averaging $24,000 per year) were awarded; Federal Work-Study, institutionally sponsored loans, scholarships/grants, traineeships, health care benefits, tuition waivers, unspecified assistantships, and health benefits (for PhD candidates only) also available. Financial award applicants required to submit FAFSA. *Faculty research:* Cardiovascular physiology, aging physiology, developmental physiology, endocrine physiology, neurophysiology, cell biology. *Unit head:* Dr. Carl I. Thompson, Director, 914-594-4106, Fax: 914-594-4966, E-mail: carl_thompson@nymc.edu. *Application contact:* Valerie Romeo-Messana, Admission Coordinator, 914-594-4110, Fax: 914-594-4944, E-mail: v_romeomessana@nymc.edu.

New York University, School of Medicine, New York, NY 10012-1019. Offers biomedical sciences (PhD), including biomedical imaging, cellular and molecular biology, computational biology, developmental genetics, medical and molecular parasitology, microbiology, molecular oncobiology and immunology, neuroscience and physiology, pathobiology, pharmacology, structural biology; clinical investigation (MS); medicine (MD); MD/MA; MD/MPA; MD/MS; MD/PhD. *Accreditation:* LCME/AMA (one or more programs are accredited). *Degree requirements:* For master's, comprehensive exam, thesis; for doctorate, comprehensive exam, thesis/dissertation. *Entrance requirements:* MCAT. Additional exam requirements/recommendations for international students: Required—TOEFL. *Expenses:* Contact institution. *Faculty research:* AIDS, cancer, neuroscience, molecular biology, neuroscience, cell biology and molecular genetics, structural biology, microbial pathogenesis and host defense, pharmacology, molecular oncology and immunology.

New York University, School of Medicine and Graduate School of Arts and Science, Sackler Institute of Graduate Biomedical Sciences, Department of Neuroscience and Physiology, New York, NY 10012-1019. Offers PhD, MD/PhD. *Degree requirements:* For doctorate, one foreign language, comprehensive exam, thesis/dissertation, qualifying exam. *Entrance requirements:* For doctorate, GRE General Test. Additional exam requirements/recommendations for international students: Required—TOEFL. *Faculty research:* Synaptic transmission, retinal physiology, signal transduction, CNS intrinsic properties, cerebellar function.

North Carolina State University, Graduate School, College of Agriculture and Life Sciences and College of Veterinary Medicine, Program in Physiology, Raleigh, NC 27695. Offers MP, MS, PhD. *Degree requirements:* For master's, thesis (for some programs); for doctorate, thesis/dissertation. *Entrance requirements:* For master's and doctorate, GRE General Test.

Physiology

North Carolina State University (continued)

Electronic applications accepted. *Faculty research:* Neurophysiology, gastrointestinal physiology, reproductive physiology, environmental/stress physiology, cardiovascular physiology.

Northwestern University, The Graduate School, Judd A. and Marjorie Weinberg College of Arts and Sciences, Department of Neurobiology and Physiology, Evanston, IL 60208. Offers MS. Admissions and degrees offered through The Graduate School. Part-time programs available. *Degree requirements:* For master's, thesis. *Entrance requirements:* For master's, GRE General Test and MCAT (strongly recommended). Additional exam requirements/recommendations for international students: Required—TOEFL. Electronic applications accepted. *Expenses:* Contact institution. *Faculty research:* Sensory neurobiology and neuroendocrinology, reproductive biology, vision physiology and psychophysics, cell and developmental biology.

Nova Scotia Agricultural College, Research and Graduate Studies, Truro, NS B2N 5E3, Canada. Offers agriculture (M Sc), including air quality, animal behavior, animal molecular genetics, animal nutrition, animal technology, aquaculture, botany, crop management, crop physiology, ecology, environmental microbiology, food science, horticulture, nutrient management, pest management, physiology, plant biotechnology, plant pathology, soil chemistry, soil fertility, waste management and composting, water quality. Program offered jointly with Dalhousie University. Part-time programs available. *Degree requirements:* For master's, thesis, ATC Exam Teaching Assistantship. *Entrance requirements:* For master's, honors B Sc, minimum GPA of 3.0. Additional exam requirements/recommendations for international students: Required—TOEFL (minimum score 580 paper-based; 237 computer-based; 92 iBT), IELTS, Michigan English Language Assessment Battery, CanTEST, CAEL. *Faculty research:* Bio-product development, organic agriculture, nutrient management, air and water quality, agricultural biotechnology.

The Ohio State University, College of Veterinary Medicine, Department of Veterinary Biosciences, Columbus, OH 43210. Offers anatomy and cellular biology (MS, PhD); pathobiology (MS, PhD); pharmacology (MS, PhD); toxicology (MS, PhD); veterinary physiology (MS, PhD). *Faculty:* 45. *Students:* 4 full-time (all women), 7 part-time (5 women); includes 1 Black or African American, non-Hispanic/Latino, 3 international. Average age 30. In 2010, 2 master's, 7 doctorates awarded. *Entrance requirements:* For master's and doctorate, GRE General Test. Additional exam requirements/recommendations for international students: Required—TOEFL. *Application deadline:* Applications are processed on a rolling basis. Application fee: $40 ($50 for international students). Electronic applications accepted. *Expenses:* Tuition, state resident: full-time $10,605. Tuition, nonresident: full-time $26,535. Tuition and fees vary according to course load and program. *Faculty research:* Microvasculature, muscle biology, neonatal lung and bone development. *Unit head:* Dr. Michael J. Oglesbee, Graduate Studies Committee Chair, 614-292-5661, Fax: 614-292-6473, E-mail: oglesbee.1@osu.edu. *Application contact:* Graduate Admissions, 614-292-9444, Fax: 614-292-3895, E-mail: domestic.grad@osu.edu.

Ohio University, Graduate College, College of Arts and Sciences, Department of Biological Sciences, Athens, OH 45701-2979. Offers biological sciences (MS, PhD); cell biology and physiology (MS, PhD); ecology and evolutionary biology (MS, PhD); exercise physiology and muscle biology (MS, PhD); microbiology (MS, PhD); neuroscience (MS, PhD). *Students:* 32 full-time (9 women), 5 part-time (2 women); includes 2 minority (1 Black or African American, non-Hispanic/Latino; 1 Hispanic/Latino), 9 international. 51 applicants, 37% accepted, 7 enrolled. In 2010, 2 master's, 9 doctorates awarded. Terminal master's awarded for partial completion of doctoral program. *Degree requirements:* For master's, comprehensive exam, thesis, 1 quarter of teaching experience; for doctorate, comprehensive exam, thesis/dissertation, 2 quarters of teaching experience. *Entrance requirements:* For master's, GRE General Test, names of three faculty members whose research interests most closely match the applicant's interest; for doctorate, GRE General Test, essay concerning prior training, research interest and career goals, plus names of three faculty members whose research interests most closely match the applicant's interest. Additional exam requirements/recommendations for international students: Required—TOEFL (minimum score 620 paper-based; 105 iBT) or IELTS (minimum score 7.5). *Application deadline:* For fall admission, 1/15 for domestic and international students. Application fee: $50 ($55 for international students). Electronic applications accepted. *Financial support:* In 2010–11, 1 fellowship with full tuition reimbursement (averaging $18,957 per year), 10 research assistantships with full tuition reimbursements (averaging $18,957 per year), 42 teaching assistantships with full tuition reimbursements (averaging $18,957 per year) were awarded; Federal Work-Study and institutionally sponsored loans also available. Financial award application deadline: 1/15. *Faculty research:* Ecology and evolutionary biology, exercise physiology and muscle biology, neurobiology, cell biology, physiology. Total annual research expenditures: $2.8 million. *Unit head:* Dr. Ralph DiCaprio, Chair, 740-593-2290, Fax: 740-593-0300, E-mail: dicapri r@ohio.edu. *Application contact:* Dr. Patrick Hassett, Graduate Chair, 740-593-4793, Fax: 740-593-0300, E-mail: hassett@ohio.edu.

Oregon Health & Science University, School of Medicine, Graduate Programs in Medicine, Program in Molecular and Cellular Biosciences, Department of Physiology and Pharmacology, Portland, OR 97239-3098. Offers PhD. *Faculty:* 18. *Students:* 11 full-time (7 women); includes 1 Black or African American, non-Hispanic/Latino; 1 American Indian or Alaska Native, non-Hispanic/Latino; 1 Asian, non-Hispanic/Latino, 2 international. Average age 28. In 2010, 3 doctorates awarded. *Degree requirements:* For doctorate, comprehensive exam, thesis/dissertation. *Entrance requirements:* For doctorate, GRE General Test (minimum scores: 500 Verbal/600 Quantitative/4.5 Analytical) or MCAT (for some programs). Additional exam requirements/recommendations for international students: Required—TOEFL. Electronic applications accepted. *Financial support:* Full tuition and stipends available. *Unit head:* Dr. Beth Habecker, Program Director, 503-494-6252, E-mail: habecker@ohsu.edu. *Application contact:* Julie Walvatne, Program Coordinator, 503-494-6252.

Penn State Hershey Medical Center, College of Medicine, Graduate School Programs in the Biomedical Sciences, The Huck Institutes of the Life Sciences, Intercollege Graduate Program in Physiology, Hershey, PA 17033. Offers MS, PhD, MD/PhD. *Students:* 40 applicants, 23% accepted, 6 enrolled. In 2010, 2 master's, 4 doctorates awarded. Terminal master's awarded for partial completion of doctoral program. *Degree requirements:* For master's, thesis or alternative; for doctorate, comprehensive exam, thesis/dissertation, oral exam. *Entrance requirements:* For master's, GRE General Test or MCAT; for doctorate, GRE General Test or MCAT, minimum GPA of 3.0. Additional exam requirements/recommendations for international students: Required—TOEFL (minimum score 500 paper-based; 213 computer-based). *Application deadline:* For fall admission, 1/31 priority date for domestic students, 2/1 priority date for international students. Applications are processed on a rolling basis. Application fee: $65. Electronic applications accepted. *Financial support:* In 2010–11, research assistantships with full tuition reimbursements (averaging $22,260 per year); fellowships with full tuition reimbursements, career-related internships or fieldwork, scholarships/grants, traineeships, health care benefits, and unspecified assistantships also available. Financial award applicants required to submit FAFSA. *Faculty research:* Gene expression, diabetes obesity and insulin resistance, DNA repair and carcinogenesis, telomerase cell senescence and cancer, ion channels and cardiovascular function. *Unit head:* Dr. Leonard S. Jefferson, Chair, 717-531-8566, Fax: 717-531-7667, E-mail: physio-grad-hmc@psu.edu. *Application contact:* Lisa Harman, Secretary, 717-531-8566, Fax: 717-531-7667, E-mail: physio-grad-hmc@psu.edu.

Penn State University Park, Graduate School, Intercollege Graduate Programs, Intercollege Graduate Program in Physiology, State College, University Park, PA 16802-1503. Offers MS, PhD. *Unit head:* Dr. Leonard Jefferson, Chair, 717-531-8567, Fax: 814-865-9451. *Application contact:* Dr. Leonard Jefferson, Chair, 717-531-8567, Fax: 814-865-9451.

Purdue University, School of Veterinary Medicine and Graduate School, Graduate Programs in Veterinary Medicine, Department of Basic Medical Sciences, West Lafayette, IN 47907. Offers anatomy (MS, PhD); pharmacology (MS, PhD); physiology (MS, PhD). Part-time programs available. Terminal master's awarded for partial completion of doctoral program. *Degree requirements:* For master's, thesis; for doctorate, thesis/dissertation. *Entrance requirements:* For master's and doctorate, GRE General Test. Additional exam requirements/recommendations for international students: Required—TOEFL. Electronic applications accepted. *Faculty research:* Development and regeneration, tissue injury and shock, biomedical engineering, ovarian function, bone and cartilage biology, cell and molecular biology.

Queen's University at Kingston, School of Graduate Studies and Research, Faculty of Health Sciences, Department of Physiology, Kingston, ON K7L 3N6, Canada. Offers M Sc, PhD. *Degree requirements:* For master's, thesis; for doctorate, comprehensive exam, thesis/dissertation. *Entrance requirements:* For master's, minimum upper B average. Additional exam requirements/recommendations for international students: Required—TOEFL. *Faculty research:* Cardiovascular and respiratory physiology, exercise, gastrointestinal physiology, neuroscience.

Rocky Mountain University of Health Professions, Doctor of Science Program in Clinical Electrophysiology, Provo, UT 84606. Offers D Sc. *Students:* 14 part-time (1 woman); includes 1 Black or African American, non-Hispanic/Latino. Average age 43. *Degree requirements:* For doctorate, thesis/dissertation. *Entrance requirements:* For doctorate, clinical entry-level master's or doctorate degree; professional licensure as a chiropractor, nurse practitioner, occupational therapist, physical therapist, physician or physician assistant; minimum of 100 hours experience in electroneuromyography. *Application deadline:* For fall admission, 7/26 for domestic students. *Expenses:* Tuition: Full-time $15,600; part-time $650 per credit. Required fees: $50 per course. *Unit head:* Dr. Lisa DePasquale, Co-Director, 801-375-5125, E-mail: ldepasquale@rmuohp.edu. *Application contact:* Bryce Greenberg, Director of Admissions, 801-734-6832, Fax: 801-734-6833, E-mail: bgreenberg@rmuohp.edu.

Rosalind Franklin University of Medicine and Science, School of Graduate and Post-doctoral Studies—Interdisciplinary Graduate Program in Biomedical Sciences, Department of Physiology and Biophysics, North Chicago, IL 60064-3095. Offers MS, PhD, MD/PhD. Terminal master's awarded for partial completion of doctoral program. *Degree requirements:* For master's, comprehensive exam, thesis; for doctorate, comprehensive exam, thesis/dissertation. *Entrance requirements:* For master's and doctorate, GRE General Test. Additional exam requirements/recommendations for international students: Required—TOEFL, TWE. *Faculty research:* Membrane transport, mechanisms of cellular regulation, brain metabolism, peptide metabolism.

Rush University, Graduate College, Department of Molecular Biophysics and Physiology, Chicago, IL 60612-3832. Offers physiology (PhD); MD/PhD. *Degree requirements:* For doctorate, thesis/dissertation. *Entrance requirements:* For doctorate, GRE General Test. Additional exam requirements/recommendations for international students: Required—TOEFL. *Faculty research:* Physiological exocytosis, raft formation and growth, voltage-gated proton channels, molecular biophysics and physiology.

Rutgers, The State University of New Jersey, New Brunswick, Graduate School-New Brunswick, Program in Endocrinology and Animal Biosciences, Piscataway, NJ 08854-8097. Offers MS, PhD. Terminal master's awarded for partial completion of doctoral program. *Degree requirements:* For master's, thesis; for doctorate, comprehensive exam, thesis/dissertation. *Entrance requirements:* For master's and doctorate, GRE General Test. Additional exam requirements/recommendations for international students: Required—TOEFL. Electronic applications accepted. *Expenses:* Tuition, state resident: full-time $7200; part-time $600 per credit. Tuition, nonresident: full-time $11,124; part-time $927 per credit. *Faculty research:* Comparative and behavioral endocrinology, epigenetic regulation of the endocrine system, exercise physiology and immunology, fetal and neonatal developmental programming, mammary gland biology and breast cancer, neuroendocrinology and alcohol studies, reproductive and developmental toxicology.

Saint Louis University, Graduate Education and School of Medicine, Graduate Program in Biomedical Sciences and Graduate Education, Department of Pharmacological and Physiological Science, St. Louis, MO 63103-2097. Offers PhD. *Degree requirements:* For doctorate, comprehensive exam, thesis/dissertation, departmental qualifying exams. *Entrance requirements:* For doctorate, GRE General Test (GRE Subject Test optional), letters of recommendation, resume, interview. Additional exam requirements/recommendations for international students: Required—TOEFL (minimum score 525 paper-based; 194 computer-based). Electronic applications accepted. *Faculty research:* Molecular endocrinology, neuropharmacology, cardiovascular science, drug abuse, neurotransmitter and hormonal signaling mechanisms.

Salisbury University, Graduate Division, Program in Applied Health Physiology, Salisbury, MD 21801-6837. Offers MS. Part-time and evening/weekend programs available. *Faculty:* 5 full-time (0 women), 2 part-time/adjunct (0 women). *Students:* 27 full-time (12 women), 20 part-time (10 women); includes 6 minority (4 Black or African American, non-Hispanic/Latino; 1 Hispanic/Latino; 1 Two or more races, non-Hispanic/Latino), 1 international. Average age 26. 41 applicants, 73% accepted, 9 enrolled. In 2010, 20 master's awarded. *Degree requirements:* For master's, fieldwork. *Entrance requirements:* For master's, minimum GPA of 2.75, undergraduate course work in anatomy and physiology. Additional exam requirements/recommendations for international students: Required—TOEFL (minimum score 550 paper-based; 213 computer-based; 79 iBT). *Application deadline:* For fall admission, 8/1 for domestic students; for spring admission, 1/1 for domestic students. Applications are processed on a rolling basis. Application fee: $45. *Financial support:* In 2010–11, 20 students received support. Applicants required to submit FAFSA. *Faculty research:* Body image and self-concept, muscle physiology, pulmonary rehabilitation, non-invasive ventilation. *Unit head:* Dr. Sidney R. Schneider, 410-543-6409, Fax: 410-548-9185, E-mail: srschneider@salisbury.edu. *Application contact:* Dr. Sidney R. Schneider, 410-543-6409, Fax: 410-548-9185, E-mail: srschneider@salisbury.edu.

San Francisco State University, Division of Graduate Studies, College of Science and Engineering, Department of Biology, Program in Physiology and Behavioral Biology, San Francisco, CA 94132-1722. Offers MS. *Application deadline:* Applications are processed on a rolling basis. *Unit head:* Dr. Megumi Fuse, Coordinator, 415-405-0728, E-mail: fuse@sfsu.edu. *Application contact:* Dr. Robert Patterson, Graduate Coordinator, 415-338-1100, E-mail: patters@sfsu.edu.

San Jose State University, Graduate Studies and Research, College of Science, Department of Biological Sciences, San Jose, CA 95192-0001. Offers biological sciences (MA, MS); molecular biology and microbiology (MS); organismal biology, conservation and ecology (MS); physiology (MS). Part-time programs available. *Entrance requirements:* For master's, GRE. Electronic applications accepted. *Faculty research:* Systemic physiology, molecular genetics, SEM studies, toxicology, large mammal ecology.

Southern Illinois University Carbondale, Graduate School, Graduate Program in Medicine, Department of Physiology, Carbondale, IL 62901-4701. Offers MS, PhD. Terminal master's awarded for partial completion of doctoral program. *Degree requirements:* For master's, thesis; for doctorate, thesis/dissertation. *Entrance requirements:* For master's, GRE General Test, minimum GPA of 3.0; for doctorate, GRE General Test, minimum GPA of 3.25. Additional exam requirements/recommendations for international students: Required—TOEFL. *Faculty research:* Hormones, neurotransmitters, cell biology, membrane protein, membranes transport.

Southern Illinois University Carbondale, Graduate School, Graduate Program in Medicine, Program in Molecular, Cellular and Systemic Physiology, Carbondale, IL 62901-4701. Offers MS.

Stanford University, School of Medicine, Graduate Programs in Medicine, Department of Molecular and Cellular Physiology, Stanford, CA 94305-9991. Offers PhD. *Degree requirements:* For doctorate, thesis/dissertation, qualifying exams. *Entrance requirements:* For doctorate, GRE General Test, GRE Subject Test. Additional exam requirements/recommendations for international students: Required—TOEFL. Electronic applications accepted. *Expenses:* Tuition: Full-time $38,700; part-time $860 per unit. One-time fee: $200 full-time. *Faculty research:* Signal transduction, ion channels, intracellular calcium, synaptic transmission.

State University of New York Upstate Medical University, College of Graduate Studies, Program in Physiology, Syracuse, NY 13210-2334. Offers MS, PhD, MD/PhD. Terminal master's awarded for partial completion of doctoral program. *Degree requirements:* For master's, thesis; for doctorate, comprehensive exam, thesis/dissertation. *Entrance requirements:* For master's, GRE General Test, interview; for doctorate, GRE General Test, telephone interview. Additional exam requirements/recommendations for international students: Required—TOEFL. Electronic applications accepted.

Stony Brook University, State University of New York, Stony Brook University Medical Center, School of Medicine and Graduate School, Graduate Programs in Medicine, Department of Physiology and Biophysics, Stony Brook, NY 11794. Offers PhD. *Faculty:* 16 full-time (5 women). *Students:* 11 full-time (6 women); includes 1 Black or African American, non-Hispanic/Latino, 4 international. Average age 29. 46 applicants, 33% accepted. In 2010, 2 doctorates awarded. *Degree requirements:* For doctorate, comprehensive exam, thesis/dissertation. *Entrance requirements:* For doctorate, GRE General Test, GRE Subject Test, BS in related field, minimum GPA of 3.0. Additional exam requirements/recommendations for international students: Required—TOEFL. *Application deadline:* For fall admission, 1/15 for domestic students. Application fee: $100. *Expenses:* Tuition, state resident: full-time $8370; part-time $349 per credit. Tuition, nonresident: full-time $13,780; part-time $574 per credit. Required fees: $994. *Financial support:* In 2010–11, 10 research assistantships, 1 teaching assistantship were awarded; fellowships, Federal Work-Study also available. Financial award application deadline: 3/15. *Faculty research:* Cellular electrophysiology, membrane permeation and transport, metabolic endocrinology. Total annual research expenditures: $5.1 million. *Unit head:* Dr. Peter Brink, Chair, 631-444-2299, Fax: 631-444-3432, E-mail: peter.brink@stonybrook.edu. *Application contact:* Dr. Raafat El-Maghrabi, Graduate Program Director, 631-444-3049, Fax: 631-444-3432, E-mail: raafat.el-maghrabi@stonybrook.edu.

Teachers College, Columbia University, Graduate Faculty of Education, Department of Biobehavioral Studies, Program in Applied Physiology, New York, NY 10027. Offers Ed M, MA, Ed D. *Faculty:* 5 full-time (2 women), 2 part-time/adjunct (1 woman). *Students:* 6 full-time (2 women), 31 part-time (15 women); includes 9 minority (5 Black or African American, non-Hispanic/Latino; 1 Asian, non-Hispanic/Latino; 3 Hispanic/Latino), 3 international. Average age 31. In 2010, 7 master's awarded. *Degree requirements:* For master's, final project; for doctorate, comprehensive exam (for some programs), thesis/dissertation. *Application deadline:* For fall admission, 1/15 for domestic students. Applications are processed on a rolling basis. Application fee: $65. *Expenses:* Tuition: Full-time $28,272; part-time $1178 per credit. Required fees: $756; $378 per semester. *Faculty research:* Modulators of autonomic outflow, the effects of aerobic improvements on autonomic and blood pressure regulation, the role of physical activity in the prevention and treatment of chronic diseases, rehabilitation and cerebral palsy. *Unit head:* Prof. Carol Ewing Garber, Program Coordinator, 212-678-3891, E-mail: ceg2140@columbia.edu. *Application contact:* Morgan Oakes, Admissions Counselor, 212-678-6613, E-mail: meo2142@columbia.edu.

Temple University, Health Sciences Center, School of Medicine and Graduate School, Doctor of Medicine Program, Department of Physiology, Philadelphia, PA 19122-6096. Offers PhD, MD/PhD. *Faculty:* 13 full-time (1 woman). *Students:* 23 full-time (7 women), 2 part-time (both women); includes 1 Black or African American, non-Hispanic/Latino; 2 Asian, non-Hispanic/Latino; 1 Hispanic/Latino, 9 international. 22 applicants, 59% accepted, 9 enrolled. In 2010, 3 doctorates awarded. *Degree requirements:* For doctorate, thesis/dissertation, research seminars. *Entrance requirements:* For doctorate, GRE General Test, minimum GPA of 3.0. Additional exam requirements/recommendations for international students: Required—TOEFL (minimum score 550 paper-based; 213 computer-based; 79 iBT). *Application deadline:* For fall admission, 12/15 for international students. Applications are processed on a rolling basis. Application fee: $50. Electronic applications accepted. *Financial support:* Fellowships available. Financial award application deadline: 1/15; financial award applicants required to submit FAFSA. *Faculty research:* Pulmonary, microvascular, and molecular physiology; cardiac electrophysiology. *Unit head:* Dr. Steven Houser, Chair, 215-707-4045, Fax: 215-707-0170, E-mail: srhouser@temple.edu. *Application contact:* Dr. Steven Houser, Chair, 215-707-4045, Fax: 215-707-0170, E-mail: srhouser@temple.edu.

Texas A&M University, College of Veterinary Medicine and Biomedical Sciences, Department of Veterinary Physiology and Pharmacology, College Station, TX 77843. Offers biomedical science (MS, PhD); toxicology (PhD). *Faculty:* 17. *Students:* 25 full-time (15 women); includes 1 Black or African American, non-Hispanic/Latino; 2 Asian, non-Hispanic/Latino; 1 Hispanic/Latino, 10 international. Average age 30. In 2010, 1 doctorate awarded. *Entrance requirements:* For master's and doctorate, GRE General Test. Additional exam requirements/recommendations for international students: Required—TOEFL. Application fee: $50 ($75 for international students). *Financial support:* Fellowships, research assistantships, teaching assistantships available. Financial award application deadline: 4/1; financial award applicants required to submit FAFSA. *Faculty research:* Gamete and embryo physiology, endocrinology, equine laminitis. *Unit head:* Glen Laine, Head, 979-845-7261, E-mail: glaine@tamu.edu. *Application contact:* Graduate Admissions, 979-845-1044, E-mail: admissions@tamu.edu.

Tufts University, Sackler School of Graduate Biomedical Sciences, Integrated Studies Program, Medford, MA 02155. Offers PhD. *Students:* 10 full-time (7 women); includes 1 Asian, non-Hispanic/Latino, 2 international. Average age 25. 333 applicants, 6% accepted. *Entrance requirements:* For doctorate, GRE General Test, 3 letters of reference. Additional exam requirements/recommendations for international students: Required—TOEFL. *Application deadline:* For fall admission, 12/15 for domestic and international students. Applications are processed on a rolling basis. Application fee: $70. Electronic applications accepted. *Expenses:* Tuition: Full-time $39,624; part-time $3962 per course. Required fees: $40 per year. Full-time tuition and fees vary according to degree level, program and student level. Part-time tuition and fees vary according to course load. *Financial support:* In 2010–11, 10 students received support, including 10 research assistantships with tuition reimbursements available (averaging $28,250 per year); scholarships/grants and health care benefits also available. *Unit head:* Dr. Karina Meiri, Program Director, 617-636-6707, E-mail: james.dice@tufts.edu. *Application contact:* Kellie Johnston, Associate Director of Admissions, 617-636-6767, Fax: 617-636-0375, E-mail: sackler-school@tufts.edu.

Tulane University, School of Medicine and School of Liberal Arts, Graduate Programs in Biomedical Sciences, Department of Physiology, New Orleans, LA 70118-5669. Offers MS, PhD, MD/PhD. MS and PhD offered through the Graduate School. *Degree requirements:* For master's, one foreign language, thesis; for doctorate, 2 foreign languages, thesis/dissertation. *Entrance requirements:* For master's, GRE General Test, minimum B average in undergraduate course work; for doctorate, GRE General Test. Additional exam requirements/recommendations for international students: Required—TOEFL. Electronic applications accepted. *Faculty research:* Renal microcirculation, neurophysiology, NA+ transport, renin/angio tensin system, cell and molecular endocrinology.

Universidad Central del Caribe, School of Medicine, Program in Biomedical Sciences, Bayamón, PR 00960-6032. Offers anatomy and cell biology (MA, MS); biochemistry (MS); biomedical sciences (MA); cellular and molecular biology (PhD); microbiology and immunology (MA, MS); pharmacology (MS); physiology (MS).

Université de Montréal, Faculty of Medicine, Department of Physiology, Montréal, QC H3C 3J7, Canada. Offers neurological sciences (M Sc, PhD); physiology (M Sc, PhD). Terminal master's awarded for partial completion of doctoral program. *Degree requirements:* For master's, thesis; for doctorate, thesis/dissertation, general exam. *Entrance requirements:* For master's and doctorate, proficiency in French, knowledge of English. Electronic applications accepted. *Faculty research:* Cardiovascular, neuropeptides, membrane transport and biophysics, signaling pathways.

Université de Sherbrooke, Faculty of Medicine and Health Sciences, Graduate Programs in Medicine, Department of Physiology and Biophysics, Sherbrooke, QC J1H 5N4, Canada. Offers M Sc, PhD. Terminal master's awarded for partial completion of doctoral program. *Degree requirements:* For master's, thesis; for doctorate, thesis/dissertation. Electronic applications accepted. *Faculty research:* Ion channels, neurological basis of pain, insulin resistance, obesity.

Université Laval, Faculty of Medicine, Department of Anatomy and Physiology, Québec, QC G1K 7P4, Canada. Offers M Sc, PhD. Terminal master's awarded for partial completion of doctoral program. *Degree requirements:* For master's, thesis (for some programs); for doctorate, comprehensive exam, thesis/dissertation. Electronic applications accepted.

Université Laval, Faculty of Medicine, Graduate Programs in Medicine, Programs in Physiology-Endocrinology, Québec, QC G1K 7P4, Canada. Offers M Sc, PhD. Terminal master's awarded for partial completion of doctoral program. *Degree requirements:* For master's, thesis; for doctorate, comprehensive exam, thesis/dissertation. Electronic applications accepted.

University at Buffalo, the State University of New York, Graduate School, School of Medicine and Biomedical Sciences, Graduate Programs in Medicine and Biomedical Sciences, Department of Physiology and Biophysics, Buffalo, NY 14260. Offers biophysics (MS, PhD); physiology (MA, PhD). Terminal master's awarded for partial completion of doctoral program. *Degree requirements:* For master's, thesis, oral exam, project; for doctorate, thesis/dissertation, oral and written qualifying exam or 2 research proposals. *Entrance requirements:* For master's and doctorate, GRE General Test. Additional exam requirements/recommendations for international students: Required—TOEFL (minimum score 600 paper-based; 250 computer-based; 100 iBT). Electronic applications accepted. *Faculty research:* Neurosciences, ion channels, cardiac physiology, renal/epithelial transport, cardiopulmonary exercise.

University of Alberta, Faculty of Graduate Studies and Research, Department of Biological Sciences, Edmonton, AB T6G 2E1, Canada. Offers environmental biology and ecology (M Sc, PhD); microbiology and biotechnology (M Sc, PhD); molecular biology and genetics (M Sc, PhD); physiology and cell biology (M Sc, PhD); plant biology (M Sc, PhD); systematics and evolution (M Sc, PhD). Terminal master's awarded for partial completion of doctoral program. *Degree requirements:* For master's, thesis; for doctorate, thesis/dissertation. *Entrance requirements:* Additional exam requirements/recommendations for international students: Required—TOEFL.

University of Alberta, Faculty of Medicine and Dentistry and Faculty of Graduate Studies and Research, Graduate Programs in Medicine, Department of Physiology, Edmonton, AB T6G 2E1, Canada. Offers M Sc, PhD. Terminal master's awarded for partial completion of doctoral program. *Degree requirements:* For master's, thesis; for doctorate, thesis/dissertation. *Entrance requirements:* For master's and doctorate, minimum GPA of 3.0. Additional exam requirements/recommendations for international students: Required—TOEFL (minimum score 580 paper-based; 237 computer-based). Electronic applications accepted. *Faculty research:* Membrane transport, cell biology, perinatal endocrinology, neurophysiology, cardiovascular.

The University of Arizona, Graduate Interdisciplinary Programs, Graduate Interdisciplinary Program in Physiological Sciences, Tucson, AZ 85721. Offers MS, PhD. *Faculty:* 16 full-time (6 women). *Students:* 33 full-time (20 women), 13 part-time (3 women); includes 2 Black or African American, non-Hispanic/Latino; 3 Hispanic/Latino; 3 Two or more races, non-Hispanic/Latino, 7 international. Average age 26. 37 applicants, 57% accepted, 19 enrolled. In 2010, 10 master's, 6 doctorates awarded. *Degree requirements:* For doctorate, thesis/dissertation. *Entrance requirements:* For master's, GRE General Test, 3 letters of recommendation, statement of purpose; for doctorate, GRE General Test, 3 letters of recommendation. Additional exam requirements/recommendations for international students: Required—TOEFL (minimum score 600 paper-based). *Application deadline:* For fall admission, 3/15 for domestic and international students. Applications are processed on a rolling basis. Application fee: $65. Electronic applications accepted. *Expenses:* Tuition, state resident: full-time $7692. *Financial support:* In 2010–11, 3 research assistantships with full tuition reimbursements (averaging $20,867 per year), 13 teaching assistantships with full tuition reimbursements (averaging $27,699 per year) were awarded; health care benefits and unspecified assistantships also available. *Faculty research:* Cellular transport and signaling, receptor and messenger modulation, neural interaction and biomechanics, fluid network regulation, environmental adaptation. *Unit head:* Dr. Ronald Lynch, Department Chair, 520-626-2472, E-mail: rlynch@u.arizona.edu. *Application contact:* Holly Lopez, Information Contact, 520-626-2898, Fax: 520-626-2382, E-mail: idp@ccit.arizona.edu.

University of Arkansas for Medical Sciences, Graduate School, Graduate Programs in Biomedical Sciences, Department of Physiology and Biophysics, Little Rock, AR 72205-7199. Offers MS, PhD, MD/PhD. *Degree requirements:* For master's, thesis; for doctorate, thesis/dissertation. *Entrance requirements:* For master's and doctorate, GRE General Test. Additional exam requirements/recommendations for international students: Required—TOEFL. *Faculty research:* Gene transcription, protein targeting, membrane biology, cell-cell communication.

The University of British Columbia, Faculty of Medicine, Department of Cellular and Physiological Sciences, Division of Physiology, Vancouver, BC V6T 1Z1, Canada. Offers M Sc, PhD. Terminal master's awarded for partial completion of doctoral program. *Degree requirements:* For master's, thesis, oral defense; for doctorate, comprehensive exam, thesis/dissertation, oral defense. *Entrance requirements:* Additional exam requirements/recommendations for international students: Required—TOEFL (minimum score 550 paper-based; 213 computer-based), IELTS (minimum score 6.2). Electronic applications accepted. Tuition charges are reported in Canadian dollars. *Expenses:* Tuition, area resident: Full-time $4179 Canadian dollars. International tuition: $7344 Canadian dollars full-time. *Faculty research:* Neurophysiology, gastroenterology, endocrinology, cardiovascular physiology.

University of California, Berkeley, Graduate Division, College of Letters and Science, Group in Endocrinology, Berkeley, CA 94720-1500. Offers MA, PhD. *Degree requirements:* For doctorate, thesis/dissertation, oral qualifying exam. *Entrance requirements:* For master's, GRE General Test or the equivalent (MCAT), minimum GPA of 3.0, 3 letters of recommendation; for doctorate, GRE General Test or the equivalent (MCAT), minimum GPA of 3.4, 3 letters of recommendation. Additional exam requirements/recommendations for international students: Required—TOEFL.

University of California, Davis, Graduate Studies, Molecular, Cellular and Integrative Physiology Graduate Group, Davis, CA 95616. Offers MS, PhD. *Degree requirements:* For master's, comprehensive exam (for some programs), thesis (for some programs); for doctorate, thesis/dissertation. *Entrance requirements:* For master's and doctorate, GRE General Test. Additional exam requirements/recommendations for international students: Required—TOEFL (minimum score 550 paper-based; 213 computer-based). Electronic applications accepted. *Faculty research:* Systemic physiology, cellular physiology, neurophysiology, cardiovascular physiology, endocrinology.

University of California, Irvine, School of Medicine and School of Biological Sciences, Department of Physiology and Biophysics, Irvine, CA 92697. Offers biological sciences (PhD); MD/PhD. Students apply through the Graduate Program in Molecular Biology, Genetics, and Biochemistry. *Students:* 11 full-time (6 women); includes 5 minority (4 Asian, non-Hispanic/Latino; 1 Hispanic/Latino). Average age 28. In 2010, 1 doctorate awarded. *Degree requirements:* For doctorate, thesis/dissertation. *Entrance requirements:* For doctorate, GRE General Test, GRE Subject Test, minimum GPA of 3.0. Additional exam requirements/recommendations for international students: Required—TOEFL (minimum score 550 paper-based; 213 computer-based). *Application deadline:* For fall admission, 1/15 priority date for domestic students, 1/15 for international students. Application fee: $80 ($100 for international students). Electronic applications accepted. *Financial support:* Fellowships, research assistantships with full tuition reimbursements, teaching assistantships, institutionally sponsored loans, traineeships, health care benefits, and unspecified assistantships available. Financial award application deadline: 3/1; financial award applicants required to submit FAFSA. *Faculty research:* Membrane physiology, exercise physiology, regulation of hormone biosynthesis and action, endocrinology, ion channels and signal transduction. *Unit head:* Prof. Michael Cahalan, Chairman, 949-824-

Physiology

University of California, Irvine (continued)

7776, Fax: 949-824-3143, E-mail: mcahalan@uci.edu. *Application contact:* Vicki C. Ledray, Chief Administrative Officer, 949-824-5865, Fax: 949-824-0019, E-mail: ledray@uci.edu.

University of California, Los Angeles, David Geffen School of Medicine and Graduate Division, Graduate Programs in Medicine, Department of Physiology, Los Angeles, CA 90095. Offers PhD. *Faculty:* 15 full-time (3 women). In 2010, 2 doctorates awarded. *Degree requirements:* For doctorate, thesis/dissertation, oral and written qualifying exams. *Entrance requirements:* For doctorate, GRE General Test, GRE Subject Test. Application fee: $70 ($90 for international students). *Financial support:* In 2010–11, 2 research assistantships were awarded; fellowships, teaching assistantships, scholarships/grants also available. Financial award application deadline: 3/1. *Faculty research:* Membrane physiology, cell physiology, muscle physiology, neurophysiology, cardiopulmonary physiology. *Unit head:* Dr. Barnett Schlinger, Chair, 310-825-5716, E-mail: schlinge@lifesci.ucla.edu. *Application contact:* Mike Carr, Student Affairs Officer, 310-825-3891, E-mail: mcarr@physci.ucla.edu.

University of California, Los Angeles, Graduate Division, College of Letters and Science, Department of Physiological Science, Los Angeles, CA 90095. Offers physiological science (MS). *Faculty:* 18 full-time (4 women). *Students:* 28 full-time (15 women); includes 18 minority (2 Black or African American, non-Hispanic/Latino; 13 Asian, non-Hispanic/Latino; 1 Hispanic/Latino; 2 Two or more races, non-Hispanic/Latino), 1 international. Average age 25. 21 applicants, 48% accepted, 9 enrolled. In 2010, 13 master's awarded. *Degree requirements:* For master's, thesis. *Entrance requirements:* For master's, GRE General Test or MCAT, minimum GPA of 3.0, bachelor's degree in biological or physical sciences. *Application deadline:* For fall admission, 6/30 for domestic and international students. Application fee: $70 ($90 for international students). Electronic applications accepted. *Financial support:* In 2010–11, 12 fellowships with full and partial tuition reimbursements, 9 research assistantships with full and partial tuition reimbursements, 21 teaching assistantships with full and partial tuition reimbursements were awarded; Federal Work-Study, institutionally sponsored loans, scholarships/grants, health care benefits, tuition waivers (full and partial), and unspecified assistantships also available. Financial award applicants required to submit FAFSA. *Faculty research:* Diet and exercise in the prevention and management of degenerative diseases, neuromuscular physiology and plasticity, neural control of movement and homeostasis. *Unit head:* Dr. Arthur Arnold, Chair, 310-825-9340, E-mail: arnold@ucla.edu. *Application contact:* Departmental Office, 310-825-3891, E-mail: mcarr@physci.ucla.edu.

University of California, Los Angeles, Graduate Division, College of Letters and Science and David Geffen School of Medicine, UCLA ACCESS to Programs in the Molecular, Cellular and Integrative Life Sciences, Los Angeles, CA 90095. Offers biochemistry and molecular biology (PhD); biological chemistry (PhD); cellular and molecular pathology (PhD); human genetics (PhD); microbiology, immunology, and molecular genetics (PhD); molecular biology (PhD); molecular toxicology (PhD); molecular, cellular and integrative physiology (PhD); neurobiology (PhD); oral biology (PhD); physiology (PhD). ACCESS is an umbrella program for first-year coursework in 12 PhD programs. *Students:* 48 full-time (28 women), 6 international. Average age 24. 388 applicants, 27% accepted, 48 enrolled. *Degree requirements:* For doctorate, thesis/dissertation, oral and written qualifying exams. *Entrance requirements:* For doctorate, GRE General Test, minimum undergraduate GPA of 3.0. Additional exam requirements/recommendations for international students: Required—TOEFL. *Application deadline:* For fall admission, 12/15 for domestic and international students. Application fee: $70 ($90 for international students). Electronic applications accepted. *Financial support:* In 2010–11, 31 fellowships with full and partial tuition reimbursements, 13 research assistantships with full and partial tuition reimbursements, 2 teaching assistantships with full and partial tuition reimbursements were awarded; Federal Work-Study, institutionally sponsored loans, scholarships/grants, health care benefits, tuition waivers (full and partial), and unspecified assistantships also available. Financial award application deadline: 3/1; financial award applicants required to submit FAFSA. *Faculty research:* Molecular, cellular, and developmental biology; immunology; microbiology; integrative biology. *Unit head:* Jody Spillane, Project Coordinator, 310-206-1845, E-mail: jspillane@mednet.ucla.edu. *Application contact:* UCLA Access Admissions, 310-206-1845, E-mail: uclaaccess@mednet.ucla.edu.

University of California, San Diego, School of Medicine and Office of Graduate Studies, Graduate Studies in Biomedical Sciences, Physiology Program, La Jolla, CA 92093. Offers PhD. *Degree requirements:* For doctorate, thesis/dissertation, qualifying exam. *Entrance requirements:* For doctorate, GRE General Test. Additional exam requirements/recommendations for international students: Required—TOEFL. Electronic applications accepted. *Faculty research:* Cell and organ physiology, eukaryotic regulatory and molecular biology, molecular and cellular pharmacology.

University of California, San Francisco, Graduate Division, Biomedical Sciences Graduate Group, San Francisco, CA 94143. Offers anatomy (PhD); endocrinology (PhD); experimental pathology (PhD); physiology (PhD). *Degree requirements:* For doctorate, thesis/dissertation. *Entrance requirements:* For doctorate, GRE General Test.

University of Chicago, Division of Biological Sciences, Neuroscience Graduate Programs, Department of Integrative Neuroscience, Chicago, IL 60637-1513. Offers cell physiology (PhD); pharmacological and physiological sciences (PhD). *Degree requirements:* For doctorate, thesis/dissertation, preliminary exam. *Entrance requirements:* For doctorate, GRE General Test. Additional exam requirements/recommendations for international students: Required—TOEFL. Electronic applications accepted. *Faculty research:* Psychopharmacology, neuropharmacology.

University of Cincinnati, Graduate School, College of Medicine, Graduate Programs in Biomedical Sciences, Department of Molecular and Cellular Physiology, Cincinnati, OH 45221. Offers physiology (PhD). *Degree requirements:* For doctorate, comprehensive exam, thesis/dissertation, publication. *Entrance requirements:* For doctorate, GRE General Test, GRE Subject Test. Additional exam requirements/recommendations for international students: Required—TOEFL (minimum score 560 paper-based; 220 computer-based). Electronic applications accepted. *Faculty research:* Endocrinology, cardiovascular physiology, muscle physiology, neurophysiology, transgenic mouse physiology.

University of Colorado Boulder, Graduate School, College of Arts and Sciences, Department of Integrative Physiology, Boulder, CO 80309. Offers MS, PhD. *Faculty:* 22 full-time (7 women). *Students:* 59 full-time (19 women), 5 part-time (4 women); includes 6 minority (1 American Indian or Alaska Native, non-Hispanic/Latino; 2 Asian, non-Hispanic/Latino; 2 Hispanic/Latino; 1 Two or more races, non-Hispanic/Latino), 3 international. Average age 27. 68 applicants, 15 enrolled. In 2010, 15 master's, 8 doctorates awarded. *Degree requirements:* For master's, comprehensive exam, thesis or alternative; for doctorate, thesis/dissertation. *Entrance requirements:* For master's, GRE General Test, minimum undergraduate GPA of 2.75. *Application deadline:* For fall admission, 1/15 priority date for domestic students, 12/15 for international students. Applications are processed on a rolling basis. Application fee: $50 ($60 for international students). *Financial support:* In 2010–11, 24 fellowships (averaging $15,189 per year), 33 research assistantships (averaging $6,975 per year) were awarded. Financial award application deadline: 2/1. *Faculty research:* Integrative or cellular kinesiology. Total annual research expenditures: $8.6 million.

University of Colorado Denver, School of Medicine, Program in Physiology, Denver, CO 80217-3364. Offers PhD. *Students:* 9 full-time (0 women), 4 international. Average age 27. 6 applicants, 17% accepted, 1 enrolled. In 2010, 2 doctorates awarded. *Degree requirements:* For doctorate, comprehensive exam, thesis/dissertation, 30 semester credit hours each of coursework and thesis, 3 lab rotations within 1st year. *Entrance requirements:* For doctorate, GRE General Test, 2 transcripts, 4 letters of recommendation; minimum GPA of 3.2; completion of college-level mathematics through calculus, one year each of organic chemistry, physical chemistry, and physics, and two years of biology. Additional exam requirements/recommendations for international students: Required—TOEFL (minimum score 550 paper-based; 213 computer-based). *Application deadline:* For fall admission, 1/1 for domestic students. Application fee: $50 ($75 for international students). Electronic applications accepted. *Expenses:* Contact institution. *Financial support:* In 2010–11, 1 fellowship with full tuition reimbursement (averaging $25,000 per year) was awarded; health care benefits, tuition waivers (full), and stipend also available. Financial award application deadline: 3/15; financial award applicants required to submit FAFSA. *Faculty research:* Nicotonic receptors, immunity, molecular structure, function and regulation of ion channels, calcium influx in the function of cytotoxic T lymphocytes. *Unit head:* Dr. Sukumar Vijayaraghavan, Director, 303-724-4531, E-mail: sukumar.v@ucdenver.edu.

University of Connecticut, Graduate School, College of Liberal Arts and Sciences, Department of Physiology and Neurobiology, Storrs, CT 06269. Offers comparative physiology (MS, PhD); endocrinology (MS, PhD), including comparative physiology (MS), neurobiology (MS); neurobiology (MS, PhD). Terminal master's awarded for partial completion of doctoral program. *Degree requirements:* For master's, comprehensive exam; for doctorate, thesis/dissertation. *Entrance requirements:* For master's and doctorate, GRE General Test, GRE Subject Test. Additional exam requirements/recommendations for international students: Required—TOEFL (minimum score 550 paper-based; 213 computer-based). Electronic applications accepted.

See Display on next page and Close-Up on page 455.

University of Delaware, College of Arts and Sciences, Department of Biological Sciences, Newark, DE 19716. Offers biotechnology (MS); cancer biology (MS, PhD); cell and extracellular matrix biology (MS, PhD); cell and systems physiology (MS, PhD); developmental biology (MS, PhD); ecology and evolution (MS, PhD); microbiology (MS, PhD); molecular biology and genetics (MS, PhD). Terminal master's awarded for partial completion of doctoral program. *Degree requirements:* For master's, thesis, preliminary exam; for doctorate, comprehensive exam, thesis/dissertation, preliminary exam. *Entrance requirements:* For master's and doctorate, GRE General Test. Additional exam requirements/recommendations for international students: Required—TOEFL (minimum score 600 paper-based; 250 computer-based); Recommended—TWE. Electronic applications accepted. *Faculty research:* Microorganisms, bone, cancer metastasis, developmental biology, cell biology, DNA.

University of Delaware, College of Health Sciences, Department of Health, Nutrition, and Exercise Sciences, Newark, DE 19716. Offers exercise science (MS), including biomechanics, exercise physiology, motor control; health promotion (MS); human nutrition (MS). Part-time programs available. *Degree requirements:* For master's, thesis. *Entrance requirements:* For master's, GRE General Test, interview, minimum GPA of 3.0. Additional exam requirements/recommendations for international students: Required—TOEFL (minimum score 550 paper-based; 213 computer-based). Electronic applications accepted. *Faculty research:* Sport biomechanics, rehabilitation biomechanics, vascular dynamics.

University of Delaware, College of Health Sciences, Department of Kinesiology and Applied Physiology, Newark, DE 19716. Offers MS, PhD.

University of Florida, College of Medicine, Department of Physiology and Functional Genomics, Gainesville, FL 32611. Offers PhD. *Degree requirements:* For doctorate, thesis/dissertation. *Entrance requirements:* For doctorate, GRE General Test, minimum GPA of 3.0. Additional exam requirements/recommendations for international students: Required—TOEFL. Electronic applications accepted. *Expenses:* Tuition, state resident: full-time $10,916. Tuition, nonresident: full-time $28,309. *Faculty research:* Cell and general endocrinology, neuroendocrinology, neurophysiology, respiration, membrane transport and ion channels.

University of Florida, College of Medicine and Graduate School, Interdisciplinary Program in Biomedical Sciences, Concentration in Physiology and Pharmacology, Gainesville, FL 32611. Offers PhD. *Degree requirements:* For doctorate, thesis/dissertation. *Entrance requirements:* For doctorate, GRE General Test, minimum GPA of 3.0. Electronic applications accepted. *Expenses:* Tuition, state resident: full-time $10,916. Tuition, nonresident: full-time $28,309.

University of Florida, Graduate School, College of Health and Human Performance, Department of Applied Physiology and Kinesiology, Gainesville, FL 32611. Offers athletic training/sport medicine (MS); biobehavioral science (MS, PhD); clinical exercise physiology (MS); exercise physiology (MS, PhD); health and human performance (PhD); human performance (MS). *Faculty:* 10 full-time (3 women), 1 (woman) part-time/adjunct. *Students:* 131 full-time (60 women), 16 part-time (4 women); includes 5 Black or African American, non-Hispanic/Latino; 5 Asian, non-Hispanic/Latino; 11 Hispanic/Latino, 38 international. Average age 26. 250 applicants, 26% accepted, 44 enrolled. In 2010, 22 master's, 13 doctorates awarded. *Degree requirements:* For master's, comprehensive exam, thesis (for some programs); for doctorate, comprehensive exam, thesis/dissertation. *Entrance requirements:* For doctorate, GRE General Test. Additional exam requirements/recommendations for international students: Required—TOEFL (minimum score 550 paper-based; 213 computer-based; 80 iBT), IELTS (minimum score 6). *Application deadline:* For fall admission, 6/1 priority date for domestic students, 6/1 for international students; for spring admission, 9/15 for domestic and international students. Applications are processed on a rolling basis. Application fee: $30. Electronic applications accepted. *Expenses:* Tuition, state resident: full-time $10,916. Tuition, nonresident: full-time $28,309. *Financial support:* In 2010–11, 100 students received support, including 21 fellowships, 48 research assistantships (averaging $15,503 per year), 31 teaching assistantships (averaging $14,956 per year); unspecified assistantships also available. Financial award application deadline: 2/1; financial award applicants required to submit FAFSA. *Faculty research:* Cardiovascular disease; basic mechanisms that underlie exercise-induced changes in the body at the organ, tissue, cellular and molecular level; development of rehabilitation techniques for regaining motor control after stroke or as a consequence of Parkinson's disease; maintaining optimal health and delaying age-related declines in physiological function; psychomotor mechanisms impacting health and performance across the life span. Total annual research expenditures: $1.3 million. *Unit head:* Dr. Michael Delp, Chair, 352-392-0584 Ext. 1338, E-mail: mdelp@hhp.ufl.edu. *Application contact:* Christopher M. Janelle, Graduate Coordinator, 352-392-0584 Ext. 1270, Fax: 352-392-5262, E-mail: cjmj@ufl.edu.

University of Georgia, College of Veterinary Medicine and Graduate School, Graduate Programs in Veterinary Medicine, Department of Physiology and Pharmacology, Athens, GA 30602. Offers pharmacology (MS, PhD); physiology (MS, PhD). *Faculty:* 12 full-time (4 women), 1 part-time/adjunct (0 women). *Students:* 19 full-time (9 women); includes 1 Asian, non-Hispanic/Latino; 1 Hispanic/Latino, 9 international. 19 applicants, 26% accepted, 3 enrolled. In 2010, 1 master's, 1 doctorate awarded. *Degree requirements:* For master's, thesis; for doctorate, one foreign language, thesis/dissertation. *Entrance requirements:* For master's and doctorate, GRE General Test. *Application deadline:* For fall admission, 7/1 priority date for domestic students; for spring admission, 11/15 for domestic students. Application fee: $50. Electronic applications accepted. *Expenses:* Tuition, state resident: full-time $7200; part-time $344 per credit hour. Tuition, nonresident: full-time $21,900; part-time $944 per credit hour. Tuition and fees vary according to course load and program. *Financial support:* Fellowships, research assistantships, teaching assistantships, unspecified assistantships available. *Unit head:* Dr. Gaylen L. Edwards, Acting Head, 706-542-3014, Fax: 706-542-3015, E-mail: gedwards@uga.edu. *Application contact:* Dr. John Wagner, Graduate Coordinator, 706-542-6428, Fax: 706-542-3015, E-mail: jwagner@uga.edu.

University of Guelph, Ontario Veterinary College and Graduate Studies, Graduate Programs in Veterinary Sciences, Department of Biomedical Sciences, Guelph, ON N1G 2W1, Canada. Offers morphology (M Sc, DV Sc, PhD); neuroscience (M Sc, DV Sc, PhD); pharmacology (M Sc, DV Sc, PhD); physiology (M Sc, DV Sc, PhD); toxicology (M Sc, DV Sc, PhD). Part-time programs available. *Degree requirements:* For master's, thesis; for doctorate, comprehensive exam, thesis/dissertation. *Entrance requirements:* For master's, honors B Sc, minimum 75% average in last 20 courses; for doctorate, M Sc with thesis from accredited institution. Additional exam requirements/recommendations for international students: Required—TOEFL (minimum score 550 paper-based; 213 computer-based; 89 iBT). Electronic applications accepted. *Faculty*

Physiology

research: Cellular morphology; endocrine, vascular and reproductive physiology; clinical pharmacology; veterinary toxicology; developmental biology, neuroscience.

University of Hawaii at Manoa, John A. Burns School of Medicine, Program in Developmental and Reproductive Biology, Honolulu, HI 96813. Offers MS, PhD. Part-time programs available. *Faculty:* 24 full-time (7 women). *Students:* 12 full-time (7 women), 8 part-time (3 women); includes 12 minority (8 Asian, non-Hispanic/Latino; 3 Native Hawaiian or other Pacific Islander, non-Hispanic/Latino; 1 Two or more races, non-Hispanic/Latino), 3 international. Average age 29. 22 applicants, 68% accepted, 11 enrolled. In 2010, 1 master's, 1 doctorate awarded. *Degree requirements:* For doctorate, thesis/dissertation. *Entrance requirements:* For doctorate, GRE General Test, GRE Subject Test. Additional exam requirements/recommendations for international students: Recommended—TOEFL (minimum score 560 paper-based; 83 computer-based), IELTS (minimum score 5). *Application deadline:* For fall admission, 3/1 for domestic and international students. Application fee: $50. *Financial support:* In 2010–11, 2 fellowships (averaging $4,577 per year), 10 research assistantships (averaging $16,328 per year) were awarded; teaching assistantships. *Faculty research:* Biology of gametes and fertilization, reproductive endocrinology. Total annual research expenditures: $5.4 million. *Application contact:* Steve Ward, Graduate Chair, 808-956-1412, Fax: 808-956-9722, E-mail: wward@hawaii.edu.

University of Illinois at Chicago, College of Medicine and Graduate College, Graduate Programs in Medicine, Department of Physiology and Biophysics, Chicago, IL 60607-7128. Offers MS, PhD. Terminal master's awarded for partial completion of doctoral program. *Degree requirements:* For master's and doctorate, GRE General Test. Additional exam requirements/recommendations for international students: Required—TOEFL. Electronic applications accepted. *Faculty research:* Neuroscience, endocrinology and reproduction, cell physiology, exercise physiology, NMR.

University of Illinois at Urbana–Champaign, Graduate College, College of Liberal Arts and Sciences, School of Integrative Biology, Program in Physiological and Molecular Plant Biology, Champaign, IL 61820. Offers PhD. *Students:* 7 full-time (3 women), 5 international. 1 applicant, 0% accepted, 0 enrolled. In 2010, 3 doctorates awarded. *Entrance requirements:* For doctorate, GRE, minimum GPA of 3.0. Additional exam requirements/recommendations for international students: Required—TOEFL (minimum score 570 paper-based; 230 computer-based; 89 iBT). *Application deadline:* Applications are processed on a rolling basis. Application fee: $75 ($90 for international students). Electronic applications accepted. *Financial support:* In 2010–11, 1 fellowship, 4 research assistantships, 4 teaching assistantships were awarded; tuition waivers (full and partial) also available. *Unit head:* Stephen Moose, Director, 217-244-6308, Fax: 217-244-1224, E-mail: smoose@illinois.edu. *Application contact:* Carol Hall, Office Manager, 217-333-8208, Fax: 217-244-1224, E-mail: cahall@illinois.edu.

University of Illinois at Urbana–Champaign, Graduate College, College of Liberal Arts and Sciences, School of Molecular and Cellular Biology, Department of Molecular and Integrative Physiology, Champaign, IL 61820. Offers MS, PhD. *Faculty:* 13 full-time (5 women). *Students:* 39 full-time (21 women); includes 2 Black or African American, non-Hispanic/Latino; 2 Asian, non-Hispanic/Latino; 3 Hispanic/Latino; 1 Two or more races, non-Hispanic/Latino, 14 international. In 2010, 5 master's, 5 doctorates awarded. *Entrance requirements:* For master's and doctorate, GRE, minimum GPA of 3.0. Additional exam requirements/recommendations for international students: Required—TOEFL (minimum score 590 paper-based; 243 computer-based). *Application deadline:* Applications are processed on a rolling basis. Application fee: $75 ($90 for international students). Electronic applications accepted. *Financial support:* In 2010–11, 2 fellowships, 33 research assistantships, 20 teaching assistantships were awarded; tuition waivers (full and partial) also available. *Unit head:* Byron Kemper, Head, 217-333-1146, Fax: 217-333-1133, E-mail: byronkem@illinois.edu. *Application contact:* Penny Morman, Office Manager, 217-333-8275, Fax: 217-333-1133, E-mail: morman@illinois.edu.

The University of Iowa, Roy J. and Lucille A. Carver College of Medicine and Graduate College, Graduate Programs in Medicine, Department of Molecular Physiology and Bio-

physics, Iowa City, IA 52242-1316. Offers MS, PhD. *Faculty:* 17 full-time (3 women), 16 part-time/adjunct (2 women). *Students:* 20 full-time (6 women); includes 3 Asian, non-Hispanic/Latino, 3 international. Average age 25. 8 applicants, 100% accepted, 8 enrolled. In 2010, 1 master's, 8 doctorates awarded. Terminal master's awarded for partial completion of doctoral program. *Degree requirements:* For master's, comprehensive exam; for doctorate, comprehensive exam, thesis/dissertation, teaching experience. *Entrance requirements:* For master's, GRE; for doctorate, GRE General Test, minimum GPA of 3.0. Additional exam requirements/recommendations for international students: Required—TOEFL. *Application deadline:* For fall admission, 4/1 for domestic students, 3/1 for international students; for spring admission, 10/1 for domestic students, 9/1 for international students. Applications are processed on a rolling basis. Application fee: $60 ($80 for international students). Electronic applications accepted. *Financial support:* In 2010–11, 4 fellowships with full tuition reimbursements (averaging $24,250 per year), 13 research assistantships with full tuition reimbursements (averaging $24,250 per year) were awarded; traineeships also available. Financial award application deadline: 4/1. *Faculty research:* Cellular and molecular endocrinology, membrane structure and function, cardiac cell electrophysiology, regulation of gene expression, neurophysiology. *Unit head:* Dr. Kevin P. Campbell, Head, 319-335-7800, Fax: 319-335-7330, E-mail: kevin-campbell@uiowa.edu. *Application contact:* Dr. Michael Anderson, Director of Graduate Studies, 319-335-7839, Fax: 319-335-7330, E-mail: michael-g-anderson@uiowa.edu.

The University of Kansas, University of Kansas Medical Center, School of Medicine, Department of Molecular and Integrative Physiology, Kansas City, KS 66160. Offers molecular and integrative physiology (MS, PhD); neuroscience (MS, PhD); MD/PhD. *Faculty:* 43. *Students:* 28 full-time (15 women); includes 2 minority (1 Black or African American, non-Hispanic/Latino; 1 Hispanic/Latino), 14 international. Average age 28. 4 applicants, 100% accepted, 4 enrolled. In 2010, 4 doctorates awarded. Terminal master's awarded for partial completion of doctoral program. *Degree requirements:* For master's, thesis; for doctorate, comprehensive exam, thesis/dissertation. *Entrance requirements:* For doctorate, GRE. Additional exam requirements/recommendations for international students: Required—TOEFL. *Application deadline:* For fall admission, 1/15 priority date for domestic and international students. Applications are processed on a rolling basis. Application fee: $10. Electronic applications accepted. *Expenses:* Tuition, state resident: full-time $7092; part-time $295.50 per credit hour. Tuition, nonresident: full-time $16,590; part-time $691.25 per credit hour. Required fees: $858; $71.49 per credit hour. Tuition and fees vary according to course load, campus/location and program. *Financial support:* Scholarships/grants and unspecified assistantships available. Financial award application deadline: 2/14; financial award applicants required to submit FAFSA. *Faculty research:* Male reproductive physiology and contraception, ovarian development and regulation by pituitary and hypothalamus, neural control of movement and stroke recovery, pulmonary physiology and hypoxia, plasticity of the autonomic nervous system. Total annual research expenditures: $6.8 million. *Unit head:* Dr. Paul D. Cheney, Chairman, 913-588-7400, Fax: 913-588-7430, E-mail: pcheney@kumc.edu. *Application contact:* Dr. Michael W. Wolfe, Director of Graduate Studies, 913-588-7418, Fax: 913-588-7430, E-mail: mwolfe2@kumc.edu.

University of Kentucky, Graduate School, Graduate School Programs from the College of Medicine, Program in Physiology, Lexington, KY 40506-0032. Offers MS, PhD. *Degree requirements:* For doctorate, comprehensive exam, thesis/dissertation. *Entrance requirements:* For master's, GRE General Test, minimum undergraduate GPA of 2.75; for doctorate, GRE General Test, minimum undergraduate GPA of 2.75, graduate 3.0. Additional exam requirements/recommendations for international students: Required—TOEFL (minimum score 550 paper-based; 213 computer-based). Electronic applications accepted.

University of Louisville, School of Medicine, Department of Physiology and Biophysics, Louisville, KY 40292-0001. Offers MS, PhD, MD/PhD. *Faculty:* 23 full-time (0 women). *Students:* 31 full-time (17 women), 6 part-time (1 woman); includes 6 Black or African American, non-Hispanic/Latino; 4 Asian, non-Hispanic/Latino; 1 Hispanic/Latino; 1 Two or more races, non-Hispanic/Latino, 6 international. Average age 27. 36 applicants, 58% accepted, 18 enrolled.

Physiology

University of Louisville (continued)

In 2010, 13 master's, 8 doctorates awarded. Terminal master's awarded for partial completion of doctoral program. *Degree requirements:* For master's, thesis; for doctorate, comprehensive exam, thesis/dissertation. *Entrance requirements:* For master's and doctorate, GRE General Test (minimum score of 1000 verbal and quantitative), minimum GPA of 3.0. Additional exam requirements/recommendations for international students: Required—TOEFL. *Application deadline:* For fall admission, 1/15 priority date for domestic students. Applications are processed on a rolling basis. Application fee: $50. Electronic applications accepted. *Expenses:* Tuition, state resident: full-time $9144; part-time $508 per credit hour. Tuition, nonresident: full-time $19,026; part-time $1057 per credit hour. Tuition and fees vary according to program and reciprocity agreements. *Financial support:* Fellowships with full tuition reimbursements, research assistantships with full tuition reimbursements available. Financial award application deadline: 4/15. *Faculty research:* Control of microvascular function during normal and disease states; mechanisms of cellular adhesive interactions on endothelial cells lining blood vessels; changes in blood rheological properties and mechanisms associated with increased blood fibrinogen content; role of nutrition in microvascular control mechanisms; mechanism of cardiovascular-renal remodeling in hypertension, diabetes, and heart failure. *Unit head:* Dr. Irving G. Joshua, Chair, 502-852-5371, Fax: 502-852-6239, E-mail: igjosh01@gwise.louisville.edu. *Application contact:* Dr. William Wead, Director of Admissions, 502-852-7571, Fax: 502-852-6849, E-mail: wbwead01@gwise.louisville.edu.

The University of Manchester, Faculty of Life Sciences, Manchester, United Kingdom. Offers adaptive organismal biology (M Phil, PhD); animal biology (M Phil, PhD); biochemistry (M Phil, PhD); bioinformatics (M Phil, PhD); biomolecular sciences (M Phil, PhD); biotechnology (M Phil, PhD); cell biology (M Phil, PhD); cell matrix research (M Phil, PhD); channels and transporters (M Phil, PhD); developmental biology (M Phil, PhD); Egyptology (M Phil, PhD); environmental biology (M Phil, PhD); evolutionary biology (M Phil, PhD); gene expression (M Phil, PhD); genetics (M Phil, PhD); history of science, technology and medicine (M Phil, PhD); immunology (M Phil, PhD); integrative neurobiology and behavior (M Phil, PhD); membrane trafficking (M Phil, PhD); microbiology (M Phil, PhD); molecular and cellular neuroscience (M Phil, PhD); molecular biology (M Phil, PhD); molecular cancer studies (M Phil, PhD); neuroscience (M Phil, PhD); ophthalmology (M Phil, PhD); optometry (M Phil, PhD); organelle function (M Phil, PhD); pharmacology (M Phil, PhD); physiology (M Phil, PhD); plant sciences (M Phil, PhD); stem cell research (M Phil, PhD); structural biology (M Phil, PhD); systems neuroscience (M Phil, PhD); toxicology (M Phil, PhD).

University of Manitoba, Faculty of Medicine and Faculty of Graduate Studies, Graduate Programs in Medicine, Department of Physiology, Winnipeg, MB R3T 2N2, Canada. Offers M Sc, PhD, MD/PhD. Terminal master's awarded for partial completion of doctoral program. *Degree requirements:* For master's, one foreign language, thesis; for doctorate, one foreign language, thesis/dissertation. *Entrance requirements:* For master's, minimum GPA of 3.5; for doctorate, minimum GPA of 3.5, M Sc. *Faculty research:* Cardiovascular research, gene technology, cell biology, neuroscience, respiration.

University of Massachusetts Amherst, Graduate School, Interdisciplinary Programs, Program in Plant Biology, Amherst, MA 01003. Offers biochemistry and metabolism (MS, PhD); cell biology and physiology (MS, PhD); environmental, ecological and integrative (PhD); environmental, ecological and integrative biology (MS); genetics and evolution (MS, PhD). *Students:* 18 full-time (8 women); includes 1 minority (Asian, non-Hispanic/Latino), 7 international. Average age 29. 27 applicants, 41% accepted, 6 enrolled. In 2010, 3 doctorates awarded. *Degree requirements:* For master's, thesis; for doctorate, 2 foreign languages, comprehensive exam, thesis/dissertation. *Entrance requirements:* For master's and doctorate, GRE General Test. Additional exam requirements/recommendations for international students: Required—TOEFL (minimum score 550 paper-based; 213 computer-based; 80 iBT), IELTS (minimum score 6.5). *Application deadline:* For fall admission, 12/15 for domestic and international students; for spring admission, 10/1 for domestic and international students. Applications are processed on a rolling basis. Application fee: $50 ($65 for international students). Electronic applications accepted. *Expenses:* Tuition, state resident: full-time $2640. Required fees: $8282. One-time fee: $357 full-time. *Financial support:* In 2010–11, 12 research assistantships with full tuition reimbursements (averaging $11,651 per year) were awarded; fellowships, teaching assistantships, career-related internships or fieldwork, Federal Work-Study, scholarships/grants, traineeships, health care benefits, tuition waivers (full), and unspecified assistantships also available. Support available to part-time students. Financial award application deadline: 12/15; financial award applicants required to submit FAFSA. *Unit head:* Dr. Elsbeth L. Walker, Graduate Program Director, 413-577-3217, Fax: 413-545-3243. *Application contact:* Jean M. Ames, Supervisor of Admissions, 413-545—0722, Fax: 413-577-0010, E-mail: gradadm@grad.umass.edu.

University of Medicine and Dentistry of New Jersey, Graduate School of Biomedical Sciences, Graduate Programs in Biomedical Sciences–Newark, Department of Pharmacology and Physiology, Newark, NJ 07107. Offers PhD. *Degree requirements:* For doctorate, thesis/dissertation, qualifying exam. *Entrance requirements:* For doctorate, GRE General Test. Additional exam requirements/recommendations for international students: Required—TOEFL. Electronic applications accepted.

University of Medicine and Dentistry of New Jersey, Graduate School of Biomedical Sciences, Graduate Programs in Biomedical Sciences–Piscataway, Program in Physiology and Integrative Biology, Piscataway, NJ 08854-5635. Offers MS, PhD, MD/PhD. *Entrance requirements:* Additional exam requirements/recommendations for international students: Required—TOEFL. *Application deadline:* For fall admission, 1/5 for domestic students. Applications are processed on a rolling basis. Application fee: $40. Electronic applications accepted. *Unit head:* Dr. Jianjie Ma, Director, 732-235-4494, Fax: 732-235-4483, E-mail: maj2@umdnj.edu. *Application contact:* University Registrar, 973-972-5338.

University of Miami, Graduate School, Miller School of Medicine, Graduate Programs in Medicine, Department of Physiology and Biophysics, Coral Gables, FL 33124. Offers PhD, MD/PhD. *Degree requirements:* For doctorate, thesis/dissertation, qualifying exam. *Entrance requirements:* For doctorate, GRE General Test, minimum GPA of 3.0 in sciences. Additional exam requirements/recommendations for international students: Required—TOEFL. *Faculty research:* Cell and membrane physiology, cell-to-cell communication, molecular neurobiology, neuroimmunology, neural development.

University of Michigan, Rackham Graduate School, Program in Biomedical Sciences (PIBS), Department of Molecular and Integrative Physiology, Ann Arbor, MI 48109. Offers PhD. *Faculty:* 32 full-time (12 women), 1 part-time/adjunct (0 women). *Students:* 24 full-time (12 women); includes 8 minority (2 Black or African American, non-Hispanic/Latino; 6 Asian, non-Hispanic/Latino). Average age 27. 31 applicants, 39% accepted, 6 enrolled. In 2010, 6 doctorates awarded. *Degree requirements:* For doctorate, thesis/dissertation, oral defense of dissertation, preliminary exam. *Entrance requirements:* For doctorate, GRE General Test, 3 letters of recommendation, research experience. Additional exam requirements/recommendations for international students: Required—Michigan English Language Assessment Battery or TOEFL (minimum iBT score 84). *Application deadline:* For fall admission, 12/1 for domestic and international students. Application fee: $60 ($75 for international students). Electronic applications accepted. *Expenses:* Tuition, state resident: full-time $17,784; part-time $1116 per credit hour. Tuition, nonresident: full-time $35,944; part-time $2125 per credit hour. International tuition: $35,994 full-time. Required fees: $95 per semester. Tuition and fees vary according to course load, degree level and program. *Financial support:* In 2010–11, 24 students received support, including 24 fellowships with full tuition reimbursements available (averaging $26,500 per year); scholarships/grants, health care benefits, tuition waivers (full), unspecified assistantships, and departmental funding also available. Financial award application deadline: 12/1. *Faculty research:* Ion transport, cardiovascular physiology, gene expression, hormone action, gastrointestinal physiology, endocrinology, muscle, signal transduction. Total annual research expenditures: $8.9 million. *Unit head:* Dr. Bishr Omary, Chair, 734-764-4376, Fax: 734-936-

8813, E-mail: mbishr@umich.edu. *Application contact:* Michelle S. Melis, Director of Student Life, 734-615-6538, Fax: 734-647-7022, E-mail: msmtegan@umich.edu.

University of Minnesota, Duluth, Medical School, Graduate Program in Physiology, Duluth, MN 55812-2496. Offers MS, PhD. MS, PhD offered jointly with University of Minnesota, Twin Cities Campus. Terminal master's awarded for partial completion of doctoral program. *Degree requirements:* For master's, thesis; for doctorate, thesis/dissertation. *Entrance requirements:* For master's, GRE or MCAT; for doctorate, GRE or MCAT, 1 year of course work in each calculus, physics, and biology; 2 years of course work in chemistry; minimum GPA of 3.0 in science. Additional exam requirements/recommendations for international students: Required—TOEFL. *Faculty research:* Neural control of posture and locomotion, transport and metabolic phenomena in biological systems, control of organ blood flow, intracellular means of communication.

University of Minnesota, Twin Cities Campus, Graduate School, Department of Integrative Biology and Physiology, Minneapolis, MN 55455-0213. Offers PhD. Part-time programs available. *Degree requirements:* For doctorate, comprehensive exam, thesis/dissertation. *Entrance requirements:* For doctorate, GRE General Test. Electronic applications accepted. *Faculty research:* Cardiovascular physiology.

University of Mississippi Medical Center, School of Graduate Studies in the Health Sciences, Department of Physiology and Biophysics, Jackson, MS 39216-4505. Offers MS, PhD, MD/PhD. *Degree requirements:* For master's, thesis; for doctorate, thesis/dissertation, first authored publication. *Entrance requirements:* For master's and doctorate, GRE General Test, minimum GPA of 3.0. *Faculty research:* Cardiovascular, renal, endocrine, and cellular neurophysiology; molecular physiology.

University of Missouri, School of Medicine and Graduate School, Graduate Programs in Medicine, Department of Medical Pharmacology and Physiology, Columbia, MO 65211. Offers pharmacology (MS, PhD); physiology (MS, PhD). *Degree requirements:* For master's, thesis; for doctorate, thesis/dissertation. *Entrance requirements:* For master's and doctorate, GRE General Test, minimum GPA of 3.0. Additional exam requirements/recommendations for international students: Required—TOEFL (minimum score 500 paper-based; 173 computer-based; 61 iBT). *Faculty research:* Endocrine and metabolic pharmacology, biochemical pharmacology, neuropharmacology, receptors and transmembrane signaling.

University of Nebraska Medical Center, Graduate Studies, Department of Cellular and Integrative Physiology, Omaha, NE 68198. Offers physiology (MS, PhD). *Faculty:* 18 full-time (4 women). *Students:* 6 full-time (3 women), 6 part-time (4 women); includes 1 Hispanic/Latino, 4 international. Average age 28. 10 applicants, 20% accepted, 2 enrolled. In 2010, 1 doctorate awarded. Terminal master's awarded for partial completion of doctoral program. *Degree requirements:* For master's, comprehensive exam, thesis optional; for doctorate, comprehensive exam, thesis/dissertation, at least one first-author research publication. *Entrance requirements:* For master's and doctorate, GRE General Test or MCAT, course work in biology, chemistry, mathematics, and physics. Additional exam requirements/recommendations for international students: Required—TOEFL (minimum score 600 paper-based; 250 computer-based; 100 iBT). *Application deadline:* For fall admission, 4/1 priority date for domestic students, 4/1 for international students. Applications are processed on a rolling basis. Application fee: $45. Electronic applications accepted. *Expenses:* Tuition, state resident: part-time $198.25 per semester hour. Required fees: $63 per semester. *Financial support:* In 2010–11, 6 students received support, including 1 fellowship with full tuition reimbursement available (averaging $21,000 per year), 2 research assistantships with full tuition reimbursements available (averaging $21,000 per year); health care benefits and unspecified assistantships also available. Financial award application deadline: 2/15. *Faculty research:* Cardiovascular, renal and visual physiology, neuroscience, reproductive endocrinology. Total annual research expenditures: $3.7 million. *Unit head:* Dr. Pamela K. Carmines, Chair, Graduate Committee, 402-559-9343, Fax: 402-559-4438, E-mail: pcarmines@unmc.edu. *Application contact:* Dan Teet, Graduate Studies Associate, 402-559-6531, Fax: 402-559-7845, E-mail: unmcgraduatestudies@unmc.edu.

University of Nevada, Reno, Graduate School, Interdisciplinary Program in Cellular and Molecular Pharmacology and Physiology, Reno, NV 89557. Offers PhD. *Degree requirements:* For doctorate, one foreign language, thesis/dissertation. *Entrance requirements:* For doctorate, GRE General Test or MCAT, minimum GPA of 3.0. Additional exam requirements/recommendations for international students: Required—TOEFL (minimum score 500 paper-based; 173 computer-based; 61 iBT), IELTS (minimum score 6). Electronic applications accepted. *Expenses:* Tuition, state resident: full-time $2219; part-time $246 per credit. Tuition, nonresident: part-time $510 per credit. International tuition: $9009 full-time. Required fees: $59 per term. One-time fee: $101. Tuition and fees vary according to course load. *Faculty research:* Neuropharmacology, toxicology, cardiovascular pharmacology, neuromuscular pharmacology.

University of New Mexico, School of Medicine, Biomedical Sciences Graduate Program, Albuquerque, NM 87131-5196. Offers biochemistry and molecular biology (MS, PhD); cell biology and physiology (MS, PhD); clinical and translational science (Certificate); molecular genetics and microbiology (MS, PhD); neuroscience (MS, PhD); pathology (MS, PhD); toxicology (MS, PhD); university science teaching (Certificate). Part-time programs available. *Faculty:* 33 full-time (14 women), 3 part-time/adjunct (1 woman). *Students:* 94 full-time (57 women), 14 part-time (8 women); includes 24 minority (3 Black or African American, non-Hispanic/Latino; 1 American Indian or Alaska Native, non-Hispanic/Latino; 6 Asian, non-Hispanic/Latino; 13 Hispanic/Latino; 1 Two or more races, non-Hispanic/Latino), 20 international. Average age 30. 135 applicants, 14% accepted, 19 enrolled. In 2010, 2 master's, 19 doctorates, 3 other advanced degrees awarded. Terminal master's awarded for partial completion of doctoral program. *Degree requirements:* For master's, thesis; for doctorate, comprehensive exam, thesis/dissertation. *Entrance requirements:* For master's and doctorate, GRE General Test, minimum undergraduate GPA of 3.0. Additional exam requirements/recommendations for international students: Required—TOEFL. *Application deadline:* For fall admission, 1/1 priority date for domestic students. Applications are processed on a rolling basis. Application fee: $50. Electronic applications accepted. *Expenses:* Tuition, state resident: full-time $5991; part-time $251 per credit hour. Tuition, nonresident: full-time $14,405; part-time $800.20 per credit hour. Tuition and fees vary according to course level, course load, program and reciprocity agreements. *Financial support:* In 2010–11, 99 students received support, including 5 fellowships (averaging $75 per year), 96 research assistantships with full tuition reimbursements available (averaging $17,401 per year), 2 teaching assistantships with full tuition reimbursements available (averaging $2,415 per year); career-related internships or fieldwork, Federal Work-Study, institutionally sponsored loans, scholarships/grants, traineeships, health care benefits, and unspecified assistantships also available. Financial award application deadline: 1/1; financial award applicants required to submit FAFSA. *Faculty research:* Signal transduction, infectious disease, biology of cancer, structural biology, neuroscience. *Unit head:* Laurie G. Hudson, Director, 505-272-1887, Fax: 505-272-8738, E-mail: lhudson@salud.unm.edu. *Application contact:* Angel Cooke-Jackson, Coordinator, 505-272-1887, Fax: 505-272-8738, E-mail: acooke-jackson@salud.unm.edu.

University of North Dakota, Graduate School and Graduate School, Graduate Programs in Medicine, Department of Pharmacology, Physiology, and Therapeutics, Grand Forks, ND 58202. Offers pharmacology (MS, PhD); physiology (MS, PhD). *Faculty:* 14 full-time (2 women), 2 part-time/adjunct (0 women). *Students:* 14 full-time (5 women), 2 part-time (1 woman); includes 1 minority (Asian, non-Hispanic/Latino), 5 international. Average age 28. 23 applicants, 17% accepted, 4 enrolled. In 2010, 3 doctorates awarded. *Degree requirements:* For master's, comprehensive exam, thesis; for doctorate, thesis/dissertation, written and oral exams. *Entrance requirements:* For master's, GRE General Test or MCAT, minimum GPA of 3.0; for doctorate, GRE General Test, minimum GPA of 3.5. Additional exam requirements/recommendations for international students: Required—TOEFL (minimum score 550 paper-based; 213 computer-based; 79 iBT), IELTS (minimum score 6.5). *Application deadline:* For fall admission, 2/1 priority date for domestic and international students. Application fee: $35. Electronic applications accepted. *Expenses:* Tuition, state resident: full-time $5857; part-time $306.74 per credit.

Tuition, nonresident: full-time $15,666; part-time $729.77 per credit. Required fees: $53.42 per credit. Tuition and fees vary according to course load, program and reciprocity agreements. *Financial support:* In 2010–11, 14 students received support, including 14 research assistantships with full tuition reimbursements available (averaging $13,997 per year); fellowships with full and partial tuition reimbursements available, teaching assistantships with full tuition reimbursements available, Federal Work-Study, institutionally sponsored loans, scholarships/grants, health care benefits, tuition waivers (full and partial), and unspecified assistantships also available. Support available to part-time students. Financial award application deadline: 3/15; financial award applicants required to submit FAFSA. Total annual research expenditures: $3.4 million. *Unit head:* Dr. James Hasselton, Graduate Director, 701-777-4683, Fax: 701-777-4490, E-mail: hasselton@medicine.nodak.edu. *Application contact:* Matt Anderson, Admissions Specialist, 701-777-2947, Fax: 701-777-3619, E-mail: matthew.anderson@gradschool.und.edu.

University of North Texas Health Science Center at Fort Worth, Graduate School of Biomedical Sciences, Fort Worth, TX 76107-2699. Offers anatomy and cell biology (MS, PhD); biochemistry and molecular biology (MS, PhD); biomedical sciences (MS, PhD); biotechnology (MS); forensic genetics (MS); integrative physiology (MS, PhD); medical science (MS); microbiology and immunology (MS, PhD); pharmacology (MS, PhD); science education (MS); DO/MS; DO/PhD. Terminal master's awarded for partial completion of doctoral program. *Degree requirements:* For master's, thesis; for doctorate, thesis/dissertation. *Entrance requirements:* For master's and doctorate, GRE General Test. Additional exam requirements/recommendations for international students: Required—TOEFL. *Expenses:* Contact institution. *Faculty research:* Alzheimer's disease, aging, eye diseases, cancer, cardiovascular disease.

University of Notre Dame, Graduate School, College of Science, Department of Biological Sciences, Notre Dame, IN 46556. Offers aquatic ecology, evolution and environmental biology (MS, PhD); cellular and molecular biology (MS, PhD); genetics (MS, PhD); physiology (MS, PhD); vector biology and parasitology (MS, PhD). Terminal master's awarded for partial completion of doctoral program. *Degree requirements:* For master's, comprehensive exam, thesis; for doctorate, comprehensive exam, thesis/dissertation, candidacy exam. *Entrance requirements:* For master's and doctorate, GRE General Test. Additional exam requirements/recommendations for international students: Required—TOEFL (minimum score 600 paper-based; 250 computer-based; 80 iBT). Electronic applications accepted. *Faculty research:* Tropical disease, molecular genetics, neurobiology, evolutionary biology, aquatic biology.

University of Oklahoma Health Sciences Center, College of Medicine and Graduate College, Graduate Programs in Medicine, Department of Physiology, Oklahoma City, OK 73190. Offers MS, PhD. Part-time programs available. Terminal master's awarded for partial completion of doctoral program. *Degree requirements:* For master's, thesis (for some programs); for doctorate, thesis/dissertation. *Entrance requirements:* For master's, GRE General Test, statement of career goals, 3 letters of recommendation; for doctorate, GRE General Test, 3 letters of recommendation. Additional exam requirements/recommendations for international students: Required—TOEFL. *Faculty research:* Cardiopulmonary physiology, neurophysiology, exercise physiology, cell and molecular physiology.

University of Oregon, Graduate School, College of Arts and Sciences, Department of Human Physiology, Eugene, OR 97403. Offers MS, PhD. *Degree requirements:* For master's, thesis optional; for doctorate, one foreign language, thesis/dissertation. *Entrance requirements:* For master's, GRE General Test, minimum GPA of 2.75 in undergraduate course work; for doctorate, GRE General Test. *Faculty research:* Balance control, muscle fatigue, lower extremity function, knee control.

University of Pennsylvania, Perelman School of Medicine, Biomedical Graduate Studies, Graduate Group in Cell and Molecular Biology, Philadelphia, PA 19104. Offers cancer biology (PhD); cell biology and physiology (PhD); developmental stem cell regenerative biology (PhD); gene therapy and vaccines (PhD); genetics and gene regulation (PhD); microbiology, virology, and parasitology (PhD); MD/PhD; VMD/PhD. *Faculty:* 299. *Students:* 315 full-time (166 women); includes 13 Black or African American, non-Hispanic/Latino; 1 American Indian or Alaska Native, non-Hispanic/Latino; 44 Asian, non-Hispanic/Latino; 18 Hispanic/Latino, 37 international. 579 applicants, 21% accepted, 49 enrolled. In 2010, 53 doctorates awarded. *Degree requirements:* For doctorate, thesis/dissertation. *Entrance requirements:* For doctorate, GRE General Test. Additional exam requirements/recommendations for international students: Required—TOEFL. *Application deadline:* For fall admission, 12/8 priority date for domestic and international students. Applications are processed on a rolling basis. Application fee: $70. Electronic applications accepted. *Expenses:* Tuition: Full-time $25,660; part-time $4758 per course. Required fees: $2152; $270 per course. Tuition and fees vary according to course load, degree level and program. *Financial support:* In 2010–11, 315 students received support; fellowships, research assistantships, scholarships/grants, traineeships, and unspecified assistantships available. Financial award application deadline: 12/8. *Unit head:* Dr. Daniel Kessler, Graduate Group Chair, 215-898-2180, E-mail: raperj@mail.med.upenn.edu. *Application contact:* Meagan Schofer, Coordinator, 215-898-9536, Fax: 215-573-2104, E-mail: camb@mailmed.upenn.edu.

University of Prince Edward Island, Atlantic Veterinary College, Graduate Program in Veterinary Medicine, Charlottetown, PE C1A 4P3, Canada. Offers anatomy (M Sc, PhD); bacteriology (M Sc, PhD); clinical pharmacology (M Sc, PhD); clinical sciences (M Sc, PhD); epidemiology (M Sc, PhD), including reproduction; fish health (M Sc, PhD); food animal nutrition (M Sc, PhD); immunology (M Sc, PhD); microanatomy (M Sc, PhD); parasitology (M Sc, PhD); pathology (M Sc, PhD); pharmacology (M Sc, PhD); physiology (M Sc, PhD); toxicology (M Sc, PhD); veterinary science (M Vet Sc); virology (M Sc, PhD). Part-time programs available. *Degree requirements:* For master's, thesis; for doctorate, thesis/dissertation. *Entrance requirements:* For master's, DVM, B Sc honors degree, or equivalent; for doctorate, M Sc. Additional exam requirements/recommendations for international students: Required—TOEFL (minimum score 550 paper-based; 213 computer-based; 80 iBT). *Expenses:* Contact institution. *Faculty research:* Animal health management, infectious diseases, fin fish and shellfish health, basic biomedical sciences, ecosystem health.

University of Puerto Rico, Medical Sciences Campus, School of Medicine, Division of Graduate Studies, Department of Physiology, San Juan, PR 00936-5067. Offers MS, PhD. Terminal master's awarded for partial completion of doctoral program. *Degree requirements:* For master's, one foreign language, thesis; for doctorate, one foreign language, comprehensive exam, thesis/dissertation. *Entrance requirements:* For master's and doctorate, GRE General Test, GRE Subject Test, interview; course work in biology, chemistry and physics; minimum GPA of 3.0; 3 letters of recommendation. Electronic applications accepted. *Faculty research:* Respiration, neuroendocrinology, cellular and molecular physiology, cardiovascular, exercise physiology and neurobiology.

University of Rochester, School of Medicine and Dentistry, Graduate Programs in Medicine and Dentistry, Department of Pharmacology and Physiology, Programs in Physiology, Rochester, NY 14627. Offers MS, PhD. Terminal master's awarded for partial completion of doctoral program. *Degree requirements:* For master's, thesis; for doctorate, thesis/dissertation, qualifying exam. *Entrance requirements:* For master's and doctorate, GRE General Test.

University of Saskatchewan, College of Medicine, Department of Physiology, Saskatoon, SK S7N 5A2, Canada. Offers M Sc, PhD. *Degree requirements:* For master's, thesis; for doctorate, thesis/dissertation. *Entrance requirements:* Additional exam requirements/recommendations for international students: Required—TOEFL.

University of Saskatchewan, Western College of Veterinary Medicine and College of Graduate Studies and Research, Graduate Programs in Veterinary Medicine, Department of Veterinary Biomedical Sciences, Saskatoon, SK S7N 5A2, Canada. Offers veterinary anatomy (M Sc); veterinary biomedical sciences (M Vet Sc); veterinary physiological sciences (M Sc, PhD). *Faculty:* 12 full-time (4 women), 4 part-time/adjunct (0 women). *Students:* 49 full-time (24 women); includes 2 Black or African American, non-Hispanic/Latino; 47 American Indian or Alaska Native, non-Hispanic/Latino. In 2010, 8 master's, 4 doctorates awarded. *Degree requirements:* For master's, thesis; for doctorate, comprehensive exam (for some programs), thesis/dissertation. *Entrance requirements:* Additional exam requirements/recommendations for international students: Required—TOEFL (minimum score 80 iBT); Recommended—IELTS (minimum score 6.5). Electronic applications accepted. *Faculty research:* Toxicology, animal reproduction, pharmacology, chloride channels, pulmonary pathobiology. *Unit head:* Dr. Barry Blakley, Head, 306-966-7350, Fax: 306-966-7376, E-mail: barry.blakley@usask.ca. *Application contact:* Application Contact.

The University of South Dakota, School of Medicine and Health Sciences and Graduate School, Biomedical Sciences Graduate Program, Physiology and Pharmacology Group, Vermillion, SD 57069-2390. Offers MS, PhD. Terminal master's awarded for partial completion of doctoral program. *Degree requirements:* For master's, thesis; for doctorate, comprehensive exam, thesis/dissertation. *Entrance requirements:* For master's and doctorate, GRE General Test, minimum GPA of 3.0. Additional exam requirements/recommendations for international students: Required—TOEFL (minimum score 550 paper-based; 213 computer-based; 80 iBT), IELTS (minimum score 6). Electronic applications accepted. *Expenses:* Contact institution. *Faculty research:* Pulmonary physiology and pharmacology, drug abuse, reproduction, signal transduction, cardiovascular physiology and pharmacology.

University of Southern California, Keck School of Medicine and Graduate School, Graduate Programs in Medicine, Department of Physiology and Biophysics, Los Angeles, CA 90089. Offers MS, PhD, MD/PhD. *Faculty:* 16 full-time (5 women). *Students:* 7 full-time (3 women); includes 1 Asian, non-Hispanic/Latino, 5 international. Average age 28. 12 applicants, 17% accepted, 1 enrolled.Terminal master's awarded for partial completion of doctoral program. *Degree requirements:* For master's, thesis optional; for doctorate, comprehensive exam, thesis/dissertation. *Entrance requirements:* For master's and doctorate, GRE General Test, minimum GPA of 3.0. Additional exam requirements/recommendations for international students: Required—TOEFL (minimum score 600 paper-based; 250 computer-based; 100 iBT). *Application deadline:* For fall admission, 2/1 priority date for domestic and international students. Application fee: $85. Electronic applications accepted. *Expenses:* Tuition: Full-time $31,240; part-time $1420 per unit. Required fees: $600. One-time fee: $35 full-time. Full-time tuition and fees vary according to degree level and program. *Financial support:* In 2010–11, 1 student received support, including 5 research assistantships with full tuition reimbursements available; Federal Work-Study, institutionally sponsored loans, scholarships/grants, traineeships, health care benefits, and unspecified assistantships also available. Financial award application deadline: 5/5. *Faculty research:* Endocrinology and metabolism, neurophysiology, mathematical modeling, cell transport, autoimmunity and cancer immunotherapy. Total annual research expenditures: $2.1 million. *Unit head:* Dr. Richard N. Bergman, Chair, 323-442-1920, Fax: 323-442-1918, E-mail: rbergman@usc.edu. *Application contact:* Elena Camarena, Graduate Coordinator, 323-442-1039, Fax: 323-442-2283, E-mail: physiol@hsc.usc.edu.

The University of Tennessee, Graduate School, College of Agricultural Sciences and Natural Resources, Department of Animal Science, Knoxville, TN 37996. Offers animal anatomy (PhD); breeding (MS, PhD); management (MS, PhD); nutrition (MS, PhD); physiology (MS, PhD). Part-time programs available. *Degree requirements:* For master's, thesis; for doctorate, thesis/dissertation. *Entrance requirements:* For master's and doctorate, GRE General Test, minimum GPA of 2.7. Additional exam requirements/recommendations for international students: Required—TOEFL. Electronic applications accepted. *Expenses:* Tuition, state resident: full-time $7440; part-time $414 per credit hour. Tuition, nonresident: full-time $22,478; part-time $1250 per credit hour. Required fees: $922; $43 per credit hour. Tuition and fees vary according to program.

The University of Texas Health Science Center at San Antonio, Graduate School of Biomedical Sciences, Department of Physiology, San Antonio, TX 78229-3900. Offers MS, PhD. *Faculty:* 21 full-time (4 women). *Students:* 17 full-time (7 women), 2 part-time (1 woman); includes 8 Asian, non-Hispanic/Latino; 1 Hispanic/Latino, 2 international. Average age 25. In 2010, 2 doctorates awarded. *Degree requirements:* For master's, thesis; for doctorate, comprehensive exam, thesis/dissertation. *Entrance requirements:* For master's, GRE General Test, MAT; for doctorate, GRE General Test. Additional exam requirements/recommendations for international students: Required—TOEFL (minimum score 560 paper-based; 220 computer-based; 68 iBT). *Application deadline:* For fall admission, 1/15 priority date for domestic and international students. Applications are processed on a rolling basis. Electronic applications accepted. *Expenses:* Tuition, state resident: full-time $3072; part-time $128 per credit hour. Tuition, nonresident: full-time $11,928; part-time $497 per credit hour. Required fees: $1078; $1078 per year. One-time fee: $60. *Financial support:* In 2010–11, 16 teaching assistantships (averaging $26,000 per year) were awarded; Federal Work-Study, institutionally sponsored loans, and health care benefits also available. Financial award application deadline: 6/30; financial award applicants required to submit FAFSA. *Faculty research:* Ion channels, cardiovascular function, neuroscience and aging. Total annual research expenditures: $6.8 million. *Unit head:* John Johnson, Professor and Interim Chair, 210-567-4324, Fax: 210-567-4326. *Application contact:* Shane Rea, Chairman, Committee on Graduate Studies, 210-567-4324, Fax: 210-567-4410, E-mail: physiologygrad@uthscsa.edu.

The University of Texas Medical Branch, Graduate School of Biomedical Sciences, Program in Cellular Physiology and Molecular Biophysics, Galveston, TX 77555. Offers MS, PhD. *Degree requirements:* For master's, thesis or alternative; for doctorate, thesis/dissertation. *Entrance requirements:* For master's and doctorate, GRE General Test. Additional exam requirements/recommendations for international students: Required—TOEFL (minimum score 550 paper-based; 213 computer-based). Electronic applications accepted.

University of Toronto, School of Graduate Studies, Life Sciences Division, Department of Physiology, Toronto, ON M5S 1A1, Canada. Offers M Sc, PhD. *Degree requirements:* For master's, thesis; for doctorate, thesis/dissertation. *Entrance requirements:* For master's and doctorate, minimum B+ average in final year, 2 letters of reference. Additional exam requirements/recommendations for international students: Required—TOEFL (600 paper-based, 250 computer-based), Michigan English Language Assessment Battery (95), IELTS (8) or COPE (5).

University of Utah, School of Medicine and Graduate School, Graduate Programs in Medicine, Department of Physiology, Salt Lake City, UT 84112-1107. Offers PhD. *Degree requirements:* For doctorate, thesis/dissertation, comprehensive qualifying exam, preliminary exam. *Entrance requirements:* For doctorate, GRE General Test, GRE Subject Test, minimum GPA of 3.0. Additional exam requirements/recommendations for international students: Required—TOEFL (minimum score 650 paper-based; 250 computer-based; 100 iBT); Recommended—TWE (minimum score 6). Electronic applications accepted. *Expenses:* Tuition, area resident: Part-time $179.19 per credit hour. Tuition, state resident: full-time $4384. Tuition, nonresident: full-time $16,684; part-time $630.67 per credit hour. Required fees: $350 per semester. Tuition and fees vary according to course load, degree level and program. *Faculty research:* Cell neurobiology, chemosensory systems, cardiovascular and kidney physiology, endocrinology.

University of Virginia, School of Medicine, Department of Molecular Physiology and Biological Physics, Program in Physiology, Charlottesville, VA 22903. Offers PhD, MD/PhD. *Students:* 13 full-time (6 women), 1 part-time (0 women); includes 2 Black or African American, non-Hispanic/Latino. Average age 29. In 2010, 1 doctorate awarded. *Entrance requirements:* For doctorate, GRE General Test, 2 letters of recommendation. Additional exam requirements/recommendations for international students: Required—TOEFL. *Application deadline:* For fall admission, 1/15 for domestic and international students. Applications are processed on a rolling basis. Application fee: $60. Electronic applications accepted. *Financial support:* Fellowships, research assistantships, teaching assistantships available. Financial award applicants required to submit FAFSA. *Unit head:* Dr. Mark Yeager, Chair, 434-924-5108, Fax: 434-982-1616, E-mail: my3r@virginia.edu. *Application contact:* Dr. Mark Yeager, Chair, 434-924-5108, Fax: 434-982-1616, E-mail: my3r@virginia.edu.

Physiology

University of Washington, Graduate School, School of Medicine, Graduate Programs in Medicine, Department of Physiology and Biophysics, Seattle, WA 98195. Offers PhD. *Degree requirements:* For doctorate, thesis/dissertation. *Entrance requirements:* For doctorate, GRE General Test. Additional exam requirements/recommendations for international students: Required—TOEFL (minimum score 580 paper-based; 237 computer-based; 70 iBT). *Faculty research:* Membrane and cell biophysics, neuroendocrinology, cardiovascular and respiratory physiology, systems neurophysiology and behavior, molecular physiology.

The University of Western Ontario, Faculty of Graduate Studies, Biosciences Division, Department of Physiology and Pharmacology, London, ON N6A 5B8, Canada. Offers M Sc, PhD. *Degree requirements:* For master's, thesis, seminar course; for doctorate, comprehensive exam, thesis/dissertation. *Entrance requirements:* For master's, minimum B average, honors degree; for doctorate, minimum B average, honors degree, M Sc. *Faculty research:* Reproductive and endocrine physiology, neurophysiology, cardiovascular and renal physiology, cell physiology, gastrointestinal and metabolic physiology.

University of Wisconsin–La Crosse, Office of University Graduate Studies, College of Science and Health, Department of Biology, La Crosse, WI 54601-3742. Offers aquatic sciences (MS); biology (MS); cellular and molecular biology (MS); clinical microbiology (MS); microbiology (MS); nurse anesthesia (MS); physiology (MS). Part-time programs available. *Faculty:* 31. *Students:* 23 full-time (14 women), 42 part-time (25 women); includes 4 minority (1 Asian, non-Hispanic/Latino; 3 Hispanic/Latino), 1 international. Average age 28. 100 applicants, 34% accepted, 29 enrolled. In 2010, 20 master's awarded. *Degree requirements:* For master's, comprehensive exam, thesis. *Entrance requirements:* For master's, GRE General Test, minimum GPA of 2.85. Additional exam requirements/recommendations for international students: Required—TOEFL (minimum score 550 paper-based; 213 computer-based; 79 iBT). *Application deadline:* For fall admission, 2/1 priority date for domestic and international students; for spring admission, 1/4 priority date for domestic and international students. Applications are processed on a rolling basis. Application fee: $56. Electronic applications accepted. *Expenses:* Tuition, state resident: full-time $7121; part-time $395.61 per credit. Tuition, nonresident: full-time $16,891; part-time $938.41 per credit. Part-time tuition and fees vary according to course load, program and reciprocity agreements. *Financial support:* In 2010–11, 14 research assistantships with partial tuition reimbursements (averaging $10,124 per year) were awarded; Federal Work-Study, scholarships/grants, health care benefits, and tuition waivers (partial) also available. Support available to part-time students. Financial award application deadline: 3/15; financial award applicants required to submit FAFSA. *Unit head:* Dr. Thomas Volk, Coordinator of Graduate Studies, 608-785-6972, Fax: 608-785-6959, E-mail: volk.thom@uwlax.edu. *Application contact:* Kathryn Kiefer, Director of Admissions, 608-785-8939, E-mail: admissions@uwlax.edu.

University of Wisconsin–Madison, School of Medicine and Public Health, Endocrinology-Reproductive Physiology Program, Madison, WI 53706-1380. Offers MS, PhD. Terminal master's awarded for partial completion of doctoral program. *Degree requirements:* For master's, comprehensive exam, thesis, oral defense of thesis; for doctorate, comprehensive exam, thesis/dissertation, oral defense of dissertation. *Entrance requirements:* For master's, GRE, resume, 3 letters of recommendation; for doctorate, GRE, resumé, 3 letters of recommendation. Additional exam requirements/recommendations for international students: Required—TOEFL (minimum score 550 paper-based; 213 computer-based). Electronic applications accepted. *Expenses:* Tuition, state resident: full-time $9887; part-time $617.96 per credit. Tuition, nonresident: full-time $24,054; part-time $1503.40 per credit. Required fees: $67.63 per credit. Tuition and fees vary according to reciprocity agreements. *Faculty research:* Ovarian physiology and endocrinology, fertilization and gamete biology, hormone action and cell signaling, placental function and pregnancy, embryo and fetal development.

University of Wisconsin–Madison, School of Medicine and Public Health and Graduate School, Graduate Programs in Medicine, Department of Physiology, Madison, WI 53706-1380. Offers PhD. *Faculty:* 18 full-time (5 women). *Students:* 11 full-time (0 women); includes 1 Black or African American, non-Hispanic/Latino; 6 Asian, non-Hispanic/Latino; 2 Hispanic/Latino. Average age 22. 40 applicants, 8% accepted, 2 enrolled. In 2010, 7 doctorates awarded. *Degree requirements:* For doctorate, thesis/dissertation, written exams. *Entrance requirements:* For doctorate, GRE, minimum GPA of 3.0. Additional exam requirements/recommendations for international students: Required—TOEFL (minimum score 580 paper-based; 237 computer-based). *Application deadline:* For fall admission, 1/15 priority date for domestic and international students. Applications are processed on a rolling basis. Application fee: $45. Electronic applications accepted. *Expenses:* Tuition, state resident: full-time $9887; part-time $617.96 per credit. Tuition, nonresident: full-time $24,054; part-time $1503.40 per credit. Required fees: $67.63 per credit. Tuition and fees vary according to reciprocity agreements. *Financial support:* In 2010–11, fellowships with tuition reimbursements (averaging $24,000 per year), research assistantships with tuition reimbursements (averaging $24,000 per year), teaching assistantships with tuition reimbursements (averaging $24,000 per year) were awarded. *Faculty research:* Studies in molecular cellular systems, cardiovascular, neuroscience. *Unit head:* Dr. Tom C. T. Yin, Interim Chair, 608-262-0368, Fax: 608-265-5512, E-mail: tcyin@wisc.edu. *Application contact:* Sue S. Krey, Program Assistant 4, 608-262-9114, Fax: 608-265-5512, E-mail: sskrey@wisc.edu.

University of Wyoming, College of Arts and Sciences, Department of Zoology and Physiology, Laramie, WY 82070. Offers MS, PhD. Part-time programs available. *Degree requirements:* For master's, comprehensive exam (for some programs), thesis; for doctorate, comprehensive exam (for some programs), thesis/dissertation. *Entrance requirements:* For master's and doctorate, GRE General Test, minimum GPA of 3.0. Additional exam requirements/recommendations for international students: Required—TOEFL. Electronic applications accepted. *Faculty research:* Cell biology, ecology/wildlife, organismal physiology, zoology.

Virginia Commonwealth University, Medical College of Virginia-Professional Programs, School of Medicine, School of Medicine Graduate Programs, Department of Physiology and Biophysics, Richmond, VA 23284-9005. Offers physical therapy (PhD); physiology (MS, PhD); MD/PhD. *Faculty:* 34 full-time (7 women). *Students:* 30 full-time (13 women), 1 part-time (0 women); includes 13 minority (3 Black or African American, non-Hispanic/Latino; 9 Asian, non-Hispanic/Latino; 1 Two or more races, non-Hispanic/Latino), 9 international. 21 applicants, 33% accepted, 7 enrolled. In 2010, 17 master's, 4 doctorates awarded. Terminal master's awarded for partial completion of doctoral program. *Degree requirements:* For master's, thesis; for doctorate, thesis/dissertation, comprehensive oral and written exams. *Entrance requirements:* For master's, GRE General Test, MCAT, or DAT; for doctorate, GRE, MCAT or DAT. Additional exam requirements/recommendations for international students: Required—TOEFL (minimum score 600 paper-based; 250 computer-based; 100 iBT). *Application deadline:* For fall admission, 12/15 priority date for domestic students. Application fee: $50. Electronic applications accepted. *Expenses:* Tuition, state resident: full-time $4308; part-time $479 per credit hour. Tuition, nonresident: full-time $8942; part-time $994 per credit hour. Required fees: $2000; $85 per credit hour. Tuition and fees vary according to course level, course load, degree level, campus/location and program. *Financial support:* Fellowships, research assistantships, teaching assistantships, career-related internships or fieldwork and tuition waivers (full) available. *Unit head:* Dr. Diomedes E. Logothetis, Chair, 804-828-5878, Fax: 804-828-7382, E-mail: delogothetis@vcu.edu. *Application contact:* Dr. Diomedes E. Logothetis, Chair, 804-828-5878, Fax: 804-828-7382, E-mail: delogothetis@vcu.edu.

Virginia Commonwealth University, Program in Pre-Medical Basic Health Sciences, Richmond, VA 23284-9005. Offers anatomy (CBHS); biochemistry (CBHS); human genetics (CBHS); microbiology (CBHS); pharmacology (CBHS); physiology (CBHS). *Students:* 86 full-time (43 women), 2 part-time (1 woman); includes 42 minority (5 Black or African American, non-Hispanic/Latino; 29 Asian, non-Hispanic/Latino; 5 Hispanic/Latino; 3 Two or more races, non-Hispanic/Latino). 314 applicants, 64% accepted. In 2010, 70 CBHSs awarded. *Entrance requirements:* For degree, GRE, MCAT or DAT, course work in organic chemistry, minimum undergraduate GPA of 2.8. Additional exam requirements/recommendations for international students: Required—TOEFL (minimum score 600 paper-based). *Application deadline:* For fall admission, 6/1 for domestic students. Application fee: $50. Electronic applications accepted. *Expenses:* Tuition, state resident: full-time $4308; part-time $479 per credit hour. Tuition, nonresident: full-time $8942; part-time $994 per credit hour. Required fees: $2000; $85 per credit hour. Tuition and fees vary according to course level, course load, degree level, campus/location and program. *Unit head:* Dr. Louis J. De Felice, Director, 804-828-9501, E-mail: premedcert@vcu.edu. *Application contact:* Zack McDowell, Administrator, 804-828-9501, E-mail: premedcert@vcu.edu.

Wake Forest University, School of Medicine and Graduate School of Arts and Sciences, Graduate Programs in Medicine, Program in Physiology and Pharmacology, Winston-Salem, NC 27109. Offers pharmacology (PhD); physiology (PhD); MD/PhD. *Degree requirements:* For doctorate, thesis/dissertation. *Entrance requirements:* For doctorate, GRE General Test. Additional exam requirements/recommendations for international students: Required—TOEFL. Electronic applications accepted. *Faculty research:* Aging, substance abuse, cardiovascular control, endocrine systems, toxicology.

Wayne State University, School of Medicine, Department of Physiology, Detroit, MI 48202. Offers MS, PhD, MD/PhD. *Faculty:* 10 full-time (1 woman). *Students:* 33 full-time (20 women), 5 part-time (2 women); includes 11 minority (4 Black or African American, non-Hispanic/Latino; 5 Asian, non-Hispanic/Latino; 1 Hispanic/Latino; 1 Two or more races, non-Hispanic/Latino), 10 international. Average age 29. 18 applicants, 83% accepted, 7 enrolled. In 2010, 2 master's, 1 doctorate awarded. *Degree requirements:* For master's, thesis; for doctorate, thesis/dissertation. *Entrance requirements:* For master's, GRE General Test, GRE Subject Test, minimum GPA of 2.6; for doctorate, GRE General Test, GRE Subject Test, minimum GPA of 3.0. *Application deadline:* For fall admission, 6/1 for international students; for winter admission, 10/1 for international students; for spring admission, 2/1 for international students. Applications are processed on a rolling basis. Application fee: $30 ($50 for international students). Electronic applications accepted. *Expenses:* Tuition, state resident: full-time $7662; part-time $478.85 per credit hour. Tuition, nonresident: full-time $16,920; part-time $1057.55 per credit hour. Required fees: $571; $35.70 per credit hour. $188.05 per semester. Tuition and fees vary according to course load and program. *Financial support:* In 2010–11, 5 fellowships (averaging $25,989 per year), 20 research assistantships (averaging $22,870 per year) were awarded; teaching assistantships. Support available to part-time students. Financial award application deadline: 4/1. *Faculty research:* Regulation of brain blood flow, mechanism of hormone action, regulation of pituitary hormone secretion, regulation of cellular membranes, nano biotechnology. *Unit head:* David Lawson, Chair, 313-577-1520, Fax: 313-577-5494, E-mail: aa2923@wayne.edu. *Application contact:* James Rillema, Professor, 313-577-1524, E-mail: ad0702@wayne.edu.

Western Michigan University, Graduate College, College of Education and Human Development, Department of Health, Physical Education and Recreation, Kalamazoo, MI 49008. Offers exercise and sports medicine (MS), including athletic training, exercise physiology; physical education (MA), including coaching sport performance, pedagogy, special physical education, sport management.

West Virginia University, Davis College of Agriculture, Forestry and Consumer Sciences, Division of Animal and Nutritional Sciences, Program in Animal and Nutritional Sciences, Morgantown, WV 26506. Offers breeding (MS); food sciences (MS); nutrition (MS); physiology (MS); production management (MS); reproduction (MS). Part-time programs available. *Degree requirements:* For master's, thesis, oral and written exams. *Entrance requirements:* For master's, GRE, minimum GPA of 2.5. Additional exam requirements/recommendations for international students: Required—TOEFL. *Faculty research:* Animal nutrition, reproductive physiology, food science.

West Virginia University, Davis College of Agriculture, Forestry and Consumer Sciences, Interdisciplinary Program in Reproductive Physiology, Morgantown, WV 26506. Offers MS, PhD. Part-time programs available. Terminal master's awarded for partial completion of doctoral program. *Degree requirements:* For master's, thesis; for doctorate, comprehensive exam, thesis/dissertation. *Entrance requirements:* For master's, minimum GPA of 2.75; for doctorate, minimum GPA of 3.0. Additional exam requirements/recommendations for international students: Required—TOEFL. Electronic applications accepted. *Faculty research:* Uterine prostaglandins, luteal function, neural control of luteinizing hormone and follicle-stimulating hormone, follicular development, embryonic and fetal loss.

West Virginia University, School of Medicine, Graduate Programs at the Health Sciences Center, Interdisciplinary Graduate Programs in Biomedical Sciences, Program in Cellular and Integrative Physiology, Morgantown, WV 26506. Offers MS, PhD, MD/PhD. *Degree requirements:* For doctorate, comprehensive exam, thesis/dissertation. *Entrance requirements:* For doctorate, GRE General Test, minimum GPA of 3.0. Additional exam requirements/recommendations for international students: Required—TOEFL. Electronic applications accepted. *Faculty research:* Cell signaling and development of the microvasculature, neural control of reproduction, learning and memory, airway responsiveness and remodeling.

Wright State University, School of Graduate Studies, College of Science and Mathematics, Department of Neuroscience, Cell Biology, and Physiology, Dayton, OH 45435. Offers anatomy (MS); physiology and biophysics (MS). *Degree requirements:* For master's, thesis optional. *Entrance requirements:* Additional exam requirements/recommendations for international students: Required—TOEFL. *Faculty research:* Reproductive cell biology, neurobiology of pain, neurohistochemistry.

Yale University, School of Medicine and Graduate School of Arts and Sciences, Combined Program in Biological and Biomedical Sciences (BBS), Physiology and Integrative Medical Biology Track, New Haven, CT 06520. Offers PhD, MD/PhD. *Entrance requirements:* Additional exam requirements/recommendations for international students: Required—TOEFL.

Youngstown State University, Graduate School, College of Science, Technology, Engineering and Mathematics, Department of Biological Sciences, Youngstown, OH 44555-0001. Offers environmental biology (MS); molecular biology, microbiology, and genetic (MS); physiology and anatomy (MS). Part-time programs available. *Degree requirements:* For master's, comprehensive exam, thesis, oral review. *Entrance requirements:* For master's, GRE General Test, minimum GPA of 2.7. Additional exam requirements/recommendations for international students: Required—TOEFL. *Faculty research:* Cell biology, neurophysiology, molecular biology, neurobiology, gene regulation.

CASE WESTERN RESERVE UNIVERSITY

Case School of Medicine
Department of Physiology and Biophysics

Programs of Study

The Department's Ph.D. training programs in cellular and molecular physiology, structural biology and biophysics, and systems and integrated physiology are tailored to prepare students for successful careers in biomedical, pharmaceutical, and/or industrial research. The Department of Physiology and Biophysics ranks among the best physiology departments in the country. The Ph.D. programs feature individual attention from committed faculty members, are tuition-free, carry a stipend, and provide health insurance. The training programs are designed to provide a mentored training environment that maximizes faculty-student interaction and emphasizes the use of state-of-the art experimental approaches. Prospective students should visit the Department's Web sites (http://physiology.cwru.edu or http://biophysics.cwru.edu) for additional information on the Department, individual investigators, and graduate programs.

The Ph.D. program in cellular and molecular physiology embraces investigation that seeks to understand the fundamental organizational and physiological functions of the cell utilizing state-of-the-art scientific methodology and conceptual approaches. The Ph.D. program in structural biology and biophysics emphasizes biophysics and bioengineering concepts and technologies and seeks to develop the students' quantitative skills. The Ph.D. program in systems integrative physiology embraces the concepts of cell and molecular physiology, biochemistry, and allied sciences but seeks to understand the function of the organism at the organ system level. The M.D./Ph.D. program consists of core medical training plus advanced graduate research training, in any of the disciplines outlined above, thereby leading to a combined degree. The Ph.D. for M.D.'s program is specifically designed for individuals who already have an M.D. degree. It can be linked to research-oriented residency programs, such as the clinical investigator pathway, approved by the American Board of Internal Medicine, and other similar programs.

The Master of Science in Medical Physiology program is a 1–3 year post-baccalaureate program designed to prepare students for admission to medical or dental school or careers in the biomedical industry. The Master of Science in Physiology and Biophysics program (Tech Master's program) is designed for research assistants working at the University, area hospitals, or biotechnology companies that want to expand their critical research knowledge and skills. This program provides an excellent foundation for careers in biomedical professions including academia or industrial research.

Research Facilities

The Department is housed in newly renovated, state-of-the-art laboratory and office space on the fifth and sixth floors of the School of Medicine. These areas were specifically designed to facilitate faculty-student interaction. They are fully equipped with modern research instruments for sophisticated spectroscopic studies, video-enhanced light microscopy with image processing, molecular biology, structural biology, and extensive computer facilities. Interdisciplinary programs with other departments enable students to have access to additional specialized equipment.

Financial Aid

As long as the students in the Ph.D. programs are in good standing, they receive full tuition, a $25,000-per-year cost-of-living stipend, and health insurance. Tuition for the M.S. in Physiology and Biophysics program (Tech Master's program) is usually paid by the students' employer. Students in the M.S. in Medical Physiology program should contact the University's Office of Financial Aid to identify appropriate financial assistance programs.

Cost of Study

Tuition at Case Western Reserve University Graduate School is approximately $34,000 per year.

Living and Housing Costs

Single rooms are available on campus, and a large variety of off-campus housing is available within 2 miles for married and single students. The cost of living in Cleveland is among the lowest in the United States.

Location

Case Western Reserve University is located 4 miles from downtown Cleveland in University Circle, a 500-acre area containing more than thirty educational, scientific, medical, cultural, and religious institutions. The parklike setting of University Circle contains the world-renowned Cleveland Museum of Art and Severance Hall, home of the famous Cleveland Orchestra. Metropolitan Cleveland has a population of approximately 2 million people and offers a wide array of recreational and cultural activities, including national sports events, theater, ballet, and cinema.

The University and The School

Case Western Reserve University is a private, nonprofit institution created in 1967 by the federation of the adjacent Western Reserve University (founded in 1826) and Case Institute of Technology (founded in 1880). The Case School of Medicine ranks among the top twenty-five schools nationally. It is part of the dynamic and innovative consortium of biomedical research centers that include University hospitals, the MetroHealth Center, and the Cleveland Clinic Foundation. This consortium creates an exceptional array of research and learning opportunities.

Applying

Requirements for admission are an undergraduate degree with a strong background in the natural sciences from an accredited college or university, GRE General Test scores or MCAT scores, a personal statement, and three letters of recommendation. Competitive candidates are invited to visit the Department to view the facility and meet the faculty members. For the Ph.D. and Tech Master's programs, applications should be submitted by January 1, but late applications are also considered. The deadline for application to the M.S. in Medical Physiology program is June 1.

Correspondence and Information

Coordinator, Graduate Degree Programs
Department of Physiology and Biophysics
Case School of Medicine
Case Western Reserve University
Cleveland, Ohio 44106-4970

Phone: 216-368-2084
Fax: 216-368-5586
E-mail: PHOL-INFO@case.edu
Web site: http://physiology.cwru.edu
          http://biophysics.cwru.edu

Case Western Reserve University

THE FACULTY AND THEIR RESEARCH

Mary Barkley, Professor; Ph.D., California, San Diego, 1964. Structure and function of reverse transcriptase.

Venkaiah Betapudi, Assistant Professor; Ph.D., Devi Ahilya University, Indore (India), 1995. Cell cytoskeleton and cancer development; myosin II ubiquitination from basic mechanism to disease development.

Walter Boron, Professor and Chairman; M.D./Ph.D., Washington (St. Louis), 1977. Regulation of intracellular pH; molecular physiology and structural biology of HCO_3 transporters; control of renal proximal-tubule HCO_3 transport; CO_2/HCO_3 receptors; gas channels.

Matthias Buck, Associate Professor; D.Phil., Oxford, 1996. Protein structure and dynamics in transmission of signals in cells.

Cathleen Carlin, Professor; Ph.D., North Carolina at Chapel Hill, 1979. Regulation of ErbB receptor tyrosine kinase membrane protein sorting.

Sudha Chakrapani, Assistant Professor; Ph.D., SUNY at Buffalo, 2004. Understanding atomic level details of ion channel functioning.

Margaret Chandler, Assistant Professor; Ph.D., Kent State, 1998. Myocardial energy metabolism in the pathophysiology of heart failure and diabetes.

Calvin Cotton, Associate Professor; Ph.D., North Carolina at Chapel Hill, 1984. Regulation of ion transport in cells of respiratory, gastrointestinal, and renal epithelia.

Isabelle Deschenes, Assistant Professor; Ph.D., Laval, 1999. Cellular and molecular mechanisms of cardiac arrhythmias.

Paul DiCorleto, Professor; Ph.D., Cornell, 1978. Regulation of growth factor and leukocyte adhesion molecule genes by the endothelium.

Anthony F. DiMarco, Professor; M.D., Tufts, 1974. Restoration of respiratory muscle function in spinal cord injury.

J. Kevin Donahue, Associate Professor; M.D., Washington (St. Louis), 1992. Cardiac electrophysiology; cardiac arrhythmias.

George Dubyak, Professor; Ph.D., Pennsylvania, 1979. Extracellular ATP release and metabolism in inflammation.

Mark Dunlap, Associate Professor; M.D., Tennessee Health Sciences, 1982. Nicotinic acetylcholine receptors; autonomic nervous system; heart failure; parasympathetic/sympathetic physiology; baroreceptors; reflexes; neurohumoral abnormalities.

Dominique Durand, Professor; Ph.D., Toronto, 1982. Electrical stimulation of neural tissue and biomagnetism.

Thomas Egelhoff, Associate Professor; Ph.D., Stanford, 1987. Signaling pathways that control actin/myosin motility during cell migration in wound healing and cancer.

Christopher Ford, Assistant Professor; Ph.D., Alberta, 2003. Regulation of synaptic transmission in the dopamine system of the VTA.

Joan E. B. Fox, Professor; Ph.D., McMaster, 1979; D.Sc., Southampton (UK), 1993. Molecular basis of integrin-mediated migration in the cardiovascular system.

Harindarpal (Harry) Gill, Assistant Professor; Ph.D., UCLA, 2001. X-ray crystallographic studies on the sodium-bicarbonate cotransporter NBCe1-A.

Brian Hoit, Professor; M.D., Illinois, 1979.

Ulrich Hopfer, Professor Emeritus; M.D., Göttingen (Germany), 1966; Ph.D., Johns Hopkins, 1970. Cell biology, physiology, and pathology of epithelial transport.

Arie Horowitz, Assistant Professor; Ph.D., Technion (Israel), 1988. Enodothelial cell signaling and motility in angiogenesis; molecular mechanisms of blood vessel sprouting; membrane trafficking.

Mukesh K. Jain, Ellery Sedgwick Jr. Professor and Director, Case Cardiovascular Research Institute; M.D., Buffalo, SUNY, 1991. Transcriptional regulation of cardiovascular cell function.

Stephen Jones, Professor; Ph.D., Cornell, 1980. Voltage-dependent ion channels; mechanisms of channel gating, permeation, and modulation.

John P. Kirwan, Associate Professor; Ph.D., Ball State, 1987. Insulin signaling; glucose transport; protein expression, activity, and phosphorylation; intramyocellular lipid content; exercise; low-glycemic diet; body composition.

Joseph LaManna, Professor; Ph.D., Duke, 1975. Control of adaptation to hypoxia and the pathophysiology of stroke; CNS function in cardiac arrest.

Carole Liedtke, Professor; Ph.D., Case Western Reserve, 1980. Regulation of Na-K-2Cl cotransport during fluid and electrolyte balance in epithelia.

Richard Martin, Professor; M.B.B.S., Sydney (Australia), 1970. Respiratory control; lung injury/maturation; airway reactivity; nitric oxide; apnea of prematurity; developmental pulmonology; airway maturation; desaturation; hyperoxia; lung parenchyma; cardiorespiratory monitoring; pulmonary function monitoring; pulse oximetry; multiple intraluminal impedance monitoring; RTPCR; Western blotting; immunohistochemistry; in vivo physiological recording; assays; patch clamping.

Sam Mesiano, Assistant Professor; Ph.D., Monash (Australia), 1988. Hormonal control of human parturition and the interaction of estrogen and progesterone receptors in the control of reproduction.

R. Tyler Miller, Professor; M.D., Case Western Reserve, 1980. The calcium-sensing receptor and G-protein–coupled signaling.

Robert H. Miller, Professor and Vice Dean for Research; Ph.D., UCL, London, 1981. Biology of neural diseases; cellular and molecular control of nervous system glial specification.

Saurav Misra, Assistant Professor; Ph.D., Illinois, 1997. Molecular basis of protein quality control.

Vera Moiseenkova-Bell, Assistant Professor; Ph.D., Texas Medical Branch, 2004. Structural and functional analysis of TRP ion channels.

Tingwei Mu, Assistant Professor; Ph.D., Caltech, 2005. Understanding ion channel protein homeostasis in the cell.

Thomas M. Nosek, Professor; Ph.D., Ohio State, 1973. Control of muscle contraction; cellular basis of muscle fatigue.

Mark Parker, Instructor; Ph.D., Bristol (UK), 2000. Causes and consequences of structural and functional diversity among Na^+-coupled HCO_3-transporters.

Xin Qi, Assistant Professor; Ph.D., Hokkaido (Japan), 2005. Mitochondrial dysfunction in disease.

Rajesh Ramachandran, Assistant Professor; Ph.D., Texas A&M, 2004. Molecular biophysics of membrane remodeling in membrane fusion and fission.

Andrea Romani, Associate Professor; M.D., Siena (Italy), 1984; Ph.D., Turin, 1990. Regulation of transmembrane Mg^{2+} transport and the role of Mg^{2+} transport in metabolism.

David Rosenbaum, Professor; M.D., Illinois at Chicago, 1983. Mechanisms of arrhythmias in myocytes.

William Schilling, Professor; Ph.D., Medical University of South Carolina, 1981. Mammalian TRP channel function; role of Ca^{2+} channels in cell death.

John Sedor, Professor; M.D., Virginia, 1978. Clinical, cellular, and genetic basis of kidney disease.

Daniel I. Simon, Professor; M.D., Harvard, 1987. Inflammation in vascular injury.

Corey Smith, Associate Professor; Ph.D., Colorado Health Sciences Center, 1996. Release of transmitter molecules from adrenal chromaffin cells and the sympathetic stress response.

Julian E. Stelzer, Assistant Professor; Ph.D., Oregon State, 2002. Cellular and molecular mechanisms of cardiac muscle contraction in health and disease.

Kingman P. Strohl, Professor; M.D., Northwestern, 1974. Respiratory physiology and sleep disorders.

Ben W. Strowbridge, Professor; Ph.D., Yale, 1991. Synaptic physiology; hippocampus; modeling; computational neuroscience; olfactory bulb.

Witold Surewicz, Professor; Ph.D., Lodz (Poland), 1982. Structure and function of prion proteins.

Richard Walsh, Professor; M.D., Georgetown, 1972. The heart and cardiovascular disease.

Christopher Wilson, Associate Professor; Ph.D., California, Davis, 1996. Neural control of autonomic function which incorporates cardio-respiratory integration at the level of the brain stem.

Patrick Wintrode, Assistant Professor; Ph.D., Johns Hopkins, 1997. Hydrogen exchange and mass spectrometry to study protein structure and function.

Xin Yu, Associate Professor; Sc.D., Harvard/MIT, 1996. Magnetic resonance imaging and spectroscopy; cardiac biomechanics of genetically manipulated mice using MRI tagging; systems biology of metabolism; cardiovascular physiology; myocardial structural characterization in diseased hearts using diffusion tensor MRI; cardiac metabolism in diabetic hearts using MRI spectroscopy and systems biology.

Assem Ziady, Assistant Professor; Ph.D., Case Western Reserve, 1999. Cystic fibrosis; proteomic integration of CF and non-CF cells to determine differential protein expression; redox-mediated inflammatory signaling; use of nonviral gene therapy to address defects in CF at the genetic level.

Yuehan Zhou, Instructor; M.D., Third Military Medical University (China), 1984. CO2/HCO3-sensing mechanism in the proximal tubules.

UCONN

UNIVERSITY OF CONNECTICUT

College of Liberal Arts and Sciences
Department of Physiology and Neurobiology

Programs of Study	The Department offers course work and research programs leading to M.S. and Ph.D. degrees in physiology and neurobiology with concentration in areas of neurobiology, endocrinology, and comparative physiology. In addition, the Department of Molecular and Cell Biology, the Department of Ecology and Evolutionary Biology, and the Biotechnology Center provide the opportunity for students to obtain a comprehensive background in biological sciences and offer the possibility of collaborative research.
	Graduate programs are designed to fit the individual student's background and scientific interests. In the first year, students take two courses on the foundations of physiology and neurobiology. Through the first two years, and occasionally into the third year of training, students select from a number of additional seminars and courses in their area of major interest and related areas. By the end of the first year, the student selects the area of dissertation research, and a committee consisting of a major adviser and 3 associate advisers is formed. Students may begin dissertation research during the first year.
Research Facilities	The Department of Physiology and Neurobiology is located primarily in the new state-of-the-art Pharmacy/Biology Building. The Department houses both shared and individual laboratories for behavioral, cellular, electrophysiological, and molecular research in physiology. The Department also houses the University's electron microscopy facility, which contains equipment for scanning and transmission EM as well as electron probe analysis. Departmental faculty members also utilize the Marine Research Laboratories at Noank and Avery Point, Connecticut.
Financial Aid	Several types of financial support are available to graduate students. Most students are supported either on teaching assistantships or research assistantships from faculty grants. In 2011–12, full-time assistantships (nine months) pay $19,384 for beginning graduate students, $20,396 for those with an M.S. or the equivalent, and $22,676 for those who have passed the Ph.D. general examination. Both half and full graduate assistantships come with a tuition waiver, and students may purchase excellent health-care coverage, heavily subsidized by the University of Connecticut. In addition, the Graduate School provides the Outstanding Scholar Award to as many as 10 incoming Ph.D. candidates during the first year of study. Several additional research fellowships and University fellowships are awarded on a competitive basis. Many labs also provide additional funding for summer research (up to $4000).
Cost of Study	In 2011–12, tuition is $5112 per semester for legal residents of Connecticut and $13,266 per semester for nonresidents, plus fees. Tuition is waived for graduate assistants; however, they pay the full-time University fees of $953 per semester. Tuition is prorated for students registering for fewer than 9 credits per semester. University fees are subject to change without notice.
Living and Housing Costs	Dormitory rooms are available for unmarried graduate students. University-owned and privately owned apartments are available near the campus at moderate rents. Houses and apartments for rent may also be found in the surrounding communities. In 2011–12, the fee for accommodations in graduate residence halls range upward from $3886 per semester; meal plans are separate. Yearly expenses, including books and travel, for a single student living off campus are upward from $19,000.
Student Group	Approximately 17,345 undergraduates and 8,153 graduate students are enrolled at the main campus at Storrs. Eighty percent of the undergraduate students and 73 percent of the graduate students are from Connecticut. The rest of the students come from many other states and more than 100 countries. The Department of Physiology and Neurobiology has about 40 graduate students.
Location	The University is located in a scenic countryside setting of small villages, streams, and rolling hills. There is easy access by car and bus to major urban and cultural centers, including Hartford, New Haven, Boston, and New York, and to other educational institutions, such as Yale, Harvard, and MIT. Recreational opportunities include skiing, fishing, sailing, hiking, ice-skating, and athletic events. Cultural opportunities available at the Storrs campus include film series, plays, symphony and chamber music series, public lectures, and art exhibits. A small shopping center is within walking distance of the campus, and several large shopping centers are nearby.
The University	Perennially ranked the top public university in New England, the University of Connecticut now stands among the best public institutions in the nation. The University was founded in 1881 and is a state-supported institution. The 1,800-acre main campus at Storrs is the site of vigorous undergraduate and graduate programs in agriculture, liberal arts and sciences, fine arts, engineering, education, business administration, human development and family relations, physical education, pharmacy, nursing, and physical therapy. Extensive cultural and recreational programs and athletic facilities are available.
Applying	For admission to the fall semester, it is suggested that applications be submitted by January 15. To be considered for financial support, students must submit applications by March 15 for admission the following September. U.S. applicants must submit scores on the General Test of the Graduate Record Examinations and must have maintained at least a 3.0 quality point ratio (QPR) for admission as graduate students with regular status. Applications and credentials from international students must be received by March 1 for admission in the fall semester or by October 1 for the spring semester and must include TOEFL scores. The University does not discriminate in admission on the basis of race, gender, age, or national origin. Students can apply online at http://www.grad.uconn.edu/applications.html.
Correspondence and Information	Graduate Admissions Committee Department of Physiology and Neurobiology University of Connecticut Box U-3156 Storrs, Connecticut 06269-3156 Phone: 860-486-3304 Fax: 860-486-3303 E-mail: kathleen.kelleher@uconn.edu Web site: http://www.pnb.uconn.edu

University of Connecticut

THE FACULTY AND THEIR RESEARCH

Lawrence E. Armstrong, Professor (primary appointment in Kinesiology); Ph.D., Ball State. Research focuses on human physiological responses to exercise, dietary intervention (i.e., caffeine, low-salt diet, glucose-electrolyte solutions, amino acid supplementation), pharmacological agents, heat tolerance, and acclimatization to heat. Laboratory measurements of local sweat production; skin blood flow; and metabolic, ventilatory, cardiovascular, fluid-electrolyte, and strength perturbations are complemented by field observations. This research includes illnesses that arise in association with exercise in hot environments.

Marie E. Cantino, Associate Professor; Ph.D., Washington (Seattle). Research in this laboratory is directed toward understanding the mechanisms of contraction in striated muscle. In particular, the lab is using electron microscopy and biochemical and mechanical assays to study the structure and organization of proteins in the contractile filaments and the mechanisms by which calcium regulates the interactions of these proteins.

William D. Chapple, Professor; Ph.D., Stanford. The interests of the laboratory center on the cellular mechanisms by which arthropods generate and control movement despite varying external forces. The model system is the hermit crab abdomen, which is used to support the animal's shell. To understand the interactions between local and global mechanisms that produce this control, identified motoneurons and interneurons are studied electrophysiologically and their properties are incorporated into a control systems model.

Thomas T. Chen, Professor (primary appointment in Molecular and Cell Biology); Ph.D., Alberta; postdoctoral study at Queen's. Structure, evolution, regulation, and molecular actions of growth hormone and insulin-like growth factor genes; regulation of foreign genes in transgenic fish; development of model transgenic fish.

Joanne Conover, Assistant Professor; Ph.D., Bath (England). Research in the laboratory focuses on neurogenesis and neuronal migration in the adult mouse brain. A combination of techniques including cell culture of neural stem cells, RT-PCR-based gene expression analysis, and examination of mouse genetic models for neurodegenerative diseases aid us in understanding neuronal proliferation, differentiation, and migration in the adult brain.

Joseph F. Crivello, Professor (joint appointment in Marine Sciences); Ph.D., Wisconsin. Research is centered in two areas. One area examines the impact of pollution on marine organisms at a biochemical and genetic level. The other area examines pollution as a selective pressure altering the genetic diversity of marine organisms.

Angel L. de Blas, Professor; Ph.D., Indiana. Research mainly focuses on the brain receptors for the inhibitory transmitter GABA. Studies are being conducted on elucidating the molecular structure of the receptors and the molecular interactions with other proteins that determine the synaptic localization of the GABA receptors. Effects of drugs and aging on GABAergic synaptic transmission are also studied. Techniques include recombinant DNA, monoclonal antibodies, cell culture, and light, electron, and laser confocal microscopy.

Robert V. Gallo, Professor; Ph.D., Purdue. The objective of the research program is to understand the neuroendocrine mechanisms regulating luteinizing hormone release during different physiological conditions. In particular, the research examines the involvement of CNS neurotransmitters and endogenous opioid peptides in this process.

Rahul N. Kanadia, Assistant Professor, Ph.D., Florida. Research is focused on deciphering the role of alternative splicing in neural development. The neural mouse retina is employed as a model system to investigate this question. Various techniques such as in situ hybridizations and molecular biology techniques are used to detect different forms of RNA. Since this is studied in development, live imaging is also used to document changes in splice pattern and its impact on cell fate determination and differentiation.

William J. Kraemer, Professor (primary appointment in Kinesiology); Ph.D., Wyoming. Research focus is directed at the neuroendocrine responses and adaptations with exercise as it relates to target tissues of muscle, bone, and immune cells. Current studies utilize receptor techniques and hormonal immunoassays and bioassays to better understand androgen, adrenal, and pituitary hormone interactions with target cells and their relationship to outcome variables of physiological function and physical performance.

Joseph J. LoTurco, Professor; Ph.D., Stanford. Research in the laboratory focuses on understanding mechanisms that direct development of the neocortex. Currently, a combination of molecular genetics, patch clamp electrophysiology, and cell culture are being used to study the mechanisms that regulate neurogenesis in the cerebral cortex.

Carl M. Maresh, Professor and Director, Human Performance Laboratory (primary appointment in Kinesiology, Department Head); Ph.D., Wyoming. Research focus is directed at the neuroendocrine, body fluid, and substrate responses and adaptations to environmental stress and training in humans. Current projects examine the efficacy of different methods of rehydration, muscle and bone adaptations to physical training in women, and exercise interventions in children at risk for obesity and diabetes.

Andrew Moiseff, Professor; Ph.D., Cornell. The laboratory is interested in the extraction and processing of sensory information by the nervous system. At present, research is concentrated on how the nervous system of the barn owl analyzes interaural time and intensity differences to obtain spatial information. Another line of research is the behavioral analysis of synchronous flashing by fireflies with an aim toward the understanding of the neural mechanisms controlling this communication behavior.

Daniel K. Mulkey, Assistant Professor; Ph.D., Wright State. Research focuses on the cellular and molecular mechanisms by which the brain controls breathing, in particular, understanding the molecular mechanism by which respiratory chemoreceptors sense changes in pH to drive breathing and the cellular mechanisms that modulate activity of these cells. Another interest is the role of nitric oxide on state-dependent modulation of respiratory motor neurons for a better understanding of the mechanisms underlying respiratory control, leading to new therapeutic approaches for the treatment of disorders such as sudden infant death syndrome and sleep apnea. Techniques include cellular electrophysiology in brain slices, cell culture, and single-cell RT-PCR.

Akiko Nishiyama, Professor; M.D., Nippon Medical School; Ph.D., Niigata (Japan). Research focuses on the biology of glial progenitor cells identified by the NG2 proteoglycan in normal and mutant mice and in demyelinating and excitotoxic lesions. Current studies employ immunohistochemical, tissue culture, biochemical, and molecular biological techniques to understand the mechanisms that regulate proliferation and differentiation of these glial cells and to explore their function.

Linda S. Pescatello, Associate Professor and Director, Center for Health Promotion (primary appointment in School of Allied Health); Ph.D., Connecticut. Research focus is on the interaction between the environment, neurohormones, and genetics on the exercise response in order to determine for whom exercise works best as a therapeutic modality. Current projects examine humoral, nutritional, and genetic explanations for postexercise hypotension, the exercise dose response for postexercise hypotension, and the influence of genetics on the muscle strength and hypertrophy response to resistance exercise training.

J. Larry Renfro, Professor and Department Head; Ph.D., Oklahoma. The research program is concerned with the mechanisms and regulation of epithelial transport. Current research deals with transepithelial transport and excretion of sulfate, and phosphate and environmental pollutants in tissues isolated from the urinary systems of a variety of vertebrates, including rats, birds, and fishes. Work has concentrated on ion secretion and its regulation in primary monolayer cultures of renal epithelium and choroid plexus. The laboratory also studies transport by renal tubule brush border and basolateral membrane vesicles.

Daniel Schwartz, Assistant Professor; Ph.D., Harvard. Research is focused on computational and experimental techniques to discover, catalog, and functionally understand short linear protein motifs. Specific projects include: (1) the continued improvement of the motif-x and scan-x web-tools, (2) the development of experimental methodologies to uncover kinase motifs, and (3) the analysis of motif signatures on viral protein primary structure toward the goal of elucidating mechanisms of viral propagation and developing therapeutic agents.

Anastasios Tzingounis, Assistant Professor; Ph.D., Oregon Health & Science. Research in the laboratory concentrates on the cellular and molecular mechanisms that control neuronal excitability in the mammalian brain. To study the molecules and signaling networks that tune the brain's innate ability to prevent epilepsy, a multidisciplinary approach is used that combines molecular and genetic techniques with optical imaging and electrophysiology.

Randall S. Walikonis, Associate Professor; Ph.D., Mayo. Research is directed at studying the postsynaptic signal transduction systems of excitatory synapses. The laboratory uses biochemical and molecular biological techniques to identify proteins associated with NMDA receptors and to determine their specific roles in the function of excitatory synapses. The lab also studies the role of growth factors in modifying excitatory synapses.

Steven A. Zinn, Associate Professor (primary appointment in Animal Science); Ph.D., Michigan State. The laboratory is interested in the somatotropic axis and its influence on growth and lactation. Specifically, the laboratory is investigating the influence of exogenous somatotropin on insulin-like growth factor I and the insulin-like growth factor birding proteins and their role in growth.

Adam Zweifach, Professor (primary appointment in Molecular and Cell Biology); Ph.D., Yale. Research focuses on the physiology of cytotoxic T lymphocytes (CTLs) and natural killer cells (NKs), cells that kill virus-infected cells, tumor cells, and transplanted tissues. The long-term goal is to understand signal transduction in these cells, which play critical roles in the immune response to viruses and cancers, and which are also involved in transplant rejection and the etiology of many autoimmune diseases.

Section 19
Zoology

This section contains a directory of institutions offering graduate work in zoology. Additional information about programs listed in the directory may be obtained by writing directly to the dean of a graduate school or chair of a department at the address given in the directory.

For programs offering related work, see also in this book *Anatomy; Biochemistry; Biological and Biomedical Sciences; Cell, Molecular, and Structural Biology; Ecology, Environmental Biology, and Evolutionary Biology; Entomology; Genetics, Developmental Biology, and Reproductive Biology; Microbiological Sciences; Neuroscience and Neurobiology;* and *Physiology.* In the other guides in this series:

Graduate Programs in the Physical Sciences, Mathematics, Agricultural Sciences, the Environment & Natural Resources

See *Agricultural and Food Sciences, Environmental Sciences and Management,* and *Marine Sciences and Oceanography*

Graduate Programs in Engineering & Applied Sciences

See *Agricultural Engineering and Bioengineering* and *Ocean Engineering*

Graduate Programs in Business, Education, Health, Information Studies, Law & Social Work

See *Veterinary Medicine and Sciences*

CONTENTS

Program Directories

Animal Behavior

Arizona State University, College of Liberal Arts and Sciences, School of Life Sciences, Tempe, AZ 85287-4601. Offers animal behavior (PhD); applied ethics (biomedical and health ethics) (MA); biological design (PhD); biology (MS, PhD); biology (biology and society) (MS, PhD); environmental life sciences (PhD); evolutionary biology (PhD); human and social dimensions of science and technology (PhD); microbiology (PhD); molecular and cellular biology (PhD); neuroscience (PhD); philosophy (history and philosophy of science) (MA); sustainability (PhD). *Faculty:* 102 full-time (26 women), 4 part-time/adjunct (1 woman). *Students:* 188 full-time (95 women), 45 part-time (29 women); includes 31 minority (3 Black or African American, non-Hispanic/Latino; 2 American Indian or Alaska Native, non-Hispanic/Latino; 12 Asian, non-Hispanic/Latino; 12 Hispanic/Latino; 2 Two or more races, non-Hispanic/Latino), 39 international. Average age 30. 203 applicants, 41% accepted, 60 enrolled. In 2010, 17 master's, 21 doctorates awarded. Terminal master's awarded for partial completion of doctoral program. *Degree requirements:* For master's, thesis (for some programs), interactive Program of Study (iPOS) submitted before completing 50 percent of required credit hours; for doctorate, variable foreign language requirement, comprehensive exam, thesis/dissertation, interactive Program of Study (iPOS) submitted before completing 50 percent of required credit hours. *Entrance requirements:* For master's and doctorate, GRE, minimum GPA of 3.0 or equivalent in last 2 years of work leading to bachelor's degree. Additional exam requirements/recommendations for international students: Required—TOEFL (minimum score 600 paper-based; 250 computer-based; 100 iBT). *Application deadline:* For fall admission, 12/15 for domestic and international students. Application fee: $70 ($90 for international students). Electronic applications accepted. *Expenses:* Tuition, state resident: full-time $8510; part-time $608 per credit. Tuition, nonresident: full-time $16,542; part-time $919 per credit. Required fees: $339; $110 per credit. Part-time tuition and fees vary according to course load. *Financial support:* In 2010–11, 80 research assistantships with full and partial tuition reimbursements (averaging $17,888 per year), 101 teaching assistantships with full and partial tuition reimbursements (averaging $17,327 per year) were awarded; fellowships with full tuition reimbursements, career-related internships or fieldwork, Federal Work-Study, institutionally sponsored loans, scholarships/grants, and tuition waivers (full and partial) also available. Financial award application deadline: 3/1; financial award applicants required to submit FAFSA. Total annual research expenditures: $29.3 million. *Unit head:* Dr. Robert E. Page, Director, 480-965-0803, E-mail: robert.page@asu.edu. *Application contact:* Graduate Admissions, 480-965-6113.

Bucknell University, Graduate Studies, College of Arts and Sciences, Department of Animal Behavior, Lewisburg, PA 17837. Offers MA, MS. Part-time programs available. *Degree requirements:* For master's, thesis. *Entrance requirements:* For master's, GRE General Test, GRE Subject Test, minimum GPA of 2.8. Additional exam requirements/recommendations for international students: Required—TOEFL (minimum score 550 paper-based; 213 computer-based). *Expenses:* Tuition: Full-time $36,992; part-time $4624 per course.

Cornell University, Graduate School, Graduate Fields of Agriculture and Life Sciences, Field of Neurobiology and Behavior, Ithaca, NY 14853-0001. Offers behavioral biology (PhD), including behavioral ecology, chemical ecology, ethology, neuroethology, sociobiology; neurobiology (PhD), including cellular and molecular neurobiology, neuroanatomy, neurochemistry, neuropharmacology, neurophysiology, sensory physiology. *Faculty:* 46 full-time (8 women). *Students:* 31 full-time (15 women); includes 1 Black or African American, non-Hispanic/Latino; 1 Asian, non-Hispanic/Latino; 1 Hispanic/Latino, 2 international. Average age 27. 52 applicants, 27% accepted, 5 enrolled. In 2010, 7 doctorates awarded. *Degree requirements:* For doctorate, comprehensive exam, thesis/dissertation, 1 year of teaching experience, seminar presentation. *Entrance requirements:* For doctorate, GRE General Test, GRE Subject Test (biology), 3 letters of recommendation. Additional exam requirements/recommendations for international students: Required—TOEFL (minimum score 550 paper-based; 213 computer-based; 77 iBT). *Application deadline:* For fall admission, 12/1 for domestic students. Application fee: $70. Electronic applications accepted. *Expenses:* Tuition: Full-time $29,500. Required fees: $76. Tuition and fees vary according to degree level and program. *Financial support:* In 2010–11, 11 fellowships with full tuition reimbursements, 8 research assistantships with full tuition reimbursements, 10 teaching assistantships with full tuition reimbursements were awarded; institutionally sponsored loans, scholarships/grants, health care benefits, tuition waivers (full and partial), and unspecified assistantships also available. Financial award applicants required to submit FAFSA. *Faculty research:* Cellular neurobiology and neuropharmacology, integrative neurobiology, social behavior, chemical ecology, neuroethology. *Unit head:* Director of Graduate Studies, 607-254-4340, Fax: 607-254-4340. *Application contact:* Graduate Field Assistant, 607-254-4340, Fax: 607-254-4340, E-mail: nbb_field@cornell.edu.

Emory University, Laney Graduate School, Department of Psychology, Atlanta, GA 30322-1100. Offers clinical psychology (PhD); cognition and development (PhD); neuroscience and animal behavior (PhD). *Accreditation:* APA. *Degree requirements:* For doctorate, comprehensive exam, thesis/dissertation. *Entrance requirements:* For doctorate, GRE General Test, minimum GPA of 3.25. Additional exam requirements/recommendations for international students: Required—TOEFL. Electronic applications accepted. *Expenses:* Tuition: Full-time $33,800. Required fees: $1300. *Faculty research:* Neuroscience and animal behavior; adult and child psychopathology, cognition development assessment.

Hunter College of the City University of New York, Graduate School, School of Arts and Sciences, Department of Psychology, New York, NY 10021-5085. Offers animal behavior and conservation (MA); applied and evaluative psychology (MA); biopsychology and behavioral neuroscience (PhD); biopsychology and comparative psychology (MA); social, cognitive, and developmental psychology (MA). Part-time and evening/weekend programs available. *Faculty:* 9 full-time (1 woman), 1 part-time/adjunct (0 women). *Students:* 10 full-time (7 women), 79 part-time (61 women); includes 3 Black or African American, non-Hispanic/Latino; 7 Asian, non-Hispanic/Latino; 9 Hispanic/Latino, 2 international. Average age 27. 151 applicants, 34% accepted, 21 enrolled. In 2010, 13 master's awarded. *Degree requirements:* For master's, comprehensive exam, thesis. *Entrance requirements:* For master's, GRE General Test, minimum 12 credits of course work in psychology, including statistics and experimental psychology; 2 letters of recommendation. Additional exam requirements/recommendations for international students: Required—TOEFL. *Application deadline:* For fall admission, 4/1 for domestic students, 2/1 for international students; for spring admission, 11/1 for domestic students, 9/1 for international students. Applications are processed on a rolling basis. Application fee: $125. *Financial support:* Federal Work-Study, scholarships/grants, and tuition waivers (partial) available. Support available to part-time students. *Faculty research:* Personality, cognitive and linguistic development, hormonal and neural control of behavior, gender and culture, social cognition of health and attitudes. *Unit head:* Dr. Jeffrey Parsons, Chairperson, 212-772-5550, Fax: 212-772-5620, E-mail: jeffrey.parsons@hunter.cuny.edu. *Application contact:* Martin Braun, Acting Program Director, 212-772-4482, Fax: 212-650-3336, E-mail: cbraun@hunter.cuny.edu.

Illinois State University, Graduate School, College of Arts and Sciences, Department of Biological Sciences, Normal, IL 61790-2200. Offers animal behavior (MS); bacteriology (MS); biochemistry (MS); biological sciences (MS); biology (PhD); biophysics (MS); biotechnology (MS); botany (MS, PhD); cell biology (MS); conservation biology (MS); developmental biology (MS); ecology (MS, PhD); entomology (MS); evolutionary biology (MS); genetics (MS, PhD); immunology (MS); microbiology (MS, PhD); molecular biology (MS); molecular genetics (MS); neurobiology (MS); neuroscience (MS); parasitology (MS); physiology (MS, PhD); plant biology (MS); plant molecular biology (MS); plant sciences (MS); structural biology (MS); zoology (MS, PhD). Part-time programs available. *Degree requirements:* For master's, thesis or alternative; for doctorate, variable foreign language requirement, thesis/dissertation, 2 terms of residency. *Entrance requirements:* For master's, GRE General Test, minimum GPA of 2.6 in last 60 hours of course work; for doctorate, GRE General Test. *Faculty research:* Redoc balance and drug development in schistosoma mansoni, control of the growth of listeria monocytogenes at low temperature, regulation of cell expansion and microtubule function by SPRI, CRUI: physiology and fitness consequences of different life history phenotypes.

University of California, Davis, Graduate Studies, Graduate Group in Animal Behavior, Davis, CA 95616. Offers PhD. *Degree requirements:* For doctorate, thesis/dissertation. *Entrance requirements:* For doctorate, GRE General Test. Additional exam requirements/recommendations for international students: Required—TOEFL (minimum score 550 paper-based; 213 computer-based), IELTS (minimum score 7). Electronic applications accepted. *Faculty research:* Wildlife behavior, conservation biology, companion animal behavior, behavioral endocrinology, animal communication.

University of Colorado Boulder, Graduate School, College of Arts and Sciences, Department of Ecology and Evolutionary Biology, Boulder, CO 80309. Offers animal behavior (MA); biology (MA, PhD); environmental biology (MA, PhD); evolutionary biology (MA, PhD); neurobiology (MA); population biology (MA); population genetics (PhD). *Faculty:* 32 full-time (10 women). *Students:* 71 full-time (36 women), 17 part-time (11 women); includes 10 minority (1 American Indian or Alaska Native, non-Hispanic/Latino; 2 Asian, non-Hispanic/Latino; 7 Hispanic/Latino), 4 international. Average age 30. 176 applicants, 20 enrolled. In 2010, 11 master's, 8 doctorates awarded. Terminal master's awarded for partial completion of doctoral program. *Degree requirements:* For master's, comprehensive exam, thesis or alternative; for doctorate, comprehensive exam, thesis/dissertation. *Entrance requirements:* For master's, GRE General Test, GRE Subject Test, minimum undergraduate GPA of 3.0; for doctorate, GRE General Test, GRE Subject Test. *Application deadline:* For fall admission, 12/30 priority date for domestic students, 12/1 for international students. Application fee: $50 ($60 for international students). *Financial support:* In 2010–11, 25 fellowships (averaging $17,876 per year), 27 research assistantships (averaging $15,070 per year) were awarded; Federal Work-Study, institutionally sponsored loans, and tuition waivers (full) also available. *Faculty research:* Behavior, ecology, genetics, morphology, endocrinology, physiology, systematics. Total annual research expenditures: $3.5 million.

University of Massachusetts Amherst, Graduate School, Interdisciplinary Programs, Program in Neuroscience and Behavior, Amherst, MA 01003. Offers animal behavior and learning (PhD); molecular and cellular neuroscience (PhD); neural and behavioral development (PhD); neuroendocrinology (PhD); neuroscience and behavior (MS); sensorimotor, cognitive, and computational neuroscience (PhD). *Students:* 31 full-time (19 women); includes 5 minority (2 Asian, non-Hispanic/Latino; 3 Hispanic/Latino), 2 international. Average age 26. 77 applicants, 30% accepted, 10 enrolled. In 2010, 2 master's, 4 doctorates awarded. Terminal master's awarded for partial completion of doctoral program. *Degree requirements:* For master's, thesis or alternative; for doctorate, comprehensive exam, thesis/dissertation. *Entrance requirements:* For master's and doctorate, GRE General Test. Additional exam requirements/recommendations for international students: Required—TOEFL (minimum score 550 paper-based; 213 computer-based; 80 iBT), IELTS (minimum score 6.5). *Application deadline:* For fall admission, 1/2 for domestic and international students. Applications are processed on a rolling basis. Application fee: $50 ($65 for international students). Electronic applications accepted. *Expenses:* Tuition, state resident: full-time $2640. Required fees: $8282. One-time fee: $357 full-time. *Financial support:* In 2010–11, 8 fellowships with full tuition reimbursements (averaging $11,100 per year), 3 research assistantships with full tuition reimbursements (averaging $1,529 per year) were awarded; teaching assistantships, career-related internships or fieldwork, Federal Work-Study, scholarships/grants, traineeships, health care benefits, tuition waivers (full), and unspecified assistantships also available. Support available to part-time students. Financial award application deadline: 1/2; financial award applicants required to submit FAFSA. *Unit head:* Dr. Neil Berthier, Graduate Program Director, 413-545-2046, Fax: 413-545-3243. *Application contact:* Jean M. Ames, Supervisor of Admissions, 413-545-0722, Fax: 413-577-0010, E-mail: gradadm@grad.umass.edu.

University of Massachusetts Amherst, Graduate School, Interdisciplinary Programs, Program in Organismic and Evolutionary Biology, Amherst, MA 01003. Offers animal behavior (PhD); ecology (PhD); evolutionary biology (PhD); organismal biology (PhD); organismic and evolutionary biology (MS). Part-time programs available. *Students:* 30 full-time (16 women), 3 part-time (all women); includes 4 minority (3 Hispanic/Latino; 1 Native Hawaiian or other Pacific Islander, non-Hispanic/Latino), 6 international. Average age 29. 51 applicants, 33% accepted, 6 enrolled. In 2010, 2 master's, 5 doctorates awarded. Terminal master's awarded for partial completion of doctoral program. *Degree requirements:* For master's, thesis or alternative; for doctorate, comprehensive exam, thesis/dissertation. *Entrance requirements:* For master's and doctorate, GRE General Test, 3 letters of recommendation. Additional exam requirements/recommendations for international students: Required—TOEFL (minimum score 550 paper-based; 213 computer-based; 80 iBT), IELTS (minimum score 6.5). *Application deadline:* For fall admission, 12/1 for domestic and international students. Applications are processed on a rolling basis. Application fee: $50 ($65 for international students). Electronic applications accepted. *Expenses:* Tuition, state resident: full-time $2640. Required fees: $8282. One-time fee: $357 full-time. *Financial support:* In 2010–11, 4 fellowships (averaging $2,657 per year), 2 teaching assistantships with full tuition reimbursements (averaging $7,607 per year) were awarded; research assistantships, career-related internships or fieldwork, Federal Work-Study, scholarships/grants, traineeships, health care benefits, tuition waivers (full), and unspecified assistantships also available. Support available to part-time students. Financial award application deadline: 12/1; financial award applicants required to submit FAFSA. *Unit head:* Dr. Elizabeth M. Jakob, Graduate Program Director, 413-545-0928, Fax: 413-545-3243. *Application contact:* Jean M. Ames, Supervisor of Admissions, 413-545-0722, Fax: 413-577-0010, E-mail: gradadm@grad.umass.edu.

University of Minnesota, Twin Cities Campus, Graduate School, College of Biological Sciences, Department of Ecology, Evolution, and Behavior, St. Paul, MN 55418. Offers MS, PhD. Terminal master's awarded for partial completion of doctoral program. *Degree requirements:* For master's, comprehensive exam, thesis or projects; for doctorate, comprehensive exam, thesis/dissertation. *Entrance requirements:* For master's and doctorate, GRE General Test, minimum GPA of 3.0. Additional exam requirements/recommendations for international students: Required—TOEFL (minimum score 550 paper-based; 79 iBT), Michigan English Language Assessment Battery. Electronic applications accepted. *Faculty research:* Behavioral ecology, community ecology, community genetics, ecosystem and global change, evolution and systematics.

The University of Montana, Graduate School, College of Arts and Sciences, Department of Psychology, Missoula, MT 59812-0002. Offers clinical psychology (PhD); experimental psychology (PhD), including animal behavior psychology, developmental psychology; school psychology (MA, PhD, Ed S). *Accreditation:* APA (one or more programs are accredited). Terminal master's awarded for partial completion of doctoral program. *Degree requirements:* For master's, thesis; for doctorate, thesis/dissertation. *Entrance requirements:* For master's, doctorate, and Ed S, GRE General Test. Additional exam requirements/recommendations for international students: Required—TOEFL.

The University of Tennessee, Graduate School, College of Arts and Sciences, Department of Ecology and Evolutionary Biology, Knoxville, TN 37996. Offers behavior (MS, PhD); ecology (MS, PhD); evolutionary biology (MS, PhD). Part-time programs available. *Degree requirements:* For master's, thesis; for doctorate, thesis/dissertation. *Entrance requirements:* For master's and doctorate, GRE General Test, minimum GPA of 2.7. Additional exam requirements/recommendations for international students: Required—TOEFL. Electronic applications accepted. *Expenses:* Tuition, state resident: full-time $7440; part-time $414 per credit hour. Tuition, nonresident: full-time $22,478; part-time $1250 per credit hour. Required fees: $922; $43 per credit hour. Tuition and fees vary according to program.

The University of Texas at Austin, Graduate School, College of Natural Sciences, School of Biological Sciences, Program in Ecology, Evolution and Behavior, Austin, TX 78712-1111.

Offers MA, PhD. *Entrance requirements:* For doctorate, GRE General Test. Additional exam requirements/recommendations for international students: Required—TOEFL. Electronic applications accepted.

University of Washington, Graduate School, College of Arts and Sciences, Department of Psychology, Seattle, WA 98195. Offers animal behavior (PhD); child psychology (PhD); clinical psychology (PhD); cognition and perception (PhD); developmental psychology (PhD); quantitative psychology (PhD); social psychology and personality (PhD). *Accreditation:* APA. *Degree requirements:* For doctorate, thesis/dissertation. *Entrance requirements:* For doctorate, GRE General Test, minimum GPA of 3.0. Electronic applications accepted. *Faculty research:* Addictive behaviors, artificial intelligence, child psychopathology, mechanisms and development of vision, physiology of ingestive behaviors.

Wesleyan University, Graduate Programs, Department of Biology, Middletown, CT 06459. Offers animal behavior (PhD); bioformatics/genomics (PhD); cell biology (PhD); developmental biology (PhD); evolution/ecology (PhD); genetics (PhD); neurobiology (PhD); population biology

(PhD). *Faculty:* 12 full-time (4 women). *Students:* 20 full-time (12 women); includes 1 Black or African American, non-Hispanic/Latino; 3 Asian, non-Hispanic/Latino. Average age 26. 24 applicants, 29% accepted, 2 enrolled. *Degree requirements:* For doctorate, variable foreign language requirement, thesis/dissertation. *Entrance requirements:* For doctorate, GRE. Additional exam requirements/recommendations for international students: Required—TOEFL. *Application deadline:* For fall admission, 1/15 for domestic and international students. Applications are processed on a rolling basis. Application fee: $0. *Expenses:* Tuition: Full-time $43,404. Required fees: $830. *Financial support:* In 2010–11, 5 research assistantships with full tuition reimbursements, 16 teaching assistantships with full tuition reimbursements were awarded; stipends also available. Financial award application deadline: 4/15; financial award applicants required to submit FAFSA. *Faculty research:* Microbial population genetics, genetic basis of evolutionary adaptation, genetic regulation of differentiation and pattern formation in *drosophila*. *Unit head:* Dr. Sonia E. Sultan, Chair/Professor, 860-685-3493, E-mail: jnaegele@wesleyan.edu. *Application contact:* Marjorie Fitzgibbons, Information Contact, 860-685-2140, E-mail: mfitzgibbons@wesleyan.edu.

Zoology

Auburn University, Graduate School, College of Sciences and Mathematics, Department of Biological Sciences, Auburn University, AL 36849. Offers botany (MS, PhD); microbiology (MS, PhD); zoology (MS, PhD). *Faculty:* 33 full-time (8 women), 1 (woman) part-time/adjunct. *Students:* 42 full-time (17 women), 60 part-time (36 women); includes 4 Black or African American, non-Hispanic/Latino; 1 American Indian or Alaska Native, non-Hispanic/Latino; 3 Asian, non-Hispanic/Latino; 1 Hispanic/Latino, 21 international. Average age 28. 134 applicants, 20% accepted, 18 enrolled. In 2010, 22 master's, 11 doctorates awarded. *Entrance requirements:* For master's and doctorate, GRE General Test. Additional exam requirements/recommendations for international students: Required—TOEFL. *Application deadline:* For fall admission, 7/7 for domestic students; for spring admission, 11/24 for domestic students. Application fee: $50 ($60 for international students). Electronic applications accepted. *Expenses:* Tuition, state resident: full-time $7002. Tuition, nonresident: full-time $21,898. International tuition: $22,116 full-time. Required fees: $892. Tuition and fees vary according to course load and program. *Financial support:* Research assistantships, teaching assistantships available. Financial award applicants required to submit FAFSA. *Unit head:* Dr. James M. Barbaree, Chair, 334-844-7511, Fax: 334-844-1645. *Application contact:* Dr. George Flowers, Dean of the Graduate School, 334-844-2125.

Colorado State University, Graduate School, College of Natural Sciences, Department of Biology, Fort Collins, CO 80523-1878. Offers botany (MS, PhD); zoology (MS, PhD). Post-baccalaureate distance learning degree programs offered (no on-campus study). *Faculty:* 25 full-time (10 women). *Students:* 27 full-time (16 women), 22 part-time (12 women); includes 6 minority (2 Asian, non-Hispanic/Latino; 3 Hispanic/Latino; 1 Two or more races, non-Hispanic/Latino), 7 international. Average age 29. 13 applicants, 46% accepted, 5 enrolled. In 2010, 6 master's, 2 doctorates awarded. Terminal master's awarded for partial completion of doctoral program. *Degree requirements:* For master's, comprehensive exam (for some programs), thesis (for some programs); for doctorate, comprehensive exam, thesis/dissertation. *Entrance requirements:* For master's, GRE General Test, minimum GPA of 3.0; 3 letters of recommendation; for doctorate, GRE General Test, minimum GPA of 3.0; statement of purpose; 2 transcripts; 3 letters of recommendation. Additional exam requirements/recommendations for international students: Required—TOEFL (minimum score 550 paper-based; 213 computer-based; 80 iBT). *Application deadline:* For fall admission, 1/15 priority date for domestic and international students; for spring admission, 11/1 priority date for domestic and international students. Applications are processed on a rolling basis. Application fee: $50. Electronic applications accepted. *Expenses:* Tuition, state resident: full-time $7434; part-time $413 per credit. Tuition, nonresident: full-time $19,022; part-time $1057 per credit. Required fees: $1729; $88 per credit. *Financial support:* In 2010–11, 14 fellowships (averaging $31,623 per year), 36 research assistantships with full tuition reimbursements (averaging $10,921 per year), 58 teaching assistantships with full tuition reimbursements (averaging $12,196 per year) were awarded; health care benefits also available. Financial award application deadline: 1/15; financial award applicants required to submit FAFSA. *Faculty research:* Aquatic and terrestrial ecology, cell biology and genetics, plant/animal physiology, developmental biology, evolutionary biology. Total annual research expenditures: $5.9 million. *Unit head:* Dr. Daniel R. Bush, Chair, 970-491-7013, Fax: 970-491-0649, E-mail: dbush@colostate.edu. *Application contact:* Dorothy Ramirez, Graduate Coordinator, 970-491-1923, Fax: 970-491-0649, E-mail: dorothy.ramirez@colostate.edu.

Cornell University, Graduate School, Graduate Fields of Agriculture and Life Sciences, Field of Zoology and Wildlife Conservation, Ithaca, NY 14853-0001. Offers animal cytology (MS, PhD); comparative and functional anatomy (MS, PhD); developmental biology (MS, PhD); ecology (MS, PhD); histology (MS, PhD). *Faculty:* 20 full-time (5 women). *Students:* 5 full-time (all women); includes 1 Hispanic/Latino, 1 international. Average age 31. 17 applicants, 18% accepted, 1 enrolled. *Degree requirements:* For doctorate, comprehensive exam, thesis/dissertation, 2 semesters of teaching experience. *Entrance requirements:* For doctorate, GRE General Test, GRE Subject Test (biology), 2 letters of recommendation. Additional exam requirements/recommendations for international students: Required—TOEFL (minimum score 550 paper-based; 213 computer-based; 77 iBT). *Application deadline:* For fall admission, 2/1 priority date for domestic students. Application fee: $70. Electronic applications accepted. *Expenses:* Tuition: Full-time $29,500. Required fees: $76. Tuition and fees vary according to degree level and program. *Financial support:* In 2010–11, 1 fellowship with full tuition reimbursement, 4 research assistantships with full tuition reimbursements were awarded; teaching assistantships with full tuition reimbursements, institutionally sponsored loans, scholarships/grants, health care benefits, tuition waivers (full and partial), and unspecified assistantships also available. Financial award applicants required to submit FAFSA. *Faculty research:* Organismal biology, functional morphology, biomechanics, comparative vertebrate anatomy, comparative invertebrate anatomy, paleontology. *Unit head:* Director of Graduate Studies, 607-253-3276, Fax: 607-253-3756. *Application contact:* Graduate Field Assistant, 607-253-3276, Fax: 607-253-3756, E-mail: graduate_edcvm@cornell.edu.

Eastern New Mexico University, Graduate School, College of Liberal Arts and Sciences, Department of Biology, Portales, NM 88130. Offers applied ecology (MS); cell, molecular biology and biotechnology (MS); education (non-thesis) (MS); microbiology (MS); plant biology (MS); zoology (MS). Part-time programs available. *Faculty:* 8 full-time (0 women). *Students:* 11 full-time (8 women), 7 part-time (4 women); includes 7 minority (5 Hispanic/Latino; 2 Two or more races, non-Hispanic/Latino), 4 international. Average age 25. 21 applicants, 14% accepted, 3 enrolled. In 2010, 4 master's awarded. *Degree requirements:* For master's, comprehensive exam, thesis optional. *Entrance requirements:* For master's, GRE, minimum GPA of 3.0, 2 letters of recommendation, statement of research interest, bachelor's degree related to field of study or proof of common knowledge. Additional exam requirements/recommendations for international students: Required—TOEFL (minimum score 550 paper-based; 213 computer-based; 79 iBT), IELTS (minimum score 6). *Application deadline:* For fall admission, 7/20 priority date for domestic students, 6/20 priority date for international students; for spring admission, 12/15 priority date for domestic students, 11/15 priority date for international students. Applications are processed on a rolling basis. Application fee: $10. Electronic applications accepted. *Expenses:* Tuition, state resident: full-time $3210; part-time $130 per credit hour. Tuition, nonresident: full-time $8652; part-time $360.50 per credit hour. Required fees:

$1212; $50.50 per credit hour. Tuition and fees vary according to course load. *Financial support:* In 2010–11, 11 teaching assistantships with partial tuition reimbursements (averaging $8,500 per year) were awarded; unspecified assistantships also available. Support available to part-time students. Financial award applicants required to submit FAFSA. *Unit head:* Dr. Zach Jones, Graduate Coordinator, 575-562-2723, Fax: 575-562-2192, E-mail: zach.jones@enmu.edu. *Application contact:* Sharon Potter, Department Secretary, Biology/Physical Sciences, 575-562-2174, Fax: 575-562-2192, E-mail: sharon.potter@enmu.edu.

Emporia State University, Graduate School, College of Liberal Arts and Sciences, Department of Biological Sciences, Emporia, KS 66801-5087. Offers botany (MS); environmental biology (MS); general biology (MS); microbial and cellular biology (MS); zoology (MS). Part-time programs available. *Faculty:* 13 full-time (3 women). *Students:* 14 full-time (8 women), 19 part-time (9 women); includes 2 minority (1 Black or African American, non-Hispanic/Latino; 1 Hispanic/Latino), 6 international. 9 applicants, 100% accepted, 9 enrolled. In 2010, 4 master's awarded. *Degree requirements:* For master's, comprehensive exam or thesis. *Entrance requirements:* For master's, GRE, appropriate undergraduate degree, interview, letters of reference. Additional exam requirements/recommendations for international students: Required—TOEFL (minimum score 520 paper-based; 133 computer-based; 68 iBT). *Application deadline:* For fall admission, 8/15 priority date for domestic students. Applications are processed on a rolling basis. Application fee: $30 ($75 for international students). Electronic applications accepted. *Expenses:* Tuition, state resident: full-time $4382; part-time $183 per credit hour. Tuition, nonresident: full-time $13,572; part-time $566 per credit hour. Required fees: $1022; $62 per credit hour. Tuition and fees vary according to course level, course load and campus/location. *Financial support:* In 2010–11, 10 research assistantships with full tuition reimbursements (averaging $7,353 per year), 9 teaching assistantships with full tuition reimbursements (averaging $7,809 per year) were awarded; career-related internships or fieldwork, Federal Work-Study, institutionally sponsored loans, health care benefits, and unspecified assistantships also available. Financial award application deadline: 3/15; financial award applicants required to submit FAFSA. *Faculty research:* Fisheries, range, and wildlife management; aquatic, plant, grassland, vertebrate, and invertebrate ecology; mammalian and plant systematics, taxonomy, and evolution; immunology, virology, and molecular biology. *Unit head:* Dr. R Brent Thomas, Chair, 620-341-5311, Fax: 620-341-5608, E-mail: rthomas2@emporia.edu. *Application contact:* Dr. Scott Crupper, Graduate Coordinator, 620-341-5621, Fax: 620-341-5607, E-mail: scrupper@emporia.edu.

Illinois State University, Graduate School, College of Arts and Sciences, Department of Biological Sciences, Normal, IL 61790-2200. Offers animal behavior (MS); bacteriology (MS); biochemistry (MS); biological sciences (MS); biology (PhD); biophysics (MS); biotechnology (MS); botany (MS, PhD); cell biology (MS); conservation biology (MS); developmental biology (MS); ecology (MS, PhD); entomology (MS); evolutionary biology (MS); genetics (MS, PhD); immunology (MS); microbiology (MS, PhD); molecular biology (MS); molecular genetics (MS); neurobiology (MS); neuroscience (MS); parasitology (MS); physiology (MS, PhD); plant biology (MS); plant molecular biology (MS); plant sciences (MS); structural biology (MS); zoology (MS, PhD). Part-time programs available. *Degree requirements:* For master's, thesis or alternative; for doctorate, variable foreign language requirement, thesis/dissertation, 2 terms of residency. *Entrance requirements:* For master's, GRE General Test, minimum GPA of 2.6 in last 60 hours of course work; for doctorate, GRE General Test. *Faculty research:* Redoc balance and drug development in schistosoma mansoni, control of the growth of listeria monocytogenes at low temperature, regulation of cell expansion and microtubule function by SPRI, CRUI: physiology and fitness consequences of different life history phenotypes.

Indiana University Bloomington, University Graduate School, College of Arts and Sciences, Department of Biology, Bloomington, IN 47405. Offers biology teaching (MAT); biotechnology (MA); evolution, ecology, and behavior (MA, PhD); genetics (PhD); microbiology (MA, PhD); molecular, cellular, and developmental biology (PhD); plant sciences (MA, PhD); zoology (MA, PhD). *Faculty:* 58 full-time (15 women), 21 part-time/adjunct (6 women). *Students:* 163 full-time (98 women), 7 part-time (2 women); includes 17 minority (3 Black or African American, non-Hispanic/Latino; 1 American Indian or Alaska Native, non-Hispanic/Latino; 7 Asian, non-Hispanic/Latino; 5 Hispanic/Latino; 1 Native Hawaiian or other Pacific Islander, non-Hispanic/Latino), 52 international. Average age 27. 346 applicants, 15% accepted, 24 enrolled. In 2010, 17 master's, 24 doctorates awarded. Terminal master's awarded for partial completion of doctoral program. *Degree requirements:* For master's, thesis, oral defense; for doctorate, thesis/dissertation, oral defense. *Entrance requirements:* For master's and doctorate, GRE General Test. Additional exam requirements/recommendations for international students: Required—TOEFL (minimum score 100 iBT). *Application deadline:* For fall admission, 1/5 priority date for domestic students, 12/1 priority date for international students. Application fee: $55 ($65 for international students). Electronic applications accepted. *Financial support:* In 2010–11, 170 students received support, including 64 fellowships with tuition reimbursements available (averaging $19,484 per year), 44 research assistantships with tuition reimbursements available (averaging $20,300 per year), 62 teaching assistantships with tuition reimbursements available (averaging $20,521 per year); scholarships/grants, traineeships, health care benefits, and unspecified assistantships also available. Financial award application deadline: 1/5. *Faculty research:* Evolution, ecology and behavior; microbiology; molecular biology and genetics; plant biology. *Unit head:* Dr. Roger Innes, Chair, 812-855-2219, Fax: 812-855-6082, E-mail: rinnes@indiana.edu. *Application contact:* Tracey D. Stohr, Graduate Student Recruitment Coordinator, 812-856-6303, Fax: 812-855-6082, E-mail: gradbio@indiana.edu.

Miami University, Graduate School, College of Arts and Science, Department of Zoology, Oxford, OH 45056. Offers biological sciences (MAT); zoology (MS, PhD). Part-time programs available. *Students:* 45 full-time (27 women), 132 part-time (106 women); includes 15 minority (2 Black or African American, non-Hispanic/Latino; 1 American Indian or Alaska Native, non-Hispanic/Latino; 5 Asian, non-Hispanic/Latino; 4 Hispanic/Latino; 1 Native Hawaiian or other Pacific Islander, non-Hispanic/Latino; 2 Two or more races, non-Hispanic/Latino), 21 international. Average age 33. In 2010, 11 master's, 7 doctorates awarded. *Entrance requirements:* For master's, minimum undergraduate GPA of 3.0 during previous 2 years or 2.75 overall; for doctorate, minimum undergraduate GPA of 2.75, 3.0 graduate. Additional exam requirements/

Zoology

Miami University (continued)
recommendations for international students: Required—TOEFL. Application fee: $50. *Expenses:* Tuition, state resident: full-time $11,616; part-time $484 per credit hour. Tuition, nonresident: full-time $25,656; part-time $1069 per credit hour. Required fees: $528. *Financial support:* Fellowships with full tuition reimbursements, research assistantships with full tuition reimbursements, teaching assistantships with full tuition reimbursements, Federal Work-Study, health care benefits, tuition waivers (full), and unspecified assistantships available. Financial award application deadline: 3/1; financial award applicants required to submit FAFSA. *Unit head:* Dr. Douglas Meikle, Chair, 513-529-3103, E-mail: meikled@muohio.edu. *Application contact:* Dr. Paul F. James, Graduate Advisor, 513-529-3129, E-mail: jamespf@muohio.edu.

Michigan State University, The Graduate School, College of Natural Science, Department of Zoology, East Lansing, MI 48824. Offers zoo and aquarium management (MS); zoology (MS, PhD); zoology-environmental toxicology (PhD). *Entrance requirements:* Additional exam requirements/recommendations for international students: Required—TOEFL. Electronic applications accepted.

North Carolina State University, Graduate School, College of Agriculture and Life Sciences, Department of Zoology, Raleigh, NC 27695. Offers MS, MZS, PhD. Terminal master's awarded for partial completion of doctoral program. *Degree requirements:* For master's, thesis (for some programs), oral exam; for doctorate, thesis/dissertation, oral and written exams. *Entrance requirements:* For master's and doctorate, GRE General Test, minimum GPA of 3.0. Additional exam requirements/recommendations for international students: Required—TOEFL. Electronic applications accepted. *Faculty research:* Acquatic and terrestrial ecology, herpetology, behavioral biology, neurobiology, avian ecology.

North Dakota State University, College of Graduate and Interdisciplinary Studies, College of Science and Mathematics, Department of Biological Sciences, Fargo, ND 58108. Offers biology (MS); botany (MS, PhD); cellular and molecular biology (PhD); environmental and conservation sciences (MS, PhD); genomics (PhD); natural resources management (MS, PhD); zoology (MS, PhD). *Students:* 18 full-time (8 women), 5 part-time (3 women); includes 2 American Indian or Alaska Native, non-Hispanic/Latino, 2 international. 17 applicants, 35% accepted. In 2010, 12 master's, 9 doctorates awarded. *Degree requirements:* For master's, thesis; for doctorate, thesis/dissertation. *Entrance requirements:* For master's and doctorate, GRE General Test. Additional exam requirements/recommendations for international students: Required—TOEFL. *Application deadline:* For fall admission, 3/15 priority date for domestic students; for spring admission, 10/30 priority date for domestic students. Applications are processed on a rolling basis. Application fee: $45 ($60 for international students). Electronic applications accepted. *Financial support:* Fellowships with full tuition reimbursements, research assistantships with full tuition reimbursements, teaching assistantships with full tuition reimbursements, career-related internships or fieldwork, Federal Work-Study, institutionally sponsored loans, scholarships/grants, tuition waivers (full), and unspecified assistantships available. Support available to part-time students. Financial award application deadline: 4/15; financial award applicants required to submit FAFSA. *Faculty research:* Comparative endocrinology, physiology, behavioral ecology, plant cell biology, aquatic biology. Total annual research expenditures: $675,000. *Unit head:* Dr. Marinus L. Otte, Head, 701-231-7087, E-mail: marinus.otte@ndsu.edu. *Application contact:* Dr. Marinus L. Otte, Head, 701-231-7087, E-mail: marinus.otte@ndsu.edu.

Oklahoma State University, College of Arts and Sciences, Department of Zoology, Stillwater, OK 74078. Offers MS, PhD. *Faculty:* 21 full-time (6 women), 1 (woman) part-time/adjunct. *Students:* 4 full-time (3 women), 56 part-time (28 women); includes 1 Black or African American, non-Hispanic/Latino; 3 American Indian or Alaska Native, non-Hispanic/Latino; 3 Asian, non-Hispanic/Latino; 1 Hispanic/Latino, 5 international. Average age 29. 36 applicants, 44% accepted, 13 enrolled. In 2010, 9 master's, 3 doctorates awarded. *Degree requirements:* For master's, thesis; for doctorate, comprehensive exam, thesis/dissertation. *Entrance requirements:* For master's and doctorate, GRE General Test. Additional exam requirements/recommendations for international students: Required—TOEFL (minimum score 550 paper-based; 79 iBT). *Application deadline:* For fall admission, 3/1 priority date for international students; for spring admission, 8/1 priority date for international students. Applications are processed on a rolling basis. Application fee: $40 ($75 for international students). Electronic applications accepted. *Expenses:* Tuition, state resident: full-time $3716; part-time $154.85 per credit hour. Tuition, nonresident: full-time $14,892; part-time $621 per credit hour. Required fees: $2044; $85.20 per credit hour. One-time fee: $50. Tuition and fees vary according to course load and campus/location. *Financial support:* In 2010–11, 12 research assistantships (averaging $17,784 per year), 41 teaching assistantships (averaging $16,221 per year) were awarded; career-related internships or fieldwork, Federal Work-Study, scholarships/grants, health care benefits, tuition waivers (partial), and unspecified assistantships also available. Support available to part-time students. Financial award application deadline: 3/1; financial award applicants required to submit FAFSA. *Unit head:* Dr. Loren Smith, Head, 405-744-5555, Fax: 405-744-7824. *Application contact:* Dr. Gordon Emslie, Dean, 405-744-6368, Fax: 405-744-0355, E-mail: grad-i@okstate.edu.

Oregon State University, Graduate School, College of Science, Department of Zoology, Corvallis, OR 97331. Offers MA, MAIS, MS, PhD. Terminal master's awarded for partial completion of doctoral program. *Degree requirements:* For doctorate, thesis/dissertation. *Entrance requirements:* For master's and doctorate, GRE General Test, GRE Subject Test, minimum GPA of 3.0 in last 90 hours. Additional exam requirements/recommendations for international students: Required—TOEFL. *Faculty research:* Cell and developmental biology, population biology and marine community ecology, behavioral physiology, comparative immunology, plant-herbivore interaction.

Southern Illinois University Carbondale, Graduate School, College of Science, Department of Zoology, Carbondale, IL 62901-4701. Offers MS, PhD. *Degree requirements:* For master's, thesis; for doctorate, thesis/dissertation. *Entrance requirements:* For master's, GRE, minimum GPA of 2.7; for doctorate, GRE, minimum GPA of 3.25. Additional exam requirements/recommendations for international students: Required—TOEFL. *Faculty research:* Ecology, fisheries and wildlife, systematics, behavior, vertebrate and invertebrate biology.

Texas A&M University, College of Science, Department of Biology, College Station, TX 77843. Offers biology (MS, PhD); botany (MS, PhD); microbiology (MS, PhD); molecular and cell biology (PhD); neuroscience (MS, PhD); zoology (MS, PhD). *Faculty:* 39. *Students:* 107 full-time (60 women), 4 part-time (3 women); includes 1 Black or African American, non-Hispanic/Latino; 5 Asian, non-Hispanic/Latino; 5 Hispanic/Latino, 47 international. Average age 28. In 2010, 3 master's, 6 doctorates awarded. *Degree requirements:* For master's, thesis or alternative; for doctorate, comprehensive exam, thesis/dissertation. *Entrance requirements:* For master's and doctorate, GRE General Test. Additional exam requirements/recommendations for international students: Required—TOEFL. *Application deadline:* For fall admission, 1/15 for domestic students. Applications are processed on a rolling basis. Application fee: $50 ($75 for international students). Electronic applications accepted. *Financial support:* Fellowships, research assistantships, teaching assistantships available. Financial award application deadline: 4/1; financial award applicants required to submit FAFSA. *Unit head:* Dr. Jack McMahan, Department Head, 979-845-2301, E-mail: granster@mail.bio.tamu.edu. *Application contact:* Dr. Jack McMahan, Department Head, 979-845-2301, E-mail: granster@mail.bio.tamu.edu.

Texas Tech University, Graduate School, College of Arts and Sciences, Department of Biological Sciences, Lubbock, TX 79409-3131. Offers biology (MS, PhD); microbiology (MS); zoology (MS, PhD). Part-time programs available. *Faculty:* 28 full-time (6 women). *Students:* 115 full-time (63 women), 12 part-time (5 women); includes 1 Asian, non-Hispanic/Latino; 6 Hispanic/Latino; 2 Two or more races, non-Hispanic/Latino, 66 international. Average age 28. 79 applicants, 32% accepted, 20 enrolled. In 2010, 14 master's, 6 doctorates awarded. *Degree requirements:* For master's, thesis or alternative; for doctorate, thesis/dissertation. *Entrance requirements:* For master's and doctorate, GRE General Test. Additional exam requirements/recommendations for international students: Required—TOEFL (minimum score 550 paper-based; 213 computer-based; 79 iBT). *Application deadline:* For fall admission, 6/1 priority date for domestic students, 1/15 priority date for international students; for spring admission, 9/1 priority date for domestic students, 6/15 priority date for international students. Applications are processed on a rolling basis. Application fee: $50 ($75 for international students). Electronic applications accepted. *Expenses:* Tuition, state resident: full-time $5496; part-time $228.99 per credit hour. Tuition, nonresident: full-time $12,936; part-time $538.99 per credit hour. Required fees: $2674; $36 per credit hour. $905 per semester. *Financial support:* In 2010–11, 123 students received support, including 14 research assistantships with partial tuition reimbursements available (averaging $6,332 per year), 49 teaching assistantships with partial tuition reimbursements available (averaging $7,121 per year). Financial award application deadline: 4/15; financial award applicants required to submit FAFSA. *Faculty research:* Biodiversity and evolution, climate change in arid ecosystems, plant biology and biotechnology, animal communication and behavior, zoonotic and emerging diseases. Total annual research expenditures: $2.3 million. *Unit head:* Dr. Llewellyn D. Densmore, Chair, 806-742-2715, Fax: 806-742-2963, E-mail: lou.densmore@ttu.edu. *Application contact:* Dr. Randall M. Jeter, Graduate Adviser, 806-742-2710 Ext. 270, Fax: 806-742-2963, E-mail: randall.jeter@ttu.edu.

Uniformed Services University of the Health Sciences, School of Medicine, Graduate Programs in the Biomedical Sciences and Public Health, Bethesda, MD 20814. Offers emerging infectious diseases (PhD); medical and clinical psychology (PhD), including clinical psychology, medical and clinical psychology (clinical/dual track), medical and clinical psychology (research track); molecular and cell biology (PhD); neuroscience (PhD); preventive medicine and biometrics (MPH, MSPH, MTMH, Dr PH, PhD), including environmental health science (PhD), medical zoology (PhD), public health (MPH, MSPH, Dr PH), tropical medicine and hygiene (MTMH). *Faculty:* 372 full-time (119 women), 4,044 part-time/adjunct (908 women). *Students:* 176 full-time (96 women); includes 6 Black or African American, non-Hispanic/Latino; 4 American Indian or Alaska Native, non-Hispanic/Latino; 14 Asian, non-Hispanic/Latino; 7 Hispanic/Latino, 11 international. Average age 28. 278 applicants, 20% accepted, 47 enrolled. In 2010, 36 master's, 17 doctorates awarded. Terminal master's awarded for partial completion of doctoral program. *Degree requirements:* For master's, comprehensive exam, thesis or alternative; for doctorate, comprehensive exam, thesis/dissertation, qualifying exam. *Entrance requirements:* For master's, GRE General Test; for doctorate, GRE General Test, minimum GPA of 3.0. Additional exam requirements/recommendations for international students: Required—TOEFL. *Application deadline:* For fall admission, 1/1 priority date for domestic and international students. Applications are processed on a rolling basis. Application fee: $0. Electronic applications accepted. *Financial support:* In 2010–11, fellowships with full tuition reimbursements (averaging $26,000 per year), research assistantships with full tuition reimbursements (averaging $26,000 per year) were awarded; career-related internships or fieldwork, scholarships/grants, health care benefits, and tuition waivers (full) also available. *Unit head:* Dr. Eleanor S. Metcalf, Associate Dean, 301-295-1104, E-mail: emetcalf@usuhs.mil. *Application contact:* Elena Marina Sherman, Graduate Program Coordinator, 301-295-3913, Fax: 301-295-6772, E-mail: elena.sherman@usuhs.mil.

Uniformed Services University of the Health Sciences, School of Medicine, Graduate Programs in the Biomedical Sciences and Public Health, Department of Preventive Medicine and Biometrics, Program in Medical Zoology, Bethesda, MD 20814-4799. Offers PhD. *Degree requirements:* For doctorate, comprehensive exam, thesis/dissertation, qualifying exam. *Entrance requirements:* For doctorate, GRE General Test, GRE Subject Test, minimum GPA of 3.0, U.S. citizenship. Additional exam requirements/recommendations for international students: Required—TOEFL. *Faculty research:* Epidemiology, biostatistics, tropical public health, parasitology, vector biology.

University of Alaska Fairbanks, College of Natural Sciences and Mathematics, Department of Biology and Wildlife, Fairbanks, AK 99775-6100. Offers biological sciences (MS, PhD), including biology, botany, wildlife biology (PhD), zoology; biology (MAT, MS); wildlife biology (MS). Part-time programs available. *Faculty:* 22 full-time (10 women). *Students:* 80 full-time (46 women), 42 part-time (26 women); includes 13 minority (2 American Indian or Alaska Native, non-Hispanic/Latino; 3 Asian, non-Hispanic/Latino; 2 Hispanic/Latino; 6 Two or more races, non-Hispanic/Latino), 6 international. Average age 31. 53 applicants, 30% accepted, 15 enrolled. In 2010, 11 master's, 10 doctorates awarded. *Degree requirements:* For master's, comprehensive exam, thesis, oral exam, oral defense; for doctorate, comprehensive exam, thesis/dissertation, oral exam, oral defense. *Entrance requirements:* For master's and doctorate, GRE General Test, GRE Subject Test (biology). Additional exam requirements/recommendations for international students: Required—TOEFL (minimum score 550 paper-based; 213 computer-based; 80 iBT), TWE. *Application deadline:* For fall admission, 6/1 for domestic students, 3/1 for international students; for spring admission, 10/15 for domestic students, 9/1 for international students. Applications are processed on a rolling basis. Application fee: $60. Electronic applications accepted. *Expenses:* Tuition, state resident: full-time $5688; part-time $316 per credit. Tuition, nonresident: full-time $11,628; part-time $646 per credit. Required fees: $289 per semester. Tuition and fees vary according to course load and reciprocity agreements. *Financial support:* In 2010–11, 38 research assistantships with tuition reimbursements (averaging $11,087 per year), 20 teaching assistantships with tuition reimbursements (averaging $8,587 per year) were awarded; fellowships with tuition reimbursements, career-related internships or fieldwork, Federal Work-Study, scholarships/grants, health care benefits, and unspecified assistantships also available. Support available to part-time students. Financial award application deadline: 7/1; financial award applicants required to submit FAFSA. *Faculty research:* Plant-herbivore interactions, plant metabolic defenses, insect manufacture of glycerol, ice nucleators, structure and functions of arctic and subarctic freshwater ecosystems. *Unit head:* Christa Mulder, Department Chair, 907-474-7671, Fax: 907-474-6716, E-mail: fybio@uaf.edu. *Application contact:* Christa Mulder, Department Chair, 907-474-7671, Fax: 907-474-6716, E-mail: fybio@uaf.edu.

The University of British Columbia, Faculty of Science, Department of Zoology, Vancouver, BC V6T 1Z1, Canada. Offers M Sc, PhD. *Degree requirements:* For master's, thesis, final defense; for doctorate, comprehensive exam, thesis/dissertation, final defense. *Entrance requirements:* For master's and doctorate, faculty support. Additional exam requirements/recommendations for international students: Required—TOEFL. Electronic applications accepted. Tuition charges are reported in Canadian dollars. *Expenses:* Tuition, area resident: Full-time $4179 Canadian dollars. International tuition: $7344 Canadian dollars full-time. *Faculty research:* Cell and developmental biology; community, environmental, and population biology; comparative physiology and biochemistry; fisheries; ecology and evolutionary biology.

University of California, Davis, Graduate Studies, Graduate Group in Avian Sciences, Davis, CA 95616. Offers MS. *Degree requirements:* For master's, comprehensive exam (for some programs), thesis (for some programs). *Entrance requirements:* For master's, GRE General Test, minimum GPA of 3.0. Additional exam requirements/recommendations for international students: Required—TOEFL (minimum score 550 paper-based; 213 computer-based). Electronic applications accepted. *Faculty research:* Reproduction, nutrition, toxicology, food products, ecology of avian species.

University of Chicago, Division of Biological Sciences, Darwinian Sciences Cluster: Ecological, Integrative and Evolutionary Biology, Department of Organismal Biology and Anatomy, Chicago, IL 60637-1513. Offers functional and evolutionary biology (PhD); organismal biology and anatomy (PhD). *Degree requirements:* For doctorate, thesis/dissertation, ethics class, 2 teaching assistantships. *Entrance requirements:* For doctorate, GRE General Test. Additional exam requirements/recommendations for international students: Required—TOEFL (minimum score 600 paper-based; 250 computer-based; 104 iBT), IELTS (minimum score 7). Electronic applications accepted. *Faculty research:* Ecological physiology, evolution of fossil reptiles, vertebrate paleontology.

University of Connecticut, Graduate School, College of Liberal Arts and Sciences, Department of Ecology and Evolutionary Biology, Storrs, CT 06269. Offers botany (MS, PhD); ecology

(MS, PhD); entomology (MS, PhD); zoology (MS, PhD). Terminal master's awarded for partial completion of doctoral program. *Degree requirements:* For master's, comprehensive exam; for doctorate, thesis/dissertation. *Entrance requirements:* For master's and doctorate, GRE General Test, GRE Subject Test. Additional exam requirements/recommendations for international students: Required—TOEFL (minimum score 550 paper-based; 213 computer-based). Electronic applications accepted.

University of Florida, Graduate School, College of Liberal Arts and Sciences, Department of Zoology, Gainesville, FL 32611. Offers botany (MS, MST); zoology (MS, MST, PhD). *Faculty:* 37 full-time (9 women), 1 part-time/adjunct (0 women). *Students:* 79 full-time (40 women), 5 part-time (2 women); includes 2 Asian, non-Hispanic/Latino; 8 Hispanic/Latino, 20 international. Average age 29. 102 applicants, 29% accepted, 22 enrolled. In 2010, 8 master's, 11 doctorates awarded. *Degree requirements:* For master's, comprehensive exam (for some programs), thesis; for doctorate, comprehensive exam, thesis/dissertation, teaching experience. *Entrance requirements:* For master's and doctorate, GRE General Test (minimum score of 1000), minimum GPA of 3.0. Additional exam requirements/recommendations for international students: Required—TOEFL (minimum score 550 paper-based; 213 computer-based; 80 iBT), IELTS (minimum score 6). *Application deadline:* For fall admission, 12/1 for domestic and international students. Applications are processed on a rolling basis. Application fee: $30. Electronic applications accepted. *Expenses:* Tuition, state resident: full-time $10,916. Tuition, nonresident: full-time $28,309. *Financial support:* In 2010–11, 95 students received support, including 39 fellowships, 14 research assistantships (averaging $23,199 per year), 42 teaching assistantships (averaging $22,469 per year); unspecified assistantships also available. Financial award application deadline: 12/15; financial award applicants required to submit FAFSA. *Faculty research:* Ecology, evolution, genetics, molecular and cellular biology, physiology. Total annual research expenditures: $4.8 million. *Unit head:* Dr. Alice Harmon, Chair, 352-273-0127, E-mail: harmon@ufl.edu. *Application contact:* Dr. Rebecca T. Kimball, Graduate Coordinator, 352-846-3737, Fax: 352-392-3704, E-mail: rkimball@ufl.edu.

University of Guelph, Graduate Studies, College of Biological Science, Department of Integrative Biology, Botany and Zoology, Guelph, ON N1G 2W1, Canada. Offers botany (M Sc, PhD); zoology (M Sc, PhD). Part-time programs available. *Degree requirements:* For master's, thesis, research proposal; for doctorate, thesis/dissertation, research proposal, qualifying exam. *Entrance requirements:* For master's, minimum B average during previous 2 years of course work. Additional exam requirements/recommendations for international students: Required—TOEFL (minimum score 550 paper-based; 213 computer-based), IELTS (minimum score 6.5). Electronic applications accepted. *Faculty research:* Aquatic science, environmental physiology, parasitology, wildlife biology, management.

University of Hawaii at Manoa, Graduate Division, College of Natural Sciences, Department of Zoology, Honolulu, HI 96822. Offers MS, PhD. Part-time programs available. *Faculty:* 39 full-time (10 women), 2 part-time/adjunct (1 woman). *Students:* 83 full-time (43 women), 8 part-time (4 women); includes 25 minority (1 Black or African American, non-Hispanic/Latino; 12 Asian, non-Hispanic/Latino; 3 Hispanic/Latino; 2 Native Hawaiian or other Pacific Islander, non-Hispanic/Latino; 7 Two or more races, non-Hispanic/Latino), 12 international. Average age 30. 86 applicants, 35% accepted, 27 enrolled. In 2010, 6 master's, 11 doctorates awarded. *Degree requirements:* For master's, one foreign language, thesis optional; for doctorate, one foreign language, comprehensive exam, thesis/dissertation, seminar. *Entrance requirements:* For master's and doctorate, GRE General Test, GRE Subject Test. Additional exam requirements/recommendations for international students: Required—TOEFL (minimum score 600 paper-based; 250 computer-based; 100 iBT), IELTS (minimum score 7). *Application deadline:* For fall admission, 12/31 for domestic and international students. Applications are processed on a rolling basis. Application fee: $60. *Financial support:* In 2010–11, 14 fellowships (averaging $1,126 per year), 44 research assistantships (averaging $20,768 per year), 27 teaching assistantships (averaging $15,699 per year) were awarded; tuition waivers (full) also available. Financial award application deadline: 2/1. *Faculty research:* Molecular evolution, reproductive biology, animal behavior, conservation biology, avian biology. Total annual research expenditures: $231,000. *Application contact:* Leslie E. Watling, Graduate Chairperson, 808-956-8621, Fax: 808-956-9812, E-mail: watling@hawaii.edu.

University of Illinois at Urbana–Champaign, Graduate College, College of Liberal Arts and Sciences, School of Integrative Biology, Department of Animal Biology, Champaign, IL 61820. Offers animal biology (ecology, ethology and evolution) (MS, PhD). *Faculty:* 9 full-time (5 women). *Students:* 14 full-time (10 women), 3 part-time (1 woman); includes 1 minority (Two or more races, non-Hispanic/Latino), 3 international. 11 applicants, 27% accepted, 1 enrolled. *Entrance requirements:* For master's and doctorate, GRE. Additional exam requirements/recommendations for international students: Required—TOEFL (minimum score 570 paper-based; 230 computer-based; 88 iBT). *Application deadline:* Applications are processed on a rolling basis. Application fee: $75 ($90 for international students). Electronic applications accepted. *Financial support:* In 2010–11, 2 fellowships, 8 research assistantships, 13 teaching assistantships were awarded; tuition waivers (full and partial) also available. *Unit head:* Ken Paige, Head, 217-244-6606, Fax: 217-244-4565, E-mail: k-paige@illinois.edu. *Application contact:* Lisa Smith, Office Administrator, 217-333-7802, Fax: 217-244-4565, E-mail: ljsmith1@illinois.edu.

University of Maine, Graduate School, College of Natural Sciences, Forestry, and Agriculture, Department of Biological Sciences, Program in Zoology, Orono, ME 04469. Offers MS, PhD. *Faculty:* 15 full-time (4 women). *Students:* 2 full-time (1 woman), 1 (woman) part-time. Average age 26. 13 applicants, 0% accepted, 0 enrolled. In 2010, 1 degree awarded. Terminal master's awarded for partial completion of doctoral program. *Degree requirements:* For master's, variable foreign language requirement, thesis; for doctorate, one foreign language, thesis/dissertation. *Entrance requirements:* For master's and doctorate, GRE General Test. Additional exam requirements/recommendations for international students: Required—TOEFL. *Application deadline:* For fall admission, 2/1 priority date for domestic students. Applications are processed on a rolling basis. Application fee: $65. Electronic applications accepted. *Expenses:* Tuition, state resident: full-time $400. Tuition, nonresident: full-time $1050. *Financial support:* Career-related internships or fieldwork available. Financial award application deadline: 3/1. *Unit head:* Dr. Stellos Tavantiz, Coordinator, 207-581-2986. *Application contact:* Scott G. Delcourt, Associate Dean of the Graduate School, 207-581-3291, Fax: 207-581-3232, E-mail: graduate@maine.edu.

University of Manitoba, Faculty of Graduate Studies, Faculty of Science, Department of Biological Sciences, Winnipeg, MB R3T 2N2, Canada. Offers botany (M Sc, PhD); ecology (M Sc, PhD); zoology (M Sc, PhD).

The University of Montana, Graduate School, College of Arts and Sciences, Division of Biological Sciences, Program in Organismal Biology and Ecology, Missoula, MT 59812-0002. Offers MS, PhD. Terminal master's awarded for partial completion of doctoral program. *Degree requirements:* For master's, one foreign language, thesis; for doctorate, 2 foreign languages, thesis/dissertation. *Entrance requirements:* For master's and doctorate, GRE General Test. *Faculty research:* Conservation biology, ecology and behavior, evolutionary genetics, avian biology.

University of New Hampshire, Graduate School, College of Life Sciences and Agriculture, Department of Biological Sciences, Program in Zoology, Durham, NH 03824. Offers MS, PhD. Part-time programs available. *Faculty:* 25 full-time. *Students:* 16 full-time (8 women), 13 part-time (8 women), 2 international. Average age 33. 21 applicants, 33% accepted, 4 enrolled. In 2010, 5 master's, 4 doctorates awarded. Terminal master's awarded for partial completion of doctoral program. *Degree requirements:* For master's, thesis; for doctorate, one foreign language, thesis/dissertation. *Entrance requirements:* For master's and doctorate, GRE General Test, GRE Subject Test. Additional exam requirements/recommendations for international students: Required—TOEFL (minimum score 550 paper-based; 213 computer-based; 80 iBT). *Application deadline:* For fall admission, 6/1 priority date for domestic students, 4/1 for international students; for spring admission, 12/1 for domestic students. Applications are processed on a rolling basis. Application fee: $65. Electronic applications accepted. *Financial support:* In 2010–11, 19 students received support, including 1 fellowship, 3 research assistantships, 12 teaching assistantships; career-related internships or fieldwork, Federal Work-Study, scholarships/grants, and tuition waivers (full and partial) also available. Support available to part-time students. Financial award application deadline: 2/15. *Faculty research:* Behavior development, ecology, endocrinology, fisheries, invertebrates. *Unit head:* Dr. Christopher Neefus, Chairperson, 603-862-2105. *Application contact:* Diane Lavalliere, Administrative Assistant, 603-862-2100, E-mail: zoology.dept@unh.edu.

University of North Dakota, Graduate School, College of Arts and Sciences, Department of Biology, Grand Forks, ND 58202. Offers botany (MS, PhD); ecology (MS, PhD); entomology (MS, PhD); environmental biology (MS, PhD); fisheries/wildlife (MS, PhD); genetics (MS, PhD); zoology (MS, PhD). *Faculty:* 17 full-time (5 women), 6 part-time/adjunct (1 woman). *Students:* 19 full-time (6 women), 8 part-time (2 women); includes 4 minority (3 American Indian or Alaska Native, non-Hispanic/Latino; 1 Asian, non-Hispanic/Latino), 1 international. Average age 28. 21 applicants, 33% accepted, 4 enrolled. In 2010, 1 master's awarded. Terminal master's awarded for partial completion of doctoral program. *Degree requirements:* For master's, thesis, final exam; for doctorate, comprehensive exam, thesis/dissertation, final exam. *Entrance requirements:* For master's, GRE General Test, GRE Subject Test, minimum GPA of 3.0; for doctorate, GRE General Test, GRE Subject Test, minimum GPA of 3.5. Additional exam requirements/recommendations for international students: Required—TOEFL (minimum score 550 paper-based; 213 computer-based; 79 iBT), IELTS (minimum score 6.5). *Application deadline:* For fall admission, 2/15 for domestic and international students; for spring admission, 10/15 for domestic and international students. Application fee: $35. Electronic applications accepted. *Expenses:* Tuition, state resident: full-time $5857; part-time $306.74 per credit. Tuition, nonresident: full-time $15,666; part-time $729.77 per credit. Required fees: $53.42 per credit. Tuition and fees vary according to course load, program and reciprocity agreements. *Financial support:* In 2010–11, 22 students received support, including 5 research assistantships with full and partial tuition reimbursements available (averaging $11,375 per year), 17 teaching assistantships with full and partial tuition reimbursements available (averaging $10,813 per year); fellowships with full and partial tuition reimbursements available, Federal Work-Study, institutionally sponsored loans, scholarships/grants, health care benefits, tuition waivers (full and partial), and unspecified assistantships also available. Support available to part-time students. Financial award application deadline: 3/15; financial award applicants required to submit FAFSA. *Faculty research:* Population biology, wildlife ecology, RNA processing, hormonal control of behavior. Total annual research expenditures: $736,510. *Unit head:* Dr. Brett Goodwin, Graduate Director, 701-777-2621, Fax: 701-777-2623, E-mail: brett.goodwin@mail.und.edu. *Application contact:* Matthew Anderson, Admissions Specialist, 701-777-2947, Fax: 701-777-3619, E-mail: matthew.anderson@gradschool.und.edu.

University of Oklahoma, College of Arts and Sciences, Department of Zoology, Norman, OK 73019. Offers cellular and behavioral neurobiology (PhD); ecology and evolutionary biology (PhD); zoology (M Nat Sci, MS, PhD), including natural science (M Nat Sci), zoology (MS, PhD). Part-time programs available. *Faculty:* 40 full-time (10 women), 3 part-time/adjunct (1 woman). *Students:* 35 full-time (16 women), 21 part-time (11 women); includes 4 minority (2 Asian, non-Hispanic/Latino; 1 Hispanic/Latino; 1 Two or more races, non-Hispanic/Latino), 18 international. Average age 28. 34 applicants, 53% accepted, 11 enrolled. In 2010, 6 master's, 4 doctorates awarded. Terminal master's awarded for partial completion of doctoral program. *Degree requirements:* For master's, thesis defense; for doctorate, dissertation defense, general exam. *Entrance requirements:* For master's and doctorate, GRE General Test, GRE Subject Test, 3 letters of recommendation. Additional exam requirements/recommendations for international students: Required—TOEFL (minimum score 550 paper-based; 213 computer-based; 79 iBT). *Application deadline:* For fall admission, 12/15 for domestic students, 4/1 for international students; for spring admission, 10/15 for domestic students, 9/1 for international students. Applications are processed on a rolling basis. Application fee: $40 ($90 for international students). Electronic applications accepted. *Expenses:* Tuition, state resident: full-time $3893; part-time $162.20 per credit hour. Tuition, nonresident: full-time $14,167; part-time $590.30 per credit hour. Required fees: $2523; $94.60 per credit hour. Tuition and fees vary according to course load and degree level. *Financial support:* In 2010–11, 3 fellowships with tuition reimbursements (averaging $4,667 per year), 6 research assistantships with tuition reimbursements (averaging $15,646 per year), 36 teaching assistantships (averaging $14,420 per year) were awarded; institutionally sponsored loans, scholarships/grants, health care benefits, and unspecified assistantships also available. Financial award applicants required to submit FAFSA. *Faculty research:* Cell signaling, ecology and evolution biology, neurobiology, animal behavior, development. Total annual research expenditures: $1.4 million. *Unit head:* Bill Matthews, Chair, 405-325-4821, Fax: 405-325-6202, E-mail: wmatthews@ou.edu. *Application contact:* Dr. Rosemary Knapp, Associate Professor and Director of Graduate Studies, 405-325-4389, Fax: 405-325-6202, E-mail: rknapp@ou.edu.

The University of Western Ontario, Faculty of Graduate Studies, Biosciences Division, Department of Zoology, London, ON N6A 5B8, Canada. Offers M Sc, PhD. *Degree requirements:* For master's, thesis; for doctorate, thesis/dissertation.

University of Wisconsin–Madison, Graduate School, College of Letters and Science, Department of Zoology, Madison, WI 53706-1380. Offers MA, MS, PhD. Part-time programs available. *Degree requirements:* For master's, thesis; for doctorate, one foreign language, thesis/dissertation. *Entrance requirements:* For master's and doctorate, GRE General Test. Additional exam requirements/recommendations for international students: Required—TOEFL. Electronic applications accepted. *Expenses:* Tuition, state resident: full-time $9887; part-time $617.96 per credit. Tuition, nonresident: full-time $24,054; part-time $1503.40 per credit. Required fees: $67.63 per credit. Tuition and fees vary according to reciprocity agreements. *Faculty research:* Developmental biology, ecology, neurobiology, aquatic ecology, animal behavior.

University of Wisconsin–Oshkosh, The Office of Graduate Studies, College of Letters and Science, Department of Biology and Microbiology, Oshkosh, WI 54901. Offers biology (MS), including botany, microbiology, zoology. *Degree requirements:* For master's, comprehensive exam, thesis. *Entrance requirements:* For master's, GRE General Test, minimum GPA of 3.0, BS in biology. Additional exam requirements/recommendations for international students: Required—TOEFL (minimum score 550 paper-based; 213 computer-based; 79 iBT). Electronic applications accepted.

University of Wyoming, College of Arts and Sciences, Department of Zoology and Physiology, Laramie, WY 82070. Offers MS, PhD. Part-time programs available. *Degree requirements:* For master's, comprehensive exam (for some programs), thesis; for doctorate, comprehensive exam (for some programs), thesis/dissertation. *Entrance requirements:* For master's and doctorate, GRE General Test, minimum GPA of 3.0. Additional exam requirements/recommendations for international students: Required—TOEFL. Electronic applications accepted. *Faculty research:* Cell biology, ecology/wildlife, organismal physiology, zoology.

Washington State University, Graduate School, College of Sciences, School of Biological Sciences, Department of Zoology, Pullman, WA 99164. Offers MS, PhD. *Faculty:* 33. *Students:* 27 full-time (13 women), 1 international. Average age 30. 40 applicants, 20% accepted, 8 enrolled. In 2010, 4 master's, 4 doctorates awarded. *Degree requirements:* For master's, comprehensive exam (for some programs), thesis (for some programs), oral exam; for doctorate, comprehensive exam, thesis/dissertation, oral exam, written exam. *Entrance requirements:* For master's and doctorate, GRE General Test, GRE Subject Test, three letters of recommendation, official transcripts from each university-level school attended, minimum GPA of 3.0. Additional exam requirements/recommendations for international students: Required—TOEFL, IELTS. *Application deadline:* For fall admission, 1/10 priority date for domestic students, 1/10 for international students; for spring admission, 7/1 for domestic and international students. Applications are processed on a rolling basis. Application fee: $50. *Expenses:* Tuition, state resident: full-time $8552; part-time $443 per credit. Tuition, nonresident: full-time $21,650; part-time $1083 per credit. Required fees: $846. *Financial support:* In 2010–11, 4 fellowships

Zoology

Washington State University (continued)
(averaging $4,500 per year), 3 research assistantships with full and partial tuition reimbursements (averaging $13,917 per year), 21 teaching assistantships with full and partial tuition reimbursements (averaging $13,056 per year) were awarded; Federal Work-Study, institutionally sponsored loans, and tuition waivers (partial) also available. Financial award application deadline: 4/1; financial award applicants required to submit FAFSA. *Unit head:* Dr. Gary H. Thorgaard, Director, 509-335-7438, Fax: 509-335-3184, E-mail: thorglab@wsu.edu. *Application contact:* Graduate School Admissions, 800-GRADWSU, Fax: 509-335-1949, E-mail: gradsch@wsu.edu.

Western Illinois University, School of Graduate Studies, College of Arts and Sciences, Department of Biological Sciences, Macomb, IL 61455-1390. Offers biological sciences (MS); environmental geographic information systems (Certificate); zoo and aquarium studies (Certificate). Part-time programs available. *Students:* 64 full-time (41 women), 31 part-time (22 women); includes 10 minority (4 Black or African American, non-Hispanic/Latino; 1 Asian, non-Hispanic/Latino; 4 Hispanic/Latino; 1 Two or more races, non-Hispanic/Latino), 7 international. Average age 26. 60 applicants, 67% accepted. In 2010, 23 master's, 15 other advanced degrees awarded. *Degree requirements:* For master's, thesis or alternative. *Entrance requirements:* Additional exam requirements/recommendations for international students: Required—TOEFL (minimum score 550 paper-based; 213 computer-based; 80 iBT); Recommended—IELTS. *Application deadline:* Applications are processed on a rolling basis. Application fee: $30. Electronic applications accepted. *Expenses:* Tuition, state resident: full-time $6370; part-time $265.40 per credit hour. Tuition, nonresident: full-time $12,740; part-time $530.80 per credit hour. Required fees: $75.67 per credit hour. *Financial support:* In 2010–11, 28 students received support, including 10 research assistantships with full tuition reimbursements available (averaging $7,280 per year), 18 teaching assistantships with full tuition reimbursements available (averaging $8,400 per year). Financial award applicants required to submit FAFSA. *Unit head:* Dr. Michael Romano, Chairperson, 309-298-1546. *Application contact:* Evelyn Hoing, Assistant Director of Graduate Studies, 309-298-1806, Fax: 309-298-2345, E-mail: grad-office@wiu.edu.

APPENDIXES

Institutional Changes
Since the 2011 Edition

Following is an alphabetical listing of institutions that have recently closed, merged with other institutions, or changed their names or status. In the case of a name change, the former name appears first, followed by the new name.

Alliance Theological Seminary (Nyack, NY): now listed as a unit of Nyack College (Nyack, NY)

American InterContinental University (Houston, TX): name changed to American InterContinental University Houston

American InterContinental University Buckhead Campus (Atlanta, GA): closed

American InterContinental University Dunwoody Campus (Atlanta, GA): name changed to American InterContinental University Atlanta

American InterContinental University–London (London, United Kingdom): name changed to American InterContinental University London

Arkansas State University - Jonesboro (State University, AR): name changed to Arkansas State University

Bard Graduate Center for Studies in the Decorative Arts, Design, and Culture (New York, NY): name changed to Bard Graduate Center: Decorative Arts, Design History, Material Culture

Birmingham-Southern College (Birmingham, AL): no longer offers graduate degrees

California School of Podiatric Medicine at Samuel Merritt College (Oakland, CA): name changed to California School of Podiatric Medicine at Samuel Merritt University

Church of God Theological Seminary (Cleveland, TN): name changed to Pentecostal Theological Seminary

Clarke College (Dubuque, IA): name changed to Clarke University

College of Santa Fe (Santa Fe, NM): name changed to Santa Fe University of Art and Design and no longer offers graduate degrees

Dongguk Royal University (Los Angeles, CA): name changed to Dongguk University Los Angeles

Embry-Riddle Aeronautical University (Prescott, AZ): name changed to Embry-Riddle Aeronautical University–Prescott

Embry-Riddle Aeronautical University (Daytona Beach, FL): name changed to Embry-Riddle Aeronautical University–Daytona

Embry-Riddle Aeronautical University Worldwide (Daytona Beach, FL): name changed to Embry-Riddle Aeronautical University—Worldwide

Emily Carr Institute of Art & Design (Vancouver, BC, Canada): name changed to Emily Carr University of Art & Design

Emmanuel School of Religion (Johnson City, TN): name changed to Emmanuel Christian Seminary

Everest University (Clearwater, FL): no longer a campus of Everest University

Framingham State College (Framingham, MA): name changed to Framingham State University

Hannibal-LaGrange College (Hannibal, MO): name changed to Hannibal-LaGrange University

Hebrew Union College–Jewish Institute of Religion (Los Angeles, CA): merged into a single entry for Hebrew Union College–Jewish Institute of Religion (New York, NY) by request from the institution

Hebrew Union College–Jewish Institute of Religion (Cincinnati, OH): merged into a single entry for Hebrew Union College–Jewish Institute of Religion (New York, NY) by request from the institution

Jesuit School of Theology at Berkeley (Berkeley, CA): now listed as a unit of Santa Clara University (Santa Clara, CA)

Johnson Bible College (Knoxville, TN): name changed to Johnson University

Keller Graduate School of Management (Long Island City, NY): now listed as a unit of DeVry College of New York (Long Island City, NY)

Keller Graduate School of Management (New York, NY): now listed as a unit of DeVry University Manhattan Extension Site (New York, NY)

Lancaster Bible College & Graduate School (Lancaster, PA): name changed to Lancaster Bible College

Medical College of Georgia (Augusta, GA): name changed to Georgia Health Sciences University

Mennonite Brethren Biblical Seminary (Fresno, CA): name changed to Fresno Pacific Biblical Seminary and now a unit of Fresno Pacific University (Fresno, CA)

Meritus University (Fredericton, NB, Canada): closed

Mount Mercy College (Cedar Rapids, IA): name changed to Mount Mercy University

Mount Sinai School of Medicine of New York University (New York, NY): name changed to Mount Sinai School of Medicine

Northeastern Ohio Universities College of Medicine and Pharmacy (Rootstown, OH): name changed to Northeastern Ohio Universities Colleges of Medicine and Pharmacy

Polytechnic University of the Americas–Miami Campus (Miami, FL): name changed to Polytechnic University of Puerto Rico, Miami Campus

Polytechnic University of the Americas–Orlando Campus (Winter Park, FL): name changed to Polytechnic University of Puerto Rico, Orlando Campus

Salem State College (Salem, MA): name changed to Salem State University

Sherman College of Straight Chiropractic (Spartanburg, SC): name changed to Sherman College of Chiropractic

Union Theological Seminary and Presbyterian School of Christian Education (Richmond, VA): name changed to Union Presbyterian Seminary

University of Colorado at Boulder (Boulder, CO): name changed to University of Colorado Boulder

University of Phoenix–Western Washington Campus (Tukwila, WA): merged into a single entry for University of Phoenix–Washington Campus (Seattle, WA)

Vassar College (Poughkeepsie, NY): no longer offers graduate degrees

Western New England College (Springfield, MA): name changed to Western New England University

Western States Chiropractic College (Portland, OR): name changed to University of Western States

Westfield State College (Westfield, MA): name changed to Westfield State University

Westminster Choir College of Rider University (Princeton, NJ): name changed to Westminster Choir College and now a unit of Rider University (Lawrenceville, NJ)

West Suburban College of Nursing (Oak Park, IL): name changed to Resurrection University

Worcester State College (Worcester, MA): name changed to Worcester State University

Abbreviations Used in the Guides

The following list includes abbreviations of degree names used in the profiles in the 2012 edition of the guides. Because some degrees (e.g., Doctor of Education) can be abbreviated in more than one way (e.g., D.Ed. or Ed.D.), and because the abbreviations used in the guides reflect the preferences of the individual colleges and universities, the list may include two or more abbreviations for a single degree.

Degrees

A Mus D	Doctor of Musical Arts
AC	Advanced Certificate
AD	Artist's Diploma Doctor of Arts
ADP	Artist's Diploma
Adv C	Advanced Certificate
Adv M	Advanced Master
AGC	Advanced Graduate Certificate
AGSC	Advanced Graduate Specialist Certificate
ALM	Master of Liberal Arts
AM	Master of Arts
AMBA	Accelerated Master of Business Administration Aviation Master of Business Administration
AMRS	Master of Arts in Religious Studies
APC	Advanced Professional Certificate
APMPH	Advanced Professional Master of Public Health
App Sc	Applied Scientist
App Sc D	Doctor of Applied Science
Au D	Doctor of Audiology
B Th	Bachelor of Theology
CAES	Certificate of Advanced Educational Specialization
CAGS	Certificate of Advanced Graduate Studies
CAL	Certificate in Applied Linguistics
CALS	Certificate of Advanced Liberal Studies
CAMS	Certificate of Advanced Management Studies
CAPS	Certificate of Advanced Professional Studies
CAS	Certificate of Advanced Studies
CASPA	Certificate of Advanced Study in Public Administration
CASR	Certificate in Advanced Social Research
CATS	Certificate of Achievement in Theological Studies
CBHS	Certificate in Basic Health Sciences
CBS	Graduate Certificate in Biblical Studies
CCJA	Certificate in Criminal Justice Administration
CCSA	Certificate in Catholic School Administration
CCTS	Certificate in Clinical and Translational Science
CE	Civil Engineer
CEM	Certificate of Environmental Management
CET	Certificate in Educational Technologies
CGS	Certificate of Graduate Studies
Ch E	Chemical Engineer
CM	Certificate in Management
CMH	Certificate in Medical Humanities
CMM	Master of Church Ministries
CMS	Certificate in Ministerial Studies
CNM	Certificate in Nonprofit Management
CP	Certificate in Performance
CPASF	Certificate Program for Advanced Study in Finance
CPC	Certificate in Professional Counseling Certificate in Publication and Communication
CPH	Certificate in Public Health
CPM	Certificate in Public Management
CPS	Certificate of Professional Studies
CScD	Doctor of Clinical Science
CSD	Certificate in Spiritual Direction
CSS	Certificate of Special Studies
CTS	Certificate of Theological Studies
CURP	Certificate in Urban and Regional Planning
D Admin	Doctor of Administration
D Arch	Doctor of Architecture
D Com	Doctor of Commerce
D Couns	Doctor of Counseling
D Div	Doctor of Divinity
D Ed	Doctor of Education
D Ed Min	Doctor of Educational Ministry
D Eng	Doctor of Engineering
D Engr	Doctor of Engineering
D Ent	Doctor of Enterprise
D Env	Doctor of Environment
D Law	Doctor of Law
D Litt	Doctor of Letters
D Med Sc	Doctor of Medical Science
D Min	Doctor of Ministry
D Miss	Doctor of Missiology
D Mus	Doctor of Music
D Mus A	Doctor of Musical Arts
D Phil	Doctor of Philosophy
D Prof	Doctor of Professional Studies
D Ps	Doctor of Psychology
D Sc	Doctor of Science
D Sc D	Doctor of Science in Dentistry
D Sc IS	Doctor of Science in Information Systems
D Sc PA	Doctor of Science in Physician Assistant Studies
D Th	Doctor of Theology

D Th P	Doctor of Practical Theology	
DA	Doctor of Accounting	
	Doctor of Arts	
DA Ed	Doctor of Arts in Education	
DAH	Doctor of Arts in Humanities	
DAOM	Doctorate in Acupuncture and Oriental Medicine	
DAST	Diploma of Advanced Studies in Teaching	
DBA	Doctor of Business Administration	
DBH	Doctor of Behavioral Health	
DBL	Doctor of Business Leadership	
DBS	Doctor of Buddhist Studies	
DC	Doctor of Chiropractic	
DCC	Doctor of Computer Science	
DCD	Doctor of Communications Design	
DCL	Doctor of Civil Law	
	Doctor of Comparative Law	
DCM	Doctor of Church Music	
DCN	Doctor of Clinical Nutrition	
DCS	Doctor of Computer Science	
DDN	Diplôme du Droit Notarial	
DDS	Doctor of Dental Surgery	
DE	Doctor of Education	
	Doctor of Engineering	
DED	Doctor of Economic Development	
DEIT	Doctor of Educational Innovation and Technology	
DEL	Doctor of Executive Leadership	
DEM	Doctor of Educational Ministry	
DEPD	Diplôme Études Spécialisées	
DES	Doctor of Engineering Science	
DESS	Diplôme Études Supérieures Spécialisées	
DFA	Doctor of Fine Arts	
DGP	Diploma in Graduate and Professional Studies	
DH Ed	Doctor of Health Education	
DH Sc	Doctor of Health Sciences	
DHA	Doctor of Health Administration	
DHCE	Doctor of Health Care Ethics	
DHL	Doctor of Hebrew Letters	
	Doctor of Hebrew Literature	
DHS	Doctor of Health Science	
DHSc	Doctor of Health Science	
Dip CS	Diploma in Christian Studies	
DIT	Doctor of Industrial Technology	
DJ Ed	Doctor of Jewish Education	
DJS	Doctor of Jewish Studies	
DLS	Doctor of Liberal Studies	
DM	Doctor of Management	
	Doctor of Music	
DMA	Doctor of Musical Arts	
DMD	Doctor of Dental Medicine	

DME	Doctor of Manufacturing Management	
	Doctor of Music Education	
DMEd	Doctor of Music Education	
DMFT	Doctor of Marital and Family Therapy	
DMH	Doctor of Medical Humanities	
DML	Doctor of Modern Languages	
DMP	Doctorate in Medical Physics	
DMPNA	Doctor of Management Practice in Nurse Anesthesia	
DN Sc	Doctor of Nursing Science	
DNAP	Doctor of Nurse Anesthesia Practice	
DNP	Doctor of Nursing Practice	
DNS	Doctor of Nursing Science	
DO	Doctor of Osteopathy	
DOT	Doctor of Occupational Therapy	
DPA	Doctor of Public Administration	
DPC	Doctor of Pastoral Counseling	
DPDS	Doctor of Planning and Development Studies	
DPH	Doctor of Public Health	
DPM	Doctor of Plant Medicine	
	Doctor of Podiatric Medicine	
DPPD	Doctor of Policy, Planning, and Development	
DPS	Doctor of Professional Studies	
DPT	Doctor of Physical Therapy	
DPTSc	Doctor of Physical Therapy Science	
Dr DES	Doctor of Design	
Dr OT	Doctor of Occupational Therapy	
Dr PH	Doctor of Public Health	
Dr Sc PT	Doctor of Science in Physical Therapy	
DRSc	Doctor of Regulatory Science	
DS	Doctor of Science	
DS Sc	Doctor of Social Science	
DSJS	Doctor of Science in Jewish Studies	
DSL	Doctor of Strategic Leadership	
DSW	Doctor of Social Work	
DTL	Doctor of Talmudic Law	
DV Sc	Doctor of Veterinary Science	
DVM	Doctor of Veterinary Medicine	
DWS	Doctor of Worship Studies	
EAA	Engineer in Aeronautics and Astronautics	
ECS	Engineer in Computer Science	
Ed D	Doctor of Education	
Ed DCT	Doctor of Education in College Teaching	
Ed L D	Doctor of Education Leadership	
Ed M	Master of Education	
Ed S	Specialist in Education	
Ed Sp	Specialist in Education	
EDB	Executive Doctorate in Business	
EDM	Executive Doctorate in Management	

EDSPC	Education Specialist
EE	Electrical Engineer
EJD	Executive Juris Doctor
EMBA	Executive Master of Business Administration
EMFA	Executive Master of Forensic Accounting
EMHA	Executive Master of Health Administration
EMIB	Executive Master of International Business
EML	Executive Master of Leadership
EMPA	Executive Master of Public Administration
EMPP	Executive Master's of Public Policy
EMS	Executive Master of Science
EMTM	Executive Master of Technology Management
Eng	Engineer
Eng Sc D	Doctor of Engineering Science
Engr	Engineer
Ex Doc	Executive Doctor of Pharmacy
Exec Ed D	Executive Doctor of Education
Exec MBA	Executive Master of Business Administration
Exec MPA	Executive Master of Public Administration
Exec MPH	Executive Master of Public Health
Exec MS	Executive Master of Science
G Dip	Graduate Diploma
GBC	Graduate Business Certificate
GCE	Graduate Certificate in Education
GDM	Graduate Diploma in Management
GDPA	Graduate Diploma in Public Administration
GDRE	Graduate Diploma in Religious Education
GEMBA	Global Executive Master of Business Administration
GEMPA	Gulf Executive Master of Public Administration
GM Acc	Graduate Master of Accountancy
GMBA	Global Master of Business Administration
GPD	Graduate Performance Diploma
GSS	Graduate Special Certificate for Students in Special Situations
IEMBA	International Executive Master of Business Administration
IM Acc	Integrated Master of Accountancy
IMA	Interdisciplinary Master of Arts
IMBA	International Master of Business Administration
IMES	International Master's in Environmental Studies
Ingeniero	Engineer
JCD	Doctor of Canon Law
JCL	Licentiate in Canon Law
JD	Juris Doctor
JSD	Doctor of Juridical Science
	Doctor of Jurisprudence
	Doctor of the Science of Law
JSM	Master of Science of Law

L Th	Licenciate in Theology
LL B	Bachelor of Laws
LL CM	Master of Laws in Comparative Law
LL D	Doctor of Laws
LL M	Master of Laws
LL M in Tax	Master of Laws in Taxation
LL M CL	Master of Laws (Common Law)
M Ac	Master of Accountancy
	Master of Accounting
	Master of Acupuncture
M Ac OM	Master of Acupuncture and Oriental Medicine
M Acc	Master of Accountancy
	Master of Accounting
M Acct	Master of Accountancy
	Master of Accounting
M Accy	Master of Accountancy
M Actg	Master of Accounting
M Acy	Master of Accountancy
M Ad	Master of Administration
M Ad Ed	Master of Adult Education
M Adm	Master of Administration
M Adm Mgt	Master of Administrative Management
M Admin	Master of Administration
M ADU	Master of Architectural Design and Urbanism
M Adv	Master of Advertising
M Aero E	Master of Aerospace Engineering
M AEST	Master of Applied Environmental Science and Technology
M Ag	Master of Agriculture
M Ag Ed	Master of Agricultural Education
M Agr	Master of Agriculture
M Anesth Ed	Master of Anesthesiology Education
M App Comp Sc	Master of Applied Computer Science
M App St	Master of Applied Statistics
M Appl Stat	Master of Applied Statistics
M Aq	Master of Aquaculture
M Arc	Master of Architecture
M Arch	Master of Architecture
M Arch I	Master of Architecture I
M Arch II	Master of Architecture II
M Arch E	Master of Architectural Engineering
M Arch H	Master of Architectural History
M Bioethics	Master in Bioethics
M Biomath	Master of Biomathematics
M Ch	Master of Chemistry
M Ch E	Master of Chemical Engineering
M Chem	Master of Chemistry
M Cl D	Master of Clinical Dentistry
M Cl Sc	Master of Clinical Science

M Comp	Master of Computing
M Comp E	Master of Computer Engineering
M Comp Sc	Master of Computer Science
M Coun	Master of Counseling
M Dent	Master of Dentistry
M Dent Sc	Master of Dental Sciences
M Des	Master of Design
M Des S	Master of Design Studies
M Div	Master of Divinity
M Ec	Master of Economics
M Econ	Master of Economics
M Ed	Master of Education
M Ed T	Master of Education in Teaching
M En	Master of Engineering
	Master of Environmental Science
M En S	Master of Environmental Sciences
M Eng	Master of Engineering
M Eng Mgt	Master of Engineering Management
M Engr	Master of Engineering
M Ent	Master of Enterprise
M Env	Master of Environment
M Env Des	Master of Environmental Design
M Env E	Master of Environmental Engineering
M Env Sc	Master of Environmental Science
M Fin	Master of Finance
M Geo E	Master of Geological Engineering
M Geoenv E	Master of Geoenvironmental Engineering
M Geog	Master of Geography
M Hum	Master of Humanities
M Hum Svcs	Master of Human Services
M IBD	Master of Integrated Building Delivery
M IDST	Master's in Interdisciplinary Studies
M Kin	Master of Kinesiology
M Land Arch	Master of Landscape Architecture
M Litt	Master of Letters
M Mat SE	Master of Material Science and Engineering
M Math	Master of Mathematics
M Mech E	Master of Mechanical Engineering
M Med Sc	Master of Medical Science
M Mgmt	Master of Management
M Mgt	Master of Management
M Min	Master of Ministries
M Mtl E	Master of Materials Engineering
M Mu	Master of Music
M Mus	Master of Music
M Mus Ed	Master of Music Education
M Music	Master of Music
M Nat Sci	Master of Natural Science
M Oc E	Master of Oceanographic Engineering
M Pet E	Master of Petroleum Engineering
M Pharm	Master of Pharmacy
M Phil	Master of Philosophy
M Phil F	Master of Philosophical Foundations
M Pl	Master of Planning
M Plan	Master of Planning
M Pol	Master of Political Science
M Pr Met	Master of Professional Meteorology
M Prob S	Master of Probability and Statistics
M Psych	Master of Psychology
M Pub	Master of Publishing
M Rel	Master of Religion
M S Ed	Master of Science Education
M Sc	Master of Science
M Sc A	Master of Science (Applied)
M Sc AHN	Master of Science in Applied Human Nutrition
M Sc BMC	Master of Science in Biomedical Communications
M Sc CS	Master of Science in Computer Science
M Sc E	Master of Science in Engineering
M Sc Eng	Master of Science in Engineering
M Sc Engr	Master of Science in Engineering
M Sc F	Master of Science in Forestry
M Sc FE	Master of Science in Forest Engineering
M Sc Geogr	Master of Science in Geography
M Sc N	Master of Science in Nursing
M Sc OT	Master of Science in Occupational Therapy
M Sc P	Master of Science in Planning
M Sc Pl	Master of Science in Planning
M Sc PT	Master of Science in Physical Therapy
M Sc T	Master of Science in Teaching
M SEM	Master of Sustainable Environmental Management
M Serv Soc	Master of Social Service
M Soc	Master of Sociology
M Sp Ed	Master of Special Education
M Stat	Master of Statistics
M Sys Sc	Master of Systems Science
M Tax	Master of Taxation
M Tech	Master of Technology
M Th	Master of Theology
M Tox	Master of Toxicology
M Trans E	Master of Transportation Engineering
M Urb	Master of Urban Planning
M Vet Sc	Master of Veterinary Science
MA	Master of Accounting
	Master of Administration
	Master of Arts
MA Missions	Master of Arts in Missions

MA Comm	Master of Arts in Communication
MA Ed	Master of Arts in Education
MA Ed Ad	Master of Arts in Educational Administration
MA Ext	Master of Agricultural Extension
MA Islamic	Master of Arts in Islamic Studies
MA Military Studies	Master of Arts in Military Studies
MA Min	Master of Arts in Ministry
MA Miss	Master of Arts in Missiology
MA Past St	Master of Arts in Pastoral Studies
MA Ph	Master of Arts in Philosophy
MA Psych	Master of Arts in Psychology
MA Sc	Master of Applied Science
MA Sp	Master of Arts (Spirituality)
MA Th	Master of Arts in Theology
MA-R	Master of Arts (Research)
MAA	Master of Administrative Arts
	Master of Applied Anthropology
	Master of Applied Arts
	Master of Arts in Administration
MAAA	Master of Arts in Arts Administration
MAAAP	Master of Arts Administration and Policy
MAAE	Master of Arts in Art Education
MAAT	Master of Arts in Applied Theology
	Master of Arts in Art Therapy
MAB	Master of Agribusiness
MABC	Master of Arts in Biblical Counseling
	Master of Arts in Business Communication
MABE	Master of Arts in Bible Exposition
MABL	Master of Arts in Biblical Languages
MABM	Master of Agribusiness Management
MABS	Master of Arts in Biblical Studies
MABT	Master of Arts in Bible Teaching
MAC	Master of Accountancy
	Master of Accounting
	Master of Arts in Communication
	Master of Arts in Counseling
MACC	Master of Arts in Christian Counseling
	Master of Arts in Clinical Counseling
MACCM	Master of Arts in Church and Community Ministry
MACCT	Master of Accounting
MACD	Master of Arts in Christian Doctrine
MACE	Master of Arts in Christian Education
MACFM	Master of Arts in Children's and Family Ministry
MACH	Master of Arts in Church History
MACI	Master of Arts in Curriculum and Instruction
MACIS	Master of Accounting and Information Systems
MACJ	Master of Arts in Criminal Justice
MACL	Master of Arts in Christian Leadership
MACM	Master of Arts in Christian Ministries
	Master of Arts in Christian Ministry
	Master of Arts in Church Music
	Master of Arts in Counseling Ministries
MACN	Master of Arts in Counseling
MACO	Master of Arts in Counseling
MAcOM	Master of Acupuncture and Oriental Medicine
MACP	Master of Arts in Counseling Psychology
MACS	Master of Arts in Catholic Studies
MACSE	Master of Arts in Christian School Education
MACT	Master of Arts in Christian Thought
	Master of Arts in Communications and Technology
MAD	Master in Educational Institution Administration
	Master of Art and Design
MADR	Master of Arts in Dispute Resolution
MADS	Master of Animal and Dairy Science
	Master of Applied Disability Studies
MAE	Master of Aerospace Engineering
	Master of Agricultural Economics
	Master of Agricultural Education
	Master of Architectural Engineering
	Master of Art Education
	Master of Arts in Education
	Master of Arts in English
MAEd	Master of Arts Education
MAEL	Master of Arts in Educational Leadership
MAEM	Master of Arts in Educational Ministries
MAEN	Master of Arts in English
MAEP	Master of Arts in Economic Policy
MAES	Master of Arts in Environmental Sciences
MAET	Master of Arts in English Teaching
MAF	Master of Arts in Finance
MAFE	Master of Arts in Financial Economics
MAFLL	Master of Arts in Foreign Language and Literature
MAFM	Master of Accounting and Financial Management
MAFS	Master of Arts in Family Studies
MAG	Master of Applied Geography
MAGU	Master of Urban Analysis and Management
MAH	Master of Arts in Humanities
MAHA	Master of Arts in Humanitarian Assistance
	Master of Arts in Humanitarian Studies
MAHCM	Master of Arts in Health Care Mission
MAHG	Master of American History and Government
MAHL	Master of Arts in Hebrew Letters
MAHN	Master of Applied Human Nutrition
MAHSR	Master of Applied Health Services Research
MAIA	Master of Arts in International Administration
MAIB	Master of Arts in International Business
MAICS	Master of Arts in Intercultural Studies

MAIDM	Master of Arts in Interior Design and Merchandising
MAIH	Master of Arts in Interdisciplinary Humanities
MAIOP	Master of Arts in Industrial/Organizational Psychology
MAIPCR	Master of Arts in International Peace and Conflict Management
MAIS	Master of Arts in Intercultural Studies Master of Arts in Interdisciplinary Studies Master of Arts in International Studies
MAIT	Master of Administration in Information Technology Master of Applied Information Technology
MAJ	Master of Arts in Journalism
MAJ Ed	Master of Arts in Jewish Education
MAJCS	Master of Arts in Jewish Communal Service
MAJE	Master of Arts in Jewish Education
MAJS	Master of Arts in Jewish Studies
MAL	Master in Agricultural Leadership
MALA	Master of Arts in Liberal Arts
MALD	Master of Arts in Law and Diplomacy
MALER	Master of Arts in Labor and Employment Relations
MALM	Master of Arts in Leadership Evangelical Mobilization
MALP	Master of Arts in Language Pedagogy
MALPS	Master of Arts in Liberal and Professional Studies
MALS	Master of Arts in Liberal Studies
MALT	Master of Arts in Learning and Teaching
MAM	Master of Acquisition Management Master of Agriculture and Management Master of Applied Mathematics Master of Arts in Management Master of Arts in Ministry Master of Arts Management Master of Avian Medicine
MAMB	Master of Applied Molecular Biology
MAMC	Master of Arts in Mass Communication Master of Arts in Ministry and Culture Master of Arts in Ministry for a Multicultural Church Master of Arts in Missional Christianity
MAME	Master of Arts in Missions/Evangelism
MAMFC	Master of Arts in Marriage and Family Counseling
MAMFCC	Master of Arts in Marriage, Family, and Child Counseling
MAMFT	Master of Arts in Marriage and Family Therapy
MAMHC	Master of Arts in Mental Health Counseling
MAMI	Master of Arts in Missions
MAMS	Master of Applied Mathematical Sciences Master of Arts in Ministerial Studies Master of Arts in Ministry and Spirituality
MAMT	Master of Arts in Mathematics Teaching
MAN	Master of Applied Nutrition

MANP	Master of Applied Natural Products
MANT	Master of Arts in New Testament
MAOL	Master of Arts in Organizational Leadership
MAOM	Master of Acupuncture and Oriental Medicine Master of Arts in Organizational Management
MAOT	Master of Arts in Old Testament
MAP	Master of Applied Psychology Master of Arts in Planning Master of Psychology Master of Public Administration
MAP Min	Master of Arts in Pastoral Ministry
MAPA	Master of Arts in Public Administration
MAPC	Master of Arts in Pastoral Counseling Master of Arts in Professional Counseling
MAPE	Master of Arts in Political Economy
MAPL	Master of Arts in Pastoral Leadership
MAPM	Master of Arts in Pastoral Ministry Master of Arts in Pastoral Music Master of Arts in Practical Ministry
MAPP	Master of Arts in Public Policy
MAPPS	Master of Arts in Asia Pacific Policy Studies
MAPS	Master of Arts in Pastoral Counseling/Spiritual Formation Master of Arts in Pastoral Studies Master of Arts in Public Service
MAPT	Master of Practical Theology
MAPW	Master of Arts in Professional Writing
MAR	Master of Arts in Religion
Mar Eng	Marine Engineer
MARC	Master of Arts in Rehabilitation Counseling
MARE	Master of Arts in Religious Education
MARL	Master of Arts in Religious Leadership
MARS	Master of Arts in Religious Studies
MAS	Master of Accounting Science Master of Actuarial Science Master of Administrative Science Master of Advanced Study Master of Aeronautical Science Master of American Studies Master of Applied Science Master of Applied Statistics Master of Archival Studies
MASA	Master of Advanced Studies in Architecture
MASD	Master of Arts in Spiritual Direction
MASE	Master of Arts in Special Education
MASF	Master of Arts in Spiritual Formation
MASJ	Master of Arts in Systems of Justice
MASL	Master of Arts in School Leadership
MASLA	Master of Advanced Studies in Landscape Architecture
MASM	Master of Aging Services Management Master of Arts in Specialized Ministries
MASP	Master of Applied Social Psychology Master of Arts in School Psychology

MASPAA	Master of Arts in Sports and Athletic Administration
MASS	Master of Applied Social Science Master of Arts in Social Science
MAST	Master of Arts in Science Teaching
MASW	Master of Aboriginal Social Work
MAT	Master of Arts in Teaching Master of Arts in Theology Master of Athletic Training Master's in Administration of Telecommunications
Mat E	Materials Engineer
MATCM	Master of Acupuncture and Traditional Chinese Medicine
MATDE	Master of Arts in Theology, Development, and Evangelism
MATDR	Master of Territorial Management and Regional Development
MATE	Master of Arts for the Teaching of English
MATESL	Master of Arts in Teaching English as a Second Language
MATESOL	Master of Arts in Teaching English to Speakers of Other Languages
MATF	Master of Arts in Teaching English as a Foreign Language/Intercultural Studies
MATFL	Master of Arts in Teaching Foreign Language
MATH	Master of Arts in Therapy
MATI	Master of Administration of Information Technology
MATL	Master of Arts in Teacher Leadership Master of Arts in Teaching of Languages Master of Arts in Transformational Leadership
MATM	Master of Arts in Teaching of Mathematics
MATS	Master of Arts in Theological Studies Master of Arts in Transforming Spirituality
MATSL	Master of Arts in Teaching a Second Language
MAUA	Master of Arts in Urban Affairs
MAUD	Master of Arts in Urban Design
MAURP	Master of Arts in Urban and Regional Planning
MAWSHP	Master of Arts in Worship
MAYM	Master of Arts in Youth Ministry
MB	Master of Bioinformatics Master of Biology
MBA	Master of Business Administration
MBA-AM	Master of Business Administration in Aviation Management
MBA-EP	Master of Business Administration–Experienced Professionals
MBAA	Master of Business Administration in Aviation
MBAE	Master of Biological and Agricultural Engineering Master of Biosystems and Agricultural Engineering
MBAH	Master of Business Administration in Health
MBAi	Master of Business Administration–International

MBAICT	Master of Business Administration in Information and Communication Technology
MBATM	Master of Business Administration in Technology Management
MBC	Master of Building Construction
MBE	Master of Bilingual Education Master of Bioengineering Master of Bioethics Master of Biological Engineering Master of Biomedical Engineering Master of Business and Engineering Master of Business Economics Master of Business Education
MBET	Master of Business, Entrepreneurship and Technology
MBiotech	Master of Biotechnology
MBIT	Master of Business Information Technology
MBL	Master of Business Law Master of Business Leadership
MBLE	Master in Business Logistics Engineering
MBMI	Master of Biomedical Imaging and Signals
MBMSE	Master of Business Management and Software Engineering
MBOE	Master of Business Operational Excellence
MBS	Master of Biblical Studies Master of Biological Science Master of Biomedical Sciences Master of Bioscience Master of Building Science
MBT	Master of Biblical and Theological Studies Master of Biomedical Technology Master of Biotechnology Master of Business Taxation
MC	Master of Communication Master of Counseling Master of Cybersecurity
MC Ed	Master of Continuing Education
MC Sc	Master of Computer Science
MCA	Master of Arts in Applied Criminology Master of Commercial Aviation
MCAM	Master of Computational and Applied Mathematics
MCC	Master of Computer Science
MCCS	Master of Crop and Soil Sciences
MCD	Master of Communications Disorders Master of Community Development
MCE	Master in Electronic Commerce Master of Christian Education Master of Civil Engineering Master of Control Engineering
MCEM	Master of Construction Engineering Management
MCH	Master of Chemical Engineering
MCHE	Master of Chemical Engineering
MCIS	Master of Communication and Information Studies Master of Computer and Information Science Master of Computer Information Systems

MCIT	Master of Computer and Information Technology
MCJ	Master of Criminal Justice
MCJA	Master of Criminal Justice Administration
MCL	Master in Communication Leadership Master of Canon Law Master of Comparative Law
MCM	Master of Christian Ministry Master of Church Music Master of City Management Master of Communication Management Master of Community Medicine Master of Construction Management Master of Contract Management Master of Corporate Media
MCMP	Master of City and Metropolitan Planning
MCMS	Master of Clinical Medical Science
MCN	Master of Clinical Nutrition
MCP	Master of City Planning Master of Community Planning Master of Counseling Psychology Master of Cytopathology Practice Master of Science in Quality Systems and Productivity
MCPC	Master of Arts in Chaplaincy and Pastoral Care
MCPD	Master of Community Planning and Development
MCR	Master in Clinical Research
MCRP	Master of City and Regional Planning
MCRS	Master of City and Regional Studies
MCS	Master of Christian Studies Master of Clinical Science Master of Combined Sciences Master of Communication Studies Master of Computer Science Master of Consumer Science
MCSE	Master of Computer Science and Engineering
MCSL	Master of Catholic School Leadership
MCSM	Master of Construction Science/Management
MCST	Master of Science in Computer Science and Information Technology
MCTP	Master of Communication Technology and Policy
MCTS	Master of Clinical and Translational Science
MCVS	Master of Cardiovascular Science
MD	Doctor of Medicine
MDA	Master of Development Administration Master of Dietetic Administration
MDB	Master of Design-Build
MDE	Master of Developmental Economics Master of Distance Education Master of the Education of the Deaf
MDH	Master of Dental Hygiene
MDM	Master of Design Methods Master of Digital Media
MDP	Master of Development Practice
MDR	Master of Dispute Resolution
MDS	Master of Dental Surgery

ME	Master of Education Master of Engineering Master of Entrepreneurship Master of Evangelism
ME Sc	Master of Engineering Science
MEA	Master of Educational Administration Master of Engineering Administration
MEAP	Master of Environmental Administration and Planning
MEBT	Master in Electronic Business Technologies
MEC	Master of Electronic Commerce
MECE	Master of Electrical and Computer Engineering
Mech E	Mechanical Engineer
MED	Master of Education of the Deaf
MEDS	Master of Environmental Design Studies
MEE	Master in Education Master of Electrical Engineering Master of Energy Engineering Master of Environmental Engineering
MEEM	Master of Environmental Engineering and Management
MEENE	Master of Engineering in Environmental Engineering
MEEP	Master of Environmental and Energy Policy
MEERM	Master of Earth and Environmental Resource Management
MEH	Master in Humanistic Studies Master of Environmental Horticulture
MEHS	Master of Environmental Health and Safety
MEIM	Master of Entertainment Industry Management
MEL	Master of Educational Leadership Master of English Literature
MELP	Master of Environmental Law and Policy
MEM	Master of Ecosystem Management Master of Electricity Markets Master of Engineering Management Master of Environmental Management Master of Marketing
MEME	Master of Engineering in Manufacturing Engineering Master of Engineering in Mechanical Engineering
MENG	Master of Arts in English
MENVEGR	Master of Environmental Engineering
MEP	Master of Engineering Physics
MEPC	Master of Environmental Pollution Control
MEPD	Master of Education–Professional Development Master of Environmental Planning and Design
MER	Master of Employment Relations
MES	Master of Education and Science Master of Engineering Science Master of Environment and Sustainability Master of Environmental Science Master of Environmental Studies Master of Environmental Systems Master of Special Education

MESM	Master of Environmental Science and Management
MET	Master of Educational Technology Master of Engineering Technology Master of Entertainment Technology Master of Environmental Toxicology
Met E	Metallurgical Engineer
METM	Master of Engineering and Technology Management
MF	Master of Finance Master of Forestry
MFA	Master of Fine Arts
MFAM	Master in Food Animal Medicine
MFAS	Master of Fisheries and Aquatic Science
MFAW	Master of Fine Arts in Writing
MFC	Master of Forest Conservation
MFCS	Master of Family and Consumer Sciences
MFE	Master of Financial Economics Master of Financial Engineering Master of Forest Engineering
MFG	Master of Functional Genomics
MFHD	Master of Family and Human Development
MFM	Master of Financial Mathematics
MFMS	Master's in Food Microbiology and Safety
MFPE	Master of Food Process Engineering
MFR	Master of Forest Resources
MFRC	Master of Forest Resources and Conservation
MFS	Master of Food Science Master of Forensic Sciences Master of Forest Science Master of Forest Studies Master of French Studies
MFST	Master of Food Safety and Technology
MFT	Master of Family Therapy Master of Food Technology
MFWB	Master of Fishery and Wildlife Biology
MFWCB	Master of Fish, Wildlife and Conservation Biology
MFWS	Master of Fisheries and Wildlife Sciences
MFYCS	Master of Family, Youth and Community Sciences
MG	Master of Genetics
MGA	Master of Global Affairs Master of Governmental Administration
MGC	Master of Genetic Counseling
MGD	Master of Graphic Design
MGE	Master of Geotechnical Engineering
MGEM	Master of Global Entrepreneurship and Management
MGH	Master of Geriatric Health
MGIS	Master of Geographic Information Science Master of Geographic Information Systems
MGM	Master of Global Management
MGP	Master of Gestion de Projet

MGPS	Master of Global Policy Studies
MGREM	Master of Global Real Estate Management
MGS	Master of Gerontological Studies Master of Global Studies
MH	Master of Humanities
MH Ed	Master of Health Education
MH Sc	Master of Health Sciences
MHA	Master of Health Administration Master of Healthcare Administration Master of Hospital Administration Master of Hospitality Administration
MHA/MCRP	Master of Healthcare Administration/Master of City and Regional Planning
MHAD	Master of Health Administration
MHB	Master of Human Behavior
MHCA	Master of Health Care Administration
MHCI	Master of Human-Computer Interaction
MHCL	Master of Health Care Leadership
MHE	Master of Health Education Master of Human Ecology
MHE Ed	Master of Home Economics Education
MHEA	Master of Higher Education Administration
MHHS	Master of Health and Human Services
MHI	Master of Health Informatics Master of Healthcare Innovation
MHIIM	Master of Health Informatics and Information Management
MHIS	Master of Health Information Systems
MHK	Master of Human Kinetics
MHL	Master of Hebrew Literature
MHM	Master of Healthcare Management
MHMS	Master of Health Management Systems
MHP	Master of Health Physics Master of Heritage Preservation Master of Historic Preservation
MHPA	Master of Heath Policy and Administration
MHPE	Master of Health Professions Education
MHR	Master of Human Resources
MHRD	Master in Human Resource Development
MHRIR	Master of Human Resources and Industrial Relations
MHRLR	Master of Human Resources and Labor Relations
MHRM	Master of Human Resources Management
MHS	Master of Health Science Master of Health Sciences Master of Health Studies Master of Hispanic Studies Master of Human Services Master of Humanistic Studies
MHSA	Master of Health Services Administration
MHSM	Master of Health Systems Management
MI	Master of Instruction

MI Arch	Master of Interior Architecture
MI St	Master of Information Studies
MIA	Master of Interior Architecture Master of International Affairs
MIAA	Master of International Affairs and Administration
MIAM	Master of International Agribusiness Management
MIB	Master of International Business
MIBA	Master of International Business Administration
MICM	Master of International Construction Management
MID	Master of Industrial Design Master of Industrial Distribution Master of Interior Design Master of International Development
MIE	Master of Industrial Engineering
MIH	Master of Integrative Health
MIHTM	Master of International Hospitality and Tourism Management
MIJ	Master of International Journalism
MILR	Master of Industrial and Labor Relations
MiM	Master in Management
MIM	Master of Industrial Management Master of Information Management Master of International Management
MIMLAE	Master of International Management for Latin American Executives
MIMS	Master of Information Management and Systems Master of Integrated Manufacturing Systems
MIP	Master of Infrastructure Planning Master of Intellectual Property
MIPER	Master of International Political Economy of Resources
MIPP	Master of International Policy and Practice Master of International Public Policy
MIPS	Master of International Planning Studies
MIR	Master of Industrial Relations Master of International Relations
MIS	Master of Industrial Statistics Master of Information Science Master of Information Systems Master of Integrated Science Master of Interdisciplinary Studies Master of International Service Master of International Studies
MISE	Master of Industrial and Systems Engineering
MISKM	Master of Information Sciences and Knowledge Management
MISM	Master of Information Systems Management
MIT	Master in Teaching Master of Industrial Technology Master of Information Technology Master of Initial Teaching Master of International Trade Master of Internet Technology
MITA	Master of Information Technology Administration
MITM	Master of Information Technology and Management
MITO	Master of Industrial Technology and Operations
MJ	Master of Journalism Master of Jurisprudence
MJ Ed	Master of Jewish Education
MJA	Master of Justice Administration
MJM	Master of Justice Management
MJS	Master of Judicial Studies Master of Juridical Science
MKM	Master of Knowledge Management
ML	Master of Latin
ML Arch	Master of Landscape Architecture
MLA	Master of Landscape Architecture Master of Liberal Arts
MLAS	Master of Laboratory Animal Science Master of Liberal Arts and Sciences
MLAUD	Master of Landscape Architecture in Urban Development
MLD	Master of Leadership Development
MLE	Master of Applied Linguistics and Exegesis
MLER	Master of Labor and Employment Relations
MLHR	Master of Labor and Human Resources
MLI Sc	Master of Library and Information Science
MLIS	Master of Library and Information Science Master of Library and Information Studies
MLM	Master of Library Media
MLRHR	Master of Labor Relations and Human Resources
MLS	Master of Leadership Studies Master of Legal Studies Master of Liberal Studies Master of Library Science Master of Life Sciences
MLSP	Master of Law and Social Policy
MLT	Master of Language Technologies
MLTCA	Master of Long Term Care Administration
MM	Master of Management Master of Ministry Master of Missiology Master of Music
MM Ed	Master of Music Education
MM Sc	Master of Medical Science
MM St	Master of Museum Studies
MMA	Master of Marine Affairs Master of Media Arts Master of Musical Arts
MMAE	Master of Mechanical and Aerospace Engineering
MMAS	Master of Military Art and Science
MMB	Master of Microbial Biotechnology
MMBA	Managerial Master of Business Administration
MMC	Master of Manufacturing Competitiveness Master of Mass Communications Master of Music Conducting

MMCM	Master of Music in Church Music
MMCSS	Master of Mathematical Computational and Statistical Sciences
MME	Master of Manufacturing Engineering
	Master of Mathematics Education
	Master of Mathematics for Educators
	Master of Mechanical Engineering
	Master of Medical Engineering
	Master of Mining Engineering
	Master of Music Education
MMF	Master of Mathematical Finance
MMFT	Master of Marriage and Family Therapy
MMG	Master of Management
MMH	Master of Management in Hospitality
	Master of Medical Humanities
MMI	Master of Management of Innovation
MMIS	Master of Management Information Systems
MMM	Master of Manufacturing Management
	Master of Marine Management
	Master of Medical Management
MMME	Master of Metallurgical and Materials Engineering
MMP	Master of Management Practice
	Master of Marine Policy
	Master of Medical Physics
	Master of Music Performance
MMPA	Master of Management and Professional Accounting
MMQM	Master of Manufacturing Quality Management
MMR	Master of Marketing Research
MMRM	Master of Marine Resources Management
MMS	Master of Management Science
	Master of Management Studies
	Master of Manufacturing Systems
	Master of Marine Studies
	Master of Materials Science
	Master of Medical Science
	Master of Medieval Studies
	Master of Modern Studies
MMSE	Master of Manufacturing Systems Engineering
MMSM	Master of Music in Sacred Music
MMT	Master in Marketing
	Master of Management
	Master of Math for Teaching
	Master of Music Teaching
	Master of Music Therapy
	Master's in Marketing Technology
MMus	Master of Music
MN	Master of Nursing
	Master of Nutrition
MN NP	Master of Nursing in Nurse Practitioner
MNA	Master of Nonprofit Administration
	Master of Nurse Anesthesia
MNAL	Master of Nonprofit Administration and Leadership
MNAS	Master of Natural and Applied Science
MNCM	Master of Network and Communications Management

MNE	Master of Network Engineering
	Master of Nuclear Engineering
MNL	Master in International Business for Latin America
MNM	Master of Nonprofit Management
MNO	Master of Nonprofit Organization
MNPL	Master of Not-for-Profit Leadership
MNpS	Master of Nonprofit Studies
MNR	Master of Natural Resources
MNRES	Master of Natural Resources and Environmental Studies
MNRM	Master of Natural Resource Management
MNRS	Master of Natural Resource Stewardship
MNS	Master of Natural Science
MO	Master of Oceanography
MOD	Master of Organizational Development
MOGS	Master of Oil and Gas Studies
MOH	Master of Occupational Health
MOL	Master of Organizational Leadership
MOM	Master of Oriental Medicine
MOR	Master of Operations Research
MOT	Master of Occupational Therapy
MP	Master of Physiology
	Master of Planning
MP Ac	Master of Professional Accountancy
MP Acc	Master of Professional Accountancy
	Master of Professional Accounting
	Master of Public Accounting
MP Aff	Master of Public Affairs
MP Th	Master of Pastoral Theology
MPA	Master of Physician Assistant
	Master of Professional Accountancy
	Master of Professional Accounting
	Master of Public Administration
	Master of Public Affairs
MPAC	Master of Professional Accounting
MPAID	Master of Public Administration and International Development
MPAP	Master of Physician Assistant Practice
	Master of Public Affairs and Politics
MPAS	Master of Physician Assistant Science
	Master of Physician Assistant Studies
MPC	Master of Pastoral Counseling
	Master of Professional Communication
	Master of Professional Counseling
MPD	Master of Product Development
	Master of Public Diplomacy
MPDS	Master of Planning and Development Studies
MPE	Master of Physical Education
	Master of Power Engineering
MPEM	Master of Project Engineering and Management
MPH	Master of Public Health
MPH/MCRP	Master of Public Health/Mster of Community and Regional Planning

MPHE	Master of Public Health Education	**MRS**	Master of Religious Studies
MPHTM	Master of Public Health and Tropical Medicine	**MRSc**	Master of Rehabilitation Science
MPIA	Master in International Affairs	**MS**	Master of Science
	Master of Public and International Affairs	**MS Cmp E**	Master of Science in Computer Engineering
MPM	Master of Pastoral Ministry	**MS Kin**	Master of Science in Kinesiology
	Master of Pest Management	**MS Acct**	Master of Science in Accounting
	Master of Policy Management	**MS Accy**	Master of Science in Accountancy
	Master of Practical Ministries	**MS Aero E**	Master of Science in Aerospace Engineering
	Master of Project Management	**MS Ag**	Master of Science in Agriculture
	Master of Public Management	**MS Arch**	Master of Science in Architecture
MPNA	Master of Public and Nonprofit Administration	**MS Arch St**	Master of Science in Architectural Studies
MPO	Master of Prosthetics and Orthotics	**MS Bio E**	Master of Science in Bioengineering
MPOD	Master of Positive Organizational Development		Master of Science in Biomedical Engineering
MPP	Master of Public Policy	**MS Bm E**	Master of Science in Biomedical Engineering
MPPA	Master of Public Policy Administration	**MS Ch E**	Master of Science in Chemical Engineering
	Master of Public Policy and Administration	**MS Chem**	Master of Science in Chemistry
MPPAL	Master of Public Policy, Administration and Law	**MS Cp E**	Master of Science in Computer Engineering
MPPM	Master of Public and Private Management	**MS Eco**	Master of Science in Economics
	Master of Public Policy and Management	**MS Econ**	Master of Science in Economics
MPPPM	Master of Plant Protection and Pest Management	**MS Ed**	Master of Science in Education
MPRTM	Master of Parks, Recreation, and Tourism Management	**MS El**	Master of Science in Educational Leadership and Administration
MPS	Master of Pastoral Studies	**MS En E**	Master of Science in Environmental Engineering
	Master of Perfusion Science	**MS Eng**	Master of Science in Engineering
	Master of Planning Studies	**MS Engr**	Master of Science in Engineering
	Master of Political Science	**MS Env E**	Master of Science in Environmental Engineering
	Master of Preservation Studies	**MS Exp Surg**	Master of Science in Experimental Surgery
	Master of Prevention Science	**MS Int A**	Master of Science in International Affairs
	Master of Professional Studies	**MS Mat E**	Master of Science in Materials Engineering
	Master of Public Service	**MS Mat SE**	Master of Science in Material Science and Engineering
MPSA	Master of Public Service Administration	**MS Met E**	Master of Science in Metallurgical Engineering
MPSRE	Master of Professional Studies in Real Estate	**MS Mgt**	Master of Science in Management
MPT	Master of Pastoral Theology	**MS Min**	Master of Science in Mining
	Master of Physical Therapy	**MS Min E**	Master of Science in Mining Engineering
MPVM	Master of Preventive Veterinary Medicine	**MS Mt E**	Master of Science in Materials Engineering
MPW	Master of Professional Writing	**MS Otal**	Master of Science in Otalrynology
	Master of Public Works	**MS Pet E**	Master of Science in Petroleum Engineering
MQM	Master of Quality Management	**MS Phys**	Master of Science in Physics
MQS	Master of Quality Systems	**MS Poly**	Master of Science in Polymers
MR	Master of Recreation	**MS Psy**	Master of Science in Psychology
	Master of Retailing	**MS Pub P**	Master of Science in Public Policy
MRA	Master in Research Administration	**MS Sc**	Master of Science in Social Science
MRC	Master of Rehabilitation Counseling	**MS Sp Ed**	Master of Science in Special Education
MRCP	Master of Regional and City Planning	**MS Stat**	Master of Science in Statistics
	Master of Regional and Community Planning	**MS Surg**	Master of Science in Surgery
MRD	Master of Rural Development	**MS Tax**	Master of Science in Taxation
MRE	Master of Real Estate	**MS Tc E**	Master of Science in Telecommunications Engineering
	Master of Religious Education		
MRED	Master of Real Estate Development		
MREM	Master of Resource and Environmental Management		
MRLS	Master of Resources Law Studies		
MRM	Master of Resources Management		
MRP	Master of Regional Planning		

MS-R	Master of Science (Research)
MSA	Master of School Administration
	Master of Science Administration
	Master of Science in Accountancy
	Master of Science in Accounting
	Master of Science in Administration
	Master of Science in Aeronautics
	Master of Science in Agriculture
	Master of Science in Anesthesia
	Master of Science in Architecture
	Master of Science in Aviation
	Master of Sports Administration
MSA Phy	Master of Science in Applied Physics
MSAA	Master of Science in Astronautics and Aeronautics
MSAAE	Master of Science in Aeronautical and Astronautical Engineering
MSABE	Master of Science in Agricultural and Biological Engineering
MSAC	Master of Science in Acupuncture
MSACC	Master of Science in Accounting
MSaCS	Master of Science in Applied Computer Science
MSAE	Master of Science in Aeronautical Engineering
	Master of Science in Aerospace Engineering
	Master of Science in Applied Economics
	Master of Science in Applied Engineering
	Master of Science in Architectural Engineering
	Master of Science in Art Education
MSAH	Master of Science in Allied Health
MSAL	Master of Sport Administration and Leadership
MSAM	Master of Science in Applied Mathematics
MSANR	Master of Science in Agriculture and Natural Resources Systems Management
MSAPM	Master of Security Analysis and Portfolio Management
MSAS	Master of Science in Applied Statistics
	Master of Science in Architectural Studies
MSAT	Master of Science in Accounting and Taxation
	Master of Science in Advanced Technology
	Master of Science in Athletic Training
MSB	Master of Science in Bible
	Master of Science in Business
MSBA	Master of Science in Business Administration
	Master of Science in Business Analysis
MSBAE	Master of Science in Biological and Agricultural Engineering
	Master of Science in Biosystems and Agricultural Engineering
MSBC	Master of Science in Building Construction
MSBE	Master of Science in Biological Engineering
	Master of Science in Biomedical Engineering
MSBENG	Master of Science in Bioengineering
MSBIT	Master of Science in Business Information Technology
MSBM	Master of Sport Business Management
MSBME	Master of Science in Biomedical Engineering

MSBMS	Master of Science in Basic Medical Science
MSBS	Master of Science in Biomedical Sciences
MSC	Master of Science in Commerce
	Master of Science in Communication
	Master of Science in Computers
	Master of Science in Counseling
	Master of Science in Criminology
MSCC	Master of Science in Christian Counseling
	Master of Science in Community Counseling
MSCD	Master of Science in Communication Disorders
	Master of Science in Community Development
MSCE	Master of Science in Civil Engineering
	Master of Science in Clinical Epidemiology
	Master of Science in Computer Engineering
	Master of Science in Continuing Education
MSCEE	Master of Science in Civil and Environmental Engineering
MSCF	Master of Science in Computational Finance
MSChE	Master of Science in Chemical Engineering
MSCI	Master of Science in Clinical Investigation
	Master of Science in Curriculum and Instruction
MSCIS	Master of Science in Computer and Information Systems
	Master of Science in Computer Information Science
	Master of Science in Computer Information Systems
MSCIT	Master of Science in Computer Information Technology
MSCJ	Master of Science in Criminal Justice
MSCJA	Master of Science in Criminal Justice Administration
MSCJPS	Master of Science in Criminal Justice and Public Safety
MSCJS	Master of Science in Crime and Justice Studies
MSCL	Master of Science in Collaborative Leadership
MSCLS	Master of Science in Clinical Laboratory Studies
MSCM	Master of Science in Church Management
	Master of Science in Conflict Management
	Master of Science in Construction Management
MScM	Master of Science in Management
MSCM	Master of Supply Chain Management
MSCNU	Master of Science in Clinical Nutrition
MSCP	Master of Science in Clinical Psychology
	Master of Science in Computer Engineering
	Master of Science in Counseling Psychology
MSCPE	Master of Science in Computer Engineering
MSCPharm	Master of Science in Pharmacy
MSCPI	Master in Strategic Planning for Critical Infrastructures
MSCR	Master of Science in Clinical Research
MSCRP	Master of Science in City and Regional Planning
	Master of Science in Community and Regional Planning

MSCS	Master of Science in Clinical Science
	Master of Science in Computer Science
MSCSD	Master of Science in Communication Sciences and Disorders
MSCSE	Master of Science in Computer Science and Engineering
MSCTE	Master of Science in Career and Technical Education
MSD	Master of Science in Dentistry
	Master of Science in Design
	Master of Science in Dietetics
MSDR	Master of Dispute Resolution
MSE	Master of Science Education
	Master of Science in Economics
	Master of Science in Education
	Master of Science in Engineering
	Master of Science in Engineering Management
	Master of Software Engineering
	Master of Special Education
	Master of Structural Engineering
MSECE	Master of Science in Electrical and Computer Engineering
MSED	Master of Sustainable Economic Development
MSEE	Master of Science in Electrical Engineering
	Master of Science in Environmental Engineering
MSEH	Master of Science in Environmental Health
MSEL	Master of Science in Educational Leadership
MSEM	Master of Science in Engineering Management
	Master of Science in Engineering Mechanics
	Master of Science in Environmental Management
MSENE	Master of Science in Environmental Engineering
MSEO	Master of Science in Electro-Optics
MSEP	Master of Science in Economic Policy
MSEPA	Master of Science in Economics and Policy Analysis
MSES	Master of Science in Embedded Software Engineering
	Master of Science in Engineering Science
	Master of Science in Environmental Science
	Master of Science in Environmental Studies
MSESM	Master of Science in Engineering Science and Mechanics
MSET	Master of Science in Educational Technology
	Master of Science in Engineering Technology
MSEV	Master of Science in Environmental Engineering
MSEVH	Master of Science in Environmental Health and Safety
MSF	Master of Science in Finance
	Master of Science in Forestry
	Master of Spiritual Formation
MSFA	Master of Science in Financial Analysis
MSFAM	Master of Science in Family Studies
MSFCS	Master of Science in Family and Consumer Science
MSFE	Master of Science in Financial Engineering
MSFOR	Master of Science in Forestry

MSFP	Master of Science in Financial Planning
MSFS	Master of Science in Financial Sciences
	Master of Science in Forensic Science
MSFSB	Master of Science in Financial Services and Banking
MSFT	Master of Science in Family Therapy
MSGC	Master of Science in Genetic Counseling
MSH	Master of Science in Health
	Master of Science in Hospice
MSHA	Master of Science in Health Administration
MSHCA	Master of Science in Health Care Administration
MSHCI	Master of Science in Human Computer Interaction
MSHCPM	Master of Science in Health Care Policy and Management
MSHE	Master of Science in Health Education
MSHES	Master of Science in Human Environmental Sciences
MSHFID	Master of Science in Human Factors in Information Design
MSHFS	Master of Science in Human Factors and Systems
MSHI	Master of Science in Health Informatics
MSHP	Master of Science in Health Professions
	Master of Science in Health Promotion
MSHR	Master of Science in Human Resources
MSHRL	Master of Science in Human Resource Leadership
MSHRM	Master of Science in Human Resource Management
MSHROD	Master of Science in Human Resources and Organizational Development
MSHS	Master of Science in Health Science
	Master of Science in Health Services
	Master of Science in Health Systems
	Master of Science in Homeland Security
MSHT	Master of Science in History of Technology
MSI	Master of Science in Information
	Master of Science in Instruction
MSIA	Master of Science in Industrial Administration
	Master of Science in Information Assurance and Computer Security
MSIB	Master of Science in International Business
MSIDM	Master of Science in Interior Design and Merchandising
MSIDT	Master of Science in Information Design and Technology
MSIE	Master of Science in Industrial Engineering
	Master of Science in International Economics
MSIEM	Master of Science in Information Engineering and Management
MSIID	Master of Science in Information and Instructional Design
MSIM	Master of Science in Information Management
	Master of Science in International Management

MSIMC	Master of Science in Integrated Marketing Communications
MSIR	Master of Science in Industrial Relations
MSIS	Master of Science in Information Science Master of Science in Information Systems Master of Science in Interdisciplinary Studies
MSISE	Master of Science in Infrastructure Systems Engineering
MSISM	Master of Science in Information Systems Management
MSISPM	Master of Science in Information Security Policy and Management
MSIST	Master of Science in Information Systems Technology
MSIT	Master of Science in Industrial Technology Master of Science in Information Technology Master of Science in Instructional Technology
MSITM	Master of Science in Information Technology Management
MSJ	Master of Science in Journalism Master of Science in Jurisprudence
MSJC	Master of Social Justice and Criminology
MSJE	Master of Science in Jewish Education
MSJFP	Master of Science in Juvenile Forensic Psychology
MSJJ	Master of Science in Juvenile Justice
MSJPS	Master of Science in Justice and Public Safety
MSJS	Master of Science in Jewish Studies
MSK	Master of Science in Kinesiology
MSL	Master of School Leadership Master of Science in Leadership Master of Science in Limnology Master of Strategic Leadership Master of Studies in Law
MSLA	Master of Science in Landscape Architecture Master of Science in Legal Administration
MSLD	Master of Science in Land Development
MSLFS	Master of Science in Life Sciences
MSLP	Master of Speech-Language Pathology
MSLS	Master of Science in Library Science
MSLSCM	Master of Science in Logistics and Supply Chain Management
MSLT	Master of Second Language Teaching
MSM	Master of Sacred Ministry Master of Sacred Music Master of School Mathematics Master of Science in Management Master of Science in Mathematics Master of Science in Organization Management Master of Security Management
MSMA	Master of Science in Marketing Analysis
MSMAE	Master of Science in Materials Engineering
MSMC	Master of Science in Mass Communications
MSME	Master of Science in Mathematics Education Master of Science in Mechanical Engineering

MSMFE	Master of Science in Manufacturing Engineering
MSMFT	Master of Science in Marriage and Family Therapy
MSMIS	Master of Science in Management Information Systems
MSMIT	Master of Science in Management and Information Technology
MSMOT	Master of Science in Management of Technology
MSMS	Master of Science in Management Science Master of Science in Medical Sciences
MSMSE	Master of Science in Manufacturing Systems Engineering Master of Science in Material Science and Engineering Master of Science in Mathematics and Science Education
MSMT	Master of Science in Management and Technology Master of Science in Medical Technology
MSMus	Master of Sacred Music
MSN	Master of Science in Nursing
MSN-R	Master of Science in Nursing (Research)
MSNA	Master of Science in Nurse Anesthesia
MSNE	Master of Science in Nuclear Engineering
MSNED	Master of Science in Nurse Education
MSNM	Master of Science in Nonprofit Management
MSNS	Master of Science in Natural Science Master of Science in Nutritional Science
MSOD	Master of Science in Organizational Development
MSOEE	Master of Science in Outdoor and Environmental Education
MSOES	Master of Science in Occupational Ergonomics and Safety
MSOH	Master of Science in Occupational Health
MSOL	Master of Science in Organizational Leadership
MSOM	Master of Science in Operations Management Master of Science in Organization and Management Master of Science in Oriental Medicine
MSOR	Master of Science in Operations Research
MSOT	Master of Science in Occupational Technology Master of Science in Occupational Therapy
MSP	Master of Science in Pharmacy Master of Science in Planning Master of Science in Psychology Master of Speech Pathology
MSPA	Master of Science in Physician Assistant Master of Science in Professional Accountancy
MSPAS	Master of Science in Physician Assistant Studies
MSPC	Master of Science in Professional Communications Master of Science in Professional Counseling
MSPE	Master of Science in Petroleum Engineering
MSPG	Master of Science in Psychology
MSPH	Master of Science in Public Health

MSPH/M Ed	Master of Science in Public Health/Master of Education
MSPH/MCRP	Master of Science in Public Health/Msater of City and Regional Planning
MSPH/MSIS	Master of Science in Public Health/Master of Science in Information Science
MSPH/MSLS	Master of Science in Public Health/Master of Science in Library Science
MSPHR	Master of Science in Pharmacy
MSPM	Master of Science in Professional Management Master of Science in Project Management
MSPNGE	Master of Science in Petroleum and Natural Gas Engineering
MSPS	Master of Science in Pharmaceutical Science Master of Science in Political Science Master of Science in Psychological Services
MSPT	Master of Science in Physical Therapy
MSpVM	Master of Specialized Veterinary Medicine
MSR	Master of Science in Radiology Master of Science in Reading
MSRA	Master of Science in Recreation Administration
MSRC	Master of Science in Resource Conservation
MSRE	Master of Science in Real Estate Master of Science in Religious Education
MSRED	Master of Science in Real Estate Development
MSRLS	Master of Science in Recreation and Leisure Studies
MSRMP	Master of Science in Radiological Medical Physics
MSRS	Master of Science in Rehabilitation Science
MSS	Master of Science in Software Master of Social Science Master of Social Services Master of Software Systems Master of Sports Science Master of Strategic Studies
MSSA	Master of Science in Social Administration
MSSCP	Master of Science in Science Content and Process
MSSD	Master of Science in Sustainable Design
MSSE	Master of Science in Software Engineering Master of Science in Space Education Master of Science in Special Education
MSSEM	Master of Science in Systems and Engineering Management
MSSI	Master of Science in Security Informatics Master of Science in Strategic Intelligence
MSSL	Master of Science in School Leadership Master of Science in Strategic Leadership
MSSLP	Master of Science in Speech-Language Pathology
MSSM	Master of Science in Sports Medicine
MSSP	Master of Science in Social Policy
MSSPA	Master of Science in Student Personnel Administration

MSSS	Master of Science in Safety Science Master of Science in Systems Science
MSST	Master of Science in Security Technologies
MSSW	Master of Science in Social Work
MSSWE	Master of Science in Software Engineering
MST	Master of Science and Technology Master of Science in Taxation Master of Science in Teaching Master of Science in Technology Master of Science in Telecommunications Master of Science Teaching
MSTC	Master of Science in Technical Communication Master of Science in Telecommunications
MSTCM	Master of Science in Traditional Chinese Medicine
MSTE	Master of Science in Telecommunications Engineering Master of Science in Transportation Engineering
MSTM	Master of Science in Technical Management
MSTOM	Master of Science in Traditional Oriental Medicine
MSUD	Master of Science in Urban Design
MSW	Master of Social Work
MSWE	Master of Software Engineering
MSWREE	Master of Science in Water Resources and Environmental Engineering
MSX	Master of Science in Exercise Science
MT	Master of Taxation Master of Teaching Master of Technology Master of Textiles
MTA	Master of Tax Accounting Master of Teaching Arts Master of Tourism Administration
MTCM	Master of Traditional Chinese Medicine
MTD	Master of Training and Development
MTE	Master in Educational Technology
MTESOL	Master in Teaching English to Speakers of Other Languages
MTHM	Master of Tourism and Hospitality Management
MTI	Master of Information Technology
MTIM	Master of Trust and Investment Management
MTL	Master of Talmudic Law
MTM	Master of Technology Management Master of Telecommunications Management Master of the Teaching of Mathematics
MTMH	Master of Tropical Medicine and Hygiene
MTOM	Master of Traditional Oriental Medicine
MTP	Master of Transpersonal Psychology
MTPC	Master of Technical and Professional Communication
MTR	Master of Translational Research
MTS	Master of Theological Studies
MTSC	Master of Technical and Scientific Communication

MTSE	Master of Telecommunications and Software Engineering
MTT	Master in Technology Management
MTX	Master of Taxation
MUA	Master of Urban Affairs
MUD	Master of Urban Design
MUEP	Master of Urban and Environmental Planning
MUP	Master of Urban Planning
MUPDD	Master of Urban Planning, Design, and Development
MUPP	Master of Urban Planning and Policy
MUPRED	Master of Urban Planning and Real Estate Development
MURP	Master of Urban and Regional Planning Master of Urban and Rural Planning
MURPL	Master of Urban and Regional Planning
MUS	Master of Urban Studies
MVM	Master of VLSI and Microelectronics
MVP	Master of Voice Pedagogy
MVPH	Master of Veterinary Public Health
MVS	Master of Visual Studies
MWC	Master of Wildlife Conservation
MWE	Master in Welding Engineering
MWPS	Master of Wood and Paper Science
MWR	Master of Water Resources
MWS	Master of Women's Studies Master of Worship Studies
MZS	Master of Zoological Science
Nav Arch	Naval Architecture
Naval E	Naval Engineer
ND	Doctor of Naturopathic Medicine
NE	Nuclear Engineer
Nuc E	Nuclear Engineer
OD	Doctor of Optometry
OTD	Doctor of Occupational Therapy
PBME	Professional Master of Biomedical Engineering
PD	Professional Diploma
PGC	Post-Graduate Certificate
PGD	Postgraduate Diploma
Ph L	Licentiate of Philosophy
Pharm D	Doctor of Pharmacy
PhD	Doctor of Philosophy
PhD Otal	Doctor of Philosophy in Otalrynology
PhD Surg	Doctor of Philosophy in Surgery
PhDEE	Doctor of Philosophy in Electrical Engineering
PM Sc	Professional Master of Science
PMBA	Professional Master of Business Administration
PMC	Post Master Certificate
PMD	Post-Master's Diploma

PMS	Professional Master of Science Professional Master's
Post-Doctoral MS	Post-Doctoral Master of Science
Post-MSN Certificate	Post-Master of Science in Nursing Certificate
PPDPT	Postprofessional Doctor of Physical Therapy
PSM	Professional Master of Science Professional Science Master's
Psy D	Doctor of Psychology
Psy M	Master of Psychology
Psy S	Specialist in Psychology
Psya D	Doctor of Psychoanalysis
Re Dir	Director of Recreation
Rh D	Doctor of Rehabilitation
S Psy S	Specialist in Psychological Services
Sc D	Doctor of Science
Sc M	Master of Science
SCCT	Specialist in Community College Teaching
ScDPT	Doctor of Physical Therapy Science
SD	Doctor of Science Specialist Degree
SJD	Doctor of Juridical Science
SLPD	Doctor of Speech-Language Pathology
SM	Master of Science
SM Arch S	Master of Science in Architectural Studies
SM Vis S	Master of Science in Visual Studies
SMBT	Master of Science in Building Technology
SP	Specialist Degree
Sp C	Specialist in Counseling
Sp Ed	Specialist in Education
Sp LIS	Specialist in Library and Information Science
SPA	Specialist in Arts
SPCM	Special in Church Music
Spec	Specialist's Certificate
Spec M	Specialist in Music
SPEM	Special in Educational Ministries
SPS	School Psychology Specialist
Spt	Specialist Degree
SPTH	Special in Theology
SSP	Specialist in School Psychology
STB	Bachelor of Sacred Theology
STD	Doctor of Sacred Theology
STL	Licentiate of Sacred Theology
STM	Master of Sacred Theology
TDPT	Transitional Doctor of Physical Therapy
Th D	Doctor of Theology
Th M	Master of Theology
VMD	Doctor of Veterinary Medicine

WEMBA	Weekend Executive Master of Business Administration	**XMBA**	Executive Master of Business Administration
XMA	Executive Master of Arts		

INDEXES

Close-Ups and Displays

Directories and Subject Areas

Following is an alphabetical listing of directories and subject areas. Also listed are cross-references for subject area names not used in the directory structure of the guides, for example, "Arabic (*see* Near and Middle Eastern Languages)."

Graduate Programs in the Humanities, Arts & Social Sciences

Addictions/Substance Abuse Counseling

Administration (*see* Arts Administration; Public Administration)

African-American Studies

African Languages and Literatures (*see* African Studies)

African Studies

Agribusiness (*see* Agricultural Economics and Agribusiness)

Agricultural Economics and Agribusiness

Alcohol Abuse Counseling (*see* Addictions/Substance Abuse Counseling)

American Indian/Native American Studies

American Studies

Anthropology

Applied Arts and Design—General

Applied Behavior Analysis

Applied Economics

Applied History (*see* Public History)

Applied Psychology

Applied Social Research

Arabic (*see* Near and Middle Eastern Languages)

Arab Studies (*see* Near and Middle Eastern Studies)

Archaeology

Architectural History

Architecture

Archives Administration (*see* Public History)

Area and Cultural Studies (*see* African-American Studies; African Studies; American Indian/Native American Studies; American Studies; Asian-American Studies; Asian Studies; Canadian Studies; Cultural Studies; East European and Russian Studies; Ethnic Studies; Folklore; Gender Studies; Hispanic Studies; Holocaust Studies; Jewish Studies; Latin American Studies; Near and Middle Eastern Studies; Northern Studies; Pacific Area/ Pacific Rim Studies; Western European Studies; Women's Studies)

Art/Fine Arts

Art History

Arts Administration

Arts Journalism

Art Therapy

Asian-American Studies

Asian Languages

Asian Studies

Behavioral Sciences (*see* Psychology)

Bible Studies (*see* Religion; Theology)

Biological Anthropology

Black Studies (*see* African-American Studies)

Broadcasting (*see* Communication; Film, Television, and Video Production)

Broadcast Journalism

Building Science

Canadian Studies

Celtic Languages

Ceramics (*see* Art/Fine Arts)

Child and Family Studies

Child Development

Chinese

Chinese Studies (*see* Asian Languages; Asian Studies)

Christian Studies (*see* Missions and Missiology; Religion; Theology)

Cinema (*see* Film, Television, and Video Production)

City and Regional Planning (*see* Urban and Regional Planning)

Classical Languages and Literatures (*see* Classics)

Classics

Clinical Psychology

Clothing and Textiles

Cognitive Psychology (*see* Psychology—General; Cognitive Sciences)

Cognitive Sciences

Communication—General

Community Affairs (*see* Urban and Regional Planning; Urban Studies)

Community Planning (*see* Architecture; Environmental Design; Urban and Regional Planning; Urban Design; Urban Studies)

Community Psychology (*see* Social Psychology)

Comparative and Interdisciplinary Arts

Comparative Literature

Composition (*see* Music)

Computer Art and Design

Conflict Resolution and Mediation/Peace Studies

Consumer Economics

Corporate and Organizational Communication

Corrections (*see* Criminal Justice and Criminology)

Counseling (*see* Counseling Psychology; Pastoral Ministry and Counseling)

Counseling Psychology

Crafts (*see* Art/Fine Arts)

Creative Arts Therapies (*see* Art Therapy; Therapies—Dance, Drama, and Music)

Criminal Justice and Criminology

Cultural Anthropology

Cultural Studies

Dance

Decorative Arts

Demography and Population Studies

Design (*see* Applied Arts and Design; Architecture; Art/Fine Arts; Environmental Design; Graphic Design; Industrial Design; Interior Design; Textile Design; Urban Design)

Developmental Psychology

Diplomacy (*see* International Affairs)

Disability Studies

Drama Therapy (*see* Therapies—Dance, Drama, and Music)

Dramatic Arts (*see* Theater)

Drawing (*see* Art/Fine Arts)

Drug Abuse Counseling (*see* Addictions/Substance Abuse Counseling)

Drug and Alcohol Abuse Counseling (*see* Addictions/Substance Abuse Counseling)

East Asian Studies (*see* Asian Studies)

East European and Russian Studies

Economic Development

Economics

Educational Theater (*see* Theater; Therapies—Dance, Drama, and Music)

Emergency Management

English

Environmental Design

Ethics

Ethnic Studies

Ethnomusicology (*see* Music)

Experimental Psychology

Family and Consumer Sciences—General

Family Studies (*see* Child and Family Studies)

Family Therapy (*see* Child and Family Studies; Clinical Psychology; Counseling Psychology; Marriage and Family Therapy)

Filmmaking (*see* Film, Television, and Video Production)

Film Studies (*see* Film, Television, and Video Production)

Film, Television, and Video Production

Film, Television, and Video Theory and Criticism

Fine Arts (*see* Art/Fine Arts)

Folklore

Foreign Languages (*see* specific language)

Foreign Service (*see* International Affairs; International Development)

Forensic Psychology

Forensic Sciences

Forensics (*see* Speech and Interpersonal Communication)

French

Gender Studies

General Studies (*see* Liberal Studies)

Genetic Counseling

Geographic Information Systems

Geography

German

Gerontology

Graphic Design

Greek (*see* Classics)

Health Communication

Health Psychology

Hebrew (*see* Near and Middle Eastern Languages)

Hebrew Studies (*see* Jewish Studies)

Hispanic and Latin American Languages

Hispanic Studies

Historic Preservation

History

History of Art (*see* Art History)

History of Medicine

History of Science and Technology

Holocaust and Genocide Studies

Home Economics (*see* Family and Consumer Sciences—General)

Homeland Security

Household Economics, Sciences, and Management (*see* Family and Consumer Sciences—General)

Human Development

Humanities

Illustration

Industrial and Labor Relations

Industrial and Organizational Psychology

Industrial Design

Interdisciplinary Studies

Interior Design

International Affairs

International Development

International Economics

International Service (*see* International Affairs; International Development)

International Trade Policy

Internet and Interactive Multimedia

Interpersonal Communication (*see* Speech and Interpersonal Communication)

Interpretation (*see* Translation and Interpretation)

Islamic Studies (*see* Near and Middle Eastern Studies; Religion)

Italian

Japanese

Japanese Studies (*see* Asian Languages; Asian Studies; Japanese)

Jewelry (*see* Art/Fine Arts)

Jewish Studies

Journalism

Judaic Studies (*see* Jewish Studies; Religion)

Labor Relations (*see* Industrial and Labor Relations)

Landscape Architecture

Latin American Studies

Latin (*see* Classics)

Law Enforcement (*see* Criminal Justice and Criminology)

Liberal Studies

Lighting Design

Linguistics

Literature (*see* Classics; Comparative Literature; specific language)

Marriage and Family Therapy

Mass Communication

Media Studies

Medical Illustration

Medieval and Renaissance Studies

Metalsmithing (*see* Art/Fine Arts)

Middle Eastern Studies (*see* Near and Middle Eastern Studies)

Military and Defense Studies

Mineral Economics

Ministry (*see* Pastoral Ministry and Counseling; Theology)

Missions and Missiology

Motion Pictures (*see* Film, Television, and Video Production)

Museum Studies

Music

Musicology (*see* Music)

Music Therapy (*see* Therapies—Dance, Drama, and Music)

National Security

Native American Studies (*see* American Indian/Native American Studies)

Near and Middle Eastern Languages

Near and Middle Eastern Studies

Near Environment (*see* Family and Consumer Sciences)

Northern Studies

Organizational Psychology (*see* Industrial and Organizational Psychology)

Oriental Languages (*see* Asian Languages)

Oriental Studies (*see* Asian Studies)

Pacific Area/Pacific Rim Studies

Painting (*see* Art/Fine Arts)

Pastoral Ministry and Counseling

Philanthropic Studies

Philosophy

Photography

Playwriting (*see* Theater; Writing)

Policy Studies (*see* Public Policy)

Political Science

Population Studies (*see* Demography and Population Studies)

Portuguese

Printmaking (*see* Art/Fine Arts)

Product Design (*see* Industrial Design)

Psychoanalysis and Psychotherapy

Psychology—General

Public Administration

Public Affairs

Public History

Public Policy

Public Speaking (*see* Mass Communication; Rhetoric; Speech and Interpersonal Communication)

Publishing

Regional Planning (*see* Architecture; Urban and Regional Planning; Urban Design; Urban Studies)

Rehabilitation Counseling

Religion

Renaissance Studies (*see* Medieval and Renaissance Studies)

Rhetoric

Romance Languages

Romance Literatures (*see* Romance Languages)

Rural Planning and Studies

Rural Sociology

Russian

Scandinavian Languages

School Psychology

Sculpture (*see* Art/Fine Arts)

Security Administration (*see* Criminal Justice and Criminology)

Slavic Languages

Slavic Studies (*see* East European and Russian Studies; Slavic Languages)

Social Psychology

Social Sciences

Sociology

Southeast Asian Studies (*see* Asian Studies)

Soviet Studies (*see* East European and Russian Studies; Russian)

Spanish

Speech and Interpersonal Communication

Sport Psychology

Studio Art (*see* Art/Fine Arts)

Substance Abuse Counseling (*see* Addictions/Substance Abuse Counseling)

Survey Methodology

Sustainable Development

Technical Communication

Technical Writing

Telecommunications (*see* Film, Television, and Video Production)

Television (*see* Film, Television, and Video Production)

Textile Design

Textiles (*see* Clothing and Textiles; Textile Design)

Thanatology

Theater

Theater Arts (*see* Theater)

Theology

Therapies—Dance, Drama, and Music

Translation and Interpretation

Transpersonal and Humanistic Psychology

Urban and Regional Planning

Urban Design

Urban Planning (*see* Architecture; Urban and Regional Planning; Urban Design; Urban Studies)

Urban Studies

Video (*see* Film, Television, and Video Production)

Visual Arts (*see* Applied Arts and Design; Art/Fine Arts; Film, Television, and Video Production; Graphic Design; Illustration; Photography)

Western European Studies

Women's Studies

World Wide Web (*see* Internet and Interactive Multimedia)

Writing

Graduate Programs in the Biological Sciences

Anatomy

Animal Behavior

Bacteriology

Behavioral Sciences (*see* Biopsychology; Neuroscience; Zoology)

Biochemistry

Biological and Biomedical Sciences—General

Biological Chemistry (*see* Biochemistry)

Biological Oceanography (*see* Marine Biology)

Biophysics

Biopsychology

Botany

Breeding (*see* Botany; Plant Biology; Genetics)

Cancer Biology/Oncology

Cardiovascular Sciences

Cell Biology

Cellular Physiology (*see* Cell Biology; Physiology)

Computational Biology

Conservation (*see* Conservation Biology; Environmental Biology)

Conservation Biology

Crop Sciences (*see* Botany; Plant Biology)

Cytology (*see* Cell Biology)

Developmental Biology

Dietetics (*see* Nutrition)

Ecology

Embryology (*see* Developmental Biology)

Endocrinology (*see* Physiology)

Entomology

Environmental Biology

Evolutionary Biology

Foods (*see* Nutrition)

Genetics

Genomic Sciences

Histology (*see* Anatomy; Cell Biology)

Human Genetics

Immunology

Infectious Diseases

Laboratory Medicine (*see* Immunology; Microbiology; Pathology)

Life Sciences (*see* Biological and Biomedical Sciences)

Marine Biology

Medical Microbiology

Medical Sciences (*see* Biological and Biomedical Sciences)

Medical Science Training Programs (*see* Biological and Biomedical Sciences)

Microbiology

Molecular Biology

Molecular Biophysics

Molecular Genetics

Molecular Medicine

Molecular Pathogenesis

Molecular Pathology

Molecular Pharmacology

Molecular Physiology

Molecular Toxicology

Neural Sciences (*see* Biopsychology; Neurobiology; Neuroscience)

Neurobiology

Neuroendocrinology (*see* Biopsychology; Neurobiology; Neuroscience; Physiology)

Neuropharmacology (*see* Biopsychology; Neurobiology; Neuroscience; Pharmacology)

Neurophysiology (*see* Biopsychology; Neurobiology; Neuroscience; Physiology)

Neuroscience

Nutrition

Oncology (*see* Cancer Biology/Oncology)

Organismal Biology (*see* Biological and Biomedical Sciences; Zoology)

Parasitology

Pathobiology

Pathology

Pharmacology

Photobiology of Cells and Organelles (*see* Botany; Cell Biology; Plant Biology)

Physiological Optics (*see* Physiology)

Physiology

Plant Biology

Plant Molecular Biology

Plant Pathology

Plant Physiology

Pomology (*see* Botany; Plant Biology)

Psychobiology (*see* Biopsychology)

Psychopharmacology (*see* Biopsychology; Neuroscience; Pharmacology)

Radiation Biology

Reproductive Biology

Sociobiology (*see* Evolutionary Biology)

Structural Biology

Systems Biology

Teratology

Theoretical Biology (*see* Biological and Biomedical Sciences)

Therapeutics (*see* Pharmacology)

Toxicology

Translational Biology

Tropical Medicine (*see* Parasitology)

Virology

Wildlife Biology (*see* Zoology)

Zoology

Graduate Programs in the Physical Sciences, Mathematics, Agricultural Sciences, the Environment & Natural Resources

Acoustics

Agricultural Sciences

Agronomy and Soil Sciences

Analytical Chemistry

Animal Sciences

Applied Mathematics

Applied Physics

Applied Statistics

Aquaculture

Astronomy

Astrophysical Sciences (*see* Astrophysics; Atmospheric Sciences; Meteorology; Planetary and Space Sciences)

Astrophysics

Atmospheric Sciences

Biological Oceanography (*see* Marine Affairs; Marine Sciences; Oceanography)

Biomathematics

Biometry

Biostatistics

Chemical Physics

Chemistry

Computational Sciences

Condensed Matter Physics

Dairy Science (*see* Animal Sciences)

Earth Sciences (*see* Geosciences)

Environmental Management and Policy

Environmental Sciences

Environmental Studies (*see* Environmental Management and Policy)

Experimental Statistics (*see* Statistics)

Fish, Game, and Wildlife Management

Food Science and Technology

Forestry

General Science (*see* specific topics)

Geochemistry

Geodetic Sciences

Geological Engineering (*see* Geology)

Geological Sciences (*see* Geology)

Geology

Geophysical Fluid Dynamics (*see* Geophysics)

Geophysics

Geosciences

Horticulture

Hydrogeology

Hydrology

Inorganic Chemistry

Limnology

Marine Affairs

Marine Geology

Marine Sciences

Marine Studies (*see* Marine Affairs; Marine Geology; Marine Sciences; Oceanography)

Mathematical and Computational Finance

Mathematical Physics

Mathematical Statistics (*see* Applied Statistics; Statistics)

Mathematics

Meteorology

Mineralogy

Natural Resource Management (*see* Environmental Management and Policy; Natural Resources)

Natural Resources

Nuclear Physics (*see* Physics)

Ocean Engineering (*see* Marine Affairs; Marine Geology; Marine Sciences; Oceanography)

Oceanography

Optical Sciences

Optical Technologies (*see* Optical Sciences)

Optics (*see* Applied Physics; Optical Sciences; Physics)

Organic Chemistry

Paleontology

Paper Chemistry (*see* Chemistry)

Photonics

Physical Chemistry

Physics

Planetary and Space Sciences

Plant Sciences

Plasma Physics

Poultry Science (*see* Animal Sciences)

Radiological Physics (*see* Physics)

Range Management (*see* Range Science)

Range Science

Resource Management (*see* Environmental Management and Policy; Natural Resources)

Solid-Earth Sciences (*see* Geosciences)

Space Sciences (*see* Planetary and Space Sciences)

Statistics

Theoretical Chemistry

Theoretical Physics

Viticulture and Enology

Water Resources

Graduate Programs in Engineering & Applied Sciences

Aeronautical Engineering (*see* Aerospace/Aeronautical Engineering)

Aerospace/Aeronautical Engineering

Aerospace Studies (*see* Aerospace/Aeronautical Engineering)

Agricultural Engineering

Applied Mechanics (*see* Mechanics)

Applied Science and Technology

Architectural Engineering

Artificial Intelligence/Robotics

Astronautical Engineering (*see* Aerospace/Aeronautical Engineering)

Automotive Engineering

Aviation

Biochemical Engineering

Bioengineering

Bioinformatics

Biological Engineering (*see* Bioengineering)

Biomedical Engineering

Biosystems Engineering

Biotechnology

Ceramic Engineering (*see* Ceramic Sciences and Engineering)

Ceramic Sciences and Engineering

Ceramics (*see* Ceramic Sciences and Engineering)

Chemical Engineering

Civil Engineering

Computer and Information Systems Security

Computer Engineering

Computer Science

Computing Technology (*see* Computer Science)

Construction Engineering

Construction Management

Database Systems

Electrical Engineering

Electronic Materials

Electronics Engineering (*see* Electrical Engineering)

Energy and Power Engineering

Energy Management and Policy

Engineering and Applied Sciences

Engineering and Public Affairs (*see* Technology and Public Policy)

Engineering and Public Policy (*see* Energy Management and Policy; Technology and Public Policy)

Engineering Design

Engineering Management

Engineering Mechanics (*see* Mechanics)

Engineering Metallurgy (*see* Metallurgical Engineering and Metallurgy)

Engineering Physics

Environmental Design (*see* Environmental Engineering)

Environmental Engineering

Ergonomics and Human Factors

Financial Engineering

Fire Protection Engineering

Food Engineering (*see* Agricultural Engineering)

Game Design and Development

Gas Engineering (*see* Petroleum Engineering)

Geological Engineering

Geophysics Engineering (*see* Geological Engineering)

Geotechnical Engineering

Hazardous Materials Management

Health Informatics

Health Systems (*see* Safety Engineering; Systems Engineering)

Highway Engineering (*see* Transportation and Highway Engineering)

Human-Computer Interaction

Human Factors (*see* Ergonomics and Human Factors)

Hydraulics

Hydrology (*see* Water Resources Engineering)

Industrial Engineering (*see* Industrial/Management Engineering)

Industrial/Management Engineering

Information Science

Internet Engineering

Macromolecular Science (*see* Polymer Science and Engineering)

Management Engineering (*see* Engineering Management; Industrial/Management Engineering)

Management of Technology

Manufacturing Engineering

Marine Engineering (*see* Civil Engineering)

Materials Engineering

Materials Sciences

Mechanical Engineering

Mechanics

Medical Informatics

Metallurgical Engineering and Metallurgy

Metallurgy (*see* Metallurgical Engineering and Metallurgy)

Mineral/Mining Engineering

Modeling and Simulation

Nanotechnology

Nuclear Engineering

Ocean Engineering

Operations Research

Paper and Pulp Engineering

Petroleum Engineering

Pharmaceutical Engineering

Plastics Engineering (*see* Polymer Science and Engineering)

Polymer Science and Engineering

Public Policy (*see* Energy Management and Policy; Technology and Public Policy)

Reliability Engineering

Robotics (*see* Artificial Intelligence/Robotics)

Safety Engineering

Software Engineering

Solid-State Sciences (*see* Materials Sciences)

Structural Engineering

Surveying Science and Engineering

Systems Analysis (*see* Systems Engineering)

Systems Engineering

Systems Science

Technology and Public Policy

Telecommunications

Telecommunications Management

Textile Sciences and Engineering

Textiles (*see* Textile Sciences and Engineering)

Transportation and Highway Engineering

Urban Systems Engineering (*see* Systems Engineering)

Waste Management (*see* Hazardous Materials Management)

Water Resources Engineering

Graduate Programs in Business, Education, Health, Information Studies, Law & Social Work

Accounting

Actuarial Science

Acupuncture and Oriental Medicine

Acute Care/Critical Care Nursing

Administration (*see* Business Administration and Management; Educational Administration; Health Services Management and Hospital Administration; Industrial and Manufacturing Management; Nursing and Healthcare Administration; Pharmaceutical Administration; Sports Management)

Adult Education

Adult Nursing

Advanced Practice Nursing (*see* Family Nurse Practitioner Studies)

Advertising and Public Relations

Agricultural Education

Alcohol Abuse Counseling (*see* Counselor Education)

Allied Health—General

Allied Health Professions (*see* Clinical Laboratory Sciences/Medical Technology; Clinical Research; Communication Disorders; Dental Hygiene; Emergency Medical Services; Occupational Therapy; Physical Therapy; Physician Assistant Studies; Rehabilitation Sciences)

Allopathic Medicine

Anesthesiologist Assistant Studies

Archival Management and Studies

Art Education

Athletics Administration (*see* Kinesiology and Movement Studies)

Athletic Training and Sports Medicine

Audiology (*see* Communication Disorders)

Aviation Management

Banking (*see* Finance and Banking)

Bioethics

Business Administration and Management—General

Business Education
Child-Care Nursing (*see* Maternal and Child/Neonatal Nursing)
Chiropractic
Clinical Laboratory Sciences/Medical Technology
Clinical Research
Communication Disorders
Community College Education
Community Health
Community Health Nursing
Computer Education
Continuing Education (*see* Adult Education)
Counseling (*see* Counselor Education)
Counselor Education
Curriculum and Instruction
Dental and Oral Surgery (*see* Oral and Dental Sciences)
Dental Assistant Studies (*see* Dental Hygiene)
Dental Hygiene
Dental Services (*see* Dental Hygiene)
Dentistry
Developmental Education
Distance Education Development
Drug Abuse Counseling (*see* Counselor Education)
Early Childhood Education
Educational Leadership and Administration
Educational Measurement and Evaluation
Educational Media/Instructional Technology
Educational Policy
Educational Psychology
Education—General
Education of the Blind (*see* Special Education)
Education of the Deaf (*see* Special Education)
Education of the Gifted
Education of the Hearing Impaired (*see* Special Education)
Education of the Learning Disabled (*see* Special Education)
Education of the Mentally Retarded (*see* Special Education)
Education of the Physically Handicapped (*see* Special Education)
Education of Students with Severe/Multiple Disabilities
Education of the Visually Handicapped (*see* Special Education)
Electronic Commerce
Elementary Education
Emergency Medical Services
English as á Second Language
English Education
Entertainment Management
Entrepreneurship
Environmental and Occupational Health
Environmental Education
Environmental Law
Epidemiology
Exercise and Sports Science
Exercise Physiology (*see* Kinesiology and Movement Studies)
Facilities and Entertainment Management
Family Nurse Practitioner Studies
Finance and Banking
Food Services Management (*see* Hospitality Management)
Foreign Languages Education

Forensic Nursing
Foundations and Philosophy of Education
Gerontological Nursing
Guidance and Counseling (*see* Counselor Education)
Health Education
Health Law
Health Physics/Radiological Health
Health Promotion
Health-Related Professions (*see* individual allied health professions)
Health Services Management and Hospital Administration
Health Services Research
Hearing Sciences (*see* Communication Disorders)
Higher Education
HIV/AIDS Nursing
Home Economics Education
Hospice Nursing
Hospital Administration (*see* Health Services Management and Hospital Administration)
Hospitality Management
Hotel Management (*see* Travel and Tourism)
Human Resources Development
Human Resources Management
Human Services
Industrial Administration (*see* Industrial and Manufacturing Management)
Industrial and Manufacturing Management
Industrial Education (*see* Vocational and Technical Education)
Industrial Hygiene
Information Studies
Instructional Technology (*see* Educational Media/Instructional Technology)
Insurance
Intellectual Property Law
International and Comparative Education
International Business
International Commerce (*see* International Business)
International Economics (*see* International Business)
International Health
International Trade (*see* International Business)
Investment and Securities (*see* Business Administration and Management; Finance and Banking; Investment Management)
Investment Management
Junior College Education (*see* Community College Education)
Kinesiology and Movement Studies
Laboratory Medicine (*see* Clinical Laboratory Sciences/Medical Technology)
Law
Legal and Justice Studies
Leisure Services (*see* Recreation and Park Management)
Leisure Studies
Library Science
Logistics
Management (*see* Business Administration and Management)
Management Information Systems
Management Strategy and Policy
Marketing

Marketing Research

Maternal and Child Health

Maternal and Child/Neonatal Nursing

Mathematics Education

Medical Imaging

Medical Nursing (*see* Medical/Surgical Nursing)

Medical Physics

Medical/Surgical Nursing

Medical Technology (*see* Clinical Laboratory Sciences/Medical Technology)

Medicinal and Pharmaceutical Chemistry

Medicinal Chemistry (*see* Medicinal and Pharmaceutical Chemistry)

Medicine (*see* Allopathic Medicine; Naturopathic Medicine; Osteopathic Medicine; Podiatric Medicine)

Middle School Education

Midwifery (*see* Nurse Midwifery)

Movement Studies (*see* Kinesiology and Movement Studies)

Multilingual and Multicultural Education

Museum Education

Music Education

Naturopathic Medicine

Nonprofit Management

Nuclear Medical Technology (*see* Clinical Laboratory Sciences/ Medical Technology)

Nurse Anesthesia

Nurse Midwifery

Nurse Practitioner Studies (*see* Family Nurse Practitioner Studies)

Nursery School Education (*see* Early Childhood Education)

Nursing Administration (*see* Nursing and Healthcare Administration)

Nursing and Healthcare Administration

Nursing Education

Nursing—General

Nursing Informatics

Occupational Education (*see* Vocational and Technical Education)

Occupational Health (*see* Environmental and Occupational Health; Occupational Health Nursing)

Occupational Health Nursing

Occupational Therapy

Oncology Nursing

Optometry

Oral and Dental Sciences

Oral Biology (*see* Oral and Dental Sciences)

Oral Pathology (*see* Oral and Dental Sciences)

Organizational Behavior

Organizational Management

Oriental Medicine and Acupuncture (*see* Acupuncture and Oriental Medicine)

Orthodontics (*see* Oral and Dental Sciences)

Osteopathic Medicine

Parks Administration (*see* Recreation and Park Management)

Pediatric Nursing

Pedontics (*see* Oral and Dental Sciences)

Perfusion

Personnel (*see* Human Resources Development; Human Resources Management; Organizational Behavior; Organizational Management; Student Affairs)

Pharmaceutical Administration

Pharmaceutical Chemistry (*see* Medicinal and Pharmaceutical Chemistry)

Pharmaceutical Sciences

Pharmacy

Philosophy of Education (*see* Foundations and Philosophy of Education)

Physical Education

Physical Therapy

Physician Assistant Studies

Physiological Optics (*see* Vision Sciences)

Podiatric Medicine

Preventive Medicine (*see* Community Health and Public Health)

Project Management

Psychiatric Nursing

Public Health—General

Public Health Nursing (*see* Community Health Nursing)

Public Relations (*see* Advertising and Public Relations)

Quality Management

Quantitative Analysis

Radiological Health (*see* Health Physics/Radiological Health)

Reading Education

Real Estate

Recreation and Park Management

Recreation Therapy (*see* Recreation and Park Management)

Rehabilitation Sciences

Rehabilitation Therapy (*see* Physical Therapy)

Religious Education

Remedial Education (*see* Special Education)

Restaurant Administration (*see* Hospitality Management)

School Nursing

Science Education

Secondary Education

Social Sciences Education

Social Studies Education (*see* Social Sciences Education)

Social Work

Special Education

Speech-Language Pathology and Audiology (*see* Communication Disorders)

Sports Management

Sports Medicine (*see* Athletic Training and Sports Medicine)

Sports Psychology and Sociology (*see* Kinesiology and Movement Studies)

Student Affairs

Substance Abuse Counseling (*see* Counselor Education)

Supply Chain Management

Surgical Nursing (*see* Medical/Surgical Nursing)

Sustainability Management

Systems Management (*see* Management Information Systems)

Taxation

Teacher Education (*see* specific subject areas)

Teaching English as a Second Language (*see* English as a Second Language)

Technical Education (*see* Vocational and Technical Education)

Teratology (*see* Environmental and Occupational Health)

Therapeutics (*see* Pharmaceutical Sciences; Pharmacy)

Transcultural Nursing

Transportation Management
Travel and Tourism
Urban Education
Veterinary Medicine
Veterinary Sciences

Vision Sciences
Vocational and Technical Education
Vocational Counseling (*see* Counselor Education)
Women's Health Nursing

Directories and Subject Areas in This Book

Special Advertising Section

Thomas Jefferson University School of Population Health

University of Medicine & Dentistry of New Jersey

Saint Louis University

St. Mary's University

The Winston Preparatory Schools

Learn from a National Leader in
Population Health

Jefferson School of Population Health

- Master of Public Health (MPH); CEPH accredited

- PhD in Population Health Sciences

Online programs

- Master of Science in Health Policy (MS-HP)

- Master of Science in Healthcare Quality and Safety (MS-HQS)

- Master of Science in Chronic Care Management (MS-CCM)

- Certificates in Public Health, Health Policy, Healthcare Quality and Safety, Chronic Care Management

Population health – putting health and health care together

215-503-0174

www.jefferson.edu/population_health/ads.cfm

Jefferson.
School of Population Health

THOMAS JEFFERSON UNIVERSITY

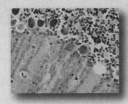

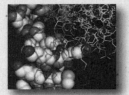
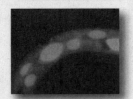

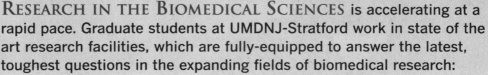
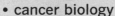

+ AMIT SOOD | sports business major

BE A BILLIKEN

Find out how the breadth and depth of the fully accredited undergraduate and graduate programs at Saint Louis University's **JOHN COOK SCHOOL OF BUSINESS** will give you the knowledge and tools necessary for success in today's global and highly technical business world.

——— + Visit **BeABilliken.com** for more information on our undergraduate business programs and to see what life is like as a Billiken.

To learn about our graduate business programs, attend an open house or visit **gradbiz.slu.edu.** + ———

SAINT LOUIS UNIVERSITY

CONCENTRATIONS IN THE JOHN COOK SCHOOL OF BUSINESS

Accounting

Economics

Entrepreneurship

Finance

Information Technology Management

International Business

Leadership and Change Management

Marketing

Sports Business

GRADUATE PROGRAMS IN THE JOHN COOK SCHOOL OF BUSINESS

One-Year MBA

Part-Time MBA

Master of Supply Chain Management

Master of Accounting

Executive Master of International Business

Post-MBA Certificate

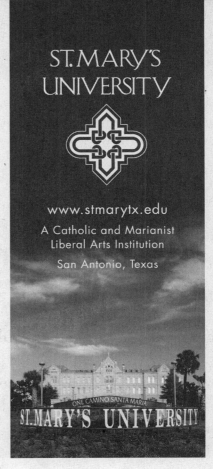